Teacher's Edition

In Association with
AmericanHeritage®

PRENTICE HALL
AMERICA
PATHWAYS TO
THE PRESENT

also available
RESOURCE PRO®
ELECTRONIC TEACHING RESOURCES
with Planning Express®

Prentice Hall

ISBN 0–13–053626–1

1 2 3 4 5 6 7 8 9 10   04 03 02 01 00

Needham, Massachusetts   Upper Saddle River, New Jersey   Glenview, Illinois

The program you need to reach today's

Student Edition (Survey)

Teacher's Edition (Survey)

Student Edition (Modern American History)

Teacher's Edition (Modern American History)

Teaching Resources with Test Bank CD-ROM

    Lesson Plans with Rubrics

    Big Idea Graphic Organizers

    Guided Reading and Review

    Why Study History? Activities

    Biography Activities

    Primary Source Activities

    Literature Activities

    Skills for Life Activities

    Debating the Future Activities

    Geography and History Activities

    History's Lasting Impact Activities

    Visual Learning Activities

    Decision-Making Activities

    Learning with Documents

    Great Debates

    Learning Styles Lesson Plans

    Section Quizzes

    Chapter Tests

    Test Bank CD-ROM

    Why Study History? poster

Student Performance Pack

    Interactive Student Tutorial CD-ROM

    Guide to the Essentials of U.S. History (English)

    Guide to the Essentials of U.S. History (Spanish)

    Guide to the Essentials Teacher's Guide

    Guided Reading Audiotapes (English)

    Guided Reading Audiotapes (Spanish)

    Standardized Test Prep Handbook

Humanities Pack

Transparencies

Resource Pro® with Planning Express® CD-ROM

America: Pathways to the Present on Audiotapes

Listening to Music, The American Experience Audio CD

Classroom Literature Library

American History Block Scheduling Support File

Perspectives: Reading in American History in the 20th Century

American History Historical Outline Map Book

Nystrom Atlas of Our Country

Constitution Study Guide/Teacher's Manual

American History Customized Reader Catalog

Brief Review in U.S. History and Government

History Alive!™ Activity Pack

Visions of America Videotapes/Videodiscs

United States History Video Collection™ Videodiscs/Videotapes

American Heritage® History of the United States CD-ROM

Decision America Videodiscs/Videotapes

Close Up Foundation Bill of Rights Videotape Series

Our Times Multimedia Encyclopedia CD-ROM

students

Program Highlights

- Balanced content that's authoritative and comprehensive
- More ways to make history relevant for today's students
- More ways to make history accessible—for every reading level and learning style
- Flexible and easy to manage for every teaching style

Now *America: Pathways to the Present* is the nation's premier American history

AmericanHeritage®

You already rely on Prentice Hall for accurate and authoritative history content. Now the excitement of history comes right into your classroom, with the support of the nation's premier American history magazine. Students and teachers alike benefit from the rich scholarship and vast archives of *American Heritage*® magazine and its classic books.

SUPER MARIO NATION: VIDEO GAMES TURN 25
RIDING THE RANGE WITH THE LAST REAL COWBOYS

AmericanHeritage

SEPTEMBER 1997 $4.95

HOW OUR GOVERNMENT GOT SO BIG

DON'T BLAME THE WELFARE STATE OR THE MILITARY THE TRUTH IS MUCH MORE INTERESTING

Washington: A Frenchman in the Revolution
From Brooklyn to Korea—Coming of Age Fast in the 1950s

AmericanHeritage

FEBRUARY • MARCH 1997 $4.95

Learning From the Last 2,000 Years

THE LESSONS OF WAR

1947—WHEN BASKETBALL CO...
LINDBERGH: THE TROUBLE W...

AmericanHe...

MAY • JUNE 1997 $4.95

TELEVISION GROWS UP

SUNDAY, 8 P.M.: TV'S GREATEST SHOW
INVENTING THE COMMERCIAL
THE FOUR DAYS THAT MADE TV NEWS

American Heritage® Magazine

American Heritage® magazine features compelling accounts and historical scholarship that add a new dimension to the way your students perceive their American history studies.

infused with the vitality of magazine.

American Heritage®

My Brush with History

BY TOM FLEMING

INTRODUCTION Both the boom times of the 1920s and the hard times of 1930s produced numerous heroes and other celebrities. Thanks to advances such as radio, these national heroes were familiar to Americans all across the country. Seeing one in person was an a day Fleming, then a young boy, saw three of the best-known Americans of the period: the President, the man who would become the next President, and the greatest baseball player of his era.

My Brush with History

This popular feature from *American Heritage®* magazine—first-person, eyewitness accounts of major historical events—inspires fascinating and accessible program features that get students to think, and to feel involved.

American Heritage®
The History of the United States CD-ROM

An interactive, in-depth software program enriches instruction with a wide array of multimedia, including live-action video, hundreds of photographs, and an audio track with music.

From the Archives of
American Heritage®

About the Presidents

Abraham Lincoln (1861–1865) faced a multitude of problems in 1862. McClellan, his difficult general, was only one. On the one hand, abolitionists called for a total war on slavery. On the other, defeatists said that peace was more important than the Union. Lincoln's cabinet was divided, too. Many members had personal ambitions. (Secretary Seward, for example, had challenged Lincoln's experience and authority.) Desertions from the army were constant. To make matters worse, Lincoln faced terrible personal grief: the death of his eleven-year old son, Willie.

Point-of-use teaching notes

Point-of-use teaching notes from *American Heritage®* books and magazines—woven throughout the text—help your class see history as they've never seen it before.

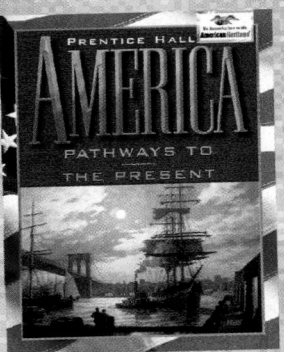

The only high school program where it matters most—in the

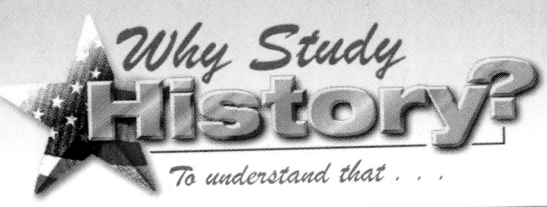

Why Study History?
To understand that . . .

The Generation Gap Is Not New

Today, as in the 1920s, the American youth culture is markedly different from that of the older generation.

Slang terms, clothing styles, musical tastes—these are areas in which young people traditionally set themselves apart from their parents and grandparents. To many older Americans, the pastimes and attitudes of youth are sad proof that the nation's morals have decayed.

Jazz record from the 1920s

Yet a "generation gap" has divided older and younger people for centuries, and society has always managed to survive.

The Impact Today

In the 1920s such trends as short skirts and jazz music troubled some Americans. Today an increasing number of Americans are disturbed by the rise in obscene language and sexual and violent images in popular music, movies, television, and the Internet. These aspects of youth culture have prompted calls for government, schools, and parents to regulate these undesirable influences.

Public and private institutions have heeded the call. For example, many school systems have decided to adopt dress codes or school uniforms to promote order and decrease violent behavior. Television networks have adopted a coding system that indicates the content of programs and their appropriateness for younger audiences.

How many Americans support actions such as these? A clear majority of those interviewed in one nationwide poll approved of greater restrictions on television programming, as well as on the lyrics to popular songs. A whopping 93 percent of interviewees favored stricter parental supervision of different forms of youth entertainment.

Some Americans, however, caution that restrictions on entertainment could go too far and become a form of censorship. These people often point out that, while every generation has its rebellions, most young people grow up to be responsible adults.

The Impact on You

Ask five people in your community to evaluate the following statement: "Warning labels on popular music and television coding systems are needed to protect young people from harmful influences and ideas." Decide what you think. Then write an editorial for your school newspaper that explains your point of view. Your editorial should deal with the arguments raised by the five people you interviewed.

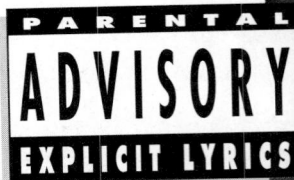

Warning label placed on CDs with explicit lyrics

627

that puts relevance classroom.

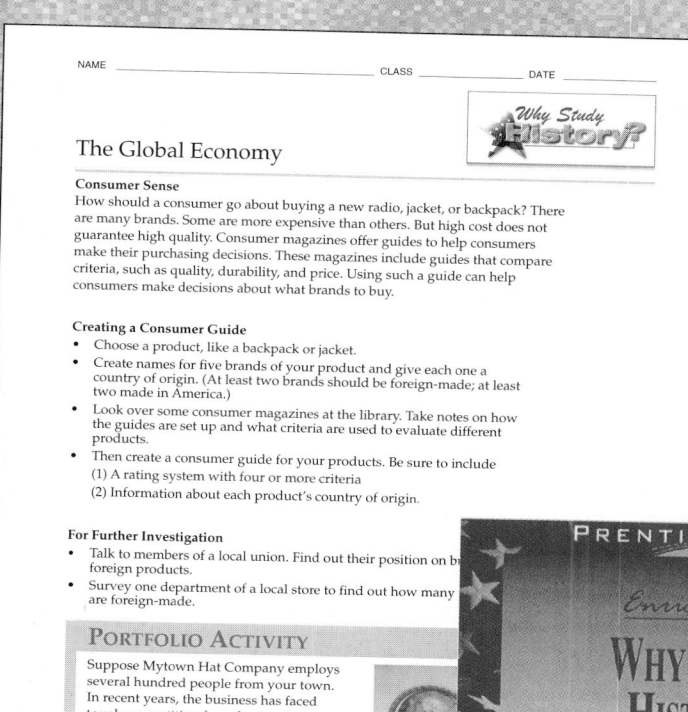

NAME _____ CLASS _____ DATE _____

The Global Economy

Consumer Sense
How should a consumer go about buying a new radio, jacket, or backpack? There are many brands. Some are more expensive than others. But high cost does not guarantee high quality. Consumer magazines offer guides to help consumers make their purchasing decisions. These magazines include guides that compare criteria, such as quality, durability, and price. Using such a guide can help consumers make decisions about what brands to buy.

Creating a Consumer Guide
- Choose a product, like a backpack or jacket.
- Create names for five brands of your product and give each one a country of origin. (At least two brands should be foreign-made; at least two made in America.)
- Look over some consumer magazines at the library. Take notes on how the guides are set up and what criteria are used to evaluate different products.
- Then create a consumer guide for your products. Be sure to include
  (1) A rating system with four or more criteria
  (2) Information about each product's country of origin.

For Further Investigation
- Talk to members of a local union. Find out their position on b___ foreign products.
- Survey one department of a local store to find out how many ___ are foreign-made.

PORTFOLIO ACTIVITY

Suppose Mytown Hat Company employs several hundred people from your town. In recent years, the business has faced tough competition from foreign hat manufacturers. What if your city council decided to give Mytown Hat Company a large tax break? Would you support this decision? Write a letter to the editor of your town newspaper, stating your opinions and reasoning.

© Prentice-Hall, Inc.

Chapt___
Chapter 1 *Modern Amer___*

PRENTICE HALL
SURVEY AND MODERN AMERICAN HISTORY EDITIONS

Enrichment

WHY STUDY HISTORY?

- **Chapter-by-Chapter Connections Between Past and Present**

- **Ready-to-Use Student Activities**

AMERICA
PATHWAYS TO THE PRESENT

In the Teaching Resources

Additional activities extend the lesson strand with activities for each chapter.

In the Teacher's Edition

Why Study History? lesson plans support and enrich instruction, encouraging students to respond and participate.

Class Discussion

Discuss with the class why and how Americans commemorate history. For a more thorough examination of the issue, see the activity folder in the Resource Options below.

ACTIVITY
STUDENT PARTICIPATION

Planning a Commemoration
Ask students to read the text. Then divide the class into small groups. Have each group consider a fitting way that your town might commemorate the 150th anniversary of the Civil War (in the year 2015). Each project should:
- **include a finished product, such as an activity, skit, monument design, or presentation**
- **reflect what the war meant to your town**
- **show what the war has come to mean today**

Have each group present its project to the class.

Follow up Discuss how students celebrated the past Memorial Day.

Using the Internet
Students can learn more about commemorating history by exploring links in the *America: Pathways to the Present* Web site at:

http://www.Pathways.phschool.com

Assessment
See the Lesson Plans folder, pp. 24–27, for rubrics on assessing Class Participation Projects.

More ways to make key conten[t]

With more kinds of learning support than any other program gives them, students of all ability levels benefit from the features of *America: Pathways to the Present*. Right in the Student Edition, reading strategies and a rich variety of visual learning tools focus students' attention on key content. Read the text and compare: our writers have constructed a narrative that is powerful and engaging, and truly conveys the impact of the key events.

SECTION PREVIEW

Objectives

1 Analyze the causes and effects of the red scare and the labor strikes of 1919.
2 Describe key features of the Republican administrations of the 1920s.
3 Compare the Harding and Coolidge presidencies.
4 *Key Terms* Define: communism; red scare; isolationism; disarmament; quota; Teapot Dome scandal; Kellogg-Brand Pact.

Main Idea

Republican administrations of the 1920s pursued pro-business economic policies and an isolationist foreign policy.

Reading Strategy

Creating an Outline Copy the headings in this section. As you read, write down at least two key points under each heading.

Main Idea CONNECTIONS

What caused the increased demand for electric power in the 1920s?

Reading Strategies

America: Pathways to the Present is the only program with reading strategies built right into the Student Edition. Key points throughout every section are reinforced with thinking exercises that focus student attention, develop sophisticated study skills, and keep students involved in the narrative.

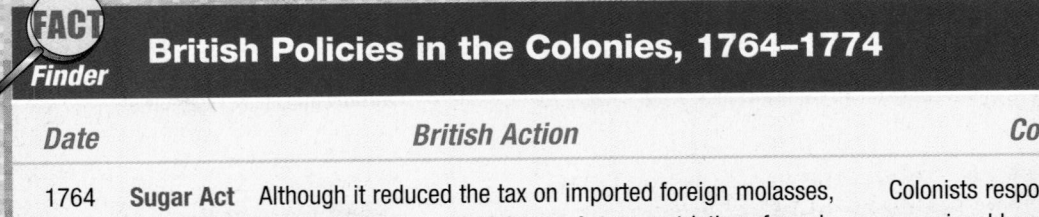

FACT Finder

British Policies in the Colonies, 1764–1774

Date	British Action	Col...
1764	**Sugar Act** Although it reduced the tax on imported foreign molasses, the law, unlike its predecessor the Molasses Act, was strictly enforced.	Colonists respon... occasional boyco...
1765	**Stamp Act** The first direct taxation of colonists, the Stamp...	

Information Graphics

Clear charts, graphs, and timelines reinforce concepts and event sequences for visual learners. Careful instruction teaches graphic comprehension and ties historical and social topics to related subjects across the curriculum.

Tea Imported from England, 1764–1775

ccessible.

 ## TURNING POINT: *The Declaration of Independence*

The Declaration of Independence states that governments derive their power from "the consent of the governed." As the time line below indicates, the right of the people to vote has been steadily broadened.

1776
The Declaration of Independence is signed.

1870
The Fifteenth Amendment grants African American males the right to vote.

1965
The Voting Rights Act of 1965 protects the voting rights of African Americans.

1971
The Twenty-sixth Amendment lowers the voting age to 18.

| 1800 | 1900 | 2000 |

1818
Constitutions of new western states, unlike earlier state constitutions, do not limit the vote to owners of property.

1920
The Nineteenth Amendment grants women the right to vote.

Leslie's

6

Benny Goodman's Clarinet

Known as the "King of Swing," Goodman began his jazz career in 1923. His "big band" helped make jazz popular with white audiences, but he preferred small groups. Goodman was also a classical performer who made recordings with leading symphony orchestras.

7 1920s Jazz Band

This band, which was photographed in St. Louis, is unidentified. The band played New Orleans-style jazz.

American **ARTIFACTS**

FROM EXHIBITIONS AND COLLECTIONS
AT THE SMITHSONIAN INSTITUTION'S
NATIONAL MUSEUM OF AMERICAN HISTORY

THE GROWTH OF JAZZ

Today rock or hip hop might be your musical choice, but in the 1920s and 1930s, jazz shook the walls of dance clubs. Have you heard of Duke Ellington? Dizzy Gillespie? Benny Goodman? They were just a few of the musicians whose trumpets, saxophones, and clarinets blended to create one of music's most popular styles—jazz. See **1** and **2**.

One reason for jazz's popularity was that its offbeat, spontaneous rhythms reflected the lively spirit of the generation. Young people hungry for expression flocked to the dance halls. The flapper with her jazz-style clothes became a symbol of what came to be known as the Jazz Age. The short dresses and fake ... were new and daring, shocking many in the

More options for instruction than any

Easy-to-access, **fully indexed**, chapter-by-chapter organization of *Teaching Resources* saves you time: it's simple to find what you need. Whether you have specific curricular requirements, your students have special needs, or you want to enrich instruction with additional primary sources or visual learning tools, you'll know where to look.

All Teaching Resources are also available electronically on CD-ROM when you get **Resources Pro®** with Planning Express®

History Alive! United States History Activity Pack

Developed in partnership with Teachers' Curriculum Institute (TCI), provides chapter-by-chapter correlation for unique, student-centered approach to history instruction.

Block Scheduling Support

No other program provides the detailed block scheduling support that comes with our kit.

...ther program.

Teaching Resources

Investigate history with documents such as Primary Sources, Visual Learning activities, Decision Making, Great Debates and History's Lasting Impact.

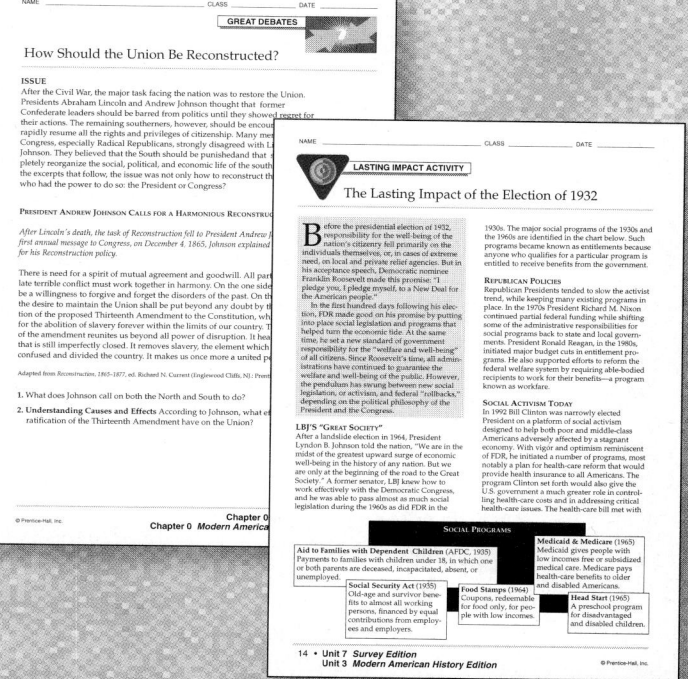

BACKGROUND

Recent Scholarship

Feared and revered Confederate general Thomas Jackson earned his nickname *Stonewall* at the First Battle of Bull Run. Confederate General Bee, attempting to rally his men in a sea of swirling chaos, shouted out, "There is Jackson, standing like a stonewall!" At the time, most people assumed that Bee was praising Jackson for his courage and steadfastness. Immediately after the war, however, some Jackson critics offered another interpretation: They contend that Bee wanted Jackson to advance and that his comment was filled with disdain and dismay. James I. Robertson Jr, in *Stonewall Jackson: The Man, The Soldier, the Legend,* attempts to put that interpretation to rest.

Teacher's Edition

Recent Scholarship notes are provided at point of use, so students understand the vigorous and dynamic process of interpretation that makes history live. Throughout each chapter, inset notes support customized lesson features right where you need them—so it's simple to meet the needs of all your students.

Customize for
English Language Learners

Ask students to write the following column headings on a piece of paper: Union Tactics, Confederate Tactics, Union Victories, Confederate Victories. As they read, have them fill in details from the text in the appropriate column.

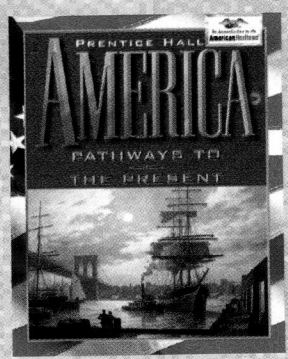

Exclusive Student Performance succeed in three key areas.

Not offered by any other program, this specially developed Student Performance Pack for *America: Pathways to the Present* enhances performance with resources in the areas of reading, test taking, and English language development.

Student Performance Pack

STUDENT PERFORMANCE PACK

PRENTICE HALL
AMERICA
PATHWAYS TO THE PRESENT

PRENTICE HALL
SOCIAL STUDIES

STANDARDIZED TEST PREP HANDBOOK

◆ SAT and ACT Activities and Practice, including:
   Critical Reading
   Analogies
   Sentence Completion
   English Language Usage and Mechanics
◆ Effective Study Skills
◆ Test-Taking Tips
◆ Writing Composition Activities

IMPROVE YOUR TEST SCORES

PRENTICE HALL
AMERICA
PATHWAYS TO THE PRESENT
Guided Reading Audiotapes
English Version
Teaching Guide

Interactive Student Tutorial
PRENTICE HALL
AMERICA
PATHWAYS TO THE PRESENT

PRENTICE HALL
AMERICA
PATHWAYS TO THE PRESENT
Guide to the Essentials

INCLUDES:

■ Easy-to-follow text and graphic organizers
■ At-a-glance correlation and Modern America
■ Key Events in America
■ Key Vocabulary
■ Chapter Tests

PRENTICE HALL
AMERICA
PATHWAYS TO THE PRESENT
Guide to the Essentials, Spanish Edition

...DES:

...chart for Survey ...istory editions

...istory

ESSENTIAL CONTENT AT A GLANCE

TEACHER'S MANUAL
AMERICA
PATHWAYS TO THE PRESENT
Guide to the Essentials, English *and* Spanish

INCLUDES:

■ Answers to all review and test questions in Guide to the Essentials and Spanish Resources
■ Strategies for reaching students of varying abilities
■ Letter Home in English and Spanish

PLUS...
The entire text of the Student Edition is available separately in an exclusive series of audiotapes.

PRENTICE HALL

Pack helps students

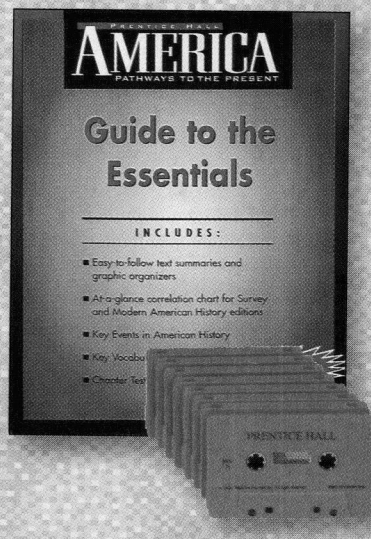

1 Reading

Guide to the Essentials of U.S. History, English and Spanish
For every section of the student book you'll find

- a narrative summary
- a graphic summary
- a review of critical content
- review tests assess student comprehension for each chapter

Guided Reading Audiotapes, English and Spanish
For every section of the student book you'll find

- section-by-section summaries
- easy use with the Guide to the Essentials of American History

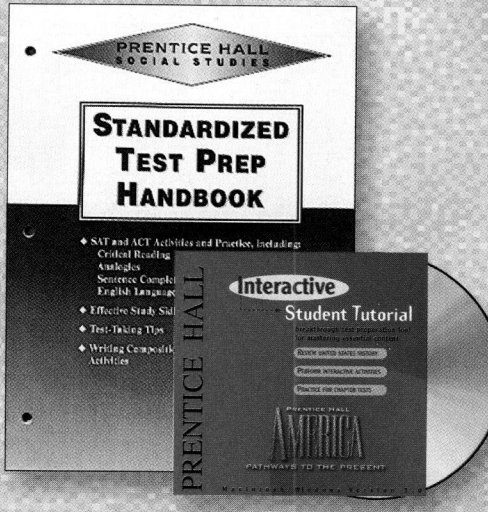

2 Test Taking

Interactive Student Tutorial CD-ROM allows student to
- review American history content
- perform interactive activities
- take practice chapter tests

Standardized Test Prep Handbook
- prepares students for standardized tests and other critical assessment
- provides students with study tips and practice tests

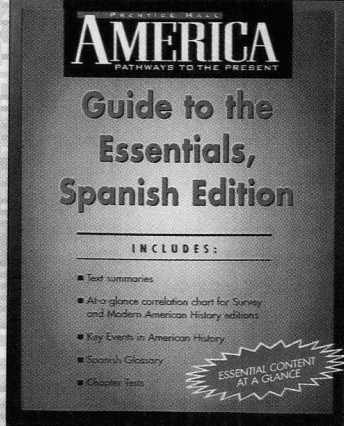

3 English Language Development

Guide to the Essentials of U.S. History
- available in Spanish

Block Scheduling support throughout

America: Pathways to the Present provides a comprehensive array of resources to meet your block scheduling needs. Flexibility is the key to your success in extended class periods. The variety of materials available in the Teacher's Edition, Teaching Resources, Student Performance Pack, Resource Pro® CD-ROM, multimedia packages and on the companion Web site provide numerous opportunities for you to expand coverage of every topic or to cover essential content in limited time.

Block Scheduling

Pacing Suggestions

For 90-minute Blocks

- Teach sections 1 and 2 using Transparency B–9, and the Extended Class Periods Activity on p. 828.
- Teach sections 3 and 4 using the Big Idea Graphic Organizer from Teaching Resources and the Background note on p. 834 for class discussion.

Additional Resources

- Prentice Hall's **American History Block Scheduling Support File** covers over 40 major topics in American history. Included are lesson plans, strategies, primary sources, literature, biographies, Great Debates, art history, simulations, and songs.
- Prentice Hall **United States History Video Collection™** contains 20 videotapes covering American history from beginnings to present.

RESOURCE OPTIONS

Teaching Resources

American History Block Scheduling Support To Arms! The Revolution Begins, found in the Forging a New Nation folder, includes interdisciplinary lesson suggestions and activities for Geography and History, Primary Sources, Biography, and Literature.

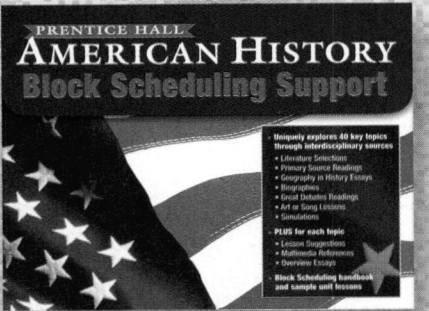

Block Scheduling Support

Lesson plans, Primary Source readings, Literature, Geography and History Essays, Biographies, Great Debates Readings, Art, Simulation Activities, and Songs.

ACTIVITY
EXTENDED CLASS PERIODS

Time: 90 minutes.
Activity: Make a collage depicting the civil rights movement.
Grouping: Groups of three students.
Purpose: Have each student in the group find or make three images relating to the civil rights movement to include in the collage. The group should decide on a title for the artwork, perhaps borrowing a film or television series title (*Mississippi Burning* or *Eyes on the Prize*), using a line from a speech ("I have a dream"), or making up a title. One student from each group should present the finished collage to the class.
Roles: Art designers, caption writers, presenters.
Outcome: Students will identify images that express the goals, attitudes, controversies, and sentiments surrounding the civil rights movement in the 1960s.

Companion Web site

The companion Web site offers online links for all chapter review activities. It also provides key content links and structured support for this chapter for both teachers and students. Visit http:/www.Pathways.phschool.com

Pacing Guide for American History

You can use this pacing guide to plan your American history course. It is based on a total of 88 days of instruction. This guide is just a model. You may need to modify it to meet the needs of your class or your block schedule configuration.

Topics	Periods
Exploration & Discovery (1492–1607)	4
Colonization (1607–1763)	4
Revolution (1763–1789)	4
Federalism (1789–1801)	5
Jeffersonian Democracy (1801–1829)	5
Jacksonian Democracy (1829–1841)	4
Expansion & Slavery (1841–1850)	4
Troubled Decade (1850–1861)	4
The War Between the States (1861–1865)	6
Reconstruction (1865–1877)	4
The West (1865–1890)	4
The Age of Big Business (1865–1890)	4
Imperialism (1890–1901)	3
Progressivism (1901–1917)	4
The Great War (1917–1921)	4
Between Two Wars (1921–1941)	8
World War Two (1941–1945)	5
Cold War and the 1960s (1948–1968)	6
Continuity and Change (1968–Present)	6

Resource Pro® CD-ROM

Plan your lessons to fit your block scheduling needs. Award-winning Resource Pro® with Planning Express® CD-ROM lets you customize daily lesson plans at the touch of a button.

Improve reading comprehension

One problem teachers frequently face is that many students—perhaps even a majority—approach their reading assignments without a positive attitude. As a result, even students who read at average or better rates often fail to fully comprehend what they have read without class discussions or lectures for support. One way to improve student reading comprehension is to encourage the use of basic features in this program designed to make students more active and aware in their approach to the text.

Objectives

1 Describe how the growth of a consumer economy changed American life.
2 Explain how Henry Ford made automobiles affordable for average Americans.
3 Explain why American businesses boomed in the 1920s.
4 *Key Terms* Define: consumer economy; installment plan; assembly line.

Main Idea

During the 1920s, new products and Americans' power to purchase them grew rapidly, producing a decade of enormous business growth.

Reading Strategy

Recognizing Cause and Effect As you read, make a list of factors that caused a business boom in the 1920s.

① Preview

At the beginning of every section students will find:

- Objectives correlate directly to the major subheadings of the text
- A Main Idea that condenses the central implication of the section
- A Reading Strategy that offers a basic method aid students in their reading.

Main Idea
CONNECTIONS

How was Ford able to make cars affordable to many Americans?

② View

While reading, the following text features will help students with comprehension.

- Main Idea Connection questions that link specific content to the section's main idea

SECTION 2 REVIEW

Comprehension

1. *Key Terms* Define: (a) consumer economy; (b) installment plan; (c) assembly line.
2. *Summarizing the Main Idea* Write a paragraph summarizing the main reasons for the business boom of the 1920s.
3. *Organizing Information* Create a cause-and-effect chart on the growth of car production in the 1920s.

Critical Thinking

4. *Analyzing Time Lines* Refer to the time line at the start of the section. Choose three

entries and explain how they influenced modern American life.

5. *Recognizing Ideologies* From what you read about Henry Ford, what conclusions can you draw about what he believed in and valued?

Writing Activity

6. *Writing a Persuasive Essay* Write a newspaper column that might have appeared in the late 1920s. Explain why the government's laissez-faire approach to the economy seems to be working. Support your case with statistics from this section.

③ Review

After reading, students use the followin to understand key content:

- Comprehension questions that return to the section's Key Terms, Main Idea and Reading Strategy
- Writing Activities that allow students to present their understanding of the section in more creative and personal ways.

Text Organized to Aid Student Comprehension

Reading specialists all agree that textbooks should have clear, logical organization, made apparent to the reader through previews, headings and subheadings, main ideas, and topic sentences. The text should also be coherent, connected, and appropriate.

ORGANIZATION How well organized is the text?

1. Does the outline formed by the headings and subheadings convey the main content of the chapter in a clear and logical manner?	See section headings pages 597–602
2. Are the main ideas clear and explicit?	See pages 597–601
3. Is the organization apparent?	See Reading Strategy on page 597

COHERENCE How well are the ideas in the text integrated?

1. Do chapter previews and reviews show how particular content is related to other content in the book?	See Why Study History? Chapter Preview page 596 and Chapter Review pages 628–629
2. Are there transition statements that help the reader move from topic to topic?	See page 600
3. Are there obvious connectives (especially causal connectives) included in the text's explanations?	See pages 610–611
4. Are graphics clearly related to the text?	See Model T Production Plant diagram on pages 604–605

AUDIENCE How well does the text match the reader's prior knowledge and interests?

1. Is content explained adequately for the reader?	See Chapter Summary and Why Study History? on page 628
2. Is the vocabulary level appropriate for the audience?	See Key Terms isolationism and disarmament on page 600 and Section Review Comprehension on page 626
3. Does the text attempt to relate to the reader's experiences?	See Why Study History? on page 628
4. Is the writing interesting and engaging?	See page 603

The examples above are from *America: Pathways to the Present* survey edition Chapter 21.

Connections to literature

History is often described as a series of dramatic stories. Learning history through literature is a perfect match for American history. Reading and analyzing literature—stories, letters, speeches, news articles, eyewitness accounts, excerpts from books—all add to our library of stories, our American history.

The at-a-glance chart to the right offers correlations between text topics and Prentice Hall's *Listening to Literature* audiotapes as well as additional literature activities that are available in the Teaching Resources and **Resource Pro® CD-ROM.**

Other Prentice Hall materials include:

Listening to Music Audio CD

Bring American history to life with period music.

Topic
Exploration & Discovery (1492–1607)
Colonization (1607–1763)
Revolution (1763–1789)
Federalism (1789–1801)
Jeffersonian Democracy (1801–1829)
Jacksonian Democracy (1829–1841)
Expansion and Slavery (1841–1850)
Troubled Decade (1850–1861)
The War Between the States (1861–1865)
Reconstruction (1865–1877)
The West (1865–1890)
The Age of Big Business (1865–1890)
Imperialism (1890–1901)
Progressivism (1901–1917)
The Great War (1917–1921)
Between Two Wars (1921–1941)
World War Two (1941–1945)
The Cold War and Modern Times (1945–present)

Literature Connections

Listening to Literature re audiotapes	Literature Activities
"A Journey Through Texas," by Alvar Núñez Cabeza de Vaca	"Corn Mother," found on **Resource Pro® CD-ROM**
from *The Interesting Narrative of the Life of Olaudah Equiano*, by Olaudah Equiano	Puritan Poetry, found on **Resource Pro® CD-ROM**
from *The Autobiography*, by Benjamin Franklin	Common Sense, found on **Resource Pro® CD-ROM**
"Letter to Her Daughter From the White House," by Abigail Adams	On America, Units 1-2 Teaching Resources folder
"The Devil and Tom Walker," by Washington Irving	American Literature, Units 1-2 Teaching Resources folder
from *Self-Reliance* by Ralph Waldo Emerson	The Pioneers, Units 1-2 Teaching Resources folder
from *Civil Disobedience* by Henry David Thoreau	What Happened in Texas, Units 3-4 Teaching Resources folder
from *My Bondage* and *My Freedom* by Frederick Douglass	Life as a Freeman, found on **Resource Pro® CD-ROM**
"An Occurrence at Owl Creek Bridge," by Ambrose Bierce	The First Battle of Bull Run, Units 3-4 Teaching Resources folder
"An Account of an Experience With Discrimination," by Sojourner Truth	The Story of Free Joe, Units 3-4 Teaching Resources folder
"I Will Fight No More Forever," by Chief Joseph	"The Californian's Tale," Units 3-4 Teaching Resources folder
"Richard Corey," by Edward Arlington Robinson	The Stories of Horatio Alger, Units 5-6 Teaching Resources folder
"This Is Just to Say," by William Carlos Williams	"You're All Right, Teddy," Units 5-6 Teaching Resources folder
"Chicago," by Carl Sandburg	The "New" Woman, found on **Resource Pro® CD-ROM**
"In Another Country," by Ernest Hemingway	A Poet Describes War, found on **Resource Pro® CD-ROM**
"Dust Tracks on a Road," by Zora Neale Hurston	In Search of Work: Migrant Farmers, found on **Resource Pro® CD-ROM**
"The Death of the Ball Turret Gunner," by Randall Jarrell	Hiroshima, Units 7-8 Teaching Resources folder
"Average Waves in Unprotected Waters," by Anne Tyler	Unraveling the Story of Watergate, Units 9-10 Teaching Resources folder

Visit http:/www.Pathways.phschool.com

The companion Web site offers online links for additional literature activities for each chapter. It also provides key content links and structured support for this chapter for both teachers and students.

Themes in American History: A Development Guide

This guide presents the scope and sequence for the seven key themes developed in *America: Pathways to the Present.* These themes are introduced and explained in the beginning of the textbook, and are also highlighted in beginning of every unit. The themes are also addressed in the Teacher's Edition, the Teaching Resources, in the multimedia packages including Resource Pro™ CD-ROM and the Interactive Student Tutorial CD-ROM. The following charts identify their special treatment throughout the entire *America: Pathways to the Present* student textbook.

Government

Student Text
Pathways to the Future, p. 1006
Gun Control and Crime, p. 1016

Turning Points
Declaration of Independence, p. 99

Why Study History?
Your Freedom of Religion is Guaranteed, p. 81
You Have a Voice in Government, p. 115
Government Requires Checks and Balances, p. 927
Government Efficiency Can Be Improved, p. 975

Skills for Life
Expressing Problems Clearly, p. 97
Making Comparisons, p. 179
Distinguishing Fact from Opinion, p. 671

Connections to American Literature
Benjamin Franklin Campaigns for the Constitution, p. 1074
"Battle Hymn of the Republic," by Julia Ward Howe and the Gettysburg Address by Abraham Lincoln, p. 1078
"Letter from the Birmingham Jail," by Martin Luther King, p. 1088

American Heritage®: My Brush with History
Bruce Killebrew & Joan Musbach, p. 900

Geography

Student Text
Pathways to the Future, p. 1006
The Debate over Trade, p. 1039

Turning Points
The Louisiana Purchase, p. 186

Why Study History?
Your Region Has a Unique Economy, p. 255
The Frontier Still Exists Today, p. 307
The Debate over States' Rights Continues, p. 337

Skills for Life
Using Population Density Maps, p. 206
How Maps Show Change Over Time, p. 384
Using a Time Zone Map, p. 526

Connections to American Literature
Hungry Hearts, by Anzia Yezierska, p. 1080

American Heritage®: My Brush with History
James Hall, p. 226

Diversity

Student Text
Pathways to the Future, p. 1006
Immigration and the Golden Door, p. 1008

Turning Points
Civil Rights Act of 1964, p. 833
The Fourteenth Amendment, p. 386

Why Study History?
Your Culture Interacts with Others, p. 55
You Can Join a Political Party, p. 197
Immigration Continues Today, p. 483
Most Women Are in the Work Force, p. 737

Skills for Life
Using Time Lines, p. 50
Reading Tables and Analyzing Statistics, p. 478
Using Autobiography and Biography, p. 825

Connections to American Literature
Incidents in the Life of a Slave Girl, by Harriet Ann Jacobs, p. 1076
Night, by Elie Wiesel, p. 1086
"Straw into Gold," by Sandra Cisneros, p. 1090

American Heritage®: My Brush with History
William M. Dorr, p. 310
An African American Woman in the South, p. 510

Learning in the Information Age

Unlike other programs, the award-winning technology for *America: Pathways to the Present* is designed to offer both options for teachers and innovative learning opportunities for students. All technology is fully correlated to every chapter in the student edition.

Interactive Student Tutorial CD-ROM

A breakthrough test preparation tool, this dual-platform CD-ROM reviews all the essential content of American history, with interactive exercises and practice tests for every chapter.

Listening to Music: The American Experience Audio CD

Bring American history to life with period music.

American Heritage® History of the United States CD-ROM

Co-developed for Prentice Hall, this great resource is the first CD-ROM package that delivers an in-depth, interactive journey through American history.

Visions of America multimedia package

Award-winning videodiscs and videotapes, developed in partnership with WGBH public television in Boston, bring further depth of content and truly dynamic instruction opportunities into your classroom.

United States History Video Collection™

The most comprehensive video collection available today—20 videotapes or 10 videodiscs—provides an engaging, in-depth view of American history.

Decision America multimedia package

Visual explorations of 13 enduring American political issues develop critical thinking skills as well as political participation.

Resource Pro® CD-ROM

Award-winning Resource Pro® with Planning Express® CD-ROM creates and customizes daily lesson plans at the touch of a button.

Test Bank CD-ROM

Our Test Bank CD-ROM makes it simple to tailor assessment tools to the needs of your class.

America: Pathways to the Present Companion website

This exclusive companion Web site—at www.Pathways.phschool.com—features online links for all chapter review activities, with assessment options, as well as numerous history-related sites. Content is updated regularly, so you can stay current on key issues, and is fully correlated to student chapters.

Go to the 'Net with
America: Pathways to the Present

The companion Web site is an integral part of *America: Pathways to the Present.* It provides both teachers and students with comprehensive and structured online support for core content in each chapter of the textbook.

Netscape: Welcome to Prentice Hall's Companion Web Sites

Back | Forward | Home | Reload | Images | Open | Print | Find | Stop

Location: http:www.ph.Pathways.phschool.com

What's New? | What's Cool? | Destinations | Net Search | People | Software

COMPANION WEB PAGES

PRENTICE HALL

TEACHER PAGES

BOOKS
RESOURCES
ASK-AN-EXPERT
FACULTY FORUM
HELP
REMOTE

Pick a chapter:
Chap. 1
GO

AMERICA
PATHWAYS TO THE PRESENT

Why Study History?
activities, with assessment, for each chapter. Each topic examines a key issue or main idea, which helps students understand why the past matters in their lives today.

Turning Point
activities, with assessment. Critical events in the nation's history and their lasting impact.

Chapter Review
activities with assessment options.

American Biographies
for each chapter.

Point-of-use activities,
with assessment, in the Teacher's Edition for each chapter.

Recent Scholarship
with annonated links for each chapter. New information and points of view on historical topics.

Key Documents
with annotated links. Important speeches, amendments, and other documents.

Key Supreme Court Cases
with annotated links.

Learning Styles Lesson Plans
for each chapter. Lesson strategies for various learning styles.

Big Idea Lesson Plans
for each chapter. Strategies to focus on essential content.

Current Events Updates
with annotated links.

Online Quizzes
with self-scoring for each chapter.

Document: Done.

In Association with
AmericanHeritage®

PRENTICE HALL

AMERICA

PATHWAYS TO
THE PRESENT

Andrew Cayton

Elisabeth Israels Perry

Linda Reed

Allan M. Winkler

Prentice
Hall

Needham, Massachusetts
Upper Saddle River, New Jersey
Glenview, Illinois

About the Authors

Andrew Cayton, Ph.D.

Andrew Cayton is Professor of History at Miami University in Oxford, Ohio. He received his B.A. from the University of Virginia and his M.A. and Ph.D from Brown University. Dr. Cayton is an early American historian, specializing in political and social history. He is author of *Frontier Republic: Ideology and Politics in the Ohio Country, 1780–1825* and co-author of *The Midwest and the Nation: Rethinking the History of an American Region.* His most recent book is *Frontier Indiana.*

Linda Reed, Ph.D.

Linda Reed directs the African American Studies Program at the University of Houston. She received her B.S. from Alabama A&M University, her M.A. from the University of Alabama, and her Ph.D. from Indiana University. Dr. Reed's specialization is twentieth-century African American history, particularly the modern-day civil rights era. She is the author of *Simple Decency and Common Sense: The Southern Conference Movement, 1938–1963.*

Elisabeth Israels Perry, Ph.D.

Elisabeth Israels Perry is Research Professor of History at Vanderbilt University in Nashville, Tennessee. She received her Ph.D. in history from the University of California at Los Angeles. Dr. Perry's period of specialization is the late nineteenth and early twentieth centuries. She is the author and coeditor of a number of books, among them *Belle Moskowitz: Feminine Politics and the Exercise of Power in the Age of Alfred E. Smith* and *Women in Action: Rebels and Reformers, 1920–1980.*

Allan M. Winkler, Ph.D.

Allan M. Winkler is Professor of History at Miami University in Oxford, Ohio. He received his B.A. from Harvard University, his M.A. from Columbia University, and his Ph.D. from Yale University. Dr. Winkler's specialization is twentieth-century political and social history. He is author of eight books, including *Home Front U.S.A.: America During World War II* and *Life Under a Cloud: American Anxiety About the Atom.*

American Heritage® *American Heritage* magazine was founded in 1954, and it quickly rose to the position it occupies today: the country's preeminent magazine of history and culture. Dedicated to presenting the past in incisive, entertaining narratives underpinned by scrupulous scholarship, *American Heritage* today goes to more than 300,000 subscribers and counts the country's very best writers and historians among its contributors. Its innovative use of historical illustration and its wide variety of subject matter have gained the publication scores of honors across more than 40 years, among them the National Magazine Awards. American Heritage is also known for the classic illustrated histories it has published over the years.

Cover: Painted in 1996, William G. Muller's *Night Docking at South Street, New York 1895* re-creates the scene around the Brooklyn Bridge, which spanned the East River to link Manhattan and Brooklyn. (Collection of Richard Hastings)

Prentice Hall

ISBN 0-13-053625-3

2 3 4 5 6 7 8 9 10   05 04 03 02 01

Program Reviewers

HISTORIAN REVIEWERS

Program Reviewers

Contents

unit TWO

Balancing Liberty and Order, 1776–1830

120

unit THREE

An Emerging New Nation, 1800–1860   228

Chapter 8   **The Market Revolution, 1812–1845** 230
     1   A Market Economy 231
        American Artifacts: Engines of Change 234
     2   The Northern Section 236
     3   The Southern Section 240
     4   The Growth of Nationalism 244
     5   The Age of Jackson 250
 ★   **Why Study History?** Your Region Has a Unique Economy 255
    Chapter Review 256

Chapter 9   **Religion and Reform, 1800–1850** 258
     1   Middle-Class Reform 259
     2   The Antislavery Movement 266
     3   The Movement for Women's Rights 274
    Turning Point: The Seneca Falls Convention 277
     4   Growing Divisions 279
 ★   **Why Study History?** You Can Help Reform Society 283
    Chapter Review 284

Chapter 10   **Beyond the Mississippi, 1800–1860** 286
     1   The Plains Indians 287
     2   Hispanic North America 291
     3   Trails to the West 297
     4   From Sea to Sea 301
 ★   **Why Study History?** The Frontier Still Exists Today 307
    Chapter Review 308

AmericanHeritage®*My Brush with History* 310

unit FOUR

Division and Uneasy Reunion, 1848–1877

312

unit FIVE

Expansion: Rewards and Costs, 1850–1915   404

unit SIX

The United States on the Brink of Change, 1890–1920 512

unit SEVEN

Boom Times to Hard Times, 1919–1938   594

Table of Contents

unit NINE

The Upheaval of the Sixties, 1960–1975   794

unit
TEN

Continuity and Change, 1968–Present   902

unit ELEVEN

Pathways to the Future   1006

Reference Section

Special Features

American Heritage®
My Brush with History

Eyewitness accounts from American Heritage magazine of ordinary Americans and extraordinary events

AMERICAN BIOGRAPHY

Profiles describing the lives and accomplishments of prominent Americans

Sandra Day O'Connor
(b. 1930)

TURNING POINT

Critical events in the nation's history and their lasting impact

Why Study History?

To understand that . . .

Links between events of the chapter and present-day issues

ECONOMICS CONCEPTS

Historical context and present-day application of important economics concepts

GOVERNMENT CONCEPTS

Historical context and present-day application of important government concepts

SKILLS FOR LIFE

Step-by-step lessons to learn and practice important skills

Notable PRESIDENTS

Biographies of some of the most highly respected Presidents

1861–1865

exploring TECHNOLOGY

Detailed drawings of key advances in technology

**Artifacts from the Smithsonian
Institution's National Museum
of American History**

**An in-depth look at the links between
geography and history**

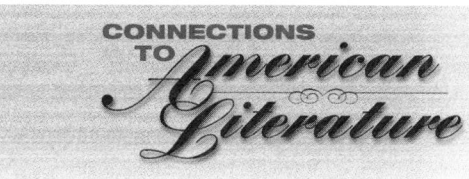

**A collection of literature, songs,
speeches, and memoirs**

Time Lines

**More than 140 time lines that highlight
the critical events in American history**

| 1700 | 1800 | 1900 |

PRIMARY SOURCES

Primary source quotations from famous and ordinary Americans

> ❝They who profess to favor freedom, and yet deprecate [criticize] agitation, are men who want crops without plowing up the ground. . . .❞
>
> —*Frederick Douglass*

PRIMARY SOURCES

"We preach freedom around the world, and we mean it, and we cherish our freedom, here at home. . . . The time has come for this nation to fulfill its promise."

—*President Kennedy*

PRIMARY SOURCES

VOICES FROM ABROAD
Primary source quotations from around the world

Political Cartoons

Cartoons are visual historical documents, which appear in every chapter of the textbook.

PRIMARY SOURCES

Important speeches, amendments, and other documents

> **❝I believe that it must be the policy of the United States to support free peoples who are resisting attempted subjugation.❞**
>
> —*Truman Doctrine,*
> *Harry S. Truman*

COMPARING PRIMARY SOURCES

Primary source quotations on controversial issues of the period

Maps

MAP skills

Grant's stubbornness and Sherman's campaign of total war brought the Civil War to a bloody close. Compare the relative forces of the Union and the Confederacy in the final months of the Civil War. *Movement Why do you think Sherman met with little resistance?*

Final Battles of the Civil War, 1863–1865

Area of main map

Ohio
Pa.
Washington, D.C.
N.J.
W. Va.
Md.
Del.

3. The Wilderness, May 5–6, 1864
4. Spotsylvania, May 8–19, 1864
5. Cold Harbor, June 3, 1864
11. Lee surrenders to Grant, April 9, 1865.
Richmond
6. Petersburg, besieged June 18, 1864– April 2, 1865.

Ohio R.
Kentucky
0   100   200 Miles
0   100   200 Kilometers
Appomattox Court House
Grant
Lee
Grant
Virginia

12. Johnston surrenders to Sherman, April 26, 1865.
Durham Station
Johnston
10. Bentonville, Mar. 19, 1865

2. Chattanooga, Nov. 23–25, 1863
North Carolina
APPALACHIAN MTS.
Sherman
Tennessee

South Carolina
9. Columbia, captured Feb. 17, 1865.

1. Chickamauga, Sept. 19–20, 1863
Georgia
Sherman
Charleston
ATLANTIC OCEAN

7. Atlanta, occupied Sept. 2, 1864.
8. Savannah, captured Dec. 21, 1864.
Alabama

Union states
Confederate states
Union forces
Confederate forces
Union victory
Confederate victory
Inconclusive
Union blockade

Town Pound

North Field

Mill Pond

Pond

Cart Path

Mill Rd.

Great River Meadow

Cow Common

Cart Path

Sudbury R.

Schuylkill R.

Gov. Penn's house

0   1/4   1/2 Mile

0   1/4   1/2 Kilometer

New England towns were more close-knit than those of Pennsylvania.

Fields held in common   House   Schoolhouse

Meeting house   Mill

0   1   2 Miles

0   1   2 Kilometers

Graphs, Charts, and Tables

FACT Finder

National Republicans vs. Jacksonian Democrats, 1820s

National Republicans/Whigs	Jacksonian Democrats
Federal government should take a leadership role	Federal government should remain as inactive as possible
Federal government should support internal improvements, such as roads and bridges	The individual states should be responsible for internal improvements
In favor of national bank	Against national bank
Tended to be middle-class or well-established Protestants	Tended to be slaveholders, small farmers, non-Protestants, and working class

Work Stoppages, 1882–1900

Year

Source: *Historical Statistics of the United States, Colonial Times to 1970*

Reasons for Work Stoppages

Source: *Historical Statistics of the United States, Colonial Times to 1970*

Interpreting Graphs A severe economic depression helped cause a steep decline in union membership in the 1870s. But the 1880s and 1890s saw growth in the number of members and in the number of work stoppages. *Economics* *What were the major reasons for work stoppages in the late 1800s?*

HOW TO USE THIS BOOK
Chapters and Sections

CHAPTER FOCUS
Every chapter begins with a brief summary of the important content to be covered in the chapter.

WHY STUDY HISTORY?
This statement previews the issue that will be covered in the Why Study History? connections page at the end of the chapter.

CHAPTER 18 Becoming a World Power
1890-1913

CHAPTER FOCUS

This chapter describes the years when the United States grew to be a world power. Growth in American industry pushed business and political leaders to look for new markets abroad. Some Americans, inspired by grand dreams of an empire, pursued new territory as well.

The Why Study History? page at the end of this chapter explores the connection between United States participation in world affairs in the early 1900s and its role in the global community today.

VIEWING HISTORY
Edward Moran captured the triumph of the Great White Fleet in his 1899 painting *Return of the Conquerors*. **Foreign Relations Why did the United States expand its influence overseas?**

514

1867
United States buys Alaska and annexes Midway Islands

1875
United States signs trade agreement with Hawaii

1881
Congress establishes Naval Advisory Board

1884
American business-man granted long-term lease in Costa Rica

1890
Alfred Mahan publishes The Influence of Sea Power Upon History

1865	1875	1885	1895

1 The Pressure to Expand

SECTION PREVIEW

Objectives

1. Explain some of the reasons for the growth of imperialism around the world.
2. Summarize the American view regarding imperialism prior to 1890.
3. *Key Terms* Define: imperialism; nationalism; annex; banana republic.

Main Idea

In the late 1800s, as European nations took over vast areas in Africa and Asia, American leaders looked to expand American influence abroad.

Reading Strategy

Reinforcing Main Ideas As you read, create a list of the pressures that led the United States to adopt a policy of political and economic expansion overseas.

By the late 1800s, the industrialists, inventors, and workers of the United States had built a powerful industrial economy. But the overproduction of food and goods led to financial panic and depression. Labor and farmers protested their plight, helping to convince business and political leaders that the United States must secure new markets abroad. Some people also began to believe that the United States had a duty to carry democratic values and Christianity to others around the globe.

Growth of Imperialism

Meanwhile, as the maps on the next page show, Europe had reached new heights in its quest for territories to rule. The late 1800s marked the peak of European imperialism, with much of Africa and Asia under foreign domination. Under **imperialism,** stronger nations attempt to create empires by dominating weaker nations—economically, politically, culturally, or militarily.

Why Imperialism Grew Several factors accounted for the burst of imperialistic activity in the late 1800s.

(1) *Economic factors.* The growth of industry in Europe created an increased need for natural resources, such as rubber and petroleum. Manufacturing nations also required new markets in which to sell their manufactured goods.

(2) *Nationalist factors.* Competition among European nations for large empires was the result of **nationalism,** or devotion to one's nation. For example, when France acquired colonies in West Africa in the late 1800s, rival nations Great Britain and Germany seized lands nearby to stop French expansion.

(3) *Military factors.* Advances in military technology produced European armies and navies that were far superior to those in Africa and Asia. Europe's growing navies

BEST QUALITY · GRAPEFRUIT
PACIFIC EXPORTER
BRAND

Businesses, such as this fruit grower, eagerly sought new markets abroad.

SECTION 1 REVIEW

Comprehension

1. *Key Terms* Define: (a) imperialism; (b) nationalism; (c) annex; (d) banana republic.
2. *Summarizing the Main Idea* Why did United States policymakers feel the need to secure new markets abroad in the late 1800s?
3. *Organizing Information* Create a web diagram that describes the major arguments for American expansionism. Label the center circle *Arguments for Expansionism.* Include supporting details in at least three surrounding circles.

Critical Thinking

4. *Analyzing Time Lines* Review the time line at the start of the section. Which event, in your opinion, best reflects American expansionist policies?
5. *Drawing Conclusions* What factors aided European imperialism in the late 1800s?

Writing Activity

6. *Writing an Expository Essay* Research and write a brief essay tracing the history of American expansionism before 1880. Be sure to include specific examples of expansionism in your essay.

HOW TO USE THIS BOOK
Technology and Learning

The Internet and the World Wide Web

The **Internet** is a global computer network that began in the 1960s as a U.S. Department of Defense project linking university computer science departments. The Internet has since grown to include millions of business, governmental, educational, and individual computers around the world. The **World Wide Web,** or "the Web" for short, is a collection of linked electronic files. Using programs called browsers, Internet users can find out what files are available on the Web and then access those files.

How to Search the Internet

There are two basic ways to find information on the Internet.

- **Use the URL.** If you know the address of the Web site you want to visit, you can go there directly by typing in the site's URL. (URL stands for Universal Resource Locator; each Web site has its own URL.)
- **Use a search engine.** You can search for information using a search engine, such as Yahoo! or Infoseek, by typing key words representing the topic you want to research. The search engine will then scan the Internet and list all of the Web sites with information on your topic.

Whichever method you use, you will encounter Web sites containing **hyperlinks.** These appear on your screen as colored or underlined text or as

CD-ROM SUPPORT

*The **Interactive Student Tutorial CD-ROM** provides section-by-section review of chapter content through interactive review activities and practice tests.*

Chapter 18 Review

Chapter Summary

The major concepts of Chapter 18 are presented below. See also *Guide to the Essentials of American History* or *Interactive Student Tutorial CD-ROM,* which contains interactive review activities, time lines, helpful hints, and test practice for Chapter 18.

Reviewing the Main Ideas
By the 1890s, farms and factories in the United States were producing more than the nation could consume. Soon, many business and political leaders began to pursue new markets abroad. Inspired by dreams of an empire, some Americans pushed for new territory as well. American expansion caused some citizens to raise doubts about the morality of imperialism.

Section 1: The Pressure to Expand
In the late 1800s, as European nations took over vast areas in Africa and Asia, American leaders looked to expand American influence abroad.

Section 2: The Spanish–American War
A swift American victory in the Spanish-American War confirmed the nation's status as a world power, but it left some people arguing over how to govern newly acquired territories.

Section 3: Expansion Under Roosevelt and Taft
President Theodore Roosevelt conducted a vigorous foreign policy that suited the new status of the United States as a world power. Although President William Howard Taft continued Roosevelt's policies, he preferred a more subtle approach to influencing other nations.

Section 4: Debating America's New Role
After the Spanish-American War, the debate intensified over whether it was appropriate for the United States to build an empire.

Why Study History?

Since the 1890s, the United States has played an active role in world affairs. On numerous occasions, Americans have provided military and economic aid to countries in need.

538

Key Terms

For each of the terms below, write a sentence explaining how it relates to this chapter.

1. annex
2. Open Door Policy
3. Great White Fleet
4. Roosevelt Corollary
5. imperialism
6. sphere of influence
7. nationalism
8. dollar diplomacy
9. jingoism
10. banana republic

Comprehension

1. Briefly explain the arguments of Alfred T. Mahan, Henry Cabot Lodge, and Albert J. Beveridge regarding expansionism.
2. Describe how the 1895 dispute between the United States and Great Britain reaffirmed the Monroe Doctrine.
3. Why did the American public favor war with Spain in 1898?
4. What was the Open Door Policy, and why was it important for the United States?
5. Describe Theodore Roosevelt's approach to foreign policy.
6. How did the Roosevelt Corollary affect United States policy in Latin America?
7. Explain President Taft's policy of dollar diplomacy.
8. Explain why anti-imperialists believed that imperialism betrayed basic American principles.

Using Graphic Organizers

On a separate sheet of paper, copy the multi-flow map to show the causes and effects of American expansion during the late 1800s and early 1900s. Provide at least three causes and three effects.

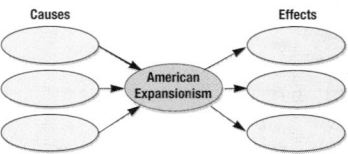

Causes   American Expansionism   Effects

icons. Hyperlinks act as doorways to other documents. When you click your mouse on hyperlinked text or graphics, a new document appears on your screen. That document may come from the same computer as the Web site you just left, or from one thousands of miles away.

Tips for Successful Searches

- **Keep your search focused.** Because the Internet contains so much interesting information, it is easy to "wander off" and lose track of your goal in searching. To avoid this, you should establish a specific research goal before your begin your Internet search.

- **Make bookmarks for your favorite Web sites.** A bookmark is a note to your computer to "remember" the location of the Web site. You can reach any bookmarked site from any other site with a simple click of your mouse.

- **Use specific key words.** If your key words are too general, your search might turn up thousands of Web sites. Many search engines have useful tips on searching with key words.

- **Evaluate the quality of Internet information.** Not all of the information available on the Internet is appropriate for your research. Ask a teacher, parent, or librarian for help in evaluating the reliability and appropriateness of Web sites and information.

Analyzing Political Cartoons ▶

1. The caption to this 1904 political cartoon was: "HIS 128th BIRTHDAY. 'Gee but this is an awful stretch!'" (a) Whose birthday is it? (b) How do you know? (c) What is the "awful stretch" referring to? (d) How do you know?

2. What is the cartoonist's view on United States imperialsim?

Critical Thinking

1. *Applying the Chapter Skill* Review the time zone map on page 526. Name two cities on the map that are in the same time zone as New York City.

2. *Identifying Central Issues* How did the popular philosophy of social Darwinism make it easier for some Americans to embrace imperialist policies in the late 1800s?

3. *Drawing Conclusions* During the late 1800s, the press fanned the flames of the Spanish-American War by publishing sensational stories about Spanish cruelties in Cuba. On what current issues has the press played a major role in influencing public opinion?

4. *Distinguishing Fact from Opinion* President McKinley's Secretary of State, John Hay, referred to the Spanish-American War as "a splendid little war." Can you think of any Americans, in addition to anti-imperialists, who might disagree with Hay?

INTERNET ACTIVITY

For your portfolio:
CREATE A TIME LINE

Access Prentice Hall's *America: Pathways to the Present* site at **www.Pathways.phschool.com** for the specific URL to complete the activity. Additional resources and related Web sites are also available.

Read the biography of William Howard Taft and create a time line of his career. Write a paragraph summarizing Taft's professional life. How would you characterize his career? What do you consider his most important achievement? What did Taft consider his most important achievement?

INTERNET ACTIVITY

*Every Chapter Review has an Internet activity based on key content of the chapter. A **Companion Web Site** (shown below) featuring online links and assessment activities provides structured chapter-by-chapter support for all Chapter Review activities and important review material for key content.*

ANALYZING DOCUMENTS ◀ ▶ INTERPRETING DATA

Turn to the "American Voices" quotation on page 528.

1. Theodore Roosevelt is suggesting that his policies made it (a) impossible to build the canal. (b) possible to return Panama to Colombia. (c) easier to build the canal. (d) necessary to submit a State paper to Congress.

2. What is the most likely reason Roosevelt felt he had to justify his policies regarding the Panama Canal even after he left office?

(a) Colombia was asking for the return of the Canal Zone. (b) Anti-imperialists were complaining about his high-handed methods. (c) Panama was asking for more money. (d) Congress was considering returning the land to Panama.

3. *Writing* Do you think Roosevelt's argument justifies his actions? Explain your reasoning.

Connecting to Today

Essay Writing The United States still intervenes in foreign countries when its interests are threatened. Write a letter to the editor of a newspaper in which you argue either for or against an interventionist foreign policy. Research recent examples of United States actions in foreign countries and use them to support your arguments.

Why Study History?

To understand that . . .

"*I know no way of judging the future but by the past,*" wrote Patrick Henry in 1775. *The four boldfaced statements on these pages help explain the continuing relevance and drama of historical events. To explore the many links between the issues of yesterday and today, every chapter in this textbook contains a Why Study History? page immediately before the Chapter Review.*

History Is Everyone's Story

American history is not only the story of famous heroes but also that of ordinary people. Remarkable leaders like Washington and Lincoln have guided the country well in times of crisis, while other men and women have been outstanding in business, science, and education. But America's greatness also rests on the hard work and dedicated effort of countless others. Since the country began, they have plowed the fields, built the cities, raised the families, fought the wars, and done all the everyday things that add up to a country's history. While we may never know all their names, we know these people's stories—because they are our story, too.

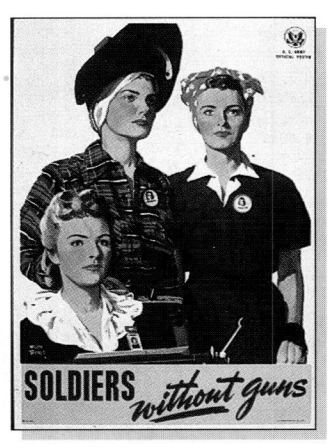

SOLDIERS *without guns*

The Present Is Linked to the Past

Throughout history, Americans have looked for new frontiers. Pioneers pushed westward into unknown territory, across rugged mountains and wide prairies. They built new towns and added new states to the nation. The frontier spirit has stayed with us, giving Americans a strong sense of energy, personal freedom, and individualism. More recently, Americans have looked toward farther frontiers, pioneering in space with the first moon landing and probes to distant planets.

History Is Unpredictable

You might mistakenly think of history as a collection of cut-and-dried facts—names, dates, laws, statistics. But in fact, history is full of unexpected twists and turns, situations that could easily have turned out differently and so changed the course of many people's lives. The Pilgrims' first landfall in America, for instance, was due to a storm that blew their ship off course. President Harry Truman's election victory in 1948 was an upset that surprised almost everyone. Like many other events, it showed that history is never predictable and often has surprise endings.

Real People Change the Course of History

History is not only about yesterday's events—it is about today's headlines and tomorrow's news. As you are reading this, someone in the United States is taking an action that could change history. That person may not be famous or powerful, but may be just an ordinary citizen, like one of the marchers at the March on Washington in 1963. Ordinary people from many different backgrounds—like you and your friends and neighbors—are the people who really write history. And that is one answer to the question, Why study history? Because you are a part of it.

THEMES IN AMERICAN HISTORY

Much of what you learn about American history can be better understood if you view events as part of a larger pattern. The themes listed below apply to all periods of American history and can help you link events across time. You will see these themes throughout this textbook, at the start of each unit and in the captions that accompany photographs and other graphics.

Government

The United States was founded on such ideals as human equality, limited government, and democratic representation. For more than two centuries, Americans have worked to make their form of government live up to those ideals. Formerly excluded groups such as women and African Americans, for example, have demanded and won equal rights.

Geography

Geography has shaped the growth of American power and prosperity, as Americans have benefited from their nation's large size and many natural resources. In addition, because the United States faces both the Atlantic and Pacific oceans, it has had profitable trade with both Europe and Asia.

Diversity

People from many nations, representing an extraordinary range of ethnic, racial, national, and religious groups, have come to the United States and become Americans. This diversity is a source of tremendous strength for the United States, but also produces conflict.

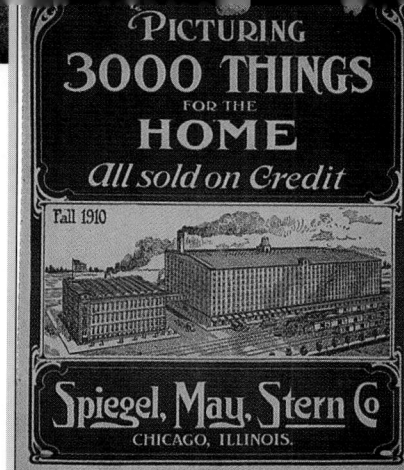

Economics

Abundant natural resources, combined with an economic system that encourages individual initiative, have made the American economy staggeringly successful. Throughout our nation's history, economic opportunity has attracted immigrants to the United States.

Culture

American culture is as diverse as American people, drawing on the traditions of the nation's many immigrants. American culture also reflects the nation's democratic ideals, as Americans have pioneered in forms of entertainment, such as baseball and movies, that are aimed at mass audiences.

Foreign Relations

In its early history the United States, focusing its energies on westward expansion, sought to remain free from European entanglements. By the twentieth century, however, this nation had become a major world power, with worldwide commitments and responsibilities.

Science & Technology

Innovations in science and technology have played critical roles in American history. These innovations—the cotton gin, the airplane, nuclear power, the polio vaccine, and the computer, to name just a few—have contributed to this nation's security and prosperity.

THE FIVE GEOGRAPHIC THEMES

*L*ike history, geography can be divided into themes. Geographers use five themes, described below, to organize their study of the world. You will find these themes in the captions that accompany the maps in this textbook. In addition, a Geography and History feature in each unit explores one of the themes in greater depth.

Location

The most basic of the geographic themes, location tells where a place is. Location can be expressed in two ways. *Absolute location* describes a place's position on the globe as determined by latitude and longitude. *Relative location* describes a place's position in relation to other places. While each place can have only one absolute location, its relative location can be expressed in a number of ways. For example, the relative location of the Smithsonian Institution can be described as "west of the Capitol," "at the Mall," or "east of the Washington Monument."

Place

Place describes the characteristics that make a location distinctive. There are two kinds of characteristics. *Physical characteristics* include landforms, vegetation, and climate. *Human characteristics* include the culture, economy, and government of the people who live in a place. Each place in the United States—indeed, on Earth—has a unique combination of physical and human characteristics.

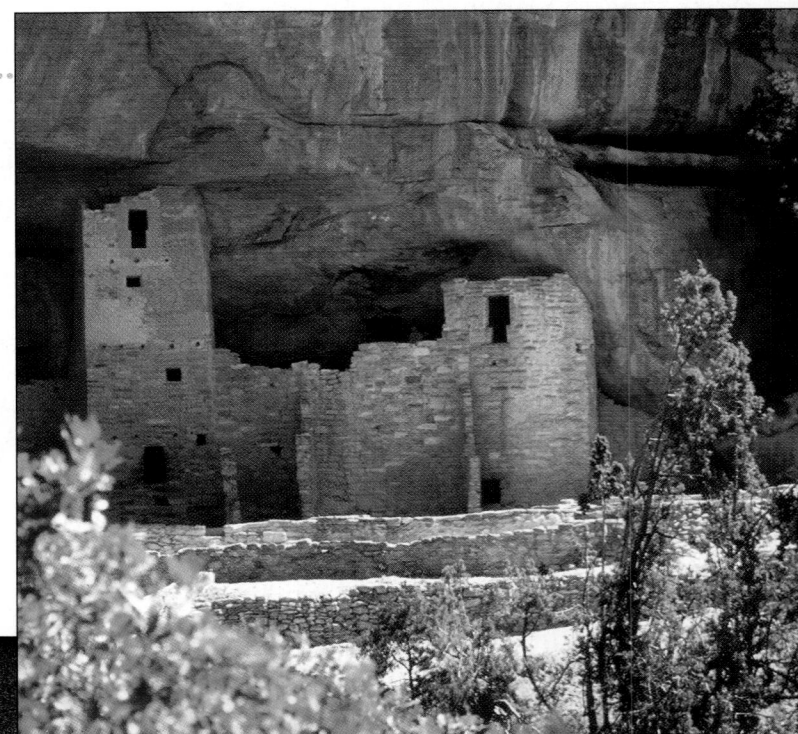

Movement

People, goods, and ideas regularly travel from one place to another. Examples from American history include the continuing immigration of new Americans, the westward migration of Americans through the 1800s, and the spread of American ideals of individual liberty through the world following the American Revolution. Today's advances in communication and transportation make movement easier and more common than ever.

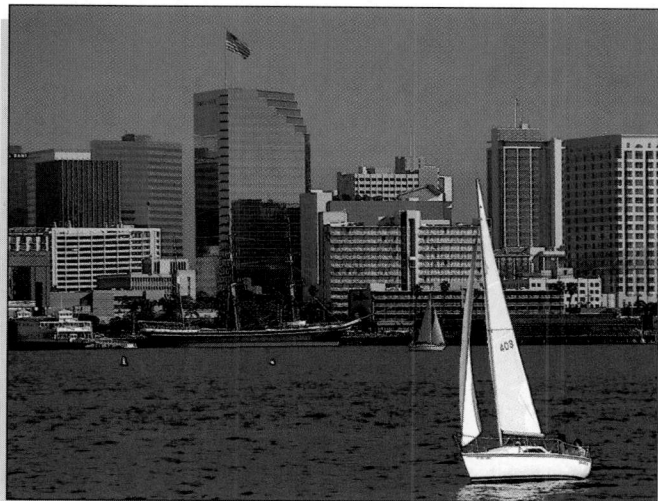

Regions

A region is any group of places with at least one common characteristic. Regions can be any size, and a single place can belong to several different regions. The city of San Diego, for example, is part of California (a political region), the Sunbelt (a demographic region), and the Pacific Rim (an economic region).

Human-Environment Interaction

Human-environment interaction explores the ways in which people use and modify their environment. The Brooklyn Bridge, the coal mines of West Virginia, the wheat fields of the Plains states, Hoover Dam—all are examples of Americans modifying their environment in order to produce or extract needed resources or to make movement more efficient.

Origins of a New Society to 1783

Introducing the Unit

Using Historical Evidence

Have students examine the painting on the right. Explain that Europeans were fascinated by Native Americans, and that they interpreted the scanty information they received about the inhabitants of the Americas according to images and patterns familiar to them.

Ask students what event is portrayed in the painting. What incorrect impressions of an encounter between Europeans and Native Americans does the painting present? How might a Native American artist have portayed this event?

Themes in American History

Direct students' attention to the Unit Themes. Point out that each chapter in this unit has its own theme. To teach this unit thematically, you may wish to use the Forging a New Nation folder in **American History Block Scheduling Support.**

Using the Time Line

To provide students with practice in using a time line to connect key events in the United States with key events in the world, ask questions such as these: (1) When did Spain establish a settlement in St. Augustine, Florida? *(1565)* (2) What other regions did Europeans explore or colonize in the 1400s and 1500s? *(Africa, Mexico, South America.)* (3) When did the France lose control of its North American colonies? *(1763)*

unit ONE

Origins of a New Society

TO 1783

W hen the American colonists overthrew British rule in the American Revolution, the new nation they created was already a society peopled from different parts of the world. Native Americans and European colonizers and the people they forcibly removed from Africa shaped the growth and direction of the United States. Their rich and varied pasts and their sometimes violent interactions can be felt throughout our nation's history.

Chapter 1	The Atlantic World *c.700 B.C.– A.D.1600*	
Chapter 2	European Colonization of the Americas *1492–1752*	
Chapter 3	Growth of the American Colonies *1689–1754*	
Chapter 4	The Road to Independence *1754–1783*	

UNIT THEMES

Diversity North America was home to a variety of Native American groups.

Economics The competition between European countries for trading partners led directly to European settlement in North America.

Government American colonists, unhappy with British rule, fought for and won complete independence.

EVENTS IN THE UNITED STATES

1492 Columbus sails to the Americas

1565 Spanish settle St. Augustine, Florida

1607 English settle Jamestown, Virginia

1450   1500   1550   1600

EVENTS IN THE WORLD

1498 Vasco da Gama completes voyage around Africa

1521 Hernando Cortés conquers Mexico's Aztec empire

1533 Francisco Pizarro destroys the Inca empire

1614 Dutch East India Company founded

▶ RESOURCE OPTIONS

Teaching Resources

 Units 1–2 folder Contains instructional materials organized by chapter.

● **VIEWING HISTORY** *Europeans Encountering Indians*, painted around 1700, captures the stark contrasts between the cultures brought together by European exploration. ***Diversity* Compare and contrast the cultures of Native Americans, Europeans, and West Africans.**

Lexington battle drum

1739
Slaves revolt in North Carolina's Stono Rebellion

1763
Britain defeats France for control of eastern North America

1776
Turning Point: Declaration of Independence (p. 99)

1781
British surrender at Battle of Yorktown

1650   1700   1750   1800

1689
England's Glorious Revolution produces a bill of rights

1756
Start of the Seven Years' War between France and Britain

1781
Peruvians revolt against Spanish rule

 RESOURCE OPTIONS

Media and Technology

Color Transparencies Specific transparencies are referenced throughout the chapters at appropriate points of use. For this unit, see American Photo, B-1; Our Multicultural Heritage, C-1; Time Lines, E-1 and E-2; Links Across Time, J-1; Political Cartoons, K-1; and Historical Maps, L-1.

 Visions of America "Scenes of an Era: Origins of a New Society" located on videodisc side 1 and on videotape 1. Lesson plans for "Scenes of an Era" can be found in the Visions of America Guidebook.

Side 1, Chapter 2

Answer to . . .

Viewing History *Answers will vary but students should consider how communities worked, and various attitudes toward religion, trade, and government.*

1

The Atlantic World, c. 700 B.C. – C. A.D. 1600

Managing Time and Instruction

INSTRUCTION SUPPORT

These materials for instruction are provided for **each section** in the **Teaching Resources.** See **Units 1–2 folder** for Enrichment Support:

- Reproducible Lesson Plans in Lesson Plans folder • Learning Styles Lesson Plans in Learning Styles Lesson Plans folder • Big Idea Graphic Organizers in Big Idea Graphic Organizer folder
- Guided Reading and Review • Quizzes • Test Preparation Practice booklet

DAILY LESSON	ENRICHMENT SUPPORT
1 The Native American World *(pp. 3–7)*	• Critical Thinking Activity, Determining Relevance: Solving an Archaeological Puzzle, found on **Resource Pro** • Nystrom *Atlas of Our Country*, The Americas Before Columbus, pp. 10–11 • Literature Activity, "Corn Mother," found on **Resource Pro** • Skills for Life Activity, Units 1–2 folder, pp. 15
2 The European World *(pp. 9–14)*	• Literature Activity, The Koran, Units 1–2 folder, p. 14 • Key Documents, *Magna Carta,* Learning with Documents folder, p. 79 • Visual Learning Activity, Mapmakers, Learning with Documents folder, p. 43 • Nystrom *Atlas of Our Country*, Early European Exploration, pp. 12–13 • Biography, Isabella I, Queen of Castile, Units 1–2 folder, p. 11
3 The World of the West Africans *(pp. 15–18)*	• Visual Learning Activity, Slave Factories, found on **Resource Pro** • Biography, Askia Muhammad, found on **Resource Pro** • Primary Source Activity, The Portuguese in West Africa, found on **Resource Pro**
4 The Atlantic World Is Born *(pp. 19–24)*	• Primary Source Activity, Europeans Encounter Native Americans, Learning with Documents folder, p. 7 • Comparing Primary Sources, On Celebrating Columbus Day, Units 1–2 folder, pp. 12–13 • You Are Part of the Global Economy, Why Study History? folder, p. 2

Running Out of Time?

- Use Tape 1, "Origins of a New Society, to 1783," from **Visions of America** videotapes series.
- Use Chapter 1 Summary, from **Guide to the Essentials of American History (English and Spanish).**

Companion Web Site

The companion Web site offers online links for all chapter review activities. It also provides key content links and structured support for this chapter for both teachers and students.

http://www.Pathways.phschool.com

Teaching in the Information Age

 ## Media and Technology

For the Student

Interactive Student Tutorial CD-ROM Chapter 1

Student Edition on Audiotape Chapter 1

American Heritage® CD-ROM

Guided Reading Audiotapes (English and Spanish) Chapter 1

For the Teacher

Resource Pro CD-ROM Chapter 1

Test Bank CD-ROM Chapter 1

Listening to Literature Audiotapes *Timeless Voices, Timeless Themes* "The Earth on Turtle's Back" by Michael J. Caduto and Joseph Bruchac

Listening to Music CD "Navajo Night Chant"

Color Transparencies K-1, D-2, F-1

 ## Assessment Options

Chapter Test Forms A&B Test Bank CD-ROM booklet

Test Bank CD-ROM Chapter 1

Standardized Test Preparation Handbook

 ## Block Scheduling

Pacing Suggestions

For 90-minute Blocks

- Teach sections 1 and 2 using Transparencies C-4, D-1, and H-1 and the Recent Scholarship note on p. 7 for class discussions.
- Teach sections 3 and 4 using the Big Idea Graphic Organizers from Teaching Resources.

Additional Resources

- Prentice Hall's **American History Block Scheduling Support File** covers over 40 major topics in American history. Included are lesson plans, strategies, primary sources, literature, biographies, Great Debates, art history, simulations, and songs.
- **Prentice Hall United States History Video Collection™** contains 20 videotapes covering American history from beginnings to present.
- **Decision America Videotapes and Videodiscs**

 ## Connections to American Literature

from Prentice Hall

Prentice Hall Literature *Timeless Voices, Timeless Themes* Journal of the First Voyage to America, pp. 15–17

Prentice Hall Literature Library "The Mountain Chant," Literature of the American Southwest collection

Additional Resources

For the Student

Basil Davidson and editors of Time-Life Books. *African Kingdoms.* Time-Life, 1966.

For the Teacher

Philip Kopper and the editors of Smithsonian Books. *The Smithsonian Book of North American Indians Before the Coming of the Europeans.* Smithsonian Books, 1986.

 Prentice Hall brings into the classroom the vast archives and scholarship of the nation's premier American history magazine. See "From the Archives of American Heritage®" teaching notes in this chapter.

 History Alive!

Teacher's Curriculum Institute, in partnership with Prentice Hall, provides unique materials that engage students with diverse learning styles. See History Alive!® unit on Geography of America from Past to Present.

 Student Performance Pack

Ensures success in the three critical areas of Reading, Test Taking, and English Language Development with the following materials:
- Guide to the Essentials of American History in English and Spanish
- Guided Reading Audiotapes in English and Spanish
- Interactive Student Tutorial CD-ROM
- Test Preparation Handbook
- Test Preparation Practice booklet

The Atlantic World
c. 700 B.C.–c. A.D. 1600

Introducing the Chapter

Five hundred years ago, frequent contact began among Native Americans, Europeans, and West Africans on the shores of North America. The resulting conflicts and interactions among these different cultures had far-reaching effects, sometimes tragic and destructive, for the people of these three worlds.

Themes in American History

The theme for this chapter, Diversity, is listed at the beginning of this unit. An alternate theme for the chapter is Culture. To teach this unit thematically, you may wish to use the Forging a New Nation folder in American History Block Scheduling Support.

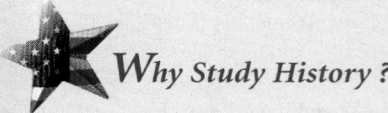

Why Study History ?

Have students explore suggested ways of connecting the past to the present on page 25.

Answer to . . .

Viewing History Students should use this question as an aid in reading the chapter. By portraying the Native Americans as eager participants in the encounter, the artist suggests that the arrival of European colonists was a good, even providential, event. The scene suggests that the native peoples had been waiting for the colonists to arrive.

CHAPTER
1 The Atlantic World
c. 700 B.C.–c. A.D. 1600

CHAPTER FOCUS

This chapter traces the development of three cultures that lived on continents encircling the Atlantic Ocean: the Americas, Europe, and Africa. These cultures came into contact when Europeans began to explore and colonize the Americas after 1492.

The Why Study History? page at the end of this chapter explores the connection between the early trade among the Atlantic continents and today's global trade network.

▲ **VIEWING HISTORY** *The Landing of Henry Hudson is Robert W. Weir's 1838 conception of the British explorer's expedition to the Americas.* **Culture What do you think the artist suggests about the contact between these peoples?**

▶ RESOURCE OPTIONS

Teaching Resources

📁 **Big Idea Graphic Organizer** folder
Graphic summary of the main idea of the chapter.

📁 **Learning Styles Lesson Plans** folder
Alternate lesson plans for diverse learning styles for each chapter.

Media and Technology

🦅 **AmericanHeritage® CD-ROM**
Time Tour A Meeting of Different Worlds: The First Americans *and* Europeans Reach the Americas

 Prentice Hall United States History Video Collection™ Volume 1 *Three Worlds Meet*

c. 700 B.C. Rise of mound builders		c. 800 Mississippian culture formed	c. 900 Anasazi build cliff dwellings		c. 1600 Iroquois League formed
800 B.C.	B.C. A.D.		800		1600

1 The Native American World

SECTION PREVIEW

Objectives

1 Describe how humans settled the Americas and adapted to a variety of environments in North America.
2 Compare the shared beliefs of Native Americans.
3 Explain the role of trade and land in Native American economies.
4 *Key Terms* Define: nomadic; kinship; clan; oral history; barter.

Main Idea

Native American societies, which populated North America for thousands of years, had shared beliefs, different ways of life, and a wide trading network.

Reading Strategy

Organizing Information Create a two-column table comparing and contrasting Native American culture groups. In the first column, list similarities among the groups. In the second column, list differences.

No one knows exactly when people first came to the Americas, but they left some fascinating clues. In New Mexico, someone left fingerprints in mud that hardened 28,000 years ago. Woven baskets found in Pennsylvania may be 19,000 years old. Other evidence suggests that the first Americans arrived as early as 40,000 years ago.

Settlement of the Americas

We know that these people came from the continent of Asia—but how? Today, North America and Asia are separated by the Bering Strait, a waterway off Alaska's west coast. During the last Ice Age, glaciers trapped much of Earth's ocean water, causing global sea levels to drop. This exposed a "land bridge." Most experts believe that Asians, perhaps following migrating herds of big game animals, walked across this bridge to North America.

Gradually the human population spread out across the Western Hemisphere, from the Arctic Circle to the southernmost tip of South America. These ancient Americans and their descendants are called Native Americans.

Over thousands of years, Native American societies settling in different regions developed a variety of distinct languages and customs. These lifestyles would be forever changed when Native Americans, Europeans, and Africans came into contact with one another just 500 years ago.

By the late 1400s, when this trans-Atlantic encounter began, some eight to ten million people may have lived in what is now the United States. Some scholars say the figure is more like 700,000 to 800,000.

North American Life

The North American environment varies greatly from region to region. It includes the surf-swept beaches of the West Coast, the hot, windy plains of the Midwest and Canada, and the rocky New England Coast. The people who first inhabited this land adapted their ways of life to fit their local environments.

The North On the coastal edges of North America lived two northern peoples, the Inuit and Aleut. They were skilled at hunting on ice

Native American artists in what is now Kentucky sculpted the spare, crisp lines and curves of this stone face.

 RESOURCE OPTIONS

Teaching Resources

📁 **Reproducible Lesson Plan** Lesson Plans folder, p. 34

📁 **Learning Styles Lesson Plan** Learning Styles Lesson Plans folder, p. 4

📁 **Big Idea Graphic Organizer** Big Idea Graphic Organizer folder, p. 6

📁 **Guided Reading and Review** Units 1–2 folder, p. 3

The Native American World

Objectives

You may wish to call students' attention to the objectives in the Section Preview. The objectives are reflected in the main headings of the section.

Bellringer

Ask students to name any Native American groups that are familiar to them from movies, television, reading, or local influences (such as geographical names). Ask them to recall any facts they know about the group, such as their location or way of life.

Reading Strategy

Organizing Information Refer to the Reading Strategy in the Section Preview. You may wish to model the main headings of the table on the chalkboard. Have students use their completed table to review section content.

LESSON PLAN
Connecting to the Main Idea

1. Focus Explain that the Native American world included a diversity of peoples. Across the continent, these peoples established kinship groups, traded, and shared religious beliefs and ceremonies.

2. Instruct Display a map of North America and point out the location of some of the Native American groups discussed in the section. List the landforms, climate, and resources of each location on the chalkboard. Then discuss how location affected the way of life of the Native Americans who lived there. Do any of these patterns still persist today?

3. Close Pair students and ask them to compare their completed tables. Ask for volunteer pairs to present their tables to the rest of the class.

Navajo Language

Changes in the language of the Navajo people dramatically demonstrate how culture and environment interact. The Navajos once lived in eastern Alaska, where they adapted to snow and cold by gathering wild food and hunting. Later they migrated to the more temperate Southwest, where they grew corn as a basic food. The Navajos chose the corn plant as a symbol of life and incorporated it into their religious beliefs and creation stories. Because they needed a word for seed, they adapted their old word for snowflake.

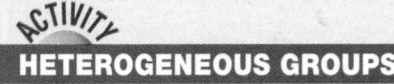

ACTIVITY
HETEROGENEOUS GROUPS

Have students create a chart that allows them to compare visually the Native American groups in different regions, using these criteria: social organization and kinship patterns, food supply, religious beliefs and observations, trading patterns. *(Reteaching)*

Answer to . . .

Viewing History Racks of fish are suspended from the ceiling, hung on drying racks; the group around the fire is cooking fish.

Main Idea Connections Answers should include examples of the ways in which the environment affected aspects of culture such as food, farming techniques, and home building.

This 1784 engraving shows a multifamily dwelling typical of the Nootka, a culture group of the Northwest Coast. Study the engraving. *Economics How does the engraving show the importance of fish in the Nootka diet?*

and snow, on shores and plains, in mild summers and bitter winters. Other northern groups such as the Koyukon and Ingalik were **nomadic**. That is, they moved their homes regularly in search of food. These groups hunted, fished, and gathered food in huge forests and along the shores of lakes and waterways of what is today Canada and Alaska.

Main Idea
CONNECTIONS

How did the various environments of North America affect the development of Native American culture?

The Northwest Coast Waterways were also the primary source of food for Native Americans of the Northwest Coast. Here rivers, fed by heavy rainfall, poured into a rich ocean fishing ground. The Coos, Coast Salish, Makah, and others in the Northwest developed remarkable fishing and food storage technologies.

California Farther south along the Pacific Coast lies what is now the state of California. During the 1400s, about 300,000 people lived in its mountains and valleys, including the Chumash, Yurok, and other people. They spoke more than a hundred variations of 20 basic languages, and they generally lived in small bands. Depending on their location, they ate deep-sea fish, acorns from mountain oaks, or beans from the desert mesquite plant.

The Plateau Inland from the Northwest Coast, between the Cascade Mountains and the Rocky Mountains, stretches a plateau of dry plains crisscrossed by rivers. Dozens of groups in this area, including the Chinook and Cayuse, fished the rivers for salmon and dug in the plains for edible roots. They often built villages that looked down from high riverbanks and dominated the waters below.

The Great Basin The map on page 5 shows the Great Basin, a region that lies between the Rockies and another mountain range, the Sierra Nevada. In this mostly dry land, food was scarce. Most people in this region, including the Paiute, Ute, and Shoshoni, lived in small groups. Members of a group worked together hunting and gathering food, including roots, pine nuts, rabbits, and insects.

The Southwest As little as four inches of rain falls annually in some parts of the Southwest region. Groups such as the Hopi and Zuñi lived settled lives and developed farming techniques to suit the dry environment. Others, such as the Apache, were nomadic. The Navaho moved to this region from the North, adapting their way of life as they did so.

The Anasazi people lived in apartment-like cliff dwellings of hundreds of rooms. The Anasazi, whose descendants are the Pueblo people, built their cliff homes starting in about A.D. 900. In the late 1100s, they abandoned these dwellings, in part because of a long drought in the region.

The Plains In villages along the rivers that drain the central area of the continent, the Mandans, Wichita, Pawnee, and other groups planted corn, beans, and squash. They also traveled great distances on foot, hunting the vast herds of buffalo that grazed on the Plains. The buffalo fulfilled many of their needs, from food to clothing and shelter.

The Northeast Vast woodlands and ample rainfall influenced the way of life of the Native Americans in the Northeast. Many people gathered wild plants, hunted, and grew corn and other crops. They fished in fresh water and salt water. In groups such as the Seneca and the Lenape, women managed the dwelling and the gardens around it. Men hunted deer, bear, moose, and other game in the woods. (See the Lenape Longhouse, on page 6.)

RESOURCE OPTIONS

Media and Technology

AmericanHeritage® CD-ROM

Explorer Activity 1 American Rivers, CD-ROM Guidebook, pp. 21–22, helps students write an outline for a TV documentary about North American rivers.

Time Tour A Meeting of Different Worlds: The First Americans

Native American Culture Groups and Trade Routes, c. 1500

 MAP Skills This map shows the main cultural areas of the peoples living in North America in the 1400s. Also shown is a sampling of specific cultural groups and their trade routes.

Place Which region has a small number of culture groups spread out over a large area? Why do you think this settlement pattern occurred?

The Iroquois people lived in the northeastern woodlands from the Atlantic Coast to the Great Lakes. Iroquois groups frequently made war on one another. However, in the late 1500s, five Iroquois groups with similar cultures and language agreed to stop the wars. They formed a well-organized political alliance called the Iroquois League.

The Southeast Vegetation ranged from swamp to seacoast in the Southeast, but the region was mostly wooded. Its inhabitants depended on growing corn and hunting. They knew what plants to use to make rope, medicine, clothing, even poison to catch fish.

As early as 700 B.C., Native American cultures were emerging in the Ohio and

RESOURCE OPTIONS

Teaching Resources

American History Block Scheduling Support The First Americans, found in the Forging a New Nation folder, includes interdisciplinary lesson suggestions and activities for Geography and History, Primary Sources, Biography, and Literature.

Answer to . . .

Map Skills The North; the cold climate in this region deterred settlement by large numbers of Native Americans.

Connections to Today

A new interest in and respect for Native American cultures has developed in recent years. One result is the establishment of a new museum in the Smithsonian Institution complex—the National Museum of the American Indian (NMAI). The new museum will be built on the last open site on the Mall in Washington, D.C., east of the National Air and Space Museum. Native Americans have played major roles in creating the museum's collections and displays of artifacts, with sensitivity to tribal feelings. They have also been leaders of the group planning the architecture and landscaping, whose design reflects the symbolic importance of the circle and other traditional Native American values.

Customize for
More Advanced Students

Much of what we know about earlier Native American cultures comes from the work of archaeologists and anthropologists. Have students choose one Native American group—perhaps one with a connection to your community—and find out what has been discovered about its history and way of life. What is its status today?

Answer to . . .

Exploring Technology Sample answer: The entry in the East symbolized birth; the exit in the West symbolized death.

Main Idea Connections All groups regarded trade as a way to show hospitality, friendliness, and respect. Land could not be owned and deserved respect.

Mississippi river valleys. One group, the Hopewell, built huge earthen monuments in various shapes, such as cones and animals. Hence, the Hopewell and similar groups are called the mound builders.

After about A.D. 800, the Mississippian culture developed. It included a variety of groups from Louisiana to Wisconsin with a shared a way of life. The Mississippians built towns of increasing size, the largest of which was Cahokia, in present-day Illinois. By the year 1200, Cahokia had a population of about 40,000 and more than 60 mounds.

The Natchez people settled the lower Mississippi River. Several thousand people lived in each Natchez town. Townspeople built magnificent temples on raised mounds of earth. East of the Natchez, other Mississippian cultures, such as the Creek and Cherokee, built similar towns. In the Cherokee town of Etowah (in modern-day Georgia) stood a pyramid more than 60 feet high.

Main Idea CONNECTIONS

What attitudes toward trade and land did all Native American groups share?

Shared Customs and Beliefs

Despite their different lifestyles, Native American peoples held to traditions handed down to them through generations. This shared culture included a common social structure and religion.

Social Structure Native American societies were not organized according to social classes, location, wealth, or age, as many cultures are today. Instead, family relationships, called **kinship**, determined the social structure. Individuals relied on their kin, or family, to fulfill many of their social needs. Kinship groups provided many of the services we expect today from governments, churches, and private organizations. Such services included medical care, child care, settlement of disputes, and education.

Native American kinship groups were based on what is called a clan. A **clan** is made up of groups of families who are all descended from a common ancestor. The Lenape people, who lived along the mid-Atlantic Coast, included at least three clans. The diagram on this page illustrates how Lenape clans gathered together for social and religious ceremonies, as did clans across the continent.

Religion Native Americans shared the belief that the most powerful forces in the world are spiritual. They performed religious ceremonies that recognized the power of those spiritual forces.

Whether they were planting crops, choosing a mate, or burying their dead, Native Americans strictly followed traditional religious practices, or rituals. They believed that failure to perform these rituals caused disasters such as invasions, disease, or bad harvests.

exploring TECHNOLOGY

The Lenape Longhouse

Oval Floor
The shape represented the back of the turtle that was believed to form the Earth.

Central Post
This post was a symbolic link to the sky, home of the Creator.

Carvings
These carvings represented 12 sky spirits.

Entry at East
This entry symbolized birth.

Drummers

Circle of Men

Circle of Women

Exit at West
This exit symbolized death.

The design of the longhouse, and everything in it, reflected the Lenape view of relationships in the universe. For example, in this thanksgiving ceremony men sat within a circle of women, who headed the clans. *Culture* **Describe some other symbolism you see in the longhouse.**

RESOURCE OPTIONS

Teaching Resources

 Nystrom *Atlas of Our Country* The Americas Before Columbus, pp. 10–11

Prentice Hall Literature Library "The Mountain Chant," Literature of the American Southwest collection

Media and Technology

 Listening to Music CD "Navajo Night Chant"

Color Transparencies Our Multicultural Heritage, C-4; Fine Art, D-1, D-2; The Way It Works, H-1

Preserving Culture To keep their beliefs and customs alive, Native Americans relied on **oral history**, the traditions passed from generation to generation by word of mouth. Elders told young people stories, songs, and instructions for ceremonies, and they then passed this knowledge on to their children.

Native American Trade

Large or small, all Native American groups traded food or goods within their group and outside it. They traded not only for items they needed or wanted, but also to show hospitality and friendliness. Among Native Americans sharing was seen as a sign of respect.

Native American trading routes crisscrossed North America. (See the map on page 5.) The Inuit traded copper from the Copper River in southern Alaska for sharks' teeth collected by people living at the mouth of the Columbia River in Washington. Shells harvested by the Northwest Coast groups found their way to central California and North Dakota.

The Mohave of the Great Basin carried out **barter,** or trade, with people on the California coast, and then traded the coastal goods to the Pueblo in what is now Arizona. Rocky Mountain groups took obsidian, a volcanic glass, eastward into Ohio. The Iroquois east of the Great Lakes bartered with groups from Minnesota to get stone for tobacco pipes. In the Southeast, Native Americans traded salt and copper from the Appalachian Mountains.

Although Native Americans used natural trade routes such as the Mississippi River and the Great Lakes, they also built a network of trading paths. These routes often led to centers where Native Americans held trade gatherings during the summer.

Native Americans and Land

One item that Native Americans never traded was land. In their view, the land could not be owned. They believed that people had a right to use land and could grant others the right to use it, too. To buy and sell land, as peoples have done throughout history, was unthinkable to them. Land, like all of nature, deserved respect, according to Native American religious beliefs. One well-known leader explained their beliefs this way:

> **AMERICAN VOICES** ❝The country was made without lines of demarcation [boundary lines], and it is no man's business to divide it. . . . I never said the land was mine to do with it as I chose. The one who has the right to dispose of it is the one who has created it.❞
>
> —*Chief Joseph of the Nez Percé, late 1800s*

As you will read in the next section, the Europeans who arrived on North American soil in the 1400s had quite a different idea about land ownership.

This Etowah neck ornament is made of shell, a sure sign that it was a trade item from a distant seacoast.

BACKGROUND

Recent Scholarship

Where did the first Americans come from and when did they arrive? Scholars have debated the question for years. Most believe the first Americans were northeast Asians who crossed the Bering Strait. Some say this happened 40,000 years ago, some say only 8,000. University of São Paulo anthropologist Walter Neves broadens the debate. He doesn't believe that the first Americans necessarily came from northeastern Asia. Anthropologists Jospeh Powell and Erik Ozolins of the University of New Mexico agree. They believe that the first people migrated from the South Pacific, at least 11,500 years ago. These anthropologists believe that northeast Asians did migrate to North America, but they don't believe they were the first Americans.

SECTION 1 REVIEW

Comprehension

1. **Key Terms** Define: (a) nomadic; (b) kinship; (c) clan; (d) oral history; (e) barter.

2. **Summarizing the Main Idea** What were some of the most significant features of Native American culture, and why were they important?

3. **Organizing Information** Create a two-column table to show similarities and differences among Native American groups.

Critical Thinking

4. **Analyzing Time Lines** Review the time line at the start of the section. How does it show Native American development?

5. **Drawing Conclusions** Do you think that the diversity of Native American groups encouraged or discouraged trade? Explain your reasoning.

Writing Activity

6. **Writing an Expository Essay** Assume that you are writing down an oral history of Native American beliefs that has been passed down to you. Write an essay to describe some of the customs and ideas that are important to your people.

Answers to
SECTION 1 REVIEW

1. (a) nomadic, see p. 4; (b) kinship, see p. 6; (c) clan, see p. 6; (d) oral history, see p. 7; (e) barter, see p. 7.

2. Answers may include adaptation to environment, a common kinship structure and religious beliefs, and trade ties.

3. Similarities include kinship and clan structure, religion, oral history as a way of preserving culture, and beliefs about land. Differences include food gathering, home building, and trade goods.

4. The entries show the growth of complex dwellings and alliances.

5. Students should support their answers with facts from the section.

6. Essays should include specific cultural details from the section.

RESOURCE OPTIONS

Teaching Resources

 Quiz Units 1–2 folder, p. 4

Student Performance Pack

 Guide to the Essentials Chapter 1, Section 1 (English and Spanish)

Media and Technology

 RESOURCE PRO

Literature Activity "Corn Mother," found on Resource Pro, uses a Penobscot folktale to portray the Native American view of land use.

SKILLS FOR LIFE

Historical Evidence

Using Artifacts

Focus Interpret artifacts and use them to evaluate a historical theory.
Instruct Show students a mysterious object, such as a toast gripper or a small spring from a toy. Brainstorm facts about the item by asking questions such as the following: What is it made of? Can you tell how old it is? What does the object tell you about the people who made it or used it?

List conclusions about the artifact on the chalkboard. Ask if any of the conclusions listed require additional evidence. What sort of evidence would support those conclusions?
Extend See the Skills for Life Activity in Resource Options below.

Answers

1. (a) Flint spear points and stone tools. (b) Hunting. (c) The age of artifacts is a reliable indicator of when humans lived at that site.

2. (a) Two archaeologists. (b) Alaska's North Slope. (c) Between 11,000 and 12,000 years old. (d) They resemble Paleoindian weapons common in the lower 48 states.

3. (a) Two different cultures lived in Alaska between 11,000 and 12,000 years ago. (b) Two different forms of stone tools were found. (c) The Paleoindian style originated in Asia and came with the migrants, or the style originated in Alaska and spread through North America. (d) A group of hunting people lived in Alaska 11,000 to 12,000 years ago and were probably culturally different from those who lived in other parts of North America.

TEST FOR SUCCESS

Students should demonstrate an understanding of the analytical process described in the three steps.

Using Artifacts

Artifacts are objects made by humans, such as tools, pottery, jewelry, or the spear point shown below. They provide evidence about people and events of the past that helps support historians' theories about history.

Some historians have theorized that humans first entered North America about 12,000 years ago in a single migration from Asia to Alaska. However, other experts now believe that waves of Asians migrated to North America at various times, as much as 40,000 years ago. A growing body of historical evidence seems to support this theory.

Historical evidence must be analyzed to see if it supports a given theory. To analyze an artifact, use the following three steps:

1. Identify the artifact. For example, read the excerpt below. (a) What type of artifacts were found? (b) What were the artifacts probably used for? (c) Why was it important to be certain about their age?

2. Determine what facts are known about the artifacts. (a) Who found the artifacts? (b) Where were they found? (c) About how old are they? (d) How do they compare to other artifacts of this type?

3. Determine whether the facts support a given theory. To help decide whether the archaeologists' theory of migration is based on fact, answer the following questions. (a) What theory do they propose? (b) Which facts support their theory? (c) Do the facts support any other possible theories? Explain. (d) What conclusions can be drawn about the artifacts and their makers?

TEST FOR SUCCESS

Study the artifact on page 7 and read the caption. Apply the three steps described above to determine whether you can use the evidence to support an historical theory.

The often-challenged theory that humans first entered the New World around twelve thousand years ago in a single migration from Asia into Alaska has taken another blow. Two archaeologists say that they have found evidence of two different cultures coexisting in Alaska between eleven thousand and twelve thousand years ago. . . .

The new find consists of several flint spear points and other stone tools found atop a small mesa that looks out over a vast plain where bison and mammoths would have roamed. "It was a hunting lookout," says Michael Kunz, an archaeologist with the Bureau of Land Management who discovered the site in 1978 when surveying Alaska's North Slope before it was opened to oil drillers.

The age of the stone weapons has only just been established by radiocarbon dating of charcoal found with them. . . . What makes the spear points remarkable is that they resemble "Paleoindian" [early American hunting people] weapons common in the lower forty-eight states.

Yet nothing like a Paleoindian weapon had been found in Alaska in a context that could be reliably dated [until now]. Instead, the state's only other culture of comparable antiquity, called the Nenana complex, made use of very different forms of stone tools. When the various tool types made by cultures differ significantly, archaeologists tend to think the peoples who made them belonged to different cultures.

Richard Reanier, a University of Washington archaeologist who is collaborating with Kunz, says it is possible that the Paleoindian weapon style originated in Asia and came with the migrants; but no such points have been found in Asia. He says it also is possible that the style originated in Alaska and spread into the rest of North America.

—Excerpt from Boyce Rensberger, "Pointing to a Shift in Migration Theories," The Washington Post, National Weekly Edition, April 5–11, 1993, p. 38.

RESOURCE OPTIONS

Teaching Resources

 Skills for Life Activity Using Artifacts, Units 1–2 folder, p. 15, takes students 2,000 years into the future to enhance their understanding of the science of archaeology.

Media and Technology

RESOURCE⊙PRO

Critical Thinking Activity Determining Relevance: Solving an Archaeological Puzzle, found on Resource Pro, helps students apply this skill by analyzing a Neanderthal tool.

500	750	1000	1250	1500

c. 500 Early Middle Ages begin

c. 1000 Late Middle Ages begin

1096 Crusades begin

c. 1300 Renaissance begins

1488 Dias sails around southern tip of Africa

2 The European World

SECTION PREVIEW

Objectives

1. Summarize life in Europe during the Early Middle Ages.
2. Describe the changes that began in the Late Middle Ages.
3. Analyze the changes brought about by the Renaissance.
4. *Key Terms* Define: Middle Ages; feudalism; Crusades; middle class; monarch; Renaissance; Reformation.

Main Idea

The Middle Ages, a period when Europe was isolated from the rest of the world, was followed by the Renaissance, a period when Europeans sought knowledge of the world and began to explore it.

Reading Strategy

Reading for Supporting Details As you read, write down details that support this statement: Europe experienced political, social, economic, and cultural change when it moved from the Middle Ages to the Renaissance.

Driven by burning curiosity, a desire for wealth, and a duty to spread their religion, European explorers in the 1400s set sail for foreign lands. But why the 1400s? Why didn't this encounter happen hundreds of years earlier? Since ancient Roman times, Europeans had known of continents beyond their own. Roman women draped themselves in Chinese silk. Wheat from Egypt fed the Roman empire. Italian merchants traded salt for African gold.

When the Roman empire collapsed in the A.D. 400s, European life changed drastically, and the foreign contacts enjoyed by the Romans largely ended. Europe would remain sheltered from the world for nearly a thousand years.

The Early Middle Ages

This era in European history, from about A.D. 500 to 1300, is known as the **Middle Ages**, or the "medieval" period. It is the historical era that came after ancient times and before the modern era. The period from 500 to 1000 is often called the Early Middle Ages.

European Invasions The Early Middle Ages was a time of instability in Europe. Germanic tribes such as the Franks surged across the borders of the former Roman empire and settled across much of Europe. From the north, fierce Viking warriors came not to settle, but to loot and burn villages.

Out of Arabia, a powerful empire arose in the A.D. 600s. It was based on a new religion: Islam, inspired by the teachings of the prophet Muhammad. The followers of Islam, called Muslims, sought to spread their religion. Within 200 years, the Muslim empire spread across North Africa and into what is now Spain, bringing the highly advanced Arab civilization to these regions.

Feudalism To protect themselves against these threats, Europeans created a political and economic system known as **feudalism.** Under feudalism a powerful noble, or lord, divided his large landholdings among lesser lords, who in return owed him military service and other favors.

▶ RESOURCE OPTIONS

Teaching Resources

📁 **Reproducible Lesson Plan** Lesson Plans folder, p. 35

📁 **Big Idea Graphic Organizer** Big Idea Graphic Organizer folder, p. 7

📁 **Guided Reading and Review** Units 1–2 folder, p. 5

📁 **Literature Activity** The Koran, Units 1–2 folder, p. 14

Objectives

You may wish to call students' attention to the objectives in the Section Preview. The objectives are reflected in the main headings of the section.

Bellringer

Have students list the major nations of Western Europe today. Which do they think were important in the 1400s? Then ask them to underline the names of nations they believe made contact with Native American cultures in North America. Have them revise their lists as they read the chapter.

Reading Strategy

Reading for Supporting Details
Refer to the Reading Strategy in the Section Preview. Have students write the statement on a sheet of paper. Encourage them to record supporting details in list form.

LESSON PLAN

Connecting to the Main Idea

1. Focus Explain that Europeans in the 1400s were ready to expand and explore. Have students think about what factors in European society influenced and motivated this desire.

2. Instruct Discuss how the European world view changed during the Renaissance. Ask students whether they think all levels of European society shared this changing point of view. Have them consider why the growth of a middle class was significant.

Have students locate England, France, Portugal, and Castille (Spain) on the map on page 13. Ask why these nations were likely to lead in developing a transatlantic trade.

3. Close Ask students to review the lists they made in the Bellringer activity. Help them conclude that Europeans were to be the prime movers in the coming encounters of the three cultures in the Atlantic World.

people in medieval Europe. They alone could read and study the Bible and other holy writings of Christianity, so they controlled how the faith was interpreted and communicated to the people. Every Christian was expected to show unquestioning obedience to Church authority.

The Late Middle Ages

Around the year 1000, Europe's economy entered a period of new growth that produced social changes. New farming methods increased food supplies. More food led to population growth and competition for land.

At the same time, new trade ties to Asia promoted interest in the world outside Europe's borders. In time, trade also led to the growth of cities and a weakening of the feudal system.

The basis of feudal society in Europe was the manor, the large estate of a lord. Peasants called serfs farmed the land and gave their lord a portion of the harvest in exchange for his shelter and protection. Born into lifetime servitude, serfs received no education. They knew little about the world outside the manor, which they were forbidden to leave.

The manor system produced everything a feudal society needed for survival. As a result, Europe's trade ties to foreign lands largely died out during the Middle Ages, and even the use of money declined.

Medieval Religion The Roman Catholic Church governed the spiritual life and daily life of medieval Christians, both rich and poor. The head of the Church, the pope, claimed authority over emperors and kings, and often appointed them. The clergy, or Church officials who were authorized to perform religious ceremonies, often owned large tracts of land and were lords of their own manors.

Much of the clergy's power came from the fact that they were virtually the only educated

The Crusades Church power grew, and so did the might of the Muslim empire. In about the year 1077, Muslims from Turkey seized Jerusalem, a holy city to both Christians and Muslims that previously had been shared by the two faiths. From 1096 to 1291 the Church organized a series of military campaigns to take Jerusalem from the Turks. These holy wars were called the **Crusades.**

Ultimately, the Christians failed to oust the Turks from Jerusalem. The Crusades' real impact on Europe was that they increased Europeans' awareness of the world beyond their borders and accelerated economic change. Returning to their homes in Europe, Crusaders brought back spices, perfumes, fabrics, and other Asian goods looted in war. Europeans quickly developed a taste for them. This growing demand for Asian products revived Europe's trade with the outside world, which had nearly ceased during the Middle Ages.

In 1271, a group of merchants from the Italian city of Venice became the first known

Europeans to reach China. Upon their return, one member of the group, Marco Polo, wrote an account of his experiences that sent European merchants scrambling to set up trading missions to the East.

The Growth of Cities Merchants sold their foreign goods at trade fairs set up along water routes and trade routes. These centers of trade grew into bustling towns and cities, particularly in northern Italy and in northern France. Growing cities needed men and women with skills in trades such as weaving, baking, and metalworking. Many places attracted workers by allowing runaway serfs to obtain their freedom.

The growth of cities and trade in Europe had three major effects:

(1) It created a new **middle class** of merchants, traders, and artisans who made and sold goods to the manors.

(2) It revived a money economy.

(3) It contributed to the eventual breakdown of the feudal system.

The Rise of Monarchs Europe's growing wealth increased the power of **monarchs**—those who rule over a kingdom—to expand their control. Monarchs attracted the loyalty of the new middle class by protecting trade routes and keeping the peace.

Strong monarchs sometimes clashed with one another. In 1066, the Duke of Normandy, a region in modern-day France, conquered England. This event, called the Norman Conquest, led to a gradual blending of French and Anglo-Saxon cultures that became part of the English and American heritage.

Monarchs also clashed with their own nobles. Disputes often arose from a king's attempts to impose heavy taxes in order to fund Crusades or simply to get richer. In 1215, England's King John, a greedy and cruel leader, was forced by his nobles to sign a document granting them various legal rights. That document, the Magna Carta, or "Great Charter," not only shaped British government, but became the foundation for future American ideals of liberty and justice. One important clause declared:

KEY DOCUMENTS ❝ No freeman shall be arrested or imprisoned or dispossessed or . . . in any way harmed . . . except by the lawful judgment of his peers or by the law of the land. ❞

—*Magna Carta, 1215*

Key Events in Europe, c. 500–1600

c.500–1000	Breakup of the Roman empire opens Europe to invasions
600s	Rise of the Muslim empire
700s	Feudal system evolves; trade and money economy dissolve
1066	Norman Conquest leads to blending of Anglo-Saxon and French cultures
1096–1204	Crusades draw Europe from isolation and help revive trade
1100s	Rise of universities
1215	King John signs the Magna Carta
1275	Merchant group including Marco Polo arrives in China
1347	Bubonic plague reaches Europe
1300s	Renaissance begins in Italy
1418	Prince Henry of Portugal starts navigation school
1455	Gutenberg prints Bible using movable type
1469	Marriage of Queen Isabella and King Ferdinand creates nation of Spain
1488	Portugal's Bartolomeu Dias sails around the tip of Africa
1492	Muslim empire driven from Spain
1500s	Northern Renaissance begins
1517	Reformation begins

 Interpreting Charts Europe experienced enormous changes during the medieval era. *Culture Compare life in Europe both before and after the Crusades. How did it change?*

Ambitious rulers such as King John also came into conflict with the Church.[†] For a time, strong popes prevailed in these struggles, but by the 1200s, monarchies were growing stronger as papal supremacy declined.

[†] King John feuded with Pope Innocent II over who should be named to the key post of Archbishop of Canterbury. John's attacks on the Church brought upon him the severest punishment: The Pope excommunicated him—that is, expelled him from the Church.

Graphing the Main Idea

To make sure students understand the main idea of this section, you may wish to use the flow map graphic organizer below.

Tell students that a flow map shows a sequence of steps or events unfolding. Ask students to use the flow map to record the sequence of historical events in Europe from the Middle Ages to the Renaissance.

Teaching Tip A template for this graphic organizer can be found in the Color Transparencies, G-4.

BACKGROUND

Geography in History

During the Middle Ages, spices from Southeast Asia traveled overland to the Mediterranean, where Italian merchants monopolized sales to Europe. Wealth from trade allowed Italian cities to sponsor the great artists and architects of the Renaissance. When the Portuguese rounded the Cape of Good Hope in 1488, they challenged the Italian monopoly. Lost income contributed to Italy's decline, and the great Renaissance centers of the 1500s were regions that profited from new trade routes: Spain and the Netherlands.

Answer to . . .

Viewing History Both works convey realism and the study of the human form and features.

Donatello's *St. Mark* (left) conveys the artist's use of humanism. Leonardo's *Mona Lisa* (right) demonstrates the techniques of painting that earned Leonardo his enduring reputation. *Culture In what ways are these artworks products of the Renaissance?*

The Rise of Universities As monarchies grew, so did the need for educated people to run these governments. Young men of the nobility and the middle class began to enroll in the universities that arose in the 1100s. Graduates hoped to get high posts in governments or the Church.

At the same time, new sources of knowledge became available in Europe. Ancient writings of the Greeks and Romans, preserved for centuries by both Catholic monks and Muslim scholars, began to be translated into Latin, the language of Christian scholars. Arab knowledge of science and mathematics ignited Europeans' interest. Latin literature was being translated into everyday languages that all could understand. A revival of Roman architecture could be seen in grand cathedrals that arose across the European landscape. These were the beginnings of a cultural revolution soon to sweep the continent.

The "Black Death" In the 1300s, however, European growth was cut down by a new, invisible enemy. It was called the plague, and it brought rapid and ugly death to one third of Europe's entire population. Europeans called the plague the "Black Death."

Carried by fleas on the rats that infested nearly every home, a global epidemic of bubonic plague ravaged China, India, and the Middle East before arriving in an Italian port in 1347. In just a few years, the plague seized all of Europe, turning entire cities into graveyards and causing starvation, riots, and economic collapse. The disease struck nobles and serfs alike. It spared no one, even the priests to whom people turned to stop the horror. Some people even began to have doubts about Church teachings.

The Renaissance

The final, fertile centuries of the Middle Ages gave birth to a new era. The **Renaissance**, a French word meaning "rebirth," was an era of enormous creativity and rapid change that began in Italy in the 1300s. From there the movement spread throughout western Europe, reaching its height in the 1500s.

The Pursuit of Learning The Renaissance was a quest for knowledge in nearly every field of study: art, literature, science, philosophy, economics, and political thought. The period produced many of the giant figures of Western civilization, such as Michelangelo, Leonardo da Vinci, and Shakespeare.

Compared to the chaos of the medieval period, the Renaissance brought order and unity in Europe. Yet it also was a rebellion against the rigid thinking of the past. Following the models of the Greeks, Romans, and Muslims, European thinkers began using reason and experimentation to understand the physical world.

Cultural Change in Italy The Renaissance was born amid the ruins of ancient Rome in Italy. Unlike most of Europe, Italy's ancient cities survived the Middle Ages. In cities such as Milan, Venice, Genoa, and Florence, a wealthy merchant class dominated local political and economic life. These nobles valued individual achievement and a well-rounded education. They studied the arts and became generous supporters of them.

Renaissance artists gained work by attracting the support of such a rich patron—a noble, a king, or even a pope. Sculptors, poets, and architects all worked in the service of their patrons, creating whatever was desired. In the city of Florence, the rich and powerful Medici family became the most famous Renaissance patrons. They made possible the work of Leonardo da Vinci, the legendary sculptor, painter, poet, inventor, and scientist.

A Golden Age Many of the greatest artists of all time lived and worked in Italy during the Renaissance. The 1400s and 1500s became a golden age in the arts. Although the movement drew inspiration from ancient models, it also

 RESOURCE OPTIONS

Teaching Resources

 Visual Learning Activity Mapmakers, Learning with Documents folder, p. 43

Media and Technology

Decision America Videotapes and Videodiscs Issue 11 *Can Government Be Too Democratic?*

produced new artistic forms and ideas. Renaissance art explored the physical world and the individual's role in it. This core philosophy of the period is called *humanism.*

Artistic subjects in the humanist world were heroic, full of emotion, and realistically physical. Poets such as Petrarch wrote about romantic love. Michelangelo's famous *Pietà* is a massive sculpture of the biblical Mary, serene and sorrowful, cradling the body of her dead son Jesus. Leonardo da Vinci studied the anatomy of the human body in order to sculpt it. He even dissected corpses to view the muscles, skeleton, and organs, making contributions to both art and science.

The Northern Renaissance As the plague died out and the rest of Europe began to prosper again, the Renaissance spread northward. By the late 1500s the Renaissance was in bloom in the Netherlands, Belgium, France, Spain, England, and Germany.

This cultural period is called the Northern Renaissance. It produced its own geniuses, including several Dutch painters who warmly depicted everyday peasant life.

The period also produced the English playwright and poet William Shakespeare, generally regarded as the most gifted writer in history. His subjects ranged from a Danish prince, Hamlet, to the Roman emperor Julius Caesar. His characters were soldiers, innkeepers, and British monarchs.

The Printing Press In medieval times, books were rare, and most dealt with religious topics. Christian monks carefully copied each one by hand. Then, as Renaissance writers were putting new ideas onto paper, a German man figured out how to put them into print. In 1455, Johann Gutenberg produced a Bible made on a printing press. The words were set in movable metal type. Books could then be printed over and over. The invention set off a communications revolution over the next century, as some 200 million books came off European printing presses.

Main Idea CONNECTIONS

What role did the printing press play in the Renaissance?

European States and Trade Routes, c. 1450

Legend:
— Trade route
- Major center of trade
Christian territory
Muslim territory

NORWAY · Bergen · SWEDEN · SCOTLAND · Novgorod · PRINCIPALITY OF MOSCOW · Moscow · IRELAND · Dublin · North Sea · DENMARK · ENGLAND · Lübeck · Danzig · London · Antwerp · Cologne · GERMAN EMPIRE · POLAND · ATLANTIC OCEAN · Paris · Ulm · Caspian Sea · FRANCE · VENETIAN REPUBLIC · Vienna · Lyon · Milan · HUNGARY · Bordeaux · Venice · Black Sea · PORTUGAL · CASTILLE · Marseille · Florence · ARAGON · PAPAL STATES · Lisbon · IBERIAN PENINSULA · Barcelona · Rome · Naples · Tabriz · Seville · Valencia · NAPLES · Constantinople · OTTOMAN SULTANATE · GRANADA · Aleppo · Baghdad · Mediterranean Sea

0   500   1000 Miles
0   500   1000 Kilometers

MAP Skills Europe at this time was divided into numerous states, which competed for control of the limited trade and land available on the continent. *Movement* What religion challenged Christianity in the Mediterranean region?

Have students suppose that they are European merchants who want royal support for voyages of exploration. Ask them to list reasons they would give to persuade the monarch that such voyages will benefit the state.

Customize for Less Proficient Readers

BACKGROUND

Biography

Between 1480 and 1780, European voyagers explored all the seas in the world except for the polar regions, giving this period the name, "Age of Discovery." In Spain's search for new land and markets, Vasco Núñez de Balboa (1475–1519) became the first European to see the Pacific Ocean. Balboa came to the Americas in 1500 and settled on Hispaniola. Later he traveled to what is now Panama. Looking for gold, in 1513 Balboa led an expedition across the Isthmus of Panama to the western coast, where he climbed a mountain ridge and saw the great ocean. He named it the Sea of the South (Mar del Sur), since he thought it was south of Asia. In fact, it was near the site of the present-day Panama Canal.

Answer to . . .

Map Skills Islam
Main Idea Connections The printing press set off a communications revolution.

Answers to

SECTION 2 REVIEW

1. (a) Middle Ages, see p. 9;
(b) feudalism, see p. 9; (c) Crusades, see p. 10; (d) middle class, see p. 11;
(e) monarch, see p. 11;
(f) Renaissance, see p. 12;
(g) Reformation, see p. 14.

2. After the fall of the Roman Empire, waves of invaders caused a breakdown in trade and forced people to form small, isolated communities for protection. The Crusades and the rise of universities helped revive European interest in ideas and trade goods from abroad.

3. Possible entries include: political—rise of monarchies, decline in Church authority; cultural—revival of Greek and Roman art, focus on humanism, printing press; social—rise of a middle class; economic—growth of trade, merchant wealth.

4. Students should provide a clear link between the items they choose.

5. Answers include protection of trade routes; wars among monarchs; the Magna Carta; disputes with popes; the breakdown of feudalism; competition on the seas.

6. Essays may point to today's Greek and Roman heritage; the Magna Carta as a model of law; and the creation of modern-day European nations.

The Reformation New ideas now traveled rapidly in print. The Bible circulated among a widening audience. The printing revolution occurred at a time when critics, angry at corruption among the clergy, were calling for reform of the Church. In 1517, criticism flared into a revolt known as the **Reformation**. It was led by Martin Luther, a German monk who declared that the Bible, not the Church, was the true authority. His followers called themselves Protestants, because they protested Church authority. From northern Germany the Reformation spread to England, where it became official under a popular Protestant queen, Elizabeth I.

This statue, which decorates Queen Isabella's tomb, shows her praying.

The Rise of Nations During the Renaissance, government by local nobles and the Church gradually declined. Instead monarchs began to combine smaller areas into the larger nation-states of Europe that we know today. For the first time, Europeans thought of themselves as members of nations such as France, England, or Portugal.

Seafaring Technology The young nations soon started to compete with one another for the highly profitable Asian trade. In 1400, the only way to reach Asia was still by land. Europeans did not have the technology to explore the faster sea route. Sailors who ventured out of sight of land often disappeared. They had no way to calculate their position and had trouble sailing against the wind.

With the help of instruments developed by Renaissance scientists, however, long-range sea travel finally became possible. Sailors could use a compass to determine direction when neither the coastline nor the sun was visible. The astrolabe and the quadrant now allowed ship captains to find their location far from visible land.

Portugal Takes to the Seas In 1418, Prince Henry of Portugal, later called Prince Henry the Navigator, established a mariners' school at Sagres, on the southwestern tip of Portugal. There, his seamen developed the final tool necessary for long-range voyages: the caravel, a ship that could sail against the wind as well as with it. In 1488, a Sagres-trained navigator, Bartolomeu Dias, sailed around the southernmost cape of Africa, the Cape of Good Hope. Nine years later, another Portuguese mariner, Vasco da Gama, sailed from Portugal to India. The first sea route from Europe to Asia was now open.

Competition on the Seas About this time, a new nation arose to challenge Portugal on the high seas. In 1469 two strong Christian monarchs, Queen Isabella of Castile and King Ferdinand of Aragon, were married, uniting their kingdoms into what is now Spain. Their combined forces then launched a successful crusade to drive the Muslim empire out of Spain in 1492 and create a Christian nation.

Isabella was not content with military victory, however. She had two other goals: to surpass Portugal in the race to explore new sea routes, and to bring Christianity to new lands. So, as her ships dropped anchor along the west coast of Africa, they carried not only trade goods, but Christian missionaries as well.

SECTION 2 REVIEW

Comprehension

1. *Key Terms* Define: (a) Middle Ages; (b) feudalism; (c) Crusades; (d) middle class; (e) monarch; (f) Renaissance; (g) Reformation.

2. *Summarizing the Main Idea* Why did Europe become isolated from the world, and what caused it to emerge from isolation?

3. *Organizing Information* Construct a web diagram called *Effects of the Renaissance*. Create the following categories: *Political Change, Cultural Change, Social Change,* and *Economic Change.* Complete the web by adding items to these categories.

Critical Thinking

4. *Analyzing Time Lines* Review the time line at the start of the section. Choose one event and explain how it affected another event.

5. *Drawing Conclusions* List three effects that occurred when monarchies and nations replaced local governments led by the Church.

Writing Activity

6. *Writing an Expository Essay* Write an essay that explains why the Renaissance is called the beginning of the modern era.

▶ **RESOURCE OPTIONS**

Teaching Resources

 Biography Isabella I, Queen of Castille, Units 1–2 folder, p. 11

📁 **Quiz** Units 1–2 folder, p. 6

Student Performance Pack

 Guide to the Essentials Chapter 1, Section 2 (English and Spanish)

c. 1050 Islam comes to West Africa	late 1200s Kingdom of Benin founded	1400s Portuguese build trading forts along West African coast	1464 Rise of the Songhai empire	c. 1500 European slave raids begin
1000	**1200**	**1400**	**1600**	

3 The World of the West Africans

SECTION PREVIEW

Objectives

1 Describe the initial meetings between West Africans and Europeans.
2 Describe how a trading relationship developed between Europe and the kingdoms of West Africa.
3 Summarize how African slavery differed from the way Europeans began to practice slavery.
4 *Key Terms* Define: savanna; lineage; scarce.

Main Idea

At the time of their first contact with Europeans, West Africans had wealthy kingdoms with strong governments, unique cultures, and traditional religious beliefs.

Reading Strategy

Formulating Questions Before you read, make a list of questions you might have about the contact between Europe and West Africa. As you read the section, fill in answers to your questions.

The Atlantic Ocean that washed against the Americas and Europe broke also on the shores of Africa. During the 1400s, the Atlantic was already a highway over which Europeans traveled to reach Africa and the ancient, wealthy kingdoms that lay beyond its coast.

West Africans and Europeans Meet

Europeans and Africans first met in ancient times, when a wide trading network of land and sea routes thrived throughout the Mediterranean region. Much of this contact ceased during the Middle Ages but resumed during the Renaissance. European traders began to trade salt for gold from North African middlemen, who in turn obtained it from their trading partners in the interior of West Africa.

Europeans wanted to get around the middlemen and go directly to these sources of gold. This was the prize for which Spain and Portugal competed in the 1400s as their ships explored Africa's Atlantic coast.

Early relations between the two cultures were mostly peaceful. Portugal established trade ties with wealthy coastal kingdoms, which produced much of the gold. The Portuguese built a string of forts along the coast for their ships to load and unload trade goods. Africans ran the trading operations and set their own prices. The Netherlands, France, and England soon launched expeditions to the region to set up similar trade arrangements.

West African Cultures

At the time of European contact, West Africa was home to a great variety of peoples and ways of life. As with all societies, Africans adapted their culture to their geographic surroundings.

Geography and Livelihoods In West Africa, three main types of vegetation regions influenced how people made a living, raised families, and worshipped. Rain forests covered a large band

The forest kingdoms of Guinea were known for their gold. The Baule people made this gold pendant, which is shown full size.

Objectives

You may wish to call students' attention to the objectives in the Section Preview. The objectives are reflected in the main headings of the section.

Bellringer

Ask students to list as many facts as they can about the continent of Africa. You may want to display a map of Africa and point out both the places they name and those mentioned in this section.

Reading Strategy

Formulating Questions Refer to the Reading Strategy in the Section Preview. Encourage students to generate questions by skimming the section headings and turning them into questions.

LESSON PLAN

Connecting to the Main Idea

1. Focus Explain that the first interactions between European and African cultures came in the 1400s along the coast of West Africa, where great kingdoms had prosperous, complex cultures. Have students think about what those cultures were like and what factors influenced their contact with European cultures.

2. Instruct Have students locate Songhai and Benin on the map on page 17 and notice trading posts and routes. How far did West African trade routes extend?

Point out that trade often brings new ideas and technology as well as goods to buy and sell. Discuss ways that Islam set Songhai apart from other cultures in West Africa at the time.

3. Close Review with students the main ideas they have learned about the complex cultures of West Africa with their rich trade and centers of learning.

ARRIVAL AT TIMBUKTU.

In this engraving from the 1800s, a caravan arrives at the city of Timbuktu. Ideas spread along the trade routes along with trade goods. *Geography How did Timbuktu's role as a trade center help lead to its development into a center of learning?*

To help students better understand trade in West Africa, have them trace the route of a trader going from Benin to Songhai to North Africa. Have them use the map on page 17 to answer these questions: What direction will the trader travel from Benin to Songhai? About how far is it from the city of Benin to Timbuktu? From Timbuktu to Fez in North Africa? What kind of terrain will the trader have to cross? *(Reteaching)*

Customize for
More Advanced Students

Have students use current travel guides and almanacs, along with information from tourist bureaus, to prepare an itinerary for a present-day traveler to West Africa. Itineraries might include visits to major cities, archaeological sites, and scenic or historic places. Ask students to present their itineraries to the class and explain their choices.

of coastal land along the southern part of the region. Africans had migrated there from central Africa over hundreds of years. Some of the continent's earliest societies and cities evolved in the resource-rich region, where people hunted, fished, mined, and farmed the land.

Farther north lay a wide expanse of **savanna**, a region near the equator with tropical grasslands and scattered trees. The savanna has a dry season and a wet season, rather than hot and cold seasons. The wet season supported limited farming. Year round, nomadic peoples hunted and raised livestock. Merchants did a brisk business obtaining gold and other goods from the forest regions and trading them to merchants farther north. From cities such as Gao and Timbuktu, on the fringes of the great Sahara, trading expeditions crossed the desert to reach the northern markets.

Desert is the third major vegetation region in West Africa. The world's largest desert, the Sahara, remained largely uninhabited. Scattered towns arose at major watering holes, where camel caravans loaded with trade goods stopped to rest.

Family Life As in the Americas, societies throughout West Africa were organized according to kinship groups. Often, all the residents of a town or city belonged to kinship groups that traced their line of origin to a common ancestor. This type of organization is called a lineage. African **lineage** groups provided the types of support that modern governments and churches do in the United States. West Africa's ruling classes generally came from powerful lineage groups.

Religion From ancient times, a great variety of religious customs and ceremonies existed in Africa. Yet traditional cultures generally shared certain religious beliefs. People worshipped a Supreme Being as well as many lesser gods and goddesses, or spirits. As in most early religions, these spirits were thought to inhabit everything in the natural world, from animals to trees to stones. Humans also were thought to be living spirits both before and after death. Africans appealed to the spirits of their ancestors for help.

Information concerning religious beliefs, family stories, and laws was handed down from generation to generation through oral tradition. As in the Americas, oral histories gave kinship groups a distinct sense of identity and unity.

Kingdoms and Trade

Africans also left a historical record in exquisite works of art. These treasures tell the story of governments that ruled for centuries.

Benin One such government ruled Benin, a coastal forest kingdom that arose in the late 1200s. There, artists left a record of their society in a series of bronze plaques that once decorated the palace of the king, or Oba. From the capital city, also called Benin, the Obas ruled surrounding lands. Through a network of administrators, Benin's rulers waged war, directed agriculture, and regulated trade.

A European traveler who had visited the capital several times made this observation: "This city is about a league [three miles] long from gate to gate; it has no wall but is surrounded by a large

Answer to . . .

Viewing History Islamic scholars who settled there helped turn Timbuktu into a center of learning.

▶ RESOURCE OPTIONS

Media and Technology

RESOURCE⊙PRO

Biography Askia Muhammad, found on Resource Pro, profiles the brilliant ruler of the West African kingdom of Songhai.

Visual Learning Activity Slave Factories, found on Resource Pro, helps students understand slavery through illustration.

moat, very wide and deep, which suffices for its defense. . . . Its houses are made of mud walls covered with palm leaves." The streets of Benin were wide and clean, and they led to a grand palace.

Benin's wealth came from trade. The kingdom produced goods such as palm oil, ivory, and beautiful woods. Groups of artisans, such as those who worked in bronze or brass or ivory, each had their own organization.

The kingdom produced some of the finest artwork of the time, especially sculpted heads created in a unique artistic style. Before long, sculptors started creating figures with beards and helmets. These figures represented the Portuguese. A strong Oba had come to the throne in 1481, and had established friendly and profitable trade relations with the Portuguese.

Songhai In the 1400s, as European monarchs began to make plans for building empires, one of the largest empires in the world was being created in the West African savanna. The Songhai empire, located between the coastal rain forest region and the dry Sahara, stretched across much of West Africa. The Songhai empire would exist from 1464 to 1590.

Songhai's most famed monarch, Askia Muhammad, created a complex government with separate departments for defense, banking, and farming. A bureaucracy of paid officials enforced laws, collected taxes, negotiated with other nations, and kept the peace.

African States and Trade, c. 1500

In the plaque on the left, an Oba, attended by servants, is offered merchandise by Portuguese traders. By 1500, extensive trade routes existed across West Africa. **Movement** Why do you think the Portuguese trading posts were located along the African coast?

Peace and prosperity supported the growth of education in Songhai. The capital city, Timbuktu, was a center of learning with about 150 schools for a population of 100,000. A famous Arab traveler and writer of the time, Leo Africanus wrote of Timbuktu:

> **"A great store of doctors, judges, priests, and other learned men . . . are bountifully maintained at the King's cost and charges. And hither [here] are brought various manuscripts of books from North Africa, which are sold for more money than any other merchandise."**
>
> —*Leo Africanus,* The History and Description of Africa, *c. 1526*

As in medieval Europe, most scholars studied religion. Islam had reached West Africa in about the year 1050, through trade and by invasion from the north. Askia Muhammad, a devout Muslim, had made Songhai a Muslim empire. Yet most people, especially outside the cities, still followed traditional African beliefs.

Songhai's location made it a major player in the growing trade with North Africa and Europe. From forest kingdoms such as Benin, Songhai traders obtained gold, ivory, and kola nuts (used to flavor drinks). They also bought pepper, a rare and much-desired spice in those days. Traders paid heavy fees to move their goods northward across Songhai. In caravans of as many as 12,000 camels, the groups continued north across the Sahara. On their return trip, they brought books, paper, weapons, cloth, horses, and salt.

Slavery in Africa

Africans, like Europeans, believed in the private ownership of goods and property. Yet Africans differed from Europeans in their attitudes toward land and people. In Europe, land was **scarce**—in short supply—and thus was very valuable. Europeans' wealth, in fact, was determined by the amount of land they possessed.

In Africa, land was plentiful, so no one could become wealthy and powerful by claiming a large area of land. Yet while land was plentiful, people were not. Leaders' power rested on the number of people they ruled rather than the amount of land they controlled.

Main Idea
CONNECTIONS

Why did West African leaders place more value on population than on land?

Growing kingdoms such as Benin and Songhai needed increasing numbers of workers. As in many other societies, slaves provided the labor. They made or grew much of what was traded. In addition, slaves themselves had value as items of trade.

People cut off from their lineage were the most likely to be enslaved in Africa. Most probably had been captured in war. The slave population also included orphans, criminals, and other people rejected by society. Many people were kidnapped in slave raids carried out by rival ethnic groups.

Africans' concept of slavery differed from slavery as it developed in the Americas. In Africa, for example, slaves became adopted members of the kinship group that enslaved them. Frequently they married into a lineage, even into the high ranks of society. Slaves also could move up in society and out of their slave role. Children of slaves were not presumed to be born into slavery. Finally, enslaved people carried out a variety of roles, not limited to tough physical labor. While most women and many men labored in the fields, some men became soldiers or administrators.

In the 1500s, Europeans began to exchange valuable goods, such as guns, for slaves sold by coastal societies such as Benin. Both sides profited greatly. The Africans obtained advanced technology, and the Europeans obtained labor for use in large farming operations in the Americas and elsewhere.

As time wore on, the Europeans demanded more and more slaves. Those who resisted dealing in the human cargo became themselves the victims of bloody slave raids.

SECTION 3 REVIEW

Comprehension

1. Key Terms Define: (a) savanna; (b) lineage; (c) scarce.

2. Summarizing the Main Idea Describe key features of early West African cultures.

3. Organizing Information Make a chart comparing West African and European customs.

Critical Thinking

4. Analyzing Time Lines Review the time line at the start of the section. Choose two entries and show how they affected West Africa.

5. Recognizing Cause and Effect What geographic and economic factors made Songhai wealthy? Explain.

Writing Activity

6. Writing a Persuasive Essay Consider the choices facing African monarchs who were meeting Europeans for the first time. Take a position either for or against establishing trade with the newcomers. Write an essay stating your view and support it with reasons. Think about both the benefits and the risks of trade.

▶ RESOURCE OPTIONS

Teaching Resources

📁 **Quiz** Units 1–2 folder, p. 8

Student Performance Pack

 Guide to the Essentials Chapter 1, Section 3 (English and Spanish)

1492	1494	1499	1507
Columbus sails to Americas	Spain and Portugal divide the non-Christian world	Amerigo Vespucci explores the American coast	"America" first appears on map

1490   **1495**   **1500**   **1505**   **1510**

4 The Atlantic World Is Born

SECTION PREVIEW

Objectives

1. Identify Columbus and describe the circumstances that led to his explorations.
2. Describe the challenges the expedition faced.
3. Describe the positive and negative impact of Columbus's journeys.
4. *Key Terms* Define: Columbian Exchange; Treaty of Tordesillas; plantation; cash crop.

Main Idea

Columbus's voyages to the Americas permanently reshaped American, European, and African history.

Reading Strategy

Analyzing Cause and Effect As you read, write down specific details that explain why Europeans came to the Americas.

Until quite recently, schoolbooks on American history repeated a famous but false legend about Christopher Columbus's voyage to America. According to the legend, Columbus believed that Earth was round, while everyone else thought it was flat. As he sailed west across the Atlantic Ocean, his crew nearly mutinied, thinking that they would fall off the edge of Earth. Just then, the story goes, the crew spotted land. Columbus had discovered America, the old histories claimed. He was the first European to set foot on American soil.

This legend is wrong in a number of ways. First, Renaissance scholars of Columbus's time studied the work of ancient Greek and Arab scientists, who had shown that the Earth is a sphere. Second, Native Americans had discovered the uninhabited Western Hemisphere thousands of years before. Third, Norsemen led by Leif Ericsson had landed and briefly settled on what is now Newfoundland, Canada, about 500 years before Columbus's famous journey.

The truth itself is amazing enough. Columbus was an experienced navigator who undertook a highly dangerous voyage into unknown waters. Other mariners had attempted the trip across the Atlantic. They never returned. Columbus did, and his accomplishment changed the course of history.

Christopher Columbus

AMERICAN BIOGRAPHY Columbus wrote volumes about his journeys to the Americas. Yet we know very little about his early life. Columbus, or Cristoforo Colombo in Italian, was born in 1451 in the bustling merchant city of Genoa, Italy. His father, Domenico, did a modest business as a merchant and worked in the wool industry. His mother, Susanna Fontanaroosa, was the daughter of a wool weaver.

Columbus grew up determined to make his fortune and join the ranks of the wealthy nobility. Young Columbus had a variety of interests, spending some time as a mapmaker and a trader. His love, however, was the ocean. So he went where any aspiring mariner of that time would go: to Portugal, for navigator's training.

Much of the rest of Columbus's life was spent at sea. In 1476, at age 25, he

Christopher Columbus (1451–1506)

 RESOURCE OPTIONS

Teaching Resources

📁 **Reproducible Lesson Plan** Lesson Plans folder, p. 37

📁 **Learning Styles Lesson Plan** Learning Styles Lesson Plans folder, p. 5

📁 **Big Idea Graphic Organizer** Big Idea Graphic Organizer folder, p. 9

📁 **Guided Reading and Review** Units 1–2 folder, p. 9

Media and Technology

 Prentice Hall United States History Video Collection™
Volume 1 *Three Worlds Meet*

Objectives
You may wish to call students' attention to the objectives in the Section Preview. The objectives are reflected in the main headings of the section.

Bellringer
Ask students to recall facts or stories they know about the first voyage of Columbus. What if he had not made the journey? Was interaction within the Atlantic World inevitable, considering what students have learned about Europeans' motivations and technology?

Reading Strategy
Analyzing Cause and Effect Refer to the Reading Strategy in the Section Preview. Model it by making a two-column table on the chalkboard. Label the first column Causes and the second column Effects.

LESSON PLAN
Connecting to the Main Idea

1. Focus Discuss how the voyage of Columbus created what is termed the Atlantic World. The three cultures of that world—Native American, European, and African—began centuries of interaction, which brought great changes to each. Ask students how those changes affected each culture.

2. Instruct Point out that the Atlantic World was based on elements from all three cultures, although historically it appears that the Europeans were dominant. Ask students to suggest ways in which the other cultures influenced and contributed to the interchange.

3. Close Discuss the three reasons Europeans wanted to conquer the Americas. *(Land, resources, conversion to Christianity.)* Ask how technology and disease helped them.

Cabot Drops By On June 24, 1497, the Genoa-born English mariner John Cabot became the first European since Viking days to set foot in North America, when he landed on what is now called Newfoundland. At least, that's the story. In actuality, an event resembling Cabot's voyage did take place in 1497, but virtually every detail is subject to question. Cabot left no written record of his journey, and the few surviving secondhand sources contradict one another. Even the basic biographical facts are skimpy. Cabot's point of disembarkation elicits the most controversy. Based on a few scraps of maddeningly vague description, historians have located the site everywhere from Labrador down to Maine, with Newfoundland the most popular choice. Source: Frederic D. Schwarz, "The Time Machine," *American Heritage* magazine, May/June 1997

*C*ustomize for

Less Proficient Readers

Tell students that in this section they will read about the early interactions among the three cultures of the Atlantic World. As they read, have them take notes on the effects of this interaction on the people of each of the three cultures.

Answer to . . .

Viewing History People thought the journey was hazardous.
Main Idea Connections Columbus was motivated by his religion and his desire to succeed where others had failed.

In this 1594 painting, Atlantic winds, whales, and flying fish alarm the crew of a Portuguese ship. *Geography What does this painting suggest about people's attitude toward the westward journey across the Atlantic Ocean?*

survived a shipwreck off the coast of Portugal. With a fearlessness that would serve him well later on, he went right back to the sea. He joined Portuguese crews that sailed to Iceland and Ireland in 1477. After spending some time as a sugar buyer for an Italian company in Spain, the restless sailor traveled to West Africa to trade along the forested coast. On these voyages Columbus developed a genius for navigation. He also learned much about the geography and wind currents of the eastern Atlantic Ocean.

Main Idea CONNECTIONS

What motivated Columbus to set sail for "the Indies"?

Columbus was a complex man, moody and distant from others, ambitious and stubborn. He was also highly religious and well-schooled in the Bible. Columbus believed absolutely that he could succeed where others had failed and that God had given him a heroic mission.

A Daring Expedition

As his skills matured, Columbus became more eager to seek a westward sea route to the "Indies," meaning China, India, and other Asian lands. He did not think of *attempting* it. He would *do* it. But he did not have the personal wealth to fund such an undertaking. For years he petitioned various European monarchs to sponsor his risky project.

Columbus's pleas were answered in January 1492, when he appeared before the Spanish court of Queen Isabella and King Ferdinand. They authorized Columbus to make contact with the people of "the lands of India." Much to his pleasure, they granted him the title of a noble and made him "High Admiral of the Ocean Sea and . . . Governor of the islands and continent which I should discover," as Columbus wrote later. His sons and grandsons would inherit his title and the conquered lands, he said.

TEST PREPARATION

Have students read the first paragraph under the heading *A Daring Expedition* and then answer the question below.

What is the main idea of the passage?

A Columbus was a mature navigator.

B Columbus was poor.

C Columbus was determined to succeed in finding a westward sea route to the Indies.

D Columbus tried for years to find a sponsor to fund his expedition.

Reasons for the Voyage Spanish nobles and clergy strongly supported Columbus's voyage. All had reasons for wanting the mission to succeed:

(1) Columbus hoped to enrich his family and to gain honor and fame. Yet Columbus also planned to conquer non-Catholic lands and convert their peoples to Catholicism. He held the belief, widespread at that time, that other cultures were inferior to his own. In the very year of his voyage, Columbus witnessed the final battle of Queen Isabella's crusade to reconquer Spain from the Muslims. This he saw as proof that God wanted him to bring Christianity to other lands.

(2) Columbus's royal patrons shared his desire to spread Catholicism. They had economic motives as well. The Crusades had failed to retake Jerusalem, and Muslims still controlled the overland trade routes connecting Europe and Asia. Europeans wanted to bypass the Muslims and find a way to trade directly for the eastern spices and herbs that Europeans needed for cooking and for medicine.

(3) Spain's rivalry with Portugal gave the Spanish an extra reason for backing the voyage. Portuguese sailors had found an eastern route to India by sailing around Africa. If Spain could find an easier, western route to Asia, it might gain an advantage over Portuguese traders.

Destination: Asia Shortly before sunrise on Friday, August 3, 1492, three ships under Columbus's command set sail from the seaport of Palos, in the Spanish kingdom of Castile. They bore Spanish names: *Niña*, *Pinta*, and *Santa María*. Before them stretched the blue curve of the horizon. Awaiting them were dangers such as ocean storms, starvation, and the sailor's enemy: rickets, a painful disease resulting from lack of fresh fruits and vegetables.

Columbus showed his navigational skills by first heading south, then west, avoiding the Atlantic storms that had blown other ships to pieces. However, the voyage was on a course for disaster, because Columbus had underestimated the size of the planet.† His ships had not brought enough food or water for a voyage all the way to Asia. Columbus's journals of the voyage suggest that as the tense weeks

---

†Columbus's flawed measurements put China roughly where the city of San Diego, California, is today. He figured that Japan was on the same line of longitude as what we now call the Virgin Islands.

---

passed, the admiral did not reveal to his crews how far they had actually traveled, wisely avoiding a scare.

On October 12 the thankful crew of the *Pinta* spotted land. The explorers' actual landing place is disputed, but it certainly was not China. Many scholars believe it to be the island of San Salvador, in the Bahamas.

A Historic Meeting Fortunately for Columbus and his crew, they received a warm welcome from the first Native Americans they met, the Tainos. The Tainos greeted the newcomers with gifts. This astonished Columbus, who was not familiar with the Native American view of trade as an exchange of gifts. Columbus later wrote about the Tainos to Isabella and Ferdinand:

> ❝They are so ingenuous [innocent] and free with all they have, that no one would believe it who has not seen it; of anything that they possess, if it be asked of them, they never say no; on the contrary, they invite you to share it and show as much love as if their hearts went with it.❞

—*letter from Columbus to Queen Isabella and King Ferdinand of Spain, 1493*

Continuing on to other islands, Columbus and his crew collected—often by force—other gifts to give to the queen. These "gifts" included some Native Americans, whom Columbus brought back to Spain to present to the Spanish monarchs. Columbus called these people "Indians," because he believed that he had reached the Indies. The term is still sometimes used today.

Heading Home When the return trip to Spain began, on January 16, 1493, only two ships set sail. The *Santa María* had accidentally run aground. The crew used the ship's battered planks to help build a small fort, where they stored what treasure they couldn't carry. Columbus left part of the crew behind to guard the stockade until he could return.

Numerous disasters followed the voyagers home. Upon his return, Columbus received the honors he had sought, including the governorship of the present-day island of Hispaniola in the Caribbean. He did not stay long to enjoy his fame. In only six months he was on his way back to the Americas.

Early sailors sighted the North Star and used an astrolabe such as this one to calculate their latitude.

RESOURCE OPTIONS

Media and Technology

 AmericanHeritage® CD-ROM

History Makers Christopher Columbus

 Color Transparencies Political Cartoons, K-1

▼ BACKGROUND

Interdisciplinary

Educated Europeans in the 1400s accepted the calculations made by the Greek scholar Eratosthenes (3rd century B.C.). Measuring differences in the lengths of shadows, he had estimated the circumference of Earth at what would be calculated today as 25,000 miles. What educated people feared about sailing west, therefore, was not falling off the edge of the world, but having to travel too long without fresh water and food before reaching Asia. Columbus took a calculated risk because he believed the less accurate figures of the later scientist Ptolemy of Alexandria (A.D. 100s), who estimated that Earth was only 18,000 miles around. When Columbus reached the islands of the Caribbean, he named them the West Indies, believing they lay off the coast of Asia. He died without understanding that he had encountered a separate landmass.

ACTIVITY
LEARNING STYLES

Ask students to use or trace an outline map of the world and draw lines to represent the major interactions among the three cultures of the Atlantic World. Have them use symbols or icons to show the major items that were interchanged: foods and crops; animals; diseases; slaves; gold and silver. *(Visual/Spatial)*

Later Voyages Columbus led a total of four trips to the Americas. Not all were profitable. In addition, Columbus proved to be a far better admiral than governor. The Spanish settlers on Hispaniola, where Columbus and his two brothers ruled, complained to the Spanish government of harsh and unfair treatment. Columbus lost his governorship, as well as his prestige at court. Furthermore, despite increasing evidence that he had found a new continent, Columbus clung to his claim that he had reached the "Indies."

The aging explorer returned from his fourth and last voyage in 1504, the same year Isabella died. Columbus asked Ferdinand to restore his governorship, but the king refused. Columbus died a disappointed man in 1506, never knowing how much he had changed the course of history.

A New Continent Others, however, realized the importance of Columbus's findings. In 1499, a merchant from Italy named Amerigo Vespucci made the first of two voyages to the Caribbean Sea. After sailing along the coast of South America, Vespucci suggested that these lands might be a continent previously unknown to Europeans, "what we may rightly call a New World." A German mapmaker named Waldseemüller read Vespucci's account and took it to heart. In 1507 he printed the first map showing the "New World" to be separate from Asia. He named the unfamiliar lands "America," after Amerigo Vespucci.

Columbus's Impact

In recent years, considerable public debate has arisen over the long-term effects of Columbus's voyages to the Americas. Most historians agree that the effects were both good and bad.

The Columbian Exchange Columbus's journeys launched a new era of transatlantic trade known as the **Columbian Exchange**, explained in the chart (left). European ships returned with exciting new foods from the Americas, including peanuts, pineapples, and tomatoes. One new item, cocoa, set off a craze in Europe. Another food, the potato, quickly became the new food of Europe's poor, helping to save them from famines.

Europeans brought to the Americas crops such as wheat, and domesticated animals such as the cow and the horse. They brought firearms and the wheel and axle, technologies that Native Americans did not have. Finally, Europeans introduced their culture to the Americas, including European laws, languages, and customs.

Native Americans Devastated Any benefits the Native Americans received, however, were far outweighed by the misery brought upon them. The greatest source of this misery was disease. The Columbian Exchange brought together people who had been isolated from one another and thus had no resistance to one another's diseases.

Europeans had already experienced a severe decline in their population due to plague and other diseases. Now Europeans brought similar disasters to the Americas. Passing germs through even the most casual contact, explorers and soldiers infected Native Americans with smallpox, typhus, measles, and other deadly diseases.

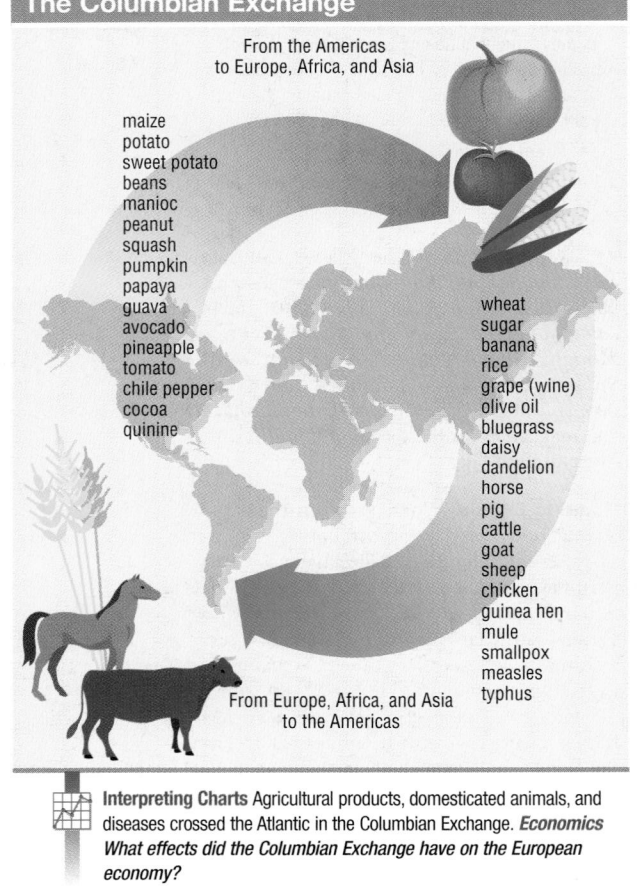

The Columbian Exchange

From the Americas to Europe, Africa, and Asia

maize
potato
sweet potato
beans
manioc
peanut
squash
pumpkin
papaya
guava
avocado
pineapple
tomato
chile pepper
cocoa
quinine

wheat
sugar
banana
rice
grape (wine)
olive oil
bluegrass
daisy
dandelion
horse
pig
cattle
goat
sheep
chicken
guinea hen
mule
smallpox
measles
typhus

From Europe, Africa, and Asia to the Americas

Interpreting Charts Agricultural products, domesticated animals, and diseases crossed the Atlantic in the Columbian Exchange. *Economics* *What effects did the Columbian Exchange have on the European economy?*

The diseases spread rapidly along the extensive Native American trade network. One man, the son of a Native American woman and a Spanish captain, described what explorers found in 1540 when they first reached the Native American town of Talomeca in present-day Georgia: "The Castilians found the town of Talomeco without any people at all, because [of] the recent pestilence [disease] . . . [Near] the rich temple, it is said they found four longhouses filled with bodies from the plague."

Europeans Gain Wealth At first, Europeans were unaware that they were passing on disease to the Native Americans. Many Europeans believed that the "pestilence" that ravaged the Native American population was a sign that God favored Europeans over Native Americans. God, these Europeans believed, had sent Europeans to conquer the Americas.

The rival nations of Europe all wanted a part of this sudden opportunity to gain land and wealth. The Portuguese, whose navigational technology made Columbus's voyage possible, resented Spain's claim to the Western Hemisphere. So Portugal sent a complaint to the Pope.

European Catholics believed that the Pope had the authority to divide up any newly conquered non-Christian lands. In 1494, at the urging of Pope Alexander, Portugal and Spain signed the **Treaty of Tordesillas.** Under the treaty, the two countries divided all lands on Earth not already claimed by other Christians. They did this by drawing an imaginary line around the world called the Line of Demarcation. Spain was to rule over lands west of the line, including most of the Americas. Portugal would control the rest, including Brazil and the sea route around Africa.[†]

At first, Spain and Portugal were able to control much of the regions they claimed. In the 1500s, however, France, England, and the Netherlands began to move into North America. In the first century after Columbus's voyage, the amount of gold and silver in Europe's economy increased eight times over, much of it made out of ore from mines in the Americas.

[†] The effects of this 500-year-old treaty can be seen today. People in most of South America, the part given to Spain, speak Spanish. In Brazil, the area set aside for Portugal, most people speak Portuguese.

A Native American in Mexico drew this picture of a smallpox victim being comforted by a healer. The squiggle near the healer's mouth symbolizes spoken words. *Geography* How did European diseases such as smallpox travel throughout the Americas?

Africans Enslaved To supply the American foods that Europeans demanded, Portugal and Spain established **plantations**, the large farming operations that produced crops not for their own use but for sale. Such products are called **cash crops**. Plantation farming of tropical cash crops such as sugar and pineapple required huge numbers of workers who labored long hours in hot climates.

At first, soldiers kidnapped Native Americans and forced them to work on the plantations. Unaccustomed to that type of work and weakened by disease, these slaves did not provide a reliable labor force. Europeans then turned to West Africa.

As you read in Section 3, a West African slave trade began to emerge in the 1400s. In 1517, the first enslaved Africans arrived in the Americas. The huge need for labor in the Western Hemisphere turned this grim business into an industry.

Main Idea
CONNECTIONS

How was Africa changed by the introduction of cash crops in the Americas?

Using the Internet

Create a Diary Entry

Objective Use the Internet to create a diary entry by a West African living during the time of the first interactions between Africans and Europeans. Have students follow these instructions:

1. See the *America: Pathways to the Present* Web site at

http://www.Pathways.phschool.com

for the URL for the Mali Interactive Site.

2. Follow the link to Jenne-jeno, an ancient African city. Read the text, taking notes on aspects of daily life, geography, and trade that the archaeological evidence reveals.

3. Write a diary entry as if you are an inhabitant of Jenne-jeno during the 1400s and 1500s. Your entry should include the type of tasks you do, clothing you make or wear, what your house is like, and how you get food and items you can't make. Add any supporting details available from the text, such as those related to art and religion.

4. Share and compare your diary entry with that of a classmate.

Answer to . . .

Viewing History The diseases spread from Europeans along the trade routes of the Columbian Exchange.
Main Idea Connections Europeans abducted West Africans to create a labor force to grow cash crops, decreasing the native population.

CAUSE AND EFFECT : European Exploration

CAUSES
- *Desire to accumulate wealth through trade*
- *Rebirth of a spirit of inquiry*
- *Improved seafaring technology*

EUROPEANS EXPLORE THE AMERICAS

EFFECTS
- *An exchange of goods and ideas between Europe and the Americas begins.*
- *European diseases devastate Native American populations.*
- *Europeans enter the West African slave trade.*

 Interpreting Charts European exploration of the Americas set off a chain of events that would forever change life for not only Europeans, but for Native Americans and West Africans as well. *Diversity What was the nature of these changes?*

From Benin and dozens of other thriving cultures and kingdoms, Europeans began trading for slaves. The West Africans who were forced into slavery generally included the healthiest people, those who would be well suited for conditions on American plantations and in other enterprises.

Historians continue to debate the number of Africans enslaved. Some estimate that during the 1500s, about 275,000 West Africans were taken against their will across the Atlantic Ocean. That number grew to about 6 million in the 1700s, these historians say. Estimates of the total number of West Africans abducted from their homeland and taken to North and South America range from roughly 9 million to more than 11 million.

Mere numbers, however, cannot portray the full horror of slavery for West Africans. Europeans constructed a uniquely cruel system to supply slaves to the Americas. They regarded slaves as mere property and treated them no better than farm animals. Slavery was a lifetime sentence—often a death sentence—from which there was no escape.

A New Culture Explorers and settlers from other European nations soon followed the Spanish. The Europeans would adopt ideas and customs from the Native Americans and from one another as well. While the United States derives its basic constitutional and legal institutions from Europeans, particularly the English, American culture today reflects the impact of centuries of exchange among many people.

SECTION 4 REVIEW

Comprehension

1. *Key Terms* Define: (a) Columbian Exchange; (b) Treaty of Tordesillas; (c) plantation; (d) cash crop.

2. *Summarizing the Main Idea* Reread the Main Idea statement in the Section Preview. Rewrite and expand it into a paragraph of your own words.

3. *Organizing Information* Create a two-column chart entitled *Columbus's Challenges*. Label the left column *Problem* and the right column *Strategy*. Fill in the chart with at least four entries in each column.

Critical Thinking

4. *Analyzing Time Lines* Review the time line at the start of the section. Choose any four entries and explain who benefited from each event and who was harmed by it.

5. *Recognizing Bias* What specific beliefs influenced Europeans' views of themselves and other cultures? How did these beliefs affect their actions?

Writing Activity

6. *Writing a Persuasive Essay* From the point of view of Columbus, write an essay to try to persuade Queen Isabella and King Ferdinand to fund your expensive voyage to the Indies.

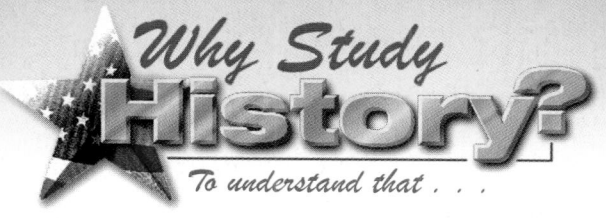
Why Study History?
To understand that . . .

You Are Part of the Global Economy

The voyages of exploration described in this chapter were an early step in the creation of today's global economy.

Read the headlines in the Sunday paper. Listen to the evening news. You will likely find at least one story about the "global economy"—the binding economic ties between countries worldwide.

The global economy is even closer than the news. You can see it in your school lunchroom, clothes closet, and local shopping mall. Check your radio and running shoes to see where they were made. You may be surprised by how many items that you use or wear every day are made in other countries.

Arab trading ship, c. 1500

The Impact Today

Two key aspects of the global economy are foreign trade and investments. Foreign trade plays a significant role in the U.S. economy. In 1995, the United States exported about $578 billion of goods. The value of imported goods was even greater: about $751 billion.

Thriving foreign trade gives Americans several benefits. We have markets throughout the world in which to sell our farm products and consumer goods. We also can buy from a wide choice of merchandise, imported from all over the world.

Growing foreign investments tie the U.S. economy closely to the economies of other countries. When foreign economies are strong, American investments prosper. Yet problems that affect other nations in the global economy affect the United

States as well. For example, the collapse of a foreign stock market could hurt thousands of American investors. The slowdown of a foreign economy, which causes foreign citizens to lose purchasing power, could threaten the jobs of Americans whose companies make goods to sell abroad.

The global economy is in your job future. A number of manufacturing industries, which rely on unskilled and semi-skilled labor, have moved to countries where they can pay workers less money. As a result, many Americans who once worked in manufacturing industries have lost their jobs. (Industries that rely on highly educated workers, such as the weapons and pharmaceutical industries, have tended to remain in the United States.) You will need more high-tech skills than did workers in the past.

Fast-food restaurant in Indonesia

The Impact on You

Consumers can encourage manufacturers to keep their operations in the United States by buying only American-made products. Do you want to buy only products made in the United States? Jot down a response. Then search your house for 15 items you use every day. List them and their country of origin. Return to your response. Do you want to maintain or revise it? Write a one-minute opinion piece for a radio program explaining your position.

RESOURCE OPTIONS

Teaching Resources

Why Study History? Activity You Are Part of the Global Economy, found in the Why Study History? folder, p. 2, provides an activity to help students become more responsible consumers.

Media and Technology

AmericanHeritage® CD-ROM

Time Tour The Nation Today and Tomorrow: Toward a New Century

Class Discussion

Discuss with the class Americans' role in the global economy. For a more thorough examination of the issue, see the activity folder in the Resource Options below.

ACTIVITY
STUDENT PARTICIPATION

Creating a Poster

Ask students to read the text. Then divide the class into two groups. Have each group create a poster to be used in a debate on this question: Which shoes should we buy—an inexpensive pair made by nonunion workers in China or an expensive pair made by U.S. union workers? Posters should address these issues:
- **cost**
- **local jobs**
- **competition**
- **expected Chinese reaction**

Have groups present their posters. Encourage debate.

Follow up Ask what difference the issue of child labor in a foreign country would make in the debate.

Using the Internet

Students can learn more about the global economy by exploring links in the *America: Pathways to the Present* Web site at

http://www.Pathways.phschool.com

Assessment

See the Lesson Plans folder, pp. 24–27, for rubrics on assessing Class Participation Projects.

Key Terms
Students should refer to the definitions of the key terms in the chapter to write sentences that show the relation of each word to the events covered in this chapter.

Comprehension
1. They developed various types of dwellings and food-gathering methods; they traded for what they did not have.
2. They had similar religious beliefs, kinship structures, trading methods, and attitudes about land.
3. Life on the manor offered protection but was isolated; everyone was born into certain roles for life; each person owed loyalty and service to another. The Church oversaw all aspects of medieval life; it had the power to excommunicate; it exercised authority over kings.
4. The Crusades helped break Europe's isolation by exposing Europeans to ideas and goods from abroad.
5. Answers should focus on topics such as these: contacts with the outside world; Church authority; the role of monarchs; culture; social structure; education; trade.
6. In the three major regions—the coastal rain forests, the savanna, and the desert—ways of living, natural resources, and trade varied greatly.
7. Yes. Powerful monarchs ruled in kingdoms such as Benin and Songhai.
8. Spain wanted to conquer non-Christians, acquire new lands and wealth, and compete for power with Portugal.
9. Positive effects include new products, wealth, and power for Europeans; new products for Native Americans. Negative effects include diseases, enslavement and conquests of Native Americans; enslavement of Africans.

Chapter Summary

The major concepts of Chapter 1 are presented below. See also *Guide to the Essentials of American History* or *Interactive Student Tutorial CD-ROM,* which contains interactive review activities, time lines, helpful hints, and test practice for Chapter 1.

Reviewing the Main Ideas
Three cultures—Native American, European, and African—built unique societies with differing customs and beliefs. These groups came into contact when Europeans explored and then colonized the Americas.

Section 1: The Native American World
Native American societies, which populated North America for thousands of years, had shared beliefs, different ways of life, and a wide trading network.

Section 2: The European World
The Middle Ages, a period when Europe was isolated from the rest of the world, was followed by the Renaissance, a period when Europeans sought knowledge of the world and began to explore it.

Section 3: The World of the West Africans
At the time of their first contact with Europeans, West Africans had wealthy kingdoms with strong governments, unique cultures, and traditional religious beliefs.

Section 4: The Atlantic World Is Born
Columbus's voyage to the Americas permanently reshaped American, European, and African history.

The voyages of exploration described in this chapter were an early step in the creation of today's global economy. Two of the main links in that economy are foreign trade and investment.

Key Terms
Use each of the terms below in a sentence that shows how it relates to either Native American, European, or West African culture.

1. Renaissance
2. oral history
3. plantation
4. kinship
5. cash crop
6. savanna
7. lineage
8. monarch
9. Crusades
10. middle class
11. Middle Ages
12. Reformation
13. nomadic
14. scarce
15. feudalism
16. clan
17. Columbian Exchange
18. Treaty of Tordesillas
19. barter

Comprehension
1. In what ways did Native American groups adapt to their environments?
2. What beliefs and customs did the many Native American groups have in common?
3. Describe how the manor system and the Church affected medieval life.
4. How did the Crusades change Europe?
5. Compare and contrast the Middle Ages and the Renaissance.
6. What effects did geography have on the development of West African cultures?
7. Did West African cultures have organized governments at the time that they came into contact with Europeans? Explain.
8. Why did Spain finally agree to sponsor Columbus's voyage?
9. What positive and negative effects did Columbus's voyages have?

Using Graphic Organizers
On a separate sheet of paper, copy the chart below. In each box write a sentence summarizing information from the chapter.

	Native Americans	Europeans	Africans
Organization of Society			
Beliefs About Land			
Religion			
Trade Goods			

Using Graphic Organizers
- Native Americans had strong kinship ties; believed that land should be used but not owned; worshipped nature and respected ancestors; traded shell and stone, minerals, and foods such as corn, potatoes, and cocoa.
- Europeans based their society on feudal ties; believed that land represented wealth; were Christians; traded foods such as wheat and rice, weapons, and livestock.
- Africans based their society on kinship ties; did not regard the land as valuable because it was so plentiful; respected ancestors and worshipped according to traditional beliefs in spirits; traded in gold, forest products, and slaves.

Analyzing Political Cartoons

1. The topic of this modern-day cartoon is the current debate over whether the United States should place new restrictions on immigration. (a) Who does the man in the center represent? (b) Who do the people on the left represent? Who does the man on the right represent?

2. What point is the cartoonist making? Do you agree with the cartoonist's view? Explain your reasoning.

Critical Thinking

1. *Applying the Chapter Skill* Discuss how Europeans' opinions about Native Americans and Africans differed from the facts about these cultures.

2. *Predicting Consequences* Explain how values, beliefs, and customs differed among the three Atlantic cultures. Choose one way in which the three cultures differed, and explain how this difference could have led to conflict.

3. *Recognizing Cause and Effect* In the early days of trade between West Africans and Europeans, the Africans controlled the exchange of goods. Within a century they had become victims of European slave-raiders. What do you think caused this change?

4. *Drawing Conclusions* How do you think the ideas of the Renaissance influenced the culture of modern-day America?

INTERNET ACTIVITY

For your portfolio:
PREPARE A REPORT

Access Prentice Hall's *America: Pathways to the Present* site at **www.Pathways.phschool.com** for the specific URL to complete the activity. Additional resources and related Web sites are also available.

Use the links provided to find out about the earliest inhabitants of your state or region. Write a brief report on the archaeological activity in the area and what it has revealed about the first people to live there.

ANALYZING DOCUMENTS ◀ ▶ INTERPRETING DATA

Turn to the excerpt from Columbus's letter to Isabella and Ferdinand on page 21.

1. Which statement best represents the meaning of the quotation? (a) The Tainos are innocent, generous, and obedient. (b) The Tainos loved the Europeans. (c) The Tainos are loving but possessive.

2. What conclusion do you think the king and queen might have drawn from Columbus's description of the Tainos? Choose from the following statements, and explain your reasoning: (a) The Tainos should be treated with the respect that they showed Columbus. (b) The Tainos would provide no resistance to Spanish conquest. (c) The Tainos must be wiped out.

3. *Writing* Assume the role of Queen Isabella or King Ferdinand and respond to Columbus's letter. Give him specific instructions on how to develop a relationship with the Tainos. The letter should reflect what you know about the values and beliefs of Renaissance Europe.

Connecting to Today

Essay Writing Write a persuasive essay in which you make the argument for going on a modern-day exploration, perhaps into space or down to the ocean floor. Include answers to these questions: (a) What are the possible benefits of the trip? (b) What are the risks? (c) Why are the benefits worth the risks?

Analyzing Political Cartoons

1. (a) A politician. (b) Americans of European descent. (c) A Native American.

2. Everyone immigrated to America at some point in history. Answers should show an understanding of the issues raised in the cartoon.

Critical Thinking

1. Answers should focus on this point: Europeans thought that these cultures were inferior to theirs, in part because they were non-Christian.

2. Students might choose examples such as views on gift-giving, attitudes about slavery, religious differences, and attitudes about land.

3. Possible answers include the superior weaponry of the Europeans and the high European demand for slaves.

4. Sample answer: The focus on humanism, the influence of classical art, and the political and economic changes of the Renaissance are all reflected in our society today.

Analyzing Documents

1. a

2. b or c—accept suitable reasoning

3. Responses might include instructions to trade with, conquer, convert, or enslave the Tainos, reflecting the belief that they were inferior to the Spanish.

Connecting to Today

Students' arguments must include answers to a, b, and c.

INTERNET ACTIVITY

Answers will vary. Reports should show an understanding of how the archaeological record is used in developing an understanding of past cultures.

European Colonization of the Americas, 1492–1752

Managing Time and Instruction

INSTRUCTION SUPPORT

These materials for instruction are provided for **each section** in the **Teaching Resources.** See **Units 1–2 folder** for Enrichment Support:

- Reproducible Lesson Plans in Lesson Plans folder   • Learning Styles Lesson Plans in Learning Styles Lesson Plans folder   • Big Idea Graphic Organizers in Big Idea Graphic Organizer folder
- Guided Reading and Review   • Quizzes   • Test Preparation Practice booklet

DAILY LESSON	ENRICHMENT SUPPORT
1 **Spanish Explorers and Colonies** *(pp. 29–33)*	• Critical Thinking Activity, Determining Relevance: Native American Words, found on **Resource Pro** • Biography, Bartolomé de Las Casas, Units 1–2 folder, p. 24 • Nystrom *Atlas of Our Country*, Early European Exploration, pp. 12–13 and Colonies in the South and West, pp. 18–19 • Biography, Popé, Medicine Man of the Pueblos, found on **Resource Pro**
2 **The Jamestown Colony** *(pp. 36–41)*	• Primary Source Activity, Cultural Clashes in the Jamestown Colony, Learning with Documents folder, p. 8 • Primary Source Activity, Native American Customs, found on **Resource Pro** • Comparing Primary Sources, On Life in Jamestown, Units 1–2 folder, pp. 25–26
3 **The New England Colonies** *(pp. 42–49)*	• Literature Activity, Puritan Poetry, found on **Resource Pro** • Key Documents, The Mayflower Compact, Learning with Documents folder, p. 80 • Visual Learning Activity, A Lasting Stereotype, Learning with Documents folder, p. 44 • Lasting Impact Activity, The Lasting Impact of King Philip's War, History's Lasting Impact folder, pp. 2–3 • Visual Learning Activity, The Pequot War, found on **Resource Pro**
4 **The Middle and Southern Colonies** *(pp. 51–54)*	• Skills for Life Activity, Units 1–2 folder, p. 28 • Your Culture Interacts with Others, Why Study History? folder, p. 3

Running Out of Time?

- Use Tape 1, "Origins of a New Society, to 1783," from **Visions of America** videotapes series.
- Use Chapter 2 Summary, from **Guide to the Essentials of American History** (English and Spanish).

Companion Web Site

The companion Web site offers online links for all chapter review activities. It also provides key content links and structured support for this chapter for both teachers and students.

http://www.Pathways.phschool.com

Teaching in the Information Age

Media and Technology

For the Student

Interactive Student Tutorial CD-ROM Chapter 2

Student Edition on Audiotape Chapter 2

American Heritage® CD-ROM

Guided Reading Audiotapes (English and Spanish) Chapter 2

For the Teacher

Resource Pro CD-ROM Chapter 2

Test Bank CD-ROM Chapter 2

Listening to Music CD from the *Bay Psalm Book*, Psalm 100

Listening to Literature Audiotapes *Timeless Voices, Timeless Themes* "A Journey Through Texas" by Alvar Nuñez Cabeza de Vaca

Assessment Options

Chapter Test Forms A&B Test Bank CD-ROM booklet

Test Bank CD-ROM Chapter 2

Standardized Test Preparation Handbook

Block Scheduling

Pacing Suggestions

For 90-minute Blocks

- Teach sections 1 and 2 using Transparencies E-1, F-1, B-1, and the Recent Scholarship note on p. 37 for class discussions.
- Teach sections 3 and 4 using the Big Idea Graphic Organizers from Teaching Resources.

Additional Resources

- Prentice Hall's **American History Block Scheduling Support File** covers over 40 topics in American history.
- **Prentice Hall United States History Video Collection™** contains 20 videotapes covering American history from beginnings to present.
- **Decision America Videotapes and Videodiscs**
- **Visions of America Videotapes and Videodiscs**

Connections to American Literature

from Prentice Hall

Prentice Hall Literature *Timeless Voices, Timeless Themes* from *Sinners in the Hands of an Angry God* by Jonathan Edwards, p. 98

Additional Resources

For the Student

Washington Irving. *"Philip of Pakanoket."* In *Rip van Winkle, The Legend of Sleepy Hollow and Other Stories.* Easton Press, 1967.

For the Teacher

Bruce Catton. *The Bold and Magnificent Dream: America's Founding Years, 1492–1815.* Doubleday, 1978.

Prentice Hall brings into the classroom the vast archives and scholarship of the nation's premier American history magazine. See "From the Archives of American Heritage®" teaching notes in this chapter.

 History Alive!

Teacher's Curriculum Institute, in partnership with Prentice Hall, provides unique materials that engage students with diverse learning styles. See History Alive!® unit on Colonial Life and the American Revolution.

 Student Performance Pack

Ensures success in the three critical areas of Reading, Test Taking, English Language Development with the following materials:
- Guide to the Essentials of American History in English and Spanish
- Guided Reading Audiotapes in English and Spanish
- Interactive Student Tutorial CD-ROM
- Test Preparation Handbook
- Test Preparation Practice booklet

European Colonization of the Americas
1492–1752

Introducing the Chapter
Each group of Europeans in North America formed a distinct society, and each group disrupted the Native American societies it encountered. By the end of the seventeenth century, New England was dominated by a single European group—the English.

Themes in American History
The theme for this chapter, Economics, is listed at the beginning of this unit. An alternate theme for the chapter is Geography. To teach this unit thematically, you may wish to use the Forging a New Nation folder in American History Block Scheduling Support.

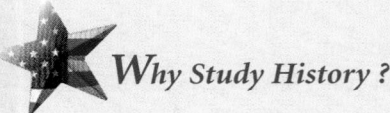

Why Study History ?

Have students explore suggested ways of connecting the past to the present on page 55.

Answer to . . .

Using Historical Evidence Students should use this question as an aid in reading the chapter. Generally, the pattern was for the colonizers to settle on land as they wanted, with little regard for native peoples. This caused open conflict in many cases.

CHAPTER 2 European Colonization of the Americas
1492–1752

CHAPTER FOCUS
This chapter describes the early explorations and settlements of the Spanish, English, French, and Dutch in North America. Because each of these groups had its own way of settling the land, regional differences emerged in the Northeast, Middle, and Southern colonies of North America.

 Why Study History? page at the end of this chapter explores the connection between European colonization of North America and the cultural diversity that continues to shape American society today.

▲ **USING HISTORICAL EVIDENCE** Although an idealized and imaginative portrait of English settlers reaching American shores, *Landing of the Pilgrims* shows the imminent meeting of two cultures. *Culture* **How did European colonizers interact with Native Americans?**

 RESOURCE OPTIONS

Teaching Resources

📁 **Big Idea Graphic Organizer** folder
Graphic summary of the main idea of the chapter.

📁 **Learning Styles Lesson Plans** folder
Alternate lesson plans for diverse learning styles for each chapter.

Media and Technology

 AmericanHeritage® CD-ROM
Time Tour A Meeting of Different Worlds: Europeans Reach the Americas *and* The Thirteen English Colonies

 Prentice Hall United States History Video Collection™ Volume 2 *The Era of Colonization (1585–1763)*

| 1513 | 1521 | 1528 | | 1680 |
| Ponce de León explores Florida | Cortés conquers the Aztec empire | Cabeza de Vaca and Estevanico explore the coastal region of Texas | 1565 The Spanish settle St. Augustine, Florida | Pueblo Revolt in New Mexico |

1500   **1550**   **1600**   **1650**   **1700**

1 Spanish Explorers and Colonies

SECTION PREVIEW

Objectives

1. Explain how Spanish explorers built an empire in the Americas.
2. Describe why the Spanish encouraged settlement in regions of North America.
3. Summarize the causes and effects of Native American resistance to the Spanish.
4. **Key Terms** Define: hidalgo; conquistador; isthmus; colony; mestizo; presidio; mission; Pueblo Revolt of 1680.

Main Idea

Between 1492 and 1650, the Spanish built an empire in Central and South America as well as the Southeast and Southwest regions of North America.

Reading Strategy

Organizing Information Sketch a map of North, Central, and South America. As you read, shade in the regions explored by the Spanish. Record key events, people, and places on your map.

Christopher Columbus made four voyages to the Americas between 1492 and 1504. His reports of lands and peoples, as well as his stories of pearls and other hints of wealth, soon drew other explorers after him. While Columbus had once been mocked as a dreamer, now he had many imitators.

Building a Spanish Empire

Like Columbus, the later Spanish explorers who sailed to the Americas had three major motives for conquering the region. They wanted to spread the Christian religion, gain wealth, and win fame. In other words, they went to the Americas for "God, gold, and glory." For centuries, adventurous young Spanish gentlemen, or **hidalgos**, had led expeditions against Muslims in Spain for these same three motives. The **conquistadors**, or Spanish conquerors of the Americas, were continuing that tradition.

Spain's Major Explorers In the first fifty years after Columbus's death, Spanish explorers expanded European knowledge of lands from Florida in the East to the shores of the

Pacific Ocean in the West. Some of Spain's most important explorers are described below.

Juan Ponce de León. One of the earliest explorers, Ponce de León, was a typical hidalgo. He was born into an upper class family in Spain and fought against the Muslims. Ponce de León then took his military skills to the Americas, perhaps as early as 1493. In the early 1500s, he heard tales of a spring with amazing powers somewhere in the Caribbean. Anyone who drank the waters from this spring would become young again. While searching in vain for this "fountain of youth," Ponce de León explored and named Florida in 1513.

A silent witness to the Spanish attempt to conquer Florida, this soldier's helmet was lost in the 1500s at Palm Beach and discovered in recent times.

Vasco Núñez de Balboa. Balboa was born to an upper class family in the Estremadura, a poor region of Spain with a harsh climate. Seeking better opportunities for wealth in the Americas, he eventually arrived on the isthmus of Panama. An **isthmus** is a narrow strip of land that joins two larger land areas, in this

---

RESOURCE OPTIONS

Teaching Resources

📁 **Reproducible Lesson Plan** Lesson Plans folder, p. 38

📁 **Big Idea Graphic Organizer** Big Idea Graphic Organizer folder, p. 10

📁 **Guided Reading and Review** Units 1–2 folder, p. 16

Media and Technology

AmericanHeritage® CD-ROM

Explorer Activity 2 The Incas, CD-ROM Guidebook, pp. 23–24, helps students create a brochure about the Incas.

Time Tour A Meeting of Different Worlds: Europeans Reach the Americas

---

Objectives

You may wish to call students' attention to the objectives in the Section Preview. The objectives are reflected in the main headings of the section.

Bellringer

Ask students to list facts that they already know about Native Americans of the Southwest and about Spanish conquest of the Americas. Students may add to and revise their lists as they read the section.

Reading Strategy

Organizing Information Refer to the Reading Strategy in the Section Preview. You may wish to have students review each other's finished maps.

LESSON PLAN

Connecting to the Main Idea

1. Focus Explain that the Spanish were the first Europeans to build an empire in the Americas. It included the Southwest and Southeast regions of North America. Ask students if they can think of any place names that reflect a Spanish heritage. (*Florida, Santa Fe, El Paso, San Antonio.*)

2. Instruct Remind students that European Christians thought it was their duty to spread their religion throughout the world. Discuss how this belief affected their dealings with Native Americans. Ask students to compare the pattern of conquest in other parts of the Spanish empire with the pattern that emerged in New Mexico in the 1700s.

3. Close The Spanish pattern of conquest was designed to acquire wealth and convert Native Americans to Christianity. In the scattered Spanish settlements in the Southwest, this pattern met with Native American resistance.

A Diverse Nation

Europeans adopted many Native American words to describe some of the animals and plants they found in the Americas, including *caribou, skunk, maize, avocado,* and *tapioca.* The English colonists had already picked up several Native American words that had entered English via Spanish, such as the Mayan *cigar* and the Taino *potato.*

European Exploration of the Americas, 1492–1682

For more than a century after Columbus's voyages, explorers sailed on behalf of any power that would sponsor them. Cabot and Verrazano were Italian, and Hudson was English. Estevanico was originally an African slave who was later freed to explore the Southwest.
Movement What nations sponsored Cabot, Verrazano, Hudson, and Estevanico?

 Ask students to look at the map of European exploration of the Americas on this page. What nations sponsored explorations? (*Spain, Portugal, England, and France.*) In what areas were the Spanish explorations focused? (*In Central and South America and the Southwest and Southeast regions of North America.*) (**Visual/Spatial**)

case North and South America. In 1513 Balboa led a group of Spaniards and Native Americans across the narrowest part of the isthmus. After crossing rivers, slashing their way through thick forests, and scaling rugged mountains, Balboa and his Spanish companions became the first known Europeans to see the Pacific Ocean from the American continent.

Ferdinand Magellan. While Balboa may have been the first European explorer to see the mysterious "South Sea," the first to cross it starting from the Americas was Magellan. Though Portuguese, not Spanish, Magellan explored in Spanish ships on behalf of the Spanish king. Starting from Spain in September 1519, Magellan and his crew sailed to Brazil, then south around the stormy tip of South America, known today as the Strait of Magellan. Magellan steered the ship boldly west from the coast of South America on a course that would take him across the Pacific Ocean for 99 days without fresh food or water. As the voyage wore on, his starving men were forced to eat the leather on the rigging of their ships. Finally, having crossed the Pacific Ocean, Magellan spotted the island of Guam. Though he later was killed in a fight with the people of the Philippine Islands, some of his crew continued on. After a three year voyage, they became the first humans known to have circumnavigated, or sailed around, the entire Earth.

Cortés and Pizarro Hernán Cortés was another explorer who left his harsh homeland, Spain's Estremadura, for the opportunities of the Americas. He was especially eager for wealth. "I and my companions," he once remarked, "suffer from a disease of the heart which can be cured only by gold." In 1519, Cortés was sent by the Spanish governor of Cuba to conquer the vast empire ruled by the Aztec people in Mexico.

Cortés's plan was so bold as to seem impossible. The Aztec capital, Tenochtitlán, had 400,000 inhabitants and was one of the world's largest urban centers. From this splendid city in the mountains of Mexico,† the Aztecs governed 20 million people, a population twice the size of Spain's at that time. All Cortés could gather for his effort was a force of about 600 soldiers.

After landing in Mexico, Cortés quickly learned that many Native Americans in the area hated the Aztecs. Not only had the Aztecs conquered their neighbors, they had sacrificed untold numbers of them in brutal ceremonies. With the help of a Native American princess known as Malinche or Doña Marina, Cortés played on the divisions among Native Americans and rallied thousands of them to his side.

By 1521 Cortés and his soldiers had destroyed Tenochtitlán, and Cortés became conqueror of one of the largest empires in the world. Like Cortés, the conquistador Francisco Pizarro set out to conquer the empire of the Incas, centered in what is now Peru in South America. The Inca continued to resist as the Spanish attempted to take control of more and more of their empire.

Control of the Spanish Empire As the Spanish conquistadors explored and conquered, they started settlements in favorable locations. They intended these settlements to grow into **colonies,** areas settled by immigrants who continue to be ruled by their parent country. By the 1550s, the Spanish colonies amounted to a large empire in Mexico, Central America, South America, and the islands of the Caribbean Sea.

The economic activity that took place in the colonies made the Spanish wealthy. Using the labor of enslaved Native Americans and Africans, the Spanish mined vast amounts of silver and gold from the mountains of Mexico and Peru. They also established farms and ranches that produced a variety of goods.

The success of this economic system required the Spanish to control the local population. They dealt with Native Americans differently than did other European conquerors in the Americas. They did not try to drive Indians out of their lands. Instead they forced them to become a part of the colonial economy. One method they used was known as the *encomienda* system. Under this system, Native Americans were required to farm, ranch, or mine for the profit of an individual Spaniard. In return, the Spaniard was supposed to ensure the well-being of the workers.

Because the Spanish and Native Americans lived together on the same land, in time a population arose that was a mixture of both peoples. These people of mixed descent were called **mestizos,** which is Spanish for "mixed."

The Spanish Push North

Cortés and Pizarro strengthened Spain's grip on Mexico and Peru. Other conquistadors explored the southern parts of what would become the United States.

Alvar Núñez Cabeza de Vaca and *Estevanico.* Cabeza de Vaca and Estevanico were part of a group of explorers who were shipwrecked near what is now Galveston, Texas, in 1528. Cabeza de Vaca was yet another hidalgo from Spain's Estremadura; Estevanico was an enslaved African. With two other survivors they wandered through the Gulf Coast region of Texas for eight years. After enduring extreme hunger and difficulty, they were rescued by Spanish raiders in northern Mexico. From the Native Americans with whom they had lived, they had heard stories of seven golden cities somewhere to the north. As these stories spread among the Spanish in the area, other explorers were inspired to press northward. Estevanico himself later traveled into what is now the southwestern United States in search of the seven cities.††

Francisco Vásquez de Coronado. Coronado, too, searched what is now the southwestern United States for the fabled golden cities. Between 1540 and 1542 he traveled through what is now Texas and pushed north as far as Kansas. Though he expected to come upon a rich city called Quivira at journey's end, instead he found only the camp of some nomadic Native Americans.

Hernán de Soto. De Soto, another hidalgo from the Estremadura, landed near what is now Tampa Bay, Florida, in 1539. He had with him about 600 soldiers. Over the next few years he traveled through much of what was the northern part of the Spanish empire. His route included parts of Florida, Alabama, Tennessee, Mississippi, Arkansas, and Oklahoma. He and his men were probably the first Spaniards to cross the Mississippi River. Yet when de Soto died of fever in Louisiana in 1542, he still had not found the golden cities he had been seeking.

Forts for Defense The regions explored by Cabeza de Vaca, Estevanico, de Soto, and others did not seem to offer much in riches or

---

Main Idea
CONNECTIONS

Which region of North America did Coronado explore?

---

† Tenochtitlán was located on the site of present-day Mexico City.

†† Some Spaniards finally realized that the stories of the seven golden cities were most likely exaggerated stories about Pueblo villages to the north.

 RESOURCE OPTIONS

Teaching Resources

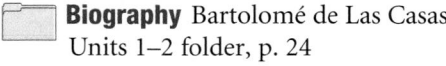 **Biography** Bartolomé de Las Casas, Units 1–2 folder, p. 24

Media and Technology

 Prentice Hall United States History Video Collection™ Volume 1 *Three Worlds Meet*

Answer to . . .

Main Idea Connections The Southwest.

Time: 90 minutes.

Activity: Produce a guidebook description for a first-time visitor to New Mexico today.

Grouping: Four to six students.

Purpose: The group will produce a guidebook that describes a site in present-day New Mexico and provides an understanding of the interaction between Spanish and Native American cultures there. An example is the village of Isleta, a surviving Native American village rebuilt after its destruction in the 1680 Pueblo revolt. Groups should consult travel guides, atlases, and historical maps such as those produced by the National Geographic Society.

Roles: Students should assign the following roles: researcher, cartographer, writer, editor, publisher, and reader.

Outcome: Students will understand how New Mexican sites reveal Native American and Spanish interactions.

Spanish Settlements and Native American Groups in the South, 1500s–1600s

MAP Skills An adviser to the Spanish king in the 1500s remarked: "It is towards the south, not towards the frozen north, that those who seek their fortune should bend their way; for everything at the Equator is rich." *Location* Cite evidence from the map to show that Spanish settlers followed this policy.

farming possibilities. For this reason, few of the 450,000 Spanish immigrants to the Americas before 1650 settled in the lands that are now the United States. As a result, the Spanish government felt the need to encourage settlement in three neglected areas, each for a particular reason:

(1) *The Southeast Coast.* Fleets loaded with silver and gold from the Americas sailed from Cuba to Spain along the Gulf Stream, a powerful current that crosses the Atlantic Ocean. The Spanish government wanted to safeguard these fleets by building defensive bases, particularly in Florida.

In 1565, Pedro Menéndez de Avilés, a conquistador, established the settlement of St. Augustine in Florida for this purpose. In the next few years, he built a half-dozen other outposts. But the Spanish did not commit themselves to maintaining these forts. Only St. Augustine survived from this first wave of Spanish settlement in Florida.

(2) *The Southwest.* The Spanish hoped to stretch the profitable mining industry of

Main Idea CONNECTIONS

Why did the Spanish encourage settlement in the Southeast and Southwest regions of North America?

Mexico into what is now the southwestern United States. In January 1598, the conquistador Juan de Oñate and about 400 men, women, and children claimed an area they called New Mexico. (Spanish New Mexico included parts of what are now Arizona and Texas.) Oñate's New Mexican colony grew to include more than 2,000 Spanish people over the next 80 years.

(3) *The West Coast.* The Spanish were also interested in establishing trade routes across the Pacific Ocean, but they realized that anyone living in California would be able to interfere with this trade. Thus they began to consider settlements in California in the hopes of keeping their European rivals out of the region. Major efforts to colonize this region, however, did not begin until the 1700s.

Missionaries The Spanish settlements that eventually dotted the South and West were forts, or **presidios,** most of them occupied by a few soldiers. The survival of these Spanish outposts was due not to the soldiers, but to the persistence and hard work of a few dozen

Answer to . . .

Map Skills Most of their settlements were south of 30°N.
Main Idea Connections To build forts to protect their fleets and to extend the mining industry.

RESOURCE OPTIONS

Teaching Resources

Nystrom *Atlas of Our Country* Early European Exploration, pp. 12–13; Colonies in the South and West, pp. 18–19

American History Block Scheduling Support Settling the New World, found in the Forging a New Nation folder, includes interdisciplinary lesson suggestions and activities for Geography and History, Primary Sources, Biography, and Literature.

Franciscans. These priests and nuns, members of a Catholic group dedicated to the work of St. Francis of Assisi, settled in Florida and New Mexico as missionaries. Missionaries are people who are sent out by their church to teach people their religion. In North America, the Franciscans converted Native Americans to Christianity and established dozens of **missions**—headquarters where the missionaries lived and worked.

In addition to converting Native Americans, the Spanish also wanted to make them follow European customs. With the help of soldiers, the Spanish forced the Native Americans into settled villages, or *congregacions*, where they would farm and worship like Catholic Europeans.

In 1634, one missionary, Fray Alonso de Benavides, reported the following:

 "[Many Native Americans] are now converted, baptized, and very well ministered to. . . . The whole land is dotted with churches, convents, and crosses along the roads. The people are so well taught that they now live like perfect Christians."

—*Fray Alonso de Benavides*

Resistance to the Spanish

While priests such as Benavides might sometimes feel they were achieving their goals, overall they were not as successful as they wanted to be. Some Native Americans, particularly nomadic groups like the Apache of the Southwest, refused to cooperate with the Spanish. Even those who sometimes cooperated, fiercely resisted at other times. Such resistance broke out as early as 1597 and continued occasionally throughout the 1600s.

Native American fighting against the Spanish was generally disorganized. In Mexico, however, following years of drought that weakened Spanish power, the Pueblo people united in what is called the **Pueblo Revolt of 1680.** By the 1670s, widespread sickness and drought had reduced the Pueblo population to about 17,000 people. Seeking to reverse this decline, the Pueblo began to turn back to their traditional religious practices, which the Spanish tried to stamp out. In August of 1680 the Pueblo people in New Mexico rose under the leadership of a man named Popé and drove the Spanish out of Santa Fe. During the fighting the Pueblo killed priests, colonists, and soldiers, and destroyed the Spanish missions. Years passed before the Spanish were able to return and rebuild.

In Florida, similar Native American rebellions occurred in the late 1600s, as the Spanish were trying once again to establish presidios. Some Native Americans combined forces with the English in North America, who were at war with Spain at that time. With Native American assistance, the English mounted crushing attacks on Spanish presidios in Florida from their own colony in South Carolina. This combined attack by the English and the Native Americans limited the Spanish to a total of two new presidios, San Marcos de Apalachee and Pensacola.

SECTION 1 REVIEW

Comprehension

1. *Key Terms* Define: (a) hidalgo; (b) conquistador; (c) isthmus; (d) colony; (e) mestizo; (f) presidio; (g) mission; (h) Pueblo Revolt of 1680.

2. *Summarizing the Main Idea* Describe how and where the Spanish built an empire in the Americas.

3. *Organizing Information* Create a graphic organizer showing three reasons why the Spanish government encouraged settlement in the Southeast, Southwest, and West Coast regions of North America. Include an additional box illustrating the missionaries' reasons for settlement in these regions.

Critical Thinking

4. *Analyzing Time Lines* Review the time line at the start of the section. Which regions of what is now the United States are included in this time line?

5. *Recognizing Cause and Effect* How did legends and rumors play a part in building European knowledge of the Americas?

Writing Activity

6. *Writing an Expository Essay* Write an essay in which you comment on the following motto printed in a Spanish book in 1599: "By the sword and the compass, more and more and more and more."

Answers to SECTION 1 REVIEW

1. (a) hidalgo, see p. 29; (b) conquistador, see p. 29; (c) isthmus, see p. 29; (d) colony, see p. 31; (e) mestizo, see p. 31; (f) presidio, see p. 32; (g) mission, see p. 33; (h) Pueblo Revolt of 1680, see p. 33.

2. How: by raiding lands, complying with the Church, forcing Native Americans to labor. Where: parts of South and Central America; Mexico; the Southeast, Southwest, and West Coast of North America.

3. Southeast: to build forts; Southwest: to make money from mining; West: to create trade routes; Missionaries: to convert Native Americans.

4. The Southeast (Florida) and the Southwest (Texas and New Mexico).

5. Legends of a fountain of youth led Ponce de León to explore Florida; rumors of gold led Cortés to conquer the Aztecs and inspired later explorers to press north.

6. Essays will vary but should be supported with facts from the section.

RESOURCE OPTIONS

Teaching Resources

 Quiz Units 1–2 folder, p. 17

Student Performance Pack

Guide to the Essentials Chapter 2, Section 1 (English and Spanish)

Media and Technology

 RESOURCE PRO

Biography Popé, Medicine Man of the Pueblos, found on Resource Pro, illustrates Pueblo attachment to ancient beliefs and traditions.

Santa Clara Pueblo

This pueblo retains many features of the pueblos built centuries earlier. Stone or adobe houses are grouped around small plazas. Within each plaza is a kiva, or ceremonial chamber.

THE CHANGING PUEBLO

Focus Remind students that the conquistadores forced Native Americans to adopt the religion, customs, and practices of their Spanish culture. Recall the efforts of the Pueblo people to maintain their own cultural identity, including the Pueblo Revolt of 1680.

Instruct Ask students to examine the examples of Pueblo artifacts presented in the American Artifacts display. What aspects of Pueblo culture are familiar to them? *(Responses will vary according to where students live, as well as according to their individual experiences.)* Ask students to read the captions and discuss the significance of each artifact for the Pueblo lifestyle, religion, and culture.

Extend You might encourage students to research Pueblo life today. Topics for research include working pueblos in New Mexico, such as the Taos Pueblo; weaving and pottery making; or ancient rituals associated with religious ceremonies, such as the kachina dance in which people in costume represent the spirits of earth, sky, and water.

Archangel St. Michael

This Spanish sculpture was made for the church at Zuni Pueblo.

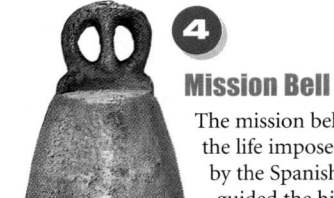

Mission Bell

The mission bell was a symbol of the life imposed on the Pueblo by the Spanish. The ringing bell guided the highly structured day of work, meals, instruction, and prayer.

Rock Painting

This painting of a missionary pierced by a lance depicts the Revolt of 1680, which drove the Spanish out of New Mexico for twelve years.

Rio Grande Blanket

This blanket is typical of the work of weavers in New Mexico in the late 1800s.

▶ RESOURCE OPTIONS

Teaching Resources

American History Block Scheduling Support The First Americans, found in the Forging a New Nation folder, includes interdisciplinary lesson suggestions and activities for Geography and History, Primary Sources, Biography, and Literature.

Storage Jar

Pottery making was a family activity among the Pueblo.

3 **Bowl**

The Pueblo traded the goods they made, such as this bowl, with other Indian peoples. In return, they received a wide range of goods, such as shells, coral, and baskets.

American ARTIFACTS

FROM EXHIBITIONS AND COLLECTIONS AT THE SMITHSONIAN INSTITUTION'S NATIONAL MUSEUM OF AMERICAN HISTORY

THE CHANGING PUEBLO

They came in search of God, gold, and glory, but they would find much more. When Spanish settlers first arrived in the land that is now New Mexico in 1598, they discovered more than a hundred separate, self-governing communities. Here was the land of the Pueblo Indians. (*Pueblo*, the Spanish word for town, can refer either to the Native American group or to the kind of town they built.) From that moment on, the Spanish presence would forever change the course of Native American life. See **1** .

The Pueblo had created a culture brimming with art, ritual, religion, and trade. Pottery making and weaving were family as well as economic practices. Mothers taught children distinctive family styles of pottery making. The pottery was created for everyday or ceremonial use or for trade with peoples from as far away as the coast of California. See **2** and **3** .

The Spanish arrival disrupted the Pueblo economy. It also affected their religion. Spanish priests set up missions to convert the Pueblo to Christianity. While many accepted Christianity, the Pueblo rarely gave up their traditional beliefs. See **4** and **5** .

Many Pueblo fought hard against the Spanish to maintain their cultural identity. As with other encounters between Native Americans and settlers, intolerance and misunderstanding led to violence.

By 1680, sickness and drought had decimated the Pueblo population. The Pueblo believed that by driving the Spanish out, they would have enough food and their community would regain its strength. The Revolt of 1680 was one of the most famous Native American wars of resistance. It kept the community free of Spanish influence for several years. See **6** .

Ultimately, the Spanish and Pueblo would coexist. The Pueblo would struggle to resist domination, to change and adapt, and to maintain their unique character and values. See **7** .

1. Summarize What do the objects and painting tell you about the Spanish effect on Pueblo life?

2. Connecting to Today Find a painting, museum display, or piece of architecture in your community that shows a blending of two cultures. Report the following to your class: (a) a description of the site; (b) the date of the site (if available); (c) why you think so many communities still retain past cultural influences.

Answers to . . .

1. Spanish settlers brought Christianity and Spanish crafts to the Pueblo. They also introduced a fixed schedule that required the Pueblo to work, pray, and eat at specific times.

2. (a) Answers will vary depending on the site selected, but should demonstrate an understanding of the cultures that influenced the site. (b) Answers will vary depending on the site selected. (c) Communities retain past cultural influences because families, schools, and churches pass on language, art, and religious traditions to the next generation.

RESOURCE OPTIONS

Media and Technology

 Prentice Hall United States History Video Collection™ Volume 1 *Three Worlds Meet*

AmericanHeritage® CD-ROM Time Tour A Meeting of Different Worlds: The First Americans

The Jamestown Colony

1497 Cabot reaches North America	1586 Drake raids St. Augustine, Florida	1607 The English settle Jamestown, Virginia	1609 Hudson explores the Hudson River	1676 Bacon's Rebellion

| 1450 | 1500 | 1550 | 1600 | 1650 | 1700 |

Objectives

You may wish to call students' attention to the objectives in the Section Preview. The objectives are reflected in the main headings of the section.

Bellringer

Ask students to think about why people want to own things such as land and other forms of property. What image does ownership convey?

Reading Strategy

Reinforcing Main Ideas Refer to the Reading Strategy in the Section Preview. You may wish to model the strategy on the chalkboard by creating a table with two columns, one marked Reasons to Settle and the other marked Challenges.

LESSON PLAN

Connecting to the Main Idea

1. Focus Explain that in its early days the Jamestown colony nearly failed, and many of its first settlers died. The discovery of a popular kind of tobacco ensured the colony's future, led to its domination by a few rich planters, and to the use of enslaved Africans as laborers.

2. Instruct Discuss the challenges of the Jamestown settlement. How did the settlers eventually solve the problems of troubled leadership, hunger, disease, and strained relations with Native Americans? How did tobacco solve some problems and create others?

3. Close After years of failure, hunger, and disease, the Virginia Colony began to thrive because of the popularity of its tobacco in Europe. A few rich planters dominated Virginia once tobacco sparked the colony's growth. In the next section, students will learn how Europeans formed settlements in New England.

2 The Jamestown Colony

SECTION PREVIEW

Objectives

1. List reasons why England was interested in exploring and colonizing the Americas.
2. Describe the English colonies of Roanoke and Jamestown, and Native American reactions to these settlements.
3. Explain the role of tobacco in Virginia and how it contributed to Bacon's Rebellion.
4. *Key Terms* Define: privateer; charter; joint-stock company; royal colony; legislature; House of Burgesses; indentured servant; Bacon's Rebellion.

Main Idea

Hunger, disease, and Native American resistance all contributed to the near failure of the English colony in Virginia. The discovery of tobacco as a cash crop, however, saved the colony.

Reading Strategy

Reinforcing Main Ideas As you read, list reasons why the English wanted to settle Virginia as well as the many challenges they faced in doing so.

England's Sir Francis Drake became the first sea captain to sail his own ship around the globe.

In the race to take advantage of the opportunities of the Atlantic World, the Spanish were soon far ahead. Other European nations tried to catch up, in the hope that they too could gain a share of the Americas' wealth. Of these nations, England was the most determined and, in time, the most successful.

English Explorers

Several explorers sailed to the Americas for England before the 1600s. Though none discovered fabulous riches as the Spanish had, they did greatly expand England's knowledge of the North American coast.

John Cabot. An Italian, whose original name was Giovanni Caboto, Cabot was the first known explorer sailing for the English to cross the Atlantic. Historians do not agree exactly where he landed, but he may have reached what is now Newfoundland, Canada, in 1497. Though the English were excited by his success,

Cabot never returned from his second voyage to the Americas and many years passed before England sponsored another American voyage.

Sir Martin Frobisher. Frobisher sailed three voyages across the Atlantic Ocean—in 1576, 1577, and 1578. Like Cabot, he was searching for a trade route to Asia that went past or through the continent of North America. This route, called the Northwest Passage, does exist north of Canada. It is extremely hazardous, however, and was not successfully navigated until 1906.

John Davis. Davis, too, made three voyages to North America in search of a Northwest Passage, in 1585, 1586, and 1587. Davis's voyages took him along the west coast of Greenland and the east coasts of Baffin Island and Labrador.

Henry Hudson. Hudson explored for both the English and the Dutch. On his third voyage, in 1609, he reached the river now known as the Hudson, in what is now New York. He sailed 150 miles (240 km) upstream, but finally realized that the river was not the Northwest Passage and turned back.

▶ RESOURCE OPTIONS

Teaching Resources

📁 **Reproducible Lesson Plan** Lesson Plans folder, p. 39

📁 **Learning Styles Lesson Plan** Learning Styles Lesson Plans folder, p. 6

📁 **Big Idea Graphic Organizer** Big Idea Graphic Organizer folder, p. 11

📁 **Guided Reading and Review** Units 1–2 folder, p. 18

Sir Francis Drake. While English explorers were looking for a shortcut to Asia through the Northwest Passage, English adventurers were taking their own shortcut to wealth. Sailing as **privateers,** they raided Spanish treasure ships and cities in the Americas. Privateers are privately owned ships hired by a government to attack foreign ships. Elizabeth I, the Protestant queen of England from 1558 to 1603, had authorized these raids against Catholic Spain.

The most famous of Queen Elizabeth's "sea dogs," as the English privateers were called, was Sir Francis Drake. On one expedition in 1586, Drake raided St. Augustine in Florida and several other Spanish port cities in the Americas. His thefts severely weakened the finances of the Spanish empire.

Drake was more than a pirate, however. As an explorer in 1577–1580, he became the first English captain to sail around the world. On his voyage he sailed into San Francisco Bay and continued as far north as the Pacific coast of what is now Canada.

The Roanoke Disaster

By Drake's time, many of the English had decided that they, too, should establish a colony in the Americas. There were several reasons for their interest in permanent settlements.

(1) Privateers were sailing far from England in search of riches. They wanted a base in the Americas from which they could attack Spanish ships and cities.

(2) Europeans were still convinced that they could find a Northwest Passage through the American continents to the Indies beyond. When they did find such a passage, they reasoned, they would need supply stations in North America for trading ships.

(3) English merchants also wanted new markets. Some thought that Native Americans would buy their goods. Others hoped that a growing population in the colonies would someday become buyers of English cloth and other products.

(4) Some of the English believed that their homeland was becoming too crowded. The Americas would be a good place to send those who could not find work or homes in England.

With these reasons in mind, a sea dog named Sir Walter Raleigh tried twice to start a colony on Roanoke Island in the 1580s. Roanoke is one of a chain of islands called the Outer Banks that run along the coast of what is now North Carolina.

Early Southern Colonies, 1580–1680

MAP skills England struggled to establish colonies on the Atlantic coast of North America.
Place Examine the map. What features of the region do you think attracted settlers? What is one drawback of the region?

Raleigh's first attempt, in 1585, ended when the starving settlers abandoned the colony and returned home. How the second attempt, made two years later, ended remains a mystery even today. Its settlers seem to have vanished. A supply expedition from England in 1590 found only empty buildings at the settlement. On a doorpost was carved the only clue to the fate of the settlers—the word *Croatoan,* an early form of the name of a nearby Native American group. Whether the settlers joined the Indians, or fought and were defeated by them, is not known.

The Jamestown Settlement

After the Roanoke disaster, years passed before the English tried again to settle on the Atlantic Coast of North America. Finally, in 1606, several Englishmen made plans to establish another colony.

To do so, these businessmen first had to get a **charter,** or certificate of permission, from the king. The charter allowed them to form what is now called a **joint-stock company**—a company funded and run by a group of

Jamestown began as a heavily palisaded settlement huddled on a peninsula deep within Chesapeake Bay. The James River flowed nearby. *Geography* *What advantages and disadvantages did this location have?*

investors who share the company's profits and losses. The English investors called their company the Virginia Company and started plans to build a colony in the Americas.

In early 1607 the Virginia Company sent about a hundred colonists to Virginia, the region that Raleigh had reached and named two decades earlier. The colonists started a settlement about 60 miles from the mouth of the James River, in the Chesapeake Bay region. (See the map on the previous page.) The settlers called the new village Jamestown in honor of their king, James I.

The Settlers' Hardships Although the Virginia Company had high hopes for the Jamestown settlement, the colony nearly failed. There were several reasons for this.

First, most of the settlers were not used to doing the hard work required to start a settlement. Many had come to get rich quickly. For instance, some were goldsmiths who expected to find gold they could work into jewelry for quick sale back home. Others had been born into wealthy families and had no experience with manual labor, such as growing crops or building houses. For these reasons, many of the settlers ignored the daily tasks necessary for their survival and instead searched feverishly for gold.

The site chosen for the settlement was another factor in Jamestown's near failure. The village was little better than a swamp swarming with disease-bearing mosquitoes. Many of Jamestown's settlers died of disease.

Lastly, leadership in the Jamestown colony was poor. The settlers squabbled about minor matters even when they were in danger of starving. In early 1608, however, a colonist named John Smith emerged as a strong leader in the colony. Smith, a brave and experienced soldier, could be blunt when necessary. He warned the settlers:

Main Idea
CONNECTIONS

Why did the colony at Jamestown nearly fail?

AMERICAN VOICES ❝You must obey this now for a law, that he that will not work shall not eat . . . for the labors of thirty or forty honest and industrious men shall not be consumed to maintain a hundred and fifty idle loiterers.❞

—*John Smith*

Unfortunately for the colonists, Smith soon left the Virginia colony because of an injury and sailed back to England.

Despite the continued backing of the Virginia Company back in London, the colony suffered from starvation and sickness for its first ten years. One particularly difficult period from October 1609 to March 1610 was remembered as the Starving Time. (See Comparing Primary Sources on this page.) If Native Americans had not given the English help in the form of food and water, the settlers surely would have died.

Meanwhile, back in England, writers were publishing pamphlets calling Virginia a paradise. Ministers gave sermons praising the colony. As a result, by 1623 approximately 5,500 English and other Europeans had migrated to Virginia. Yet life in this new "paradise" was so hard that about 4,000 of these settlers died within a short time of arriving in the colony.

Governing the Colony As the colony struggled, the Virginia Company tried to improve its governing system. In 1609 the company received a new charter, under which the Virginia Company could appoint a governor who would actually live in the colony. When the Virginia Company proved unable to turn a steady profit, King James took away the company's charter and shut it down in 1624. Instead of a corporate colony, Virginia became a **royal colony,** with a governor appointed by the king.

In addition to its royal governor, Virginia also had a **legislature,** or lawmaking assembly, beginning in 1619. The legislature was made up of representatives from the colony. Because the representatives were called burgesses, the assembly itself came to be called the **House of Burgesses.** Though no one understood it in these terms at the time, we see this legislature as the first instance of limited self-government in the English colonies.

Native Americans React

Besides troubled leadership, another source of hardship for the colonists was warfare with the Native Americans. Shortly after the arrival of the English, about 200 Native Americans attacked the Jamestown settlement. Only an English cannon forced them to retreat. Within weeks of that attack, several Englishmen traveled to neighboring Native American villages to make peace. Their efforts produced a tense, uneasy truce.

In March 1622, this truce broke down completely. The leader of the Native Americans, Opechancanough, carefully planned and carried out a surprise attack on Jamestown with the intention of wiping out the English. Although the attack failed, he and his men did kill about 350 of the colonists, more than 10 percent of the population at that time. Within days, the settlers struck back, killing as many or more Native Americans. Again an uneasy truce was patched up between the English and the Native Americans.

Opechancanough's people made their last major attack on the English in the Chesapeake in 1644. Opechancanough took part again, still active and defiant at more than 70 years of age. This attack also failed, and Opechancanough was shot in the streets of Jamestown.

COMPARING PRIMARY SOURCES

LIFE IN JAMESTOWN

Many English settlers were lured to the Americas by descriptions of an easy life. The realities of settlement life were very different, however.

Dreams of Riches	Realities of Jamestown
"I tell thee golde is more plentifull there than copper is with us. . . . Why man all their dripping pans and their chamber pottes are pure golde; . . . and as for rubies and diamonds, they goe forth on holy dayes and gather them by the seashore to hang on their children's coates and sticke in their cappes."	"Of five hundred within six months after Captain Smith's departure, there remained not past sixtie men, women and children, most miserable and poore creatures; and those were preserved for the most part, by roots, herbes, acornes, walnuts, berries, now and then a little fish. . . yea even the skinnes of our horses. . . . [S]o great was our famine, that a Savage [Native American] we slew and buried, the poorer sorte took him up again and eat him. . . . [I]t were too vile to say, and scarce to be beleeved, what we endured."
—Description of Virginia from *Eastward Ho!, a popular London play, 1605*	—*A survivor's record of the Starving Time in Jamestown, October 1609 to March 1610*

ANALYZING VIEWPOINTS **What motivated some of the English in London to describe America in such positive terms?**

The Jamestown Massacre The Powhatan Indians and the Jamestown settlers mingled freely. In fact, the Powhatans often ate and slept in the settlers' houses and borrowed their possessions, even firearms. So when Jamestown and its surrounding plantations began to stir that fateful Good Friday morning, the presence of Indian guests and traders drew no particular attention. Then, at the prearranged hour of eight o'clock, Indians throughout the widely spaced settlements suddenly attacked their hosts with clubs, tomahawks, and the settlers' own fowling pieces. Others descended from the woods to join the slaughter and cut off escape routes. Most of the outlying settlements were destroyed. Only a timely warning from a Christianized Indian saved the town of Jamestown from complete destruction. Source: Frederic D. Schwarz, "The Time Machine," *American Heritage* magazine, February 1997.

RESOURCE OPTIONS

Teaching Resources

Comparing Primary Sources On Life in Jamestown, Units 1–2 folder, pp. 25–26

Answer to . . .

Comparing Primary Sources Some were investors in or owners of the new colonies. They stood to gain financially if the settlements produced a profit, so they enticed settlers with false images of wealth and ease.

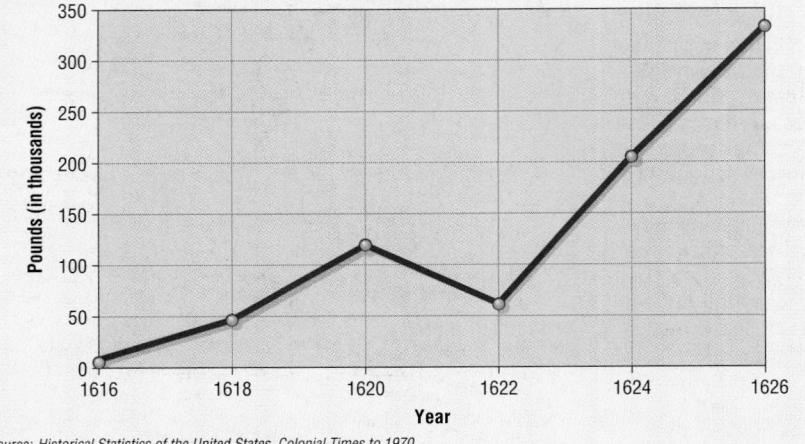

American Tobacco Imported by England, 1616–1626

Source: *Historical Statistics of the United States, Colonial Times to 1970*

Interpreting Graphs When John Rolfe introduced a mild tobacco to England, he saved the struggling Virginia colony. *Economy How much more tobacco did England import from America in 1626 than in 1616?*

ACTIVITY
HETEROGENEOUS GROUPS

List with students three problems faced by settlers of the Jamestown colony in its early days. Ask students to review the section to find a cause and the ultimate resolution for each problem. *(Reteaching)*

ACTIVITY
LEARNING STYLES

Have pairs of students improvise a debate between William Berkeley and Nathaniel Bacon about Bacon's reasons for rebelling and his plans for the western lands of the colony. Each pair of students should take a point and illustrate it through argument. *(Verbal/Linguistic)*

Customize for
More Advanced Students

You might ask students to propose alternatives to using enslaved Africans in the Virginia colony. What other crops might they have planted? What else could they have done with the land?

Answer to . . .

Interpreting Graphs About 330,000 more pounds.
Main Idea Connections Money from the sale of tobacco in England supplied colonists with an income.

Growing Tobacco

During the early years of their settlement one thing saved the Virginia colonists from failing completely. This was tobacco, a plant native to the Western Hemisphere but unknown in Europe. In 1614 colonist John Rolfe shipped some tobacco to Europe, where it quickly became popular. Soon tobacco was the basis of the colony's economy. In 1616, Virginians sent 2,500 pounds of the plant to England. By 1618, this amount had increased to nearly 50,000 pounds. By 1640, Virginia and its neighbor colony, Maryland, were sending home 3 million pounds a year.

In order to cash in on the tobacco boom, settlers moved out from Jamestown. They carved out

Main Idea
CONNECTIONS

How did tobacco contribute to the success of England's colony in Virginia?

The labor of indentured servants included bundling and packing dried tobacco leaves.

plantations on the banks of the James, York, Rappahannock, and Potomac rivers, and along the shores of Chesapeake Bay. Settlers established their plantations close to waterways, so that they could grow and transport their tobacco more easily.

The Promise of Land To produce large crops of tobacco, planters needed laborers to work the fields. One way of persuading people to come to Virginia was to promise them land when they arrived. Over time, the custom developed of giving each "head," or person who came to the colony, the right to fifty acres of land. This system became known as the headright system.

The promise of land helped attract new colonists from England. So did changes that were taking place in England at the time. English landowners had found that they could make more money from raising livestock than they could from renting land to farmers. The landowners therefore forced the farmers off the land and turned their fields into animal pastures by enclosing them with fences. Many farmers lost their homes as a result of this enclosure movement. England was swarming with young people in search of food and work. They were called "masterless" men and women because they did not have a master, or patron.

Indentured Servants One of the few choices open to the masterless people was to sail to Virginia. Many, however, did not have the money for the voyage. To pay for the crossing, they became **indentured servants.** These were people who had to work for a master for a period of time, usually seven years, under a contract called an indenture. In return for their work, their master paid the cost of their voyage to Virginia and gave them food and shelter. Some indentures promised a

RESOURCE OPTIONS

Teaching Resources

 Literature Activity The Fate of an Indentured Servant, Units 1–2 folder, p. 27

piece of land to the servant at the end of the indenture period. Others gave the servant's headright to the master.

Historians estimate that between 100,000 and 150,000 men and women came as servants to work in the fields of Virginia and neighboring Maryland during the 1600s. Most of them were 18 to 22 years of age, unmarried, and poor. Few indentured servants lived long enough to claim their land at the end of their service. The hot climate and diseases of Chesapeake Bay killed them in large numbers.

Among Virginia's indentured servants were some Africans, the first to settle in what is now the United States. The first group of about 20 Africans arrived in 1619. Their numbers remained small, however.

Nathaniel Bacon, shown at left, declared that he meant "not only to ruin ... all Indians in General but all Manner of Trade and Commerce with them."

Bacon's Rebellion

As the population of Virginia increased, settlers pushed farther west in search of new farmland. Many were former indentured servants who, lacking the money to buy farmland, tried to take it from the Indians instead. Clashes between settlers and Native Americans took place along Virginia's western frontier.

In 1676 one planter, Nathaniel Bacon, raised an army to fight the Native Americans. Governor William Berkeley, angry that Bacon was acting without his permission, declared him a rebel and gathered an army to stop him.

Suddenly, however, Bacon turned his army around. Complaining that Berkeley had failed to protect the western settlers, and charging that those western settlers had too little voice in colonial government, Bacon and his supporters attacked and burned Jamestown. For a time Bacon controlled nearly all of Virginia. He died suddenly, probably from illness, and with his death **Bacon's Rebellion** crumbled.

Bacon's Rebellion is important for two reasons. First, it showed that the frontier settlers were frustrated with a government concerned only about the interests of a small group of wealthy planters. Second, it showed that the poorer colonists were unwilling to tolerate such a government.

SECTION 2 REVIEW

Comprehension

1. **Key Terms** Define: (a) privateer; (b) charter; (c) joint-stock company; (d) royal colony; (e) legislature; (f) House of Burgesses; (g) indentured servant; (h) Bacon's Rebellion.

2. **Summarizing the Main Idea** Describe the challenges the English faced in settling Virginia.

3. **Organizing Information** Create a graphic organizer showing the reasons the English wanted to settle in North America.

Critical Thinking

4. **Analyzing Time Lines** Review the time line at the start of the section. How are the second and third events related?

5. **Identifying Central Issues** North America was a difficult, dangerous place for both the Spanish and the English. Why did they want to settle there?

Writing Activity

6. **Writing a Persuasive Essay** Write an essay from the point of view of Nathaniel Bacon, arguing that the government in Virginia should protect western planters from Native American attacks.

RESOURCE OPTIONS

Teaching Resources

 Quiz Units 1–2 folder, p. 19

Student Performance Pack

 Guide to the Essentials Chapter 2, Section 2 (English and Spanish)

Answers to
SECTION 2 REVIEW

1. (a) privateer, see p. 37; (b) charter, see p. 37; (c) joint-stock company, see p. 37; (d) royal colony, see p. 39; (e) legislature, see p. 39; (f) House of Burgesses, see p. 39; (g) indentured servant, see p. 40; (h) Bacon's Rebellion, see p. 41.

2. Challenges faced by the English include: colonists did not have experience with manual labor and other necessary skills, the settlement site was swampy with disease-bearing mosquitoes, leadership was poor, and there was resistance from Native Americans.

3. Graphic organizers should include the following points: privateers wanted a base in the Americas, supply stations for ships traveling the Northwest Passage to Asia, new markets for English goods, and new land for those who could not find work or homes in England.

4. Privateers like Drake wanted to have a base in the Americas. This need encouraged the settlement of Jamestown.

5. Both the English and Spanish were lured to the Americas with hopes of finding gold and other resources with which to gain great wealth.

6. Students' essays should include reference to Bacon's claim that Virginia's government represented only the interests of the wealthy planters to the east and was therefore not interested in protecting poorer settlers in the west from Native American attacks.

| 1535 Cartier explores the St. Lawrence River | 1608 Champlain settles Quebec | 1620 Pilgrims settle Plymouth Colony | 1630 Puritans settle Massachusetts Bay Colony | 1673 Joliet and Marquette explore the Mississippi | 1675 King Philip's War begins |

| 1500 | 1550 | 1600 | 1650 | 1700 |

Objectives

You may wish to call students' attention to the objectives in the Section Preview. The objectives are reflected in the main headings of the section.

Bellringer

Ask students to suppose that an unfamiliar group suddenly took over their classrooms. How would they react?

Reading Strategy

Formulating Questions Refer to the Reading Strategy in the Section Preview. You may model the strategy on the chalkboard by listing questions and having students answer them as they read.

LESSON PLAN

Connecting to the Main Idea

1. Focus Ask students how the French and English interacted with Native Americans. Explain that in 1675, Native Americans in New England fought back against English settlers in King Philip's War. Discuss the impact of the war on settlers and Native Americans.

2. Instruct Ask why the French had good relations with Native Americans, while the Puritans provoked resentment. Discuss the difficulty of a life such as Metacom's, moving between two societies that were at odds. Ask why Metacom gave up trying to maintain peace. What were the long-term causes of King Philip's War?

3. Close The French and English created different types of settlements in the Northeast. The French exploited the trading system of the Native Americans, while the English tried to transform their culture. King Philip's War, a desperate attempt by Native Americans to stop the destruction of their way of life, weakened both settlers and Native Americans.

3 The New England Colonies

SECTION PREVIEW

Objectives

1 Summarize French exploration and colonization in North America.
2 Describe the Plymouth and Massachusetts Bay colonies in New England.
3 Explain why war broke out between the Indians and the Puritans.
4 *Key Terms* Define: New England Colonies; Puritan; persecute; Pilgrim; Mayflower Compact; Great Migration; religious tolerance; Salem witch trials; sachem; Pequot War; King Philip's War.

Main Idea

With both help and resistance from Native Americans, English colonists succeeded in establishing permanent settlements in New England.

Reading Strategy

Formulating Questions Write three questions about each of the following colonies and look for answers to these questions as you read the section: New France, Plymouth, Massachusetts Bay.

The English were not the only Europeans interested in the East Coast of North America. The French, too, had been exploring the region for decades, looking for trading opportunities. These voyages would lead to the creation of a French North American colony. Eventually they would also lead to conflict between France and England for control of eastern North America.

Wampum belts, made of shell beads, served as currency in the trade between Native Americans and Europeans. This one belonged to an Iroquois.

The French in North America

Like their long-time rivals the English, the French sponsored several voyages of exploration to North America.

Giovanni da Verrazano. Verrazano was an Italian who sailed for the French in 1523–1524. Searching for the Northwest Passage, he explored the coast of North America from what is now North Carolina to Newfoundland. Verrazano also entered New York harbor.

Jacques Cartier. Cartier made three voyages to Canada, in 1534, 1535, and again in 1541–1542. On the basis of Cartier's explorations, the French king claimed a region called New France for his nation. New France included not only the land covered by present-day Canada, but also parts of what is now the northern United States. Though he explored the St. Lawrence River as far as the modern-day city of Montreal, he did not succeed in establishing a permanent colony in North America.

Samuel de Champlain. Champlain founded the first successful French colony in North America, in 1608. The site he chose was at Quebec, on high ground above a narrow stretch of the St. Lawrence River in what is now Canada. Champlain also mapped the Atlantic shores as far as Massachusetts, and traveled inland to the lakes now known as Lake Huron and Lake Champlain.

Louis Joliet and *Jacques Marquette.* Explorers Joliet and Marquette traveled together from the Great Lakes to the Mississippi River

▶ RESOURCE OPTIONS

Teaching Resources

📁 **Reproducible Lesson Plan** Lesson Plans folder, p. 40

📁 **Learning Styles Lesson Plan** Learning Styles Lesson Plans folder, p. 7

📁 **Big Idea Graphic Organizer** Big Idea Graphic Organizer folder, p. 12

📁 **Guided Reading and Review** Units 1–2 folder, p. 20

in 1673. Hoping that the Mississippi emptied into the Pacific Ocean, they canoed south along the waterway as far as what is now Arkansas. There they learned from Native Americans that the river flowed into the Gulf of Mexico. Realizing they had not found the Northwest Passage, they returned to New France.

The Fur Trade The French did not need the Northwest Passage to grow rich from their exploits in New France. They discovered that a local product, fur, could be sold for great gain in Europe. Clothing made from the skins of deer, beaver, and other animals became highly fashionable in France and elsewhere in Europe in the 1600s. Native Americans trapped these animals, collected their furs, and traded them to the French.

The fur trade determined the shape of New France. By the late 1600s, New France was a long, narrow colony stretching far into the interior of Canada, along the St. Lawrence and the Great Lakes. The colony clung to the waterways because, as in Virginia, water was vital for transporting goods.

The Iroquois The fur trade linked the Native Americans of northeastern North America with the trade of the Atlantic World. Native Americans gathered furs for European markets and became eager consumers of European goods, including guns, cloth, and jewelry. Many Native Americans learned of the Christian religion from Catholic missionaries. Many also suffered and died from European diseases.

The fur trade with the French also ignited an increase in warfare among Native Americans, as different groups fought over hunting territory. In response, several Indian nations joined together during the late 1500s to form the Iroquois League. The Iroquois lived in what is now New York State between the Hudson River and Lake Erie. Having ended warfare among themselves, the Iroquois nations fought a series of wars against other Native Americans in the middle and late 1600s. In the end, the Iroquois pushed their rivals out of their homelands, forcing them to migrate west of the Great Lakes.

Plymouth Colony

While the French were building the fur trade in New France, the English were beginning new colonies along the Atlantic Coast in what is

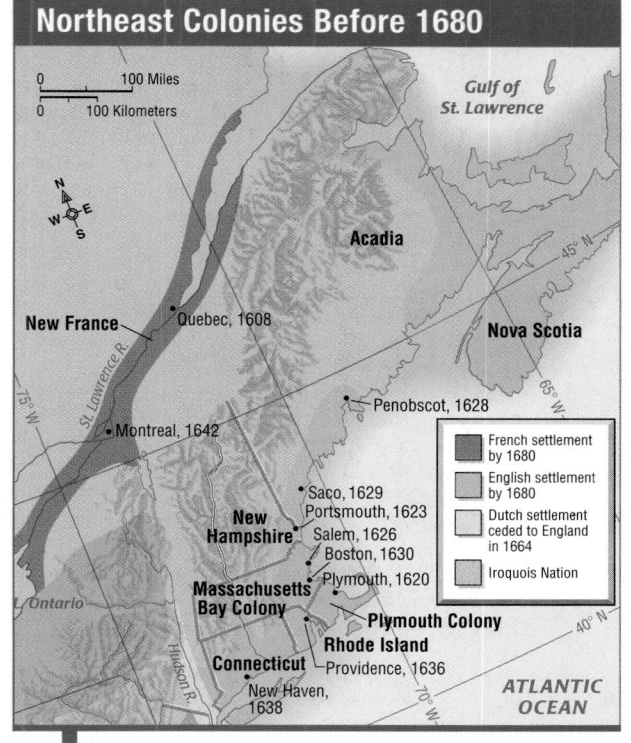

Northeast Colonies Before 1680

French settlement by 1680
English settlement by 1680
Dutch settlement ceded to England in 1664
Iroquois Nation

 Both the French and the Dutch were more interested in the fur trade than they were in the establishment of permanent settlements. *Location How does the resulting settlement pattern of the French and Dutch differ from that of the English?*

now the northeast region of the United States. Known as New England, this region included land that became the states of Connecticut, Rhode Island, Massachusetts, Vermont, New Hampshire, and Maine. (See the map on this page.) The colonies in this region were called the **New England Colonies.**

Puritans and Separatists The first successful colony in New England was founded as a result of religious conflicts in England. In 1534 England's King Henry VIII had broken with the Catholic Church and had founded the Anglican Church, England's national Protestant church. Some of the English, however, complained that the Anglican Church continued too many of the Catholic practices and traditions. Because they wanted what they

BACKGROUND

Geography in History

The journey taken by the Pilgrims from England to the coast of North America was much longer than we sometimes remember. Members of the English Separatist Church, some of whom would later be the first English settlers of Massachusetts, first left Great Britain in 1609 and sailed to the Netherlands. They stayed for a decade before they began to formulate a plan for founding a colony in the New World. It is worth noting, too, that they were not the only persecuted religious minority to seek refuge in the Netherlands. Among others were Jews whose ancestors had been persecuted in, and exiled from, Spain.

The English in Plymouth wore shoes like these reproductions as they worked to turn the forests of New England into fields.

considered a "purer" kind of church, they were called **Puritans.** Some of the Puritans started separate churches of their own and were called Separatists. Both Puritans and Separatists were **persecuted,** or attacked because of their beliefs.

The Voyage of the *Mayflower* One group of Separatists, those who came to be called the **Pilgrims,** decided to make a new home in North America, where they hoped they would be free to worship as they wanted. In 1620 a group of roughly 100 Pilgrims sailed to New England on the *Mayflower.*

Some non-Separatists were also on board the *Mayflower,* and as the ship neared shore, these settlers threatened to go off and live by themselves. Afraid that the group would break up, the Pilgrims made a compact, or agreement, called the **Mayflower Compact.** In the agreement, the settlers agreed to obey all of their government's laws. As they put it:

> **KEY DOCUMENTS**
> "We . . . do . . . combine ourselves together into a civil body politic, for our better ordering and preservation . . . and . . . to . . . frame such just and equal laws . . . as shall be thought most [fitting] and convenient for the general good of the colony, unto which we promise all due . . . obedience."
>
> —*The Mayflower Compact*

The compact succeeded in keeping the Pilgrims together. It also showed that the Pilgrims expected to decide for themselves how they would be governed. Later this belief in self-government would become one of the founding principles of the United States.

One of the men who drew up the Mayflower Compact was William Bradford, who went on to be elected governor of the colony 30 times between 1621 and 1656. Bradford helped create a form of government in which the people guided their own affairs. Bradford later wrote a moving history of the colony, *History of Plymouth Plantation,* in which he recounted the many difficulties faced by the early settlers.

Early Difficulties The Pilgrims started their colony at a harbor they called New Plymouth, or simply Plymouth, after the English port from which they had sailed. Like the Jamestown settlers in Virginia, the Pilgrims at Plymouth Colony endured tremendous hardships. Half of them died in the first winter alone. The next summer the colonists had the help of a Native American, Squanto, who taught them how to plant corn. They harvested plenty of corn and held a great feast of thanksgiving in the fall of 1621.[†]

The Massachusetts Bay Colony

In 1630 a thousand English settlers braved a voyage across the Atlantic to found the Massachusetts Bay Colony just a few miles north of the Plymouth Colony in New England. These were the first of a flood of colonists who came to New England in a movement called the **Great Migration.** By 1643 the Massachusetts Bay Colony had grown to roughly 20,000 people living in twenty towns, including its capital, Boston.

Reasons for Migrating Many of these new settlers were Puritans hoping to live where they could worship as they wanted. However, they did not believe in **religious tolerance**—the idea that people of different religions should live in peace together. They came from England in part because they wanted to leave a society where their beliefs were ridiculed and they were persecuted. But also they had no desire to live among people who held beliefs different from their own. By law, everyone in the Massachusetts Bay Colony had to attend the Puritan church and pay taxes to support it.

For the Puritans, the Massachusetts Bay Colony was not just an opportunity to make a living on new farmland. They believed that they were creating a new, pure society to serve the will of God. John Winthrop, a founder of the colony and later its governor, summarized the colonists' goals in a lay sermon he delivered on board the ship *Arbella* in 1630. To succeed, he said:

> **KEY DOCUMENTS**
> "We must be knit together in this work, as one man. We must entertain each other in brotherly affection. . . . We must delight in each other; make others' condition our own; rejoice together, mourn together, labor and suffer together. . . . For we must consider that we shall be as a city on a hill. The eyes of all people are upon us."
>
> —*A Model of Christian Charity*

[†] The American holiday Thanksgiving is held in memory of the Pilgrims' feast.

▶ RESOURCE OPTIONS

Teaching Resources

📁 **Key Documents** The Mayflower Compact, Learning with Documents folder, p. 80

Media and Technology

🦅 **American**Heritage® CD-ROM

Explorer Activity 3 Trade in New France, CD-ROM Guidebook, pp. 25–26, helps students write a story about a fur trader in New France.

History Makers Pocahontas

Winthrop's sermon voiced a belief that many on board the ship, and many Americans since that time, have shared. America would be an example to people throughout the world.

A Well-Ordered Community As a result of their shared goals, the Puritans were united and strong. When Puritan settlers established a new town, they left a large area of open land as a "common" to be used by all. Facing the common was the church or meeting house, and nearby was the house for the minister, as well as a schoolhouse. The rest of the land near the common was divided into house lots. Outside the town, each family had a strip of farmland. The Puritan plan was to have well-ordered families in well-ordered towns in a well-ordered colony.

In general it was a successful plan. The Puritans worked hard, took care of themselves and one another, and enjoyed relatively good health. Children born in the colony could be expected to live at least twice as long as children born in early Virginia. By 1700, New England was home to over 93,000 people living fairly comfortable lives.

The Salem Witch Trials Yet life in the Puritans' ideal community had its dark moments. In 1692, several girls and young women in Salem, Massachusetts, claimed that the devil had taken control of them. They also accused three townspeople of being witches. In the public uproar that followed, neighbors fearfully accused one another of dealing with the devil. Trials were held to determine if the accused townspeople really were witches. As a result of these **Salem witch trials,** the Massachusetts authorities ordered twenty men and women to die by hanging. However, after a few months the community regained its balance, and the trials and hangings came to a stop.

Some historians believe that the witch trials reflected colonists' fears about political changes taking place at the time.

As you will read in the next chapter, a revolution known as the Glorious Revolution had recently occurred in England. The year before the trials, England's new monarchs, William and Mary, had joined the Massachusetts Bay Colony and the Plymouth Colony into one. They were now a single royal colony, known as Massachusetts.

Other Puritan Colonies As the population of New England increased, farmland in Massachusetts grew scarce. Some Puritans were given permission to search for better farmland and to establish new communities in New England.

Connecticut. Puritan minister Thomas Hooker led a group of settlers from Massachusetts in the mid-1630s to Connecticut. In 1639 representatives from several Connecticut towns wrote a new plan of government for their colony. They called it the Fundamental Orders.

New Hampshire and *Maine.* Similarly, settlements in Maine and New Hampshire were populated by Puritans, some from England and some from Massachusetts. New Hampshire became a separate colony in 1680. Maine was a part of Massachusetts until it became a separate state in 1820.

Plate III. Fig. I. page 114

This engraving of an English hanging gives a good idea of the scene in Salem on September 22, 1692, when seven women and one man were hanged as witches. *Culture How do the Salem witch trials reflect the Puritans' passion for social order?*

David, Joanna, and Abigail Mason posed for this portrait about 1670. Like other Puritan children, they could expect to live twice as long as children in colonies where life was harder. *Culture* *What evidence of prosperity do you see in this painting?*

Other Separatist Colonies Not all of the people leaving the Massachusetts Bay Colony left simply to find new farmland. Some left because of religious conflicts with the colony's Puritan leaders.

Rhode Island. In 1636 Roger Williams, a Separatist minister, was banished from Massachusetts after quarreling with Puritan authorities. He started a settlement called Providence, in Rhode Island. In 1644 Providence joined with several other Separatist communities in Rhode Island and received permission to be a self-governing colony. Roger Williams's colony was remarkable because it guaranteed religious tolerance to all settlers.

New Haven. In 1638, a new group of Separatists came from England and founded New Haven, in what is now Connecticut. In 1662, New Haven and the Connecticut colony were combined into a single royal colony.

Exeter. Also in 1638, John Wheelwright founded the settlement of Exeter, in what is now New Hampshire. He, too, had disagreed with Puritans on religious matters. Exeter soon became a part of the New Hampshire colony.

Wheelwright was the brother-in-law of an even more famous opponent of the Puritan authorities in Massachusetts—a deeply religious woman by the name of Anne Hutchinson.

Anne Hutchinson

AMERICAN BIOGRAPHY Born in England in 1591, Anne Marbury married a wealthy merchant named William Hutchinson in 1612. Over the next thirty years she bore fourteen children, of whom twelve survived. In 1634 the Hutchinson family moved to Boston to escape religious persecution in England and to join other Puritans living there.

Hutchinson, however, did not accept Puritan authority. She believed that it was wrong to obey the church if by doing so a person felt he or she was disobeying God. Her home soon became a center for those in the colony who wanted to think for themselves. Critics of John Winthrop and the Massachusetts government gathered there, as did women interested in studying the Bible.

The Puritan authorities called Hutchinson to trial in November 1637 to explain her actions. At the trial, Hutchinson skillfully defended herself with references to law and the Bible. She proved to be more than a match for her chief accuser and judge, the learned Governor Winthrop. Still, the judges rejected her claim that her own beliefs about God could override the authority of Puritan laws and leaders. The court declared Hutchinson "unfit for our society" and banished her from the colony.

Early the next year, the Hutchinsons left for land on Narragansett Bay in what is now Rhode Island. In 1642, after the death of her husband, Hutchinson and her family moved to Long Island, now a part of New York State. In 1643, Indians engaged in a war against the Europeans murdered Hutchinson and her family.■

Anne Hutchinson (1591–1643)

FACT Finder

The Colonies in America, 1607–1776

Colony	European Settlement	Reason for Settlement	Leaders	Charter[1]	Economic Activities
NEW ENGLAND COLONIES					
Massachusetts Plymouth (1620–1691)	1620	Escape religious persecution	William Bradford	Mayflower Compact 1620–1621; joint-stock 1621–1691	Fishing, lumber, shipbuilding, triangular trade, rum, whaling
Massachusetts Bay Colony (1630–1691)		Establish a Puritan commonwealth	John Winthrop	Joint-stock 1630–1684; royal 1684–1691 Two colonies merged in 1691; royal 1691	
New Hampshire	1623	Profit from trade and fishing	Benning Wentworth; John Wentworth	Proprietary 1622–1641; joint-stock (part of Massachusetts) 1641–1679; royal 1679–1776	Trade, fishing
Exeter (1638)		Escape religious persecution	John Wheelwright		
Connecticut	1636	Establish a Puritan settlement; establish a fur trade route	Thomas Hooker	Self-governing 1636–1662; royal 1662–1776	Triangular trade
Rhode Island[2]	1636	Escape religious intolerance of Massachusetts Bay	Roger Williams	Self-governing 1636–1644; joint-stock 1644–1663; royal 1663–1776	Shipping, livestock, agriculture
MIDDLE COLONIES					
New York[3]	1625	Expansion	James, Duke of York; Richard Nicolls; Thomas Dongan; John Montgomerie	Colony of Dutch West Indian Co. 1625–1664; proprietary (English) 1664–1685; royal 1685–1776	Wheat, milling, lumber, furs, sugar refining, distilling, shipbuilding, trade
Delaware[4]	1638	Trade	Johan Pritz; Johan Rising; William Penn	Proprietary (Swedish) 1638–1682; part of Penn. (proprietary) 1682–1704; royal 1704–1776	Trade, farming
New Jersey	1664	Trading post; refuge for Quakers from England	John Berkeley; John Carteret	Proprietary 1664–1702; royal 1702–1776	Trade, farming
Pennsylvania[5]	1637	Establish a Quaker colony, tolerance of religion	William Penn	Proprietary 1681–1692; royal 1692–1694; proprietary 1694–1776	Trade, farming
SOUTHERN COLONIES					
Virginia	1607	Search for gold; English outpost against Spain	John Smith; John Rolfe; Thomas Dale	Joint-stock 1607–1624; royal 1625–1776	Tobacco
Maryland	1632	Establish a Catholic settlement; escape religious persecution	George Calvert (Lord Baltimore); Cecilius Calvert	Proprietary 1632–1691; royal 1691–1716; proprietary 1716–1776	Tobacco
The Carolinas North Carolina (1712) South Carolina (1712)	1663	Land wealth, refuge for small farmers; strengthen English possessions in the Americas	William Berkeley; Anthony Ashley-Cooper; John Locke	Proprietary 1712–1729; royal 1729–1776 Proprietary 1670–1719; royal 1719–1776	Ship supplies, rice, indigo, tobacco
Georgia[6]	1732	Settlement for debtors; buffer Carolinas from Spanish Florida	James Oglethorpe	Proprietary 1732–1752; royal 1752–1776	Rice, indigo, lumber, beef, pork, ship supplies, trade

[1]Corporate colonies were organized by a joint-stock company, or corporation, for the benefit of shareholders. Such colonies could only be formed when the English king issued a charter, or certificate of his approval. In a royal colony, a governor appointed by the king served as its chief official, though a colonial assembly approved laws before they could go into effect. Self-governing colonies were independent of the king or a corporation. Proprietary colonies were granted by the king to a proprietor, or owner, whether one person or a small group of people.
[2]The four original settlements of Providence, Portsmouth, Warwick, and Newport created a united government in 1647 under the name "Providence Plantations."
[3]Called New Netherland until 1664 when the English took it over from the Dutch.
[4]Settled in 1638 by Swedes and called New Sweden. Seized by Dutch in 1655 and became part of New Netherland. Conquered by English in 1664.
[5]First settled by Swedes in 1637. Part of New Sweden until 1655, when seized by Dutch and became part of New Netherland. Conquered by English in 1664.
[6]Originally part of South Carolina.

Interpreting Tables The thirteen colonies developed different characteristics because of their differing economic activities, government structures, reasons for settlement, and variations in the ethnic groups in each region. *Geography What regional patterns can you find in the table?*

Using the Internet

Create a Chart

Objective Use the Internet to create a cause-and-effect chart of the 1680 Pueblo revolt. Have students follow these instructions:

1. See the *America: Pathways to the Present* Web site at

http://www.Pathways.phschool.com

for the URL of the 1680 Pueblo revolt.

2. Read the letter by New Mexico's governor. List and take notes on the events he describes. Ask yourself: Why is this event important? What were its consequences? Did it cause a later event?

3. Prepare a cause-and-effect chart of the events you have listed. Compare your chart with a classmate's.

RESOURCE OPTIONS

Teaching Resources

Nystrom *Atlas of Our Country* Colonies in the North and East, pp. 14–15

Visual Learning Activity A Lasting Stereotype, Learning with Documents folder, p. 44

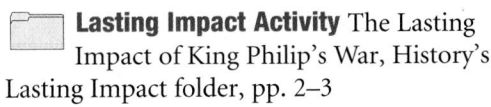

Lasting Impact Activity The Lasting Impact of King Philip's War, History's Lasting Impact folder, pp. 2–3

Answer to . . .

Interpreting Tables Sample answer: The New England Colonies sought to establish religion-based settlements. The economy of the Middle Colonies was based on trade and farming. The economy of the Southern Colonies was based on farming, especially tobacco.

Connections to Today

By 1675, tuberculosis and smallpox had reduced the southern New England population of Native Americans to about 20,000—against the approximately 50,000 settlers who had displaced them. This put the Native Americans at a disadvantage before King Philip's War had even begun. In fact, one present-day writer regards King Philip's defeat as "America's first war of ethnic cleansing." Today, there are approximately 12,000 Wampanoags living in Massachusetts—many on Cape Cod and on the Gay Head reservation on Martha's Vineyard.

ACTIVITY
HETEROGENEOUS GROUPS

Ask students to stage an interview with Metacom in the style of *Meet the Press*. Ask them to write two or three questions for Metacom about King Philip's War. Ask for volunteers to take turns answering in the role of Metacom. **(Enrichment)**

Answer to . . .

Map Skills The center of the region, where there were primarily Native American villages.

Main Idea Connections They didn't want the colonists to wear out the land, cut down the trees, and overhunt the animals and fish.

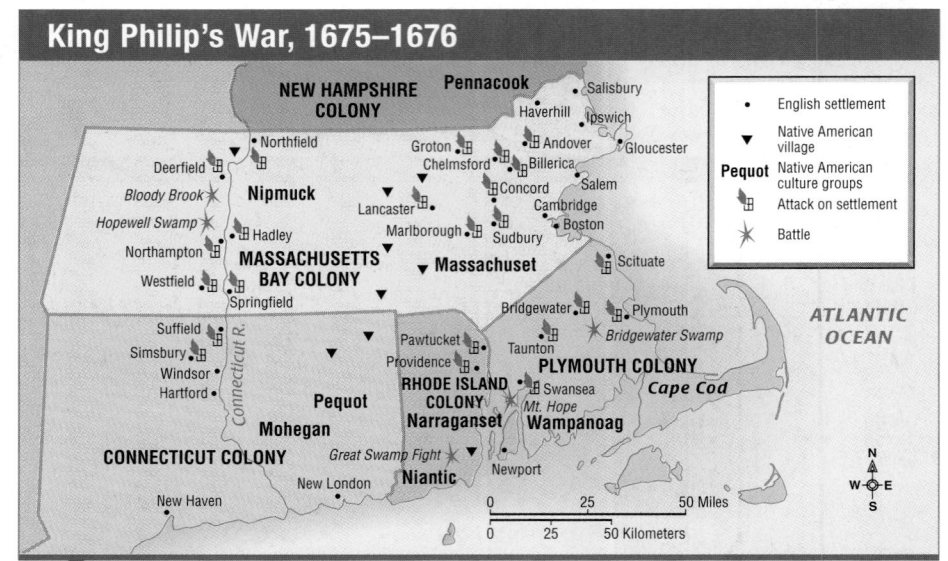

King Philip's War, 1675–1676

Legend:
- • English settlement
- ▼ Native American village
- **Pequot** Native American culture groups
- Attack on settlement
- ✴ Battle

 MAP skills Attacks on English settlements during King Philip's War are well recorded in history. The exact locations of Native American villages attacked by English settlers are in many cases unclear. It is known, however, that Native Americans and settlers lived close to one another within the region. *Location According to the map, which area saw the least amount of fighting?*

War with the Indians

Main Idea
CONNECTIONS

Why did Native Americans resist English settlement?

The war that killed Hutchinson was just one of several between English settlers and Indians in the 1600s. The cause of these wars was simple: English settlers were pushing Native Americans out of their homelands. As one **sachem,** or Native American leader, explained in 1642:

> **AMERICAN VOICES** "Our fathers had plenty of deer and skins, our plains were full of deer, as also our woods, and of turkies, and our coves full of fish and fowl. But these English having gotten our land, they with scythes cut down the grass, and with axes fell the trees; their cows and horse eat the grass, and their hogs spoil our clam banks, and we shall be starved."
>
> —*Miantonomo*

The Pequot War The Pequot people of Connecticut were among the first to strike back against the English settlers. In 1637 the Massachusetts Bay Colony responded to several violent incidents by sending an army to attack them in what is known as the **Pequot War.** The Puritans burned down a Pequot fort near Mystic, Connecticut, killing over 500 people inside. The Puritans then went on to hunt down and kill or capture the rest of the Pequot. Although a handful of the Pequot did survive, their strength as a people had been shattered.

King Philip's War In the 1660s, a strong leader arose among one of the Algonquin peoples of New England. This was Metacom, also known by his English name, King Philip. Like many Native Americans of the 1600s, Metacom had spent much of his life moving between Native American and white society. He was the son of Massasoit, the leader of the Pokanokets, who had helped the Pilgrims of Plymouth Colony survive in the first years of settlement. In the years that followed, trade developed between the Indians and the English. But trade could not erase the basic tension between the two groups.

By 1670 some 45,000 English people were living in about ninety towns in New England. They were cutting down forests, putting up fences, and creating pasture. All of these actions threatened the livelihood of Native Americans. In 1675 Metacom united Indian groups from Rhode Island to Maine in a determined effort to

This incident in Hadley, Massachusetts, is one of the legends that grew up around King Philip's War. Supposedly, William Goffe, a Puritan hero and fugitive from England, came out of hiding to lead the English against a Native American attack. Whether the story is true or not, the engraving reflects the violent nature of the struggle. *Geography What was the outcome of King Philip's War?*

drive out the English once and for all. In what became known as **King Philip's War,** he and his warriors destroyed 112 English towns, attacked 52 others, and killed about 600 settlers. In addition, they ruined fields, slaughtered cattle, and kidnapped dozens of people.

Yet the English struck back, killing or wounding about 4,000 Native Americans. In August of 1676 soldiers caught Metacom sleeping in his hideout near Mount Hope, Rhode Island. As he jumped up and tried to escape, he was shot through the heart.

Even without Metacom, the war raged on for nearly a year and devastated the economy in northern New England. When it was over, the English conquest of the region was nearly complete.

SECTION 3 REVIEW

Comprehension

1. *Key Terms* Define: (a) New England Colonies; (b) Puritan; (c) persecute; (d) Pilgrim; (e) Mayflower Compact; (f) Great Migration; (g) religious tolerance; (h) Salem witch trials; (i) sachem; (j) Pequot War; (k) King Philip's War.

2. *Summarizing the Main Idea* What challenges did the Puritan colonists face and why do you think they succeeded in establishing permanent settlements in New England?

3. *Organizing Information* Create a graphic organizer that compares the main characteristics of the following colonies: New France, Plymouth, and Massachusetts Bay Colony.

Critical Thinking

4. *Analyzing Time Lines* Review the time line at the start of the section. Which of the events on the time line contributed to the outbreak of King Philip's War?

5. *Drawing Conclusions* What was the Mayflower Compact and why was it important?

Writing Activity

6. *Writing an Expository Essay* Write an essay in which you compare the French and English settlers' relationships with Native Americans.

RESOURCE OPTIONS

Teaching Resources

 Quiz Units 1–2 folder, p. 21

Student Performance Pack

Guide to the Essentials Chapter 2, Section 3 (English and Spanish)

Media and Technology

RESOURCE◉PRO

Visual Learning Activity The Pequot War, found on Resource Pro, presents a drawing from 1638 that will enhance students' understanding of the settlers' battle with the Pequots of Connecticut.

Answers to
SECTION 3 REVIEW

1. (a) New England Colonies, see p. 43; (b) Puritan, see p. 44; (c) persecute, see p. 44; (d) Pilgrim, see p. 44; (e) Mayflower Compact, see p. 44; (f) Great Migration, see p. 44; (g) religious tolerance, see p. 44; (h) Salem witch trials, see p. 45; (i) sachem, see p. 48; (j) Pequot War, see p. 48; (k) King Philip's War, see p. 49.

2. Challenges include: war with Native Americans, harsh climate, disagreements among themselves. Reasons for success include: common goal; plan for strong government and well-ordered society; united, strong community; hard work.

3. New France: based on fur trade, located along St. Lawrence River and Great Lakes; Plymouth: settled by Pilgrims from England in 1620, led by William Bradford, agreed to Mayflower Compact; Massachusetts Bay: settled by Puritans from England in 1630, led by John Winthrop, strict rules and religious intolerance.

4. The settlements of Plymouth and Massachusetts Bay.

5. The Mayflower Compact was an agreement in which the Pilgrims agreed to obey their government's laws. It shows that the Pilgrims expected to decide for themselves by whom they would be governed.

6. Essays should include these points: the French settled in the Americas in small numbers; they traded with the Native Americans rather than displacing them; the English settled in large numbers and took over much Native American land.

Answer to . . .

Viewing History Metacom was killed, and the English successfully conquered the region.

SKILLS FOR LIFE

Graphs and Charts

Using Time Lines

Focus Tell students that a time line, either standard or condensed, can illustrate the significance of a date or period relative to other events.

Instruct Allow students to work through the exercise on time lines. Invite them to work in pairs to explore the relationship between events on the time line on this page and those on the section time line at the beginning of section 3. How many years passed between the settlement of Plymouth Colony and the settlement of the Massachusetts Bay Company? *(ten)*

Extend See the Skills for Life Activity in the Resource Options below.

Answers

1. (a) 1565; 1715 (b) 150 years. (c) 1608; 1616 (d) Eight years.

2. (a) 25-year intervals. (b) Two-year intervals.

3. (a) 1609 (b) Until 1701, or 92 years. (c) The alliance formed by Champlain with the Algonquins and Hurons against the Iroquois in 1609–1610 had been in effect for years by the time the English settled Plymouth in 1620 and the Dutch settled New Amsterdam in 1625. The English and Dutch probably sought an alliance with the Iroquois in order to gain leverage against the French and their Native American allies, whose control of the inland fur trade had expanded into the midcontinent by 1615.

TEST FOR SUCCESS

Students' time lines will vary. Events should be in chronological order.

Using Time Lines

Time lines are visual presentations of events in the order in which they happened. When studying history, seeing events set out in chronological order can help you understand the events and their relationship to each other.

In the seventeenth century, Europe's major powers were greatly interested in North America. By the early 1600s, the Spanish, English, French, and Dutch were scrambling to establish colonies there and fighting to secure their claims against rivals—both European and Native American.

The two time lines below set out in chronological order several events that occurred during this period. The upper one, a standard time line, covers major events within a broad time frame. The condensed time line, the lower of the two, works something like a microscope. It magnifies a short time segment from the standard time line and looks in more detail at just one event—in this case, the explorations of Samuel de Champlain of France.

Practice using and comparing the two time lines by following these steps.

1. *Identify the time period covered by each time line.* Study the time lines to discover the span of history each covers. (a) What are the earliest and the latest dates shown on the upper time line? (b) How many years are covered by the upper time line? (c) What are the earliest and the latest dates on the lower time line? (d) How many years does the lower time line cover?

2. *Determine how each time line has been divided.* Time lines are divided into equal periods of time, such as 10-year, 25-year, or 100-year intervals. (a) Study the dates on the standard time line. Into what intervals is this time line divided? (b) Into what intervals is the condensed time line divided?

3. *Study the time lines to see whether events might be related.* Explore the possible relationship between two events on the two time lines. (a) When did hostilities between the French and the Iroquois begin? (b) How long did the hostilities last? (c) What events on the time lines help explain why the Dutch and English settlers both allied themselves with the Iroquois?

TEST FOR SUCCESS

Conduct library research and create a time line showing the key events in the early history of your state.

RESOURCE OPTIONS

Teaching Resources

Skills for Life Activity Units 1–2 folder, p. 28, uses a time line of significant events during the cold war (1945–1992).

1664	1681	1702	1704	1712	1729	
English take New Amsterdam from the Dutch	Penn receives land grant for Pennsylvania	New Jersey becomes a royal colony	Delaware becomes a royal colony	South Carolina becomes a royal colony	North Carolina becomes a royal colony	1732 Georgia colony founded

1650	1675	1700	1725	1750

4 The Middle and Southern Colonies

SECTION PREVIEW

Objectives

1 Explain the early history of the Dutch in New York.
2 Describe the founding of the other Middle Colonies.
3 Compare the reasons for settlement of the Southern Colonies.
4 *Key Terms* Define: Middle Colonies; diversity; synagogue; proprietary colony; Quaker; haven; Southern Colonies; trustee.

Main Idea

The Middle and Southern Colonies were settled for a variety of political, economic, and religious reasons.

Reading Strategy

Organizing Information As you read the section, create a chart in which you list important facts about each of the Middle and Southern Colonies.

The colonies to the south of New England developed differently for a variety of reasons. The settlers of the **Middle Colonies,** for example, came from several countries. These colonies included New York, New Jersey, Pennsylvania, and Delaware. They are called the Middle Colonies because they are in the middle of the Atlantic coast of North America. New York in particular was a colony with great **diversity,** or variety of people.

The Dutch in New York

The first Europeans to settle in the area that is now New York were the Dutch. They came from Holland, also called the Netherlands. In 1621 Dutch investors formed the Dutch West India Company to develop trade in the Americas. The company started a colony, New Netherland, in the Hudson and Delaware river valleys.

A Thriving Colony In 1625, the Dutch began building a trading station they called New Amsterdam at the mouth of the Hudson River. They quickly realized that the best spot for their homes was the beautiful island of Manhattan.

The director of the colony, Peter Minuit, traded goods with the local Native Americans for the right to use it. Meanwhile, the company also built Fort Orange upstream, not far from the site of Albany, the modern capital of New York State.

The settlers soon built up a prosperous trade in furs and other goods with Europe. In 1655 the Dutchman Adriaen Van der Donck gave three reasons for Dutch trading success in New Netherland:

This hand-carved trunk, with its tulip motif, was probably brought from Holland or made by a Dutch artisan in America.

❝First, it is a fine fruitful country. Secondly, it has fine navigable rivers extending far inland, by which the productions of the country can be brought to places of [sale]. [Thirdly,] the Indians, without our labor or trouble, bring to us their fur trade, worth tons of gold, which may be increased, and is like goods found.❞

—*Adriaen Van der Donck*

Farmers also grew wheat and rye on their Manhattan lands, and more crops as their

RESOURCE OPTIONS

Teaching Resources

📁 **Reproducible Lesson Plan** Lesson Plans folder, p. 41

📁 **Big Idea Graphic Organizer** Big Idea Graphic Organizer folder, p. 13

📁 **Guided Reading and Review** Units 1–2 folder, p. 22

Objectives

You may wish to call students' attention to the objectives in the Section Preview. The objectives are reflected in the main headings of the section.

Bellringer

Have students examine a present-day map of the mid-Atlantic states. How do place names still reflect the Dutch, Swedes, Germans, and other groups who settled there?

Reading Strategy

Organizing Information Refer to the Reading Strategy in the Section Preview. You may wish to model the chart on the chalkboard, asking students to list facts as they go along.

LESSON PLAN

Connecting to the Main Idea

1. Focus Tell students that the colonies to the south of New England were not settled by the Puritans. The Middle and Southern colonies developed differently because of the beliefs of the people who settled there. Unlike the Puritan colonies, many of these colonies showed religious tolerance.

2. Instruct Explain that most colonies that developed in the South and mid-Atlantic region were proprietary, which meant that an individual or group "owned" the colony and could make all its laws. An example was the Dutch colony of New Netherland, renamed New York by the Duke of York after he decided to take over the colony.

3. Close Remind students that people from Sweden settled in Delaware and that Quakers settled in Pennsylvania. Pennsylvania grew out of William Penn's philosophy of religious tolerance. All the southern colonies, like Virginia, began as proprietary colonies. Discuss how settlers shaped the land they claimed.

Shortly after this painting was made, about 1650, the English took over New Amsterdam, renaming it New York. **Culture** *How did the English interaction with Native Americans differ from Dutch interaction with Native Americans?*

holdings expanded along the Hudson and Delaware rivers. The settlers shipped most of these products to other colonies.

New Amsterdam became a port where Dutch, Swedes, French, German, English and many others carried on peaceful business together. Some eighteen different languages were spoken in its streets. Religious tolerance was a firm rule. The town even boasted the first **synagogue,** or house of Jewish worship, on the North American continent.

Though Dutch rule was generally mild, the last governor, Peter Stuyvesant, was often at odds with the colonists. They wanted more self-government, and the hot-tempered Stuyvesant refused to grant it.

England Takes Over The English looked on the prosperity of the Dutch colony with envious eyes. In 1664 the English king, Charles II, decided to make a move. He declared that the entire region of the Dutch colonies belonged to his brother, the Duke of York.

The Duke of York sent a fleet of four ships and several hundred soldiers to New Amsterdam. The town had no fort or other defenses, and the Dutch realized at once that they could do nothing to stop the English. Though Stuyvesant stormed and raged, they would not fight, and in the end he was forced to give up the town. New Amsterdam was immediately renamed New York and became an English colony. Soon the rest of New Netherland surrendered to the English.

Main Idea
CONNECTIONS

Why did the English want to take over New Netherland?

The Other Middle Colonies

The colony of New York was a **proprietary colony**—a colony granted by a king or queen to an individual or group who had full governing rights. (*Proprietor* means "owner.") The colony of New York was owned by the Duke of York. He could make laws and rule it as he wished. The other Middle Colonies were also proprietary.

New Jersey. The Duke of York's charter included land in what is now Maine, New York, New Jersey, and Delaware. He signed some of it over to two English noblemen. This land was divided into East Jersey and West Jersey. East Jersey was closely linked to New York, while West Jersey developed close ties to Pennsylvania. In 1702, both East and West Jersey became a single royal colony called New Jersey.

Delaware In 1638, settlers from Sweden started the first permanent colony in what is now Delaware. They built Fort Christina on the site of modern-day Wilmington. The Dutch under Peter Stuyvesant captured this trading village from the Swedes, and the Duke of York captured it from the Dutch. In 1682 he turned it over to an Englishman named William Penn. Penn allowed Delaware to become a separate colony in 1704.

Pennsylvania Delaware was not Penn's only colony. He had received a huge land grant from King Charles II of England in 1681. He called it Pennsylvania, which means "Penn's woods." Like the Puritans, he saw his colony as a "Holy Experiment," but unlike the Puritans, he wanted his colonists to practice religious tolerance.

Penn made agreements with the Native Americans about land use and then brought over the first of many settlers from England.

These settlers, like Penn, were **Quakers,** members of a Protestant group that had suffered persecution in England. Quakers believed firmly that all people should be treated as equals, not only in church but in society and government. Along with Delaware and West New Jersey, which Penn also owned at that time, Pennsylvania became a **haven,** or safe place, for people of every faith.

Soon Pennsylvania was drawing Quakers from other American colonies, as well as from Wales, Germany, and other lands. The colony also invited non-Quakers. Protestant groups such as the German Lutherans, Scotch-Irish Presbyterians, and Swiss Mennonites built large settlements in Pennsylvania. So many Germans settled in the colony that they came to be known as the Pennsylvania Dutch, after the German word *Deutsch*, which means "German."

The Southern Colonies

Virginia was the first-settled of the **Southern Colonies.** The others were Maryland, the Carolinas, and Georgia. All of these settlements began as proprietary colonies.

Maryland Maryland started as the idea of George Calvert, an English lord who had become a Roman Catholic after growing up in the Anglican Church. He saw Roman Catholics being persecuted in England, and wanted to establish a safe place for them to live. He had also been a member of the Virginia Company, and was convinced that well-run colonies could be profitable. In the early 1630s Calvert asked the king for a charter to establish a colony in the Chesapeake Bay area. The king approved his plan, but Calvert died before the charter could be written up. Thus it was issued in the name of his son, Lord Baltimore.

The first settlers arrived in Maryland in 1634. Though Maryland was supposed to be a haven for Roman Catholics, Puritans also moved to the colony. In fact, they outnumbered the Catholics from the very beginning. Therefore Lord Baltimore ordered adoption of a law that would protect Catholics from persecution in the colony. This Maryland Toleration Act was important as part of a general trend toward religious tolerance in the English colonies. The law said that no one who believed in Jesus would be "any ways troubled," that is,

persecuted. The act was severely limited, however, in that it did not provide protection for non-Christians. Puritans in Maryland's assembly amended the law to state that non-Christians would be put to death.

The planters of Maryland, like those in Virginia, grew prosperous during the 1600s by growing tobacco. Like the Virginians, as time went on they began to use enslaved Africans to work their fields. The Africans were brought to the colonies by slave traders. By 1704, roughly 15,000 of the 90,000 people in the two colonies were African slaves. Planters considered the Africans as property and both these colonies and others passed laws aimed at protecting the planters' "property" rights. For example, a Virginia law passed in 1642 penalized people for sheltering runaway slaves or indentured servants. A 1664 Maryland law specified that

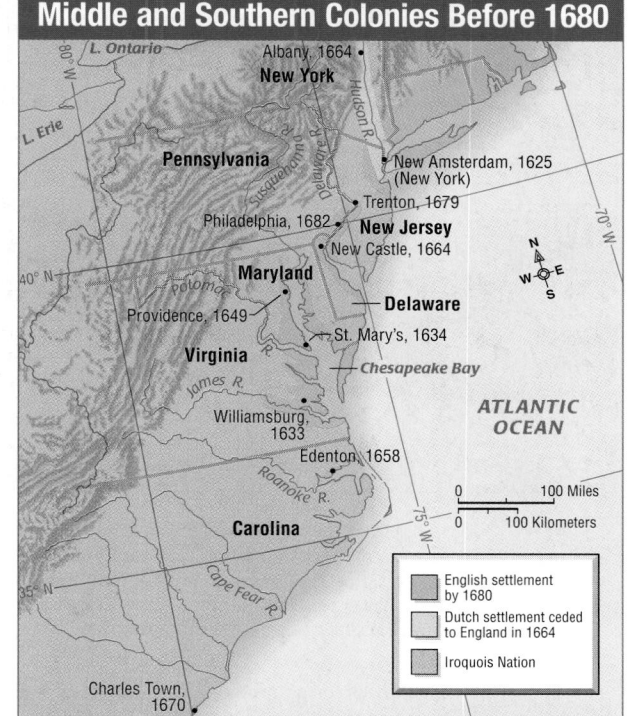

Middle and Southern Colonies Before 1680

Albany, 1664
New York
New Amsterdam, 1625 (New York)
Trenton, 1679
Pennsylvania
Philadelphia, 1682
New Jersey
New Castle, 1664
Maryland
Delaware
Providence, 1649
St. Mary's, 1634
Virginia
Chesapeake Bay
ATLANTIC OCEAN
Williamsburg, 1633
Edenton, 1658
Carolina
Charles Town, 1670

L. Ontario
L. Erie
Hudson R.
Susquehanna
Delaware
Potomac
James R.
Roanoke R.
Cape Fear R.

0   100 Miles
0   100 Kilometers

- English settlement by 1680
- Dutch settlement ceded to England in 1664
- Iroquois Nation

MAP Skills
The English were a strong presence along the mid-Atlantic coast by 1680. Not even the thriving Dutch settlements could resist England's colonizing zeal.
Movement *Why do you think the English avoided settling farther inland?*

Answers to
SECTION 4 REVIEW

1. (a) Middle Colonies, see p. 51; (b) diversity, see p. 51; (c) synagogue, see p. 52; (d) proprietary colony, see p. 52; (e) Quaker, see p. 53; (f) haven, see p. 53; (g) Southern Colonies, see p. 53; (h) trustee, see p. 54.

2. Reasons include: to escape religious persecution, to gain profits from trade and fishing, to establish a fur trade, to escape religious intolerance in Massachusetts, to seek gold, to establish an outpost against the Spanish, to establish a Catholic settlement, to gain land wealth, to create a settlement for debtors.

3. New York: practiced religious tolerance for all; Pennsylvania: practiced religious tolerance for all; Maryland: religious tolerance limited to Christians; Georgia: religious tolerance for all Protestants, not Catholics.

4. New Amsterdam was renamed New York after the British took over the lucrative trading colony in 1664.

5. The fact that so many colonies began as proprietary colonies set the precedent for self-rule in North America. The American Revolution was, in part, a consequence of this precedent.

6. Answers will vary. Students' essays could include some of the following points: religious tolerance, good farmland, good trade, peaceful relationship with Native Americans.

James Oglethorpe, a general as well as a member of Parliament, carefully planned the city of Savannah, Georgia, as a series of squares. He intended the colony to be a haven for debtors, but also realized its strategic value. *Geography* *What was the strategic value of the Georgia colony?*

all black people imported to the colony were to be given the status of slaves.

The Carolinas South of Maryland and Virginia was a region known as Carolina. Although there had been earlier claims on the land, King Charles II granted its ownership to a group of English noblemen in 1663.

The large area called Carolina was first split into North and South Carolina in 1691, when two different governors were appointed. In 1721, South Carolina became a royal colony. North Carolina became a royal colony in 1729. Despite threats from the Spanish and Native Americans, both colonies thrived on trade with Native Americans and tobacco profits.

Georgia Though Georgia was set up like a proprietary colony in 1732, it was actually managed not by owners but by **trustees.** A trustee is someone entrusted to look after a business.

The trustees, led by James Oglethorpe, wanted to make a haven for people who had been in jail in England because they could not pay their debts. They also accepted another duty the English government had insisted upon: helping to protect the Southern Colonies against attack from Spanish raiders based in Florida.

Oglethorpe and the trustees ruled Georgia strictly. No one was allowed to own enslaved workers or drink hard liquor. Although the trustees did not allow Catholics to live in Georgia, all types of Protestants were permitted. Thanks to Oglethorpe's careful negotiations, the settlers lived at peace with the Native Americans.

Gradually, however, the colonists forced the trustees to change their rules. Settlers were allowed to use and sell liquor, and enslaved Africans were brought in to work the land. After twenty years, the trustees gave their charter back to the king, and Georgia became a royal colony in 1752.

SECTION 4 REVIEW

Comprehension

1. *Key Terms* Define: (a) Middle Colonies; (b) diversity; (c) synagogue; (d) proprietary colony; (e) Quaker; (f) haven; (g) Southern Colonies; (h) trustee.

2. *Summarizing the Main Idea* List some of the reasons people settled in the Middle and Southern Colonies of North America.

3. *Organizing Information* Create a chart showing the degree of religious tolerance in New York, Pennsylvania, Maryland, and Georgia.

Critical Thinking

4. *Analyzing Time Lines* Review the time line at the start of the section. When and why was the Dutch colony of New Amsterdam renamed New York?

5. *Predicting Consequences* Proprietors were able to make their own laws in the colonies. What do you think might be the consequences of this fact?

Writing Activity

6. *Writing a Persuasive Essay* Write an essay in which you try to persuade a relative in Germany to join you in Pennsylvania as a settler in 1740.

Answer to . . .

Viewing History It served as a buffer between the Spanish in Florida and the Southern Colonies.

▶ RESOURCE OPTIONS

Teaching Resources

📁 **Quiz** Units 1–2 folder, p. 23

📁 **Chapter Tests Forms A and B** Chapter Test folder

Student Performance Pack

⭐ **Guide to the Essentials** Chapter 2, Section 4 (English and Spanish)

Standardized Test Preparation Handbook

Media and Technology

🎧 **Guided Reading Audiotapes** Chapter 2 Summary (English and Spanish)

Student Edition on Audiotape Chapter 2

 Test Bank CD-ROM; Interactive Student Tutorial CD-ROM Chapter Test

Why Study History?
To understand that . . .

Your Culture Interacts with Others

European colonization added greatly to the cultural diversity of North America, a diversity that continues to shape American society today.

Check out the restaurants in any major American city. Chinese, Italian, Indian, French, Mexican,

Meeting between Native Americans and Europeans

Thai, Vietnamese . . . the variety of cuisines reflects the diversity of cultures in the United States. Read the names in the telephone directory of a city such as Dallas, New York, or San Francisco: "Goldstein," "Reyes," "Bennett," "O'Donnell," "Petringa," "Moskos," "Khalsa." These names represent cultural ancestries that span the world. Listen to your friends talk. Their speech contains many words of diverse origins—words like pasta (Italian), hurricane (Spanish), khaki (Urdu), canoe (Arawak), pretzel (German), and assassin (Arabic).

The Impact Today

Americans take pride in our nation's cultural diversity as shown by the richness of our language and the variety of our foods. Different cultural groups often struggle, however, over resources and jobs and for power to define what it means to be an American.

For more than 100 years, Latino and "Anglo" (European) cultures have interacted in the United States. Latino Americans live mainly in large cities and in Florida, California, Texas, and the Southwest—an area first colonized by

Spain but taken over by the United States in the mid-1800s.

In 1990 more than 22 million Americans were of Latino ancestry, and many spoke Spanish as their first language. Today Latinos are the fastest-growing ethnic minority in the United States. As the Latino population has increased, some people have argued that Latinos are not adapting to American culture but instead are creating a separate, competing culture.

Political resistance to Latino culture revolves most intensely around language. A number of Americans support "English Only" policies. Their strategy is to make English the official language of the United States. Yet many Spanish-speaking Americans feel a strong connection to their roots. They want to preserve the links to their cultural heritage.

Diversity in the classroom today

The Impact on You

Should English be declared the official language of the United States? List three effects that you believe such a law would have. Then write one paragraph explaining your position.

RESOURCE OPTIONS

Teaching Resources

 Why Study History? Activity Your Culture Interacts with Others, found in the Why Study History? folder, p. 3, provides an activity to help students better understand cultural diversity.

Media and Technology

 AmericanHeritage® CD-ROM

Time Tour The Nation Today and Tomorrow: Toward a New Century

---

Class Discussion

Discuss with the class cultural diversity in the United States. For a more thorough examination of the issue, see the activity folder in the Resource Options below.

ACTIVITY
STUDENT PARTICIPATION

Conducting Immigrant Interviews

Ask students to read the text. Then divide the class into small groups. Have each group brainstorm a list of questions they might ask an adult for whom English is a second language. They should address these issues:

- **how they learned English**
- **the "English only" movement**
- **bilingual education**
- **the experience of being a new immigrant**

Have the groups share their ideas. Encourage students to conduct real interviews. Put these together in an "Immigrant Interviews" notebook.

Follow up Discuss the variety of responses to interview questions. Did factors such as country of origin or job status affect answers?

Using the Internet

Students can learn more about interactions among cultures by exploring links in the *America: Pathways to the Present* Web site at

http://www.Pathways.phschool.com

Assessment

See the Lesson Plans folder, pp. 24–27, for rubrics on assessing Class Participation Projects.

Key Terms

Students should refer to the definitions of the key terms in the chapter to write sentences that show the relation of each word to European colonization of the Americas.

Comprehension

1. Southeast: to build forts to defend the Spanish ships; Southwest: to make money from mining; West Coast: to build trade routes across the Pacific and protect against foreign countries.
2. The Pueblo people of New Mexico drove the Spanish out of Santa Fe, killed priests, colonists, and soldiers, and destroyed missions. The revolt came in response to widespread sickness among the Pueblo population and resentment over forced conversion.
3. Lack of experience with manual labor and other necessary skills, swampy site with disease-bearing mosquitoes, poor leadership, Native American resistance.
4. Along the St. Lawrence River and Great Lakes.
5. To escape religious persecution in England.
6. The Puritans wanted to transform the land into farmland and pasture, but Native Americans depended on large amounts of land for hunting.
7. A movement of people from Europe to New England beginning in 1630.
8. Charles II wanted the colonists to trade only with Britain.
9. Quakers, Scotch-Irish Presbyterians, and Swiss Mennonites.
10. As a haven for English debtors.

Chapter Summary

The major concepts of Chapter 2 are presented below. See also *Guide to the Essentials of American History* or *Interactive Student Tutorial CD-ROM,* which contains interactive review activities, time lines, helpful hints, and test practice for Chapter 2.

Reviewing the Main Ideas
In the 1500s and 1600s, Spain, England, and France established colonies in North America. Each European nation had a different relationship with Native Americans, as well as its own way of settling the land. As a result, there was great variety among the European colonies in the Americas.

Section 1: Spanish Explorers and Colonies
Between 1492 and 1650, the Spanish built an empire in Central and South America as well as the Southeast and Southwest regions of North America.

Section 2: The Jamestown Colony
Hunger, disease, and Native American resistance all contributed to the near failure of the English colony in Virginia. The discovery of tobacco as a cash crop, however, saved the colony.

Section 3: The New England Colonies
With both help and resistance from Native Americans, English colonists succeeded in establishing permanent settlements in New England.

Section 4: The Middle and Southern Colonies
The Middle and Southern Colonies were settled for a variety of political, economic, and religious reasons.

European colonization added greatly to the cultural diversity of North America, a diversity that continues to shape American society today. Different cultural groups often struggle, however, over resources and jobs and for power to define what it means to be an American.

Key Terms

For each of the terms below, write a sentence explaining how it relates to this chapter.

1. conquistador
2. mission
3. joint-stock company
4. royal colony
5. legislature
6. House of Burgesses
7. indentured servant
8. Puritan
9. Pilgrim
10. Mayflower Compact
11. sachem
12. proprietary colony

Comprehension

1. Why did the Spanish encourage settlement in the Southeast, Southwest, and West Coast regions of North America?
2. Describe the Pueblo Revolt of 1680.
3. List the reasons for Jamestown's near failure.
4. Where was New France located?
5. Why did English Pilgrims come to New England?
6. Why did conflicts develop between Native Americans and the English settlers?
7. What was the Great Migration?
8. Why did the British want to take over New Amsterdam?
9. Describe the groups that settled Pennsylvania.
10. Why was the colony of Georgia established?

Using Graphic Organizers

On a separate sheet of paper, copy the graphic organizer below. As you review the chapter, fill in the locations of major settlements for each of the following countries.

Spain	England	France

Using Graphic Organizers

- Spain: Southeast, Southwest, and West Coast.
- England: Jamestown, New England, New York (after 1664), Plymouth, Massachusetts Bay Colony.
- France: Quebec, Montreal, along St. Lawrence River and Great Lakes.

Analyzing Political Cartoons ▶

1. This Puritan cartoon expresses sentiments about behavior in Massachusetts in the early colonial period. (a) What does the labeling in the two panels suggest? (b) What does the book in the top panel represent? (c) What do the dice, cards, cup, and pipe in the lower panel represent?

2. What is the message of this cartoon?

3. Given what you know about Puritans, what is the cartoonist's view of the situation?

Critical Thinking

1. *Applying the Chapter Skill* Create a time line for the chapter that includes key dates for the Spanish, English, and French settlement of North America.

2. *Drawing Inferences* Review the excerpt from "A Model of Christian Charity" on page 44. How might the ideals expressed in this sermon have contributed to the success of the New England settlers?

3. *Identifying Central Issues* In what ways did religion contribute to the founding of some of the North American colonies?

4. *Demonstrating Reasoned Judgment* Review the excerpt from the Mayflower Compact on page 44. How might the ideas in this document have contributed to the colonists' eventual fight for independence from England?

ANALYZING DOCUMENTS ▶ INTERPRETING DATA

Turn to the graph of tobacco exports on page 40.

1. Which statement best summarizes the information on the graph? (a) England imported very little tobacco between 1622 and 1624. (b) English tobacco imports increased steadily after 1622. (c) English tobacco imports decreased steadily after 1622. (d) English tobacco imports reached their highest levels in 1620.

2. The amount of American tobacco imported by England in 1622 (a) nearly equalled the amount imported in 1618, (b) was double the amount imported in 1618, (c) was half the amount imported in 1624, (d) nearly equalled the amount imported in 1626.

3. *Writing* What events in Jamestown and Virginia allowed the colonists to export more and more tobacco to England during the period from 1616 to 1626?

INTERNET ACTIVITY

For your portfolio:
PREPARE A SUMMARY

Access Prentice Hall's *America: Pathways to the Present* site at **www.Pathways.phschool.com** for the specific URL to complete the activity. Additional resources and related Web sites are also available.

Select and summarize an excerpt from the accounts of Coronado's expeditions. Describe the expedition's objectives, difficulties, people encountered, and outcome. Based on this account, how would you characterize Coronado?

Connecting to Today

Essay Writing In the United States, the First Amendment to the Constitution guarantees people the right to practice their religion as they wish. Which early American colonies set precedents for such a law? Which did not?

INTERNET ACTIVITY

Answers will vary. Summaries should include expedition objectives, difficulties, and people encountered. Characterizations of Coronado should reflect his behavior during the expedition.

Analyzing Political Cartoons

1. (a) Change over time. (b) The Bible. (c) Immoral behavior.
2. Society has abandoned religious principles and adopted social vices.
3. Disapproval.

Critical Thinking

1. See section time lines for sections 1, 2, 3, and 4.
2. The excerpt reflects the idea that the colonists must work together in order to survive. Working together would have enabled them to solve problems more easily than working alone.
3. Many of those who founded colonies were fleeing religious persecution.
4. The excerpt reveals that the colonists at Plymouth intended to form their own political unit and make their own laws. Ideas similar to these fueled the American Revolution.

Interpreting Data

1. b
2. a
3. The use of indentured servants allowed farmers to grow more tobacco. Also, settlers opened up more lands to the west for growing tobacco.

Connecting to Today

Colonies setting precedents for religious freedom include Rhode Island, New York, Pennsylvania, Maryland (partial), and Georgia (partial). Colonies setting precedents for religious intolerance include Massachusetts.

Growth of the American Colonies, 1689–1754

Managing Time and Instruction

INSTRUCTION SUPPORT
These materials for instruction are provided for **each section** in the **Teaching Resources**. See **Units 1–2 folder for Enrichment Support:**

- Reproducible Lesson Plans in Lesson Plans folder • Learning Styles Lesson Plans in Learning Styles Lesson Plans folder • Big Idea Graphic Organizers in Big Idea Graphic Organizer folder
- Guided Reading and Review • Quizzes • Test Preparation Practice booklet

DAILY LESSON	ENRICHMENT SUPPORT
1 **An Empire and Its Colonies** (pp. 59–63)	• Nystrom *Atlas of Our Country*, Colonies in the North and East, pp. 14–15 • Biography, Hannah Callowhill Penn, found on **Resource Pro** • Skills for Life Activity, Units 1–2 folder, p. 41
2 **Life in Colonial America** (pp. 65–69)	• Literature Activity, The Captivity of Mary Rowlandson, found on **Resource Pro** • Literature Activity, As Poor Richard Says, Units 1–2 folder, p. 40 • Visual Learning Activity, The First American Schoolbook, Learning with Documents folder, p. 45 • Primary Source Activity, A Marriage Agreement, Learning with Documents folder, p. 9 • Critical Thinking Activity, Identifying Central Issues: The Status of Colonial Women, found on **Resource Pro** 11
3 **African Americans in the Colonies** (pp. 72–76)	• Geography and History Activity, Changing Economic Patterns in the South, Geography and History folder, pp. 2–3 • Nystrom *Atlas of Our Country*, Unwilling Immigrants and Native Americans, pp. 16–17 • Visual Learning Activity, Education as a Step Toward Freedom, found on **Resource Pro**
4 **Emerging Tensions** (pp. 77–80)	• Comparing Primary Sources, On Expansion into Native American Lands, Units 1–2 folder, pp. 38–39 • Nystrom *Atlas of Our Country*, Early Expansion of the United States, pp. 20–21 • Biography, Jonathan Edwards, Units 1–2 folder, p. 37 • Primary Source Activity, The Great Awakening, found on **Resource Pro** • Your Freedom of Religion Is Guaranteed, Why Study History? folder, p. 4

Running Out of Time?

- Use Tape 1, "Origins of a New Society, to 1783," from **Visions of America** videotapes series.
- Use Chapter 3 Summary, from **Guide to the Essentials of American History (English and Spanish).**

Companion Web Site

The companion Web site offers online links for all chapter review activities. It also provides key content links and structured support for this chapter for both teachers and students.

http://www.Pathways.phschool.com

Teaching in the Information Age

Media and Technology

For the Student

Interactive Student Tutorial CD-ROM Chapter 3
Student Edition on Audiotape Chapter 3
American Heritage® CD-ROM
Guided Reading Audiotapes (English and Spanish) Chapter 3

For the Teacher

Resource Pro CD-ROM Chapter 3
Test Bank CD-ROM Chapter 3
Listening to Literature Audiotapes *Timeless Voices, Timeless Themes* from *The Interesting Narrative of the Life of Olaudah Equiano* by Olaudah Equiano
Color Transparencies Our Multicultural Heritage, C-1, C-5

Assessment Options

Chapter Test Forms A&B Test Bank CD-ROM booklet
Test Bank CD-ROM Chapter 3
Standardized Test Preparation Handbook

Block Scheduling

Pacing Suggestions

For 90-minute Blocks

- Teach sections 1 and 2 using Transparencies E-2, L-1, H-2, H-3, J-1, and D-3 and the Recent Scholarship note on p. 66 for class discussions.
- Teach sections 3 and 4 using the Big Idea Graphic Organizers from Teaching Resources and the Extended Class Periods Activity on p. 74.

Additional Resources

- Prentice Hall's **American History Block Scheduling Support File** covers over 40 major topics in American history.
- **Prentice Hall United States History Video Collection**ᴛᴍ contains 20 videotapes covering American history from beginnings to present.
- **Visions of America Videotapes and Videodiscs**

Connections to American Literature

from Prentice Hall

Prentice Hall Literature *Timeless Voices, Timeless Themes*

- "To My Dear and Loving Husband" by Anne Bradstreet, p. 90
- from *Poor Richard's Almanac* by Benjamin Franklin, p. 188

Additional Resources

For the Student
Colonial America. C.A.I. Software. Video.
Nathaniel Hawthorne. *The Scarlet Letter.* Silver Burdett Classics, 1985.

For the Teacher
Sidney Kaplan and Emma Nagrady Kaplan. *The Black Presence in the Era of the American Revolution.* University of Massachusetts, 1989.

Prentice Hall brings into the classroom the vast archives and scholarship of the nation's premier American history magazine. See "From the Archives of American Heritage®" teaching notes in this chapter.

 History Alive!

Teacher's Curriculum Institute, in partnership with Prentice Hall, provides unique materials that engage students with diverse learning styles. See History Alive!® unit on Colonial Life and the American Revolution.

 Student Performance Pack

Ensures success in the three critical areas of Reading, Test Taking, and English Language Development with the following materials:
- Guide to the Essentials of American History in English and Spanish
- Guided Reading Audiotapes in English and Spanish
- Interactive Student Tutorial CD-ROM
- Test Preparation Handbook
- Test Preparation Practice booklet

Introducing the Chapter
The years up to 1754 were a defining period for the American colonies. Varied landforms and climate, a steady stream of immigrants from different regions of the world, and England's policy of salutary neglect gave rise to a future hallmark of America: diversity of belief, economy, and people. A spirit of independence also spread among the colonists during this period; not just independence from England, but also from each other.

Themes in American History
The theme for this chapter, Diversity, is listed at the beginning of this unit. An alternate theme for the chapter is Economics. To teach this unit thematically, you may wish to use the Forging a New Nation folder in American History Block Scheduling Support.

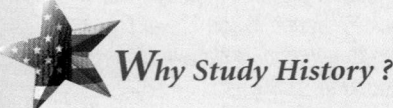

Have students explore suggested ways of connecting the past to the present on page 81.

Answer to . . .

Viewing History Students should use this question as an aid in reading the chapter. The British government was often too preoccupied to pursue a very active colonial policy, instead following a policy of salutary neglect. With this freedom, the colonies grew quickly and prospered. They also developed their own local governments.

CHAPTER 3
Growth of the American Colonies
1689-1754

CHAPTER FOCUS

This chapter discusses the changes that took place in the British colonies of North America in the years between 1689 and 1754. Settlers from Britain and other European nations, along with African slaves, poured into the colonies. As they developed ways of making a living in the new land, they formed distinct colonial societies. They also began to develop a taste for independence.

The Why Study History? page at the end of this chapter explores the connection between the growth of religious pluralism in colonial America and the guarantee of freedom of worship in the United States today.

VIEWING HISTORY In 1757 Bethlehem, Pennsylvania, displayed all the characteristics of a self-sufficient community. *Government How did British colonial policy affect the development of colonial societies?*

RESOURCE OPTIONS

Teaching Resources

 Big Idea Graphic Organizer folder Graphic summary of the main idea of the chapter.

 Learning Styles Lesson Plans folder Alternate lesson plans for diverse learning styles for each chapter.

Media and Technology

AmericanHeritage® CD-ROM
Time Tour A Meeting of Different Worlds: The Thirteen English Colonies

Prentice Hall United States History Video Collection™ Volume 2 *The Era of Colonization (1585–1763)*

1660				1686	1688	1689

1660 Navigation Act strengthened

1686 Dominion of New England established

1688 Glorious Revolution in England

1689 Rebellion in Boston against Dominion of New England

1660   **1670**   **1680**   **1690**

1 An Empire and Its Colonies

An Empire and Its Colonies

SECTION PREVIEW

Objectives

1 Understand how the English Civil War and mercantilism affected colonial development.
2 Explain how English policies allowed the colonies to develop on their own in the early 1700s.
3 Describe the economic and social differences that developed in each region.
4 *Key Terms* Define: mercantilism; balance of trade; duty; salutary neglect; staple crop; triangular trade.

Main Idea

The English colonies in the mid-1600s and early 1700s grew and prospered with little direct interference from the English government.

Reading Strategy

Reinforcing Main Ideas As you read the section, look for evidence to support the statement above that the colonies ". . . grew and prospered with little direct interference from the English government."

In the late 1600s and early 1700s, England prized its cluster of colonies on the Atlantic coast of North America for two reasons. The colonies supplied food and raw materials, and they bought large amounts of English goods. The colonists were, in general, loyal to their parent country. Thus England got what it wanted from its colonies—raw materials and a place to sell its goods—by leaving them alone.

The English Civil War

From 1640 to 1660, England had another reason for ignoring the colonies. In the 1640s, tensions that had long simmered in England boiled over in a civil war. The nation became so preoccupied with conflicts within its own borders that it could pay little attention to its North American colonies.

Two opponents faced off in the clash: King Charles I and Parliament. Parliament, made up of representatives of the people, had the power to make laws and approve new taxes. Many of its members believed that Charles was attempting to limit the powers of Parliament and of English property owners.

After defeating the king's army in a series of battles, Parliament ordered the execution of Charles in January 1649. Oliver Cromwell, the commander of the Parliamentary armies, then governed England until his death in 1658. After two decades of upheaval, Parliament recognized the need for stability. In 1660 it restored Charles II, the son of the executed king, to the throne.

Mercantilism

Before 1660, the people of England were too busy fighting a civil war to be concerned with a group of colonies on the other side of the Atlantic. As the political situation in England settled down, England's focus shifted to economic matters.

The Theory of Mercantilism By 1650, many nations in western Europe were working to improve their economies, spurred on by a new theory called **mercantilism**. Mercantilism held that a country should try to get and keep as much bullion, or gold and silver, as possible. The more gold and silver a country had, argued mercantilists, the wealthier and more powerful it would be.

▶ RESOURCE OPTIONS

Teaching Resources

📁 **Reproducible Lesson Plan** Lesson Plans folder, p. 42

📁 **Big Idea Graphic Organizer** Big Idea Graphic Organizer folder, p. 14

📁 **Guided Reading and Review** Units 1–2 folder, p. 29

Objectives
You may wish to call students' attention to the objectives in the Section Preview. The objectives are reflected in the main headings of the section.

Bellringer
Ask students to define the term *empire* as broadly as they can. Encourage students to think about why a country would want an empire. What obligations and responsibilities does an empire bring with it?

Reading Strategy
Reinforcing Main Ideas Refer to the Reading Strategy in the Section Preview. You may wish to model the strategy by writing details on the chalkboard to support the statement.

LESSON PLAN
Connecting to the Main Idea

1. Focus Explain that the relationship between England and its colonies in the late 1600s and early 1700s was generally peaceful but distant. Ask students why England purposely neglected its colonies. How did the colonies develop into prosperous but distinct regions?

2. Instruct Emphasize to students the basic goal of mercantilism: to accumulate as much gold and silver as possible, using foreign trade and colonies. Discuss England's economic approach to its colonies as evidenced by the Navigation Act, which brought in additional money to the English treasury. Also discuss why England adopted a colonial policy of salutary neglect in the 1700s.

3. Close Ask students to describe the effects of the policy of salutary neglect (under which the colonies prospered and developed distinct regional differences).

For countries without mines like those Spain controlled in the Americas, the only way to obtain more bullion was through trade. If a country sold more goods to other countries than it bought from them, it would end up with more bullion. In other words, a country's **balance of trade,** or the difference in value between imports and exports, should show more exports than imports.

Mercantilists believed a nation should have colonies where it could buy raw materials and sell products. The colonies should not be allowed to sell products to other nations or even to manufacture goods. The right to make goods for sale was reserved exclusively for the parent country, since manufacturing was a major source of profit. To maintain control over trade and to increase profits, the parent country required the colonies to use its ships for transporting their raw materials.

Effects on Trade Laws Mercantilism appealed to English rulers. They came to realize that colonies could provide raw materials such as tobacco, furs, and perhaps gold for England to sell to other countries. Furthermore, the colonies would have to buy England's manufactured goods. This exchange would greatly improve England's balance of trade. English leaders therefore decided that it was necessary to have as many colonies as possible and to control colonial trade to provide the maximum profit to England.

In 1660 Charles II approved a stronger version of a previous law called the Navigation Act. Together with other legislation, the Navigation Act tightened control over colonial trade. The new laws required the colonies to sell certain goods, including sugar, tobacco, and cotton, only to England. Moreover, if colonists wanted to sell anything to people in other parts of the world, they had to take the crop or product to England first and pay a **duty,** or tax, on it. They also had to use English ships for all their trade.

Effects on War and Politics As European countries adopted mercantilism, the relations between them began to change. More and more, European countries fought each other over territory and trade routes rather than over religion. In the 1500s, for example, Protestant England's major enemy had been Catholic Spain. But from 1652 to 1654, and again from 1665 to 1667, the English fought wars against the Protestant Dutch over control of trade and land in North America. To eliminate the Dutch as a major trade rival in North America, the English conquered the Dutch colony of New Netherland in 1664, renaming it New York in honor of James, Duke of York and brother of King Charles II.

During the next two decades, Charles II and James tried in several ways to tighten their control over the colonies. Their actions reached a peak in 1686 when James, now king, attempted to take direct control over New York and the New England Colonies by creating the Dominion of New England. This action abolished colonial legislatures within the Dominion and replaced them with a governor and a council appointed by King James II.

Anger in the Colonies Colonists up and down the Atlantic seaboard deeply resented James's grab for power. Edmund Andros, whom James II had appointed governor of the Dominion, made matters worse. From his headquarters in Boston, he collected taxes without the approval of either the king or the colonists and demanded payment of an annual land tax. He also declared a policy of religious tolerance, or respect for different religious beliefs. The Puritans felt these heavy-handed actions were a blow both to their freedom from English influence and to their tight control over religious affairs in their own colony.

Meanwhile, James II was making enemies in England. News reached North America in the spring of 1689 that Parliament had replaced James II with his daughter Mary and her husband William of Orange, a change of rulers known as the Glorious Revolution. New England citizens promptly held their own mini-rebellion against the Andros government, imprisoning Governor Andros and his associates.

In response to this protest, William and Mary dissolved the Dominion of New England and reestablished the colonies that James had abolished. When they restored Massachusetts's charter, however, they revised the organization of the government. The new charter allowed the king to appoint a royal governor of the colony.

Britain's Colonial Policy in the Early 1700s

In the early 1700s the British government rarely interfered directly in the affairs of its North American colonies.[†] By not interfering, Britain allowed colonial legislatures such as the House of Burgesses in Virginia to gain extensive power over local affairs.

Origins of Self-Government
As you recall, England established three different types of colonies in North America: royal, proprietary, and charter. Over time, England transformed several of the charter and proprietary colonies into royal colonies and appointed royal governors for them. By the early 1700s, therefore, the colonial governments shared a similar pattern of government. In most colonies a governor, appointed by the king, acted as the chief executive. A colonial legislature served under the governor. Most colonial assemblies consisted of an advisory council, or upper house of prominent colonists appointed by the king, and a lower house elected by qualified voters. Only male landowners were allowed to vote. However, most adult white males did own land and thus could vote.

In theory, the royal governor had a great amount of power. He decided when to call the legislature together and when to end its sessions. He could veto any laws that the legislature passed. The governor also appointed local officials, such as the treasurer and colonial judges.

In reality, it was the colonial legislatures, not the governors, that came to dominate the

[†] In 1707, England joined with Scotland to form Great Britain.

The colonies supplied England with food and raw materials. This detail from a map of 1751 shows tobacco being loaded at a southern dock for shipment to England. **Economics** Why did England require the colonies to supply it with raw materials?

colonial governments. The legislatures created and passed laws regarding defense and taxation. Later they took over the job of setting salaries for royal officials. Colonial assemblies also influenced local appointments of judges and other officials because the governor usually accepted their recommendations. Even the governor's council came to be dominated by prominent local leaders who served the interests of the legislature rather than those of the royal government.

Salutary Neglect Why did the British government allow its colonies freedom in governing themselves—far more than was allowed in Spanish or French colonies? One reason is that England had a long tradition of strong local government and weak central power. Another reason is that the British government lacked the resources and the bureaucracy to enforce its wishes. Then, too, colonists recognized the authority of the king and Parliament without being forced to. Most were proud to be British subjects.

Finally, Britain allowed its colonies freedom because the existing economy and politics of the colonists already served British interests.

Virginia's Tobacco Economy

By the 1700s, it was said that "the Establishment [of Virginia] is indeed Tobacco." This staple was the crop around which much of the colony's economy revolved. Clergymen, for example, were paid in tobacco. In 1695, the annual salary of a clergyman was legally fixed at 16,000 pounds of tobacco. In addition, the money value of a minister's salary depended on the quality of the local crop. Ministers, often from England, were most easily lured to the colony by offers from regions growing the higher-priced "Sweet Scented" tobacco.

Using physical and climate maps, discuss the geographical features that helped the colonies grow into distinct regions. Have students trace the long rivers of the Southern Colonies and compare them to those of New England. Point out the sea islands and coastal marshes of South Carolina and Georgia, where rice grew well. Compare the regions' climates. *(Visual/Spatial)*

Answer to . . .

Map Skills African Americans; along the Virginia coast, in North Carolina, and in the region spanning Savannah, Georgia, and Charleston, South Carolina.

Main Idea Connections The colonies provided Britain with needed supplies while Britain allowed the colonies relative freedom from government interference.

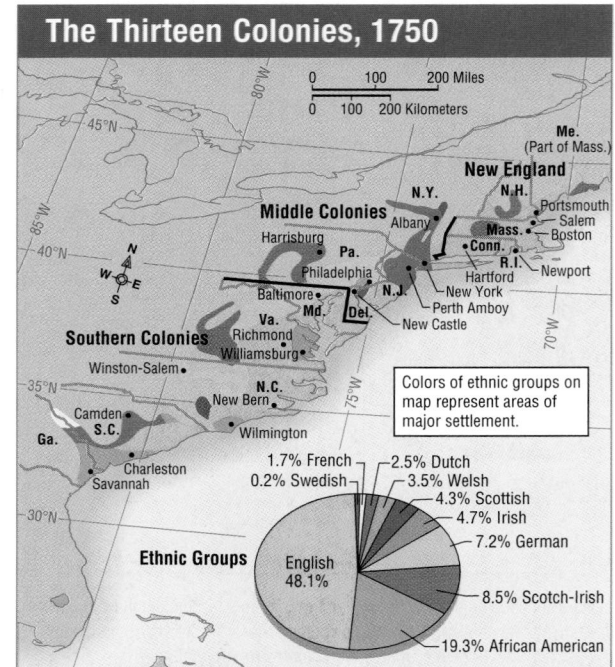

The Thirteen Colonies, 1750

Colors of ethnic groups on map represent areas of major settlement.

Ethnic Groups

- English 48.1%
- 1.7% French
- 0.2% Swedish
- 2.5% Dutch
- 3.5% Welsh
- 4.3% Scottish
- 4.7% Irish
- 7.2% German
- 8.5% Scotch-Irish
- 19.3% African American

MAP Skills English settlements in North America in the 1700s generally clung to the Eastern seaboard and its rivers. In this narrow strip, however, lived a wide variety of ethnic groups. *Regions After the English, which was the largest ethnic group? Where did they live?*

Main Idea CONNECTIONS

Why was the relationship between England and the colonies prosperous for both sides?

The British realized that the most salutary, or beneficial, policy was to neglect their colonies. Thus later historians would call British colonial policy during the early 1700s **salutary neglect**. In the early 1700s, Great Britain rarely enforced its trade regulations, such as the Navigation Act, because neglect served British economic interests better than strict enforcement. As a result, the colonies prospered, as did their trade with Britain, without much government interference.

Diverse Colonial Economies

By the early 1700s the economic foundations of Britain's American colonies were in place. While the Spanish colonies focused on mining silver and growing sugar, and New France focused on the fur trade, the British regions of eastern North America developed diverse economies. Each region's geography affected its economy.

For the most part, English-speaking settlements continued to hug the Atlantic Ocean and the deep rivers that empty into it, as shown on the map to the left. Most commerce took place on water. It was simply too expensive and too difficult to carry crops and goods long distances over land. Even water traffic on rivers, however, was blocked at the waterfalls and rapids of the fall line, where the inland hills meet the coastal plain. Roads were little more than footpaths or rutted trails. The Atlantic Ocean remained so vital to travel that there was more contact between Boston and London than between Boston and Virginia.

The Southern Colonies In the Southern Colonies of Virginia, Maryland, South Carolina, North Carolina, and Georgia, the economy was based on growing **staple crops**—crops that are in constant demand. In Virginia and North Carolina, the staple crop was tobacco. In the warm and wet coastal regions of South Carolina and Georgia, it was rice. In the early 1730s, these two colonies were exporting 16.8 million pounds of rice per year; by 1770, the figure was 76.9 million. Meanwhile, the number of pounds of tobacco exported per year by Virginia, Maryland, and Delaware rose from 32 million in 1700 to 83.8 million in 1770.

Throughout the Southern Colonies, African slaves supplied most of the labor on tobacco and rice plantations. Virginia planters began to purchase large numbers of Africans in the mid-1600s. In 1650, Africans in Virginia numbered only about 500, which accounted for 3 percent of the colony's population. By 1700, enslaved Africans totaled 16,000, or 28 percent of the colony. About 1750, the figure was 40 percent. In South Carolina, Africans outnumbered Europeans throughout the 1700s.

To produce staple crops, planters needed huge amounts of land and labor but very little else. As a result, the Southern Colonies remained a region of plantations strung out along rivers and coastlines. Except for the cities of Charles Town (Charleston), South Carolina, and Williamsburg, Virginia, the South had few towns and only a small group of people who could be called merchants.

The Middle Colonies From Maryland north to New York, the economy of the Middle Colonies was a mixture of farming and commerce. The long stretch of the Delaware and Hudson rivers and their tributaries allowed colonists to move into the interior and establish farms on rich, fertile soil. There they specialized in growing grains, including wheat, barley, and rye. This kind of farming was very profitable.

Commerce, however, was just as important as agriculture in the Middle Colonies. New York and Philadelphia were already among the largest cities in North America. Home to growing numbers of merchants, traders, and craftspeople, these cities teemed with people in the business of buying and selling goods. Ships from all over the Atlantic World arrived regularly in these ports. Philadelphia became the major port of entry for Germans and Scotch-Irish people coming to North America as indentured servants.

The populations of both New York and Pennsylvania were ethnically diverse. They included English, Dutch, French, Scots, Irish, Scotch-Irish, Germans, Swedes, Portuguese Jews, Welsh, Africans, and Native Americans. No wonder a traveler in the late 1750s despaired of ever discovering "any precise or determinate character" in the population of New York—it was made up of "different nations, different languages, and different religions."

The New England Colonies In the 1700s, the New England Colonies were a region of small, self-sufficient farms and of towns dependent on long-distance trade. Unlike the merchants of Philadelphia and New York, those in Boston, Salem, and Newport, Rhode Island, did not rely heavily on local crops for their commerce.

Unlike the plantations of the South, New England's farms were small. *Economics How did the differing economies of New England and the Southern colonies result in different styles of farming?*

Instead, they carried crops and goods from one place to another—a "carrying trade." They hauled china, books, and cloth from England to the West Indies in the Caribbean Sea. From the Caribbean they would transport sugar back to New England, where it was usually distilled into rum. They traded the rum and firearms for slaves in West Africa and then carried slaves to the West Indies for more sugar. This trade between three points in the Atlantic World—the Americas, Europe, and Africa—was called **triangular trade**.

SECTION 1 REVIEW

Comprehension

1. *Key Terms* Define: (a) mercantilism; (b) balance of trade; (c) duty; (d) salutary neglect; (e) staple crop; (f) triangular trade.

2. *Summarizing the Main Idea* What was the British government's policy toward the colonies after the rule of King James II had ended?

3. *Organizing Information* Create a multi-flow web diagram to organize the causes and effects of England's policy of salutary neglect toward its colonies. Give four causes contributing to salutary neglect and then show three effects.

Critical Thinking

4. *Analyzing Time Lines* Review the time line at the start of the section. Choose an entry that demonstrates England's mercantilist policy. Explain the reasons behind your choice.

5. *Making Comparisons* How were the economies of the Southern, Middle, and New England colonies similar? How did they differ?

Writing Activity

6. *Writing a Persuasive Essay* Do you think the American colonies would have been positively or negatively affected if the British had strictly enforced the Navigation Act of 1660? Write an essay explaining your opinion. Support it with specific examples.

SKILLS FOR LIFE

Geography

Interpreting an Economic Activity Map

Focus Identify the purpose of an economic activity map, interpret its symbols, and analyze the relationships indicated by the information displayed.

Instruct Ask students to define the term *region* as it is used by geographers and historians. (*A group of places bound together by one or more similar characteristics.*) Ask students what on the map justifies classifying the colonies into three regions. (*The symbols and color-coded key indicate the distinct economic activities of each region.*)

Ask students to find current economic activity maps in a geography textbook or encyclopedia showing the same regions. Have them compare the maps and name at least three things in each area that have changed.

Extend See the Skills for Life Activity in the Resource Options below.

Answers

1. (a) General farming. (b) Fishing and whaling. (c) North Carolina. (d) General farming.

2. (a) Southern Colonies. (b) Lumber production enabled the New England Colonies to build ships that could be used for fishing and whaling. (c) New York and Georgia appear to have provided the best opportunities for raising livestock.

TEST FOR SUCCESS

The New England Colonies, because they depended on both general farming and industry.

Interpreting an Economic Activity Map

An economic activity map shows how the land in a particular region is used and helps demonstrate the ways that geography can influence historical events and developments. Economic activity maps also illustrate ways in which regions are similar or different.

Often a region's economic activity is related to its natural resources and climate. For example, mining can take place only in regions where enough minerals are present to make this activity profitable. By the mid-1700s, clear patterns of economic activity were emerging among the British colonies in North America. This map uses symbols and a color-coded key to communicate basic information about land use in the colonies.

Use the following steps to analyze the economic activity map.

1. *Identify the economic activities shown on the map.* Use the map and key to answer the following questions. (a) What was the major economic activity in Delaware? (b) What were the major economic activities north of Massachusetts? (c) Which colony produced tobacco, rice, and indigo? (d) According to the map, what economic activity supported residents of Pennsylvania and New Jersey?

2. *Look for relationships or patterns among the colonies and their economic activities.* (a) As shown on the map, was farmland more extensive in the Southern or the New England colonies? (b) What other economic activities in the New England Colonies encouraged shipbuilding? (c) If you had been a livestock herder in Britain planning to move to the colonies, which of the American colonies do you think would have offered you the most opportunity for making a living?

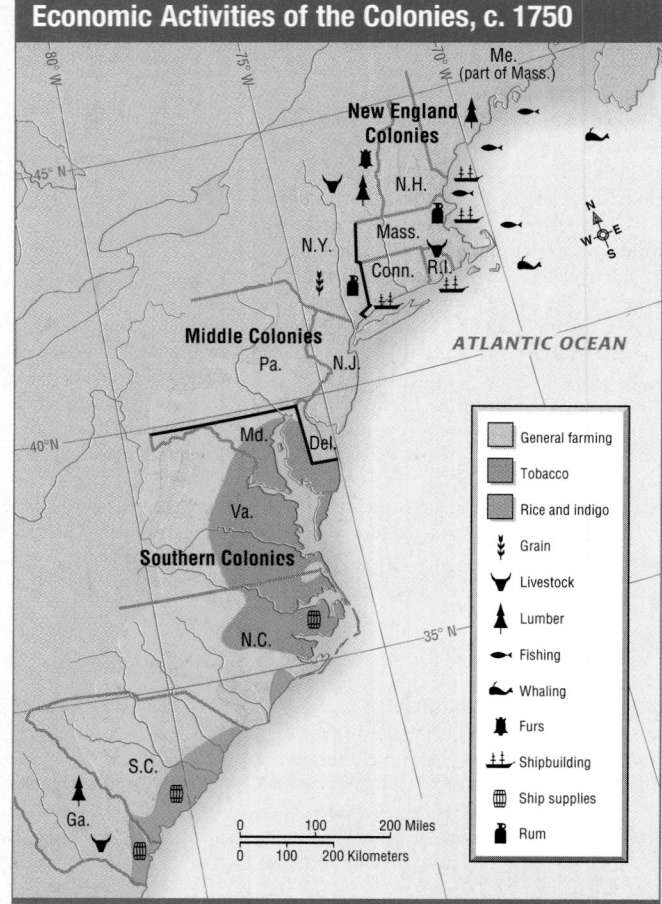

Economic Activities of the Colonies, c. 1750

ATLANTIC OCEAN

New England Colonies

Me. (part of Mass.)

N.H.

Mass.

Conn. R.I.

N.Y.

Middle Colonies

Pa.   N.J.

Md.   Del.

Va.

Southern Colonies

N.C.

S.C.

Ga.

Key:
- General farming
- Tobacco
- Rice and indigo
- Grain
- Livestock
- Lumber
- Fishing
- Whaling
- Furs
- Shipbuilding
- Ship supplies
- Rum

0   100   200 Miles
0   100   200 Kilometers

TEST FOR SUCCESS

Review the symbols and color-coded key. Which region appears to have had a mixed economy? Explain your answer.

 RESOURCE OPTIONS

Teaching Resources

Skills for Life Activity Units 1–2 folder, p. 41, gives a present-day application of the skill of interpreting an economic activity map.

1701
Yale College founded in
New Haven, Connecticut

1732
Benjamin Franklin
begins publishing Poor
Richard's Almanac

1734
John Peter Zenger
arrested for libel

1700   1710   1720   1730   1740

2 Life in Colonial America

SECTION PREVIEW

Objectives
1   Describe the structure of colonial American society and its distribution of wealth.
2   List contributions that tradespeople and women made to colonial society.
3   Describe the working lives of the average colonists and the colonial education system.
4   *Key Terms*   Define: gentry; apprentice; almanac; indigo; self-sufficient.

Main Idea
The social groups that made up colonial society had different roles and ways of living.

Reading Strategy
Outlining Information Skim the section and use the heads and subheads to create an outline. As you read, fill in supporting evidence under each head.

It is common to speak of what "the American colonists" said or thought or did. Yet colonial society, like any society, consisted of a variety of groups with widely varying lives. A person's wealth or gender or race went a long way toward determining his or her place in society.

Colonial Society

American colonists brought many ideas and customs from Europe. Among these was the belief that people are not equal. Most colonists accepted the notion that the wealthy were superior to the poor, that men were superior to women, and that whites were superior to blacks. They accepted too the idea that society was made up of different ranks or levels, with some groups having more wealth and power than others. In the words of one New Englander, "ranks and degrees" were as much a part of this world as "Mountains and Plains, Hills and Vallies."

The differences between social ranks could easily be seen in colonial clothes, houses, and manners. **Gentry,** or men and women wealthy enough to hire others to work for them, set themselves apart by their clothing:

wigs, silk stockings, lace cuffs, and the latest fashions in suits, dresses, and hats. Ordinary people wore plain breeches and shirts or dresses. Wigs were an unmistakable sign of status, power, and wealth.

"Gentle folk," a colonial term for the gentry class, were the most important members of colonial society. To be considered "gentle," one had to be wealthy.

Wealth in Land

For English colonists the foundation of real wealth was land. Land was plentiful and most white men owned some land. Although adult, single women and free African Americans could legally own land, very few did. The majority of landowners were white men. In each colony a small group of elite, landowning men dominated politics. Lawyers, planters, and merchants held most of the seats in the colonial assemblies, or lawmaking bodies.

HAIR POWDER

Of the first Quality, *Manufactured and Sold by* HUGH HENRY, No. 38, *Chesnut-street,* PHILADELPHIA: Where Merchants, Captains and Dealers may be supplied on the shortest Notice.

☞ *Starch put up for Exportation.*

A white wig—or hair powdered to look like one—was the hallmark of a gentleman in colonial society.

In the early 1700s gentry devoted much of their time to displaying their status. The gentry socialized most with people of a similar class, especially in the Southern Colonies. In many cases they were related to one another by blood or marriage. To impress others, they had mansions and townhouses built for themselves. To refine their manners, the gentry eagerly read newspapers and books from England. They sent their sons to expensive schools and taught their daughters how to manage a household. They supervised, but they did not actually perform physical labor.

Main Idea CONNECTIONS

Describe the lives of the gentry in the British colonies.

We know from *The Diary, and Life, of William Byrd II of Virginia, 1674–1744* that gentlemen tried to live their lives according to a refined, well-mannered routine. William Byrd owned several plantations in the colony of Virginia. In his diary, Byrd relates that every day he read Greek or Latin, said his prayers, and "danced his dance" (performed a series of exercises) in the garden of his home.

Byrd rarely varied from these regular habits. Although he did have to keep an eye on his plantations, such labor was not the focus of his life. Like many other colonial gentlemen, Byrd wished to demonstrate to the world his refinement and self-control and to prove that he deserved the respect of others.

Benjamin Franklin was so interested in electricity that he sold his businesses in order to have more time to study it. In 1752 he flew a kite in a thunderstorm in a famous experiment proving the electrical nature of lightning.
Science and Technology How did people like Benjamin Franklin help the development of the colonies?

Trades and Occupations

Everyone recognized, however, that the colonies needed people from all walks of life, not just gentlemen. Those who were not gentry had the opportunity to develop specialized skills and trades.

Artisans At a very early age, boys from most families became **apprentices,** or persons placed under a legal contract to work for another person in exchange for learning a trade. Silversmith Paul Revere and artisans like him prospered by creating some of the items that the gentry desired. Cabinetmakers, such as John Goddard of Newport, Rhode Island, produced high-quality furniture with a distinctive colonial style. Other tradespeople provided equally important goods, such as tinware, pottery, and glassware.

Printers Colonial printers, who were respected members of colonial society, gathered and circulated local news and information. Printers, however, had to be cautious when deciding which stories to report. In 1734, authorities arrested John Peter Zenger, printer and publisher of the *New York Weekly Journal,* for printing libelous (false) stories critical of the governor of New York. Zenger's lawyer argued that if the stories were true then they could not be considered libel. Zenger won his case, a landmark victory for freedom of the press in America.

One of America's most famous printers from the 1700s was Benjamin Franklin. Among his best known works is *Poor Richard's Almanac,* which was printed annually from 1732 to 1757. An **almanac** is a book containing information such as calendars, weather predictions, proverbs, and advice. Franklin also published several newspapers and magazines. After his successful career as a printer, Franklin retired when he was only in his early forties. In retirement, Franklin dabbled in science and politics and spent much of his time in Europe. He is perhaps most famous for his experiments and inventions. Through his scientific work, Franklin invented the lightning rod, the Franklin stove, and bifocal eyeglasses. He also wrote his *Autobiography,* which set forth a number of rules for controlling oneself and behaving in a respectable manner.

Farmers and Fishermen Farms in the colonies varied in size from large cash-crop plantations in the Southern Colonies to small subsistence farms in the New England and

RESOURCE OPTIONS

Teaching Resources

📁 **Literature Activity** As Poor Richard Says, Units 1–2 folder, p. 40

📁 **Visual Learning Activity** The First American Schoolbook, Learning with Documents folder, p. 45

📁 **Primary Source Activity** A Marriage Agreement, Learning with Documents folder, p. 9

Prudence Punderson, a Connecticut housewife, created in needlework this symbolic view of the life of a colonial woman. The symbols, from right to left, indicate birth, work, and death. *Economics How does this needlework reflect the role of women in the colonial economy?*

Middle Colonies. New England farmers who worked the thin, rocky soil gained a reputation for being tough, thrifty, and conservative.

Many coastal settlers turned their backs on the poor soil and earned their living from the sea. North America's shores abounded with haddock, bass, clams, mussels, and crabs. Colonists ate some of the bounty, but most was dried, salted, and shipped out from busy harbor cities. Fishing quickly became a main industry and promoted growth in the related industry of shipbuilding.

Indentured Servants Many immigrants, both male and female, came to the colonies as indentured servants. Indentured servants agreed to work for a master for a set amount of time, up to seven years. In exchange the master agreed to pay for travel costs to the colonies. Masters had total authority over indentured servants and sometimes treated them as if they were slaves. Those servants who served out their time were granted their freedom and in some cases a piece of land.

Colonial Women

The status of colonial women was determined by the men in their lives. Most women were legally the dependents of men and had no legal or political standing. Married women could not own property. Laws prevented women from voting or holding office or serving on a jury. Even a widowed woman did not have any political rights, although she could inherit her husband's property and conduct business.

Women and the Law Under English common law, a woman was under her husband's control. According to the English writer William Blackstone in his influential *Commentaries on the Laws of England,* published in the 1760s:

❝ By marriage, the husband and wife are one person in law; that is, the very being or legal existence of the woman is suspended during the marriage, or at least is incorporated and consolidated into that of the husband. ❞

—William Blackstone

▶ RESOURCE OPTIONS

Media and Technology

 AmericanHeritage® **CD-ROM**

History Makers Anne Hutchinson

RESOURCE⊙PRO

Critical Thinking Activity Identifying Central Issues: The Status of Colonial Women, found on Resource Pro, enhances students' understanding of complex issues through summarizing excerpts from colonial authors.

BACKGROUND

Women Inventors

In the early 1700s, women were not allowed to hold patents for scientific inventions. Sybilla Masters, a Quaker mother of four children, invented a way to make cornmeal by stamping rather than grinding corn. In June 1712, she journeyed to London to get a patent for her invention. Three years later, a government patent was granted to Masters's husband for "the sole use and benefit of 'a new invention . . . by Sybilla, his wife, for cleaning and curing the Indian Corn growing in the several colonies in America.'" Sybilla Masters later returned to Philadelphia and sold her cornmeal, which she called "Tuscarora Rice."

ACTIVITY
HETEROGENEOUS GROUPS

With fundamental beliefs based on inequality, colonial society paid close attention to social status expressed in clothing, homes, and manners. Wigs, for example, were a sign of wealth and power. Though society in the United States today is based on a fundamental belief in equality, economic and social status are still reflected in homes, cars, clothing, manners, and behavior. Have students work in small groups to list descriptions of homes, cars, clothing, manners, and behavior and to explain what status they represent in society today. *(Enrichment)*

Answer to . . .

Viewing History The needlework reflects the fact that women's lives consisted primarily of the duties necessary to running a household.

Graphing the Main Idea

To make sure students understand the main idea of this section, you may wish to use the double web graphic organizer below.

Tell students that a double web can be used to compare and contrast information about colonial gentry and colonial workers.

Teaching Tip A template for this graphic organizer can be found in the Color Transparencies, G-2.

Ask students to correct any of the following incorrect statements.
• The most powerful people in the English colonies were bankers, because they controlled the money supply.
• Any woman could own land in the colonies, but only unmarried women without fathers could vote.
• Most colonists did not work hard.
• Colonial women had few rights.
• Any colonists could become one of the gentry. *(Reteaching)*

Answer to . . .

Viewing History The goal was to be self-sufficient.

VIEWING HISTORY In most of colonial American society all members of the household worked, even children (above). Women of lesser means in colonial society also spent many hours at their spinning wheels (left). Nearly all enslaved women, too, learned to spin.
Economics What was the economic goal of a typical colonial household?

washing, cleaning, weaving cloth, and sewing. They supported one another by helping in childbirth and sharing equipment and tools. They also trained their daughters in the traditional duties of women.

Women sometimes took on many tasks before marriage. One example is Eliza Lucas Pinckney of South Carolina, who as a teenager managed her father's plantations in the late 1730s and early 1740s. This duty fell to Pinckney because, as she wrote to a friend, "Mama's bad state of health prevents her going thro' any fatigue," and her father, the governor of the Caribbean island of Antigua, was usually absent. As she wrote to her friend:

AMERICAN VOICES " I have the business of 3 plantations to transact, which requires much writing and more business and fatigue of other sorts than you can imagine, but lest you should imagine it too burdensome to a girl at my early time of life, give me leave to assure you I think myself happy that I can be useful to so good a father. "

—*Eliza Lucas Pinckney*

Pinckney was more than just a stand-in for her father. She was one of the people responsible for promoting the growing of **indigo,** a type of plant used in making a blue dye for cloth. Indigo became a major staple crop in South Carolina.

In spite of their hard work and dedication, women remained legally inferior to men. They might argue with their fathers or husbands, but women almost never directly challenged the basic structure of colonial society.

The Nature of Work

By the mid-1700s, life was better for most white colonists than it would have been in Europe. They ate better, lived longer, and had more children to help them with their work. They also had many more opportunities to advance in wealth and status than average Europeans did. Still, whether they were skilled artisans in cities or small farmers in the countryside, colonists had to labor very hard to keep themselves and their families alive.

Everyone in a household, including children and servants, worked to maintain the household by producing food and goods. In fact, the basic goal of the household was to be **self-sufficient,** or able to make everything needed to maintain itself.

Men held nearly unlimited power in colonial households. English law, for example, allowed husbands to beat their wives without fear of prosecution. Divorces, although legal, were rare. Surprisingly, the easiest place to obtain a divorce was Puritan New England. The Puritans were so concerned about order and stability that they preferred to allow a bad marriage to end rather than let it continue to create disorder among them.

Women's Duties In practice, however, men and women depended heavily on one another. In colonial America, women juggled a number of duties that contributed to the well-being of the household and also of the community. Women managed the tasks that kept a household operating, such as cooking, gardening,

While men grew crops or made goods such as shoes, guns, or candles, the rest of the household was equally busy. Wives often assisted in whatever work their husbands did, from planting crops to managing the business affairs of the family. Children helped both parents from an early age. Almost all work was performed in or around the home. Even artisans worked out of shops in the front of their houses.

Colonial Education

During the colonial period, attendance at school was not required by law, and most children received very little formal education. The New England Colonies, however, became early leaders in the development of public education. The main reason was that the Protestant settlers believed everyone should be able to read the Bible. As a result, literacy rates were higher in New England than anywhere else in British North America.

In 1647, Massachusetts passed a law requiring every town with at least 50 families to hire a schoolmaster to teach basic reading, writing, and arithmetic. Towns with 100 or more families were expected to establish a grammar school that offered instruction in Greek and Latin. Boys attended the grammar school to prepare for college. Girls did not go to school. They were expected to learn everything they needed to know from their mothers at home.

Public schools did not develop as quickly outside New England. If there were no schools in the area, parents taught their children at home. In the Southern Colonies, plantation owners often hired private instructors to teach their children.

 Harvard College, now Harvard University, was the nation's first institution of higher learning. It was founded in 1636 by Massachusetts Bay Colony with the help of John Harvard, a minister who left the college his library and a portion of his estate upon his death in 1638. *Culture* How does the establishment of Harvard reflect colonial Massachusetts society?

Colonial colleges were primarily training grounds for ministers and lawyers and generally only the very wealthy attended. Up until the 1740s there were only three colleges in the colonies, Harvard, in Massachusetts (established in 1636), William and Mary in Virginia (1693), and Yale in Connecticut (1701). By 1769, five more colleges had been founded in the Middle and New England colonies.

SECTION 2 REVIEW

Comprehension

1. *Key Terms* Define: (a) gentry; (b) apprentice; (c) almanac; (d) indigo; (e) self-sufficient.
2. *Summarizing Main Ideas* How did the legal status of women differ from their actual importance in colonial society?
3. *Organizing Information* Create a chart that organizes information about the structure of colonial society.

Critical Thinking

4. *Analyzing Time Lines* Review the time line at the start of the section. Pick an entry and explain how it continues to impact society today.
5. *Identifying Central Issues* Why did everyone in the average colonial household have to work?

Writing Activity

6. *Writing an Expository Essay* Use information from the section to write a one-page essay comparing the lives of the gentry with the lives of artisans and tradespeople.

GEOGRAPHY AND HISTORY

Two Settlement Patterns in the Colonies

Focus Explain that the colonists from England settled colonies in New England and Pennsylvania. They were rapidly joined by settlers from other parts of Europe. The result was two unique places that were not only unlike England, but also unlike each other.

Instruct Divide the class into groups and assign each group either New England or Pennsylvania. Ask students to suppose that they are in a plane flying over their assigned region—in 1750. Tell each group to use physical and historical maps of the colonies to write a description of their assigned colony from the air. Have students first decide on three or four landmarks or cities to use as anchors for their descriptions and then determine where to begin and end their description. Suggest that they use the information in the feature about the types and sizes of towns and farms.

Extend Ask students to analyze the advantages that each mode of settlement gave its colonists. In New England, people moved into new territory as a group to start a town. How did this help the colonists survive? *(Security from attack, ability to help one another quickly.)* How did the pattern of large farms help the settlers of Pennsylvania? *(It provided ample crops to feed the settlers.)*

GEOGRAPHY AND HISTORY

Two Settlement Patterns in the Colonies

The geographic theme of place explores how physical and human characteristics make one environment different from another. In the American colonies, New England and Pennsylvania reflected the diversity of the American settlers. In what ways were these two places different?

Corn husk doll

By 1750, several distinct settlements had emerged in colonial North America. New England and Pennsylvania, for example, had vastly different physical and human landscapes. As you will see, the religion and culture of the people who settle in a place also help to shape its features.

Puritan Values Shape New England

The Puritan settlers of 1620 influenced the character of the New England Colonies. Puritans valued both family and church. Their close-knit settlements were rooted in community and in faith.

Despite the fact that they had come to America to escape religious persecution, the Puritans were intolerant of others. They excluded all those who believed in a different form of worship from their communities.

A Close-knit Settlement

Typically, an immigrating Puritan group was granted a town by the colonial legislature. A town was a piece of land about 6 square miles in size, usually divided into 36 lots. The group would establish a village near the

> The Puritan settlers of 1620 influenced the character of the New England Colonies.

town center. There, the meetinghouse or church, the public school, and other public buildings were built. Each family in the group received a house lot in the village and some acres to farm in the town lands nearby. They also had the right to use any of the town's common land.

Puritan settlements were first established in the area around Boston, Massachusetts, and the Connecticut River valley. The map of Sudbury shows the typical settlement characteristics of New England by 1750: a homogeneous population, one in which nearly all members had a common origin; clusters of closely linked towns with small family farms; and village centers built around a piece of public, or common, land and dominated by a single church.

Quaker Values Shape Pennsylvania

The Quakers were a religious group who fled persecution in England, as had the Puritans before them. Unlike the Puritans, however, the Quakers valued individuality. They practiced tolerance for others.

In 1681 William Penn, a Quaker, received a huge land grant from King Charles II of England on the west

---

RESOURCE OPTIONS

Teaching Resources

 Geography and History Activity
Changing Economic Patterns in the South, Geography and History folder, pp. 2–3

Nystrom *Atlas of Our Country*
Colonies in the North and East, pp. 14–15

Sudbury, Massachusetts, 1656

Germantown, Pennsylvania, 1772

New England towns were more close-knit than those of Pennsylvania.

Fields held in common House Schoolhouse Meeting house Mill

side of the lower Delaware River. Penn founded Pennsylvania, which he saw as a "Holy Experiment," a place of religious freedom and social equality. Penn negotiated land treaties with Native Americans and then brought over Quaker settlers from England.

A Diverse Settlement

Pennsylvania drew Quakers from Wales, Germany, and other American colonies. Many moved to Philadelphia, the fast-growing city and the nucleus of the colony. Others came to farm the rich lands in the Great Valley to the west of Philadelphia.

The colony soon started recruiting non-Quakers interested in cheap land and religious tolerance. The German Lutherans, Scotch-Irish Presbyterians, and Swiss Mennonites tended to settle on farms some distance apart in the southeastern region of the colony. As the map of Germantown shows, the large villages and towns that dotted the region differed in one important way from New England towns—they featured churches or meetinghouses of several different Christian groups.

By 1750 Pennsylvania had developed a character marked by prosperity, individualism, and religious tolerance. It also reflected the cultural diversity of several ethnic groups. The colony differed greatly from Puritan New England, where the population was homogeneous, more rooted in the doctrines of a single church, and less tolerant of religious variation of any kind.

GEOGRAPHIC CONNECTIONS

1. Explain how the Puritan settlers influenced the character of the New England Colonies.

2. What was the main difference between the New England and Pennsylvania colonies?

Themes in Geography

3. *Place* Look at the settlement pattern on each map. How are the religious and cultural values of each region reflected in the location of people's houses?

RESOURCE OPTIONS

Media and Technology

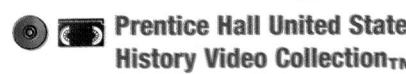 **Prentice Hall United States History Video Collection**™
Volume 2 *The Era of Colonization*

African Americans in the Colonies

Objectives
You may wish to call students' attention to the objectives in the Section Preview. The objectives are reflected in the main headings of the section.

Bellringer
Ask students what makes up a family. What needs do families fill in people's lives?

Reading Strategy
Reinforcing Key Ideas Refer to the Reading Strategy in the Section Preview. You may want to model the chart on the chalkboard and ask students to suggest ideas.

LESSON PLAN
Connecting to the Main Idea

1. Focus Point out that about 20 percent of the colonists were Africans or of African descent. Ask students what their lives were like. What contributions did they make to colonial society?

2. Instruct Discuss why slave traders treated Africans so poorly. Compare the lives of enslaved Africans and their descendants in the southern coastal colonies with the lives of those in the New England and Middle colonies. Ask whether plantation owners consciously allowed enslaved Africans to maintain some of their traditions. What factors enabled them to maintain a language with roots in Africa, for example? Why were their lives most varied in the New England and Middle colonies? Why were the revolts of enslaved African Americans unsuccessful?

3. Close African Americans played an important role in the development of American society, in spite of the fact that they came to the colonies in slavery.

1661 Virginia passes first slave code	1735 Slavery banned in Georgia	1739 Stono Rebellion	1740 South Carolina revises and strengthens slave laws	1750 Georgia ban on slavery lifted

1650	1700	1750	1800

3 African Americans in the Colonies

SECTION PREVIEW

Objectives

1. Describe how slave traders brought Africans to the Americas.
2. Describe the lives of African Americans (free and enslaved) in the colonies.
3. Explain how slaves reacted to laws restricting their actions.
4. *Key Terms* Define: Middle Passage; mutiny; Stono Rebellion.

Main Idea

Africans, brought across the Atlantic Ocean as slaves, helped build England's American colonies while enduring harsh and often brutal treatment.

Reading Strategy

Reinforcing Key Ideas Create a chart with the following regions as headings: South Carolina and Georgia; Virginia and Maryland; New England and Middle Colonies. As you read the section, fill in information about the lives of slaves in each of the regions.

Not counting Native Americans, about one out of every five people living in British North America by the middle of the 1700s was of African descent. As in the case of all immigrants, the experiences of African Americans in the colonies varied depending on where they lived. Yet the stories of Africans, uprooted from their homeland and sold into slavery, had many elements in common. One African who later told his story was Olaudah Equiano.

Olaudah Equiano

AMERICAN BIOGRAPHY Olaudah Equiano was born around 1745 in the country of Benin. He wrote in his autobiography decades later that the land of his youth was "uncommonly rich and fruitful" and "a nation of dancers, musicians and poets." As a child, he learned "the art of war" and proudly wore "the emblems of a warrior" made by his mother.

When Equiano was ten, his world was shattered. Two men and a woman kidnapped him and one of his sisters while their parents were working. Separated from his sister, Equiano was enslaved to a series of African masters. About six months after he was kidnapped, Equiano was sold and put aboard a British slave ship bound for the Americas. In his autobiography, he wrote:

> **"** The first object which saluted my eyes when I arrived on the coast was the sea, and a slave ship which was then riding at anchor and waiting for its cargo. These filled me with astonishment, which was soon converted into terror when I was carried on board. **"**
>
> —Equiano's Travels, *1789*

Olaudah Equiano (1745?–1797)

During the **Middle Passage,** Equiano witnessed many scenes of brutality. (The Middle Passage was one leg of the triangular trade

---

▶ RESOURCE OPTIONS

Teaching Resources

📁 **Reproducible Lesson Plan** Lesson Plans folder, p. 44

📁 **Learning Styles Lesson Plan** Learning Styles Lesson Plans folder, p. 8

📁 **Big Idea Graphic Organizer** Big Idea Graphic Organizer folder, p. 16

📁 **Guided Reading and Review** Units 1–2 folder, p. 33

Media and Technology

◉ 📼 **Prentice Hall United States History Video Collection™** Volume 3 *Slavery and Freedom*

"No eye pities; no hand helps," said a slaver describing the treatment of his human cargo. An eyewitness painted this scene aboard a slave ship in 1846. *Geography* *What was the Middle Passage?*

between the Americas, Europe, and Africa. The Middle Passage is also used to refer to the forced transport of slaves from Africa to the Americas.) Although historians differ on the actual figures, from 10 to 40 percent of the Africans on a slave ship typically died in the crossing. Sick and frightened about what lay ahead, they were forced to endure chains, heat, disease, and the overpowering odor caused by the lack of sanitation and their cramped, stuffy quarters. As Equiano wrote, "Many a time we were near suffocation from the want [absence] of fresh air, which we were often without for whole days together." Conditions were so grim on Equiano's voyage that two people committed suicide. A third was prevented from doing so and then whipped.

Occasionally, enslaved Africans physically resisted during the Middle Passage by staging a **mutiny,** or revolt. The slave traders lived in continual fear of mutinies, and crews were heavily armed. Statistics about the British slave trade show that a rebellion occurred every two years on the average. Many of these were successful.

Equiano's ship finally arrived at a port on the island of Barbados, in the West Indies, where the Africans were sold at a public auction. Most went to work and die in the sugar plantations of the West Indies. Equiano noted that the sale separated families, leaving people grief-stricken and alone.

❝ In this manner, without scruple [concern], are relations and friends separated, most of them never to see each other again. I remember in the vessel in which I was brought over, in the men's apartment there were several brothers who, in the sale, were sold in different lots; and it was very moving on this occasion to see and hear their cries at parting. O, ye nominal Christians [Christians in name only]! might not an African ask you, Learned you this from your God, who says unto you, Do unto all men as you would men should do unto you?❞

—*Olaudah Equiano*

In 1766 Equiano was taken to Virginia, where he later bought his freedom. Migrating to Great Britain, he found work as a barber and a personal servant and became active in the antislavery movement. ■

Slavery in the Colonies

The experiences of Africans varied greatly in colonial times. Slavery was legal everywhere, but the number of slaves in each region and the kind of labor they performed differed widely from region to region.

South Carolina and Georgia Much of the seaboard region of South Carolina and Georgia is formed by a coastal plain called the low country. Planters found the low country ideal for growing rice and indigo. Slaves there labored under especially brutal conditions. High temperatures and dangerous diseases

This authentic watercolor depicts a scene at a South Carolina plantation in the late 1700s. The musical instruments and the dance form were derived from the Yoruba people of West Africa. *Culture How does this painting document the character of African American culture on South Carolina plantations?*

made life particularly difficult. Charles Ball, an African American whose account was published in 1836, described the situation as it had existed for well over a century:

> **AMERICAN VOICES** " The general features of slavery are the same every where; but the utmost rigor [strictness] of the system, is only to be met with on the cotton plantations of Carolina and Georgia, or in the rice fields which skirt the deep swamps and morasses of the southern rivers. "
>
> —*Charles Ball*

African Americans made up the majority of the population in South Carolina and Georgia. Because rice was grown most efficiently on large estates, this region had more plantations with more than one hundred slaves than anywhere else in the colonies. Since wealthy planters often chose to spend most of their time away from their isolated estates, slaves generally had regular contact with only a handful of white colonists.

The lack of interaction allowed slaves in South Carolina and Georgia to preserve some of their cultural traditions. Many had come to the region directly from Africa. They continued to make the crafts of their homeland, such as baskets and pottery. They played the music they loved and told the stories their parents and grandparents had passed down to them. In some cases, they kept their culture alive in their speech. The most well-known example is the Gullah language, a combination of English and African languages. As late as the 1940s, speakers of Gullah were using four thousand words from the languages of more than twenty-one separate groups in West Africa.

The skills that African Americans brought with them to South Carolina and Georgia also deeply affected the lives of their masters. African Americans had superior knowledge of cattle herding and fishing. Because many had grown rice in their homelands, they had practical know-how about its cultivation.

Strong African kinship networks helped people not only survive slavery but also preserve their traditions. Africans highly valued family relationships. When separated from their blood relatives, slaves created new relationships with one another by acting as substitute kin. In these relationships, people behaved as if they were brothers or sisters or aunts or uncles, though in fact they were not.

In these and many other ways, the slaves in South Carolina and Georgia made the best of a horrible situation. Forced to come to North America, they found strength in each other's company and in the memory of their African origins.

Virginia and Maryland The lives of slaves in Virginia and Maryland differed from those of African Americans in South Carolina and Georgia in four ways:

(1) Slaves in Virginia and Maryland made up a minority rather than a majority of the population.

(2) Relatively few slaves came to Virginia and Maryland directly from Africa.

(3) Slaves performed different work. Cultivating tobacco, the major crop, did not take as much time as growing rice, so slave-owners put enslaved African Americans to work at a variety of other tasks.

(4) African Americans in Virginia and Maryland had more regular contact with European Americans. The result was greater integration of European American and African American cultures than in South Carolina and Georgia. In the latter half of the 1700s, slaves in Virginia and Maryland blended the customs of African and European origin. They mingled the African and the European in everything from food and clothes to religion.

The high costs of importing slaves from Africa led some Virginia and Maryland planters to encourage their slaves to raise families. It was in their economic interest to allow African Americans a fuller family and community life. Over time, therefore, some slaves were able to form fairly stable family lives, though they still lived in constant fear of being sold and separated from their families.

Some male slaves in Virginia worked away from plantations as artisans or laborers in Richmond and other towns. As long as they sent back part of their wages to the plantations, they lived fairly independently of their master's control. They were, however, still subject to harsh laws that controlled what they could do. In addition, their children were born enslaved.

New England and the Middle Colonies About 400,000 African Americans lived in the Southern Colonies by the late 1700s. In contrast, there were only about 50,000 African Americans in the New England and Middle colonies combined. These colonies north of Maryland had a more diverse economy than that of the Southern Colonies. As a result, African Americans in the New England and Middle colonies had more freedom to choose their occupations than did African Americans in the Southern Colonies.

Throughout the 1700s, farms in the New England and Middle colonies were much smaller than those in the Southern Colonies and did not require as many slaves for field work. It was more common to find slaves in this region working in the cities as cooks, housekeepers, or personal servants. Male slaves often worked in manufacturing and trading or as skilled artisans. They also worked in the forests as lumberjacks. Because shipbuilding and shipping were major economic activities, some African American men worked along the seacoast. As dockworkers, merchant sailors, fishermen, whalers, and privateers, they contributed to the growth of the Atlantic economy.

Free Blacks

Most African Americans in the colonies were enslaved. It was not until after the American Revolution that the free black population in the Northern and Southern colonies grew significantly. Some slave laws discouraged people from freeing slaves. Owners had to get permission from the legislature before freeing any of their slaves. The laws also demanded that freed slaves leave a colony within six months of gaining freedom. Despite the obstacles, those slaves who earned money as artisans or laborers had the possibility of saving enough to purchase their freedom.

Free African Americans did much of the same kind of work as enslaved African Americans. They were, however, probably worse off materially. Free blacks endured poorer living conditions and more severe discrimination than slaves who were identified with specific white households. Free blacks also faced limited rights. They could not vote, testify in court against whites, or marry whites.

African-American Population, 1690–1750

Year	New England Colonies	Middle Colonies	Southern Colonies
1690	905	2,472	13,307
1700	1,680	3,361	22,476
1710	2,585	6,218	36,063
1720	3,956	10,825	54,058
1730	6,118	11,683	73,220
1740	8,541	16,452	125,031
1750	10,982	20,736	204,702

Source: *Historical Statistics of the United States, Colonial Times to 1970*

Interpreting Tables The growth in the number of African Americans, although relatively small in the 1600s, jumped considerably in the early 1700s. *Geography* In which group of colonies did the number of African Americans increase most sharply?

Using the Internet

Write an Article

Objective Use the Internet to write an article on the experiences of enslaved Africans. Have students follow these instructions:

1. See the *America: Pathways to the Present* Web site at

http://www.Pathways.phschool.com

for the URL that contains excerpts from slave narratives.

2. Skim through the headings, choosing a topic that interests you. Follow the links to the excerpts under that topic. Choose one of the narratives to report on.

3. Write an article about the narrator's story. Include specific details and quotes from the narrative. To make your article complete, try to fill in additional details. Use these questions to guide you: What is the narrator's perspective and how does that affect his or her story? How much time elapsed between the events that took place and the recording of them? What is the historical context behind the narration? Collect each class member's article and compile them into a newspaper.

TO BE SOLD on Thursday next, at publick vendue,
TEN LIKELY GOLD COAST NEW NEGROES, Juſt imported from the Weſt-Indies, Conſiſting of eight ſtout men and two women. To prevent their receiving the infection of the ſmallpox, they have been kept conſtantly on board the veſſel ſince they arrived, where they will be ſold.—Any perſon inclining to purchaſe them at private ſale may apply to Meſſrs. Johnſon and Wylly.

RUN AWAY from the ſubſcriber, a NEGROE MAN named FRANK, who carried off a gun and ſhot pouch with him. He is a likely well made ſtout fellow, ſpeaks broken Engliſh, with the Spaniſh accent, having been ſeveral years at the Havana.—Whoever will deliver him to Mr. George Baillie in Savannah, or to me in Auguſta, ſhall receive 20s. reward, beſides all charges. JAMES GRAY.

VIEWING HISTORY These advertisements, which appeared in the *Georgia Gazette* in 1764, reflect the status of slaves as property as well as the rebellious spirit of many of the enslaved. *Economics* **How were economic incentives used to reclaim runaway slaves?**

Laws and Revolts

Laws controlling the lives of slaves varied from region to region. Every colony passed its own slave laws, and colonies revised these laws over time. Settlers in Georgia, for example, barred slavery from the colony in 1735 but lifted the ban in 1750. Virginia enacted its first slave code in 1661. South Carolina passed fairly weak regulations in 1690 and then revised its laws in 1696, 1712, and 1740, each time strengthening the restrictions placed on slaves.

Generally, slaves could not go aboard ships or ferries or leave the town limits without a written pass. Crimes for slaves ranged from owning hogs and carrying canes to disturbing the peace and striking a white person. Punishments included whipping, banishment to the West Indies, and death. Many of these laws also applied to free African Americans and to Native Americans.

Laws restricting the movement of slaves made organizing slave rebellions extremely difficult. Because slaves could not travel or meet freely, they had only limited contact with slaves in other areas. A few early documented cases of slave revolts do stand out. In 1739, several dozen slaves near Charleston, South Carolina, killed more than twenty whites in what is known as the **Stono Rebellion**. The slaves burned an armory and began to march toward Spanish Florida, where a small colony of runaway slaves lived. Armed planters captured and killed the rebels. In New York City, brutal laws passed to control African Americans led to rebellions in 1708, 1712, and 1741. After the 1741 revolt, thirteen African Americans were burned alive in punishment. African Americans undertook almost fifty documented revolts between 1740 and 1800.

More commonly, African Americans resisted slavery through a series of silent acts, such as pretending to misunderstand orders or faking illness. While these actions could not give them freedom, they did grant the slaves a small degree of control over their own lives.

SECTION 3 REVIEW

Comprehension

1. *Key Terms* Define: (a) Middle Passage; (b) mutiny; (c) Stono Rebellion.
2. *Summarizing the Main Idea* In what way did the skills that slaves brought from Africa allow the colonies of South Carolina and Georgia to prosper?
3. *Organizing Information* Create a Venn diagram comparing the lives of slaves in South Carolina and Georgia with the lives of slaves in Virginia and Maryland.

Critical Thinking

4. *Analyzing Time Lines* Review the time line at the start of the section. Write a phrase or sentence that connects each entry to the entry that follows it.
5. *Identifying Central Issues* In what ways was Olaudah Equiano's experience similar to that of other enslaved Africans?

Writing Activity

6. *Writing an Expository Essay* Slaves did not often openly rebel against their situation. Write a brief essay explaining some of the reasons for their actions.

▶ RESOURCE OPTIONS

Teaching Resources

📁 **Quiz** Units 1–2 folder, p. 34

Student Performance Pack

 Guide to the Essentials Chapter 3, Section 3 (English and Spanish)

1730s	1738	1749	1752
Beginning of religious revival sparked by Jonathan Edwards	George Whitefield begins tour of New England	French send troops to seize Ohio Valley	French build Ft. Presque Isle

1725   **1735**   **1745**   **1755**

4 Emerging Tensions

SECTION PREVIEW

Objectives

1. Explain why British settlers in the mid-1700s wanted to move west of the thirteen colonies.
2. Analyze the impact of British westward migration on Native Americans and the French.
3. Summarize the effects that the religious movement known as the Great Awakening had on colonial society.
4. *Key Terms* Define: immigrant; Great Awakening; itinerant; dissent.

Main Idea

In the mid-1700s, the American colonies experienced a growing population and a powerful religious revival.

Reading Strategy

Formulating Questions Reread the Main Idea above. Then rewrite it as a question. As you read the section, take notes to help answer that question.

By the mid-1700s, thirteen prosperous British colonies hugged the Atlantic Coast. Colonial settlers had transformed the Atlantic colonies into a world of thriving farms, towns, and plantations. The success of the colonies came at a price, however. The growth of the colonies, both in population and territory, raised new issues in colonial life.

Western Expansion

In the mid-1700s the colonial population increased rapidly, almost doubling every twenty-five years, as the birth rate grew faster than the death rate. In addition to a rising birth rate, the colonies experienced a growth in the number of **immigrants**, or people who enter a new country to settle. While colonists continued to come from England, they also began to arrive from Ireland and Germany. Those people immigrating from Ireland were often called Scotch-Irish, for they had originally traveled from Scotland across the Irish Sea to settle in Ireland before moving on to the North American colonies. As the population grew, the colonists began to feel crowded, especially in the smaller colonies of New England.

According to English custom, fathers tried to provide their sons with some land of their own. New Englanders now found it increasingly difficult to do so. Maintaining a family required about 45 acres and since colonists were having many children, there was simply not enough fertile land to go around. Benjamin Franklin and others feared a land shortage would make it more difficult for American men to secure their independence by owning private property.

Clearly the colonies could not continue to flourish if forced to remain confined to the land along the Atlantic Ocean. By the mid-1700s, European settlers were moving into the interior of North America. Scotch-Irish and Germans settled central Pennsylvania and the Shenandoah Valley of Virginia. Farther to the north, colonists spread into the Mohawk River valley in New York and the Connecticut River valley in what is now Vermont. In southern

Main Idea CONNECTIONS

Aside from needing land for farming, why did American men fear a land shortage?

▶ RESOURCE OPTIONS

Teaching Resources

📁 **Reproducible Lesson Plan** Lesson Plans folder, p. 45

📁 **Learning Styles Lesson Plan** Learning Styles Lesson Plans folder, p. 9

📁 **Big Idea Graphic Organizer** Big Idea Graphic Organizer folder, p. 17

📁 **Guided Reading and Review** Units 1–2 folder, p. 35

SECTION 4

Emerging Tensions

Objectives

You may wish to call students' attention to the objectives in the Section Preview. The objectives are reflected in the main headings of the section.

Bellringer

Ask students to think about what land ownership signifies. What are the reasons for wanting land today? What were they in colonial times?

Reading Strategy

Formulating Questions Refer to the Reading Strategy in the Section Preview. Encourage students to skim the headings in the section and turn them into questions.

LESSON PLAN

Connecting to the Main Idea

1. **Focus** Explain that by the mid-1700s, conflicts emerged in colonial society. Ask what tensions arose from the desire of colonists to move westward. How did a revival of religious feeling challenge colonial society and British government?
2. **Instruct** Review why the French and Native Americans did not welcome English settlers. How did settlers disrupt Native Americans' lives? How did British settlement affect the French fur trade? Explain how religion both maintained order and threatened it. How did Great Awakening preachers stress each person's importance?
3. **Close** Westward movement and the doctrines taught by preachers of the Great Awakening created tensions in colonial society and set the stage for conflicts.

Answer to . . .

Main Idea Connections Because of all the new immigrants.

The Inoculation Controversy

Around three o'clock on the morning of November 4, 1721, a crude grenade made of black powder and turpentine sailed through a window of Cotton Mather's house in Boston. It failed to explode but the attempted bombing was the most lurid episode in a campaign of intimidation aimed at Mather and his ally Dr. Zabdiel Boylston, whom mobs had threatened to hang. What offenses had these two men committed to enrage the masses so violently? They had inoculated their fellow citizens against smallpox. Mather heard of the African practice of inoculation from his slave Onesimus. When smallpox struck Boston in 1721, Mather and Boylston began an aggressive inoculation campaign. Instead of being hailed as saviors, the two were reviled by many Bostonians for interfering with God's will and spreading disease. Factors unrelated to medicine were at work in the dispute. Bostonians were losing their customary reverence for the clergy. Class-based resentment accounted for some anticlerical feeling, and Mather had recently made enemies by taking sides in a fight over the establishment of a new church.

Source: Frederic D. Schwarz, "The Time Machine," *American Heritage* magazine, November 1996

COMPARING PRIMARY SOURCES

EXPANSION INTO NATIVE AMERICAN LANDS

Colonial efforts to purchase Native American lands in Pennsylvania created a difference of opinions.

Opposed to Expansion	In Favor of Expansion
"We know our Lands are now become more valuable. The white People think we do not know their Value; but we are sensible [aware] that the Land is everlasting, and the few Goods we receive for it are soon worn out and gone. . . . Besides, we are not well used [treated] with respect to the lands still unsold by us. Your people daily settle on these lands, and spoil our hunting. . . . Your horses and cows have eaten the grass our deer used to feed on." —*Canassatego, Iroquois leader, July 7, 1742*	"It is very true that lands are of late becoming more valuable; but what rises their value? Is it not entirely owing to the industry and labor used by the white people in their cultivation and improvement? Had not they come among you, these lands would have been of no use to you, any further than to maintain you. . . . The value of the land is no more than it is worth in money." —*Governor of Pennsylvania, July 7, 1742*

ANALYZING VIEWPOINTS How does each of the speakers above describe the value of the land?

Pennsylvania and the Carolinas, settlements sprang up as far west as the Appalachian Mountains. In a few cases, settlers pushed through the Appalachians and began cultivating land in Indian territory. People migrated, or moved, in search of land on which they could stake their independence and maintain their households.

Native American and French Reaction

The colonists' desire for more land raised tensions between the settlers and those groups who already lived on the land—the French and the Native Americans. Contact between the groups was rare at first, but interactions continued to increase as greater numbers of colonists looked for new places to settle.

Native American Response Just ahead of the westward-moving English migrants were Native Americans. In the Ohio and Susquehanna river valleys lived a number of groups, including the Delaware, the Shawnee, and the Huron. They were moving west, too. As white settlers migrated into Native American territory, they forced the Indians to relocate into lands already occupied by other Native American groups.

By the mid-1700s, disease and wars over trade had taken a toll on Native Americans, especially in New England. The Iroquois, for example, were no longer as strong militarily as they had been in the 1600s. The southern frontier, however, remained a stronghold for Native Americans. There the Cherokees, Creeks, Chickasaws, and Chocktaws created a powerful barrier to westward colonial expansion. In addition, Native Americans remained skilled at playing on the rivalry between the French in Canada and the British in New York and Pennsylvania.

French Actions The steady migration of the English settlers alarmed the French as well as the Native Americans. In 1749, disturbed by the expansion of British trading posts in the Ohio Valley, the French sent defenders to strengthen the settlement of Detroit and to seize the Ohio Valley. Tensions continued to rise in the summer of 1752 when the French built Fort Presque Isle (where Erie, Pennsylvania, is now located) and attacked and killed the men defending an English trading post in the valley.

By the early 1750s, it was clear that some kind of explosion was rapidly approaching. The most likely setting was western Pennsylvania. There the interests of the colonies of Pennsylvania and Virginia conflicted with the Native Americans and the French. Whoever controlled the forks of the Ohio River, the place where the Allegheny and Monongahela rivers meet to form the Ohio, could dominate the entire region. This was, in other words, an area worth fighting for.

Religious Tensions

While tensions built along the outer edges of the British colonies, unrest was also increasing within them. Nowhere was this more obvious than in colonial religious life.

While the British colonies were overwhelmingly Protestant (aside from a small number of Jews in cities and some Catholics in Maryland), no single group of Protestants was more powerful than any other. Southern planters and northern merchants and professionals tended to belong to the Church of England. Most New Englanders were either

Answer to . . .

Comparing Primary Sources
The Iroquois leader says that the land is made less valuable by settlers and their cattle. The governor says that the land is made more valuable by the labor of the settlers.

78 Chapter 3 • Section 4

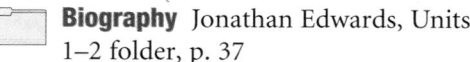

RESOURCE OPTIONS

Teaching Resources

 Comparing Primary Sources On Expansion into Native American Lands, Units 1–2 folder, pp. 38–39

ATLAS **Nystrom *Atlas of Our Country*** Early Expansion of the United States, pp. 20–21

Biography Jonathan Edwards, Units 1–2 folder, p. 37

Congregationalists or Presbyterians. Quakers were strong in Pennsylvania, as were Lutherans and Mennonites. The Dutch Reformed Church thrived in the colony of New York.

In the early 1700s, many ministers, especially Congregationalists, believed that the colonists had fallen away from the faith of their Puritan ancestors. In the 1730s and 1740s, they led a series of revivals designed to renew religious enthusiasm and commitment. Their preaching especially touched women of all ages and young men. This revival of religious feeling is now known as the **Great Awakening.**

The Great Awakening was not a single event that began or ended all at one time. It did not even take place in every colony. Revivals had begun in scattered New England towns as early as the 1720s and continued through the 1760s. Most historians, however, date the beginning of the Great Awakening to the great explosion of religious feeling that arose in the 1730s in response to the preaching of Jonathan Edwards, a minister in Northampton, Massachusetts.

News of Edwards's success spread throughout the colonies and even to Britain. It encouraged other ministers to increase their efforts to energize their followers. These ministers sought to remind people of the power of God and, at least in the beginning, to remind them of the authority of their ministers as well. In a well-known fiery sermon, "Sinners in the Hands of an Angry God," Edwards gave his congregation a terrifying picture of their situation:

AMERICAN VOICES "O sinner! Consider the fearful danger you are in: it is a great furnace of wrath, a wide and bottomless pit, full of the fire of wrath, that you are held over in the hand of that God, whose wrath is provoked and incensed as much against you, as against many of the damned in hell. You hang by a slender thread."

—*Jonathan Edwards*

Edwards would eventually be eclipsed in popularity by George Whitefield, a young English minister who toured the colonies seven times between 1738 and 1770. Whitefield's tour of New England in 1740 was a great triumph. In Boston, he preached to vast crowds packed into churches. Later he held open-air meetings at which thousands of listeners at a time could hear his ringing sermons.

As time went on, however, the Great Awakening did more than revive people's religious convictions. It energized them to speak for themselves and to rely less on the traditional authority of ministers and books. As George Whitefield said,

"The Generality of Preachers talk of an unknown, unfelt Christ. And the Reason why Congregations have been so dead, is because dead Men preach to them."

—*George Whitefield*

In some areas the Great Awakening was led by ministers in established congregations. Many people flocked to revival leaders, such as Whitefield, who were **itinerant**, or traveling, preachers. If welcomed by the local minister, the itinerants would preach inside the church as a "visiting minister." If unwelcome, they

"The bow of God's wrath is bent, and the arrow made ready on the string." Such warnings peppered Jonathan Edwards's fiery sermon (below).

SINNERS IN THE HANDS OF AN ANGRY GOD. A SERMON Preached at ENFIELD, July 8th, 1741. At a Time of great Awakenings; and attended with remarkable Impressions on many of the Hearers. By JONATHAN EDWARDS, A.M. Pastor of the Church of CHRIST, in Northampton.

BOSTON, Printed; NEW-YORK, Re-printed, and Sold by JOHN HOLT, at the Exchange, 1769.

Preachers such as George Whitefield, shown here, were known for their "pathetical," or emotional, style. They used their powerful oratorical skills to encourage ordinary people to believe that they, too, could reach out to God. *Culture What prompted the religious revivals of the Great Awakening?*

Answers to
SECTION 4 REVIEW

1. (a) immigrant, see p. 77; (b) Great Awakening, see p.79; (c) itinerant, see p. 79; (d) dissent, see p. 80.

2. Ordinary people wondered: if they could question the authority of the ministers, could they not also question the authority of the British government?

3. Population increases lead to westward migration of British settlers in search of land, which lead to tensions with Native Americans and French settlers.

4. Sample answer: The Great Awakening had the greatest long-term impact by fostering a spirit of independence and democracy.

5. Because of the strategically important forks of the Ohio River.

6. In support of expansion: more land needed due to high birth rate and immigration; need to deter French. Against expansion: land already occupied by Native Americans and French; conflict inevitable.

Answer to . . .

Interpreting Graphs The number of Congregational churches far outnumbered churches of other denominations.

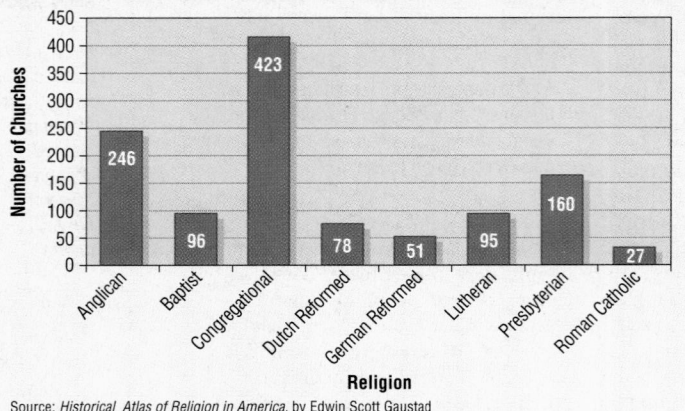

Colonial Churches, 1740

Number of Churches

- Anglican: 246
- Baptist: 96
- Congregational: 423
- Dutch Reformed: 78
- German Reformed: 51
- Lutheran: 95
- Presbyterian: 160
- Roman Catholic: 27

Religion

Source: *Historical Atlas of Religion in America*, by Edwin Scott Gaustad

Interpreting Graphs Traveling preachers of the Great Awakening led to the increase in Baptist churches and to the creation of Methodist churches by the late 1700s. *Diversity What information in the graph helps explain why Congregationalists were so influential during the Great Awakening?*

preached in fields and barns to anyone who would come to hear their sermons.

These ministers, some of whom had had little formal education, preached that anyone could have a personal relationship with Jesus Christ. The infinitely great power of God did not put Him beyond the reach of ordinary people, they argued. Faith and sincerity, rather than wealth or education, were the major requirements needed to understand the Gospel.

One sign of the new religious independence brought about by the Great Awakening was the shift of many New Englanders to the Baptist faith in the 1740s and 1750s. In the South, both the Baptist and, later, the Methodist churches drew new followers. Evangelical Baptists attracted followers among the common people who settled in the southern backcountry. The appeal of these two particular churches lay in their powerful, emotional ceremonies and their celebration of ordinary people.

While some churches grew, others split. Revivals caused several churches to break apart as some church members embraced, while others rejected, the new emotionalism. Yet some of these splinter groups were more tolerant of **dissent,** or difference of opinion, than the organizations from which they had split. This helped make religion in the colonies more democratic.

Though it was a religious movement, the Great Awakening had long-term social and political effects as well. Methodists and Baptists tended to be people at the middle or bottom of colonial society. When they claimed that individuals could act on their own faith and not rely on a minister or other authority, they were indirectly attacking the idea that some people are better than others. Such talk of equality would, in time, have revolutionary consequences.

SECTION 4 REVIEW

Comprehension

1. *Key Terms* Define: (a) immigrant; (b) Great Awakening; (c) itinerant; (d) dissent.

2. *Summarizing the Main Idea* Why was the Great Awakening an indirect challenge to the hierarchical social order of the British colonies?

3. *Organizing Information* Create a cause-effect chart showing the impact of colonial expansion.

Critical Thinking

4. *Analyzing Time Lines* Review the time line at the start of the section. Which event, in your opinion, had the greatest long-term importance?

5. *Drawing Conclusions* Why was western Pennsylvania a likely hot spot for confrontation between the French, English, and Native Americans?

Writing Activity

6. *Writing a Persuasive Essay* In your view, was it necessary for British colonists to expand westward in the mid-1700s? Write an essay explaining your opinion. Support your ideas with specific examples.

Why Study History?

To understand that . . .

Your Freedom of Religion Is Guaranteed

The search for freedom of worship has brought people of many faiths to America, from colonial times to the present day.

Person speaking at a Quaker meeting

Five times each day, American Muslims face eastward and pray to Allah. On Saturdays American Jews gather for worship at local synagogues. Millions of Catholics and Protestants attend Sunday worship services across the United States. Buddhists, Hindus, and people of other faiths also practice their religion here.

The Impact Today

Since early colonial times, people have come to America for religious freedom. Today the United States is home to more than 150 religious denominations or sects. The smallest, such as the Primitive Advent Christian Church, have only a few hundred members. The largest, the Roman Catholic Church, has more than 60 million members.

The First Amendment of the United States Constitution protects all religious groups, regardless of size. "Congress shall make no law," it states, " . . . prohibiting the free exercise of religion."

In many parts of the world, including Northern Ireland, Bosnia, Tibet, and the Middle East, religious differences have provoked war or persecution. Our nation's long tradition of

respecting people's right to worship as they choose has kept religious differences from erupting into war.

Yet Americans often disagree over issues related to religion, and religious organizations have played an important role in American politics. Religious groups participated on both sides of the debate over slavery in the 1800s, for example. Black churches helped organize the civil rights movement of the 1950s and 1960s, and fundamentalist Christians spearheaded the growth of the conservative movement of the 1980s. In these and other cases, Americans' religious values have helped shape their political views.

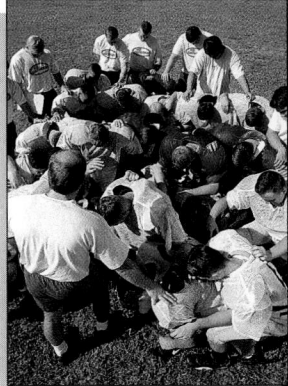

Football players at a Baptist high school praying before practice

The Impact on You

Consider both sides of an issue that has been debated in recent years: Should organized prayer be allowed in public schools? Brainstorm a list of three reasons why it should be allowed and three reasons why it should not. Then decide which position you favor. Use your list as the basis for a letter to the editor of a newspaper. Write the letter, listing the arguments on both sides of the issue and explaining your position.

▶ RESOURCE OPTIONS

Teaching Resources

 Why Study History? Activity Your Freedom of Religion Is Guaranteed, found in the Why Study History? folder, p. 4, provides an activity to help students better understand freedom of religion.

Media and Technology

 Decision America Videotapes and Videodiscs Issue 1 *Can One Voice Make a Difference?*

Class Discussion

Discuss freedom of religion with the class. For a more thorough examination of the issue, see the activity folder in the Resource Options below.

ACTIVITY
STUDENT PARTICIPATION

Organizing a Tolerance Forum

Ask students to read the text. Then divide the class into three groups to discuss the following topic: How can we increase religious tolerance in our school? Each group might concentrate on one of these issues:

- **understanding differences**
- **fighting prejudice**
- **guidelines for promoting tolerance**

Have the groups share their ideas in a forum. Then ask them to create a checklist of positive actions students can take to increase religious tolerance in school.

Follow up Discuss religious differences within the classroom. Include students who do not practice a religion. Encourage volunteers to share aspects of their religion such as worship services.

💻 Using the Internet

Students can learn more about freedom of religion by exploring links in the *America: Pathways to the Present* Web site at

http://www.Pathways.phschool.com

Assessment

See the Lesson Plans folder, pp. 24–27, for rubrics on assessing Class Participation Projects.

Key Terms

Students should refer to the definitions of key terms in the chapter to write sentences that show an understanding of the colonial societies in North America.

Comprehension

1. Tradition of strong central government and weak central power; lacked the resources to enforce their wishes overseas; most colonists recognized British authority without force; economy and politics of the colonies served them as they were.

2. Southern Colonies—agriculture; Middle Colonies—commerce and agriculture; New England—self-sufficient farms and long-distance trade.

3. New Englanders shipped goods from England to the West Indies, transported sugar from the West Indies to New England to distill into rum, traded rum and firearms for slaves in West Africa, then carried slaves to the West Indies for more sugar.

4. Cooking, gardening, washing, cleaning, weaving, and sewing; helping each other in childbirth; assisting husbands' work; training daughters in the traditional responsibilities of women.

5. Work was the central focus in most people's lives.

6. Slaves were forced to endure chains, oppressive heat, disease, and a lack of fresh air and sanitation.

7. They were the majority of the population, mostly came directly from Africa, had little contact with colonists, and created new kinship networks.

8. A rising birth rate and immigration caused population growth.

9. It encouraged them to speak for themselves and question the traditional authority of ministers, books, and ultimately of the existing political and social order.

Chapter Summary

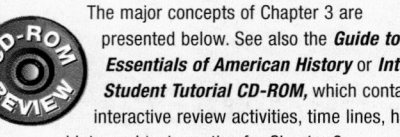

The major concepts of Chapter 3 are presented below. See also the *Guide to the Essentials of American History* or *Interactive Student Tutorial CD-ROM,* which contains interactive review activities, time lines, helpful hints, and test practice for Chapter 3.

Reviewing the Main Ideas

The early 1700s was a time of growth and change for the British colonies in North America. Colonists, largely left alone by the British government, gained confidence and independence. The colonial economy grew and society became more diverse. Yet sources of tension, from slavery to conflicts with the colonies' neighbors, remained.

Section 1: An Empire and Its Colonies

The English colonies in the mid-1600s and early 1700s grew and prospered with little direct interference from the English government.

Section 2: Life in Colonial America

The social groups that made up colonial society had different roles and ways of living.

Section 3: African Americans in the Colonies

Africans, brought across the Atlantic Ocean as slaves, helped build England's American colonies while enduring harsh and often brutal treatment.

Section 4: Emerging Tensions

In the mid-1700s, the American colonies experienced a growing population and a powerful religious revival.

Why Study History?

The search for freedom of worship has brought many people to America, from colonial times to the present day. The United States today is home to more than 150 religious denominations or sects.

Key Terms

For each of the terms below, write a sentence explaining how it relates to this chapter.

1. gentry
2. triangular trade
3. salutary neglect
4. Stono Rebellion
5. balance of trade
6. mercantilism
7. indigo
8. Great Awakening
9. Middle Passage
10. duty
11. itinerant
12. staple crop

Comprehension

1. Give four reasons why the British were able to neglect their colonies in the 1700s.
2. What was the main economic activity in the Southern Colonies? In the Middle Colonies? In the New England Colonies?
3. Describe the system of triangular trade used by New Englanders in the 1700s.
4. What duties did women perform in colonial America?
5. Describe the importance of work in colonial America.
6. Describe the conditions of the Middle Passage.
7. Give four reasons why slaves in South Carolina and Georgia were able to preserve many of their cultural traditions.
8. Why did the colonists feel pressure to expand westward in the mid-1700s?
9. Besides energizing religious feeling, what effect did the Great Awakening have on colonial people and society?

Using Graphic Organizers

On a separate sheet of paper, copy the web diagram to organize the main ideas of the chapter. Provide four reasons for the growing spirit of independence in the colonies.

Rising Spirit of Independence

Using Graphic Organizers

Possible answers:
- Immigration from a variety of countries.
- English policy of salutary neglect.
- Regional differences in land, climate, and economy.
- Great Awakening encouraged independence of thought.

Analyzing Political Cartoons ▶

1. Examine this Puritan cartoon. (a) Describe the scene shown in the drawing. (b) What information does the caption add?
2. What is the message of the cartoon?
3. How is the message of the cartoon characteristic of Puritan culture?

Severall Young men playing at foote-ball on the Ice upon the Lords-Day are all Drownd

Critical Thinking

1. *Applying the Chapter Skill* Review the economic activity map on page 64. Based on the crops you see listed, where do you think large-scale slavery existed?
2. *Recognizing Ideologies* Today many people consider it wrong for a nation to have colonies. How does this view of colonies contrast with that held by the British in the late 1600s and early 1700s?
3. *Making Comparisons* How did the life of a slave differ in the New England and the Southern Colonies?
4. *Distinguishing False from Accurate Images* Would it be correct to state that colonial society was dominated by men? Explain your answer.

INTERNET ACTIVITY

For your portfolio:
CREATE A PIE CHART

Access Prentice Hall's *America: Pathways to the Present* site at **www.Pathways.phschool.com** for the specific URL to complete the activity. Additional resources and related Web sites are also available.

Read about how historians determine the number of Africans that were enslaved for the Atlantic slave trade. Create a pie chart showing the percent of enslaved Africans who reached America and those that died along the way. Provide a caption to explain these deaths.

ANALYZING DOCUMENTS ◀ INTERPRETING DATA

Turn to the "American Voices" quotation on page 68.

1. How did Eliza Pinckney feel about her work on the plantations? (a) She thought it was too great a burden. (b) She was overwhelmed by the amount of writing involved. (c) She was happy and proud to be able to help her father. (d) She did not seem to like the work.
2. Why might Eliza Pinckney's friend have thought that the workload was too much for Eliza? (a) Eliza was in poor health. (b) It was rare for a girl to carry so much responsibility. (c) Most girls only managed one plantation at a time. (d) Eliza's letter complains about the amount of work.
3. *Writing* Write a brief letter responding to Eliza. You may want to comment on the amount of work she has taken on or ask about plantation life.

Connecting to Today

Essay Writing Reread the section on Diverse Colonial Economies that begins on page 62. Research and write an essay that describes the important economic activities in your region of the country today. What changes have there been in your region's economy in recent years?

Analyzing Political Cartoons

1. **a.** Men are falling in the water while playing a game. **b.** That the scene takes place on Sunday.
2. The men are "treading on the thin ice" by playing a game on Sunday instead of going to church.
3. It shows how Puritan culture emphasized rules, punishment, and strict religious observation.

Critical Thinking

1. Georgia, South and North Carolina.
2. The British believed that nations should have colonies and exploit them for wealth.
3. Slaves in New England worked on small farms or as domestic help, interacting with whites frequently. Slaves in the South worked on huge plantations, interacting with whites less often.
4. Students who agree that men dominated society should provide examples of colonial laws and politics. Students who disagree should support their stance with examples of women's vital roles on the farm and in the community.

Analyzing Documents

1. c
2. b
3. Answers will vary but should demonstrate an understanding of plantation life.

Connecting to Today

Answers will vary but should demonstrate an understanding of students' regional economy.

INTERNET ACTIVITY

Answers will vary. Charts and captions should show an understanding of historical data on the slave trade.

CHAPTER 4

The Road to Independence, 1754–1783

Managing Time and Instruction

INSTRUCTION SUPPORT

These materials for instruction are provided for **each section** in the **Teaching Resources.** See **Units 1–2 folder for Enrichment Support:**

- Reproducible Lesson Plans in Lesson Plans folder • Learning Styles Lesson Plans in Learning Styles Lesson Plans folder • Big Idea Graphic Organizers in Big Idea Graphic Organizer folder
- Guided Reading and Review • Quizzes • Test Preparation Practice booklet

DAILY LESSON	ENRICHMENT SUPPORT
1 **The French and Indian War** (pp. 85–88)	• Nystrom *Atlas of Our Country,* Colonies in the North and East, pp. 14–15 • Primary Source Activity, Braddock's Defeat, Learning with Documents folder, p. 10
2 **Issues Behind the Revolution** (pp. 89–96)	• Biography, Pontiac, found on **Resource Pro** • Visual Learning Activity, The American Rattlesnake, found on **Resource Pro** • Visual Learning Activity, Boycotting Tea, Learning with Documents folder, p. 46 • Skills for Life Activity, Units 1–2 folder, p. 56
3 **Ideas Behind the Revolution** (pp. 98–101)	• Key Documents, Patrick Henry, Speech to the Virginia Provincial Convention, Learning with Documents folder, p. 81 • Literature Activity, To the King, Units 1–2 folder, p. 55 • Literature Activity, *Common Sense,* found on **Resource Pro** • Comparing Primary Sources, On Rule by the People, Units 1–2 folder, pp. 53–54
4 **Fighting for Independence** (pp. 106–110)	• Critical Thinking Activity, Checking Consistency: Lexington and Concord, found on **Resource Pro** • Primary Source Activity, War Diary of Margaret Hill Morris, found on **Resource Pro**
5 **Winning Independence** (pp. 111–114)	• Biography, Deborah Sampson Gannett, Units 1–2 folder, p. 52 • You Have a Voice in Government, Why Study History? folder, p. 5

Running Out of Time?

- Use Tape 1, "Origins of a New Society, to 1783," from **Visions of America** videotapes series.
- Use Chapter 4 Summary, from **Guide to the Essentials of American History (English and Spanish).**

Companion Web Site

The companion Web site offers online links for all chapter review activities. It also provides key content links and structured support for this chapter for both teachers and students.

http://www.Pathways.phschool.com

Teaching in the Information Age

Media and Technology

For the Student

Interactive Student Tutorial CD-ROM Chapter 4
Student Edition on Audiotape Chapter 4
American Heritage® CD-ROM
Guided Reading Audiotapes (English and Spanish) Chapter 4

For the Teacher

Resource Pro CD-ROM Chapter 4
Test Bank CD-ROM Chapter 4
Listening to Music CD William Billings, "Chester"
Color Transparencies Critical Thinking, I-1; Fine Art, D-4 and D-5

Assessment Options

Chapter Test Forms A&B Test Bank CD-ROM booklet
Test Bank CD-ROM Chapter 4
Standardized Test Preparation Handbook

Block Scheduling

Pacing Suggestions

For 90-minute Blocks

- Teach sections 2 and 3 using Transparencies E-2, H-4, F-2, and H-5 and the Recent Scholarship note on p. 100 for class discussions.
- Teach sections 1, 4, and 5 using the Big Idea Graphic Organizers from Teaching Resources and the Extended Class Periods Activity found on p. 86.

Additional Resources

- Prentice Hall's **American History Block Scheduling Support File** covers over 40 major topics in American history.
- **Prentice Hall United States History Video Collection**TM contains 20 videotapes covering American history from beginnings to present.
- **Decision America Videotapes and Videodiscs**

Connections to American Literature

from Prentice Hall

America: Pathways to the Present
Howard Fast, *April Morning*, pp. 1072–1073

Prentice Hall Literature *Timeless Voices, Timeless Themes*

- from *The Autobiography* by Benjamin Franklin, p. 131
- from The Iroquois Constitution, p. 28
- from "The Crisis, Number 1" by Thomas Paine, p. 144

Additional Resources

For the Student

A. J. Lagguth. *Patriots: The Men Who Started the American Revolution.* Simon & Schuster, 1988.
Milton Meltzer. *The American Revolutionaries: A History in Their Own Words.* Crowell, 1987.

For the Teacher

Irving Kristol, Martin Diamond, and G. Warren Nutter. *The American Revolution: Three Views.* American Brands, 1975.
Page Smith. *A New Age Now Begins: A People's History of the American Revolution.* McGraw-Hill, 1976.

Prentice Hall brings into the classroom the vast archives and scholarship of the nation's premier American history magazine. See "From the Archives of American Heritage®" teaching notes in this chapter.

History Alive!

Teacher's Curriculum Institute, in partnership with Prentice Hall, provides unique materials that engage students with diverse learning styles. See History Alive!® unit on Colonial Life and the American Revolution.

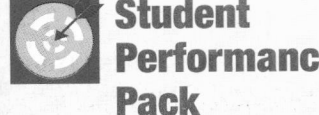
Student Performance Pack

Ensures success in the three critical areas of Reading, Test Taking, and English Language Development with the following materials:
- Guide to the Essentials of American History in English and Spanish
- Guided Reading Audiotapes in English and Spanish
- Interactive Student Tutorial CD-ROM
- Test Preparation Handbook
- Test Preparation Practice booklet

Introducing the Chapter

The American Revolution was more than a war for independence. The struggle reflected the development of a unique American identity that was fueled by colonists' personal definitions of democracy and equality. This new consciousness inspired a war that led to independence from Great Britain and the creation of a radically new society.

Themes in American History

The theme for this chapter, Government, is listed at the beginning of this unit. An alternate theme for the chapter is Economics. To teach this unit thematically, you may wish to use the Forging a New Nation folder in American History Block Scheduling Support.

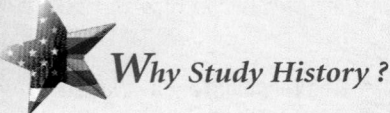

Why Study History?

Have students explore suggested ways of connecting the past to the present on page 115.

Answer to . . .

Viewing History Students should use this question as an aid in reading the chapter. The "spirit" that led the colonists to rebel was in part a growing confidence in their capacity for self-government combined with a shrinking respect for the government in Britain.

84

CHAPTER FOCUS

This chapter describes the Americans' protests against British rule and their successful struggle to win independence from Great Britain. The revolution that swept the colonies encouraged powerful ideas about democracy.

The Why Study History? page at the end of this chapter explores the connection between the cries for representative government during the American Revolution and the issue of representative government today.

▲ **VIEWING HISTORY**
Archibald Willard painted *The Spirit of '76* in 1875 for Pennsylvania's centennial celebration. He originally called the painting *Yankee Doodle*. *Culture* **What was this "spirit" that led American colonists to rebel against England?**

▶ RESOURCE OPTIONS

Teaching Resources

 Big Idea Graphic Organizer folder
Graphic summary of the main idea of the chapter.

Learning Styles Lesson Plans folder
Alternate lesson plans for diverse learning styles for each chapter.

Media and Technology

 AmericanHeritage® CD-ROM
Time Tour From Revolution to Republic: The Road to Revolution *and* The American Revolution

 Prentice Hall United States History Video Collection™ Volume 4 *The American Revolution*

| 1754 French and Indian War begins | 1758 British seize Louisbourg | 1759 British take Quebec | 1761 British seize Fort Detroit | 1763 Treaty of Paris ends French and Indian War |

1750 **1755** **1760** **1765**

1 The French and Indian War

SECTION PREVIEW

Objectives

1. Summarize the causes of the French and Indian War.
2. Describe how the British won the French and Indian War.
3. Analyze how the war weakened the colonists' loyalty to Britain.
4. **Key Terms** Define: French and Indian War; Albany Plan of Union; militia; prime minister; siege; Treaty of Paris (1763).

Main Idea

The war that the colonists fought against the French and Indians caused them to rethink their relationship with Britain.

Reading Strategy

Organizing Information As you read, create a graphic organizer showing the causes and effects of the French and Indian War.

After ambushing a French scouting party in western Pennsylvania in May 1754, a small force of British colonists built a stronghold named Fort Necessity. There they waited for the French to try to retake the Ohio Valley, which both Britain and France claimed. The French, who far outnumbered the British, soon surrounded the fort and forced a surrender. The colonists returned to Virginia defeated and disgraced. It was not a good start for their 21-year-old commander, George Washington. One day, however, his achievements would make him a hero.

Causes of War

George Washington's unsuccessful expedition into western Pennsylvania was the first minor battle of a war that lasted until 1763. It was called the **French and Indian War** because the British and their American colonists waged it against the French and their Indian allies. This nine-year conflict was the final chapter in a long struggle among the French, the British, and various groups of Native Americans for control of eastern North America.

Rivalry Between Britain and France The rivalry among European nations for control of North America began soon after they began to explore and colonize the continent. While English colonists built their settlements along the eastern seacoast during the 1600s, the French explored farther inland: along the St. Lawrence River, the Great Lakes, and the Mississippi River. From these explorations the French claimed a vast region stretching from the Appalachian Mountains in the east to the Rocky Mountains in the west. Conflict arose because the English claimed some of this territory as well.

British and French colonization of North America followed different patterns. British settlers founded towns and cleared land for planting crops, while French colonists established forts to protect their land claims. The French forts also served as centers for trade with Native Americans. As a result of these differences, French relations with Native Americans were generally better than were British-Indian relations. In 1718 the deputy governor of Virginia noted the French threat in a report to his superiors in England:

RESOURCE OPTIONS

Teaching Resources

📁 **Reproducible Lesson Plan** Lesson Plans folder p. 46

📁 **Big Idea Graphic Organizer** Big Idea Graphic Organizer folder, p. 18

📁 **Guided Reading and Review** Units 1–2 folder, p. 42

Media and Technology

AmericanHeritage® CD-ROM
Time Tour From Revolution to Republic: The Road to Revolution

---

By . . . the forts [the French] have already built, the British Plantations [settlements] are in a manner Surrounded by [French] Commerce with the numerous Nations of Indians. . . . [The French] may, when they please, send out such Bodys of Indians on the back [outskirts] of these Plantations as may greatly distress [threaten] his Majesty's Subjects here.

—*Deputy governor of Virginia*

Main Idea CONNECTIONS

Why was the Albany Plan of Union important?

Beginning in the late 1600s, Great Britain and France were often at war. When they battled over issues in Europe, their colonists often fought in America. Increasingly, however, these conflicts focused on the rivalry in North America. The last of them, the French and Indian War, actually started in the colonies and spread to Europe. Because the European phase began in 1756, about two years after the fighting was under way in America, in Europe it was called the Seven Years' War.

The Albany Plan of Union At the time George Washington and his small force held out at Fort Necessity, a meeting of delegates from seven northern colonies convened at Albany, New York, in June 1754. The delegates hoped to strengthen ties with the Iroquois League. British officials saw the powerful Iroquois as important potential allies.

Another reason for the Albany meeting was to work out a unified war effort in the northern colonies. With this in mind Benjamin Franklin, a Pennsylvania delegate, offered an ambitious plan for a permanent union of the colonies. Named the **Albany Plan of Union,** it called for a grand council of delegates from each colony, elected by their colonial legislatures. Heading the council would be a president general, appointed by the British crown. Franklin believed that just as the Iroquois nation had strengthened itself by forming the Iroquois League, the British colonies would benefit from greater unity.

Although the delegates approved Franklin's plan, the colonies themselves rejected it. Colonists were unwilling to surrender that much power to a central government. The Albany Plan of Union is important, however, because it provided a model for the later government of the United States.

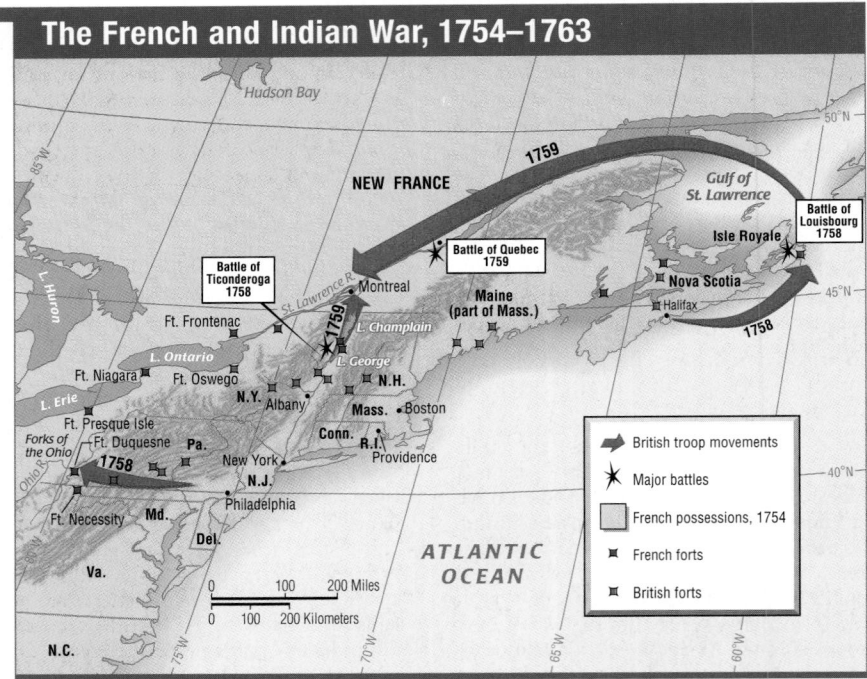

The French and Indian War, 1754–1763

MAP skills

The three main thrusts of British strategy are shown here. In 1758, British forces struck in two directions—at French strongholds in the west and against Louisbourg in the east. Finally, in 1759 they attacked Quebec and Montreal. *Movement Why was it necessary to capture Louisbourg before attacking Quebec?*

Hudson Bay

NEW FRANCE

1759

Gulf of St. Lawrence

Isle Royale

Battle of Louisbourg 1758

Battle of Quebec 1759

Nova Scotia

Battle of Ticonderoga 1758

Montreal

Maine (part of Mass.)

Halifax

St. Lawrence R.

Ft. Frontenac

L. Champlain

1759

L. George

L. Huron

L. Ontario

Ft. Niagara

Ft. Oswego

N.Y.

N.H.

Albany

Mass.

Boston

L. Erie

Ft. Presque Isle

Conn.

R.I.

Providence

Forks of the Ohio

Ft. Duquesne

Pa.

New York

Ohio R.

1758

N.J.

Philadelphia

Ft. Necessity

Md.

Del.

Va.

ATLANTIC OCEAN

N.C.

0   100   200 Miles
0   100   200 Kilometers

→ British troop movements
★ Major battles
◻ French possessions, 1754
⚑ French forts
⚑ British forts

Early British Defeats At first the French and Indian War went poorly for the British. The badly outnumbered French and their Indian allies won important victories. The most impressive of these victories took place once again in the forests of western Pennsylvania. On July 9, 1755, about 900 French and Native Americans surprised a force of nearly 1,500 British troops and 450 colonial **militia,** armed citizens who serve as soldiers during an emergency.

British soldiers had been trained to fight in the open and in straight lines, as was done in Europe. They were no match for an enemy who hid behind rocks and trees. In the fierce three-hour battle about a third of the British force was killed or wounded. Among those killed was the British commander, General Edward Braddock. "We shall better know how to deal with them another time," Braddock is reported to have said of the French as he died.

Among the colonists who survived was wagon driver Daniel Boone, later to become known for his exploits on the Kentucky frontier. Another was Braddock's aide, George Washington, who had two horses killed under him and ended the battle with four bullet holes in his coat. Washington, who organized the British retreat, later reported that the colonists "showed a great deal of Bravery" and "were exposed to almost certain death" because of the "dastardly behavior" of the British soldiers who "broke and run [sic] as Sheep pursued by dogs."

The British Win the War

In 1756 Great Britain formally declared war on France. As fighting spread to Europe and Asia, the British repeated their American military disasters. In 1757 William Pitt became Britain's **prime minister,** the highest official of a parliamentary government. Believing that the entire British Empire could be at stake, Pitt persuaded Parliament to raise taxes and borrow huge sums of money to fight the war.

The Tide of War Turns Pitt's efforts soon paid off. In 1758, better-prepared and better-led British troops began to overwhelm French

By compressing space and time, the painter of this view of the British attack on Quebec was able to illustrate several events at once. *Movement* *What British actions are shown?*

and Indian forces in western Pennsylvania and Canada. They first attacked the long line of forts and settlements that the French had built. (See the map on the previous page.) In July 1758, British forces seized Louisbourg, an important French fortress on the Gulf of St. Lawrence. In November they captured Fort Duquesne in Pennsylvania. (The fort, renamed Fort Pitt for the British leader, eventually became the city of Pittsburgh.) In July 1759 British troops took Fort Niagara.

The British victories put the French on the defensive. They abandoned their forts in New York and retreated into Canada. The Iroquois, who had cleverly been playing each side against the other, now decided that the French cause was hopeless. They began to support the British actively.

The Fall of Quebec In the late spring of 1759, the British began a campaign to invade Canada and capture Quebec, the capital of New France. The city sat high on the cliffs overlooking the St. Lawrence River. General James Wolfe commanded about 9,000 British troops. Some 7,500 French forces led by the Marquis de Montcalm defended Quebec.

After suffering heavy losses in a direct attack in July 1759, Wolfe settled down to a **siege** of the city. Laying siege to a stronghold is a tactic by which enemy forces are trapped in their position and starved into surrendering.

Answers to
SECTION 1 REVIEW

1. (a) French and Indian War, see p. 85; (b) Albany Plan of Union, see p. 86; (c) militia, see p. 87; (d) prime minister, see p. 87; (e) siege, see p. 87; (f) Treaty of Paris (1763), see p. 88.

2. As a result of the French and Indian War, Americans lost respect for the British. They also came to believe that the British did not respect them and that their values differed from those of Britain. Many Americans saw no reason why they should not expand and prosper on their own, without British help.

3. Major causes: conflict between French and British over territory in North America; British fears of relationship between French and Indians. Major effects: weakened loyalty of colonists to Britain; Britain incurred huge debts; France turned Canada over to the British and surrendered its claim to all lands east of the Mississippi River (except for New Orleans); the British returned Cuba to Spain in exchange for Florida.

4. As a result of the Treaty of Paris (1763), France turned Canada over to the British and surrendered its claim to all lands east of the Mississippi River (except for New Orleans). The British returned Cuba to Spain in exchange for Florida.

5. British prime minster William Pitt persuaded Parliament to raise taxes and borrow money to fight the war. This enabled the British to improve their army.

6. Students' essays will vary. Essays should point out that Pitt believed the future of the British Empire was at stake. Britain gained money from the colonists in the form of trade and taxes.

Wolfe, however, had only limited time for the siege to work. The British warships that supported his army needed to withdraw from the river as winter approached. By September, he was ready to try a daring tactic.

On the night of September 12, Wolfe began moving his troops up a narrow, undefended path on the side of Quebec's cliffs. By dawn about 4,500 troops were in position to threaten the French defenders of the city. Without waiting for some 3,000 reinforcements to arrive, Montcalm moved his 4,500 troops out of the city to battle the enemy. The British turned back his attack, inflicting heavy losses on the French. Both Wolfe and Montcalm were killed in the fighting. A few days later, the city surrendered.

With the fall of Quebec the war was nearly over. The following September, British forces took the city of Montreal, giving Great Britain control over all of Canada. By 1761, the British had seized Fort Detroit and other French posts along the Great Lakes.

The Treaty of Paris In 1763, representatives of Great Britain, France, and France's ally Spain signed a treaty in Paris, France. The **Treaty of Paris (1763)** ended the French and Indian War in America and the Seven Years' War in Europe. In the treaty, France turned Canada over to Britain and surrendered its claim to all lands east of the Mississippi River. The only exception was the city of New Orleans, which France had given to Spain in a secret treaty the year before. The British returned Cuba, captured during the war, to Spain in exchange for Florida.

Weakened Loyalty to Britain

Despite the victory, the French and Indian War seriously strained relations between the British and the American colonists. The British thought the colonists did not provide enough support for the long and costly war that Britain had fought to protect them.

For their part, the Americans were shocked by the weakness of British military tactics. They demanded to be led by colonial officers, which the British viewed as treason. One militiaman expressed amazement at his British commander during the battle for Fort Ticonderoga:

 AMERICAN VOICES ❝The . . . roar of [muskets] terrified me. . . . Our regiment formed among the trees, behind which the men kept stepping from their ranks for shelter. Colonel Preble . . . swore he would knock the first man down who should step out of his ranks, which greatly surprised me, to think that I must stand still to be shot at.❞

—*Massachusetts militiaman*

The end of the war left many colonists with two strong beliefs. One was a loss of respect for British military power. The other was a belief that the British did not share the same values as Americans or treat them with appropriate respect. Now that the French no longer held Canada or the region west of the Appalachian Mountains, the colonists saw no reason why they should not expand and prosper on their own, without British help. These feelings would soon combine with events to deepen the split between Britain and its colonies.

SECTION 1 REVIEW

Comprehension

1. *Key Terms* Define: (a) French and Indian War; (b) Albany Plan of Union; (c) militia; (d) prime minister; (e) siege; (f) Treaty of Paris (1763).

2. *Summarizing the Main Idea* How did the French and Indian War cause the colonists to rethink their relationship with Britain?

3. *Organizing Information* Outline the major causes and effects of the French and Indian War.

Critical Thinking

4. *Analyzing Time Lines* Review the time line at the start of the section. Why was the Treaty of Paris significant?

5. *Drawing Conclusions* What made it possible for the British to win the French and Indian War?

Writing Activity

6. *Writing a Persuasive Essay* Write a speech by William Pitt persuading Parliament to raise taxes and borrow money in order to fight the war. Think about why the war in North America was so important to the British.

▶ RESOURCE OPTIONS

Teaching Resources

📁 **Quiz** Units 1–2 folder, p. 43

Student Performance Pack

 Guide to the Essentials Chapter 4, Section 1 (English and Spanish)

| 1763 | 1765 | 1770 | 1774 | 1775 |
| Pontiac's Rebellion | Stamp Act Congress | Boston Massacre | First Continental Congress | Fighting at Lexington and Concord, Massachusetts |

| 1760 | 1765 | 1770 | 1775 | 1780 |

2 Issues Behind the Revolution

SECTION PREVIEW

Objectives

1. Explain how and why British policies in the colonies changed after 1763.
2. Summarize the causes and effects of the Stamp Act.
3. Describe how rising tensions in the colonies led to fighting at Lexington and Concord, Massachusetts.
4. *Key Terms* Define: Pontiac's Rebellion; Proclamation of 1763; Stamp Act; boycott; Boston Massacre; First Continental Congress; Battles of Lexington and Concord; Revolutionary War.

Main Idea

The colonists, believing they should not be taxed without representation, protested new British taxes.

Reading Strategy

Outlining Information As you read this section, create an outline of the major events leading to the outbreak of the Revolutionary War.

Shortly after 7:00 A.M. on October 25, 1760, a servant entered the bedroom of Britain's King George II. He gently awakened the 77-year old monarch and offered some hot chocolate. The king rose and looked out the window. Noting that it was a fine day, the ruler announced he would take a walk. The page bowed and turned to leave. As he reached the door he heard a deep sigh behind him, and then the king fell to the floor.

The king's grandson, Prince George, was riding a horse on the palace grounds that morning. Anxious servants located the prince and told him he was needed in the palace. There a messenger handed him a note addressed "To His Majesty." In this way the prince learned that he was now king of England.

Changing British Policy

At age 22, George III was very young to assume the leadership of an empire. Stubborn and insecure, the king replaced William Pitt as prime minister with his personal adviser, John Stewart,

Earl of Bute. The new king promised a quick end to the long and expensive war with France which Lord Bute accomplished in the Treaty of Paris of 1763. However, the British government's problems in North America were far from over.

The Proclamation of 1763 As the end of the war approached, British traders and land speculators showed increased interest in the Great Lakes region and the Ohio River valley. Native Americans in these regions became alarmed. These British colonists were not hunters and traders like the French. As farmers, they represented a much greater threat to Indian lands and resources.

When Native Americans approached government officials with their concerns, they discovered another difference between the British and the French. General Jeffrey Amherst, the British military commander in North America, despised the Indians. Not only did Amherst ignore Indian protests, he ended the flow of trade goods on which they had come to depend under French rule.

 RESOURCE OPTIONS

Teaching Resources

📁 **Reproducible Lesson Plan** Lesson Plans folder, p. 47

📁 **Big Idea Graphic Organizer** Big Idea Graphic Organizer folder, p. 19

📁 **Guided Reading and Review** Units 1–2 folder, p. 44

Media and Technology

AmericanHeritage® CD-ROM

Explorer Activity 5 British Policies in the American Colonies, CD-ROM Guidebook, pp. 29–30, helps students compose an interview with an American colonist in the 1760s.

Objectives

You may wish to call students' attention to the objectives in the Section Preview. The objectives are reflected in the main headings of the section.

Bellringer

Ask students to jot down a list of items that the state and/or federal government singles out for taxation. Ask students if they think these taxes are fair or unfair and whether they feel that they restrict individual freedom in any way.

Reading Strategy

Outlining Information Refer to the Reading Strategy in the Section Preview. You may want to model creating an outline on the chalkboard. Have students fill in the outline as they read the section.

LESSON PLAN

Connecting to the Main Idea

1. Focus Tell students that the French and Indian War left Great Britain in debt. In order to increase tax revenues, it tried to tighten its control over the colonies. The colonists resisted fiercely.

2. Instruct Review British policy toward the colonies up until the 1760s. Ask why Great Britain felt justified in exerting more control over the colonies after the French and Indian War. Why did the colonists react so strongly? Ask why the passage of the Sugar Act was significant. What led Americans to believe that the British were going to take away their freedom?

3. Close As Great Britain tried to increase its authority over the American colonies, the colonists became convinced that the British were trying to take away their liberty. Americans decided at the Second Continental Congress that war against the British was their only option if they wanted to keep their freedom.

To demonstrate the British policy of forcing the colonists to share in the cost of running the colonies (and the colonists' reaction to it), have students list their most cherished privileges at home. Responses may include using the phone, driving the family car, watching TV, and so on. Then announce that students will be taxed for such privileges. Divide the class into two groups—parents (Tories) and students (colonists). Have the groups informally debate this new taxation policy. *(Verbal/Linguistic)*

Customize for
Less Proficient Readers

Tell students that by 1770, growing numbers of Americans were convinced that British politicians were engaged in nothing less than a deliberate plot to rob them of their personal independence through taxation. As they read, students should list and briefly describe specific British actions that led so many Americans to feel this way.

Answer to . . .

Map Skills 1754: Britain, France, Spain. After 1763: Britain, Spain.

European Land Claims in North America, 1754–1763

In 1754

In 1763

British territory
French territory
Spanish territory
Disputed territory

Proclamation Line of 1763 prohibited colonial settlement west of the Appalachians.

MAP Skills The Proclamation of 1763 prohibited settlement west of a line through the Appalachian Mountains. *Regions What European countries claimed land in North America in 1754? After 1763?*

In response, Ottawa, Huron, Potawatomi, and other Indians in the Great Lakes region rebelled against the British in the spring of 1763. Europeans named the uprising **Pontiac's Rebellion,** after one of its Ottawa leaders. By the end of the year, Native Americans had destroyed every British fort in the area west of the Appalachians except Fort Pitt and Fort Detroit. Some 2,000 colonists had been killed or captured. Thousands more hurried back east to safer areas.

As its army in America reeled from these setbacks, the British government acted to restore peace. In October, King George issued the **Proclamation of 1763.** This order closed the region west of the Appalachian Mountains to all settlement by colonists. The area, which had just been given up by the French, was placed under the control of the British military.

Between 1764 and 1766, Britain signed peace treaties with the Indian groups that had taken part in the rebellion. Yet despite the Proclamation of 1763, colonists continued to move west into the forbidden territory. Britain's lack of success in halting the colonists' migration further undermined its authority in America.

Britain's Financial Problems By 1763 the British were among the most heavily taxed people in the world. The costs of governing and defending Britain's vast empire contributed greatly to this burden. These costs had skyrocketed during the French and Indian War. In early 1763 the creation of yet another tax, this time on cider, caused riots throughout the apple-growing regions of England.

In April, Lord Bute resigned and finance minister George Grenville became the prime minister. Although a brilliant money manager, Grenville was self-centered and rude. The king hated him, and he had few friends in political circles.

While Britain struggled with its heavy debts and taxes, its colonies in America were prospering. "What a land of wealth, plenty, and contentment this is among all ranks, vastly improved within the last ten years," wrote a Massachusetts colonist in 1760. With British

RESOURCE OPTIONS

Media and Technology

Biography Pontiac, found on Resource Pro, profiles the chief of the Ottawa who headed a Native American confederation to stop the spread of the British colonies.

Color Transparencies Time Lines, E-2

citizens so burdened, Grenville asked, why shouldn't these colonists begin to pay some of the costs of their own government and defense?

In early 1764, Richard Jackson, a member of Parliament, wrote to his old friend Benjamin Franklin in Philadelphia. He advised Franklin that Grenville planned to raise money in the colonies with some new form of taxation. This would be in addition to enforcing the duties, or taxes on imports, which had been in place for years.

The Sugar and Quartering Acts The passage of the Sugar Act in 1764 marked the start of a new British policy designed to raise more income from the colonies.The law actually cut the duty on foreign molasses in half. Grenville predicted that the lower tax would encourage Americans to buy imported molasses and pay the tax rather than risk smuggling (illegally importing) molasses, as they had been doing. The result, he hoped, would be increased tax collections.

To enforce this tax and others, Grenville issued a flurry of rules. Ship owners were told that their ships would be seized if they "forgot" to pay their duties. The British navy was ordered to patrol the American coast to further discourage smuggling.

Most upsetting to colonists was Grenville's requirement that smuggling cases be tried in British rather than colonial courts. Under British law, such cases were decided by a judge alone, not by a jury. In addition, the judge received a 5 percent commission on all illegal cargoes and fines. This encouraged judges to find accused smugglers guilty.

Another of Grenville's reforms was the Quartering Act, which Parliament passed in early 1765. This law required the colonies to provide housing and supplies for the British troops who remained in America after the French and Indian War.

Although colonists complained about these British changes, most went along with them. Opposition to the next step in Grenville's program was much stronger, however.

The Stamp Act Crisis

In March 1765 the British Parliament passed the **Stamp Act.** This law placed a tax on newspapers, pamphlets, legal documents, and most other printed materials. It required that an official government stamp be printed on or attached to these materials to show the tax had been paid. Grenville estimated that this tax would raise enough money to pay the cost of keeping British troops in America.

The Stamp Act marked the first time that the British government had taxed the colonists for the clear purpose of raising money. Of course, the Sugar Act was really a way to raise money, too. It, however, had been presented to the American colonists as a way to regulate trade rather than to raise money.

People in England had been paying a stamp tax since 1694. Yet, because the law represented such a radical change for the colonists, Grenville was cautious about introducing the tax. Before putting the law into effect he talked with agents of the colonies and gave them time to suggest alternatives. He also allowed the colonists to distribute the stamps themselves. Having taken these careful steps, Grenville was unprepared for the firestorm of protest that followed.

The Stamp Act Congress For a number of reasons, the reaction in the colonies against the Stamp Act was widespread and extreme. Most importantly, this measure touched almost all Americans in every colony. It was not like a trade measure, which might only apply to New England shippers or to southern tobacco growers, for example. In addition, the new law directly affected some of the most powerful people in the colonies—printers, merchants, and lawyers.

In October 1765, delegates from seven colonies met in New York to hold a meeting that became known as the Stamp Act Congress. Among them was the main organizer of the meeting, James Otis of Massachusetts. As early as 1761 Otis had claimed that Britain had no right to force laws on the colonies, because the colonists had no representatives in the British Parliament. In 1764 he had used the same "no taxation without representation" argument to protest the Sugar Act.

Otis and other delegates now made this argument again in petitions, or letters, they sent to the king and Parliament. In a series of resolutions they claimed that colonists should have the same rights and liberties that the people of Great Britain enjoyed. Some of the resolutions of the Stamp Act Congress read as follows:

Colonists who poured their tea from this pot bolstered their resistance to the Stamp Act.

Women's Boycott

Women played a central role in the movement to boycott British goods. Instead of tea, Patriot women served coffee and herbal brews. Refusing to buy British cotton, they dressed themselves and their families in homespun. At times women took more direct action. One Boston man described a "Female Riot" in which a large mob of women attacked a merchant who was overcharging for coffee, "and demanded the Keys to his Store, which he refusing to deliver, they immediately placed him in a Cart and threatened to Cart him out of Town."

Customize for
English Language Learners

Work with students to help them understand the Key Documents quotation on this page. Ask volunteers to provide definitions or synonyms of difficult terms. Once students are comfortable with the main ideas of the passage, have them make a simple outline of the three main points.

Answer to . . .

Interpreting Tables *To reassert its dominion over the colonies and to punish the colonies for resisting government acts.*

British Policies in the Colonies, 1764–1774

Date	British Action	Colonial Action
1764	**Sugar Act** Although it reduced the tax on imported foreign molasses, the law, unlike its predecessor the Molasses Act, was strictly enforced.	Colonists responded with written protests, occasional boycotts, and cries of "No taxation without representation!"
1765	**Stamp Act** The first direct taxation of colonists, the Stamp Act taxed legal and commercial documents and printed matter, such as newspapers.	Colonists protested violently. The Stamp Act Congress met and a boycott of British goods began.
	Quartering Act Following the French and Indian War, England maintained a standing army in the colonies. The Quartering Act required colonial assemblies to house and provision the British soldiers.	Most colonial legislatures refused to pay for supplies as required by the Quartering Act.
1766	**Declaratory Act** England repealed the Stamp Act in the face of colonial protest. To reassert its authority over the colonies it passed the Declaratory Act—a statement of England's right to rule the colonies in any way it saw fit.	Colonists were pleased with the repeal of the Stamp Act, but continued to protest other British-imposed laws, such as the Quartering Act.
1767	**Townshend Acts** Import taxes on lead, paper, tea, paint, and glass were collected at port. Revenue from the Townshend duties were used to support British troops, royal governors, and royal judges, taking the power of the purse away from colonial assemblies. The Townshend Acts also created a customs commission and suspended the New York assembly for failing to comply with the 1765 Quartering Act.	"Letters from a Farmer in Pennsylvania," a widely read series of letters protesting the act, were published in nine colonial newspapers. Colonists resumed boycotting British goods, cutting trade in half.
1773	**Tea Act** The Tea Act was created to save the ailing East India Company. It allowed the company to sell its surplus tea in the American colonies. The act retained the import tax on tea—the only remaining tax of the nearly defunct Townshend Acts.	A group of Boston patriots destroyed a shipment of tea in a protest known as the Boston Tea Party.
1774	**Intolerable Acts** Also called the Coercive Acts, this series of punitive acts targeted Massachusetts. The Port Bill closed Boston Harbor until Boston paid for the tea destroyed by the Boston Tea Party. Other acts nearly eliminated self-government in Massachusetts. New provisions to the Quartering Act required colonists to house British soldiers in private homes as necessary.	Delegates from twelve colonies met as the First Continental Congress. They created the Continental Association to boycott British goods. They also sent a petition to the king, outlining what they considered the rights of the colonists and their assemblies.

Interpreting Tables The years between 1764 and 1774 were beset with unrest in the American colonies. **Government** *Why did England continue to pass controversial acts in the face of colonial protest?*

KEY DOCUMENTS " II. That His Majesty's . . . subjects in these colonies are [entitled] to all the inherent rights and liberties of his natural born subjects within the kingdom of Great Britain.

III. That it is inseparably essential to the freedom of a people, and the undoubted right of Englishmen, that no taxes be imposed on them but with their own consent, given personally or by their representatives.

V. That the only representatives of the people of these colonies are persons chosen therein by themselves, and that no taxes ever have been, or can be constitutionally imposed on them, but by their respective legislatures. "

—*Declaration of Rights and Grievances*

The Sons of Liberty Americans did not protest the Stamp Act with words alone. Merchants and others organized a **boycott** of British goods. A boycott is a refusal to buy certain products or use certain services. Groups sprang up throughout the colonies to enforce

---

TEST PREPARATION

Have students read the excerpt from the Declaration of Rights and Grievances on this page and then answer the question below.

The word *inherent* in the passage means—

(A) essential and unquestionable.

B given by a government.

C equal.

D traditional.

the boycott and to organize other ways to resist British policies. The groups were known as the Sons of Liberty and the Daughters of Liberty.

Among the most active of these groups was the Boston Sons of Liberty. One of its founders was Samuel Adams. In August, members of the Sons of Liberty called on the person who distributed stamps in Boston. They warned him that unless he resigned "his House would be immediately Destroyed and his Life in Continual Danger." Several nights later a mob attacked the home of his brother-in-law, Thomas Hutchinson, who was lieutenant governor of the colony. After telling Hutchinson and his family to leave the house or be killed, the mob destroyed or carried off everything that was inside.

Throughout the colonies, other groups followed Boston's example. A New Jersey mob attacked the house of the colony's governor. Only the bravery of Deborah Franklin, the governor's wife, saved their home. She reported the event in a letter to her husband, who was away at the time:

AMERICAN VOICES ❝I ordered some sort of defense upstairs such as I could manage myself. I said when I was advised to remove [leave] that I was very sure you had done nothing to hurt anybody, . . . nor would I stir [move] or show the least uneasiness, but if anyone came to disturb me I would show a proper resentment.❞

—*Deborah Franklin*

By November 1765, when the Stamp Act was to take effect, most stamp distributors had resigned or fled, leaving no one to sell the stamps. In Britain, merchants also howled in protest as the colonists' boycott threatened their profitable trade with America. After Grenville was forced from power, Parliament repealed the Stamp Act in March 1766.

Rising Tensions in the Colonies

The colonists celebrated wildly when news arrived that the Stamp Act had been repealed. However, the larger issue had not gone away. Could Parliament tax the colonists without their being represented in that body? Few colonists paid much attention to the fact that Parliament had also addressed this issue. On the very day the Stamp Act was repealed, Parliament had passed the Declaratory Act. This measure stated that Parliament had the authority to make laws that applied to the colonists "in all cases whatsoever."

The Townshend Acts In 1767 Parliament reasserted its power by placing duties on certain imported goods, including glass and tea. These laws were named after the British government's chief financial officer, Charles Townshend. After the Stamp Act disaster, Townshend hoped to satisfy the colonists by raising money through duties rather than direct taxes. However, the Townshend Acts clearly stated that the money would be used for "the support of civil government" in the colonies.

The protests and violence began again. It made little difference, Americans said, whether Britain raised money through trade duties or direct taxes. Either way, the colonists were being taxed without their consent. And either way, Britain would use this money to pay the salaries of royal governors in America, who then would not have to turn to the colonial legislatures for their pay. This change would weaken the legislatures and undermine self-government in the colonies.

Pennsylvania lawyer John Dickinson warned that the Townshend Acts presented a choice between freedom and slavery:

AMERICAN VOICES ❝Countrymen, ROUSE yourselves, and behold the ruin hanging over your heads. . . . [If] parliament can legally take money out of our pockets, without our consent . . . our boasted liberty is but . . . a sound and nothing else.❞

—*John Dickinson*

Tea Imported from England, 1764–1775

Source: *Historical Statistics of the United States, Colonial Times to 1970*

Interpreting Graphs Compare the data in this graph with the table on page 92. *Economics How might this data reflect the success of colonial boycotts?*

 BACKGROUND

Townshend Acts

The goods on which the Townshend Acts placed small customs duties—including paper and paint—were valued imports from Britain. Chancellor of the Exchequer Charles Townshend insisted that the duties were merely regulations of trade and, he argued, the colonists had agreed such regulation was within Parliament's rights. But the colonists saw the acts for what they were: taxes to raise money for England, not duties to control trade. The Townshend Duties encouraged the colonists to manufacture goods themselves rather than import them from England. Suddenly it became more fashionable to use colonial-made goods than English luxury goods.

Customize for

More Advanced Students

Have students analyze the American colonists' growing resentment of British authority. Ask them to explain the words of John Dickinson when he said, "[If] Parliament can legally take money out of our pockets. . . our boasted liberty is but a sound and nothing else."

▶ **RESOURCE OPTIONS**

Teaching Resources

American History Block Scheduling Support To Arms! The Revolution Begins, found in the Forging a New Nation folder, includes interdisciplinary lesson suggestions and activities for Geography and History, Primary Sources, Biography, and Literature.

Answer to . . .

Interpreting Graphs The large dips in tea imports correspond to periods of colonial boycotts, showing them to be quite successful.

2 A mob, drawn by news of trouble, floods into the street from a nearby square.

3 Responding to a call for help, a British captain brings seven soldiers from headquarters.

4 Attacked by the mob, soldiers fire on citizens, killing five.

1 Boys throw ice at a sentry guarding the Customs House.

Paul Revere used the Boston Massacre to arouse anger toward the British. His engraving (left) shows the end result—troops firing on citizens—but omits the events leading up to the shooting (above). A handful of soldiers attacked by hundreds of angry citizens fired without orders; they and their commanding officer were charged with murder but were later acquitted. *Government Why had England sent troops to Boston?*

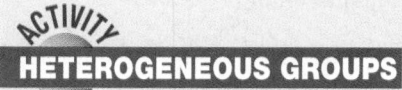

The boycott, which had proven so successful against the Stamp Act, was also renewed. Women pledged to weave their own cloth rather than buy cloth made in England. Many also boycotted British tea.

The Boston Massacre To put down violent resistance to the Townshend Acts, Britain sent troops to Boston, where officials feared a rebellion was at hand. A series of minor clashes occurred as the Sons of Liberty openly opposed the presence of these troops.

On the evening of March 5, 1770, an unruly crowd threatened a squad of British soldiers. The soldiers opened fire on the crowd, leaving an African American named Crispus Attucks and four other colonists dead or dying in the snow. The shooting added to an already tense situation. The incident became known as the **Boston Massacre.**

The next day a British officer and eight soldiers were arrested and charged with murder. Samuel Adams's cousin, John Adams, and another Boston lawyer agreed to defend them. John Adams was also a harsh critic of British policy. However, he believed the soldiers had a right to a fair trial. Seven of the accused were found not guilty, while two were convicted of lesser crimes. Their thumbs were branded as punishment and they were released.

Soon after the Boston Massacre, Parliament canceled the Townshend taxes. It kept only the duty on tea as a reminder of its authority over the colonies. With this move, the general boycott of British goods collapsed. Only the boycott of tea continued.

The colonies now entered a quiet period. Most Americans hoped the crisis had passed. Yet Samuel Adams and other Boston leaders continued to remind the colonists of British offenses. In 1772 Adams, James Otis, and other Bostonians formed a Committee of Correspondence to coordinate resistance throughout the colonies. By 1774 nearly all the colonies had such committees.

The Boston Tea Party The Committees of Correspondence were soon put into action. In May 1773, in a move to help the struggling British East India Company, Parliament passed the Tea Act. The law gave that company the right to sell its tea in America without paying the normal taxes. Colonists had been smuggling much of their tea in order to avoid paying these taxes. Now, however, the Tea Act would make the British East India Company's tea even less expensive than smuggled tea, thereby driving the American tea merchants out of business.

Colonists, especially tea merchants, protested. The British East India Company's sales agents in America were pressured to resign. When the tea began to arrive in November 1773, several colonial port cities refused to let the ships dock in their harbors. On the night of December 16, 1773, a group of colonists disguised as Indians boarded three tea ships in Boston. As a large crowd watched, they broke open every crate on board and threw the tea into the harbor.

The Intolerable Acts To punish Boston and all of Massachusetts, in the spring of 1774 Parliament passed a series of laws known as the Coercive Acts. Because the measures seemed so harsh, the colonists labeled them the Intolerable Acts. (See the Fact Finder chart earlier in this section.)

Another "intolerable" new law, though it was not part of the Coercive Acts, extended Canada's boundary south to the Ohio River. This action stripped Massachusetts, Connecticut, and Virginia of their claims to western lands. In addition, General Thomas Gage, the commander of British forces in America, was named the new governor of Massachusetts. Committees of Correspondence in several colonies called for a meeting to plan a united response to these developments. This gathering became known as the **First Continental Congress.**

Tea chests were lined with lead to make them water-tight. Patriots at the Boston Tea Party (above) hacked open each chest to make sure every last tea leaf was destroyed. *Economics Why did the colonists want to prevent the tea from landing?*

The First Continental Congress On September 5, 1774, a gathering of 56 delegates met at Carpenter's Hall in Philadelphia. Delegates came from every colony but Georgia, and they had a wide range of viewpoints. George Washington from Virginia was a leading figure, as were Patrick Henry and Richard Henry Lee. Samuel Adams was the most rebellious of the delegates. Among those with moderate points of view were John Dickinson of Delaware and New York's John Jay.

Main Idea
CONNECTIONS

Describe some of the ways the colonists protested British taxes.

The First Continental Congress adopted a number of measures. Among these were a renewed boycott and a call to the people of all the English colonies to arm themselves and form militias. At the same time, the delegates made a direct appeal to the king, outlining their grievances and asking for understanding:

KEY DOCUMENTS "The foundation of English liberty, and of all free government, is a right of the people to participate in their legislative council: and as the English colonists are not represented, and . . . cannot properly be represented in the British parliament, they are entitled to a free and exclusive power of legislation in their several provincial legislatures, where their right of representation can alone be preserved."

—*Declaration and Resolves of the First Continental Congress*

From the Archives of

American Heritage

The *Gaspée* Incident On June 9, 1772, the British revenue schooner *Gaspee* ran aground in Rhode Island's Narragansett Bay while chasing a suspected smuggler. Word quickly spread among the merchants, sailors, and smugglers of nearby Providence, who, like all Rhode Islanders, hated anything to do with duties and tariffs. That evening John Brown, a wealthy merchant, rounded up about a hundred men. Shortly after midnight they piled into longboats and rowed out to the *Gaspée*. The Providence men boarded the ship and set it on fire. When the king decreed that anyone implicated in the attack would be taken to Britain for trial, rage over this violation of the right to a trial by one's peers spread through all the colonies. In March 1773, Virginia's House of Burgesses, angered at the flagrant attack upon "American liberty" established the first Committee of Correspondence. Similar committees sprang up in the other colonies to circulate information and coordinate responses. The *Gaspée* incident brought America another step closer to open revolt.
Source: Frederic D. Schwarz, "The Time Machine," *American Heritage* magazine, May/June 1997.

Answer to . . .

Viewing History To protest the Tea Act and prevent the British East India Company from selling tea in the colonies.
Main Idea Connections Petitions, boycotts, forming militias.

On October 26 the Congress ended, though its members vowed to meet again in the spring if the crisis was not resolved. However, George III remained stubborn and firm. On November 18 he wrote, "The New England colonies are in a state of rebellion, blows must decide."

Fighting at Lexington and Concord

The Americans that King George had labeled "rebels" (they preferred to call themselves *Patriots*) followed the advice of the First Continental Congress. Massachusetts Patriots formed militias and began to gather guns and ammunition. A major stockpile of weapons was stored in Concord, a town about 20 miles from Boston.

Late at night on April 18, 1775, a force of about 700 British troops moved out of Boston and marched toward Concord with orders to seize these supplies. The plan was supposed to be secret. However, Boston Patriots learned of it and sent Paul Revere, William Dawes, and Dr. Samuel Prescott on horseback through the countryside aiming to get the news to Patriot leaders. Revere arrived in Lexington, about five miles from Concord, near midnight. Samuel Adams and John Hancock were there, and Revere warned them that the British soldiers were coming.

The main British force reached Lexington at about dawn on April 19. There they encountered 70 armed militia, known as minutemen, blocking their path on the village green. "Throw down your arms and you shall come to no harm," the British commander ordered. The colonists began to obey. Then someone fired a shot, though to this day no one knows for sure who it was. The troops fired a volley into the militia. Within minutes eight Americans lay dead on the green and another ten were wounded.

The British marched on to Concord, where they burned the militia's stockpile of supplies. As the troops returned to Boston, some 4,000 Patriots gathered along the road to shoot at them from behind trees and stone walls. When the **Battles of Lexington and Concord** were over, what had seemed an easy British victory at dawn had turned into an exhausting and costly defeat. More than 70 British soldiers were killed and over 170 wounded before the force reached the safety of Boston. The **Revolutionary War,** which would last until 1783, had begun.

Just days before this fateful clash, Patrick Henry had warned his fellow Virginians to prepare for what was soon to come:

AMERICAN VOICES "Gentlemen may cry, 'Peace! Peace!'—but there is no peace. . . . The next gale that sweeps from the north will bring to our ears the clash of resounding arms! . . . Is life so dear, or peace so sweet, as to be purchased at the price of chains and slavery? Forbid it, Almighty God! I know not what course others may take; but as for me, give me liberty or give me death!"

—*Patrick Henry*

SECTION 2 REVIEW

Comprehension

1. *Key Terms* Define: (a) Pontiac's Rebellion; (b) Proclamation of 1763; (c) Stamp Act; (d) boycott; (e) Boston Massacre; (f) First Continental Congress; (g) Battles of Lexington and Concord; (h) Revolutionary War.

2. *Summarizing the Main Idea* Why did the colonists protest new British taxes, and in what ways did they protest?

3. *Organizing Information* Create a graphic organizer showing the causes and effects of the Stamp Act.

Critical Thinking

4. *Analyzing Time Lines* Review the time line at the start of the section. How was the fighting at Lexington and Concord related to the First Continental Congress?

5. *Identifying Alternatives* Why did Britain change its colonial policies after 1763? What alternative policies, if any, might Britain have adopted?

Writing Activity

6. *Writing a Persuasive Essay* Write a newspaper article encouraging colonists to boycott English tea. Be sure to include reasons for supporting the boycott.

Critical Thinking

Geography

Graphs and Charts

Historical Evidence

Expressing Problems Clearly

The ability to express a problem clearly means being able to describe the nature of a situation or a question that is difficult, puzzling, or open to debate. When you express a problem clearly, you are taking the first step toward understanding and solving it.

Following Parliament's passage of the Stamp Act in 1765, articles like those excerpted on this page appeared in American and British newspapers.

Use the following steps to practice expressing problems clearly.

1. Analyze the information. When you are confronted with a problem, study the information involved. Read excerpts A and B. (a) What was the nature of the case made by the American colonist in excerpt A? (b) What information was given by the British writer in excerpt B?

2. Identify the basic concepts involved. Problems usually arise out of a specific set of circumstances. However, they often revolve around a general principle, such as fairness. To identify this concept, try to express the problem in terms of what each side wants for itself. (a) What benefit did the American writer want to achieve for the colonists? (b) What did the British writer want?

3. Identify the function of the supporting details. In any problem, details often are presented that may not be basic to the problem itself. (a) The British writer characterizes the colonists'

opposition to an act of Parliament as "an alarming crisis." Is this a basic part of the problem? Why or why not? (b) What other details in these excerpts did not relate to the basic issue of disagreement?

4. Express the problem clearly. Now that you have identified the main area of dispute and stripped away irrelevant details, you are ready to express the problem clearly. How would you describe the dispute between the British supporters of the Stamp Act and its American opponents?

TEST FOR SUCCESS

Why did John Adams consider the Stamp Act to be unconstitutional?

A *"In all the calamities which have ever befallen this country, we have never felt so great a concern, or such alarming apprehensions, as on this occasion. . . . We [find] this tax to be unconstitutional. We have always understood it to be a grand and fundamental principle of the [British] constitution, that no freeman should be subject to any tax to which he has not given his own consent, in person or by proxy [representation]. And . . . that no freeman can be separated from his property but by his own act or fault. We take it clearly, therefore, to be inconsistent with the spirit of the . . . principles of the British constitution, that we should be subject to any tax imposed by the British Parliament; because we are not represented in that assembly in any sense, unless it be by a fiction of law."*

John Adams, *Instructions of the Town of Braintree Massachusetts on the Stamp Act*, October 14, 1765

B *"The question now is, Whether those American subjects are, or are not, bound by the resolutions of a British parliament? If they are not, they are entirely a separate people from us. On the other hand, if the people of America are bound by the proceedings of the English legislature, . . . [then] the present crisis . . . is really an alarming one. The people of the colonies know very well that the taxes of the Mother country are every day increasing; and can they expect that no addition whatsoever will be made to theirs? . . . In assisting the colonies we had an eye to our own interest. It would be ridiculous otherwise to squander away our blood and our treasure in their defense. But surely the benefit was mutual; and consequently the disadvantage [of taxes] should be mutual too."*

"William Pym" to the *London General Evening Post*, August 20, 1765, reprinted in the *Newport Mercury*, October 28, 1765

RESOURCE OPTIONS

Teaching Resources

📁 **Skills for Life Activity** Units 1–2 folder, p. 56, gives students practice expressing problems clearly by analyzing excerpts from contemporary colonial and British newspapers.

Media and Technology

Color Transparencies Critical Thinking, I-1

Ideas Behind the Revolution

Objectives

You may wish to call students' attention to the objectives in the Section Preview. The objectives are reflected in the main headings of the section.

Bellringer

Write the word *idealistic* on the chalkboard. Ask students to briefly define the word and list some attributes of an idealistic person.

Reading Strategy

Organizing Information Refer to the Reading Strategy in the Section Preview. Model by creating a graphic organizer on the chalkboard.

LESSON PLAN

Connecting to the Main Idea

1. Focus Tell students that the War for Independence was fueled by more than British actions. Powerful new ideas inspired Americans to challenge authority in hopes of creating a different kind of society. Ask students what these new ideas were.

2. Instruct Have students discuss the war in terms of the ideas of Thomas Paine and Thomas Jefferson. Why might these men be considered idealists? You might want to refer to the attributes students listed in the Bellringer activity. Discuss how the ideas that fueled the War for Independence also helped create a new society. Ask why *Common Sense* was important to the development of democracy.

3. Close The beliefs that people were born equal and could rule themselves took a passionate hold on colonial thinking. The ideals of equality and liberty for all people encouraged Americans to rebel against Great Britain in the hope of creating a new society.

1775 Second Continental Congress	1775 Olive Branch Petition	1776 Common Sense published	1776 Declaration of Independence

1774   **1775**   **1776**

3 Ideas Behind the Revolution

SECTION PREVIEW

Objectives

1. Describe the importance of Thomas Paine's *Common Sense*.
2. Identify the four parts of the Declaration of Independence.
3. *Key Terms* Define: *Common Sense;* Second Continental Congress; Olive Branch Petition; Declaration of Independence; Enlightenment; natural rights.

Main Idea

New ideas about equality and self-government contributed to the outbreak of the American Revolution.

Reading Strategy

Organizing Information Create a graphic organizer describing the four parts of the Declaration of Independence.

The American Revolution really took place on two levels. At one level it was a struggle for power between the American colonists and Great Britain over the question of who would rule them. The winner of this struggle was decided on the battlefield. The other level on which the Revolution took place was the level of ideas. The colonists were rethinking the proper role of citizens, government, and the relationship between the two. It was during the Revolution, and the years leading up to it, that Americans learned to demand that government respect citizens' rights.

Common Sense

One important document that expressed both levels of the Revolution was **Common Sense,** a 47-page pamphlet written by Thomas Paine. *Common Sense* first appeared in Philadelphia in January 1776. Paine's direct writing style suggested that anyone could understand the conflict between Great Britain and the colonies. To simplify his writing Paine avoided the references to Greek and Latin literature that were common at the time:

Main Idea CONNECTIONS

How did Common Sense *contribute to the outbreak of the Revolution?*

KEY DOCUMENTS "The period of debate is closed. Arms as the last resource decide the contest. . . . Every thing that is right or reasonable pleads for separation. The blood of the slain, the weeping voice of nature cries, 'TIS TIME TO PART."

—Common Sense, *1776*

Within a year some 500,000 copies of *Common Sense* were sold. The pamphlet convinced many readers, including those who had favored a peaceful settlement of differences with the British government, to support a complete break with Britain instead.

Turning Point: The Declaration of Independence

Common Sense appeared at a time when the **Second Continental Congress** was meeting in Philadelphia. The Congress had first gathered in May 1775, less than a month after British troops and colonial militia clashed at Lexington and Concord. Most of the delegates to the First Continental Congress returned for the meeting. However, there were some important newcomers. Among the

▶ RESOURCE OPTIONS

Teaching Resources

📁 **Reproducible Lesson Plan** Lesson Plans folder, p. 48

📁 **Learning Styles Lesson Plan** Learning Styles Lesson Plans folder, p. 10

📁 **Big Idea Graphic Organizer** Big Idea Graphic Organizer folder, p. 20

📁 **Guided Reading and Review** Units 1–2 folder, p. 46

new faces were Benjamin Franklin of Pennsylvania and John Hancock of Massachusetts. In June another new delegate, Thomas Jefferson, arrived from Virginia.

At first the delegates, like the American people, were deeply divided. Members such as Samuel Adams, John Adams, Patrick Henry, and Richard Henry Lee leaned toward independence. Moderates, led by John Dickinson, favored seeking some compromise with Britain that would increase colonial self-rule.

In November 1775, the Congress learned that George III had refused the **Olive Branch Petition.** Written by Dickinson, the document had expressed the colonists' continued loyalty to the monarch and their desire for peace. It begged the king to halt the fighting until a solution could be found.

Drafting a Declaration In June 1776, after more than a year of war, the Congress decided it was time for the colonies to cut their ties with Britain. The Congress appointed a committee to prepare a statement of the reasons for the separation—a **Declaration of Independence.** (See the full text of the Declaration on the pages following this section.) Members of the committee were lawyer and planter Thomas Jefferson; Boston lawyer John Adams; Roger Sherman, a judge from Connecticut; Robert Livingston, the lawyer son of a wealthy New York family; and the well-known Benjamin Franklin. The committee chose Jefferson to draft the statement.

Jefferson's political ideas were influenced by the **Enlightenment,** an 18th-century movement that emphasized science and reason as key to improving society. He also drew ideas from earlier political thinkers, such as John Locke. In this Englishman's writing, Jefferson found support for revolution. Locke wrote:

KEY DOCUMENTS
"Governments are dissolved . . . when such a single person or prince sets up his own arbitrary will in place of the laws. . . . Secondly, when the prince hinders the legislative [legislature] from . . . acting freely. . . . Thirdly, when by the arbitrary power of the prince, the electors, or ways of election are altered, without the consent, and contrary to the common interest of the people.**"**

—*John Locke,*
Second Treatise of Government, *1689*

 TURNING POINT : *The Declaration of Independence*

The Declaration of Independence states that governments derive their power from "the consent of the governed." As the time line below indicates, the right of the people to vote has been steadily broadened.

1776
The Declaration of Independence is signed.

1870
The Fifteenth Amendment grants African American males the right to vote.

1965
The Voting Rights Act of 1965 protects the voting rights of African Americans.

1971
The Twenty-sixth Amendment lowers the voting age to 18.

1800   1900   2000

1818
Constitutions of new western states, unlike earlier state constitutions, do not limit the vote to owners of property.

1920
The Nineteenth Amendment grants women the right to vote.

RESOURCE OPTIONS

Teaching Resources

 Literature Activity To the King, Units 1–2 folder, p. 55

Key Documents Patrick Henry, Speech to the Virginia Provincial Convention, Learning with Documents folder, p. 81

Media and Technology

 RESOURCE PRO

Literature Activity *Common Sense,* found on Resource Pro, uses excerpts from Thomas Paine's famous pamphlet to enhance students' understanding of the pro-independence faction's arguments.

The Foundations of Democracy

Ancient Greece (c. 500 B.C.)	Democratic government originated in ancient Greek city-states 2,500 years ago. The word *democracy* comes from the Greek words *demos*, "the people," and *kratein*, "to rule."
Magna Carta (1215)	In 1215, English barons forced King John to sign a charter guaranteeing certain civil and political freedoms. Over time, these protections became the rights of all English people.
The Petition of Right (1626)	In 1626, the English Parliament forced Charles I to sign the Petition of Right, a document that limited the power of the monarchy. It included protections against (1) imprisonment without jury trial, (2) the institution of martial law during peacetime, (3) the mandatory quartering of troops, and (4) taxation without the permission of Parliament.
English Bill of Rights (1689)	This document forbade the crown from suspending or passing laws and from raising taxes without Parliament's consent, guaranteed the right to a fair and speedy trial, and forbade cruel and unusual punishment.
Social Contract Theory (1651)	Philosopher Thomas Hobbes described the relationship between the state and the governed as a social contract. Individuals surrendered their will to the state, which saved the people from anarchy.
Natural Rights (1690)	Political philosopher John Locke put forth an opposing view of the social contract. Locke maintained that the state exists to preserve the natural rights of its citizens—the right to life, liberty, and property. If the government fails in its duty to the citizens, the citizens then have the right to resist or rebel against that government.

Interpreting Tables Democracy has evolved into a delicate balance between the rights of individuals and the need for social order. *Government How are limits on government power a part of that balancing act?*

The Parts of the Declaration Jefferson divided the Declaration of Independence into four sections: an introduction, a declaration of rights, a list of complaints against the king, and a resolution of independence.

1. In the introduction, or preamble, Jefferson explained the purpose of the Declaration.

2. In the second section, Jefferson explained the political ideas on which the document was based. Here is where he drew most heavily on the writings of John Locke. Locke believed that people had **natural rights**— rights which belonged to them simply because they were human, not because kings or governments had granted them these rights. Jefferson used the expression "inalienable rights"—meaning, rights that could not be taken away. Then he listed some of them: "Life, Liberty, and the pursuit of happiness."

According to Locke's theory, people formed governments to protect their natural rights. If a government failed to act in the best interests of the people it governed, then the people had the right to revolt and replace the government with a new one.

3. Following the statement on rights was a third section that laid out a long list of wrongs the colonists believed had been committed by the British king. "The history of the present King of Great Britain is a history of repeated injuries," Jefferson wrote, "all having in direct object the establishment of an absolute Tyranny."

4. Jefferson concluded the Declaration with a fourth section, titled "Resolution of Independence by the United States." In it he wrote, "these United Colonies are . . . and of Right ought to be Free and Independent States."

The Declaration Is Adopted On July 4, the date now celebrated as Independence Day, delegates joined in voting to approve the Declaration. Jefferson's document did much more than declare a nation's independence, however. It also defined the basic principles on which American government and society would rest. The United States would be a nation in which ordinary citizens would have a strong voice in their own government.

Abigail Adams

AMERICAN BIOGRAPHY Abigail Smith, born on November 22, 1744, grew up in a Massachusetts household. Her youth was a comfortable one. Shortly before her twentieth

Abigail Adams (1744–1818)

birthday, Abigail married 29-year-old John Adams. She entered her husband's family and, following the laws and customs of the time, she became subject to his authority.

In the 1770s, as John Adams became one of the leaders of the opposition to British rule, Abigail remained shut off from public debate because she was a woman. However, she did not hesitate to express her opinions to her husband. Several weeks before John was named to the committee to write the Declaration of Independence, Abigail sent him a letter in Philadelphia, where he was attending the Continental Congress:

 AMERICAN VOICES "I long to hear that you have declared an independency— and by the way in the new Code of Laws which I suppose it will be necessary for you to make I desire you would Remember the Ladies, and be more generous and favorable to them than your ancestors. Do not put unlimited power into the hands of the Husbands. Remember all Men would be tyrants if they could. If particular care and attention is not paid to the Ladies we are determined to foment [stir up] a rebellion, and will not hold ourselves bound by any Laws in which we have no voice, or Representation."

—*Abigail Adams, March 31, 1776*

Some of Abigail's comments were intended to tease John. She was serious, however, in her complaints about the status of women in American society. She employed the very ideas that men were using against Britain to suggest that it was time to rethink the relationship between men and women.

COMPARING PRIMARY SOURCES

RULE BY THE PEOPLE

In trying to decide whether or not to declare independence, colonists debated whether people were capable of ruling themselves.

For Rule by the People	Against Rule by the People
"The American Congress derives all its power, wisdom, and justice, not from scrolls of parchment signed by kings but from the people. A more august [respectable] and a more equitable legislative body never existed in any quarter of the globe."	"Suppose we were to revolt from Great Britain, declare ourselves independent, and set up a republic of our own—what would be the consequence? I stand aghast at the prospect; my blood runs chill when I think of the calamities."
—*Anonymous newspaper editorial, November 14, 1774*	—*Rev. Charles Inglis*, The True Interest of America, *1776*

ANALYZING VIEWPOINTS **What are the assumptions behind each writer's statement?**

John did not attempt to follow through on Abigail's request. However, the two had an affectionate relationship and truly respected each other. The humor and friendship that can be seen in their letters remained a part of their marriage through bad times and good, until her death in 1818. Together they weathered the Revolution and eventually became the first presidential couple to live in the White House.

SECTION 3 REVIEW

Comprehension

1. **Key Terms** Define: (a) *Common Sense;* (b) Second Continental Congress; (c) Olive Branch Petition; (d) Declaration of Independence; (e) Enlightenment; (f) natural rights.

2. **Summarizing the Main Idea** Describe some of the political ideas that influenced the outbreak of the American Revolution.

3. **Organizing Information** Make a list of reasons why Thomas Paine's pamphlet, *Common Sense*, was so important.

Critical Thinking

4. **Analyzing Time Lines** Review the time line at the start of the section. How did the king's rejection of the Olive Branch Petition contribute to the Declaration of Independence?

5. **Making Comparisons** Compare and contrast Thomas Paine's *Common Sense* with the Declaration of Independence.

Writing Activity

6. **Writing an Expository Essay** Write an essay in which you explain the four parts of the Declaration of Independence.

THE DECLARATION OF Independence

THE DECLARATION OF Independence

DECLARATION OF INDEPENDENCE

Focus Write the following quotation on the chalkboard: "We must all hang together, or assuredly we shall all hang separately." Explain that Benjamin Franklin spoke these words at the signing of the Declaration of Independence. Ask students what they think Franklin meant.

Instruct Explain how the ideals that inspired the American Revolution are embodied in the Declaration of Independence. Have students read the first paragraph of the Declaration and explain its purpose. Why was the Declaration such a revolutionary document in its time? How does it define the basic principles upon which American society is based? Ask a volunteer to read from "We hold these truths to be self-evident" to ". . . effect their safety and happiness." Discuss why this section forms the heart of the Declaration.

Close The Declaration describes the basic rights on which the nation was founded, the wrongs committed by Britain, and the colonists' intentions to cut ties with Britain. The men who signed it made a brave commitment to pursue revolutionary ideals regarding human rights.

In Congress, July 4, 1776

THE UNANIMOUS DECLARATION OF THE THIRTEEN UNITED STATES OF AMERICA,

When in the Course of human events, it becomes necessary for one people to dissolve the political bands which have connected them with another, and to assume among the Powers of the earth, the separate and equal station to which the Laws of Nature and of Nature's God entitle them, a decent respect to the opinions of mankind requires that they should declare the causes which impel them to the separation.

We hold these truths to be self-evident, that all men are created equal, that they are endowed by their Creator with certain unalienable Rights, that among these are Life, Liberty and the pursuit of Happiness. That to secure these rights, Governments are instituted among Men, deriving their just powers from the consent of the governed, That whenever any Form of Government becomes destructive of these ends, it is the Right of the People to alter or to abolish it, and to institute new Government, laying its foundation on such principles and organizing its powers in such form, as to them shall seem most likely to effect their Safety and Happiness. Prudence, indeed, will dictate that Governments long established should not be changed for light and transient causes; and accordingly all experience hath shown, that mankind are more disposed to suffer, while evils are sufferable, than to right themselves by abolishing the forms to which they are accustomed. But when a long train of abuses and usurpations, pursuing invariably the same Object evinces a design to reduce them under absolute Despotism, it is their right, it is their duty, to throw off such Government, and to provide new Guards for their future security.—Such has been the patient sufferance of these Colonies; and such is now the necessity which constrains them to alter their former Systems of Government. The history of the present King of Great Britain is a history of repeated injuries and usurpations, all having in direct object the establishment of an absolute Tyranny over these States. To prove this, let Facts be submitted to a candid world.

He has refused his Assent to Laws, the most wholesome and necessary for the public good.

He has forbidden his Governors to pass Laws of immediate and pressing importance, unless suspended in their operation till his Assent should be obtained; and when so suspended, he has utterly neglected to attend to them.

He has refused to pass other Laws for the accommodation of large districts of people, unless those people would relinquish the right of Representation in the Legislature, a right inestimable to them and formidable to tyrants only.

 RESOURCE OPTIONS

Teaching Resources

 Comparing Primary Sources On Rule by the People, Units 1–2 folder, pp. 53–54

He has called together legislative bodies at places unusual, uncomfortable, and distant from the depository of their Public Records, for the sole purpose of fatiguing them into compliance with his measures.

He has dissolved Representative Houses repeatedly, for opposing with manly firmness his invasions on the rights of the people.

He has refused for a long time, after such dissolutions, to cause others to be elected; whereby the Legislative powers, incapable of Annihilation, have returned to the People at large for their exercise; the State remaining in the mean time exposed to all the dangers of invasions from without, and convulsions within.

He has endeavored to prevent the population of these States; for that purpose obstructing the Laws for Naturalization of Foreigners; refusing to pass others to encourage their migration hither, and raising the conditions of new Appropriations of Lands.

He has obstructed the Administration of Justice, by refusing his Assent to Laws for establishing Judiciary powers.

He has made Judges dependent on his Will alone for the tenure of their offices, and the amount and payment of their salaries.

He has erected a multitude of New Offices, and sent hither swarms of Officers to harass our people and eat out their substance.

He has kept among us in time of peace, Standing Armies, without the Consent of our legislature.

He has affected to render the Military independent of and superior to the Civil power.

He has combined with others to subject us to a jurisdiction foreign to our constitutions, and unacknowledged by our laws; giving his Assent to their Acts of pretended Legislation:

For Quartering large bodies of armed troops among us:

For protecting them, by a mock Trial, from Punishment for any Murders which they should commit on the Inhabitants of these States:

For cutting off our Trade with all parts of the world:

For imposing Taxes on us without our Consent:

For depriving us in many cases, of the benefits of Trial by Jury:

For transporting us beyond Seas to be tried for pretended offenses:

For abolishing the free System of English Laws in a neighbouring Province, establishing therein an Arbitrary government, and enlarging its Boundaries so as to render it at once an example and fit instrument for introducing the same absolute rule into these Colonies:

For taking away our Charters, abolishing our most valuable Laws, and altering fundamentally the Forms of our Governments;

For suspending our own Legislature, and declaring themselves invested with Power to legislate for us in all cases whatsoever.

He has abdicated Government here, by declaring us out of his Protection, and waging War against us.

He has plundered our seas, ravaged our Coasts, burned our towns, and destroyed the lives of our people.

He is at this time transporting large Armies of foreign mercenaries to compleat the works of death, desolation and tyranny, already begun with circumstances of Cruelty and perfidy scarcely paralleled in the most barbarous ages, and totally unworthy the Head of a civilized nation.

He has constrained our fellow Citizens taken Captive on the high Seas to bear Arms against their Country, to become the executioners of their friends and Brethren, or to fall themselves by their Hands.

DECLARATION OF INDEPENDENCE

Customize for
More Advanced Students

Have students research the ideas of John Locke and the English tradition of government. Then ask students to correlate these ideas with specific ideas in the Declaration. They may present the results of their project in essay or chart form.

Customize for
English Language Learners

Ask students to make a list of sentences from the Declaration that they find challenging. Have them work together to restate the sentences in their own words.

Customize for
Less Proficient Readers

Have students draw cartoons representing main ideas from the Declaration. Have them share their cartoons with the class and explain their meaning. You may want to collect their cartoons in a class political cartoon booklet.

RESOURCE OPTIONS

Media and Technology

 AmericanHeritage® CD-ROM

Time Tour From Revolution to Republic: The American Revolution (*Independence Declared*)

Library Declaration of Independence

 Prentice Hall United States History Video Collection™ Volume 4 *The American Revolution*

Have students suppose that they are television or newspaper commentators on the day of the signing of the Declaration of Independence. Have small groups write a short commentary explaining the importance of the event, where the ideas of the Declaration came from, and what is likely to happen next. Groups may place newspaper articles on a class bulletin board or appoint a TV anchorperson to report the event to the class. (*Reteaching*)

DECLARATION OF INDEPENDENCE

He has excited domestic insurrections amongst us, and has endeavored to bring on the inhabitants of our frontiers the merciless Indian Savages, whose known rule of warfare, is an undistinguished destruction of all ages, sexes, and conditions.

In every stage of these Oppressions We have Petitioned for Redress in the most humble terms. Our repeated Petitions have been answered only by repeated injury. A Prince, whose character is thus marked by every act which may define a Tyrant, is unfit to be the ruler of a free People.

Nor have We been wanting in attentions to our British brethren. We have warned them from time to time of attempts by their legislature to extend an unwarrantable jurisdiction over us. We have reminded them of the circumstances of our emigration and settlement here. We have appealed to their native justice and magnanimity, and we have conjured them by the ties of our common kindred to disavow these usurpations, which, would inevitably interrupt our connections and correspondence. They too have been deaf to the voice of Justice and of consanguinity. We must, therefore, acquiesce in the necessity, which denounces our Separation, and hold them, as we hold the rest of mankind, Enemies in War, in Peace Friends.

We, therefore, the Representatives of the United States of America, in General Congress, Assembled, appealing to the Supreme Judge of the world for the rectitude of our intentions, do, in the Name, and by the Authority of the good People of these Colonies, solemnly publish and declare, That these United Colonies are, and of Right ought to be Free and Independent States; that they are Absolved from all Allegiance to the British Crown, and that all political connection between them and the State of Great Britain, is and ought to be totally dissolved, and that as Free and Independent States, they have full Power to levy War, conclude Peace, contract Alliances, establish Commerce, and to do all other Acts and Things which Independent States may of right do. And for the support of this Declaration, with a firm reliance on the protection of Divine Providence, we mutually pledge to each other our Lives, our Fortunes and our sacred Honor.

JOHN HANCOCK
President of the Continental Congress 1775–1777

NEW HAMPSHIRE
Josiah Bartlett
William Whipple
Matthew Thornton
MASSACHUSETTS BAY
Samuel Adams
John Adams
Robert Treat Paine
Elbridge Gerry
RHODE ISLAND
Stephen Hopkins
William Ellery
CONNECTICUT
Roger Sherman
Samuel Huntington
William Williams
Oliver Wolcott
NEW YORK
William Floyd

NEW JERSEY
Richard Stockton
John Witherspoon
Francis Hopkinson
John Hart
Abraham Clark
DELAWARE
Caesar Rodney
George Read
Thomas McKean
MARYLAND
Samuel Chase
William Paca
Thomas Stone
Charles Carroll
of Carrollton

VIRGINIA
George Wythe
Richard Henry Lee
Thomas Jefferson
Benjamin Harrison
Thomas Nelson, Jr.
Francis Lightfoot Lee
Carter Braxton
PENNSYLVANIA
Robert Morris
Benjamin Rush
Benjamin Franklin
John Morton
George Clymer
James Smith
George Taylor
James Wilson
George Ross
NORTH CAROLINA

SOUTH CAROLINA
Edward Rutledge
Thomas Heyward, Jr.
Thomas Lynch, Jr.
Arthur Middleton
GEORGIA
Button Gwinnett
Lyman Hall
George Walton

Using the Internet

Write a Letter

Objective Use the Internet to create a letter from one of the signers of the Declaration to his family at home. Have students follow these instructions:

1. Access *America: Pathways to the Present* Web site at **http://www.Pathways.phschool.com** for the URL to complete the activity.

2. Use links to research information on the signers of the Declaration of Independence.

3. Choose a signer of the Declaration and write a letter from his point of view. Include information about why the signer chose to sign the Declaration, how he felt the day of the signing, the mood of the other signers, and his thoughts about the risks he is taking by signing and about the future of the colonies.

Reviewing the Declaration

VOCABULARY

Choose ten words in the Declaration with which you are unfamiliar. Look them up in the dictionary. Then, on a piece of paper, copy the sentence in the Declaration in which each unfamiliar word is used, and after the sentence write the definition of the unfamiliar word.

COMPREHENSION

1. Which truths in the second paragraph are "self-evident"?

2. Name the three unalienable rights listed in the Declaration.

3. From what source do governments derive their "just powers"?

4. What right do people have when their government becomes destructive?

5. In the series of paragraphs beginning, "He has refused his Assent," to whom does the word "He" refer?

6. Which phrase in the Declaration expresses the colonists' opposition to taxation without representation?

7. According to the Declaration, what powers does the United States have "as Free and Independent States"?

8. List the colonies that the signers of the Declaration represented.

CRITICAL THINKING

1. *Cause and Effect* Why do you think the colonists were unhappy with the fact that their judges' salaries were paid by the king?

2. *Drawing Conclusions* As Section 3 of this chapter explains, the Declaration was divided into four parts. Write down the first phrase of each of those four parts.

3. *Identifying Assumptions* Do you think that the statement "all men are created equal" was intended to apply to all human beings? Explain your reasoning.

4. *Recognizing Bias* What reference do you see to Native Americans? What attitudes toward Native Americans does this express?

5. *Drawing Conclusions* What evidence is there that the colonists had already unsuccessfully voiced concerns to the King?

ISSUES PAST AND PRESENT

1. Write a letter to the Continental Congress from the perspective of a woman or an African American who has just read the Declaration in 1776. In your letter, comment on the Declaration's statement that "all men are created equal" and also express your attitude toward American independence.

2. What evidence in the Declaration is there of religious faith? How do you think this religious faith influenced the ideals expressed in the Declaration?

3. Examine the unalienable rights of individuals as stated in the Declaration. Do you think these rights are upheld today? Give examples to support your answer.

ANALYZING POLITICAL CARTOONS

1. This cartoon was published in 1779.
(a) Read the caption and identify the horse.
(b) Who is the master being thrown? (c) How do you know?

2. Examine the figure on the horse. (a) What is he holding? (b) What does it represent?

3. What is the cartoonist's overall message?

THE HORSE AMERICA, *throwing his Master.*

Issues Past and Present

1. Answers will vary. Women may discuss the use of "men" in the quote. An African American might read "all men are created equal" and hope that American independence would bring freedom.
2. It asserts that the right to life, liberty, and the pursuit of happiness comes from God. The signatories put their trust in "the protection of Divine Providence."
3. Answers may mention current issues such as censorship, children's rights, religion, gun control, abortion, or the death penalty.

Analyzing Political Cartoons

1. (a) America (b) King George (c) Britain was America's master, and the rider is dressed like King George.
2. (a) A whip made of swords, bayonets and axes. (b) The British Army.
3. Because Britain used force to control the colonies, Americans became angry and tried to throw off British control.

Vocabulary

Answers should reflect an understanding of the words selected.

Comprehension

1. That all men are created equal, and all are endowed by their Creator with certain rights.
2. Life, liberty, and the pursuit of happiness.
3. The consent of the governed.
4. The people may change or abolish the government.
5. King George III.
6. "imposing taxes on us without our consent."
7. Powers to declare war, conclude peace, contract alliances, and establish commerce.
8. New Hampshire, Massachusetts Bay, Rhode Island, Connecticut, New York, New Jersey, Delaware, Maryland, Virginia, Pennsylvania, North Carolina, South Carolina, and Georgia.

Critical Thinking

1. Judges were likely to favor the king over the colonists in court.
2. "When in the Course of human events"; "We hold these truths to be self-evident"; "The history of the present King of Great Britain is a history of repeated injuries and usurpations"; "We, therefore, the Representatives of the United States of America."
3. No. Many of the signers, including Thomas Jefferson, owned slaves and were unwilling to extend these basic rights to African Americans. Laws limited the rights of women and Native Americans, who were denied the right to live and govern themselves on their own land.
4. The Declaration accuses King George of encouraging "merciless Indian Savages" to attack colonists on the frontier. Colonists considered Native Americans barbarians who attacked indiscriminately.
5. The Declaration claims that the colonists had petitioned the king many times.

1775	1776	1776	1777	1777
Battle of Bunker Hill	The American Crisis *is published*	Battle of Trenton	Battle of Princeton	Battle of Saratoga; Burgoyne surrenders

1775	1776	1777	1778

Objectives

You may wish to call students' attention to the objectives in the Section Preview. The objectives are reflected in the main headings of the section.

Bellringer

Read students this quote by Thomas Paine: "These are the times that try men's souls." What is Paine referring to? What are the conditions that try men's and women's souls?

Reading Strategy

Reinforcing Main Ideas Refer to the Reading Strategy in the Section Preview. You may want to model the chart on the chalkboard. Label the first column American Victories and the second column Reasons.

LESSON PLAN

Connecting to the Main Idea

1. Focus Explain that in the fight for independence, both the British and American forces had strengths and weaknesses.

2. Instruct Tell students that not all the colonists supported the Revolution. In general, colonists were split in their loyalties. Some were Patriots, others were Loyalists or Tories, and the rest were neutral. Discuss the fact that more African Americans served in the Patriot cause than supported the British. Explain that important battles took place in the North, including the British victory at Bunker Hill, and the American victory at Saratoga.

3. Close Despite many weaknesses, the Americans won important battles against the British between 1775 and 1777. The next section tells how they went on to defeat the British and gain their independence.

4 Fighting for Independence

SECTION PREVIEW

Objectives

1 Describe the siege of Boston and its outcome.
2 List the strengths and weaknesses of the British and American forces.
3 Explain the importance of battles in the North between 1776 and 1777, including the American victory at Saratoga.
4 *Key Terms* Define: Battle of Bunker Hill; casualty; Loyalist; mercenary; Battle of Trenton; Battle of Saratoga.

Main Idea

Despite considerable weaknesses, the Americans won important battles against the British between 1775 and 1777.

Reading Strategy

Reinforcing Main Ideas As you read the section, create a chart listing the major American victories in one column and the reasons for these victories in the other.

While the Declaration of Independence was not issued until July 4, 1776, Britain and the American colonists had been fighting since the Battles of Lexington and Concord in April 1775. King George III had not expected a war, much less a long one. "Once these rebels have felt a smart blow, they will submit," he had vowed after the clashes at Lexington and Concord. After all, the nation he ruled was the most powerful on Earth. But the fighting continued, and even intensified.

The Siege of Boston

Following the clashes at Lexington and Concord in April 1775, as many as 20,000 armed Patriots surrounded Boston. Though the Patriots were disorganized, their presence prevented the 6,000 British troops under General Thomas Gage from quickly crushing the rebellion.

With the main British force bottled up in Boston, the Patriots turned their attention to gathering badly needed military equipment. In May a group of Vermont militia under Colonel Ethan Allen crossed Lake Champlain and surprised the British troops at Fort Ticonderoga in northern New York. The capture of the fort provided the Patriots with cannons and other supplies.

The Battle of Bunker Hill In June 1775 the Americans occupied two hills north of Boston. General Gage decided that the rebels must be driven from these strategic high grounds. On June 17, 1775, the British army attacked. In an awesome display of power, the tightly packed lines of red-coated troops marched up Breed's Hill with battle flags flying and drummers tapping out the beat. But as the British neared the American position, 1,600 Patriots poured unending musket fire into their ranks. The advancing troops slowed, stopped, and then fell back.

The British launched another assault. Again, heavy Patriot fire from the top of the hill drove them back. Determined, the British commander General William Howe ordered yet a third attack. This time, picking their way over the bodies of their fallen comrades, the troops succeeded in taking Breed's Hill. The Patriots, having used all of their ammunition, were forced to retreat. British forces then quickly overran the second, weaker Patriot position on nearby Bunker Hill.

▶ RESOURCE OPTIONS

Teaching Resources

📁 **Reproducible Lesson Plans** Lesson Plans folder, p. 49

📁 **Learning Styles Lesson Plan** Learning Styles Lesson Plans folder, p. 11

📁 **Big Idea Graphic Organizer** Big Idea Graphic Organizer folder, p. 21

📁 **Guided Reading and Review** Units 1–2 folder, p. 48

Media and Technology

 AmericanHeritage® CD-ROM
Time Tour From Revolution to Republic: The American Revolution

In a costly attempt to intimidate American forces, waves of British troops climb Breed's Hill toward the waiting enemy. **Geography** *Why did General Gage target Breed's Hill?*

The British emerged victorious from the **Battle of Bunker Hill,** but at a tremendous cost. Nearly 1,100 of 2,400 British soldiers had been killed or wounded. Patriot **casualties**—that is, persons killed, wounded, or missing—amounted to fewer than 400. "You can never conquer us," wrote a defiant Patriot after the battle. "All America will revenge our cause."

The British Leave Boston Warning that the Americans "are now spirited up by a rage and enthusiasm as great as ever people were possessed of," General Gage asked for permission to march on Rhode Island or New York. Yet General Howe, still confident of an easy victory, advised against it. So for the next nine months Gage's small army remained pinned down in Boston.

In July George Washington arrived from Philadelphia, where the Congress had named him commanding general of the Patriot forces. While Gage's troops remained in Boston, Washington worked to transform the Patriot militia groups into the Continental Army.

In January 1776, General Henry Knox arrived outside Boston. He brought with him cannons his Patriots had hauled through the snowy forests from Fort Ticonderoga. Washington placed these big guns on Dorchester Heights, south of Boston. From there he could shell the British forces in the city and the British ships in Boston Harbor.

Realizing that they could no longer defend their position, the British abandoned Boston in March 1776. The British fleet moved the army to the Canadian city of Halifax, taking along some 1,000 **Loyalists,** or people who remained loyal to Great Britain. The Loyalists had no desire to be left behind with no one to protect them from the rebels.

Strengths and Weaknesses

According to John Adams, about one third of colonists were Patriots. Another third were Loyalists, or Tories as the Patriots called them. Adams believed that the remaining third of Americans were neutral in the war. While the population may have been divided, each of the two sides in the war had its own strengths and weaknesses.

The British Britain's main strength was its well-equipped, disciplined, and trained army. In addition, the British navy was the world's finest. It provided support by transporting and landing troops and protecting supply lines at sea.

The British also received help from a number of sources. Roughly 50,000 Loyalists fought with the British army. Some African Americans, largely in the South, also helped Great Britain. The British promised freedom to all slaves who served their cause.

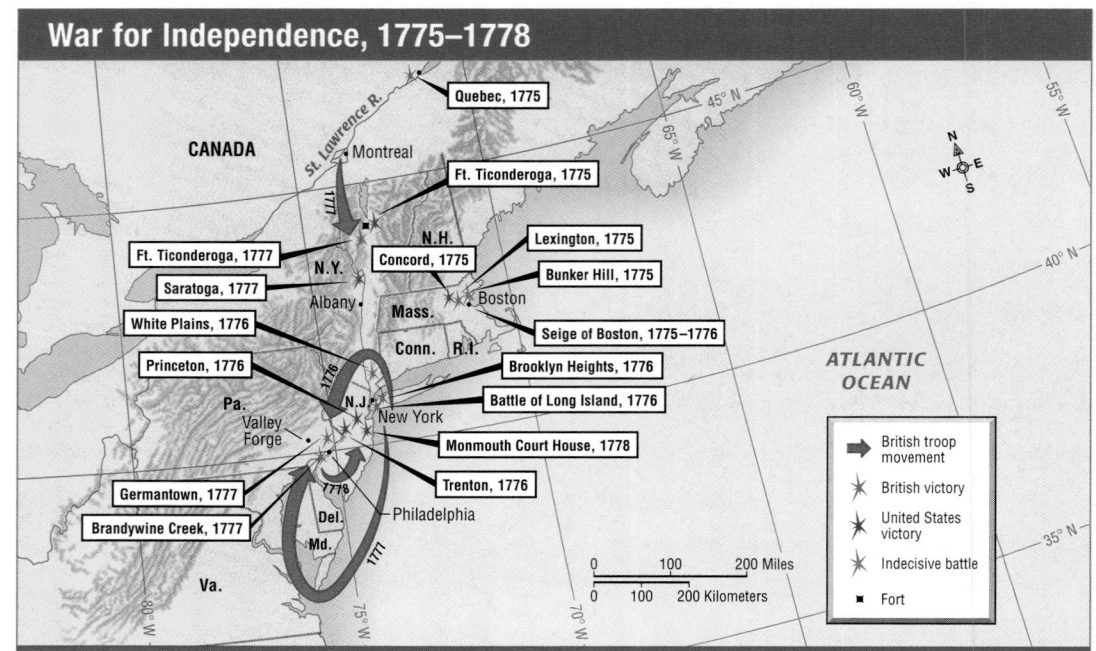

War for Independence, 1775–1778

MAP Skills The major battles of the early part of the war took place in the North. **Location** *Where were most of these battles fought?*

Additional help came from Native Americans. Most Indian nations believed an American victory would be harmful to their interests. In the South and West, the Creeks, Cherokees, and Shawnees fought alongside British and Loyalist forces. In the North the Mohawks, led by Joseph Brant, and most other Iroquois nations sided with the British.

The British also hired about 30,000 **mercenaries,** foreign soldiers who fight for pay. The colonists called these troops "Hessians" because most of their officers came from the German province of Hesse.

On the other hand, the British also had their problems. The war was not popular in Great Britain. Many British citizens resented paying taxes to fight the war and sympathized with the Americans. British troops had to fight in hostile territory and British commanders resisted adapting their tactics to conditions in America.

The Americans The very things that were British weaknesses were American strengths. Patriot forces were fighting on their own territory. Many of their officers were familiar with the tactics that had worked in the French and Indian War. George Washington, in particular, proved to be an exceptional commander.

For much of the war, the Americans lacked a well-supplied, stable, and effective fighting force. New recruits were constantly arriving while experienced soldiers, their time of service up, were heading home. As he tried to plan strategy, Washington never could be sure how many troops he would have.

More African Americans served in the Patriot cause than supported the British. Washington's army had some all-black units, but more often, African Americans served in white units.

Fighting in the North

In the summer of 1776, General Howe and a large British army appeared off the New York coast. The British had decided to concentrate on the Middle Colonies, where many Loyalists lived. In a series of battles, including the Battle of Long Island, some 32,000 British and German troops battered Washington's poorly trained and poorly equipped army.

Retreat from New York By October the British had captured New York City and driven the Continental Army into Pennsylvania. Many troops deserted Washington. By the winter of 1776 the entire Patriot cause seemed on the point of collapse. Fearing for their safety, members of the Continental Congress fled Philadelphia.

In December 1776 Thomas Paine produced another pamphlet to inspire Americans once again to the cause of freedom. He called this work *The Crisis*. It began with this eloquent statement:

 "These are the times that try men's souls. The summer soldier and the sunshine patriot will, in this crisis, shrink from the service of their country; but he that stands it NOW, deserves the love and thanks of man and woman. Tyranny, like hell, is not easily conquered; yet we have this consolation with us, that the harder the conflict, the more glorious the triumph."

—*Thomas Paine, The Crisis*

Trenton and Princeton Desperate times called for heroic measures. Washington and his troops met the challenge. Abandoning the tradition that armies did not fight during winter, on Christmas night of 1776 Washington left his Pennsylvania camp and went on the attack. Some 2,400 troops were ferried across the ice-choked Delaware River in small boats. Early the next morning they surprised about 1,400 Hessians stationed in Trenton, New Jersey. Nearly the entire Hessian force was captured, while the Americans suffered only five casualties in the **Battle of Trenton.**

A few days later Washington made a similar attack on nearby Princeton. Leaving fires burning so the local Tories would think his troops were still in camp, he led some 5,000 troops on a difficult nighttime march. One of the soldiers later described the ordeal:

 "The horses attached to our cannon were without shoes, and when passing over the ice they would slide in every direction. . . . Our men, too, were without shoes or other comfortable clothing; and as traces of our march towards Princeton, the ground was literally marked with the blood of the soldiers' feet."

—*Soldier at the Battle of Princeton*

The next morning, British troops under General Charles Cornwallis spotted Washington's army and attacked. However, the Americans drove them back, inflicting heavy losses, and captured the town.

The victories in December 1776 and January 1777 greatly boosted Patriot morale and convinced more Americans to support the Patriot cause. "Volunteer companies are collecting in every county," a British traveler observed after the battles. "In a few months the rascals will be stronger than ever."

Emanuel Gottlieb Leutze's *George Washington Crossing the Delaware* captures the patriotic feelings inspired by Washington's victories at Trenton and Princeton. *Geography What difficulties did fighting in winter pose?*

TEST PREPARATION

Have students read the quotation from Thomas Paine on this page and then answer the question below.

"Summer soldiers" and "sunshine patriots" are those who—
A are eternally optimistic about the outcome.
B agree to fight only during the summer months.
C are prepared to fight only when circumstances are favorable.
D join the battle eagerly at any time.

Answer to . . .

Viewing History Cold weather; difficult travel for troops and horses.

Answers to
SECTION 4 REVIEW

1. (a) Battle of Bunker Hill, see p. 107; (b) casualties, see p. 107; (c) Loyalists, see p. 107; (d) mercenaries, see p. 108; (e) Battle of Trenton, see p. 109; (f) Battle of Saratoga, see p. 110.

2. Boston: cannon from Ticonderoga, British general's unwillingness to march on Rhode Island or New York; Trenton: surprise attack caught British off guard; Princeton: deception tactics; Saratoga: Americans slowed British army advance by burning bridges and felling trees on roads, giving the Americans time to assemble larger forces. Washington's ability to outsmart British leaders and foreign aid contributed to all four victories.

3. Students' maps should label the following battles: Lexington and Concord, Bunker Hill, Boston, Battle of Long Island, New York City, Trenton, Princeton, Brandywine Creek, Philadelphia, Germantown, Saratoga.

4. Patriot victories boosted morale and convinced more Americans, as well as foreigners, to support the American cause.

5. Answers will vary, but might include: fighting tactics, General Washington's expertise, fighting on own territory.

6. Students' essays will vary, but should include the Battles of Lexington and Concord.

Answer to . . .

Main Idea Connections It marked the turning point of the war.

Victory at Saratoga

Despite the increasing Patriot numbers, the months that followed held no success for the Continental Army. In July 1777 Howe moved his 15,000-man army from New York to attack the rebel capital at Philadelphia. Washington's 10,500 defenders were defeated at Brandywine Creek, on the outskirts of the city, in early September. Late in the month, the British occupied Philadelphia, as the Congress once again fled. In early October, Washington counterattacked to drive the British from the city, but lost again at the Battle of Germantown.

Main Idea
CONNECTIONS

Why was the American victory at Saratoga important?

A British Attack from the North While Howe was advancing to capture Philadelphia, another British army was on the move in northern New York. Led by General John Burgoyne, its objective was to cut New England off from the rest of the colonies. In June Burgoyne moved out of Canada with a mixed force of about 8,000 British and German troops, Loyalists, Canadians, and Native Americans. The force quickly recaptured Fort Ticonderoga and then moved south through the dense New York forest toward Albany.

As the Americans retreated in Burgoyne's path, they destroyed bridges and felled trees across the road to slow his advance. Burgoyne's slow progress caused his army to run low on supplies. Meanwhile, the colonial force continued to grow, as the Continental Army and Patriot militias assembled to confront the invaders.

In mid-September the Americans, led by General Horatio Gates, attacked Burgoyne's forces. This series of American victories, which

took place around Saratoga, New York, is called the **Battle of Saratoga.** Finally, on October 17, 1777, surrounded by a force now much larger than his own, Burgoyne surrendered his army. It was the biggest American victory yet and it marked the turning point of the war.

Help from Abroad A few months after the Continental Congress declared independence, it sent Benjamin Franklin on a mission to Paris. Although France secretly aided the Americans in their struggle against its longtime enemy, Franklin pushed for an open alliance. The British defeat at Saratoga convinced the French that the Americans had a real chance of winning the war. On February 6, 1778, France and the United States signed a treaty of alliance.

The alliance with France helped the Americans tremendously. It meant not only more supplies, but loans of money, French troops, and a navy. In addition, Britain now had to defend itself in Europe. A year later Spain joined the war as France's ally, followed by the Netherlands in 1780. From Louisiana, Spanish governor Bernardo de Gálvez, who also had been secretly aiding the Patriots, attacked British outposts in Florida and along the Mississippi River.

Even before France and Spain entered the war, a number of Europeans volunteered to help the American cause against the British. Among them were the Marquis de Lafayette and Johann de Kalb from France. Both became generals in the Americans' Continental Army. Polish military engineer Thaddeus Kosciusko helped American forces build effective defenses. German Baron Friedrich von Steuben was largely responsible for training the Continental Army and transforming it into an effective fighting force.

SECTION 4 REVIEW

Comprehension

1. *Key Terms* Define: (a) Battle of Bunker Hill; (b) casualty; (c) Loyalist; (d) mercenary; (e) Battle of Trenton; (f) Battle of Saratoga.

2. *Summarizing the Main Idea* Outline the factors that contributed to important American victories at Boston, Trenton, Princeton, and Saratoga.

3. *Organizing Information* Using the map in this section, sketch a map of the American colonies and label the major battles described in this section.

Critical Thinking

4. *Analyzing Time Lines* Explain how Patriot victories at Trenton and Princeton contributed to victory at Saratoga.

5. *Demonstrating Reasoned Judgment* What do you think were the Americans' greatest strengths in the early years of the war?

Writing Activity

6. *Writing an Expository Essay* Write an essay outlining the events that led up to the siege of Boston.

RESOURCE OPTIONS

Teaching Resources

📁 **Quiz** Units 1–2 folder, p. 49

Student Performance Pack

Guide to the Essentials Chapter 4, Section 4 (English and Spanish)

1778	1778		1780		
Continental Army spends winter at Valley Forge	British seize Savannah, Georgia	**1779** Colonel Clark recaptures Vincennes	British seize Charleston, South Carolina	**1781** British surrender at Yorktown	

1778	1780	1782

5 Winning Independence

SECTION PREVIEW

Objectives

1 Explain the hardships the Americans endured during the war.
2 Describe the American victories in the West and South that led to an end to the war.
3 Summarize the impact of the American Revolution.
4 *Key Terms* Define: blockade; profiteering; inflation; Battle of Yorktown; Treaty of Paris (1783).

Main Idea

Americans won their independence militarily by outlasting the British in one of the longest and costliest wars in American history.

Reading Strategy

Outlining Information As you read this section, create an outline by filling in main ideas for each of the headings and subheadings.

The British lost their colonies in the end because Americans had the determination to outlast their rulers. George Washington understood this better than anyone. He never gave up, even in the face of repeated military defeats. Although Britain seized New York, Philadelphia, and almost every other important colonial city, Washington knew the secret to winning the war. The British might capture territory, he said, but they could never win the war as long as Americans were willing and able to continue fighting them.

Americans Endure Hardships

There may be no better symbol of Americans' determination to be free than the Continental soldiers who spent the winter of 1777–1778 at Valley Forge in Pennsylvania. While British troops remained warm and well-fed in Philadelphia, about 20 miles away, Patriot soldiers huddled in huts with few blankets, ragged clothing, and almost no food. Washington reported to Congress that nearly one third of his 10,000 soldiers were unfit for duty because they lacked coats or shoes.

Financing the War Part of the problem was that the Continental Congress had little real power. It asked the states to provide troops, money, and supplies, but with no taxing power it could not force them to do so.

Congress did issue paper money that the army could use to purchase supplies. Yet these bills were not backed by gold or silver, and if Britain were to win the war they would become worthless. So while Washington's army starved at Valley Forge, nearby farmers sold their crops in Philadelphia, where the British army paid in gold.

Disruptions of Trade Civilians suffered hardships, too. The British navy **blockaded,** or isolated from outside contact, the Atlantic Coast and severely disrupted American trade. Measured in the British monetary units of pounds sterling, the combined value of American imports and exports fell from about £2,700,000 in 1775 to £110,000 in 1777.

Nearly everyone felt the pinch of shortages during the war. Even necessities often were scarce. A few colonists took advantage of these shortages by **profiteering,** or selling

▶ RESOURCE OPTIONS

Teaching Resources

📁 **Reproducible Lesson Plan** Lesson Plans folder, p. 50

📁 **Big Idea Graphic Organizer** Big Idea Graphic Organizer folder, p. 22

📁 **Guided Reading and Review** Units 1–2 folder, p. 50

Objectives

You may wish to call students' attention to the objectives in the Section Preview. The objectives are reflected in the main headings of the section.

Bellringer

Ask students if they can recall a time in their life when they felt hopelessly defeated but kept going in spite of their feelings and were eventually successful. What techniques did they use to boost their morale?

Reading Strategy

Outlining Information Refer to the Reading Strategy in the Section Preview. Model it by creating an outline on the chalkboard. Ask students to suggest main ideas as they read. Write them in the outline.

LESSON PLAN

Connecting to the Main Idea

1. Focus Explain that the War for Independence was a long and costly war that caused people great hardship. In the end, Americans won their independence from Great Britain.

2. Instruct Tell students that Americans made great sacrifices during the war. Why were they willing to sacrifice so much? What kinds of hardships did Americans suffer during the war? Discuss the course of the war, and ask why it took the colonists so long to win.

3. Close Victories in the West and South led to the end of the war. Now that Americans had won their independence, they faced the challenge of establishing a new society based on their ideals.

ECONOMICS CONCEPTS

inflation and deflation: Inflation is a steady rise in prices; deflation is a steady drop in prices

▼ **The Historical Context:** Inflation, which has been described as "too much money chasing too few goods," plagued the American economy during the Revolutionary War. As Congress printed more and more Continental dollars, and the war limited the supply of goods available to consumers, the price of goods rose.

▼ **The Concept Today:** Government officials, knowing that inflation could hurt economic growth, keep a close watch over consumer prices. The federal government has several tools to fight inflation, such as reducing the supply of money and limiting government spending.

scarce items at unreasonably high prices. Washington suggested that profiteers should be hanged. "No punishment in my opinion is too great for the man who can build his greatness upon his country's ruin," he said.

Even when goods were available, it was not always possible to purchase them. **Inflation,** a steady increase in prices over time, reduced people's ability to buy goods. In Massachusetts, for example, the price of a bushel of corn rose from less than one dollar in 1777 to almost eighty dollars in 1779.

Victories in the West and South

In June 1778, hearing that a French fleet was sailing for America, the British abandoned Philadelphia and returned to reinforce New York. Trying unsuccessfully to stop the British from reaching New York, Washington's forces

Wholesale Price Index, 1775–1784

Source: Historical Statistics of the United States, Colonial Times to 1970

Interpreting Graphs Economists often use a price index to demonstrate inflation. A wholesale price index measures changes in the wholesale prices of goods over time. *Economics* What caused the huge rise in prices beginning in 1778?

fought the British at Monmouth, New Jersey, and inflicted more casualties than they suffered.

Fighting in the West In the spring of 1778, Patriot militia under Colonel George Rogers Clark began fighting the British. By late summer, with the help of French settlers, Clark and his 175 soldiers had captured all the British posts in what are now Indiana and Illinois.

A few months later a British force of roughly 500, about half of them Native Americans, returned to Vincennes, a fort in Indiana. Clark then gathered nearly 200 French and American colonists and left his winter quarters near the Mississippi River. Marching through mud and icy water, the group reached Vincennes in late February 1779. After persuading most of the Indians to abandon their British allies, Clark recaptured the fort. This success strengthened the Patriots' claim to the Ohio River valley.

The War in the South In 1779 the focus of the war shifted to the South where the British hoped to draw on Loyalist sympathies. Supported by the Royal Navy, British forces from New York seized Savannah, Georgia, in December 1778 and Charleston, South Carolina, in May 1780.

The southern phase of the Revolution was especially vicious. It pitted Americans against Americans, because Tories did much of the fighting for the British. Although many battles in the South were fought on a smaller scale than the northern engagements, they proved just as important to the war's outcome.

In August 1780, some 2,400 British troops defeated Patriot militia and Continental Army troops at Camden, South Carolina. British general Lord Cornwallis then began a campaign to invade North Carolina. At the Battle of Kings Mountain on the Carolina border that October, the Patriots defeated an army made up entirely of Tories. About 1,000 Patriots stopped Cornwallis again at the Battle of Cowpens in the same area in January 1781.

Despite the defeat, Cornwallis continued into North Carolina and defeated the Patriots at the Battle of Guilford Court House in March 1781. After stopping in Wilmington, North Carolina, to be resupplied by sea, Cornwallis advanced north into Virginia. His army was now much larger than the Patriot forces commanded by the Marquis de Lafayette.

Patriot reinforcements soon arrived, however, and Cornwallis marched his army to the coast, where it too could be reinforced with additional troops arriving by sea. In August he set up camp at Yorktown, on a peninsula between the York and James rivers, and waited for the Royal Navy to arrive. Lafayette positioned his troops to block an overland escape from the peninsula.

Victory at Yorktown To the north, Washington at once saw the opportunity to deal the British a fatal blow. A French army had just joined the Continental Army in New York. Washington quickly moved the combined American-French force south, while the French fleet set up a blockade off the Virginia coast. When the British navy arrived in early September, the French ships drove it off.

A few days later Washington's troops arrived to reinforce Lafayette's force and the **Battle of Yorktown** began. In early October the American and French artillery began to pound Yorktown. Cornwallis now faced an army more than twice the size of his own, blocking his escape from the peninsula. The French fleet prevented him from being reinforced or removed by sea. He realized that escape was impossible. On October 18 Cornwallis surrendered to Washington.

The Treaty of Paris Nearly two years passed between the surrender of Cornwallis and the signing of the peace treaty that formally ended the war.[†] Because four nations (Great Britain, France, Spain, and the United States) were involved in the peace process, negotiations were long and complex. Finally, in September 1783 the **Treaty of Paris (1783)** was signed. It contained these major provisions:

(1) Great Britain recognized the independence of the United States of America.

(2) The northern border between the United States and British Canada was set from New England to the Mississippi River, primarily along the Great Lakes.

(3) The Mississippi River was established as the boundary between the new United States and Spanish territory to the west. Navigation on the river was to be forever open to American and British citizens.

(4) Florida, which Britain had gained from the Spanish after the French and Indian War, was returned to Spain. The border between Florida and the United States was set.

(5) Great Britain agreed to withdraw its remaining troops from United States territory.[††]

[†] King George stubbornly wanted to continue the war, despite the public's and Parliament's protests.
[††] British troops remained in some forts near the Great Lakes in violation of this provision.

War for Independence, 1778–1781

MAP Skills

Fighting shifted south during the latter part of the war. *Movement* How was General Washington able to trap the British at Yorktown?

Legend:
- British troop movement
- British victory
- United States victory
- Fort
- British blockade

General Nathanael Greene wears out the British in the South with cautious but determined warfare.

Using the Internet

Analyze Quotations

Objective Use the Internet to analyze the words of Thomas Jefferson. Have students follow these instructions:

1. See the *America: Pathways to the Present* Web site at

http://www.Pathways.phschool.com

for the URL for Thomas Jefferson on Politics and Government.

2. Select one of the quotations in the section "The Nature and Source of Our Rights."

3. Write an essay explaining in your own words what Jefferson meant by the quote. Tell whether you agree or disagree with Jefferson's position. Support your analysis with other quotes provided at this site or with details from other links to this site.

RESOURCE OPTIONS

Teaching Resources

Biography Deborah Sampson Gannett
Units 1–2 folder, p. 52

Answer to . . .

Map Skills The British were located on a peninsula, so Washington set up a successful blockade by the French fleet.

Biography

Elizabeth Freeman (1744–1829) was a Massachusetts slave who in 1781 sued for her freedom under the new state constitution that declared all people "free and equal" under the law. She won her case and went free, setting a legal precedent that would help to end slavery in Massachusetts. Freeman, who lived into her eighties, became widely admired. Her lawyer once said of her, "Having known this woman, I cannot believe in the moral or physical inferiority of the race to which she belonged."

---

(6) Congress pledged to recommend to the states that the rights and property of American Loyalists be restored and that no future action be taken against them. Persecution of the Tories continued after the war, however.

The Impact of the Revolution

In 1776 the American people had declared their independence to the world, and in 1783 Great Britain accepted American independence. The effects of the Revolution would be felt in different ways by different groups of Americans, and would shape American society to the present day.

Main Idea
CONNECTIONS

What impact did the American Revolution have on women?

For women the Revolution did not produce any immediate gain in political or legal power. Yet experiences during the war did challenge some of the traditional ideas about women. As men set off for war, women took charge of family farms and businesses. Many women also followed their husbands and fathers into battle and cared for them.

For African Americans, the results of the Revolution were mixed. On the one hand, the Revolution promoted the antislavery cause in the North. As Abigail Adams put it, "It always appeared a most evil scheme to me to fight ourselves for what we are daily robbing and plundering from those who have as good a right to freedom as we have." Most northern states abolished slavery in the late 1700s and early 1800s. On the other hand, these states

also passed laws severely limiting the legal rights and political power of African Americans. In the South, if the Revolution brought about any change in slavery at all, that change was to make it more restrictive.

For Native Americans the war's outcome was a disaster. The power of the Iroquois League was destroyed and the nations were essentially pushed out of New York. For decades after the Revolution, Americans justified their attacks on Cherokees, Shawnees, and other southern and western Indians by pointing to these nations' support for the British.

Perhaps the greatest effect of the Revolution was to spread the idea of liberty, both at home and abroad. In 1776 the Congress had used Thomas Jefferson's assertion that "all men are created equal" to help justify a revolution. This was a radical concept in a world that had long accepted the idea of human inequality.

Jefferson, like most members of the Continental Congress, probably had no thought of applying this principle to people other than white men. However, he had set in motion a powerful idea that no one could long control. Over the next two centuries many groups in the United States, such as women and African Americans, would demand and win greater equality. At the same time, the principles for which the Patriots fought would also inspire people around the world. Indeed, in the United States and many other parts of the world, people today are still discovering the full meaning of those principles.

SECTION 5 REVIEW

Comprehension

1. *Key Terms* Define: (a) blockade; (b) profiteering; (c) inflation; (d) Battle of Yorktown; (e) Treaty of Paris (1783).

2. *Summarizing the Main Idea* Summarize the hardships Americans had to overcome to win the war against Britain.

3. *Organizing Information* Create a map of the United States that shows the territorial changes made by the Treaty of Paris (1783). Label the map to explain these changes.

Critical Thinking

4. *Analyzing Time Lines* Review the time line at the start of the section. Which of the battles listed do you think was most important? Explain your answer.

5. *Recognizing Cause and Effect* What powerful idea did the American Revolution set in motion? What effect did this idea have over time?

Writing Activity

6. *Writing an Expository Essay* Write an essay in which you analyze the qualities of George Washington's leadership.

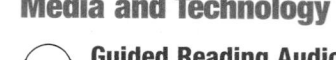

RESOURCE OPTIONS

Teaching Resources

 Quiz Units 1–2 folder, p. 51

Chapter Tests Forms A and B Chapter Test folder

Student Performance Pack

 Guide to the Essentials Chapter 4, Section 5 (English and Spanish)

Standardized Test Preparation Handbook

Media and Technology

Guided Reading Audiotapes Chapter 4 Summary (English and Spanish)

Student Edition on Audiotape Chapter 4

 Test Bank CD-ROM; Interactive Student Tutorial CD-ROM Chapter Test

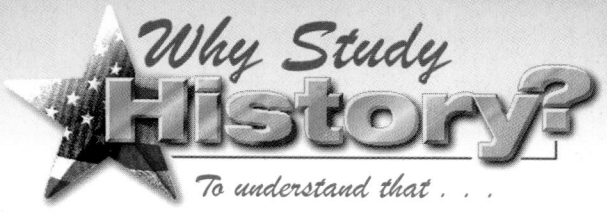

Why Study History?

To understand that . . .

You Have a Voice in Government

Lack of representation in Parliament fueled the conflicts that caused the American colonists to take up arms. Representation remains a fundamental right to Americans—a right that we can exercise by voting.

"No taxation without representation!" So strong was American colonists' demand for a voice in government that they fought to secure it. Representation means that we choose our public officials and expect them to express our needs and wishes.

The Patriots' victory did not bring representation to all Americans. Only white men who owned a certain amount of property could vote. Women, African Americans, Native Americans, and many white men had little voice in government. Expansion of voting rights to include all adult citizens occurred only after a long and painful struggle.

American colonists pulling down a statue of King George III

The Impact Today

The percentage of eligible voters has increased tremendously since our nation's founding, yet the percentage of Americans who exercise their voting rights has declined. In the late 1800s, voter participation averaged more than 70 percent. By the 1960s it had fallen to around 60 percent. In 1996, a presidential election year, fewer than 50 percent of those eligible bothered to vote. (In non-presidential election years, voting rates are usually even lower!)

Some people say that the decline in voter participation reflects a growing unhappiness with government. According to this view,

Americans see government leaders as corrupt or powerless to deal with the nation's problems.

Other people assert an opposite point of view. They claim that many Americans see no need to vote because they are generally satisfied with their lives and with the direction in which the nation is headed.

To reverse the decline in voter participation, people have proposed different strategies. Some want to limit the number of terms that elected officials can serve. Term limits, they suggest, would increase voters' interest by giving voters new candidates from which to choose. Others suggest that Americans be allowed to decide more issues themselves, by voting "yes" or "no" on ballot questions instead of leaving the most important issues to elected officials.

Teenager voting in Texas

The Impact on You

Do you think that government should act decisively to increase voter participation? Imagine that a vote will be held, in your community, on a law that requires eligible voters to vote. Decide where you stand on the proposed law. Write a slogan that could be used on a poster to convince other people to support your view.

▶ RESOURCE OPTIONS

Teaching Resources

 Why Study History? Activity, You Have a Voice in Government, found in the Why Study History? folder, p. 5, provides an activity to help students understand the importance of participation in government.

Media and Technology

 Decision America Videotapes and Videodiscs Issue 3 *Why Vote?*

Why Study History?

Class Discussion

Discuss with the class voter participation and the government's role in promoting it. For a more thorough examination of the issue, see the activity folder in the Resource Options below.

ACTIVITY
STUDENT PARTICIPATION

Taking a Survey of Voters

Ask students to read the text. Then encourage them to participate in a voter survey. Each student should interview three adults and ask the following questions:

- **Did you vote in the last national election?**
- **Why or why not?**
- **What is your age group?**
- **What is your education?**

Divide the class into four groups and give the survey results to each group. Have each group create a graph or table that analyzes one of the factors addressed in the questions above.

Follow up Have a classroom discussion about factors that influence voting.

Using the Internet

Students can learn more about voter participation by exploring links in the *America: Pathways to the Present* Web site at

http://www.Pathways.phschool.com

Assessment

See the Lesson Plans folder, pp. 24–27, for rubrics on assessing Class Participation Projects.

Key Terms

Students should refer to the definitions of the key terms in the chapter to write sentences that show an understanding of the ideals and events that shaped the Revolution.

Comprehension

1. Americans lost respect for the British, believing that the British did not respect them and that their values differed.
2. The British had incurred heavy debts fighting the French and Indian War and so began to tax the colonists more heavily to help pay those debts.
3. It caused widespread protests among the colonists. They issued their Declaration of Rights and Grievances, boycotted British goods, and formed protest groups.
4. French and Spanish aid, in the form of money, supplies, troops, ships, and military expertise, enabled the Americans to fight the British effectively.
5. To explain the political ideas on which the document was based, to list the wrongs the colonists believed had been committed by the British king, and to declare the colonies' independence as a new country.
6. Strengths: help from Loyalists, some African Americans and Native Americans, mercenaries, and a well-equipped, disciplined, and trained army and navy. Weaknesses: unpopularity of war in Britain; fighting in hostile territory; inability of British generals to adapt their tactics to the Americans' tactics.
7. The British attacked two hills occupied by the Americans. Though they eventually succeeded, they suffered heavy casualties in comparison with the Patriots so that the Patriot cause was strengthened.
8. It disrupted colonial trade, caused shortages of goods, and contributed to inflation.

Chapter Summary

The major concepts of Chapter 4 are presented below. See also **Guide to the Essentials of American History** or **Interactive Student Tutorial CD-ROM,** which contains interactive review activities, time lines, helpful hints, and test practice for Chapter 4.

Reviewing the Main Ideas
Struggling for their rights and protesting against what they saw as British wrongs, colonists in the Americas demanded and won their independence from Britain.

Section 1: The French and Indian War
The war that the colonists fought against the French and Indians caused them to rethink their relationship with Britain.

Section 2: Issues Behind the Revolution
The colonists, believing they should not be taxed without representation, protested new British taxes.

Section 3: Ideas Behind the Revolution
New ideas about equality and self-government contributed to the outbreak of the American Revolution.

Section 4: Fighting for Independence
Despite considerable weaknesses, the Americans won important victories against the British between 1775 and 1777.

Section 5: Winning Independence
Americans won their independence militarily by outlasting the British in one of the longest and costliest wars in American history.

Lack of representation in Parliament fueled the conflicts that caused the American colonists to take up arms. Representation remains a fundamental right to Americans—a right that we can exercise by voting.

Key Terms

For each of the terms below, write a sentence explaining how it relates to this chapter.

1. Albany Plan of Union
2. siege
3. inflation
4. boycott
5. First Continental Congress
6. Boston Massacre
7. *Common Sense*
8. Treaty of Paris (1783)
9. Enlightenment
10. Loyalist
11. Battle of Yorktown
12. mercenary
13. blockade
14. profiteering

Comprehension

1. Describe how the French and Indian War weakened the colonists' loyalty to Britain.
2. Why did British policies in the colonies change after 1763?
3. Summarize the effects of the Stamp Act.
4. Why was foreign aid important to the Patriot cause during the American Revolution?
5. What was the purpose of the Declaration of Independence?
6. Describe the strengths and weaknesses of the British at the start of the war.
7. What happened at the Battle of Bunker Hill?
8. How did the British blockade affect the colonists?

Using Graphic Organizers

On a separate sheet of paper, copy the graphic organizer below showing causes of the American Revolution. Fill in at least two examples of colonists' actions or reactions for each of the headings.

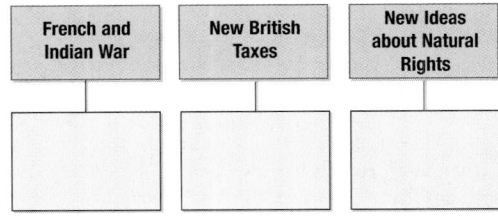

Using Graphic Organizers

- French and Indian War: Colonists lose sense of loyalty to British; lose respect for British military power
- New British Taxes: Colonists enact boycotts; form groups to organize protest, such as the Sons and Daughters of Liberty.
- New Ideas about Natural Rights: Declaration of Independence; *Common Sense.*

Analyzing Political Cartoons ▶

JOIN, or DIE.

1. This cartoon by Benjamin Franklin appeared in several versions during the American Revolution. (a) What do the segments of the snake represent? (b) How do you know?
2. What is the message of the cartoon?
3. What makes this an effective cartoon?

Critical Thinking

1. *Applying the Chapter Skill* What problems did the British army face at Yorktown?
2. *Determining Relevance* Colonial politicians had never lobbied to send representatives to the British Parliament. Also, a majority of men in Britain were not entitled to vote for representatives in Parliament because they did not own enough property. Given these facts, do you think the colonists were justified in protesting British taxes? Explain your reasoning.
3. *Identifying Assumptions* What assumptions underlay the British decisions to raise new taxes in the colonies?
4. *Identifying Central Issues* Review the excerpt from the Declaration and Resolves of the First Continental Congress on page 95. Are the colonists asking for representation in the British Parliament?

INTERNET ACTIVITY

For your portfolio:
PREPARE A SUMMARY

Access Prentice Hall's *America: Pathways to the Present* site at **www.Pathways.phschool.com** for the specific URL to complete the activity. Additional resources and related Web sites are also available.

Read Thomas Paine's words on the origins and design of government and summarize his views. How does society differ from government? Why does Paine consider government a "necessary evil"? What form should government take, and why? What objections does Paine have to the English Constitution?

ANALYZING DOCUMENTS ◀▷ *INTERPRETING DATA*

Turn to excerpt by John Locke on page 99.

1. The word *arbitrary* in this passage means: (a) weakened (b) unreasonable (c) absolute, based on one's own preference (d) careful.
2. *Which statement best summarizes the excerpt?* (a) People can dissolve a government when the ruler ignores the laws. (b) Government by an arbitrary ruler interferes with elections.
   (c) The common people must not act against the elected ruler. (d) Rulers will often interfere with the legislature.
3. *Writing* Find a passage in the Declaration of Independence that states an idea very similar to the idea presented in the quotation by John Locke. Explain how the two excerpts are similar.

Connecting to Today

Recognizing Cause and Effect Review the Turning Point time line on page 99. Research and write an essay on one of the last two events shown on the time line.

INTERNET ACTIVITY

Answers will vary. Reports should show an understanding of how Thomas Paine felt about the conditions of war.

Analyzing Political Cartoons

1. (a) The Thirteen Colonies.
(b) Each segment is labeled with the initial of a state or states.
2. The colonies must unite to survive.
3. The imagery is easy to understand, but makes a powerful impression.

Critical Thinking

1. They were badly outnumbered by the forces of Washington and Lafayette. They were trapped and could not be reinforced or escape by sea because of a French fleet off the shore of Virginia.
2. Answers will vary. Students may suggest that the colonists should have used legal tactics to gain representation in the British Parliament or that the property requirements should have been equally applied both in Britain and in the Americas, or not at all.
3. George Grenville assumed the colonists would not object to the Sugar Act. He thought they would buy the imported molasses and pay the taxes.
4. No. The document states that the English colonists "cannot properly be represented in the English Parliament."

Analyzing Documents

1. c
2. a
3. The Declaration of Independence states: "Whenever . . . Government becomes destructive. . ., it is the Right of the People to alter or to abolish it. . . ." Both passages state people can dissolve government when the ruler no longer follows the law.

Connecting to Today

Students' should include causes and effects of either the Voting Rights Act of 1965 or the Twenty-sixth Amendment in 1971.

My Brush with History

American Heritage®

Focus Have students find the meaning of each of these words in a dictionary before they begin to read: *acquaintance, conjectured, prophesy, procure.* Explain that Israel Putnam was an American general from Connecticut. Ask them to think, as they read, about the advantages of fighting on one's home soil.

Instruct Review the account of the battles at Trenton and Princeton in Chapter 4. Discuss details that make this a factual, objective account of the battle. Then discuss how the information provided in the diary entries differs from the description in Chapter 4. Ask volunteers for words and phrases describing the point of view of the diary entries. *(Personal, emotional.)* Have students explain how the diary entries enhance their understanding of the Revolution.

Analyzing the Document

Use this additional question to generate class discussion:

CRITICAL THINKING: MAKING INFERENCES
How does Margaret Hill Morris regard Count Donop? Give evidence from the document to support your answer. *(At first, Morris resents Donop for ignoring her town's request to remain neutral but later comes to respect him. After his death, Morris observes that the Hessians "have lost a brave and humane commander.")*

My Brush with History

BY MARGARET HILL MORRIS

INTRODUCTION Fought in the towns and farms of the American colonies, the battles of the American Revolution dominated the lives not only of soldiers but of the unlucky civilians who lived nearby. The editors of *American Heritage* magazine have selected entries from the diary of Margaret Hill Morris. Morris lived in New Jersey, site of the Battle of Princeton and other battles.

December 22, 1776: It is said Putnam with 1,000 men [600 New Jersey militia and Virginia artillerymen] are at Mount Holly. All the women removed from the town, except one widow of our acquaintance. This evening we hear the sound of much hammering at Bristol, and it is conjectured that a fortification is carrying on there. More cannon are said to be planted on the island. We hear this afternoon that the gentlemen who went last to the Count Donop [Col. Carl von Donop, Hessian] with a request that our town might be allowed to remain a neutral one, are returned, and report that he had too many affairs of greater consequence in hand to attend to them, or give an answer. I think we don't like the Count quite so well today as we did yesterday. . . .

We hear this afternoon that our officers are afraid their men will not fight and wish they may all run home again. A peaceable man ventured to prophesy today that if the war is continued through the winter, the British troops will be scared at the sight of our men, for as they never fought with naked men, the novelty of it will terrify them and make them retreat faster than they advanced to meet them; for he says, from the present appearance of our ragged troops, he thinks it probable they will not have clothes to cover them a month or two hence. . . .

Battle of Princeton

Dec. 29: This morning the soldiers at the next house prepared to depart, and as they passed my door, they stopped to bless and thank me for the food I sent them, which I received, not as my due, but as belonging to my Master who had reached a morsel to them by my hands. A great number of soldiers are in town today. Another company took possession of the next house when the first left it. The inhabitants are much straitened for bread to supply the soldiers and firewood to keep them warm. This seems to be only one of the many calamities of war.

TEST PREPARATION

Have students use the excerpt on these pages to answer the following question.

What point of view does this document provide on the battles of Trenton and Princeton?

A That of an observant civilian.

B That of an objective reporter.

C That of a historian.

D That of a misinformed civilian.

Dec. 30: A number of poor soldiers sick and wounded brought into town today, and lodged in the court-house; some of them in private houses. Today I hear several of our town's men have agreed to procure wood for the soldiers; but they found it was attended with considerable difficulty, as most of the wagons usually employed to bring in wood were pressed to take the soldiers' baggage.

Dec. 31: We have been told of an engagement between the two armies, in which it was said the English had 400 taken prisoners, and 300 killed and wounded. The report of the evening contradicts the above intelligence, and there is no certain account of a battle.

American flag from the Revolution

January 1, 1777: This New Year's day has not been ushered in with the usual ceremonies and rejoicing; indeed, I believe it will be the beginning of a sorrowful year to very many people. Yet the flatterer—hope—bids me look forward with confidence and trust in Him who can bring order out of this great confusion. I do not hear that any messengers have been in town from the camp.

Jan. 3: This morning between 8 and 9 o'clock we heard very distinctly a heavy firing of cannon. The sound came from toward Trenton. About noon a number of [American] soldiers, upwards of 1,000, came into town in great confusion with baggage and some cannon. From these soldiers we learn there was a smart engagement yesterday at Trenton, and that they left them engaged near Trenton Mill, but were not able to say which side was victorious. . . .

    Several of those who lodged in Col. Cox's house last week returned tonight, and asked for the key, which I gave them. At about bedtime I went into the next house to see if the fires were safe, and my heart was melted with compassion to see such a number of my fellow creatures lying like swine on the floor, fast asleep, and many of them without even a blanket to cover them. It seems very strange to me that such a number should be allowed to come from the camp at the very time of the engagements, and I shrewdly suspect they have run away—for they can give no account why they came, nor where they are to march next.

Jan. 4: The accounts hourly coming in are so contradictory and various that we know not which to give credit to. We have heard our people have gained another victory [Battle of Princeton], that the English are fleeing before them, some at Brunswick, some at Princeton. We hear today that Sharp Delany, Anthony Morris, and others of the Philadelphia militia are killed, and that the Count Donop is numbered with the dead; if so, the Hessians have lost a brave and humane commander. The prisoners taken by our troops are sent to Lancaster jail. A number of sick and wounded were brought into town—calls upon us to extend a hand of charity towards them. Several of my soldiers left the next house, and returned to the place from whence they came. Upon my questioning them pretty close, I brought several to confess they had run away, being scared at the heavy firing on the 3rd. There were several innocent looking lads among them, and I sympathised with their mothers when I saw them preparing to return to the army.

Source: *Weathering the Storm: Women of the American Revolution* by Elizabeth Evan, Scribner's, 1975.

ADDITIONAL READING

To learn more about the topics discussed in this selection, you might want to read the following books:

- *Angel in the Whirlwind: The Triumph of the American Revolution,* by Benson Bobrick (New York: Simon & Schuster, 1997)
- *Founding Mothers: Women in America in the Revolutionary Era,* by Linda Grant Depauw (Boston: Houghton Mifflin, 1975)
- *The Spirit of 'Seventy-Six: The Story of the American Revolution as Told by Participants,* edited by Henry Steele Commager and Richard B. Morris (New York: Harper & Row, 1967)
- *Writings,* by George Washington (New York: Library of America, 1997)

Customize for

English Language Learners

Students may need help with the following words and phrases:

a fortification is carrying on soldiers are building military defenses

canteen container for water

straitened for lacking sufficient supplies of

smart engagement brisk battle

hand of charity help and kindness

Customize for

Less Proficient Readers

As students read the selection, write these topics on the chalkboard: Preparations at Mount Holly, Challenges of Lodging Soldiers, A Funny Prophecy, A False Rumor, and The Soldiers' Confession. Have students make a two-column chart titled Margaret Hill Morris Diary. In the first column, have students write the topics listed on the chalkboard. In the second column, have them write details from the document to explain each topic.

Customize for

More Advanced Students

Have students write three diary entries for a soldier garrisoned in Morris's town. Entries should be set between December 22, 1776, and January 4, 1777.

TEST PREPARATION

Have students use the excerpt on these pages to answer the following question.

From what you have read, which statement best describes Margaret Hill Morris?

A She hates the enemy soldiers who were captured.

(B) She is deeply compassionate.

C She despairs at humankind.

D She is prejudiced against soldiers.

Balancing Liberty and Order 1776–1830

Introducing the Unit

Using Historical Evidence

In the painting on the right, John L. Krimmel depicts the American enthusiasm for politics. Divide the class into small groups, and have members of each group take turns writing one sentence that describes the painting. Have a volunteer from each group read the collective description to the class. What might an artist include in an election day painting today?

Themes in American History

Direct students' attention to the Unit Themes. Point out that each chapter in this unit has its own theme. To teach this unit thematically, you may wish to use the Forging a New Nation folder in **American History Block Scheduling Support.**

Using the Time Line

To provide students with practice in using a time line to connect key events in the United States with key events in the world, ask questions such as these: (1) How long did it take to draft and adopt the Constitution? *(3 years.)* (2) Which European country abolished the slave trade during Washington's presidency? *(Denmark)* (3) Who was President during the War of 1812? *(Madison)*

---

unit
TWO

Balancing Liberty and Order

1776 – 1830

*N*ow that it had won independence, the young nation needed to find a way to turn its democratic ideals into effective government. Its greatest challenge lay in achieving balance between liberty and order. The central government created by the Articles of Confederation granted liberty, but did little to provide stability. Amid alarming signs of social unrest, 55 of the most distinguished citizens of the day met to address the crisis. Together they crafted the United States Constitution—the set of governing principles by which the nation hoped to achieve liberty while maintaining order.

		UNIT THEMES
Chapter 5 **The Constitution of the United States**	The Constitution of the United States *1776–1800*	**Government** In 1787 the Constitutional Convention crafted a plan of government that would strike a balance between liberty and order.
Chapter 6	The Origins of American Politics *1789–1820*	**Diversity** Native Americans resisted U.S. expansion.
Chapter 7	Life in the New Nation *1783–1830*	**Science and Technology** A spirit of improvement led to new inventions and innovations.

EVENTS IN THE UNITED STATES

1787 Constitutional Convention

1789
- Bill of Rights proposed
- Washington takes office as President

1790 Final state approves Constitution

1794 Whiskey Rebellion

1803 Turning Point: Louisiana Purchase *(p. 186)*

Presidents | Washington | J. Adams | Jefferson

1780   1790   1800

EVENTS IN THE WORLD

1789 French Revolution begins

1791 Haitians revolt against French rule

1792 Denmark abolishes slave trade

1804 Haiti wins independence from France

▶ RESOURCE OPTIONS

Teaching Resources

 Units 1–2 folder Contains instructional materials organized by chapter.

VIEWING HISTORY John L. Krimmel painted *Election Day in Philadelphia* in 1815. **Culture** *What do you think explains the emotional intensity of the crowd?*

E pluribus unum — *"from many, one"*— was chosen as the nation's motto in 1776.

1812
War of 1812 begins

1820
Missouri Compromise

1825
Erie Canal opens

Madison	Monroe	J. Q. Adams

1810 **1820** **1830**

1815
Brazil declares independence from Portugal

1821
Mexico declares independence from Spain

1829
James Smithson bequeaths money to found Smithsonian Institution

 RESOURCE OPTIONS

Media and Technology

Color Transparencies Specific transparencies are referenced throughout the chapters at appropriate points of use. For this unit, see American Photo, B-2; Fine Art, D-6; The Way It Works, H-6; Links Across Time, J-2; and Political Cartoons, K-2.

 Visions of America "Scenes of an Era: Balancing Liberty and Order" located on videodisc side 1 and on videotape 1. Lesson plans for "Scenes of an Era" can be found in the Visions of America Guidebook.

Side 1, Chapter 5

TECHNOLOGY CENTER

Listed below are the technology resources that *America: Pathways to the Present* offers:

RESOURCE PRO

America: Pathways to the Present Teaching Resources on CD-ROM offers lesson planning flexibility, test generation capability, and additional enrichment support.

Using the Internet
Prentice Hall's *America: Pathways to the Present* companion Web site offers student-appropriate Internet activities and links as well as resources for teachers. Visit us at
http://www.Pathways.phschool.com

AmericanHeritage®
History of the United States CD-ROM This interactive, multimedia exploration of the American experience provides a journey through historical, political, and social aspects of American history. Includes Time Tours, Presidents, and History Makers.

Visions of America
This award-winning integrated multimedia package offers Scenes of an Era, Turning Point stories, and historians' viewpoints on core content.

Our Times Multimedia Encyclopedia of the 20th Century **CD-ROM**

INTERACTIVE STUDENT TUTORIAL CD-ROM

GUIDED READING AUDIOTAPES

STUDENT EDITION ON AUDIOTAPE

PRENTICE HALL LISTENING TO MUSIC THE AMERICAN EXPERIENCE AUDIO CD

Answer to . . .

Viewing History Sample answer: Early Americans believed strongly in democracy and took a personal interest in politics.

121

The Constitution of the United States, 1776–1800

Managing Time and Instruction

> **INSTRUCTION SUPPORT**
> These materials for instruction are provided for **each section** in the **Teaching Resources**. See **Units 1–2 folder for Enrichment Support:**

- Reproducible Lesson Plans in Lesson Plans folder   • Learning Styles Lesson Plans in Learning Styles Lesson Plans folder   • Big Idea Graphic Organizers in Big Idea Graphic Organizer folder
- Guided Reading and Review   • Quizzes   • Test Preparation Practice booklet

DAILY LESSON	ENRICHMENT SUPPORT
1 **Government by the States** (pp. 123–128)	• Comparing Primary Sources, On the United States as an Independent Nation, Units 1–2 folder, pp. 66–67 • Key Documents, Virginia Statute of Religious Liberty, Learning with Documents folder, p. 82 • Nystrom *Atlas of Our Country,* Early Expansion of the United States, pp. 20–21 • Literature Activity, *The Contrast,* found on **Resource Pro** • Biography, Captain Daniel Shays, found on **Resource Pro**
2 **The Constitutional Convention** (pp. 132–138)	• Skills for Life Activity, Units 1–2 folder, p. 69 • Literature Activity, On America, Units 1–2 folder, p. 68 • Primary Source Activity, Hamilton and Jefferson, Learning with Documents folder, p. 11 • Decision-Making Activity, Redistributing Government Power, Decision-Making Activities folder, pp. 6–7 • Critical Thinking Activity, Determining Relevance: Checks and Balances, found on **Resource Pro**
3 **Ratifying the Constitution** (pp. 139–142)	• Key Documents, *The Federalist,* no. 71, Learning with Documents folder, p. 83 • Visual Learning Activity, The First United States Coins, Learning with Documents folder, p. 47
4 **The New Government** (pp. 143–146)	• Primary Source Activity, A Department of Peace, found on **Resource Pro** • Visual Learning Activity, A Portrait of a President, found on **Resource Pro** • Biography, Benjamin Banneker, Units 1–2 folder, p. 65 • Primary Source Activity, Meeting President and Mrs. Washington, found on **Resource Pro** • The Bill of Rights Protects You, Why Study History? folder, p. 6

Running Out of Time?

- Use Tape 1, "Balancing Liberty and Order, 1781–1830," from **Visions of America** videotapes series.
- Use Chapter 5 Summary, from **Guide to the Essentials of American History (English and Spanish).**

Companion Web Site

The companion Web site offers online links for all chapter review activities. It also provides key content links and structured support for this chapter for both teachers and students.

http://www.Pathways.phschool.com

Teaching in the Information Age

Media and Technology

For the Student

Interactive Student Tutorial CD-ROM Chapter 5

Student Edition on Audiotape Chapter 5

American Heritage® CD-ROM

Guided Reading Audiotapes (English and Spanish) Chapter 5

For the Teacher

Resource Pro CD-ROM Chapter 5

Test Bank CD-ROM Chapter 5

Listening to Literature Audiotapes *Timeless Voices, Timeless Themes* "Letter to Her Daughter from the New White House" by Abigail Adams

Color Transparencies Critical Thinking, I-1

Assessment Options

Chapter Test Forms A&B Test Bank CD-ROM booklet

Test Bank CD-ROM Chapter 5

Standardized Test Preparation Handbook

Block Scheduling

Pacing Suggestions

For 90-minute Blocks

- Teach sections 2 and 4 using Transparencies K-2, E-3, J-2, and B-2 and the Extended Class Periods Activity on p. 145.
- Teach sections 1 and 2 using the Big Idea Graphic Organizers from Teaching Resources and the Recent Scholarship note on p. 141 for class discussions.

Additional Resources

- Prentice Hall's **American History Block Scheduling Support File** covers over 40 major topics in American history, from beginnings to present.
- **Prentice Hall United States History Video Collection™** contains 20 videotapes covering American history from beginnings to present.
- **Decision America Videotapes and Videodiscs**

Connections to American Literature

from Prentice Hall

America: Pathways to the Present Ben Franklin Campaigns for the Constitution, pp. 1076–1077

Prentice Hall Literature *Timeless Voices, Timeless Themes* "To His Excellency, General Washington" by Phillis Wheatley, pp. 150–151

Additional Resources

For the Student
Catherine D. Bowen. *Miracle at Philadelphia: The Story of the Constitution, May to September, 1787.* Little Brown, 1986.

For the Teacher
Lessons on the Federalist Papers: Supplement to High School Courses in American History, Government and Civics. Organization of American Historians, 1987.

Prentice Hall brings into the classroom the vast archives and scholarship of the nation's premier American history magazine. See "From the Archives of American Heritage®" and "About the Presidents" teaching notes in this chapter.

History Alive!

Teacher's Curriculum Institute, in partnership with Prentice Hall, provides unique materials that engage students with diverse learning styles. See History Alive!® unit on The Constitution in a New Nation.

Student Performance Pack

Ensures success in the three critical areas of Reading, Test Taking, and English Language Development with the following materials:
- Guide to the Essentials of American History in English and Spanish
- Guided Reading Audiotapes in English and Spanish
- Interactive Student Tutorial CD-ROM
- Test Preparation Handbook
- Test Preparation Practice booklet

Introducing the Chapter

A group of powerful men succeeded in writing and winning approval of the federal Constitution and in establishing a strong central government. The conflict generated by their efforts resulted in safeguards in the form of the Bill of Rights to protect Americans' liberty from government infringement.

Themes in American History

The theme for this chapter, Government, is listed at the beginning of this unit. An alternate theme for the chapter is Diversity. To teach this unit thematically, you may wish to use the Forging a New Nation folder in American History Block Scheduling Support.

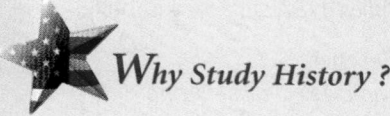

Why Study History ?

Have students explore suggested ways of connecting the past to the present on page 147.

Answer to . . .

Viewing History Students should use this question as an aid in reading the chapter. In portraying the Constitutional Convention, the artist has emphasized the gravity and nobility of the event. The faces and bearing of the men in the painting suggest that such a group would produce a worthy form of government.

122

CHAPTER 5 The Constitution of the United States

1776–1800

CHAPTER FOCUS

This chapter describes the struggle of the young United States to form a lasting government. Recognizing the weaknesses of the Articles of Confederation, delegates met in Philadelphia in 1787 to draft a new plan of government. The resulting Constitution was approved by the states, and a Bill of Rights was added to protect individual freedoms. George Washington, as the nation's first President, set the tone of the new federal government.

The **Why Study History?** page at the end of this chapter explores the effect of the Bill of Rights on the lives of Americans today.

▲
VIEWING HISTORY This painting shows George Washington heading the Constitutional Convention in Philadelphia in 1787. *Government What impressions did the artist try to convey about this historic gathering?*

RESOURCE OPTIONS

Teaching Resources

📁 **Big Idea Graphic Organizer** folder Graphic summary of the main idea of the chapter.

📁 **Learning Styles Lesson Plans** folder Alternate lesson plans for diverse learning styles for each chapter.

Media and Technology

 AmericanHeritage® CD-ROM Time Tour From Revolution to Republic: Creating a Republic; *also* The New Republic: The New Government

 Prentice Hall United States History Video Collection™ Volume 5 *A New Nation (1776–1815)*

Timeline

1776 Pennsylvania Constitution written

1777 Articles of Confederation adopted

1783 Washington retires from army

1786 Shays' Rebellion begins

1787 Constitutional Convention

1775 — 1780 — 1785 — 1790

1 Government by the States

SECTION PREVIEW

Objectives

1. Describe the early government of the United States.
2. List the reasons for opposition to the Articles of Confederation.
3. Evaluate the causes and effects of Shays' Rebellion.
4. **Key Terms** Define: Articles of Confederation; legislative branch; executive branch; judicial branch; constitution; republic; Shays' Rebellion; specie.

Main Idea

In the government under the Articles of Confederation, political power rested mostly with the states, while the national government was weak.

Reading Strategy

Organizing Information As you read, list the arguments for and against the Articles of Confederation.

O n December 23, 1783, a month after watching the British army leave New York, George Washington performed perhaps the most important act of his life: He voluntarily gave up power.

The triumphant general was easily the country's most popular and best-known figure. Many people expected him to move into a new role as head of the new nation, maybe even its king. But Washington had other plans.

Having helped Americans win their freedom from a king, he believed that the nation did not need another supreme ruler. In an act that stunned the world, he gave up his commission as commander of the American army and headed home to Mount Vernon to retire.

Early Government

Americans now faced a new challenge. Could they enjoy their hard-won freedoms without a strong, unified, national government? Could they keep their new liberty and maintain order at the same time? In short, what kind of government should a free people have?

The Continental Congress that had approved the Declaration of Independence in 1776 was simply a loose collection of delegates from 13 separate states. Almost no one wanted a powerful national government. Most people saw Congress as only a wartime necessity.

Americans at that time generally thought of themselves as citizens of individual states, not of a nation. In fact, when referring to the United States, most Americans wrote "the United States *are*" (plural) rather than "the United States *is*" (singular) as people do today. They believed that the country as a whole was less important than its 13 parts. It was not a nation as much as it was a *confederation,* an alliance of separate governments that work together.

The Articles of Confederation In 1777 the Continental Congress adopted a set of laws to govern the United States. These laws were called the **Articles of Confederation.** Approved in

Paul Revere crafted this bowl to honor a general who crushed a rebellion against increased taxes in 1787.

RESOURCE OPTIONS

Teaching Resources

📁 **Reproducible Lesson Plan** Lesson Plans folder, p. 51

📁 **Big Idea Graphic Organizer** Big Idea Graphic Organizer folder, p. 23

📁 **Guided Reading and Review** Units 1–2 folder, p. 57

Media and Technology

 AmericanHeritage® CD-ROM

Time Tour From Revolution to Republic: Creating a Republic

Objectives

You may wish to call students' attention to the objectives in the Section Preview. The objectives are reflected in the main headings of the section.

Bellringer

Ask students on what occasions, or for what reasons, people turn to the federal government. Why do people expect the federal government to help after natural disasters? Discuss the differences between a dictatorship and a democracy, including the pros and cons of each.

Reading Strategy

Organizing Information Refer to the Reading Strategy in the Section Preview. You may wish to model the headings For and Against on the chalkboard. Have students use their completed table to review section content.

LESSON PLAN
Connecting to the Main Idea

1. Focus Explain that the years after the American Revolution were difficult ones for the new United States, which was disorganized and suffered from economic and political problems. Some Americans, known as Nationalists, demanded a stronger national government. Ask why Nationalists saw this as beneficial.

2. Instruct Review the ideas that fueled the American Revolution. Have students explain how the United States government before 1788 reflected these ideas. Ask why many Americans were happy with a weak national government.

3. Close After the war, the United States suffered a variety of political and economic problems. To save the new nation, a small group made plans to restructure the government.

Both the stern General Washington and his officers were overcome by emotion on the day he left the army. With Washington's resignation, the country lost one of its few nationally known and admired leaders.
Government *Why did Washington resign his commission?*

1781, the Articles established a limited national government. Most of the political power lay with the states.

The national government created by the Articles had only one branch: a legislature, or Congress, made up of delegates from the states. Today, Congress is one of the three separate branches of the American government. The **legislative branch,** which includes Congress, is the part of the government that is responsible for making laws. The **executive branch,** headed by the President, executes, or puts in action, the laws passed by the Congress. The third part of the government is the **judicial branch,** made up of the courts and judges who interpret and apply the laws in cases brought before them.

By contrast, under the Articles of Confederation, the Congress carried out the duties of both the legislative and executive branches. The Articles did not create a judicial branch. Each state maintained its own court system.

The Congress set up by the Articles differed in several ways from today's Congress. For example, it lacked the power to tax. To carry out its tasks, Congress had to petition the states for money. It had no power to force the states to do what it wanted.

The Articles of Confederation allowed states to send as many representatives to Congress as they wished. However, each of the thirteen states had only one vote in Congress. Passage of any measure involving money required 9 votes out of the 13, not just a simple majority of 7. Changes in the Articles themselves could only be made if all 13 states agreed.

State Constitutions Far more powerful than the Articles in the country's early years were the individual state constitutions, which created the states' governments. A **constitution** is a plan of government that describes the different parts of the government and their duties and powers. Not every state adopted a constitution during the Revolution, but most did.

GOVERNMENT CONCEPTS

three branches of government: the legislative branch makes the laws; the executive branch enforces the laws; the judicial branch interprets the laws

▼ **The Historical Context** The national government created by the Articles of Confederation did not include an executive or judicial branch. This omission, which reflected Americans' fear of a strong central government, made it difficult for the national government to operate effectively.

▼ **The Concept Today** The Constitution of the United States, which later replaced the Articles, did provide for three separate branches of government. All three branches remain strong and vital parts of the federal government.

In its constitution the state of Pennsylvania introduced bold new ideas about democratic government. Written in 1776, the Pennsylvania constitution gave voting rights to all white men 21 years of age or older who paid taxes. Thus, the state became the first to open the voting process to ordinary people, not just wealthy gentlemen.

The Pennsylvania constitution also created a state legislature that was *unicameral.* That is, it had just one house, or body of representatives. Today, most state legislatures, as well as the United States Congress, are *bicameral,* having two houses. Congress, for example, has a House of Representatives and a Senate.

Finally, representatives in Pennsylvania's legislature had to run for election every year. This provision made state lawmakers very responsive to the people's wishes.

Opposition to the Articles

Americans generally agreed that their new nation should be a democracy, or government by the people. Specifically, they favored the creation of a **republic,** a government run by the people through their elected representatives. Yet people held widely differing views on how much influence ordinary citizens should have in the governing of the republic.

Economic Problems Wealthy, educated gentlemen worried that the Articles had given too much power to ordinary citizens, who were generally less educated. These gentlemen were more interested in preserving order than expanding freedom, and they had plenty of disorder to point to.

By 1786, three years after the American Revolution, the nation still had a debt of about $50 million, an unthinkably huge sum at that time. State governments and the national government had borrowed money from foreign countries and from their own citizens to pay for the war.

Debt was such a problem everywhere that some state governments printed cheap paper money to help their citizens pay off their loans. This created economic chaos. Desperate for money, states with good seaports put heavy taxes on goods destined for neighboring states, stirring up hostilities.

Upper-class critics of the Articles believed that these troubles had arisen because citizens had too much power in their state legislatures. They feared that this was not always the best way to run a government.

Concerns About Weak Government By the early 1780s, a group called the Nationalists sought to strengthen the national government. They wanted to restrain what they saw as the unpredictable behavior of the states. The Nationalists included several former military officers, many members of Congress, merchants, planters, and lawyers, and some whose names are now familiar: George Washington, Benjamin Franklin, James Madison, and Alexander Hamilton.

In newspaper articles and private letters, Nationalists expressed their views about the dangers of a weak national government. They pointed out that Congress sometimes was unable to act because so many lawmakers failed to attend the sessions. They predicted that the lack of a national court system and national economic policies would create chaos. They feared that the United States would not command respect from the rest of the world.

Most of all, they worried that Americans' fondness for challenging authority and for demanding individual rights was getting out of hand. Nationalists saw this period, from 1781 to 1787, as a dangerous time of indecision about how to govern the new nation.

Main Idea
CONNECTIONS

What did the Nationalists see as the dangers of a weak national government?

FACT Finder
Weaknesses in the Articles of Confederation

Weaknesses
One vote for each state, regardless of size
Congress cannot collect taxes
Congress powerless to regulate foreign and interstate commerce
No separate executive branch to enforce acts of Congress
No national court system to interpret laws
Amendment only with consent of all the states
A 9/13 majority required to pass laws
Articles only a "firm league of friendship"

Interpreting Tables The confederation entered into by the 13 states gave little real power to the national government. *Government* How did the Articles limit the power of Congress?

ACTIVITY
LEARNING STYLES

In 1776, a loose confederation of thirteen states met to establish the Articles of Confederation. State governments, however, resisted this attempt to centralize government. To demonstrate this struggle, divide the class into thirteen "states," each of which should write its own constitution of three laws. Then have each state send a representative to the "First Constitutional Congress" to establish ten federal laws that do not conflict with their state constitutions. *(Verbal/Linguistic)*

RESOURCE OPTIONS

Teaching Resources

📁 **Comparing Primary Sources** On the United States as an Independent Nation, Units 1–2 folder, pp. 66–67

📁 **Key Documents** Virginia Statute of Religious Liberty, Learning with Documents folder, p. 82

Media and Technology

🦅 **AmericanHeritage® CD-ROM**

History Makers Benjamin Franklin

Answer to . . .

Main Idea Connections Disorganization due to lack of national court systems and economic policies; lack of respect from other nations.

Interpreting Tables They did not give Congress the power to raise money, regulate commerce, or enforce the laws it passed.

Though the Revolution was over, many Americans were still challenging authority. In this engraving, a crowd puts an end to a county meeting by throwing a government official into a brook. *Government How did incidents such as this one bolster the arguments of the Nationalists?*

 AMERICAN VOICES "Every man of sense must be convinced that our disturbances have arisen more from the want of [government] power than the abuse of it."

—*Fisher Ames, Nationalist from Massachusetts*

Most Americans did not agree with this view. The state constitutions and the Articles of Confederation were doing exactly what they were supposed to be doing: maintaining a democratic republic. So what if government was disorderly? So what if mistakes were made?

It was better to have mistakes under a government of the people than order under the rule of tyrants. Besides, the government established by the Articles had won independence from Britain. This showed that the government was strong enough, the supporters reasoned.

Learning from History The Nationalists were well educated in European history. They knew that in Europe, attempts to establish republican governments had failed, dissolving into chaos and then tyranny. Nationalists pointed out that this had happened to the Roman republic, over 1800 years earlier, and it could happen to the United States as well.

The Nationalists said that history had shown that people were not naturally wise enough to have so much power over their own affairs. George Washington expressed it this way: "We have . . . had too good an opinion of human nature in forming our confederation."

America as a Model Finally, the Nationalists agreed with Thomas Paine that America was a model for the world. It would be irresponsible, they believed, to allow the nation to fall into political violence. One Englishman commented that if this happened:

> **"The fairest experiment ever tried in human affairs will miscarry; and . . . a REVOLUTION which had revived the hopes of good men and promised an opening to better times, will become a discouragement to all future efforts in favor of liberty, and prove only an opening to a new scene of human degeneracy and misery."**
>
> —*Richard Price, 1785*

In fact, it was General Washington's understanding of history and his respect for this greater cause that had led him to give up his command to the civilian government so promptly. He did not want to play the role of Julius Caesar of ancient Rome, a general who became a symbol of tyranny by replacing a republican government with a dictatorship.

The Annapolis Convention In 1786, Nationalists held a convention in Annapolis, Maryland, to discuss economic problems that could not be solved under the limits of the Articles. These included issues such as interstate and foreign trade. But the convention failed to rally interest in dealing with the weaknesses in the Articles. Only 12 delegates from five states attended the convention. Those who came took only one step, but it would be an important one: They agreed to call another convention in Philadelphia the following year, 1787, to try to fix the government.

Shays' Rebellion

In the meantime, a crisis occurred in Massachusetts that would boost support for the Nationalists' cause. It is known as **Shays' Rebellion.**

The Causes of the Rebellion In the years following the war, merchants and wealthy people who had loaned money to the states started to demand their money back. They pressed the impoverished states to pass high taxes in order to collect the money to pay off their debts.

In Massachusetts, legislators passed the heaviest direct tax ever. It was to be paid in **specie**—gold or silver coin—rather than in paper money. Compared to paper money, specie was far more scarce, and worth much more.

COMPARING PRIMARY SOURCES

THE STRENGTH OF THE NEW NATION

Amid the social and political upheaval of the 1770s, observers differed on whether the United States would continue as a country.

Unfavorable Opinion	Favorable Opinion
"I [see] insurmountable causes for weakness that will prevent America from being a powerful state. . . . In short, such is the difference of character, manners, religion and interest of the different colonies that if they were left to themselves, there would soon be a civil war from one end of the continent to another." —*British clergyman Andrew Burnaby,* Burnaby's Travels Through North America, *1775*	"Let us view [America] as it now is—an independent state that has taken an equal station amid the nations of the earth. . . . It is a vitality [living thing], liable, indeed, to many disorders, many dangerous diseases; but it is young and strong, and will struggle . . . against those evils and surmount them. . . . Its strength will grow with its years." —*Former Massachusetts governor Thomas Pownall,* The New Relation Between the Old and the New World, *1780*

ANALYZING VIEWPOINTS Compare the main arguments made by the two writers.

The lawmakers and merchants who supported the tax generally lived in eastern coastal regions of the state. Opposition came from farmers in the western part of the state most hard-hit by the new tax. To these citizens the situation brought back memories of the British taxes that had helped spark the American Revolution.

Farmers complained bitterly to the state legislature to take back the tax. The state refused. Overloaded with debt, farmers grew desperate as the courts seized their possessions.

Like many farmers in the region, Daniel Shays was a war veteran who now found himself facing jail for his debts. In 1786 he led a rebellion that quickly spread through the local area. Citizens drove off tax collectors and protested the new taxes with petitions and public meetings. When the state courts rejected their petitions, the rebels forced the courts to close.

Main Idea
CONNECTIONS

Why did Shays come into conflict with the Massachusetts government?

Answers to
SECTION 1 REVIEW

1. (a) Articles of Confederation, see p. 123; (b) legislative branch, see p. 124; (c) executive branch, see p. 124; (d) judicial branch, see p. 124; (e) constitution, see p. 124; (f) republic, see p. 125; (g) Shays' Rebellion, see p. 127; (h) specie, see p. 127.

2. Supporters believed that only a limited national government was needed once the war had ended. They feared that a strong national government might take away states' authority and individuals' freedoms. Opponents believed that the Articles did not give the national government the authority it needed to settle political and economic problems.

3. Sample answers: causes—high taxes to be paid in specie, farmers drowning in debt; effects—showed the resolve of citizens to fight heavy-handed government, supported Nationalists' claim that stronger government was needed to avoid chaos.

4. Students should support their answers with facts from the text.

5. Facts include: created limited national government, gave most powers to the states. Opinions include: the Articles were too weak, they would not hold the union together, they needed to be reformed but not replaced.

6. The strongest essays will state an opinion, support it with facts, and rebut opposing views.

Liberty and order clashed in Shays' Rebellion. Protesters, shown here blocking a courthouse, refused to pay taxes—and the government insisted that laws be obeyed. *Government* *Why do you think the rebels felt justified in challenging the government?*

Angry crowds rioted. Shays and a small army marched to the city of Springfield, where guns were stored at an arsenal. As open conflict raged, Congress could only look on helplessly. It had no money to raise an army and no way to force states to pay for one. Finally, the state government gathered an army and sent it to the western part of Massachusetts, where it quieted the rebellion in January 1787.

Many rebels and their families left Massachusetts for Vermont or New York, states with lower taxes. Shays and a few others were arrested and sentenced to death. Shays appealed the sentence and eventually regained his freedom.

Effects of the Rebellion For the rebels themselves, Shays' Rebellion demonstrated their commitment to defy the authority of any government when it acted against people's wishes. Far more important, the rebellion demonstrated to many prominent Americans that steps had to be taken to strengthen the national government and avoid civil unrest.

In May 1787, the convention called by the delegates at Annapolis opened in the city of Philadelphia. This time, convinced of the urgent need for government reform, 12 states (all but Rhode Island) sent delegates. The business at hand, wrote key delegate James Madison, was to "decide forever the fate of republican government."

SECTION 1 REVIEW

Comprehension

1. **Key Terms Define:** (a) Articles of Confederation; (b) legislative branch; (c) executive branch; (d) judicial branch; (e) constitution; (f) republic; (g) Shays' Rebellion; (h) specie.

2. **Summarizing the Main Idea** Why did some people support the Articles of Confederation, and why did some oppose it?

Critical Thinking

3. **Organizing Information** Create a cause-and-effect chart on Shays' Rebellion.

4. **Analyzing Time Lines** Review the time line at the start of the section. Choose any two entries and show how they are related.

5. **Distinguishing Fact from Opinion** Write two major facts and two opinions about the Articles of Confederation.

Writing Activity

6. **Writing a Persuasive Essay** If you had lived at the time of Shays' Rebellion, would you have supported it or opposed it? Write an essay that might appear in a newspaper of the time.

 RESOURCE OPTIONS

Teaching Resources

🗀 **Quiz** Units 1–2 folder, p. 58

Student Performance Pack

✪ **Guide to the Essentials** Chapter 5, Section 1 (English and Spanish)

Answer to . . .

Viewing History They felt they were being taxed unfairly, and that as western farmers they were carrying a heavier burden than eastern merchants.

SKILLS FOR LIFE

Critical Thinking

Geography

Graphs and Charts

Historical Evidence

Identifying Central Issues

Identifying central issues means recognizing the main topics or problems in a piece of information. Usually, all the problems a writer discusses are connected in some way with the central issues.

The excerpt below appeared in a newspaper in Rhode Island, the only state that did not send delegates to the Constitutional Convention. It is a parable, a story in which a lesson is set forth in symbols. The symbols provide clues to the central issues being discussed.

Read the excerpt and use these steps to identify the central issues.

1. *Identify the subject of the excerpt.* (a) What is the subject of the excerpt, and when was it published? (b) Given the subject and date, what historical period or event is the writer referring to?

2. *Identify the meaning of the symbols in the story.* (a) Who or what do the parents and the sons represent? (b) What historical period or event is symbolized by the events that occur between the building of the house and the addition to the house? (c) Who or what do the three rooms of the house represent? (d) Who or what does the "thirteenth son" represent?

3. *Summarize the message or main idea and identify the central issue of the excerpt.* (a) What central issue does this excerpt from a 1787 newspaper article address? (b) Explain how the parable illustrates this point. (c) What point does the parable make about failing to join in a common effort?

TEST FOR SUCCESS

(a) What do you think "repairing the house" symbolizes? (b) What might the addition of the two rooms represent? (c) How do these symbols relate to the central issue of the parable?

Philadelphia, August 25, 1787

The conduct of the United States, with respect to their governments, may be illustrated by the following story:—An old man arrived, after a long and dangerous voyage, upon the coast of America, with a family consisting of a wife, a few choice old servants, and *thirteen* sons. As soon as they landed, they joined and built a large and commodious dwelling-house, where they lived in safety for several years. The sons, however, grew weary of the company of their parents, and each of them built a cabin for himself, at a distance from the family mansion-house. They had not lived long in this way, before they began to suffer many difficulties and wants. . . . At last *twelve* of them met by agreement upon a plain, and agreed to petition their father to be admitted again under his protection. The venerable [honorable] old man

opened his doors to them, and they again became members of his family. They first joined in repairing and fortifying the old mansion-house. They, moreover, added *two* more rooms to it, for the separate use of the old man and his wife, in order thereby to preserve their dignity and authority. From this time the whole family became respectable, happy, and prosperous. . . .

The *thirteenth* son, who refused to accompany his brothers to his father's house, after living a miserable life . . . by himself in the woods, was found *hanging* . . . to the limb of a tree near his cabin.

—Providence Gazette and Country Journal, *Vol. 24 Saturday, September 8, 1787, p. 2*

RESOURCE OPTIONS

Teaching Resources

Skills for Life Activity, Units 1–2 folder, p. 69, encourages students to apply the skill of identifying central issues by writing a parable to reflect the political status of the District of Columbia.

Media and Technology

 Color Transparencies Critical Thinking, I-2

SKILLS FOR LIFE

Critical Thinking

Identifying Central Issues

Focus Students will identify the central issues of a parable.

Instruct Explain that a symbol is a word or sign that stands for something other than itself. Ask students to read the parable and discuss the symbols. After identifying the central issue, ask why they think the writer chose these symbols and how they communicate the central issue.

Extend See the Skills for Life Activity in the Resource Options below.

Answers

1. (a) The behavior of the states toward their government; September 8, 1787. (b) The Constitutional Convention.

2. (a) The parents represent a strong central government. The thirteen sons represent the thirteen states. (b) The Critical Period, the Constitutional Convention, and the twelve states' recommitment to the concept of a unified national government. (c) Possible answer: The three branches of government. (d) The state of Rhode Island, which refused to send delegates to the Constitutional Convention.

3. (a) The importance of a strong, unified, national government. (b) It compares the states to sons who learned that they must live and work together as one unit. (c) Those who don't participate would suffer like the thirteenth son.

TEST FOR SUCCESS

Sample answers: (a) Strengthening the national government. (b) Adding two more branches to the national government. (c) The writer argues that in order to be happy and prosperous, states should support the provisions of the new Constitution.

129

GEOGRAPHY AND HISTORY

The Northwest Territory

Focus Point out that the location of Marietta, Ohio—the first settlement in the western lands of the United States—contributed to its success. Then explain that Marietta was the first of a number of Ohio towns begun by New Englanders and that the New Englanders who settled Marietta left their stamp throughout the region.

Instruct Ask students if any of them have lived in another part of the country. Discuss the differences between their former and present communities. What might account for such differences? What differences exist today between New England and the Midwest?

Ask students to find place names in Ohio that seem to be based on place names in New England. What places in their own region might have been named by immigrants or by people migrating from other parts of the country?

Extend Explain that new settlers formed covenants that resembled those made by their ancestors upon first reaching Massachusetts. The New England settlers of Oberlin, Ohio, for example, pledged themselves to "a life of simplicity, to special devotion to church and school, and to earnest labor in the missionary cause." Ask students to suppose that a small group of settlers from their community is emigrating to an undeveloped, isolated section of Alaska. Ask each student to list at least five institutions that they would expect to see in the new settlement. On what principles would they hope to see the community based?

GEOGRAPHY AND HISTORY

The Northwest Territory

A compass

The geographic theme of regions examines the characteristics that set one area apart from others. The region called the Northwest Territory was the first public land for sale after the American Revolution. How did the government divide it up?

To help pay off Revolutionary War debt, the Continental Congress decided to sell off an area of public lands northwest of the Ohio River. This land was known as the Northwest Territory. As shown on the map on the next page, the Northwest Territory was a huge region so legislators needed to develop a system of dividing it up into affordable segments.

How Land Was Divided

To achieve its goal, Congress passed the Land Ordinance of 1785. This law stated that before land in the Northwest Territory could be sold, it had to be surveyed and divided up into townships. This system was based on the principles used in the laying out of New England towns.

As you can see on the map, the size of each township was 36 square miles. Townships were subdivided into 36 lots (now called sections), with one lot set aside for a public school. Lots were the smallest unit for sale. Each lot was a square mile, or about 640 acres. The minimum price was $1.00 per acre. The undivided townships were bought by groups wishing to start communities in the New England tradition, or by people pooling their resources to buy a township, which they themselves would later divide into individual farm units.

Congress chose a tract of land on the Ohio River as the first to be sold in the Northwest Territory. The area labeled "Area of First Survey" on the map is part of that tract, which totaled about 5 million acres.

New Englanders Buy Western Land

The first tract of land was purchased by the Ohio Company, a group of New Englanders who persuaded others in their region to move to Ohio with them. They founded the town of Marietta, where the Muskingum River flows into the Ohio River.

As General George Washington noted, "Information, property, and strength will be [the town's] characteristics. I know many of the settlers personally, and there never were men better calculated to promote the welfare of such a community." Indeed, Marietta became a successful, even thriving settlement.

> *The first tract of land was purchased by the Ohio Company, a group of New Englanders who persuaded others in their region to move to Ohio with them.*

▶ RESOURCE OPTIONS

Teaching Resources

 Geography and History Activity
Moving the City to the Country, Geography and History folder, pp. 4–5

 Nystrom *Atlas of Our Country*
Early Expansion of the United States, pp. 20–21

Each range, as determined by surveyors, was a strip of land between two meridians six miles apart. Each range made up a row of townships. Townships were divided into 36 1-square-mile sections and sold for a minimum of $1 per acre.

The First Settlement Succeeds

Marietta grew rapidly because it was a magnet for new settlers. It was also a jumping off point for travel farther west, and thus developed a thriving trade. Between 1788 and 1790, nearly 900 boats carrying some 20,000 settlers passed along Marietta's shores on their way west.

Despite the influences of the many travelers who passed through Marietta, the New England character of the town lasted well into the 1800s. Voting records of the settlers and their descendants show that for years Marietta's residents voted as New Englanders did in national elections, rather than as people in other settlements in Ohio and nearby Kentucky did.

GEOGRAPHIC CONNECTIONS

1. How was the Northwest Territory divided up?

2. What factors contributed to the success of the town of Marietta, Ohio?

Themes in Geography

3. *Regions* How was public education promoted in this region?

Objectives

You may wish to call students' attention to the objectives in the Section Preview. The objectives are reflected in the main headings of the section.

Bellringer

Ask students to define the word *compromise* and recall a time in their life when they compromised about an important issue.

Reading Strategy

Organizing Information Refer to the Reading Strategy in the Section Preview. Have students share their lists with one another.

2 The Constitutional Convention

SECTION PREVIEW

Objectives

1 Describe the role of James Madison at the Constitutional Convention.
2 Identify divisions at the convention and the agreements that produced a lasting document.
3 Analyze the structure of the government under the Constitution.
4 *Key Terms* Define: amend; veto; Great Compromise; Three-Fifths Compromise; federal; separation of powers; checks and balances; Electoral College.

Main Idea

In 1787, delegates to a convention in Philadelphia created a new plan of government, the Constitution of the United States.

Reading Strategy

Organizing Information As you read, list ways that the Constitutional Convention addressed the weaknesses of the Articles of Confederation.

LESSON PLAN

Connecting to the Main Idea

1. Focus Explain that delegates to the Constitutional Convention struggled over how much power to leave with the states and how much to give the national government. Ask how the new government was structured.

2. Instruct Explain that crafting a lasting national government was an arduous process of debate and compromise. Ask why compromise was so important to the success of the convention.

Discuss the major divisions among the delegates. What was the Great Compromise? The Three-Fifths Compromise?

3. Close Writing the Constitution was an important step in creating a lasting nation. But before the Constitution could become law, it had to be approved by the states.

During the convention, Benjamin Franklin wondered if the decoration on Washington's chair represented a sun setting or rising on America.

The air outside the Pennsylvania State House was hot and sticky, smelling of animals and rotten garbage. Around the modest brick building, which is now called Independence Hall, soldiers kept curious onlookers at a distance. Despite the withering heat, the windows of one room were closed so no one could eavesdrop on the voices within. Gathered in the Assembly Room, men in powdered wigs and heavy clothing labored through the long summer. They were building a government.

The Convention Assembles

This historic meeting is known as the Constitutional Convention. In only four months, the Philadelphia convention produced the document that has governed the United States for more than 200 years,

the United States Constitution. (See the complete text of the Constitution following this chapter.)

The Constitutional Convention grew out of an unsuccessful meeting in Annapolis, Maryland, in 1786. Failing to stir up support for addressing the problems of the Articles of Confederation, the Annapolis delegates had decided to tackle the issue again the next year. They called for a convention in Philadelphia to begin in May 1787, and invited states to send delegates.

During the passing months, disputes among states and violent outbreaks such as Shays' Rebellion raised fears that the fragile nation might collapse. This time, states responded to the call to fix the national government.

The Constitutional Convention drew 55 delegates from all the states except Rhode Island, which chose not to attend. Half of the men were over age 42. A few were very rich, but some had no more than a comfortable living. Many were well educated and familiar with the theories of European political thinkers.

▶ RESOURCE OPTIONS

Teaching Resources

📁 **Reproducible Lesson Plan** Lesson Plans folder, p. 52

📁 **Learning Styles Lesson Plan** Learning Styles Lesson Plans folder, p. 12

📁 **Big Idea Graphic Organizer** Big Idea Graphic Organizer folder, p. 24

📁 **Guided Reading and Review** Units 1–2 folder, p. 59

Media and Technology

 AmericanHeritage® CD-ROM

 Time Tour From Revolution to Republic: Creating a Republic

James Madison

One man made it his business to attend every meeting of the convention. During these sessions, he could be seen busily taking the notes that later would become our best record of the proceedings. His name was James Madison. Later generations would call him "the father of the Constitution."

James Madison (1751–1836)

Man of Knowledge Madison was a quiet bachelor of only 36 when he arrived in Philadelphia to help rescue the struggling government. Yet few men came better prepared for the task.

In his home at the foot of the Blue Ridge Mountains of Virginia, Madison had spent evenings poring over books of history, government, and law. By the time of the Constitutional Convention, he had invested a year thinking specifically about how to craft a new government.

Madison had a superb foundation of knowledge to build upon. The son of a wealthy landowner, he grew up on a plantation in Orange County, Virginia. There he studied European political thought under a Scottish tutor. In 1769 he left home for the College of New Jersey (now Princeton University), finishing the four-year program in two years.

Education, talent, and hard work made Madison the "best-informed Man of any point in debate," as a fellow delegate noted. Yet the Virginian remained "a Gentleman of great modesty—with a remarkable sweet temper."

A small-boned man with a thin voice and sometimes frail health, Madison was shy and polite. He did not marry until he was 43, but found a good match in the lively and sociable Dolley Payne Todd, a 26-year-old widow. They were happily married for 42 years.

Man of Politics Despite his shyness and dislike for public speaking, Madison became an early leader in the independence movement. He served in the Continental Congress in 1780, served in the Virginia legislature, and helped draft the Articles of Confederation.

After his work on the Constitution, Madison would serve in the new House of Representatives and hold other key jobs in the early government. Madison became President in 1809 and served until 1817. He remained active in politics well into his eighties.

Man of Philosophy Madison's studies of philosophy had led him to believe that people are naturally selfish creatures driven by powerful emotions and personal interests. That did not mean there was no hope for order in society, however. Madison drew from the writings of European philosophers who argued that, through proper government, humans could take control of themselves.

Madison believed that constitutions could establish political institutions that encouraged the best in people while restraining the worst. A dream of devising just such a constitution was exactly what brought James Madison to the Philadelphia Convention. ■

Divisions at the Convention

The first act of the Constitutional Convention in 1787 was to unanimously elect George Washington as its president. Other business proved far more divisive.

The major division was between those who wanted to **amend,** or revise, the Articles of Confederation and those who wanted to abandon them altogether. Nearly everyone agreed on the need for a stronger national government, but some saw no need to start from scratch. In fact, the Philadelphia convention had been empowered only to amend the Articles. In order to replace them, the convention would have to overstep its authority. That is what it did.

In the end, Madison and others who wanted a new government managed to dominate the meetings by bringing a plan with them. Their Virginia Plan became the focus of discussion against which all other ideas were weighed.

The Virginia Plan Submitted by Edmund Randolph of Virginia, the Virginia Plan called for the creation of a bicameral, or two-house, national legislature. Each state would send representatives in proportion to the number of its citizens. A state with a large population thus would have more representatives, and greater voting power, than a state with a small population.

The Virginia Plan addressed the shortcomings of the Articles in several ways:

BACKGROUND

The Writers of the Constitution

The men who wrote and supported the Constitution are often thought of as wise old men. But the nine leading Federalists were, on average, 10 to 12 years younger than the Antifederalists. George Washington, at 55, was the oldest of the leading Federalists in 1787. James Madison—"father of the Constitution"—was only 36, and Alexander Hamilton was 30. Antifederalist leaders reflected the generational split among the founders. Samuel Adams, for example, was 67 in 1787.

Customize for

English Language Learners

Ask students to write the following section headings on a piece of paper: *James Madison, Divisions at the Convention, Government Structure.* Have students scan the section for subheadings under each heading and fill in details from the text as they read.

As they signed the Constitution at Philadelphia's Independence Hall on September 17, 1787, the delegates finally agreed on a framework for the nation. *Government What finally broke the deadlock over legislative representation?*

(1) The new legislature would have added powers, including the right to tax and to regulate foreign and interstate commerce.

(2) The national legislature would have the power to **veto,** or prohibit from becoming law, any act of a state legislature. Should a state defy national authority, the national government would have the power to use force against the state. Such proposals frightened some people because they would give the national government greater power than the states.

(3) In addition to the legislative branch, the proposed government would have an executive branch and a judicial branch.

States with large populations stood to benefit from the Virginia Plan, because they would get the most representatives in the legislature. Thus the larger states championed the Virginia Plan.

The New Jersey Plan Opposition to the Virginia Plan came from small states, which feared they would have little power in the new government. They proposed an alternative, the New Jersey Plan. Proposed by New Jersey's William Paterson, the New Jersey Plan had these key features:

(1) It would give Congress the power to tax and to regulate foreign and interstate commerce.

(2) It would create executive and judicial branches.

(3) It would give every state an equal vote in a unicameral Congress. Smaller states thus would have the same voting power as larger states.

Like the Articles of Confederation, the New Jersey Plan aimed to keep state governments more powerful than the national government. The plan also ensured that heavily populated states would not overpower the others.

Reaching Agreements

A central difference between the Virginia and New Jersey plans was representation in the legislature. To put it simply, should states with more people have more representatives in Congress? On July 2, the convention voted on this issue. The vote was split and the convention deadlocked. For a while, matters seemed hopeless.

The Great Compromise Within several days, a solution finally emerged. It is called the **Great Compromise.** It created a legislative branch made up of two houses, as called for in the Virginia Plan. In one house, the Senate, each state, regardless of its size, would have the same number of representatives. (That number is now two per state.) This pleased the small states. In the House of Representatives, the number of seats would be based on each state's population. This won the support of the large states. The Great Compromise was approved on July 16, 1787.

The Three-Fifths Compromise Another difficult issue remained: When calculating a state's population, should enslaved people be included? Many of the Framers (creators) of the Constitution, including James Madison, owned slaves. Madison and others considered slavery immoral. Yet they were unable to bring themselves to do anything about this contradiction.

If slaves were to be included in a state's population count, the southern states, with their many slaves, would gain great power in the House of Representatives. If slaves were not counted, southern states would be weak in the House. Once again the delegates compromised, adopting a formula that became known as the **Three-Fifths Compromise.** Under this plan, three fifths of a state's slave population would be counted when determining representation.

The Three-Fifths Compromise did not mean that enslaved African Americans would be allowed to vote or that their interests would be represented in Congress. They, like Native Americans, were excluded from participating in the government, although in this early period some free African Americans in some states could vote.

Although many features of Madison's Virginia Plan survived these compromises, the delegates never went as far in strengthening the national government as Madison would have liked. For example, they refused to give Congress the right to veto laws passed by the states. Yet the plan did create a stronger government.

A Lasting Document

After further debate over the various provisions, the convention approved the final draft of the United States Constitution on September 17, 1787. Remarkably, this written plan of government has remained basically the same for over two hundred years.

The Constitution has many strengths that have helped it to endure. On certain issues it is specific enough not to be misinterpreted by later generations. Yet it has been flexible enough to adapt to social, economic, political, and technological changes that its creators could scarcely have imagined. Perhaps the best proof of this flexibility is the fact that the Constitution has been amended just 27 times in this nation's history.

The United States Constitution continues to inspire people around the world. Many nations have modeled their own governments after it, borrowing ideas not only about the structure of government, but also about its goals. The Constitution's goals are set forth in its introduction, called the Preamble:

KEY DOCUMENTS

"We the People of the United States, in Order to form a more perfect Union, establish Justice, insure domestic Tranquility, provide for the common defence, promote the general Welfare, and secure the Blessings of Liberty to ourselves and our Posterity, do ordain and establish this Constitution for the United States of America."

—*Preamble to the Constitution, 1787*

Over the years, Americans have come to see the first three words of the Constitution, "We the People," as the most important. Everything else in the document follows from the basic idea that in the United States it is the people who govern.

Government Structure

The Framers of the Constitution knew that while government needed power in order to be effective, too much power could lead to abuses. So they kept government under control by dividing power, in two ways.

Federal and State Powers The Constitution created what some leaders began to call a **federal** government, in which power is shared among state and national authorities. Some powers, such as establishing an

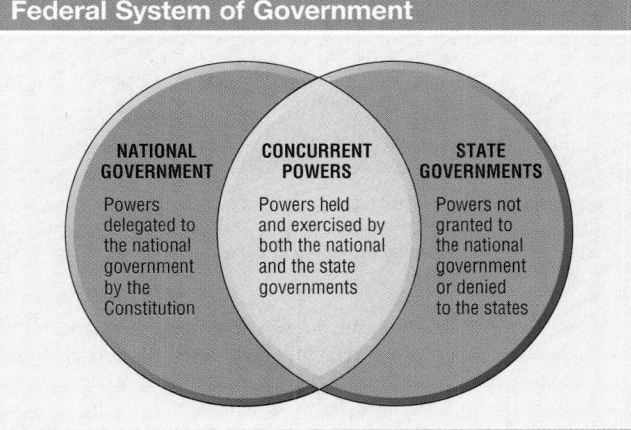

Federal System of Government

NATIONAL GOVERNMENT	CONCURRENT POWERS	STATE GOVERNMENTS
Powers delegated to the national government by the Constitution	Powers held and exercised by both the national and the state governments	Powers not granted to the national government or denied to the states

Interpreting Charts Powers not granted to the federal government or denied to the states are reserved for state government. *Government Some powers are exercised by both federal and state governments. What are these powers called?*

Using the Internet

Create a Diary Entry

Objective Use the Internet to create a diary entry of one of the delegates to the Constitutional Convention. Have students follow these instructions:

1. Access *America: Pathways to the Present* Web site at

http://www.Pathways.phschool.com

for the URL for the National Archives and Records Administration's The Constitution of the United States.

2. Open the link to the article on "A More Perfect Union." Read it.

3. Study the text under the heading The First Draft. Choose a delegate and write three diary entries, each one describing an event that took place during this time. Choose from: George Mason, Gouverneur Morris, Benjamin Franklin, Edmund Randolph, Alexander Hamilton.

4. Be sure your entry contains facts told in chronological order. Post it in the classroom or read it out loud.

TEST PREPARATION

Have students read the excerpt from the Preamble to the Constitution on this page and then answer the question below.

What did the writers of the Constitution mean by "ourselves and our Posterity"?

A The men who wrote the Constitution.

B All the land and wealth the writers had accumulated.

C The writers and their immediate families.

D Americans and their future descendants.

Answer to . . .

Interpreting Charts Concurrent powers.

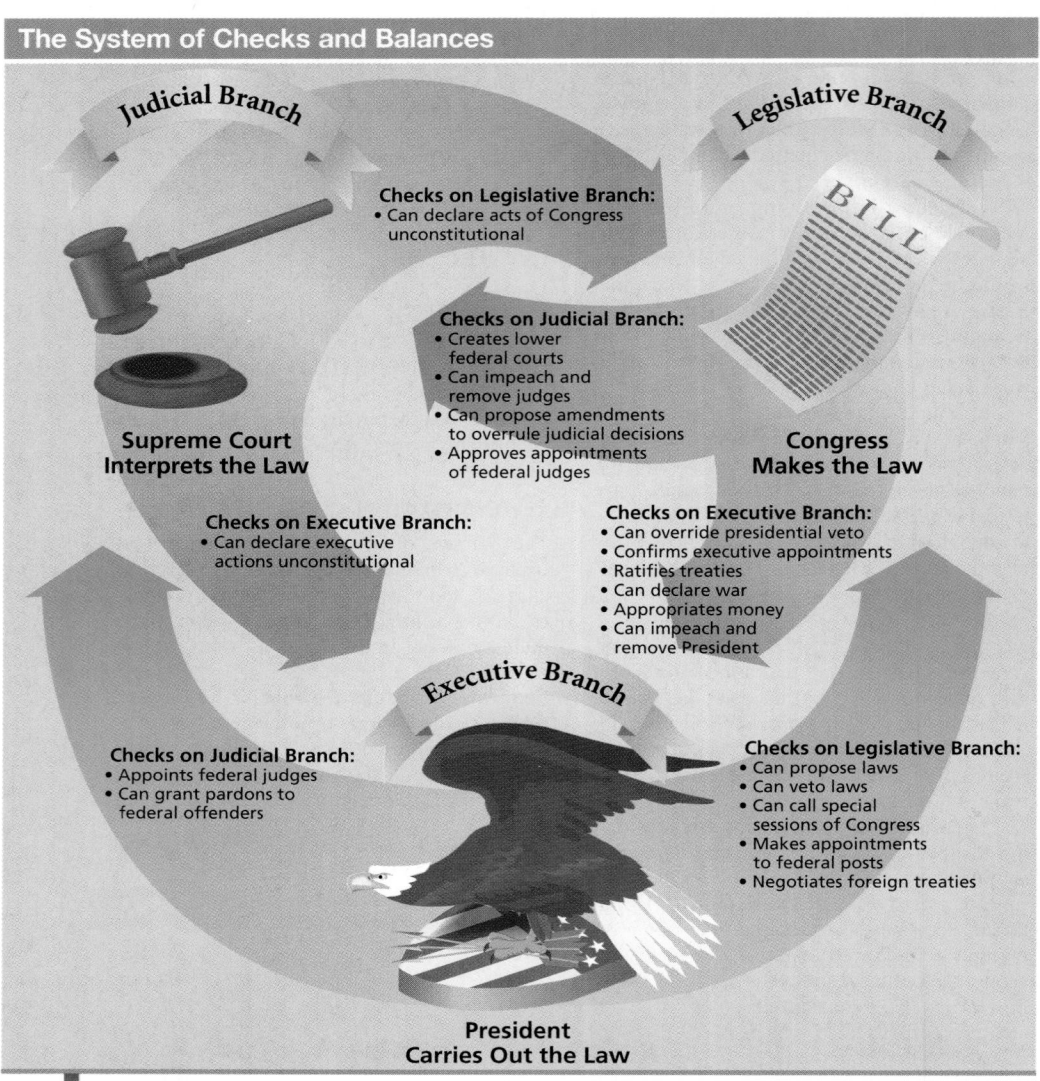

Judicial Branch

Supreme Court
Interprets the Law

Checks on Legislative Branch:
• Can declare acts of Congress unconstitutional

Checks on Judicial Branch:
• Creates lower federal courts
• Can impeach and remove judges
• Can propose amendments to overrule judicial decisions
• Approves appointments of federal judges

Checks on Executive Branch:
• Can declare executive actions unconstitutional

Legislative Branch

Congress
Makes the Law

Checks on Executive Branch:
• Can override presidential veto
• Confirms executive appointments
• Ratifies treaties
• Can declare war
• Appropriates money
• Can impeach and remove President

Executive Branch

President
Carries Out the Law

Checks on Judicial Branch:
• Appoints federal judges
• Can grant pardons to federal offenders

Checks on Legislative Branch:
• Can propose laws
• Can veto laws
• Can call special sessions of Congress
• Makes appointments to federal posts
• Negotiates foreign treaties

 Interpreting Charts "You must first enable the government to control the governed," wrote Madison, "and in the next place, oblige it to control itself." This control is found in the Constitution's system of checks and balances *Government How does the legislative branch check the executive branch?*

Customize for
More Advanced Students

Have students analyze the Constitution and the new government it created. How did the Constitution combine popular sovereignty with a strong national government? Why did delegates to the convention impose limits on presidential power? Are there problems today that the Constitution fails to address?

---

educational system, are called *reserved powers* because they are reserved for the states. Others, such as declaring war, are called *delegated powers* because they are delegated to the federal government. Still other powers, such as collecting taxes, are called *concurrent powers* because the federal and state governments hold them at the same time, or concurrently.

Separation of Federal Powers To keep power under control within the national government, the Constitution created what is called a **separation of powers** among the three branches. That is, the legislative, executive, and judicial branches would all have their own areas of authority.

In addition, the Constitution set up a system of **checks and balances,** which gave each

---

Answer to . . .

Interpreting Charts It can override a presidential veto and can impeach and remove a President, among other powers.

RESOURCE OPTIONS

Teaching Resources

📁 **Decision–Making Activity** Redistributing Government Power, Decision-Making Activities folder, pp. 6–7

Media and Technology

Color Transparencies Political Cartoons, K-2; Time Lines, E-3

branch the power to *check,* or stop, the others in certain ways. For instance, the President, as the head of the executive branch, can veto acts of Congress. This executive power is balanced, however, by Congress's power to overturn the veto with a two-thirds vote of each house. (See the chart on the previous page.)

Congress By creating a federal system with a separation of powers, the Framers both preserved and limited the people's control over the government. A comparison of the House of Representatives and the Senate demonstrates this effort at balance.

Population size determined the number of seats that each state received in the House of Representatives. This made the House directly responsible to the people. Its members served two-year terms so that voters could change the membership of the House quickly if they wanted to.

The Senate, on the other hand, was elected by the state legislatures, not by the voters.[†] Furthermore, unlike representatives in the House, senators served six-year terms. Every two years, only one third of the Senate would come up for reelection. Thus it was harder for voters to have a direct and sudden impact on the membership of the Senate.

The Framers made the Senate more removed from the people so that it would be less likely to follow the whims of popular opinion. Since no bill could become law without the Senate's approval, voters were less likely to succeed in forcing the passage of a bad law. The Framers also granted to the Senate certain powers that they did not give the House, such as giving advice and consent to the President.

On the other hand, the Framers gave the House some powers that the Senate did not have. For example, bills about raising money must be introduced in the House of Representatives alone. This provision came about because the large states were afraid of losing their influence over tax matters that could affect them greatly.

The House and the Senate, when combined as the Congress of the United States, became the most powerful legislative body in the nation. Only the Congress could coin money, declare

---

[†] In 1913, the Seventeenth Amendment changed this procedure, establishing direct election of senators by the people. The Senate originally met in closed sessions, but public pressure persuaded the Senate to construct a visitors' gallery in 1795.

FACT Finder — Electoral College Today

1. Political parties choose electors. Each state has as many presidential electors as it does senators and representatives in Congress.

2. Voters cast votes for electors, who will support their popular vote for President and Vice President.

3. Electors cast the official votes for President and Vice President.

Interpreting Tables The Constitution does not provide for direct popular election of the President. Instead, voters elect representatives who then cast the actual votes for President. *Government Why were the Framers opposed to direct popular elections?*

---

war, raise an army, provide for a navy, and regulate commerce. In a sweeping statement now known as the Elastic Clause because it fits so many situations, the Constitution declares that the Congress can do the following:

> **KEY DOCUMENTS** "Make all Laws which shall be necessary and proper for carrying into Execution the foregoing Powers, and all other Powers vested by this Constitution in the Government of the United States, or in any Department or Officer thereof."
>
> —U.S. Constitution, Article 1, Section 8, Clause 18, 1787

In other words, Congress would have the authority to pass any laws reasonably necessary to carry out its duties. This gave Congress great power, especially compared to its earlier role under the Articles of Confederation.

The President The Constitution created a strong executive officer, the President of the United States. Notable among the President's powers were overall command of the armed forces and the power to veto acts of Congress. His term was to be only four years, but he could be reelected as many times as the people wished. (Today, however, the President is limited to two terms in office, a change made by the Twenty-second Amendment in 1951.)

Main Idea CONNECTIONS

Why did the Framers of the Constitution decide to make the election of the President indirect rather than direct?

Once again, the Framers placed a shield between the government and the people by making the election of the President indirect. The President would be chosen by a vote of electors from each state. Each state would get as many electors as it had members of Congress. The candidate with the majority of the votes in the **Electoral College,** or group of electors, would become President.

The Framers knew that George Washington was likely to be the nation's first President. But Washington was unique in having support across the country. Later candidates for President, the Framers believed, would have difficulty winning the required majority of electoral votes.

Main Idea CONNECTIONS

Why did the Constitution make it difficult to remove federal judges from their posts?

Thus the Constitution provided for the House of Representatives to be the final decision maker in the presidential election. If the Electoral College failed to produce a clear majority for one candidate, the election would move to the House.

In the House of Representatives each state would have one vote, and the representatives would continue voting until one of the candidates received a majority. As it turned out, only twice in American history did the House need to vote to break a deadlock of the electors, in the elections of 1800 and 1824.

The Constitution gave the President enormous powers. He was to be commander in chief of the armed forces. In the system of checks and balances, he also had the power to veto acts of Congress.

Federal Courts The Constitution called for a national court system. Its members would be chosen by the President with the advice and consent of the Senate. Thus the choice of judges was two steps removed from the people—the President, indirectly chosen by the people, chose the judges. In addition, removing judges was made difficult so that the people could not directly control them. Federal judges would hold office for life, as long as they did not act dishonorably.

Although the Constitution called for one Supreme Court and several lesser ones, the details of the federal court system were left intentionally vague. Congress later developed the federal court system to fit the needs of the growing nation.

The Road Ahead This, then, was the outline of the new government as set forth in the Constitution, completed by the delegates in months of intense work during the summer of 1787. In order to take effect, however, the Constitution required the approval of nine of the 13 states. Supporters of the new Constitution knew that winning approval for it would not be easy.

SECTION 2 REVIEW

Comprehension

1. *Key Terms* Define: (a) amend; (b) veto; (c) Great Compromise; (d) Three-Fifths Compromise; (e) federal; (f) separation of powers; (g) checks and balances; (h) Electoral College.

2. *Summarizing the Main Idea* What were the most important features of the Constitution?

3. *Organizing Information* Reread your answer to Question 2. Create a web diagram that shows which features strengthened the national government and which gave the people control over it.

Critical Thinking

4. *Analyzing Time Lines* Review the time line at the start of the section. Write a sentence for each entry explaining its historical significance.

5. *Identifying Assumptions* What assumptions might have influenced the convention's decision *not* to allow the American people to directly choose their President, senators, and federal judges?

Writing Activity

6. *Writing a Persuasive Essay* Take the position of James Madison at the Constitutional Convention. Write a short essay in support of the Constitution. Address the concerns of the Antifederalists.

1787 Constitution submitted to states for approval	1787 Publication of The Federalist begins	1788 Constitution approved by the required number of states	1789 Bill of Rights proposed	1790 Final state approves the Constitution

1787   **1788**   **1789**   **1790**

3 Ratifying the Constitution

SECTION PREVIEW

Objectives

1 Compare and contrast the positions of the Federalists and the Antifederalists.
2 Identify the reasons that the Federalists won approval of the Constitution.
3 Outline the arguments for and against a Bill of Rights.
4 *Key Terms* Define: ratify; Federalist; Antifederalist; faction; Bill of Rights.

Main Idea

The states debated and then approved the new Constitution. A Bill of Rights soon was added to protect individual liberties.

Reading Strategy

Formulating Questions As you read, make a list of questions that you would want to ask the Federalists and Antifederalists if you were trying to decide how to vote on the Constitution.

A s the ink was still drying on the final draft of the new Constitution, proponents and opponents of it were busy trying to line up support for their positions. For the Constitution to become law, 9 of the 13 states had to **ratify,** or approve, it. Ratification votes would be cast not by state legislatures but by special conventions called in each state. The Framers of the Constitution bypassed the state legislatures because they feared the legislatures would never approve a document that reduced their powers.

The Federalist View

Those who favored the Constitution were called **Federalists.** They wanted the strong national government the Constitution provided. Those who opposed the Constitution were called the **Antifederalists.** They believed that the Federalists' plan posed a threat to state governments and to the rights of individuals.

The Federalists included many Nationalists, such as George Washington, James Madison, and Alexander Hamilton. They argued that even if there were problems with the document, it had to be approved. To make their case for the

Constitution, several supporters wrote a series of 85 essays called *The Federalist.* These articles appeared in New York City newspapers between October 1787 and August 1788. The authors were Hamilton, Madison, and John Jay, a Nationalist from New York.[†]

Written to win approval of the Constitution in New York, the Federalist essays are today recognized as perhaps the most sophisticated explanation of the new American political system ever written. Hamilton and Madison offered a defense of the Constitution that was also a commentary on human nature and the role of government.

For example, in *The Federalist,* No. 10, Madison answered those who feared that a federal government could come under the control of one powerful **faction,** a group that is concerned only with its own interests.

The Constitution's supporters rallied around a new national symbol: a ship in full sail.

[†] The essays were signed with the fictitious name "Publius." Scholars have argued over the identity of the writers. Today, however, computer analyses and other historical evidence have led most experts to agree on who wrote which essays.

RESOURCE OPTIONS

Teaching Resources

📁 **Reproducible Lesson Plan** Lesson Plans folder p. 53

📁 **Learning Styles Lesson Plan** Learning Styles Lesson Plans folder, p. 13

📁 **Big Idea Graphic Organizer** Big Idea Graphic Organizer folder, p. 25

📁 **Guided Reading and Review** Units 1–2 folder, p. 61

Objectives

You may wish to call students' attention to the objectives in the Section Preview. The objectives are reflected in the main headings of the section.

Bellringer

Ask students if they think the United States government infringes too much on individual liberty. Possible examples include taxes or military service.

Reading Strategy

Formulating Questions Refer to the Reading Strategy in the Section Preview. Encourage students to generate questions by skimming the headings and turning them into questions.

LESSON PLAN

Connecting to the Main Idea

1. Focus Explain that at the time the Constitution was written it was controversial. The Antifederalists feared it meant the end of liberty, and it was approved by only a narrow margin. Why did the Federalists believe that a strong central government was so important?

2. Instruct Explain that writing the Constitution was only half the battle. Now the Federalists had to get it approved by all the states. Why did so many Americans think the Constitution betrayed the ideas behind the American Revolution? Review the debate between the Federalists and Antifederalists. Have students explain the two opposing positions. How did the Federalists win ratification of the Constitution? Why did the Antifederalists insist on adding the Bill of Rights?

3. Close With the ratification of the Constitution, the United States combined a powerful central government with a respect for individual liberty.

FACT Finder — Ratification of the Constitution

State	Date	Vote
Delaware	December 7, 1787	30-0
Pennsylvania	December 12, 1787	46-23
New Jersey	December 19, 1787	38-0
Georgia	January 2, 1788	26-0
Connecticut	January 9, 1788	128-40
Massachusetts	February 6, 1788	187-168
Maryland	April 28, 1788	63-11
South Carolina	May 23, 1788	149-73
New Hampshire	June 21, 1788	57-46
Virginia	June 25, 1788	89-79
New York	July 26, 1788	30-27
North Carolina	November 21, 1789	184-77
Rhode Island	May 29, 1790	34-32

Interpreting Tables For the Constitution to become law, ratification by only nine states was needed. Patrick Henry opposed ratification, fearing that "a proposal of establishing nine states into a confederacy [would lead] to the eventual exclusion of four states." *Government Why was it important, however, for all 13 states to ratify the Constitution?*

Because the United States was so big, Madison wrote, no single faction would be able to control the government. Factions based on regional or economic or other interests would fight with each other within the federal government, but no single faction would be able to dominate the others for long. As Madison put it:

> **KEY DOCUMENTS** "Extend the sphere [that is, enlarge the territory of the nation] and you take in a greater variety of parties and interests; you make it less probable that a majority of a whole will have a common motive to invade the rights of other citizens; or if such a common motive exists, it will be more difficult for all who feel it to discover their own strength and to act in unison with each other."

—*The Federalist*, No. 10

The Antifederalist View

The Antifederalists rallied behind the leadership of older revolutionary figures, such as Patrick Henry of Virginia. This group picked up support in more isolated regions where protecting commerce was not a major concern. People in these areas had less need for the leadership and laws of a strong national government. The Antifederalists also included some former Nationalists who still wanted a national government but were unhappy with the Constitution as written.

Most Antifederalists saw the Constitution as a betrayal of the American Revolution. A President would be nothing but a king, they warned. Had American patriots fought and died to create yet another government to tax them and tell them what to do?

While the Federalists feared the people more than government, the Antifederalists feared government more than the people. Many objected not only to the presidency, but to the new federal court system. They also worried that those governments closest to the people, the local and state authorities, would be crushed by this new federal monster. Finally, they feared for Americans' individual liberties. Two New York Antifederalists argued:

> **KEY DOCUMENTS** "A general government, however guarded by declarations of rights, . . . must unavoidably, in a short time, be productive of the destruction of the civil liberty of such citizens who could be effectively coerced [dominated] by it."

—*Letter from Robert Yates and John Lansing to the Governor of New York, 1787*

Why the Federalists Won

The Constitution was officially submitted to the states for approval on September 28, 1787. From the start, the Federalists had several advantages in their campaign to promote it.

(1) The Federalists drew on the widespread feeling that the Articles of Confederation had serious flaws. The young nation's economic problems and Shays' Rebellion convinced many Americans that something had to be done.

(2) The Federalists were united around a specific plan—the Constitution. The Antifederalists, in contrast, were united only in their opposition to the Constitution. They had no constructive plan of their own to offer.

TEST PREPARATION

Have students read the excerpt from *The Federalist* on this page and then answer the question below.

Which is the best summary of the passage?

(A) A strong national government discourages factionalism and protects the rights of all citizens.

B The larger the nation, the more parties and interests will result.

C People with a common motive can invade the rights of others.

D A large nation makes it difficult for people to act in unison.

(3) The Federalists were a well-organized national group in regular contact with one another. The Antifederalists tended to be local and state politicians who could not coordinate their activities on the national level.

(4) Finally, the Federalists had George Washington. In 1786 Washington had foreseen the type of chaos that would erupt in Shays' Rebellion. "Something must be done," he warned his countrymen, "or the fabric [the Union] must fall, for it is certainly tottering." The following year, 1787, Washington had served as head of the Constitutional Convention. Federalists could point out that the Constitution had been crafted under the leadership of the nation's greatest hero and most respected public figure.

Washington's support was crucial for another reason. Everyone expected Washington to be the first President. That made people more willing to accept the idea of a stronger government and a powerful executive. During the war, Washington had proved his ability to lead, through defeat and discouragement. More significant, he had voluntarily given up his power at the end of the war. This was seen as a sign of his commitment to act within the law.

Delaware, New Jersey, and Connecticut ratified quickly. They were relatively small states whose citizens could benefit from being part of a large federal structure. Georgia ratified quickly as well. The Georgians feared a war with Native Americans and wanted a national government for support. In Pennsylvania, Federalists had come to power, and they readily agreed to the new Constitution. All these states acted in December 1787 and January 1788.

Then Massachusetts narrowly voted to ratify. Maryland and South Carolina soon fell into line. New Hampshire Federalists managed to delay the vote in their state until they had a majority. In June 1788, New Hampshire had the honor of being the ninth state and final state needed to ratify the Constitution.

Yet everyone knew the new nation would not succeed without the backing of the highly populated states of Virginia and New York. Loud debates and quiet maneuvers during the summer of 1788 produced narrow Federalist victories in both these states. North Carolina first rejected the Constitution but reversed itself and voted in favor in November 1789. In May 1790, Rhode Island similarly reversed its position and became the last of the original thirteen states to approve the new government.

The Bill of Rights

The states did adopt the Constitution. Yet the voting was close, and they might easily have rejected it. What turned the tide in close states like Massachusetts, Virginia, and New York? The skills of men such as Madison and Hamilton certainly had an impact. The most important factor, however, was the Federalist offer to support several amendments to the Constitution.

In September 1789, Congress proposed twelve constitutional amendments designed to protect citizens' rights. The states ratified ten of the amendments, and they took effect on December 15, 1791. These first ten amendments to the Constitution are known today as the **Bill of Rights.**

Main Idea
CONNECTIONS

Why was a Bill of Rights added to the Constitution?

Against the Bill of Rights Most Federalists saw no need for these amendments. Members of the Constitutional Convention had talked about protecting freedom of speech, the press, and religion. But they decided such measures were unnecessary. They were building a government of, for, and by the people. Under the Constitution, the people and the government were the same. So why did the people need to protect their rights from themselves?

In *The Federalist*, No. 84, Hamilton quoted the Preamble of the Constitution to claim that

United we stand—Divided we fall

This cartoon shows the states as pillars, with nine upright and a tenth being raised. Nine states had to approve the new Constitution before it became law. *Government* What is the message of the words in the cartoon?

Customize for
English Language Learners

Ask students to scan the section, and create *who, what, when, where,* and *why* questions for the text. Have them exchange papers and answer the questions as they read.

RESOURCE OPTIONS

Teaching Resources

Key Documents The Federalist, no. 71, Learning with Documents folder, p. 83

American History Block Scheduling Support The Birth of the Constitution: The Philadelphia Convention, and Taking Sides: The Creation of Political Parties, found in the Forging a New Nation folder, include interdisciplinary lesson suggestions and activities for Geography and History, Primary Sources, Biography, and Literature.

Answer to . . .

Main Idea Connections To help win the support of those who were concerned that the Constitution did not adequately protect individual liberties.
Viewing History That the future of the nation depends on the ratification of the Constitution.

Answers to
SECTION 3 REVIEW

1. (a) ratify, see p. 139;
(b) Federalist, see p. 139;
(c) Antifederalist, see p. 139;
(d) faction, see p. 139; (e) Bill of Rights, see p. 141.

2. The Federalists carried out an organized campaign that tapped people's fear of disunion and played up Washington's role in the Constitutional Convention.

3. Charts might compare views on the role of the national and state governments and the need for a Bill of Rights.

4. Students should support their choice with facts from the section.

5. Sample answers: Quotation #1—As the nation grows, it becomes unlikely that a majority of citizens will want to take away the rights of others or be able to unite to do so. Quotation #2—The national government might promise to protect citizens' rights, but before long it will inevitably take those rights away.

6. Essays should clearly state the argument and back it up with examples either from history or from the present day.

FACT Finder   The Bill of Rights

1st Amendment	Guarantees freedom of religion, speech, press, assembly, and petition
2nd Amendment	Guarantees the right to bear arms
3rd Amendment	Restricts the manner in which the federal government may house troops in the homes of citizens
4th Amendment	Protects individuals against unreasonable searches and seizures
5th Amendment	Provides that a person must be accused by a grand jury before being tried for a serious federal crime; protects individuals against self-incrimination and against being tried twice for the same crime; prohibits unfair actions by the federal government; prohibits the government from taking private property for public use without paying a fair price for it
6th Amendment	Guarantees persons accused of a crime the right to a swift and fair trial
7th Amendment	Guarantees the right to a jury trial in civil cases tried in federal courts
8th Amendment	Protects against cruel and unusual punishment and excessive bail
9th Amendment	Establishes that the people have rights beyond those stated in the Constitution
10th Amendment	Establishes that all powers not guaranteed to the federal government and not withheld from the states are held by each of the states, or their citizens

Interpreting Tables The Bill of Rights was intended to protect Americans from the strong national government the Constitution created. *Government* Which amendment protects people's right to express their views?

"the people surrender nothing" under the new system. That is, they keep all the power. "Here is a better recognition of popular rights" than any added list of rights, he argued.

For the Bill of Rights Many Americans did not accept Hamilton's reasoning. Thomas Jefferson favored the Constitution but insisted

that it include a Bill of Rights. He wanted the "unalienable rights" he wrote of in the Declaration of Independence to be guaranteed in the Constitution.

Jefferson had not been a delegate at the Constitutional Convention. He was in Paris, serving as United States ambassador to France. Instead he corresponded with friends back home to keep abreast of events.

In one letter he urged Madison to agree to specific protections for freedom of religion and of the press as well as protections from armies and unjust courts. "A bill of rights is what the people are entitled to against every government on earth," the ambassador wrote.

Jefferson unsuccessfully pushed for clearer, more detailed language in the Bill of Rights. For instance, he wanted it to specify the number of days a person could be held under arrest without a trial. He also believed it was important to ensure that the army would disband immediately after its service. Yet, upon returning home from France at the end of 1789, he threw his full support behind the Bill of Rights as written.

Facing overwhelming pressure for the Bill of Rights, the Federalists gave in. This compromise led them to victory.

SECTION 3 REVIEW

Comprehension

1. **Key Terms** Define: (a) ratify; (b) Federalist; (c) Antifederalist; (d) faction; (e) Bill of Rights.
2. **Summarizing the Main Idea** How were the Federalists able to win ratification of the Constitution?
3. **Organizing Information** Make a chart to compare and contrast the views of the Federalists and Antifederalists.

Critical Thinking

4. **Analyzing Time Lines** Review the time line at the start of the section. Choose one date and explain why it was a turning point in the nation's history.
5. **Summarizing Information** Reread the excerpts from the Federalist and Antifederalist papers. Summarize them in your own words.

Writing Activity

6. **Writing a Persuasive Essay** Choose two amendments from the Bill of Rights chart above. Make the case for passage of them.

Answer to . . .

Interpreting Tables The First Amendment, which guarantees freedom of speech.

RESOURCE OPTIONS

Teaching Resources

📁 **Quiz** Units 1–2 folder, p. 62

📁 **Visual Learning Activity** The First United States Coins, Learning with Documents folder, p. 47

Student Performance Pack

Guide to the Essentials Chapter 5, Section 3 (English and Spanish)

1789
Washington takes office

1789
Jefferson and Hamilton get key government posts

1792
Washington reelected

1799
Washington dies; capital named for him

1800
Government moves into Washington, D.C.

1785   1790   1795   1800

4 The New Government

SECTION PREVIEW

Objectives

1 List some of the new leaders of President Washington's government, and compare and contrast the views of Jefferson and Hamilton.
2 Describe the precedents set by Washington.
3 Explain why and how the new capital of Washington, D.C., was built.
4 *Key Terms* Define: inauguration; Cabinet; domestic affairs; administration; precedent.

Main Idea

President Washington led the effort to create an effective federal government that would earn the respect of the American people and of other nations.

Reading Strategy

Making an Outline Make a list of all the headings in this section. As you read, write down at least one key fact under each heading.

On April 30, 1789, a crowd of thousands surrounded Federal Hall, an elegant building on New York City's Wall Street that served as the temporary home of the new government. From windows and rooftops, people strained to catch a glimpse of the tall figure with freshly powdered hair that now appeared on the front balcony of the building.

Those within earshot listened as George Washington repeated the oath of office of President of the United States and kissed a Bible. The crowd roared its approval.

The French ambassador observed this joyous **inauguration,** or official swearing-in ceremony. "Never," he wrote, "has [a] sovereign [a ruler] reigned more completely in the hearts of his subjects than did Washington in those of his fellow-citizens. . . . He has the soul, look, and figure of a hero united in him."

New Leaders

Washington had been elected in early 1789 by a unanimous vote of the new Electoral College. (*Unanimous* means having the agreement of everyone.) Massachusetts patriot John Adams, a leading Federalist, became Vice President. As the

nation celebrated this peaceful inauguration of leaders, difficult tasks lay ahead. The infant nation had a huge war debt. It lacked a permanent capital. It had no federal officers beyond Washington, Adams, and the newly elected Congress.

Immediately, President Washington began selecting officials to head the major departments of the executive branch. This group of federal leaders is called the **Cabinet.** Besides running their own agencies, Cabinet officers advise the President.

President Washington selected prominent Americans to fill these new posts. Edmund Randolph of Virginia was named Attorney General, the nation's chief law officer and legal adviser. Henry Knox, who had been Secretary of War under the Articles of Confederation, continued in the job under Washington.

Washington called on two of the nation's most respected patriots to fill his most crucial Cabinet posts. Thomas Jefferson was named to head the Department of State, which handles relations with foreign countries. Alexander Hamilton accepted the job of Secretary of the Treasury.

An inauguration souvenir proclaims "silence to the tongue that will utter a calumny [insult] against the immortal Washington."

RESOURCE OPTIONS

Teaching Resources

📁 **Reproducible Lesson Plan** Lesson Plans folder, p. 54

📁 **Big Idea Graphic Organizer** Big Idea Graphic Organizer folder, p. 26

📁 **Guided Reading and Review** Units 1–2 folder, p. 63

Media and Technology

AmericanHeritage® CD-ROM

Time Tour The New Republic: The New Government Begins

The New Government

Objectives
You may wish to call students' attention to the objectives in the Section Preview. The objectives are reflected in the main headings of the section.

Bellringer
Ask students to recall magazine, newspaper, or television pictures of Washington, D.C. What are their impressions of the capital?

Reading Strategy
Making an Outline Refer to the Reading Strategy in the Section Preview. You may wish to model the headings on the chalkboard and ask students to suggest facts for each heading.

LESSON PLAN
Connecting to the Main Idea

1. Focus Explain that with the ratification of the Constitution, strengthening the central government had only begun. Now the Federalists had to make the new government work.

2. Instruct Explain that although the Constitution provided a framework for the new government, it was untested. Washington and the members of Congress were charting new territory when they took office. Ask students about the challenges they faced. How did Washington choose his Cabinet members? Was there provision for a Cabinet in the Constitution? What impression did government officials hope to give the people?

3. Close Federalists worked hard in the first few years to make the government impressive. A growing number of Americans were disturbed by their expensive displays of power. They worried that the ideals of the Revolution were being lost.

Using Historical Evidence This painting of a reception during the Washington administration is titled *The Republican Court*. Culture How does the scene reflect Federalist plans for the new government?

A sense of duty made Jefferson a politician, but he much preferred the life of a gentleman farmer. Like many other southern planters of his day, Jefferson relied on slave labor. He well knew that slavery was wrong, and he wrote eloquently about it as a moral evil. Yet he could never bring himself to free more than a few of his slaves.

President Washington chose Jefferson to head the Department of State because of his experience in dealing with France, the United States' closest ally. In the bargain the President also got a man who never fully trusted the new government. Jefferson later would become one of Washington's harshest critics.

Secretary of State Jefferson Despite his role as chief author of the Declaration of Independence, Thomas Jefferson had not achieved great fame yet when he became Secretary of State. He had just spent several years out of the spotlight, serving as ambassador to France.

Upon his return from France in 1789, Jefferson quickly became involved again in **domestic affairs**—that is, the country's internal matters, as opposed to foreign issues. He eventually supported the Federalists' efforts to ratify the Constitution. Yet Jefferson was not a strict Federalist. His passionate concern for individuals' rights led him to press for the Bill of Rights.

Jefferson, later to become the nation's third President, was one of this nation's most gifted public figures.[†] Besides being a planter, lawyer, and diplomat, Jefferson was a writer, inventor, and violinist. He made contributions to philosophy, mathematics, agricultural science, linguistics, and archaeology. Jefferson's love of learning led him to found the University of Virginia. A lover of architecture, Jefferson built several homes for himself. The most famous is Monticello, a gracious house near Charlottesville, Virginia.

Main Idea
CONNECTIONS

What qualities made Jefferson a good choice for Secretary of State?

Today's campaign buttons are the offspring of these buttons from Washington's inauguration.

[†] Generations later, the nation's thirty-fifth President, John F. Kennedy, was hosting a supper at the White House for Nobel Prize winners. Kennedy joked that his guests were the greatest gathering of talent ever to dine in the building, except when Thomas Jefferson ate there alone.

Treasury Secretary Hamilton Alexander Hamilton, the new head of the Department of the Treasury, was an intellectually brilliant man. He attended King's College (now Columbia University) in New York City. He soon became involved in politics, supporting the Patriot cause. As an officer in the Continental Army during the Revolution, Hamilton served as private secretary to General Washington.

Now Hamilton headed the government's largest department. In contrast to Jefferson, who never really trusted government, Hamilton believed that governmental power, properly used, could accomplish great things.

Despite the strong contrasts between Jefferson and Hamilton, the first months, even years, of the new government went fairly smoothly. The economic problems brought on by the war eased, and the adoption of the Constitution gave the nation much-needed stability.

Washington's Government

The largest problems and the smallest details came to Washington's attention during his first **administration,** or term of office. (The word *administration* can also refer to the members and agencies of the executive branch as a whole.) With every decision, every action, every inaction, Washington and his officials were establishing precedents for how to govern. A **precedent** is something done or said that becomes an example, rule, or tradition to be followed.

For example, how should Congress and the President interact with each other? What was the role of the Cabinet? Nobody yet knew.

  RESOURCE OPTIONS

Media and Technology

RESOURCE PRO

Primary Source Activity A Department of Peace, found on Resource Pro, helps demonstrate the ideals people had for the development of their new country.

Visual Learning Activity A Portrait of a President, found on Resource Pro, uses a 1789 print of George Washington to illustrate some images and ideals prevalent at the time.

 Color Transparencies Links Across Time, J-2; American Photo, B-2

Typical of this experimental period was the debate in the Senate over what to call the President. "Your Majesty" was too kingly, yet "Mr. Washington" sounded too plain. A Senate committee suggested "His Highness the President of the United States of America and Protector of the Rights of the Same." But the House of Representatives rejected that title, and the issue died for the time being. (Today we use the simple and democratic "Mr. President.")

Meanwhile, President Washington, aware of the precedents he was setting, worked to establish a tone of dignity in his administration. His own appearance and personality helped. More than six feet tall, Washington made an impressive figure. By nature he was solemn, reserved, and very formal.

Washington was also intensely private. A man named Gouverneur Morris had found this out the hard way: During the Constitutional Convention, some of Morris's fellow delegates had dared him to put his hand on Washington's shoulder. According to one account of the incident:

AMERICAN VOICES
&&Washington withdrew his hand, stepped suddenly back, [and] fixed his eye on Morris for several minutes with an angry frown, until the latter retreated abashed, and sought refuge in the crowd.&&

Throughout his first term Washington remained a popular figure, and in 1792 he won unanimous reelection. Reluctantly, he accepted. As you will read in the next section, his second administration would prove to be more difficult, marked by criticism and controversy.

During his eight years in the capital, Washington lived in grand style. Soldiers escorted his carriage, which was pulled by a team of six horses. The President and his wife, Martha, held regular Friday afternoon parties to entertain government officials and ambassadors. Every year, government officials celebrated the President's birthday with elaborate ceremonies.

Washington believed that such pomp was necessary to command the respect of the American public and the rest of the world. To some people, however, such activities made Washington seem like a king with a lavish court.

The need to make the government appear both powerful and democratic at the same time presented quite a challenge. Yet such issues were important because they would set precedents for generations to come.

Notable PRESIDENTS

George Washington

1789–1797

"To be prepared for war is one of the most effectual means of preserving peace."
—First Annual Address, 1790

George Washington was not only the nation's first President, but the person for whom the office was created. A former Virginia planter and surveyor, he had fought in the French and Indian War and had led the Continental Army during the Revolutionary War. Washington's successful leadership in the fight for independence made the tall and imposing 57-year-old easily the nation's leading public figure.

Washington was famous too for his honesty, dignity, and self-control. In 1787 the Framers of the Constitution created the office of President with him in mind, confident that he could be trusted with the enormous powers of the presidency. Washington backed the Constitution during the debate over ratification, and as President he acted with dignity and restraint, thus easing many people's fears about the new government.

Washington could not, however, make the new government universally popular. Many Americans distrusted the new, stronger government and disliked Alexander Hamilton's economic plans. Washington's pro-British foreign policy angered those Americans who thought the United States should support France instead. Convinced that Washington was leading the nation away from the ideals of the Revolution, these opponents rallied behind Thomas Jefferson, who had resigned as secretary of state in 1793. Washington tried to keep the nation politically united under his leadership, but ultimately, divisions occurred. Offended and tired, in 1796 he refused to run for a third term.

When Washington died in 1799, Americans put aside the bitter conflicts of his presidency. They remembered instead his years of steadfast service to the nation, first as a general fighting a difficult war and later as a President seeking a workable balance between order and liberty.

Connecting to Today

Do you believe that characteristics such as dignity and restraint are as important for American Presidents today as they were in Washington's era? Explain your answer.

Answers to
SECTION 4 REVIEW

1. (a) inauguration, see p. 143; (b) Cabinet, see p. 143; (c) domestic affairs, see p. 144; (d) administration, see p. 144; (e) precedent, see p. 144.

2. He carried himself with dignity; he chose talented administrators; he insisted upon a certain amount of ceremony and style that he felt was befitting a respectable government.

3. Possible entries: government structure—Cabinet created, Jefferson and Hamilton get key posts; government style—formal, ceremonial, expensive; national capital—designed by L'Enfant, formal, European-style layout, White House, Capitol, monuments.

4. Possible answer: 1789 was the first year of the new United States government; it was a year in which many precedents were set.

5. Possible answers: (a) Yes, there is still much formality and ceremony, such as inaugurations and state dinners at the White House. New monuments such as the Vietnam War Memorial and the Roosevelt Memorial have been built. (b) No, today's leaders act and dress much more casually. They can be seen in hard hats touring factories, swimming or playing golf, and helping to build houses for the poor.

6. Students should state their case clearly, supporting it with details from the chapter, such as the desire to rival the European capitals.

The Capitol in 1800 was no more than one wing in a muddy wilderness, but its lavishness stood in sharp contrast to the drab surroundings. *Culture* **Why do you think the young United States needed an impressive Capitol?**

Planning a Capital City

A new nation needed a new capital, one that could equal the beauty and stature of Europe's grand capital cities. New York City was home to the government during Washington's first year. In 1790 the capital was moved to Philadelphia. There it would remain for a decade, while a brand-new capital could be planned and built.

That effort began with the Residence Act of 1790. It specified that the capital would be a 10-square-mile stretch of land on the Potomac River near Washington's home at Mount Vernon.

The city would be situated along the Maryland-Virginia border, but it would be governed by federal authorities, not by either state. The new capital was called the District of Columbia. (After President Washington's death in 1799, the city was renamed Washington, District of Columbia.)

At the suggestion of the knowledgeable Jefferson, Washington appointed Benjamin Banneker, an African American mathematician and inventor, to the commission to survey the city. Pierre-Charles L'Enfant, a French artist and architect who had fought for the United States during the Revolution, developed the city plan.

L'Enfant designed a spacious capital with broad streets laid out in an elegant, European-style pattern. He created plans for the official residence of the President, a mansion now called the White House, as well as Congress's new home, the Capitol building.[†] The federal government moved to the District in 1800, decades before the plan was fully realized.

Today, Washington, D.C., with its great boulevards, marble buildings in the Roman style, and public monuments, is the most visible legacy of the Federalists' grand plans for the United States. It was meant to display the power and dignity of the new federal government that they had fought to build.

[†] Notice that *capital* refers to the city, while the *Capitol* is a specific building. To this day, no building in the District of Columbia may be taller than the Capitol.

SECTION 4 REVIEW

Comprehension

1. *Key Terms* Define: (a) inauguration; (b) Cabinet; (c) domestic affairs; (d) administration; (e) precedent.

2. *Summarizing the Main Idea* How did President Washington carry out his goal of creating a respected government?

3. *Organizing Information* Create a web diagram with *Establishing a New Government* in the center circle. The circles coming out of the center might be labeled *Government Structure, Government Style,* and *National Capital.*

Critical Thinking

4. *Analyzing Time Lines* Review the time line at the start of the section. Why do you think 1789 was such a unique year in American history?

5. *Drawing Conclusions* Do you think that the precedents set by Washington still influence our government today? Explain your reasoning.

Writing Activity

6. *Writing a Persuasive Essay* From the point of view of L'Enfant, try to persuade President Washington to approve your design for a new capital. Show why such an expensive project is necessary.

Answer to . . .

Viewing History To symbolize the power of the federal government, to serve as a source of pride for citizens, and to impress foreign governments.

▶ RESOURCE OPTIONS

Teaching Resources

📁 **Quiz** Units 1–2 folder, p. 64

📁 **Chapter Tests Forms A and B** Chapter Test folder

Student Performance Pack

Guide to the Essentials Chapter 5, Section 4 (English and Spanish)

Standardized Test Preparation Handbook

Media and Technology

🎧 **Guided Reading Audiotapes** Chapter 5 Summary (English and Spanish)

Student Edition on Audiotape Chapter 5

◉ **Test Bank CD-ROM; Interactive Student Tutorial CD-ROM** Chapter Test

The Bill of Rights Protects You

By agreeing to a Bill of Rights, the Federalists ensured ratification of the United States Constitution. The Bill of Rights has endured for more than 200 years, guaranteeing individual freedoms to Americans.

You can criticize the President without being put in jail. You can say or write what you think about any issue. You and your friends can hold public meetings or organize marches to express your views. You also have the right to worship freely.

These and other individual freedoms are expressed in the Bill of Rights, which makes up the first ten Amendments to the Constitution. The Bill of Rights speaks mainly in general principles. For example, the Eighth Amendment forbids but does not define "cruel and unusual punishment." Does "freedom of speech" include the right to threaten to kill someone? The Bill of Rights does not say.

Wedding party entering a church in colonial America

In 1998, supporters of this viewpoint in the U.S. Congress proposed a Religious Freedom Amendment to the Constitution. The amendment promises "to secure the people's right to acknowledge God according to the dictates of conscience . . . [and guarantee] the people's right to pray and to recognize their religious beliefs." The amendment failed to receive the necessary two-thirds majority in Congress.

Supporters of the proposed amendment say that it would protect Americans' right to religious speech. Opponents argue that the First Amendment already guarantees freedom of religion. They fear that the Religious Freedom Amendment would allow one group of Americans to impose their views on others.

Mosque in Michigan

The Impact Today

Because the Bill of Rights is open to interpretation, Americans often argue about what it means. In recent years, controversy has arisen over religious freedom. Some Christians say that, since the 1960s, the federal government has been hostile to religion. They contend that laws and Supreme Court decisions designed to separate church and state have infringed on their right to worship freely.

The Impact on You

Examine both sides of the controversy over the Religious Freedom Amendment. Reread the First Amendment, paying close attention to what it says about religious freedom. Prepare arguments for and against the proposed amendment. Present your arguments as you participate in a class discussion on the issue.

RESOURCE OPTIONS

Teaching Resources

📁 **Why Study History? Activity** The Bill of Rights Protects You, found in the Why Study History? folder, p. 6, provides an activity to help students better appreciate the freedoms guaranteed under the Bill of Rights.

Media and Technology

💿📼 **Decision America Videotapes and Videodiscs** Issue 2 *Should Privacy Be Protected?*; Issue 9 *How Much Does Free Speech Cost?*

Why Study History?

Class Discussion

Discuss with the class freedoms protected under the Bill of Rights. For a more thorough examination of the issue, see the activity folder in the Resource Options below.

ACTIVITY
STUDENT PARTICIPATION

The Bill of Rights and You

Ask students to read the text. Then divide the class into several groups. Tell the groups to discuss this question: How would our country be different if there were no Bill of Rights? Have each group write an "obituary" memorializing one freedom. (A possible opening: "Freedom of speech died this morning . . .") Obituaries should include these points:

- **an appreciation of the freedom**
- **an understanding of why this freedom was included in the Bill of Rights**
- **a recognition of what its loss would mean**

Have the groups present their work to the class. Encourage discussion.

Follow up Ask students to write short stories or poems about an America without a Bill of Rights.

🖥 Using the Internet

Students can learn more about the Bill of Rights by exploring links in the *America: Pathways to the Present* Web site at

http://www.Pathways.phschool.com

Assessment

See the Lesson Plans folder, pp. 24–27, for rubrics on assessing Class Participation Projects.

Key Terms

Students should refer to the definitions of the key terms in the chapter to write sentences that show an understanding of the writing of the Constitution and the founding of the new nation's central government.

Comprehension

1. A weak national government, with most powers going to the states.

2. It supported the Federalists' claim that the national government must be strengthened.

3. The historic debate over the structure and powers of the American government was resolved.

4. Established a government with three branches; gave them separate powers and checks and balances; created a process for selecting the President, Congress, and federal judges.

5. Madison is known as "the father of the Constitution." His talents, education, and preparation qualified him to shape the writing of the Constitution.

6. They drew on people's confidence in Washington's leadership and his endorsement of the Constitution. They also drew on people's fear that the Union would dissolve unless the government was strengthened. They benefited from being well organized.

7. Thomas Jefferson believed that a strong national government would infringe on the rights of the people unless those rights were spelled out in the Constitution.

8. Jefferson became Secretary of State because of his experience as ambassador to France. Hamilton became Secretary of the Treasury.

9. He created a panel called the Cabinet, made up of the heads of the departments of the executive branch. He set a formal, dignified style for the presidency in order to command the respect of Americans and other nations.

Chapter Summary

The major concepts of Chapter 5 are presented below. See also *Guide to the Essentials of American History* or *Interactive Student Tutorial CD-ROM,* which contains interactive review activities, time lines, helpful hints, and test practice for Chapter 5.

Reviewing the Main Ideas

During the 1780s, the government under the Articles of Confederation faced economic and other problems. A new and stronger plan of government, the Constitution of the United States, was created in 1787. By 1789 the United States had approved this new Constitution and elected its first President, George Washington.

Section 1: Government By the States

In the government under the Articles of Confederation, political power rested mostly with the states, while the national government was weak.

Section 2: The Constitutional Convention

In 1787, delegates to a convention in Philadelphia created a new plan of government, the Constitution of the United States.

Section 3: Ratifying the Constitution

The states debated and then approved the new Constitution, later adding a Bill of Rights to protect individual liberties.

Section 4: The New Government

President Washington led the effort to create an effective federal government that would earn the respect of the American people and of other nations.

Why Study History?

By agreeing to a Bill of Rights, the Federalists ensured ratification of the Constitution. Today, the Bill of Rights provides important protections as well as generating controversy over how to interpret it.

Key Terms

For each of the terms below, write a sentence explaining how it relates to this chapter.

1. Articles of Confederation
2. legislative branch
3. executive branch
4. judicial branch
5. constitution
6. amend
7. veto
8. federal
9. separation of powers
10. checks and balances
11. Electoral College
12. Federalist
13. Antifederalist
14. ratify
15. Bill of Rights
16. Cabinet

Comprehension

1. What kind of government structure did the Articles of Confederation create?
2. What were the effects of Shays' Rebellion?
3. Why was the year 1787 a turning point in American history?
4. Describe the structure of the government created by the Constitution.
5. Who was James Madison, and what role did he have at the Constitutional Convention?
6. How did the Federalists win ratification of the Constitution?
7. Name a supporter of the Bill of Rights and explain his argument for it.
8. What roles did Jefferson and Hamilton have in Washington's administration?
9. What precedents did Washington set during his terms in office?

Using Graphic Organizers

On a separate sheet of paper, copy the chart below. In each box write a sentence summarizing information from the chapter.

	Arguments For	Arguments Against
Articles of Confederation		
Constitution		
Bill of Rights		

Using Graphic Organizers

- Articles: for—creates proper relationship between national and state government; against—creates weak national government lacking necessary power.
- Constitution: for—strengthens power of national government while providing checks on each branch; against—limits states' rights and takes away civil liberties.
- Bill of Rights: for—ensures people's rights won't be taken away; against—if government created for people by people, their rights are safe.

Analyzing Political Cartoons ▶

1. This engraving shows the celebration of New York's ratification of the Constitution. (a) What does the ship represent? (b) How do you know? (c) In this engraving, who is identified with the success of ratification? (d) How do you know?

2. Was the cartoonist a Federalist or an Antifederalist? Explain your answer.

Critical Thinking

1. *Applying the Chapter Skill* Reread the Notable Presidents feature in Section 4. Identify the central issues in the passage.

2. *Distinguishing Fact from Opinion* Write two facts and two opinions about the Articles of Confederation.

3. *Demonstrating Reasoned Judgment* Do you think that Shays' Rebellion was a sign that the nation was slipping into disorder? Explain your answer.

4. *Testing Conclusions* Jefferson and his supporters believed that a Bill of Rights was absolutely crucial to the protection of liberty. Do you think this conclusion has proven to be correct? Use examples from history or from the present to show your reasoning.

INTERNET ACTIVITY

For your portfolio:
WRITE AN ESSAY

Access Prentice Hall's *America: Pathways to the Present* site at **www.Pathways.phschool.com** for the specific URL to complete the activity. Additional resources and related Web sites are also available.

Read Thomas Jefferson's words on rights and the need for a bill of rights. Write an essay describing what rights you believe are inalienable and whether you think a bill of rights or other constitutional protections are necessary to guarantee them. Include present-day examples in your argument.

ANALYZING DOCUMENTS ◀ ▶ *INTERPRETING DATA*

Turn to the Preamble to the Constitution on page 135.

1. What document was designed to "secure the Blessings of Liberty"? (a) the Constitution (b) *The Federalist,* No. 1 (c) the Cabinet (d) the Bill of Rights.

2. Why were the Framers attempting to "form a more perfect Union"? (a) Under the Articles of Confederation, the national government had little power to resolve problems among states. (b) Smaller states threatened to leave the Union because they feared a strong national government. (c) Shays' Rebellion had shown Americans that their national government was too powerful. (d) The Articles of Confederation did not give people enough say in their government.

3. *Writing* Why did the Framers begin the Constitution with the words "We the People. . ."? Why do you think this phrase is important to Americans today?

Connecting to Today

Essay Writing The Constitution is often referred to as "The Living Constitution." Write an essay that shows how the Constitution is "alive" today. Include answers to these questions: (a) What features of the Constitution make it flexible enough to apply to the nation's needs today? (b) What freedoms do you enjoy because of the Constitution?

Analyzing Political Cartoons

1. (a) The Federalists. (b) It is named *Hamilton,* a leading Federalist. (c) Hamilton. (d) The ship is named for him.
2. Federalist; the people are celebrating ratification.

Critical Thinking

1. Possible answers: The office of the presidency was created with Washington in mind; Washington was not universally popular because he represented a strong central government.
2. Sample answers: Facts—They created a weak national government; they gave most powers to the states. Opinions—They did not give the national government enough authority; they needed to be replaced, not simply amended.
3. Answers should be supported with facts from the chapter.
4. Conclusions should be clearly stated and supported with examples.

Analyzing Documents

1. a
2. a
3. Answers should reflect an understanding of the early nation's desire for popular sovereignty and fear of a tyrannical government. Many Americans cherish these words because they are proud of the country's tradition of democratic government.

Connecting to Today

(a) Essays should mention that the Constitution can be amended as needed. (b) Essays should reflect an understanding of some of the provisions of the Bill of Rights.

INTERNET ACTIVITY

Answers will vary. Students should present reasoned arguments that indicate an understanding of Jefferson's argument for a bill of rights.

THE CONSTITUTION
OF THE
United States

Focus Ask students to describe their student government. Is there a constitution? If so, what is its purpose? What is the procedure for making changes? If there is no constitution, would student government benefit from one? Why or why not? Explain that student governments and other organizations often use the Constitution of the United States as their model.

Instruct Review the issues that divided Federalists and Antifederalists. Discuss how the Constitution preserves popular sovereignty and limits the powers of government while avoiding the weaknesses of the Articles of Confederation. Write the Six Basic Principles of the Constitution listed on this page on the chalkboard. Ask students to explain each one in their own words. Then ask them to find examples of each principle within the Constitution.

Discuss how the Bill of Rights protects Americans' basic rights. Ask students to make a list of examples of the rights that are protected in their own lives.

Close The Constitution provides a broad explanation of the limits of government, based on six basic principles. It has protected the rights of Americans for over 200 years.

THE CONSTITUTION
OF THE
United States

THE SIX BASIC PRINCIPLES

The classic textbook *Magruder's American Government* outlines the six basic principles of the Constitution. Below is a description of these principles:

1 POPULAR SOVEREIGNTY

The Preamble to the Constitution begins with the bold phrase, "We the people. . . ." These words announce that in the United States, the people are sovereign. The government receives its power from the people and can govern only with their consent.

2 LIMITED GOVERNMENT

Because the people are the ultimate source of all government power, the government has only as much authority as the people give it. Government's power is thus limited. Much of the Constitution, in fact, consists of specific limitations on government power.

3 SEPARATION OF POWERS

Government power is not only limited, but also divided. The Constitution assigns certain powers to each of the three branches: the legislative (Congress), executive (President), and judicial (federal courts). This separation of government's powers was intended to prevent the misuse of power.

4 CHECKS AND BALANCES

The system of checks and balances gives each of the three branches of government the ability to restrain the other two. Such a system makes government less efficient but also less likely to trample on the rights of citizens.

5 JUDICIAL REVIEW

Who decides whether an act of government violates the Constitution? Historically, the courts have filled this function. The principle of judicial review means that federal courts have the power to review acts of the federal government and to cancel any acts that are unconstitutional, or violate a provision in the Constitution.

6 FEDERALISM

A federal system of government is one in which power is divided between a central government and smaller governments. This sharing of powers is intended to ensure that the central government is powerful enough to be effective yet not so powerful as to threaten states or individuals.

▶ RESOURCE OPTIONS

Teaching Resources

American History Block Scheduling Support Checks and Balances: The Rise of the American Judiciary, found in the Forging a New Nation folder, includes interdisciplinary lesson suggestions and activities for Geography and History, Primary Sources, Biography, and Literature.

Media and Technology

Prentice Hall United States History Video Collection™ Volume 5 *A New Nation*

Decision America Videotapes and Videodiscs Issue 2 *Should Privacy Be Protected?*; Issue 5 *How Are We Represented?*; Issue 13 *What Is a Fair Trail?*

PARTS OF THE CONSTITUTION

A Note on the Text of the Constitution

The complete text of the Constitution, including amendments, appears on the pages that follow. Spelling, capitalization, and punctuation have been modernized, and headings have been added. Portions of the Constitution altered by later amendments or that no longer apply have been crossed out. Commentary appears in the outside column of each page.

THE CONSTITUTION

Customize for
English Language Learners

Ask a volunteer to read the Preamble to the Constitution aloud. Then have students paraphrase the Preamble in their own words.

Customize for
Less Proficient Readers

Help students begin reading the Constitution by having volunteers read the first several sections and clauses aloud, then read the appropriate paraphrase in the Commentary. Point out that students can look to the Commentary to help them understand the reading.

Customize for
More Advanced Students

Have students research one amendment to the Constitution and give a report to the class on the importance of the amendment and its impact on American society.

 Using the Internet

Write a Court Opinion

Objective Use the Internet to research a Supreme Court case that has affected young people. Write a court "opinion" describing how the case should have been decided. Have students follow these instructions.

1. See the *America: Pathways to the Present* Web site at **http://www.Pathways.phschool.com** for the URL for U.S. Supreme Court cases.

2. Use links to read about In re *Gault; Hazelwood School District* v. *Kuhlmeier; Tinker* v. *Des Moines School District,* and other cases that interest you.

3. Write an opinion from the point of view of the judge in one of the cases.

The Preamble describes the purpose of the government set up by the Constitution. Americans expect their government to defend justice and liberty and provide peace and safety from foreign enemies.

The Constitution gives Congress the power to make laws. Congress is divided into the Senate and the House of Representatives.

Clause 1 *Electors* refers to voters. Members of the House of Representatives are elected every two years. Any citizen allowed to vote for members of the larger house of the state legislature can also vote for members of the House.

Clause 2 A member of the House of Representatives must be at least 25 years old, an American citizen for 7 years, and a resident of the state he or she represents.

Clause 3 The number of representatives each state elects is based on its population. An *enumeration*, or census, must be taken every 10 years to determine population. Today, the number of representatives in the House is fixed at 435.

This clause contains the famous Three-Fifths Compromise worked out at the Constitutional Convention. *Persons bound to service* meant indentured servants. *All other persons* meant slaves. All free people in a state were counted. However, only three fifths of the slaves were included in the population count. This three-fifths clause became meaningless when slaves were freed by the Thirteenth Amendment.

Clause 4 *Executive authority* means the governor of a state. If a member of the House leaves office before his or her term ends, the governor must call a special election to fill the seat.

Clause 5 The House elects a Speaker. Today, the Speaker is usually chosen by the party that has a majority in the House. Also, only the House has the power to *impeach*, or accuse, a federal official of wrongdoing.

PREAMBLE

We the people of the United States, in order to form a more perfect union, establish justice, insure domestic tranquillity, provide for the common defense, promote the general welfare, and secure the blessings of liberty to ourselves and our posterity, do ordain and establish this Constitution for the United States of America.

Article I. Legislative Branch

Section 1. Legislative Powers; The Congress

All legislative powers herein granted shall be vested in a Congress of the United States, which shall consist of a Senate and House of Representatives.

Section 2. House of Representatives

1. Election of Members The House of Representatives shall be composed of members chosen every second year by the people of the several states, and the electors in each state shall have the qualifications requisite for electors of the most numerous branch of the state legislature.

2. Qualifications No person shall be a representative who shall not have attained to the age of twenty-five years, and been seven years a citizen of the United States, and who shall not, when elected, be an inhabitant of that state in which he shall be chosen.

3. Apportionment Representatives and direct taxes shall be apportioned among the several states which may be included within this Union, according to their respective numbers, which shall be determined by adding to the whole number of free persons, including those bound to service for a term of years and excluding Indians not taxed, three fifths of all other persons. The actual enumeration shall be made within three years after the first meeting of the Congress of the United States, and within every subsequent term of ten years, in such manner as they shall by law direct. The number of representatives shall not exceed one for every thirty thousand, but each state shall have at least one representative; and until such enumeration shall be made, the state of New Hampshire shall be entitled to choose three, Massachusetts eight, Rhode Island and Providence Plantations one, Connecticut five, New York six, New Jersey four, Pennsylvania eight, Delaware one, Maryland six, Virginia ten, North Carolina five, South Carolina five, and Georgia three.

4. Filling Vacancies When vacancies happen in the representation from any state, the executive authority thereof shall issue writs of election to fill such vacancies.

5. Officers; Impeachment The House of Representatives shall choose their Speaker and other officers; and shall have the sole power of impeachment.

Section 3. Senate

1. Composition; Term The Senate of the United States shall be composed of two senators from each state ~~chosen by the legislature thereof,~~ for six years, and each senator shall have one vote.

2. Classification; Filling Vacancies Immediately after they shall be assembled in consequence of the first election, they shall be divided as equally as may be into three classes. The seats of the senators of the first class shall be vacated at the expiration of the second year, of the second class at the expiration of the fourth year, and of the third class at the expiration of the sixth year, so that one third may be chosen every second year; ~~and if vacancies happen by resignation, or otherwise, during the recess of the legislature of any State, the executive thereof may make temporary appointments until the next meeting of the legislature, which shall then fill such vacancies.~~

3. Qualifications No person shall be a senator who shall not have attained to the age of thirty years, and been nine years a citizen of the United States, and who shall not, when elected, be an inhabitant of that state for which he shall be chosen.

4. President of the Senate The Vice President of the United States shall be president of the Senate, but shall have no vote, unless they be equally divided.

5. Other Officers The Senate shall choose their other officers, and also a president *pro tempore*, in the absence of the Vice President, or when he shall exercise the office of the President of the United States.

6. Impeachment Trials The Senate shall have the sole power to try all impeachments. When sitting for that purpose, they shall be on oath or affirmation. When the President of the United States is tried, the Chief Justice shall preside; and no person shall be convicted without the concurrence of two thirds of the members present.

7. Penalty on Conviction Judgment in cases of impeachment shall not extend further than to removal from office, and disqualification to hold and enjoy any office of honor, trust or profit under the United States: but the party convicted shall nevertheless be liable and subject to indictment, trial, judgment, and punishment, according to law.

Section 4. Elections and Meetings

1. Election of Congress The times, places, and manner of holding elections for senators and representatives, shall be prescribed in each state by the legislature thereof; but the Congress may at any time by law make or alter such regulations, except as to the places of choosing senators.

2. Sessions The Congress shall assemble at least once in every year, ~~and such meeting shall be on the first Monday in December, unless they shall by law appoint a different day.~~

Clause 1 Each state has two senators. Senators serve for six-year terms. The Seventeenth Amendment changed the way senators were elected.

Clause 2 Every two years, one third of the senators run for reelection. Thus, the makeup of the Senate is never totally changed by any one election. The Seventeenth Amendment changed the way of filling *vacancies*, or empty seats. Today, the governor of a state must choose a senator to fill a vacancy that occurs between elections.

Clause 3 A senator must be at least 30 years old, an American citizen for 9 years, and a resident of the state he or she represents.

Clause 4 The Vice President presides over Senate meetings, but he or she can vote only to break a tie.

Clause 5 *Pro tempore* means temporary. The Senate chooses one of its members to serve as president *pro tempore* when the Vice President is absent.

Clause 6 The Senate acts as a jury if the House impeaches a federal official. The Chief Justice of the Supreme Court presides if the President is on trial. Two thirds of all senators present must vote for conviction, or finding the accused guilty. No President has ever been convicted. The House impeached President Andrew Johnson in 1868, but the Senate acquitted him of the charges. In 1974, President Richard Nixon resigned before he could be impeached.

Clause 7 If an official is found guilty by the Senate, he or she can be removed from office and barred from holding federal office in the future. These are the only punishments the Senate can impose. However, the convicted official can still be tried in a criminal court.

Clause 1 Each state legislature can decide when and how congressional elections take place, but Congress can overrule these decisions. In 1842, Congress required each state to set up congressional districts with one representative elected from each district. In 1872, Congress decided that congressional elections must be held in every state on the same date in even-numbered years.

Clause 2 Congress must meet at least once a year. The Twentieth Amendment moved the opening date of Congress to January 3.

THE CONSTITUTION

Clause 1 Each house decides whether a member has the qualifications for office set by the Constitution. A *quorum* is the smallest number of members who must be present for business to be conducted. Each house can set its own rules about absent members.

Clause 2 Each house can make rules for the conduct of members. It can only expel a member by a two-thirds vote.

Clause 3 Each house keeps a record of its meetings. *The Congressional Record* is published every day with excerpts from speeches made in each house. It also records the votes of each member.

Clause 4 Neither house can *adjourn*, or stop meeting, for more than three days unless the other house approves. Both houses of Congress must meet in the same city.

Clause 1 *Compensation* means salary. Congress decides the salary for its members. While Congress is in session, a member is free from arrest in civil cases and cannot be sued for anything he or she says on the floor of Congress. This allows for freedom of debate. However, a member can be arrested for a criminal offense.

Clause 2 *Emolument* also means salary. A member of Congress cannot hold another federal office during his or her term. A former member of Congress cannot hold an office created while he or she was in Congress. An official in another branch of government cannot serve at the same time in Congress. This strengthens the separation of powers.

Clause 1 *Revenue* is money raised by the government through taxes. Tax bills must be introduced in the House. The Senate, however, can make changes in tax bills. This clause protects the principle that people can be taxed only with their consent.

Clause 2 A *bill,* or proposed law, that is passed by a majority of the House and Senate is sent to the President. If the President signs the bill, it becomes law.

A bill can also become law without the President's signature. The President can refuse to act on a bill. If Congress is in session at the time, the bill becomes law 10 days after the President receives it.

Section 5. Legislative Proceedings

1. Organization Each house shall be the judge of the elections, returns, and qualifications of its own members, and a majority of each shall constitute a quorum to do business; but a smaller number may adjourn from day to day, and may be authorized to compel the attendance of absent members, in such manner, and under such penalties, as each house may provide.

2. Rules Each house may determine the rules of its proceedings, punish its members for disorderly behavior, and with the concurrence of two thirds, expel a member.

3. Record Each house shall keep a journal of its proceedings, and from time to time publish the same, excepting such parts as may in their judgment require secrecy; and the yeas and nays of the members of either house on any question shall, at the desire of one fifth of those present, be entered on the journal.

4. Adjournment Neither house, during the session of Congress, shall, without the consent of the other, adjourn for more than three days, nor to any other place than that in which the two houses shall be sitting.

Section 6. Compensation, Immunities, and Disabilities of Members

1. Salaries; Immunities The senators and representatives shall receive a compensation for their services, to be ascertained by law, and paid out of the Treasury of the United States. They shall in all cases, except treason, felony, and breach of the peace, be privileged from arrest during their attendance at the session of their respective houses, and in going to and returning from the same; and for any speech or debate in either house, they shall not be questioned in any other place.

2. Restrictions on Other Employment No senator or representative shall, during the time for which he was elected, be appointed to any civil office under the authority of the United States, which shall have been created, or the emoluments whereof shall have been increased during such time; and no person holding any office under the United States shall be a member of either house during his continuance in office.

Section 7. Revenue Bills, President's Veto

1. Revenue Bills All bills for raising revenue shall originate in the House of Representatives; but the Senate may propose or concur with amendments as on other bills.

2. How a Bill Becomes Law; the Veto Every bill which shall have passed the House of Representatives and the Senate shall, before it become a law, be presented to the President of the United States; if he approve, he shall sign it, but if not, he shall return it, with his objections, to that house in which it shall have originated, who shall enter the objections at large on their journal, and proceed to reconsider it. If after such reconsideration two thirds of that house shall agree to pass the bill, it shall be sent, together with the objections, to the other house, by which it shall likewise be reconsidered, and if approved by two thirds of that house, it shall become a law. But in all such cases the votes of both houses shall be determined by yeas and nays, and the names of the persons voting for and against the bill shall be entered on the journal of each house respectively. If any bill shall not be returned by the President within ten days (Sundays excepted) after it shall have been presented to him, the same shall be a law, in like manner as if he had signed it, unless the Congress by their adjournment prevent its return, in which case it shall not be a law.

3. Resolutions Passed by Congress Every order, resolution, or vote to which the concurrence of the Senate and House of Representatives may be necessary (except on a question of adjournment) shall be presented to the President of the United States; and before the same shall take effect, shall be approved by him, or being disapproved by him, shall be repassed by two thirds of the Senate and House of Representatives, according to the rules and limitations prescribed in the case of a bill.

Section 8. Powers of Congress

The Congress shall have power

1. To lay and collect taxes, duties, imposts, and excises, to pay the debts and provide for the common defense and general welfare of the United States; but all duties, imposts and excises shall be uniform throughout the United States;

2. To borrow money on the credit of the United States;

3. To regulate commerce with foreign nations, and among the several states, and with the Indian tribes;

4. To establish an uniform rule of naturalization, and uniform laws on the subject of bankruptcies throughout the United States;

5. To coin money, regulate the value thereof, and of foreign coin, and fix the standard of weights and measures;

6. To provide for the punishment of counterfeiting the securities and current coin of the United States;

7. To establish post offices and post roads;

8. To promote the progress of science and useful arts by securing for limited times to authors and inventors the exclusive right to their respective writings and discoveries;

The President can *veto*, or reject, a bill by sending it back to the house where it was introduced. Or if the President refuses to act on a bill and Congress adjourns within 10 days, then the bill dies. This way of killing a bill without taking action is called the *pocket veto*.

Congress can override the President's veto if each house of Congress passes the bill again by a two-thirds vote. This clause is an important part of the system of checks and balances.

Clause 3 Congress can pass resolutions or orders that have the same force as laws. Any such resolution or order must be signed by the President (except on questions of adjournment). Thus, this clause prevents Congress from bypassing the President simply by calling a bill by another name.

Clause 1 *Duties* are tariffs. *Imposts* are taxes in general. *Excises* are taxes on the production or sale of certain goods. Congress has the power to tax and spend tax money. Taxes must be the same in all parts of the country.

Clause 2 Congress can borrow money for the United States. The government often borrows money by selling bonds, or certificates that promise to pay the holder a certain sum of money on a certain date.

Clause 3 Only Congress has the power to regulate foreign and interstate trade, or trade between states. Disagreements over interstate trade were a major problem with the Articles of Confederation.

Clause 4 *Naturalization* is the process whereby a foreigner becomes a citizen. *Bankruptcy* is the condition in which a person or business cannot pay its debts. Congress has the power to pass laws on these two issues. The laws must be the same in all parts of the country.

Clause 5 Congress has the power to coin money and set its value. Congress has set up the National Bureau of Standards to regulate weights and measures.

Clause 6 *Counterfeiting* is the making of imitation money. *Securities* are bonds. Congress can make laws to punish counterfeiters.

Clause 7 Congress has the power to set up and control the delivery of mail.

Clause 8 Congress may pass copyright and patent laws. A *copyright* protects an author. A patent makes an inventor the sole owner of his or her work for a limited time.

COMMENTARY

Clause 9 Congress has the power to set up **inferior**, or lower, federal courts under the Supreme Court.

Clause 10 Congress can punish **piracy**, or the robbing of ships at sea.

Clause 11 Only Congress can declare war. Declarations of war are granted at the request of the President. **Letters of marque and reprisal** were documents issued by a government allowing merchant ships to arm themselves and attack ships of an enemy nation. They are no longer issued.

Clauses 12, 13, 14 These clauses place the army and navy under the control of Congress. Congress decides on the size of the armed forces and the amount of money to spend on the army and navy. It also has the power to write rules governing the armed forces.

Clauses 15, 16 The **militia** is a body of citizen soldiers. Congress can call up the militia to put down rebellions or fight foreign invaders. Each state has its own militia, today called the National Guard. Normally, the militia is under the command of a state's governor. However, it can be placed under the command of the President.

Clause 17 Congress controls the district around the national capital. In 1790, Congress made Washington, D.C., the nation's capital. In 1973, it gave residents of the District the right to elect local officials.

Clause 18 Clauses 1–17 list the powers delegated to Congress. The writers of the Constitution added Clause 18 so that Congress could deal with the changing needs of the nation. It gives Congress the power to make laws as needed to carry out the first 17 clauses. Clause 18 is sometimes called the elastic clause because it lets Congress stretch the meaning of its power.

Clause 1 **Such persons** means slaves. This clause resulted from a compromise between the supporters and the opponents of the slave trade. In 1808, as soon as Congress was permitted to abolish the slave trade, it did so. The $10 import tax was never imposed.

Clause 2 A **writ of habeas corpus** is a court order requiring government officials to bring a prisoner to court and explain why he or she is being held. A writ of habeas corpus protects people from unlawful imprisonment. The government cannot suspend this right except in times of rebellion or invasion.

Clause 3 A **bill of attainder** is a law declaring that a person is guilty of a particular crime. An **ex post facto law** punishes

CONSTITUTION

9. To constitute tribunals inferior to the Supreme Court;

10. To define and punish piracies and felonies committed on the high seas and offenses against the law of nations;

11. To declare war, grant letters of marque and reprisal, and make rules concerning captures on land and water;

12. To raise and support armies, but no appropriation of money to that use shall be for a longer term than two years;

13. To provide and maintain a navy;

14. To make rules for the government and regulation of the land and naval forces;

15. To provide for calling forth the militia to execute the laws of the Union, suppress insurrections, and repel invasions;

16. To provide for organizing, arming, and disciplining the militia, and for governing such part of them as may be employed in the service of the United States, reserving to the states, respectively, the appointment of the officers, and the authority of training the militia according to the discipline prescribed by Congress;

17. To exercise exclusive legislation in all cases whatsoever, over such district (not exceeding ten miles square) as may, by cession of particular states, and the acceptance of Congress, become the seat of the government of the United States, and to exercise like authority over all places purchased by the consent of the legislature of the state in which the same shall be, for the erection of forts, magazines, arsenals, dock-yards, and other needful buildings; —and

18. To make all laws which shall be necessary and proper for carrying into execution the foregoing powers, and all other powers vested by this Constitution in the government of the United States, or in any department or officer thereof.

Section 9. Powers Denied to Congress

1. The Slave Trade ~~The migration or importation of such persons as any of the states now existing shall think proper to admit, shall not be prohibited by the Congress prior to the year one thousand eight hundred and eight, but a tax or duty may be imposed on such importation, not exceeding ten dollars for each person.~~

2. Writ of *Habeas Corpus* The privilege of the writ of *habeas corpus* shall not be suspended, unless when in cases of rebellion or invasion the public safety may require it.

3. Bills of Attainder; *Ex Post Facto* Laws No bill of attainder or *ex post facto* law shall be passed.

4. Apportionment of Direct Taxes No capitation, ~~or other direct,~~ tax shall be laid, unless in proportion to the census or enumeration herein before directed to be taken.

5. Taxes on Exports No tax or duty shall be laid on articles exported from any state.

6. Special Preference for Trade No preference shall be given by any regulation of commerce or revenue to the ports of one state over those of another; nor shall vessels bound to, or from, one state, be obliged to enter, clear, or pay duties in another.

7. Spending No money shall be drawn from the Treasury, but in consequence of appropriations made by law; and a regular statement and account of the receipts and expenditures of all public money shall be published from time to time.

8. Titles of Nobility No title of nobility shall be granted by the United States; and no person holding any office of profit or trust under them, shall, without the consent of the Congress, accept of any present, emolument, office, or title, of any kind whatever, from any king, prince or foreign state.

Section 10. Powers Denied to the States

1. Unconditional Prohibitions No state shall enter into any treaty, alliance, or confederation; grant letters of marque and reprisal; coin money; emit bills of credit; make any thing but gold and silver coin a tender in payment of debts; pass any bill of attainder, *ex post facto* law, or law impairing the obligation of contracts, or grant any title of nobility.

2. Powers Conditionally Denied No state shall, without the consent of the Congress, lay any imposts or duties on imports or exports, except what may be absolutely necessary for executing its inspection laws; and the net produce of all duties and imposts, laid by any state on imports or exports, shall be for the use of the Treasury of the United States; and all such laws shall be subject to the revision and control of the Congress.

3. Other Denied Powers No state shall, without the consent of Congress, lay any duty of tonnage, keep troops, or ships of war in time of peace, enter into any agreement or compact with another state, or with a foreign power, or engage in war, unless actually invaded, or in such imminent danger as will not admit of delay.

Article II. Executive Branch
Section 1. President and Vice President

1. Chief Executive; Term The executive power shall be vested in a President of the United States of America. He shall hold his

an act which was not illegal when it was committed. Congress cannot pass a bill of attainder or *ex post facto* laws.

Clause 4 A *capitation tax* is a tax placed directly on each person. *Direct taxes* are taxes on people or on land. They can be passed only if they are divided among the states according to population. The Sixteenth Amendment allowed Congress to tax income without regard to the population of the states.

Clause 5 This clause forbids Congress to tax exports. In 1787, southerners insisted on this clause because their economy depended on exports.

Clause 6 Congress cannot make laws that favor one state over another in trade and commerce. Also, states cannot place tariffs on interstate trade.

Clause 7 The federal government cannot spend money unless Congress *appropriates* it, or passes a law allowing it. This clause gives Congress an important check on the President by controlling the money he or she can spend. The government must publish a statement showing how it spends public funds.

Clause 8 The government cannot award titles of nobility, such as Duke or Duchess. American citizens cannot accept titles of nobility from foreign governments without the consent of Congress.

Clause 1 The writers of the Constitution did not want the states to act like separate nations. So they prohibited states from making treaties or coining money. Some powers denied to the federal government are also denied to the states. For example, states cannot pass *ex post facto* laws.

Clauses 2, 3 Powers listed here are forbidden to the states, but Congress can lift these prohibitions by passing laws that give these powers to the states.

Clause 2 forbids states from taxing imports and exports without the consent of Congress. States may charge inspection fees on goods entering the states. Any profit from these fees must be turned over to the United States Treasury.

Clause 3 forbids states from keeping an army or navy without the consent of Congress. States cannot make treaties or declare war unless an enemy invades or is about to invade.

Clause 1 The President is responsible for *executing*, or carrying out, laws passed by Congress.

Clauses 2, 3 Some writers of the Constitution were afraid to allow the people to elect the President directly. Therefore, the Constitutional Convention set up the electoral college. Clause 2 directs each state to choose electors, or delegates to the electoral college, to vote for President. A state's electoral vote is equal to the combined number of senators and representatives. Each state may decide how to choose its electors. Members of Congress and federal officeholders may not serve as electors. This much of the original electoral college system is still in effect.

Clause 3 called upon each elector to vote for two candidates. The candidate who received a majority of the electoral votes would become President. The runner-up would become Vice President. If no candidate won a majority, the House would choose the President. The Senate would choose the Vice President.

The election of 1800 showed a problem with the original electoral college system. Thomas Jefferson was the Republican candidate for President, and Aaron Burr was the Republican candidate for Vice President. In the electoral college, the vote ended in a tie. The election was finally decided in the House, where Jefferson was chosen President. The Twelfth Amendment changed the electoral college system so that this could not happen again.

Clause 4 Under a law passed in 1792, electors are chosen on the Tuesday following the first Monday of November every four years. Electors from each state meet to vote in December.

Today, voters in each state choose *slates*, or groups, of electors who are pledged to a candidate for President. The candidate for President who wins the popular vote in each state wins that state's electoral vote.

Clause 5 The President must be a citizen of the United States from birth, at least 35 years old, and a resident of the country for 14 years. The first seven Presidents of the United States were born under British rule, but they were allowed to hold office because they were citizens at the time the Constitution was adopted.

Clause 6 The powers of the President pass to the Vice President if the President leaves office or cannot discharge his or her duties. The wording of this clause caused confusion the first time a President died in office. When President William Henry Harrison died, it was uncertain whether Vice President John Tyler should remain Vice President and act

---

office during the term of four years, and, together with the Vice President, chosen for the same term, be elected as follows:

2. Electoral College Each state shall appoint, in such manner as the legislature thereof may direct, a number of electors, equal to the whole number of senators and representatives to which the state may be entitled in the Congress: but no senator or representative, or person holding an office of trust or profit under the United States, shall be appointed an elector.

3. Former Electoral Method ~~The electors shall meet in their respective states, and vote by ballot for two persons, of whom one at least shall not be an inhabitant of the same state with themselves. And they shall make a list of all the persons voted for, and of the number of votes for each; which list they shall sign and certify, and transmit sealed to the seat of the government of the United States, directed to the president of the Senate. The president of the Senate shall, in the presence of the Senate and House of Representatives, open all the certificates, and the votes shall then be counted. The person having the greatest number of votes shall be the President, if such number be a majority of the whole number of Electors appointed; and if there be more than one who have such majority, and have an equal number of votes, then the House of Representatives shall immediately choose by ballot one of them for President; and if no person have a majority, then from the five highest on the list the said House shall in like manner choose the President. But in choosing the President, the votes shall be taken by states, the representation from each state having one vote; a quorum for this purpose shall consist of a member or members from two thirds of the states, and a majority of all the states shall be necessary to a choice. In every case, after the choice of the President, the person having the greatest number of votes of the electors shall be the Vice President. But if there should remain two or more who have equal votes, the Senate shall choose from them by ballot the Vice President.~~

4. Time of Elections The Congress may determine the time of choosing the electors, and the day on which they shall give their votes; which day shall be the same throughout the United States.

5. Qualifications for President No person except a natural-born citizen, ~~or a citizen of the United States at the time of the adoption of this Constitution,~~ shall be eligible to the office of President; neither shall any person be eligible to that office who shall not have attained to the age of thirty-five years, and been fourteen years a resident within the United States.

6. Presidential Succession ~~In case of the removal of the President from office, or of his death, resignation, or inability to discharge the powers and duties of the said office, the same shall devolve on the Vice President,~~ and the Congress may by law provide for the case of removal, death, resignation or inability, both of the President and Vice President, declaring what officer shall then act as President, and such officer shall act accordingly, until the disability be removed, or a President shall be elected.

7. Salary The President shall, at stated times, receive for his services, a compensation, which shall neither be increased nor diminished during the period for which he shall have been elected, and he shall not receive within that period any other emolument from the United States, or any of them.

8. Oath of Office Before he enter on the execution of his office, he shall take the following oath or affirmation:—"I do solemnly swear (or affirm) that I will faithfully execute the office of the President of the United States, and will to the best of my ability, preserve, protect, and defend the Constitution of the United States."

Section 2. Powers of the President

1. Military Powers The President shall be commander in chief of the army and navy of the United States, and of the militia of the several states, when called into the actual service of the United States; he may require the opinion, in writing, of the principal officer in each of the executive departments, upon any subject relating to the duties of their respective offices, and he shall have power to grant reprieves and pardons for offenses against the United States, except in cases of impeachment.

2. Treaties; Appointments He shall have power, by and with the advice and consent of the Senate, to make treaties, provided two thirds of the senators present concur; and he shall nominate, and by and with the advice and consent of the Senate, shall appoint ambassadors, other public ministers and consuls, judges of the Supreme Court, and all other officers of the United States, whose appointments are not herein otherwise provided for, and which shall be established by law: but the Congress may by law vest the appointment of such inferior officers, as they think proper, in the President alone, in the courts of law, or in the heads of departments.

3. Temporary Appointments The President shall have power to fill up all vacancies that may happen during the recess of the Senate, by granting commissions which shall expire at the end of their next session.

Section 3. Duties of the President

He shall from time to time give to the Congress information of the state of the Union, and recommend to their consideration such measures as he shall judge necessary and expedient; he may, on extraordinary occasions, convene both houses, or either of them, and in case of disagreement between them, with respect to the time of adjournment, he may adjourn them to such time as he shall think proper; he shall receive ambassadors and other public ministers; he shall take care that the laws be faithfully executed, and shall commission all the officers of the United States.

as President or whether he should be sworn in as President. Tyler persuaded a federal judge to swear him in. So he set the precedent that the Vice President assumes the office of President when it becomes vacant. The Twenty-fifth Amendment replaced this clause.

Clause 7 The President is paid a salary. It cannot be raised or lowered during his or her term of office. The President is not allowed to hold any other federal or state position while in office. Today, the President's salary is $200,000 a year.

Clause 8 Before taking office, the President must promise to protect and defend the Constitution. Usually, the Chief Justice of the United States administers the oath of office to the President.

Clause 1 The President is head of the armed forces and the state militias when they are called into national service. So the military is under *civilian*, or nonmilitary, control.

The President can get advice from the heads of executive departments. In most cases, the President has the power to grant a reprieve or pardon. A *reprieve* suspends punishment ordered by law. A *pardon* prevents prosecution for a crime or overrides the judgment of a court.

Clause 2 The President has the power to make treaties with other nations. Under the system of checks and balances, all treaties must be approved by two thirds of the Senate. Today, the President also makes agreements with foreign governments. These executive agreements do not need Senate approval.

The President has the power to appoint ambassadors to foreign countries and to appoint other high officials. The Senate must *confirm*, or approve, these appointments.

Clause 3 If the Senate is in *recess,* or not meeting, the President may fill vacant government posts by making temporary appointments.

The President must give Congress a report on the condition of the nation every year. This report is now called the State of the Union Address. Since 1913, the President has given this speech in person each January.

The President can call a special session of Congress and can adjourn Congress if necessary. The President has the power to receive, or recognize, foreign ambassadors.

The President must carry out the laws. Today, many government agencies oversee the execution of laws.

Section 4. Impeachment

The President, Vice President and all civil officers of the United States, shall be removed from office on impeachment for, and conviction of, treason, bribery, or other high crimes and misdemeanors.

Article III. Judicial Branch
Section 1. Courts, Terms of Office

The judicial power of the United States shall be vested in one Supreme Court, and in such inferior courts as the Congress may from time to time ordain and establish. The judges, both of the Supreme and inferior courts, shall hold their offices during good behavior, and shall, at stated times, receive for their services, a compensation, which shall not be diminished during their continuance in office.

Section 2. Jurisdiction

1. Scope of Judicial Power The judicial power shall extend to all cases, in law and equity, arising under this Constitution, the laws of the United States, and treaties made, or which shall be made, under their authority;—to all cases affecting ambassadors, other public ministers and consuls;—to all cases of admiralty and maritime jurisdiction;—to controversies to which the United States shall be a party;—to controversies between two or more states; between a state and citizens of another state; —between citizens of different states;—between citizens of the same state claiming lands under grants of different states, and between a state, or the citizens thereof, and foreign states, citizens, or subjects.

2. Supreme Court In all cases affecting ambassadors, other public ministers and consuls, and those in which a state shall be a party, the Supreme Court shall have original jurisdiction. In all the other cases before mentioned, the Supreme Court shall have appellate jurisdiction, both as to law and fact, with such exceptions, and under such regulations as the Congress shall make.

3. Trial by Jury The trial of all crimes, except in cases of impeachment, shall be by jury; and such trial shall be held in the state where the said crimes shall have been committed; but when not committed within any state, the trial shall be at such place or places as the Congress may by law have directed.

Section 3. Treason

1. Definition Treason against the United States shall consist only in levying war against them, or in adhering to their enemies, giving them aid and comfort. No person shall be convicted of treason unless on the testimony of two witnesses to the same overt act, or on confession in open court.

2. Punishment The Congress shall have power to declare the punishment of treason, but no attainder of treason shall work corruption of blood or forfeiture except during the life of the person attained.

Civil officers include federal judges and members of the Cabinet. **High crimes** are major crimes. **Misdemeanors** are lesser crimes. The President, Vice President, and others can be forced out of office if impeached and found guilty of certain crimes. Andrew Johnson and Bill Clinton are the only two Presidents to have been impeached.

Judicial power means the right of the courts to decide legal cases. The Constitution creates the Supreme Court but lets Congress decide on the size of the Supreme Court. Congress has the power to set up inferior, or lower, courts. The Judiciary Act of 1789 set up a system of district and circuit courts, or courts of appeal. All federal judges serve for life.

Clause 1 **Jurisdiction** refers to the right of a court to hear a case. Federal courts have jurisdiction over cases that involve the Constitution, federal laws, treaties, foreign ambassadors and diplomats, naval and maritime laws, disagreements between states or between citizens from different states, and disputes between a state or citizen and a foreign state or citizen.

In *Marbury v. Madison*, the Supreme Court established the right to judge whether a law is constitutional.

Clause 2 **Original jurisdiction** means the power of a court to hear a case where it first arises. The Supreme Court has original jurisdiction over only a few cases, such as those involving foreign diplomats. More often, the Supreme Court acts as an appellate court. An **appellate** court does not decide guilt. It decides whether the lower court trial was properly conducted and reviews the lower court's decision.

Clause 3 This clause guarantees the right to a jury trial for anyone accused of a federal crime. The only exceptions are impeachment cases. The trial must be held in the state where the crime was committed.

Clause 1 Treason is clearly defined. An **overt act** is an actual action. A person cannot be convicted of treason for what he or she thinks. A person can be convicted of treason only if he or she confesses or two witnesses testify to it.

Clause 2 Congress has the power to set the punishment for traitors. Congress may not punish the children of convicted traitors by taking away their civil rights or property.

Article IV. Relations Among the States

Section 1. Full Faith and Credit

Full faith and credit shall be given in each state to the public acts, records, and judicial proceedings of every other state. And the Congress may by general laws prescribe the manner in which such acts, records, and proceedings shall be proved, and the effect thereof.

Each state must recognize the official acts and records of any other state. For example, each state must recognize marriage certificates issued by another state. Congress can pass laws to ensure this.

Section 2. Privileges and Immunities of Citizens

1. Privileges The citizens of each state shall be entitled to all privileges and immunities of citizens in the several states.

Clause 1 All states must treat citizens of another state in the same way it treats its own citizens. However, the courts have allowed states to give residents certain privileges, such as lower tuition rates.

2. Extradition A person charged in any state with treason, felony, or other crime, who shall flee from justice, and be found in another state, shall on demand of the executive authority of the state from which he fled, be delivered up, to be removed to the state having jurisdiction of the crime.

Clause 2 *Extradition* means the act of returning a suspected criminal or escaped prisoner to a state where he or she is wanted. State governors must return a suspect to another state. However, the Supreme Court has ruled that a governor cannot be forced to do so if he or she feels that justice will not be done.

3. Fugitive Slaves ~~No person held to service or labor in one state, under the laws thereof, escaping into another, shall in consequence of any law or regulation therein, be discharged from such service or labor, but shall be delivered up on claim of the party to whom such service or labor may be due.~~

Clause 3 *Persons held to service or labor* refers to slaves or indentured servants. This clause required states to return runaway slaves to their owners. The Thirteenth Amendment replaces this clause.

Section 3. New States and Territories

1. New States New states may be admitted by the Congress into this Union; but no new states shall be formed or erected within the jurisdiction of any other state; nor any state be formed by the junction of two or more states, or parts of states, without the consent of the legislatures of the states concerned as well as of the Congress.

Clause 1 Congress has the power to admit new states to the Union. Existing states cannot be split up or joined together to form new states unless both Congress and the state legislatures approve. New states are equal to all other states.

2. Federal Lands The Congress shall have power to dispose of and make all needful rules and regulations respecting the territory or other property belonging to the United States; and nothing in this Constitution shall be so construed as to prejudice any claims of the United States, or of any particular state.

Clause 2 Congress can make rules for managing and governing land owned by the United States. This includes territories not organized into states, and federal lands within a state.

Section 4. Protection Afforded to States by the Nation

The United States shall guarantee to every state in this Union a republican form of government, and shall protect each of them against invasion; and on application of the legislature, or of the executive (when the legislature cannot be convened) against domestic violence.

In a *republic,* voters choose representatives to govern them. The federal government must protect the states from foreign invasion and from *domestic,* or internal, disorder if asked to do so by a state.

THE CONSTITUTION

The Constitution can be *amended*, or changed, if necessary. An amendment can be proposed by (1) a two-thirds vote of both houses of Congress or (2) a national convention called by Congress at the request of two thirds of the state legislatures. (This second method has never been used.) An amendment must be *ratified*, or approved, by (1) three fourths of the state legislatures or (2) special conventions in three fourths of the states. Congress decides which method will be used.

The United States government promised to pay all debts and honor all agreements made under the Articles of Confederation.

Under the Constitution, federal laws and treaties that the Senate have ratified are the *supreme,* or highest, law of the land. A judge must overturn a state law if he or she believes that it conflicts with the Constitution or a federal law that he or she deems constitutional.

State and federal officeholders take an *oath,* or solemn promise, to support the Constitution. However, this clause forbids the use of religious tests for officeholders. During the colonial period, every colony except Rhode Island required a religious test for officeholders.

During 1787 and 1788, states held special conventions. By October 1788, the required nine states had ratified the Constitution.

Article V. Provisions for Amendment

The Congress, whenever two thirds of both houses shall deem it necessary, shall propose amendments to this Constitution, or, on the application of the legislatures of two thirds of the several states, shall call a convention for proposing amendments, which, in either case, shall be valid to all intents and purposes, as part of this Constitution, when ratified by the legislatures of three fourths of the several states, or by conventions in three fourths thereof, as the one or the other mode of ratification may be proposed by the Congress; provided ~~that no amendment which may be made prior to the year one thousand eight hundred and eight shall in any manner affect the first and fourth clauses in the ninth section of the first Article; and~~ that no state, without its consent, shall be deprived of its equal suffrage in the Senate.

Article VI. National Debts, Supremacy of National Law, Oath

Section 1. Validity of Debts

All debts contracted and engagements entered into, before the adoption of this Constitution, shall be as valid against the United States under this Constitution, as under the Confederation.

Section 2. Supremacy of National Law

This Constitution, and the laws of the United States which shall be made in pursuance thereof, and all treaties made, or which shall be made, under the authority of the United States, shall be the supreme law of the land; and the judges in every state shall be bound thereby, anything in the constitution or laws of any state to the contrary notwithstanding.

Section 3. Oaths of Office

The senators and representatives before mentioned, and the members of the several state legislatures, and all executive and judicial officers, both of the United States and of the several states, shall be bound by oath or affirmation, to support this Constitution; but no religious test shall ever be required as a qualification to any office or public trust under the United States.

Article VII. Ratification of Constitution

The ratification of the conventions of nine states shall be sufficient for the establishment of this Constitution between the states so ratifying the same.

Done in convention by the unanimous consent of the states present the seventeenth day of September, in the year of our Lord one thousand seven hundred and eighty-seven, and of the independence of the United States of America the twelfth. *In Witness* whereof, we have hereunto subscribed our names.

Attest:
> William Jackson, SECRETARY
> George Washington,
> PRESIDENT and deputy from
> Virginia

NEW HAMPSHIRE
> John Langdon
> Nicholas Gilman

MASSACHUSETTS
> Nathaniel Gorham
> Rufus King

CONNECTICUT
> William Samuel Johnson
> Roger Sherman

NEW YORK
> Alexander Hamilton

NEW JERSEY
> William Livingston
> David Brearley
> William Paterson
> Jonathan Dayton

PENNSYLVANIA
> Benjamin Franklin
> Thomas Mifflin
> Robert Morris
> George Clymer
> Thomas Fitzsimons
> Jared Ingersoll
> James Wilson
> Gouverneur Morris

DELAWARE
> George Read
> Gunning Bedford, Jr.
> John Dickinson
> Richard Bassett
> Jacob Broom

MARYLAND
> James McHenry
> Dan of St. Thomas Jennifer
> Daniel Carroll

VIRGINIA
> John Blair
> James Madison, Jr.

NORTH CAROLINA
> William Blount
> Richard Dobbs Spaight
> Hugh Williamson

SOUTH CAROLINA
> John Rutledge
> Charles Cotesworth Pinckney
> Charles Pinckney
> Pierce Butler

GEORGIA
> William Few
> Abraham Baldwin

AMENDMENTS

First Amendment
(1791) Freedom of Religion, Speech, Press, Assembly, and Petition

Congress shall make no law respecting an establishment of religion, or prohibiting the free exercise thereof; or abridging the freedom of speech, or of the press; or the right of the people peaceably to assemble, and to petition the government for a redress of grievances.

First Amendment The First Amendment protects five basic rights: freedom of religion, speech, the press, assembly, and petition. Congress cannot set up an established, or official, church or religion for the nation. During the colonial period, most colonies had established churches. However, the authors of the First Amendment wanted to keep government and religion separate.

Congress may not **abridge**, or limit, the freedom to speak and write freely. The government may not censor, or review, books and newspapers before they are printed. This amendment also protects the right to assemble, or hold public meetings. **Petition** means ask. **Redress** means to correct. **Grievances** are wrongs. The people have the right to ask the government for wrongs to be corrected.

Second Amendment
(1791) Bearing Arms

A well-regulated militia being necessary to the security of a free state, the right of the people to keep and bear arms shall not be infringed.

Second Amendment The meaning of this amendment is highly controversial. Some experts believe that it guarantees individuals the right to bear arms while others contend that it guarantees the individual states the right to maintain a militia.

Third Amendment
(1791) Quartering of Troops

No soldier shall, in time of peace, be quartered in any house, without the consent of the owner; nor in time of war, but in a manner to be prescribed by law.

Third Amendment During the colonial period, the British **quartered,** or housed, soldiers in private homes without the permission of the owners. This amendment limits the government's right to use private homes to house soldiers.

THE CONSTITUTION

Fourth Amendment This amendment protects Americans from unreasonable searches and seizures. Search and seizure are permitted only if a judge has issued a *warrant*, or written court order. A warrant is issued only if there is probable cause. This means an officer must show that it is probable, or likely, that the search will produce evidence of a crime. A search warrant must name the exact place to be searched and the things to be seized.

In some cases, courts have ruled that searches can take place without a warrant. For example, police may search a person who is under arrest.

Fifth Amendment This amendment protects the rights of the accused. *Capital crimes* are those that can be punished with death. *Infamous crimes* are those that can be punished with prison or loss of rights. The federal government must obtain an *indictment*, or formal accusation, from a grand jury to prosecute anyone for such crimes. A *grand jury* is a panel of between 12 and 23 citizens who decide if the government has enough evidence to justify a trial. This procedure prevents the government from prosecuting people with little or no evidence of guilt. (Soldiers and the militia in wartime are not covered by this rule.)

Double jeopardy is forbidden by this amendment. This means that a person cannot be tried twice for the same crime. However, if a court sets aside a conviction because of a legal error, the accused can be tried again. A person on trial cannot be forced to *testify,* or give evidence, against himself or herself. A person accused of a crime is entitled to *due process of law*, or a fair hearing or trial.

Finally, the government cannot seize private property for public use without paying the owner a fair price for it.

Sixth Amendment In criminal cases, the jury must be *impartial*, or not favor either side. The accused is guaranteed the right to a trial by jury. The trial must be speedy. If the government purposely postpones the trial so that it becomes hard for the person to get a fair hearing, the charge may be dismissed. The accused must be told the charges against him or her and be allowed to question prosecution witnesses. Witnesses who can help the accused can be ordered to appear in court.

The accused must be allowed a lawyer. Since 1942, the federal government has been required to provide a lawyer if the accused cannot afford one. In 1963, the Supreme Court decided that states must also provide lawyers for a defendant too poor to pay for one.

Fourth Amendment
(1791) Searches and Seizures

The right of the people to be secure in their persons, houses, papers, and effects, against unreasonable searches and seizures, shall not be violated, and no warrants shall issue, but upon probable cause, supported by oath or affirmation, and particularly describing the place to be searched, and the persons or things to be seized.

Fifth Amendment
(1791) Criminal Proceedings; Due Process; Eminent Domain

No person shall be held to answer for a capital, or otherwise infamous, crime, unless on a presentment or indictment of a grand jury, except in cases arising in the land or naval forces, or in the militia, when in actual service in time of war or public danger; nor shall any person be subject for the same offense to be twice put in jeopardy of life and limb; nor shall be compelled, in any criminal case, to be a witness against himself; nor be deprived of life, liberty, or property, without due process of law; nor shall private property be taken for public use, without just compensation.

Sixth Amendment
(1791) Criminal Proceedings

In all criminal prosecutions, the accused shall enjoy the right to a speedy and public trial, by an impartial jury of the state and district wherein the crime shall have been committed, which district shall have been previously ascertained by law, and to be informed of the nature and cause of the accusation; to be confronted with the witnesses against him; to have compulsory process for obtaining witnesses in his favor, and to have the assistance of counsel for his defense.

Seventh Amendment
(1791) Civil Trials

In suits at common law, where the value in controversy shall exceed twenty dollars, the right of trial by jury shall be preserved, and no fact tried by a jury shall be otherwise re-examined in any court of the United States, than according to the rules of the common law.

Eighth Amendment
(1791) Punishment for Crimes

Excessive bail shall not be required, nor excessive fines imposed, nor cruel and unusual punishments inflicted.

Ninth Amendment
(1791) Unenumerated Rights

The enumeration in the Constitution, of certain rights, shall not be construed to deny or disparage others retained by the people.

Tenth Amendment
(1791) Powers Reserved to the States

The powers not delegated to the United States by the Constitution, nor prohibited by it to the states, are reserved to the states respectively, or to the people.

Eleventh Amendment
(1798) Suits Against States

The judicial power of the United States shall not be construed to extend to any suit in law or equity, commenced or prosecuted against one of the United States by citizens of another state, or by citizens or subjects of any foreign state.

Twelfth Amendment
(1804) Election of President and Vice President

The electors shall meet in their respective states, and vote by ballot for President and Vice President, one of whom, at least, shall not be an inhabitant of the same state with themselves; they shall name in their ballots the person voted for as President, and in distinct ballots the person voted for as Vice President, and they shall make distinct lists of all persons voted for as President, and of all persons voted for as Vice President, and of the number of votes for each, which lists they shall sign and certify, and transmit sealed to the seat of the government of the United States, directed to the president of the Senate; the president of the Senate shall, in the presence of the Senate and the House of Representatives, open all the certificates and the votes shall then be counted;—the person having the greatest number of votes for

Seventh Amendment *Common law* refers to rules of law established by judges in past cases. This amendment guarantees the right to a jury trial in lawsuits where the sum of money at stake is more than $20. An appeals court cannot change a verdict because it disagrees with the decision of the jury. It can set aside a verdict only if legal errors made the trial unfair.

Eighth Amendment *Bail* is money the accused leaves with the court as a pledge that he or she will appear for trial. If the accused does not appear for trial, the court keeps the money. *Excessive* means too high. This amendment forbids courts to set unreasonably high bail. The amount of bail usually depends on the seriousness of the charge and whether the accused is likely to appear for the trial. The amendment also forbids cruel and unusual punishments such as mental and physical abuse.

Ninth Amendment The people have rights that are not listed in the Constitution. This amendment was added because some people feared that the Bill of Rights would be used to limit rights to those actually listed.

Tenth Amendment This amendment limits the power of the federal government. Powers not given to the federal government belong to the states. The powers reserved to the states are not listed in the Constitution.

Eleventh Amendment This amendment changed part of Article 3, Section 2, Clause 1. As a result, a private citizen from one state cannot sue the government of another state in federal court. However, a citizen can sue a state government in a state court.

Twelfth Amendment This amendment changed the way the electoral college voted. Before the amendment was adopted, each elector simply voted for two people. The candidate with the most votes became President. The runner-up became Vice President. In 1800, however, a tie vote resulted between Thomas Jefferson and Aaron Burr.

In such a case, the Constitution required the House of Representatives to elect the President. Federalists had a majority in the House. They tried to keep Jefferson out of office by voting for Burr. It took 35 ballots in the House before Jefferson was elected President.

To keep this from happening again, the Twelfth Amendment was passed and ratified in time for the election of 1804.

This amendment provides that each elector choose one candidate for President and one candidate for Vice President. If no candidate for President receives a majority of electoral votes, the House of Representatives chooses the President. If no candidate for Vice President receives a majority, the Senate elects the Vice President. The Vice President must be a person who is eligible to be President.

This system is still in use today. However, it is possible for a candidate to win the popular vote and lose in the electoral college. This happened in 1876.

Thirteenth Amendment The Emancipation Proclamation (1863) freed slaves only in areas controlled by the Confederacy. This amendment freed all slaves. It also forbids *involuntary servitude*, or labor done against one's will. However, it does not prevent prison wardens from making prisoners work. Congress can pass laws to carry out this amendment.

Fourteenth Amendment, Section 1 This section defines citizenship for the first time in the Constitution, and it extends citizenship to blacks. It also prohibits states from denying the rights and privileges of citizenship to any citizen. This section also forbids states to deny due process of law.

Section 1 guarantees all citizens "equal protection under the law." For a long time, however, the Fourteenth Amendment did not protect blacks from discrimination. After Reconstruction, separate facilities for blacks and whites sprang up. In 1954, the Supreme Court ruled that separate facilities for blacks and whites were by their nature unequal. This ruling, in the case of *Brown* v. *Board of Education*, made school segregation illegal.

Fourteenth Amendment, Section 2 This section replaced the three-fifths clause. It provides that representation in the House of Representatives is decided on the basis of the number of people in the state. It also provides that states which deny the vote to male citizens over age 21 will be punished by losing part of their representation in the

President shall be the President, if such number be a majority of the whole number of electors appointed; and if no person have such a majority, then from the persons having the highest numbers not exceeding three on the list of those voted for as President, the House of Representatives shall choose immediately, by ballot, the President. But in choosing the President, the votes shall be taken by states, the representation from each state having one vote; a quorum for this purpose shall consist of a member or members from two thirds of the states, and a majority of all the states shall be necessary to a choice. And if the House of Representatives shall not choose a President whenever the right of choice shall devolve upon them, ~~before the fourth day of March next following,~~ then the Vice President, shall act as President, as in the case of the death or other constitutional disability of the President.—The person having the greatest number of votes as Vice President, shall be the Vice President, if such number be a majority of the whole number of electors appointed, and if no person have a majority, then from the two highest numbers on the list, the Senate shall choose the Vice President; a quorum for the purpose shall consist of two thirds of the whole number of senators, and a majority of the whole number shall be necessary to a choice. But no person constitutionally ineligible to the office of President shall be eligible to that of Vice President of the United States.

Thirteenth Amendment
(1865) Slavery and Involuntary Servitude

Section 1. Outlawing Slavery Neither slavery nor involuntary servitude, except as a punishment for crime whereof the party shall have been duly convicted, shall exist within the United States, or any place subject to their jurisdiction.

Section 2. Enforcement Congress shall have power to enforce this article by appropriate legislation.

Fourteenth Amendment
(1868) Rights of Citizens

Section 1. Citizenship All persons born or naturalized in the United States, and subject to the jurisdiction thereof, are citizens of the United States and of the state wherein they reside. No state shall make or enforce any law which shall abridge the privileges or immunities of citizens of the United States; nor shall any state deprive any person of life, liberty, or property, without due process of law; nor deny to any person within its jurisdiction the equal protection of the laws.

Section 2. Apportionment of Representatives Representatives shall be apportioned among the several states according to their respective numbers, counting the whole number of persons in each state, excluding Indians not taxed. But when the right to vote at any election for the choice of electors for President and Vice President of the United States, representatives in Congress, the executive and judicial officers of a state, or the members of the legislature thereof, is denied to any of the male inhabitants of such state, being twenty-one years of age, and citizens of the United States, or in any way abridged, except for participation in rebellion, or other crime, the basis of representation therein shall be reduced in the proportion which the number of such male citizens shall bear to the whole number of male citizens twenty-one years of age in such state.

Section 3. Former Confederate Officials No person shall be a senator or representative in Congress, or elector of President and Vice President, or hold any office, civil or military, under the United States, or under any state, who, having previously taken an oath, as a member of Congress, or as an officer of the United States, or as a member of any state legislature, or as an executive or judicial officer of any state, to support the Constitution of the United States, shall have engaged in insurrection or rebellion against the same, or given aid or comfort to the enemies thereof. But Congress may, by a vote of two thirds of each house, remove such disability.

Section 4. Public Debt The validity of the public debt of the United States, authorized by law, including debts incurred for payment of pensions and bounties for services in suppressing insurrection or rebellion, shall not be questioned. But neither the United States nor any state shall assume or pay any debt or obligation incurred in aid of insurrection or rebellion against the United States, or any claim for the loss or emancipation of any slave; but all such debts, obligations and claims shall be held illegal and void.

Section 5. Enforcement The Congress shall have power to enforce, by appropriate legislation, the provisions of this article.

Fifteenth Amendment
(1870) Right to Vote—Race, Color, Servitude

Section 1. Extending the Right to Vote The right of citizens of the United States to vote shall not be denied or abridged by the United States or by any state on account of race, color, or previous condition of servitude.

Section 2. Enforcement The Congress shall have power to enforce this article by appropriate legislation.

Sixteenth Amendment
(1913) Income Tax

The Congress shall have power to lay and collect taxes on incomes, from whatever source derived, without apportionment among the several states, and without regard to any census or enumeration.

Seventeenth Amendment
(1913) Popular Election of Senators

Section 1. Method of Election The Senate of the United States shall be composed of two senators from each state, elected by the people thereof, for six years; and each senator shall have one vote.

House. This provision has never been enforced.

Despite this clause, black citizens were often prevented from voting. In the 1960s, federal laws were passed to end voting discrimination.

Fourteenth Amendment, Section 3 This section prohibited people who had been federal or state officials before the Civil War and who had joined the Confederate cause from serving again as government officials. In 1872, Congress restored the rights of former Confederate officials.

Fourteenth Amendment, Section 4 This section recognized that the United States must repay its debts from the Civil War. However, it forbade the repayment of debts of the Confederacy. This meant that people who had loaned money to the Confederacy would not be repaid. Also, states were not allowed to pay former slave owners for the loss of slaves.

Fourteenth Amendment, Section 5 Congress can pass laws to carry out this amendment.

Fifteenth Amendment, Section 1 *Previous condition of servitude* refers to slavery. This amendment gave blacks, both former slaves and free blacks, the right to vote. In the late 1800s, southern states used grandfather clauses, literacy tests, and poll taxes to keep blacks from voting.

Fifteenth Amendment, Section 2 Congress can pass laws to carry out this amendment. The Twenty-fourth Amendment barred the use of poll taxes in national elections. The Voting Rights Act of 1965 gave federal officials the power to register voters where there was voting discrimination.

Sixteenth Amendment Congress has the power to collect taxes on people's income. An income tax can be collected without regard to a state's population. This amendment changed Article 1, Section 9, Clause 4.

Seventeenth Amendment, Section 1 This amendment modified Article 1, Section 3, Clause 1. Before it was adopted, state legislatures chose senators. This amendment provides that senators are directly elected by the people of each state.

Seventeenth Amendment, Section 2 When a Senate seat becomes vacant, the governor of the state must order an election to fill the seat. The state legislature can give the governor power to fill the seat until an election is held.

The electors in each state shall have the qualifications requisite for electors of the most numerous branch of the state legislatures.

Section 2. Vacancies When vacancies happen in the representation of any state in the Senate, the executive authority of such state shall issue writs of election to fill such vacancies: provided, that ɪne legislature of any state may empower the executive thereof to make temporary appointments until the people fill the vacancies by election as the legislature may direct.

Seventeenth Amendment, Section 3 Senators who had already been elected by the state legislatures were not affected by this amendment.

Section 3. Those Elected Under Previous Procedure ~~This amendment shall not be so construed as to affect the election or term of any senator chosen before it becomes valid as part of the Constitution.~~

Eighteenth Amendment
(1919) Prohibition of Intoxicating Liquors

Eighteenth Amendment, Section 1 This amendment, known as Prohibition, banned the making, selling, or transporting of alcoholic beverages in the United States. Later, the Twenty-first Amendment *repealed,* or canceled, this amendment.

Section 1. Ban on Alcohol ~~After one year from the ratification of this article, the manufacture, sale, or transportation of intoxicating liquors within, the importation thereof into, or the exportation thereof from the United States and all territory subject to the jurisdiction thereof for beverage purposes is hereby prohibited.~~

Eighteenth Amendment, Section 2 Both the states and the federal government had the power to pass laws to enforce this amendment.

Section 2. Enforcement ~~The Congress and the several states shall have concurrent power to enforce this article by appropriate legislation.~~

Eighteenth Amendment, Section 3 This amendment had to be approved within seven years. The Eighteenth Amendment was the first amendment to include a time limit for ratification.

Section 3. Method of Ratification ~~This article shall be inoperative unless it shall have been ratified as an amendment to the Constitution by the legislatures of the several states, as provided in the Constitution, within seven years from the date of the submission hereof to the states by Congress.~~

Nineteenth Amendment
(1920) Women's Suffrage

Nineteenth Amendment, Section 1 Neither the federal government nor state governments can deny the right to vote on account of sex. Thus, women won *suffrage,* or the right to vote. Before 1920, some states had allowed women to vote in state elections.

Section 1. The Right to Vote The right of citizens of the United States to vote shall not be denied or abridged by the United States or by any state on account of sex.

Nineteenth Amendment, Section 2 Congress can pass laws to carry out this amendment.

Section 2. Enforcement Congress shall have power to enforce this article by appropriate legislation.

Twentieth Amendment
(1933) Commencement of Terms; Sessions of Congress; Death or Disqualification of President-Elect

Twentieth Amendment, Section 1 The date for the President and Vice President to take office is January 20. Members of Congress begin their terms of office on January 3. Before this amendment was adopted, these terms of office began on March 4.

Section 1. Beginning of Terms The terms of the President and Vice President shall end at noon on the 20th day of January, and the terms of senators and representatives at noon on the 3d day of January, of the years in which such terms would have ended if this article had not been ratified; and the terms of their successors shall then begin.

Twentieth Amendment, Section 2 Congress must meet at least once a year. The new session of Congress begins

Section 2. Congressional Sessions The Congress shall assemble at least once in every year, and such meeting shall begin at noon on the 3rd day of January, unless they shall by law appoint a different day.

Section 3. Presidential Succession If, at the time fixed for the beginning of the term of the President, the President-elect shall have died, the Vice President-elect shall become President. If a President shall not have been chosen before the time fixed for the beginning of his term, or if the President-elect shall have failed to qualify, then the Vice President-elect shall act as President until a President shall have qualified; and the Congress may by law provide for the case wherein neither a President-elect nor a Vice President-elect shall have qualified, declaring who shall then act as President, or the manner in which one who is to act shall be selected, and such person shall act accordingly until a President or Vice President shall have qualified.

Section 4. Elections Decided by Congress The Congress may by law provide for the case of the death of any of the persons from whom the House of Representatives may choose a President whenever the right of choice shall have devolved upon them, and for the case of the death of any of the persons from whom the Senate may choose a Vice President whenever the right of choice shall have devolved upon them.

Section 5. Date of Implementation ~~Sections 1 and 2 shall take effect on the 15th day of October following the ratification of this article.~~

Section 6. Ratification Period ~~This article shall be inoperative unless it shall have been ratified as an amendment to the Constitution by the legislatures of three fourths of the several states within seven years from the date of its submission.~~

Twenty-first Amendment
(1933) Repeal of Prohibition

Section 1. Repeal The eighteenth article of amendment to the Constitution of the United States is hereby repealed.

Section 2. State Laws The transportation or importation into any state, territory, or possession of the United States for delivery or use therein of intoxicating liquors, in violation of the laws thereof, is hereby prohibited.

Section 3. Ratification Period ~~This article shall be inoperative unless it shall have been ratified as an amendment to the Constitution by conventions in the several states, as provided in the Constitution, within seven years from the date of the submission hereof to the states by the Congress.~~

Twenty-second Amendment
(1951) Presidential Tenure

Section 1. Two-Term Limit No person shall be elected to the office of the President more than twice, and no person who has held the office of President, or acted as President, for more than two years of a term to which some other person was elect-

on January 3. Before this amendment, members of Congress who had been defeated in November continued to hold office until the following March. Such members were known as lame ducks.

Twentieth Amendment, Section 3 If the President-elect dies before taking office, the Vice President-elect becomes President. If no President has been chosen by January 20 or if the elected candidate fails to qualify for office, the Vice President-elect acts as President, but only until a qualified President is chosen.

Finally, Congress has the power to choose a person to act as President if neither the President-elect nor Vice President-elect is qualified to take office.

Twentieth Amendment, Section 4 Congress can pass laws in cases where a presidential candidate dies while an election is being decided in the House. Congress has similar power in cases where a candidate for Vice President dies while an election is being decided in the Senate.

Twentieth Amendment, Section 5 Section 5 sets the date for the amendment to become effective.

Twentieth Amendment, Section 6 Section 6 sets a time limit for ratification.

Twenty-first Amendment, Section 1 The Eighteenth Amendment is repealed, making it legal to make and sell alcoholic beverages. Prohibition ended December 5, 1933.

Twenty-first Amendment, Section 2 Each state was free to ban the making and selling of alcoholic drink within its borders. This section makes bringing liquor into a "dry" state a federal offense.

Twenty-first Amendment, Section 3 Special state conventions were called to ratify this amendment. This is the only time an amendment was ratified by state conventions rather than state legislatures.

Twenty-second Amendment, Section 1 Before Franklin Roosevelt became President, no President served more than two terms in office. Roosevelt broke with this custom and was elected to four terms. This amendment provides that no President may serve more than two terms. A President who has already served more than half of someone else's term can serve only one more full term. However, the amendment did not apply to Harry Truman, who had become President after Franklin Roosevelt's death in 1945.

Twenty-second Amendment, Section 2 A seven-year time limit is set for ratification.

Twenty-third Amendment, Section 1 This amendment gives residents of Washington, D.C., the right to vote in presidential elections. Until this amendment was adopted, people living in Washington, D.C., could not vote for President because the Constitution had made no provision for choosing electors from the nation's capital. Washington, D.C., has three electoral votes.

Twenty-third Amendment, Section 2 Congress can pass laws to carry out this amendment.

Twenty-fourth Amendment, Section 1 A *poll tax* is a tax on voters. This amendment bans poll taxes in national elections. Some states used poll taxes to keep African Americans from voting. In 1966, the Supreme Court struck down poll taxes in state elections, also.

Twenty-fourth Amendment, Section 2 Congress can pass laws to carry out this amendment.

Twenty-fifth Amendment, Section 1 If the President dies or resigns, the Vice President becomes President. This section clarifies Article 2, Section 1, Clause 6.

Twenty-fifth Amendment, Section 2 When a Vice President takes over the office of President, he or she appoints a

ed President shall be elected to the office of the President more than once. ~~But this article shall not apply to any person holding the office of President when this article was proposed by the Congress, and shall not prevent any person who may be holding the office of President, or acting as President, during the term within which this article becomes operative from holding the office of President or acting as President during the remainder of such term.~~

Section 2. Ratification Period ~~This article shall be inoperative unless it shall have been ratified as an amendment to the Constitution by the legislatures of three fourths of the several states within seven years from the date of its submission to the states by the Congress.~~

Twenty-third Amendment
(1961) Presidential Electors for the District of Columbia

Section 1. Determining the Number of Electors The district constituting the seat of government of the United States shall appoint in such manner as the Congress may direct:

A number of electors of President and Vice President equal to the whole number of senators and representatives in Congress to which the district would be entitled if it were a state, but in no event more than the least populous state; they shall be in addition to those appointed by the states, but they shall be considered, for the purposes of the election of President and Vice President, to be electors appointed by a state; and they shall meet in the district and perform such duties as provided by the twelfth article of amendment.

Section 2. Enforcement The Congress shall have power to enforce this article by appropriate legislation.

Twenty-fourth Amendment
(1964) Right to Vote in Federal Elections—Tax Payment

Section 1. Poll Tax Banned The right of citizens of the United States to vote in any primary or other election for President or Vice President, for electors for President or Vice President, or for senator or representative in Congress, shall not be denied or abridged by the United States or any state by reason of failure to pay any poll tax or other tax.

Section 2. Enforcement The Congress shall have the power to enforce this article by appropriate legislation.

Twenty-fifth Amendment
(1967) Presidential Succession, Vice Presidential Vacancy, Presidential Inability

Section 1. President's Death or Resignation In case of the removal of the President from office or of his death or resignation, the Vice President shall become President.

Section 2. Vacancies in Vice Presidency Whenever there is a vacancy in the office of the Vice President, the President shall nominate a Vice President who shall take office upon confirmation by a majority vote of both houses of Congress.

Section 3. Disability of the President Whenever the President transmits to the president *pro tempore* of the Senate and the Speaker of the House of Representatives his written declaration that he is unable to discharge the powers and duties of his office, and until he transmits to them a written declaration to the contrary, such powers and duties shall be discharged by the Vice President as acting President.

Section 4. Vice President as Acting President Whenever the Vice President and a majority of either the principal officers of the executive departments or of such other body as Congress may by law provide, transmit to the President *pro tempore* of the Senate and the Speaker of the House of Representatives their written declaration that the President is unable to discharge the powers and duties of his office, the Vice President shall immediately assume the powers and duties of the office as acting President.

Thereafter, when the President transmits to the president *pro tempore* of the Senate and the Speaker of the House of Representatives his written declaration that no inability exists, he shall resume the powers and duties of his office unless the Vice President and a majority of either the principal officers of the executive department or of such other body as Congress may by law provide, transmit within four days to the president *pro tempore* of the Senate and the Speaker of the House of Representatives their written declaration that the President is unable to discharge the powers and duties of his office. Thereupon Congress shall decide the issue, assembling within forty-eight hours for that purpose if not in session. If the Congress, within twenty-one days after receipt of the latter written declaration, or, if Congress is not in session, within twenty-one days after Congress is required to assemble, determines by two thirds vote of both Houses that the President is unable to discharge the powers and duties of his office, the Vice President shall continue to discharge the same as acting President; otherwise, the President shall resume the powers and duties of his office.

Twenty-sixth Amendment
(1971) Right to Vote—Age
Section 1. Lowering of Voting Age The right of citizens of the United States, who are eighteen years of age or older, shall not be denied or abridged by the United States or by any state on account of age.

Section 2. Enforcement The Congress shall have the power to enforce this article by appropriate legislation.

Twenty-seventh Amendment
(1992) Congressional Pay
No law, varying the compensation for the services of the senators and representatives, shall take effect until an election of representatives shall have intervened.

Vice President who must be approved by a majority vote of both houses of Congress. This section was first applied after Vice President Spiro Agnew resigned in 1973. President Richard Nixon appointed Gerald Ford as Vice President.

Twenty-fifth Amendment, Section 3 If the President declares in writing that he or she is unable to perform the duties of office, the Vice President serves as acting President until the President recovers.

Twenty-fifth Amendment, Section 4 Two Presidents, Woodrow Wilson and Dwight Eisenhower, have fallen gravely ill while in office. The Constitution contained no provision for this kind of emergency.

Section 3 provided that the President can inform Congress that he or she is too sick to perform the duties of office. However, if the President is unconscious or refuses to admit to a disabling illness, Section 4 provides that the Vice President and Cabinet may declare the President disabled. The Vice President becomes acting President until the President can return to the duties of office. In case of a disagreement between the President and the Vice President and Cabinet over the President's ability to perform the duties of office, Congress must decide the issue. A two-thirds vote of both houses is needed to find the President is disabled or unable to fulfill the duties of office.

Twenty-sixth Amendment, Section 1 In 1970, Congress passed a law allowing 18-year-olds to vote. However, the Supreme Court decided that Congress could not set a minimum age for state elections. So this amendment was passed and ratified.

Twenty-sixth Amendment, Section 2 Congress can pass laws to carry out this amendment.

Twenty-seventh Amendment If members of Congress vote themselves a pay increase, it cannot go into effect until after the next congressional election. This amendment was proposed in 1789. In 1992, Michigan became the thirty-eighth state to ratify it.

Comprehension: Articles I–III

1. The Senate and the House of Representatives.

2. Seats in the House of Representatives are apportioned by population. Senate seats are divided equally among states, with each receiving two seats.

3. Congress can impose taxes and import duties. Congress regulates trade between states, foreign countries, and with Native Americans.

4. The President must be a native-born citizen who has lived in the United States for fourteen years and reached the age of 35.

5. The President commands the armed forces and the state militias.

6. Treason, bribery, or other high crimes and misdemeanors.

7. The Supreme Court and any other courts established by Congress.

8. Federal judges are given life terms. Judges can be removed earlier if they are unfit to serve.

9. Cases involving the United States government, ambassadors and foreign ministers, and admiralty and maritime jurisdiction; also cases between different states, between citizens of different states, and between American citizens (or states) and foreign citizens (or countries).

Comprehension: Articles IV–VII and Amendments

10. No. Clause 1 of Article IV, Section 2 requires each state to respect the rights of all American citizens equally.

11. Clause 2 of Article IV, Section 2 requires states to return criminals to the state where they will stand trial.

12. The federal government.

13. Both houses of Congress must approve the amendment by a two-thirds majority.

14. By calling a special convention.

15. Three fourths.

16. Federal law.

17. An oath to support the Constitution.

18. The first ten amendments.

19. The Fourteenth Amendment.

20. The Twenty-sixth Amendment; 18.

Reviewing the Constitution

SUMMARY OF THE CONSTITUTION

The Constitution is the set of fundamental laws of the United States. Drafted by the Constitutional Convention in 1787, the document was approved by all thirteen original states by 1790. Twenty-seven amendments have been added to the Constitution since then.

ARTICLE I. Legislative Branch
The Congress constitutes the legislative, or law-making, branch of the federal government. The Congress consists of the Senate and the House of Representatives.

ARTICLE II. Executive Branch
The President heads the executive branch, which enforces the laws of the federal government.

ARTICLE III. Judicial Branch
A Supreme Court and other federal courts make up the judicial branch, which interprets the laws.

ARTICLE IV. Relations Among the States
This article describes states' obligations toward each other and each other's residents, procedures for creating new states, and the obligations of the federal government toward the states.

ARTICLE V. Provisions for Amendment
This article describes the procedure by which the Constitution may be amended.

ARTICLE VI. National Debts, Supremacy of National Law, Oath
This article discusses the debts acquired prior to the Constitution, asserts the supremacy of national over state law, and requires oaths of state and federal officials.

ARTICLE VII. Ratification of Constitution
This article states that the approval of nine of the thirteen states was necessary for ratification of the Constitution.

AMENDMENTS
The 27 amendments to the Constitution include the Bill of Rights (amendments 1–10) plus other amendments on such topics as slavery, women's suffrage, and prohibition.

COMPREHENSION: Articles I–III

1. Name the two bodies that constitute the legislative branch.

2. How are the seats in these two bodies divided among the states?

3. What powers does Congress have regarding taxes? Regarding trade?

4. What are the qualifications for President?

5. What are the President's military powers?

6. For what acts may the President be removed from office?

7. Which courts make up the national judicial branch?

8. How long do federal judges serve in office?

9. What kinds of cases do federal courts handle?

COMPREHENSION: Articles IV–VII and Amendments

10. Do states have the power to discriminate against citizens of other states? Why or why not?

11. How does the Constitution ensure that fugitives cannot escape prosecution by fleeing from one state to another?

12. Which level of government is responsible for protecting the states against foreign invasion?

13. What must happen before Congress can propose an amendment to the Constitution?

14. How can the state legislatures propose an amendment to the Constitution?

15. What fraction of the states must approve an amendment before it becomes law?

16. Which is the supreme law of the land: state or federal law?

17. What oath must state and federal officials take?

18. Which amendments make up the Bill of Rights?

19. Which amendment prevents states from denying any citizen the "equal protection of the laws"?

20. Which amendment changed the minimum voting age? What is the minimum voting age?

ANALYZING POLITICAL CARTOONS

1. This cartoon appeared during Bill Clinton's presidential administration. Clinton is the figure on the left. (a) What does the figure on the right represent? (b) How do you know?

2. Note the scene. (a) What activity are the two figures engaged in? (b) What happens if one figure lets go of the rope he is holding?

3. What comment does this cartoon make on the separation of powers and federal system of checks and balances?

CRITICAL THINKING

1. *Recognizing Cause and Effect* Which Article and Section of the Constitution describe the infamous Three-Fifths Compromise? Why has that part of the Constitution been struck out?

2. *Identifying Assumptions* Why, do you think, are the qualifications for the Senate more strict than those for the House?

3. *Drawing Conclusions* Do the American voters directly elect the President? Explain your answer.

4. *Expressing Problems Clearly* Though the Constitution limits the terms of Congress and the President to a specific number of years, it does not set such a limit for federal judges. Why do you think this is so?

5. *Demonstrating Reasoned Judgment* Restate the First Amendment in your own words.

6. *Making Comparisons* Which constitutional amendment do you believe is the most important? Justify your choice.

ACTIVITIES

1. *Organizing a Class Debate* Hold a class debate on the following resolution: *Resolved, that the Constitution be amended to provide for a single, six-year term of office for the President, with no eligibility for reelection.* To organize the debate, divide the class into two equal teams. The debate should begin with a five-minute presentation by each team, after which team members are free to rebut the other team's arguments.

2. *Reporting on Constitutional Issues* Find a current newspaper story that concerns a constitutional issue, such as an important court case. Then prepare a five-minute oral report in which you (a) provide the background of the issue, (b) describe the outcome, and (c) analyze the importance of the issue.

3. *Creating a Time Line* Connect several sheets of construction paper end-to-end. Then create a time line showing all 27 amendments to the Constitution. For each amendment, include the year in which it was ratified and a brief description of the amendment.

YOU NEED MY SUPPORT!!

CONGRESS

INTERNET ACTIVITY

For your portfolio:
PREPARE A REPORT

Access Prentice Hall's *America: Pathways to the Present* site at **www.Pathways.phschool.com** for the specific URL to complete the activity. Additional resources and related Web sites are also available.

Use the links to find the text of the United States Constitution and your state's constitution. Compare the Preamble of the national Constitution to your state's. How do they compare in spirit? In language? Write a brief report analyzing the similarities and differences between the two.

INTERNET ACTIVITY

Answers should show a careful reading of both the United States Constitution and the student's state constitution.

REVIEWING THE CONSTITUTION

Analyzing Political Cartoons

1. (a) Congress. (b) It is written on his shirt.
2. (a) Tightrope walking. (b) Both will fall.
3. The system of checks and balances forces the different branches of government to work together.

Critical Thinking

1. Article I, Section 2. The Thirteenth Amendment abolished slavery in 1865, and the Fourteenth Amendment gave former slaves the same rights enjoyed by other citizens. Since all people were now free, everyone was now counted equally for congressional representation.
2. Since all but a few states have more members of Congress than senators, each senator has far more power than each member of Congress.
3. No, they vote for electors who promise to vote for a candidate.
4. The Framers wanted to keep the judicial system free of politics.
5. Answers should refer to freedom of speech, religion, assembly, and petition.
6. Answers should demonstrate an understanding of the amendment and explain how this amendment has shaped the country.

Activities

1. Arguments for might include: discourages people from becoming career politicians; eliminates the advantage of a sitting President; saves money by spacing elections over many years. Arguments against might include: makes the President unresponsive to voters since he need not worry about reelection; restricts opportunities to choose a leader.
2. Reports should follow steps a, b, and c.
3. Projects should demonstrate an accurate reading of the amendments.

The Origins of American Politics, 1789–1820

Managing Time and Instruction

INSTRUCTION SUPPORT
These materials for instruction are provided for **each section** in the **Teaching Resources**. See **Units 1–2 folder** for Enrichment Support:

- Reproducible Lesson Plans in Lesson Plans folder
- Learning Styles Lesson Plans in Learning Styles Lesson Plans folder
- Big Idea Graphic Organizers in Big Idea Graphic Organizer folder
- Guided Reading and Review
- Quizzes
- Test Preparation Practice booklet

DAILY LESSON	ENRICHMENT SUPPORT
1 Liberty Versus Order in the 1790s *(pp.175–178)*	• Literature Activity, American Literature, Units 1–2 folder, pp. 83–85 • Critical Thinking Activity, Recognizing Bias: The Seeds of Nationalism, found on **Resource Pro** • Skills for Life Activity, Units 1–2 folder, p. 86
2 The Government Takes a New Course *(pp.180–183)*	• Biography, Noah Webster, Units 1–2 folder, p. 80 • Lasting Impact Activity, The Lasting Impact of the Election of 1800, History's Lasting Impact folder, pp. 4–5
3 The Jefferson Administration *(pp. 184–188)*	• Visual Learning Activity, Honoring Thomas Jefferson, found on **Resource Pro** • Primary Source Activity, Napoleon Sells Louisiana, found on **Resource Pro** • Nystrom *Atlas of Our Country*, Early Expansion of the United States, pp. 20–21
4 Native American Resistance *(pp. 189–191)*	• Primary Source Activity, Native American Politics, Learning with Documents folder, p. 12
5 The War of 1812 *(pp.192–196)*	• Visual Learning Activity, "The Present State of Our Country," Learning with Documents folder, p. 48 • Comparing Primary Sources, For and Against the War of 1812, Units 1–2 folder, pp. 81–82 • Key Documents, "The Star-Spangled Banner," Learning with Documents folder, p. 85 • Biography, Francis Scott Key, found on **Resource Pro** • You Can Join a Political Party, Why Study History? folder, p. 7

Running Out of Time?

- Use Tape 1, "Balancing Liberty and Order, 1781–1830," from **Visions of America** videotapes series.
- Use Chapter 6 Summary, from **Guide to the Essentials of American History (English and Spanish).**

Companion Web Site

The companion Web site offers online links for all chapter review activities. It also provides key content links and structured support for this chapter for both teachers and students.

http://www.Pathways.phschool.com

Teaching in the Information Age

Media and Technology

For the Student

Interactive Student Tutorial CD-ROM Chapter 6
Student Edition on Audiotape Chapter 6
American Heritage® CD-ROM
Guided Reading Audiotapes (English and Spanish) Chapter 6

For the Teacher

Resource Pro CD-ROM Chapter 6
Test Bank CD-ROM Chapter 6
Listening to Literature Audiotapes *Timeless Voices, Timeless Themes* "Speech in the Convention" by Benjamin Franklin
Color Transparencies Fine Art, D-2

Assessment Options

Chapter Test Forms A&B Test Bank CD-ROM booklet
Test Bank CD-ROM Chapter 6
Standardized Test Preparation Handbook

Block Scheduling

Pacing Suggestions

For 90-minute Blocks

- Teach sections 1 and 3 using Transparencies I-3 and C-9.
- Teach sections 2, 4, and 5 using the Big Idea Graphic Organizers from Teaching Resources and the Recent Scholarship note on p. 182 for class discussions.

Additional Resources

- Prentice Hall's **American History Block Scheduling Support File** covers over 40 major topics in American history.
- **Prentice Hall United States History Video Collection**™ contains 20 videotapes covering American history from beginnings to present.
- **Visions of America Videotapes and Videodiscs**

Connections to American Literature

from Prentice Hall

Prentice Hall Literature *Timeless Voices, Timeless Themes*

- from *Letters from an American Farmer* by Michel-Guillaume Jean de Crèvecoeur, p. 197
- "Old Ironsides" by Oliver Wendell Holmes, p. 262
- "Crossing the Great Divide" by Merriwether Lewis, p. 276

Additional Resources

For the Student
Electing the President. Encyclopedia Britannica. Film/Video.
Milton Meltzer. *American Politics: How It Really Works.* William Morrow, 1989.

For the Teacher
D. Boorstin. *The Lost World of Thomas Jefferson.* University of Chicago Press, 1981.
Stanley I. Kutler, ed. *John Marshall.* Prentice Hall, 1972.

Prentice Hall brings into the classroom the vast archives and scholarship of the nation's premier American history magazine. See "From the Archives of American Heritage®" and "About the Presidents" teaching notes in this chapter.

History Alive!

Teacher's Curriculum Institute, in partnership with Prentice Hall, provides unique materials that engage students with diverse learning styles. See History Alive!® unit on The Constitution in a New Nation.

Student Performance Pack

Ensures success in the three critical areas of Reading, Test Taking, and English Language Development with the following materials:
- Guide to the Essentials of American History in English and Spanish
- Guided Reading Audiotapes in English and Spanish
- Interactive Student Tutorial CD-ROM
- Test Preparation Handbook
- Test Preparation Practice booklet

The Origins of American Politics
1789–1820

Introducing the Chapter
In the years following the ratification of the Constitution, American leaders fought passionately over the formation of the new government. Some groups that were not represented in the legislatures, including Native Americans and African Americans, tried to acquire or maintain liberty by other means. The new nation enjoyed prosperity and political harmony for only a brief period following the War of 1812.

Themes in American History
The theme for this chapter, Government, is listed at the beginning of this unit. An alternate theme for the chapter is Foreign Relations. To teach this unit thematically, you may wish to use the Forging a New Nation folder in American History Block Scheduling.

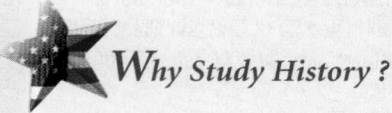

Why Study History?

Have students explore suggested ways of connecting the past to the present on page 197.

Answer to . . .

Viewing History Students should use this question as an aid in reading the chapter. As federal policies were debated, the nation became sharply divided over whether to strengthen the central government or to retain strong local and state governments. Parties formed around these issues as advocates on both sides pressed their cause publicly.

174

CHAPTER
6
The Origins of American Politics
1789–1820

☆UNDER ☆MY☆ ☆WINGS☆ ☆ ☆ ☆EVERY☆ ☆THING☆ ☆ ☆ PROSPERS

CHAPTER FOCUS

This chapter describes the period following the ratification of the Constitution, during which Americans continued to debate how much power the federal government should have. Despite this ongoing internal debate, the young nation once again defeated the British and continued to expand west.

 The *Why Study History?* page at the end of this chapter explores the role of political parties in the life of the country today.

▲
VIEWING HISTORY
This 1803 painting reflects Americans' pride in the nation's growing prosperity. *Government* **How did the debate over the role of the federal government lead to the rise of political parties?**

 RESOURCE OPTIONS

Teaching Resources

📁 **Big Idea Graphic Organizer** folder
Graphic summary of the main idea of the chapter.

📁 **Learning Styles Lesson Plans** folder
Alternate lesson plans for diverse learning styles for each chapter.

Media and Technology

 AmericanHeritage® CD-ROM
Time Tour The New Republic: The New Government *and* The Jefferson Era

 Prentice Hall United States History Video Collection™ Volume 5 *A New Nation (1776–1815)*

1 Liberty Versus Order in the 1790s

SECTION PREVIEW

Objectives

1 Describe Alexander Hamilton's program for dealing with national and state debt.
2 Explain how the French Revolution divided Americans.
3 Describe the causes and effects of the Whiskey Rebellion.
4 Summarize the debate over Jay's Treaty and the resulting rise of political parties.
5 *Key Terms* Define: tariff; interest; strict construction; loose construction; neutral; Whiskey Rebellion; Jay's Treaty; political party.

Main Idea

Americans became sharply divided in the 1790s over whether order or liberty was more important.

Reading Strategy

Reinforcing Main Ideas As you read, list some of the specific actions of the federal government that angered Jefferson and many Americans.

In the 1790s Americans had a new Constitution and a new government, but the debate over the proper role of government had by no means ended. Most Americans, Federalists and Antifederalists alike, hoped that this debate would not lead to the establishment of rival political groups. Struggles between such groups elsewhere in the world had often led to civil war.

Hamilton's Program

Secretary of the Treasury Hamilton was a keen supporter of strong national power. He had little faith in the people. The Constitution, he believed, was not enough in itself to preserve the new nation. In his view, the government had to expand its role and actively direct the development of the American economy.

To this end, Hamilton proposed a complicated plan. In 1790, after months of debate, Congress approved Hamilton's plan for the national government to take on the debts acquired by the states during the Revolution.

Congress's vote was a controversial one. Southern states did not want to be responsible for northern debts. Yet Hamilton managed to win the support of the southern states through a deal: If southern states would back Hamilton's debt plan, Hamilton would gain northern support for a plan to locate the nation's capital in the South. Thus in 1790 Congress approved both the debt plan and a plan to locate the capital on the banks of the Potomac River.

Hamilton's debt plan was controversial for another reason. As critics pointed out, the federal government already had a huge debt of about $50 million. Why would the government want to add to this burden?

Hamilton's Strategy The answer is simpler than one might think. Most of the state and national debt was owed to European banks and to American merchants and speculators,

Alexander Hamilton participated in framing the Constitution and favored a strong central government.

RESOURCE OPTIONS

Teaching Resources

📁 **Reproducible Lesson Plan** Lesson Plans folder, p. 55

📁 **Learning Styles Lesson Plan** Learning Styles Lesson Plans folder, p. 14

📁 **Big Idea Graphic Organizer** Big Idea Graphic Organizer folder, p. 27

📁 **Guided Reading and Review** Units 1–2 folder, p. 70

SECTION 1

Liberty Versus Order in the 1790s

Objectives

You may wish to call students' attention to the objectives in the Section Preview. The objectives are reflected in the main headings of the section.

Bellringer

Ask students if they consider themselves Republicans, Democrats, Independents, or members of a minor political party. Have them define the different political goals of these parties.

Reading Strategy

Reinforcing Main Ideas Refer to the Reading Strategy in the Section Preview. You may wish to have volunteers share their lists with the rest of the class.

LESSON PLAN

Connecting to the Main Idea

1. Focus As the Federalists tried to institute their vision of government, their opponents created a new political party to stop them. What were the major differences between the Federalist party and the Jeffersonian Republicans?

2. Instruct Explain that although the Federalists had a majority in both houses of Congress during its first session, there were strong regional differences within the party. Ask students how much of Hamilton's and Jefferson's respective policies can be deduced from the following information: Hamilton favored Great Britain and industry, while Jefferson favored France and rural life.

3. Close Hamilton, Jefferson, and their respective followers disagreed about how much power the national government should have and about with whom it should ally itself. Many people believed that the election of 1800, described in the next section, would decide the nation's future.

Interdisciplinary

The federal government may manipulate money in order to produce a desired economic effect within the American economy. In the 1790s the government sought to pay off war debts from the Revolution completely; by assuming the debts of the states, it aimed to restore national credit, create wealth, and promote new business. During the Great Depression the government, following Keynesian economics, purposely ran up large deficits to get money into circulation, promote private spending, and hasten the return of prosperity.

ACTIVITY
LEARNING STYLES

Assign volunteers one of the following roles: a farmer from western Pennsylvania, a French revolutionary, a Dutch banker, John Adams, John Marshall, the wife of a Virginia tobacco planter, a wealthy Boston merchant, or a tavern keeper from upper New York State. Ask students to state their point of view (Federalist or Jeffersonian), giving two reasons in support of their chosen party. *(Interpersonal)*

Answer to . . .

Main Idea Connections Hamilton's plan, by calling for a stronger national government, aimed for order.

---

or people who take a financial risk in the hope of future profit. Hamilton knew that these creditors (or lenders) did not want any government that owed them money to collapse. If the states owed creditors money, Hamilton reasoned, creditors would care about the states. But if the United States owed creditors the money, they would be less interested in the individual states and more concerned with the future of the United States as a whole.

Why would creditors go along with this plan? To satisfy their concerns, Hamilton outlined a specific budget and set up a regular payment plan. Two measures would help to raise money to pay off the debts. In 1789, Congress had created a **tariff**—a tax on imported goods. In 1791, Congress placed a tax on whiskey.

Most of the money raised by these two taxes went to pay the expenses of the government, such as the salaries of officials. Hamilton, however, also put some of it into a special fund used to pay creditors a little money every year. He did not intend to pay them off right away; if he did, they would have no reason to care what happened to the United States. Instead, the government paid them **interest**—an extra sum of money that borrowers pay creditors in return for the loan. To handle these complicated financial matters, Congress established the Bank of the United States in 1791.

Hamilton thus transformed the debts of the state governments into what amounted to a long-term investment in the United States government. The country's creditors now held an interest in the stable functioning of the government.

Hamilton's Opponents Many Americans did not like Hamilton's plan. They objected to the interference of the federal government in local and state affairs. They also disliked Hamilton's new taxes.

Opponents of the Washington administration regarded Hamilton's policy of taxation and regulation similar to the one the British had proposed in the 1760s. Combined with the elegant style of Washington's presidency, the Federalist program suggested to opponents a return to aristocracy and monarchy. Many people saw this as an all-out assault on the hard-won liberty of the American people.

Secretary of State Jefferson was particularly opposed to Hamilton's plans. President

Main Idea
CONNECTIONS

Did Hamilton's program aim more at achieving liberty or order?

Washington usually sided with Hamilton, and Jefferson increasingly found himself a minority opinion in the President's Cabinet. At the end of 1793, Jefferson resigned as Secretary of State.

One way to contrast Jefferson and Hamilton is in terms of their construction, or view of, the Constitution. Jefferson favored a **strict construction.** That is, he believed that the government should not do anything—such as start a national bank—that the Constitution did not specifically say it could do. Hamilton preferred a **loose construction.** He thought the Constitution was only a loose framework of laws on which the government could build the nation as it saw fit. The government, in other words, could do anything that the Constitution did not say it could not do.

The differences between the two men went deeper than this, however. Jefferson believed that Hamilton and his Federalist allies were betraying the American Revolution. They were, he told Thomas Paine in 1792, "a sect preaching up and pouting after an English constitution of king, lords, & commons." Jefferson had more faith in the people than in their government. He took pride in *not* being one of those men who preferred "the calm of despotism [tyranny] to the boisterous sea of liberty."

The French Revolution

That "boisterous sea" threw a tidal wave over France in 1789, when the people of France started the French Revolution. According to their public declaration, the revolution was committed to "liberty, fraternity, and equality." By the early 1790s, disagreement over how to make these ideals reality led not to fraternity, or brotherhood, but to a prolonged period of violence called the Reign of Terror. During this time the revolutionary government executed thousands of people, including King Louis XVI and Queen Marie Antoinette.

American Reactions The French Revolution sharply divided Americans. Federalists tended to oppose it, seeing it as an example of a democratic revolution gone wrong. Jefferson's supporters, on the other hand, generally viewed the French Revolution as an extension of the American Revolution. Though upset by its violence, they applauded its rejection of government by kings and its acceptance of republican government. Even during the Reign of Terror, Jefferson said that he "would have seen half the

---

▶ RESOURCE OPTIONS

Teaching Resources

Literature Activity American Literature, Units 1–2 folder, pp. 83–85

Media and Technology

RESOURCE○PRO

Critical Thinking Activity Recognizing Bias: The Seeds of Nationalism, found on Resource Pro, helps students apply the skill by analyzing a patriotic song written in the 1800s.

earth desolated [ruined] rather than see the French Revolution fail."

Choosing Sides While Americans debated the French Revolution, the outbreak of a war between Britain and France created more immediate practical problems. Whose side should the United States take? The nation could not afford to offend the British, whose navy dominated the oceans. Few people, however, wanted to abandon the French, who had helped Americans during the War for Independence.

The most sensible strategy was to remain **neutral,** or not take either side. In April 1793, after having been reelected for a second term as President, Washington issued a Proclamation of Neutrality. The United States would not take sides in the struggle.

The Whiskey Rebellion

Meanwhile, resistance to Hamilton's economic program grew. In western Pennsylvania and other frontier areas, many people refused to pay the tax on whiskey. Whiskey was of critical importance to the frontier economy. It was not just a traditional beverage—it was one of the only products that farmers could make out of corn that could be transported to market without spoiling. Whiskey was even used as a kind of currency, like tobacco leaves in colonial Virginia. In 1794 opposition to the whiskey tax was so strong that western Pennsylvania appeared to be in a state of rebellion against the authority of the federal government.

The **Whiskey Rebellion** followed the tradition of the Stamp Act and Shays' Rebellion. The rebels closed courts and attacked tax collectors. But President Washington and Secretary Hamilton were determined to end the rebellion. They saw the rebellion as an opportunity to demonstrate the power of the United States government. Hamilton himself declared that a government can never be said to be established until it has proved itself by exerting its military force.

In the summer of 1794, Washington gathered an army of over 12,000 men. General "Light Horse Harry" Lee, accompanied by Alexander Hamilton, led the army to the Pittsburgh area. The rebellion soon dissolved. Washington's tough response had demonstrated to American citizens and the world that the young American government was committed to enforcing its laws.

Jay's Treaty

In 1794 the debate over whether the United States should be neutral in the war between Great Britain and France rose to a fever pitch. Washington and Hamilton believed that the long-term interests of the United States would be served better by siding with Britain rather than with France. Therefore Washington sent Chief Justice John Jay to London to negotiate an agreement with the British. In the agreement, called **Jay's Treaty,** Britain agreed to leave the forts it occupied in the Northwest Territory. Other provisions aimed at expanding trade between the two nations. Jay was unable, however, to convince the British to end their practice of stopping American ships on the high seas and searching them for British subjects.

About the time of the Whiskey Rebellion, farmers' protests against Federalist economic plans included this rough drawing. It shows a government agent collecting taxes—in the form of two kegs of whiskey.

Jay's Treaty unleashed a storm of controversy throughout the United States. Critics complained that the treaty contained no protection for American shipping. More broadly, many Americans saw the treaty as a betrayal of revolutionary ideals, a sell-out to the hated British. Despite the anger, however, Congress ratified the treaty in 1795.

The Federalists had established their economic program, suppressed the Whiskey Rebellion, and ensured peace with Great Britain. Yet in so doing, they had lost the support of a great many Americans.

The Jeffersonian Republicans

As early as 1793, artisans and professional men were forming what were called Democratic Societies to oppose the Federalists. Meanwhile, Jefferson, and various state leaders were furiously promoting resistance to the Federalists in letters to one another. Some leaders also encouraged newspaper attacks on the Washington administration.

Originally these critics of the Federalists were called Republicans or Democratic-Republicans because they stood for a more democratic republic. To avoid confusing them with the modern Republican party, historians

ACTIVITY
HETEROGENEOUS GROUPS

Ask students to mark with the letter *H* each statement that correctly identifies one of Alexander Hamilton's beliefs or policies.
• Hamilton believed that national government should have strong powers.
• Hamilton had little faith in the people's ability to make good decisions.
• Hamilton wanted the individual states to pay their debts.
• Hamilton did not want the government to impose taxes on its citizens.
• Hamilton thought that the national debt could be a source of strength. *(Reteaching)*

*C*ustomize for
More Advanced Students

Tell students that in 1969, President Richard Nixon announced a policy that he called the "New Federalism." Ask students to write a description, based on what they have learned about Federalist beliefs and programs, of what such a policy might entail. Students might also research and report on the "New Federalism."

 RESOURCE OPTIONS

Media and Technology

 AmericanHeritage® CD-ROM

History Makers Alexander Hamilton

Time Tour The New Republic: The New Government Begins

Answers to
SECTION 1 REVIEW

1. (a) tariff, see p. 176; (b) interest, see p. 176; (c) strict construction, see p. 176; (d) loose construction, see p. 176; (e) neutral, see p. 177; (f) Whiskey Rebellion, see p. 177; (g) Jay's Treaty, see p. 177; (h) political party, see p. 178.

2. Many Americans—slaveholders, planters, commercial farmers, and people distant from urban areas—opposed the Federalists because they objected to the interference of the national government in local and state affairs. They thought the United States had no business regulating the economy, and they disliked taxes.

3. Major government actions include:

1791	Tax on whiskey
1791	Bank of the United States established
1792	Tariff on imported goods
1793	Proclamation of Neutrality
1794	Government ends Whiskey Rebellion
1794	Jay's Treaty

4. The entries for 1792 and 1796 show Washington and Adams, both Federalists, being elected President.

5. The federal government demonstrated its power and its willingness to use force against those who defied federal laws. Hamilton had stated that a government can never be said to be established until it has shown its power by exerting its military force.

6. Speeches should include grievances against Federalist actions prior to 1796.

George Washington, shown here reviewing troops gathered to put down the Whiskey Rebellion, declined to run for a third term in office. *Government Why did Washington warn against the formation of political parties?*

ington chose not to run for a third term. He thus set a precedent followed in later times. Instead, Washington's Vice President, John Adams, ran for President against Thomas Jefferson in 1796. Adams gained a majority of electoral votes and was elected President. Because Jefferson finished second in the electoral vote race, Jefferson became the new Vice President under the election system established by the Constitution.

In his Farewell Address of 1796, Washington warned against competing political parties:

 "[A system of political parties] agitates the Community with ill-founded jealousies and false alarms, kindles the animosity of one part against another, [and] foments [stirs up] occasional riot and insurrection.**"**

—*George Washington, Farewell Address, 1796*

The coming election of 1800 would prove Washington correct.

call them Jeffersonian Republicans. They, along with the Federalists, were the first political parties in the United States.[†] A **political party** is a group of people who seek to win elections and hold public office in order to control government policy and programs.

In the midst of criticism from the Jeffersonian Republicans, President Wash-

[†] Today politics in the United States is dominated by two major political parties. One is the Republican party, which was founded in the 1850s. The other is the Democratic party, which is descended from the Jeffersonian Republicans. The Democratic party is one of the oldest continuous political parties in the world.

SECTION 1 REVIEW

Comprehension

1. *Key Terms* Define: (a) tariff; (b) interest; (c) strict construction; (d) loose construction; (e) neutral; (f) Whiskey Rebellion; (g) Jay's Treaty; (h) political party.

2. *Summarizing the Main Idea* Who opposed the Federalists, and why?

3. *Organizing Information* Create an outline listing the major actions of the federal government between 1791 and 1796.

Critical Thinking

4. *Analyzing Time Lines* Review the time line at the start of the section. Which entry on the time line indicates that a majority of Americans probably did not oppose the Federalists?

5. *Drawing Conclusions* What did the federal government demonstrate in its reaction to the Whiskey Rebellion?

Writing Activity

6. *Writing a Persuasive Essay* Taking the part of a Jeffersonian Republican, write a campaign speech stating reasons why voters should elect Jefferson over Adams in 1796.

RESOURCE OPTIONS

Teaching Resources

Quiz Units 1–2 folder, p. 71

Student Performance Pack

 Guide to the Essentials Chapter 6, Section 1 (English and Spanish)

Answer to . . .

Viewing History He thought that parties created disagreement and promoted riots.

Critical Thinking

Geography

Graphs and Charts

Historical Evidence

Making Comparisons

Making comparisons means examining two or more ideas, objects, events, or people to discover ways that they are alike and ways they are different. When studying history, being able to make comparisons allows you to evaluate more fully historical periods and specific events or viewpoints.

One way to evaluate an event, idea, or historical period is to compare the views that different people have about it. At right are excerpts from an article by James Madison that appeared in the *National Gazette*, an Antifederalist newspaper, and from a statement by Robert Goodloe Harper, a Federalist. Use the following steps to compare their points of view.

1. Identify the basis on which you will make the comparison. It is not possible to compare two or more items that are fundamentally different. Making a comparison is possible only when items share a common concept or characteristic. Read the excerpts at right, and then answer the following questions. (a) What subject do the statements have in common? (b) When was each statement written? (c) What purpose would a comparison of these statements serve?

2. Determine the ways in which the statements are alike. Making comparisons includes finding similarities between two or more items. Are the statements at right similar in their views on the potential value or potential harm of political parties? If so, in what ways are they similar?

3. Determine the ways in which the statements are different. Making comparisons also includes finding any differences that may exist between items. In what fundamental ways do the statements below differ from one another in their views about political parties?

4. Summarize and evaluate your comparison of the statements. Complete the comparison based on similarities and differences. (a) Why does Robert Goodloe Harper view political parties as beneficial? (b) How does Madison imply that parties are a negative influence on government?

TEST FOR SUCCESS

In your opinion, which of the statements below more accurately describes the state of political parties today?

James Madison

" In every political society, parties are unavoidable. A difference of interests, real or supposed, is the most natural and fruitful source of them. The great object should be to combat the evil: (1) by establishing a political equality among all; (2) by withholding unnecessary opportunities for a few to increase the equality of property . . . ; (3) by the silent operation of laws, which, without violating the rights of property, reduce extreme wealth toward a state of mediocrity [averageness] and raise extreme [poverty] toward a state of comfort; (4) by abstaining from measures which . . . favor one interest at the expense of another; (5) by making one party a check on the other. . . . If this is not the language of reason it is that of republicanism. "

From "Parties," in the National Gazette, *January 23, 1792*

Robert Goodloe Harper

" While opposite parties in the Government . . . [struggle] for preeminence, they . . . [are] like persons engaged in an exhibition before the public, who are obliged to display superior merit and superior excellence in order to gain the prize. The republic is the judge . . . and that party which possesses power must employ it properly, must conduct the government wisely, in order to insure public [approval] and retain their power. In this [competition], while the two parties draw different ways, a middle course is produced generally comfortable to public good. "

From Annals of Congress, Fifth Congress, 2d session, January 1798

RESOURCE OPTIONS

Teaching Resources

Skills for Life Activity Making Comparisons, Units 1–2 folder, p. 86, helps students compare the relative strengths of present and past political parties.

Media and Technology

 Color Transparencies Critical Thinking, I-3

SKILLS FOR LIFE

Critical Thinking

Making Comparisons

Focus Compare historical statements presenting different sides of an issue to learn more about the period and the reasons for people's actions.
Instruct Ask students to look for examples of two or more statements about the same topic in newspapers, magazines, or newsletters. Point out grounds for comparison and contrast, and have students evaluate them.
Extend See the Skills for Life Activity in the Resource Options below.

Answers

1. (a) Both express views on political parties. (b) Madison, 1792; Harper, 1798. (c) A comparison could clarify some of the positive and negative aspects of political parties from the perspective of individuals who were involved in the debate at the time.

2. The statements both admit that political parties are an inevitable part of American politics.

3. Madison thinks that political parties are unavoidable, but ultimately harmful. Harper thinks that political parties benefit government.

4. (a) Harper believes that in order to gain the public's confidence and retain the public's approval, the party in power will act in ways that display excellence and merit and will select a moderate course for the country. (b) Madison writes that "the great object should be to combat the evil," the "evil" being political parties.

TEST FOR SUCCESS

Answers will vary, but should be supported with appropriate current examples.

1796	1798	1800	1802

1797 XYZ Affair

1798 Alien and Sedition Acts

1800 Gabriel Prosser's Rebellion

1800 Jefferson wins popular vote for President

1801 House elects Jefferson President

Objectives
You may wish to call students' attention to the objectives in the Section Preview. The objectives are reflected in the main headings of the section.

Bellringer
Ask students to rate (on a scale of 1–5, with 1 being the lowest possible score) the importance of the following conditions to presidential campaigns: length of the campaign, honesty of the campaign, relevance of issues raised during the campaign.

Reading Strategy
Outlining Information Refer to the Reading Strategy in the Section Preview. You may wish to have students trade their completed outlines with one another as a way to review.

LESSON PLAN
Connecting to the Main Idea

1. Focus Although the election of 1800 was bitter and raucous, power was peacefully transferred from the Federalists to the Jeffersonians. Ask students to describe how this was accomplished.

2. Instruct Explain that Jefferson called the election of 1800 "as real a revolution in the principles of our government as that of 1776 was in its form."

Ask students to summarize the reasons behind the Alien and Sedition Acts and the effects of those laws. Then have them describe the Jeffersonian response to the acts. Discuss the reasons for Prosser's Rebellion. Ask students to list reasons why Prosser failed.

3. Close The bitter and closely contested election of 1800 showed that power could peacefully pass from one party to another. In the next section, students will learn how President Jefferson performed in office.

2 The Government Takes a New Course

SECTION PREVIEW

Objectives
1 Summarize the actions of John Adams as President.
2 Describe the events of Gabriel Prosser's Rebellion.
3 Explain the outcome and the importance of the election of 1800.
4 *Key Terms* Define: XYZ Affair; Alien and Sedition Acts; Virginia and Kentucky resolutions; nullification.

Main Idea
With the election of 1800, Americans peacefully accomplished the nation's first transfer of power from one party to another.

Reading Strategy
Outlining Information As you read this section, create an outline of the major headings and write main idea statements for each heading.

In 1800, as public sentiment turned away from Federalism and back toward the principles of 1776, an unknown artist painted Liberty feeding the American eagle.

Despite having served as a leader during the American Revolution and as the Vice President for eight years, John Adams lacked the prestige of George Washington. As President, Adams faced the difficult task of trying to govern a young country where party differences were growing wider and wider. He also faced the threat of war from abroad.

John Adams as President
From the beginning of the Adams administration, the United States began to drift toward war with France. The French were angry about Jay's Treaty with the British and began seizing American ships in French harbors. Trying to avoid war, Adams sent officials to Paris to negotiate with the revolutionary government.

The XYZ Affair Once in Paris, the American officials were met by secret agents sent by the French foreign minister. These agents were later identified only as X, Y, and Z. The French agents demanded a bribe of $250,000 and a loan to the French of $10 million before the Americans would even be allowed to see the French foreign minister. Though such a request was common practice in European diplomacy, it outraged Americans and became known as the **XYZ Affair.**

Refusing to pay the bribe, the American diplomats quickly returned home. They were met with public cries of patriotism, war, and defiance against the French. The slogan "Millions for defense, but not one cent for tribute [bribery]" rang out in the United States. Unable to resolve their differences, by 1798 France and the United States were involved in what amounted to an undeclared war. Both sides fired on and seized each other's ships.

The Alien and Sedition Acts The Federalists took advantage of the war crisis and Adams's popularity to push important new measures through Congress. Among these were an

▶ RESOURCE OPTIONS

Teaching Resources

📁 **Reproducible Lesson Plan** Lesson Plans folder, p. 56

📁 **Learning Styles Lesson Plan** Learning Styles Lesson Plans folder, p. 15

📁 **Big Idea Graphic Organizer** Big Idea Graphic Organizer folder, p. 28

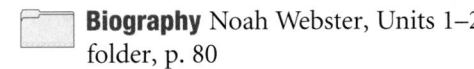

📁 **Guided Reading and Review** Units 1–2 folder, p. 72

📁 **Biography** Noah Webster, Units 1–2 folder, p. 80

increase in the size of the army, higher taxes to support the army and navy, and the **Alien and Sedition Acts** of 1798. Under the Alien Act, the President gained the right to imprison or deport citizens of other countries residing in the United States. Under the Sedition Act, persons who wrote, published, or said anything "of a false, scandalous, and malicious" nature against the American government or its officials could be fined or jailed. In other words, it was against the law to criticize government officials unless you could prove everything you said. The Federalists used the Sedition Act to silence Republican opposition. Under the act ten Republicans were convicted and many others were tried.

The Virginia and Kentucky Resolutions Jefferson, James Madison, and other Republicans believed that the Sedition Act violated the constitutional protection of freedom of speech. Yet the Constitution did not spell out who had the authority to judge whether an act of Congress went beyond the powers stated in the Constitution.

Jefferson and Madison believed that the states should make that judgment. They responded to the Alien and Sedition Acts with the **Virginia and Kentucky resolutions.** These resolutions, adopted by the legislatures of Virginia and Kentucky, argued that the states had the right to judge whether federal laws agreed with the Constitution. If a state decided that a law was unconstitutional, it could declare that law "null and void" within the state. This principle of **nullification** remained unresolved. Neither Virginia nor Kentucky tried to enforce the resolutions. Still, their defiance of federal power was clear.

Increasing Tensions Tensions between Federalists and Jeffersonian Republicans continued to grow during the late 1790s. Members of Congress attacked each other in the House of Representatives. Crowds taunted President Adams, at times forcing him to enter the presidential residence in Philadelphia through the back door.

As the presidential election of 1800 loomed, many people believed that the future of the nation was at stake. Would the nation tilt toward what Jefferson called "the Spirit of 1776," and the idea of liberty found in the Declaration of Independence? Or would the nation choose the Spirit of 1787, with an emphasis on order as stated in the Constitution?

During the presidential campaign of 1800, each side attacked the other bitterly. In this Federalist cartoon, Thomas Jefferson is about to destroy the Constitution and lead the nation into violence like that of the French (Gallic) Revolution. *Government* How did Jeffersonian Republicans characterize John Adams (pictured at right)?

Gabriel Prosser's Rebellion

Before the election took place, however, another event in the summer of 1800 demonstrated the conflict surrounding, the unresolved issue of slavery. In the area around Richmond, Virginia, a blacksmith named Gabriel Prosser and several other slaves planned a rebellion. The leaders intended to take over Richmond and win freedom.

Prosser's small-scale rebellion failed. The rebels were caught and tried, and at least twenty of them, including Prosser, were executed. At the trial, one defendant said, "I have adventured my life in endeavoring [trying] to obtain the liberty of my countrymen, and am a willing sacrifice to their cause."

The Election of 1800

The personal attacks and negative campaigning of elections today are nothing new. The election of 1800 was

Main Idea CONNECTIONS

Summarize the tensions between Federalists and Jeffersonian Republicans in your own words.

Customize for

English Language Learners

Ask students to find five or more words in the section that are new to them. Have them define the words by using context clues or by looking them up in a dictionary.

Answer to . . .

Viewing History The Jeffersonian Republicans characterized Adams as a monarchist.

Main Idea Connections Sample answer: The political opponents resorted to personal attack and smear tactics as they tried to win the population to their respective sides.

BACKGROUND

Recent Scholarship

One of the most important developments in the early American Republic was the rapid expansion in the number of newspapers, periodicals, books, and other forms of "print culture." Suddenly, it became possible for people in Massachusetts to read about what people were doing and saying in South Carolina, and vice versa. David Waldstreicher's *In the Midst of Perpetual Fetes: The Making of American Nationalism, 1776–1829* shows how these new forms of communication created a national language through which Americans began to celebrate diverse local identities as expressions of the greatness of their nation as a whole.

EXTENDED CLASS PERIODS

Time: 90 minutes.

Activity: Simulate live television coverage of the House balloting for President during the election of 1800.

Grouping: Four to six students.

Purpose: To re-create the tension and impact of the balloting for President in the House of Representatives, reporters should interview Jefferson, Hamilton, and members of the House.

Roles: Reporters, members of the House, Jefferson, Hamilton, a producer.

Outcome: Students will identify key issues of the election of 1800 through interviews with Jefferson, Hamilton, and members of the House.

Notable PRESIDENTS

Thomas Jefferson

"We hold these truths to be self-evident; that all men are created equal"
—Declaration of Independence

1801–1809

Thomas Jefferson had impressive qualifications for the presidency. The Virginia-born planter and lawyer had not only drafted the Declaration of Independence, but had served as ambassador to France, Secretary of State, and Vice President. Jefferson promised a more democratic government, one that would leave most decisions in the hands of the people.

During his first term, from 1801 to 1805, Jefferson had considerable success. He trimmed the federal government's size and cost and acted as President in a simple, democratic manner. When given the chance to buy the Louisiana Territory from France, Jefferson approved the purchase. The Louisiana Purchase of 1803 considerably increased the country's size.

Jefferson failed, however, in his effort to reduce the power of the federal courts. Jefferson feared the power of federal judges, who were appointed for life and thus were beyond the reach of voters. The federal courts, led by Chief Justice John Marshall, gained power during Jefferson's administration.

Jefferson's second term, from 1805 to 1809, was far less successful than his first. His Embargo of 1807, which halted trade with European nations until they promised to stop harassing American ships on the high seas, was a disaster. Americans ignored the embargo and it was repealed before a disappointed Jefferson left office.

Jefferson died on July 4, 1826, the fiftieth anniversary of the Declaration of Independence. In his time, Jefferson's commitment to equality among white men, as well as his opposition to slavery, were brave and radical ideas. Today, Jefferson remains a puzzle for historians, for the author of some of the most eloquent words ever written about human freedom was himself the owner of slaves.

Connecting to Today

Find an issue in the news today in which one or both sides might use the famous phrase from the Declaration, "all men are created equal," to support its case. Then describe how the idea of equality affects that issue.

---

truly a nasty campaign. Jeffersonian newspapers accused Adams of being a monarchist, which was a terrible insult at the time. Federalists, on the other hand, asserted that Jefferson was a godless man who would lead the United States into chaos.

Jefferson won the popular vote in December 1800. He was unable to get a majority in the Electoral College, however. Therefore the House of Representatives would have to choose the new President. Though Jeffersonians had won most of the seats in the congressional elections of 1800, these new members had not yet entered office. The vote for President would be taken by the old House, which the Federalists controlled. Even before the voting began in the House on February 11, 1801, it was clear that no candidate could get a majority immediately.

On February 17, only a few days before the end of Adams's term, the House of Representatives finally elected Jefferson as the third President of the United States on the thirty-sixth ballot.

Why Adams Lost In a way, John Adams's defeat was an unfair judgment of his abilities. Adams was more devoted to public service and, some historians believe, more honest than most Presidents. Rising above Federalist hostility to France, he had sent a second diplomatic mission to that country in 1799. This mission had cooled tensions between the United States and France considerably. Like most decisive Presidents, however, Adams failed to quiet his critics and angered many of his supporters.

Why Jefferson Won By 1800 Thomas Jefferson was the clear leader of those who preferred local to national government. Jefferson and his followers believed it was better to risk too much liberty than suffer from too much government. Jefferson always denied that he was a politician. He never saw himself as working to build a permanent political party. Nevertheless, that is exactly what he did.

A Peaceful Transfer of Power

Washington, D.C., in 1801 seemed very much like the Federalists' plans in general: grand but unfinished. The new capital, designed by L'Enfant to feature broad boulevards and

---

 RESOURCE OPTIONS

Teaching Resources

American History Block Scheduling Support Taking Sides: The Creation of American Political Parties, found in the Forging a New Nation folder, includes interdisciplinary lesson suggestions and activities for Geography and History, Primary Sources, Biography, and Literature.

Media and Technology

AmericanHeritage® CD-ROM

Explorer Activity 8 The Election of 1800, CD-ROM Guidebook, pp. 35–36, helps students create a homepage for one of the two parties in this election.

Presidents John Adams

Roman buildings, was little more than a swamp with muddy, rutted roads and half-completed structures. Here, on March 4, 1801, Thomas Jefferson took the oath of office administered by one of Adams's appointees, Chief Justice John Marshall.

With this inauguration, the Federalist leaders of the young country proved that they could do what so many leaders in other times and places in history had refused to do. Although few on either side could forget their bitter disagreements, the Federalists did step down and let the Jeffersonian Republicans take over. Whether they stood for individual liberty or a strong, central government, Americans had proved that they could transfer power from one party to another—and do it peacefully. Jefferson recognized the significance of this peaceful transfer of power. He also understood that his administration would not succeed, nor the nation survive, unless Americans were willing to disagree peacefully. As he stated in his First Inaugural Address:

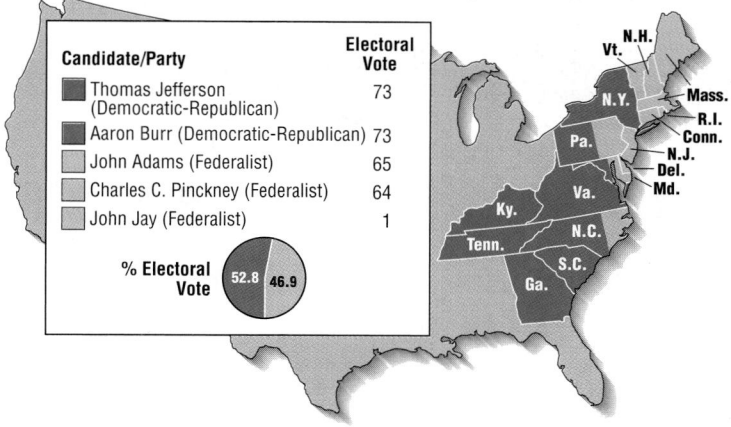

Election of 1800

Candidate/Party	Electoral Vote
Thomas Jefferson (Democratic-Republican)	73
Aaron Burr (Democratic-Republican)	73
John Adams (Federalist)	65
Charles C. Pinckney (Federalist)	64
John Jay (Federalist)	1

% Electoral Vote 52.8 46.9

The political divisions within the country were made clear by the election of 1800. **Place** *How does this map show the regional differences in the nation in 1800?*

KEY DOCUMENTS **"**Every difference of opinion is not a difference of principle. We have called by different names brethren of the same principle. We are all republicans—we are all federalists. If there be any among us who would wish to dissolve this Union or to change its republican form, let them stand undisturbed as monuments of the safety with which error [difference] of opinion may be tolerated where reason is left free to combat it. **"**

—*Thomas Jefferson, First Inaugural Address, 1801*

SECTION 2 REVIEW

Comprehension

1. **Key Terms** Define: (a) XYZ Affair; (b) Alien and Sedition Acts; (c) Virginia and Kentucky resolutions; (d) nullification.

2. **Summarizing the Main Idea** Why was the election of 1800 significant in the history of the United States?

3. **Organizing Information** Create a list of the Federalists' actions that angered many Americans and caused them to elect Jeffersonian Republicans in 1800.

Critical Thinking

4. **Analyzing Time Lines** Review the time line at the start of the section. How are the first two events on the time line related?

5. **Recognizing Ideologies** How does the Sedition Act reflect the Federalists' position in the controversy between those who favored liberty and those who favored order?

Writing Activity

6. **Outlining an Essay** Write an outline for a response to the following essay question: "What did Federalists and Jeffersonian Republicans fear most about each other's ideas prior to the election of 1800?"

▶ RESOURCE OPTIONS

Teaching Resources

Lasting Impact Activity The Lasting Impact of the Election of 1800, History's Lasting Impact folder, pp. 4–5, allows students to discover the relevance of the principles of order and liberty in their lives through a mock council election and debate.

Quiz Units 1–2 folder, p. 73

Student Performance Pack

Guide to the Essentials Chapter 6, Section 2 (English and Spanish)

Answers to SECTION 2 REVIEW

1. (a) XYZ Affair, see p. 180; (b) Alien and Sedition Acts, see p. 181; (c) Virginia and Kentucky resolutions, see p. 181, (d) nullification, see p. 181.

2. It was the first time citizens of the United States had peacefully transferred the power of the presidency from one party to another. In order for this to occur, the party in power had to peacefully step down from the office and turn it over to the winner from another party. Americans take this for granted today, but in many parts of the world such an orderly transfer is still unusual.

3. Students' lists should include the Alien and Sedition Acts, expansion of the army, and higher taxes.

4. The Federalists took advantage of the war crisis created by the XYZ Affair to push the Alien and Sedition Acts through Congress.

5. The Sedition Act made it illegal to criticize government officials, thereby silencing the opposition. It therefore greatly limited an individual's freedom of expression in the interest of increasing the power and stability of the government.

6. Students' outlines may include the following points: Jeffersonian Republicans feared the growing power of the government in people's lives in the form of taxes and limits on freedom; Federalists feared the loss of order and the end of the rule of law if no government stood ready to enforce the laws.

Answer to . . .

Map Skills *The Democratic-Republicans received the most votes from people in the South, while people in the Northeast voted for the Federalists.*

Objectives
You may wish to call students' attention to the objectives in the Section Preview. The objectives are reflected in the main headings of the section.

Bellringer
Have students consider the following question: Under what circumstances might reversing one's opinion be a sign of flexibility and strength? When might sticking to an opinion be a sign of weakness?

Reading Strategy
Formulating Questions Refer to the Reading Strategy in the Section Preview. You may wish to model this strategy on the chalkboard, using one of the headings in the section.

LESSON PLAN

Connecting to the Main Idea

1. Focus Although Jefferson was able to carry out much of his agenda to limit the national government, he was also willing to use and even expand his powers as President. Ask for what purposes Jefferson used the powers of government.

2. Instruct Discuss the steps Jefferson took to limit the role of government and why they were almost guaranteed to make him popular with voters. Now ask students to list the ways in which Jefferson used and expanded the power of the national government. Ask students to state in their own words Jefferson's dilemma concerning the Louisiana Purchase.

3. Close While Jefferson was successful in undoing some of the Federalists' programs, he also used the power of his office to make the Louisiana Purchase and to restrict trade with European countries. The next section discusses Native American resistance to the expansion of the United States into their territory.

1801 Jefferson takes office as President	1803 Marbury v. Madison	1803 Louisiana Purchase	1804 Jefferson reelected President		1807 Embargo Act	
1800	**1802**		**1804**	**1806**		**1808**

3 The Jefferson Administration

SECTION PREVIEW

Objectives

1 Describe how Jefferson both reduced and expanded the power of the national government.
2 Understand the Supreme Court's power to review laws.
3 Identify important foreign policies of the Jefferson administration.
4 *Key Terms* Define: agenda; bureaucracy; *Marbury* v. *Madison;* judicial review; Louisiana Purchase; Lewis and Clark expedition; embargo.

Main Idea

As President, Jefferson sought to reduce the power of the federal government. Yet he also demonstrated the government's power when he bought new lands and restricted foreign trade.

Reading Strategy

Formulating Questions Write two questions for each of the headings in this section and look for answers to those questions as you read.

Thomas Jefferson entered office with a straightforward **agenda,** or list of things that he wanted to accomplish. His goal was to reduce the influence of the national government in the lives of the American people. Jefferson believed:

AMERICAN VOICES "The sum of good government is a wise and frugal Government, which shall restrain men from injuring one another, shall leave them otherwise free to regulate their own pursuits of industry and improvement, and shall not take from the mouth of labor the bread it has earned. "

—*Thomas Jefferson*

Jefferson's informal presidential style extended to his clothing—casual by the standards of the day.

Reducing Government

To accomplish his goals, Jefferson reversed much of what the Federalists had done, starting with matters of presidential style. He refused to deliver speeches to Congress, claiming that to do so would seem too much like the act of a king. He also resolved a question that had troubled Congress for many years—what to call the President. Jefferson asked to be addressed simply as "Mr. President."

Domestic Changes Of course, Jefferson's effect on government went beyond style. Together with Congress, he reduced the amount of taxes paid by the American people and severely cut the size of the federal **bureaucracy**—the departments and workers that make up the federal government. The Attorney General, for instance, was not even allowed a clerk. Jefferson also slashed the size of the army from 12,000 soldiers to only 3,000. Jefferson's goal was to limit the national government's presence in people's lives.

Jefferson, however, did not intend to destroy the government created by the Constitution, or even to undo all the acts of the Federalists. For example, he let the Bank of the United States continue to function, knowing that its twenty-year term would run out in 1811.

 RESOURCE OPTIONS

Teaching Resources

📁 **Reproducible Lesson Plan** Lesson Plans folder, p. 57

📁 **Big Idea Graphic Organizer** Big Idea Graphic Organizer folder, p. 29

📁 **Guided Reading and Review** Units 1–2 folder, p. 74

Media and Technology

American Heritage® CD-ROM

Explorer Activity 9 Lewis and Clark, CD-ROM Guidebook, pp. 37–38, helps students write a movie script based on the experiences of Lewis and Clark.

Time Tour The New Republic: The Jefferson Era

Jefferson's program made him an extremely popular President during his first term. In 1804, when he easily won reelection, he even received the electoral votes of Massachusetts, a state dominated by Federalists.

Hamilton and Burr Jefferson's greatest rivals were his ambitious Vice President, Aaron Burr, and Alexander Hamilton, now a lawyer in New York. In the summer of 1804, Burr killed Hamilton in a duel. With one shot, Burr removed the leader of the Federalists and wrecked his own political future. Although he was never tried, and even continued to preside over the Senate after the duel, Burr was never again a serious challenge to Jefferson.

The Judiciary Acts The most controversial part of Jefferson's first term was his relationship with the judicial branch, particularly the Supreme Court. The Constitution had not fully explained either the organization or the role of this branch of government. With the Judiciary Act of 1789, Congress had filled in the missing details. The act created a national court system with three circuit courts and thirteen district courts, all headed by the Supreme Court. The act also stated that the Supreme Court would settle differences between state and federal laws.

Just before the end of its term, Congress passed the Judiciary Act of 1801. This act decreased the number of Supreme Court justices and increased the number of federal judges. Outgoing members of Congress, in cooperation with President Adams, were trying to limit Jefferson's opportunity to appoint judges to the Supreme Court. They were also working to leave behind a powerful group of Federalist judges whose terms were made for life. Adams quickly filled the new judicial posts just before leaving office. These last-minute appointments, known as the midnight judges, angered Jefferson, who believed that he had the right to appoint judges from his own party.

John Marshall

AMERICAN BIOGRAPHY One of Adams's judicial appointments was John Marshall, a long-time Federalist leader. At the time of his appointment, Marshall was serving as Secretary of State.

Marshall became Chief Justice (the leading judge of the Supreme Court) on January 31, 1801. He held that post for 34 years, until his death in 1835. While on the Supreme Court, Marshall helped establish many important principles of constitutional law. Marshall also helped build the prestige and authority of the Supreme Court in such cases as the historic *Marbury* v. *Madison*.[†]

Marbury v. Madison The case of **Marbury v. Madison** (1803) arose when President Jefferson tried to block the activities of Federalist judges. Just before he left office, President Adams had appointed William Marbury as justice of the peace for the District of Columbia. But Secretary of State James Madison, under orders from President Jefferson, never delivered the official papers giving Marbury his authority. Marbury sued Madison, demanding that the Supreme Court order the Secretary of State to let him take his office. According to the Judiciary Act of 1789, the Court had the power to give such an order.

Judicial Review Chief Justice John Marshall ruled against Marbury, declaring that it was against the Constitution for the Supreme Court to give this order to the executive branch. In other words, Marshall declared part of the Judiciary Act of 1789 unconstitutional—the first time a federal court had been so bold.

The Court's ruling was a victory for the Jefferson administration. Yet in a much larger sense it was a victory for the Supreme Court, for the case established the power of **judicial review.** The power of judicial review enables federal courts to review state laws and state court decisions to determine if they are in keeping with the federal Constitution.[††] Judicial review also allows federal courts to decide whether laws passed by Congress are constitutional, as in the case of *Marbury* v. *Madison*.

*John Marshall
(1755–1835)*

[†] Marshall's other landmark Supreme Court cases include: *Fletcher v. Peck* (1810), the *Dartmouth College Case* (1819), *Ogden v. Saunders* (1827), *McCulloch v. Maryland* (1819) and *Gibbons v. Ogden* (1824).

[††] In this way, the Court plays an important role in preserving the federal union. Marshall, a Federalist, wanted to establish the supremacy of the national government over the states.

Main Idea CONNECTIONS

Why did Jefferson want to limit the power of the federal government?

TEST PREPARATION

Have students read the paragraph on this page under the heading "*Marbury* v. *Madison*," then answer the question below.

When did Marbury sue Madison?

A After President Adams appointed Marbury justice of the peace.

B After President Jefferson appointed Marbury justice of the peace.

(C) After Secretary of State Madison withheld the official papers giving Marbury authority to hold the office of justice of the peace.

D Before President Adams left office.

Answer to . . .

Main Idea Connections
Jefferson believed that the goal of the federal government should be to ensure people's liberty, not to regulate their lives.

About the Presidents

Thomas Jefferson (1801–1809) had a definite understanding with Aaron Burr during the election of 1800: Jefferson was running for President, Burr for Vice President. Nevertheless, Burr stayed in the competition when they both received the same number of electoral votes for President. Hamilton swung the vote in Jefferson's favor—only because he hated Jefferson less than Burr. Jefferson never trusted Burr again. In his second term, Jefferson chose New York governor George Clinton as running mate. Still blinded by dreams of glory, Burr led an unsuccessful revolt of western states in 1807. He was tried for treason. Before the verdict, Jefferson made it clear he thought Burr should be found guilty. But Burr was acquitted under the anti-Jefferson Chief Justice John Marshall. Source: Wilson Sullivan, "Thomas Jefferson," *The American Heritage® Pictorial History of the Presidents of the United States*, vol. 1, 1968

Customize for
Less Proficient Readers

Have students reread the text on judicial review and answer the following questions. Why is the power of the Supreme Court to judge a law's constitutionality important to the United States system of government? How does this power help the Supreme Court check the power of Congress? What would happen without the power of judicial review?

Judical review is not clearly stated anywhere in the Consitition. Yet thanks in part to *Marbury* v. *Madison*, it remains a vital power of the judicial branch today.

Turning Point:
The Louisiana Purchase

As a strict constructionist, Jefferson opposed the development of a strong central government. In issues concerning American expansion west of the Appalachians, however, Jefferson and his supporters used the power and money of the national government as boldy as the Federalists had ever dared.

The Land Act of 1800 The Northwest Ordinance of 1787 established a process by which territories, as lands in the West were called, could become states. The Jeffersonians sped the development of the frontier—which now extended only as far west as the Mississippi—through a new federal land policy. Under the Land Act of 1800, Americans were able to buy land in small parcels and on credit. Federal land offices appeared across the West, making easier the transfer of land from government to its citizens.

Napoleon and the French American farmers in the West depended on the Mississippi River to transport their crops to foreign markets. When the French ruler Napoleon took over much of the Spanish land in the West, he gained control of the mouth of the Mississippi at New Orleans. The French used this control to extract large sums of money from American traders who had no choice but to travel the Mississippi.

Fearing this French control and Napoleon's ambitions, Jefferson in 1803 sent James Monroe to Paris to buy the city of New Orleans. Congress instructed Monroe along with the American minister in Paris, Robert Livingston, that they could pay up to $10 million for the land. What happened next was one of the most fateful events in American history.

Napoleon did in fact have ambitions to create a new French Empire in the Americas. When his attempt to quell a rebellion on the French island of Haiti failed, however, he quickly changed his mind. Napoleon refused

TURNING POINT : *The Louisiana Purchase*

The Louisiana Purchase was a historic step in the United States' westward expansion. While the nation's territorial expansion has ended, the westward movement of people continues to this day.

1803 The United States buys the Louisiana Territory from France.

1846 In a treaty with Britain, the United States gains claim to the Pacific Northwest.

1912 Arizona and New Mexico, the newest of the "lower 48" states, join the Union.

| 1800 | 1850 | 1900 | 1950 | 2000 |

1845 The United States annexes Texas.

1848 Following the Mexican War, Mexico cedes southwestern territories to the United States.

1980 For the first time, the mean population center of the United States lies west of the Mississippi River.

 RESOURCE OPTIONS

Exploration of the American West, 1804–1807

Nov. 1805 Lewis and Clark sight the Pacific.

June 1805 Party reaches the Great Falls of the Missouri — proof that they have followed the right course.

Nov. 1804 The party builds Ft. Mandan, where they spend the winter, Nov. 1804 to Apr. 1805.

July 1805 The party crosses the Continental Divide.

Sept. 1804 Party narrowly avoids skirmish with the Teton Sioux.

Aug. 1804 Meeting with friendly Yankton Sioux.

Feb. 1807 Pike and his men captured by Spanish cavalry.

May 1804 Lewis and Clark depart St. Louis with party of about 40 men.

Nov. 1806 Pike tries to reach the summit that now bears his name.

July 1806 Pike's expedition departs St. Louis.

Pike's reports on Santa Fe stimulate expansion into Texas.

July 1807 Pike and his men taken to Chihuahua, then to Louisiana and released.

Legend:
- United States
- Louisiana Purchase
- Oregon Country
- Spanish territory
- British territory
- *Oto* Native American lands
- — Lewis and Clark expedition
- – – Lewis and Clark (return)
- – – Lewis
- – – Clark
- — Pike expedition
- ■ Fort

MAP Skills In their two-year expedition, Louis and Clark explored thousands of miles and collected information on the lands, peoples, and plant and animal species they encountered. Their crossing of the Continental Divide proved once and for all that a water route to the Pacific did not exist. *Movement Study the map above. What difficulties did the exploring parties face?*

---

to sell New Orleans to the United States but offered instead to sell *all* of the French claims known as Louisiana. Not daring to ask him to wait for weeks or months for an answer, Monroe and Livingston offered Napoleon $15 million for the **Louisiana Purchase.**[†] They desperately hoped that Congress and the President would support their decision.

When Jefferson heard of the agreement with the French, he was troubled. The Constitution did not mention the purchase of foreign lands. He was also wary of spending large amounts of public money. Jefferson overcame his doubts, however, and urged Congress to approve the sale. With the stroke of a pen, the Louisiana Purchase dramatically increased both

the national debt and the size of United States. As the time line on the previous page shows, the Louisiana Purchase was to have an enormous impact on the history of the United States.

The Lewis and Clark Expedition Congress agreed to finance Jefferson's call for an expedition to explore the area included in the Louisiana Purchase. Jefferson chose his private secretary, Meriwether Lewis, to lead the expedition. Lewis in turn chose William Clark as his companion officer.

[†] The actual cost of Louisiana was $11.25 million. The remainder was for covering debts of France to United States citizens.

Using the Internet

Prepare a Summary

Objective Use the Internet to write a summary of the treaties that formalized the Louisiana Purchase. Have students follow these instructions:

1. See the *America: Pathways to the Present* Web site at

http://www.Pathways.phschool.com

for the URL of the National Archives and Records Administration.

2. Follow the links to the pages containing the three documents that recorded the Louisiana Purchase. Take notes as you read. Consider questions such as: Which nations were affected by the treaties? Were the concerns of Native Americans met? How much money was involved, and which lands?

3. Write a summary of the Louisiana Purchase based on these documents and your notes. Include specific quotes wherever possible.

RESOURCE OPTIONS

Teaching Resources

 Primary Source Activity Napoleon Sells Louisiana, Learning with Documents folder, p. 12

ATLAS **Nystrom *Atlas of Our Country*** Early Expansion of the United States, pp. 20–21

 American History Block Scheduling Support Checks and Balances: The Rise of the American Judiciary, found in the Forging a New Nation folder, includes interdisciplinary lesson suggestions and activities for Geography and History, Primary Sources, Biography, and Literature.

Answer to . . .

Map Skills Getting lost, straying into foreign territory, conflicts in Native American territory, rugged terrain, wild animals, weather.

The **Lewis and Clark expedition** began in the spring of 1804. Their goals were to search for river routes to the western ocean, make contact with the Native Americans living in the territory, and gather information about the region's natural resources. To help in this task, the expedition hired a French-Canadian fur trapper and his wife Sacajawea, a Shoshone Indian, as interpreters.

The expedition reached the Pacific Ocean late in 1805 and returned east by September 1806. The journey, that had lasted two years, four months, succeeded in filling in many of the details of the vast lands to the west. Additional information about the West was gathered by Zebulon Pike, who traveled as far west as the Rockies and then south into Spanish-held territory between 1806 and 1807.

Jefferson's Foreign Policy

During Jefferson's first term, a brief peace settled on European nations. When the European wars resumed, so too did troubles between Europe and the United States.

The Chesapeake Jay's Treaty, under which the United States had remained at peace with Great Britain, expired in 1805. By then, Europeans were back at war with each other. French warships began harassing American ships trading with Britain, and British ships interfered with American ships trading with France. The British also kidnapped American sailors to serve in their navy. In 1807 a British ship, the *Leopard*, attacked the U.S.S. *Chesapeake*, inflicted twenty-one casualties, and boarded it to search for deserters from His Majesty's navy.

The Embargo of 1807 Like other Americans, Jefferson was outraged by these acts and believed that they should not go unpunished. Yet he rejected the use of force, in part because of the small size of the American navy. Instead Jefferson chose an economic weapon against the British and French. At his insistence, Congress passed the Embargo Act of 1807, which outlawed almost all trade with foreign countries. An **embargo** is a restriction on trade. Britain's trade, however, had grown too strong to be severely injured by the embargo. The French, too, were largely unaffected.

Many Americans, on the other hand, hated the embargo—particularly New Englanders who made their living through trade. They now smuggled goods to Great Britain and other countries in defiance of the President and Congress. With the authority of the national government at stake, Jefferson had no alternative but to use his small navy and federal agents to enforce the law.

The embargo ruined Jefferson's second term. Many Americans despised the direct interference of the national government in the economy. Federalists exploited this anger, and the party enjoyed a revival. While Jefferson was able to see his Secretary of State, James Madison, elected President in 1808, the nation's third President retired to his home at Monticello as an unpopular figure.

SECTION 3 REVIEW

Comprehension

1. **Key Terms** Define: (a) agenda; (b) bureau-cracy; (c) *Marbury* v. *Madison*; (d) judicial review; (e) Louisiana Purchase; (f) Lewis and Clark expedition; (g) embargo.

2. **Summarizing the Main Idea** Describe the changes Jefferson tried to make in the rela-tionship between government and the people.

3. **Organizing Information** Create an outline of Jefferson's major accomplishments as President.

Critical Thinking

4. **Analyzing Time Lines** Review the time line at the start of the section. How do each of the events for 1803 conflict with Jefferson's principles?

5. **Making Comparisons** How was the enforce-ment of the Embargo Act of 1807 like the sup-pression of the Whiskey Rebellion?

Writing Activity

6. **Writing a Persuasive Essay** Write a per-suasive letter to Thomas Jefferson from a Northeast merchant explaining why the Embargo Act should be lifted.

RESOURCE OPTIONS

Teaching Resources

Quiz Units 1–2 folder, p. 75

Student Performance Pack

Guide to the Essentials Chapter 6, Section 3 (English and Spanish)

4 Native American Resistance

SECTION PREVIEW

Objectives

1 Describe the condition of Native Americans in the Old Northwest around 1790.
2 Summarize the ideas of Native American leaders about dealing with the United States.
3 *Key Terms* Define: Treaty of Greenville; reservation; assimilation; Battle of Tippecanoe.

Main Idea

As the United States continued to expand onto their land, Native Americans responded in various ways, from acceptance to war.

Reading Strategy

Reinforcing Main Ideas As you read, take notes on the ways in which Indian leaders dealt with the advance of Americans of European descent.

Before the American colonies gained independence from Britain, relations between Native Americans and colonists were often marked by violence. If anything, the creation of the United States worsened the situation as large numbers of American settlers now moved westward onto Indian lands.

War in the Old Northwest

The American Revolution had broken the power of the Iroquois nations in the North and beaten back the Cherokee in the South. In the early 1790s, however, many Miami, Delaware, Shawnee, and other Native American groups came together to fight American expansion. Assisted by the British in Canada and led by warriors such as Little Turtle and Blue Jacket, they defeated a United States army at Miamitown (now Fort Wayne, Indiana) in 1790. Then they defeated an expedition commanded by Northwest Territory governor Arthur St. Clair, inflicting one of the biggest defeats ever suffered by a United States army.

The British soon deserted the Native Americans, however. To add to their woes, Native Americans now faced a new national

army known as the Legion of the United States. In 1794, General "Mad Anthony" Wayne led the Legion to victory over the Native Americans at the Battle of Fallen Timbers in what is now northwestern Ohio. As a result of this battle, the Miami, Delaware, Shawnee, and other Native Americans were forced in 1795 to accept the **Treaty of Greenville,** in which they lost the southern two thirds of Ohio. The treaty also forced them to accept that the Ohio River was no longer a permanent boundary between their lands and those of American settlers. From New York to Indiana to Mississippi, Native Americans ended the 1700s in a greatly weakened condition.

Native American Reactions

In the early 1800s, several Native American leaders proposed different ways to deal with the United States. The options they suggested included four broad strategies: accepting white culture, blending Indian and

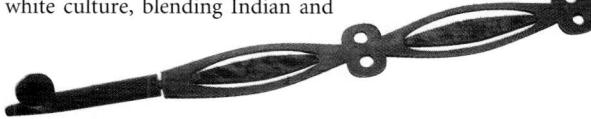

Native American custom dictated that negotiating parties take turns smoking a "peace pipe."

SECTION 4

Native American Resistance

Objectives
You may wish to call students' attention to the objectives in the Section Preview. The objectives are reflected in the main headings of the section.

Bellringer
Ask students to define *accommodation* and *assimilation*. Ask whether they have ever accommodated to the wishes of a stronger power, such as an institution, or tried to become assimilated into a new group.

Reading Strategy
Reinforcing Main Ideas Refer to the Reading Strategy in the Section Preview. List the names Little Turtle, Handsome Lake, Tenskwatawa, and Tecumseh on the chalkboard. Ask students to focus on these leaders as they take notes on the ways Native Americans dealt with the advance of European Americans.

LESSON PLAN
Connecting to the Main Idea

1. **Focus** As settlers continued to move into Native American lands, different groups tried to deal with the United States in different ways. Ask what those ways were. How successful were they?
2. **Instruct** Explain why it was difficult for Native American groups to adopt a united policy for dealing with the United States. *(Groups spoke different languages, observed different customs, and some had been enemies for generations.)*
   Discuss the major Native American leaders. Ask students to identify each leader's group and highlight the ideas of each for dealing with the United States.
3. **Close** Review the different ways in which Native American leaders responded to the encroachment on their land.

Main Idea CONNECTIONS

What was Tenskwatawa's response to United States expansion?

American cultures, returning to Indian religious traditions, and taking military action.

Accepting White Culture Some Native Americans followed the path of Little Turtle, a leader of the Miami people. Little Turtle was a brilliant military leader who had engineered the great victories of the early 1790s. After making peace with white settlers, he lived in northern Indiana on annual payments from the government. Over time Little Turtle adopted some of the Americans' customs. After devoting much of his life to fighting the Americans, Little Turtle tried to live peacefully with white American settlers.

Blending Indian and American Cultures In western New York a Seneca named Handsome Lake followed a different course. Handsome Lake had fought with the British against the Americans during the Revolutionary War. Later, he had suffered the humiliation of being con-

fined to a **reservation,** an area that the federal government set aside for Native Americans who had lost their homelands. In 1799, Handsome Lake called for a rebirth of Seneca culture that would blend Native American customs with those of the Americans.

Handsome Lake urged Native Americans to abandon war and instead to give more attention to traditional Indian rituals. While holding on to age-old beliefs, Handsome Lake and his followers adopted American notions about land, agriculture, and family life. While Little Turtle's way was acceptance, Handsome Lake's was acceptance on Native American terms. As he told President Jefferson:

AMERICAN VOICES "Our lands are decaying because we do not think on [about] the Great Spirit, but we are now going to renew our Minds and think on the great Being who made us all. . . . Dear Brother, the Lord has confidence in your people as well as ours, provided we can settle all our Business."

—*Handsome Lake*

 The Shawnee prophet, Tenskwatawa, called on his followers to return to their ancient ways and obey the Master of Life. He said the Master of Life had told him: "If you Indians will do everything which I have told you, I will overturn the land, so that all the white people will be covered and you alone shall inhabit the land." *Culture According to Tenskwatawa, how did assimilation threaten Native Americans?*

Returning to Indian Traditions In Indiana another leader arose, among the Shawnee, Delaware, and Miami. Tenskwatawa, also known simply as "the Prophet," called for a return to traditional Native American ways and a total rejection of European values. He strongly opposed **assimilation,** the process by which people of one culture merge into and become part of another culture.

In 1808 Tenskwatawa established Prophetstown on the Wabash River (near present-day Lafayette, Indiana). There Tenskwatawa offered his followers a sense of dignity and the promise of a stable life together. He also adopted an increasingly warlike attitude toward the United States. In this he was aided by his older brother, Tecumseh.

Taking Military Action Born in 1768, Tecumseh had fought against the United States in the 1780s and 1790s and had earned a reputation as a talented war chief. In 1795, he refused to participate in the negotiations that led to the Treaty of Greenville.

Tecumseh believed that Indians' only hope of resisting American expansion was to unite by overcoming local and group differences. He and Tenskwatawa acted on this belief by rallying opposition to the Treaty of Fort Wayne. In this treaty, negotiated in 1809 by Governor William Henry Harrison of the Indiana

Territory, Native Americans had given up much of south-central Indiana. Like many treaties with Native Americans, this made use of a legal trick. Because Native Americans held their land in common, they all had to agree before the status of the land could change. United States government officials would first persuade a few individuals to sign away their people's land, and then ignore protests from the rest of the group.

In August 1810, Tecumseh and several dozen warriors met with Governor Harrison to protest such a trick. Tecumseh warned that if the government continued to purchase lands: "it will produce war among the different tribes and at last I do not know what will be the consequence to the white people." Governor Harrison took the warning and moved first. While Tecumseh was in Alabama and Mississippi trying to get the Choctaw and the Creek to join in the resistance, Harrison marched north from Vincennes to Prophetstown with roughly one thousand militia and soldiers.

Just before sunrise on November 7, 1811, after a day of negotiations, Tenskwatawa sent his warriors to attack Harrison and his men. The **Battle of Tippecanoe** lasted about two hours. Neither side won, but the battle shattered Native American morale and eroded confidence in Tenskwatawa's leadership. Within a few days, Harrison burned an abandoned Prophetstown to the ground.

Native American military resistance was not over, however. During the War of 1812 between the United States and Britain, Tecumseh rallied warriors to fight with the

VIEWING HISTORY William Henry Harrison reported that Tecumseh (pictured at left) wished to "form a combination of all the Indian Tribes … to put a stop to the encroachments of the white people." *Diversity What difficulties do you think Tecumseh faced in trying to unite the various Native American nations?*

British in Canada. (See the next section.) When a British officer began to talk of retreat, Tecumseh responded:

AMERICAN VOICES
"If you have an idea of going away, give [your weapons] to us, and you may go and welcome. As for us, our lives are in the hands of the Great Spirit. We are determined to defend our lands, and if it be his will we wish to leave our bones upon them."

—Tecumseh

A few weeks later, Tecumseh died in the Battle of the Thames in Ontario, Canada, on October 5, 1813. Although Tecumseh and his brother did not accomplish their objectives, they left a vital legacy of defiance and respect for their people and their culture.

SECTION 4 REVIEW

Comprehension

1. *Key Terms* Define: (a) Treaty of Greenville; (b) reservation; (c) assimilation; (d) Battle of Tippecanoe.

2. *Summarizing the Main Idea* How did the paths proposed by Handsome Lake and Tenskwatawa differ?

3. *Organizing Information* Create a chart comparing and contrasting the views of Little Turtle, Handsome Lake, Tenskwatawa, and Tecumseh.

Critical Thinking

4. *Analyzing Time Lines* Review the time line at the start of the section. What was the significance of the Battle of Tippecanoe?

5. *Making Comparisons* How did Native American and European American ideas about land ownership differ?

Writing Activity

6. *Writing an Expository Essay* Write an essay in which you outline the basic sources of conflict between Native Americans and Americans of European descent.

Answer to . . .

Viewing History Sample answer: Tecumseh had to convince the various Native American groups to disregard their cultural differences and forget any existing conflicts. Also, he had to convince all groups to agree with his approach to dealing with U.S. expansion.

Objectives

You may wish to call students' attention to the objectives in the Section Preview. The objectives are reflected in the main headings of the section.

Bellringer

Ask students to think of times when they have had to compromise. When is compromise necessary? What elements are required for a compromise to work?

Reading Strategy

Outlining Information Refer students to the Reading Strategy in the Section Preview. You may wish to model this strategy on the chalkboard by filling in the main ideas for one heading.

LESSON PLAN

Connecting to the Main Idea

1. Focus Discuss the reasons that Congress declared war on Great Britain in 1812. Ask students to identify what the United States hoped to gain and what it actually accomplished.

2. Instruct Ask students to create a time line of major events in the War of 1812. Then have them write newspaper headlines on why the Battle of New Orleans unified the country and restored patriotism.

Have students review Jefferson's comment at the end of the section about the Missouri Compromise. Ask students what they think Jefferson meant.

3. Close Point out that the War of 1812 was mostly a series of discouraging losses for the United States, yet was followed by a period of national pride and prosperity. Ask students what dampened these political good feelings.

1812 War of 1812 begins	1814 Battle of Horseshoe Bend	1814 Treaty of Ghent signed	1815 Battle of New Orleans	1816 Monroe elected President	1820 Missouri Compromise
1810		**1815**			**1820**

5 The War of 1812

SECTION PREVIEW

Objectives

1 Explain the causes and results of the War of 1812.
2 Describe the events leading to the economic panic of 1819.
3 Understand the issues that led to the Missouri Compromise.
4 *Key Terms* Define: impressment; War of 1812; Treaty of Ghent; Battle of New Orleans; depression; Missouri Compromise.

Main Idea

Americans emerged from the War of 1812 with a new sense of national pride, but economic and moral conflicts continued to trouble the country.

Reading Strategy

Outlining Information Make an outline using the headings in this section. As you read, fill in main idea statements under each heading.

This "star-spangled banner" inspired the national anthem as it flew bravely through a British attack on Baltimore in 1814.

Following the Battle of Tippecanoe in November 1811, Native Americans increased their attacks against settlers who were moving onto their lands. Most Americans believed that the Indians were being encouraged and armed by the British.

War Breaks Out

Among those who blamed the British for the frontier violence were some members of Congress. Congress in 1812 included many new members from the South and West who represented the interests of farmers moving west onto Indian lands. The new members included Henry Clay of Kentucky and John C. Calhoun of South Carolina. The leaders of this new group were known as the War Hawks. They favored a war with Britain to push the British out of North America and thereby put a stop to Native American attacks in the West.

Anger Toward Britain In June 1812, President Madison sent a message urging Congress to declare war against the British. Madison argued that the British had not only encouraged the Indians to attack American settlers, but had also interfered with United States shipping. For years, the American government had tried without success to stop the British practice of **impressment.** Impressment is the act of forcing people into military service. British ships regularly stopped American ships at sea and removed men, including American citizens, to serve in the British navy. Congress approved Madison's call for war. The war that followed became known as the **War of 1812.**

In many ways, the declaration of war was a foolhardy action. The United States had only a small army and navy, and no offers of help from foreign countries. The nation would have to deal not only with the powerful British, but with Native Americans to the north and south who were angered by western expansion.

▶ RESOURCE OPTIONS

Teaching Resources

📁 **Reproducible Lesson Plan** Lesson Plans folder, p. 59

📁 **Big Idea Graphic Organizer** Big Idea Graphic Organizer folder, p. 31

📁 **Guided Reading and Review** Units 1–2 folder, p. 78

📁 **Visual Learning Activity** "The Present State of Our Country," Learning with Documents folder, p. 48

The Land War Despite these disadvantages, Americans believed that the United States could strike swiftly and effectively at Britain by invading British-held Canada. To their surprise, American troops—poorly equipped and led—were beaten by the British in the summer of 1812.

The United States did manage some victories on land. William Henry Harrison defeated the British and Native Americans, including Tecumseh's forces, at the Battle of the Thames in October 1813. Andrew Jackson, a general who (like Harrison) would later be President, defeated the Creek Indians at Horseshoe Bend in Alabama in March 1814. But these modest successes were not about to convince a great power like Britain to give up.

The Naval War Despite the fact that British ships outnumbered American vessels by about twenty to one, Americans at first won a number of victories at sea. The United States had a half-dozen frigates, or medium-sized sailing warships, that won several battles against the British. American victories fought by the crews of the *Constitution* ("Old Ironsides"), the *Wasp,* and the *United States* raised the country's morale. In addition, American privateers captured more than a thousand British ships.

The Americans did suffer a number of naval defeats, however. In 1813 a British warship fought and captured the American warship *Chesapeake* off the coast of Massachusetts. The dying order of *Chesapeake* captain James Lawrence, "Don't give up the ship," became the battle cry of the United States Navy.

The war's most important naval victory took place in the summer of 1813. Master Commandant Oliver Hazard Perry defeated a small British fleet on Lake Erie, enabling the United States to control that lake and protect a vital stretch of its northern border. "We have met the enemy, and he is ours," Perry reported after more than three hours of the war's bloodiest naval battle.

In time, the superiority of the British navy began to have an effect on the United States. The British blockaded the American coast, strangling trade and putting a stop to the attacks of American frigates.

The Burning of Washington, D.C. In 1814 the British ended a difficult and dangerous war they had been fighting against the French emperor Napoleon in Europe. They then turned their full attention and resources to the

war in the United States. Some 14,000 British troops tried to invade the United States from Canada in the late summer of 1814. To the surprise of the British, however, a much smaller American force drove them back across the border.

By contrast, a fleet of British ships that arrived in Chesapeake Bay at about the same time scored a major success. About 4,000 British troops left the ships and descended on Washington, D.C., meeting little serious opposition. On August 24, President James Madison and his wife, Dolley Madison, were warned of the approach of the British and fled. Toward evening, the British entered the capital and started fires that consumed the city. Even the Capitol and the White House were gutted by flames.

From Washington the British troops moved on toward Baltimore. An all-night British bombardment of Fort McHenry, at the entrance to Baltimore harbor, was witnessed by lawyer Francis Scott Key. Key wrote the following words as a testimony to the American's determination to stand strong against an overwhelming enemy:

COMPARING PRIMARY SOURCES

FOR AND AGAINST THE WAR OF 1812

The War of 1812 was promoted by the War Hawks, mostly from the South and West, and opposed by leaders from New England and the Middle Atlantic states.

For War with Britain	Against War with Britain
"We shall drive the British from our continent—they will no longer have an opportunity of intriguing [conspiring] with our Indian neighbors, and setting on the ruthless savage to tomahawk our women and children." —Representative Felix Grundy of Kentucky, December 1811	"It was our own thirst for territory, our own want [lack] of moderation that had driven these sons of nature [Native Americans] to desperation, of which we felt the effects.... Go! March to Canada! ...The coast is to be left defenseless, while men of the interior are reveling in conquest and spoil." —Representative John Randolph of Virginia, December 1811

ANALYZING VIEWPOINTS **Compare the main arguments made by the two writers.**

BACKGROUND

Connections to Today

An intense spirit of nationalism ensued after both the American Revolution and the War of 1812. This unifying spirit, which usually accompanies times of conflict, was conspicuously absent during the Vietnam War in the 1960s and 1970s. Many citizens protested openly against the war on a grand scale, and many refused to join the armed forces.

Graphing the Main Idea

To make sure students understand the main idea of this section, you may wish to use the flow map graphic organizer below.

Tell students that a flow map shows a sequence of events unfolding. Ask students to use it to record the events that led to the Missouri Compromise.

Teaching Tip A template for this graphic organizer can be found in the Color Transparencies, G-4.

RESOURCE OPTIONS

Teaching Resources

Comparing Primary Sources For and Against the War of 1812, Units 1–2 folder, pp. 81–82

Key Documents "The Star-Spangled Banner," Learning with Documents folder, p. 85

Media and Technology

 AmericanHeritage® CD-ROM

History Makers Henry Clay

Presidents James Madison

Time Tour The New Republic: The Jefferson Era

Answer to . . .

Comparing Primary Sources Grundy argues that the British should be attacked for inciting the Native Americans against American settlers. Randolph argues that war should not be waged because American actions forced Native Americans to retaliate; further, the East Coast would be left defenseless.

About the Presidents

James Madison (1809–1817) understood clearly that Americans were divided about waging a war with Britain. But he had already tried diplomacy, embargo, and threats. American ships and seamen were still being harassed. The war vote in Congress reflected the nation's disunity—79 to 49 in the House, 19 to 13 in the Senate. Not surprisingly, Congress was slow to approve funds for fighting the war. And though the frontier states were united in the war effort, the New England states refused to be involved. In fact, the Treaty of Ghent settled few of the issues that started the war. But the President's prestige was enhanced for standing up to the world's strongest empire. Source: Vincent Buranelli, "James Madison," *The American Heritage® Pictorial History of the Presidents of the United States*, vol. 1, 1968

"And the rocket's red glare, the bombs bursting in air Gave proof through the night that our flag was still there. O say, does that Star-Spangled Banner yet wave O'er the land of the free and the home of the brave?"

—*Francis Scott Key*
"The Star-Spangled Banner"

The "star-spangled banner" did indeed still wave over the fort. The citizens of Baltimore had been strengthening their defenses, and American forces were able to turn back the enemy.

The War Ends

The British retreat from Baltimore lifted American spirits. But not all Americans felt as patriotic about the War of 1812 as did Francis Scott Key. "Mr. Madison's War," others bitterly called it, while pointing to the harm it had done to the country. The national treasury was empty, the Capitol lay in ruins, and the British blockade had brought trade to a standstill.

The Hartford Convention In December 1814, New Englanders, who had suffered tremendous losses in trade during the war, sent delegates to a meeting in Hartford, Connecticut, to consider the possibility of leaving the nation. In the end, the Hartford Convention called only for constitutional amendments to increase New England's political power.

The Treaty of Ghent Meanwhile, both the British and the Americans had recognized that this was a war no one wanted, and the British realized they could not win. On December 24,

The War of 1812

9. Harrison defeats the British in the **Battle of the Thames**, Oct. 1813.

3. Hull surrenders **Detroit** without a fight, Aug. 1812.

4. **Fort Dearborn Massacre**, Aug. 1812.

8. Perry defeats British fleet at **Put-in-Bay**, Sept. 1813.

1. Harrison defeats the Shawnee at the **Battle of Tippecanoe**, Nov. 1811.

10. Jackson defeats the Creek at the **Battle of Horseshoe Bend**, Mar. 1814.

14. Jackson defeats the British in the **Battle of New Orleans**, Jan. 1815, before news of the peace treaty arrives.

12. **Battle of Lake Champlain**, Sept. 1814.

2. *Constitution* defeats *Guerrière*, Aug. 1812.

7. *Shannon* defeats *Chesapeake*, June 1813.

6. *United States* captures *Macedonian*, Oct. 1812.

11. British capture **Washington**, burn White House, Aug. 1814.

13. American defense of **Fort McHenry**, Sept. 1814, inspires the "Star-Spangled Banner."

5. *Wasp* captures *Frolic*, Oct. 1812.

	Legend
	United States
	British territory
	Spanish territory
→	British troop movement
→	United States troop movement
✳	British victory
✳	United States victory
✳	Indecisive battle
✳	Indian battle
■	Fort
‡‡	British blockade

0   150   300 Miles
0   150   300 Kilometers

Although the United States considered the War of 1812 a victory over England, in the end neither side gained nor lost any territory. *Movement Why was the British naval blockade such a threat?*

Answer to . . .

Map Skills It not only threatened the United States economy, but also allowed British troops access to the United States capital.

► RESOURCE OPTIONS

Teaching Resources

American History Block Scheduling Support Proud to Be American: A New Spirit of Nationalism, found in the Forging a New Nation folder, includes interdisciplinary lesson suggestions and activities for Geography and History, Primary Sources, Biography, and Literature.

Media and Technology

RESOURCE PRO

Biography Francis Scott Key, found on Resource Pro, profiles the man who wrote "The Star-Spangled Banner" after witnessing the battle at Fort McHenry.

1814, representatives of the two nations met in Belgium and signed the **Treaty of Ghent,** ending the war. All the old boundaries between the United States and British territory in North America were restored.

The Battle of New Orleans Although the Treaty of Ghent officially ended the war, the greatest victory for the United States came two weeks after the treaty was signed. This final twist to a strange war was the result of the slow communication of the times.[†]

On December 23, 1814, a British force of 11,000 men tried to take New Orleans from the south. General Andrew Jackson and 4,500 soldiers and volunteers from all over the Mississippi Valley, including two battalions of free African Americans, defended the city.

On January 8, the overconfident British, fresh from victories over the French in Europe, foolishly threw their troops against the Americans' well-protected positions. Without cover, the advancing British were easy targets for American riflemen. The battle was finished in just over an hour; in fact, most of the shooting took place in about twenty minutes. The British suffered 2,036 casualties; the Americans, 21.

The **Battle of New Orleans** was a remarkable victory for the United States. The battle allowed Americans to end an unhappy war on a powerful, positive note. The battle unified the country, restored patriotism, and made Andrew Jackson a national hero.

Post-War Boom and Panic

In 1815 the United States entered a period of growth and prosperity. Republican James Monroe, the former governor of Virginia, easily won election as the fifth President of the United States in 1816. Monroe and the Republican party dominated American politics, as the Federalists faded out of existence.

Congress, in an attempt to deal with financial problems resulting from the war, created the Second Bank of the United States in 1816.[††] Encouraged by abundant credit from this bank and others, as well as by federal land laws, Americans began moving westward at an incredible rate. Meanwhile, American ships were busy carrying farm products and other goods to Europe.

Then, in 1819, the United States experienced the first great **depression,** or severe economic downturn, in its history. Known as the

United States Exports, 1800–1820

Source: *Historical Statistics of the United States, Colonial Times to 1970*

Interpreting Graphs The Embargo of 1807 sharply cut United States export trade. The British blockade during the War of 1812 nearly brought U.S. trade income to a halt. *Economics What was the status of U.S. export income before the embargo? By how much had it decreased by 1814?*

Panic of 1819, it began across the Atlantic when London banks demanded that banks in the United States pay money owed to them. American banks in turn demanded the money that they had loaned to the American public. Many of the Americans who had borrowed too much in the days of easy loans after 1815 were financially ruined.

The Missouri Compromise

While the economy would eventually rebound from the depression, another problem that year would pose a far greater long-term danger to the nation. In 1819 Congress began debating the admission of the state of Missouri to the United States. The basic issue at stake was slavery.

The Northwest Ordinance of 1787 had established that no state northwest of the Ohio River could be a slave state (that is, a state where slavery was legal). But because Missouri was not

Main Idea
CONNECTIONS

What conflict was temporarily solved by the Missouri Compromise?

[†] News of the Treaty of Ghent did not reach America until mid-February 1815.
[††] The first bank, having dissolved in 1811, had left the country with no central financing for the war.

TEST PREPARATION

Have students read the three paragraphs under the heading "Post-War Boom and Panic," and then answer the question below.

The word *abundant* in the passage means—

(A) plentiful.

B insufficient.

C scarce.

D unavailable.

Answer to . . .

Interpreting Charts Before the embargo the United States made about 110 million dollars in export trade; by 1814, that had decreased by about 100 million dollars.
Main Idea Connections *The Missouri Compromise temporarily solved the conflict over slavery and political power in Congress.*

1. (a) impressment, see p. 192; (b) War of 1812, see p. 192; (c) Treaty of Ghent, see p. 195; (d) Battle of New Orleans, see p. 195; (e) depression, see p. 195; (f) Missouri Compromise, see p. 196.

2. The War of 1812 ended with the Treaty of Ghent in which all old boundaries between the United States and British territory in North America were restored. News of the treaty did not reach the United States for several weeks, however, and so the Battle of New Orleans was fought, and won, by the Americans, greatly boosting the morale and patriotism of the country. Also, Andrew Jackson became a national hero.

3. Charts should include some of the following points. Strengths: fighting to defend own land, located close to fighting, pride. Weaknesses: small army and navy, no foreign assistance, no central bank to finance war, two enemies, poorly equipped and led army, regional opposition to the war.

4. The time line shows battles against both Native Americans and Britain.

5. The Missouri Compromise avoided making a decision on whether slavery would be legal or illegal.

6. Essays should include some of the following points. For war: drive out British, who are encouraging attacks on western settlers; make West safer for settlers; put an end to impressment. Against war: will leave East Coast unprotected, will disrupt trade with Britain, army and navy too small to win.

Answer to . . .

Map Skills New free states.

The Missouri Compromise, 1820

Oregon Country (Occupied by U.S. and Great Britain)

Unorganized Territory

NEW SPAIN

States formed by Missouri Compromise

Free states and territories closed to slavery

Slave states and territories open to slavery

36° 30' N Missouri Compromise Line

Under the terms of the Missouri Compromise, Maine was admitted as a free state, Missouri was admitted as a slave state, and slavery was prohibited north of 36° 30' N latitude. *Region* Which would cover more land under the compromise, new free states or new slave states?

northwest of the Ohio River, it was not covered by this definition. Several members of Congress from the North objected to admitting Missouri as a slave state. They were not simply concerned about the liberty of African Americans; they worried that another slave state would increase the power of the southern states in the Senate. Southern members of Congress replied that the federal government had no business dictating to states what they could and could not do. They feared that if the federal government could forbid slavery in Missouri, it could do so elsewhere.

After months of bitter debate, Congress reached what is now called the **Missouri Compromise.** It was signed into law in 1820. The Missouri compromise had two main points: (1) Slavery would be permitted in Missouri; at the same time, Maine was carved out of what had been northern Massachusetts and admitted to the Union as a free, or nonslave, state. This arrangement kept the balance in the Senate between slave and free states. (2) Furthermore, Congress agreed that as the United States expanded westward, states north of 36° 30' N latitude would be free states, as the map above shows.

To Thomas Jefferson, still a keen observer of the national scene, the Missouri controversy "filled [him] with terror." Could compromises enable the United States to avoid confronting the issue of slavery indefinitely? As Jefferson had written earlier about the existence of slavery in a democratic republic: "I tremble for my country when I reflect that God is just: that His justice cannot sleep forever."

SECTION 5 REVIEW

Comprehension

1. *Key Terms* Define: (a) impressment; (b) War of 1812; (c) Treaty of Ghent; (d) Battle of New Orleans; (e) depression; (f) Missouri Compromise.

2. *Summarizing the Main Idea* Describe how the War of 1812 ended.

3. *Organizing Information* Create a chart comparing the strengths and weaknesses of the Americans during the war.

Critical Thinking

4. *Analyzing Time Lines* Review the time line at the start of the section. How does the time line reveal that the Americans faced two enemies during the War of 1812?

5. *Predicting Consequences* What issue was left unresolved by the Missouri Compromise?

Writing Activity

6. *Writing a Persuasive Essay* Write an essay persuading members of Congress either to vote for or against war with Britain in 1812.

RESOURCE OPTIONS

Teaching Resources

Quiz Units 1–2 folder, p. 79

Chapter Tests Forms A and B Chapter Test folder

Student Performance Pack

Guide to the Essentials Chapter 6, Section 5 (English and Spanish)

Standardized Test Preparation Handbook

Media and Technology

Guided Reading Audiotapes Chapter 6 Summary (English and Spanish)
Student Edition on Audiotape Chapter 6

Test Bank CD-ROM; Interactive Student Tutorial CD-ROM Chapter Test

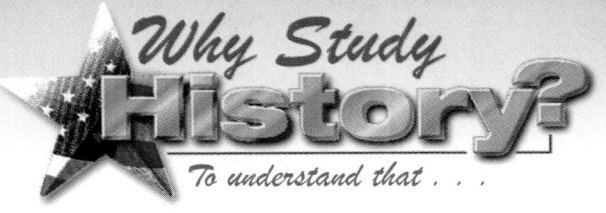

Why Study History?

To understand that . . .

You Can Join a Political Party

Political parties arose, over President Washington's opposition, in the 1790s. A two-party system dominates American political life today.

Women voted alongside men in New Jersey's early history.

The first Tuesday in November, millions of Americans enter voting booths to elect candidates for local, state, and national office. As they pull a lever or mark a paper ballot, they may be voting on the basis of the candidates' qualifications or ideas. Alternatively, they may be voting on the basis of candidates' political party affiliation. Political parties play a leading role in the American political system—a much greater role than the founders of the nation ever intended.

The Impact Today

The nation's early leaders initially opposed political parties. (For example, James Madison argued that parties would fill Congress with unqualified candidates who would use their position to pursue selfish goals.) Yet during George Washington's presidency these same men actively encouraged the rise of parties. Washington's Cabinet was bitterly divided into two groups that took opposite sides on important issues. The two opposing groups formed political parties to win support for their views.

For most of our history, two major parties have dominated American politics. In the 1790s, the two parties were the Federalists and Republicans. Since the mid-1800s they have been the Democrats and Republicans. From time to time, however, an independent candidate or third party challenges the two-party system. One recent example occurred in 1992, when Texas entrepreneur Ross Perot received almost 19 percent of the popular vote for President.

Many nations in the world have multiple parties—sometimes as many as two dozen or more. Some people argue that a multiple-party system allows more views to be represented. With only two strong parties, they say, voters have less of a choice.

Other people argue that multiple parties create confusion. Reaching agreement is already difficult in the American Congress, which is dominated by only two parties. Think how much harder it must be for legislators to compromise when they represent a dozen or more competing parties!

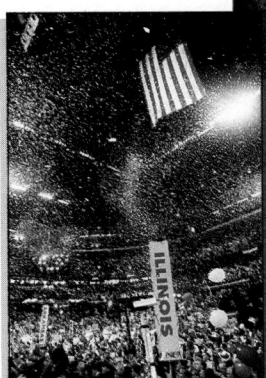

Delegates cheer at a national political convention.

The Impact on You

Choose a political issue (for example, the driving age) that interests you. Think of five positions on the issue. Assign each position to a separate, fictitious political party. Ask your classmates to vote on the position that they support. Note the results. What do they suggest about a system with many political parties?

RESOURCE OPTIONS

Teaching Resources

 Why Study History? Activity You Can Join a Political Party, found in the Why Study History? folder, p. 7, provides an activity to help students understand political parties and platforms.

Media and Technology

 AmericanHeritage® CD-ROM

Time Tour The New Republic: The New Government Begins (*Rise of Political Parties*)

Class Discussion

Discuss with the class the role of political parties. For a more thorough examination of the issue, see the activity folder in the Resource Options below.

ACTIVITY
STUDENT PARTICIPATION

Creating a Chart

Ask students to read the text. Then divide the class into three groups. Have each group make a chart showing the strengths and weaknesses of a one-party, two-party, or multiple-party system. Each chart should address these issues:

- **ability to represent many points of view**
- **tendency toward dictatorship**
- **efficiency of government**
- **stability of government**
- **quality of candidates**

Have the groups present their charts. Encourage discussion.

Follow up Have students vote on which system they would choose if they were setting up a new government.

Using the Internet

Students can learn more about political parties by exploring links in the *America: Pathways to the Present* Web site at

http://www.Pathways.phschool.com

Assessment

See the Lesson Plans folder, pp. 24–27, for rubrics on assessing Class Participation Projects.

Key Terms

Students should refer to the definitions of the key terms in the chapter to write sentences that show an understanding of the events that took place in the United States following the ratification of the Constitution.

Comprehension

1. Hamilton transformed the debts of all the states into a long-term investment in the United States government by the country's creditors. He did this by having the federal government take on the states' debts.
2. They knew that federal laws would not mean anything to people unless they were enforced by the federal government.
3. Federalists believed in a strong central government to maintain order in the country. Jeffersonian Republicans favored a weaker central government and stronger state governments as well as protection of individual rights and freedoms.
4. The goal of Prosser's Rebellion was freedom from slavery.
5. The goals of the Lewis and Clark expedition were to search for river routes to the western ocean, make contact with the Native Americans living in the territory, and gather information about the region's natural resources.
6. Tenskwatawa strongly opposed assimilation by Native Americans to European culture. He called for a return to traditional Native American ways. Tecumseh favored united military action against American settlers.
7. Many members of Congress believed that the British were inciting and arming Native Americans in the West to attack American settlers. Americans were also offended by Britain's ongoing practice of impressment.

Chapter Summary

The major concepts of Chapter 6 are presented below. See also *Guide to the Essentials of American History* or *Interactive Student Tutorial CD-ROM,* which contains interactive review activities, time lines, helpful hints, and test practice for Chapter 6.

Reviewing the Main Ideas

During the 1790s two political parties emerged: the Federalists, who favored a strong central government, and the Jeffersonian Republicans, who favored a smaller and weaker central government. Despite the tensions between these two parties, the nation's first peaceful transfer of power took place with the election of 1800. The United States increased its size with the Louisiana Purchase in 1803, but its new boundaries brought the nation into conflict with both Native Americans and the British.

Section 1: Liberty Versus Order in the 1790s

Americans became sharply divided in the 1790s over whether order or liberty was more important.

Section 2: The Government Takes a New Course

With the election of 1800, Americans peacefully accomplished the nation's first transfer of power from one party to another.

Section 3: The Jefferson Administration

As President, Jefferson sought to reduce the power of the federal government. Yet he also demonstrated the government's power when he bought new lands and restricted foreign trade.

Section 4: Native American Resistance

As the United States continued to expand onto their lands, Native Americans responded in various ways, from acceptance to war.

Section 5: The War of 1812

Americans emerged from the War of 1812 with a new sense of national pride, but economic and moral conflicts continued to trouble the country.

You Can Join a Political Party Political parties arose, over President Washington's opposition, in the 1790s. A two-party system dominates American political life today.

Key Terms

For each of the terms below, write a sentence explaining how it relates to this chapter.

1. strict construction
2. tariff
3. Whiskey Rebellion
4. XYZ Affair
5. Alien and Sedition Acts of 1798
6. *Marbury* v. *Madison*
7. judicial review
8. Louisiana Purchase
9. embargo
10. Jay's Treaty
11. Missouri Compromise
12. War of 1812
13. Battle of New Orleans
14. Lewis and Clark expedition

Comprehension

1. How was Alexander Hamilton able to change the national debt from a weakness to a strength?
2. Why was the federal government determined to crush the Whiskey Rebellion?
3. Summarize the views of Federalists and Jeffersonian Republicans in the 1790s.
4. What was the goal of Gabriel Prosser's Rebellion?
5. What were the goals of the Lewis and Clark expedition?
6. Explain Tenskwatawa's and Tecumseh's beliefs about the path that Native Americans should follow.
7. What were the causes of the War of 1812?

Using Graphic Organizers

On a separate sheet of paper, copy the graphic organizer below to organize the main ideas of the chapter. Fill in at least one choice or action taken by the group identified in the heading.

Problems and Choices, 1789–1820		
White Americans	African Americans	Native Americans

Using Graphic Organizers

Students should include some of the following points in their tree map.
- In choosing between order and liberty Federalists chose to assert order.
- Jeffersonian Republicans chose a return to individual liberties.
- Whiskey Rebels chose armed resistance.
- In reaction to slavery some African Americans chose armed resistance during Gabriel Prosser's Rebellion.
- In reaction to losing control over their lands, Little Turtle chose accommodation, Handsome Lake chose spiritual renewal, Tenskwatawa and Tecumseh chose spiritual renewal and armed resistance.

Analyzing Political Cartoons ▶

1. During the Embargo of 1807, smuggling increased dramatically. (a) How do you know the man with the barrel is a smuggler? (b) What is *Ograbme* spelled backwards? (c) What does the turtle represent?

2. How does Ograbme depict the embargo's effect on traders?

3. What is the cartoonist's view of the Embargo of 1807?

Critical Thinking

1. *Applying the Chapter Skill* Compare Jefferson's enforcement of the Embargo Act of 1807 to Washington's reaction to the Whiskey Rebellion. In what ways were they similar?

2. *Identifying Assumptions* Today we expect a peaceful transfer of power when Americans vote to change political parties in a presidential election. Why were people unable to make this assumption in the election of 1800?

3. *Predicting Consequences* Thomas Jefferson said that the Missouri Compromise "filled [him] with terror." Why might Jefferson have viewed the compromise with such fear?

ANALYZING DOCUMENTS ◀ ▶ INTERPRETING DATA

Turn to the graph of United States exports on page 195.

1. In which year was the value of United States exports the highest? (a) 1801 (b) 1807 (c) 1810 (d) 1818

2. Which of the following events explains the drop in trade between 1810 and 1814? (a) the Embargo of 1807 (b) the Missouri Compromise (c) the War of 1812 (d) the Louisiana Purchase

3. *Writing* Write an essay in which you describe the causes of the low points on this graph. Be sure to include examples of political effects.

INTERNET ACTIVITY

For your portfolio:
CREATE A TIME LINE

Access Prentice Hall's *America: Pathways to the Present* site at **www.Pathways.phschool.com** for the specific URL to complete the activity. Additional resources and related Web sites are also available.

Use excerpts from the journals of Meriwether Lewis and William Clark to create an annotated time line of their journey.

Connecting to Today

Recogizing Cause and Effect Review the Turning Point time line on page 186. Research and write an essay on one of the last two events shown on the time line.

Analyzing Political Cartoons

1. (a) Because he is carrying goods to a British ship (seen in harbor). (b) Embargo. (c) The Embargo of 1807.
2. It is hurting the tradesman (smuggler) and restraining him from conducting business.
3. The cartoonist is opposed to the embargo because it hurts trade.

Critical Thinking

1. Both were situations in which the leaders of the federal government used force to ensure compliance with unpopular federal laws.
2. Presidential elections prior to 1800 were won by members of the party that was in power.
3. The compromise put off for the future the important debate over slavery and failed to resolve this important issue. Jefferson feared that the unresolved issue of slavery could lead to war or the dissolution of the country.

Interpreting Data

1. b
2. c

Students' essays should include some of the following points. 1808: Embargo of 1807 cut off all foreign trade, enforced by Jefferson. 1814: War of 1812 blockade by British virtually halted all trade.

Connecting to Today

Answers should demonstrate an understanding of the event that students have chosen.

INTERNET ACTIVITY

Answers will vary. Students may create a time line of the entire expedition, or of a particular leg of the journey.

Life in the New Nation, 1783–1830

Managing Time and Instruction

INSTRUCTION SUPPORT

These materials for instruction are provided for **each section** in the **Teaching Resources.** See **Units 1–2 folder** for Enrichment Support:

- Reproducible Lesson Plans in Lesson Plans folder • Learning Styles Lesson Plans in Learning Styles Lesson Plans folder • Big Idea Graphic Organizers in Big Idea Graphic Organizer folder
- Guided Reading and Review • Quizzes • Test Preparation Practice booklet

DAILY LESSON	ENRICHMENT SUPPORT
1 **Crossing the Appalachians** *(pp. 201–205)*	• Nystrom *Atlas of Our Country,* Early Expansion of the United States, pp. 20–21 • Critical Thinking Activity, Making Comparisons: Population Boom, found on **Resource Pro** • Primary Source Activity, Moving West, found on **Resource Pro** • Literature Activity, The Pioneers, Units 1–2 folder, pp. 96–97 • Skills for Life Activity, Units 1–2 folder, p. 98
2 **Inventions and Innovations** *(pp. 207–213)*	• Biography, Catherine Littlefield Greene, Units 1–2 folder, p. 93 • Comparing Primary Sources, On Educating the People, Units 1–2 folder, pp. 94–95 • Literature Activity, The Natural World, found on **Resource Pro** • Biography, Anne Newport Royall, found on **Resource Pro**
3 **Social and Religious Life** *(pp. 216–222)*	• Visual Learning Activity, "Married Mum?" found on **Resource Pro** • Visual Learning Activity, "Do They Miss Me at Home?" Learning with Documents folder, p. 49 • Primary Source Activity, The American Spirit, Learning with Documents folder, p. 13 • You Live in the Information Age, Why Study History? folder, p. 8

Running Out of Time?

- Use Tape 2, "Balancing Liberty and Order, 1781–1830," from **Visions of America** videotapes series.
- Use Chapter 7 Summary, from **Guide to the Essentials of American History (English and Spanish).**

Companion Web Site

The companion Web site offers online links for all chapter review activities. It also provides key content links and structured support for this chapter for both teachers and students.

http://www.Pathways.phschool.com

Teaching in the Information Age

Media and Technology

For the Student

Interactive Student Tutorial CD-ROM Chapter 7

Student Edition on Audiotape Chapter 7

American Heritage® CD-ROM

Guided Reading Audiotapes (English and Spanish) Chapter 7

For the Teacher

Resource Pro CD-ROM Chapter 7

Test Bank CD-ROM Chapter 7

Listening to Literature Audiotapes *Timeless Voices, Timeless Themes* from *Life on the Mississippi* by Mark Twain

Listening to Music CD Aaron Copland, from *Appalachian Spring*

Color Transparencies Our Multicultural Heritage, C-7

Assessment Options

Chapter Test Forms A&B Test Bank CD-ROM booklet

Test Bank CD-ROM Chapter 7

Standardized Test Preparation Handbook

Block Scheduling

Pacing Suggestions

For 90-minute Blocks

- Teach sections 1 and 2 using Transparencies I-3, C-10, D-6, H-6, and H-7 and the Recent Scholarship note on p. 202 for class discussions.
- Teach section 3 using the Big Idea Graphic Organizer from Teaching Resources and the Extended Class Periods Activity found on p. 221.

Additional Resources

- Prentice Hall's **American History Block Scheduling Support File** covers over 40 major topics in American history. Included are lesson plans, strategies, primary sources, literature, biographies, Great Debates, art history, simulations, and songs.
- **Prentice Hall United States History Video Collection™** contains 20 videotapes covering American history from beginnings to present.

Connections to American Literature

from Prentice Hall

America: Pathways to the Present from *April Morning* by Howard Fast, p. 1074

Prentice Hall Literature *Timeless Voices, Timeless Themes* "The Devil and Tom Walker," by Washington Irving, pp. 236–245

Additional Resources

For the Student

Constance Green. *Eli Whitney and the Birth of American Technology.* Scott Foresman, 1956.

Washington Irving. *The Sketch Book of Geoffrey Crayton.* Penguin, 1988.

For the Teacher

Nancy F. Cott. *The Bonds of Womanhood: "Woman's Sphere" in New England, 1780–1835.* Yale University Press, 1977.

Prentice Hall brings into the classroom the vast archives and scholarship of the nation's premier American history magazine. See "From the Archives of American Heritage®" and "About the Presidents" teaching notes in this chapter.

History Alive!

Teacher's Curriculum Institute, in partnership with Prentice Hall, provides unique materials that engage students with diverse learning styles. See History Alive!® unit on Manifest Destiny in a Growing Nation.

Student Performance Pack

Ensures success in the three critical areas of Reading, Test Taking, and English Language Development with the following materials:

- Guide to the Essentials of American History in English and Spanish
- Guided Reading Audiotapes in English and Spanish
- Interactive Student Tutorial CD-ROM
- Test Preparation Handbook
- Test Preparation Practice booklet

Life in the New Nation
1783–1830

Introducing the Chapter
Dramatic population growth and movement, as well as new technology, brought both opportunities and uncertainties to the people of the new republic. Americans responded to the changes with growing confidence in material progress and religious salvation.

Themes in American History
The theme for this chapter, Science and Technology, is listed at the beginning of this unit. An alternate theme for the chapter is Geography. To teach this unit thematically, you may wish to use the Forging a New Nation folder in American History Block Scheduling Support.

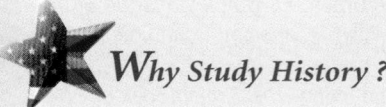

Why Study History ?

Have students explore suggested ways of connecting the past to the present on page 223.

Answer to . . .

Viewing History Students should use this question as an aid in reading the chapter. Americans were experiencing explosive population growth, with a doubling in population every 20 years. Also, technology and industry were booming, and religious movements were sweeping the country.

200

CHAPTER 7
Life in the New Nation
1783-1830

CHAPTER FOCUS

This chapter describes the changes in culture and lifestyle in the United States during the early years of the republic. In this period, the nation's population grew rapidly. Americans faced many challenges and made great advances in technology. Some experienced a new awakening in their spiritual life.

 The Why Study History? page at the end of this chapter explores the connection between inventions that transformed American life in the late 1700s and the technological revolution occurring today.

▲
VIEWING HISTORY John Hull's 1830s engraving shows the Erie Canal, one of the developments in transportation that led to changes in the young republic. *Culture* **In what other areas of life were Americans experiencing change?**

 RESOURCE OPTIONS

Teaching Resources

📁 **Big Idea Graphic Organizer** folder
Graphic summary of the main idea of the chapter.

📁 **Learning Styles Lesson Plans** folder
Alternate lesson plans for diverse learning styles for each chapter.

Media and Technology

 AmericanHeritage® **CD-ROM**
Time Tour The New Republic: The New Government *and* The Jefferson Era

  Prentice Hall United States History Video Collection™ Volume 6
Expansionism

1775 Wilderness Road constructed	1787 Northwest Ordinance	1795 Pinckney Treaty		1819 Adams-Onís Treaty	1827 Cherokee declare themselves an independent nation

1775	1790	1805	1820	1835

1 Crossing the Appalachians

SECTION PREVIEW

Objectives

1. List the major reasons why the nation's population became larger and younger between 1780 and 1830.
2. Describe the westward movement of white and African American pioneers to west of the Appalachians.
3. Explain how Native Americans were forced west of the Mississippi.
4. *Key Terms* Define: infant mortality rate; median age; trans-Appalachia; Wilderness Road; Pinckney Treaty; Adams-Onís Treaty; cede.

Main Idea

In the early years of the republic, a young and energetic population migrated west over the Appalachians and settled in the Ohio and Mississippi valleys and the Gulf Coast.

Reading Strategy

Outlining Information Skim the section and create an outline using the headings and subheadings. As you read, fill in your outline using supporting evidence from the section.

By the late 1700s and early 1800s, Americans were bursting with energy and enthusiasm about their new country. Many left their homes in the coastal states and headed inland in search of land, independence, and prosperity. In 1828, James Hall, who traveled through the Mississippi Valley as a circuit court judge, captured the mood of a nation on the move in a travel book called *Letters from the West.* Hall observed that "the innumerable caravans of adventurers who are daily crowding to the West in search of homes . . . produce a constant succession of visitors of every class and of almost every nation."

A Growing and Young Nation

That surge of people on the move was partly the result of a rapidly growing population. About 2.7 million people lived in the original thirteen states in 1780. By 1830, the population had grown to 12 million people in 24 states. The graph on the next page shows this

explosive increase in population. As the graph indicates, between 1780 and 1830 the population doubled about every twenty years. In fact, in the first half of the 1800s the American population grew more than twice as fast as that of any other nation.

Causes of Growth Unlike in other periods of American history, immigration did not play a very big role in the rapid growth of the American population during the early 1800s. As you will read later, the great rise in the number of immigrants from Germany and Ireland did not take place until the 1830s and 1840s. In addition, the arrival of Africans slowed during this time with a law, which took effect in 1808, that made it illegal to import slaves. Although some slave traders continued

This cradle from around 1800 symbolizes the young nation's population growth.

SECTION 1

Crossing the Appalachians

Objectives

You may wish to call students' attention to the objectives in the Section Preview. The objectives are reflected in the main headings of the section.

Bellringer

Tell students that in 1810 only one seventh of the American population of 7.2 million lived west of the Alleghenies; by 1840 more than one third of 17.2 million Americans lived there. Have them consider the impact of such rapid population growth.

Reading Strategy

Outlining Information Refer to the Reading Strategy in the Section Preview. You may wish to model the outline on the chalkboard. Have students use their outlines to keep track of the section.

LESSON PLAN

Connecting to the Main Idea

1. **Focus** Tell students that a young, energetic generation of Americans of both European and African heritage crossed the Appalachians during this period and moved into the river valleys from the Ohio to the mouth of the Mississippi. Ask what effect this migration had on the original inhabitants of these regions.

2. **Instruct** Call students' attention to the quotation on the following page. How could it be said that "Old America seems to be breaking up"? What was the "Old America" to which Morris Birkbeck referred? What ideals, concerns, and dreams caused this upheaval? Ask why Native Americans were forced to move at this time.

3. **Close** A young, restless United States population was on the move in the early Republic. As described in the next section, this energy would also be expressed in efforts to become an educated, disciplined, and technological society.

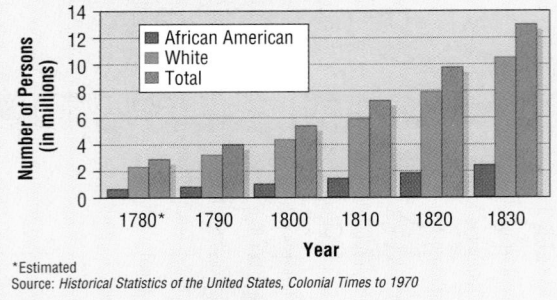

Number of Persons (in millions)

- African American
- White
- Total

1780* 1790 1800 1810 1820 1830

Year

*Estimated
Source: *Historical Statistics of the United States, Colonial Times to 1970*

Interpreting Graphs The census, a national head count taken every ten years, recorded the startling population growth of the United States. *Diversity Which group grew more rapidly, whites or African Americans? About how much did the total population increase between 1780 and 1830?*

to smuggle Africans into the United States, by the early 1800s the slave trade had mostly become internal.

Immigration, therefore, accounted for only about 10 percent of the American population growth during this period. The other 90 percent of the growth came from an astonishing increase in the number of children born to each family. Between 1800 and 1849, the average American woman had nearly five children. By comparison, in the decade after 1870 the average woman would have only about three children.

During the early 1800s the white population grew a good deal faster than the black population. As a result, the percentage of the American population that was of African descent began to change from a high of 20 percent in 1790. By the early 1900s, only 10 percent of Americans were of African descent.

The huge growth of the population is all the more amazing in view of the high **infant mortality rate** at the time. The infant mortality rate is the rate at which infants (babies less than one year old) die. It is often given in terms of a certain number of deaths per thousand births. During the early 1800s, the infant mortality rate was probably at least 130 deaths per thousand births. By comparison, the rate at the end of the 1900s was only about 8 deaths per thousand births. More babies died in the early 1800s than now because people then did not

know how to treat infant illnesses. Yet because of the high birth rate, large numbers of infants did survive, and the population boomed.

Low Median Age The large number of children meant that most of the population was young. The **median age** of Americans in 1820 was about 17. That is, half of the population was under the age of seventeen, and half was over that age. By comparison, today the median age is about 33.

With a growing and youthful population, America was buzzing with energy. Young couples dreamed of working hard to make a good future for themselves and their families. The place to make those dreams come true, many of them felt, was the area west of the Appalachian Mountains, a region known as **trans-Appalachia.**

Pioneers Move West

In the late 1780s, only a few hundred white Americans lived north of the Ohio River. By 1830 there were hundreds of thousands of Americans living in the region, which by then consisted of Michigan Territory and three new states. These new states were Ohio (with close to 1,000,000 residents), Indiana (with almost 350,000 residents), and Illinois (with over 150,000 residents).

Life on the Frontier Most of the settlers in the region north of the Ohio River had traveled down the river from western Pennsylvania and Virginia, or northward from Kentucky and Tennessee. In either case, the journey was long and difficult. Settlers usually moved as families, although young men often traveled west alone. An English traveler crossing the Appalachians in the spring of 1817 described the scene on the road:

❝Old America seems to be breaking up and moving westward. We are seldom out of sight, as we travel on this grand track towards the Ohio, of family groups behind and before us, some [intending to go] to a particular spot, close to a brother perhaps, or [to] a friend who has gone before and reported well of the country.❞

—*Morris Birkbeck*

Once the newcomers settled on a piece of land, they faced a heavy burden of work. Families toiled to clear the land, plant a crop, and build a house, all with hand tools and muscle power. To survive, they developed quick methods for building shelter and clearing the land. Until they had time to build a better home, settlers found shelter in a rough log cabin or a lean-to. Instead of wasting energy chopping down trees, they scarred the bark so that the trees died, a method called girdling. Settlers also used fire to clear the undergrowth. Here in rough fields among the leafless trunks they planted corn, counting on a good harvest to feed them through the next winter.

Daniel Boone People from many different backgrounds settled the trans-Appalachian region. One settler, Daniel Boone, became a legend in his own lifetime, though in many ways he was no different from thousands of other pioneers. In 1775, the Transylvania Company employed Boone and a group of men to cut the **Wilderness Road** through the Cumberland Gap, a low spot in the Appalachian Mountains.[†] This road began in eastern Tennessee and ended in what is now Louisville, Kentucky. It became the main route to trans-Appalachia for countless Americans, including Boone's own family.

After the Revolution, Boone became a leading citizen of the Ohio Valley. He was a member of the Kentucky state legislature as well as a hunter and a trapper. Moving west with the growing nation, he migrated to Missouri in 1799. When he died there in 1820, his fame as a bold and tough pioneer had spread across the nation.

Expansion into Florida Boone's Kentucky was just one area south of the Ohio River that drew settlers. They also swarmed into other lands in the South. The population in Alabama, Mississippi, and Louisiana swelled as settlers moved to the region. Even Florida, which only became part of the United States in 1819, gained 35,000 American settlers by 1830.

The story of how the United States acquired Florida begins in 1795. In that year the United States and Spain agreed to the **Pinckney Treaty,** named after the

---

[†] The Transylvania Company wanted to establish Kentucky as the fourteenth colony, but the Revolutionary War started before the colony was organized.

American diplomat who arranged it, Thomas Pinckney. The treaty settled several points, including the following:

(1) The southern boundary of the United States was set at 31° N latitude, leaving Florida firmly in Spanish hands.

(2) United States citizens would be allowed free use of the Mississippi River through Spanish territory.

(3) Spain and the United States agreed to control the Native Americans living within each country's territories and to prevent them from attacking the other country's territory.

During the 1810s, Spain faced rebellions in its South American colonies. Fearing that it would lose its empire, the Spanish government tried desperately to put down these uprisings. In the meantime, it paid little attention to its two colonies of East and West Florida. The Seminoles, a Native American group living in the Floridas, took advantage of the lax control and stepped up their raids on settlers in southern Georgia. The Seminoles also angered American officials by allowing escaped slaves to live among them.

The general in charge of protecting the settlers was the tough veteran of the War of 1812, Andrew Jackson. When told to put an end to the attacks, Jackson noted that he would have to cross into the Spanish Floridas. "Let it be signified to me," Jackson wrote President Monroe, "that the possession of the Floridas would be desirable to the United States, and in sixty days it will be accomplished." Though Monroe did not openly encourage him, Jackson decided to go ahead with his plan to invade the Floridas.

General Jackson was as good as his promise. Setting out in March 1818 with only 2,000 men,

Starting a new home in Ohio was tough work for most of the nearly 1 million people who settled there by 1830. *Economics* *What tasks are shown in the picture?*

RESOURCE OPTIONS

Teaching Resources

American History Block Scheduling Support No Neighbors for Miles: The Northwest Territory, found in the Forging a New Nation folder, includes interdisciplinary lesson suggestions and activities for Geography and History, Primary Sources, Biography, and Literature.

Media and Technology

 AmericanHeritage® **CD-ROM**

History Makers Daniel Boone

Presidents James Monroe

 Listening to Music CD Aaron Copland, from *Appalachian Spring*

Hundreds of thousands of enslaved African Americans settled with their owners in the area west of the Appalachians. This sketch by Louis Miller shows a group on the march from Virginia to Tennessee. **Government** *What factors limited African American migration north of the Ohio River?*

he swept across the border and within a few weeks claimed possession of the entire western part of the territory. Spain was outraged and Congress threatened to condemn Jackson. Most Americans, however, applauded Jackson's move.

Monroe and his Secretary of State, John Quincy Adams, decided to make the best of the situation. Refusing to apologize for Jackson's actions, Adams accused Spain of breaking the Pinckney Treaty by failing to control the Seminoles.

The Spanish were not in a good position to argue. If the United States recognized and supported the new nations forming in South America, Spain would have no hope of holding onto its colonies there. Besides, the Americans were already in possession of the two Floridas. The Spanish decided they might as well try to get something for the land they had already lost.

Spain's representative in Washington, Don Luiz de Onís y Gonzales, spent weeks working out a treaty with Adams. Finally, in 1819, the two men agreed on what has since been called the Transcontinental Treaty, or **Adams-Onís Treaty.** Spain agreed to **cede,** or give up, Florida to the United States. Spain also gave up its long-held claim on the Pacific Northwest. Now for the first time the United States stretched from the Atlantic to the Pacific Ocean.

The Adams-Onís Treaty also fixed the boundary between the Louisiana Purchase and Spanish territory in the West. To settle the dispute over this boundary, the United States agreed to cede its claims to a huge territory in what is now the southwestern United States, including part of Texas.

African American Pioneers

While the majority of new settlers in Florida and other areas of the South were white, many were African Americans. An estimated 98,000 slaves moved west with their owners between 1790 and 1810. When the people brought directly from Africa or from the West Indies are added in, some 194,000 African Americans settled in Kentucky, Tennessee, and the Gulf Coast states. Another 144,000 followed between 1810 and 1820.

North of the Ohio River, slavery had been forbidden by the Northwest Ordinance of 1787. Supposedly, African Americans who gained their freedom could live in this region. Yet many settlers north of the Ohio did not want free African Americans in their states. In particular, they feared that African Americans would compete for land and jobs. Therefore they made laws to discourage African Americans from moving in. In Illinois, for example, one law required African American immigrants to post a $1,000 security bond unless they already owned land.

Native Americans Forced West

Native Americans, too, were moving during the early 1800s. In most cases, they were forced to move. Native Americans gradually lost their land to the United States government in one treaty after another. As they lost their homelands, Indians were compelled to make long and dangerous journeys to new areas west of the Mississippi River.

No matter where Native Americans lived, their numbers continued to shrink. The main cause of their decline continued to be diseases brought by white settlers. Devastating epidemics regularly swept through Indian villages on both sides of the Mississippi River.

Native American Land Transfer Before 1850

A map can only hint at the hardship and turmoil of being forced to move. For instance, the Seminole people fought United States troops well into the 1840s to avoid being removed from their homeland. Some remain in their homeland even today. *Place Where is the Seminole homeland?*

Though many Native Americans fought to preserve their way of life, one group, the Cherokee, chose to adapt instead. Under leaders such as John Ross, the Cherokee created a legal system and government that blended Cherokee and European traditions.

Many of the Cherokee gave up the practice of owning property in common and accepted the custom of private property. The Cherokee practiced slavery and held 1,300 African American slaves. They became farmers and produced a variety of goods. They published their own newspaper, using an alphabet invented by one of their leaders, Sequoyah. In 1827 the Cherokee even declared themselves an independent nation.

However, neither adopting the ways of white people nor insisting on their independence would save the Cherokee. Too many white settlers were hungry for their land.

SECTION 1 REVIEW

Comprehension

1. **Key Terms** Define: (a) infant mortality rate; (b) median age; (c) trans-Appalachia; (d) Wilderness Road; (e) Pinckney Treaty; (f) Adams-Onís Treaty; (g) cede.

2. **Summarizing the Main Idea** What area did Americans settle in the early 1800s?

3. **Organizing Information** Create a web diagram that shows the causes of American population growth in the early 1800s.

Critical Thinking

4. **Analyzing Time Lines** Review the time line at the start of the section. Pick an entry and explain how it influenced the settlement of the trans-Appalachian region.

5. **Making Comparisons** How were the migrations of Native Americans different from those of people of European descent?

Writing Activity

6. **Writing a Persuasive Essay** In your view, would a young population be more likely to migrate than an older population? Write an essay explaining your opinion.

RESOURCE OPTIONS

Teaching Resources

 Quiz Units 1–2 folder, p. 88

Student Performance Pack

 Guide to the Essentials Chapter 7, Section 1 (English and Spanish)

Media and Technology

AmericanHeritage® CD-ROM

History Makers Sequoyah

SKILLS FOR LIFE

Geography

Using Population Density Maps

Focus Analyze and draw conclusions from a population density map.

Instruct Review the concept of population density. Ask: Is your school in a densely populated region? Is your county or township densely populated? What parts of your state are more densely populated than others? Have students read the text on this page.

Extend See Skills for Life Activity in the Resource Options below.

Answers

1. (a) A range of population densities. (b) Darkest: a population density of 90 or more persons per square mile; lightest: a population density of two or fewer persons per square mile. (c) No. Rhode Island had more people per square mile than any other state, but it had the least land area.

2. (a) 1790: Mass., Rhode Island, Conn., New York, Penn., New Jersey, Virginia; 1830: Maine, New Hampshire, Mass., Rhode Island, Conn., New York, Penn., New Jersey, Virginia, Ohio, Indiana, Kentucky, Tenn. (b) New York, Penn., Ohio, Indiana, Kentucky, Tennessee, Louisiana, Alabama, and Georgia.

3. (a) Land in the South was taken up with crops—not people. The North's economy was more diversified. (b) Rivers, because nearby land was fertile, and they could be used to transport goods. Mountains probably discouraged settlement, because their rugged terrain was difficult to farm.

TEST FOR SUCCESS

Sample answer: Differences—in 1790 people settled largely along the East Coast, by 1830 they had migrated westward. Similarities—in both years the Northeast was the most densely populated.

Using Population Density Maps

Figures for population density indicate the average number of people living in a given area—usually a square mile or square kilometer. Population density maps can show density for a small area, such as a city, or a very large area, such as a continent or the entire world.

Overall patterns of human settlement at a particular period of time can also be shown on a population density map. The population density maps on this page, for example, provide a broad picture of the number of white and black people living in the United States at two different points in time—1790 and 1830. These maps are based on United States census counts, which at that time did not include Native Americans.

Use the following steps to read and analyze the population density maps below.

1. Determine what information the maps provide. To interpret the population data, first look at the map key and then at the maps. (a) What kind of information is represented by the color-coded key on each map? (b) What do the darkest and lightest colors on each key represent? (c) You can tell at a glance that Rhode Island was the most densely populated state in 1790. Do you think that it also had the largest total population of any state? Explain.

2. Analyze population density patterns. Study the maps and answer the following questions. (a) Which states on each map had population densities of 45 or more people per square mile? (b) Which states experienced the greatest and most widespread increase in population density between 1790 and 1830?

3. Study the maps to draw conclusions. Relate what you know from your reading to what you see on the maps. (a) What economic factors do you think accounted for the difference between the population densities of the North and South, both in 1790 and 1830? (b) What geographical factors probably contributed to the overall pattern of settlement in 1830? Explain.

TEST FOR SUCCESS

What differences and similarities are apparent in the human settlement patterns in the United States in 1790 and 1830?

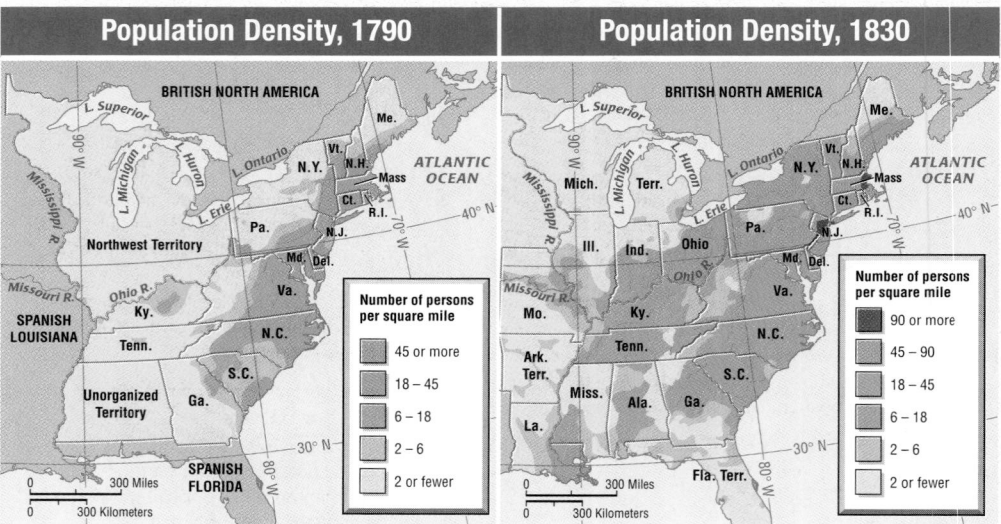

RESOURCE OPTIONS

Teaching Resources

Skills for Life Activity Units 1–2 folder, p. 98, provides an opportunity for students to apply the skill by examining a 1990 population density map of the western United States.

1793	1793	1807		
Samuel Slater opens first textile mill in Rhode Island	Eli Whitney invents the cotton gin	Robert Fulton's steamboat makes first commercially successful steamboat trip	**1811** Construction begins on the Cumberland Road	**1825** Erie Canal opens

1790	1800	1810	1820	1830

2 Inventions and Innovations

SECTION PREVIEW

Objectives

1. Describe the spirit of improvement in American society during the early 1800s, including women's role in promoting virtue.
2. Show how the Industrial Revolution affected the nation's economy through inventions such as the cotton gin.
3. Provide examples of the advances that produced "revolutions" in transportation and communication.
4. *Key Terms* Define: republican virtues; Industrial Revolution; emigrate; interchangeable parts; cotton gin; Erie Canal; Cumberland Road; turnpike.

Main Idea

A new sense of freedom pushed Americans to experiment and invent new and better ways to do tasks.

Reading Strategy

Reinforcing Main Ideas As you read, look for evidence of the "spirit of improvement" during the late 1700s and early 1800s. Make a list of specific ways in which Americans tried to improve their lives.

O ne of the great themes in American history has been the search to make life better. The need to survive and the hope of making a profit led many Americans to invent and innovate, or find new ways of doing things. This spirit of improvement is not unique to the United States. It reflects, in part, the ideals of the Enlightenment. Yet it has been especially strong and widespread in the United States.

The Spirit of Improvement

One way to better the general condition of humankind, Americans believed, was through education. In this spirit, Americans began to focus on the importance of learning.

Cultural Leaders As a result of increased prosperity, a growing number of people had the time to devote themselves to scholarship. Many well-educated men and women contributed to the development of American learning.

Mercy Otis Warren. Warren was friendly with many of the well-known Americans who were active during the Revolution, including Martha Custis Washington, George Washington's wife. Believing she had a duty to participate during the war, Warren hosted political meetings at her home in Plymouth, Massachusetts. She also wrote several patriotic plays encouraging the cause of independence, and in 1805 she wrote a book titled *History of the American Revolution*. She actively encouraged other women to take up scholarly interests, but cautioned them to balance their intellectual pursuits with domestic duties.

Benjamin Rush. A doctor, scientist, and revolutionary, Rush signed the Declaration of Independence and represented Pennsylvania in the Continental Congress. He also published numerous books on chemistry,

This 1839 traveling library was published for settlers in the West.

RESOURCE OPTIONS

Teaching Resources

📁 **Reproducible Lesson Plan** Lesson Plans folder, p. 61

📁 **Big Idea Graphic Organizer** Big Idea Graphic Organizer folder, p. 33

📁 **Guided Reading and Review** Units 1–2 folder, p. 89

SECTION 2

Inventions and Innovations

Objectives

You may wish to call students' attention to the objectives in the Section Preview. The objectives are reflected in the main headings of the section.

Bellringer

Have students list ways in which they or other people try to change either their own lives or society in general. Do people always respond favorably to efforts toward change? Why or why not?

Reading Strategy

Reinforcing Main Ideas Refer to the Reading Strategy in the Section Preview. You may wish to model students' lists on the chalkboard.

LESSON PLAN

Connecting to the Main Idea

1. Focus To many Americans, the Revolution seemed to mark a new era of experimentation and invention. Ask students what kinds of social change this new attitude brought about.

2. Instruct Point out that the ideas of rapid change, progress, and improvement of humankind are concepts most Americans take for granted today. This was not always the case, but after the Revolutionary War, a sense of new possibilities began to take hold among the nation's citizens. Discuss what caused this change in people's thinking. How did society's values change? What was the connection between changes in people's attitudes and changes in technology?

3. Close The post-Revolutionary period marked a time of invention, social progress, and material improvement. These changes, however, also brought uncertainty for many Americans. The next section describes the search for new rules to guide social relationships.

medicine, and mental illness. In a time when many thought mental illness was caused by the devil, Rush suggested that it was often the result of physical disease. His medical lectures in Philadelphia, which he began in 1790, attracted a wide audience.

Benjamin Banneker. Banneker was an African American writer, inventor, mathematician, and astronomer. Largely self-educated, Banneker used his skills in many tasks, including surveying (mapping out) the site of the nation's new capital of Washington, D.C. In 1791 he began publishing an almanac detailing the motions of the moon, sun, planets, and stars. He presented a copy to Thomas Jefferson, along with a letter calling for better treatment of enslaved Africans. Jefferson was so impressed that as President he asked Banneker to be one of his advisers.

Charles Willson Peale. Peale was a skilled artist who painted over a thousand portraits in his long life. Yet he was also a soldier in the Revolution, a representative in the Pennsylvania legislature, a scientist, an inventor, and the father of seventeen children. In 1786, he started the first major museum in the nation. Peale's Museum, as it was called, soon housed about 100,000 objects. Among its features was a series of Peale's own paintings of heroes of the Revolution. For Peale, the various objects in his museum were not simply curiosities. Before Peale's time, people had thought of art and science as luxuries for the wealthy. His museum proved that these fields could be a source of enjoyment and education for ordinary citizens of the new republic.

Phillis Wheatley. Bought by the Wheatley family of Boston in 1761, the young woman from Senegal, West Africa, was recognized early on for her intelligence and was allowed to learn to read and write. Wheatley published her first poem in 1770. Her reputation spread to Europe in 1773 when her collection, *Poems on Various Subjects, Religious and Moral,* was published in England under the direction of the Countess of Huntingdon. Wheatley gained further recognition and acclaim when a poem she wrote and dedicated to George Washington was published in 1776.

Education As interest in learning increased, some Americans called for better education for all. One such spokesman was Noah Webster, who dedicated much of his life to promoting education. In 1790 he wrote:

> **AMERICAN VOICES** "Americans, unshackle your minds, and act like independent beings. . . . You have an empire to raise and support by your exertions, and a national character to establish and extend by your wisdom and virtues. To effect these great objects, it is necessary to [build] a broad system of education."
>
> —Noah Webster

Webster's primary contribution to establishing America's "national character" was in the field of language. Webster called for establishing standards for the national language and backed up this call by compiling the first major dictionary of American English. It had a tremendous influence on later dictionary makers. In fact, some Americans today still use the word *Webster's* as a synonym for *dictionary.* Webster also wrote *The American Spelling Book.* It remained in print well into the 1900s, selling an estimated total of 100 million copies.

The growing republic offered a good market for Webster's speller. Many state constitutions required free public education for all children. Even though few state governments actually provided free education in those early years, academies, or private high schools, often filled the gap.

American schools had a big responsibility. In 1789 the Massachusetts legislature stated that the task of the state's schoolteachers was to teach students "the principles of piety, justice, and a sacred regard to truth, love to their

Here, women study music and geography at a school for young ladies around 1810. *Culture How was education part of the spirit of improvement?*

RESOURCE OPTIONS

Teaching Resources

📁 **Biography** Catherine Littlefield Greene, Units 1–2 folder, p. 93

Media and Technology

🦅 **AmericanHeritage® CD-ROM**

History Makers Benjamin Banneker, Phillis Wheatley

country, . . . chastity, moderation and temperance, and those other virtues which are the ornaments of human society, and the basis upon which the Republican Constitution is structured."

Like the Massachusetts legislature, many Americans were concerned about developing character by promoting certain virtues. The virtues the American people would need to govern themselves in the new republic were called **republican virtues.** They included sacrificing individual needs for the good of the community, self-reliance, industry, frugality, and harmony.

The Role of Women

In the early 1800s, Americans began to look to women to set the standard for republican virtues. After all, they reasoned, women were mothers, wives, and sometimes teachers. Thus women had a powerful influence on the men who would vote in, and rule, the nation. If women had such virtues as honesty, self-restraint, and discipline, they could teach these qualities to men.

To serve as examples of these virtues, however, women had to learn them first. In the late 1700s, the vast majority of schools were for boys only. As people began to see the value in educating girls, many academies added "female departments" to help girls become "republican women." A republican woman was one who had the virtues that would help her contribute to the success of the republic.

P. W. Jackson was a graduate of a women's academy in Connecticut. In 1809 she described her belief in the importance of education for women as follows:

> **AMERICAN VOICES** **❝**A woman who is skilled in every useful art, who practices every domestic virtue . . . may, by her [teaching] and example, inspire her brothers, her husband, or her sons, with such a love of virtue, such just ideas of the true value of civil liberty . . . that future heroes and statesmen, when arrived at the summit of military or political fame, shall exaltingly declare, it is to my mother I owe this [success].**❞**
>
> —*P. W. Jackson*

Jackson, like other men and women of her time, believed that republican women should play only a supporting role in the new nation. Though this attitude limited opportunities for

women, it was still a significant change. People were now beginning to think about the importance of women in the life of the republic.

The Industrial Revolution

Americans pursued profit with the same energy with which they pursued self-improvement and virtue. As the young republic expanded, Americans developed and profited from a variety of inventions that produced goods and materials faster and more cheaply.

Many of the inventions grew out of what is now known as the **Industrial Revolution.** This revolution was an ongoing effort over many decades to increase production by using machines powered by sources other than humans or animals. Several key British inventions sparked the Industrial Revolution in the 1700s. They were all built for the textile, or

---

Graphing the Main Idea

To make sure students understand the effects of the cotton gin, you may wish to use the web graphic organizer below.

Tell students that a web graphic organizer shows the effects or characteristics of an event. Ask students to use it to record the several points listed in the section.

Teaching Tip A template for this graphic organizer can be found in the Color Transparencies, G-1.

cloth-weaving, business. One invention in particular, however, led to improvements in many other fields besides textiles. This was James Watt's steam engine, developed in Britain between 1765 and 1785. It worked by harnessing the tremendous force given off by expanding steam.

The British jealously guarded all knowledge of their new technology. Anyone who knew about the design of new machines was forbidden to **emigrate,** or move out of the nation. However, Britain's secrets and its technological lead were spoiled by a man named Samuel Slater.

Samuel Slater

Samuel Slater was born in Derbyshire, England, in 1768. As a boy, he became an apprentice to a mill builder, Jedediah Strutt, who was a pioneer in the use of the new British textile technology.

Spending almost seven years working for Strutt, Slater learned how the machinery operated and how it was built and repaired. When his apprenticeship ended, Slater decided to emigrate to the United States. He had heard of rewards being offered to anyone who could bring the new technology from Britain, and he hoped to prosper in the new nation. Hiding his background from the British authorities, Slater left Britain for the United States in 1789.

Samuel Slater (1768–1835)

Once he was safe in his new country, Slater found a company to back him financially. Working from memory alone, he directed skilled mechanics who reproduced the complicated machinery of the British mills. Soon he was made a partner in the company. In 1793, he and his partners established the first successful textile mill in the United States in Pawtucket, Rhode Island. They chose the spot because of a waterfall in the river there, which provided power for their new mill.

In 1798, Slater started a new company of his own. He made his own machines and built another mill in Pawtucket. Within a few years, he was expanding his business throughout New England. After he had been in the United States about 40 years, Slater estimated his wealth at close to $1 million. When he died in 1835, he owned all or part of thirteen textile mills.

Others, meanwhile, had been copying Slater's methods. By 1814 there were about 240 mills operating in the United States, most of them in Pennsylvania, New York, and New England. It was no wonder that Slater and these other mill builders became wealthy. The United States needed more and more cloth for its growing population. Slater and his imitators gave Americans what they needed when they needed it. ■

Industrial Innovation in America

Although the Industrial Revolution began in Great Britain, American inventors were not far behind. In some cases, Americans built on ideas developed in Britain. One American, Eli Whitney, is credited with developing an idea that changed industry forever.

Interchangeable Parts Whitney was an inventor from New England. In 1796 he signed a contract with the federal government to make 10,000 guns in a little over two years. It was a bold promise. In those days, a gunmaker made parts for one gun at a time. He assembled the gun as he went, fitting the parts together carefully, and then starting again. The process took weeks, because each part fit only one gun. No part could be swapped with similar parts from other guns.

Whitney realized that if all the parts were made exactly alike, they could be used on any of the guns. The gunmaker would not have to spend days making the individual parts fit together. He could assemble the parts rapidly, which would translate into higher production and greater profit.

Though Whitney worked hard on his new system, it took him ten years to make the 10,000 guns, and the parts were never truly interchangeable. However, other inventors later perfected what is now called the system of **interchangeable parts,** where all parts are made to an exact standard. By 1824, the nation had a reliable system for producing the guns it needed. Other industries, too, gradually adopted the system, and today it is almost unthinkable to make factory goods in any other way.

The Cotton Gin Another of Whitney's inventions also had a lasting effect on the United States. While visiting a Georgia plantation in 1793, Whitney noted the time and effort needed to clean cotton seeds from the cotton fibers. Working by hand, a laborer could only clean one pound of cotton per day. Whitney devised a solution to the problem: the **cotton gin,** a machine that separates the seeds from raw cotton fibers. (The word *gin* means an "engine" or "machine.") With a gin operated by water power, one worker could now clean 1,000 pounds per day. See the diagram of a hand-operated model to the right.

Whitney's invention had several important effects:

(1) Profit per pound of cotton skyrocketed, and with it the amount of cotton planted for harvest. United States exports in cotton boomed as a result, rising 6,000 percent between 1790 and 1815.

(2) Many southern planters began to depend on cotton as their only major crop, because it was so profitable.

(3) Planters began looking for new land where they could grow ever larger crops of cotton. They bought up and quickly settled large areas in Alabama, Mississippi, Louisiana, and finally Texas.

(4) To keep up with the increased demand for raw cotton, planters bought more enslaved Africans to work on the new and expanded cotton plantations. The enslaved population of the South more than doubled between 1790 and 1820, rising from 700,000 to 1.5 million. Many Americans had expected slavery to fade away gradually, but the cotton gin put an end to that dream.

Thus the cotton gin helped keep the southern states a land of slavery and of farming, while the northern states became a land of free labor and of industry. Time after time, these fundamental differences between North and South would cause friction between the two regions. Ultimately they would lead to civil war.

A Transportation Revolution

The Industrial Revolution was not the only "revolution" of the early 1800s in the United States. New, advanced technologies and new building projects produced a revolution in transportation.

Steam Power Though James Watt had first used his steam engine to make textiles, American inventor Robert Fulton proved it could also be used to power a ship. His steamboat *Clermont* chugged up the Hudson River in 1807. The *Clermont* demonstrated the great advantage of the steamboat: It could travel upriver, against the current. Although Fulton's was not the first steamboat to navigate the waters of an American river, it was the first to successfully complete a round trip.

Before long, hundreds of steamboats were plying the rivers of America's West. Steam power made it possible for western farmers and southern planters to ship their goods to markets around the world.

exploring TECHNOLOGY

The Cotton Gin

5 The **clearer** brushes clean cotton fibers off the cylinder.

2 The **movable bar** forces raw cotton against the grate.

1 The **hopper** holds raw cotton.

6 The **clearer compartment** catches cleaned cotton.

3 The cotton seeds are too large to pass through the **grate**.

4 Teeth on the **cylinder** catch cotton fibers and pull them through the grate. Cotton seeds are left in the hopper.

By hand, a worker could clean, or remove the seeds from, only one pound of cotton per day. With a hand-operated gin like the one shown here, a worker could clean 50 pounds of cotton per day. *Economics How did the invention of the cotton gin lead to the expansion of slavery?*

Main Idea CONNECTIONS

What effect did the invention of the steamboat have on the American economy?

Up the River On April 21, 1823, the riverboat *Virginia* steamed out of St. Louis with a few passengers and a cargo of military supplies bound for Fort St. Anthony, an army post on the site of present-day St. Paul, Minnesota. Its departure marked the first time a steamboat was going to travel up the Mississippi River all the way to the head of navigation. The low-pressure steam engine employed by Robert Fulton in his famous *Clermont* had been of little use against the powerful currents, treacherous rapids, islands, and shoals that characterized western rivers like the upper Mississippi, so a new type of engine with much higher pressure had to be developed. Although *Virginia's* voyage was slow, it proved that a steamboat could conquer the upper Mississippi. Before long a fleet of steamers was carrying lead, furs, and grain down the Mississippi and settlers up it. Source: Frederic D. Schwarz, "The Time Machine," *American Heritage* magazine, April 1998.

RESOURCE OPTIONS

Media and Technology

 Listening to Literature Mark Twain, from *Life on the Mississippi*

 Color Transparencies The Way It Works, H-6, H-7

Answer to . . .

Exploring Technology Because the cotton gin made cotton so profitable, planters wanted to grow more and more of it, requiring greater amounts of slave labor.

Main Idea Connections Steamboats allowed farmers and planters to ship their goods to market more easily.

Geography in History

Although the early trains solved some problems, they created many of their own. Routes were frequently unfenced or single-tracked, leading trains to collide with livestock or each other. Wood-burning locomotives threw out sparks that set fire to passengers' clothing and nearby forests. Some trains even included a car stuffed with cotton to protect passengers from locomotive explosions. Train travel became safe and viable only with the introduction of closed cars and new safety devices in the 1850s.

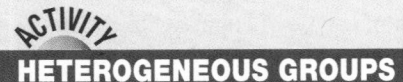

HETEROGENEOUS GROUPS

Ask students to correct any of the following incorrect statements.
• The cotton gin ended slavery and farming in the South.
• Waterways were the most expensive way to carry goods.
• Most early railroad technology was brought over from Britain.
(Reteaching)

*C*ustomize for

English Language Learners

Have each student create a poster entitled "New Types of Transportation." Posters should use text and drawings to illustrate how these types of transportation helped America prosper.

Answer to . . .

Map Skills Buffalo and Albany.

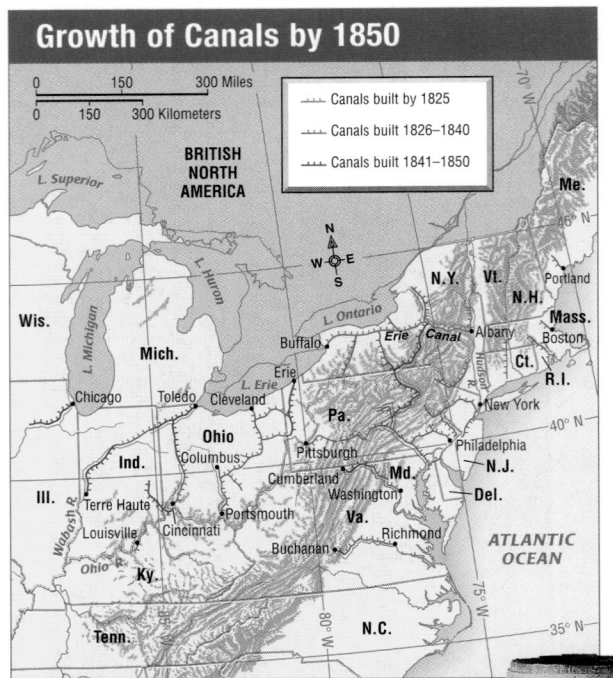

Growth of Canals by 1850

Canals built by 1825
Canals built 1826–1840
Canals built 1841–1850

Americans built canals with great enthusiasm during the early 1800s. During the celebration that marked the opening of the Erie Canal, the governor of New York poured water into the Atlantic Ocean from the keg at right. *Location* *What two cities did the Erie Canal connect?*

Canals Waterways were the cheapest way to carry goods. Unfortunately, they did not go everywhere that Americans wanted to go. To solve this problem, American innovators built artificial waterways, or canals. By 1840 the nation had some 3,000 miles of canals.

The best-known of these canals, and the one that had the greatest impact, was the **Erie Canal,** which opened in 1825. Built by the state of New York, this 363-mile waterway connected the Hudson River with Lake Erie. People and goods could now travel easily between the Atlantic Coast and the Great Lakes. The Erie Canal thus increased the rate of settlement and development of the entire Great Lakes region. Farmers of that area could now ship their products quickly and inexpensively to profitable markets as far away as New York City and beyond.

Roads Though canal building boomed in the early republic, it did not equal road building. Americans used roads to move goods, migrate west, communicate, even run their government. At first road-builders simply carved routes out of forests, throwing down the cut trees to surface the roadway. When they used whole logs, the roads were called corduroy roads, because they looked like ribbed cloth. Travel over corduroy roads was rather bumpy and uncomfortable. When road-builders used boards, the roads were called plank roads. Both types of surfacing soon rotted away and were replaced with stone and gravel.

By contrast, the National or **Cumberland Road** was built to last. Financed by the federal government, construction began in Cumberland, Maryland, in 1811. By 1833 it had reached Columbus, Ohio, and in later years it was gradually continued westward. Today it is known as U.S. Route 40.

Despite government interest, most of the new roads were privately built. Companies constructed their own highways and expected to make a profit by collecting tolls. At key locations on the road they put up a gate with a bar called a pike that blocked the way. After collecting the toll, the attendant would turn the pike aside. Thus the highways came to be known as **turnpikes.**

Railroads While better roads aided transportation, railroads proved far more durable and efficient for moving goods and people. Like textile technology, most early railroad technology was brought over from Britain. Several inventors in England and the United States adapted Watt's steam engine technology to build a steam locomotive—a self-propelled vehicle used for pulling railroad cars.

In 1828, construction on the first American railroad began in Baltimore, Maryland. It came to be known as the Baltimore and Ohio (B & O) line. By 1840, the nation had over 3,300 miles of track on

▶ RESOURCE OPTIONS

Media and Technology

RESOURCE PRO

Literature Activity The Natural World, found on Resource Pro, uses William Cullen Bryant's "Inscription for the Entrance to a Wood" to reveal how this poet and journalist viewed nature.

several different lines, more than any other country in the world.

Advances in Communication

Along with the revolution in transportation came advances in communication. The federal government led the way by expanding its postal service. The number of post offices in the nation leaped from 75 in 1790 to 8,450 in 1830. Regular mail delivery made it easier for people in distant places to communicate with one another. The mail also created a national network of information, since it carried newspapers, magazines, and books.

Before the Revolution, a relatively small number of newspapers had been published in the colonies. Most often, these papers were published on a weekly basis. By the 1820s, however, more than 500 newspapers and magazines of all sorts were being published daily in the United States. Advances in education had increased the nation's literacy rate. Newspapers and magazines now made information available to large numbers of people. Improved communication and the free exchange of ideas helped tie together the different parts of the country as it grew in both size and population.

FACT Finder

The Industrial Revolution in America

Date	Invention or Innovation
1787	John Fitch launches the first American steamboat.
1790	Samuel Slater invents water-powered cotton-processing machines.
1793	Eli Whitney invents the cotton gin.
1795	Robert Fulton invents the steam shovel (for digging canals).
1798	Eli Whitney mass produces muskets with standard measures and interchangeable parts.
1807	Robert Fulton launches the *Clermont*, the first commercially successful steamboat.
1814	Frances C. Lowell opens the first completely mechanized cotton mill.
1820	William Underwood opens a canning factory.
1826	Samuel Morey patents an internal combustion engine.
1828	Joseph Henry invents the electromagnet.

Interpreting Tables The early years of the nation saw advances in engineering, medicine, science, agriculture, and, especially, technology. Even the word *technology* was coined in 1829. *Science and Technology* *Examine the sampling of inventions in the table above. What similarities can you identify?*

SECTION 2 REVIEW

Comprehension

1. **Key Terms** Define: (a) republican virtues; (b) Industrial Revolution; (c) emigrate; (d) interchangeable parts; (e) cotton gin; (f) Erie Canal; (g) Cumberland Road; (h) turnpike.
2. **Summarizing the Main Idea** Name at least three inventions or innovations that changed the way Americans lived during the early republic.
3. **Organizing Information** Create a two-column chart that organizes information about *transportation* and *communication*. List at least four developments in transportation and two developments in communication.

Critical Thinking

4. **Analyzing Time Lines** Review the time line at the start of the section. Which event on the time line, in your opinion, had the greatest long-term importance?
5. **Identifying Central Issues** How did Americans demonstrate a spirit of improvement in the early republic?

Writing Activity

6. **Writing an Expository Essay** Use information from the section to write an essay on the ways in which the Industrial Revolution affected the nation's economy.

LIFE AFTER THE AMERICAN REVOLUTION

Focus Explain that Americans lived a variety of lifestyles in the 1790s. Discuss how for many people life involved a great deal of hard work and discomfort.

Instruct Ask students what the artifacts on these pages reveal about the working life of early Americans. Note the "freedom suit"; ask what a young man who completed job training today might receive instead. Have students look at the engraving captioned "Venerate the Plough." Ask volunteers what "venerate" means (*revere, respect, honor*) and what the caption might mean. Why might this engraving be considered a romanticized depiction of farm life? What impact did this idealized view of farming have on the settlement of the United States?

Extend Ask students to list the chores they and other family members do around the house. Have volunteers read their lists and compare and contrast their chores with those of people in the early Republic. What artifacts and symbols would they use in a display depicting life today?

Blacksmith's Anvil and Hammer

A blacksmith heated metal until it was glowing and soft, then shaped it with a hammer on the anvil.

Liberty Jug

This practical creamware jug celebrates the nation by listing the populations of the new American states.

Respect for the Land

This magazine engraving shows the popular link between American liberty and hardworking farmers.

Freedom Suit

Many young apprentices, bound in service to one master for years, received a "freedom suit" of new clothes at the end of training.

Dairying

This engraving titled "Straining and Skimming" shows an idealized view of two women preparing dairy products from whole milk.

Gravestones

These matching stones mark the graves of a husband and wife who were born in Africa. Brought to America to work as slaves, they eventually purchased their own freedom.

▶ RESOURCE OPTIONS

Teaching Resources

American History Block Scheduling Support Proud to Be American: A New Spirit of Nationalism, found in the Forging a New Nation folder, includes interdisciplinary lesson suggestions and activities for Geography and History, Primary Sources, Biography, and Literature.

6 Gridiron

One of the most common household objects, a gridiron was used to broil food in an open fireplace.

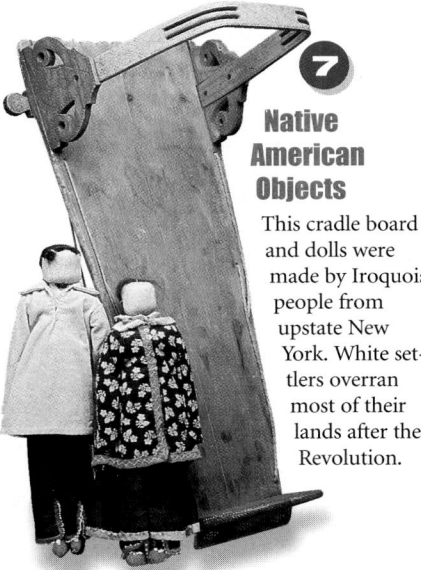

7 Native American Objects

This cradle board and dolls were made by Iroquois people from upstate New York. White settlers overran most of their lands after the Revolution.

VIEWING HISTORY

1. Summarize What do the objects and engravings tell you about daily life after the American Revolution?

2. Connecting to Today Think about the working life of individuals today. How does it compare to that of people after the Revolution? Report the following to your class: (a) how earning a living after the Revolution differs from earning a living today; (b) whether you think that advances in technology have made work life easier or harder.

American ARTIFACTS

FROM EXHIBITIONS AND COLLECTIONS AT THE SMITHSONIAN INSTITUTION'S NATIONAL MUSEUM OF AMERICAN HISTORY

LIFE AFTER THE AMERICAN REVOLUTION

The winds of change swept across the young United States, promising new freedoms. But not everyone benefited equally. People's opportunities depended on their ethnic identity, where they lived, and whether or not they were free.

As America's population grew rapidly in the late 1700s and early 1800s, many families headed west to lands beyond the Appalachian Mountains. Families found themselves building new lives surrounded by strangers. See **1**.

Most everyday objects were handmade by artisans using fairly simple tools, such as an anvil and hammer. Young men learned crafts by apprenticing for several years to a master craftsman. Often, poor girls used their sewing abilities to earn money for their families. See **2** and **3**.

Food came not from the store but from the family farm. Farmers spent long, hot days plowing, seeding, and harvesting their fields. Family members prepared dairy products like butter and cheese from whole milk. (Unlike milk, these products did not spoil quickly.) Green vegetables were considered food for animals, and were rarely eaten by humans. Foods were cooked over an open fireplace. See **4**, **5**, and **6**.

For African Americans and Native Americans, the United States was not yet a place of opportunity. African Americans who gained freedom might be able to purchase their own land, but whites' prejudice still denied them equal rights and an equal chance at success in life. Native Americans fared hardly better. Some became farmers and artisans, owning land and producing goods. But ultimately, there was little that Native Americans could do to protect their ways of life. See **7** and **8**.

Social and Religious Life

1816
African Methodist
Episcopal Church
established

1825
American Unitarian
Association organized

1830
Joseph Smith publishes
The Book of Mormon

1815   **1820**   **1825**   **1830**

Objectives

You may wish to call students' attention to the objectives in the Section Preview. The objectives are reflected in the main headings of the section.

Bellringer

Write the word *evangelist* on the chalkboard and ask students to define it. Then ask students to think about what draws people to evangelism. Ask who some of today's evangelists are and where they can be seen.

Reading Strategy

Formulating Questions Refer to the Reading Strategy in the Section Preview. You may want to model writing questions from headings on the chalkboard.

3 Social and Religious Life

SECTION PREVIEW

Objectives

1. Explain how people responded to social changes in the early 1800s, including such areas as courtship and marriage.
2. Describe the religious revival movement known as the Second Great Awakening.
3. Summarize the changes in the religious lives of African Americans.
4. *Key Terms* Define: mobile society; Second Great Awakening; evangelical; congregation; revival; denomination; spiritual.

Main Idea

Social changes during the early 1800s forced Americans to search for new rules to guide their relationships. Many found hope in a new religious revival, based on the idea that salvation was open to everyone.

Reading Strategy

Formulating Questions Skim the section, noting the headings and subheadings. Then rewrite the headings as questions and answer the questions as you read.

LESSON PLAN

Connecting to the Main Idea

1. Focus As America changed, so did the rules of society. Ask how these changes affected people's lives. Explain that the Second Great Awakening was a religious movement that said everyone was equal in the search for salvation.

2. Instruct Discuss how the expansion and the mobility of the population put a strain on Americans in the early 1800s. Discuss the conditions that made the United States ripe for the Second Great Awakening. In what ways did the new religious denominations reflect a truly American outlook? Why did the Great Awakening hold particular appeal for women?

3. Close The rules governing social behavior caused uncertainty for many Americans. The Second Great Awakening grew because it offered people comfort and purpose. New Christian denominations arose during this period, attracting many women and African Americans.

The rapid growth of population, expansion of territory, and improvements in the early republic brought with them sudden changes in American society. Just as Americans were inventing new mills, engines, and machines, they were also inventing a new way of living. Americans had to learn how to survive and thrive in a rapidly changing world.

Social Changes

Americans in the early republic knew they were living in a time of rapid change. The clash between old and new presented them with constant challenges. They often responded by using old traditions in new ways.

A Mobile Society The United States was (and remains) what is now called a **mobile society**—one in which people are constantly moving from place to place. Yet they were not just moving from one place to another. They were also able to move upward in society from one social class to another. This new mobility had two major effects:

(1) White Americans had an opportunity perhaps greater than that of any people in the history of the world up to that time. They were not tied to the land, as people were in Europe. White Americans could pack up their belongings and head west, where land was available and where society placed no limits on their success. For example, the son of a poor farmworker in Vermont could become a successful store owner in Ohio. Of course not everyone had an equal chance to get ahead, and opportunity was not a guarantee of success.

(2) Moving from place to place people often found themselves living among strangers, and were lonely as a result. Some historians believe that this loneliness led to increased suicide and drunkenness during the early republic. Previously, people had enjoyed the company of family and friends in the villages where they had lived all their lives. Now they had left those old acquaintances behind. People had to develop friendships with people whom they had never known before. Thus they had to learn new skills and make up new rules about getting along with others.

▶ RESOURCE OPTIONS

Teaching Resources

📁 **Reproducible Lesson Plan** Lesson Plans folder, p. 62

📁 **Learning Styles Lesson Plan** Learning Styles Lesson Plans folder, p. 17

📁 **Big Idea Graphic Organizer** Big Idea Graphic Organizer folder, p. 34

📁 **Guided Reading and Review** Units 1–2 folder, p. 91

In the upheaval of society in the early republic, American males took up the old European custom of dueling. Andrew Jackson owned this set of dueling pistols. *Culture* Why do you think Americans were trying to imitate Europeans?

Defending One's Honor One social skill that became more important was the ability to judge strangers. This involved knowing what role a stranger played in society. Yet because people were constantly moving, their places in society were not clear. As a result, people were more likely to question one another's position.

Many men responded with violence when others questioned their social position or insulted them. They would defend to the death their honor, or reputation for courage and honesty. This concern with honor is a good example of an old tradition being put to new use in the United States. In Europe, upper-class men defended their honor in duels, or formal one-on-one fights with weapons such as swords or pistols. In the early American republic, men of all social classes took up this tradition.

Andrew Jackson, the hero of the Battle of New Orleans and President from 1829 to 1837, was one well-known American who had a reputation for defending his honor in this way. On various occasions in the late 1790s and early 1800s, he dueled with a walking stick, a horsewhip, and a .70-caliber pistol.

New Rules for Courtship and Marriage

Women, too, had to deal with uncertainty about others in the changing world of the early republic. One of the few decisions in life that a young woman had some control over was her choice of a marriage partner. If she was thinking of marrying a man, it was vital that she learn as much as she could about him.

Moralizing Novels Many women looking for guidance about how to evaluate a future marriage partner found it in books. Some turned to advice manuals, but moralizing novels were much more popular.

By far the most popular of these works was the 1794 novel *Charlotte Temple,* by Susanna Haswell Rowson. Rowson herself had married an irresponsible man and was forced to support her family as a writer. Rowson's novel tells the sad story of Charlotte Temple, a 15-year-old girl who is carried off by a handsome man in a splendid military uniform. He soon leaves Charlotte penniless and desperate. She bears the child that results from this affair and then dies in the arms of her forgiving father, who arrives just in time to care for his grandchild. The moral of the story is that appearances do not provide enough clues to a person's character.

Courtship As American society became less ordered and certain, women became increasingly cautious about marriage. They preferred a long period of getting acquainted before they committed themselves. This period, called a courtship, was not new but had a new importance. Women used it not only to get to know a potential partner, but also to negotiate the terms of their future life together.

Consider, for example, the proposal of Zadoc Long, a 24-year-old storekeeper in Buckfield, Maine. After a year of courtship, he wrote a letter to Julia Davis asking her to be his wife. No one knows what their courtship was like. However, his offer—which she accepted—sounds like a response to a long list of demands that Davis may have made:

AMERICAN VOICES "I feel sad when I don't see you. Be married, why won't you? And come to live with me. I will make you as happy as I can. You shall not be obliged to work hard; and when you are tired, you may lie in my lap, and I will sing you to rest. . . . I will play a tune upon the violin as often as you ask and as well as I can; and leave off smoking, if you say so. . . . I would be always very kind to

Answer to . . .

Viewing History Sample answer: Unable to deal with the rapidly changing culture, Americans fell back on established customs.

Whether rushed or carefully considered, courtship led to the marriages that were building the new nation. *Country Wedding*, a painting of about 1819, gently pokes fun at young love and informal country life. *Culture Describe the activities of the participants in the wedding.*

you, I think, because I love you so well. I will not make you bring in wood and water, or feed the pig, or milk the cow, or go to the neighbors to borrow milk. Will you be married?"

—*Zadoc Long*

For most women getting married was a matter of survival, since decent employment opportunities hardly existed. Nevertheless, women had other concerns besides marriage. For one thing, they were becoming increasingly interested in religion. In the early 1800s, a new wave of religious feeling swept the United States. Many Americans, especially women, were soon participating in a religious movement.

The Second Great Awakening

Main Idea
CONNECTIONS

Why was the Second Great Awakening democratic?

During the colonial era, many churches had received financial support from state governments. Congregational churches in New England continued to receive government aid well into the 1800s. Backing for this practice was declining, however, due in part to a drop in church membership. The 1790 census showed that only about one out of ten Americans was a member of a church. Yet in the early 1800s the pressures of a changing society led many people to renew their religious faith.

An Evangelical Movement The great religious movement of the early 1800s is known as the **Second Great Awakening.** The movement began in the backcountry of Kentucky and Tennessee and attracted large numbers of people. Like the Great Awakening of the 1730s and 1740s, it took place among Protestant Christians and was an **evangelical** movement. A Christian religious movement is evangelical when it emphasizes these three ideas:

(1) The Scripture is the final authority.

(2) Salvation can only be achieved through a personal belief in Jesus Christ.

(3) People demonstrate true faith by leading a transformed life and by performing good deeds. This is sometimes called "witnessing for Christ."

In addition to being evangelical, the Second Great Awakening was democratic. Anyone, rich or poor, could win salvation if he or she chose to do so. Evangelical religions generally stressed the importance of the **congregation,** or the people of the church, rather than ministers.

One common feature of the Second Great Awakening was the **revival.** This was a gathering where people were "revived," or brought back to a religious life, by listening to preachers and accepting belief in Jesus Christ. Revivals were also called camp meetings because they were often held outdoors in temporary shelters such as tents. One participant described a camp meeting in New Haven, Connecticut, in 1804:

 "The power increased during the whole meeting. . . . Triumphing, . . . weeping, people falling, the voice of joy and sorrow mingling, prayer, praise, and shouting, shouting, shouting filled the groves around.**"**

—*William Thacher*

New Denominations Partly as a result of the Second Great Awakening, during the early 1800s several Protestant **denominations,** or religious subgroups, experienced rapid growth. The United States soon had more different Christian denominations than any other nation.

By 1850, Presbyterians and Congregationalists, once the most popular denominations, had taken third and fourth place. Some of the fastest-growing denominations were:

Baptists. Baptists got their name from their beliefs about baptism, a Christian ceremony by which a person is made a member of the church. Unlike other denominations, which tended to baptize people as infants, Baptists believed that only those who were old enough to understand Christian beliefs should be baptized. Also, instead of baptizing people by sprinkling them with water, as other denominations did, Baptists baptized by immersion, or dipping people completely underwater.

Baptist churches had existed in what became the United States since the 1600s. The Baptists grew rapidly during the Second Great Awakening because of their evangelical beliefs and their frequent camp meetings. By 1850, Baptists were the nation's second-largest denomination.

American Baptists also spread their beliefs to other countries through foreign missionaries. In 1814, a General Convention was organized to support missions abroad. In time it came to be known as the American Baptist Foreign Mission Society.

VIEWING HISTORY

The lantern above lit the way to a camp meeting like the one at the left. **Culture** *Describe the reactions of the crowd to the speaker at this meeting.*

*C*ustomize for

English Language Learners

Ask students to skim the section, noting any unfamiliar words. Help them define these words using context clues or a dictionary.

▶ RESOURCE OPTIONS

Teaching Resources

📁 **Visual Learning Activity** "Do They Miss Me at Home?" Learning with Documents folder, p. 49

Answer to . . .

Viewing History Some are fainting or showing signs of emotion; some are more interested in the crowd than in the speaker; some are paying little attention at all.

Methodists, on their way to a camp meeting, carry bundles of food and clothing in this painting by Jacques Gerard Milbert. **Culture** *Why did Methodism grow so large so quickly?*

Methodists. Methodism grew out of the beliefs of a British minister, John Wesley, who lived from 1703 to 1791.† His ideas came to the United States in the 1780s and spread rapidly after 1800. By 1850, the Methodists had become the largest Protestant denomination in the United States.

The growth of Methodism had four main causes. First, it focused on a person's personal relationship with God rather than religious doctrines that might be hard to understand. Second, compared to ministers in other denominations who were highly educated scholars, Methodist preachers had more in common with their congregations. Thus they tended to understand the needs of the people in the rough-and-tumble frontier world. Third, the Methodists spread their message through a system of traveling ministers called circuit riders. Traveling on horseback in sweeping routes or "circuits" through the wilderness, these circuit riders won many new members. Finally, Methodists put on frequent and exciting camp meetings. In 1820 alone, they held a thousand revivals across the country.

---

† The name *Methodist* arose when Wesley as a young man formed a small group to study religion. Other students made fun of the group for following strict methods of study.

†† The name *Unitarian* comes from the belief that God is a unity. Many other Christian groups believe that God is a trinity, or made up of three parts.

Unitarians. Although Unitarianism gained strength during the Second Great Awakening, it was not an evangelical faith.†† Unitarians believed that Jesus Christ was only a human messenger of God, not divine himself. They saw God not as a stern judge, but as a loving father.

Unitarianism took root not on the frontier, like other new denominations, but in New England. In the early 1800s, Boston was leaving its Puritan beginnings behind, and many elite churchgoers were looking for a religion that was less old-fashioned. They wanted a faith that was moderate, calm, and rational, in contrast to the emotion and enthusiasm of many evangelical religions. Unitarianism fulfilled that need.

Boston minister William Ellery Channing was the perfect spokesperson for the rising denomination. In 1825, he organized a conference of Congregational ministers that became the American Unitarian Association. Calm and compassionate, Channing said that the world was a place where God was training people, as a father would, "by aids and obstructions, by conflicts of reason and passion. . . for union with himself." This Unitarian idea that people were on Earth to improve themselves had a great effect on the movement for social reform in New England.

Mormons. Another region of great activity during the Second Great Awakening was central New York State. This region was swept so often by fiery religious movements, led by ministers such as Charles Grandison Finney, that it became known as the Burned-Over District. Here, in 1830, Joseph Smith published *The Book of Mormon.* According to Smith, the book was a translation of the writing on gold plates that had been given to him by an angel. The book foretold that God would soon restore a truer, simpler church, free of ministers. This was to take place not in the faraway Holy Land, but in North America. Smith went on to start a religion based on the book. He called it the Church of Jesus Christ of Latter-day Saints. In time people began calling members of the church Mormons.

Millennialists. Many evangelical ministers believed that America was leading the world into the millennium, or Earth's final thousand years of glory before the Day of Judgment. They looked for signs of the coming event in everyday life.

One Vermont farmer, William Miller, determined by studying the Bible that Jesus Christ would return to the world in 1843. This return was called the Advent, or the Second Coming. Miller preached that only the people who knew of the Advent ahead of time and believed in it would be saved and go to heaven. His followers, called Millerites, numbered between 50,000 and 100,000, according to his estimate. When 1843 passed without any sign of Jesus' arrival, the date of the Advent was changed to October 21, 1844.

Millerites continued to believe that Jesus would soon return despite the disappointment in 1844. In the 1860s, they formed several churches, including the Seventh Day Adventist Church and the Advent Christian Church.

Women in the Awakening Women were extremely active in the Second Great Awakening. In part this may have reflected the loneliness and unhappiness of many women on the frontier. Religion offered them a chance to connect with others. They might work together to help widows and orphans, to spread the Christian religion, or to improve conditions for mothers. For example, in Oneida County, New York, religious women founded the Female Missionary Society in 1814, hoping to encourage the revival of religion. Their letters to one another are full of what they called "heartfelt communications of hope, joy, and gratitude." In a world of strangers, they were especially grateful for the company of "beloved sisters" who shared their religious views.

Few women actually preached or took leadership roles in the Second Great Awakening. One exception was Jarena Lee, an African American who frequently preached to congregations in the Philadelphia area. The revival movement did bring women increased power, but it was indirect power. For example, they had a greater voice in choosing ministers for their churches. In this way, women gained an opportunity to influence the beliefs and standards of behavior in their community.

African American Worship

In the 1700s and early 1800s, Methodists and other evangelical churches included whites and blacks. As African Americans joined in Christian churches, the black and white traditions were blended together. One example is the call-and-response method of worship, in which the congregation responds together to a statement made by one member. This is a feature of both older Protestant worship and African music.

Spirituals Both white and black Christians also sang **spirituals,** or folk hymns. African American singers, however, often focused on themes that held a double meaning. For example, in the Bible, Moses led the Israelites to freedom from slavery under the Pharaoh, the ruler of Egypt. African Americans made this a symbol for winning both spiritual salvation and freedom from physical slavery. One spiritual put it this way:

> When Israel was in Egypt's Land
>   (Let my people go)
>
> Oppressed so hard they could not stand
>   (Let my people go)
>
> Go down, Moses, way down in Egypt's land,
>
> Tell ol' Pharaoh to let my people go. . . .
>
> O let us all from bondage flee
>   (Let my people go)
>
> And let us all in Christ be free
>   (Let my people go). . . .

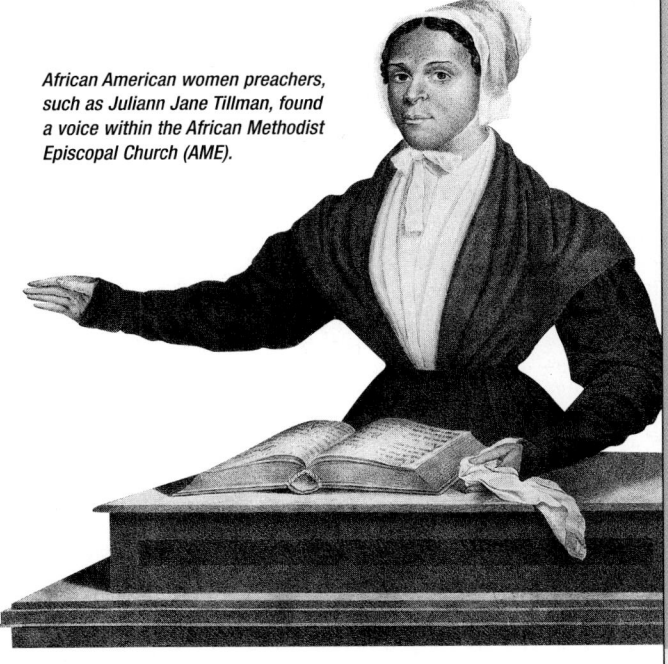

African American women preachers, such as Juliann Jane Tillman, found a voice within the African Methodist Episcopal Church (AME).

ACTIVITY

EXTENDED CLASS PERIODS

Time: 90 minutes.
Activity: Reenact the confrontation at the St. George Methodist Church in Philadelphia in 1792. Students should prepare scripts for their skits or perform them as improvisational role-plays. They should include the feelings and reactions of the African Americans at the St. George Methodist Church and explain why African Americans formed their own congregation under Richard Allen.
Grouping: Groups of six students.
Purpose: To role-play the event that prompted African Americans, led by Richard Allen, to organize the African Methodist Episcopal Church.
Roles: Richard Allen, white and African American church members.
Outcome: Students will identify issues of religious conflict and understand how tension between white Methodists and African Americans led to the organization of a new denomination.

ACTIVITY

LEARNING STYLES

Have students take the perspective of a woman during the Second Great Awakening and write a diary entry describing her life. *(Verbal/Linguistic)*

▶ **RESOURCE OPTIONS**

Teaching Resources

 Primary Source Activity The American Spirit, Learning with Documents folder, p. 13

Media and Technology

Color Transparencies Our Multicultural Heritage, C-7; Graphic Organizer, G-3

Richard Allen was a key figure in organizing African American churches in the early republic. One such church, the Bethel Church of Baltimore, celebrated its good relationship with the minister of a neighboring white congregation in 1845. *Diversity How did white and African American worshippers influence each other's religious traditions?*

AMERICAN VOICES "Our only design is to secure to ourselves our rights and privileges, to regulate our own affairs, [worldly] and spiritual, the same as if we were white people."

—*Richard Allen*

African Americans in other cities soon followed Allen's example and started their own churches. In 1816, sixteen congregations joined to form the African Methodist Episcopal Church (AME). They elected Allen as their first bishop. By 1831, the AME included 86 churches with about 8,000 members.

Like white Americans, great numbers of African Americans turned to evangelical religion during the period of the early republic because they believed their souls were at risk. They found a strong sense of community in Methodism and other Protestant denominations. In addition, African Americans were attracted to the democratic aspects of evangelical Christianity. As Richard Allen explained, "The plain and simple gospel suits best for any people; for the unlearned can understand, and the learned are sure to understand."

By themselves, the revivals could not establish real equality or overcome racial prejudice. Yet they did remind Americans of every background that what mattered in the United States was not wealth or education or color, but what Martin Luther King, Jr., would later call "the content of one's character."

A Black Denomination African Americans sometimes felt unwelcome in white-dominated churches. The tensions between whites and blacks increased as African Americans became more assertive about sharing in democratic liberty. In 1792, white worshippers at the St. George Methodist Church in Philadelphia asked the African Americans in the congregation to leave the main floor and sit up in the gallery. They refused. Under the leadership of Richard Allen, the black worshippers left and started a new church of their own. Allen, an African American minister, explained their purpose:

SECTION 3 REVIEW

Comprehension

1. ***Key Terms*** Define: (a) mobile society; (b) Second Great Awakening; (c) evangelical; (d) congregation; (e) revival; (f) denomination; (g) spiritual.

2. ***Summarizing the Main Idea*** What changes did Americans make addressing the social uncertainties of the United States in the early decades of the 1800s?

3. ***Organizing Information*** Create a five-column chart that describes the new denominations active during the Second Great Awakening.

Critical Thinking

4. ***Analyzing Time Lines*** Review the time line at the start of the section. What do the entries suggest about religious diversity in the United States in the early 1800s?

5. ***Making Comparisons*** Compare and contrast the Great Awakening and the Second Great Awakening.

Writing Activity

6. ***Writing an Expository Essay*** Research and write a brief essay explaining the role of the African Methodist Episcopal Church in the evangelical revivals.

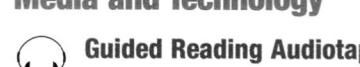

RESOURCE OPTIONS

Teaching Resources

📁 **Quiz** Unit 1–2 folder, p. 92

📁 **Chapter Tests Forms A and B** Chapter Test folder

Student Performance Pack

⭐ **Guide to the Essentials** Chapter 7, Section 3 (English and Spanish)

Standardized Test Preparation Handbook

Media and Technology

🎧 **Guided Reading Audiotapes** Chapter 7 Summary (English and Spanish)

Student Edition on Audiotape Chapter 7

💿 **Test Bank CD-ROM; Interactive Student Tutorial CD-ROM** Chapter Test

Why Study History? To understand that . . .

You Live in the Information Age

Beginning in the late 1700s, the United States experienced a wave of invention and innovation that transformed American life. Yet that period of change pales in comparison to the technological revolution occurring today.

Colonial printing press

At the start of every workday, Ms. Ruth Banta, vice president of a large insurance agency, boots her computer. She checks her voice mail and e-mail. She reviews faxes that arrived overnight. Computers, fax machines, telephone answering machines, and modems are just a few of the recent innovations that regulate Americans' work lives. Outside the office, microwaves prepare our meals and cable televisions, VCRs, and Internet surfing fill our leisure time.

The Impact Today

Computers launched the Information Age in the 1970s. They remain a technological frontier today. Like other frontiers, the technological frontier holds both promise and peril.

In 1985 an estimated 21.5 million computers operated in the United States. Ten years later, the number had increased to about 96 million. Today, more than 50 percent of jobs in the United States involve using computers to organize, analyze, and store information. Businesses use computers to handle payrolls and store customer and employee records. Many workers, who once commuted by car to office buildings, now "telecommute." That is, they work at home

and use computers to communicate with employers, clients, or employees. Technology affects students and retired people, too. Computers and Internet connections are available for their use at many schools and libraries.

The development of sophisticated computer technology has made information on almost any topic widely available. Yet new problems have surfaced in the Information Age. For example, many computer databases show the health, employment, or credit history of individuals. The unauthorized use of such personal information has become a widespread concern. Breaking into computer systems to steal, alter, or destroy data is another problem of the Information Age.

The Impact on You

Some Americans believe that government agencies should regulate the Internet, setting guidelines for its contents and limiting access to databases containing personal information. Discuss this idea with friends and relatives. Determine your opinion. List reasons why you support or oppose regulation of the Internet. Use your list as the basis for a letter explaining your position on this issue to the editor of a computer magazine.

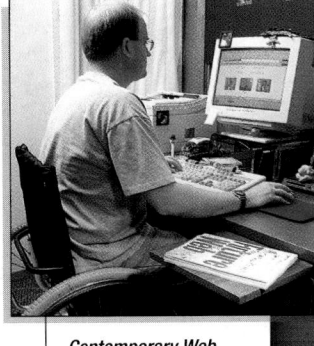

Contemporary Web page designer

RESOURCE OPTIONS

Teaching Resources

📁 **Why Study History? Activity** You Live in the Information Age, found in the Why Study History? folder, p. 8, provides an activity to help students better understand the changes brought by the Information Revolution.

Media and Technology

 AmericanHeritage® CD-ROM

Time Tour The Nation Today and Tomorrow: Toward a New Century

Class Discussion

Discuss with the class the Information Age and government regulation. For a more thorough examination of the issue, see the activity folder in the Resource Options below.

ACTIVITY
STUDENT PARTICIPATION

Comparing Information Sources
Ask students to read the text. Then divide the class into groups of three. Assign each group a topic to research. Include both current and historical topics, such as the Industrial Revolution and global warming. Each student should compile a bibliography using one of the following sources:

- **traditional (library books, magazines)**
- **computer media search services**
- **Internet**

Have the groups present their findings on posters. Encourage class discussion.

Follow up Ask students to make generalizations about the strengths and weaknesses of each method of research, using evidence to support their ideas.

🖥 Using the Internet

Students can learn more about the Information Age by exploring links in the *America: Pathways to the Present* Web site at

http://www.Pathways.phschool.com

Assessment

See the Lesson Plans folder, pp. 24–27, for rubrics on assessing Class Participation Projects.

Key Terms

Students should refer to the definitions of key terms in the chapter to write sentences that show an understanding of the relation of each word to life in the new nation.

Comprehension

1. Although immigration and continued importation of slaves fueled population growth, the most important factor was the high number of births.

2. African Americans participated in the development of the region by clearing the land and supporting homesteads.

3. People considered education extremely important and began to insist that it be made more widely available to both men and women.

4. Samuel Slater's re-creation of British textile machinery vastly increased production capacity. This expansion inspired many American inventions, such as the cotton gin and steam power.

5. The cotton gin was largely responsible for the continued growth of slavery, because as profits from cotton grew, the demand for slave labor increased.

6. Because of the population's mobility during this period, a woman was less likely to know much about the status and family background of a potential partner; courtship became an opportunity to get to know him better before making a final commitment.

7. Many people were attracted by the democratic nature of the movement. They were also attracted to the movement's promise of meaning and community.

8. Women were seeking a sense of community; they also wanted to influence the moral development of their communities.

Chapter Summary

The major concepts of Chapter 7 are presented below. See also the *Guide to the Essentials of American History* or *Interactive Student Tutorial CD-ROM,* which contains interactive review activities, time lines, helpful hints, and test practice for Chapter 7.

Reviewing the Main Ideas

During the early republic, the nation grew dramatically, and its young population faced a multitude of challenges. Pioneers poured over the Appalachians, settling new states and territories. Advances in industry, transportation, and communication dramatically changed people's lives. Yet change also brought uncertainty. Some Americans responded with a renewed commitment to their spiritual life.

Section 1: Crossing the Appalachians

In the early years of the republic, a young and energetic population migrated west over the Appalachians and settled in the Ohio and Mississippi valleys and the Gulf Coast.

Section 2: Inventions and Innovations

A new sense of freedom pushed Americans to experiment and invent new and better ways to do tasks.

Section 3: Social and Religious Life

Social changes during the early 1800s forced Americans to search for new rules to guide their relationships. Many found hope in a new religious revival, based on the idea that salvation was open to everyone.

Beginning in the late 1700s, the United States experienced a wave of invention and innovation that transformed American life. Yet that period of change pales in comparison to the technological revolution occurring today. Computers, fax machines, and modems are just a few of the recent innovations that affect Americans' lives.

Using Graphic Organizers

- Education and Learning: first standardized dictionary of American English compiled; many states required free public education for all children.
- Inventions Lead to Economic Growth: Slater's mills boosted the textile industry; Whitney's cotton gin promoted the cotton industry.

Key Terms

For each of the terms below, write a sentence explaining how it relates to this chapter.

1. republican virtues
2. cotton gin
3. turnpike
4. Second Great Awakening
5. Industrial Revolution
6. trans-Appalachia
7. Erie Canal
8. Adams-Onís Treaty
9. revival
10. Wilderness Road
11. denomination
12. interchangeable parts

Comprehension

1. What was the main cause of the great increase in the United States' population before 1830?
2. How did African Americans participate in the development of the trans-Appalachian region?
3. Describe the attitude toward education in the early republic.
4. Explain how the Industrial Revolution that began in Great Britain affected the United States.
5. What was the effect of the cotton gin on slavery?
6. Why did courtship gain in importance during the early republic?
7. What attracted Americans to the Second Great Awakening?
8. Why were women drawn to the evangelical movement?

Using Graphic Organizers

On a separate sheet of paper, copy the tree-map organizer to organize information about the ways in which Americans joined in the spirit of improvement during the early republic. Provide at least two supporting details for each main idea.

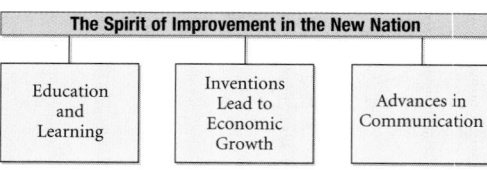

The Spirit of Improvement in the New Nation		
Education and Learning	Inventions Lead to Economic Growth	Advances in Communication

- Advances in Communication: federal postal service expanded; number of newspapers and magazines increased.

LIVING MADE EASY.

Revolving Hat
Which by a slight touch presents its wearer with Eye-Glass, Cigar, Scent-Box, Spectacles, Hearing-Trumpet, without the intolerable trouble of holding them.

Analyzing Political Cartoons ▶

1. One cartoonist got into the spirit of improvement of the early republican era. Examine the gentlemen's hats. What "improvements" has the artist made to the ordinary hat?

2. Read the title and caption of the cartoon. What do you think is the cartoonist's attitude toward the technological improvements of the era?

Critical Thinking

1. *Applying the Chapter Skill* Review the population density maps on page 206. In 1830, which states or territories had the greatest amount of land with a density of two or fewer persons?

2. *Recognizing Cause and Effect* How did the ideals of the American Revolution continue to influence social developments in the early republic?

3. *Distinguishing Fact from Opinion* Explain why you agree or disagree with the statement, "The industrial and transportation revolutions had little effect on the economy of the United States in the early republic."

4. *Predicting Consequences* You have read that the population of the United States doubled every twenty years during the era of the new republic. What might be the effects on your town or city if its population doubled in the next twenty years?

ANALYZING DOCUMENTS ◀ **INTERPRETING DATA**

Turn to the chart *United States Population, 1780–1830* on page 202.

1. What was the change in total population between 1790 and 1810? (a) increase of 2 million persons (b) no change (c) increase of 3 million persons (d) decrease of 4 million persons

2. In which decade did the number of white Americans increase by the greatest amount? (a) 1780–1790 (b) 1800–1810 (c) 1810–1820 (d) 1820–1830

3. *Writing* Use information from the text to explain the reasons for the rapid rise in population between 1780 and 1830.

INTERNET ACTIVITY

For your portfolio:
Write an Essay

Access Prentice Hall's *America: Pathways to the Present* site at **www.Pathways.phschool.com** for the specific URL to complete the activity. Additional resources and related Web sites are also available.

Examine Ohio's black codes of 1804. Write an essay describing how these laws burdened both free blacks and those who would assist free blacks or escaped slaves.

Connecting to Today

Essay Writing Reread the section beginning on page 216 about the effects mobility had on society. Research and write an essay that answers the following question: "Have recent technological changes made the United States more, or less, a nation of strangers?" Include evidence to support your conclusions.

INTERNET ACTIVITY

Answers will vary. Essays should show an understanding of how the black codes burdened both free blacks and those assisting free blacks or escaped slaves.

Analyzing Political Cartoons

1. The hat has been automated and accessories have been attached.
2. That they are sometimes ridiculous and make people lazy.

Critical Thinking

1. Michigan Territory, Arkansas Territory, Florida Territory, Missouri.
2. The ideal of democracy manifested itself in the evangelical movement; the ideal of beginning a new era was seen in new inventions and faith in human progress.
3. Students should disagree. The Industrial Revolution had a profound effect on the economy. Large mills were built in New England. Inventions like the steam engine and the cotton gin forever changed the way people did work. Developments in transportation increased the speed with which farmers and industrialists could get their products to market. Canals connected the interior of the country to cities on the coast. The steamboat allowed products to be moved upstream.
4. Answers will vary. Students should cite the need for more schools, jobs, housing, and increased city services; strain on public resources; and expansion of markets.

Interpreting Data

1. c
2. d
3. Population increased rapidly during this period because of an increase in the birth rate and an increase in immigration, especially from Germany and Ireland.

Connecting to Today

Answers will vary. Students may suggest that population growth and mobility have increased a feeling of being a "nation of strangers."

My Brush with History

Focus Have students find the meaning of each of these words in a dictionary before they begin to read: *destitute, benefaction, improvidence, motley, pestilential, sanguine, advent, desponding, incessant.* Ask them to consider, as they read, what personal qualities helped a settler prosper.

Instruct Divide the class into eight groups and assign each group one paragraph from the selection. Ask groups to study their paragraph closely and discuss what it means. Have groups explain their paragraphs as other students refer to the selection. Allow time for students to ask questions after each explanation.

Point out any elements essential to understanding the selection that groups neglected. Then have students make a sketch or write a poem, perhaps a ballad, about foreigners who migrated to the western frontier in the early 1800s.

Analyzing the Document

Use this additional question to generate class discussion:

CRITICAL THINKING: DRAWING CONCLUSIONS What does Hall mean when he says that "All [emigrants] are deceived, as well the desponding as the enthusiastic"? *(Some emigrants are afraid and pessimistic about what they might encounter on the frontier, while others anticipate instantly achieving success there. Both expectations are unrealistic.)*

American Heritage®

My Brush with History

BY JAMES HALL

INTRODUCTION The editors of *American Heritage* magazine have selected these impressions of James Hall, a settler in the Mississippi Valley. Hall contrasted the various backgrounds of the new arrivals and the different expectations they had of life in the West.

Crossing the Ohio River

The foreigners whom I met were in much worse circumstances than our own citizens. These arrive on our shores in a destitute condition, and undertake the journey without money enough to accomplish half the distance, and some without a cent to pay their entrance, confiding in the protection of heaven and the benefactions of the charitable. This confidence is not so often deceptive as might be expected, for an American is never seen to turn a houseless wanderer from his door or to refuse a morsel to the hungry. It is surprising to see to what a dreary plight some of these adventurers are reduced by their poverty or improvidence; and yet many of them will trudge along with light hearts and empty purses, apparently forgetful of the past and regardless of the future.

At Pittsburgh, where the emigrants generally embark on the Ohio, they may be seen in larger numbers than at any other place; and here may be remarked, not only their number but, in some degree, their various characters and as various expectations. Some arrive with furniture, farming utensils, and servants, and push forward, confident in their ability to overcome every obstacle; some come burdened with large families and but little worldly gear; and others, happy at such a time in their "single blessedness," come alone, errant knights, leaving all their cares behind them. Upon observing these motley collections, I have been reminded of the invitation in a camp-meeting song which I have heard, and which I think is about as follows:

> Come hungry, come thirsty, come ragged, come bare,
> Come filthy, come lousy, come just as you are.

For, to be brief, here you see all sorts of folks crowding to the West.

Those who are driven by misfortune from their homes go like exiles from the land, to which fond recollection attaches a thousand charms, to a wilderness, which fancy clothes

T E S T   P R E P A R A T I O N

Have students use the excerpt on these pages to answer the following question.

According to James Hall, what drew emigrants to the western frontier?

A The products of nature or the cheapness of the land.

B A thirst for adventure or a wilderness with a thousand terrors.

C The good folks of the West or wealth, honor, and pleasure.

D Misfortune at home or hope of a better life in a new land.

with a thousand terrors. Every sympathy is awakened and every tender feeling thrilled with anguish, when they exchange the comforts of society, the scenes of their youth, and the friends of their hearts for the nameless and unknown difficulties which appear in the dark perspective. They dream of interminable forests and pestilential swamps, and at every step fancy themselves surrounded by noxious vermin and beasts of prey. Thus, anticipating no good and fearing every evil, they go into banishment with sorrowful hearts.

While some settlers brought bulky possessions like furniture on their journey west, others carried only a few lightweight belongings, like this leather shooting bag.

But there is a more sanguine class of emigrants to whom a different picture is presented. They have been allured by interest or ambition, or led by choice, to a new country, and hope arrays their future abodes with every charm. . . . The old men are to be blessed with wealth, the young men with honor, and the girls with husbands—and, I suppose, with wealth, and honor, and pleasure into the bargain; and, to crown all, the good folks of the West will feel so delighted and so flattered by their advent that they will crowd about them like the friends of Job, and everyone will give them "an earring and a piece of gold!"

All these are deceived, as well the desponding as the enthusiastic. The advantages of the Western country consist in the great fertility of the soil, the profusion of all the products of nature, whether of the animal, vegetable, or mineral kingdom, the cheapness of lands, and the newness of the country, which affords room and opportunity for enterprise. These, together with its commercial advantages, the total exemption from all taxes and political burdens, and the comparatively small portion of labor requisite to procure the necessaries of life, certainly render this a desirable home. But . . . slow and persevering industry is not less necessary here than elsewhere. . . .

[F]ew here are raised to eminent public stations without a long and intimate acquaintance with the people. In the West there is no jealousy or unfriendliness to strangers, who are generally received with open arms and treated with kindness and respect; but political honors are more sparingly bestowed and are seldom lavished upon foreigners, who, whatever may be their pretensions, can hardly be supposed to know or to feel the interests of the country.

The desponding emigrant, on the other hand, is agreeably surprised at finding every plain, substantial comfort which a reasonable man can wish; and, though he discovers no attempt at luxury or style, he sees hospitality, plenty, and intelligence. Instead of a vast wilderness he finds large settlements which, though thinly scattered, are now sufficiently dense to afford the comforts and civilities of life, to ensure protection, and to enforce municipal regulations. . . .

Well, and when the emigrant has reached his journey's end, what then? Why, then, my dear sir, he very often finds that he had better have stayed at home. Labor, labor, labor, hard, heavy, incessant labor, is the lot of him who proclaims war against the forest; but the victory is certain, and the conqueror's reward is rich and ample.

Source: *Letters from the West* by James Hall, published in London, 1828.

ADDITIONAL READING

To learn more about the topics discussed in this selection, you might want to read the following books:

- *The Americans: The National Experience,* by Daniel J. Boorstin (New York: Random House, 1965)
- *Daniel Boone: The Life and Legend of an American Pioneer,* by John Mack Faragher (New York: Holt, 1992)
- *Frontier Indiana,* by Andrew R. L. Cayton (Bloomington: Indiana University Press, 1996)
- *Twilight of Empire,* by Allan W. Eckert (Boston: Little, Brown, 1988)

Customize for
English Language Learners

Students may need help with the following words and phrases:

emigrant person who leaves one place to settle permanently in another

deceptive misleading

camp-meeting song hymn

noxious vermin small dangerous animals

eminent public stations positions of power and responsibility in a community

Customize for
Less Proficient Readers

Discuss with students how the emigrants that Hall describes differ in motivations, expectations, economic means, number of settlers per family, and so on. Have students create an emigrant character, jotting down on paper his or her motivations, economic means, etc. Then ask students to write a diary entry depicting the fears or dreams of their character when the character arrives on the western frontier.

Customize for
More Advanced Students

Ask students to write an article for a newspaper published in 1828. Tell them to begin with Hall's assertion, "At Pittsburgh, you see all sorts of folks crowding to the West." Have them use additional observations and information from the selection.

TEST PREPARATION

Have students use the excerpt on these pages to answer the following question.

Based on the passage, how is the western frontier like other places where people make new lives for themselves?

A People must overcome noxious vermin and beasts of prey.

(B) People must work long and hard to build a satisfying life.

C The reward of hard work is rich and ample.

D Newcomers are warmly welcomed.

An Emerging New Nation 1800–1860

Introducing the Unit

Using Historical Evidence

The Erie Canal was a marvelous work of engineering and an effective means of providing access to the nation's interior. Like the artist who painted the scene of Lockport reproduced on the right, Americans enjoyed the vitality and excitement of their growing nation.

Ask students what the name *Lockport* tells them about the village. Have students locate the five locks in the painting and explain how they worked. Ask half the class to find out how many people live in Lockport today and the other half to locate Lockport on a map.

Themes in American History

Direct students' attention to the Unit Themes. Point out that each chapter in this unit has its own theme. To teach this unit thematically, you may wish to use the Expansion, Reconstruction, Immigration folder in **American History Block Scheduling Support.**

Using the Time Line

To provide students with practice in using a time line to connect key events in the United States with key events in the world, ask questions such as these: (1) According to the time line, which two future states received waves of settlers in the 1840s? *(Oregon, California)* (2) What problem did Ireland face during this time period? *(Famine)* (3) How many years passed between the abolition of slavery in England and its abolition in Mexico? *(22)*

unit THREE

An Emerging New Nation

1800 – 1860

*I*n the 1800s new ways of doing business changed the political, economic, and social landscape of the nation. The appearance of textile mills in New England signaled the beginning of industrialization. Small towns blossomed into bustling urban centers. Regional and class divisions deepened, and urban pressures developed. Some citizens, concerned over the accompanying social changes, poured their energies into reform movements. Others flocked to newly acquired territories in the West. As the United States expanded from sea to sea, the economic and political focus of the nation gradually shifted from the local to the national level.

Chapter 8	The Market Revolution *1812–1845*
Chapter 9	Religion and Reform *1800–1850*
Chapter 10	Beyond the Mississippi *1800–1860*

UNIT THEMES

Economics The nation moved from a household economy to a market economy.

Culture Reformers focused national attention on social problems such as alcoholism, poor education, and inhumane prisons.

Geography As the United States expanded westward, white settlers displaced Native Americans from their homelands.

EVENTS IN THE UNITED STATES

1808 Congress bans importation of slaves

1813 Textile mill built at Waltham, Massachusetts

1822 American colonists settle in Texas

1823 Monroe Doctrine

Presidents	Jefferson	Madison	Monroe

1800   **1810**   **1820**

EVENTS IN THE WORLD

1807 England bans slave trade

1819 12-hour workday for juveniles established in England

1822 The American Colonization Society founds Liberia

RESOURCE OPTIONS

Teaching Resources

Units 3–4 folder Contains instructional materials organized by chapter.

● **VIEWING HISTORY** Lockport, New York, painted in 1836 by an unknown artist, owed its very existence to the Erie Canal. The town arose out of a "rattlesnake–infested wilderness" when the canal opened in 1825. *Geography* **Why did urban centers develop near waterways?**

Commercial loom and textile worker

1830
Indian Removal Act

1833
William Lloyd Garrison founds American Anti-Slavery Society

1843
Mass migration to Oregon begins

1846
Mexican War begins

1848
Turning Point: Seneca Falls Convention (p. 277)

1849
California Gold Rush

| Jackson | Van Buren | Harrison | Tyler | Polk | Taylor | Fillmore | Pierce |

1830 | **1840** | **1850**

1829
Slavery abolished in Mexico

1840
Female delegates are excluded from the World Anti-Slavery Convention in London

1845
Irish Potato Famine

1848
The Communist Manifesto published

▶ RESOURCE OPTIONS

Media and Technology

Color Transparencies Specific transparencies are referenced throughout the chapters at appropriate points of use. For this unit, see American Photo, B-3; Fine Art, D-8; Links Across Time, J-3; Political Cartoons, K-3; and Historical Maps, L-2.

◉ ▭ **Visions of America** "Scenes of an Era: An Emerging New Nation" located on videodisc side 1 and on videotape 2. Lesson plans for "Scenes of an Era" can be found in the Visions of America Guidebook.

Side 1, Chapter 10

Answer to . . .

Viewing History Before railroads, most goods were shipped by water. Cities could not sell or ship goods without easy access to a canal, river, or ocean.

229

The Market Revolution, 1812–1845

Managing Time and Instruction

INSTRUCTION SUPPORT

These materials for instruction are provided for **each section** in the **Teaching Resources**. See **Units 3–4 folder** for Enrichment Support:

- Reproducible Lesson Plans in Lesson Plans folder • Learning Styles Lesson Plans in Learning Styles Lesson Plans folder • Big Idea Graphic Organizers in Big Idea Graphic Organizer folder • Guided Reading and Review • Quizzes • Test Preparation Practice booklet

DAILY LESSON	ENRICHMENT SUPPORT
1 A Market Economy (pp. 231–233)	• Literature Activity, Preacher to the World, found on **Resource Pro**
2 The Northern Section (pp. 236–239)	• Nystrom *Atlas of Our Country*, A Divided Nation, pp. 26–27 • Primary Source Activity, New England Mill Women, found on **Resource Pro** • Biography, Sarah Todd Astor, found on **Resource Pro**
3 The Southern Section (pp. 240–243)	• Critical Thinking Activity, Making Comparisons, found on **Resource Pro** • Comparing Primary Sources, On Slavery, Units 3–4 folder, pp. 14–15 • Critical Thinking Activity, Identifying Alternatives: Reacting to Slave Uprisings, found on **Resource Pro**
4 The Growth of Nationalism (pp. 244–248)	• Visual Learning Activity, The Jackson Ticket, Learning with Documents folder, p. 50 • Literature Activity, The Life of Washington, Units 3–4 folder, pp. 16–17 • Key Documents, The Monroe Doctrine, Learning with Documents folder, p. 86 • Nystrom *Atlas of Our Country*, The Second Wave of Immigration, pp. 24–25 • Skills for Life Activity, Units 3–4 folder, p. 18
5 The Age of Jackson (pp. 250–254)	• Primary Source Activity, President Jackson's Inauguration, Learning with Documents folder, p. 14 • Key Documents, Cherokee Address to the American People, Learning with Documents folder, p. 84 • Decision-Making Activity, Native American Fishing Rights, Decision-Making Activities folder, pp. 8–9 • Visual Learning Activity, The Presidential Election of 1840, found on **Resource Pro** • Your Region Has a Unique Economy, Why Study History? folder, p. 9

Running Out of Time?

- Use Tape 2, "An Emerging New Nation, 1800–1860," from **Visions of America** videotapes series.
- Use Chapter 8 Summary, from **Guide to the Essentials of American History** (English and Spanish).

Companion Web Site

The companion Web site offers online links for all chapter review activities. It also provides key content links and structured support for this chapter for both teachers and students.

http://www.Pathways.phschool.com

Teaching in the Information Age

Media and Technology

For the Student

Interactive Student Tutorial CD-ROM Chapter 8

Student Edition on Audiotape Chapter 8

American Heritage® CD-ROM

Guided Reading Audiotapes (English and Spanish) Chapter 8

For the Teacher

Resource Pro CD-ROM Chapter 8

Test Bank CD-ROM Chapter 8

Listening to Music CD "Swing Low, Sweet Chariot" and "Go Down, Moses"

Listening to Literature Audiotapes *Timeless Voices, Timeless Themes* from *Self-Reliance* by Ralph Waldo Emerson

Color Transparencies Political Cartoons, K-3; Critical Thinking, I-4

Assessment Options

Chapter Test Forms A&B Test Bank CD-ROM booklet

Test Bank CD-ROM Chapter 8

Standardized Test Preparation Handbook

Block Scheduling

Pacing Suggestions

For 90-minute Blocks

- Teach sections 1, 2, and 3 using Transparencies B-3, C-6, C-8, M-2, M-3, M-4, M-6, J-3, and H-8 and the Extended Class Periods Activity note on p. 232.
- Teach sections 4 and 5 using the Big Idea Graphic Organizers from Teaching Resources and the Background note on p. 247 for class discussions.

Additional Resources

- Prentice Hall's **American History Block Scheduling Support File** covers over 40 major topics in American history. Included are lesson plans, strategies, primary sources, literature, biographies, Great Debates, art history, simulations, and songs.
- **Prentice Hall United States History Video Collection™** contains 20 videotapes covering American history from beginnings to present.

Connections to American Literature

from Prentice Hall

Prentice Hall Literature *Timeless Voices, Timeless Themes* My Bondage and My Freedom by Frederick Douglass, pp. 458–463

Additional Resources

For the Student

John Ehle. *Trail of Tears: The Rise and Fall of the Cherokee Nation.* Anchor, 1988.

For the Teacher

Gerda Lerner. *Black Women in White America: A Documentary History.* Vintage, 1972.

Barbara M. Wertheimer. *We Were There: The Story of Working Women in America.* Pantheon, 1977.

Prentice Hall brings into the classroom the vast archives and scholarship of the nation's premier American history magazine. See "From the Archives of American Heritage®" and "About the Presidents" teaching notes in this chapter.

History Alive!

Teacher's Curriculum Institute, in partnership with Prentice Hall, provides unique materials that engage students with diverse learning styles. See History Alive!® unit on Manifest Destiny in a Growing Nation.

Student Performance Pack

Ensures success in the three critical areas of Reading, Test Taking, and English Language Development with the following materials:
- Guide to the Essentials of American History in English and Spanish
- Guided Reading Audiotapes in English and Spanish
- Interactive Student Tutorial CD-ROM
- Test Preparation Handbook
- Test Preparation Practice booklet

The Market Revolution
1812–1845

Introducing the Chapter

During the first half of the 1800s, expanding markets and thriving industries and businesses transformed American life. The Market Revolution, as this transformation was called, made the making of money the chief goal of most Americans. The change also created divisions between the poor and the wealthy, and between those in different regions of the country.

Themes in American History

The theme of this chapter, Economics, is listed at the beginning of this unit. An alternate theme is Geography. To teach this unit thematically, you may wish to use the Expansion, Reconstruction, Immigration folder in American History Block Scheduling Support.

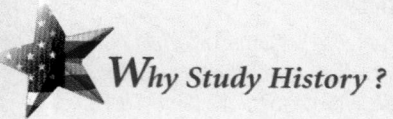

Why Study History?

Have students explore suggested ways of connecting the past to the present on page 255.

Answer to . . .

Viewing History Students should use this question as an aid in reading the chapter. The Northeast was home to huge textile mills in part because lands on the frontier were coming under cultivation. This freed up land and potential employees for manufacturing enterprises in the Northeast. Also, water power provided by the region's rivers served the industry well.

CHAPTER 8 The Market Revolution
1812-1845

CHAPTER FOCUS

This chapter examines the coming of industry and the economic changes that reached into every corner of America in the early 1800s. Industry brought manufactured goods to average households. It triggered the growth of banks and drew factory workers to cities. Industrial growth also shifted the balance of wealth and launched political battles over the role of government in the nation's growth.

The Why Study History? page at the end of this chapter explores the differences in regional economies today.

VIEWING HISTORY This painting shows a large wool mill in the 1830s. *Critical Thinking Why do you think textile mills arose in the northeastern United States?*

RESOURCE OPTIONS

Teaching Resources

Big Idea Graphic Organizer folder
Graphic summary of the main idea of the chapter.

Learning Styles Lesson Plans folder
Alternate lesson plans for diverse learning styles for each chapter.

Media and Technology

AmericanHeritage® CD-ROM
Time Tour The New Republic: Years of Growth and Expansion; *also,* An Expanding Nation: The Worlds of North and South

Prentice Hall United States History Video Collection™ Volume 8 *Causes of the Civil War*

| 1813 Textile mill built at Waltham, Massachusetts | c. 1830 Most clothing made outside the home | c. 1830 Banking industry is well established | 1837 Panic causes economic depression |

| 1810 | 1820 | 1830 | 1840 |

1 A Market Economy

SECTION PREVIEW

Objectives

1 Analyze the ways in which the American economy changed in the early 1800s.
2 Describe how banks influenced the country's economic growth.
3 *Key Terms* Define: Market Revolution; manufacturing; centralized; free enterprise system; capital; bank note.

Main Idea

In the early 1800s a new kind of economy emerged, in which goods were produced in factories and sold for money instead of being made in households.

Reading Strategy

Reinforcing Main Ideas As you read, refer back to the Main Idea from time to time and list details from the section that support it.

I n a very basic way water transformed the young economy of the United States. The waters of the Northeast gathered strength as they descended from mountaintops, surged through valleys, and plunged over waterfalls. The power harnessed from these moving waters ran the new machines in factories that sprang up in the early 1800s.

Products started rolling out of water-powered factories at an astounding rate. This increased supply of goods forever changed the patterns of American life. The self-sufficient household, where family members spun their own thread or made their own soap, was beginning to disappear.

An Expanding Economy

In the decades after the War of 1812, the American economy soared. While the United States remained mostly a nation of farmers, a new generation of Americans began buying and selling goods, borrowing and circulating money, and creating wealth. This change in the way Americans made, bought, and sold goods is known as the **Market Revolution.**

The Rise of Manufacturing The Market Revolution was fueled by the American genius for invention, which resulted in new and better ways to make and transport goods. Farmers started putting more and more frontier lands into production, and some of these lands were ideal for growing wheat and corn. Land in New England could then be put to other uses including **manufacturing,** the making of products by machinery.

In 1813 a group of businessmen led by a Boston merchant named Francis Cabot Lowell built a factory in Waltham, Massachusetts, to manufacture textiles. Lowell's was the world's first truly **centralized** textile factory. That is, all the tasks involved in making a product (in this case, cloth) were carried out in one place. Lowell's Waltham mill and the many later mills that were built along rivers in New

As this bank note shows, people began to earn a living outside the home in the early 1800s.

Objectives
You may wish to call students' attention to the objectives in the Section Preview. The objectives are reflected in the main headings of the section.

Bellringer
Ask students if they have ever come up with a plan for making money, such as taking on a paper route or selling T-shirts they've designed, and, if so, ask them to describe its success or failure.

Reading Strategy
Reinforcing Main Ideas Refer to the Reading Strategy in the Section Preview. You may wish to have volunteers share their lists of details with the class and, as they do, make a composite list on the chalkboard.

LESSON PLAN

Connecting to the Main Idea

1. Focus The American economy underwent a fundamental change in the early 1800s. Ask how this change altered the focus of American life.
2. Instruct Review the characteristics of the American economy during colonial times. Ask what factors led to economic change during the early 1800s. Then discuss the expansion of the free enterprise system and the changes it created. Ask students to describe the Market Revolution. How did the relationship between Americans and their work change as a result of the Market Revolution? What role did banks play in fueling the new economy?
3. Close The Market Revolution radically altered life throughout the United States. The next section explains how this revolution affected the northern region of the country.

BACKGROUND

Global Connections

The economic and territorial growth of the United States relied heavily on a sophisticated banking system, similar in structure to the one that had been established in the United Kingdom. The Rothschild family of financiers had funded Britain's war against Napoleon by making it possible for the British government to raise money by selling securities. The United States government applied the same principle, and between 1816 and 1821 it raised sufficient funds to create six new states, equal in size to six countries in Europe.

ACTIVITY
EXTENDED CLASS PERIODS

Time: 90 minutes.
Activity: Devise a plan for convincing Americans to buy a factory-made household item.
Grouping: Groups of four students.
Purpose: Through the efforts of entrepreneurs, products that were traditionally made in the household began to be manufactured in factories in the early 1800s. Have groups select a household product from the early 1800s and devise a scheme to persuade Americans to purchase it.
Roles: Entrepreneurs.
Outcome: Students will demonstrate the effects of manufactured goods on the household economy.

Answer to . . .

Interpreting Charts Household economy: people produce goods at home for private use; market economy: people work outside the home to produce goods for a business in exchange for money.

FACT Finder: Comparing Household and Market Economies

	Household Economy	Market Economy
Producers	Households	Industries
Labor	Members of the household produce a variety of goods at home.	Workers specialize in producing a certain product outside the home. They exchange their labor for cash.
Goods	Goods are made primarily to be used by the household.	Goods are sold on the open market for a profit.

Interpreting Charts The market revolution changed not only how goods were produced and used, but changed the nature of labor as well. *Economics How did household economy labor differ from market economy labor?*

England brought together all the tasks of spinning, weaving, and dyeing that turned raw, cleaned cotton into finished cloth.

From the 1820s through the 1840s, manufacturing industries arose in New England and spread across the Northeast and parts of the Northwest Territory, such as the Ohio River valley. Manufacturing would soon become the backbone of the North's economy.

Centralizing work dramatically increased production. In 1817 New England's textile mills produced 4 million yards of cotton cloth. By 1840 the amount was 323 million yards.

The changes of the Market Revolution were based on a **free enterprise system,** an economic system in which companies compete for profits. (See the *Economics Concepts* feature at left.) This system, also called capitalism, rewarded people who could find better, faster, and more efficient ways of running their businesses. It encouraged the creation of new industries, jobs, and wealth.

ECONOMICS CONCEPTS

free enterprise system: an economic system based on privately owned firms competing for profits

▼ **The Historical Context** Adam Smith's *The Wealth of Nations*, published in 1776, outlined the principles of the free enterprise system. Smith argued that businesses should follow the market forces of supply and demand rather than government regulation. Free enterprise expanded greatly in the United States during the early 1800s.

▼ **The Concept Today** The federal and state governments now play important roles in the economy, such as regulating business to protect workers and consumers. Yet free enterprise remains the heart of the American economy and the foundation of American prosperity.

Working Outside the Home For most Americans, "going to work" in the 1700s generally meant working in the home or around the farm. Of course, some skilled artisans did produce goods such as books or glass that could not be made easily at home. Others were employed in the shipping industry or legal or financial professions. Most people, however, simply labored to make the food, clothing, and shelter they needed. In the 1800s the building of new factories sharply increased the demand for people to work outside the home, for a specific number of hours each day and for a certain amount of money.

The Rise of Shopping As products became available and people worked for money, Americans began to shop. In colonial America, only the houses of wealthy planters and merchants had been full of goods. But the relatively simple homes of the 1700s gave way to much more decorated and furnished homes of the 1800s.

By the mid-1800s the homes of many average Americans were full of purchased items. Families bought reproductions of paintings to hang on their walls. They bought manufactured furniture and silverware. Household spinning wheels and looms fell silent as women purchased fabrics to make clothing.

Banks Spark Rapid Economic Growth

New types of businesses thrived during the Market Revolution. Banks quickly rose to the top as the most influential of the new enterprises. They provided **capital,** wealth that can be invested to produce goods and make money. Businesses used this capital to buy land or to invest in money-making projects.

The Rise of the Banking Industry The first real banks appeared in the United States in the 1780s and 1790s. By the 1830s hundreds of new banks had cropped up.

Generally, a group of private investors would obtain a charter from the state to start a bank. The bank made money by charging interest for the loans it made. It made these loans using the money that customers deposited in the bank for safekeeping. Banks thus helped the economy grow by providing the money that businesses needed to expand. The system generally worked out well. However, disasters could, and did, occur.

▶ RESOURCE OPTIONS

Teaching Resources

American History Block Scheduling Support On the Job: Industrialism in America, found in the Expansion, Reconstruction, Immigration folder, includes interdisciplinary lesson suggestions and activities for Geography and History, Primary Sources, Biography, and Literature.

Media and Technology

RESOURCE PRO

Literature Activity Preacher to the World, found on Resource Pro, features excerpts from the journals of Ralph Waldo Emerson to give students a glimpse of other reactions to American materialism.

Uncontrolled Lending Today, most deposits are insured by the government. Banks are required to keep a certain amount of cash on hand instead of lending it all out. In the 1800s, states did not restrict banks' runaway lending. The new banks often made bad loans to people who could not pay them back.

The banks then lacked the cash to give to depositors who wanted to take their money out. Customers would panic, rushing to the banks to get their money out before the banks went broke.

As a result, the American economy experienced wild booms followed by panics, bank failures, and depressions. Panics occurred in 1819 and later in 1837, the latter so severe that it disrupted the economy well into the 1840s.

Bank Notes Money in the early republic was not what it is today. The government did not issue paper money. Most people preferred to deal in specie, or coin, mainly of gold or silver. Specie was scarce, however, and difficult to carry around. The most common form of money was the **bank note,** a piece of paper that banks issued to their customers. People generally used bank notes to pay for goods and services.

Similar to modern-day checks, bank notes were promises to pay specie on demand. Anyone possessing a note could in theory walk into the bank anytime and cash it in for specie.

The problem with these notes was that banks simply printed more of them whenever

The well-to-do city merchant and his wife who posed for this scene in 1843 wanted to be shown in their "best room"—the parlor. *Culture* What objects in the engraving reveal the new American passion for buying goods?

they needed money, so the value of this money was unpredictable. A farmer, for instance, might sell some corn and receive in payment a $100 bank note that could be worth anything from $50 to $200 in specie, depending on the time and place he tried to cash it.

Despite such economic growing pains, banks were essential to the expansion of the economy during the 1800s. While different areas of the country grew at different rates, the United States as a whole achieved a new level of prosperity.

SECTION 1 REVIEW

Comprehension

1. **Key Terms** Define: (a) Market Revolution; (b) manufacturing; (c) centralized; (d) free enterprise system; (e) capital; (f) bank note.

2. **Summarizing the Main Idea** How did factories change the American economy in the early 1800s?

3. **Organizing Information** Make a chart that lists changes that occurred in the 1800s in the following categories: *Production of Goods, Types of Labor, Obtaining Goods,* and *Availability of Money.*

Critical Thinking

4. **Analyzing Time Lines** Review the time line at the start of the section. Choose any two entries and write a sentence for each describing its effects.

5. **Recognizing Cause and Effect** How might the rise in the number of factory workers affect the demand for manufactured goods? Explain your reasoning.

Writing Activity

6. **Writing an Expository Essay** How was the Market Revolution a "revolution"? Support your essay with facts from the section.

ENGINES OF CHANGE

Focus Remind students how new machines changed the way Americans worked, traveled, and shopped in the early 1800s. Advances in shipping and the invention of interchangeable parts led to new factories and a national market for manufactured goods.

Instruct Have students create a wish list of new products currently available that they or their parents would like to own. List students' suggestions on the chalkboard, noting next to each product whether it is used mainly for work, daily life, or entertainment and recreation. Repeat these steps for the items shown in the American Artifacts display. Then compare the two lists and discuss the ways in which work and nonwork activities have changed during the last 150 years.

Extend Students may be asked to research a town that flourished because of inventions of the early 1800s. Possibilities include food processing centers like Cincinnati, Ohio, or textile cities like Lowell, Massachusetts or Paterson, New Jersey.

Colt Revolver

Samuel Colt patented his revolving pistol in 1836. Later models were made using the "American system of manufacture," including interchangeable parts. The revolver had a single barrel and six chambers in a small, revolving cylinder.

Consumer Goods

The adjustable wrench and level were among the new consumer items that became available in the mid-1800s.

Harvesting Machine

This model shows the reaper invented by Cyrus McCormick in 1831. McCormick built a factory in Chicago in 1847 and used many new marketing methods to sell his product.

The John Bull

The Camden & Amboy Railroad imported this locomotive from England in 1831.

▶ RESOURCE OPTIONS

Teaching Resources

American History Block Scheduling Support On the Job: Industrialization in America, found in the Expansion, Reconstruction, and Immigration folder, includes interdisciplinary lesson suggestions and activities for Geography and History, Primary Sources, Biography, and Literature.

Safe Lock

This patented safe lock is one of the hundreds of new locks that were invented in the 1800s.

5

6

Office Safe

This office safe had separate compartments for company records and cash.

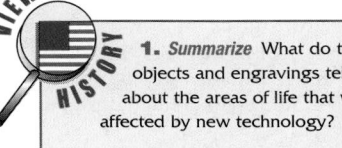

1. *Summarize* What do the objects and engravings tell you about the areas of life that were affected by new technology?

2. *Connecting to Today* What "engines of change" might be displayed to show the advances in technology in the past decade?

FROM EXHIBITIONS AND COLLECTIONS
AT THE SMITHSONIAN INSTITUTION'S
NATIONAL MUSEUM OF AMERICAN HISTORY

ENGINES OF CHANGE

When Englishman Samuel Slater moved to the United States in 1789 and began duplicating British textile machinery, he probably didn't know his work would transform the American economy. In fact, Slater's textile mills helped launch America's Industrial Revolution. The United States began to change from a country of farmers and artisans to an urban, industrial nation.

The Industrial Revolution gave Americans the tools and machinery to create new products and improve existing ones. No longer limited by human or animal power, a new system of manufacturing was born. This system used interchangeable parts, division of labor, and special-purpose tools. Companies were now able to produce goods in large quantities. *See* **1** *and* **2**.

Inventors' ideas became reality, as thousands of new patents were approved and manufactured. New harvesting machines allowed faster grain production. The steam engine increased the power available to manufacturers. The steamboat and locomotive not only sped passengers across the country more quickly, but also increased the market for manufactured products. The nature of work changed as more and more Americans worked in factories, for wages. *See* **3**, **4**, *and* **5**.

The 1800s produced more than new products and sources of power. Techniques to market and sell products now included testimonials, demonstrations, guarantees, and easy-payment plans. As businesses grew, financing, management, and record keeping became increasingly important. *See* **6**.

Answers to . . .

1. Farms and businesses benefited from new technology. People did not need to work as hard as they did in the 1700s to harvest crops or build furniture. Railroads decreased the cost and time needed to ship goods.

2. Answers will vary, but students should refer to advances in computing, communications, and transportation. Examples may include a personal computer, a cellular phone, a satellite, and a modem.

RESOURCE OPTIONS

Media and Technology

 Prentice Hall United States History Video CollectionTM Volume 7 *Democracy and Freedom*

 AmericanHeritage® CD-ROM

Time Tour The New Republic: Years of Growth and Expansion

The Northern Section

Objectives
You may wish to call students' attention to the objectives in the Section Preview. The objectives are reflected in the main headings of the section.

Bellringer
Ask students to list the pros and cons of living in a large city. As students share their lists, make a composite list on the chalkboard.

Reading Strategy
Formulating Questions Refer to the Reading Strategy in the Section Preview. When students have finished the reading, you may wish to have volunteers play the role of factory workers and other students use their questions to interview them.

LESSON PLAN
Connecting to the Main Idea

1. Focus The Market Revolution affected regions of the country in different ways. Although most northerners remained farmers, the region underwent significant economic and social changes. Ask students to describe these changes.

2. Instruct Discuss the changes brought about by the Market Revolution in the Old Northwest and in the Northeast. Ask how farmers in the Northwest contributed to the growth of cities in the Northeast. How did the changing nature of work affect the entire way of life in northern cities? What problems resulted in these cities?

Have students analyze the plight of factory and mill workers in the first half of the 1800s. Why did they feel powerless to change their working conditions?

3. Close Although the Old Northwest remained largely a region of farmers, in the Northeast the Market Revolution spurred industrialization and rapid urban growth. The next section describes the development of the southern region.

1832 Cholera epidemic	1834 National Trades Union formed	1840 About 12 percent of Americans live in cities	1850 New York City population reaches a half million

| 1830 | 1835 | 1840 | 1845 | 1850 |

2 The Northern Section

SECTION PREVIEW

Objectives

1 Trace the development of farming and industries in the North.
2 Describe the growth of cities in the North.
3 Explain how labor disputes arose in northern factories.
4 *Key Terms* Define: section; urban; population density; industrialization; tenement; strike; labor union.

Main Idea
Between 1800 and 1850, cities and industries expanded in the North, bringing new wealth but also new problems such as conflicts between factory workers and owners.

Reading Strategy
Formulating Questions Before you read, make a list of questions you might ask a northern factory worker about city life in the early 1800s.

In the early 1800s, Americans became more and more aware that their nation was divided into regions or **sections,** with distinct geographic, economic, and cultural differences. The two main sections during this period were the North and the South.

The North was made up of two parts. One was the Northeast, composed of New England, New York, New Jersey, and Pennsylvania. This area had once been the New England and Middle Colonies. The other part was the region north and west of the Ohio River. Historians call it the Old Northwest to distinguish it from the Northwest of today. It included land that is now Ohio, Indiana, Illinois, Michigan, Wisconsin, and part of Minnesota.

A woman going to work in one of the busy mills of the North carried her noon-day meal in this tin and wood lunch pail.

Farming in the Northwest
The fertile hills of the Old Northwest were ideal for growing corn, wheat, and other grains. Grains were profitable, but they tended to spoil. Farmers had to get them to market quickly or turn them into a product that would not spoil.

For example, corn could be used to raise pigs. Pigs could then be slaughtered and sold not just for meat, but also for fat, which was used to make soap, and bristles for brushes. Similarly, wheat and other crops were fed to cattle. Farm families also sold wheat, oats, barley, and corn to brewers and distillers, who used these crops to make beer and whiskey, products that were easy to store.

Many specialized businesses arose to handle the processing, transport, and selling of farm products. They included banks, slaughterhouses, distilleries, merchants, and shipping companies. From Ohio west into Illinois, agriculture fueled the growth of large cities such as Cincinnati and later Chicago. Cincinnati, for example, was known as "Porkopolis." Some 162,000 hogs were slaughtered there in 1835.

In the early 1800s, farmers sent flour, meal, pork products, whiskey, and other products by river to New Orleans to be sold in the Caribbean islands, the eastern United States, and Europe.

RESOURCE OPTIONS

Teaching Resources

 Reproducible Lesson Plan Lesson Plans folder, p. 64

Big Idea Graphic Organizer Big Idea Graphic Organizer folder, p. 36

Guided Reading and Review Units 3–4 folder, p. 5

Nystrom *Atlas of Our Country* A Divided Nation, pp. 26–27

Media and Technology

Prentice Hall United States History Video Collection™ Volume 11 *Industrialization and Urbanization*

Industries of the Northeast

The pork, beef, and beer of the Old Northwest were sold into a market where, increasingly, people no longer raised their own food. Although most people in the Northeast still lived on farms, many others now worked in factories in **urban** areas, places made up mostly of one or more cities.

These urban areas had fast-growing populations. As more people came to the cities to work, the Northeast's **population density,** or the amount of people living within a given space, increased as well. **Industrialization,** or the growth of industry, increased rapidly in Connecticut with the help of Eli Whitney, the inventor of the cotton gin. In 1797, Whitney built a factory in Hamden, Connecticut, to manufacture muskets using his concept of interchangeable parts. Other water-powered factories produced furniture, clocks, glass, and tin ware. By 1850 more people in Connecticut worked in manufacturing than in farming.

Pennsylvania's huge coal-mining industry got its start in 1820. The state also became a top producer of ships, lumber, iron, leather, and textiles. By 1850, the industrial city of Pittsburgh had 40 glass factories.

In Massachusetts, new industries produced shoes, carpet, and bricks. The town of Lynn, north of Boston, was to become the shoemaking capital of the country.

When Francis Cabot Lowell built the first totally centralized textile mill in Waltham, Massachusetts, in 1813, he launched an industry. New mills went up along many of New England's rivers. In 1826, the mill town of Lowell, Massachusetts, was founded and named for Francis Cabot Lowell. It would become a booming industrial center.

The Lowell mills hired young, unmarried women from New England farms to run the spinning and weaving machines. The women were promised a moral environment and a stable income. They enjoyed being able to earn and save money before they married. The women made about $3.25 for a 73-hour week in the 1830s. After deducting $1.25 for room

exploring TECHNOLOGY
A Textile Mill

New England mill builders adopted a system of belts to harness river power. On the first floor, cotton was combed; on the second floor it was spun into thread; on the third, thread was woven into cloth; and on the fourth, the cloth was dressed, or finished. *Geography Why was the Northeast a suitable place to build a factory?*

Urban and Rural Populations, 1800–1850

A bar graph titled "Urban and Rural Populations, 1800–1850" shows Number of Persons (in millions) on the y-axis (0 to 20) and Year on the x-axis (1800, 1810, 1820, 1830, 1840, 1850), with bars for Urban and Rural.

Source: *Historical Statistics of the United States, Colonial Times to 1970*

Interpreting Charts The changes in the United States economy led to changes in its population. **Geography** About how many Americans lived in cities in 1830? In 1850? Which grew faster during this period, the urban or rural population?

The Northeast was full of young people looking for work. Farming opportunities now were limited, because the population in the region had outgrown the available land in the region. Some young workers went west, but thousands went to the cities of the Northeast. In 1810 only about 6 percent of Americans lived in cities. By 1840, 12 percent lived in cities, an increase shown in the graph on the left.

The largest cities in colonial North America had had no more than 30,000 residents. By contrast, in the early United States, the population of New York City (Manhattan only) soared from about 33,000 in 1790 to 131,000 in 1820, and about 516,000 by 1850. The populations of Boston and Philadelphia also rose, as did those in smaller cities such as Baltimore.

Urban life differed greatly from colonial times, when human needs such as medical care, education, and care for the elderly took place within the household. Now, as workers spent more and more time away from the household, they could no longer supply these needs to their families at home. Children, sick relatives, and elderly family members in northern cities often had no support in times of trouble. Gradually, public institutions such as hospitals and schools began to fill this gap.

A growing number of urban poor people lived in areas where housing was cheap. By the 1830s, for example, the Five Points area in lower Manhattan had become notorious for its **tenements,** crowded apartments with poor standards of sanitation, safety, and comfort. Two decades later, a group of middle-class Methodist women described Five Points as "miserable-looking buildings, liquor-stores innumerable, neglected children by scores, playing in rags and dirt."

Cities were simply unable to handle the rapid increases in their populations. Police and fire services were primitive at best. Many cities lacked sewage systems and reliable supplies of fresh water. In 1832 and 1833, thousands of people were killed or sickened by a major outbreak of cholera, an intestinal disease caused by contaminated water.

and board, the average woman made about $2 per week, a good wage at a time when many basic goods cost only pennies.

Part of the reason the mill owners hired women laborers was that they were willing to work for about half the pay that men demanded. Most factory workers were women until the 1840s, when they were replaced by men, mainly Irish immigrants who were unable to find better-paying jobs.

Main Idea CONNECTIONS

What was life like for women mill workers?

Woman mill workers usually lived in boardinghouses run by the mill owners. Six days a week, twelve hours a day, from dawn till seven at night, they tended the grinding, clattering machines. In the evening they might attend lectures or classes, or gather in sewing or reading circles. Although the work was boring, the women valued the friendships they made. One mill worker recalled her work in the mill:

AMERICAN VOICES "There was a great deal of play mixed with it. We were not occupied more than half the time. The intervals were spent frolicking around among the spinning frames, teasing and talking to the older girls, or entertaining ourselves with games and stories in a corner."

—Mill worker Lucy Larcom

TEST PREPARATION

Have students read the passage on this page by Lucy Larcom and then answer the question below.

How did Lucy characterize her work days?

A They were long and boring.

(B) They had plenty of free time for play and games.

C She had to spend all day at the spinning frames.

D She had no other girls to talk to.

Labor Disputes in Factories

The Lowell mills treated their employees quite well in comparison to other early industries. Most factory owners of that time paid their employees little and did not provide benefits such as housing or food. Before long, workers began to demand more from their bosses.

Workers Go on Strike   While workers toiled for almost nothing, they saw factory owners grow rich. They began to want a slice of the wealth that their hard labor produced.

Workers' main complaints were about long hours and low wages. Since the government set no minimum wage, workers could not go to the legislatures or the courts for help. In fact, they only had one real weapon: They could call for a **strike,** or work stoppage.

Strikes had occurred as early as the 1700s, when sailors and dockworkers walked off their jobs. Shoemakers also launched strikes in the first decade of the 1800s. From 1834 through 1836, more than 150 strikes took place in the United States, mainly for shorter hours and higher pay. Even in Lowell, one out of every six women workers went on strike in 1834 when employers cut wages by 15 percent because of poor sales.

The First Labor Unions   In 1834, during this period of growing labor activity, workers organized the first national **labor union,** the National Trades Union (NTU). A labor union is an organization of workers formed to protect the interests of its members, usually by negotiating to resolve issues such as wages, hiring practices,

and working conditions. Close to 300,000 people joined the NTU or other labor unions in the 1830s, a large number for that period.

These early unions soon died out, however. Factory owners went to court and obtained rulings that outlawed labor organizations. Workers were also hard hit by the economic depressions of 1837 and 1839, which caused higher unemployment and lower wages.

Despite its failures, the early labor movement showed that some workers were willing to take action against their employers. One mill worker recalled her response when some women hesitated to strike during a protest against wage cuts:

> **AMERICAN VOICES**   "Not one of them having the courage to lead off, I . . . became impatient and started on ahead, saying, with childish bravado, 'I don't care what you do, I am going to turn out [strike], whether any one else does or not'; and I marched out, and was followed by the others. As I looked back at the long line that followed me, I was more proud than I have ever been since at any success I may have achieved."
>
> —*Lowell mill worker Harriet Robinson, 1836*

In time the labor movement would build on the pride of people such as Robinson. By the 1840s, the North had a booming and complex economy with a mix of industry and agriculture. It was increasingly a region of cities and towns, banks and factories, with all the benefits and problems that come with growth.

SECTION 2 REVIEW

Comprehension

1. *Key Terms*   Define: (a) section; (b) urban; (c) population density; (d) industrialization; (e) tenement; (f) strike; (g) labor union.

2. *Summarizing the Main Idea*   In what ways did the economy of the North change from 1800 to 1850?

3. *Organizing Information*   Make a web diagram of the North's economy. Include circles for the *Northeast* and the *Old Northwest*.

Critical Thinking

4. *Analyzing Time Lines*   Review the time line at the start of the section. Describe one effect that each entry might have caused.

5. *Drawing Conclusions*   (a) In what ways did economic change in the North link people together? (b) In what ways did it push them apart from one another?

Writing Activity

6. *Writing an Expository Essay*   As a journalist in the 1840s, write an essay describing the life of mill workers and efforts to improve conditions.

RESOURCE OPTIONS

Teaching Resources

 Quiz Units 3–4 folder, p. 6

Student Performance Pack

 Guide to the Essentials Chapter 8, Section 2 (English and Spanish)

Media and Technology

 AmericanHeritage® CD-ROM

Time Tour   An Expanding Nation: The Worlds of North and South

---

ACTIVITY
LEARNING STYLES

Assume the role of a worker who is trying to persuade his co-workers to strike, while students role-play the following: a male worker with a large family and a sick wife at home; an unmarried woman with no children; a woman with a large family and no husband; and a young, unmarried male. Ask students to explain their reasons for wanting or not wanting to strike. *(Interpersonal)*

Answers to
SECTION 2 REVIEW

1. (a) section, see p. 236; (b) urban, see p. 237; (c) population density, see p. 237; (d) industrialization, see p. 237; (e) tenement, see p. 238; (f) strike, see p. 239; (g) labor union, see p. 239.

2. The Northeast became industrialized and urban, and workers began to form unions. With new transportation systems, wheat and corn farming flourished in the Old Northwest, as did the livestock trade.

3. Diagrams should include information in the answer to question 2.

4. Sample answers: 1832—death or illness of people due to polluted waters; 1834—some improvement in pay or working conditions; 1840—cities becoming more crowded; 1850—inadequate housing and health care, business boom.

5. Sample answers: (a) People and industries in the North relied on farm products from the South, while the South needed northern markets. (b) Southerners resented the North's wealth and its dependence on banks, while northerners increasingly opposed slavery in the South.

6. Essays should show an understanding of the benefits and drawbacks of factory life.

1808
Congress bans importation of slaves

1820
Slave population reaches 1.5 million

1822
Vesey's revolt

1831
Turner's Rebellion

1850
Slave population reaches 3.2 million

3 The Southern Section

SECTION 3

The Southern Section

Objectives

You may wish to call students' attention to the objectives in the Section Preview. The objectives are reflected in the main headings of the section.

Bellringer

Ask students to describe a southern or a northern accent. Next ask them to explain the phrase *regional difference.* Then ask students what regional differences exist between the North and the South today.

Reading Strategy

Analyzing Cause and Effect Refer to the Reading Strategy in the Section Preview. You may wish to model a composite list on the chalkboard and have students discuss the significance of each effect.

LESSON PLAN
Connecting to the Main Idea

1. Focus Explain that most of the South's economy centered on commercial agriculture. Yet it was also a dynamic society based on a free enterprise system. Ask what made its economy flourish.

2. Instruct Discuss the South's economy. Ask how agriculture differed in the North and South. In what ways were southern planters and farmers as capitalistic as their northern counterparts? How did the Market Revolution affect the South?

Analyze the role enslaved people played in the southern economy. Would southern commercial agriculture have been possible without slavery?

3. Close The Market Revolution created deep divisions between the North and South. Although no less vital, the South's economy was very different from that of the North. The next section describes the growth of nationalism and the division in United States politics.

3 The Southern Section

SECTION PREVIEW

Objectives

1. Compare the South's economy to that of the North.
2. Compare slave life on small farms and large plantations.
3. Describe the slave revolts of the early 1800s.
4. *Key Terms* Define: rural; Turner's Rebellion.

Main Idea

In the early 1800s cotton farming became the South's main economic activity. This boosted the slave trade, triggering slave revolts in 1822 and 1831.

Reading Strategy

Analyzing Cause and Effect As you read, list the effects of increased cotton farming in the South.

One famous phrase sums up the economy of the South in the first half of the 1800s: "King Cotton."† Why cotton? The answer could be found in the closets and dresser drawers of people in Europe and the Americas. They were giving up their wool and linen clothing for the more comfortable cotton.

In 1820, the South produced 160 million pounds of raw cotton. By 1830, the harvest had doubled. The 1850 crop surpassed a billion pounds. In 1860 King Cotton made up two thirds of the total value of American exports, and had created enormous wealth in the South.

Loading and unloading cotton shipments at the port city of New Orleans in 1883.

The Economy of the South

The South consisted of six of the original thirteen states: Delaware, Maryland, Virginia (including what would become West Virginia), North Carolina, South Carolina, and Georgia. It also included newer states carved out of former Indian lands south of Ohio that stretched from the Appalachian Mountains to the Mississippi River: Kentucky, Tennessee, Alabama, Mississippi, Louisiana, and Arkansas. Most of these southern states had economies based on cotton.

The Geography of Southern Farming While urban centers developed in the North, the South remained mostly **rural,** made up of farms and countryside instead of cities. The physical geography of the South made farming extremely profitable. Farmers could count on 200 to 290 frost-free days a year in which to grow crops. Fertile soil and plentiful rain encouraged the spread of agriculture.

The development of industry progressed slowly in the early 1800s. In fact, although southerners resented being dependent on northern

---

† The term "King Cotton" first appeared in an 1855 book, *Cotton Is King,* by David Christy.

RESOURCE OPTIONS

Teaching Resources

📁 **Reproducible Lesson Plan** Lesson Plans folder, p. 65

📁 **Big Idea Graphic Organizer** Big Idea Graphic Organizer folder, p. 37

📁 **Guided Reading and Review** Units 3–4 folder, p. 7

Media and Technology

 Color Transparencies Geographic Setting, M-4; Links Across Time, J-3

banks, shipping companies, and textile mills, few southerners entered into these industries. Even lawyers, doctors, and preachers hoped to retire eventually and become plantation farmers.

Most plantation farmers of this period did not inherit their wealth from the gentlemen farmers of the 1700s. Typically, this new gentry descended from small farmers who had lived in log cabins. During this period perhaps 15,000 families owned plantations, and most earned their wealth through hard work.

By contrast, hundreds of thousands of farm families owned a few slaves, or none, and raised their own cash crops, food crops, and livestock. During the early 1800s, half of the cotton crop was produced on farms with six slaves or fewer.

With the invention of the cotton gin in 1793, southerners scrambled to put more land into cotton production. Small farmers seized this new opportunity, streaming west into uncultivated parts of the trans-Appalachian region. Within a generation, however, most of these farmers had been bought out by the big plantation owners, who acquired huge tracts of land for cotton production.

Not all southern states changed over to cotton, however. Virginia and North Carolina continued to be mainly tobacco states. Sugar and rice crops thrived in hot and wet places such as South Carolina. Kentucky developed a varied rural economy that included the breeding of thoroughbred horses.

Slow Urban Growth Although the South was mainly rural, cities did develop gradually. They included New Orleans, Louisiana; Charleston, South Carolina; and Richmond, Virginia. These cities had smaller populations than those in the North. Yet they shared some of the problems that plagued New York and Boston, such as poor housing and sanitation.

During this period, fewer than 8 percent of white southerners lived in towns of more than 4,000 people. On the other hand, southern towns and cities were home to large numbers of free African Americans. By 1850, of the 3.7 million blacks nationwide, 12 percent were free. Some lived in the North, but most resided in southern cities or rural areas away from the large plantations.

The Slavery System

By 1804, all the northern states had either banned slavery or passed laws to end it gradually. The Constitution had specified that

Five generations of an African American family—all enslaved—posed for this photograph outside their plantation home in 1862. *Culture* Could this photograph be used as evidence of living conditions during the 1840s? Explain your answer.

Congress could not end the slave trade before 1808, so in that year Congress banned all further importation of slaves to the United States.

In the South, however, the slave trade increased sharply for the next half-century due to population growth among people already enslaved. In 1820, the slave population numbered about 1.5 million. Just 30 years later, in 1850, the population had more than doubled, to about 3.2 million. By 1860, African American slaves made up more than half of the population of South Carolina and of Mississippi as well as two fifths of the population in Florida, Georgia, Alabama, and Louisiana.

> **Main Idea**
> **CONNECTIONS**
> What happened to the slave population in the South after the importation of slaves was banned?

Slavery on Small and Large Farms The life of enslaved Americans varied. On small farms, slaves often worked side by side with their owners in the fields. They sometimes ate together and slept in the same house. But just as often, enslaved workers endured all manner of cruelties without family or friends to turn to for support and protection.

Most slaves, however, did not live on small farms but on the large cotton plantations. By 1850, cotton farming employed nearly 60 percent of the enslaved African Americans in the United States. These people lived in a sizable community of slaves, usually 20 or more. On

Graphing the Main Idea

To make sure students understand the main idea of this section, you may wish to use the multiflow map graphic organizer below.

Tell students that a multiflow map shows the causes and effects of a development. Ask students to use the multiflow map to record the causes and effects of the South's flourishing cotton economy.

Teaching Tip A template for this graphic organizer can be found in the Color Transparencies, G-5.

COMPARING PRIMARY SOURCES

SLAVERY

The quotations below reflect opposing views of slavery that fueled the nation's divisive debate on the issue.

In Support of Slavery	In Opposition to Slavery
"A merrier being does not exist on the face of the globe than the Negro slave of the United States. They are happy and contented, and the master is much less cruel than is generally imagined. Why then . . . should we attempt to disturb his contentment by planting in his mind a vain and indefinite desire for liberty—something which he cannot understand?" —*Prof. Thomas R. Dew, speech to the Virginia legislature, 1832*	"I thank God I am not property now, but am regarded as a man like yourself. . . . You may perhaps think hard of us for running away from slavery, but as for myself, I have but one apology to make for it, which is this: I have only to regret that I did not start at any early period." —*Henry Bibb, who escaped from slavery with his family, in a letter to his former master, 1844*

ANALYZING VIEWPOINTS Compare the main arguments made by the two writers.

the plantations, life was generally harsher than on small farms. Workers often toiled in gangs under the supervision of foremen.

For women in particular, life could be extremely difficult. In addition to bearing and caring for their own children and taking care of their households, they cooked and served food, cleaned houses and clothes, and labored in the fields. In addition, some women had to endure the threat of physical or sexual abuse by slave owners.

Main Idea CONNECTIONS

What conditions led to slave revolts?

Slaves as Property Farming was a business, and most owners saw slaves as mere property that performed labor. In a bill of sale from 1811, a slave named Eve and her child, at a price of $156, are listed between a plow for $1.60 and "Eight Fancy Chairs" for $9.25.

As the demand for slaves rose, so did the prices that slave traders demanded. A "prime" field worker between 18 and 25 years old cost about $500 in 1832. By 1837 the price had soared to $1,300, a huge amount at that time. Starting a plantation, therefore, was very expensive and out of the reach of

most farmers. Yet after the initial investment, slaves cost only $15 to $60 a year to support.

Because replacing a slave was so costly, slaveowners generally kept their slaves healthy enough to work. But the system provided little else. One enslaved man, Moses Grandy, was standing in the street when he saw his wife go by in a group of African Americans who had been sold to a slaveholder named Rogerson. Grandy later recalled:

AMERICAN VOICES "Mr. Rogerson was with them on his horse, armed with pistols. I said to him, "For God's sake, have you bought my wife?" He said he had: when I asked him what she had done, he said she had done nothing, but that her master wanted money. He drew out a pistol and said that if I went near the wagon on which she was, he would shoot me. I asked for leave to shake hands with her, which he refused, but said I might stand at a distance and talk with her. My heart was so full that I could say very little. . . . I have never seen or heard from her that day to this. I loved her as I love my life."

—*Narrative of the Life of Moses Grandy, 1844*

Slave Revolts

Only a small percentage of slaves ever managed to escape their captivity or to win their freedom. Rebellion, especially on a large scale, stood little chance of success. While historians have documented scores of slave rebellions, most were small, spontaneous responses to cruel treatment and ended in tragic failure.

Vesey's Plan In 1800, the year of Gabriel Prosser's revolt, a young slave named Denmark Vesey bought his freedom with $600 he won in a street lottery. He worked as a carpenter and became a preacher at the local African Methodist Episcopal Church. Vesey was self-educated and read anti-slavery literature. He grew increasingly angry at the sufferings of his fellow African Americans.

Vesey preached against slavery, quoting the Declaration of Independence and the Bible. He criticized African Americans who would not stand up to whites.

In 1822 Vesey's anger turned to action. He laid plans for the most ambitious slave revolt in American history. In a conspiracy that reportedly involved hundreds or even thousands of

---

Answer to . . .

Comparing Primary Sources Dew argues that slaves are already content and can't do without masters; Bibb argues that slavery turns men into property and must be escaped.
Main Idea Connections Sample answer: Slaves were viewed as property, without basic human rights.

 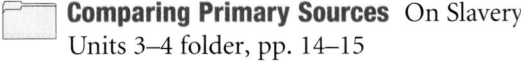 **RESOURCE OPTIONS**

Teaching Resources

 Comparing Primary Sources On Slavery, Units 3–4 folder, pp. 14–15

ATLAS **Nystrom** *Atlas of Our Country* A Divided Nation, pp. 26–27

Media and Technology

 RESOURCE PRO

Critical Thinking Activity Identifying Alternatives: Reacting to Slave Uprisings, found on Resource Pro, allows students to apply this skill by assuming the role of a Virginia legislator after Turner's Rebellion.

rebels, Vesey plotted to seize the city of Charleston in July 1822. Later accounts said that he intended to raid the arsenal, kill all the white residents, free the slaves, and burn the city to the ground.

Like Gabriel Prosser, Vesey was betrayed by some of his followers. In June, South Carolina troops smashed the rebellion before it could get started. Thirty-five African Americans were hanged, including Vesey. Another 32 were expelled from South Carolina. Four white men received fines and prison terms for aiding the rebels.

Turner's Rebellion Nat Turner, a 31-year-old African American preacher, planned and carried out a violent uprising in August 1831 known as **Turner's Rebellion.** Acting under what he believed was divine inspiration, he led up to 70 slaves in raids on white families in southeastern Virginia. In attacks on four plantations, the rebels killed 57 white people.

Eventually, local militia captured most of the rebels. The state of Virginia hanged about 20 of the slaves, including Turner. Crowds of frightened and angry whites rioted, slaughtering about a hundred African Americans who had had no part in the revolt.

White Southerners Alarmed Slave revolts were a white southerner's nightmare, since in many communities African Americans outnumbered the white population. Virginia, which was not a cotton state, briefly considered

African American Nat Turner claimed that an eclipse of the sun in 1831 was a sign that "I should arise and prepare myself, and slay my enemies with their own weapons." This etching depicts his capture. *Government How did Virginia respond to Turner's Rebellion?*

ending slavery in order to ease this threat. But instead, it joined other southern states in tightening restrictions on slaves following the Vesey and Turner rebellions. Virginia and North Carolina passed laws against teaching enslaved people to read. Some states prevented African Americans from moving freely or meeting.

SECTION 3 REVIEW

Comprehension

1. *Key Terms* Define: (a) rural; (b) Turner's Rebellion.
2. *Summarizing the Main Idea* How did cotton growing change the South?
3. *Organizing Information* Make a chart to compare and contrast the economic activities of the North and South.

Critical Thinking

4. *Analyzing Time Lines* Review the time line at the start of the section. Choose any three entries and explain how they are related to each other.
5. *Drawing Conclusions* Why, do you think, did some southerners retire from their professions to become plantation owners? How might this help to explain southerners' strong defense of the slave system?

Writing Activity

6. *Writing an Expository Essay* From the point of view of a European visitor traveling through the South in 1840, write an essay describing slave life. Include observations of slavery on plantations and on small farms.

The Growth of Nationalism

| 1819 McCulloch v. Maryland | 1819 Dartmouth College v. Woodward | 1823 Monroe Doctrine | 1824 Gibbons v. Ogden | 1825 John Quincy Adams becomes President | 1828 Andrew Jackson elected President |

1815 · 1820 · 1825 · 1830

Objectives

You may wish to call students' attention to the objectives in the Section Preview. The objectives are reflected in the main headings of the section.

Bellringer

Ask students with which they feel a stronger identification—the state they live in or the United States. Have them explain their responses.

Reading Strategy

Arranging Events in Order Refer to the Reading Strategy in the Section Preview. You may wish to have students convert their lists into a time line to reinforce section content.

LESSON PLAN

Connecting to the Main Idea

1. Focus As American leaders sought to strengthen the national government in order to give it more power over the country's growing economy, a deep split in American politics resulted. Ask what new nationalist policies the government adopted.

2. Instruct Ask how Jackson's defeat in 1824 contributed to the development of the second American party system. What role did the National Republicans believe the government should play in the economy? What position did Jacksonian Democrats take?

Ask students to analyze the role of specific economic interests in the second party system. How does the debate over the role of the national government in the economy continue in politics today?

3. Close The growth of nationalism created a split in American politics that resulted in the development of two distinct parties. In 1828, the people elected Andrew Jackson as their new leader. The next section discusses his term in office.

4 The Growth of Nationalism

SECTION PREVIEW

Objectives

1 Give examples of the rise of nationalism at home and abroad.
2 Describe why the election of 1824 was controversial.
3 Compare the views of the National Republicans and the Jacksonian Democrats.
4 **Key Terms** Define: *McCulloch* v. *Maryland; Dartmouth College* v. *Woodward; Gibbons* v. *Ogden;* Monroe Doctrine.

Main Idea

The rise of nationalism among Americans could be seen in key Supreme Court rulings and in government policies at home and abroad. Nationalism also affected the growth of new political parties.

Reading Strategy

Arranging Events in Order As you read, jot down the key events of the presidential elections of 1824 and 1828. Then review your list to make sure it is in chronological order.

Supreme Court Chief Justice John Marshall

In 1800, a resident of Georgia might have called himself a citizen of Georgia, and a resident of Pennsylvania probably saw himself as a citizen of that state. But, if questioned again in the mid-1820s, these men might have replied that they were citizens of the United States of America.

During the 1820s, Americans underwent a shift in thinking toward the modern view of ourselves as belonging to a country under a national government, instead of an association of states under separate governments. Reflecting this shift, a new generation of American leaders sought to exercise the powers of the federal government to unite the country.

Nationalism at Home

After the War of 1812, the nation was weary of conflict, both with Europe and among its own regions. It adopted new nationalist policies to resolve political struggles at home and abroad. In domestic affairs, the Supreme Court under Chief Justice John Marshall made key decisions that strengthened the federal government's role in the nation's economic business.

Supporting the National Bank The Constitution did not specifically grant the federal government the right to charter a national bank. Those who strictly interpreted the Constitution maintained that such a bank was merely a convenience, not a necessity. In 1819, the issue made its way to the Supreme Court. The case involved Maryland's attempt to wipe out the National Bank by levying heavy taxes on it. Maryland's action challenged Congress's authority to create such an institution.

In *McCulloch* v. *Maryland,* Chief Justice Marshall ruled that Congress did have the authority to charter the bank. The powers of the federal government were greater than those spelled out in the Constitution, Marshall said. He based his argument on Article I, Section 8, which states that Congress has the right "to

▶ RESOURCE OPTIONS

Teaching Resources

📁 **Reproducible Lesson Plan** Lesson Plans folder, p. 66

📁 **Big Idea Graphic Organizer** Big Idea Graphic Organizer folder, p. 38

📁 **Guided Reading and Review** Units 3–4 folder, p. 9

make all laws necessary and proper" for carrying out the powers granted it under the Constitution. Thus Congress had the power to create such a bank if it wished.

Furthermore, Chief Justice Marshall stressed that because the national government had created the bank, no state had the power to tax it. "The power to tax is the power to destroy," he pointed out. No state could destroy by taxes what the federal government under the Constitution had created.

Protecting Contracts In another 1819 ruling, the Court prohibited New Hampshire from changing the charter of Dartmouth College. The college had been chartered during colonial times. In *Dartmouth College v. Woodward,* the Court ruled that states cannot interfere in such contracts. The long-term effect of the ruling was to protect business contracts, providing further stability to the economy.

Regulating Commerce A man named Aaron Ogden purchased a state license giving him exclusive rights to operate a New York-to-New Jersey steamboat line. When a competitor, Thomas Gibbons, started a business on the same route, Ogden sued him. Gibbons said he operated under federal license.

In the 1824 case *Gibbons v. Ogden,* Chief Justice Marshall declared that states could not regulate commerce on interstate waterways. In effect, the ruling gave the federal government authority over all types of interstate business.

Nationalism Abroad

As the Supreme Court was strengthening federal authority, American Presidents were strengthening the nation's foreign policy. The new policies took shape under the leadership of President James Monroe and his Secretary of State, John Quincy Adams, the son of Abigail and John Adams.

One of Monroe's main concerns was to ease tensions with Britain, which remained high following the War of 1812. In 1817 the United States and Britain signed the Rush-Bagot Agreement, which called on both sides to reduce the number of warships in the Great Lakes region. The following year the two

countries agreed to extend the northern border of the United States westward along the 49° N latitude from the Great Lakes to the Rocky Mountains.

A second concern for Monroe was that European countries, which were recovering from several years of warfare,[†] would resume their efforts to colonize the Western Hemisphere. Starting in 1815, Spain's colonies in South America had rebelled and won independence. Monroe had to decide what type of relations to have with these new nations.

American policy on these urgent matters was spelled out firmly by President Monroe in his yearly address to Congress on December 2, 1823. The speech, influenced by Adams, established a policy that has been followed to some degree by every President since Monroe. The **Monroe Doctrine,** as it is called, had four main parts:

(1) The United States would not get involved in the internal affairs of European countries, nor would it take sides in wars among them.

[†] From 1792 to 1815, the armies of the French general Napoleon Bonaparte marched through Europe, bringing much of the continent under his control. After Napoleon's empire crumbled in 1815, European nations struggled to regain their former strength.

Main Idea
CONNECTIONS

How was the Monroe Doctrine an example of nationalism?

Nationalist Supreme Court Decisions, 1819–1824

Case	Issues	Outcome
McCulloch v. Maryland (1819)	Does the government have the power to create a national bank? Do states have the right to tax institutions created by the federal government?	Reinforced (1) the doctrine of implied powers and (2) the principle of the power of the national government over state governments.
Dartmouth College v. Woodward (1819)	Was Dartmouth's contract protected by the Constitution? Was New Hampshire interfering with the contract?	Prevented state interference in business contracts. Gave stability to the economy by encouraging growth of corporations.
Gibbons v. Ogden (1824)	Who has the power to regulate navigation, the states or the federal government?	Established the federal government's right to regulate all aspects of interstate commerce.

Interpreting Tables Chief Justice John Marshall made several decisions that strengthened the authority of the federal government. *Government How do these decisions reflect the shift toward nationalism?*

---

(2) The United States recognized the existing colonies and states in the Western Hemisphere and would not interfere with them.

(3) The United States would not permit any further colonization of the Western Hemisphere.

(4) Any attempt by a European power to control any nation in the Western Hemisphere would be viewed as a hostile action toward the United States.

These points are summed up in this quotation from Monroe's address:

KEY DOCUMENTS "Our policy in regard to Europe . . . is, not to interfere in the internal concerns of any of its powers; to consider the government de facto [in power] as the legitimate government for us; to cultivate friendly relations with it, and to preserve those relations by a frank, firm, and manly policy, meeting in all instances the just claims of every power, submitting to injuries [aggression] from none. . . . It is impossible that the allied [European] powers should extend their political system to any portion of either continent without endangering our peace and happiness. . . . "

—*The Monroe Doctrine, speech by President James Monroe to Congress, December 2, 1823*

The United States did not have the armed forces necessary to make the Monroe Doctrine anything but a paper declaration of policy. Still, the declaration was a bold one for a young nation whose Capitol had been burned to the ground by a foreign army only a decade earlier.

The Election of 1824

On July 4, 1826, the 50th anniversary of the Declaration of Independence, former Presidents Thomas Jefferson and John Adams both died. This was just one among many signs that the founding generation of American leaders had passed into history. Adams had lived just long enough to see his son, John Quincy Adams, reach the height of his political career by winning the 1824 race for President.

This was the first presidential election in which no candidate could boast of having been a leader during the Revolution. Besides Adams, the main candidates in the election of 1824 were two brilliant political leaders, John C. Calhoun of South Carolina and Henry Clay of Kentucky, as well as the popular General Andrew Jackson of Tennessee.

Main Idea
CONNECTIONS

How did Calhoun's political role change during his career?

John C. Calhoun

AMERICAN BIOGRAPHY John Caldwell Calhoun is remembered as a champion of the South. Born to a prominent South Carolina family on March 18, 1782, Calhoun trained as a lawyer. In 1811 he married a wealthy heiress, which allowed him to give up his practice and become a statesman and gentleman farmer. At Fort Hill, his 500-acre plantation in South Carolina, Calhoun had about 70 slaves.

As a statesman for four decades, Calhoun was one of the towering figures in Washington. He served in the House of Representatives; as Monroe's Secretary of War; as Vice President under Presidents Adams and Jackson; as Secretary of State for President James K. Polk; and finally in the Senate.

In the House, Calhoun allied himself with the great statesman Henry Clay, whom he would later run against for President. Calhoun developed a close friendship with another future opponent, John Quincy Adams, who was then Secretary of State. Adams hailed Calhoun's support for nationalism, stating that Calhoun "is above all sectional and factious prejudices more than any other statesman of this Union with whom I have ever acted."

John C. Calhoun (1782–1850)

Early on, Calhoun was an outspoken advocate of nationalism. In Congress he sponsored a variety of economic measures to help unify the nation. He headed committees that created the Second Bank of the United States, a national road system, a modernized navy, and protective tariffs to boost American businesses.

During the 1820s, Calhoun's attention turned more toward defending southern sectional interests. Yet even his fierce support for slavery stemmed from his concern for holding the Union together. He despaired of seeing the slavery issue tear the nation in two. He threw his efforts into keeping the North from controlling the national government and pushing the South toward secession. Yet in 1850 he correctly predicted the future breakup of the Union. On his deathbed March 31, he cried, "The South! The poor South!"

Devoted as he was to the United States, Calhoun was even more devoted to his principles. He once wrote: "My politics, I think I may say with perfect truth, has . . . been founded on certain fixed principles; and to carry them into effect has been my highest ambition." ■

A Controversial Race

Calhoun withdrew from the crowded 1824 race, instead running for Vice President, where he stood a better chance of success. This left Adams to face two other American heroes, Henry Clay and Andrew Jackson.

Clay, a Passionate Orator   Henry Clay, former Speaker of the House and United States senator from Kentucky, was the most colorful politician of his generation. Known as "Harry of the West," Clay loved to drink and gamble, popular pastimes in his frontier homeland. He was energetic and charming, with a magnificent gift for speech-making.

Like Calhoun, Clay married into wealth and bought a plantation. Clay owned slaves but shared Jefferson's discomfort with slavery. He tried and failed to bring slavery in Kentucky to a gradual end, and in his will, Clay freed his own slaves.

Quick-witted and quick-tempered, Clay survived two duels with politicians who had offended him. He had once claimed that he would "rather be right than be President." In 1824, however, he wanted to be President. He made no secret of his ambition, and he was willing to make political deals to get there.

Jackson, Man of the People   Finally, the 1824 election had a wild card: Andrew Jackson. Jackson had served in the Senate in the 1790s and was a wealthy plantation owner near Nashville, Tennessee. A brilliant general, Jackson's victories in the War of 1812 and his attacks on the Seminole Indians in Florida won him widespread popularity, as did his colorful personality. His opponents, on the other hand, saw him as poorly educated and ill-tempered.

The "Corrupt Bargain"   In the 1824 election Jackson won the most popular votes, but none of the candidates received the required majority of Electoral College votes. Thus in February 1825, as the Constitution required, the House of Representatives voted to decide the election.

Clay managed to swing Kentucky's votes to Adams to give him the victory. Just days later, Adams made Clay his Secretary of State.

Jackson supporters charged that Adams and Clay had made a "corrupt bargain" to deny Jackson the win.

Two New Parties Face Off

Adams and Clay wanted to use federal power to strengthen the nation's economy, as Adams declared:

> **AMERICAN VOICES** "The spirit of improvement is abroad upon the earth. . . . Let us not be unmindful that liberty is power; and that the tenure [holding] of power by man is . . . upon condition that it shall be exercised . . . to improve the condition of himself and his fellow men."
>
> —*President John Quincy Adams, 1825*

Internal Improvements   Adams supported the building of roads, canals, bridges, lighthouses, universities, and many other public improvements. Adams and Clay both favored protective tariffs to make foreign goods more expensive and encourage the purchase of American-made goods.

This 1828 election poster praises Andrew "Old Hickory" Jackson for honoring the constitutional election system in 1824 even though it cost him the presidency. *Government Describe the meaning of the words in lines 4 and 5: "He who could not barter nor bargain for the presidency!"*

TEST PREPARATION

Have students read the passage on this page by John Quincy Adams and then answer the question below.

Adams clearly felt that power—

A had nothing to do with liberty.

B blocked the spirit of improvement.

C had no particular purpose for the nation.

Ⓓ should be used to improve the conditions of Americans.

Answer to . . .

Viewing History They refer to the "corrupt bargain" of 1824, when Adams became President and made Clay Secretary of State.

Answers to
SECTION 4 REVIEW

1. (a) *McCulloch* v. *Maryland*, see p. 244; (b) *Dartmouth College* v. *Woodward*, see p. 245; (c) *Gibbons* v. *Ogden*, see p. 245; (d) Monroe Doctrine, see p. 245.

2. Under Presidents Monroe and Adams, nationalist measures were seen as a way to promote commerce and assert American interests. Andrew Jackson led a backlash against these policies, which were seen as fueled by banking and other business interests of the North and an infringement on the powers of states.

3. Sample answer: Adams—favored nationalist policies, national bank, protective tariffs; Calhoun—supported nationalism, sought to preserve Union, defended South's interests; Clay—supported nationalism, tried to end slavery in Kentucky, favored protective tariffs; Jackson—favored limited federal powers, opposed national bank and tariffs.

4. The entries show a rise of nationalism followed by a backlash against it.

5. Possible answers: successful, because Adams had a successful diplomatic career; unsuccessful, because as President he was thwarted by Jackson supporters.

6. Answers should emphasize National Republicans' support for active federal policies or Democrats' call for limited government.

National Republicans vs. Jacksonian Democrats, 1820s

FACT Finder

National Republicans/Whigs	Jacksonian Democrats
Federal government should take a leadership role	Federal government should remain as inactive as possible
Federal government should support internal improvements, such as roads and bridges	The individual states should be responsible for internal improvements
In favor of national bank	Against national bank
Tended to be middle-class or well-established Protestants	Tended to be slaveholders, small farmers, non-Protestants, and working class

Interpreting Tables National Republicans and Jacksonian Democrats disagreed on the federal government's role in the economy. *Government How did each party want to make internal improvements?*

Jackson supporters in Congress blocked Adams' plans at every turn. Meanwhile Jackson prepared for the coming election—and for revenge.

The Election of 1828 Both Jackson and Adams had once been Jeffersonian Republicans, members of the party that had quarreled with Federalists, largely over constitutional issues. Now economic issues were forcing politicians to choose sides.

Supporters of Adams and Clay adopted a new name: the National Republicans. They believed they were true to the Jeffersonian spirit of improvement. Jackson's followers called themselves Democrats. (Historians refer to them as Jacksonian Democrats.) They believed that they were true to Jefferson's ideal of limited government.

Unlike most previous elections, the 1828 campaign offered voters a choice between candidates of sharply differing views. (See chart at left.) More than twice as many men voted in 1828 than had voted in 1824. Most of these new voters threw their support to the man of the people, Andrew Jackson. With this sizable following, Jackson trounced Adams, winning 178 electoral votes to Adams's 83.

French writer Alexis de Tocqueville visited the United States three years later, in 1831. In his book *Democracy in America,* he noted that "liberty is generally born in stormy weather, growing with difficulty amid civil discords, and only when it is already old does one see the blessings it has brought." The rise of opposition parties in America would indeed produce "discords." But the party system would bring "blessings" as well. It would stir healthy debates on key issues and strengthen the democratic process.

SECTION 4 REVIEW

Comprehension

1. **Key Terms** Define: (a) *McCulloch* v. *Maryland;* (b) *Dartmouth College* v. *Woodward;* (c) *Gibbons* v. *Ogden;* (d) Monroe Doctrine.

2. **Summarizing the Main Idea** Why did nationalism become popular, and why did it later become unpopular?

3. **Organizing Information** Make a chart comparing the views of John Quincy Adams, John C. Calhoun, Henry Clay, and Andrew Jackson.

Critical Thinking

4. **Analyzing Time Lines** Review the time line at the start of the section. Explain how the entries in the time line show political change between 1819 and 1828.

5. **Demonstrating Reasoned Judgment** Would you say that the political career of John Quincy Adams was successful or unsuccessful? Explain your reasoning.

Writing Activity

6. **Writing a Persuasive Essay** Taking the position of either a National Republican or a Jacksonian Democrat, write an essay to persuade voters to support your candidate in the 1828 election.

Answer to . . .

Interpreting Tables National Republicans: strengthen national government and create national bank; Jacksonian Democrats: strengthen the power of the states.

▶ RESOURCE OPTIONS

Teaching Resources

 Quiz Units 3–4 folder, p. 10

Visual Learning Activity The Jackson Ticket, Learning with Documents folder, p. 50

 Nystrom *Atlas of Our Country* The Second Wave of Immigration, pp. 24–25

Student Performance Pack

 Guide to the Essentials Chapter 8, Section 4 (English and Spanish)

Determining Relevance

Determining relevance means discovering whether a logical connection exists between one item of information and another. For instance, you have seen that the Market Revolution expanded the American economy. You have also seen that the debate over federal efforts to promote economic growth helped shape a new political party system in the 1820s. So you know that the Market Revolution was relevant to the politics of this decade.

Use the tables on this page and the following steps to practice determining the relevance of different pieces of information.

1. *Identify the main purpose of each table.* Study each table, including titles and headings. (a) What purpose does Table A serve? (b) What is the purpose of Table B? (c) What is the purpose of Table C?

2. *Determine the relevance of the tables.* Examine each table in the light of a specific need. (a) If you wanted to find out how people who favored slavery voted in 1828, which tables would be relevant? (b) If you wanted to know which candidates in 1824 favored tariffs, which tables would be most relevant? (c) You would use Table A to find the total votes cast for Jackson and Adams in 1828. Now, however, you want to know how each section of the country voted in that election. Which table would now be relevant to your needs?

3. *Use your understanding of the relevance of the tables to support an observation.* (a) Generally speaking, northerners favored the American System of tariffs and internal improvements more than southerners because the North had more industry. Explain how the tables support this generalization. (b) You want to demonstrate to someone that in an election the popular vote is often closer than the vote in the Electoral College. Explain how the tables could be used to demonstrate this.

TEST FOR SUCCESS

Review the table on the previous page. Use this and a relevant table on this page to support the statement that western states tended to be against a national bank.

A. Presidential Elections, 1824 and 1828

| Year | Candidate | Political Party | Votes Cast | | |
			Popular	Electoral	House of Representatives
1824	John Quincy Adams	No distinct party designations	108,740	84	13
	Andrew Jackson		153,544	99	7
	Henry Clay		47,136	37	0
	W. H. Crawford		46,618	41	4
1828	Andrew Jackson	Democratic	647,826	178	No vote needed
	John Quincy Adams	National Republican	508,064	83	

Source: *World Almanac & Book of Facts, 1993; Historical Statistics of the United States, Colonial Times to 1970*

B. State Electoral Votes Cast for President, 1828

| | Slave States | | Free States | | |
	South	West	North	West	Total
Number of States	9	3	9	3	24
Number of Electoral Votes	86	28	123	24	261
Number of Democratic Electoral Votes	77	28	49	24	178
Number of National Republican Electoral Votes	9	0	74	0	83

Source: *Historical Statistics of the United States, Colonial Times to 1970*

C. Candidate Profiles

Issue	Adams	Jackson
Slavery	Against	For
National Bank	For	Against
Protective Tariffs	For	Generally against
Federally Funded Internal Improvements	For	Against
Voting Rights for Propertyless Workers	Against	For

1830 Indian Removal Act	1832 South Carolina threatens to secede over tariff	1832 President Jackson vetoes national bank	1836 Martin Van Buren elected President	1840 William Henry Harrison elected President

| 1830 | 1832 | 1834 | 1836 | 1838 | 1840 |

Objectives

You may wish to call students' attention to the objectives in the Section Preview. The objectives are reflected in the main headings of the section.

Bellringer

Ask students to recall a recent President whose personality played a major role in his popularity and to explain what it was that the public found so appealing.

Reading Strategy

Analyzing Cause and Effect Refer to the Reading Strategy in the Section Preview. You may wish to have students quiz each other by naming an effect on their list and having a partner cite its cause as a way to review the section.

LESSON PLAN

Connecting to the Main Idea

1. **Focus** Explain that Jackson's terms in office were marked by a commitment to minimize the role of government. Ask what events characterized Jackson's presidency.

2. **Instruct** Explain that Jackson's actions as President were consistent with the political views he expressed before his election. Ask how these views gave the common man hope and encouraged the spirit of capitalism.

Ask students to analyze Jackson's actions in terms of the ideals of the Market Revolution, including the relocation of thousands of Native Americans. Why might it be said that Jackson embodied the best and the worst of the capitalist spirit?

3. **Close** Jackson's presidency was marked by a commitment to the interests of the common man and the belief that it was the right of every white American male to compete and make money.

5 The Age of Jackson

SECTION PREVIEW

Objectives

1 Describe the link between Jackson's presidency and the expansion of democracy.
2 Explain the crises over the tariff and Native Americans.
3 Summarize the battle over the Bank of the United States.
4 *Key Terms* Define: patronage; spoils system; Tariff of 1828; secede; Indian Removal Act; Trail of Tears.

Main Idea

Jackson's presidency strengthened the political power of voters and of the West, brought about a more limited government, and revived the two-party system.

Reading Strategy

Analyzing Cause and Effect As you read, make a list of Jackson's policies and the effects that they caused.

A navy ship bore this figurehead of Andrew Jackson in 1834.

One incident sheds light on the man who in 1829 became the nation's seventh President: In 1781, 14-year-old Andrew Jackson was taken prisoner by the British, who had invaded his homeland in the western Carolinas. Refusing to shine a British officer's boots, the young patriot was slashed in the face by a sabre.

This and other acts of courage made Andrew Jackson a larger-than-life figure, a tough, stubborn man who embodied the spirit of the frontier. As the country would soon learn, Jackson was a man of strong opinions, accustomed to making tough decisions and fiercely defending them.

Jackson as President

The rise of Andrew Jackson signaled several changes in American politics. One was the growing power of the West. Jackson was the first President from west of the Appalachian Mountains. Another change was the start of a new era in American democracy. Jackson came to the presidency not through party politics but on a wave of popular support.

Jacksonian Democracy Jackson's support came from thousands of new, less-wealthy voters. State laws requiring voters to be property holders had been repealed in the previous decade, and new states such as Indiana and Maine allowed all white adult men to vote. Some states had begun to let voters, rather than state legislatures, choose presidential electors. As a result of these changes, the votes cast for President tripled between 1824 and 1828, from roughly 356,000 to more than 1.1 million.

The Spoils System For many years, newly elected officials had given government jobs to friends and supporters. This practice, known as **patronage,** became official when Andrew Jackson took office. He dismissed more than 200 previous presidential appointees and nearly 2,000 other officeholders and replaced them with Jacksonian Democrats. While Jackson replaced less than 20 percent of federal workers during his eight years as President, this was more than previous Presidents had done.

RESOURCE OPTIONS

Teaching Resources

 Reproducible Lesson Plan Lesson Plans folder, p. 67

Learning Styles Lesson Plan Learning Styles Lesson Plans folder, p. 19

Big Idea Graphic Organizer Big Idea Graphic Organizer folder, p. 39

Guided Reading and Review Units 3–4 folder, p. 11

Media and Technology

 Prentice Hall United States History Video Collection™

Volume 7 *Democracy and Reform*

Patronage under Jackson became known as the **spoils system.** In this case, the spoils, or loot taken from a conquered enemy, were jobs for party supporters.

Jackson defended the spoils system on the grounds that any intelligent person could be a competent public official. He also argued that "rotation in office" would prevent a small group of wealthy, well-connected people from controlling the government. His support for the spoils system contributed to Jackson's image as the champion of the common man.

Limited Government Jackson shared the beliefs of Americans who feared the power of the federal government. He attacked politicians whom he considered corrupt and laws that he thought would limit people's liberty. He used his veto power to restrict federal activity as much as possible, rejecting more acts of Congress than the six previous Presidents combined.

For example, Congress voted to provide money to build a road from the town of Maysville, Kentucky, along the Ohio River, southward to the growing city of Lexington, in Kentucky's horse-breeding region. In 1830, when the bill came to Jackson's desk, he vetoed it. Jackson did not object to the road. He just thought the state of Kentucky, not the national government, should build it.

The Tariff and Indian Crises

While Jackson sought to limit federal power, he did not shy away from strong federal action when he thought it necessary. This can be seen in two emotionally charged crises that arose during his first term.

The Tariff Crisis Prior to Jackson's first term, Congress had passed the **Tariff of 1828,** a heavy tax on imports designed to discourage foreign imports and encourage American manufacturing. The tariff greatly benefited the industrial North but forced southerners to pay higher prices for manufactured goods. They called the import tax the "Tariff of Abominations." (*Abomination* refers to something especially horrible or monstrous.)

The tariff prompted South Carolina to declare that states had the right to judge when the federal government had exceeded its authority and that states could nullify, or reject, federal laws they judged to be unconstitutional. The issue continued to smolder, finally igniting a famous debate on the floor of the Senate.

In January 1830, Senators Robert Hayne of South Carolina and Daniel Webster of Massachusetts engaged in a debate that quickly leapt to the broader question of the fate of the Union. The debate peaked on January 26, when Webster, the great orator, delivered a thrilling defense of the Union.

"While the Union lasts we have high, exciting, gratifying prospects spread out before us, for us and our children," Webster declared. He attacked Hayne's claim that liberty (meaning, in Hayne's view, the rights of states) was more important than the Union.

In 1832, after passage of yet another tariff, South Carolina declared the tariffs "null, void, and no law, nor binding upon this State, its officers or citizens." The state threatened to **secede,** or withdraw, from the Union if its nullification were not respected.

The issue of nullification burst on the national scene in 1830, in a debate between Massachusetts senator Daniel Webster (standing) and South Carolina senator Robert Hayne (seated, hands before him). Webster rejected nullification, claiming it would make the Constitution "a rope of sand" that would not hold the states together. *Government Why was President Jackson, a believer in limited federal government, so enraged by the nullification issue?*

*C*ustomize for

More Advanced Students

Ask students to research the Cherokee or Seminole people, especially their cultural contributions and important leaders, and prepare a report to present orally to the class.

ACTIVITY
LEARNING STYLES

Ask students to create an editorial cartoon for or against one of the following policies:
• Jackson institutionalizes the spoils system (champion of the common man or despotic politician).
• The Bank War (an eye for an eye or for the good of the nation).
• The Trail of Tears (in the name of progress or a cruel exile).
(Visual/Spatial)

Answer to . . .

Viewing History Jackson believed that the state was defying the will of the people.

RESOURCE OPTIONS

Teaching Resources

Primary Source Activity President Jackson's Inauguration, Learning with Documents folder, p. 14

Media and Technology

Color Transparencies Political Cartoons, K-3

 AmericanHeritage® CD-ROM

Explorer Activity 11 The Age of Andrew Jackson, CD-ROM Guidebook, pp. 41–42, helps students simulate a conversation between Jackson and Sequoyah.

About the Presidents

Martin Van Buren (1837–1841) faced the Panic of 1837 just days after his inauguration. "The less government interferes with private pursuits the better for the general prosperity," he said. Van Buren pressed Congress for an independent treasury to deal with the nation's finances. But the permanent independent treasury he hoped for was not established until 1846. Source: Wilson Sullivan, "Martin Van Buren," *The American Heritage® Pictorial History of the Presidents,* vol. 1, 1968

When **William Henry Harrison** (1841) ran for President, a Baltimore, Maryland, newspaper insulted his lack of intellectual depth. They said he'd be content with a log cabin and a barrel of hard cider. The Whigs turned the insult to their advantage by giving out log cabin songbooks and cider. Although the Whigs ignored real issues, their "log cabin campaign" won Harrison the presidency. Source: David Jacobs, "William Henry Harrison," *The American Heritage® Pictorial History of the Presidents,* vol. 1, 1968

VIEWING HISTORY

Jackson claimed that his Indian removal policy would "place a dense and civilized population in large tracts of country now occupied by a few savage hunters." **Culture** *How did the lifestyle of the Cherokee, shown here on the Trail of Tears, contradict Jackson's claim?*

South Carolina's defiance of federal law enraged the President. Jackson believed that the state was defying the will of the people. At his urging, in 1833 Congress passed the Force Bill, which required South Carolina to collect the tariff. Jackson threatened to send 50,000 federal troops to enforce the law.

The crisis eased when Kentucky senator Henry Clay engineered a compromise. Congress reduced some of the import duties, and South Carolina canceled its nullification act. Yet in an act of continued defiance it nullified the Force Bill at the same time.

Main Idea
CONNECTIONS

How did Jackson's response to the tariff crisis reflect his belief that power belongs to the people?

Indian Relocation In the 1820s, wealthy plantation owners were buying up much of the best cotton-farming land in the South. There were soaring profits to be made in cotton farming, and large and small planters alike wanted to expand westward into Native American lands. The Cherokee, Creek, Choctaw, Chickasaw, and Seminole peoples lived on about 100 million acres of fertile land in western parts of the Carolinas and in Georgia, Florida, Alabama, Mississippi, and Tennessee. These Native Americans were known as the "Five Civilized Tribes." The Cherokees, the Creek, and the Chickasaw practiced farming and led a settled lifestyle.

Just after Jackson took office, Georgia, Alabama, and Mississippi began to take control of the Indian lands within their states, breaking federal treaties. The President supported these actions. In 1830 he encouraged Congress's passage of the **Indian Removal Act,** which authorized him to give Native Americans land in parts of the Louisiana Purchase in exchange for lands taken from them in the East.

Under the Indian Removal Act and later acts, Jackson forcibly relocated about 100,000 members of the Five Tribes. For their 100 million acres of largely cultivated land, the Native Americans received about 32 million acres of prairie land in what is now Oklahoma.

The situation of the Cherokees was unique. More than any other Native American people, they had adopted white culture. Many Cherokees had taken up the farming methods, home styles, clothing styles, and religion of their white neighbors. Their government was modeled upon that of the United States. In 1821, a Cherokee named Sequoyah devised a writing system using symbols to represent syllables. In a very short time, nearly all the Cherokee people became literate.

In 1829, however, gold was found on Cherokee land in western Georgia. White miners and farmers flooded Indian lands. Violent confrontation between settlers and Indians seemed almost inevitable. The state seized about 9 million acres of Indian land that lay within its borders, violating treaties with the Cherokees.

The Cherokees sued. But Chief Justice John Marshall ruled that they had no legal standing in American courts, because the Cherokees

Answer to . . .

Viewing History The Cherokees lived settled lives very similar to those of white Americans.
Main Idea Connections He disagreed with the state, which he thought was defying the people's will.

▶ RESOURCE OPTIONS

Teaching Resources

■ **American History Block Scheduling Support** The Trail of Tears: Native Americans During the Jackson Presidency, found in the Expansion, Reconstruction, Immigration folder, include interdisciplinary lesson suggestions and activities for Geography and History, Primary Sources, Biography, and Literature.

Media and Technology

 AmericanHeritage® CD-ROM

Presidents Andrew Jackson, Martin Van Buren, William Henry Harrison

Time Tour An Expanding Nation: The Jackson Era

were neither United States citizens nor a foreign country. The Cherokees also sought help in the United States Senate. When that failed, they issued a public statement, trying (unsuccessfully) to win the support of the American people:

 "We wish to remain on the land of our fathers. We have a perfect and original right to remain without interruption. . . . It cannot be that the community we are addressing, remarkable for its intelligence and religious sensibilities, and preeminent [unmatched] for its devotion to the rights of man, will lay aside this appeal."

—*Cherokee public appeal, July 17, 1830*

In 1832, the Cherokees pursued their case again through a missionary from Vermont, Samuel Austin Worcester. This time, in *Worcester* v. *Georgia,* Chief Justice John Marshall ruled that Georgia had no authority over Cherokee territory. Georgia, however, simply ignored the ruling.

President Jackson sided firmly with Georgia in defiance of the United States Supreme Court. "John Marshall has made his decision. Now let him enforce it!" Jackson is said to have declared. Of course, the Court had no power to enforce its decisions.

Jackson stated his reasons for supporting the Indian relocation in an 1835 speech:

"All preceding experiments for the improvement of the Indians have failed. It seems now to be an established fact they they can not live in contact with a civilized community and prosper. . . . No one can doubt the moral duty of the Government of the United States to protect and if possible to preserve and perpetuate the scattered remnants of this race which are left within our borders."

—*President Jackson, annual address to Congress, December 7, 1835*

In 1838 the United States Army rounded up more than 15,000 Cherokees into camps, while settlers burned their homes and farms. Then, in a nightmare journey that the Cherokees called the **Trail of Tears,** men, women, and children, most on foot, began a 116-day forced march westward in groups of about 1,000.

The poorly organized and undersupplied effort took place in the fall and winter of 1838 and 1839. One out of every four Cherokees died of cold or disease, as troops refused to let them pause to rest. Afterward, the $6 million spent by the federal government to relocate the Cherokees was subtracted from the $9 million payment to the Cherokees for their lands.

The Bank War

The defining moment of Jackson's presidency came in 1832. Like many Americans, Jackson believed the Bank of the United States was a "monster" institution controlled by a small group of wealthy easterners. He held it responsible for the Panic of 1819 and the hard times that had followed.

Under its charter, the Bank of the United States could only operate until 1836, unless Congress extended the life of the bank by issuing it a new charter. Supporters of the bank, including Senators Henry Clay and Daniel Webster of Massachusetts, and the president of the bank, Nicholas Biddle, decided to recharter it four years early, in 1832. If Jackson vetoed the bank, Jackson's opponents planned to use that veto against him in the 1832 election.

Jackson, however, did not bend to the political pressure. He vetoed the bill to recharter the bank, dooming it to close in 1836. Jackson justified his action as a protection of the rights of ordinary citizens. He attacked the bank as a tool of greedy aristocrats:

"When the laws undertake . . . to make the rich richer and the potent more powerful, the humble members of society—the farmers, mechanics, and laborers—who have neither the time nor the means of securing like favors to themselves, have a right to complain of the injustice of their Government."

—*President Jackson, veto message, 1832*

The bank's supporters underestimated Jackson. He won reelection in 1832 by a huge margin, defeating National Republican Henry Clay. In the process, a distinct two-party system was reestablished, consisting of Jackson's Democratic party and the National Republicans. Later the National Republicans would take the name Whigs, after the party in the British parliament that had opposed the king in the 1700s. These American Whigs saw themselves as defenders of liberty against an executive so powerful they dubbed him "King Andrew I."

Using the Internet

Create a Diary Entry

Objective Use the Internet to write a diary entry from Andrew Jackson. Have students follow these instructions:

1. See the *America: Pathways to the Present* Web site at

http://www.Pathways.phschool.com

for the URL of the United States Presidents.

2. Use links to research information on Andrew Jackson and his presidential inaugurations.

3. Write a diary entry by Andrew Jackson on the day of his first or second inauguration. Include information about how Jackson felt, the mood of the attendees, and thoughts about what Jackson hoped to accomplish during his term of office.

In this cartoon, Andrew Jackson drags Henry Clay behind him as he attacks the monster national bank. *Government How does the artist suggest that the danger is imaginary?*

order, called the Specie Circular, weakened the "pet banks" and helped cause the Panic of 1837, which occurred during Van Buren's first year in office. In this severe depression, thousands of Americans lost their jobs and poverty grew worse in American cities.

Prolonged by a second panic in 1839, the depression dragged on into the 1840 election year. Taking a lesson from the Democrats' success with Jackson, the Whigs chose military hero William Henry Harrison as their presidential candidate. They boasted that Harrison was a plain man of the people who had lived in a log cabin. In fact, he was the son of an aristocratic family and had grown up in a mansion.

More than 80 percent of eligible voters cast ballots in the election. Many voted in hopes that a change might end the depression.

Harrison defeated President Van Buren, only to be defeated himself by illness. Just one month after taking office, he died of pneumonia. Vice President John Tyler, who took over as President, was more of a Jacksonian Democrat than a Whig, and his term was largely one of fruitless quarreling between the parties.

Jackson's Successors

In frail health, Jackson chose not to run for a third term in 1836. The next President, Martin Van Buren, whom Jackson had supported as a candidate, was not as popular as the general.

Jackson was at least in part to blame. Even before killing off the Bank of the United States, Jackson had begun withdrawing federal funds from the bank and depositing them in various "pet banks" around the country. These banks printed and lent paper money recklessly. As a result, in 1836 Jackson was forced to declare that the federal government would accept only gold or silver in payment for public lands. Jackson's

---

SECTION 5 REVIEW

Comprehension

1. *Key Terms* Define: (a) patronage; (b) spoils system; (c) Tariff of 1828; (d) secede; (e) Indian Removal Act; (f) Trail of Tears.

2. *Summarizing the Main Idea* In what ways did Jackson's presidency represent a change from the past?

3. *Organizing Information* Create a chart showing issues that Jackson favored and those that he opposed.

Critical Thinking

4. *Analyzing Time Lines* Review the time line at the start of the section. Choose any three events and write a sentence for each that describes an effect of that event.

5. *Checking Consistency* Jackson favored strong state governments and a weak national government. Yet he blocked the exercise of states' power in the nullification crisis. How do you explain this seeming contradiction?

Writing Activity

6. *Writing a Persuasive Essay* Write a newspaper editorial either for or against Jackson's use of patronage. Support your opinion with facts from the section.

Answers to

SECTION 5 REVIEW

1. (a) patronage, see p. 250; (b) spoils system, see p. 251; (c) Tariff of 1828, see p. 251; (d) secede, see p. 251; (e) Indian Removal Act, see. p. 252; (f) Trail of Tears, see p. 253.

2. Jackson represented voters rather than established institutions, and he shifted political power toward states and western and southern interests.

3. Sample answers: opposed—nationalism, South Carolina nullification, national bank; favored—patronage, limited government, Indian relocation.

4. Indian Removal Act stripped Native Americans of homelands and caused many deaths. South Carolina's secession threat brought strong opposition from Jackson but did not settle argument over state vs. federal powers. Jackson's bank veto killed the bank, raised Jackson's popularity. Van Buren had a difficult presidency plagued by economic disasters. Harrison's election was a brief Whig victory, but his subsequent death brought to power the Democratic-leaning Tyler.

5. Although Jackson opposed the expansion of federal power under Monroe and Adams, he also opposed states' efforts to defy the federal government's constitutionally delegated powers.

6. Essays should be supported with facts from the section.

Answer to . . .

Viewing History The bank is represented by a mythical creature and the action is highly exaggerated.

 RESOURCE OPTIONS

Teaching Resources

📁 **Quiz** Units 3–4 folder, p. 12

📁 **Chapter Tests Forms A and B** Chapter Test folder

Student Performance Pack

⭐ **Guide to the Essentials** Chapter 8, Section 5 (English and Spanish)

Standardized Test Preparation Handbook

Media and Technology

🎧 **Guided Reading Audiotapes** Chapter 8 Summary (English and Spanish)

Student Edition on Audiotape Chapter 8

💿 **Test Bank CD-ROM; Interactive Student Tutorial CD-ROM** Chapter Test

---

Why Study History?

To understand that . . .

Your Region Has a Unique Economy

During the first half of the 1800s, significant economic differences emerged between the industrializing North and agricultural South. Economic differences persist today among the regions of the United States.

Advertisement for an early factory

Suppose you ride a bus around the United States. Accents change as the bus lets off passengers from the South and picks up passengers from the Northeast. Geographical features also change as the bus moves from one region to another. A kaleidoscope of landforms, including the majestic Rocky Mountains in the West, the deserts of the Southwest, the endless expanse of the Great Plains, and the rolling Appalachian Mountains in the East, unfolds before your eyes.

Less noticeable, but just as important, are the economic differences between different parts of the country. Agriculture predominates in the Midwest, where acres of corn fields reflect the United States' status as the world's largest corn producer. Manufacturing dominates in other areas.

The Impact Today

The nature of sectional economic differences has changed since the early 1800s. No longer an overwhelmingly agricultural region, the South led the nation in total value of manufactured goods by the 1990s. The Midwest, meanwhile, has become the nation's leading agricultural region.

The South's rise as a manufacturing center has been helped by the relatively low cost of labor there. To cut labor costs and increase profits, many companies from the Northeast have moved to southern states. The loss of these companies has hurt economies in the older industrial centers. Meanwhile, economic growth in the South has raised families' incomes, but has also created suburban sprawl and related problems formerly associated with other regions of the country.

The Impact on You

Find out how your area has changed economically in recent years. You might begin by consulting with your parents or neighbors to learn about changes that they have seen. Make a list of companies or businesses that have moved into and out of your area. Use your list, and the information from parents or neighbors, to prepare an economic overview of your area for people moving there from other regions.

Modern textile factory in the South

Class Discussion

Discuss with the class the economy of your region and how it has changed. For a more thorough examination of the issue, see the activity folder in the Resource Options below.

ACTIVITY
STUDENT PARTICIPATION

Promoting Community Development
Ask students to read the text. Then ask them to suppose that a large enterprise (such as a community college, theme park, shopping mall, or home supply center) is thinking about locating in your area. Divide the class into four groups. Have each group create a chart to use as part of a presentation to encourage location of the enterprise in your area. Each chart should address these issues:

• **land/resources available**
• **size of city (or cities) nearby**
• **labor pool**
• **markets for their "product"**

Have each group make a presentation.

Follow up Discuss the community benefits (such as jobs, new sources of entertainment) each enterprise would provide.

Using the Internet

Students can learn more about regional economies by exploring links in the *America: Pathways to the Present* Web site at

http://www.Pathways.phschool.com

Assessment

See the Lesson Plans folder, pp. 24–27, for rubrics on assessing Class Participation Projects.

Key Terms

Students should refer to the definitions of the key terms in the chapter to write sentences that show the relation of each word to the Market Revolution and the Age of Jackson.

Comprehension

1. Prior to 1800, most people worked at home, growing and making whatever they needed. The rise of manufacturing in the North created a need for people to work in factories.

2. It dramatically increased production.

3. Banks provided the capital entrepreneurs needed to build new factories and other businesses.

4. Southern land was ideal for cotton farming, which was extremely profitable. This increased the region's dependence on slave labor. The North, with its many rivers, was ideal for manufacturing, which created urban growth.

5. Low pay, long hours, unhealthy conditions.

6. Maintaining secrecy while organizing a large revolt was very difficult.

7. At home—Supreme Court decisions supporting federal control of commerce, federal improvement projects; foreign policy—Monroe Doctrine.

8. None of the candidates received a majority of electoral votes, so the House of Representatives had to choose the President. Clay swung Kentucky's votes to Adams, giving him the win. When Adams then chose Clay to be Secretary of State, Jackson supporters accused the two of making a "corrupt bargain."

9. Jackson urged Congress to pass the Force Bill, which required South Carolina to pay the Tariff of 1823 and threatened force if the state did not comply; he vetoed the bill to recharter the bank.

Chapter Summary

The major concepts of Chapter 8 are presented below. See also **Guide to the Essentials of American History** or **Interactive Student Tutorial CD-ROM**, which contains interactive review activities, time lines, helpful hints, and test practice for Chapter 8.

Reviewing the Main Ideas

From 1800 to 1850, the economy expanded with the growth of industry in the North and cotton farming in the South. The government's nationalist policies promoted commerce. Later, Jackson set a new course for limited government.

Section 1: A Market Economy

In the early 1800s a new kind of economy emerged, in which goods were produced in factories and sold for money instead of being made in households.

Section 2: The Northern Section

Between 1800 and 1850, cities and industries expanded in the North, bringing new wealth but also new problems such as conflicts between factory workers and owners.

Section 3: The Southern Section

In the early 1800s cotton farming became the South's main economic activity. This boosted the slave trade, triggering slave revolts in 1822 and 1831.

Section 4: The Growth of Nationalism

A rise of nationalism was reflected in key Supreme Court rulings and in government policies at home and abroad. Nationalism also affected the growth of new political parties.

Section 5: The Age of Jackson

Jackson's presidency strengthened the political power of voters and of the West, brought about a more limited government, and revived the two-party system.

In the early 1800s, economic differences emerged between the industrializing North and the agricultural South. Regional economic differences still persist today.

Key Terms

Use each of the terms below in a sentence that shows how it relates to this chapter.

1. *McCulloch* v. *Maryland*
2. labor union
3. spoils system
4. secede
5. Indian Removal Act of 1830
6. urban
7. free enterprise system
8. Market Revolution
9. industrialization
10. Monroe Doctrine

Comprehension

1. How and why did the concept of "going to work" change in parts of the North?
2. What benefits did centralized manufacturing offer?
3. What role did banks have in the economic growth of the early 1800s?
4. How did geography cause the North and the South to develop different economic systems?
5. What conditions led to the formation of labor unions?
6. Why did most slave rebellions fail?
7. Give examples of nationalism in foreign policy and at home during the early 1820s.
8. Why was the election of 1824 controversial?
9. Explain President Jackson's response to the nullification crisis and to the rechartering of the national bank.

Using Graphic Organizers

On a separate sheet of paper, copy the cause-and-effect chart below. In the top box, fill in at least three causes of the Market Revolution. In the bottom box, fill in at least three effects of it.

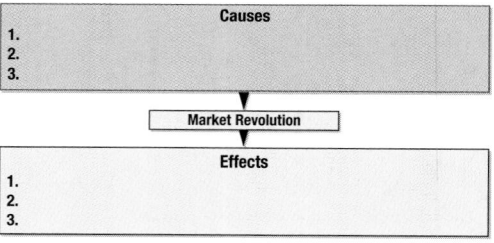

Causes
1.
2.
3.

Market Revolution

Effects
1.
2.
3.

Using Graphic Organizers

- Causes include development of manufacturing, growth of banking, nationalist policies, better transportation, inventions, westward expansion.
- Effects include more people working in factories, urbanization, people buying products instead of making them, more goods available to buy, economic growth in the North.

Analyzing Political Cartoons ▶

1. This cartoon is titled "King Andrew the First." (a) Who is "King Andrew"? (b) What is he holding in his left hand? (c) What is he standing on?

2. The other document on the floor is labeled "Internal Improvements" and "U.S. Bank." The book in the foreground is labeled "Judiciary of the United States." To what do these items refer?

3. Why do you think the cartoonist used the image of a king to criticize Jackson?

Critical Thinking

1. *Applying the Chapter Skill* How is the topic of shopping in the early 1800s relevant to a discussion of the free enterprise system?

2. *Summarizing Information* What economic changes took place in the frontier lands west of the Appalachians during the first half of the 1800s?

3. *Recognizing Ideologies* How did the Supreme Court rulings of Chief Justice John Marshall reflect his nationalist beliefs?

4. *Making Comparisons* How did Andrew Jackson's views on the role of government compare with the views of his predecessor, John Quincy Adams?

5. *Identifying Alternatives* With southern states seizing Indian lands illegally and white settlers pouring into these areas, how might President Jackson have handled the situation other than to forcibly remove the Native Americans?

ANALYZING DOCUMENTS ◀ ▶ INTERPRETING DATA

Turn to the excerpt from the Monroe Doctrine on page 246.

1. Which statement best represents the meaning of the quotation? (a) The United States considers European governments to have legitimate claims in both North and South America. (b) The United States will not take sides in European conflicts and will not allow European aggression in the Americas. (c) European powers have injured the peace and prosperity of the United States by engaging in aggressive acts. (d) It is impossible for the United States to have friendly relations with de facto European governments, because they are not legitimate.

2. Monroe's message stated that American foreign policy regarding European conflicts would be (a) neutral (b) de facto (c) nationalist (d) firm but friendly.

3. *Writing* The last sentence in the excerpt gives the hint of a threat. Rewrite the sentence in one or two sentences of your own words, and state the threat directly.

INTERNET ACTIVITY

For your portfolio:
WRITE AN ARTICLE

Access Prentice Hall's *America: Pathways to the Present* site at **www.Pathways.phschool.com** for the specific URL to complete the activity. Additional resources and related Web sites are also available.

View the Lowell National Historic Park's virtual slide show. Write an article describing how the textile industry shaped the city and the people who lived there.

INTERNET ACTIVITY

Articles should describe how the city's canal system, trolley system, and buildings were connected to the early textile mills. They should also describe how the need for canal builders and textile workers affected the make-up of the city's population.

Connecting to Today

Essay Writing The role of the federal government in promoting economic prosperity has continued to the present day. Write an essay describing ways that the federal government tries to influence economic growth today. Compare today's policies to the policies of Presidents John Quincy Adams and Andrew Jackson.

Analyzing Political Cartoons

1. (a) Andrew Jackson. (b) Paper saying "veto." (c) The U.S. Constitution.

2. Jackson vetoed the rechartering of the National Bank and money for internal improvements. The book on the floor is a reminder that Jackson ignored the Court in its ruling that opposed Cherokee relocation.

3. Many Americans believed that Jackson was abusing the power of the presidency.

Critical Thinking

1. As the supply of manufactured goods increased in the early 1800s, people began shopping for goods instead of making them, fueling a demand for products.

2. As transportation networks reached into the Old Northwest, livestock and grain became big business. In the South, settlement and cotton farming spread westward, displacing Native Americans.

3. Some of his decisions favored the right of the federal government to regulate interstate commerce.

4. Jackson favored limited government and reversed many of Adams's nationalist policies.

5. He might have sent troops to protect Native Americans, or he might have ensured better compensation for the Indians and safer conditions for their removal.

Analyzing Documents

1. b
2. a
3. The United States will respond with force to any acts of aggression by European countries in the Western Hemisphere.

Connecting to Today

Like Adams, the federal government carries out improvement projects, regulates banks, makes business loans, and gives tax breaks to foster growth. Like Jackson, federal policymakers today are "downsizing" the government to eliminate wasteful government programs.

Religion and Reform, 1800–1850

Managing Time and Instruction

INSTRUCTION SUPPORT

These materials for instruction are provided for **each section** in the **Teaching Resources**. See **Units 3–4 folder for Enrichment Support:**

- Reproducible Lesson Plans in Lesson Plans folder
- Learning Styles Lesson Plans in Learning Styles Lesson Plans folder
- Big Idea Graphic Organizers in Big Idea Graphic Organizer folder
- Guided Reading and Review
- Quizzes
- Test Preparation Practice booklet

DAILY LESSON	ENRICHMENT SUPPORT
1 **Middle-Class Reform** (pp. 259–264)	• Critical Thinking Activity, Recognizing Ideologies: Transcendentalism, found on **Resource Pro** • Primary Source Activity, Protecting Society's Outcasts, found on **Resource Pro** • Visual Learning Activity, Utopian Communities, found on **Resource Pro**
2 **The Antislavery Movement** (pp. 266–271)	• Skills for Life Activity, Units 3–4 folder, p. 31 • Visual Learning Activity, Countrymen in Chains, Learning with Documents folder, p. 51 • Nystrom *Atlas of Our Country*, A Divided Nation, pp. 26–27 • Biography, William Lloyd Garrison, found on **Resource Pro** • Literature Activity, Life as a Freeman, found on **Resource Pro**
3 **The Movement for Women's Rights** (pp. 274–278)	• Literature Activity, Advice on Marriage, Units 3–4 folder, p. 30 • Decision-Making Activity, Promoting Women's Rights, Decision-Making Activities folder, pp. 10–11 • Lasting Impact Activity, The Lasting Impact of Women in Public Life, History's Lasting Impact folder, pp. 6–7 • Key Documents, Seneca Falls Declaration, Learning with Documents folder, p. 87 • Biography, Maria Mitchell, Units 3–4 folder, p. 27
4 **Growing Divisions** (pp. 279–282)	• Nystrom *Atlas of Our Country*, The Second Wave of Immigration, pp. 24–25 • Primary Source Activity, Plantation Life, Learning with Documents folder, p. 15 • Comparing Primary Sources, On Southern and Northern Women, Units 3–4 folder, pp. 28–29 • You Can Help Reform Society, Why Study History? folder, p. 10

Running Out of Time?

- Use Tape 2, "An Emerging New Nation, 1800–1860," from **Visions of America** videotapes series.
- Use Chapter 9 Summary, from **Guide to the Essentials of American History (English and Spanish).**

Companion Web Site

The companion Web site offers online links for all chapter review activities. It also provides key content links and structured support for this chapter for both teachers and students.

http://www.Pathways.phschool.com

Media and Technology

For the Student

Interactive Student Tutorial CD-ROM Chapter 9
Student Edition on Audiotape Chapter 9
American Heritage® CD–ROM
Guided Reading Audiotapes (English and Spanish) Chapter 9

For the Teacher

Resource Pro CD-ROM Chapter 9
Test Bank CD-ROM Chapter 9
Listening to Literature Audiotapes *Timeless Voices, Timeless Themes* from *Civil Disobedience* by Henry David Thoreau
Color Transparencies Our Multicultural Heritage, C-13; Critical Thinking, I-5

Assessment Options

Chapter Test Forms A&B Test Bank CD-ROM booklet
Test Bank CD-ROM Chapter 9
Standardized Test Preparation Handbook

Block Scheduling

Pacing Suggestions

For 90-minute Blocks

- Teach sections 1 and 2 using Transparencies I-11 and C-5 and the Extended Class Periods Activity on p. 264.
- Teach sections 3 and 4 using the Big Idea Graphic Organizers from Teaching Resources and the Recent Scholarship note on p. 276 for class discussions.

Additional Resources

- Prentice Hall's **American History Block Scheduling Support File** covers over 40 major topics in American history.
- **Prentice Hall United States History Video Collection™** contains 20 videotapes covering American history from beginnings to present.
- **Visions of America Videotapes and Videodiscs**

Connections to American Literature

from Prentice Hall

America: Pathways to the Present
Incidents in the Life of a Slave Girl by Harriet Ann Jacobs, p. 1055

Prentice Hall Literature *Timeless Voices, Timeless Themes* "The Minister's Black Veil" by Nathaniel Hawthorne, p. 318

Additional Resources

For the Student

Frances Fitzgerald. *Cities on a Hill.* Simon & Schuster, 1986.
John Anthony Scott. *Woman Against Slavery: The Story of Harriet Beecher Stowe.* Crowell, 1978.

For the Teacher

Charles L. Blockson. *The Underground Railroad: First-Person Narratives of Escape to Freedom in the North.* Prentice Hall, 1987.

Prentice Hall brings into the classroom the vast archives and scholarship of the nation's premier American history magazine. See "From the Archives of American Heritage®" and "About the Presidents" teaching notes in this chapter.

 History Alive!

Teacher's Curriculum Institute, in partnership with Prentice Hall, provides unique materials that engage students with diverse learning styles. See History Alive!® unit on The Civil War and Reconstruction.

 Student Performance Pack

Ensures success in the three critical areas of Reading, Test Taking, and English Language Development with the following materials:
- Guide to the Essentials of American History in English and Spanish
- Guided Reading Audiotapes in English and Spanish
- Interactive Student Tutorial CD-ROM
- Test Preparation Handbook
- Test Preparation Practice booklet

Religion and Reform
1800–1850

Introducing the Chapter

The young republic sped through rapid social change in the early 1800s—change that brought not only new benefits but also new regional and cultural tensions. A growing and dynamic reform movement urged Americans to seek both personal and social improvements, shaping society and the nation for generations to come.

Themes in American History

The theme for this chapter, Culture, is listed at the beginning of this unit. An alternate theme for the chapter is Diversity. To teach this unit thematically, you may wish to use the Expansion, Reconstruction, Immigration folder in American History Block Scheduling Support.

Have students explore suggested ways of connecting the past to the present on page 283.

Answer to . . .

Viewing History Students should use this question as an aid in reading the chapter. Abolitionists used pamphlets and newspapers, and campaigned for public office. Some abolitionists also used illegal means to advance their cause, such as helping escaped slaves travel north to freedom.

258

CHAPTER 9 Religion and Reform

1800–1850

CHAPTER FOCUS

This chapter describes how reform-minded Americans, disturbed by the effects of industrialization and called to action by the Second Great Awakening, led a charge to improve society and protect those in need.

The Why Study History? page at the end of this chapter explores how Americans today carry on the tradition of morality-based reform.

VIEWING HISTORY
A mother and child are being sold into slavery in front of the courthouse in St. Louis, Missouri.
Culture **What tactics did abolitionists use to oppose slavery?**

▶ RESOURCE OPTIONS

Teaching Resources

 Big Idea Graphic Organizer folder Graphic summary of the main idea of the chapter.

 Learning Styles Lesson Plans folder Alternate lesson plans for diverse learning styles for each chapter.

Media and Technology

AmericanHeritage® CD-ROM
Time Tour An Expanding Nation: A Reforming Age

Prentice Hall United States History Video Collection™ Volume 7
Democracy and Reform; Volume 8 *Causes of the Civil War*

1815	1821	1825	1837	1841	1845
Temperance movement begins	Charles Grandison Finney becomes an evangelist	Utopian community founded in New Harmony, Indiana	Horace Mann begins school reforms in Massachusetts	Dorothea Dix begins prison reform work	Henry David Thoreau goes to Walden Pond

1815   1825   1835   1845

1 Middle-Class Reform

SECTION PREVIEW

Objectives

1. Explain how revivalists and transcendentalists influenced the reform movement.
2. Describe reform efforts in such areas as temperance, public education, and prisons.
3. Explain why utopian communities were formed and why most did not last long.
4. *Key Terms* Define: transcendentalism; temperance movement; abstinence; segregate; utopian community.

Main Idea

Revivalists and transcendentalists urged Americans to improve themselves and society as a whole. Reformers set out to battle social problems such as alcoholism, poor education, and inhumane prisons.

Reading Strategy

Recognizing Cause and Effect As you read, make a list of the reformers mentioned and explain briefly what caused them to get involved in their work.

Poverty, alcoholism, illiteracy, overcrowded housing, poor health care, abuse of women, declining moral values—this reads like a list of typical problems in urban areas today. In fact, these were the growing pains that began to plague America's young cities in the early decades of the 1800s. Because these growing pains occurred first in the urban North, it was there that a powerful movement to reform American society first took hold.

Protestant Revivalists

The reform movement was largely rooted in religious faith. Most reformers based their arguments on Protestant principles, whether they preached fiery sermons at camp meetings, risked their lives to help slaves escape, or made speeches to hostile crowds to demand women's right to vote. Their faith gave them purpose and courage.

The democratic principles of the Second Great Awakening stirred the reform movements of the 1830s and 1840s. Reformers generally rejected the Puritan belief that God predetermined people's lives and placed them in rigid social ranks. They believed that God was all-powerful but that God allowed people to make their own destinies.

Charles Grandison Finney This message reached Americans through the preaching of several popular revivalists. The central figure in the revivalist movement was Charles Grandison Finney. A lawyer in Adams, New York, Finney became a Presbyterian minister following a powerful conversion experience in 1821. He addressed his audiences as he had pleaded with juries, with passion and fire.

Finney sparked revivals in upstate New York before moving to New York City in 1832, where he drew enormous crowds. His common-sense sermons emphasized individuals' power to reform themselves.

Lyman Beecher Another major revivalist came from New England but later set out to evangelize the West. Lyman Beecher, son of a blacksmith, attended Yale University and became a popular preacher in Boston. In 1832 he moved to Cincinnati to become president of the Lane Theological Seminary, a religion college.

SECTION 1

Middle-Class Reform

Objectives

You may wish to call students' attention to the objectives in the Section Preview. The objectives are reflected in the main headings of the section.

Bellringer

Ask students to describe their ideal society. Would it have rules and standards? If so, what kind? What kinds of values might it seek to promote among its members?

Reading Strategy

Recognizing Cause and Effect Refer to the Reading Strategy in the Section Preview. You may wish to list the reformers on the chalkboard and, as a way to review, have volunteers explain the issue(s) that concerned each reformer.

LESSON PLAN
Connecting to the Main Idea

1. Focus Many Americans were concerned about the problems that accompanied the growth and development of the United States. Ask students how Americans reacted to these problems.

2. Instruct Explain that although both Protestant reformers and transcendentalists believed that people were responsible for their own destiny, their beliefs differed in other ways. Discuss the ways in which the two groups' spiritual beliefs differed. Then ask students how Protestant reformers and transcendentalists influenced reform efforts in temperance, public education, and prisons.

3. Close Social reformers attempted to remedy problems brought about by the nation's rapid growth. One of the main problems reformers tackled was slavery. The next section describes the antislavery movement in the 1830s.

This painting of a baptism ceremony captures the emotional intensity of a typical religious revival during the Second Great Awakening. *Culture How was the Second Great Awakening a move away from Puritan beliefs?*

In writings and lectures from about 1830 to 1855, transcendentalists declared that humans are naturally good. They rejected outward rituals and group worship in favor of private, inward searching. They urged people to be self-reliant and to have the courage to act on their own beliefs. In this way, one could lead a moral, meaningful life. To many, a moral life involved helping to reform society.

Ralph Waldo Emerson The leader of the Transcendental movement was Ralph Waldo Emerson (1803–1882), a Boston-area lecturer and writer who became one of America's greatest thinkers. Following the family tradition passed down from his Puritan ancestors, Emerson entered the ministry, becoming pastor of a Unitarian church in Boston in 1829.

When his young wife died of tuberculosis in 1831, the grieving Emerson began to question his beliefs. He resigned his ministry the following year. He then pursued his growing conviction that people can transcend the material world and become conscious of the spirit that is in all of nature.

In 1834, Emerson settled in Concord, where he started a writing career that would help launch what historians call an "American renaissance" in literature. He gathered his public lectures into two volumes called *Essays,* which gained him worldwide fame. In 1846 Emerson published his first collection of poems. He is now recognized as a major American poet.

Like other transcendentalists, Emerson supported various reform causes and urged others to do so. "What is man born for," Emerson wrote, "but to be a Reformer, a Reformer of what man has made; a renouncer of lies; a restorer of truth and good . . . ?"

Emerson's work attracted a generation of young thinkers and writers. Among them was a neighbor of Emerson's from Concord, Henry David Thoreau.

Henry David Thoreau Just down the road from the town of Concord is a pine forest surrounding a small pond. This serene setting produced one of the best-known works of American literature: *Walden, or Life in the Woods*. Its author was a friend and admirer of Emerson's, Henry David Thoreau (1817–1862), who would become an equally renowned figure among the New England transcendentalists.

Main Idea CONNECTIONS

What was the main message of the revivalist reformers?

America, Beecher warned, was threatened by "the vast extent of territory, our numerous and increasing population, . . . diversity of local interests, the power of selfishness, and the fury of sectional jealousy and hate." He taught in simple terms that good people would make a good country.

Living up to his own teachings, Beecher himself raised a flock of 13 children, many of whom became major figures in various reform movements. The most famous were the preacher and lecturer Henry Ward Beecher; the writer and antislavery activist Harriet Beecher Stowe; and Catharine Beecher, a key figure in women's education. (See Section 3.)

The Transcendentalists

The reform movement drew inspiration not only from Protestant revivalists, but also from a group of philosophers and writers who rejected traditional religion. The group, centered in Concord, Massachusetts, founded a philosophical movement known as **transcendentalism.** (To *transcend* means to "rise above.") Transcendentalism taught that the process of spiritual discovery and insight would lead a person to truths more profound than he or she could reach through reason.

Like Emerson, Thoreau suffered tragedy in his life. An early attempt at teaching failed miserably. A wedding engagement fell through in 1840, and two years later Thoreau's brother died. After trying to break into the literary trade in New York City, Thoreau, unhappy with city life, returned to Concord in 1843.

In 1845 Thoreau began his famous stay at Walden Pond, which was located on land owned by Emerson. Thoreau built a small cabin for himself and spent the next two years in a mostly solitary life of thinking, reading, writing, and observing nature. Published in 1854, *Walden* contains 18 essays that describe his experiment in living simply. Among his themes, Thoreau explores the value of leisure and the benefits of living closely with nature:

AMERICAN VOICES ❝Why should we be in such desperate haste to succeed, and in such desperate enterprises? If a man does not keep pace with his companions, perhaps it is because he hears a different drummer. Let him step to the music which he hears, however measured or far away.❞

—*Henry David Thoreau*, Walden, *1854*

A strong opponent of the war with Mexico, Thoreau, true to his beliefs, protested in 1846 by refusing to pay his taxes. He was jailed for this act of conscience, and later described the episode in his most famous essay, *Civil Disobedience*. In his later years, Thoreau devoted much of his time to the antislavery movement, personally helping escaped slaves to flee northward.

The Temperance Movement

Reformers went to work on numerous social problems in the early 1800s. The first and most widespread of these reform efforts was the **temperance movement,** an organized campaign to eliminate alcohol consumption.

In the early 1800s Americans consumed more alcoholic beverages per person than at any other time in the country's history. Drinking was so popular that the Greene and Delaware Moral Society warned in 1815 that the United States was "actually threatened with becoming a nation of drunkards."

Valuing self-control and self-discipline, reformers opposed alcohol consumption because it tended to make people lose control. Women reformers in particular saw drinking as a threat to family life. All too often wives and children suffered abuse at the hands of drunken men.

The Reform Effort Between 1815 and the 1840s, thousands of local temperance societies were formed. By 1834 the American Temperance Society boasted 7,000 local organizations with 1,250,000 members.

Members urged people to take pledges to practice **abstinence**—that is, to not drink alcohol. The societies also established alcohol-free hotels and passenger boats, encouraged employers to require their workers to sign antidrinking pledges, and worked for political candidates who promised to ban the sale of alcohol. Reformers promoted the moral, social, and health benefits of abstinence as well as its economic benefits (because it reduced employee absenteeism).

Speaking in Springfield, Illinois, in 1842, 33-year-old lawyer Abraham Lincoln equated the temperance revolution with the American Revolution. Lincoln looked forward to the "happy day when . . . the victory shall be complete—when there shall be neither a slave nor a drunkard on the earth."

Impact of the Temperance Movement In 1851 Maine became the first state to ban the manufacture and sale of all alcoholic beverages. Although several other states passed similar laws around this time, the protests of brewers, distillers, and other citizens soon led to the repeal of most of these laws.

Nevertheless, the temperance movement did have a significant impact on Americans'

Main Idea
CONNECTIONS

Why did reformers take up the temperance issue?

Alcohol Consumption, 1800–1860

Gallons per capita (y-axis: 0–8)
Year (x-axis): 1800, 1810, 1820, 1830, 1840, 1850, 1860

Interpreting Graphs Temperance societies relied primarily on persuasion to discourage drinking. *Culture Based on the information in this graph, how successful was the temperance movement?*

ACTIVITY
EXTENDED CLASS PERIODS

Time: 90 minutes.
Activity: Create a political platform.
Grouping: Groups of three students.
Purpose: Have students start a new political party called the Reform party. Ask them to draft a document stating their key positions and goals.
Roles: Transcendentalist, temperance leader, education reformer.
Outcome: Students will write position statements, evaluate them, rank them in importance, and combine them into a party platform.

TEST PREPARATION

Have students read the quotation by Thoreau on this page and then answer the question below.

By "desperate enterprises," Thoreau means—

A pursuits that are destined to fail.

Ⓑ attempts to achieve success and keep up with others.

C actions that are attempted too hastily.

D pursuits taken out of desperation.

Answer to . . .

Main Idea Connections They believed alcohol made people lose control and caused societal problems.
Interpreting Graphs Very successful, since the consumption of alcohol decreased dramatically.

Girls Get a School The autumn of 1821 saw the opening of two pioneering educational institutions: the Troy Female Seminary, in Troy, New York, and the English Classical School, in Boston. The Troy Female Seminary, founded by the formidable Emma Willard, is generally called the country's first secondary school for girls. It offered course work in everything from zoology to geography, trigonometry to Greek. The English Classical School, in Boston, is usually considered the first truly public high school in the United States. Public education dated back to 1635, when the Boston Latin School was founded, but that institute and its successors were meant only for college-bound boys. The English Classical School (renamed English High School in 1824), was meant to "give a child an education that shall fit him for active life, and shall serve as a foundation for eminence in his profession, whether Mercantile or Mechanical." Source: Frederic D. Schwarz, "The Time Machine," *American Heritage* magazine, Sept. 1996.

VIEWING HISTORY This 1857 photograph shows a class at a school in Massachusetts, the home of public education. *Government What were the arguments for and against tax-supported public schools?*

drinking habits. Between the 1830s and the 1860s, alcohol consumption in the United States dropped dramatically, as the graph on the previous page shows.

Public Education

Although reformers stressed the need for self-improvement, they sought to reform America's social institutions as well. Of particular concern was the lack of public education in the nation. Even in New England, where colonial laws had required towns to provide elementary schools, support for public education had declined. Many school buildings were old, textbooks and other materials were scarce, and the quality of teaching was often inadequate.

The geography of the mid-Atlantic and southern states further discouraged the building of schools. People in these regions lived on isolated farms separated by poor roads.

Horace Mann Leads Reforms Beginning in the 1820s, many working-class and middle-class citizens began demanding tax-supported public schools. They argued that a democracy could not survive without literate, informed voters and morally upright citizens.

This demand ran into strong opposition. Taxpayers with no children, or whose children attended private schools, objected to supporting public schools. Many parents did not want to entrust their children's education to the government. Also, many parents relied on their children's labor for their families' survival. They opposed any measures that would keep their children in school until a certain age.

Still, the movement for educational reform gained strength in the 1830s. It owed much of its eventual success to a tireless reformer from Massachusetts, Horace Mann.

Mann grew up in poverty and eventually educated himself at his hometown library. He later earned a law degree and practiced law before winning a seat in the Massachusetts legislature. In 1837 he became that state's first secretary of the Board of Education.

Mann believed in "the absolute right to an education of every human being that comes into the world." He supported the raising of taxes to provide for free public education. Under his leadership, Massachusetts pioneered school reform. He began a system in which schools were divided into grade levels. He established consistent curricula and teacher training.

Mann's accomplishments encouraged reformers in other states to establish public schools. By the 1850s most northern states had free public elementary schools.

Massachusetts established the nation's first public high school in 1821. By 1860 the number of public high schools in the United States had risen to 300.

In 1848 Mann took over the United States Senate seat of John Quincy Adams and became a fierce opponent of slavery. Later, as president of Antioch College in Ohio, he delivered this advice to his students:

AMERICAN VOICES ❝I beseech you to treasure up in your hearts these my parting words: Be ashamed to die until you have won some victory for humanity.❞

—*Horace Mann, speech to graduating class of Antioch College, Yellow Springs, Ohio, June 1859*

Two months later Mann died. Presumably, he was unashamed.

Moral Education Like other middle-class reformers of his time, Horace Mann had a particular kind of education in mind, an education that promoted self-discipline and good citizenship. In Mann's day, public schools taught students how to behave, stand in line and wait their turn, deal with each other politely, and respect authority.

Students learned many of these skills through a series of popular textbooks called the *McGuffey's Readers*. Their creator, William Holmes McGuffey, largely educated himself as a boy and became a teacher in Ohio's frontier schools at age 13. McGuffey became a respected educator, and published his first *McGuffey's Readers* in 1836. Like other textbooks of the day, McGuffey's books promoted evangelical Protestant values. Besides teaching children to read, the books taught moral values such as thrift, obedience, honesty, and temperance.

The Limits of Reform Not all parts of the country moved toward free public education at the same pace. Schools were more common in the North than in the South, and were more common in urban areas than in rural areas.

Where schools did exist, girls often were discouraged from attending, or were denied an education beyond learning to read and write. Schools frequently excluded free black students. In places where African Americans could enroll, such as Boston and New York, students often were **segregated,** or separated according to race. African Americans were placed in inferior schools. Opportunities for women and African Americans in higher education were even more limited.

Several private colleges, such as Oberlin, Amherst, and Dartmouth, did open their doors to a small number of African American students. Three black colleges—Avery, Lincoln, and Wilberforce—were founded during this period. In addition, Oberlin, Grinnell, and several other private colleges were coeducational. For the most part, however, white males were the only students welcome at public universities.

Reforming Prisons

In the early 1800s many states built prisons to house those who had committed crimes. Rather than punish criminals by branding them or putting them on display in public stocks, the states isolated them in institutions for a period of years. The hope was that prisoners would use their time in jail to lead regular, disciplined lives, reflect on their sins, and perhaps become law-abiding citizens.

By the time a Boston schoolteacher named Dorothea Dix visited a Massachusetts jail in 1841, that idealism had given way to a night-

School Enrollment, 1840–1870

Source: *American Education, The National Experience, 1783–1876*, by Lawrence A. Cremin

 Interpreting Graphs Thanks to the efforts of Horace Mann and other educational reformers, school enrollment in the United States increased rapidly in the mid-1800s. *Diversity What group do you think is most represented by these figures?*

mare. Dix discovered men and women, young and old, sane and insane, first-time offenders and hardened criminals, all crowded together in shocking conditions. Many of the inmates were dressed in rags, poorly fed, and chained together in unheated cells.

Dix spent the next two years visiting every prison in Massachusetts. She then submitted a vividly detailed report on her findings to the Massachusetts legislature. Treating the mentally ill as criminals rather than patients "is to condemn them to mental death," she stated. Her powerful testimony convinced the state to improve prison conditions and create separate institutions for the mentally ill. Dix's efforts led 15 other states to build hospitals for the mentally ill.

Dorothea Dix

Utopian Communities

While most reformers worked to improve society at large, some formed **utopian communities,** small societies dedicated to perfection in social and political conditions.

The idea of a Utopia had appeared in literature centuries earlier. It described a fictional place where human greed, sin, and egotism did not exist, and people lived in prosperity as equals. Utopian reformers, disturbed by the ill effects of urban and industrial growth, believed that it was truly possible to create a place that was free from these troubles.

most of the utopias, however, New Harmony fell victim to laziness, selfishness, and quarreling.

Brook Farm, a utopian community near Boston, attracted some of the country's top intellectuals and writers, including transcendentalists from nearby Concord. Its supporters included Bronson Alcott, the father of author Louisa May Alcott, and the novelist Nathaniel Hawthorne. Founded in 1841, Brook Farm won considerable fame before dissolving six years later.

Most utopian communities were religiously oriented. Examples include the Ephrata Cloister in Pennsylvania, founded in 1732, and others established in the 1800s: the Oneida community in Putney, Vermont; the Zoar community in Ohio, and the Amana Colony in Iowa.

Far more numerous were the Shakers, an offshoot of the Quakers, who established their first community at New Lebanon, New York, in 1787. The Shakers strived to lead lives of productive labor, moral perfection, and equality among women and men. They are best known today for their simply styled, well-crafted furniture. The Shaker population peaked at about 6,000 in 1840. A few members still survived in the late 1900s.

This 1844 painting of Brook Farm conveys the sense of peace and perfection that were the goals of most utopian communities. *Culture How were utopian communities an outgrowth of the reform movements of the era?*

Short-Lived Experiments In the first half of the 1800s more than 100 utopian communities arose in the United States. Among the most famous was New Harmony, Indiana, founded in 1825 by Scottish industrialist and social reformer Robert Owen. Owen envisioned a town in which well-educated and hardworking people would share property in common and live in harmony. Like

SECTION 1 REVIEW

Comprehension

1. *Key Terms* Define: (a) transcendentalism; (b) temperance movement; (c) abstinence; (d) segregate; (e) utopian community.

2. *Summarizing the Main Idea* How did new ideas in the early 1800s encourage the growth of the reform movement?

3. *Organizing Information* Make a two-column chart. List social problems of the first half of the 1800s, and explain what reformers did to solve each of these problems.

Critical Thinking

4. *Analyzing Time Lines* Refer to the time line at the start of the section. Select the name of one Protestant reformer and one transcendentalist. Explain the importance of both persons.

5. *Drawing Inferences* From what you know about the goals of utopian communities, what can you infer about the problems they faced?

Writing Activity

6. *Writing a Persuasive Essay* Choose one of the social problems mentioned in this section. In the role of a reformer, write a newspaper essay that describes the problem for your readers and tries to persuade them to join your cause. Remember to address any possible objections your opponents might raise.

Customize for

Less Proficient Readers

Have students construct a chart showing the major reform movements covered in the section, who their leaders were, what their goals were, and the methods they used to try to accomplish their goals.

Answers to

SECTION 1 REVIEW

1. (a) transcendentalism, see p. 260; (b) temperance movement, see p. 261; (c) abstinence, see p. 261; (d) segregate, see p. 263; (e) utopian communities, see p. 263.

2. Revivalists and transcendentalists believed humans could improve themselves and help others to reform.

3. Sample answers: alcoholism—encouraged abstinence; slavery—helped slaves to escape; poor education—built new public schools; hazardous prisons—passed laws to improve conditions, created hospitals for the mentally ill.

4. Sample answer: Charles Grandison Finney was a revivalist minister who emphasized an individual's power to change. Henry David Thoreau was an influential thinker, writer, and activist.

5. Sample answers: not everybody contributed equally to the community; disagreements frequently arose; people got discouraged.

6. Answers should be supported with facts from the section.

Answer to . . .

Viewing History They were a reaction to the same ills of society that concerned reformers.

RESOURCE OPTIONS

Teaching Resources

 Quiz Units 3–4 folder, p. 20

Student Performance Pack

 Guide to the Essentials Chapter 9, Section 1 (English and Spanish)

Media and Technology

RESOURCE PRO

Visual Learning Activity Utopian Communities, found on Resource Pro, uses the title page from Robert Owen's *The Crisis* to describe the unhappiness that Owen felt about the state of society in the early 1800s.

264 Chapter 9 • *Section 1*

SKILLS FOR LIFE

Critical Thinking

Geography

Graphs and Charts

Historical Evidence

Formulating Questions

To think critically you need to be able to formulate questions as you read. Asking questions about what you read helps you to focus on the facts and determine how reliable or significant they are. Questioning helps you identify the writer's purpose and point of view. In short, formulating questions sharpens your understanding of what you read.

To formulate good questions, keep in mind the question words used by reporters: Who? What? When? Where? Why? How? The first four words help you gather the facts. The last two help you to interpret those facts.

Use the following steps to formulate questions about the excerpt on the right.

1. Identify the topic and the speaker. To guide your reading, first think of a question about the topic of the material. Sometimes you can do this by rephrasing the title in the form of a question. (a) The title of this excerpt is "The Scourge of Intemperance." *Scourge* is another word for a cause of serious trouble. What question can you formulate by rephrasing the title of the excerpt to focus on the writer's main topic? (b) What questions would you like to see answered about this topic?

2. Locate the major points. To discover how the writer is going to support his or her premise, skim the first paragraph to get a sense of the problem areas the writer identifies and the sources used to support the facts. (a) What questions can you formulate to help you identify the problem areas? (b) What questions can you ask to evaluate the writer's sources of information?

3. Identify the writer's point of view. Use the information you have about the writer, the source of the excerpt, and the purpose of the excerpt to help you identify the writer's ideology or view of the world. (a) What questions can help you determine the writer's point of view? (b) What questions can you ask to determine how the writer's viewpoint affects the reliability of the facts he includes?

TEST FOR SUCCESS

Refer to the passage on Dorothea Dix in Section 1. If you had been a member of the Massachusetts legislature reading her report on prisons, what questions could you have formulated to (a) identify her point of view, and (b) determine the reliability of the information in her report?

The Scourge of Intemperance

What are the statistics of [intemperance]? Ask the records of mad-houses and they will answer that one-third of all their wretched inmates were sent there by intemperance. Ask the keepers of our prisons and they will testify that, with scarcely an exception, their horrible population is from the schools of intemperance. Ask the history of the 200,000 paupers now burdening the hands of public charity and you will find that two-thirds of them have been the victims, directly or indirectly, of intemperance. Inquire at the gates of death and you will learn that no less than 30,000 souls are annually passed for the judgment bar of God, driven there by intemperance.

How many slaves [to intemperance] are at present among us? . . . They are estimated at 480,000! And what does the nation pay for the honor and happiness of this whole system of ruin? Five times as much every year as for the annual support of its whole system of government. These are truths, so often published, so widely sanctioned [approved], so generally received, and so little doubted, that we need not detail the particulars by which they are made out.

—Bishop Charles P. McIlvaine, Protestant Episcopal Church, *Tracts of the American Tract Society*, c. 1835

SKILLS FOR LIFE

Critical Thinking

Formulating Questions

Focus Analyze a reading selection using questions that demonstrate critical thinking skills.

Instruct Explain that just as detectives ask thoughtful questions and make careful observations when solving a crime, readers need to ask careful questions about a selection. Only then can they determine what kind of information is available from the passage and whether or not the information is reliable.

Extend See the Skills for Life Activity in the Resource Options below.

Answers

1. Possible questions: (a) Why is intemperance a scourge? What is the scourge of intemperance? How bad is the scourge of intemperance? What forms does the scourge of intemperance take? (b) What proofs are offered that intemperance is a scourge? What are the supposed effects of this scourge?

2. Possible questions: (a) What problems does intemperance create? (b) What sources does the writer use for his facts? How knowledgeable is he likely to be about the facts? How reliable might his reporting be?

3. Possible questions: (a) Who is the writer? For what purpose has he written the piece? (b) How honest is the writer? How likely is he to color the facts to make his point?

TEST FOR SUCCESS

Sample answers: (a) What is Dix's occupation and education? Does she have a reputation for honesty? (b) How did Dix gather her information, from firsthand observation or from hearsay? How recently did she obtain this information?

 RESOURCE OPTIONS

Teaching Resources

📁 **Skills for Life Activity** Units 3–4 folder, p. 31, gives a present-day application of this skill with an excerpt from the report to Congress on smoking and health.

Media and Technology

📄 **Color Transparencies** Critical Thinking, I-5

| 1817 | 1833 | 1841 | 1843 | 1849 |
| American Colonization Society founded | William Lloyd Garrison founds American Anti-Slavery Society | Frederick Douglass joins abolition movement | Sojourner Truth joins abolition movement | Harriet Tubman flees slavery, joins Underground Railroad |

| 1810 | 1820 | 1830 | 1840 | 1850 |

The Antislavery Movement

Objectives

You may wish to call students' attention to the objectives in the Section Preview. The objectives are reflected in the main headings of the section.

Bellringer

Ask students for what act the biblical Moses is most remembered. How do they think the name "Black Moses" might apply to Harriet Tubman? Ask them to explain what they think the nickname means.

Reading Strategy

Identifying Supporting Details Refer to the Reading Strategy in the Section Preview. You may wish to list the statements in the Main Idea on the chalkboard and have students copy them. Tell them to refer to the statements as they read.

LESSON PLAN

Connecting to the Main Idea

1. **Focus** Explain that in the 1830s the slavery debate created tensions within both the nation and the abolition movement itself. Ask students to describe the nature of the divisions within the movement.
2. **Instruct** Discuss some of the arguments for and against abolition. What were people's motives for supporting or rejecting abolition?

   Ask students to identify people or groups who favored immediate abolition, gradual abolition, or slavery. Have them analyze which approach they think would have been best for the nation and why.
3. **Close** The antislavery movement caused divisions in United States society. It also inspired another social group—women—to fight for greater freedoms. The next section describes the birth of the women's rights movement in the 1840s.

2 The Antislavery Movement

SECTION PREVIEW

Objectives

1. Summarize the growth of the abolitionist movement, including divisions among abolitionists.
2. Explain the operation of the Underground Railroad.
3. Describe the types of resistance that abolitionists met in the North and the South.
4. *Key Terms* Define: abolitionist movement; emancipation; Underground Railroad; gag rule.

Main Idea

A small but committed antislavery movement arose in the North in the early- to mid-1800s. Leaders of the movement, both African American and white, used a variety of tactics to combat slavery, while facing conflicts within the movement and dangerous attacks by opponents.

Reading Strategy

Identifying Supporting Details As you read, write down facts that support the various statements in the Main Idea above.

David Walker found a creative way to spread his antislavery message.

From his modest secondhand clothing store near Boston Harbor, a 44-year-old free black man named David Walker fought slavery in a unique way. He bought clothes from sailors returning to port. In the pockets of the pants and jackets, he placed copies of his 1829 antislavery pamphlet, *Appeal to the Colored Citizens of the World*. Then he resold the garments to other sailors departing for southern ports.

Walker's message began to circulate: White people should cooperate so that all Americans could "live in peace and happiness together." But if they would not listen, he warned, then "We must and shall be free . . . in spite of [white people], for America is as much our country as it is yours."

Growth of the Movement

In response to this and other antislavery activities, enraged southern states banned antislavery publications and made it illegal to teach slaves to read. Yet fighters in the **abolitionist movement,** the movement to end slavery, continued their work in the face of southern opposition and even personal danger. In 1830, the year after he published his essay, Walker died in the streets of Boston, possibly poisoned to death.

Walker became one of the heroes of the abolitionist movement. Started by a group of free African Americans and whites, the movement gained momentum in the 1830s. The debate over ending slavery created steadily increasing tensions between the North and the South.

The Roots of Abolitionism The movement against slavery did not spring up overnight. Even during colonial times, a few Americans in both the North and the South had spoken out against slavery. In addition, some slaves petitioned colonial legislatures for their freedom—without success.

The earliest known antislavery protest came from the Mennonites, a Christian sect of German immigrants, who declared in 1688:

RESOURCE OPTIONS

Teaching Resources

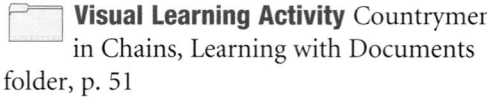

Reproducible Lesson Plan Lesson Plans folder, p. 69

Big Idea Graphic Organizer Big Idea Graphic Organizer folder, p. 41

Guided Reading and Review Units 3–4 folder, p. 21

Visual Learning Activity Countrymen in Chains, Learning with Documents folder, p. 51

 Nystrom *Atlas of Our Country* A Divided Nation, pp. 26–27

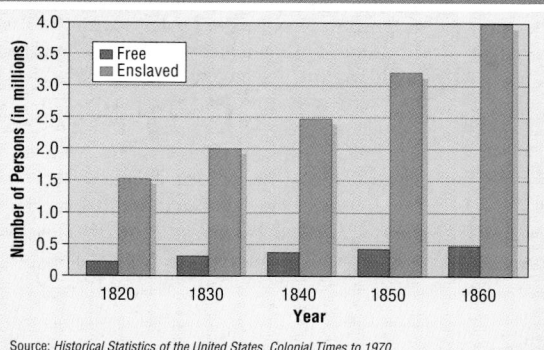

Free and Enslaved Black Population, 1820–1860

Source: *Historical Statistics of the United States, Colonial Times to 1970*

THE LIBERATOR
COMMENCED JANUARY 1st 1831.

W.L.G.

"I am in earnest! I will not equivocate! I will not excuse! I will not retreat a single inch. And *I WILL BE HEARD!*"

Interpreting Graphs The banner at right celebrates the founding of William Lloyd Garrison's famous antislavery newspaper, *The Liberator*. The population of both free and enslaved African Americans rose in the early 1800s. *Diversity Which rose more rapidly?*

AMERICAN VOICES

❝There is a saying, that we should do to all men like as we will be done ourselves; making no difference of what generation, descent, or colour they are. And those who steal or rob men, and those who buy or purchase them, are they not all alike?❞

—*Resolutions of Germantown Mennonites, 1688*

During the late 1700s, several antislavery societies formed in the North, while abolitionist newspapers appeared in both the North and the South. From 1774 to 1807, every state north of Maryland passed laws that gradually abolished slavery. The importing of slaves to the United States also ended in 1808.

At first, most antislavery activists favored a moderate approach. One of the most important of these early abolitionists was a Quaker named Benjamin Lundy. In 1821 Lundy founded an antislavery newspaper in Ohio called *The Genius of Universal Emancipation*. The newspaper called for a gradual program for the **emancipation,** or freeing, of enslaved persons. He favored stopping the spread of slavery to new states and ending the slave trade within the United States as first steps toward full emancipation.

Free blacks had actively opposed slavery long before white reformers became involved in the abolitionist movement. By the end of the 1820s, nearly 50 African American antislavery groups had formed throughout the nation.

The Colonization of Liberia In the early 1800s, some abolitionists favored colonization, a program to send free blacks and emancipated slaves to Africa. Convinced that African Americans would never receive equal treatment in American society, these antislavery advocates founded the American Colonization Society in 1817. To pursue their plan of colonization, the society established the West African country of Liberia (its name taken from liberty) in 1822.[†]

White supporters of colonization did not all believe in racial equality. Many were eager to rid the United States of both slavery and African Americans. Some southern planters backed colonization as a way to eliminate the threat of free blacks who might encourage slaves to revolt.

The colonization plan offended most African Americans. They considered themselves and their children to be as American as any white people. They wanted to improve their lives in their homeland, not on a faraway continent they had never seen.

Such opposition doomed colonization to failure. By 1831, only about 1,400 free blacks and former slaves had migrated to Liberia. By that time, both black and white abolitionists were adopting a more aggressive tone in their fight against slavery.

Radical Abolitionism One of the most famous of the radical abolitionists was a white Bostonian named William Lloyd

---

[†] Liberia was founded by a white American, Jehudi Ashmun. In six years he formed a trading state with a government and a set of laws. Liberia's first black governor was Joseph Jenkins Roberts, a free black born in Virginia in 1809.

RESOURCE OPTIONS

Media and Technology

AmericanHeritage® CD-ROM

Explorer Activity 15 Slavery in the Western Territories, CD-ROM Guidebook, pp. 49–50, helps students write a description of how the issue of slavery affected four Presidents' administrations.

Out of Africa! On December 1, 1822, in what is now Monrovia, Liberia, three dozen former American slaves desperately fought off an armed assault by 1,000 native-born Africans determined to reclaim their land. In 1821 the American Colonization Society had forced a local king at gunpoint to deed them a 130-mile strip of coastland in return for a few cartloads of hardware and household goods (including place settings for twelve, complete with wineglasses). Ever since, his subjects had been waiting for a chance to expel the interlopers. When fever had killed or weakened a sufficient number, they struck. Some of the warriors carried spears. Others bore large-caliber muskets, which they loaded with foot-long copper and iron slugs for close-range use. But the settlers had artillery, which made up for their numerical disadvantage. Despite repeated attacks, the colony continued for three more decades until the Civil War made it irrelevant. By that time a mere 15,000 blacks had been resettled. Source: Frederic D. Schwarz, "The Time Machine," *American Heritage* magazine, Dec. 1997.

Answer to . . .

Interpreting Graphs The enslaved population rose more rapidly.

While some slaves escaped to the North, others were sent southward from Virginia and Maryland. Two centuries of tobacco farming had worn out Virginia's soil, and plantations there sold many of their slaves to estates in the deep South where laborers were needed. A common punishment for slaves who tried to revolt or escape was to be "sold South" where the climate was hotter and free territory too far away to encourage runaways.

BACKGROUND

Recent Scholarship

Recent research, including Philip D. Morgan's *Black Culture in the Eighteenth-Century Chesapeake and Lowcountry* and Ira Berlin's *Many Thousands Gone: The First Two Centuries of Slavery in North America* is shedding new light on the variations among regions in the practice of slavery. For instance, the lives of slaves in the Chesapeake Bay region were painful and demeaning, but not nearly so difficult as the lives of slaves in South Carolina's Low Country. There, slaves were likely to have worse food, clothing, shelter, and far shorter lives. Yet in one way the slave populations of both regions were much alike. In both places they struggled to live decent, full lives under the dehumanizing order of slavery.

Garrison. In 1831 Garrison began publishing *The Liberator*, an antislavery newspaper supported largely by free African Americans. Garrison denounced moderation in the fight against slavery:

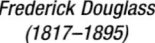

> **"**I do not wish to think, or speak, or write, with moderation . . . . I am in earnest—I will not equivocate—I will not excuse—I will not retreat a single inch—AND I WILL BE HEARD.**"**
>
> —*William Lloyd Garrison, in the first issue of* The Liberator, *1831*

In 1833, with the support of both white and African American abolitionists, Garrison founded the American Anti-Slavery Society. As the decade progressed, more middle-class white northerners began to support the immediate end of slavery. By 1835 the American Anti-Slavery Society had some 1,000 local chapters with roughly 150,000 members. With agents traveling throughout the North, the society distributed more than 1 million antislavery pamphlets a year.

Frederick Douglass

AMERICAN BIOGRAPHY Cruel experiences toughened the will of Frederick Douglass and made him into the nation's most influential African American abolitionist. Douglass was born Frederick Augustus Washington Bailey in Maryland, a slave state, in 1817. Educating slaves was forbidden there, so the young boy taught himself and coaxed white children to teach him to read. Later he worked on a plantation where the owner's wife tutored him, disregarding the law.

At 17, Douglass was considered unruly, so he was sent to a "slave breaker," a man skilled in punishing unruly slaves to make them passive and cooperative. Submitted to whippings and back-breaking labor for endless hours and days, Douglass did indeed become broken in body and spirit. But after one particularly brutal beating, Douglass reached what he called a "turning point" in his life. He fought back, attacking the slave-breaker with such ferocity that the man never again laid a whip to him. This, Douglass said later, was the story of "how a man became a slave and a slave became a man."

Frederick Douglass (1817–1895)

In 1838, the 21-year-old Douglass, working in a shipyard, disguised himself as a sailor and escaped to New Bedford, Massachusetts. There he changed his name from Bailey to Douglass to avoid capture. Asked to describe his experiences as a slave to an antislavery convention in 1841, Douglass spoke with passion and eloquence. This was the start of his lifelong work as an agent of the American Anti-Slavery Society.

In 1845 Douglass published his autobiography, *Life and Times of Frederick Douglass,* which sold thousands of copies. Douglass's speeches in the United States and Great Britain convinced many people of the evils of slavery and helped form close ties among abolition groups in the two countries.

While abroad, Douglass raised the money to purchase his freedom. He then started an abolitionist newspaper, the *North Star*, which he published from 1847 to 1860. Although Douglass opposed the use of violence, he also believed that slavery should be fought with deeds as well as words:

> **"**They who profess to favor freedom, and yet deprecate [criticize] agitation, are men who want crops without plowing up the ground, they want rain without thunder and lightning. They want the ocean without the awful roar of its many waters.**"**
>
> —*Frederick Douglass*

During the Civil War, Douglass served as an adviser to President Abraham Lincoln. After the war he fought for the rights of freed slaves, of poor people, and of women, causes he supported until his death in 1895.

Divisions Among Abolitionists

While abolitionists shared a common goal, they came from diverse backgrounds and favored a variety of tactics. It is not surprising, therefore, that divisions appeared within the antislavery movement.

(1) Divisions over Women's Participation. One of the first splits occurred over women's participation in the American Anti-Slavery Society. At the time, Americans in general did not approve of women's involvement in political gatherings. When Garrison insisted that female abolitionists be allowed to speak at antislavery meetings, some members resigned in protest.

▶ RESOURCE OPTIONS

Media and Technology

RESOURCE ⊙ PRO

Biography William Lloyd Garrison, found on Resource Pro, profiles the man known as the conscience of the abolitionist movement.

Literature Activity Life as a Freeman, found on Resource Pro, presents a passage from

Narrative of the Life of Frederick Douglass to give insight into the views of this prominent African American abolitionist.

AmericanHeritage® CD-ROM

History Makers Frederick Douglass

Biography William Lloyd Garrison

Two of the most prominent women speakers were Sarah and Angelina Grimké, white sisters from South Carolina who moved north, became Quakers, and devoted their lives to abolitionism. In 1836, Angelina's pamphlet, *An Appeal to the Christian Women of the South,* and Sarah's *Epistle to the Clergy of the Southern States* prompted southern officials to ban and burn the publications.

In the 1840s, a powerful crusader joined the abolition cause. She called herself Sojourner Truth.

Truth was born Isabella Baumfree in Ulster County, New York, in 1797. Freed from slavery in 1827, she found work as a domestic servant in New York City and soon became involved in various religious and reform movements. In 1843 she took the name Sojourner Truth because she believed her life's mission was to sojourn, or "travel up and down the land," preaching the truth about God at revival meetings. That same year she visited a utopian community in Northampton, Massachusetts, where she learned of the abolition movement and took up the cause.

(2) Divisions over Race. Racial tensions further divided the movement. For African Americans the movement to end slavery had a personal dimension and an urgency that many white people could never fully understand. In addition, some black reformers felt that white abolitionists regarded them as inferior.

This treatment insulted Martin Delany, an abolitionist who also was one of the first black students to graduate from Harvard Medical School. In the 1840s, Delany founded a highly respected newspaper, the *Mystery,* and worked closely with Frederick Douglass. A supporter of colonization and a frequent critic of white abolitionists, Delany noted:

AMERICAN VOICES ❝We find ourselves occupying the very same position in relation to our Anti-Slavery friends, as we do in relation to the pro-slavery part of the community —a mere secondary, underling position.❞

—*Dr. Martin Delany, African American abolitionist*

Tensions such as these helped lead Frederick Douglass to break with Garrison in 1847 and found, with Delany, his antislavery newspaper, the *North Star.*

(3) Divisions over Tactics. A third source of tension among abolitionists was political action. Garrison believed that the Constitution

Sojourner Truth's commanding presence and powerful speaking style captured people's attention at many slavery and women's rights meetings. *Diversity Why was women's participation in the abolition movement controversial?*

supported slavery. Thus, he reasoned, attempting to win emancipation by passing new laws would be pointless, because any such laws would be unconstitutional.

Abolitionists who disagreed, such as Arthur and Lewis Tappan, broke with Garrison to follow a course of political action. Together with former slaveowner and abolitionist James Birney, the Tappans formed the Liberty party in 1840. The Liberty party received only a fraction of the presidential vote in 1840 and in 1844. Yet it drew off enough support from the Whig party in such key states as Ohio and New York to give the 1844 election to James K. Polk, a Democrat.

The Underground Railroad

Some abolitionists insisted on using only legal methods, such as protest and political action. But with tremendous human suffering going on, other people could not wait for long-term legal strategies to work. They attacked slavery in every way they could, legal and illegal.

"There's two things I've got a right to…death or liberty," said Harriet Tubman (above, far left), shown here with former slaves she led to freedom. Many slave-owners went to great lengths to recapture escaped slaves. *Government What personal risks did Underground Railroad conductors undertake?*

Risking arrest, and sometimes risking their lives, abolitionists created the **Underground Railroad,** a network of escape routes that provided protection and transportation for slaves fleeing north to freedom. The term *railroad* referred to the paths that Africans Americans traveled, either on foot or in wagons, across the North-South border and finally into Canada, where slave-hunters could not go.

Underground meant that the operation was carried out in secret, usually on dark nights in deep woods. Men and women known as conductors acted as guides. They opened their homes to the fugitives and gave them money, supplies, and medical attention. Historians' estimates on the number of slaves rescued vary widely, from about 40,000 to 100,000. (See the Geography and History feature "The Underground Railroad," following this section.)

African Americans, some with friends and family still enslaved, made up the majority of the conductors. By far the most famous was a courageous former slave named Harriet Tubman.

Tubman herself escaped from a plantation in Maryland in 1849 and fled north on the Underground Railroad. Remarkably, she returned just the next year to rescue family members and lead them to safety. Thereafter, she made frequent trips to the South, rescuing more than 300 slaves and gaining the nickname "the Black Moses."[†]

Enraged slave owners offered a $40,000 reward for Tubman's capture. Yet she continued. Armed with devout faith—and a handy revolver—she required strict discipline among her escapees, even threatening those who wavered. Tubman later boasted: "I never run my train off the track, and I never lost a passenger."

Resistance to Abolitionism

The activities of the Underground Railroad generated a great deal of publicity and sympathy. Yet the abolition movement as a whole did not receive widespread support. In fact, it provoked intense opposition in both the North and the South.

Opposition in the North In the decades before the Civil War, most white Americans viewed abolitionism as a radical idea, even in the North. Northern merchants, for example, worried that the antislavery movement would

---

[†] Tubman's nickname refers to the Bible story of the prophet Moses leading Jewish slaves out of captivity in Egypt.

Main Idea
CONNECTIONS

How was the Underground Railroad organized?

further sour relations between North and South, harming trade between the two regions. White workers and labor leaders feared competition from escaped slaves willing to work for lower wages. Most northerners, including some who opposed slavery, did not want African Americans living in their communities. They viewed blacks as socially inferior to whites.

Opposition to the abolitionists eventually boiled over into violence. At public events on abolition, people hurled stones and rotten eggs at the speakers or tried to drown them out with horns and drums. In 1835, an angry Boston mob assaulted William Lloyd Garrison and paraded him around the city with a rope around his neck. A new hall built by abolitionists in Philadelphia was burned down, as were homes of black residents.

The most brutal act occurred in Alton, Illinois, where Elijah P. Lovejoy edited the *St. Louis Observer*, a Presbyterian weekly newspaper. In his editorials, Lovejoy denounced slavery and called for gradual emancipation. Opponents repeatedly destroyed his printing presses, but each time Lovejoy resumed publication. On the night of November 7, 1837, rioters again attacked the building. Lovejoy, trying to defend it, was shot and killed.

Opposition in the South Most southerners were outraged by the criticisms that the antislavery movement leveled at slavery. Attacks by northern abolitionists such as Garrison, together with Nat Turner's 1831 slave rebellion, made many southerners even more determined to defend slavery. During the 1830s, it became increasingly dangerous and

Elijah Lovejoy might have used a printing press similar to the one shown at right to print the *St. Louis Observer*. Lovejoy was killed and his offices destroyed (above) by anti-abolitionists. *Economics Why were some northern merchants opposed to abolitionism?*

rare for southerners to speak out in favor of freeing the slaves.

Public officials in the South also joined in the battle against abolitionism. Southern postmasters, for example, refused to deliver abolitionist literature. In 1836, moreover, southerners in Congress succeeded in passing the so-called **gag rule,** which for the next eight years prohibited antislavery petitions from being read or acted upon in the House. Abolitionists pointed to the gag rule as proof that slavery threatened the rights of all Americans, white as well as black.

SECTION 2 REVIEW

Comprehension

1. *Key Terms* Define: (a) abolitionist movement; (b) emancipation; (c) Underground Railroad; (d) gag rule.

2. *Summarizing the Main Idea* What tactics did the abolitionist movement use to battle slavery?

3. *Organizing Information* Create a chart that identifies important abolitionists and lists the contributions of each.

Critical Thinking

4. *Analyzing Time Lines* Copy the time line at the start of the section. Then add as many other events from the section as you can, in their proper chronology.

5. *Formulating Questions* What questions might you ask African Americans who risked their lives working on the Underground Railroad?

Writing Activity

6. *Writing an Expository Essay* Assume the role of a journalist for an abolitionist newspaper. Write an essay describing and comparing the types of resistance that abolitionists are facing in the North and the South.

Answers to SECTION 2 REVIEW

1. (a) abolitionist movement, see p. 266; (b) emancipation, see p. 267; (c) Underground Railroad, see p. 270; (d) gag rule, see p. 271

2. Protest, political action, creating newspapers, forming groups and societies, developing a colonization program, using the Underground Railroad.

3. Charts may include: Benjamin Lundy—founded antislavery newspaper, *The Genius of Universal Emancipation;* William Lloyd Garrison—founded *The Liberator,* the American Anti-Slavery Society; Frederick Douglass—published his autobiography, started the *North Star;* the Grimkés—devoted lives to abolitionism; Sojourner Truth—involved in various religious and reform movements; Arthur and Lewis Tappan—formed the Liberty party; Harriet Tubman—rescued over 300 slaves on the Underground Railroad; Nat Turner—led a slave rebellion; Elijah Lovejoy—edited *St. Louis Observer* and denounced slavery.

4. Answers should include a full sampling of important people, dates, and events from the section.

5. Sample questions: What were your working conditions? Why did you risk your life? How many people did you save? How did you help people escape? Were you ever caught?

6. Essays will vary but should reflect an understanding of the types of resistance abolitionists were facing in the North and South.

Answer to . . .

Viewing History They feared it would harm trade relations with the South.

GEOGRAPHY AND HISTORY

The Underground Railroad

Focus Ask students if they always travel to and from a location by the shortest possible route. Have them think about other factors that affect their choice of routes to and from a known location, such as school or the grocery store. Tell students that in this feature they will learn why enslaved Americans took the tortuous routes they did as they fled to freedom along the underground railroad.

Instruct After students have read the feature, divide the class into small groups. Ask each group to choose one of the following actual starting points for recorded passengers on the underground railroad: Portsmouth, Virginia; South Florence, Alabama; Martin, Tennessee; Wadesboro, North Carolina; or Eastport, Mississippi. Then, using the map on the following page, additional atlas maps, and the material in the feature, have each group plan a route northward for a group of enslaved people. Groups should prepare a detailed map of their route, including stops of any length.

Extend Ask students to research the escape of one enslaved African American and present the story to the class.

GEOGRAPHY AND HISTORY

The Underground Railroad

The geographic theme of movement explores ways in which people, goods, and ideas travel from one place to another. The Underground Railroad, a network of routes out of the South, carried thousands of slaves to freedom. How did these particular routes help move people to a safer place in the North?

Behind this cupboard was a space for hiding escaped slaves.

The Underground Railroad was not underground. Nor was it strictly a railroad. It was a network of paths, roads, rivers, and railways by which African Americans escaped out of slavery. On a map, the routes of the Underground Railroad look like a tangled clump of lines. Why did escaping slaves take these particular routes?

River out of the South

In the West, the valley of the Mississippi River offered a natural escape route. Some slaves managed to book riverboat passages northward. If they were lucky, they could reach the Underground Railroad routes that started in western Illinois. The Mississippi River route was dangerous, however, since slave hunters stalked the riverboat towns and boarded the ships looking for slaves on the run.

Eastern Swamps Lead North

The East Coast, by contrast, had a physical feature that offered protection from human pursuers, but posed serious natural dangers. This was the string of low-lying swamps stretching along the Atlantic Coast from southern Georgia to southern Virginia. Fugitives who traveled north through the swamps could link up with one of the eastern Underground Railroad routes to Canada, shown on the map on the next page. The travelers would face hazards, however, such as poisonous snakes and disease-bearing mosquitoes.

> *The Underground Railroad was not underground. Nor was it strictly a railroad. It was a network of paths, roads, rivers, and railways by which African Americans escaped out of slavery.*

The Mountain Route

The physical feature that most influenced the choice of a route was the Appalachian Mountains. The mountain chain, extending from northern Georgia into Pennsylvania, has narrow, steep-sided valleys separated by forested ridges.

The Appalachians served as an escape route for two reasons. First, the forests and limestone caves sheltered fugitives as they avoided capture on their way north. Second, the Appalachians acted as a barrier for western runaways, pushing them northward into a region of intense Underground Railroad activity.

RESOURCE OPTIONS

Teaching Resources

Geography and History Activity The Sanctuary Movement in the United States, Geography and History folder, pp. 6–7

Nystrom *Atlas of Our Country* A Divided Nation, pp. 26–27

The Underground Railroad

Frederick Douglass established a print shop in Rochester that became a depot.

John Brown led fugitives on a midwinter journey from Missouri to Canada via Chicago.

Portuguese fishermen and Native Americans of the Shinnecock group helped transport escaped slaves from Long Island to New England.

Dorchester County was the birthplace of Harriet Tubman. She rescued about 300 slaves on 19 trips to the South.

The home of Presbyterian minister John Rankin in Ripley was one of the most active depots.

Levi Coffin, a Quaker, helped more than 3,000 slaves to escape.

Harriet Beecher Stowe maintained a depot in Walnut Hills.

Slaveholders looked upon the Underground Railroad as organized theft.

Seminoles in Florida offered safe havens for escaped slaves.

Somewhere between 50,000 and 100,000 escaped slaves made their way to freedom with the help of "conductors" on the Underground Railroad.

Map Legend:
- Slavery prohibited
- Slaveholding states
- Swamps
- Underground Railroad
- 1850 Boundaries
- Depot

0   150   300 Miles
0   150   300 Kilometers

A Refuge for Runaways

The center of Underground Railroad activity included Ohio and parts of two states that border it, Indiana and Pennsylvania. This region shared a long boundary with two slave states, Virginia and Kentucky.

Once the fugitives crossed into Ohio, they found themselves in a region with a very different attitude toward slavery. Southern Ohio was home to Quakers and others who volunteered their houses as depots, or stations. There, too, lived free blacks, as well as whites who had left the South because they opposed slavery. Many white people in the northern and eastern parts of Ohio were antislavery New Englanders.

Ohio's support for escaped slaves frustrated southern slave owners. "It is evident," wrote one, "that there exist some eighteen or nineteen thoroughly organized thoroughfares through the State of Ohio for the transportation of runaway and stolen slaves."

Southern Illinois, on the other hand, was a dangerous region for fugitives. Settled largely by Southerners, this region remained proslavery. Abolitionists in that area often ticketed fugitives on a real railroad, the Illinois Central, for transit to Chicago. From there they continued on toward Canada, often on foot, following the North Star as it marked their route to freedom.

GEOGRAPHIC CONNECTIONS

1. What physical features in the South offered escaped slaves protection from pursuers?

2. Why did so many of the Underground Railroad routes run through Ohio?

Themes in Geography

3. *Movement* Of the three main routes north, which do you think was the best for families or large groups, and which was best for individual fugitives? Explain your reasoning.

RESOURCE OPTIONS

Media and Technology

Prentice Hall United States History Video Collection™ Volume 8 *Causes of the Civil War*

1840	1841	1841	1845	1848
Women barred from public role at abolition conference	Catharine Beecher's A Treatise on Domestic Economy	Lydia Child becomes editor of National Anti-Slavery Standard	Margaret Fuller's Woman in the Nineteenth Century	Seneca Falls Convention on women's rights

| 1840 | 1842 | 1844 | 1846 | 1848 |

Objectives

You may wish to call students' attention to the objectives in the Section Preview. The objectives are reflected in the main headings of the section.

Bellringer

Have students speculate on how a woman of the early 1800s would react if she were somehow transported to the present day. Which aspects of society might she enjoy? Which would she dislike?

Reading Strategy

Making an Outline Refer to the Reading Strategy in the Section Preview. You may want to model the headings on the chalkboard and have volunteers share facts under each to create a composite list.

LESSON PLAN

Connecting to the Main Idea

1. Focus Women in the early 1800s were expected to dedicate themselves to home and family. Many women, however, were not content with this role. Ask students why people began questioning society's expectations.

2. Instruct Explain that radical reform often comes about through a series of changes. Entrenched attitudes such as discrimination are slowly broken down over time as a result of many people's actions. Discuss how some of Catharine Beecher's peers might have considered her views "radical." Compare her views to those of Elizabeth Cady Stanton. In what ways do Stanton's views represent a further development of Beecher's ideas?

3. Close Inspired by the antislavery movement, women began fighting for equality. Their demands often met with bitter resistance. The next section describes the resentments of some segments of society toward reform movements.

3 The Movement for Women's Rights

SECTION PREVIEW

Objectives

1 Describe how women used their private roles to influence American society.
2 Explain how reform movements increased the public role for women.
3 Summarize the Seneca Falls Convention for women's rights.
4 *Key Terms* Define: Seneca Falls Convention; suffrage.

Main Idea

Although women were expected to devote their energies to home and family in the early 1800s, some women organized a women's rights movement in the 1840s.

Reading Strategy

Making an Outline Make a list of all the headings in the text of this section. As you read, write down one important fact under each heading.

Catharine Beecher had the spirit of reform in her blood. Daughter of the revivalist Lyman Beecher, Catharine, like her talented siblings, identified a need in society and set about fulfilling it. Like Emerson and Thoreau, Beecher overcame personal tragedy to lead a productive life. In 1823 her fiancé drowned at sea. Beecher never married. Instead she dedicated herself to a career of teaching, writing, and helping.

This anti-slavery logo made many white abolitionist women begin thinking about women's rights.

Private Roles for Women

In the new age of urbanization and industrialization, Beecher was one of many reformers to examine the role of women in American society. Like other reformers, she believed that women were central to the success of a strong, democratic nation. However, while other women of her time were beginning to demand new rights and freedoms, Beecher took a traditional stand. She advised women on how to reform society from within their roles in the home.

Cultural and Legal Limits on Women As industrialization and urbanization took hold in the United States, women, especially in the North, felt the impact. Many lower-class women took jobs in factories. Middle-class women, however, were freed from chores such as growing their own food and making clothes, as more products appeared on store shelves.

How, then, should these women spend their energies? Most people believed that women should remain in the home. Middle-class women were expected to raise and educate their children, entertain guests, serve their husbands, do community service, and engage in at-home activities such as needlework and quilting.

In this division of labor, men engaged in public activities such as politics, law, and public speaking. Most people, traditionally minded or not, would have been shocked at the idea of women doing these things. A lady simply did not behave in this way. Even Dorothea Dix, the champion of prison reform, did not present her research on prison conditions to state legislatures. She had to have men make these public presentations.

▶ RESOURCE OPTIONS

Teaching Resources

📁 **Reproducible Lesson Plan** Lesson Plans folder, p. 70

📁 **Big Idea Graphic Organizer** Big Idea Graphic Organizer folder, p. 42

📁 **Guided Reading and Review** Units 3–4 folder, p. 23

🖥 **American History Block Scheduling Support** The Reformers: A Struggle for Women's Rights, found in the Prosperity, Depression, and War folder, includes interdisciplinary lesson suggestions and activities for Geography and History, Primary Sources, Biography, and Literature.

Although some women defied these cultural limits, they still faced strict legal restrictions. For example, the law denied women the right to vote. In most states, married women could not own property or make a will. Despite the increasing number of women working outside the home, women generally could not keep the money they earned. Instead they had to turn it over to a husband or father.

Reform at Home Catharine Beecher sought reform within the rules of her time and culture. She tried to win respect for women's contributions as wives, mothers, and teachers.

Just a year after her fiancé died, Catharine and her sister Mary Beecher established the Hartford Female Seminary. Teaching was considered a proper occupation for a young woman because it was an extension of the role of mother.

While teaching, Catharine Beecher also started writing about and lobbying for the education of women. She published several books that earned her a national reputation.

Beecher's most popular and important work was *A Treatise on Domestic Economy*. It offered practical advice and household tips and inspired women to help build a strong American society.

"The success of democratic institutions . . . ," she wrote, "depends upon the intellectual and moral character of the mass of the people." In particular, "the formation of the moral and intellectual character of the young is committed mainly to the female hand." Here, then, was the reason why women were so critically important to the nation's welfare:

Catharine Beecher

AMERICAN VOICES ❝The mother forms the character of the future man; . . . the wife sways the heart, whose energies may turn for good or for evil the destinies of a nation. . . . Let the women of a country be made virtuous and intelligent, and the men will certainly be the same. The proper education of a man decides the welfare of an individual; but educate a woman, and the interests of a whole family are secured.❞

—*Catharine Beecher,*
A Treatise on Domestic Economy, 1841

Public Roles for Women

Even as Beecher instructed women in their private roles, a restlessness was stirring among a small number of American women. As more women became educated, they grew eager to apply their knowledge and skills beyond the home. They also became increasingly dissatisfied with the laws and attitudes that prohibited them from doing so.

Fighting for Reform The religious revivals and reform movements of the early 1800s heightened women's sense of their potential and power. For some, participation in a reform movement was a first, satisfying taste of the world outside the family. Women played a prominent role in nearly every avenue of reform, from temperance to abolition. They marched in parades to support their causes. They participated in economic boycotts. They even gave lectures at public assemblies.

Through these activities, many northern middle-class women became more conscious of their inferior position in American society. At the same time, they formed strong intellectual and emotional ties with other women in similar positions.

Fighting for Abolition The battle to end slavery was the primary means by which women emerged into the public world of politics. By the 1840s, some women were protesting their second-class position within both the antislavery movement and society in general.

Women who participated in the abolition movement saw parallels between the plight of enslaved African Americans and the status of women. Neither group could vote or hold office, for instance, and both were denied the full rights of American citizens.

The fight to end slavery also provided women with a political platform from which they could assert power over public opinion. For example, one famous abolitionist and writer, South Carolina–born Angelina Grimké, demanded that the women of the South fight slavery:

Main Idea
CONNECTIONS
What problems did slaves and women share in society?

Recent Scholarship

Women dominated the anti-slavery movement. Historians have long known about white women who took up the cause in alliance with their demands for equal rights. More recently, they have begun to write about the important roles played by the large community of free women of color. Shirley J. Yee's *Black Women Abolitionists: A Study in Activism, 1828–1860* illuminates the contributions of African American women and reminds us that free blacks had to deal with racism and inequalities even among radical opponents of slavery.

Have students design a logo that might have been used by women and African Americans to illustrate their common bonds in the fight against oppression. (*Visual/Spatial*)

Answer to . . .

Viewing History They found themselves excluded from public forums and resented the lack of women's rights under the law.

Elizabeth Cady Stanton (left) issued a manifesto declaring that "all men and women are created equal." More than 300 delegates gathered for the first women's rights convention in 1848. The document above is one of the results of the meeting. **Diversity** *How did their involvement in abolitionism lead women activists to seek women's rights?*

AMERICAN VOICES ❝If you really suppose you can do nothing to overthrow slavery, you are greatly mistaken. . . . You can read. . . . You can pray. . . .You can speak. . . .You can act.❞

—*Abolitionist Angelina Grimké, 1836*

Black women such as Sojourner Truth and white women such as the Grimké sisters began to attend meetings, gather petitions, give public talks, and write pamphlets and books. Abolitionist Lydia Child served on the executive committee of the American Anti-Slavery Society. In 1841 she became editor of the group's publication, the *National Anti-Slavery Standard.*

Women writers had an enormous influence on public opinion about slavery. Harriet Beecher Stowe, sister of Catharine Beecher, opened the eyes of many northerners with her 1852 abolitionist novel *Uncle Tom's Cabin.* Harriet Ann Jacobs authored the 1861 book *Incidents in the Life of a Slave Girl.* Sojourner Truth could not read or write, but she dictated her experiences to an author to produce *The Narrative of Sojourner Truth.* In 1869, *The Life of Harriet Tubman* detailed Tubman's dangerous activities with the Underground Railroad.

Men's Opposition Many male abolitionists were horrified rather than pleased with women's role in the movement. Some men found it distasteful for women to take part in public meetings. Although many people believed that women were more virtuous than men, they felt that women should use their influence only within their families.

A Women's Rights Movement In 1840, many American abolitionists attended the first World Anti-Slavery Convention in London, England. The attendees included women delegates from the American Anti-Slavery Society. Despite American women's achievements and devotion to the cause, the convention, after much debate, voted to prohibit women from participating. The action angered and humiliated the American women. Two of the delegates later turned their anger into action.

Born in 1793, Lucretia Mott had taken up teaching at age 15, earning only half the wages of male teachers. Mott became a Quaker minister in 1821. She and her husband became abolitionists and sheltered fugitive slaves in their home.

Elizabeth Cady Stanton was the daughter of a United States congressman who later became a judge on the New York Supreme Court. She studied law in her father's office and became aware of the legal limits that the law placed on women. She later married an abolitionist lawyer.

Mott and Stanton both attended the 1840 antislavery convention and resented their exclusion from it. Eight years later, the women organized a convention on women's rights.

TEST PREPARATION

Have students read the quotation by Grimké on this page and then answer the question below.

Grimké's purpose in using simple, repetitive phrases in the passage is—

A to make sure that even less intelligent women understand her.

B to make her speech easier to remember.

C to make her words more "catchy."

D to make it clear that even the simplest actions have an effect.

Turning Point: Seneca Falls Convention

The meeting took place in Stanton's hometown of Seneca Falls, New York, in July 1848. The **Seneca Falls Convention** was the first women's rights convention in United States history.

At the convention, Stanton herself wrote and presented a historic set of resolutions called a Declaration of Sentiments. The document echoed the language of the Declaration of Independence:

 KEY DOCUMENTS 66The history of mankind is a history of repeated injuries and usurpations [seizure of power] on the part of man toward woman, . . . [to establish] absolute tyranny over her. . . . [B]ecause women do feel themselves aggrieved, oppressed, and fraudulently deprived of their most sacred moral rights, we insist that they have immediate admission to all the rights and privileges which belong to them as citizens of the United States.99

—Elizabeth Cady Stanton,
Declaration of Sentiments, 1848

The convention passed 12 resolutions altogether. Signed by 68 women and 32 men, they protested the lack of legal and political rights for women. It urged women to demand these rights.

The ninth resolution proved to be controversial. It called for women's **suffrage,** or the right to vote. (See Government Concepts, next page.) At Stanton's insistence the convention passed the resolution. Mott, however, disapproved of the suffrage demand, and so did others at the convention, many of whom withdrew their support for the movement. The resolution also subjected the convention to considerable public criticism.

Slow Progress for Women's Rights The lasting impact of the Seneca Falls Convention is shown in the Turning Point feature below. The Convention did not trigger an avalanche of support for women's rights. Most Americans still shared Catharine Beecher's view that women should influence public affairs indirectly, through their work in the home.

Yet the convention marked the beginning of the organized movement for women's rights

TURNING POINT : The Seneca Falls Convention

Following the Seneca Falls Convention, women played an increasingly visible role in the nation's public life.

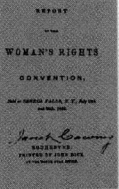

1848 First women's rights convention is held at Seneca Falls, N.Y.

1879 Belva Lockwood becomes first woman to practice law before the Supreme Court.

1972 Congress passes the Equal Rights Amendment, but ratification effort fails.

1840	1880	1920	1960	2000

1869 Wyoming territory grants women full suffrage.

1920 On August 26, the Nineteenth Amendment becomes law, giving women the right to vote.

1981 Sandra Day O'Connor becomes the first woman member of the Supreme Court.

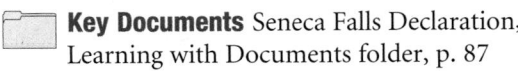

Interdisciplinary

Astronomer Maria Mitchell (1818–1889) was born in the busy whaling port of Nantucket, Massachusetts. As a child, she helped her father record an eclipse of the sun and was encouraged to use his telescope. In 1847, she discovered a comet, which was later named for her. As a teacher, she advised her students to question everything: "We especially need imagination in science. It is not all mathematics, nor all logic, it is somewhat beauty and poetry."

Answers to
SECTION 3 REVIEW

1. (a) Seneca Falls Convention, see p. 277; (b) suffrage, see p. 277.

2. Changed: women became consumers more than producers; lower class women took jobs in factories; middle class women freed from home chores; some became active in reform. Did not change: managed home and family; discouraged from public activities; could not vote or keep their earnings.

3. Sample chart: Cause—Seneca Falls Convention; Effect—Wyoming grants suffrage, Nineteenth Amendment becomes law.

4. *A Treatise on Domestic Economy;* women could contribute to society by supporting their men and raising sons to be upstanding citizens.

5. Beecher—women should make the most of their role in the home by influencing men; Stanton—women should make their voices heard through voting; should have equal rights.

6. Essays should be supported with facts from the section.

GOVERNMENT CONCEPTS

suffrage: *the right to vote*

▼ **The Historical Context** The Seneca Falls *Declaration of Sentiments* of 1848 included a resolution calling on women to fight for "their sacred right to the elective franchise," or right to vote. Under the Constitution, each state set its own voting requirements and thus could deny suffrage to any group it chose, such as women or African Americans.

▼ **The Concept Today** Suffrage in the United States has steadily broadened. Constitutional amendments have guaranteed the vote to African Americans (Fifteenth Amendment, ratified 1870), women (Nineteenth Amendment, ratified 1920), and citizens age 18 or older (Twenty-sixth Amendment, ratified 1971).

and for the women's suffrage movement in the United States.

Whereas no college in the United States admitted women in 1820, by 1890 more than 2,500 women a year graduated from American colleges and universities. Educated women began appearing in professions from which they once had been excluded.

After becoming the first American woman to earn a medical diploma, Elizabeth Blackwell began practicing medicine in New York City in 1850. Seven years later she founded the first school of nursing in the United States. Maria Mitchell made history by becoming the nation's first woman astronomer. Mitchell discovered a new comet in 1847 and in 1848 became the first woman elected to the American Academy of Arts and Sciences.

In 1845 Margaret Fuller, the editor of an important philosophical journal, also wrote a book, *Woman in the Nineteenth Century*, in which she criticized cultural traditions that restricted women's roles in society. As editor of

the popular magazine *Godey's Lady's Book*, Sarah Josepha Hale published articles about women's issues for almost 50 years.

The Role of African American Women No African American women attended the Seneca Falls Convention, and only a handful came to most other women's rights conventions. For most African American women, the abolition of slavery was a more pressing issue.

A frequent participant in such meetings, however, was abolitionist and former slave Sojourner Truth. She reminded white women that African American women also had a place in the movement for women's rights. Truth also became one of a small number of black women in the 1840s and 1850s who were active in the movement for women's rights.

In 1852, the 54-year-old Truth walked into a convention of white women in Akron, Ohio. Over the objections of many delegates, convention president Frances Dana Gage allowed Truth to speak. Truth walked slowly to the front and addressed the group:

 AMERICAN VOICES ❝I am a woman's rights. I have as much muscle as any man, and can do as much work as any man. . . . I can carry as much as any man, and can eat as much too . . . I have heard the Bible and have learned that Eve caused man to sin. Well, if woman upset the world, do give her a chance to set it right side up again.❞

—*Speech by Sojourner Truth, 1852*

SECTION 3 REVIEW

Comprehension

1. *Key Terms* Define: (a) Seneca Falls Convention; (b) suffrage.

2. *Summarizing the Main Idea* How did the role of women change in the mid-1800s, and in what ways did it not change?

3. *Organizing Information* Create a cause and effect chart on the Seneca Falls Convention.

Critical Thinking

4. *Analyzing Time Lines* Refer to the time line at the start of the section. Which publication shown on the time line dealt with women's

private contributions to American society? Describe the message of that publication.

5. *Recognizing Ideologies* Compare Catharine Beecher's views on women and reform with those of Elizabeth Cady Stanton.

Writing Activity

6. *Writing an Expository Essay* How did the various reform movements lead to a greater public role for women? Describe this connection in an expository essay.

 ### RESOURCE OPTIONS

Teaching Resources

📁 **Biography** Maria Mitchell, Units 3–4 folder, p. 27

📁 **Quiz** Units 3–4 folder, p. 24

📁 **Literature Activity** Advice on Marriage, Units 3–4 folder, p. 30

Student Performance Pack

Guide to the Essentials Chapter 9, Section 3 (English and Spanish)

1840	1844	1845	1845	1848
Major rise in immigration begins	Ethnic, religious riots in Philadelphia	North-South split in Baptist church	Irish Potato Famine leads to increased immigration	Failed German revolution leads to increased immigration

1840   **1845**   **1850**

4 Growing Divisions

SECTION PREVIEW

Objectives

1. Describe the causes and effects of the huge rise in immigration to the United States in the 1830s and 1840s.
2. Analyze why the reform movement deepened cultural differences between the North and the South.
3. *Key Terms*   Define: Irish Potato Famine; naturalize; discrimination.

Main Idea

The United States grew increasingly diverse due to the arrival of new groups of immigrants and the growing cultural differences between the North and South.

Reading Strategy

Compare and Contrast As you read, make notes on the beliefs and traditions of groups of Americans mentioned. Then note what the groups have in common, and how they differ.

People do not always want to hear advice, no matter how sincerely it is offered. Reformers of the early 1800s found this out. From revivalism to temperance to abolition to women's rights, reform movements often did as much to divide American society as to improve it.

One reason was that the nation was becoming more culturally diverse. The North and the South were becoming more distinct. Differences between working people and the middle class were widening. In addition, the young, prosperous nation was attracting immigrants from a variety of European cultures. Some segments of this diverse population did not share the reformers' vision of America.

Rising Immigration

The economic changes of the early 1800s created a growing demand for cheap labor in factories and in the building of canals and railroad lines. These jobs attracted immigrants, most of whom arrived hungry, penniless, and eager to work.

In the entire decade of the 1820s, only about 129,000 immigrants arrived in the United States. During the 1830s, however, the number of new immigrants rose to 540,000, and in the 1850s, the figure skyrocketed to 2.8 million. Nearly all of these new arrivals settled in the North and West, because the use of slave labor in the South offered few job opportunities.

Almost all of the immigrants to the United States from 1820 to 1860 came from northern Europe. While some immigrated from Scandinavia and England, most were from Ireland and Germany. The graph on the next page shows the number and origin of these immigrants.

The Irish Irish immigration soared in the mid-1840s when Ireland suffered a horrible disaster known as the **Irish Potato Famine.** The famine, which lasted from 1845 to 1849,

This poster from an English travel office targeted potential emigrants.

RESOURCE OPTIONS

Teaching Resources

 Reproducible Lesson Plan Lesson Plans folder, p. 71

 Learning Styles Lesson Plan Learning Styles Lesson Plans folder, p. 21

Big Idea Graphic Organizer Big Idea Graphic Organizer folder, p. 43

Guided Reading and Review Units 3–4 folder, p. 25

Media and Technology

Color Transparencies Our Multicultural Heritage, C-13

Immigration to the United States, 1821–1860

Source: *Historical Statistics of the United States, Colonial Times to 1970*

Year

 Interpreting Graphs Seeking to escape famine and revolution in Europe, several million immigrants came to the United States in the 1840s and 1850s, changing the character of the United States population in the process. *Culture From which nation came the largest number of immigrants to the United States in the period from 1846 to 1855?*

caused hundreds of thousands of Irish to flee to the United States.[†] Most settled in northeastern cities such as Boston and New York.

Like other immigrant groups, after settling in the United States the Irish became **naturalized.** That is, they applied for and were granted American citizenship. Irish men filled manual labor jobs in factories or on canals or railroads. Once established, the newcomers sent for relatives to join them. Irish communities in northern cities grew steadily.

As their numbers grew, Irish Americans became a political force. Most were Jacksonian Democrats. The Democratic party had reached out to these potential new voters when they first arrived. The tactic paid off. In 1855, for example, 34 percent of all New York City voters were first-generation Irish immigrants.

The Germans Many Germans came to America seeking political freedom after a series

[†] The causes of the Irish famine are the subject of scholarly debate today. In the 1840s, under British rule, three-quarters of Irish farmland produced crops to be sold to England. When disease wiped out the potato crops that were the main source of food for the Irish, famine spread across the country. Still, British landowners refused to put more land into production of other food, such as wheat or oats, for the Irish population. Nearly 1.1 million Irish died of starvation and related diseases. Between the deaths and flight from the famine, Ireland's total population of 8.4 million in 1844 dropped to 6.6 million by 1851.

of failed rebellions across Europe in 1848. The majority of the German immigrants were peasants who bought up large tracts of farmland in the Midwest, especially in Wisconsin and Missouri. German artisans and intellectuals tended to settle in northern cities such as New York, Chicago, and Milwaukee.

New Cultures These immigrants brought new cultural traditions. Most of the Irish and many of the Germans were Roman Catholic. Like Catholics in other countries, they respected the authority of the Pope in Rome as the head of the Church. They looked to Church laws for guidance. Their celebrations followed Church traditions and those of their home country.

Like other laborers, the new immigrants worked long hours in tedious jobs. After work the men gathered in taverns, often the social centers of the neighborhood. Boxing matches, horse races, and new team sports such as baseball were inexpensive diversions from the grind of daily life.

Immigrants Face Hostility Irish and German immigrants often faced **discrimination,** the unequal treatment of a group of people because of their nationality, race, sex, or religion. Discrimination came from Americans who felt threatened by the presence of the newcomers or disapproved of their culture.

One source of tension was economics. The Irish, for example, arrived just as new, struggling labor unions were launching strikes to obtain higher wages and better working conditions. Because the Irish would work for lower wages, companies used them as strike breakers. Many of the New England "mill girls" lost their jobs to Irish men in the 1830s and 1840s.

A second source of tension was religion. Many Protestants disapproved of the Catholic religion. They believed that Catholicism's emphasis on rituals and on the Pope's authority discouraged individual thinking.

Catholics protested when their children in public schools were forced to read the Protestant version of the Bible (the King James Version). Textbooks of the time also required students to learn Protestant values. Catholics fought efforts by reformers to enact laws restricting drinking, gambling, and sports, which they did not view as immoral.

In 1843, anti-immigrant citizens formed the American Republican party. The party unsuccessfully pushed for a new naturalization law requiring immigrants to live in the United States for 21 years before being eligible for citizenship. When the Philadelphia school board allowed Catholic students to use the Catholic (Douay) version of the Bible and to be excused from religious activities, the American Republicans protested.

In 1844, Irish Catholics attacked American Republicans who were attempting to vote in Philadelphia's Irish districts. This led to riots in the city in May 1844, in which armed mobs burned down Irish homes and churches and 30 people were killed.

North-South Tensions

Reform movements produced conflict not only in the North. They increased ill will between the North and the South as well. Southerners bitterly resented abolitionists' efforts to prevent the spread of slavery and to shelter escaped slaves. They felt stung by the charge that slaveholders were immoral.

Divided Churches For southern churches, slavery presented a painful dilemma. As southern revivalists began claiming that the Bible supported slavery, their audiences

In this 1885 painting, Irish immigrants disembark in New York. *Economics* Why did companies use Irish workers as strike breakers?

began to grow. Catholic and Episcopal churches in the South, on the other hand, were largely silent on the issue.

As the abolition movement intensified, it produced deep rifts in the Methodist and Baptist churches. In 1842 the Methodist Church demanded that one of its southern bishops free his slaves. That action snapped the bonds that had unified northern and southern members for decades. Churches in the slaveholding states left the national organization. They then formed the Methodist Episcopal Church South, which endorsed slavery.

The national membership of the Baptist Church had worked closely together for many years. But it, too, finally splintered, as about 300 churches withdrew in 1845 to form the Southern Baptist Convention.[†]

South Holds on to Traditions Reformers' calls for public schools and equal rights for women further offended many white southerners. These southern men saw these "reforms" as suggestions that they did not properly care for

Main Idea
CONNECTIONS

How did abolition cause divisions in some churches?

[†]In 1995, the Southern Baptists adopted a historic resolution condemning the church's past support of slavery and racial discrimination.

Using the Internet

Making a Graph

Objective Use the Internet to make a graph of information comparing two historical documents. Have students follow these instructions:

1. See the *America: Pathways to the Present* Web site at

http://www.Pathways.phschool.com

for the URL of the U.S. Department of Labor.

2. Compare the Seneca Falls Declaration with the Declaration of Independence. As you read through it, take detailed notes. How does Stanton deliberately mimic the Declaration of Independence? In what ways does she depart from it, and why?

3. Make a Venn diagram to compare the two documents. Include similarities and differences. Be sure to include supporting details.

4. Share your graph with the class. If students challenge some of your points, support them with quotes from the documents.

RESOURCE OPTIONS

Teaching Resources

📁 **Comparing Primary Sources** On Southern and Northern Women, Units 3–4 folder, pp. 28–29

📁 **Primary Source Activity** Plantation Life, Learning with Documents folder, p. 15

Answer to . . .

Viewing History Because they would work for lower wages.
Main Idea Connections Southern churches, whose members believed in slavery, broke off from national organizations.

Answers to
SECTION 4 REVIEW

1. (a) Irish Potato Famine, see
p. 279; (b) naturalize, see p. 280;
(c) discrimination, see p. 280.
2. The arrival of new groups of
immigrants; growing cultural differences between the North and South;
tensions created by the reform
movements.
3. Causes: growing demand for
cheap labor; Irish potato famine;
Germans sought freedom after a
series of failed rebellions across
Europe. Effects: Catholic population
grew; Democratic party grew; many
New England "mill girls" lost their
jobs to Irish men; growing Catholic
population created religious rifts;
Republican party formed by anti-immigrant citizens; riots between
Irish Catholics and Republicans.
4. Sample answers: Major rise in
immigration begins—economic
changes caused demand for cheap
labor in factories and in the building
of canals and railroad lines; North-South split in Baptist churches—
caused by a rift over slavery.
5. Southerners resented abolitionists'
efforts to prevent the spread of slavery and shelter escaped slaves, and
the charge that slavery was immoral.
Reformers' calls for public schools
and women's rights offended white
southerners who took it as an accusation that they did not properly
honor their families.
6. Answers should be supported by
facts from the section.

Answer to . . .

Comparing Primary Sources
*Olmsted argues that white women
in the South may work for wages
but should leave the demanding
work to slaves. The Harbinger
report argues that northern women
work as hard as slaves, but their
work is more profitable.*

COMPARING PRIMARY SOURCES

WORKING WOMEN, NORTH AND SOUTH

In the excerpts below, writers compare the work done by poor
women in the North and the South with work done by slaves.

Southern Women	Northern Women
"Poor white girls never hired [themselves] out to do servants' work, but they would come and help another white woman with her sewing or quilting, and take wages for it. . . . That their condition is not as unfortunate by any means as that of Negroes, however, is most obvious, since among them, people may sometimes elevate themselves to positions and habits of usefulness and respectability."	"Thirteen hours per day of monotonous labor are exacted from these young women. So fatigued are the girls that they go to bed soon after their evening meal. It would be a poor bargain from the industrial point of view to own these workers. . . . The greater number of fortunes accumulated by people in the North in comparison with the South shows that hired labor is more profitable than slave labor."
—Frederick Law Olmsted, A Journey in the Seaboard Slave States, 1856	—Report on a visit to the Lowell, Massachusetts, textile mills, published in The Harbinger, 1846

ANALYZING VIEWPOINTS **Compare the main arguments
made by the two writers.**

their families. In the South, where personal
honor was particularly important, such suggestions provoked offense and outrage.

Most of the South remained untouched by
the social turmoil that came with urbanization
and industrialization in the North. Thus,
southerners saw no need to reform their society. Families held fast to their traditional family relationships and roles. From small farmers
to wealthy planters, for example, southern
men had authority over not only their farms
and businesses, but their households as well.
The master of the plantation was also master of
his wife and children.

A few southern white women saw parallels
between their role and that of slaves. A South
Carolina woman, Mary Boykin Chesnut, confided to her diary that her husband was "master
of the house." "To hear is to obey. . . ," she
wrote. "All the comforts of my life depend upon
his being in a good humor." At times Chesnut
was sure that "there is no slave . . . like a wife."

Southern women had important roles to
play. The wives of small farmers often worked
with their husbands in the fields. The wives of
plantation owners supervised large households
and sometimes helped manage the plantation.
Many of these women, rich and poor, oversaw
their children's education.

Because farms and plantations were often
miles apart, however, opportunities to participate in public organizations and community
meetings were rare. The message of reformers
such as Elizabeth Cady Stanton and Sojourner
Truth did not reach the ears of many southern
women, who generally played a less public role
than their northern counterparts.

Clearly, the bonds that had united
Americans were slipping. As emotions intensified, the North and the South found it increasingly difficult to resolve differences through
negotiation and compromise.

SECTION 4 REVIEW

Comprehension

1. **Key Terms** Define: (a) Irish Potato Famine;
(b) naturalize; (c) discrimination.

2. **Summarizing the Main Idea** Why did
Americans become less united in the 1830s
and 1840s?

3. **Organizing Information** Create a cause-and-effect chart that identifies some of the causes
and effects of immigration in the 1840s.

Critical Thinking

4. **Analyzing Time Lines** Refer to the time line
at the start of the section. Choose two entries
and describe what caused each of them.

5. **Expressing Problems Clearly** Summarize
how the reform movement deepened hostilities between the North and South.

Writing Activity

6. **Writing an Persuasive Essay** Write a
newspaper column from the 1840s that
identifies a problem that divides Americans
and proposes constructive solutions.

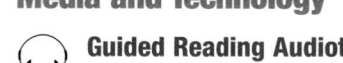

RESOURCE OPTIONS

Teaching Resources

 Quiz Units 3–4 folder, p. 26

Chapter Tests Forms A and B Chapter
Test folder

Student Performance Pack

 Guide to the Essentials Chapter 9,
Section 4 (English and Spanish)

Standardized Test Preparation Handbook

Media and Technology

Guided Reading Audiotapes Chapter 9
Summary (English and Spanish)
Student Edition on Audiotape Chapter 9

**Test Bank CD-ROM; Interactive Student
Tutorial CD-ROM** Chapter Test

To understand that . . .

You Can Help Reform Society

In the 1800s, the temperance movement aimed to improve society by changing people's behavior. Today, several organizations formed to eliminate drunk driving carry on the tradition of morality-based reform.

Banner from 1851 praising the virtues of temperance

In Los Angeles, students and teachers listen silently as a mother describes how her teenage son was hit and killed by a drunk driver. In Washington, D.C., another school assembly hears a student describe an automobile accident in which his girlfriend lost her life while driving under the influence of alcohol.

Many school assemblies about the dangers of drunk driving are organized each year by SADD (Students Against Driving Drunk), a club with more than 4 million members nationwide. SADD promotes the use of "designated drivers." It also urges teens not to drink and drive.

The Impact Today

SADD emerged in the early 1980s as part of a movement to deal with the injustices suffered by the victims of drunk drivers. SADD members sign a "contract for life" in which they promise to call a parent, neighbor, or car service for a safe ride should the need arise. SADD members also pledge to help others in situations involving alcohol and driving.

A similar organization, MADD (Mothers Against Drunk Driving), focuses on reducing the number of persons who drive drunk. MADD supports a minimum drinking age of 21, laws against open containers of alcohol in motor vehicles, and sobriety checkpoints on highways.

Despite the efforts of groups such as SADD and MADD, drunk driving remains a devastating problem. In 1996 approximately 17,000 people were killed in alcohol-related crashes in the United States. Many victims were young people, between 15 and 20 years old. In addition to the tragedy of lost life, drunk driving imposes an enormous financial burden on society. The economic costs of alcohol-related accidents are an estimated $45 billion per year.

The Impact on You

Do research to learn about some of the public awareness campaigns that SADD and MADD have organized. In class discussion, evaluate the tactics of SADD and MADD along with other strategies that can prevent drunk driving. Then write three paragraphs explaining the strategy that you believe is most effective.

MADD rally, including photos of victims of drunk driving

RESOURCE OPTIONS

Teaching Resources

Why Study History? Activity
You Can Help Reform Society, found in the Why Study History? folder, p. 10, provides an activity to help students explore ways they can help solve social problems.

Media and Technology

 AmericanHeritage® CD-ROM

Time Tour An Expanding Nation: A Reforming Age

Class Discussion

Discuss with the class drunk driving and public awareness campaigns. For a more thorough examination of the issue, see the activity folder in the Resource Options below.

Performing a Skit

Ask students to read the text. Then have the class brainstorm problems related to excessive drinking, for example:
- **fights**
- **problems with dates**
- **illness**
- **destructive behavior**

Next divide the class into small groups. Have each group create a skit on a problem related to excessive drinking, including alcohol and driving. Have the groups present their skits. Encourage discussion.

Follow up Have students investigate how to set up a chapter of SADD in your school.

Using the Internet

Students can learn more about reform movements by exploring links in the *America: Pathways to the Present* Web site at

http://www.Pathways.phschool.com

Assessment

See the Lesson Plans folder, pp. 24–27, for rubrics on assessing Class Participation Projects.

Key Terms

Students should refer to the definitions of the key terms in the chapter to write sentences that show the relation of each word to the reform movements and the growing divisions between North and South from 1815 to 1860.

Comprehension

1. Emerson—people can transcend the material world and become conscious of the spirit in nature; Thoreau—people should live simply and close to nature.
2. Mann pioneered school reform, establishing the grade level system, making curricula consistent, and instituting teacher training. Dix's appeals for prison reform led to the improvement of prison conditions and separate institutions for the mentally ill.
3. Garrison—published a newspaper, denounced moderation in fighting slavery, founded American Anti-Slavery Society; Douglass—great speaker and writer, started newspaper, opposed violence; Grimké sisters—involved women in the movement through speaking and writing pamphlets.
4. Answers may include: involved women in public life; further split the North and South; ultimately led to emancipation.
5. Women should exercise their power by influencing their husbands and sons.
6. It marked the beginning of the battle for suffrage.
7. A growing need for cheap labor in the United States; economic and political conditions in Ireland and Germany.
8. Reform movements sparked conflict; while the North became industrial, the South remained largely rural; slavery further split the nation; southern women held to tradition while northern women became active in reform movements.

Chapter Summary

 The major concepts of Chapter 9 are presented below. See also *Guide to the Essentials of American History* or *Interactive Student Tutorial CD-ROM,* which contains interactive review activities, time lines, helpful hints, and test practice for Chapter 9.

Reviewing the Main Ideas
Responding to changes brought about by industrialization, a movement to reform society arose in the early 1800s. Reformers were mainly northern, middle class, white, and Protestant. They sought to end slavery, prohibit drinking, win voting rights for women, and reform education.

Section 1: Middle-Class Reform
Revivalists and transcendentalists urged Americans to improve themselves and society as a whole. Reformers set out to battle social problems such as alcoholism, poor education, and inhumane prisons.

Section 2: The Antislavery Movement
A small but committed antislavery movement arose in the North in the early- to mid-1800s. Strong leaders, both black and white, used a variety of tactics to combat slavery, facing conflicts from within and attacks by opponents.

Section 3: The Movement for Women's Rights
Although women were expected to devote their energies to home and family in the early 1800s, some women organized a women's rights movement in the 1840s.

Section 4: Growing Divisions
The United States grew increasingly diverse due to the arrival of new groups of immigrants and the growing cultural differences between the North and South.

In the 1800s, the temperance movement aimed to improve society by changing individuals' behavior. Today, organizations formed to eliminate drunk driving carry on the tradition of morality-based reform.

Key Terms

Use each of the terms below in a sentence that shows how it relates to the chapter.

1. segregate
2. emancipation
3. utopian community
4. suffrage
5. temperance movement
6. discrimination
7. abolitionist movement
8. Seneca Falls Convention
9. naturalize
10. Underground Railroad
11. gag rule

Comprehension

1. Name two major transcendentalists and summarize their beliefs.
2. Describe the contributions of Horace Mann and Dorothea Dix.
3. Name three important abolitionists and describe the tactics they used to combat slavery.
4. Describe several effects of the abolitionist movement.
5. What was Catharine Beecher's main message to women?
6. Why was the Seneca Falls Convention important?
7. Why did immigration to the United States increase after the 1820s?
8. In what ways were the North and the South growing apart in the mid-1800s?

Using Graphic Organizers

On a separate sheet of paper, copy the web diagram below. Fill in the empty circles as shown in the sample.

Using Grapic Organizers
- Abolition: Tubman, Douglass, Garrison.
- Protestant reformers: revivalists, Transcendentalists.
- Public education: Mann.
- Women's rights: Beecher, Stanton.

Analyzing Political Cartoons ▶

THE DRUNKARDS PROGRESS.

1. Analyze the message of this temperance movement cartoon. (a) What is the title of the cartoon? (b) Characterize the people shown in Steps 1–3. (c) Characterize the people shown in Steps 4–5. (d) Characterize the people shown in Steps 6–9.

2. How does this cartoon help explain why members of the temperance movement were opposed to all alcohol consumption?

3. (a) Who are the figures under the steps? (b) What additional message do they provide?

4. Is this an effective political cartoon? Why or why not?

Critical Thinking

1. *Applying the Chapter Skill* Reread the Key Documents excerpt from the Declaration of Sentiments in Section 3. Make a list of questions you could ask in order to better understand and evaluate the excerpt.

2. *Making Comparisons* How did the goals of the abolitionist movement and the women's movement differ?

3. *Recognizing Bias* What issues led to conflict between some Protestants and Catholics?

ANALYZING DOCUMENTS ◀ ▶ INTERPRETING DATA

Refer to the chart entitled "Free and Enslaved Black Population, 1820–1860" in Section 2 to answer the following questions:

1. About how many more enslaved African Americans were there in 1860 than in 1820? (a) 4,000 (b) 1,000 (c) 1,500 (d) 2,500

2. In 1860 the number of enslaved African Americans was about how many times larger than that of free African Americans?

 (a) two times (b) five times (c) eight times (d) eleven times

3. *Writing* Assume the role of an abolitionist in 1860. Write a letter to your senator calling for an end to slavery. Use data from this chart to support your position.

INTERNET ACTIVITY

For your portfolio:
PREPARE A REPORT

Access Prentice Hall's *America: Pathways to the Present* site at **www.Pathways.phschool.com** for the specific URL to complete the activity. Additional resources and related Web sites are also available.

Read about the start of the antislavery movement and visit three stops on the Underground Railroad. Compare the abolitionists. What motivated them? What approach did each abolitionist believe in?

Connecting to Today

Essay Writing Choose a reform discussed in this chapter and write an essay on the impact of that reform on American society today. Include answers to these questions: (a) What successes did the reform achieve? (b) How did the reform affect you or someone you know? (c) What work still needs to be done to improve conditions?

INTERNET ACTIVITY

Answers will vary but reports should include historical facts from the Web site on abolitionists and their motivations.

Analyzing Political Cartoons

1. (a) "The Drunkards Progress." (b) Happy and social. (c) Drunk and rowdy. (d) Filthy, ill, violent, suicidal.

2. It shows that even social drinking will lead to ruin.

3. (a) A women and child left widowed and orphaned by a man ruined by alcohol. (b) A man's fall to alcohol affects more than himself; it affects his dependents, too.

4. Possible response: Effective, because the message is both clear and dramatic.

Critical Thinking

1. Questions may include: What moral rights were women deprived of? What rights should they be given as citizens of the United States? Which repeated injuries are referred to?

2. Abolitionist movement: freedom from slavery, not necessarily full equality; women's movement: to vote and hold office and to have full rights of American citizens.

3. Protestants disapproved of Catholicism, feared the United States would become a Catholic nation; Catholics protested when their children in public schools were forced to read the Protestant version of the Bible, fought efforts by reformers to enact laws restricting drinking, gambling, and sports.

Interpreting Data

1. d
2. c
3. Answers will vary but should be based on data from the chart.

Connecting to Today

Essays should include facts from the chapter on the particular reform movement and a comparison of its impact on present-day society.

CHAPTER 10

Beyond the Mississippi, 1800–1860

Managing Time and Instruction

INSTRUCTION SUPPORT

These materials for instruction are provided for **each section** in the **Teaching Resources.** See **Units 3–4 folder for Enrichment Support:**

- Reproducible Lesson Plans in Lesson Plans folder
- Learning Styles Lesson Plans in Learning Styles Lesson Plans folder
- Big Idea Graphic Organizers in Big Idea Graphic Organizer folder
- Guided Reading and Review
- Quizzes
- Test Preparation Practice booklet

DAILY LESSON	ENRICHMENT SUPPORT
1 **The Plains Indians** (pp. 287–290)	• Biography, York, Units 3–4 folder, p. 40 • Nystrom *Atlas of Our Country*, The Second Wave of Immigration, pp. 24–25 • Literature Activity, Native American Legends: Hiawatha, found on **Resource Pro**
2 **Hispanic North America** (pp. 291–296)	• Nystrom *Atlas of Our Country*, Early Expansion of the United States, pp. 20–21 • Literature Activity, What Happened in Texas, Units 3–4 folder, p. 43
3 **Trails to the West** (pp. 297–299)	• Primary Source Activity, Traveling West, found on **Resource Pro** • Literature Activity, Song of the Pioneers, found on **Resource Pro** • Critical Thinking Activity, Determining Relevance, found on **Resource Pro** • Skills for Life Activity, Units 3–4 folder, p. 44
4 **From Sea to Sea** (pp. 301–306)	• Key Documents, Declaration of "Manifest Destiny," Learning with Documents folder, p. 88 • Visual Learning Activity, The Annexation of Texas, Learning with Documents folder, p. 52 • Comparing Primary Sources, On Expanding into Mexican Territory, Units 3–4 folder, pp. 41–42 • Primary Source Activity, Gold! Gold! Gold!, Learning with Documents folder, p. 16 • Visual Learning Activity, Living Dead in Califor-nee, found on **Resource Pro** • Biography, Kamiakin, found on **Resource Pro** • The Frontier Still Exists Today, Why Study History? folder, p. 11

Running Out of Time?

- Use Tape 2, "An Emerging New Nation, 1800–1860," from **Visions of America** videotapes series.
- Use Chapter 10 Summary, from **Guide to the Essentials of American History (English and Spanish).**

Companion Web Site

The companion Web site offers online links for all chapter review activities. It also provides key content links and structured support for this chapter for both teachers and students.

http://www.Pathways.phschool.com

Media and Technology

For the Student

Interactive Student Tutorial CD-ROM Chapter 10
Student Edition on Audiotape Chapter 10
American Heritage® CD-ROM
Guided Reading Audiotapes (English and Spanish) Chapter 10

For the Teacher

Resource Pro CD-ROM Chapter 10
Test Bank CD-ROM Chapter 10
Listening to Literature Audiotapes *Timeless Voices, Timeless Themes* "I Will Fight No More" by Chief Joseph
Color Transparencies D-7, D-8, D-9, E-4

 ## Assessment Options

Chapter Test Forms A&B Test Bank CD-ROM booklet
Test Bank CD-ROM Chapter 10
Standardized Test Preparation Handbook

 ## Block Scheduling

Pacing Suggestions

For 90-minute Blocks

- Teach sections 3 and 4 using Transparencies H-9, H-10, L-2, M-7, M-8 and F-4 and the Extended Class Periods Activity on p. 299.
- Teach sections 1 and 2 using the Big Idea Graphic Organizers from Teaching Resources and the Recent Scholarship note on p. 293 for class discussions.

Additional Resources

- Prentice Hall's **American History Block Scheduling Support File** covers over 40 major topics in American history. Included are lesson plans, strategies, primary sources, literature, biographies, Great Debates, art history, simulations, and songs.
- **Prentice Hall United States History Video Collection™** contains 20 videotapes covering American history from beginnings to present.

 ## Connections to American Literature

from Prentice Hall

Prentice Hall Literature *Timeless Voices, Timeless Themes* "Heading West" by Miriam Davis Colt, p. 546

Prentice Hall Literature Library Literature of the Expanding Frontier

Additional Resources

For the Student
J. Jeffrey. *Frontier Women: The Trans-Mississippi West, 1840–1880.* Hill & Wang, 1979.

For the Teacher
Francis Parkman. *The Oregon Trail.* The University of Wisconsin Press, 1969.
José Enrique de la Peña. *With Santa Anna in Texas.* Translated and edited by Carmen Perry. Texas A&M Press, 1975.

Prentice Hall brings into the classroom the vast archives and scholarship of the nation's premier American history magazine. See "From the Archives of American Heritage®" and "About the Presidents" teaching notes in this chapter.

 History Alive!

Teacher's Curriculum Institute, in partnership with Prentice Hall, provides unique materials that engage students with diverse learning styles. See History Alive!® unit on Manifest Destiny in a Growing Nation.

 Student Performance Pack

Ensures success in the three critical areas of Reading, Test Taking, and English Language Development with the following materials:
- Guide to the Essentials of American History in English and Spanish
- Guided Reading Audiotapes in English and Spanish
- Interactive Student Tutorial CD-ROM
- Test Preparation Handbook
- Test Preparation Practice booklet

Introducing the Chapter
Americans pushed westward into Texas, New Mexico, California, and Oregon in search of new opportunities. As their numbers grew, tensions developed between the new settlers and the peoples who already claimed these lands as their home.

Themes in American History
The theme for this chapter, Geography, is listed at the beginning of this unit. An alternate theme for the chapter is Government. To teach this unit thematically, you may wish to use the Expansion, Reconstruction, Immigration folder in American History Block Scheduling Support.

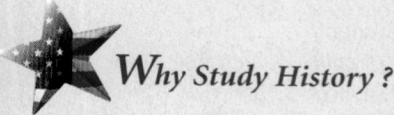

Why Study History ?

Have students explore suggested ways of connecting the past to the present on page 307.

CHAPTER
10 Beyond the Mississippi
1800–1860

CHAPTER FOCUS

This chapter describes the push to settle the lands west of the Mississippi. Although many people found new opportunities in the West, they were invading land that the Native Americans and Mexicans had lived on for centuries. The tensions that resulted from these encounters led eventually to conflict with Native Americans and a war with Mexico.

The Why Study History? page at the end of this chapter explores the connection between the shifting frontier in the 1800s and the new frontier in space today.

VIEWING HISTORY
Mouth of the Platte River, 900 Miles above St. Louis, was one of many scenes George Catlin painted of the American West. **Geography What peoples inhabited western lands before settlers began moving there?**

Answer to . . .

Viewing History Students should use this question as an aid in reading the chapter. Before the settlers from the United States began to make their way into western lands, the region was largely inhabited by Native Americans and, especially in the Southwest, Mexicans.

RESOURCE OPTIONS

Teaching Resources

Big Idea Graphic Organizer folder Graphic summary of the main idea of the chapter.

Learning Styles Lesson Plans folder Alternate lesson plans for diverse learning styles for each chapter.

Media and Technology

 AmericanHeritage® CD-ROM
Time Tour An Expanding Nation: From Sea to Shining Sea

  Prentice Hall United States History Video Collection™ Volume 6
Expansionism

The Plains Indians

Objectives

You may wish to call students' attention to the objectives in the Section Preview. The objectives are reflected in the main headings of the section.

Bellringer

Ask students to try to recall from films, books, and other sources the names of Native American groups who lived on the Great Plains. Ask them to write down their names and to consider the cultural images that these sources created.

Reading Strategy

Reading for Evidence Refer to the Reading Strategy in the Section Preview. You may wish to ask students to list the details they find.

1806 Lewis and Clark return from Louisiana Territory

1825 United States forces Indians west of Mississippi

1837 Mandan culture destroyed

c. 1850 Nomadic Indians dominate Great Plains

1806 **1817** **1828** **1839** **1850**

1 The Plains Indians

SECTION PREVIEW

Objectives

1 Identify ways the horse changed life for Indians on the Great Plains.
2 Describe the changing roles of Native American men and women.
3 Explain the decline of Plains Indians who lived in villages.
4 *Key Terms* Define: Great Plains; middleman; nomad.

Main Idea

Life for Native Americans on the Great Plains changed with the arrival of horses and white traders.

Reading Strategy

Reading for Evidence As you read, identify details that support the idea that European animals and goods affected Native American societies of the Great Plains.

The explorers Lewis and Clark returned from their journey of discovery in 1806. They brought back maps of the northern section of the Louisiana Purchase and descriptions of the Indians in the territory. That information would help open the region to white settlers.

Lewis and Clark were by no means the first white people to venture west of the Mississippi River. The Spanish and French had explored and claimed parts of the **Great Plains,** the vast grassland that lies between the Mississippi River and the Rocky Mountains. Fur traders had established business ties with Plains Indians. By this time, animals and goods from Europe had been affecting Plains cultures for more than two centuries.

The Coming of the Horse

One European animal, the horse, had a profound impact on the everyday lives of the Native Americans of the Plains. The Spanish brought horses to their colonies in northern Mexico in the 1500s. Native Americans acquired them through trading and also through raids. By the mid-1700s, horses had

spread as far north as the Missouri Valley, the Dakotas, and parts of what are now Oregon and Washington.

Before the arrival of the horse, Native Americans had generally relied on another four-legged animal, the dog. Dogs could hunt, and they could also transport a small load when harnessed to a *travois* [truh VOY], a platform supported by two poles that dragged along the ground. The strong and agile horse made hunting and transportation much easier, but it did far more. Horses changed almost every part of Native American life, from the nature of warfare to the division of labor between men and women.

Effects on Farming and Commerce Many Native Americans took advantage of the horse without allowing it to transform their cultures. The Pawnee, Mandan, and other Native American nations continued to live primarily as farmers, hunters, and gatherers. As in most

The flags and horses on this Sioux beaded vest document the increasing contact among Native Americans, Europeans, and white Americans.

LESSON PLAN

Connecting to the Main Idea

1. Focus Explain that Native Americans living on the Great Plains had contact with Europeans, principally the Spanish, long before the coming of white Americans. Ask how this contact altered their lives.

2. Instruct Discuss the effect of the introduction of the horse. Ask how it changed the traditional lives of some groups of Native Americans living on the Great Plains. Discuss how the shift from being settled villagers to living as nomads changed male and female roles. How did the horse affect the relationship between nomadic and village peoples?

3. Close By the time white Americans began to explore the territory west of the Mississippi River, contact with the Spanish had already changed traditional Native American life in the Great Plains region. The next section discusses the growing tensions between Mexico and the United States as settlers pushed into areas inhabited by Native Americans and Mexicans.

▶ RESOURCE OPTIONS

Teaching Resources

📁 **Reproducible Lesson Plan** Lesson Plans folder, p. 72

📁 **Learning Styles Lesson Plan** Learning Styles Lesson Plans folder, p. 22

📁 **Big Idea Graphic Organizer** Big Idea Graphic Organizer folder, p. 44

📁 **Guided Reading and Review** Units 3–4 folder, p. 32

📁 **Biography** York, Units 3–4 folder, p. 40

📖 **Nystrom *Atlas of Our Country*** The Second Wave of Immigration, pp. 24–25

This Navajo wall painting shows the Spanish bringing horses and other animals into the Southwest. Horses quickly spread north onto the Great Plains. *Culture How did the arrival of the horse change the lifestyle of the Plains Indians?*

Native American societies, the women in these villages did most of the farming, while the men were in charge of the hunting.

The Mandan lived in several villages along the Missouri River in the present-day Dakotas. French traders visited them as early as the 1730s, bringing manufactured goods, including blankets, beads, tools, and guns. They exchanged these goods for beaver pelts and buffalo hides. By the late 1700s, the Mandan had become part of an international trading system. They served as **middlemen** in the fur trade—that is, they bought items from one source (Indian trappers) and then sold them to others (white traders). This trade had a far greater impact on their way of life than did the horse.

The Pawnee, on the other hand, became somewhat more mobile than the Mandan following the arrival of the horse. They began to use horses to travel from their homes in the river valleys onto the plains for semiannual buffalo hunts. Although these hunts became an important part of the year, the Pawnee always returned to their villages afterward. There they continued to farm, hunt, and gather food.

Main Idea CONNECTIONS

In what way did the horse change the lives of the Pawnee?

The Rise of the Nomads For other Native Americans, the horse completely changed their way of life. They became **nomads**—people who continually migrate instead of living permanently in one place. Carrying their possessions on the backs of horses, they followed the vast herds of buffalo that crisscrossed the Great Plains.

By 1800 the Plains Indians had hunted the buffalo on horseback for more than half a century. During that time they discovered countless uses for the buffalo. James R. Walker, a doctor who lived for a time among the Oglala Sioux, described how the buffalo had become an important resource for Native Americans:

AMERICAN VOICES ❝[They used] the hair for making ropes and pads and for ornamental and ceremonial purposes; the horns and hoofs for making implements and utensils; the bones for making soup and articles to be used in their various occupations and games; the sinews [tendons] for making their sewing thread and their stronger cords such as bowstrings; the skins for making ropes, tipis, clothing . . . ; the flesh and viscera [intestines] for food.❞

—*James R. Walker*

Most of the nomads who lived on the Great Plains in the early 1800s were newcomers to that region. The Crow had long lived on the Plains, but the Cheyenne, the Sioux, the Comanche, and the Blackfeet all migrated to that area after horses made it possible for them to live on the move. The seemingly endless herds of buffalo were only one reason these Indian nations migrated to the Plains. Another was the need to avoid the wave of settlers who were pushing westward toward the Mississippi River and beyond.

Changing Roles

The nomadic Indians of the Plains differed sharply in many respects, but they did have some things in common. They depended heavily on skilled riding, hunting, and fighting, which only men learned formally. For this reason, nomadic societies granted men higher status than women. Men had to be aggressive warriors in dealing with other Native Americans as well as in hunting buffalo. In the early 1800s, Native Americans often conducted raids on one another to obtain horses or to defeat rivals.

Men also found more opportunities to gain wealth or power in a nomadic society than they had living in a farming village. Wealth was determined by the number of horses one had, and power by the skill and daring one showed in battle or during the hunt.

A young Cheyenne warrior named Wilkis remembered when his uncle taught him how to hunt buffalo and gave him the following advice:

 "Ride your horse close up to the buffalo, as close as you can, and then let fly the arrow with all your force. If the buffalo turns to fight, your horse will take you away from it; but, above all things, do not be afraid; you will not kill buffalo if you are afraid to get close to them."

—*Wilkis*

Eventually Wilkis became exactly what a grown man was supposed to be, according to Cheyenne culture. "I was a good hunter," he explained. "I had been to war, and had been well spoken of by the leaders whose war parties I went with."

Women had gained influence in farming villages partly because their responsibilities kept them close to home. When the men left for long periods of hunting or fighting, the women ran the village.

Women in nomadic cultures generally had less influence and less wealth than women in settled cultures. These Indians rarely stayed in one place long enough to farm the land. After Indian nations such as the Sioux and Comanche had adopted a nomadic way of life, women followed their husbands and fathers on an endless buffalo hunt. Therefore, women spent their time either preparing for the hunt or drying buffalo meat and tanning buffalo hides after the hunt was over. Power had shifted from the farming village, where females had some authority, to the male-dominated hunting camp.

The Decline of Villages

Before the arrival of the horse, the nomadic and village people of the Great Plains lived fairly peacefully together. But as the 1700s wore on, some nomadic groups developed into warrior cultures. To gain power in their group, Indians joined war parties and rode into battle. Warfare, as much as the buffalo hunt, became a way of life.

Nomadic Indians engaged in destructive raids on more settled Native American groups.

 Alfred Jacob Miller's painting illustrates the nomadic life adopted by many Native Americans of the Plains. Both horses and dogs provided hauling power. Using a travois, or sled, a dog could pull a 40-pound load five or six miles a day. *Economics How did the nomadic lifestyle affect the roles of men and women?*

Ⅱ ▼ **BACKGROUND**

Connections to Today

Before the arrival of white settlers, about one million Native Americans lived in the continental United States. By the early 1900s, that number had been reduced to a mere 300,000. By 1960, the numbers had climbed back up to about 800,000—half of whom lived on reservations. Today, nearly 2 million Native Americans live in the United States; according to the Census Bureau, about four in ten are either Cherokee, Sioux, Navajo, or Chippewa.

*C*ustomize for
More Advanced Students

Ask students to analyze the horse as a source of power for Native Americans. How did the horse contribute to creating a hierarchy both within and among Native American societies? What factors contribute to status in society today?

Answer to . . .

Viewing History Men, who traditionally were hunters and warriors, found increased status as dependence on the buffalo increased. Women, whose status was based on farming and other activities of a settled lifestyle, suffered a loss of status.

Graphing the Main Idea

To make sure students understand the main idea of this section, you may wish to use the multiflow map graphic organizer below.

Tell students that a multiflow map shows causes and effects. Ask students to use it to show how life changed for Native Americans on the Great Plains.

Teaching Tip A template for this graphic organizer can be found in the Color Transparencies, G-5.

Artist George Catlin lived with and observed the Native Americans of the Plains for many years, producing more than 500 sketches and paintings of the Native American way of life. The painting to the left is titled *Buffalo Chase—Single Death*. **Geography** How did the buffalo hunt affect the settled Native American groups of the region?

To the south, the Comanche drove the Apache and Navajo west into Spanish New Mexico. In the north, the Sioux—in alliance with the Arapaho and Cheyenne—emerged as the dominant Indian group in the region by the early 1800s.

Caught between white Americans who were pushing from the east and their nomadic neighbors to the west, agricultural Native Americans suffered greatly. The diseases brought by white traders and settlers added to the tragic effects. No group was hit harder by European diseases than the Mandan. From a population of close to 10,000 in the mid-1700s, the number of Mandan already had fallen to a total of around 2,000 in the summer of 1837. By the end of the year, after the smallpox epidemic, only 100 or so were left.

American artist George Catlin later suggested that disease was not the only cause of the Mandan tragedy. The Mandan died in such large numbers, he claimed, because they were trapped in their villages and could not escape the surrounding war parties.

By roughly 1850 about 75,000 nomadic Indians dominated the Great Plains. They swept across the grasslands, trailing the buffalo and pursuing their enemies. In addition to these nomads, roughly 84,000 Native Americans from the East lived in what is now Oklahoma. Beginning in 1825 the United States government had decided to force them to relocate west of the Mississippi. Together, these two groups made up about 40 percent of the Native American population of North America.

SECTION 1 REVIEW

Comprehension

1. *Key Terms* Define: (a) Great Plains; (b) middleman; (c) nomad.

2. *Summarizing the Main Idea* How did horses and traders change the way of life of the Plains Indians?

3. *Organizing Information* Create a cause and effect diagram that shows how the roles of Native American men and women changed with the switch from an agricultural culture to a nomadic way of life.

Critical Thinking

4. *Analyzing Time Lines* Review the time line at the start of the section. How much time passed between the return of Lewis and Clark and the destruction of the Mandan culture? Are the two events linked? Explain.

5. *Drawing Inferences* Why do you think the Mandan chose not to adopt the nomadic way of life?

Writing Activity

6. *Writing a Persuasive Essay* Write an essay to persuade a friend that the arrival of the horse had a positive effect, overall, on Indians of the Great Plains.

RESOURCE OPTIONS

Teaching Resources

📁 **Quiz** Units 3–4 folder, p. 33

Student Performance Pack

 Guide to the Essentials Chapter 10, Section 1 (English and Spanish)

Media and Technology

 AmericanHeritage® CD-ROM

History Makers George Catlin

🖨 **Color Transparencies** Fine Art, D-8

| 1769 First California mission founded | 1821 Mexico wins independence from Spain | 1822 First colony of Americans set up in Texas | 1836 Republic of Texas established |

1765　　　　1790　　　　1815　　　　1840

2 Hispanic North America

SECTION PREVIEW

Objectives

1 Summarize Spain's efforts to strengthen its North American empire and the effects of Mexican independence.
2 Explain the rise of trade between the United States and Mexico's northern territories.
3 Describe the events that led to Texas independence.
4 *Key Terms* Define: presidio; secularize; Santa Fe Trail; Texas War for Independence; Battle of the Alamo.

Main Idea

The movement of traders and settlers from the United States into northern Mexico led to economic and political changes.

Reading Strategy

Question Writing Read the section's boldfaced headings. Write a question about each heading and look for the answers as you read.

T he United States government assumed that the Louisiana Purchase would remain part of "Indian Country." Thousands of migrating Americans had other ideas. By the 1830s, many white settlers already were pushing west into Indian Country. In the north the stream of migrants was so large and steady that it led to the creation of three new states: Iowa (1846), Wisconsin (1848), and Minnesota (1858). Long before these states came into the Union, however, many Americans in the southern part of the United States were moving west along the coast of the Gulf of Mexico.

Spain's North American Empire

Spain's commitment to controlling what is now the southwestern United States had always been weak. After the Pueblo revolted against Spanish settlers in present-day New Mexico in the late 1600s, this commitment grew even weaker. In the 1700s, surrounded by increasingly powerful Indians, the Spanish limited settlement to a string of small towns along the Rio Grande and in present-day Texas.

Spanish weakness in its control over New Mexico and Texas reflected the larger weakness of the empire as a whole. No longer the most powerful nation in Europe, Spain in the late 1700s faced growing threats to its North American territory from other European nations.

To meet these various threats, the Spanish government tried to establish better relations with the Comanche and Apache. These efforts achieved an uneasy peace with these Native American groups.

Securing California More dramatic was the Spanish effort to secure the area that is now the state of California. The Spanish feared that this land would fall into the hands of either the British or the Russians. In the late 1700s, Spanish soldiers and priests began building a

These Spanish mission bells were rung at religious services to indicate key points in the Mass.

RESOURCE OPTIONS

Teaching Resources

📁 **Reproducible Lesson Plan** Lesson Plans folder, p. 73

📁 **Big Idea Graphic Organizer** Big Idea Graphic Organizer folder, p. 45

📁 **Guided Reading and Review** Units 3–4 folder, p. 34

Media and Technology

🦅 **American**Heritage® **CD-ROM**

Time Tour An Expanding Nation: From Sea to Shining Sea

Objectives
You may wish to call students' attention to the objectives in the Section Preview. The objectives are reflected in the main headings of the section.

Bellringer
Provide a map of the United States and ask students to list at least five cities in California, Texas, and New Mexico with names that are Spanish in origin. Ask them if, based on what they know, Mexican and American cultures would be likely to clash.

Reading Strategy
Question Writing Refer to the Reading Strategy in the Section Preview. You may wish to have student pairs review by quizzing each other with their questions.

LESSON PLAN
Connecting to the Main Idea

1. Focus The movement of settlers and traders into Texas, New Mexico, and California caused tension between Mexico and the United States. Ask how Mexico reacted to these new immigrants.

2. Instruct Discuss the settlement of Hispanic North America. Encourage discussion with questions such as: What was Spain trying to do by establishing missions in California? What role did economics play in the American colonization of Mexico's northern territories? How did Mexico unwittingly encourage the American takeover of Texas?

3. Close At first Mexico welcomed American settlers into its northern territories, particularly Texas. But as the settlers' numbers increased, tensions developed and led to war. The next section discusses Americans' push westward over the Oregon Trail after acquiring Texas.

Geography in History

Spanish missions along the California coast enjoyed an unusually hospitable climate. The southern coast receives approximately 300 days of sun each year, but cold ocean currents from Alaska produce ocean breezes and moderate weather. Further inland, coastal mountains cut off moisture, and crops must endure drought and extreme temperatures. The conditions of California's fertile coast led the Spanish to establish missions along a narrow north-south corridor.

You may wish to have students add the following to their portfolios. To assess student work, refer to the generic rubrics in the Program Overview in the Teaching Resources.

Tell students that while Native Americans in California allowed missions to flourish, New Mexico's Native Americans made the establishment of missions difficult. Ask students to research and write an essay comparing the cultures of the Native Americans in these regions and explaining the factors that contributed to or undermined Spanish colonization.

Answer to . . .

Viewing History By the labor, sometimes forced, of their Native American workers.

Main Idea Connections Answers should take one or more of the following perspectives: the Spanish government, priests, or Native Americans.

network of missions and **presidios,** or forts, along the rugged California coastline. They created a chain of 21 missions running north from San Diego to San Francisco.

From the Spanish point of view, the colonizing efforts in California were a great success. While their settlements in present-day New Mexico and Texas remained small, the presidios and missions in California grew and thrived. However, from the point of view of many coastal Indians, the settlements were a disaster.

Main Idea
CONNECTIONS

Were the California missions successful? Explain.

Enthusiastic Franciscan missionaries devoted themselves to converting Native Americans to Christianity. One such missionary, Father Junípero Serra, founded the first of the California missions, at San Diego, in 1769. By 1782 he had founded eight more missions farther north. One goal of all the missions was to make the local Indian groups a part of the Spanish culture. Some of the Indians entered the mission community willingly. Others had to be forced.

The missions became visible symbols of Spanish authority in the region. They also became lively centers of trade. Serra brought Mexican cattle, sheep, fruits, and grains into California. As a result the missions, located on fertile farm and ranch lands, produced wine, olive oil, grain, hides, and tallow, a waxy substance used to make candles and soap.

The missions owed much of their success, however, to the Indians who labored for them. Indians tended the cattle and sheep, farmed the land, built the missions, and wove clothing. In return for their efforts, they usually received only food, clothing, and shelter. The priests often treated the Indians as harshly as the soldiers did. Those who refused to work might be whipped or locked in chains.

For these reasons, some Native Americans chose to leave when the chance to escape arose. Those who stayed often endured poor living conditions and limited medical care. These contributed to tragic epidemics of measles and smallpox. Between 1769 and 1848, the population of Indians in California fell from about 300,000 to about 150,000.

While the number of Indians declined, the number of Mexicans grew. These colonists from the south settled along the coast, usually around the missions and presidios. Monterey was the capital of the territory of California. Other important Spanish settlements included Santa Barbara, San Diego, and Los Angeles.

New Mexico Grows Meanwhile, change also had come to the settlements in northern Mexico, known as New Mexico. Thanks to long stretches of peace and more attention from Spain, the Mexican population in the

Franciscan friars lead a religious procession in this painting of a California mission in the early 1880s (right). The Native American pictograph (above) captures another view of a Spanish mission.
Economics How were the missions able to develop into centers of trade?

Teaching Resources

 Nystrom *Atlas of Our Country* Early Expansion of the United States, pp. 20–21

Media and Technology

 Color Transparencies Fine Art, D-9

region increased from 3,800 in 1750 to 19,000 by 1800. Unlike settlers in eastern North America, those in the New Mexico region did not spread over the countryside in small farms. Instead, the presence of powerful nomadic Indians and the harsh landscape of New Mexico encouraged the new Mexicans to live close together in large settlements, such as Albuquerque.

As New Mexico's population grew and its trade thrived, social changes took place. Women in this colony gained a great deal of independence. Wives were able to run businesses, divorce their husbands, own property, and sue in courts of law. In fact, women actually lost rights and influence when the region of New Mexico became part of the United States in 1848.

Effects of Mexican Independence

Mexico won its independence from Spain in 1821, after a thirteen-year struggle. The independence movement started with demands for self-government and a few local uprisings. In 1810 one of those uprisings, led by a priest named Miguel Hidalgo, triggered a rebellion that spread throughout southern Mexico. Spanish authorities crushed the early rebel groups, but the idea of independence stayed alive. In 1821, when a respected army officer named Agustín de Iturbide joined forces with the remaining rebels, victory came quickly. The Treaty of Córdoba, signed August 24, 1821, officially granted Mexico its independence from Spain.

California, New Mexico, and Texas were far from the fighting. Still, independence had an effect on their residents. As citizens of Mexico, the men in these territories were now free to elect representatives to the new government in Mexico City.

Because Mexico's new government was hostile to the Roman Catholic Church, it **secularized** the missions, meaning it put them under the control of the state rather than the Church. By the 1830s, only a handful of priests remained in northern Mexico. In addition, economic reforms designed to bolster the Mexican economy actually widened the gap between rich and poor in Mexico's northern territories. But these reforms also encouraged trade with the United States.

Traders blast their guns in celebration as they reach the outskirts of Santa Fe in this drawing from the 1840s. The journey from Independence, Missouri, was a dry and dangerous trip more than a month long. Unable to negotiate through the mountains, wagon trains took the Cimarron Cutoff, discovered by William Becknell in 1821. *Economics How did trade strengthen U.S. relations with Texas, New Mexico, and California?*

Trade with the United States

In 1821 William Becknell, a nearly bankrupt American, brought a load of goods from Missouri to the New Mexican capital of Santa Fe, where he sold them for mules and silver coins. Other Americans followed, taking advantage of the commercial opening created by Mexican independence and economic reforms. The high quality and low prices of American goods nearly replaced New Mexico's trade with the rest of Mexico.

By the early 1830s, caravans of wagons traveled regularly along the **Santa Fe Trail,** which linked Independence, Missouri, and Santa Fe, New Mexico. According to one of the most active American merchants, these caravans shaped the character of Santa Fe: "One now sees everywhere the bustle, noise, and activity of a lively market town."

American fur traders and merchants took advantage of economic openings in other parts of northern Mexico. New Englanders who sailed around South America to reach the West soon dominated the trade with California in fur, cattle hides, and tallow. In return, Californians bought finished goods from the New Englanders. According to one resident of Monterey in the 1840s, "There is not a yard of tape, a pin, or a piece

Bowing to his father's dying wish, Stephen Austin (above) established the first colony of American settlers in Texas in 1822.

of domestic cotton or even thread that does not come from the United States."

Thus the United States had strong economic ties with Texas, New Mexico, and California long before it gained political control over these areas. When the Mexican government loosened the rules affecting trade with American merchants, it ensured that Mexico's northern territories would trade more with the United States than with the rest of Mexico. More important, stronger commercial ties encouraged some Americans to settle in northern Mexico.

Texans Seek Independence

Nowhere was the flow of Americans into Mexican territory more apparent in the 1820s than in Texas. Stephen Austin, carrying out the plan begun by his father, Moses, received permission from the Mexican government to found a colony of several hundred families in east Texas. Austin, 29 years old and a member of the Missouri territorial legislature, led the first organized group of American settlers into Texas in 1822. By 1824, some 2,000 immigrants were living in Austin's colony.

American Demands Grow When Americans first started moving into what is now eastern Texas, the new Mexican government adopted policies that favored immigration. The Mexican Colonization Law of 1824 promised American immigrants cheap land, the protection of the Mexican government, and a four-year tax break if they settled in Texas.

Soon land agents were arranging contracts for hundreds of Americans to settle in Texas. By 1830 about 7,000 Americans lived there, more than twice the number of Mexicans in the territory. Worried that they were losing Texas through immigration, Mexico passed a law in 1830 prohibiting any more Americans from settling there. Equally important, it outlawed the importation of slaves. Still, Americans continued to flow across the border, and they brought their slaves with them.

By 1835 more than 30,000 Americans lived in Texas. As their numbers swelled, these Americans demanded more political control. In particular, they wanted slavery to be guaranteed under Mexican law. At the time, some 3,000 African American slaves labored for settlers in Texas. Through his diplomatic efforts, Stephen Austin blocked a proposed ban on slavery in the territory. The newcomers continued to call for the same rights from the Mexican government that they had possessed in the United States.

Tension Erupts into War The settlers were divided between those led by Austin, who preferred to work within the Mexican system, and those led by a lawyer from Alabama named William Travis, who wanted to fight for independence. Events in Mexico City soon helped Travis's supporters gain the upper hand. The ambitious General Antonio López de Santa Anna declared himself dictator of Mexico. Later, he stripped Texas and other territories of their remaining rights of self-government.

These actions united the Texans in the cause of independence. Not only settlers from the United States, but also Mexican settlers in Texas sought self-government. In November 1835 these independence-minded settlers clashed with Mexican troops, beginning the **Texas War for Independence.** The settlers named Sam Houston, a recent immigrant from Tennessee, as their commander in chief.

Sam Houston

AMERICAN BIOGRAPHY Before Sam Houston arrived in Texas in 1832, he had already led an exciting life. Born in Virginia in 1793, Houston moved west with his family to a farm in the Tennessee wilderness. He left home as a teenager to live with a nearby group of Cherokee Indians, with whom he stayed for almost three years. Houston took the name Black Raven and educated himself in the Cherokee language and way of life.

Sam Houston (1793–1863)

During the War of 1812 Houston fought under Andrew Jackson. In 1817, Jackson helped him get a job managing the removal of Cherokee from Tennessee to a reservation in the Arkansas Territory. Houston left this position the next year after the Secretary of War scolded him for wearing his Indian clothes in the Secretary's office.

Houston went on to study law and become a district attorney before running successfully for Congress. In 1827, at age 34, he won election as governor of Tennessee. Houston did not run for a second term, instead deciding to follow the Cherokee to Arkansas. He traded with them and became their adviser, using his knowledge of government to fight for Cherokee rights.

In 1832 President Jackson sent Houston to Texas to work out treaties with the Indians there to protect American traders crossing the border. He settled in Texas the next year and soon became a leader of the independence movement. ▪

Texas Wins Independence

The settlers' defiance of Mexico provoked General Santa Anna into action. He led an army of several thousand men north to subdue the rebellion. After crossing the Rio Grande, the Mexican general headed for the Alamo, a walled fortress built on the ruins of a Spanish mission in San Antonio. In December 1835 a group of Texas rebels had ousted Mexican troops from the fortress.

The Texans at the Alamo, numbering fewer than 200 men, prepared to meet Santa Anna. Their leaders, William Travis and James Bowie, hoped to be able to slow the general's advance long enough to allow their fellow rebels to assemble an army.

The **Battle of the Alamo** lasted 13 days. Under siege by a vastly larger Mexican force, Travis sent this plea for help "to the People of Texas and all the Americans in the World":

AMERICAN VOICES ❝Fellow citizens & compatriots, I am besieged by a thousand or more of the Mexicans under Santa Anna. . . . I call on you in the name of Liberty, of patriotism & everything dear to the American character to come to our aid, with all dispatch. . . . If this call is neglected, I am determined to sustain myself as long as possible & die like a soldier who never forgets what is due to his own honor or that of his country.❞

—*Colonel William B. Travis*

The courageous Texans inflicted heavy casualties on the roughly 4,000 Mexican troops, but on the morning of March 6 Santa Anna's men forced their way inside the walls. The Mexican general ordered his men to take no prisoners. When the fighting stopped, more than 180 Texans lay dead, including Travis, Bowie, and the legendary frontiersman Davy Crockett.[†]

The slaughter of the Alamo defenders was followed two weeks later by another shocking event. Texans occupying the presidio at Goliad surrendered to a larger Mexican force, which agreed to treat them as prisoners of war. Santa Anna later rejected that agreement and had all the Texans shot, more than 300 soldiers in all. These two events enraged and energized Texans to mighty actions for their cause.

[†] All the Texans in the Alamo did not die. The Mexicans spared around 15 people, mostly women and children. An estimated 1,000 to 1,600 Mexican soldiers died in the battle.

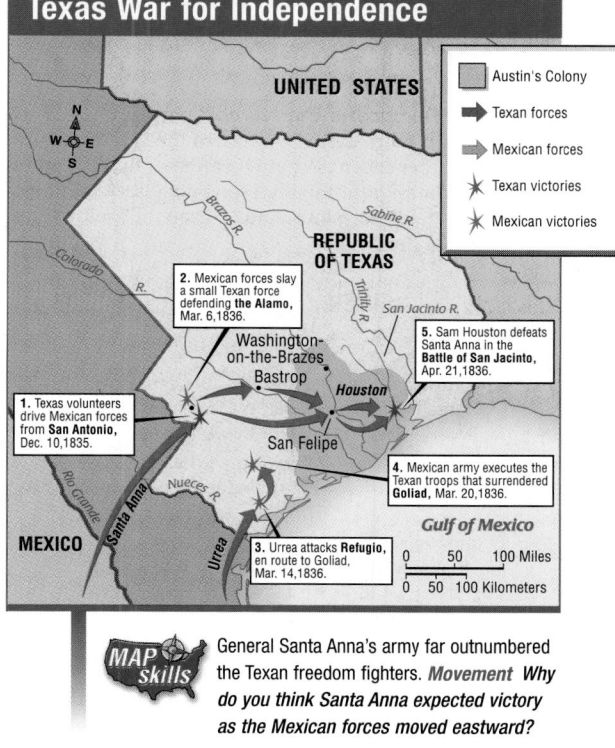

Texas War for Independence

UNITED STATES

- Austin's Colony
- ➡ Texan forces
- ➡ Mexican forces
- ✶ Texan victories
- ✶ Mexican victories

REPUBLIC OF TEXAS

2. Mexican forces slay a small Texan force defending **the Alamo**, Mar. 6,1836.

Washington-on-the-Brazos
Bastrop
Houston

5. Sam Houston defeats Santa Anna in the **Battle of San Jacinto**, Apr. 21,1836.

1. Texas volunteers drive Mexican forces from **San Antonio**, Dec. 10,1835.

San Felipe

4. Mexican army executes the Texan troops that surrendered **Goliad**, Mar. 20,1836.

MEXICO

3. Urrea attacks **Refugio**, en route to Goliad, Mar. 14,1836.

Gulf of Mexico

0   50   100 Miles
0 50 100 Kilometers

MAP Skills General Santa Anna's army far outnumbered the Texan freedom fighters. *Movement* Why do you think Santa Anna expected victory as the Mexican forces moved eastward?

Graphing the Main Idea

To make sure students understand the main idea of the section, you may wish to use the flow map graphic organizer below.

Tell students that a flow map shows students a sequence of events or steps unfolding. Ask students to use the flow map to record the events that led to increasing American settlement in northern Mexico.

Teaching Tip A template for this graphic organizer can be found in the Color Transparencies, G-4.

Customize for
English Language Learners

List the following terms on the chalkboard and have a volunteer read each one aloud: mission, Mexico's northern territories, Santa Fe Trail, Stephen Austin, William Travis, the Alamo, General Antonio López de Santa Anna, and Sam Houston. Then ask volunteers to use each term in a sentence that relates to the section content. You may wish to direct students to where the term first appears in the text.

Answer to . . .

Map Skills Sample answer: The Texans had suffered heavy losses and he assumed they were fleeing.

TEST PREPARATION

Have students read the quotation by Colonel Travis on this page and then answer the question below.

Travis's main means of attracting Americans to his cause is—

A by exaggerating the numbers of Mexicans he is up against.

B by highlighting his own willingness to die.

Ⓒ by appealing to their sense of loyalty and patriotism.

D by making them feel guilty for not joining his cause.

Answers to
SECTION 2 REVIEW

1. (a) presidio, see p. 292; (b) secularize, see p. 293; (c) Santa Fe Trail, see p. 293; (d) Texas War for Independence, see p. 294; (e) Battle of the Alamo, see p. 295.

2. They wanted more political control and the right to own slaves, forbidden by Mexican law.

3. California: Spanish establish missions and presidios, bringing trade; their diseases decimate Native Americans, lowering their population. New Mexico: Mexican population increases; women gain independence and rights; settlements grow. Texas: Americans settle in Texas in large numbers; tensions erupt between them and Mexican government; the War for Independence breaks out.

4. Sample answer: Mexico wins independence from Spain, because Mexico is now an independent nation, with its own set of problems and benefits.

5. The Santa Fe Trail was established, linking the countries economically and culturally; Americans began to settle in northern Mexico.

6. Essays will vary but should be supported by examples from the text.

Answer to . . .

Interpreting Tables Santa Anna's declaration of dictatorship and his removal of all Texan self-government.

FACT Finder

Events Leading to the Texas War for Independence

Date	Event
1821	Moses Austin receives a 200,000 acre land grant from the Spanish government to colonize Texas, in northeastern Mexico. He dies before he organizes the colony.
	Mexico achieves independence from Spain.
	Stephen Austin, Moses's son, receives permission from Mexico to carry out his father's plan.
1825	Mexico opens Texas to American settlement. American population in Texas swells.
1829	Mexico abolishes slavery.
1830	Mexico stops American settlement. Differences between American settlers and the Mexican government increase.
1834	General Santa Anna declares himself dictator.
1835	Mexico rejects Texas application for statehood.
1836	Texas declares independence.

Interpreting Tables At first, many settlers were willing to seek diplomatic solutions to resolve the disputes between Texas and the Mexican government. *Government What finally united settlers to declare Texan independence?*

"Remember the Alamo!" On March 2, 1836, the rebels formally declared the founding of an independent Republic of Texas. By the end of the month, the young republic seemed about to fall to Santa Anna's army. Thousands of Texans were fleeing eastward in what became known as the Runaway Scrape. Sure that victory was near, Santa Anna divided his force to finish off the rebels.

Just when all seemed lost, about 800 Texans regrouped at the San Jacinto River under Sam Houston. There, on April 21, they surprised the overconfident Santa Anna. Rallying to cries of "Remember the Alamo!" they routed the Mexican troops in a matter of minutes. The map on the previous page illustrates the Texas war for independence.

The Texans captured Santa Anna and forced him to sign a treaty recognizing the Republic of Texas. Mexico later denounced that treaty but did not try to retake Texas. In the fall of 1836, the citizens of Texas elected Sam Houston as their first president. They then drafted a constitution modeled on that of the United States. The constitution included a provision that forbade the Texas Congress from interfering with slavery. The slavery provision would raise difficult issues in the years to come.

By the end of the 1830s, with almost no help from the United States government, American traders and settlers had established a firm presence in Hispanic North America. They had also succeeded in prying away a large piece of territory from Mexico. The loss of Texas continued to enrage the Mexican government. Meanwhile, however, Americans kept on pushing west, threatening even more Mexican territory. With these issues unresolved, tensions between Mexico and the United States grew to the point that war became a possibility.

SECTION 2 REVIEW

Comprehension

1. *Key Terms* Define: (a) presidio; (b) secularize; (c) Santa Fe Trail; (d) Texas War for Independence; (e) Battle of the Alamo.

2. *Summarizing the Main Idea* Why did the settlers in Texas want independence from Mexico?

3. *Organizing Information* Make a table showing the important changes that took place in the areas of California, New Mexico, and Texas during this period.

Critical Thinking

4. *Analyzing Time Lines* Review the time line at the start of the section. Which event do you think had the greatest effect on the people of Mexico? Explain.

5. *Recognizing Cause and Effect* Name two effects of increased trade between the United States and northern Mexico.

Writing Activity

6. *Writing an Expository Essay* Write an essay explaining how Mexican independence from Spain affected California, New Mexico, and Texas.

 ## RESOURCE OPTIONS

Teaching Resources

 Quiz Units 3–4 folder, p. 35

Student Performance Pack

 Guide to the Essentials Chapter 10, Section 2 (English and Spanish)

1818
Convention of 1818 allows
American migration to Oregon

1834
First missionaries
arrive in Oregon

1843
Mass migration
to Oregon begins

1846
United States
and Britain
divide
Oregon

1818   1825   1832   1839   1846

3 Trails to the West

SECTION PREVIEW

Objectives

1. Explain how the United States obtained part of the Oregon Country.
2. Describe the role of fur traders and missionaries in opening Oregon to settlers.
3. Describe what it was like to travel along the overland trails.
4. *Key Terms* Define: mountain man; trek; Oregon Trail; pass.

Main Idea

In the 1840s thousands of Americans migrated to Oregon and California.

Reading Strategy

Predicting Content Before you read, predict the kinds of challenges American settlers faced as they moved west. As you read, look for details to support your predictions.

While some Americans were pushing into Texas in the early 1820s, others back East began to hear stories of a beautiful land beyond the Rocky Mountains. This vast territory, known as the Oregon Country, stretched from northern California to the southern border of Alaska. Now called the Pacific Northwest, the area had magnificent mountains, endless forests, and fertile valleys.

The Oregon Country

A variety of Native American groups had lived in Oregon for centuries. Still, by the early 1800s four different nations—the United States, Great Britain, Russia, and Spain—claimed rights to the territory. In 1818, the United States and Britain signed a treaty agreeing to joint occupation of the Oregon Country. Called the Convention of 1818, the treaty ignored the Native Americans who already lived there.

Distracted by other problems, Russia and Spain withdrew their claims to the area in the mid-1820s. By that time a small but increasing number of enterprising Americans had made their way into Oregon.

Traders and Missionaries

Yankee merchants from New England, traveling by ship, first traded for furs with the Native Americans of Oregon in the late 1700s. After Lewis and Clark completed their expedition in 1806, growing numbers of American fur traders, such as Jedediah Smith and Jim Beckwourth, began to roam the Rocky Mountains in search of beaver pelts. Dubbed **mountain men,** these hardy trappers were some of the toughest and most colorful characters in the country's history. The mountain men generally adopted Indian ways, and many of them married Indian women. They also used the Indian trails that led through the Rockies to California and Oregon.

As news of the Oregon Country filtered back to the East, a few churches decided to

This journal recorded the adventures of one pioneer who braved the western trails.

RESOURCE OPTIONS

Teaching Resources

 Reproducible Lesson Plan Lesson Plans folder, p. 74

Learning Styles Lesson Plan Learning Styles Lesson Plans folder, p. 23

Big Idea Graphic Organizer Big Idea Graphic Organizer folder, p. 46

 Guided Reading and Review Units 3–4 folder, p. 36

Media and Technology

 RESOURCE PRO

Primary Source Activity Traveling West, found on Resource Pro, includes firsthand accounts of westward migration.

SECTION 3

Trails to the West

Objectives

You may wish to call students' attention to the objectives in the Section Preview. The objectives are reflected in the main headings of the section.

Bellringer

Ask students if they have ever taken a long and difficult trip. If so, ask them to describe how long it took and why it was difficult.

Reading Strategy

Predicting Content Refer to the Reading Strategy in the Section Preview. You may wish to ask volunteers to share their predictions with the class and list them on the chalkboard. When students have finished reading, ask them to share details that support their predictions.

LESSON PLAN

Connecting to the Main Idea

1. Focus Attracted by stories of fertile land beyond the Rocky Mountains, settlers began to travel west to the Oregon Country. Ask what the journey west was like for these pioneers.

2. Instruct Discuss the journey across the Oregon Trail and the settlement of the Oregon Country. Ask what kinds of people the Oregon Country attracted. Why was a woman like Narcissa Whitman, who led a comfortable middle-class life, willing to risk the challenges of a trip over the Oregon Trail? What difficulties did settlers encounter?

3. Close By 1845 thousands of pioneers had survived the Oregon Trail and settled in the Oregon Country. The next section discusses growing tensions between American settlers and the Mexicans and Native Americans who already lived there.

California Dreaming On November 4, 1841, after nearly seven months on the trail, the Bidwell-Bartleson caravan crossed the Stanislaus River and reached Mount Diablo, 50 miles from San Francisco, becoming the first train of Western emigrants to enter the new California Territory. The original party had left Sapling Grove, Missouri (now Kansas), in the spring. In July they had divided in half. Part of the expedition headed along the Oregon Trail. The rest, led by John Bartleson and John Bidwell, pushed westward. Among them was Nancy Kelsey, the only remaining woman on the trip, who was carrying her baby with her. Wagons had to be abandoned during the remaining trek over deserts and mountains. The 32 travelers were butchering pack mules by the time they emerged from the Sierra Mountains in late October and were saved from starvation when they discovered a herd of deer. After feasting, they made the final leg of their journey to Mount Diablo. Source: Nathan Ward, "The Time Machine," *American Heritage* magazine, November 1991.

The Overland Trails to the West, 1840s

Between 1842 and 1848 approximately 11,500 people migrated to Oregon.

Between 1842 and 1848 approximately 2,700 people migrated to California.

In 1847 and 1848 approximately 4,600 people migrated to Utah.

— 1845 boundaries
≍ Mountain pass
■ Fort

0   200 Miles
0   200 Kilometers

MAP skills Thousands of settlers headed west along various overland trails in the 1840s, facing dry, barren country in some parts of the journey and tall, rugged mountains in others. *Movement Along what important river did the final leg of the Oregon Trail run?*

send missionaries to the territory to convert Native Americans to Christianity. The first of these missionaries, a Methodist minister named Jason Lee, arrived in Oregon in 1834. He promptly built a mission school for Indians in the Willamette Valley.

Encouraged by his example, four Presbyterian missionaries joined Lee in Oregon in 1836. Among them was one of the first white women to cross the Rocky Mountains, Narcissa Prentiss Whitman. Whitman and her husband, a doctor, lived and worked among the Cayuse and Nez Percé. Neither Narcissa nor the other missionaries who settled in Oregon had much success in converting the region's Indians. In fact, by acting superior to the native peoples, many of them created more hostility than goodwill.

Overland Trails

Starting in 1843, organized wagon trains carried masses of migrants to Oregon along Indian trails opened up by mountain men. Groups met at a small town in western Missouri called Independence. From there they began the grueling, 2,000-mile **trek,** or journey, across the Great Plains and the Rocky Mountains along the **Oregon Trail.** The Santa Fe Trail to Texas also started at Independence, but the Mormon Trail started at Nauvoo, Illinois.

Why did people head west? The most common reason was land, which could be settled and farmed or bought and sold at a profit. Trade was another reason, and as the western population grew, the region's attractiveness to merchants grew as well. Beyond these economic factors, many of the pioneers also enjoyed the challenge and independence of life on the frontier.

The journey along the Oregon Trail could take from four to six months, and it was expensive. A typical family paid between $500 and $1,000 to make the trip. Normally, these pioneers traveled along the Platte River in present-day Nebraska and through the South Pass in what is now Wyoming. A **pass** is a low spot in a mountain range that allows travelers to

Answer to . . .

Map Skills The Columbia River.

cross over to the other side. People heading for California would turn southwest at the Snake River. Those bound for Oregon would continue following the Snake to the northwest.

Most of the pioneers who traveled the Oregon Trail went west as part of a family. Some were free African Americans, but the majority were white settlers from states along the Mississippi. Often, the trip was the second or third major move in their lives.

Most migrants traveling the Oregon Trail enjoyed the beauty of the plains and the mountains. Still, the trip was long and difficult. Getting the heavy covered wagons across rivers, through muddy bogs, and up steep hills was exhausting, backbreaking work.

As the months passed and the travelers became more frustrated with the demands of the long journey, people's nerves began to fray. As Oregon Trail traveler Enoch Conyers reported in his diary, "If there is anything in this world that will bring to the surface a man's bad traits, it is a trip across the continent with an ox team." The need to cross over the dangerous Rocky Mountains before the early winter snows arrived only added to the tension.

Movies and television westerns would have us believe that western pioneers and Indians continually fought with each other. In fact, they spent more time trading than fighting. Serious conflict did not develop until the 1850s. Before then, white travelers regularly received food and other items from Indians in return for clothing and tools. Disease was a far more deadly threat than the Indian. For example, cholera killed as

Pausing for a photograph in front of their covered wagon, this family was one of many that headed west in the 1840s in search of a better life. *Culture* Why do you think fictional portrayals of the westward journey differ so much from the facts?

many as 10,000 pioneers (about 4 percent of the total) between 1840 and 1860.

By 1845 more than 5,000 Americans had migrated to the Oregon Country. American settlers there began to outnumber the British. The next year, in the Treaty of 1846, the United States and Great Britain agreed to divide the Oregon Country along the 49th parallel (line of latitude). Because of the growing threat of war with Mexico, this peaceful solution proved to be in the best interest of the United States.

Main Idea CONNECTIONS

What posed the greatest threat to those who migrated to California and Oregon?

SECTION 3 REVIEW

Comprehension

1. **Key Terms** Define: (a) mountain man; (b) trek; (c) Oregon Trail; (d) pass.

2. **Summarizing the Main Idea** What caused thousands of Americans to begin migrating to the Oregon Country in the 1840s?

3. **Organizing Information** Make a web diagram that describes the various types of pioneers who followed trails to the West.

Critical Thinking

4. **Analyzing Time Lines** Review the time line at the start of the section. Which of the first three events is a cause of the last event? Explain.

5. **Distinguishing Fact from Opinion** Recall the statement quoted in this section, "If there is anything in this world that will bring to the surface a man's bad traits, it is a trip across the continent with an ox team." Is this fact or opinion? Explain.

Writing Activity

6. **Writing a Persuasive Essay** Write an essay that might have appeared in a newspaper or magazine in the 1840s. Try to persuade your readers that the trek to Oregon either is or is not worth making.

SKILLS FOR LIFE

Historical Evidence

Analyzing Tombstones

Focus Students analyze epitaphs as historical evidence of the physical conditions, hardships, and human emotions connected with a particular event in history.

Instruct Explain that artifacts left behind at historical sites can provide important historical evidence about an event. Ask students why artifacts such as gravestones, which are associated with the highly emotional experience of death, can be particularly illuminating.

Extend See the Skills for Life Activity in the Resources Options below.

Answers

1. (a) From 1845 to 1863, the Oregon Trail's most traveled period.
(b) Cholera, conflict with Native Americans, thirst.

2. (a) Her family's frustration at their inability to save her and their plea for people who followed to keep up her grave both demonstrate great loss.
(b) His sons took the time and probably considerable trouble to have a commemorative tablet made and placed on his grave.

3. (a) Cholera. (b) The Ellis and Martess epitaphs both show the death of infants. (Note: Childbirth along the Oregon Trail was also a common cause of death, for mother and child.)
(c) Cholera was epidemic, Native Americans posed a threat, good water was hard to find, and illness and accidents were common.

TEST FOR SUCCESS

Epitaphs will vary but should reflect an understanding of the steps for analysis presented in this feature.

Analyzing Tombstones

Have you ever passed an old cemetery and tried to figure out the stories its tombstones and other grave markers tell? They tell you when people lived, how long they lived, and sometimes even how they died and how they were remembered by those they left behind. Whether made for husbands or wives mourned by their spouses, beloved children who died too soon, or brave soldiers killed in battle, these markers also offer clues about the times in which the people they honor lived.

In a way, the overland trails west were also cemeteries. As one traveler along the Oregon Trail put it, "The road from Independence to Ft. Laramie is a graveyard." Another observer remarked that there was "one dead person every 80 yards along the Oregon Trail." Estimates of the number of people who died on this trek range from 20,000 to 45,000.

Use the following steps to analyze a few of the epitaphs, or inscriptions, that appeared on gravestones along the Oregon Trail.

1. *Identify the time in which the people lived and, if possible, how they met their deaths.* (a) What is the time period in which the people remembered met their deaths? (b) What were the various causes of their deaths?

2. *Evaluate what their lives meant to others who knew them.* (a) How does the Martess epitaph reflect a deep sense of loss on the part of those who survived her? (b) What tells you that George Winslow was well remembered?

3. *Study the grave markers to see what clues they offer about the historical period.* (a) According to many of the epitaphs, the Oregon Trail was plagued with an epidemic. What was it? (b) What clues can you find to tell you that the Oregon Trail was hard on small children? (c) What clues can you find to help you identify the dangers of the Oregon Trail?

TEST FOR SUCCESS

Create an epitaph for a fictional person from this period. Then draw a gravestone and write the epitaph on it. To get started, prepare a brief character sketch of the person. Be prepared to tell how the epitaph reflects the person's life as well as the historical period.

Died: Of Cholera

(This was the most frequent epitaph found on grave sites along the way.)

Mary Ellis
Died May 7th, 1845
Aged two months

(This epitaph was found on a piece of plank standing up from a grave site, its letters traced by a red-hot piece of iron.)

Marlena Elizabeth Martess
Died Aug. 9th, 1863
Born July 7th, 1862
Friends nor physician could save her from the grave

(This epitaph was followed by a plea to all who might pass to keep the grave in good repair.)

IN MEMORY OF GEORGE WINSLOW
who died on this great highway June 8, 1849
and was buried here by his comrades. . . .
This tablet is affectionately placed by his sons,
George Edward and Orrin Henry Winslow.

Rachel E. Pattison
Aged 18
June 19, '49

(This was a rock, hand-lettered.)

Rebecca Winters,
age 50 years

(This was crudely carved on a wagon wheel, which served as the grave's headstone.)

In Memory
of Charles Hatch HO
Died June 12, 1850

(Scratched on this carved tombstone is "Killed by Indians.")

Pioneer Grave of
John D. Henderson
Died of Thirst
August 9, 1852
Unaware of Nearness of the Malheur River Leaving Independence, Missouri, in May 1852, Mr. Henderson and Companion Name Unknown, Had completed Only Part of the Journey When Their Team Died. They were Compelled to Continue on Foot Carrying Their Few Possessions. The Twenty Miles of Desert Separating the Snake and Malheur Rivers Proved too Great a Struggle for the Weary Travelers

(This marker replaced a stone that gave Henderson's name and date of death.)

RESOURCE OPTIONS

Teaching Resources

Skills for Life Activity Units 3–4 folder, p. 44, helps students understand what information about a society can be learned from death notices.

| 1845 United States annexes Texas | 1846 Mexican War begins | 1846 Bear Flag Revolt | 1847 Mormons migrate to Utah | 1848 Treaty of Guadalupe Hidalgo | 1849 California Gold Rush |

1845   **1846**   **1847**   **1848**   **1849**

SECTION 4

From Sea to Sea

4 From Sea to Sea

SECTION PREVIEW

Objectives

1. Explain how the United States annexed Texas.
2. Describe the war with Mexico and its effects.
3. Identify the causes and effects of migration to Utah, California, and other parts of the West, including the Native American reaction.
4. *Key Terms* Define: manifest destiny; annex; Mexican War; Treaty of Guadalupe Hidalgo; Gadsden Purchase; California Gold Rush; boom town; ghost town.

Main Idea

The Mexican War of 1846–1848 extended the boundaries of the United States from the Atlantic to the Pacific, and migration to the West increased.

Reading Strategy

Reading for Evidence As you read, find evidence to support the following statement: "In the 1840s, Americans believed that no other nation should be allowed to keep the United States from fulfilling its destiny."

Objectives

You may wish to call students' attention to the objectives in the Section Preview. The objectives are reflected in the main headings of the section.

Bellringer

Write the word *destiny* on the chalkboard. Ask students to define it and to think about what the word might have to do with the expanding United States in the mid-1840s.

Reading Strategy

Reading for Evidence Refer to the Reading Strategy in the Section Preview. You may wish to write the statement on the board and tell students to glance at it as they read.

Migration from the United States into western territories surged in the 1830s and 1840s. That started some Americans dreaming of an empire stretching from the Atlantic to the Pacific. These Americans believed that the United States had a divine mission to spread liberty across the continent. A New York journalist named John L. O'Sullivan captured this sense of mission when he coined the phrase **manifest destiny,** meaning "obvious or undeniable fate."

Writing in 1845, O'Sullivan claimed that it was the nation's "manifest destiny to overspread and to possess the whole of the continent which Providence has given us for the development of the great experiment of liberty and federated self-government entrusted to us." In the 1840s, Americans believed that no other nation should be allowed to keep the United States from fulfilling its destiny.

Annexation of Texas

In 1836, after winning independence from Mexico, Texans voted to be **annexed** by the United States. To annex means to "join" or "attach." Texans encouraged the United States to absorb their new republic, partly to protect themselves from invasion by Mexico.

Americans, however, were far from united on the question of annexation. Most southerners and Democrats supported it. They looked forward to carving one or more slave states out of the Texas territory. Northerners and Whigs generally opposed it. They feared that the addition of even one slave state would shift the balance of power to the South.

Many people in both the North and the South worried that annexation would lead to war with Mexico. Their fear proved justified in August 1843, when Mexican leader Santa Anna warned that annexation would be "equivalent to a declaration of war against the Mexican Republic." Despite this warning, President John Tyler signed a treaty of annexation with Texas in April 1844. Two months later the Whig-controlled Senate defeated the treaty.

Later that year Democrat James K. Polk won the presidency. The victory of Polk, a strong advocate of expansion, suggested that the

The Texas flag reflected the new republic's informal name: the Lone Star Republic.

LESSON PLAN

Connecting to the Main Idea

1. Focus As settlers streamed into the West, growing numbers of Americans began to believe it was the destiny of the United States to extend from the Atlantic to the Pacific. Ask how the United States realized its dream of a continental empire.

2. Instruct Discuss the idea of manifest destiny. Why did Americans feel justified in fulfilling their destiny, despite the costs to other nations? What major historical events between 1845 and 1860 illustrate the American drive toward a continental empire? How did westward expansion heighten the tension between North and South over the issue of slavery? How did westward migration affect Native Americans?

3. Close American expansion across the continent resulted in conflicts with Mexico and Native Americans. Still, the United States was determined to fulfill its dream of stretching from the Atlantic to the Pacific.

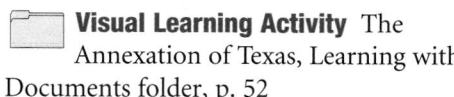

RESOURCE OPTIONS

Teaching Resources

📁 **Reproducible Lesson Plan** Lesson Plans folder, p. 75

📁 **Big Idea Graphic Organizer** Big Idea Graphic Organizer folder, p. 47

📁 **Guided Reading and Review** Units 3–4 folder, p. 38

📁 **Visual Learning Activity** The Annexation of Texas, Learning with Documents folder, p. 52

📁 **Key Documents** Declaration of "Manifest Destiny," Learning with Documents folder, p. 88

Customize for

English Language Learners

Have students pantomime the meaning of *manifest destiny* with the aid of a large map of the United States.

Answer to . . .

Map Skills Students should infer that the Americans won the war, as the map shows far more American victories than Mexican.

majority of Americans wanted to acquire more territory. Legislators' views on the Texas question began to shift. In February 1845, before Polk even took the oath of office, Congress approved annexation. In December 1845, after Texas voters added their approval, Texas became the twenty-eighth state in the Union.

War with Mexico

In March 1845, one month after Congress approved annexation, Mexico broke off diplomatic relations with the United States. The Mexican government had taken the first step toward war. Even if the United States could persuade Mexico to accept the annexation, a dispute about the southern boundary of Texas remained an explosive issue. The United States claimed that the Rio Grande was the official American-Mexican border. Mexico claimed that the Nueces River, located quite a few miles farther north, was the border.

President Polk and other southern Democrats wanted much more from Mexico than just Texas. Polk had dreams of acquiring the entire territory stretching from Texas to the Pacific. In a final attempt to avoid war, he sent Ambassador John Slidell to Mexico City in November 1845 with an offer to buy New Mexico and California for $30 million. But the Mexican government refused even to receive Slidell, let alone consider his offer.

Determined to have his way, Polk sent more than 3,000 American troops under General Zachary Taylor into the disputed area of southern Texas. Taylor crossed the Nueces in March 1846 and set up camp near the Rio Grande. Mexico considered Taylor's advance an invasion of Mexican territory and prepared to take action.

Mexican troops engaged in a skirmish with Taylor's forces in late April 1846. Several Americans were killed. This was the excuse Polk had been waiting for. Expressing outrage at the loss of "American blood on American soil," the President pushed for a declaration of war. Despite some opposition, Congress gave it to him on May 13, 1846, and the **Mexican War** was declared. Meanwhile, an American expedition under the command of Captain John C. Frémont moved into California, probably under orders from President Polk.[†]

Bear Flag Revolt Before news of the war with Mexico even reached California, a group of American settlers took matters into their own hands. Led by William B. Ide, these settlers launched a surprise attack on the town of Sonoma on June 14 and proclaimed the Republic of California. The settlers' flag pictured a grizzly bear and a single star, so the uprising became known as the Bear Flag Revolt. Frémont quickly assumed control of the rebel forces and then drove the Mexican army out of northern California.

In July 1846, United States troops under General Stephen Kearny crossed into New Mexico. Meeting little resistance, American forces occupied Santa Fe by mid-August. Kearny then took part of his army and marched west to California to join Frémont. Together

[†] Frémont was a mapmaker and explorer prior to the war. In 1843 he surveyed the Columbia River with mountainmen Kit Carson and Thomas Fitzpatrick.

The Mexican War

Oregon Country

ROCKY MOUNTAINS

Unorganized Territory

UNITED STATES

Iowa

Ft. Leavenworth

Mo.

Colorado R.

2. Bear Flag Revolt June 14, 1846

San Francisco

3. Monterey occupied July 7, 1846

8. San Gabriel Jan. 8, 1847

6. San Pasqual Dec. 6, 1846

4. Santa Fe occupied Aug. 18, 1846

San Diego

30° N

Rio Grande

7. El Brazito Dec. 25, 1846

Texas

1. Palo Alto May 8, 1846

10. Sacramento Feb. 28, 1847

5. Monterrey Sept. 20–25, 1846

Nueces R.

Corpus Christi

120° W

9. Buena Vista Feb. 22–23, 1847

Santa Anna

Gulf of Mexico

12. Cerro Gordo Apr. 18, 1847

Mazatlán

MEXICO

Tampico

Disputed territory

American forces

Mexican forces

American victory

Mexican victory

20° N

110° W

13. Chapultepec Sept. 13, 1847

PACIFIC OCEAN

0   200 Miles

0   200 Kilometers

14. Mexico City entered Sept. 14, 1847

11. Veracruz Mar. 29, 1847

MAP Skills

Many Americans, including President Polk, viewed the Mexican War as an opportunity for the United States to expand its boundaries across the continent.

Movement Looking at this map, what information can you use to make a judgment about who probably won the war?

they defeated the Mexican army. By January 1847 the United States had taken control of the territories of New Mexico and California.

Fighting in Mexico While Frémont and Kearny were securing Mexico's northern territories, General Taylor had taken the war into Mexico. After crossing the Rio Grande, Taylor won a series of victories, leading finally to the Battle of Buena Vista in February 1847.

Here he met Santa Anna, who had brought an army of 20,000 Mexican troops north from Mexico City. Taylor's army won the hard-fought battle, which left hundreds killed and wounded on both sides. When it was over, Santa Anna chose to declare victory and return to Mexico City rather than continue the struggle.

Santa Anna abandoned northeastern Mexico to Taylor in part because of a serious threat to his capital. Pressing for complete victory, Polk had dispatched forces under General Winfield Scott to take Mexico City. In March 1847 Scott captured the port city of Veracruz. Then he marched his army of 10,000 men toward Mexico City along the route once taken by Spanish conquistador Hernán Cortés. After fierce fighting, Scott defeated Santa Anna's forces and captured the Mexican capital on September 14, bringing the war to an end.

The Treaty of Guadalupe Hidalgo With the defeat of its troops and the fall of the country's capital, the Mexican government sought peace. The terms of the **Treaty of Guadalupe Hidalgo,** signed on February 2, 1848, reflected Mexico's weak bargaining position:

(1) Mexico gave up its claim to Texas and recognized the Rio Grande as the southern border of Texas.

(2) Mexico gave New Mexico and California, which together made up more than two fifths of its territory, to the United States.

(3) The United States paid Mexico $15 million.

(4) The United States agreed to pay claims made by American citizens against Mexico, which would amount to more than $3 million.

Five years later, in 1853, the Mexican government sold 30,000 square miles of what is now southern New Mexico and Arizona to the United States for $10 million. Known as the **Gadsden Purchase,** this land eventually provided a route for the southern transcontinental railroad.

Although the Mexican War is less well known than other wars the United States has

fought, the American victory over Mexico had important effects. The Treaty of Guadalupe Hidalgo, together with the 1846 division of Oregon and the Gadsden Purchase, established the boundaries of the continental United States as we now know them. Referred to by Mexicans as the North American Invasion, the war also left many Mexicans deeply bitter toward the United States and led to decades of poor relations and misunderstandings. Finally, the acquisition of a vast expanse of territory in the West opened the doors for an even larger wave of western migration.

The Wilmot Proviso Possibly the most important effect of the Mexican War was helping to bring the question of slavery to the forefront of American politics. Politicians had long avoided dealing with the question of slavery within existing states. But they had to confront the slavery issue directly when they created new territories or states.

A central issue facing Congress in the 1840s and 1850s was whether or not to allow

Answer to . . .

Interpreting Charts It was a success because it increased the size of the United States; it intensified the debate over the expansion of slavery.

CAUSE AND EFFECT: The Mexican War

CAUSES
- United States annexes Texas.
- United States and Mexico disagree about the southern border of Texas.
- Mexico refuses to sell California and New Mexico to the United States.
- Polk sends troops to establish the Rio Grande as the U.S.-Mexico border.
- Polk sends troops to California.

THE MEXICAN WAR

EFFECTS
- Rio Grande is established as the U.S.-Mexico border.
- United States acquires California and New Mexico.
- Debate over the expansion of slavery intensifies.

Interpreting Charts The Mexican War was the result of Polk's desire to expand the United States. *Government In what way was the Mexican War a success? What new problems did it cause the United States?*

slavery in the territories acquired by the United States from Mexico. Any states carved out of slave territories would, one day, probably become slave states. Likewise, free territories would become free states.

Depending on what Congress did, the balance of political power between North and South (or between free and slave states) could shift. The Senate, where each state had equal representation, would feel the greatest shock as a result of such a power shift. Northerners also feared that adding slave states could cause an economic shift to the South. They did not want to compete with plantation owners, whose use of slavery drove wages down.

In 1846 a bill came before Congress to provide funds for negotiating with Mexico. Pennsylvania Democrat David Wilmot attached a proviso, or amendment, to the bill. The Wilmot Proviso stated that slavery would not be permitted in any of the territory acquired from Mexico. Congress defeated the amendment.

Northerners continued to attach this proviso to bills related to the new territories, but it never became law. Each time it came up for discussion, however, the Wilmot Proviso revealed the growing gap between the North and the South over slavery.

Mormons Settle Utah

At the time of the Mexican War, the Mormons, one of the largest groups of migrants to head west in the 1840s, were finding a new home in present-day Utah. Mormons, or members of the Church of Jesus Christ of Latter-day Saints, had been looking for a permanent home ever since Joseph Smith founded the religion in western New York in 1830. Harassed by neighbors who were suspicious of their beliefs, the Mormons moved to Ohio and then to Missouri before finding a home in Nauvoo, Illinois.

For a while, the Mormons prospered in Illinois. Relations with neighbors broke down, however, after Smith revealed in 1843 that the Mormons allowed men to have more than one wife at the same time. After a hostile mob killed Smith and his brother in 1844, the Mormons were forced to move on once again.

The religion's new leader, Brigham Young, decided that the Mormons' only hope was to live beyond the borders of the United States. He and other leaders chose the Great Salt Lake Basin as the Mormons' new home, largely because it was located nearly a thousand miles from other Americans.

Starting in 1847, hundreds of Mormons left their temporary camps in Iowa for new homes near the Great Salt Lake. Within three years, more than 11,000 Mormons had settled in the region. By 1860, about 30,000 Mormons lived in Salt Lake City and more than 90 other towns in present-day Utah.

Despite many difficulties, these settlements were orderly and prosperous. The Mormons skillfully irrigated their desert region and devoted themselves primarily to farming. They also made money from trade with the wagon trains traveling to California and Oregon.

At first the leaders of the Mormon church established their own system of government. With the end of the Mexican War, however, Utah became an official territory of the United States and Brigham Young its first governor. Utah eventually entered the Union in 1896 as the forty-fifth state.

The Gold Rush in California

In January 1848 a carpenter who was building a sawmill for John Sutter, a Swiss immigrant living in California, discovered gold on Sutter's land. The Mexican governor of California had granted

---

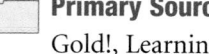

RESOURCE OPTIONS

Teaching Resources

Primary Source Activity Gold! Gold! Gold!, Learning with Documents folder, p. 16

Prentice Hall Literature Library Literature of the Expanding Frontier

American History Block Scheduling Support Along the Oregon Trail, found in the Expansion, Reconstruction, Immigration folder, includes interdisciplinary lesson suggestions and activities for Geography and History, Primary Sources, Biography, and Literature.

Sutter the land to build a colony for settlers. By August of that year, some 4,000 gold-crazed prospectors swarmed over the property, destroying the colony and bankrupting Sutter. The **California Gold Rush** had begun. No event was more important in attracting settlers to the West than the gold strike at Sutter's Mill.

The news filled the papers in the eastern United States, and Americans touched by gold fever rushed west by the thousands. California had 14,000 residents in 1848. A year later the population exploded to 100,000 and it reached 200,000 by 1852. Some traveled by ship around the tip of South America or by a combination of ship, rail, and foot via Central America. Most, however, took the direct route, west across the overland trails.

A majority of the new immigrants were unmarried men. In fact, only 5 percent of the "forty-niners" who went to California in the 1849 gold rush were women or children. African Americans, both slave and free, also took part in the gold rush. Slaves worked as servants or searched for gold on their owners' work crews. Some free African Americans became independent miners. The gold rush brought settlers not only from the United States but also from Europe and Asia. By 1852 about 10 percent of Californians were Chinese. Chinese immigrants mainly labored in mines and as servants.

The gold rush had a tremendous impact on life in California. For Native Americans, the flood of immigrants was a disaster. The tens of thousands of miners forced Indian men to work in the mines and the women to work in their households.

The gold rush shattered Native American societies, but it brought commercial prosperity to cities along the Pacific Coast. The growth of San Francisco was the most impressive. Richard Henry Dana first visited San Francisco in 1835, and he wrote of the port's potential in his book *Two Years Before the Mast.* Yet when he returned to San Francisco in 1859, Dana was stunned by its transformation into a center of trade:

AMERICAN VOICES

❝We bore round the point toward the old anchoring-ground of the hide-ships, and there, covering the sand-hills and the valleys, stretching from the water's edge to the base of the great hills, and from the old Presidio to the Mission, flickering all over with the lamps of its streets and houses, lay a city of one hundred thousand inhabitants.❞

—*Richard Henry Dana*

The Mining Frontier

In the wake of the California Gold Rush came news of more gold strikes. Miners rushed to Cripple Creek in Colorado in the late 1850s, to the Fraser River in western Canada in 1858, to the Comstock Lode in Nevada in 1859, and to smaller strikes in Montana and Idaho in the early 1860s.

Whenever reports of a strike went out, new towns appeared almost overnight. Men and women came to mine, to open stores, or to run saloons. Some stories have exaggerated the number of fights and murders that took place in these **boom towns,** but many of the towns were truly wild and violent places.

Mining towns usually had short lives. During the boom, hundreds of new residents arrived and built scores of houses and businesses with amazing speed. Then, when the mines stopped producing, the towns went bust and people moved on. Many mining communities slowly decayed and died, turning into abandoned **ghost towns.** A few of the luckier mining towns were reborn in the late 1900s as tourist and skiing centers.

Main Idea CONNECTIONS

What was the impact of the Gold Rush on California?

 This gold miner was one of thousands who traveled to California to find his fortune. *Culture Describe the typical "forty-niner."*

Using the Internet

Prepare a Report

Objective Use the Internet to prepare a report on a topic related to the history and culture of the Sioux Indians. Have students follow these instructions.

1. See the *America: Pathways to the Present* Web site at

http://www.Pathways.phschool.com

for the URL of the Cheyenne River Sioux Tribal History page.

2. Explore the Web site, listing the topics that are covered, such as cultural stereotypes, different tribes within the Sioux, history, modern views, and legends.

3. From your list, choose a topic that interests you. Read all of the text relating to your topic, taking detailed notes.

4. Prepare a report from your notes and share it with the class. From the reports, the class can form a summary of the Sioux.

RESOURCE OPTIONS

Media and Technology

RESOURCE **PRO**

Visual Learning Activity Living Dead in Califor-nee, found on Resource Pro, uses a contemporary cartoon to illustrate the fate of some who sought gold in the California Gold Rush.

Biography Kamiakin, found on Resource Pro, profiles the influential Native American chief during the time the Native American groups of the Northwest were being forced off their land and onto reservations.

Answer to . . .

Viewing History The average miner was an unmarried white man from the East.

Main Idea Connection: It brought hundreds of thousands of people to the state, transformed San Francisco into a major commercial center, and destroyed much of what remained of Native American cultures.

Answers to
SECTION 4 REVIEW

1. (a) manifest destiny, see p. 301; (b) annex, see p. 301; (c) Mexican War, see p. 302; (d) Treaty of Guadalupe Hidalgo, see p. 303; (e) Gadsden Purchase, see p. 303; (f) California Gold Rush, see p. 305; (g) boom town, see p. 305; (h) ghost town, see p. 305.

2. By adding Texas, New Mexico, and California, it greatly increased the nation's territory.

3. Before: Texas annexed, Polk elected; during: Bear Flag Revolt, fighting in Mexico, Treaty of Guadalupe Hidalgo; after: Utah settled, California Gold Rush, western migration.

4. Mormons migrate to Utah and the California Gold Rush. Without the war, people may not have flocked to the West in such numbers if it were still Mexican territory.

5. Sample answer: no, because they were heavily populated by American settlers.

6. Essays will vary but should be supported by facts from the text.

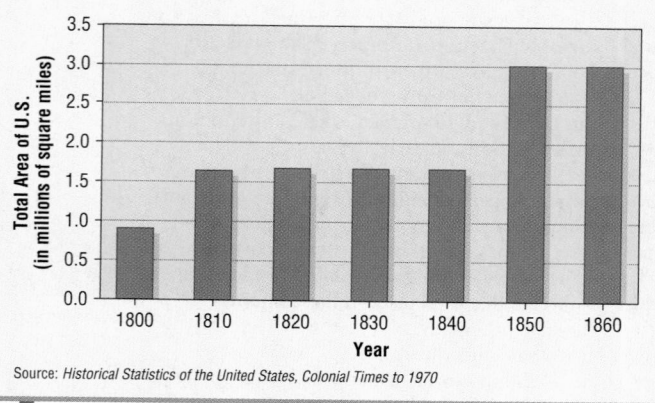

Expansion of the United States, 1800–1860

Total Area of U.S. (in millions of square miles)

Year

Source: *Historical Statistics of the United States, Colonial Times to 1970*

Interpreting Graphs The United States more than tripled in size between 1800 and 1860. *Diversity How did expansion of the United States affect Native Americans?*

numbers of Americans migrated west, however, the United States built new military posts farther and farther west.

The government established the Bureau of Indian Affairs, or BIA, in 1824. It became part of the newly created Department of the Interior in 1849. The Bureau attempted to "extinguish" Indian land claims through treaties and annuities, or yearly payments. In the 1850s the government increasingly championed the idea of reservations as the ultimate solution to the "Indian problem."

Indians in Oregon and Washington refused to be herded onto reservations. In 1855, led by the Yakima chief Kamiakin, they fought to preserve their way of life. Still, through treaties, thousands of Indians ended up confined to reservations. In California, eight reservations were in place by 1858.

Nomadic Indians proved to be the most successful at resisting government efforts to control them. Despite peace treaties signed in the early 1850s, tension grew with every group of settlers that crossed the Mississippi. Increasing numbers of Americans wanted to carve farms out of the rugged lands beyond the Mississippi River. Indians wanted to follow the buffalo on the wide-open plains as they had for decades. With neither side willing to yield or compromise, tragic violence resulted.

Indians and Western Migration

Until the Mexican War, the United States had proclaimed all land west of the 95th meridian, or line of longitude, to be Indian Country. Along this "permanent Indian frontier," running from Minnesota to Louisiana, the United States Army built a series of forts. As growing

SECTION 4 REVIEW

Comprehension

1. *Key Terms* Define: (a) manifest destiny; (b) annex; (c) Mexican War; (d) Treaty of Guadalupe Hidalgo; (e) Gadsden Purchase; (f) California Gold Rush; (g) boom town; (h) ghost town.

2. *Summarizing the Main Idea* How did the war against Mexico help the United States achieve its "manifest destiny"?

3. *Organizing Information* Prepare a flowchart to show the sequence of key events before, during, and after the Mexican War.

Critical Thinking

4. *Analyzing Time Lines* Review the time line at the start of the section. Which two events were not directly related to the Mexican War? Might either of those events have turned out differently if there had been no Mexican War? Explain.

5. *Identifying Alternatives* Do you think that it would have been possible for Texas or Utah to have remained separate from the United States? Why?

Writing Activity

6. *Writing a Persuasive Essay* Write an essay that might have appeared in a Mormon newspaper in the 1850s urging Mormons to come to Utah.

▶ RESOURCE OPTIONS

Teaching Resources

 Quiz Units 3–4 folder, p. 39

Chapter Tests Forms A and B Chapter Test folder

Student Performance Pack

Guide to the Essentials Chapter 10, Section 4 (English and Spanish)

Standardized Test Preparation Handbook

Media and Technology

 Guided Reading Audiotapes Chapter 10 Summary (English and Spanish)

Student Edition on Audiotape Chapter 10

Test Bank CD-ROM; Interactive Student Tutorial CD-ROM Chapter Test

Answer to . . .

Interpreting Graphs It forced them off of their lands and onto reservations.

Why Study History?

To understand that . . .

The Frontier Still Exists Today

The frontier has shifted many times in American history, from the lands west of the Mississippi River in the 1800s to outer space today.

Wagon trains heading toward the frontier

"Life Discovered on Mars!" "Astronauts Retrieve Wayward Satellite!" Newspaper headlines such as these, which would have been dismissed as science fiction just a few decades ago, are commonplace today. They tell us that while the western frontier may have disappeared, the frontier of outer space remains.

On July 20, 1969, astronauts Neil Armstrong and Edwin Aldrin, Jr., planted an American flag on the moon. More recently, the National Aeronautics and Space Administration (NASA) sent space probes to Mars and Venus. The probes took close-up photographs of these planets and gathered data on their climate, atmosphere, and soil. Other probes have been sent toward the more distant planets of Saturn and Jupiter.

The Impact Today

For today's pioneers, as for those who traveled the Oregon Trail in the 1840s, survival depends on careful planning. Space-age technology is allowing people to live in space for months and even years at a time, which will be necessary if humans are ever to journey to distant planets. Beginning in 1986, the Russian space station *Mir* served as a temporary space home and research base for American as well as Russian astronauts.

In addition, the United States and Russia are working together to create *Alpha*, which is an international space station that is scheduled for completion by 2003.

The exploration of space has brought us new and fascinating information about the universe. It has other, less obvious benefits as well. Practical applications derived from the space program include improvements in weather forecasting, global communications, resource mapping, and navigational aids, as well as food packaging and clothing materials. Economic opportunities on "the last frontier" of space abound.

Yet space exploration is expensive. It costs billions of dollars, at a time when pressing problems here on Earth are also demanding attention. While supporters of the space program point to the vast potential for discoveries in space, opponents assert that the American people's immediate needs should receive public funds.

Astronaut Edwin E. Aldrin, Jr., on the moon

The Impact on You

Should federal funds be used for space research and exploration? List three reasons to support your opinion. If you oppose federal funding of the space program, list at least two alternative uses for these funds.

RESOURCE OPTIONS

Teaching Resources

 Why Study History? Activity The Frontier Still Exists Today, found in the Why Study History? folder p. 11, provides an activity to help students understand issues surrounding the newest frontier.

Media and Technology

AmericanHeritage® CD-ROM

Time Tour Reshaping the Nation: The Frontier West

Why Study History?

Class Discussion

Discuss with the class space exploration and whether and how it should be funded. For a more thorough examination of the issue, see the activity folder in the Resource Options below.

ACTIVITY
STUDENT PARTICIPATION

Creating a Plan for Space

Ask students to read the text. Then divide the class into two groups. Have each group create a plan explaining why the exploration and development of the moon should (or should not) be regulated in the future. Each plan should address these questions:

- **Should people be allowed to exploit the moon?**
- **How should decisions about the moon be made?**
- **Should any people or nations be allowed to own part of the moon?**

Follow up Ask whether an international organization should be involved in questions of space exploration.

Using the Internet

Students can learn more about space as the last frontier by exploring links in the *America: Pathways to the Present* Web site at

http://www.Pathways.phschool.com

Assessment

See the Lesson Plans folder, pp. 24–27, for rubrics on assessing Class Participation Projects.

Key Terms

Students should refer to the definitions of key terms in the chapter to write sentences that show an understanding of the causes of western migration and the nature of the conflicts that arose.

Comprehension

1. Village societies were decimated by the push of white settlers and their diseases, as well as by the increasingly warlike nomadic groups.

2. They migrated on horse in search of buffalo, carrying their possessions with them. Their societies were increasingly male-dominated, as males gained wealth and status from horses. As they became less dependent on farming, women had less and less influence.

3. They built a network of missions and presidios, strengthened trade, and attempted to convert the Native Americans to Christianity.

4. It opposed Mexican laws prohibiting American immigration and the importation of slaves. Texans also wanted the same political rights as they had had in the United States.

5. They first used the old Indian trails, which the wagon trains would later use, and their successes as traders attracted other people to Oregon as well.

6. Congress approved a treaty to annex Texas; war with Mexico broke out one month later.

7. Mexico gave up New Mexico, California, and Texas, recognizing the Rio Grande as the southern border of Texas. The United States paid Mexico $15 million and agreed to pay claims by American citizens against Mexico, amounting to more than $3 million.

8. The California Gold Rush.

Chapter Summary

The major concepts of Chapter 10 are presented below. See also *Guide to the Essentials of American History* or *Interactive Student Tutorial CD-ROM,* which contains interactive review activities, time lines, helpful hints, and test practice for Chapter 10.

Reviewing the Main Ideas

During the 1830s and 1840s, American settlers moved west into Texas, New Mexico, California, and Oregon. The United States acquired those territories through war with Mexico and through various treaties. This expansion created tensions between settlers and Indians over land, and between North and South over extending slavery into the territories.

Section 1: The Plains Indians

Life for Native Americans on the Great Plains changed greatly with the arrival of horses and white traders.

Section 2: Hispanic North America

The movement of traders and settlers from the United States into northern Mexico led to economic and political changes.

Section 3: Trails to the West

In the 1840s thousands of Americans migrated to Oregon and California.

Section 4: From Sea to Sea

The Mexican War of 1846–1848 extended the boundaries of the United States from the Atlantic to the Pacific, and migration to the West increased.

The frontier has shifted many times in American history, from the lands west of the Mississippi in the 1800s to outer space today. Travel to the new frontier requires careful planning and a large amount of money.

Key Terms

For each of the terms below, write a sentence explaining how it relates to the chapter.

1. presidio
2. annex
3. Great Plains
4. Texas War for Independence
5. boom town
6. Santa Fe Trail
7. nomad
8. mountain man
9. Gadsden Purchase
10. Battle of the Alamo
11. California Gold Rush
12. Oregon Trail
13. manifest destiny

Comprehension

1. What caused the decline of village societies on the Great Plains?
2. Describe the way of life of the nomadic Plains Indians.
3. How did the Spanish try to strengthen their hold on California in the late 1700s?
4. Why did Texas declare its independence from Mexico?
5. How did fur traders help open the Oregon Country to settlement?
6. What action by the United States Congress helped lead to the Mexican War?
7. List the basic terms of the Treaty of Guadalupe Hidalgo.
8. What event attracted a huge number of settlers to California?

Using Graphic Organizers

On a separate sheet of paper, copy the web diagram to organize the main ideas of the chapter. In the first set of circles, name at least four migrating groups and where they went. Add circles to the web as needed to show more groups and to describe the effects of each group's migration.

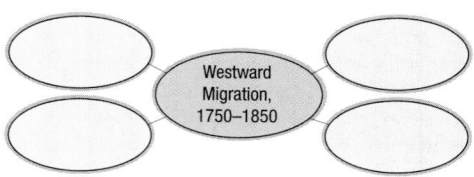

Westward Migration, 1750–1850

Using Graphic Organizers

- Stephen Austin and American families—Texas.
- Mountain men—Rocky Mountains.
- Missionaries—Oregon.
- Wagon train families—Oregon.
- Mormons—Utah.
- Miners—California.

Analyzing Political Cartoons ▶

1. This cartoon appeared in 1847. (a) What does the eagle represent? (b) How do you know? (c) To what war does the cartoon refer?

2. Compare the eagle before and after the war. What does the cartoonist mean by "Plucked"?

3. Describe the cartoonist's attitude.

PLUCKED:

THE MEXICAN EAGLE BEFORE THE WAR!   THE MEXICAN EAGLE AFTER THE WAR!

Critical Thinking

1. *Applying the Chapter Skill* Use an encyclopedia or other resource to find more information about a person from the chapter. Then write an epitaph for the person that offers clues about the time in which the person lived.

2. *Making Comparisons* Why were the Spanish missionaries in California more successful than the American missionaries in Oregon?

3. *Recognizing Ideologies* While the United States referred to the conflict with Mexico as the Mexican War, Mexicans called the war the North American Invasion. What do these different names suggest about each country's perspective on the war?

4. *Expressing Problems Clearly* Explain why the addition of Mexico's northern territories to the Union created a problem for the United States.

ANALYZING DOCUMENTS ▶ INTERPRETING DATA

Turn to the map of the overland trails on page 298.

1. About how far apart were the forts on the Oregon Trail? (a) 3 miles (b) 30 miles (c) 300 miles (d) 3,000 miles

2. Through which pass in the Sierra Nevada did the California Trail proceed? (a) South (b) Cajon (c) Donner (d) Raton

3. *Writing* Imagine that you just traveled from Independence, Missouri, to Los Angeles, California, in the 1840s. Write a letter to a friend describing the routes you took and the natural features you encountered along the way.

INTERNET ACTIVITY

For your portfolio:
WRITE AN ARTICLE

Access Prentice Hall's *America: Pathways to the Present* site at **www.Pathways.phschool.com** for the specific URL to complete the activity. Additional resources and related Web sites are also available.

Read about how Plains Indians felt and continue to feel toward the buffalo. Describe the buffalo's importance to Plains culture, the historical impact of settlers on the buffalo and Plains Indians' lives, and the buffalo and Plains Indians today.

Connecting to Today

Essay Writing Americans remain an extremely mobile people, with most families moving several times in their lifetime. Write an essay in which you describe at least two similarities and two differences between American migration today and migration in the mid-1800s.

INTERNET ACTIVITY

Answers will vary but should reflect an understanding of the buffalo's importance to Plains Indians in terms of culture, economy, and spirituality. They should also show an appreciation of how the decline of the buffalo and the dwindling Native American population were related.

Analyzing Political Cartoons

1. (a) The eagle represents Mexico. (b) The caption refers to the eagle as Mexican. (c) The Mexican War.

2. Before the war, the eagle looks strong and is perched on a cactus. After, it has lost all its feathers. By "plucked," the cartoonist means that Mexico had to give up Texas, New Mexico, and California.

3. Sample answer: The cartoonist's attitude is that without these territories, Mexico is weak and pathetic.

Critical Thinking

1. Epitaphs will vary but should synthesize information students find with themes from the text.

2. The Spanish used Native American labor to ensure that their missions succeeded; they also fostered a lively network of trade. The missionaries in Oregon focused on converting the Native Americans, which failed.

3. The name Mexican War suggests that, to those in the United States, war was fought because Mexico was causing problems for Americans. The name North American Invasion suggests that to Mexicans, they were being forced to defend their territory by invaders from the north.

4. It brought up the slavery issue, as a decision had to be made whether new territories would be slave or free states. Though new bills addressed the problem, the issue remained unresolved.

Interpreting Data

1. c
2. c
3. Letters will vary but should include information from the map.

Connecting to Today

Essays will vary but might include similarities such as people seeking new opportunities, and differences such as the lack of unsettled land today.

My Brush with History

Focus Have students find the meaning of each of these words in a dictionary before they begin to read: *boarder, verandah.* Ask them to consider, as they read, the risks that Dorr's great-great-grandfather took by helping people in the Underground Railroad.

Instruct Ask volunteers to identify and describe a big change or trauma that they experienced long ago yet whose effects persist in their lives. Then have students compare their feelings about their experience to Grandma's feelings about the "secret" of her grandfather's involvement in the underground railroad. How are they similar or different? Suggest that students write about their experience either as a journal entry or a memoir.

Analyzing the Document

Use this additional question to generate class discussion:
CRITICAL THINKING: CHECKING CONSISTENCY Is the pride that Grandma feels toward her grandfather's helping runaway slaves consistent with her warning the speaker not to tell anyone? *(Answers will vary. Students should recognize that Grandma can be simultaneously proud of her grandfather and insecure about her social standing.)*

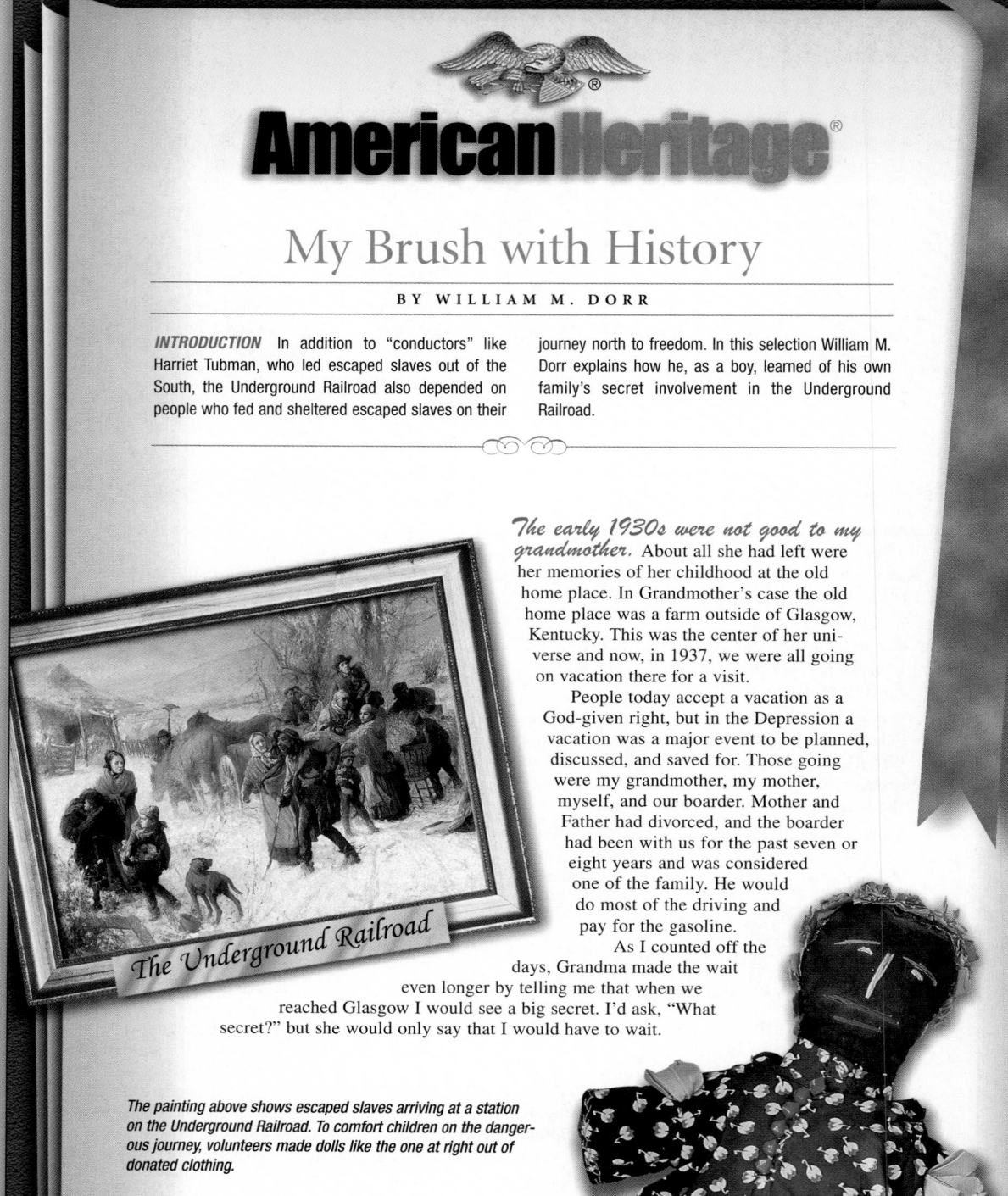

American Heritage®

My Brush with History

BY WILLIAM M. DORR

INTRODUCTION In addition to "conductors" like Harriet Tubman, who led escaped slaves out of the South, the Underground Railroad also depended on people who fed and sheltered escaped slaves on their journey north to freedom. In this selection William M. Dorr explains how he, as a boy, learned of his own family's secret involvement in the Underground Railroad.

The early 1930s were not good to my grandmother. About all she had left were her memories of her childhood at the old home place. In Grandmother's case the old home place was a farm outside of Glasgow, Kentucky. This was the center of her universe and now, in 1937, we were all going on vacation there for a visit.

People today accept a vacation as a God-given right, but in the Depression a vacation was a major event to be planned, discussed, and saved for. Those going were my grandmother, my mother, myself, and our boarder. Mother and Father had divorced, and the boarder had been with us for the past seven or eight years and was considered one of the family. He would do most of the driving and pay for the gasoline.

As I counted off the days, Grandma made the wait even longer by telling me that when we reached Glasgow I would see a big secret. I'd ask, "What secret?" but she would only say that I would have to wait.

The Underground Railroad

The painting above shows escaped slaves arriving at a station on the Underground Railroad. To comfort children on the dangerous journey, volunteers made dolls like the one at right out of donated clothing.

TEST PREPARATION

Have students use the excerpt on these pages to answer the following question.

Which word best describes the speaker's feelings about his great-great-grandfather's involvement in the underground railroad?

(A) pride

B shame

C horror

D fear

I'd like to say that the trip down to Glasgow from Louisville was all fun and excitement, but that would be far from the truth. Less than twenty miles out of Louisville, the family found out that I had car sickness.

By the time we reached Glasgow I was a hot, sick, and irritable little boy who was making life miserable for all around him. Then the second blow fell: I saw the old home place. I had expected it to look like a Georgia plantation with high columns and wide verandahs. But the house was none of this. Its current owners had not been able to spare a lot of money for upkeep, and to a city boy used to urban newness, it seemed shabby and rundown.

Symbols of the hated institution of slavery, these tags were worn by slaves to identify their owners.

But there was a cold pitcher of lemonade and an electric fan in the living room. Grandma asked if I would like to see the bedroom. I didn't really want to see a bedroom, but I was pushed upstairs and into a chamber dominated by a large bed and little else. The headboard of the bed stood solid into the rear wall, and my grandmother told me I was to push against the top left of it. After one missed push, I made part of the headboard slide back into the wall.

The owner of the house came upstairs with a flashlight, and I looked into my first secret panel. I was told I could go in, but all I could see was cobwebs, and I decided I could see all I wanted from the bed. As I shone the light in, Grandma told me that this passage went around the chimney and was three feet wide by three and a half feet tall. The only way in or out was by way of the bed.

Grandma explained that after thinking hard on the subject, her granddaddy had decided that slavery was wrong. Being a man who acted on his beliefs, he had built this room and become part of the Underground Railroad, helping runaway slaves to freedom.

Then Grandma gave a warning. Although the Civil War (or rather the War between the States) had been over for more than seventy years, feelings for the lost cause still ran high. If the purpose of the secret passage were known, we might no longer be socially accepted in Glasgow. I had to promise never to say a word about it.

That night and for a number of nights after, I dreamed of being Great-Great-Granddaddy's helper taking those slaves toward freedom. Mother and Grandma promised that we could come back again to see more of the farm's secrets; but it was not to be.

The 1930s kept us too poor for another vacation, and then came Pearl Harbor. The boarder was drafted and later came home to marry my mother. Grandma did not get back to Glasgow until the late 1940s. By then the owners had sold the property, and the house had been torn down for an industrial plant. Granddaddy's secret passage was gone forever.

I never knew my grandmother's granddaddy, or any of the blacks he helped to spirit North; but occasionally in dreams I still go back to Glasgow to help Great-Great-Granddaddy.

Source: *American Heritage* magazine, September 1993.

ADDITIONAL READING

To learn more about the topics discussed in this selection, you might want to read the following books:

- *American Slavery, 1619–1877,* by Peter Kolchin (New York: Hill and Wang, 1993)
- *Escape from Slavery: Five Journeys to Freedom,* by Doreen Rappaport (New York: HarperCollins, 1991)
- *North Star to Freedom: The Story of the Underground Railroad,* by Geena K. Gorrell (New York: Delacorte Press, 1997)
- *The Underground Railroad,* by Charles L. Blockson (New York: Prentice-Hall Press, 1987)

TEST PREPARATION

Have students use the excerpt on these pages to answer the following question.

Which statement best describes the boarder's relationship with the narrator's family?

A The boarder was basically a servant who did things like drive the car and fill it with gasoline.

B The boarder helped the family in hard times by paying rent.

Ⓒ The boarder grew close to the family and eventually became the speaker's stepfather.

D The boarder would have married the speaker's mother if he had been socially accepted in both Glasgow and Louisville.

Division and Uneasy Reunion 1848–1877

Introducing the Unit

Using Historical Evidence

Have students examine the picture on the right. Read the caption out loud or ask a volunteer to do so. Ask students how the caption establishes that the Battle of Gettysburg was a key event in the Civil War. (*The caption identifies the battle as the bloodiest battle of the war.*) Point out that key battles of the Civil War were often memorialized in large-scale paintings. Ask students in what chapter they will read about this major battle. (*Chapter 12*)

Themes in American History

Direct students' attention to the Unit Themes. Point out that each chapter in this unit has its own theme. To teach this unit thematically, you may wish to use the Extended Unit Lesson Plan for the Civil War, p. 11, in the To the Teacher folder in **American History Block Scheduling Support.**

Using the Time Line

To provide students with practice in using the time line to connect key events in the United States with key events in the world, ask questions such as these: (1) When did the Civil War begin? When did it end? (*1861, 1865*) (2) What two events on the time line took place in Europe during the Civil War? (*Serfdom abolished in Russia; International Red Cross founded.*) (3) Who was President during passage of the Fifteenth Amendment? (*Grant*)

unit FOUR

Division and Uneasy Reunion

1848 – 1877

A series of fragile political compromises between the North and the South in the early 1800s could not prevent the United States from exploding into war in 1861. Although the North ultimately prevailed in the Civil War, President Lincoln's goal of healing the nation's regional and racial divisions ended with his assassination. The period of Reconstruction that followed the war enjoyed limited success, but ultimately failed to achieve political, social, or economic justice for African Americans.

Chapter 11 The Coming of the Civil War *1848–1861*

Chapter 12 The Civil War *1861–1865*

Chapter 13 Reconstruction *1865–1877*

UNIT THEMES

Government The nation's debate over slavery erupted into a full-scale civil war.

Economics The North's superior economic strength helped it defeat the South in the Civil War.

Diversity During Reconstruction, black southerners sought full participation in the political life of their region.

EVENTS IN THE UNITED STATES

1850 Compromise of 1850

1860
• Lincoln elected President
• South Carolina becomes the first state to secede

1861 Civil War begins

1863
• Emancipation Proclamation
• Battle of Gettysburg

| Presidents | Fillmore | Pierce | Buchanan | Lincoln |

| 1850 | 1855 | 1860 |

EVENTS IN THE WORLD

1855 Florence Nightingale improves military hospitals

1856 Bessemer steel-making process

1861 Serfdom abolished in Russia

1863 International Red Cross founded

▶ RESOURCE OPTIONS

Teaching Resources

📁 **Units 3–4 folder** Contains instructional materials organized by chapter.

VIEWING HISTORY The bloodiest battle of the Civil War was fought in July 1863, in Gettysburg, Pennsylvania. *Geography* **What was the significance of the Union victory at Gettysburg?**

African American regimental flag

1865
- Civil War ends
- Thirteenth Amendment ends slavery

1868
Turning Point: Fourteenth Amendment (p. 386)

1870
Fifteenth Amendment

1877
Reconstruction ends

Johnson	Grant	Hayes
1865	**1870**	**1875**

1867
Russia sells Alaska to the United States

1871
Britain legalizes labor unions

1873
Slave markets are abolished in Zanzibar

▶ RESOURCE OPTIONS

Media and Technology

Color Transparencies Specific transparencies are referenced at points of use. See American Photo, B-4; Cause and Effect, F-5; Links Across Time, J-4; Political Cartoons, K-4; Historical Maps, L-3; and Geographic Setting, M-3 and M-4.

Visions of America "Scenes of an Era: Division and Uneasy Reunion," located on videodisc side 2 and on videotape 2. Lesson plans for "Scenes of an Era" can be found in the Visions of America Guidebook.

Side 2, Chapter 13

Answer to . . .

Viewing History The South was now on the defensive.

CHAPTER 11

The Coming of the Civil War, 1848–1861

Managing Time and Instruction

INSTRUCTION SUPPORT

These materials for instruction are provided for **each section** in the **Teaching Resources**. See **Units 3–4 folder** for Enrichment Support:

- Reproducible Lesson Plans in Lesson Plans folder • Learning Styles Lesson Plans in Learning Styles Lesson Plans folder • Big Idea Graphic Organizers in Big Idea Graphic Organizer folder
- Guided Reading and Review • Quizzes • Test Preparation Practice booklet

DAILY LESSON	ENRICHMENT SUPPORT
1 Two Nations? (pp. 315–319)	• Literature Activity, An Antislavery Bestseller, Units 3–4 folder, pp. 56–57 • Literature Activity, "A Poem in Defense of Slavery," found on **Resource Pro** • Nystrom *Atlas of Our Country*, A Divided Nation, pp. 26–27
2 New Political Parties (pp. 320–326)	• Nystrom *Atlas of Our Country*, Settling the West, pp. 28–29 • Visual Learning Activity, Anthony Burns and the Fugitive Slave Law, found on **Resource Pro** • Skills for Life Activity, Units 3–4 folder, p. 58
3 The System Fails (pp. 328–332)	• Nystrom *Atlas of Our Country*, Settling the West, pp. 28–29 • Visual Learning Activity, Free Soiler Chokes on Slavery, Learning with Documents folder, p. 53 • Primary Source Activity, An Interview with John Brown, Learning with Documents folder, p. 17 • Primary Source Activity, Lincoln-Douglas Senate Campaign, found on **Resource Pro** • Biography, John Anthony Copeland, Jr., found on **Resource Pro**
4 A Nation Divided Against Itself (pp. 333–336)	• Comparing Primary Sources, On the Southern Secession, Units 3–4 folder, pp. 54–55 • Biography, General P.G.T. Beauregard, Units 3–4 folder, p. 53 • Critical Thinking Activity, Identifying Assumptions: War Begins, found on **Resource Pro** • The Debate over States' Rights Continues, Why Study History? folder, p. 12

Running Out of Time?

- Use Tape 2, "Division and Uneasy Reunion, 1848–1877," from **Visions of America** videotapes series.
- Use Chapter 11 Summary, from **Guide to the Essentials of American History (English and Spanish).**

Companion Web Site

The companion Web site offers online links for all chapter review activities. It also provides key content links and structured support for this chapter for both teachers and students.

http://www.Pathways.phschool.com

Media and Technology

For the Student

Interactive Student Tutorial CD-ROM Chapter 11
Student Edition on Audiotape Chapter 11
American Heritage® CD-ROM
Guided Reading Audiotapes (English and Spanish) Chapter 11

For the Teacher

Resource Pro CD-ROM Chapter 11
Test Bank CD-ROM Chapter 11
Listening to Literature Audiotapes *Timeless Voices, Timeless Themes* from *My Bondage and My Freedom* by Frederick Douglass

Assessment Options

Chapter Test Forms A&B Test Bank CD-ROM booklet
Test Bank CD-ROM Chapter 11
Standardized Test Preparation Handbook

Block Scheduling

Pacing Suggestions

For 90-minute Blocks

- Teach sections 1 and 2 using Transparencies H-11 and L-3 and the Recent Scholarship note on p. 318 for class discussions.
- Teach sections 3 and 4 using the Big Idea Graphic Organizers from Teaching Resources and the Extended Class Periods Activity found on p. 334.

Additional Resources

- Prentice Hall's **American History Block Scheduling Support File** covers over 40 major topics in American history. Included are lesson plans, strategies, primary sources, literature, biographies, Great Debates, art history, simulations, and songs.
- **Prentice Hall United States History Video Collection™** contains 20 videotapes covering American history from beginnings to present.

Connections to American Literature

from Prentice Hall

America: Pathways to the Present
Incidents in the Life of a Slave Girl, found on p. 1078

Prentice Hall Literature *Timeless Voices, Timeless Themes* "Letter to His Son" by Robert E. Lee, pp. 482–483

Prentice Hall Literature Library Southern Writers

Additional Resources

For the Student

Harold Holzer, ed. *Dear Mr. Lincoln: Letters to the President.* Addison-Wesley, 1993.
Mark E. Neely, Jr. *The Last Best Hope of Earth: Abraham Lincoln and the Promise of America.* Harvard University Press, 1993.

For the Teacher

Bruce Catton. *The Coming Fury.* Washington Square Press, 1972.

Prentice Hall brings into the classroom the vast archives and scholarship of the nation's premier American history magazine. See "From the Archives of American Heritage®" and "About the Presidents" teaching notes in this chapter.

History Alive!

Teacher's Curriculum Institute, in partnership with Prentice Hall, provides unique materials that engage students with diverse learning styles. See History Alive!® unit on The Civil War and Reconstruction.

Student Performance Pack

Ensures success in the three critical areas of Reading, Test Taking, and English Language Development with the following materials:
- Guide to the Essentials of American History in English and Spanish
- Guided Reading Audiotapes in English and Spanish
- Interactive Student Tutorial CD-ROM
- Test Preparation Handbook
- Test Preparation Practice booklet

Introducing the Chapter
The middle of the nineteenth century was a time of deep distrust and escalating hostility between the North and the South. Many Americans no longer believed that the federal government could settle their differences, and the Union finally shattered.

Themes in American History
The theme for this chapter, Government, is listed at the beginning of this unit. An alternate theme for the chapter is Economics. To teach this unit thematically, you may wish to use the Expansion, Reconstruction, Immigration folder in American History Block Scheduling Support.

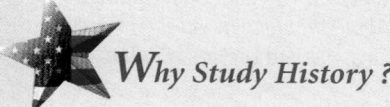

*W**hy Study History ?*

Have students explore suggested ways of connecting the past to the present on page 337.

Answer to . . .

Viewing History Students should use this question as an aid in reading the chapter. At the heart of the attempt at compromise was legislation that acknowledged the legality of slavery in southern states, but that sought to limit the expansion of slavery into the western territories. In the end, successful compromise proved impossible.

CHAPTER
11 The Coming of the Civil War
1848-1861

CHAPTER FOCUS

By the 1850s, deep distrust divided Northerners and Southerners. Under the strain of conflict between North and South, the great web of law, compromise, and tradition that had held the United States together for over 70 years snapped. The nation broke apart and began its darkest and most painful trial: the Civil War.

The Why Study History? page at the end of this chapter explores the issue of states' rights versus the power of the federal government—the same issue that played a role in the outbreak of the Civil War.

▲
VIEWING HISTORY
Abolitionists and pro-slavery forces clash in the "Battle of Hickory Point," about 25 miles outside of Lawrence, Kansas. *Government* **How did the nation attempt to compromise on the issue of slavery?**

 RESOURCE OPTIONS

Teaching Resources

📁 **Big Idea Graphic Organizer** folder
Graphic summary of the main idea of the chapter.

📁 **Learning Styles Lesson Plans** folder
Alternate lesson plans for diverse learning styles for each chapter.

Media and Technology

 AmericanHeritage® **CD-ROM**
Time Tour The Nation Torn Apart: The Road to Civil War

◉ ▭ **Prentice Hall United States History Video Collection**™ Volume 8 *Causes of the Civil War*

1852	1857	1860		
Uncle Tom's	Cannibals All!	110,000 factories	1861	
Cabin *published*	*published*	in the North; 20,000	*Civil War begins*	
		in the South		

| 1850 | 1855 | 1860 | 1865 |

1 Two Nations?

SECTION PREVIEW

Objectives

1 Summarize historians' views on whether the Civil War could have been avoided.
2 Describe the Northern and Southern views on slavery, including the views of Harriet Beecher Stowe.
3 Identify the differences between the North and South.
4 **Key Terms** Define: Union; prejudice; obsolete.

Main Idea

In the 1850s growing numbers of Americans were convinced that the North and South were moving in different directions. Each side saw the other as a threat to the American way of life.

Reading Strategy

Organizing Information As you read this section, create a chart comparing and contrasting the North's and South's views on slavery, as well as the level of economic development in the two regions.

Starting in 1861, states of the North clashed with states of the South in a brutal conflict that Americans call the Civil War. The outcome of the war would determine whether the **Union,** as the unified nation was called, would continue to exist or whether the country would be permanently split into two nations.

The causes of the Civil War were many and complex, and have been debated by historians for decades. This section describes some of the growing cultural and economic differences between the North and South in the decade before the outbreak of war.

Historians and the Civil War

Some historians have suggested that the Civil War could have been avoided. If the United States had elected better leaders and established stronger political institutions, they believe, wild-eyed extremists on both sides would never have been able to force the nation into war. This view is based on the belief that Americans of the mid-1800s were fairly similar and therefore could have settled their differences.

Whether in Alabama, Oregon, Indiana, or Massachusetts, according to this belief, Americans agreed in their support of democracy and free enterprise. Likewise, in earlier chapters you have read about Americans' general commitment to democratic government, social equality, and a market economy.

Other historians—especially more recent ones—do not accept the idea that American society was similar everywhere. They tend to emphasize differences, including differences between geographic regions, racial groups, and social classes. Although these historians do not claim that the events of the Civil War had to have happened the way they did, they do believe that some kind of major conflict was bound to occur. In this section you will read more about growing regional differences.

The Case Against Slavery

Many Americans during the early 1800s noticed contrasts between North and South. They said that the two great sections amounted to distinct nations within the United States.

RESOURCE OPTIONS

Teaching Resources

Reproducible Lesson Plan Lesson Plans folder, p. 76

Learning Styles Lesson Plan Learning Styles Lesson Plans folder, p. 24

Big Idea Graphic Organizer Big Idea Graphic Organizer folder, p. 48

Guided Reading and Review Units 3–4 folder, p. 45

Media and Technology

 AmericanHeritage® CD-ROM

Time Tour The Nation Torn Apart: The Road to Civil War

Two Nations?

Objectives

You may wish to call students' attention to the objectives in the Section Preview. The objectives are reflected in the main headings of the section.

Bellringer

Ask students to discuss what they know about differences among regions in the United States today. What effect might these differences have on the nation as a whole?

Reading Strategy

Organizing Information Refer to the Reading Strategy in the Section Preview. You may want to model the chart on the chalkboard and ask volunteers to suggest ideas as they read the section.

LESSON PLAN

Connecting to the Main Idea

1. Focus Explain that in the 1850s, differences between the North and the South increasingly divided the two regions. Ask what these key differences between the North and the South were.

2. Instruct Review the economies of the North and the South. Ask students to compare the two regions in terms of their economic and material differences. Discuss the way in which slavery divided the North and the South. Ask why so many Northerners found slavery morally offensive. Why did Southerners accuse Northerners of hypocrisy regarding slavery?

3. Close Despite their common political roots, by the 1850s more and more Americans saw the North and the South as two distinct regions with very different values, especially concerning slavery. The next section discusses the new political parties that arose on either side of the issues that divided the nation.

Biography

Harriet Beecher Stowe (1811–1896), author of *Uncle Tom's Cabin*, lived in the shadow of two famous men in her family—her father, the Calvinist minister Lyman Beecher, and her brother Henry Ward Beecher, an outspoken and well-known clergyman and orator. Her father wrote to a friend, "Hattie is a genius. I would give a hundred dollars if she was a boy."

Customize for
Less Proficient Readers

Ask students to find and list evidence as they read the section supporting the belief that the differences between the North and the South were so great that these two regions were really distinct nations within the United States.

ACTIVITY
HETEROGENEOUS GROUPS

In 1852, the publication of *Uncle Tom's Cabin* ignited the antislavery movement. The author, Harriet Beecher Stowe, created one character who evoked sympathy and a contrasting, despicable character. To help students understand both sides of the slavery issue, divide the class into small groups. Ask each group to develop a theme for a book and to create two main characters who would evoke the reader's sympathies toward the South. *(Enrichment)*

Harriet Beecher Stowe's novel Uncle Tom's Cabin *offered antislavery forces new encouragement in resisting the slavery system.*

The key difference between North and South, and the difference to which all the other differences were connected in some way, was slavery.

By the 1850s many white Northerners had come to believe that slavery violated the basic principles not only of the United States, but also of the Christian religion. Most white opponents of slavery were members of the democratic Protestant faiths that had been on the rise since the Second Great Awakening. The members of these faiths believed that all humans had the right to choose their own destiny and follow God's laws.

Slavery's white opponents did not necessarily believe that blacks and whites were equal. Many, in fact, were deeply prejudiced against African Americans. (A **prejudice** is an unreasonable, usually unfavorable opinion of another group that is not based on fact.) Nevertheless, for these people slavery was simply an evil that could not be tolerated. Without question, the most popular statement about the impact of slavery was a novel by Harriet Beecher Stowe.

Harriet Beecher Stowe

AMERICAN BIOGRAPHY "If I could use my pen as you can, I would write something that would make this whole nation feel what an accursed thing slavery is," wrote Harriet Beecher Stowe's sister. Born in Connecticut in 1811 and part of the well-known Beecher family, Stowe would become one of the best-known writers of the antislavery movement.

Harriet Beecher Stowe (1811–1896)

Uncle Tom's Cabin Stowe took her sister's advice and published a novel, *Uncle Tom's Cabin*, in 1852. The book became an instant bestseller and sold millions of copies in the United States and abroad.

The story is set in the pre–Civil War South. In the novel, a slave named Eliza Harris escapes from her home on Shelby plantation in Kentucky when her child is about to be sold. As Eliza heads north, she eludes the hired slave catchers and finds help along the Underground Railroad. Another slave, Uncle Tom, is "sold down the river" and is eventually killed by his brutal master, Simon Legree.†

Stowe did not depend only on the sharp contrast between a kind slave and his cruel master to make her case against slavery. She also tried to show that slavery was opposed to beliefs that many Northerners cherished: the importance of women and the ideal of the family. In the novel, the neat, orderly world of Uncle Tom's cabin, formed around his happy family, comes to a tragic end when Uncle Tom's owner has to sell him. Eventually Uncle Tom falls into the hands of another slaveholder, Simon Legree.

By contrast with the saintly Uncle Tom, Simon Legree is everything Stowe's audience in the North feared and despised: an unmarried, anti-Christian, heavy-drinking brute who cares only about satisfying his desires and his greed. Not only does he brutalize the enslaved women of his plantation, but in the end he beats Uncle Tom to death with a whip. It was not a mistake that Stowe made Legree a Northerner who lived in the South. She wanted to show that slavery could corrupt even those born outside the system.

To contrast these stark images of the immoral effects of slavery, Stowe wrote powerful scenes in which northern women influence their husbands to do what is right. For example, in one scene set in a house in Ohio, a wife persuades her husband, a senator, to permit some escaped slaves to continue their journey to Canada. When her husband tries to argue with her, she replies:

> **"**I don't know anything about politics, but I can read my Bible; and there I see that I must feed the hungry, clothe the naked, and comfort the desolate; and that Bible I mean to follow.**"**

Her husband points out that to help escaped slaves would involve breaking the law. But the wife steadily replies:

> **"**Obeying God never brings on public evils. I know it can't. It's always safest, all round, to do as He bids us.**"**

---

† Today, many readers are offended by Stowe's portraits of the enslaved Uncle Tom and his wife, Aunt Chloe. Stowe seems to us now to have been condescending and biased in describing these characters. In fact, "Uncle Tom" has become an insulting nickname for an African American man who passively accepts unequal status. Stowe, however, regarded Uncle Tom as a sympathetic character.

RESOURCE OPTIONS

Teaching Resources

📁 **Literature Activity** An Antislavery Bestseller, Units 3–4 folder, pp. 56–57

Media and Technology

AmericanHeritage® CD-ROM

Explorer Activity 13 The Cotton Kingdom, CD-ROM Guidebook, pp. 45–46, helps students plan a dramatic presentation about life in the South before 1861.

History Makers Harriet Beecher Stowe

Impact of *Uncle Tom's Cabin* Although a work of fiction, *Uncle Tom's Cabin* had as powerful an effect in Stowe's time as Thomas Paine's *Common Sense* had in his. According to a family story, when Stowe met President Lincoln during the Civil War he said, "So this is the little lady who made this big war?"

Stowe's novel presented northern readers with a vivid picture of both slavery and the South that they could adopt as accurate, even if it was in fact exaggerated. As they read *Uncle Tom's Cabin*, many Northerners became convinced that slavery would be the ruin of the United States. They worried about the impact of slavery not just on African Americans, but on whites and American society in general. Of this they were sure: they would never allow the United States to become a land of Simon Legrees. ▪

Southern Views on Slavery

Southern intellectuals and politicians saw *Uncle Tom's Cabin* as a book of insulting lies. They admitted that some masters did treat enslaved people badly. But the South was hardly home to thousands of Legrees. White Southerners had their own exaggerated view of slavery: to them, plantation households were like large and happy families.

Southerners did more than protest northern insults. Many began to justify the institution of slavery and attack the evils they saw in the North. They claimed that most planters took a personal interest in the well-being of the enslaved people who labored for them, providing them with the basic necessities of life. Northern industrialists, on the other hand, took no personal responsibility for their workers. Nor did they care whether the meager wages they paid could buy decent food, clothing, and shelter. Most Southerners believed that northern business owners were motivated solely by profit.

Perhaps the most direct statement of this point of view appeared in a book by George Fitzhugh published in 1857, titled *Cannibals All!* Attacking northern industrialists, whom he saw as no better than cannibals, Fitzhugh wrote:

> **❝**You, with the command over labor which your capital gives you, are a slave owner—a master, without the obligations of a master. They who work for you, who create your income, are slaves, without the rights of slaves. Slaves without a master!**❞**

Outraged by antislavery Northerners who pretended to be better than Southerners, Fitzhugh exclaimed:

Main Idea
CONNECTIONS
Describe southern views on slavery.

THE NEGRO IN HIS OWN COUNTRY.

THE NEGRO IN AMERICA.

Southern proslavery writers promoted the myth that slavery "raised Africans from savagery" and "civilized" them. These before-and-after pictures are from a pamphlet titled *Bible Defence of Slavery*. *Culture* What other claims did proslavery activists make to justify slavery?

Answer to . . .

Viewing History They claimed that slave owners took a personal interest in the well being of the people they enslaved and that slaves were better off than northern industrial workers.

Main Idea Connections Slavery was viewed as "civilizing" for enslaved workers, who were seen as well cared for by their masters.

Advantages and Disadvantages of the North and South

	Northern States	Southern States
Population	21.5 million	9 million
Railroad Mileage	21.7 thousand miles	9 thousand miles
Manufacturing		
Number of Factories	110.1 thousand	20.6 thousand
Number of Workers	1.17 million	111 thousand
Value of Products	$1.62 billion	$155 million
Finance		
Bank Deposits	$207 million	$47 million
Specie	$56 million	$27 million
Agriculture		
Corn (bushels)	446 million	280 million
Wheat (bushels)	132 million	31 million
Oats (bushels)	150 million	20 million
Cotton (bales)	4 thousand	5 million
Tobacco (pounds)	229 million	199 million
Rice (pounds)	50 thousand	187 million
Livestock		
Horses	4.2 million	1.7 million
Donkeys and Mules	300 thousand	800 thousand
Milk Cows	5.7 million	2.7 million
Beef Cattle	6.6 million	7 million
Sheep	16 million	5 million
Swine	16.3 million	15.5 million

Highlight indicates advantage

Source: *The American Heritage Picture History of the Civil War,* edited by Richard M. Ketchum

Interpreting Tables As a war between the North and South threatened to erupt, a Northerner warned his southern friend, "You are bound to fail." ***Economics Which advantages would allow the North to raise a larger, better equipped army than the South?***

❝What is falsely called Free Society is a very recent invention. It proposes to make the weak, ignorant, and poor, free, by turning them loose in a world owned exclusively by the few . . . to get a living.❞

White Southerners argued that they represented the true spirit of the American Revolution. They believed that their households possessed an order, a grace, and a sense of liberty that Northerners could not begin to understand. On this point Southerners were agreed: they were not about to let Northerners, whom they saw as haughty and self-righteous, tell them how to live.

Differences Between North and South

The differences between North and South were not simply a product of exaggerated fiction and propaganda. Hard facts also told the story. They showed that the North was becoming still more urban, still more industrial than the South. Its population, already more than twice as large as the South's, was becoming even larger and more diverse as Irish and German immigrants crowded into northern cities. By 1860, nine of the country's ten largest cities were located in the North.

Like immigration, new technology had a heavier impact on the North than on the South. The biggest technological change was the appearance of railroads. The most efficient form of transportation the world had yet known, railroads made canals **obsolete,** or outdated, in a matter of years.

By 1840 more than 3,300 miles of track had been laid in the United States. African American and Irish immigrant workers added another 5,000 miles during the 1840s. It was in the 1850s, however, that the railroads truly came into their own. More than 20,000 miles of track were laid in that decade.

During this railroad boom, remote places suddenly became the centers of bustling trade. The small trading village of Chicago grew incredibly fast. Why? Because railroads helped make Chicago a central location through which people both to the east and to the west transported goods such as corn and wheat.

The railroads, however, had a positive effect primarily in the North. In 1860 the North had 70 percent of the railroad track in the United States. Railroads in the South did contribute to the growth of cities such as Atlanta, Georgia. But southern planters and farmers were still more likely to transport their crops by water than by rail.

Like the railroad, the telegraph magnified differences between North and South. This historic advance in communication was developed

A train thunders past smoking metal forges in this late-1850s print of Bridgewater, Massachusetts. Though the North was still largely a land of farms, its landscape increasingly resembled this scene. *Economics How did the growth of railroads contribute to the growth of cities?*

by Samuel F. B. Morse in 1844. The telegraph allowed people to send messages over wire by using a code of short and long pulses of electricity that represented the alphabet. Because telegraph wires were strung along the ever-growing network of railroad tracks, the communications revolution in the North advanced more quickly than in the South.

Railroads and improved communications nourished the booming industries of the North. In 1860 the North had 110,000 factories, compared to 20,000 in the South; it produced over $1.6 billion

worth of goods, compared to the South's $155 million. In fact, in terms of numbers, the South outdid the North in only two notable ways: it had more enslaved people and it had more cotton.

Certainly, the North and the South in 1860 had much in common. They both cherished their democratic tradition. Even on the issue of the status of African Americans, whites in both the North and South displayed tremendous prejudice. But despite these similarities, they differed greatly in their beliefs about what American society should be.

SECTION 1 REVIEW

Comprehension

1. **Key Terms** Define: (a) Union; (b) prejudice; (c) obsolete.

2. **Summarizing the Main Idea** How did slavery affect the views that Northerners and Southerners had of each other?

3. **Organizing Information** Create a chart listing the major economic contrasts between the North and South in 1860.

Critical Thinking

4. **Analyzing Time Lines** Review the time line at the start of the section. What impact did *Uncle Tom's Cabin* have on northern views of slavery?

5. **Drawing Inferences** Describe the two main views held by historians on the issue of whether the Civil War could have been avoided. What can you infer about each group's views of people's abilities to deal with differences?

Writing Activity

6. **Writing an Expository Essay** Write an essay in which you describe Harriet Beecher Stowe's use of contrast in *Uncle Tom's Cabin* to make her case against slavery.

1848	1850	1852	1854	1854
Zachary Taylor elected President	Compromise of 1850	Franklin Pierce elected President	Kansas-Nebraska Act	Republican party founded

1845　　　　　　　　　　　1850　　　　　　　　　　　1855

SECTION 2

New Political Parties

Objectives

You may wish to call students' attention to the objectives in the Section Preview. The objectives are reflected in the main headings of the section.

Bellringer

Ask students whether, considering past efforts to compromise on the slavery issue, it was reasonable to expect that the Compromise of 1850 would continue to maintain peace in the United States. Why or why not?

Reading Strategy

Organizing Information Refer to the Reading Strategy in the Section Preview. You may want to model the graphic organizer on the chalkboard, dividing students into Northerners and Southerners and asking them to suggest actions and ideas.

LESSON PLAN

Connecting to the Main Idea

1. Focus Explain that existing political organizations in the 1850s failed to deal with the question of slavery. New political parties emerged in order to try to solve the problem.

2. Instruct Discuss the inability of politicians to deal with slavery. Ask why the Compromise of 1850 provided only a temporary solution. Why did Senator John C. Calhoun think it was impossible for southern interests to be protected by the existing government? How were both Northerners and Southerners able to justify their stand on slavery in terms of the United States Constitution? Why did the Kansas-Nebraska Act outrage Northerners?

3. Close New political parties emerged during the 1850s to address the issues of the times. The next section discusses the continuing failure of the political system to solve the biggest issue, slavery, and the growing hostility between proslavery and antislavery forces.

---

2 New Political Parties

SECTION PREVIEW

Objectives

1. Explain the effects of the Missouri Compromise, and how the Compromise of 1850 tried to deal with them.
2. Summarize the changes in political parties in the 1850s.
3. Describe the causes and effects of the Kansas-Nebraska Act, including its role in the creation of the Republican party.
4. *Key Terms* Define: Compromise of 1850; Fugitive Slave Act; states' rights; nativism; Kansas-Nebraska Act; popular sovereignty.

Main Idea

A compromise during the 1850s failed to end disagreement over slavery in the territories. Meanwhile, the existing political party system broke down as new political parties arose.

Reading Strategy

Organizing Information As you read this section, create a graphic organizer that lists the actions and ideas of Northerners and Southerners in two separate columns.

So what if there were differences between North and South? Perhaps the differences were bound to cause political conflict, but did they have to lead to a lengthy war that would kill hundreds of thousands of people? The answer to this question requires an understanding of politics in the 1850s. The war came *when* it did and *how* it did because politicians could not solve the question of slavery. The rest of this chapter explains that political breakdown.

Effects of the Missouri Compromise

Politicians might have been able to keep slavery from tearing the nation apart if Americans had not settled new lands to the west of the Mississippi. This newly acquired land forced an old question back into politics: whether or not slavery would be allowed in the territories.

Congress had made its first attempt to address this question with the Missouri Compromise of 1820. In the short run, the compromise maintained the balance in the Senate between slave and free states so that neither North nor South would have more power.[†] It also sought to address the long-term issue of westward expansion by stating that newly formed states north of 36° 30' N latitude would be free states. The compromise did not, however, settle the issue of whether slavery would be legal while the lands to the west were still territories.

After the Mexican War, the Treaty of Guadalupe Hidalgo of 1848 gave the United States a large piece of land that had been part of Mexico. Because much of this new territory was south of the line set by the Missouri Compromise, Northerners feared that it would eventually be divided into several slave states. This would give the South a majority vote in the Senate and perhaps in the Electoral College. The best way to prevent the creation

---

[†]Balance in the Senate was especially important to the southern states which were already outnumbered in the House because of the North's larger population.

▶ RESOURCE OPTIONS

Teaching Resources

📁 **Reproducible Lesson Plan** Lesson Plans folder, p. 77

📁 **Big Idea Graphic Organizer** Big Idea Graphic Organizer folder, p. 49

📁 **Guided Reading and Review** Units 3–4 folder, p. 47

of more slave states, reasoned antislavery Northerners, was to keep slavery out of these areas while they were still territories.

Southerners were equally firm in insisting that the national government had no business telling its free citizens they could not take their property to the territories if they wanted to. Property, after all, was what they considered enslaved people to be.

In the presidential election of 1848, both major parties hoped to gain voters from all sides of the slavery debate. Thus they avoided discussing the slavery issue and nominated non-controversial candidates. The Democrats chose Governor Lewis Cass of Michigan, while the Whigs chose Mexican War general Zachary Taylor.

Angered by their parties' unwillingness to deal with the slavery issue, some members from both parties split off and formed their own Free Soil party to oppose slavery in the territories.

The Free Soilers did not win any states in the 1848 election, but they did take enough votes away from Cass to give Taylor a narrow victory.

The Compromise of 1850

Westward expansion once again raised the issue of slavery in 1849. In that year the thousands of Americans who had rushed into California during the Gold Rush requested admission to the United States as a free state. Admitting California as a free state would upset the fragile balance between free and slave states in the Senate. The stage was set for one of the most dramatic events in American history.

Clay Proposes a Compromise At the center of this drama were three of the most respected senators of that (or any) era: John C. Calhoun of South Carolina, Henry Clay of Kentucky, and Daniel Webster of Massachusetts. All three

 During the debate that led to the Compromise of 1850, all the great speakers of Congress had their say. Among them was Henry Clay, shown here in February 1850 as he warned that a failure to compromise would lead to "furious" and "bloody" war. *Government What led Clay to propose a compromise?*

Customize for

Less Proficient Readers

Have students read the section's main headings and then write a question based on each, filling in the answers as they read.

RESOURCE OPTIONS

Teaching Resources

Nystrom *Atlas of Our Country* Settling the West, pp. 28–29

Media and Technology

AmericanHeritage® CD-ROM

Presidents Zachary Taylor

Answer to . . .

Viewing History Westward expansion reopened the debate over slavery; Clay's proposal sought to keep a balance between northern and southern interests.

men had begun their long political careers in Congress prior to the War of 1812. When the Senate convened in 1849, the 73-year-old Clay, who was called "Gallant Harry of the West," tried to solve the nation's dilemma with words rather than blood.

Clay's plan for a compromise over slavery would become known as the **Compromise of 1850.** Seeking a middle ground on the slavery debate, Clay proposed five separate laws, two of which favored the North and two of which favored the South:

(1) Congress would admit California as a free state.

(2) The people of the territories of New Mexico and Utah would decide for themselves whether slavery would be legal.

(3) Congress would abolish the sale of enslaved people in Washington, D.C.

(4) Slavery itself would remain legal in Washington, D.C.

(5) A **Fugitive Slave Act** would order all citizens of the United States to assist in the return of enslaved people who had escaped from their owners. It would also deny a jury trial to escaped slaves.

Calhoun Opposes Compromise Debate over the compromise dragged on for months. On March 4, 1850, the Senate gathered to hear the opinion of John C. Calhoun of South Carolina. Calhoun was a direct and dynamic orator. As it turned out, Calhoun's speech was one of the great summaries of the southern view of the crisis.

Many in the Senate felt great emotion when it was Calhoun's turn to present his views. Everyone knew that the 67-year-old senator was ill and that he probably did not have long to live. He was so weak that he asked James Mason of Virginia to read his speech for him.

As the speech began, Calhoun—through Senator Mason—stated the problem the nation faced:

The "great and primary" cause of the crisis, Calhoun said, was that the North now had "the exclusive power of controlling the Government, which leaves the [South] without any adequate means of protecting itself against . . . encroachment and oppression."

Over the years, the North had indeed gained power—not only through its greater wealth, but also through its larger population, which gave it more representatives in the House and more votes in the Electoral College. Like many other Southerners, Calhoun had responded to the growth in northern power by embracing the theory of **states' rights.** According to this theory, states have the right to nullify acts of the federal government and even to leave the Union if they wish to do so.

In his speech, Calhoun made clear that the South did not want to leave the Union. He also stated, however, that the South would not give up its liberty to save the Union: "The South asks for justice, simple justice, and less she ought not to take," he stated. "She has no compromise to offer, but the Constitution; and no concession or surrender to make."

Today Americans believe that slavery is morally wrong, because it robs people of their liberty. Calhoun and other white southern planters believed that stopping slavery was morally wrong, because it interfered with their liberty to own enslaved people as property. Government, they believed, should protect this basic liberty.

Southern planters held that if the federal government intended to reduce their rights or threaten their property, then it was no longer a government worthy of their respect. From the point of view of Calhoun, it was the northern section, not the southern section, that was twisting the Constitution and the intentions of the Framers. The ringing finale of his speech made this clear: "I have exerted myself . . . with the intention of saving the Union, if it could be done; and if it could not, [with saving] the section . . . which I sincerely believe has justice and the Constitution on its side."

Webster Favors Compromise Three days after Calhoun's speech, Daniel Webster, the nation's leading orator, stood to speak. Webster was a large man with dark, intense eyes. His voice was both magnetic and persuasive. During his speech, Webster surprised his audience with a reversal of opinion. Senator Webster had previously opposed any extension of slavery. Now, fearing for the existence of the Union, Webster supported each of Clay's proposals:

> ❝I wish to speak today, not as a Massachusetts man, nor as a northern man, but as an American. . . . I speak today for the preservation of the Union. 'Hear me for my cause.'❞
>
> —*Daniel Webster*

Webster went on to speak for several hours. Believing that slavery would never be practical in New Mexico, he supported Clay's compromise. He also maintained that it was a constitutional duty to return fugitive slaves. Webster's speech outraged northern abolitionists and many of his long-time supporters. They accused Webster of putting financial matters ahead of issues of freedom and humanity. Northern business owners, however, supported Webster's stance because they feared the loss of valuable southern trade if the Union was dissolved.

Congress Approves the Compromise As the debate continued over the Compromise of 1850, President Taylor made his own set of proposals and many feared a presidential veto. Taylor's sudden death in July 1850, however, brought Millard Fillmore to the presidency. Working with Senator Stephen A. Douglas of Illinois, who had taken over for an exhausted Clay, Congress eventually passed the Compromise of 1850.

As Calhoun had foreseen, Southerners were not satisfied with the compromise, although the legislation did bring a brief calm to the nation. In reality, it solved nothing beyond determining that California would be a free state. The compromise did not settle the issue of slavery in the new area acquired from Mexico. Part of the compromise, the Fugitive Slave Act, actually made the situation worse by infuriating many Northerners—including Harriet Beecher Stowe, who expressed her outrage in *Uncle Tom's Cabin*.

Changes in Political Parties

During the early 1850s, the American party system began to break down. One sign of this breakdown was the decline of the Whig party. In 1852 the Whigs, rejecting President Fillmore because of his support for the Compromise of 1850, instead nominated Winfield Scott, a general from the Mexican War. The Democrats nominated Franklin Pierce of New Hampshire, and Pierce won the election in a landslide.

Decline of the Whigs The Whigs never won another presidential contest, and by the end of the 1850s the Whig party had largely disappeared. The slavery issue badly hurt the Whigs. Many of their northern voters were Protestants who were disgusted with the politicians' fondness for compromise.

Another reason the Whigs faded away was that the old issues that had divided political parties in the 1830s now seemed largely resolved. Why argue about banks? The United States was prosperous and expanding. The

Massachusetts senator Daniel Webster used his powerful oratorical skill to persuade Congress to adopt the Compromise of 1850. *Economics Why did northern businessmen favor the compromise?*

From the Archives of
American Heritage®

About the Presidents

Millard Fillmore (1850–1853) took advantage of the brief period of calm following the Compromise of 1850. He secured grants for railroad construction in the West and, by promoting a good neighbor policy, he sought to open new markets abroad. To the south, his efforts led to railroad links with Mexico and negotiations to cut a canal through Nicaragua. In the Pacific, his letters urging trade helped to break down barriers. But Fillmore's accomplishments abroad came at the expense of long-term domestic tranquillity. The issue of slavery continued to simmer and get worse.

Franklin Pierce (1853–1857) threw his support behind the Kansas-Nebraska Act. He helped to bring enough Democratic dissenters in line to win its passage. At the time, he believed he had won a great victory, but the Kansas-Nebraska Act proved to be the great tragedy of the administration. First, it cost him control of the Democratic party. Then, it cost the Democrats the control of the House. Source: David Jacobs, "Millard Fillmore"; Martin Luray, "Franklin Pierce," *The American Heritage® Pictorial History of the United States*, vol. 1, 1968.

 RESOURCE OPTIONS

Media and Technology

 AmericanHeritage® CD-ROM

Presidents Millard Fillmore, Franklin Pierce

Answer to . . .

Viewing History They thought that if the Union dissolved, they would lose valuable southern trade.

The Kansas and Nebraska Territories

The desire to build a railroad all the way across the continent to unite East and West was the American Dream of the 1850s. No American city could hope for a greater prize than to be chosen as the eastern terminus of the nation's transcontinental railway. New Orleans, Memphis, and St. Louis were among many towns competing with Chicago to be selected and thereby become the bustling headquarters for reaching the wealth and commerce of the West. But Senator Douglas knew that a railroad through the unsettled land of the West could be built only with the aid of government land grants. And these land grants could be made only if the region the railroad passed through was already surveyed and organized politically. With this in mind, Douglas introduced a bill to organize the lands west of Iowa and Missouri—the bill which in its final form provided for a Kansas Territory and a Nebraska Territory.

FREEDOM OF THE ELECTIVE FR...

WELL! LET EM COME ON, WE'RE ARM'D.

POPULAR SOVEREIGNTY

THE MAJORITY RULE

Stephen Douglas champions popular sovereignty in this 1858 cartoon. Douglas believed that slavery in the territories would no longer be a national issue if it were decided by voters in the territories themselves. *Government What role did Douglas's political ambitions play in his proposal of the Kansas-Nebraska Act?*

men at the center of the Jacksonian-Whig struggles—Jackson, Clay, Webster, Calhoun—were either dead or dying. Political parties seemed to be lumbering onward only to keep their hold on government jobs and contracts.

The time had come for a new generation of leaders to come forward, and during the 1850s, they did emerge. Whether they would be able to deal with the new issues facing the nation was another question.

Rise of the Know-Nothings Slavery and unhappiness with politics were not the only issues that brought down the Whigs. The equally powerful issue of **nativism** also played a part. Nativism is a movement to ensure that native-born Americans receive better treatment than immigrants. It arose in response to a surge in immigration: between 1846 and 1854, close to 3 million Europeans arrived in

the United States. Many evangelical Protestants were particularly disturbed by the Catholic immigrants among them.

Fear about immigrants led in 1849 to the formation of a secret nativist society called the Order of the Star-Spangled Banner. Within a few years, its membership totaled around one million. The order insisted on complete secrecy from its members, who used passwords and special handshakes. They always replied to questions about the organization with the answer, "I know nothing."

In 1854, nativists went public by forming a political organization, the American party. It pledged to work against Irish Catholic candidates and for laws requiring immigrants to wait longer before they could become citizens. Because it was closely associated with the Order of the Star-Spangled Banner, the American party came to be called the Know-Nothings.

Know-Nothings claimed that they were committed to "the great work of Americanizing Americans." They declared:

AMERICAN VOICES ❝[E]very American and naturalized Protestant citizen throughout the Union, [should] use his utmost exertions to aid the cause by organizing and freeing the country from that monster [Catholicism] which . . . is only waiting . . . to approach to plant its flag of tyranny, persecution, and oppression among us.❞

—*The American party*

The Know-Nothings did very well in local elections in northern states. Their main supporters were Americans worried that immigration would lead to crime and vice, and working men fearful of losing jobs to Irish and German immigrants.

The Kansas-Nebraska Act

As if the growing turmoil among the parties were not enough trouble for the nation, Senator Stephen Douglas of Illinois again raised the issue of slavery in the territories. Douglas had two conflicting ambitions. First, he wanted Chicago to benefit from the development of the West. The sooner the territories of Kansas and Nebraska became states, the sooner railroads could be built across them to link Chicago with the West. Second, Douglas wanted to run for President. To do that, he needed the support of southern Democrats. Pushing statehood for Kansas and Nebraska was not the way to gain supporters in the

Answer to . . .

Viewing History Douglas hoped to be President one day. He saw the act, by its repeal of the Missouri Compromise, as a way to gain the votes of southern Democrats.

TEST PREPARATION

Have students read the excerpt from the American party on this page and then answer the question below.

From the passage, you can infer that the only people the Know-Nothings welcomed, besides Protestants born in the United States, were—

A Catholic immigrants.

Ⓑ Protestant immigrants who had become naturalized.

C Catholic immigrants who had become naturalized.

D immigrants who were neither Protestant nor Catholic.

A banner of one of the new political parties of the 1850s—the Republicans—shows John Frémont, candidate for President in 1856. *Culture Read the proclamations on the banner. How do they reflect the members of the party?*

BACKGROUND

Voting Patterns

Because today more than 80 percent of them favor Democratic candidates, African Americans are strongly identified with that party. But until the 1930s, African Americans in the North generally voted Republican. In 1856 a gathering of voters resolved: "That we, the colored citizens of Boston, will support with our voices and our votes, John C. Frémont, of California, as President of the United States. . . . [T]hat while we regard the Republican party as the people's party . . . and while we are willing to unite with them to resist the aggressions of the Slave Power, we do not pledge ourselves to go further with the Republicans than [they] will go with us."

South. Under the terms of the Missouri Compromise of 1820, Kansas and Nebraska would become free states. The North would then become still more powerful, and Southerners would blame Douglas.

Trying to win the support of both Northerners and Southerners, Douglas introduced the **Kansas-Nebraska Act** in the Senate in January 1854. The act supported the practice of **popular sovereignty,** or letting the people in a territory decide whether slavery would be allowed there. In effect, Douglas was asking the nation to repeal the Missouri Compromise and its boundary line of 36° 30' N and rely instead on popular sovereignty. As Douglas wrote to a Southerner in April 1854:

> **AMERICAN VOICES**
> ❝The great principle of self-government is at stake, and surely the people of this country are never going to decide that the principle upon which our whole republican system rests is vicious and wrong.❞
>
> —Stephen A. Douglas

Douglas knew that the Kansas-Nebraska Act would make Southerners happy. After all, it raised the possibility that Kansas and Nebraska might become slave states, which would have been impossible under the Missouri Compromise. Douglas also thought that Northerners would back his proposal. Northerners, he believed, would decide that slavery would never take hold on the Great Plains, where cotton could not grow. The people of Kansas and Nebraska would no doubt vote peacefully to become free states.

After nine months of debate, Congress passed the Kansas-Nebraska Act. But instead of applauding the bill, as Douglas had expected, Northerners were outraged by it. Northern members of Douglas's own party, the Democrats, denounced Douglas for what they saw as a sellout to the South. As you will read, Douglas was also wrong about a peaceful vote in the territories.

Main Idea
CONNECTIONS

Why did the Kansas-Nebraska Act anger Northerners?

RESOURCE OPTIONS

Media and Technology

Color Transparencies Historical Maps, L-3

ACTIVITY
HETEROGENEOUS GROUPS

Ask students to write a paragraph summarizing how the failure of politicians to solve the important issues of the day led to the rise of new political parties in the 1850s. *(Reteaching)*

Answer to . . .

Viewing History The party was made up mostly of Northerners. The North was largely industrial, and the party was formed to oppose the extension of slavery.

Main Idea Connections Northerners believed Douglas was selling out to the South.

Answers to
SECTION 2 REVIEW

1. (a) Compromise of 1850, see p. 322; (b) Fugitive Slave Act, see p. 322; (c) states' rights, see p. 322; (d) nativism, p. 324; (e) Kansas-Nebraska Act, see p. 325; (f) popular sovereignty, see p. 325.

2. The Whigs didn't want to compromise on the slavery issue; fears about immigration led to nativism and the Know-Nothing party.

3. Favoring the North: California admitted as a free state; the sale of slaves in Washington, D.C., abolished. Favoring the South: slavery to remain legal in Washington, D.C.; Fugitive Slave Act. In addition, the people of New Mexico and Utah would decide the slavery issue for themselves.

4. The Republican party grew in response to the Kansas-Nebraska Act.

5. It did not address the issue of whether slavery would be legal while the lands to the west were still territories; Northerners feared the South would have a majority rule in the Senate; it addressed only the issue of California. Southerners were not satisfied because it did not address the new area acquired from Mexico; the Fugitive Slave Act made the situation worse.

6. Answers will vary. Speeches should include: Southerners were happy because Kansas and Nebraska could become slave states; Northerners were unhappy because they thought Douglas sold out to the South.

FACT Finder — Political Parties of the 1850s

Party	Views	Supporters
Democrats (North)	Favored deciding issue of slavery in the territories by popular sovereignty	A variety of backgrounds, but particularly northern voters in urban areas and Catholics; some of those born in the South who had moved to the Old Northwest
Democrats (South)	Favored expanding slavery in territories	Those living in southern areas undergoing growth in economy and population
Republicans	Opposed to slavery, supported nativist movement	People in New England and people born in New England living in the Old Northwest; Protestant English, Scotch-Irish immigrants; former American party followers
American Party	Known as "Know-Nothings"; anti-Catholic, fearing "Papal Power"; nativist, favoring a longer naturalization period for immigrants; antislavery	Supporters were generally northern Protestants born in the United States

Interpreting Tables During the 1850s, three major parties jostled for power in the North, but only one major party represented the South. *Culture* Why did the Republicans lack support in the South? What views did the Republican party share with the American party that enabled it to win over American party members?

The Creation of the Republican Party

During the summer of 1854, people throughout the North held meetings to protest the Kansas-Nebraska bill. During one of these meetings in Michigan, disgusted Northerners launched a new Republican party. This party is the direct ancestor of today's party by the same name. Members of the new Republican party dedicated themselves to stopping the "Slave Power," or the South. They declared that slavery was a great moral evil and vowed to fight against its extension into new territories. They also demanded the repeal of the Kansas-Nebraska Act and the Fugitive Slave Act.

The new Republicans drew their support almost entirely from antislavery Democrats, Whigs, and Free Soilers in the North. Farmers, professionals, small business owners, craftworkers—these were the Republicans.

New parties appear frequently in American history. Few last very long. In the mid-1850s, however, the disappearance of the Whigs and the emotional issues of nativism and slavery produced two strong parties, the Know-Nothings and the Republicans. It remained to be seen which would become the more powerful.

SECTION 2 REVIEW

Comprehension

1. *Key Terms* Define: (a) Compromise of 1850; (b) Fugitive Slave Act; (c) states' rights; (d) nativism; (e) Kansas-Nebraska Act; (f) popular sovereignty.

2. *Summarizing the Main Idea* List the reasons why the Whig party declined and the Know-Nothing party was created.

3. *Organizing Information* Create a list of the main points of the Compromise of 1850. Indicate which points favored the North and which points favored the South.

Critical Thinking

4. *Analyzing Time Lines* Review the time line at the start of the section. How are the last two events on the time line related?

5. *Identifying Central Issues* Describe why neither Northerners nor Southerners were satisfied with the Missouri Compromise. Did the Compromise of 1850 satisfy them? Explain.

Writing Activity

6. *Writing a Persuasive Essay* Write a persuasive speech from the point of view of either a Southerner or Northerner supporting or opposing the Kansas-Nebraska Act.

RESOURCE OPTIONS

Teaching Resources

Quiz Units 3–4 folder, p. 48

Student Performance Pack

Guide to the Essentials Chapter 11, Section 2 (English and Spanish)

Answer to . . .

Interpreting Tables Because they were opposed to slavery; both were nativist and abolitionist.

Analyzing Political Speeches

Political speeches are as old as government itself. Their goal has always been to persuade listeners to take a particular view. Such speeches can be about almost anything—whom citizens should vote for, what new law they should support, what action the government should take, or what policy it should adopt. Political speeches can also serve as valuable evidence about people and events in history.

Political speakers use a variety of techniques to win over their listeners. Sometimes they appeal to the self-interest of their audience: "See how doing what I propose will make your life better." Sometimes they appeal to their listeners' social conscience: "See how doing what I propose will benefit the community or the nation as a whole." Often they appeal to patriotism.

Use the following steps to analyze the excerpts from a speech made by Henry Clay during the debate over the Compromise of 1850.

1. *Identify the main topic of the speech and the speaker's stand on it.* Recall what you already know about the speaker and his political ideas. Skim through the speech to get a general idea of the speaker's topic and aims in making the speech. (a) What is the main topic of the speech? (b) Cite evidence in the speech that Clay believes the compromise will work. (c) What is Clay's stand on the measure?

2. *Analyze the techniques the speaker uses to persuade listeners.* Political speakers appeal to both the minds and the hearts of their listeners. Evaluate the speaker's persuasiveness and how he or she achieves it. (a) What does Clay tell his listeners to disregard and forget? (b) Give evidence that Clay appeals to reason in his speech. (c) Give evidence that Clay appeals to his listeners' feelings of patriotism. (d) How would you evaluate Clay's persuasiveness in this speech?

3. *Study the speech for clues to what the historical period was like.* (a) What does the speech tell you about how serious the tensions between North and South seemed to people at that time? (b) What does it tell you about the style of speeches during that period?

TEST FOR SUCCESS

Compare and contrast this speech with any modern speeches you have heard or read.

To the Senate, July 22, 1850

I believe from the bottom of my soul that this measure is the reunion of the Union. And now let us disregard all resentments, all passions, all petty jealousies, all personal desires, all love of place, all hungering after the guilded crumbs which fall from the table of power. Let us forget popular fears, from whatever quarter they may spring. Let us . . . think alone of our God, our country, our conscience, and our glorious Union; that Union without which we shall be torn into hostile fragments, and sooner or later become the victims of military despotism, or foreign domination. . . .

What is an individual man? An atom, almost invisible without a magnifying glass—a mere speck upon the surface of the immense universe—not a second in time, compared to immeasurable, never-beginning, and never-ending eternity; a drop of water in the great deep, which evaporates and is borne off by the winds; a grain of sand, which is soon gathered to the dust from which it sprung. Shall a being so small, so petty, so fleeting, so evanescent [quick to disappear], oppose itself to the onward march of a great nation? . . . Let us look at our country and our cause; elevate ourselves to the dignity of pure and disinterested patriots, wise and enlightened statesmen, and save our country from all impending dangers. . . . What are we—what is any man worth who is not ready and willing to sacrifice himself for the benefit of his country when it is necessary?

—*Henry Clay, United States senator from Kentucky*

 RESOURCE OPTIONS

Teaching Resources

Skills for Life Activity Units 3–4 folder, p. 58, gives a present-day applicaton of the skill of analyzing speeches for content and technique.

1856	1856	1857	1858	1859	
Violence erupts in Kansas	Buchanan elected President	Scott v. Sandford	Lincoln-Douglas debates	John Brown's raid on Harpers Ferry	

| **1855** | **1856** | **1857** | **1858** | **1859** | **1860** |

SECTION 3

The System Fails

Objectives

You may wish to call students' attention to the objectives in the Section Preview. The objectives are reflected in the main headings of the section.

Bellringer

Ask students to make a list of controversial issues in the United States that have incited groups to violence in recent years. Ask when and why people adopt violence to achieve political ends.

Reading Strategy

Arranging Events in Order Refer to the Reading Strategy in the Section Preview. You may want to model the time line on the chalkboard. As students read, ask them to suggest key events.

3 The System Fails

SECTION PREVIEW

Objectives

1 Summarize the causes of violence in Kansas and in Congress in 1856.
2 Explain how slavery dominated national politics from 1856 to 1858.
3 Describe how the Lecompton constitution, Lincoln-Douglas debates, and John Brown's raid reflected national divisions over slavery.
4 *Key Terms* Define: free soiler; *Scott* v. *Sandford;* arsenal.

Main Idea

A series of violent clashes between antislavery and proslavery forces took place between 1856 and 1860. Americans on each side of the slavery issue became convinced that the other side was acting against law and morality.

Reading Strategy

Arranging Events in Order As you read this section, create a time line of events. Write a statement for each event summarizing its impact on the North and/or South.

LESSON PLAN

Connecting to the Main Idea

1. Focus Explain that between 1856 and 1860, hostilities between antislavery and proslavery forces escalated. Ask what events took place to increase the tension between the North and the South.

2. Instruct Discuss the breakdown of law and the political process brought about by the government's inability to solve the slavery issue. Ask students why Kansas became a battleground for proslavery and antislavery forces. What was John Brown's role in the escalating violence over the slavery issue? How did Brooks's attack on Sumner illustrate the growing failure of the political process? How did the Supreme Court decision in Dred Scott and the Lecompton constitution contribute to the breakdown of trust in the law?

3. Close After the passage of the Kansas-Nebraska Act, the web of order that held the nation together began to unravel. The next section discusses the nation's final descent into war.

After passage of the Kansas-Nebraska Act in 1854, national attention turned to the Kansas Territory. According to this law, voters in the territory would decide whether to become a free or slave state. Both proslavery and antislavery groups organized to make sure that they would have a majority of voters in the region.

Violence Begins

Antislavery groups in the Northeast set up so-called Emigrant Aid societies in 1854–1855 to send some 1,200 New Englanders to Kansas to fight against slavery. The new settlers were known as **free soilers.** Like the Free Soil party founded in 1848, free soilers worked to end slavery in the territories. Meanwhile, proslavery settlers in Missouri organized secret societies to oppose the free soilers. Many proslavery settlers crossed into Kansas to vote illegally in territorial elections. By 1855, Kansas had an antislavery capital at Topeka and a proslavery capital at Lecompton.

In 1856 tensions in Kansas escalated into open violence. The clashes began on May 21, when a group of Southerners, with the support of a proslavery federal marshal, looted newspaper offices and homes in Lawrence, Kansas, a center of free-soiler activity.

"Bleeding Kansas" The action of the proslavery looters stirred a swift response from Connecticut-born and Ohio-raised John Brown, a stern evangelical who believed that he was God's chosen instrument to end slavery. On the night of May 24–25, Brown led several New Englanders to a proslavery settlement near Pottawatomie Creek. There, Brown and his men roused five men from their beds, dragged them from their homes, and killed them with swords in front of their families.

The looting in Lawrence and Brown's brutal reaction to it sparked a summer of murderous raids and counterraids throughout Kansas, shown on the map on the next page. The violence won the territory the grim nickname: "Bleeding Kansas."

▶ RESOURCE OPTIONS

Teaching Resources

📁 **Reproducible Lesson Plan** Lesson Plans folder, p. 78

📁 **Big Idea Graphic Organizer** Big Idea Graphic Organizer folder, p. 50

📁 **Guided Reading and Review** Units 3–4 folder, p. 49

🦅 **American**Heritage® **CD-ROM**

Time Tour The Nation Torn Apart: The Road to Civil War

"Bleeding Sumner" Violence was not confined to Kansas. On May 22 it appeared in the United States capital. On May 19 and 20, Senator Charles Sumner of Massachusetts had given a fiery speech later titled "The Crime Against Kansas." Sumner, a leading Republican and one of the most powerful antislavery voices in Congress, bitterly attacked Southerners for forcing slavery on the territory. In particular, he made bold insults against Senator Andrew Butler of South Carolina.

Preston Brooks, who was both a member of the House of Representatives and Butler's nephew, was angered by Sumner's remarks and determined to defend the honor of the South. Two days after Sumner's speech, Brooks approached Sumner at his Senate desk and began beating him with his cane.

Sumner survived the caning, but was never completely healthy again. Brooks resigned his House seat, but was immediately reelected. People across the South voiced their support for Brooks. One Southerner sent him a cane inscribed with the words "Hit him again." Northerners were outraged by Brooks's action and the support he received. Sumner's empty Senate seat served as a reminder of that hatred.

Slavery and National Politics

The violence of 1856 did not last. Still, slavery continued to dominate national politics, from presidential contests to Supreme Court cases to proposed state constitutions.

The Election of 1856 At their convention in Cincinnati, Democrats nominated for President, James Buchanan, who had been out of the country and had no connection with the violence in Kansas. Similarly, the Republicans chose John C. Frémont, a dynamic Mexican War hero with no experience in politics. The American party, or Know-Nothings, nominated former President Millard Fillmore.

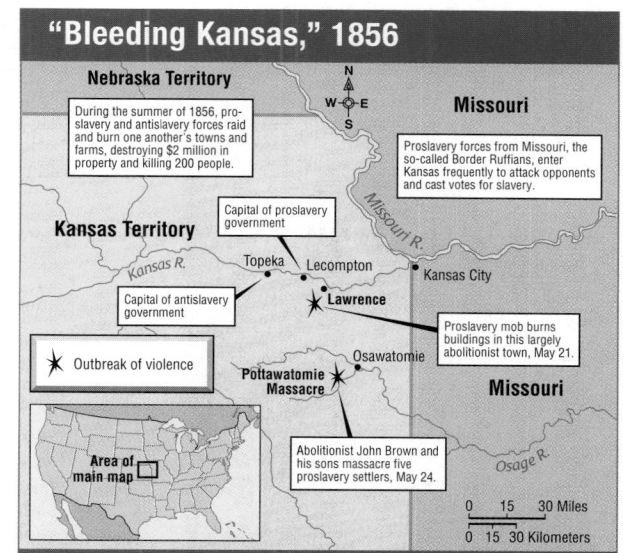

"Bleeding Kansas," 1856

Nebraska Territory

During the summer of 1856, pro-slavery and antislavery forces raid and burn one another's towns and farms, destroying $2 million in property and killing 200 people.

Missouri

Proslavery forces from Missouri, the so-called Border Ruffians, enter Kansas frequently to attack opponents and cast votes for slavery.

Kansas Territory

Capital of proslavery government

Kansas R.
Topeka Lecompton
★ Lawrence   Kansas City

Capital of antislavery government

Proslavery mob burns buildings in this largely abolitionist town, May 21.

★ Outbreak of violence

Osawatomie
Pottawatomie Massacre

Missouri

Abolitionist John Brown and his sons massacre five proslavery settlers, May 24.

Osage R.

Area of main map

0   15   30 Miles
0   15 30 Kilometers

MAP Skills Outsiders from both slave and free states meddled aggressively in Kansas politics. In one election, 5,000 proslavery men from Missouri crossed the border to vote. The final tally totaled four times as many votes as there were registered voters. *Location How far is the abolitionist stronghold Lawrence from the Missouri border?*

During the campaign, the Democrats supported the Compromise of 1850 and the Kansas-Nebraska Act. In direct opposition, the Republicans declared the federal government's right to restrict slavery in the territories and called for the admission of Kansas as a free state.

While the Republicans received strong northern support, Buchanan won the election. He pledged to his supporters in the South that as President he would stop "the agitation of the slavery issue" in the North.

In fact Buchanan stated that the slavery issue was now "approaching its end." Buchanan expressed his hope that the Supreme Court would use its power to resolve the slavery issue for good. Two days after Buchanan's inauguration, however, the Supreme Court did just the opposite. It handed down a decision that would outrage Northerners even more and further divide the country over the issue of slavery.

The Dred Scott Decision In March 1857 the Supreme Court handed down one of the most controversial decisions in its history, ***Scott v. Sandford.*** The case had started when Dred Scott, an enslaved man living in Missouri, had

ACTIVITY
HETEROGENEOUS GROUPS

Many Northerners, including the great New England philosopher and poet Ralph Waldo Emerson, revered the abolitionist John Brown, while Southerners vilified him as one of the world's most evil men. Ask students to research the life of this controversial abolitionist and to write a short essay describing his character and explaining his motives. *(Enrichment)*

RESOURCE OPTIONS

Teaching Resources

 Nystrom *Atlas of Our Country* Settling the West, pp. 28–29

Media and Technology

 AmericanHeritage® **CD-ROM**

Presidents James Buchanan

Answer to . . .

Map Skills About 30 miles.

Graphing the Main Idea

To make sure students understand the main idea of this section, you may wish to use the flow map graphic organizer below.

Tell students that a flow map is often used to show cause and effect. Ask students to use the flow map to show how government's inability to deal with the slavery issue led to a breakdown of trust in the law and in violent clashes throughout the country.

Teaching Tip A template for this graphic organizer can be found in the Color Transparencies, G-4.

Customize for
More Advanced Students

Ask students to analyze why the beliefs, principles, and government that had held the United States together for seven decades broke down over the issue of slavery. What led some Americans to abandon the democratic process in favor of violence to settle the slavery issue? Is it possible that a similar situation could happen today in the United States?

VIEWING HISTORY

Dred Scott lost his suit for freedom because the Supreme Court viewed slaves as property and not as people. *Government* Why was the Dred Scott decision a blow not just for Scott, but for antislavery forces in general?

filed suit against his owner. Scott argued that because he and his wife, Harriet, had once lived in states and territories where slavery was illegal, the couple was in fact free.

The Supreme Court ruled 7 to 2 against Scott. The justices held that Scott, and therefore all slaves, were not citizens and therefore had no right to sue in court. The Court also ruled that Scott was not free simply because he had lived for a time in free territory. Finally, the Court found that the Missouri Compromise was unconstitutional. Slaves were the property of their owners, reasoned the Court, and Congress could not deprive people of their property without due process of law according to the Fifth Amendment.

**Main Idea
CONNECTIONS**

How did antislavery forces respond to the Dred Scott decision?

In his written opinion on the case, Chief Justice Roger Taney stated that "the right of property in a slave is distinctly and expressly affirmed in the Constitution." Furthermore, he added:

> **AMERICAN VOICES** "No word can be found in the Constitution, which gives Congress a greater power over slave property, or which entitles property of that kind to less protection than property of any other description. The only power conferred [granted] is the power coupled with the duty of guarding and protecting the owner in his rights."
>
> —*Chief Justice Roger Taney*

Antislavery forces were disgusted with the Dred Scott decision. It meant that Congress had no power to ban slavery anywhere, including the territories. President Buchanan, however, supported the Court's decision. He hoped that the national government would no longer be required to deal with the slavery issue.

The Lecompton Constitution

Events soon proved, however, that the political fight over slavery had not ended. In the fall of 1857, a small proslavery group in Kansas elected members to a convention to write their own constitution. A constitution was required to attain statehood. Called the Lecompton constitution, it was as proslavery as its namesake, the proslavery capital. Most Kansans were opposed to slavery and refused even to vote on the constitution when it was offered for their approval. Yet President Buchanan, hoping that the problem of slavery in Kansas would go away as soon as the territory became a state, endorsed the Lecompton constitution.

Though Buchanan was a Democrat, his total disregard for popular sovereignty and the rule of law was too much for northern Democrats to swallow. Democratic leader Stephen Douglas spoke sharply against the Lecompton constitution and criticized Buchanan for accepting it. Congress returned the constitution to Kansas for another vote, and the people soundly defeated it in August 1858. For the time being, Kansas remained a territory where slavery was legal according to the Dred Scott decision. In reality, however, the free-soiler majority prohibited it.

The Lincoln-Douglas Debates

Senator Douglas denounced the Lecompton constitution in part out of principle and in part because he had to be responsive to public opinion. He faced a difficult reelection campaign in Illinois in 1858, where opinion on slavery was sharply divided.

A short, stout man, Douglas was known as "the Little Giant." Like many whites in the 1850s, he believed that white Americans were superior to African Americans. He went even further, however, and tolerated slavery, because he believed in the absolute right of white citizens to choose the kind of society and government they wanted.

Though Douglas was one of the most important senators in the nation's history, today he is overshadowed by the man the Republican party nominated to run against him, Abraham Lincoln. The campaign drew nationwide attention when Douglas and Lincoln met in a series of seven debates on the issue of slavery in the territories.

Abraham Lincoln had been born in a log cabin in Kentucky in 1809. As a young man, he studied law and worked at various jobs, including postmaster and rail splitter. In 1837 he settled in Springfield, Illinois, where he practiced law. He served one term in Congress in the 1840s. Known for his strength of character, Lincoln won further recognition for his skillful performance in the Lincoln-Douglas debates.

The debates between Lincoln and Douglas were covered in newspapers throughout the country. Many reporters commented on the great difference in appearances of the two candidates. While Douglas was stout, Lincoln was tall, awkward, and thin. While Douglas dressed in an elegant new suit, Lincoln purposely wore plain, everyday clothes.

The Lincoln and Douglas debates highlighted two important principles in American government, majority rule and minority rights. Douglas supported popular sovereignty. He believed that the majority of people of a state or territory could do anything they wished, including making slavery legal. Lincoln, on the other hand, did not believe that a majority should have the power to deny a minority of their rights to life, liberty, and the pursuit of happiness.

Despite this fundamental difference, Lincoln actually shared many of Douglas's views on African Americans. During one of the debates Lincoln stated: "I am not nor ever have been in favor of bringing about in any way the social and political equality of the white and black races." He did not even propose forbidding slavery in the South because he thought the federal government did not have that power. He hoped that if slavery were confined to the states in which it already existed, it would eventually die out.

Yet Lincoln, like millions of other Northerners, knew that slavery was wrong. Lincoln considered slavery a moral issue. During the debates against Douglas, he quoted both the Bible and the Declaration of Independence to justify his stand:

AMERICAN VOICES ❝The Savior [Jesus] . . . said, 'As your Father in Heaven is perfect, be ye also perfect.' He set that up as a standard, and [whoever] did most towards reaching that standard attained the highest degree of moral perfection. So I say in relation to the principle that all men are created equal, let it be as nearly reached as we can.❞

—*Abraham Lincoln*

In a now-famous speech in Springfield in June 1858, Lincoln foresaw the confrontation that the country would soon face. He stated:

AMERICAN VOICES ❝A house divided against itself cannot stand. I believe this government cannot endure, permanently half slave and half free. I do not expect the Union to be dissolved—I do not expect the house to fall—but I do expect it will cease to be divided. It will become all one thing, or all the other.❞

—*Abraham Lincoln*

Though Lincoln gained a large following in 1858, Douglas won the election. In a letter to a friend after losing the election Lincoln wrote that he was glad to have participated in the election. "It gave me a hearing on the great and durable question of the age. . . . I believe I have made some marks which will tell for the cause of

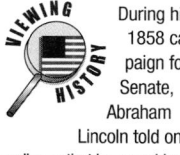
During his 1858 campaign for the Senate, Abraham Lincoln told one audience that he was driven "by something higher than an anxiety for office"—desire to defend the principle of equality established by the Declaration of Independence. **Government** *How did Lincoln's political stance on slavery differ from his personal belief?*

Using the Internet

Prepare a Summary

Objective Use the Internet to prepare a summary of newspaper articles about John Brown.

1. See the *America: Pathways to the Present* Web site at

http://www.Pathways.phschool.com

for the URL of the master list of John Brown articles.

2. Use links to explore the articles. Choose three or four that you like.

3. Take detailed notes on each article. Pay attention to the attitude of the writer. Is the depiction of John Brown favorable or unfavorable? How do you know?

4. Prepare a summary on the general themes of these articles. Use quotations from the articles to support your ideas. Compare your summary with your classmates'.

Answer to . . .

Viewing History Politically, Lincoln was not opposed to the existence of slavery, believing the government had no power to forbid it. Personally, he felt slavery was immoral.

Behind John Brown's "glittering, gray-blue eyes" lurked a cool willingness to break the law in order to end slavery. *Culture How did John Brown's raid deepen the divisions between the North and South?*

John Brown's Raid

On October 16, 1859, an event took place that raised the worst fears of the South. Three years after his raid along Pottawatomie Creek in Kansas, John Brown attacked the federal **arsenal** at Harpers Ferry, Virginia. (An arsenal is a place where weapons are made or stored.) With him were 21 men, including five African Americans. Supported by abolitionists in the North, Brown and his followers hoped to seize the weapons and give them to enslaved people. They had a dream of an uprising of enslaved Americans that would end slavery, punish slaveholders, and lead the United States to moral renewal.

Alerted to the attack, United States troops under the command of Colonel Robert E. Lee surrounded the arsenal. The troops killed half of Brown's men, including two of his sons, before the rest surrendered. Convicted of treason, John Brown was sentenced to be hanged.

Just before his execution, Brown wrote a brief note. Although he had failed as a soldier, his final message proved him a prophet:

> **AMERICAN VOICES** ❝I John Brown am now quite certain that the crimes of this guilty land will never be purged away; but with Blood.❞
>
> —*John Brown*

Northerners hailed Brown as a martyr to the cause of justice and celebrated him in song. Southerners denounced Brown as a tool of Republican abolitionists. In short, Brown's raid only deepened the division, distrust, and anger between North and South.

civil liberty long after I am gone." To another friend he wrote, "The cause of civil liberty must not be surrendered at the end of one, or even, one hundred defeats." Despite his defeat, the tall, gaunt lawyer from Springfield earned a reputation for eloquence and moral commitment that would serve him and the Republicans well just two years later.

SECTION 3 REVIEW

Comprehension

1. **Key Terms** Define: (a) free soiler; (b) *Scott v. Sandford;* (c) arsenal.

2. **Summarizing the Main Idea** What impact did the violent clashes between 1856 and 1860 have on the antislavery and proslavery forces in the United States?

3. **Organizing Information** Create a graphic organizer comparing and contrasting the views of Lincoln and Douglas on slavery.

Critical Thinking

4. **Analyzing Time Lines** Review the time line at the start of the section. What were the main points of the Supreme Court's decision in *Scott v. Sandford?*

5. **Testing Conclusions** Explain how the events in Kansas and Congress in 1856 support the message of this section's title: "The System Fails."

Writing Activity

6. **Writing an Expository Essay** Write an essay describing what you think was the greatest impact of John Brown's raid.

▶ RESOURCE OPTIONS

Teaching Resources

📁 **Quiz** Units 3–4 folder, p. 50

Student Performance Pack

💫 **Guide to the Essentials** Chapter 11, Section 3 (English and Spanish)

Media and Technology

Biography John Anthony Copeland, Jr., found on Resource Pro, profiles one of the five African Americans who helped John Brown in his famous raid.

1860 Lincoln elected President	1860 South Carolina becomes the first state to secede	1861 Confederacy created	1861 Confederate forces bombard Fort Sumter

1860   **1861**   **1862**

4 A Nation Divided Against Itself

SECTION PREVIEW

Objectives

1 Describe the outcome and the importance of the election of 1860.
2 Explain why states of the Lower South seceded from the Union.
3 Summarize events leading to the start of the war at Fort Sumter.
4 **Key Terms** Define: Border States; Lower South; secessionist; Confederate States of America; Fort Sumter; Upper South.

Main Idea

Seven southern states left the Union after Abraham Lincoln was elected as President. While politicians and the people debated how to respond, the first shots were fired, and the nation plunged into civil war.

Reading Strategy

Outlining Information As you read the section, create an outline of the events leading up to the outbreak of war.

A s the year 1860 began, it was clear that the majority of Northerners would not accept leadership by a Southerner. Southerners, likewise, announced that they would not accept a leader from the ranks of the antislavery Republicans in the North. The next presidential election was looming. Could the Union survive it?

The Election of 1860

When the Democratic party met in Charleston, South Carolina, in April 1860 to nominate its candidate for President, it was still a national party. For ten days, delegates from both North and South debated the issue that had divided the nation for a decade: slavery in the territories. Southern Democrats argued that the party should support protection of slavery in the territories, while Democrats from the North stood by the doctrine of popular sovereignty.

Unable to gain control of the voting, delegates from eight southern states left the convention and agreed to meet separately to nominate their own candidate. In the months ahead the split within the Democratic party became official. Southern Democrats nominated as their candidate John C. Breckinridge, who was committed to an aggressive policy of expanding slavery in the territories. Northern Democrats nominated Stephen Douglas of Illinois, who supported popular sovereignty.

In the meantime, moderate Southerners who had belonged to the Whig and American parties met in Baltimore to form their own new party. These Southerners, along with a few politicians from the **Border States** (Delaware, Maryland, Kentucky, and Missouri), formed the Constitutional Union party. They chose John Bell of Tennessee, a moderate slaveholder, as their presidential nominee.

When the Republican party convened in Chicago to nominate their candidate, the man favored to win was William Henry Seward of New York. As the days went by, however, many delegates began to worry that Seward was too extreme in his antislavery views to attract the voters they needed.

Another Republican candidate, Abraham Lincoln, offered more moderate views on slavery while at the same time standing firmly

A Nation Divided Against Itself

Objectives

You may wish to call students' attention to the objectives in the Section Preview. The objectives are reflected in the main headings of the section.

Bellringer

Ask students for names of nations that are currently fighting or have recently fought a civil war, along with the reasons for the conflict. List responses on the chalkboard as a focus for discussion.

Reading Strategy

Outlining Information Refer to the Reading Strategy in the Section Preview. You may wish to model the outline on the chalkboard. Ask students to suggest events as they read.

LESSON PLAN

Connecting to the Main Idea

1. Focus Point out that the election of a Republican President in 1860 was too much for the South to bear. One by one the southern states seceded from the Union. Ask how the nation finally broke apart.

2. Instruct Discuss why the southern states seceded from the Union. Ask why Southerners felt it was impossible to trust any Republican President. Why were Southerners so outraged by the election of Lincoln? Why did the secessionists feel that it was their legitimate right to withdraw from the Union?

3. Close With the election of Abraham Lincoln in 1860, the southern states no longer felt represented in the Union and decided to secede. After a decade of growing hostility between the North and the South, civil war finally broke out.

Time: 90 minutes.
Activity: Create a political campaign.
Grouping: Groups of four to six students.
Purpose: To help students understand that the primary consideration for presidential candidates in 1860 was how to win in a divided nation, have them select a candidate from this election and develop a political campaign for him.
Roles: Candidates and members of the campaign team (campaign manager, secretary, and personal consultants).
Outcome: Students will define and portray the political strategy of one of the candidates in the 1860 presidential campaign.

Answer to . . .

Comparing Primary Sources
Heyward argues that the election of an abolitionist President means that the South must secede immediately; the merchant argues that it is in the interests of both sides to support the country and the President.

COMPARING PRIMARY SOURCES

SOUTHERN SECESSION

Lincoln's election in November 1860 led South Carolina to plan secession.

For Secession	Against Secession
"In January next we shall take leave of the Union and shall construct with our sister Cotton States a government for ourselves. The condition of affairs at the North since the election of an Abolitionist for President makes it necessary for us to get away as quickly as possible." —*E. B. Heyward, South Carolina cotton planter, letter to a friend in Connecticut, November 20, 1860*	"I am for the preservation of the Union; I desire to witness no separation of the States; I have a pecuniary [financial] interest both in the South and in the North. . . . Men of South Carolina . . . No harm will come to you. Mr. Lincoln and his party are your safest and best friends. They will do what is right." —*Anonymous northern merchant, New York Tribune, November 22, 1860*

ANALYZING VIEWPOINTS Compare the main arguments made by the two writers.

against its spread. Though Lincoln was little-known outside his own state, the convention-goers nominated him for President.

The November election made absolutely clear that there were no longer any national political parties. The division between North and South was beyond repair. In the South, the race was between Bell and Breckinridge. (Lincoln's name did not even appear on many southern ballots.) In the North, voters chose between Lincoln and Douglas. Lincoln won in every free state except New Jersey, which he split with Douglas. Breckinridge, meanwhile, won North Carolina, Arkansas, Delaware, Maryland, and the states of the **Lower South**—Texas, Louisiana, Mississippi, Alabama, Florida, Georgia, and South Carolina. Bell carried three Border States, Tennessee, Kentucky, and Virginia. Douglas took Missouri.

Lincoln captured the presidency without winning a single electoral vote in the South. While gaining only 39 percent of the popular vote, Lincoln had won 180 electoral votes—the majority he needed to win. His was a decisive victory, but a sectional one.

The Lower South Secedes

Southerners were outraged that a President could be elected without any southern electoral votes. The government of the nation, it seemed, had passed completely out of their hands. Planters and others who backed slavery called for the South to secede, or withdraw, from the Union. Wrote an Augusta, Georgia, newspaper editor:

AMERICAN VOICES "[The Republican party] stands forth today, hideous, revolting, loathsome, a menace not only to the Union of these states, but to Society, to Liberty, and to Law."

—*Augusta, Georgia, newspaper editor*

The **secessionists,** or those who wanted the South to secede, argued that since the states had voluntarily joined the United States, they also could choose to leave it. Edmund Ruffin of Virginia, a typical secessionist, stated that because the Republicans controlled the federal government, they could act constitutionally and legally "to produce the most complete subjection and political bondage, degradation, and ruin of the South."

South Carolina left the Union officially on December 20, 1860. Over the next few weeks, so did six other states of the Lower South. In early February 1861, delegates from the seven states met in Montgomery, Alabama. There they created a new nation, the **Confederate States of America,** also called the Confederacy, shown on the map at the end of this section. As their president they elected Jefferson Davis of Mississippi.

The War Starts

The question on everyone's mind as the winter dragged on was what the federal government would do about the secession of seven of its member states. President Buchanan believed that secession from the Union was illegal. Still, he declared in his message to Congress that he would not try to prevent secession by force.

Last-Minute Compromises Fail Some politicians proposed compromises with the South, including Senator John J. Crittenden of Kentucky. Crittenden proposed a plan by which slavery would be recognized in territories south of 36° 30' N. President-elect Lincoln opposed the plan, however, and convinced the Senate to reject it.

TEST PREPARATION

Have students read the paragraphs under "The Lower South Secedes," including the quotation, on this page and then answer the question below.

Based on the writings of the secessionists, you can tell that—

A they liked the North, but disliked Republicans.

B they felt that since Lincoln had been legally elected, they had to accept him.

C they felt a Republican President would support their interests.

(D) they believed that one of the Republican party's goals was to ruin the South as they knew it.

FACT Finder
Events Leading to the Civil War

Date	Event
November 6, 1860	Abraham Lincoln is elected President without the support of the southern states.
December 18, 1860	Senator John J. Crittenden of Kentucky proposes a plan that would recognize slavery in territories south of 36°30′ N. The Senate rejects the plan on Lincoln's advice.
December 20, 1860 to February 8, 1861	South Carolina secedes from the United States, followed by Mississippi, Florida, Alabama, Georgia, Louisiana, and Texas. They form the Confederate States of America.
February 9, 1861	Jefferson Davis is elected as the Confederacy's provisional president.
March 4, 1861	Lincoln is sworn into office. He refuses to recognize the Confederacy.
April 12–13, 1861	Confederate General P.G.T. Beauregard opens fire on Fort Sumter. Major Robert Anderson surrenders.
April 15, 1861	Lincoln declares a state of insurrection, or rebellion, and calls for volunteers to fight.

Interpreting Tables By the time Lincoln was elected President, tension between the North and the South was already high. No single event led to the Civil War. *Government At what point did Lincoln declare a state of civil war?*

Other Americans, including Horace Greeley, editor of the *New York Tribune*, proposed that the seceding states be allowed to go in peace. Many opposed this option, especially those who believed strongly in the Union. Northern businesspeople also objected to secession, fearing that profits from their business with the South would be lost. They insisted that the southern states should be forced to return to the Union. After all, how could the United States continue to function as a country if its members could come and go as they pleased?

The only man in the nation who could decide the government's response left his home in Springfield, Illinois, in early 1861, bound for the White House. Abraham Lincoln believed secession was wrong. He was also strongly committed to stopping the expansion of slavery. Rather than focus on the reasons behind the South's secession, however, the President-elect emphasized his duty to enforce the laws of the United States.

In his Inaugural Address on March 4, 1861, Lincoln spoke directly to the Southerners. He stated, "In your hands, my dissatisfied fellow-countrymen, and not in mine, is the momentous issue of civil war. . . . You have no oath . . . to destroy the government, while I shall have the most solemn one to preserve, protect, and defend it." Lincoln concluded his address with the following plea:

KEY DOCUMENTS "We must not be enemies. Though passion may have strained, it must not break our bonds of affection. The mystic chords of memory, stretching from every battlefield and patriot grave to every living heart . . . will yet swell the chorus of the Union when again touched, as surely they will be, by the better angels of our nature."

—*Abraham Lincoln*, First Inaugural Address

Fort Sumter As Lincoln spoke those words, the attention of the nation was on **Fort Sumter,** a federal fort in the harbor of Charleston, South Carolina. A federal ship sent to supply the fort in January had been forced to retreat when Confederate forces fired on it. Now federal soldiers under the command of Major Robert Anderson were running out of supplies. If Lincoln did not resupply the fort, it would have to be abandoned, thus leaving it to the Confederates.

Lincoln struggled over a decision. He had pledged to Southerners in his Inaugural Address that "the government will not assail you. You can have no conflict without being yourselves the aggressors." But he had also taken an oath to defend the property of the government. Fort Sumter stood as a vital symbol of the Union he had sworn to preserve. To fight to keep the fort, or even to send new troops there, might make

Main Idea CONNECTIONS
Why was Fort Sumter a symbol of the Union?

Answers to
SECTION 4 REVIEW

1. 1. (a) Border States, see p. 333; (b) Lower South, see p. 334; (c) secessionist, see p. 334; (d) Confederate States of America, see p. 334; (e) Fort Sumter, see p. 335; (f) Upper South, see p. 336.

2. These states felt that since they had voluntarily joined the United States, they also could leave it. They refused to remain in a Union run by the antislavery Republicans.

3. Lower South: Texas, Louisiana, Mississippi, Alabama, Florida, Georgia, and South Carolina; Upper South: Virginia, North Carolina, Tennessee, and Arkansas; Border States: Delaware, Maryland, Kentucky, and Missouri.

4. The southern states began to secede, or leave the Union. They soon formed the Confederacy.

5. The Second War for Independence: Southerners felt they needed to gain independence from the Union and govern themselves. The War of the Rebellion: The Northerners felt no state had the power to defy the Constitution; they branded all who tried as rebels.

6. Answers will vary but essays should include the fact that many saw Fort Sumter as a vital symbol of the Union. By firing on this federal property, the Confederate states had committed an undeniable act of open rebellion.

Answer to . . .

Map Skills Virginia, North Carolina, Tennessee, and Arkansas.

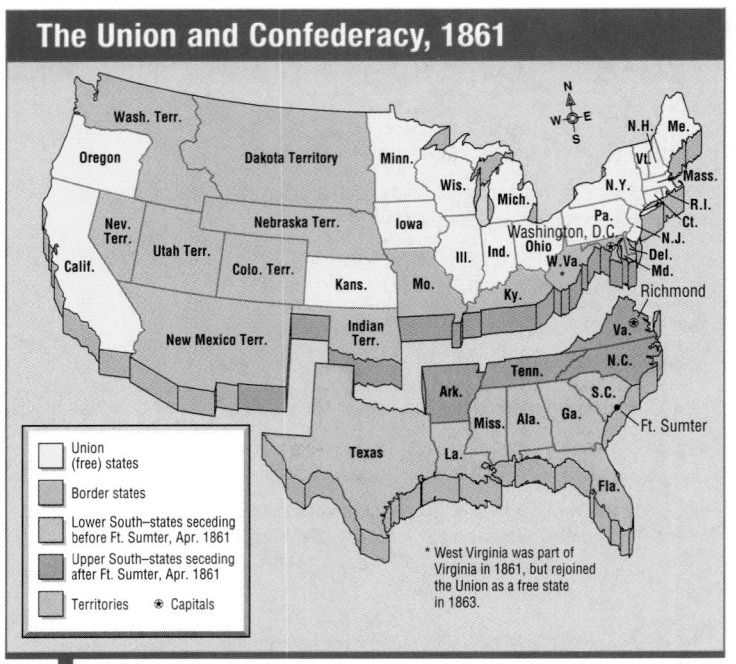

The Union and Confederacy, 1861

* West Virginia was part of Virginia in 1861, but rejoined the Union as a free state in 1863.

Legend:
- Union (free) states
- Border states
- Lower South—states seceding before Ft. Sumter, Apr. 1861
- Upper South—states seceding after Ft. Sumter, Apr. 1861
- Territories ● Capitals

MAP skills South Carolina was the first state to secede from the Union. It was soon joined by other states, however, making the Confederate republic one of the largest republics in the world. *Place* Name the states that seceded after the surrender of Fort Sumter.

Carolina that he was sending food, but no soldiers or arms, to Fort Sumter. On April 10, before supplies could arrive, Confederate president Davis ordered General P.G.T. Beauregard to demand that Fort Sumter surrender. If Anderson refused, Beauregard was to take it by force.

Anderson did refuse, and on April 12, 1861, Beauregard opened fire on the fort. After a 24-hour bombardment, Anderson surrendered Fort Sumter to Confederate troops.

By firing on federal property, the Confederate states had committed an act of open rebellion. As the defender of the Constitution, Lincoln had no choice but to respond. When he called for volunteers, Southerners saw his action as an act of war against them. The **Upper South** states of Virginia, North Carolina, Tennessee, and Arkansas, now joined the lower South in the Confederacy. For the time being, the four Border States remained uncommitted to either side in the struggle.

Eighty-four years after it had declared its independence, the United States had come apart. The fighting at Fort Sumter in April 1861 proved that the division between the North and South could not be settled peacefully. Now a new question was raised: Could the Union be restored by force?

him responsible for starting the war. Yet to abandon the fort would mean acknowledging the authority of the Confederate government.

Remaining true to both of his pledges, on April 6 Lincoln told the governor of South

SECTION 4 REVIEW

Comprehension

1. *Key Terms* Define: (a) Border States; (b) Lower South; (c) secessionist; (d) Confederate States of America; (e) Fort Sumter; (f) Upper South.

2. *Summarizing the Main Idea* Summarize why the southern states seceded from the Union.

3. *Organizing Information* Create a graphic organizer listing the states included in each of the following categories: the *Lower South*, the *Upper South*, and the *Border States*.

Critical Thinking

4. *Analyzing Time Lines* Review the time line at the start of this section. What impact did Lincoln's election in 1860 have on the South?

5. *Recognizing Ideologies* Southerners called the Civil War the Second War for Independence. Northerners called it the War of the Rebellion. Explain how each name reflects the point of view of the people who used it.

Writing Activity

6. *Writing an Expository Essay* Write an essay highlighting the importance of what took place at Fort Sumter.

RESOURCE OPTIONS

Teaching Resources

📁 **Quiz** Units 3–4 folder, p. 52

📁 **Chapter Tests Forms A and B** Chapter Test folder

Student Performance Pack

⊕ **Guide to the Essentials** Chapter 11, Section 4 (English and Spanish)

Standardized Test Preparation Handbook

Media and Technology

🎧 **Guided Reading Audiotapes** Chapter 11 Summary (English and Spanish)

Student Edition on Audiotape Chapter 11

💿 **Test Bank CD-ROM; Interactive Student Tutorial CD-ROM** Chapter Test

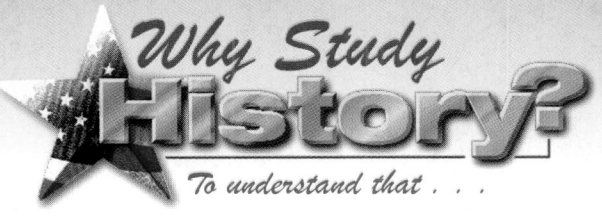

Why Study History?

To understand that . . .

The Debate over States' Rights Continues

A controversy over public land use focuses on states' rights, the issue that divided the United States in the mid-1800s.

The debate over federal power led to violence in Kansas in 1856.

Stunning snow-covered peaks and alpine flowers reward hikers in Colorado's Rocky Mountain National Park. Ancient Indian ruins and petrified sand dunes amaze visitors to Arizona's Canyon de Chelly. Mountains and seashore compete for tourists' attention in Maine's Acadia National Park. Each year, millions of people from all over the world experience the wilderness areas preserved in our national parks and monuments.

Who would imagine that these beautiful areas could be the subject of a bitter political struggle? Yet the federal government is caught in a tug-of-war with western states for control over public lands.

The Impact Today

Throughout American history, there have been two different views on the relationship between the states and the federal government. One view, generally called states' rights, argues that the federal government's powers are limited to the powers that the Constitution specifically gives to it and that states hold all powers that the Constitution does not specifically deny to them. (In the past, some believers in states' rights have also argued that states have the right to nullify federal laws or even to secede from the Union.) The other view, in contrast, tends to favor national power over that of the states.

Across the nation, states exercise their rights in areas such as education, public safety, and highway construction. In the West, many states are also trying to determine the use of public lands. The federal government owns more than 50 percent of land in the West, which it administers as national parks, forests, and monuments. The western states have no control over this land, even though it lies within their borders.

A "sagebrush rebellion" has been brewing in the West for a number of years. Many westerners seek control over the public lands within their states and over laws regulating land use. The issue exploded in 1996, when President Clinton set aside 1.7 million acres of Utah's desert plateaus and canyonlands to create the Grand Staircase-Escalante National Monument. Some Americans called the action a federal "land grab" that deprived Utah of its rights. Others applauded the move because it preserved a beautiful wilderness area.

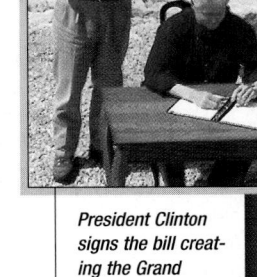

President Clinton signs the bill creating the Grand Staircase-Escalante National Monument.

The Impact on You

What control, if any, should states have over the use of federal lands within their borders? Discuss the issue with a small group of classmates and see if your group can agree on a common position.

Class Discussion

Discuss public land use and states' rights with the class. For a more thorough examination of the issue, see the activity folder in the Resource Options below.

ACTIVITY
STUDENT PARTICIPATION

Writing a Proposal
Ask students to read the text. Then divide the class into three groups. Have each group create a proposal (pro or con) on one of the following topics:

- **making more land available for multiple uses, such as logging and hunting**
- **transferring control of all park lands to the states**
- **turning more public lands into national parks**

Have each group discuss the pros and cons of its issue before writing.

Follow up Ask groups to present their work for classroom debate. Then take a vote on each issue.

Using the Internet
 Students can learn more about the public lands debate by exploring links in the *America: Pathways to the Present* Web site at:

http://www.Pathways.phschool.com

Assessment
See the Lesson Plans folder, pp. 24–27, for rubrics on assessing Class Participation Projects.

RESOURCE OPTIONS

Teaching Resources

Why Study History? Activity The Debate over States' Rights Continues, found in the Why Study History? folder, p. 12, provides an activity to help students better understand the controversy over public lands.

Media and Technology

 AmericanHeritage® CD-ROM

Time Tour The Nation Today and Tomorrow: Toward a New Century

Key Terms

Students should refer to the definitions of the key terms in the chapter to write sentences that show an understanding of the events that broke the nation apart and sent it to war.

Comprehension

1. It violated the basic principles of the United States and denied people their right to make choices.

2. Southerners viewed slaves as property. They thought stopping slavery was morally wrong because it interfered with the right to own property, and that the government should protect this right.

3. The North was more urban and industrial and had nine out of the nation's ten largest cities; in the North, railroads transported goods, while in the South, crops were transported by water; telegraph wires allowed faster communications in the North; the North had about five times more factories, fewer slaves, and less cotton.

4. It addressed only the issue of California. Stephen Douglas went on to undo the Compromise of 1850 by reopening the issue of slavery in the territories with the Kansas-Nebraska Act.

5. They adopted the nativist ideas of the American party and drew voters away from that party.

6. Because of a series of murderous raids and violent acts in the territory.

7. For Lincoln, slavery was a moral issue. He knew slavery was wrong and hoped it would die out if confined. Douglas tolerated slavery. He believed in the absolute right of white citizens to choose the society and government they wanted.

8. Lincoln won by a majority of electoral votes, but won no votes in the Lower South.

9. Lincoln was an antislavery President elected by Northerners. The South no longer felt it had a voice in government.

Chapter Summary

The major concepts of Chapter 11 are presented below. See also *Guide to the Essentials of American History* or *Interactive Student Tutorial CD-ROM*, which contains interactive review activities, time lines, helpful hints, and test practice for Chapter 11.

Reviewing the Main Ideas

During the 1850s, politicians could not resolve the tensions that emerged between North and South over the issue of slavery—especially the issue of slavery in the new territories to the west. By 1860, neither side was willing to compromise. The following year the Civil War broke out.

Section 1: Two Nations?

In the 1850s growing numbers of Americans were convinced that the North and South were moving in different directions. Each side saw the other as a threat to the American way of life.

Section 2: New Political Parties

A compromise during the 1850s failed to end disagreement over slavery in the territories. Meanwhile, the existing political party system broke down as new political parties arose.

Section 3: The System Fails

A series of violent clashes between antislavery and proslavery forces took place between 1856 and 1860. Americans on each side of the slavery issue became convinced that the other side was acting against law and morality.

Section 4: A Nation Divided Against Itself

Seven southern states left the Union after Abraham Lincoln was elected President. While politicians and the people debated how to respond, the first shots were fired, and the nation plunged into civil war.

A controversy over public land use focuses on states' rights, the issue that divided the United States in the mid-1800s and led to the Civil War. Today the federal government is caught in a tug-of-war with western states for control over public lands.

Using Graphic Organizers

• Lincoln elected President.
• Southerners refuse to accept outcome of election.
• Southern states begin to leave Union.
• Southern states create the Confederate States of America.
• Violence occurs at Fort Sumter.
• Civil War begins.

Key Terms

For each of the terms below, write a sentence explaining how it relates to this chapter.

1. Fugitive Slave Act
2. nativism
3. states' rights
4. Kansas-Nebraska Act
5. *Scott* v. *Sandford*
6. free soiler
7. Border States
8. Lower South
9. Upper South
10. arsenal
11. prejudice
12. Confederate States of America

Comprehension

1. Why did slavery seem threatening to Northerners?

2. How did Southerners respond to Northerners' attacks on slavery?

3. Compare the economic development of the North and South.

4. Why was the Compromise of 1850 a failure?

5. What issues helped the Republicans in the 1850s?

6. Why was Kansas called "Bleeding Kansas"?

7. How did Lincoln and Douglas differ in their views?

8. Lincoln's victory in the election of 1860 was "a decisive victory, but a sectional one." Explain this statement.

9. Why did Lincoln's election prompt the secession of southern states?

Using Graphic Organizers

On a separate sheet of paper, copy the graphic organizer below. Fill in the empty boxes with at least one effect from the preceding box and/ or cause relating to the following box.

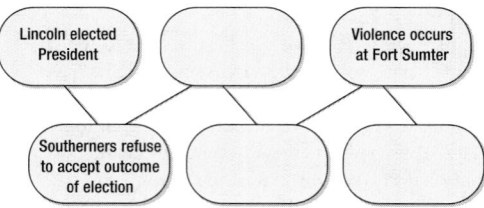

Analyzing Political Cartoons ▶

1. Examine the images in the cartoon.
   (a) What is the eagle's nest?
   (b) What do the eggs represent?
   (c) Why are some eggs rotten?
   (d) Why are they hatching?

2. Explain the action of the eagle and what it symbolizes.

3. Read the caption and state the cartoonist's message.

Critical Thinking

1. *Applying the Chapter Skill* Review the excerpt from Lincoln's First Inaugural Address on page 335. (a) What is the main topic of the excerpt? (b) Give evidence that Lincoln is trying to appeal to the patriotic feelings of his listeners.

2. *Determining Relevance* The idea that states have the right to secede did not spring from out of nowhere. What other beliefs concerning government that you have read about are related to it?

3. *Demonstrating Reasoned Judgment* Lincoln was elected only by voters from the North. How might voters in the United States respond today if a President were elected by only one region? What challenges might a future President encounter if he or she had only regional support?

4. *Identifying Central Issues* How did the Supreme Court's Dred Scott decision further inflame the slavery issue?

THE EAGLE'S NEST.
"THE UNION—IT MUST AND SHALL BE PRESERVED"

INTERNET ACTIVITY

For your portfolio:
CREATE A TIME LINE

Access Prentice Hall's *America: Pathways to the Present* site at **www.Pathways.phschool.com** for the specific URL to complete the activity. Additional resources and related Web sites are also available.

Read the account of Dred Scott's life and the Supreme Court ruling on *Scott* v. *Sandford*. Create a time line chronicling Dred Scott's life. Then write a paragraph explaining how the events of Scott's life and the ruling reflect the attitudes toward slavery prevailing in the early to mid-1800s.

ANALYZING DOCUMENTS ◀▶ INTERPRETING DATA

Turn to the map on page 336.

1. According to this map, southern states seceded from the Union (a) before the attack on Ft. Sumter. (b) after the attack on Ft. Sumter. (c) before and after the attack on Ft. Sumter. (d) before the election of 1860.

2. Which of the following states was part of the Upper South?

   (a) Alabama (b) Kentucky
   (c) Tennessee (d) South Carolina.

3. *Writing* Washington, D.C., the capital of the Union, was surrounded on three sides by the Border State of Maryland. Describe why this might have been a difficult situation for the Union.

Connecting to Today

Making Comparisons
During his campaign in 1860, Lincoln was portrayed as an ordinary American who was honest, self-made, and hard-working. Compare this portrayal to that of a candidate in a recent presidential election. Are there any similarities? If so, what does this reveal about American values?

INTERNET ACTIVITY

Answers will vary. Paragraphs should show an understanding of how Scott's suit, the support he received during the case, and his ultimate freedom reflect the fact that many people were opposed to slavery. The Supreme Court ruling reflected the prevailing attitude that slaves were property and were denied human rights.

Analyzing Political Cartoons

1. (a) The United States. (b) The individual states. (c) They are slave-holding states. (d) Slavery and rebellion.

2. It is protecting its nest; the government is protecting the Union.

3. The federal government must preserve the Union.

Critical Thinking

1. (a) His duty to enforce the laws of the country, but his preference for working out differences peacefully. (b) He refers to past battles and soldiers who have died for the unification of the country.

2. The social contract, nullification, and states' rights.

3. Voters would probably feel that they had lost their voice in government. A President with only regional appeal would encounter great difficulties getting bills through Congress.

4. Antislavery forces were opposed to the Dred Scott decision because it sent the message that the federal government had no power to keep the territories slavery-free.

Interpreting Data

1. c
2. c
3. The city could have been surrounded by a Confederate army, making it impossible to get Union troops in and out of the capital.

Connecting to Today

Students' answers will vary. They should discuss the way candidates are portrayed today in the media.

The Civil War, 1861–1865

Managing Time and Instruction

INSTRUCTION SUPPORT
These materials for instruction are provided for **each section** in the **Teaching Resources.** See **Units 3–4 folder for Enrichment Support:**

- Reproducible Lesson Plans in Lesson Plans folder
- Learning Styles Lesson Plans in Learning Styles Lesson Plans folder
- Big Idea Graphic Organizers in Big Idea Graphic Organizer folder
- Guided Reading and Review
- Quizzes
- Test Preparation Practice booklet

DAILY LESSON	ENRICHMENT SUPPORT
1 From Bull Run to Antietam *(pp. 341–348)*	• Comparing Primary Sources, On the Purpose of the Civil War, Units 3–4 folder, pp. 68–69 • Literature Activity, The First Battle of Bull Run, Units 3–4 folder, p. 70 • Visual Learning Activity, A British View of the Civil War, found on **Resource Pro** • Biography, General Robert E. Lee, Units 3–4 folder, p. 67 • Critical Thinking Activity, Recognizing Bias: Six Months on the Potomac, found on **Resource Pro**
2 Life Behind the Lines *(pp. 349–356)*	• Biography, Mary Elizabeth Bowser, found on **Resource Pro** • Key Documents, Emancipation Proclamation, Learning with Documents folder, p. 89 • Literature Activity, Diary from Dixie, found on **Resource Pro**
3 The Tide of War Turns *(pp. 360–366)*	• Skills for Life Activity, Units 3–4 folder, p. 71 • Nystrom *Atlas of Our Country,* A Divided Nation, pp. 26–27 • Lasting Impact Activity, The Lasting Impact of the Siege of Vicksburg, History's Lasting Impact folder, pp. 8–9
4 A New Birth of Freedom *(pp. 367–372)*	• Visual Learning Activity, Defending Atlanta, Learning with Documents folder, p. 54 • Primary Source Activity, A Teenager's Account of War, found on **Resource Pro** • Americans Remember the Civil War, Why Study History? folder, p. 13

Running Out of Time?

- Use Tape 2, "Division and Uneasy Reunion, 1848–1877," from **Visions of America** videotapes series.
- Use Chapter 12 Summary, from **Guide to the Essentials of American History (English and Spanish).**

Companion Web Site

The companion Web site offers online links for all chapter review activities. It also provides key content links and structured support for this chapter for both teachers and students.

http://www.Pathways.phschool.com

Media and Technology

For the Student

Interactive Student Tutorial CD-ROM Chapter 12

Student Edition on Audiotape Chapter 12

American Heritage® CD-ROM

Guided Reading Audiotapes (English and Spanish) Chapter 12

For the Teacher

Resource Pro CD-ROM Chapter 12

Test Bank CD-ROM Chapter 12

Listening to Literature Audiotapes *Timeless Voices, Timeless Themes* "An Occurrence at Owl Creek Bridge" by Ambrose Bierce

Listening to Music CD "Bonnets of Blue," by Frank Johnson

Color Transparencies Fine Art, D-10
The Way It Works, H-12
Cause and Effect, F-5

Assessment Options

Chapter Test Forms A&B Test Bank CD-ROM booklet

Test Bank CD-ROM Chapter 12

Standardized Test Preparation Handbook

Block Scheduling

Pacing Suggestions

For 90-minute Blocks

- Teach sections 3 and 4 using Transparencies H-13, M-3, M-4, B-4, J-4, and D-11 and the Extended Class Periods Activity on p. 370.
- Teach sections 1 and 2 using the Big Idea Graphic Organizers from Teaching Resources and the Recent Scholarship note on p. 342 for class discussions.

Additional Resources

- Prentice Hall's **American History Block Scheduling Support File** covers over 40 major topics in American history.
- **Prentice Hall United States History Video Collection**™ contains 20 videotapes covering American history from beginnings to present.
- **Visions of America Videotapes and Videodiscs**

Connections to American Literature

from Prentice Hall

America: Pathways to the Present
Classics from the Civil War, pp. 78–79

Prentice Hall Literature *Timeless Voices, Timeless Themes* Recollections of a Private by Warren Lee Goss, p. 499

Prentice Hall Literature Library *The Red Badge of Courage* by Stephen Crane

Additional Resources

For the Student

Bruce Catton, ed. *The American Heritage Picture History of the Civil War.* Outlet Book Co., 1985.

For the Teacher

Benjamin Quarles. *The Negro in the Civil War.* Little, Brown, 1989.

Garry Wills. *Lincoln at Gettysburg: The Words That Remade America.* Simon & Schuster, 1993.

Prentice Hall brings into the classroom the vast archives and scholarship of the nation's premier American history magazine. See "From the Archives of American Heritage®" and "About the Presidents" teaching notes in this chapter.

History Alive!

Teacher's Curriculum Institute, in partnership with Prentice Hall, provides unique materials that engage students with diverse learning styles. See History Alive!® unit on The Civil War and Reconstruction.

Student Performance Pack

Ensures success in three the critical areas of Reading, Test Taking, and English Language Development with the following materials:
- Guide to the Essentials of American History in English and Spanish
- Guided Reading Audiotapes in English and Spanish
- Interactive Student Tutorial CD-ROM
- Test Preparation Handbook
- Test Preparation Practice booklet

The Civil War
1861–1865

Introducing the Chapter

"The Civil War," wrote historian Page Smith, "took place because the southern states felt that they could no longer tolerate their status as members of the Union." After the bloodiest war in the western world in the nineteenth century, enslaved African Americans gained their freedom, while the federal government became a strong force in citizens' lives.

Themes in American History

The theme for this chapter, Economics, is listed at the beginning of this unit. An alternate theme for the chapter is Government. To teach this unit thematically, you may wish to use the Expansion, Reconstruction, Immigration folder in American History Block Scheduling Support.

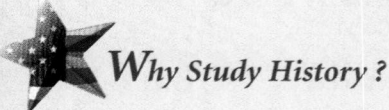 *Why Study History?*

Have students explore suggested ways of connecting the past to the present on page 373.

Answer to . . .

Viewing History Students should use this question as an aid in reading the chapter. The North's economy was based on industry and shipping, while the South's was largely agricultural.

340

CHAPTER FOCUS

This chapter describes the years of the Civil War, the period between 1861 and 1865 when the nation divided and North fought South. The Confederate states of the South struggled to gain self-government and to retain a way of life supported by the institution of slavery. The Northern or Union states battled to maintain the unity of the nation.

 The Why Study History? page at the end of this chapter explores the ways in which Americans today remember the Civil War.

▲
VIEWING HISTORY
Union soldiers practice a drill in this 1861 painting by James Walker. *Culture What regional differences between the North and the South contributed to the Civil War?*

▶ RESOURCE OPTIONS

Teaching Resources

📁 **Big Idea Graphic Organizer** folder Graphic summary of the main idea of the chapter.

📁 **Learning Styles Lesson Plans** folder Alternate lesson plans for diverse learning styles for each chapter.

Media and Technology

 AmericanHeritage® CD-ROM
Time Tour The Nation Torn Apart: Torn by War

  Prentice Hall United States History Video Collection™ Volume 9 *The Civil War*

| July 21, 1861 *First Battle of Bull Run* | March 9, 1862 *Battle between the Merrimack and the Monitor* | April 6–7, 1862 *Battle of Shiloh* | September 17, 1862 *Battle of Antietam* |

| 1861 | 1862 | 1863 |

1 From Bull Run to Antietam

SECTION PREVIEW

Objectives

1 Describe the First Battle of Bull Run and the war preparations of the two sides.
2 Explain the importance of Union victories in the western part of the Confederacy during 1862.
3 Describe the outcome of the battles in the East during 1862.
4 *Key Terms* Define: Civil War; First Battle of Bull Run; casualty; war of attrition; shell; canister; Battle of Shiloh; Battle of Antietam.

Main Idea

Bloody fighting during the first two years of the Civil War made it clear to both the North and the South that the struggle would be long and difficult.

Reading Strategy

Formulating Questions Reread the Main Idea above. Then rewrite it as a question. As you read, take notes about events that help answer the question.

In May 1861, after the Upper South (Virginia, North Carolina, Tennessee, and Arkansas) seceded from the Union, the Confederate states shifted their capital from Montgomery, Alabama, to Richmond, Virginia. By July, some 35,000 northern volunteers were training in Washington, D.C., just 100 miles away. "Forward to Richmond!" urged a headline in the *New York Tribune*. Many Northerners believed that capturing the Confederate capital would bring a quick end to the **Civil War.** No one predicted that this war between the Northern (Union) and Southern (Confederate) states would last from 1861 to 1865.

The First Battle of Bull Run

General Irvin McDowell, commander of the Union troops, was not yet ready to fight. Most of his troops, however, had volunteered for just 90 days and their term of service was nearly finished. "This is not an army," he told the President. "It will take a long time to make an army." Despite this warning, Lincoln ordered his general into action.

On July 16, McDowell marched his poorly prepared army into Virginia. His objective was the town of Manassas, an important railroad junction southwest of Washington. Opposing him was a smaller Confederate force under General P.G.T. Beauregard, the officer who had captured Fort Sumter. The Confederates were camped along Bull Run, a stream that passed about four miles north of Manassas.

The Union army took nearly four days to march 25 miles to Manassas. The soldiers' lack of training contributed to their slow pace. McDowell later explained, "They stopped every moment to pick blackberries or get water. . . . They would not keep in the ranks, order as much as you pleased."

Beauregard had no trouble keeping track of McDowell's progress. Accompanying the troops was a huge crowd of reporters, politicians, and other civilians from Washington, planning to picnic and watch the battle.

McDowell's delays allowed Beauregard to strengthen his army. Some 11,000 additional Confederate troops were packed into freight cars and sped to the scene. (This was the first

More than 90 percent of all battle wounds in the Civil War were caused by bullets such as the newer, more accurate type shown here.

RESOURCE OPTIONS

Teaching Resources

📁 **Reproducible Lesson Plan** Lesson Plans folder, p. 80

📁 **Big Idea Graphic Organizer** Big Idea Graphic Organizer folder, p. 52

📁 **Guided Reading and Review** Units 3–4 folder, p. 59

Media and Technology

🦅 **American**Heritage® **CD-ROM**
Time Tour The Nation Torn Apart: Torn by War

Objectives

You may wish to call students' attention to the objectives in the Section Preview. The objectives are reflected in the main headings of the section.

Bellringer

Tell students that at the start of the Civil War, many Northerners expected the war to be over quickly. Some even called it "the six months' war." Write the words new tactics and new technology on the chalkboard. Ask students to predict how these two factors changed Northerners' expectations.

Reading Strategy

Formulating Questions Refer to the Reading Strategy in the Section Preview. Ask volunteers to share their questions with the class.

LESSON PLAN

Connecting to the Main Idea

1. Focus In the first two years of the Civil War, Union forces tried unsuccessfully to capture the Confederate capital. They did succeed, however, in blockading the coasts of the South and seizing control of the river valleys of its midwestern states.
2. Instruct Discuss with students how the expectations of both sides were called into question in the early days of the war. Why did the Union want to capture the Confederate capital? How did the First Battle of Bull Run affect those calling for a short war? Ask students to discuss the tactics of the war. How did tactics lag behind technology? What caused the lag?
3. Close The first two years of the Civil War were bloody and in some ways indecisive. The Union victories in the west, however, were crucial. In the next section, students will see how the war changed American lives on both sides.

Recent Scholarship

Feared and revered Confederate general Thomas Jackson earned his nickname Stonewall at the First Battle of Bull Run. Confederate General Bee, attempting to rally his men in a sea of swirling chaos, shouted out, "There is Jackson, standing like a stonewall!" At the time, most people assumed that Bee was praising Jackson for his courage and steadfastness. Immediately after the war, however, some Jackson critics offered another interpretation: they contend that Bee wanted Jackson to advance and that his comment was filled with disdain and dismay. James I. Robertson, Jr., in *Stonewall Jackson: The Man, the Soldier, the Legend,* attempts to put that interpretation to rest. Robertson acknowledges that we may never truly know (as Bee was killed that day), but he offers evidence to support the idea that Bee was praising Jackson and his stand.

COMPARING PRIMARY SOURCES

THE AIMS OF THE CIVIL WAR

Throughout the years of quarreling between North and South, Southerners protested repeatedly that Northerners were trampling on their rights, including the right to own slaves as property.

The Aims of the South	The Aims of the North
"We have vainly endeavored to secure tranquillity and obtain respect for the rights to which we were entitled. . . . If . . . the integrity of our territory and jurisdiction [legal authority] be assailed [attacked], it will but remain for us with firm resolve to appeal to arms."	"This war is not waged upon our part in any spirit of oppression, nor for any purpose of conquest or subjugation, nor purpose of overthrowing or interfering with the rights or established institutions of those [seceding] States, but to defend and maintain the supremacy of the Constitution and to preserve the Union."
—President Jefferson Davis, Inaugural Address, February 18, 1861	—House of Representatives, Crittenden Resolution, July 25, 1861

ANALYZING VIEWPOINTS **How did the war aims of each side reflect their quarrel, as described above?**

---

time in the history of warfare that troops were moved by train.) When McDowell finally attacked on July 21, he faced a force nearly the size of his own. Beyond the Confederate lines lay the road to Richmond.

After hours of hard fighting, the Union soldiers appeared to be winning. Their slow advance pushed the Southerners back. However, some Virginia soldiers commanded by General Thomas Jackson refused to give up. Seeing this, another Confederate officer rallied his retreating troops, shouting: "Look! There is Jackson standing like a stone wall! Rally behind the Virginians!" The Union advance was stopped, and "Stonewall" Jackson had earned his nickname.

Tired and discouraged, in late afternoon the Union forces began to fall back. Then a trainload of fresh Confederate troops arrived and launched a counterattack. The orderly Union retreat fell apart. Hundreds of soldiers dropped their weapons and started to run north. They stampeded into the sightseers who had followed them to the battlefield.

As the army disintegrated, soldiers and civilians were caught in a tangle of carriages, wagons, and horses on the narrow road. Terrified that the Confederate troops would catch them, they ran headlong for the safety of Washington. The Confederates, however, were also disorganized and exhausted, and they did not pursue the Union army.

The first major battle of the Civil War thus ended. It became known as the **First Battle of Bull Run,** because the following year another bloody battle occurred at almost exactly the same site.[†]

Compared to what would come, this battle was not a huge action. About 35,000 were involved on each side. The Union suffered about 2,900 **casualties,** the military term for those killed, wounded, captured, or missing in action. Confederate casualties were fewer than 2,000. Later battles would prove much more costly.

Preparing for War

Bull Run caused some Americans on both sides to suspect that winning the war might not be easy. "The fat is in the fire now," wrote Lincoln's private secretary. "The preparations for the war will be continued with increased vigor by the Government." Congress quickly authorized the President to raise a million three-year volunteers. In Richmond, a clerk in the Confederate War Department began to worry, "We are resting on our oars, while the enemy is drilling and equipping 500,000 or 600,000 men."

Strengths and Weaknesses In several respects, the North was much better prepared for war than was the South. For example, the North had more than double the South's miles of railroad track. This made the movement of troops, food, and supplies quicker and easier in the North. More than twice as many factories were in the North as in the South. The North was thus better able to produce the guns, ammunition, shoes, and other items it needed for its army. The North's economy was well balanced between farming and industry, and the North had far more money in its banks than the South. Finally, the North already had a functioning government and, although they were small, an existing army and navy.

[†] Many Civil War battles have two names, one given by the South and the other given by the North. The South tended to connect a battle with the nearest town, the North with some physical feature close by the battlefield.

RESOURCE OPTIONS

Teaching Resources

Comparing Primary Sources On the Purpose of the Civil War, Units 3–4 folder, p. 68–69

Literature Activity The First Battle of Bull Run, Units 3–4 folder, p. 70

Most importantly, two thirds of the nation's population lived in Union states. This made more men available to the Union army, but allowed for a sufficient labor force to remain behind for farm and factory work.

The Confederates had some advantages, too. Because seven of the nation's eight military colleges were in the South, a majority of the nation's trained officers were Southerners. When the war began, most of these officers sided with the Confederacy. In addition, the southern army did not need to initiate any military action to win the war. All they needed to do was maintain a defensive position and keep from being beaten. In contrast, to restore unity to the nation the North would have to attack and conquer the South. Southerners had the added advantage of fighting to preserve their way of life and, they believed, their right to self-government.

Union Military Strategies After the fall of Fort Sumter, President Lincoln ordered a naval blockade of the seceded states. By shutting down the South's ports along the Atlantic Coast and the Gulf of Mexico, Lincoln hoped to keep the South from shipping its cotton to Europe. He also wanted to prevent Southerners from importing the manufactured goods they needed.

Lincoln's blockade was part of a strategy developed by General Winfield Scott, the hero of the Mexican War and commander of all U.S. troops in 1861. The general realized it would take a long time to raise and train an army that was big enough and strong enough to invade the South successfully. Instead, he proposed to choke off the Confederacy with the blockade and to use troops and gunboats to gain control of the Mississippi River. Scott believed this would pressure the South to seek peace and would restore the nation without a bloody war.

Northern newspapers sneered at Scott's strategy. They scornfully named it the Anaconda Plan, after a type of snake that coils around its victims and crushes them to death. Despite the Union defeat at Bull Run, political pressure for action and a quick victory remained strong in 1861. This public clamor for results led to several more attempts to capture Richmond.

Confederate War Strategies The South's basic war plan was to prepare and wait. Many Southerners hoped that Lincoln would let them go in peace. "All we ask is to be let alone," announced Confederate president Jefferson Davis, shortly after secession. He planned for a defensive war.

Southern strategy called for a **war of attrition.** In this type of war, one side inflicts continuous losses on the enemy in order to wear down its strength. Southerners counted on their forces being able to turn back Union attacks until Northerners lost the will to fight. However, this strategy did not take into account the North's tremendous advantage in the resources needed to fight a long war. In the end, it was the North that waged a war of attrition against the South.

Southern strategy in another area also backfired. The South produced some 75 percent of the world's cotton. Historically, much of this cotton supplied the textile mills of Great Britain and France. However, Confederate leaders convinced most southern planters to stop exporting cotton. The South believed that the sudden loss of southern cotton would cause problems for the textile industries in Great Britain and France. They hoped that European industrial leaders would then pressure their governments to help the South gain its independence in exchange for restoring the flow of cotton.

Gunboats gave Union forces a great advantage in river warfare. One Union naval commander was reported to have preached a Sunday sermon to his sailors in which he said, "Let not your heart be troubled. Ye believe in God; believe also in gunboats." **Geography** *Why did the Union want to control the Mississippi River?*

Interdisciplinary

Hot air balloons, first employed in warfare by France in 1794, were used by American balloonist Thaddeus Lowe to provide the Union army with information on Confederate troop movements. Lowe conducted the first airborne operation of the recently invented telegraph. He also brought aloft cameras, which were just coming into popular use, to provide panoramic shots of military positions.

ACTIVITY
LEARNING STYLES

Have each student select four generals discussed in this section and write a first-person statement identifying each general on one side of an index card and listing the general's name on the other side. An example might be "My soldiers stopped the Union advance at the First Battle of Bull Run."— Stonewall Jackson. When students have completed their clues, hold a brief contest to see how many leaders students can identify. *(Kinesthetic)*

Answer to . . .

Map Skills *Memphis and New Orleans.*

Main Idea Connections *They had been trained in these tactics in previous wars, before the new technology.*

Civil War in the West, July 1861–May 1863

Area of main map

Pa.

Indiana   Ohio

Ill.   Louisville   Virginia

Kentucky   N.C.

Mo.   Paducah   Nashville

1. Ft. Henry, Feb. 6, 1862

2. Ft. Donelson, Feb. 16, 1862

6. Murfreesboro, Dec. 31, 1862–Jan. 2, 1863

5. Memphis, captured June 6, 1862.

Tenn.   Chattanooga   S.C.

Corinth   Johnston   Atlanta

Ark.   3. Shiloh, April 6–7, 1862   Ga.

Alabama

Vicksburg   Jackson   Mississippi

Texas   Port Hudson   Mobile   Fla.

Louisiana

4. New Orleans, captured April 25, 1862.   Farragut   Gulf of Mexico

0   100   200 Miles
0   100   200 Kilometers

	Union states
	Confederate states
←	Union forces
←	Confederate forces
✦	Union victory
⚓	Union blockade

MAP Skills Union generals in the West focused their attention on the Mississippi River. "That Mississippi ruins us, if lost," worried southern observer Mary Boykin Chesnut in 1862. *Place What two key cities on the Mississippi had the Union captured by the summer of 1862?*

Instead the Europeans turned to India and Egypt for their cotton. By the time Southerners recognized the failure of this strategy, the Union blockade had become so effective that little cotton could get out. With no income from cotton exports, the South lost the money it needed to buy guns and maintain its armies.

Tactics and Technology For generations, European commanders had fought battles by concentrating their forces, assaulting a position, and driving the enemy away. Cannons and muskets in early times were neither accurate nor capable of repeating fire very rapidly. Generals relied on masses of charging troops to overwhelm the enemy.

Main Idea CONNECTIONS

Why did Civil War generals use outdated tactics?

Most generals in the Civil War had been trained in these methods. Many on both sides had seen such tactics work well in the Mexican War. However, the technology that soldiers faced in the 1860s was much improved over what these officers had faced on the battlefields of the 1840s.

By the Civil War, gun makers knew that bullet-shaped ammunition drifted less as it flew through the air than a round ball, the older type of ammunition. They had also learned that rifling, a spiral groove cut on the inside of a gun barrel, would make a fired bullet pick up spin, causing it to travel farther and straighter.

Older muskets, which had no rifling, were accurate only to about 100 yards. Bullets fired from rifles, as the new guns were called, hit targets at 500 yards. In addition, they could be reloaded and fired much faster.

Improvements in artillery were just as deadly. Instead of relying only on iron cannon balls, gunners could also fire **shells,** devices that exploded in the air or when they hit something. Artillery often fired **canister,** a special type of shell filled with bullets. This turned cannons into giant shotguns.

Thousands of soldiers went to their deaths by following orders to cross open fields against such weapons. Commanders on both sides, however, were slow to recognize that traditional methods exposed their troops to slaughter.

War in the West

After the disaster at Bull Run, President Lincoln named General George McClellan to build and command a new army. While McClellan was involved with this task, Union forces in the west invaded the Confederacy.

The states of Arkansas, Louisiana, Mississippi, and Tennessee held the key to control of the Mississippi River. Although some battles did take place farther west, the fighting in these four states is generally referred to as the "war in the West."

The most successful Union forces in the West were led by General Ulysses S. Grant. A graduate of the United States Military Academy at West Point, Grant had left the military after serving in the Mexican War. Over the next several years he tried and failed at a number of civilian jobs. After the fall of Fort Sumter, Grant organized a group of Illinois volunteers and became a colonel. His success at organizing and training troops caused Lincoln to promote him to general. He was assigned to command the Union forces based in Paducah, Kentucky, where the Ohio and Tennessee rivers meet.

▶ **RESOURCE OPTIONS**

Media and Technology

 Prentice Hall United States History Video Collection™ Volume 9
The Civil War

RESOURCE PRO

Visual Learning Activity A British View of the Civil War, found on Resource Pro, depicts European hopes for the war in a political cartoon.

 Color Transparencies Fine Art, D-10

Forts Henry and Donelson In February 1862, Grant advanced south along the Tennessee River with more than 15,000 troops and several gunboats. Powered by steam and built to navigate shallow bodies of water, these gunboats were basically small floating forts fitted with cannons.

Grant's objectives were Fort Henry and Fort Donelson, located just over the border in the Confederate state of Tennessee. The forts protected the Tennessee and Cumberland rivers, important water routes into the western Confederacy.

On February 6 the Union gunboats pounded Fort Henry into surrender before Grant's troops arrived. The general then marched his army east and attacked Fort Donelson on the Cumberland River. Following three days of shelling by the gunboats, Fort Donelson also gave up.

The battles caused a sensation in both North and South. Northerners rejoiced that at last the Union had an important victory. Southerners worried that loss of the forts exposed much of the region to attack. Indeed Nashville soon fell to another Union army. Meanwhile, Grant and some 42,000 soldiers pushed farther south along the Tennessee River to threaten Mississippi and Alabama.

The Battle of Shiloh In late March, Grant's army neared Corinth, Mississippi, an important railroad center near the Tennessee-Mississippi border. Confederate general Albert Sidney Johnston gathered troops from throughout the region to halt the Union advance. As Grant's forces approached, Johnston had assembled an army of about 40,000 to oppose them.

Grant, however, stopped at Pittsburg Landing, Tennessee, a small river town about 20 miles north of Corinth. Here he waited for more Union troops that General Don Carlos Buell was bringing from Nashville. Johnston decided to launch an attack against Grant's army before it got any larger.

On April 6, 1862, Johnston's Confederates surprised some of Grant's troops, who were camped at Shiloh Church outside Pittsburg Landing. Fighting quickly spread along a battle line six miles long. By the end of the first day of the **Battle of Shiloh,** the Southerners had driven the Union forces back, nearly into the Tennessee River. That night, some of Grant's officers advised a retreat before the Confederates could renew their attack the next

day. "Retreat?" Grant scoffed. "No. I propose to attack at daylight and whip them."

Fortunately for Grant, Buell's troops arrived during the night. The next day, Union forces counterattacked and defeated Johnston's army. However, the cost to both sides was high. The Union suffered more than 13,000 casualties, the Confederates nearly 11,000. Johnston was among the Confederate dead.

Shiloh was the bloodiest single battle that had taken place on the North American continent to that time. It shattered on both sides any remaining illusions about the glory of war and destroyed northern hopes that the Confederacy would be soon defeated.

Action on the Mississippi While Grant advanced into the Confederacy from the north, Union forces were also moving up the Mississippi River from the Gulf of Mexico. In late April 1862, a naval squadron commanded by David Farragut fought its way past two forts in the Louisiana swamps to force the surrender of New Orleans. Pushing upriver, Farragut soon captured Baton Rouge, Louisiana, and Natchez, Mississippi. In her diary, Southerner Mary Chesnut voiced her concerns about the Confederate losses:

U.S. Grant demanded "unconditional and immediate surrender" of Fort Donelson, earning himself the nickname "Unconditional Surrender Grant."

AMERICAN VOICES ❝Battle after battle—disaster after disaster. How can I sleep? The power they are bringing to bear against our country is tremendous. . . . Are we not cut in two? . . . The reality is hideous.❞

—*Mary Chesnut*

On June 6, the Union navy seized Memphis, Tennessee. Only two major posts on the Mississippi River now remained in

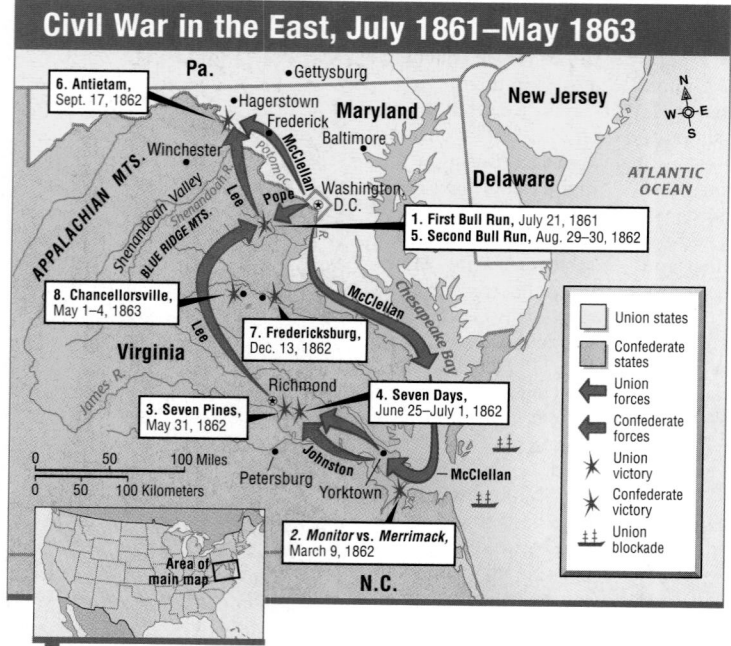

Civil War in the East, July 1861–May 1863

6. Antietam, Sept. 17, 1862
1. First Bull Run, July 21, 1861
5. Second Bull Run, Aug. 29–30, 1862
8. Chancellorsville, May 1–4, 1863
7. Fredericksburg, Dec. 13, 1862
3. Seven Pines, May 31, 1862
4. Seven Days, June 25–July 1, 1862
2. Monitor vs. Merrimack, March 9, 1862

Pa. • Gettysburg
Hagerstown
Frederick
Maryland
Winchester
Baltimore
Washington, D.C.
New Jersey
Delaware
ATLANTIC OCEAN
APPALACHIAN MTS.
Shenandoah Valley
BLUE RIDGE MTS.
Virginia
Richmond
Petersburg
Yorktown
Johnston
James R.
Chesapeake Bay
McClellan
Lee
Pope
N.C.
Area of main map

Union states
Confederate states
Union forces
Confederate forces
Union victory
Confederate victory
Union blockade

0 50 100 Miles
0 50 100 Kilometers

 MAP skills McClellan's extreme caution was his own worst enemy. "No one but McClellan would have hesitated to attack," said Confederate general Joseph Johnston during McClellan's slow advance toward Richmond before the Seven Days' Battles. *Movement* What action did Lee take following the Seven Days' Battles?

Confederate hands. These were Vicksburg, Mississippi, and Port Hudson, Louisiana. If northern forces could find some way to capture them, the entire Mississippi River valley would finally be under Union control. The Confederacy would be split into two parts.

War in the East

While the Union army marched through the western Confederate states, Union warships maintained the blockade of Virginia's coast. The Confederates, however, had developed a secret weapon with which to fight the blockade. In early March 1862, a Confederate ship that resembled a floating barn roof steamed out of the James River. When the Union warships guarding the mouth of the river opened fire on the strange-looking vessel, their cannon shots bounced off it like rubber balls. In hours, the Confederate vessel destroyed or heavily damaged three of the most powerful ships in the Union navy.

The *Monitor* and the *Merrimack* Southerners had created the strange-looking vessel by bolting iron plates to an old wooden steamship called the *Merrimack*. (Although the ship was renamed the *Virginia*, it is still called the *Merrimack* in most historical accounts.) The Union's wooden navy was no match for this powerful ironclad warship. Northern leaders feared the new weapon might soon break apart the entire blockade.

Fortunately for the Union, early reports of the Confederates' work on the *Merrimack* had reached the North. Reacting to the threat of a powerful weapon, President Lincoln had ordered construction of a similar Union warship. It was made entirely of iron and was rushed to completion in about 100 days. Named the *Monitor*, it looked like a tin can on a raft.

On March 9, the *Monitor* arrived off the Virginia coast to confront the Confederate ironclad. Neither ship was able to do serious damage to the other. After several hours of fighting, the *Merrimack* finally withdrew.

The two ships never met again. The Confederates blew up the *Merrimack* at its base in Norfolk, Virginia, in May 1862. The following December the *Monitor* sank in a storm. Their one encounter, however, changed the history of warfare. In a single day, the wooden navies of the world became obsolete.

The Peninsular Campaign The Confederates destroyed the *Merrimack* because they feared it would fall into Union hands. They knew that Union general George McClellan had landed troops nearby, launching the North's second attempt to capture Richmond.

At 36 years old, McClellan was young for a commanding general. However, he was an outstanding organizer and an excellent strategist. In addition, he was well liked by his troops. McClellan's great weakness was that he was very cautious and never seemed quite ready to fight. This irritated Lincoln and other northern leaders, who were impatient to avenge the Union's defeat at Bull Run.

In March 1862, McClellan finally ordered the Army of the Potomac out of Washington. Because he thought that marching to Manassas again would be a mistake, he transported some 100,000 soldiers by boat to a peninsula southeast of Richmond. As the Union troops moved up the peninsula, they encountered some 15,000 Southerners at Yorktown, Virginia, about 60 miles from the Confederate capital.

Although the enemy force was much smaller than his own, McClellan asked for more troops. Lincoln dispatched a stern message to his general:

 "It is indispensable to you that you strike a blow. . . . The country will not fail to note—and is now noting—that the present hesitation to move upon an entrenched enemy is but the story of Manassas repeated. . . . I have never written you . . . in greater kindness of feeling than now. . . . But you must act."

—*President Lincoln*

McClellan, however, waited outside Yorktown for about a month. When he was finally ready to advance, the defenders abandoned their positions and retreated toward Richmond.

On May 31, as they neared the capital, the Southerners suddenly turned and attacked McClellan's army. Although the North claimed victory at the Battle of Seven Pines, both sides suffered heavy casualties. Among the wounded was the Confederate commander, General Joseph Johnston. Command of his army fell to Robert E. Lee.

Robert E. Lee

AMERICAN BIOGRAPHY A warm and charming southern gentleman, Robert E. Lee came from an old, distinguished Virginia family. Among his relatives were two signers of the Declaration of Independence. His father, Henry Lee, was a hero of the American Revolution. After falling into debt, however, his father fled the country, leaving Robert to be raised by his mother.

In 1829 Lee graduated second in his class from West Point. During the next 17 years, he became expert in designing defensive military fortifications. His outstanding service in the Mexican War caught the attention of the army's top officers, and in the early 1850s he served a short time as the head of West Point.

As the southern states seceded, Lincoln offered Lee command of Union forces. Although he was opposed to slavery and secession, Lee refused, explaining "I cannot raise my hand against my birthplace, my home, my children." Instead, he resigned from the army and became the top military advisor to Confederate president Jefferson Davis. In May 1862 he took command of the Army of Northern Virginia, a post he held for the rest of the war. After the war Lee served as president of what is now Washington and Lee University in Lexington, Virginia, until his death in 1870 at age 63.

Robert E. Lee (1807–1870)

As a commander, Lee earned the loyalty and trust of his troops. "I would follow him onto the battlefield blindfolded," Stonewall Jackson said. Like all great generals, Lee believed in good training and planning. However, he also understood that victory sometimes depends on the willingness to take chances. ■

The South Attacks

With McClellan's forces still threatening Richmond, Lee had his opportunity to take a chance. In early June he divided his 55,000-man army, sending several thousand troops to strengthen Stonewall Jackson's forces in western Virginia. The Seven Pines battle had reduced McClellan's army to about 80,000 soldiers. Lee was gambling that the overly cautious McClellan, who was awaiting reinforcements, would not attack Richmond while the Confederate army was weakened.

General Jackson then began to act as though he intended to attack Washington. This tactic caused Lincoln to cancel the order for McClellan's additional troops, keeping them in Washington to protect the Union capital. Jackson then slipped away to join Lee outside Richmond. In late June their combined forces attacked McClellan's larger army in a series of encounters called the Seven Days' Battles. Although the Confederates lost more than 20,000 soldiers, to the Union's nearly 16,000, McClellan decided to retreat.

The Second Battle of Bull Run With McClellan having failed, Lincoln turned to General John Pope, who was organizing a new army outside Washington. The President

Answers to
SECTION 1 REVIEW

1. (a) Civil War, see p. 341; (b) First Battle of Bull Run, see p. 342; (c) casualty, see p. 342; (d) war of attrition, see p. 343; (e) shell, see p. 344; (f) canister, see p. 344; (g) Battle of Shiloh, see p. 345; (h) Battle of Antietam, see p. 348.

2. Despite the Union army's superior strength, they were unable to overcome the Confederate forces in the first two years of the war. Several battles had seen very high casualty rates, including Antietam, the bloodiest battle of all.

3. Union Strategies: Implement Anaconda Plan by blockading the South and gaining control of the Mississippi River. Confederate Strategies: Fight a war of attrition; apply pressure on Great Britain and France to help gain independence by stopping cotton exports. Union Victories: Forts Henry and Donelson, Battle of Shiloh, Battle of New Orleans, Battle of Antietam. Confederate Victories: First Battle of Bull Run, Seven Days' Campaign, Second Battle of Bull Run.

4. Possible answer: The First Battle of Bull Run. This battle was a big victory for the South. It boosted morale and made many believe it would be a short war.

5. New military technologies such as bullets, rifle guns, exploding shells, and canisters turned the tactic of attacking a position with massed troops into an act of slaughter. However, political pressure for success on the battlefield on both sides drove generals to continue using this old tactic.

6. Answers will vary. Students' essays should state an opinion and support it with specific examples.

ordered McClellan's troops back to Washington and put Pope in overall command. Lee knew that he must draw Pope's army into battle before McClellan's soldiers joined it. Otherwise, the size of the Union force would be overwhelming.

Lee again divided his army. In late August he sent Jackson's troops north in a sweeping movement around Pope's position. After marching 50 miles in two days, they struck behind Pope's army and destroyed some of his supplies, which were stored at Manassas. Enraged, Pope ordered his 62,000 soldiers into action to smash Jackson. On August 29, while Pope's force was engaged, Lee also attacked it with the main body of the Confederate army.

The battle was fought on virtually the same ground where McDowell had been defeated the year before. Pope met the same fate at this Second Battle of Bull Run. After Pope's defeat, McClellan was returned to command. "We must use what tools we have," Lincoln said in defense of his decision. "If he can't fight himself, he excels in making others ready to fight."

The Battle of Antietam With Richmond no longer threatened, Lee decided that the time had come to invade the North. Lee hoped that a victory on Union soil would arouse support in Europe for the South and turn northern public opinion against the war.

In early September 1862, Lee's army bypassed the Union troops guarding Washington and slipped into western Maryland.

McClellan had no idea where the Confederates were. Then one of his soldiers found a copy of Lee's orders wrapped around some cigars near an abandoned Confederate camp. Now that he knew the enemy's strategy, McClellan crowed, "If I cannot whip Bobbie Lee, I will be willing to go home."

True to his nature, however, McClellan delayed some 16 hours before ordering his troops after Lee. This gave the Confederate general, who had learned that his plans were in enemy hands, time to prepare for the Union attack. The two armies met at Antietam Creek near Sharpsburg, Maryland, on September 17. Lee had about 40,000 troops, McClellan over 75,000, with nearly 25,000 more in reserve.

Union troops attacked throughout the day, suffering heavy losses. In the first three hours of fighting, some 12,000 soldiers from both sides were killed or wounded. By day's end Union casualties had grown to over 12,000. Lee's nearly 14,000 casualties amounted to more than a third of his army.

The next day the battered Confederates retreated back into Virginia. Lincoln telegraphed McClellan, "Destroy the rebel army if possible." But the ever-cautious general did not take advantage of his opportunity to destroy the Army of Northern Virginia.

The **Battle of Antietam** became the bloodiest day of the Civil War. "God grant these things may soon end and peace be restored," wrote a Pennsylvania soldier after the battle. "Of this war I am heartily sick and tired."

SECTION 1 REVIEW

Comprehension

1. *Key Terms* Define: (a) Civil War; (b) First Battle of Bull Run; (c) casualty; (d) war of attrition; (e) shell; (f) canister; (g) Battle of Shiloh; (h) Battle of Antietam.

2. *Summarizing the Main Idea* Why was it clear by the end of 1862 that the Civil War would be a long and bloody struggle ?

3. *Organizing Information* Write the following column headings on a piece of paper: *Union Strategies, Confederate Strategies, Union Victories, Confederate Victories.* Then fill in details from the text in the appropriate column.

Critical Thinking

4. *Analyzing Time Lines* Review the time line at the start of the section. Choose one battle that you think would have been encouraging for the Confederacy. Explain why you chose that event.

5. *Recognizing Cause and Effect* How did the development of new military technologies affect the Civil War?

Writing Activity

6. *Writing a Persuasive Essay* In your view, was the North or the South more prepared to fight a war? Write an essay explaining your opinion. Support your ideas with specific examples.

Teaching Resources

📁 **Quiz** Units 3–4 folder, p. 60

Student Performance Pack

 Guide to the Essentials Chapter 12, Section 1 (English and Spanish)

November 1861	April 1862	July 1862	July 1862	January 1863
The Trent affair	Confederate draft law passed	Pacific Railroad Act	Internal Revenue Act	Emancipation Proclamation takes effect

1861　　　　　**1862**　　　　　**1863**

2 Life Behind the Lines

SECTION PREVIEW

Objectives

1 Compare the effects of wartime politics on the Confederate and Union governments.
2 Describe the Emancipation Proclamation and its effects, especially on African Americans.
3 List the hardships that befell the North and the South during the war.
4 *Key Terms* Define: draft; recognition; greenback; martial law; Copperhead; writ of *habeas corpus;* Emancipation Proclamation; contraband.

Main Idea

The Union and Confederate governments struggled to support their armies and care for their citizens. The Union government also moved to abolish slavery.

Reading Strategy

Problem Solving List some possible solutions to the problems that the Union and Confederate governments faced during the war. As you read, take specific notes on how both sides actually responded.

Objectives

You may wish to call students' attention to the objectives in the Section Preview. The objectives are reflected in the main headings of the section.

Bellringer

Ask students to think about how the power of the federal government in the United States changed during its first century as a nation. Ask them to consider the effects of war on the power of government.

Reading Strategy

Problem Solving Refer to the Reading Strategy in the Section Preview. You may wish to model two headings, Problems and Solutions, on the board. Have students discuss both lists.

In early 1862 the South faced a crisis. As Grant moved toward Mississippi and McClellan's army threatened Richmond, many Confederate soldiers neared the end of their enlistments. Few seemed ready to reenlist. "If I live this twelve months out, I intend to try mighty hard to keep out [of the army]," pledged one Virginia soldier.

Politics in the South

The branches and powers of the Confederate government were similar to those of the government of the United States. However, the framers of the Confederate constitution made certain that it recognized states' rights and slavery. These two differences caused difficulties for the South throughout the war.

Like the government of the North, the Confederate government had to persuade individual citizens to sacrifice their personal interests for the common good. Confederate leaders had to find a way to build Southerners' loyalty to their new government. Furthermore, because the South had fewer resources than

the North, its war effort depended more on making the best possible use of what it had. Since the southern state governments were strong and sometimes fiercely independent, meeting these objectives would prove difficult.

Mobilizing for War Fearing the war would be lost if there were not enough soldiers to fight, General Lee called for a **draft,** or required military service. Opponents of strong central government claimed that the proposal violated the principles the South was fighting for. One Texas senator disagreed with such arguments:

AMERICAN VOICES ❝Cease this child's play. . . . The enemy are in some portions of almost every state in the Confederacy. . . . We need a large army. How are you going to get it? . . . No man has any individual rights, which come into conflict with the welfare of the country.❞

—*Senator Louis Wigfall*

Medals of Honor like this one were awarded to many Civil War soldiers, both white and African American.

LESSON PLAN
Connecting to the Main Idea

1. Focus The Civil War brought many changes to Northerners and Southerners. The national governments of both sides grew in power. How did the war affect African Americans?
2. Instruct Discuss the strengths and weaknesses of the Confederate government. List the ways the federal government increased its power during the war. Was Lincoln justified in taking on extraordinary powers to keep the Border States in the Union?
3. Close During the Civil War, the governments of both the North and the South took steps that increased their power. Even before the Emancipation Proclamation, enslaved African Americans acted to free themselves, and many of them fought to free others. Have students explain the effects of the Emancipation Proclamation on African Americans in the North and the South.

▶ RESOURCE OPTIONS

Teaching Resources

📁 **Reproducible Lesson Plan** Lesson Plans folder, p. 81

📁 **Big Idea Graphic Organizer** Big Idea Graphic Organizer folder, p. 53

📁 **Guided Reading and Review** Units 3–4 folder, p. 61

In April 1862 the Confederate congress passed a draft law requiring three years of military service for white men between the ages of 18 and 35. This automatically extended the service of all volunteers for two more years. After the horrible losses at the Battle of Antietam, the upper age for the draft became 45. Later it was raised again to 50. Owners of 20 or more slaves were excused from serving, and so were Southerners wealthy enough to hire a substitute to serve in their place.

The Confederate government took charge of the South's economy. It determined the amount of production of wool, cotton, and leather, and seized control of southern railroads from private owners. Farmers were required to contribute one tenth of their produce to the war effort.

To help raise money for the war, the Confederate congress imposed a tax on personal incomes. The Confederate government also authorized the army to seize male slaves for military labor. Though they were paid a monthly fee for borrowed slaves, planters resented this practice because it disrupted work on their plantations.

The Impact of States' Rights A fierce commitment to states' rights worked against the Confederate government and harmed the war effort in many ways. Georgia governor Joseph Brown proclaimed, "I entered into this revolution . . . to sustain the rights of the states . . . and I am *still* a rebel . . . no matter who may be in power."

Many Southerners shared the governor's point of view. Local authorities sometimes refused to cooperate with draft officials. Whole counties in some states were ruled by armed bands of draft-dodgers and deserters. It is estimated that perhaps half of Confederate men eligible for the draft failed to cooperate. "If we are defeated," warned an Atlanta newspaper, "it will be by the people at home."

Seeking Help from Europe Although the blockade effectively prevented southern cotton from reaching Great Britain and France, Southerners continued to hope for British and French intervention in the war. In May 1861 the Confederate government sent representatives to both nations. Even though the Confederacy failed to gain **recognition,** or official acceptance, as an independent nation, it did receive some help.

Main Idea
CONNECTIONS

In what way was the Confederate government both strong and weak?

Great Britain agreed to allow its ports to be used to build Confederate privateers. One of these vessels, the *Alabama,* captured more than 60 northern merchant ships. In all, 11 British-built Confederate privateers forced most Union shipping from the high seas for much of the war.

Recognition did seem possible for a time in 1862. Napoleon III, the ruler of France, had sent troops into Mexico, trying to rebuild a French empire in the Americas. He welcomed the idea of an independent Confederate States of America on Mexico's northern border. However, France would not give the Confederacy open support without Great Britain's cooperation.

British opinion about the war was divided. Some leaders clearly sympathized with the Southerners. Many believed an independent South would be a better market for British products. Others, however, questioned whether the Confederacy would be able to win the war. The British government adopted a wait-and-see attitude. To get foreign help, the South would have to first prove itself on the battlefield.

Politics in the North

After early losses to Confederate forces, President Lincoln and his government had to convince some northern citizens that maintaining the Union was worth the sacrifices they were being asked to make. In addition, the federal government found itself facing international crises as it worked to strengthen civilian support for the war.

Tensions with Great Britain British talks with the South aroused tensions between Great Britain and the United States. Late in 1861 Confederate president Davis again sent two representatives from the Confederacy to England and France. After evading the Union blockade, John Slidell and James Mason boarded the British mail ship *Trent* and steamed for Europe.

Soon a Union warship stopped the *Trent* in international waters, removed the two Confederates, and brought them to the United States. An outraged British government sent troops to Canada and threatened war unless Slidell and Mason were freed. President Lincoln ordered the release of the Confederates. "One war at a time," he said.

The Union vigorously protested Great Britain's support of the Confederacy. Lincoln demanded $19 billion compensation from

Great Britain for damages done by the privateers, and for other British actions on the South's behalf. This demand strained relations between the United States and Great Britain for nearly a decade after the war.

Republicans in Control With southern Democrats out of the United States Congress, the Republicans had little opposition. The Civil War Congresses thus became among the most active in American history. Republicans were able to pass a number of laws during the war that would have a lasting impact on the United States.

Southerners had opposed building a rail line across the Great Plains since Illinois senator Stephen Douglas first proposed it in the early 1850s. In July 1862, however, Congress passed the Pacific Railroad Act with little resistance. The law allowed the federal government to give land and money to companies for construction of a railroad line from Nebraska to the Pacific Coast. The Homestead Act, passed in the same year, offered free government land to people willing to settle on it.

The disappearance of southern opposition allowed Congress to raise tariff rates as well. The tariff became more a device to protect northern industries than to provide revenue for the government. Union leaders turned to other means to raise money for the war.

Financial Measures In 1861 the Republican-controlled Congress passed the first federal tax on income in American history. It collected 3 percent of the income of people earning more than $800 a year. The Internal Revenue Act of 1862 imposed taxes on items such as liquor, tobacco, medicine, and newspaper ads. Nearly all these taxes ended when the war was over.

During the war, Congress reformed the nation's banking system. Since 1832, when President Jackson vetoed the recharter of the Second Bank of the United States, Americans had relied on state banks. In 1862 Congress passed an act that created a national currency, called **greenbacks** because of their color. This paper money was not backed by gold, but was declared by Congress to be acceptable for legal payment of all public and private debts.

Emergency Wartime Actions Like the government of the Confederacy, the United States government exercised great power during the Civil War. As in the South, efforts focused on raising troops and uniting the nation behind the war effort.

Notable PRESIDENTS

Abraham Lincoln

"A house divided against itself cannot stand."
—Speech in 1858

1861–1865

Abraham Lincoln entered the White House with little training in national politics. Before being elected in 1860, he had been a successful lawyer in Illinois and a member of the House of Representatives for a single term. Nothing, however, could have prepared him for the extraordinary challenges he would face as President.

Lincoln confronted crises on every side. Southern states began seceding from the Union even before he took office. The border states somehow had to be kept in the Union. Many Northerners, while opposing secession, did not want to fight the South, and white Northerners disagreed among themselves about slavery.

Lincoln's actions as President all pointed toward one goal: preserving the Union. He changed commanding generals again and again in a desperate search for one who could defeat the Confederate army. He suppressed freedom of speech and assembly. He issued the Emancipation Proclamation to free the slaves living behind Confederate lines, and in 1863 he called on free blacks to join the Union army. All of these actions brought a torrent of criticism on Lincoln. To some critics he was a power-hungry tyrant; to others he was weak and indecisive.

Along with his commitment to preserving the Union, Lincoln's greatest strengths were his sense of compassion and his ability to express powerful ideas in simple yet moving language. In fact, his words have come to help define the Civil War, from his warning before the war that "A house divided against itself cannot stand" to his hope in 1865 that Americans would face the future "with malice toward none, with charity for all." Assassinated shortly before the war's end, Lincoln would not live to work for the compassionate peace he favored. But he had done more than any other single person to preserve the nation at its time of greatest danger.

Connecting to Today

Lincoln is remembered for leading the nation through a time of crisis. His ability to express ideas clearly created support for maintaining a unified nation. ***How important is it that the President be able to rally the people behind a cause? Defend your opinion.***

Customize for

More Advanced Students

Have students copy the following statement: "The Civil War forever changed the relationship between Americans and their government and gave a new meaning to American citizenship." After reading the section, have them discuss and analyze reasons to support this statement.

RESOURCE OPTIONS

Media and Technology

Prentice Hall United States History Video Collection™ Volume 9 *The Civil War*

Answer to . . .

Connecting to Today *Answers will vary but should be defended and supported with examples from the text.*

Four slave states remained in the Union—Delaware, Maryland, Missouri, and Kentucky. Because of their locations, the continued loyalty of these border states was critical to the Union. Lincoln considered Delaware, where few citizens held slaves, to be secure. In nearby Maryland, however, support for secession was strong. In September 1861 Lincoln ordered that all "disloyal" members of the Maryland state legislature be arrested. This action prevented a vote on secession and assured that Washington would not be surrounded by the Confederacy.

The North needed the loyalty of Kentucky and Missouri in order to keep control of the Ohio and Mississippi rivers. In Missouri, Lincoln supported an uprising to overthrow the pro-Confederate state government. To secure Kentucky, he put the state under **martial law** for part of the war. This is emergency rule by military authorities, during which some Bill of Rights guarantees are suspended. Although Jefferson Davis imposed martial law on parts of the Confederacy, Lincoln is the only United States President ever to exercise this power.

The Union also established a draft. In March 1863 President Lincoln signed a law requiring military service of all white males age 20 to 45. Like the southern law, there were exceptions. To avoid the draft, a Northerner could pay the government $300 or he could hire a substitute to serve in his place.

Opposition to the War Riots broke out in the North after the draft law was passed. Mobs of whites in New York City vented their rage at the draft in July 1863. More than 100 people died during four days of destruction. At least 11 of the dead were African Americans, who seemed to be targeted by the rioters.

Although Democrats could not control Congress, some raised their voices in protest against the war. Nicknamed **Copperheads,** after a type of poisonous snake, these Democrats warned that Republican policies would bring a flood of freed slaves to the North. They predicted these freed slaves would take jobs away from whites. Radical Copperheads tried to persuade Union soldiers to desert the army and other Northerners to resist the draft.

To silence the Copperheads and other opponents of the war, Lincoln resorted to extreme measures. He used the army to shut down opposition newspapers and denied others the use of the mails.

In some places Lincoln suspended the **writ of habeas corpus.** This is a legal protection requiring that a court determine if a person is lawfully imprisoned. Without it, people can be held in jail for indefinite periods without even being charged with a crime. The Constitution allows suspension of the writ during a rebellion.

More than 13,000 Americans who objected to the Union government's policies were imprisoned without trial during the war. They included newspaper editors and elected state officials, plus southern sympathizers and some who actually did aid the Confederacy. Most Northerners approved of Lincoln's actions as necessary to restore the Union.

Emancipation and the War

While the Copperheads attacked Lincoln for making war on the South, abolitionists and others attacked him for not making it a war to end slavery. As the Union's battlefield casualties mounted, many Northerners began to question whether it was enough to simply restore the nation. Some, including a group in the Republican party called Radical Republicans, wanted the Confederacy punished for causing so much suffering. No punishment could be worse, the Radical Republicans argued, than freeing the slaveholders' "property."

Lincoln and Slavery At first, the President resisted pressure to make the abolition of slavery a Union war goal. He insisted that under the Constitution he was bound only to preserve and protect the nation. Lincoln explained this view in a letter to Horace Greeley, an abolitionist newspaper editor:

"My paramount object in this struggle is to save the Union, and is not to either save or to destroy slavery. If I could save the Union without freeing any slave, I would do it, and if I could save the Union by freeing all the slaves, I would do it; and if I could save it by freeing some and leaving others alone, I would also do that."

—*President Lincoln*

Although Lincoln personally opposed slavery, he did not believe that he had the legal authority to abolish it. He also worried about the effect such an action would have on the loyalty of the border states. However, Lincoln recognized the importance of slavery to the South's war effort. Every slave working in a field or factory freed a white Southerner to fire a gun at Union soldiers. Gradually, he came to regard ending slavery as one more strategy for winning the war.

The Emancipation Proclamation In the fall of 1862, as Lee retreated south from Antietam, Lincoln proclaimed that on January 1, 1863, slaves in areas of rebellion against the government would be free. Then, on New Year's Day, 1863, he issued the final **Emancipation Proclamation:**

KEY DOCUMENTS

"I, Abraham Lincoln, President of the United States, by virtue of the power in me vested as Commander-in-Chief, of the Army and Navy of the United States . . . as a fit and necessary war measure for suppressing said rebellion . . . do order and declare that all persons held as slaves within said designated States, and parts of States, are and henceforward shall be free. . . ."

—*The Emancipation Proclamation, January 1863*

Reaction to the Proclamation The decree had little direct impact on slavery because it applied only to places that were under Confederate control. Nevertheless, it was condemned in the South and debated in the North. Some abolitionists criticized Lincoln for not having gone far enough. The proclamation did nothing to free people enslaved in the border states, nor did it free slaves living in Confederate areas controlled by Union forces.

Other Northerners, fearing that freed people coming north would cause unemployment, criticized even this limited action. After Lincoln's September announcement, the Democratic party made gains in the congressional elections of November 1862.

The response of black Northerners was much more positive. "We shout for joy that we live to record this righteous decree," abolitionist Frederick Douglass exclaimed. Even if the proclamation brought no immediate end to slavery, it promised that an enslaved people would be free when the North won the war.

Perhaps the most significant reaction occurred in Europe. The abolition movement was strong in England. The Emancipation Proclamation, coupled with news of Lee's defeat at Antietam, ended any real chance that France and Great Britain would intervene in the war.

African Americans Fight

The Emancipation Proclamation had two immediate effects. It inspired southern slaves who heard about it to free themselves by escaping to the protection of Union troops. It also encouraged African Americans to serve in the Union army.

The Contraband Issue Southern slaveholders usually fled with their slaves when the Union

VIEWING HISTORY

Over the course of the Civil War, nearly 180,000 African Americans wore the Union uniform. *Government How did the Emancipation Proclamation change the role of African Americans in the military?*

BACKGROUND

Connections to Today

Students can see the story of the 54th Massachusetts Regiment retold in the film *Glory*. The film, which won three Academy Awards in 1989, also won praise for its attention to historical detail. Historian Peter Burchard wrote: "It took great heart . . . to tell the story of the 54th as it is told in *Glory*—from the point of view of the regiment's rank and file."

ACTIVITY
HETEROGENEOUS GROUPS

Have students analyze the following statement by Viscount Palmerston, a contemporary British observer, that in the Emancipation Proclamation, Lincoln attempted "to abolish slavery where he was without power to do so, while protecting it where he had power to destroy it." Ask students to explain and then agree or disagree with the statement. Did Lincoln accomplish his purpose with the Emancipation Proclamation? *(Enrichment)*

RESOURCE OPTIONS

Teaching Resources

Key Documents The Emancipation Proclamation, Learning with Documents folder, p. 89

Answer to . . .

Viewing History It encouraged freed African Americans to enlist in the Union army.

A Diverse Nation

When African American soldiers joined the Union Army, they were paid only $7 a month, compared to the $13 a month paid other soldiers. James Gooding, an African American soldier, wrote to President Lincoln, "We have done a soldier's duty. Why can't we have a soldier's pay?"

Based on what they are learning in the section, ask students to identify the following changes in the federal government as temporary or permanent.
• A draft law supplied troops for the army.
• Congress passed new tax laws, including a federal tax on income.
• Congress created a national currency.
• The President suspended the writ of *habeas corpus*.
• The President shut down newspapers that disagreed with his policies.
(Reteaching)

Answer to . . .

Viewing History Some women had to take the place of men who were off fighting; others left home to serve as nurses in the war.

army approached. Frequently, however, slaves remained behind or escaped to the safety of nearby Union forces. Believing they had no choice, some Union officers gave these slaves back to slaveholders who demanded return of their "property."

Early in the war, Union general Benjamin Butler devised a legal argument that allowed the Union army to free captured and escaped slaves. During war, one side's possessions may be seized by its enemy. Called **contraband,** these captured items become property of the enemy government. Butler maintained that if slaves were property then they could be considered contraband of war. The Union government, as their new owner, could then let the slaves go.

At first, the army employed these African Americans to build fortifications, drive wagons, and perform countless other noncombat jobs. After the Emancipation Proclamation, however, many enlisted to fight the Confederacy.

African American Soldiers When the Civil War began, black volunteers were not allowed to join the Union army. In July 1862, following McClellan's defeats in Virginia, Congress authorized Lincoln to accept African Americans in the army. Several months later, he made the announcement in the Emancipation Proclamation.

Given this encouragement, African Americans rushed to join the fight. By 1865 nearly 180,000 African Americans had enlisted in the Union army. More than half were black Southerners who had been freed from slavery by the fighting. For these soldiers, fighting to help free others who were still enslaved held special meaning. Many African Americans viewed the chance to fight against slavery as a milestone in their history. In total, African Americans composed almost 10 percent of the troops who served the North during the war.

On warships, black and white sailors served together. African American soldiers, however, served in all-black regiments under the command of white officers. Until June 1864 African Americans also earned less pay than white soldiers.

In July 1863, an African American regiment earned a place in history at Fort Wagner, a stronghold that protected the harbor at Charleston, South Carolina. On July 18, the 54th Massachusetts Infantry, commanded by Colonel Robert Gould Shaw, led the attack on the fort. The regiment's charge across a narrow spit of sand cost it nearly half its men. Frederick Douglass's two sons were among the survivors; so was Sergeant William Carney, who became the first African American to earn the Congressional Medal of Honor.

The actions of the 54th Massachusetts demonstrated what Frederick Douglass wrote in his newspaper the following month:

"All that has been said by orators and poets since the creation of the world in praise of women ... would not do them justice for their conduct during the war," said Abraham Lincoln. This woman cared for her children and her soldier husband in a Union camp in 1862. *Culture In what other ways did women's lives change during the war?*

AMERICAN VOICES ❝Once let a black man get upon his person the brass letters, U.S.; let him get an eagle on his button, and a musket on his shoulder and bullets in his pocket, and there is no power on earth which can deny that he has earned the right to citizenship.❞

—*Frederick Douglass*

The Hardships of War

The Union's changing policies regarding slavery in the South prompted thousands of slaves to escape to freedom. This development hurt the Confederacy in two ways. It depleted the South's labor force, and it provided the North with even greater numerical advantages in the war effort.

The war produced drastic changes in the lives of Northerners and Southerners. With the majority of men off fighting, women on both sides took on new responsibilities. Wives and mothers lived with the fear that every day could bring news of the loss of a loved one. In addition, both sides faced labor shortages, inflation, and other economic problems during the war. By 1863, however, it was clear that the North's greater resources were allowing it to meet these challenges, while the South could not.

The Southern Economy Among the problems the Confederacy faced during the war was a food shortage. Invading armies disrupted the South's food-growing regions as well as its production of cotton. In parts of the South not threatened by Union forces, the Confederate draft pulled large numbers of white males out of rural areas. Southern women worked the land, oversaw slaves, and tried to keep farms and plantations operating. However, food production declined in the South as the war progressed.

Many planters made the problem worse by resisting the central government's pleas to shift from raising cotton to growing food crops. While cotton piled up in warehouses, due to the Union blockade, food riots erupted in southern cities. The worst of these occurred in Richmond, where nearly 1,000 women looted bakeries and other shops in April 1863.

Although the Confederacy never was able to provide all the manufactured goods its army needed, southern industry grew during the war. The Confederate government supervised construction of factories to make railroad track, guns and ammunition, and many other items. Women filled many of the jobs in these factories.

The labor shortage and lack of goods contributed to inflation. By late 1862 a bag of salt that cost $2 before the war was selling for $60 in some places. The hardships at home increased desertions in the Confederate army. "We are poor men and are willing to defend our country but our families [come] first," a Mississippi soldier declared.

Conditions at Georgia's Andersonville prison evoked outrage from Northerners and calls for prisoner exchanges. *Economy How did the state of the South's economy contribute to the horrible conditions of Confederate prison camps?*

The Northern Economy The war hurt industries that depended heavily on southern markets or southern cotton. However, most northern industries boomed. Unlike the Confederacy, the North had the farms and factories to produce nearly everything its army and civilian population needed. War-related industries fared especially well. Philip Armour made a fortune packaging pork to feed Union soldiers. Samuel Colt ran his factory night and day producing guns for the army.

As in the South, when men went off to war, women filled critical jobs in factories and on farms. Many factory owners preferred women employees because they were paid less. This hiring practice kept wages down overall. Prices rose faster than pay during the war.

A few manufacturers made their profits even greater by selling the Union government inferior products: rusty rifles, boats that leaked, hats that dissolved in the rain. Uniforms made from compressed rags quickly fell apart. The soles came off some boots after a few miles of marching.

Prison Camps Captured Confederate soldiers were sent to prison camps throughout the North, including Point Lookout in

Using the Internet

Prepare a Report

Objective Use the Internet to prepare a report on Letters from the Soldiers of the Civil War. Have students follow these instructions:

1. See the *America: Pathways to the Present* Web site at

http://www.Pathways.phschool.com

for the URL for Letters from the Soldiers of the Civil War.

2. Use links to explore the letters written by the different Civil War soldiers.

3. Take detailed notes on the concerns, issues, and tone of each letter. Is there anything that surprises you? If so, what is it?

4. Prepare a report on the general themes of these letters. Use quotes from the letters to support your ideas. Compare your reports with those of your classmates.

RESOURCE OPTIONS

Media and Technology

Listening to Music CD "Bonnets of Blue," Frank Johnson

Answer to . . .

Viewing History Food shortages throughout the region resulted in starvation in the prison camps.

Clara Barton organized an agency to bring relief to wounded soldiers.

Maryland and Camp Chase in Ohio. The Ohio Penitentiary also housed some Confederate prisoners. The South's prison camps were located wherever there was room. Andersonville, its most notorious camp, was in a field in Georgia. Richmond's Libby Prison was a converted tobacco warehouse.

The North and South generally treated their prisoners about the same. In most cases officers received better treatment than other prisoners. Andersonville was the exception. Built to hold 10,000 Northerners, it eventually confined nearly 35,000 men in a fenced, 26-acre open area. About 100 prisoners a day died, usually of starvation or exposure. The camp's commander was the only Confederate to be later tried for war crimes. He was convicted and hanged.

Improving Medical Conditions While soldiers faced miserable conditions in prison camps, life was not much better in the battle camps. Health and medical conditions on both sides were frightful. About one in four Civil War soldiers did not survive the war. A Union soldier was three times more likely to die in camp or in a hospital than he was to be killed on the battlefield. In fact, about one in five Union soldiers wounded in battle later died from their wounds. While most doctors were aware of the relationship between cleanliness and infection, they did not know how to sterilize their equipment. Surgeons sometimes went for days without even washing their instruments.

On both sides, thousands of women volunteered to care for the sick and wounded. Government clerk Clara Barton quit her job in order to provide needed supplies and first aid to Union troops in camp and during battle. Known to soldiers as the "angel of the battlefield," Barton continued her service after the war by founding the American Red Cross. Mental health reformer Dorothea Dix volunteered to organize and head the Union army's nursing corps. Some 4,000 women served as nurses for the northern army. By the end of the war, nursing was no longer only a man's profession.

Sanitation in most army camps was nonexistent. Rubbish and rotting food littered the ground. Human waste and heaps of animal manure polluted water supplies. Epidemics of contagious diseases, such as mumps and measles, swept through camps. Sick lists were lengthy. Sometimes only half the troops in a regiment were available for battle.

The United States Sanitary Commission, created in June 1861, attempted to combat these problems. Thousands of volunteers, mostly women, inspected army hospitals and camps. They organized cleanups and provided advice about controlling infection, disease prevention, sewage disposal, and nutrition. Despite these and similar Confederate efforts, about twice as many soldiers on each side died from disease as from the guns of the enemy.

SECTION 2 REVIEW

Comprehension

1. *Key Terms* Define: (a) draft; (b) recognition; (c) greenback; (d) martial law; (e) Copperhead; (f) writ of *habeas corpus;* (g) Emancipation Proclamation; (h) contraband.

2. *Summarizing the Main Idea* Give some examples of steps the Confederate and Union governments took to support the war effort.

3. *Organizing Information* Create a web diagram showing the legislation passed by the Republican Congress during the war. Label the center circle *Republican Legislation 1861–1862.* Note three or four pieces of legislation in surrounding circles.

Critical Thinking

4. *Analyzing Time Lines* Review the time line at the start of the section. Which event on the time line, in your opinion, had the greatest impact on the Civil War?

5. *Determining Relevance* In what ways did the Emancipation Proclamation affect the war?

Writing Activity

6. *Writing an Expository Essay* Use information from the section to write a one-page essay describing the effects the war had on the economies of the North and the South.

Historical Evidence

Geography

Graphs and Charts

Critical Thinking

Using Letters as Primary Sources

When people write letters, they report firsthand about something of interest to themselves. For this reason, letters are a valuable source of historical evidence. Not only do they present factual information about a subject, but they also give clues to the attitudes of people in a particular historical period.

Use the following steps to analyze the historical evidence in the letters on this page.

1. Lay the groundwork for analyzing the letters by asking who, when, where, and what. (a) What clues do the letters give about the identity of the writers? (b) To whom were the letters written? (c) When were they written? (d) Where were they written? (e) What are the topics of the letters?

2. Analyze the information in each letter. Study the letters to identify their main points. (a) What specific problems does the writer of letter A describe? (b) What tasks does the writer of letter B perform?

3. Study each letter to see what it reveals about conditions and attitudes during the period in which it was written. (a) What general difficulties did farm wives face when their husbands were away at war? (b) Summarize what conditions were like for the wounded after Civil War battles. (c) Generalize about the contribution to the war effort made by women during the Civil War.

TEST FOR SUCCESS

How do you think the writer of letter A would carry on if her husband did not return from war? Give evidence from the letter to support your answer.

Lowndes County, Alabama, June 1, 1862   **A**

Dear husband,

I now take my pen in hand [to] drop you a few lines to let you know that we are all well as common and I am in about the same health that I was when you left. I hopes these lines may find you the same. The boys [her sons] has come home to see me on a furlough [leave from the army] and stayed 10 days. They started back yesterday to the camp. . . . John, my corn is out now and I have not drawed [harvested] any thing yet but hope I will. My crop is nice but Pane [a hired man] has quit and left my crop in bad fix, but the neighbors says they will help us. You said you wanted me to pray for you. As for prayers, I pray for you all the time. I pray for you nearly every breath I draw. . . . Your baby is the prettyest thing you ever saw in your life. She can walk by herself and your little grandson is pretty as pink and grows the fastest in the world. You must come home and see all of your babies and kiss them. I have got the rye cut. . . . Your old mare is gone blind in one eye and something is the matter with one of her feet so that she can't hardly walk. Your hogs and cows is coming on very well, I want you to come home for I want to see you so bad I don't know what to do. I must come to a close by saying I remain your loving wife until death. You must write to me as soon as you get this letter. Goodbye to you.

Lucy Lowe to John P. Lowe

Adapted from Katherine P. Jones, Heroines of Dixie, *1955*

Gettysburg, Pennsylvania, July 8, 1863   **B**

My Dear Cousin,

I am very tired tonight; have been on the field all day. . . . There are no words in the English language to express the sufferings I witnessed today. The men lie on the ground; their clothes have been cut off them to dress [bandage] their wounds; they . . . have nothing but hardtack [biscuit] to eat only as Sanitary Commissioners, Christian Associations [volunteer workers], and so forth give them. . . . To give you some idea of the extent and numbers of the wounds, four surgeons, none of them whom were idle fifteen minutes at a time, were busy all day amputating legs and arms. I gave to every man that had a leg or arm off a gill [measure] of wine, to every wounded in the Third Division, one glass of lemonade, some bread and preserves and tobacco—as much as I am opposed to the latter. . . . I would get on first rate [remain in good spirits] if they would not ask me to ask to write to their wives; that I cannot do without crying, which is not pleasant to either party.

Cornelia

Cornelia Hancock, South After Gettysburg, *1956*

SKILLS FOR LIFE

Historical Evidence

Using Letters as Primary Sources

Focus Students analyze letters as a source of historical evidence.

Instruct After students have read the feature, discuss how the information in letters contributes to our understanding of the Civil War. Discuss how different sorts of letters provide different sorts of historical evidence. Ask students what types of evidence might take the place of letters in the future.

Extend See the Skills for Life Activity in the Resource Options below.

Answers

1. (a) Letter A refers to a husband and children and to farm matters; it is from a wife and mother living on a farm. Letter B refers to nursing work on the battlefield; it is from a nurse. (b) Letter A was written to a husband; Letter B was written to a cousin. (c) Letter A was written on June 1, 1862; Letter B was written on July 8, 1863. (d) Letter A: Lowndes County, Alabama (the South); Letter B: Gettysburg, Pennsylvania (the North). (e) Letter A discusses crops, children, farm animals, and the writer's sadness about the absence of her husband. Letter B discusses the conditions of wounded men and the writer's duties.

2. (a) A hired worker has quit and a horse has gone blind and lame. (b) She gives food and drink to the wounded and writes letters for them.

3. (a) They had difficulties raising the crops and caring for livestock without help, in addition to their usual task of raising children. (b) They suffered intensely, lying on the ground in rags with only biscuits to eat, and many had to have their limbs amputated. (c) Women contributed both by maintaining business at home and by nursing and working at battle sites.

TEST FOR SUCCESS

Answers will vary, but should be based on evidence from the letter.

LIFE AT WAR

Focus Explain that the Civil War has been endlessly fascinating to Americans, almost from the moment the smoke cleared from the battlefields. At Gettysburg and other battle sites, souvenir seekers prowled the fields as soon as the armies retreated.

Instruct Have students study the photos and captions in the feature and discuss how the objects shown give us information about the Civil War that we would not otherwise have known. Then divide the class into small groups. Have each group write a letter from a Union or Confederate soldier in which one of the items displayed is mentioned. Ask a spokesperson from each group to read the group's letter to the class.

Extend You may wish to ask students to do further research on the equipment, medical treatment, and camp life of the Civil War and report their findings to the class.

② Bullet in Shoulder Belt Plate

The soldier who wore this shoulder plate was very lucky. The plate saved his life by stopping a musket bullet.

① Confederate Uniform

John Singleton Mosby, a Confederate scout and guerrilla leader, wore this jacket. Mosby and his Partisan Rangers often operated behind enemy lines in Virginia and Maryland.

③ Civil War Musket

Many soldiers used a musket, but the rifled musket soon replaced it as the standard weapon. A rifle was more accurate over long distances.

④ Bowie Knife

Some Confederate soldiers carried Bowie knives—named after frontiersman Jim Bowie, who died defending the Alamo during the Texas War for Independence in 1836.

⑤ Field Hospital

More soldiers died from disease and from infections caused by wounds than were killed in battle. Field hospitals were ill-equipped to treat the wounded.

⑥ Bottle of Quinine

Many soldiers suffered from the disease of malaria. Quinine relieved some symptoms, but did not cure soldiers of the disease.

▶ RESOURCE OPTIONS

Teaching Resources

American History Block Scheduling Support Experiences of the Civil War Soldier, found in the Expansion, Reconstruction, Immigration folder, includes interdisciplinary lesson suggestions and activities for Geography and History, Primary Sources, Biography, and Literature.

Mess Tins

A soldier carried his own eating implements with him. Most had only a cup, knife, fork, spoon, and metal plate. This more-elaborate mess kit was privately purchased.

Hard Tack

Although not very tasty, this chewy bread lasted a long time without spoiling and was easy to carry.

1. Summarize What do the objects and illustrations tell you about the life of the ordinary soldier during the Civil War?

2. Connecting to Today Find a monument, museum display, statue, or name of street or highway that is related to the Civil War in your community or some other place and report the following to your class: (a) a description of the site; (b) when it was created; (c) why you think so many communities have a Civil War memorial.

American ARTIFACTS

FROM EXHIBITIONS AND COLLECTIONS
AT THE SMITHSONIAN INSTITUTION'S
NATIONAL MUSEUM OF AMERICAN HISTORY

LIFE AT WAR

When Union and Confederate soldiers set off to war in 1861, both sides expected it to last only a short time. They soon realized that the struggle would not be settled quickly, and that they would have to adapt to long years of war.

As in most wars, much of what the soldiers did was boring or uncomfortable—training for battle, securing food, idling with their fellow soldiers, and marching. Soldiers far preferred these daily activities, however, to the deadly horrors they faced from battle and disease.

Scarcity of clothing was also a problem, especially for the Confederates because of the Union blockade. It was common to see Confederate soldiers barefoot or wearing the blue uniforms taken from Union soldiers killed in battle. See **1**.

Technological advances changed the way the war was fought. While both sides relied on older weapons such as knives, bayonets, and muskets at the start of the war, rifles became more common as the war progressed. The greater range and accuracy of rifles enabled defenders to cut down attacking troops with terrible efficiency. See **2**, **3** and **4**.

Medical care on the battlefield was crude. Surgeons routinely cut off injured arms and legs of wounded soldiers. Without medicines to fight infection, minor wounds often became infected. Diseases like pneumonia and malaria killed more men than guns or cannons. See **5** and **6**.

The armies survived mainly on hard tack, a kind of biscuit that, with bacon and coffee, was the main part of the soldiers' diet. See **7** and **8**.

By the war's end, more than 600,000 people had died—the greatest number of Americans ever to die in a war. Four of every ten men who went off to the Civil War were killed or wounded.

Answers to . . .

1. The life of ordinary soldiers was difficult and dangerous, with poor food and medical care, and the threat of disease.

2. (a) Answers will vary depending on the site selected. (b) Answers will vary depending on the site selected. (c) Students may mention the fascination that many Americans have for the Civil War and the need to remember the past.

RESOURCE OPTIONS

Media and Technology

 Prentice Hall United States History Video Collection™ Volume 9 *The Civil War*

 AmericanHeritage® CD-ROM

Time Tour The Nation Torn Apart: Torn by War

December 13, 1862	May 1–4, 1863	July 1–3 1863	July 4, 1863	November 19, 1863
Battle of Fredericksburg	Battle of Chancellorsville	Battle of Gettysburg	Vicksburg surrenders	Lincoln presents Gettysburg Address

1863   **1864**

Objectives

You may wish to call students' attention to the objectives in the Section Preview. The objectives are reflected in the main headings of the section.

Bellringer

Ask students if they can remember being without electricity for any length of time. If so, ask them to describe how they spent that time. Then ask them how that experience would compare to living in a cave for several months while an enemy army shelled their city.

Reading Strategy

Reinforcing Key Ideas Refer to the Reading Strategy in the Section Preview. You may want to model the headings on the chalkboard. After students read the section, discuss with them the importance of each battle before they write about it.

LESSON PLAN

Connecting to the Main Idea

1. Focus Explain that the turning point of the war came in 1863 with the battles of Vicksburg and Gettysburg. Ask why those battles were so important.

2. Instruct The capture of Vicksburg was part of the Anaconda Plan, by which the Union intended to divide and squeeze the Confederacy. Tell students that Lincoln said, "Vicksburg is the key. The war cannot be brought to a close until the key is in our pocket." Tell students that General Lee hoped that invading Pennsylvania might encourage foreign countries to recognize and assist the Confederacy and might also dishearten northern civilians.

3. Close The turning point of the Civil War came with Union victories at Vicksburg in the west and Gettysburg in the east. The next section describes the war's end.

3 The Tide of War Turns

SECTION PREVIEW

Objectives

1 Analyze the importance of Lee's victories at Fredericksburg and Chancellorsville.
2 Explain how the Battles of Gettysburg and Vicksburg turned the war in the North's favor.
3 Describe the importance of 1863 and the message of the Gettysburg Address.
4 *Key Terms* Define: Battle of Fredericksburg; Battle of Chancellorsville; Battle of Gettysburg; Pickett's Charge; siege; Gettysburg Address.

Main Idea

Despite southern victories at Fredericksburg and Chancellorsville, the tide of war turned in the summer of 1863, when the North won important battles at Gettysburg and Vicksburg.

Reading Strategy

Reinforcing Key Ideas Write the headings *Gettysburg* and *Vicksburg* on a sheet of paper and take notes about each battle as you read. When finished reading the section, write briefly about why each battle was important in turning the tide of the war.

The Emancipation Proclamation may have renewed enthusiasm for the war among some Northerners, but it had little effect on the battlefield. When General George McClellan delayed in following up on his victory over Robert E. Lee at the Battle of Antietam, Lincoln again removed the general from command.

Victories for Lee

In November 1862 the President named General Ambrose Burnside to replace McClellan. Sadly for Lincoln, Burnside was better known for his thick whiskers, the origin of the term "sideburns," than for his skills as a military strategist. He soon proved that his poor reputation was justified.

The Battle of Fredericksburg Knowing that McClellan had been fired for being too cautious, Burnside quickly advanced into Virginia. His plan was simple—to march his army of some 122,000 men straight toward Richmond. In response, Lee massed his army of nearly 79,000 at Fredericksburg, Virginia, on the south bank of the Rappahannock River. Lee spread his troops along a ridge called Marye's Heights, behind and overlooking the town.

Incredibly, instead of crossing the river out of range of the Confederate artillery, Burnside decided to cross directly in front of Lee's forces. "The enemy will be more surprised [by this move]," he explained. Lee was surprised only by the poor strategy of Burnside's plan.

Union troops poured across the river on specially constructed bridges and occupied the town. Lee let them cross. He knew that his artillery had the area well covered. Lee believed that if Burnside's army attacked, the Confederate forces could easily deal it a crushing defeat.

On December 13, 1862 the **Battle of Fredericksburg** began. Throughout the day Burnside ordered charge after charge into the Confederate gunfire. Some Union army units lost more than half their men. When the

 ## RESOURCE OPTIONS

Teaching Resources

Reproducible Lesson Plan Lesson Plans folder, p. 82

Learning Styles Lesson Plan, Learning Styles Lesson Plans folder, p. 26

Big Idea Graphic Organizer Big Idea Graphic Organizer folder, p. 54

Guided Reading and Review Units 3–4 folder, p. 63

fighting ceased at nightfall, the Union had suffered nearly 13,000 casualties. Confederate losses were just over 5,000. A demoralized Burnside soon asked to be relieved of his command.

The Battle of Chancellorsville After accepting Burnside's resignation, a worried Lincoln turned to yet another general, Joseph "Fighting Joe" Hooker. The general's plan was to move the Union army around Fredericksburg and attack the Confederates' strong defenses from behind. "May God have mercy on General Lee, for I will have none," Fighting Joe promised.

In late April 1863, Hooker put his plan into action. Leaving about a third of his 115,000-man army outside Fredericksburg, he marched the rest of his troops several miles upriver and slipped across the Rappahannock. Lee soon became aware of Hooker's actions. Confederate cavalry commanded by General J.E.B. "Jeb" Stuart discovered Hooker's force camped about ten miles west of Fredericksburg, near a road crossing called Chancellorsville.

Dividing his forces, Lee sent more than 40,000 Confederate soldiers westward to meet Hooker. About 10,000 troops remained in Fredericksburg. Lee ordered them to build many fires at night, so the enemy across the river would not realize most of the army was gone.

The **Battle of Chancellorsville** began on May 1, 1863. When the Union troops started their march toward Fredericksburg, they suddenly saw Lee's army in front of them. After a brief clash, Fighting Joe ordered them to pull back into the thick woods and build defenses.

The next day, when the Confederates did not attack, Hooker assumed they were in retreat. Instead, Lee had daringly divided his forces a second time. He sent General Stonewall Jackson and 26,000 men on a 12-mile march around the Union army for a late-afternoon attack on its right side. The movement of Jackson's troops was concealed by heavy woods that covered the area.

Again, Hooker was taken by surprise. The only warning was a wave of rabbits and deer that poured into the Union camp moments ahead of the Confederate charge. If darkness had not halted his attack, Jackson would have crushed the Union army.

That night, Jackson and some other officers left the Confederate camp to scout the Union positions for a renewed attack. As they returned, in the darkness some Confederate

The Last Meeting of Lee and Jackson depicts the two great generals before Lee sends Jackson and his troops to outflank Union forces at Chancellorsville. **Geography** *How did the terrain aid the Confederate plan?*

soldiers mistook them for enemies and opened fire. Three bullets hit Jackson, one shattering his left arm so badly that it had to be amputated.

On May 3, with Stuart now leading Jackson's command, the Confederate army completed its victory. On May 5, Hooker's badly beaten troops withdrew back across the river. Chancellorsville was Lee's most brilliant victory, but it was also his most costly one. On May 10, Jackson died of complications from his wounds. Stonewall Jackson was probably Lee's most brilliant general. His popularity with the troops was exceeded only by Lee's. His death deprived Lee of a man he called his "strong right arm."

Main Idea
CONNECTIONS

Why was the death of Stonewall Jackson at the Battle of Chancellorsville a major blow to the Confederate army?

The Battle of Gettysburg

The crushing defeats at Fredericksburg and Chancellorsville were the low point of the war for the Union. The mood in Washington was dark. Rumors swept the capital that Lincoln would resign as President. Some northern leaders began to talk seriously of making peace with the South. "If there is a worse place than Hell," Lincoln said, "I am in it."

In June 1863 Lee marched his forces northward. The Union blockade and the South's lack of resources were beginning to weaken his army. With all the fighting in Virginia, supplies there had become scarce. Lee hoped to find some in Pennsylvania. More importantly, he

RESOURCE OPTIONS

Teaching Resources

 Nystrom _Atlas of Our Country_ A Divided Nation, pp. 26–27

American Literature

Connections to American Literature Classics from the Civil War, pp. 1078–1079.

ACTIVITY
HETEROGENEOUS GROUPS

Have students create a fact file on each of the following battles: Fredericksburg, Chancellorsville, Gettysburg, and Vicksburg. Fact files should include the significance of the battle and a brief summary of what took place. **(Reteaching)**

ACTIVITY
LEARNING STYLES

Have students use a map to explain why Vicksburg was so critical to Union strategy. Ask students to trace Lee's route to Gettysburg. **(Visual/Spatial)**

BACKGROUND

Geography in History

Roads and railways were poor in the Upper South, so rivers played an important role in Union planning. Armies covered the most ground in the west, where north-south rivers like the Mississippi, Tennessee, and Cumberland offered an easy route into the Confederacy. In Virginia, however, most rivers flow east from the Appalachians into the Atlantic Ocean. These formed a natural defense for Confederate troops, since the Union army had to stop to build pontoon bridges across the wider rivers.

Answer to . . .

Viewing History The heavy woods concealed Lee's troops.
Main Idea Connections He was Lee's most popular and able general.

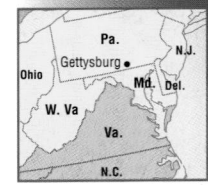

Battle of Gettysburg, July 1–3, 1863

MAP Skills

The Battle of Gettysburg was fought over three days. Notice the changes in troop positions over the course of the battle. *Human-Environment Interaction* How did each side attempt to use the terrain to gain an advantage?

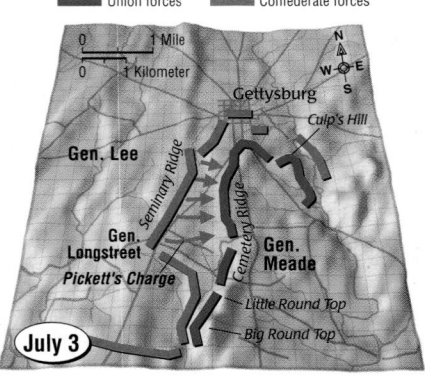

hoped that a major Confederate victory on northern soil would finally push the Union into giving up the war.

As Lincoln prepared to replace Hooker, the Union army moved north, too, staying between the Confederates and Washington. On July 1, some Confederate troops entered the town of Gettysburg, Pennsylvania. Many of them were barefoot, and a supply of shoes was rumored to be stored in the town. There the Confederates encountered a unit of Union cavalry and a fight developed. From this skirmish grew the greatest battle ever fought in North America, the three-day **Battle of Gettysburg.**

July 1, 1863 Hearing the gunfire coming from Gettysburg, units of both armies rushed to the scene. At first, the Confederates outnumbered the Union forces. Fighting through the day, they pushed the Northerners back onto some hills south of town. Meanwhile, troops on both sides continued to gather. Among the Union soldiers to arrive that night was General George Meade, the new head of the Union army. He had been in command for less than a week.

As units arrived, both armies took up positions on a series of hills. Each army's lines stretched from the outskirts of town, in a southerly direction, for about four miles. The center of the Union line was a long hill called Cemetery Ridge. Another series of hills, called Seminary Ridge, was the center of the Confederate position. Between these ridges was a large field several hundred yards wide.

That evening, Lee discussed his battle plan with General James Longstreet, his second-in-command since Jackson's death. Having won the day's fighting, and fresh from his victory at Chancellorsville, Lee's confidence in his troops was high. He proposed to continue the battle the next day. Longstreet advised against attacking such a strong Union position, but Lee had made up his mind. "The enemy is there," said Lee, pointing to Cemetery Ridge, "and I am going to attack him there." He ordered Longstreet to lead an attack on the southern end of the Union line the next morning.

July 2, 1863 Although a graduate of West Point, Longstreet preferred more peaceful endeavors. An accountant, he wanted to be in charge of the Confederate army's payroll. Lee made him a field commander instead. "Longstreet is a very good fighter when he . . . gets everything ready," Lee said of him, "but he is so slow."

On this second day of the battle, Longstreet was not ready to attack until about 4:00 P.M. His delays gave Meade the chance to bring up reinforcements. The battle raged into the early evening. Heavy fighting took place in a peach orchard, a wheat field, and a mass of boulders known locally as the Devil's Den.

At one point, some Alabama soldiers noticed that one of the hills in the Union position, called Little Round Top, was almost undefended. They rushed to capture the hill. From it, Confederate artillery could have bombarded the Union lines.

However, Union commanders also had noticed Little Round Top's weakness. About 350 Maine soldiers under Colonel Joshua Chamberlain, a college professor before the war, were ordered to defend the position. They arrived on the hill just before the Alabamans' assault and then held off repeated attacks until they ran out of ammunition. Unwilling to give up, Chamberlain ordered a bayonet charge. The surprised Confederates retreated back down the hill. The Maine soldiers' heroic act likely saved the Union army from defeat. At the end of the day, the Union lines remained intact.

July 3, 1863 The third day of battle began with a brief Confederate attack on the north end of the Union line. Then the battlefield fell quiet. Finally, in the early afternoon, about 150 Confederate cannons began the heaviest artillery barrage of the war. Some Union generals thought the firing might be to protect a Confederate retreat. However, they were wrong. Lee had decided to risk everything on an infantry charge against the center of the Union position. As he had two days before, Longstreet opposed such a direct attack. Again Lee overruled him.

After a two-hour artillery duel, the Union guns stopped returning fire. Thinking that the Confederate artillery had destroyed the enemy's guns, Longstreet reluctantly ordered the direct attack. Actually, the Union artillery commander had ceased fire only to save ammunition. Now, however, northern soldiers on Cemetery Ridge saw nearly 15,000 Confederates, formed in a line a mile long and three rows deep, coming toward them.

Although this event is known in history as **Pickett's Charge,** General George Pickett was only one of three southern commanders on the field that day. Each led an infantry division of about 5,000 men. As the Confederates marched across about a mile of open ground between the two ridges, the Union artillery resumed firing. Hundreds of canister shells rained down on the soldiers, tearing huge gaps in their ranks. When they closed to within about 200 yards of the Union lines, northern soldiers poured rifle fire into those who remained standing.

Only a few hundred Confederates reached the Union lines—at a bend in a stone wall that became known as the Angle. A survivor described the fighting there:

> **AMERICAN VOICES** ❝ Men fire into each other's faces, not five feet apart. There are bayonet-thrusts, sabre-strokes, pistol-shots; . . . men going down on their hands and knees, spinning round like tops, throwing out their arms, falling; legless, armless, headless. There are ghastly heaps of dead men. ❞
>
> —Soldier at Gettysburg

In about 30 minutes it was over. Scarcely half the Confederate force returned to Seminary Ridge. Lee ordered Pickett to reform his division

Confederate troops in George Pickett's charge at Gettysburg temporarily broke the Union line in the action shown here, at a bend in a stone wall called the Angle. *Science and Technology How was Pickett's Charge an example of old and new war tactics? How did this combination of warfare result in Confederate defeat?*

To make sure students understand the main idea of this section, you may wish to use the flow map graphic organizer below.

Tell students that a flow map shows the sequence of events or steps unfolding. Ask students to use the flow map to record the battles and significant changes that led up to Lincoln's Gettysburg Address.

Teaching Tip A template for this graphic organizer can be found in the Color Transparencies, G-4.

Answer to . . .

Viewing History The charge was an example of old-fashioned tactics because a huge rank and file of men advanced on the enemy. The new weapon technology of the war, however, made it much easier for the Union forces to cut down the advancing Confederate troops.

In order for Grant to capture Vicksburg, navy gunboats under Commander David Porter had to sail past the city at night under heavy fire. "It was as if hell itself were loose," said one observer. The gunboats survived their mad dash past Vicksburg and linked up with Grant's forces south of the city.
Geography Why was it important for the Union to capture Vicksburg?

in case Meade counterattacked. "General Lee, I have no division," Pickett replied.

Pickett's Charge ended the bloodiest battle of the Civil War. Losses on both sides were staggering. The Union army of about 85,000 suffered over 23,000 casualties. Of some 75,000 Southerners, about 28,000 were casualties. For the second time, Lee had lost more than a third of his army. The next day, July 4, the Confederates began their retreat back to Virginia.

Vicksburg

While armies clashed in the East, a Union army in the West struggled to capture the city of Vicksburg, Mississippi. Only this stronghold and a fortress at Port Hudson, Louisiana, prevented the Union from having complete control of the Mississippi River.

Vicksburg seemed safe from attack. It sat on a bluff, high above a sharp bend in the river. From this bluff, Confederate artillery could lob shells at any Union ships that approached the city. In addition, much of Vicksburg was surrounded by swamps. The only approach to the city over dry land was from the east and Confederate forces held that territory.

Grant Attacks The Union general who faced these challenges was Ulysses S. Grant. Between December 1862 and April 1863 he made several attempts to either capture or bypass the city.

First, he sent General William Tecumseh Sherman and several thousand troops in an unsuccessful attack on Vicksburg from the north. Next he had his army dig a canal across the bend in the river, so Union boats could bypass the city's guns. However, the canal turned out to be too shallow. Then he tried to attack from the north by sending gunboats down another river. This too failed.

An attempt to approach the city through a swampy backwater called Steele's Bayou nearly ended in disaster. The Confederates cut down trees to slow the boats and fired on them from shore. Finally, Sherman's troops had to come and rescue the fleet.

By mid-April 1863, the ground had dried out enough for Grant to try a daring plan. He marched his army down the Louisiana side of the river and crossed into Mississippi south of Vicksburg. Then he moved east and attacked Jackson, the state capital. This drew out the Confederate forces from Vicksburg, commanded by General John Pemberton, to help defend the capital. Before they could arrive, Grant captured Jackson. Then he turned his troops west to fight Pemberton.

On May 16 the two armies clashed at Champion's Hill halfway between Jackson and Vicksburg. Although Grant won another victory, he could not trap Pemberton's army. The Confederates were able to retreat back to Vicksburg's fortifications. In late May, after two more unsuccessful attacks, Grant began a **siege,** a tactic in which an enemy is surrounded and starved in order to make it surrender.

The Siege of Vicksburg When Union cannons opened fire on Vicksburg from land and water, a bombardment began that would average 2,800 shells a day. For more than a month, citizens of Vicksburg endured a nearly constant pounding from some 300 guns. The constant schedule of shelling took over everyday life.

Residents dug caves in hillsides, some complete with furniture and attended by slaves. "It was living like plant roots," one cave dweller said. As the siege dragged on, residents and soldiers alike were reduced to eating horses, mules, and dogs. Rats appeared for sale in the city's butcher shops.

By late June, Confederate soldiers' daily rations were down to one biscuit and one piece of bacon per day. On July 4, some 30,000 Confederate troops marched out of Vicksburg and laid down their arms. Pemberton thought he could negotiate the best terms for the surrender on the day that celebrated the Union's independence.

The Importance of 1863

For the North, 1863 had begun disastrously. However, the Fourth of July 1863 was the most joyous Independence Day since the first one 87 years earlier. Thousands of former slaves for the first time could truly celebrate American independence. The holiday marked the turning point of the Civil War.

In the West, Vicksburg was in Union hands. For a time, the people of that city had been sustained by the hope that President Jefferson Davis would send some of Lee's troops to rescue them. But Lee had no reinforcements to spare. His weakened army had begun its retreat into Virginia, never again seriously to threaten Union soil.

Four days later, Port Hudson surrendered to Union forces. The Mississippi River was in Union hands, cutting the Confederacy in two. "The Father of Waters again goes unvexed [undisturbed] to the sea," announced Lincoln in Washington, D.C.

In Richmond there began to be serious talk of making peace. Although the war would continue for nearly two years more, for the first time the end seemed in sight.

The Gettysburg Address

On November 19, 1863, some 15,000 people gathered at Gettysburg. The occasion was the dedication of a cemetery to honor the Union soldiers who had died there just four months before. The featured guest was Edward Everett

Siege of Vicksburg

1 Grant's camp at Millikens Bend, Dec. 1862–April 1863

2 Route of Grant's army past Vicksburg, Mar. 29– early April

3 Route of Union navy past Vicksburg, April 14 & 22

4 Navy ferries army to eastern bank, April 30

5 Vicksburg to Jackson rail line cut, May 13

6 Grant captures and destroys Jackson, Mississippi, May 14

7 Grant defeats Confederate forces at Champion's Hill, May 16

8 Siege of Vicksburg, begins, May 22

Raymond
Auburn
Cayuga
Rocky Springs
Crystal Springs
Pine Bluff
Bruinsburg

Mississippi R.
New Orleans and Jackson R.R.

→ Grant's Route

MAP Skills Lincoln called capturing Vicksburg "the key" to winning the war. Jefferson Davis considered the city to be "the nailhead that holds the South's two halves together." Grant spent eight months trying to capture it. *Movement* Trace Grant's route on the map and explain the strategy behind it.

RESOURCE OPTIONS

Teaching Resources

Lasting Impact Activity The Lasting Impact of the Siege of Vicksburg, History's Lasting Impact folder, pp. 8–9

Media and Technology

Color Transparencies The Way It Works, H-13; Geographic Setting, M-3, M-4

Customize for
More Advanced Students

Ask students to respond to the following statement by Josiah Gorgas, the chief of Confederate ordnance in 1863: "One brief month ago we were apparently at the point of success. Lee was in Pennsylvania. . . . Vicksburg seemed to laugh all Grant's efforts to scorn. . . . Yesterday we rode on the pinnacle of success—today absolute ruin seems to be our portion." Students should explain why Union victories at Vicksburg and Gettysburg meant ruin for the Confederacy.

ACTIVITY
LEARNING STYLES

Ask students to deliver a brief monologue on the celebration of July 4, 1863, by one of the following figures: a formerly enslaved African American, a citizen of Vicksburg, or a Union soldier. Have students choose their character, do research to prepare the monologue, and present the monologue in front of the class. (*Verbal/Linguistic, Interpersonal*)

Answer to . . .

Map Skills *Because of the terrain, Grant chose to attack Vicksburg from the south. He moved his army west of the city, as the Confederates controlled the east. He then moved overland toward Jackson to avoid fire from Vicksburg's protected location on a bluff at a bend in the river. By destroying Jackson and cutting its rail line to Vicksburg, Grant cut Vicksburg off from incoming supplies, enabling the siege.*

Answers to
SECTION 3 REVIEW

1. (a) Battle of Fredericksburg, see p. 360; (b) Battle of Chancellorsville, see p. 361; (c) Battle of Gettysburg, see p. 362; (d) Pickett's Charge, see p. 363; (e) siege, see p. 364; (f) Gettysburg Address, see p. 366.

2. Possible answers: They defined how each side would be able to operate thereafter. After Gettysburg, Lee was restricted to operating defensively within the South. After Vicksburg, the Union gained control of the Mississippi River and access to a huge part of the Confederacy.

3. Fredericksburg: Lee; Burnside; Confederate victory. Chancellorsville: Lee, Jackson, Stuart; Hooker; Confederate victory. Gettysburg: Lee, Longstreet, Pickett; Meade, Chamberlain; Union victory. Vicksburg: Pemberton; Grant, Sherman; Union victory.

4. Possible answers: early 1863— Confederate victories at Fredericksburg and Chancellorsville demoralize Union. Summer— Union victories at Gettysburg and Vicksburg boost North's morale. Fall— Lincoln's speech redefines meaning of Union.

5. It reminded Americans that their country was founded on the ideals of freedom and equality, and that these were the rights of all Americans.

6. Students' essays will vary but should suggest that Union victories at Vicksburg and Gettysburg turned the outcome of the war in favor of the North.

Answer to . . .

Viewing History They stress the importance of the nation. Lincoln's primary goal in the war was to preserve the nation by any means necessary.

"In times like the present," Lincoln said, "men should utter nothing for which they would not willingly be responsible through time. . . ." *Government How do Lincoln's words at Gettysburg represent his goals in the Civil War?*

of Massachusetts, the most famous public speaker of the times. President Lincoln was invited to deliver "a few appropriate remarks" to help fill out the program.

Everett delivered a grand crowd-pleasing speech that lasted two hours. Then it was the President's turn to speak. In his raspy, high-pitched voice, Lincoln delivered his remarks,

which became known as the **Gettysburg Address.** In a short, two-minute speech he eloquently explained the meaning of the Civil War. The speech began simply and ended with a statement that redefined the meaning of the United States:

KEY DOCUMENTS "Fourscore and seven years ago our fathers brought forth on this continent, a new nation, conceived in Liberty, and dedicated to the proposition that all men are created equal. . . .

[T]hat this nation, under God, shall have a new birth of freedom—and that government of the people, by the people, for the people, shall not perish from the earth."

—*Lincoln's Gettysburg Address, November 19, 1863*

Lincoln spoke with a wisdom ahead of his time. Most Americans in 1863 did not like his speech. They thought it was too short and simple. But in the years since then, people have come to appreciate that Lincoln's words marked a dramatic new definition of the United States. Freedom and equality no longer belonged to a few, as they had in 1776. They were the right of everyone. Democracy and the Union did not exist to serve the interests of only white men. They existed to preserve freedom for all. Lincoln's Gettysburg Address marked a great milestone in the expansion of liberty to all Americans.

SECTION 3 REVIEW

Comprehension

1. *Key Terms* Define: (a) Battle of Fredericksburg; (b) Battle of Chancellorsville; (c) Battle of Gettysburg; (d) Pickett's Charge; (e) siege; (f) Gettysburg Address.

2. *Summarizing the Main Idea* In what ways were the Battles of Gettysburg and the siege of Vicksburg turning points in the Civil War?

3. *Organizing Information* Create a chart that details the major battles discussed in this section. In the first column, write the *names of the battles*. In the next column note the important *Confederate officers* for each battle. In the third column note the *Union officers*, and in the last column write if the battle is considered a *Confederate* or *Union victory*.

Critical Thinking

4. *Analyzing Time Lines* Review the time line at the start of the section. Write a sentence or phrase that connects each entry to the entry that follows it.

5. *Identifying Central Issues* Explain how the Gettysburg Address redefined the concept of freedom for Americans.

Writing Activity

6. *Writing an Expository Essay* The events of 1863 are considered to be vital in determining the outcome of the Civil War. Write a one-page essay explaining why. Support your essay with specific examples.

▶ RESOURCE OPTIONS

Teaching Resources

 Quiz Units 3–4 folder, p. 64

Student Performance Pack

 Guide to the Essentials Chapter 12, Section 3 (English and Spanish)

May 5–6, 1864	June 3, 1864	Sept. 2, 1864	Dec. 21, 1864	April 9, 1865	April 14, 1865
Battle of the Wilderness	Battle of Cold Harbor	Sherman occupies Atlanta	Sherman captures Savannah	Lee surrenders to Grant at Appomattox	President Lincoln assassinated

1864 **1865** **1866**

4 A New Birth of Freedom

SECTION PREVIEW

Objectives

1. Explain Grant's and Sherman's strategies for defeating the South.
2. Summarize the issues and the outcome of the election of 1864.
3. Describe the end of the war and the assassination of President Lincoln.
4. *Key Terms* Define: Battle of the Wilderness; Battle of Spotsylvania; Battle of Cold Harbor; Thirteenth Amendment; guerrilla.

Main Idea

After years of fighting and countless casualties, the South surrendered in April 1865.

Reading Strategy

Arranging Events in Order As you read, create a time line that lists in order the major events in the section. Beneath each entry write a brief sentence or phrase that connects each event to the entry that follows it.

The Confederates' war strategy for 1864 was a simple one—to hold on. They knew the North would have a presidential election in November. If the war dragged on and casualties mounted, northern voters might replace Lincoln with a President willing to grant the South its independence. "If we can only subsist," wrote an official in the Confederate War Department, "we may have peace."

Grant Takes Command

President Lincoln understood that his chances for reelection in 1864 depended on the Union's success on the battlefield. In March he summoned Ulysses S. Grant to Washington and gave him command of all Union forces. Grant's plan was to confront and crush the Confederate army and end the war before the November election.

Placing General William Tecumseh Sherman in charge in the West, Grant remained in the East to battle General Lee. He realized that Lee was running short of men and supplies. Grant now proposed to use the North's superiority in population and industry

to wear down the Confederates. In the West he ordered Sherman to do the same.

Battle of the Wilderness In early May 1864 Grant moved south across the Rapidan River in Virginia with a force of some 120,000 men. Lee had about 65,000 troops. The Union army headed directly toward Richmond. Grant knew that to stop the Union advance, Lee would have to fight. In May and June the Union and Confederate armies clashed in three major battles. This was exactly what Grant wanted.

The fighting began on May 5 with the two-day **Battle of the Wilderness.** This battle occurred on virtually the same ground as the Battle of Chancellorsville the year before.[†] The two armies met in a dense forest. The fighting was so heavy that the woods caught fire, causing many of the wounded to be

---

[†] The Confederate forces felt a sense of repetition when General Longstreet, Lee's second-in-command, was accidentally shot and wounded by his own soldiers only three miles from where Stonewall Jackson had been shot the year before.

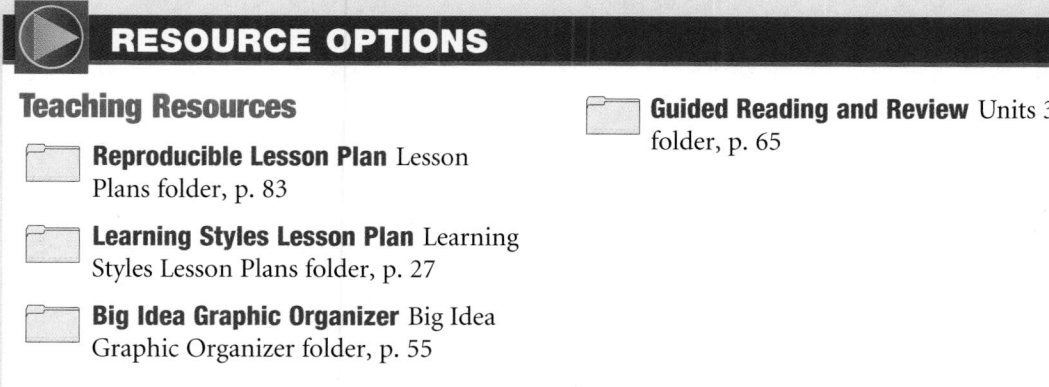

RESOURCE OPTIONS

Teaching Resources

📁 **Reproducible Lesson Plan** Lesson Plans folder, p. 83

📁 **Learning Styles Lesson Plan** Learning Styles Lesson Plans folder, p. 27

📁 **Big Idea Graphic Organizer** Big Idea Graphic Organizer folder, p. 55

📁 **Guided Reading and Review** Units 3–4 folder, p. 65

A New Birth of Freedom

Objectives

You may wish to call students' attention to the objectives in the Section Preview. The objectives are reflected in the main headings of the section.

Bellringer

Ask students to think about what it means to surrender. Have them describe the feeling of giving up a fight. How does it feel to win a long-fought struggle?

Reading Strategy

Arranging Events in Order Refer to the Reading Strategy in the Section Preview. You may wish to model the time line on the chalkboard. Ask students to suggest dates and descriptions as they read.

LESSON PLAN

Connecting to the Main Idea

1. Focus Explain that Lee finally surrendered at Appomattox Court House, Virginia, in April 1865. Ask students to consider the costs of the Civil War. What were its major results?

2. Instruct Have students trace Sherman's route through Georgia. Ask how Sherman's march and Grant's dogged pursuit of Lee show commitment of both generals to the idea of total war. Discuss how Lincoln's reelection led to the passage of the Thirteenth Amendment.

3. Close The Civil War ended in 1865, after Sherman's brutal march through Georgia and Grant's fierce hammering of Lee's exhausted troops. The nation emerged from the war an undivided democracy, with slavery abolished.

Connections to Today

While there are hundreds of monuments commemorating those who fought in the Civil War, there is one that stands apart. Unveiled in July 1998, "The Spirit of Freedom" is an 11-foot bronze statue, part of the first national monument honoring the role of African American soldiers in the Civil War. "The Spirit of Freedom" depicts an African American soldier leaving for war, and his family members. The monument is part of an ongoing movement by African Americans to publicize history often excluded from textbooks, movies, and popular culture and to foster pride among young people in African American history.

ACTIVITY
HETEROGENEOUS GROUPS

Ask students to prepare an oral reading of one of the following: the Gettysburg Address, selections from Stephen Vincent Benet's "John Brown's Body," or Walt Whitman's poem mourning the death of Lincoln, "O Captain! My Captain!" *(Enrichment)*

Answer to . . .

Map Skills The South was already weakened by years of fighting.

---

burned to death. Unable to see in the smoke-filled forest, units got lost and fired on friendly soldiers, mistaking them for the enemy.

Grant took heavy losses at the Wilderness. However, instead of retreating as previous Union commanders had done after defeats, he moved his army around the Confederates and again headed south. Despite the high number of casualties, Union soldiers were proud that under Grant's leadership they would not retreat so easily.

Spotsylvania and Cold Harbor Two days later, on May 8, the Confederates caught up to the Union army near the little town of Spotsylvania Court House. The series of clashes that followed over nearly two weeks are called the **Battle of Spotsylvania.**

The heaviest fighting took place on May 12. In some parts of the battlefield the Union dead were piled four deep. When Northerners began to protest the huge loss of life, a determined Grant notified Lincoln, "I propose to fight it out on this line [course of action] if it takes all summer." Then he moved the Union army farther south.

In early June the armies clashed yet again at the **Battle of Cold Harbor,** just eight miles from Richmond. In a dawn attack on June 3, Grant launched two direct charges on the Confederates, who were behind strong fortifications. Some 7,000 Union soldiers fell in less than an hour.

The Siege of Petersburg Unable to reach Richmond or defeat Lee's army, Grant moved his army around the capital and attacked Petersburg, a railroad center south of the city. He knew that if he could cut off shipments of food to Richmond, the city would have to surrender. The attack failed, however.

In less than two months, Grant's army had suffered some 65,000 casualties. The toll had a chilling effect on the surviving Union troops. At Cold Harbor, many soldiers pinned their names and addresses on their uniforms so their bodies could be identified.

Grant then turned to the tactic he had successfully used at Vicksburg. On June 18, 1864, he began the siege of Petersburg. Lee responded by building defenses. While he had lost many fewer men than Grant, it was becoming difficult for Lee to replace all his casualties. He was willing to stay put and wait for the northern election in November.

Final Battles of the Civil War, 1863–1865

MAP Skills

Grant's stubbornness and Sherman's campaign of total war brought the Civil War to a bloody close. Compare the relative forces of the Union and the Confederacy in the final months of the Civil War. *Movement* Why do you think Sherman met with little resistance?

Ohio

Pa.

N.J.

Washington, D.C.

W. Va.

Del.

Md.

3. The Wilderness, May 5–6, 1864

4. Spotsylvania, May 8–19, 1864

Area of main map

11. Lee surrenders to Grant, April 9, 1865.

Richmond

Grant

5. Cold Harbor, June 3, 1864

Kentucky

Ohio R.

Appomattox Court House

Lee

Grant Virginia

6. Petersburg, besieged June 18, 1864– April 2, 1865.

0   100   200 Miles
0   100   200 Kilometers

12. Johnston surrenders to Sherman, April 26, 1865.

Durham Station

Johnston

10. Bentonville, Mar. 19, 1865

2. Chattanooga, Nov. 23–25, 1863

North Carolina

Sherman

Tennessee

APPALACHIAN MTS.

South Carolina

9. Columbia, captured Feb. 17, 1865.

Georgia

Sherman

1. Chickamauga, Sept. 19–20, 1863

Charleston

ATLANTIC OCEAN

7. Atlanta, occupied Sept. 2, 1864.

Alabama

8. Savannah, captured Dec. 21, 1864.

	Union states
	Confederate states
←	Union forces
←	Confederate forces
✶	Union victory
✶	Confederate victory
✶	Inconclusive
‡‡	Union blockade

▶ RESOURCE OPTIONS

Media and Technology

Color Transparencies American Photo, B-4; Links Across Time, J-4; Fine Art, D-11

Sherman in Georgia

As Grant's army advanced against Lee, Sherman began to move south from Chattanooga, Tennessee, to threaten the city of Atlanta. Sherman's strategy was identical to Grant's in Virginia. He would force the main Confederate army in the West to attempt to stop his advance. If the southern general took the bait, Sherman would destroy the enemy with his huge 98,000-man force. If the Confederates refused to fight, he would seize Atlanta, an important rail and industrial center.

The Capture of Atlanta Sherman's opponent was General Joseph Johnston, the Confederate commander who had been wounded at the Battle of Seven Pines in Virginia in 1862. Johnston's tactics were similar to Lee's. He would engage the Union force to block its progress. At the same time, he would not allow Sherman to deal him a crushing defeat. In this way, he hoped to delay Sherman from reaching Atlanta before the presidential elections could take place in the North.

Despite Johnston's best efforts, by mid-July 1864 the Union army was just a few miles from Atlanta. Wanting more aggressive action, Confederate president Jefferson Davis replaced Johnston with General James Hood.

The new commander gave Davis—and Sherman—exactly what they wanted. In late July, Hood engaged the Union force in a series of battles. With each clash the southern army lost thousands of soldiers. Finally, with the Confederate forces reduced from some 62,000 to less than 45,000, General Hood retreated to Atlanta's strong defenses. Like Grant at Petersburg, Sherman laid siege to the city. Throughout the month of August, Sherman's forces bombarded Atlanta. In early September the Confederate army pulled out and left the city to the Union general's mercy.

Sherman Marches to the Sea "War is cruelty," Sherman once wrote. "There is no use trying to reform it. The crueler it is, the sooner it will be over." It was from this viewpoint that

the tough Ohio soldier conducted his military campaigns. Although a number of Union commanders considered Sherman to be mentally unstable, Grant stood by him. As a result, Sherman was fiercely loyal to his commander.

Now, Sherman convinced Grant to permit a daring move. Vowing to "make Georgia howl," in November 1864, Sherman led some 62,000 Union troops on a march to the sea to capture Savannah, Georgia. Before abandoning Atlanta, however, he ordered the city evacuated and then burned.

After leaving Atlanta in ruins, Sherman's soldiers cut a nearly 300-mile long path of destruction across Georgia. The troops destroyed bridges, factories, and railroad lines. They seized and slaughtered livestock. Grain that had recently been harvested for the Confederate troops went to Union soldiers instead.

As the Northerners approached Savannah, the small Confederate force there fled. On December 21 the Union army entered the city without a fight. "I beg to present you, as a Christmas gift, the city of Savannah," read General Sherman's message to Lincoln. For the President, it was the second piece of good news since the November election.

The Election of 1864

"I am going to be beaten," Lincoln said of his reelection chances in 1864, "and unless some great change takes place, *badly* beaten." In an attempt to broaden Lincoln's appeal, the Republicans dumped Vice President Hannibal Hamlin and nominated Andrew Johnson of

FACT Finder

	Killed and Mortally Wounded	Dead of Disease	Prisoner-of-War Dead	Wounded	Total Casualties
Union	110,100	224,580	30,192	275,175	640,047
Confederacy	94,000	164,000	31,000	194,026	483,026
Total	204,100	388,580	61,192	469,201	1,123,073

Source: *Blood Brothers: A Short History of the Civil War*, by Frank E. Vandiver

Interpreting Tables After four years and more than 10,500 engagements, the Civil War claimed well over a million casualties. *Science and Technology* What was the leading cause of death in the Civil War? What role did science and technology play in the high death tolls of this war?

RESOURCE OPTIONS

Teaching Resources

 Visual Learning Activity Defending Atlanta, Learning with Documents folder, p. 54

Media and Technology

 RESOURCE PRO

Primary Source Activity A Teenager's Account of War, found on Resource Pro, uses excerpts from Emma LeDonte's diary to show how young Southerners viewed and experienced the war.

ACTIVITY
HETEROGENEOUS GROUPS

Remind students that war is really about individual people, and that relationships between individuals often affect the lives of thousands. Sherman and Grant had a relationship built on loyalty. Despite what other Union commanders thought, Grant stood by Sherman. Divide students into groups. Have them research the lives of both men. Then have each group prepare and present a short skit demonstrating the personalities and philosophies of both men as Sherman convinces Grant to permit a daring move and "make Georgia howl."
(Enrichment)

Answer to . . .

Interpreting Charts Disease; new weapons technology made warfare more deadly; lack of medical knowledge and technology contributed to the high number of deaths from disease.

Tennessee to run with the President. Johnson was a Democrat and a pro-Union Southerner.

The Democrats nominated General George McClellan as their candidate. McClellan was only too happy to oppose Lincoln, who had twice fired him. The general was still loved by his soldiers, and Lincoln feared that McClellan would find wide support among the troops. McClellan promised that if elected, he would negotiate an end to the war.

Sherman's capture of Atlanta, however, changed the political climate in the North. Sensing victory, Northerners became less willing to support a negotiated settlement. In November, with the help of ballots cast by Union soldiers, Lincoln won an easy victory, gathering 212 out of a possible 233 electoral votes.

By reelecting Lincoln, voters not only showed their approval of his war policy, but also their increasing acceptance of his stand against slavery. Three months later, in February 1865, Congress joined him in that stand and passed the **Thirteenth Amendment** to the Constitution. It was ratified by the states and became law on December 18, 1865. In a few words, the amendment ended slavery in the United States forever:

"Neither slavery nor involuntary servitude, except as a punishment for crime whereof the party shall have been duly convicted, shall exist within the United States, or any place subject to their jurisdiction."

—*Thirteenth Amendment to the Constitution*

As President Lincoln prepared to begin his second term, it was clear to most Northerners that the war was nearly over. In his Second Inaugural Address, in March 1865, Lincoln reflected on the meaning of the previous four years:

"Both [North and South] read the same Bible and pray to the same God, and each invokes His aid against the other. It may seem strange that any men should dare ask a just God's assistance in wringing their bread from the sweat of other men's faces; but let us judge not that we be not judged. The prayers of both could not be answered. That of neither has been answered fully. The Almighty has His own purposes."

—*Lincoln's Second Inaugural, March 1865*

The End of the War

As Grant strangled Richmond and Sherman prepared to move north from Savannah to join him, Southerners' gloom deepened. President Davis claimed that he had never really counted on McClellan's election, or on a negotiated peace. "The deep waters are closing over us," Mary Chesnut observed in her diary.

Sherman Moves North In February 1865 General Sherman's troops left Savannah and headed for South Carolina. As the first state to secede, many Northerners regarded it as the heart of the rebellion. "Here is where the treason began and, by God, here is where it shall end," wrote one Union soldier as the army marched northward.

Unlike Virginia and many other Confederate states, the Carolinas had seen relatively little fighting. Sherman had two goals as he moved toward Grant's position at

---

CAUSE AND EFFECT: The Civil War

CAUSES

- Regional differences between the largely industrial North and the agrarian South grow stronger.
- The question of slavery in the territories widens the gap between Northern and Southern interests.
- The Compromise of 1850 and the Kansas-Nebraska Act inflame passions on both sides of the slavery issue.
- An antislavery candidate, Abraham Lincoln, is elected President.
- The Lower South secedes to form the Confederate States of America.
- The Confederacy attacks Fort Sumter.

THE CIVIL WAR

EFFECTS

- The Union is preserved.
- Slavery is abolished.
- More than half a million people are dead.

Interpreting Charts Slavery was at the center of the dispute between Northern and Southern interests. The central issue of the Civil War, according to President Lincoln, was the preservation of the Union. In the end, the Union prevailed. *Government How did the Civil War resolve the question of slavery? Do you think the war could have ended without a resolution of the issue?*

TEST PREPARATION

Have students read the passage on this page from Lincoln's Second Inaugural Address, and then answer the question below.

Based on the passage, it is clear that

(A) Lincoln believed the war had a greater purpose than either side knew.

B Lincoln thought Northerners were more religious than Southerners.

C Lincoln thought the North was winning because people there prayed more often.

D the North and the South had nothing in common.

Petersburg: to destroy the South's remaining resources and to crush Southerners' remaining will to fight. In South Carolina he did both. The Confederate army could do little but retreat in front of Sherman's advancing force.

South Carolina was treated even more harshly than Georgia. In Georgia, for example, Union troops burned very few of the houses that were in their path. In South Carolina, few houses were spared.

On February 17 the Union forces entered the state capital, Columbia. That night a fire burned nearly half of the city to the ground. Although no one could prove who started the fire, South Carolinians blamed Sherman's troops for the destruction. When the Union army moved into North Carolina, all demolition of civilian property ceased.

Surrender at Appomattox By April 1865, daily desertions had shrunk the Confederate army defending Richmond to less than 35,000 starving men. Realizing that he could no longer protect the city, on April 2 Lee tried to slip around Grant's army. He planned to unite his troops with those of General Johnston, who was retreating before Sherman's force in North Carolina. Lee hoped that together they would be able to continue the war.

Units of General Grant's army tracked the Confederates as they moved west. Each time Lee tried to turn his soldiers south, Grant's troops cut them off. On April 9, Lee's army arrived at the small Virginia town of Appomattox Court House. There the Confederates were surrounded by a much larger Union force. Some of Lee's officers suggested that the army could scatter and continue to fight as **guerrillas**—soldiers who use hit-and-run tactics. Lee rejected this idea, fearing it would bring more devastation to Virginia. Reluctantly he admitted, "There is nothing left for me to do but go and see General Grant, and I would rather die a thousand deaths." He knew the war was over.

That afternoon Lee and Grant met in a private home in the town. General Lee was in his dress uniform, a sword at his side. Grant, wearing his usual private's uniform, was splattered with mud. They briefly chatted about the weather and their service in the Mexican War.

Then Lee asked Grant about the terms of the surrender. These were generous. Southern soldiers could take their horses and mules and go home. They would not be punished as traitors as long as they obeyed the laws where

Lee's surrender to Grant was both solemn and civil. *Government* *How would you characterize the terms of the surrender?*

they lived. Grant also offered to feed the starving Confederate army. After the two men signed the surrender papers, they talked for a few more minutes. Then Lee mounted his horse and rode away.

As news of the surrender spread through the Union army, soldiers began firing artillery salutes. Grant ordered the celebration stopped. He did not want rejoicing at the Southerners' misfortune because, as he pointed out, "the rebels are our countrymen again."

Main Idea **CONNECTIONS** Why was Lee finally forced to surrender?

Lincoln's Assassination

A few weeks after Lee's surrender, General Johnston surrendered to Sherman in North Carolina. Throughout May, other Confederate forces large and small also gave up.

Tragically, Abraham Lincoln did not live to see the official end of the war. Throughout the winter of 1864–1865 a group of southern conspirators in Washington, D.C., had worked on a plan to aid the Confederacy. Led by John Wilkes Booth, a Maryland actor with strong southern sympathies, the group plotted to kidnap Lincoln and exchange him for Confederate prisoners of war. After several unsuccessful attempts, Booth revised his plan. He assigned members of his group to kill top Union officials, including General Grant and Vice President Johnson. Booth himself would murder the President.

On April 14, 1865, Booth slipped into the back of the President's unguarded box at

Answers to
SECTION 4 REVIEW

1. (a) Battle of the Wilderness, see p. 367; (b) Battle of Spotsylvania, see p. 368; (c) Battle of Cold Harbor, see p. 368; (d) Thirteenth Amendment, see p. 370; (e) guerrilla, see p. 371.

2. Grant planned to attack Lee's army directly until he exhausted it. By marching through Georgia, Sherman planned to show that the Union had a power that the Confederacy could not resist.

3. Possible battles include: Battle of the Wilderness, May, 1864; Spotsylvania and Cold Harbor, May and June, 1864; the Siege of Petersburg, began June, 1864; Sherman captures Atlanta, September, 1864; Sherman takes Savannah, December, 1864; Sherman burns through South Carolina, February, 1865; Lee surrenders at Appomattox, April, 1865.

4. Possible answer: Sherman occupies Atlanta. This event demoralized the South.

5. Possible answer: He thought war was cruel and best ended quickly, prompting his destructive march through Georgia. Once the war ended, he could be generous.

6. Students' essays will vary, but might suggest that continued southern victories on the battlefield would have likely spelled defeat for Lincoln. The North was tired of war by 1864. If there had been no chance for victory, Northerners may have decided to cut their losses and bring the war to an end under the direction of a new leader.

Answer to . . .

Viewing History Sample answers: He was respected for bringing the war to an end; an elaborate funeral was a display of Union solidarity.

Lincoln's body was displayed in several major cities, such as New York shown here, on its way from Washington, D.C., to its resting place in Springfield, Illinois. *Culture Why do you think Lincoln was given such an elaborate and lengthy funeral?*

Ford's Theater in Washington, D.C. Inside, the President and Mrs. Lincoln were watching a play. Booth pulled out a pistol and shot Lincoln in the head. Leaping over the railing, he fell to the stage, breaking his leg in the process. Booth then limped off the stage and escaped out a back alley.

The army tracked Booth to his hiding place in a tobacco barn in Virginia. When he refused to surrender, they set the barn on fire. In the confusion that followed, Booth was shot to death, either by a soldier or by himself.

Mortally wounded, the unconscious President was carried to a boarding-house across the street from the theater. While doctors and family stood by helplessly, Lincoln lingered through the night. He died early the next morning without regaining consciousness.

In the North, citizens mourned for the loss of the man who had led them through the war. Lincoln's funeral train took 14 days to travel from the nation's capital to his hometown of Springfield, Illinois. As the procession passed through towns and cities, people lined the tracks to show their respect.

Both the North and the South had suffered great losses during the war, but they also both gained by it. They gained an undivided nation, a democracy that would continue to seek the equality Lincoln had promised for it. They also gained new fellow citizens—the African Americans who had broken the bonds of slavery and claimed their right to be free and equal, every one.

SECTION 4 REVIEW

Comprehension

1. *Key Terms* Define: (a) Battle of the Wilderness; (b) Battle of Spotsylvania; (c) Battle of Cold Harbor; (d) Thirteenth Amendment; (e) guerrilla.

2. *Summarizing the Main Idea* What strategies did Grant and Sherman use to finally bring victory to the Union?

3. *Organizing Information* Create a flowchart that shows the battles leading up to Lee's surrender at Appomattox. Label the first box *Battle of the Wilderness*. Label the last box *Lee surrenders at Appomattox Court House.*

Critical Thinking

4. *Analyzing Time Lines* Review the time line at the start of the section. Which event, in your opinion, had the greatest impact on the outcome of the Civil War?

5. *Drawing Conclusions* At the end of the Civil War, General Sherman was called a traitor to the North because of his generosity to the defeated South. Yet many people believe his hatred for the South prompted Sherman's destructive actions in South Carolina. How could the same person be so unforgiving during the war yet generous after it?

Writing Activity

6. *Writing a Persuasive Essay* In your view, would Lincoln have won the election of 1864 if the South had continued to triumph on the battlefield? Write an essay explaining your opinion. Support it with specific examples.

RESOURCE OPTIONS

Teaching Resources

📁 **Quiz** Units 3–4 folder, p. 66

📁 **Chapter Tests Forms A and B** Chapter Test folder

Student Performance Pack

⭐ **Guide to the Essentials** Chapter 12, Section 4 (English and Spanish)

Standardized Test Preparation Handbook

Media and Technology

🎧 **Guided Reading Audiotapes** Chapter 12 Summary (English and Spanish)

Student Edition on Audiotape Chapter 12

💿 **Test Bank CD-ROM; Interactive Student Tutorial CD-ROM** Chapter Test

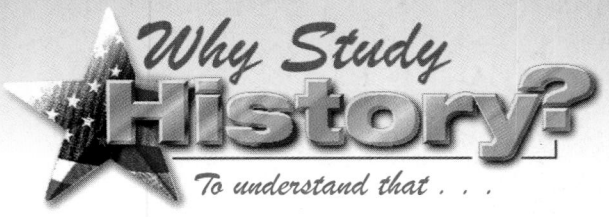

Why Study History?

To understand that . . .

Americans Remember the Civil War

More than a century after the Civil War, Americans in both northern and southern states remember that tragic conflict in a variety of ways.

Confederate and Union soldiers, their rifles drawn, clash in an open field near Sharpsburg, Maryland, on a crisp September day. The battle is not real. It is a reenactment of the Battle of Antietam.

Each year thousands of Americans witness or take part in reenactments of famous Civil War battles such as Antietam, Vicksburg, and Gettysburg. Civil War reenactments are staged with historically accurate uniforms and firearms. They are often organized alongside other activities such as parades, talks, and demonstrations of military camp life during the Civil War.

Battle of Missionary Ridge, Tennessee, in 1863

The Impact Today

The Civil War's enduring power to engage Americans' memory and imagination reflects the impact of the war on the nation. The Civil War pitted American against American, dividing families and causing an enormous amount of death and destruction.

Reenactments are just one way in which Americans remember the conflict. Civil War novels, histories, feature films, and documentaries remain extremely popular among Americans. Towns across the nation have established memorials to Union and Confederate soldiers. Monuments mark almost every Civil War battle site. Literally thousands of Web sites offer information on the conflict.

The oldest intact Civil War monument is a stone cemetery at the Stones River Battlefield near Murfreesboro, Tennessee. It was erected in 1863 to honor a Union brigade led by Colonel William B. Hazen of Ohio. One of the newest monuments, dedicated in 1998, is the African American Civil War Memorial in Washington, D.C. It honors the 235,000 African Americans who fought bravely for freedom. The Gettysburg National Military Park, perhaps the best-known Civil War site, receives more than 1.5 million visitors each year.

The Impact on You

Research the history of a particular military unit in the Civil War, such as a unit consisting of men from your community or state. Write a report describing when the unit was formed, where it fought, what casualties it suffered, and whether there are any monuments commemorating its achievements.

Confederate soldiers in a battle reenactment

Why Study History?

Class Discussion

Discuss with the class why and how Americans commemorate history. For a more thorough examination of the issue, see the activity folder in the Resource Options below.

ACTIVITY
STUDENT PARTICIPATION

Planning a Commemoration

Ask students to read the text. Then divide the class into small groups. Have each group consider a fitting way that your town might commemorate the 150th anniversary of the Civil War (in the year 2015). Each project should:

- **include a finished product, such as an activity, skit, monument design, or presentation**
- **reflect what the war meant to your town**
- **show what the war has come to mean today**

Have each group present its project to the class.

Follow up Discuss how students celebrated the past Memorial Day.

Using the Internet

Students can learn more about commemorating history by exploring links in the *America: Pathways to the Present* Web site at:

http://www.Pathways.phschool.com

Assessment

See the Lesson Plans folder, pp. 24–27, for rubrics on assessing Class Participation Projects.

 RESOURCE OPTIONS

Teaching Resources

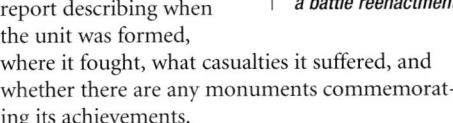 **Why Study History? Activity**

Americans Remember the Civil War, found in the Why Study History? folder, p. 13, provides an activity to help students understand reasons for and ways of commemorating history.

Media and Technology

AmericanHeritage® CD-ROM

Time Tour The Nation Torn Apart: Torn by War

 Prentice Hall United States History Video Collection™

Volume 9 *The Civil War*

GEOGRAPHY AND HISTORY

The Shenandoah Valley

Focus Tell students that one skill a military leader needed in the Civil War was the ability to use a piece of land to its best advantage. Both the Confederate and the Union armies used the Shenandoah Valley for military advantage, although in different ways.

Instruct Have the class make a map of the Shenandoah Valley like the one that belonged to Stonewall Jackson. Then ask students to describe how Jackson used the Valley to protect Richmond. How did Sheridan's treatment of the Valley differ from Jackson's? How did Sheridan's policy of total destruction serve the Union's strategy?

Ask students to suppose that they lived on a small farm near Winchester. How would they have responded to Jackson's constant raids? To Sheridan's destruction?

Extend Ask students to research and report on the use of computer technology in modern warfare. How do military strategists use computers to plan their attacks? How do modern weapons render less vital the skill of seeing how to use a piece of land for military advantage?

The Shenandoah Valley

The geographic theme of location explores where a place is, not only in absolute terms but in relation to other places. The location of the Shenandoah Valley affected the way the North and South treated it during the Civil War. What made this valley the site of so many battles?

A confederate flag and soldier's cap

Great generals study the geography of the land where they are fighting and use it to their advantage. Like geographers, they pay careful attention to location. Because of its location, the Shenandoah Valley played a crucial role in the Civil War.

Location of the Valley

One of the Southern general Stonewall Jackson's deadliest weapons was a detailed map of the Shenandoah Valley. The Valley is a corridor about 150 miles long and 25 miles wide between the Blue Ridge Mountains and the Alleghenies. Swift and decisive movement was the secret of the Confederate military strategy. Southern armies were able to travel up through the Valley toward the Northern capital of Washington, D.C.

As a Union route, the corridor proved less useful. Union armies traveling south through the Valley would end up in the mountains, far away from the Southern capital of Richmond. Eventually, however, Northern armies would devise another tactic.

The Southern Advantage

As a valley, the Shenandoah formed an excellent corridor for Confederate movement. Its slopes, though

> *Great generals study the geography of the land where they are fighting and use it to their advantage.*

forested, were not too steep or rocky for troops on foot or horseback. Furthermore, the Valley Pike, the main road through the Shenandoah, allowed even a large army like that of Confederate general Robert E. Lee to travel rapidly from the heart of Virginia to the borders of the North. And the many gaps in the Blue Ridge mountain chain allowed Southern forces like those led by Stonewall Jackson to duck easily in and out of the Shenandoah Valley as it suited their purposes.

The special characteristics of the Valley also made it valuable to the South for another reason. The population of the Valley was mostly sympathetic to the Confederacy, so Union invaders had to endure constant attacks by armed raiders. Even more helpful to the South were the Valley's splendid pastures and fields, which supplied the Confederate army in Virginia with meat and grain.

The North Fights Back

Confederate control of the Valley posed an ongoing threat to Union forces. As Union troops marched toward Richmond, Confederate armies would sneak up through the Shenandoah. Union commanders would then have to send part of their troops to defend

---

▶ RESOURCE OPTIONS

Teaching Resources

📁 **Geography and History Activity** A Cold War Confrontation, Geography and History folder, pp. 8–9

 Nystrom *Atlas of Our Country* East Central U.S., pp. 64–65

Shenandoah Valley and the Civil War

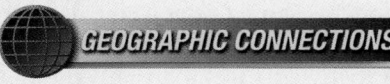

Major roads

Railroads

Lee's Invasion of the North, June–July 1863

Sheridan's Valley Campaign, Fall 1864

Union victory

Capitals

ATLANTIC OCEAN

Bordered by the Alleghenies to the west and the Blue Ridge Mountains to the east, the Shenandoah Valley provided the Confederate Army with a corridor to Washington, D.C.

Cedar Creek, Oct. 19, 1864

0   50   100 Miles

0   50   100 Kilometers

Answers to . . .

GEOGRAPHIC CONNECTIONS

1. Its slopes were not too steep or rocky for troops on foot or horseback. The Valley Pike allowed a large army to travel rapidly from Virginia to the borders of the North. The many gaps in the Blue Ridge mountain chain allowed southern forces to duck easily in and out.

2. The Valley was supplying the army in northern Virginia with food.

3. The Valley led southern troops toward their target of Washington, D.C., making it an extremely useful route. For northern troops, it led into the mountains, away from their target, Richmond.

Washington, thus diminishing the main part of their army. Hoping to put an end to this, Northern generals repeatedly tried to take control of the Shenandoah during the early years of the war. Even though they did win parts of the Valley at times, they were soon forced to give up their conquests. One key town in the upper Shenandoah Valley, Winchester, changed hands 72 times between 1861 and 1865. The Shenandoah was soon known to Northerners as the "Valley of Humiliation."

The North Wins the Valley

This was not the end of the story. The commander of Union forces, General Grant, decided in the summer of 1864 that the Southern source of supply had to be shut down once and for all.

He gave these specific instructions to General Phil Sheridan: "Do all the damage to railroads and crops you can. . . . If the war is to last another year, we want the Shenandoah Valley to remain a barren waste."

Sheridan carried out these orders to the letter. In the fall of 1864 he wrote Grant: "The people here are getting sick of the war." Grant answered: "Keep on, and your good work will cause the fall of Richmond."

In the spring of the next year, Grant's words came true. As one Confederate soldier wrote, "There are a good many of us who believe that this shooting match has been carried on long enough. A government that has run out of rations [food for its army] can't expect to do much more fighting."

Early in April 1865, Lee abandoned Richmond and surrendered. In some respects, the war had been lost months before—in the Shenandoah Valley.

GEOGRAPHIC CONNECTIONS

1. How did the Valley's geographical characteristics help Southerners?

2. Why did Grant want to make the Shenandoah Valley "a barren waste"?

Themes in Geography

3. *Location* How did the Valley's relative location to Richmond and Washington affect its value to both sides during the war?

RESOURCE OPTIONS

Media and Technology

Prentice Hall United States History Video CollectionTM

Volume 8 *Causes of the Civil War;* Volume 9 *The Civil War*

Key Terms

Students should refer to the definitions of the key terms in the chapter to write sentences that show the relation of each word to the events of the Civil War.

Comprehension

1. Union forces took control of the Cumberland and Tennessee rivers, pushed nearly to Mississippi and Alabama, and captured New Orleans and Memphis.

2. Union troops under Irvin McDowell were repulsed at Manassas in 1861; troops under McClellan were repulsed by Lee in 1862; troops under Burnside were beaten at Fredericksburg in 1862; troops under Hooker were beaten at Chancellorsville in 1863.

3. He sought to imprison anyone who interfered with the war effort without having to justify his actions.

4. Possible answer: The Pacific Railroad Act provided for the construction of transcontinental railways that linked East and West.

5. Doctors did not sterilize equipment between operations, sanitation was nonexistent, rotting garbage and human waste covered the ground, epidemics of contagious diseases swept through battle camps.

6. Lee's army was forced to retreat; Both sides suffered staggering casualties.

7. Sherman's march brought destruction to the South and made the hatred between North and South more difficult to heal.

8. Sheridan cut off Lee's supplies, forcing him to abandon Petersburg and Richmond. Then, hemmed in by Union forces, Lee surrendered at Appomattox Court House.

Chapter Summary

The major concepts of Chapter 12 are presented below. See also the *Guide to the Essentials of American History* or *Interactive Student Tutorial CD-ROM,* which contains interactive review activities, time lines, helpful hints, and test practice for Chapter 12.

Reviewing Main Ideas

Between the years 1861 and 1865, the North and the South fought a violent Civil War that set neighbor against neighbor and father against son. Hundreds of thousands of Americans were killed or maimed, and property worth billions of dollars was destroyed. By the end of the conflict, African Americans had won their freedom and the Union was preserved.

Section 1: From Bull Run to Antietam

Bloody fighting during the first two years of the Civil War made it clear to both the North and the South that the struggle would be long and difficult.

Section 2: Life Behind the Lines

The Union and Confederate governments struggled to support their armies and care for their citizens. The Union government also moved to abolish slavery.

Section 3: The Tide of War Turns

Despite southern victories at Fredericksburg and Chancellorsville, the tide of war turned in the summer of 1863 when the North won important battles at Gettysburg and Vicksburg.

Section 4: A New Birth of Freedom

After years of fighting and countless casualties, the South surrendered in April 1865.

More than a century after the Civil War, Americans remember that tragic conflict in a variety of ways. People take part in or witness battle reenactments, read novels or histories, watch films and documentaries, and honor the dead at memorials.

376

Using Graphic Organizers

- Causes: conflicts among new political parties, disagreement over the issue of slavery, economic depression, secession of lower South.
- Effects: slavery abolished, nation reunited, African Americans given equality.

Key Terms

For each of the terms below, write a sentence explaining how it relates to this chapter.

1. Copperhead
2. Pickett's Charge
3. canister
4. siege
5. martial law
6. Thirteenth Amendment
7. Emancipation Proclamation
8. war of attrition
9. Gettysburg Address
10. writ of *habeas corpus*
11. Civil War
12. greenback

Comprehension

1. What gains did Union forces make in the western part of the Confederacy in the first two years of the Civil War?
2. Briefly summarize Union efforts to capture the southern capital of Richmond in 1861–1863.
3. Why did Lincoln suspend the writ of *habeas corpus*?
4. What laws did the Republican Congress pass during the Civil War to support economic development?
5. Describe the medical and health conditions faced by Union and Confederate soldiers.
6. What was the result of the Battle of Gettysburg?
7. What were the immediate and the long-term effects of Sherman's march to the sea?
8. Briefly describe the events of 1865 that led to Lee's surrender.

Using Graphic Organizers

On a separate piece of paper, copy the multi-flow map to organize the main ideas of the chapter. On the left side note the causes leading to the Civil War. On the right side note the effects of the Civil War.

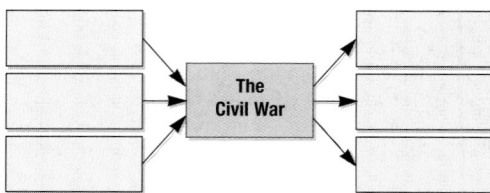

Analyzing Political Cartoons ▶

1. England and France look on as a pair of combatants fight. Identify the two fighters. (a) What does the figure on the left, labeled "Secession," represent? (b) What does the figure on the right, labeled "The People shall Rule!" represent?

2. What additional threat does the figure on the right face? Explain how you know.

3. What is being trampled? What does it stand for?

4. Identify the political leanings of the cartoonist.

Critical Thinking

1. **Applying the Chapter Skill** Review the Using Letters as Primary Sources skill on page 357. How does the writer of letter B feel about the duties she performs for the soldiers?

2. **Making Comparisons** Compare the Union and Confederate military strategies.

3. **Identifying Alternatives** What alternatives did President Lincoln have at the start of the Civil War? How might United States history have been different if he had chosen a different course of action?

4. **Testing Conclusions** Lincoln came to believe that the Union could not survive if slavery were preserved. Give evidence to support this conclusion.

INTERNET ACTIVITY

For your portfolio:
CREATE A PHOTO ESSAY

Access Prentice Hall's *America: Pathways to the Present* site at **www.Pathways.phschool.com** for the specific URLs to complete the activity. Additional resources and related Web sites are also available.

Select a Civil War topic from the links provided at the sites. Choose from the available photographs to create a photographic essay on your topic. Write detailed captions to explain each photograph and its importance in the Civil War. Include an introductory paragraph describing the theme of your photo essay.

ANALYZING DOCUMENTS ◀ ▶ INTERPRETING DATA

Turn to the "Civil War Casualties" chart on page 369.

1. Which statement best describes Union deaths due to disease? (a) Twice as many soldiers died from diseases than were killed and mortally wounded. (b) Fewer Union soldiers died from disease than died in prison. (c) Disease killed more Confederate than Union soldiers. (d) More Union soldiers died of disease than were wounded.

2. Which statement best describes the total number of Civil War casualties? (a) Confederate casualties made up the greatest part of the total war casualties. (b) The total number of killed and wounded equaled half the total casualties. (c) Total casualties were split evenly between both sides. (d) Union soldiers made up a greater number of the total casualties.

3. **Writing** How do you think the deaths from disease affected soldiers' morale? Explain your opinion.

Connecting to Today

Essay Writing Read the Gettysburg Address on page 1079. Think about how President Lincoln redefined the meaning of the United States in his speech. Then rewrite the Gettysburg Address in your own words, making sure to include a definition of the United States today.

377

INTERNET ACTIVITY

Answers will vary. Essays should have a unified theme and show an understanding of the main issues of the Civil War.

Analyzing Political Cartoons

1. (a) The seceding states, or the Confederacy. (b) The Union.
2. Copperheads, or anti-war Democrats, symbolized by the snake wrapped around the figure's leg.
3. The American flag; the United States and its ideals.
4. The cartoonist expresses the sentiments of a Union Democrat who supports the war.

Critical Thinking

1. The writer is happy to help the soldiers, although she feels great sadness when she is asked to write letters home to their wives.
2. The Union implemented the Anaconda Plan, blockading the Confederacy and gaining control of the Mississippi River to cut the Confederacy in two. The Confederacy fought a defensive war, hoping to wear down the Union's appetite for battle.
3. Possible answer: Lincoln might have chosen to allow the Confederacy to secede from the United States. The entire course of United States history would have changed. The Union and Confederacy might have battled for territory across North America.
4. Possible answer: Northerners were no longer content to let the slave system stand, even in the states in which it had originally been legal under the Missouri Compromise. Lincoln knew that slavery would be an enduring source of friction even if the South could be brought back into the Union if slavery were intact in the southern states.

Interpreting Data

1. a

2. d

3. Answers will vary, but should demonstrate an understanding of the miserable medical conditions during the war.

Connecting to Today

Answers will vary, but should demonstrate an understanding of the Address.

Reconstruction, 1865–1877

Managing Time and Instruction

INSTRUCTION SUPPORT

These materials for instruction are provided for **each section** in the **Teaching Resources.** See **Units 3–4 folder for Enrichment Support:**

- Reproducible Lesson Plans in Lesson Plans folder • Learning Styles Lesson Plans in Learning Styles Lesson Plans folder • Big Idea Graphic Organizers in Big Idea Graphic Organizer folder
- Guided Reading and Review • Quizzes • Test Preparation Practice booklet

DAILY LESSON	ENRICHMENT SUPPORT
1 Presidential Reconstruction (pp. 379–383)	• Biography, Thaddeus Stevens, found on **Resource Pro** • Great Debates, How Should the Union Be Reconstructed? Decision-Making Activities folder, pp. 26–27 • Critical Thinking Activity, Identifying Central Issues: Granting Amnesty, found on **Resource Pro** • Literature Activity, The Story of Free Joe, Units 3–4 folder, pp. 83–85 • Visual Learning Activity, A Symbol of Freedom, Learning with Documents folder, p. 55 • Biography, Charlotte Forten Grimké, Units 3–4 folder, p. 80
2 Congressional Reconstruction (pp. 385–390)	• Primary Source Activity, The Trial of President Johnson, found on **Resource Pro** • Comparing Primary Sources, On Voting Rights for African Americans, Units 3–4 folder, pp. 81–82 • Key Documents, Blanche K. Bruce, Speech in the Senate, Learning with Documents folder, p. 90 • Skills for Life Activity, Units 3–4 folder, p. 86
3 Birth of the "New South" (pp. 391–394)	• Primary Source Activity, A Bleak Future for Freedmen, Learning with Documents folder, p. 19 • Nystrom *Atlas of Our Country,* Settling the West, pp. 28–29
4 The End of Reconstruction (pp. 395–398)	• Key Documents, Frederick Douglass, Speech to the Congregational Church, Learning with Documents folder, p. 91 • Visual Learning Activity, America's Birthday Party, found on **Resource Pro** • Congress Represents All Americans, Why Study History? folder, p. 14

Running Out of Time?

- Use Tape 2, "Division and Uneasy Reunion, 1848–1877," from **Visions of America** videotapes series.
- Use Chapter 13 Summary, from **Guide to the Essentials of American History (English and Spanish).**

Companion Web Site

The companion Web site offers online links for all chapter review activities. It also provides key content links and structured support for this chapter for both teachers and students.

http://www.Pathways.phschool.com

Teaching in the Information Age

Media and Technology

For the Student

Interactive Student Tutorial CD-ROM Chapter 13
Student Edition on Audiotape Chapter 13
American Heritage® CD-ROM
Guided Reading Audiotapes (English and Spanish) Chapter 13

For the Teacher

Resource Pro CD-ROM Chapter 13
Test Bank CD-ROM Chapter 13
Listening to Literature Audiotapes *Timeless Voices, Timeless Themes* "An Account of an Experience With Discrimination" by Sojourner Truth

Assessment Options

Chapter Test Forms A & B Test Bank CD-ROM booklet
Test Bank CD-ROM Chapter 13
Standardized Test Preparation Handbook

Block Scheduling

Pacing Suggestions

For 90-minute Blocks

- Teach sections 2 and 3 using Transparencies K-4 and M-4 and the Recent Scholarship note on p. 393 for class discussions.
- Teach sections 1 and 4 using the Big Idea Graphic Organizers from Teaching Resources.

Additional Resources

- Prentice Hall's **American History Block Scheduling Support File** covers over 40 major topics in American history.
- **Prentice Hall United States History Video Collection™** contains 20 videotapes covering American history from beginnings to present.
- **Visions of America Videotapes and Videodiscs**

Connections to American Literature

from Prentice Hall

Prentice Hall Literature *Timeless Voices, Timeless Themes* "Reaction to the Emancipation Proclamation" by Reverend Henry M. Turner, p. 502

Additional Resources

For the Student

Gay Wilson Allen. *The Solitary Singer: A Critical Biography of Walt Whitman.* University of Chicago Press, 1985.
Julius Lester. *This Strange New Feeling.* Scholastic, 1985.

For the Teacher

W. E. B. Du Bois. *Black Reconstruction.* Krause-Thomason, 1976.

Prentice Hall brings into the classroom the vast archives and scholarship of the nation's premier American history magazine. See "From the Archives of American Heritage®" and "About the Presidents" teaching notes in this chapter.

 History Alive!

Teacher's Curriculum Institute, in partnership with Prentice Hall, provides unique materials that engage students with diverse learning styles. See History Alive!® unit on The Civil War and Reconstruction.

 Student Performance Pack

Ensures success in the three critical areas of Reading, Test Taking, and English Language Development with the following materials:
- Guide to the Essentials of American History in English and Spanish
- Guided Reading Audiotapes in English and Spanish
- Interactive Student Tutorial CD-ROM
- Test Preparation Handbook
- Test Preparation Practice booklet

Reconstruction
1865–1877

Introducing the Chapter
Though the outcome of the Civil War cemented the Union, the years that followed plunged the nation into dramatic social and economic changes. While African Americans obtained their liberty and southern society was transformed, Reconstruction involved a redefinition of social, economic, and political relationships between the North and the South as well as between the races.

Themes in American History
The theme for this chapter, Diversity, is listed at the beginning of this unit. An alternate theme for the chapter is Government. To teach this unit thematically, you may wish to use the Expansion, Reconstruction, Immigration folder in American History Block Scheduling Support.

Have students explore suggested ways of connecting the past to the present on page 399.

Answer to . . .

Viewing History Students should use this question as an aid in reading the chapter. Many of the South's political leaders and institutions were blamed for secession, and so were discredited at the end of the war. To reintegrate the South into the Union, southern political life would have to be rebuilt according to standards dictated by the federal government.

378

CHAPTER
13 Reconstruction
1865-1877

VIEWING HISTORY
Richmond, Virginia, like the South in general, faced an enormous rebuilding task following the Civil War. *Government In what ways did the South's political institutions need to be "rebuilt" as well?*

CHAPTER FOCUS

This chapter describes Reconstruction, the period following the Civil War, in which efforts were made to rebuild the southern states. In Washington, the nation's leaders argued bitterly over how best to reunify the nation. In the South, meanwhile, African Americans began exercising their newly won freedom, and southerners worked to rebuild the region's economy.

The Why Study History? page at the end of this chapter explores the connection between black voting rights, which African Americans won during Reconstruction, and black representation in Congress today.

 RESOURCE OPTIONS

Teaching Resources

Big Idea Graphic Organizer folder Graphic summary of the main idea of the chapter.

Learning Styles Lesson Plans folder Alternate lesson plans for diverse learning styles for each chapter.

Media and Technology

 AmericanHeritage® CD-ROM
Time Tour The Nation Torn Apart: Rebuilding the Nation

 Prentice Hall United States History Video Collection™ Volume 10
Reconstruction and Segregation (1865–1910)

1863 Lincoln's Reconstruction plan	1864 Wade-Davis Act		1865 Freedmen's Bureau created	1865 Civil War ends	1865 Johnson's Reconstruction plan
1862	**1863**	**1864**	**1865**		**1866**

1 Presidential Reconstruction

SECTION PREVIEW

Objectives

1. Describe the condition of the South in the aftermath of the Civil War.
2. Compare the Reconstruction plans of Lincoln and Johnson.
3. Explain how newly freed slaves began to rebuild their lives and how the federal government helped them.
4. *Key Terms* Define: Reconstruction; pardon.

Main Idea

During the Reconstruction era, the federal government put forth plans to allow southern states to resume participation in the Union.

Reading Strategy

Organizing Information As you read, list the main headings of the section in a chart. Beneath each heading, list at least two key facts.

The South was the main battleground of the Civil War and its largest casualty. Hardly a farm or family remained unscarred by the time soldiers began straggling home. A northern journalist described the once-gracious city of Charleston, South Carolina: "A city of ruins, of desolation, of vacant houses, of widowed women, of rotting wharves, of deserted warehouses, of weed-wild gardens, of grass-grown streets."

The federal government's controversial effort to repair the damage to the South and to restore southern states to the Union is known as **Reconstruction.** The Reconstruction program was carried out from 1865 to 1877 and involved four American Presidents.

The War's Aftermath

At the start of Reconstruction, it was clear that the nation—especially the South—had been changed forever by the war. The changes reached into families and farms.

The Physical Toll War had destroyed two thirds of southern shipping and 9,000 miles of railroads. It had devoured farmland, farm buildings,

and farm machinery; work animals and one third of all livestock; bridges, canals, and levees; and thousands of miles of roads. Factories, ports, and cities lay smoldering. The value of southern farm property had plunged 70 percent.

The Human Toll The Civil War destroyed a generation of young, healthy men—fathers, brothers, and husbands. The North lost 364,000 soldiers, including more than 38,000 African Americans. The South lost roughly 290,000 soldiers, one fifth of its adult white men. One out of three southern men were killed or wounded. Many of the survivors were permanently scarred in mind or body.

In addition, the North's decision to destroy southern homes and property resulted in countless civilian deaths. Children were made orphans; brides became widows.

Southerners' Hardships The postwar South was made up of three major groups of people. Each group faced its own hardships and fears.

(1) *Black southerners.* Some 4 million freed people were starting their new lives in a poor region with slow economic activity. As slaves, they had received food and shelter, however

In the final days of the Civil War, Lincoln visited Richmond, Virginia, the captured Confederate capital. In this painting he is shown being greeted by war-weary residents of the city. *Economics How does the painting show the damage that Richmond suffered during the war?*

inadequate. Now, after a lifetime of forced labor, many found themselves homeless, jobless, and hungry.

(2) *Plantation owners.* Planters lost slave labor worth about $3 billion. In addition the Captured and Abandoned Property Act of 1863 allowed the federal government to seize $100 million in southern plantations and cotton. With worthless Confederate money, some farmers couldn't afford to hire workers. Others had to sell their property to cover debts.

(3) *Poor white southerners.* Many white laborers could not find work any more because of the new job competition from freedmen. Poor white families began migrating to frontier lands such as Mississippi and Texas to find new opportunities.

The Changing Plantation The history of one southern plantation illustrates the complex issues brought about by the war and its aftermath. In 1824, Richard Arnold bought a rice plantation near Savannah, Georgia, which he called White Hall. The Arnolds were among 360,000 white northerners who lived and worked in the South in 1860.

Main Idea CONNECTIONS

What temporary and permanent changes did the Civil War bring to southern life?

Richard opposed secession. He sold the plantation to his son Thomas, a Confederate supporter, so the Confederacy would not seize it. At the war's end, Richard's northern connections saved White Hall from being seized by the federal government. In 1865 Richard bought White Hall back from Thomas and put him in charge of the rebuilding effort.

The White Hall plantation had suffered considerable damage. But more shocking to Thomas was the attitude of the plantation's freed slaves. They were unreliable, he reported; they refused even to speak to him. Thomas brought in a Union colonel to tell the freedmen that they would be wise to trust Arnold and agree to work for pay. But, Thomas said, one slave spoke up and "said they had made up their minds never to work for me again."

Yet throughout the South, some freed slaves chose to continue working for their former masters. Amos Morel and his wife, Cretia, did stay on to help rebuild the plantation. By the early 1870s, White Hall was one of the largest rice plantations in the South.

Two Reconstruction Plans

Most southerners accepted the war's outcome and focused on rebuilding their lives. In Washington, however, peacetime launched new battles so fierce that some historians call Reconstruction an extension of the Civil War.

The fall of the Confederacy and the end of slavery raised tough questions. How and when should southern states be allowed to resume their role in the Union? Should the South be punished for its actions, or be forgiven and allowed to recover quickly? Now that black southerners were free, would the races have equal rights? If so, how might those rights be protected? Did the Civil War itself point out a need for a stronger federal government?

At stake were basic issues concerning the nation's political system. Yet it was not even clear which branch of government had the authority to decide these matters.

On these key questions, the Constitution was silent. The Framers had made no provisions for solving the problems raised by the Civil War.

Lincoln's Plan With no road map for the future, Lincoln had begun postwar planning as early as December 1863, when he proposed a Ten Percent Plan for Reconstruction. The plan was forgiving to the South:

(1) It offered a **pardon,** an official forgiveness of a crime, to any Confederate who would take an oath of allegiance to the Union and accept federal policy on slavery.

(2) It denied pardons to all Confederate military and government officials and to southerners who had killed African American war prisoners.

(3) It permitted each state to hold a constitutional convention only after 10 percent of voters in the state had sworn allegiance to the Union.

(4) States could then hold elections and resume full participation in the Union.

Lincoln's plan did not require the new constitutions to give voting rights to black Americans. Nor did it "readmit" southern states to the Union, since in Lincoln's view, their secession had not been constitutional.

Lincoln set a tone of forgiveness for the postwar era in his Second Inaugural Address:

KEY DOCUMENTS   ❝With malice toward none; with charity for all; with firmness in the right, as God gives us to see the right, let us strive on to finish the work we are in; to bind up the nation's wounds . . . to do all which may achieve and cherish a just, and a lasting peace, among ourselves, and with all nations.❞

—*Lincoln's Second Inaugural Address, March 1865*

Congress, however, saw Lincoln's Reconstruction plan as a threat to congressional authority. The Republican leadership warned that Lincoln "should confine himself to his executive duties—to obey and execute, not make the laws . . . and leave political reorganization to Congress."

Much of Lincoln's opposition came from a group of congressmen from his own party. The group, known as the Radical Republicans, believed that the Civil War had been fought over the moral issue of slavery. Therefore the Radicals insisted that the main goal of Reconstruction should be a total restructuring of society to guarantee black people true equality.

The Radical Republicans viewed Lincoln's plan as too lenient. In July 1864 Congress passed its own, stricter Reconstruction plan, the Wade-Davis Act. Among its provisions, it required

ex-Confederate men to take an oath of past and future loyalty and to swear that they had never willingly borne arms against the United States. Lincoln let the bill die in a pocket veto.

Lincoln's hopes came to a violent end less than six weeks after his second inauguration. As discussed in the previous chapter, Lincoln was murdered on April 14, 1865, by John Wilkes Booth. The assassination plunged the nation into grief and its politics into chaos.

Johnson's Plan With Lincoln's death, Reconstruction was now in the hands of a one-time slave owner from the South: the former Vice President, Andrew Johnson. Born poor in North Carolina, Johnson grew up to become a tailor. He learned to read and write with the help of his wife and later entered politics in Tennessee as a Democrat.

Johnson had a profound hatred of rich planters and found strong voter support among poor white southerners. He served Tennessee first as governor, then in Congress. Johnson was the only southern senator to remain in Congress after secession. Hoping to attract Democratic voters, the Republican party chose Johnson as Lincoln's running mate in 1864.

When Johnson took office in April 1865, Congress was in recess until December.[†] During those eight months, Johnson pursued his own plan for the South. His plan, known as Presidential Reconstruction, included these provisions:

(1) It pardoned southerners who swore allegiance to the Union.

(2) It permitted each state to hold a constitutional convention (without Lincoln's 10 percent allegiance requirement).

(3) States were required to void secession, abolish slavery, and ratify the Thirteenth Amendment.

(4) States could then hold elections and resume participation in the Union.

Presidential Reconstruction reflected the spirit of Lincoln's Ten Percent Plan but was more generous to the South. Although officially it denied pardons to all Confederate leaders, in reality Johnson often issued pardons to those who asked him personally. In 1865 alone, he pardoned 13,000 southerners.

Main Idea
CONNECTIONS

How did Johnson's Reconstruction plan differ from Lincoln's?

[†] Until the mid-1900s, a typical session of the United States Congress lasted only four or five months. Today, Congress remains in session throughout most of the year.

Customize for
Less Proficient Readers

Have students construct a chart showing the major points of the two Reconstruction plans. Headings should include Lincoln's Plan at the top of one column and Johnson's Plan at the top of the other.

 BACKGROUND

Biography

With the end of the Civil War, American leaders looked outward. Secretary of State William H. Seward became the champion of expansionism. When the Russians asked whether the United States might want to buy Alaska, he jumped at the chance. In spite of a Civil War debt of $3 billion, the Senate approved the purchase of Alaska for $7.2 million. The purchase turned out to be a bargain—the gold taken from the Yukon Valley since 1897 has paid for Alaska many times over.

RESOURCE OPTIONS

Teaching Resources

📁 **Great Debates** How Should the Union Be Reconstructed? Decision-Making Activities folder, pp. 26–27

Media and Technology

RESOURCE ⦿ PRO

Critical Thinking Activity Identifying Central Issues: Granting Amnesty, found on Resource Pro, helps students understand why Andrew Johnson granted a general amnesty to former Confederates.

Answer to . . .

Main Idea Connections It was a similar plan, but more generous to the South than Lincoln's.

VIEWING HISTORY

Freedom opened new opportunities for African Americans, such as forming choirs (top left), preaching (above), and getting an education (right). *Culture Why do you think northerners volunteered to teach at freedmen's schools?*

The Taste of Freedom

As politicians debated, African Americans celebrated their new freedom. No longer were they mere property, subject to the whims of white slave owners.

The feeling was overwhelming. "Everybody went wild," said Charles Ames, a Georgia freedman. "We all felt like horses. . . . We was free. Just like that, we was free."

Booker T. Washington, a future leader in black education, was nine years old when the news came: "[W]e were told that we were all free and could go when and where we pleased. My mother, who was standing by my side, leaned over and kissed her children, while tears of joy ran down her cheeks."

Freedom of Movement During the war, enslaved people had simply walked away from the plantations upon hearing that a northern army approached. "Right off colored folks started on the move," said James, a freed cowhand from Texas. "They seemed to want to get closer to freedom, so they'd know what it was like—like it was a place or a city."

Many freed people took to the roads looking for family members who had been torn from them by slavery. Not all were successful in finding loved ones, but many joyful reunions did occur. In addition, many couples who had been forbidden to marry under slavery now found each other and got legally married.

Freedom to Own Land Black leaders knew that emancipation—physical freedom—was only a start. True freedom would come only with economic independence, the ability to get ahead through hard work.

Freed people urged the federal government to redistribute southern land. They argued that they were entitled to the land that slaves had cleared and farmed for generations.

A Virginia freedman put it this way: "We have a right to the land where we are located. For why? I tell you. Our wives, our children, our husbands, have been sold over and over again to purchase the lands we now locate upon; for that reason we have a divine right to the land."

Proposals to give white-owned land to freedmen got little political support.[†] Instead, small-scale, unofficial land redistribution took place. For example, in 1871 Amos Morel, the freedman who stayed on at the White Hall plantation, used his wages to buy more than 400 acres of land. He sold pieces to other freedmen and later bought land for his daughter.

[†] In 1865, Union general William Tecumseh Sherman had set up a land-distribution experiment in South Carolina. He divided confiscated coastal lands into 40-acre plots and gave them to black families. Soon the South buzzed with rumors that the government was going to give all freedmen "forty acres and a mule." Sherman's project was highly successful. However, President Johnson eventually returned much of the land to its original owners, forcing the freedmen out.

Freedom to Worship In their struggle to survive, African Americans looked to each other for help. New black organizations arose throughout the South. The most visible were churches. African Americans throughout the South withdrew from racially mixed congregations to form their own churches. They also started thousands of voluntary groups, including mutual aid societies, debating clubs, drama societies, and trade associations.

Freedom to Learn Historians estimate that in 1860, 90 percent of black adults were illiterate, partly because many southern states had banned the educating of slaves.

One supporter of black education was Charlotte Forten, a wealthy black woman from Philadelphia. In 1862, after Union troops occupied Port Royal, South Carolina, Forten went there to teach. She observed:

AMERICAN VOICES ❝I never before saw children so eager to learn. Coming to school is a constant delight and recreation to them. . . . Many of the grown people [also] are desirous of learning to read. It is wonderful how a people who have been so long crushed to the earth . . . can have so great a desire for knowledge, and such a capability for attaining it.❞

—*Charlotte Forten*

Help came from several directions. White teachers, often young women, went south to start schools. Some freed people taught themselves and one another. Between 1865 and 1870, black educators founded thirty African American colleges.

Near the White Hall plantation, two former slaves purchased property in 1870. There they created a center of education and vocational training for African Americans.

The Freedmen's Bureau To help black southerners adjust to freedom, Congress created the Freedmen's Bureau in March 1865, just prior to Lincoln's death. It was the first major federal relief agency in United States history.

The Freedmen's Bureau lacked strong support in Congress, and the agency was largely dismantled in 1869. Yet in its short existence the bureau gave out clothing, medical supplies, and millions of meals to both black and white war refugees. More than 250,000 African American students received their first formal education in bureau schools.

For a time, the bureau also distributed confiscated Confederate land to farmers. However, when President Johnson returned these properties to their white owners, black farmers again found themselves landless.

This child proudly displays clothes and a book furnished by the Freedmen's Bureau.

SECTION 1 REVIEW

Comprehension

1. **Key Terms** Define: (a) Reconstruction; (b) pardon.
2. **Summarizing the Main Idea** How did Johnson's Reconstruction plan differ from Lincoln's?
3. **Organizing Information** Create a chart that describes the challenges faced by three different groups of southerners after the Civil War.

Critical Thinking

4. **Analyzing Time Lines** Review the time line at the start of the section. Which event on that time line, in your opinion, had the greatest long-term importance? Explain your reasoning.
5. **Determining Relevance** Why was it more difficult for freedmen to exercise their freedom to own land than it was for them to exercise their freedoms to worship or to become educated?

Writing Activity

6. **Writing a Persuasive Essay** Should the federal government have taken land from white southerners and given it to former slaves? Write an essay in support of or in opposition to this idea.

▶ **RESOURCE OPTIONS**

Teaching Resources

📁 **Quiz** Units 3–4 folder, p. 73

📁 **Biography** Charlotte Forten Grimké, Units 3–4 folder, p. 80

Student Performance Pack

⭐ **Guide to the Essentials** Chapter 13, Section 1 (English and Spanish)

SKILLS FOR LIFE

Geography

How Maps Show Change Over TIme

Focus Compare two historical maps to identify changes in the cultural landscape over time.

Instruct Explain that historical maps provide information about the cultural, or human-made, traits of a place. Ask students to use visual evidence from the maps, along with information they already have about the time periods, to suggest at least one cultural change that may have taken place. Then ask students what a map of this same area might be likely to show today.

Extend See the Skills for Life Activity in the Resource Options below.

Answers

1. (a) The Barrow Plantation in Oglethorpe County, Georgia. (b) 1860 and 1881. (c) The borders of the plantation, a road crossing it, and bodies of water.

2. (a) Pre–Civil War slave quarters. (b) Sharecroppers' houses. (c) The church has a cross.

3. (a) The 21 years between 1860 and 1881. (b) In 1860 they were concentrated in a single area; by 1881 they had spread out across the entire plantation. (c) A church and a school. (d) The Civil War emancipated slaves, eliminating the need for slave quarters. By 1881, many former slaves had become sharecroppers, who worked scattered plots of land.

TEST FOR SUCCESS

Answers should show an understanding of how the symbols, namely for slave quarters and sharecroppers, indicate different time periods.

SKILLS FOR LIFE

How Maps Show Change over Time

An important task of historians is identifying change over time. One far-reaching change that took place in American life after the Civil War was the breakup of plantations. Maps can show important evidence of such a development.

The historical maps below show the changes to 2,000 acres of land in the post–Civil War South. Use the following steps to identify the changes for which the maps provide evidence.

1. Identify the location, time period, and subject matter covered by the maps. (a) What specific area of land do the maps show, and where is it located? (b) What dates are given on the maps? (c) What physical features do the maps show?

2. Analyze the key to determine the type of data that it provides. Map keys use symbols and colors to illustrate specific data. (a) What do the brown squares represent in the map on the left? (b) What do the green squares represent in the map on the right? (c) How is the symbol for a church distinguishable from the symbol for a schoolhouse?

3. Analyze the data in the maps. Now compare these maps to draw conclusions about the change over time that they indicate. (a) Over what period of time has the change taken place? (b) How has the location of dwellings on the plantation changed during this period? (c) What new buildings have been added? (d) What historical events and trends helped to produce the changes that these maps illustrate?

TEST FOR SUCCESS

If the years of the maps were not labeled, would you be able to tell which map showed the plantation in 1860 and which showed the land in 1881? Explain your answer.

The Barrow Plantation, Oglethorpe County, Georgia

1860

1881

Branch Creek

Syll's Fork

Road

"The House"

Wright's Branch

Little River

Slave quarters

Source: Eric Foner, *A Short History of Reconstruction, 1863–1877,* New York: Harper & Row, 1990

0   1/2   1 Mile
0   1/2   1 Kilometer

Branch Creek

Syll's Fork

"The House"

Road

Wright's Branch

Little River

Sharecroppers' houses
Church
Schoolhouse

0   1/2   1 Mile
0   1/2   1 Kilometer

384

▶ RESOURCE OPTIONS

Teaching Resources

Skills for Life Activity Units 3–4 folder, p. 86, helps students draw conclusions about the effect of legislation by comparing maps of African American voters.

1865	1866	1867	1868	1869	1870

1865
Southern states
pass black codes

1867
Radical
Reconstruction

1868
President Johnson
impeached

1868
Fourteenth
Amendment ratified

1870
Fifteenth
Amendment
ratified

2 Congressional Reconstruction

SECTION PREVIEW

Objectives

1 Describe the relationship between the black codes and Fourteenth Amendment.
2 Summarize the effects of Radical Reconstruction and of the Fifteenth Amendment.
3 Analyze conditions in the South under Republican government.
4 *Key Terms* Define: black codes; Fourteenth Amendment; civil rights; impeach; Fifteenth Amendment; carpetbagger; scalawag.

Main Idea

As southern states moved to limit freedmen's rights, Congress took over Reconstruction and passed new laws to protect African Americans' freedom.

Reading Strategy

Problem Solving In the late 1860s, southern states were putting ex-Confederates back in power and trying to keep freedmen in slavelike conditions. List some possible solutions to this problem. As you read, take specific notes on how Congress actually responded.

Black southerners in 1865 faced unseen dangers on the road to freedom. For many African Americans, the initial surge of joy quickly turned to a thousand worrisome questions.

How would freedmen feed and house themselves? Who would take care of the old, the sick, and the orphaned? How could families leave the plantation to seek a better life? Where could they get help in a place where some angry ex-Confederates still carried a gun and a grudge?

Black Codes

Defeat in war had not changed the fact that white people still dominated southern society. As one white Georgian noted: "[The freedman] has no land; he can make no crops except the white man gives him a chance. . . . He can scarcely get work anywhere but in the rice-fields and cotton plantations. . . . What sort of freedom is that?"

Indeed, one of the main goals of the Civil War, freedoms for enslaved people, was being

rolled back. One by one, southern states met Johnson's Reconstruction demands and were restored to the Union. The first order of business in these new, white-run governments was to enact **black codes,** laws that restricted freedmen's rights. The black codes established virtual slavery with provisions such as these:

Curfews. Generally, black people could not gather after sunset.

Vagrancy laws. Freedmen convicted of vagrancy—that is, not working—could be fined, whipped, or sold for a year's labor.

Labor contracts. Freedmen had to sign agreements in January for a year of work. Those who quit in the middle of a contract often lost all the wages they had earned.

Limits on women's rights. Mothers who wanted to stay home and care for their families were forced instead to do farm labor.

Land restrictions. Freed people could rent land or homes only in rural areas. This forced them to live on plantations.

Southern defiance of Reconstruction enraged northern Republicans in Congress.

RESOURCE OPTIONS

Teaching Resources

📁 **Reproducible Lesson Plan** Lesson Plans folder, p. 85

📁 **Big Idea Graphic Organizer** Big Idea Graphic Organizer folder, p. 57

📁 **Guided Reading and Review** Units 3–4 folder, p. 74

Media and Technology

AmericanHeritage® CD-ROM

Explorer Activity 17 Reconstruction, CD-ROM Guidebook, pp. 53–54, helps students research and create a test on Reconstruction.

Objectives

You may wish to call students' attention to the objectives in the Section Preview. The objectives are reflected in the main headings of the section.

Bellringer

Ask students to think about times in their lives when they experienced change. How did they and others react to the change? Did they want to go back to the way it had been before the change?

Reading Strategy

Problem Solving Refer to the Reading Strategy in the Section Preview. You may wish to discuss possible solutions with students before they begin the reading.

LESSON PLAN

Connecting to the Main Idea

1. Focus Explain that once southern state governments were reestablished under Johnson's plan, they began to undermine the plan. Ask students what southern states did to undermine Reconstruction. How did Congress respond?

2. Instruct Discuss how Republicans were able to bring radical political and social changes to the South. Ask students why Congress wanted to take over Reconstruction. How did the dissatisfaction of Congress with Johnson eventually lead to his impeachment? What was Congress hoping to accomplish by passing the Fourteenth and Fifteenth Amendments? What impact did the Fifteenth Amendment have on Reconstruction legislatures?

3. Close The Reconstruction policy of the Republicans brought great changes to the South. The next section describes the economic impact of Reconstruction on the region.

They blamed President Johnson for southern Democrats' return to power. Determined to bypass Johnson, Congress used one of its greatest tools: the power to amend the Constitution.

Turning Point: Fourteenth Amendment

In early 1866 Congress passed a Civil Rights Act that outlawed the black codes. Johnson vetoed the measure. As President, Johnson was head of the Republican party. Yet instead of leading congressional Republicans, he was often at odds with them.

As an unelected former Democrat, Johnson had no mandate to govern. A mandate is voter approval of a politician's policies that is implied when he or she wins an election. Lack of a mandate limited Johnson's ability to influence Congress.

Congress overrode the President's veto. Then it took further action. Concerned that courts might strike down the Civil Rights Act, Congress decided to build equal rights into the Constitution. In June 1866 Congress passed the **Fourteenth Amendment,** which was ratified by the states in 1868. The amendment states:

> **KEY DOCUMENTS** "All persons born or naturalized in the United States . . . are citizens of the United States and of the State wherein they reside. No State shall make or enforce any law which shall abridge the privileges or immunities of citizens of the United States; nor shall any State deprive any person of life, liberty, or property, without due process of law; nor deny to any person within its jurisdiction the equal protection of the laws. . . . "

—Fourteenth Amendment, Section 1

 TURNING POINT : *The Fourteenth Amendment*

Ratification of this landmark amendment made possible future victories for American citizens seeking "equal protection of the laws," as the time line below illustrates.

1868
The Fourteenth Amendment is ratified.

1938
Congress passes the Fair Labor Standards Act, banning child labor and setting a minimum wage and maximum hours.

In the 1960s and beyond, women and minorities sought "equal protection" in jobs, housing, and other areas.

| 1850 | 1900 | 1950 | 2000 |

1920
American women gain the right to vote with passage of the Nineteenth Amendment. Photo (left) shows women filling in a map to show states that had approved the amendment.

1992
Carol Moseley-Braun becomes the first African American woman elected to the United States Senate.

TEST PREPARATION

Have students read the excerpt from the Fourteenth Amendment on this page and then answer the question below.

The word *abridge* in the passage means—

A enforce.

B take away.

C connect.

D grant.

The full text of the Fourteenth Amendment is on page 166–167. Its effects have echoed throughout American history, as shown in the time line on the previous page.

Radical Reconstruction

The congressional Republicans who drafted the Fourteenth Amendment consisted of two major groups. One group was the Radical Republicans. Radicals were small in number but increasingly influential. Most Republicans, however, saw themselves as moderates. In politics, a moderate is someone who supports the mainstream views of the party, not the more extreme positions.

Moderates and Radicals both opposed Johnson's Reconstruction policies, opposed the spread of black codes, and favored the expansion of the Republican party in the South. But moderates were less enthusiastic over the Radicals' goal of granting African Americans their **civil rights,** citizens' personal liberties guaranteed by law, such as voting rights and equal treatment. (See Government Concepts at right.) Racial inequality was still common in the North, and moderates did not want to impose stricter laws on the South than those in the North.

The North Grows Impatient This reluctance began to dissolve in early 1866, as word spread of new violence against African Americans. In April, the famous Civil War nurse Clara Barton gave graphic testimony in Congress about injured black victims she had treated. During the next three months, white rioters went on rampages against African Americans in Memphis, Tennessee; New Orleans, Louisiana; and New York City. White police joined in the stabbings, shootings, and hangings that killed hundreds.

Despite public outrage against the brutality, Johnson continued to oppose equal rights for African Americans. In the 1866 congressional elections, he gave speeches urging states not to ratify the Fourteenth Amendment. Angry northern voters responded by sweeping Radical Republicans into Congress. Now, Radicals could put their own Reconstruction plans into action.

Strict Laws Imposed Calling for "reform, not revenge," Radicals in Congress passed the Reconstruction Act of 1867. Historians note that this was indeed a "radical" act in American history. These are its key provisions:

(1) It put the South under military rule, dividing it into five districts, each governed by a northern general. (See map on the next page.)

(2) It ordered southern states to hold new elections for delegates to create new state constitutions.

(3) It required states to allow all qualified male voters, including African Americans, to vote in the elections.

(4) It temporarily barred southerners who had supported the Confederacy from voting.

(5) It required southern states to guarantee equal rights to all citizens.

(6) It required the states to ratify the Fourteenth Amendment.

Congress and the President The stage was now set for a showdown that pitted Johnson against two powerful Radical Republicans in Congress. Massachusetts Senator Charles Sumner, a founder of the Republican party, was a passionate abolitionist who sought voting rights for black Americans.

In the House, Johnson faced Thaddeus Stevens, a Pennsylvania congressman with a stern face and a personality to match. Stevens led the charge that threatened to bring down Johnson's presidency.

At face value, the contest was a test of wills between the President and his congressional adversaries. Yet it was also a power struggle between the legislative and executive branches of government, a test of the system of checks and balances established by the Constitution.

A Power Struggle The crisis began in early 1868, when Johnson tried to fire Secretary of War Edwin Stanton, a Lincoln appointee. Johnson wanted Stanton out because, under the new Reconstruction Act, Stanton, a friend of the Radicals, would preside over military rule of the South.

GOVERNMENT CONCEPTS

civil rights: **the rights to which every citizen is entitled**

▼ **The Historical Context:** The first Civil Rights Act, in 1866, guaranteed citizenship to African Americans. The second, in 1875, guaranteed them equal rights in public places. More fundamentally, in 1868 the Fourteenth Amendment made protection of civil rights part of the Constitution.

▼ **The Concept Today:** Violations of African Americans' civil rights continued and even increased following Reconstruction. Nearly a century later, the civil rights movement of the 1950s and 1960s fought to erase laws that discriminated against African Americans. Today it is illegal to discriminate on the basis of race.

Main Idea CONNECTIONS

What were the main goals of Radical Reconstruction?

About the Presidents

Andrew Johnson (1865–1869) was impeached after two days of one-sided debate. The charges against the President were politically motivated. As his Secretary of the Navy wrote, "Those who may vote to convict . . . would as readily vote to impeach the President had he been accused of stepping on a dog's tail." The Senate had responsibility for conducting the trial. Members of Johnson's Cabinet were not allowed to testify on his behalf, and Radicals pressured undeclared Republican senators to convict Johnson. Among them, Senator Grimes buckled under the pressure and had a stroke. The Radicals even postponed the final vote to exert more pressure. In the end, however, seven Republican senators gave up their legislative careers to vote for Johnson's acquittal. Source: David Jacobs, "Andrew Johnson," *The American Heritage® Pictorial History of the Presidents of the United States,* vol. 1, 1968

Radical Rule of the South

 MAP Skills President Lincoln had hoped to restore southern state governments to "successful operation, with order prevailing and the Union reestablished," by December 1865. Under Radical Republican rule, however, this did not happen for more than a decade. *Place* Which state was the first to rejoin the Union? Which states rejoined in 1870?

The firing of Stanton directly challenged the Tenure of Office Act just passed by Congress in 1867. The act placed limits on the President's power to hire and fire government officials.

Under the Constitution, the President must seek Senate approval for candidates to fill certain jobs, such as Cabinet posts. The Tenure of Office Act demanded that the Senate approve the firing of those officials as well, thereby limiting the President's power to create an administration to his own liking. The act also took away the President's constitutional powers as commander in chief of the armed forces.

Johnson Impeached Led by the fiery Stevens, the House found that Johnson's firing of Stanton was unconstitutional. On February 24, 1868, House members voted to **impeach** him—to charge him with wrongdoing in office. Johnson became the first President to be impeached.

As called for by the Constitution, in May 1868 the Senate tried President Andrew Johnson for "high crimes and misdemeanors." If two thirds of the senators were to vote for conviction, Johnson would become the first and only President ever removed from office.

The historic vote took place on May 16, 1868. When all the "ayes" and "nays" were counted, Johnson had escaped by the closest of margins: one vote.[†] The crisis set the precedent that only the most serious crimes, and not merely a dispute with Congress, could remove a President from office.

Grant Is Elected President Johnson, as the saying goes, "won the battle but lost the war." He served the remaining months of his term, but with no mandate and no real power. Rejected by the party that had never really embraced him, Johnson went back to Tennessee and regained his Senate seat—as a Democrat.

In the 1868 election, Republicans chose a trusted candidate who was one of their own: the victorious Civil War general, Ulysses S. Grant. In a close race, Grant beat Democrat Horatio Seymour, former governor of New York. Now, Congress and the President were allies, not enemies.

The Fifteenth Amendment

Across the South, meanwhile, freedmen were beginning to demand the rights of citizenship: to vote, to hold public office, to serve on juries, and to testify in court. In a letter to the Tennessee constitutional convention dated January 9, 1865, Nashville freedmen eloquently presented the case for black voting rights:

[†] All but one senator had declared their votes even before the trial had begun. The lone holdout was Kansas Republican Edmund G. Ross, an opponent of Johnson. His yes vote would have given Radicals the two-thirds majority needed to convict. Despite bribes and threats, Ross insisted on hearing the evidence before deciding. In the end he felt there was insufficient evidence, and he voted with the Democrats and six other Republicans not to convict. For following his conscience, Ross was severely condemned and eventually forced out of office.

AMERICAN VOICES "If [freedmen] are good law-abiding citizens, praying for its prosperity, rejoicing in its progress, paying its taxes, fighting its battles, making its farms, mines, work-shops and commerce more productive, why deny them the right to have a voice in the election of its rulers?"

—The "black citizens of Nashville"

The letter received no known response. Yet African Americans, and their supporters in Congress, pressed on. (See Comparing Primary Sources on the right.)

In February 1869, at the peak of Radical power, Congress passed the **Fifteenth Amendment** to the Constitution. It stated that no citizen may be denied the right to vote "by the United States or by any State on account of race, color, or previous condition of servitude." Ratified in March 1870, the Fifteenth Amendment was one of the last major pieces of Reconstruction legislation.

The Supreme Court added its weight to the federal Reconstruction effort in 1869. In *Texas v. White*, the Court upheld Congress's right to restructure southern governments. The ruling added new support for federal power over states' rights.

In 1870, with federal troops stationed across the South and with the Fifteenth Amendment in place, southern black men proudly voted. Most voted Republican, while many angry white voters stayed home. The unique situation swept Republicans, including hundreds of freedmen, into public office in the South.

More than 600 African Americans were elected to southern legislatures. Louisiana gained a black governor, P.B.S. Pinchback. Sixteen black men went to Congress. In 1874, Mississippi sent to the Senate a former slave, Blanche Bruce.

Blanche K. Bruce

AMERICAN BIOGRAPHY A boy born into slavery in 1841 could expect little more than a life of servitude. Blanche K. Bruce was more fortunate than some. Growing up in Virginia and Missouri, he shared a tutor with his master's son. Bruce later attended Oberlin College in Ohio, until his money ran out.

Bruce then moved to Mississippi and recruited Republicans from among freedmen

on the plantations. In 1871 he ran for sheriff of Bolivar County, Mississippi. In a debate, his opponent, a white Democrat, called Bruce "a slave who did nothing but wait on his master."

"It is true that I was a house slave," Bruce replied. "But I freed myself, educated myself, and raised myself up in the world. If my opponent had started out where I did, he would still be there."

Bruce won the sheriff's post, and held other government jobs as well. He worked to ease racial and political tensions, earning respect from Radical and moderate Republicans—even white planters who opposed Reconstruction. In 1874 Bruce won election to the United States Senate.

In Congress Bruce worked to help African Americans. He opposed moves

Blanche K. Bruce (1841–1898)

COMPARING PRIMARY SOURCES

VOTING RIGHTS FOR AFRICAN AMERICANS

The question of whether to extend voting rights to African Americans was hotly debated in the 1860s.

In Favor of Voting Rights

"If impartial suffrage is excluded in rebel States, then every one of them is sure to send a solid rebel representative delegation to Congress, and cast a solid rebel electoral vote. They . . . would always elect the President and control Congress. . . . I am for negro suffrage in every rebel state. If it be just, it should not be denied; if it be necessary, it should be adopted; if it is a punishment to traitors, they deserve it."

—Speech by Thaddeus Stevens, Radical Republican, January 3, 1867

Opposed to Voting Rights

"Most of the whites are disenfranchised [not legally able to vote] and ineligible for office, whilst the Negroes are [granted] the right of voting. The political power is therefore thrown into the hands of a mass of human beings who, having just emerged from a state of servitude [slavery], are ignorant of the forms of government and totally unfit to exercise this, the highest privilege of a free people."

—Henry William Ravenel, South Carolina planter, journal entry for February 24, 1867

ANALYZING VIEWPOINTS Compare the main arguments made by the two writers.

Using the Internet

Prepare a Summary

Objective Use the Internet to have students prepare a summary of the history of impeachment. Tell students to follow these directions.

1. See the *America: Pathways to the Present* Web site at

http://www.Pathways.phschool.com

for the URL for The American Presidency.

2. Use links to find information about impeachment.

3. Write a summary of the history of impeachment. Include information from the Constitution on procedures for impeachment in your summary.

▶ RESOURCE OPTIONS

Teaching Resources

Comparing Primary Sources On Voting Rights for African Americans, Units 3–4 folder, pp. 81–82

Key Documents Blanche K. Bruce, Speech in the Senate, Learning with Documents folder, p. 90

Answer to . . .

Comparing Primary Sources Stevens argues that voting rights should be extended so that the black vote can temper the white Southern influence in Congress; Ravenel argues that, having just been slaves, African Americans are not fit to participate in government.

Tell students that a multiflow organizer shows causes and effects. Ask students to use it to record the causes and effects of congressional Reconstruction and Radical Reconstruction.

Teaching Tip A template for this graphic organizer can be found in the Color Transparencies, G-5.

Answers to
SECTION 2 REVIEW

1. (a) black codes, see p. 385; (b) Fourteenth Amendment, see p. 386; (c) civil rights, see p. 387; (d) impeach, see p. 388; (e) Fifteenth Amendment, see p. 389; (f) carpetbagger, see p. 390; (g) scalawag, see p. 390.

2. To eradicate black codes and unequal/violent treatment of African Americans; Reconstruction Act of 1867.

3. Causes: Johnson's policies, black codes, violence toward African Americans, civil rights denied; Effects: Reconstruction Act of 1867, 14th Amendment ratified, Johnson impeached, Tenure of Office Act, 15th Amendment ratified.

4. Sample entry: Southern states passed black codes, resulting in an opposition movement to implement Radical Reconstruction, which sought to give African Americans equal treatment.

5. Congress used its power to impeach a President accused of acting unconstitutionally.

6. Essays will vary but should be supported by facts from the section.

---

to encourage black people to relocate in the West African country of Liberia. Instead he urged freedmen to stay, get an education, and fight for equality. At his death in 1898, Blanche Bruce was said to be second only to Frederick Douglass as a leader of African Americans.

The Republican South

During Radical Reconstruction, the Republican party was a mixture of people who had little in common but a desire to prosper in the postwar South. This strong bloc of voters included freedmen and two other groups.

Carpetbaggers Northern Republicans who moved to the postwar South became known as **carpetbaggers.** Southerners gave them this insulting nickname, which referred to a type of cheap suitcase made from carpet scraps. The name implied that these northerners had stuffed some clothes into a carpetbag and rushed in to profit from southern misery.

The carpetbag became a symbol of corruption and greed.

Carpetbaggers were often depicted as greedy men seeking to grab power or make a fast buck. Certainly the trainloads of northerners who disembarked in southern cities included some profiteers and swindlers. Yet historians point out that most carpetbaggers were honest, educated men. They included former union soldiers, black northerners, Freedmen's Bureau officials, businessmen, clergy, and political leaders.

Scalawags In the postwar South, to be white and a southerner and a Republican was to be seen as a traitor. Southerners had an unflattering name for white southern Republicans as well: **scalawag,** originally a Scottish word meaning "scrawny cattle." Some scalawags were former Whigs who had opposed secession. Some were small farmers who resented the planter class. Still others were former planters. Many scalawags, but not all, were poor.

Many Southern whites, resenting the power of freedmen, carpetbaggers, and scalawags, criticized the Reconstruction governments as corrupt and incompetent. In reality, Reconstruction legislatures included honest men and dishonest men, qualified politicians and incompetent ones, literate men and a few illiterate ones. Today, most historians agree that these officials were no worse and no better than officials in other regions of the country at this time.

SECTION 2 REVIEW

Comprehension
1. *Key Terms* Define: (a) black codes; (b) Fourteenth Amendment; (c) civil rights; (d) impeach; (e) Fifteenth Amendment; (f) carpetbagger; (g) scalawag.
2. *Summarizing the Main Idea* Why did Congress take over Reconstruction, and what policies did it create?
3. *Organizing Information* Create a cause-and-effect chart on Radical Reconstruction.

Critical Thinking
4. *Analyzing Time Lines* Review the time line at the start of the section. Write a phrase or sentence that connects each entry to the entry that follows it.
5. *Drawing Conclusions* How was the impeachment of Andrew Johnson a test of the nation's system of checks and balances?

Writing Activity
6. *Writing an Expository Essay* From the perspective of a journalist traveling in the postwar South, write an expository essay describing the effects of Republican government on the region.

 RESOURCE OPTIONS

Teaching Resources

📁 **Quiz** Units 3–4 folder, p. 75

Student Performance Pack

⭐ **Guide to the Essentials** Chapter 13, Section 2 (English and Spanish)

3 Birth of the "New South"

SECTION PREVIEW

Objectives

1. Summarize the post–Civil War changes in southern agriculture.
2. Explain the achievements and limitations of urban and industrial growth in the South.
3. List the beneficial and the harmful ways in which Reconstruction funds were used.
4. *Key Terms* Define: sharecropping; tenant farming; infrastructure.

Main Idea

Reconstruction transformed the South's economy, as plantations adjusted to the loss of slave labor and the region began to attract investment and industry.

Reading Strategy

Formulating Questions Reread the Main Idea above. Then rewrite it as a question. As you read, take notes that help answer that question.

No man can work another man's land [without getting] poorer and poorer every year," a black southerner wrote during Reconstruction. One black family in postwar Alabama found this out the hard way.

The Holtzclaw family worked on the cotton farm of a white planter. Every year at harvest time they received part of the cotton crop as payment for their work. But you can't eat cotton, and most years the Holtzclaws' share of the harvest didn't earn them enough money to feed themselves.

Some years the planter gave them nothing at all. So the mother worked as a cook. The father hauled logs at a sawmill for 60 cents a day. The children would wade knee-deep in swamps gathering anything edible. This was not the freedom they had hoped for.

Changes in Farming

The Holtzclaws were part of an economic reorganization in the "New South" of the 1870s. It was triggered by the ratification of the Thirteenth Amendment in 1865, which ended slavery and shook the economic foundations of the South.

The loss of slave labor raised grave questions for southern agriculture. Would cotton still be king? If so, who would work the plantations? Would freed people flee the South or stay? How would black emancipation affect the poor white laborers of the South? No one really knew.

Wanted: Workers Although the Civil War left southern plantations in tatters, the destruction was not permanent. Many planters managed to hang on to their land, and others regained theirs after climbing out of debt.

Planters complained, however, that they couldn't find people willing to work for them. Nobody liked picking cotton in the blazing sun. It seemed too much like slavery. Workers often disappeared to look for better, higher-paying jobs. For instance, railroad workers in Virginia in the late 1860s earned $1.75 to $2.00 a day. Plantation wages came to 50 cents a day at best. Women in the fields earned as little as 6 cents a day.

In simple terms, planters had land but no laborers, while freedmen had their own labor but no land. Out of these needs came new patterns of farming in the South.

With shovels and pickaxes, workers built railroads that crisscrossed the New South.

RESOURCE OPTIONS

Teaching Resources

📁 **Reproducible Lesson Plan** Lesson Plans folder, p. 86

📁 **Learning Styles Lesson Plan** Learning Styles Lesson Plans folder, p. 29

📁 **Big Idea Graphic Organizer** Big Idea Graphic Organizer folder, p. 58

📁 **Guided Reading and Review** Units 3–4 folder, p. 76

Media and Technology

🦅 **AmericanHeritage® CD-ROM**

Time Tour A Nation Torn Apart: Rebuilding the Nation

SECTION 3

Birth of the "New South"

Objectives

You may wish to call students' attention to the objectives in the Section Preview. The objectives are reflected in the main headings of the section.

Bellringer

Ask students to think about the term economic reorganization. What do they suppose it means? Ask students if they know of any countries that have undergone economic reorganization in the last decade.

Reading Strategy

Formulating Questions Refer to the Reading Stategy in the Section Preview. When students have finished the reading, you may wish to ask them to write a one-paragraph answer to their question.

LESSON PLAN

Connecting to the Main Idea

1. Focus Explain that the passage of the Thirteenth Amendment in 1865 and Reconstruction brought great economic changes to the South. Ask students what these changes were.

2. Instruct Discuss economic reorganization in the South. How did the end of slavery bring about new patterns of farming? Ask students why state governments poured money into creating infrastructure. What were the good and bad effects of this kind of business development? Why didn't the South become as industrialized as the North?

3. Close Reconstruction policies transformed the South but white Southerners resented the changes. The next section describes how some white Southerners struck back violently to reverse these changes, as well as the Republicans' retreat from Reconstruction.

CAUSES
- *Slavery is abolished.*
- *Small farmers lack capital to buy land.*
- *Planters need a stable work force.*

↓

SHARECROPPING AND TENANT FARMING

↓

EFFECTS
- *Farmers are caught in a cycle of debt.*
- *Planters and merchants prosper.*
- *Agricultural focus shifts from food crops to cash crops.*

 Interpreting Charts Whether white or black, most southern farmers remained poor in the years following the Civil War—as did this Florida family (right), thought to be sharecroppers or tenant farmers. The chart (left) shows some of the problems that poor families faced. *Economics How did farmers get caught in a cycle of debt?*

Sharecropping The most common new farming arrangement was **sharecropping.** A sharecropping family, such as the Holtzclaws, farmed some portion of a planter's land. As payment the family was promised a share of the crop at harvest time, generally one third or one half of the yield. The planter usually provided housing for the family.

Sharecroppers worked under close supervision and under the threat of harsh punishment. They could be fined for missing a single workday. After the harvest, some dishonest planters simply evicted the sharecroppers without pay. Others charged the families for housing and other expenses, so that the sharecroppers often wound up in debt at the end of the year. Since they could not leave before paying the debt, these sharecroppers were trapped on the plantation.

Main Idea CONNECTIONS

In what ways did Reconstruction change agriculture in the South?

Tenant Farming If a sharecropper saved enough money, he might try **tenant farming.** Like sharecroppers, tenant farmers did not own the land they farmed. Unlike sharecroppers, however, tenant farmers paid to rent the land, just as you might rent an apartment today. Tenants chose what to plant and when to work. Thus they had a higher social status than sharecroppers.

The Holtzclaws managed to move from sharecropping to tenant farming. They rented 40 acres of land. They bought a mule, a horse, and a team of oxen. William Holtzclaw was a child at the time. "We were so happy at the prospects of owning a wagon and a pair of mules, and having only our father for boss, that we shouted and leaped for joy," he later recalled.

Effects on the South Changes in farming during Reconstruction affected the South's economy in several important ways:

Changes in the labor force. Before the Civil War, 90 percent of the South's cotton was harvested by slaves. By 1875, white laborers, mostly tenant farmers, picked 40 percent of the crop.

Emphasis on cash crops. Sharecropping and tenant farming encouraged planters to grow cash crops, such as cotton, tobacco, and sugar cane, rather than food crops. The South's postwar cotton production soon surpassed prewar levels. As a result of the focus on cash crops, the South had to import much of its food.

Cycle of debt. By the end of Reconstruction, rural poverty was deeply rooted in the South, among blacks and whites alike. They remained in a cycle of debt, in which this year's profits went to pay last year's bills. The Southern Homestead Act of 1866 attempted to break that cycle by offering low-cost land to southerners, black or white, who would farm it. By 1874, black farmers in Georgia

---

owned 350,000 acres. Still, most landless farmers could not afford to participate. In the cotton states, only about one black family in 20 owned land after a decade of Reconstruction.

Rise of merchants. Tenant farming created a new class of wealthy southerners: the merchants. Throughout the South, stores sprang up around plantations to sell supplies on credit. "We have stores at almost every crossroad," a journalist observed. By 1880 the South had more than 8,000 rural stores.

Some merchants were honest; others were not. Landlords frequently ran their own stores and forced their tenants to buy there at high prices.

After four years of tenant farming, the Holtzclaws watched as creditors carted away everything they owned. "They came and took our corn and, finally, the vegetables from our little garden, as well as the chickens and the pig," Holtzclaw said. The family had no choice but to return to sharecropping.

Cities and Industry

Southerners who visited the North after the Civil War were astounded at how industrialized the North had become. The need for large-scale production of war supplies had turned small factories into big industries that dominated the North's economy. Industrialization had produced a new class of wage earners. It had ignited city growth and generated wealth. Could all this happen in the South?

Some southern leaders saw a unique opportunity for their region. They urged the South not simply to rebuild its old agricultural economy but to build a new, industrialized one. One of the pro-business voices was Henry Grady, editor of the *Atlanta Constitution.* He called for a "New South" of growing cities and thriving industries.

The Growth of Cities Atlanta, the city so punished by Sherman's army, took Grady's advice. Only months after the war, the city was on its way to becoming a major metropolis of the South, as one observer noted:

❝A new city is springing up with marvelous rapidity. The narrow and irregular and numerous streets are alive from morning till night . . . with a never-ending throng of . . . eager and excited and enterprising men, all bent on building and trading and swift fortune-making.❞

—*Visitor to Atlanta, 1865*

A major focus of Reconstruction, and one of its greatest successes, was the rebuilding and extension of southern railroads. By 1872, southern railroads were totally rebuilt and about 3,300 miles of new track laid, a 40 percent increase.

Railroads turned southern villages into towns, and towns into cities. Commerce and population rose not only in Atlanta, but also in Richmond, Nashville, Memphis, Louisville, Little Rock, Montgomery, and Charlotte. On the western frontier, the Texas towns of Dallas, Houston, and Fort Worth were on the rise.

Limits of Industrial Growth Despite these changes, Reconstruction did not transform the South into an industrialized, urban region like the North. Most southern factories did not make finished goods such as furniture. They handled only the early, less profitable stages of manufacturing, such as making lumber or pig iron. These items were shipped north to be made into finished products and sold.

Most of the South's postwar industrial growth came from cotton mills. New factories began to spin and weave cotton into undyed fabric. The value of cotton mill production in South Carolina rose from about $713,000 in 1860 to nearly $3 million by 1880. However, the big profits went to northern companies that dyed the fabric and sold the finished product.

Still, the growth of southern industry planted seeds of economic change. For example, Alabama, already the nation's biggest iron producer, would become a major producer of steel.

American Cotton Production, 1860–1870

Source: *Historical Statistics of the United States, Colonial Times to 1970*

Interpreting Graphs Cotton production was the South's main economic activity until 1930. *Economics* **What accounts for the drop in production in the middle of this chart?**

Answer to . . .

Interpreting Graphs The Civil War.

Answers to
SECTION 3 REVIEW

1. (a) sharecropping, see p. 392;
(b) tenant farming, see p. 392;
(c) infrastructure, see p. 394

2. Agriculture: changes in labor force resulted in more white laborers; emphasis on cash crops led to the need to import much of the food, creating a cycle of debt and rural poverty; tenant farming created a new class of wealthy southerners. Industry: rebuilding of southern railroads led to the growth of villages into cities, population rose in these places.

3. Sharecropper harvests crops; planter charges sharecropper for housing and other expenses; sharecropper can't pay so goes into debt; sharecropper trapped on plantation for another season.

4. Southern Homestead Act: unsuccessful because, while it attempted to offer low-cost land to Southerners, most landless farmers still could not participate. Rebuilding of southern railroads: successful because with a 40 percent increase in miles of track, railroads turned villages into highly populated cities.

5. Infrastructure, especially railroads, was rebuilt quickly and at great expense. Funding for programs such as the Freedmen's Bureau received little support.

6. Essays will vary but should be supported by facts from the section.

Funding Reconstruction

The Republicans who led Congress agreed with southern legislatures on the importance of promoting business. The strong conviction that the growth of business would bring better times for everyone was called the "gospel of prosperity." It guided the Reconstruction efforts of Congress and the Reconstruction legislatures throughout the 1870s.

Raising Money In a sense, the postwar South was one giant business opportunity. The region's **infrastructure,** the public property and services that a society uses, had to be almost completely rebuilt. That included roads, bridges, canals, railroads, and telegraph lines.

In addition to the rebuilding effort, some states used Reconstruction funds to expand services to their citizens. For instance, following the North's example, all southern states created public school systems by 1872.

Reconstruction legislatures poured money into infrastructure. Some of the money came from Congress and from private investors. The rest, however, was raised by levying heavy taxes on individuals, many of whom were still in deep debt from the war. White southerners, both wealthy and poor, resented this added financial burden.

Spending by Reconstruction legislatures added another $130 million to southern debt. What further angered southerners was evidence that much of this big spending for infrastructure was being lost to corruption.

Corruption Today, corruption in government and business is vigorously uncovered and prosecuted. That was not the case a century ago. Government officials in both the North and South regularly used their positions for personal profit.

During Reconstruction, a time of many large and costly government projects, enormous sums of money changed hands rapidly in the form of loans and grants.

The worst cases of fraud involved the railroads. A crooked businessman might bribe a key state senator to win a government contract for construction of a new railroad. The businessman would then collect the construction money, use it for personal investments or even a vacation, then declare bankruptcy. In this way numerous railroads were never built, and millions of dollars raised to rebuild the South evaporated without a trace.

Participants in such schemes included blacks and whites, Republicans and Democrats, southerners and northern carpetbaggers. "You are mistaken if you suppose that all the evils . . . result from the carpetbaggers and negroes," a Louisiana man wrote to a northern fellow Democrat. Democrats and Republicans cooperated "whenever anything is proposed which promises to pay," he observed. The South Carolina legislature even gave $1,000 to the speaker of the House to cover his loss on a horse race!

Not every politician or businessman gave in to temptation. Yet those who did gave Reconstruction a reputation for waste and corruption.

SECTION 3 REVIEW

Comprehension

1. **Key Terms** Define: (a) sharecropping; (b) tenant farming; (c) infrastructure.
2. **Summarizing the Main Idea** What effects did Reconstruction have on agriculture and industry in the South?
3. **Organizing Information** Create a diagram to illustrate sharecroppers' cycle of debt. Begin with this entry: "Sharecropper signs one-year contract with planter."

Critical Thinking

4. **Analyzing Time Lines** Review the time line at the start of the section. Pick one event that was largely successful and one that was not. Write a sentence to explain each of your choices.
5. **Drawing Conclusions** Do you think more Reconstruction money was spent on rebuilding infrastructure, or on housing, jobs, and education for freed people? Explain your answer.

Writing Activity

6. **Writing an Expository Essay** Write an essay explaining how southern farming changed after the Civil War.

RESOURCE OPTIONS

Teaching Resources

📁 **Quiz** Units 3–4 folder, p. 77

Student Performance Pack

Guide to the Essentials Chapter 13, Section 3 (English and Spanish)

1866	1870	1872	1877
Ku Klux Klan formed	Anti-Klan laws; last states rejoin Union	Grant reelected President	Hayes wins presidency. Reconstruction ends

1865   **1870**   **1875**   **1880**

4 The End of Reconstruction

SECTION PREVIEW

Objectives

1 Assess the impact of racial terrorism on the South.
2 Explain why the Reconstruction period came to an end.
3 List the major successes and failures of Reconstruction.
4 *Key Terms* Define: solid South; Compromise of 1877.

Main Idea

In the 1870s, white Democrats regained power in the South, and public interest in Reconstruction declined. The program was both a success and a failure.

Reading Strategy

Analyzing Cause and Effect Create a cause-and-effect chart entitled "Why Reconstruction Ended," using the chart in Section 3 as a model. As you read, add information to your chart.

I n March 1870 the last southern states were restored to the Union. Yet the United States was still far from united. From 1868 through 1871, groups of white southerners launched a violent backlash against Radical Reconstruction. At the head of the campaign was an organization that started in 1866 as a social club in Tennessee: the Ku Klux Klan, or KKK.

The Klan quickly evolved into a terrorist organization. Klansmen pledged to "defend the social and political superiority" of whites against what they called the "aggressions of an inferior race." The membership consisted largely of ex-Confederate officers and plantation owners who had been excluded from politics. The group also attracted merchants, lawyers, and other professionals. The Klan was supposed to be a "secret society," but in fact most members' identities were well known to their local communities.

Spreading Terror

During Radical Reconstruction, the Klan sought to eliminate the Republican party in the South by intimidating Republican voters,

both white and black. The Klan's long-term goal was to keep African Americans in the role of submissive laborers. This motive still drives Klan activity today.

The Klan's terror tactics varied. Often, horsemen in long robes and hoods appeared suddenly at night, carrying guns and whips. They encircled the homes of their victims, and planted huge burning crosses in their yards. People were dragged from their homes and harassed, tortured, kidnapped, or murdered.

Anyone who didn't share the Klan's goals and hatreds could be a victim: carpetbaggers, scalawags, freedmen who had become prosperous—even those who had merely learned to read. With chilling frequency, black women went to claim the dead bodies of their husbands and sons.

The Federal Response The violence kindled northern outrage. At President Grant's request, Congress passed a series of anti-Klan laws in 1870 and 1871. The Force Act of 1870 banned the use of

The Klan left miniature coffins like this, containing written death threats, at the doors of many freedmen and their white supporters.

The First Grand Wizard In May 1867 the ex-Confederate general and guerrilla leader Nathan Bedford Forrest took his place as the first Grand Wizard in the recently formed Ku Klux Klan in Pulaski, Tennessee. In June, the Klan held its first parade and proved something of a bewilderment even to the sympathetic Pulaski citizens. "They conversed in Dutch, Hebrew, or some other language which we couldn't comprehend. No two of them dressed alike, all having on masks and some sort of fanciful costume," reported one person. As the 1868 elections approached, violence against freedmen hoping to vote became general throughout Tennessee. By the next spring, Grand Wizard Forrest oversaw an empire with toeholds in fourteen southern states. The Klan led riots against black suffragists in Mississippi, burned schools and whipped or lynched northern schoolteachers, who were blamed for the freedmen's new political interest, and sent out its now-familiar night armies to frighten former slaves. Testifying before Congress in 1871, Forrest explained, "this organization was got up to protect the weak, with no political intention at all. . . ."
Source: Nathan Ward, "The Time Machine," *American Heritage* magazine, May/June 1992

terror, force, or bribery to prevent people from voting because of their race. Other laws banned the KKK entirely and strengthened military protection of voters and voting places.

Using troops, cavalry, and the power of the courts, the government arrested and tried thousands of Klansmen. Within a year the KKK was virtually wiped out. Still, the thinly spread federal army could not be everywhere at once. As federal troops gradually withdrew from the South, black suffrage all but ended.

Reconstruction Ends

President Grant, who won reelection in 1872, continued to pursue the goals of Reconstruction, sometimes with energy. However, the widespread corruption in his administration reminded voters of all that was wrong with Reconstruction.

A Dying Issue By the mid-1870s, voters had grown weary of Republicans and their decade-long concern with Reconstruction. Historians cite several reasons for this shift:

(1) Reconstruction legislatures taxed and spent heavily, putting southern states into deeper debt.

(2) Reconstruction came to symbolize corruption, greed, and poor government.

(3) As federal troops withdrew from the South, more and more freedmen were prevented from voting, allowing white southerners to regain control of state governments.

(4) White-dominated southern states blocked many federal Reconstruction policies.

(5) Northern voters never fully supported the Radicals' goal of racial equality.

(6) A nationwide economic downturn in 1873 diverted public attention from the movement for equal rights.

The era of Republican control of the South was coming to a close. In 1872 the last ex-Confederates had been pardoned. They combined with other white southerners to form a new bloc of Democratic voters known as the **solid South.** Democrats of the solid South reversed many reforms of the Reconstruction legislatures.

The Compromise of 1877 Reconstruction politics took a final, sour turn in the presidential election of 1876. Republican Rutherford B. Hayes lost the popular vote to Democrat Samuel Tilden, who had the support of the solid South. The electoral vote, however, was disputed. The map on the left shows the results.

Hayes claimed victory based partly on wins in Florida, Louisiana, and South Carolina. Those states were still under Republican and federal control. Democrats submitted another set of tallies showing Tilden as the winner in those states, and thus in the presidential race.

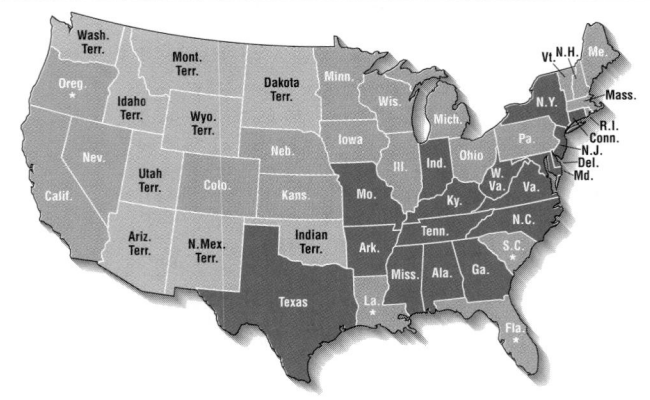

Presidential Election of 1876

Candidate/Party	Electoral Vote	Popular Vote	% Electoral Vote	% Popular Vote
Rutherford B. Hayes (Republican)	185	4,034,311	49.9 / 50.1	51.0 / 48.0
Samuel J. Tilden (Democrat)	184	4,288,546		
Peter Cooper (Greenback)		75,973		1.0
★ States with disputed results				

MAP Skills In the tarnished election of 1876, the electoral votes in three states under federal control were disputed, but went to Hayes when he promised to end Reconstruction. *Location In which states were election results disputed?*

RESOURCE OPTIONS

Teaching Resources

Key Documents Frederick Douglass, Speech to the Congregational Church, Learning with Documents folder, p. 91

Media and Technology

RESOURCE PRO

Visual Learning Activity America's Birthday Party, found on Resource Pro, shows a list published in 1876 in the children's magazine *St. Nicholas,* citing major events in the first hundred years of the American Republic.

Answer to . . .

Map Skills Louisiana, Florida, South Carolina, and Oregon.

Congress set up a special commission to resolve the election crisis. Not surprisingly, the commission, which included more Republicans than Democrats, named Hayes the victor. However, Democrats had enough strength in Congress to reject the commission's decision.

Finally the two parties made a deal. In the **Compromise of 1877,** the Democrats agreed to give Hayes the victory in the presidential election he had not clearly won. In return, the new President agreed to remove the remaining federal troops from southern states. He also agreed to give huge subsidies to southern railroads. The compromise opened the way for Democrats to regain control of southern politics and marked the end of Reconstruction.

Effects of Reconstruction

Until quite recently, historians saw Reconstruction as a dismal failure, a time simply of corrupt and incompetent government in the South. Today most historians argue that the truth is more complex.

Successes of Reconstruction The Reconstruction era included several important accomplishments:

(1) Republicans carried out their two main goals, to rebuild the Union and to help repair the war-torn South.

(2) Reconstruction stimulated economic growth in the South and created new wealth in the North.

(3) The Fourteenth and Fifteenth amendments guaranteed African Americans the rights of citizenship, equal protection under the law, and suffrage. African Americans gained the right to testify in court and to sit on juries.

(4) The Freedmen's Bureau and other organizations helped many black families obtain housing, jobs, and schooling.

(5) Southern states adopted the system of tax-supported, mandatory education practiced in the North. Increased access to education would benefit whites and blacks alike.

Failures of Reconstruction Yet the Reconstruction era had a number of failures as well:

(1) As in the era of slavery, most black southerners remained in a cycle of poverty that allowed almost no escape. African Americans still lacked property, economic opportunity, and political power.

Atlanta, Georgia, rose from the devastation left by the Civil War to become a bustling commercial center, as this 1887 picture shows. *Government In what other ways was Reconstruction successful?*

(2) After the withdrawal of federal troops from the South, southern state governments and terrorist organizations such as the Ku Klux Klan effectively denied African Americans the right to vote.

(3) Racist attitudes toward African Americans continued, in both the South and the North.

(4) Reconstruction left a lasting bitterness among many white southerners toward the federal government and the Republican party.

(5) While Reconstruction programs resulted in the rebuilding and expansion of southern infrastructure, the region was slow to industrialize. The southern economy continued to emphasize agriculture and to lag far behind the industrialized economy of the North.

(6) Reconstruction did not address concerns of groups such as farmers wanting regulation of railroads, workers seeking safer conditions, and advocates of woman suffrage.

Civil Rights Battles Continue Members of the women's suffrage movement were angry and disappointed when some Radical Republicans refused to endorse voting rights for women. "Either the theory of our government is false, or women have a right to vote," suffrage worker Lydia Maria Child told the Senate's Radical Republican leader, Charles Sumner, in 1872.

Main Idea CONNECTIONS

- What trends in the South helped bring about the end of Reconstruction?
- Why do most historians now believe that Reconstruction was not a complete failure?

ACTIVITY
HETEROGENEOUS GROUPS

The Radical Republicans' dream of social equality and justice was abandoned in 1877. Ask student groups to write a slogan for a modern bumper sticker reflecting the feelings of betrayal African Americans might have felt at this time. *(Reteaching)*

TEST PREPARATION

Have students read the first paragraph under Civil Rights Battles Continue and then answer the question below.

Lydia Maria Child believed that—

A the American theory of government was wrong.

B denying women rights was a natural part of the American plan of government.

C the American theory of government needed to be changed.

D denying women equal rights betrayed the ideals of government on which the nation was founded.

Answer to . . .

Viewing History Important laws and organizations were instituted.

Main Idea Connections Tactics to block Reconstruction policies; a new bloc of solid Southern voters. Because it rebuilt the Union, repaired the South, and enacted important laws.

Graphing the Main Idea

To make sure students understand the main idea of this section, you may wish to use the tree map graphic organizer below.

Tell students that a tree map shows an outline of a main topic, ideas, and supporting details. Ask students to use it to outline Section 4.

Teaching Tip A template for this graphic organizer can be found in the Color Transparencies, G-3.

FACT Finder: Major Reconstruction Legislation

Date	Legislation	Purpose
1865	13th Amendment	Abolishes slavery
1865, 1866	Freedmen's Bureau	Provides services for war refugees and newly freed people
1867	Reconstruction Acts	Establishes Radical Reconstruction
1868	14th Amendment	Defines citizenship; guarantees due process of law and equal protection
1870	15th Amendment	Guarantees that voting rights are not denied on the basis of race
1875	Civil Rights Act	Protects African Americans' rights in public

Interpreting Tables The political cartoon at right shows President Hayes "plowing under" the Reconstruction program. During Reconstruction, the federal government struggled to create a new social and political order in the South. *Government What purpose do most of these laws have in common?*

In the decades before the Civil War, women had played prominent roles in the abolitionist movement. During Reconstruction, women's leaders had backed equal rights for African Americans. In both struggles, women pointed out the parallels between the denial of equal rights to blacks and to women. When Reconstruction legislation avoided the issue of women's voting rights, it severed the longtime alliance between abolitionists and the suffrage movement.

For African Americans in the South, Reconstruction's promise of freedom and opportunity would not begin to be realized until the civil rights movement of the 1950s and 1960s. In the words of African American leader W.E.B. du Bois, "The slave went free; stood a brief moment in the sun; then moved back again toward slavery." Or as historian Samuel Eliot Morison concluded, "The North may have won the war, but the white South won the peace."

SECTION 4 REVIEW

Comprehension

1. *Key Terms* Define: (a) solid South; (b) Compromise of 1877.

2. *Summarizing the Main Idea* What were some of the major successes and failures of Reconstruction?

3. *Organizing Information* Create a cause-and-effect chart of the events that led to the Compromise of 1877.

Critical Thinking

4. *Analyzing Time Lines* Review the time line at the start of the section. Choose one entry and explain why it was a turning point in the Reconstruction period.

5. *Identifying Alternatives* What tactics did some white southerners use to challenge Reconstruction? What might they have done to try to improve Reconstruction governments?

Writing Activity

6. *Writing a Persuasive Essay* In your view, did Reconstruction's successes outweigh its failures? Write an essay explaining your opinion. Support it with specific examples.

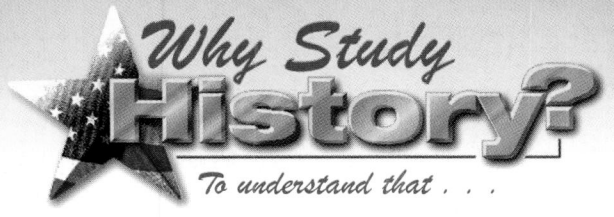

To understand that . . .

Congress Represents All Americans

Although the first African American representatives to Congress were elected during Reconstruction, only in recent years has their number increased substantially.

African American congressmen during Reconstruction

"The right of citizens of the United States to vote shall not be denied or abridged by the United States or by any state on account of race, color, or previous condition of servitude." With ratification of the Fifteenth Amendment in 1870, African Americans won the right to vote. Between 1870 and 1877 sixteen African Americans, including one senator, were elected to Congress.

Many southern whites mobilized against Reconstruction. Through terror and intimidation, the Ku Klux Klan prevented black men from exercising their right to vote. After Reconstruction, the number of black representatives dropped sharply. Only after the civil rights movement secured legal protection of black voting rights in 1965 did the number of black representatives rise again.

The Impact Today

The number of black representatives rose in the 1990s—in part because several states redrew congressional boundaries to create districts with a large percentage of black voters. Supporters of these "majority-minority districts" see them as a way to give African Americans an equal voice in

government. (The percentage of black representatives in Congress is lower than that of African Americans in the population as a whole.) Opponents of the new districts claim that they violate white voters' rights. The Supreme Court has ruled that some of these new districts must be redrawn.

As the number of black representatives has grown, so has the diversity of their views. For example, recent black representatives have disagreed on the degree to which race affects their role in Congress. Democratic senator Carol Moseley-Braun of Illinois, for example, defended government programs that encourage the hiring of minorities. "As a minority," said Moseley-Braun, "I have seen first-hand the benefits" of such programs. By contrast, Republican representative J. C. Watts of Oklahoma stated that he "didn't come to Congress to be a black leader or a white leader but a leader."

Representative J. C. Watts of Oklahoma

The Impact on You

Should voters take race into account when choosing a candidate? Write an essay explaining how you, as a future voter, will or will not consider race in elections. As you write your essay, address arguments against your position.

Class Discussion

Discuss with the class the issue of the ethnic composition of Congress. For a more thorough examination of the issue, see the activity folder in the Resource Options below.

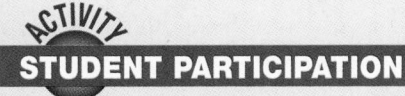

Making a Class Chart

Ask students to read the text. Then assign pairs of students each a state to research. Using an almanac and other sources, pairs should find:

- **the composition of the state's population (percent white, African American, Hispanic, Asian)**
- **the composition of the state's delegation in Congress (percent white, African American, Hispanic, Asian)**

Have each pair record its findings on a class chart.

Follow up Discuss disparities between population and representation among different groups. Consider differences in various regions.

Using the Internet

Students can learn more about congressional representation by exploring links in the *America: Pathways to the Present* Web site at:

http://www.Pathways.phschool.com

Assessment

See the Lesson Plans folder, pp. 24–27, for rubrics on assessing Class Participation Projects.

RESOURCE OPTIONS

Teaching Resources

 Why Study History? Activity Congress Represents All Americans, found in the Why Study History? folder, p. 14, provides an activity to help students better understand congressional representation.

Media and Technology

Decision America Videotapes and Videodiscs Issue 3 *Why Vote?*; Issue 12 *Is Politics for Professionals Only?*

Key Terms

Students should refer to the definitions of key terms in the chapter to write sentences that show an understanding of the issues of Reconstruction.

Comprehension

1. Strict laws imposed, cycle of debt, and loss of labor on plantations.

2. Lincoln's plan was tougher on the South. He supported a 10 percent allegiance requirement.

3. They attempted to create a new social order in the South and gain equal rights as citizens.

4. Congress blamed Johnson for southern Democrats' return to power and the southern defiance of Reconstruction. Johnson violated the Tenure of Office Act.

5. Equal protection for African Americans under the law and the right to vote.

6. Through Reconstruction efforts, a Supreme Court decision that upheld Congress's right to restructure southern governments, and through the Republican votes of freedmen who were benefiting from the Fifteenth Amendment.

7. They were filled with government-sanctioned corruption.

8. The South became more industrialized and had to adjust to a new labor system. Still, it remained largely a farming economy.

9. It ended with the Compromise of 1877, which created an understanding between Democrats and Republicans. By then, however, many viewed it as representing corruption and incompetent government. Hayes removed federal troops from southern states and opened the way for Democrats to regain control of southern politics.

Chapter Summary

The major concepts of Chapter 13 are presented below. See also *Guide to the Essentials of American History* or *Interactive Student Tutorial CD-ROM,* which contains interactive review activities, time lines, helpful hints, and test practice for Chapter 13.

Reviewing the Main Ideas

The end of the Civil War was the beginning of a massive program to repair the South, restructure its economy, reshape its society, and reunite it with the North. Reconstruction forced the nation to grapple with two key issues: the control of southern wealth and political power, and the role and rights of newly freed African Americans.

Section 1: Presidential Reconstruction

Presidents Lincoln and Johnson sought to pardon the South, not to punish it, as freedmen pursued education and jobs.

Section 2: Congressional Reconstruction

Southern defiance of Reconstruction provoked a showdown between President Johnson and Congress and led to major new civil rights laws and Republican control of the South.

Section 3: Birth of the "New South"

Corruption-plagued programs to repair southern war damage brought about limited economic growth.

Section 4: The End of Reconstruction

White southerners undid many Republican reforms, as dwindling northern support brought Reconstruction to an end.

The first African American representatives to Congress were elected during Reconstruction. However, only in recent years has their number increased substantially.

Key Terms

For each of the terms below, write a sentence explaining how it relates to the post–Civil War period.

1. Reconstruction
2. pardon
3. black codes
4. impeach
5. carpetbagger
6. scalawag
7. sharecropping
8. tenant farmer
9. infrastructure
10. solid South

Comprehension

1. Name three major problems the South faced at the end of the Civil War.
2. How did Lincoln's plan for Reconstruction compare to Johnson's?
3. How did African Americans try to improve their lives after emancipation?
4. Why did Johnson and Congress clash over Reconstruction?
5. What were the goals of the Fourteenth and Fifteenth amendments?
6. How did Republicans gain control of southern governments?
7. How were Reconstruction legislatures unique in American history?
8. How did the economy of the South change after the Civil War, and in what ways did it remain unchanged?
9. When and why did Reconstruction end?

Using Graphic Organizers

On a separate sheet of paper, copy the chart below to organize the main ideas of each section in this chapter. Provide at least two supporting details for each main idea.

Reconstruction			

Using Graphic Organizers

Box 1: Federal government puts forth plans to allow southern states to resume participation in the Union—Lincoln's Ten Percent Plan; Johnson's plan. **Box 2:** Congress takes over Reconstruction and passes new laws to protect African Americans' freedom—Fourteenth and Fifteenth Amendments are passed. **Box 3:** Reconstruction transforms southern economy as plantations adjust to loss of slave labor and the region begins to attract investment and industry—southern railroads rebuilt, resulting in the growth of cities; sharecropping and tenant farming become common.

Box 4: Democrats regain power in the South and Reconstruction declines—Union rebuilt; repaired; white Southerners left with a bitterness toward the federal government and the Republican party.

Analyzing Political Cartoons ▶

1. This cartoon depicts President Grant riding in a carpetbag. (a) What does Grant represent? (b) What do the soldiers represent? (c) What does the woman represent?

2. State in a sentence or two the message of this cartoon.

3. What was the bias of the cartoonist, and how can you tell?

Critical Thinking

1. **Applying the Chapter Skill** Evaluate Reconstruction from the point of view of (a) a black sharecropper, (b) an ex-Confederate, (c) a carpetbagger, (d) a Radical Republican.

2. **Identifying Assumptions** Congress accused President Johnson of abusing his presidential powers, and Johnson thought that Congress overstepped its authority in carrying out Radical Reconstruction. What differing assumptions led to these conclusions?

3. **Identifying Central Issues** In what ways was Reconstruction basically a struggle for political power?

4. **Recognizing Ideologies** Why were the strong policies of Radical Reconstruction largely ineffective in changing the attitudes of white southerners toward African Americans?

THE "STRONG" GOVERNMENT 1869—1877.

INTERNET ACTIVITY

For your portfolio:
PREPARE A REPORT

Access Prentice Hall's *America: Pathways to the Present* site at **www.Pathways.phschool.com** for the specific URL to complete the activity. Additional resources and related Web sites are also available.

Write a report about Tennessee's Reconstruction experience. Begin by describing Reconstruction in general, then in Tennessee. How did that state's experience differ from Reconstruction elsewhere in the South? How did Reconstruction politics affect Tennessee's African Americans?

ANALYZING DOCUMENTS ◀ ▷ INTERPRETING DATA

Turn to the "American Voices" quotation in Section 2.

1. Which statement best represents the meaning of the quotation? (a) Freedmen are responsible citizens. (b) Freedmen deserve the right to vote because they earn money for the country. (c) Freedmen deserve the right to vote because they are fulfilling the responsibilities of citizenship. (d) Freedmen deserve to rule themselves.

2. What is the most likely reason the writers never received a response? (a) White Tennesseans did not want freedmen to vote. (b) White Tennesseans did not want freedmen to become citizens. (c) White Tennesseans thought freedmen should have economic rights, not political rights.

3. **Writing** Do you think the authors emphasized the most important arguments in their letter? Explain your reasoning.

Connecting to Today

Essay Writing Refer to the Turning Point in Section 2. Research and write an essay on one group of Americans today that has benefited from the Fourteenth Amendment. Address these questions: (a) What equal protections have they sought? (b) In the last 50 years, what laws have been passed to grant them equal rights?

INTERNET ACTIVITY

Answers will vary, but should be based on an understanding of Tennessee's Reconstruction experience.

Analyzing Political Cartoons
1. (a) Republican government. (b) Bayonet rule. (c) A suffragist.
2. Grant is oppressing the South.
3. The bias of the cartoonist is toward economic growth, because under Grant the South is prospering.

Critical Thinking
1. (a) Reconstruction efforts helped to provide aid but sharecropping resulted in greater debt for farmers; (b) Confederates may have reluctantly accepted Reconstruction or turned to activities such as Klan membership; (c) Carpetbaggers benefited from southern poverty; (d) Much was accomplished despite the corruption and blockage of policies by southern states.
2. Both sides assumed that the other was overstepping boundaries and should have limited power.
3. It was a struggle for power between the North and South, between Radical and Moderate Republicans, and between the legislative and executive branches of government.
4. White Southerners believed African Americans were inferior and that the government was treating them better than they, themselves, were treated. Plantation owners resented the changes because they lost their work force.

Analyzing Documents
1. c
2. b
3. Answers will vary. Responses should be based on a careful reading of the passage.

Connecting to Today
Answers will vary but should show an understanding of "equal protection" and a knowledge of legislation enacted in the last 50 years.

My Brush with History

American Heritage ®

My Brush with History

BY DAVID CONYNGHAM

INTRODUCTION The editors of *American Heritage* magazine have selected eyewitness accounts of David Conyngham, an officer in the army of William T. Sherman. Conyngham was also a newspaper correspondent who vividly described his Civil War experiences.

Union Lieutenant George A. Custer (right) is shown with his friend and prisoner, Confederate Major James Washington.

It was no unusual thing to see our pickets and skirmishers enjoying themselves very comfortably with the rebels, drinking bad whiskey, smoking and chewing worse tobacco, and trading coffee and other little articles. The rebels had no coffee, and our men plenty, while the rebels had plenty of whiskey; so they very soon came to an understanding. It was strange to see these men, who had been just pitted in deadly conflict, trading, and bantering, and chatting, as if they were the best friends in the world. They discussed a battle with the same gusto they would a cock-fight, or horse-race, and made inquiries about their friends, as to who was killed, and who not, in the respective armies. Friends that have been separated for years have met in this way. Brothers who parted to try their fortune have often met on the picket line, or on the battle-field.

I once met a German soldier with the head of a dying rebel on his lap. The stern veteran was weeping, whilst the boy on his knee looked pityingly into his face. They were speaking in German, and from my poor knowledge of the language, all I could make out was, that they were brothers; that the elder had come out here several years before; the younger followed him, and being informed that he was in Macon, he went in search of him, and got conscripted; while the elder brother, who was in the north all the time, joined our army. The young boy was scarcely twenty, with light hair, and a soft, fair complexion. The pallor of death was on his brow, and the blood was flowing from his breast, and gurgled in his throat and mouth, which the other wiped away with his handkerchief. When he could speak, the dying youth's conversation was of the old home in Germany, of his brothers and sisters, and dear father and mother, who were never to see him again.

In those improvised truces, the best possible faith was observed by the men. These truces were brought about chiefly in the following manner. A rebel, who was heartily tired of his crippled position in his pit, would call out, "I say, Yank!"

"Well, Johnny Reb," would echo from another hole or tree.

"I'm going to put out my head; don't shoot."

"Well, I won't."

TEST PREPARATION

Have students use the excerpt on these pages to answer the following question.

What two main topics does Conyngham treat in this selection?

A The German brothers' sad reunion and Sherman's campaign.

B Friendly interactions between northern and southern soldiers and the northern campaign through central Georgia and South Carolina.

C Soldiers' abuse of alcohol and tobacco and the campaign through central Georgia.

D The Civil War and its effects on soldiers' morale.

The reb would pop up his head; the Yank would do the same.

"Hain't you got any coffee, Johnny?"

"Na'r a bit, but plenty of rot-gut."

"All right; we'll have a trade."

They would meet, while several others would follow the example, until there would be a regular bartering mart established. In some cases the men would come to know each other so well, that they would often call out,—

"Look out, reb; we're going to shoot," or "Look out, Yank, we're going to shoot," as the case may be.

On one occasion the men were holding a friendly reunion of this sort, when a rebel major came down in a great fury, and ordered the men back. As they were going back, he ordered them to fire on the Federals. They refused, as they had made a truce. The major swore and stormed, and in his rage he snatched the gun from one of the men, and fired at a Federal soldier, wounding him. A cry of execration at such a breach of faith rose from all the men, and they called out, "Yanks, we couldn't help it." At night these men deserted into our lines, assigning as a reason, that they could not with honor serve any longer in an army that thus violated private truces. . . .

Our campaign all through Central Georgia was one delightful picnic. We had little or no fighting, and good living. The farm-yards, cellars, and cribs of the planters kept ourselves and animals well stored with provisions and forage. . . .

In passing through the camp one night, I saw a lot of jolly soldiers squatted outside the huts . . . , and between them a table richly stocked with meats and fowls of different kinds, flanked by several bottles of brandy. . . . They thought campaigning in Georgia about the pleasantest sort of life out, and they wondered what would become of the poor dog-gone folks they had left with their fingers in their mouths, and little else to put in them.

Many of our foragers, scouts, and hangers-on of all classes, thought, like Cromwell, that they were doing the work of the Lord, in wantonly destroying as much property as possible. Though this was done extensively in Georgia, it was only in South Carolina that it was brought to perfection. . . .

A planter's house was overrun in a jiffy; boxes, drawers, and escritoires were ransacked with a laudable zeal, and emptied of their contents. If the spoils were ample, the depredators were satisfied, and went off in peace; if not, everything was torn and destroyed, and most likely the owner was tickled with sharp bayonets into a confession where he had his treasures hid. . . . Sorghum barrels were knocked open, bee hives rifled, while their angry swarms rushed frantically about. Indeed, I have seen a soldier knock a planter down because a bee stung him. Hogs are bayonetted, and then hung in quarters on the bayonets to bleed; chickens, geese, and turkeys are knocked over and hung in garlands from the saddles . . . ; cows and calves, so wretchedly thin that they drop down and perish on the first day's march, are driven along, or, if too weak to travel, are shot, lest they should give aid to the enemy.

Should the house be deserted, the furniture is smashed in pieces, music is pounded out of four hundred dollar pianos with the ends of muskets. . . . After all was cleared out, most likely some set of stragglers wanted to enjoy a good fire, and set the house, debris of furniture, and all the surroundings, in a blaze. This is the way Sherman's army lived on the country. They were not ordered to do so, but I am afraid they were not brought to task for it much either.

Source: *Sherman's March Through the South* by David Conyngham, Sheldon & Co., 1865.

Potter House, Atlanta

Blasted by Union artillery fire, the Potter house was one of countless buildings damaged or destroyed by Sherman's forces.

ADDITIONAL READING

To learn more about the topics discussed in this selection, you might want to read the following books:

- *For Cause and Comrades: The Will to Combat in the Civil War,* by James M. McPherson (New York: Oxford University, 1997)
- *Marching Through Georgia: The Story of Soldiers and Civilians During Sherman's Campaign,* by Lee B. Kennett (New York: HarperCollins, 1995)
- *Mary Chesnut's Civil War,* edited by C. Vann Woodward (New Haven: Yale University Press, 1981)

Customize for
English Language Learners

Students may need help with the following words and phrases:

pickets soldiers guarding an army from surprise attack

skirmishers soldiers sent out ahead of the main army to slow down the enemy and warn their own troops when an attack was coming

crippled position uncomfortably cramped posture

rot-gut bad whiskey

cry of execration curse or condemnation

Customize for
Less Proficient Readers

After students read the selection, divide them into three groups. Assign each group one scene: The German Brothers' Reunion, Improvised Truces, or Campaigning in Georgia. Have groups create a skit depicting their assigned scene. Allow time for groups to rehearse before performing their skits in front of the class.

Customize for
More Advanced Students

After students read the selection, have them review the information on Sherman's March in Chapter 12. Ask them to evaluate the textbook's assertion that Sherman's March "would make the hatred between North and South still more difficult to heal." Then have students write a monologue of a Southern planter or family member who lived through the campaign.

T E S T   P R E P A R A T I O N

Have students use the excerpt on these pages to answer the following question.

Which statement best describes the speaker's view of Sherman's March?

A Sherman's army behaved badly in destroying private property.

B Sherman's army acted as soldiers normally do in war.

C Sherman's March gave the army a much-needed break from combat.

D Sherman's army got carried away in teaching the South a lesson.

Expansion: Rewards and Costs 1850–1915

Introducing the Unit

Using Historical Evidence

After the Civil War, industry radically changed American life. Ask students to study the photograph on the right. Then write two column headings on the chalkboard, Rewards and Costs. Ask students to list the rewards that the railroads brought to the sight-seers shown in the photograph and to their neighbors. Then ask them to identify the environmental costs of the railroad construction visible in the photograph.

Themes in American History

Direct students' attention to the Unit Themes. Point out that each chapter in this unit has its own theme. To teach this unit thematically, you may wish to use the Expansion, Reconstruction, Immigration folder in **American History Block Scheduling Support.**

Using the Time Line

To provide students with practice in using a time line to connect key events in the United States with key events in the world, ask questions such as these: (1) Who was President when the Haymarket Riot occurred? *(Cleveland)* (2) What freedom did the people of France gain during the period shown on the time line? *(Freedom of the press.)* (3) What transportation landmarks were completed in the United States? *(Transcontinental railroad, Brooklyn Bridge.)*

Expansion: Rewards and Costs

1850 – 1915

*T*he explosive growth of the post–Civil War era transformed the nation. The promise of new opportunities attracted thousands of settlers to the West, set off a dramatic wave of immigration, and swelled the populations of cities. Expansion brought important rewards, such as technological advances, but at a high cost. Along with expansion came urban poverty, labor unrest, and the displacement of Native Americans.

Chapter 14	The Expansion of American Industry **1850–1900**
Chapter 15	Looking to the West **1860–1900**
Chapter 16	Politics, Immigration, and Urban Life **1870–1915**
Chapter 17	Daily Life in the Gilded Age **1870–1915**

UNIT THEMES

Science and Technology New technologies led to rapid industrial growth.

Diversity White settlement of western lands devastated Native American cultures.

Economics Powerful and unregulated businesses brought wealth to the national economy, but many began to question their aggressive practices.

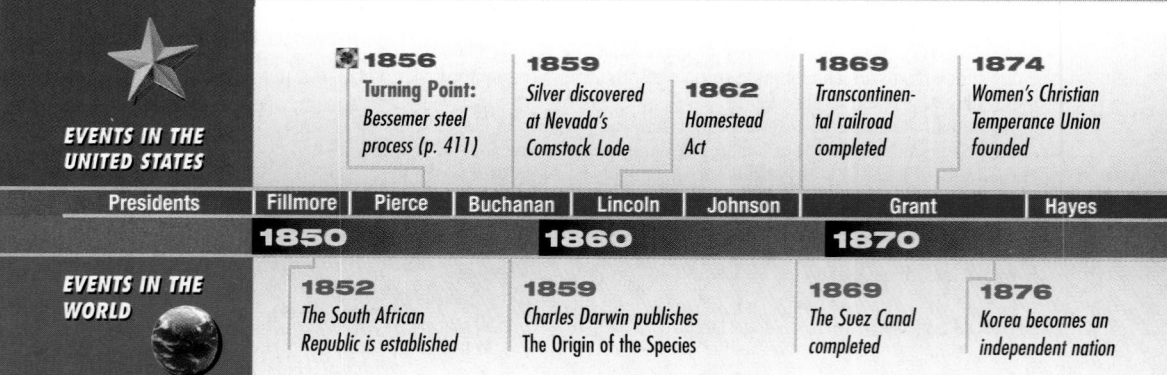

EVENTS IN THE UNITED STATES

1856 Turning Point: Bessemer steel process (p. 411)	**1859** Silver discovered at Nevada's Comstock Lode	**1862** Homestead Act	**1869** Transcontinental railroad completed	**1874** Women's Christian Temperance Union founded

Presidents	Fillmore	Pierce	Buchanan	Lincoln	Johnson	Grant	Hayes

1850   1860   1870

EVENTS IN THE WORLD

1852 The South African Republic is established	**1859** Charles Darwin publishes The Origin of the Species	**1869** The Suez Canal completed	**1876** Korea becomes an independent nation

▶ RESOURCE OPTIONS

Teaching Resources

📁 **Units 5–6 folder** Contains instructional materials organized by chapter.

● **VIEWING HISTORY** An excursion party, reveling in the newfound technologies of the era, stops for a photograph on Devil's Gate Bridge in Utah.
Geography How does the photo capture both rewards and costs of the nation's growth?

Assiniboine war shirt

1883
Brooklyn
Bridge
completed

1886
Haymarket
Riot

1890
Sherman
Antitrust Act
passed

1892
Ellis Island immigration center opened

1896
Plessy v. Ferguson

| Garfield | Arthur | Cleveland | Harrison | Cleveland | Roosevelt |

1880   **1890**   **1900**

1881
Freedom of the press
established in France

1889
French Panama Canal
Company goes bankrupt

1891
Building of Trans-
Siberian Railroad begins

1904
10-hour workday
established in France

RESOURCE OPTIONS

Media and Technology

Color Transparencies Specific transparencies are referenced at points of use. See American Photo, B-5; Our Multicultural Heritage, C-2 and C-10; Fine Art, D-12 and D-13; Links Across Time, J-5; and Political Cartoons, K-5.

◉▣ **Visions of America** "Scenes of an Era: Expansion: Rewards and Costs" located on videodisc side 2 and on videotape 2. Lesson plans for "Scenes of an Era" can be found in the Visions of America Guidebook.
Side 2, Chapter 16

Answer to . . .

Viewing History People and goods could now easily cross a difficult river. However, many trees were cut down.

405

CHAPTER 14

The Expansion of American Industry, 1850–1900

Managing Time and Instruction

INSTRUCTION SUPPORT

These materials for instruction are provided for **each section** in the **Teaching Resources.** See **Units 5–6 folder for Enrichment Support:**

- Reproducible Lesson Plans in Lesson Plans folder • Learning Styles Lesson Plans in Learning Styles Lesson Plans folder • Big Idea Graphic Organizers in Big Idea Graphic Organizer folder
- Guided Reading and Review • Quizzes • Test Preparation Practice booklet

DAILY LESSON	ENRICHMENT SUPPORT
1 A Technological Revolution *(pp. 407–412)*	• Primary Source Activity, Working on the Railroad, found on **Resource Pro** • Nystrom *Atlas of Our Country,* Settling the West, pp. 28–29 • Biography, Washington A. Roebling, found on **Resource Pro** • Skills for Life Activity, Units 5–6 folder, p. 15
2 The Growth of Big Business *(pp. 414–418)*	• Primary Source Activity, Pestilence in the Cigar, Learning with Documents folder, p. 20 • Primary Source Activity, Carnegie's Gospel of Wealth, found on **Resource Pro** • Great Debates, How Did Business Leaders Affect the Economy? Decision-Making Activities folder, pp. 30–31 • Critical Thinking Activity, Making Comparisons: Business Consolidations, found on **Resource Pro**
3 Industrialization and Workers *(pp. 419–422)*	• Nystrom *Atlas of Our Country,* The Second Wave of Immigration, pp. 24–25; The Third Wave of Immigration, pp. 30–31 • Visual Learning Activity, The Noble Face of Labor, Learning with Documents folder, p. 56 • Literature Activity, The Stories of Horatio Alger, Units 5–6 folder, p. 14
4 The Great Strikes *(pp. 423–428)*	• Literature Activity, *Sister Carrie*, found on **Resource Pro** • Comparing Primary Sources, On Labor Unions, Units 5–6 folder, pp. 12–13 • Biography, Mary Kenney O'Sullivan, Units 5–6 folder, p. 11 • Lasting Impact Activity, The Lasting Impact of the Great Strikes, History's Lasting Impact folder, pp. 10–11 • You Live in a Post-Industrial Society, Why Study History? folder, p. 15

Running Out of Time?

- Use Tape 3, "Expansion: Rewards and Costs, 1860–1920," from **Visions of America** videotapes series.
- Use Chapter 14 Summary, from **Guide to the Essentials of American History (English and Spanish).**

Companion Web Site

The companion Web site offers online links for all chapter review activities. It also provides key content links and structured support for this chapter for both teachers and students.

http://www.Pathways.phschool.com

Media and Technology

For the Student

Interactive Student Tutorial CD-ROM Chapter 14

Student Edition on Audiotape Chapter 14

American Heritage® CD-ROM

Guided Reading Audiotapes (English and Spanish) Chapter 14

For the Teacher

Resource Pro CD-ROM Chapter 14

Test Bank CD-ROM Chapter 14

Listening to Literature Audiotapes *"Timeless Voices, Timeless Themes"* "Richard Cory" by Edward Arlington Robinson

Block Scheduling

Pacing Suggestions

For 90-minute Blocks

- Teach sections 1 and 2 using Transparencies E-5, H-11, H-14, H-16, B-5, K-5, and F-6 and the Recent Scholarship note on p. 415 for class discussions.
- Teach sections 3 and 4 using the Big Idea Graphic Organizers from Teaching Resources and the Extended Class Periods Activity found on p. 421.

Additional Resources

- Prentice Hall's **American History Block Scheduling Support File** covers over 40 major topics in American history.
- **Prentice Hall United States History Video Collection™** contains 20 videotapes covering American history from beginnings to present.
- **Decision America Videotapes and Videodiscs**
- **Visions of America Videotapes and Videodiscs**

Assessment Options

Chapter Test Forms A&B Test Bank CD-ROM booklet

Test Bank CD-ROM Chapter 14

Standardized Test Preparation Handbook

Connections to American Literature

from Prentice Hall

Prentice Hall Literature *Timeless Voices, Timeless Themes* "Douglass" and "We Wear the Mask" by Paul Lawrence Dunbar, p. 600

Additional Resources

For the Student

Jacob Riis. *How the Other Half Lives.* Dover, 1971.

For the Teacher

Daniel J. Boorstin. *The Americans: The Democratic Experience.* Random House, 1964.

Prentice Hall brings into the classroom the vast archives and scholarship of the nation's premier American history magazine. See "From the Archives of American Heritage®" and "About the Presidents" teaching notes in this chapter.

History Alive!

Teacher's Curriculum Institute, in partnership with Prentice Hall, provides unique materials that engage students with diverse learning styles. See History Alive!® unit on The Rise of Industrial America.

Student Performance Pack

Ensures success in the three critical areas of Reading, Test Taking, and English Language Development with the following materials:
- Guide to the Essentials of American History in English and Spanish
- Guided Reading Audiotapes in English and Spanish
- Interactive Student Tutorial CD-ROM
- Test Preparation Handbook
- Test Preparation Practice booklet

Introducing the Chapter

Beginning before the Civil War, rapid industrial progress transformed the United States, but relations between those who managed the industries and those who labored in them were filled with tensions. Conditions for workers grew worse.

Themes in American History

The theme for this chapter, Science and Technology, is listed at the beginning of this unit. An alternate theme for the chapter is Economics. To teach this unit thematically, you may wish to use the Expansion, Reconstruction, Immigration folder in American History Block Scheduling Support.

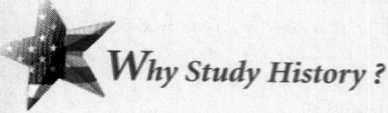

Why Study History?

Have students explore suggested ways of connecting the past to the present on page 429.

Answer to . . .

Viewing History Students should use this question as an aid in reading the chapter. Railroad growth encouraged industry by greatly improving the nation's transportation system. It also depended on industrial products like high-quality air brakes and mass-produced steel.

CHAPTER FOCUS

*I*n this chapter you will read about a revolution of new inventions and ideas that transformed the United States after the Civil War. Industrial growth led to more work and wealth for men, women, and business owners. It also led to rising tensions between workers and employers, however.

The **Why Study History?** page at the end of this chapter explores the connection between today's service economy and the industrial economy that arose in the United States after the Civil War.

VIEWING HISTORY
Citadel Rock looms over the construction of the Union Pacific Railroad through Wyoming Territory in 1868. *Economics*
How was the growth of railroads related to the growth of industry?

RESOURCE OPTIONS

Teaching Resources

Big Idea Graphic Organizer folder
Graphic summary of the main idea of the chapter.

Learning Styles Lesson Plans folder
Alternate lesson plans for diverse learning styles for each chapter.

Media and Technology

AmericanHeritage® CD-ROM
Time Tour Reshaping the Nation: The Rise of Industry

Prentice Hall United States History Video Collection™ Volume 11
Industrialization and Urbanization

1844	1856	1869	1876	1880	1883
First Morse code telegraph message sent	Bessemer process patented	Transcontinental railroad completed	Bell patents the telephone	Edison develops a new light bulb	Brooklyn Bridge completed

1840   **1850**   **1860**   **1870**   **1880**   **1890**

1 A Technological Revolution

SECTION PREVIEW

Objectives

1 Identify some of the changes in people's daily lives in the decades following the Civil War.
2 Describe how advancements in transportation, communication, and electric power affected people and businesses.
3 Explain the effects of the development of the Bessemer process.
4 **Key Terms** Define: patent; productivity; transcontinental railroad; Bessemer process; mass production.

Main Idea

In the years after the Civil War, new technology revolutionized American life.

Reading Strategy

Reinforcing Key Ideas You will be reading about daily life in the United States between 1865 and 1900. As you read, list the ways in which the United States changed in those 35 years.

Objectives
You may wish to call students' attention to the objectives in the Section Preview. The objectives are reflected in the main headings of the section.

Bellringer
Write the following list of inventions on the chalkboard: typewriter, phonograph, telegraph, telephone. Ask students to decide which they consider the most important.

Reading Strategy
Reinforcing Key Ideas Refer to the Reading Strategy in the Section Preview. You may wish to ask volunteers to contribute to a composite list that you write on the chalkboard.

I n the years after the Civil War, the United States developed into an industrial powerhouse. Inventors and scientists, backed by business leaders, created an explosion of inventions and improvements. Their efforts brought about a technological revolution that energized American industry and forever changed people's daily lives.

Changes in Daily Life

Most Americans today can flip a switch for light, turn a faucet for water, and talk to a friend a thousand miles away just by pressing a few buttons. It is hard for us to imagine life without these conveniences. In 1865, however, daily life was vastly different.

Daily Life in 1865 Indoor electric lighting did not exist in 1865. Instead, the rising and setting of the sun dictated the rhythm of a day's work. After dark, people lit candles or oil lamps if they could afford them. If they could not, they simply went to sleep, to rise at the first light of dawn.

Imagine summers without the benefits of refrigeration! Ice was available in 1865, but only at great cost. People sawed blocks of ice out of frozen ponds during the winter, packed them in sawdust, and stored them in icehouses for later use.

By modern standards, long-distance communication was agonizingly slow. In 1860, most mail from the East Coast took ten days to reach the Midwest and three weeks to get to the West. An immigrant living on the frontier would wait months for news from relatives in Europe.

Daily Life in 1900 By 1900, this picture of daily life had changed dramatically for millions of Americans. A combination of factors made this change possible.

The post–Civil War years saw tremendous growth in new ideas and inventions. Between 1790 and 1860, the Patent and Trademark Office of the federal government issued just 36,000

Inventions such as this Singer sewing machine changed daily life for many Americans.

LESSON PLAN
Connecting to the Main Idea

1. **Focus** Explain that the transformation of the United States in the late nineteenth century was due in large part to inventions that changed the way Americans lived and worked. Ask about the impact of the electric light.
2. **Instruct** Explain that conditions were ideal for a great surge in technology. Business leaders had capital to invest, and human and natural resources were abundant. Discuss how one invention often leads to others. Have students describe some of the inventions and refinements that resulted from new technology and explain how they affected people and industry. Ask students to link the growth of the railroads, the development of the Bessemer process, and a new age of building.
3. **Close** Many inventions of this period changed daily life—as well as business. The next section describes how American business became "big business" and brought the country's inventions to market.

RESOURCE OPTIONS

Teaching Resources

Media and Technology

 AmericanHeritage® CD-ROM

 Time Tour Reshaping the Nation: The Rise of Industry

Railroads

Not everyone greeted the improvements in railroad transportation and travel with enthusiasm. The Boston *Courier* printed the following assertion as part of an editorial in 1827: "The project of a railroad from Boston to Albany is impracticable, as every one knows who knows the simplest rule of arithmetic, and the expense would be little less than the market value of the whole of Massachusetts; and which, if practicable, every person of common sense knows would be as useless as a railroad from Boston to the moon."

ACTIVITY

STUDENT PORTFOLIO

You may wish to have students add the following to their portfolios. To assess student work, refer to the generic rubrics in the Program Overview in the Teaching Resources.

Many popular American folk songs concern the building of the railroads. Ask students to research the history of railroad songs and to prepare a written report or an oral presentation using an audiotape of the songs they researched. Suggest that students begin their research with books of American folk songs, such as Carl Sandburg's *The American Songbag.*

Answer to . . .

Viewing History Women played a significant role in producing the inventions of the era.

This drawing appeared in the April 1890 edition of a journal called *The Woman Inventor. Science and Technology* **What does it suggest about women's contributions to the industrial growth of the late 1800s?**

patents—licenses to make, use, or sell an invention. In contrast, between 1860 and 1890 500,000 patents were issued for inventions such as the typewriter, sewing machine, and phonograph.

European investors and American business leaders began to invest heavily in new inventions. This combination of American ingenuity and financial backing helped create new industries and expand old ones. By 1900 Americans' standard of living was among the highest in the world. So too was the nation's industrial **productivity**—the amount of goods and services created in a given period of time.

Railroads Improve Transportation

In 1850 steam-powered ships still provided much of the nation's transportation. Over the following decades, however, improvements in train and track design, plus the construction of new rail lines, gave railroads a big boost.

Before the Civil War most of the nation's railroad tracks were in short lines that connected neighboring cities, mainly in the East. Since there was no standard track width, or gauge, each train could only travel on certain tracks. As a result, goods and passengers often had to be moved to different trains, which caused costly delays. To make matters worse, train travel was dangerous. No system of standard signals existed, and train brakes were unreliable.

The Transcontinental Railroad The rail business improved greatly after the Civil War. The key event was the building of the **transcontinental railroad,** a railway extending from coast to coast. The project began in 1862. By this time rail lines already reached from the East Coast to the Mississippi River.

Now new rails had to be laid between Omaha, Nebraska, and Sacramento, California.

Government involvement was vital. The project was too big for most private investors, who in any event did not consider building railroads beyond the line of settlement to be profitable. Thus federal government awarded huge loans and land grants to two private companies. The Central Pacific Railroad began laying track eastward out of Sacramento. The Union Pacific Railroad began work toward the west in Omaha.

Most of the workers on the transcontinental railroad were immigrants. Irish workers on the Union Pacific line used pickaxes to dig and level rail beds across the Great Plains at the rate of up to six miles a day. Chinese workers that the Central Pacific had brought to the United States chiseled, plowed, and dynamited their way through the Sierra Nevada mountains.

Finally, after seven years of grueling labor, the two crews approached each other in what is now Utah. On May 10, 1869, at a place called Promontory Point, Central Pacific president Leland Stanford raised his hammer to drive the final, golden spike. A telegraph operator beside the track tapped out a message to crowds throughout the country: "Almost ready now. Hats off. Prayer is being offered. . . . Done!" The nation had its first transcontinental railroad.

Rail Problems and Solutions By 1870 railroads could carry goods and passengers from coast to coast, but they still had problems. Trains were often noisy, dirty, and uncomfortable for travelers. The huge engines, spewing smoke and cinders as they thundered through the countryside, aroused fear and distrust.

In spite of the problems, train travel continued to expand and improve. Steel rails replaced iron rails, and track gauges and signals became standardized. Railroad companies also took steps to improve safety. In 1869 George Westinghouse developed more effective air brakes. In 1887 Granville Woods patented a telegraph system for communicating with moving trains, thus reducing the risk of collision.

Railroads and Time Zones Scheduling proved to be another problem for railroads. In the 1800s most towns set their clocks independently, according to solar time. When trains started regular passenger service, they had to be "on time." Time differences from town to town created chaos. In 1883 the railroads adopted a national system of time zones to improve

RESOURCE OPTIONS

Media and Technology

Prentice Hall United States History Video Collection™ Volume 11
Industrialization and Urbanization

RESOURCE PRO

Primary Source Activity Working on the Railroad, found on Resource Pro, introduces students to a folk song by Thomas Casey about the hard life of an 1880s worker.

Time Zones and the Growth of the Railroads, 1870–1890

Pacific Time
Mountain Time
Central Time
Eastern Time

CANADA

ATLANTIC OCEAN

PACIFIC OCEAN

MEXICO

Railroads built by 1870
Railroads built, 1870–1890

0   500   1000 Miles
0   500   1000 Kilometers

MAP Skills Following the Civil War railroads expanded rapidly across the United States, making necessary the introduction of standard time zones. Workers such as those pictured here performed the dangerous, backbreaking construction. *Movement In what ways did the nation's growing transportation system help promote industrial growth?*

scheduling. As a result, clocks in broad regions of the country showed the same time.

Rail improvements such as this made life easier not only for passengers but also for businesses that shipped goods. By the end of the century, some 190,000 miles of rails linked businesses and their customers. Shipping costs dropped enormously. In 1865 shipping a barrel of flour from Chicago to New York cost $3.45. In 1895 it cost just 68 cents.

Advances in Communications

In the late 1800s thousands of people left their homes in Europe and the eastern United States to seek a new life in the West. One of the greatest hardships for these migrants was leaving their loved ones behind. Would they ever hear from family and friends again? By 1900, thanks to many advances in communications, such fears of isolation had diminished.

The Telegraph The idea of sending messages over wires had occurred to inventors in the early 1700s. Several inventors actually set up working telegraph systems well before an American, Samuel F. B. Morse, took out a patent on telegraphy.

Morse may not have invented the telegraph, but he perfected it. Morse devised a code of short and long electrical impulses to represent the letters of the alphabet. Using this system, later called Morse code, he sent his first message in 1844. His success signaled the start of a communications revolution.

After the Civil War, several telegraph companies joined together to form the Western Union Telegraph Company. In 1870 Western Union had more than 100,000 miles of wire, over which some 9 million telegraph messages were transmitted. By 1900 the company owned more than 900,000 miles of wire and was sending roughly 63 million telegraph messages a year.

▼ **BACKGROUND**

Biography

African American engineer Elijah McCoy (1843–1929) was born in Canada to escaped slaves. He studied in Edinburgh, Scotland, before settling in the United States. In 1872, while working for the Michigan Central Railroad, McCoy invented the lubricating cup—a device that continuously oiled the moving parts of factory machinery. Over the years he invented and sold 57 kinds of devices and machine parts. It is sometimes said that the expression "the real McCoy," meaning the genuine article, came about because people insisted that the machinery they bought be equipped with McCoy's invention.

Customize for
Less Proficient Readers

Ask students to construct a cause-and-effect chart showing the effects of the growth of railroads, improved communications, the availability of electric power, and the discovery of the Bessemer process.

Answer to . . .

Map Skills Railroads opened vast new regions for American settlement and allowed manufacturers to ship more raw materials and goods to more places.

▶ **RESOURCE OPTIONS**

Teaching Resources

 American History Block Scheduling Support Linking the Nation: The Railroads, found in the Expansion, Reconstruction, Immigration folder, includes interdisciplinary lesson suggestions and activities for Geography and History, Primary Sources, Biography, and Literature.

 Nystrom *Atlas of Our Country* Settling the West, pp. 28–29

Media and Technology

 Color Transparencies Time Lines, E-5; The Way It Works, H-11, H-14, H-16

Graphing the Main Idea

To make sure students understand the main idea of this section, you may wish to use the multiflow graphic organizer below.

Tell students that a multiflow graphic organizer shows causes and effects. Ask them to use it to record the causes and effects of changes in American life after the Civil War.

Teaching Tip A template for this graphic organizer can be found in the Color Transparencies, G-5.

Answer to . . .

Main Idea Connections *Homes and businesses were linked throughout entire cities, meaning that people could communicate with each other at any time.*

Main Idea CONNECTIONS

How did the telephone revolutionize American life?

The Telephone In 1871 Alexander Graham Bell of Scotland immigrated to Boston, Massachusetts, to teach people with hearing difficulties. After experimenting for several years with an electric current to transmit sounds, Bell patented the "talking telegraph" on March 7, 1876. He had just turned 29. In 1885, Bell and a group of partners set up the American Telephone and Telegraph Company to build long-distance telephone lines.

The earliest local phone lines could connect only two places, such as a home and a business. Soon central switchboards with operators could link an entire city. The first commercial telephone exchange began serving 21 customers on January 28, 1878, in New Haven, Connecticut. That same year President Rutherford B. Hayes had a telephone installed at the White House. By 1900, 1.5 million telephones were in use.

Electric Power

The blossoming of American inventive genius in the late 1800s had a profound effect on millions of people's lives. For example, scientists began developing new uses for petroleum, including fuels such as gasoline that would help power new machines. Electricity proved to be another productive energy source. It led to many important advances in the nation's industrial development and changed people's eating, working, and even sleeping habits.

Edison, a Master of Invention The work of Thomas A. Edison helped make electric power widely available. Born in 1847, Edison grew up tinkering with electricity. While working for a New York company, he improved the stock tickers that sent stock and gold prices to other offices. When his boss awarded him a $40,000 bonus, the 23-year-old Edison left his job and set himself up as an inventor.

In 1876 Edison moved into his "invention factory" in Menlo Park, New Jersey. The young genius, who had never received any formal science training, claimed that he could turn out "a minor invention every ten days and a big thing every six months or so."

Edison's favorite invention, the phonograph, recorded sounds on metal foil wrapped around a rotating cylinder. The first words Edison recorded and then replayed on his phonograph were "Mary had a little lamb." This wondrous machine, introduced in 1877, gained Edison the nickname "Wizard of Menlo Park."

Edison also experimented with electric lighting. His goal was to develop affordable, in-home lighting to replace oil lamps and gaslights. Starting around 1879, Edison and his fellow inventors tried different ways to produce light within a sealed glass bulb. They needed to find a material that would glow without quickly burning up when heated with an electric current.

The team experimented with various threadlike filaments with little success. In 1880 they finally found a workable filament made of bamboo fiber. This filament glowed, Edison said, with "the most beautiful light ever seen."

Other inventors later improved upon Edison's work. Lewis Latimer, the son of an escaped slave, patented an improved method for producing the filament in light bulbs. He worked in Edison's laboratories, where he helped develop new advances in electricity. He later wrote a landmark book about electric lighting.

Until the early 1880s people who wanted electricity had to produce it with their own generator. Hoping to provide affordable lighting to many customers, Edison developed the idea of a central power station. In 1882, to attract investors, Edison built a power plant that lit dozens of buildings in New York City. Investors were impressed, and Edison's idea spread. By 1890 power stations across the country provided electricity for lamps, fans, printing presses, and many other newly invented appliances.

Westinghouse and Alternating Current At first Edison used a form of electricity called direct current to transmit power from his stations. Direct current was expensive to generate and could travel only a mile or two.

In 1885 George Westinghouse began to experiment with alternating current, which could be produced and transmitted more cheaply and efficiently. Westinghouse also used a device called a transformer to boost power levels at a station so that electricity could be sent over long distances. Another transformer at a distant substation could reduce power levels as needed. These aspects of Westinghouse's system made home use of electricity practical.

By the early 1890s, investors had used Edison's and Westinghouse's ideas and inventions to create two companies, General Electric and Westinghouse Electric. These companies' products encouraged the spread of the use of electricity. By 1898 nearly 3,000 power stations were lighting some 2 million light bulbs across the land.

Electricity's Impact on Daily Life Household use of electric current revolutionized many aspects of daily life. To take but one example, electricity made the refrigerator possible. This invention reduced food spoilage and the need to cut, distribute, and store ice.

Electricity also transformed the world of work and created new jobs. For example, people powered early sewing machines by pushing on a foot pedal. The electric sewing machine, first made in 1889, led to the rapid growth of the ready-made clothing industry. Many of the country's new immigrants, especially women and children, found work making clothing in factories powered by electricity.

Yet the benefits of electricity were not felt equally by all Americans. Rural areas, especially, went without electricity for many decades. Even where electric power was available, many people could not afford the home appliances or other conveniences that ran on electricity.

Turning Point: The Bessemer Process

Through the mid-1800s, the nation depended on iron for railroad rails and the frames of large buildings. But in the 1850s, Henry Bessemer in England and William Kelly in Kentucky independently developed a new process for making steel. In 1856 Bessemer received the first patent for the **Bessemer process.** Steel had long been produced by melting iron, adding carbon, and removing impurities. The Bessemer process made it much easier and cheaper to remove the impurities.

Steel is lighter, stronger, and more flexible than iron. The Bessemer process made possible the **mass production,** or production in great amounts, of steel. As a result, a new age of building began. A majestic symbol of this new age was the Brooklyn Bridge.

The Brooklyn Bridge After the Civil War, New York City grew in size as well as population. Many people who worked on the island of Manhattan lived in nearby Brooklyn. The only way to travel between Brooklyn and Manhattan was by ferry across the East River. In winter, ice or winds often shut down the ferry service. Could a bridge high enough to clear river traffic be built across such a large distance? Engineer John A. Roebling, a German immigrant, thought it could.

Roebling designed a suspension bridge with thick steel cables suspended from high towers to hold up the main span. That span,

TURNING POINT: *The Bessemer Steel Process*

The Bessemer process led to the use of steel in a variety of products, as the time line below indicates.

1856
Development of Bessemer process encourages mass production of steel

1914
Method developed for producing stainless-steel cutlery

1931
Design of the Empire State Building calls for structural skeleton of steel girders

1850   **1900**   **1950**   **2000**

1883
Brooklyn Bridge completed, using steel cables to suspend a long bridge span

1948
Steel-belted radial tires introduced

1998
Ultra-light steel frame for autos unveiled

Answers to
SECTION 1 REVIEW

1. (a) patent, see p. 408; (b) productivity, see p. 408; (c) transcontinental railroad, see p. 408; (d) Bessemer process, see p. 411; (e) mass production, see p. 411.

2. Changes may include higher standard of living; improved train travel; advances in communications; electric power; new bridges and buildings.

3. Charts may include: transcontinental railroad—people could travel coast to coast; telegraph—started communications revolution; telephone—connected people instantly; electric power—improved industry and daily life; Bessemer process—made mass production possible.

4. Transportation: transcontinental railroad and Brooklyn Bridge completed, Bessemer process patented; communication: first telegraph sent, Bell patents telephone; electric power: Edison patents new light bulb.

5. Sample answer: It meant that people could work in Manhattan, making it the center of the business world, and still live in the suburbs.

6. Essays will vary but should include descriptions of problems people faced in the mid-1800s and how various inventions solved those problems.

exploring TECHNOLOGY — The Brooklyn Bridge

Water Shaft Earth was removed by scoops inside these shafts. Water in the shafts prevented loss of air pressure.

Supply Shaft These shafts allowed workers to get supplies to the work area.

Air Lock These chambers let workers enter and leave the caisson without a loss of air.

Boom Derrick

Granite Blocks

Timber Caisson Each tower was built atop a timber shell, or caisson, under which workers removed earth.

The Brooklyn Bridge included two massive towers, one of which is shown being built here. As workers removed earth beneath the tower and piled granite blocks above it, the tower sank into the ground. When completed, the two towers supported the steel cables that in turn held up the span.
Science and Technology How did the Bessemer process for manufacturing steel make possible the construction of the Brooklyn Bridge?

arching 1,595 feet above the river, would be the longest in the world. Roebling died shortly after construction of the Brooklyn Bridge began in 1869, so his son Washington took over the project. Washington was disabled in 1872 by a severe attack of decompression sickness ("the bends") while inspecting a foundation deep under the river. Other disasters followed, from explosions and fires to dishonest dealings by a greedy steel-cable contractor.

A Symbol of American Success Despite these problems, the Brooklyn Bridge was completed and opened on May 24, 1883. At nightfall crowds gasped as electric light bulbs, which had been strung along the bridge, lit up the darkness and shimmered on the river below. The city celebrated with a magnificent fireworks display. Indeed, the entire United States celebrated, its inventive genius and hard work plainly visible for all the world to see.

SECTION 1 REVIEW

Comprehension

1. **Key Terms** Define: (a) patent; (b) productivity; (c) transcontinental railroad; (d) Bessemer process; (e) mass production.
2. **Summarizing the Main Idea** How did Americans' daily lives change between 1865 and 1900?
3. **Organizing Information** Create a chart to describe the major inventions in this section and explain the impact they had on Americans.

Critical Thinking

4. **Analyzing Time Lines** Review the time line at the start of the section. Which events involved advances in transportation? In communication? In electric power?
5. **Predicting Consequences** What long-term impact do you think the Brooklyn Bridge had on the people of the New York City area?

Writing Activity

6. **Writing an Expository Essay** Write an essay about the inventiveness of Americans in the last half of the 1800s.

▶ RESOURCE OPTIONS

Teaching Resources

 Quiz Units 5–6 folder, p. 4

Student Performance Pack

 Guide to the Essentials Chapter 14, Section 1 (English and Spanish)

Media and Technology

 Color Transparencies The Way It Works, H-14

Answer to . . .

Exploring Technology It produced lighter, stronger, more flexible steel and allowed for inexpensive mass production.

Using Cross-Sectional Maps

Sometimes it is necessary to use more than one type of map to understand the way a particular piece of land looks. Cross-sectional maps show how an area of land would look if viewed from the side. The cross-sectional map below shows the changes in elevation along the route of the first transcontinental railroad, completed in 1869. These changes in elevation appear on the map as the rising and falling of the bold line. In contrast, physical-political maps show Earth's surface as if viewed from above. The physical political map below gives a bird's-eye view of the vast horizontal distances covered by the railroad.

Snowstorms, floods, and extreme heat all posed great challenges to the workers who built the transcontinental railroad, but the greatest challenges arose from the changes in elevation of the terrain. Follow the steps below to study the cross-sectional map.

1. *Study the region shown on the maps.* (a) Which landforms on the physical-political map correspond to those on the cross-sectional map? (b) Does the cross-sectional map show the same land area as the political map? Explain.

2. *Analyze the information shown on the cross-sectional map.*

(a) What were the highest and lowest elevations of each railroad route? (b) Where did the sharpest and the most gradual changes occur? (c) Write a paragraph comparing the length and elevation changes of the Central Pacific and Union Pacific routes.

TEST FOR SUCCESS

Think about the route you follow to school or some other familiar route. Would a cross-sectional map like the one shown below help you explain your route to a stranger? Or would a physical-political map provide all the necessary information? Explain.

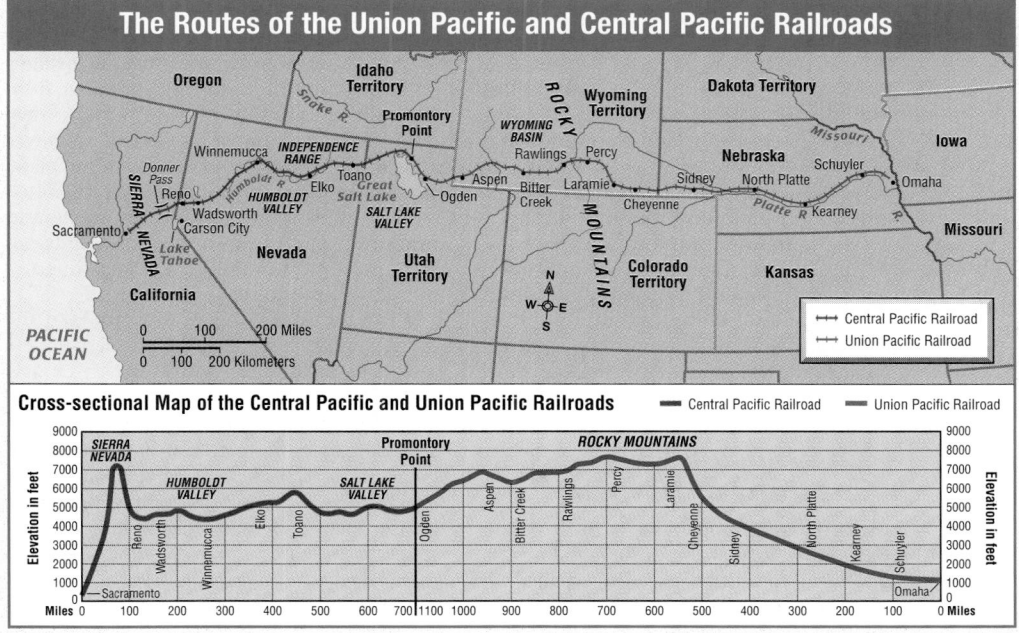

The Routes of the Union Pacific and Central Pacific Railroads

Cross-sectional Map of the Central Pacific and Union Pacific Railroads

413

Focus Compare the data provided in the cross-sectional map with that in the physical-political map.

Instruct To be sure students understand the information presented in the cross-sectional map, ask them to identify the locations on the map at elevation 1,000 feet and 7,000 feet. Have them indicate the elevation at Bitter Creek. Ask students to think about some other useful subjects for cross-sectional maps. (*The ocean floor, rivers and other waterways.*)

Extend See the Skills for Life Activity in the Resource Options below.

Answers

1. (a) The Rocky Mountains, Salt Lake Valley, Humboldt Valley, and the Sierra Nevada are on the physical-political and cross-sectional maps. (b) No. The cross-sectional maps do not show the land area that lies north or south of the railroads.

2. (a) Union Pacific—the highest elevation was about 7,500 feet above sea level; the lowest about 1,000 feet. Central Pacific—the highest elevation was just over 7,000 feet above sea level, the lowest about 300 feet. (b) The sharpest changes occurred heading east from Sacramento; the most gradual occurred heading west from Omaha. (c) Paragraphs should demonstrate an understanding of the information in the cross-sectional and physical-political maps.

TEST FOR SUCCESS

Answers will vary but should be supported by conclusions drawn from questions 1 and 2.

| 1859 Titusville oil strike | 1870 Standard Oil founded | 1882 Standard Oil Trust set up | 1889 Carnegie Steel founded | 1890 Sherman Antitrust Act passed |

| 1850 | 1860 | 1870 | 1880 | 1890 |

SECTION 2

The Growth of Big Business

Objectives

You may wish to call students' attention to the objectives in the Section Preview. The objectives are reflected in the main headings of the section.

Bellringer

Have students describe a "mom and pop" business. Then have them write a definition of "big business" and explain how the two differ.

Reading Strategy

Finding Evidence Refer to the Reading Strategy in the Section Preview. You may wish to have students make a list of the evidence they find.

LESSON PLAN

Connecting to the Main Idea

1. Focus Explain that the business organization changes of the late nineteenth century brought both great wealth and great hardship to the country. Ask students what those changes were and how they affected Americans.

2. Instruct Explain that in order to control the large amounts of money needed to produce new inventions and build railroads, bridges, and factories, American businesses grew into giant enterprises. Ask students how industrialists expanded their businesses. Discuss how the powerful industrialists of the late 1800s were both captains of industry and robber barons. Ask students who they think would be most likely to advocate the theory of social Darwinism—industrialists or workers.

3. Close The inventions and discoveries of the late 1800s needed business people to market them. Businesses grew and consolidated, becoming huge corporations; however, the methods they used to do this were controversial. The next section describes the struggles of the American worker during the age of big business.

2 The Growth of Big Business

SECTION PREVIEW

Objectives

1. Explain why American industrialists of the late 1800s were called both "robber barons" and "captains of industry."
2. Describe the theory of social Darwinism and its connection to big business.
3. Summarize the ways that industrialists gained a competitive edge over rivals, and the effects that big businesses had on American society.
4. *Key Terms* Define: social Darwinism; monopoly; cartel; trust; Sherman Antitrust Act; horizontal consolidation; vertical consolidation; economies of scale; business cycle.

Main Idea

Big business created wealth for its owners and also for the nation, but it also prompted controversy and concern over its methods.

Reading Strategy

Finding Evidence Read the paragraphs under the heading "Robber Barons or Captains of Industry?" on this page. Look for evidence to support both of these views of industrialists of the late 1800s.

Industrial growth required the contributions of both workers and business owners, as this illustration suggests.

The period of invention after the Civil War set the stage for great industrial growth. Still, it would take more than technology to transform the United States. It would take shrewd business-people and wealthy investors willing to gamble on new products. Without huge amounts of capital, businesses could not build factories or market their inventions. To succeed, business leaders often combined funds and resources into large companies. Thus was born the age of big business.

Robber Barons or Captains of Industry?

Historians have adopted the terms "robber barons" and "captains of industry" to describe the powerful industrialists who established large businesses in the late 1800s. The two terms suggest strikingly different images.

"Robber barons" implies that the business leaders built their fortunes by stealing from the public. According to this view, they drained the country of its natural resources and persuaded public officials to interpret laws in their favor. At the same time, these industrialists ruthlessly drove their competitors to ruin. They paid their workers meager wages and forced them to toil under dangerous and unhealthful conditions.

The term "captains of industry," on the other hand, suggests that the business leaders served their nation in a positive way. This view credits them with increasing the supply of goods by building factories, raising productivity, and expanding markets. In addition, the giant industrialists created the jobs that enabled many Americans to buy their new goods. They also founded and funded outstanding museums, libraries, and universities, many of which still thrive today.

Most historians believe that both views of America's early big business contain elements

 RESOURCE OPTIONS

Teaching Resources

📁 **Reproducible Lesson Plan** Lesson Plans folder, p. 89

📁 **Big Idea Graphic Organizer** Big Idea Graphic Organizer folder, p. 61

📁 **Guided Reading and Review** Units 5–6 folder, p. 5

Media and Technology

AmericanHeritage® CD-ROM

Explorer Activity 19 Business and Industry, CD-ROM Guidebook, pp. 57–58, helps students write an editorial supporting or opposing child labor laws.

History Makers Andrew Carnegie

of the truth. For example, consider the story of Andrew Carnegie, one of the United States' first great industrialists.

Andrew Carnegie

AMERICAN BIOGRAPHY Born in Scotland in 1835, Andrew Carnegie knew something about the harsh side of industrialization. His father was a skilled weaver, but the coming of the power loom caused the market for skilled craftsworkers to collapse. Carnegie's family faced hard times. As a result, they immigrated to the United States in 1848, settling near Pittsburgh, Pennsylvania.

Andrew Carnegie (1835–1919)

Though he was only 13 years old, Carnegie found work in a cotton mill at $1.20 a week. At age 18 he won the post of secretary to the superintendent in the Pennsylvania Railroad Company. When his boss went to work at the War Department during the Civil War, Carnegie was promoted to his job.

Captain of the Steel Industry By the time he was 30, in 1865, Carnegie was making $50,000 a year, and he wanted to invest his wealth. The development of the Bessemer process persuaded Carnegie that steel would soon replace iron in many industries. During the early 1870s, near Pittsburgh, he founded the first steel plants to use the Bessemer process. These holdings would eventually grow into the Carnegie Steel Company, which he established in 1889.

Carnegie's business prospered. This enabled him to cut his prices until he had driven his competitors out of the market. Carnegie soon controlled the American steel industry, from the mines that produced iron ore to the furnaces and mills that made pig iron and steel. He even bought up the shipping and rail lines necessary to transport his products to market.

Carnegie the Philanthropist While expanding his business, Carnegie became a major public figure. Through books and speeches, he preached a "gospel of wealth." The essence of his message was simple: People should be free to make as much money as they can. After they make it, however, they should give it away.

By the turn of the century, Carnegie had donated the money for roughly 3,000 free public libraries, supported artistic and research institutes, and set up a fund to study how to abolish war. By the time he died in 1919, Carnegie had given away some $350 million.

Still, not everyone approved of Carnegie's methods. As you will read later in this chapter, workers at his steel plants protested against his company's labor practices. Many others questioned the sincerity of his good works. In reply, Carnegie argued that the success of men like him helped the nation as a whole:

AMERICAN VOICES " It will be a great mistake for the community to shoot the millionaires, for they are the bees that make the most honey, and contribute most to the hive even after they have gorged themselves full."

—Andrew Carnegie ■

Social Darwinism

In statements such as these, Carnegie also suggested that the wealthy were somehow better than other people. This idea, popular in the late 1800s, was based on Charles Darwin's theory of evolution, first published in 1859. According to

---

CAUSE AND EFFECT: Growth of Big Business

CAUSES
- Railroad boom lowers the cost of shipping.
- New inventions make businesses more efficient.
- Nation has rich supply of natural resources.
- Small firms merge to form giant companies.

↓

GROWTH OF BIG BUSINESS

↓

EFFECTS
- Steel and oil become giant industries.
- Monopolies, cartels, and trusts dominate major industries.
- Factory workers face harsh working and living conditions.
- Labor unions grow.

Interpreting Charts Technological advances and aggressive business practices combined to form big business. *Economics* **What effects did the growth of big business have on workers?**

Main Idea CONNECTIONS

Why was the government concerned about monopolies?

Darwin, all animal life had evolved by a process of "natural selection" through which only the fittest survived to reproduce.

A theory soon emerged that applied Darwin's theory to the struggle between workers and employers. Called **social Darwinism,** it held that society should do as little as possible to interfere with people's pursuit of success. If government would stay out of the affairs of business, the theory went, those who were most "fit" would succeed and become rich. Society as a whole would benefit from the success of the fit and the weeding out of the unfit.

Most Americans agreed that the government should not interfere with private businesses. As a result, the government neither taxed businesses' profits nor regulated their relations with their workers.

Gaining a Competitive Edge

Industrialists used whatever means necessary, fair or unfair, to gain a competitive edge. They paid as little as they could for raw materials, labor, and shipping. Sometimes they sought to take control of their entire industry.

PUCK.

THE PROTECTORS OF OUR INDUSTRIES.

Some Americans were offended by the argument that business leaders protected jobs. *Economics What does this cartoon suggest about the relationship of workers to business leaders?*

Monopolies and Cartels Some companies set out to gain a **monopoly,** or complete control of a product or service. To do this, a business bought its competitors or drove them out of business. Once consumers had no other place to turn for a given product or service, the sole remaining company would be free to raise its prices.

Toward the end of the 1800s, federal and state governments passed laws to prevent certain monopolistic practices. Those laws did not prevent or destroy all monopolies, however. One reason was that political leaders refused to attack the powerful business leaders.

Forming monopolies was not the only way to control an industry. Sometimes industrialists prospered by taking steps to limit competition with other firms. One way was to form a **cartel**—a loose association of businesses that make the same product. Members of a cartel agreed to limit the supply of their product and thus keep prices high.

Neither monopolies nor cartels were foolproof. Monopolies faced the threat of government action, and cartels tended to fall apart during hard economic times. To achieve a more reliable arrangement, Samuel Dodd, a lawyer for oil tycoon John D. Rockefeller, invented yet another strategy.

The Standard Oil Trust Oil had become a major industry after Edwin L. Drake proved that it could be extracted from the ground through a well. Drake set up his well at Titusville, Pennsylvania, in 1858. A year later he struck oil, and Titusville soon became one of several boom towns in the northwestern part of the state.

Events in Pennsylvania excited John D. Rockefeller. He had become rich from a grain and meat partnership during the Civil War, and he saw the oil business as a way to become even richer. In 1863 Rockefeller built an oil refinery near Cleveland, Ohio. The refinery expanded rapidly. In 1870 Rockefeller and several associates formed the Standard Oil Company of Ohio.

Rockefeller persuaded his railroad friends to give him refunds on part of the cost of transporting his oil. As a result

Horizontal Consolidation

Purchased by Rockefeller

Independent Oil Refineries → Standard Oil Company

Vertical Consolidation

Coke fields	purchased by Carnegie
Iron ore deposits	purchased by Carnegie
Steel mills	purchased by Carnegie
Ships	purchased by Carnegie
Railroads	purchased by Carnegie

Carnegie Steel Company — Owns all phases of production

Interpreting Charts In the late 1800s large businesses dominated industry. Some companies grew more powerful through horizontal consolidation, in which companies simply bought competitors in their field (above). Other companies grew more powerful through vertical consolidation. By controlling all phases of production, they could lower the costs of making their product and charge less than their competitors (right). *Economics What problems might a business face when trying to compete with a company with a vertical monopoly? With a horizontal monopoly?*

of these refunds, Rockefeller could set Standard Oil's prices lower than those of his competitors. As Rockefeller's company sold more oil, he was able to undersell his competitors by charging even less.

Rockefeller soon had enough money to buy out his competitors, but the law stood in his way. State laws prohibited one company from owning the stock of another. This practice reduced competition and therefore "restrained," or held back, free trade.

Samuel Dodd had an idea to get around this ban. In 1882 the owners of Standard Oil and companies allied with it agreed to combine their operations. They would turn over their assets to a board of nine trustees. In return, they were promised a share of the profits of the new organization. The board of trustees, which Rockefeller controlled, managed the companies as a single unit called a **trust.**

In time, 40 companies joined the trust. Because the companies did not officially merge, no laws were violated. Rockefeller's trust, a new kind of monopoly, controlled almost all of the nation's oil-refining capacity.

Trusts proved an effective means of limiting industrial competition. As a result, many Americans began to demand government action to break up these industrial giants. In 1890 Congress responded by passing the **Sherman Antitrust Act.** This law outlawed any combination of companies that restrained interstate trade or commerce.

The act, however, proved ineffective against trusts for nearly 15 years, because the federal government rarely enforced it. Besides,

the law's vague wording made it hard to apply in court. The act was applied successfully against labor unions. Federal officials argued that labor unions restrained trade because workers were combining to gain an advantage.

Methods of Industrial Control Rockefeller's use of the Standard Oil Trust to create a giant company was an example of **horizontal consolidation.** This method involved bringing together many firms that were in the same business. Other industrialists practiced **vertical consolidation,** or gaining control of the many different businesses that make up all phases of a product's development. Andrew Carnegie used this method in the steel business. He purchased not only steel plants but also the mines that supplied the iron and the railroads that transported the finished products.

By controlling all stages of steel production, Carnegie could lower his costs and drive competitors out of business. He could charge less because of **economies of scale.** That is, as production increases, the cost of each item produced is often lower. As Carnegie Steel expanded, its cost per item went down.

Effects on American Society

Few people truly liked trusts and other large business organizations. In 1873 a New

Graphing the Main Idea

To make sure students understand the main idea of the section, you may wish to use the double web graphic organizer below.

Tell students that a double web compares information about two main ideas. Ask students to use it to show how big business both helped and hurt American society.

Teaching Tip A template for this graphic organizer can be found in the Color Transparencies, G-2.

Answer to . . .

Interpreting Charts Too many goods were produced, resulting in wage cuts and worker layoffs.

Business Cycles

Interpreting Charts Although business cycles have no regular intervals, they typically follow the pattern shown above. A recession is a temporary decline in business activity. A prolonged recession is a depression. *Economics How did rapid industrial growth result in a depression between 1893 and 1897?*

Englander painted a bleak picture of industrialization:

> **AMERICAN VOICES** ❝It is only too evident that the cause now at work in Lynn may render it rich and prosperous as a city, but with a population of overworked, underpaid hirelings, hopelessly dependent upon employers who act upon the good old rule, the simple plan—that they may take who have the power, and they may keep who can.❞
>
> —*Resident of Lynn, Massachusetts*

Despite their questionable practices, industrial giants continued to sidestep the law. Politicians did not have the will to crack down on them. After all, these firms contributed mightily to the United States' rising level of wealth. By the turn of the century, such mammoth companies as American Telephone and Telegraph, Swift and Armour, General Electric, Westinghouse, and DuPont were some of America's greatest success stories.

Rapid industrial growth did place strains on the economy. Big businesses sometimes churned out more goods than consumers wanted or could afford. Then they had to lower prices in order to sell their products. To cover their losses, they often cut wages and laid off workers. The resulting shock to the economy could be severe. In 1893, for example, a period of expansion suddenly ended. By the end of the year, nearly 500 banks and more than 15,000 businesses had failed, and the economy sank into a four-year depression.

Economists call such a "boom and bust" period the **business cycle.** One cause of the depression that began in 1893 was a panic. Panics occurred when investors feared that key businesses, heavily in debt, might not be able to repay their loans. Investors rushed to sell stock, stock prices fell, and companies went bankrupt. The resulting unemployment caused widespread misery, especially among workers and their families.

SECTION 2 REVIEW

Comprehension

1. *Key Terms* Define: (a) social Darwinism; (b) monopoly; (c) cartel; (d) trust; (e) Sherman Antitrust Act; (f) horizontal consolidation; (g) vertical consolidation; (h) economies of scale; (i) business cycle.

2. *Summarizing the Main Idea* Describe some of the methods that companies used to dominate their markets, and explain why some people questioned those methods.

3. *Organizing Information* Make a two-column chart with columns headed *Robber Baron* and *Captain of Industry*. Now list people, events, and methods from the section in the appropriate column, along with a brief explanation of why each entry appears where it does.

Critical Thinking

4. *Analyzing Time Lines* Review the time line at the start of the section. Which events could be causes of the Sherman Antitrust Act? Which one event is the likeliest cause? Explain.

5. *Formulating Questions* Write a question that would help you or another reader better understand the information about Andrew Carnegie in this section.

Writing Activity

6. *Writing a Persuasive Essay* Write an essay in which you explain your agreement or disagreement with the theory of social Darwinism and attempt to convince others to accept your viewpoint.

 RESOURCE OPTIONS

Teaching Resources

📁 **Quiz** Units 5–6 folder, p. 6

Student Performance Pack

 Guide to the Essentials Chapter 14, Section 2 (English and Spanish)

1864 Contract Labor Act	1868 Eight-hour day for government employees		1881 First time and motion studies of workers	1887 Major drought ruins many farmers	1893 Illinois limits child labor
1860		**1880**			**1900**

3 Industrialization and Workers

SECTION PREVIEW

Objectives

1. Identify the sources of the growing American work force and the reasons why entire families worked.
2. Describe factory work in the late 1800s.
3. Explain the roles that women and children played in the work force.
4. *Key Terms* Define: piecework; division of labor.

Main Idea

Industry relied on its laborers, who worked for low wages and often in unsafe factories.

Reading Strategy

Predicting Content Look at the pictures and the main headings in this section. Write a prediction of what life was like for factory workers. As you read, compare your predictions with the information presented in the text.

The United States was ripe for economic prosperity after the Civil War. Its abundant natural resources, inventive minds, and risk-taking entrepreneurs all played central roles in the nation's industrial expansion. This expansion would not have been possible, however, without the millions of workers who toiled in the factories.

The Growing Work Force

Around 14 million people immigrated to the United States between 1860 and 1900. Most came in the hope of finding work in America's booming industrial centers. During the Civil War, when labor was scarce, the federal government encouraged immigration by passing what has been called the Contract Labor Act. This law, passed in 1864, allowed employers to enter into contracts with immigrants. Employers would pay their cost of passage, and in return, immigrants had to work for a certain amount of time, up to a year. Employers soon began actively recruiting foreign laborers.

In another dramatic population shift, some 8 or 9 million Americans moved to cities during the late 1800s. (See graph at right.)

Most of them fled poor economic conditions on the nation's farms. A long drought beginning in 1887, combined with low prices and more competition from foreign wheat producers, left many farm families penniless. Plentiful work in the factories lured the former farmers, as did the faster-paced life of the city.

Shifts in U.S. Labor Force, 1860–1900

Percent of Total Labor Force

- ■ Agricultural workers
- ■ Industrial workers (mining, construction, manufacturing)

Year

Source: *Historical Statistics of the United States, Colonial Times to 1970*

 Interpreting Graphs The growth of industry in the mid- to late 1800s changed the distribution of the work force. *Economics Compare the percentage of the labor force engaged in agricultural work with the percentage engaged in industrial work for 1860 and 1900.*

 RESOURCE OPTIONS

Teaching Resources

📁 **Reproducible Lesson Plan** Lesson Plans folder, p. 90

📁 **Learning Styles Lesson Plan** Learning Styles Lesson Plans folder, p. 31

📁 **Big Idea Graphic Organizer** Big Idea Graphic Organizer folder, p. 62

📁 **Guided Reading and Review** Units 5–6 folder, p. 7

📁 **Nystrom *Atlas of Our Country*** The Second Wave of Immigration, pp. 24–25; The Third Wave of Immigration, pp. 30–31

During the 1800s, few African Americans took part in this migration. Although some moved into southern cities, the better job opportunities there were closed to them.

Working Families

For those who labored in the factories, work was a family affair. Every family member worked in some way. Because wages were low, no one person could earn enough to provide for a household.

As a result, children often left school at the age of 12 or 13 to work. Girls sometimes took factory jobs so that their brothers could stay in school. If a mother could not make money working at home, she might take a factory job, leaving her children with relatives or neighbors. If an adult became ill, died, or could not find or keep a job, children as young as 6 or 7 had to bring in cash or go hungry.

In the 1800s needy families were largely on their own. During that century Americans did not believe that government should provide public assistance, except in rare cases. Unemployment insurance, for example, did not exist, so workers received no payments as a result of layoffs or factory closings. The popular theory of social Darwinism held that poverty resulted from personal weakness. Many thought offering relief to the unemployed would encourage idleness.

Families in need relied on private charities. These charities could not afford to help everyone, however. They had limited resources, so only the neediest received the food, clothing, and shelter that charities had to offer.

Factory Work

By 1860 most states had established a ten-hour workday, yet they rarely enforced it. Thus, most laborers worked twelve hours, six days a week—and even more when they had to meet production goals. An 1868 federal law granted government employees an eight-hour day, but this did not affect private industry. In fact, workers would fight for the eight-hour day well into the 1900s.

In many industries, employers paid workers not by the time worked but by what they produced. Workers received a fixed amount for each finished piece they produced—for example, a few cents for a garment or a number of cigars. This system of **piecework** meant that those who worked fastest and produced the most pieces earned the most money. Piecework favored young and strong workers; older or less able workers suffered.

Increasing Efficiency In 1881 Frederick Winslow Taylor set out to improve worker efficiency in the steel plant where he was chief engineer. He began to study the workers, trying to see how much time it took to do various jobs. Then he broke down each task into a number of steps and determined how long each step should take. In the same way he also studied each motion needed in a task. The goal of Taylor's time and motion studies was to get workers to produce more in less time.

Workers hated Taylor's ideas, which imposed an outside control on the way they did their work. They also feared that increased efficiency would result in layoffs or a lower rate of pay for each piece of work.

By the early years of the 1900s, Taylor had used his studies as the foundation of an entire system for the scientific management of workers. In 1911, in his book *The Principles of Scientific Management,* he described his system:

AMERICAN VOICES "The work of every workman is fully planned out by the management at least one day in advance, and each man receives in most cases complete written instructions, describing in detail the task which he is to accomplish, as well as the means to be used in doing the work . . . and the exact time allowed for doing it."

—*Frederick Winslow Taylor*

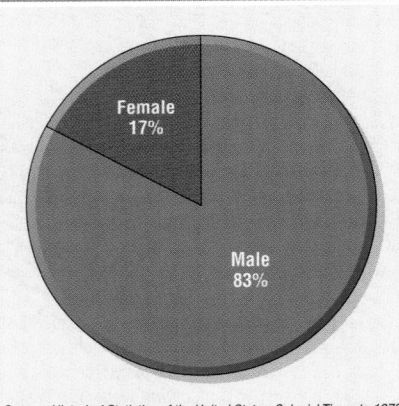

Interpreting Graphs In 1890 women formed 17 percent of the labor force. Most of these female workers were unmarried. *Economics What obstacles to employment did women industrial workers face?*

Male and Female Workers, 1890

Female 17%

Male 83%

Source: *Historical Statistics of the United States, Colonial Times to 1970*

▶ RESOURCE OPTIONS

Teaching Resources

📁 **Visual Learning Activity** The Noble Face of Labor, Learning with Documents folder, p. 56

American History Block Scheduling Support On the Job: Industrialism in America, found in the Expansion, Reconstruction, Immigration folder, includes interdisciplinary lesson suggestions and activities for Geography and History, Primary Sources, Biography, and Literature.

John Furguson Weir's painting *Gun Foundry* presents a vivid image of the nation's industrial might. *Economics* *What does the painting suggest about the conditions faced by workers?*

Some employers had their own, unscientific methods of improving efficiency. They simply increased the speed of factory machines or gave each employee more work. Yet they rarely increased workers' pay. The additional workload could endanger workers' health and safety.

A Strict Work Environment The routines of factory work differed greatly from those of earlier kinds of work. Factory workers were ruled by the clock, which told them when to start, take any breaks, and stop work. On the farm, in contrast, workers had labored at their own pace.

Less obvious, but equally important, was a change in the relationship between the worker and the product. Craftsworkers traditionally made a product from start to finish, which required them to perform a variety of tasks. Factory workers performed only one small task, over and over, and rarely even saw the finished product. This **division of labor** into separate tasks proved to be efficient, but it took much of the joy out of the work.

Owners seldom visited the factory floor where their workers toiled. Called "hands" or "operatives," the workers were viewed as interchangeable parts in a vast and impersonal machine. One factory manager in 1883 declared, "I regard my people as I regard my machinery. So long as they can do my work for what I choose to pay them, I keep them, getting out of them all I can."

Discipline was strict. To make a profit, factory managers needed to run an efficient operation. Thus they might fine or fire workers for a range of offenses, such as being late or refusing to do a task. Workplaces were not always safe. The noise of the machines was deafening. Lighting and ventilation were poor. Fatigue, faulty equipment, and careless training resulted in frequent fires and accidents. In 1882, the average number of workers killed on the job each week was 675—compared to about 120 today. Despite the harsh conditions, employers suffered no shortage of labor. Factory work offered higher pay and more opportunities than most people could hope to find elsewhere.

Working Women and Children

Employers in industry excluded women from the most-skilled and highest-paying jobs. Of course, not all men had good jobs, either. But factory owners usually assigned women to the operation of simple machines. More complex machines required machinists and engineers. These were almost always men, for only they had access to training in such fields.

Women had almost no chance to advance in factory work. In the garment industry, for example, running the machines that cut large stacks of fabric was defined as a man's job. Typically, women performed only one part of the process of sewing a garment.

In the 1880s, children made up more than 5 percent of the industrial labor force. For many households, children's wages meant the difference between going hungry or having food on the table.

Main Idea
CONNECTIONS

Why did women have little chance for advancement in factory work?

Many children worked under hazardous conditions. The boys at left worked in coal mines. The grime that covers their faces also clogged their lungs, leading to disease. Industrial growth created jobs for African Americans, though opportunities were limited. The men at right were hired for the low-paying job of carrying bricks. White men got the higher-paying jobs as masons. *Economics* **Why were so many children put to work?**

Laboring in factories or mines and performing dangerous work was unhealthful for all workers. But it especially threatened growing children. Many children became stunted in both body and mind. In 1892 social reformer Jacob Riis tried to explain the impact of factory work on children in a book titled *Children of the Poor*. Riis wrote that people who spent their whole childhood on the factory floor grew "to manhood and womanhood . . . with the years that should have prepared them for life's work gone in hopeless and profitless drudgery." Thanks to Riis and others, the practice of child labor came under broad attack in the 1890s and early 1900s when states began curbing this practice through legislation[†].

[†] Illinois limited children's time at work to 8 hours a day and 48 hours a week in 1893. By 1912, three fourths of the states had similar laws.

SECTION 3 REVIEW

Comprehension

1. **Key Terms** Define: (a) piecework; (b) division of labor.
2. **Summarizing the Main Idea** What made factory work difficult in the late 1800s?
3. **Organizing Information** Create a web diagram to show the two major sources of the growing work force. Use smaller circles to provide details about each of these sources.

Critical Thinking

4. **Analyzing Time Lines** Review the time line at the start of the section. Which of the events do you think helped factory owners the most? Explain.
5. **Identifying Alternatives** Would the problems faced by women and children in the work force, as described in this section, have been solved by a law banning women and children from working? Explain your answer.

Writing Activity

6. **Writing an Expository Essay** Write an essay describing the day-to-day life of a typical factory worker in the late 1800s.

RESOURCE OPTIONS

Teaching Resources

 Quiz Units 5–6 folder, p. 8

Student Performance Pack

 Guide to the Essentials Chapter 14, Section 3 (English and Spanish)

Media and Technology

 Prentice Hall United States History Video Collection™ Volume 12
Immigration and Cultural Change

The Great Strikes

Timeline

1866 National Labor Union organized	1877 Nationwide rail strike	1886 Haymarket Riot	1886 American Federation of Labor organized	1892 Homestead Strike	1894 Pullman Strike

1860   1870   1880   1890   1900

4 The Great Strikes

SECTION PREVIEW

Objectives

1 Summarize the growing gulf between rich business owners and poor workers.
2 List some of the early labor unions and their activities.
3 Describe the causes and outcomes of the major strikes of the late 1800s.
4 *Key Terms* Define: socialism; collective bargaining; scab; anarchist; Haymarket Riot; Homestead Strike; Pullman Strike.

Main Idea

In the late 1800s workers organized labor unions to improve their wages and working conditions.

Reading Strategy

Reinforcing Key Ideas Make a table with two columns on a sheet of paper. Label one column *Successes* and the other *Failures*. As you read, use the table to keep track of the successes and failures of labor unions.

Industrialization had lowered the prices of consumer goods, but in the late nineteenth century most factory workers did not earn enough to buy them. The successful entrepreneurs of the era had worked hard. Many, like Carnegie, had used their wealth to provide money for good works. Still, in hard times only the poor went hungry. Increasingly, working men and woman took their complaints directly and forcefully to their employers.

Gulf Between Rich and Poor

The 1890 census revealed that the richest 9 percent of Americans held nearly 75 percent of the national wealth. In the best of times, the average worker could earn only a few hundred dollars a year. Many workers resented the extravagant lifestyles of many factory owners.

Poor families had little hope of relief when hard times hit. Some suffered in silence, trusting that tomorrow would be better. Others became politically active in an effort to improve their lives. A few of these individuals were drawn to the idea of socialism, which was then gaining popularity in Europe.

Socialism is an economic and political philosophy that favors public (or social) control of property and income, not private control. Socialists believe that society at large, not just private individuals, should take charge of a nation's wealth. That wealth, they say, should be distributed to everyone.

Socialism began in the 1830s as an idealistic movement. Early Socialists believed that people should cooperate, not compete, in producing goods. Socialism then grew more radical, reflecting the ideas of a German philosopher named Karl Marx. In 1848 Marx, along with Friedrich Engels, wrote a famous pamphlet called the *Communist Manifesto*. In it they denounced the capitalist economic system and predicted that workers would one day overturn it.

Most Americans opposed socialism. The wealthy saw it as a threat to their fortunes. Politicians saw it as a threat to public order. Americans in general, including most workers, saw it as a threat to the deeply rooted

Workers in many industries formed unions in the late 1800s.

RESOURCE OPTIONS

Teaching Resources

📁 **Reproducible Lesson Plan** Lesson Plans folder, p. 91

📁 **Big Idea Graphic Organizer** Big Idea Graphic Organizer folder, p. 63

📁 **Guided Reading and Review** Units 5–6 folder, p. 9

Media and Technology

RESOURCE⊙PRO

Literature Activity *Sister Carrie,* found on Resource Pro, introduces students to factory life in the late 1800s with an excerpt from Theodore Dreiser's novel.

The Great Strikes

Objectives
You may wish to call students' attention to the objectives in the Section Preview. The objectives are reflected in the main headings of the section.

Bellringer
Have student pairs choose several possible courses of action in the following situation: Restaurant workers are told that unless they agree to work four additional evening hours each week for no extra pay, they will be fired. As students read, have them circle any option that uses collective bargaining.

Reading Strategy
Reinforcing Key Ideas Refer to the Reading Strategy in the Section Preview. You may wish to make a table on the chalkboard and have volunteers fill it in.

LESSON PLAN
Connecting to the Main Idea

1. Focus Explain to students that industrialization caused great inequalities in wealth in the late nineteenth century. Big business owners grew wealthy, while workers toiled for low wages. Ask students how workers tried to improve their wages and working conditions.

2. Instruct Discuss why workers resented the wealth of business owners. Ask how socialism, anarchism, and labor unions were all efforts to solve the problems of workers. Ask how socialism promised to improve workers' lives but ran counter to some American ideals. What did labor unions do to address workers' problems? Ask students to describe public reaction to the strikes. What pattern of events did the Pullman Strike set in motion?

3. Close Although unions were organized to improve workers' conditions in the late 1800s, opposition from employers resulted in violent strikes and great suffering.

Many workers lived in crowded boarding-houses (far right). Many wealthy industrialists, on the other hand, enjoyed great personal wealth and luxurious comforts (left). *Economics How did many workers respond to the contrast between the rich and poor?*

American ideals of private property, free enterprise, and individual liberty.

The Rise of Labor Unions

A small percentage of American workers did become Socialists and called for an end to free enterprise. Far more workers, however, chose to work within the system by uniting to form labor unions.

Early Labor Unions Workers formed a few local labor unions during the early years of industrialization. These were called trade unions, and they were organized for workers in specific trades. The Federal Society of Journeymen Cordwainers (shoemakers), founded in Philadelphia in 1794, was the strongest of these early unions. Still, it lasted only until 1806, when it was outlawed for engaging in a strike.

Philadelphians took the labor movement to the next level in 1827, when several craft groups joined to form the Mechanics' Union of Trade Societies. This city-wide form of trade union spread quickly to other cities in the East. In 1834 a number of these groups, representing about 21,000 members, organized the National Trades Union. Open to workers from all crafts, the National Trades Union was the first national labor organization. It lasted only a few years before being destroyed by the panic and depression that began in 1837.

Main Idea
CONNECTIONS

What was the National Trades Union?

Strong local unions resurfaced after the Civil War. They began as a way to provide help for their members in bad times, but soon became the means for expressing workers' demands to employers. These demands included shorter workdays, higher wages, and better working conditions.

In the 1860s and 1870s labor activists again began organizing nationally. In Baltimore in 1866 they formed the National Labor Union, representing some 60,000 members. In 1872 this union nominated a candidate for President. It failed, however, to survive a depression that began the following year. Indeed, unions in general suffered a steep decline in membership as a result of the poor economy.

The Knights of Labor Another national union, the Noble Order of the Knights of Labor, was formed in Philadelphia in 1869. The Knights hoped to organize all working men and women, skilled and unskilled, into a single union. Membership included farmers and factory workers as well as shopkeepers and office workers. The union actively recruited African Americans, 60,000 of whom joined.

Under the leadership of former machinist Terence Powderly, the Knights pursued broad social reforms. These included equal pay for equal work, the eight-hour day, and an end to child labor. They did not emphasize higher wages as their primary goal.

The leaders of the Knights preferred not to use the strike as a tool. Most members, however, differed with their leadership on this issue. In fact, it was a strike that helped the Knights achieve their greatest strength. In 1885, when unions linked to the Knights forced railroad owner Jay Gould to give up a wage cut, membership quickly soared to 700,000. Yet a series of failed strikes followed, some of them violent. Membership dropped off, and public support for the Knights waned. By the 1890s the Knights had largely disappeared as a national force.

The American Federation of Labor A third national union, the American Federation of Labor (AFL), followed the leadership of Samuel Gompers, a London-born cigar maker. Formed in 1886, the AFL had different objectives than the Knights of Labor. The AFL sought to organize only skilled workers in a network of smaller unions, each devoted to a specific craft.

Between 1886 and 1892, the AFL gained some 250,000 members. Yet they still represented only a tiny portion of the nation's total labor force. Few African Americans joined. In theory the AFL was open to African Americans, but local unions often found ways to exclude them from membership. Women, too, were not welcome in the AFL. Gompers opposed the membership of women because he believed that their presence in the work force would drive wages down, as he stated:

AMERICAN VOICES ❝We know to our regret that too often are wives, sisters and children brought into the factories and workshops only to reduce the wages and displace the labor of men—the heads of families.❞

—*Samuel Gompers*

Gompers and the AFL focused mainly on issues of workers' wages, hours, and working conditions. This so-called bread-and-butter unionism set the AFL apart from the Knights of Labor. The Knights had sought to help their members through political activity and education. The AFL relied on economic pressure, such as strikes and boycotts, against employers.

Through these tactics the AFL tried to force employers to participate in **collective bargaining,** a process in which workers negotiate as a group with employers. Workers acting as a group had more power than a single worker acting alone. To strengthen its collec-

tive bargaining power, the AFL pressed for a "closed shop," a workplace in which only union members would be hired.

The Wobblies The AFL's policies did not suit all workers. In 1905 in Chicago, 43 groups opposed to the AFL founded the Industrial Workers of the World (IWW), or Wobblies. The IWW, which focused on unskilled workers, was a radical union that included many Socialists among its leadership. A number of IWW strikes were violent on both sides. During World War I, many IWW leaders were convicted of promoting strikes in war-related industries.

Reaction of Employers By and large, employers disliked and feared unions. They preferred to deal with employees as individuals instead of in powerful groups. Employers took several measures to stop unions:
(1) They forbade union meetings.
(2) They fired union organizers.
(3) They forced new employees to sign "yellow dog" contracts, in which workers

---

COMPARING PRIMARY SOURCES

LABOR UNIONS

In 1883 the Senate Committee on Education and Labor held a series of hearings concerning the relationship between workers and management. The committee heard these opposing views about the need for labor unions.

Testimony of a Labor Leader	Testimony of a Factory Manager
"The laws written [by Congress] and now in operation to protect the property of the capitalist and the moneyed class generally are almost innumerable, yet nothing has been done to protect the property of the workingmen, the only property that they possess, their working power, their savings bank, their school, and trades union." —*Samuel Gompers, labor leader*	"I think that . . . in a free country like this . . . it is perfectly safe for at least the lifetime of this generation to leave the question of how a man shall work, and how long he shall work, and what wages he shall get to himself." —*Thomas L. Livermore, manager of a manufacturing company*

ANALYZING VIEWPOINTS **Compare the main arguments made by the two speakers.**

About the Presidents

Rutherford B. Hayes (1877–1881) seemed old-fashioned: he always wore a silk hat, frock coat, and black shoes. But in some ways, he was ahead of his times. He ended Reconstruction and turned away from the politics of the past. Declaring that the old spoils system should be abolished, he pleaded for a merit system instead. Though Congress didn't pass civil service reform under Hayes, reform would be the wave of the future. What's more, Hayes traveled more than any of his predecessors. He became the first President to see the West Coast. Source: Donald Young, "Rutherford B. Hayes," *The American Heritage® Pictorial History of the Presidents of the United States,* vol. 2, 1968.

promised never to join a union or participate in a strike.

(4) They refused to bargain collectively when strikes did occur.

(5) They refused to recognize unions as their workers' legitimate representatives.

In 1902 George F. Baer, the president of a mining company, reflected the opinions of many business leaders when he wrote: "Rights and interests of the laboring man will be protected and cared for—not by the labor agitators, but by the Christian men to whom God has given control of the property interests of the country."

The Railroad Strike of 1877

The first major case of nationwide labor unrest in the United States occurred in the railroad industry. The strike began on July 14, 1877, when the Baltimore and Ohio Railroad announced a wage cut of 10 percent in the midst of a depression. This was the second wage cut in eight months. Railroads elsewhere imposed similar cuts, along with orders to run "double headers," trains with two engines and twice as many cars as usual. The unusually long trains increased the risk of accidents and the chance of worker layoffs.

Railway workers in Baltimore reacted with violence. Rioting spread rapidly to Pittsburgh, Chicago, St. Louis, and other cities. In Martinsburg, West Virginia, strikers turned back the local militia. President Rutherford B. Hayes sent in federal troops to put down a

strike, the first time this had been done in American history.

A week later in Pittsburgh, soldiers fired on rioters, killing and wounding many. A crowd of 20,000 angry men and women reacted to the shootings by setting fire to railroad company property, causing more than $5 million in damage. President Hayes again chose to send in federal troops.

From the 1877 strike on, employers relied on federal and state troops to repress labor unrest. A new and violent era in labor relations had begun.

Strikes Rock the Nation

From 1881 to 1900 the United States faced one industrial crisis after another. Some 24,000 strikes erupted in the nation's factories, mines, mills, and rail yards during those two decades alone. Three events were particularly violent: the Haymarket Riot and the Homestead and Pullman strikes.

Haymarket, 1886 On May 1, 1886, groups of workers mounted a national demonstration for an eight-hour workday. "Eight hours for work, eight hours for rest, eight hours for what we will," ran the cry. Strikes then erupted in a number of cities.

On May 3 at Chicago's McCormick reaper factory, police broke up a fight between strikers and scabs. (A **scab** is a negative term for a worker called in by an employer to replace striking laborers. Using scabs allows a company to continue operating

Work Stoppages, 1882–1900

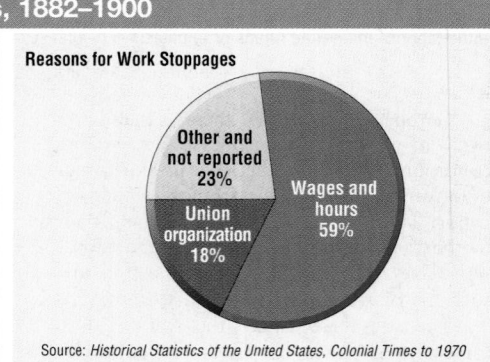

Source: *Historical Statistics of the United States, Colonial Times to 1970*

Source: *Historical Statistics of the United States, Colonial Times to 1970*

 Interpreting Graphs A severe economic depression helped cause a steep decline in union membership in the 1870s. But the 1880s and 1890s saw growth in the number of members and in the number of work stoppages. *Economics* What were the major reasons for work stoppages in the late 1800s?

Answer to . . .

Interpreting Charts Disputes over wages and hours.

---

and avoid having to bargain with the union.) The police action caused several casualties among the workers.

Union leaders called for a protest rally on the evening of May 4 in Chicago's Haymarket Square. A group of **anarchists,** radicals who violently oppose all government, joined the strikers. Anarchists, such as newspaper editor August Spies, knew how to whip up anger among the workers. He stated:

AMERICAN VOICES ❝You have endured the pangs of want and hunger; your children you have sacrificed to the factory-lords. In short, you have been miserable and obedient slaves all these years. Why? To satisfy the insatiable greed, to fill the coffers of your lazy thieving master!❞

—*August Spies*

At the May 4 event someone threw a bomb into a police formation, killing seven officers. In the riot that followed, gunfire between police and protesters killed dozens on both sides. Investigators never found the bomb thrower, yet eight anarchists were tried for conspiracy to commit murder. Four were hanged. Another committed suicide in jail. Governor John P. Altgeld of Illinois decided later that the convictions resulted from public outrage rather than evidence. He pardoned the remaining three anarchists.

To many unionists, the anarchists who took part in the **Haymarket Riot** forever would be heroes. To employers, however, they remained vicious criminals determined to undermine law and order. Much of the American public came to associate unions in general with violence and radical ideas.

Homestead, 1892 In the summer of 1892, while Andrew Carnegie was in Europe, his partner Henry Frick tried to cut workers' wages at Carnegie Steel. The union at the Carnegie plant in Homestead, Pennsylvania, called a strike.

Frick intended to crush the union. On July 1 he called in the Pinkertons, a private police force known for their ability to break strikes. Under cover of darkness, some 300 Pinkertons moved up the Monongahela River on barges. In a shootout with strikers on shore, several people died and many were wounded.

At first Americans generally sympathized with the striking workers. Then, on July 23,

The violence of the Haymarket Riot, depicted here, troubled many Americans. *Culture Did the incident at Haymarket help or hurt the union cause?*

anarchist Alexander Berkman tried and failed to assassinate Frick. Although Berkman was not connected with the strike, the public associated his act with the rising tide of labor violence.

The union admitted defeat and called off the **Homestead Strike** on November 20. Homestead reopened under militia protection. "I will never recognize the union, never, never!" Frick cried. Carnegie believed in unions and accepted their right to strike, as long as no violence took place.[†]

Pullman, 1894 Like the strike of 1877, the last of the great strikes also involved the railroad industry. This strike also marked a shift in the federal government's involvement with labor-employer relations.

Sleeping-car maker George Pullman considered himself a caring industrialist. Near Chicago he built a town for his workers that boasted a school, bank, water and gas systems, and comfortable homes. Conditions in the town, however, took a turn for the worse after

---

[†] Carnegie Steel (and its successor, U.S. Steel) remained nonunionized until the late 1930s.

Using the Internet

Create a Diary Entry

Objective Use the Internet to write a diary entry from the point of view of August Spies, one of the anarchists convicted of inciting the Haymarket Riot. Have students follow these instructions:

1. See the *America: Pathways to the Present* Web site at

http://www.Pathways.phschool.com

for the URL for Chicago Historical Information.

2. Use links to read about the Haymarket Riot and the anarchists convicted of inciting it, and to view related photographs.

3. Write a diary entry from the point of view of anarchist August Spies. Include his account of the riot, his arrest, and his feelings about the trial and his pending execution.

RESOURCE OPTIONS

Teaching Resources

📁 **Biography** Mary Kenney O'Sullivan, Units 5–6 folder, p. 11

📁 **Lasting Impact Activity** The Lasting Impact of the Great Strikes, History's Lasting Impact folder, pp. 10–11

Answer to . . .

Viewing History It hurt the union cause because the public came to associate unions with violence and radicalism.

Answers to
SECTION 4 REVIEW

1. (a) socialism, see p. 423; (b) collective bargaining, see p. 425; (c) scab, see p. 426; (d) anarchist, see p. 427; (e) Haymarket Riot, see p. 427; (f) Homestead Strike, see p. 427; (g) Pullman Strike, see p. 428.

2. The Knights of Labor wanted to organize all workers, skilled and unskilled, into a single union. They strove for broad social reform and preferred not to use strikes. The AFL included only skilled workers in its many small unions, addressed specific workers' issues, and used strikes and collective bargaining.

3. Sample chart entry: Railroad Strike of 1877—workers began strike, accompanied by violence, to protest 10 percent wage cut. Federal troops sent to dispel the workers, setting a precedent for how the government would deal with later strikes.

4. The AFL was formed at the time of the Haymarket Riot.

5. Socialism proposed to end private control of property and income, so that all Americans would share equally in the nation's wealth. The labor movement strove to work within the free enterprise system, to ensure that neither workers nor owners were unfairly favored.

6. Letters will vary but should be supported with examples from the text.

Eugene Debs was a successful labor organizer in the late 1800s. Later, Debs would combine his energetic style and his belief in socialism to conduct several unsuccessful presidential campaigns as the leader of the Socialist party.
Government **Why did the government interfere with the Pullman Strike?**

the Panic of 1893. Pullman laid off workers and cut wages by 25 percent. Meanwhile, he kept rent and food prices in his town at the same levels.

In May 1894 a delegation of workers went to him to protest. In response Pullman fired three of the workers, causing the local union to go on strike. Pullman refused to bargain and instead shut down the plant. The American Railway Union, led by popular labor organizer Eugene V. Debs, called for a boycott of Pullman cars throughout the country. Widespread local strikes followed.

By June 1894 some 120,000 railway workers had joined in the **Pullman Strike.** Debs instructed strikers not to interfere with the nation's mail, but the strike got out of hand. It completely disrupted western railroad traffic, including delivery of the mail.

Railroad owners turned to the federal government for help, and Attorney General Richard Olney came to their rescue. By arguing that the mail had to get through and citing the Sherman Antitrust Act, Olney won a court order forbidding all union activity that halted railroad traffic. Two days later, on July 4, President Grover Cleveland sent in 2,500 federal troops to ensure that strikers obeyed the court order. A week later the strike was over.

The Pullman strike and its outcome set an important pattern. In the years ahead, factory owners appealed frequently for court orders against unions. The federal government regularly approved these appeals, denying unions recognition as legally protected organizations. This official government opposition helped limit union gains for more than 30 years.

SECTION 4 REVIEW

Comprehension

1. *Key Terms* Define: (a) socialism; (b) collective bargaining; (c) scab; (d) anarchist; (e) Haymarket Riot; (f) Homestead Strike; (g) Pullman Strike.

2. *Summarizing the Main Idea* Compare the goals and policies of the Knights of Labor and the American Federation of Labor.

3. *Organizing Information* Create a two-column chart to summarize information about the major strikes of the late 1800s.

Critical Thinking

4. *Analyzing Time Lines* Review the time line at the start of the section. Which national union got started in the midst of a period of great turmoil? Explain.

5. *Making Comparisons* Compare socialism and the labor movement as two different responses to the growing gulf between rich and poor. How did they differ in their proposed solution to the problem?

Writing Activity

6. *Writing a Persuasive Essay* Write a letter to President Hayes regarding the strike in Martinsburg, West Virginia, in 1877. In your letter, try to persuade the President either to send troops in to stop the strike or to refuse to intervene.

Answer to . . .

Viewing History Railroad owners appealed for government help. The Attorney General, citing the disruption of mail service, won a court order forbidding all union activity that halted railroad traffic.

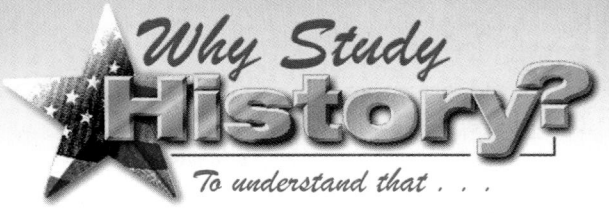

Why Study History?

To understand that . . .

You Live in a Post-Industrial Society

A service economy is replacing the industrial economy that arose in the United States in the decades following the Civil War.

Factory workers in the late 1800s

Suppose your great-grandfather worked in a steel mill. Your grandfather worked in a steel mill. Your father works in a computer-repair shop. Why?

Family work histories like the one above are common today. They reflect a historic change in the American economy: the decline of manufacturing and the rise of services. We live, in other words, in a post-industrial age.

The Impact Today

Services existed even before the rise of industry in the 1800s. In colonial times, people provided such services as shoeing horses, selling cloth, and importing tea. Most Americans, however, lived and worked on farms.

After the Civil War, millions of Americans left farming for factory jobs. Industry powered the nation's economy and employed its workers from the post–Civil War era through most of the twentieth century. It helped create a large and vital middle class and made the United States the world's wealthiest, most powerful economy.

Today the steel, railroad, automotive, and other industries have decreased in economic importance. Meanwhile, the service sector,

which includes banking, tourism, food services, recreation, data processing, and health care, has grown enormously. The number of Americans employed in services has more than doubled since 1970. More than 40 million Americans now work in the service sector.

The full impact of the post-industrial age remains to be seen, yet it has already created many changes in our society. More Americans are self-employed. Labor unions have declined. Education and skills have become increasingly important for people seeking jobs. According to some analysts, the loss of manufacturing jobs and the rise of low-paying service jobs (for example, in fast-food restaurants) have widened the gap between rich and poor.

Workers in a semiconductor factory today

The Impact on You

Interview two young or middle-aged adults, perhaps your parents, about their work. Find out what they like and dislike about their jobs. Then interview two older adults. Ask them to explain whether the economy is better or worse today than it was when they were young. Use your interviews to write a feature article about the post-industrial society.

RESOURCE OPTIONS

Teaching Resources

📁 **Why Study History? Activity** You Live in a Post-Industrial Society, found in the Why Study History? folder, p. 15, provides an activity to help students better understand today's service economy.

Media and Technology

🦅 **AmericanHeritage® CD-ROM**

Time Tour The Nation Today and Tomorrow: Toward a New Century

Why Study History?

Class Discussion

Discuss with the class life in a post-industrial society. For a more thorough examination of the issue, see the activity folder in the Resource Options below.

ACTIVITY
STUDENT PARTICIPATION

Analyzing Data

Ask students to read the text. Then brainstorm services that students and their families use during a typical day at home, at school, or at work. If necessary, provide some examples, such as:
- **bus service**
- **public transportation**
- **car repair**
- **restaurants**
- **teachers**
- **doctors**

Ask students to create a services checklist from their brainstorming session. They can use the list as a survey, tally results, and discuss findings.

Follow up Have students survey senior citizens about services that were available when they were teenagers. Discuss changes that have occurred since then.

💻 Using the Internet

Students can learn more about our post-industrial society by exploring links in the *America: Pathways to the Present* Web site at:

http://www.Pathways.phschool.com

Assessment

See the Lesson Plans folder, pp. 24–27, for rubrics on assessing Class Participation Projects.

Key Terms

Students should refer to the definitions of key terms in the chapter to write sentences that show an understanding of the impact of new technology on industry, daily life, and working life.

Comprehension

1. Business could ship goods farther and faster; railway technology could be used by other industries, promoting economic growth.

2. Large amounts of capital were needed to market new products and inventions, which small companies could not provide.

3. To get around the law prohibiting one company from buying another. It was successful; however, public reaction eventually led to antitrust laws.

4. It made the United States wealthy, but businesses often made more goods than they could sell; to make a profit, they laid off workers or cut wages. Eventually, this hurt the economy and caused depressions.

5. Most came hoping to find work; many were attracted by contracts under which they would work in exchange for passage to the United States.

6. Women were paid lower wages than men and had access only to unskilled jobs; women and children worked in poor, unhealthy conditions.

7. They disallowed union meetings; fired union organizers; forced new employees to promise never to strike or join a union; refused to participate in collective bargaining or recognize unions as workers' legitimate representatives.

8. The side of the factory owners by sending in troops, putting striking anarchists on trial, and obtaining court orders against strikers.

Chapter Summary

The major concepts of Chapter 14 are presented below. See also *Guide to the Essentials of American History* or *Interactive Student Tutorial CD-ROM,* which contains interactive review activities, time lines, helpful hints, and test practice for Chapter 14.

Reviewing the Main Ideas

New technologies such as electric power and the Bessemer process greatly changed American life after the Civil War. Industrialists applied new technologies to create wealth, but most factory workers did not feel that their pay was adequate. To improve their wages and working conditions, workers organized labor unions.

Section 1: A Technological Revolution

In the years after the Civil War, new technology revolutionized American life.

Section 2: The Growth of Big Business

Big business created wealth for owners and also for the country, but it also prompted controversy and concern over its methods.

Section 3: Industrialization and Workers

Industry relied on its laborers, who worked for low wages and often in unsafe factories.

Section 4: The Great Strikes

In the late 1800s workers organized labor unions to improve their wages and working conditions.

A service economy is replacing the industrial economy that arose in the United States after the Civil War. The number of Americans employed in services has more than doubled since 1970.

Key Terms

For each of the terms below, write a sentence explaining how it relates to the chapter.

1. trust
2. anarchist
3. social Darwinism
4. economies of scale
5. mass production
6. socialism
7. horizontal consolidation
8. vertical consolidation
9. division of labor
10. monopoly
11. business cycle
12. collective bargaining
13. Bessemer process
14. transcontinental railroad

Comprehension

1. How did new railroads and improvements in railway technology help spur economic growth?
2. Why did increasing the size of companies make sense in the expanding economy of the late 1800s?
3. Why was the Standard Oil Trust formed, and was it successful?
4. How did rapid industrial growth affect the country?
5. Why did most immigrants come to the United States in the late 1800s?
6. What problems did women and children workers face in industrialized America?
7. What steps did employers take to fight labor unions?
8. Which side did the federal government take in the major strikes of the late 1800s? Explain.

Using Graphic Organizers

On a separate sheet of paper, copy the cause-and-effect flowchart below. In each empty box, write an effect. Add more boxes to show more effects.

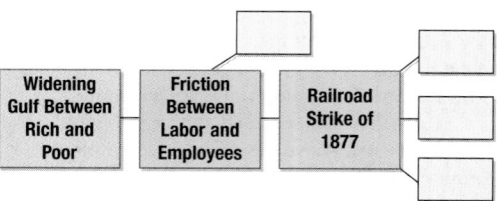

Using Graphic Organizers

- Widening Gulf Between Rich and Poor— some people turn to socialism; some people form unions.
- Friction Between Labor and Employees— Knights of Labor formed, AFL formed, workers strike in response to wage cuts and working conditions.
- Railroad Strike of 1877—riots result, federal troops sent in, violent era in labor relations begun.

Analyzing Political Cartoons ▶

1. In the background of this cartoon, a concerned citizen tries to alert Uncle Sam to the dangerous scene in the foreground. (a) What is the snake a symbol of ? (b) How do you know? (c) Who is the woman? (d) How do you know?
2. What is the snake doing?
3. What is the cartoon's overall message?

Critical Thinking

1. *Applying the Chapter Skill* Use map resources to plot a route across the Appalachian Mountains, from Raleigh, North Carolina, to Columbus, Ohio. Then draw a cross-sectional map of your route.
2. *Distinguishing False from Accurate Images* In your opinion, was Andrew Carnegie more a "captain of industry" or a "robber baron"? Explain.
3. *Expressing Problems Clearly* What problems did labor unions have to overcome in order to reach their main goals?
4. *Making Comparisons* How have the inventions of the past thirty years changed daily life for you?
5. *Demonstrating Reasoned Judgment* Choose two visuals from the chapter and explain why they demonstrate the inequality of labor and business in the late 1800s.

ANALYZING DOCUMENTS ◀▶ INTERPRETING DATA

Turn to the Work Stoppages graphs on page 426.

1. Which statement best summarizes the information shown in the graphs? (a) The number of work stoppages fell steadily from 1870 to 1900. (b) The number of work stoppages rose between 1882 and 1900. (c) Work stoppages dropped after 1900. (d) The number of work stoppages fell steadily from 1882 to 1900.

2. What was the main reason for work stoppages in the late 1800s? (a) wages and hours (b) union organization (c) child labor (d) panics

3. *Writing* Use the data in the graphs to write a notice inviting workers to a union-organizing meeting. Then create a notice that presents an opposing view to such a meeting.

INTERNET ACTIVITY

For your portfolio:
WRITE AN ARTICLE

Access Prentice Hall's *America: Pathways to the Present* site at **www.Pathways.phschool.com** for the specific URL to complete the activity. Additional resources and related Web sites are also available.

Explore the links to read about the life and works of Thomas Alva Edison. Write an article describing what you think were Edison's most important inventions and why. In what ways does Edison's career reflect the times in which he lived?

Connecting to Today

Essay Writing The Bessemer process helped create what has been termed the "age of steel" in the United States. Is the United States still in the age of steel? If not, how might you describe the present era? Write an essay expressing your view. Include specific examples.

INTERNET ACTIVITY

Articles will vary but should explore themes introduced in the text and be supported with facts or quotations from the Web site.

Analyzing Political Cartoons
1. (a) Monopolies. (b) It is labeled Monopoly. (c) Liberty. (d) Lady Liberty is a common political symbol.
2. The snake has control of the Capitol and is attacking liberty.
3. That monopolies control the government and threaten freedom.

Critical Thinking
1. Maps should make use of the technology and transportation options available at the time.
2. Sample answers: He was a "captain of industry" because he donated money for 3,000 public libraries, supported the arts and research, and gave away about $350 million. Or, he was a "robber baron" because he drove out his competitors, monopolized the steel industry, and bought up shipping and rail lines to have total control over his products.
3. They had to overcome their differences in order to stay united; deal with hostile employers who attempted to stop all union activity; and face disapproval by the federal government.
4. Answers will vary. Students might mention the impact of computers or other new electronic inventions.
5. Answers will vary but should be supported with facts from the section.

Interpreting Data
1. b
2. a
3. Advertisements will vary but should contain data from the graphs.

Connecting to Today
Essays will vary but should include specific examples from the text and from current events.

Looking to the West, 1860–1900

Managing Time and Instruction

INSTRUCTION SUPPORT

These materials for instruction are provided for **each section** in the **Teaching Resources.** See **Units 5–6 folder for Enrichment Support:**

• Reproducible Lesson Plans in Lesson Plans folder • Learning Styles Lesson Plans in Learning Styles Lesson Plans folder • Big Idea Graphic Organizers in Big Idea Graphic Organizer folder

• Guided Reading and Review • Quizzes • Test Preparation Practice booklet

DAILY LESSON	ENRICHMENT SUPPORT
1 Moving West (pp. 433–435)	• Critical Thinking Activity, Formulating Questions, found on **Resource Pro** • Nystrom *Atlas of Our Country,* Settling the West, pp. 28–29 • Primary Source Activity, African American Settlers, Learning with Documents folder, p. 21
2 Conflict with Native Americans (pp. 436–439)	• Visual Learning Activity, Western Expansion into Native American Land, Learning with Documents folder, p. 57 • Nystrom *Atlas of Our Country,* Later Expansion of the United States, pp. 32–33 • Primary Source Activity, Talks with Otoe Chiefs, found on **Resource Pro** • Comparing Primary Sources, On Land Use, Units 5–6 folder, pp. 27–28
3 Farming, Mining, and Ranching (pp. 440–443)	• Literature Activity, "The Californian's Tale," Units 5–6 folder, pp. 29–31
4 Populism (pp. 446–451)	• Great Debates, Should the Government Control the Supply of Money?, Decision-Making Activities folder, pp. 32–33 • Visual Learning Activity, The Farmers' Complaint, found on **Resource Pro** • Biography, Mary Elizabeth Lease, found on **Resource Pro** • Key Documents, William Jennings Bryan, Cross of Gold Speech, Learning with Documents folder, p. 92
5 Frontier Myths (pp. 453–456)	• Skills for Life Activity, Units 5–6 folder, p. 32 • Nystrom *Atlas of Our Country,* Later Expansion of the United States, pp. 32–33 • Biography, Nat Love (alias Deadwood Dick), Units 5–6 folder, p. 26 • Americans Are on the Move, Why Study History? folder, p. 16

Running Out of Time?

• Use Tape 3, "Expansion: Rewards and Costs, 1860–1920," from **Visions of America** videotapes series.
• Use Chapter 15 Summary, from **Guide to the Essentials of American History (English and Spanish).**

Companion Web Site

The companion Web site offers online links for all chapter review activities. It also provides key content links and structured support for this chapter for both teachers and students.

http://www.Pathways.phschool.com

Teaching in the Information Age

Media and Technology

For the Student

Interactive Student Tutorial CD-ROM Chapter 15

Student Edition on Audiotape Chapter 15

American Heritage® CD-ROM

Guided Reading Audiotapes (English and Spanish) Chapter 15

For the Teacher

Resource Pro CD-ROM Chapter 15

Test Bank CD-ROM Chapter 15

Listening to Literature Audiotapes *Timeless Voices, Timeless Themes* "The Outcasts of Poker Flat" by Bret Harte

Color Transparencies Fine Art, D–13
The Way It Works, H–9, H–15; Cause and Effect, F–4; Critical Thinking, I–12

Assessment Options

Chapter Test Forms A&B Test Bank CD-ROM booklet

Test Bank CD-ROM Chapter 15

Standardized Test Preparation Handbook

Block Scheduling

Pacing Suggestions

For 90-minute Blocks

- Teach sections 1, 2 and 5 using Transparencies I–5, C–10, D–8, L–4, and J–5 and the Recent Scholarship note on p. 455 for class discussions.
- Teach sections 3 and 4 using the Big Idea Graphic Organizers from Teaching Resources.

Additional Resources

- Prentice Hall's **American History Block Scheduling Support File** covers over 40 major topics in American history. Included are lesson plans, strategies, primary sources, literature, biographies, Great Debates, art history, simulations, and songs.
- **Prentice Hall United States History Video Collection**™ contains 20 videotapes covering American history from beginnings to present.

Connections to American Literature

from Prentice Hall

Prentice Hall Literature *Timeless Voices, Timeless Themes*
- from *Lonesome Dove* by Larry McMurty, p. 579
- "The Notorious Jumping Frog of Calaveras County" by Mark Twain, p. 525

Prentice Hall Literature Library *My Antonia* by Willa Cather

Additional Resources

For the Student
Time-Life Books Editors. *Time-Life Books: The Old West.* Prentice Hall, 1990.

For the Teacher
John D. Unruh, Jr. *The Overland Emigrants and the Trans-Mississippi West, 1840–60.* University of Illinois Press, 1993.

Prentice Hall brings into the classroom the vast archives and scholarship of the nation's premier American history magazine. See "From the Archives of American Heritage®" and "About the Presidents" teaching notes in this chapter.

History Alive!

Teacher's Curriculum Institute, in partnership with Prentice Hall, provides unique materials that engage students with diverse learning styles. See History Alive!® unit on Manifest Destiny in a Growing Nation.

Student Performance Pack

Ensures success in the three critical areas of Reading, Test Taking, and English Language Development with the following materials:
- Guide to the Essentials of American History in English and Spanish
- Guided Reading Audiotapes in English and Spanish
- Interactive Student Tutorial CD–ROM
- Test Preparation Handbook
- Test Preparation Practice booklet

Looking to the West
1860–1900

Introducing the Chapter

After the Civil War, Americans moved west of the Mississippi River, taking over the land for farms, ranches, and mines, and forcing out the original users, the Native Americans. The taming of the West became one of the great American myths.

Themes in American History

The theme for this chapter, Diversity, is listed at the beginning of this unit. An alternate theme for the chapter is Economics. To teach this unit thematically, you may wish to use the Expansion, Reconstruction, Immigration folder in American History Block Scheduling Support.

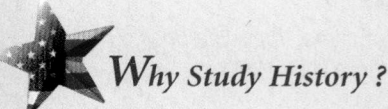

Why Study History ?

Have students explore suggested ways of connecting the past to the present on page 457.

Answer to . . .

Viewing History Students should use this question as an aid in reading the chapter. The painting shows that the way west was a difficult journey through rugged, remote lands. In addition, the painting suggests that many people, including the artist, also saw the land as beautiful and inviting.

CHAPTER

15 Looking to the West

1860-1900

CHAPTER FOCUS

This chapter describes the continued westward expansion in the last decades of the 1800s. Following the Civil War, thousands of settlers poured into the region west of the Mississippi River, looking for land and a place to call their own. Conflicts arose, however, when settlers clashed with Native American peoples living in the newly opened territories.

 The Why Study History? page at the end of this chapter explores the connection between the homesteaders who moved west in the late 1800s and Americans who move in search of new opportunities today.

VIEWING HISTORY The prospect of prosperity in the West lured many Americans along the Oregon Trail, as in this 1867 painting by Albert Bierstadt. *Geography* ***What does this painting tell you about the journey?***

▶ RESOURCE OPTIONS

Teaching Resources

📁 **Big Idea Graphic Organizer** folder
Graphic summary of the main idea of the chapter.

📁 **Learning Styles Lesson Plans** folder
Alternate lesson plans for diverse learning styles for each chapter.

Media and Technology

 AmericanHeritage® CD-ROM
Time Tour Reshaping the Nation: The Frontier West

 Prentice Hall United States History Video Collection™ Volume 11
Industrialization and Urbanization

1 Moving West

SECTION PREVIEW

Objectives

1 Explain how settlers acquired land in the West.
2 Describe how settlers worked with each other to overcome the hardships of the West.
3 Describe the experiences of women and African Americans in the West.
4 *Key Terms* Define: Morrill Land-Grant Act; land speculator; Homestead Act; Exoduster.

Main Idea

With the encouragement of the federal government, settlers took up the challenges of life in the West.

Reading Strategy

Problem Solving As you read the section, list possible solutions to the following problems: how to obtain land, how to locate water, how to work prairie sod.

As the nation swelled with new inventions and businesses during the late 1800s, it also expanded across the continent. The story of this expansion is one of rugged frontier families, big businesses, and bold individuals who were willing to take a chance on the unknown.

Lands for Settlement

By the Civil War, Americans already had settled areas west of the Mississippi and along parts of the West Coast. Following the war, they began filling in the areas in between—the Great Plains, the Pacific Northwest, and the Southwest.

Americans and European immigrants wanted to settle in the West for many reasons. Most hoped for a new start in life. They looked forward to the chance to own a farm and be their own boss, an increasingly difficult goal in the crowded East.

Big Business Receives Land Much of the western land to which people were flocking belonged to big businesses. Under the Pacific Railway Acts of 1862 and 1864, the Union Pacific and Central Pacific railroad companies received huge grants of land from the federal government. The original act granted 10 square miles of public land on each side of the track for every mile of track laid.

As settlers flocked to the West, the railroads profited by selling the land to arriving settlers. Especially profitable were the lands close to the tracks, since farmers needed the railroads to transport their goods to the cities.

Settling Government Lands In 1862 the federal government passed two important laws to encourage settlement of the West. The **Morrill Land-Grant Act** of 1862 was created to provide support for state colleges. Under the act, the federal government distributed millions of acres of western lands to state governments. States could then sell the land to fund agricultural "land-grant" colleges. The states sold their land grants at fifty cents an acre to bankers and **land speculators,** people who bought up large areas of land in the hope of later selling it for a profit.

The federal government also gave land directly to settlers through the **Homestead Act,** signed by President Lincoln in 1862. This act offered 160 acres of public land to anyone who met the following requirements:

Only the settlers' most cherished possessions made the trip west.

Breaking and turning the thick sod required special plows.

Wind was an abundant energy source. Homesteaders often built windmills to power their water pumps.

Homesteaders burned dried buffalo or cattle dung, corn cobs and stalks, even bundles of grass to keep warm.

Sod also covered the roof, which leaked terribly.

All members of the household worked the gardens and fields.

Dirt floors were difficult to keep clean.

Three-foot strips of sod were stacked like bricks to form the walls.

Wells could be more than a hundred feet deep.

The geography of the West made homesteading a challenge. Timber was often scarce, so settlers built their first shelters out of the endless expanse of sod. Special plows were required to break through the mass of roots holding the sod together. *Science and Technology* What other kinds of technology did homesteaders use to adapt to life on the prairie?

(1) All applicants had to be at least 21 years of age or the head of a family.

(2) Applicants had to be American citizens or immigrants who had filed for citizenship.

(3) Applicants had to pay a ten-dollar registration fee.

(4) Settlers had to build a house and live on the claim at least six months of the year.

(5) Settlers had to farm the land actively for five consecutive years before they could claim ownership.

By 1900, individual homesteading families had filed 600,000 claims for more than 80 million acres. There were, however, problems with the Homestead Act. Many eager settlers could not meet all of the law's requirements. Others received their claims but were unable to survive economically. Total costs to make a homestead livable could easily reach $1,000, far beyond the reach of many immigrants.

Moreover, most settlers who moved from cities had no farming experience. The tough prairie sod was hard to plow, water was scarce, and the climate ranged from blistering heat to bitter cold. Many farmers gave up before their five years were over.

Fraud was another shortcoming of the Homestead Act. The goal of the act was not simply to distribute land, but to give land to people who would then settle and farm it. Underhanded speculators wheeled portable cabins from plot to plot or built miniature shelters on several plots and then filed phony claims. Land office agents seldom visited the claims, as distances were too great and new claims were being filed daily.

Settlers Work Together

Even the basic necessities did not come without a struggle for the western settlers. If their claims were not near water, they had to use buckets or cisterns to collect rainwater for drinking, bathing, and cooking. Such open water supplies

Customize for
More Advanced Students

Explain that pressure for a homestead law began long before 1862. Ask students to discuss why Northerners opposed such a law until the Civil War. What factors might have made life easier for African Americans in the West?

EXTENDED CLASS PERIODS

Time: 90 minutes.
Activity: As a group, decide where to homestead.
Grouping: Groups of three to six students.
Purpose: Propose the following opportunity: An adventurous group of Vermont farmers has decided to homestead in the West in the late 1800s. The group must decide whether to settle in Tucson (Arizona), Boise (Idaho), Lecompton (Kansas), Jackson (Minnesota), Helena (Montana), Nebraska City (Nebraska), or Cheyenne (Wyoming). To make the best decision, the group must study physical, climate, and rainfall maps.
Roles: Have students assume the following responsibilities: physical map and atlas researcher, climate researcher, rainfall researcher, collator, and reporter.
Outcome: Students will learn about the decisions made by homesteaders as they prepared to go west.

Answer to . . .

Exploring Technology They used windmills to pump water from deep wells.

 RESOURCE OPTIONS

Teaching Resources

 Nystrom *Atlas of Our Country* Settling the West, pp. 28–29

Media and Technology

 Color Transparencies Critical Thinking, I-5; Our Multicultural Heritage, C-10

AmericanHeritage® CD-ROM

Explorer Activity 18 On the Plains, CD-ROM Guidebook, pp. 55–56, helps students write a diary entry about life on the Plains.

Time Tour Reshaping the Nation: The Frontier West

often carried "prairie fever," or typhoid. A safer source of water could be found underground by digging wells. Until the 1880s, when well-digging machinery became available, digging a well was a difficult and dangerous task.

Working the tough prairie sod also required backbreaking labor. Even after the plowing and planting was done, men often had to spend months away from the homestead earning cash for their families' survival while they waited for their crops to come in. Women, meanwhile, made most of the articles that their families needed, such as clothing, soap, candles, and preserved foods.

In such an unforgiving land, settlers came to rely heavily on each other. Families cooperated in raising houses and barns, sewing quilts, husking corn, and providing many other forms of support.

African Americans

The majority of settlers who traveled to the West were white. There were, however, thousands of African Americans who moved westward after the Civil War. In many cases they migrated to escape the violence and exploitation that followed Reconstruction. In 1879, Benjamin "Pap" Singleton became the leader of a group of southern African Americans planning a mass "Exodus," similar to the biblical account of the Israelites' flight from Egypt to the promised land. For this reason, these settlers called themselves **Exodusters.**

Life was not easy for the almost 50,000 Exodusters who migrated to western lands. Many came with little money and few possessions. Even after finding work, only a few earned enough to support a homestead. Many resettled farmers lacked experience with the crops, such as wheat and corn, widely grown on the plains. In addition, the Exodusters could not completely escape racial hatred. In spite of these difficulties, Exodusters with farming skills managed to make a living and in general met with better treatment than they had in the South.

A Frontier for Women

Although most homesteaders went west as families, women were able to file claims on their own. Homesteading alone was, however, an enormous challenge for both women and men.

Even for married women, homesteading often meant long periods of solitude. While many men were away from the homestead earning money, women often stayed behind to prevent squatters from taking the land. (Squatters are people who move onto land that does not belong to them.) Such lonely experiences increased western women's eagerness for opportunities outside the home.

Western women launched an active campaign to gain the vote at the city and state level. They succeeded in making the West a pioneer in granting women's suffrage. In 1887 two Kansas towns, Syracuse and Argonia, passed women's suffrage. Syracuse then elected an all-female town council, and Argonia the nation's first female mayor. Wyoming, which entered the union in 1890, became the first state whose constitution granted women the right to vote.

Main Idea CONNECTIONS

How did western women overcome some of the challenges they faced?

SECTION 1 REVIEW

Comprehension

1. *Key Terms* Define: (a) Morrill Land-Grant Act; (b) land speculator; (c) Homestead Act; (d) Exoduster.

2. *Summarizing the Main Idea* Describe some of the challenges homesteaders faced and some hardships they endured.

3. *Organizing Information* Create a chart that organizes information about the three federal acts dealing with the distribution of public lands in the West.

Critical Thinking

4. *Analyzing Time Lines* Review the time line at the start of the section. Which event, in your opinion, had the greatest long-term impact on the settlement of the West?

5. *Formulating Questions* Based on what you have read, write four questions to ask new homesteaders about their life in the West.

Writing Activity

6. *Writing an Expository Essay* Use information from the section to write an essay on the challenges and opportunities women and African Americans found in the West.

RESOURCE OPTIONS

Teaching Resources

Primary Source Activity African American Settlers, Learning with Documents folder, p. 21

Quiz Units 5–6 folder, p. 17

Prentice Hall Literature Library *My Antonia*, Willa Cather

Student Performance Pack

Guide to the Essentials Chapter 15, Section 1 (English and Spanish)

Conflict with Native Americans

1876
Battle of Little Bighorn

1877
Nez Percé surrender to U.S. government

1887
Dawes Act divides Indian lands

1889
Indian Territory opened for white settlement

1890
Massacre at Wounded Knee

1870   **1880**   **1890**

Objectives

You may wish to call students' attention to the objectives in the Section Preview. The objectives are reflected in the main headings of the section.

Bellringer

Ask students to read Lord Bryce's observation at the end of the section under Comparing Primary Sources. Ask them how such a policy might affect Native American land.

Reading Strategy

Outlining Information Refer to the Reading Strategy in the Section Preview. You may wish to have students use their outlines to review the content of this section.

---

2 Conflict with Native Americans

SECTION PREVIEW

Objectives

1. Summarize the causes and effects of the Indian Wars of the late 1800s.
2. Explain how Indian cultures were weakened by wars and government reforms.
3. Describe the division and settlement of Indian Territory.
4. *Key Terms* Define: reservation; Battle of Little Bighorn; Massacre at Wounded Knee; Dawes Act; boomer; sooner.

Main Idea

American expansion into the West led to the near destruction of the Native American nations there.

Reading Strategy

Outlining Information Use the headings and subheadings to create an outline of the section. As you read, fill in supporting details.

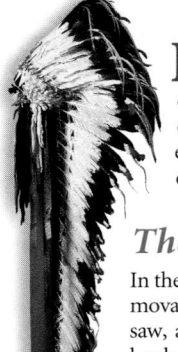

For generations, many Americans viewed the West as a wild, empty expanse, freely available to those brave enough to tame it. But the West was not empty. Others had been living there for centuries.

The Indian Wars

In the 1830s, President Jackson supported the removal of the Cherokee, Choctaw, Creek, Chickasaw, and Seminole peoples living in the East to lands west of the Mississippi. They were crowded into Indian Territory in present-day Oklahoma. By the end of the Civil War, the surviving Native American groups on United States land lived throughout the Great Plains and the West.

This elaborate feather headdress belonged to a Plains Indian.

Railroads and Settlers Following the Civil War, the railroad companies began pushing their way deeper into the West. With each mile of track laid, the Native Americans' chances for survival became bleaker. The Plains soon swarmed with settlers, many of whom felt justified in taking Native American lands. Settlers believed they had a greater right

to the land because they improved it by producing more food and wealth than did the Native Americans.

To Native Americans, on the other hand, the oncoming settlers were simply invaders. The Indian peoples wanted to continue to live off their lands as they had been doing, free of the influence of outsiders.

Some Native Americans tried to initiate friendly contacts. Others, however, resisted violently. Many groups, realizing that they were outgunned and outnumbered, eventually signed treaties that sold their lands. These nations accepted federal government demands that they live within **reservations,** or federal lands set aside for Native Americans.

Often these agreements fell apart. One reason was that many had been signed without the full approval of the affected Indian groups. In addition, Native Americans and white settlers had widely different concepts of owning land. When Native Americans signed treaties, they often did not realize that settlers would not let them continue using the land. Isolated acts of violence on both sides set off cycles of revenge and counter-revenge.

LESSON PLAN

Connecting to the Main Idea

1. Focus Explain that as settlers from both the eastern United States and Europe poured into the West, they took up land that had been home to Native Americans for many generations. Ask students how Native Americans of the West were affected.

2. Instruct Discuss how cultural beliefs can lead to misunderstandings and even war. How did beliefs about land use and government differ between Native American groups and settlers? What role did they play in the Indian Wars of the late 1800s? How did attempts to "civilize" Native Americans help ruin them?

Ask students to consider the results of dividing up Native American land. What was the effect of the homesteading rush by boomers and sooners in 1889?

3. Close Native Americans of the West lost access to their lands and their traditions, as settlers encroached and reform laws broke up their holdings. The next section describes how technology and industry transformed the West again.

▶ RESOURCE OPTIONS

Teaching Resources

📁 **Reproducible Lesson Plan** Lesson Plans folder, p. 93

📁 **Learning Styles Lesson Plan** Learning Styles Lesson Plans folder, p. 32

📁 **Big Idea Graphic Organizer** Big Idea Graphic Organizer folder, p. 65

📁 **Guided Reading and Review** Units 5–6 folder, p. 18

📁 **Visual Learning Activity** Western Expansion into Native American Land, Learning with Documents folder, p. 57

The Final Destruction One by one, Native American groups fell. (See the map below.) The Navajo and Apache wars began in the Southwest in 1861 and continued on and off for 25 years until the Indians were finally all forced onto reservations, starved, or killed in battle. The Navajo agreed to settle on a reservation in New Mexico in 1865. Some Apache leaders also surrendered between 1871 and 1873, but large numbers of warriors continued their raids on whites until their leader Geronimo surrendered in 1886.

In the 1860s and 1870s, the Cheyenne were devastated. The first blow came in 1864, with Colonel John M. Chivington's massacre of men, women, and children in a peaceful village at Sand Creek in present-day Colorado. Some reports put the number of dead as high as 450. The following year the Cheyenne surrendered their claims and agreed to move to reservations.

The Sioux resisted white expansion as fiercely as any Native American group. The First Sioux War was triggered in 1865 by the federal government's decision to build a road through Sioux lands to connect the East with the mining towns of Bozeman and Virginia City. In response, Sioux warriors ambushed and slaughtered more than 80 soldiers under Captain W. J. Fetterman near Fort Phil Kearny in December 1866.

Sitting Bull and the Fall of the Sioux
The First Sioux War ended in 1868, when the Sioux agreed to live on a reservation in the Dakota Territory. In 1875, however, the Second Sioux War began when the federal government allowed miners to go into the Black Hills, in what is now South Dakota, in search of gold. As a result, a number of the Sioux joined Chief Sitting Bull and left their Black Hills reservation.

In June 1876, Lieutenant Colonel George Armstrong Custer was sent to locate and round up the Indians. He moved his cavalry toward the

Main Idea CONNECTIONS
How did the Sioux react to the decision to allow settlers to expand into their territory?

Graphing the Main Idea
To make sure students understand the main idea of this section, you may wish to use the flow map graphic organizer below.

Tell students that a flow map shows a sequence of events or steps unfolding. Ask students to use the flow map to record the events that led to the near-destruction of Native Americans in the West.

Teaching Tip A template for this graphic organizer can be found in the Color Transparencies, G-4.

ACTIVITY
LEARNING STYLES

Ask students to research and write a brief biography of one of the following Native American leaders of the West: Red Cloud, Sitting Bull, Black Kettle, Crazy Horse, Cochise, or Geronimo. Ask students to include the leader's dates and, if possible, a quotation.
(Verbal/Linguistic)

Native American Territory and Major Battles, 1860–1890

Land ceded by Native Americans:
- Before 1850
- 1850–1870
- 1870–1890
- Native American reservations, 1890
- ★ Major battle sites

MAP Skills Though Native Americans won occasional victories in isolated battles, they were vastly outnumbered by United States troops. *Location* What pattern can you see in the location of the remaining Native American reservations in 1890?

RESOURCE OPTIONS

Teaching Resources

Nystrom *Atlas of Our Country* Later Expansion of the United States, pp. 32–33

Media and Technology

AmericanHeritage® CD-ROM

Time Tour Reshaping the Nation: The Frontier West

Prentice Hall United States History Video Collection™

Volume 11 *Industrialization and Urbanization*

Answer to . . .

Main Idea Connections They resisted violently, by means of ambush and attack.

Map Skills Most were in the central part of the continent, an area settlers were not interested in.

A Diverse Nation

The town of Wounded Knee has become a continuing symbol of Native American suffering. In March 1973, more than 200 members of the American Indian Movement (AIM) seized the trading post at Wounded Knee in an attempt to draw national attention to their platform. AIM leaders wanted reforms in the tribal government and demanded Senate hearings on United States treaties with Native American nations. In response, federal law officers surrounded the area. "You have here," said one government official, "an arguable case of treason." The AIM occupation ended in surrender to the federal authorities, but it mobilized other Native American groups and focused attention on recovering title to their tribal territories.

Customize for
Less Proficient Readers

Ask students to rewrite the following incorrect statements:
• In the massacres at Sand Creek and Wounded Knee, Native Americans killed large numbers of United States cavalry.
• Reformers thought that Native Americans should farm individual plots to earn money and become "civilized."

Little Bighorn River in what is now Montana. There he met a larger-than-expected Sioux force. In the clash that followed—the **Battle of Little Bighorn**—Custer and more than 200 American soldiers were killed. This victory proved to be the Indians' last, as the federal government flooded the region with troops. By the end of 1876, most of the Sioux had returned to their reservations. Sitting Bull escaped to Canada, but returned to a Sioux reservation five years later.

In 1890, following the death of Sitting Bull, soldiers of the Seventh Cavalry tried to arrest a group of the chief's followers who had left their reservation. While the Indians were handing over their weapons in surrender, someone fired a shot. The soldiers then opened fire, killing more than 200 unarmed Sioux (including nearly 70 women and children) in what later became known as the **Massacre at Wounded Knee.**

Chief Joseph

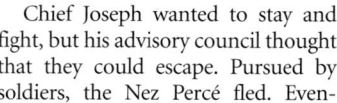 The Nez Percé inhabited a large area in the northwest region of the United States. In the 1850s and 1860s, some Nez Percé signed treaties agreeing to sell their lands to the federal government. But the largest group refused. They lived in the Wallowa Valley at the crossroads of present-day Idaho, Oregon, and Washington. As the chief of this group lay dying in 1871, he made his son and successor, Joseph, swear never to sell their homeland.

Fulfilling that promise proved impossible. After pressuring Chief Joseph for five years, General Oliver Otis Howard finally ordered him and his people to leave Wallowa Valley for a reservation in Idaho. Faced with the threat of superior force, Chief Joseph decided that he must give in. Before he could do so, however, a group of Nez Percé youths attacked some settlers who had been accused of stealing Nez Percé horses. The Nez Percé and the United States government were now at war.

*Chief Joseph
(1840?–1904)*

Chief Joseph wanted to stay and fight, but his advisory council thought that they could escape. Pursued by soldiers, the Nez Percé fled. Eventually, Chief Joseph's group reached Montana. Exhausted, they set up camp at Big Hole Basin, but in a surprise raid, American soldiers attacked, killing men, women, and children.

The surviving Nez Percé looked to Canada as their last hope for freedom. On September 30, 1877, less than 40 miles from Canada, they were charged by Colonel Nelson Miles's cavalry. Heavily outnumbered, Chief Joseph surrendered. "I am tired of fighting," he is reported to have said.

The federal government sent Chief Joseph's people to Indian Territory. There, due to heat and malaria, many more Nez Percé died, including all of Joseph's children. In 1885 Chief Joseph and the remaining Nez Percé were permitted to leave for a reservation in present-day Washington State. ■

Native Cultures Destroyed

As Native Americans lost land and battles to American troops, many aspects of Indian cultures also disappeared. The peoples of the Great Plains, for example, relied on the buffalo for food, clothing, shelter, fuel, and tools. By the 1870s, the great buffalo herds began to disappear. At first the herds were hunted by the railroad companies to feed their workers. Later they were targeted by settlers to clear the range, to satisfy a craze for hides, and even for sport. The federal government encouraged this slaughter as a means to wipe out the Plains peoples' food supply.

Some white Americans found such acts horrifying. Inspired in part by Helen Hunt Jackson's 1881 publication *A Century of Dishonor*, a national "Indian rights" movement arose. Protesting what she saw as the government's broken promises and treaties, Jackson said, "It makes little difference . . . where one opens the record of the history of the Indians; every page and every year has its dark stain."

As sincere as reformers were, however, most believed that Native Americans still needed to be "civilized." Christian missionaries, who ran schools on the reservations, shared this belief. The government supported this opinion and passed a criminal code in 1884 forbidding Indians to practice their religions.

Other reformers sought to break Native American traditions by requiring Indians to farm individual plots. The **Dawes Act** of 1887 gave separate plots of land to each Native American family headed by a male. Much of the land was not suitable for farming, however, and many Native Americans had no interest or experience in agriculture. Many simply sold their lands to speculators. In fact, between 1887 and 1934 the amount of land owned by Native Americans shrank by 65 percent.

The Fate of Indian Territory

For the nearly 70 Indian nations that had been forced into Indian Territory, worse was to come. Following the Civil War, a flood of settlers began to enter the territory. Many were squatters, tempted by the territory's farmland.

Although Native Americans protested and the government tried to stop them, squatters continued to come. Other would-be settlers pressured Congress to allow legal settlement in the territory. In 1889 Congress responded, opening for homesteading nearly 2 million acres in Indian Territory that had not yet been assigned to Native Americans. At noon on April 22, soldiers signaled with their pistols, and hundreds of homesteaders rushed across the border to stake their claims as described:

AMERICAN VOICES ❝Along the line as far as the eye could reach, with a shout and a yell the swift riders shot out, then followed the light buggies or wagons and last the lumbering prairie schooner and freighters' wagons, with here and there even a man on a bicycle and many too on foot,—above all a great cloud of dust hovering like smoke over a battlefield.❞

—*Newspaper reporter, 1889*

Within a few hours these settlers, called **boomers,** had staked off hundreds of claims. Oklahoma City had over 10,000 residents by the end of the first day. Many boomers were unhappy to discover that some of the best lands had been reserved by **sooners,** or those

people who had sneaked past the government officials earlier to mark their claims.

Under continued pressure from settlers, Congress created the Oklahoma Territory on May 2, 1890. In the following years, the remainder of Indian Territory was opened to settlement.

COMPARING PRIMARY SOURCES

ATTITUDES TOWARD THE ENVIRONMENT

As settlers pushed west, it became clear that they and the Native Americans held different attitudes toward the land.

In Favor of Respecting the Environment	In Favor of Conquering the Environment
"The ground says, the Great Spirit has placed me here to produce all that grows on me, trees and fruit. The same way the ground says, It was from me man was made. The Great Spirit, in placing men on the earth, desired them to take good care of the ground and to do each other no harm."	"To open the greatest number of mines and extract the greatest quantity of ore, to scatter cattle over a thousand hills, to turn the flower-spangled prairies . . . into wheatfields, . . . to force from nature the most she can be made to yield . . . is preached by Western newspapers as a kind of religion."
—*Young Chief of the Cayuse, on opposing selling land in Washington Territory, 1855*	—*Britain's Lord James Bryce, after visiting the American West in the 1880s*

ANALYZING VIEWPOINTS **Which of the attitudes expressed above do you think is more common today? Explain.**

SECTION 2 REVIEW

Comprehension

1. *Key Terms* Define: (a) reservation; (b) Battle of Little Bighorn; (c) Massacre at Wounded Knee; (d) Dawes Act; (e) boomer; (f) sooner.

2. *Summarizing the Main Idea* Describe the pattern of conflict between the United States government and Native Americans.

3. *Organizing Information* Create a chart that organizes information about the devastation of various Native American groups. Include the Navajo, the Apache, the Cheyenne, the Sioux, and the Nez Percé.

Critical Thinking

4. *Analyzing Time Lines* Review the time line at the start of the section. Select one event and write a paragraph on how it relates to the conquest of the Native Americans.

5. *Expressing Problems Clearly* By what means were Native American cultures destroyed in the late 1800s?

Writing Activity

6. *Writing a Persuasive Essay* Write a letter to a friend defending or attacking the United States government's decision to open up Indian Territory for settlement. Support your arguments with information from the text.

Answers to SECTION 2 REVIEW

1. (a) reservation, see p. 436; (b) Battle of Little Bighorn, see p. 438; (c) Massacre at Wounded Knee, see p. 438; (d) Dawes Act, see p. 438; (e) boomer, see p. 439; (f) sooner, see p. 439.

2. The government treated the Native Americans brutally, ignoring the fact that they had a prior claim to the land.

3. Sample entry: Sioux—resisted surrender and attacked U.S. soldiers. Had great victory at Battle of Little Bighorn. Finally forced onto reservation and massacred at Wounded Knee.

4. Sample answer: The Opening of Indian Territory—Congress completely dishonored Native Americans by selling lands it had set aside for them to white settlers, leaving them displaced and unprotected.

5. By destroying the buffalo; by "civilization"; by taking away their lands and granting them land that was unfarmable.

6. For: white settlers felt crowded and wanted to farm the land. Against: the government backed down on promises made to the Native Americans.

▶ RESOURCE OPTIONS

Teaching Resources

📁 **Quiz** Units 5–6 folder, p. 19

📁 **Comparing Primary Sources** On Land Use, Units 5–6 folder, p. 27–28

Student Performance Pack

 Guide to the Essentials Chapter 15, Section 2 (English and Spanish)

Media and Technology

 Color Transparencies Fine Art, D-8; Historical Maps, L-4

Answer to . . .

Comparing Primary Sources Sample answer: Bryce's view is more common today, as countries around the world depend on industry and agriculture to increase their wealth, and often fail to agree on environmental regulations.

1859	1862	1867	1874	1886
Silver discovered at Nevada's Comstock Lode	Congress establishes the Department of Agriculture	J. G. McCoy establishes Abilene, Kansas, as a cow town	Joseph Glidden invents barbed wire	Harsh winter damages cattle industry

1859	1869	1879	1889

3 Farming, Mining, and Ranching

SECTION PREVIEW

Objectives

1 List the changes that transformed farming on the Great Plains.
2 Explain the changing mining industry in the West.
3 Describe the growth and decline of the cattle industry.
4 *Key Terms* Define: dry farming; bonanza farm; placer mining; long drive.

Main Idea

Modern farming methods, the discovery of mineral deposits, and ranching made the West attractive to many individual settlers and big businesses.

Reading Strategy

Reinforcing Main Ideas Write the following column headings on a piece of paper: *Farming, Mining,* and *Ranching*. As you read, note in the appropriate column how each of these industries had changed by the late 1800s.

By the late 1800s, machines like these performed many harvesting tasks.

The pioneers who first settled the West recognized its great potential. Farmers, miners, and ranchers all searched for ways to unlock that potential and make the land fruitful.

Farming on the Plains

Despite the hopes of many settlers, the Great Plains was not a farmer's paradise. Rainfall was unpredictable, and never enough. The weather swung from one extreme to the other, with summer temperatures exceeding 100°F and winter bringing raging blizzards and bone-chilling cold. Drought and hot winds fed dust storms and prairie fires. Grasshoppers, locusts, and boll weevils ravaged crops and destroyed property.

These challenging conditions weeded out all but the hardiest settlers. But the same inventiveness that had helped spur industrial expansion in the East helped confront such troubles in the West.

New Technology on the Farm The dry climate in parts of the West greatly reduced the land's productivity. In response, farmers practiced what is called **dry farming.** This involved techniques such as planting crops that do not require a great deal of water and keeping the fields free of weeds.

Because western farms were very large, farmers welcomed any machines that would save them time and effort. During the 1870s, improvements in farm implements multiplied. Soon farmers were riding behind a plow that made several furrows at once. Other inventions included harrows, equipped with spring teeth to dislodge debris and break up the ground before planting, and automatic drills to spread grain. Steam-powered threshers arrived on the scene by 1875, and corn-huskers and cornbinders by the 1890s.

Agricultural Knowledge Grows Congress had established the federal Department of Agriculture in 1862 as part of the Morrill Land-Grant Act. In the 1880s and 1890s, the department gathered statistics on markets, crops, and plant diseases. Government publications helped spread information on new farming techniques, including such topics as crop rotation, hybridization (the crossing of different plants to produce new varieties), and the preservation of water and topsoil.

The Big Business of "Bonanza" Farms
New machines and farm techniques increased farm output enormously. Owners of large farms now hoped to reap a "bonanza" by supplying food to the growing populations of the East. They began applying to farming the same organizational ideas then taking hold in industry. As one observer noted:

> ❝It is no longer left to the small farmer, taking up 160 acres of land, building a log cabin and struggling to secure himself a home. Organized capital is being employed in the work, with all the advantages which organization implies. Companies and partnerships are formed for the cultivation precisely as they are for building railroads, manufactures, etc.❞

—Commercial and Financial Chronicle, *1879*

The result was **bonanza farms**—farms controlled by large businesses and managed by professionals. Specializing in single cash crops raised for sale in massive quantities, bonanza farms promised enormous profits to their investors.

The farms' massive output caused problems, however. When the supply of a certain product rose faster than the demand, the market became glutted and prices fell. Such dips in prices were common. To compensate for falling prices, farmers produced ever larger amounts of wheat, but this only made the oversupply problem worse.

The Problem of Debt Falling prices contributed to a constant worry for farmers: debt. Once farmers invested in machines, they had to raise only the crop for which the machines were designed. If prices for that crop dipped, farmers could not pay off their debts.

In some cases, land speculation contributed to farmers' debts. Hoping to profit from rising land prices, some farmers bought more land than they could manage. The burden of a heavy mortgage became unbearable when the bottom fell out of the market.

---

† Comstock did not reveal its greatest riches until 1873, when quartz mills and other mining machinery were brought in. From 1859 to 1879 Comstock mines produced $350 million, of which 55 percent was in silver and 45 percent in gold.

Boom and Bust on the Mining Frontier

"Gold!" Since the California Gold Rush of 1849, this word alone has conjured up the image of lucky prospectors striking it rich. The reality, however, was far more complicated.

"Pikes Peak or Bust!" The gold strike at Sutter's Mill, California, in 1848 was the first of several large strikes in the West. In 1859, rumors of gold strikes in the area of Pikes Peak, Colorado, brought on a stampede of wagons with the words "Pikes Peak or Bust!" scrawled on their sides. Also in 1859, a silver strike in Nevada's famed "Comstock Lode" brought on another rush.†

The lure of quick wealth brought people of all colors, ethnic backgrounds, and levels of education into mining towns. Asians, especially men from China who had left railway work, often became miners. While an overwhelming majority of settlers on the mining frontier were men, some women became miners as well.

Miners worked and played hard. Widespread gambling and drunkenness gave mining towns reputations for vice. Actually, most towns settled down quickly. In many cases, the arrival of big mining companies brought stability to the settlement.

Mining Techniques Miners, working alone or in small groups, searched for metal that was close to the surface. Using a technique called **placer mining,** they shoveled loose dirt into boxes and then ran water over it, causing the heavy minerals to sink to the bottom. Placer mining worked well for finding the loose gold that had washed out of rock and into the streams.

Yet before long, all the easily gathered precious metal was gone. By the late 1850s and early 1860s, in fact, most of the precious metals that remained in the West lay locked in quartz and deeply buried. At this point

It is unlikely that this man struck it rich panning for gold. Far more successful were those who "mined the miners," or sold goods to the fortune-seekers.

East to the Slaughter On September 5, 1867, the first of many thousands of Texas longhorns were packed into twenty waiting cattlecars of the Kansas Pacific Railway and left Abilene, Kansas, for eastern slaughterhouses. The event marked the birth of the era of great cattle drives along the Chisholm Trail and the culmination of Joseph McCoy's work. He had bought the 480-acre town for twenty-four hundred dollars, then made a deal with the railway company and persuaded ranchers to drive their herds to his northern shipping point. The route followed by most of the drivers came to be known for an Indian trader, Jesse Chisholm, whose wagon ruts had worn it over the years. By 1871, seven hundred thousand cattle had followed the Chisholm Trail to be packed off at Abilene and slaughtered in Kansas City and Chicago.

Source: Nathan Ward, "The Time Machine," *American Heritage* magazine, September 1992.

Mining and Ranching Boom, c. 1860

The mining and ranching boom of the early to mid-1800s was short-lived but intense. In its peak year, the Chisholm Trail alone saw 600,000 head of cattle driven to market. *Regions Judging from the map, why do you think the cattle trails followed the routes they did?*

Demand Spurs Growth During the 1860s and 1870s, cattle ranching boomed. The destruction of the buffalo and removal of Native Americans to reservations emptied the land for grazing cattle. The open plains offered a rancher limitless pasture that was free for the taking. At the same time, the growing population of eastern cities drove up the demand for beef. By the end of the Civil War, cattle that sold for $3 to $5 a head in Texas could bring $30 to $50 a head in the meat markets of Chicago and St. Louis.

At first, Texas cattlemen reached these markets by gathering up their herds and driving them northward across the open range. Railroads, however, promised a far easier and faster route to market. In 1867, J. G. McCoy established Abilene, Kansas, on the Hannibal and St. Joe Railroad. The first town built specifically for receiving cattle, it included pens where ranchers held their cattle until they could be shipped out by railroad. Other so-called "cow towns," including Cheyenne in Wyoming Territory and Dodge City and Ellsworth in Kansas, soon sprang up on the rail lines.

most prospectors straggled home, leaving many mining cities deserted ghost towns.

Large corporations then moved in. Only they could afford the large investments in machinery, mine shafts, and tunnels required to reach these riches. Like so many other industries, mining became the realm of big business.

The Cattle Industry

When American settlers began to arrive in Texas in the early 1800s, they learned the cattle ranching ways of the Mexicans living there. It was not long before Americans had adopted Mexican ranching equipment and dress as their own. Americans also learned from Mexican cattlemen the advantages of raising the hardy Texas longhorn cattle that thrived on the dry, grassy plains.

Along the Cattle Trails A series of routes or trails linked the San Antonio region of Texas with the cow towns to the north. One of the most famous, the Chisholm Trail, ended at Abilene. The Goodnight-Loving Trail followed a twisting route farther west and terminated in Cheyenne.

Managing the **long drive,** or the transporting of cattle from ranges to the cow towns, was the job of the cowboys. The work was neither easy nor pleasant. Pay varied greatly depending on experience. Cowboys braved rough, muddy trails, pounding thunderstorms, and attacks by cattle thieves. Stampedes were another constant danger. Recalled a cowboy after one stampede, "We found 341 dead cattle, two dead horses, one

Main Idea
CONNECTIONS

Describe the cattle industry in the late 1800s.

Answer to . . .

Map Skills They took the most direct routes from Texas ranches to midwestern "cow towns."
Main Idea Connections It was booming as growing eastern cities demanded more meat, and the removal of the buffalo left open plains for cattle grazing.

dead cowboy and two more with broken legs after the herd had passed."

As the cattle moved along the trail, two experienced cowboys rode in front of the herd, guiding the animals along the route. Other cowboys rode beside the herd to keep the cattle all together, and still others rode in the dust at the rear, pushing along the stragglers. A cowboy could spend up to 18 hours a day in the saddle and had to be on constant alert.

Fencing the Open Range   The cattle boom ended in the mid-1880s as a result of several factors. One was Joseph Glidden's 1874 invention of barbed wire, which he claimed was "Light as air. . . . Cheaper than dirt. All steel and miles long. The cattle ain't born that can get through it." Farmers on the Great Plains lacked a supply of trees or rocks with which to build fences. With the invention of barbed wire, farmers could fence their land and keep out grazing cattle that had caused much conflict between farmers and ranchers. Slowly the open range, on which ranchers had freely grazed their huge herds, began to disappear.

Cattlemen contributed to their own downfall by overstocking the market with cattle. They also allowed their herds to overgraze what remained of the range, seriously damaging the prairie grasses. In 1885 beef prices began to fall.

The final death knell sounded with the harsh winter of 1885–1886. Some ranchers lost up to 85 percent of their cattle to freezing temperatures and starvation. That tough winter was followed by a summer of drought that destroyed the grasses and weakened the cattle. The winter of 1886–1887 was even worse than the previous one and wiped out much of the remaining herds. Thousands of individual ranchers, and even many of the larger corporations, were ruined. Cattle ranching survived, but on a much smaller scale and with new breeds of cattle that largely replaced the Texas longhorn.

Population Growth of the West, 1860–1900

Source: *Historical Statistics of the United States, Colonial Times to 1970*

Interpreting Graphs The American West saw steady and dramatic population growth during the latter part of the 19th century. **Geography** *What attracted people to the western states?*

SECTION 3 REVIEW

Comprehension

1. **Key Term** Define: (a) dry farming; (b) bonanza farm; (c) placer mining; (d) long drive.

2. **Summarizing the Main Idea** What were some of the key developments in farming, mining, and ranching that attracted settlers to the West?

3. **Organizing Information** Create two cause-and-effect charts that organize information about the growth and decline of the cattle industry in the late 1800s.

Critical Thinking

4. **Analyzing Time Lines** Review the time line at the start of the section. Which entries are related to the decline of the ranching industry?

5. **Identifying Central Issues** Briefly describe the benefits and drawbacks of new farm machinery and farming methods.

Writing Activity

6. **Writing an Expository Essay** Reread the section "Boom and Bust on the Mining Frontier." Then write a brief essay explaining why most individuals did not "strike it rich" in the mining booms of the late 1800s.

 RESOURCE OPTIONS

Teaching Resources

 Quiz Unit 5–6 folder, p. 21

Student Performance Pack

 Guide to the Essentials Chapter 15, Section 3 (English and Spanish)

Answers to SECTION 3 REVIEW

1. (a) dry farming, see p. 440; (b) bonanza farms, see p. 441; (c) placer mining, see p. 441; (d) long drive, see p. 442.

2. Farming: mechanized means for cultivation and harvesting; the introduction of the Department of Agriculture and agricultural colleges that developed new cultivation techniques. Mining: discovery of gold and silver; new mining machinery that allowed access to deeply buried minerals. Ranching: extension of railroads provided for cattle transportation; large-scale ranching operations emerged.

3. Growth: increased population leads to increased demand for beef; destruction of buffalo and removal of Native Americans opens up range for cattle; extended railroad lines and development of "cow towns" permit easy shipment of cattle to markets. Decline: Overproduction of cattle; overgrazing; invention of barbed wire closes off open range; beef prices fall.

4. Glidden invents barbed wire; Harsh winter damages cattle industry.

5. Mechanization increased productivity but also caused price declines, hurting farmers. It reduced the need for farm labor, increased start-up costs for farmers, and required crop specialization.

6. Essays will vary but should note that most of the gold and silver was buried deep underground. Most riches from America's mines went to large corporations that could afford the costs of deep mining operations.

Answer to . . .

Interpreting Graphs *The farming, ranching, and mining boom.*

GEOGRAPHY AND HISTORY

The End of the Open Range

GEOGRAPHY AND HISTORY

The End of the Open Range

A cowboy's spur

The geographic theme of human-environment interaction examines ways in which people affect their natural environment. In the 1800s, conflicts arose between farmers and ranchers over how to use the western plains. Who would win control of the open range?

How people interact with their environment is largely determined by its natural resources and climate. For instance, if you were a farmer seeking a place to plant crops, you would choose a region with good soil, enough water, and a long growing season. The map on the next page shows land use in the American West today.

Generally, only one land use dominates a region. This is because a single economic activity can use up an area's resources. If there is more than one land use in a place, conflicts may arise. That is what happened when farmers met ranchers on the vast grasslands between the Mississippi River and the Rocky Mountains.

Free-ranging cattle and cattle being driven to market trampled the farmers' crops. Because the prairie had no trees or stones, there were no materials for fences to keep the cattle out.

Ranchers Settle the Plains

Before they were driven from the land, Native Americans hunted great buffalo on the open plains. They knew the value of this rich and expansive land. But until the 1850s, most white settlers from the East hurried right through the plains on their way to the West. Then they discovered the value of the land.

The plains were covered in seemingly limitless grassland. Ranchers soon found that the open range was a perfect place to raise cattle. So began the growth of open-range ranching.

Ranchers were especially attracted to Texas, with its herds of free-roaming longhorns. They fed their cattle on the grass and watered them in the streams and rivers that meandered through the plains. Then they rounded them up for market.

Railroads Help Ranchers

The ranchers' biggest problem was getting cattle to customers in the Northeast. The long journey could be dangerous. Still, the big demand and the high prices paid for beef convinced cattlemen to take the risk. They found they could drive their cattle several hundred miles north to the railroads. The first of these long drives went from Texas to Sedalia, Missouri, in 1866.

As the miles of railroad extended further west and south, the distance between grazing land and the railroads decreased. "Cow towns" sprang up on the Great Plains next to the rail lines. Ellsworth, Wichita, and Dodge City in Kansas, Cheyenne and Laramie in Wyoming, and other towns processed millions of head of cattle during the late 1870s and early 1880s.

Farmers Claim the Plains

Ranchers were not the only ones interested in the land. Soon, farmers discovered that beneath the grassy surface of the plains was not sand but as much as six feet of fertile topsoil. This would be excellent land on which to grow crops.

The prairie grasses, however, imprisoned this topsoil with a layer of dense roots called sod. Before land could be farmed, the tough, centuries-old sod had to be broken up. Although "sod busting" required the most advanced and expensive plows, farmers arrived by the thousands, encouraged by the federal government and the railroads to make the plains their home. The railroads could transport the farmers' products to be sold in the Northeast.

Yet all was not well on the plains. Farming and ranching interfered with each other. Free-ranging cattle and cattle being driven to market trampled the farmers' crops. Because the prairie had no trees or stones, there were no materials for fences to keep the cattle out. Barbed wire, introduced in 1874, solved this problem but created another.

Farmers Win the Range War

Angered by the farmers' attempts to fence off the land, some ranchers started to enclose huge areas of their own. The ranchers' illegal fences sometimes cut farmers off from roads and water supplies. Farmers fought back by cutting the barbed wire and seeking government help. The ranchers fixed their fences and protected them with gunfire.

But even with their fenced ranches, cattlemen were crowded out by the farmers. Farmers could make a living with much less land than cattle ranchers. Because the federal government had a land policy that tried to benefit the largest number of people, it helped the many small farmers more than it helped

the few cattle ranchers. Government land-use laws increasingly made open-range ranching impossible. Finally, several years of harsh weather all but destroyed the herds.

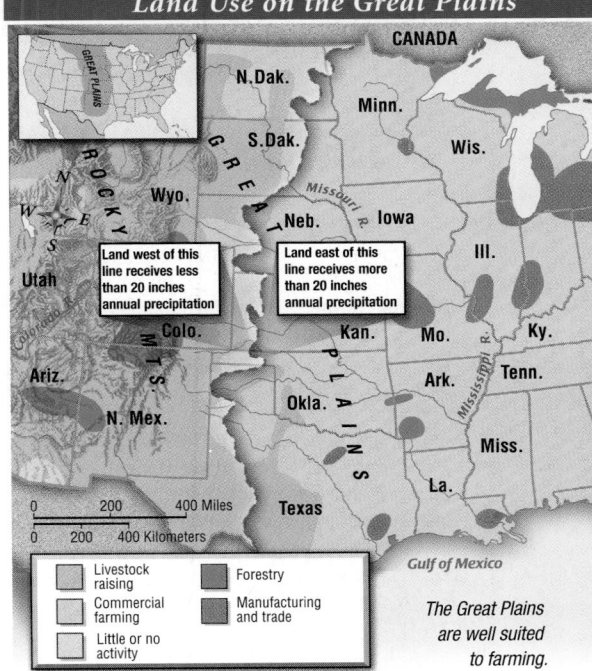

Land Use on the Great Plains

Land west of this line receives less than 20 inches annual precipitation

Land east of this line receives more than 20 inches annual precipitation

Legend:
- Livestock raising
- Commercial farming
- Little or no activity
- Forestry
- Manufacturing and trade

The Great Plains are well suited to farming.

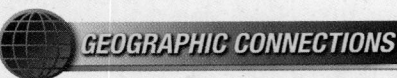

GEOGRAPHIC CONNECTIONS

1. How did the spread of railroads throughout the South and West help both ranchers and farmers?

2. Before the invention of barbed wire, what problem did the ranchers' cattle cause for the farmers?

Themes in Geography

3. *Human-Environment Interaction* The map shows that the western plains generally receive less than half the rainfall of those parts closest to the Mississippi River. How does this help explain the ways that people interact with and use the land?

RESOURCE OPTIONS

Media and Technology

 Prentice Hall United States History Video Collection™
Volume 11 *Industrialization and Urbanization*

 Color Transparencies Cause and Effect, F-4

Answers to . . .

GEOGRAPHIC CONNECTIONS

1. The railroads provided the transportation that both farmers and ranchers needed to sell their products in the Northeast.

2. Cattle being driven to market and free-ranging cattle trampled the farmers' unprotected crops. Because there was no material for fencing, farmers had no way to keep the cattle out.

3. The map shows that the western part of the region is used today for livestock ranching and the eastern part for farming. The western part does not get enough rainfall to grow crops, so ranching is still the primary way for people to make a living there.

Objectives

You may wish to call students' attention to the objectives in the Section Preview. The objectives are reflected in the main headings of the section.

Bellringer

Ask students why merchants and service industries accept paper money or coins in return for goods and services. What gives these items value?

Reading Strategy

Problem Solving Refer to the Reading Strategy in the Section Preview. You may wish to extend this activity by asking students how the organizations that they identified promised help.

LESSON PLAN
Connecting to the Main Idea

1. **Focus** Explain that as farmers' incomes declined, they began to join together, many by supporting the Populist party. Ask students what the farmers' complaints were. What reforms did the Populist party promise to help them institute?

2. **Instruct** Discuss why Americans in the late 1800s were divided over the issue of tariffs. Ask how industrialists profited from tariffs and why farmers ultimately protested against them.

   Ask students why the federal government did not do more to help farmers. What did farmers do to help themselves? Discuss the reforms promised by the Populist party. How would a graduated income tax and government ownership of the railroads have helped farmers?

3. **Close** In the late 1800s, American farmers banded together to protest their economic plight. Many farmers supported the short-lived Populist party. The next section examines the popular vision of the Old West and the realities it ignored.

1873 Congress puts nation's currency on a gold standard		**1878** Bland-Allison Act	**1887** Interstate Commerce Act	**1887** Texas Seed bill	**1890** Sherman Silver Purchase Act

1870   **1880**   **1890**

4 Populism

SECTION PREVIEW

Objectives

1 Describe farmers' economic complaints during the late 1800s.
2 List the key organizations formed to protest problems faced by farmers.
3 Understand *populism,* the people behind the movement, and its legacy.
4 *Key Terms* Define: deflation; monetary policy; Bland-Allison Act; the Grange; Interstate Commerce Act; Populist; progressive income tax.

Main Idea

By the late 1800s, declining incomes for American farmers created fertile ground for a farmers' protest movement.

Reading Strategy

Problem Solving Imagine you are a farmer in the late 1800s. List some of the problems you face and identify some of the organizations that promise to help you.

Farmers in the late 1800s were in trouble. Farm production was up, but so too was debt, as farmers bought expensive new equipment. At the same time, crop prices were down. In 1890 a Congregational minister described the plight of the farmer in this way:

AMERICAN VOICES
"The farmers . . . are the bone and sinew of the nation; they produce the largest share of its wealth; but they are getting, they say, the smallest share for themselves. The American farmer is steadily losing ground. His burdens are heavier every year and his gains are more meager [smaller]."

—*Washington Gladden*

The Farmers' Complaint

Farmers in the late 1800s were suffering from a long-term decline in crop prices that had begun after the Civil War. Moreover, competition from farmers in other nations had increased. Finally, they complained about the power of big business and the government's refusal to help. Their solution was to unite.

Farmers and Tariffs A federal policy of particular concern to farmers was tariffs. Tariffs on imported goods discourage people from buying imports by making them more expensive. Thus, tariffs encourage the sale of goods produced at home.

Americans in the late 1800s were divided on the benefit of tariffs. Industrialists claimed that tariffs protected American factory jobs—and their own profits. However, because tariffs reduced foreign competition, they also encouraged American firms to raise their prices, which was not good for workers.

Tariffs helped farmers in one way: by protecting them against competition from farm imports. But tariffs hurt farmers in two ways. First, they raised the prices of manufactured goods. Second, they prevented foreigners from earning the American currency they needed to buy American crops. Thus, tariffs indirectly reduced the international market for American farm products.

▶ RESOURCE OPTIONS

Teaching Resources

📁 **Reproducible Lesson Plan** Lesson Plans folder, p. 95

📁 **Learning Styles Lesson Plan** Learning Styles Lesson Plans folder, p. 33

📁 **Big Idea Graphic Organizer** Big Idea Graphic Organizer folder, p. 67

📁 **Guided Reading and Review** Units 5–6 folder, p. 22

Whenever the government raised tariffs to benefit industry, farmers protested. They saw this high-tariff policy as proof that the government was favoring eastern manufacturers over western farmers. Yet tariffs were not the only concern of the agriculture industry in the late 1800s. The dominant issue for many farmers was "free silver."

The Money Issue The value of money is linked to the amount in circulation. If the government increases the money supply, the value of every dollar drops. This drop in value shows up as inflation, a widespread rise in prices on goods of all kinds.

People who borrow money benefit from inflation because the money they pay back to the lender is worth less than the money they borrowed. Inflation also helps people who sell things, such as farm goods, because inflation allows sellers to charge higher prices.

In contrast, if the government reduces the money supply, the value of each dollar becomes greater. This causes **deflation,** or a drop in the prices on goods. People who lend money are helped by deflation because the money they receive in payment of a loan is worth more than the money they lent out.

In the years following the Civil War, the nation's money supply shrank as the federal government took out of circulation the paper money that had been issued during the war. As a result, the nation experienced a prolonged period of deflation.

Monetary policy, the federal government's plan for the makeup and quantity of the nation's money supply, thus emerged as a major political issue. Supporters of inflation pushed for an increase in the money supply. Supporters of deflation wanted a "tight money" policy of less currency in circulation.

Gold bugs In 1873 the supporters of tight money won a victory. Until that time, United States currency had been on a bimetallic standard. That is, currency consisted of gold or silver coins or United States treasury notes that could be traded in for gold or silver. In 1873, in order to prevent inflation and ensure economic stability, Congress put the nation's currency on a gold standard. This move reduced the amount of money in circulation because the money supply would be limited by the amount of gold held by the government.

Conservative "gold bugs" were pleased. Many of them were big lenders, and they liked the idea of being repaid in currency backed by the gold standard.

Silverites "Silverites," mostly silver-mining interests and western farmers, were furious at the nation's move to a gold standard. They claimed that the end of silver as a monetary standard would depress the prices of farm produce. Silverites called instead for free silver— the unlimited coining of silver dollars as a means of increasing the money supply.

The **Bland-Allison Act** of 1878, was, for the silverites, a step in the right direction. This act required the federal government to purchase and coin more silver, increasing the money supply and causing inflation.

Passed by Congress, the Bland-Allison Act was vetoed by President Hayes because he opposed the inflation it would create. Congress then overrode Hayes's

FACT Finder

Gold Standard vs. Free Silver

	Gold Standard	Free Silver
Supporters	Gold Bugs: bankers and wealthy industrialists	Silverites: silver miners, farmers, and debtors
Position	A gold standard would limit the amount of money in circulation and deflate prices.	The unlimited coinage of silver would increase the money supply and inflate prices.
Benefits	The economy would be more stable. The wealthy would have protection for their money.	The economy would be stimulated. Farmers would get more money for their goods; debtors would more easily repay loans.

Interpreting Tables One of the biggest concerns of the Populists was the nation's monetary policy. *Economics* Why were farmers supportive of free silver?

ECONOMICS CONCEPTS

monetary policy: the federal government's plan for the size of the nation's money supply

▼ **The Historical Context:** Farmers in the late 1800s called for an increase in the money supply, which would cause higher prices and thus raise their incomes. Their opponents called for a continued "tight money" policy, in which the money supply is kept low.

▼ **The Concept Today:** The Federal Reserve System, established in 1913, controls the nation's money supply today. Led by its chairman the "Fed" seeks to promote steady economic growth without causing high inflation.

Using the Internet

Organize a Debate

Objective Use the Internet to organize a debate on populism and The Wizard of Oz. Have students follow these instructions:

1. See the *America: Pathways to the Present* Web site at

http://www.Pathways.phschool.com

for the URL of the essay on *The Wizard of Oz* and populism.

2. Read the essay, taking detailed notes on the ideas presented by various scholars. Organize a debate on how the story should be interpreted.

3. Support your position with quotes from the scholars and historians presented in the site. Be able to demonstrate how the person you are quoting makes the most sense in terms of the facts you have studied about populism.

RESOURCE OPTIONS

Teaching Resources

Great Debates Should the Government Control the Supply of Money? Decision-Making Activities folder, pp. 32–33

Media and Technology

 AmericanHeritage® CD-ROM

Time Tour Reshaping the Nation: The Rise of Industry

Answer to . . .

Interpreting Tables The resulting inflation would allow them to get more money for their goods and repay their loans.

About the Presidents

Grover Cleveland (1885–1889 and 1893–1897) devoted his annual message to Congress to the tariff issue in December 1887. He called tariff laws "vicious" and harshly criticized trusts. Before his address, Cleveland was considered a shoo-in for reelection. But powerful business interests mobilized against him. He won the popular vote; however, the tariff cost Cleveland the electoral vote. He never did win his fight for a tariff reduction.

Source: Charles L. Mee, Jr., "Grover Cleveland," *The American Heritage® Pictorial History of the Presidents of the United States,* vol. 2, 1968.

Answer to . . .

Viewing History They include images of cooperation among farmers and images supporting people working in industry and trade.

veto. Yet the act had only a limited effect because the Treasury Department refused to buy more than the minimum silver required under the act. The Treasury also refused to circulate the silver dollars that the law required it to mint.

In 1890, Congress passed the Sherman Silver Purchase Act. While not authorizing the free and unlimited coinage of silver that the silverites wanted, it did increase the amount of silver the government was required to purchase every month. The law required the Treasury to buy the silver with notes that could be redeemed for either silver or gold. Yet as people turned in their silver Treasury notes for gold dollars, the gold reserves of the government began to be depleted. To protect the nation's gold supply, President Cleveland oversaw the repeal of the Silver Purchase Act in 1893.

Organizing Farmer Protest

Because farmers lived far from one another and usually relied on their own efforts, they tended not to organize protests against policies that hurt them. In the late nineteenth century, however, farmers began to take advantage of improvements in communication and transportation. They united to form several powerful protest groups.

The Grange   In 1866 the Department of Agriculture sent Oliver H. Kelley on an inspection tour of southern farms. Disturbed by farmers' isolation, the following year he founded the Patrons of Husbandry, or **the Grange.**

The Grange soon began helping farmers form cooperatives, in which farmers saved money by buying goods in large quantities. The Grange also pressured state legislators to regulate the businesses on which farmers depended—for example, the grain elevators that stored the farmers' crops and the railroads that shipped them. The railroads, which gave better rates to powerful eastern industrialists than unorganized western farmers, received the brunt of farmers' anger.

Although the Grange was popular, by the mid-1870s farmers were turning to other political outlets. A Greenback party, which argued for the circulation of more paper money as a means to cause inflation, elected fourteen members to Congress in 1878. Its power quickly faded, however, as more farmers adopted the free silver position in the currency debate.

Farmers' Alliances   In the 1880s many farmers joined a network of Farmers' Alliances that were formed around the nation. The alliances launched harsh attacks on monopolies, such as those that controlled the railroads. Alliance lecturer Napoleon B. Ashby accused the nation's millionaires of having made their fortunes by preying upon "the mighty rivers of commerce which the farmers have set flowing."

VIEWING HISTORY

Farmers' Alliances provided an important channel for farmer protest and political action in the late 1800s. This illustration comes from a book of songs for these organizations. *Culture What do the images on this songbook cover reveal about the ideals of the Farmers' Alliances?*

The Farmers' Alliance in the South, formed in Texas in the mid-1870s, grew especially powerful.[†] It emphasized themes that many of the nation's farmers could support: federal regulation of the railroads, more money in circulation, creation of state departments of agriculture, antitrust laws, and farm credit.

Farmer's Alliances held special importance for women, who served as officers and won support for women's political rights. One of the most popular speakers was Kansas lawyer Mary Elizabeth Lease, who bluntly urged farmers to raise "less corn and more Hell!"

African Americans worked through a separate but parallel "Colored Farmers' Alliance." Formed in 1886 in Lovelady, Texas, the group had a quarter of a million members by 1891.

A series of natural disasters gave special urgency to Farmers' Alliance programs. The Mississippi River flooded in 1882. In 1886–1887, twenty-one consecutive months of drought in Texas impoverished 30,000 people. Terrible blizzards, which killed thousands of cattle, struck the West in 1887. The increasingly angry farmers asked, Why was the federal government unwilling to respond to these disasters?

An Inactive Government In every election from 1880 to 1892, no candidate won a majority of the popular vote. Only rarely did the President's party command a majority in Congress. Presidents thus lacked the power to take bold action.

In addition, some Presidents were influenced by promises of support from powerful business interests. In return, these Presidents protected American industry, angering many farmers.

The federal government did take some actions. In 1887 Congress passed the Texas Seed bill, which provided seed grain to aid drought victims. But Democratic President Grover Cleveland vetoed the bill, expressing the commonly held view that "though the people support the government, the government should not support the people."

Cleveland did sign the **Interstate Commerce Act** of 1887, a response to the many complaints against the railroad companies. It regulated the prices that railroads charged to move freight between states, requiring the rates to be set in proportion to the distance traveled. The law also made it illegal to give special rates to some customers. While the act did not control the monopolistic practices of the railroads that so angered farmers, it did establish the principle that Congress could regulate the railroads. The act also set up the Interstate Commerce Commission (ICC) to enforce the laws.

Finally, in 1890 President Benjamin Harrison approved the Sherman Antitrust Act. This act was meant to curb the power of trusts and monopolies. But during its first decade, enforcement was lax.

The Populists

In 1890 the various small political parties associated with the Farmers' Alliances began to enjoy success at the ballot box, especially in the South. In 1891 the Alliances founded the People's party, a new national party that demanded radical changes in federal economic and social policies. The **Populists,** as followers of the new party were known, built their platform around the following issues:

(1) They called for an increased circulation of money.

(2) They urged the unlimited minting of silver.

(3) They supported a **progressive income tax,** in which the percentage of taxes owed increases with income. This would place a greater tax burden on wealthy industrialists and a lesser one on farmers.

(4) They called for government ownership of the country's communications and transportation systems.

(5) In an effort to attract urban support, they endorsed an eight-hour work day. They also opposed the use of Pinkertons, the private police force that had been involved in the bloody Homestead Strike of 1892, as strikebreakers.

Breaking through deeply rooted racial prejudice, Populists sought a united front of African American and white farmers. The poor of both races had a common cause, they argued. As one of the party's leaders explained:

Mary Elizabeth Lease won fame as a Farmers' Alliance speaker.

[†] Hundreds of thousands of farmers joined the Farmers' Alliances. One estimate placed the number of members at close to 3 million.

Main Idea
CONNECTIONS

The Populist party grew out of what farmers' protest group?

From the Archives of

American Heritage®

About the Presidents

Benjamin Harrison (1889–1893) filled his Cabinet with businessmen. His domestic policy, for the most part, reflected the influence of business interests. In foreign affairs, however, he was more independent. His administration concentrated on improving Pan-American relations. Toward that end, the International Bureau of American Republics was established. (It was later renamed the Pan-American Union.) Harrison also took strong, decisive actions that helped diffuse difficult situations, first with Italy (1890) and later with Chile (1891). Because his Secretary of State was ill during much of his term, Harrison often had to implement policies himself.
Source: David Jacobs, "Benjamin Harrison," *The American Heritage® Pictorial History of the Presidents of the United States,* vol. 2, 1968.

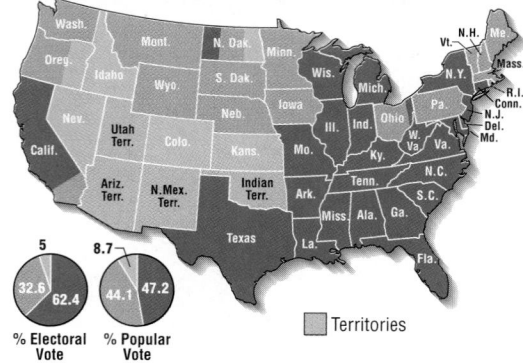

About the Presidents

William McKinley (1897–1901) enjoyed a big advantage over William Jennings Bryan in his first election: a well-financed campaign. Businessman Marcus A. Hanna raised millions of dollars on McKinley's behalf. McKinley's campaign chest paid for pamphlets, posters, and buttons, as well as train fare for those wishing to visit McKinley in his home town of Canton, Ohio. On one day alone, McKinley spoke to some 30,000 visitors. By contrast, Bryan's campaign had little money. Although Bryan crossed the country with his "silverite" message, warning Americans not to "crucify mankind upon a cross of gold," McKinley beat Bryan with a comfortable electoral margin. Source: Donald Young, "William McKinley," *The American Heritage® Pictorial History of the Presidents of the United States,* vol. 2, 1968.

Customize for

Less Proficient Readers

Ask students to make a chart with the headings The Farmers and The Populists. On one side students should list the complaints of farmers in 1896 about the money supply, the transportation system, and the disparity between the incomes of the rich and the poor. On the other side they should list the promises of the Populist party that answered those complaints.

Answer to . . .

Map Skills They had no success in the states of the North and East.

Election of 1892

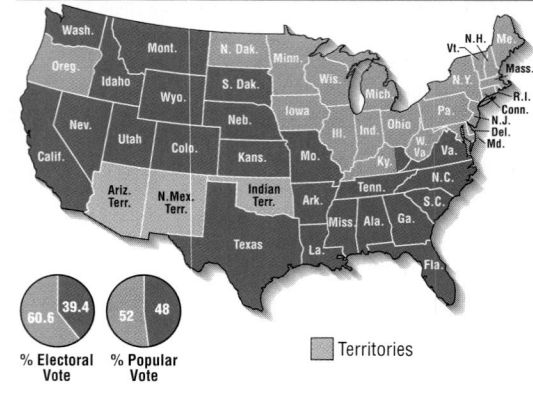

Candidate/Party	Electoral Vote	Popular Vote
Grover Cleveland (Democrat)	277	5,554,414
Benjamin Harrison (Republican)	145	5,190,802
James Weaver (People's)	22	1,027,329

Election of 1896

Candidate/Party	Electoral Vote	Popular Vote
William McKinley (Republican)	271	7,035,638
William J. Bryan (Democrat)	176	6,497,946

 MAP Skills In their first presidential election, the People's party ran poorly against both the Democrats and Republicans. In 1896, they shared candidate William Jennings Bryan with the Democrats. *Regions What pattern can you identify in the limited success of the Populists in the presidential elections of 1892 and 1896?*

AMERICAN VOICES "Now, the People's Party says to [whites and African Americans], 'You are kept apart that you may be separately fleeced of your earnings. You are made to hate each other because upon that hatred is rested the keystone of the arch of financial despotism [absolute power] which enslaves you both. You are deceived and blinded that you may not see how this race antagonism perpetuates a monetary system which beggars both.'"

— *Tom Watson*

During the 1892 campaign, populism generated great excitement among its followers. But the party's presidential candidate, Iowan James B. Weaver, won barely a million votes. Democrat Grover Cleveland returned to the presidency.

Back in office, Cleveland alienated labor when he put down the Pullman Strike. He angered farmers with his support for a gold standard and manufacturers when he tried to lower the tariff. The 1893 depression, which had started before he took office, threw millions out of work. When marchers promoting Populist ideas flocked to Washington in 1894, Americans added "hayseed Socialists" to their list of frightening agitators.

Bryan's "Cross of Gold"

Populists saw in Cleveland's troubles the promise of success in the 1896 presidential campaign. In an election that focused mainly on currency issues, the Republicans ran William McKinley on a gold-standard platform. William Jennings Bryan, a former silverite congressman from Nebraska and a powerful speaker, captured the Democratic nomination with an emotional plea for free silver. Using images from the Bible, he stood with head bowed and arms outstretched and cried out at the climax of his speech, "You shall not press down upon the brow of labor this crown of thorns. You shall not crucify mankind upon a cross of gold!" So stunning was Bryan's speech that he captured the nomination of the Populists as well as the Democrats.

The 1896 campaign was one of marked contrasts. Bryan was a whirlwind of activity, traveling all over the country and making speeches at every stop. McKinley ran a more traditional campaign. He remained in his hometown of

TEST PREPARATION

Have students read the quotation by Watson on this page and then answer the question below.

The word *beggars* in this passage means —

Ⓐ makes poor.

B separates.

C empowers.

D enslaves.

Canton, Ohio, greeting visitors and making a few speeches from his front porch.

Despite his best efforts, Bryan lost the election. He carried the Democratic West and South but not one of the urban and industrial midwestern and northern states. In these states, factory workers feared that free silver might cause inflation, which would eat away the buying power of their wages. Thus, despite populism's broad appeal, it could not bridge the ever-widening gap between America's cities and farms. Nor could populism slow America's transition from an agricultural nation to an industrial nation.

Populism's Legacy

By 1897 McKinley's administration had raised the tariff to new heights. In 1900, after gold strikes in South Africa, the Canadian Yukon, and Alaska had added more than $100 million worth of gold to the world's supply, Congress returned the nation to a gold standard. To the surprise of many farmers, crop prices began a slow rise that would last until 1920. The silver movement died, as did populism.

The goals of populism, however, lived on. In the decades ahead, other reformers known as progressives applied populist ideas to urban and industrial problems. In so doing, they launched a new wave of reform that shifted the course of United States history.

THE SACRILEGIOUS CANDIDATE.

This cartoon shows William Jennings Bryan wielding the crown of thorns and cross of gold—Biblical images that he used in a famous speech. *Culture Is this cartoon presenting Bryan in a positive or a negative light?*

SECTION 4 REVIEW

Comprehension

1. *Key Terms* Define: (a) deflation; (b) monetary policy; (c) Bland-Allison Act; (d) the Grange; (e) Interstate Commerce Act; (f) Populist; (g) progressive income tax.

2. *Summarizing the Main Idea* By what means did farmers organize to protest and present their views?

3. *Organizing Information* Create a web diagram that presents information about the organizations farmers formed to solve their problems. Label the center circle *Organizing Farmer Protest.* Include at least three organizations in your diagram.

Critical Thinking

4. *Analyzing Time Lines* Review the time line at the start of the section. Choose one entry and explain how it supported the needs of farmers.

5. *Drawing Conclusions* Populism appealed to people in many parts of the country. How can you explain, then, the failure of the Populist party to win the presidential election of 1896?

Writing Activity

6. *Writing a Persuasive Essay* Imagine that you are a farmer in the late 1800s. Write a letter to Congress asking for support of economic policies that would help solve some of your problems. Explain how you feel about tariffs and the issues surrounding the gold standard and free silver.

SKILLS FOR LIFE

Critical Thinking

Drawing Conclusions

Focus Summarize, compare, and draw conclusions about two primary source passages dealing with the same topic. **Instruct** Ask for volunteers to read the passages to the class. Divide the class into small groups to study the facts of each passage and to draft a summary statement for each one. Then have the whole class attempt to compare the passages. Ask students if the passages basically deal with the same issue. Ask what is different about the passages. Finally, ask students what happens if historians make faulty conclusions. **Extend** See the Skills for Life Activity in the Resource Options below.

Answers

1. (a) Farming is unprofitable; although they work hard, farmers are in debt; mortgages keep increasing; in Connecticut, farmers earn only $181.31 a year, far less than factory laborers. (b) Political parties mislead farmers into thinking that their problems are their own fault. The problems are actually caused by government practices.

2. (a) That the farmers' problems are caused by conditions beyond their control, regardless of their hard work. (b) That the government has not been sympathetic.

3. (a) Students may conclude that farmers would support the Populists' ideas and candidates because the party was sympathetic to their plight and suggested solutions to it. (b) Students may conclude that the major political parties were part of the farmers' economic problems, not part of the solution.

Gladden is concerned about the farmers' problems.

452

Drawing Conclusions

Drawing conclusions means reaching an answer or forming an opinion based on information that is suggested but not stated directly. When you read about history or any subject, it is important to be able to draw conclusions. Then you can go beyond what is presented in textbooks and other sources and form new insights about a historical period or event.

Use the following steps and the two passages from the late 1800s that appear on this page to practice drawing conclusions.

1. Study the facts and ideas that the author presents. Read the two passages below, and then answer the following questions about them. (a) What facts does Washington Gladden present to describe the farmers' problems? (b) What factors does Mary Elizabeth Lease cite to explain the farmers' problems as she perceives them?

2. Make a summary statement as a conclusion about a group of details. A statement that summarizes the major points of an argument is one type of conclusion. Clarify each person's position by summarizing the basic information contained in the two passages. Then answer the following questions. (a) From passage A, what can you conclude about the farmers' plight? Would farming be more profitable if farmers worked as hard as laborers? Or, are the farmers' problems beyond their control? (b) From the information in passage B, what can you conclude about the government's response to the problems the farmers are experiencing? Explain your reasoning.

3. Decide whether or not you can draw a conclusion based on what is stated. If an argument does not contain sufficient information, it is possible to jump to a faulty conclusion. Comparing the information in the two passages should raise some questions in your mind. As you answer these questions, you are deciding whether you have enough information to draw conclusions. (a) Given what you read in both passages, what conclusion can you draw about the relationship between farmers and the Populist party? Explain your answer. (b) Based on Lease's ideas in passage B, what conclusion can you draw concerning the ideas of the Populist party and the ideas of the major political parties?

Reread passage A. Based on Gladden's statement, is he concerned or unconcerned about the plight of the farmer?

Passage A	Passage B
"The business of farming has become, for some reasons, extremely unprofitable. With the hardest work and with the sharpest economy, the average farmer is unable to make both ends meet; every year closes with debt, and the mortgage grows till it devours the land. The Labor Bureau of Connecticut has shown, by an investigation of 693 representative farms, that the average annual reward of the farm proprietor of that state for his expenditure of muscle and brain is $181.31, while the average annual wages of the ordinary hired man is $386.36."	"The parties lie to us and the political speakers mislead us. We were told two years ago to go to work and raise a big crop, that was all we needed. We went to work and plowed and planted; the rains fell, the sun shone, nature smiled, and we raised the big crop that they told us to. . . . Then the politicians said we suffered from over-production. . . . We want money, land, and transportation. We want the abolition of the national banks, and we want the power to make loans direct from the government. We want the accursed foreclosure system wiped out."
—Washington Gladden, Congregational minister, 1890	—Mary Elizabeth Lease, Populist leader

RESOURCE OPTIONS

Teaching Resources

📁 **Skills for Life Activity** Units 5–6 folder, p. 32, uses two discourses on the North American Free Trade Agreement to give students a present-day application of this skill.

Media and Technology

Color Transparencies Critical Thinking, I-12

1872	1883	1893	1912
Congress establishes Yellowstone National Park	"Buffalo Bill" Cody begins his Wild West shows	Historian Frederick Turner develops frontier thesis	Juliette Low founds the American Girl Scouts

1872 **1882** **1892** **1902** **1912**

Frontier Myths

5 Frontier Myths

SECTION PREVIEW

Objectives

1 Explain why Americans, by 1900, believed that the American frontier no longer existed.
2 Compare the myths and the realities of frontier life.
3 Understand how frontier myths have affected this nation's identity and why they remain important today.
4 *Key Terms* Define: Turner thesis; buffalo soldier; stereotype.

Main Idea

The story of the "Wild West" has always captured Americans' imagination, but the myths disregard many other experiences that helped shape the nation.

Reading Strategy

Reinforcing Key Ideas As you read, make a list of myths about the American frontier on the left side of a piece of paper. Then, to the right of each myth, write a sentence about the reality of life on the frontier.

As the 1800s came to a close, Americans faced a situation that few could have imagined. After decades of expansion the American frontier seemed to be disappearing. An era of special meaning seemed to be ending. But what, exactly, did the era mean? The answer to that question is surrounded by many myths—and is responsible for many of the nation's most cherished images of itself.

The West by 1900

One by one, areas of the West became United States territories. Residents then wrote constitutions and applied for statehood. A decline in the amount of unorganized territory created the sense that the opportunities of the frontier were fading.

Long before 1900, American observers of the West noticed ominous signs of change. The number of tenant farmers had risen, along with the number of large farms owned by corporations. Many farmers were deep in debt. In 1872 the federal government established Yellowstone National Park to preserve western lands. Located in northwestern

Wyoming, southern Montana, and eastern Idaho, the park was the nation's first national park. Despite this step, in 1890 the superintendent of the census announced the end of the frontier. The country's so-called "unsettled area has been so broken into by isolated bodies of settlement," he declared, "that there can hardly be said to be a frontier line."

Turner's Frontier Thesis

In 1893 a young historian named Frederick Jackson Turner delivered a speech in which he claimed that the frontier had played a central role in forming the American character. The West had forced its Anglo-American and European settlers to shed their old ways and adapt, innovate, and invent, he said. To the frontier, Turner claimed, "American intellect owes its striking characteristics." He described these as:

William F. "Buffalo Bill" Cody became famous by playing up the myths of the American West.

BACKGROUND

Connections to Today

In the 1870s, store owner Levi Strauss and tailor Jacob Davis found a way to answer the need for stronger work clothes. They used tent canvas to make pants with double-stitched seams and small copper rivets pounded into the corners of the front and back pockets. The new clothes were an immediate success and became even more popular when Strauss and Davis switched from canvas to tougher, softer, dyed-blue denim. In the 1950s and 1960s, blue jeans were seen as the symbol of restless youth. By the 1990s, international designers had turned them into high-fashion clothing. An example of the original "Levi's" now hangs in the Smithsonian Institution in Washington, D.C.

FACT Finder — The West Joins the Union

State	Year Admitted
California	1850
Oregon	1859
Kansas	1861
Nevada	1864
Nebraska	1867
Colorado	1876
North Dakota	1889
South Dakota	1889
Montana	1889
Washington	1889
Wyoming	1890
Idaho	1890
Utah	1896
Oklahoma	1907
New Mexico	1912
Arizona	1912

Interpreting Tables In the late 1800s and early 1900s, one western territory after another achieved statehood. *Geography Why do you think that the interior of the country was settled later than most of the West Coast?*

KEY DOCUMENTS "That coarseness and strength combined with acuteness [keen insight] and inquisitiveness [curiosity]; that practical, inventive turn of mind, quick to find expedients [ways to achieve goals]; . . . that restless, nervous energy; that dominant individualism, working for good and for evil, and withal that buoyancy [liveliness] and exuberance which comes with freedom."

—*Frederick Jackson Turner*

To Turner, it was the frontier that had produced the highly individualistic, restless, and socially mobile American. Frontier life created Americans who were ready for adventure, bent on self-improvement, and committed to democracy.

Turner's Critics The **Turner thesis,** as his view came to be called, made certain assumptions that historians have since modified. Turner defined settlers as whites only and saw no difference in the experiences of women and men. His theory was not a complete picture of frontier life because it did not consider the important contributions African Americans and immigrants from Japan and China made to the West. Nor did Turner consider the impact of settlement on Native American and Spanish-speaking inhabitants.

Turner concentrated on the effects that individuals had on development, but played down the government subsidies and big business investments that were critical to farming, cattle ranching, and mining. Finally, he disregarded the traditions that immigrants had brought from their homelands and used in helping build the nation.

Frontier Realities

A far more complex view of the West now prevails. This view more accurately reflects the reality of the settlement of the West.

Diverse Western Settlers The West did appeal to the restless, adventurous man, but it also appealed to adventurous women. While many women regretted their family's decision to go west, others embraced the more open society and thrived on the frontier.

Still, the West was hardly a land of unlimited opportunity for either men or women. Boom inevitably led to bust, especially when prices fell for the items that settlers produced.

Western settlers were not always eastern whites. Chinese and Japanese settlers farmed the fertile lands of the West Coast. Chinese and African American railway workers went into mining and established businesses in western towns. About 9,000 African Americans worked as cowhands on ranches. Thousands of black Exodusters settled the West. Thousands more African Americans served there as soldiers in the United States Army, most notably in the all-black Ninth and Tenth Cavalry Regiments, which Native Americans named the **"buffalo soldiers."**

A Limited View of Democracy Frontier life encouraged certain democratic values. As noted earlier, western states gave women the vote before their eastern counterparts did the same. Yet many settlers rode roughshod over

TEST PREPARATION

Have students read the quotation by Turner on this page and then answer the question below.

The main point of the passage is that—

A Americans have a lot of different characteristics.

B individualism can lead to good or evil.

C characteristics formed on the frontier shape a free society.

D people who aren't free can't be exuberant.

the rights of the Native American peoples they displaced. On the West Coast, white settlers treated Asian immigrants with scorn, isolating them in separate neighborhoods and prohibiting them from owning land.

The Impact on the Land Although in the popular mind the settlement of the West meant progress, the costs to the environment were high. Settlers treated the vast natural resources of the West as if they were limitless. Railroad tunnels destroyed mountains. The construction of huge mines scarred the land and leveled forests. Overcultivation eroded fields, and senseless slaughter nearly wiped out the buffalo.

Frontier Myths and National Identity

Despite today's deeper understanding of the history of the American West, frontier myths linger on. Through literature, film, and song, they continue to influence how Americans think about themselves.

Creating the Myths The romantic image of the American cowboy began as early as the 1870s, in the dime novels of writers like Edward L. Wheeler. In *Deadwood Dick, The Prince of the Road: or, the Black Rider of the Black Hills,* Wheeler painted a hero who was, at various times, outlaw, miner, gang leader, or cowboy and who dealt out righteous justice against evil.

> ❝Mounted upon his midnight steed, and clad in the weird suit of black, he makes an imposing spectacle as he comes fearlessly up. . . .
>
> Close up to the side of the coach rides the daring young outlaw, his piercing orbs peering out from the eye-holes in his black mask, one hand clasping the bridle-reins, the other a nickel-plated seven-shooter.❞
>
> —*Scene from* Deadwood Dick

Scenes like these kept alive the idea that the West saw little else but stagecoach robberies and killings. Although Wheeler's *Deadwood Dick* was based on a real person, the cowboy of that name was no outlaw. He was an African American named Nat Love. Entering a rodeo contest in a Dakota Territory mining town named Deadwood, Love won several roping and shooting contests. In his autobiography, Love wrote, "Right there the assembled crowd named me 'Deadwood Dick'

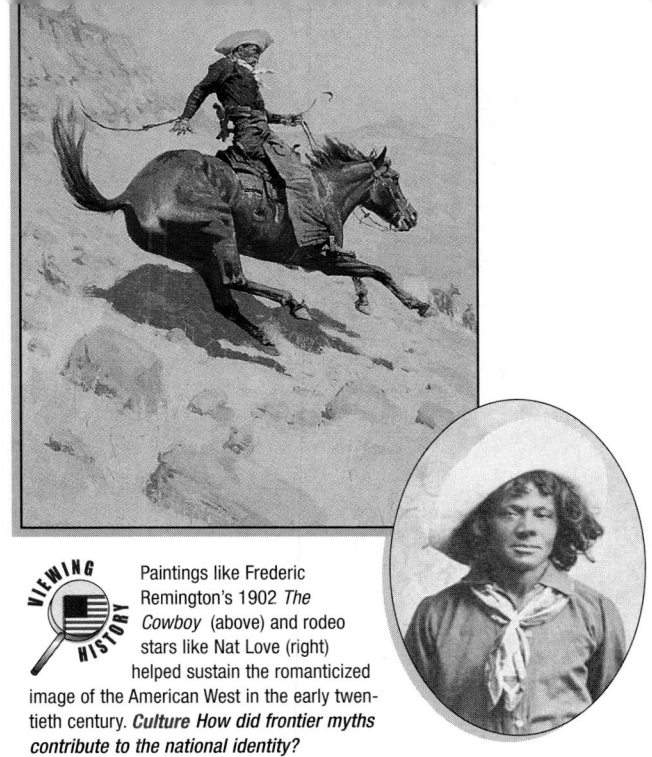

Paintings like Frederic Remington's 1902 *The Cowboy* (above) and rodeo stars like Nat Love (right) helped sustain the romanticized image of the American West in the early twentieth century. **Culture** *How did frontier myths contribute to the national identity?*

and proclaimed me champion roper of the Western cattle country."

In 1883 William F. ("Buffalo Bill") Cody began his Wild West shows, contributing further to frontier myths. These events drew thousands of spectators to steer-roping contests, rodeos, and staged battles between "good" cavalry regiments and "bad" Native Americans.

Writers transformed other real figures from the West, such as Wild Bill Hickok and Calamity Jane, into larger-than-life characters. This is Wheeler again:

> "Who was that chap?" asked Redburn, not a little bewildered.
> "That?—why that's Calamity Jane!"
> "Calamity Jane? What a name."
> "Yes, she's an odd one. Can ride like the wind, shoot like a sharp-shooter, and swear like a trooper. . . . Owns this coop and two or three other lots in Deadwood; a herding ranch at Laramie; an interest in a paying placer claim [mine] near Elizabeth City, and the Lord only knows how much more."
> "But it is not a woman?"
> "Reckon 'tain't nothin' else."

Main Idea CONNECTIONS

How have the myths of the American West been perpetuated?

BACKGROUND

Recent Scholarship

African American women played a role on every American frontier, including the West. Some traveled west in pioneer wagons; others were born among Native American nations. These women continued in the roles of mothers and daughters, while assisting in the building of communities, schools, and churches. For example, in 1781 forty-four people founded Los Angeles, California. Twenty-six of those people were of African descent. The children of these African American homesteaders eventually became poets, civil rights activists, teachers, nurses, and landowners. William Loren Katz's *Black Women of the Old West* is filled with fascinating stories about black women's roles in the development of the West.

▶ RESOURCE OPTIONS

Teaching Resources

📁 **Biography** Nat Love (alias Deadwood Dick), Units 5–6 folder, p. 26

Media and Technology

AmericanHeritage® CD-ROM

Time Tour Reshaping the Nation: The Frontier West

🖼 **Color Transparencies** Links Across Time, J-5

🎧 **Listening to Literature** Bret Harte, "The Outcasts of Poker Flat"

Answer to . . .

Viewing History By celebrating images of wide-open spaces, courage, and opportunity.

Main Idea Connections Through literature, Wild West shows, films, and songs.

CAUSE AND EFFECT: Westward Expansion

CAUSES

- Big businesses put western land up for sale.
- Morrill Land-Grant Act provides state governments with millions of acres to sell.
- Homestead Act gives land to settlers willing to farm.
- European immigrants, people seeking opportunity, and people fleeing racial prejudice in the East seek land in the West.
- California Gold Rush draws thousands of fortune seekers.

WESTWARD EXPANSION

EFFECTS

- Violence erupts between settlers and Native Americans.
- Many Native American groups are destroyed or displaced.
- Challenges of prairie farming lead to increased mechanization.
- Bonanza farms and cattle ranching industries develop.
- Frontier myths influence national identity.

 Interpreting Charts Westward expansion of the United States changed the human geography of North America. Immigrants, fortune-seekers, and people fleeing racial prejudice soon displaced the original inhabitants of the West. *Government Why do you think the government offered so many incentives to settlers?*

This sketch suggested that a woman had to act masculine and be "mean with a pistol" in order to survive in the West. Thus it helped create one of the several **stereotypes,** or fixed ideas held by people, about the West.

The "Strenuous Life" of the West Most stories from the West supported stereotypes about men. The West was the place where a young man could find freedom and opportunity. He could lead a virtuous life and resist the forces of civilization that had made easterners soft. Many writers praised the West for having toughened the bodies and souls of young men. In his histories of the West, future President Theodore Roosevelt urged American men to experience the "strenuous life" of the West before they became too weak from the comforts of modern civilization.

Some male themes also appealed to women. In 1912 Juliette Low founded the American Girl Scouts in part because she feared that civilization had made girls too soft. Praising women homesteaders for their strength and intelligence, she made the scouting techniques of tracking, woodcraft, and wilderness survival the core of her program.

National Identity Frontier myths have left permanent marks on the nation's character. How many classic American songs arose from the cowboy era? "Home on the Range," where the buffalo roam, and "Don't Fence Me In" both suggest enduring images of wide-open spaces and freedom from civilization. When Americans hear these songs, they celebrate the richness of their land and the courage of their ancestors.

Reality, however, is much more complex than the myth. It is a balance, for example, between the dream of endless opportunities and the fact that opportunities were not equal for all. Although our image of the West is much simpler and perhaps more heroic than the reality, the myths remain imbedded in the spirit of the nation.

SECTION 5 REVIEW

Comprehension

1. *Key Terms* Define: (a) Turner thesis; (b) buffalo soldier; (c) stereotype.

2. *Summarizing the Main Idea* Explain how the myths about the Wild West disregard many other experiences that also helped shape the nation.

3. *Organizing Information* Create a chart that organizes information about the myths and realities of life on the American frontier.

Critical Thinking

4. *Analyzing Time Lines* Review the time line at the start of the section. Which entry helped to reinforce certain myths about the West in the American imagination?

5. *Identifying Central Issues* What did observers mean when they said that the frontier was "closed" in the late 1800s?

Writing Activity

6. *Writing a Persuasive Essay* Write a brief essay explaining the Turner thesis and some of the criticisms of it.

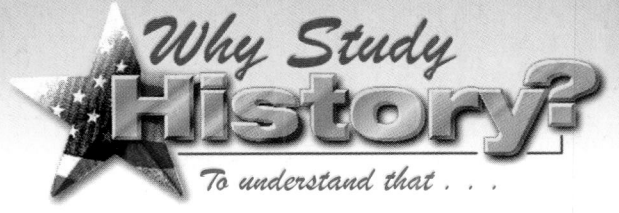

To understand that . . .

Americans Are on the Move

Like the homesteaders who moved west in the late 1800s, many Americans today are seeking opportunity by moving to new places.

Family of Nebraska homesteaders in front of their sod house

Housing developments and shopping malls spring up where cattle once grazed. Country roads are widened into multi-lane highways. Signs of growth such as these have characterized the United States since the 1950s. Since the 1970s, most such growth has occurred in an area that stretches across the nation's southernmost states. Because of its warm and sunny climate, this area has been nicknamed the Sunbelt. Between 1970 and 1980, population in the Sunbelt grew almost twice as fast as in the nation as a whole.

The Impact Today

Americans have always been on the move. In the mid-1800s thousands headed west to the frontier to build farms or ranches or mine for precious metals.

The shift to the Sunbelt continues the American tradition of migration. Individuals are drawn to the region for various reasons, including a warm climate, low taxes, plentiful jobs, and a low crime rate. Industry and manufacturing have also moved to the Sunbelt from the so-called "Rustbelt," or older industrial areas in the North and Midwest. While many Rustbelt communities have suffered economic hardship as a result of the loss of jobs, this movement has fueled impressive economic growth in the Sunbelt. With growth has come some problems, however, such as strains on public services and increased traffic and pollution.

Growth in the Sunbelt has also affected American politics. The increase in population of Sunbelt states has given the region additional seats in Congress. Between 1970 and 1990, for example, California rose from 43 to 52 representatives in the House of Representatives. The growth of the Sunbelt, a politically conservative region, has helped create a more conservative political climate in the United States.

The Impact on You

If you were to decide to move to another region of the country, to which region might you move? Choose a state in that region as your destination and find out about its climate and economy. Write a paragraph comparing that state to your current state and describing the advantages and disadvantages that your destination offers.

New home construction in Texas, part of the growing Sunbelt

Class Discussion

Discuss with the class migration and regional differences. For a more thorough examination of the issue, see the activity folder in the Resource Options below.

ACTIVITY
STUDENT PARTICIPATION

Diagramming Regional Change
Ask students to read the text. Then ask the class to discuss the following question: What are the advantages and disadvantages of dramatic growth in a region? Next, have students work in small groups to create before-and-after diagrams, illustrating how growth changes a region. Their diagrams should show effects on a region's:

- **economy**
- **population**
- **environment**
- **culture**
- **housing costs**
- **living costs**
- **cities**
- **general atmosphere**

Follow up Have students debate whether or not local government should regulate development.

Using the Internet
Students can learn more about migration patterns by exploring links in the *America: Pathways to the Present* Web site at:

http://www.Pathways.phschool.com

Assessment
See the Lesson Plans folder, pp. 24–27, for rubrics on assessing Class Participation Projects.

 RESOURCE OPTIONS

Teaching Resources

 Why Study History? Activity
Americans Are on the Move, found in the Why Study History? folder, p. 16, provides an activity to help students better understand American migration patterns.

Media and Technology

 AmericanHeritage® CD-ROM

Time Tour The Nation Today and Tomorrow: Toward a New Century

Prentice Hall United States History Video Collection™ Volume 20

Post-War USA

Key Terms

Students should refer to the definitions of key terms in the chapter to write sentences that show an understanding of the causes of westward expansion and the resulting conflicts.

Comprehension

1. Settlers bought lands from large corporations, who had bought them from state governments or received them as grants from the federal government. Settlers also bought lands through the Homestead Act.

2. Families cooperated in building houses and barns, making quilts, husking corn, and providing many other forms of support.

3. Sooners sneaked in before being officially allowed entry. Settlement by boomers and sooners led to the eventual dominance of the territory by American settlers and the displacement of Native Americans.

4. Machines helped farmers farm more land. However once they invested in machines, they had to produce the crop for which the machines were designed. When prices for that crop declined, farmers went into debt. Machines also contributed to unemployment for farm workers.

5. The destruction of the buffalo and the removal of the Native Americans freed up land for grazing. The extension of railroads into the West allowed ranchers to ship cattle to markets throughout the country.

6. Supporters of inflation fought for an increase in the amount of currency, or money, in circulation. Supporters of deflation wanted less currency in circulation.

7. They formed powerful farm protest groups, including the Grange and the Farmers' Alliances.

8. Turner claimed that the frontier played a central role in forming the American character—ready for adventure, bent on self-improvement, and commited to democracy.

Chapter Summary

The major concepts of Chapter 15 are presented below. See also **Guide to the Essentials of American History** or **Interactive Student Tutorial CD-ROM,** which contains interactive review activities, time lines, helpful hints, and test practice for Chapter 15.

Reviewing the Main Ideas

After the Civil War, Americans accelerated their settlement of lands west of the Mississippi River. Leaving behind the world they knew, adventurous people tried to build new lives on the great frontier. For Native Americans of the West, however, this period was one of defeat and devastation.

Section 1: Moving West

With the encouragement of the federal government, settlers took up the challenges and the hardships of life in the West.

Section 2: Conflict with Native Americans

American expansion into the West led to the near destruction of the Native American nations there.

Section 3: Farming, Mining, and Ranching

Modern farming methods, the discovery of mineral deposits, and ranching made the West attractive to many individual settlers and big businesses.

Section 4: Populism

By the late 1800s, declining incomes for American farmers created fertile ground for a farmers' protest.

Section 5: Frontier Myths

The story of the "Wild West" has always captured Americans' imagination, but the myths disregard many other experiences that also helped shape the nation.

Like the homesteaders who moved west in the late 1800s, many Americans today are seeking opportunity by moving to new places. This mobility has caused a shift in population from older industrial areas in the North and Midwest to an area in the South known as the Sunbelt.

Using Graphic Organizers

• Agriculture: mechanization; new agricultural knowledge; bonanza farms.
• Mining: gold rushes; mining towns; growth of corporations.
• Ranching: large-scale ranches; cattle drives; end of the cattle boom.

Key Terms

For each of the terms below, write a sentence explaining how it relates to this chapter.

1. Morrill Land-Grant Act
2. speculator
3. Homestead Act
4. Battle of Little Bighorn
5. boomer
6. squatter
7. bonanza farm
8. long drive
9. deflation
10. monetary policy
11. the Grange
12. buffalo soldier

Comprehension

1. How did settlers acquire lands in the West?
2. Describe some ways settlers relied on each other.
3. What was the result of the decision to allow settlement in Indian Territory?
4. How did the development of new machines affect farming?
5. Describe several factors that led to the cattle ranching boom of the 1860s and 1870s.
6. Summarize the two opposing arguments in the monetary policy debate of the late 1800s.
7. How did farmers protest their hardships in the late 1800s?
8. What was the message of Frederick Jackson Turner's frontier thesis?

Using Graphic Organizers

On a separate sheet of paper, copy the tree map organizer on the main ideas about developing the West. Provide at least two supporting details for each main idea.

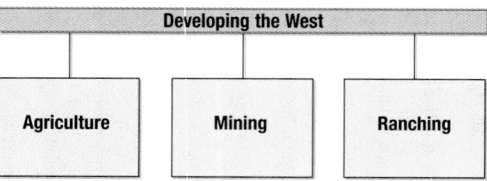

Developing the West		
Agriculture	Mining	Ranching

Analyzing Political Cartoons ▶

1. This hot air balloon holds aloft several Populist figures. (a) How do you know these men are Populists? (b) What is the balloon made of? (c) What does this composition suggest?

2. What is the message of the words on the basket ("Platform of Lunacy")?

3. Analyze the elements of this hot air balloon and state the cartoonist's overall message.

Critical Thinking

1. *Applying the Chapter Skill* Reread the two passages on page 452. Based on the information in the two passages, what were some of the problems that western farmers faced in the late 1800s?

2. *Distinguishing False from Accurate Images* Myths about the frontier led people to believe that the West was a lawless, dangerous place, but one in which everyone could strike it rich. In what ways is this a false image?

3. *Formulating Questions* Based on what you have read in the chapter, write three questions to ask farmers about new machinery and farming techniques that helped them farm the Great Plains.

4. *Recognizing Cause and Effect* How did settlement in the West contribute to the decline of Native American cultures?

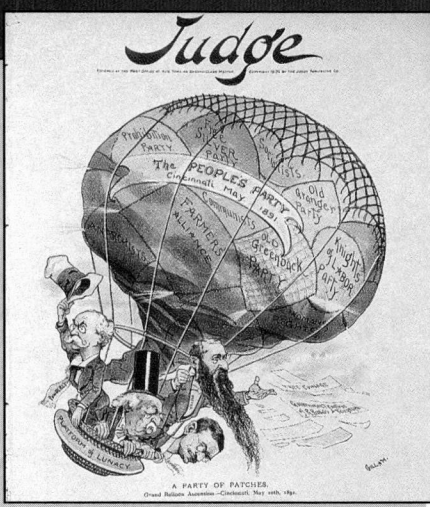

Judge

A PARTY OF PATCHES.

ANALYZING DOCUMENTS ◀ ▶ *INTERPRETING DATA*

Turn to the "American Voices" quotation on page 439.

1. Which statement best describes the opening of Indian Territory to settlement? (a) It was an orderly process. (b) Few people took part in settlement of Indian Territory. (c) It was chaotic. (d) All settlers into Indian Territory traveled by foot.

2. What was the most likely reaction of Native Americans to the opening of Indian Territory for settlement? (a) Native Americans welcomed the newcomers. (b) Native Americans felt betrayed by the opening of Indian Territory. (c) Native Americans lobbied Congress to open the territory for settlement. (d) Native Americans moved farther east to avoid settlers.

3. *Writing* Do you think the reporter exaggerated the description of the events on the day Indian Territory was opened for settlement? Explain your answer.

INTERNET ACTIVITY

For your portfolio:
PREPARE A SUMMARY

Access Prentice Hall's *America: Pathways to the Present* site at **www.Pathways.phschool.com** for the specific URL to complete the activity. Additional resources and related Web sites are also available.

Read the first-hand account of the Massacre at Wounded Knee. Summarize the events described by Alice Ghost Horse. How old was she at the time of the massacre? How did the soldiers behave before the attack? How did they behave afterward? How did Alice Ghost Horse feel about them?

INTERNET ACTIVITY

Summaries will vary but should include specific details and quotations from the chapter, and should answer the questions listed.

Connecting to Today

Essay Writing Reread the sections on the Populists and the elections of 1892 and 1896 in Section 4. Then research and write an essay on the central platform issues of a political party today. Does the platform represent the interests of a single group or many different groups?

Analyzing Political Cartoons

1. (a) The balloon is labeled "The People's Party," which was the Populist party. (b) Patchwork labeled with the names of different Populist groups and causes. (c) That the party is a hodgepodge of unrelated causes.
2. The balloon's label suggests that the Populists support crazy ideas.
3. Populists are full of hot air, expounding a patchwork of unrelated, unrealistic ideals.

Critical Thinking

1. Despite working hard, farmers were falling into debt, some farmers were losing their land, and they faced falling crop prices from overproduction.
2. The frontier was much more complicated. Large corporations made much more money on mining that did individuals. While some towns were chaotic when first settled, many became stable.
3. Possible questions: How much more land can you farm with the new equipment? How do falling crop prices affect your decisions to plant? Have you been helped by the Department of Agriculture?
4. The disappearance of the buffalo eventually destroyed Native Americans' ability to build lives on reservations. Much of the land given to Native Americans was unsuitable for farming; in addition, many Native Americans had no interest in farming and sold their land.

Analyzing Documents

1. c
2. b
3. The account was probably accurate considering the historical evidence.

Connecting to Today

Answers will vary but should indicate that the student has researched the selected party's platform and understands the central issues.

CHAPTER 16

Politics, Immigration, and Urban Life, 1870–1915

Managing Time and Instruction

INSTRUCTION SUPPORT

These materials for instruction are provided for **each section** in the **Teaching Resources.** See **Units 5–6 folder** for Enrichment Support:

• Reproducible Lesson Plans in Lesson Plans folder • Learning Styles Lesson Plans in Learning Styles Lesson Plans folder • Big Idea Graphic Organizers in Big Idea Graphic Organizer folder • Guided Reading and Review • Quizzes • Test Preparation Practice booklet

DAILY LESSON	ENRICHMENT SUPPORT
1 **Politics in the Gilded Age** *(pp. 461–466)*	• Critical Thinking Activity, Distinguishing False from Accurate Images: Honest Graft, found on **Resource Pro**
2 **People on the Move** *(pp. 467–472)*	• Nystrom *Atlas of Our Country,* The Third Wave of Immigration, pp. 30–31 • Visual Learning Activity, Passage to America, Learning with Documents folder, p. 58 • Literature Activity, The Statue of Liberty, Units 5–6 folder, p. 44 • Visual Learning Activity, The Chinese Question, found on **Resource Pro** • Comparing Primary Sources, On Cultural Ties, Units 5–6 folder, pp. 42–43
3 **The Challenge of the Cities** *(pp. 473–477)*	• Primary Source Activity, New York Gangs, Learning with Documents folder, p. 22 • Biography, Thomas Nast, Units 5–6 folder, p. 41 • Skills for Life Activity, Units 5–6 folder, p. 45
4 **Ideas for Reform** *(pp. 479–482)*	• Nystrom *Atlas of Our Country,* The Third Wave of Immigration, pp. 30–31 • Biography, Lillian Wald, found on **Resource Pro** • Primary Source Activity, Hull House, found on **Resource Pro** • Immigration Continues Today, Why Study History? folder, p. 17

Running Out of Time?

• Use Tape 3, "Expansion: Rewards and Costs, 1860–1920," from **Visions of America** videotapes series.

• Use Chapter 16 Summary, from **Guide to the Essentials of American History (English and Spanish).**

Companion Web Site

The companion Web site offers online links for all chapter review activities. It also provides key content links and structured support for this chapter for both teachers and students.

http://www.Pathways.phschool.com

Teaching in the Information Age

Media and Technology

For the Student

Interactive Student Tutorial CD-ROM Chapter 16

Student Edition on Audiotape Chapter 16

American Heritage® CD-ROM

Guided Reading Audiotapes (English and Spanish) Chapter 16

For the Teacher

Resource Pro CD-ROM Chapter 16

Test Bank CD-ROM Chapter 16

Listening to Music CD "Drill, Ye Tarriers," Anonymous

Listening to Literature Audiotapes *Timeless Voices, Timeless Themes* "The First Seven Years" by Bernard Malamud

Color Transparencies Cause and Effect, F-3

Assessment Options

Chapter Test Forms A&B Test Bank CD-ROM booklet

Test Bank CD-ROM Chapter 16

Standardized Test Preparation Handbook

Block Scheduling

Pacing Suggestions

For 90-minute Blocks

- Teach sections 1 and 2 using Transparencies J-7, C-2, C-11, and L-5 and the Extended Class Periods Activity on p. 465.
- Teach sections 3 and 4 using the Big Idea Graphic Organizers from Teaching Resources and the Recent Scholarship note on p. 480 for class discussions.

Additional Resources

- Prentice Hall's **American History Block Scheduling Support File** covers over 40 major topics in American history. Included are lesson plans, strategies, primary sources, literature, biographies, Great Debates, art history, simulations, and songs.
- **Prentice Hall United States History Video Collection™** contains 20 videotapes covering American history from beginnings to present.

Connections to American Literature

from Prentice Hall

America: Pathways to the Present *Hungry Hearts* by Anzia Yezierska, p. 1080

Prentice Hall Literature *Timeless Voices, Timeless Themes* "The Tropics in New York" by Claude McKay, p. 843

Additional Resources

For the Student

Jane Addams. *Twenty Years at Hull–House.* University of Illinois, 1989

Kenneth C. Martis. *The Historical Atlas of Political Parties in the United States Congress.* Macmillan, 1989.

For the Teacher

Blake McKelvey. *The Urbanization of America, 1860–1915.* Rutgers, 1963.

Kerby A Miller. *Emigrants and Exile: Ireland and the Irish Exodus to North America.* Oxford University Press, 1985.

Prentice Hall brings into the classroom the vast archives and scholarship of the nation's premier American history magazine. See "From the Archives of American Heritage®" and "About the Presidents" teaching notes in this chapter.

 History Alive!

Teacher's Curriculum Institute, in partnership with Prentice Hall, provides unique materials that engage students with diverse learning styles. See History Alive!® unit on The Rise of Industrial America.

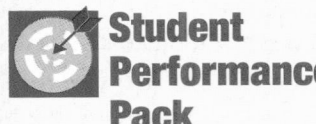 **Student Performance Pack**

Ensures success in the three critical areas of Reading, Test Taking, and English Language Development with the following materials:
- Guide to the Essentials of American History in English and Spanish
- Guided Reading Audiotapes in English and Spanish
- Interactive Student Tutorial CD–ROM
- Test Preparation Handbook
- Test Preparation Practice booklet

Introducing the Chapter

The years from 1870 to 1915 saw a continuation of the social, economic, and political divisions that had characterized the nation even before the Civil War. This was not a "nation united" as much as it was a collection of political factions and machines, ghettos, neighborhoods, ethnic enclaves, and extremes of rich and poor all competing to realize their version of the "American Dream."

Themes in American History

The theme for this chapter, Diversity, is listed at the beginning of this unit. An alternate theme for the chapter is Government. To teach this unit thematically, you may wish to use the Expansion, Reconstruction, Immigration folder in American History Block Scheduling Support.

Why Study History?

Have students explore suggested ways of connecting the past to the present on page 483.

Answer to . . .

Viewing History Students should use this question as an aid in reading the chapter. The photo suggests that immigrants viewed their entry into the United States with determination and optimism.

460

CHAPTER FOCUS

This chapter examines political developments around the turn of the century, including issues of political corruption and economic development. It also looks at changes in American cities brought about in part by the influx of immigrants.

The **Why Study History?** page at the end of this chapter analyzes the effects of immigration and immigration policy in the United States today.

▲ **VIEWING HISTORY**
Immigrants had their hands full as they arrived at Ellis Island to begin a new life in the United States. *Culture What does this photo reveal about their feelings?*

 RESOURCE OPTIONS

Teaching Resources

 Big Idea Graphic Organizer folder
Graphic summary of the main idea of the chapter.

Learning Styles Lesson Plans folder
Alternate lesson plans for diverse learning styles for each chapter.

Media and Technology

 AmericanHeritage® CD-ROM
Time Tour Reshaping the Nation: The Rise of Industry *and* A Diverse Nation; *also*, A New Role in the World: Progressives and Reformers

 Prentice Hall United States History Video Collection™ Volume 12
Immigration and Cultural Change

Timeline

1877 Munn v. Illinois

1881 President Garfield assassinated

1883 Pendleton Civil Service Act

1887 Interstate Commerce Act

1894 Coxey's army marches to Washington, D.C.

1901 President McKinley assassinated

1875 — 1885 — 1895 — 1905

1 Politics in the Gilded Age

SECTION PREVIEW

Objectives

1 Explain how business influenced politics during the Gilded Age.
2 Describe the government efforts to reform the spoils system and regulate railroads.
3 Explain how the cycle of depression and prosperity hurt the Democrats and helped the Republicans in the 1890s.
4 *Key Terms* Define: Gilded Age; laissez-faire; subsidy; blue law; civil service; Pendleton Civil Service Act; *Munn* v. *Illinois*.

Main Idea

From 1877 to 1900, national politics was dominated by issues of corruption and reform.

Reading Strategy

Structured Overview Write the following headings from the section on a sheet of paper, leaving room under each: *The Business of Politics; Reforming the Spoils System; Regulating Railroads; Depression to Prosperity.* As you read, list important details under each of these headings.

Many labels have been used to describe the post-Reconstruction era (1877–1900). The most famous is the **Gilded Age,** a term coined by writer Mark Twain. *Gilded* means "covered with a thin layer of gold," and "Gilded Age" suggests that a thin but glittering layer of prosperity covered the poverty and corruption of much of society.

It is an unflattering picture of this era, but it is accurate. This was a golden period for America's industrialists. Their wealth helped hide the problems of immigrants, laborers, and farmers. It also helped cover up the widespread abuse of power in business and government.

The Business of Politics

The United States faced great challenges as it emerged from Reconstruction. Industrial expansion raised the output of the nation's factories and farms. Some Americans, such as speculators in land and stocks, quickly rose "from rags to riches." At the same time, depressions, low wages, and rising farm debt con-

tributed to discontent among working people.

Laissez-faire Policies
In the late 1800s, businesses operated largely without government regulation. This hands-off approach to economic matters, known by the French phrase **laissez-faire,**[†] holds that government should play a very limited role in business. Supporters of this strategy maintain that if government does not interfere, the strongest businesses will succeed and bring wealth to the nation as a whole.

In the late 1800s, most Americans accepted this idea in theory. In practice, however, many champions of laissez-faire supported government involvement when it benefited

Monopolies and trusts control the government in this political cartoon.

[†] The term, meaning "allow to be," may have originated with French economists as early as the 1750s.

RESOURCE OPTIONS

Teaching Resources

 Reproducible Lesson Plan Lesson Plans folder, p. 97

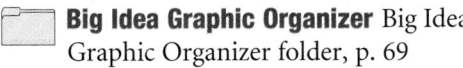 **Learning Styles Lesson Plan** Learning Styles Lesson Plans folder, p. 34

Big Idea Graphic Organizer Big Idea Graphic Organizer folder, p. 69

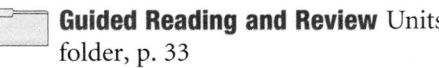 **Guided Reading and Review** Units 5–6 folder, p. 33

Media and Technology

 AmericanHeritage® CD-ROM

Time Tour Reshaping the Nation: The Rise of Industry

Objectives

You may wish to call students' attention to the objectives in the Section Preview. The objectives are reflected in the main headings of the section.

Bellringer

Ask students to list ideas they associate with the word *reformer.* In what areas of life are reformers trying to make changes today? What factors work against them?

Reading Strategy

Structured Overview Refer to the Reading Strategy in the Section Preview. You may want to model the headings on the chalkboard. After students have finished reading, have volunteers compose a list of details.

LESSON PLAN

Connecting to the Main Idea

1. Focus National politics during the Gilded Age were uninspired at best. Ask how business affected politics during the Gilded Age. Why were reformers unable to end corruption in politics and business?

2. Instruct Review with students the reasons some Americans demanded reform. Discuss the positions of the two major political parties. Which party was favored by wealthy Americans? Which party opposed blue laws? How did the cycle of depression hurt Democrats and help Republicans in the 1890s?

Ask students to list the efforts of Presidents Hayes and Arthur to end the spoils system. How did President Garfield's assassination contribute to the end of the spoils system?

3. Close During the Gilded Age, a series of ineffective Presidents failed to deal with economic problems and corruption. The next section describes the lives of the many immigrants entering the United States during this period.

Political Corruption

The corruption of this period is illustrated in the story of the Johnstown Flood of 1889. The developer who purchased the South Fork Dam and its reservoir from the Commonwealth of Pennsylvania in 1879 had the right friends and political connections. He turned the property into an exclusive fishing and hunting club that counted among its members the entrepreneurs Andrew Mellon and Andrew Carnegie.

Officials in the nearby industrial center of Johnstown, about 12 miles east of Stony Creek, persistently warned that the reservoir lake, which could hold approximately 5 billion gallons of water, was unsafe. They were told by the club's owners: "You and your people are in no danger from our enterprise." However, on May 31, 1889, the South Fork Dam collapsed. One witness described the scene: "In an instant the deserted street became black with people running for their lives. The flood came and licked them up with one eager and ferocious lap." More than 2,000 people died in the Johnstown Flood.

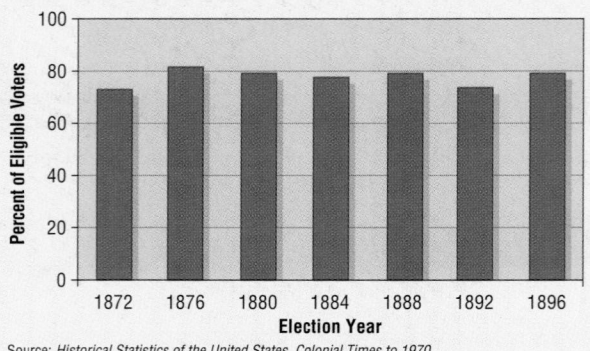

Turnout in Presidential Vote, 1872–1896

Source: *Historical Statistics of the United States, Colonial Times to 1970*

Interpreting Graphs Voter turnout was high during the late 1800s compared with later eras. By 1920, it had dropped below 50 percent and has never again risen as high as 65 percent. *Government What factors might help explain the high turnout in the late 1800s?*

them. For example, American businesses favored high tariffs on imported goods to encourage people to buy American goods instead. American businesses also willingly accepted government land grants and subsidies. A **subsidy** is a payment made by the government to encourage the development of certain key industries, such as railroads.

Business giants during the Gilded Age supported friendly politicians with gifts of money. Some of these contributions were legal and some were illegal. Between 1875 and 1885, the Central Pacific Railroad reportedly budgeted $500,000 each year for bribes. Central Pacific co-founder Collis P. Huntington explained, "If you have to pay money to have the right thing done, it is only just and fair to do it."

The Spoils System American politics also suffered from its reliance on the spoils system, in which elected officials appointed friends and supporters to government jobs, regardless of their qualifications. Introduced by President Jackson in 1829, the system had since flourished. By the Gilded Age, government swarmed with unqualified, dishonest employees.

The spoils system appealed to many politicians because it ensured them a loyal group of supporters in future elections. Both Democrats and Republicans handed out jobs to pay off the

Main Idea
CONNECTIONS

What were the effects of the spoils system?

people who had helped them get elected. But the system led to corruption when dishonest appointees used their jobs for personal profit.

Opposing Political Parties During the Gilded Age, the Democratic and Republican parties had roughly the same number of supporters. They differed greatly, however, in who those supporters were and in the positions that the parties took on major issues.

Republicans appealed to industrialists, bankers, and farmers. The party was strongest in the North and the upper Midwest and was weak to nonexistent in the South. In general, Republicans favored:

(1) a tight money supply backed by gold;
(2) high tariffs to protect American business;
(3) generous pensions for Union soldiers;
(4) government aid to the railroads;
(5) strict limits on immigration;
(6) enforcement of **blue laws,** regulations that prohibited certain private activities (such as drinking alcoholic beverages on Sundays).

As a rule, the Democratic party attracted those in American society who were less privileged, or at least felt that way. These groups included northern urban immigrants, laborers, southern planters, and western farmers. Claiming to represent the interests of ordinary people, Democrats favored:

(1) an increased money supply backed by silver;
(2) lower tariffs on imported goods;
(3) higher farm prices;
(4) less government aid to big business;
(5) fewer blue laws.

Reforming the Spoils System

Since the two parties had roughly equal strength, presidential candidates needed the votes of almost all members of their party in order to win an election. To avoid offending any of them, candidates generally avoided taking strong stands on controversial issues.

Republicans, especially, whipped up support by "waving the bloody shirt." This meant recalling the bloodshed of the Civil War, a conflict they blamed on the Democrats. This tactic helped Republicans hold on to the presidency for much of the post-Reconstruction era.

Presidents of this period did make some efforts to exercise leadership. Indeed, the Gilded Age witnessed some important reforms in such areas as the spoils system and the railroads.

RESOURCE OPTIONS

Media and Technology

RESOURCE PRO

Critical Thinking Activity Distinguishing False from Accurate Images: Honest Graft, found on Resource Pro, helps students apply this skill by examining a politician's attempted justification of "honest graft."

Hayes Fights the Spoils System After his election in 1877, Rutherford B. Hayes surprised many supporters by refusing to use the patronage system. Instead he appointed qualified political independents to Cabinet posts and fired employees who were not needed. By these actions Hayes began to reform the **civil service,** or the government's non-elected workers.

Hayes undertook these reforms without congressional backing, even from members of his own Republican party. He further angered his party on July 11, 1878, when he removed fellow Republican Chester A. Arthur from an important patronage position in New York. Then, with the help of congressional Democrats, he replaced Arthur with one of his own appointments. These moves especially upset Senator Roscoe Conkling, who had used patronage to control the Republican party in New York State.

Hayes had announced at the beginning of his presidency that he would not seek a second term. After his bold attack on the spoils system, he probably could not have won his party's nomination in any case. That attack strengthened the government but also helped weaken the Republicans.

Garfield's Term Cut Short As the 1880 presidential election approached, the Republican party was split into three factions. The Stalwarts, followers of Senator Conkling, defended the spoils system. The Half-Breeds, who followed Maine senator James G. Blaine, hoped to reform the spoils system while remaining loyal to the party. Independents opposed the spoils system altogether.

James A. Garfield, a congressman from Ohio, won the party's presidential nomination. Garfield was linked to the Half-Breeds. To balance the ticket, the Republicans chose as their vice-presidential candidate Chester A. Arthur, the New York Stalwart whom Hayes had fired two years earlier.

In the 1880 election Garfield won a narrow victory over the Democratic candidate, General Winfield S. Hancock. Garfield's term was cut short, however, by an assassin's bullet. On July 2, 1881, a mentally unstable lawyer named Charles Guiteau shot Garfield as the President walked through the Washington, D.C., railroad station. When he fired his fatal shot, Guiteau cried out, "I am a Stalwart and Arthur is President now!" Garfield suffered for nearly three months before dying.

It was later revealed that Guiteau, a loyal Republican, had expected to win a job through the spoils system. When Garfield passed him over, Guiteau became so enraged that he decided to murder the President. Guiteau's senseless act caused a public outcry against the spoils system.

Arthur Ends the Spoils System Upon Garfield's death, Vice President Chester Arthur became President. Arthur had fought for (and benefited from) patronage in New York. Once in office, however, he urged Congress to support reform of the spoils system. With Garfield's assassination fresh in the nation's mind, President Arthur was able to obtain congressional support for this reform. As a result, the **Pendleton Civil Service Act** became law in 1883.

> A GREAT NATION IN GRIEF
>
> PRESIDENT GARFIELD SHOT BY AN ASSASSIN.
>
> THOUGH SERIOUSLY WOUNDED HE STILL SURVIVES.
>
> THE WOULD-BE MURDERER LODGED IN PRISON.
>
> THE PRESIDENT OF THE UNITED STATES ATTACKED AND TERRIBLY WOUNDED BY A FANATICAL OFFICE-SEEKER ON THE EVE OF INDEPENDENCE DAY—THE NATION HORRIFIED AND THE WHOLE CIVILIZED WORLD SHOCKED—THE PRESIDENT STILL ALIVE AND HIS RECOVERY POSSIBLE.

President Garfield's assassination by a disappointed office seeker roused the nation to the need for reform of the spoils system. *Government How did President Arthur end the spoils system?*

From the Archives of

AmericanHeritage®

About the Presidents

James Abram Garfield (1881) had just appointed a new Postmaster General when *The New York Times* brought the "Star Route Frauds" to light. The *Times* investigation revealed that thousands of dollars were being spent for deliveries to places that received mail no more than three times a year. With Garfield's approval, the Postmaster General began a thorough public investigation. In the scandal that unfolded, several high-ranking Republicans were implicated. Nevertheless, Garfield called on the Postmaster General to continue releasing his report. As it turned out, the scandal outlived Garfield. In time, it helped lead to civil service reform. Source: David Jacobs, "James Abram Garfield," *The American Heritage® Pictorial History of the Presidents of the United States,* vol. 2, 1968.

ACTIVITY

STUDENT PORTFOLIOS

You may wish to have students add the following to their portfolios. To assess student work, refer to the generic rubrics in the Program Overview in the Teaching Resources.

Have students research the lives of the very wealthy during the Gilded Age. Students may select one person and present their findings in a report or skit that shows some of the details of the person's daily activities.

RESOURCE OPTIONS

Media and Technology

AmericanHeritage® **CD-ROM**

Presidents James A. Garfield

Answer to . . .

Viewing History By passage of the Pendleton Civil Service Act.

Customize for
More Advanced Students

Ask students to write a paragraph explaining why the passage of the Interstate Commerce Act was a hollow victory for reformers and analyzing why it was so difficult to get political support to curb railroad company abuses.

Powerful Union Pacific Railroad executives are shown here holding a meeting in the lavish surroundings of a private car. **Government** *What prompted the government to start regulating the railroad industry?*

was an Algonquin word meaning "important chief.") The editor was suggesting that the independents were little men who wanted to be big chiefs. His insult did not keep the Mugwumps from helping to put Cleveland in office.

Cleveland favored tight money policies, so most business interests backed him. Yet not all his policies were pro-business. He opposed high tariffs and took back from the railroads and other interests some 80 million acres of federal land that had been granted to them. In addition, Cleveland supported more government regulation of the powerful railroad companies.

Regulating Railroads

Railroad regulation had begun in 1869, when Massachusetts investigated charges that railroad companies were overcharging customers. By 1880, about 14 states had railroad commissions to look into complaints about railroad practices. One of those practices was charging more for a short haul than for a long haul over the same track. Others included keeping rates secret and charging different rates to different people for the same service. These practices kept farmers and businesses from predicting their shipping costs.

In 1877 the Supreme Court, in ***Munn v. Illinois,*** allowed states to regulate certain businesses within their borders, including railroads. But railroad traffic often crossed state boundaries. Lawyers for the railroads argued that under the Constitution only the federal government could regulate interstate commerce. In 1886, in the *Wabash* case, the Supreme Court agreed. Interstate railroad traffic thus remained unregulated.

Pressure mounted on Congress to curb railroad company abuses. As you read in the last chapter, in 1887 Congress responded by passing the Interstate Commerce Act. The act required that rates be set in proportion to the distance traveled and that rates be made public. It also outlawed the practice of giving special rates to powerful customers. Finally, it set up the nation's first federal regulatory board, the Interstate Commerce Commission (ICC), to enforce the act.

The Interstate Commerce Act failed, however, to give the ICC the power to set railroad rates. Also, to enforce its rulings the ICC had to take the railroads to court. Of the 16 cases involving the ICC that came before the Supreme Court between 1887 and 1905, the Court ruled against the ICC 15 times.

The act created a Civil Service Commission, which classified government jobs and tested applicants' fitness for them. It also stated that federal employees could not be required to contribute to campaign funds and could not be fired for political reasons.

Democrats Take Power In 1884 the Republicans nominated James G. Blaine, a former Secretary of State and senator from Maine, for President. The Democrats chose Grover Cleveland, former mayor of Buffalo and governor of New York.

Serious issues confronted the nation, such as high tariffs, unfair business practices, and unregulated railroads. Yet the campaign focused mostly on scandals. Had James G. Blaine received railroad stock options in return for favorable votes while he was in Congress? No one could prove it. Had Cleveland fathered a child out of wedlock while a bachelor in Buffalo? Cleveland admitted it was true. Republicans jeered, "Ma, Ma, where's my Pa?" Democrats responded, "Going to the White House, ha, ha, ha!" In spite of his admission, Cleveland won the election, thereby becoming the first Democrat to capture the presidency since 1856.

Cleveland owed at least some of his success to Republican independents who bolted their party to vote for him. These independents had decided that Blaine was too corrupt to support. An unsympathetic newspaper editor started calling them "Little Mugwumps." (*Mugwump*

Main Idea
CONNECTIONS
How did Cleveland gain political support?

Answer to . . .

Viewing History Growing numbers of complaints about railroad practices.

Main Idea Connections He gained the support of Republican independents and big business.

RESOURCE OPTIONS

Teaching Resources

American History Block Scheduling Support Linking the Nation: The Railroads, found in the Expansion, Reconstruction, Immigration folder, includes interdisciplinary lesson suggestions and activities for Geography and History, Primary Sources, Biography, and Literature.

Media and Technology

AmericanHeritage® CD-ROM

Time Tour A New Role in the World: Progressives and Reformers

Presidents Chester A. Arthur

Depression to Prosperity

Boosted by vigorous industrial growth, American business generally grew during the late 1880s and into the 1890s. But in 1893 a depression struck, and prosperity did not return until around 1900. These ups and downs made the economy the hottest political issue of this period.

Focus on Tariffs Cleveland lost the 1888 election to Republican Benjamin Harrison. The campaign had focused on tariffs. Cleveland favored a minor reduction in tariffs, while Harrison wanted an increase. Harrison's position won him plenty of business support and, ultimately, the presidency.

Among President Harrison's achievements was the signing of the Sherman Antitrust Act in 1890, described earlier. Like the Interstate Commerce Act, however, this seemingly bold action failed to curb the power of the largest corporations until well after the turn of the century.

Meanwhile, Harrison made good his campaign promise to business by approving a huge tariff increase in 1890. He also supported legislation on behalf of special business interests. Although he was thought to be conservative with public funds, Harrison dipped deep into the Treasury to award huge new pensions to dependents of Civil War soldiers.

These actions would later damage the economy, and they did not help Harrison in the election of 1892. Many new immigrants had swelled the ranks of the Democratic party. Campaigning again for lower tariffs, Grover Cleveland was returned to the presidency.

Cleveland's Second Term Cleveland's second term started badly. Thanks in part to the drained treasury, a panic hit the country in 1893. This began a four-year depression, the worst yet in American history. Millions of workers lost their jobs or had their wages slashed, yet the government offered no help.

In 1894 Jacob S. Coxey, a wealthy Ohio quarry owner who had become a Populist, demanded that government create jobs for the unemployed. Coxey called on unemployed workers to march on the nation's capital. "We will send a petition to Washington with boots on," he declared.

Many small "armies" started out on the protest march, but only Coxey's army reached Washington. Police arrested him and a few others for illegally carrying banners on the Capitol grounds and for trampling the grass. A song sung by Coxey's supporters mocked the government for worrying more about its lawns than its citizens. It was sung to the tune of "The Star-Spangled Banner":

AMERICAN VOICES "Oh, say, can you see, by the dawn's early light
That grass plot so dear to the hearts of us all?
Is it green yet and fair, in well-nurtured plight,
Unpolluted by the Coxeyites' hated foot-fall?
Midst the yells of police, and swish of clubs
    through the air,
We could hardly tell if our grass was still there.
But the green growing grass does in triumph
    yet wave,
And the gallant police with their buttons of brass
Will sure make the Coxeyites keep off the grass."

—Anonymous

One cartoonist saw trusts and monopolies as a monstrous octopus.
Government How successful was Harrison in curbing the power of trusts?

Answers to
SECTION 1 REVIEW

1. (a) Gilded Age, see p. 461; (b) laissez-faire, see p. 461; (c) subsidy, see p. 462; (d) blue law, see p. 462; (e) civil service, see p. 463; (f) Pendleton Civil Service Act, see p. 463; (g) *Munn* v. *Illinois*, see p. 464.

2. Hayes and Garfield refused to use the patronage system; Arthur signed into law the Pendleton Civil Service Act.

3. *Munn* v. *Illinois* raises question of railroad regulation; Supreme Court rules against state regulation; mounting pressure causes Congress to pass Interstate Commerce Act and set up Interstate Commerce Commission to enforce it.

4. Statements of agreement or disagreement should be supported with facts from the section.

5. Sample answer: They voted for increased tariff regulation because it would help the businessmen who had made contributions.

6. Essays will vary but should be supported with facts from the text.

Coxey's original "army" of around 100 men was joined by an additional 400 or so men as it made its way to Washington, D.C. *Government How effective was Coxey's protest?*

In his second term Cleveland managed to anger not only the unemployed but almost everyone else. In 1893 he upset farmers by repealing the Sherman Silver Purchase Act, which had become law just three years before. He enraged unions when he sent federal troops to Chicago during the Pullman strike of 1894.

By the time of his party's convention in 1896, Cleveland had turned many fellow Democrats against him. Hence, the President failed to win his party's nomination.

McKinley Wins in 1896

The Populists had emerged as a political power during the economic hard times of the early 1890s and had made gains in the 1894 elections. But in 1896 William Jennings Bryan, presidential candidate of the Populists and Democrats, lost to the Republican, William McKinley, who was supported by urban workers and the middle class.

President McKinley oversaw passage of a new tariff and strengthening of the gold standard. These actions brought Republicans an even more decisive victory against Bryan in 1900. As the economy began to climb out of the 1890s depression, Republicans claimed credit with their slogan "A Full Dinner Pail."

McKinley did not live long enough to enjoy the effects of the returning prosperity. On September 6, 1901, McKinley went on a tour of the Pan-American Exposition in Buffalo, New York. There a mentally ill anarchist named Leon Czolgosz shot the President as he greeted the public. McKinley died a few days later.

SECTION 1 REVIEW

Comprehension

1. *Key Terms* Define: (a) Gilded Age; (b) laissez-faire; (c) subsidy; (d) blue law; (e) civil service; (f) Pendleton Civil Service Act; (g) *Munn* v. *Illinois*.

2. *Summarizing the Main Idea* How did several Presidents reform the spoils system?

3. *Organizing Information* Draw a flowchart to show the sequence of events related to the regulation of railroads.

Critical Thinking

4. *Analyzing Time Lines* Review the time line at the start of the section. Decide whether you agree or disagree with the following statement: "The federal government's passage of legislation to regulate railroads paved the way for states to enact their own laws." Explain your answer.

5. *Recognizing Cause and Effect* Big businesses sought political influence by making large contributions to "friendly" politicians. How do you think these politicians voted on tariff legislation? Why?

Writing Activity

6. *Writing an Expository Essay* Write an essay exploring how economic issues affected the outcome of presidential elections during the Gilded Age.

RESOURCE OPTIONS

Teaching Resources

 Quiz Units 5–6 folder, p. 34

Student Performance Pack

Guide to the Essentials Chapter 16, Section 1 (English and Spanish)

Media and Technology

 Color Transparencies Links Across Time, J-7

Answer to . . .

Viewing History Not very effective; Cleveland did little to aid the unemployed or solve the country's economic woes.

| 1882 Chinese Exclusion Act | 1886 Statue of Liberty erected | 1892 Ellis Island immigration center opened | 1907 Gentlemen's Agreement signed | 1910 Angel Island immigration center built | 1913 Webb Alien Land Law enacted | 1921 Immigration Restriction Act |

1882　　1892　　1902　　1912　　1922

2 People on the Move

SECTION PREVIEW

Objectives

1 Describe the experiences of immigrants in the late 1800s and early 1900s.
2 Compare immigration from Europe, Asia, and Mexico.
3 Explore the experiences of two typical immigrants.
4 *Key Terms* Define: steerage; quarantine; Chinese Exclusion Act; segregation; Gentlemen's Agreement; alien.

Main Idea

Millions of immigrants, representing many different cultures, arrived in the United States during the late 1800s and early 1900s.

Reading Strategy

Formulating Questions Write down several questions you might ask about the experiences of immigrants around 1900. As you read, note answers to your questions.

It was sometimes said that America's streets were paved with gold. This myth held a grain of truth for the millions of immigrants who left a life of utter poverty behind. They came to America because it offered, if not instant wealth, then at least the chance to improve their lives. Some immigrants did get rich here, through hard work and determination. Many more managed to carve out a decent life for themselves and their families. For these immigrants, the chance to come to the United States was indeed a golden opportunity.

The Immigrant Experience

In the late 1800s, people in many parts of the world were on the move from farms to cities and from one country to another. Immigrants from around the globe were fleeing crop failures, shortages of land and jobs, rising taxes, and famine. Some were also escaping religious or political persecution.

Immigrants' Hopes and Dreams The United States received a huge portion of this

global migration. In 1860 the resident population of the United States was 31.5 million people. Between 1865 and 1920, close to 30 million additional people entered the country.

Some of these newcomers dreamed of getting rich, or at least of receiving free government land through the Homestead Act. Others yearned for personal freedoms. In America, they had heard, everyone could go to school, young men were not forced to serve long years in the army, and citizens could freely take part in a democratic government.

Millions of immigrants brought their belongings and their dreams to the United States in the late 1800s.

Crossing the Ocean In the late 1800s, steam-powered ships could cross the Atlantic Ocean in two to three weeks. By 1900, on more powerful steamships, the crossing took just one week. Even this brief journey, however, could be difficult, especially for those who could not afford cabins. Most immigrants traveled in **steerage,** a large open area beneath the ship's deck. Steerage offered limited toilet

Global Connections

Through the port of New York City alone, between 1847 and 1860 a million people came over from Ireland. That was nearly half of all Europeans who landed in New York in those years. The Irish came, in large part, because blight destroyed their country's entire potato crop, which was the mainstay of their diet. Eventually over one million people died in Ireland from starvation and disease during the potato famine. America seemed a far cry from the disaster. One new arrival wrote, "Every day [in America] is like Christmas Day."

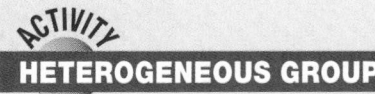

ACTIVITY
HETEROGENEOUS GROUPS

In 1892 the Office of the Superintendent of Immigration was established to determine who was "fit" for immigration into the United States. Divide students into an even number of groups and ask each group to design a test for immigration fitness. Suggest the following tests: physical fitness, intelligence, finances, and knowledge of U.S. history. Have groups administer their tests to each other. Discuss with students their feelings about being tested in this way. (Reteaching)

Answer to . . .

Interpreting Charts 1870—NW Europe; 1880—NW Europe; 1890—NW Europe; 1900—Central Europe; 1910—Central Europe; 1920—Southern Europe.

These arrivals on Ellis Island contemplate a bewildering yet promising future in their new homeland.

facilities, no privacy, and poor food, but the fare was relatively cheap.

Crossing the vast Pacific Ocean took much longer, but the arrangements were similar. Passengers traveled in steerage, with few comforts. Where a person came from, however, could make a difference in the conditions aboard ship. Immigrants from Japan, whose power in the world was growing, often received better treatment than those from China, which at that time was a weak country.

Arriving in America Information about the number and origins of the nation's immigrants is not precise. Officials often misidentified the origins of immigrants. About one third of them were "birds of passage." These were usually young, single men who worked for a number of months or years and then returned home.

Historians estimate that about 10 million immigrants arrived between 1865 and 1890.

European Immigration, 1870–1920

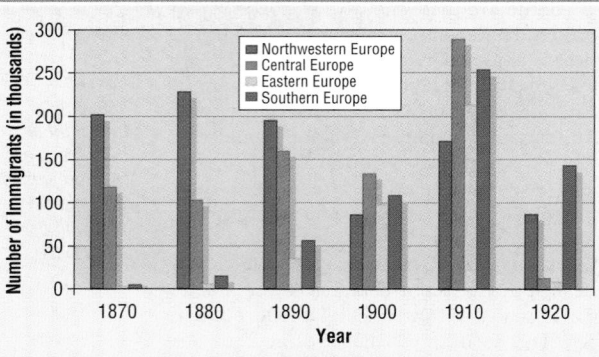

Number of Immigrants (in thousands) / *Year*

- Northwestern Europe
- Central Europe
- Eastern Europe
- Southern Europe

Source: *Historical Statistics of the United States, Colonial Times to 1970*

Interpreting Graphs The greatest number of immigrants came from Europe. *Geography Name the region from which most European immigrants came for each year shown.*

Most came from northern European countries: about 2.8 million from Germany, another 1.8 million from Great Britain, and nearly 1.4 million from Ireland.

In the 1890s, the pattern of immigration shifted dramatically. Most new immigrants came from the countries of southern and eastern Europe and the Middle East. Between 1890 and 1920 about 10 million Italians, Greeks, Slavs, Eastern Europeans, Russian Jews, and Armenians arrived. Around 3.8 million immigrants came from Italy alone. From Russia came another 3 million.

Until the 1880s, decisions about whom to allow into the country were left to the states. In 1882 the federal government began excluding certain categories of immigrants. In 1891 the Office of the Superintendent of Immigration was formed to determine who was fit for life in America and who was not.

Immigrants entered through several ports. European newcomers might come through Boston, Philadelphia, or Baltimore. Asians might enter through San Francisco or Seattle. Yet more than 70 percent of all immigrants came through New York City, the "Golden Door."

Immigrants from Europe

Throughout most of the 1800s, immigrants arriving in New York entered at the Castle Garden depot, near the southern tip of Manhattan. In 1892, the federal government opened a huge reception center for steerage passengers on Ellis Island in New York Harbor, near where the Statue of Liberty had been erected in 1886. The statue, a gift from France, celebrated "Liberty Enlightening the World." It became a symbol of the United States as a place of refuge and hope.

Physical Exams In 1892 the federal government required all new immigrants to undergo a physical examination. Those that were found to have a contagious disease such as tuberculosis faced **quarantine,** a time of isolation to prevent the spread of a disease. They could even be deported. People with trachoma, an eye disease common among immigrants, were automatically sent back to their country.

Fiorello La Guardia, who later became mayor of New York City, worked as an interpreter at Ellis Island. "It was harrowing to see families separated," he remembered in the book *The Making of an Insurgent:*

RESOURCE OPTIONS

Teaching Resources

American History Block Scheduling Support Ellis Island: Gateway to America, found in the Expansion, Reconstruction, Immigration folder, includes interdisciplinary lesson suggestions and activities for Geography and History, Primary Sources, Biography, and Literature.

Literature Activity The Statue of Liberty, Units 5–6 folder, p. 44

Media and Technology

Listening to Music CD "Drill, Ye Tarriers"

Color Transparencies Our Multicultural Heritage, C-2

Chinese Immigration, 1864–1894

Number of Immigrants (in thousands) vs. Year (1864, 1870, 1876, 1882, 1888, 1894)

1882 Chinese Exclusion Act

Source: *Historical Statistics of the United States, Colonial Times to 1970*

Japanese Immigration, 1905–1910

Number of Immigrants (in thousands) vs. Year (1905, 1906, 1907, 1908, 1909, 1910)

1907 Restrictions on Japanese immigration

Source: *Historical Statistics of the United States, Colonial Times to 1970*

Interpreting Graphs Anti-Asian pressure groups used both economic and pseudo-scientific justification to limit Asian immigration to the United States. **Diversity** *What effect did the 1882 Chinese Exclusion Act and the 1907 restrictions on Japanese immigration have on immigration?*

AMERICAN VOICES ❝Sometimes, if it was a young child who suffered from trachoma, one of the parents had to return to the native country with the rejected member of the family. When they learned their fate, they were stunned. They . . . had no homes to return to.❞

—*Fiorello La Guardia*

After their physicals, immigrants showed their documents to officials and then collected their baggage. If they had the address of friends or relatives, they headed off to find them. Those who were on their own had a harder time. Criminals hung around ports with fake offers of lodgings and jobs, stealing money and baggage from the unwary.

Where Immigrants Settled Immigrants often sought to live in communities established by previous settlers from their homelands. These communities formed not only in ports of entry, such as New York and Boston, but also in inland cities. In this way, large settlements of Poles and Italians grew in Buffalo, Cleveland, Detroit, and Milwaukee. A diverse group of immigrants found a home in Chicago, a growing port, railroad hub, and industrial center. Some immigrants continued on to mining towns of the West. Only 2 percent went to the South, an area that offered newcomers few jobs.

Once settled, immigrants looked for work. When jobs were scarce, employers (many of whom were immigrants themselves) took advantage of the newcomers. They paid them less than other workers and paid the women even less than the men. Female seamstresses, for example, did the same job as male tailors,

working up to 14 hours a day, 6 days a week, but earning only half as much as the men.

Immigrants from Asia

Most of the immigrants who entered the United States through West Coast ports came from Asia. Chinese and Japanese formed the largest groups by far. Culturally, Asians differed greatly from both Americans and Europeans, and those differences made them targets of suspicion and even hostility. Often as a result, Asian immigrants found that the path to acceptance was especially difficult.

Chinese immigrants brought distinctive styles and customs to the United States.

Chinese Excluded In the mid-1800s, American railroad companies recruited about a quarter of a million Chinese workers. Thousands of them helped build the transcontinental railroad, completed in 1869.

Like the indentured servants of the colonial era, the Chinese had

Graphing the Main Idea

To make sure students understand the main idea of this section, you may wish to use the tree map graphic organizer below.

Tell students that a tree map provides an outline to fill in topics, main ideas, and supporting details. Ask students to use it to outline the immigration experience.

Teaching Tip A template for this graphic organizer can be found in the Color Transparencies, G-3.

Answer to . . .

Comparing Primary Sources Nagy thought assimilation was important; Ribahny felt that his family's culture helped them overcome difficulties.

Main Idea Connections They were victims of racism; they made enemies of unions as they were willing to work for low wages.

COMPARING PRIMARY SOURCES

CULTURAL TIES

Many people held opinions on how immigrants could best adjust to their new lives in the United States. Some thought they should give up their own language and customs as quickly as possible. Others thought they should hold on to their heritage.

Breaking Cultural Ties

"We wanted to be Americans so quickly that we were embarrassed if our parents couldn't speak English. My father was reading a Polish paper. And somebody was supposed to come to the house. I remember sticking it under something. We were that ashamed of being foreign."

—Louise Nagy,
a Polish immigrant, 1913

Preserving Cultural Ties

"We ate the same dishes, spoke the same language, told the same stories, [as in Syria]. . . . To me the colony [neighborhood] was a habitat so much like the one I had left behind in Syria that its home atmosphere enabled me to maintain a firm hold on life in the face of the many difficulties which confronted me in those days."

—Abraham Ribahny,
on his neighborhood in
New York, 1893

ANALYZING VIEWPOINTS **Compare the statements of the two speakers.**

---

to work for their companies until they had paid the cost of their passage and upkeep. Many Chinese immigrants paid their debts, settled down, and began to work in other fields, often side by side with white Americans and European immigrants. Those occupations included mining, farming, fishing, factory work, food preparation, and laundering.

In this way the Chinese contributed to their new country, but that often was not enough to earn the respect of white society. Like many European immigrants, the Chinese tended to live in their own ethnic communities, such as the Chinatown section of San Francisco. Living in such communities was not only more comfortable for them but also safer, for it helped them avoid expressions and acts of hostility from non-Asian neighbors.

American Labor unions fought hard to exclude Chinese immigrants. Because the Chinese accepted low wages, they affected the rates of pay of all workers. The unions main-

**Main Idea
CONNECTIONS**

Why did Chinese immigrants face hostility?

---

tained that if Chinese laborers kept pouring into California, wage rates there would continue to drop.

Other groups claimed the Chinese simply were not worthy of being Americans. Using scientific-sounding but faulty reasoning, anti-Asian movements claimed that Asians were physically and mentally inferior to white Americans. These claims both reflected and helped spread racist attitudes toward Asian immigrants.

Congress responded to the demands of unions and others by passing the **Chinese Exclusion Act** in 1882. The act prohibited Chinese laborers from entering the country. It did not, however, prevent entry by those who had previously established residence or who had family already living in the United States. The act was renewed in 1892 and 1902 and then made permanent. It was not repealed until 1943.

In 1910 the federal government built an immigration center on Angel Island in San Francisco Bay, similar to the center on Ellis Island in New York Harbor. There immigrants underwent a lengthy examination. Besides having to pass medical checks, the Chinese newcomers also had to prove that they should not be excluded.

Japanese Restricted Many of the earliest Japanese to immigrate to the United States came from Hawaii. They had migrated to Hawaii to work on sugar plantations, and when the United States obtained Hawaii in 1898, a number of Japanese saw an opportunity for a better life in America.

By 1920 some 200,000 Japanese had arrived through West Coast ports. Most Japanese settled in the Los Angeles area, and soon they were producing a large percentage of southern California's fruits and vegetables. Mainly involved in private business, the Japanese did not compete with union laborers as the Chinese had. Still, labor unions and the political leaders who supported them fought to stop Japanese immigration.

More than economic motives were at work, for some acts reflected prejudice against Asians generally. In 1906, for example, the San Francisco school board ruled that all Chinese, Japanese, and Korean children should attend a separate school. The Japanese government condemned this **segregation,** or forced separation, claiming it violated an 1894 treaty that gave Japanese citizens the right to enter the

---

 RESOURCE OPTIONS

United States freely. The issue threatened to become an international crisis.

In response, President Theodore Roosevelt reached a compromise with Japanese officials in 1907. Named the **Gentlemen's Agreement** because it was not an official government document, the compromise called on San Francisco to end its school segregation and Japan to stop issuing passports to laborers.

Anti-Japanese feeling, however, did not subside. In 1913 California passed the Webb Alien Land Law, which banned **alien** (noncitizen) Asians from owning farmland.

Immigration from Mexico

In 1902 Congress passed the Newlands National Reclamation Act to promote the irrigation of southwestern lands. Over the next decade, irrigation turned millions of acres of desert into fertile farmland across Texas, Arizona, New Mexico, and California.

The new farmland meant new jobs in the sparsely populated Southwest. Employers hired Mexican laborers to work on farms as well as in mines. Roughly 50,000 Mexicans headed north between 1900 and 1910. The Mexican Revolution, which began in 1910, increased the flow north over the next decade.

When the United States entered World War I in 1917, demand increased sharply for laborers to grow and harvest food and mine the copper, coal, and other vital minerals needed for the war effort. Around a million Mexicans, 10 percent of Mexico's population, came to the United States during this decade.

When the Immigration Restriction Act of 1921 limited immigration from Europe and Asia, labor shortages again drew Mexicans across the border. By 1925 Los Angeles had the largest Spanish-speaking population of any North American city outside of Mexico.

Two Immigrant Portraits

Facts and figures tell only a part of the story of immigration in the United States. The drama behind the figures is best revealed in the accounts of ordinary people, whose lives and experiences reflect the struggles and triumphs of living day to day in a new land.

Sadie Frowne, Polish Immigrant Sadie Frowne's early years in her native Poland were happy. Her mother kept a grocer's shop and worked in the fields with her husband. Sadie

helped out with chores whenever she could. When Sadie was 10, however, her father died.

Unable to support themselves, Sadie and her mother looked to the United States, where they hoped to build a new life. Sadie's aunt, who lived in New York City, collected donations to pay for their passage to America.

In 1898, 13-year-old Sadie and her mother made the 12-day Atlantic crossing:

AMERICAN VOICES "There were hundreds of other people packed in with us, men, women and children, and almost all of them were sick. . . . We thought we should die, but at last the voyage was over, and we came up and saw the beautiful bay and the big woman with the spikes on her head and the lamp that is lighted at night in her hand."

—*Sadie Frowne*

In New York Sadie worked as a live-in servant. Her mother found a job as a garment worker. Tragedy then struck again when Sadie's mother contracted a fatal case of tuberculosis, a disease then raging through the crowded neighborhoods of New York City.

Now she would have to support herself. Sadie landed a new job as a skirt maker, earning $4 for a six-day week. She rented a room with another young woman for $1.50 a week.

By keeping her expenses down, Sadie was now able to set aside a dollar a week for "clothing and pleasure" and another dollar for savings. She went to school at night to learn English. She also worked to improve her sewing skills, found a better job, and moved to a nicer place in Brooklyn.

With constant work, sacrifice, and determination, Sadie was living out the dream of millions of immigrants. It was a dream of simple comforts, modest prosperity, and the chance for a better life.

Take Eto, Japanese Picture Bride Tameji Eto came to the United States from Japan in 1904. After working as a farmhand he became a foreman for the Pacific Coast Railroad Company. He earned enough to lease land for his own farm.

Treasured items from home, such as this stuffed bear and set of spoons, helped provide a link between an immigrant's old life and new.

Answers to
SECTION 2 REVIEW

1. (a) steerage, see p. 467; (b) quarantine, see p. 468; (c) Chinese Exclusion Act, see p. 470; (d) segregation, see p. 470; (e) Gentlemen's Agreement, see p. 471; (f) alien, see p. 471.

2. Most settled in communities established by previous immigrants; many European immigrants settled in the East and Midwest; most Asians settled along the West Coast.

3. European: came through Ellis Island, settled in East Coast cities; Asian: came to West Coast, many worked for railroads, faced racial discrimination; Mexican: people left during Mexican Revolution, hired to work on farms, not limited by immigration restrictions. Common to all three groups: left harsh conditions at home in search of better lives, left family members behind, faced difficulties in new nation.

4. Chinese Exclusion Act, Webb Alien Land Law, Immigration Restriction Act: reflect people's hostility toward immigration, racist attitudes; Ellis Island and Angel Island immigration centers opened: attitude of welcoming immigrants but also regulating who could stay; Statue of Liberty: attitude that all immigrants would be welcomed; Gentlemen's Agreement: reflects attitude of compromise.

5. Sample answer: To pack in as many passengers as possible, thereby making more money than would the same boat without steerage.

6. Letters will vary but should be supported with facts from the section.

Answer to . . .

Viewing History Sample response: making friends, overcoming language barriers.

Japanese picture brides, such as these women in traditional dress, looked with both hope and apprehension to life in a new land with new husbands they had never met. *Culture* *What other social challenges do you think new immigrants faced in the United States?*

the proposal. Clutching Tameji's photograph, her only means of identifying her future husband, she sailed for the United States.

On board ship, Take met other "picture brides," women whose marriages had been arranged through the exchange of photographs across the Pacific Ocean. Like her companions, Take spent the voyage trying to adapt to strange foods and wondering about her future.

After her arrival and a 10-day quarantine for an eye infection, Take finally met Tameji. Luckily, he looked like his picture, "straight and tall with lots of hair," and he also seemed kind. Together they set out for Tameji's land in the frontier town of Grand Arroyo, California.

For Take the frontier life posed a challenge, but one she accepted. She later told one of her eight children that farming the semiarid California land "was not easy, but it was my future as well as [Tameji's], and I wanted to be a part of it. Father never demanded I work so hard. I did it because it was necessary and I wanted to."

Tameji began to think of settling down and starting a family. Because few Japanese women had immigrated to the United States, Tameji's thoughts turned to Take, the sister of one of his school friends back in Japan. He wrote her family to ask permission to marry her.

Nineteen-year-old Take had no memory of Tameji. Yet her parents insisted that she agree to the arranged marriage, and Take accepted

The Etos' hard work paid off, and by 1919 they had enough money to buy their own farm. Because of the Webb Alien Land Law, however, they had to buy land under the name of a white friend. After some difficult years, the farm did well. Take cared for her children and cooked for a farm crew of 40 to 50 men. Finally, after 15 years of hard work, the Etos could afford a journey back to Japan to see their parents and tell them of their success in America.

SECTION 2 REVIEW

Comprehension

1. *Key Terms* Define: (a) steerage; (b) quarantine; (c) Chinese Exclusion Act; (d) segregation; (e) Gentlemen's Agreement; (f) alien.

2. *Summarizing the Main Idea* Where did various groups of immigrants settle once they had entered the United States?

3. *Organizing Information* Create a Venn diagram to compare the experiences of European, Asian, and Mexican immigrants.

Critical Thinking

4. *Analyzing Time Lines* Review the time line at the start of the section. How do the entries reflect varying attitudes toward immigration?

5. *Drawing Conclusions* Why do you think steamships have a steerage area for immigrants?

Writing Activity

6. *Writing a Persuasive Essay* Write a letter that Sadie Frowne or Take Eto might have written to persuade a relative in her former homeland that she did the right thing by coming to the United States.

 RESOURCE OPTIONS

Teaching Resources

 Quiz Units 5–6 folder, p. 36

Student Performance Pack

Guide to the Essentials Chapter 16, Section 2 (English and Spanish)

Media and Technology

Color Transparencies Our Multicultural Heritage, C-11

1871
Great Chicago Fire

1877
Reconstruction ends; segregation begins to rise

1885
Nation's first skyscraper built, in Chicago

1890
Jacob Riis's How the Other Half Lives

1897
First subway opens in Boston

1870 | 1880 | 1890 | 1900

3 The Challenge of the Cities

SECTION PREVIEW

Objectives

1. Explain why people left farms for cities in the late 1800s and early 1900s.
2. Describe some of the new developments that helped cities grow.
3. Describe urban living conditions and the results of city growth.
4. *Key Terms* Define: suburb; tenement; ghetto; restrictive covenant; political machine; graft.

Main Idea

Millions of people moved into the cities, creating new growth and new challenges.

Reading Strategy

Reading for Evidence As you read, find evidence to support the following statement: "The arrival of large numbers of newcomers, from both within and outside the nation, radically changed the face of the nation's cities."

While millions of immigrants from around the world were settling in the cities of the United States, growing numbers of Americans were moving there, too. Between 1880 and 1920, 11 million Americans left behind the economic hardship of their farms and headed for the opportunities of the cities. This migration within the country, combined with the new immigration, brought explosive growth to the nation's urban centers.

From Farms to Cities

Women and men alike took part in the migration from rural to urban America. As factories produced more of the goods that farm women had once made, the need for women's labor on farms declined. In addition, as new machines replaced manual labor on many farms, the need for male farmhands shrank. The result was a striking shift in the nation's population. Between 1880 and 1910, the percentage of the nation's population living on farms fell from 72 to 54 percent.

Many African Americans took part in this internal migration. In 1870 fewer than a half million of the nation's 5 million African Americans

lived outside the South. But after Reconstruction ended in 1877, segregation and acts of racial violence against African Americans increased. By 1890, partly as a result of these pressures, another 150,000 black southerners had left the South, and many rural African Americans had moved into nearby cities. Then, in the 1910s, the boll weevil destroyed cotton crops and floods ruined Alabama and Mississippi farmlands. These disasters drove several hundred thousand more African Americans out of the South, mostly to northern cities.

Cities like Chicago, pictured on this postcard, grew upward and outward in the late 1800s.

How Cities Grew

The arrival of large numbers of newcomers, from both within and outside the nation, radically changed the face of the nation's cities. Between 1865 and 1900 many features of modern city life, both good and bad, first appeared—from subways and skyscrapers to smog and slums.

RESOURCE OPTIONS

Teaching Resources

📁 **Reproducible Lesson Plan** Lesson Plans folder, p. 99

📁 **Big Idea Graphic Organizer** Big Idea Graphic Organizer folder, p. 71

📁 **Guided Reading and Review** Units 5–6 folder, p. 37

📁 **Primary Source Activity** New York Gangs, Learning with Documents folder, p. 22

Media and Technology

 AmericanHeritage® CD-ROM

Time Tour Reshaping the Nation: A Diverse Nation

SECTION 3

The Challenge of the Cities

Objectives

You may wish to call students' attention to the objectives in the Section Preview. The objectives are reflected in the main headings of the section.

Bellringer

Ask students to think about the expression "bright lights, big city." Then have them list the advantages and disadvantages of city life.

Reading Strategy

Reading for Evidence Refer to the Reading Strategy in the Section Preview. You may wish to ask students to list the evidence they find to support the statement.

LESSON PLAN

Connecting to the Main Idea

1. **Focus** Tell students that immigrants and migrants flocked to the nation's cities during the Gilded Age. Ask how the nation's cities changed as a result of these dramatic increases in population.
2. **Instruct** Remind students that the Industrial Revolution greatly affected how Americans lived. Ask what role it played in the human migration from farm to city. Discuss new developments, such as motorized transportation, that helped cities grow. Ask why skyscrapers were built.

Tell students that between the Civil War and 1900, many features of modern city life first appeared—skyscrapers, noise, traffic, slums, air pollution, and sanitation and health problems. Ask how the increasing population contributed.
3. **Close** Immigrants and migrants poured into the rapidly changing cities. Living conditions for the poor deteriorated, and political bosses took control in many cities. The next section describes the efforts of reformers to improve American cities and life.

Two Fires On the evening of October 7, Chicago firemen encountered the latest and biggest in a series of fires the city had seen during an unusually dry summer and fall. The next evening, around a quarter of nine, a fresh load of hay caught on fire in Catherine and Patrick O'Leary's barn at the corner of DeKoven and Jefferson streets. A tale sprang up almost instantly that one of their milk cows had kicked over a lantern, but there is no evidence for this; other possible explanations include arson, spontaneous combustion, and a discarded cigar or cigarette. Whatever the cause, high winds swiftly spread the flames, and the fire department, weary from the previous night's marathon effort, was slow to respond. The first company to reach the site attacked the wrong end of the fire, while the second one found its steam pumper broken and without fuel. By the time the whole department could be mobilized, the blaze was out of control. A couple of hours later a gasworks exploded, intensifying the conflagration, and then at 7:00 a.m. hydrants ran dry when the city waterworks caught fire. From then on, all anyone could do was pray for rain. Source: Frederic D. Schwarz, "The Time Machine," *American Heritage* magazine, October 1996.

 Growing cities lured migrants from within the United States as people left rural areas to find work. This woman found a job as a porter in a subway, itself a product of urban expansion. *Geography* How did transportation change city settlement patterns?

Main Idea CONNECTIONS

In what ways did cities grow in the late 1800s, and why?

Before the Civil War, cities were small in area, rarely extending more than 3 or 4 miles across. Most people lived near their workplace, and they walked wherever they had to go. The introduction of public, horse-drawn carriages that traveled on rails began to change this pattern. Introduced in 1832 in New York City, they allowed people who could afford the fares to move outside the cities. Those people made their homes in the **suburbs,** or residential communities surrounding the cities.

Later in the 1800s, motorized methods of transportation made commuting much easier and speeded suburban growth. The first elevated trains, built in 1868 in New York, allowed commuters to bypass the congested streets. Cable cars, introduced in San Francisco in 1873, allowed quick access to the city's steep hills. Electric trolleys, first used in Richmond, Virginia, in 1888, replaced horse-drawn cars and reached even farther into the suburbs. Subway trains first appeared in Boston in 1897. Finally, the automobile, invented in 1893 and mass-produced beginning in the 1910s, guaranteed that expansion into the suburbs would continue.

Cities grew upward as well as outward. Before the Civil War, buildings stood no more than five stories high. Yet as urban space became scarce, buildings were made taller and taller. To build these mammoth structures, engineers relied on the strength of Bessemer steel girders.

To reach the upper floors, people relied on the speed and efficiency of elevators. In 1853 Elisha Graves Otis, an American, invented a safety device that made passenger elevators possible. The first one went into operation four years later. The first skyscraper, Chicago's Home Insurance Company Building, appeared in 1885. Ten stories tall, it was built with a framework of iron and steel and had four passenger elevators.

As cities expanded, specialized areas emerged within them. Banks, financial offices, law firms, and government offices located in one central area. Retail shops and department stores located in another. Industrial, wholesale, and warehouse districts formed a ring around the center of the city.

Urban Living Conditions

Some urban workers moved into housing built especially for them by mill and factory owners. The rest found apartments wherever they could. Many middle-class residents who moved to the suburbs left empty buildings behind. Owners converted these buildings into multi-family units for workers and their families.

Speculators also built many **tenements,** low-cost apartment buildings designed to house as many families as the owner could pack in. A group of dirty, run-down tenements could transform an area into a slum.

Conditions in the Slums Before long, because of poverty, overcrowding, and neglect, the old residential neighborhoods of cities gradually declined. Trees and grass disappeared beneath the new, cheaply built tenements. Hundreds of people were crammed into spaces meant for a few families. Soot from coal-fired steam engines and boilers made the air seem dark and foul even in daylight. Open sewers attracted rats and other disease-spreading vermin.

In 1905 journalist Eleanor McMain quoted a university student who described a block of tenements in the Italian district of New Orleans as "death traps, closely built, jammed together, with no side openings. Twenty-five per cent of the yard space is damp and gloomy. . . . Where the houses are three or more rooms in depth, the middle ones are dark, without outside ventilator. . . . There is no fire protection whatever."

Fire was a constant danger in cities. With tenement buildings so closely packed together, even a small fire could quickly consume a neighborhood. Once a fire started, it leaped easily from roof to roof. As a result, most large cities had major fires during this period.

Chicago experienced one of the most devastating: the Great Chicago Fire of 1871. Nobody knows for sure what started it, but before it was over, 18,000 buildings had burned, leaving some 250 people dead and 100,000 homeless.

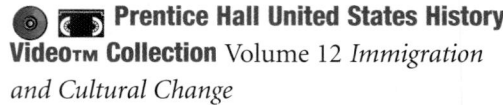
RESOURCE OPTIONS

Media and Technology

AmericanHeritage® CD-ROM

Explorer Activity 20 In the City, CD-ROM Guidebook, pp. 59–60, helps students create an illustrated chart about American city life in the late 1800s and early 1900s.

Prentice Hall United States History Video™ Collection Volume 12 *Immigration and Cultural Change*

Property damage estimates reached $200 million, the equivalent of $2 billion today. A similar fire in Boston the following year caused the equivalent of nearly $1 billion damage.

Contagious diseases, including cholera, malaria, tuberculosis, diphtheria, and typhoid, thrived in crowded tenement conditions. Epidemics, such as the yellow fever that swept through Memphis, Tennessee, in the late 1870s and through New Orleans, Louisiana, in the early 1900s, took thousands of lives. Children were especially vulnerable to disease. In New York City, in one district of tenements, 6 out of 10 babies died before their first birthday.

Ghettos Some urban neighborhoods became **ghettos,** areas in which one ethnic or racial group dominated. Many newly arrived immigrants chose to live near others of their ethnic group because of the comfort of familiar language and traditions. These ethnic communities strongly reflected the culture of the homeland. In 1904 Emily Dinwiddie, a tenement-house inspector, wrote a joyful description of Philadelphia's "Little Italy:"

AMERICAN VOICES "The black-eyed children rolling and tumbling together, the gaily colored dresses of the women and the crowds of street vendors all give the neighborhood a wholly foreign appearance."

—*Emily Dinwiddie*

Dinwiddie's delight with the neighborhood did not lessen her distress at the slum conditions and poverty that she saw.

Other ghettos formed when ethnic groups isolated themselves, often because of threats from whites. San Francisco's Chinatown had well-known street boundaries: "From Kearny to Powell, and from California to Broadway," recalled one resident. "If you ever passed them and went out there, the white kids would throw stones at you."

Still other urban ghettos resulted from **restrictive covenants.** These were agreements among homeowners not to sell real estate to certain groups of people. Covenants often prevented African Americans, Mexicans, Asian Americans, and Jews from buying land or houses in the better neighborhoods.

Immigrant Neighborhoods in Chicago, 1900

German
Irish
Italian
Czechoslovak
Scandinavian
Polish
Other East Europeans

Hungarian
NORTH AVE.
ELSTON
CLYBOURN AVE.
LINCOLN AVE.
CLARK ST.
MILWAUKEE AVE.
N. Branch
Jewish
CHICAGO AVE.
Ukrainian
MADISON AVE.
CRAWFORD
KEDZIE
WESTERN
ASHLAND
OGDEN AVE.
Jewish
Greek
HALSTED
STATE ST.
Chicago R.
12TH ST.
BLUE IS. AVE.
22ND ST.
Jewish
Chicago R.
S. Branch
ARCHER AVE.
Lake Michigan

N W E S

0 1/2 1 Mile
0 1/2 1 Kilometer

Chicago
Lake Michigan
Illinois

MAP Skills As this map of Chicago shows, immigrants often settled in communities that had been established by others from their homeland, creating ethnic neighborhoods within cities. *Place* What advantages and disadvantages might ethnic neighborhoods have offered their residents?

RESOURCE OPTIONS

Teaching Resources

American History Block Scheduling Support Ellis Island: Gateway to America, found in the Expansion, Reconstruction, Immigration folder, includes interdisciplinary lesson suggestions and activities for Geography and History, Primary Sources, Biography, and Literature.

Media and Technology

Listening to Literature Bernard Malamud, "The First Seven Years"

Jacob Riis

AMERICAN BIOGRAPHY

**Jacob Riis
(1849–1914)**

Some reformers worked to improve the lives of the urban poor. One was Jacob Riis. A native of Denmark, Riis had boarded a steamship bound for America in 1870 at the age of 21 and settled in New York City. There he personally experienced the dreadful conditions in which many new Americans lived.

Riis held various jobs before he landed a position as a police reporter in 1873. Riis honed his writing skills while covering New York's Lower East Side, a tenement slum bursting with immigrant families. He worked for the New York *Tribune* from 1877 to 1888 and the New York *Evening Sun* from 1888 to 1899.

While still a reporter at the *Sun,* Riis began writing books about what he had seen. In *How the Other Half Lives,* published in 1890, Riis exposed the horrors of tenement life to a shocked American public. Hoping to generate public support for reform of the tenement "system," he painted a bleak picture of New York's future:

AMERICAN VOICES 66Today three-fourths of [New York's] people live in the tenements. . . . We know now that there is no way out; that the 'system' that was the evil offspring of public neglect and private greed has come to stay, a storm-centre forever of our civilization. Nothing is left but to make the best of a bad bargain.99

—*Jacob Riis,* How the Other Half Lives, *1890*

In order to document his reporting, Riis mastered the new technology of flash photography. Drawings based on those photographs appeared in his books, and he showed the actual photographs of overcrowded rooms and run-down buildings in his lectures on the plight of immigrants. As a result of Riis's work, New York State passed the nation's first meaningful laws to improve tenements. ■

The Results of City Growth

Some city residents could avoid urban problems simply by leaving the cities. The middle and upper classes began moving to the suburbs in the late 1800s. As a result, the gap between the well-to-do and the poor widened.

A few cities preserved areas for the most wealthy residents near the city center. These areas include Boston's Beacon Hill, Chicago's Gold Coast, and San Francisco's Nob Hill. Often, people living in these neighborhoods also owned country estates and were quite isolated from the nearby poverty.

Political Divisions Rapid urban growth put pressure on city officials to improve police and fire protection, transportation systems, sewage disposal, electrical and water service, and health care. To deliver these services, cities raised taxes and set up offices to deal with people's needs.

Increased revenue and responsibilities gave city governments more power. Competition among groups for control of city government grew more intense. Some groups represented the remaining middle and upper classes. Others represented new immigrants and workers.

The Rise of Political Bosses Out of these clashing interests, the **political machine** was born. This was an unofficial city organization

VIEWING HISTORY

This photograph by Jacob Riis shows the kind of cramped, unsafe apartments in which many immigrants were forced to live. *Government How did city governments address the problems of urban living conditions?*

---

designed to keep a particular party or group in power and usually headed by a single, powerful "boss." Sometimes the boss held public office. More often he handpicked others to run for office and then helped them win.

Political machines worked through the exchange of favors. Machines used an army of ward leaders, each of whom managed a city district, to hand out city jobs and contracts to residents of their ward and do other favors for them. In return, those residents supported the machine's candidates on election day. Similarly, individuals or companies wanting a favor from the city could get it by first paying some money to the machine. **Graft,** or the use of one's job to gain profit, was a major source of income for the machines.

Many people blamed the success of political machines on the large number of urban immigrants. They charged that immigrants, poorly educated and with little experience in democracy, were being taken advantage of by corrupt politicians. Immigrants tended to support political machines, because they helped poor people at a time when neither government nor private industry would.

Cincinnati's George B. Cox, a former saloon owner, was an unusual example of a fairly honest political boss. A Republican, in 1879 he won election to the city council. In true machine fashion he used this post to guarantee election victories and business contracts for the party faithful. But he also worked with local reformers to improve the quality of police officers and city services.

Perhaps the most notorious boss was William Marcy Tweed. "Boss" Tweed controlled Tammany Hall, the political club that ran New York City's Democratic party. Once Tweed and his pals gained access to the city treasury in 1870, they used various illegal methods to plunder it, including padding bills and submitting false receipts.† Tweed also used his power to persuade businesses to pay him for nonexistent services. Through countless such instances of fraud and graft, the Tweed ring amassed many millions of dollars.

Cartoonist Thomas Nast illustrated "The 'Brains'" of Boss Tweed in 1871.

The brilliant political cartoons of German immigrant Thomas Nast helped bring Tweed down by exposing his methods to the public. Convicted of crimes in 1873, Tweed eventually died in jail. Under new leaders, however, Tammany Hall dominated New York politics for another half century.

---

† Urban disasters, such as the great fires in Chicago and Boston, pointed out the need for better city government. Galveston, Texas, demolished by a hurricane in 1900, completely restructured its government under a commission to run the major municipal agencies. Other cities hired professional managers.

SECTION 3 REVIEW

Comprehension

1. *Key Terms* Define: (a) suburb; (b) tenement; (c) ghetto; (d) restrictive covenant; (e) political machine; (f) graft.

2. *Summarizing the Main Idea* What were living conditions like for new immigrants in cities?

3. *Organizing Information* Make a graphic organizer that shows the different reasons that people moved from farms to cities.

Critical Thinking

4. *Analyzing Time Lines* Review the time line at the start of the section. In 1890 Jacob Riis published his book *How the Other Half Lives.* Which other event in the time line most directly relates to the theme of Riis's book? Explain.

5. *Demonstrating Reasoned Judgment* Do you think that the political machine helped or hurt cities overall? Explain.

Writing Activity

6. *Writing an Expository Essay* Describe the inventions and developments that helped cities grow both outward and upward.

▶ RESOURCE OPTIONS

Teaching Resources

 Quiz Units 5–6 folder, p. 38

Biography Thomas Nast, Units 5–6 folder, p. 41

Student Performance Pack

 Guide to the Essentials Chapter 16, Section 3 (English and Spanish)

Media and Technology

 Color Transparencies Cause and Effect, F-3

Right column teaching material.

Graphing the Main Idea

To make sure students understand the main idea of this section, you may wish to use the multiflow graphic organizer below.

Tell students that a multiflow graphic organizer shows causes and effects. Ask students to use it to show the causes and effects of the growth of cities in the late 1800s and early 1900s.

Teaching Tip A template for this graphic organizer can be found in the Color Transparencies, G-5.

Answers to
SECTION 3 REVIEW

1. (a) suburb, see p. 474; (b) tenement, see p. 474; (c) ghetto, see p. 475; (d) restrictive covenant, see p. 475; (e) political machine, see p. 476; (f) graft, see p. 477.

2. There was often overcrowding, disease, poor housing and sanitation, and threat of fire.

3. Reasons include: declining need for women's labor on farms drew them to work in cities; new machinery lessened need for farmhands; black southerners fled poverty in rural South for the cities.

4. Sample answer: Great Chicago Fire, because threat of fire was one of the poor conditions facing tenement families that concerned Riis.

5. Sample answer: They hurt the cities because by skimming millions of dollars from the cities' income, they limited city services, affecting rich and poor residents alike.

6. Essays will vary but should be supported with facts from the section.

Reading Tables and Analyzing Statistics

SKILLS FOR LIFE

Graphs and Charts

Reading Tables and Analyzing Statistics

Focus Analyze statistics to see what they show, what they distort, and what they hide.

Instruct After students have worked through the excercises in the activity, ask them to change the chart in this way: (1) Add the figures for immigrants from central Europe, eastern Europe, and southern Europe, and head the new column New Immigrants. (2) Change the heading Northwestern Europe to Old Immigrants. Ask students if the focus of the chart changed. Does the chart give a valid representation of old and new immigration?

Extend See the Skills for Life Activity in the Resource Options below.

Answers

1. (a) Estimated Number of Immigrants to the United States, by Region, 1871–1920. (b) Five. (c) *Historical Statistics of the United States.* (d) Yes, because the source is reliable.

2. (a) 65,727 (b) Largest: northwestern Europe; smallest: Africa.

3. (a) Central Europe. (b) 1881–1890 (c) The actual number of immigrants from the Americas increased the most —by 422,019—when comparing 1871 to 1920; but proportionally, Africa had the largest increase with a more than tenfold growth in immigrants.

4. When the U.S. unemployment rate was high, the immigration rate was relatively low. When unemployment was low, the immigration rate increased dramatically. A low unemployment rate may have signaled the availability of jobs in the United States and attracted immigrants.

TEST FOR SUCCESS

Sample answer: changes in numbers of immigrants from different regions.

Statistical tables present large amounts of numerical data clearly and concisely. The patterns suggested by statistics must be carefully analyzed, however, and their sources evaluated for reliability. Statistics should be verified by other historical evidence. Use the following steps to read and interpret the data below.

1. *Determine what type of information is presented and decide whether the source is reliable.* The title of the table and the labels for the rows and columns tell you what information is presented. The source is usually found below the table. (a) What is the table's title? (b) How many decades are covered? (c) What is the source of the statistics in the table? (d) Can the data be used as historical evidence?

2. *Read the information in the table.* Note that the table provides the total number of immigrants for each region for a given five-year period. (a) Between 1871 and 1875, how many immigrants came from Asia? (b) Between 1881 and 1885, which region provided the largest number of immigrants? The smallest?

3. *Find relationships among the statistics.* You can use the data in this table to compare the immigrant populations from different regions or to trace changes in one region's immigration pattern over time. (a) Which region had the largest total number of immigrants between 1871 and 1920? (b) During which decade did the region called The Americas show the sharpest drop in number of immigrants? (c) Which region in the table showed the largest increase in number of immigrants from 1871 to 1920?

4. *Use the data in the table to draw conclusions.* Between 1891 and 1900 the unemployment rate in the United States averaged 10.5 percent. Between 1901 and 1910, it averaged 4.5 percent. Using the data in the table, what conclusions can you draw about the relationship between the unemployment rate and the immigration rate for those time periods?

TEST FOR SUCCESS

Imagine that you are preparing a report on immigration during this period. What kinds of information would you look for in the table to make your report more interesting?

Estimated Number of Immigrants to the United States, by Region, 1871–1920								
	North-western Europe	Central Europe	Eastern Europe	Southern Europe	Asia [1]	The Americas [2]	Africa	Oceania
1871–1875	858,325	549,610	15,580	37,070	65,727	193,354	205	6,312
1876–1880	493,866	254,511	24,052	39,248	58,096	210,690	153	4,602
1881–1885	1,193,819	1,128,528	63,443	120,297	60,432	403,977	331	4,406
1886–1890	1,131,844	729,967	157,749	211,399	7,948	22,990	526	8,168
1891–1895	745,433	762,216	251,405	314,625	19,255	14,734	163	2,215
1896–1900	392,907	432,363	270,421	389,608	51,981	24,238	187	1,750
1901–1905	761,527	1,121,234	711,546	1,050,721	115,941	63,774	1,829	6,134
1906–1910	807,020	1,365,530	1,058,024	1,260,424	127,626	298,114	5,539	6,890
1911–1915	652,189	1,027,138	978,931	1,137,539	123,719	528,098	5,847	6,126
1916–1920	201,304	23,276	33,547	322,640	68,840	615,373	2,596	7,301

[1] No record of immigration from Korea prior to 1948. [2] No record of immigration from Mexico for 1886 to 1893.
Source: *Historical Statistics of the United States*

RESOURCE OPTIONS

Teaching Resources

Skills for Life Activity Units 5–6 folder, p. 45, helps students find information and identify relationships in tables of data.

| 1869
Prohibition
party
founded | 1874
Woman's Christian
Temperance Union
founded | 1882
New York Charity
Organization
Society formed | 1889
Hull House
founded | 1893
Anti-Saloon
League
founded | 1894
Immigration
Restriction
League formed |

1865   **1875**   **1885**   **1895**

4 Ideas for Reform

SECTION PREVIEW

Objectives

1 Describe the efforts in the late 1800s to control immigration and personal behavior.
2 Explain how different movements helped the needy.
3 *Key Terms* Define: nativism; temperance movement; prohibition; vice; social gospel movement; settlement house.

Main Idea

A variety of groups worked to improve social, economic, and political conditions in the cities.

Reading Strategy

Reinforcing Key Ideas Write down these headings: *Controlling Immigrants* and *Helping the Needy*. As you read, list under the correct heading strategies used to reform cities.

In 1890 New York City had as many Italians as the city of Naples, Italy, and as many Germans as Hamburg, Germany. It had twice as many Irish as Dublin, Ireland, and twice as many Jews as Warsaw, Poland. Other cities around the country also attracted large numbers of immigrants. The many Americans migrating from the countryside boosted urban populations further. This steady stream of people to the cities brought serious problems that needed solutions.

Controlling Immigration and Behavior

Many Americans linked all the problems of the cities to the new immigrants. By controlling immigrants, they hoped to restore what they believed was a past of purity and virtue. Groups were formed to pursue this goal. Some sought to keep immigrants out, while others wanted to control their behavior.

Nativism In the 1850s the Know-Nothing party had gained many followers by vowing to restrict immigration. Thirty years later this policy of **nativism,** or favoring native-born

Americans over immigrants, reappeared. The rise of immigrants to positions of power in the cities helped provoke this new wave of antiforeign bias. Passage of the Chinese Exclusion Act in 1882 showed how politically effective the new nativists were.

Nativists did not oppose only Asian immigration. The American Protective Association, a nativist group founded in 1887, also targeted immigrants in general. It called for the teaching of only American culture and the English language in schools and demanded tighter rules on citizenship and employment of aliens.

Nativists won a victory in 1885, when Congress repealed the Contract Labor Act. Passed in 1864, the law had allowed employers to recruit foreign laborers. Even after the law's repeal, however, employers often illegally brought in foreign workers to replace striking

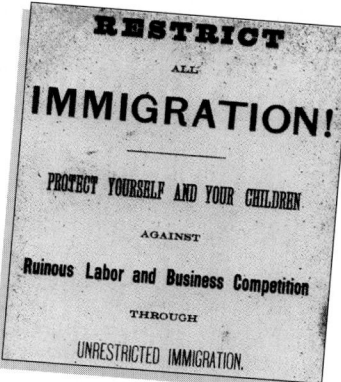

This 1885 brochure reflects the fear that hiring immigrants would lower wages.

▶ RESOURCE OPTIONS

Teaching Resources

 Reproducible Lesson Plan Lesson Plans folder, p. 100

 Big Idea Graphic Organizer Big Idea Graphic Organizer folder, p. 72

Guided Reading and Review Units 5–6 folder, p. 39

 Nystrom *Atlas of Our Country* The Third Wave of Immigration, pp. 30–31

Media and Technology

 AmericanHeritage® **CD-ROM**

Time Tour A New Role in the World: Progressives and Reformers

---

Ideas for Reform

Objectives

You may wish to call students' attention to the objectives in the Section Preview. The objectives are reflected in the main headings of the section.

Bellringer

Ask students to list what they consider to be the most effective ways to help needy people. Ask them to consider the pros and cons of each.

Reading Strategy

Reinforcing Key Ideas Refer to the Reading Strategy in the Section Preview. You may wish to model the headings of the chart on the chalkboard. Have students use their charts to review section content.

LESSON PLAN
Connecting to the Main Idea

1. Focus Point out that the rapid growth of the nation's cities led to many urban problems. Reformers worked to improve social, economic, and political conditions in the cities. How successful were they?

2. Instruct Discuss the events and trends that made some Americans wary of immigration. Examples include the assassination of President McKinley, corruption in city governments, and poor conditions in slums. How did groups like nativists and the temperance movement try to control immigration and personal behavior?

Have students compare reformers who tried to outlaw certain behaviors with those who developed a "helping" approach. Which group more successfully achieved its goals?

3. Close Shocked by the terrible conditions in the nation's cities, reformers took various approaches to improving urban conditions, depending on their ideas about what caused the problems.

BACKGROUND

Recent Scholarship

Were settlement movement founders altruists who respected the cultural pluralism of immigrant communities? Or were they "social controllers" trying to check the chaos of a rapidly urbanizing society and bent on Americanization? Solely focusing on the nationally important settlement houses can be misleading, suggests Ruth Crocker in *Social Work and Social Order: The Settlement Movement in Two Industrial Cities, 1889–1930.* Crocker looks at "second-tier" settlements, notably those founded by religious groups in Indiana. By highlighting the evangelical side of the movement and the support it received from the business community, she reveals a conservatism that historians often do not discuss.

The caption on this cartoon reads "Uncle Sam is a man of strong features." *Diversity What does the cartoon suggest about the artist's view of immigration?*

employees. Such actions only heightened nativist feelings among workers.

There were nativists among the wealthy as well. The Immigration Restriction League was organized in 1894 by some recent graduates of Harvard College. The League hoped to exclude immigrants considered unfit by forcing them to pass literacy tests. Its main targets were immigrants from southern and eastern Europe, whose cultures differed greatly from those of League members.

Main Idea
CONNECTIONS

How did some Americans want to change the customs of immigrants?

Prohibition Like nativism, another movement begun before the Civil War saw a revival later in the 1800s: the **temperance movement,** an organized campaign to eliminate alcohol consumption. Three groups dominated the new temperance movement: the Prohibition party, founded in 1869, the Woman's Christian Temperance Union, founded in 1874, and the Anti-Saloon League, founded in 1893. These groups opposed drinking on the grounds that it led to personal tragedies. They supported **prohibition,** a ban on the manufacture and sale of alcoholic beverages.

Prohibition groups also opposed drinking because of what they saw as the links among saloons, immigrants, and political bosses. Immigrant men often used saloons as social clubs, where they could relax and also pick up information about jobs. Prohibitionists believed that saloons undermined public morals. Some prohibitionists even claimed that saloons formed the center of a movement to take over the United States.

"Foreign control or conquest is rapidly making us un-Christian, with immorality throned in power," one prohibitionist wrote in 1908. Had foreigners used "armies and fleets," he declared, they could not have achieved greater control.

Purity Crusaders As cities grew, drugs, gambling, prostitution, and other forms of vice became big business. **Vice** (immoral or corrupt behavior) was not unique to the cities. But large urban populations made vice highly visible and very profitable. Then as now, many residents fought to rid their communities of unwholesome and illegal activities.

"Purity crusaders" led the way. In 1873 Anthony Comstock founded the New York Society for the Suppression of Vice. The following year he won passage of a law that prohibited sending obscene materials through the United States mail. Material deemed obscene included descriptions of methods to prevent unwanted pregnancy. For decades the Comstock Law, as it came to be known, slowed the distribution of information about birth control.

Other purity crusaders attacked urban political machines, saying that machine-controlled police forces profited from vice. Police were known to demand payment from gamblers, for example, in return for ignoring illegal activities.

On occasion, purity crusaders joined forces with other reformers to run for public office. By campaigning on an anti-vice platform, some succeeded in throwing machine candidates out of office. Usually the political machines regained power in later elections by mocking the self-righteous tone of many purists and by arguing that morality was a personal issue.

▶ RESOURCE OPTIONS

Teaching Resources

American History Block Scheduling Support Ellis Island: Gateway to America, found in the Expansion, Reconstruction, Immigration folder, includes interdisciplinary lesson suggestions and activities for Geography and History, Primary Sources, Biography, and Literature.

Answer to . . .

Viewing History That the many immigrant groups give the nation strength and character.
Main Idea Connections By controlling their behavior and imposing their own values on them.

Helping the Needy

Another group of reformers, moved by social conscience or religious idealism, preferred to improve society by helping the needy. They argued that prosperous Americans should fight poverty and improve unwholesome social conditions in cities.

The Charity Organization Movement In 1882 Josephine Shaw Lowell founded the New York Charity Organization Society (COS). The COS tried to make charity a scientific enterprise. Members kept detailed files on those who received help. In this way COS leaders could more easily determine how to serve their clients. Yet keeping detailed files also allowed COS leaders to distinguish between the poor whom they considered worthy of help and those whom they deemed unworthy. This attitude sometimes led to unkind treatment of the needy.

Some charity reformers interfered in the lives of immigrants. One clergyman who worked in a southern Italian neighborhood claimed that social workers burst into homes of immigrant women. There they "upset the usual routine of their lives, opening windows, undressing children, giving orders not to eat this and that, not to wrap babies in swaddling clothes."

Many COS members wanted immigrants to adopt American, middle-class standards of child-raising, cooking, and cleaning. They did not care how strange these customs seemed to people with different cultural backgrounds. This disturbed some immigrants, but others were grateful for the advice and assistance.

The Social Gospel Movement In the 1880s and 1890s, urban churches began to provide social services for the poor who now surrounded them. They also tried to aim prohibition and purity campaigns in new directions. Instead of blaming immigrants for drinking, gambling, and other behaviors, the churches sought to treat the misfortunes that drove people into such activities.

Soon a social reform movement developed within religious institutions. Called the **social gospel movement,** it sought to apply the gospel (teachings) of Jesus directly to society and focused on the gospel ideals of charity and justice, especially by seeking labor reforms. In 1908, followers of such views formed the Federal Council of the Churches of Christ. This organization supported improved living conditions and a larger share in the national

Some reformers focused their efforts on helping immigrants adjust to life in the United States. This immigrant is learning English. *Culture* **What else is she learning?**

wealth for all workers. Other religious organizations, including some Jewish synagogues, adapted the social gospel ideal for themselves.

The Settlement Movement Thousands of young, educated women and men put the social gospel into practice in an innovative reform program called the settlement movement. These young reformers would move into a house in the midst of a poor neighborhood. From this **settlement house,** a kind of community center, they offered social services.

The settlement movement had begun in Britain. Its founders believed that simply giving money to the poor never really helped them. In order to find out what would be most helpful, social workers had to live in poor neighborhoods. There they could witness the effects of poverty firsthand.

In 1889, inspired by the British settlement movement, Jane Addams and Ellen Gates Starr bought the rundown Charles Hull mansion in Chicago. They repaired it and opened its doors to their immigrant neighbors. At first, Starr and Addams simply wanted to get to know them, offering help when needed. Soon they began anticipating and responding to the needs of the community as a whole.

Over the decades that followed, Addams and Starr turned Hull House into a center of community activity. At Hull House, neighbors

Answers to
SECTION 4 REVIEW

1. (a) nativism, see p. 479; (b) temperance movement, see p. 480; (c) prohibition, see p. 480; (d) vice, see p. 480; (e) social gospel movement, see p. 481; (f) settlement house, see p. 481.

2. Prohibition groups and purity crusaders focused on banning alcohol and crime. The other groups focused on improving society by helping the needy.

3. Sample entry: Corrupt political and personal behavior—Prohibition groups want to ban alcohol; purity crusaders attack political machines and ban obscene materials.

4. All of these groups targeted alcohol as society's greatest ill.

5. Sample answer: Less wealthy nativists might have argued to restrict immigration so they wouldn't have to compete for jobs.

6. Letters will vary but should be supported with facts from the text.

Reformers offered help to newcomers by watching over their children while they worked. *Economics* *What other services did settlement houses offer?*

could attend cultural events, take classes, or display exhibits of crafts from their home countries. The settlement set up child-care centers, playgrounds, clubs and summer camps for boys and girls; employment and legal-aid bureaus; and health-care clinics. It also launched investigations of city economic, political, and social conditions. These actions laid the foundation for many later reforms.

Settlement houses like Hull House sprang up across the country. Each was unique. The Henry Street Settlement, founded by Lillian Wald on New York's Lower East Side, was originally a nurses' settlement. Wald's plan was to develop a system to offer home care to the poor. Its programs soon expanded to resemble many of those at Hull House. Missionaries, too, founded settlement houses, in part to gain converts but also to apply the social gospel in practical ways.

By 1910 there were more than 400 settlement houses. Most were supported by donations and staffed by volunteers or people willing to work for low wages and free room and board. Hundreds of college graduates, especially women excluded from other professions, became settlement workers. Except for leaders, such as Addams and Wald, most workers spent only a few years in these jobs. Many moved on to professional careers in social work, education, or government.

They moved on, but few ever forgot their settlement experience. "I don't know that my attitude changed," wrote one former settlement worker, "but my point of view certainly did, or perhaps it would be more true to say that now I have several points of view." By helping its workers see social issues in new ways, the settlement houses energized the reform movement while improving the lives of the urban poor.

SECTION 4 REVIEW

Comprehension

1. *Key Terms* Define: (a) nativism; (b) temperance movement; (c) prohibition; (d) vice; (e) social gospel movement; (f) settlement house.

2. *Summarizing the Main Idea* How did Prohibition groups and purity crusaders differ from charity, social gospel, and settlement movements?

3. *Organizing Information* Create a two-column chart listing the key urban problems and the solutions offered by various reform groups.

Critical Thinking

4. *Analyzing Time Lines* Review the time line at the start of the section. How are the entries for 1869, 1874, and 1893 related?

5. *Demonstrating Reasoned Judgment* How might the anti-immigrant arguments of wealthy nativists have differed from those of less-wealthy nativists?

Writing Activity

6. *Writing a Persuasive Essay* Write a letter to the editor (around 1910) about the need for government or private funding to set up a settlement house. Show why such programs help strengthen communities.

Answer to . . .

Viewing History Cultural events, diversions for children, employment and legal-aid bureaus, health-care clinics.

482 Chapter 16 • Section 4

RESOURCE OPTIONS

Teaching Resources

📁 **Quiz** Units 5–6 folder, p. 40

📁 **Chapter Tests Forms A and B** Chapter Test folder

Student Performance Pack

⭐ **Guide to the Essentials** Chapter 16, Section 4 (English and Spanish)

Standardized Test Preparation Handbook

Media and Technology

🎧 **Guided Reading Audiotapes** Chapter 16 Summary (English and Spanish)
Student Edition on Audiotape Chapter 16

💿 **Test Bank CD-ROM; Interactive Student Tutorial CD-ROM** Chapter Test

Immigration Continues Today

Since the great surge of immigration in the late 1800s and early 1900s, millions of people from dozens of nations have moved to the United States.

Family of immigrants arriving at Ellis Island in 1905

Look around your classroom. What ethnic and racial backgrounds are reflected in the faces of your classmates? Listen to conversations on the streets of a large city. You may hear people speaking languages such as Spanish, Vietnamese, French, Russian, and Japanese.

The United States has always benefited from the intelligence and hard work of its immigrants. Yet some Americans have felt threatened by the continued arrival of immigrants and have called for measures to restrict immigration.

The Impact Today

More than 20 million people came to the United States between 1890 and 1920. Some Americans viewed this surge of immigration as a threat to their way of life. Most Americans at that time were of northern and western European ancestry, and an increasing share of the new immigrants came from eastern and southern Europe, China, and Japan.

In the 1920s, widespread fear of foreigners prompted Congress to pass laws limiting immigration, especially from countries outside northern and western Europe. These laws set quotas, or numerical limits, on the number of immigrants allowed from certain countries.

This country-based quota system remained in effect until 1965. A new immigration law in that year established broader quotas of 120,000 immigrants from the Western Hemisphere, 170,000 from the Eastern Hemisphere, and 20,000 from any one nation.

Immigration policy continues to be debated and revised. The Immigration Act of 1990 raised the overall immigration quota. Laws passed in 1986 and 1996 sought to halt the tide of illegal immigration, for example by toughening the penalties for smuggling people into the country. Many Americans call for additional changes in immigration policy. Some want to reduce the immigration quotas dramatically. Others just want to make immigration laws fair.

The Impact on You

Do you think immigration is good or bad for the United States? Make a list of its benefits and drawbacks. Write a "law" on immigration, based on your views. Specify the various elements of your law and explain how they should be enforced.

Family of newly naturalized American citizens

Class Discussion

Discuss with the class immigration to the United States today. For a more thorough examination of the issue, see the activity folder in the Resource Options below.

ACTIVITY
STUDENT PARTICIPATION

Determining Priorities

Ask students to read the text. Then divide the class into two groups. Have each group discuss factors used in determining immigration status, including:

- **flight from political repression**
- **flight from war**
- **flight from drought or famine**
- **reunion with family**
- **ability to make an economic contribution**
- **ability to make a scientific contribution**
- **ability to make an artistic contribution**

Have each group prioritize factors that the government should consider when determining immigration status, from most important to least important. Then have the two groups discuss and debate their ideas.

Follow up Students could compare their lists with actual immigration priorities.

Using the Internet

 Students can learn more about immigration by exploring links in the *America: Pathways to the Present* Web site at:

http://www.Pathways.phschool.com

Assessment

See the Lesson Plans folder, pp. 24–27, for rubrics on assessing Class Participation Projects.

▶ RESOURCE OPTIONS

Teaching Resources

📁 **Why Study History? Activity**

Immigration Continues Today, found in the Why Study History? folder, p. 17, provides an activity to help students better understand today's immigration patterns.

Media and Technology

🦅 **AmericanHeritage® CD-ROM**

Time Tour The Nation Today and Tomorrow: Toward a New Century

◉ 📼 **Prentice Hall United States History Video Collection™** Volume 12
Immigration and Cultural Changes

Key Terms

Students should refer to the definitions of key terms in the chapter to write sentences that show an understanding of politics, immigration, and urban life in the Gilded Age.

Comprehension

1. With gifts and money they tried to influence politicians to vote in their interests.

2. The hiring of unqualified and often dishonest government employees.

3. Immigrants fled poor farming, working, and living conditions in their home countries.

4. More new immigrants during this period came from southern and eastern Europe and the Americas.

5. Middle-class residents moved to the suburbs, leaving empty buildings, which owners converted into cheap tenements. The tenements were neglected and became overcrowded, turning them into slums.

6. Advantages: They helped poor people and immigrants when no help was offered from the government or private industry. Disadvantages: They skimmed money from the city's income illegally and hurt businesses.

7. They influenced politicians to pass the Chinese Exclusion Act and to repeal the Contract Labor Act. They founded the Immigration Restriction League and called for the teaching of only the English language and American culture in schools.

8. By offering social services in community centers, such as classes, child care, and health care. They also launched investigations of city economic, political, and social conditions, laying the foundation for later reforms.

Chapter Summary

The major concepts of Chapter 16 are presented below. See also *Guide to the Essentials of American History* or *Interactive Student Tutorial CD-ROM,* which contains interactive review activities, time lines, helpful hints, and test practice for Chapter 16.

Reviewing the Main Ideas

During the Gilded Age, powerful and unregulated businesses amassed great wealth with the help of corrupt politicians. The economic boom attracted millions of immigrants to the United States. Most of them settled in cities, which led to overcrowding and other problems. Reformers worked to improve conditions in the cities.

Section 1: Politics in the Gilded Age

From 1877 to 1900, national politics was dominated by issues of corruption and reform.

Section 2: People on the Move

Millions of immigrants, representing many different cultures, arrived in the United States during the late 1800s and early 1900s.

Section 3: The Challenge of the Cities

Millions of people moved into the cities, creating new growth and new challenges.

Section 4: Ideas for Reform

A variety of groups worked to improve social, economic, and political conditions in the cities.

Why Study History?

Since the big waves of immigration around the turn of the century, millions more immigrants have come to America, raising new controversies about immigration policy.

Using Graphic Organizers

- Urban problems: Reformers develop programs to help.
- Cities expand: suburbs grow; specialized areas within cities develop.
- People react to increasing numbers of immigrants: Legislation passed to restrict immigration; immigrants develop own communities within cities.

Key Terms

For each of the terms below, write a sentence explaining how it relates to this chapter.

1. suburb
2. graft
3. political machine
4. Chinese Exclusion Act
5. prohibition
6. steerage
7. laissez-faire
8. tenement
9. civil service
10. nativism
11. Gilded Age
12. segregation
13. settlement house
14. ghetto
15. blue law

Comprehension

1. How did business influence politicians during the Gilded Age?
2. What problems did the spoils system create?
3. Why did so many people want to come to the United States in the late 1800s and early 1900s?
4. Starting in the 1890s, where did large numbers of immigrants come from?
5. How did slums develop in cities?
6. What were the advantages and disadvantages of political machines for urban residents?
7. What actions did nativists take to restrict immigration?
8. How did the settlement movement seek to help the needy?

Using Graphic Organizers

On a large sheet of paper, copy the web diagram below. Add as many connecting circles as you need, and fill them with information from the chapter.

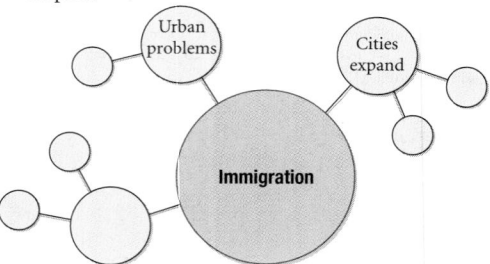

Analyzing Political Cartoons ▶

1. This scene shows a strength contest once popular at fairs. The goal was to test one's strength in an attempt to ring the bell at the top of the column. Examine the scene. Who are the contestants?

2. Examine the game. (a) What are the contestants hitting? (b) What is the bell? (c) What is the mallet?

3. Read the caption. Describe the cartoonist's message in a brief paragraph.

Try Your Strength, Gents!
The Harder You Hit It, The Higher It Goes.

Critical Thinking

1. *Applying the Chapter Skill* Look back at the table on the Skills for Life page. World War I was fought between 1914 and 1918. How does the table reflect the influence of the war on immigration to the United States?

2. *Drawing Inferences* What character trait did President Rutherford B. Hayes exhibit by his actions regarding the spoils system? Explain your answer.

3. *Drawing Conclusions* What conclusion can you draw from the fact that Tammany Hall dominated New York City politics for more than 50 years?

4. *Predicting Consequences* What might have been the effect if the United States had adopted all the ideas of the nativists?

═══ INTERNET ACTIVITY ═══

For your portfolio:
CREATE A DIARY ENTRY

Access Prentice Hall's *America: Pathways to the Present* site at **www.Pathways.phschool.com** for the specific URL to complete the activity. Additional resources and related Web sites are also available.

Study the photographs of immigrants arriving at Ellis Island. How did people arrive? Where did they come from? What did they do at Ellis Island? Select a country of origin and create a fictional diary entry recounting an immigrant's experience at Ellis Island.

ANALYZING DOCUMENTS ◀ ▶ INTERPRETING DATA

Turn to the map titled "Immigrant Neighborhoods in Chicago, 1900," in Section 3.

1. Which group formed the largest immigrant neighborhood in Chicago at this time? (a) Polish (b) German (c) Italian (d) Irish

2. Which group seemed to be concentrated in just one distinct neighborhood? (a) Jewish

(b) Scandinavian
(c) Czechoslovak (d) German

3. *Writing* Write a tour guide to the immigrant neighborhoods of Chicago. In the guide, describe the route that visitors might take to explore the main ethnic neighborhoods.

Connecting to Today

Essay Writing Today, the Democratic and Republican parties both try to appeal to the large American middle class. Write an essay comparing and contrasting the major parties of today with those in the Gilded Age. Be sure to address this question: Did all levels of society have a political voice in both eras?

485

═══ INTERNET ACTIVITY ═══

Diary entries will vary but should be supported with research and should explore themes introduced in the text. Diaries might address these topics: the voyage; who they encountered on the trip; what sorts of tests they had to take at Ellis Island; the different cultures, languages, and foods they encountered.

Analyzing Political Cartoons

1. Trusts.
2. (a) Consumers. (b) Profits. (c) A tariff.
3. Powerful trusts are being assisted by tariffs. These trusts are abusing consumers in order to reap high profits.

Critical Thinking

1. In the later years of the war, immigration from most parts of the world had decreased significantly.
2. Sample answer: Integrity, because he refused to use the patronage system even though he angered his fellow Republicans and ensured that he could not win reelection.
3. That political machines, though corrupt, were entrenched in city politics and economics and successful enough that there was no organized public outcry against them.
4. Sample answer: Immigration from some countries would have declined greatly; society would be less multicultural and less tolerant.

Interpreting Data

1. a
2. c
3. Answers will vary but should be based on the map of Chicago.

Connecting to Today

Essays will vary but should be supported with facts from the section. Sample answer to question: Many segments of society in the Gilded Age had much less of a political voice than today. Women in the Gilded Age still could not vote; African Americans still faced various forms of social, political, and economic discrimination; and many immigrant groups were discriminated against and not considered citizens.

Daily Life in the Gilded Age, 1870–1915

Managing Time and Instruction

INSTRUCTION SUPPORT

These materials for instruction are provided for each section in the **Teaching Resources**. See **Units 5–6 folder** for Enrichment Support:

• Reproducible Lesson Plans in Lesson Plans folder • Learning Styles Lesson Plans in Learning Styles Lesson Plans folder • Big Idea Graphic Organizers in Big Idea Graphic Organizer folder • Guided Reading and Review • Quizzes • Test Preparation Practice booklet

DAILY LESSON	ENRICHMENT SUPPORT
1 The Expansion of Education *(pp. 487–491)*	• Literature Activity, The Promised Land, found on **Resource Pro** • Key Documents, Pledge of Allegiance, Learning with Documents folder, p. 93 • Visual Learning Activity, The Ideal Public School, found on **Resource Pro** • Primary Source Activity, The Washington–Du Bois Debate, Learning with Documents folder, p. 23
2 New Forms of Entertainment *(pp. 492–495)*	• Biography, George M. Cohan, Units 5–6 folder, p. 54 • Critical Thinking Activity, Recognizing Cause and Effect: America's Game, found on **Resource Pro** • Literature Activity, Around the World in 72 Days, Units 5–6 folder, p. 57
3 The World of Jim Crow *(pp. 498–501)*	• Nystrom *Atlas of Our Country,* The Third Wave of Immigration, pp. 30–31 • Decision-Making Activity, Can Separate Be Equal? Decision-Making Activities folder, pp. 14–15 • Primary Source Activity, Lynchings and Mob Law, found on **Resource Pro** • Skills for Life Activity, Units 5–6 folder, p. 58
4 Women in the Late 1800s *(pp. 503–506)*	• Visual Learning Activity, The New Woman and the New Man, Learning with Documents folder, p. 59 • Biography, Lucy Stone, found on **Resource Pro** • Comparing Primary Sources, On the Woman Question, Units 5–6 folder, pp. 55–56 • Education Is the Key to Success, Why Study History? folder, p. 18

Running Out of Time?

• Use Tape 3, "Expansion: Rewards and Costs, 1860–1920," from **Visions of America** videotapes series.
• Use Chapter 17 Summary, from **Guide to the Essentials of American History (English and Spanish).**

Companion Web Site

The companion Web site offers online links for all chapter review activities. It also provides key content links and structured support for this chapter for both teachers and students.

http://www.Pathways.phschool.com

Teaching in the Information Age

Media and Technology

For the Student

Interactive Student Tutorial CD-ROM Chapter 17

Student Edition on Audiotape Chapter 17

American Heritage® CD-ROM

Guided Reading Audiotapes (English and Spanish) Chapter 17

For the Teacher

Resource Pro CD-ROM Chapter 17

Test Bank CD-ROM Chapter 17

Listening to Literature Audiotapes *Timeless Voices, Timeless Themes* "The Story of an Hour" by Kate Chopin

Block Scheduling

Pacing Suggestions

For 90-minute Blocks

- Teach sections 1 and 2 using Transparencies D-14 and C-9 and the Recent Scholarship note on p. 490 for class discussions.
- Teach sections 3 and 4 using the Big Idea Graphic Organizers from Teaching Resources and the Extended Class Periods Activity on p. 504.

Additional Resources

- Prentice Hall's **American History Block Scheduling Support File** covers over 40 major topics in American history.
- **Prentice Hall United States History Video Collection™** contains 20 videotapes covering American history from beginnings to present.
- **Decision America Videotapes and Videodiscs**

Assessment Options

Chapter Test Forms A & B Test Bank CD-ROM booklet

Test Bank CD-ROM Chapter 17

Standardized Test Preparation Handbook

Connections to American Literature

from Prentice Hall

Prentice Hall Literature *Timeless Voices, Timeless Themes*
- "I Hear America Singing" by Walt Whitman, p. 413
- "I Too" by Langston Hughes, p. 419
- "To Walt Whitman" by Angela de Hoyos, p. 420

Additional Resources

For the Student
Blacks and the Constitution. PBS Video, 1987.
Carol Hymnowitz and Michaele Weissman. *A History of Women in America.* Bantam, 1978.

For the Teacher
Roger D. Abrahams. *Singing the Master: The Emergence of African Culture in the Plantation South.* Penguin USA, 1993.
David Levering Lewis. *W.E.B. Du Bois: 1868–1919, Biography of a Race.* Holt, 1993.

 Prentice Hall brings into the classroom the vast archives and scholarship of the nation's premier American history magazine. See "From the Archives of American Heritage®" and "About the Presidents" teaching notes in this chapter.

 History Alive! Teacher's Curriculum Institute, in partnership with Prentice Hall, provides unique materials that engage students with diverse learning styles. See History Alive!® unit on The United States Coming of Age: 1890–1920.

 Student Performance Pack Ensures success in the three critical areas of Reading, Test Taking, and English Language Development with the following materials:
- Guide to the Essentials of American History in English and Spanish
- Guided Reading Audiotapes in English and Spanish
- Interactive Student Tutorial CD–ROM
- Test Preparation Handbook
- Test Preparation Practice booklet

Daily Life in the Gilded Age
1870–1915

Introducing the Chapter
The growth of industry and urban areas in the late 1800s brought many cultural and social transformations to the United States. At the same time, many Americans feared change and clung to old ideas about social roles, particularly those that affected women and African Americans.

Themes in American History
The theme for this chapter, Diversity, is listed at the beginning of this unit. An alternate theme for the chapter is Culture. To teach this unit thematically, you may wish to use the Expansion, Reconstruction, Immigration folder in American History Block Scheduling Support.

Why Study History?

Have students explore suggested ways of connecting the past to the present on page 507.

Answer to . . .
Viewing History Students should use this question as an aid in reading the chapter. Sports and popular amusements like trolley parks and vaudeville acts met the needs of city workers who wanted fun things to do when they were not working.

486

CHAPTER
17 Daily Life in the Gilded Age
1870-1915

▲
VIEWING HISTORY
These spectators are enjoying the thrill of race car driving at the Indianapolis Motor Speedway. *Culture What role did sports and entertainment play in the Gilded Age?*

CHAPTER FOCUS

This chapter describes social and cultural changes that took place in society in the period following Reconstruction through the early 1900s. While education expanded and new forms of entertainment were invented, many people in society resisted changes, especially in the status of African Americans and women.

The Why Study History? page at the end of this chapter explores the connection between the surge in educational opportunities in the late 1800s and the role of education today.

 RESOURCE OPTIONS

Teaching Resources

 Big Idea Graphic Organizer folder
Graphic summary of the main idea of the chapter.

 Learning Styles Lesson Plans folder
Alternate lesson plans for diverse learning styles for each chapter.

Media and Technology

AmericanHeritage® CD-ROM
Time Tour Reshaping the Nation: A Diverse Nation; *also,* A New Role in the World: Progressives and Reformers

Prentice Hall United States History Video Collection™ Volume 11
Immigration and Cultural Change

1881	1895	1905	1910
Tuskegee Institute founded	Booker T. Washington delivers Atlanta Exposition speech	W.E.B. Du Bois establishes Niagara Movement	Nearly 60 percent of American children attend school

| 1870 | 1880 | 1890 | 1900 | 1910 |

1 The Expansion of Education

SECTION PREVIEW

Objectives

1. List reasons why public schools expanded during the late 1800s.
2. Describe the higher education opportunities that were available after the Civil War.
3. Examine the views of W.E.B. Du Bois on civil rights and education for African Americans.
4. *Key Terms* Define: literacy; assimilation; philanthropist; Niagara Movement.

Main Idea

Education was a lofty goal that was out of reach for most nineteenth-century Americans. As the century came to a close, however, more and more Americans gained the opportunity to learn.

Reading Strategy

Reinforcing Main Ideas As you read the section, make a list of examples of how educational opportunities expanded between 1870 and 1910.

Americans had long understood that a democratic society functioned best when its citizens could read and write. By the late 1800s, however, an education had become more than just a worthy goal. For a growing number of Americans, it was a necessary first step toward economic and social success. In recognition of this fact and in response to public demand, educational opportunities expanded.

The Growth of Public Schools

By the time of the Civil War, more than half of the nation's white children were attending the nation's free public schools. Because most children had to help their families earn a living, however, many left school at an early age. A high school diploma was still the exception. In 1870, only 2 percent of all 17-year-olds graduated from high school. An even lower percentage of students went on to college.

The vast majority of American children attended school for only a few years and acquired only basic skills. As industries grew

after the Civil War, young people came to realize that they needed more than basic skills to advance in life. Parents began pressuring local governments to increase school funding and lengthen the school year. At the same time, reformers pressured state governments to limit child labor.

By 1900, 31 states had laws that required children between the ages of 8 and 14 to attend school. Although unevenly enforced, these laws had a powerful effect. By 1910 nearly 60 percent of American children attended school, with more than a million students in high school.

Immigrants and Education Many immigrants placed a high value on American public education. In the mid-1890s, the Russian immigrant father of author Mary Antin was proud to send his children to a Boston public school, convinced "there was no surer way to their advancement and happiness."

One of the most important functions of the public schools was to teach literacy skills. **Literacy** is the ability to read and write. For many immigrants, learning to read and write English was an important achievement in their

---

▶ **RESOURCE OPTIONS**

Teaching Resources

📁 **Reproducible Lesson Plan** Lesson Plans folder, p. 101

📁 **Big Idea Graphic Organizer** Big Idea Graphic Organizer folder, p. 73

📁 **Guided Reading and Review** Units 5–6 folder, p. 46

Media and Technology

(RESOURCE ◉ **PRO**)

Literature Activity The Promised Land, found on Resource Pro, uses an excerpt from the autobiography of Mary Antin, a Jewish immigrant living in Boston, to show the importance of education to immigrant families.

Objectives

You may wish to call students' attention to the objectives in the Section Preview. The objectives are reflected in the main headings of the section.

Bellringer

Ask students if they think changes need to be made in American education in order to better prepare students for their future roles. Ask them to explain what they think these changes should be.

Reading Strategy

Reinforcing Main Ideas Refer to the Reading Strategy in the Section Preview. You may wish to have volunteers contribute to a composite list that you write on the chalkboard.

LESSON PLAN

Connecting to the Main Idea

1. Focus Explain that as the United States became more industrialized and urbanized after the Civil War, Americans needed more education.

2. Instruct Discuss the expansion of education after the Civil War. What was the result of compulsory school laws? How did education encourage immigrants to assimilate? Who benefited from increased opportunities for higher education?

Ask students to analyze the impact of educational expansion on African Americans, women, and on American society as a whole. How did Booker T. Washington's and W.E.B. Du Bois's approach toward education for African Americans differ?

3. Close As urbanization and industrialization increased in the late 1800s, a growing number of Americans took advantage of the country's expanding educational opportunities. The next section describes new opportunities for recreation and leisure time.

Some parents resisted Americanization. Fearing that their children would forget their heritage, many parents sent their children to religious schools where they could learn their own cultural traditions in their native languages. For example, Polish parents in Chicago in the early 1900s sent their children to Roman Catholic schools. There, Polish history and religion were taught in Polish, and American history, bookkeeping, and algebra were taught in English.

Of course, the process of Americanization was not a one-way street. The contact between Americans and newer immigrants, both in public schools and in the wider society, allowed for a constant sharing of cultural traditions. As immigrants shared customs and habits from their homelands, they enriched their new country and helped to redefine American culture itself.

Uneven Support for Schools Though state and local government support for education was expanding, not everyone benefited equally. This is because most schools throughout the country were segregated. Compared to white schools, schools for African Americans received far less money. Writing of her upbringing in Durham, North Carolina, in the 1910s, civil rights activist Pauli Murray remembered vividly the contrast between "what we had and what the white children had." She noted:

❝We got the greasy, torn, dog-eared books; they got the new ones. They had field day in the city park; we had it on a furrowed, stubby hillside. They got wide mention in the newspaper; we got a paragraph at the bottom. . . . We came to know that whatever we had was always inferior.❞

—*Pauli Murray*

Mexican Americans in parts of the Southwest and many Asians in California were also sent to separate schools that were less well funded than those for white children. In 1900, only a small percentage of Native American children were receiving any formal schooling at all.

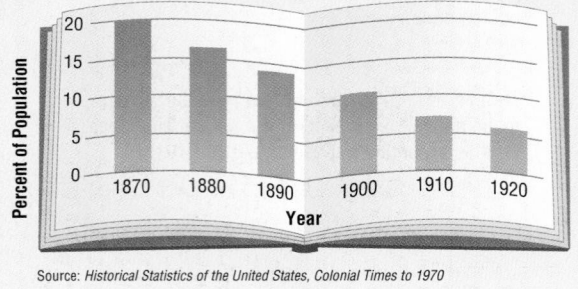

Illiteracy in the United States, 1870–1920

Source: *Historical Statistics of the United States, Colonial Times to 1970*

Interpreting Graphs The expansion of education meant more students in classrooms, such as this one in Nebraska in 1895. *Culture How do the illiteracy figures above show the success of the push for expanding education?*

quest to succeed in the United States. Adults attended school at night to learn English and civics, which they needed to qualify for citizenship.

Beyond teaching basic literacy skills, public schools also played a role in assimilating immigrants into the American way of life. **Assimilation** is the process by which people of one culture become part of another culture. Public school teachers taught their students about American standards of thrift, patriotism, and hard work. Students also learned how to cook traditional American foods and play American games like baseball. As a result of their schooling, many immigrant children became Americanized.

Higher Education Expands

Between 1880 and 1900, more than 250 new American colleges and universities opened to train people in the skills needed by a growing industrial economy. Wealthy Americans often endowed, or gave money or property to, institutions of higher learning. For example, in 1885 Leland Stanford, the entrepreneur who had helped build the transcontinental railroad, and his wife, Jane Lathrop Stanford, founded Stanford University in memory of their son. John D. Rockefeller made donations to the University of Chicago that eventually totaled $40 million.

With the opening of these new schools, college enrollment more than doubled between 1890 and 1910. Even with this growth in enrollment, however, only a small percentage of Americans went to college. In the 1890s annual family incomes averaged under a thousand dollars and parents were hard-pressed to meet college costs. A few less fortunate but gifted students won scholarships or worked their way through college.

By 1915 some middle-income families began to aspire to and attain college educations for their children. The availability of advanced education would distinguish the United States from other industrialized countries.

Women and Higher Education After the Civil War, some women called for greater educational opportunities. In response, educators and **philanthropists,** people who give donations to worthy causes, established private women's colleges with high academic standards. The first was New York's Vassar College, which opened in 1865.

Pressure also increased on men's colleges in the 1880s and 1890s to admit women.

Rather than do so, some schools founded separate institutions for women that were related to the men's schools. Tulane University in Louisiana became the only major southern university to take this step when it established Sophie Newcomb College in 1886. Shortly thereafter, Columbia in New York opened Barnard (1889), Brown in Rhode Island started Pembroke (1891), and Harvard University in Massachusetts established Radcliffe (1879).

Opportunities for men and women to study together—coeducation—also increased. A number of religiously based colleges, including Oberlin, Knox, Antioch, Swarthmore, and Bates, had been coeducational since long before the Civil War. In the postwar years, they were joined by institutions such as Cornell. Boston University announced in 1873 that it welcomed women not only as students but also as professors.

Because most scholarships went to men, women had a harder time obtaining a college education. Even those who could afford the cost faced prejudice against educating women.

Main Idea
CONNECTIONS
What factors led to the expansion of higher education?

The women in this 1880 Smith College chemistry class were among the first to benefit from new higher education opportunities. *Cultures* *What obstacles did women face in seeking higher education?*

Bachelor's Degrees Conferred, 1870–1920

Source: *Historical Statistics of the United States, Colonial Times to 1970*

Interpreting Graphs The number of women earning bachelor's degrees rose dramatically between 1870 and 1920. Even by 1920, however, nearly twice as many degrees were earned by male students. *Culture In what ways was the call for women's access to higher education answered?*

Parents feared that college made daughters too independent or "unmarriageable" or brought them in contact with unacceptable friends. When Martha "Minnie" Carey Thomas finally persuaded her Quaker father to allow her to take the Cornell University entrance exams, he said to her, "Well, Minnie, I am proud of thee, but this university is an awful place to swallow thee up."

Women had to struggle to gain access to most state-funded institutions. For example, in 1863 the coeducational University of Wisconsin required women to stand until all male students had found seats. After 1867 Wisconsin directed women into a "Female College." In 1873, however, when women refused to attend segregated classes, the university was forced to reestablish coeducation.

Booker T. Washington encouraged African Americans to use education to achieve economic success.

African Americans and Higher Education African Americans also had to fight prejudice in institutions of higher learning. A few colleges, such as Oberlin, Bates, and Bowdoin, did accept blacks. Most did not. In 1890 only 160 African Americans were attending white colleges.

Many more were studying at the nation's African American institutions. Several predominantly black colleges, including Atlanta, Fisk, Hampton Institute, and Howard, were founded through the efforts of the American Missionary Association. Wilberforce University, incorporated in 1856 in Ohio, is the nation's oldest private African American school. By 1900, more than 2,000 students had graduated from 34 African American colleges.

Schools founded for African Americans after the Civil War generally accepted both women and men. The number of women attending remained small, however, because most of the scholarships went to men. Anna Julia Cooper, an Oberlin graduate who later became an educator, estimated that there were only 30 black women studying in college in the United States in 1891.

Booker T. Washington Among the black college graduates was Booker T. Washington. Born into slavery in 1856, Washington began his studies at Hampton Institute in Virginia in 1872. His education there inspired him to spend his life promoting the growth of a similar institution, Tuskegee Institute, which he founded in Alabama in 1881.

Washington taught his students the skills and attitudes that he thought would help them succeed in society. Washington told his students to temporarily put aside their desire for political equality and instead to focus on building economic security by gaining vocational skills. He urged them to prepare for productive, profitable work and to bring their intellect "to bear upon the everyday practical things of life, upon something that is needed to be done, and something which they will be permitted to do in the community in which they reside." African Americans could win white acceptance eventually, he predicted, by succeeding economically.

Washington spelled out his ideas in a speech he delivered in 1895 at the Atlanta Exposition:

AMERICAN VOICES "To those of my race who depend on bettering their condition . . . I would say: 'Cast down your bucket where you are'—cast it down . . . in agriculture, mechanics, in commerce, in domestic service, and in the professions. . . . No race can prosper till it learns that there is as much dignity in tilling a field as in writing a poem. . . . In all things that are purely social we can be as separate as the fingers, yet one as the hand in all things essential to mutual progress."

—*Booker T. Washington*

In addition to appealing to many African Americans, Washington's ideas relieved those whites who worried that educated African Americans would seek more equality within society. Whites began to consult him on all issues concerning race relations. President Theodore Roosevelt invited Washington to the White House in 1901. Washington's autobiography, *Up From Slavery* (1901), became a classic, and he became a dominant force in the African American community.

W.E.B. Du Bois

 W.E.B. Du Bois led the next generation of African Americans in a different direction. Born in Massachusetts, Du Bois graduated from Tennessee's Fisk University and then in 1895 became the first African American to earn a Ph.D. from Harvard. Du Bois taught economics, history, and sociology at Atlanta University and in 1905 helped found the **Niagara Movement.** This was a group of African Americans that called for full civil liberties, an end to racial discrimination, and recognition of human brotherhood.

Du Bois rejected Washington's message, which he mockingly called the Atlanta Compromise. Instead, Du Bois argued that the brightest African Americans had to step forward to lead their people in their quest for political and social equality and civil rights. He urged those future leaders to seek an advanced liberal arts education rather than a vocational education as Washington promoted. Only when they had developed "intelligence, broad sympathy, knowledge of the world that was and is, and of the relation of men to it," he wrote, would they be equipped to lead "the Negro race."

In a collection of articles published in 1903 called *The Negro Problem*, Du Bois wrote:

W.E.B. Du Bois (1868–1963)

 "I insist that the true object of all true education is not to make men carpenters, it is to make carpenters men. . . . The Talented Tenth of the Negro race must be made leaders of thought and missionaries of culture among their people. No others can do this work and Negro colleges must train men for it."

— *W.E.B. Du Bois*

In writings such as *The Souls of Black Folk*, Du Bois urged blacks not to define themselves as whites saw them. Instead, he insisted that they take pride in both their African and their American heritages.

In 1910 Du Bois left his teaching post at Atlanta University to work as publications director at the National Association for the Advancement of Colored People (Section 3). He would remain associated with the NAACP for many years, becoming perhaps the best-known black leader of the first half of the twentieth century.

SECTION 1 REVIEW

Comprehension

1. **Key Terms** (a) literacy; (b) assimilation; (c) philanthropist; (d) Niagara Movement.

2. **Summarizing the Main Idea** Give examples of how educational opportunities expanded between 1870 and 1910.

3. **Organizing Information** Make a list of reasons why public schools expanded during the late 1800s.

Critical Thinking

4. **Analyzing Time Lines** How did Washington's ideas, as portrayed in his speech at Atlanta, differ from the ideas of Du Bois and the members of the Niagara Movement?

5. **Drawing Inferences** Why do you think education was so important to many immigrants?

Writing Activity

6. **Writing an Expository Essay** Write an essay outlining the higher education opportunities that were available after the Civil War.

1884		1891		1899	1903
Mark Twain publishes The Adventures of Huckleberry Finn		Basketball invented		Scott Joplin composes "Maple Leaf Rag"	The Great Train Robbery released

1884   **1894**   **1904**

Objectives

You may wish to call students' attention to the objectives in the Section Preview. The objectives are reflected in the main headings of the section.

Bellringer

Ask students how they like to entertain themselves during their free time. Ask them if they spend money on entertainment.

Reading Strategy

Formulating Questions Refer to the Reading Strategy in the Section Preview. You may wish to have students exchange questions and quiz each other as a way to review the section content.

LESSON PLAN

Connecting to the Main Idea

1. Focus Explain that urbanization and industrialization brought in their wake a new commercial entertainment industry. Ask students what the new forms of amusement were in the late 1800s. Did men and women prefer different forms of entertainment?

2. Instruct Discuss the kinds of popular amusements that emerged in the late 1800s. Ask what part sports played in mass entertainment. What was the influence of African American art on popular entertainment?

3. Close In response to the demand of the urban working class for inexpensive recreational activities, a mass entertainment industry emerged in the late 1800s. The next section describes how African Americans confronted repression and discrimination.

2 New Forms of Entertainment

SECTION PREVIEW

Objectives

1. Describe the popular amusements that emerged in the late 1800s.
2. Summarize the influence of African American musical styles on mass culture.
3. *Key Terms* Define: vaudeville; yellow journalism; ragtime.

Main Idea

New forms of entertainment and sports emerged during the late 1800s.

Reading Strategy

Formulating Questions Before you read, write a question about each heading in the section. As you read, look for answers to these questions.

Basketball and other sports were popular forms of recreation at the turn of the century.

In rural America, time spent in play was considered time wasted. Only after the harvest was in or during special celebrations would rural people allow themselves to enjoy leisure activities at family and community gatherings. These activities tended to be free, with people providing their own food and music.

In contrast, factory laborers worked by the clock. After long hours on the job, they wanted fun things to do. A commercial recreation industry emerged to meet the need for inexpensive entertainment for all Americans.

Popular Amusements in the Late 1800s

Of all the places where working people gathered in the late 1800s, saloons were the most popular. Denver (population 133,859) had nearly 500 saloons by 1900; New York City (population 3,437,202) had an estimated 10,000. Besides providing entertainment, saloons served as places for forging neighborhood and ethnic ties and political alliances. Most saloon customers were men. Women preferred to attend dance halls and cabarets, where they could watch musical shows and dance the latest dances.

Trolley parks—amusement parks built at the ends of trolley lines—were popular with the whole family. Moving pictures also appeared during this era. *The Great Train Robbery*, released in 1903, was a huge success and demonstrated very clearly the profits that could be made from movies. By 1908 the nation had 8,000 nickelodeons, theaters set up in converted stores or warehouses that charged a nickel admission. They showed slapstick comedies and other films to as many as 200,000 people daily.

Vaudeville Live theatrical performances also attracted large crowds in this era. **Vaudeville,** a type of inexpensive variety show that first appeared in the 1870s, was the most popular. Vaudeville performances consisted of comic sketches based on ethnic or racial humor, song-and-dance routines, ventriloquists, jugglers, and trapeze artists.

Vaudeville was strictly for the family. Theater owners insisted on keeping everything

RESOURCE OPTIONS

Teaching Resources

Reproducible Lesson Plan Lesson Plans folder, p. 102

Learning Styles Lesson Plan Learning Styles Lesson Plans folder, p. 36

Big Idea Graphic Organizer Big Idea Graphic Organizer folder, p. 74

Guided Reading and Review Units 5–6 folder, p. 48

Biography George M. Cohan, Units 5–6 folder, p. 54

on a "high plane of respectability and moral cleanliness." A "Notice to Performers" posted on the backstage wall of a prominent vaudeville house in 1899 warned:

AMERICAN VOICES "Such words as Liar, Slob, Son-of-a-Gun, Devil . . . and all other words unfit for the ears of ladies and children, also any reference to questionable streets, resorts, localities, and bar-rooms, are prohibited under fine of instant discharge."

—"Notice to Performers"

Sports As leisure time expanded in the late 1800s, sporting events also became a favorite pastime. Boxing and horse racing were widely enjoyed spectator sports, but baseball was by far the most popular.

By 1860, groups such as firefighters, police officers, and teachers had formed baseball clubs in many American cities. When audiences for these games grew, entrepreneurs enclosed fields and charged admission. Teams formed into leagues and began to play championship games. In 1869 the nation's first true professional team, the Cincinnati Red Stockings, was formed. By the 1870s the sport's best players were paid. The most popular leagues included Native American and white immigrant players. African Americans were included only for a short time. After their exclusion, even the best African Americans had to play in segregated leagues until the late 1940s.

What Americans loved most about baseball was the speed, daring, and split-second timing of the game. Pitcher Christy Mathewson commented, "The American public wants its excitement rolled up in a package and handed out quickly." Baseball fulfilled that desire.

Two other games also took hold of the American public during the late 1800s. Football emerged as a popular American game when Walter Camp began adapting the European game of rugby during the 1880s. Basketball, the only major sport of exclusively American origin, was invented in 1891. A physical education instructor, Dr. James Naismith of Springfield, Massachusetts, invented the game to keep athletes fit during winter.

Women, too, took up sports. Ice-skating had long been a favorite recreation of women. The national bicycling fad of the late 1800s also became popular among women. Bicycling required practical clothing, and so brought about changes in women's clothing styles. "For muscle-play, freedom is the first requisite," a doctor advised in an 1896 article entitled "Bicycling for Women: The Puzzling Question of Costume." Women athletes abandoned corsets, which wrapped tightly around their torsos and restricted breathing. Women's involvement in sports also led to the popularity and acceptance of shirtwaists (ready-made blouses) that were tucked into shorter or split skirts.

Women students also played basketball. Assuming that stiff competition and hard physical exertion were unhealthy for women, recreation specialists devised less demanding rules for them. Women athletes also learned gymnastics and swam, although society's strict dress codes required them to wear black cotton stockings under short dresses or bloomers.

Newspapers For city residents, newspapers always had been a vital source of information. In the late 1800s, they became a popular form of entertainment as well. Taking advantage of new typesetting machinery that allowed printers to set whole lines of type quickly, publishers created larger and more interesting

Baseball was a well-established spectator sport by 1886, when the picture of this team was taken. **Geography** *Why was commercial recreation largely an urban phenomenon?*

Main Idea CONNECTIONS

What impact did the emergence of sports have on women?

Interdisciplinary

By 1905 the phonograph, an Edison invention, did for sound what the film projector did for film. Before radio, the phonograph gave the greatest impetus to the spread of popular music, much of it ragtime and jazz, and by 1914 more than half a million phonographs were manufactured each year. Ragtime was, according to African American writer LeRoi Jones (now known as Imamu Amiri Baraka), "a music the Negro came to in imitating white imitations of Negro music."

You may wish to have students add the following to their portfolios. To assess student work, refer to the generic rubrics in the Program Overview in the Teaching Resources.

Tell students that many middle- and upper-class Americans lived by Victorian morals that dictated proper behavior. These people had long been offended by popular amusements. Have students research Victorianism and write an essay contrasting the kinds of behavior embraced by forms of entertainment like dance hall, vaudeville, and sports with the code of behavior dictated by Victorianism.

Answer to . . .

Viewing History News coverage done in a sensational style.

Newspapers such as the *Chicago Daily News* offered readers both information and entertainment. Magazines also expanded in this era, assisted by lowered postal rates. **Culture** What is "yellow journalism"?

publications. They introduced new features, such as comics, sports sections, Sunday editions, women's pages, stories "hot off the wires," and graphic pictures.

Between 1870 and 1900, newspaper circulation soared from 2.6 to 15.1 million copies a day. Competing heatedly with one another, publishers urged reporters to discover fresh news sources and lurid details of murders, vice, and scandal—anything to sell more papers. Such "sensational" news coverage came to be called **yellow journalism,** a reference to the yellow ink used in a popular comic strip of the era.

Several publishers became national figures. Hungarian-born Joseph Pulitzer, who owned the *St. Louis Post-Dispatch* and in 1883 bought the *New York World,* hoped to "expose all fraud and sham, fight all public evils and abuses." Californian William Randolph Hearst used his father's gold-mining millions to put out the even more sensational *New York Journal.*

Yellow journalism troubled many people. Critics charged that the "yellow press" intruded into private lives, invented facts, and sensationalized the ordinary with exaggeration.

Magazines and Popular Fiction It was also during the late 1800s that magazines came into wide circulation. This increase in circulation resulted in part from a law passed by Congress in 1879 lowering the postal rates for periodicals. Some of the popular magazines included *McClure's, Cosmopolitan,* and *Munsey's.*

Many of the stories that appeared weekly or monthly in popular magazines were written to appeal to the dreams and aspirations of American readers. The main character in Horatio Alger's *Ragged Dick,* which appeared in magazines in 1867 and the following year as a book, embodied the American dream of rising from "rags to riches" through cheerfulness, honesty, and hard work. *Ragged Dick* and other stories reminded the working poor of the seemingly boundless opportunities available to them in the nation's industrial cities.

Other writers, including Samuel Langhorne Clemens (whose pen name was Mark Twain), chose to write about the more corrupt side of industrialization and Gilded Age politics. Twain's novel *The Gilded Age,* written with his neighbor Charles Dudley Warner, began a trend that continued into the twentieth century of using the novel as a vehicle for social protest.

In addition to political writings, Twain is known for his classic American tales of youthful adventure and life along the Mississippi River. These include *The Adventures of Tom Sawyer* (1876), and *The Adventures of Huckleberry Finn* (1884). Twain's descriptions of the Mississippi and his humor captivated his audiences' hunger for information about distant parts of the country.

Like Twain, popular writers during the late 1800s were admired for their ability to describe the people and places of specific regions of the United States with great color and detail. While Sarah Orne Jewett wrote about the people of Maine and many of New England's disappearing traditions, Bret Harte described the excitement of the California Gold Rush. Other "local color" writers included George Washington Cable, Joel Harris, and Kate Chopin in the South, Edward Eggleston in Indiana, and O. Henry, who wrote about both Texas and New York City.

African American Influence

As the entertainment culture expanded, it absorbed many forms of African American art.

In the process, the culture also transformed African American culture in order to meet the tastes of white audiences.

The Negro Spiritual In 1871 nine Fisk University students went on a singing tour to raise money for their struggling school. When the Fisk Jubilee Singers began to concentrate solely on spirituals, or African American religious folk songs, they excited such interest that triumphal tours of the United States, England, and Europe resulted. Britain's Queen Victoria was so impressed that she had a group portrait of them painted.

In the process of making the spiritual acceptable to white audiences, the Fisk group and others like it transformed the musical form. It acquired characteristics of the European musical tradition with which whites were familiar. This new spiritual became identified as an American art form, as opposed to a purely African American one.

Minstrel Shows Other forms of African American culture were also absorbed into the white entertainment world. The minstrel show began when white actors discovered they could captivate audiences with exaggerated imitations of African American music, dance, and humor. The shows perpetuated racist stereotypes, generally portraying African Americans as foolish imitators of a white culture they could not understand.

White actors in minstrel shows performed in "blackface"—that is, they blackened their faces and hands and painted on wide grins. African Americans also performed in minstrel shows, as minstrel jobs were often the only stage work they could get.

Ragtime and Jazz A type of music known as **ragtime** originated among black musicians playing in saloons in the South and Midwest in the 1880s. Consisting of melodies with shifting accents over a steady, marching-band beat, it became a rage in the 1890s. Ragtime composer Scott Joplin, who came from St. Louis, Missouri, became famous for his "Maple Leaf Rag" composed in 1899.

Jazz grew out of the vibrant musical culture of New Orleans, a city with a popular marching-band tradition. After the Civil War, African American bands experimented with new styles of playing, including "raggy" rhythms and call-and-response forms in which singers or instruments respond to a single leader. They also played jazzed-up versions of familiar melodies, such as hymns or the mournful "blues" songs of southern sharecroppers.

New Orleans jazz styles from the 1890s slowly worked their way northward through towns along the Mississippi River. By 1915, thanks in part to the success of the phonograph, jazz and the dances associated with it were becoming a national passion.

The music of ragtime composer Scott Joplin remains popular today.

SECTION 2 REVIEW

Comprehension
1. **Key Terms** (a) vaudeville; (b) yellow journalism; (c) ragtime.
2. **Summarizing the Main Idea** Describe some of the new forms of entertainment that emerged in the late 1800s.
3. **Organizing Information** Make a chart describing the three forms of African American music that were absorbed into the mass culture in the late 1800s.

Critical Thinking
4. **Analyzing Time Lines** Review the time line at the start of the section. What categories of popular entertainment are included?
5. **Drawing Inferences** What role do you think compulsory education played in bringing about a larger market for newspapers, magazines, and novels?

Writing Activity
6. **Writing an Expository Essay** Write an essay explaining how the growth of cities helped make possible the growth of entertainment and recreation.

RESOURCE OPTIONS

Teaching Resources
 Quiz Units 5–6 folder, p. 49

Student Performance Pack
 Guide to the Essentials Chapter 17, Section 2 (English and Spanish)

Media and Technology
Color Transparencies Fine Art, D-14; Our Multicultural Heritage, C-9

Graphing the Main Idea
To make sure students understand the main idea of this section, you may wish to use the web graphic organizer below.

Tell students that a web shows a main idea and its supporting details. Ask students to use it to record details on the emergence of new forms of entertainment and sports during the 1800s.

Teaching Tip A template for this graphic organizer can be found in the Color Transparencies, G-1.

Answers to
SECTION 2 REVIEW

1. (a) vaudeville, see p. 492; (b) yellow journalism, see p. 494; (c) ragtime, see p. 495.

2. Answers should include: vaudeville, baseball, football, and basketball; newspapers, magazines, and popular fiction; moving pictures.

3. The spiritual blended classical European musical tradition with African religious folk songs; ragtime began in saloons and mixed shifting melodies with marching-band beats; jazz originated in New Orleans, combined various styles of music.

4. Popular fiction, sports, music, and film.

5. Sample answer: increased literacy expanded the need for magazines, newspapers, and fiction.

6. Essays will vary but should point out city workers having more regulated working hours with blocks of free time; entertainment industry grew to cater to city customers.

THE GROWTH OF SPORTS

Focus Remind students that the popularity of sports at the turn of the century was a result of prosperity and increased leisure time for Americans.

Instruct Using the artifacts and captions as a basis for discussion, ask students what changes in American society were indicated by the growing appeal of sports. Then divide students into small groups and ask each group to make a list of artifacts to include in an American Artifacts display about sports today. How do their selections reflect changes in American society since the turn of the century?

Extend Ask students to write about the effects of technology, communications, and business on sports at the turn of the century and today. Is the influence of business on sports good or bad? Is there as much criticism of sports today as there was at the turn of the century?

Early Baseball

Many songs, such as the polka tune shown on this sheet music cover, celebrated the heroes of baseball. Fans of Georgetown University's baseball team dyed the ball (in the mitt) dark blue and painted in the score to honor their team's victory over Yale in 1899.

Football at the Turn of the Century

1

This football card shows that players wore much less protection than modern players. The only protection came from padded pants (also worn by some basketball players of the time), which protected players from bruises.

Women Cyclists

5

By the 1890s women had joined the bicycle craze and entered into this active, public sport. On this 1870 bicycle, the pedals connect directly to the front wheels at the axle. The introduction of a chain and foot brakes in the 1890s made pedaling much easier and gave the cyclist more control.

▶ RESOURCE OPTIONS

Teaching Resources

American History Block Scheduling Support The Reformers: A Struggle for Women's Rights, found in the Prosperity, Depression, and War folder, includes interdisciplinary lesson suggestions and activities for Geography and History, Primary Sources, Biography, and Literature.

Ice Skating

A common winter sport before the 1800s, ice skating became a "mania" in the 1860s.

3

4 Skiing

Skiing began in Norway in the mid-1800s when the addition of bindings made it possible for skiers to turn and jump. Norwegian immigrants then brought the sport to Minnesota, from where it spread to other snowy areas in the United States.

VIEWING HISTORY

1. *Summarize* Which objects shown here look the most like their present-day counterparts?

2. *Connecting to Today* Think about the role of sports today. Then write an editorial on one of the following topics: (a) how participating in sports can benefit people; (b) whether professional athletes should be seen as role models; (c) whether girls and women currently have enough opportunities to participate in sports.

American
ARTIFACTS

FROM EXHIBITIONS AND COLLECTIONS AT THE SMITHSONIAN INSTITUTION'S NATIONAL MUSEUM OF AMERICAN HISTORY

THE GROWTH OF SPORTS

Fun for fun's sake was the new way of thinking at the turn of the twentieth century. The great rise in sports reflected the changes sweeping across America. The nation's growing wealth and workers' demands allowed for more leisure time than ever before. Also, while Americans had earlier shunned activities that did not create wealth or improve character, it was now morally acceptable to pursue interests for simple enjoyment.

Sporting became a form of recreation as well as entertainment. Baseball and skating became widely popular. The game of American football grew out of rugby and soccer. Collegians developed a new set of rules, such as the system of downs and the position of quarterback. Baseball achieved its status as the great American pastime in the last third of the 1800s. In 1903 the first World Series was played. *See* **1** *and* **2**.

Sports provided year-round entertainment, even in colder parts of the country. Ice skating grew in popularity with the introduction of low-priced, store-bought skates. Skiing came to the United States from Scandinavia, and in later decades would become widely popular with the creation of the ski tow. *See* **3** *and* **4**.

Sports engaged women as well as men. Before the late 1800s, outdoor sports activities for women were limited. But women's steady struggle for legal and political rights advanced their freedom. For example, in the bicycling fad of the late 1800s, many women no longer wore restrictive clothing. The athletic demands of riding a bicycle required more practical apparel. This angered many people, but neither an opinion nor a peculiar piece of clothing would stop the enthusiasts. *See* **5**.

American men and women would continue to ride, play, and swim their way through the twentieth century. Sports were here to stay. They had become a necessary part of life, one that contributed to health and quality of life.

VIEWING HISTORY

Answers to . . .

1. Students may mention the baseball and the skis.

2. (a) Students may mention such factors as stress reduction, cardiovascular health, and other physical and mental benefits. (b) Students may mention specific sports figures whose actions have made them either good or poor role models. (c) Answers will vary, but should be based on specific examples of women in sports at the school, local, or national levels.

Objectives

You may wish to call students' attention to the objectives in the Section Preview. The objectives are reflected in the main headings of the section.

Bellringer

Ask students to define the words *discriminate* and *discrimination*. Ask how a discriminating person is different from a discriminatory one.

Reading Strategy

Organizing Information Refer to the Reading Strategy in the Section Preview. You may wish to make a composite list on the chalkboard and have students discuss which methods they think were the most difficult to combat.

LESSON PLAN

Connecting to the Main Idea

1. Focus Tell students that although African Americans were free, white society found many ways to suppress them. Despite this, many reached high levels of achievement after Reconstruction. Ask in what ways white society denied African Americans their freedom.

2. Instruct Review discrimination after Reconstruction. Which tactics did whites use to legally prohibit African Americans from doing certain things, and which inhibited them from exercising their full rights? Have students analyze the African American response to discrimination. How did "community" help them overcome discrimination?

3. Close Despite the fact that African Americans were denied their most basic constitutional freedoms in the era following Reconstruction, many reached high levels of achievement. The next section discusses attitudes and changes regarding the status of women.

1883	1896	1908	1909
Supreme Court overturns Civil Rights Act of 1875	Plessy v. Ferguson	Race riots in Springfield, Illinois	NAACP founded

1880   **1890**   **1900**   **1910**

3 The World of Jim Crow

SECTION PREVIEW

Objectives

1. List the means by which African Americans were discriminated against after Reconstruction.
2. Describe how African Americans responded to discrimination.
3. *Key Terms* Define: poll tax; grandfather clause; Jim Crow; *Plessy* v. *Ferguson;* lynching; National Association for the Advancement of Colored People (NAACP).

Main Idea

African Americans found their hopes dashed in the years after Reconstruction. Yet many not only resisted discrimination, but achieved success in spite of the obstacles placed before them.

Reading Strategy

Organizing Information As you read this section, make a list of the methods white society used to prevent African Americans from achieving equality.

Within a few years after the end of Reconstruction in the 1870s, African Americans began to see many of their newly won freedoms disappear. In the South, black Americans were prevented from voting and were subjected to segregation laws and random violence. Discrimination was also widespread in the North.

African American voters faced intimidation at the polls.

Post-Reconstruction Discrimination

Booker T. Washington's belief that white Americans would accept hard-working African Americans into equal citizenship was proving too optimistic. Some southern whites, who in the past had used slavery to repress African Americans, now turned to other vicious methods of oppression.

Voting Restrictions In many southern communities, whites were concerned that African Americans would gain too much political power by exercising their right to vote. As a result, southern states used several tactics during the 1890s to deny the vote to blacks. Some southern states began to require voters to own property and to pay a **poll tax,** or special fee, before they could vote. Both of these requirements were beyond the financial reach of most African Americans. Voters also had to demonstrate minimum standards of knowledge by passing literacy tests. These tests were specifically designed to keep African Americans from voting. In fact, blacks were often given much more difficult tests than whites.

To ensure that the literacy tests did not keep too many whites from voting, some states passed special laws. These laws exempted men from certain voting restrictions if they themselves had voted, or had ancestors who had voted, prior to black suffrage. African Americans, therefore, were not exempted from the literacy tests. Such laws are examples of **grandfather clauses.** A grandfather clause is a passage in a piece of legislation that exempts a group of people

---

 RESOURCE OPTIONS

Teaching Resources

📁 **Reproducible Lesson Plan** Lesson Plans folder, p. 103

📁 **Big Idea Graphic Organizer** Big Idea Graphic Organizer folder, p. 75

📁 **Guided Reading and Review** Units 5–6 folder, p. 50

🗺 **Nystrom *Atlas of Our Country*** The Third Wave of Immigration, pp. 30–31

Media and Technology

◉ 📼 **Prentice Hall United States History Video Collection™** Volume 10
Reconstruction and Segregation

from obeying a law provided they met certain conditions before that law was passed.

Segregation During this period many states also instituted a system of legal segregation that further degraded African Americans. This system was called **Jim Crow,** after a minstrel song-and-dance routine.

Although Jim Crow laws usually are associated with the South, they first appeared in the 1830s, when Massachusetts allowed railroad companies to separate black and white passengers. It was in the South, however, that Jim Crow became firmly established. Jim Crow laws began to appear in the South a few years after the end of Reconstruction and were solidly in place by 1900.

Jim Crow dominated almost every aspect of daily life by the early 1900s. The laws required the separation of blacks and whites in schools, parks, public buildings, hospitals, and on transportation systems. African Americans and whites could not use the same water fountains or public toilets. They could not sit in the same sections of theaters. Facilities designated for blacks were almost always inferior.

Plessy* v. *Ferguson With its rulings, the Supreme Court upheld many of the Jim Crow laws. In 1883 the Court overturned the Civil Rights Act of 1875, which had guaranteed African American rights in public places. According to the Supreme Court, the Fourteenth Amendment could not prevent private organizations from discriminating against individuals.

Perhaps the greatest setback to African American equality came with the Court's establishment of the "separate-but-equal" doctrine with the case of ***Plessy* v. *Ferguson*** in 1896. In this case, African American Homer Plessy argued that his right to "equal protection of the laws" was violated by a Louisiana law that required separate seating for white and black citizens on public railroads. In its decision, the Court held that segregation was legal as long as the separate facilities provided for blacks were equal to those provided to whites. The Fourteenth Amendment, the Court stated, was "not intended to give Negroes social equality but only political and civil equality."[†] The ruling in *Plessy* proved hard to enforce, and African American schools and other facilities in the South were rarely if ever made equal.

Adoption of Voting Restrictions in the South, 1889–1908

Year	Poll Tax	Literacy Test	Property Test	Grand-father Clause	Other*
1889	FL				TN, FL
1890	MS, TN	MS			MS
1891					AR
1892	AR				
1893					AL
1894					SC, VA
1895	SC	SC			SC
1896					
1897					LA
1898	LA	LA	LA	LA	
1899					NC
1900	NC	NC	NC	NC	
1901	AL	AL	AL	AL	
1902	VA, TX	VA	VA		VA
1903					TX
1904					
1905					
1906					
1907					
1908		GA	GA	GA	GA

*Registration, multiple-box, secret ballot, understanding clause
Source: *The American Record: Images of the Nation's Past*, Volume Two, edited by William Graebner and Leonard Richards

Interpreting Tables As shown above, southern states began to adopt discriminatory voting laws in the late 1800s. Though the laws varied in their techniques, the effect was always the same— African Americans were denied the vote. *Government* *Which states had the widest variety of voting restrictions?*

Violence The worst feature of the post-Reconstruction decline in conditions for African Americans was **lynching.** The term refers to a mob's illegal seizure and execution of a person. Between 1882 and 1892, an estimated 1,200 black people were lynched. Sometimes the victims were suspected criminals. Often

[†] Segregated public facilities were permitted until *Plessy* was overturned by the *Brown* v. *Board of Education* case in 1954, which stated that separate facilities were inherently unequal.

Using the Internet

Prepare a Report

Objective Use the Internet to prepare a television news report on the *Plessy* v. *Ferguson* trial. Have students follow these instuctions:

1. See the *America: Pathways to the Present* Web site at

http://www.Pathways.phschool.com

for the URLs on the Jim Crow Laws and *Plessy* v. *Ferguson*.

2. Use links to research the trial and its background. Take detailed notes.

3. Suppose you are a news reporter at the Supreme Court during the trial. Describe to the class the background of the trial, the arguments presented, and the results.

Answer to . . .

Interpreting Charts Louisiana, North Carolina, Alabama, and Virginia.

Lynching of African Americans, 1886–1920

Years	Number of Persons Lynched
1886–1890	392
1891–1895	639
1896–1900	493
1901–1905	407
1906–1910	345
1911–1915	279
1916–1920	275

Source: *Historical Statistics of the United States, Colonial Times to 1970*

Interpreting Tables Violence against African Americans was an alarmingly frequent phenomenon in the late 1800s. In spite of vocal protests, mobs had killed more than 3,000 African Americans by the 1920s. **Government** *Why do you think lynch mobs were rarely pursued or caught?*

they were merely individuals who were unlucky enough to be in the wrong place at the wrong time. The seizure sometimes included a mock trial, torture, and even mutilation, before the victim was hanged and riddled with bullets. Those who carried out these horrors were rarely pursued or caught, much less punished. Although most lynchings took place in the South, African Americans in the North were sometimes lynched as well.

Conditions in the North Decline Many African Americans, though realizing that life in the North was far from perfect, moved there in part to escape legal segregation. What they found instead was de facto discrimination, or discrimination "in fact" instead of by law. Northern schools, housing, and employment were effectively segregated. As many African Americans moved north, they began to compete with white Americans and recent immigrants for work in the industrial cities. Whites' fears of racial equality erupted in the form of race riots in 1900 in New York City and in 1908 in Springfield, Illinois. The Springfield riot was touched off when authorities refused to release a black prisoner charged with rape to a crowd of white citizens. After learning that the prisoner had

been secretly transferred to another city, a mob of several thousand white citizens attacked, looted, and burned black businesses and homes and killed two elderly African Americans. The Illinois state militia gained control of the mob only after two days.

African Americans Resist Discrimination

As conditions for African Americans deteriorated, black leaders began to seek new approaches to race problems. For example, Bishop Henry M. Turner of the African Methodist Episcopal church advocated black pride and emigration to Africa. Others criticized Booker T. Washington for his silence on such issues as lynching. Such attacks ignored Washington's quiet support for legal cases against segregation and his financial support for civil rights and black businesses.

As you read in Section 1, a number of outspoken African Americans came together under the leadership of W.E.B. Du Bois in 1905 to denounce all discrimination. Meeting in Niagara Falls, Ontario, Canada, they vowed never to accept "inferiority," bow to "oppression," or apologize "before insult." "We do not hesitate to complain, and to complain loudly and insistently," they warned.

The Niagara Movement, as this group came to be called, gained only about 400 members and won few victories. After the 1908 Springfield race riot, however, its members joined with concerned white citizens to discuss solutions to the conflict between the races.

The NAACP Mary White Ovington, a white social worker who had worked in black neighborhoods, was among the concerned individuals. She helped organize a national conference on the "Negro Question" to be held on Lincoln's birthday in 1909. Niagara Movement leaders attended. This event marked the founding of the **National Association for the Advancement of Colored People (NAACP).**

By 1914 the NAACP had 50 branches and 6,000 members. Its magazine, *Crisis*, edited by Du Bois, reached more than 30,000 readers. The organization worked primarily through the courts. It won its first major victory when the Supreme Court declared grandfather clauses in voting restriction laws unconstitutional in 1915. In the decades ahead, the NAACP would remain a vital force in the fight for civil rights.

African American Achievement African American mutual aid and benefit societies also multiplied in this period. Social workers and church groups founded settlement houses in black neighborhoods. The Young Men's and Young Women's Christian Associations developed separate recreational and guidance programs for African American youth. The National Urban League, founded in 1911, improved job opportunities and housing for blacks.

Also during this period, African American intellectuals began to publish literature, history, and groundbreaking sociological studies. Black-owned businesses appeared everywhere. To help them, Booker T. Washington founded the National Negro Business League in 1900. By 1907 it had 320 branches.

In 1912 Madam C. J. Walker spoke at the annual meeting of the Negro Business League. She was a notable example of African American achievement at the turn of the century. Born Sarah Breedlove, Walker came from a family of ex-slaves and sharecroppers. Her first seven years were spent on a Louisiana cotton plantation. Then, after the death of her parents, she moved to Vicksburg, Mississippi, to work as a servant. She later moved to St. Louis, where she worked for 17 years laundering clothes.

"I got myself a start by giving myself a start," Walker would later say. She did so by developing her own preparations to style the hair of African American women. Walker moved to Denver, Colorado, in 1905, where

she married C. J. Walker, a newspaper sales agent. There she set up a prosperous mail-order business for her hair products. She also established a chain of beauty parlors and training schools. By 1916 her company claimed 20,000 employees.

Her business was a great success and Walker moved to Harlem, in New York City, an area that had begun to attract African American residents. Her Harlem town house and later her estate in Irvington-on-Hudson, New York, became gathering places for the country's African American leaders. Walker supported black welfare, education, and civil rights work with large contributions. She also made many speeches for the antilynching drives of the NAACP and for African American women's organizations. "The girls and women of our race must not be afraid to take hold of business endeavor," she said in her 1913 speech to the Negro Business League. "I want to say to every Negro woman present, don't sit down and wait for the opportunities to come. . . . Get up and make them!"

George Washington Carver rose from slavery to become an important agricultural scientist. He is most famous for his work on peanuts.

SECTION 3 REVIEW

Comprehension

1. **Key Terms** Define: (a) poll tax; (b) grandfather clause; (c) Jim Crow; (d) *Plessy* v. *Ferguson;* (e) lynching; (f) National Association for the Advancement of Colored People (NAACP).

2. **Summarizing the Main Idea** List some of the methods that white society used to discriminate against African Americans after Reconstruction.

3. **Organizing Information** Make a graphic organizer showing the actions African Americans took in response to discrimination.

Critical Thinking

4. **Analyzing Time Lines** Review the time line at the start of the section. Which two events on the time line represent actions taken by African Americans to combat discrimination?

5. **Expressing Problems Clearly** How did the Supreme Court's decision in *Plessy* v. *Ferguson* contribute to the denial of African American rights?

Writing Activity

6. **Writing an Expository Essay** Write an expository essay outlining three methods used by white society to restrict black voting rights.

Answers to
SECTION 3 REVIEW

1. (a) poll tax, see p. 498; (b) grandfather clause, see p. 498; (c) Jim Crow, see p. 499; (d) *Plessy* v. *Ferguson,* see p. 499; (e) lynching, see p. 499; (f) NAACP, see p. 500.

2. States required voters to own property and pay poll taxes that African Americans couldn't afford; required literacy tests were specifically designed to exclude them; Jim Crow laws were passed to instigate segregation and supported by *Plessy* v. *Ferguson;* lynching was widespread; race riots were carried out in the North.

3. Actions included advocating black pride; emigrating to Africa; forming protest groups such as the Niagara Movement and NAACP; developing aid societies, business groups, and settlement houses.

4. *Plessy* v. *Ferguson* (1896); NAACP founded (1910).

5. By saying that segregation was legal as long as black facilities were equal to white facilities, the Supreme Court denied African Americans their civil rights.

6. Essays will vary but should be supported with facts from the section. Methods outlined might include: requirements to own property and pay poll taxes; literacy tests; Jim Crow laws; court decisions like overturning the Civil Rights Act and *Plessy* v. *Ferguson;* violence.

SKILLS FOR LIFE

Historical Evidence

Reading a Political Cartoon

Focus Analyze a political cartoon as historical evidence of ideas and attitudes about a past event.

Instruct Explain that political cartoons usually take as their theme a topical and highly controversial event. Ask students to consider that this cartoon comes from a southern newspaper. Does the cartoon reinforce or reject southern sentiment regarding Jim Crow laws? How?

Extend See the Skills for Life Activity in the Resource Options below.

Answers

1. (a) A ballot marked "Republican vote"; the white men are holding firearms. (b) Both an old Civil War fort and a polling station. (c) The African American man represents all African Americans who try to vote; the white men represent those who prevent them from doing so.

2. (a) "The Constitution gives the Negro the right to vote but what care we for the Constitution." "Voting done inside by whites only. K.K.K." "Vote Inside /No Negro Votes Taken." (b) Preventing African Americans from exercising their right to vote.

3. (a) That Jim Crow laws were unfair, since those who prevent the African American from entering the polls are portrayed as mean, violent scoundrels. (b) By applauding the African American for being righteous and condemning the whites for being mean. (c) As self-interested bigots, giving them unflattering labels, and dressing some as members of the KKK. It is not sympathetic.

TEST FOR SUCCESS

Answers will vary, but should reflect an understanding of the steps shown on this page.

Reading a Political Cartoon

Political cartoons can tell you a great deal about the past. For many years, cartoonists have tried to influence public feeling about important issues. To do so, they use visual images to exaggerate or highlight certain details about the facts. This is one reason why cartoons often can make a point more strongly than words alone can.

Study the cartoon below, published in 1892. Ask yourself what point about Jim Crow laws the cartoonist was trying to make. Then answer the following questions.

1. *Identify the symbols used in the cartoon.* Cartoons often use symbols, visual images that stand for some other idea or event. For example, a skull and crossbones is a commonly used symbol for death. A dove is a symbol for peace. To understand a cartoon, you must be able to identify the symbols it uses.

Decide what the symbols in this cartoon are. (a) What is the figure on the left holding in his right hand? What are the men on the right holding? (b) What is the building at the right meant to be? (c) Based on these symbols, what groups do these people represent?

2. *Analyze the meaning of the symbols.* Use your reading of this chapter and the cartoon to decide what the symbols refer to. (a) What do the signs on the building say? (b) What practice is being referred to in this cartoon?

3. *Interpret the cartoon.* Draw conclusions about the cartoonist's point of view. (a) What do you think the cartoonist thought of Jim Crow laws? Give evidence to support your answer. (b) How is the cartoonist trying to influence the public's attitude toward the practice? (c) How does the cartoonist portray the white figures? Is this a sympathetic portrayal?

TEST FOR SUCCESS

Locate a political cartoon in a newspaper or news magazine. Use the steps on this page to identify and analyze any symbols used in the cartoon and to interpret and identify the central issue of the cartoon.

THE POLITICAL PINKERTONS.

RESOURCE OPTIONS

Teaching Resources

Skills for Life Activity Units 5–6 folder, p. 58, focuses on a cartoon about the 1964 Civil Rights Act to enhance students' understanding of the power of cartoons.

1873	1874	1890	1896		
Association for the Advancement of Women is founded	Woman's Christian Temperance Union is formed	General Federation of Women's Clubs and the National American Woman Suffrage Association are formed	Rural free delivery begins		

1870	1880	1890	1900	1910

4 Women in the Late 1800s

SECTION PREVIEW

Objectives

1. Describe the debate over women's equality in the late 1800s.
2. List ways in which women's work in the home changed in the late 1800s.
3. Describe women's work outside the home during the late 1800s.
4. *Key Terms* Define: department store; rural free delivery; mail-order catalog.

Main Idea

Changes in women's lives, including new jobs, new educational opportunities, and new roles in the home, fueled a debate on the proper role of women in society at the turn of the century.

Reading Strategy

Reinforcing Main Ideas As you read this section, look for evidence to support the following statement: "Although much had changed in women's lives by the turn of the century, much had stayed the same."

Objectives

You may wish to call students' attention to the objectives in the Section Preview. The objectives are reflected in the main headings of the section.

Bellringer

Ask students if they think women have full equality with men in American society today. Encourage them to explain their answers.

Reading Strategy

Reinforcing Main Ideas Refer to the Reading Strategy in the Section Preview. You may wish to draw a web diagram on the chalkboard. Have students copy the diagram and fill it in with the evidence they find to support the statement.

Women hain't no business a votin'," pronounced Josiah Allen, a fictional creation of the popular turn-of-the-century humorist Marietta Holley. "They had better let the laws alone, and tend to their housework. The law loves wimmin and protects 'em." Replied his wife, Samantha, "If the law loves wimmin so well, why don't he give her as much wages as men get for doin' the same work?"

The Debate over Women's Equality

Most Americans around 1900 would have known exactly what Samantha and Josiah were arguing about. They would have called it *the woman question*, a wide-ranging debate about the social role of women that grew out of several major developments of the era.

For women like Samantha Allen, the woman question boiled down to a few key demands: Women should be able to vote. They should be able to control their own property and income, and they should have access to higher education and professional jobs.

Women's rights advocates were countered by those who insisted that giving women economic and political power would upset the social order. Some argued that allowing women any public roles would destroy their femininity.

What was the reality of women's lives at the turn of the century? Women worked in most sectors of the economy and in many areas of public life. Their work at home continued to be essential. At the same time a small number of women were earning advanced degrees and entering professions. Others were building voluntary organizations that took leading roles in reforming education, labor relations, public health, and other areas of society.

New technologies, such as this washing machine, helped ease women's housekeeping burdens.

LESSON PLAN

Connecting to the Main Idea

1. Focus Explain that women's lives were undergoing rapid changes in the late 1800s. Ask what women's rights advocates wanted. Why were they opposed by people with more traditional views?

2. Instruct Discuss the ways in which women's lives were different in the late 1890s from in the 1840s. Why did women want more economic and political rights?

Ask students why the demand for equal economic and political rights for women stirred up so much controversy. Why did many men feel threatened by the demands of women's rights advocates? How might some women feel threatened? Why does the gender question continue to inspire emotional debate today?

3. Close The changing role of women spurred women's rights advocates to demand greater economic and political rights for women. These demands were resisted by traditionalists, who were afraid of upsetting the social order.

 RESOURCE OPTIONS

Teaching Resources

Reproducible Lesson Plan Lesson Plans folder, p. 104

Big Idea Graphic Organizer Big Idea Graphic Organizer folder, p. 76

Learning Styles Lesson Plan Learning Styles Lesson Plans folder, p. 37

Guided Reading and Review Units 5–6 folder, p. 52

Visual Learning Activity The New Woman and the New Man, Learning with Documents folder, p. 59

Women's Roles

The notion that women should not depend on men for survival did not, as some believe, originate with the women's movements of the twentieth century. In her 1898 book, *Women and Economics,* Charlotte Perkins Gilman argued that, "If there should be built and opened. . . [an] apartment house for professional women with families, it would be filled at once. . . . It would be a home where the cleaning was done by [hired] workers . . . and [a] day nursery, and kindergarten, under well-trained professional nurses and teachers, would insure proper care of the children."

Time: 90 minutes.
Activity: Choose a club focus.
Grouping: Groups of four to six students.
Purpose: For many women in the late 1800s, club membership provided the means to involvement in public life for the first time. Have groups choose a focus for a club and develop an agenda of activities around that focus. Have a recorder from each group report to the class, and discuss common activities.
Roles: Members of a women's club.
Outcome: Students will portray the potential of clubs as a stepping-stone for women's broader participation in American society.

Answer to . . .

Viewing History *They worked at jobs inside and outside of the home; they were consumers of new goods.*

New technology reduced the time many women spent performing household chores. New responsibilities as household consumers, as suggested in the ad above, emerged along with these changes. *Economics In what ways were women engaged in the economy at the end of the 19th century?*

they began to shop for these items at stores and through the mail.

Growing urban populations, an abundance of manufactured goods, public transportation, and electric lighting led to the development of **department stores.** Department stores are retail establishments that carry a wide variety of goods. Unlike small general stores, which carried only a few items at high prices, department stores could offer their customers lower prices because they were able to buy larger quantities from manufacturers. Some of the earliest department stores included Marshall Field in Chicago, which opened in 1865, and Macy's in New York City, which opened in 1858.

Of course, farming families in rural areas of the Midwest also wanted access to manufactured items at low prices. Despite the protests of local shopkeepers, the United States Post Office began offering **rural free delivery** (RFD) in 1896 to any group of farmers who petitioned their congressman. By 1905, the Post Office was delivering mail on over 32,000 RFD routes. This free service gave farm families access to big-city goods through the use of **mail-order catalogs,** or printed materials advertising a wide range of goods that could be purchased by mail. Two of the largest mail-order companies were Montgomery Ward and Sears, Roebuck and Company. Both of these companies worked hard to gain their customers' trust by offering money-back guarantees.

Women's Work in the Home

As they had for centuries, women continued to perform most of the jobs in the home. Thanks to the era's technological revolution, some aspects of this work became less time-consuming. However, women still had much to do. In households that could not afford the benefits of technology, housework continued to be strenuous. Many homes were without indoor plumbing. Even as late as 1917, only one quarter of American homes had electricity. Though technology was not available to all people, it did free many women to pursue wage work, careers, and voluntary activity.

By 1900, fewer women were making their own bread or butchering and preserving their own meat. The number of foods available in tin cans increased fourfold between 1870 and 1880. Few women produced their family's clothing from start to finish anymore. Instead,

Working Outside the Home

In 1870 nearly two million women and girls, or one in every eight over the age of 10, worked outside the home. Women worked in each of the 338 occupations listed in the United States census. Most of these working women were single. In the decades that followed, however, a rising proportion of married women would go to work.

Most single female workers were between the ages of 16 and 24. Employers assumed they would leave upon marriage and rarely gave them supervisory jobs or advanced training. They also paid women $3 to $5 a week less than men—about 30 to 60 percent less—on average.

Domestic work was an important source of income for many women. In 1900 about one in fifteen American homes employed live-in servants. Most were women from foreign countries or African Americans. Working from dawn to dusk, six-and-a-half days a week, these women cooked, cleaned, washed, ironed, and cared for children. Many supported their own families who lived elsewhere.

American society accepted the stereotype that women did not have the mental capacity for professional training. In 1873 retired Harvard Medical School professor Edward H. Clarke warned in his famous book *Sex in Education* that young women could not engage in studying and learning while at the same time retaining "uninjured health and a future secure from [sickness], hysteria, and other derangements of the nervous system."

Three years before Clarke made this warning, the United States had 525 physicians, 67 ministers, and 5 lawyers who were women. Still, most Americans believed that for women, careers and married life did not go together. Self-supporting women were allowed to train for professions but were discouraged from entering fields that put them in competition with men. Women professionals found opportunities mostly in women's colleges and hospitals.

Volunteering for a Larger Role in Society
Women in both the North and South had performed important voluntary service during the Civil War. Afterward, there was an explosion of interest among many women in voluntary associations.

Women joined these organizations primarily for intellectual and social reasons. They studied subjects of common interest, gave talks on selected topics, or heard lectures by distinguished guests. Some organizations, such as the New England Woman's Club, founded in 1868, pursued specific causes such as temperance and girls' education. Others worked to establish new libraries and playgrounds. African American club women in Atlanta studied a national adult education program. The Chicago Woman's Club read Karl Marx's writings and other theoretical works.

Whatever their focus, clubs gave women invaluable experience in speaking, writing, and financial skills. They helped women increase their self-confidence and take their first steps toward public life.

As the number of clubs for women increased, the idea of joining them into national associations took hold. In 1873 the Association for the Advancement of Women came into being, and in 1890 the General Federation of Women's Clubs was formed. These groups took on increasingly ambitious projects, including suffrage and the correction of political abuses. In doing so, they joined with other groups founded to pursue specific reforms, such as the Woman's Christian

Main Idea CONNECTIONS

Describe the prevailing attitudes toward women's work outside the home in the late 1800s.

During this era, more women moved out of the home and into the workplace. Some, such as the telephone operators at left, worked in the new industries that came with industrialization. *Economics Why did employers routinely deny young women supervisory jobs or advanced training?*

RESOURCE OPTIONS

Teaching Resources

Comparing Primary Sources On the Woman Question, Units 5–6 folder, pp. 55–56

Media and Technology

AmericanHeritage® CD-ROM

History Makers Margaret Sanger

Explorer Activity 21 The Suffragists, CD-ROM Guidebook, pp. 61–62, helps students create a historical tour of the suffragist movement.

RESOURCE PRO

Biography Lucy Stone, found on Resource Pro, profiles the fervent abolitionist and pioneer in the struggle for women's rights.

Answer to . . .

Main Idea Connections Most people assumed that women could not sustain a marriage while working outside the home.

Viewing History They assumed that women would get married and quit their jobs.

Graphing the Main Idea

To make sure students understand the main idea of this section, you may wish to use the double web graphic organizer below.

Tell students that a double web graphic organizer compares information about two main ideas, topics, or groups. Ask students to use it to examine the role of women at the turn of the century.

Teaching Tip A template for this graphic organizer can be found in the Color Transparencies, G-2.

Answer to . . .

COMPARING PRIMARY SOURCES

EQUALITY FOR WOMEN

Americans debated the social, political, and economic roles of women in the late 1800s and early 1900s.

For Women's Rights	Against Women's Rights
"These things the women want to do and be and have are not in any sense masculine. They do not belong to men. They never did. They are departments of our social life, hitherto monopolized [until now controlled] by men." —*Charlotte Perkins Gilman,* "Are Women Human Beings?" Harper's Weekly, *May 25, 1912*	"So I say deliberately that the so-called woman movement is an attempt to escape the function of woman, a revolt against the fact that woman is not a man. . . . It is a rising against nature. It is a revolt against God." —*Dr. Cyrus Townsend Brady, from a sermon given October 17, 1915*

ANALYZING VIEWPOINTS **Summarize the arguments presented in the excerpts above.**

Temperance Union, formed in 1874, and the National American Woman Suffrage Association, formed in 1890. This last group would carry the cause of women's suffrage to victory some 30 years later.

New Women, New Ideas During this period of change, women struggled to agree on a proper focus for their activities. By the early 1900s, the woman question had grown to include a number of issues besides economic and political rights.

One issue was the question of lifestyle: How should women dress and behave? As more women entered the work force or went to college, they took this matter into their own hands. In search of more convenient hair styles, they began to shorten their hair. They raised hemlines and wore skirts and blouses that were more suited to their new activities. The New England Woman's Club even opened a store where women could buy the new styles of clothing.

Courting and marriage customs also changed. For example, instead of entertaining a man at home, many women now went out on dates without supervision. "New women," as they were sometimes called, still hoped to marry. Yet they seemed to have higher expectations of fulfillment in marriage. As a result, the divorce rate rose from one in twelve in 1900 to one in nine by 1916. Many married "new women" began to push for the legalized spread of information about birth control, a campaign led by New York nurse Margaret Sanger. Such developments were shocking to more traditional Americans.

What was the consensus among women on the woman question? Though the majority agreed with the principle of greater rights, most women still saw domestic fulfillment as their chief goal. The right to vote was another matter. The issue of the vote prompted huge numbers of women to support the suffrage movement in some way. Soon the vote would be the one issue on which women from many walks of life would unite.

SECTION 4 REVIEW

Comprehension

1. *Key Terms* Define: (a) department store; (b) rural free delivery; (c) mail-order catalog.

2. *Summarizing the Main Idea* What arguments were used by those Americans who did not want to expand women's roles in the economy and society in the late 1800s?

3. *Organizing Information* List the main characteristics of women's work outside the home in this period.

Critical Thinking

4. *Analyzing Time Lines* Review the time line at the beginning of this section. What do the organizations on this time line represent?

5. *Determining Relevance* How did the growth in women's employment and volunteer activity outside the home support the demands by women for greater political and social roles?

Writing Activity

6. *Writing an Expository Essay* Write an essay detailing some of the ways women benefited from membership in clubs.

Why Study History?

To understand that . . .

Education Is the Key to Success

Educational opportunity in the United States surged in the late 1800s. Today a good education is the gateway to economic success.

North Dakota classroom around 1910

What are your plans after high school? Will you work for a while to earn money for college? Go straight on to school? Take any job you can find? Times have changed since the late 1800s, when fewer than 10 percent of Americans graduated from high school. Today, more than 80 percent of Americans are high school graduates.

Recent statistics show that a good education has become an economic necessity, leading to higher wages and more stable employment. Between 1970 and 1994, for example, the hourly earnings of workers without college degrees declined. Hourly earnings of workers with college degrees rose. In 1998, the unemployment rate of high school dropouts was almost twice the rate for high school graduates and more than three times the rate for college graduates. A 1998 survey by the Bureau of Labor Statistics found that nearly 20 percent of high school dropouts ages 16 to 24 were unemployed.

The Impact Today

In preparing for life after high school, young people have many options. Some students take Advanced Placement courses in history, chemistry, calculus, or other subjects. By doing well on an Advanced Placement examination, high school students can get credit for introductory college courses.

Some students take courses in auto mechanics, bookkeeping, secretarial work, or other trades. Many high school students receive valuable on-the-job training through summer or part-time jobs.

A number of special programs help students prepare for work or further academic study after high school. For example, a government-sponsored program called Job Corps gives disadvantaged youth the academic, vocational, and social training that they need to obtain good jobs. Summer study programs, such as the Institute for the Academic Advancement of Youth at Johns Hopkins University, introduce students to the academic workload they can expect in college.

The Impact on You

Think about educational programs, work or apprenticeship programs, and other activities that might help you prepare for life after high school. Formulate a five-year plan for achieving your goals. You might ask guidance counselors, teachers, and librarians for help.

High school student learning auto repair

RESOURCE OPTIONS

Teaching Resources

Why Study History? Activity
Education Is the Key to Success, found in the Why Study History? folder, p. 18, provides an activity to help students better understand the link between education and success in the job market.

Media and Technology

AmericanHeritage® CD-ROM

Time Tour The Nation Today and Tomorrow: Toward a New Century

Why Study History?

Class Discussion

Discuss with the class the role of education in preparing students for future success. For a more thorough examination of the issue, see the activity folder in the Resource Options below.

ACTIVITY
STUDENT PARTICIPATION

Making a Poster
Ask students to read the text. Then have small groups create posters on volunteer opportunities, internships, and "learn while you earn" programs in these fields:
- **medicine**
- **journalism**
- **computer sciences**
- **veterinary medicine**
- **business**
- **teaching**

Encourage discussion about work-study programs that give practical experience to students.

Follow up Have groups share their findings with the class.

Using the Internet
Students can learn more about education and employment by exploring links in the *America: Pathways to the Present* Web site at:

http://www.Pathways.phschool.com

Assessment
See the Lesson Plans folder, pp. 24–27, for rubrics on assessing Class Participation Projects.

Chapter 17 Review

Key Terms

Students should refer to the definitions of the key terms in the chapter to write sentences that show an understanding of the social and cultural changes that took place following Reconstruction.

Comprehension

1. Child labor laws resulted in more children going to school rather than working; education laws mandated more schools and thus more students; newly arrived immigrants sent their children to public schools.

2. Women and African Americans were excluded from many schools, faced prejudice in higher education, and were denied scholarships. Both groups profited from colleges founded just for them.

3. Amusement parks, movie theaters, vaudeville, spectator and participatory sports, newspapers, magazines, and popular literature.

4. Ragtime evolved in the saloons of the South and Midwest, by combining shifting melodies with marching-band beats; jazz originated in New Orleans and synthesized a variety of different musical styles, including traditional hymns and the newer ragtime rhythms.

5. The NAACP worked through the courts system to gain civil rights for African Americans; the National Urban League improved job opportunities and housing for urban blacks.

6. The Supreme Court's "separate but equal" ruling meant that segregation was legal as long as the separate facilities for blacks were equal to those for whites.

7. Voting restrictions such as poll taxes and literacy tests; legal segregation such as Jim Crow laws; violence.

8. They joined volunteer organizations and clubs to enhance their practical and intellectual skills. The skills and self-confidence they gained in these groups compelled them to form national groups with more specific political and social goals.

Chapter Summary

The major concepts of Chapter 17 are presented below. See also *Guide to the Essentials of American History* or *Interactive Student Tutorial CD-ROM,* which contains interactive review activities, time lines, helpful hints, and test practice for Chapter 17.

Reviewing the Main Ideas

Between 1870 and 1915, more children began to attend school, and college became an attainable goal for a growing number of students. A recreation industry, which borrowed heavily from African American culture, also emerged. Yet some segments of society refused to grant African Americans and women an equal chance at success.

Section 1: The Expansion of Education

Education was a lofty goal that was out of reach for most nineteenth-century Americans. As the century came to a close, however, more and more Americans gained the opportunity to learn.

Section 2: New Forms of Entertainment

New forms of entertainment and sports emerged during the late 1800s.

Section 3: The World of Jim Crow

African Americans found their hopes dashed in the years after Reconstruction. Yet many not only resisted discrimination, but achieved success in spite of the obstacles placed before them.

Section 4: Women in the Late 1800s

Changes in women's lives, including new jobs, new educational opportunities, and new roles in the home, fueled a debate on the proper role of women in society at the turn of the century.

Educational opportunity surged in the late 1800s. Today education is the gateway to economic success. A number of special programs help students prepare for work or further academic study after high school.

Key Terms

For each of the terms below, write a sentence explaining how it relates to this chapter.

1. literacy	**7.** poll tax
2. assimilation	**8.** grandfather clause
3. philanthropist	**9.** rural free delivery
4. vaudeville	**10.** ragtime
5. yellow journalism	**11.** NAACP
6. Niagara Movement	**12.** Jim Crow

Comprehension

1. Why did public schools gain more students in the late 1800s?

2. In what ways were the experiences of women and African Americans similar with regard to higher education?

3. What entertainment was available to enjoy during the late 1800s?

4. Where and how did ragtime and jazz originate?

5. How did the NAACP and the National Urban League help African Americans during the early 1900s?

6. What was the Supreme Court's ruling in *Plessy* v. *Ferguson*?

7. What methods were used to prevent African Americans from voting?

8. Describe how women achieved greater social equality by the early 1900s.

Using Graphic Organizers

On a separate sheet of paper, copy the tree map to organize information about the expansion of education. Fill in at least two main idea statements for each heading.

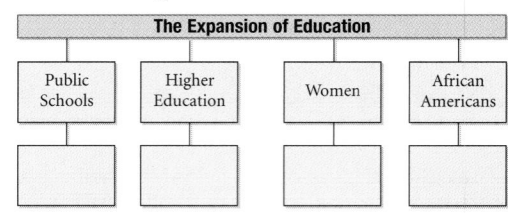

The Expansion of Education
- Public Schools
- Higher Education
- Women
- African Americans

Using Graphic Organizers

- Public schools: education laws require school attendance, immigrants send children to schools in large numbers.
- Higher education: New schools open to meet needs of growing industrial society, enrollment doubles in the last decade of the 19th century.
- Women: Philanthropists help establish private women's colleges, coeducational opportunities increase; still face discrimination.
- African Americans: Black colleges founded, debate over how blacks should use their education ensues; colleges still often unequal to those of whites, and few black women attend.

Analyzing Political Cartoons ▶

1. Read the words at the top of the cartoon. To what government do they refer?

2. Identify the figures. (a) What does each figure represent? (b) How do you know?

3. Analyze the woman on the right. (a) Why is she shackled? (b) Why is she appealing to the man on the left? (c) What is the purpose of representing the woman in the middle as supporting the woman on the right?

4. Read the words at the bottom of the cartoon. Explain the cartoonist's message.

Critical Thinking

1. *Applying the Chapter Skill* Locate a political cartoon in a newspaper or weekly news magazine. Identify and analyze the meanings of the symbols in the cartoon and then write a statement summarizing the cartoon's main point.

2. *Making Comparisons* As greater numbers of people sought entertainment during the late 1800s, a commercial recreation industry emerged. How are the types of activities available today similar to the types of activities available during the late 1800s?

3. *Expressing Problems Clearly* Jim Crow required the segregation of whites and African Americans. Aside from the fact that facilities for African Americans were inferior, how might segregation have harmed African Americans?

ANALYZING DOCUMENTS ▶ INTERPRETING DATA

Turn to the graph of illiteracy in the United States in Section 1.

1. In which year were illiteracy rates the highest? (a) 1870 (b) 1880 (c) 1890 (d) 1920

2. Which of the following statements best summarizes the information in this graph? (a) Few people were able to read and write in the late 1800s. (b) About 10 percent of the United States population was illiterate in 1900. (c) During the period from 1870 to 1920, illiteracy rates dropped in the United States. (d) Literacy was an important requirement for citizenship in the United States.

3. *Writing* Write an essay in which you describe some of the likely causes for a decrease in illiteracy in the United States between 1870 and 1920.

A GOVERNMENT OF THE PEOPLE BY THE PEOPLE FOR THE PEOPLE

ARE NOT THE WOMEN HALF THE NATION?

INTERNET ACTIVITY

For your portfolio:
WRITE AN ESSAY

Access Prentice Hall's *America: Pathways to the Present* site at **www.Pathways.phschool.com** for the specific URL to complete the activity. Additional resources and related Web sites are also available.

Read about the life of African American entrepreneur Sarah Breedlove (Madam C. J.) Walker. How does her life and work exemplify the social changes of the era in which she lived?

Connecting to Today

Making Comparisons
During the 1890s local storekeepers protested rural free delivery by the Post Office because they feared competition from mail-order businesses that offered a greater variety of goods at lower prices. Describe the challenges faced by local storeowners today. How are they similar to the challenges faced by local storekeepers in the 1890s?

INTERNET ACTIVITY

Essays will vary but should address her ability to overcome her family's slave and sharecropping background and succeed as an entrepreneur in the mail-order business. Details might include: her domestic work; her business; her real-estate investments in Harlem; her support for the NAACP and other groups; her efforts to expand black rights.

Analyzing Political Cartoons

1. The United States government.
2. (a) The seated woman represents American women, the standing woman represents justice, and the man represents the government. (b) The seated woman wears a banner reading "unenfranchised" to indicate that she is an American woman who cannot vote; the standing woman wears a banner reading "Justice"; the man wears clothes representing the government.
3. (a) Because her rights are limited. (b) She appeals to the government to grant women liberty and justice. (c) That justice for women is a natural right even though the man is not granting it.
4. That women are shackled to inequality by the power of men, even though equality is their natural right.

Critical Thinking

1. Answers will vary but should indicate an understanding of the cartoon selected.
2. Sample answer: Theme parks and movies have replaced trolley parks and vaudeville. Sports have been important in both eras.
3. It made it clear to African Americans that they were thought to be different from and inferior to whites, undermining their self-confidence; they limited African Americans' chances to advance in society or even obtain adequate housing and education; they gave whites excessive power over blacks.

Interpreting Data

1. a
2. c
3. Essays will vary but should be based on facts from the section.

Connecting to Today

Storekeepers today still face competition from mail-order companies, as well as competition from companies on the Internet, and from large national chains.

My Brush with History

Focus Have students find the meaning of each of these words in a dictionary before they begin to read: *vehement, rookery, hovel, locality, consternation, glimpse.* Ask them to think, as they read, about how segregation shaped the attitudes of blacks and whites toward one another. Explain the allusion to Spanish-American heroes. *(In 1898, the United States declared war on Spain. African American troops served with distinction in the Spanish-American War, which the United States won resoundingly in just three months.)*

Instruct Ask students to think about a typical day in their family's life. Discuss with students how the presence of Jim Crow would affect such a day. Elicit specific examples.

To ensure that students grasp the speaker's subtle points, call on volunteers to explain sentences such as the following:

- "There is no wonder that we die; the wonder is that we persist in living."
- "We had ruined his neighborhood of poor people; poor as we, poorer in manners at least."

Analyzing the Document

Use this additional question to generate class discussion:
CRITICAL THINKING: DEMONSTRATING REASONED JUDGMENT Give evidence to support the speaker's statement, "I have seen very small white children hang their black dolls. It is not the child's fault, he is simply an apt pupil . . ." *(Adult whites hanged African Americans under Jim Crow.)*

American Heritage®

My Brush with History

BY AN AFRICAN AMERICAN WOMAN IN THE SOUTH

INTRODUCTION The editors of *American Heritage* magazine have selected this account, published in 1902 and written by an unnamed African American woman living in the South. In it she described the world of Jim Crow—the daily frustrations and humiliations that African Americans had to endure as they struggled to build successful lives.

I am a colored woman, wife and mother. I have lived all my life in the South, and have often thought what a peculiar fact it is that the more ignorant the Southern whites are of us the more vehement they are in their denunciation of us. They boast that they have little intercourse with us, never see us in our homes, churches or places of amusement, but still they know us thoroughly.

They also admit that they know us in no capacity except as servants, yet they say we are at our best in that single capacity. What philosophers they are! The Southerners say we Negroes are a happy, laughing set of people, with no thought of tomorrow. How mistaken they are! The educated, thinking Negro is just the opposite. There is a feeling of unrest, insecurity, almost panic among the best class of Negroes in the South. In our homes, in our churches, wherever two or three are gathered together, there is a discussion of what is best to do. Must we remain in the South or go elsewhere? Where can we go to feel that security which other people feel? Is it best to go in great numbers or only in several families? These and many other things are discussed over and over. . . .

I know of houses occupied by poor Negroes in which a respectable farmer would not keep his cattle. It is impossible for them to rent elsewhere. All Southern real estate agents have "white property" and "colored property." In one of the largest Southern cities there is a colored minister, a graduate of Harvard, whose wife is an educated, Christian woman, who lived for weeks in a tumble-down rookery because he could neither rent nor buy in a respectable locality.

Many colored women who wash, iron, scrub, cook or sew all the week to help pay the rent for these miserable hovels and help fill the many small mouths, would deny themselves some of the necessaries of life if they could take their little children and teething babies on the cars to the parks of a Sunday afternoon and sit under trees, enjoy the cool breezes and breathe God's pure air for only two or three hours; but this is denied them. Some of the parks have signs, "No Negroes allowed on these grounds except as servants." Pitiful, pitiful customs and laws that make war on women and babes! There is no wonder

Educated African Americans were often restricted to low-paying jobs.

510

TEST PREPARATION

Have students use the excerpt on these pages to answer the following question.

What sentence below best summarizes the excerpt?

A Southern whites believed themselves to be superior.

B Southern whites restricted African Americans to housing not fit for cattle or pigs.

C Southern whites had no respect for an African American minister and Harvard graduate.

Ⓓ Southern whites humiliated African Americans through their continuing practice of Jim Crow.

that we die; the wonder is that we persist in living.

Fourteen years ago I had just married. My husband had saved sufficient money to buy a small home. On account of our limited means we went to the suburbs, on unpaved streets, to look for a home, only asking for a high, healthy locality. Some real estate agents were "sorry, but had nothing to suit," some had "just the thing," but we discovered on investigation that they had "just the thing" for an unhealthy pigsty. Others had no "colored property." One agent said that he had what we wanted, but we should have to go to see the lot after dark, or walk by and give the place a casual look; for, he said, "all the white people in the neighborhood would be down on me." Finally, we bought this lot. When the house was being built we went to see it. Consternation reigned. We had ruined his neighborhood of poor people; poor as we, poorer in manners at least. The people who lived next door received the sympathy of their friends. When we walked on the street (there were no sidewalks) we were embarrassed by the stare of many unfriendly eyes.

Two years passed before a single woman spoke to me, and only then because I helped one of them when a little sudden trouble came to her. Such was the reception, I a happy young woman, just married, received from people among whom I wanted to make a home. Fourteen years have now passed, four children have been born to us, and one has died in this same home, among these same neighbors. Although the neighbors speak to us . . . , not one woman has ever been inside of my house, not even at the times when a woman would doubly appreciate the slightest attention of a neighbor. . . .

White agents and other chance visitors who come into our homes ask questions that we must not dare ask their wives. They express surprise that our children have clean faces and that their hair is combed. . . .

We were delighted to know that some of our Spanish-American heroes were coming where we could get a glimpse of them. Had not black men helped in a small way to give them their honors? In the cities of the South, where these heroes went, the white school children were assembled, flags waved, flowers strewn, speeches made, and "My Country, 'tis of Thee, Sweet Land of Liberty," was sung. Our children who need to be taught so much, were not assembled, their hands waved no flags, they threw no flowers, heard no thrilling speech, sang no song of their country. And this is the South's idea of justice. Is it surprising that feeling grows more bitter, when the white mother teaches her boy to hate my boy, not because he is mean, but because his skin is dark? I have seen very small white children hang their black dolls. It is not the child's fault, he is simply an apt pupil. . . .

Source: Anonymous, *Independent* magazine, 1902.

Laundry day in Birmingham, Alabama

In the Jim Crow South, even laundry services were segregated by race.

ADDITIONAL READING

To learn more about the topics discussed in this selection, you might want to read the following books:

- *The Crucible of Race: Black/White Relations in the American South Since Emancipation,* by Joel Williamson (New York: Oxford University Press, 1984)
- *The Souls of Black Folk,* by W.E.B. Du Bois (New York: Library of America, 1986)
- *Trouble in Mind: Black Southerners in the Age of Jim Crow,* by Leon Litwak (New York: Alfred A. Knopf, 1998)
- *Up from Slavery,* by Booker T. Washington (New York: Oxford University Press, 1995)

TEST PREPARATION

Have students use the excerpt on these pages to answer the following question.

Which of her neighbors' slights gave the speaker most pain?

A The neighbors' allowing their children to hang their black dolls.

B The neighbors' failing to call on the speaker after her child died.

C The neighbors' expressing surprise that the speaker's children are clean and well cared for.

(D) The neighbors' unfriendliness and lack of even slight attention.

The United States on the Brink of Change

1890–1920

Introducing the Unit

Using Historical Evidence

Direct students to the photograph on the right and point out the Brooklyn Bridge in the background. Ask students to list the kinds of transportation shown in the picture. Then divide the class into discussion groups and ask each group to explain why a vigorously expanding economy continually needs new markets. Ask students to identify the overseas market advertised by the steamship company in the picture.

Themes in American History

Direct students' attention to the Unit Themes. Point out that each chapter in this unit has its own theme. To teach this unit thematically, you may wish to use the Prosperity, Depression, and War folder in **American History Block Scheduling Support.**

Using the Time Line

To provide students with practice in using a time line to connect key events in the United States with key events in the world, ask questions such as these: (1) How many years after World War I began did the United States enter the war? *(3 years.)* (2) What event occurred in Russia during World War I? *(The Russian Revolution.)* (3) Who was President during the Spanish-American War? *(McKinley)*

---

unit SIX

The United States on the Brink of Change

1 8 9 0 – 1 9 2 0

*T*he industrial boom at the turn of the century had far-reaching effects. It created serious problems that inspired a reform movement known as progressivism. It also led the United States to join the scramble for new territories as it searched for new markets. Both the ambitions of the imperialists and the ideals of the progressives contributed to the nation's growing role as a world power. This role eventually drew the United States into the horrors of World War I.

Chapter 18	Becoming a World Power *1890–1913*
Chapter 19	The Era of Progressive Reform *1890–1920*
Chapter 20	The World War I Era *1914–1920*

UNIT THEMES

Foreign Relations Pursuit of new markets and territory fueled United States expansion.

Culture Progressive reformers sought governmental solutions to the problems that resulted from rapid industrialization.

Science and Technology New forms of weaponry and warfare contributed to a devastating stalemate in World War I.

EVENTS IN THE UNITED STATES

1890 National American Woman Suffrage Association formed

1898 Turning Point: The Spanish-American War (p. 521)

1899 John Hay announces Open Door Policy

1904 Roosevelt Corollary to the Monroe Doctrine

Presidents	Cleveland	Harrison	Cleveland	McKinley	
1885		**1890**	**1895**	**1900**	

EVENTS IN THE WORLD

1895
• Japan defeats China in Sino-Japanese War
• Cubans rebel against Spanish rule

1900 Boxer Rebellion breaks out in China

▶ RESOURCE OPTIONS

Teaching Resources

📁 **Units 5–6 folder** Contains instructional materials organized by chapter.

VIEWING HISTORY New York City's docks were teeming with activity in the early 1900s. Spurred by an economic boom, the United States reached across the Atlantic Ocean in its quest to become an economic and political world power. *Geography* **How did expansion overseas draw the United States into international conflicts?**

Suffrage poster

1906 Upton Sinclair publishes The Jungle

1913 Sixteenth and Seventeenth amendments ratified

1914 Panama Canal completed

1917 United States declares war on Germany

1918 Wilson announces Fourteen Points

1920 Nineteenth Amendment ratified

T. Roosevelt | Taft | Wilson

1905 | **1910** | **1915** | **1920**

1905 Japan defeats Russia in Russo-Japanese War

1914 World War I begins

1917 Russian Revolution

1918 Germany surrenders

1919 League of Nations formed

THE VOTE
GIVE YOUR CHILDREN EQUAL RIGHTS
VOTE YES Nov. 2
On the Amendment Enabling Woman to Vote

RESOURCE OPTIONS

Media and Technology

Color Transparencies Specific transparencies are referenced at points of use. See American Photo, B-6; Fine Art, D-16; Cause and Effect, F-5; Links Across Time, J-6; Political Cartoons, K-6; and Geographic Setting, M-9.

Visions of America "Scenes of an Era: The United States on the Brink of Change" located on videodisc side 2 and on videotape 3. Lesson plans for "Scenes of an Era" can be found in the Visions of America Guidebook.

Side 2, Chapter 21

Answer to . . .

Viewing History The United States competed with countries like Japan and Spain for influence and markets.

Becoming a World Power, 1890–1913

Managing Time and Instruction

INSTRUCTION SUPPORT

These materials for instruction are provided for each section in the **Teaching Resources**. See **Units 5–6 folder for Enrichment Support**:

- Reproducible Lesson Plans in Lesson Plans folder • Learning Styles Lesson Plans in Learning Styles Lesson Plans folder • Big Idea Graphic Organizers in Big Idea Graphic Organizer folder
- Guided Reading and Review • Quizzes • Test Preparation Practice booklet

DAILY LESSON	ENRICHMENT SUPPORT
1 **The Pressure to Expand** (pp. 515–518)	• Nystrom *Atlas of Our Country,* Later Expansion of the United States, pp. 32–33 • Visual Learning Activity, Expansionism, found on **Resource Pro**
2 **The Spanish–American War** (pp. 519–525)	• Literature Activity, "The Open Boat," found on **Resource Pro** • Critical Thinking Activity, Drawing Conclusions: The Explosion of the *Maine*, found on **Resource Pro** • Visual Learning Activity, Wartime Propaganda, Learning with Documents folder, p. 60 • Primary Source Activity, Teddy Roosevelt: Letters Home, found on **Resource Pro** • Biography, Walter Reed, Units 5–6 folder, p. 67 • Great Debates, Should the United States Have Colonies? Decision-Making Activities folder, pp. 34–35
3 **Expansion Under Roosevelt and Taft** (pp. 527–531)	• Skills for Life Activity, Units 5–6 folder, p. 71 • Nystrom *Atlas of Our Country,* Later Expansion of the United States, pp. 32–33 • Primary Source Activity, The Panamanian Revolution, Learning with Documents folder, p. 24 • Literature Activity, "You're All Right, Teddy," Units 5–6 folder, p. 70 • Key Documents, "The Strenuous Life," Learning with Documents folder, p. 94
4 **Debating America's New Role** (pp. 534–536)	• Comparing Primary Sources, On the Race for Empire, Units 5–6 folder, pp. 68–69 • Biography, Juliette Gordon Low, found on **Resource Pro** • Your Nation Is a World Power, Why Study History? folder, p. 19

Running Out of Time?

- Use Tape 3, "The United States on the Brink of Change, 1890–1920," from **Visions of America** videotapes series.
- Use Chapter 18 Summary, from **Guide to the Essentials of American History (English and Spanish)**.

Companion Web Site

The companion Web site offers online links for all chapter review activities. It also provides key content links and structured support for this chapter for both teachers and students.

http://www.Pathways.phschool.com

Teaching in the Information Age

Media and Technology

For the Student

Interactive Student Tutorial CD-ROM Chapter 18
Student Edition on Audiotape Chapter 18
American Heritage® CD-ROM
Guided Reading Audiotapes (English and Spanish) Chapter 18

For the Teacher

Resource Pro CD-ROM Chapter 18
Test Bank CD-ROM Chapter 18
Listening to Literature Audiotapes *Timeless Voices, Timeless Themes* from "This Is Just to Say" by William Carlos Williams

Assessment Options

Chapter Test Forms A&B Test Bank CD-ROM booklet
Test Bank CD-ROM Chapter 18
Standardized Test Preparation Handbook

Block Scheduling

Pacing Suggestions

For 90-minute Blocks

- Teach sections 1 and 2 using Transparencies C–11, K–6, F-7, I-12, D-15, and M-9 and the Recent Scholarship note on p. 520 for class discussions.
- Teach sections 3 and 4 using the Big Idea Graphic Organizers from Teaching Resources and the Extended Class Periods Activity on p. 536.

Additional Resources

- Prentice Hall's **American History Block Scheduling Support File** covers over 40 major topics in American history.
- **Prentice Hall United States History Video Collection™** contains 20 videotapes covering American history from beginnings to present.
- **Decision America Videotapes and Videodiscs**

Connections to American Literature

from Prentice Hall

Prentice Hall Literature *Timeless Voices, Timeless Themes* "Gulf War Journal" from *A Woman at War* by Molly Moore, p. 507

Additional Resources

For the Student
G. J. A. O'Toole. *The Spanish War: An American Epic—1898.* Norton, 1986.
Judith St. George. *Panama Canal: Gateway to the World.* Putnam's, 1989.

For the Teacher
George P. Marks III, ed. *The Black Press Views American Imperialism (1898–1900).* Arno Press and the New York Times, Inc., 1971.
David McCullough. *The Path Between the Seas: The Creation of the Panama Canal, 1870–1914.* Simon & Schuster, 1977.

Prentice Hall brings into the classroom the vast archives and scholarship of the nation's premier American history magazine. See "From the Archives of American Heritage®" and "About the Presidents" teaching notes in this chapter.

History Alive!

Teacher's Curriculum Institute, in partnership with Prentice Hall, provides unique materials that engage students with diverse learning styles. See History Alive!® unit on The United States Coming of Age: 1890–1920.

Student Performance Pack

Ensures success in the three critical areas of Reading, Test Taking, and English Language Development with the following materials:
- Guide to the Essentials of American History in English and Spanish
- Guided Reading Audiotapes in English and Spanish
- Interactive Student Tutorial CD–ROM
- Test Preparation Handbook
- Test Preparation Practice booklet

Becoming a World Power

1890–1913

Introducing the Chapter

By the 1890s, businesses and political leaders with dreams of empire were pushing into new markets and seizing control of territory abroad. Imperialism on the part of a country founded on freedom from colonialism troubled many United States citizens. The responsibilities of a world power brought conflicting domestic and international agendas of the government to the forefront.

Themes in American History

The theme for this chapter, Foreign Relations, is listed at the beginning of this unit. An alternate theme for the chapter is Government. To teach this unit thematically, you may wish to use the Prosperity, Depression, and War folder in American History Block Scheduling Support.

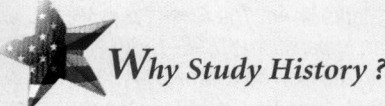

Why Study History?

Have students explore suggested ways of connecting the past to the present on page 537.

Answer to . . .

Viewing History Students should use this question as an aid in reading the chapter. Economic pressures, such as meeting the nation's increasing need for natural resources, encouraged the expansion of United States influence overseas.

CHAPTER 18 Becoming a World Power

1890–1913

CHAPTER FOCUS

This chapter describes the years when the United States grew to be a world power. Growth in American industry pushed business and political leaders to look for new markets abroad. Some Americans, inspired by grand dreams of an empire, pursued new territory as well.

The *Why Study History?* page at the end of this chapter explores the connection between United States participation in world affairs in the early 1900s and its role in the global community today.

VIEWING HISTORY
Edward Moran captured the triumph of the Great White Fleet in his 1899 painting *Return of the Conquerors. Foreign Relations* **Why did the United States expand its influence overseas?**

 RESOURCE OPTIONS

Teaching Resources

Big Idea Graphic Organizer folder
Graphic summary of the main idea of the chapter.

Learning Styles Lesson Plans folder
Alternate lesson plans for diverse learning styles for each chapter.

Media and Technology

 AmericanHeritage® CD-ROM
Time Tour A New Role in the World: Expanding Overseas

 Prentice Hall United States History Video Collection™ Volume 15 *The United States and the World*

1867
United States buys Alaska and annexes Midway Islands

1875
United States signs trade agreement with Hawaii

1881
Congress establishes Naval Advisory Board

1884
American businessman granted long-term lease in Costa Rica

1890
Alfred Mahan publishes The Influence of Sea Power Upon History

1865   1875   1885   1895

1 The Pressure to Expand

SECTION PREVIEW

Objectives

1. Explain some of the reasons for the growth of imperialism around the world.
2. Summarize the American view regarding imperialism prior to 1890.
3. *Key Terms* Define: imperialism; nationalism; annex; banana republic.

Main Idea

In the late 1800s, as European nations took over vast areas in Africa and Asia, American leaders looked to expand American influence abroad.

Reading Strategy

Reinforcing Main Ideas As you read, create a list of the pressures that led the United States to adopt a policy of political and economic expansion overseas.

By the late 1800s, the industrialists, inventors, and workers of the United States had built a powerful industrial economy. But the overproduction of food and goods led to financial panic and depression. Labor and farmers protested their plight, helping to convince business and political leaders that the United States must secure new markets abroad. Some people also began to believe that the United States had a duty to carry democratic values and Christianity to others around the globe.

Growth of Imperialism

Meanwhile, as the maps on the next page show, Europe had reached new heights in its quest for territories to rule. The late 1800s marked the peak of European imperialism, with much of Africa and Asia under foreign domination. Under **imperialism,** stronger nations attempt to create empires by dominating weaker nations—economically, politically, culturally, or militarily.

Why Imperialism Grew Several factors accounted for the burst of imperialistic activity in the late 1800s.

(1) *Economic factors.* The growth of industry in Europe created an increased need for natural resources, such as rubber and petroleum. Manufacturing nations also required new markets in which to sell their manufactured goods.

(2) *Nationalist factors.* Competition among European nations for large empires was the result of **nationalism,** or devotion to one's nation. For example, when France acquired colonies in West Africa in the late 1800s, rival nations Great Britain and Germany seized lands nearby to stop French expansion.

(3) *Military factors.* Advances in military technology produced European armies and navies that were far superior to those in Africa and Asia. Also, Europe's growing navies required bases around the world for taking on fuel and supplies.

(4) *Humanitarian factors.* Humanitarian and religious goals spurred on imperialists. Colonial officials, doctors, and missionaries believed they had a duty to spread the blessings of Western civilization, including its law, medicine, and Christian religion.

Businesses, such as this fruit grower, eagerly sought new markets abroad.

RESOURCE OPTIONS

Teaching Resources

Reproducible Lesson Plan Lesson Plans folder, p. 105

Big Idea Graphic Organizer Big Idea Graphic Organizer folder, p. 77

Guided Reading and Review Units 5–6 folder, p. 59

 Nystrom *Atlas of Our Country* Later Expansion of the United States, pp. 32–33

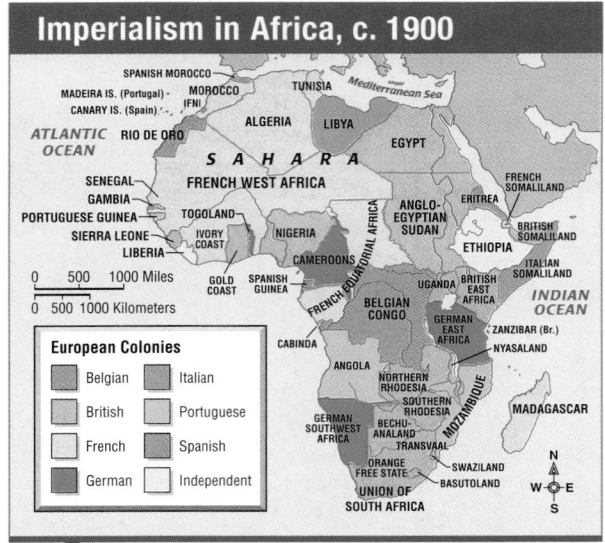

Imperialism in Africa, c. 1900

European Colonies
- Belgian
- British
- French
- German
- Italian
- Portuguese
- Spanish
- Independent

By 1900, European imperialist nations controlled vast amounts of territory in Africa. *Place* Which African nations retained their independence from imperialist control?

Imperialism in Asia, c. 1900

Spheres of Influence
- American
- British
- French
- German
- Japanese
- Russian
- Independent
- Treaty port

The United States and Japan joined European nations in exerting economic control, or "spheres of influence," in Asian nations. *Location* Where was the American sphere of influence?

Europe Leads the Way Improved transportation and communication made it easier for Great Britain, France, and Russia, all with long imperialist traditions, to extend their grip to far-flung lands. Great Britain, in particular, acquired so much new territory around the globe that the saying "The sun never sets on the British Empire" became popular. Competition for new territory grew even more intense when Germany, unified in 1871, seized colonies in Africa and Asia.

By 1890 the United States was eager to join the competition for new territories. Supporters of expansion denied that the United States sought to **annex** foreign lands. (To annex is to join a new territory to an existing country.) Yet annexation did take place.

The United States and Imperialism

In his Farewell Address in 1796, President George Washington had advised Americans to "steer clear of permanent alliances" with other countries. For the next century, Americans generally followed Washington's advice. The nation's rapid economic growth along with the settlement of the West left the United States with little interest in foreign affairs.

There were instances, however, when Americans "looked outward." In 1866, for example, Secretary of State Seward sent 50,000 troops to the Mexican border after France placed an emperor on the Mexican throne. In the face of this army, the French abandoned their colonial venture. Then, in 1867, Seward bought Alaska from Russia. Most Americans ridiculed the venture. Seward, they said, was buying "walrus-covered icebergs" in a "barren, worthless, God-forsaken region." Seward, however, waged a successful campaign to educate the nation about Alaska's rich resources. In the end, the Senate ratified the purchase, and the United States took possession of "Seward's Folly."

Americans also showed their interest in the Pacific. In 1853 an American fleet led by Commodore Matthew C. Perry sailed into Tokyo Bay and convinced Japan to open trade relations with the United States. By the 1860s the United States and several European countries had signed a series of treaties that allowed for expanded trade with China.

Now the United States government wanted control of some Pacific islands to use as refueling and repair stations for its naval vessels. To this end, Seward annexed the uninhabited

Midway Islands in 1867. Eight years later the United States government signed a treaty with Hawaii. This agreement allowed Hawaiians to sell sugar in the United States duty free, as long as they did not sell or lease territory to any foreign power.

By the 1890s, American attitudes toward foreign affairs had changed. A debate arose over what foreign policy would best serve the United States. Some argued that the country should continue to avoid foreign entanglements. Others offered a variety of reasons for increased American involvement in international affairs.

Promoting Economic Growth A chief argument in favor of expansion was economic. By the late 1800s, Americans simply could not consume all of the food and other goods that their nation produced. In 1890, James G. Blaine, Secretary of State under President Harrison, summarized the situation as follows:

 AMERICAN VOICES ❝We have developed a volume of manufactures which, in many departments, overruns the demands of the home market. . . . Our great demand is expansion . . . of trade with countries where we can find profitable exchanges.❞

—*James G. Blaine*

Many business leaders agreed that the economic problems of the nation could only be solved by expanding its markets. For this reason, they threw their support behind expansionist policies. Some American businesses already dominated international markets. In the 1880s and 1890s, firms such as Rockefeller's Standard Oil and American Telephone and Telegraph had all became popular internationally. So had products such as McCormick farm machinery, Singer sewing machines, Kodak cameras, and Sherwin-Williams paint.

Other American business leaders had gone a step further and invested directly in the economies of other countries. In some cases their investments gave them political influence in those countries. In Central America, for example, an American named Minor C. Keith provided financial services to the Costa Rican government. In return, in 1884 he won long-term leases for lands and railroad lines. By 1913 Keith's United Fruit Company not only exported 50 million bunches of bananas a year to the United States, but also dominated the governments

Value of United States Exports, 1870–1920

Source: *Historical Statistics of the United States, Colonial Times to 1970*

Interpreting Graphs The expansion of American businesses into international markets in the late 1800s and early 1900s led to the rapid rise in U.S. exports during this period. *Economics By how much did U.S. exports increase between 1870 and 1920?*

and economies of Costa Rica, Guatemala, and Honduras. As a result, some people began to refer to the Central American nations as **banana republics.**

Protecting American Security Lobbyists who favored a strong United States Navy formed a second force pushing for expansion. By the 1880s, United States warships left over from the Civil War were rusting and rotting. Naval officers joined with business interests to convince Congress to build modern steam-powered, steel-hulled ships to protect overseas trade.

The most influential of these officers was Captain (later Admiral) Alfred T. Mahan. In his 1890 book, *The Influence of Sea Power Upon History, 1660–1783,* Mahan argued that the nation's economic future hinged on gaining new markets abroad. In his view, the United States needed a powerful navy to protect these markets from foreign rivals.

Influenced by supporters of an expanded navy, Congress established a Naval Advisory Board in 1881. The board pushed to increase the navy's budget. Two years later, Congress authorized the building of three cruisers and two battleships, including the U.S.S. *Maine.* Finally, the Naval Act of 1890 called for the construction of more battleships, gunboats, torpedo boats, and cruisers. By 1900, the United States had one of the most powerful navies in the world. The expanded fleet suggested that the United

Main Idea
CONNECTIONS
Why did Alfred T. Mahan think it was necessary for the United States to build a strong navy?

Customize for
Less Proficient Readers

Have students write at least one cause for each of these effects:
• U.S. companies began to dominate the affairs of banana republics.
• Congress authorized an expansion of the United States Navy.
• Public opinion gradually warmed to the idea of expansionism.

As this 1901 political cartoon suggests, the United States relied on the principles of the Monroe Doctrine to block European involvement in Latin America. *Foreign Relations* *How did expansion of trade lead to the expansion of the United States Navy?*

States was willing and able to confront an enemy on the open sea.

Preserving American Spirit A third force for expansion consisted of people who feared that the United States was losing its vitality. Among them were Massachusetts senator Henry Cabot Lodge, historian Frederick Jackson Turner, and a rising young politician from New York named Theodore Roosevelt. Worried that the closing of the frontier would sap the nation's energy, they argued that a quest for empire might restore the country's pioneer spirit.

These and other leaders of the day also drew on the doctrine of social Darwinism to justify the takeover of new territories, just as they had done earlier to defend the conquest of Native Americans. In the opinion of respected leaders such as Congregationalist minister Josiah Strong and Indiana senator Albert J. Beveridge, the civilizations produced by Anglo-Saxon and Teutonic (Germanic) peoples were superior to the societies they conquered.

Thus, social Darwinists believed that expansionism was not only this nation's destiny but a noble pursuit as well, for it introduced Christianity and modern civilization to other peoples around the world. It is important to remember that this was an era before scientific studies showed that no racial or national group is superior to any other.

Public Opinion Leans Toward Expansion Gradually public opinion warmed to the idea of expansionism. Most Americans did not see themselves as potential rulers of oppressed foreign peoples, but they did want new markets abroad and favorable trade relations. What they soon discovered was that political and military entanglements tended to follow. The United States would find itself in difficult, bloody, and painful foreign conflicts.

Answers to
SECTION 1 REVIEW

1. (a) imperialism, see p. 515; (b) nationalism, see p. 515; (c) annex, see p. 516; (d) banana republic, see p. 517.

2. The nation needed foreign markets to provide a place to sell its surplus products.

3. Details may include: the need for natural resources and new markets; protecting American territory and keeping pace with European expansion; fulfilling the nation's destiny according to such philosophies as social Darwinism.

4. Sample answer: U.S. annexes Midway Islands, because they could be used as a port for the expanded U.S. Navy, and they were a stepping stone for future expansion.

5. Industrial growth; advances in military technology; humanitarian and religious goals.

6. Essays will vary but should be supported with facts from the section.

SECTION 1 REVIEW

Comprehension

1. *Key Terms* Define: (a) imperialism; (b) nationalism; (c) annex; (d) banana republic.

2. *Summarizing the Main Idea* Why did United States policymakers feel the need to secure new markets abroad in the late 1800s?

3. *Organizing Information* Create a web diagram that describes the major arguments for American expansionism. Label the center circle *Arguments for Expansionism.* Include supporting details in at least three surrounding circles.

Critical Thinking

4. *Analyzing Time Lines* Review the time line at the start of the section. Which event, in your opinion, best reflects American expansionist policies?

5. *Drawing Conclusions* What factors aided European imperialism in the late 1800s?

Writing Activity

6. *Writing an Expository Essay* Research and write a brief essay tracing the history of American expansionism before 1880. Be sure to include specific examples of expansionism in your essay.

RESOURCE OPTIONS

Teaching Resources

Quiz Units 5–6 folder, p. 60

Student Performance Pack

Guide to the Essentials Chapter 18, Section 1 (English and Spanish)

Answer to . . .

Viewing History The Navy was expanded to protect overseas trade.

| 1891 United States demands compensation from Chile | 1895 United States demands Britain acknowledge Monroe Doctrine | 1898 U.S.S. Maine explodes in Havana harbor | 1898 Congress approves annexation of Hawaii | 1899 John Hay publishes Open Door Policy |

1891   **1893**   **1895**   **1897**   **1899**

2 The Spanish-American War

SECTION PREVIEW

Objectives

1. Describe the ways in which the United States took advantage of several incidents in Latin America to reaffirm the Monroe Doctrine.
2. Analyze the events leading up to and following the Spanish-American War.
3. Identify the areas after the war where the United States gained influence and new territories.
4. *Key Terms* Define: arbitration; jingoism; sphere of influence; Open Door Policy.

Main Idea

A swift American victory in the Spanish-American War confirmed the nation's status as a world power, but it left some people arguing over how to govern newly acquired territories.

Reading Strategy

Organizing Information Create a two-column chart entitled *United States Foreign Policy.* In the left-hand column, list countries where the United States pursued expansionist policies. In the right-hand column list the effects of United States policies.

Those in the United States who dreamed of expansion looked to three main areas of the world in the late 1800s: Latin America, the islands of the Pacific, and China. In the 1890s, the United States established a pattern of intervention in these three areas that changed its status in world politics. In the process of expanding and becoming a world power, however, the United States increasingly found itself in conflict with other nations.

Involvement in Latin America

American expansionists paid close attention to the political and economic actions of countries in the Western Hemisphere. During the 1890s, the United States played an active role in several diplomatic and military conflicts in Latin America.

United States in Latin America In 1891 an angry Chilean mob attacked a group of American sailors on shore leave in Valparaíso.

They killed two Americans and injured seventeen others. The United States government reacted strongly, forcing Chile to pay $75,000 to the families of those sailors who were killed or injured. Two years later, when a rebellion threatened the friendly republican government of Brazil, President Cleveland ordered naval units to Rio de Janeiro to protect United States shipping interests. This show of force broke the back of the rebellion.

In the third and most important incident of the era, the United States confronted the nation then considered the most powerful in the world, Great Britain. Since the 1840s, Britain and Venezuela had disputed ownership of a piece of territory located at the border between Venezuela and British Guiana. In the 1880s, the dispute intensified when rumors surfaced of mineral wealth in this border area. President Cleveland's Secretary of State, Richard Olney, demanded in July 1895 that Britain acknowledge the Monroe Doctrine and submit the boundary dispute to **arbitration.** (Arbitration is the settlement of a dispute by a person chosen

RESOURCE OPTIONS

Teaching Resources

📁 **Reproducible Lesson Plan** Lesson Plans folder, p. 106

📁 **Learning Styles Lesson Plan** Learning Styles Lesson Plans folder, p. 38

📁 **Big Idea Graphic Organizer** Big Idea Graphic Organizer folder, p. 78

📁 **Guided Reading and Review** Units 5–6 folder, p. 61

FACT Finder

Morning Journal Sales

Date	Amount
1895	30,000
1897	400,000
1898	1,000,000

Source: *American Heritage,* February 1957

Interpreting Tables Sale of William Randolph Hearst's *Morning Journal* soared in 1898 thanks to sensational stories before and during the Spanish-American War. **Culture** How did yellow journalism influence U.S. participation in the Spanish-American War?

to listen to both sides and come to a decision.) The British government replied that the doctrine had no standing in international law.

Eventually Britain backed down and agreed to arbitration. Concerned about the rising power of Germany in Africa, the British government realized that it needed to stay on friendly terms with the increasingly powerful United States.

The Cuban Rebellion

By the mid-1890s the United States had not only reaffirmed the Monroe Doctrine, it had also forced the world's most powerful nation to bow to its will. Events in Cuba soon paved the way for a far more spectacular display of American power.

An island nation off the coast of Florida, Cuba first rebelled against Spain in 1868. After ten years of fighting the rebels, Spain finally put in place a few meager reforms to appease the Cuban people. In 1895, after the island's economy had collapsed, Cubans rebelled again.[†] This time Spain sent 150,000 troops and its best general, Valeriano Weyler, to put down the rebellion. In a desperate attempt to prevent civilians from aiding the rebels, Weyler instituted a policy of "reconcentration." He forced hundreds of thousands of Cubans into guarded camps. The prisoners, including women, children, and the elderly, lived in miserable conditions with little food or sanitation. Over two years, disease and starvation killed an estimated 200,000 Cubans.

Cuban exiles living in the United States, led by the journalist José Martí, urged the United States to intervene. Both Presidents Cleveland and McKinley refused. They were unwilling to spend the money that intervention would require and feared the United States would be saddled with colonial responsibilities it could not handle. Frustrated,

[†] A Spanish decision to impose increased taxes and to restrict trade was responsible for the collapse of the Cuban economy.

Cuban guerrillas turned to the one tactic they knew would attract the United States government's attention: the destruction of American sugar plantations and mills in Cuba. As a result, business owners increased their pressure on the government to act.

Demands for United States intervention in Cuba also came from an unexpected source—American newspapers. In the 1890s a fierce competition for readers broke out between two New York City newspapers, the *New York World* and the *New York Morning Journal.* Both newspapers reported exaggerated and sometimes false stories about the events in Cuba in order to increase circulation. The battle pitted the *World's* established publisher, Joseph Pulitzer, against a newcomer to the city, the *Journal's* William Randolph Hearst.

William Randolph Hearst

AMERICAN BIOGRAPHY Hearst, the son of a gold-mining tycoon, grew up in California. His first venture into newspaper publishing came in 1887, when he took control of the *San Francisco Examiner,* a faltering paper owned by his father. Hearst used a combination of investigative reporting and sensationalist stories to increase circulation. His methods turned the struggling paper around, and within two years he was showing a profit.

In 1895 Hearst expanded his efforts into the New York City market when he bought the *New York Morning Journal.* He set about improving the paper by luring experienced journalists from other papers, including the *World.* Hearst used a variety of other techniques to increase the *Journal's* circulation, including printing sensational crime stories, using illustrations and vivid headlines to draw in the reader, and lowering the price to one penny.

William R. Hearst (1863–1951)

Newspaper publishers Hearst and Pulitzer both took advantage of the horrifying stories coming from Cuba about the "Butcher"

RESOURCE OPTIONS

Teaching Resources

American History Block Scheduling Support The Spanish-American War: Door to Imperialism, found in the Prosperity, Depression, and War folder, includes interdisciplinary lesson suggestions and activities for Geography and History, Primary Sources, Biography, and Literature.

Media and Technology

RESOURCE PRO

Literature Activity "The Open Boat," found on Resource Pro, describes the harrowing experience of Stephen Crane, who survived the sinking of a munitions supply steamer returning from Cuba in 1897.

Weyler and his barbed-wire concentration camps. Their sensational headlines and stories, known as yellow journalism, whipped up the American public in favor of the rebels. The intense burst of national pride and the desire for an aggressive foreign policy that followed came to be known as **jingoism.** The name came from a line in a British song of the 1870s: "We don't want to fight, yet by Jingo! if we do, We've got the ships, we've got the men, and got the money too."

Hearst went on to serve briefly in the United States House of Representatives. He continued to expand his publishing empire, acquiring newspapers in cities throughout the country. By 1935 he owned 28 major newspapers, 18 magazines, and several radio stations and news services. Although the era of rabid yellow journalism declined following the turn of the century, the innovations of Hearst and his competitors continue to influence journalism today. ■

Turning Point: The Spanish-American War

The stories printed in newspapers such as the *Journal* strengthened American sympathy for the Cuban rebels. Slowly the demand for United States intervention began to build.

Steps to War Early in 1898 riots erupted in Havana, the capital of Cuba. In response, President McKinley moved the battleship U.S.S. *Maine* into the city's harbor to protect American citizens and property. A few weeks later, in early February 1898, United States newspapers published a letter stolen from the Spanish ambassador to Washington, Dupuy de Lôme. The de Lôme letter, which described McKinley as "weak and a bidder for the admiration of the crowd," caused an outcry in the United States.

Then, on February 15, an explosion sank the *Maine,* killing more than 250 American sailors. Even though the blast probably had been caused by a fire that set off ammunition, an enraged American public blamed the Spanish for the disaster and called for war. Still, McKinley hesitated.

On the other side of the world, the people of another of Spain's last remaining possessions, the Philippine Islands, also were rebelling. In the view of Theodore Roosevelt, then Assistant Secretary of the Navy, the Philippines could become a key base from which the United States might protect its Asian trade. On February 25, while his boss, the Secretary of the Navy, was out of the office, Roosevelt cabled naval commanders in the Pacific to prepare for military action against

 TURNING POINT : *The Spanish-American War*

As you can see from the time line, after the Spanish-American War the United States became involved in many foreign conflicts, some thousands of miles from home.

1898 The United States enters the Spanish-American War.

 1941 After Japan bombs Pearl Harbor, the United States enters World War II against the Axis.

 1964 Congress passes the Gulf of Tonkin Resolution, authorizing the use of American military force in the war in Vietnam.

| 1900 | 1925 | 1950 | 1975 | 2000 |

 1917 After a time of neutrality, the United States reacts against German submarine warfare by entering World War I on the side of the Allies.

1950 After North Korea's invasion of South Korea, President Truman calls on American troops to defend South Korea.

 1991 The United States and its allies free Kuwait from Iraqi occupation in the Gulf War.

RESOURCE OPTIONS

Media and Technology

 RESOURCE PRO

Critical Thinking Activity Drawing Conclusions: The Explosion of the *Maine,* found on Resource Pro, presents contemporary reports about the mysterious explosion of the *Maine* to help students apply this skill.

Spain. When President McKinley discovered what Roosevelt had done, he ordered most of the cables withdrawn, but he made an exception in the case of the cable directed to Admiral George Dewey. Dewey was told to attack the Spanish fleet in the Philippines if war broke out with Spain.

Late in March, in a final attempt at a peaceful solution, McKinley sent a list of demands to Spain. These included compensation for the *Maine,* an end to the concentration camps, a truce in Cuba, and Cuban independence. Eager to find a peaceful settlement to the crisis, Spain accepted most of the American demands. Still, McKinley decided he could not resist the growing cries for war. On April 11, he sent a war message to Congress. A few days later, rallying to the cry of "Remember the *Maine!*" Congress recognized Cuban independence and authorized force against Spain.

"A Splendid Little War" The war's first action took place, not in Cuba, but in the Philippines as shown on the map on this page. On May 1, 1898, Admiral Dewey launched a surprise attack on Spanish ships anchored in Manila Bay, destroying Spain's entire Pacific fleet in just seven hours. In Cuba, meanwhile, United States warships quickly bottled up Spain's Atlantic fleet in the harbor at Santiago.

American army troops gathered in Tampa, Florida, to prepare for an invasion of Cuba. The group that received the most publicity was the 1st Volunteer Cavalry, known as the Rough Riders. Its leader, Theodore Roosevelt, had resigned his position as Assistant Secretary of the Navy and recruited an eclectic group of volunteers that included cowboys, miners, policemen, and college athletes. On July 1, 1898, Roosevelt led the Rough Riders in a charge up San Juan Hill, which became the most famous incident of the war. Several units of African American troops also performed superbly in the land war. A white soldier later wrote the *Washington Post* that "if it had not been for the Negro cavalry, the Rough Riders would have been exterminated."

The Spanish fleet made a desperate attempt to escape Santiago harbor on July 3. In the ensuing battle, the United States Navy sank every Spanish ship, setting off wild Independence Day celebrations back in the United States.

It had all seemed quite simple. Although 2,500 Americans had died in the short war, fewer than 400 died in battle. The remainder

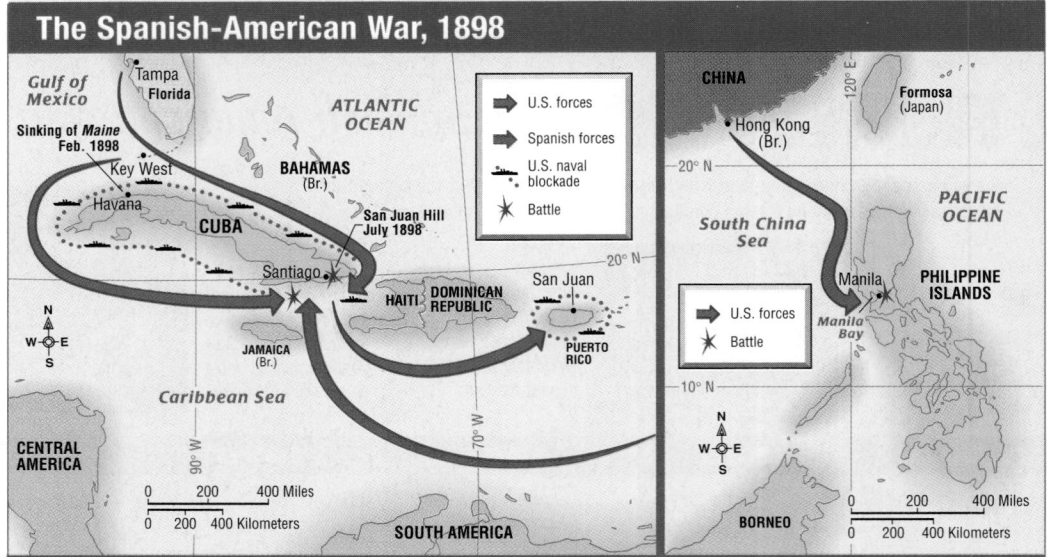

The Spanish-American War, 1898

Although the Spanish-American War was fought in two locations on opposite sides of the world, the United States defeated Spain in just nine weeks. *Location At what specific sites were the major battles of the war fought?*

Filipinos were encouraged by the United States to fight Spain for independence, only to find themselves under U.S. domination following the Spanish-American War. Filipino civilians suffered extremely high casualty rates during the three-year war between the United States and the Philippines. *Economics What economic motive did the United States have to take over the Philippines?*

died from food poisoning, yellow fever, malaria, and inadequate medical care. Future Secretary of State John Hay captured the public mood when he wrote his friend Teddy Roosevelt that it had been "a splendid little war."

After the War

The United States signed the Treaty of Paris with Spain in December 1898. In the treaty the Spanish government recognized Cuba's independence. In return for a payment of $20 million, Spain also gave up the Philippines, Puerto Rico, and the Pacific island of Guam to the United States. These became "unincorporated" territories of the United States, which meant that their residents would not become American citizens.

Dilemma in the Philippines Although many Americans supported the treaty, others were deeply troubled by it. How could the United States become a colonial power without violating the nation's most basic principle—that all people have the right to liberty? Forced to justify this departure from American ideals, President McKinley explained that rebels in the Philippines were on the edge of war with one another and that the Filipino people were "unfit for self-government." If the United States did not act first, moreover, European powers might seize the islands.

After a heated debate, the Senate ratified the treaty in February 1899.

Filipino rebels had fought with American troops in the war against Spain with the expectation that victory would bring independence. But when rebel leader Emilio Aguinaldo issued a proclamation in January 1899 declaring the Philippines a republic, the United States ignored him. Mounting tensions between the rebel forces and American soldiers finally erupted into war in February. In the bitter three-year war that followed, 4,200 Americans were killed and 2,800 more wounded. Fighting without restraint—and sometimes with great brutality—American forces killed some 16,000 Filipino rebels and as many as 200,000 Filipino civilians. Occasional fighting continued for years. The Philippines did not gain complete independence until 1946.

The Fate of Cuba and Puerto Rico Supporters of Cuban independence had attached an amendment, called the Teller Amendment, to Congress's 1898 war resolution against Spain. The document promised that the United States would not annex Cuba. Yet American involvement in Cuba did not end with the victory over Spain. In order to protect American business interests in the chaotic environment

Main Idea
CONNECTIONS

Why did the United States continue to intervene in Cuba after the Spanish-American War?

that followed the war, President McKinley installed a military government in Cuba led by General Leonard Wood. The military government would rule for three years. This government organized a school system and restored economic stability. It also established a commission led by Major Walter Reed of the Army Medical Corps that found a cure for the deadly disease yellow fever.

In 1900 the military government authorized the Cubans to begin to draft a constitution. The new constitution was modeled on the United States Constitution and did not allow for continued American involvement in Cuba. The United States government, however, insisted that the Cubans include provisions outlined in a document called the Platt Amendment. The Platt Amendment stipulated that the Cuban government could not enter any foreign agreements, must allow the United States to establish two naval bases on the island, and must give the United States the right to intervene whenever necessary. The Platt Amendment remained in force until 1934.

Unlike Cuba, Puerto Rico did not become independent. In an attempt to stem a growing independence movement, the United States government granted Puerto Ricans United States citizenship in 1917.

Queen Liliuokalani was Hawaii's last monarch. By the time she came into power, Hawaii was already dominated by U.S. business concerns. *Economics* **What finally caused the fall of Hawaii's monarchy?**

Other Gains in the Pacific

The United States government was intervening in other parts of the Pacific at the same time that the Spanish-American War was brewing. This intervention eventually brought about changes in the American relationship with Hawaii, Samoa, and China.

Annexation of Hawaii Hawaii had become increasingly important to United States business interests in the late 1800s. In 1887 Hawaii and the United States renewed a trade treaty that allowed Hawaiian sugar to be sold duty free in the United States. Hawaii also leased Pearl Harbor to the United States as a fueling and repair station for naval vessels. That same year, white Hawaiian-born planters forced the Hawaiian king, Kalakaua, to accept a new constitution that, in effect, gave them control of the government.

When the king died in 1891, his sister Liliuokalani came to the throne. A strong nationalist, Queen Liliuokalani opposed United States control of the islands and sought to reduce the power of foreign merchants. In 1893, with the help of the United States Marines, pineapple planter Sanford B. Dole removed Queen Liliuokalani from power. In addition he proclaimed a republic and requested that Hawaii be annexed by the United States.

When William McKinley was elected President, he supported the annexation. "We need Hawaii just as much and a good deal more than we did California. It is manifest destiny," McKinley said in early 1898. After briefly considering whether the Hawaiian people wished to be annexed, Congress was swayed by arguments that the United States needed naval stations in Hawaii in order to be a world power. In 1898 Congress approved the annexation of Hawaii.

Samoa The Polynesian islands of Samoa represented another possible stepping-stone to the growing trade with Asia. Back in 1878, the United States had negotiated a treaty with Samoa offering protection in return for a lease on Samoa's fine harbor at Pago Pago. When Britain and Germany began competing for control of these islands in the 1880s, tension between these European powers and the United States almost led to war. Eventually the three nations arranged a three-way protectorate of Samoa in 1889. The withdrawal of Great Britain from Samoa in 1899 left Germany and the

United States to divide up the islands. A year after the annexation of Hawaii, the United States had acquired the harbor at Pago Pago as well.

An Open Door to China China's huge population and its vast markets were increasingly important to American trade by the late 1800s. But the United States was not the only nation interested in China. Countries such as Russia, Germany, Britain, France, and Japan were seeking **spheres of influence,** or areas of economic and political control, in China. In 1899 John Hay, President McKinley's Secretary of State, wrote notes to the major European powers trying to persuade them to keep an "open door" to China. He wanted to ensure through his **Open Door Policy** that the United States would have equal access to China's millions of consumers. Hay's suggestions met with a cool response from the other countries.

Meanwhile, many Chinese resented foreign influence of any kind. A secret society called the Righteous and Harmonious Fists (the western press called them "Boxers") started a rebellion in the spring of 1900 that led to the massacre of 300 foreigners and Christian Chinese. Although the European powers eventually defeated the Boxers,

Competition for trade in China led to Secretary Hay's Open Door Policy. *Foreign Relations According to this cartoon, who holds the "key" to China's open door?*

Secretary Hay feared that these imperialist nations would use the rebellion as an excuse to seize more Chinese territory. Thus, he issued a second series of Open Door notes. These notes reaffirmed the principle of open trade in China and made an even stronger statement about the intention of the United States to preserve it.

SECTION 2 REVIEW

Comprehension

1. *Key Terms* Define: (a) arbitration; (b) jingoism; (c) sphere of influence; (d) Open Door Policy.
2. *Summarizing the Main Idea* What actions led to the Spanish-American War?
3. *Organizing Information* Create a flowchart that organizes information about the events that led the United States into war with Spain. Begin your chart with *1895: Cuban Rebellion flares after economic collapse* and end with *December 1898: United States signs treaty with Spain.*

Critical Thinking

4. *Analyzing Time Lines* Review the time line at the start of the section. Pick one event where the United States intervened in another country and explain why this event was typical of United States foreign policy.
5. *Recognizing Cause and Effect* Describe how the 1895 dispute between the United States and Great Britain reaffirmed the validity of the Monroe Doctrine.

Writing Activity

6. *Writing a Persuasive Essay* Write an essay that supports or refutes the following statement: *United States expansionist policies in the Pacific earned the nation new territories and increased its influence in the region.*

RESOURCE OPTIONS

Teaching Resources

 Quiz Units 5–6 folder, p. 62

Student Performance Pack

 Guide to the Essentials Chapter 18, Section 2 (English and Spanish)

Media and Technology

 Color Transparencies Geographic Setting, M-9

Answers to SECTION 2 REVIEW

1. (a) arbitration, see p. 519; (b) jingoism, see p. 521; (c) sphere of influence, see p. 525; (d) Open Door Policy, see p. 525.

2. The American government forced Chile to pay an indemnity for the deaths of American soldiers, intervened to prevent the overthrow of a friendly government in Brazil, and forced Great Britain to accept arbitration in a Venezuelan border dispute; hostilities with Cuba and the explosion of the *Maine.*

3. Yellow journalism leads to jingoism in the 1890s; early 1898: McKinley moves battleship *Maine* to Cuba; Feb.: American newspapers print letter from Spanish ambassador; Feb. 15: an explosion sinks the *Maine;* Feb. 25: Roosevelt signals Pacific commanders to prepare for war; March: McKinley sends demands to Spain; April: McKinley calls for war; May: first action takes place in Philippines; July: San Juan Hill incident; July 3: battle ensues in which United States sinks all Spanish ships.

4. Sample event: Congress approves annexation of Hawaii. Americans used the idea of manifest destiny to justify their actions; they considered American economic and military interests to be more important than the wishes of Hawaiians.

5. Great Britain's consent to subject its territorial dispute with Venezuela to arbitration gave the Monroe Doctrine international validity, setting a precedent for future disputes.

6. Essays will vary but should be supported with facts from the section.

Answer to . . .

Viewing History Uncle Sam (the United States).

SKILLS FOR LIFE

Geography

Using a Time Zone Map

Focus Students will use a time zone map to calculate times in various locations in the world.

Instruct Ask students if they have seen pictures of Earth from space. Do they show a clear dividing line between day and night? Explain that as areas of Earth pass out of darkness and into sunlight, people experience sunrise. We say that sunrise occurs at a specific time in a certain area, but that time is arbitrarily assigned, since sunrise occurs continuously as Earth turns. Ask why people on Earth need agreed-upon times and time zones.

Extend See the Skills for Life Activity in the Resource Options below.

Answers

1. (a) Moscow: 2:00 P.M.; Denver: 5:00 A.M. (b) 9:00 P.M.; 10:00 A.M.

2. Answers will vary depending on students' time zones. Answers are given for the time zones labeled –5 through –10, which include those for the United States.

(a) Karachi: Zone –5: 11:00 A.M.; Zone –6: 12:00 noon; Zone –7: 1:00 P.M.; Zone –8: 2:00 P.M.; Zone –9: 3:00 P.M.; Zone –10: 4:00 P.M. Guangzhou: 3 hours later (b) Zone –5: 10:00 A.M.; Zone –6: 9:00 A.M.; Zone –7: 8:00 A.M.; Zone –8: 7:00 A.M.; Zone –9: 6:00 A.M.; Zone –10: 5:00 A.M. (c) Zone –5: 12:00 noon on Thurs.; Zone –6: 1:00 P.M. on Thurs.; Zone –7: 2:00 P.M. on Thurs.; Zone –8: 3:00 P.M. on Thurs.; Zone –9: 4:00 P.M. on Thurs.; Zone –10: 5:00 P.M. on Thurs.

TEST FOR SUCCESS

Seven hours back.

SKILLS FOR LIFE

Using a Time Zone Map

Until the late 1800s, communities around the world calculated local time by the sun. When railroads began providing rapid long-distance train service between many communities—each with its own version of local time—this method began to cause scheduling nightmares.

In 1884 delegates from 27 nations met in Washington, D.C., to discuss the problem. They eventually agreed on a system of worldwide standard time. Under this system, the world is divided into 24 time zones, shown by colored bands on the map below. Time is the same throughout each zone.

The Prime Meridian, which passes through Greenwich, England, at 0° longitude, is the starting point for calculating the time in each zone. The International Date Line—located in the Pacific Ocean at 180° longitude—is where the date changes. The calendar date to the east of this line is one day earlier than that to the west.

Use the following steps to read the time zone map below.

1. Study the information on the map. The numbers at the bottom of the map indicate the number of hours each time zone differs from Greenwich time at the Prime Meridian. For example, a value of +3 means that the time in that zone is three hours later than Greenwich time; –3 means it is three hours earlier. The numbers at the top of the map provide examples of how this system works. (a) If it is 12:00 noon, Greenwich time, what time is it in Moscow? In Denver? (b) If it is 2:00 P.M. in Abidjan, Côte d'Ivoire, what time is it in the zone labeled +7? In the zone labeled –4?

2. Compare the time in your zone with other zones around the world. Find your time zone on the map. (a) If it is 1:00 A.M. in the time zone where you live, what time is it in Karachi, Pakistan? In Guangzhou, China? (b) If it is 12:00 noon in São Paulo, Brazil, what time is it where you live? (c) If it is 9:00 P.M. on Wednesday where you live, what time and day is it in Brisbane, Australia?

TEST FOR SUCCESS

If you flew west from Cairo, Egypt, to Lima, Peru, how many hours forward or back would you have to set your watch?

World Time Zones

RESOURCE OPTIONS

Teaching Resources

Skills for Life Activity Units 5–6 folder, p. 71, allows students to apply the skill by answering questions about global travel.

| 1901 Theodore Roosevelt becomes President when William McKinley is assassinated | 1904 President Roosevelt issues Roosevelt Corollary to the Monroe Doctrine | 1904 Construction begins on Panama Canal | 1905 Roosevelt mediates settlement of Russo-Japanese War | 1908 William Howard Taft elected President |

1900   1902   1904   1906   1908

3 Expansion Under Roosevelt and Taft

SECTION PREVIEW

Objectives

1. Explain why the United States built the Panama Canal and the impact that it had.
2. Compare American foreign policy in the early 1900s in Latin America and in Asia.
3. Describe President Taft's use of "dollar diplomacy," including its legacy as an American foreign policy.
4. *Key Terms* Define: concession; Roosevelt Corollary; dollar diplomacy.

Main Idea

President Theodore Roosevelt conducted a vigorous foreign policy that suited the new status of the United States as a world power. Although President William Howard Taft continued Roosevelt's policies, he preferred a more subtle approach to influencing other nations.

Reading Strategy

Formulating Questions Reread the Main Idea above. Then rewrite it as two questions. As you read the section, take notes that help answer the questions.

By 1900 the United States had emerged as a genuine world power. It controlled several overseas territories and had a large and vigorous economy. These circumstances contributed to William McKinley's decisive victory in the presidential election of 1900. One year later McKinley was dead, cut down by an assassin's bullet. Theodore Roosevelt, McKinley's Vice President, was now President. The new President developed a foreign policy to support the nation's new role in the world. Under his leadership, the United States continued to intervene in the affairs of countries that were of economic and strategic interest to the nation.

The Panama Canal

The Spanish-American War brought home to Americans the need for a shorter route between the Pacific and Atlantic oceans. A canal built across Central America would link the Atlantic and Pacific oceans, making global shipping much faster. It would also allow the United States Navy to move quickly from one ocean to the other in time of war.

Building the Canal The Isthmus of Panama was an ideal location for such a route. At that time Panama was a province of the South American nation of Colombia. In 1879 a French company headed by Ferdinand de Lesseps had bought a 25-year **concession** from Colombia to build a canal across Panama. (A concession is a grant for a piece of land in exchange for a promise to use the land for a specific purpose.) Defeated by yellow fever and severe mismanagement, the company abandoned the project 10 years later. It offered its

The Panama Canal cut through the Isthmus of Panama—the strip of land separating the Atlantic and Pacific oceans.

RESOURCE OPTIONS

Teaching Resources

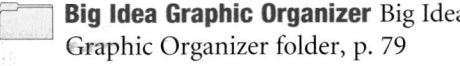 **Reproducible Lesson Plan** Lesson Plans folder, p. 107

 Big Idea Graphic Organizer Big Idea Graphic Organizer folder, p. 79

Guided Reading and Review Units 5–6 folder, p. 63

 Nystrom *Atlas of Our Country* Later Expansion of the United States, pp. 32–33

Graphing the Main Idea

To make sure students understand the main idea of this section, you may wish to use the double web graphic organizer below.

Tell students that a double web is useful for comparing and contrasting information. Ask students to use the double web to compare and contrast Presidents Roosevelt and Taft's foreign policies.

Teaching Tip A template for this graphic organizer can be found in the Color Transparencies, G-2.

Answer to . . .

Map Skills By 8,900 miles.
Main Idea Connections He hoped that an independent Panama would seek United States protection and offer the isthmus of Panama at a low price.

Cross Section of the Panama Canal Zone

Because of the uneven elevation in the canal zone, engineers had to design a series of locks (above) to raise and lower the ships so that they could pass through the canal. Compare the sea route from New York City to San Francisco (left) with and without the canal. *Movement* By how many miles did the Panama Canal reduce the journey?

remaining rights to the United States for $100 million. When the price fell to $40 million, Congress passed the Spooner Act in 1902 that authorized the purchase of the French assets. The act required that the United States work out a treaty with Colombia for a lease on the land.

Treaty negotiations went nowhere. Colombia was waiting for the French concession to expire in 1904 so that it could offer the isthmus at a higher price. Roosevelt was enraged by this attempt by Colombian "bandits" to "rob" the United States. He secretly made it clear to Philippe Bunau-Varilla, an official with the French company, that the United States would not interfere if the company organized a Panamanian revolution against Colombia.

Main Idea
CONNECTIONS

Why did President Roosevelt secretly support the revolution in Panama?

The revolt took place in November 1903 with United States warships waiting offshore to provide support for the rebels. The United States immediately recognized an independent Panama and became its protector. In return, Panama ratified the Hay–Bunau-Varilla Treaty in February 1904. The treaty gave the United States a permanent grant of a 10-mile-wide strip of land for a Canal Zone. The United States had complete sovereignty over this zone. The Panamanians received $10 million.

Construction of the canal began in 1904. To complete this mammoth task, workers were brought in from several countries. Many of them had no construction experience whatsoever. After receiving proper training, the workers surpassed all expectations. They finished the canal in 1914, six months ahead of schedule and $23 million under budget.

Reaction to the Canal Roosevelt's opponents did not appreciate the methods he had used to secure the Canal Zone. A newspaper published by William Hearst commented, "Besides being a rough-riding assault upon another republic over the shattered wreckage of international law . . . it is a quite unexampled instance of foul play in American politics."

Most Americans, however, approved of President Roosevelt's actions in Panama. They were convinced that the canal was vital to national security and prosperity. Two years after leaving office, Theodore Roosevelt gave a speech at the University of California at Berkeley in which he justified his methods:

AMERICAN VOICES "If I had followed traditional, conservative methods I would have submitted a dignified State paper of probably 200 pages to Congress and the debates on it would have been going on yet; but I took the Canal Zone and let Congress debate; and while the debate goes on the canal does also."

—*Theodore Roosevelt*

RESOURCE OPTIONS

Teaching Resources

 Primary Source Activity The Panamanian Revolution, Learning with Documents folder, p. 24

Media and Technology

AmericanHeritage® CD-ROM

Presidents Theodore Roosevelt

Time Tour A New Role in the World: Expanding Overseas

Despite its success as a link between the Atlantic and Pacific, the Panama Canal left a long heritage of ill will among Latin Americans toward the United States. In recognition of the illegal means used to acquire the Canal Zone, Congress voted to pay $25 million to Colombia in 1921, after TR had died.

Foreign Policy in the Early 1900s

In 1901 Roosevelt reminded an audience at the Minnesota State Fair of an old African proverb: "Speak softly and carry a big stick; you will go far." In his view, the "big stick" was the United States Navy. Indeed, the threat of military force allowed Roosevelt to conduct an aggressive foreign policy.

The Roosevelt Corollary In December 1904, Roosevelt issued a message to Congress that became known as the **Roosevelt Corollary** to the Monroe Doctrine. Roosevelt began this corollary, or extension of a previously accepted idea, by denying that the United States wanted any more territory.

> **KEY DOCUMENTS** "It must be understood that under no circumstances will the United States use the Monroe Doctrine as a cloak for territorial aggression. We desire peace with all the world, but perhaps most of all with the other peoples of the American continent. . . . It is always possible that wrong actions toward this nation . . . may result in our having to take action to protect our rights; but such action will not be taken with a view to territorial aggression."
>
> —*Roosevelt Corollary to the Monroe Doctrine, Theodore Roosevelt, 1904*

The United States wanted only "to see neighboring countries stable, orderly, and prosperous," he said. But if the countries engaged in activities harmful to the interests of the United States or if their governments collapsed, inviting intervention from stronger nations, then the United States would be forced to exercise "an international police power." In other words, the United States government would intervene to prevent intervention from other powers. This was the central point of the Roosevelt Corollary.

The first test of the Roosevelt Corollary concerned the small Caribbean island republic of Santo Domingo (now the Dominican

Notable PRESIDENTS

1901–1909

Theodore Roosevelt

"Speak softly and carry a big stick; you will go far."
—1901 speech at the Minnesota State Fair

Born into a wealthy New York family, Theodore Roosevelt had asthma as a child, but at his father's insistence he overcame it with rigorous physical exercise. "TR" developed a stocky body, a fighter's toughness, and a love for strenuous living.

As a Republican politician in New York in the 1880s, TR called for a larger government role in the economy, a stand that made him leader of the Progressives. TR believed in honest as well as active government. During a six-year term on the U.S. Civil Service Commission, he enforced the merit system. TR later attacked corruption as head of the New York City Police Board.

In 1897 TR was appointed Assistant Secretary of the Navy. There he built up a two-ocean fleet and urged a tougher American foreign policy. When the Spanish-American War was declared in 1898, TR, though nearly 40 and with poor eyesight, demanded to see combat. He organized the "Rough Riders" and led them on a famous charge up Cuba's San Juan Hill.

The war made TR a national hero. Returning to New York, he won the governorship in 1898. Two years later President McKinley chose TR as his running mate. (Conservative New York Republicans, unhappy at TR's Progressive policies, were not sorry to see him leave New York.) In 1901 McKinley was assassinated. Roosevelt became, at age 42, the nation's youngest President to that time.

TR saw the presidency as a "bully pulpit," or a wonderful stage from which to win public support for his brand of strong leadership. His economic policies included regulating big business and encouraging labor unions. His foreign policies reflected the "big stick" approach described in the quotation above. TR was also a vocal conservationist, acting to preserve the nation's natural resources and wildlife. Most importantly, TR's boldness and constant activity helped create the modern image of the President.

Connecting to Today

Do you think that American foreign policy today should be guided by the principle of "speak softly and carry a big stick"? Explain your answer.

About the Presidents

William Howard Taft (1909–1913) hoped to establish a system for working out disagreements between nations. Under Taft, treaties were drafted with Great Britain and France in 1911. These treaties included provisions for negotiating issues that might lead to war, but the Senate made important changes. One of Taft's main opponents in this disagreement was Theodore Roosevelt. Just back from an African safari, Roosevelt was ready to jump into politics again. In the end, Taft refused to sign the new Senate version.

Source: Michael Harwood, "William Howard Taft," *The American Heritage® Pictorial History of the Presidents of the United States*, vol. 2, 1968.

Customize for
More Advanced Students

Next to Washington, Jefferson, and Lincoln, the fourth stony face on the slopes of Mount Rushmore is that of Theodore Roosevelt. Have students write one or two paragraphs explaining why some people might have wanted Roosevelt to be on this monument, while others felt that he did not belong.

Answer to . . .

Map Skills They provided stepping stones to Asian markets and stations for repairing vessels.

Viewing History By claiming that the U.S. was interested in peace, not in acquiring territory.

United States Acquisitions and Annexations, 1857–1903

United States possessions (with date of acquisition)

Spheres of influence of the United States

Alaska 1867
ASIA
PACIFIC OCEAN
Midway Is. 1867
UNITED STATES
Philippine Is. 1898
Wake I. 1899
Hawaiian Is. 1898
Puerto Rico 1898
CUBA · HAITI
Johnston I. 1858
DOMINICAN REPUBLIC
Guam 1898
Palmyra I. 1898
GUATEMALA
HONDURAS
NICARAGUA
PANAMA
Howland I. Baker I. 1857
Jarvis I. 1857
Panama Canal Zone 1903
SOUTH AMERICA
American Samoa 1899

MAP Skills Between 1857 and 1903, the United States acquired many new territorial possessions around the globe. *Location* Why do you think so many of these new possessions were islands located in the Pacific Ocean?

Republic). When the island went bankrupt, European nations threatened to intervene to collect their money. Roosevelt moved quickly to establish American supervision of customs collections. Bankers in the United States took over the country's finances and paid its European debt. Roosevelt's actions were initially blocked by Congress. The President was able to get around congressional opposition by creating an executive agreement with Santo Domingo's president.

Under Roosevelt, United States intervention in Latin America became common. This development angered many Latin Americans. Congress also was displeased with Roosevelt's single-handed foreign policies that seemed to strengthen the President's powers while weakening their own.

Roosevelt as Peacemaker In Asia, the President's chief concern was to preserve an "open door" to trade with China. In order for this to happen, Roosevelt believed that both Japan and Russia had to be kept in check. In 1904 the two nations went to war. Roosevelt feared that a Japanese victory would upset the balance of power in Asia. Working in secret through friends in the diplomatic corps, the President looked for a way to end the war.

In 1905 Roosevelt mediated a peace agreement to the Russo-Japanese War. He invited delegates from the two nations to Portsmouth, New Hampshire, where he persuaded Japan to

THE WORLD CONSTABLE.

Published after the announcement of the Roosevelt Corollary, this political cartoon depicts Teddy Roosevelt as the world's police officer, using his "big stick" to maintain order and stability in Latin America. *Foreign Relations* How did Roosevelt justify U.S. interventions in Latin America?

▶ **RESOURCE OPTIONS**

Teaching Resources

📁 **Literature Activity** "You're All Right, Teddy," Units 5–6 folder, p. 70

📁 **Key Documents** Theodore Roosevelt, The Strenuous Life, Learning with Documents folder, p. 94

American History Block Scheduling Support The Spanish-American War: Door to Imperialism, and Through Mud and Disease: Building the Panama Canal, found in the Prosperity, Depression, and War folder, includes interdisciplinary lesson suggestions and activities for Geography and History, Primary Sources, Biography, and Literature.

be satisfied with small grants of land and control over Korea instead of a huge payment of money. He also secured a promise from Russia to vacate Manchuria, which remained part of China. Roosevelt succeeded in keeping trade in China open to all nations. His role as mediator won him the Nobel Peace Prize.

Taft and Dollar Diplomacy

William Howard Taft, elected to the presidency in 1908, was not as aggressive as Roosevelt in pursuing foreign policy aims. A distinguished lawyer from Ohio, Taft had served as Roosevelt's Secretary of War and had headed the commission that governed the Philippines.

Taft's main foreign policy goals were to maintain the open door to Asia and preserve stability in Latin America. As for the rest, he preferred "substituting dollars for bullets." By this he meant maintaining orderly societies abroad by increasing American investment in foreign economies. Although some of Taft's contemporaries mocked his approach, calling it **dollar diplomacy,** Taft himself later used this term with pride.

Dollar diplomacy did not succeed as well as Taft had hoped. Although it increased the level of United States financial involvement abroad, the results were not always profitable. For example, when Taft's Secretary of State, Philander Knox, persuaded bankers from the United States to invest in railroad projects in China and Manchuria, Russia and Japan united in an effort to block the influence of the Americans. In addition, many United States investments in China

Although President William Howard Taft shared Teddy Roosevelt's policy goals, he adopted a less aggressive approach to foreign policy.
Foreign Relations *What was Taft's dollar diplomacy?*

were lost when the country's government collapsed in revolution in 1911.

Dollar diplomacy also created enemies in Latin America, especially in the Caribbean and Central America, where local revolutionary movements opposed American influence. Although the United States reached new heights as an international power under Roosevelt and Taft, anti-colonialism abroad and anti-imperialism at home provided a growing check to further expansion.

SECTION 3 REVIEW

Comprehension

1. **Key Terms** Define: (a) concession; (b) Roosevelt Corollary; (c) dollar diplomacy.

2. **Summarizing the Main Idea** How was President Taft's dollar diplomacy both similar to and different from the approach to foreign policy taken by Theodore Roosevelt?

3. **Organizing Information** Create a chart that compares information about American foreign policy in the early 1900s. Label one column *Latin America* and the other *Asia.* In each column describe American foreign policy in general terms. Provide at least one example to support your description.

Critical Thinking

4. **Analyzing Time Lines** Review the time line at the start of the section. Choose one entry and explain how it is an example of American foreign policy in the early 1900s.

5. **Identifying Central Issues** How did the United States secure the rights to build a canal through Panama?

Writing Activity

6. **Writing an Expository Essay** Write a brief essay explaining President Taft's main foreign policy goals. Include his plan for accomplishing these goals.

GEOGRAPHY AND HISTORY

The Panama Canal

The geographic theme of place explores how physical and human characteristics make one environment different from another. On a world map it is hard to see these characteristics. The Isthmus of Panama, for example, seems a thread of land. But up close, it is miles wide, formed of violent rivers, dense forests, and towering mountains. How did these characteristics and others affect the effort to build the canal?

Workers digging the Panama Canal

Three factors affected the building of the Panama Canal. First, engineers had to decide where the canal should be located. Second, they had to cope with environmental hazards to workers. Finally, massive amounts of earth had to be moved to complete the project. The canal was to become the greatest engineering accomplishment of its era.

Cutting Across the Continental Divide

When the construction team arrived in Panama in 1904, the end points of the canal already had been decided. The canal would begin at Colón on the Atlantic Ocean side and end close to Panama City on the Pacific Ocean side, as the map on the next page shows.

Two major obstacles impeded its path, however. One was the Continental Divide, a ridge across Central America that separates rivers that flow west from rivers that flow east. A decision was made to cut through the Divide. Engineers soon realized that some of the work had already been done. In the 1880s, a French company trying to build a canal had

> *The canal was to become the greatest engineering accomplishment of its era.*

scooped out 19 million cubic yards of dirt and rock from the Divide near Culebra. At the time, no one would have guessed that this excavation, the Culebra Cut, would require digging another 96 million cubic yards before it was finished.

Taming the Chagres River

The other geographic obstacle was the wild and unpredictable Chagres River. It had to be tamed if the canal was to be built.

Taming the river had been a challenge for ages. The French had never really solved the problem. The American solution was to "drown" it.

Drowning the river meant that a huge earthen dam would be laid across the river valley at Gatún (see map opposite). This section of the Chagres would then overflow, creating the largest artificial lake in the world at that time. The Chagres would become the only river in the world to cross a continental divide and flow into two oceans at once.

From the entrance at Colón Harbor, ships using the new canal would sail 7 miles up a channel and ascend through three locks to a height of 85 feet

---

above sea level. Then they would cross the new and sprawling Gatún Lake for 24 miles, pass through the 9 miles of the Culebra Cut, and descend by one lock to a smaller lake about 1 mile long. Another set of two locks would bring them to sea level and the final 8-mile leg of the canal to the open Pacific.

An Environmental Problem Solved

While engineers were wrestling with the location of the canal, army physician William Gorgas wrestled with an environmental hazard that threatened workers: the mosquito. Medical science had learned only a few years before that two of the deadliest tropical diseases, yellow fever and malaria, were transmitted by mosquitoes.

The secret of mosquito control, Gorgas found, was to cover, destroy, or drain every place where mosquitoes could lay their eggs. This meant every tank, jar, hollow, and puddle, indoors or out, had to be covered. Dividing the cities on the canal route into districts, he assigned an inspector to check every house on a daily basis for uncovered or standing water. He also gave orders that any pools that could not be drained were to be covered with a film of oil or kerosene.

Gorgas's methods wiped out yellow fever before the end of 1905. Malaria, which was carried by a tougher mosquito, was not eliminated, but was much reduced.

Solving Problems of Movement

When it came to actually digging the canal, the chief engineer, John F. Stevens, viewed the project as a simple problem of movement: dirt—lots of it—had to be moved. As an experienced builder of railroads, he knew that the cheapest, fastest way to move anything on land was by railroad.

Within a week after his arrival, the new chief engineer had ordered double tracks laid. To get the dirt from the ditch to the train cars, Stevens brought in monster steam shovels. President Theodore Roosevelt, on an inspection visit to Panama, wrote, "Now we have taken hold of the job. . . . The huge steam shovels are hard at it, scooping huge masses of rock and gravel and dirt." The shovels were so efficient they filled five hundred trains with debris every day.

The highly efficient railway system could not solve another problem, however. Panama could not provide enough supplies to keep tens of thousands of

Panama Canal Zone

The 40-mile-long Panama Canal cuts north-south through the isthmus of Panama.

workers fed and busy. Thus, ships traveled frequently between Colón and the United States. Ships brought in workers as well, some 45,000 of them, from 97 different nations. By 1914, the geographic obstacles had been overcome and the "big ditch" was completed.

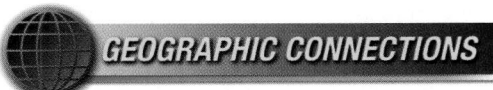

GEOGRAPHIC CONNECTIONS

1. What two problems of movement did the building of the canal entail, and how were they solved?

2. How did Dr. Gorgas change the environment of Panama, and what effect did his work have?

Themes in Geography

3. *Place* Describe how engineers solved one geographical problem in locating the canal.

Objectives

You may wish to call students' attention to the objectives in the Section Preview. The objectives are reflected in the main headings of the section.

Bellringer

Write the following sentence on the chalkboard: The Constitution must follow the flag. Ask students what it might mean in relation to the American control of other nations.

Reading Strategy

Outlining Information Refer to the Reading Strategy in the Section Preview. You may wish to have students go over their outlines together in small groups to be sure they have included all the important details.

LESSON PLAN

Connecting to the Main Idea

1. Focus After the Spanish-American War, anti-imperialists launched heated debates over United States foreign policy. Ask what arguments these anti-imperialists used to support their case. How persuasive were they?

2. Instruct Discuss the arguments for and against imperialism. Why did professionals, southern Democrats, labor leaders, and African Americans oppose imperialism? Who supported imperialism? What role did the "frontier mentality" play? Discuss with students the way racism entered into the arguments of both imperialists and anti-imperialists.

Ask students how imperialism created a love-hate relationship between the United States and some countries.

3. Close After the Spanish-American War, the debate over imperialism intensified. Strong arguments by anti-imperialists, however, failed to dampen the appeal of imperialism to the American imagination.

| 1898 Anti-Imperialist League established | 1907 Roosevelt sends the "Great White Fleet" on trip around the world | 1910 Boy Scouts formed in the United States | 1914 Construction of the Panama Canal is completed |

| 1895 | 1905 | 1915 |

4 Debating America's New Role

SECTION PREVIEW

Objectives

1. Describe the main arguments raised by the anti-imperialists.
2. Explain why imperialism appealed to many Americans.
3. Understand how imperialism made the United States both welcome and unpopular around the world.
4. *Key Terms* Define: racism; compulsory; Great White Fleet.

Main Idea

After the Spanish-American War, the debate intensified over whether it was appropriate for the United States to build an empire.

Reading Strategy

Outlining Information Skim the section and use the headings and subheadings to create an outline. As you read the section, fill in supporting details.

efore the Spanish-American War, United States citizens were already debating the consequences of an expanded role in world affairs. Walter Gresham, President Cleveland's Secretary of State in 1894, cautioned against "the evils of interference in affairs that do not specially concern us." Until the annexation of the Philippines in 1898, however, most citizens supported overseas involvement.

This 1870 weathervane shows pride in the United States' new role as a world power.

The Anti-Imperialists

After the annexation, opposition to imperialism grew. In November 1898, opponents of United States policy in the Philippines established the Anti-Imperialist League. Most of its organizers were well-to-do professionals. They included editor E. L. Godkin, Democratic politician William Jennings Bryan, settlement house leader Jane Addams, and novelist Mark Twain.

Moral and Political Arguments The anti-imperialists used a variety of arguments to support their position. The strongest of these were moral and political in nature. Expansionist behavior, the anti-imperialists asserted, was a rejection of the nation's foundation of "liberty for all." As one prominent Republican and former senator explained in 1899:

AMERICAN VOICES **"** We regret that it has become necessary in the land of Washington and Lincoln to reaffirm that all men, of whatever race or color, are entitled to life, liberty, and the pursuit of happiness. **"**

—*Carl Schurz*

Other anti-imperialists argued that the United States already had enough difficulties at home and should not take on more responsibilities. Finally, anti-imperialists noted that imperialism threatened the nation's democratic foundations. The large standing armies that were employed to bring other nations under American control could be used just as easily to crush dissent at home.

Racial Arguments Other anti-imperialists saw **racism** at work in imperialism. Racism is a belief that differences in character or intelligence

---

RESOURCE OPTIONS

Teaching Resources

Reproducible Lesson Plan Lesson Plans folder, p. 108

Learning Styles Lesson Plan Learning Styles Lesson Plans folder, p. 39

Big Idea Graphic Organizer Big Idea Graphic Organizer folder, p. 80

Guided Reading and Review Units 5–6 folder, p. 65

Media and Technology

 Listening to Literature William Carlos Williams, "This is Just to Say"

are due to one's race. Many Americans of this period believed that people of Anglo-Saxon heritage were superior to other races. The public officials who developed the country's policies shared these sentiments.

African Americans were at first torn about imperialistic issues. As United States citizens, they wanted to support their country. But they recognized the racism that underlay imperialism. A leader of the A.M.E. Zion Church had this to say in 1899:

AMERICAN VOICES ❝Had the Filipinos been white and fought as bravely as they have, the war would have been ended and their independence granted a long time ago.❞

—*Bishop Alexander Walters*

Although most southern Democrats also opposed imperialism, they did so for different reasons. Many southern politicians feared the effects of having to absorb more people of different races into the United States. Consequently, southern Democrats led the movement in the Senate against ratifying the treaty with Spain after the Spanish-American War. A number of anti-imperialists outside the South also opposed imperialist policies because of the fear that they would encourage people of different racial backgrounds to move to the United States.

Economic Arguments Finally, anti-imperialists raised economic objections to expansionist policies. In the view of these thinkers, it was not a good time for the United States to expand. First, expansion involved too many costs. Maintaining the necessary armed forces required more taxation, debt, and possibly even **compulsory,** or required, military service.

Samuel Gompers raised another concern. He argued that laborers coming to the United States from annexed territories would compete with American workers for jobs. Since these immigrants would work for lower wages, their presence would drive all wages down.

Imperialism's Appeal

Despite the strength of these arguments, imperialism maintained a powerful hold on the American imagination. Some people looked to a new frontier abroad to keep Americans from losing their competitive edge. The director of the census had declared the frontier "closed" in the 1890 census. Imperialism offered a new kind of frontier for American expansion.

The growth and popularity of youth scouting programs during this period shows that many Americans shared a "frontier mentality." Sir Robert Baden-Powell, an army officer of the

Main Idea CONNECTIONS

What was the connection between imperialism and the closing of the American frontier?

United States Interventions, 1898–1933

MAP Skills

This map shows how frequently the United States intervened in the affairs of Latin American countries in the early 1900s. The United States government defended these interventions as necessary for the protection of the nation's economic and political interests. *Place* What form did most of these interventions take?

U.S. expeditionary force, 1916–1917

Parral

MEXICO

Tampico

Mexico City

Veracruz

U.S. occupation, 1898–1902, 1906–1909, 1912, 1917–1922

U.S. seizure, 1914

Havana
CUBA

U.S. leased naval base, 1903

Guantánamo

HAITI

Bahamas (Br.)

DOMINICAN REPUBLIC

U.S. occupation, 1915–1934

U.S. possession, 1898

Purchased from Denmark, 1917

Puerto Rico

Virgin Is.

Antigua (Br.)

PACIFIC OCEAN

BR. HONDURAS

GUATEMALA

HONDURAS

United Fruit Co. organized for banana trade, 1899

EL SALVADOR

NICARAGUA

U.S. leased Corn Is., 1914

Jamaica (Br.)

U.S. occupation, 1916–1924

Guadeloupe (Fr.)
Dominica (Br.)
Martinique (Fr.)
St. Lucia (Br.)
Barbados (Br.)
Grenada (Br.)

Trinidad (Br.)

VENEZUELA

U.S. occupation, 1924–1925

COSTA RICA

PANAMA

U.S. occupation, 1909–1910, 1912–1925, 1926–1933 Canal proposed, 1916

U.S. acquired Canal Zone, 1904 Canal completed, 1914

COLOMBIA

0   250   500 Miles
0   250   500 Kilometers

ATLANTIC OCEAN

UNITED STATES

RESOURCE OPTIONS

Teaching Resources

📁 **Comparing Primary Sources** On the Race for Empire, Units 5–6 folder, pp. 68–69

Media and Technology

RESOURCE⊙PRO

Biography Juliette Gordon Low, found on Resource Pro, profiles the woman who founded the Girl Scouts in 1912.

Answer to . . .

Main Idea Connections As the American frontier became settled, people looked to frontiers abroad to maintain the American spirit.
Map Skills Military seizures and occupations.

Time: 90 minutes.

Activity: Role-play interviews on imperialism.

Grouping: Four to six students.

Purpose: To conduct interviews with students playing various types of citizens. Interviewees assume imperialist or anti-imperialist positions.

Roles: Reporter, a Filipino immigrant, a social worker, a U.S. general, a coal miner, a fruit grower.

Outcome: Students understand different perspectives on imperialism.

Answers to
SECTION 4 REVIEW

1. (a) racism, see p. 534; (b) compulsory, see p. 535; (c) Great White Fleet, see p. 536.

2. Imperialism went against the ideal of liberty and was racist; building up armies threatened democracy; expansion was expensive.

3. Welcome: countries that were worried about their independence welcomed help. Unpopular: United States support of unpopular governments created conflict.

4. 1907: Roosevelt sends Great White Fleet, was meant to impress other nations and Americans undecided about imperialism.

5. Defender of democratic ideals and institutions around the world.

6. Essays will vary but should be supported with facts from the section.

Answer to . . .

Comparing Primary Sources
Sumner's point that other people should be free to practice their customs is more in keeping with American political ideals.

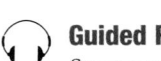

COMPARING PRIMARY SOURCES

IMPERIALISM

The Spanish-American War heightened the debate between imperialist and anti-imperialist factions at home.

Anti-Imperialist

"We assume that what we like and practice, and what we think better, must come as a welcome blessing to Spanish-Americans and Filipinos. This is grossly and obviously untrue. They hate our ways. They are hostile to our ideas. Our religion, language, institutions, and manners offend them."

—*William G. Sumner, Yale University professor, in an 1898 speech*

Pro-Imperialist

"Think of the tens of thousands of Americans who will invade mine and field and forest in the Philippines when a liberal government, protected and controlled by this republic, if not the government of the republic itself, shall establish order and equity there!"

—*Albert J. Beveridge, leading imperialist and later United States senator, in an 1898 speech*

ANALYZING VIEWPOINTS Which of the viewpoints do you think best represents the political ideals of liberty and equality on which the United States was founded?

British Empire, had used scouting techniques (tracking, woodcraft, and wilderness survival) to great success in a battle in South Africa. A few years after he returned to Britain as a war hero, Baden-Powell founded the Boy Scout movement. Scouting appeared in the United States in 1910 and soon became immensely popular.

Many people were swayed by the practical advantages of imperialism. They agreed with the economic arguments that emphasized the need to gain access to foreign markets. Others embraced the strategic reasons for expansion.

In December 1907 Roosevelt sent part of the United States Navy on a cruise around the world. The trip was designed to demonstrate the nation's impressive naval power to the world. The **Great White Fleet,** as the gleaming white ships were called, made a big impression everywhere it sailed. For American citizens, the fleet clearly showed the benefits of having a powerful navy.

Two Sides of Imperialism

Having begun a pattern of international involvement, shown on the map on the previous page, the United States discovered that these actions frequently took on a life of their own. In the Caribbean and Central America, for example, the United States often had to defend governments that were unpopular with local inhabitants. In Latin America, the cry "Yankee, Go Home!" began to be heard. Even before the Panama Canal was completed in 1914, Panamanians began to complain that they suffered from discrimination.

On the other hand, other countries—even those fearful about maintaining their independence—began to turn to the United States for help. Both welcomed and rejected, the United States would spend the rest of the century trying to decide the best way to reconcile its growing power and national interests with its relationships with other nations.

SECTION 4 REVIEW

Comprehension

1. *Key Terms* Define: (a) racism; (b) compulsory; (c) Great White Fleet.

2. *Summarizing Main Ideas* Name some of the major arguments of the anti-imperialists.

3. *Organizing Information* Create a two-column chart that shows how imperialism made the United States both welcome and unpopular around the world.

Critical Thinking

4. *Analyzing Time Lines* Review the time line at the start of the section. Choose an entry and explain why it reflects the debate over America's new role.

5. *Identifying Assumptions* Based on the arguments they used against imperialism, what kind of role do you think the anti-imperialists believed the United States should play in world affairs?

Writing Activity

6. *Writing an Expository Essay* Write a brief essay explaining why imperialism appealed to many Americans. Support your essay with examples from the section.

RESOURCE OPTIONS

Teaching Resources

 Quiz Units 5–6 folder, p. 66

Chapter Tests Forms A and B Chapter Test folder

Student Performance Pack

Guide to the Essentials Chapter 18, Section 4 (English and Spanish)

Standardized Test Preparation Handbook

Media and Technology

Guided Reading Audiotapes Chapter 18 Summary (English and Spanish)

Student Edition on Audiotape Chapter 18

Test Bank CD-ROM; Interactive Student Tutorial CD-ROM Chapter Test

Why Study History?

To understand that . . .

Your Nation Is a World Power

Since the Spanish-American War, the United States has played an increasingly active role in events around the world.

Teddy Roosevelt and the Rough Riders, 1898

"U.S. Air Assault Pounds Iraq." "U.S. Peacekeepers Arrive in Bosnia." "U.S. Food Shipments Reach North Korea." Headlines such as these reflect the extent of American involvement in distant parts of the world, as well as the many different types of involvement. As the United States has grown into a world power, its participation in world affairs has increased dramatically.

The Impact Today

In 1796 President George Washington warned Americans against involvement with foreign nations. For roughly a century American leaders heeded Washington's advice, avoiding foreign entanglements as much as possible.

That policy ended in the 1890s. The Spanish-American War marked the beginning of a more active foreign policy, in which the United States participated in foreign conflicts and acquired overseas territories, such as the Philippines.

American overseas involvement became especially widespread after the end of World War II in 1945. For the next half-century the United States and the Soviet Union, the world's two most powerful nations, fought a cold war for influence in Europe, Africa, Asia, and Latin America. To fight communism in other nations, the United States supplied large amounts of economic and military aid. American military forces fought large, costly wars in Korea and Vietnam and intervened in other nations such as the Dominican Republic and Grenada.

The cold war ended in the early 1990s with the collapse of the Soviet Union. Still, the United States remains committed to an active international role. In 1991, for example, American military forces liberated Kuwait from Iraqi occupation. Two years later, American troops went to Bosnia as part of a United Nations peacekeeping force aimed at ending the ethnic conflict raging there. The United States has assisted former Communist nations in their transition to democratic governments and market economies. Finally, the United States has played a leading role in international efforts to expand trade and promote economic growth around the world.

The Impact on You

What guidelines should American leaders use in deciding whether to become involved in the affairs of other countries? Discuss the issue with your classmates, friends, and family. Then write a "policy statement" outlining your conclusions about United States involvement abroad.

Marine comforts a Somali child during an American relief effort in 1992

Class Discussion

Discuss with the class United States involvement in world events. For a more thorough examination of the issue, see the activity folder in the Resource Options below.

ACTIVITY
STUDENT PARTICIPATION

Writing a Congressional Report

Ask students to read the text. Then divide the class into groups. Have each group act as a congressional committee member writing a report on the benefits of extending U.S. influence through:

- **economic aid**
- **medical aid**
- **economic boycotts**
- **food and supplies**
- **technological expertise**
- **special programs (like the Peace Corps)**

Each group should discuss one of the items above before writing its report on that topic.

Follow up Have students discuss situations where nonmilitary intervention is the most effective method of solving international issues.

Using the Internet

Students can learn more about the United States as a world power by exploring links in the *America: Pathways to the Present* Web site at:

http://www.Pathways.phschool.com

Assessment

See the Lesson Plans folder, pp. 24–27, for rubrics on assessing Class Participation Projects.

RESOURCE OPTIONS

Teaching Resources

Why Study History? Activity Your Nation Is a World Power, found in the Why Study History? folder, p. 19, provides an activity to help students better understand the role of the United States in today's world.

Media and Technology

Decision America Videotapes and Videodiscs Issue 7 *Is America Still the Free World Leader?*

Key Terms

Students should refer to the definitions of key terms in the chapter to write sentences that show an understanding of the causes of American imperialism and how it affected countries around the world.

Comprehension

1. Mahan: the economic future of the United States depended on new markets abroad and a navy to protect them. Lodge: worried about the effects of a disappearing frontier. Beveridge: expansionism was necessary because it introduced the ideas and customs of "superior" races to "primitive" societies.

2. By backing down, Great Britain in effect validated the Monroe Doctrine and set a precedent for future conflicts.

3. Yellow journalism played on human rights abuses in Cuba and fanned public outrage over the destruction of American property. The public blamed the Spanish for the explosion aboard the *Maine*.

4. The Open Door Policy, initiated by John Hay, called for open trade in China. It was important for Americans because European nations and Japan were establishing spheres of influence in China, threatening to shut out American influence.

5. He conducted an aggressive foreign policy, often dealing with other countries in a high-handed manner, assuming that what he wanted for each country was in its best interests.

6. It caused United States military intervention to become standard policy in Latin America.

7. It increased American investment in foreign economies, thus expanding American interests while at the same time maintaining orderly societies abroad.

8. Anti-imperialists believed that imperialism betrayed the ideal of liberty for all people.

Chapter Summary

The major concepts of Chapter 18 are presented below. See also *Guide to the Essentials of American History* or *Interactive Student Tutorial CD-ROM*, which contains interactive review activities, time lines, helpful hints, and test practice for Chapter 18.

Reviewing the Main Ideas

By the 1890s, farms and factories in the United States were producing more than the nation could consume. Soon, many business and political leaders began to pursue new markets abroad. Inspired by dreams of an empire, some Americans pushed for new territory as well. American expansion caused some citizens to raise doubts about the morality of imperialism.

Section 1: The Pressure to Expand

In the late 1800s, as European nations took over vast areas in Africa and Asia, American leaders looked to expand American influence abroad.

Section 2: The Spanish–American War

A swift American victory in the Spanish-American War confirmed the nation's status as a world power, but it left some people arguing over how to govern newly acquired territories.

Section 3: Expansion Under Roosevelt and Taft

President Theodore Roosevelt conducted a vigorous foreign policy that suited the new status of the United States as a world power. Although President William Howard Taft continued Roosevelt's policies, he preferred a more subtle approach to influencing other nations.

Section 4: Debating America's New Role

After the Spanish-American War, the debate intensified over whether it was appropriate for the United States to build an empire.

Since the 1890s, the United States has played an active role in world affairs. On numerous occasions, Americans have provided military and economic aid to countries in need.

Using Graphic Organizers

*   Causes: pressure to find new markets abroad; growth of European imperialism; United States tradition of expansionism, manifest destiny, Monroe Doctrine; wish to keep frontier spirit alive.
*   Effects: purchase of Alaska from Russia; trade treaty with Hawaii and annexation of Midway Islands; trading relationships established with Japan and China; political and military entanglements, war.

Key Terms

For each of the terms below, write a sentence explaining how it relates to this chapter.

1. annex
2. Open Door Policy
3. Great White Fleet
4. Roosevelt Corollary
5. imperialism
6. sphere of influence
7. nationalism
8. dollar diplomacy
9. jingoism
10. banana republic

Comprehension

1. Briefly explain the arguments of Alfred T. Mahan, Henry Cabot Lodge, and Albert J. Beveridge regarding expansionism.

2. Describe how the 1895 dispute between the United States and Great Britain reaffirmed the Monroe Doctrine.

3. Why did the American public favor war with Spain in 1898?

4. What was the Open Door Policy, and why was it important for the United States?

5. Describe Theodore Roosevelt's approach to foreign policy.

6. How did the Roosevelt Corollary affect United States policy in Latin America?

7. Explain President Taft's policy of dollar diplomacy.

8. Explain why anti-imperialists believed that imperialism betrayed basic American principles.

Using Graphic Organizers

On a separate sheet of paper, copy the multi-flow map to show the causes and effects of American expansion during the late 1800s and early 1900s. Provide at least three causes and three effects.

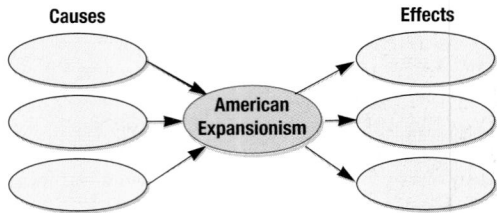

Analyzing Political Cartoons ▶

1. The caption to this 1904 political cartoon was: "HIS 128th BIRTHDAY. 'Gee but this is an awful stretch!'" (a) Whose birthday is it? (b) How do you know? (c) What is the "awful stretch" referring to? (d) How do you know?

2. What is the cartoonist's view on United States imperialism?

Critical Thinking

1. *Applying the Chapter Skill* Review the time zone map on page 526. Name two cities on the map that are in the same time zone as New York City.

2. *Identifying Central Issues* How did the popular philosophy of social Darwinism make it easier for some Americans to embrace imperialist policies in the late 1800s?

3. *Drawing Conclusions* During the late 1800s, the press fanned the flames of the Spanish-American War by publishing sensational stories about Spanish cruelties in Cuba. On what current issues has the press played a major role in influencing public opinion?

4. *Distinguishing Fact from Opinion* President McKinley's Secretary of State, John Hay, referred to the Spanish-American War as "a splendid little war." Can you think of any Americans, in addition to anti-imperialists, who might disagree with Hay?

INTERNET ACTIVITY

For your portfolio:
CREATE A TIME LINE

Access Prentice Hall's *America: Pathways to the Present* site at **www.Pathways.phschool.com** for the specific URL to complete the activity. Additional resources and related Web sites are also available.

Read the biography of William Howard Taft and create a time line of his career. Write a paragraph summarizing Taft's professional life. How would you characterize his career? What do you consider his most important achievement? What did Taft consider his most important achievement?

ANALYZING DOCUMENTS ◀ INTERPRETING DATA

Turn to the "American Voices" quotation on page 528.

1. Theodore Roosevelt is suggesting that his policies made it (a) impossible to build the canal. (b) possible to return Panama to Colombia. (c) easier to build the canal. (d) necessary to submit a State paper to Congress.

2. What is the most likely reason Roosevelt felt he had to justify his policies regarding the Panama Canal even after he left office?

(a) Colombia was asking for the return of the Canal Zone. (b) Anti-imperialists were complaining about his high-handed methods. (c) Panama was asking for more money. (d) Congress was considering returning the land to Panama.

3. *Writing* Do you think Roosevelt's argument justifies his actions? Explain your reasoning.

Connecting to Today

Essay Writing The United States still intervenes in foreign countries when its interests are threatened. Write a letter to the editor of a newspaper in which you argue either for or against an interventionist foreign policy. Research recent examples of United States actions in foreign countries and use them to support your arguments.

INTERNET ACTIVITY

Time lines and paragraphs will vary but should include Taft's professional work before he became President (lawyer, government positions under Roosevelt), as well as the policies he implemented as President and how successful they were.

Analyzing Political Cartoons

1. (a) The birthday of the United States. (b) The eagle with the banner is a common cartoon symbol of the nation. (c) U.S. imperialism. (d) The eagle's wings stretch from Puerto Rico and Panama to the Philippines—places of strong U.S. involvement.

2. Sample response: The cartoonist may be suggesting that the United States is not justified in its involvements far from home.

Critical Thinking

1. Toronto and Lima.

2. Social Darwinism promoted the idea that modern, European-style cultures and peoples were more civilized than and superior to other cultures and peoples. Social Darwinists thought that imperialism was noble because civilization could be brought to the "inferior" countries.

3. Answers will vary. Students might cite press coverage of any issue currently in the news. Students may point out that the degree of sensationalism usually depends on the source that is covering the story.

4. The families of people who were injured or killed in the war would probably disagree with Hay, as would anyone who suffered as a result of the war.

Analyzing Documents

1. c
2. b
3. Answers will vary, but should be based on the quotation.

Connecting to Today

Students' letters should take into account the imperialist and anti-imperialist arguments advanced in Sections 1 and 4.

The Era of Progressive Reform, 1890–1920

Managing Time and Instruction

INSTRUCTION SUPPORT

These materials for instruction are provided for **each section** in the **Teaching Resources**. See **Units 5–6 folder for Enrichment Support:**

- Reproducible Lesson Plans in Lesson Plans folder • Learning Styles Lesson Plans in Learning Styles Lesson Plans folder • Big Idea Graphic Organizers in Big Idea Graphic Organizer folder
- Guided Reading and Review • Quizzes • Test Preparation Practice booklet

DAILY LESSON	ENRICHMENT SUPPORT
1 **The Origins of Progressivism** (pp. 541–545)	• Biography, Ida Tarbell, Units 5–6 folder, p. 80 • Literature Activity, Horrors of the Meat-packing Industry, Units 5–6 folder, pp. 83–84 • Visual Learning Activity, A Different Kind of "Wild West" Show, Learning with Documents folder, p. 61 • Skills for Life Activity, Units 5–6 folder, p. 85
2 **Progressive Legislation** (pp. 547–551)	• Nystrom *Atlas of Our Country,* The Third Wave of Immigration, pp. 30–31 • Primary Source Activity, The Shame of the People, Learning with Documents folder, p. 25 • Primary Source Activity, Giving the Child a Chance, found on **Resource Pro** • Decision-Making Activity, Marching for Child Labor Laws, Decision-Making Activities folder, pp. 16–17
3 **Progressive Presidents** (pp. 552–556)	• Critical Thinking Activity, Distinguishing False from Accurate Images, found on **Resource Pro** • Biography, Louis D. Brandeis, found on **Resource Pro**
4 **Suffrage at Last** (pp. 557–560)	• Lasting Impact Activity, The Lasting Impact of the Nineteenth Amendment, History's Lasting Impact folder, pp. 12–13 • Comparing Primary Sources, On the Nineteenth Amendment, Units 5–6 folder, pp. 81–82 • Visual Learning Activity, When Women Have Rights, found on **Resource Pro** • Literature Activity, The "New" Woman, found on **Resource Pro** • You Can Make a Difference, Why Study History? folder, p. 20

Running Out of Time?

- Use Tape 3, "The United States on the Brink of Change, 1890–1920," from **Visions of America** videotapes series.
- Use Chapter 19 Summary from **Guide to the Essentials of American History (English and Spanish).**

Companion Web Site

The companion Web site offers online links for all chapter review activities. It also provides key content links and structured support for this chapter for both teachers and students.

http://www.Pathways.phschool.com

Media and Technology

For the Student

Interactive Student Tutorial CD-ROM Chapter 19

Student Edition on Audiotape Chapter 19

American Heritage® CD-ROM

Guided Reading Audiotapes (English and Spanish) Chapter 19

For the Teacher

Resource Pro CD-ROM Chapter 19

Test Bank CD-ROM Chapter 19

Listening to Literature Audiotapes *Timeless Voices, Timeless Themes* "Chicago" by Carl Sandburg

Color Transpariences Critical Thinking I–16

 ## Block Scheduling

Pacing Suggestions

For 90-minute Blocks

- Teach sections 3 and 4 using Transparencies I-8 and B–6, and the Recent Scholarship note on p. 559 for class discussions.

- Teach sections 1 and 2 using the Big Idea Graphic Organizers from Teaching Resources and the Extended Class Periods Activity on p. 549.

Additional Resources

- Prentice Hall's **American History Block Scheduling Support File** covers over 40 major topics in American history.

- **Prentice Hall United States History Video Collection**TM contains 20 videotapes covering American history from beginnings to present.

- **Decision America Videotapes and Videodiscs**

- **Visions of America Videotapes and Videodiscs**

 ## Assessment Options

Chapter Test Forms A&B Test Bank CD-ROM booklet

Test Bank CD-ROM Chapter 19

Standardized Test Preparation Handbook

 ## Connections to American Literature

from Prentice Hall

Prentice Hall Literature *Timeless Voices, Timeless Themes* "A Wagner Matinée" by Willa Cather, p. 614

Additional Resources

For the Student

Life History of the United States, Vols. 8–10.
The Progressive Era. 1964
The Women Get the Vote. McGraw Hill Films.

For the Teacher

Nancy F. Cott. *Root of Bitterness: Documents of the Social History of American Women.* Dutton, 1972.

Prentice Hall brings into the classroom the vast archives and scholarship of the nation's premier American history magazine. See "From the Archives of American Heritage®" and "About the Presidents" teaching notes in this chapter.

 History Alive!

Teacher's Curriculum Institute, in partnership with Prentice Hall, provides unique materials that engage students with diverse learning styles. See History Alive!® unit on The Rise of Industrial America.

 Student Performance Pack

Ensures success in the three critical areas of Reading, Test Taking, and English Language Development with the following materials:

- Guide to the Essentials of American History in English and Spanish
- Guided Reading Audiotapes in English and Spanish
- Interactive Student Tutorial CD-ROM
- Test Preparation Handbook
- Test Preparation Practice booklet

Introducing the Chapter

At the turn of the century, many Americans hoped to change American society for the better. These reform-minded citizens, who were called progressives, worked for many different causes at the national, state, and local levels. Many of their reforms had lasting effects on American society.

Themes in American History

The theme for this chapter, Culture, is listed at the beginning of this unit. An alternate theme for the chapter is Government. To teach this unit thematically, you may wish to use the Prosperity, Depression, and War folder in American History Block Scheduling Support.

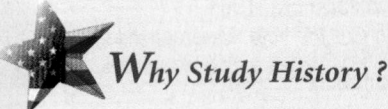

Why Study History?

Have students explore suggested ways of connecting the past to the present on page 561.

Answer to . . .

Viewing History Students should use this question as an aid in reading the chapter. Reforms included: improvement of the civil service system, workplace safety legislation, antitrust laws, public health regulations in the meat industry, and an expansion of environmental preservation and protection.

CHAPTER 19 The Era of Progressive Reform
1890–1920

CHAPTER FOCUS

At the turn of the century, a spirit of reform known as progressivism took hold of many Americans. Less a united movement than a loose collection of informal alliances among reform groups, progressivism targeted the challenges of an urban, industrialized nation.

The *Why Study History?* page at the end of this chapter explores the rise of volunteer organizations during the Progressive Era and community service activities today.

▲
VIEWING HISTORY
These women cheer the passage of the Nineteenth Amendment, which extended the vote to women. *Government What other lasting reforms originated in the Progressive Era?*

▶ RESOURCE OPTIONS

Teaching Resources

 Big Idea Graphic Organizer folder
Graphic summary of the main idea of the chapter.

Learning Styles Lesson Plans folder
Alternate lesson plans for diverse learning styles for each chapter.

Media and Technology

AmericanHeritage® CD-ROM
Time Tour A New Role in the World: Progressives and Reformers

  Prentice Hall United States History Video Collection™ Volume 14 *The Progressive Movement*

1879	1888	1899	1906
Henry George writes Progress and Poverty	Edward Bellamy writes Looking Backward	National Consumers' League founded	Upton Sinclair publishes The Jungle

| 1870 | 1880 | 1890 | 1900 | 1910 |

1 The Origins of Progressivism

SECTION PREVIEW

Objectives

1 Describe the new reform ideas that took hold at the turn of the century.
2 Summarize the methods muckrakers used to bring about reforms.
3 List the goals that most progressive reformers had in common.
4 *Key Terms* Define: municipal; injunction; home rule; muckraker; Progressive Era; social welfare program.

Main Idea

At the end of the 1800s, many citizens recognized the need to solve problems resulting from rapid industrialization and urban growth. The appearance of many reform movements caused historians to refer to the period as the Progressive Era.

Reading Strategy

Organizing Information As you read the section, create a list of the reforms that Progressives worked to bring about.

During the last part of the 1800s, rapid industrialization had contributed to the growth of the nation's cities, population, and wealth. This growth had come at a cost, however. Unemployment, unsafe working conditions, and political corruption continued to plague the nation. Many citizens realized that private efforts to address these issues, such as charity and settlement houses, were inadequate. Some argued that the government needed to become more involved in solving the nation's problems.

New Reform Ideas

The 1880s and 1890s were filled with lively debates about how to reform society. The ideas of journalists Henry George and Edward Bellamy were among the most popular. Socialists, labor leaders, and city government reformers also had many followers.

Two Leading Reformers In 1879 Henry George wrote *Progress and Poverty* in an effort to explain why poverty continued to flourish in

such an advanced civilization. George concluded that poverty arose because some people bought and held on to land until its price went up. This practice, known as speculation, prevented others from using the land productively.

To solve this problem, George proposed that the government charge landowners a single tax on the value of the land itself. In the past, landowners had been taxed on improvements to the land, such as houses and cultivation. A single tax would make speculation in land less attractive by increasing the cost of holding land without using it. George's ideas had a powerful effect. "Single-tax" clubs sprang up everywhere. In 1894, club members from Iowa, Ohio, Minnesota, and Pennsylvania migrated to Fairhope, Alabama, to establish a single-tax colony.

In 1888 newspaper editor Edward Bellamy published *Looking Backward*. In this novel a man undergoes hypnosis in 1887 and wakes up in the year 2000. Upon waking, the man finds the United States transformed. In place of harsh working conditions, poverty, and political corruption, he finds a country where

---

▶ RESOURCE OPTIONS

Teaching Resources

📁 **Reproducible Lesson Plan** Lesson Plans folder, p. 109

📁 **Learning Styles Lesson Plan** Learning Styles Lesson Plans folder, p. 40

📁 **Big Idea Graphic Organizer** Big Idea Graphic Organizer folder, p. 81

📁 **Guided Reading and Review** Units 5–6 folder, p. 72

Media and Technology

 AmericanHeritage® **CD-ROM**

Time Tour A New Role in the World: Progressives and Reformers

---

SECTION 1

The Origins of Progressivism

Objectives

You may wish to call students' attention to the objectives in the Section Preview. The objectives are reflected in the main headings of the section.

Bellringer

Ask students what cues they look for to determine whether they are making progress, possibly in a course or with a project. How does a society or a nation measure its progress? In what areas would students like to see the United States make progress today?

Reading Strategy

Organizing Information Refer to the Reading Strategy in the Section Preview. You may wish to have volunteers contribute to a composite list that you write on the chalkboard.

LESSON PLAN

Connecting to the Main Idea

1. Focus In the 1880s and 1890s, many concerned citizens worked to reform American society. Their efforts became known as progressivism. How did progressivism affect American life?

2. Instruct Discuss the theme of reform. In what ways does progressivism resemble populism? What reform ideas were new? Ask students to compare the ideas of Henry George and Edward Bellamy. What actions did each think the government should take to transform society?

Discuss the various progressive movements. How did journalists work to bring about reform? What kinds of reforms did women and labor unions hope to effect?

3. Close At the turn of the century, a spirit of reform known as progressivism swept the country, especially in cities. The next section discusses progressive bills passed by local, state, and federal legislatures.

the government has taken over the largest companies. In the novel, the government has also reorganized the companies with the goal of meeting human needs rather than making profits. Wrote Bellamy:

 AMERICAN VOICES "In a word, the people of the United States concluded to assume the conduct of their own business, just as . . . years before they had assumed the conduct of their own government."

—*Edward Bellamy,* Looking Backward

Bellamy's novel was a phenomenal best seller. In response to its ideas, hundreds of "Nationalist" clubs formed.

Socialists Bellamy's views were related to the widely discussed ideas of socialism. Socialism is an economic and political philosophy favoring public or government control of property and income. Many American socialists in this era wanted to end the capitalist system, distribute wealth more equally, and nationalize American industries. They wished to do so through the ballot box, not through revolution. In 1901 they formed the Socialist Party of America. By 1912 the party had won more than 1,000 **municipal,** or city government, offices.

The Labor Movement Like members of the Socialist party, some union members also hoped for fundamental economic change. Unions, however, focused their efforts on the goals of reducing hours and gaining better wages and working conditions.

The union movement grew in the 1890s, but only slowly. Employers discouraged union membership, preferring to deal with individual workers. If unions were successful despite this discouragement, business leaders could count on courts to issue **injunctions,** or court orders, prohibiting workers from going on strike.

Municipal Reform The spirit of reform was also felt within city governments. Municipal reformers opposed the influence of political bosses. They argued that only a civil service system based on merit instead of favors would keep political appointees out of important jobs enforcing labor laws. Reformers also worked for **home rule,** a system by which cities exercise a limited degree of self-rule. Home rule allowed cities to escape from domination by state governments, which often were controlled by political machines or rural interests.

Municipal reformers sometimes appeared naive in their belief that they could abolish corruption. Some of them also held negative views of immigrants, whom they felt were

 VIEWING HISTORY

In spite of the obstacles facing unions, the International Ladies Garment Workers Union (ILGWU) formed in 1900. After a strike in 1909, which included 20,000 New York City women garment workers, the ILGWU won the right to bargain collectively, or negotiate contracts with employers. *Economics How did businesses prevent workers from striking?*

responsible for many city problems. Still, their ideas formed an important element of the era's spirit of reform.

The Muckrakers

Many reformers at the turn of the century worked to bring about change in a systematic manner. Relying heavily on scientific data and expert testimony, they first investigated issues of concern, such as slum or sweatshop conditions. Next, they publicized the results of their investigations. Readers could then put pressure on legislators to pass and enforce new laws. Women's clubs and charitable groups provided a key means of increasing support for reform and pressuring officials to take action.

Journalists also alerted the public to wrongdoing in politics and business. Theodore Roosevelt called such writers **muckrakers.** He took the term *muckraker* from John Bunyan's 1678 book *Pilgrim's Progress,* in which one of the characters was too busy raking filth on Earth to lift his eyes to heaven. While Roosevelt approved of legitimate exposure of wrongdoing, he condemned those who "earn their livelihood by telling . . . scandalous falsehoods about honest men."

Despite Roosevelt's criticism, the muckrakers included many respected writers who identified and exposed real abuses. Lincoln Steffens exposed political corruption in St. Louis and other cities. Ida Tarbell revealed the abuses committed by the huge Standard Oil trust. *The Jungle,* a novel by Upton Sinclair published in 1906, described the horrors of the meatpacking industry. Publication of the book led to the creation of a federal meat inspection program. Wrote Sinclair of the nation's filthy canneries:

AMERICAN VOICES ❝It seemed they must have agencies all over the country, to hunt out old and crippled and diseased cattle to be canned. . . . It was stuff such as this that made the 'embalmed beef' that had killed several times as many United States soldiers as all the bullets of the Spaniards [in the Spanish-American War].❞

—*Upton Sinclair,* The Jungle

This cartoon shows that TR himself was willing to wield the muckrake to attack difficult problems. Here, TR tries to clean up the nation's meatpacking industry. *Culture How did muckrakers use the media to advance reform?*

The Goals of the Progressives

Americans read the muckrakers' novels and newspaper accounts with enthusiasm. Whether angered or sickened by what they read, many Americans were inspired to take action by joining reform organizations. Many of these new reform movements had their roots in earlier reform groups. These included nativists, prohibitionists, purity crusaders, charity reformers, social gospel adherents, settlement house workers, and Populists. Because all these groups were working to bring about "progress" in society, historians refer to the period from about 1890 to 1920 as the **Progressive Era.**

Unlike the socialists and some other reformers, most Progressives did not support sweeping economic and political changes. Many deeply feared the violence of revolution. Most Progressives were Americans of average wealth. They did not want to lose the high standard of living and personal liberty that democracy and a free-enterprise system had given them. Instead Progressives wanted to free the existing government of corruption so that it could be more efficient in an expanded role as guardian of workers and the poor.

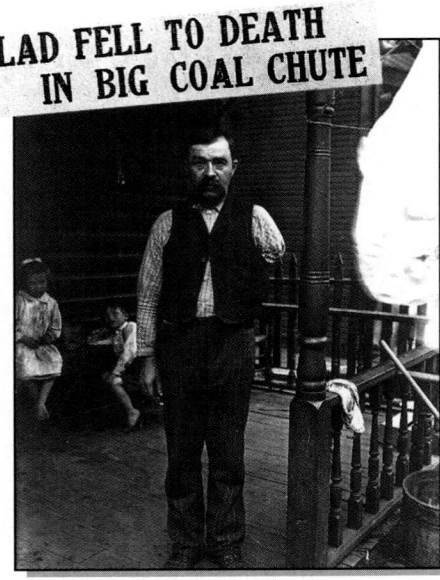

LAD FELL TO DEATH IN BIG COAL CHUTE

VIEWING HISTORY

Workers of all ages had little protection against workplace hazards—and few benefits when accidents befell them on the job. The fate of injured or killed workers aroused public sympathy and demands for reform. *Government Why did Progressives push for social welfare programs?*

Main Idea CONNECTIONS

Why did many Progressives argue that government must play a larger role in regulating economic activity?

An Expanded Role for Government Many Progressives also argued that government must play a larger role in regulating economic activity. This regulation would prevent businesses from treating workers and competing companies unfairly. Progressives opposed government control of businesses, except for those companies that supplied essential services such as water, electricity, and transportation. They wanted most businesses to operate independently—provided they took workers' needs into account.

Progressives also believed that government ought to increase its responsibility for human welfare, or well-being. Workers had little protection against low wages, unemployment, or workplace hazards. Progressives proposed that government protect workers from such circumstances. They also wanted government to develop more **social welfare programs,** which would help ensure a basic standard of living for

all Americans. These programs included unemployment, accident, and health insurance. Some also favored a social security system that would aid the disabled and the elderly. Progressives expected that government would rely on experts and scientists to plan efficient programs, which professionals, not politicians, would manage.

Women Work for Reforms As social worker Jane Addams explained in a 1910 *Ladies' Home Journal* article, women had a special interest in the reform of American society:

AMERICAN VOICES "Women who live in the country sweep their own dooryards and may either feed the refuse [trash] of the table to a flock of chickens or allow it innocently to decay in the open air and sunshine. In a crowded city quarter, however, if the street is not cleaned by the city authorities no amount of private sweeping will keep the tenement free from grime; if the garbage is not properly collected and destroyed a tenement house mother may see her children sicken and die of diseases."

—*Jane Addams*

In short, Addams argued that women in cities could not care for their families without government help. Progressive women did not all agree on how to reform society. Many focused on outlawing alcohol; others on reforming conditions in the workplace. Whatever their focus, many women agreed that they needed the right to vote. The cause of women's suffrage was important to many Progressives.

Because women and their children were workers, labor issues were also important to progressive women. Florence Kelley became a leader in the work for labor reform. She came from a prominent Pennsylvania family. Her father, William Darrah Kelley, was a fifteen-term member of Congress. Her great-aunt, Sarah Pugh, had a strong influence on her. An abolitionist and suffragist, Pugh had once refused to use cotton and sugar because slave labor produced them.

After completing her education at Cornell University in New York, and at the University of Zurich in Switzerland, Kelley became a resident in Jane Addams's Hull House in Chicago. When federal officials asked Addams to investigate labor conditions in the neighborhood, Addams recommended Kelley for the job. "Hull House was . . . surrounded in every direction by home

▶ RESOURCE OPTIONS

Teaching Resources

📁 **Biography** Ida Tarbell, Units 5–6 folder, p. 80

📁 **Literature Activity** Horrors of the Meat-Packing Industry, Units 5–6 folder, pp. 83–84

📁 **Visual Learning Activity** A Different Kind of "Wild West" Show, Learning with Documents folder, p. 61

Media and Technology

 AmericanHeritage® CD-ROM

History Makers Ida Tarbell, Jane Addams

work carried on under the sweating system," Kelley wrote later. "From the age of eighteen months few children able to sit in high chairs at tables were safe from being required to pull basting threads." Once, Kelley reported, a public official who was supposed to visit a sweatshop refused to enter, fearing contamination from one of the many diseases, such as tuberculosis, that raged through the tenements at that time.

Largely through her efforts, in 1893 Illinois passed a law prohibiting child labor, limiting working hours for women, and regulating sweatshop conditions. The governor put Kelley in charge of enforcing it. She became so frustrated by the district attorney's refusal to prosecute cases that she earned a law degree in order to take legal action herself.

In 1897 a new governor replaced Kelley as factory inspector with a political friend who did nothing to enforce the 1893 law. It was this experience that drew Kelley into municipal reform. Kelley believed that a civil service system would keep unqualified political appointees out of important regulatory jobs.

Kelley also served as general secretary of the National Consumers' League (NCL). The NCL was organized in 1899 to unite local consumers' leagues. Through the leagues, women investigated the conditions under which goods were made and sold. They also encouraged consumers to purchase goods only at shops that did not employ children or require overtime. Leagues insisted that factories obey state factory inspection laws. Later they insisted that they pay a minimum wage. Under Kelley's leadership,

the NCL spearheaded national movements to outlaw child labor and protect workers, especially women. When criticized over this issue, Kelley would ask why "seals, bears, reindeer, fish, wild game in the national parks, buffalo" and numerous other creatures were worthy of government protection, "but not the children of our race and their mothers."

Kelley's legacy lasted long after her death in 1932. In 1954 Supreme Court justice Felix Frankfurter said that Florence Kelley "had probably the largest single share in shaping the social history of the United States during the first thirty years of this century."

Florence Kelley

Resistance to Progressive Reforms To protect vulnerable citizens, Progressives backed increased levels of government control over people's lives. They thought government should have some say in housing, health care, and even in the content of the movies people watched. This aspect of progressivism aroused resistance, often among the very people Progressives hoped to help. For example, Progressives saw child labor laws as critical to social progress. Employers who relied on cheap child labor, however, opposed the laws. In addition, poor families who could not survive without sending their children to work also objected. Such disputes added to the perception that Progressives were insensitive to the poor.

SECTION 1 REVIEW

Comprehension

1. *Key Terms* Define: (a) municipal; (b) injunction; (c) home rule; (d) muckraker; (e) Progressive Era; (f) social welfare program.

2. *Summarizing the Main Idea* Summarize the diverse goals of the progressive reformers.

3. *Organizing Information* Create a chart with two columns, one labeled *Problem* and the other labeled *Progressive Solution.* Complete the chart using information from this section.

Critical Thinking

4. *Analyzing Time Lines* Review the time line at the start of the section. How does each of the events on this time line reflect the spirit of the Progressive Era?

5. *Recognizing Ideologies* What beliefs about the role of government lay at the heart of the Progressive Era?

Writing Activity

6. *Writing a Persuasive Essay* Write a letter to the editor of a 1905 newspaper arguing why it is important for the paper to publish the muckrakers' articles.

SKILLS FOR LIFE

Critical Thinking

Testing Conclusions

Focus Students test the validity of conclusions by checking to see if the conclusions are supported by known data.

Instruct Divide students into groups and ask each group to decide what kind of data they would need to test the validity of the following conclusions, each made by a prominent historian:
"The United States has had the bloodiest and most violent labor history of any industrial nation in the world." (Philip Taft and Philip Ross)
"The railroads . . . gave an enormous stimulus to industrial growth." (Page Smith)
"A good index of the industrial development of the Middle West is the rise of ship tonnage passing through the 'Soo' [Sault Ste. Marie] Canal between Lakes Superior and Huron." (Samuel Eliot Morison)
Compare responses from different groups.

Extend See the Skills for Life Activity in the Resource Options below.

Answers

1. (a) The work force, labor union membership, and earnings between 1900 and 1920. (b) Yes, the conclusions appear to be based on the data provided.

2. (a) Conclusion 1 requires data over a period of time because it is based on a trend. (b) No.

3. (a) contradict (b) No. No data is given that indicates the earnings that were lost due to work stoppages. Therefore, conclusion 4 is not a valid conclusion.

TEST FOR SUCCESS

Valid according to the data.

Testing Conclusions

Testing conclusions means checking statements or opinions to see whether or not they are supported by known data. Data that are known to be valid can be used as criteria for testing a conclusion. If the data support the conclusion, then you have reason to believe that the conclusion is sound. Use the following steps to test the validity of conclusions.

1. *Study the conclusions to recognize the type of data that is necessary to verify them.* If supporting data are provided, decide if they are useful for testing the conclusions. Read the conclusions at right, examine the data in the tables, and answer the following questions: (a) Upon what information are the conclusions based? (b) Is there a relationship between the conclusions and the evidence provided?

2. *Decide on the criteria by which the conclusions could be tested.* Some conclusions are based upon trends and must be tested against data that cover a period of time. Other conclusions are more specific and may need exact data for verification. (a) Does Conclusion 1 deal with a trend or with a specific point in time? (b) Would data covering a period of time be needed to support Conclusion 2?

3. *Test the conclusions by comparing them with the data.* Decide if the data support or contradict the conclusions and whether additional information is needed to determine the validity of some conclusions. (a) Do the facts support or contradict Conclusion 3? (b) Do you agree with Conclusion 4?

Conclusions:

1. The twenty-year period between 1900 and 1920 saw a steady and significant growth in union membership.

2. By 1920, union workers earned more money than nonunion workers while working fewer hours.

3. In terms of a percent of the work force, more workers were union members in 1910 than in 1920.

4. The reason why the vast majority of workers did not join labor unions in the early 1900s was that work stoppages led to pay stoppages and decreased earnings.

TEST FOR SUCCESS

According to the data, is the following conclusion valid or not? "In 1900 builders claimed more union members than any other industry."

Work Force and Labor Union Membership			
Year	Total Workers	Total Union Membership	Percentage of Work Force in Unions
1900	29,073,000	868,000	3.0
1910	37,371,000	2,140,000	5.7
1920	42,434,000	5,048,000	11.9

Union Membership by Industry			
Year	Building	Textiles	Public Service
1900	153,000	8,000	15,000
1910	459,000	21,000	58,000
1920	888,000	149,000	161,000

Average Union and Nonunion Hours and Earnings in Manufacturing Industries				
	Union		Nonunion	
Year	Weekly Hours	Hourly Earnings	Weekly Hours	Hourly Earnings
1900	53.0	$0.341	62.1	$0.152
1910	50.1	$0.403	59.8	$0.188
1920	45.7	$0.884	53.5	$0.561

Source: *Historical Statistics of the United States, Colonial Times to 1970*

 RESOURCE OPTIONS

Teaching Resources

Skills for Life Activity Units 5–6 folder, p. 85, provides further practice in interpreting quantitative data to examine conclusions.

Media and Technology

 Color Transparencies Critical Thinking, I–16

1902	1905		1911	1913		
United Mine	United States	1908	Triangle	Sixteenth and	1913	
Workers strike	Forest Service	Muller v.	Shirtwaist	Seventeenth	Department of	
over low wages	established	Oregon	Factory fire	amendments ratified	Labor formed	

1900   **1910**   **1920**

2 Progressive Legislation

SECTION PREVIEW

Objectives

1   Describe urban reforms that took place during the Progressive Era.
2   Summarize the reforms made in state government that gave voters more power.
3   List the reforms that took place at the federal level.
4   *Key Terms* Define: direct primary; initiative; referendum; recall; holding company.

Main Idea

Because of public demand, local, state, and federal legislatures enacted a number of progressive reforms in the early 1900s.

Reading Strategy

Organizing Information As you read this section, create a chart listing the major progressive reforms made at the local, state, and federal levels.

P ublic demand for change led to a tremendous amount of legislation in the early 1900s. Reform took place at all levels of government—city, state, and federal.

Urban Reforms

Many of the earliest progressive reforms were made at the city level. Cities were home to most of the settlement workers, club members, and professionals who were pushing many of the reforms. Thus, they were on hand to maintain the pressure for change.

Attacking the Bosses Political machines and bosses sustained heavy criticism during the Progressive Era. For the most part, they were able to survive such attacks. New York City provides a good example. In 1896 Columbia University president Seth Low ran for mayor, supported by municipal reformers. To help his campaign against Tammany Hall's ward bosses, settlement houses sent children out to post handbills in their neighborhoods. Low lost the election, but he tried again in 1901 and won. But the Tammany Hall machine returned to power in the next elec-

tion. Over the following decades, New York voters switched back and forth between reformers and old political bosses.

In some cities, voter support for reforms prompted machine politicians to work with reformers. Together they registered voters, improved city services, established public health programs, and enforced tenement codes. Such alliances brought about astonishing improvements in urban life in some places.

Cities Take Over Utilities Reformers made efforts to regulate or dislodge the monopolies that provided city utilities such as water, gas, and electricity. Reform mayors Hazen S. Pingree of Detroit (1889–1897), Samuel M. "Golden Rule" Jones of Toledo (1897–1904), and Tom Johnson of Cleveland (1901–1909) pioneered city control or ownership of utilities. City control provided residents with more affordable services. By 1915, nearly two out of three cities had some form of city-owned utilities.

Providing Welfare Services Some reform mayors led movements for city-supported welfare services. Hazen Pingree provided public baths, parks, and a work-relief program.

RESOURCE OPTIONS

Teaching Resources

📁 **Reproducible Lesson Plan** Lesson Plans folder, p. 110

📁 **Big Idea Graphic Organizer** Big Idea Graphic Organizer folder, p. 82

📁 **Guided Reading and Review** Units 5–6 folder, p. 74

 Nystrom *Atlas of Our Country* The Third Wave of Immigration, pp. 30–31

About the Presidents

Theodore Roosevelt (1901–1909) accomplished several "firsts" as President. He was the first Vice President to become President and then to be elected in his own right. He was the first Republican President from the East. He set up the first White House press room. Roosevelt was the first President to invite an African American—Booker T. Washington—to dinner at the White House. He was the first to leave U.S. soil while in office, on a visit to the Panama Canal in 1908. What's more, he was the first President to fly in an airplane. The purchase of a Wright brothers' airplane during his presidency led to the U.S. Army Air Force. Source: Wilson Sullivan, "Theodore Roosevelt," *The American Heritage® Pictorial History of the Presidents of the United States,* vol. 2, 1968.

Women workers crowd the floor of this Progressive Era factory. *Economics Why did Florence Kelley consider labor issues to be women's issues?*

"Golden Rule" Jones opened playgrounds, free kindergartens, and lodging houses for the homeless. "Nobody has a right to rule anybody else," he once said. In his view, all people would be good if social conditions were good.

State Reforms

Some governors and state legislators also were active in promoting progressive reforms. Governors Robert "Battling Bob" La Follette in Wisconsin and Hiram Johnson in California, among others, introduced reforms to give voters a more direct voice in government. They also worked for reforms in the workplace.

More Power to Voters Progressive reformers believed they could put an end to corruption in government by limiting the power of party bosses and politicians. One way to do this was to give voters more direct say in lawmaking and in choosing candidates. Five important gains were made by voters during the Progressive Era:

> **Main Idea**
> **CONNECTIONS**
>
> Why did Progressive reformers want to give voters more power?

(1) *Direct Primaries.* Throughout the country, party leaders had long handpicked who would run for office. By 1904 Governor La Follette had instituted a **direct primary** in Wisconsin. A direct primary is an election in which voters cast ballots to select nominees for upcoming elections. By 1916 all but three states had direct primaries.

(2) *The Seventeenth Amendment.* In 1904 Oregon began allowing voters, rather than the state legislature, to choose their United States senator. By 1913 more than enough states were electing their senators in this way to ratify the Seventeenth Amendment to the Constitution. This amendment allows for the popular election of senators.

(3) *Initiative.* Many states also passed laws allowing citizens to use an **initiative** process. Through this process, citizens can propose new laws by obtaining a certain percentage of voters' signatures on a petition. Once the required number of signatures is gathered, the proposed law is then placed on the ballot in the next election.

(4) *Referendum.* The **referendum** process also gave voters a more direct role in legislation. Using this process, citizens may demand via petition that a law passed by the legislature be "referred" to voters for their approval or rejection.

(5) *Recall.* The **recall** procedure gave voters the ability to remove public officials from office before the next election.

Reforms of the Workplace Workplace tragedies also led to demands for reform. Late in the afternoon on Saturday, March 25, 1911, a match or cigarette ignited a fire on the eighth floor of the Triangle Shirtwaist Company in New York City. Because many of the exit doors were locked to prevent employee theft, 146 people died in the blaze.

The horror of the Triangle fire roused the public to action. The day after the tragedy, the Women's Trade Union League and the Red Cross formed a committee to improve fire safety standards. The committee called on the city to appoint fire inspectors, to make fire drills compulsory, and to unlock and fireproof exits.

Motivated in part by this disaster, state reformers also worked toward ending unsafe working conditions. Some states established labor departments to provide information and dispute-resolution services to employers and employees. Other states developed workers' accident insurance programs and compensation systems. By 1920 all but five states had taken steps to make it easier for workers to collect payment for workplace accidents.

Government efforts to control working conditions met legal opposition at every turn. In the case of *Lochner* v. *New York* (1905), for example, the Supreme Court struck down a law setting maximum hours for bakers. The law was declared void on the ground that it was

Answer to . . .

Viewing History Because women and their children were workers and urban women faced difficult living conditions.

Main Idea Connections They thought that if voters had more say in the political process, corruption could be reduced.

RESOURCE OPTIONS

Teaching Resources

Primary Source Activity The Shame of the People, Learning with Documents folder, p. 25

Media and Technology

AmericanHeritage® **CD-ROM**

Presidents Theodore Roosevelt

"an illegal interference with the rights of individuals . . . to make contracts."

After this setback, reformers tried to convince the courts that government had to control conditions to protect women. This approach worked. In the 1908 case of *Muller* v. *Oregon,* the United States Supreme Court upheld an Oregon law that limited hours for women laundry workers to ten hours a day.

Labor reformers were successful on some other fronts as well. By 1907 the National Child Labor Committee had convinced some thirty states to abolish child labor. Child labor was often defined as employment of children under age 14. Minimum wage legislation for women and children also made headway, with Florence Kelley leading a national campaign. After Massachusetts adopted a minimum wage in 1912, eight other states followed.

Federal Reforms

A number of important progressive reforms were also made at the federal level. Beginning with Theodore Roosevelt, the White House became a powerful voice for change.

Theodore Roosevelt's "Square Deal" As President, Theodore Roosevelt was determined to use his powers vigorously. He got his chance in May 1902, when the United Mine Workers called a strike to protest their low wages. As winter approached and mine owners continued to refuse to talk to the union, TR decided to intervene. Lacking coal, the nation would be without a key source of heating fuel.

Roosevelt insisted that both sides submit to arbitration, in which an impartial third party decides on a legally binding solution. To encourage mine owners to accept this step, TR threatened to use the army to seize and operate the mines. In 1903 arbitrators granted the miners a 10 percent raise and reduced their hours from 10 to 9. They did not grant official recognition of their union, however. When Roosevelt called this a "square deal" for both sides, the phrase became a slogan of his presidency.

After his reelection in 1904, Roosevelt urged Congress to pass laws to regulate the food and drug industries and the railroads. In 1906 the Hepburn Act authorized the Interstate Commerce Commission to limit rates if shippers complained of unfair treatment. Also in 1906 the Pure Food and Drug Act and the Meat Inspection Act required accurate labeling of ingredients, strict sanitary conditions, and a rating system for meats.

Antitrust Activism Although the Sherman Antitrust Act in 1890 was in place as a check on big business, it had never been vigorously enforced. Reversing this trend, Roosevelt's Attorney General used the act to sue the Northern Securities Company. Northern Securities was a holding company. A **holding company** buys up stocks and bonds of smaller companies. In doing so, it creates a monopoly. Northern Securities had brought about a slight dip in railroad rates by forming such a monopoly. But in 1904 the government convinced the Supreme Court that the company was in violation of the Sherman Act. The Court dissolved the company.

By the time Roosevelt had completed his second term in 1909, the government had filed 42 antitrust actions. The beef trust, Standard Oil, and the American Tobacco Company were either broken up or forced to reorganize. TR was not antibusiness. He did not wish to destroy trusts that he deemed "good," or not harmful to the public. But he believed that they should be supervised and controlled.

Protecting the Environment Roosevelt also urged Congress to extend the earlier steps that

This 1904 political cartoon compared Standard Oil to an octopus with a stranglehold on government. *Economics What was TR's attitude toward monopolies?*

Date	Legislation	Purpose
1890	Sherman Antitrust Act	Outlawed monopolies and practices that result in restraint of trade, such as price fixing.
1902	National Reclamation Act	Created to plan and develop irrigation projects.
1905	United States Forest Service	Created to manage the nation's water and timber resources.
1906	Hepburn Act	Required railroads to obtain permission from the Interstate Commerce Commission before raising rates.
1906	Pure Food and Drug Act	Outlawed interstate transportation of impure or diluted foods and the deliberate mislabeling of foods and drugs.
1906	Meat Inspection Act	Required federal inspection of meat processing to ensure sanitary conditions.
1913	Department of Labor	Cabinet department created to protect and promote the welfare and employment of working people. Began with four existing bureaus, including the Children's Bureau.
1913	16th Amendment	Gave Congress the power to levy an income tax.
1913	17th Amendment	Provided for the direct election of senators.
1916	National Park Service	Created to take over the administration of the nation's parks.
1919	18th Amendment	Prohibited the manufacture and sale of liquor. (Repealed in 1933.)
1920	Women's Bureau	Created within the Department of Labor to promote the status of working women.

Interpreting Tables Progressive reform touched many aspects of life, including business, natural resources, labor, and consumer protection. *Government Which reforms required constitutional amendments?*

From the Archives of American Heritage

The Start of Prohibition The official date for the enforcement of Prohibition—midnight, January 16, 1920—came and went quietly. The American temperance movement was nothing new. Thirteen states were completely dry at the time the amendment was proposed; Michigan had been dry from 1856 to 1875. In the 1880s schoolchildren signed pledges showing their contempt for the "Cup of Death." "There is a happy time, not far away," children were taught to sing, "When Temp'rance truth shall shine, bright as day." Similarly, saloon patrons sang "Good-bye, whiskey, good-bye, gin" when the Eighteenth Amendment finally triumphed. Prohibition lived on into the Depression, when on April 7, 1933, President Franklin Roosevelt toasted the return of legal drink with a beer. Source: Nathan Ward, "The Time Machine," *American Heritage* magazine, December 1992.

---

had been taken to protect the nation's natural environment and resources. For example, at the urging of explorers and nature writers such as John Wesley Powell and John Muir, Congress had established Yellowstone in Wyoming as the nation's first national park in 1872. In 1890 Yosemite in California was also established as a national park. Presidents Harrison and Cleveland preserved some 35 million acres of forest land.

Now, in the early 1900s, the federal government called in experts to develop a policy for land and water use based on scientific data. In 1905 Roosevelt named Gifford Pinchot, a forester, to head a new United States Forest Service. At Pinchot's recommendation, TR set aside more than 200 million acres of land for national forests, mineral reserves, and water projects. The National Reclamation Act, passed in 1902, set aside money from the sale of public lands to fund the construction of irrigation systems in arid states.

A New Labor Department In response to pressure from women's clubs and labor organizations, in 1912 the government established a Children's Bureau. The following year, the Department of Labor was added as a new Cabinet department. A Women's Bureau was formed in 1920. These two bureaus, both part of the Department of Labor, supported legislation that would benefit women and children. Julia Lathrop and Mary Anderson, the heads of these bureaus, became the first female bureau heads at the federal level.

New Constitutional Amendments Like the Seventeenth Amendment ratified in the same year, progressive reformers fought for the ratification of the Sixteenth Amendment in 1913. The Sixteenth Amendment authorized Congress to collect income taxes. Prior to this amendment, the government relied on income from tariffs. Progressives argued that tariffs pushed up the prices of goods purchased by

---

RESOURCE OPTIONS

Teaching Resources

Decision-Making Activity Marching for Child Labor Laws, Decision-Making Activities folder, pp. 16–17

Answer to . . .

Interpreting Tables Creation of an income tax, direct election of senators, prohibition of alcohol.

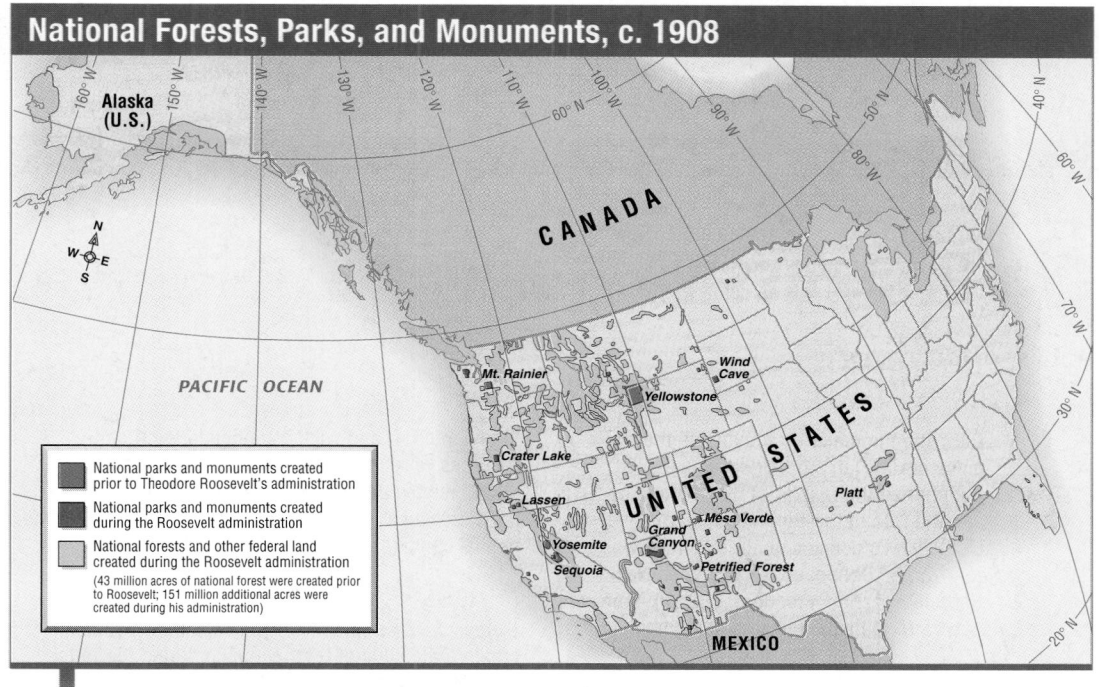

National Forests, Parks, and Monuments, c. 1908

Legend:
- National parks and monuments created prior to Theodore Roosevelt's administration
- National parks and monuments created during the Roosevelt administration
- National forests and other federal land created during the Roosevelt administration
  (43 million acres of national forest were created prior to Roosevelt; 151 million additional acres were created during his administration)

MAP Skills TR was convinced that "vigorous action must be taken" to save the nation's natural environment. *Location* *What do you notice about the location of the nation's parks, monuments, and forests?*

the working poor. In contrast, the Sixteenth Amendment allowed the government to derive more of its income from the wealthy.

The Eighteenth Amendment was also pushed forward by progressive reformers and was ratified in 1919. The amendment made it illegal for Americans to make, sell, or import liquor. Although not all Progressives favored prohibition, many thought it would protect society from the poverty and violence associated with drinking. As you will read, this amendment proved to be controversial.

SECTION 2 REVIEW

Comprehension

1. **Key Terms** Define: (a) direct primary; (b) initiative; (c) referendum; (d) recall; (e) holding company.

2. **Summarizing the Main Idea** Briefly describe the progressive reforms that were made at the city, state, and federal levels.

3. **Organizing Information** Create a diagram showing the changes that gave voters a more direct role in democracy.

Critical Thinking

4. **Analyzing Time Lines** Which events on the time line are related to labor reforms?

5. **Testing Conclusions** Provide evidence to support the conclusion that progressivism was not a single, unified movement.

Writing Activity

6. **Writing a Persuasive Essay** Write a letter to city officials in New York asking for specific workplace reforms.

Answers to
SECTION 2 REVIEW

1. (a) direct primary, see p. 548; (b) initiative, see p. 548; (c) referendum, see p. 548; (d) recall, see p. 548; (e) holding company, see p. 549.

2. City: control of utilities; provision for welfare. State: voter and workplace legislation. Federal: regulation of food and drug industries, railroads; antitrust legislation; child and environment protection; constitutional amendments.

3. Diagrams should include direct primaries; Seventeenth Amendment; intitiative, referendum, and recall.

4. 1902—United Mine Workers strike; 1908—*Muller* v. *Oregon*; 1911—Triangle Shirtwaist fire; 1913—Department of Labor formed.

5. Sample answer: Reforms were made at all levels of government—local, state, and federal. Areas covered included labor, public welfare, politics, and countless other unrelated ideas.

6. Letters will vary but should be supported with facts from the section.

RESOURCE OPTIONS

Teaching Resources

Quiz Units 5–6 folder, p. 75

Student Performance Pack

Guide to the Essentials Chapter 19, Section 2 (English and Spanish)

Answer to . . .

Map Skills *Most of them are in the western half of the nation, a part of the country that has historically been sparsely populated.*

Progressive Presidents

1908	1910	1912	1913	1914	1916
Taft elected President	Ballinger-Pinchot Affair	Wilson elected President	Federal Reserve system established	Clayton Antitrust Act	Wilson reelected President

1905   **1910**   **1915**   **1920**

Objectives

You may wish to call students' attention to the objectives in the Section Preview. The objectives are reflected in the main headings of the section.

Bellringer

Have students consider an election for class president with four students running for office. Who would win if all the girls agreed to vote for one nominee and the boys voted for several? Explain how the election of 1912 was determined in a similar fashion.

Reading Strategy

Organizing Information Refer to the Reading Strategy in the Section Preview. You may wish to draw a timeline from 1904–1916 on the chalkboard and have volunteers label the dates of reforms.

LESSON PLAN

Connecting to the Main Idea

1. Focus In 1912, many groups associated with the progressive movement established a political party. Ask students why. Although the Progressive candidate did not win the election, the new President, Woodrow Wilson, continued to institute progressive reforms.

2. Instruct Explain that while Roosevelt said, "I believe in a strong executive. I believe in power," Taft felt that the President should use restraint. Discuss Taft's unwillingness or inability to influence Congress. In what ways did Taft disappoint Roosevelt and his followers? How did Wilson increase the powers of the federal government?

3. Close Presidents Taft and Wilson continued the flow of reforms even as some progressives formed their own party. The next section discusses a turning point in American life: women's suffrage.

3 Progressive Presidents

SECTION PREVIEW

Objectives

1. Describe the major controversies that took place during Taft's presidency.
2. Summarize the results of the election of 1912 and the role of the Bull Moose party.
3. List Wilson's policies as President.
4. *Key Terms* Define: conservationist; New Nationalism; New Freedom; Clayton Antitrust Act; Federal Reserve system.

Main Idea

Presidents Taft and Wilson continued to promote progressive reforms. Some Progressives were dissatisfied with Taft's policies and formed their own party. Roosevelt ran as the Progressive party's presidential candidate in 1912.

Reading Strategy

Organizing Information As you read this section, create a time line of reforms made during the Taft and Wilson presidencies.

William H. Taft

Progressivism had always been a series of informal alliances among like-minded reform groups. In 1912, however, a number of progressive reformers created their own political party. Though this party did not win the presidential election that year, its ideas continued to hold the attention of American voters and politicians.

Taft's Presidency

The day after his election in 1904, Theodore Roosevelt announced he would not seek another presidential term. As the campaign of 1908 neared, Roosevelt handpicked his Secretary of War, William Howard Taft, to be the next Republican presidential nominee. On the Democratic side, William Jennings Bryan tried for a third and last time to win the office. Taft won easily.

President Taft had pledged to carry on TR's progressive program. He fulfilled that promise. Taft pursued some 90 antitrust cases and supported numerous other reforms. As President, however, Taft had neither Roosevelt's energy nor strength of personality. He gave in to the Republican "old guard," which resisted many progressive programs. One such issue in which Taft compromised on his support for progressivism was tariff reduction. Progressives favored lowering tariffs because higher tariffs hurt consumers and favored business. Taft's failure to reduce tariffs angered Progressives in his own party. As a result, a faction of Progressives who disliked Taft's policies developed within the Republican party.

The Ballinger-Pinchot Affair A party crisis in 1910 only worsened matters for Taft. Taft compromised on yet another important progressive cause when he ignored the protests of **conservationists.** (Conservationists are people concerned with the care and protection of natural resources.) Taft's Secretary of the Interior, Richard A. Ballinger, allowed a private group of business people to obtain several million acres of Alaskan public lands. The lands con-

RESOURCE OPTIONS

Teaching Resources

 Reproducible Lesson Plan Lesson Plans folder, p. 111

 Big Idea Graphic Organizer Big Idea Graphic Organizer folder, p. 83

 Guided Reading and Review Units 5–6 folder, p. 76

Media and Technology

 AmericanHeritage® CD-ROM
Time Tour A New Role in the World: Progressives and Reformers

tained rich coal deposits. Roosevelt's appointee to head the Forest Service, Gifford Pinchot, felt that Ballinger had shown special preference to the purchasing group. When Pinchot protested to a congressional committee, Taft fired him.

Upset over Taft's handling of the affair, the progressive faction within the Republican party rebelled against him. They joined with Democrats in a vote to investigate Ballinger. Although never found guilty of wrongdoing, Ballinger eventually resigned.

The progressive faction also took action against the Republican old guard. Because the old guard controlled the House Rules Committee, they had been able to block much reform legislation.[†] In 1910, the progressive faction amended the House rules so that the powerful old guard member and House Speaker, Joseph G. Cannon, would no longer appoint the committee. Instead the committee would be elected by the House. In addition, the Speaker of the House was barred from serving on the committee.

The Midterm Elections of 1910 Following Taft's election in 1908, Roosevelt had set off on a long hunting trip to East Africa. On his trip home from Africa, Roosevelt was hailed as a hero throughout Europe. He returned to the United States to a wildly cheering crowd in New York and a storm of protest against Taft. At first Roosevelt remained silent. Soon, however, he could not resist entering the political battle between Taft and the Progressives. Roosevelt began speaking in support of progressive candidates in the 1910 midterm elections. He called for more federal regulation of business, welfare legislation, and progressive reforms. He favored stronger workplace protections for women and children, income and inheritance taxes, direct primaries, and the initiative, referendum, and recall. TR called this program the **New Nationalism.**

Republicans lost seats in the election while Democrats captured a majority in the House of Representatives. Progressive Democrats and

---
[†] The House Rules Committee decides whether or not, and under what conditions, a bill will be taken up by the House.

In spite of his respectable record on progressive issues, Taft's presidency became entangled in controversy and conflict with Congress. *Government* *What does this cartoon suggest about TR's reaction to Taft's difficulties?*

Republicans dominated the Senate. By early 1912 Roosevelt announced that he would oppose Taft for the Republican presidential nomination.

Taft's Record Taft did not have a bad record on progressive causes. He had reserved more public lands and brought more antitrust suits in four years than TR had in seven. He also had supported the Children's Bureau, the Sixteenth and Seventeenth amendments, and the Mann-Elkins Act of 1910. This act gave the Interstate Commerce Commission the power to regulate telephone and telegraph rates. In the end, however, Taft never gained the full support of the progressive Republicans.

The Election of 1912

Roosevelt and Taft both vied for the Republican presidential nomination at the party's Chicago convention in 1912. Taft, who controlled the central party machinery, won the nomination handily. Charging Taft's group with fraud, the Progressives marched out vowing to form their own party. In August they held their own convention and formed the Progressive party with Roosevelt as their

Main Idea
CONNECTIONS

Why did Progressives form their own party in 1912?

About the Presidents

Woodrow Wilson (1913–1921) met with Louis D. Brandeis in August 1912. It may have been the most important event of his campaign. Brandeis helped to convert Wilson to a progressive agenda. During his campaign, Wilson articulated the New Freedom, as preached to him by Brandeis. After Wilson's inauguration, progressivism took the form of far-reaching reforms. Lowering the tariff was one top priority. To emphasize its importance, the new President called a special session of Congress. The result was a tariff reform bill. As it turned out, however, a law attached to that bill had a more far-reaching effect: the first U.S. income tax. Source: Joseph L. Gardner, "Woodrow Wilson," *The American Heritage® Pictorial History of the Presidents of the United States,* vol. 2, 1968.

FACT Finder

Presidential Election of 1912

Candidate and Party	Popular Vote	Percent	Electoral Vote
Woodrow Wilson/Democrat	6,296,547	41.8	435
Theodore Roosevelt/Progressive	4,118,571	27.4	88
William H. Taft/Republican	3,486,720	23.2	8
Eugene V. Debs/Socialist	900,672	6.0	—
Eugene Chafin/Prohibition	206,275	1.4	—
Arthur E. Reimer/Socialist Labor	28,750	0.8	—

Interpreting Tables In the 1912 election, progressive ideas played a part in the platforms of the Democrats, Progressives, Republicans, and Socialists. *Government* What would have happened if TR had not run and Taft had received TR's votes?

on the Socialist ticket. Woodrow Wilson, governor of New Jersey, headed the Democratic ticket. Like Roosevelt, Wilson ran on a reform platform. Unlike Roosevelt, he criticized both big business and big government. As part of his **New Freedom** policy, he promised to enforce antitrust laws without threatening free economic competition.

Despite gaining only about 42 percent of the popular vote, Wilson won the election. This was in part because the Republican vote was split between Roosevelt and Taft. The Democrats also took control of both houses of Congress.

Wilson's Policies as President

As the governor of New Jersey, Wilson had acquired a reputation as a reformer. As he explained during the 1912 campaign, "We used to think . . . that all that government had to do was to put on a policeman's uniform, and say, 'Now don't anybody hurt anybody else.'" But life in the early 1900s had become so complex that Wilson believed government had to "step in and create new conditions."

Government did "step in" in 1914 when Congress passed the **Clayton Antitrust Act** to strengthen the Sherman Antitrust Act of 1890. The Clayton Act spelled out specific activities big businesses could not do. For example, the act stated that companies could not use contracts to prevent their buyers from purchasing goods from their competitors. The Clayton Act also stated that members of unions could not be "held or construed to be illegal combinations in restraint of trade under the antitrust laws." The act lent further support to unions by making strikes, peaceful picketing, and boycotts legal. As a result, courts were prevented from issuing injunctions unless union activities led to "irreparable injury to property."

With the Clayton Act passed, the government was now committed to regulating business. To help in this task, Wilson and the Congress created a Federal Trade Commission (FTC) in 1914. Its purpose was to set up fair trade laws and to enforce antitrust laws. The FTC could punish companies by issuing "cease and desist orders" if they followed unfair business practices.

candidate. California's progressive crusader, Hiram Johnson, was TR's running mate. When TR was asked about his physical readiness for a campaign, he said, "I feel fit as a bull moose!" The Bull Moose party became the nickname of the Progressive party.

ROOSEVELT AND JOHNSON

The new Progressive party took the Bull Moose as its symbol.

The Bull Moose Party The Bull Moose platform included tariff reduction, women's suffrage, more regulation of business, and an end to child labor. The platform also called for an eight-hour workday, a federal workers' compensation system, and the popular election of senators. Many women joined the party and campaigned for progressive candidates. In those states where women had already won the right to vote, women ran for state and local offices.

TR ran a vigorous campaign that became legendary. During one speech in Milwaukee, Roosevelt was shot by a would-be assassin. Despite bleeding from a chest wound, Roosevelt continued to speak for an hour and a half before seeking medical aid. "It takes more than this to kill a bull moose," he said as he showed the crowd his bloodstained shirt.

A Four-Way Election Four men sought the presidency in 1912. Taft was the Republican candidate. Roosevelt represented his Bull Moose Progressives. Labor leader Eugene V. Debs ran

RESOURCE OPTIONS

Media and Technology

RESOURCE PRO

Biography Louis D. Brandeis, found on Resource Pro, profiles the progressive Supreme Court justice.

American Heritage® CD-ROM

Presidents Woodrow Wilson

Color Transparencies American Photo, B-6

The Federal Reserve System Wilson also lowered many tariffs and instituted major financial reforms. In 1913 he helped establish the **Federal Reserve system,** which reorganized the federal banking system as follows:

1. The system created eight to twelve regional Federal Reserve Banks throughout the country. All national banks were required to become members of these banks. The Federal Reserve Banks were the central banks for their districts. Member banks stored some of their capital and their cash reserves at the Federal Reserve Bank in their district.

2. All of the Federal Reserve Banks were supervised by a Federal Reserve Board appointed by the President.

3. Each of the regional Federal Reserve Banks allowed member banks to borrow money to meet short-term demands. This helped to prevent bank failures that occurred when large numbers of depositors withdrew funds during an economic panic. Such bank failures could cause widespread job loss and misery.

4. The system also created a new national currency known as Federal Reserve notes. This allowed the Federal Reserve to expand or contract the amount of money in circulation according to business needs.

Another Wilson financial reform was the establishment of the Federal Farm Loan Board in 1916. This board and a system of Farm Loan Banks made loans available to farmers. Farmers could borrow money for five to forty years at rates lower than those offered by commercial banks.

Wilson was less active in social justice legislation. He allowed his Cabinet officers to extend the Jim Crow practice of separating the races in federal offices. This was a practice that had begun under Taft. Wilson also opposed a constitutional amendment on women's suffrage because his party platform had not endorsed it.

Brandeis to the Supreme Court Early in 1916 Wilson nominated progressive lawyer Louis D. Brandeis to the Supreme Court. Born in 1856 in Louisville, Kentucky, Brandeis was known for his brilliance and for fighting many public causes. His work earned him the name "the people's lawyer."

Brandeis supported Wilson in 1912 and advised him during the campaign. When Wilson nominated him to the Supreme Court, the action drew a storm of protest. Opponents, who included former President Taft, accused

This 1916 Wilson campaign truck publicizes Wilson's record during his first term as President. *Government Which of his policies contributed most to Wilson's reelection?*

Brandeis of being too radical. Anti-Semitism also played a part in opposition to Brandeis. He was the first Jewish Supreme Court nominee. Nevertheless, Brandeis won his seat on the Court and served with distinction until 1939. His appointment marked the peak of progressive reform at the federal level.

Wilson projected a winning attitude with this presidential campaign button.

Wilson Wins a Second Term Wilson ran for reelection in 1916. By then, progressivism had lost some of its appeal. TR did not want to run again. Instead, he endorsed Wilson's Republican opponent, Charles Evans Hughes, a former governor of New York and Supreme Court justice. The campaign was dominated by debate over the war then raging in Europe. Wilson won a narrow victory by promising to keep the country out of war.

The Limits of Progressivism

By the mid-1910s, Progressives could take pride in the many changes they had helped bring about. They had redefined the role of

Using the Internet

Prepare a Report

Objective Use the Internet to prepare a report on Booker T. Washington's views of African American rights. Have students follow these instructions:

1. See the *America: Pathways to the Present* Web site at

http://www.Pathways.phschool.com

for the URL of Washington's biography.

2. Read the biography, taking detailed notes.

3. Write a report on Washington's views of slavery, education, work, whites, and stereotypes. Include quotes and information about his life that support your report.

T E S T   P R E P A R A T I O N

Have students read the passages under "Brandeis to the Supreme Court" and then answer the question below.

Brandeis was most likely nicknamed "the people's lawyer" because—

A he was the first Jewish Supreme Court nominee.

B he was a brilliant lawyer.

Ⓒ he pushed for progressive reform.

D he was nominated by Wilson, who was popular with the people.

Answer to . . .

Viewing History His foreign policy of isolationism.

President Roosevelt met with Booker T. Washington at the White House in 1901. *Government What was Roosevelt's record on African American rights?*

government in business and politics. There were limits to what they had accomplished, however. For example, Progressives focused primarily on the problems of cities. They did little to address the plights of tenant and migrant farmers and of nonunionized workers in general. Some supported immigration restriction and literacy tests.

In addition, many Progressives supported the government's imperialistic policies abroad. Just as they believed in their ability to uplift the slums in American cities, they favored the "civilizing" of undeveloped nations.

African Americans and Progressivism What seems progressive to one class, race, or region might seem regressive, even repressive, to another. For example, many African Americans felt ignored by Progressives. Only a tiny group of Progressives, those who helped found the NAACP, concerned themselves with the worsening race relations of the era. Although Roosevelt invited Booker T. Washington to the White House in 1901, he did little else to support African American rights during his presidency. At the 1912 Progressive party convention, Roosevelt declined to seat African American delegates from the South for fear of alienating white southern supporters. In addition, some white southern Progressives who favored the women's vote did so for racist reasons. They realized that the white vote would double if suffrage passed. African Americans, on the other hand, would fall further behind because of their lower population and the effectiveness of voting restrictions in the South.

The End of Progressivism In August 1914, war broke out in Europe, and many nations began to assemble troops and supplies. Americans worried about how long they could remain uninvolved in the European conflict. Soon, calls to prepare for war drowned out calls for reform in the United States. By the end of 1916 the reform spirit had sputtered out, but the drive for women's suffrage remained.

SECTION 3 REVIEW

Comprehension

1. *Key Terms* Define: (a) conservationist; (b) New Nationalism; (c) New Freedom; (d) Clayton Antitrust Act; (e) Federal Reserve system.

2. *Summarizing the Main Idea* In what areas did President Taft back away from progressive reform? What happened when he did this?

3. *Organizing Information* Wilson and Roosevelt both favored progressive reforms. Use the table on page 554 to determine what percentage of American voters voted for the two progressive candidates in 1912.

Critical Thinking

4. *Analyzing Time Lines* Review the time line at the start of the section. How are the second and third events on the time line related?

5. *Identifying Central Issues* Based on the actions he took as President, summarize Wilson's view of the proper role of government.

Writing Activity

6. *Writing an Expository Essay* Write an essay describing some of the ways in which the goals of the Progressives were limited.

| 1890 | 1900 | | 1913 | 1920 |
National American Woman Suffrage Association (NAWSA) formed | Carrie Chapman Catt leads NAWSA | | Alice Paul and Lucy Burns lead a suffrage rally in Washington, D.C. | Nineteenth Amendment ratified

1890 **1900** **1910** **1920**

4 Suffrage at Last

SECTION PREVIEW

Objectives

1   List some of the efforts Susan B. Anthony and other women made in their quest to win suffrage at the turn of the century.
2   Summarize the different strategies that suffragists used to win the vote.
3   Analyze the factors that led to a final victory for the suffragists.
4   *Key Terms* Define: civil disobedience; National American Woman Suffrage Association (NAWSA); Congressional Union.

Main Idea

While demonstrating their skills as organizers and activists, women finally won the right to vote with the ratification of the Nineteenth Amendment in 1920.

Reading Strategy

Reinforcing Main Ideas As you read this section, list and briefly describe the methods women used to win the right to vote.

American women activists first formally demanded the right to vote in 1848 at a meeting in Seneca Falls, New York. Their struggle for suffrage and other rights continued throughout the second half of the century. One of the leaders in the fight was Susan B. Anthony.

Susan B. Anthony

 Like her father, a Quaker abolitionist, Susan B. Anthony was a crusader. Throughout her life she worked for radical change. In her thirties Anthony fought to give women a stronger voice in the temperance movement. She also joined the fight to abolish slavery. From 1856 to 1861 she served as an agent of the American Anti-Slavery Society. Following the Civil War, Anthony demanded that women be given the same rights as African Americans under the Fourteenth and Fifteenth amendments. Although this effort failed, Anthony continued her tireless campaign for women's rights as head of the National Woman Suffrage Association. In 1872 she led a group of women to the polls in Rochester, New York, where she insisted on voting. Anthony was arrested for this act of civil disobedience. (**Civil disobedience** is a nonviolent refusal to obey a law in an effort to change the law.) While Anthony awaited her trial, she set out on a highly publicized lecture tour. During one of these lectures she asserted:

AMERICAN VOICES ❝The preamble of the Federal Constitution says: 'We, the people of the United States. . . . ' It was we, the people; not we, the white male citizens; nor yet we, the male citizens; but we, the whole people, who formed the Union. And we formed it, not to give the blessings of liberty, but to secure them; not to the half of ourselves and the half of our posterity, but to the whole people—women as well as men.❞

—*Susan B. Anthony*

Susan B. Anthony (1820–1906)

Biography

Born into slavery, Ida Bell Wells-Barnett (1862–1931) founded what was probably the first African American women's suffrage group, Chicago's Alpha Suffrage Club. As a journalist she was a strident crusader against the lynching of African Americans in the South, and in 1909 she helped organize the National Association for the Advancement of Colored People (NAACP). Her memoirs, *Crusade for Justice,* were published posthumously in 1970.

COMPARING PRIMARY SOURCES

THE NINETEENTH AMENDMENT

In the early 1900s, the debate over women's suffrage heated up.

Pro-Women's Suffrage	Anti-Suffrage
"The great doctrine of the American Republic that 'all governments derive their just powers from the consent of the governed' justifies the plea of one-half of the people, the women, to exercise the suffrage. The doctrine of the American Revolutionary War that taxation without representation is unendurable justifies women in exercising the suffrage."	"In political warfare, it is perfectly fitting that actual strife and battle should be apportioned [given out] to man, and that the influence of woman, radiating from the homes of our land, should inspire to lofty aims and purposes those who struggle for the right. I am thoroughly convinced that woman can in no better way than this usefully serve the cause of political betterment."
—*Robert L. Owen,* senator from Oklahoma, 1910	—*Grover Cleveland,* Ladies' Home Journal, *October 1905*

ANALYZING VIEWPOINTS Summarize the arguments presented in the primary sources above.

Although Anthony was convicted at her trial, she refused to pay the $100 fine. In 1890 veteran leaders of the suffrage movement, including Anthony, Elizabeth Cady Stanton, and Lucy Stone, were joined by a younger generation of leaders in forming the **National American Woman Suffrage Association (NAWSA).** Anthony served as president of NAWSA from 1892 until 1900. ■

Suffrage at the Turn of the Century

By the time of NAWSA's founding, women had won many rights. For example, married women could now buy, sell, and will property. Yet legal efforts to win suffrage had failed. Perhaps more troubling to suffrage workers were the widely held attitudes about women and their proper social roles. When lawyer Myra Bradwell of Chicago was denied a state license to practice law in 1869, she took her case to the Supreme Court. In *Bradwell* v. *Illinois* (1873), the Court upheld the denial, reaffirming the "wide difference in the respective spheres and destinies of man and woman."

Although Illinois had given Bradwell her license by 1890, most Americans believed that woman's proper sphere remained the home, not the workplace.

By 1900, however, growing numbers of women were demanding the vote. Some were participating in voluntary organizations that were investigating social conditions. These women were publicizing their findings, suggesting reforms, lobbying officials, and monitoring enforcement of new laws. Working women were becoming more active in unions, picketing, and getting arrested. To many of these women, it seemed ridiculous to deny women the vote.

As the suffrage movement became more energetic, an antisuffrage movement mobilized. People opposed to women's suffrage made two basic arguments. The first was that women were powerful enough without the vote. The second was the old notion that giving women the vote would blur the distinctions between the sexes and make women more masculine. Suffrage opponents also included liquor interests, who assumed that women voters would quickly establish prohibition.

Suffragist Strategies

Suffragists followed two paths toward their goal. One path was to press for a constitutional amendment. The most commonly used method of amending the Constitution required two thirds of each house of Congress to pass a measure. The measure then had to be ratified by three fourths of the state legislatures.

The other path pursued by suffragists was to get individual states to permit women to vote. At first this approach was more successful, especially in the western states. There, survival on the frontier required the combined efforts of men and women and encouraged a greater sense of equality.

Pushing for a federal amendment proved the more difficult approach. The first amendment introduced in Congress in 1868 stalled. In 1878 suffragists introduced a new amendment that adopted the wording of suffrage leader Susan B. Anthony:

KEY DOCUMENTS "The right of citizens of the United States to vote shall not be denied or abridged by the United States or by any state on account of sex."

—*The Nineteenth Amendment*

RESOURCE OPTIONS

Answer to . . .

Comparing Primary Sources Owen: *Women should be allowed to vote because they are citizens and pay taxes.* Cleveland: *Women serve best, in politics as in war, by supporting the men who participate.*

With this language, the proposed amendment received its first committee hearing. Elizabeth Cady Stanton described the chair of the committee, Senator Wadleigh of New Hampshire, as a picture of "inattention and contempt." "He stretched, yawned, gazed at the ceiling, cut his nails, sharpened his pencil, changing his occupation and position every two minutes."

Stalled again, the bill was not debated until 1887. It was then defeated in the Senate by a vote of 16 for, 34 against, and 26 absent. Supporters reintroduced the "Anthony Amendment," as the bill came to be called, every year until 1896. Then it disappeared, and did not resurface again until 1913.

The Movement Strengthens in the 1910s
At the turn of the century, the idea of votes for women had become more acceptable. The suffrage movement, however, was at a low point. New leadership and new techniques were desperately needed to give it momentum.

One of these new leaders was Carrie Chapman Catt. Catt was a former high school principal and superintendent of schools in Mason City, Iowa. A talented speaker and organizer, she headed NAWSA from 1900 to 1904, and then again after 1915. As head of NAWSA, Catt insisted on close, precinct-by-precinct political work.

Alice Paul also emerged as a leader in the women's suffrage movement. She had experienced the aggressive English suffrage movement while she was a student in England. In January 1913, she and a friend, Lucy Burns, took over the NAWSA committee that was working on congressional passage of the federal suffrage amendment.

Two months later, the two women had organized a parade of 5,000 women in Washington, D.C. The parade took place on the day before Woodrow Wilson's inauguration. It drew so much attention that no crowd greeted Wilson when he arrived at the train station. After this success, Paul transformed her committee into a new organization, the **Congressional Union (CU).**

A Split in the Movement Following Paul's action, a split occurred within the suffrage movement. Paul's CU called for an aggressive, militant campaign for the constitutional amendment. She planned to enter different states, bypass the suffrage organizations there, and set up new ones.

The leadership of NAWSA did not agree with Paul's plan. In February 1914 they expelled her group from the organization. The CU went on to stage militant protests. They demonstrated in front of the White House, burned copies of President Wilson's speeches and even a life-size dummy made to look like Wilson. CU members were sent to prison for their demonstrations, where they went on hunger strikes to protest prison conditions. NAWSA condemned the CU, not their treatment.

Meanwhile, NAWSA's state suffrage campaigns continued. Hopes had centered on winning the vote in four eastern states, New York, Pennsylvania, Massachusetts, and New Jersey. In 1915 the suffrage campaigns failed in all four states. At that point, Catt was reinstated as NAWSA president and was given free rein to bring about victory. Out of this challenge came her "Winning Plan."

Main Idea CONNECTIONS

How did NAWSA and the CU differ in their strategies for winning women's suffrage?

Colorful parades became a favorite technique of suffragists in the 1910s. Suffragists in this 1912 parade in New York City offered a suffrage "plank" for political party platforms. *Culture What caused the split in the suffrage movement?*

Graphing the Main Idea

To make sure students understand the main idea of this section, you may wish to use the flow map graphic organizer below.

Tell students that a flow map shows a sequence of events unfolding. Ask students to use the flow map to record the events that led up to the ratification of the Nineteenth Amendment.

Teaching Tip A template for this graphic organizer can be found in the Color Transparencies, G-4.

Answer to . . .

Map Skills *Suffrage was passed throughout the West; it was not supported in the South or Northeast.*

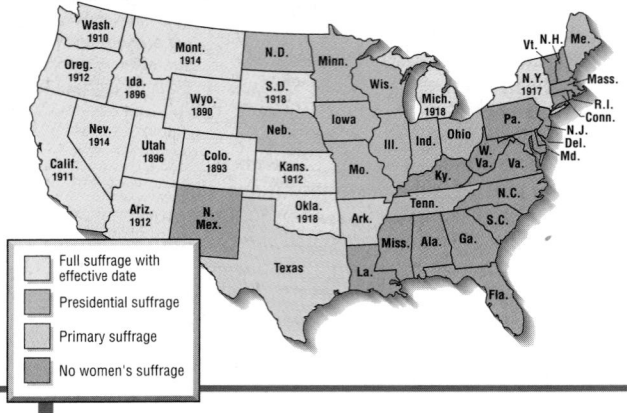

Women's Suffrage Before 19th Amendment

Legend:
- Full suffrage with effective date
- Presidential suffrage
- Primary suffrage
- No women's suffrage

MAP Skills Women's suffrage was already in place in many states by the time the Nineteenth Amendment was ratified. *Location* *What pattern do you notice in the locations of states that did and did not pass suffrage at the state level?*

This plan consisted of developing a large group of full-time leaders to work in "red-hot" campaigns for six years. In addition, NAWSA decided to focus on getting Congress to propose the federal amendment.

By 1917, NAWSA had 2 million members. It was the largest voluntary organization in the country. In the fall, New York State finally voted for women's suffrage.

Impact of World War I The United States entered World War I in April 1917. Women hastened to do their patriotic duty by volunteering for ambulance corps and medical work and by taking on jobs left by men. Arguments of separate spheres for women and men were forgotten during wartime. In addition, Congress adopted the Eighteenth Amendment prohibiting the sale of liquor. As a result of this action, liquor interests no longer had reason to fight suffrage.

The Final Victory for Suffrage

In 1918 Congress formally proposed the suffrage amendment. Its members finally succumbed to the political forces of states that had passed suffrage and to the unrelenting work of NAWSA. They also had been keenly embarrassed and disturbed by the treatment the women of Paul's CU had received in jail. After the amendment was proposed in Congress the ratification battle began. It would end on August 24, 1920, when Tennessee became the necessary thirty-sixth state to ratify the suffrage amendment.

As Carrie Chapman Catt commented when the exhausting fight was all over, "It is doubtful that any man . . . ever realized what the suffrage struggle came to mean to women. . . . It leaves its mark on one, such a struggle." The Nineteenth Amendment marked the last major reform of the Progressive Era.

SECTION 4 REVIEW

Comprehension

1. *Key Terms* Define: (a) civil disobedience; (b) National American Woman Suffrage Association (NAWSA); (c) Congressional Union.

2. *Summarizing the Main Idea* What were the two main strategies of the suffrage movement during the late 1800s and early 1900s?

3. *Organizing Information* Make a list of the events that finally led to victory in the fight for women's suffrage.

Critical Thinking

4. *Analyzing Time Lines* Review the time line at the start of the section. How many years passed between the formation of NAWSA and the ratification of the Nineteenth Amendment?

5. *Recognizing Ideologies* Recall what you have read about the reasons for the passage of suffrage in the West and at the national level. In the end, what seemed to "prove" women's fitness to vote?

Writing Activity

6. *Writing an Expository Essay* Write an essay describing the major accomplishments of Susan B. Anthony.

To understand that . . .

You Can Make a Difference

The spirit of progressive reform remains alive today in the volunteer community service activities performed by Americans of all ages.

Nurse visiting an immigrant household around 1915

A youth group in Cape Cod, Massachusetts, adopts a stretch of highway and keeps it litter-free. High school cheerleaders in Houston, Texas, organize an aluminum can drive to fund a Mother's Day luncheon in a local nursing home. A support group made up of teens in San Francisco serves dinner at a local soup kitchen.

In urban and rural communities throughout the United States, millions of Americans participate regularly in some form of volunteer service. They are taking steps to tackle such important and difficult problems as hunger, illiteracy, pollution, and poverty.

The Impact Today

Reformers of the Progressive Era targeted issues such as child labor, women's suffrage, workplace hazards, poverty, and political corruption. Great progress has been made on some of these issues. Others, such as corruption and poverty, remain a concern. In addition, problems such as cleanup of hazardous waste have emerged as major issues since the Progressive Era. Today individual volunteers, along with various private, public, and

non-profit organizations, have mobilized to address both old and new issues.

Young Americans play a vital role as volunteers. Millions of youths participate in the volunteer programs of Youth Service America (YSA). Founded in 1986, this alliance of organizations works to build healthy communities and foster citizenship through volunteerism. YSA includes more than 100 organizations, representing more that 15 million young Americans.

Each year YSA observes National Youth Service Day, when young people kick off a year-long commitment to volunteer service and meet new friends engaged in a common cause. The day includes activities such as planting gardens, picking up roadside litter, and delivering meals to senior citizens.

The Impact on You

Choose one problem in your community that troubles you—for example, homelessness, air or water pollution, substance abuse, or toxic waste disposal. Discuss the problem with family, friends, and neighbors to get ideas for dealing with it. Write a one-page proposal for a volunteer service project that you would like to create to address the problem you chose.

Teenage volunteer tutoring a young student

RESOURCE OPTIONS

Teaching Resources

Why Study History? Activity You Can Make a Difference, found in the Why Study History? folder, p. 20, provides an activity to help students better understand volunteerism in America.

Media and Technology

AmericanHeritage® CD-ROM

Time Tour A New Role in the World: Progressives and Reformers; *and* The Nation Today and Tomorrow: A Time for Turmoil

Class Discussion

Discuss voluntary community service with the class. For a more thorough examination of the issue, see the activity folder in the Resource Options below.

ACTIVITY
STUDENT PARTICIPATION

Designing Creative Solutions
Ask students to read the text. Then have the class brainstorm a list of school issues that volunteers might address, such as:

- **litter on school grounds or in hallways**
- **graffiti in the bathrooms**
- **missing books in the library**

Assign partners or small groups to discuss one of these issues. Ask them to list some creative solutions for each one. Have these groups present their ideas to the class.

Follow up Turn the best ideas into school volunteer projects.

Using the Internet
Students can learn more about volunteerism by exploring links in the *America: Pathways to the Present* Web site at:

http://www.Pathways.phschool.com

Assessment
See the Lesson Plans folder, pp. 24–27, for rubrics on assessing Class Participation Projects.

561

Key Terms

Students should refer to the definitions of key terms in the chapter to create sentences that show an understanding of the dynamics and goals of the Progressive Movement.

Comprehension

1. Progressives valued the high standard of living and personal liberty of the free enterprise system. However, they wanted to change the unfair aspects of the system.

2. Progressives typically studied a social problem using scientific methods. Then they publicized their results to put pressure on lawmakers. Muckraking journalists helped publicize many progressive causes.

3. State reformers aimed at making government more responsive and efficient, for example, through direct primaries. They also championed labor and factory legislation. Urban reformers attacked political machines, took over utilities, and expanded welfare services.

4. Roosevelt went after certain "bad" trusts and sought to conserve the nation's natural resources. The federal government also established the Women's Bureau and the Children's Bureau.

5. Taft achieved many progressive goals, such as increased prosecution of antitrust cases. Yet he lost progressive support because of events such as the Ballinger-Pinchot affair and his failure to lower the tariff.

6. Preparations for war began to occupy the nation.

7. Early campaigns met with the greatest success on the state level, mostly in the West, since survival there depended on the efforts of both men and women.

8. The CU's strategy, calling for an all-out campaign for a constitutional amendment, was more militant than that of NAWSA, which planned long-term (six-year) campaigns focused on getting Congress to propose the amendment.

Chapter Summary

The major concepts of Chapter 19 are presented below. See also *Guide to the Essentials of American History* or *Interactive Student Tutorial CD-ROM*, which contains interactive review activities, time lines, helpful hints, and test practice for Chapter 19.

Reviewing the Main Ideas

Progressive reformers at the turn of the century worked to meet the challenges of an urban, industrialized society. In spite of opposition, Progressives were able to redefine government's role in American life, and to enact such lasting reforms as women's suffrage.

Section 1: The Origins of Progressivism

At the end of the 1800s, many citizens recognized the need to solve problems resulting from rapid industrialization and urban growth. The appearance of many reform movements caused historians to later refer to the period as the Progressive Era.

Section 2: Progressive Legislation

Because of public demand, local, state, and federal legislatures enacted a number of progressive reforms in the early 1900s.

Section 3: Progressive Presidents

Presidents Taft and Wilson continued to promote progressive reforms. Some Progressives were dissatisfied with Taft's policies and formed their own party. Roosevelt ran as the Progressive party's presidential candidate in 1912.

Section 4: Suffrage at Last

While demonstrating their skills as organizers and activists, women finally won the right to vote with the ratification of the Nineteenth Amendment in 1920.

The spirit of progressive reform remains alive today in the volunteer community service activities performed by Americans of all ages. Millions of Americans participate regularly in some form of volunteer service.

Key Terms

Use each of the terms below in a sentence that shows how it relates to the chapter.

1. Federal Reserve system
2. injunction
3. home rule
4. social welfare program
5. direct primary
6. initiative
7. referendum
8. recall
9. Clayton Antitrust Act
10. holding company
11. conservationist
12. New Nationalism
13. New Freedom

Comprehension

1. What did Progressives see as good about the United States? What did they want to reform?
2. What were the typical methods of progressive reformers?
3. Summarize progressive reforms at the municipal and state levels.
4. Briefly describe progressive reforms at the national level.
5. What were the successes and failures of the Taft presidency?
6. Why did progressivism come to an end?
7. Where did campaigns to achieve suffrage first meet with success?
8. How did the Congressional Union and the National American Woman Suffrage Association differ in their strategies?

Using Graphic Organizers

On a separate sheet of paper, copy the tree map below to organize information about progressive legislation at the city, state, and national levels. In the lower boxes, fill in examples of city, state, and federal reforms.

Progressive Era Reforms		
City	State	Federal

Using Graphic Organizers

- City: improved city services; took over utilities; provided welfare services; allied with political bosses in some cases.
- State: became more efficient and responsive to voters; championed labor and factory legislation; instituted direct primaries; abolished child labor in some states; instituted minimum wage laws for women and children.

- Federal: Roosevelt negotiated Square Deal for miners; antitrust actions filed; land water policy intitiated; Children's Bureau and Women's Bureau established; Prohibition passed.

Analyzing Political Cartoons ▶

1. Examine the images in the cartoon. (a) What is the woman holding? (b) What does it represent? (c) In what manner is she holding it?
2. Notice the woman's clothing. What point is the cartoonist trying to make with her clothing?
3. What is the "delusion" referred to in the cartoon?

Critical Thinking

1. *Applying the Chapter Skill* Based on the election results in 1912, is it reasonable to conclude that most Americans favored some amount of progressive reform? Explain.
2. *Identifying Central Issues* What was the Clayton Antitrust Act and why was it important to progressive reformers?
3. *Expressing Problems Clearly* What was the purpose of the Federal Reserve system?
4. *Demonstrating Reasoned Judgment* Progressives were sometimes criticized for being insensitive to the needs of the poor. Do you think that this criticism was justified?
5. *Identifying Central Issues* What does the fate of Taft's presidency suggest about the nature of the presidency and presidential leadership?

HUGGING A DELUSION

COPYRIGHTED BY LIFE PUBLISHING CO.

INTERNET ACTIVITY

For your portfolio:
WRITE AN ESSAY

Access Prentice Hall's *America: Pathways to the Present* site at **www.Pathways.phschool.com** for the specific URLs to complete the activity. Additional resources and related Web sites are also available.

Use the links provided to read biographies of famous suffragists and a time line of the women's rights movement. Write an essay describing the suffrage movement. Who were suffragists? How would you characterize the suffrage movement? How did it differ from other struggles for liberty?

ANALYZING DOCUMENTS ◀▶ INTERPRETING DATA

Turn to the map of women's suffrage on page 560.

1. Which of the following states had given women full suffrage prior to the passage of the Nineteenth Amendment? (a) Iowa (b) North Dakota (c) Colorado (d) Kentucky.
2. Which of the following statements best summarizes the information on the map? (a) States throughout the nation refused to grant women suffrage. (b) Many states in the West had granted women full suffrage prior to passage of the Nineteenth Amendment. (c) Many states in the Southeast had granted women full suffrage prior to passage of the Nineteenth Amendment. (d) States in the Midwest generally supported full suffrage for women.
3. *Writing* What factors contributed to the granting of full suffrage to women in the western states?

Connecting to Today

Florence Kelley led a campaign to investigate labor conditions in the United States. Consumers pressured owners to comply with laws. Today, similar work is being done on an international level. Conduct research and write a brief essay on one or more of the groups monitoring international labor issues.

INTERNET ACTIVITY

Students should identify the suffrage movement as a nonviolent social and political movement, unlike the American Revolution, Shays' Rebellion, John Brown's Raid, or the Civil War.

Analyzing Political Cartoons

1. (a) The ballot. (b) Woman's suffrage. (c) As though it were an infant.
2. That women will turn into men if they have the vote.
3. That women will be as fulfilled by participating in democracy as they are by motherhood.

Critical Thinking

1. Yes. Roosevelt and Wilson, who both supported progressivism, between them gained almost 70 percent of the popular vote.
2. The Clayton Antitrust Act strenghtened the Sherman Antitrust Act by specifying actions businesses could not do and by supporting unions. It showed that government was committed to regulating business and protecting workers.
3. To reorganize and improve the federal banking system.
4. Answers should acknowledge that Progressives focused mainly on cities and did little to address the plight of farm and other nonunionized workers.
5. A President needs the full support of the dominant wing of his party.

Interpreting Data

1. c
2. b
3. In the West, the nature of frontier survival had encouraged greater equality between men and women.

Connecting to Today

Essays will vary but should be based on facts from the chapter.

CHAPTER 20

The World War I Era, 1914–1920

Managing Time and Instruction

INSTRUCTION SUPPORT
These materials for instruction are provided for **each section** in the **Teaching Resources.** See **Units 5–6 folder for Enrichment Support:**

- Reproducible Lesson Plans in Lesson Plans folder • Learning Styles Lesson Plans in Learning Styles Lesson Plans folder • Big Idea Graphic Organizers in Big Idea Graphic Organizer folder
- Guided Reading and Review • Quizzes • Test Preparation Practice booklet

DAILY LESSON	ENRICHMENT SUPPORT
1 **The Road to War** (pp. 565–568)	• Primary Source Activity, Thoughts on the War, Learning with Documents folder, p. 26 • Skills for Life Activity, Units 5–6 folder, p. 100
2 **The United States Declares War** (pp. 570–572)	• Critical Thinking Activity, Identifying Central Issues: Provocations of War, found on **Resource Pro** • Visual Learning Activity, Uncle Sam's Pledge, found on **Resource Pro**
3 **Americans on the European Front** (pp. 573–577)	• Primary Source Activity, Women on the War Front, found on **Resource Pro** • Literature Activity, A War Song, Units 5–6 folder, p. 99 • Biography, Henry Johnson, found on **Resource Pro** • Literature Activity, A Poet Describes War, found on **Resource Pro**
4 **On the Home Front** (pp. 578–581)	• Literature Activity, Selling the War, found on **Resource Pro** • Nystrom *Atlas of Our Country,* The Third Wave of Immigration, pp. 30–31 • Visual Learning Activity, Women's Roles in World War I, Learning with Documents folder, p. 62
5 **Global Peacemaker** (pp. 584–588)	• Key Documents, Woodrow Wilson, The Fourteen Points, Learning with Documents folder, p. 95 • Comparing Primary Sources, On the League of Nations, Units 5–6 folder, pp. 97–98 • Primary Source Activity, Mrs. Wilson's Role, found on **Resource Pro** • Modern Warfare Poses Grave Dangers, Why Study History? folder, p. 21

Running Out of Time?

- Use Tape 3, "The United States on the Brink of Change, 1890–1920," from **Visions of America** videotapes series.
- Use Chapter 20 Summary from **Guide to the Essentials of American History (English and Spanish).**

Companion Web Site

The companion Web site offers online links for all chapter review activities. It also provides key content links and structured support for this chapter for both teachers and students.

http://www.Pathways.phschool.com

Media and Technology

For the Student

Interactive Student Tutorial CD-ROM Chapter 20
Student Edition on Audiotape Chapter 20
American Heritage® CD-ROM
Guided Reading Audiotapes (English and Spanish) Chapter 20

For the Teacher

Resource Pro CD-ROM Chapter 20
Test Bank CD-ROM Chapter 20
Listening to Literature Audiotapes *Timeless Voices, Timeless Themes* "In Another Country" by Ernest Hemingway
Color Transparencies E-6, D–16, D–17

Assessment Options

Chapter Test Forms A&B Test Bank CD-ROM booklet
Test Bank CD-ROM Chapter 20
Standardized Test Preparation Handbook

Block Scheduling

Pacing Suggestions

For 90-minute Blocks

- Teach sections 2, 3, and 4 using Transparencies F-8, H-17, I-15, and J-6 and the Recent Scholarship note on p. 580 for class discussions.
- Teach sections 1 and 5 using the Big Idea Graphic Organizers from Teaching Resources and the Extended Class Periods Activity on p. 567.

Additional Resources

- Prentice Hall's **American History Block Scheduling Support File** covers over 40 major topics in American history.
- **Prentice Hall United States History Video Collection**™ contains 20 videotapes covering American history from beginnings to present.
- **Decision America Videotapes and Videodiscs**

Connections to American Literature

from Prentice Hall

America: Pathways to the Present "Over There" and "K-K-K-Katy," pp. 1082–1083
Prentice Hall Literature *Timeless Voices, Timeless Themes* "The Love Song of J. Alfred Prufrock" by T. S. Eliot

Additional Resources

For the Student

Erich Maria Remarque. *All Quiet on the Western Front.* Fawcett, 1987.
Laurence Stallings. *The Doughboys.* Harper & Row, 1963.

For the Teacher

Barbara Tuchman. *The Guns of August.* Macmillan, 1962.

Prentice Hall brings into the classroom the vast archives and scholarship of the nation's premier American history magazine. See "From the Archives of American Heritage®" teaching notes in this chapter.

History Alive!

Teacher's Curriculum Institute, in partnership with Prentice Hall, provides unique materials that engage students with diverse learning styles. See History Alive!® unit on The United States Coming of Age: 1890–1920.

Student Performance Pack

Ensures success in the three critical areas of Reading, Test Taking, and English Language Development with the following materials:
- Guide to the Essentials of American History in English and Spanish
- Guided Reading Audiotapes in English and Spanish
- Interactive Student Tutorial CD-ROM
- Test Preparation Handbook
- Test Preparation Practice booklet

Introducing the Chapter

In the second decade of the twentieth century, a terrible war began in Europe, with the death toll eventually totaling an estimated 8 million combatants—and many times more civilians. At first the United States vowed to maintain its neutrality. However, the nation finally declared war in order to support its allies and defend its commercial interests.

Themes in American History

The theme for this chapter, Science and Technology, is listed at the beginning of this unit. An alternate theme for the chapter is Foreign Relations. To teach this unit thematically, you may wish to use the Prosperity, Depression, and War folder in American History Block Scheduling Support.

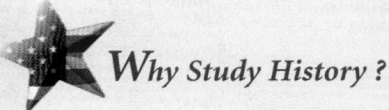

Why Study History ?

Have students explore suggested ways of connecting the past to the present on page 589.

Answer to . . .

Viewing History Students should use this question as an aid in reading the chapter. Americans were divided in their sympathies, with a substantial minority, especially German Americans and Irish Americans, supporting the Central Powers early in the war. Also, there was a strong peace movement in the country, with deep roots in the progressive and populist traditions.

CHAPTER FOCUS

This chapter discusses the World War I era, during which much of Europe became embroiled in conflict. Despite American reluctance, powerful forces pulled the nation into battle. With the end of the war, President Wilson sought a peace treaty and a new international organization to prevent world-wide conflict from ever happening again.

 The *Why Study History?* page at the end of this chapter explores the connection between the advances in weaponry during World War I and the continued horrors of modern warfare.

▲
VIEWING HISTORY
United States infantrymen charge out of their trench and into battle in this 1918 photograph.
Foreign Relations **Why had the United States been reluctant to join the World War?**

▶ RESOURCE OPTIONS

Teaching Resources

 Big Idea Graphic Organizer folder Graphic summary of the main idea of the chapter.

Learning Styles Lesson Plans folder Alternate lesson plans for diverse learning styles for each chapter.

Media and Technology

 AmericanHeritage® **CD-ROM**
Time Tour A New Role in the World: World War I

 Prentice Hall United States History Video Collection™ Volume 16 *The Great War*

June 28, 1914	July 28, 1914	August 1, 1914	August 4, 1914
Assassination of Archduke Francis Ferdinand	Austria-Hungary declares war on Serbia	Germany declares war on Russia	Britain declares war on Germany

1914   **1915**

1 The Road to War

SECTION PREVIEW

Objectives

1 Identify the main causes of World War I.
2 Describe how the conflict expanded to draw in much of Europe.
3 Describe the American response to the war in Europe.
4 *Key Terms* Define: militarism; mobilization; Central Powers; Allies; stalemate; autocrat.

Main Idea

As World War I began and then expanded to much of Europe, the United States remained neutral.

Reading Strategy

Formulating Questions Rewrite the Main Idea above as a question. As you read the section, write down answers to your question.

On June 28, 1914, Archduke Francis Ferdinand and his wife Sophie made a state visit to Sarajevo, the capital of Bosnia. Bosnia was a new province within the Austro-Hungarian Empire, and Francis Ferdinand was heir to the empire's throne.

That morning a bomb thrown by a terrorist bounced off the archduke's car and exploded, injuring two officers in another car. Unfazed, Francis Ferdinand attended a state ceremony and then rode to the hospital to see the wounded officers. Gavrilo Princip, a second terrorist, just 19 years old, happened to spot the car as it slowly moved down a narrow street. He pulled out his pistol and shot the archduke and his wife to death.

Princip, a Bosnian nationalist, believed that Austria-Hungary had no right to rule Bosnia. Little did he know that his act of terrorism would have such grave consequences.

Causes of World War I

The assassination of Archduke Francis Ferdinand ignited what was called the Great War, later known as World War I. But the main causes of the war existed well before 1914. Those causes included imperialism, militarism, nationalism, and alliances.

(1) *Imperialism*. A great scramble for colonies took place in the late 1800s. European powers rushed to beat each other to the remaining uncolonized areas of the world, particularly in Africa and China. This surge of imperialism sharpened rivalries within Europe. Japan joined the roster of colonial powers when it won the Sino-Japanese War in 1895 and acquired Korea, Taiwan, and territory on China's mainland.

(2) *Militarism*. By the early 1900s in Europe, diplomacy had taken a back seat to **militarism.** This policy involved aggressively building up a nation's armed forces in preparation for war. Under this policy the military gained more authority. The great powers of Europe—Austria-Hungary, France, Germany, Great Britain, and Russia—all engaged in militarism. Their endless planning for war made war much more likely.

Soldiers in World War I wore gas masks to protect against poison gas, a horrible new weapon introduced in the war.

RESOURCE OPTIONS

Teaching Resources

📁 **Reproducible Lesson Plan** Lesson Plans folder, p. 113

📁 **Learning Styles Lesson Plan** Learning Styles Lesson Plans folder, p. 42

📁 **Big Idea Graphic Organizer** Big Idea Graphic Organizer folder, p. 85

📁 **Guided Reading and Review** Units 5–6 folder, p. 86

Media and Technology

 AmericanHeritage® CD-ROM
Time Tour A New Role in the World: World War I

SECTION 1

The Road to War

Objectives
You may wish to call students' attention to the objectives in the Section Preview. The objectives are reflected in the main headings of the section.

Bellringer
Ask students to define the word *neutral*. Ask them to think of situations in which they chose to remain neutral and others in which they took a stand. What conditions encouraged their choices?

Reading Strategy
Formulating Questions Refer to the Reading Strategy in the Section Preview. You may wish to have students answer each other's questions after they read the section.

LESSON PLAN
Connecting to the Main Idea

1. Focus Explain that when war first broke out in Europe, most Americans wished to remain neutral. However, as the war continued, the United States moved toward more active involvement. Ask what prompted this change in direction.

2. Instruct Remind students that World War I did not erupt overnight. Ask them what the long-standing causes were. Discuss the reasons why each of the European nations became involved in the early days of the war. Why did the system of secret European alliances fail to maintain peace?

Discuss the possibility of being both neutral and prepared. Did building up arms and troops ensure United States entry into the war? Why or why not?

3. Close When war began in Europe in 1914, the United States resolved to stay neutral. Given the nation's many interests abroad, this policy would be difficult to maintain. The next section describes how the nation finally joined the war.

566 Chapter 20 • Section 1

---

(3) *Nationalism.* Two kinds of nationalism contributed to World War I. The first was the tendency for countries such as the great powers to act in their own national interest. When such action went against the national interest of another nation, warfare could result. The second kind of nationalism occurred in countries with diverse populations. In such countries the longing of an ethnic minority for independence often led to violence.

(4) *Alliances.* A complicated system of alliances developed among the nations of Europe during the late nineteenth century. Designed to bolster each nation's security, the alliances bound the great powers to come to each other's aid in the event of attack. In 1914 the fragile balance of power that had kept the peace for decades led its creators into war.

The Conflict Expands

At the time of the assassination, Bosnia was the focal point of a nationalist dispute between Austria-Hungary, which had recently annexed Bosnia, and its neighbor Serbia. Convinced that Serbia was behind the assassination, Austria-Hungary used the event as an excuse to crush its small enemy. On July 28, 1914, Austria-Hungary declared war on Serbia.

This declaration of war set off a chain reaction that worked its way through Europe's complex web of alliances. On July 29, Russia, as Serbia's protector, began **mobilization**—the readying of troops for war. Germany, Austria-Hungary's chief ally, demanded that Russia stop mobilizing. Russia refused. At that point, Russia's ally, France, began to ready its troops, as did Germany.

On August 1, Germany declared war on Russia. Germany's military leaders had long prepared for this day. Their country lay between France to the west and Russia to the east. To avoid being trapped by advancing French and Russian armies, Germany had developed a first-strike strategy. Known as the Schlieffen Plan, it called for a quick sweep through France to knock the French out of the war. Then the German army would concentrate on Russia.

Germany put the plan into action. To reach France as fast as possible, the German army had to pass through Belgium. To Germany's dismay, this invasion brought Great Britain, Belgium's protector, into the conflict on August 4. Germany had hoped that Britain, with its powerful navy, would stay neutral.

One week after the war started, all the great powers of Europe had been drawn into it. The conflict divided them into two sides. Germany and Austria-Hungary made up the **Central Powers.** Russia, France, Serbia, and Great Britain were called the **Allies.**

Stalemate Each side felt confident of swift victory. Six weeks, experts said, and it would all be over. The experts were wrong. Relatively equal in size and strength, the two sides reached a bloody **stalemate,** a situation in which neither side is able to gain the advantage.

In earlier wars a forceful offense led by a heroic cavalry often was enough to secure victory in battle. Now defensive forces could use modern firepower, such as machine guns and long-range artillery, to stop such advances. In September 1914 the German army, following the Schlieffen Plan, advanced to within 30 miles of Paris. There, at the river Marne, a combined French and British force stopped their progress. Both sides then dug in.

Holed up in lines of muddy, rat-infested trenches, the two sides faced each other across an empty "no-man's land." For months each side tried to reach the other's lines to destroy or at least push back the enemy. But neither side

European Alliances in World War I

Allied Powers / Central Powers / Neutral nations

Before the war, Europe was a land of empires and alliances. When Austria-Hungary declared war on Serbia, much of the continent was drawn into the conflict. *Location* **Based on this map, which side, if any, had a geographical advantage in the war? Explain.**

---

was able to gain more than a few miles, and that only at appalling human cost.

Meanwhile, an Austrian army captured Belgrade, the Serbian capital. Combined German and Austro-Hungarian forces pushed the Russian lines back. At the end of 1914, the Ottoman Empire, centered in what is now Turkey, entered the war on the side of the Central Powers. In the spring of 1915, Italy joined the Allies.

Modern Warfare In 1914 the youth of Europe had marched off to fight, eager for a chance to be heroic. They came up against new killing machines of amazing efficiency. Ripped apart by machine guns, hand grenades, or artillery shells, and choked by poison gases, soldiers found that heroism came at a ghastly price.

If soldiers charging across no-man's land toward the enemy survived the artillery shells that rained down upon them, the enemy's machine guns, firing 450 rounds a minute, mowed them down. The generals, unaccustomed to the new weaponry, repeatedly gave the order to attack. That strategy, however, produced only a mounting pile of dead infantry. In the Battle of the Somme in 1916, for example, the British suffered some 20,000 deaths in a single day of combat.

Morale sank. Desperate, the armies began using any tactic available. Erasing the distinction between soldier and civilian, they burned fields, killed livestock, and poisoned wells. They tunneled under the no-man's land to plant bombs below enemy trenches. German submarines torpedoed any ship they believed to be carrying arms to the Allies. A British naval blockade slowly starved the German people. None of these tactics brought a quick end to the conflict.

The American Response

Newspapers in the United States had recorded the march toward war in bold headlines. "Austria Declares War, Rushes Vast Army into Serbia; Russia Masses 80,000 Men on Border."

Americans read the news with mounting alarm. How could all these great countries of beauty and culture be at war with one another?

Some Americans felt personally involved. More than a third of the nation's 92 million people were first- or second-generation immigrants. They still identified with their old countries. About a quarter of these were German American, and another eighth were

Trench warfare ranged from crudely dug foxholes (above) to a series of elaborate trenches stretching for miles. Trench networks allowed armies to fire on the enemy, obtain supplies and reinforcements, and take cover from enemy fire. *Science and Technology How did trench warfare contribute to a stalemate in World War I?*

Irish American. Both of these groups felt hostility toward Great Britain because of past conflicts and the current war in Europe. For this reason, they favored the Central Powers over the Allies.

Most Americans, however, opposed the Central Powers. One reason was Kaiser Wilhelm, the ruler of Germany. The Kaiser, or emperor, was an **autocrat**—a ruler with unlimited power. Also, Americans saw the Germans as a people of frightening militarism and cold-blooded efficiency. Reporters who had rushed to Belgium in August 1914 to witness the German advance toward France fueled this view. Richard Harding Davis described the event for New York *Tribune* readers as "not men marching, but a force of nature like a tidal wave, an avalanche, or a river flooding its banks."

American Neutrality Trade strongly influenced the American position on the war. Between 1897 and 1914 United States commercial investments overseas had increased fivefold, from $700 million to $3.5 billion. Now German submarines and a British naval

> **Main Idea**
> ## CONNECTIONS
>
> What were the reactions in the United States to the outbreak of World War I?

This "peace ship" journeyed to Europe in 1915 with hopes of ending the war. Suffragist and social reformer Jane Addams, second from the left in the front row, joined the delegation. **Foreign Relations** *How did the peace movement differ from the preparedness movement?*

if necessary. In December 1914 preparedness supporters organized a National Security League to "promote patriotic education and national sentiment and service among people of the United States."

By the late summer of 1915, the movement's leaders had persuaded the government to set up camps to train American men for combat. By the summer of 1916, Wilson had worked out an agreement with Congress for large increases in the armed forces.

The Peace Movement When World War I broke out, a peace movement also swung into gear. Its members consisted primarily of former Populists, Midwest progressives, and social reformers.

Women were particularly active in the movement. On August 29, 1914, suffragists dressed in black and carrying a banner of a dove marched down New York City's Fifth Avenue. In November 1915 a group of female and male social reformers founded the American Union Against Militarism.

Congress also included some peace advocates. They insisted on paying for preparedness through a tax on the makers of arms and through higher income taxes. Claude Kitchin, member of Congress from North Carolina, predicted that when people discovered "that the income tax will have to pay for the increase in the army and navy, . . . preparedness will not be so popular with them as it now is." Congress did increase taxes, but the preparedness movement remained strong.

blockade of the North Sea were putting those investments at risk. To protect the investments, President Wilson on August 4, 1914, officially proclaimed the United States a neutral country. The American government protested the actions of both sides and tried to act as peacemaker.

The Preparedness Movement American business leaders welcomed the proclamation of neutrality. Still, those who had strong commercial ties to Great Britain urged that the United States get ready for war. Their watchword was "preparedness." They wanted their country to be in a position to aid Great Britain

SECTION 1 REVIEW

Comprehension

1. **Key Terms** Define: (a) militarism; (b) mobilization; (c) Central Powers; (d) Allies; (e) stalemate; (f) autocrat.
2. **Summarizing the Main Idea** What was the main reason that the United States stayed neutral at the start of World War I?
3. **Organizing Information** Create a cause-and-effect chart that shows why World War I started and what some of its effects were.

Critical Thinking

4. **Analyzing Time Lines** Review the time line at the start of the section. What clue suggests to

you that the major powers expected the crisis between Austria-Hungary and Serbia to lead to war?

5. **Checking Consistency** The alliance system in Europe in 1914 was designed to maintain peace. Yet it seemed to make the conflict worse once the fighting began. Explain this apparent inconsistency.

Writing Activity

6. **Writing a Persuasive Essay** Write an essay in which you express your support for the preparedness movement. Persuade your readers that the United States has no choice but to be ready to go to war.

RESOURCE OPTIONS

Teaching Resources

Quiz Units 5–6 folder, p. 87

Student Performance Pack

Guide to the Essentials Chapter 20, Section 1 (English and Spanish)

Identifying Alternatives

I dentifying alternatives means finding one or more possible solutions to a problem. In the previous section, you read about the conflict in the United States over how to react to the war raging in Europe. The passages on this page make the case for two responses the United States might have made. Passage A presents the views of then President Woodrow Wilson, as stated in August 1914. Passage B, which was published in January 1915, presents the thoughts of former President Theodore Roosevelt.

Use the following steps to identify and analyze the alternatives presented in the passages.

1. Identify the nature of the problem under discussion. Before you can identify alternative solutions to a problem, you must understand what the problem is. (a) What is the issue that both passages address? (b) Does each passage present the same approach to the problem?

2. Identify the solutions proposed in the two passages. (a) What does Passage A suggest is the proper response of the United States to the war raging in Europe? (b) How does Passage B propose that the United States respond to the war? (c) In what ways are these two viewpoints similar or different?

3. Evaluate the potential effectiveness of each view. Consider the strengths and weaknesses of each proposal. For example, you might ask the following questions about Passages A

and B: (a) What difficulties do you see in Wilson's suggestion that the United States not judge the actions of other nations? (b) What might happen if the United States acts in a "disinterested" way, as Wilson suggests? (c) Does Roosevelt make clear what he means when he refers to a nation that "does ill"? (d) Does Roosevelt explain the basis by which nations should be judged "highly civilized" or "well behaved"?

4. Consider other alternatives. Recall the nature of the problem under discussion. Then, using insights you

gained above, think of other possible solutions. Ask: (a) What should be the goal of the United States in responding to the war in Europe? (b) What steps are most likely to achieve that goal?

TEST FOR SUCCESS

Do you think President Wilson or President Roosevelt would have been the first to declare war on a nation that provoked the United States? Explain your answer, based on Passages A and B.

A

"My thought is of America. . . . [T]his great country of ours . . . should show herself in this time of peculiar trial a nation fit beyond others to exhibit the fine poise of undisturbed judgment, the dignity of self-control, the efficiency of dispassionate [unemotional] action; a nation that neither sits in judgment upon others nor is disturbed in her own counsels and which keeps herself fit and free to do what is honest and disinterested and truly serviceable for the peace of the world."

Woodrow Wilson, *Appeal for Neutrality,* August 19, 1914

B

"Our true course should be to judge each nation on its conduct, unhesitatingly to antagonize every nation that does ill [at the point] it does ill, and equally without hesitation to act. . . .

One of the greatest of international duties ought to be the protection of small, highly civilized, well-behaved and self-respecting states from oppression and conquest by their powerful military neighbors. . . .

I feel in the strongest way that we should have interfered, at least to the extent of the most emphatic diplomatic protest and at the very outset—and then by whatever further action was necessary—[when Germany invaded Belgium]."

Theodore Roosevelt, *America and the World War,* 1915

RESOURCE OPTIONS

Teaching Resources

 Skills for Life Activity Identifying Alternatives, Units 5–6 folder, p. 100, extends students' opportunity to practice this skill by analyzing American policy proposals for response to the war in Bosnia-Herzegovina.

Media and Technology

 Color Transparencies Critical Thinking, I–15

May 1915 Lusitania sunk	March 1916 Sussex sunk	November 1916 Wilson reelected	February 1917 Germany resumes unrestricted submarine warfare; Zimmermann note	March 1917 Russian Revolution; City of Memphis, Illinois, and Vigilancia sunk	April 1917 United States declares war on Germany

1915   **1916**   **1917**   **1918**

SECTION 2

The United States Declares War

Objectives

You may wish to call students' attention to the objectives in the Section Preview. The objectives are reflected in the main headings of the section.

Bellringer

Ask students what makes a country one of the great nations of the world. What domestic conditions and foreign alliances characterize a great nation? What countries are great nations today? Why?

Reading Strategy

Organizing Information Refer to the Reading Strategy in the Section Preview. You may wish to have volunteers share their decision and the reasons for it with the class.

LESSON PLAN

Connecting to the Main Idea

1. Focus Explain that from 1915 to 1917, relations between the United States and Germany deteriorated. Ask why the United States finally declared war on the Central Powers.

2. Instruct Discuss why Germany's use of submarines caused outrage among Americans. Ask students to respond to the German argument that they should not be denied their weapon of surprise.

Discuss the events that moved the United States toward war with Germany. How did Germany violate the Sussex pledge? Ask students how they think the Zimmermann note affected American public opinion. What roles did the Russian Revolution, British propoganda, big business, and idealism play in the American decision to enter the war?

3. Close Although the United States tried to maintain its neutrality, events pushed Congress into a declaration of war. The next section describes the role of Americans overseas in the war.

---

2 The United States Declares War

SECTION PREVIEW

Objectives

1 Describe German submarine tactics during World War I.
2 Identify events that moved the United States toward war.
3 *Key Terms* Define: U-boat; Sussex pledge; filibuster; Zimmermann note; Russian Revolution.

Main Idea

German submarine warfare helped push the United States into World War I.

Reading Strategy

Organizing Information Imagine that you are a member of Congress in 1917. You must decide whether the United States should go to war against Germany and the other Central Powers. As you read the section, list the events that influence your decision.

This German poster urged U-boats on their mission. The translation is, "Submarine: come out!"

From 1915 to 1917 friction between the United States and Germany increased. The preparedness movement continued to gain support in the United States, and the pressure to join in the war intensified. Ultimately, actions by the Central Powers pushed Congress and the President into entering the war on the side of the Allies.

German Submarine Warfare

One action that provoked angry calls for war in the United States was the German use of submarine warfare. This tactic was effective militarily, but it cost the Germans dearly in terms of American public opinion.

The German **U-boat,** short for *Unterseeboot,* or submarine, was a terrifying new weapon that changed the rules of naval warfare. Passenger and merchant ships had no defense against the submarine, which could go undetected nearly anywhere in the ocean. Submarine attacks depended on the element of surprise. Unlike other naval ships, U-boats issued no warning to their targets. This struck many Americans as uncivilized.[†]

The British encouraged such anti-German feelings. Shortly after the war began, the British cut the transatlantic cable connecting Germany and the United States. All news of the European front henceforth flowed through London. Its pro-Allied bias helped shape the opinion of the people in the United States in favor of punishing Germany for its use of the submarine.

American public opinion of the Germans sank even lower on May 7, 1915, when a U-boat sighted the *Lusitania*, a British passenger liner, in the Irish Sea. Suspecting correctly that the ship carried weapons for the Allies, the U-boat fired on the liner. Eighteen minutes later the *Lusitania* disappeared beneath the waves along with its almost 1,200 passengers. Included among the dead were 128 Americans, who had

---

[†] Americans did not react the same way to the British blockade of Germany, even though it threatened freedom of the seas and was slowly starving the German people. They generally thought that such a blockade was reasonable during wartime. In contrast, German attempts to break the blockade with submarines seemed unfair.

 RESOURCE OPTIONS

Teaching Resources

📁 **Reproducible Lesson Plan** Lesson Plans folder, p. 114

📁 **Big Idea Graphic Organizer** Big Idea Graphic Organizer folder, p. 86

📁 **Guided Reading and Review** Units 5–6 folder, p. 88

Media and Technology

🖳 **Color Transparencies** Cause and Effect, F-8

NOTICE!

TRAVELLERS intending to embark on the Atlantic voyage are reminded that a state of war exists between Germany and her allies and GreatBritian and her allies; that the zone of war includes the waters adjacent to the British Isles; that, in accordance with formal notice given by the Imperial German Government, vessels flying the flag of Great Britian, or of any of her allies, are liable to destruction in those waters and that travellers sailing in the war zone on ships of Great Britian or her allies do so at their own risk.

IMPERIAL GERMAN EMBASSY,
WASHINGTON, D. C., APRIL 22, 1915.

CUNARD

EUROPE VIA LIVERPOOL

LUSITANIA

Fastest and Largest Steamer now in Atlantic Service Sails
SATURDAY, MAY 1, 10 A. M.
Transylvania - Fri., May 7, 5P.M.
Orduna, - - - Tues., May 18, 10 A.M.
Tuscania, - - - Fri., May 21, 5 P.M.
LUSITANIA, - Sat., May 29, 10 A.M.
Transylvania, - - - - 5P.M.

American public opinion was extremely critical of Germany and its use of U-boats. The cartoon (right) suggests that Germany felt no remorse for the loss of American lives. Germany, however, did warn travelers—including passengers of the *Lusitania*—to stay out of the war zone (left). *Foreign Relations* *What does this cartoon suggest about Wilson's response to the sinking of the* Lusitania?

boarded the *Lusitania* in spite of German warnings to stay off British ships. Nevertheless, the American press went wild over what they called Germany's act of "barbarism."

Wilson urged patience. He demanded that Germany stop its submarine warfare and make payments to the victims' families. Germany's reply that the ship carried small arms and ammunition did not quiet American anger. Wilson sent a second, stronger note of protest. In response, Germany promised to stop sinking passenger ships without warning, as long as the ship's crew offered no resistance to German search or seizure.

Still, U-boats continued to torpedo Allied ships. On March 24, 1916, a German submarine sank the *Sussex,* a French passenger steamship. The United States threatened to cut diplomatic ties to Germany. In what came to be called the **Sussex pledge,** the German government again promised that U-boats would warn ships before attacking.

The series of demands and broken promises that led up to the Sussex pledge frustrated Wilson. He could not threaten force without entering the war. During this time, however, Wilson did embrace the concept of preparedness. He also authorized New York bankers to

make a huge loan to the Allies. American neutrality was beginning to weaken.

Moving Toward War

In the presidential election of 1916, Wilson ran on the slogan "He kept us out of war." The Republicans, who nominated Supreme Court justice Charles Evans Hughes, criticized Wilson for not taking a stronger stand against Germany. American voters gave Wilson a narrow victory.

Germany soon tested Wilson's patience. On February 1, 1917, Germany violated the Sussex pledge by resuming unrestricted submarine warfare. German strategists knew that it might bring the United States into the war. But they felt fairly confident that they could defeat Britain and win the war before American entry could make a difference.

Germany's action dashed Wilson's hope of maintaining freedom of the seas—and American neutrality. On February 3 the United States broke off diplomatic relations with Germany. Wilson asked Congress for permission to arm American merchant ships.

Main Idea
CONNECTIONS

What was the impact of Germany's unrestricted submarine warfare?

President Woodrow Wilson reluctantly led the nation into World War I.

President Woodrow Wilson reluctantly led the nation into World War I.

The Zimmermann Note In the Senate, a group of antiwar senators tried to prevent action on Wilson's request by using a **filibuster.** (A filibuster is a tactic in which senators take the floor, begin talking, and refuse to stop talking to prevent a vote on a measure.) While this was taking place, the British revealed the contents of an intercepted German telegram. In the note Arthur Zimmermann, Germany's foreign secretary, made a secret offer to Mexico.

> **"**We shall endeavor to keep the United States neutral. In the event of this not succeeding, we make Mexico a proposal of alliance. . . : Make war together, make peace together, . . . and . . . Mexico is to reconquer the lost territory in Texas, New Mexico, and Arizona.**"**
>
> —*Arthur Zimmermann*

Neither Wilson nor Mexico took the **Zimmermann note** seriously. Its release, however, scored another public relations victory for Great Britain. The United States edged closer to war.

Revolution in Russia By early 1917 Russia already had suffered enormous casualties in the war: more than 1.5 million killed, roughly 2.5 million taken prisoner, and millions more wounded. Austrian and German forces had advanced deep into Russian territory. Poorly fed and miserably equipped, the Russians fell back farther and farther into their interior.

Then, in March 1917, Czar Nicholas II, Russia's autocratic leader, was forced to give up power. The Russian monarchy was replaced with a republican government. This **Russian Revolution** elated the prowar faction in the United States. Concern over being allied with the czar had helped slow the nation's move toward entry into the war. The fall of the czar removed a last stumbling block to a full American commitment to the Allies.

The War Resolution Between March 16 and March 18, Germany sank the United States ships *City of Memphis, Illinois,* and *Vigilancia.* On March 20 Wilson's Cabinet voted unanimously for war. Casting the issue in idealistic terms, Wilson told Congress on April 2 that "the world must be made safe for democracy." He stated:

> **AMERICAN VOICES** **"**It is a fearful thing to lead this great peaceful people into war, the most terrible and disastrous of all wars, civilization itself seeming to be in the balance. But the right is more precious than peace.**"**
>
> —*Woodrow Wilson*

A war resolution passed 82 to 6 in the Senate and 373 to 50 in the House. On April 6, 1917, the President signed it.

SECTION 2 REVIEW

Comprehension

1. **Key Terms** Define: (a) U-boat; (b) Sussex pledge; (c) filibuster; (d) Zimmermann note; (e) Russian Revolution.
2. **Summarizing the Main Idea** Why did German submarine warfare upset Americans so much?
3. **Organizing Information** Create a flowchart that shows the events leading up to American entrance into World War I. Charts might consist of a series of boxes connected by arrows.

Critical Thinking

4. **Analyzing Time Lines** Review the time line at the start of the section. Which event do you think most directly caused the United States to declare war on Germany? Explain.
5. **Identifying Alternatives** Consider the causes that brought the United States into World War I. What would the United States have had to do to avoid the conflict altogether? For what reasons did the United States not take such steps?

Writing Activity

6. **Writing a Persuasive Essay** Choose one of the events that led to American involvement in World War I. Imagine that the event has just taken place. Write an essay to try to persuade the President and Congress that the United States should enter the war now, based on that one event.

Answers to SECTION 2 REVIEW

1. (a) U-boat, see p. 570; (b) Sussex pledge, see p. 571; (c) filibuster, see p. 572; (d) Zimmermann note, see p. 572; (e) Russian Revolution, see p. 572.

2. Ships had no warning or defense against it; submarines attacked American and other neutral ships; the German government broke its promises about restricting its submarines.

3. Sample events: Sinking of the *Lusitania* and *Sussex;* German resumption of open submarine warfare; Zimmermann note; Russian Revolution; sinking of the *City of Memphis,* the *Illinois,* and the *Vigilancia.*

4. Sample answer: The sinking of the *City of Memphis,* the *Illinois,* and the *Vigilancia* triggered the declaration.

5. Sample answer: The United States would have had to keep its commercial vessels out of waters patrolled by U-boats. This would have been politically unpopular and economically damaging.

6. Essays should focus on an event, describe it, and explain why it is cause enough for the United States to enter the war.

RESOURCE OPTIONS

Teaching Resources

📁 **Quiz** Units 5–6 folder, p. 89

📁 **Biography** Jeannette Rankin, Units 5–6 folder, p. 96

Student Performance Pack

 Guide to the Essentials Chapter 20, Section 2 (English and Spanish)

Media and Technology

Visual Learning Activity Uncle Sam's Pledge, found on Resource Pro, uses a Library of Congress drawing to show how symbols were used to promote public support for World War I.

May 1917	June 1917	March 1918	June 1918	August 1918	November 1918
Selective Service Act; Convoy system put in place	American troops arrive in France	Russia exits war	Battle of Château-Thierry	Allied counteroffensive	Cease-fire ends fighting

1917   **1918**   **1919**

3 Americans on the European Front

SECTION PREVIEW

Objectives

1 Describe how the United States prepared to take part in World War I.
2 Explain how American troops helped turn the tide of the war.
3 Describe the war's end and its costs.
4 *Key Terms* Define: Selective Service Act; American Expeditionary Force; convoy; armistice; genocide.

Main Idea

American troops helped the Allies defeat the Central Powers in World War I.

Reading Strategy

Predicting Content Create a list of this section's bold-face headings and subheadings. Under each one, write a one-sentence prediction of what the content will be. Then check your predictions against the actual text.

By the time the United States entered the war in April 1917, the Allies desperately needed replacement troops. In June, President Wilson agreed to send a small force to Europe under the command of General John J. Pershing. A veteran of the Spanish-American War, the general had also taught for a time at West Point. Pershing would need all his experience and skills to lead the American forces against a determined German army.

Preparing for Action

Despite the success of the preparedness movement, in April 1917 the United States was far from ready to send an army to the European front. Instead, a cautious Congress sent naval support, supplies, arms, and $3 billion in loans. The token force of 14,500 men led by General Pershing served mainly to boost Allied morale. After landing in France, Pershing realized that he needed more troops. He recommended that the army should number 1 million men by 1918 and 3 million the year after that.

Draftees and Volunteers When the United States entered World War I, the armed forces

had only 120,000 enlisted men and 80,000 National Guardsmen. In May 1917 Congress passed a **Selective Service Act,** authorizing a draft of young men for military service.

During the Civil War the draft had sparked riots. Now, however, the general feeling that this would be the "war to end all wars" resulted in wide acceptance of the program. By November 1918 more than 24 million men had registered for the draft. From those, a lottery picked 3 million draftees to serve in the war. Volunteers and National Guardsmen made up the remainder of what was called the **American Expeditionary Force** (AEF).

Among the Americans who served their country were thousands of women. Some 11,000 women volunteered to serve in uniform as nurses, drivers, and clerks. Another 14,000 women served abroad, as civilians

In 1917 American soldiers marched off to war, carrying items such as this shaving kit.

Interdisciplinary

One of the inventions that revolutionized twentieth-century warfare was the tank. By mounting the body of an armored car onto a tractor, the British improvised the first armored, tracked vehicle in July 1915. The prototype tank, called "Little Willie," was quickly succeeded by "Big Willie." The new weapon proved itself at the Battle of Cambrai in late 1917, where 474 British tanks breached German lines. But the tanks were too slow to exploit the victory, necessitating the development of faster armored vehicles.

LEARNING STYLES

Ask students to locate the lyrics and music, or a recording, of some of the songs popular with troops and civilians during the war. Possibilities include "Over There," "It's a Long Way to Tipperary," and "Pack Up Your Troubles." Ask students to work together to present a cabaret featuring the music of World War I. *(Musical/Rhythmic)*

Denied combat opportunity by the United States, these New York National Guardsmen fought with the French as the 369th Infantry Regiment. Though facing combat for the first time, they performed with such skill and bravery that they were awarded the French Croix de Guerre. *Diversity Why do you think African Americans suffered discrimination in the armed forces?*

working for the government or for private agencies.

The Convoy System In addition to building a fighting force, the War Department had to worry about transporting its troops overseas. In April 1917 alone, German U-boats had sunk more than 400 Allied and neutral ships.

Starting in May 1917 all merchant and troop ships traveled in a **convoy.** A convoy consisted of a group of unarmed ships surrounded by a ring of destroyers, torpedo boats, and other armed naval vessels. The torpedo boats were specially equipped to track and destroy submarines. Between April and December 1917, merchant marine losses dropped by half.

American Soldiers in Europe From the time the AEF arrived in France in June 1917, Pershing kept them independent of the Allied armies. In Pershing's view the Allies had become too accustomed to defensive action. He wanted to save his men's strength for offensive moves.†

---

† American infantrymen were called *doughboys.* This term originated during the Civil War in reference to the dumpling-shaped buttons on Union infantry uniforms.

American and Allied units fought separately, but a further division existed within the American ranks. The more than 300,000 African Americans who volunteered or were drafted into service were kept apart from white troops. Though many African Americans fought with distinction and nearly 4,000 died or were wounded, most never saw combat. The marines refused to accept African Americans altogether, and the navy used them for minor tasks only. The army, too, used African Americans mostly for manual labor.

These assignments distressed many African Americans. The 369th Infantry Regiment, who came to be known as the Harlem Hell Fighters, was especially eager to fight. Its members persuaded their white officers to loan the regiment to the French, who integrated the regiment into the French army. Because of their distinguished service, the entire regiment received France's highest combat medal, the Croix de Guerre.

Turning the Tide of War

As American involvement in the war expanded, a major development occurred within the alliance. In November 1917 followers of Vladimir Lenin, called Bolsheviks, violently overthrew Russia's government. Lenin had been living in Switzerland and had promised to make peace with Germany if he ever gained control in Russia. For this reason Germany had helped arrange his return to Russia in April 1917. By November, Lenin had taken over the country.

Lenin made peace with Germany on March 3, 1918. Russia's exit from the war freed the Germans from the two-front war they had been forced to fight. From March through May 1918, German forces turned all their energies toward pounding the French and British lines. They finally broke through, and by June 3 were about 50 miles from Paris.

Americans Save Paris American forces came to the rescue. Marching out from Paris, the men received this word from their leader, Brigadier

RESOURCE OPTIONS

Teaching Resources

Literature Activity A War Song, Units 5–6 folder, p. 99

American Literature

Connections to American Literature "Over There" and "K-K-K-Katy," pp. 1082–1083

Media and Technology

RESOURCE PRO

Biography Henry Johnson, found on Resource Pro, profiles the most famous African American soldier of World War I.

Major Battles of World War I, 1914–1917

☐ Allied Powers	➡ Central Powers' offensives
☐ Central Powers	— Farthest advance of Central Powers
☐ Neutral nations	---- Line of trench warfare, 1915–1917
☐ German submarine warfare zone	★ Major battles
➡ Allied offensives	

Lusitania sunk May 7, 1915

Battles of Ypres Oct.–Nov. 1914, Apr.–May 1915

Tannenberg Aug. 1914

Battle of the Somme July–Nov. 1916

Caporetto Oct.–Dec. 1917

First Battle of the Marne Sept. 1914

Battle of Verdun Feb.–Dec. 1916

Gallipoli Apr. 1915–Jan. 1916

MAP Skills After the Germans advanced through Belgium, the French prevented them from capturing Paris in the First Battle of the Marne. The war, however, was far from over. A deadly stalemate ensued. *Location* Locate the line of trench warfare. What was its strategic value? Why didn't it extend across Switzerland?

General James G. Harbord: "We dig no trenches to fall back on. The Marines will hold where they stand." At the battle of Château-Thierry in early June, they did just that. At a loss of over half of their troops, they helped the French save Paris, blunted the edge of the German advance, and began to turn the tide of the war.

Allied Counterattack After turning back the Germans outside Paris, the Allies took heart. Using a new weapon, the tank, which could cross trenches and roll through barbed wire, they began to break the German lines. On August 8 at the battle of Amiens, the Allied armies stopped the German advance once and for all.

On August 11, German general Erich von Ludendorff sensed that the end was near. He advised Kaiser Wilhelm to seek a peace settlement. The Allies, however, insisted on total surrender. In September some 500,000 American troops, assisted by 100,000 French, began to hit the final German strongholds. In the battle of St. Mihiel, the first major military effort entirely in American hands, General Pershing and his troops ousted the Germans

from a long-held position. Soon after, the German army was in full retreat.

The Allies also began to use airplanes to drop bombs. Aerial dogfights already had taken place. Each side had its "aces," such as the American captain Eddie Rickenbacker, who downed 26 enemy fighters. Now Colonel Billy Mitchell organized a fleet of over 1,400 bomb-carrying planes. Although not very effective at first, bombing raids would become a devastating weapon in the future.

Corporal Alvin York

AMERICAN BIOGRAPHY The final Allied assault, the Meuse-Argonne Offensive, began on September 26, 1918. Over a million AEF troops began the drive to expel the Germans from France and cut their supply lines. Many acts of heroism shone during these final months. But the bravery of Corporal Alvin York stood out above the rest.

Born in 1887, York grew up in the mountains of Tennessee, where he learned to shoot by hunting wild turkeys. York did not volun-

Main Idea CONNECTIONS

What were some of the military innovations introduced during World War I?

Using the Internet

Write an Article

Objective Use the Internet to write an article on the life of a World War I recruit at Camp Funston. Have students follow these instructions:

1. See the *America: Pathways to the Present* Web site at **http://www.Pathways.phschool.com** for the URL of Reflections of Army Sergeant Charles L. Johnston.

2. Read the letters of Sergeant Charles Johnston.

3. Write an article describing what life was like for a recruit at Camp Funston during World War I.

4. Include an illustration with your article.

TEST PREPARATION

Have students read the passage under "Americans Save Paris" and then answer the question below.

You can tell from General Harbord's quotation that—

Ⓐ his tactic was to hold his line without retreating, at whatever the cost.

B he would only use trenches as a last resort.

C the Marines disliked digging trenches.

D he believed in defensive tactics.

Answer to . . .

Map Skills It was the last line of defense against France; Switzerland was neutral.
Main Idea Connections Submarines, torpedo boats, the convoy system, machine guns, hand grenades, poison gases.

Graphing the Main Idea

Graphing the Main Idea

To make sure students understand the main idea of this section, you may wish to use the flow map graphic organizer below.

Tell students that a flow map shows a sequence of events unfolding. Ask students to use the flow map to record the events that took place after the United States entered World War I that led to the defeat of the Central Powers.

Teaching Tip A template for this graphic organizer can be found in the Color Transparencies, G-4.

Answer to . . .

Map Skills After turning back the Germans at Paris, the Allies took the offensive, moving into the western front.

teer to fight. In fact, he applied to be classified a conscientious objector, someone who refuses to serve in the military because of religious beliefs. His application was denied, and he was drafted.

As a member of the 82nd Infantry Division, York took part in the Meuse-Argonne Offensive. On October 8 his patrol tried to destroy a German machine-gun nest, losing half its men in the attempt. Facing heavy machine-gun fire, the remaining soldiers took cover. York continued the attack on his own, killing 25 machine-gunners with his rifle and pistol and capturing 132 German soldiers.

When a general asked about his exploits, York replied, "General, I would hate to think I missed any of them shots; they were all at pretty close range—50 or 60 yards." For his heroism above and beyond the call of duty, York received the Congressional Medal of Honor as well as the French Croix de Guerre.

Corporal Alvin York (1887–1964)

Ending the War

The Allies pressed on against their enemy. The German commanders begged for peace, still hoping to dictate some terms. The Allies refused. By the time the **armistice,** or cease-fire, came, the Kaiser had fled to Holland. On November 11, 1918, the guns finally fell silent.

More than 50,000 American soldiers died in battle, and many more died of disease, mainly influenza. The toll would have been even greater but for the efforts of volunteer nurses serving their country through the Red Cross and other agencies.

The physical and mental scars of the war ran deep. Corporal Elmer Sherwood of Indiana, just 21 years old, wrote after one bloody battle in August 1918:

AMERICAN VOICES "Hundreds of bodies of our brave boys lie on Hill 212, captured with such a great loss of blood. We will never be able to explain war to our loved ones back home even if we . . . live and return."

—*Corporal Elmer Sherwood*

American losses were tiny compared with those suffered by the Europeans. The total death toll of 8 million soldiers and sailors is only an estimate. Still, this figure averages out to more than 5,000 soldiers killed on each day of the war. Germany, Austria-Hungary, Russia, and France all suffered more than a

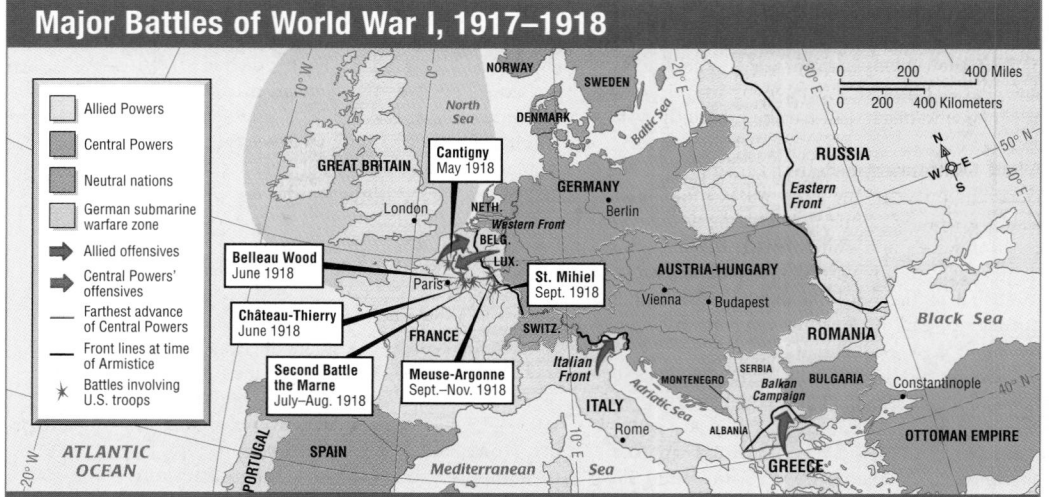

Major Battles of World War I, 1917–1918

Allied Powers
Central Powers
Neutral nations
German submarine warfare zone
Allied offensives
Central Powers' offensives
Farthest advance of Central Powers
Front lines at time of Armistice
Battles involving U.S. troops

Cantigny May 1918
Belleau Wood June 1918
Château-Thierry June 1918
St. Mihiel Sept. 1918
Meuse-Argonne Sept.–Nov. 1918
Second Battle the Marne July–Aug. 1918

 MAP skills In 1917 the United States entered the war, providing the Allies with both economic and military support. *Location* Why was the fighting concentrated on the western fronts by 1917–1918?

exploring TECHNOLOGY *World War I Tank*

- 105-horsepower, six-cylinder engine
- One of four Lewis machine guns
- One of two 57-mm pedestal-mounted guns
- Armor plating
- Driver
- Commander
- Pressed-steel track plate

The tank was another new weapon introduced in World War I. It was designed to cross rough terrain and trenches while remaining invulnerable to enemy fire. Tanks were used to launch assaults in advance of foot troops. *Science and Technology* How was the tank a response to trench warfare?

million war dead. Just under 900,000 British troops died. While most of the fighting and dying took place in Europe, there were battles in the Middle East and Africa as well.

The terrible slaughter extended beyond the battlefields. Millions of civilians died during and immediately after the fighting, from starvation, disease, or war-related injuries.

These deaths included hundreds of thousands of Armenian civilians. In a campaign of **genocide,** or the organized killing of an entire people, Ottoman forces deported and murdered Armenians, whom they suspected of disloyalty to the government. The killings of Armenians would continue into the early 1920s.

SECTION 3 REVIEW

Comprehension

1. *Key Terms* Define: (a) Selective Service Act; (b) American Expeditionary Force; (c) convoy; (d) armistice; (e) genocide.
2. *Summarizing the Main Idea* What role did American troops play in World War I?
3. *Organizing Information* Create a chart with three headings: *Preparing for Action, Turning the Tide,* and *Ending the War.* Fill in the chart with important details from the section.

Critical Thinking

4. *Analyzing Time Lines* Review the time line at the start of the section. How long did it take for the American Expeditionary Force to make a significant impact on the course of the war? Explain.

5. *Drawing Inferences* Long after Pershing's American Expeditionary Force arrived in Europe, French soldiers were still asking, "Where are the Americans?" Why do you think they asked that question?

Writing Activity

6. *Writing an Expository Essay* Write an essay focusing on the number of war deaths suffered by the main combatants in World War I.

| February 1917 Literacy test for immigrants | June 1917 Espionage Act | August 1917 Lever Food and Fuel Control Act | September 1917 Police raids against IWW members | May 1918 Sedition Act |

1917   **1918**   **1919**

SECTION 4

On the Home Front

Objectives

You may wish to call students' attention to the objectives in the Section Preview. The objectives are reflected in the main headings of the section.

Bellringer

Ask students what the term *home front* implies about the nature of American life during the war. Why could life not continue normally while the nation was involved in war?

Reading Strategy

Reading for Evidence Refer to the Reading Strategy in the Section Preview. You may wish to have volunteers add to a composite list of war sacrifices, which you write on the chalkboard.

LESSON PLAN

Connecting to the Main Idea

1. Focus Point out that World War I brought many changes at home, including unprecedented government control of the economy and of news and information. How did the war lead to the suppression of civil liberties?

2. Instruct Discuss the extent of the sacrifices that were required of Americans at home. Have students list changes in American life caused by the war and then categorize the changes.

Ask how the War Industries Board controlled industry. Have students compare the operations of a small manufacturing company before and during the war. Ask in what ways the War Labor Policies Board controlled workers. Why did business and labor cooperate with these boards? Would business and labor have cooperated with them in peacetime?

3. Close To support the war effort, the government assumed a new role. The next section describes the difficult task of shaping the peace that ended the war.

---

4 On the Home Front

SECTION PREVIEW

Objectives

1. Explain how the government financed the war and managed the wartime economy.
2. Describe how efforts to enforce loyalty led to hostility and repression.
3. Describe how the lives of Americans on the home front changed during the war.
4. *Key Terms* Define: Liberty Bond; price controls; rationing; daylight saving time; sedition; vigilante.

Main Idea

Americans and their government took extraordinary steps at home to support the war effort.

Reading Strategy

Reading for Evidence As you read, look for evidence to support the following statement, which appears on this page: "Waging war required many sacrifices at home." On a sheet of paper, list as many kinds of sacrifices described as you can.

The U.S. government used posters to whip up sentiment against the "Huns"—the Germans.

Waging war required many sacrifices at home. Despite the efforts of the preparedness movement, the American economy was not ready to meet the demands of modern warfare. In this era, war required huge amounts of money and personnel. As President Wilson explained, now "there are no armies . . . ; there are entire nations armed."

Financing the War

The government launched a vigorous campaign to raise money from the American people. It started offering **Liberty Bonds,** special war bonds sold to support the Allied cause. Like all bonds, they could later be redeemed for the original value of the bonds plus interest. Secretary of the Treasury William Gibbs McAdoo had the idea for Liberty Bonds. By selling war bonds to enthusiastic Americans, McAdoo raised more than $20 billion. This allowed the United States to loan more than $10 billion to the Allies during and just after the war.

Responding to the slogan "Every Scout to Save a Soldier," Boy Scouts and Girl Scouts set up booths on street corners and sold bonds. The government hired popular commercial artists to draw colorful posters and recruited famous screen actors to host bond rallies. An army of 75,000 "four-minute men" gave brief (four-minute) speeches before movies, plays, and school or union meetings to persuade audiences to buy bonds.

Managing the Economy

The government also called on industry to convert to the production of war goods. In 1918 Wilson won authority to set up a huge bureaucracy to manage this process. Business leaders flocked to Washington to take up posts in thousands of new agencies. Because they gave their service for a token salary, they were called "dollar-a-year" men and women.

New Agencies A War Industries Board, headed by financier Bernard Baruch, oversaw the nation's war-related production. The

---

RESOURCE OPTIONS

Teaching Resources

📁 **Reproducible Lesson Plan** Lesson Plans folder, p. 116

📁 **Big Idea Graphic Organizer** Big Idea Graphic Organizer folder, p. 88

📁 **Guided Reading and Review** Units 5–6 folder, p. 92

Media and Technology

🦅 **AmericanHeritage® CD-ROM**

Time Tour A New Role in the World: World War I

board had far-reaching powers. It doled out raw materials, told manufacturers what and how much to produce, and even fixed prices.

A War Trade Board licensed foreign trade and punished firms suspected of dealing with the enemy. A National War Labor Board, set up in April 1918 under former President Taft, worked to settle any labor disputes that might hinder the war effort. (Labor leader Samuel Gompers promised to limit labor strife in war-production industries.) A separate War Labor Policies Board, headed by Harvard law professor Felix Frankfurter, set standard wages, hours, and working conditions in the war industries. Labor unions won limited rights to organize and bargain collectively.

Regulating Food and Fuel Consumption In August 1917 Congress passed the Lever Food and Fuel Control Act. This act gave the President the power to manage the production and distribution of foods and fuels vital to the war effort.

Using the slogan "Food will win the war," the government began regulating food consumption. Under the leadership of engineer and future President Herbert Hoover, the Food Administration worked to increase agricultural output and reduce waste. Hoover had the power to impose **price controls,** a system of pricing determined by the government, on food. He also could have begun a system of **rationing,** or distributing goods to consumers in a fixed amount. But he opposed both these approaches. Hoover hoped instead that voluntary restraint and increased efficiency would accomplish the Food Administration's goals.

Women played a key role in Hoover's program. Writing to women in August 1917, he preached a "Gospel of the Clean Plate." He appealed:

> **AMERICAN VOICES** ❝Stop, before throwing any food away, and ask "Can it be used?" . . . Stop catering to different appetites. No second helpings. Stop all eating between meals. . . . One meatless day a week. One wheatless meal a day. . . . No butter in cooking: use substitutes.❞
>
> —*Herbert Hoover*

"The American woman and the American home," Hoover concluded, "can bring to a successful end the greatest national task that has ever been accepted by the American people." Eager to take part in the war effort, women across the country responded to this patriotic challenge.

The Lever Food and Fuel Control Act also created an agency called the Fuel Administration. It sponsored gasless days to save fuel. This agency also began the practice of **daylight saving time**—turning clocks ahead one hour for the summer. This new policy increased the number of daylight hours available for activities. In this way daylight saving time lessened the need for artificial light, which lowered fuel consumption.

Main Idea CONNECTIONS
In what way did the Fuel Administration agency help in the war effort?

A Progressive Victory? Thanks to the war, some hopes of progressive-era reformers had come to pass. Government now regulated American economic life to an extent most progressives had never dreamed possible. When regulation spilled over into more private areas of life, however, some progressives wondered if the growth in public power had gone too far.

In addition, to the dismay of all progressives, regulation had not lessened the power of the corporate world. Indeed, during the war the influence of business leaders grew, the government relaxed its pursuit of antitrust suits, and corporate profits tripled.

Enforcing Loyalty

News and information also came under federal control during World War I. The government imposed censorship on the press and banned some publications from the mails.

In 1917 George Creel, a Denver journalist and former muckraker, was made head of the Committee on Public Information. His job was to rally popular support for the war. Creel's office coordinated the production of short films, pamphlets explaining war aims, and posters selling recruitment and Liberty Bonds.

Fear of Foreigners As in all wars, the fear of espionage, or spying, was widespread. A few months after the sinking of the *Lusitania*, a staff member of the German embassy left his briefcase on an American train. In it were plans for weakening pro-Allied sentiment and disrupting the American economy.

The government feared that secret agents might try to undermine the war effort by destroying transportation or communication networks. The possibility of such acts of sabotage put the government on alert. It also generated calls for restrictions on immigration.

Customize for
More Advanced Students

Tell students that in 1929, Herbert Hoover said, "Absolute freedom of the press to discuss public questions is a foundation stone of American liberty." Have students write a few paragraphs explaining how Woodrow Wilson would have responded if Hoover had made that statement in 1917. They should also indicate if they agree with Hoover or with Wilson, and why.

RESOURCE OPTIONS

Media and Technology

RESOURCE ● PRO

Literature Activity Selling the War, found on Resource Pro, uses an excerpt from the propaganda booklet *Why America Fights Germany* to show how the government galvanized popular sentiment against Germany.

American Heritage® CD-ROM

Explorer Activity 23 World War I on the Home Front, CD-ROM Guidebook, pp. 65–66, helps students create a scrapbook of an American who lived through the war.

 Color Transparencies Critical Thinking, I-15; Links Across Time, J-6

Answer to . . .

Main Idea Connections It instituted daylight savings time and gasless days to lower fuel consumption.

The National Security League, having won its battle for preparedness, began to preach "100 Percent Americanism." Early in 1917 the League got Congress to pass, over Wilson's veto, a literacy test for immigrants. This test excluded those who could not read English or some other language. As it turned out, relatively few immigrants failed the test. Still, the test set the stage for a vigorous revival of nativism.

"Hate the Hun!" Once the United States declared war, alertness for spies approached hysteria. The war also spurred a general hostility toward Germans. People began calling them Huns, in reference to an Asiatic people who brutally invaded Europe in the fourth and fifth centuries. German composers and musicians were banned from symphony concerts. German measles became "liberty measles," and a hamburger (which was named after Hamburg, a German city) became a "liberty sandwich."

Yet it was a mob of Americans who showed brutality and hatred in April 1918, when they lynched German-born citizen Robert Prager near St. Louis. Despite his German heritage,

"I am afraid we are going to have a good many instances of people roughly treated on very slight evidence of disloyalty," wrote Secretary of War Newton Baker. Indeed, as this 1917 photograph shows, anti-German feeling in the United States led to the arrest of many citizens of German descent. *Government How did government policies such as the Sedition Act contribute to nativist hatred?*

Prager had in fact tried to enlist in the navy. His lynching was but one of numerous wartime attacks on people of German descent.

Repression of Civil Liberties In his message to Congress in 1917, calling for war on Germany, Wilson had claimed that the United States would be fighting for liberty and democracy. His claim offended those who suffered from wartime restrictions on their civil liberties.

In that same war message Wilson warned that disloyalty would be "dealt with with a firm hand of stern repression." Accordingly, Congress in 1917 passed the Espionage Act, which made it illegal to interfere with the draft. The Espionage Act was amended in 1918 by the Sedition Act. (**Sedition** is speech or actions that encourage rebellion.) The Sedition Act made it illegal to obstruct the sale of Liberty Bonds or to discuss anything "disloyal, profane, scurrilous, or abusive" about the American form of government, the Constitution, or the army and navy.

The government pursued more than 1,500 prosecutions and won more than 1,000 convictions. Socialist and former presidential candidate Eugene Debs drew a ten-year jail sentence for criticizing the American government and business leaders and urging people to "resist militarism."

Controlling Political Radicals Socialists such as Debs argued that the war was merely a quarrel among imperialist capitalists. This view became a rallying point for antiwar sentiment. In the elections of 1917 in New York, Ohio, and Pennsylvania, socialists made impressive gains.

The radical labor organization Industrial Workers of the World (IWW) also gained new supporters. Its membership of western miners, migrant farm workers, and other unskilled laborers supported the IWW's goal of overthrowing capitalism.

The views of socialists and the IWW distressed moderate labor leaders like Samuel Gompers, who had pledged union cooperation with the war effort. The police hounded the IWW. Raids in September 1917 led to the conviction of nearly 200 members in trials held in Illinois, California, and Oklahoma. Groups of **vigilantes,** citizens who take the law into their own hands, lynched and horsewhipped others.

Changing People's Lives

American patriotism and war fever made military styles and activities more acceptable at home. Scouting programs for boys and girls, involving military-style uniforms, marching, and patriotic exercises, grew in popularity. Military drill became part of many school programs. By the summer of 1918, all able-bodied males in colleges and universities became army privates, subject to military discipline.

Social Mobility for Minorities and Women
Americans turned away from military styles and activities after the war. But other social changes had more lasting effects. The war cut off the flow of immigrants from Europe, and the armed forces took many young men out of the labor pool. Businesses, especially war-related industries, suddenly needed workers. These wartime conditions propelled some people into higher paid jobs. Factories that used to discriminate against African Americans and Mexican Americans now actively recruited them.

The African Americans who left the South to work in northern factories added to a steady stream of migrants that had started in the late 1800s. The stream turned into a flood during the war, when some 500,000 African Americans joined what came to be called the Great Migration.

Wage-earning women, too, benefited from the diminished work force. Some women found jobs on farms, thanks to organizations such as the Women's Land Army. Others moved into jobs previously closed to them, such as telegraph messenger, elevator operator, and letter carrier. A few earned management positions.

As a result of the war, about 400,000 women joined the industrial work force for the first time. In 1917 a speaker for the Women's Trade Union League proclaimed, "At last, after centuries of disabilities and discrimination, women are coming into the labor and festival of life on equal terms with men." Such pronouncements, while premature, celebrated what seemed like a major social change.

Prohibition Finally Passes In 1917 the temperance movement was almost a century old. In that year Congress proposed the Eighteenth Amendment to the Constitution, which made it illegal to manufacture, sell, or transport alcoholic beverages in the United States. Members of Congress backed the Eighteenth Amendment in part to show patriotism during wartime. The production of alcohol used a lot of grain, which was now needed to make the bread to feed people at home and overseas. The states ratified the Prohibition Amendment in 1919.

The IWW gained strength during World War I. It also became the target of the government's effort to control political radicals.

SECTION 4 REVIEW

Comprehension

1. *Key Terms* Define: (a) Liberty Bond; (b) price controls; (c) rationing; (d) daylight saving time; (e) sedition; (f) vigilante.

2. *Summarizing the Main Idea* What special powers did new government agencies have over industry and labor during the war?

3. *Organizing Information* Create a chart to show the steps the government took to finance the war, manage the economy, and boost Americanism.

Critical Thinking

4. *Analyzing Time Lines* Review the time line at the start of the section. Which event do you think did the most to change Americans' lives? Explain.

5. *Demonstrating Reasoned Judgment* Do you think the Sedition Act was a good way to deal with critics during wartime? Explain.

Writing Activity

6. *Writing a Persuasive Essay* Write an essay in the form of a speech for one of the "four-minute men." Before you begin, decide who your audience is and craft your speech to persuade that audience to buy war bonds.

▶ RESOURCE OPTIONS

Teaching Resources

 Quiz Unit 5–6 folder, p. 93

 Visual Learning Activity Women's Roles in World War I, Learning with Documents folder, p. 62

Student Performance Pack

Guide to the Essentials Chapter 20, Section 4 (English and Spanish)

▼ BACKGROUND

Global Connections

In 1918 a devastating, worldwide epidemic of influenza—the worst outbreak of disease since the Black Death more than 500 years earlier—left some 20 million people dead, including more than 500,000 in the United States. The epidemic killed twice as many people in one year as did all four years of World War I.

Answers to SECTION 4 REVIEW

1. (a) Liberty Bond, see p. 578; (b) price controls, see p. 579; (c) rationing, see p. 579; (d) daylight saving time, see p. 579; (e) sedition, see p. 580; (f) vigilante, see p. 580.

2. The War Industries Board distributed raw materials, regulated manufacturing, and fixed prices. The National War Labor Board mediated labor disputes. The War Labor Policies Board standardized wages, hours, and working conditions in war-related industries.

3. Charts could take the form of steps, each step containing a different government policy or action, or they could be three-column charts that list steps under the categories.

4. Sample answer: The Lever Food and Fuel Control Act dealt with products—food and fuel—that affected every American.

5. Students might consider fear of espionage; special pressures on the government; and the history of free speech in the United States.

6. Students might suggest that buying Liberty Bonds is a patriotic act.

AFRICAN AMERICANS' GREAT MIGRATION

Focus Discuss why African American poet Margaret Walker called the South the "sorrow home." Remind students that before 1914 most African Americans were share-croppers or tenant farmers, and very few lived in northern cities like Chicago, New York, and Detroit.

Instruct Divide students into groups. Ask groups to plan a mural depicting items or conditions—such as those pictured on these pages—that reflect an African American family's decision to leave their home in the rural South. Students should prepare a brief description of each panel in the mural.

Extend Ask students to investigate their own family histories and to explore the reasons why their ancestors may have migrated from one part of the country to another, or from another country to the United States.

2 Plow
Sharecropping farmers walked behind a mule-drawn plow like this one to break the land.

1 Handmade Doll
Cash-poor African Americans made or grew much of what they used in the South. This doll had its own handmade cradle and blankets.

3 Store Owner's Record Book
The store owner kept track of sharecroppers' debts and payments in a ledger like this.

4 Home Schooling
In the South, African American parents frequently served as their children's teachers.

5 Suitcase and Bibles
African American families could only bring a limited number of items with them on their journey northward.

▶ RESOURCE OPTIONS

Teaching Resources

American History Block Scheduling Support The Realities of Reconstruction *and* Ellis Island: Gateway to America, found in the Expansion, Reconstruction, Immigration folder, includes interdisciplinary lesson suggestions and activities for Geography and History, Primary Sources, Biography, and Literature.

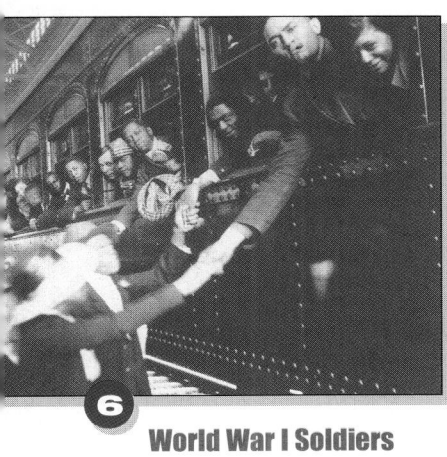

6

World War I Soldiers

Many African Americans learned about race relations in other countries when they served as soldiers during World War I. This was the first time most African Americans had traveled more than a few miles from home.

Job Opportunities **7**

Industries expanded for wartime production during World War I, and many workers were drafted into the armed forces. Thus job opportunities for African Americans rose sharply during the war.

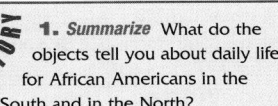

VIEWING HISTORY

1. **Summarize** What do the objects tell you about daily life for African Americans in the South and in the North?

2. **Connecting to Today** Think about the reasons people migrate today. Are they similar or different from the reasons of African Americans during the Great Migration? Report the following to your class: (a) a current example of a migration; (b) whether you think that migrating always changes life for the better.

American ARTIFACTS

FROM EXHIBITIONS AND COLLECTIONS AT THE SMITHSONIAN INSTITUTION'S NATIONAL MUSEUM OF AMERICAN HISTORY

AFRICAN AMERICANS' GREAT MIGRATION

The African American poet Margaret Walker called the South "Sorrow home." Perhaps this sentiment was shared by African Americans as they began their "Great Migration" north. Beginning in 1915, hundreds of thousands of African Americans packed up their bags, eager to take advantage of northern opportunities and leave behind the poverty and discrimination of the Jim Crow South. This move would change both the lives of the migrants and the history of race relations in the North.

Life had not been easy in the South. More than two thirds of African Americans were sharecropping farmers who paid landowners a part of their crops in exchange for rent of their land. Farming was backbreaking work for the whole family, and rarely did sharecroppers earn enough money for more than survival. Most fell deeper and deeper in debt to landlords, landowners, and store owners. See **1**, **2**, and **3**.

African Americans in the South had to rely on their own efforts to get by. Since schools for African Americans were few in number and poorly funded, many children were taught at home instead. The hope that conditions would be better in the North led many African Americans to pack their few possessions and head north. See **4** and **5**.

World War I created new opportunities. For one thing, scores of African Americans served in Europe, bringing home new ideas about race relations and civil rights. In addition, job opportunities grew in the North. African Americans streamed north to fill many of the openings. While leaving their homes would not be easy, African Americans believed a better way of life awaited them. See **6** and **7**.

VIEWING HISTORY

Answers to . . .

1. In the South, most African Americans lived in poverty as farm laborers. African American families valued education and religion. Those who moved to the North lived in cities and earned higher wages.

2. (a) Students may mention that many Americans are moving from the Northeast, Midwest, and California to states in the Sunbelt and the Pacific Northwest. Also, many Hispanics and African Americans are leaving cities for nearby suburbs. (b) Students should consider that migrants may earn more money in a new town, but must leave behind family and friends in their old communities.

RESOURCE OPTIONS

Media and Technology

 Prentice Hall United States History Video Collection™ Volume 16 *The Great War*

AmericanHeritage® CD-ROM

Time Tour Reshaping the Nation: A Diverse Nation

January 1918	January 1919	June 1919	March 1920	April 1921	July 1921
Wilson announces Fourteen Points	Paris Peace Conference opens	Versailles Treaty signed	Senate refuses to ratify Versailles Treaty	Reparations Commission announces German debt to Allies	United States declares formal end to war

1918 · 1919 · 1920 · 1921 · 1922

SECTION 5

Global Peacemaker

Objectives

You may wish to call students' attention to the objectives in the Section Preview. The objectives are reflected in the main headings of the section.

Bellringer

Ask students to explain the expression "At what cost peace?" How could this expression be applied to other wars the United States has fought?

Reading Strategy

Reinforcing Key Ideas Refer to the Reading Strategy in the Section Preview. You may wish to have students save their notes to review section content.

LESSON PLAN
Connecting to the Main Idea

1. Focus Explain that President Wilson's vision of postwar peace, summarized in his Fourteen Points, was not shared by the Allies or the United States Congress. Ask what Wilson's Fourteen Points were. What were the provisions of the Versailles Treaty?

2. Instruct Explain that Wilson made several political mistakes that cost him support for his peace plan. Ask how the loss of Republican support hurt Wilson's efforts to negotiate and fulfill his promise to "make the world safe for democracy."

Discuss why such harsh conditions were imposed on Germany. Ask students if they agree that the seeds of World War II were sown in the Versailles Treaty.

Ask why many Americans had trouble adjusting to life after the war. Why were Americans disillusioned?

3. Close Wilson's idealistic hopes for the peace settlement were dashed by the Allies and by the United States Congress. The mood of the country as it entered the 1920s was stormy and disillusioned.

---

5 Global Peacemaker

SECTION PREVIEW

Objectives

1. Describe how Wilson's vision for peace fared during the Paris Peace Conference.
2. Explain the main points of the peace treaty and describe Wilson's efforts to gain approval for the treaty.
3. Describe the difficult adjustments many Americans had to make after the war.
4. *Key Terms* Define: Fourteen Points; self-determination; spoils; League of Nations; reparations; Versailles Treaty.

Main Idea

When the fighting ended in Europe, President Wilson pressed for a treaty that would bring peace to the postwar world.

Reading Strategy

Reinforcing Key Ideas As you read, take notes on how the Versailles Treaty was created and why the United States Senate refused to ratify it.

On January 8, 1918, President Wilson stood before the Congress of the United States. The war had not ended, yet Wilson talked about peace. He hoped that the world could "be made safe for every peace-loving nation which, like our own, wishes to live its own life, determine its own institutions, be assured of justice and fair dealing by the other peoples of the world as against force and selfish aggression."

Wilson's Vision for Peace

Wilson's program for reaching these goals came to be called the **Fourteen Points,** for the number of provisions it contained. Wilson's first point called for an end to entangling alliances, a key cause of the war. He wrote:

KEY DOCUMENTS "Open covenants of peace, openly arrived at, after which there shall be no private international understandings of any kind but diplomacy shall proceed always frankly and in the public view."

—*Woodrow Wilson*

The remaining provisions of the Fourteen Points dealt with a variety of issues related to keeping the peace after the war. They included removal of trade barriers among nations and the reduction of armaments. Wilson also sought the protection of the right of Austria-Hungary's ethnic groups to **self-determination,** or the power to make decisions about one's own future.

Wilson hoped that these points would form the basis of peace negotiations. Germany assumed they would. At first, the Allies appeared to cooperate. But it soon became obvious that Wilson's colleagues did not share his idealism. After a while, the Fourteen Points began to unravel.

The Paris Peace Conference

In January 1919 an international peace conference was held in Paris. Wilson decided to head the United States delegation. With the exception of one elderly diplomat, Republican Henry White, he chose not to name any other senior Republicans to the group.

▶ RESOURCE OPTIONS

Teaching Resources

📁 **Reproducible Lesson Plan** Lesson Plans folder, p. 117

📁 **Learning Styles Lesson Plan** Learning Styles Lesson Plans folder, p. 43

📁 **Big Idea Graphic Organizer** Big Idea Graphic Organizer folder, p. 89

📁 **Guided Reading and Review** Units 5–6 folder, p. 94

📁 **Key Documents** Woodrow Wilson, The Fourteen Points, Learning with Documents folder, p. 95

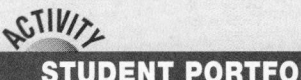

World War I Casualties

	Allies	Central Powers
Military Battle Deaths	4,889,000	3,132,000
Military Wounded	12,809,000	8,420,000
Total Casualties	17,698,000	11,552,000

Interpreting Tables The postwar years would find nations coping with the huge number of casualties. *Foreign Relations How might the casualty figures have influenced the peace plan?*

When Wilson arrived in Paris, Parisians threw flowers in his path and greeted the American President as a conquering hero. Wilson claimed that he was not interested in the **spoils,** or rewards, of war. That is, he did not expect the United States to gain any territory taken from the war's losers. His only goal was to establish a permanent agency to guarantee international stability. As Wilson had declared two years earlier, "There must be not a balance of power, but a community of power; not organized rivalries, but an organized common peace."

Wilson Forced to Compromise All would not go Wilson's way. First, the Allies were interested in spoils. In particular, they wanted to divide up Germany's colonies. The French wanted more. Determined never to be invaded again, they pressed for the total humiliation if not destruction of Germany.

Russia, although absent from the conference, was on everyone's mind. In March 1918 civil war had erupted there. British, French, and American forces had become involved in the civil war on the side of Lenin's opponents. Would Lenin's government survive? Would it present a set of war claims? As it turned out, Lenin's government held on to power, and it refused to claim any spoils of war.

Russia would, in fact, sign a Treaty of Friendship and Cooperation with Germany in 1922.

From the start of the Paris Peace Conference, Wilson was forced to compromise on the principles outlined in the Fourteen Points. He had to give up, for example, the idea of respecting the rights of native peoples in Germany's colonies. He finally agreed that the Allied powers could simply take over the colonies.

The League of Nations Wilson did, however, convince the other powers to postpone further discussion of Germany's fate and move directly to his ideas for global security. After 10 days of hard work, he produced a plan for the **League of Nations,** an organization in which the nations of the world would join together to ensure security and peace for all members. Wilson then left for home, hoping to persuade Congress and the nation to accept his plan.

For Wilson, the heart of his proposal for the League of Nations was Article 10 of the plan. This provision pledged members of the League to regard an attack on one as an attack on all. Since the League would not have any military power, the force of the article was moral only. Nevertheless, 39 Republican senators or senators-elect signed a statement rejecting it.

European Nations Created by World War I

Legend:
- New nations
- Allied-occupied zones

 MAP Skills The peace process helped lead to the transformation of the map of Europe. *Location In what ways does this map of Europe differ from the map on page 566?*

TEST PREPARATION

Have students read the quotation by Wilson on the previous page and then answer the question below.

The word *covenants* in the passage can best be defined as—

A understandings.

B secret arrangements.

C formal agreements.

D written guidelines.

Answer to . . .

Interpreting Tables The high death toll might have contributed to eagerness to end the war, calls for reparations, or calls for an end to alliances.
Map Skills It includes several new nations, such as Poland, Czechoslovakia, and Yugoslavia.

COMPARING PRIMARY SOURCES

LEAGUE OF NATIONS

The debate over joining the League of Nations often hinged on the effect that joining would have on American sovereignty or independence.

In Favor of Joining the League of Nations	Opposed to Joining the League of Nations
"The United States will, indeed, undertake . . . to 'respect and preserve as against external aggression the territorial integrity and existing political independence of all members of the League,' and that engagement constitutes a very grave and solemn moral obligation. But it is a moral, not a legal, obligation, and leaves our Congress absolutely free to put its own interpretation upon it." —President Woodrow Wilson, testifying before the Foreign Relations Committee, August 19, 1919	"Shall we go there, Mr. President, to sit in judgment, and in case that judgment works for peace join with our allies, but in case it works for war withdraw our cooperation? How long would we stand as we now stand, a great Republic commanding the respect and holding the leadership of the world, if we should adopt any such course?" —Senator William Borah (Idaho), testifying in the Senate, November 19, 1919

ANALYZING VIEWPOINTS On what basis does each speaker support or oppose American entry into the League?

The Peace Treaty

In March 1919 Wilson returned to the peace conference. The Big Four—Britain, France, Italy, and the United States—dominated the proceedings. Though the Allies accepted Wilson's plan for the League of Nations, opposition to the League from Congress and many Americans had weakened Wilson's position at the conference.

French premier Georges Clemenceau took advantage of that weakness to demand harsh penalties against Germany. Wilson feared that these demands would lead to future wars, but he could not get Clemenceau to budge.

Wilson also had to compromise elsewhere. Self-determination for the peoples of Austria-Hungary proved hard to apply. As the map on the previous page shows, the conference created the new nations of Czechoslovakia and Yugoslavia. Their borders were drawn with the ethnic populations of the region in mind. But these arrangements failed even then to resolve all ethnic tensions.[†]

Wilson had more luck opposing the demands of Vittorio Orlando, Italy's prime minister. Italy claimed several pieces of territory formerly controlled by Austria-Hungary. Wilson and the other Allied leaders refused to support Italy's claims. Because of his failure at the peace conference, Orlando had to resign as prime minister.

War Guilt and Reparations Wilson met his greatest defeat when he gave in to French insistence on German war guilt and financial responsibility. The French wanted to cripple Germany. The demands of the British, led by David Lloyd George, supported the French goal. They insisted on billing Germany for **reparations,** or payment from an enemy for economic injury suffered during a war. In 1921 a Reparations Commission ruled that Germany owed the Allies $33 billion, an amount far beyond its ability to pay. As Wilson had feared, Germany never forgot or forgave this humiliation.

Signing the Treaty The Allies presented the treaty to the Germans on May 7, 1919. Insisting that the treaty violated the Fourteen Points, the Germans at first refused to sign it. They soon gave in, however, when threatened with a French invasion. On June 28 the great powers signed the treaty at Versailles, the former home of French kings, outside of Paris. Thus, the treaty is known as the **Versailles Treaty.**

Seeking Approval at Home

On July 8, treaty in hand, Wilson returned home to great acclaim. But many legislators had doubts. Some senators opposed the treaty because it included American commitment to the League of Nations. These senators were called the "irreconcilables," because they could not be reconciled to, or made to accept, the treaty. Irreconcilables argued that joining the League would weaken American independence.

Senator Henry Cabot Lodge, chair of the Foreign Relations Committee, led another group called the "reservationists." This group wanted to impose reservations, or restrictions,

They feared that the article could be used to drag the United States into unpopular foreign wars.

Main Idea CONNECTIONS

What factors forced Wilson to compromise on his plans at the Paris Peace Conference?

---
† In the early 1990s these same ethnic tensions would contribute to the breakup of the two nations.

RESOURCE OPTIONS

Teaching Resources

📁 **Comparing Primary Sources** On the League of Nations, Units 5–6 folder, pp. 97–98

Media and Technology

🦅 **AmericanHeritage® CD-ROM**

Presidents Woodrow Wilson

on American participation in the League. In particular they wanted a guarantee that the Monroe Doctrine would remain in force. Wilson's point that compliance with League decisions was "binding in conscience only, not in law," failed to persuade them.

Wilson Tours the Country Determined to win grass roots support for the League, Wilson took to the road in September. In 23 days he delivered three dozen speeches. After this tremendous effort, he suffered a stroke that paralyzed one side of his body. He would remain an invalid, isolated from his Cabinet and visitors, for the rest of his term.

During his illness, Wilson grew increasingly inflexible. Congress would have to accept the treaty and the League as he envisioned it, or not at all. In November 1919 the Senate voted on the treaty with Lodge's reservations included. The vote was 39 for, 55 against. When the treaty came up without the reservations, it went down again, 38 to 53. In the face of popular dismay at this outcome, the Senate reconsidered the treaty in March 1920, but once again the treaty failed to win approval.

A Formal End to Hostilities On May 20, 1920, Congress voted to declare the war officially over. Steadfast to his principles, Wilson vetoed it. Finally, on July 2, 1921, another joint resolution to end the war passed. By that time a new President, Warren G. Harding, was in office, and he signed it. Congress ratified separate peace treaties with Germany, Austria, and Hungary that October.

Difficult Postwar Adjustments

The war spurred the United States economy, giving a big boost to American businesses. The United States was now the world's largest creditor nation. In 1922 a Senate debt commission calculated that European countries owed the United States $11.5 billion.

The return to peace caused problems for the country at large, however. By April 1919 about 4,000 servicemen a day were being mustered out of the armed forces. But nobody had devised a plan to help returning troops merge back into society. The federal agencies that controlled the economy during the war had abruptly canceled war contracts. As a result, jobs proved scarce.

The women who had taken men's places in factories and offices also faced readjustment. Late in 1918, Mary Van Kleeck, head of the Women in Industry Service, reported that "the question heard most frequently was whether women would now retire from industry." Many women did, either voluntarily or because they were fired.

Postwar Gloom Many artists and intellectuals in the United States entered the postwar years with a sense of gloom or disillusionment. They expressed their feelings in books, paintings, and other artistic works. Social reformers experienced similar emotions. They had been encouraged by the government-business collaboration during the war. For most of them, the end of the war marked the end of an era of optimism.

CAUSE AND EFFECT: World War I

CAUSES
- *Imperialism leads to international rivalries, particularly within Europe.*
- *Nationalism between and within countries intensifies.*
- *Military buildup in Europe intensifies.*
- *Europe develops a complicated system of alliances.*
- *Archduke Francis Ferdinand of Austria-Hungary is assassinated.*
- *Austria-Hungary declares war on Serbia.*

WORLD WAR I

EFFECTS
- *Map of Europe is redrawn.*
- *League of Nations is formed.*
- *United States economy is boosted.*
- *United States suffers post-war disillusionment.*

 Interpreting Charts The assassination of Francis Ferdinand was the spark that ignited the powder keg of imperialism, nationalism, and alliances that began a world war. **Foreign Relations** *Why was Congress opposed to the League of Nations?*

ACTIVITY
HETEROGENEOUS GROUPS

Ask students to prepare arguments for or against United States membership in the League of Nations. Ask for pairs of volunteers to present their arguments at three-minute intervals. Ask one or two students to summarize the arguments on the chalkboard. *(Enrichment)*

Answer to . . .

Interpreting Charts It seemed a repeat of the alliances that drew the world into war and a threat to American independence.

Answers to

SECTION 5 REVIEW

1. (a) Fourteen Points, see p. 584; (b) self-determination, see p. 584; (c) spoils, see p. 585; (d) League of Nations, see p. 585; (e) reparations, see p. 586; (f) Versailles Treaty, see p. 586.

2. Wilson's ideas had little impact on the final treaty, except for the founding of the League of Nations.

3. The center circle might be labeled Postwar Peace. Other circles might include the Fourteen Points, with its failures and successes; the Treaty of Versailles, with its main points; and the stance taken by the United States Senate on ratification.

4. Sample answer: "Senate refuses to ratify Versailles Treaty." After failing to sway the Allies with his Fourteen Points, Wilson could not even get his own nation's Senate to approve the peace treaty.

5. Sample answer: The Fourteen Points did not serve the ends of the other Allies, especially France and Britain; they wanted to cripple Germany by taking its territory and by collecting reparations.

6. Essays should use comparison to persuade readers of their point.

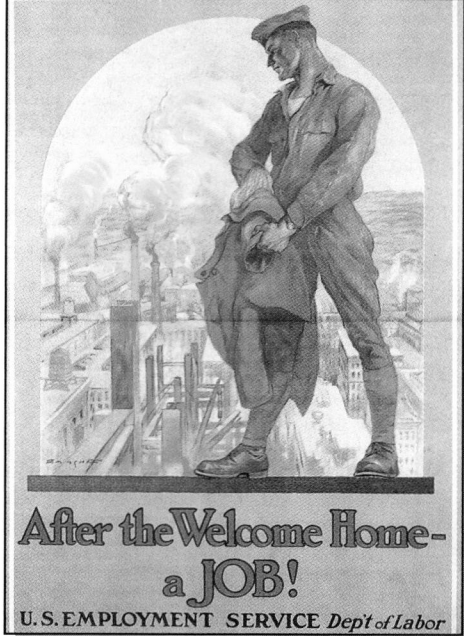

After the Welcome Home—
a JOB!

U.S. EMPLOYMENT SERVICE *Dep't of Labor*

A federal employment service kept jobs filled during the war. After the war, it had to cope with thousands of returning soldiers. *Economics* **Why were jobs scarce?**

Others felt the postwar gloom as well. The enthusiasm that had greeted the start of the Great War had faded by war's end. The realities of trench warfare, death, and destruction hit many people very hard. Alice Lord O'Brian, a military post exchange director from Buffalo who was twice decorated, expressed the views of many who were directly involved in the war. She stated:

AMERICAN VOICES ❝We all started out with high ideals. . . . [A]fter being right up here almost at the front line . . . I cannot understand what it is all about or what has been accomplished by all this waste of youth.❞

—*Alice Lord O'Brian*

African American Troops at Home Like white troops, black soldiers came home to a hero's welcome. When they went to find jobs, however, the reception was different.

W.E.B. Du Bois, editor of the NAACP's magazine, the *Crisis,* had supported the war. In July 1918 he had written, "Let us, while this war lasts, forget our special grievances and close our ranks . . . with our white citizens and the allied nations that are fighting for democracy." A year later, after more lynchings of African Americans, including some still in uniform, his message became defiant. "This country of ours, despite all its better souls have done and dreamed, is yet a shameful land," he wrote in May 1919. "It lynches. . . . It steals from us. . . . It insults us. . . . We return. We return from fighting. We return fighting."

Du Bois's views heralded a new era in the struggle for equality. The entire nation was on the threshold of a stormy era—the 1920s.

SECTION 5 REVIEW

Comprehension

1. *Key Terms* Define: (a) Fourteen Points; (b) self-determination; (c) spoils; (d) League of Nations; (e) reparations; (f) Versailles Treaty.

2. *Summarizing the Main Idea* What kind of impact did President Wilson's ideas make at the Paris Peace Conference?

3. *Organizing Information* Create a web diagram to organize information about the peace-making efforts after World War I.

Critical Thinking

4. *Analyzing Time Lines* Review the time line at the start of the section. Which event best summarizes the results of Wilson's peace efforts? Explain.

5. *Drawing Inferences* Why did the Fourteen Points fail as a basis of peace negotiations?

Writing Activity

6. *Writing a Persuasive Essay* Write an essay about the treatment of African Americans after the war. Compare the way black soldiers should have been treated with the way they were treated. Persuade your readers that despite the mistreatment, the struggle for equality will continue.

Answer to . . .

Viewing History War contracts with businesses had been canceled, limiting jobs.

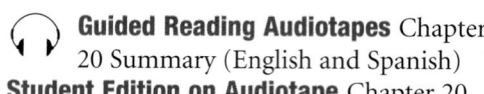

▶ RESOURCE OPTIONS

Teaching Resources

📁 **Quiz** Unit 5–6 folder, p. 95

📁 **Chapter Tests Forms A and B** Chapter Test folder

Student Performance Pack

 Guide to the Essentials Chapter 20, Section 5 (English and Spanish)

Standardized Test Preparation Handbook

Media and Technology

🎧 **Guided Reading Audiotapes** Chapter 20 Summary (English and Spanish)
Student Edition on Audiotape Chapter 20

 Test Bank CD-ROM; Interactive Student Tutorial CD-ROM Chapter Test

Modern Warfare Poses Grave Dangers

The horrors of modern warfare unleashed by World War I remain a threat to peoples around the world. Today's dangers include chemical and biological weapons.

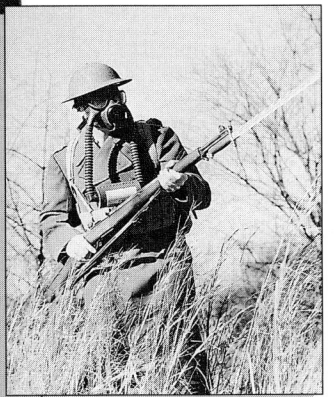

World War I soldier with protective gas mask

The weapons of World War I, such as the machine gun and chemical weapons, turned the battlefields of Europe into vast killing grounds. World War I also blurred the distinction between soldier and civilian, as troops razed enemy towns, burned fields, and poisoned water supplies. Since World War I, nations have invented even more lethal weapons, increasing the potential for destruction and the risk to civilians — even those living far from the battlefield.

The Impact Today

About 90,000 of the more than 8 million soldiers who died in World War I were poisoned or asphyxiated by chemical weapons, such as chlorine gas and mustard gas. Thousands more suffered lasting injuries. The impact of chemical weapons was so horrifying that, in the Geneva Protocol of 1925, nations outlawed the use of chemical and biological weapons in war.

Since the Geneva Protocol a number of nations have stockpiled chemical and biological weapons that could be used in war. During the Iran-Iraq War in the 1980s, Iraq unleashed chem-ical weapons on Iranian soldiers and Kurdish civilians. Thousands were killed or wounded.

Many nations have signed treaties to stop the proliferation, or spread, of chemical and biological weapons. For example, the 1972 Biological Weapons Convention prohibits the development and use of biological weapons. In addition, the 1997 Chemical Weapons Convention bans the production, stockpiling, transfer and use of chemical weapons.

Despite international efforts, chemical and biological weapons continue to pose a worldwide threat. In 1995, a radical Japanese group released sarin gas in the Tokyo subway system, killing several people and injuring thousands. The incident served as a warning that lethal agents of modern warfare can be deployed by terrorists against unsuspecting civilian populations.

The Impact on You

Look for newspaper or magazine articles about international efforts to limit nuclear, chemical, or biological weapons. Write a one-page "policy paper" in which you summarize these efforts and present your own ideas about how nations should work together to reduce the risk that these weapons will be used.

Civil defense training for Israeli children

Class Discussion

Discuss with the class ways of controlling chemical and biological weapons. For a more thorough examination of the issue, see the activity folder in the Resource Options below.

ACTIVITY STUDENT PARTICIPATION

Creating a Mural

Ask students to read the text. Then divide the class into small groups. Have the groups discuss ideas for a mural on the risks and dangers of modern warfare. They could consider the following questions:

- **What statement would you like to make?**
- **What images come to mind when you think of these dangers?**
- **How might you turn the images into a mural?**

Have the groups share their ideas. Then take a class vote on the best ones.

Follow up Organize and carry out one or more of the best mural ideas.

Using the Internet

Students can learn more about modern warfare by exploring links in the *America: Pathways to the Present* Web site at:

http://www.Pathways.phschool.com

Assessment

See the Lesson Plans folder, pp. 24–27, for rubrics on assessing Class Participation Projects.

RESOURCE OPTIONS

Teaching Resources

📁 **Why Study History? Activity** Modern Warfare Poses Grave Dangers, found in the Why Study History? folder, p. 21, provides an activity to help students better understand modern warfare.

Media and Technology

🔘📼 **Prentice Hall United States History Video Collection™** Volume 16 *The Great War*

🔘📼 **Decision America Videotapes and Videodiscs** Issue 6 *A New Role for the Military?*

Key Terms

Students should refer to the definitions of key terms in the chapter to write sentences that show an understanding of the World War I era.

Comprehension

1. Imperialism, militarism, nationalism, and alliances were the deeper causes. The triggering cause was the assassination of Archduke Francis Ferdinand.

2. Most Americans favored the Allies. President Wilson decided on a position of neutrality. Both the preparedness movement, which urged the United States to get ready for war, and the peace movement began promoting their views.

3. The triggering cause was the continued sinking of neutral ships, which harmed American commercial interests. Other causes included the Zimmermann note, the Russian Revolution, and an anti-German bias among Americans.

4. Machine guns, hand grenades, long-range artillery, poison gases, tanks, the convoy system, and the use of airplanes as fighters and bombers.

5. They stopped the German attack toward Paris and then led a counterattack that helped bring about the end of the war.

6. To be sure that the United States would produce enough for the war effort, the government established new federal agencies to oversee industry and labor, as well as food consumption.

7. There was widespread popular support for the treaty, but many senators opposed membership in the League.

Chapter Summary

The major concepts of Chapter 20 are presented below. See also *Guide to the Essentials of American History* or *Interactive Student Tutorial CD-ROM,* which contains interactive review activities, time lines, helpful hints, and test practice for Chapter 20.

Reviewing the Main Ideas

World War I began in 1914 as a European war. The United States remained neutral. After German submarine warfare drew the Americans into the war in 1917, United States troops, supplies, and loans helped the Allies defeat the Central Powers. President Wilson hoped to devise a peace treaty that would eliminate the main causes of war.

Section 1: The Road to War

As World War I began and then expanded to much of Europe, the United States remained neutral.

Section 2: The United States Declares War

German submarine warfare helped push the United States into World War I.

Section 3: Americans on the European Front

American troops helped the Allies defeat the Central Powers in World War I.

Section 4: On the Home Front

Americans and their government took extraordinary steps at home to support the war effort.

Section 5: Global Peacemaker

When the fighting ended in Europe, President Wilson pressed for a treaty that would bring peace to the postwar world.

The horrors of modern warfare unleashed by World War I continue to haunt the world. Despite efforts by the international community to stop the use of chemical and biological weapons, they pose a worldwide threat.

Key Terms

For each of the terms below, write a sentence explaining how it relates to the chapter.

1. Liberty Bond
2. Allies
3. convoy
4. American Expeditionary Force
5. militarism
6. Versailles Treaty
7. Zimmermann note
8. U-boat
9. armistice
10. sedition
11. Central Powers
12. League of Nations
13. Fourteen Points
14. stalemate

Comprehension

1. What were the main causes of World War I?
2. What were the reactions in the United States to the outbreak of the war in Europe?
3. Why did the United States declare war on Germany?
4. Name some of the military innovations introduced during World War I.
5. How did American troops help turn the tide of the war on the battlefield?
6. Why and how did the government try to control the economy at home?
7. What was the American reaction to the Versailles Treaty and to the League of Nations?

Using Graphic Organizers

On a separate sheet of paper, copy the cause-and-effect flowchart to organize the main ideas of the chapter. Fill in each box with the appropriate effect. Remember that effects sometimes also become causes.

Using Graphic Organizers

Sample flow chart: Archduke Francis Ferdinand assassinated; European alliances draw Great Powers into War; German U-boats launch attacks on Allied and neutral shipping; United States enters War; American troops help turn the tide of war; Allies win the war; Versailles Treaty favors Allies.

Analyzing Political Cartoons ▶

1. Analyze the images in this 1919 cartoon. (a) Who is the man? (b) What does the little boy represent? (c) How do you know?

2. Who does the man in the cartoon want the "child" to play with?

3. Why does the "child" want to "play by himself"?

4. Explain the meaning of the cartoon.

Critical Thinking

1. *Applying the Chapter Skill* The United States chose to go to war with Germany in 1917 largely because of continued German submarine attacks on neutral shipping. Identify alternative solutions to this problem of U-boat attacks. Discuss your alternative in a written proposal to President Wilson.

2. *Predicting Consequences* What might have happened on the European front if General Pershing had decided to mix the American troops in with the Allied armies instead of keeping them independent?

3. *Demonstrating Reasoned Judgment* Do you think women played a key role in World War I? Why or why not?

4. *Expressing Problems Clearly* It is often said that Woodrow Wilson won World War I but then "lost the peace." Explain your understanding of this statement.

TEMPLE·OF·PEACE

THE CHILD WHO WANTED TO PLAY BY HIMSELF.
President Wilson: *"Now come along and enjoy yourself with the other nice children. I promised that you'd be the life and soul of the party."*

INTERNET ACTIVITY

For your portfolio:
CREATE A GRAPH

Access Prentice Hall's *America: Pathways to the Present* site at **www.Pathways.phschool.com** for the specific URL to complete the activity. Additional resources and related Web sites are also available.

Use the statistics provided at the site to create a bar graph of the financial costs of World War I.

ANALYZING DOCUMENTS ◀▶ *INTERPRETING DATA*

Turn to the Exploring Technology diagram of a tank on page 577.

1. Tank crews felt secure against rifle fire because of the tank's (a) pressed-steel track plate. (b) armor plating. (c) commander. (d) 105-horsepower, six-cylinder engine.

2. The tank was able to cross battle-field trenches and barbed wire because of its (a) pressed-steel track plate. (b) armor plating. (c) 57-mm pedestal-mounted guns. (d) Lewis machine guns.

3. *Writing* Imagine that you were part of a tank crew at the front during World War I. Write a letter to your family describing your tank and what warfare is like from the inside of a tank.

Connecting to Today

Essay Writing Compare the ability of the United States to be a peace-maker today with its ability after the war. What characteristics does it take for a country to serve as a peacemaker? Does the United States have those characteristics today? Did it have them in Wilson's time?

INTERNET ACTIVITY

Graphs should include all the nations that participated in World War I.

Analyzing Political Cartoons
1. (a) President Wilson. (b) The United States. (c) "U.S.A." is printed on his hat.
2. He wants him to play with other children in the "Temple of Peace." In other words, Wilson wants the U.S. to join the League of Nations.
3. Congress was reluctant to involve the nation in alliances that could pull it into future international disputes.
4. Wilson looks foolish to the world because he cannot get his nation to agree to an organization he proposed.

Critical Thinking
1. Alternatives may include negotiation with the Germans, restricting American shipping, developing a convoy system, or suffering the attacks without retaliation.
2. The American troops might have adopted the Europeans' defensive posture; the Americans might not have taken the offensive against the Germans in Paris; Paris might have fallen; the war might have been lost.
3. Yes; they moved into important jobs, helped Food Administration programs succeed, served in the American Expeditionary Force at home and at the front.
4. Sample answer: Wilson had directed the United States's victorious effort in the war, yet he was unable to influence the Allies in the peace settlement.

Interpreting Data
1. b
2. a
3. Letters should include a description of the tank, using labels from the diagram. They should also include a more personal description of the experience of warfare.

Connecting to Today
Essays might focus on characteristics such as power and influence, and on the role of military might and democratic values.

My Brush with History

American Heritage®

My Brush with History

BY A WORLD WAR I PILOT

INTRODUCTION The psychological stresses of modern warfare were felt not only by soldiers in the trenches but also by those who fought in the skies overhead. The passage below, selected by the editors of *American Heritage* magazine, is from the diary of an unknown pilot in World War I.

We've lost a lot of good men. It's only a question of time until we all get it. I'm all shot to pieces. I only hope I can stick it. I don't want to quit. My nerves are all gone and I can't stop. I've lived beyond my time already.

It's not the fear of death that's done it. I'm still not afraid to die. It's this eternal flinching from it that's doing it and has made a coward out of me. Few men live to know what real fear is. It's something that grows on you, day by day, that eats into your constitution and undermines your sanity. I have never been serious about anything in my life and now I know that I'll never be otherwise again. But my seriousness will be a burlesque for no one will recognize it.

Here I am, twenty-four years old, I look forty and I feel ninety. I've lost all interest in life beyond the next patrol. No one Hun will ever get me and I'll never fall into a trap, but sooner or later I'll be forced to fight against odds that are too long or perhaps a stray shot from the ground will be lucky and I will have gone in vain. Or my motor will cut out when we are trench strafing or a wing will pull off in a dive. Oh, for a parachute! The Huns are using them now. I haven't a chance, I know, and it's this eternal waiting around that's killing me. I've even lost my taste for liquor. It doesn't seem to do me any good now. I guess I'm stale. Last week I actually got frightened in the air and lost my head. Then I found ten Huns and took them all on and I got one of them down out of control. I got my nerve back by that time

Since few pilots had parachutes, aerial "dogfights" in World War I were often fatal to the loser.

TEST PREPARATION

Have students use the excerpt on these pages to answer the following question.

Which sentence best describes the pilot's feelings about the war?
A The war is honorable.
B The war is unwinnable.
C The war is manly.
D The war is futile.

and came back home and slept like a baby for the first time in two months. What a blessing sleep is! I know now why men go out and take such long chances and pull off such wild stunts. No discipline in the world could make them do what they do of their own accord. I know now what a brave man is. I know now how men laugh at death and welcome it. I know now why Ball went over and sat above a Hun airdrome and dared them to come up and fight with him. It takes a brave man to even experience real fear. A coward couldn't last long enough at the job to get to that stage. What price salvation now?

War is a horrible thing, a grotesque comedy. And it is so useless. This war won't prove anything. All we'll do when we win is to substitute one sort of Dictator for another. In the meantime we have destroyed our best resources. Human life, the most precious thing in the world, has become the cheapest. After we've won this war by drowning the Hun in our own blood, in five years' time the sentimental fools at home will be taking up a collection for these same Huns that are killing us now and our fool politicians will be cooking up another good war. Why shouldn't they? They have to keep the public stirred up to keep their jobs and they don't have to fight and they can get soft berths for their sons and their friends' sons. To me the most contemptible cur in the world is the man who lets political influence be used to keep him away from the front. For he lets another man die in his place.

The worst thing about this war is that it takes the best. If it lasts long enough the world will be populated by cowards and weaklings and their children. And the whole thing is so useless, so unnecessary, so terrible! . . .

The devastation of the country is too horrible to describe. It looks from the air as if the gods had made a gigantic steam roller, forty miles wide and run it from the coast to Switzerland, leaving its spike holes behind as it went. . . .

I've lost over a hundred friends, so they tell me—I've seen only seven or eight killed—but to me they aren't dead yet. They are just around the corner, I think, and I'm still expecting to run into them any time. I dream about them at night when I do sleep a little and sometimes I dream that some one is killed who really isn't. Then I don't know who is and who isn't. I saw a man in Boulogne the other day that I had dreamed I saw killed and I thought I was seeing a ghost. I can't realize that any of them are gone. Surely human life is not a candle to be snuffed out. . . .

ADDITIONAL READING

To learn more about the topics discussed in this selection, you might want to read the following books:

- *The Canvas Falcons: The Men and the Planes of World War I,* by Stephen Longstreet (New York: Barnes & Noble Books, 1995)
- *The First World War: A Complete History,* by Martin Gilbert (New York: Henry Holt, 1994)
- *The Last Days of Innocence: America at War, 1917–1918,* by Meirion and Susie Harries (New York: Random House, 1997)
- *The Penguin Book of First World War Poetry,* edited by Jon Silkin (New York: Penguin Books, 1981)

More than 8 million soldiers died in World War I, making it the costliest war in history to that time.

Source: *Anonymous, War Birds: Diary of an Unknown Aviator,* Doran, 1926.

∽ *WWI Cemetery* ∽

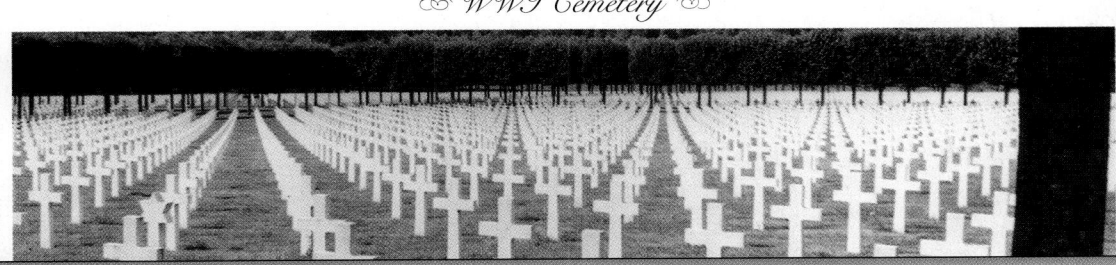

TEST PREPARATION

Have students use the excerpt on these pages to answer the following question.

Based on the passage, you can tell that—

Ⓐ The pilot's mental and emotional health are very frail.

B The pilot is mourning the loss of things that he may never experience, such as getting married and having children.

C The pilot is angry with himself for not using his family connections to stay out of the war.

D The pilot has post-traumatic stress syndrome.

Boom Times to Hard Times 1919–1938

Introducing the Unit

Using Historical Evidence

In March 1936, Dorothea Lange (1895–1965), working for the Farm Security Administration, a New Deal agency, photographed the migrant farm family seen on the right. Lange commented, "I saw and approached the hungry and desperate mother as if drawn by a magnet."

Ask students how wives and children suffered from the effects of unemployment. Students may compare Lange's photograph to images of victims of poverty, war, and natural disasters appearing today in newspapers and newsmagazines. What gave Lange's work such impact?

Themes in American History

Direct students' attention to the Unit Themes. Point out that each chapter in this unit has its own theme. To teach this unit thematically, you may wish to use the Extended Unit Lesson Plan for the Great Depression, p. 16, in the To the Teacher folder in **American History Block Scheduling Support.**

Using the Time Line

To provide students with practice in using a time line to connect key events in the United States with key events in the world, ask questions such as these: (1) Name a legislative accomplishment of Roosevelt's first term. *(Social Security Act passed.)* (2) What major setback in race relations occurred in Africa? *(The term* apartheid *was introduced in South Africa.)* (3) Who was President when Japan invaded the Chinese province of Manchuria? *(Hoover)*

---

unit SEVEN

Boom Times to Hard Times

1 9 1 9 – 1 9 3 8

Optimism and faith in business and technology characterized the United States in the 1920s. That faith was shattered with the stock market crash of October 1929. The fragile prosperity of the decade quickly gave way to a period of severe economic distress known as the Great Depression. In the election of 1932, voters chose Franklin Delano Roosevelt as the President to lead them out of hard times.

Chapter 21	The Twenties	*1920–1929*
Chapter 22	Crash and Depression	*1929–1933*
Chapter 23	The New Deal	*1933–1938*

UNIT THEMES

Culture The nation underwent a change in manners and morals during the 1920s.

Economics The stock market crash of 1929 resulted in a worldwide economic depression.

Government FDR's New Deal forged a new link between the government and the economy.

EVENTS IN THE UNITED STATES

1919
• Red scare
• Palmer raids

1924
Teapot Dome scandal

1927
Sacco and Vanzetti executed

1929
Stock market crashes

Presidents	Wilson	Harding	Coolidge

1915 — **1920** — **1925**

EVENTS IN THE WORLD

1920
Adolf Hitler helps form Nazi party in Germany

1923
Hitler fails in attempted coup

1929
The term apartheid is introduced in South Africa

 RESOURCE OPTIONS

Teaching Resources

Units 7–8 folder Contains instructional materials organized by chapter.

VIEWING HISTORY During the Great Depression, poverty and suffering were constant traveling companions to families like the one above, who were forced to move from town to town in search of work. *Culture How did the Great Depression change both the government and society?*

FDR campaign button

1931
Scottsboro Boys convicted

1932
Turning Point: The Election of 1932 (p. 653)

1933
Prohibition repealed

1935
Social Security Act passed

1939
Supreme Court outlaws sit-down strike

Hoover | F. D. Roosevelt

1930 | **1935** | **1940**

1931
Japanese troops occupy Manchuria

1933
Hitler and the Nazis take over Germany

1935
Italy invades Ethiopia

1937
Japan launches a full-scale war against China

Kick out DEPRESSION WITH A DEMOCRATIC VOTE

RESOURCE OPTIONS

Media and Technology

Color Transparencies Specific transparencies are referenced at points of use. See American Photo, B-7; Fine Art, D-8; Cause and Effect, F-9; The Way It Works, H-18; Links Across Time, J-7; and Political Cartoons, K-7.

Visions of America "Scenes of an Era: Boom Times to Hard Times" located on videodisc side 3 and on videotape 4. Lesson plans for "Scenes of an Era" can be found in the Visions of America Guidebook.

Side 3, Chapter 24

Answer to . . .

Viewing History Families broke down as people lost jobs and homes. The government's role in the economy grew.

The Twenties, 1920–1929

Managing Time and Instruction

INSTRUCTION SUPPORT

These materials for instruction are provided for **each section** in the **Teaching Resources**. See **Units 7–8 folder** for Enrichment Support:

- Reproducible Lesson Plans in Lesson Plans folder • Learning Styles Lesson Plans in Learning Styles Lesson Plans folder • Big Idea Graphic Organizers in Big Idea Graphic Organizer folder
- Guided Reading and Review • Quizzes • Test Preparation Practice booklet

DAILY LESSON	ENRICHMENT SUPPORT
1 A Republican Decade (pp. 597–602)	• Decision-Making Activity, Lobbying for Indian Immigration, Decision-Making Activities folder, pp. 18–19
2 A Business Boom (pp. 603–607)	• Visual Learning Activity, Advertising Techniques of the 1920s, Learning with Documents folder, p. 63 • Nystrom *Atlas of Our Country,* The Third Wave of Immigration, pp. 30–31 • Skills for Life Activity, Units 7–8 folder, p. 17
3 Society in the 1920s (pp. 609–613)	• Primary Source Activity, Teens and Cigarette Smoking, Learning with Documents folder, p. 27 • Primary Source Activity, Growing Up Black, found on **Resource Pro** • Biography, Lillian Moller Gilbreth, Units 7–8 folder, p. 13
4 Mass Media and the Jazz Age (pp. 614–619)	• Critical Thinking Activity, Testing Conclusions: The Jazz Age, found on **Resource Pro** • Literature Activity, Tales of the Jazz Age, found on **Resource Pro** • Literature Activity, The Weary Blues, Units 7–8 folder, p. 16 • Biography, Bessie Smith, found on **Resource Pro**
5 Cultural Conflicts (pp. 622–626)	• Comparing Primary Sources, On the Eighteenth Amendment, Units 7–8 folder, pp. 14–15 • Visual Learning Activity, The Ku Klux Klan, found on **Resource Pro** • The Generation Gap Is Not New, Why Study History? folder, p. 22

Running Out of Time?

- Use Tape 4, "Boom Times to Hard Times, 1919–1929," from **Visions of America** videotapes series.
- Use Chapter 21 Summary from **Guide to the Essentials of American History (English and Spanish).**

Companion Web Site

The companion Web site offers online links for all chapter review activities. It also provides key content links and structured support for this chapter for both teachers and students.

http://www.Pathways.phschool.com

Teaching in the Information Age

Media and Technology

For the Student

Interactive Student Tutorial CD-ROM Chapter 21

Student Edition on Audiotape Chapter 21

American Heritage® CD-ROM

Guided Reading Audiotapes (English and Spanish) Chapter 21

For the Teacher

Resource Pro CD-ROM Chapter 21

Test Bank CD-ROM Chapter 21

Listening to Music CD "Take the A Train" by Duke Ellington

Listening to Literature Audiotapes *Timeless Voices, Timeless Themes* "The Far and the Near" by Thomas Wolfe

Color Transparencies Our Multicultural Heritage, C-12; Fine Art, D-18, D-19

Assessment Options

Chapter Test Forms A&B Test Bank CD-ROM booklet

Test Bank CD-ROM Chapter 21

Standardized Test Preparation Handbook

Block Scheduling

Pacing Suggestions

For 90-minute Blocks

- Teach sections 1 and 2 using Transparencies E-6 and H-18 and the Global Connections note on p. 604 for class discussions.

- Teach sections 3, 4, and 5 using the Big Idea Graphic Organizers from Teaching Resources and the Extended Class Periods Activity on p. 615.

Additional Resources

- Prentice Hall's **American History Block Scheduling Support File** covers over 40 major topics in American history. Included are lesson plans, strategies, primary sources, literature, biographies, Great Debates, art history, simulations, and songs.

- **Prentice Hall United States History Video Collection**™ contains 20 videotapes covering American history from beginnings to present.

Connections to American Literature

from Prentice Hall

Prentice Hall Literature *Timeless Voices, Timeless Themes* "Dust Tracks on a Road" by Zora Neale Hurston, p. 830

Additional Resources

For the Student

Deborah Willis-Braithwaite. *Van Der Zee.* Harry N. Abrams, 1993.

For the Teacher

Sarah Louise and Annie Elizabeth Delany. *Having Our Say: The Delany Sisters' First 100 Years.* Kodansha, 1993.

Nicholas Lemann. *The Promised Land, The Great Black Migration and How It Changed America.* Alfred A. Knopf, Inc., 1991.

Prentice Hall brings into the classroom the vast archives and scholarship of the nation's premier American history magazine. See "From the Archives of American Heritage®" and "About the Presidents" teaching notes in this chapter.

History Alive!

Teacher's Curriculum Institute, in partnership with Prentice Hall, provides unique materials that engage students with diverse learning styles. See History Alive!® unit on The Roaring Twenties and the Great Depression.

Student Performance Pack

Ensures success in the three critical areas of Reading, Test Taking, and English Language Development with the following materials:
- Guide to the Essentials of American History in English and Spanish
- Guided Reading Audiotapes in English and Spanish
- Interactive Student Tutorial CD-ROM
- Test Preparation Handbook
- Test Preparation Practice booklet

The Twenties
1920–1929

Introducing the Chapter
American society changed in many ways following World War I. as the Jazz Age introduced a variety of new styles, tastes, and manners. Conflict arose between Americans ready to adopt these new manners and new ways and Americans who tried to resist the forces of change.

Themes in American History
The theme for this chapter, Culture, is listed at the beginning of this unit. An alternate theme for the chapter is Diversity. To teach this unit thematically, you may wish to use the Prosperity, Depression, and War folder in American History Block Scheduling Support.

Why Study History?

Have students explore suggested ways of connecting the past to the present on page 627.

Have students explore suggested ways of connecting the past to the present on page 627.

CHAPTER 21 The Twenties
1920-1929

CHAPTER FOCUS

This chapter explores the decade of the 1920s. More than just a time between two world wars, the 1920s literally set in motion much of modern America. Cars hit the roads. Business boomed. Radios crackled. Hemlines moved up. The nation moved to the new sound of jazz, while the tiny town of Hollywood gave the world motion pictures.

The Why Study History? page at the end of this chapter explores the connection between generational differences of the 1920s and those of today.

▲ **VIEWING HISTORY**
Sixth Avenue Elevated at Third Street, 1928, by John Sloan, captures the high spirits of the 1920s. *Culture* **How does this painting show changing social morals?**

 RESOURCE OPTIONS

Teaching Resources

📁 **Big Idea Graphic Organizer** folder
Graphic summary of the main idea of the chapter.

📁 **Learning Styles Lesson Plans** folder
Alternate lesson plans for diverse learning styles for each chapter.

Media and Technology

 AmericanHeritage® **CD-ROM**
Time Tour Prosperity, Depression, and War: The Jazz Age

🔘 **Prentice Hall United States History Video Collection**™ Volume 17 *The Roaring Twenties*

Answer to . . .

Viewing History *Students should use this question as an aid in reading the chapter. Women are shown as active, independent participants in nightlife, not in traditional roles as mother, wife, or daughter.*

1919	1920	1923	1924	1927	1928
Red scare; Palmer raids; widespread labor strikes	Harding elected President	Harding dies; Coolidge takes office	Teapot Dome scandal uncovered; Coolidge wins election	Sacco and Vanzetti executed	Kellogg-Briand Pact; Hoover elected President

1915   **1920**   **1925**   **1930**

1 A Republican Decade

SECTION PREVIEW

Objectives

1. Analyze the causes and effects of the red scare and the labor strikes of 1919.
2. Describe key features of the Republican administrations of the 1920s.
3. Compare the Harding and Coolidge presidencies.
4. *Key Terms* Define: communism; red scare; isolationism; disarmament; quota; Teapot Dome scandal; Kellogg-Briand Pact.

Main Idea

Republican administrations of the 1920s pursued pro-business economic policies and an isolationist foreign policy.

Reading Strategy

Creating an Outline Copy the headings in this section. As you read, write down at least two key points under each heading.

Warren G. Harding "looks like a President," said a political friend promoting the handsome, silver-haired Ohio senator for the Republican nomination in 1920. Harding sounded like a President, too. He had a deep voice and dignified speaking style and impressed people as honest and kind.

Yet Harding's speeches often left people wondering what his views were. One Democrat called Harding's speeches "an army of pompous phrases moving across the landscape in search of an idea."

Yet voters got the message when Harding declared that America needed "not heroism but healing, not nostrums [fake cures] but normalcy." In a nation weary of war abroad and sacrifice at home, the mere promise of "normalcy" gave Harding a landslide victory over Democrat James Cox and his running mate, Franklin D. Roosevelt.

The Red Scare

"Normalcy" appealed to Americans in 1920 because the times seemed anything but normal. Having suffered through World War I, Americans were soon caught up in events both in faraway Russia and at home that convinced many people that the United States was threatened by political violence.

The Russian Revolution In March 1917 Russia's absolute ruler, Czar Nicholas II, lost his popularity as a result of a series of tragically poor decisions, including leading his country into World War I. The war brought devastating casualties and severe food shortages. With riots in the streets and the army too weak to protect him, Nicholas was forced to abdicate.

After months of upheaval, a revolutionary named Vladimir I. Lenin saw his opportunity. With such slogans as "End the war! All land to the peasants!" Lenin and his followers, referred to as the Bolsheviks, took power November 6, 1917. The new Bolshevik government put all privately owned farms, industries, land, and transportation under government ownership.

In early 1918, civil war engulfed the nation. Lenin's forces were called the "Reds." His opponents, the "Whites," included former landowners, government officials, and army

Main Idea
CONNECTIONS

What events in Russia caused concern among war-weary Americans?

RESOURCE OPTIONS

Teaching Resources

📁 **Reproducible Lesson Plan** Lesson Plans folder, p. 118

📁 **Big Idea Graphic Organizer** Big Idea Graphic Organizer folder, p. 90

📁 **Guided Reading and Review** Units 7–8 folder, p. 3

Media and Technology

 AmericanHeritage® CD-ROM

Time Tour Prosperity, Depression, and War: The Jazz Age

SECTION 1

A Republican Decade

Objectives

You may wish to call students' attention to the objectives in the Section Preview. The objectives are reflected in the main headings of the section.

Bellringer

Write on the chalkboard: "The business of the American people is business." Ask students what they think the quote means and why it might have appealed to Americans after World War I.

Reading Strategy

Creating an Outline Refer to the Reading Strategy in the Section Preview. You may wish to have students compare outlines in small groups in order to develop a composite outline.

LESSON PLAN

Connecting to the Main Idea

1. Focus As the country entered the post–World War I era, the mood was one of discontent and fear. Americans turned to the Republican party for security. Ask students what policies the Republicans followed in the 1920s to encourage economic and social stability.

2. Instruct Discuss why Americans were feeling insecure and frightened about the future after World War I. Why did the Russian Revolution and postwar economic adjustments make people feel uneasy? Why did labor disputes increase?

Ask students to describe the economic and foreign policies of Harding and Coolidge. How were laws restricting immigration an attempt to restore "normalcy"?

3. Close World War I greatly affected the mood of the country, making many people fearful of change and determined to maintain stability. Yet, as the next section explains, many changes did take place in the decade that followed.

You may wish to have students add the following to their portfolios. To assess student work, refer to the generic rubrics in the Program Overview in the Teaching Resources.

In August 1924, the first of Harold Gray's comic strips about the adventures of "Little Orphan Annie" appeared in the *New York Daily News*. Ask students to find out more about "Annie's" popularity, along with the values and beliefs about the United States and business on which the strip was based. Have students create their own "Little Orphan Annie" comic strip.

ACTIVITY
HETEROGENEOUS GROUPS

To help students understand the red scare, propose that communism will replace the capitalist system. Divide students into groups and assign to each one of the following roles: factory worker, factory owner, investor, government official, consumer. From the perspective determined by each of their roles, have students decide if the new system would improve or worsen their lives. How might the wish for "normalcy" have intensified these views? *(Reteaching)*

Answers to . . .

Main Idea Connections (previous page) The revolution and the advent of communism.

Viewing History Many people believed Sacco and Vanzetti would not receive a fair trial because they were immigrants.

leaders. Britain, France, Japan, and the United States, whose investments in Russia had been seized by Bolsheviks, backed the Whites.

After two bloody years, millions of deaths, and widespread destruction, the Reds triumphed in 1920. In time their new nation became known as the Union of Soviet Socialist Republics (USSR), or the Soviet Union.

Lenin made **communism** the official ideology of the Soviet Union. As practiced in the Soviet Union, communism meant the following:

(1) The government owned all land and property.

(2) A single political party controlled the government.

(3) Individuals had no rights that the government was bound to respect.

(4) The government vowed to stir up revolutions in other countries and spread communism throughout the world.

The Communist system was openly hostile to American beliefs and values, such as capitalism, private ownership of land and business, and First Amendment freedoms. As early as 1919 a **red scare,** an intense fear of communism and other extreme ideas, gripped the United States. Americans called for known Communists to be jailed or driven out of the country.

Schenck v. U.S. A 1919 Supreme Court decision seemed to some people to justify jailing Communists. During World War I, a war opponent named Charles Schenck had mailed letters to men who were drafted, urging them not to report for duty. He was convicted of breaking the Espionage Act, a wartime law aimed at spies and people who opposed the war. He appealed the case, claiming that he was only exercising his right to speak freely.

In the Court's written opinion, Justice Oliver Wendell Holmes, Jr., said that the government was justified in silencing free speech when there is a "clear and present danger" to the nation. He compared what Schenck had done to shouting "Fire!" in a crowded theater, which would cause a dangerous panic.

The Palmer Raids As the red scare heightened, the United States government began a campaign to identify and root out groups whose activities posed a "clear and present danger" to the country. In 1919 the Justice Department, headed by Attorney General A. Mitchell Palmer, set up a special force to conduct raids and arrest suspected "subversives" (people trying to subvert, or overthrow, the government). Palmer's targets included Communists, socialists, and anarchists.

Palmer's force jailed thousands of people. Most had been born overseas. Many were innocent of any crime. More than 500 immigrants were deported, or sent back to their homelands, although they had not been convicted of any crime.

Palmer received strong support at first. The army's chief of staff urged that those deported be sent away on "ships of stone with sails of lead," and popular preacher Billy Sunday suggested that a firing squad would save money on ships.

The red scare reached such a fever that in January 1920 the New York State Assembly voted to expel five members who were socialists. Yet the five had been legally elected and had broken no rules or laws. People were outraged that the assembly had ignored the public's right to elect whomever they wanted.

Sacco and Vanzetti The red scare played a part in one of the most controversial events in United States history. The story began on April 15, 1920, when gunmen robbed and killed the guard and

The case of Sacco and Vanzetti inspired much protest, including this piece of folk art. *Government Why did the artist include a plea for a fair trial?*

RESOURCE OPTIONS

Media and Technology

 Color Transparencies Time Lines, E-6

 Prentice Hall United States History Video Collection™ Volume 16 *The Great War*

paymaster of a shoe factory in South Braintree, Massachusetts. A few weeks later, police arrested two Italian immigrants in connection with the crime.

One, Nicola Sacco, was a shoemaker, while the other, Bartolomeo Vanzetti, was a fish peddler. Both were carrying guns when they were arrested, and Sacco's was the same model used in the crime. Yet many Americans suspected that the real reason the two men were accused of the crime was that they were immigrants. The case drew international attention and controversy.

Sacco and Vanzetti were soon convicted and sentenced to die. Their case was appealed to higher courts again and again for years, but their conviction was upheld.[†] In 1927, Sacco and Vanzetti were electrocuted.

Union Membership and Work Stoppages, 1916–1920

Source: *Historical Statistics of the United States, Colonial Times to 1970*

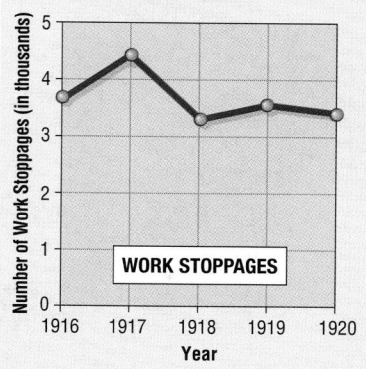

Source: *Historical Statistics of the United States, Colonial Times to 1970*

 Interpreting Graphs The post–World War I years were stormy ones for labor and business. The number of annual strikes was high and union membership was on the rise. *Economics* **Based on this information, how would you summarize the condition of organized labor in 1920?**

Labor Strikes

One cause of the red scare was a wave of labor unrest in 1919. Many Americans were convinced that Communists were behind the strikes. Most of the unrest, however, had a simpler cause. In early 1919 food prices and rents shot up, and by 1920 the cost of living was more than double prewar levels.

The Boston Police Strike Boston police officers had not received a pay increase since the start of World War I. In the fall of 1919, they decided they had had enough of sacrifice. When 19 officers were fired for union activity, the whole force voted to strike.

With police off the job, rioting soon broke out in Boston. Massachusetts governor Calvin Coolidge called out the state guard. "There is no right to strike against the public safety by anybody, anywhere, anytime," Coolidge said. The future President gained national attention for his firm response to the strike.

Steel and Coal Strikes Meanwhile, steelworkers in Gary, Indiana, and several other cities struck in 1919. Claiming that the strike was the work of Communists, the United States Steel Corporation used force to break it. The corporation's private police force killed 18 strikers and beat hundreds more.[††]

Another strike in that troubled fall of 1919 took place in the coal fields. The United Mine Workers of America (UMW) had made a no-strike agreement during the war, but they claimed the agreement ended with the armistice. The government claimed the agreement was still in effect. When the workers struck for a shorter work week and better pay, Attorney General Palmer got a court to order strikers back to work. Although the UMW canceled the strike, it did manage to get its workers a raise.

After hitting its high point in 1919, strike activity declined during the 1920s, as the economy boomed and wages rose. Union membership dropped during 1921 and 1922, and did not grow again through the rest of the decade.

[†] Investigators in 1961 reexamined Sacco's gun and found that it was indeed the murder weapon, although it had never been proven that it was Sacco who fired the gun. On the 50th anniversary of the executions, August 23, 1977, Massachusetts governor Michael Dukakis decreed that Sacco and Vanzetti had not received their right to a fair trial.

[††] A follow-up investigation produced the "Report on the Steel Strike of 1919," which helped limit working hours in the steel industry.

TEST PREPARATION

Have students read the paragraphs under "The Boston Police Strike" and then answer the question below.

Based on the passage and Governor Coolidge's quotation, you can infer that—

(A) Coolidge believed this strike should be stopped, as it presented a danger to the general public.

B Coolidge did not support strikes under any circumstances.

C Coolidge favored expanding the role of government to stop all strikes.

D Coolidge sympathized with the police officers.

Answer to . . .

Interpreting Graphs While union membership had steadily increased, work stoppages leveled off, suggesting that workers struck less often than they had in the immediate postwar years.

Immigration from Regions of Europe

Source: *Historical Statistics of the United States, Colonial Times to 1970*

Interpreting Graphs The 1921 cartoon at left satirized American immigration restriction. *Government Describe the effect of Harding's immigration policies on the number of immigrants from eastern and southern Europe as shown by the graph above.*

Republican Leadership

Strikes, arrests, revolution overseas—such events frightened Americans in the 1920s, and they turned to the Republican party to maintain stability. In a remarkable solidifying of its power, the Republican party dominated all three branches of government. Republican Presidents Warren G. Harding, Calvin Coolidge, and Herbert Hoover served from 1921 to 1933. Republicans held the majority in Congress during this time. In addition, Supreme Court decisions of the era reflected the influence of its new Chief Justice, former President William Howard Taft, appointed by Harding in 1921.

Republican leaders of this generation were united in basic goals and ideals. They favored business, and many of them were in fact businessmen. They wanted social stability, believing that it promoted economic growth.

The Harding Presidency

President Harding took office as the red scare and the labor strikes were beginning to subside. In that respect, the country did seem to be getting back to "normalcy."

Harding made some wise Cabinet appointments. The able administrator (and future President) Herbert Hoover became Secretary of Commerce. Treasury Secretary Andrew Mellon was one of the nation's most powerful businessmen. Under Harding and his Republican successors, Mellon shaped the economic policies of the 1920s. However, Harding showed terribly poor judgment in many of his appointments, giving jobs to friends, some of whom were incompetent and dishonest. These decisions would eventually overwhelm his presidency and his life.

Isolationism Harding's foreign policy reflected Americans' postwar desire for a return to **isolationism,** a policy of avoiding political or economic alliances with foreign countries. Hence Harding made no further attempt to join the League of Nations.

Yet the President did support efforts to find ways of preventing future wars. He called for **disarmament,** a program in which the nations of the world would voluntarily give up their weapons. In 1921 Harding convened the Washington Conference, at which several major nations signed treaties limiting the size of their navies.

In 1922 Congress, with Harding's support, passed the Fordney-McCumber Tariff, which raised rates on a number of imports. It especially discouraged imports that competed with goods made by new American industries, such as china, toys, and chemicals.

Limiting Immigration As Americans became more isolationist, they also became more nativist.

Answer to . . .

Interpreting Graphs Immigration was dramatically reduced beginning in 1924. Numbers of immigrants remained low throughout the decade.

As you have read, nativism is a movement favoring native-born Americans over immigrants. It had first appeared in the 1800s, but after World War I it grew stronger, for several reasons:

(1) Many Americans believed that people from foreign countries could never be fully loyal to the United States.

(2) Nativists, who were mostly Protestants, had long disliked immigrants who were Catholics, Orthodox Christians, or Jews.

(3) Americans often blamed the problems of cities, such as slums and corruption, on the immigrants who lived in them.

(4) Workers feared immigrants might take their jobs away from them.

(5) Nativists argued that some immigrants came from the most unstable parts of Europe, where World War I had started. They believed that these immigrants might hold or might adopt dangerous political ideas.

When immigration rose sharply after World War I, nativist reaction was swift. In 1921, at Harding's request, and again in 1924, Congress passed laws restricting immigration. The laws limited annual immigration to 350,000 people and set up a **quota,** or numerical limit, on immigrants from each foreign nation. The laws set low quotas for immigrants from southern and eastern European countries, including Italy, Poland, and Russia. Asian immigration was banned altogether.

The Teapot Dome Scandal At the start of 1923, the economy was bouncing back from wartime disruptions, and the President enjoyed strong popularity. Within months, however, Harding was dead.

In the months before his death, major corruption scandals in Harding's administration were coming to light. There was no evidence that the President was involved in the scandals. In fact, Harding became terribly disturbed when he heard of the scandals, and the strain may have contributed to his death, from heart problems, on August 2, 1923.

By 1924 the extent of the corruption in Harding's administration had become known. One official had stolen government funds. Others had taken bribes in return for help getting contracts approved or laws passed. Several other officials were also accused of wrongdoing, and two committed suicide.

The worst Harding scandal came to be known as the **Teapot Dome scandal.** In 1921 and 1922, Harding's Secretary of the Interior, Albert B. Fall, secretly gave oil drilling rights on government oil fields in Elk Hills, California, and Teapot Dome, Wyoming, to two private oil companies. In return, Fall received more than $300,000 in illegal payments and gifts disguised as loans. He later went to jail for his role in the scandal.

The Coolidge Presidency

Vice President Calvin Coolidge was visiting his parents in Vermont on August 3, 1923, when word arrived of Harding's death. At 2:30 A.M., by the light of a kerosene lamp, Coolidge's father, a justice of the peace, administered to him the oath of office of President of the United States.

Coolidge was still widely respected for his actions as governor of Massachusetts. He had played no part in the Harding scandals. In fact, one Democrat said that Coolidge's "great task was to restore the dignity and prestige of the Presidency when it had reached the lowest ebb in our history." After finishing Harding's term, Coolidge ran in the 1924 election, defeating Democrat John W. Davis and Progressive Robert M. La Follette with the slogan "Keep cool with Coolidge."

Coolidge had a reputation as a skilled public speaker, but in private he was a man of few words. Someone said of him that "he could be silent in five languages."†

Laissez Faire In one sentence, Coolidge summed up a major theme of the Republican decade: "The business of the American people is business." The best that the government could do, he believed, was not to interfere with the growth of business. This laissez-faire business policy helped fuel the tremendous economic boom of the 1920s. As part of his laissez-faire policy, Coolidge tried to make the federal government smaller. For example, when war veterans won a bonus payment from Congress, he vetoed the bill on the grounds

The Democrats in 1924 tried to use public anger over the Teapot Dome affair to defeat the Republicans, as this campaign artifact shows.

Main Idea
CONNECTIONS

What policies did Republican leaders pursue in the 1920s?

---

† Many funny anecdotes grew up around "Silent Cal," as he was called. His wife, Grace, told the story of a young woman who sat next to Coolidge at a dinner party. The woman told Coolidge that she had bet that she could get him to say at least three words. Without looking at her, the President said, in his typically dry wit: "You lose."

From the Archives of

American Heritage®

About the Presidents

Calvin Coolidge (1923–1929) believed in laissez faire in domestic matters, while in foreign affairs he was an active diplomat. When an earthquake devastated Japan, he sent the Pacific fleet to help. His excellent international appointments improved U.S. relations abroad. Coolidge himself set a precedent by addressing the Sixth InterAmerican Conference in Havana, Cuba. The United States took part in several conferences sponsored by the League of Nations, as well. But the isolationist tendencies of the 1920s prevented U.S. entry into the Permanent Court of International Justice, which Coolidge favored. Isolationism also led to the Immigration Act of 1924. This act included a provision, which Coolidge opposed, banning Japanese immigration. Twenty years later, this ban would help lead to war in the Pacific. Source: Michael Harwood, "Calvin Coolidge," *The American Heritage*® *Pictorial History of the Presidents of the United States,* vol. 2, 1968.

RESOURCE OPTIONS

Teaching Resources

Decision-Making Activity Lobbying for Indian Immigration, Decision-Making Activities folder, pp. 18–19

Answer to . . .

Main Idea Connections Laissez faire, isolationism, nativism, downsizing government.

Calvin Coolidge, shown here with a saxophone, was known for his support of big business. *Economics* **What does this cartoon say about big business's reaction to his policies?**

that the government could not afford it. (Congress overrode his veto in 1924.)

Coolidge's effort to have government do less drew criticism from those who saw it as a failure to take action. The noted newspaper columnist Walter Lippmann said:

 "Mr. Coolidge's genius for inactivity is developed to a very high point. It is a grim, determined, alert inactivity, which keeps Mr. Coolidge occupied constantly."

—*Columnist Walter Lippmann, 1926*

Continued Isolationism Coolidge continued the isolationist policies of Harding. He left most foreign policy up to his Secretary of State, Frank B. Kellogg.

In 1928, isolationism led to an unusual treaty worked out by Kellogg and French Foreign Minister Aristide Briand. Under the **Kellogg-Briand Pact,** 15 nations agreed not to use the threat of war in their dealings with one another. More than 60 nations eventually joined the pact. The Kellogg-Briand Pact seemed to be a good idea, but it was unrealistic and unworkable because it had no provisions for enforcement. By 1941, many of the nations that had signed the pact were at war.

The Election of 1928

As Coolidge neared the end of his first full term, he was asked about his political plans. "I do not choose to run for President in 1928," was his brief and famous reply. In his place, Republicans nominated Herbert Hoover. During and after World War I, Hoover had won respect for programs he ran in Europe to ease hunger. He had held Cabinet posts under Harding and Coolidge.

Hoover's main opponent was Alfred E. Smith of New York, a popular Democratic governor and the first Roman Catholic to be nominated for President. Americans hoped that what they called the "Coolidge prosperity" would continue under Hoover. They elected him by a large margin, about 21.4 million to 15 million.

SECTION 1 REVIEW

Comprehension

1. *Key Terms* Define: (a) communism; (b) red scare; (c) isolationism; (d) disarmament; (e) quota; (f) Teapot Dome scandal; (g) Kellogg-Briand Pact.

2. *Summarizing the Main Idea* What were the main goals of the Republican administrations of the 1920s?

3. *Organizing Information* Create two cause-and-effect charts, one on the red scare and one on the labor strikes of 1919.

Critical Thinking

4. *Analyzing Time Lines* Refer to the time line at the start of the section. Which entries show a return to "normalcy," as Harding put it, and which indicate political or social upheaval? Explain your answers.

5. *Recognizing Ideologies* What beliefs did Harding and Coolidge share? In what ways did their presidencies differ?

Writing Activity

6. *Writing a Persuasive Essay* From the perspective of a writer living during the 1920s, write a persuasive essay about events connected to the red scare. Urge your readers either to (a) support ongoing efforts to arrest suspected subversives or (b) protest the hysteria of the red scare.

| 1927 American companies spend $3.2 billion on advertising | 1927 Ford introduces the Model A | 1929 Value of electrical appliances reaches $2.3 billion | 1929 Nearly $2 billion spent on roads and bridges | 1929 Value of top 200 companies reaches $81 billion | 1930 Americans own more than 23 million cars |

| 1927 | 1928 | 1929 | 1930 |

2 A Business Boom

SECTION PREVIEW

Objectives

1. Describe how the growth of a consumer economy changed American life.
2. Explain how Henry Ford made automobiles affordable for average Americans.
3. Explain why American businesses boomed in the 1920s.
4. *Key Terms* Define: consumer economy; installment plan; assembly line.

Main Idea

During the 1920s, new products and Americans' power to purchase them grew rapidly, producing a decade of enormous business growth.

Reading Strategy

Recognizing Cause and Effect As you read, make a list of factors that caused a business boom in the 1920s.

Forget malls and food courts. Until the 1920s, you couldn't even find a shopping center. Food was not "fast." Billboards did not line the highways because there were no highways, few cars, and relatively few advertisements.

Then came the 1920s, a decade that gave birth to much of modern America. In Kansas City, the nation's first shopping center opened, giving consumers a more convenient way to shop. The first fast-food chain, A & W Root Beer, began selling burgers and soft drinks. Advertising became big business in the 1920s, with companies spending an amazing $3.2 billion on ads in 1927. And in Michigan, a young man named Ford was building an automobile empire. This was no ordinary decade.

A Consumer Economy

Despite a year or so of uncertainty after World War I, the United States economy made a rapid adjustment. The rise in incomes that had begun during the war had resumed by 1920. Between 1914 and 1926, average wages rose more than 28 percent. The number of millionaires in the United States more than doubled in the same

period. The main cause of this growth was the development of the **consumer economy,** one that depends on a large amount of buying by consumers—individuals who use (or "consume") products. During the 1920s, a consumer economy developed rapidly in the United States.

Buying on Credit Until the 1920s, Americans generally paid cash for anything they bought. Borrowing money for any purchase but a house or land was considered unthrifty, even immoral. During the 1920s, the nation eagerly adopted a new way to buy goods. Instead of paying the full price at once, consumers arranged to pay on an **installment plan,** a system that lets customers make partial payments (installments) at set intervals over a period of time until the total debt is paid. Installment plans fueled the growth of the consumer economy.

Installment plans encouraged people to buy who otherwise would not, even though they had to pay interest charges ranging from 11 to 40 percent. By 1929, Americans were using the installment plan to buy 60 percent of all cars, 70 percent of furniture, 80 percent of vacuum

Electrical appliances changed the nature of housework.

exploring TECHNOLOGY   The Model T Production Plant

Workers assembled cars as they passed on a conveyor.

Even the detailed and skillful work of upholstering seats was performed on an assembly line.

Model T bodies moved down a slide to be fitted onto the car.

Each worker on the line performed the same tasks over and over.

Henry Ford's ingenious production methods were based on two key ideas: the assembly line and uniformity of product—the making of identical cars. *Science and Technology* **How did the assembly line change the nature of work?**

cleaners, radios, and refrigerators, and 90 percent of sewing machines and washing machines.

Electric Power These new power-hungry appliances created a surge in the demand for electricity. Between 1913 and 1927, the number of electric power customers more than quadrupled. The number of people who had electric lights jumped from 16 percent to 63 percent in about the same time.

Though the cities were gaining electric power rapidly, the countryside was not. The cost of running electric lines to scattered farming communities was simply too high. By 1925, for example, only 4 percent of American farms were connected to a power plant. Still, many farm families used wind-powered generators to bring handy new electric products to their remote homes.

Main Idea CONNECTIONS

What caused the increased demand for electric power in the 1920s?

The growth of General Electric Company illustrates how the increasing use of electricity went hand in hand with the boom in consumer sales. General Electric was formed in 1892 to take over Thomas Edison's electric light business. During the 1920s, the company

grew dramatically on sales of a variety of household electrical appliances. It also sold electric motors and other products for industry. Between 1919 and 1929, the value of electrical products of this kind more than doubled, from nearly $1 billion to $2.3 billion. General Electric rode this wave of consumer buying to become one of the world's largest companies.

New Products to Buy Among the products General Electric offered were electric toasters, ovens, sewing machines, coffee pots, irons, and vacuum cleaners. Other companies, too, offered a vast array of goods, from telephones to cosmetics. Some of these were updated versions of products that had been around for centuries. Others had never been seen before.

Ford and the Automobile

Another product that was invented in the 1890s but became available to the mass market in the 1920s was the automobile. Charles and Frank Duryea of Springfield, Massachusetts, developed a model in 1892, and several other inventors soon followed their lead. Over the

Small items such as wheels were assembled separately.

Passenger Car Sales, 1920–1929

Number of Cars (in millions) vs Year

Source: *Historical Statistics of the United States, Colonial Times to 1970*

Interpreting Graphs Use of the assembly line made the growth of the automobile industry possible. *Economics* *What was the overall trend in car sales during the 1920s?*

BACKGROUND

Geography in History

American roads could scarcely keep up with Ford's assembly line. Most were intended for horses and cattle, and none were planned with a national network in mind. In 1919, Lt. Col. Dwight D. Eisenhower left Washington, D.C. with a party of 60 military trucks to test the feasibility of a coast-to-coast trip. Two months and over eighty repaired bridges later, he arrived in San Francisco, convinced of the need for government action. A concerned General Pershing proposed an 8,000 mile interstate highway system to the President and Congress in 1922, but little progress was made until Eisenhower became President in the 1950s.

next 28 years, about 8 million cars were put on the road. Yet in the ten years after that, during the 1920s, the number of registered cars rose by over 15 million. Much of this rapid growth was due to the efforts of the legendary businessman Henry Ford.

Ford and the "Model T" Ford was born on a Michigan farm during the Civil War, the son of Irish immigrants. Early in life he showed a skill with machines. In the late 1880s, he worked as an engineer with a lighting company in Detroit. In his spare time he began inventing a "horseless carriage." In 1896 Ford perfected his first version of the lightweight, gas-powered car, which he called the "quadricycle." He soon sold it to get the money to build a better one. By 1903, he had started his own automobile company. Only a few years later, in 1908, Ford sold 30,000 of an improved type that he called the Model T.

Ford's Assembly Line In those days, 30,000 was a huge number of cars. Yet Ford had even bigger dreams. He wanted to "democratize the automobile," producing even more cars and selling them at prices ordinary people could

afford. This goal was what set him apart from all other car makers and made him one of the most influential people of the century.

To achieve his goal, he adapted for his factories the revolutionary assembly line, shown in the Exploring Technology feature above. An **assembly line** is a manufacturing process in which each worker does one specialized task in the construction of the final product. In the past, an individual worker might build an entire product, such as a gun. In the automobile business, that process would have been inefficient since each worker would have to master hundreds of tasks. On an assembly line, however, one worker might install windshields on all the cars. Another might mount the tires, or weld a certain part in place, or apply the paint.

Ford did not invent the assembly line, but he made it more efficient: Ford's assembly line moved while the workers stayed in place, instead of having the workers move from

Answer to . . .

Interpreting Graphs Sales increased, more than doubling between 1920 and 1929.

The Impact of the Automobile

The automobile industry had an enormous impact on related industries during the 1920s. Petroleum producers in particular had a difficult time meeting demand as Americans took to the road.

Automobile manufacture ate up one fifth of the nation's yearly steel production.

Three quarters of all sheet-glass was installed as automobile windows.

Four fifths of the nation's rubber ended up as car tires.

Interpreting Diagrams The automobile industry not only affected related industries, but created new ones as well. Manufacturers of batteries, spark plugs, and other auto parts supplied car components. Service industries such as filling stations and mechanic shops soon became necessities. *Economics* **What role did the prosperity of the 1920s play in the automobile industry?**

vehicle to vehicle. The assembly line also used interchangeable parts to speed production. At Ford's Highland Park, Michigan, factory, the assembly line spit out a Model T every 24 seconds. Between 1908 and 1927, Ford built half of the automobiles produced in the entire world, more than 15 million cars.

By making large numbers of identical automobiles in an identical way, Ford could take advantage of economies of scale. The more automobiles he made, the less each one cost. In 1914, the first year his assembly line was in full swing, his company sold Model T's at $490 each. This was almost half of what a car had cost in 1910. The following year he actually dropped the price to $390.

Main Idea CONNECTIONS

How was Ford able to make cars affordable to many Americans?

Ford's cars were identical. He joked that his customers could get their Model T's in any color they liked, as long as it was black. However, other car makers realized that the American public wanted different colors and styles of cars. When General Motors introduced its low-priced Chevrolet in several colors, Ford lost many customers. Not until 1928 did he introduce a choice of colors in a new automobile, the Model A.

Ford's success, however, came partly from vertical consolidation, controlling the businesses that make up phases of a product's develop-

ment. Ford boasted that he could take a load of raw ore on Monday morning and sell it as a car 52 hours later on Wednesday afternoon. The ore came from Ford's own iron mines and was forged in his own blast furnaces and steel mills, which were fired by coal from his 16 coal mines. Wood used in the car came from his 700,000 acres of forests, rubber from his plantations in Brazil, glass for windshields from his own glassworks. He shipped materials over his own railroad and his own fleet of ships. Nearly all the tools used in his factories were made in his own shops. Furthermore, this entire empire was built with his own money.

A Complex Businessman Like the empire he ran, Ford was a complex man. He had both good qualities and personal failings. For example, he won praise in 1914 for introducing a $5-a-day pay rate for many of his workers. This was double what other factories paid at the time. Yet he was not always generous. He ruled his company harshly, and used violence to fight unions. Though he showed genius in giving millions of Americans a car they could afford, he stubbornly refused to keep up with their changing tastes. By 1936 the Ford Motor Company had slipped to third place in the car business.

Critics of his system claimed the assembly line was hard on the workers. Ford admitted that work on the assembly line would be boring to him, but insisted that his employees enjoyed it. In his 1922 autobiography he stated:

AMERICAN VOICES "Probably the most monotonous task in the whole factory is one in which a man picks up a gear with a steel hook, shakes it in a vat of oil, then turns it into a basket. . . . Yet the man on that job has been doing it for eight solid years . . . and he stubbornly resists every attempt to force him into a better job!"

—*Henry Ford, My Life and Work, 1922*

Another of Ford's failings was his contempt for history, which he described as "bunk," or nonsense. Because he did not understand the past, he could not understand the present. He sailed a rented ocean liner across the Atlantic in 1915 and made a hopeless effort to talk Europe out of fighting World War I. In 1920, he used his own newspaper, the *Dearborn Independent*, to blame Jews for the world's problems. However, in 1927, after being sued for slander, he apologized for these attacks and sold the paper.

Industrial Growth

Through Ford's genius, automobile making became the nation's biggest single manufacturing industry in the 1920s. By the late twenties, cars were using 15 percent of America's steel, 80 percent of its rubber, half its glass, 65 percent of its leather upholstery, and 7 billion gallons of its gasoline every year.

Thousands of new businesses arose to serve automobile travel, including garages, car dealerships, motels, campgrounds, gas stations, and restaurants. Truck lines began hauling the nation's freight, and motorized buses traveled new routes through both countryside and city. About 3.7 million people were employed directly or indirectly because of the automobile industry by 1929. In that year the nation spent nearly $2 billion to build and maintain its roads and bridges.

Other industries were growing, too. Under Republican laissez-faire policies, which limited the government's regulation of business, the value of the nation's businesses took off. Between 1919 and 1929 the 200 top American companies nearly doubled their value, which rose from $43 billion to $81 billion.

Interestingly, the power of monopolies declined even while American business was getting bigger. Rapid business expansion opened up new opportunities for competitors to the giant monopolies of the 1800s.

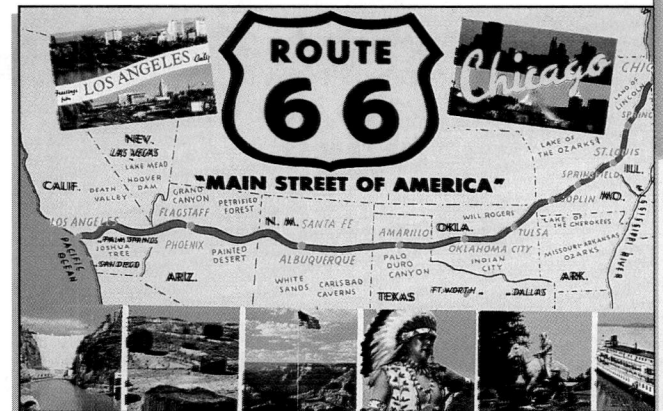

The United States Steel Corporation is a good example. When created by the powerful banker J. P. Morgan in 1901, it controlled about 60 percent of the steel business. By 1930, it had grown enormously. Yet its competitors also grew, and in that year United States Steel controlled only about 39 percent of the steel business.

Likewise, the companies that had once made up the Standard Oil Trust grew with the demand for oil products during the 1920s. Even so, by 1930 they controlled only about half of the nation's oil business.

Besides the automobile, steel, oil, and electrical industries, other businesses that boomed during the 1920s were the publishing, motion picture, and machine-making industries. People seemed eager to prove that the business of the United States truly was business.

Route 66, begun in the mid-1920s, linked urban and rural communities between Chicago and Los Angeles.

SECTION 2 REVIEW

Comprehension

1. **Key Terms** Define: (a) consumer economy; (b) installment plan; (c) assembly line.

2. **Summarizing the Main Idea** Write a paragraph summarizing the main reasons for the business boom of the 1920s.

3. **Organizing Information** Create a cause-and-effect chart on the growth of car production in the 1920s.

Critical Thinking

4. **Analyzing Time Lines** Refer to the time line at the start of the section. Choose three entries and explain how they influenced modern American life.

5. **Recognizing Ideologies** From what you read about Henry Ford, what conclusions can you draw about what he believed in and valued?

Writing Activity

6. **Writing a Persuasive Essay** Write a newspaper column that might have appeared in the late 1920s. Explain why the government's laissez-faire approach to the economy seems to be working. Support your case with statistics from this section.

SKILLS FOR LIFE

Critical Thinking

Analyzing Advertisements

Focus Analyze a period advertisement as evidence of the ideas, attitudes, and values of a historical period.

Instruct Read the following quotation from David Ogilvy, founding partner of the famous advertising firm Ogilvy and Mather: "It pays to give most products an image of quality—a First Class ticket. This is particularly true of products whose brand-name is visible to your friends, like . . . automobiles: products you 'wear.'. . . Who wants to be seen using shoddy products?" Ask students what warning Ogilvy's statement contains for those using advertising as historical evidence.

Extend See the Skills for Life Activity in the Resource Options below.

Answers

1. (a) Garters used to hold up men's socks. (b) The ad shows two available garter styles; gives price range; states that no metal can touch the wearer. (c) Men: the need to present a neat appearance and to be successful; the concern about being rejected by women. Women: the concern about having husbands who will not be embarrassments in social situations.

2. (a) Answers will vary but should be based on facts about the 1920s. (b) That men will be more desirable to women if they use Paris Garters.

3. (a) Being neat, well-dressed, successful, and attractive to the opposite sex; caring about others' opinions. (b) Sample answer: ads create a desire for products and manipulate people into buying them.

TEST FOR SUCCESS

Answers will vary but should show an understanding of the steps shown in this skill.

SKILLS FOR LIFE

Analyzing Advertisements

Advertisements offer important evidence of the consumer goods and services that were promoted during a historical period. Ads often hold clues to widely held ideas, attitudes, and values. However, when using advertisements as historical evidence, keep in mind that ads can reflect what advertisers want people to value and desire, rather than representing the reality for most of the consumers of the time.

By the 1920s, the "what-it-is, what-it-does" type of advertising was giving way to "situational" ads. These ads depicted not only the products but also the ways in which those products might increase personal satisfaction or enhance the lives of typical consumers.

One such ad from the 1920s is shown here. Use the following steps to analyze it.

1. *Identify the subject of the ad.* (a) What product or service does it promote? (b) What facts about the product does the ad provide? (c) What issue does this advertisement use to appeal particularly to men? To women?

2. *Analyze the advertisement's reliability as historical evidence.* (a) Do you think the people depicted in the ad represent typical consumers of the 1920s? Explain. (b) What is the unstated message that the advertiser is using in this case to persuade people to buy the product?

3. *Study the ad to learn more about the historical period.* (a) What social or cultural values are promoted in the advertisement? (b) In general, do you think advertisements reflect consumers' desires for products or create the desire for such products? Explain.

TEST FOR SUCCESS

Think of a modern advertisement you've seen for a specific product such as a car, a food, or a type of running shoe. Use the steps shown here to analyze the ad.

—and he wonders why she said "NO!"

Could he have read her thoughts he would not have lost her. A picture of neatness herself, she detested slovenliness. And not once, but many times, she had noticed his ungartered socks crumpling down around his shoe tops. To have to apologize to her friends for a husband's careless habits was too much to ask. So she had to say "NO"—and in spite of his pleading couldn't tell him WHY.

No SOX Appeal Without

PARIS GARTERS

NO METAL CAN TOUCH YOU

25c to $2

Dress Well and Succeed

SINGLE GRIP   DOUBLE GRIP

© 1928–A. STEIN & COMPANY–MAKERS–CHICAGO, NEW YORK, LOS ANGELES, TORONTO

RESOURCE OPTIONS

Teaching Resources

Skills for Life Activity Units 7–8 folder, p. 17, uses an advertisement of the 1990s to help students analyze visual evidence as a guide to social and cultural values.

1924
Women governors elected
in Wyoming and Texas

1926
Ederle becomes first
woman to swim
English Channel

1927
Lindbergh makes
first nonstop
transatlantic flight

1927
Babe Ruth sets
baseball's home-
run record

| 1924 | 1926 | 1928 | 1930 |

3 Society in the 1920s

SECTION PREVIEW

Objectives

1 Describe changes in women's attitudes and roles in society during the 1920s.
2 Analyze the causes for population changes in American cities and suburbs.
3 Identify some of the heroes of the 1920s and explain their popularity.
4 *Key Terms* Define: flapper; demographics; barrio.

Main Idea

The 1920s was a time of rapid social change, in which women, in particular, adopted new lifestyles and attitudes. Amid these changes many Americans admired heroes who embodied old-fashioned values.

Reading Strategy

Formulating Questions Write down three questions you might ask to help you better understand the social changes of the 1920s.

After the war ended and the nation prospered, the manners and attitudes of Americans were bound to change. A symbol of this shift was the **flapper.** The term described a new type of woman: young, rebellious, fun loving, and bold. One author depicted the flapper this way:

AMERICAN VOICES "Breezy, slangy, and informal in manner; slim and boyish in form; covered in silk and fur that clung to her as close as onion skin; with carmined [vivid red] cheeks and lips, plucked eyebrows and close-fitting helmet of hair; gay, plucky and confident."

—*Preston Slosson,*
The Great Crusade and After, *1930*

Women's Changing Roles

Actually, the flapper represented only a tiny number of American women. Yet the symbol had a wide impact on fashion and manners. More than anything else, it stood for a longing to make a break with the past.

The Flapper Image Women of the 1920s preferred shorter dresses than those of their mothers. Hemlines rose from 6 inches above the ground in 1919 to knee-length or even higher by 1927. Dresses and blouses became much simpler. Amazingly, between 1913 and 1928, the average amount of fabric used to make a woman's outfit shrank from 19.5 yards to just 7 yards.

Women also discarded other symbols of the past. While their mothers had worn their hair long, young women "bobbed," or cut short, their hair. Even the hat they preferred, the tight-fitting cloche, matched their helmet-shaped haircuts. They also began wearing makeup, which had once been considered a sign of immorality.

Women's manners changed along with their appearance. Before the 1920s, women rarely smoked or drank in public. By the end of the decade, many women were doing both. Between 1918 and 1928 the number of cigarettes produced in the United States more than doubled. Though men were smoking

Flappers defined a whole new style of dress.

Women Who Smoke Having recently secured the right to vote, America's women rose up in early 1922 to defend an even more fundamental liberty: the right to smoke. In February newspapers reported the shocking news that smoking was common among female students at Northwestern University, the University of Chicago, Columbia University's Teacher's College, and other institutions of higher learning. Barnard College even allowed unrestricted use of the devil's weed. Barnard's permissive attitude was not universal throughout New York City, however. On March 27, with no warning, police began to enforce an ordinance that banned smoking by females in restaurants, hotels, and other public gathering places. Women were outraged. The law's sponsor defended the bill saying that ". . . [Y]oung fellows go into restaurants to find women folk sucking cigarettes. What happens? The young fellows . . . vampired by these smoking women, desert their homes, their wives and children, rob their employers and even commit murder so that they can get money to lavish on these smoking women." Source: Frederic D. Schwarz, "The Time Machine," *American Heritage* magazine, February 1997.

more, too (many switching from cigars and pipes to cigarettes), a big part of the increase was due to the new woman smoker.

Women Working and Voting Despite the power of the flapper image, large numbers of young people did not rebel against traditions. While many women had their hair bobbed and wore shorter skirts, some adopted the new styles because they were more convenient, not because they admired the flapper lifestyle.

Convenience was an issue for women who were moving into office, sales, service, and some professional jobs during the 1920s. Generally only single women could get jobs, and even then they held them only until they were married. If married women did go to work, they usually had to quit if they became pregnant.

For this and other reasons, employers seldom trained women for higher positions or paid them on the same scale as men. Women in leadership positions were few. Many hospitals refused to hire women doctors, and many law firms rejected women lawyers.

> ### Main Idea
> **CONNECTIONS**
>
> *What types of social change did many women experience in the 1920s?*

To celebrate the passage of the Nineteenth Amendment in 1920, Alice Paul adds the "ratification star" to the flag of the National Woman's Party. *Culture* Why do you think more women did not turn out to vote in the early 1920s?

Like the situation of women at work, women's status in politics changed little. Although as of 1920 women could vote in national elections, they seldom did. One estimate suggested that only about 35 percent of all women voters went to the polls. When they did, their votes did not change politics as much as suffragists had hoped. In national elections especially, women voted in patterns similar to men. They seemed to have a noticeable impact, however, in local elections.

Still, women did begin to seek and win state and national political office. Jeannette Rankin of Montana had begun the trend when she was elected to the House of Representatives in 1916, becoming the first woman to serve in either house of Congress. Miriam A. Ferguson from Texas and Nellie Tayloe Ross of Wyoming, both wives of former governors, were elected governors themselves in 1924. By 1928, there were 145 women in 38 state legislatures. Thus, although women did not increase their political power as quickly as suffragists had hoped, they did lay a foundation for future participation in government.

Cities and Suburbs

The 1920s saw demographic as well as social changes. **Demographics** are the statistics that describe a population, such as data on race or income. The major demographic change of the 1920s was a movement away from the countryside. During the decade some 6 million people moved from rural areas to the cities.

African Americans in the North As you read earlier, the passage of Jim Crow laws, as well as new job opportunities in the North, produced the Great Migration of blacks from the South to northern cities from the late 1800s through World War I. The industrial boom you read about in Section 2 further encouraged this demographic shift.

Throughout the early 1900s, jobs for African Americans in the South had been scarce and low-paying. Many factory jobs simply were closed to them. As industries expanded production during the 1920s, many new job opportunities opened up for African Americans in the North. In 1860, 93 percent of all African Americans lived in the South. By 1910, this had dropped very little, to 89 percent. By 1930, it had fallen far more, to 80 percent.

Yet the North was no promised land. African American factory workers often faced

---

▶ RESOURCE OPTIONS

Teaching Resources

📁 **Biography** Lillian Moller Gilbreth, Units 7–8 folder, p. 13

Media and Technology

Primary Source Activity Growing Up Black, found on Resource Pro, provides an excerpt from Daisy Bates's autobiography describing the effects of segregation on her and her African American and white neighbors in the 1920s South.

African American Migrations, 1890–1920

Legend:
- States that had significant loss of African American population
- States that had significant gain in African American population
- 2% — Gain or loss of African Americans as a percentage of a state's total population

Map labels:
- N.Y. +1%
- Mich. +1%
- Pa. +1%
- Ill. +1%
- Ind. +1%
- Ohio +1%
- W.Va. +1%
- Del. –3%
- Md. –4%
- Va. –8%
- Ky. –5%
- Tenn. –5%
- N.C. –5%
- Okla. –1%
- Ark. –1%
- S.C. –9%
- Miss. –5%
- Ala. –7%
- Ga. –5%
- Texas –6%
- La. –11%
- Fla. –8%

MAP Skills The migration of African Americans from the South to the North helped alter the populations of both regions. This family moved from the rural South to settle in Chicago in 1912. *Movement* Which states lost the largest percentages of their black populations?

anger and hatred from whites, who feared that migrants threatened their jobs and wages. African American women often had to work as household help for whites, at wages that kept them trapped in poverty.

Other Migration As you read, the nation's immigration laws were tightened in the 1920s. As the number of immigrants from Europe decreased, employers turned to immigrants from Mexico and Canada to fill low-paying jobs. The new immigration quotas did not apply to nations in the Americas.

In the West, Mexicans supplied this labor, migrating across the border to work on the farms of California and the ranches of Texas. In the Northeast, Canadians from the French-speaking province of Quebec traveled south to work in the paper mills, potato fields, and forests of New England and New York.

The migrants also took jobs in the cities. Los Angeles, for example, became a magnet for Mexicans and developed a distinct **barrio,** or Spanish-speaking neighborhood. New York also attracted Spanish-speakers—Puerto Ricans migrating in the hope of a better life in the United States.

Growth of the Suburbs One result of the movements of Americans in the 1920s was a huge increase in the size of American suburbs. Some suburban growth had taken place earlier, as cities built transportation systems that used electric trolleys, or railway cars, that ran on rails laid in or along streets. The trolleys allowed people to get from the suburbs to jobs and stores in the city quickly and cheaply.

When automobiles were introduced, electric trolleys lost passengers. Between 1916 and 1926, about 2,500 miles of trolley track were abandoned. Yet the loss of trolleys did not slow the growth of suburbs.

About 80 percent of the old trolley routes were soon replaced by bus lines. By the middle of the 1920s, about 70,000 buses were operating throughout the United States. The automobile extended transportation lines even farther.

New York City is a good example of demographic change during the 1920s. The number of residents decreased in Manhattan, the heart of the city. Meanwhile, one of the city's suburbs, Queens, saw its population double.

American Heroes

The changing morals of the 1920s made many Americans hungry for the values of an earlier era. Their memories of the senseless brutality of World War I remained strong. In America's cities, they saw people indulging in behavior that had always been connected with immorality—smoking, drinking, wearing revealing clothing and bright make-up. The newspapers of the time were filled with sensational headlines about crimes and sins of every description.

Main Idea CONNECTIONS

Why did Americans seem to long for heroes during the 1920s?

It was no wonder, then, that the nation became fascinated with heroes, especially those who seemed to have all the virtues of the good old days. Some were sports stars. Others were experts in new fields such as aviation. None became as famous as "Lucky Lindy."

"Lucky Lindy" The sky was drizzling rain at Roosevelt Field on Long Island, New York, on the morning of May 20, 1927. A 25-year-old Minnesotan, Charles Lindbergh, climbed into the cockpit of his specially built plane, the *Spirit of St. Louis,* and revved the engine. He had not slept much, but he did not dare wait any longer.

Two other teams were waiting on the airfield, hoping to be the first to fly nonstop from New York to Paris. The prize was $25,000, and Lindbergh was determined to capture it.

In those days, flying was an infant science. Orville and Wilbur Wright had achieved the first powered, sustained, and controlled airplane flight only two decade earlier, in 1903. Radio and navigation equipment were primitive at best. Lindbergh had no copilot and no computer to fly his plane so he could rest.

The minute his plane was aloft, the news flashed by telegraph and telephone to news desks around the nation. Americans everywhere took notice and began to wait eagerly for news. The newspapers fed this hunger, printing some 27,000 columns of information about Lindbergh in the first few days after his departure.

After a brutal flight over the Atlantic Ocean, battling icy weather and fighting off sleep, Lindbergh was sighted over Ireland, then England. Finally, 33 1/2 hours after he had left New York, "Lucky Lindy" landed safely in an airfield outside Paris.

America went wild with celebration. Lindbergh was brought home on a Navy cruiser, given the Congressional Medal of Honor, and honored with parades in every state in the nation.

Charles Lindbergh, pictured here with his *Spirit of St. Louis,* not only inspired the nation but also fostered the development of commercial aviation. *Culture* Why was the nation so hungry for heroes?

Answer to . . .

Main Idea Connections In the face of war, crime, and immoral behavior, they held up people who seemed virtuous.

Yet despite this frenzy of hero-worship, Lindbergh remained modest and calm. He refused offers of millions of dollars in publicity fees. Fame and applause could not spoil him. To millions of Americans, Lindbergh was proof that the solid moral values of the old days lived on in the heartland of America.

Amelia Earhart Lindbergh's feat inspired later flyers, including Amelia Earhart, who in 1932 flew across the Atlantic alone. Three years later Earhart flew solo from Hawaii to California, a challenge that had resulted in the deaths of many aviators before her. In 1937, however, attempting to fly around the world, she disappeared somewhere in the Pacific Ocean.

Heroes of Sports In general, the 1920s were a time when Americans began to enjoy sports as never before. A highly publicized fight between boxers Jack Dempsey and Georges Carpentier in 1921 broke the record for ticket sales, taking in $1 million. Dempsey won the fight to become the heavyweight champion of the world and a new American hero.

Of all the heroes of the era, none generated more excitement than baseball legend George Herman "Babe" Ruth. Known as "the Sultan of Swat," Babe Ruth set records in hitting, pitching, and outfielding that stood for decades.

During his career, with the Boston Red Sox and then with the New York Yankees, Ruth hit 714 home runs, a record that was unbroken for nearly 40 years. In 1927 the champion enthralled Americans by setting the legendary record of 60 home runs in a 154-game season.

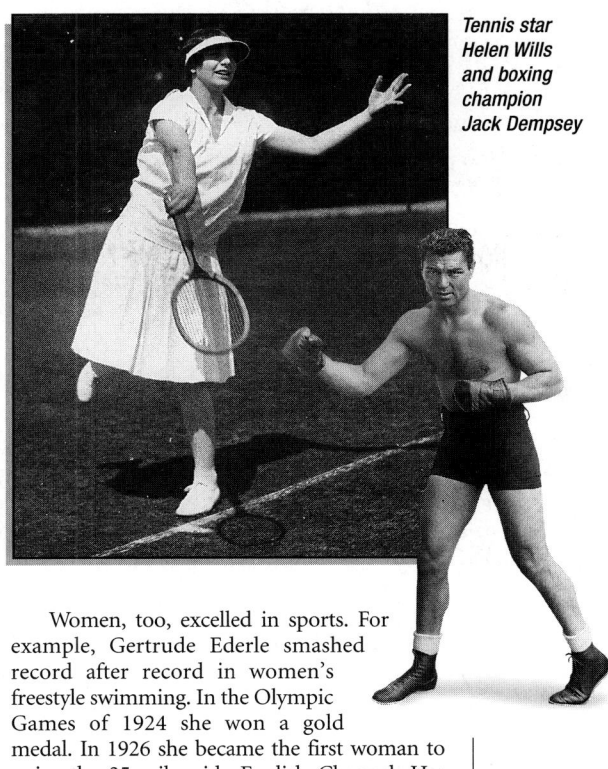

Tennis star Helen Wills and boxing champion Jack Dempsey

Women, too, excelled in sports. For example, Gertrude Ederle smashed record after record in women's freestyle swimming. In the Olympic Games of 1924 she won a gold medal. In 1926 she became the first woman to swim the 35-mile-wide English Channel. Her time beat the men's record by nearly two hours.

Besides being eager spectators, more Americans began participating in sports. With more leisure time and with the mobility of automobiles, people took up golf, tennis, swimming, and other types of recreation.

SECTION 3 REVIEW

Comprehension

1. **Key Terms** Define: (a) flapper; (b) demographics; (c) barrio.
2. **Summarizing the Main Idea** In what ways did Americans react to the changing social values of the 1920s?
3. **Organizing Information** Make a tree map entitled *Women in the 1920s.* On the first level, create categories labeled *Changes in Lifestyles, Women at Work,* and *Women in Politics.* Then fill in facts under each of these categories.

Critical Thinking

4. **Analyzing Time Lines** Refer to the time line at the start of the section. Choose three entries and explain the significance of each.
5. **Recognizing Cause and Effect** How did the business boom of the 1920s affect the nation's demographics?

Writing Activity

6. **Writing an Expository Essay** Write a magazine article titled "The Roaring Twenties." Describe some of the trends and people who gave the 1920s this name.

SECTION 4

Mass Media and the Jazz Age

Objectives
You may wish to call students' attention to the objectives in the Section Preview. The objectives are reflected in the main headings of the section.

Bellringer
Ask students what new source of information became popular in the 1990s? (*The Internet.*) How has it affected communication? In what other ways has the Internet affected life in the United States?

Reading Strategy
Organizing Information Refer to the Reading Strategy in the Section Preview. You may wish to have students share their definitions and then work together as a class to create a composite definition.

LESSON PLAN
Connecting to the Main Idea

1. Focus In the 1920s, developments in communication, entertainment, and the arts contributed to the growth of a distinctly American culture. Ask students what these developments were. How did they affect life in the United States?
2. Instruct Discuss the role of the mass media. How did newspapers and radio help to create a national culture?

Ask students how radio helped make jazz a part of American culture. Who were some of the most well-known jazz musicians during the 1920s?

Discuss the role of other art forms and artists in the 1920s. How did writers of the Lost Generation express their discontent with American culture? What was the contribution of the Harlem Renaissance to American literature?
3. Close A uniquely American culture developed in the 1920s. The next section discusses the conflicts within this culture.

614 Chapter 21 • *Section 4*

4 Mass Media and the Jazz Age

SECTION PREVIEW

Objectives
1. Analyze the impact of the growth of the nation's mass media.
2. Identify some of the major figures of the Jazz Age and other artistic figures of the 1920s.
3. Show how the Lost Generation and the Harlem Renaissance influenced American culture.
4. *Key Terms* Define: mass media; Jazz Age; Lost Generation; Harlem Renaissance.

Main Idea
Radio, movies, and jazz were some of the new forms of information, entertainment, and the arts that began in the 1920s. The decade was an especially creative period for music, art, and literature.

Reading Strategy
Organizing Information As you read, write down facts that will help you to define what the Jazz Age was. Then use your notes to write a one-sentence definition.

Lillian Gish worked in silent films and "talkies."

Before 1900, few outside of Los Angeles had even heard of the dusty little suburb northwest of the city. It had been built by a prohibitionist, who hoped it would remain a dry town, free of drinking and bad behavior.

In the early 1900s, however, filmmakers moved into the little town. They were attracted by its sunny climate, its variety of landscapes from desert to snowy mountains, and the large work force available in the area. Movies made the little town big. In time, its main avenue became a strip of expensive shops and bars. Stars drove the streets in luxurious imported cars, trailed by reporters.

By the 1920s, the whole nation knew about it. In fact, the whole world knew about it. Dusty little Hollywood had grown up.

The Mass Media

Hollywood's new fame reflected a major trend of the 1920s. Before that time, the United States had been largely a collection of regional cultures. Interests, tastes, and attitudes varied widely from one region to another. The majority of people simply did not travel about much, talk to those in other regions, or even read much of the same news as others.

The 1920s changed all that. Films, nationwide news gathering, and the new industry of radio broadcasting produced a truly national culture. Print and broadcast methods of communicating information to large numbers of people are known as the **mass media.**

Movies From their beginnings in the 1890s, motion pictures had been a wildly popular mass medium, and through the 1920s, people just kept coming. Between about 1910 and 1930, the number of theaters rose from about 5,000 to about 22,500. During the later part of the decade, the nation's theaters showed movies to roughly 90 million Americans each week—at a time when the total population was less than 125 million. Movie making had become the fourth largest business in the country.

These growth figures are even more amazing in view of the fact that before 1927, movies

▶ RESOURCE OPTIONS

Teaching Resources

📁 **Reproducible Lesson Plan** Lesson Plans folder, p. 121

📁 **Learning Styles Lesson Plan** Learning Styles Lessons Plans folder, p. 44

📁 **Big Idea Graphic Organizer** Big Idea Graphic Organizer folder, p. 93

📁 **Guided Reading and Review** Units 7–8 folder, p. 9

FACT Finder

Growth of the Mass Media, 1920–1930

Newspapers	Between 1920 and 1930 daily newspaper circulation rose from 27,791,000 to 39,589,000—an increase of 42%.
Motion Pictures	Between 1922 and 1930 the number of people attending motion pictures rose from 40 million per week to 90 million per week—an increase of 125%.
Radios	Between 1920 and 1930 the number of households with radios, like the one at right, rose from 20,000 to 13,750,000—an increase of 68,650%.

Source: *Historical Statistics of the United States, Colonial Times to 1970*

Interpreting Tables The decade of the 1920s saw an explosion in forms of mass communication, such as this radio (right). *Science and Technology Which form of mass communication grew most during this decade?*

were silent. In that year the first film with sound was introduced. Titled *The Jazz Singer,* it featured a vaudeville star named Al Jolson. Audiences loved the singing, music, and sound effects of the film. The industry boom continued as theaters everywhere changed over to the new "talkies."

Newspapers Americans followed the off-screen lives of their favorite stars in another mass medium, the newspaper. During the 1920s newspapers increased both in their size and in the number of readers. In 1900, a hefty edition of *The New York Times* totaled only 14 pages. By the mid-1920s, however, newspapers even in mid-sized American cities were totaling more than 50 pages a day, and Sunday editions were enormous. In fact, the use of newsprint roughly doubled in the United States between 1914 and 1927.

Although newspapers were getting bigger, the number of them was declining. Between 1914 and 1929, several thousand newspapers and magazines went out of business in the United States. Often, newspaper chains owned by a single individual or company bought up established papers and merged them. Between 1923 and 1927, the number of chains doubled, and the total number of newspapers they owned rose by 50 percent.

William Randolph Hearst, the legendary publisher of the *San Francisco Examiner* and the *New York Journal,*[†] gained control of newspapers in more than 20 cities. As newspapers became a mass medium, people shared the same information, read about the same events, and were influenced by the same ideas and fashions. Thus newspapers helped create a common culture.

Radio As a mass medium, radio barely existed until the 1920s. Before that time, only about 20,000 Americans had radio sets, all homemade. As an experiment, in 1920 Frank Conrad of the Westinghouse Company in East Pittsburgh tried sending recorded music and baseball scores over the radio. The response was so great that Westinghouse began broadcasting programs on a regular basis. Soon the nation had its first radio station operating as a for-profit business, Pittsburgh's KDKA.

The growth of radio was tremendous. By 1922 more than 500 stations were on the air, and Americans were eagerly buying radios to listen to them. To reach more people, networks

Main Idea CONNECTIONS

What social changes were brought about by the mass media?

[†] Hearst's life and quest for power were the basis for one of the most popular motion pictures ever, Orson Welles's 1941 classic *Citizen Kane.*

ACTIVITY
EXTENDED CLASS PERIODS

Time: 90 minutes.
Activity: Create a movie idol.
Grouping: Groups of four students.
Purpose: Through the efforts of the entertainment media, national idols were created for the first time during the 1920s. Have groups select a movie character of the 1920s and develop a campaign to make that character the newest movie idol. Students can refer to *The Story of Cinema* by David Shipman for ideas regarding movie characters of the decade.
Roles: Members of a media public relations group, such as writers, illustrators, marketing specialists.
Outcome: Students will portray the effects of the media and advertising in the 1920s.

Customize for
More Advanced Students

Have students research the roots of jazz. Than have them write a paragraph or two explaining how jazz is a uniquely American art form.

Answer to . . .

Interpreting Tables Radio.
Main Idea Connections With people sharing the same information and being influenced in the same ways, a common culture emerged.

Recent Scholarship

In the 1920s, African Americans made history through music, literature, and social movements. One of the many notable African Americans living during this time was Carter G. Woodson, generally known as the "Father of Black History," who was one of the first to point out that African Americans had a rich history worthy of significant study. Jacqueline Goggin, in *Carter G. Woodson: A Life in Black History,* explains how Woodson's work, capitalizing on the tide of the Harlem Renaissance, prompted Americans to celebrate Negro History Week in the second week of February, a week framed by the birthdays of Abraham Lincoln and Frederick Douglass. From 1926 until 1976, Americans recognized Negro History Week. In 1976, the entire month of February was designated as Black History Month.

Play a recording of one of the jazz greats, such as Duke Ellington or Louis Armstrong. Have students listen to the music and then discuss how it expresses the mood of the 1920s. *(Musical/Rhythmic, Auditory)*

---

such as the National Broadcasting Company (NBC) linked many individual stations together. Each station in the network played the same programming. Soon much of the country was listening to the same jokes, commercials, music, sports events, religious services, and news. Other companies imitated NBC, building networks of their own. Thus radio became a medium for the masses.

The Jazz Age

Radio combined with the great African American migration to the cities to produce another highlight of the 1920s—a music called jazz. This music features improvisation, a process by which musicians make up music as they are playing it rather than relying completely on printed scores. It also has a type of off-beat rhythm called syncopation.

Jazz Arrives Jazz grew out of African American music of the South, especially ragtime and blues. By early in the 1900s, bands in New Orleans were playing the new mix of styles, and many radio listeners began hearing the new sound for the first time in the 1920s. Soon jazz became a nationwide craze. Younger people in particular loved to dance to the new music. By 1929, a survey of stations showed that two thirds of all radio air time was devoted to jazz.

Jazz won over even Americans who had been horrified by it at first. It seemed to sum up the character of the decade. The great symphony conductor Leopold Stokowski declared that jazz was "an expression of the times, of the breathless, energetic, superactive times in which we are living." It was no surprise that the 1920s came to be called the **Jazz Age.**

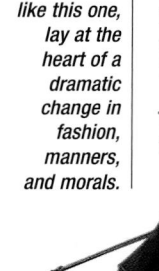
Jazz music, played on phonographs like this one, lay at the heart of a dramatic change in fashion, manners, and morals.

The Jazz Clubs One of hottest places to listen to jazz was Harlem, a district on the northern end of New York City. By one count, Harlem had some 500 jazz clubs. About a dozen clubs gave shows mostly for white visitors, including the Cotton Club, Connie's Inn, and the Saratoga Club.

Nearly all the great jazz musicians played in the Harlem clubs at one time or another. The Jelly Roll Morton Band had a smooth, modern sound. Louis

---

"Satchmo" Armstrong improvised brilliant solos on his trumpet or sang soulful tunes. One of the best remembered jazz musicians to play in Harlem, however, was "the Duke" himself—Duke Ellington.

Duke Ellington

AMERICAN BIOGRAPHY Edward Kennedy Ellington was born in Washington, D.C., in 1899. His father worked as a butler but later became a blueprint maker for the navy. The Ellingtons were able to keep up a middle-class life in a time when doing so was especially difficult for African Americans.

"Duke," as Ellington was called, showed talent at both drawing and piano from an early age. At 17 he was supporting himself by playing in clubs in Washington at night and painting signs during the day. Although he was offered a scholarship at the Pratt Institute of Fine Arts in New York City, he turned it down in favor of continuing his musical career.

Duke Ellington (1899–1974)

In 1923, jazz musician Fats Waller persuaded Ellington and several of his musician friends to move to New York. They formed a band and soon landed a job at the Hollywood Club in the downtown area. This band, under various names and in one form or another, continued to play with Ellington until his death in 1974.

In the 1920s, he worked with superb jazz musicians such as Bubber Miley on trumpet, "Tricky Sam" Nanton on trombone, and Sonny Greer on drums. Later Billy Strayhorn joined as an assistant arranger.

Though Ellington was an excellent pianist, his greatest genius was as a bandleader, arranger, and composer. For some 50 years, Ellington's music and his band's music seemed one and the same.

For example, even though "Take the A Train," the band's theme song, was written by Strayhorn, most people associate it with Ellington. Yet Ellington was also a brilliant composer in his own right, writing at least a thousand pieces in his long career, including

---

music for concerts, broadway shows, films, and operas.

Ellington's music lives on today. His old recordings are still available, and new artists continually rework such great tunes as "Mood Indigo," "Solitude," "In a Sentimental Mood," "Blue Harlem," and "Bojangles." Even a century after his birth, among jazz musicians the Duke is still the king.

Other Artists

The jazz spirit ran through all the arts of the 1920s. People spoke of "jazz poetry" and "jazz painting." Its strongest effect, of course, was on other forms of music. Composer George Gershwin, the son of Russian immigrants, won overnight success in 1924 with his *Rhapsody in Blue.* Composed for jazz bandleader Paul Whiteman, this piece was first played by Whiteman's orchestra and throbbed with jazz rhythms. Yet it was not quite jazz and not quite symphony. Instead it was a magical blend of the two.

Painting Like jazz musicians, American painters of the 1920s did not shy away from taking the pulse of American life. Painters such as Edward Hopper and Rockwell Kent showed the nation's rougher side, from cities to coal mines, from the streets to the barrooms.

By contrast, a young artist named Georgia O'Keeffe painted natural objects such as flowers, animal bones, and landscapes. Yet her simple images always suggest something greater than themselves. A range of hills, for example, seem almost to shudder with life. O'Keeffe continued to paint until her death in 1986 at the age of nearly 100.

Literature Several writers, too, began fruitful careers during the 1920s. Muckraking novelist Sinclair Lewis attacked American society with savage irony. His targets included the small town (in *Main Street*, 1920), the prosperous conformist (*Babbit*, 1922), the medical business (*Arrowsmith*, 1925), and dishonest ministers (*Elmer Gantry*, 1927). Lewis refused a Pulitzer Prize in 1926, but he did win (and accept) the Nobel Prize for Literature in 1930, the first such award to go to an American.

Edward Hopper painted this lonely scene, called *Automat,* in 1927. The Automat was a popular restaurant chain in which one could purchase a snack or a meal from a vending machine and eat it at a table. *Culture What does the painting suggest about Hopper's view of the society of the times?*

Another writer destined for the Nobel Prize was playwright Eugene O'Neill. In a career stretching from the 1920s into the 1950s, he wove dark, poetic tragedies out of the material of everyday American life. Until his time, most American theaters had shown only European plays or light comedies. The power of O'Neill's work proved to the public that the American stage could achieve a greatness rivaling that of Europe.

The Lost Generation

One set of writers during the 1920s gained the name the **Lost Generation,** because of their belief that they were lost in a greedy, materialistic world that lacked moral values. Many of these writers and thinkers flocked to Greenwich Village, part of Manhattan, in New York City. (For decades afterward, Greenwich Village would remain a cultural center for bohemians, or rebels against conventional lifestyles.)

F. Scott Fitzgerald and his wife, Zelda Sayre, lived the life of the Lost Generation.

ACTIVITY
STUDENT PORTFOLIO

You may wish to have students add the following to their portfolios. To assess student work, refer to the generic rubrics in the Program Overview in the Teaching Resources.

Ask students to research the life and writings of F. Scott Fitzgerald in order to determine whether he invented the flapper and to write a paper defending their point of view.

BACKGROUND
Art History

Edward Hopper's (1882–1967) paintings reflected the character of the people and the land realistically and objectively. Hopper saw America as a lonely place, often silhouetted in harsh shades of light, as depicted in his paintings "Early Sunday Morning" (1930) or "Room in Brooklyn" (1932). In the midst of the Depression, Hopper's works achieved national recognition when New York's Museum of Modern Art mounted a one-man retrospective show in 1933.

▶ RESOURCE OPTIONS

Media and Technology

RESOURCE PRO

Literature Activity Tales of the Jazz Age, found on Resource Pro, highlights the shallow, carefree rebellion of the flapper culture.

Listening to Music CD Duke Ellington, "Take the A Train"

Color Transparencies Our Multicultural Heritage, C-12; Fine Art, D–18

Answer to . . .

Viewing History Sample answer: It shows a view of a lonely, isolated, impersonal world.

A Diverse Nation

The Harlem Renaissance inspired many artists to create masterpieces of language and tone. Claude McKay's "The Tropics in New York," Jean Toomer's "Cane," and Georgia Douglas Johnson's "Common Dust" are among the many works that express the feelings of both urban and rural African Americans. Langston Hughes's poem "I, Too" epitomizes the sense of possibility and the deep frustrations that African Americans felt at the time. Carl Van Doren, the editor of *Century Magazine* and a Pulitzer Prize–winner for biography, observed: "What American literature decidedly needs at this moment is color, music, gusto, the free expression of gay or desperate moods. If the Negroes are not in a position to contribute to these items, I don't know what Americans are."

VIEWING HISTORY

Writers Langston Hughes (far left) and Zora Neale Hurston (top left) helped make Harlem a leading artistic center. Jazz singer Bessie Smith (bottom left) helped fill jazz nightspots in the North (above). Harlem was also a vital social hub in the 1920s. *Culture* Why do you think Harlem became the center of a literary awakening in the 1920s?

Others became expatriates, or people who live outside their homeland. Discontent with American society of the 1920s, they left the country to live in Paris, or other parts of Europe thought to be more intellectually stimulating.

The most prominent writers of the Lost Generation were John Dos Passos, Archibald MacLeish, Hart Crane, e. e. cummings, Ernest Hemingway, and F. Scott Fitzgerald. Hemingway wrote of the Lost Generation in his 1926 novel *The Sun Also Rises*. His novels and short stories are read today for their direct, simple style.

F. Scott Fitzgerald was both part of the Lost Generation and part of the flapper world. In fact, some people believe Fitzgerald had a part in creating flapper culture with his novel *This Side of Paradise*, published in 1920. His 1925 masterpiece, *The Great Gatsby*, focused on the wealthy, sophisticated Americans of the Jazz Age. Not surprisingly, this Lost Generation writer found the rich to be self-centered and shallow.

After Hemingway made the term "Lost Generation" famous, it was taken up by the flappers. They liked to imagine themselves as rebels against the culture of their time, living a life both fast and dangerous. As their motto they took the words of a popular poet of the day, Edna St. Vincent Millay:

AMERICAN VOICES

❝ My candle burns at both ends;
It will not last the night;
But ah, my foes, and oh, my friends—
It gives a lovely light! ❞

—Edna St. Vincent Millay, "First Fig," 1920

The Harlem Renaissance

For African Americans, the cultural center of the United States increasingly was New York City's Harlem. The number of African Americans living in Harlem grew from 50,000 in 1914 to about 200,000 in 1930. Not just a national center for jazz, Harlem also became the home of an

---

Answer to . . .

Viewing History It was a center for jazz and increasingly attracted other artists.

▶ RESOURCE OPTIONS

Teaching Resources

American History Block Scheduling Support The Harlem Renaissance During the Jazz Age, found in the Prosperity, Depression, and War folder, includes interdisciplinary lesson suggestions and activities for Geography and History, Primary Sources, Biography, and Literature.

Media and Technology

AmericanHeritage® CD-ROM
History Makers Langston Hughes

Biography Zora Neale Hurston

🎧 **Listening to Literature** Zora Neale Hurston, from "Dust Tracks on a Road"

African American literary awakening of the 1920s known as the **Harlem Renaissance.**

James Weldon Johnson emerged as a leading writer of the Harlem group. Johnson lived in two worlds, the political and the literary. As executive secretary of the NAACP, he led the group during an active time in its history, while pursuing a writing career that inspired younger members of the Harlem group. His most famous work, *God's Trombones* (1927), is a collection of sermons in rhythmic verse modeled after the style of traditional black preaching.

Alain Locke's 1925 book *The New Negro* celebrated the blossoming of African American culture. Locke noted that both African and American heritage could be enriching, not conflicting.

Zora Neale Hurston came to New York as a young actress, became an anthropologist, and gained fame as a Harlem writer with her poignant novel *Their Eyes Were Watching God* (1937). Dorothy West, another accomplished writer, tackled the dual themes of being black and being a woman.

The leading poets of the Harlem Renaissance were Claude McKay and Countee Cullen. McKay produced a large body of work, including *Harlem Shadows* (1922), and was a voice of protest against the sufferings of African Americans in white society.

The gifted Cullen is best known for his 1925 collection of poems called *Color*. He was also responsible for bringing to light the talents of the Harlem writers by collecting many of their works into *Caroling Dusk: An Anthology of Verse by Negro Poets* (1927).

The Harlem writer perhaps most studied today is Langston Hughes, a poet, short story writer, journalist, and playwright whose career stretched into the 1960s. Hughes spoke with a clear, strong voice about the joys and difficulties of being human, being American, and being black:

AMERICAN VOICES

" I, too, sing America.
I am the darker brother.
They send me to eat in the kitchen
When company comes,
But I laugh,
And eat well,
And grow strong. . . .

Tomorrow,
I'll be at the table
When company comes.
Nobody'll dare
Say to me,
"Eat in the kitchen,"
Then.

Besides,
They'll see how beautiful I am
And be ashamed—

I, too, am America. "

—*Langston Hughes,*
"I, Too," 1926

Main Idea
CONNECTIONS

What themes did Harlem writers deal with in their works?

SECTION 4 REVIEW

Comprehension

1. **Key Terms** Define: (a) mass media; (b) Jazz Age; (c) Lost Generation; (d) Harlem Renaissance.

2. **Summarizing the Main Idea** What types of cultural changes took place in the United States during the 1920s?

3. **Organizing Information** Create a web diagram with the label *Mass Media* in the center circle. Fill out the diagram to show the various media that developed during the 1920s and some effects these media had on American life.

Critical Thinking

4. **Analyzing Time Lines** Refer to the time line at the start of the section. Choose two people listed on the time line and explain why each was important to the Jazz Age.

5. **Analyzing Documents** Reread the poem above. (a) In a sentence, state the message of the verse. (b) How does it express the spirit of the Harlem Renaissance?

Writing Activity

6. **Writing an Expository Essay** Write an essay describing the spirit of the Jazz Age. Use supporting details from the section.

Answers to
SECTION 4 REVIEW

1. (a) mass media, see p. 614; (b) Jazz Age, see p. 616; (c) Lost Generation, see p. 617; (d) Harlem Renaissance, see p. 619.

2. Mass media created a national culture; radio combined with the African American migration produced jazz; writers of the Lost Generation explored disillusionment; the Harlem Renaissance flourished.

3. Newspapers—brought information to more people, linked regions; radio—spread jazz music to those who might not have listened to it; film—created a huge industry in America, became the fourth-largest business in the country.

4. Duke Ellington—African American pianist, bandleader, arranger and composer; his 50-year career left a legacy of music for concerts, Broadway shows, films and operas. George Gershwin—composer who won overnight success with *Rhapsody in Blue,* which for the first time blended jazz music with symphony.

5. (a) Answers will vary but should show a grasp of the poem. (b) The poem gives voice to the emerging strength and pride among African Americans embodied by the Harlem Renaissance.

6. Essays will vary but should be supported by facts from the section.

RESOURCE OPTIONS

Teaching Resources

📁 **Quiz** Units 7–8 folder, p. 10

📁 **Literature Activity** *The Weary Blues,* Units 7–8 folder, p. 16

Student Performance Pack

Guide to the Essentials Chapter 21, Section 4 (English and Spanish)

Media and Technology

RESOURCE PRO

Biography Bessie Smith, found on Resource Pro, profiles the singer whose life—from poverty, through migration, to success as an interpreter of the blues—is a microcosm of the African American experience of the times.

Answer to . . .

Main Idea Connections African American culture, being black, being American, being a woman.

American ARTIFACTS

The Growth of Jazz

Focus Remind students that the 1920s were referred to as the "Jazz Age." Discuss what this term evoked in terms of dress, art, and behavior among Americans of the time. Would students term the present time the Rap or the Rock-and-Roll Age? Why or why not?

Instruct Have students study the photographs and captions in the feature and discuss why radio was important in bringing jazz to the American public, including white audiences who were less likely to attend jazz clubs. Ask students to make a list of the artifacts they would include in an American Artifacts display about music today. Tell them to choose items that illustrate the many aspects of life that rock or rap music touches.

Extend You may wish to bring CDs or tapes of jazz from the 1920s and later for students to listen to and comment on.

MOOD INDIGO

1

Duke Ellington

Duke Ellington, pictured on the sheet music of one of his famous compositions, became one of America's greatest composers.

2 ### Dizzy Gillespie's Trumpet

Dizzy Gillespie, whose bent horn distinguished him from other trumpet players, pioneered the modern jazz and bebop styles. His career began in the 1930s and spanned seven decades.

3 ### Flapper's Dress and Beads

Flapper clothes were a must for doing the newest dances to jazz music.

4 ### Hymie Shertzer

The well-known saxophonist worked with many bands as well as in recording studios and in radio.

5 ### Shertzer's Saxophone

The saxophone was invented in Europe in 1840 but never became a popular orchestral instrument. Musicians like Shertzer, however, made the sax's smooth, easily blended sound one of the major voices of the jazz band.

▶ **RESOURCE OPTIONS**

Teaching Resources

American History Block Scheduling Support The Harlem Renaissance During the Jazz Age, found in the Poverty, Depression, and War folder, includes interdisciplinary lesson suggestions and activities for Geography and History, Primary Sources, Biography, and Literature.

6 Benny Goodman's Clarinet

Known as the "King of Swing," Goodman began his jazz career in 1923. His "big band" helped make jazz popular with white audiences, but he preferred small groups. Goodman was also a classical performer who made recordings with leading symphony orchestras.

7 1920s Jazz Band

This band, which was photographed in St. Louis, is unidentified. The band played New Orleans-style jazz.

VIEWING HISTORY

1. *Summarize* What do the objects tell you about the growth of jazz?

2. *Connecting to Today* Think about the music of today. How does it compare to that during the 1920s and 1930s? Prepare an oral report for your class in which you explain whether you think that today's music will withstand the test of time, as jazz has.

American ARTIFACTS

FROM EXHIBITIONS AND COLLECTIONS AT THE SMITHSONIAN INSTITUTION'S NATIONAL MUSEUM OF AMERICAN HISTORY

THE GROWTH OF JAZZ

Today rock or hip hop might be your musical choice, but in the 1920s and 1930s, jazz shook the walls of dance clubs. Have you heard of Duke Ellington? Dizzy Gillespie? Benny Goodman? They were just a few of the musicians whose trumpets, saxophones, and clarinets blended to create one of music's most popular styles—jazz. See **1** and **2**.

One reason for jazz's popularity was that its off-beat, spontaneous rhythms reflected the lively spirit of the generation. Young people hungry for expression flocked to the dance halls. The flapper with her jazz-style clothes became a symbol of what came to be known as the Jazz Age. The short dresses and fake jewelry were new and daring, shocking many in the older generations. See **3**.

Jazz exploded across the American music scene during a time of great excitement and change. Americans' notions of art and literature were expanding as artists experimented with new forms of expression. A surge in mass media—movies and newspapers—made information available to more people. Radio had just begun broadcasting, allowing people to hear the same styles of music across the nation. See **4** and **5**.

Jazz had its roots in the African American music of the South. Yet as its popularity grew, jazz crossed racial boundaries. Black jazz artists like Duke Ellington, Count Basie, and Jimmie Lunceford became very popular among white as well as black audiences. White artist Benny Goodman's 1936 quartet that included African American musicians Lionel Hampton and Teddy Wilson was the first popular racially mixed jazz group. See **6** and **7**.

Jazz musicians developed their own styles and signatures. Today, these styles are part of the American culture. Few musical movements have withstood the test of time like jazz. Just ask any fan.

VIEWING HISTORY

Answers to . . .

1. Sample answer: Jazz influenced changes in dress, musical instruments, and lifestyles.

2. Presentations will vary but should discuss how and why jazz has remained popular since the 1920s and apply some of the same criteria to music today.

RESOURCE OPTIONS

Media and Technology

United States History Video Collection™
Volume 12 *Immigration and Cultural Change*

AmericanHeritage® CD-ROM

Time Tour Prosperity, Depression, and War: The Jazz Age

1919	1920	1922	1925	1925
Race riots in Chicago and other cities	Prohibition takes effect	Anti-lynching law fails to pass in Congress	Scopes trial	Marcus Garvey's "Back to Africa" movement ends

| 1918 | 1920 | 1922 | 1924 | 1926 |

5 Cultural Conflicts

Objectives

You may wish to call students' attention to the objectives in the Section Preview. The objectives are reflected in the main headings of the section.

Bellringer

Ask students to consider what might happen if the making, selling, importing, and exporting of soft drinks were made illegal. Do they think all Americans would stop drinking soda? What unwanted effects might such a law have?

Reading Strategy

Problem Solving Refer to the Reading Strategy in the Section Preview. You may wish to discuss as a class the conflicts and students' possible solutions.

SECTION PREVIEW

Objectives

1 Analyze the effects of Prohibition.
2 Summarize the main issue in the Scopes trial.
3 Explain why an increase in racial tensions occurred following World War I.
4 *Key Terms* Define: bootlegger; speakeasy; fundamentalism; Scopes trial.

Main Idea

Rapid social change after World War I caused conflicts among people with differing beliefs and values.

Reading Strategy

Problem Solving As you read, list types of conflicts that divided Americans during the 1920s. Note ways these problems could have been eased.

Prohibition forced many beer companies to find new beverages to brew, as these labels show.

Prohibition of all alcoholic beverages became the law of the land when the Eighteenth Amendment to the Constitution took effect on January 16, 1920. Yet for many people, life went on as usual, including for President Harding, as the daughter of former President Theodore Roosevelt witnessed:

AMERICAN VOICES ❝Though violation of the Eighteenth Amendment was a matter of course in Washington, it was rather shocking to see the way Harding disregarded the Constitution he was sworn to uphold. . . . There were always, at least before the unofficial dinners, cocktails in the upstairs hall outside the President's room. . . .

One evening . . . a friend of the Hardings asked me if I would like to go up to the study. . . . No rumor could have exceeded the reality. . . . Trays with bottles containing every imaginable brand of whiskey stood about. . . .❞

—*Alice Roosevelt Longworth,*
Crowded Hours, 1933

Prohibition

The Volstead Act, the law passed by Congress in 1919 to enforce the Eighteenth Amendment, was ignored most of all in the cities of the East Coast. A 1924 report showed Kansans obeying the law at a rate of about 95 percent and New Yorkers at a rate of only about 5 percent. Thus Prohibition sharpened the contrast between urban and rural moral values during the 1920s.

Bootlegging Americans who defied the Volstead Act had to get their liquor, beer, and wine from somewhere. A new type of criminal now came along to supply Americans with alcohol: the bootlegger.

In the old days, **bootleggers** merely had been drinkers who hid flasks of liquor in the leg of their boots. Now the term was used to describe suppliers of illegal alcohol. Some bootleggers smuggled whiskey from the Caribbean or Canada. Others operated stills—devices that made alcohol from corn, grain, potatoes, or other fruit and vegetable sources.

Many bootleggers' customers were owners of **speakeasies,** illegal bars that flourished in

LESSON PLAN

Connecting to the Main Idea

1. Focus Explain that rapid changes in American life after World War I led to differences in values among Americans. Ask students what major conflicts arose.

2. Instruct Discuss the institution of Prohibition and its failure. How did Prohibition contribute to the expansion of organized crime? Ask students to explain why some Americans argued that even though alcohol was bad, it should be legal.

Ask students how the Scopes trial pointed up divisions in American society. Why was the trial of lasting importance?

Discuss racial tensions in the 1920s. Why did violence by whites against blacks increase in the North? Why did membership in the Klan grow? How did African Americans react to the violence?

3. Close The 1920s was a time of rapid social change in the United States, which led to the development of divisions and conflict in American society.

▶ RESOURCE OPTIONS

Teaching Resources

📁 **Reproducible Lesson Plan** Lesson Plans folder, p. 122

📁 **Learning Styles Lesson Plan** Learning Styles Lesson Plans folder, p. 45

📁 **Big Idea Graphic Organizer** Big Idea Graphic Organizer folder, p. 94

📁 **Guided Reading and Review** Units 7–8 folder, p. 11

the cities. Entrance to the speakeasies was restricted. A heavy gate usually blocked the door, to be opened only when customers showed a membership card or were recognized by a guard.

Organized Crime In several cities, criminals formed large, efficient organizations that controlled the distribution of alcohol. Individuals or gangs who tried to compete were run out of town or murdered. The streets of American cities became a battleground, as gangsters fought for control with machine guns and sawed-off shotguns.

Successful bootleggers often expanded into other illegal activities, including gambling, prostitution, and a highly profitable business called racketeering. In the typical "racket," local businesses were forced to pay a fee for "protection." Those who refused to pay might be gunned down or their businesses blown to bits. In one period of a little more than a year, 157 bombs were set off by racketeers in Chicago. Terrified citizens went along with the gangsters' demands. The supporters of Prohibition had never dreamed that their ideals would bear such evil fruit.

Al Capone The most notorious of the gangster organizations was in Chicago. There, bootlegging had added immense wealth to an already successful gambling, prostitution, and racketeering business that reached into nearly every neighborhood, police station, and government office.

In 1925 a young crime boss murdered his way to the top of Chicago's organized crime network. He was Al Capone, nicknamed "Scarface."

Capone was a ruthless criminal with a talent for avoiding jail. With so much money at his disposal ($60 million a year from bootlegging alone), Capone found it easy to buy the cooperation of police and city officials. Politicians, even judges, took orders from him.

The government fought back with improved law enforcement. The Federal Bureau of Investigation (FBI), headed by J. Edgar Hoover, became a dedicated, independent force against organized crime during the 1920s.

For years, Capone managed to slip out of any charges brought against him. Finally, in 1931 he was convicted of tax evasion and sent to prison. Bootlegging, however, remained a problem until Prohibition was ended in 1933.

COMPARING PRIMARY SOURCES

THE EIGHTEENTH AMENDMENT

Violations of Prohibition led Congress to hear testimony on whether the Eighteenth Amendment should be repealed.

In Favor of Repeal	**Against Repeal**
"I will concede that the saloon was odious [offensive], but now we have delicatessen stores, pool rooms, drug stores, millinery shops, private parlors, and 57 other varieties of speakeasies selling liquor and flourishing." —*Representative Fiorello La Guardia of New York, 1926*	"Instead of lowering our standards, we urge that the law be strengthened. . . . The closing of the open saloon . . . has resulted in better national health; children are born under better conditions, homes are better, and the mother is delivered from the fear of a drunken husband." —*Ella A. Boole, president of the National Woman's Christian Temperance Union, 1926*

ANALYZING VIEWPOINTS Compare the main arguments made by the two speakers.

Chicago gangster Al Capone (left) confers with his lawyer in this 1929 photo. *Government How was the government finally able to put Capone away?*

From the Archives of

AmericanHeritage®

Sister Aimee On January 1, 1923, in Los Angeles, Aimee Semple McPherson opened the 5,300-seat Angelus Temple, home base for her Church of the Four Square Gospel. Sister Aimee, as she was known, had a riveting stage presence, her charisma was overwhelming, and she knew how to draw a crowd. Aimee preached almost every day and on Sunday, three times. As colored lights played over her pure white gown, she spoke of love and redemption instead of sin and damnation. Vaudevillian musical acts and elaborately staged allegorical scenes rounded out her services. One observer saw the proceedings as "a sensuous debauch served up in the name of religion"; another called them "supernatural whoopee." Within five years the church had thirty thousand members. In a short time, however, scandals and lawsuits had turned off the lights on Aimee's career. Source: Frederic D. Schwarz, "The Time Machine," *American Heritage* magazine, December 1997.

William Jennings Bryan (right) and Clarence Darrow (left) faced off on the issue of evolution in Dayton, Tennessee, in 1925. *Government* *What was the constitutional issue at the heart of the matter?*

Issues of Religion

In addition to prohibition, an issue that highlighted the differences between urban and rural Americans was evolution. Specifically, should public schools teach the Biblical version of the creation of humans or the theory of evolution? The problem touched off a debate that continues to this day.

Fundamentalism Before the teaching of evolution became an issue, many Americans were already uneasy with changes in society. During the early part of the century, challenges to traditional beliefs came from several directions:

(1) Science and technology were taking a larger role in everyday life and thought.

(2) War and the widespread problems of modern society were causing more people to question whether God existed or took an active role in human affairs.

(3) Some scholars were saying that the Bible was a document written by humans and contained contradictions and even historical inaccuracies.

Main Idea
CONNECTIONS
What social changes of the early 1900s did some Americans find disturbing?

In response to these challenges, religious traditionalists published a series of 12 pamphlets called *The Fundamentals.* They stated a set of beliefs that have since come to be called **fundamentalism.** In addition to traditional Christian ideas about Jesus Christ, fundamentalists argued that the Bible was inspired by God and cannot contain contradictions or errors. They declared that the Bible is literally true and that every story in it actually took place as described.

Fundamentalism gained tremendous attention in the 1920s. The most famous fundamentalist preacher of the times was Billy Sunday. His series of more than 300 revivals attracted an estimated total attendance of 100 million. Another popular preacher of the time was Aimee Semple McPherson. Founder of the Angelus Temple, she owned her own radio station and skillfully used the power of mass media in her work.

Evolution and the Scopes Trial Fundamentalists were deeply disturbed by several ideas that were gradually gaining acceptance. One of these, the theory of evolution, stated that human beings and all other living species developed over time from simple life forms.

Fundamentalists denounced the evolution theory, saying it contradicted the history of creation as stated in the Bible. They worked for the passage of laws to prevent public schools from teaching evolution.

When Tennessee passed such a ban, a science teacher named John T. Scopes challenged it as unconstitutional and decided to test the law in the courts. He asked a friend to file suit against him for teaching evolution. Thus began the case popularly known as the **Scopes trial.**

The case became a battle between two of the country's greatest lawyers. William Jennings Bryan, a fundamentalist and former presidential candidate, volunteered to prosecute Scopes.

Answer to . . .

Viewing History The separation of church and state.
Main Idea Connections The role of science and technology, war, challenges to religion.

RESOURCE OPTIONS

Media and Technology

AmericanHeritage® CD-ROM

Time Tour A New Role in the World: Progressives and Reformers

Lawyer Clarence Darrow, agreeing with Scopes's view of the issue as a constitutional one, volunteered for the defense. Darrow had won fame for defending political and labor activists such as Eugene V. Debs.

The trial took place in the small town of Dayton, Tennessee, in the withering heat of July 1925. In this new era of mass media, journalists swarmed around the courthouse, telegraphing some 2 million words of reporting to their papers over the ten days of the trial. This was the first trial ever broadcast over American radio.

At one level, the case was a simple one. Scopes readily admitted he had taught the subject, and the jury found him guilty and fined him $100.[†] But there were more complex issues at stake, including the clash between modern beliefs and traditional values of the country.

The dramatic climax of the case came when Darrow put Bryan himself on the stand to testify as an expert on the Bible. Under Darrow's intense questioning, Bryan admitted that even he did not interpret all of the Bible literally.

Fundamentalists saw Bryan as a martyr for their cause, especially when, exhausted from the grueling battle, he died just a few days after the trial. Modernists saw Darrow as a defender of science and reason.

Although the trial was seen as a setback for fundamentalism, the movement remained active. In later decades it would grow in membership and strength.

Racial Tensions

Another clash of the 1920s had to do with race. The Great Migration of African Americans to the North in the early 1900s had been triggered not only by the growth of jobs in the North, but also by an increase in violence against African Americans in the South. Sadly, many black migrants found that they could not escape prejudice by moving north.

Violence against African Americans In what became known as the "Red Summer," race riots erupted in about 25 cities nationwide

---

[†] The Tennessee Supreme Court later threw out Scopes's fine on the grounds that it was too high. Thus the Scopes case could not be used to make an appeal to a higher court to test Tennessee's law against teaching evolution. The law remained in force until 1967, but no other teachers were prosecuted.

---

during the summer of 1919. The bloodiest of the riots occurred in Chicago, where the African American population more than doubled between 1910 and 1920. This increase led to overcrowded neighborhoods and heightened tensions between blacks and whites.

Main Idea
CONNECTIONS
Why did racial tensions increase after World War I?

The violence was touched off when a nine-year-old black boy, swimming at a beach on Lake Michigan, accidentally floated into a "whites only" area. Several whites threw stones at him, and the boy drowned. Furious blacks accused the whites of killing him, and fighting broke out.

The riot spread through the city. For 13 days, parts of Chicago were without law and order. By the end, some 23 African Americans and 15 whites were dead, another 537 people wounded, and 1,000 blacks left homeless. Similar violence broke out in 1919 in Omaha, Tulsa, and Washington, D.C.

Racial violence was also directed against individuals. During the 1920s, the lynchings of the Jim Crow era continued. Many of these new crimes were the work of an old enemy of racial harmony, the Ku Klux Klan.

Revival of the Klan During Reconstruction, President Grant's campaign against the Klan had largely eliminated it. However, in 1915 a former Methodist circuit preacher from Atlanta, Colonel William J. Simmons, revived the organization. By 1922, the Klan membership had grown to about 100,000. By 1924, it was roughly 4 million. The new Klan was no longer a southern organization. In fact, the state with the greatest number of Klansmen was Indiana.

During the early 1920s, Klan members carried out many crimes against African Americans, Catholics, Jews, immigrants, and others. They rode by night, beating, whipping, even killing their victims, terrorizing blacks and whites alike. Then, in 1925, the head of the Klan in Indiana was sentenced to life imprisonment for assaulting a girl who later poisoned herself. The nation was finally shocked into action, and police began to step up enforcement. By 1927, Klan activity had diminished once again.

This 1920s Klan poster leaves no doubt about the Ku Klux Klan's view on immigration.

Graphing the Main Idea

To make sure students understand the main idea of this section, you may wish to use the multiflow map graphic organizer below.

Tell students that a multiflow map shows causes and effects. Ask students to use it to show the conflicts caused by the rapid social changes of the 1920s and their effects.

Teaching Tip A template for this graphic organizer can be found in the Color Transparencies, G-5.

Customize for
Less Proficient Readers

Ask students to explain the following: why Prohibition divided Americans, why the Scopes trial generated heated debate among Americans, and why the Ku Klux Klan experienced a revival in the 1920s.

RESOURCE OPTIONS

Media and Technology

RESOURCE PRO

Visual Learning Activity The Ku Klux Klan, found on Resource Pro, uses a 1923 drawing from *Life* magazine to enhance students' understanding of how artists use symbols to convey political viewpoints.

Answer to . . .

Main Idea Connections Blacks had moved to the cities in huge numbers, causing overcrowding and racial conflicts.

Answers to
SECTION 5 REVIEW

1. (a) bootlegger, see p. 622; (b) speakeasy, see p. 622; (c) fundamentalism, see p. 624; (d) Scopes trial, see p. 624

2. Social and cultural changes challenged traditional beliefs; science and technology were taking a larger role; war and other issues caused people to question the role of God.

3. Cause—Americans fearful of declining moral fiber of society; many blame alcohol. Effect—18th Amendment, bootleggers, speakeasies, organized crime.

4. Accept reasonable answers supported by facts from the section.

5. African American soldiers fought for freedom abroad and were dismayed by the lack of freedoms they experienced at home.

6. Essays will vary but should be supported by facts from the section.

Marcus Garvey (right) is shown here at a Universal Negro Improvement Association equal rights parade. Although his Black Star project ended in disgrace, Garvey received a pardon from President Coolidge before completing his five-year jail sentence. *Culture Why do you think Garvey sought to bolster self-esteem among African Americans?*

to pass federal anti-lynching laws. A proposed law passed the House of Representatives in 1922, but died in the Senate. Nevertheless, because of improved law enforcement at the state level, lynchings gradually decreased to ten per year in 1929.

During the 1920s, the NAACP also worked to protect African Americans' right to vote, but again it had only limited success. A Texas law establishing a separate primary election for whites was declared unconstitutional. Yet African Americans in the South still could not gain the political power they deserved in a true democracy.

The Garvey Movement Some African Americans, frustrated by continued violence and discrimination, dreamed of a new homeland where they could live in peace. The leader of this movement was an African American named Marcus Garvey.

Garvey had come to New York from his native Jamaica in 1916 to establish a new headquarters for his Universal Negro Improvement Association (UNIA). The UNIA sought to build up African Americans' self-respect and economic power. Its message of racial pride attracted a large number of followers.

Garvey urged African Americans to return to "Motherland Africa." He gathered $10 million for a steamship line (the "Black Star") that would take his followers back to the motherland. In 1925, however, Garvey was jailed on fraud charges, and the UNIA collapsed. Still, Garvey's ideas remained an inspiration to later "black pride" movements.

Fighting Discrimination Increasing violence against African Americans rallied the efforts of the National Association for the Advancement of Colored People (NAACP). During the 1920s, the NAACP worked in vain

SECTION 5 REVIEW

Comprehension

1. *Key Terms* Define: (a) bootlegger; (b) speakeasy; (c) fundamentalism; (d) Scopes trial.

2. *Summarizing the Main Idea* Why did divisions emerge within American society during the 1920s?

3. *Organizing Information* Create a cause-and-effect chart on Prohibition.

Critical Thinking

4. *Analyzing Time Lines* Refer to the time line at the start of the section. Which events do you think had a lasting impact on society, and which did not? Explain your answer.

5. *Making Inferences* How might the participation of African Americans in World War I have influenced the racial tensions that emerged just after the war?

Writing Activity

6. *Writing an Expository Essay* From the perspective of a writer in the 1920s, write an essay that explains the key issues in the Scopes trial. Base your analysis on the facts in this section.

Answer to . . .

Viewing History Sample answer: So that they would work together to overcome discrimination and achieve economic success.

▶ RESOURCE OPTIONS

Teaching Resources

📁 **Quiz** Unit 7–8 folder, p. 12

📁 **Chapter Tests Forms A and B** Chapter Test folder

Student Performance Pack

Guide to the Essentials Chapter 21, Section 5 (English and Spanish)

Standardized Test Preparation Handbook

Media and Technology

🎧 **Guided Reading Audiotapes** Chapter 21 Summary (English and Spanish)
Student Edition on Audiotape Chapter 21

💿 **Test Bank CD-ROM; Interactive Student Tutorial CD-ROM** Chapter Test

The Generation Gap Is Not New

Today, as in the 1920s, the American youth culture is markedly different from that of the older generation.

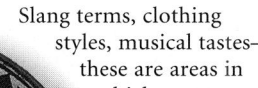

Jazz record from the 1920s

Slang terms, clothing styles, musical tastes—these are areas in which young people traditionally set themselves apart from their parents and grandparents. To many older Americans, the pastimes and attitudes of youth are sad proof that the nation's morals have decayed. Yet a "generation gap" has divided older and younger people for centuries, and society has always managed to survive.

The Impact Today

In the 1920s such trends as short skirts and jazz music troubled some Americans. Today an increasing number of Americans are disturbed by the rise in obscene language and sexual and violent images in popular music, movies, television, and the Internet. These aspects of youth culture have prompted calls for government, schools, and parents to regulate these undesirable influences.

Public and private institutions have heeded the call. For example, many school systems have decided to adopt dress codes or school uniforms to promote order and decrease violent behavior. Television networks have adopted a coding system that indicates the content of programs and their appropriateness for younger audiences.

How many Americans support actions such as these? A clear majority of those interviewed in one nationwide poll approved of greater restrictions on television programming, as well as on the lyrics to popular songs. A whopping 93 percent of interviewees favored stricter parental supervision of different forms of youth entertainment.

Some Americans, however, caution that restrictions on entertainment could go too far and become a form of censorship. These people often point out that, while every generation has its rebellions, most young people grow up to be responsible adults.

The Impact on You

Ask five people in your community to evaluate the following statement: "Warning labels on popular music and television coding systems are needed to protect young people from harmful influences and ideas." Decide what you think. Then write an editorial for your school newspaper that explains your point of view. Your editorial should deal with the arguments raised by the five people you interviewed.

Warning label placed on CDs with explicit lyrics

▶ RESOURCE OPTIONS

Teaching Resources

📁 **Why Study History? Activity** The Generation Gap is Not New found in the Why Study History? folder, p. 22, provides an activity to help students better understand the "generation gap."

Media and Technology

 AmericanHeritage® **CD-ROM**

Time Tour Prosperity, Depression, and War: The Jazz Age

◉ 📼 **Prentice Hall United States History Video Collection**™ Volume 17 *The Roaring Twenties*

Class Discussion

Discuss with the class youth culture and the "generation gap." For a more thorough examination of the issue, see the activity folder in the Resource Options below.

ACTIVITY
STUDENT PARTICIPATION

Creating a Youth-Culture Bulletin Board

Ask students to read the text. Then have them identify specific examples of youth culture, including:

- **music**
- **clothing**
- **slang**
- **hair styles**
- **books**

Invite students to each bring in one or more drawings, photographs, quotations, or objects to contribute to a bulletin board, titled "Youth Culture at (Name of Your School)."

Follow up Have small groups write songs on the topic of youth culture.

💻 Using the Internet

💻 Students can learn more about youth culture by exploring links in the *America: Pathways to the Present* Web site at:

http://www.Pathways.phschool.com

Assessment

See the Lesson Plans folder, pp. 24–27, for rubrics on assessing Class Participation Projects.

Key Terms

Students should refer to the definitions of key terms in the chapter to write sentences that show an understanding of the social changes of the 1920s.

Comprehension

1. (a) Labor strikes and terrorist acts. (b) The Palmer raids; the defeat of many progressive reforms.
2. (a) Several corruption scandals, including the Teapot Dome scandal. (b) He was already well-respected for having avoided corruption.
3. Republican laissez-faire policies caused rapid business expansion, opening up new opportunities for competitors to the giant monopolies. The automobile, steel, oil, and electrical industries boomed as did the publishing, motion picture, and machine-making industries.
4. Ford produced cars that working people could afford. Auto-making became the nation's biggest single manufacturing industry. Thousands of related new businesses arose.
5. Women started smoking, wearing makeup, and drinking. Women began moving into office jobs, but were still denied equal pay and leadership positions. Some began to seek political offices.
6. A huge number of people moved to cities; African Americans moved north; immigrants from Mexico and Canada entered the country; American suburbs greatly expanded.
7. A group of writers in the 1920s. They were troubled by what they saw as a greedy, materialistic world that lacked moral values.
8. Traditional black culture; being black; being women; being Americans; the sufferings of African Americans in white society; being human.
9. Discontent and disrespect for law in America.
10. Divisions between traditional values and modern scientific beliefs.

Chapter Summary

The major concepts of Chapter 21 are presented below. See also *Guide to the Essentials of American History* or *Interactive Student Tutorial CD-ROM,* which contains interactive review activities, time lines, helpful hints, and test practice for Chapter 21.

Reviewing the Main Ideas

The 1920s was a decade of rapid business growth under the postwar laissez-faire policies of three Republican Presidents. The 1920s brought social change as well, including new freedoms for women, a blossoming of the arts, and the effects of Prohibition.

Section 1: A Republican Decade

Republican administrations of the 1920s pursued pro-business economic policies and an isolationist foreign policy.

Section 2: A Business Boom

During the 1920s, new products and Americans' power to purchase them grew rapidly, producing a decade of enormous business growth.

Section 3: Society in the 1920s

The 1920s was a time of rapid social change, in which women, in particular, adopted new lifestyles and attitudes. Amid these changes many Americans admired heroes who embodied old-fashioned values.

Section 4: Mass Media and the Jazz Age

Radio, movies, and jazz were some of the new forms of information, entertainment, and the arts that began in the 1920s. The decade was an especially creative period for music, art, and literature.

Section 5: Cultural Conflicts

Rapid social change after World War I caused conflicts among people with differing beliefs and values.

Today, as in the 1920s, the American youth culture is markedly different from that of the older generation.

Key Terms

Use each of the terms below in a sentence that shows how it relates to the chapter.

1. bootlegger
2. communism
3. Jazz Age
4. installment plan
5. fundamentalism
6. Teapot Dome scandal
7. flapper
8. assembly line
9. mass media

Comprehension

1. (a) What events of 1919 caused the red scare? (b) How did the government respond?
2. (a) What events brought disgrace upon the Harding presidency? (b) How did Coolidge restore respect to the office?
3. How did a decade of Republican government affect the economy?
4. Describe the impact of Henry Ford on American business and society.
5. In what ways did the role of women change during the 1920s?
6. What types of demographic change occurred during the 1920s?
7. What was the Lost Generation? What trends in society did they find troubling?
8. What themes and experiences did the writers of the Harlem Renaissance explore?
9. What long-term effects did Prohibition produce?
10. What divisions in American society were reflected in the Scopes trial?

Using Graphic Organizers

On a separate sheet of paper, copy the chart below. In each box write a sentence summarizing information from the chapter.

Using Graphic Organizers

Answers will vary but may include:

- Political events in Russia spawned American suspicion of the spread of communism
- Economic change and growth resulted from a Republican laissez-faire approach to business
- The flapper reflected a new lifestyle and role of women in society.
- Artistic achievements such as jazz music reflected a more buoyant, less traditional generation.

Analyzing Political Cartoons ▶

1. This cartoon appeared in 1924. (a) Who was President in 1924? (b) What were the big news items regarding the presidential administration in 1924?

2. Describe the scene in the cartoon. What is it satirizing?

3. Why are Cabinet members for sale?

Critical Thinking

1. *Applying the Chapter Skill* Turn to the vacuum cleaner ad on page 603. From what you know about the changing attitudes of young women of the 1920s, why might this ad have appealed to them?

2. *Demonstrating Reasoned Judgment* Explain the meaning of this statement: "For many African Americans, migration to the North was a mixed success."

3. *Recognizing Ideologies* What beliefs and fears helped fuel the red scare? Were those fears justified? Explain your reasoning.

4. *Drawing Conclusions* What connection might there have been between the mass media and the flapper image?

INTERNET ACTIVITY

For your portfolio:
WRITE AN ESSAY

Access Prentice Hall's *America: Pathways to the Present* site at **www.Pathways.phschool.com** for the specific URL to complete the activity. Additional resources and related Web sites are also available.

Read about the cycles of nativism in American history and a Boston journalist's perspective on the continuing effects of the Sacco and Vanzetti trial. What factors contribute to nativism? What are the dangers of nativism? Write an essay exploring these questions, using the Sacco and Vanzetti case as an example.

ANALYZING DOCUMENTS ◀▷ INTERPRETING DATA

Turn to the excerpt from the poem "First Fig" in Section 4.

1. Which of the following best expresses the meaning of the first line? (a) She feels bright. (b) She stays up all night. (c) She is religious. (d) The pace of her life is dangerously fast.

2. Which of the following best expresses the meaning of the last line? (a) Her lifestyle is exciting while it lasts. (b) She feels bright and lovely. (c) Her friends and foes approve of her lifestyle. (d) Her life is quiet.

3. *Writing* Why do you think the flappers thought of this poem as their motto? Why do think the writer herself disapproved of this interpretation?

Connecting to Today

Essay Writing Write an essay that addresses this statement: "The 1920s laid the foundation for today's society." Use examples from the economy and from society.

INTERNET ACTIVITY

Essays will vary but should consider facts about nativism and the Sacco and Vanzetti trial discussed in the chapter and include details and quotes from the Web site.

Analyzing Political Cartoons

1. (a) Harding. (b) Financial scandals, such as the 1923 Teapot Dome scandal.

2. The scene shows the Capitol, White House, Washington Monument, the armed forces, and members of Harding's administration for sale. It is satirizing the scandals in Harding's administration.

3. In the Teapot Dome affair, a Cabinet secretary gave away oil rights on government land in exchange for money.

Critical Thinking

1. Sample answer: They might have been attracted to its apparent ease of use, and to the daintiness of the girl in the ad.

2. Although they came in search of a better life, they still met with racism. Women often had to work as household help for whites at low wages that kept them trapped in poverty.

3. The belief that communism would spread to America and the fear of violence. It was understandable to a certain extent since Lenin vowed to stir up revolutions in other countries, but the widespread paranoia that took place in America resulted in raids and arrests of many innocent people.

4. The mass media spread jazz, which was embodied in the symbol of the flapper.

Analyzing Documents

1. d
2. a
3. They liked to imagine themselves as living a fast and dangerous lifestyle and, to them, the poem embodied that sentiment. She probably disapproved because the poem had taken on a meaning other than what she intended.

Connecting to Today

Essays will vary but should be based on examples from the chapter.

Crash and Depression, 1929–1933

Managing Time and Instruction

INSTRUCTION SUPPORT

These materials for instruction are provided for **each section** in the **Teaching Resources.** See **Units 7–8 folder** for Enrichment Support:

- Reproducible Lesson Plans in Lesson Plans folder • Learning Styles Lesson Plans in Learning Styles Lesson Plans folder • Big Idea Graphic Organizers in Big Idea Graphic Organizer folder
- Guided Reading and Review • Quizzes • Test Preparation Practice booklet

DAILY LESSON	ENRICHMENT SUPPORT
1 The Economy in the Late 1920s *(pp. 631–634)*	• Critical Thinking Activity, Identifying Central Issues: Signs of Trouble, found on **Resource Pro** • Visual Learning Activity, Hard Times for Farmers, Learning with Documents folder, p. 64
2 The Stock Market Crash *(pp. 635–638)*	• Literature Activity, The Stock Market Crash, Units 7–8 folder, p. 31 • Biography, Woody Guthrie, found on **Resource Pro**
3 Social Effects of the Depression *(pp. 639–643)*	• Primary Source Activity, Hard Times in Oklahoma, Learning with Documents folder, p. 28 • Nystrom *Atlas of Our Country,* People on the Move, pp. 34–35 • Literature Activity, The Psychological Effects of the Depression, found on **Resource Pro**
4 Surviving the Great Depression *(pp. 646–648)*	• Biography, Babe Didrikson Zaharias, Units 7–8 folder, p. 28 • Primary Source Activity, "The Forgotten Man," found on **Resource Pro** • Skills for Life Activity, Units 7–8 folder, p. 32
5 The Election of 1932 *(pp. 650–654)*	• Comparing Primary Sources, On Ending the Depression, Units 7–8 folder, pp. 29–30 • Visual Learning Activity, Veterans March on Washington, found on **Resource Pro** • Lasting Impact Activity, The Lasting Impact of the Election of 1932, History's Lasting Impact folder, pp. 14–15 • Key Documents, Franklin D. Roosevelt, First Inaugural Address, Learning with Documents folder, p. 96 • Investing Involves Risk, Why Study History? folder, p. 23

Running Out of Time?

- Use Tape "Boom Times to Hard Times, 1919–1938," from **Visions of America** videotapes series.
- Use Chapter 22 Summary from **Guide to the Essentials of American History (English and Spanish).**

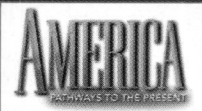

Companion Web Site

The companion Web site offers online links for all chapter review activities. It also provides key content links and structured support for this chapter for both teachers and students.

http://www.Pathways.phschool.com

Teaching in the Information Age

Media and Technology

For the Student

Interactive Student Tutorial CD-ROM Chapter 22
Student Edition on Audiotape Chapter 22
American Heritage® CD-ROM
Guided Reading Audiotapes (English and Spanish) Chapter 22

For the Teacher

Resource Pro CD-ROM Chapter 22
Test Bank CD-ROM Chapter 22
Listening to Literature Audiotapes *Timeless Voices, Timeless Themes* "Winter Dreams" by F. Scott Fitzgerald

Block Scheduling

Pacing Suggestions

For 90-minute Blocks

- Teach sections 2 and 5 using Transparencies B-7, E-6, and I-8 and the Extended Class Periods Activity on p. 637.
- Teach sections 1, 3, and 4 using the Big Idea Graphic Organizers from Teaching Resources and the Recent Scholarship note on p. 642 for class discussion.

Additional Resources

- Prentice Hall's **American History Block Scheduling Support File** covers over 40 major topics in American history.
- **Prentice Hall United States History Video Collection**™ contains 20 videotapes covering American history from beginnings to present.
- **Visions of America Videotapes and Videodiscs**

Assessment Options

Chapter Test Forms A&B Test Bank CD-ROM booklet
Test Bank CD-ROM Chapter 22
Standardized Test Preparation Handbook

Connections to American Literature

from Prentice Hall

Prentice Hall Literature *Timeless Voices, Timeless Themes* "Allentown" by Billy Joel, p. 719

Additional Resources

For the Student
The Great Depression. 420 minutes. PBS Video, 1993.
The Grapes of Wrath. 129 minutes. Zenger.

For the Teacher
T. H. Watkins. *The Great Depression: America in the 1930s.* Little Brown, 1993.

Prentice Hall brings into the classroom the vast archives and scholarship of the nation's premier American history magazine. See "About the Presidents" teaching notes in this chapter.

History Alive!

Teacher's Curriculum Institute, in partnership with Prentice Hall, provides unique materials that engage students with diverse learning styles. See History Alive!® unit on The Roaring Twenties and the Great Depression.

Student Performance Pack

Ensures success in the three critical areas of Reading, Test Taking, and English Language Development with the following materials:
- Guide to the Essentials of American History in English and Spanish
- Guided Reading Audiotapes in English and Spanish
- Interactive Student Tutorial CD-ROM
- Test Preparation Handbook
- Test Preparation Practice booklet

Crash and Depression
1929–1933

Introducing the Chapter
When the economy of the high-flying 1920s crashed in 1929, the bleak years of the Great Depression began. Behind the headlines and photos of stock-buying-and-selling frenzy and destitution grew a debate that cut to the very political, social, and economic fiber of the country and changed forever how Americans look at government.

Themes in American History
The theme for this chapter, Economics, is listed at the beginning of this unit. An alternate theme for the chapter is Government. To teach this unit thematically, you may wish to use the Prosperity, Depression, and War folder in American History Block Scheduling Support.

Why Study History?

Have students explore suggested ways of connecting the past to the present on page 655.

on page 655.

CHAPTER FOCUS

This chapter examines the events leading to the crash of the stock market in 1929 and the economic disaster it unleashed: the Great Depression. The chapter looks at how the Depression took its toll and how Americans learned to cope with it.

The Why Study History? page at the end of this chapter explores the connection between investing in the stock market in 1929 and investing in it today.

▲
VIEWING HISTORY
The effects of the Great Depression show on the weary faces of this homeless Oklahoma family. *Economics What evidence does this photo give of the depth of their poverty?*

Answer to . . .

Viewing History Students should use this question as an aid in reading the chapter. Their worn clothing, the suggestion that they are carrying all their belongings, and the weariness on their faces suggest the depth of the people's poverty.

 RESOURCE OPTIONS

Teaching Resources

Big Idea Graphic Organizer folder Graphic summary of the main idea of the chapter.

Learning Styles Lesson Plans folder Alternate lesson plans for diverse learning styles for each chapter.

Media and Technology

 AmericanHeritage® CD-ROM
Time Tour Prosperity, Depression, and War: Depression and the New Deal

 Prentice Hall United States History Video CollectionTM Volume 18 *The Great Depression and the New Deal*

| 1927 Coolidge vetoes farm relief bill | 1928 Hoover elected President | 1929 Home building falls by 25 percent | 1929 200 companies own nearly half of all industry | 1929 In October, value of stocks climbs to $87 billion |

1927   **1928**   **1929**

1 The Economy in the Late 1920s

SECTION PREVIEW

Objectives

1 Explain why the economy appeared to be healthy in the 1920s.
2 Explain why, in reality, the economy was headed into danger.
3 *Key Terms* Define: welfare capitalism; speculation; buying on margin.

Main Idea

During the 1920s, rising wealth and a booming stock market gave Americans a false sense of faith in the economy. In fact, there were signs that the economy was in trouble.

Reading Strategy

Outlining Information Use the headings and subheadings in this section to help you create an outline. As you read, add two key facts under each subheading.

The mood of most Americans in the late 1920s was optimistic, and with good reason. Medical advances had greatly reduced deaths from whooping cough, diphtheria, and other serious diseases. Since 1900 the number of infant deaths had declined, and life expectancy had lengthened more than 10 years, to 59 years for men and 63 years for women.

The brightest hopes seemed to come from the economy. In his final message to Congress, President Calvin Coolidge said that the country could "regard the present with satisfaction and anticipate the future with optimism." His successor, Herbert Hoover, predicted that "poverty will be banished from this nation."

Economy Appears Healthy

When Coolidge chose not to run in 1928, Hoover won easily, benefiting from years of prosperity under the Republicans. A self-made millionaire, Hoover was widely admired for the way he had organized food relief in Europe during and after World War I. He had also been an effective Secretary of Commerce for Presidents Harding and Coolidge. People expected that the

good times would get even better under Hoover.

"Wonderful Prosperity" As Hoover took office, the United States economy seemed to be in fine shape. In 1925, the market value of all stocks was $27 billion. Over the next few years, it soared. In 1928 alone, stock values rose by almost $11.4 billion. Because the stock market was widely regarded as the nation's economic weathervane, *The New York Times* could describe the year as one "of unprecedented advance, of wonderful prosperity." By early October 1929, stock values hit $87 billion.

Working people seemed to have prospered in the post–World War I period. Since 1914, the value of workers' wages had risen more than 40 percent. Although certain industries were troubled, and some workers lost jobs to assembly-line machinery, unemployment averaged below 4 percent. Even critics of capitalism made optimistic predictions:

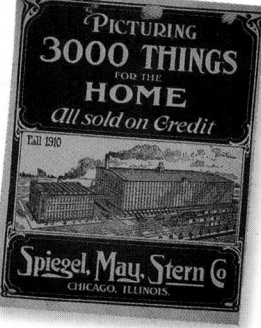

During the 1920s, catalogs brimming with exciting new goods tempted consumers to buy on credit.

▶ RESOURCE OPTIONS

Teaching Resources

 Reproducible Lesson Plan Lesson Plans folder, p. 123

Big Idea Graphic Organizer Big Idea Graphic Organizer folder, p. 95

Guided Reading and Review Units 7–8 folder, p. 18

Media and Technology

AmericanHeritage® CD-ROM

Time Tour Prosperity, Depression, and War: The Jazz Age

The Economy in the Late 1920s

Objectives

You may wish to call students' attention to the objectives in the Section Preview. The objectives are reflected in the main headings of the section.

Bellringer

Have students describe what happens when a consumer makes a purchase on credit. Have them consider factors such as how a consumer gets credit, how buying on credit affects prices, and what happens when consumers cannot make their payments.

Reading Strategy

Outlining Information Refer to the Reading Strategy in the Section Preview. You may wish to model the outline headings and subheadings on the chalkboard. Volunteers may complete the outline on the chalkboard.

LESSON PLAN
Connecting to the Main Idea

1. Focus Many Americans enjoyed great prosperity during the 1920s. Millions of others, however, did not—a sign of trouble to come. Ask what other signs pointed to flaws in the economy.

2. Instruct Discuss the reasons for the mood of optimism that existed in America in the mid-1920s. Ask students to name some of the ways in which workers were better off than they had been.

Point out the indications of trouble ahead. Ask students what percentage of American families had no savings, and how this might have affected their lives.

3. Close Most Americans were optimistic about the continued growth of the economy in 1928 and early 1929. Certain key signs, however, showed that the economy was in trouble. The next section discusses the stock market crash of October 1929.

This car advertisement from the late 1920s reflects the apparent prosperity and optimism of those years. *Economics In what other ways was prosperity apparent in the late 1920s?*

Higher Compression with *any* Gas!

BEAUTIFUL NEW COLORS

WILLYS·KNIGHT

$1295

AMERICAN VOICES

"Big business in America is producing what the Socialists held up as their goal: food, shelter and clothing for all. You will see it during the Hoover administration."

—*Journalist Lincoln Steffens, 1928*

"Everybody Ought to Be Rich" People had unusually high confidence in the business world during the 1920s. For some, business success became almost a religion. One of the decade's best-selling books was *The Man Nobody Knows* (1925). Written by Bruce Barton, an advertising executive, it told the biblical story of Jesus' life in business terms. Barton portrayed Jesus as a managerial genius who "picked up twelve men [a reference to Jesus' 12 apostles, or followers] from the bottom ranks of business and forged them into an organization that conquered the world."

Similarly, Americans trusted the advice of corporate leaders such as John J. Raskob. In a 1929 article, "Everybody Ought to Be Rich," he stated that savings of only $15 a week over 20 years could bring a $400-a-month income from investments. "I am firm in my belief," Raskob said, "that anyone not only can be rich, but ought to be rich."

The three Republican Presidents of the 1920s equated the interests of the nation with the interests of business. Although people in the late 1920s were wildly buying stocks with borrowed money, the Hoover administration did little to discourage such borrowing.

Welfare Capitalism Following the violent labor strikes of 1919, the postwar economy stabilized, and during the 1920s organized labor lost members. To keep the unions weak, many companies launched strategies to meet some of their workers' needs without demands from unions. This new approach to labor relations was known as **welfare capitalism.** Employers raised wages and provided benefits such as paid vacations, health plans, and even English classes for recent immigrants.

Economic Danger Signs

Despite the apparent prosperity, all was not well. Only later did many people recognize the warning signs of an unsound economy.

Uneven Prosperity Despite some stock market success stories, it was mainly the rich who got richer. Huge corporations rather than small businesses dominated industry. In 1929, 200 large companies controlled 49 percent of American industry.

Similarly, a small proportion of families held most of the nation's personal wealth. (See the graph on the next page.) In 1929, the richest Americans—24,000 families, or just 0.1 percent

Main Idea
CONNECTIONS

Why did Americans have so much confidence in the economy in the 1920s?

of the population—had incomes of more than $100,000. They also held 34 percent of the country's total savings.

By contrast, 71 percent of individuals and families earned less than $2,500 a year. Nearly 80 percent of all families had no savings. Many people earned so little that almost everyone in a family, including children, had to work just to get by.

Buying on Credit Another sign of trouble was an increase in personal debt. In the 1920s assembly-line production made consumer items more affordable and available. People bought radios, vacuum cleaners, refrigerators, and other exciting new products, whether or not they could afford them.

Traditionally, Americans feared debt and postponed buying goods until they had the cash to pay for them. Now, however, installment plans made expensive items irresistible.

Playing the Stock Market Fed by the optimism of the age, a "get-rich-quick" attitude prevailed during the 1920s. The dizzying climb of stock prices encouraged widespread **speculation,** the practice of making high-risk investments in hopes of getting a high gain.

Before World War I only the wealthy played the stock market. Now, the press reported stories of ordinary people who had made fortunes. Small investors entered the market, often with their life savings. To attract less-wealthy investors, stockbrokers encouraged a practice called **buying on margin.** It allowed investors to purchase a stock for only a fraction of its price (10 to 50 percent) and borrow the rest.

Brokers charged high interest and could demand payment of the loan at any time. But if the stock price went up, borrowers could sell at a price high enough to pay off loan and interest charges and still make money.

Too Many Goods, Too Little Demand By the late 1920s, the country's warehouses held piles of unbought consumer goods. Wages had risen, but people still could not afford to buy goods as fast as the assembly lines turned them out.

Although the stock market kept rising, overproduction caused some industries to slow in the late 1920s. The automobile industry, which had helped create American prosperity, slumped after 1925. Industries that depended on it—steel, rubber, and glass—also declined. Housing construction fell by 25 percent between 1928 and 1929.

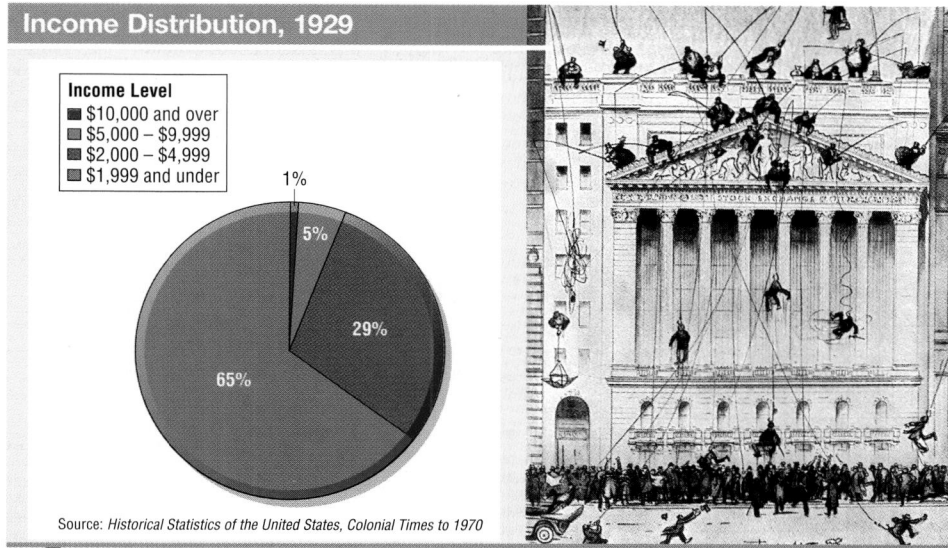

Income Distribution, 1929

Income Level
- $10,000 and over
- $5,000 – $9,999
- $2,000 – $4,999
- $1,999 and under

1%
5%
29%
65%

Source: *Historical Statistics of the United States, Colonial Times to 1970*

 Interpreting Graphs The circle graph (left) shows how unevenly the country's wealth was distributed in the 1920s. At right, greedy stockbrokers fish for new clients from the top of the New York Stock Exchange. *Economics What percentage of American families earned less than $2,000 a year in 1929?*

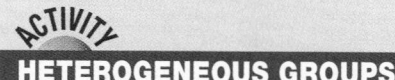

Answers to
SECTION **1** REVIEW

1. (a) welfare capitalism, see p. 632; (b) speculation, see p. 633; (c) buying on margin, see p. 633.

2. The economy seemed healthy and prosperous with a strong stock market and rising wages. People had confidence in business and in Presidents Coolidge and Hoover, and after World War I they were looking for a bright future.

3. Reasons might include: the example of self-made millionaire Hoover; the rising stock market; rising wages; high confidence in big business and business leaders; new benefits for workers.

4. (a) 1927—Coolidge vetoes farm relief bill; 1929—200 companies own nearly half of all industry; 1929—in October, value of stocks climbs to $87 billion. (b) 1927—Coolidge vetoes farm relief bill; 1928—homebuilding falls by 25 percent; 1929—200 companies own nearly half of all industry.

5. Signs might include: widening gap between rich and poor; increase in personal debt; widespread stock speculation; too many unbought consumer goods; slumps in certain key industries; troubles for farmers and factory workers.

6. Essays will vary but should be supported with facts from the section.

Farm families faced hard times in the 1920s. Many had to watch as their homes, land, and animals were sold at auction. *Economics* **Why were farmers struggling economically?**

Trouble for Farmers For some sectors of the farm economy, the 1920s brought not prosperity but devastation. Farm prices had stayed high during the war and just afterward. But when the wartime demand ended, prices, especially for wheat and cotton, plummeted. During the good times, many farmers had purchased the new tractors and other machinery now available. This allowed them to put more land under cultivation, so they bought more land as well.

Falling farm prices made farmers unable to repay their debts for land and machinery. Rural banks suffered when loans were not repaid, and about 6,000 banks went out of business.

Congress responded with the McNary-Haugen farm relief bill, a measure designed to increase the price farmers received for their crops. Congress passed the bill twice, in 1927 and 1928, but each time President Coolidge vetoed it, believing that it was not the government's job to provide such assistance.

Farmers continued to suffer. "We were in the Depression before 1929, we just didn't call it that," recalled a rural Tennessean.

Trouble for Workers Life remained exceedingly hard for many factory workers as well. While companies grew wealthy, most laborers still worked long hours for low wages. Conditions were especially bad in coal mines and southern textile mills. In the rayon mills of Elizabethton, Tennessee, for instance, women worked 56-hour weeks, earning 16 to 18 cents an hour—about $10 a week.

To some observers, these factors—uneven wealth, rising debt, stock speculation, overproduction, and the hardships of farmers and workers—clearly signaled trouble in the economy. In 1928, Belle Moskowitz, who had managed Al Smith's losing presidential campaign that year, predicted that "growing unemployment, business depression, or some false step" would soon trigger a reaction against Hoover and his policies.

SECTION **1** REVIEW

Comprehension

1. *Key Terms* Define: (a) welfare capitalism; (b) speculation; (c) buying on margin.

2. *Summarizing the Main Idea* Why did Americans unwisely trust the economy in the 1920s?

3. *Organizing Information* Create a web diagram to show the reasons that Americans in the 1920s had confidence in the health of the economy.

Critical Thinking

4. *Analyzing Time Lines* Review the time line at the start of this section. (a) Which entries indicate a booming economy? (b) Which indicate signs of trouble? Explain your reasoning. *Note:* Some may fit both (a) and (b).

5. *Identifying Supporting Details* List five signs that the economy was in danger. Explain your choices.

Writing Activity

6. *Writing a Persuasive Essay* Assume the role of the writer of a business column in a 1920s newspaper. Write an essay to persuade your readers either (a) to take advantage of the money-making opportunities in the booming economy, or (b) to show caution in their investments and avoid speculation.

RESOURCE OPTIONS

Teaching Resources

📁 **Visual Learning Activity** Hard Times for Farmers, Learning with Documents folder, p. 64

📁 **Quiz** Units 7–8 folder, p. 19

Student Performance Pack

Guide to the Essentials Chapter 22, Section 1 (English and Spanish)

Answer to . . .

Viewing History Farm machinery allowed them high yields, but falling prices meant they could not earn enough to repay their loans.

1929 (Sept. 3) Stock market reaches all-time high of 381 points	1929 (Oct. 24) Black Thursday	1929 (Oct. 29) Black Tuesday	1931 Ford shuts down Detroit factories	1932 One fourth of work force is unemployed	1933 Money in 9 million savings accounts has been wiped out

1929   1930   1931   1932   1933

2 The Stock Market Crash

SECTION PREVIEW

Objectives

1. Outline the key events of the stock market's Great Crash of 1929.
2. Analyze the effects of the Crash.
3. List the main causes of the Great Depression.
4. *Key Terms* Define: Dow Jones Industrial Average; Black Tuesday; Great Crash; business cycle; Great Depression; Gross National Product (GNP).

Main Idea

In October 1929 panic selling caused the United States stock market to crash. The crash led to a worldwide economic crisis called the Great Depression.

Reading Strategy

Arranging Events in Order Copy the time line above on a separate sheet of paper. As you read, add more information to the time line. Make notes on how one event led to the next.

In early 1928 the **Dow Jones Industrial Average,** an average of stock prices of major industries, had climbed to 191. By Hoover's inauguration day, March 4, 1929, it had risen another 122 points. On September 3, the Dow Jones Average reached an all-time high of 381.

The Market Crashes

The rising stock market dominated the news. Keeping track of prices became almost as popular as counting Babe Ruth's home runs. Eager, nervous investors filled brokerage houses to catch the latest news coming in on the ticker tape. Prices for many stocks soared far above their real value in terms of the company's earnings and assets.

Black Thursday After the peak in September, stock prices fell slowly. Some brokers began to call in loans, but others continued to lend even more. One bank official assured the nervous public: "Although in some cases speculation has gone too far, . . . the markets generally are now in a healthy condition."

When the stock market closed on Wednesday, October 23, the Dow Jones average had dropped 21 points in an hour. The next day, Thursday, October 24, worried investors began to sell, and stock prices fell. Investors who had bought General Electric stock at $400 a share sold it for $283 a share.

Again, business and political leaders told the country not to worry. Another banking executive said that only a nation as rich as the United States could "withstand the shock of a $3 billion paper loss on the Stock Exchange in a single day without serious effects to the average citizen." Hoover maintained that the nation's business "is on a sound and prosperous basis."

Black Tuesday To stop the panic, a group of bankers pooled their money to buy stock. This action stabilized prices, but only for a few days.

The Long and the Short of it

Ticker-tape machines delivered investors both good and bad news about their stocks.

RESOURCE OPTIONS

Teaching Resources

📁 **Reproducible Lesson Plan** Lesson Plans folder, p. 124

📁 **Big Idea Graphic Organizer** Big Idea Graphic Organizer folder, p. 96

📁 **Guided Reading and Review** Units 7–8 folder, p. 20

📁 **Literature Activity** The Stock Market Crash, Units 7–8 folder, p. 31

Media and Technology

 AmericanHeritage® CD-ROM

 Time Tour Prosperity, Depression, and War: Depression and the New Deal

SECTION 2

The Stock Market Crash

Objectives

You may wish to call students' attention to the objectives in the Section Preview. The objectives are reflected in the main headings of the section.

Bellringer

Ask students to take the perspective of a bank customer who wants to withdraw savings and is told by the teller that there is no money. What might be the cause of such a situation? What options would he have?

Reading Strategy

Arranging Events in Order Refer to the Reading Strategy in the Section Preview. You may wish to model the time line on the chalkboard and have volunteers fill it in.

LESSON PLAN

Connecting to the Main Idea

1. Focus Explain that the stock market crash in October 1929 brought on a depression more severe than any the nation had ever experienced. Ask what events led to the crash.

2. Instruct Have students think about conditions on the day after the crash. Explain that it took time for the effects of the crash to reach businesses and services, and few Americans understood at first how the event would affect them. Ask how a general economic failure might affect various employers.

Remind students that the economy was in a fragile state before the collapse of the stock market and the crash of 1929. Ask students to list and explain the underlying causes of the Depression.

3. Close The crash of the stock market in October 1929 brought on a severe economic depression that had repercussions around the world. The next section deals with some of the suffering endured by Americans in that bleak time.

As stock market prices fell, the ticker tape could not report market activity fast enough. Nervous investors crowded into Wall Street, hoping to hear the latest news. *Economics* **Why did President Hoover believe the economy could weather the stock market crash?**

ECONOMICS CONCEPTS

business cycle: *the periodic growth and contraction of a nation's economy*

▼ **The Historical Context:** The Crash of 1929 brought an abrupt end to the economic expansion of the 1920s and ushered in the Great Depression. Following the Crash, political leaders debated whether to fight the Depression through higher government spending or to rely on the natural operation of the business cycle to restore prosperity.

▼ **The Concept Today:** The American economy continues to alternate between periods of higher growth and periods of slower growth, or contraction. The federal government, through its policies on taxing, spending, and the money supply, seeks to prevent shocks to the economy such as the Crash of 1929.

By Monday prices were falling again. Investors all over the country raced to get their money out of the stock market. On October 29, known as **Black Tuesday,** a record 16.4 million shares were sold, compared with the average 4 million to 8 million shares a day earlier in the year.

This collapse of the stock market is known as the **Great Crash.** Despite efforts to halt it, the Crash continued beyond Black Tuesday. By November 13, the Dow Jones average had fallen from its September high of 381 to 198.7. Overall losses totaled $30 billion. The Great Crash was part of the nation's **business cycle,** periods in which the economy grows, then contracts. (See the Economics Concepts feature above.)

From Riches to Ruin It took time for people to recognize the extent of the disaster caused by the Crash. One wealthy Bostonian who lost heavily in the market wrote in his diary, "The profit in my little book melted yesterday to seven thousand. It is probably nil [nothing] today. . . . My dreams of a million—where are they?"

For people whose entire wealth did not depend on the stock market, life went on much as before, with perhaps a few cutbacks. Others, including wealthy families, lost everything. Brokers and banks called in their loans, but people did not have cash to pay them.

The Crash Affects Millions

By 1929, about 4 million people out of a population of 120 million had invested in the stock market. They were the first to suffer from the Crash, but it soon affected millions who had never owned a single share of stock.

The Crash triggered a much wider, long-term crisis called the **Great Depression,** a severe economic decline that lasted from 1929 until the United States' entry into World War II in 1941. The Great Depression was felt throughout the United States, causing millions of Americans to lose their jobs, farms, and homes. The Depression had a ripple effect, producing economic turmoil throughout the world for years.

Impact on Workers and Farmers As income and profits fell, American factories began to close. Thousands of workers lost their jobs or had their pay cut. In August 1931 Henry Ford shut down his Detroit automobile factories, putting at least 75,000 people out of work.

In some European countries, workers had government unemployment insurance, but the United States had no such program. By 1932 more than 12 million people were unemployed, about a quarter of the labor force (see graph on the next page). Others worked only part-time or had their wages cut. The **Gross National Product (GNP)**—the total value of goods and services a country produces annually—was $103 billion in 1929. By 1933 it was only $56 billion.

Economic Impact of the Great Depression

UNEMPLOYMENT 1925–1933

Source: *Historical Statistics of the United States, Colonial Times to 1970*

WHEAT PRICES 1925–1933

Source: *Historical Statistics of the United States, Colonial Times to 1970*

STOCK PRICES 1925–1933

*Based on Standard and Poor's index of common stocks
Source: *Historical Statistics of the United States, Colonial Times to 1970*

BANK SUSPENSIONS 1925–1933

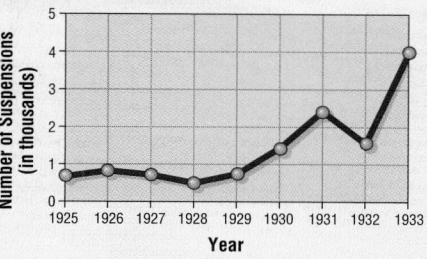

Source: *Historical Statistics of the United States, Colonial Times to 1970*

 Interpreting Graphs The stock market crash caused a series of economic disasters. It hastened the fall of farm prices, added millions of people to the ranks of the unemployed, and forced the government to suspend the activity of thousands of banks. *Economics Roughly how many workers became unemployed between 1929 and 1933?*

The effects of the Crash spread. Restaurants and other small businesses closed because customers could no longer afford to go to them. Once-wealthy families dismissed household workers. Farm prices, already low, fell even more, bringing final disaster to many families. In 1929, a bushel of wheat had sold for $1.04; in 1932 it brought a mere 38 cents. (See graph above.) Cotton dropped from 17 to 6.5 cents a pound.

Banks Close Unpaid farm loans already had ruined many rural banks. Now city banks were in trouble. Banks exist on the interest they earn from lending out their deposits. They assume that not everyone will claim their deposits at once. After the stock market crash, people with loans to repay as well as nervous depositors rushed to withdraw their money.

Thousands of banks closed their doors when they could not return their depositors' money. In just a few years, more than 5,500 banks failed. By 1933, the money from 9 million savings accounts had vanished.

Impact on the World By the 1930s, international banking, manufacturing, and trade had made nations interdependent. When the world's leading economy fell, the global economic system began to crumble.

After World War I, the United States had insisted that France and Britain, its wartime allies, repay their war debts. At the same time, Congress kept import taxes high, making it hard for European nations to sell goods in the United States. With economies weakened by the war and little chance of selling goods in the United States, the Allies had to rely on Germany's reparations payments for income.

As long as United States companies invested in Germany, reparations payments continued. But with the Depression, investments fell off. German banks failed, Germany suspended reparations, and the Allies in turn stopped

Answer to . . .
Interpreting Graphs Around 10 million.

Graphing the Main Idea

To make sure students understand the main idea of this section, you may wish to use the flow map graphic organizer below.

Tell students that a flow map shows a sequence of events unfolding. Ask students to use the flow map to record the events that led to the Great Depression.

Teaching Tip A template for this graphic organizer can be found in the Color Transparencies, G-4.

CAUSE AND EFFECT: The Great Depression

CAUSES

- *The 1920s economy is out of balance.*
- *Americans are increasingly in debt.*
- *Speculation is on the rise.*
- *Overproduction slows industrial growth.*
- *The federal government introduces a tight-money policy in order to control credit.*
- *The stock market crashes in October 1929.*

THE GREAT DEPRESSION

EFFECTS

- *Millions of workers lose their jobs.*
- *Gross National Product falls dramatically.*
- *Many banks fail.*
- *Increased poverty leads to health and social problems.*
- *Global economy suffers.*

Interpreting Charts Carefree spending and exaggerated faith in the nation's economy contributed to the Great Depression. *Economics What role did the government's monetary policy play in the Depression?*

paying their debts. Europeans no longer could afford to buy American-made goods. Thus the American stock market crash started a downward cycle in the global economy.

Causes of the Depression

The stock market crash of 1929, though devastating to investors, was only the final push that toppled the fragile structure of the American economy. Deeper problems were the real underlying causes of the Great Depression.

Overspeculation During the 1920s, speculators bought stocks with borrowed money, then pledged those stocks as collateral to buy more stocks. *Collateral* is an item of value that a borrower agrees to forfeit to the lender if the borrower cannot repay a loan. Brokers' loans went from under $5 million in mid-1928 to $850 million in September 1929. The stock market boom was based on borrowed money and optimism instead of real value.

Government Policies Mistakes in monetary policy were also to blame. During the 1920s the Federal Reserve system, which regulates the amount of money in circulation, cut interest rates to spur economic growth. Then in 1929, worried about overspeculation, the Federal Reserve limited the money supply to discourage lending. After the Crash, however, this meant that there was too little money in circulation to help the economy recover.

An Unstable Economy Overall, the seemingly prosperous economy lacked a firm base. National wealth was unevenly distributed, with the most money in the hands of a few families who tended to save or invest rather than buy goods. Industry produced more goods than most consumers wanted or could afford. Farmers and many workers had not shared in the economic boom. The unevenness of the 1920s prosperity made rapid recovery impossible.

SECTION 2 REVIEW

Comprehension

1. *Key Terms* Define: (a) Dow Jones Industrial Average; (b) Black Tuesday; (c) Great Crash; (d) business cycle; (e) Great Depression; (f) Gross National Product.

2. *Summarizing the Main Idea* What were the causes and effects of the stock market crash of 1929?

3. *Organizing Information* Use the information in the four charts on the previous page to create a web diagram. Show the effects of the Depression on unemployment, wheat prices, stock prices, and bank closings.

Critical Thinking

4. *Analyzing Time Lines* Review the time line at the start of this section. Find examples of the financial impact and the social impact of the Great Crash of 1929.

5. *Analyzing Cause and Effect* Why do you think the Great Depression had such a huge impact on economies in other countries?

Writing Activity

6. *Writing an Expository Essay* It is the day after Black Tuesday. Write a newspaper article explaining to readers what happened to the economy in the past week.

1930s	1931	1931	1932	1935
Dust storms ruin farms in the Great Plains	Scottsboro Boys convicted	Homeless in New York City number about 15,000	About 56 percent of African Americans are unemployed	Dorothea Lange begins project to photograph migrant farmers

| 1930 | 1931 | 1932 | 1933 | 1934 | 1935 |

3 Social Effects of the Depression

SECTION PREVIEW

Objectives

1. Describe the spread of poverty during the Great Depression.
2. Identify Dorothea Lange.
3. Define the social problems caused by poverty in the 1930s and explain how people struggled to survive.
4. *Key Terms* Define: Hooverville; Dust Bowl.

Main Idea

Most people were not immediately affected by the 1929 stock market crash. But by the early 1930s, wage cuts and growing unemployment brought widespread suffering and discrimination.

Reading Strategy

Reinforcing Main Ideas As you read, list examples of how the Great Depression affected different parts of American society.

Not everyone felt the impact of the Great Crash immediately. Many Americans thought the Depression that followed would not last. For them, reality hit in 1931 or 1932.

As hard times spread to all levels of society, a song from a 1932 Broadway revue became a theme song of the times:

> **AMERICAN VOICES**
> "Once I built a railroad, made it run,
> Made it race against time.
> Once I built a railroad, now it's done.
> Brother, can you spare a dime?"

Poverty Spreads

Imagine that the bank where you had a savings account suddenly closed. Your money was gone. Or your parents lost their jobs and could not pay the rent or mortgage. One day you came home to find your furniture on the sidewalk—you had been evicted.

People at all levels of society faced these situations. Professionals and white-collar workers, who had felt more secure than laborers, suddenly were laid off with no prospects of finding another job. Those whose savings disappeared found it hard to understand why banks no longer had the money they had deposited for safekeeping.

"Hoovervilles" The hardest hit were those at the bottom of the economic ladder. Some unemployed laborers, unable to pay their rent, moved in with relatives. Others drifted. In 1931, census takers estimated the homeless in New York City alone at 15,000.

Homeless people sometimes built shanty towns, with shacks of tar paper, cardboard, or scrap material. These shelters of the homeless came to be called **Hoovervilles,** mocking the President, whom people blamed for the crisis.

A woman living in Oklahoma visited one Hooverville: "Here were all these people living in old, rusted-out car bodies," she noted. "There were people living in shacks made of orange crates. One family with a whole lot of kids were living in a piano box."

The number of people without jobs rose dramatically after the Crash.

RESOURCE OPTIONS

Teaching Resources

 Reproducible Lesson Plan Lesson Plans folder, p. 125

Learning Styles Lesson Plan Learning Styles Lesson Plans folder, p. 46

Big Idea Graphic Organizer Big Idea Graphic Organizer folder, p. 97

Guided Reading and Review Units 7–8 folder, p. 22

Makeshift huts served as homes for the homeless and unemployed in this New York City Hooverville.
Economics What group of people was hardest hit by the Depression?

Farm Distress Farm families suffered as low food prices cut their income. When they could not pay their mortgages, they lost their farms to the banks, which sold them at auction. In the South, landowners expelled tenant farmers and sharecroppers. In protest against low farm prices, farmers dumped thousands of gallons of milk and destroyed other crops. These desperate actions shocked a hungry nation.

The Dust Bowl For thousands of farm families in the Midwest, the harsh conditions of the Depression were made even more extreme by another major crisis of the decade. This one was not economic, but environmental. It was the **Dust Bowl,** a region in the Great Plains where drought and dust storms took place for much of the 1930s. (See the Geography and History feature following this section.)

Low farm prices and terrible weather caused many families to sell their farms or see them taken away. More than 440,000 people left Oklahoma during the 1930s. Nearly 300,000 people left Kansas. Thousands of families in Oklahoma, Texas, Kansas, and other southwestern Plains states migrated to California. Many found work on California's farms as laborers.

About 100,000 of the Dust Bowl migrants headed to cities, such as Los Angeles, San Francisco, and San Diego.

One woman was there to witness their arrival, and to tell their story to the rest of America. She was photographer Dorothea Lange.

Dorothea Lange

AMERICAN BIOGRAPHY "The camera is an instrument that teaches people how to see without a camera," said photographer Dorothea Lange. In the 1930s and for all time, Lange taught the nation to see the realities of the Depression in the faces of suffering Americans.

Born in New Jersey in 1895, Lange decided at a young age to be a photographer. In 1918 Lange opened a portrait studio in San Francisco and did a prosperous business photographing wealthy clients.

Beyond the windows of her studio, she could see the spreading effects of the Depression: jobless men in worn-out shoes; hungry babies; desperate mothers. She thought about the vast difference "between what I was working on in the printing frames [in the studio] and what was going on in the street."

So she took to the streets, becoming a photo-journalist of sorts, long before there was such a term. Lange drew on her experience in making portraits. She could put her subjects at ease, working quietly and respectfully, in the bread lines and the soup kitchens and along the waterfronts.

Dorothea Lange (1895–1965)

Lange's first exhibition, in 1934, landed her an assignment to photograph the hundreds of migrant workers streaming into California from the Dust Bowl. Lange's photographs showed the world the desperation and bravery of whole families reduced to picking peas in the sun and sleeping in cars or makeshift shelters.

The pictures stirred public attention and helped win aid for the workers. Lange's work also captured the attention of the Farm Security Administration (FSA), an agency set up by Hoover's successor, President Franklin Delano Roosevelt, to help farmers recover from the Depression. In 1935 Lange became one of several photographers hired by the FSA to document the lives of migrant farmers.

Lange worked for the FSA until 1939. Her most famous photograph, "Migrant Mother" (1936), shown on the Unit opener, has become a symbol of the Depression. The face of the undernourished mother displays a numbness to her destitute surroundings in a peapickers' camp; a profound worry for her shy children who huddle around her; and yet, a certain determination to pull through it all.

"She told me her age, that she was thirty-two," Lange recalled. "She said that they had been living on frozen vegetables from the surrounding fields and the birds that the children killed. She had just sold the tires from her car to buy food. There she sat in that lean-to tent with her children huddled around her, and seemed to know that my pictures might help her. . . ."

Lange's work helped bring about the creation of government migrant camps. Her work also inspired John Steinbeck's Depression-era novel *The Grapes of Wrath*.

Lange went on to document the sufferings and mistreatment of other Americans until her death in 1965. But she will be forever linked in people's minds to the 1930s, and the human courage that she made a part of the nation's permanent record. ◼

Poverty Strains Society

As the Depression wore on, it took a serious physical and psychological toll on the entire nation. Unemployment and fear of losing a job caused great anxiety. People became depressed; many considered suicide, and some did take their own lives.

Impact on Health "No one has starved," President Hoover declared, but some did, and thousands more went hungry. Impoverished people who could not afford food or shelter got sick more easily. Children suffered most from the long-term effects of poor diet and inadequate medical care.

"All last winter we never had a fire except about once a day when Mother used to cook some mush or something," one homeless boy recalled. "When the kids were cold they went to bed. I quit high school, of course."

"White Angel Breadline" is one of Dorothea Lange's most famous photographs. *Culture* **What effect did her photographs have on the general public?**

Poverty was especially hard on sharecroppers in the South who had to live in improvised camps after being evicted from their farms by landowners. *Economics How did increased poverty lead to a decline in health?*

jobs," he explained. In the Depression, this practice became common. In 1931, the American Federation of Labor endorsed it. Most school districts would not hire married women teachers, and many fired those who got married.

Many women continued to find work, however, because poor-paying jobs such as domestic service, typing, and nursing were considered "women's work." The greatest job losses of the Depression were in industry and other areas that had seldom hired women.

Discrimination Increases Hard economic times put groups of Americans in competition with one another for a shrinking number of jobs. This produced a general rise in suspicions and hostilities against minorities. African Americans, Hispanics, and in the West, Asian Americans, all suffered as white laborers began to demand the low-paying jobs typically filled by these minorities.

African Americans continued to leave the South, although not as many as in the 1920s. They had jobs such as janitors or baggage carriers in northern cities, but soon lost even those jobs to whites. Black unemployment soared—about 56 percent of black Americans were out of work in 1932. Photographer Gordon Parks, who rode the trains to Harlem, later wrote:

AMERICAN VOICES 6637o most blacks who had flocked in from all over the land, the struggle to survive was savage. Poverty coiled around them and me with merciless fingers.99

—*Photographer Gordon Parks*

Because relief programs discriminated against African Americans, black churches and organizations like the National Urban League gave private help. The followers of a Harlem evangelist known as Father Divine opened soup kitchens that fed thousands every day.

Discrimination increased for African Americans in the South. Some white southerners declared openly that blacks had no right to a job if whites were out of work. African Americans were denied civil rights such as access to education, voting, and health care. Lynchings increased.

Hispanics and Asian-Americans lost not only their jobs but also their country. Thousands were deported—even those born in America.

The justice system often ignored the rights of minority Americans. In March 1931, near Scottsboro, Alabama, nine black youths who

In the country, people grew food and ate berries and other wild plants. In cities, they sold apples and pencils, begged for money to buy food, and fought over the contents of restaurant garbage cans. Families who had land planted "relief gardens" to feed themselves or to barter food for other items.

Stresses on Families Living conditions declined as families moved in together, crowding into small houses or apartments. The divorce rate dropped because people could not afford separate households. People gave up even small pleasures like an ice cream cone or a movie ticket.

Men who had lost jobs or investments often felt like failures because they could no longer provide for their families. If their wives or children were working, men thought their own status had fallen. Many were embarrassed to be seen at home during normal work hours. They were ashamed to ask friends for help.

Women faced other problems. Those who depended on a husband's paycheck worried about feeding their hungry children. Working women were accused of taking jobs away from men.

Even in the better times of the 1920s, Henry Ford had fired married women. "We do not employ married women whose husbands have had been riding the rails were arrested and accused of raping two white women on the train. Without being given the chance to hire a defense lawyer, eight of the nine were quickly convicted by an all-white jury and sentenced to die.

The case of the "Scottsboro boys" was taken up, and sometimes exploited, by northern groups, most notably the Communist party. The party helped supply legal defense and organized demonstrations, which, in the end, helped overturn the convictions.

Stories of Survival

A generation of Americans would live to tell their grandchildren how they survived the Depression. Wilson Ledford first felt the effects of the Depression in March 1930 when he was 15, living in Chattanooga, Tennessee, with his mother and younger sister. Ledford looked after the family horse and cow, chopped wood for the fireplace, tended the garden that provided family food, and raised corn to feed the animals:

"We had to raise most of what we ate since money was so scarce. . . . Sometimes I plowed for other people when I could get the work. . . . I got 15 cents an hour for plowing, and I furnished the horse and plow."

—*Wilson Ledford*

Nothing was wasted. Ledford's mother kept chickens and traded eggs at the store for things they could not raise. Overalls cost 98 cents; shoes were $2. She bought a pig for $3 and raised it for meat, and made jelly from wild blackberries. Despite the family's own poverty,

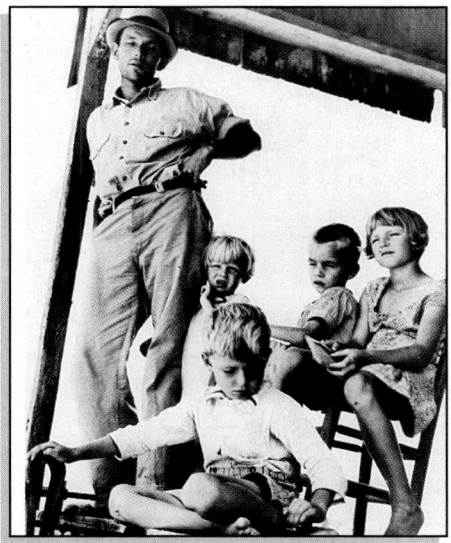
"If they come to take my farm, I'm going to fight. I'd rather be killed outright than die by starvation," said one Depression-era farmer. Although farm families were hard hit by the Depression, the fighting spirit represented by this quotation was seen across the country.

she gave extra milk and butter to "some poor people, a woman with three small children who lived in a one-room shack with a dirt floor."

Ledford never got to high school, "as survival was more important." In the summers of 1932 and 1933, Ledford hauled ice, working "12 hours a day, six days a week, and made $3.00 a week."

Later Ledford bought a truck to haul coal, cotton, and oranges, then worked nights in a woolen mill while carrying ice during the day. Finally, "I got a call from Chickamauga Dam and I went to work there. That was a good job working on the dam. I made 60 cents an hour. Times were better by then, but did not start booming until World War II started."

SECTION 3 REVIEW

Comprehension

1. *Key Terms* Define: (a) Hooverville; (b) Dust Bowl.

2. *Summarizing the Main Idea* How did the effects of the Great Crash widen into a deeper economic crisis?

3. *Organizing Information* Create a cause-and-effect chart showing the impact of poverty on Americans.

Critical Thinking

4. *Analyzing Time Lines* Review the time line at the start of the section. Choose two items and explain how they were related to the Great Depression.

5. *Analyzing Primary Sources* In your own words, rewrite the American Voices quotation by photographer Gordon Parks.

Writing Activity

6. *Writing an Expository Essay* In what ways was Dorothea Lange important to her time and to people in future generations? Write an essay addressing this question. Include supporting details from this section.

RESOURCE OPTIONS

Teaching Resources

Quiz Units 7–8 folder, p. 23

Student Performance Pack

Guide to the Essentials Chapter 22, Section 3 (English and Spanish)

Answers to
SECTION 3 REVIEW

1. (a) Hooverville, see p. 639; (b) Dust Bowl, see p. 640.

2. Failing banks and businesses gradually affected all Americans and people lost jobs and homes. Farmers were affected as low prices cut their incomes.

3. Causes: savings lost due to bank failures, unemployment, farms lost because of economic problems and natural disasters. Effects: homelessness, Hoovervilles, migration, health problems, social problems, discrimination.

4. 1931—homeless in New York: loss of jobs and savings due to Great Depression caused an increase in number of homeless. 1932—African Americans unemployed: competition for jobs meant whites renewed discrimination against African Americans and took jobs from them.

5. Answers will vary but should show an understanding of the quotation.

6. Essays will vary but should be supported with facts from the section.

The Dust Bowl

GEOGRAPHY AND HISTORY

The Dust Bowl

The geographic theme of regions examines the characteristics that set one area apart from others. Between 1933 and 1940, so much earth blew out of the central and southern Great Plains that the region became known as the Dust Bowl. What factors contributed to this environmental disaster?

A migrant worker and her children

Focus Explain that during the Great Depression a series of terrible dust storms destroyed many farms on the Great Plains. Some of the most vivid images of the Great Depression are of abandoned farms on the Great Plains, and of farm families on the road, headed for a new life.

Instruct Ask students to locate the Great Plains on a map of the United States. Then have them trace the history of farming on the Great Plains by creating a time line for the period between 1800 and 1950. Time lines should contain the following events:
- Great Plains identified as desert.
- Richness of the Great Plains discovered.
- Hard winter wheat introduced.
- World War I causes rise in wheat prices.
- Four million acres under plow.
- Prices for wheat fall.
- First dust storms.
- Rain relieves drought.

Ask students whether it was a coincidence that the dust storms came at the same time as the Depression or if the Depression helped to cause them. *(An early sign of the Depression was a drop in farm income, causing farmers to plow up more land for wheat in an effort to survive.)*

Extend Ask students to explain how each of the following factors contributed to the Dust Bowl: extensive wheat farming on the Great Plains, invention and use of tractors, drought, high winds. Students might also want to learn about current farming practices in the Great Plains to see if topsoil loss is still a problem and how current techniques help prevent erosion.

The Great Plains is called "America's breadbasket." Deep, fertile soils, a long growing season, and flat land give it its farming advantage. But the region has always experienced severe weather. Hot and humid tropical air masses come from the Gulf of Mexico. Cold polar air masses rush southward from above the Arctic Circle. When these air masses collide, powerful storms with fierce updrafts are created.

The complex root systems of the grasslands had protected the land from the weather. But as you will see, drought and human interaction during the 1930s created a near disaster.

> **The drought and winds persisted for more than seven years, bringing ruin to farmers.**

Farmers Plow the Plains

It was the dryness of the region that early settlers noticed first. For this reason, maps in the early 1800s referred to the Great Plains as the Great American Desert. By the late 1800s, however, farmers discovered an important truth about the Great American Desert. When there was water, the Great Plains was one of the world's best farming regions.

The soil of the Great Plains looked promising, but early farmers in the region faced a major obstacle. The soil was protected by a thick layer of grasses with roots that were difficult to cut. Breaking the roots required expensive steel plows and months of hard labor. Yet, from the time that hard winter wheat was first introduced in central Kansas in the mid-1870s, farmers in the plains sank their plow blades into the sod and turned it over to make wheat fields.

Wheat Replaces Grassland

In the early years of the twentieth century, wheat brought good prices, and farmers continually increased the acres of plowed land by getting rid of native grasses. In 1917 prices rose with the great demand caused by World War I. The price increases stimulated an even greater rush to plow more land to grow wheat. "Plant more wheat! Wheat will win the war!" was the slogan. By 1919, farmers had plowed under nearly 4 million acres of grassland. Though the war was over, the big plow-up continued.

It was new technology that allowed so much land to be plowed. Plowing with tractors allowed farmers to turn over far more acres in a day than they ever could have without those machines. When prices for wheat began to fall in the early 1920s, farmers responded by growing even more wheat. In the five years between 1925 and 1930 alone, more than 5 million additional acres of grassland disappeared,

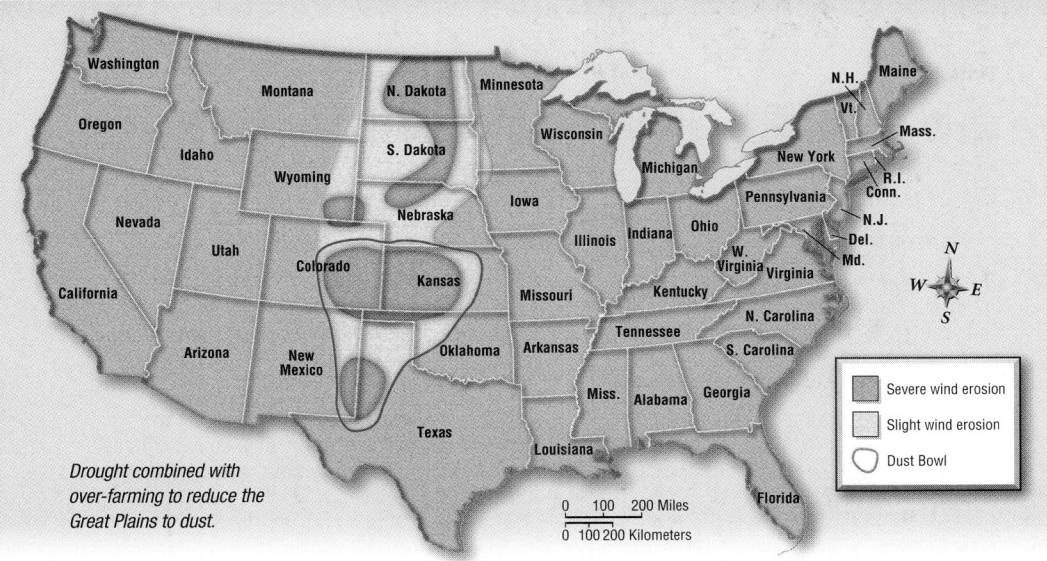

Drought combined with over-farming to reduce the Great Plains to dust.

Severe wind erosion
Slight wind erosion
Dust Bowl

0 100 200 Miles
0 100 200 Kilometers

converted to wheat fields by the relentless plow blades. But this conversion came with a cost.

Causes of Dust Storms

In the early 1930s, the dust storms began. Farmers said they were the result of the severe drought that would last through the decade. While drought was a major factor in creating the Dust Bowl, it was not the only factor. Farming practices also contributed.

As long as there was a thick layer of prairie grasses to protect the topsoil, severe weather could not harm the land. However, when farmers plowed the land, they stripped the soil of its natural protection. Winds picked up the dark, nutrient-rich topsoil and carried it eastward, sometimes for hundreds of miles, leaving behind barren, shifting dunes of grit and sand. The map above shows the extent of soil erosion across the plains.

People Lose their Farms

The most severe storms of the dry years were called "black blizzards." Time after time, dirt was sucked up and dropped by the ton over states and cities to the east. The dirt darkened the sky in New York City and Washington, D.C. It stained the snows of New England red and dropped on ships hundreds of miles off the Atlantic Coast. The drought and winds persisted for more than seven years, bringing ruin to farmers.

The combination of terrible weather and low prices for farm products caused about 60 percent of Dust Bowl families to lose their farms. Relief did not come until the early 1940s, when the rains finally arrived and World War II drove farm prices up.

GEOGRAPHIC CONNECTIONS

1. (a) What features of land and climate make the Great Plains a good farming region? (b) What features make it a poor farming region?

2. What caused the black blizzards of the 1930s?

Themes in Geography

3. *Regions* How did farmers destroy the region's natural protection against severe weather?

▶ RESOURCE OPTIONS

Media and Technology

Prentice Hall United States History Video Collection™
Volume 18 *The Great Depression and the New Deal*

1931	1931		1933	1933
Al Capone convicted of tax evasion	Empire State Building, world's tallest, opens		Twenty-first Amendment repeals Prohibition	Former President Coolidge dies

1931	**1932**	**1933**

SECTION 4

Surviving the Great Depression

Objectives

You may wish to call students' attention to the objectives in the Section Preview. The objectives are reflected in the main headings of the section.

Bellringer

Ask students to recall a time in their lives when friends, neighbors, or strangers worked together to solve a problem or helped one another through an unpleasant situation.

Reading Strategy

Problem Solving Refer to the Reading Strategy in the Section Preview. You may wish to discuss the strategies Americans used to survive during the Depression.

LESSON PLAN

Connecting to the Main Idea

1. Focus Explain that Americans who lived through the Great Depression never forgot the pain of that time, and their feelings about banks, business, government, and money changed forever. Ask what characteristics helped Americans to survive those troubled times.

2. Instruct Discuss how living through the Great Depression brought out courage, kindness, charity, and humor in many Americans. Ask why they think crises bring out these characteristics. You might want to have students share their recollections from the Bellringer activity.

Discuss the signs of changing times that gave Americans hope. Ask students to explain the impact of the repeal of Prohibition.

3. Close The Depression changed the Americans who lived through it. Above all, an era ended. The next section shows the nation taking a new direction—through the exciting election of 1932.

4 Surviving the Great Depression

SECTION PREVIEW

Objectives

1 Describe ways in which Americans pulled together to survive the Depression.
2 Analyze the signs of social change in the 1930s.
3 *Key Term* Define: Twenty-first Amendment.

Main Idea

Americans survived the Great Depression with determination and even humor. They helped one another, looked for solutions, and waited for the hard times to pass.

Reading Strategy

Problem Solving If you had lived during the Depression, what might you have done to get by? As you read, make a list of the strategies that helped Americans to survive.

This "kind-hearted woman" symbol drawn on a fence post meant that the family inside would offer handouts to a needy passer-by.

No one who lived through the Great Depression ever forgot it. Long after the economy rebounded, the "Depression generation," even those who recovered enough to live a very comfortable life, would continue to pinch pennies as if financial ruin were just around the corner. Many Americans avoided buying on credit, instead saving for years to pay cash for needed items. Others even stuffed money under their mattresses rather than trust their life savings to banks.

Americans Pull Together

Not all the memories of the Depression were bad or despairing, as one reporter noted:

"The great majority of Americans may be depressed. They may not be well pleased with the way business and government have been carried on, and they may not be at all sure that they know exactly how to remedy the trouble. They may be feeling dispirited. But there is one thing they are not, and that is—beaten."

—*Journalist Gerald W. Johnson, 1932*

People pulled together to help each other. Tenant groups formed to protest rent increases and evictions. In some farm communities, people agreed to keep bids low when foreclosed farms were auctioned. Buyers then returned the farms to their original owners.

People helped those they saw as worse off than themselves. One woman remembered:

"There were many beggars, who would come to your back door, and they would say they were hungry. I wouldn't give them money because I didn't have it. But I did take them in and put them in my kitchen and give them something to eat."

—*Depression survivor Kitty McCulloch*

McCulloch also gave one beggar a pinstripe suit belonging to her husband, who, she explained, already had three others.

Seeking Political Solutions As bad as conditions were, there were no widespread calls for radical political change. In Europe, economic problems brought riots and political upheaval, but in the United States most citizens trusted

▶ RESOURCE OPTIONS

Teaching Resources

Reproducible Lesson Plan Lesson Plans folder, p. 126

Big Idea Graphic Organizer Big Idea Graphic Organizer folder, p. 98

Guided Reading and Review Units 7–8 folder, p. 24

Media and Technology

AmericanHeritage® CD-ROM

Time Tour Prosperity, Depression, and War: Depression and the New Deal the democratic process to handle the problems. As one writer wryly observed at the time:

AMERICAN VOICES ❝Ten million unemployed continue law-abiding. No riots, no trouble, no multi-millionaires cooked and served with cranberry sauce, alas.❞

—*Writer William Saroyan, 1936*

For some Americans, however, radical and reform movements offered new solutions to the country's problems, promising a fairer distribution of wealth. The Communist party had about 14,000 members, mainly intellectuals and labor organizers. In the 1932 election, the Communist candidate polled just over 100,000 votes. Socialists, who called for gradual social and economic changes rather than revolution, did better. Their presidential candidate, Norman Thomas, won 881,951 votes in 1932, about 2.2 percent of the total vote.

Voting figures and party membership do not reflect the notable interest in radical and reform movements in the 1930s. Those who were part of those movements remember the decade as a high point of cooperation among different groups of Americans—students, workers, writers, artists, and professionals of all races. They worked together for social justice in cases such as that of the Scottsboro Boys.

Depression Humor For the most part, Americans gritted their teeth and waited out the hard times. Jokes and cartoons kept people laughing through their troubles. The term "Hooverville" was at first a joke. People who slept on park benches huddled under "Hoover blankets"—old newspapers. Empty pockets turned inside out were "Hoover flags." When Babe Ruth was criticized for requesting a salary of $80,000, higher than Hoover's, he joked, "I had a better year than he did."

People fought despair by laughing at it. In 1929 humorist Will Rogers quipped, "When Wall Street took that tail spin, you had to stand in line to get a window to jump out of." A cartoon that showed two men jumping out of a window arm-in-arm was captioned "The speculators who had a joint account."

Signs of Change

Looking back, we know that the Great Depression largely came to an end with the United States' entry into World War II in 1941. Americans suffering through the Depression,

of course, had no idea when the hard times would end. They looked for signs of change, and even in the early 1930s there were some.

Prohibition Is Repealed In February 1933, just 14 years after it passed the Eighteenth Amendment banning the sale of alcoholic beverages, Congress passed the **Twenty-first Amendment,** repealing Prohibition. The amendment was ratified by the end of the year.

Some people, including President Hoover, regretted the end of the ban, but most welcomed repeal as an end to a failed social experiment and as a curb on gangsters who profited from bootlegging. Control of alcohol returned to the states, eight of which chose to continue the ban on liquor sales.

The Empire State Building For many, a dramatic symbol of hope was the new Empire State Building, begun in 1930. John J. Raskob, the developer of the gleaming new skyscraper, won the race to build the world's tallest building.

Showing the darker side of Depression humor, an end-of-the-year cartoon in *Life* magazine summed up the hopes and disasters of 1929. *Culture* Why did Americans use humor to fight their despair?

ACTIVITY

LEARNING STYLES

The Empire State Building was designed in the Art Deco style. Ask students to bring to class copies of photographs of the Empire State Building or another building built in the same time period that illustrates the Art Deco style, and to describe its prominent features. *(Verbal/Linguistic, Visual/Spatial)*

▶ **RESOURCE OPTIONS**

Teaching Resources

📁 **Biography** Babe Didrikson Zaharias, Units 7–8 folder, p. 28

Media and Technology

RESOURCE ⚙ **PRO**

Primary Source Activity "The Forgotten Man," found on Resource Pro, uses two letters written to President Hoover during the Depression to show the way many American workers viewed their President and the economic breakdown of the country.

Answer to . . .

Viewing History Sample answer: To forget their worries and to share their misery.

Answers to
SECTION 4 REVIEW

1. Twenty-first Amendment, see p. 647.

2. People helped each other through the hard times; they continued to believe in the democratic process; humor kept peoples' spirits up.

3. Sample entries: Political solutions —communism, socialism; Social solutions—groups formed to help the needy, individual acts of kindness, Depression humor.

4. 1931—Empire State Building opens: signal of hope and inspiration. 1933—Twenty-first Amendment passed: end of a failed experiment and stimulus to the economy.

5. Sample answer: That they feared the radical change and possible chaos that would result from challenging the political and social order.

6. Essays will vary but should be supported with facts from the section.

Some 2,500 to 4,000 people worked on its construction on any given day. The cost of the construction was about $41 million (including land). Because of the Depression, projected building costs were cut in half.

The 102-story Empire State Building soared 1,250 feet into the sky and was topped with a mooring mast for blimps. The building's 67 elevators, traveling 1,000 feet per minute, brought visitors to its observation deck. On the first Sunday after it opened in 1931,[†] more than 4,000 people paid a dollar each to make the trip.

The End of an Era By 1933, it was clear that an era was ending. One by one, symbols of the 1920s faded away. In 1931 organized crime gangster Al Capone was at last brought down, convicted of tax evasion and sent to prison. Baseball legend Babe Ruth retired in 1935. The Depression-era labor policies of automaker Henry Ford, once admired for his efficiency, made him labor's prime enemy.

In 1932 the nation was horrified when the infant son of aviation hero Charles Lindbergh and Anne Morrow Lindbergh was kidnapped and murdered. Somehow this tragedy seemed to echo the nation's distressed condition and its fall from the energy and heroism of the 1920s. Finally, in January 1933, Calvin Coolidge, the frugal former President who presided over the freewheeling prosperity of the 1920s, died.

[†] On May 1, President Hoover pressed a button in Washington, D.C., and officially turned on the building lights, illuminating the New York skyline.

Despite the economic hardships of the 1930s, American architects raced to build the world's tallest building. Workers like the man shown above looked out over New York City as they labored to complete the Empire State Building. *Culture How was the Empire State Building a symbol of hope?*

SECTION 4 REVIEW

Comprehension

1. *Key Term* Define: Twenty-first Amendment.

2. *Summarizing the Main Idea* To what extent did Americans' attitudes and outlook help them survive the Depression?

3. *Organizing Information* Make a web diagram showing ways that people worked to overcome the hardships of the Depression.

Critical Thinking

4. *Analyzing Time Lines* Review the time line at the start of this section. Choose two items and explain why they seemed to signal changing times.

5. *Analyzing Primary Sources* Explain the quotation from William Saroyan. What does it suggest about people's fears during the Depression?

Writing Activity

6. *Writing an Expository Essay* In a time of crisis, the building of an expensive skyscraper such as the Empire State Building might have been seen as wasteful. Instead, many Americans found it inspiring. What might account for this view of the project?

Answer to . . .

Viewing History It symbolized progress.

RESOURCE OPTIONS

Teaching Resources

 Quiz Unit 7–8 folder, p. 25

Student Performance Pack

Guide to the Essentials Chapter 22, Section 4 (English and Spanish)

Media and Technology

 Listening to Literature F. Scott Fitzgerald, "Winter Dreams"

Critical Thinking

Geography

Graphs and Charts

Historical Evidence

Distinguishing False from Accurate Images

Distinguishing false from accurate images means examining widely held beliefs about a person, a thing, or an event to determine whether or not those beliefs are based in fact. When studying history, you may uncover source materials such as newspaper and magazine articles that use stereotypes or that put forth misleading ideas. Learning to recognize the differences between false and accurate images will help you to reach your own conclusions about a statement.

The letter excerpted below was written to President Herbert Hoover during the early years of the Depression. Practice distinguishing between false and accurate images by using the following steps.

1. *Summarize the main message of the passage.* The first step in evaluating a piece of information is to understand what its central message is. Read the excerpt at right and answer the following question: What is the main point of the letter?

2. *Look for generalizations and overstatements in the passage.* Generalizations are broad and oversimplified statements about people, events, or issues that are presented as being accurate in all cases. Overstatements exaggerate or stretch the truth. These techniques often signal claims that are unsupported by facts and, therefore, may indicate the use of false images. (a) What generalizations can you find in the letter? (b) What overstatements or unsupported claims do you find?

3. *Look for supporting facts or evidence.* Accurate statements are usually backed up by statistics, quotations, or other verifiable evidence. Facts can be fabricated and used in misleading ways, however, so always check them for accuracy. (a) What verifiable facts, if any, are given in the letter below? (b) Based on the use of facts in the letter, what can you conclude about the accuracy of its message?

TEST FOR SUCCESS

(a) What false images were created about the United States economy prior to the Great Crash? (b) Write an accurate statement about the economy at that time, based on verifiable evidence given in Section 2.

Annapolis, Maryland
September 10, 1931

My dear Mr. Hoover,

In these days of unrest and general dissatisfaction, it is absolutely impossible for a man in your position to get a clear and impartial view of the general conditions of things in America today. But, of this fact I am very positive, that there is not five per cent of the poverty, distress, and general unemployment that many of your enemies would have us believe. It is true, that there is much unrest, but this unrest is largely caused . . . by the excessive prosperity and general debauchery through which the country has traveled since the period of the war. The result being that in three cases out of four, the unemployed [person] is looking for a very light job at a very heavy pay, and with the privilege of being provided with an automobile if he is required to walk more than four or five blocks a day.

National Relief Director, Walter S. Gifford, and his committee are entirely unnecessary at this time, as it has a tendency to cause communities to neglect any temporary relief to any of their people, with the thought of passing the burden on to the National Committee. . . .

. . . Believe me to be one of your well wishers in this ocean of conflict.

Yours sincerely,
W. H. H.

SKILLS FOR LIFE

Critical Thinking

Distinguishing False from Accurate Images

Focus Students will distinguish true from false images by identifying generalizations and overstatements and by citing the presence or lack of evidence to support statements.

Instruct Ask students to generate examples of generalizations and overstatements on a given topic, such as "Television plays a harmful role in the development of American children." You might want to display W.H.H.'s letter on an overhead projector and invite students to underline generalizations and overstatements and circle verifiable evidence.

Extend See the Skills for Life Activity in the Resource Options below.

Answers

1. The majority of Americans in 1931 were not suffering economically.

2. (a) Most unemployed persons are looking for light work at high pay; people would refuse a job that required them to walk four or five blocks; local communities would neglect their responsibilities and freeload on the national government. (b) "absolutely impossible," "of this fact I am very positive," "there is not five per cent of the poverty, distress, and general unemployment," "unrest is largely caused . . . by the excessive prosperity and general debauchery," "in three cases out of four, the unemployed [person] is . . .," and "entirely unnecessary."

3. (a) None. (b) That its accuracy is suspect.

TEST FOR SUCCESS

(a) That it was booming and sound. (b) Sample statement: Though the economy seemed to be thriving, many signs pointed to its instability.

 RESOURCE OPTIONS

Teaching Resources

 Skills for Life Activity Units 7–8 folder, p. 32, uses President Clinton's presentation before Congress of his health-care plan to give students a present-day application of this skill.

Media and Technology

Color Transparencies Critical Thinking, I-8

| 1930 Construction begins on Boulder Dam | 1930 Congress passes Hawley-Smoot tariff | 1932 Hoover sets up Reconstruction Finance Corporation | 1932 Bonus Army protesters forced out of Washington | 1932 Franklin Delano Roosevelt elected President |

1930 **1931** **1932**

Objectives

You may wish to call students' attention to the objectives in the Section Preview. The objectives are reflected in the main headings of the section.

Bellringer

Ask students to consider why elections are important and to provide specific examples of how elections are an avenue of change.

Reading Strategy

Compare and Contrast Refer to the Reading Strategy in the Section Preview. You may wish to use students' notes on Hoover and Roosevelt as the basis for a class comparison of the two candidates.

5 The Election of 1932

SECTION PREVIEW

Objectives

1 Outline Hoover's responses to the Great Depression.
2 Explain what Roosevelt meant when he offered Americans a "new deal."
3 Explain why the 1932 election was a turning point in United States history.
4 *Key Terms* Define: Hawley-Smoot tariff; Bonus Army.

Main Idea

As the Depression worsened, people blamed Hoover and the Republicans for their misery. The 1932 presidential election brought a sweeping victory for Democrat Franklin D. Roosevelt and a new direction for American government.

Reading Strategy

Compare and Contrast As you read, make notes about Hoover's policies and his style of governing. Do the same for Roosevelt. Then compare the key characteristics of these two candidates in the 1932 election.

LESSON PLAN

Connecting to the Main Idea

1. Focus The 1932 presidential election presented an opportunity for change. What was the outcome of this election? How did the new administration change the direction of American government?

2. Instruct Explain that Hoover believed a positive outlook and voluntary cooperation by business leaders would end the economic crisis. His administration did, however, take more direct action than had former governments. Ask students to state the results of the Hawley-Smoot tariff and the Reconstruction Finance Corporation.

Discuss what Roosevelt meant when he offered Americans a "New Deal." What programs was he referring to? Ask why the 1932 election signaled a shift in the relationship between the people and the government.

3. Close President Hoover's attempts to curb the Depression were inadequate. In 1932 voters swept in the Democratic candidate Franklin Delano Roosevelt in the hope that he could deliver a "New Deal."

For a few months after the stock market crash, President Hoover, along with business leaders, insisted that the key to recovery was confidence. Hoover blamed the Great Depression on "world-wide economic conditions beyond our control"—not on problems in the United States economy.

Hoover's Limited Strategy

Taking Hoover's advice, business and government leaders tried to maintain public confidence in the economy. Even as factories closed, Hoover administration officials insisted that conditions would improve soon.

Voluntary Action Fails Hoover believed that voluntary controls by United States businesses were the best way to end the economic crisis. He quickly organized a White House conference of business leaders and got their promise to maintain wage rates. At first, many firms did keep wages up. By the end of 1931, however, companies were quietly cutting workers' pay.

Hoover held rigidly to this principle of voluntary action. A shy man, he was successful in business but inexperienced in politics. He could not make his plan attractive to the American people. After a year of misery, they began to blame him and the Republicans for the crisis.

The Government Acts As the hardships continued and criticisms increased, Hoover took a more active approach. To create jobs, the government spent more on new public buildings, roads, parks, and dams. Boulder Dam (later renamed Hoover Dam) was begun in 1930. A President's Emergency Committee on Employment advised local relief programs.

Trying to protect domestic industries from foreign imports, in 1930 Congress passed the **Hawley-Smoot tariff,** the highest import tax in history. The tariff backfired. European countries raised their own tariffs, bringing a sudden slowdown in international trade. Hoover suspended the Allies' payments of their war debts, but Europe's economies grew weaker.

▶ RESOURCE OPTIONS

Teaching Resources

📁 **Reproducible Lesson Plan** Lesson Plans folder, p. 127

📁 **Learning Styles Lesson Plan** Learning Styles Lesson Plans folder, p. 47

📁 **Big Idea Graphic Organizer** Big Idea Graphic Organizer folder, p. 99

📁 **Guided Reading and Review** Units 7–8 folder, p. 26

In 1932, Hoover set up the Reconstruction Finance Corporation (RFC), which gave government credit to banks so that they could extend loans. The RFC reflected the theory that prosperity at the top would help the economy as a whole. To many people, however, it seemed that the government was helping bankers while ordinary people went hungry.

Some government efforts helped, but not enough. Hoover wanted state and local governments to handle relief, but their programs never had enough money. Despite the RFC, banks continued to fail.

Hoover's Unpopularity Grows Many people blamed Hoover, not always fairly, for their problems. Hoover argued that direct federal relief would destroy people's self-respect and create a large bureaucracy. His refusal to help brought bitter public reaction and negative publicity. Although his World War I relief work had made him the "Great Humanitarian," Hoover's attitude toward Depression relief made him seem cold and hard-hearted.

While people went hungry, newspapers showed a photograph of him feeding his dog on the White House lawn. People booed when he said such things as "Our people have been protected from hunger and cold."

Private charities and local officials could not meet the demands for relief as Hoover wanted. Finally, in 1932, Hoover broke with tradition and let the RFC lend the states money for unemployment relief. But it was too little and too late.

As the Depression deepened, some economists backed the ideas of British economist John Maynard Keynes. He said that massive government spending could help a collapsing economy and encourage more private spending. This economic theory was not yet widely accepted, however.

Veterans March on Washington A low point for Hoover came in the summer of 1932, when 20,000 jobless World War I veterans and their families encamped in Washington, D.C. The **Bonus Army,** as they called themselves, wanted immediate payment of a pension bonus that had been promised for 1945. The House of Representatives agreed, but the Senate said no. Most of the Bonus Army then went home, but a few thousand stayed, living in shacks.

Although the bonus marchers were generally peaceful, a few violent incidents prompted Hoover to call in the army. General Douglas

COMPARING PRIMARY SOURCES

FIGHTING THE DEPRESSION

Sharp philosophical differences characterized the presidential campaign of 1932.

Against Drastic Measures	For Drastic Measures
"We are told by the opposition that we must have a change, that we must have a new deal. It is not the change . . . to which I object but the proposal to alter the whole foundations of our national life which have been built through generations of testing and struggle." —Herbert Hoover, speech at Madison Square Garden, October 31, 1932	"I have recounted to you in other speeches, and it is a matter of general information, that for at least two years after the Crash, the only efforts made by the [Hoover administration] to cope with the distress of unemployment were to deny its existence." —Franklin D. Roosevelt, campaign address, October 13, 1932

ANALYZING VIEWPOINTS **Compare the statements made by the two candidates.**

MacArthur's troops set fire to the Bonus Army camps after driving out the protesters. *Culture Why do you think the government's response to the Bonus Army hurt Hoover at election time?*

Election of 1932

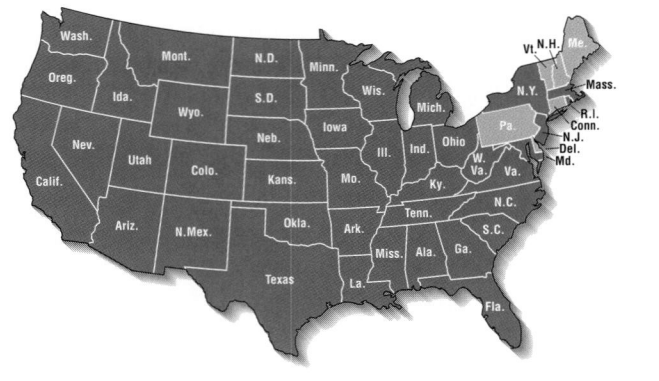

Candidate/Party	Electoral Vote	Popular Vote	% Electoral Vote	% Popular Vote
Franklin D. Roosevelt (Democrat)	472	22,821,857	88.9	57.4
Herbert Hoover (Republican)	59	15,761,841	11.1	39.7
Minor parties		1,160,615		2.9

Franklin D. Roosevelt and the Democratic party won the popular vote in 1932 as well as a huge margin of electoral votes. *Location* Which states' electoral votes did Hoover win?

MacArthur decided to use force to drive the marchers out of Washington. Armed with bricks and stones, the Bonus Army veterans faced their own country's guns, tanks, and tear gas. Many people were injured. Hoover was horrified, but he took responsibility for MacArthur's actions. In the next election, the lingering image of this ugly scene would help defeat him.

A "New Deal" for America

"I pledge myself to a new deal for the American people," announced presidential candidate Franklin Delano Roosevelt as he accepted the Democratic party's nomination at its Chicago convention in July 1932. Delegates cheered, and an organ thundered out the song "Happy Days Are Here Again."

The Republicans, in June, had again named Hoover. As the presidential campaign took shape, the differences between the two candidates became very clear.

In Franklin and Eleanor Roosevelt, the Democrats had a remarkable political couple to bring them victory. Franklin, nicknamed "FDR" by the press, was born in 1882. He graduated from Harvard University and took a job in a law firm, although his main interest was politics. He was elected twice to the New York State Senate before becoming Assistant Secretary of the Navy in President Woodrow Wilson's administration.

In 1920, FDR ran for Vice President but lost. The following summer, he came down with polio and never walked without help again. He spent much of the 1920s recovering at Warm Springs, Georgia, but kept up his political interests.

Eleanor Roosevelt, a niece of Theodore Roosevelt, was born in 1884 into a wealthy family. She married her distant cousin Franklin in 1905. During the 1920s, in New York State, Eleanor worked for public housing legislation, state government reform, birth control, and better conditions for working women. By 1928, when FDR was persuaded to run for governor of New York, Eleanor was an experienced political worker and social reformer.

After FDR's success as governor of New York (1929–1932), his supporters believed him ready to try for the presidency. With his broad smile and genial manner, he represented a spirit of optimism that the country badly needed.

Unlike Hoover, FDR was ready to experiment with governmental roles. Though from a wealthy background, he had genuine compassion for ordinary people, in part because of his disability. He was also moved by the great gap between the nation's wealthy and the poor.

As governor of New York, he had worked vigorously for Depression relief. In 1931, he set up an unemployment commission and a relief administration, the first state agencies to aid the poor in the Depression era. When, as a presidential candidate, FDR promised the country a "new deal," he had similar programs in mind.

Turning Point:
The Election of 1932

Hoover, the incumbent candidate for President, summed up the choice that voters had in 1932:

 "This campaign is more than a contest between two men. . . . It is a contest between two philosophies of government."

—*President Herbert Hoover, October 1932*

This statement also accurately describes the long-term impact of the 1932 presidential election. It was a historic battle between those who believed that the federal government could not and should not try to fix people's problems, and those who felt that large-scale problems such as the Depression required the government's help. The election would have an enormous effect on public policy for decades to come. (See the Turning Point time line below.)

Still arguing for voluntary aid to relieve the Depression, Hoover attacked the Democratic platform. If its ideas were adopted, he said, "this will not be the America which we have known in the past." He sternly resisted the idea of giving the national government more power.

Roosevelt, by contrast, called for "a reappraisal of values" and controls on business:

"I feel that we are coming to a view through the drift of our legislation and our public thinking in the past quarter century that private economic power is . . . a public trust as well."

—*Franklin Delano Roosevelt, 1932*

While statements like this showed FDR's new approach, probably any Democratic candidate could have beaten Hoover in 1932. Even longtime Republicans deserted him. A reserved man by nature, Hoover became grim and isolated. He gave few campaign speeches. Crowds jeered his motorcade.

 TURNING POINT : *The Election of 1932*

The election of FDR launched an era of greater government involvement in social welfare programs, an era that would last until the 1980s.

1932
Roosevelt is elected President after promising "a new deal for the American people."

1980
Reagan is elected President on a pledge to cut social welfare spending.

1996
Federal welfare reform gives states control over welfare programs.

| 1925 | 1950 | 1975 | 2000 |

1935
Social Security Act is passed, providing aid to retired workers, dependent mothers and children, and others.

1965
Federal medical aid programs for the elderly (Medicare) and the poor (Medicaid) are established under Johnson.

 RESOURCE OPTIONS

Teaching Resources

📁 **Lasting Impact Activity** The Lasting Impact of the Election of 1932, History's Lasting Impact folder, pp. 14-15

📁 **Key Documents** Franklin D. Roosevelt, First Inaugural Address, Learning with Documents folder, p. 96

Media and Technology

 AmericanHeritage® CD-ROM

Presidents Herbert Hoover, Franklin Delano Roosevelt

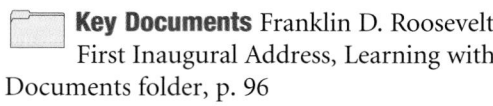

A Diverse Nation

Hardships for rural African Americans mounted during the Depression, often spurred by policies of the New Deal that were of benefit to the nation as a whole. Historian Jacqueline Jones writes in her book *The Dispossessed* that NRA (National Recovery Act) minimum-wage legislation spurred mechanization of the tobacco industry and put many African American men and women out of work. The crop-reduction programs of the AAA (Agricultural Adjustment Administration) severely cut demand for farm labor and provided ready cash for planters to invest in labor-saving machinery. The long-term effects of major development programs such as the TVA (Tennessee Valley Authority) are well known, but the fates of 841 Santee-Cooper (South Carolina) families living along the flood plain of a proposed dam are all but forgotten.

Answers to
SECTION 5 REVIEW

1. (a) Hawley-Smoot tariff, see p. 650; (b) Bonus Army, see p. 651.

2. Hoover's growing unpopularity and inability to deal with the problems of the Depression turned many Americans, including those belonging to his own party, against him.

3. Voluntary action—failed, workers began to blame Hoover. Hawley-Smoot tariff—Europe raised own tariffs and international trade slowed. Reconstruction Finance Corporation set up—not strong enough, people thought Hoover favored bankers over people. Army sent against Bonus Army—unflattering image of Hoover worsened.

4. Sample entries: 1930—Hawley-Smoot tariff passed; backfired, rival European tariffs instituted which slowed international trade. 1932—Bonus Army protestors forced out of Washington; added to Hoover's unpopularity. 1932—Roosevelt elected; new spirit of optimism, period of experimentation with roles of government begun.

5. Answers will vary but may point out that one person's policies and personality probably could not have compensated for the deep flaws in the economy. On the other hand, Hoover appeared cold and hard-hearted, unwilling to provide enough government money either for relief or to stimulate economic recovery.

6. Essays will vary but should be supported with facts from the section.

Answer to . . .

Viewing History They were disillusioned with Hoover and wanted change.

 This *New Yorker* cover drawing of FDR's inauguration clearly shows how people saw Roosevelt, the new President, in contrast with Hoover. *Culture Why did voters so overwhelmingly favor FDR?*

FDR won the presidency by a huge margin of 7 million popular votes. (See the map on page 652.) Much of his support came from groups that had begun to turn to the Democrats in 1928: urban workers, coal miners, and immigrants of Catholic and Jewish descent. Some people did not vote *for* Roosevelt as much as they voted *against* Hoover and the Republican policies.

On a rainy day in 1933, FDR stood before a Depression-weary crowd and took the oath of office of President of the United States. As reporter Thomas Stokes observed, a stirring of hope moved through the crowd when Roosevelt said, "This nation asks for action and action now."

Phrases like this foreshadowed a sweeping change in the style of presidential leadership and government response to its citizens' needs. Ultimately, such changes altered the way many Americans viewed their government and its responsibilities.

In the depths of the Great Depression, many Americans had to give up cherished traditional beliefs in "making it on their own." They turned to the government as their only hope. Thus, as you will read in the next chapter, the Roosevelt years saw the beginning of many programs that changed the role of the government in American society.

The words of FDR's Inaugural Address gave much of the country renewed hope:

 KEY DOCUMENTS "So first of all let me assert my firm belief that the only thing we have to fear is fear itself."

—*First Inaugural Address, President Franklin Delano Roosevelt, 1933*

Having overcome fear in his own life many times, Roosevelt spoke with conviction and confidence, reassuring a frightened nation.

SECTION 5 REVIEW

Comprehension

1. *Key Terms* Define: (a) Hawley-Smoot tariff; (b) Bonus Army.

2. *Summarizing the Main Idea* How did Hoover's failures bring victory for Roosevelt?

3. *Organizing Information* Make a chart listing the measures Hoover enacted to ease the Depression. For each, describe the outcome.

Critical Thinking

4. *Analyzing Time Lines* Review the time line at the start of this section. Choose three items and describe the impact of each.

5. *Distinguishing False from Accurate Images* Do you think the criticisms of Hoover were justified, or might the Depression have brought failure for any President? Explain your reasoning.

Writing Activity

6. *Writing an Expository Essay* Take the position of a reporter covering FDR's inaugural speech. Write a newspaper essay describing what the President said and analyzing the changes he will bring to American government.

▶ RESOURCE OPTIONS

Teaching Resources

📁 **Quiz** Unit 7–8 folder, p. 27

📁 **Chapter Tests Forms A and B** Chapter Test folder

Student Performance Pack

✪ **Guide to the Essentials** Chapter 22, Section 5 (English and Spanish)

Standardized Test Preparation Handbook

Media and Technology

🎧 **Guided Reading Audiotapes** Chapter 22 Summary (English and Spanish)
Student Edition on Audiotape Chapter 22

◎ **Test Bank CD-ROM; Interactive Student Tutorial CD-ROM** Chapter Test

Why Study History?
To understand that . . .

Investing Involves Risk

Today, as in the 1920s, an increasing number of Americans with various incomes are investing their money in the stock market.

Traders watch the ticker tape in 1929

In the 1980s, a group of women friends in Illinois pooled their money to share the risks and rewards of investing. They outlined their investment strategies, and their extraordinary results, in a book titled *The Beardstown Ladies.* Though doubts arose over the accuracy of their figures, the Beardstown Ladies inspired many Americans who were eager for financial reward to pool their own money in investment clubs.

The Impact Today

Before the stock market crash of 1929, most Americans were optimistic about the nation's economic strength. Not only did the wealthy invest huge amounts of money in the stock market, but small investors were entering the market in greater numbers. In 1929 about 10 percent of American households owned stocks.

For years after the 1929 crash, most Americans were wary of investing their hard-earned money in stocks. As recently as the early 1980s, only 25 percent of households held stock.

In the 1990s a new mood of optimism, similar to that of the 1920s, gripped the nation. As the stock market enjoyed several years of spectacular gains, many Americans chose to invest their savings in stocks or mutual funds. Some

hoped to get rich quickly, but most had a longer-term goal: saving money for their retirement. The number of households owning stocks or mutual funds rose from about 32 percent in 1989, to about 49 percent in 1998.

The stock market boom of the 1990s was accompanied by a surge in the formation of investment clubs. Today the National Association of Investors Corporation, a non-profit organization of clubs and individual investors, includes more than 37,000 clubs. Investment clubs on the Internet are popular, too. Some, like the Pioneer Online Investment Club, meet and conduct business entirely online. Members of other online clubs meet face to face, using World Wide Web sites as links to investment resources.

The Impact on You

Set up an imaginary investment club with three classmates. First, study the financial pages of newspapers or magazines and work together to choose four or five stocks of companies to invest in. "Buy" 100 shares of each. Write down the date of purchase, the price paid, and the symbol for each com-

In 1998, the Beardstown Ladies follow stock prices in the newspaper

pany. Keep track of your stocks, recording each day the changes in price and your profit or loss. At the end of two weeks, calculate how much money you made—or lost.

RESOURCE OPTIONS

Teaching Resources

 Why Study History? Activity Investing Involves Risk, found in the Why Study History? folder, p. 23, provides an activity to help students better understand investing.

Media and Technology

 AmericanHeritage® CD-ROM

Time Tour Prosperity, Depression, and War: The Jazz Age *and* Depression and the New Deal

 Prentice Hall United States History Video Collection™ Volume 17 *The Roaring Twenties;* Volume 18 *The Great Depression and the New Deal*

Why Study History?

Class Discussion

Discuss with the class the risks and rewards of investment. For a more thorough examination of the issue, see the activity folder in the Resource Options below.

ACTIVITY
STUDENT PARTICIPATION

Making a Chart
Ask students to read the text. Then have students work with partners or in small groups to investigate different investment strategies, such as:

- **savings accounts**
- **stocks**
- **pension plans**
- **IRA accounts**
- **insurance plans**
- **money markets**

Have each group learn about and discuss the strengths and weaknesses of one strategy. Use the information to create an "investment strategies" chart.

Follow up Ask students to each set up a short-term and long-term investment strategy for themselves.

Using the Internet
Students can learn more about investing by exploring links in the *America: Pathways to the Present* Web site at:

http://www.Pathways.phschool.com

Assessment
See the Lesson Plans folder, pp. 24–27, for rubrics on assessing Class Participation Projects.

Key Terms

Have students refer to the definitions of the key terms in the chapter to write sentences that show an understanding of the causes and effects of the Great Depression.

Comprehension

1. Crop prices fell as European farmers recovered from World War I; farmers could not meet their payments on loans for land and machinery; natural disasters such as the Dust Bowl ruined farms.

2. Americans thought that under his leadership, the government was not doing enough to relieve their problems. What assistance he did offer was too little and too late, and he was reluctant for government to expand its role.

3. It caused stock values to be overvalued; when stock values began to drop because of the overproduction of goods, panicked investors sold their stock at any price, sending shock waves throughout the system.

4. Beginning with FDR, an era of greater government involvement in social welfare programs was initiated.

5. Immediate: stock investors lost their savings and homes; banks and brokers who could not claim their loans failed. Long-term: economic decline resulted in loss of jobs and farms; GNP plummeted; economies around the world were affected and international trade stunted.

6. With the ensuing competition for jobs and relief, minorities were discriminated against and civil rights violations worsened.

7. Welfare capitalism was a system of providing benefits to workers; companies adopted it as a way to keep unions weak and prevent labor unrest.

8. Tenant groups formed to protest rent increases and evictions; soup kitchens and breadlines were set up; people agreed to keep bids on foreclosed farms low.

Chapter Summary

The major concepts of Chapter 22 are presented below. See also *Guide to the Essentials of American History* or *Interactive Student Tutorial CD-ROM,* which contains interactive review activities, time lines, helpful hints, and test practice for Chapter 22.

Reviewing the Main Ideas

The prosperity of the 1920s disguised an economy in danger. The stock market crashed in October 1929, destroying millions of dollars of wealth and triggering the Great Depression. Hoover's unpopular policies brought FDR to power and his activist approach to government.

Section 1: The Economy in the Late 1920s

During the 1920s, rising wealth and a booming stock market gave Americans a false sense of faith in the economy. In fact, there were signs that the economy was in trouble.

Section 2: The Stock Market Crash

In October 1929, panic selling caused the United States stock market to crash. The Crash led to a worldwide economic crisis called the Great Depression.

Section 3: Social Effects of the Depression

Most people were not immediately affected by the Great Crash. But by the early 1930s, wage cuts and unemployment brought widespread suffering and discrimination.

Section 4: Surviving the Great Depression

Americans survived the Great Depression with determination and even humor. They helped one another, looked for solutions, and waited for the hard times to pass.

Section 5: The Election of 1932

As the Depression worsened, people blamed Hoover and the Republicans for their misery. The 1932 election was a sweeping victory for Democrat Franklin D. Roosevelt and a new direction for American government.

Today, as in the 1920s, an increasing number of Americans are investing their money in the stock market.

Key Terms

For each of the terms below, write a sentence explaining how it relates to the Great Depression.

1. Twenty-first Amendment
2. Bonus Army
3. speculation
4. Hooverville
5. Black Tuesday
6. Great Crash
7. Dust Bowl
8. Hawley-Smoot tariff
9. Dow Jones Industrial Average
10. business cycle
11. Great Depression
12. buying on margin
13. Gross National Product (GNP)
14. welfare capitalism

Comprehension

1. Name three problems that plagued farmers during the 1920s and 1930s.
2. Why was President Hoover criticized for his handling of the Depression?
3. How did overspeculation in the stock market endanger the economy?
4. Why was the election of 1932 a turning point in the nation's history?
5. What were the immediate and the long-term effects of the Great Crash?
6. How did the Depression affect minorities?
7. What was welfare capitalism, and why did companies adopt this approach in the 1920s?
8. What did Americans do to try to help one another during the Depression?

Using Graphic Organizers

On a separate sheet of paper, copy the chain-of-events chart below and fill in the empty boxes.

| 1. Stock market hits record high. | → | 2. | → | 3. | → | 4. |

Using Graphic Organizers

2. Overspeculation causes prices to fall; on Black Thursday investors begin to panic and sell at any price.

3. Black Tuesday—overselling of stocks causes the American stock market to collapse in the Great Crash.

4. Triggered by the Great Crash, the widespread and long-term Great Depression sets in.

Analyzing Political Cartoons ▶

1. This political cartoon appeared in 1931. Who is the figure in the center of the cartoon?

2. What is the crowd doing?

3. What is the cartoonist's attitude toward Hoover's handling of the Depression?

Critical Thinking

1. *Applying the Chapter Skill* Study the cover of the *New Yorker* magazine in Section 5. (a) What point is the cartoonist trying to make? (b) Do you think the characterization of these two men is fair and accurate? Explain your reasoning.

2. *Identifying Assumptions* Why do you think so many Americans of various incomes engaged in dangerous speculation on the stock market during the 1920s?

3. *Drawing Conclusions* How did the government's response to the Bonus Army help ruin Hoover's presidency?

4. *Recognizing Ideologies* How did the political ideologies of Hoover and Roosevelt affect their decision making?

5. *Analyzing Primary Sources* What did one farmer mean when he said, "We were in the Depression before 1929, we just didn't call it that"?

INTERNET ACTIVITY

For your portfolio:
CREATE A DIARY ENTRY

Access Prentice Hall's *America: Pathways to the Present* site at **www.Pathways.phschool.com** for the specific URLs to complete the activity. Additional resources and related Web sites are also available.

Read the first-hand accounts of people who traveled illegally by railroad to find work during the Depression. Create a fictional diary entry of one such hobo. Why did you leave home? Where did you go? What people did you meet and what experiences did you have along the way?

ANALYZING DOCUMENTS ◀▶ INTERPRETING DATA

Turn to the series of four graphs in Section 2.

1. About how many banks suspended their business in 1933?
   (a) about 2,000 (b) about 2,300
   (c) about 1,500 (d) about 4,000

2. Which of the following statements best summarizes the data on the unemployment graph?
   (a) The numbers of unemployed people peaked in 1929.
   (b) Unemployment was low in 1925. (c) Unemployment increased dramatically between 1929 and 1933. (d) Unemployment decreased after 1933.

3. *Write* Imagine you are a wheat farmer. Write a letter to the President describing your situation. Use specific data from the graph in your letter.

Connecting to Today

Essay Writing Reread the Turning Point feature in Section 5. Address the following question in an essay: What evidence can you find today of the effects of the election of 1932?

INTERNET ACTIVITY

Entries will vary but should clearly answer the questions asked and be supported with facts or quotations from the section.

Analyzing Political Cartoons

1. President Hoover.
2. Blaming their problems on Hoover.
3. The cartoonist seems to be mocking the fact that Hoover is blamed for everyone's troubles, but also shows Hoover as ineffective.

Critical Thinking

1. (a) That FDR is outgoing while Hoover is quiet and withdrawn.
(b) It is fair in that this is how people had largely come to view the two men.
2. Students might point out the spirit of high optimism and economic security that Americans had at the time; the low unemployment rate; the trust in and respect for big business.
3. People viewed his use of the army to dispel the protestors as unnecessarily violent. It helped tarnish his image and decreased his popularity.
4. Hoover believed that government should be as unobtrusive as possible. With this in mind, he was hesitant to use the government to enact decisions, even during the Depression. Roosevelt believed in social welfare programs and was willing to expand the role of government to help out.
5. That farm prices had been steadily falling before the Depression and that farmers were already in a cycle of debt.

Interpreting Data

1. d
2. c
3. Letters will vary but should be supported with facts from the section.

Connecting to Today

Essays will vary but might point out recent examples of social welfare and of debates on the role of the government and states in social welfare programs.

The New Deal, 1933–1938

Managing Time and Instruction

INSTRUCTION SUPPORT

These materials for instruction are provided for **each section** in the **Teaching Resources**. See **Units 7–8 folder** for Enrichment Support:

- Reproducible Lesson Plans in Lesson Plans folder • Learning Styles Lesson Plans in Learning Styles Lesson Plans folder • Big Idea Graphic Organizers in Big Idea Graphic Organizer folder
- Guided Reading and Review • Quizzes • Test Preparation Practice booklet

DAILY LESSON	ENRICHMENT SUPPORT
1 **Forging a New Deal** (pp. 659–665)	• Nystrom *Atlas of Our Country,* People on the Move, pp. 34–35 • Primary Source Activity, A Fireside Chat: The NIRA, Learning with Documents folder, p. 29 • Great Debates, Who Is Responsible for the Elderly and Unemployed? Decision-Making Activities folder, pp. 38–39 • Primary Source Activity, Providing Emergency Relief, found on **Resource Pro** • Visual Learning Activity, Promoting the WPA, Learning with Documents folder, p. 65 • Critical Thinking Activity, Recognizing Ideologies: The Role of Government, found on **Resource Pro**
2 **The New Deal's Critics** (pp. 666–670)	• Literature Activity, In Search of Work: African Americans, Units 7–8 folder, p. 42 • Comparing Primary Sources, On the New Deal, Units 7–8 folder, pp. 40–41 • Visual Learning Activity, FDR Tries to Pack the Court, found on **Resource Pro** • Skills for Life Activity, Units 7–8 folder, p. 43
3 **Last Days of the New Deal** (pp. 672–676)	• Biography, Emma Tenayuca, Units 7–8 folder, p. 39 • Literature Activity, In Search of Work: Migrant Farmers, found on **Resource Pro** • Biography, Jacob Lawrence, found on **Resource Pro** • Americans Depend on Social Security, Why Study History? folder, p. 24

Running Out of Time?

- Use Tape 4, "Expansion: Boom Times to Hard Times, 1919–1938," from **Visions of America** videotapes series.
- Use Chapter 23 Summary from **Guide to the Essentials of American History (English and Spanish).**

Companion Web Site

The companion Web site offers online links for all chapter review activities. It also provides key content links and structured support for this chapter for both teachers and students.

http://www.Pathways.phschool.com

Media and Technology

For the Student

Interactive Student Tutorial CD-ROM Chapter 23
Student Edition on Audiotape Chapter 23
American Heritage® CD-ROM
Guided Reading Audiotapes (English and Spanish) Chapter 23

For the Teacher

Resource Pro CD-ROM Chapter 23
Test Bank CD-ROM Chapter 23
Listening to Literature Audiotapes *Timeless Voices, Timeless Themes* from *Here Is New York* by E. B. White
Color Transparencies Critical Thinking, I-6

Assessment Options

Chapter Test Forms A&B Test Bank CD-ROM booklet
Test Bank CD-ROM Chapter 23
Standardized Test Preparation Handbook

Block Scheduling

Pacing Suggestions

For 90-minute Blocks

- Teach sections 1 and 2 using Transparencies F-9 and K-7 and the Recent Scholarship note on p. 668 for class discussions.
- Teach section 3 using the Big Idea Graphic Organizers from Teaching Resources and the Extended Class Periods Activity on p. 673.

Additional Resources

- Prentice Hall's **American History Block Scheduling Support File** covers over 40 major topics in American history. Included are lesson plans, strategies, primary sources, literature, biographies, Great Debates, art history, simulations, and songs.
- **Prentice Hall United States History Video Collection™** contains 20 videotapes covering American history from beginnings to present.

Connections to American Literature

from Prentice Hall

Prentice Hall Literature *Timeless Voices, Timeless Themes* "The Jilting of Granny Weatherall" by Katherine Anne Porter, p. 776

Additional Resources

For the Student
Robert Penn Warren. *All the King's Men.* Random House, 1960.

For the Teacher
Anne E. Schraff. *The Great Depression and the New Deal: America's Collapse and Recovery.* Watts, 1990.

Prentice Hall brings into the classroom the vast archives and scholarship of the nation's premier American history magazine. See "From the Archives of American Heritage®" and "About the Presidents" teaching notes in this chapter.

History Alive!

Teacher's Curriculum Institute, in partnership with Prentice Hall, provides unique materials that engage students with diverse learning styles. See History Alive!® unit on The Roaring Twenties and the Great Depression.

Student Performance Pack

Ensures success in the three critical areas of Reading, Test Taking, and English Language Development with the following materials:
- Guide to the Essentials of American History in English and Spanish
- Guided Reading Audiotapes in English and Spanish
- Interactive Student Tutorial CD-ROM
- Test Preparation Handbook
- Test Preparation Practice booklet

Introducing the Chapter

President Roosevelt's New Deal—the name given to the vast collection of programs and policies formulated to combat the Depression—proved to be only partially successful at ending the nation's misery. But though critics were quick to point to the New Deal's many failures, it was hard to argue against its resounding success in bringing hope to a weary nation. Moreover, the New Deal influenced the social, political, and cultural life and attitudes of Americans in ways that are still apparent today.

Themes in American History

The theme for this chapter, Government, is listed at the beginning of this unit. An alternate theme for the chapter is Economics. To teach this unit thematically, you may wish to use the Prosperity, Depression, and War folder in American History Block Scheduling Support.

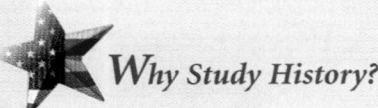

Why Study History?

Have students explore suggested ways of connecting the past to the present on page 677.

Answer to . . .

Viewing History Students should use this question as an aid in reading the chapter. The New Deal provided relief for those who suffered most from the Depression, public works programs to put people to work, and regulatory efforts in banking and other sectors of the economy.

658

CHAPTER 23 The New Deal
1933–1938

CHAPTER FOCUS

This chapter describes the New Deal, a series of programs designed by Franklin Roosevelt to help Americans during the Depression. The New Deal promised to change the relationship between the government and the economy. Critics of the program noted that many people were left out and that the Depression continued. Still, the New Deal left permanent marks on American political, social, and cultural life.

 The *Why Study History?* page at the end of this chapter explores the connection between the creation of the Social Security program and its impact on life today.

VIEWING HISTORY
Campaigning for President in 1932, Franklin Roosevelt shakes hands with a miner in Elm Grove, West Virginia. *Government* **How did the New Deal attempt to fight the Depression?**

 RESOURCE OPTIONS

Teaching Resources

📁 **Big Idea Graphic Organizer** folder
Graphic summary of the main idea of the chapter.

📁 **Learning Styles Lesson Plans** folder
Alternate lesson plans for diverse learning styles for each chapter.

Media and Technology

 AmericanHeritage® CD-ROM
Time Tour Prosperity, Depression, and War: Depression and the New Deal

Prentice Hall United States History Video Collection™ Volume 18 *The Great Depression and the New Deal*

1 Forging a New Deal

SECTION PREVIEW

Objectives

1 Identify the programs FDR created to restore the nation's hope, and explain the role of Eleanor Roosevelt.
2 Identify key New Deal personnel, and explain why the New Deal faltered.
3 Describe the Second New Deal and how the voters responded to it in the 1936 election.
4 *Key Terms* Define: New Deal; hundred days; public works program; Tennessee Valley Authority (TVA); Second New Deal; Wagner Act; Social Security system.

Main Idea

President Roosevelt sought to end the Depression through the programs of the New Deal.

Reading Strategy

Structured Overview Write two column headings on a sheet of paper: *New Deal* and *Second New Deal*. As you read, list details from the section in the appropriate column and note the significance of each detail.

Objectives
You may wish to call students' attention to the objectives in the Section Preview. The objectives are reflected in the main headings of the section.

Bellringer
Have students consider a situation where all members of their household were out of work, had no hope of finding a job, and had no government benefits. Ask them how they would want their government leaders to respond.

Reading Strategy
Structured Overview Refer to the Reading Strategy in the Section Preview. You may wish to model the column headings on the chalkboard. Have volunteers complete the chart.

When Franklin Roosevelt took office in 1933, he had big plans for the country. He had already promised "a new deal for the American people," and he kept his word. The **New Deal** became his program of relief, recovery, and reform aimed at combating problems caused by the Depression.

Even Roosevelt himself, however, was not sure exactly how the New Deal would work. Nevertheless, the new President's personality and willingness to experiment won him the support of the American people.

Restoring the Nation's Hope

Shortly after FDR took office, World War I veterans staged a second Bonus March on Washington. This time, the new administration provided campsites for the veterans. Even more astounding, Eleanor Roosevelt paid them a visit.

When she walked up to a group of marchers, "They looked at me curiously and one of them asked my name and what I wanted," she recalled. By the time she left an hour later, the veterans were waving and calling out, "Good-by and good luck to you!" The First Lady later told reporters how polite the marchers had been. By this act she both soothed popular fears about renewed radical agitation and demonstrated the new administration's approach to unrest.

FDR also soothed the public. In his Inaugural Address of March 4, 1933, he told Americans, "The only thing we have to fear is fear itself." The first Sunday after taking office, Roosevelt spoke to the nation over the radio in the first of what became regular "fireside chats." His easy manner and confidence made people feel better.

The First Hundred Days In campaigning for the White House, FDR had promised "bold, persistent experimentation." No one knew exactly what that experimentation would include, only that someone was going to do something. As reporter Arthur Krock noted,

The National Recovery Administration (NRA) was one of many new agencies combating the Depression.

LESSON PLAN
Connecting to the Main Idea

1. Focus Explain that FDR fulfilled his promise to take action to combat the Depression. Though the New Deal suffered setbacks, FDR's attitude and programs uplifted the nation.
2. Instruct Explain that the Depression had deeply demoralized the nation by the time FDR became President. Ask students to name the programs FDR created. What were the problems with this New Deal? How did the Second New Deal address the shortcomings of the first one?
Discuss FDR's choice of advisers and policymakers. How did FDR's political appointments reflect his commitment to change? Ask how Eleanor Roosevelt redefined the role of First Lady.
3. Close The New Deal gave millions of Americans new hope by its vigorous response to the Depression. The next section explores some of the criticisms of FDR and the New Deal.

RESOURCE OPTIONS

Teaching Resources

📁 **Reproducible Lesson Plan** Lesson Plans folder, p. 128

📁 **Learning Styles Lesson Plan** Learning Styles Lesson Plans folder, p. 48

📁 **Big Idea Graphic Organizer** Big Idea Graphic Organizer folder, p. 100

📁 **Guided Reading and Review** Units 7–8 folder, p. 33

Media and Technology

 AmericanHeritage® CD-ROM

Time Tour Prosperity, Depression, and War: Depression and the New Deal

About the Presidents

Franklin Delano Roosevelt (1933–1945) used two forms of public communication that contributed to his administration's success. First, he met with the press about twice a week. These free-and-easy, back-and-forth sessions put his achievements and plans in the headlines. Even more important were his radio "fireside chats." On these occasions, Roosevelt talked about his programs and purposes to the nation. His beautiful voice inspired confidence. Source: Wilson Sullivan, "Franklin Delano Roosevelt," *The American Heritage® Pictorial History of the Presidents of the United States*, vol. 2, 1968.

Reforming Society

With FDR's enactment of the New Deal, a horde of young, idealistic lawyers came to Washington eager to reform American society. These students and protégés of Harvard University's Felix Frankfurter—who were accordingly nicknamed "hot dogs"—incurred the disapproval of conservatives. One bureaucratic spokesperson complained of the "plague of young lawyers settled upon Washington."

Notable PRESIDENTS

Franklin Delano Roosevelt

1933–1945

"The only thing we have to fear is fear itself."
—First Inaugural Address

Courage in times of crisis was perhaps Franklin Roosevelt's greatest strength and most powerful legacy. His first crisis was personal rather than political. In 1921 Roosevelt was stricken with polio, which paralyzed his legs and threatened to destroy what had been a promising political career. (Roosevelt had been the Democratic vice-presidential candidate the year before.)

Refusing to quit, Roosevelt returned to politics. In 1928 he ran for governor of New York. Despite his paralysis, which meant he had to be helped or even carried onto podiums to speak, Roosevelt campaigned energetically and won the election. Four years later he ran for President. In a campaign dominated by the gloom of the Great Depression, Roosevelt's confidence helped bring him victory.

As President, Roosevelt fought the Great Depression through what he called "bold, persistent experimentation." "It is common sense to take a method and try it," he explained. "If it fails, admit it frankly and try another. But above all, try something." This commitment to government action gave the American people much-needed hope.

Roosevelt showed a similar commitment as commander in chief during World War II. After the attack on Pearl Harbor in 1941, Roosevelt rallied a shocked nation and oversaw the creation of the greatest military force in history. Elected President for a record fourth time in 1944, Roosevelt died in April 1945, just months before the victorious end of the war.

Roosevelt had plenty of faults, and plenty of critics. Yet as this nation's leader in the two great battles of the twentieth century—the Great Depression and World War II—Franklin Roosevelt's place in American history is secure.

Connecting to Today

Should government programs to help the elderly and the poor be temporary responses to crises such as the Great Depression, or should they be permanent? Defend your position.

Washington "welcomes the 'New Deal,' even though it is not sure what the New Deal is going to be."

From his inauguration in March through June 1933, a period known as the **hundred days,** FDR pushed program after program through Congress to provide relief, create jobs, and stimulate economic recovery. He based some of these programs on the work of federal agencies that had controlled the economy during World War I. Former Progressives figured prominently, inspiring New Deal legislation or administering programs.

Closing the Banks FDR's first step was to restore public confidence in the nation's banks. On March 5, 1933, he ordered all banks to close for the next four days. He then pushed Congress to pass the Emergency Banking Act, which they did on March 9. The act authorized the government to inspect the financial health of all banks.

Many Americans had been terrified by the prospect of losing all their savings in a bank failure. By his actions FDR hoped to assure the American people that their banks would not fail. Indeed, government inspectors found that most banks were healthy, and two thirds had reopened by March 15.

After the brief "bank holiday," Americans regained confidence in the banking system. They began at last to put more money back into their accounts than they took out. This allowed banks to make loans that would help stimulate the economy. In June Congress increased confidence further by establishing a Federal Deposit Insurance Corporation (FDIC) to insure bank deposits up to $5,000.

Providing Relief and Creating Jobs FDR's next step was to help overburdened local relief agencies. He persuaded Congress in May to establish a Federal Emergency Relief Administration (FERA), which sent funds to these agencies. Harry Hopkins directed this agency. He was in office barely two hours before he had given out $5 million.

Hopkins professed a strong belief in helping people find work:

AMERICAN VOICES ❝Give a man a dole [handout], and you save his body and destroy his spirit. Give him a job and pay him an assured wage and you save both the body and the spirit.❞

—*Harry Hopkins*

RESOURCE OPTIONS

Teaching Resources

Nystrom *Atlas of Our Country* People on the Move, pp. 34–35

Media and Technology

 AmericanHeritage® CD-ROM

Explorer Activity 25 The New Deal, CD-ROM Guidebook, pp. 69–70, helps students write a script for a "fireside chat" about the New Deal.

Presidents Franklin Delano Roosevelt

To help people who were out of work, the FERA also put federal money into **public works programs,** government-funded projects to build public facilities. One of these programs, set up in November 1933, was the Civil Works Administration (CWA). The CWA gave jobs building or improving roads, parks, airports, and other facilities to the unemployed. The CWA was a tremendous morale booster to its 4 million employees. As a former insurance salesman from Alabama remarked, "When I got that [CWA identification] card, it was the biggest day in my whole life. At last I could say, 'I've got a job.'"

FDR believed strongly in conservation of the environment. For this reason the Civilian Conservation Corps (CCC) was his favorite program. Established by an act of Congress in March 1933, the CCC put more than 2.5 million young, unmarried men to work restoring and maintaining forests, beaches, and parks.

CCC workers earned only $1 a day, but they lived in camps free of charge and received food and medical care as well as job training. Thanks to Eleanor Roosevelt's intervention, from 1934 to 1937 the CCC funded similar programs for young women, though only 8,500 women took part.

Public works programs also helped Native Americans. John Collier, FDR's commissioner of Indian Affairs, used New Deal funds and Native American workers to build schools, hospitals, and irrigation systems. Native Americans also benefited from the Indian Reorganization Act of 1934, which ended the sale of tribal lands begun under the Dawes Act (1887) and restored ownership of some lands to Indian groups.

A Helping Hand to Business The sharp decline of industrial prices in the early 1930s had caused many business failures and much unemployment. The National Industrial Recovery Act (NIRA) of June 1933 sought to bolster those prices. The NIRA established the National Recovery Administration (NRA), an agency that set out to balance the unstable economy through sensible planning.

This planning took the form of industry-wide codes that would spell out fair practices. The codes regulated wages, working conditions, production, and even prices. They also set a minimum wage and gave organized labor collective bargaining rights. These rights allowed workers to negotiate as a group with

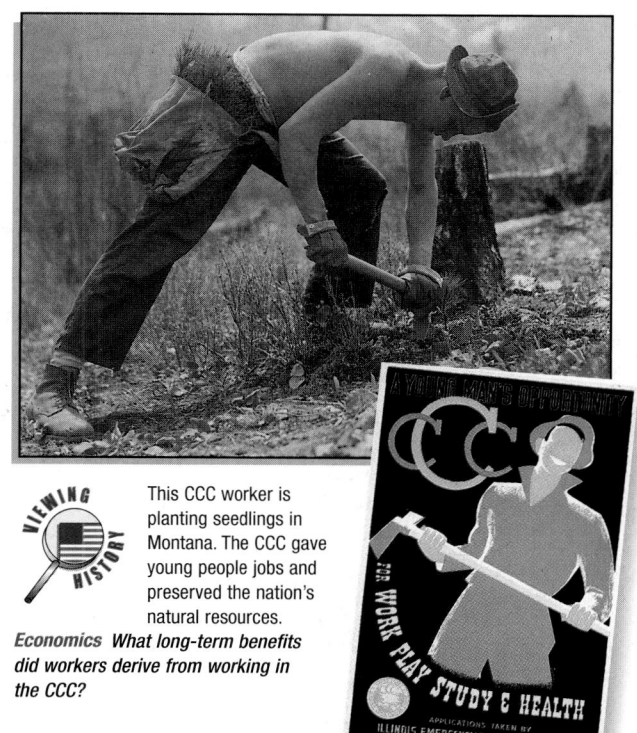

This CCC worker is planting seedlings in Montana. The CCC gave young people jobs and preserved the nation's natural resources.
Economics What long-term benefits did workers derive from working in the CCC?

employers. NRA officials wrote some of the codes, and they negotiated the details of some codes with the affected businesses. But many codes were drawn up by the largest companies in an industry, which pleased businesses but drew criticism from other people.

For a brief time, the codes stopped the tailspin of industrial prices. But by the fall of 1933, when higher wages went into effect, prices rose, too. Consumers stopped buying. The cycle of rising production and falling consumption returned, and many more businesses failed. Businesses soon complained that the codes were too complicated and that control by the NRA was too rigid.

The best part of the NIRA may have been its Public Works Administration (PWA). Directed by Secretary of the Interior Harold Ickes, the PWA launched projects ranging from the Grand Coulee Dam on the Columbia River in the state of Washington, to the causeway connecting Key West to the Florida mainland, to New York City's Triborough Bridge.

Main Idea CONNECTIONS

Why did the codes implemented by the NRA fail to balance the unstable economy?

Answer to . . .

Viewing History Job training and medical care.
Main Idea Connections When higher wages went into effect, prices rose and the cycle of falling consumption resumed.

Source: *Historical Statistics of the United States, Colonial Times to 1970*

 Interpreting Graphs One of Roosevelt's greatest challenges during the hundred days was combating unemployment. *Economics By how much did unemployment decline between 1933 and 1937?*

BACKGROUND

Interdisciplinary

In 1933, FDR established the Tennessee Valley Authority (TVA) to oversee "a land use experiment on a regional scale, one embracing many states." In spite of considerable opposition, the TVA revitalized the economic life of the Tennessee Valley. Building projects brought $500 million into the region and employed 200,000 men and women. Fertilizers produced from local minerals in river-powered factories nourished the thin soil. Exhausted corn, cotton, and tobacco fields soon became rich pastures for livestock. In the 1940s one resident of Decatur, Alabama, described the change: "Fifteen years ago we were dozing in the sunshine waiting for that once-a-year payroll brought by cotton and wearing out our second finest resource, the land. Today the cash income from all farm products in the area surrounding Decatur is $43 million."

The Federal Securities Act, passed in May 1933, required companies to provide information about their finances if they offered stock for sale. To provide further protection against economic downturns, Congress also reformed the stock market. The next year Congress set up the Securities and Exchange Commission (SEC) to regulate the stock market. The SEC was given the power to tell companies what information must be included in their financial statements. Congress also gave the Federal Reserve Board power to regulate the purchase of stock on margin—a practice that had contributed heavily to the crash of 1929.

Saving Homes and Farms Many middle-income homeowners were having trouble paying their mortgages. The Home Owners' Loan Corporation (HOLC) refinanced, or reshaped the terms of, mortgages to make the payments more manageable. Between June 1933 and June 1936, the HOLC made about one million low-interest loans.

Many farmers were losing their homes and their land because of the low prices they received for their products. An Agricultural Adjustment Administration (AAA), set up in May 1933, tried to raise farm prices through subsidies, or government financial assistance. The AAA used proceeds from a new tax to pay farmers not to raise certain crops and animals. Lower production, it was hoped, would raise prices.

Under this program some farmers plowed under growing crops. Many Americans could not understand how the federal government could encourage the destruction of food while so many were hungry.

The TVA One public works project proved especially popular. The **Tennessee Valley Authority (TVA),** created in May 1933, helped farmers and created jobs in one of the country's least developed regions. By reactivating a hydroelectric power facility started during World War I, the TVA provided cheap electric power, flood control, and recreational opportunities to the entire Tennessee River valley, as shown on the map on the next page.

New Deal Personnel

FDR surrounded himself with eager and hardworking advisers. Some, like Harry Hopkins and Harold Ickes, went directly into his Cabinet or headed one of the new agencies. Others, such as Raymond Moley, Adolf A. Berle, and Rexford G. Tugwell, were part of a so-called brain trust, an informal group of intellectuals who helped devise policies.

For the first time a woman held a Cabinet post. Frances Perkins became Secretary of Labor, a job she held until 1945. Perkins successfully pressed for laws that would help wage earners as well as the unemployed. Perkins was one of more than two dozen women who held key New Deal positions.

FDR's administration broke new ground by hiring African Americans to more than a hundred policy-making posts. One of Roosevelt's key appointees, Mary McLeod Bethune, held the highest position of any African American woman in the New Deal. Bethune was a former elementary school teacher, a college president, and the founder of the National Council of Negro Women. She entered government service with a reputation as one of the country's most influential spokespersons for African American concerns.

Appointed director of the Division of Negro Affairs of the National Youth Administration in 1936, Bethune advised FDR on programs that aided African Americans. In the process she increased her level of influence. She forged a united stand among black officeholders by organizing a Federal Council on Negro Affairs. This unofficial group, known as the black cabinet, met weekly to hammer out priorities and to increase African American support for the New Deal.

Answer to . . .

Interpreting Graphs Nearly 5 million people.

The Tennessee Valley Authority

New Deal projects included the Grand Coulee Dam, the California Central Valley Water Project, and the Tennessee Valley Authority, or TVA. The TVA linked industry, agriculture, forestry science, and flood prevention. *Human-Environment Interaction* To how many states did the TVA provide service?

Legend:
- — Tennessee River drainage basin
- / Dam
- ⚒ Power plant
- ☐ Area served by TVA

0   50   100 Miles
0   50   100 Kilometers

Area of Main Map

Eleanor Roosevelt

AMERICAN BIOGRAPHY Among FDR's most important colleagues was his wife, Eleanor Roosevelt. She threw herself into supporting the New Deal and traveled widely for her husband, whose disability made traveling difficult. She reported to him on conditions in the country and on the effects his programs were having.

Eleanor Roosevelt, a niece of Theodore Roosevelt, was born in New York City on October 11, 1884. A member of a wealthy family, Eleanor attended private schools. In 1905 she married her distant cousin Franklin, and they had six children.

During World War I Eleanor Roosevelt joined the war effort as a volunteer, aiding soldiers passing through New York City. After the war she expanded her volunteer work, involving herself with social and political reforms. In 1922 she became a member of the Women's Trade Union League and also began active service in the New York State Democratic party.

After helping FDR win the presidency, Eleanor Roosevelt began to reshape the position of First Lady. She toured the country in place of her husband, visiting coal mines, sewing rooms, and housing

Eleanor Roosevelt (1884–1962)

projects. Back in the White House she held her own press conferences for women correspondents. She gave lectures and in 1935 started a newspaper column called "My Day," in which she drummed up support for the New Deal.

At times, Mrs. Roosevelt took stands that embarrassed her husband. For example, in 1938 she attended a Birmingham, Alabama, meeting of the Southern Conference for Human Welfare, an interracial group. She knew she was expected to obey local Jim Crow laws that required African Americans and whites to sit in separate parts of the auditorium. In protest she sat in the center aisle, between the divided races. Her act received wide publicity, and no one missed its symbolism.

Eleanor Roosevelt's activities troubled some Americans. In their view a First Lady should act only as a gracious hostess at state dinners. Gradually, however, the public got used to her unconventional style, and many came to admire her for her enthusiasm, humanity, and idealism. ■

The New Deal Falters

The zeal and energy with which New Dealers attacked the Depression pleased most observers. But when the new programs failed to bring

Answer to . . .

Map Skills To seven states.

To make sure students understand the main idea of this section, you may wish to use the web graphic organizer below.

Tell students that a web shows a main idea and its supporting details. Ask students to use it to show President Roosevelt's attempt to overcome the Depression through the programs of the New Deal.

Teaching Tip A template for this graphic organizer can be found in the Color Transparencies, G-1.

Write the following words on the chalkboard: *What, Who, Where, When, Why.* Ask volunteers to make up a question about the New Deal using each of these words. For example: *What was the New Deal?* Write the questions on the chalkboard. Then help students formulate answers to these questions.

Answer to . . .

Interpreting Tables Nation: promoted economic recovery; created public works; conserved the environment. Individuals: protected unions; gave them jobs and job training; helped with debts; provided security in the forms of pensions and unemployment benefits.

FACT Finder
Some New Deal Agencies

Agency	Purpose
Civilian Conservation Corps (CCC)	Provided jobs to young, unmarried men (and, later, women) to work on conservation and resource development projects.
Works Progress Administration (WPA)	Gave the unemployed work in building construction and arts programs.
Public Works Administration (PWA)	Sponsored massive public works projects such as dams and hydroelectric plants.
National Recovery Administration (NRA)	Worked with industries to establish codes outlining fair business and labor practices.
National Labor Relations Board (NLRB)	Enforced provisions of the Wagner Act, which included the right to collective bargaining and other union rights
Federal Deposit Insurance Corporation (FDIC)	Insured bank deposits up to $5,000.
Securities and Exchange Commission (SEC)	Regulated the stock market and protected investors from dishonest trading practices.
Agricultural Adjustment Administration (AAA)	Attempted to raise farm prices by paying farmers to lower farm output.
Social Security Administration (SSA)	Provided old-age pensions, disability payments, and unemployment benefits.

Interpreting Tables New Deal zeal created dozens of federal agencies. *Government How did these agencies aim to help both the nation and individuals?*

about significant economic improvement, criticism began to mount. Many worried about the increasing power that New Deal agencies were giving to the federal government. Former President Hoover warned against "a state-controlled or state-directed social or economic system. . . . That is not liberalism; it is tyranny," he said.

FDR also found his programs under attack by the Supreme Court. In 1935 the Court declared the NIRA unconstitutional because it gave the President lawmaking powers and regulated local, rather than interstate, commerce. The following year, the Court ruled that the tax that funded AAA subsidies to farmers was also unconstitutional. Two of the most important elements of the New Deal had crumbled. It was time to reassess.

A Second New Deal

Most of the public remained behind Roosevelt. The midterm elections of 1934 showed overwhelming nationwide support for FDR's administration. In 1935 he launched a new, even bolder burst of legislative activity. Some have called this period the **Second New Deal.** In part, it was FDR's response to critics who said he was not doing enough for ordinary Americans. The Second New Deal included more social welfare benefits, stricter controls over business, stronger support for unions, and higher taxes on the rich.

New and Expanded Agencies New agencies attacked joblessness even more aggressively than before. The Works Progress Administration (WPA), an agency set up in 1935 and lasting eight years, provided work for more than 8 million citizens. The WPA constructed or improved more than 20,000 playgrounds, schools, hospitals, and airfields and supported the creative work of many artists and writers. (See Section 3.)

The Second New Deal responded to the worsening plight of agricultural workers. The original AAA had ignored many of the farm workers who did not own land. In the Southwest, for example, Mexican American farm workers struggled to survive. Many of these migrant workers were forced to return to Mexico. Others tried to form unions, causing fierce resistance from farmer associations. In the South, landlords had accepted the AAA subsidies, taken land out of production, and left tenants and sharecroppers to fend for themselves.

In May 1935 Rexford Tugwell set up a Resettlement Administration that loaned money to owners of small farms and helped resettle tenants and sharecroppers on productive land. In 1937 a Farm Security Administration (FSA) replaced Tugwell's agency. It loaned more than $1 billion to farmers and set up camps for migrant workers.

New Labor Legislation Labor unions had liked the NIRA provision known as 7a, which

RESOURCE OPTIONS

granted them the right to organize and bargain collectively. When the NIRA was declared unconstitutional, however, workers began to demand new legislation to protect their rights.

In July 1935 Congress responded. It passed a National Labor Relations Act, called the **Wagner Act** after its leading advocate, New York senator Robert Wagner. The Wagner Act legalized practices allowed only unevenly in the past. These included collective bargaining and closed shops, which are workplaces open only to union members. It also outlawed spying on union activities and blacklisting, a practice in which employers agreed not to hire union leaders. The act set up a National Labor Relations Board (NLRB) to enforce its provisions. In 1938 a Fair Labor Standards Act banned child labor and established a minimum wage for all workers covered under the act.

Social Legislation In 1935 Congress also passed the Social Security Act. The act established a **Social Security system** to provide security, in the form of regular payments, to people who could not support themselves. This system offered three types of insurance:

(1) *Old-age pensions and survivors' benefits.* Workers and their employers paid equally into a national insurance fund. Retired workers or their surviving spouses were eligible to start receiving Social Security payments at age 65. The act did not cover farm and domestic workers until amended in 1954.

(2) *Unemployment insurance.* Employers with more than eight employees funded this provision by paying a tax. The government distributed the money to workers who lost their jobs. States administered their own programs, with federal guidance and financial support.

(3) *Aid for dependent children, the blind, and the physically disabled.* The federal government sent money grants to the states to help support needy individuals in these categories.

The Social Security system, though harshly criticized, helped millions of beneficiaries feel more secure. Its success has helped inspire numerous other social welfare programs.

The Social Security Act provided a variety of benefits to many retired, disabled, and unemployed workers.

The 1936 Election

No one expected the Republican presidential candidate of 1936, Kansas governor Alfred M. Landon, to beat FDR. But few predicted the extent of FDR's landslide. FDR carried every state except Maine and Vermont, winning 523–8 in the electoral college.

FDR's landslide victory showed that most Americans supported the New Deal. Yet the New Deal still had many critics with their own sizable followings.

Objectives
You may wish to call students' attention to the objectives in the Section Preview. The objectives are reflected in the main headings of the section.

Bellringer
Write the following statement on the chalkboard: "I feel that our President is doing an outstanding job, and I agree with his policies." Do students agree? Ask them to consider the reasons people criticize their leaders.

Reading Strategy
Formulating Questions Refer to the Reading Strategy in the Section Preview. You may wish to ask volunteers to read their questions aloud.

LESSON PLAN
Connecting to the Main Idea

1. Focus Explain that the many far-reaching programs of the New Deal did not provide benefits to all people. Ask students why President Roosevelt and the New Deal sparked criticism.

2. Instruct Ask how the New Deal failed to address the problems of many women and African Americans. Ask students to describe the opposition from the right and the left, respectively. Discuss the role of anti–New Dealers such as Huey Long and Father Coughlin, and ask students to consider why such demagogues are often effective critics.

Explore the Court-packing scheme. Ask students how that episode provoked widespread public disapproval of Roosevelt and damaged his standing in Congress.

3. Close President Roosevelt and the New Deal faced criticisms from all points along the political spectrum. The next section examines how the New Deal left a permanent mark on the United States.

1932
Huey Long's Share-the-Wealth program

1934
American Liberty League founded

1934
EPIC clubs formed in California

1935
Wealth Tax Act

1937
FDR's Court-packing scheme

1932   **1934**   **1936**   **1938**

2 The New Deal's Critics

SECTION PREVIEW

Objectives
1 Identify which Americans received only limited benefits from the New Deal.
2 Describe how politicians and demagogues criticized the New Deal.
3 Explain FDR's Court-packing scheme.
4 *Key Terms* Define: American Liberty League; demagogue; nationalization.

Main Idea
A variety of critics pointed out the shortcomings of the New Deal as well as its potential for restricting individual freedom.

Reading Strategy
Formulating Questions Scan the section and note the main headings. Turn each main heading into a question. As you read, answer the questions that you have created.

Franklin Roosevelt's success at the polls in 1936 suggests complete approval of his New Deal. Indeed, many Americans benefited from the relief programs. Letters thanking the President poured into the White House. One writer said, "There ain't no other nation in the world that would have sense enough to think of WPA and all the other A's."

Yet the New Deal inspired its share of critics, too. Another letter writer said, "If you could get around the country as I have and seen the distress forced upon the American people, you would throw your darn NRA and AAA, and every other . . . A into the sea."

The Limits of the New Deal
For all its successes, the New Deal fell short of many people's expectations. The Fair Labor Standards Act, for example, covered fewer than one quarter of all gainfully employed workers. It set the minimum wage at 25 cents an hour, which was well below what most covered workers already made. New Deal agencies also were generally less helpful to women and minority groups than they were to white men.

Women Many aspects of New Deal legislation put women at a disadvantage. The NRA codes, for example, permitted lower wages for women's work in almost a quarter of all cases. In relief and job programs, men and boys received strong preference. Jobs went to male "heads of families," unless the men were unable to work.

No New Deal provision protected domestic service, the largest female occupation. In 1942 an African American domestic worker in St. Louis pleaded with the President to ask employers, the "rich people," to "give us some hours to rest in and some Sundays off and pay us more wages." Working 14-hour days, she earned only $6.50 per week. A brutally honest official wrote back to her:

 AMERICAN VOICES "State and Federal labor laws, which offer protection to workers in so many occupations, have so far not set up standards for working conditions in domestic situations. There is nothing that can be done . . . to help you and others in this kind of employment."

—Roosevelt administration official

▶ RESOURCE OPTIONS

Teaching Resources

 Reproducible Lesson Plan Lesson Plans folder, p. 129

Learning Styles Lesson Plan Learning Styles Lesson Plans folder, p. 49

Big Idea Graphic Organizer Big Idea Graphic Organizer folder, p. 101

 Guided Reading and Review Units 7–8 folder, p. 35

Literature Activity In Search of Work: African Americans, Units 7–8 folder, p. 42

WORLD'S HIGHEST STANDARD OF LIVING

There's no way like the American Way

VIEWING HISTORY

This picture, taken at a relief center in Louisville, Kentucky, highlights the struggle of African Americans to overcome both the Depression and the effects of prejudice. *Culture How does this photograph reflect the racial discrimination that was part of the New Deal relief programs?*

African Americans Federal relief programs in the South, including public works projects, reinforced racial segregation. As a rule African Americans were not offered jobs at a professional level. They were kept out of skilled jobs on dam and electric power projects, and they received lower pay than whites for the same work. Because the Social Security Act excluded both farmers and domestic workers, it failed to cover nearly two thirds of working African Americans.

African Americans in the North had not supported FDR in 1932, but by 1936 they had joined his camp. Often the last hired and first fired, they had experienced the highest unemployment rates of any group during the Depression. For this reason those who did gain employment appreciated many of the New Deal programs.

Yet the New Deal did nothing to end discriminatory practices in the North. The employment of only whites in white-owned businesses in black neighborhoods was especially troubling. In the absence of help from the federal government, African Americans took matters into their own hands. Protesters picketed and boycotted such businesses with the slogan "Don't shop where you can't work."

The early Depression had seen an alarming rise in the number of lynchings. The federal government again offered no relief. In 1935 and 1938 bills to make lynching a federal crime went down to narrow defeat. NAACP head Walter White recalled in 1948 that FDR had given this explanation for his refusal to support these measures:

> **AMERICAN VOICES** "Southerners, by reason of seniority rule in Congress, are chairmen or occupy strategic places on most of the Senate and House committees. If I come out for the anti-lynching bill now, they will block every bill I ask Congress to pass to keep America from collapsing. I just can't take that risk."
>
> *—Franklin Roosevelt*

Of course, Roosevelt's record had much that African Americans could applaud. He appointed more African Americans to policy-making posts than any President before him. The Roosevelts also seemed genuinely concerned for the fate of African Americans. These factors help to explain FDR's wide support among black voters.

Political Critics

African Americans may have supported FDR. But many others, with widely differing political views, criticized the New Deal.

BACKGROUND

A Diverse Nation

Many African Americans felt left out by the New Deal and turned to the Communist party. Hosea Hudson, for example, an African American farmer from rural Georgia, joined the party. Angered by the 1931 case of the Scottsboro Boys, Hudson organized unemployed African Americans in Birmingham, Alabama, to meet weekly and discuss social issues. The Communist party's legal arm, the International Labor Defense (ILD), defended the Scottsboro Boys.

Customize for

More Advanced Students

Ask students to analyze the difficulties of forging government programs that provide equal benefit and satisfaction to all citizens. Have students discuss what limits the democratic process places on the ability of a government to implement broad new programs, such as universal health care.

TEST PREPARATION

Have students read the quotation by Roosevelt on this page and then answer the question below.

From the passage, you can infer that—

A Southerners do not have considerable power in Congress.

B FDR opposes the anti-lynching bill.

C Southerners do not support the anti-lynching bill.

D FDR is not interested in helping African Americans.

Answer to . . .

Viewing History All of the people on the billboard, which trumpets the nation's high standard of living, are white. All the people in the relief line are African American.

New Deal Does Too Much A number of Republicans, in Congress and elsewhere, opposed Roosevelt. They knew something had to be done about the Depression, but they believed that the New Deal went too far.

These critics included many wealthy people, who regarded FDR as their enemy. Early in the New Deal, they had disapproved of programs such as the TVA, which they considered to be socialistic. The Second New Deal gave them even more to hate, as FDR pushed through a series of higher taxes aimed at the rich. One of these was the Revenue Act of 1935, also known as the Wealth Tax Act. This act raised the tax rate on individual incomes over $50,000 and also increased rates on the income and profits of corporations.

Main Idea CONNECTIONS
Why did many wealthy Americans oppose the New Deal?

The Social Security Act also aroused political opposition. Some of FDR's enemies claimed that it penalized successful, hard-working people. Others saw the assignment of Social Security numbers as the first step toward a militaristic, regimented society. They predicted that soon people would have to wear metal dog tags engraved with their Social Security numbers.

Uncle Sam is being restrained by New Deal agencies and policies created by FDR to fight the Depression. Note the flock of blue eagles—symbols of the NRA. *Economics* **What complaints did critics have with the New Deal?**

A group called the **American Liberty League,** founded in 1934, spearheaded much of the opposition to the New Deal. It was led by former Democratic presidential candidate Alfred E. Smith, the National Association of Manufacturers, and business figures such as John J. Raskob and the Du Pont family.

The league charged the New Deal with limiting individual freedom in an unconstitutional, "un-American" manner. To them, programs such as compulsory unemployment insurance smacked of "Bolshevism," referring to the political philosophy of the founders of the Soviet Union.

New Deal Does Not Do Enough Many Progressives and Socialists also attacked the New Deal. But these critics accused FDR's programs of not providing enough help.

In 1934 muckraking novelist and Socialist Upton Sinclair ran for governor of California on the Democratic ticket. His platform, "End Poverty in California" (EPIC), called for a new economic system in which the state would take over factories and farms. EPIC clubs formed throughout the state, and Sinclair won the primary. Terrified, opponents used shady tactics to discredit Sinclair. They produced fake newsreels showing people who spoke with a Russian accent praising Sinclair. Associated unfairly with communism, Sinclair lost the election.

The New Deal had only limited success in eliminating poverty. This helped lead to a revival of progressivism in Minnesota and Wisconsin. Running for the United States Senate, Wisconsin Progressive Robert La Follette, Jr., argued that "devices which seek to preserve the unequal distribution of wealth . . . will retard or prevent recovery." His brother, Philip, also took a radical stand, calling for the redistribution of income. Philip's ideas persuaded the state Socialist party to join his Progressives after he won the Wisconsin governorship in 1934.

Other Critics

Some New Deal critics were **demagogues**— leaders who manipulate people with half-truths, deceptive promises, and scare tactics. One such demagogue was Father Charles E. Coughlin (CAWG-lin), a dynamic speaker who used the radio to broadcast his message. Throughout the 1930s the so-called Radio Priest held listeners spellbound from his studio in Detroit. In 1934 Father Coughlin's weekly broadcasts reached an audience estimated at more than 10 million people.

Coughlin achieved popularity even though he sometimes contradicted himself. One time he advocated the **nationalization,** or conversion to government ownership, of banks and the redistribution of their wealth. Another time he defended the sanctity of private property, which includes banks. At first he supported FDR and the New Deal. Later he denounced them, through his radio show and the organization he formed in 1934 called the "National Union for Social Justice."

Coughlin's attacks on FDR grew increasingly reckless. In 1936 he called him Franklin "Double-crossing" Roosevelt and described him as a "great betrayer and liar."

By the end of the 1930s, Coughlin was issuing openly anti-Jewish statements. He also began showering praise on Adolf Hitler and Benito Mussolini, two menacing leaders who were then rising to power in Europe. Coughlin's actions alarmed many Americans and he lost some of his support. In 1942 Roman Catholic officials ordered him to stop broadcasting his show.

Huey Long was a different type of demagogue. A country lawyer, he won the governorship of Louisiana in 1928 and became a United States senator in 1932. Unlike many other southern Democrats, Long never used racial attacks to build a base of power. Instead, he worked to help the underprivileged, improving education, medical care, and public services. He also built an extraordinarily powerful and ruthless political machine in his home state.

Originally a supporter of FDR, Long broke with him early in the New Deal. "Unless we provide for redistribution of wealth in this country, the country is doomed," he said. While in the Senate, Long developed a program called "Share-the-Wealth." In 1932 he submitted a proposal to limit individual income to $1 million and inheritance to $5 million. The government would take the rest through taxes. In 1934 he devised a plan to give every American family a minimum $5,000 "homestead allowance" and a minimum annual income of $2,000.

Long's program for helping all Americans achieve wealth attracted many followers. His success helped push FDR to propose new taxes on wealthy Americans in the Second New

Deal. Meanwhile, Long himself began to eye the presidency. But in September 1935 the son-in-law of one of Long's political enemies shot and killed him.

Long and Coughlin never seriously threatened FDR or the New Deal. But their popularity warned Roosevelt that if he failed to solve the nation's problems, he risked losing popular support.

The Court-Packing Scheme

Roosevelt received criticism not only for his programs, but also for his actions. No act aroused more opposition than his attempt to "pack" the Supreme Court.

Throughout the early New Deal the Supreme Court had caused FDR his greatest frustration. The Court had invalidated the NIRA, the AAA, and many state laws from the progressive era. In February 1937 FDR proposed a major court reform bill.

COMPARING PRIMARY SOURCES

THE NEW DEAL

FDR's promise to improve life for all Americans with a New Deal did not win approval from all quarters.

In Favor of the New Deal	Opposed to the New Deal
"Roosevelt is the only President we ever had that thought the Constitution belonged to the pore [poor] man too. . . . Yessir, it took Roosevelt to read in the Constitution and find out them folks way back yonder that made it was talkin' about the pore man right along with the rich one. I am a Roosevelt man." —*Testimony by mill worker George Dobbin, 1939. Collected in* These Are Our Lives, *Federal Writers Project of the Works Progress Administration (1939).*	"All the prosperity he had brought to the country has been legislated and is not real. Nothing he has ever started has been finished. My common way of expressing it is that we are in the middle of the ocean like a ship without an anchor. No good times can come to the country as long as there is so much discrimination practiced. . . . I don't see much chance for our people to get anywhere when the color line instead of ability determines the opportunities to get ahead economically." —*Testimony by Sam T. Mayhew, 1939. Collected in* Such As Us *(1978)*

ANALYZING VIEWPOINTS **Compare the main arguments made by the two speakers.**

Ask students to locate speeches given by 1936 Republican presidential candidate Alf Landon or by any other prominent New Deal critic. Have students summarize the messages of the speeches and analyze the strengths and weaknesses of all the arguments. *(Verbal/Linguistic, Logical)*

Answers to
SECTION 2 REVIEW

1. (a) American Liberty League, see p. 668; (b) demagogue, see p. 668; (c) nationalization, see p. 669.

2. Upton Sinclair and midwestern Progressives criticized it for not doing enough. The wealthy and critics of Social Security felt it had gone too far. Many people deplored the Court-packing scheme; demagogues attacked FDR's policies.

3. Progressives: new economic system to take over farms and factories, redistribute wealth, end poverty. Coughlin: naturalization, denouncing of FDR's policies, racial attacks. Long: redistribution of wealth.

4. Yes, because the Second New Deal strengthened and extended the programs of the first.

5. Women: jobs and relief programs favored men. African Americans: relief programs enforced segregation; Social Security excluded most blacks.

6. Essays will vary but should be supported with facts from the section.

The Constitution had not specified the number of Supreme Court justices. Congress had last changed the number in 1869. But by Roosevelt's time, the number nine had become well established. Arguing that he merely wanted to lighten the burden of the aging justices, FDR asked Congress to pass his reform bill. The legislation would have enabled him to appoint as many as six additional justices, one for each justice over 70 years of age. Most people understood Roosevelt's real intention. He wanted to "pack" the Court with judges favorable to the New Deal.

Negative reaction came swiftly from all sides. Critics blasted the President for trying to inject politics into the judiciary. They warned Congress not to let him undermine the sacred constitutional principle of separation of powers.

With several dictators ruling in Europe, the world seemed already to be tilting toward tyranny. If Congress let FDR reshape the Supreme Court, critics worried, the United States might start heading down the same slope. Sam E. Roberts of

> **GOVERNMENT CONCEPTS**
>
> *separation of powers:* **the separation of powers within the federal government among the legislative, executive, and judicial branches**
>
> ▼ **The Historical Context:** One of the many arguments made against President Roosevelt's 1937 proposal to expand the Supreme Court was that it would weaken the separation of powers. Roosevelt, his critics stated, was trying to undermine the independence of the judicial branch of the federal government.
>
> ▼ **The Concept Today:** Conflicts between the President and the Supreme Court, as well as other conflicts between different branches of government, continue to occur today. Yet all three branches retain their independent powers.

Kansas, in a letter to his representative in Congress, expressed the fears of many:

> **AMERICAN VOICES** ❝Our liberty is much more important than any whim of the President's. He might be a kind dictator himself, but after the stage is set the next President might be a Hitler or Mussolini.❞
>
> —*Sam E. Roberts*

California's aging senator Hiram W. Johnson echoed the views of many legislators:

> **AMERICAN VOICES** ❝Shall the Congress make the Supreme Court subservient to [subject to] the presidency? The implications of this are so grave and far-reaching, I can do but one thing, and that is, . . . oppose this extraordinary legislation.❞
>
> —*Senator Hiram W. Johnson*

FDR was forced to withdraw his reform bill. He also suffered political damage. Many Republicans and Southern Democrats united against further New Deal legislation. This alliance remained a force for years to come.

FDR did wind up with a Court that tended to side with him. Some older justices retired, allowing FDR to appoint justices who favored the New Deal. Even earlier, however, the Court had begun to uphold measures from the Second New Deal, including the Wagner Act. The Court may have been reacting to public opinion, or it may have decided that those measures were better thought out and more skillfully drafted than earlier ones.

SECTION 2 REVIEW

Comprehension

1. *Key Terms* Define: (a) American Liberty League; (b) demagogue; (c) nationalization.

2. *Summarizing the Main Idea* Why did people criticize FDR and the New Deal?

3. *Organizing Information* Create a Venn diagram to compare the demands of the Progressives, Father Coughlin, and Huey Long.

Critical Thinking

4. *Analyzing Time Lines* Review the time line at the start of the section. Were most criticisms of FDR's programs aimed at the Second New Deal? Explain.

5. *Drawing Conclusions* Why did women and African Americans benefit less from the New Deal than white men?

> ### Writing Activity
> **6.** *Writing a Persuasive Essay* Write an essay about FDR's court reform bill. Defend one side of the issue in your essay.

RESOURCE OPTIONS

Teaching Resources

📁 **Quiz** Units 7–8 folder, p. 36

Student Performance Pack

 Guide to the Essentials Chapter 23, Section 2 (English and Spanish)

Distinguishing Fact from Opinion

When you read historical materials such as speeches, letters, and diaries, you will find that their authors express both facts and opinions. A fact is something that can be proved to be true by checking an encyclopedia or other source. An opinion is a judgment that reflects beliefs or feelings.

To determine the soundness of an author's ideas, you need to be able to distinguish between fact and opinion. The ability to do so will help you evaluate what you read and reach your own conclusions about historical events.

Read the excerpt criticizing the New Deal from a speech by Herbert Hoover at the Republican National Convention in 1936. Use the following steps to distinguish between fact and opinion in the speech.

1. *Determine which statements are facts.* Remember that facts can be verified in other sources. (a) For what reason is Hoover's first statement, about the Supreme Court, easily recognizable as a fact? (b) Choose two other statements of fact in the excerpt. Explain how you might prove that each statement is a fact.

2. *Determine which statements are opinions.* Sometimes authors signal opinions with phrases such as "I believe" or "I think," but often they do not. Other clues that indicate opinions are sweeping generalizations and emotion-packed words. (a) What indicates that the final sentence of the first paragraph is an opinion rather than a fact? (b) Choose two other statements

of opinion, and explain what tells you that they are opinions.

3. *Evaluate opinions as you read.* Generally, an opinion is more reliable when an author gives facts to support it. (a) How does Hoover support his opinion that many New Deal acts "were a violation of the rights of men and of self-government"? (b) Does he present any facts to support his statement that the Congress has "aban-

doned its responsibility"? (c) In your opinion, how good a job has Hoover done in supporting his opinions? Explain your answer.

TEST FOR SUCCESS

Write a paragraph about some aspect of the New Deal. Include in your paragraph one opinion based on facts and one opinion that is unreliable.

> **"**The Supreme Court has reversed some ten or twelve of the New Deal major enactments. Many of these acts were a violation of the rights of men and of self-government. Despite the sworn duty of the Executive and Congress to defend these rights, they have sought to take them into their own hands. That is an attack on the foundations of freedom.
>
> More than this, the independence of the Congress, the Supreme Court, and the Executive are pillars at the door of liberty. For three years the word 'must' has invaded the independence of Congress. And the Congress has abandoned its responsibility to check even the expenditures [spending] of money. . . .
>
> We have seen these gigantic expenditures and this torrent of waste pile up a national debt which two generations cannot repay. . . .
>
> Billions have been spent to prime the economic pump. . . . We have seen the frantic attempts to find new taxes on the rich. Yet three-quarters of the bill will be sent to the average man and the poor. He and his wife and his grandchildren will be giving a quarter of all their working days to pay taxes. Freedom to work for himself is changed into a slavery of work for the follies of government. . . .
>
> We have seen the building up of a horde of political officials. We have seen the pressures upon the helpless and destitute to trade political support for relief. Both are a pollution of the very fountains of liberty.**"**
>
> —*Herbert Hoover, excerpted from* American Ideals Versus the New Deal

671

SKILLS FOR LIFE

Critical Thinking

Distinguishing Fact from Opinion

Focus Analyze a speaker's use of facts and opinions in a political speech. **Instruct** Divide students into small groups to examine the speech and identify the various facts and opinions used by the speaker. Ask each group to report its findings. If groups draw different conclusions about which statements are facts and which are opinions, have the whole class discuss the examples. Then ask students whether or not they think the speaker in this case has made an effective argument. What facts might he have used to strengthen his points? **Extend** See the Skills for Life Activity in the Resource Options below.

Answers

1. (a) The decisions of the Supreme Court are matters of public record and can thus be easily verified. (b) Possible answer: The statements about the growth of the national debt and the growth in the number of public officials are verifiable facts.

2. (a) It is a sweeping accusation of the executive and the Congress. (b) Possible answer: The statements that Congress has abandoned its responsibility and that New Deal developments have polluted the fountain of liberty are both opinions.

3. (a) He states that they were overthrown by the Supreme Court, the guardian of constitutional rights. (b) No, he gives no specific examples—he just makes a sweeping accusation. (c) Students' answers should be based on evidence from the quotation.

TEST FOR SUCCESS

Answers will vary but should show an understanding of the steps outlined in the skill.

1935
WPA begins to fund projects in the arts

1935
CIO created

1936
Sit-down strike at GM's Flint, Michigan, auto plants

1937
Republic Steel strike

1937
Economic recession begins

1939
Supreme Court outlaws sit-down strike

1935   **1937**   **1939**

Objectives

You may wish to call students' attention to the objectives in the Section Preview. The objectives are reflected in the main headings of the section.

Bellringer

Write the term *federal government* on the chalkboard. Ask students to brainstorm a list of words they associate with the term. Explain that many modern attitudes and beliefs concerning the government stem from the New Deal era.

Reading Strategy

Reading for Evidence Refer to the Reading Strategy in the Section Preview. You may wish to have students list the evidence they find.

LESSON PLAN

Connecting to the Main Idea

1. Focus Point out that the New Deal did not succeed in ending the Depression but that it did have a great impact on the nation's political, social, and cultural life. Ask students to list ways that this impact is felt today.

2. Instruct Ask students what the Recession of 1937 revealed about the New Deal and the economy. Discuss the changes that the New Deal introduced to the nation. Ask students to describe changes affecting labor unions. Ask them to consider the role of government in helping to make union gains possible.

Discuss government support for the arts as an important part of the New Deal. Ask students to discuss the benefits and drawbacks of government funding of the arts.

3. Close The New Deal failed to bring an end to the Depression. Yet it helped bring about many important developments whose impact can still be felt today.

3 Last Days of the New Deal

SECTION PREVIEW

Objectives

1 Explain what caused the recession of 1937.
2 Identify labor union triumphs resulting from the New Deal.
3 Describe the effects of the New Deal in terms of culture and lasting achievements.
4 *Key Terms* Define: national debt; revenue; coalition; sit-down strike.

Main Idea

The New Deal had a lasting effect on many aspects of American life.

Reading Strategy

Reading for Evidence As you read, look for evidence to support the claim on this page that the New Deal led to "some profound changes in American life."

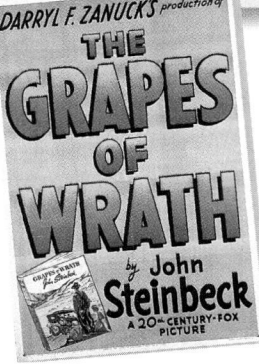

The Depression era produced many lasting works of art, including the novel The Grapes of Wrath.

The New Deal attacked the Great Depression with a barrage of programs that affected nearly every American. The New Deal did not end the nation's suffering, but it did lead to some profound changes in American life. Voters began to expect a President to formulate programs and solve problems. People accepted more government intervention in their lives, and laborers demanded more changes in the workplace.

The Recession of 1937

The New Deal did not put an end to the Depression, but its massive government spending did lead to some economic improvement. The improvement did not last long, however, as the economy collapsed again in August 1937. Industrial production fell, as did employment levels.

The new Social Security tax was partly to blame for this recession. The tax came directly out of workers' paychecks, through payroll deductions. Americans now had less money in their pockets, so they bought fewer goods.

Americans also had less money because FDR had cut way back on expensive programs such as the WPA. The President had become distressed at the rising **national debt.** This is the total amount of money the federal government has borrowed and has yet to pay back. The government borrows when its **revenue,** or income, does not keep up with its expenses. To fund the New Deal, the government had to borrow massive amounts of money. As a result, the national debt rose from $21 billion in 1933 to $43 billion by 1940.[†]

After 1937 Harry Hopkins and others persuaded FDR to expand the WPA and other programs that had been slashed. Joblessness and misery slowly decreased. Still, hard times lasted until well into the 1940s.

Unions Triumph

The New Deal changed the way Americans thought about labor unions. The Wagner Act

---

[†] The national debt is different from the federal budget deficit. The deficit is the shortfall between the amount of revenue the government takes in and the amount it spends.

RESOURCE OPTIONS

Teaching Resources

Reproducible Lesson Plan Lesson Plans folder, p. 130

Big Idea Graphic Organizer Big Idea Graphic Organizer folder, p. 102

Guided Reading and Review Units 7–8 folder, p. 37

Federal Public Debt, 1933–1940

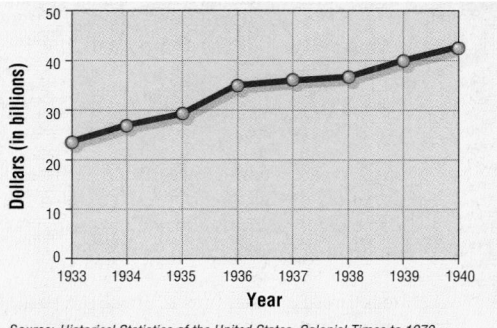

Source: *Historical Statistics of the United States, Colonial Times to 1970*

Federal Deficit, 1933–1940

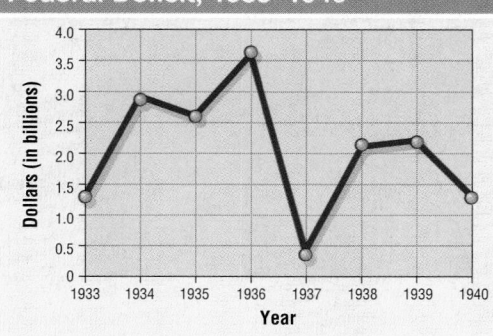

Source: *Historical Statistics of the United States, Colonial Times to 1970*

 Interpreting Graphs The New Deal was paid for by huge increases in government spending. Because of yearly federal deficits, the national debt expanded greatly during the Depression. *Economics In which year was the deficit the greatest? The lowest?*

provided federal protection for the activities of labor unions, making unions more attractive to workers. Union membership rose from about 3 million in 1933 to 10.5 million by 1941, a figure representing 11.3 percent of the nonagricultural work force. By 1945 some 36 percent were unionized, the high-water mark for unions in the United States.

A New Labor Organization Activism by powerful union leaders helped increase membership. The cautious and craft-based American Federation of Labor (AFL) had done little to attract unskilled industrial workers during its half-century of existence. In 1935 United Mine Workers president John L. Lewis joined with representatives of seven other AFL unions to try to change this situation. They created a Committee for Industrial Organization (CIO) within the AFL.

Although the AFL did not support its efforts, the CIO sought to organize the nation's unskilled workers. It sent organizers into steel mills, auto plants, and southern textile mills and welcomed all workers. The AFL suspended the CIO unions in 1936.

Nevertheless, two years later the CIO had 4 million members. In November 1938 this **coalition,** or alliance of groups with similar goals, changed its name to the Congress of Industrial Organizations. John L. Lewis became its first president. The aim of this coalition of industrial unions was to challenge conditions in industry, and their main tool was the strike.

An Era of Strikes The Wagner Act legalized collective bargaining and told management it had to bargain in good faith with certified union representatives. But the act could not force a company to accept union demands. Although the Wagner Act was designed to bring about industrial peace, in the short run it led to a wave of spectacular strikes.

Many of these work stoppages took the form of **sit-down strikes,** in which laborers stopped work but refused to leave the workplace. Supporters outside then organized picket lines. Together, the strikers and the picket lines prevented the company from bringing in scabs, or substitute workers.

The first sit-down strikes took place in early 1936 at three huge rubber-tire plants in Akron, Ohio. The success of the sit-downs led to similar strikes later in the year at several General Motors (GM) auto plants. The most famous began December 31, 1936. In this strike, laborers associated with the United Auto Workers (UAW) occupied GM's main plants in Flint, Michigan.

GM executives turned off the heat and blocked entry to the plants so that the workers could not receive food. They also called in the police against

Main Idea CONNECTIONS

In what sense did labor triumph in the 1930s?

John L. Lewis

ACTIVITY
EXTENDED CLASS PERIODS

Time: 90 minutes.
Activity: Create a newspaper special edition about the New Deal.
Grouping: Groups of four to six students.
Purpose: To have students create a newspaper that highlights the major people and events of the New Deal. The newspaper could include such features as news stories about New Deal programs or developments, profiles of key figures, political cartoons about people or events, and an editorial.
Roles: Cartoonist, editorial writer, reporters, layout and production designers.
Outcome: Students will understand the importance of prominent people and events of the New Deal.

Answer to . . .

Interpreting Graphs Greatest in 1936; lowest in 1937.
Main Idea Connections Union memberships increased and the first coalition of labor groups was formed.

The successful sit-down strike at the Fisher body plant during the winter of 1936–1937 (above) demonstrated the effectiveness of the new work stoppage technique. Here, workers guard a window during the strike. *Economics How did sit-down strikes differ from other strikes?*

the picketers outside. Violence erupted. The wife of a striker then grabbed a bullhorn and urged other wives to join the picketers.

Women later organized food deliveries to supply the strikers, set up a speakers' bureau to present the union's position to the public, and formed a Women's Emergency Brigade to take up picket duty. Governor Frank Murphy of Michigan and President Roosevelt refused to use the militia against the strike. By early February General Motors had given in.

Not all strikes were as successful. Henry Ford continued to resist unionism. In 1937 at a Ford Motor Company plant near Detroit, his men beat UAW officials when the unionists tried to distribute leaflets. Walter Reuther, a beating victim and future president of the UAW, later testified about the incident:

AMERICAN VOICES **❝**They picked me up about eight different times and threw me down on my back on the concrete. While I was on the ground they kicked me in the face, head, and other parts of my body. . . . I never raised a hand.**❞**

—*Walter Reuther*

Like Ford, the Republic Steel Company refused to sign with steelworkers' unions until war loomed in 1941. At one strike against Republic Steel on May 30, 1937, Chicago police killed 10 picketers and injured another 84. This Memorial Day tragedy showed that labor, despite its triumphs, still faced many challenges. Another sign came in the form of a Supreme Court ruling. In 1939 the Court outlawed the sit-down strike as being too potent a weapon and an obstacle to negotiation.

New Deal's Effects on Culture

Artists created enduring cultural legacies for the nation during the Depression. They were aided by federal funds allocated by Congress to support the popular and fine arts.

Literature Several works of literature destined to become classics emerged during this period. One example is Pearl Buck's novel *The Good Earth* (1931), a saga of peasant struggle in China. In 1936 Tennessee writer James Agee and photographer Walker Evans lived for a few weeks with sharecropper families in Alabama. Together they produced a masterpiece of nonfiction literature, *Let Us Now Praise Famous Men* (1941). John Steinbeck wrote *The Grapes of Wrath* (1939), a powerful tale about Dust Bowl victims who travel to California in search of a better life. In 1937 folklorist Zora Neale Hurston published *Their Eyes Are Watching God,* a novel about a strong-willed African American woman and the Florida town in which she lived.

Radio and Movies The new medium of radio became a major source of entertainment for most American families. In particular, comedy shows peaked in the 1930s, producing stars such as Jack Benny, Fred Allen, George Burns, and Gracie Allen. The first daytime dramas, called soap operas because soap companies often sponsored them, emerged in this period. These 15-minute stories, designed to provoke strong emotional responses, were meant to appeal to women who remained at home during the day. Symphony music and opera also flourished on the radio.

By 1933 the movies had recovered from the initial setback caused by the early Depression. Americans needed an escape from hard times, and the movies gave it to them—in Technicolor. This entertainment was not free, like radio broadcasts, but it was affordable. For a quarter, customers could see a double feature (introduced in 1931) or take the whole family to a drive-in theater (introduced in 1933). Federal agencies used motion pictures to publicize their work. The Farm Security Administration, for example, produced documentaries of American agricultural life.

TEST PREPARATION

Have students read the quotation by Walter Reuther on this page and then answer the question below.

You can tell from the passage that—

A Reuther's resistance encouraged more violence against him.

(B) Reuther was determined to remain passive even when being beaten.

C Ford's men did not seriously intend to harm Reuther.

D Reuther was determined to resist the men by any means necessary.

Some Hollywood studios concentrated on optimistic films about common people who triumphed over evil, such as Warner Brothers' *Mr. Smith Goes to Washington* (1939). Comedies were very popular, too. In this era the zany Marx Brothers produced such comic classics as *Monkey Business* (1931) and *Duck Soup* (1933).

The greatest box-office hits, however, transported Americans out of the gloom of Depression into a happier time. The *Wizard of Oz*, released in 1939, allowed viewers to escape to a whole different world. Moviegoers flocked to musicals that featured large orchestras and exquisitely choreographed dance numbers with dancers in luxurious costumes.

No one understood the needs of Depression-era audiences better than Walt Disney, whose Mickey Mouse cartoons delighted moviegoers everywhere. Disney also released the classic cartoon *Snow White and the Seven Dwarfs* (1937) in this period.

The WPA and the Arts FDR believed that the arts were not luxuries that people should give up in hard times. For this reason he earmarked WPA funds to support unemployed artists, musicians, historians, theater people, and writers. The Federal Writers' Project, established in 1935, assisted more than 6,000 writers, including Richard Wright, Saul Bellow, Margaret Walker,

and Ralph Ellison. Historians with the project surveyed the nation's local government records, wrote state guidebooks, and collected life stories from about 2,000 former slaves.

Other projects supported music and the visual arts. The Federal Music Project started community symphonies and organized free music lessons. It also sent music specialists to lumber camps and small towns to collect and preserve a fast-disappearing folk heritage.

The Federal Art Project, begun in 1935, put more than 10,000 artists to work. They painted some 2,000 murals, mainly in public buildings. They also produced about 100,000 other paintings, 17,000 sculptures, and many other works of art.

The Federal Theatre Project, directed by Vassar College professor Hallie Flanagan, was the most controversial. Flanagan used drama to create awareness of social problems. Her project launched the careers of many actors, playwrights, and directors who later became famous, including Burt Lancaster, Arthur Miller, John Houseman, and Orson Welles.

Accusing the Federal Theatre Project of being a propaganda machine for international communism, the House Un-American Activities Committee (HUAC) investigated the project in 1938 and 1939. In July 1939 Congress killed the project's appropriation.

Government support for the arts led to many lasting works, including this mural painted by Thomas Hart Benton in 1930 for the New School of Social Research in New York City. Audrey McMahon, New York Director of the WPA, said: "We did the best we could, and that best was very good." *Culture In what ways can art be considered a necessity, and not a luxury?*

Using the Internet

Write an Essay

Objective Use the Internet to write an essay on the Federal Writers' Project. Have students follow these instructions:

1. See the *America: Pathways to the Present* Web site at

http://www.Pathways.phschool.com

for the URL of "American Life Histories: Manuscripts from the Federal Writers' Project, 1936–1940."

2. Read the *Special Presentation* describing the background of the Federal Writers' Project and its role in collecting the life histories of thousands of Americans.

3. Use links to select and read several sample interviews from one or more states.

4. Write an essay on the lasting legacy of these life histories that answers the following question: Should the life histories recorded under the Federal Writers' Project be considered a national treasure?

RESOURCE OPTIONS

Media and Technology

RESOURCE PRO

Biography Jacob Lawrence, found on Resource Pro, profiles one of the finest artists in the WPA Federal Arts Project, long considered the foremost African American painter of his time.

 Listening to Literature E. B. White, from *Here Is New York*

Answer to . . .

Viewing History Sample answer: It provides a means of preserving history, as well as allowing individual expression.

BACKGROUND

Geography in History

The Great Depression had a catastrophic impact on the United States. It was equally damaging to economies of other nations, whose fortunes were becoming ever more tightly interconnected. Japan's burden of a rapidly growing population and a lack of territorial resources was exacerbated by the economic depression. In response, militarist Japanese leaders promoted aggressive expansion into areas rich in natural resources, such as the northern Chinese province of Manchuria. The stage was thus being set for World War II, President Roosevelt's greatest challenge.

Answers to SECTION 3 REVIEW

1. (a) national debt, see p. 672; (b) revenue, see p. 672; (c) coalition, see p. 673; (d) sit-down strike, see p. 673.

2. It provided federal protection for them, making them more attractive to workers.

3. Sample column: Cultural—arts supported; historical and literary materials collected; new period of intense creativity begun.

4. 1939—Supreme Court outlaws sit-down strike.

5. They advised resuming the suspended programs; they were proven right, as economic conditions slowly improved.

6. Essays will vary but should be supported with facts from the section.

Lasting New Deal Achievements

The New Deal did not completely vanish when the Depression ended. Its accomplishments continued in many forms. This legacy ranges from physical monuments that dot the American landscape to towering political and social achievements that still influence American life.

Public Works and Federal Agencies Many New Deal bridges, dams, tunnels, public buildings, and hospitals stand to this day. These durable public works are visible reminders of this extraordinary period of government intervention in the economy.

Some of the federal agencies from the New Deal era have also endured. The Tennessee Valley Authority remains a model of government planning. The Federal Deposit Insurance Corporation still guarantees bank deposits. The Securities and Exchange Commission continues to monitor the workings of the stock exchange. And in rural America, farmers still plant according to federal crop allotment strategies.†

Social Security Few people today seriously question the place of the Social Security system in American society. Social Security, however, has had many critics. You read about some of these critics in Section 2. Others attacked Social Security because, at first, payments were very low.

For a long time the system discriminated against women. It assumed, for example, that the male-headed household was typical. A mother could lose benefits for her children if a man, whether providing support for her or not, lived in her house. Women who went to work when their children started school rarely stayed in the work force long enough or earned high enough wages to receive the maximum benefits from the system.

A Legacy of Hope Of all of its achievements, perhaps the New Deal's greatest was to restore a sense of hope. People poured out their troubles to the President and First Lady. Eleanor and Franklin Roosevelt received thousands of letters daily in the late Depression era. Every letter contained a story of continued personal suffering. In their desperation people looked to their government for support. Indeed, government programs did mean the difference between survival and starvation for millions of Americans.

By the end of the 1930s, the event that would ultimately bring a lasting economic recovery to the United States was set in motion on the battlefields of Europe. Several years would pass before that recovery reached the United States. When it did arrive, it came in the form of another tremendous test of American character: world war.

---

† These strategies were put in place to conserve soil and reduce acreage after the Supreme Court struck down AAA crop-reduction plans.

SECTION 3 REVIEW

Comprehension

1. *Key Terms* Define: (a) national debt; (b) revenue; (c) coalition; (d) sit-down strike.

2. *Summarizing the Main Idea* How did the Wagner Act affect labor unions in the United States?

3. *Organizing Information* Create a four-column chart to show how the New Deal affected the *economic, political, social,* and *cultural* aspects of American life.

Critical Thinking

4. *Analyzing Time Lines* Review the time line at the start of the section. Which event do you think did the most to undercut the period of labor triumph?

5. *Testing Conclusions* FDR's advisers concluded that certain actions were needed to combat the recession of 1937. What action did they advise, and were they proved right or wrong? Explain.

Writing Activity

6. *Writing an Expository Essay* Write an essay that examines the legacy of the New Deal. In your essay, suggest which aspects of that legacy you think have been positive for the country and which have been negative.

RESOURCE OPTIONS

Teaching Resources

 Quiz Units 7–8 folder, p. 38

Chapter Tests Forms A and B Chapter Test folder

Student Performance Pack

 Guide to the Essentials Chapter 23, Section 3 (English and Spanish)

Standardized Test Preparation Handbook

Media and Technology

Guided Reading Audiotapes Chapter 23 Summary (English and Spanish)
Student Edition on Audiotape Chapter 23

 Test Bank CD-ROM; Interactive Student Tutorial CD-ROM Chapter Test

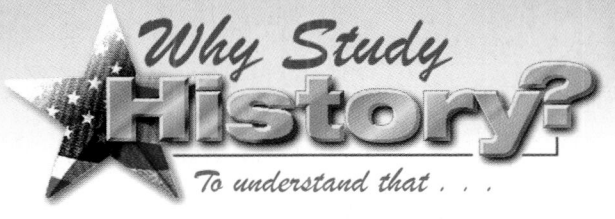

Why Study History?
To understand that . . .

Americans Depend on Social Security

Since its creation in 1935, the Social Security system has been an important safety net for millions of older Americans.

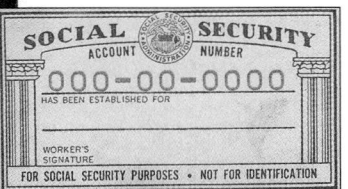

Sample Social Security card with individual account number

Few of us expect to work for the rest of our lives. Instead we plan to retire at a certain age, such as 65 or 70, and enjoy more free time—visiting relatives, traveling, learning new hobbies. Yet when jobs end, paychecks end too. Meanwhile, expenses for groceries, clothing, housing, gasoline, and health care remain. How do retired Americans pay their bills?

The Impact Today

The New Deal included a Social Security system to provide old-age pensions for retired workers. Social Security, one of the most popular programs run by the federal government, allows Americans to retire with a basic income. It also provides benefits for disabled workers and for the wives, husbands, and children of deceased workers. For many Americans, Social Security is their prime source of income.

Together, the federal government and working Americans finance the Social Security system. Unfortunately, as the retirement-age population of the United States has grown, so too has the cost of the program. Since 1970 the number of Social Security recipients has increased from about 26 million to more than 40 million. In the same period, the cost of the program has shot up from around $30 billion to more than $300 billion.

The population of working Americans is not growing quickly enough to fund continued increases in Social Security spending. At some point after the year 2000, in fact, the amount paid to retirees will exceed the amount collected to finance the program. Social Security will become an unsupportable burden unless something is done.

Many solutions to the problem have been proposed. They include raising the retirement age, cutting annual increases in Social Security benefits, raising the taxes that finance Social Security, and paying Social Security benefits only to people who earn less than a certain amount of money. There are also proposals to supplement or replace Social Security with a system of individual retirement accounts. While Americans disagree over specific solutions, they do agree that retired Americans should be able to live in dignity and comfort.

The Impact on You

Interview your parents and other adults to get their ideas on how to solve the Social Security problem. (You may ask their opinion of the ideas listed above.) Make a table showing possible solutions and the pros and cons of each. Then write a one-page report explaining which solution you support and why.

Many older Americans rely on Social Security

Class Discussion

Discuss with the class the problem of funding Social Security. For a more thorough examination of the issue, see the activity folder in the Resource Options below.

ACTIVITY
STUDENT PARTICIPATION

Making a Benefits Table

Ask students to read the text. Then divide the class into three groups. Have each group investigate one aspect of the Social Security system, including:

- **retirement benefits**
- **unemployment insurance**
- **Medicare**

Have the groups report their findings to the class, using a table for illustration.

Follow up Encourage students to find out about procedures for applying to receive different Social Security benefits.

Using the Internet

Students can learn more about Social Security by exploring links in the *America: Pathways to the Present* Web site at

http://www.Pathways.phschool.com

Assessment

See the Lesson Plans folder, pp. 24–27, for rubrics on assessing Class Participation Projects.

RESOURCE OPTIONS

Teaching Resources

 Why Study History? Activity

Americans Depend on Social Security, found in the Why Study History? folder, p. 24, provides an activity to help students better understand Social Security.

Media and Technology

 AmericanHeritage® CD-ROM

Time Tour Prosperity, Depression, and War: Depression and the New Deal

Prentice Hall United States History Video Collection™ Volume 18 *The Great Depression and the New Deal*

Chapter 23 Review

Key Terms

Students should refer to the definitions of key terms in the chapter to write sentences that show an understanding of the New Deal and its long-term effects.

Comprehension

1. To alleviate Americans' fears that the banks were unstable and would lose their savings.

2. By bolstering industrial prices; by instituting industry-wide codes to regulate industrial procedures and thus balance the unstable economy.

3. The successful reelection of FDR indicated that the American public approved of the New Deal.

4. Its programs fell short of covering many segments of society, including workers, women, and minorities.

5. Their main criticism was that New Deal policies were unconstitutional and limited individual freedom; they compared New Deal philosophy to that of the founders of the Soviet Union.

6. The Court had struck down some New Deal programs, such as the NRA and the AAA. He wanted to pack the court with justices who favored the New Deal.

7. Social Security taxes meant that workers had less money to spend and bought fewer goods; consumers also had less money because programs such as the WPA had been cut.

8. Because the New Deal legalized unions, relations between workers and employers were permanently changed, and unions became more powerful.

Chapter Summary

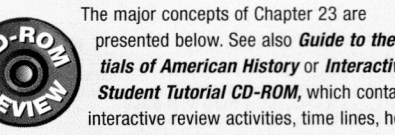

The major concepts of Chapter 23 are presented below. See also *Guide to the Essentials of American History* or *Interactive Student Tutorial CD-ROM*, which contains interactive review activities, time lines, helpful hints, and test practice for Chapter 23.

Reviewing the Main Ideas

In the 1930s Franklin Roosevelt introduced the New Deal, a set of programs aimed at ending the Great Depression. Some critics attacked the New Deal because they thought it went too far and others because they thought it did not go far enough. The New Deal did not end the Depression, but it did have a lasting effect on American life.

Section 1: Forging a New Deal

President Roosevelt sought to end the Depression through the programs of the New Deal.

Section 2: The New Deal's Critics

A variety of critics pointed out the shortcomings of the New Deal as well as its potential for restricting individual freedom.

Section 3: Last Days of the New Deal

The New Deal had a lasting effect on many aspects of American life.

Why Study History?

Since its creation in 1935, Social Security has been an important safety net for millions of Americans. A growing population of retirees, however, has placed a great strain on Social Security funding. The government is considering several solutions to the problem.

Key Terms

Use each of the terms below in a sentence that shows how it relates to the chapter.

1. New Deal
2. demagogue
3. sit-down strike
4. Social Security system
5. nationalization
6. Tennessee Valley Authority (TVA)
7. national debt
8. Second New Deal
9. hundred days
10. Wagner Act

Comprehension

1. Why did FDR begin the New Deal by closing the nation's banks?
2. How did the National Industrial Recovery Act aim to help businesses?
3. What did the 1936 election reveal about voters' attitudes toward the New Deal?
4. What were some of the limitations of the New Deal?
5. What was the main criticism of the New Deal by the American Liberty League?
6. Why did President Roosevelt attempt to "pack" the Supreme Court?
7. What factors led to the recession of 1937?
8. What permanent changes took place for labor unions as a result of the New Deal?

Using Graphic Organizers

On a separate sheet of paper, copy the tree map to organize the main ideas of the chapter. Then fill in the empty boxes with at least three important supporting details. Details for *Hundred Days* and *Second New Deal* might focus mainly on programs. Provide a variety of *Criticisms* and *Legacies*.

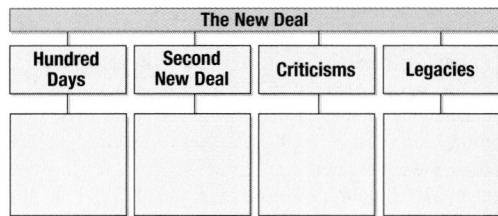

The New Deal			
Hundred Days	Second New Deal	Criticisms	Legacies

Using Graphic Organizers

- Hundred Days: bank holiday; Federal Deposit Insurance Corporation established; Federal Emergency Relief Adminstration set up; public works programs sponsored; National Industrial Recovery Act passed; organizations set up to help farmers.
- Second New Deal: Works Progress Administration set up; AAA strengthened; Wagner Act passed; Social Security system initiated.
- Criticisms: programs ignored women and African Americans; new taxes on wealthy and Social Security system unfair; programs did nothing to alleviate poverty or redistribute wealth.
- Legacies: unions more powerful; relations between workers and employers permanently changed; arts expanded; Social Security and public works still in place today; renewed hope for government.

THIS IS ONE RABBIT THAT NEVER FAILED ME!

SPENDING

OLD RELIABLE!

Analyzing Political Cartoons ▶

1. Examine the images in this New Deal era cartoon.
   (a) Who is the magician?
   (b) What is the rabbit that he is pulling out of the hat?
2. What does the caption "Old Reliable" mean?
3. Summarize the cartoon's message in a single sentence.

Critical Thinking

1. **Applying the Chapter Skill** Suppose you could use these three sources for a report on the 1936 election: (a) a speech by Alfred M. Landon, (b) a political encyclopedia, (c) Franklin Roosevelt's diary for 1936. Which source would you turn to for verifiable facts about the 1936 election? Why? Which sources would you turn to for opinions? Why?
2. **Identifying Central Issues** Do you think that the New Deal was a success or a failure? Explain, citing information from the chapter.
3. **Demonstrating Reasoned Judgment** Do you agree with the way Eleanor Roosevelt carried out the role of First Lady, or do you think she should have acted differently? Explain.

INTERNET ACTIVITY

For your portfolio:
WRITE AN ARTICLE

Access Prentice Hall's *America: Pathways to the Present* site at **www.Pathways.phschool.com** for the specific URL to complete the activity. Additional resources and related Web sites are also available.

Read about the New Deal support of the arts and view a sampling of the artwork. Write an article about the art programs of the New Deal in general and a single medium or theme in the arts during this period in detail. What were the goals of the arts at this time? Were they achieved?

ANALYZING DOCUMENTS ◀▶ INTERPRETING DATA

Turn to the "Tennessee Valley Authority" map on page 663.

1. Which section of the country was affected most by the TVA?
   (a) Northeast (b) Midwest
   (c) Southwest (d) Southeast
2. Which Tennessee city had four dams and two power plants within 25 miles of it? (a) Kingsport
   (b) Nashville (c) Oak Ridge
   (d) Chattanooga
3. *Writing* By the late 1930s the TVA was well established. Write an interview that might have taken place between a reporter and a farmer, homeowner, banker, or some other person living in the region affected by the TVA. Introduce the interview by reviewing the purpose of the TVA project.

Connecting to Today

Essay Writing Some politicians still favor large government programs as a way to eliminate social and economic problems. Choose a present-day problem. Write an essay either supporting or opposing the use of a New Deal kind of approach to solving it.

INTERNET ACTIVITY

Articles will vary. Students' descriptions of New Deal art programs should be supported with facts from the chapter. Themes or media addressed should be treated consistently throughout the article.

Analyzing Political Cartoons
1. (a) FDR. (b) New Deal spending.
2. That FDR can be relied on to think he has solved Depression-era problems.
3. FDR's answer to the ills of the Depression is always government spending.

Critical Thinking
1. For reliable facts about the election you would choose the encyclopedia as a source as it presents facts that have been checked and confirmed by many sources. For opinions, you would choose the Landon and Roosevelt sources, as they are first-person accounts and reflect the participants' personal beliefs and feelings, unconfirmed by other sources.
2. Answers will vary but should be supported with specific facts from the chapter.
3. Answers will vary but should show an understanding that Eleanor Roosevelt performed many active roles in promoting government programs and alleviating suffering.

Interpreting Data
1. d
2. c
3. Answers will vary but should show an understanding of the TVA project.

Connecting to Today
Essays will vary but should be supported with specific examples and address themes and topics introduced in the chapter.

My Brush with History

Teacher's Notes (left column)

My Brush with History

Focus Have students find the meaning of each of these words in a dictionary before they begin to read: *revered, buoyant, bunting, luster, jaunty*. Ask them to think about the selection's two themes as they read: the historic opening game of the 1932 World Series and the emergence of FDR as the front runner on the presidential "playing field."

Instruct Ask students to describe what they already know about the social, political, and economic climate of the country in 1932. Write key ideas on the chalkboard. Then ask them to explain the significance to the writer of the "bright autumn afternoon" of October 1, 1932. Ask a volunteer to read aloud the last two paragraphs of the selection. Discuss the significance to the writer of seeing then-governor Roosevelt.

Ask students to consider today's baseball heroes and their feats (for example, Mark McGwire and Sammy Sosa's 1998 shattering of Roger Maris's single-season home-run record). How might they respond to seeing a famous baseball or other sports star today?

Analyzing the Document

Use this additional question to generate class discussion:
CRITICAL THINKING: PREDICTING CONSEQUENCES Based on the passage, which candidate do you think the people of Chicago supported in the election of 1932? (*Franklin D. Roosevelt. Fleming remarks that Hoover was booed in Chicago. Americans blamed Hoover and the Republicans for the Depression.*)

Right page (student excerpt)

My Brush with History

BY TOM FLEMING

INTRODUCTION Both the boom times of the 1920s and the hard times of the 1930s produced numerous heroes and other celebrities. Thanks to advances such as radio, these national heroes were familiar to Americans all across the country. Seeing one in person was an experience that average Americans long remembered.

In the passage below, Tom Fleming recalls the "bright autumn afternoon" of October 1, 1932. On that day Fleming, then a young boy, saw three of the best-known Americans of the period: the President, the man who would become the next President, and the greatest baseball player of his era.

Like every American boy in the twenties and thirties, I revered Babe Ruth as the greatest name in baseball. What made him come alive for me was a genuine American League baseball that my father brought home after one of his trips to New York. Ruth had fouled it off, and Dad had jumped up and caught it one-handed. "Just for you," he said. That was at Yankee Stadium, the "House that Ruth built."

Of course, I wanted to see Babe Ruth play too, but this wasn't easy. Dad and I were Cub fans. Ruth was an American Leaguer with the Yankees, so when they came to Chicago, they played the White Sox in Comiskey Park on the South Side.

In the fall of 1932 it became clear that Babe would be coming to Wrigley Field (the Cubs and Yankees had reached the World Series). It was beyond expectation that I would actually get to see those games; I hoped that perhaps I could sneak into the coach's office in the high school locker room and catch a few plays on his radio before the bell rang for afternoon classes.

One evening in September Dad came home in an unusually buoyant mood. I was doing a jigsaw puzzle at the family game table in the den. I watched him take off his suit coat and drape it deliberately over the back of his desk chair. As he unbuttoned his vest, he leaned forward and took a small envelope from his inside coat pocket.

Inside the envelope was a pair of tickets to the October 1 home opener of the World Series—the Cubs and the Yankees at Wrigley Field. "Now you can see Babe Ruth," he said.

Our beloved Wrigley Field had been transformed for the Series, with red, white, and blue bunting draped everywhere. Temporary stands had been set up in the outfield to accommodate the huge crowd. Our seats were only six rows back from the playing field on the left-field side, between the end of the Cubs' dugout and third base.

"There's your man," Dad said, pointing to left field as we settled in. Sure enough, there he was warming up with his teammates—the Bambino, the Sultan of Swat, the Colossus of

TEST PREPARATION

Have students use the excerpt on these pages to answer the following question.

From what you have read, which statement best describes Tom Fleming's boyhood?

A He was a typical American boy of the 1930s.

B He disliked baseball.

C He was fascinated by politics.

D His family was too affected by the Depression to care about politics.

Clout—Babe Ruth, all six feet two inches and 215 pounds of him.

When the players left the field, the announcer introduced President Hoover, who was in the stands for the big game. The applause was scattered, and I was shocked to hear boos. (As a Boy Scout I thought you didn't do such a thing to a President.) When Governor Franklin D. Roosevelt was introduced, there was much more applause and fewer boos. Both men were on the campaign trail for the presidential election coming up that November. If I had been politically conscious, I would have known right then that Mr. Hoover was in trouble, for it seemed most fans felt Hoover wasn't having nearly as good a year as Ruth.

Charlie Root took the mound for the Cubs. He was in trouble from the first pitch. With the first two Yankees on base on a walk and a throwing error by the shortstop Billy Jurges, Ruth lumbered up to the plate. He promptly did what he was famous for—lofted one of his patented homers out to the center field seats.

The Cubs lifted our hearts with some good hitting, especially from Kiki Cuyler, but they never seemed to get real control of the game. The score was 4 to 4 when Ruth stepped into the box at the top of the fifth inning.

How lucky we were to be on the third-base side. As a left-handed batter, Ruth faced us, and we could see his every move and gesture. Root was very careful. After each strike the Babe raised his right arm, showing one finger for a strike, then two, to keep the stands posted on the duel between him and the pitcher. The crowd reacted wildly. When the count stood at 2 and 2, Ruth stepped back a bit and then pointed grandly to the outfield, making a big arc with his right hand.

Dad poked me in the ribs.

"Look at him point, son! Look at him point! He's calling a home run!"

The very air seemed to vibrate. I held my breath, digging my fingernails into my palms.

Ruth stepped back into the batter's box, ready for Root's next pitch. It came in knee-high, and the Babe connected solidly with his great swing. The crowd let out a volcanic, spontaneous gasp of awe. Everybody knew it was gone, gone, gone as it soared high and out over the center-field score board for one of the longest homers ever hit out of Wrigley Field.

The Babe started his trip around the bases. When he rounded second and came toward us, we saw a triumphant smile on his face. Past third, he leaned over and pointed into the Cub dugout. I can only guess what he said to the Cub bench jockeys, although I probably wouldn't have known all the words then.

Root and Hartnett, the Cub battery, later denied that Ruth had called his shot or pointed. I guess that as great competitors they didn't want to give Ruth any more luster than he already had. Dad and I knew that Babe Ruth had pointed though. The Yankees went on to win, 7 to 5, and four of their runs were provided by Babe Ruth. That was the Sultan of Swat at his greatest.

As we were leaving the ballpark, a loud siren wailed just below us, and we rushed over to the ramp railing to see what was going on. Below was the big white touring car of the city greeter, and beside him on the back seat was Governor Roosevelt—gray felt hat and cigarette holder at the jaunty angle cartoonists loved to draw. For a brief moment my eyes locked with his as he looked up at the people lining the railing.

At that moment I realized I was seeing a new star about to enter a more serious arena. That day was a capsule of life. I passed from my boyhood interests to those of the greater game of politics on that bright autumn afternoon of October 1, 1932.

Source: *American Heritage* magazine, November 1990.

ADDITIONAL READING

To learn more about the topics discussed in this selection, you might want to read the following books:

- *Babe Ruth: His Life and Legend,* by Kal Wagenheim (Maplewood, N.J.: Waterfront Press, 1990)
- *Baseball: An Illustrated History,* narrative by Geoffrey C. Ward, based on a filmscript by Geoffrey C. Ward and Ken Burns (New York: Alfred A. Knopf, 1994)
- *FDR: The New York Years, 1928–1933,* by Kenneth S. Davis (New York: Random House, 1985)
- *The Life of Herbert Hoover,* by George H. Nash (New York: W.W. Norton, 1983)

TEST PREPARATION

Have students use the excerpt on these pages to answer the following question.

What is the main idea of this excerpt?

A Roosevelt was a popular governor.

B Fleming's father applauded President Hoover while other spectators booed.

C Many people lost their jobs during the Depression.

(D) Seeing Roosevelt made Fleming realize that he was part of the larger world of politics.

Hot and Cold War

1939–1960

Introducing the Unit

Using Historical Evidence

During World War II, public opinion was considered as important as soldiers' morale for winning the war because civilians sustained the war effort with their labor and income. The poster on the right is designed to sell war bonds. Ask students what other messages the poster conveys. What emotions are called up by the scene? How are the individual soldiers depicted?

Themes in American History

Direct students' attention to the Unit Themes. Point out that each chapter in this unit has its own theme. To teach this unit thematically, you may wish to use the Prosperity, Depression, and War folder in **American History Block Scheduling Support.**

Using the Time Line

To provide students with practice in using a time line to connect key events in the United States with key events in the world, ask questions such as these: (1) How did the Supreme Court advance the cause of civil rights in 1956? *(It outlawed segregation on buses.)* (2) Which President approved the internment of Japanese Americans? *(F.D. Roosevelt)* (3) What event took place in Cuba in the 1950s? *(Castro overthrew Cuban dictatorship.)*

---

unit EIGHT

Hot and Cold War

1939 – 1960

Many Americans were determined to stay out of another European conflict, but Japan's attack on Pearl Harbor ended the debate on American entry into World War II. After the war, the nation barely had time to enjoy its hard-won peace before a "cold war" developed between the United States and the Soviet Union. The state of international tension and the threat of nuclear destruction cast a long shadow across the postwar era.

Chapter 24	World War II *1939–1945*
Chapter 25	World War II at Home *1941–1945*
Chapter 26	The Cold War *1945–1960*
Chapter 27	The Postwar Years at Home *1945–1960*

UNIT THEMES

Foreign Relations German, Italian, and Japanese aggression in the 1930s led to global warfare.

Culture Cold war tensions raised popular fears of Communist infiltration into American society and government.

Diversity Following World War II, African Americans began to push harder for civil rights.

EVENTS IN THE UNITED STATES	**1941** Japan attacks Pearl Harbor	**1942** Internment of Japanese Americans	**1944** D-Day invasion	**1947** Truman Doctrine	**1948** Turning Point: The Marshall Plan (p. 749)

Presidents	F. D. Roosevelt	

1935	**1940**	**1945**

EVENTS IN THE WORLD	**1939** Germany invades Poland	**1941** Germany invades USSR	**1945** Germany and Japan surrender	**1949** Communists take over China

---

RESOURCE OPTIONS

Teaching Resources

 Units 7–8 folder Contains instructional materials organized by chapter.

VIEWING HISTORY
The government used powerful images—such as the illustration on this "Buy War Bonds" poster—to encourage Americans on the home front to make their own contributions to the war effort. *Culture* **How did World War II affect American culture and America's role in world affairs?**

Army Medal of Honor

Timeline

1950 Korean War begins

1954 Brown v. Board of Education

1955 Montgomery bus boycott begins

1956
• Interstate Highway Act
• Supreme Court outlaws segregation on buses

Truman | Eisenhower

1950 | **1955** | **1960**

1954 Vietnamese win independence

1957 USSR launches Sputnik

1959 Castro overthrows Cuban dictatorship

1960 USSR shoots down U.S. spy plane

Listed below are the technology resources that *America: Pathways to the Present* offers:

RESOURCE PRO

America: Pathways to the Present Teaching Resources on CD-ROM offers lesson planning flexibility, test generation capability, and additional enrichment support.

Using the Internet
Prentice Hall's *America: Pathways to the Present* companion Web site offers student-appropriate Internet activities and links as well as resources for teachers. Visit us at
http://www.Pathways.phschool.com

AmericanHeritage®
History of the United States CD-ROM This interactive, multimedia exploration of the American experience provides a journey through historical, political, and social aspects of American history. Includes Time Tours, Presidents, and History Makers.

Visions of America
This award-winning integrated multimedia package offers Scenes of an Era, Turning Point stories, and historians' viewpoints on core content.

Our Times Multimedia Encyclopedia of the 20th Century CD-ROM

INTERACTIVE STUDENT TUTORIAL CD-ROM

GUIDED READING AUDIOTAPES

STUDENT EDITION ON AUDIOTAPE

PRENTICE HALL LISTENING TO MUSIC THE AMERICAN EXPERIENCE AUDIO CD

▶ RESOURCE OPTIONS

Media and Technology

 Color Transparencies Specific transparencies are referenced at points of use. See American Photo, B-8; Time Lines, E-7 and E-8; Cause and Effect, F-10; The Way It Works, H-19 and H-20; Links Across Time, J-8; and Political Cartoons, K-8.

Visions of America "Scenes of an Era: Hot and Cold War" located on videodisc side 3 and on videotape 4. Lesson plans for "Scenes of an Era" can be found in the Visions of America Guidebook.

Side 3, Chapter 29

Answer to . . .

Viewing History Cold war tensions permeated U.S. culture. The U. S. became leader of the "free world."

CHAPTER 24

World War II, 1939–1945

Managing Time and Instruction

INSTRUCTION SUPPORT

These materials for instruction are provided for **each section** in the **Teaching Resources**. See **Units 7–8 folder** for Enrichment Support:

- Reproducible Lesson Plans in Lesson Plans folder • Learning Styles Lesson Plans in Learning Styles Lesson Plans folder • Big Idea Graphic Organizers in Big Idea Graphic Organizer folder
- Guided Reading and Review • Quizzes • Test Preparation Practice booklet

DAILY LESSON	ENRICHMENT SUPPORT
1 **Prelude to Global War** *(pp. 685–691)*	• Great Debates, Should the United States Get Involved in World Affairs? Decision-Making Activities folder, pp. 40–41 • Visual Learning Activity, Books Are Weapons, Learning with Documents folder, p. 66 • Key Documents, Franklin D. Roosevelt, Message Asking for War Against Japan, Learning with Documents folder, p. 97
2 **The Road to Victory in Europe** *(pp. 692–699)*	• Comparing Primary Sources, On the Integration of the Military, Units 7–8 folder, pp. 53–54 • Biography, Navajo Code Talkers, Units 7–8 folder, p. 52 • Primary Source Activity, Experiences of an African American Soldier, found on **Resource Pro** • Biography, Jacqueline Cochran, found on **Resource Pro** • Critical Thinking Activity, Predicting Consequences: After the Army—What?, found on **Resource Pro** • Visual Learning Activity, The North African Front, found on **Resource Pro** • Literature Activity, Dispatches from the Battle Front, found on **Resource Pro**
3 **The War in the Pacific** *(pp. 700–705)*	• Primary Source Activity, Guadalcanal, Learning with Documents folder, p. 30 • Literature Activity, *Hiroshima,* Units 7–8 folder, p. 55 • Lasting Impact Activity, The Lasting Impact of the Atomic Bomb, History's Lasting Impact folder, pp. 16–17
4 **The Holocaust** *(pp. 707–710)*	• Skills for Life Activity, Units 7–8 folder, p. 56 • Genocide Has Happened Again, Why Study History? folder, p. 25

Running Out of Time?

- Use Tape 4, "Hot and Cold War, 1939–1960," from **Visions of America** videotapes series.
- Use Chapter 24 Summary from **Guide to the Essentials of American History (English and Spanish).**

Companion Web Site

The companion Web site offers online links for all chapter review activities. It also provides key content links and structured support for this chapter for both teachers and students.

http://www.Pathways.phschool.com

Media and Technology

For the Student

Interactive Student Tutorial CD-ROM Chapter 24
Student Edition on Audiotape Chapter 24
American Heritage® CD-ROM
Guided Reading Audiotapes (English and Spanish) Chapter 24

For the Teacher

Resource Pro CD-ROM Chapter 24
Test Bank CD-ROM Chapter 24
Listening to Literature Audiotapes *Timeless Voices, Timeless Themes* "Losses"; "The Death of the Ball Turret Gunner" by Randall Jarrell

Assessment Options

Chapter Test Forms A&B Test Bank CD-ROM booklet
Test Bank CD-ROM Chapter 24
Standardized Test Preparation Handbook

Block Scheduling

Pacing Suggestions

For 90-minute Blocks

- Teach sections 1 and 2 using Transparencies E-7 and H-19 and the Recent Scholarship note on p. 688 for class discussions.
- Teach sections 3 and 4 using the Big Idea Graphic Organizers from Teaching Resources.

Additional Resources

- Prentice Hall's **American History Block Scheduling Support File** covers over 40 major topics in American history.
- **Prentice Hall United States History Video Collection**™ contains 20 videotapes covering American history from beginnings to present.
- **Visions of America Videotapes and Videodiscs**

Connections to American Literature

from Prentice Hall

America: Pathways to the Present
Night by Elie Wiesel, p. 1086

Prentice Hall Literature *Timeless Voices, Timeless Themes* from *Hiroshima* by John Hersey, p. 1036

Additional Resources

For the Student

John Hersey. *Into the Valley: A Skirmish of the Marines.* Knopf, 1942.
Kyoko Selden and Mark Selden, eds. *The Atomic Bomb: Voices from Hiroshima and Nagasaki.* Sharpe, 1989.

For the Teacher

George Roeder. *The Censored War: American Visual Experience During World War II.* Yale University Press, 1993.

Prentice Hall brings into the classroom the vast archives and scholarship of the nation's premier American history magazine. See "From the Archives of American Heritage®" and "About the Presidents" teaching notes in this chapter.

History Alive!

Teacher's Curriculum Institute, in partnership with Prentice Hall, provides unique materials that engage students with diverse learning styles. See History Alive!® unit on The United States in World War II.

Student Performance Pack

Ensures success in the three critical areas of Reading, Test Taking, and English Language Development with the following materials:
- Guide to the Essentials of American History in English and Spanish
- Guided Reading Audiotapes in English and Spanish
- Interactive Student Tutorial CD-ROM
- Test Preparation Handbook
- Test Preparation Practice booklet

Introducing the Chapter

"The peace, freedom, and security of 90 percent of the population of the world is being jeopardized by the remaining 10 percent . . ." said President Roosevelt about the war raging in Europe. Many Americans, opposed to intervention, were convinced only after the attack on Pearl Harbor. With the American entry into World War II, there was no longer any question about the role of the United States in world affairs.

Themes in American History

The theme for this chapter, Foreign Relations, is listed at the beginning of this unit. An alternate theme for the chapter is Geography. To teach this unit thematically, you may wish to use the Prosperity, Depression, and War folder in American History Block Scheduling Support.

Why Study History?

Have students explore suggested ways of connecting the past to the present on page 711.

Answer to . . .

Viewing History Students should use this question as an aid in reading the chapter. The Japanese bombed the U.S. naval facilities at Pearl Harbor, Hawaii.

CHAPTER
24 World War II
1939-1945

CHAPTER FOCUS

This chapter describes World War II, in which the United States and the other Allies battled aggression in Europe, northern Africa, and Asia. A Japanese attack on Pearl Harbor brought an end to the hope that the United States could remain neutral. Once involved, America fully committed its material and human resources to the global conflict.

The *Why Study History?* page at the end of this chapter explores the connection between the Holocaust and the continued threat of genocide today.

▲
VIEWING HISTORY
American troops plunge into action on the French shore of Normandy in 1944.
Foreign Relations **What finally caused the United States to enter into World War II?**

▶ RESOURCE OPTIONS

Teaching Resources

 Big Idea Graphic Organizer folder
Graphic summary of the main idea of the chapter.

Learning Styles Lesson Plans folder
Alternate lesson plans for diverse learning styles for each chapter.

Media and Technology

 AmericanHeritage® CD-ROM
Time Tour Prosperity, Depression, and War: World War II

 Prentice Hall United States History Video Collection™ Volume 19
World War II

1933	1935	1938	1939	1941
Adolf Hitler becomes dictator of Germany	Italy invades Ethiopia	Germany annexes Austria and the Sudetenland	Germany invades Poland	Japan attacks Pearl Harbor

1933 **1935** **1937** **1939** **1941**

SECTION 1

Prelude to Global War

Objectives
You may wish to call students' attention to the objectives in the Section Preview. The objectives are reflected in the main headings of the section.

1 Prelude to Global War

SECTION PREVIEW

Objectives

1. Explain how Fascist and Nazi aggression led to war in Europe.
2. List the reasons that made Japan eager to build an empire.
3. Describe the American response to the war in Europe and explain how the Japanese attack on Pearl Harbor pulled the United States into the war.
4. *Key Terms* Define: totalitarian; fascism; Axis Powers; appeasement; *blitzkrieg;* Allies; Lend-Lease Act.

Main Idea
Depressed economic conditions and a desire to build powerful nations led to the rise of dictators in Germany and Italy and eventually to a second global conflict.

Reading Strategy
Organizing Information Create a concept map by drawing five large circles on a piece of paper and labeling each circle with a heading from the section. Add supporting information in smaller circles and draw lines connecting them to the large circles.

Throughout the 1930s the Depression kept a tight grip on the American economy. While Americans faced personal hardship and political upheaval at home, conditions in other countries were even worse. The United States watched warily as dictators in Europe and Asia sought to solve their nations' problems by extending their power at the expense of other nations.

Fascism and Nazism

Throughout the 1920s and 1930s brutal dictators came to power in Europe. In Germany, Italy, and the Soviet Union **totalitarian** governments controlled every aspect of life. These governments used terror to suppress individual rights and to silence all forms of opposition.

Germany's Adolf Hitler and Italy's Benito Mussolini based their governments on a philosophy called **fascism.** Fascism places the importance of the nation above the value of the individual. Hitler and Mussolini focused on the need to rebuild Germany and Italy.

Unlike communism, which calls for all society to jointly own the nation's means of production, fascism allows private business. According to Communist theory, conflicts between workers and owners will not exist in a Communist society, because the workers are the owners. In a Fascist system such conflicts are resolved by the government's power. Under both systems, however, the result is the same. Individual rights and freedoms are lost as everyone works for the benefit of society and the nation.

Mussolini Controls Italy Benito Mussolini had fought and been wounded in World War I. Along with many other Italians, Mussolini felt his country had been shortchanged in the peace settlement after the war. In 1919 he joined with other dissatisfied war veterans to organize the revolutionary Fascist party.

Calling himself *Il Duce* ("the leader"), Mussolini organized Fascist groups throughout Italy. He relied on gangs of Fascist thugs,

The official Nazi emblem, the swastika, became a symbol of terror in World War II.

Bellringer
Ask students to choose a place in the world where there is currently armed conflict, and to describe the involvement of the United States in that area, if any. Ask them to consider under what conditions the United States should intervene in a conflict between other nations.

Reading Strategy
Organizing Information Refer to the Reading Strategy in the Section Preview. You may wish to model the concept map on the chalkboard.

LESSON PLAN
Connecting to the Main Idea

1. Focus Fascist dictators seized control in several nations scarred by World War I, while military leaders in Japan pursued a policy of expansion. Ask how the United States responded to the growing worldwide conflict and what finally propelled the United States into the war.

2. Instruct Point out that Hitler and Mussolini promised to restore economic prosperity to the countries they led. Ask students to describe how they used expansion as a way to bolster national pride. How did their aggression lead to war? Have students describe the sequence of German conquests in Europe.

Ask students to explain why Japan wanted to build an empire in Asia.

Discuss why the United States was reluctant to enter the war. What were the events that overcame this reluctance?

3. Close Americans tried to remain neutral when the fascist powers began a second world war; however, they did give increasing amounts of aid to the Allies.

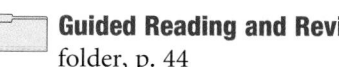

RESOURCE OPTIONS

Teaching Resources

Reproducible Lesson Plan Lesson Plans folder, p. 131

Learning Styles Lesson Plan Learning Styles Lesson Plans folder, p. 50

Big Idea Graphic Organizer Big Idea Graphic Organizer folder, p. 103

Guided Reading and Review Units 7–8 folder, p. 44

Media and Technology

 AmericanHeritage® CD-ROM
Time Tour Prosperity, Depression, and War: World War II

called Blackshirts because of the way they dressed, to terrorize and bring under control those who opposed him. By 1922 Mussolini had become such a powerful figure that when he threatened to march on Rome, the king panicked and appointed him prime minister.

Mussolini and the Fascists swiftly attempted to deal with the political and economic problems that had plagued Italy since World War I. Claiming that efficiency and order were necessary to restore the nation's greatness, they suspended elections, outlawed all other political parties, and soon established a dictatorship.

"The Country Is Nothing Without Conquest," proclaimed a Fascist slogan. In October 1935 Mussolini put those words into practice by invading Ethiopia. The Ethiopians resisted fiercely, but by March 1936 the East African nation was in Italian hands.

Hitler Rules Germany While Mussolini was gaining control in Italy, a discontented Austrian painter was rising to power in Germany. Like Mussolini, Hitler had been wounded while serving in World War I. He, too, was enraged by the outcome of the war and by the terms of the peace settlement.

In 1919 Hitler joined a small political party which soon took the name National Socialist German Workers' party, or Nazi party. His powerful public-speaking abilities quickly made him a leader. In November 1923, with some 3,000 followers, Hitler tried to overthrow the German government. Authorities easily crushed the uprising. Although Hitler was sentenced to five years in prison, he was confined for only nine months.

Adolf Hitler spoke with a charismatic passion that electrified audiences.

Most of Hitler's time in prison was devoted to writing the first volume of an autobiography titled *Mein Kampf* ("My Struggle"). In it Hitler outlined the Nazi philosophy, his views of Germany's problems, and his plans for the nation. According to *Mein Kampf,* Germany had been weakened by certain groups who lived within its borders. He was highly critical of the nation's Jewish population, which he blamed for Germany's defeat in World War I.

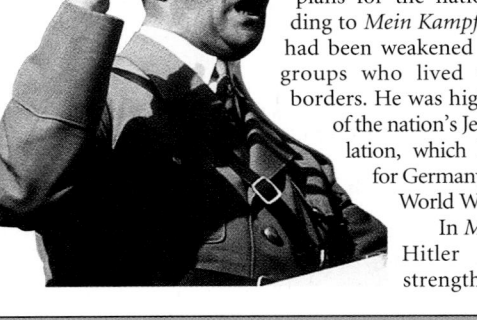

In *Mein Kampf,* Hitler proposed strengthening the nation's military and expanding its borders to include Germans living in other nations. He also called for purifying the so-called Aryan "race" (blond, blue-eyed Germans) by removing from Germany those groups he considered undesirable. In time, removal came to mean the mass murder of millions of Jews and other peoples.

Saddled with huge debts because of World War I, Germany suffered high unemployment and massive inflation during the 1920s. In the early 1930s, the effects of the Great Depression further ravaged the German people. Hitler and the Nazis promised to stabilize the country, rebuild the economy, and restore the empire that had been lost.

Because of such promises, Hitler gradually won a large following. By January 1933 the Nazi party was the largest group in the *Reichstag* (the German parliament) and Hitler became head of the German state. He soon silenced his opposition, suspended civil liberties, and convinced the *Reichstag* to give him dictatorial powers. Hitler then took for himself the title *Der Führer,* or "the leader."

Europe Goes to War

Like Mussolini, Hitler saw expansion as a way to bolster national pride. He also longed to return Germany to a dominant position in the world. On March 9, 1936, German troops moved into the Rhineland, a region in western Germany along the borders of France and Belgium. The Treaty of Versailles, signed after World War I, had expressly excluded German military forces from the region. The invasion of the Rhineland was an enormous gamble for Hitler because it clearly violated the Versailles Treaty. In addition, the German army was not yet ready to fight. Had Britain or France threatened to attack, Hitler later admitted, he would have withdrawn his forces. However, neither nation resisted him.

Also in 1936, Hitler signed an alliance with the Italian dictator, Mussolini. This created what Mussolini called an "axis" between Rome and Berlin, the capitals of the two nations. Germany and Italy, joined later by Japan, became known as the **Axis Powers.**

The German Empire Grows Encouraged by his success in the Rhineland, in March 1938 Hitler sent German troops into the neighboring nation of Austria and annexed it. When Britain and France protested, he was defiant. German-Austrian affairs were the concern of only the German people, he said.

RESOURCE OPTIONS

Media and Technology

Prentice Hall United States History Video Collection™ Volume 19 *WWII*

German Aggression, 1939–1941

Legend:
- Axis Powers
- Areas under Axis control, 1941
- Areas under Allied control, 1941
- Neutral nations
- German troop movements
- Farthest German advance
- Maginot Line

3. Aug. 1940–April 1941 Germany faces its first loss of the war in the Battle of Britain.

1. Sept. 1939 Hitler invades Poland.

2. June 1940 France surrenders to Germany.

MAP skills   Millions of people, like this Czechoslovakian woman shown reluctantly saluting the Nazis in 1938, saw their homelands conquered by the Axis Powers. *Location How does this map illustrate the dire situation of the Allies in 1941?*

Several months later, Hitler demanded the Sudetenland, a region of western Czechoslovakia with a heavily German population. In an effort to avoid war, representatives from England, France, Germany, and Italy met in Munich, Germany, in September 1938. Britain and France followed a policy of **appeasement,** or giving in to someone's demands in order to keep the peace. Neither country was prepared for war, and the peoples of both countries had not forgotten the awful costs of World War I. At the Munich Conference, therefore, Britain and France agreed to let Hitler have the Sudetenland, hoping that his appetite for territory would be satisfied. "Britain and France had to choose between war and dishonor," said Winston Churchill, a member of Parliament, of this action. "They chose dishonor. They will have war."

Churchill's prophecy came true. In March 1939, only six months after occupying the Sudetenland, Hitler annexed the rest of Czechoslovakia. British and French leaders warned him that any further German expansion risked war. On March 31, 1939, they formally pledged their support to Poland, agreeing to come to its aid if invaded by Germany. By now, however, Hitler was unconcerned about such threats. After signing a treaty with the Soviet Union so that he would face no threat from the east, Hitler invaded Poland on September 1, 1939. Two days later Britain and France declared war on Germany.

Blitzkrieg* and *Sitzkrieg In invading Poland, the German military unveiled a tactic called ***blitzkrieg,*** or "lightning war." Tanks, artillery, and soldiers, moving by truck instead of on foot, rapidly struck deep into enemy territory before the foe had time to react. Using this tactic, German troops overran Poland in less than a month. In mid-September, under the terms of his agreement with Hitler, Stalin attacked and seized eastern Poland for the Soviet Union.

After Poland fell, the war entered a quiet period. The Germans labeled the lull the *sitzkrieg,* or "sit-down war." For the next several months German troops sat and watched French forces on the Maginot Line, a massive

Main Idea CONNECTIONS

Describe Germany's strategy for overwhelming its enemies.

TEST PREPARATION

Have students read the first two paragraphs under "The German Empire Grows" and then answer the question below.

You can tell from Churchill's statement that—

(A) he thinks that France and Britain's policy is dishonorable and will lead to more trouble.

B he intends to wage war on France and Britain.

C he thinks France and Britain made the right choice.

D he blames France and Britain more than he blames Germany.

Answer to . . .

Map Skills The Axis powers have control over most of Europe and North Africa. Germany has made great inroads into Russian territory.

Main Idea Connections Germany's tactic of "lightning war" was to strike deeply and quickly before the enemy could react.

Answer to . . .

Viewing History The courage of the British forces and the British people's will to resist helped them withstand the massive German attacks.

---

system of defenses that France had built along its border with Germany. The American press called this "the phony war."

On April 9, 1940, the phony war came to an end as Hitler launched an attack on Denmark and Norway. Then, on May 10, German troops moved around the Maginot Line and launched a *blitzkrieg* on Belgium, the Netherlands, and France. All three countries were quickly overwhelmed.

In the face of this savage German attack, British forces in France retreated to the coastal city of Dunkirk. There, over a nine-day period in late May and early June, one of the greatest rescues in the history of warfare took place. While other troops fought to slow the advancing Germans, some 900 vessels were hastily assembled. The makeshift fleet consisted mainly of tugboats, yachts, and other small private craft. Braving merciless attacks by the

London's St. Paul's Cathedral (above) survived while surrounding buildings were reduced to rubble during the bombing. The cathedral became a powerful symbol of Britain's spirit of defiance. *Culture How did this spirit help defeat the* **Luftwaffe***?*

Luftwaffe (the German air force), they carried nearly 340,000 soldiers across the English Channel to Great Britain.

On June 14, German troops entered the city of Paris and a few days later France surrendered. In less than three months Hitler had conquered most of Western Europe. Of the **Allies,** the name given those countries who fought the Axis, Great Britain now stood alone. (The United States and Soviet Union would eventually join the Allies.)

The Battle of Britain As France was falling, Hitler massed troops on the French coast. His next target was Great Britain, just 20 miles away across the English Channel. Winston Churchill, now Britain's prime minister, pledged that the British would defend their island at all costs:

> **❝**We shall fight on the beaches, we shall fight on the landing grounds, we shall fight in the fields and in the streets, we shall fight in the hills; we shall never surrender.**❞**
>
> —*Winston Churchill*

Hitler turned to the *Luftwaffe* to destroy Britain's ability and will to resist. In what became known as the Battle of Britain, he launched the greatest air assault the world had yet seen. As many as 1,000 planes a day rained bombs on Britain. Although its Royal Air Force (RAF) was greatly outnumbered, RAF pilots sometimes flew six and seven missions a day, inflicting heavy losses on the attackers. "Never in the field of human conflict was so much owed by so many to so few," said Churchill, praising the courageous resistance of the RAF.

The British people were equally brave. In December 1940, German bombing of London started some 1,500 fires, setting the center of the city ablaze. Despite the massive losses, the British people held on to their will to fight. By the end of 1941, when the German raids had ended, some 20,000 Londoners had been killed and roughly 73,000 injured.

Japan Builds an Empire

Many Japanese were as unhappy with their situation in Asia in the 1920s as Italians and Germans were with their status in Europe. Located on a chain of small islands, Japan lacked sufficient raw materials and markets for its industries. It also needed land to support its

---

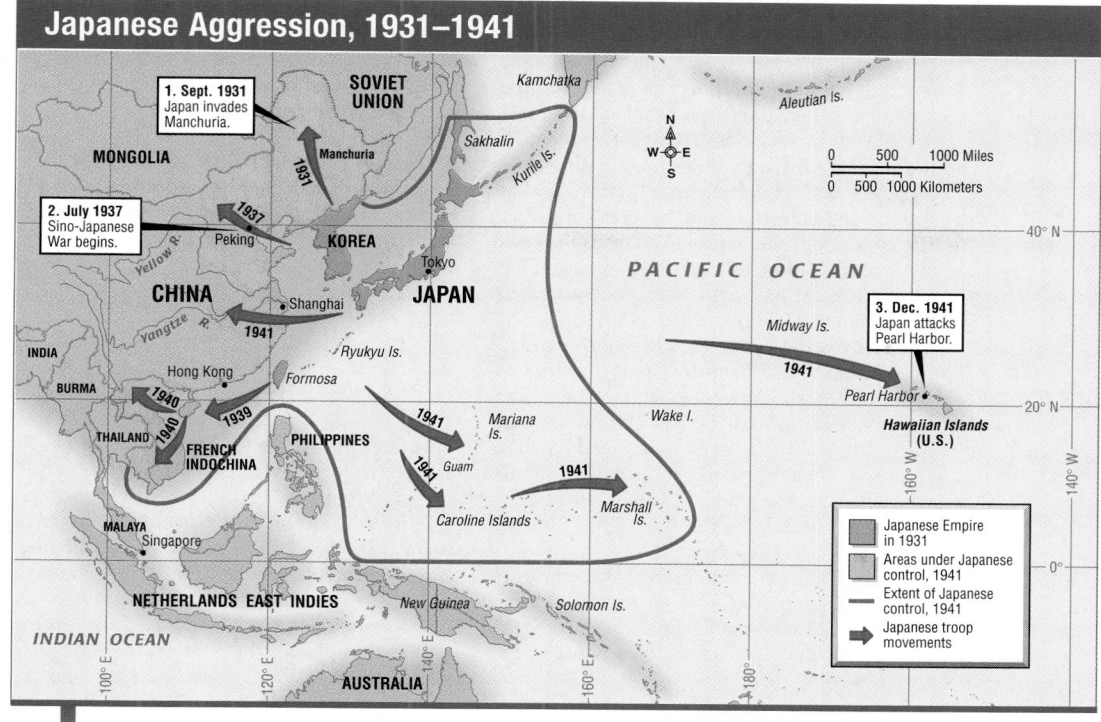

Japanese Aggression, 1931–1941

1. Sept. 1931 Japan invades Manchuria.

2. July 1937 Sino-Japanese War begins.

3. Dec. 1941 Japan attacks Pearl Harbor.

Legend:
- Japanese Empire in 1931
- Areas under Japanese control, 1941
- Extent of Japanese control, 1941
- Japanese troop movements

MAP Skills The Japanese were as eager as the Germans and Italians to build an empire.
Location Judging from this map, what regions appear to be in the greatest danger of being attacked next by Japan?

American Isolationism

American isolationism in the late 1930s had significant support. The America First Committee was not only vocal but also influential in gathering support from a cross-section of Americans against intervening in the war in Europe. Among the public figures who supported the America First Committee were former President Herbert Hoover, labor leader John L. Lewis, historian Charles Beard, architect Frank Lloyd Wright, chairman of Sears, Roebuck Robert Wood, and the most famous American of his generation—Charles Lindbergh.

growing population. For these reasons, some Japanese were eager to establish an empire.

Discontent spread after 1930, as the Great Depression added to Japan's economic woes. Yet world leaders and most Japanese were shocked in 1931, when Japan's army seized Manchuria, a mineral-rich region in northern China. During the next five years, the deepening Depression gave Japan's military a powerful voice in its government. In 1937 Japan resumed its aggression in China. Despite American help, the Chinese army of General Jiang Jieshi (jyawng jeh SHEE) was no match for the invaders.† An ongoing battle between Jiang's army and the Communist guerrilla fighters led by Mao Zedong contributed to the weakness of China. By 1940 the Japanese controlled most of eastern China.

---

† In earlier textbooks, this name is spelled Chiang Kai-shek. A newer method of spelling Chinese names with Roman letters is used today.

Japan next set its sights on Southeast Asia and the Dutch East Indies. First, it became an ally of Germany and Italy in the Tripartite Pact of September 1940. Then in April 1941 the Japanese signed a neutrality pact with the Soviet Union. The stage was now set for Japan to challenge the Europeans and Americans for supremacy in Asia.

The American Response

American officials watched Japan's actions in Asia with growing concern. In 1938 President Franklin D. Roosevelt began a naval buildup in the Pacific. The following year he moved the American Pacific Fleet from San Diego, California, to Pearl Harbor in the Hawaiian Islands.

America Remains Neutral Americans did not want to fight a war in Asia any more than they did in Europe. Most remained

Answer to . . .

Map Skills The areas on the fringes of Japanese controls: the Philippines, the Netherlands, and the rest of China.

Time: 90 minutes.

Activity: Conduct a short, simulated debate between American interventionists and isolationists in 1939.

Grouping: Groups of four students.

Purpose: Ask the members of each group to review the section and to develop arguments for isolationism and for intervention in the European and Asian conflicts.

Roles: Two students in each group can act as research staff members for two student debaters.

Outcome: Students will understand the issues faced by America's leaders as they assessed their role in the global conflict.

ACTIVITY
HETEROGENEOUS GROUPS

Historian Geoffrey Perrett begins his book *Days of Sadness, Years of Triumph: The American People, 1939–1945* with the sentence: "The war came as a surprise that was expected." Ask students to explain this seemingly contradictory statement in a brief essay or speech. **(Enrichment)**

Answer to . . .

Map Skills To the east and southeast of Ford Island.

disillusioned by World War I. They had fought to make the world safe for democracy, but now questioned whether their actions had made any difference. In addition, many believed the nation already had enough problems at home, as the American economy remained trapped in the Great Depression. These people supported a policy of isolationism, believing that American interests would be best served by staying out of other nations' quarrels. In 1940 some isolationists formed the America First Committee. At its height, this group attracted more than 800,000 members.

In the mid-1930s, Congress had responded to isolationist sentiment by passing a series of Neutrality Acts. These laws declared that the United States would withhold weapons and loans from all nations at war. Further, they required that nonmilitary goods sold to nations at war be paid for in cash and transported by the purchaser. This policy became known as "cash and carry."

Believing that war in Europe was unavoidable, Roosevelt tried without success to get these restrictions eased. After the war began, Congress passed the Neutrality Act of 1939. This law permitted Britain and France to purchase weapons on a cash-and-carry basis. A later amendment allowed American merchant ships to transport these purchases to Britain. Yet loans and purchases on credit remained illegal.

American Involvement Grows German aggression scared many Americans. Roosevelt was thus gradually able to offer Britain more help. In September 1940 he traded 50 old destroyers to Britain in return for permission to build bases on British territory in the Western Hemisphere.

That same month, Congress authorized the first peacetime draft in the nation's history. The Selective Service Act required all males ages 21 to 36 to register for military service. From this pool a limited number of men were selected to serve a year in the army.

In November 1940 Roosevelt won reelection to a third term as President. His easy victory encouraged him to push for greater American involvement in the war. In January 1941 he proposed to provide war supplies to Great Britain without any payment in return. Roosevelt explained the policy to the American people through the use of a simple comparison: if your neighbor's house is on fire, you don't sell him a hose. You lend it to him and take it back after the fire is out.

Congress responded by passing the **Lend-Lease Act** in March 1941, which authorized the President to aid any nation whose defense he believed was vital to American security. Roosevelt immediately began sending aid to Britain, and the United States became, as FDR had said in a speech in 1940, "the great arsenal of democracy."

Japan Attacks Pearl Harbor

Soon after France fell to the Germans, the Japanese demanded control of French colonies in Indochina. In mid-1941 Japanese forces occupied the region. In response, Roosevelt froze Japanese financial assets in the United States and cut off all trade with Japan. For the next few months, leaders in both nations looked for ways to avoid war.

American diplomats in Tokyo, eager to avoid a confrontation, urged the President to compromise. They warned that pushing the Japanese would result in war. Some of Roosevelt's advisers at home, however, called for a tough stance. The government had cracked secret Japanese codes and had

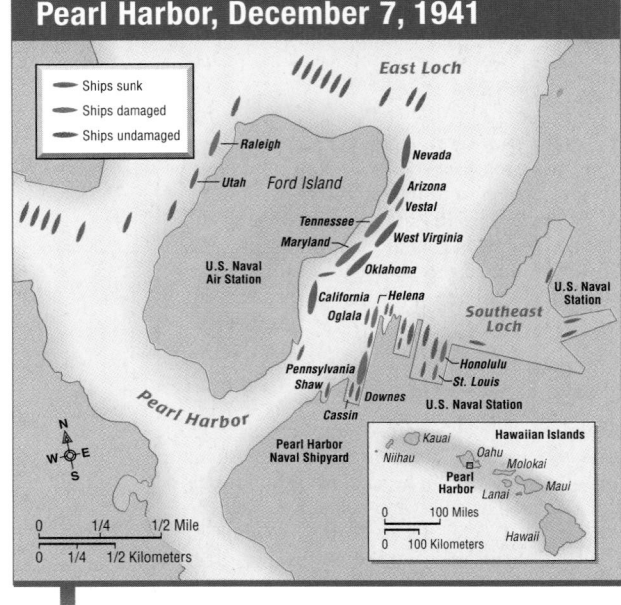

Pearl Harbor, December 7, 1941

- Ships sunk
- Ships damaged
- Ships undamaged

East Loch

Raleigh
Nevada
Utah — Ford Island
Arizona
Vestal
Tennessee
Maryland
West Virginia
U.S. Naval Air Station
Oklahoma
California — Helena
Oglala
U.S. Naval Station
Southeast Loch
Pennsylvania
Shaw
Honolulu
St. Louis
Downes
Cassin
U.S. Naval Station
Pearl Harbor
Pearl Harbor Naval Shipyard

0   1/4   1/2 Mile
0   1/4   1/2 Kilometers

Hawaiian Islands
Kauai
Niihau
Oahu
Molokai
Pearl Harbor
Lanai
Maui
0   100 Miles
0   100 Kilometers
Hawaii

MAP Skills The Japanese attack on Pearl Harbor was surprising and swift. *Location Where did the Japanese inflict the most damage?*

▶ RESOURCE OPTIONS

Teaching Resources

Visual Learning Activity Books Are Weapons, Learning with Documents folder, p. 66

been intercepting messages. American officials knew that Japan was planning to seize more territory.

In October 1941, General Hideki Tojo, who supported war with the United States, became prime minister of Japan. Yet Roosevelt still hoped for peace. He proposed to his advisers that trade could be resumed if Japan halted any further troop movements. On November 25, the American government learned that a Japanese fleet was moving toward Southeast Asia. The United States demanded that Japan withdraw from all conquered territory and from its Tripartite Pact with Germany and Italy.

Even as this tough message was being sent, a second Japanese fleet of 6 aircraft carriers and more than 20 other ships was under way. Japan's leaders had decided that their goals in Asia could not be achieved as long as the American fleet remained in Hawaii. That threat had to be destroyed.

Shortly after 7:00 A.M. on December 7, an American army radar operator on the Hawaiian island of Oahu reported to his headquarters that planes were headed toward him. The only officer on duty that Sunday morning decided they were American. "Don't worry about it," the officer told the radar operator, as he hung up the phone. Less than an hour later more than 180 Japanese warplanes streaked overhead. Most of the Pacific Fleet lay at anchor in Pearl Harbor, crowded into an area less than three miles square.

Japanese planes bombed and strafed (attacked with machine-gun fire) the fleet and the airfields nearby. By 9:45 it was over. In less than two hours some 2,400 Americans had been killed and nearly 1,200 wounded. Nearly 300 American warplanes were damaged or destroyed; 18 warships had been sunk or heavily damaged, including 8 of the fleet's 9 battleships. Japan lost just 29 planes.[†]

The attack on Pearl Harbor stunned the American people. Calling December 7, 1941, "a date which will live in infamy," Roosevelt the next day asked Congress to declare war on Japan:

> **KEY DOCUMENTS** ❝Hostilities exist. There is no blinking at the fact that our people, our territory, and our interests are in grave danger. With confidence in our armed forces—with the unbound determination of our people—we will gain the inevitable triumph—so help us God.❞
>
> —*Franklin D. Roosevelt*

Three days later, Germany and Italy declared war on the United States. For the second time in the century, Americans were part of a world war. Their contributions would make the difference between victory and defeat for the Allies.

[†] The Japanese did not achieve their main goal, which was to destroy the three aircraft carriers that were part of the American fleet. Two of the carriers, accompanied by the fleet's heavy cruisers, were at sea during the attack. The third was undergoing repairs in California.

SECTION 1 REVIEW

Comprehension

1. **Key Terms** Define: (a) totalitarian; (b) fascism; (c) Axis Powers; (d) appeasement; (e) *blitzkrieg;* (f) Allies; (g) Lend-Lease Act.

2. **Summarizing the Main Idea** What steps did Italy, Germany, and Japan take in the mid-1930s to extend their power?

3. **Organizing Information** Create a flow map to show how German and Italian aggression led to war. Begin with *October 1935: Italy invades Ethiopia* and end with *September 1939: England and France declare war on Germany.*

Critical Thinking

4. **Analyzing Time Lines** Review the time line at the start of the section. Which entry was responsible for bringing the United States into World War II?

5. **Recognizing Cause and Effect** What were some of the reasons behind Japan's desire to build an empire in Asia?

Writing Activity

6. **Writing an Persuasive Essay** Write a letter to President Roosevelt that expresses support for or opposition to the Lend-Lease Act.

▶ RESOURCE OPTIONS

Teaching Resources

 Quiz Units 7–8 folder, p. 45

 Key Documents Franklin D. Roosevelt, Message Asking for War Against Japan, Learning with Documents folder, p. 97

Student Performance Pack

Guide to the Essentials Chapter 24, Section 1 (English and Spanish)

Media and Technology

Color Transparencies Time Lines, E-7

| Sept. 1942 Battle of Stalingrad begins | Nov. 1942 British win decisive victory at El Alamein in Egypt | July 1943 American troops attack Sicily | June 1944 D-Day invasion of Western Europe begins | Dec. 1944 Battle of the Bulge begins | May 1945 Germany surrenders |

1942   **1944**   **1946**

Objectives

You may wish to call students' attention to the objectives in the Section Preview. The objectives are reflected in the main headings of the section.

Bellringer

Ask students if they have ever used the term *D-Day*. If so, what did they mean by it?

Reading Strategy

Formulating Questions Refer to the Reading Strategy in the Section Preview. You may wish to have students review the section by quizzing each other with their questions.

LESSON PLAN

Connecting to the Main Idea

1. Focus The Allies were on the defensive when the United States entered the war. Ask students to consider how the Allies planned to win victory in Europe.

2. Instruct Discuss the factors that mobilized diverse groups of Americans to enter the armed forces. Ask students to explain how Roosevelt's vision of freedom might have been a unifying force. Ask how discrimination and segregation affected some groups in the military. How did the armed forces benefit from diversity?

Ask why the Soviet Union continually pressured the Allies to open a front in western Europe. Why did Churchill insist on attacking Germany through North Africa and Italy? How were D-Day and the Battle of the Bulge significant?

3. Close In early 1941, the United States joined forces with the Allies. Aided by American military strength, the Allies eventually gained control of Europe and North Africa. Germany at last surrendered, but the war in the Pacific continued, as the next section describes.

2 The Road to Victory in Europe

SECTION PREVIEW

Objectives

1 Identify the various groups of Americans who mobilized to fight the war.
2 Understand how the Allied decision to begin fighting in North Africa and Italy affected war efforts in the Soviet Union.
3 Show how the Allied invasion of Western Europe led to the end of the war in Europe.
4 *Key Terms* Define: Atlantic Charter; GI; Battle of Stalingrad; carpet bombing; D-Day; Battle of the Bulge; Yalta Conference.

Main Idea

To secure victory in Europe, the Allies waged war in North Africa, Western Europe, and the Soviet Union between 1941 and 1945.

Reading Strategy

Formulating Questions Skim the section and write down the main headings. Then rewrite each heading as a question. As you read, note the answers to your questions.

Fatigues were standard wear for American soldiers.

In August 1941, unknown to the rest of the world, two warships quietly lay at anchor off the coast of Newfoundland. Aboard were Prime Minister Winston Churchill and President Franklin Roosevelt. Both men believed the United States would soon be allied with Britain in war, and they were meeting to agree on the war's goals. The two leaders pledged "a peace that will afford all nations the means of dwelling in safety inside their own boundaries." Roosevelt and Churchill put this and other principles into writing in the **Atlantic Charter.** The agreements reached at this meeting would form the basis for the United Nations.

Americans Mobilize for War

As the United States prepared for war, thousands of American men received official notices to enter the army or navy. After the bombing of Pearl Harbor, tens of thousands more volunteered to serve. Roosevelt shared his vision of what these troops would be asked to fight for:

AMERICAN VOICES
"We look forward to a world founded upon four essential freedoms. The first is freedom of speech and expression. . . . The second is freedom of every person to worship God in his own way. . . . The third is freedom from want [need]. . . . The fourth is freedom from fear."

—*Franklin D. Roosevelt*

The GI War World War II greatly changed the lives of the men and women who were uprooted from home and sent far away to fight for freedom. The 16 million Americans who served as soldiers, sailors, and aviators made their way through distant deserts, jungles, swamps, turbulent seas, and forbidding skies. For those on the front lines, the war was often a desperate struggle just to stay alive.

American soldiers called themselves **GIs,** after the "Government Issue" stamp that

RESOURCE OPTIONS

Teaching Resources

Reproducible Lesson Plan Lesson Plans folder, p. 132

Learning Styles Lesson Plan Learning Styles Lesson Plans folder, p. 51

Big Idea Graphic Organizer Big Idea Graphic Organizer folder, p. 104

Guided Reading and Review Units 7–8 folder, p. 46

appeared on all shoes, clothes, weapons, and other equipment provided by the military. While the "four freedoms" and the Atlantic Charter may have defined the goals of the United States in the war, most GIs served for more personal reasons. As soldiers fought in filthy foxholes overseas, they dreamed of home and a cherished way of life. When asked what he was fighting for, a young marine on the Pacific front replied, "What I'd give for a piece of blueberry pie."

Diversity in the Armed Forces Americans from all ethnic and racial backgrounds fought during World War II. Among these were more than 300,000 Mexican Americans. Most enlisted in the army. Mexican American troops fought to defend the Philippines, served in the North African campaign, and took part in the D-Day invasion of France in 1944.

Some 25,000 Native Americans also served in the army and other branches of the military. The marines recruited about 300 Navajos to serve as radio operators. They developed a code based on their language that the Japanese could not break when they eavesdropped on marine radio transmissions. The "code talkers," as they became known, provided a vitally important secure communications link in several key battles in the Pacific.

Although Japanese Americans were not accepted into the armed forces until early 1943, thousands volunteered to fight. Many came from the camps where tens of thousands of Japanese Americans were detained during the war. Eventually more than 20,000 Japanese Americans fought in the United States armed services. Most were Nisei, or citizens born in the United States of Japanese immigrant parents. The all-Nisei 442nd Regimental Combat team won so many commendations for bravery while fighting in Europe that it became the most decorated military unit in American history.

African American troops also played an important role in the war. Nearly a million African Americans volunteered or were drafted to serve in the military. At first, most black troops were limited to support roles. However, black leaders pushed to get African Americans into combat. By late 1942, faced with mounting casualties, military authorities reluctantly gave in.

Like Japanese American troops, African Americans fought in segregated units. The African American 761st Tank Battalion captured 30 major towns from the Germans in a grueling 183-day campaign. The Army Air Force 99th Fighter Squadron, known as the Black Eagles,

---

COMPARING PRIMARY SOURCES

INTEGRATION OF THE ARMED FORCES

Discussion about desegregating the armed forces during World War II aroused strong feelings on both sides. Below are two viewpoints.

In Support of Integration	In Opposition to Integration
"Though I have found no Negroes who want to see the United Nations lose this war, I have found many who, before the war ends, want to see the stuffing knocked out of white supremacy. . . . If freedom and equality are not vouchsafed [granted] the peoples of color, the war for democracy will not be won. . . . We demand the abolition of segregation and discrimination in . . . [all] branches of national defense." —A. Philip Randolph, African-American labor and civil rights leader, November 1942	"In this hour of national crisis, it is much more important that we have the full-hearted co-operation of the thirty million white southern Americans than that we satisfy the National Association for the Advancement of Colored People. . . . If they be forced to serve with Negroes, they will cease to volunteer; and when drafted, they will not serve with that enthusiasm and high morale that has always characterized the soldiers and sailors of the southern states." —W. R. Poage, Texas state representative, 1941

ANALYZING VIEWPOINTS **What arguments does each side use to support its viewpoint?**

To defeat the Japanese in the Pacific, United States Marines had to keep their strategies from the enemy. Navajo code talkers like these allowed the Allies to stay one step ahead of the Japanese. **Diversity** *How else did the armed forces benefit from diversity?*

BACKGROUND

Geography in History

The United States's "Good Neighbor Policy" paid dividends during the war. The Latin American nations provided vital war materials—rubber, quinine, tin—along with naval and air bases. Brazil sent troops to Europe, and Mexico had an air squadron in the Pacific. The Mexican and Cuban navies patrolled the Caribbean for German submarines. In return, the United States provided military equipment and loans to these nations.

Customize for
More Advanced Students

Ask students to write a short paper on what facts of the African American experience in World War II they think were the most important in beginning the movement for equality. Discuss the importance of leadership and experience in a large institution such as the military, and the significance of the contrast between the nation's stated goals and its discriminatory actions.

Answer to . . .

Comparing Primary Sources Poage argues that keeping up the morale of the southern white volunteers is more important to winning the war than serving the interests of African Americans. Randolph argues that the military is fighting for democracy and that if it remains segregated, it has won nothing.
Viewing History The Japanese American unit was the most decorated in American history; African Americans and women signed up in significant numbers.

ACTIVITY
LEARNING STYLES

Explain that the age of the typical soldier in World War II ranged from late teens to early twenties. Ask students to assume the role of a citizen of this age group during World War II. Have them write a letter to President Roosevelt explaining their views on either of the following topics: the role of women in the military or segregation in the armed forces. Letters should respectfully suggest to Roosevelt a change the students feel is acceptable. Ask why they think the government did not change its policies at the time. *(Verbal/Linguistic)*

Answer to . . .

Exploring Technology Nations develop new weapons or technology to counter the new technology of their enemies.

Main Idea Connections They worked in all areas, from clerical work to aviation, except combat.

---

exploring TECHNOLOGY   World War II Submarine

Periscopes
Radio tower
Escape hatch
Anchor
Showers & toilets
Conning tower
Bunks
Galley
Engineers' room
Electric engines
Diesel engines
Ammunition
Radio room
Control room
Batteries
Officers' quarters
Torpedoes

Both the Germans and the Allies used subs to attack enemy merchant convoys. The Allies used asdic, a form of echo-location, to detect enemy subs. *Science and Technology How does one development in war technology often lead to another?*

shot down more than 110 enemy planes over Italy. In late 1944, when heavy casualties in Europe forced the army to accept African Americans into white combat units, nearly 5,000 additional black volunteers stepped forward.

Women in the Armed Forces Not all soldiers were men. By the war's end, roughly 350,000 American women had volunteered for military service. Faced with a personnel shortage, officials were willing to use women in almost all areas except combat. About 13,000 women marines worked as clerks, typists, airfield control tower operators, mechanics, photographers, and drivers. Another 10,000 women served in the Coast Guard.

Some 1,200 WASPs (Women Air Force Service Pilots) ferried planes around the country and towed practice targets for antiaircraft gunners. The Navy had a similar organization, the WAVES (Women Accepted for Volunteer Emergency Service). One quarter of the 86,000 WAVES served in naval aviation. With nearly 100,000 officers and enlisted personnel, the Women's Army Corps (WAC) was the largest of the women's military groups. The WAC's commander, Colonel Oveta Culp Hobby, led more people than many army generals.

Main Idea
CONNECTIONS
Describe the roles that women played during World War II.

Fighting in North Africa and Italy

When the United States entered the war in 1941, the situation was critical. London and other major British cities had suffered heavy damage during the Battle of Britain. The Germans' *blitzkrieg* had extended Nazi control across most of Europe. In North Africa a German army led by General Erwin Rommel, known as the "Desert Fox" for his shrewd tactics, was equally successful. Many people feared that Germany could not be stopped.

The Battle of the Atlantic At sea a desperate struggle developed in the effort to keep German submarines from isolating Great Britain. To deliver the food and supplies that the British needed, merchant ships formed

---

▶ RESOURCE OPTIONS

Media and Technology

 Color Transparencies The Way It Works, H-19

RESOURCE PRO

Biography Jacqueline Cochran, found on Resource Pro, profiles a veteran of the World War II Women's Air Force Service Pilots.

Critical Thinking Activity Predicting Consequences: After the Army—What? found on Resource Pro, helps students apply this skill by having them explore possible postwar lifestyle changes for returning servicewomen.

convoys. American warships often served as escorts. The Germans countered with groups of as many as 30 submarines, called wolf packs, that carried out coordinated attacks on the convoys. After the United States entered the war, the Battle of the Atlantic spread as German submarines began attacking merchant ships off the American coast.

Although Allied warships used sonar (underwater sound equipment) to locate and attack submarines, the wolf packs were highly effective. In the Atlantic they sank nearly 175 ships in June 1942 alone.

The North Africa Campaign Since August 1940, a British army had been battling Italian and German troops in North Africa. In November 1942 the British, under General Bernard Montgomery, won a decisive victory at El Alamein in Egypt. The Germans began to retreat west. A few days later, British and American troops commanded by American gen-

eral Dwight D. Eisenhower landed in Morocco and Algeria and quickly pushed eastward. In May 1943 the two Allied armies came together in Tunisia, trapping Rommel's forces. Despite Hitler's instructions to fight to the death, nearly 240,000 Germans and Italians surrendered.

Churchill and Roosevelt met once again in January 1943, this time at Casablanca, Morocco. At this Casablanca Conference they planned strategy for fighting much of the rest of the war. The decision was made to continue concentrating Allied resources on Europe before trying to win the war in the Pacific. Churchill and Roosevelt also agreed to accept only the unconditional surrender of Italy, Germany, and Japan.

The Invasion of Italy In July 1943, American troops under General George S. Patton attacked Sicily, just south of the Italian mainland. When the island fell in just 38 days, Mussolini was overthrown. In September, as

Allied Advances in Europe and Northern Africa, 1942–1945

Legend:
- Axis Powers
- Areas under Axis control, 1942
- Allies and areas under Allied control, 1942
- Neutral nations
- Allied advances
- ★ Major battles

5. Dec. 1944 Battle of the Bulge begins
6. Apr. 1945 Soviet forces capture Berlin
1. Sept. 1942 Battle of Stalingrad
4. June 1944 D-Day
3. May 1944 Battle of Anzio
2. Nov. 1942 El Alamein

 MAP Skills Axis Powers controlled most of Europe by the time the United States entered the war in 1941.
Location What geographic advantage did the United Kingdom have over other European nations that helped protect it from German aggression?

 BACKGROUND

Connections To Today

The United Service Organizations (USO), founded in 1941, assembled volunteer touring companies of actors, comedians, bandleaders, singers, and dancers to entertain the armed forces overseas. USO camp shows performed wherever American troops were stationed—in the North African desert, in bombed-out opera houses in Italy, or in the steamy rain forests of New Guinea. The USO has toured in every American war zone since then. Today about 40,000 volunteers around the world keep the USO active.

Answer to . . .

Map Skills *It was an island nation and easier to defend; it shared no geographic borders with Axis nations or nations under Axis control.*

LEARNING STYLES

Ask students to work in groups to make a detailed map of the theater of war in either Europe or North Africa, including battle lines and the dates of important events. (*Visual/Spatial*)

Customize for

Less Proficient Readers

Have students work together to make a time line of the major battles and events in the European and North African theatres of war. The time line should begin in 1941 and end in 1945.

Allied troops threatened the rest of Italy, its new government surrendered.

German troops in Italy, however, continued to resist, blocking roads and destroying bridges as they retreated up the Italian peninsula. By November, German defenses stiffened and the Allied advance stalled. In January, to get it moving again, an Allied force landed behind the German lines at Anzio, just south of Rome. For the next four months Allied soldiers fought to move more than a few miles beyond the beach. Before they finally broke through German defenses in May 1944, some 72,000 American soldiers had been killed or wounded.

After winning the Battle of Anzio, the Allies quickly captured Rome. However, many more months of heavy fighting were required before the Germans in northern Italy finally surrendered in April 1945. The Americans suffered nearly 190,000 casualties during the Italian campaign. German losses approached half a million troops.

War in the Soviet Union

Meanwhile, as the Allies battled their way across northern Africa and southern Europe, an epic struggle had been developing in eastern Europe. As early as 1924 Hitler had called for conquest of the Soviet Union, claiming that Germany needed *lebensraum* (living space) to the east. After losing the Battle of Britain, he broke his pact with Stalin and launched an attack against the Soviet Union.

The Germans Advance, 1941–1942 In June 1941, nearly 3.6 million German and other Axis troops poured across the length of the Soviet border, from the Baltic Sea in the north to the Black Sea in the south. The nearly 3 million Red Army soldiers opposing this onslaught were poorly equipped and not well trained.

The Soviets were unprepared for the intensity and the brutality of the German attack. The *Luftwaffe* quickly gained control of the air, and German ground troops drove deep into Soviet territory. In lands they occupied, German troops began rounding up and executing large numbers of civilians.

The Soviets adopted a scorched earth policy, destroying everything useful to the enemy as they retreated. In the meantime, Stalin asked Roosevelt for help through the Lend-Lease program. However, Congress blocked this request for many months. American aid did not begin to flow until June 1942.

By that summer, German armies threatened major cities deep inside the Soviet Union. Stalin desperately urged his allies to launch an attack on Western Europe. He believed such an attack would take pressure off the Soviet Union's Red Army in the east by forcing Hitler to divide his forces. Churchill, however, hesitated to make such a risky invasion. At Casablanca he persuaded Roosevelt instead to invade Italy, which he called the "soft underbelly" of Europe. The Soviets would have to confront the bulk of the German army on their own.

The Battle of Stalingrad The Red Army decided to make its stand at Stalingrad, a major industrial railroad center. In mid-September 1942 the Germans began a campaign of bombing and shelling that lasted more than two months. The Soviets took up positions in the rubble that remained of Stalingrad and engaged the advancing German troops in bitter house-to-house fighting.

In mid-November, taking advantage of the harsh Russian weather, Soviet forces counterattacked and surrounded the German army. In late January, the Red Army launched a final assault on the freezing enemy. On January 31, 1943, more than 90,000 surviving Germans surrendered.

In all, Germany lost some 330,000 troops at Stalingrad; the Soviet Union never released official data on its casualties. The **Battle of Stalingrad** was the turning point of the war in the east. After their victory, Soviet forces began a long struggle to regain the territory lost to the Germans.

George Marshall

AMERICAN BIOGRAPHY As the Red Army slowly forced the German invaders back, Stalin continued to push for the long-promised invasion of Western Europe. Everyone assumed that American George Marshall would be appointed to lead the assault once it finally began. Marshall was the top American general and Roosevelt's Army Chief of Staff. In addition, he had been a strong voice in support of such an invasion long before others were willing to back it.

Thus, the Allies were shocked when Roosevelt instead tapped Dwight Eisenhower to lead the invasion. Marshall was so important to the overall war effort, the President said in explaining his decision, that he would not sleep well if the general were out of the country.

▶ RESOURCE OPTIONS

Media and Technology

 Listening to Literature Randall Jarrell, "Losses"; "The Death of the Ball Turret Gunner"

George Marshall (1880–1959)

A graduate of Virginia Military Institute, Marshall had served in France during World War I, where he aided in planning major Allied victories. Promotions were slow after the war, however, until Marshall came to Washington, D.C. There he became Deputy Chief of Staff in 1938 and was named to the army's top job just a year later.

As Army Chief of Staff, Marshall pushed the President to prepare for war by strengthening the army. Soon after America's entry into World War II, Marshall called for an invasion of Western Europe. He opposed Churchill's plan to focus on North Africa and Italy first. Churchill later credited Marshall with being "the true organizer of [the Allies'] victory."

After the war ended in 1945, Marshall resigned. However, President Harry Truman quickly called him back to public service. As Secretary of State, Marshall launched a massive effort to rebuild postwar Europe. Today that program is known as the Marshall Plan. For this work Marshall received the Nobel Peace Prize in 1953.

The Invasion of Western Europe

At every conference of Allied leaders after the United States entered the war, Marshall pushed for an attack on the German forces occupying France. Allied planes were already bombing Germany. In late 1943 the British finally agreed to go along with Marshall's proposal to launch a land invasion as well.

The Air War The RAF had begun bombing Germany in 1940. However, the *Luftwaffe* quickly forced the British to give up daylight missions for safer but less accurate nighttime raids. When the Germans started to target cities during the Battle of Britain, the RAF responded in kind. It abandoned attempts to pinpoint targets and developed a technique called **carpet bombing,** in which large numbers of bombs were scattered over a wide area. German cities suffered heavy damage as a result.

Allied bombing of Germany had intensified after the United States entered the war. In the spring of 1943 the bombing campaign was stepped up yet again in order to soften Germany for the planned Allied invasion. By 1944 British and American commanders were conducting coordinated air raids—American planes bombing by day and the RAF by night. At its height, some 3,000 planes were involved in this campaign.

Preparation for Invasion A massive buildup of troops began in southern England as American, British, and Canadian forces were joined by Polish, Dutch, Belgian, and French troops. In response, the Germans strengthened their defenses along the French coastline. As they waited for the invasion to begin, German soldiers added machine-gun emplacements, barbed wire fences on beaches, land and water mines, and underwater obstructions.

D-Day Shortly after midnight on June 6, 1944, the largest landing by sea in history began as some 4,600 invasion craft and warships slipped out of their harbors in southern England. As the ships crossed the English Channel, about 1,000 RAF bombers pounded German defenses at Normandy. Meanwhile,

General Dwight Eisenhower (left) commanded many Allied initiatives in Europe, including the D-Day landing at Normandy in 1944. *Geography* Why was Hitler expecting the main thrust of the invasion to be at Calais, and not Normandy?

Graphing the Main Idea

To make sure students understand the main idea of this section, you may wish to use the web graphic organizer below.

Tell students that a web graphic organizer is used to show a main idea and its supporting details. Ask students to use it to show that the Allies secured victory in Europe in World War II by waging war in North Africa, Western Europe, and the Soviet Union.

Teaching Tip A template for this graphic organizer can be found in the Color Transparencies, G-1.

---

some 23,000 airborne British and American soldiers, in a daring nighttime maneuver, were dropped behind enemy lines.

At dawn on **D-Day,** the code name for the day the invasion began, Allied warships in the channel began a massive shelling of the coast. Some 1,000 American planes continued the RAF's air bombardment. Then around 150,000 Allied troops and their equipment began to come ashore along 60 miles of Normandy coast.

Despite the advice of his generals to launch a counterattack, Hitler hesitated. He feared a larger invasion at the narrowest part of the English Channel near Calais. Nevertheless, German resistance at Normandy was fierce. At Omaha Beach, the code name for one landing site, the Allies suffered some 2,000 casualties.

In spite of the heavy casualties of D-Day, within a week a half million men came ashore. By late July the Allied force in France numbered some 2 million troops.

The Battle of the Bulge Bitter fighting followed as the Allies broke through German defenses at Normandy and pushed across France. In late August 1944, American troops liberated Paris. British and Canadian forces freed Brussels and Antwerp in Belgium a few days later. In mid-September, a combined Allied force attacked the Germans occupying Holland. At about the same time, Americans crossed the western border of Germany.

The Nazis fought desperately to defend their homeland. After reinforcing the army with thousands of additional draftees, some as young as 15, they launched a counterattack in Belgium and Luxembourg in December 1944. This battle came to be known as the **Battle of the Bulge.**

As the German attack overwhelmed the American forces and pushed them back, many small units became cut off from the rest of the army. The soldiers of these isolated units fought gallantly. From his headquarters near Paris, Eisenhower ordered more troops to the scene. The most spectacular of these reinforcement actions was carried out by General Patton. In just a few days he moved his entire army of 250,000 soldiers from western France to help stop the German advance.

The Battle of the Bulge was the largest battle in Western Europe during World War II and the largest ever fought by the United States Army. It involved some 600,000 GIs, of whom about 80,000 were killed, wounded, or captured. German losses totaled about 100,000 troops. After this battle, most Nazi leaders recognized that the war was lost.

War Ends in Europe

In March 1945, as Allied bombers continued to hammer German cities, American ground forces crossed the Rhine River and advanced toward Berlin from the west. Meanwhile, the Soviets pushed into Germany from the east.

The Soviets Advance The fighting between German and Soviet forces from 1941 to 1945 was the greatest conflict ever fought on a single front. At any given time it involved more than 9 million troops. The costs of this struggle were horrific. The 13.6 million Soviet and 3 million German military killed accounted for more than two thirds the total dead for all World War II. Current research in records in the former Soviet Union places the total of Soviet civilian and military deaths at 27 million.

After the hardships their nation had endured, Soviet leaders considered the capture of Berlin, Germany's capital, a matter of honor. In late April 1945 the Soviets fought their way into Berlin. They found a city more than 80 percent destroyed by Allied bombing.

While some Soviet troops attacked Berlin, other elements of the Red Army continued to

CAUSE AND EFFECT: World War II

CAUSES
- Fascism takes hold in Italy and Germany.
- Germany invades the Rhineland and annexes Austria and Czechoslovakia.
- Germany invades Poland.
- Japan aggressively builds an empire in Asia.

↓

WORLD WAR II

↓

EFFECTS
- Europe and Japan are left in ruins.
- Two thirds of Europe's Jewish population is killed.
- The United States and the Soviet Union emerge as world powers.
- The cold war begins.

Interpreting Charts Foreign aggression on both sides of the world erupted into global war. *Foreign Relations* **How was the world changed by the end of the war?**

Answer to . . .

Interpreting Charts Europe and Japan were left in ruins, two thirds of Europe's Jewish population was killed, the United States and Soviet Union emerged as world powers, the cold war began.

RESOURCE OPTIONS

Media and Technology

AmericanHeritage® **CD-ROM**

Explorer Activity 26 A Global War, CD-ROM Guidebook, pp. 71–72, helps students write an outline for a television documentary about World War II.

---

drive west. On April 25, they met American troops at the Elbe River.

Germany Surrenders In Berlin, Hitler had refused to take his generals' advice to flee as the Soviets closed in on the city. Instead he fulfilled a vow he had made in 1939: "I shall stand or fall in this struggle. I shall never survive the defeat of my people." On May 1, the German government announced that Hitler had committed suicide. A few days later, on May 8, 1945, Germany surrendered.

American soldiers rejoiced and civilians celebrated V-E Day (Victory in Europe Day) at home as the war in Europe came to an end. The war was not over yet, however, as Japan was still to be defeated.

The Yalta Conference In February 1945, two months before the fall of Berlin, Roosevelt, Churchill, and Stalin met at Yalta, a city in the Soviet Union near the Black Sea. The purpose of the **Yalta Conference** was to plan for the postwar world. The leaders agreed to split Germany into four zones, each under the control of one of the major Allies. The city of Berlin, which would lie in the Soviet zone, would be similarly divided. Stalin promised to allow elections in the nations his army liberated from the Germans. He also promised to enter the war against Japan soon after Germany surrendered.

A United States soldier and Russian soldier (left and right) share a moment of camaraderie after meeting at the Elbe River in April 1945. *Foreign Relations How did Soviet assaults in 1945 help end the war?*

The agreements at Yalta were only partially fulfilled. Stalin refused, for example, to honor his promise for free elections. Roosevelt and Churchill were accused of not doing enough to prevent Soviet domination of Eastern Europe. The issue of Eastern Europe would be at the heart of the problems that later arose between the Soviet Union and the Western Allies.

SECTION 2 REVIEW

Comprehension

1. *Key Terms* Define: (a) Atlantic Charter; (b) GI; (c) Battle of Stalingrad; (d) carpet bombing; (e) D-Day; (f) Battle of the Bulge; (g) Yalta Conference.
2. *Summarizing the Main Idea* What events helped turn the tide of war in favor of the Allies?
3. *Organizing Information* Create a four-column chart on a sheet of paper. Label the columns *1942, 1943, 1944,* and *1945*. In each column list the major battles and events in the European and North African theaters of war for that year.

Critical Thinking

4. *Analyzing Time Lines* Review the time line at the start of the section. Explain how the Allied decision to delay an invasion of Western Europe and fight instead in North Africa and Italy affected war efforts in the Soviet Union.
5. *Checking Consistency* Why do you think Americans who were denied full rights at home were eager to take part in the war against fascism?

Writing Activity

6. *Writing an Expository Essay* Joseph Stalin repeatedly asked the Allies to invade Western Europe in order to take the pressure off the Soviet Union. Write an essay convincing the Allied leaders to support this plan, or write a reply explaining why the invasion had to be delayed.

RESOURCE OPTIONS

Teaching Resources

Quiz Units 7–8 folder, p. 47

Student Performance Pack

Guide to the Essentials Chapter 24, Section 2 (English and Spanish)

Answers to SECTION 2 REVIEW

1. (a) Atlantic Charter, see p. 692; (b) GI, see p. 692; (c) Battle of Stalingrad, see p. 696; (d) carpet bombing, see p. 697; (e) D-Day, see p. 698; (f) Battle of the Bulge, see p. 698; (g) Yalta Conference, see p. 699.

2. The Battle of Stalingrad, D-Day, and the Battle of the Bulge.

3. 1942: the Battle of the Atlantic; the British victory at El Alamein; Germans retreat west. 1943: Allied armies meet in Tunisia and gain victory; Casablanca Conference; Mussolini overthrown by Allies in Italy; Battle of Stalingrad. 1944: D-Day; Battle of the Bulge. 1945: Soviet and American troops meet in Berlin; Germany surrenders; Yalta Conference.

4. The Soviets had to fight before they were adequately equipped and trained, without Allied aid.

5. Sample answer: They were eager to fight oppression since they themselves felt oppressed.

6. Essays will vary but should be supported with facts from the section.

Answer to . . .

Viewing History They struck the final blow to Berlin, already heavily damaged by Allied bombing.

Objectives

You may wish to call students' attention to the objectives in the Section Preview. The objectives are reflected in the main headings of the section.

Bellringer

Ask students to write one sentence describing what they think is the most important way the use of nuclear weapons has changed the world.

Reading Strategy

Organizing Information Refer to the Reading Strategy in the Section Preview. You may wish to point out on a classroom map the locations where fighting took place in the Pacific.

LESSON PLAN

Connecting to the Main Idea

1. Focus As Allied forces struggled to defeat the Axis Powers in Europe, they were also fighting fiercely against the Japanese in the Pacific.

2. Instruct Explain that initially the Japanese had the upper hand in the Pacific. Ask students why they think this was so. What military successes did Japan have between 1941 and 1942?

Discuss the strategies used by the Allies in the Pacific from 1943 to 1945. Why was it important that the Allies get control of the islands? Why did so many casualties result? Ask students to explain the significance of the Battle of Okinawa.

Discuss the history of the atomic bomb and have students explain the Manhattan Project. Ask them if they think Truman would have dropped the atomic bomb if he had known the bomb's delayed effects.

3. Close The United States, weary of fighting, finally ended the war by using a terrible new weapon, the atomic bomb. The next section describes another atrocity of the war—the Holocaust.

3 The War in the Pacific

SECTION PREVIEW

Objectives

1 Summarize the Japanese advance in the Pacific in 1941 and 1942 and describe Allied victories that turned the tide of the war.

2 Describe the Allied struggle for the Pacific islands, including Iwo Jima and Okinawa.

3 Describe the Manhattan Project and its effect in bringing an end to the war.

4 *Key Terms* Define: Bataan Death March; Battle of the Coral Sea; Battle of Midway; Battle of Guadalcanal; *kamikaze;* Battle of Iwo Jima; Battle of Okinawa; Manhattan Project.

Main Idea

Fierce fighting and heavy casualties characterized the war in the Pacific Ocean as the Allied forces struggled to turn back Japanese advances.

Reading Strategy

Organizing Information Sketch a map that shows the areas where fighting took place in the Pacific Ocean. As you read the section, mark the major battle sites on your map. Also note who won each battle.

The bombing of Pearl Harbor was only the first of several Japanese offensives across the Pacific. Just hours after the attack on Pearl Harbor, Japanese warplanes based in China hit Clark Field, the main American air base in the Philippine Islands. (American troops had occupied the Philippines since the Spanish-American War in 1898.) The American planes sat neatly parked along the runways at Clark Field. As Japanese planes swept over the airfield, strings of bombs fell toward their targets. Planes and buildings were blown to pieces. Returning to their base, the Japanese attackers rejoiced over their success. Many were puzzled, however. They asked, What was the matter with the enemy? Didn't the Americans know the war had started?

The Japanese Advance, 1941–1942

Although news of Pearl Harbor had reached Douglas MacArthur, the commanding general, the Americans at Clark Field had not expected an immediate attack. About half of General MacArthur's air force was destroyed as it sat on the ground.

Within days, a large Japanese force landed in the Philippines. MacArthur withdrew most of his troops to the Bataan Peninsula on Manila Bay. There he set up defenses, hoping the navy would be able to evacuate his army to safety.

The Philippines Fall For some four months, American and Filipino troops held out on the Bataan Peninsula. In March, realizing the situation was hopeless, President Roosevelt ordered MacArthur to escape to Australia. The general was reluctant to abandon his soldiers to the Japanese, but promised, "I shall return."

When the peninsula's gallant troops surrendered to Japanese forces in early April, about 2,000 soldiers and nurses escaped to the fortified island of Corregidor in Manila Bay. Joining the fort's defenders, they fought on for another month. The holdouts survived nearly constant Japanese bombing and artillery barrages by living in the rock tunnels of the

▶ RESOURCE OPTIONS

Teaching Resources

📁 **Reproducible Lesson Plan** Lesson Plans folder, p. 133

📁 **Big Idea Graphic Organizer** Big Idea Graphic Organizer folder, p. 105

📁 **Guided Reading and Review** Units 7–8 folder, p. 48

fortress. Finally, running low on ammunition and food, over 11,000 Americans and Filipinos surrendered on May 6, 1942.

As the Bataan Peninsula fell, some 76,000 Filipinos and Americans became prisoners of war. Japanese soldiers split the prisoners into groups of 500 to 1,000 and marched them some 60 miles to a railroad. Those who survived the ordeal were shipped to prison camps where they were held for the rest of the war. However, already weakened from weeks without enough food or medicine, at least 10,000 prisoners died during the 6- to 12-day march. Many were executed by the guards when they could not keep up.

Word of what became known as the **Bataan Death March** did not reach America until three years later, when three soldiers escaped from their prison camp. After the war the general blamed for organizing the march was one of six Japanese executed for war crimes.

The War at Sea As Japanese forces spread across the Pacific, the battered American navy fought desperately to stop them. In May 1942, a largely American naval group halted a Japanese advance by engaging a superior enemy fleet in the Coral Sea, northeast of Australia. The **Battle of the Coral Sea** was the first naval combat carried out entirely by aircraft. The enemy ships never came within sight of one another. Planes launched from the aircraft carriers bombed and strafed the enemy forces more than 70 miles away.

The costs of the five-day battle were high. Both sides lost more than half their aircraft. The American aircraft carrier *Lexington* was destroyed, and the *Yorktown* was badly damaged. But one Japanese carrier sank, another lost most of its planes, and a third was put out of action. Militarily the battle was probably a draw. However, it prevented the Japanese from establishing the bases they needed to bomb Australia, thus blocking the invasion of that nation.

Allied Victories Turn the Tide

While the Soviets resisted German advances and the Allies prepared to invade North Africa, two critical battles took place in the Pacific. Midway Island, near Hawaii, and Guadalcanal, in the western Pacific near the Coral Sea, were small but strategic islands. In mid-1942, the battles for these islands changed the course of the war in the Pacific.

The Battle of Midway Despite his success at Pearl Harbor, Japanese admiral Isoroku Yamamoto believed that American naval power still held the key to victory or defeat in Asia. He hoped to destroy what remained of the Pacific Fleet by luring it into battle at Midway Island, northwest of Hawaii. Yamamoto committed a large part of Japan's navy to his plan. He correctly believed that American admiral Chester Nimitz would use all his resources to protect Midway, which was vital to the defense of Hawaii.

The **Battle of Midway** erupted on June 4, 1942. Like the action in the Coral Sea, it was fought entirely from the air. The American planes found the Japanese carriers at a vulnerable time—the Japanese were still loading bombs onto their planes. The Americans swiftly demolished three of four Japanese carriers as bombs stacked up on their decks exploded in the attack. The fourth was destroyed trying to escape. The sinking of these carriers, plus the loss of some 250 planes they carried, was a devastating blow to Japanese naval power. After the Battle of Midway, Japan was unable to launch any more offensive operations.

Main Idea CONNECTIONS

Why was the Battle of Midway an important victory for the Allies?

The Battle of Guadalcanal The victory at Midway allowed the Allies to take the offensive in the Pacific. Their first goal was to capture Guadalcanal in the Solomon Islands. When more than 11,000 marines landed on

This eerie scene of Guadalcanal, painted by Kerr Eby, is called *Ghost Trail*. **Geography** What was the geographical challenge of the Battle of Guadalcanal?

RESOURCE OPTIONS

Media and Technology

AmericanHeritage® **CD-ROM**

Time Tour Prosperity, Depression, and War: World War II

Answer to . . .

Main Idea Connections It destroyed Japan's ability to launch offensive operations.

Viewing History A dense jungle in which the enemy was easily hidden.

Although it was the scene of a brutal battle, Guadalcanal Island also saw its share of gentler heroes. One was Father Frederick Gehring, Chaplain to the 1st Division of the Marine Corps. He achieved modest fame for acting as a surrogate father to a 6-year old orphan, left to die in the wake of a Japanese attack on a remote village. As he nursed her back to health, the girl came to the attention of news reporters on the island, and she became a popular symbol of hope during the dark, early days of the war. Long after the battle, Father Gehring continued to help the girl, finding her a family to live with, and even serving as priest at her wedding.

ACTIVITY
LEARNING STYLES

Ask students to find out about and visit World War II memorials in your community. Students also might interview a veteran of the war (possibly through contacting the local VFW post), and ask questions about his or her branch of service, locations of service, assignments, rank, and conditions experienced. Have them report to the class what they have learned. *(Auditory, Verbal/Linguistic, Interpersonal)*

Answer to . . .

Map Skills The arrows leading from the Hawaiian Islands show that Pearl Harbor was the base from which Allied initiatives were launched in the Pacific.

---

the island in August 1942, some 2,200 Japanese fled into the jungle. Months of fighting followed. By November the American navy controlled the waters around Guadalcanal.

The **Battle of Guadalcanal** provided the marines with their first taste of jungle warfare. As they slogged through swamps, forded rivers, and hacked through tangles of vines, they frequently encountered enemy units. The marines made easy targets for Japanese snipers hidden in the underbrush or in the tops of palm trees. When Japan's forces finally slipped off the island in February 1943, their withdrawal went undetected until the marines discovered their empty boats on the beach.

Struggle for the Islands

From Guadalcanal, American forces began island-hopping, a strategy of selectively attacking or bypassing specific enemy-held islands. The Japanese fiercely defended their positions.

Both sides suffered heavy casualties before the Allies won the war in 1945.

Island-Hopping in the Pacific In 1943 and 1944 the Allies pushed north from Australia and west across the central Pacific. As forces under General MacArthur and Admiral William Halsey leapfrogged through the Solomon Islands, other Americans led by Admiral Nimitz began a similar campaign in the Gilbert Islands. After seizing the island of Tarawa, Nimitz used it to launch bombing raids on Japan's bases in the Marshall Islands. By February 1944, these attacks had crippled Japanese air power. This allowed Nimitz's forces to seize Kwajalein and Eniwetok at the northwest end of the island group.

From the Marshalls, Nimitz captured parts of the Mariana Islands in June. American long-range bombers were able to reach Japan from this location. By the end of 1944, American planes were dropping tons of explosives on Japanese cities.

Allied Advances in the Pacific, 1942–1945

General Douglas MacArthur (left) was Allied commander of the southwest Pacific during World War II. **Location** What does the map reveal about why the Japanese attacked Pearl Harbor in 1941?

RESOURCE OPTIONS

Teaching Resources

Primary Source Activity Guadalcanal, Learning with Documents folder, p. 30

The Philippines Campaign As American forces pushed forward in the summer of 1944, military planners decided to bypass the Philippine Islands. MacArthur vigorously opposed this strategy, claiming that the United States had an obligation to free the Filipino people. The general's arguments convinced Roosevelt, who reversed the decision.

In mid-October, some 160,000 American troops invaded the Philippine island of Leyte. After the beach was secure, General MacArthur dramatically waded ashore from a landing craft. As news cameras recorded the historic event, MacArthur proclaimed, "People of the Philippines, I have returned."

While American troops fought their way inland, the greatest naval battle in world history developed off the coast. More than 280 warships were engaged during the three-day Battle of Leyte Gulf. The Japanese high command directed nearly every warship still afloat to attack the enemy. This battle saw the first use of *kamikazes,* or suicide planes.[†] Japanese pilots deliberately crashed their aircraft, which were heavily loaded with bombs, into their targets. Despite this tactic, the Japanese were badly beaten and their navy was virtually destroyed.

Japanese land forces continued to resist, however. In the more than two months it took American troops to control Leyte, some 80,000 Japanese defenders were killed. Fewer than 1,000 Japanese surrendered. The battle for Manila, the Philippines' capital city, on the island of Luzon, was equally hard fought. The nearly month-long struggle left most of Manila in ruins and some 100,000 Filipino civilians dead. Not until June 1945 were the Philippines securely in Allied hands.

Iwo Jima and Okinawa

The **Battle of Iwo Jima** was one of the bloodiest of the war. The struggle for this tiny volcanic island, less than 700 miles from Japan, was both long and intense. The island's steep rocky slopes were honeycombed with caves and tunnels. More than 600 guns, many encased in concrete bunkers, were protected by the natural terrain. In November 1944, American bombers, based in the recently conquered Marianas, began to pound Iwo Jima from the air. For 74 days

---

[†] The term *kamikaze* means "divine wind" and refers to a typhoon which reputedly saved Japan in 1281 by destroying a Mongol fleet that was sailing to invade the islands.

American planes and warships poured nearly 7,000 tons of bombs and more than 20,000 shells onto Iwo Jima's defenders.

In mid-February 1945, marines stormed the beaches from the ships offshore. They encountered furious resistance from the Japanese. After three days of combat, the marines had advanced only about 700 yards inland. Eventually nearly 110,000 American troops were involved in the campaign. Although fewer than 25,000 Japanese opposed the Americans, it took almost a month for the marines to secure the island. The enemy fought virtually to the last defender. Only 216 Japanese were taken prisoner.

The American forces suffered an estimated 25,000 casualties in capturing this 14-square-mile island. Twenty-seven Medals of Honor were awarded for actions on Iwo Jima, more than in any other single operation of the war. Admiral Nimitz described the island as a place where "uncommon valor was a common virtue."

The **Battle of Okinawa,** fought from April to June 1945, was equally bloody. Nearly 100,000 defenders occupied this island, which was little more than 350 miles from Japan itself. The Japanese troops on Okinawa knew they were the last obstacle to an Allied invasion of the Japanese home islands. Many had pledged to fight to the death to prevent their homeland from falling.

The American and British force amassed at Okinawa was second in size only to the

---

FACT Finder

World War II Deaths

Country	Military Deaths	Civilian Deaths	Total Deaths
Axis			
Germany	3,250,000	2,350,000	5,600,000
Italy	226,900	60,000	286,900
Japan	1,740,000	393,400	2,133,400
Allies			
France	122,000	470,000	592,000
Great Britain	305,800	60,600	366,400
United States	405,400	—	405,400
Soviet Union	11,000,000	6,700,000	17,700,000

Source: *World War II: A Statistical Survey,* by John Ellis

Interpreting Tables Accurate death tolls are hard to determine, and figures vary widely. Scholars do not dispute, however, the horrific human cost of the war. **Culture** *Which nation suffered the greatest human loss?*

Answer to . . .

Interpreting Tables The Soviet Union.

Normandy invasion in Europe. Some 1,300 warships and more than 180,000 combat troops were gathered to drive the enemy from the island. Japanese pilots flew nearly 2,000 *kamikaze* attacks against this fleet. On the island, defenders made equally desperate *banzai* charges—attacks designed to kill as many of the enemy as possible while dying in battle.

One GI described the long, hard-fought campaign to take Okinawa:

AMERICAN VOICES "Our attack pattern was: barrage a hill with bombs and shells, move up the foot soldiers, hold it against counterattacks, fight down the reverse slope, then start on the next one. We would attack during the day, dig in for the night—not for sleep, but for safety. A hole was never deep enough when the Japanese started their barrage. And then, at night, they would come, a screaming banzai or a single shadow."

—*An American GI at Okinawa*

In June, when the Japanese resistance finally ended after almost three months, only 7,200 defenders remained to surrender. For American forces, nearly 50,000 casualties made the Battle of Okinawa the costliest engagement of the Pacific war. At long last, however, the way was open for an invasion of Japan.

The Manhattan Project

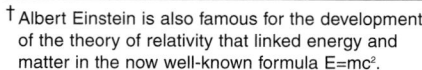

After the grueling battles at Iwo Jima and Okinawa, American soldiers began to prepare themselves for the invasion of Japan. They knew how costly such an invasion would be. Unknown to them, however, work was nearly done on a bomb that would make the invasion unnecessary.

The story begins in August 1939, when President Roosevelt received a letter from Albert Einstein, a brilliant Jewish physicist who had sought refuge in America from the Nazis.† In his letter, Einstein suggested that an incredibly powerful new type of bomb could be built. He hinted that the Germans were already at work on such a weapon. Roosevelt,

Physicist Albert Einstein

---
† Albert Einstein is also famous for the development of the theory of relativity that linked energy and matter in the now well-known formula $E=mc^2$.

concerned that Germany not develop this weapon first, organized the top secret **Manhattan Project** to develop such a bomb.

Scientists had already succeeded in splitting the nucleus of the uranium atom. However, to make an atomic bomb they had to create a controlled chain reaction. In such a reaction, particles released from the splitting of one atom would cause another atom to break apart, and so on. The theory was that the energy released when so many atoms were split would produce a massive explosion. In 1942, Enrico Fermi, a scientist who had left Fascist Italy, accomplished such a chain reaction in a laboratory at the University of Chicago.

On July 16, 1945, Manhattan Project scientists field-tested Fermi's work. In the desert of New Mexico they detonated the world's first atomic bomb. With a blinding flash of light, the explosion blew a huge crater in the earth and shattered windows some 125 miles away. As he watched, J. Robert Oppenheimer, who headed the building of the bomb, remembered the words of the *Bhagavad Gita,* the Hindu holy book: "Now I am become Death, the destroyer of worlds."

The Decision to Drop the Bomb Once the bomb was ready, the question became whether to use it. Other courses of action existed for bringing an end to the war. Allied planners had already worked out plans for a massive invasion of Japan. However, Japanese resistance to an attack on their home islands was expected to be even greater than it had been in the rest of the Pacific.

A naval blockade or continued conventional bombing could also help defeat Japan. A demonstration of the new weapon on some deserted island might show the Japanese the atomic bomb's awesome power. Some diplomats believed that Japan might give up more quickly if the United States softened its insistence on an unconditional surrender.

An advisory group of scientists, military leaders, and government officials, called the Interim Committee, formed in the spring of 1945. The committee members debated these ideas and many others. In the end, they found themselves unwilling to recommend any of the alternatives. The heavy American casualties at Iwo Jima and Okinawa were a factor in the committee's support for using the bomb.

Although the recommendation was unanimous, many other scientists who had worked on the bomb's development disagreed with the Interim Committee's endorsement of its use. The final decision, however, rested with the President. That burden fell on Harry S. Truman, President for barely three months after Roosevelt's sudden death in April 1945. Truman had no difficulty making up his mind. He considered the bomb to be a military weapon and had no doubt that it should be used. Despite the controversy that later arose over whether the bombing was justified, Truman never regretted his decision. "You should do your weeping at Pearl Harbor," he said to his critics in 1963.

Japan Surrenders On August 6, 1945, an American plane dropped an atomic bomb on Hiroshima, a city in southern Japan and the site of a large army base. No one knows for sure how many people were killed. The official Japanese estimate is that 140,000 died in the explosion or within a few months from burns or radiation poisoning. Thousands of others survived, but with horrible burns. Some 90 percent of the city's buildings were damaged or totally destroyed. A Hiroshima resident described the scene after the bombing as follows:

> **"**Wherever you went, you didn't bother to take the roads. Everything was flat, nothing was standing, no gates, pillars, walls, or fences. You walked in a straight line to where you wanted to go. Practically everywhere you came across small bones that had been left behind.**"**
>
> —*Hiroshima survivor*

A moment before the bomb code-named "Little Boy" leveled Hiroshima, the American GI above would have been standing in the midst of a thriving city. *Science and Technology How was the atomic bomb different from other war technology?*

Three days later a second bomb, dropped on Nagasaki, produced similar devastation, disfigurement, and death. The Japanese people were stunned by these developments. On August 14, the government of Japan accepted the American terms for surrender. The next day Americans celebrated what appeared to be the end of the war. The formal surrender agreement was signed on September 2, 1945, in a ceremony aboard the U.S.S. *Missouri* in Tokyo Bay. The long and destructive war had finally come to an end.

SECTION 3 REVIEW

Comprehension

1. **Key Terms** Define: (a) Bataan Death March; (b) Battle of the Coral Sea; (c) Battle of Midway; (d) Battle of Guadalcanal; (e) *kamikaze;* (f) Battle of Iwo Jima; (g) Battle of Okinawa; (h) Manhattan Project.

2. **Summarizing the Main Idea** Which two battles changed the course of the war in the Pacific?

3. **Organizing Information** Use information from the section to create a chart that identifies the Allied successes in the Pacific from 1943 to 1945.

Critical Thinking

4. **Analyzing Time Lines** Review the time line at the start of the section. Write a sentence or phrase that connects each entry to the one that follows it.

5. **Identifying Alternatives** What were some of the alternatives to dropping the atomic bomb on Japan?

Writing Activity

6. **Writing an Expository Essay** Write a brief essay that explains why the Japanese were able to advance through the Pacific so easily in 1941 and 1942. Also note how the Allies succeeded in changing the momentum of the war.

SKILLS FOR LIFE

Historical Evidence
Examining Photographs

Focus Analyze a photograph as historical evidence, taking into account the point of view of the photographer.

Instruct If possible, display collections of World War II photographs. Ask students to note the subjects, background, and qualities of light and mood in the photographs. Encourage them to try to determine the style or point of view of the photographer. Discuss the importance of being able to analyze a photographer's point of view in learning about a particular period in history.

Extend See the Skills for Life Activity in the Resource Options below.

Answers

1. (a) A group of American soldiers raising an American flag on a debris-covered hill. (b) Victory after struggle. (c) After, as the soldiers raising the flag implies that they have won the battle.

2. (a) Victory, exhaustion, struggle. (b) The dishevelment of the soldiers and disarray of the land; the men struggling against the wind to right the flag; their position on the top of a hill. (c) Black and white photos are less detailed and more abstract. They may influence the mood of a photograph—more serious, "classic," historical, and artistic. (d) Rosenthal's choices might have included where to position himself relative to the soldiers, at which point in the flag raising to take the picture, and whether to take a close-up shot or one from a distance.

3. (a) They might be proud of the soldiers, proud of their country, and they may feel patriotic. (b) They convey an emotion that written sources often lack.

TEST FOR SUCCESS

It is realistic but incomplete. Ideally, one would have access to both text and pictures for a full account.

Examining Photographs

Photographs are a form of visual evidence that can provide valuable information about an event or historical period. They show what people or places in recent history looked like and can document momentous occasions. Photographers, however, like other observers of events, have their own points of view. Therefore, you must analyze their photographs carefully.

By their choice of subject, lighting, and camera angle, photographers can influence what is seen and how it is perceived. They may choose to photograph a scene that strikes them as interesting, dramatic, or revealing but that, in reality, is not typical or representative. Photographers may also distort the appearance of objects in their pictures to create an illusion or convey a particular mood. By making these choices, photographers affect what may be learned from their pictures.

The photograph below, taken by Joe Rosenthal, is one of the most famous photographs taken during World War II. The photograph shows victorious United States Marines hoisting the American flag on the Pacific island of Iwo Jima. Use the following steps to analyze and evaluate the photograph.

1. *Study the photograph to identify the subject.* Look at the photograph as a whole, then study the details.

(a) What do you see in the picture? (b) What broad subject does the photograph seem to illustrate? (c) Was the photograph likely taken before, during, or after a battle? Explain.

2. *Analyze the reliability of the photograph as a source of information.* (a) What mood or emotion is captured in this photograph? (b) What aspects of the photograph capture this mood? (c) Is it significant that this photo is in black and white, not color? Explain. (d) What role does the photographer play in shaping this image? What choices might he have made before taking the picture?

3. *Study the photograph to learn more about the historical period.* Refer to the photograph and what you have read about World War II to answer the following questions. (a) How might Americans back home have reacted to this photograph? (b) What can photographs such as this one contribute to knowledge of an event that written sources cannot?

TEST FOR SUCCESS

From what you have read in this chapter about the fighting in the Pacific islands during World War II, do you think this photograph presents a realistic picture of the war? Explain.

RESOURCE OPTIONS

Teaching Resources

Skills for Life Activity Units 7–8 folder, p. 56, provides further opportunity for students to determine a photographer's intent and learn other information from a photograph.

| 1935 Nazis pass the Nuremberg Laws | 1937 Jewish businesses forcibly "Aryanized." | 1938 Kristallnacht violence results in destruction of Jewish synagogues and businesses | 1942 The "final solution" announced at Wannsee Conference | 1943 Warsaw ghetto uprising | 1944 Roosevelt creates the War Refugee Board | 1945 Allied troops liberate concentration camps |

1935   **1940**   **1945**

4 The Holocaust

SECTION PREVIEW

Objectives

1. Explain how persecution of Jews and other minorities increased in Germany under the Nazis during the 1930s.
2. Describe how the Nazis carried out their plans for genocide.
3. *Key Terms* Holocaust; anti-Semitism; concentration camp; *Kristallnacht;* Wannsee Conference; death camp; War Refugee Board.

Main Idea

During World War II, the Nazis carried out a brutal plan that resulted in the deaths of 6 million Jews and millions of other victims.

Reading Strategy

Arranging Events in Order As you read the section, create a time line of the events related to the Holocaust. Write a sentence to describe each event.

When Adolf Hitler came to power in 1933, he set about implementing the Nazi philosophy outlined in his book *Mein Kampf.* Chief among his goals was the removal of so-called "non-Aryans," in particular the Jews.

No persecution of Jews in world history equals the extent and brutality of the **Holocaust,** Nazi Germany's systematic murder of European Jews. In all, some six million Jews, about two thirds of Europe's Jewish population, had been massacred by the end of World War II. Some five to six million other people also died in Nazi captivity.

The Start of Persecution

Theories that European peoples, so-called Aryans, were superior to Middle Eastern peoples called Semites had developed in Germany in the mid-1800s. (Semitic peoples include Arabs, Ethiopians, and other Middle Eastern and North African groups, as well as Jews.) Although these theories were rejected by all responsible scholars at the time, others used them to justify continued persecution. By the 1880s **anti-Semitism** had come to mean hostility toward Jews. When the Nazi party gained control of Germany's government in 1933, anti-Semitism became the official policy of the nation.

The Nazis Take Action Under Nazi rule, German citizens were encouraged to stop patronizing Jewish businesses. In 1935, the Nazis passed the Nuremberg Laws, stripping Jews of their German citizenship and forbidding marriage between Jews and non-Jews.

In 1937 and 1938 the Nazis began a program to "Aryanize" Jewish businesses. They required Jews to register their property and dismissed Jewish employees and managers. Jewish doctors were banned from treating non-Jews. All German people had to carry identity cards. The Nazi government marked Jews' cards with a red letter "J" and gave all Jews new middle names—"Sarah" for women and "Israel" for men. This practice made it easier for the police to identify Jews.

When the Nazis came to power, they organized the SA, a police unit charged with silencing opposition to the Nazis. Later, Hitler formed the SS, an elite guard that became the private army of the Nazi party. In addition, a Secret

Nazis singled out Jews for persecution by forcing them to wear yellow Stars of David like this one.

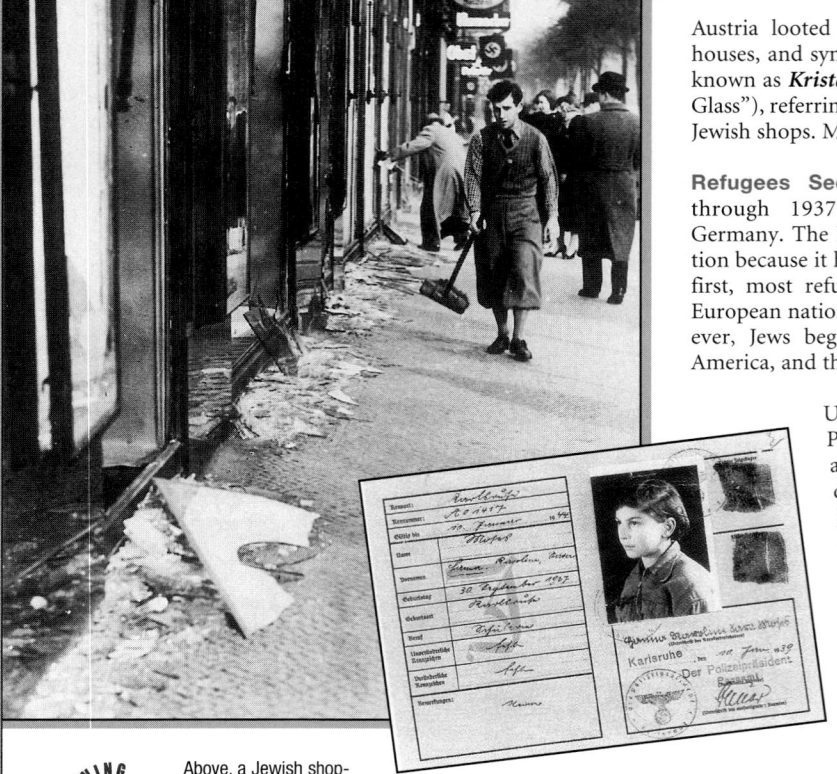

Austria looted and destroyed Jewish stores, houses, and synagogues. The incident became known as *Kristallnacht* ("Night of the Broken Glass"), referring to the broken windows of the Jewish shops. Mass arrests of Jews followed.

Refugees Seek an Escape From 1933 through 1937 about 130,000 Jews fled Germany. The Nazis encouraged this emigration because it helped to achieve their plan. At first, most refugees merely moved to other European nations. As the numbers grew, however, Jews began to go to Palestine, Latin America, and the United States.

Responding to calls for the United States to take action, President Roosevelt called for an international conference to discuss the growing numbers of Jewish refugees. However, the Evian Conference, held in France in July 1938, failed to deal with the situation. With the exception of the Dominican Republic, none of the 29 nations represented, including the United States, was willing to ease its immigration laws.

Above, a Jewish shopkeeper sweeps up shop windows left shattered by *Kristallnacht.* At right, the "J" stamp on this girl's identification paper identifies her as Jewish. *Government In what other ways did the Nazis organize the persecution of Jews?*

From Murder to Genocide

In 1939, the invasion of Poland brought some 2 million Jews under German control. In Warsaw over 350,000 Jews, about 30 percent of the Polish capital's population, were rounded up and confined in less than 3 percent of the city's area. The Warsaw ghetto was sealed off by a wall topped with barbed wire. Guards prevented movement between the ghetto and the rest of the city. Hunger, overcrowding, and a lack of sanitation brought on disease. The death rate soared as Jews were placed in ghettos throughout Poland and Eastern Europe.

The *Einsatzgruppen* Special forces called the *Einsatzgruppen,* or mobile killing units, were sent to Poland in 1939. There they systematically murdered members of Poland's upper class, along with intellectuals, priests, and influential Jews. In 1941 the *Einsatzgruppen* carried out Hitler's orders to eliminate Communist political leaders and Jews during the invasion of the Soviet Union.

While Hitler accepted mass murder by firing squad as appropriate for a war zone, he felt the method was not suitable for nations already

State Police, or Gestapo, was formed to identify and pursue those people who did not follow the new laws of the Nazi regime. Political enemies were thrown into hastily built "camps" in empty warehouses and factories guarded by SS troops.

Typically, **concentration camps** are places where prisoners of war and political prisoners are confined, usually under harsh conditions. However, the Nazi camps soon held many other people considered by them to be "undesirable," including the homeless, homosexuals, Jehovah's Witnesses, and persons with mental and physical disabilities. By the late 1930s, Gypsies were also being imprisoned.

Kristallnacht Organized attacks on Jews began in early 1938, after Hitler's annexation of Austria. On the night of November 9–10, 1938, Nazi thugs throughout Germany and conquered. In January 1942, government officials met at the **Wannsee Conference** outside Berlin to announce a plan for what one Nazi leader called the "final solution to the Jewish question." The plan called for establishing a number of special concentration camps in rural areas of Germany and elsewhere. There, the genocide, or deliberate destruction of Europe's Jewish population, was to be carried out.

The Death Camps In 1941 the Nazis had begun experimenting on Jews and Soviet prisoners of war to determine the most efficient way of killing people. They chose a poison gas, called Zyklon B, to be administered in specially designed chambers disguised as showers. In December 1941 a "model" operation was opened in western Poland. On the first day, some 2,300 Jews were killed.

Eventually the Nazis built six camps in Poland. Unlike the earlier concentration camps, where prisoners were forced to perform hard labor, these **death camps** existed only for mass murder. Jews were crammed into trains and transported to these extermination centers. Most Jews did not know where they were going when they boarded the trains.

On arrival at the camps, prisoners were organized into a line and quickly inspected. The elderly, most women with children, and those who looked too weak to work were herded into gas chambers and killed. Guards forced prisoners to carry the dead to the crematoria, where the bodies were burned in huge ovens.

Those who escaped immediate death at the extermination camps endured almost unbearable conditions. Men and women alike had their heads shaved and a registration number tattooed on their arms. Given only one set of clothes, prisoners were interned in crowded, unheated barracks. There were no bathrooms or beds. Food was usually a thin, foul-tasting soup made with rotten vegetables. Diseases swept through the camps and claimed many who were weakened by harsh labor and the lack of food. Periodic "selections" took place where the weak and ill were sent to the gas chamber.

The number of people killed in the labor and death camps is staggering. About 43,000 prisoners perished at Germany's Buchenwald labor camp, between 1937 and 1945. However, this number pales in comparison to the genocide at Auschwitz, a death camp in Poland. There, more victims were murdered than anywhere else—as many as 1.5 million people, some 90 percent of them Jews.

Fighting Back Some Jews, both in and outside the camps, fiercely resisted the Nazis. In April 1943, the Warsaw ghetto revolted against deportation to the death camp Treblinka. For some 27 days about 700 Jews armed with little more than pistols and homemade bombs held out against more than 2,000 Germans with tanks.

Revolts also erupted in the camps themselves. In August 1943, rioting Jews damaged Treblinka so badly that it had to be closed. Escape was the most common form of resistance, however. Most attempts failed, but a few people managed to bring word of the death camps to the outside world.

Rescue and Liberation American newspapers showed little interest in the Holocaust during the war years. In addition, the Jewish community in the United States was ineffective in rousing the government to take action toward rescuing Jews. Immigration quotas were not raised and existing quotas for Jews were not filled.

Finally, in January 1944, over the objection of the State Department, Roosevelt created the

Main Idea CONNECTIONS

What were conditions like in the camps?

FACT Finder — Estimated Jewish Losses in the Holocaust

Country	Estimated Minimum Loss	Percentage of Initial Jewish Population Lost
Poland	2,900,000	88–91%
Soviet Union	1,000,000	33–36%
Hungary	550,000	67–69%
Romania	271,000	44–47%
Czechoslovakia	146,150	71%
Lithuania	140,000	83–85%
Germany	134,500	24–25%
Netherlands	100,000	71%
France	77,320	22%
Latvia	70,000	77–78%
Greece	60,000	78–87%
Yugoslavia	56,200	72–81%
Austria	50,000	27%
Belgium	28,900	44%
Italy	7,680	17%

Interpreting Tables The horror of the Holocaust touched many nations. *Culture* Which country do you think was most altered by the Holocaust?

RESOURCE OPTIONS

American Literature

Connections to American Literature Elie Wiesel, *Night,* pp. 1086–1087

Answer to . . .

Main Idea Connections People not immediately killed were starved and subjected to disease and filthy living conditions. They always faced the threat of extermination.
Interpreting Tables Poland

The haunted faces of these starving prisoners reflect the horrors they experienced in a concentration camp in Ebensee, Austria. *Foreign Relations How did camp liberation lead to the Nuremberg Trials?*

at an army camp in Oswego, New York, but Roosevelt would not expand the program.[†]

As Allied armies advanced in late 1944, the Nazis abandoned concentration camps outside Germany and moved their prisoners to camps on German soil. In May 1945, as Germany collapsed, camp guards fled and American troops for the first time were able to witness the horrors of the Holocaust. A young soldier described the conditions he discovered as he entered the barracks at Buchenwald:

AMERICAN VOICES "The odor was so bad I backed up, but I looked at a bottom bunk and there I saw one man. He was too weak to get up; he could just barely turn his head. . . . He looked like a skeleton; and his eyes were deep set. He didn't utter a sound; he just looked at me with those eyes, and they still haunt me today."

—*Leon Bass, American soldier*

Sickened by the death camps, in November 1945 the Allies placed 24 leading Nazis on trial for crimes against humanity. At the Nuremberg Trials 12 of them received the death sentence. More significant than the number of convictions, the trials established an important principle—the idea that individuals were responsible for their own actions. No longer could war criminals escape punishment by saying they were only "following orders."

[†] A larger rescue was carried out by a single individual. Oskar Schindler was a Nazi industrialist who purposely employed some 1,300 Jews in his factories in Poland and Czechoslovakia. Their jobs saved them from being shipped to the gas chambers.

War Refugee Board (WRB) to try to help people threatened with murder by the Nazis. In a short time, its programs helped save some 200,000 lives. With WRB funding, for example, Swedish diplomat Raoul Wallenberg rescued thousands of Hungarian Jews by issuing them special Swedish passports. Wallenberg disappeared into Soviet-controlled Eastern Europe after the war. After he disappeared, Congress made Wallenberg an honorary U.S. citizen for his humanitarian war work.

A WRB effort to bring Jews to America was less successful. Some 1,000 refugees were held

SECTION 4 REVIEW

Comprehension

1. *Key Terms* Define: (a) Holocaust; (b) anti-Semitism; (c) concentration camp; (d) *Kristallnacht*; (e) Wannsee Conference; (f) death camp; (g) War Refugee Board.

2. *Summarizing the Main Idea* What was the Holocaust?

3. *Organizing Information* Create a web diagram that organizes information about Nazi persecution of Jews and others in Germany during the 1930s. In the center circle write *Nazi Persecution Grows*. Include at least four supporting details in the surrounding circles.

Critical Thinking

4. *Analyzing Time Lines* Review the time line at the start of the section. Explain how the first entry made it easier for the third to take place.

5. *Identifying Central Issues* How did the Nazis implement their plans for genocide?

Writing Activity

6. *Writing an Expository Essay* Several survivors of the Nazi concentration camps wrote books describing their experiences in the camps. Research and write an essay that relates the story of one survivor.

Genocide Has Happened Again

The threat of genocide did not end with the defeat of Nazi Germany. It continues to deserve worldwide attention today.

Nazis rounding up Jewish families

Entire families tortured to death. Children beaten savagely. Elderly men and women shot and buried in mass graves. In this chapter you read about the horrors of the Holocaust. Nazi Germany murdered an estimated 6 million Jews, as well as some 5 to 6 million Slavs, gypsies, Communists, homosexuals, and disabled people. Only the Allies' conquest of Germany stopped the mass killing.

In this century, and even in your own lifetime, there have been other mass murders. Between 1915 and 1923, for example, hundreds of thousands of Armenians were killed by the Turkish government. In Cambodia in the 1970s, the Communist Khmer Rouge government killed an estimated 1 million people. In 1994, Hutu soldiers and civilians in the African nation of Rwanda slaughtered at least 1 million men, women, and children of a rival tribe, the Tutsi.

Genocide was also committed during a civil war in Bosnia between 1992 and 1995. The war, fueled by long-standing ethnic and religious hatreds, claimed the lives of roughly 200,000 Bosnian Muslims, Serbs, and Croats.

The Impact Today

International laws and tribunals have condemned genocide and punished those who take part in it. In 1948, the United Nations declared genocide a crime under international law. A number of Nazis charged with "crimes against humanity" were tried and executed at the Nuremberg Trials. (Only a fraction, however, of those who participated in the killing were prosecuted.) More recently, there have been efforts to bring to trial those who committed atrocities in the Bosnian war.

Unfortunately, prosecuting war criminals cannot bring back their victims or mend the lives of loved ones who survived them. Only changes in peoples' attitudes toward others can ensure that genocide will never happen again.

The Impact on You

Brainstorm with your classmates to create a list of places in the world where serious racial, ethnic, or religious hatreds exist today. Try to find out the history behind these conflicts by doing library research. Think of ways that people in those places could help ease the hatreds. Write a short essay on what individuals can do to create greater understanding among different peoples.

Rwandan refugees fleeing violence

RESOURCE OPTIONS

Teaching Resources

Why Study History? Activity Genocide Has Happened Again, found in the Why Study History? folder, p. 25, provides an activity to help students better understand the tragedy of genocide.

Media and Technology

 AmericanHeritage® CD-ROM
Time Tour Prosperity, Depression, and War: World War II

 Prentice Hall United States History Video Collection™ Volume 19
World War II

Class Discussion

Discuss with the class the history and ongoing threat of genocide. For a more thorough examination of the issue, see the activity folder in the Resource Options below.

ACTIVITY
STUDENT PARTICIPATION

Planning Humanitarian Help
Ask students to read the text. Then discuss strategies for aiding current victims of racial, ethnic, or religious hatred; for example:
- **a letter campaign**
- **a collection of clothes, toys, food, or money**
- **a public information drive**
- **involvement in an organization, such as the Red Cross or Oxfam**

Have students divide into groups to design a plan of action based on one of these strategies.

Follow up Students could discuss their plans and vote on executing one plan.

Using the Internet
Students can learn more about genocide by exploring links in the *America: Pathways to the Present* Web site at

http://www.Pathways.phschool.com

Assessment
See the Lesson Plans folder, pp. 24–27, for rubrics on assessing Class Participation Projects.

Key Terms

Have students refer to the definitions of key terms in the chapter to write sentences that show an understanding of the events of World War II.

Comprehension

1. Germany was suffering economically at the time, especially following the Great Depression. Hitler's autobiography and Nazi propaganda attracted Germans with their promises of stabilizing the economy and restoring the German empire.
2. President Roosevelt traded American ships to convoy supplies across the Atlantic; he also supported the Lend-Lease Act to provide war supplies to Britain.
3. Japan hoped to knock out the U.S. Pacific Fleet so that nothing would stand in the way of Japanese control of the Pacific.
4. The Navajos used their language to transmit secret messages by radio and telephone.
5. In Europe: the failed German invasion of the Soviet Union and the successful Allied offensives in North Africa and Italy. In the Pacific: the Allies won key strategic victories on the islands of Midway and Guadalcanal.
6. The invasion of Allied forces at German camps in Normandy on June 6, 1944. It was the largest landing by sea in history.
7. Dropping the atomic bombs ended the war.
8. To annihilate all Jews and other "undesirables" by gathering them in concentration camps and killing them.

Chapter Summary

The major concepts of Chapter 24 are presented below. See also the *Guide to the Essentials of American History* or *Interactive Student Tutorial CD-ROM,* which contains interactive review activities, time lines, helpful hints, and test practice for Chapter 24.

Reviewing the Main Ideas

German, Italian, and Japanese aggression in the 1930s led to war in Europe and Asia. Many Americans hoped that the United States could remain neutral. They quickly changed their minds after Japan bombed the American naval base at Pearl Harbor. At the end of the war, people around the world reacted in horror as they discovered the full extent of Nazi Germany's attempt to destroy the Jews of Europe.

Section 1: Prelude to Global War

Depressed economic conditions and a desire to build powerful nations led to the rise of dictators in Germany and Italy and eventually to a second global conflict.

Section 2: The Road to Victory in Europe

To secure victory in Europe, the Allies waged war in North Africa, Western Europe, and the Soviet Union between 1941 and 1945.

Section 3: The War in the Pacific

Fierce fighting and heavy casualties characterized the war in the Pacific Ocean as the Allied forces struggled to turn back Japanese advances.

Section 4: The Holocaust

During World War II, the Nazis carried out a brutal plan that resulted in the deaths of 6 million Jews and millions of other victims.

The threat of genocide did not end with the defeat of Nazi Germany. It continues to deserve worldwide attention today. Despite international laws condemning genocide, other mass killings have taken place in the twentieth century.

Key Terms

For each of the terms below, write a sentence explaining how it relates to this chapter.

1. Lend-Lease Act
2. Battle of Midway
3. Holocaust
4. Axis Powers
5. concentration camp
6. Yalta Conference
7. *Kristallnacht*
8. totalitarian
9. GI
10. Allies
11. D-Day

Comprehension

1. How did Hitler come to power in Germany?
2. How did the United States support the Allies with economic aid while staying out of the fighting?
3. Why did Japan attack Pearl Harbor?
4. What contribution did Native Americans make to the American military effort?
5. What events in Europe and the Pacific helped turn the tide in favor of the Allies?
6. What was the D-Day operation?
7. Why did the United States not have to invade Japan to end the war?
8. What was Hitler's "final solution"?

Using Graphic Organizers

On a separate piece of paper, copy the flowchart to organize information about the events of World War II. Add additional boxes if you need to. Begin your chart with the entry *1939: Germany invades Poland.* End with *May 1945: Germany surrenders; August 1945: Japan surrenders.*

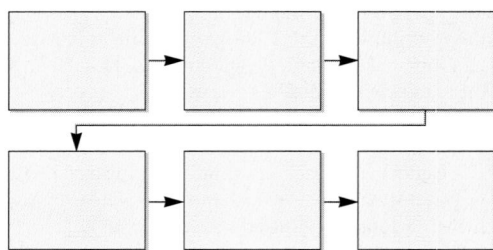

Using Graphic Organizers

- 1939: Germany invades Poland
- 1939: Britain and France declare war on Germany
- 1941: Japan attacks Pearl Harbor
- 1942: Red Army defeats Germans at Battle of Stalingrad
- 1943: Allies invade Western Europe
- May 1945: Germany surrenders
- August 1945: Japan surrenders

Analyzing Political Cartoons ▶

1. Analyze the images in the cartoon. (a) What do the two figures in the bed represent? (b) How do you know? (c) Who is the third figure joining them?

2. What is the common interest the three figures share?

3. Why is the "unexpected guest" joining the other two by circumstance?

Critical Thinking

1. *Applying the Chapter Skill* Turn to the photo on page 710. What can you learn about the Holocaust from this photograph?

2. *Expressing Problems Clearly* The Soviet Union fought on the Allied side during World War II, yet soon after became a bitter enemy of the United States. Give evidence to show that the seeds of conflict between the United States and the Soviet Union were already present during World War II.

3. *Demonstrating Reasoned Judgment* World War II propaganda influenced the way many Americans viewed the Japanese. List two reasons for American hostility toward the Japanese.

4. *Predicting Consequences* If Britain and France had not adopted a policy of appeasement, would Adolf Hitler have been as successful as he was in overrunning Europe?

DOWN WITH HITLER

INTERNET ACTIVITY

For your portfolio:
CREATE A GRAPH

Access Prentice Hall's *America: Pathways to the Present* site at **www.Pathways.phschool.com** for the specific URL to complete the activity. Additional resources and related Web sites are also available.

Create a bar graph showing the number of casualties the United States suffered in the Revolutionary War, the Civil War, World War I, and World War II. Which war claimed the most casualties? Why do you think this is so?

Connecting to Today

Essay Writing The horrible slaughter of six million Jews during the Holocaust is an example of genocide. Research and write an essay on a more recent case where one group tried to carry out a campaign of genocide against another ethnic group. In your essay, include the global community's reactions to the killings.

713

ANALYZING DOCUMENTS ◀ *INTERPRETING DATA*

Turn to the "American Voices" quotation on page 704.

1. Which phrase best describes the American campaign on Okinawa? (a) long and hard fought (b) easy (c) completely safe (d) over in one day

2. According to the description of the fighting, you can infer that the terrain on Okinawa was (a) flat and sandy. (b) heavily wooded. (c) rocky. (d) hilly.

3. **Writing** Write a brief paragraph describing how you think the GIs felt during the long nights on Okinawa.

INTERNET ACTIVITY

Graphs should clearly and accurately show the figures given, and conclusions should reflect an understanding of the graph and of topics discussed in the chapter.

Analyzing Political Cartoons

1. (a) England and the U.S. (b) By their caricatures and hats. (c) Stalin (Russia)
2. Defeat of Hitler.
3. Germany broke its nonaggression agreement with the Soviet Union, forcing it to join with the Allies.

Critical Thinking

1. Sample answer: That concentration camp victims were starved and horribly mistreated.
2. The nations had different ideas about what the postwar world should look like; the Soviets resented being exluded from the Manhattan Project; the United States had deployed the atomic bomb in part to demonstrate its strength to the Soviet Union.
3. Sample reasons: Americans felt bitterness toward the Japanese for the Americans they had killed in Pearl Harbor and the Pacific; propaganda stirred up racist feelings, making it easier to decide to use the atomic bomb.
4. Sample answer: Probably; Hitler was determined to build his empire, and France and Britain would have been no better prepared for war had they engaged in war with Germany earlier.

Analyzing Documents

1. a
2. d
3. Answers will vary, but might mention the constant threat of attack from *kamikaze* pilots or *banzai* charges.

Connecting to Today

Essays will vary, but should be supported with facts and should address topics introduced in the chapter.

World War II at Home, 1941–1945

Managing Time and Instruction

INSTRUCTION SUPPORT

These materials for instruction are provided for **each section** in the **Teaching Resources**. See **Units 7–8 folder for Enrichment Support:**

- Reproducible Lesson Plans in Lesson Plans folder • Learning Styles Lesson Plans in Learning Styles Lesson Plans folder • Big Idea Graphic Organizers in Big Idea Graphic Organizer folder
- Guided Reading and Review • Quizzes • Test Preparation Practice booklet

DAILY LESSON	ENRICHMENT SUPPORT
1 **The Shift to Wartime Production** (pp. 715–719)	• Visual Learning Activity, Campaigns on the Home Front, Learning with Documents folder, p. 67 • Critical Thinking Activity, Identifying Alternatives: Mobilizing a Wartime Labor Force, found on **Resource Pro**
2 **Daily Life on the Home Front** (pp. 720–723)	• Literature Activity, *How to Win Friends and Influence People,* Units 7–8 folder, p. 68 • Nystrom *Atlas of Our Country,* People on the Move, pp. 34–35 • Visual Learning Activity, "The Nature of the Enemy," found on **Resource Pro**
3 **Women and the War** (pp. 726–729)	• Primary Source Activity, Working Conditions for Women of Color, found on **Resource Pro** • Skills for Life Activity, Units 7–8 folder, p. 69
4 **The Struggle for Justice at Home** (pp. 731–736)	• Nystrom *Atlas of Our Country,* Later Expansion of the United States, pp. 32–33; People on the Move, pp. 34–35 • Literature Activity, *Black Boy,* found on **Resource Pro** • Biography, James Farmer, found on **Resource Pro** • Biography, Daniel K. Inouye, Units 7–8 folder, p. 65 • Comparing Primary Sources, On Japanese American Internment, Units 7–8 folder, pp. 66–67 • Primary Source Activity, Anti-Japanese Sentiment, Learning with Documents folder, p. 31 • Most Women Are in the Work Force, Why Study History? folder, p. 26

Running Out of Time?

- Use Tape 4, "Hot and Cold War, 1939–1960," from **Visions of America** videotapes series.
- Use Chapter 25 Summary from **Guide to the Essentials of American History** (English and Spanish).

Companion Web Site

The companion Web site offers online links for all chapter review activities. It also provides key content links and structured support for this chapter for both teachers and students.

http://www.Pathways.phschool.com

Teaching in the Information Age

Media and Technology

For the Student

Interactive Student Tutorial CD-ROM Chapter 25
Student Edition on Audiotape Chapter 25
American Heritage® CD-ROM
Guided Reading Audiotapes (English and Spanish) Chapter 25

For the Teacher

Resource Pro CD-ROM Chapter 25
Test Bank CD-ROM Chapter 25
Listening to Literature Audiotapes *Timeless Voices, Timeless Themes* "In a Station of the Metro" by Ezra Pound
Color Transparencies I-9

Assessment Options

Chapter Test Forms A&B Test Bank CD-ROM booklet
Test Bank CD-ROM Chapter 25
Standardized Test Preparation Handbook

Block Scheduling

Pacing Suggestions

For 90-minute Blocks

- Teach sections 1 and 2 using Transparency B-8 and the Global Connections note on p. 718 for class discussions.
- Teach sections 3 and 4 using the Big Idea Graphic Organizers from Teaching Resources and the Extended Class Periods Activity on p. 728.

Additional Resources

- Prentice Hall's **American History Block Scheduling Support File** covers over 40 major topics in American history. Included are lesson plans, strategies, primary sources, literature, biographies, Great Debates, art history, simulations, and songs.
- **Prentice Hall United States History Video Collection**™ contains 20 videotapes covering American history from beginnings to present.

Connections to American Literature

from Prentice Hall

Prentice Hall Literature *Timeless Voices, Timeless Themes* "Gold Glade" by Robert Penn Warren, p. 916

Additional Resources

For the Student

Miriam Frank, et al. *The Life and Times of Rosie the Riveter.* Clarity, 1982.

For the Teacher

Allan M. Winkler. *Home Front, U.S.A.: America During World War II.* Harlan Davidson, 1986.
Mary Penick Motley, ed. *The Invisible Soldier: The Experience of the Black Soldier, World War II.* Wayne State University Press, 1975.

Prentice Hall brings into the classroom the vast archives and scholarship of the nation's premier American history magazine. See "From the Archives of American Heritage®" and "About the Presidents" teaching notes in this chapter.

 History Alive!

Teacher's Curriculum Institute, in partnership with Prentice Hall, provides unique materials that engage students with diverse learning styles. See History Alive!® unit on The United States in World War II.

 Student Performance Pack

Ensures success in the three critical areas of Reading, Test Taking, and English Language Development with the following materials:
- Guide to the Essentials of American History in English and Spanish
- Guided Reading Audiotapes in English and Spanish
- Interactive Student Tutorial CD-ROM
- Test Preparation Handbook
- Test Preparation Practice booklet

CHAPTER 25
World War II at Home
1941–1945

Introducing the Chapter

World War II affected every aspect of American life, from jobs and wages to the kinds of food that appeared on the nation's dinner tables. Americans were asked to examine the ideals they were fighting for overseas and put them into practice, in as many ways as possible, at home.

Themes in American History

The theme for this chapter, Culture, is listed at the beginning of this unit. An alternate theme for the chapter is Government. To teach this unit thematically, you may wish to use the Prosperity, Depression, and War folder in American History Block Scheduling Support.

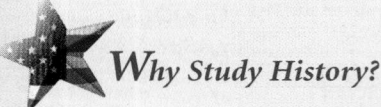 *Why Study History?*

Have students explore suggested ways of connecting the past to the present on page 737.

Answer to . . .

Viewing History Students should use this question as an aid in reading the chapter. A large number of people, especially women, were drawn into factory work to help make military materiel. Gasoline and other products were rationed, and a wave of patriotic involvement made many people purchase war bonds and plant victory gardens.

CHAPTER 25 World War II at Home
1941–1945

CHAPTER FOCUS

As war raged in Europe, the United States government faced the enormous challenge of mobilizing American businesses and civilians to help win the war. The government launched a massive campaign to remind people to conserve, participate, and sacrifice.

 The *Why Study History?* page at the end of this chapter explores the connection between women's work during World War II and their work today.

▲ **VIEWING HISTORY**
Men and women work side by side to produce war planes in this 1944 illustration from *The Saturday Evening Post*. *Culture* **How did the war change life at home?**

 RESOURCE OPTIONS

Teaching Resources

 Big Idea Graphic Organizer folder
Graphic summary of the main idea of the chapter.

 Learning Styles Lesson Plans folder
Alternate lesson plans for diverse learning styles for each chapter.

Media and Technology

AmericanHeritage® CD-ROM
Time Tour Prosperity, Depression, and War: World War II

Prentice Hall United States History Video Collection™ Volume 19
World War II

1941	1942	1943	1943
OPA sets limits on prices and rents	Income taxes are raised to finance war	FDR creates Office of War Mobilization	United Mine Workers call several strikes

1941   **1942**   **1943**   **1944**

1 The Shift to Wartime Production

SECTION PREVIEW

Objectives

1 Explain how American businesses mobilized for war.
2 Summarize how World War II affected the American work force.
3 List the methods the government used to finance the war.
4 *Key Terms* Define: Office of War Mobilization; Liberty ship; wildcat strike; war bond; deficit spending.

Main Idea

At the beginning of World War II, the government mobilized industries and workers to produce materials for the war.

Reading Strategy

Formulating Questions Before you read this section, look at the illustrations and then write one question for each of the main headings. Answer the questions as you read.

Supplying goods to the Allied forces at the start of World War II helped boost the American economy. The country began to emerge from the Depression as a result of this production. Industries were eager to start making cars, refrigerators, and washing machines again, and consumers were eager to buy them. For the sake of the war effort, however, the American economy soon had to convert full time to making war equipment.

Mobilizing the Economy for War

President Roosevelt understood that the outcome of the war ultimately depended on America's ability to produce enough bombers, tanks, uniforms, and other war materials. The war had destroyed many factories in Europe, cutting down the other Allies' production. Japan's conquests in the Pacific cut off supplies of rubber, oil, and tin.

The Government Steps In To meet the demand, FDR knew that the government would have to coordinate the production of American

businesses. Even before Pearl Harbor, new government agencies were dealing with the war economy. In April 1941, an executive order established the Office of Price Administration (OPA). Its job was to keep shortages from sending up prices and rents and causing inflation. Later the OPA oversaw rationing of scarce resources.

The War Production Board (WPB) was set up in January 1942 to direct the conversion of peacetime industries to those that made war goods. It quickly halted the production of hundreds of civilian consumer goods, from cars to lawn mowers to bird cages. The armed forces gave out contracts and scheduled production, but the WPB set priorities and allocated raw materials.

As the war went on, dozens of other agencies were set up to deal with war production, labor questions, and scarce resources. To

"At ease... for refreshment"

Many advertisements linked their products to wartime patriotism.

RESOURCE OPTIONS

Teaching Resources

📁 **Reproducible Lesson Plan** Lesson Plans folder, p. 135

📁 **Learning Styles Lesson Plan** Learning Styles Lesson Plans folder, p. 52

📁 **Big Idea Graphic Organizer** Big Idea Graphic Organizer folder, p. 107

📁 **Guided Reading and Review** Units 7–8 folder, p. 57

📁 **Visual Learning Activity** Campaigns on the Home Front, Learning with Documents folder, p. 67

The Shift to Wartime Production

Objectives
You may wish to call students' attention to the objectives in the Section Preview. The objectives are reflected in the main headings of the section.

Bellringer
Ask students to suppose they are President Roosevelt on December 8, 1941. What are the three most important things that must be done to prepare the country for war?

Reading Strategy
Formulating Questions Refer students to the Reading Strategy in the Section Preview. You may wish to have volunteers ask the class their questions as a way to review content.

LESSON PLAN

Connecting to the Main Idea

1. Focus Explain that as factories shifted into wartime production, new opportunities arose for workers and businesses. Ask students how these opportunities changed American life.

2. Instruct Discuss why it was crucial for American industries to begin making war supplies rather than consumer goods. What happened in Europe and in the Pacific to make it necessary for the United States to become the "arsenal of democracy"? Have students restate this slogan in their own words: "Production lines are battle lines."

Ask students how the government financed the war. What role did deficit spending play? Why did unemployment drop after the country entered the war?

3. Close The mobilization of industry and workers to manufacture supplies for the war helped to end the Depression. The next section describes what daily life was like for Americans during World War II.

Source: *Miracle of World War II: How American Industry Made Victory Possible*, by Francis Walton

Source: *Historical Statistics of the United States, Colonial Times to 1970*

 Interpreting Graphs Many industries were converted to military production during World War II. *Economics What overall trends in auto production and military aircraft production do these graphs show?*

centralize those agencies, in May 1943 the President organized a superagency, the **Office of War Mobilization.** James F. Byrnes, a long-time member of Congress and close presidential adviser, headed it. Working from a makeshift office in the White House, Byrnes had such broad authority that he was often called the "assistant president." Some people said that Byrnes ran the country while FDR ran the war.

Industries Convert As production of consumer goods stopped, factories converted to war production. Shirt factories made mosquito netting. Typewriter plants made machine guns. On February 1, 1942, after the last cars rolled off the assembly lines, workers began converting automobile factories to produce bombers. The OPA took over the 500,000 new cars in stock. During the war years, it carefully rationed out cars to people who really needed them, such as country doctors.

In addition to converting plants, the Ford Motor Company built a huge new factory to make B-24 Liberator bombers, using the assembly-line techniques used for cars. When the Willow Run plant, near Ann Arbor, Michigan, opened in 1942, it was the largest factory space in the world. The assembly line stretched for a mile across what was once a flat meadowland. Willow Run had production problems at first, but by late 1943 it was building 340 planes a month.

Entrepreneurs in other industries also revolutionized production. Henry J. Kaiser introduced mass production techniques to shipbuilding and set production speed records. Instead of building a ship from the keel up,

Welder Benny Chan gives the "V for Victory" sign. *Culture Why was patriotism linked to industry?*

Kaiser's engineers built sections of the ship in different parts of the shipyard. As huge cranes brought in the finished sections, welders put them together. The Kaiser shipyards also speeded up operations with crews that specialized in making one part, such as bows or bulkheads (walls).

The vessels that made Kaiser famous were called **Liberty ships** (though other shipyards also built them). They were large, sturdy merchant ships that usually carried supplies or troops, but were sometimes converted to hospital ships or other uses. In 1941 it took an average of 150 days to build one Liberty ship. As the war went on, Kaiser shipyards cut building time to an average of 46 days and even set a record of 4 days.

New Business Approaches War production demanded new approaches to business. As Secretary of War Henry L. Stimson put it, "If you are going to try to go to war, or to prepare for war, in a capitalist country, you have to let business make money out of the process." To guarantee profits, the government established the "cost-plus" system for military contracts. The military paid development and production costs, plus a percentage of costs as profit. Pride and patriotism also provided industry leaders with motivation. Factories with good production records could fly pennants bearing the Army-Navy "E" for Excellent.

Thousands of business executives went to Washington to work in the new government agencies that were coordinating war production. As government employees, they received a token "dollar-a-year" salary, while remaining on their own companies' payrolls.

Some entrepreneurs found profitable new markets for their products during the war. Robert Woodruff, head of Coca-Cola, declared in December 1941: "We will see that every man in uniform gets a bottle of Coca-Cola for five cents wherever he is and whatever it costs [the company]." By the time the war was over, American troops had drunk 5 billion bottles of Coca-Cola. At the same time, Woodruff's company had established a future "army" of civilian consumers, those who had enjoyed the drink while in uniform.

The "Great Arsenal of Democracy" In December 1940, Franklin Roosevelt had told Americans that the country must become "the great arsenal of democracy." In each year of war, the United States raised its production

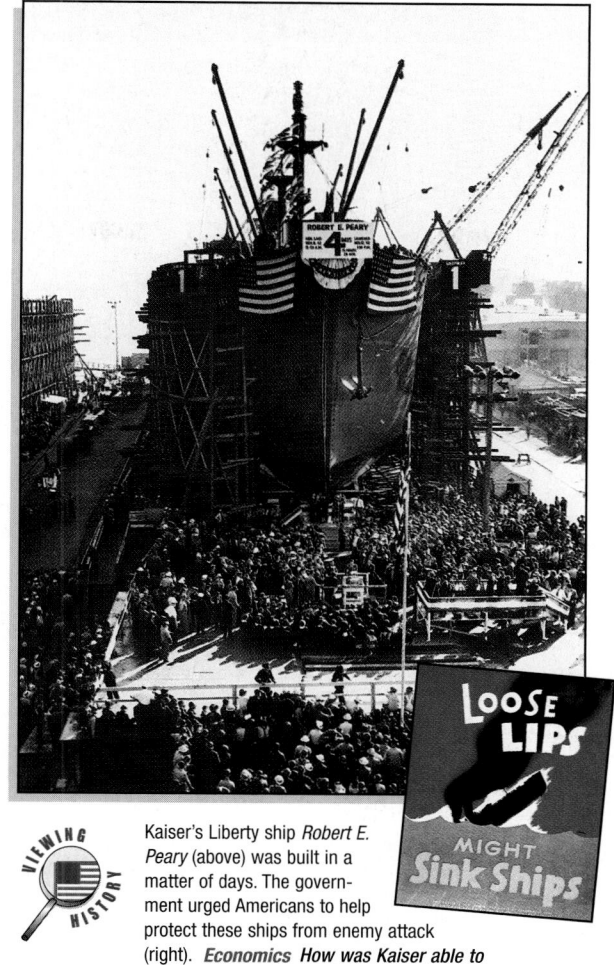

Kaiser's Liberty ship *Robert E. Peary* (above) was built in a matter of days. The government urged Americans to help protect these ships from enemy attack (right). *Economics How was Kaiser able to produce ships so fast?*

goals for military materials, and each year it met them. By the middle of 1945, the nation had produced (in rounded numbers) 300,000 airplanes; 80,000 landing craft; 100,000 tanks and armored cars; 5,600 merchant ships (including about 2,600 Liberty ships); 6 million rifles, carbines, and machine guns; and 41 billion rounds of ammunition.

The Wartime Work Force

War production benefited workers, too, ending the massive unemployment of the 1930s.

Main Idea
CONNECTIONS

What did Franklin Roosevelt mean when he said that America must be the "great arsenal of democracy"?

Graphing the Main Idea

To make sure students understand the main idea of this section, you may wish to use the tree map graphic organizer below.

Tell students that a tree map is a graphic representation of an outline and shows main ideas and their supporting details. Ask students to use it to show how the government mobilized the nation to provide materials and financial support for the war.

Teaching Tip A template for this graphic organizer can be found in the Color Transparencies, G-3.

Answer to . . .

Interpreting Graphs By about 13 percent of the labor force; by about 20 dollars.

Unemployment and Weekly Earnings, 1940–1945

 Interpreting Graphs War mobilization had a positive effect on the labor force.
Economics By how much did unemployment fall between 1940 and 1945? By how much did average weekly wages increase during the same period?

As the graphs above show, by 1943 unemployment had fallen dramatically. Average weekly wages in manufacturing, adjusted for inflation, rose by more than 50 percent between 1940 and 1945.

With more people working, union membership rose. Between 1940 and 1941, the number of workers belonging to unions increased by 1.5 million. Union membership continued to rise sharply once the United States entered the war. It went from 10.5 million in 1941 to 14.8 million in 1945.

Two weeks after the attack on Pearl Harbor, labor and business representatives agreed to refrain from strikes and "lockouts"—a tactic in which an employer keeps employees out of the workplace to avoid meeting their demands. As the cost of living rose during the war, however, the no-strike agreement became hard to honor. The government continually had to remind citizens of the importance of the agreement. A construction company superintendent recalled what happened during the building of a military base in New Jersey:

 AMERICAN VOICES "They started at one time to develop a strike there, and some big guy from the Pentagon came down, and he just laid the cards on the table: 'There'll be no strikes.' Everybody kind of buckled down, and we finished the thing in record time."

—*Leonard Williamson*

Still, the number of strikes rose sharply between 1942 and 1943, and it continued to rise in the last two years of the war. Some of the strikes were **wildcat strikes**—that is, they were organized by the workers themselves and not endorsed by the unions.

The most serious troubles with union labor were in the coal mines. There, John L. Lewis, head of the United Mine Workers union, called strikes on four occasions in 1943. Lewis and the miners watched industry profits soar while their wages stayed the same. They demanded a pay raise to compensate for the rising cost of living. Secretary of the Interior Harold L. Ickes finally negotiated an agreement with Lewis. Meanwhile, Congress passed the Smith-Connally Act in June 1943, limiting future strike activity.

Financing the War

Wartime production was so vital that the United States government was willing to spend whatever was necessary. Federal spending increased from $8.9 billion in 1939 to $95.2 billion in 1945. The Gross National Product (GNP) more than doubled in that time. Overall, the cost to the federal government between 1941 and 1945 was about $321 billion—ten times as much as World War I.

Higher taxes paid for about 41 percent of the cost of the war. The Revenue Act of 1942

▶ **RESOURCE OPTIONS**

Media and Technology

◉ 📼 **Prentice Hall United States History Video Collection**™ Volume 19 *WWII* increased the number of Americans who paid income taxes from 13 million to 50 million people. It also introduced the idea of withholding income taxes from people's paychecks, known as "pay-as-you-go." Income tax rates went up gradually during the war years, reaching a high of 94 percent for the richest taxpayers. Extra taxes were also levied on corporate profits and consumer goods.

The government borrowed the rest of the money from banks, private investors, and the public. Starting in 1941, the Treasury Department launched bond drives to encourage Americans to buy **war bonds,** government savings bonds that financed the war. Movie stars and war heroes urged the public to "buy bonds." Even schoolchildren brought their dimes or quarters to school each week, buying defense stamps that would eventually add up to the price of a bond. Total war bond sales brought in about $186 billion.

During the Depression, British economist John Maynard Keynes had argued for **deficit spending**—government spending of borrowed money—to get the economy moving. Many other economists believed the economy would recover if government left it alone. There was some deficit spending in the 1930s, but government borrowing skyrocketed during World War II. Deficit spending turned the economy around overnight, bringing wartime prosperity. It also created a huge national debt that caused economic problems later.

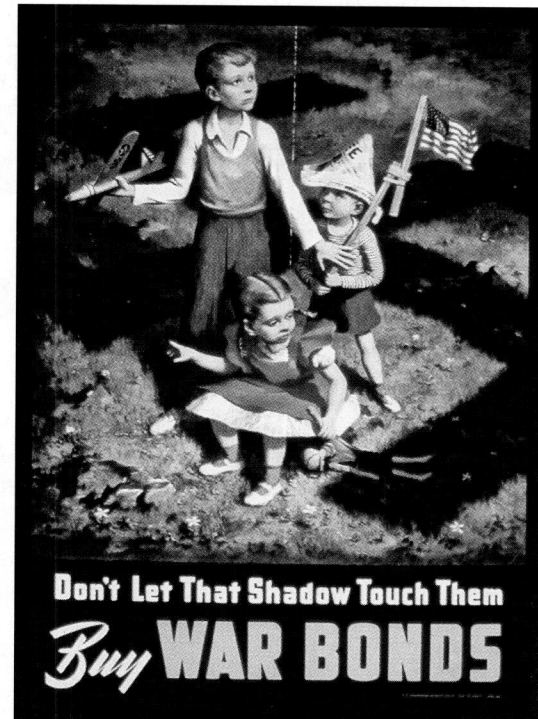

Don't Let That Shadow Touch Them

Buy WAR BONDS

This war bond poster used powerful images to convince people to buy war bonds. *Economics How else did the government raise money to pay for the war?*

SECTION 1 REVIEW

Comprehension
1. *Key Terms* Define: (a) Office of War Mobilization; (b) Liberty ship; (c) wildcat strike; (d) war bond; (e) deficit spending.
2. *Summarizing the Main Idea* What steps did the government take to mobilize industries and labor for war production?
3. *Organizing Information* Create a web diagram to organize the different types of actions taken by government and business to convert the American economy into a wartime economy.

Critical Thinking
4. *Analyzing Time Lines* Review the time line at the start of the section. Choose one entry and explain its consequences.
5. *Formulating Questions* Imagine that you are a government planner in 1942. Draw up a list of "nonessential" civilian goods that will be rationed or not produced at all.

Writing Activity
6. *Writing a Persuasive Essay* You are making a speech at a bond drive, trying to persuade people to buy war bonds. Write a draft of the speech you will give.

Answers to SECTION 1 REVIEW

1. (a) Office of War Mobilization, see p. 716; (b) Liberty ship, see p. 717; (c) wildcat strike, see p. 718; (d) war bond, see p. 719; (e) deficit spending, see p. 719.

2. Several agencies were set up to control inflation and regulate war production, actions were taken to limit strikes, and government spending was increased to boost wartime production.

3. Webs may include: OPA, WPB, and Office of War Mobilization set up; industries convert production from consumer to war materials; new business appoaches taken; labor strikes dealt with in new ways; federal spending increased.

4. Sample entry: 1941—OPA sets limits: inflation controlled; first of many similar agencies set up to deal with war economy.

5. Answers may include examples of luxury and other nonessential goods.

6. Speeches will vary but should be supported with facts from the section.

Answer to . . .

Viewing History *Increasing the number of people paying income taxes, raising taxes, withholding income taxes from paychecks, levying additional taxes on corporate profits and consumer goods.*

Daily Life on the Home Front

Objectives

You may wish to call students' attention to the objectives in the Section Preview. The objectives are reflected in the main headings of the section.

Bellringer

Ask students to think about how their lives would change if their family could buy only three gallons of gasoline a week—the amount that was allowed under rationing during World War II.

Reading Strategy

Formulating Questions Refer students to the Reading Strategy in the Section Preview. You may want to have students quiz each other using their questions as a way to review content.

LESSON PLAN

Connecting to the Main Idea

1. Focus Explain that constant effort was required to support the war. Ask students how daily life changed as a result of these efforts.

2. Instruct Explain that during the war, jobs were plentiful and workers made good wages. Ask students to describe the forms of entertainment that Americans enjoyed with their extra money. Also note that many basic necessities were not available. Have students explain why rationing was instituted and how it supported the war effort.

Discuss the reasons the government wanted to maintain high morale among its citizens. What government-sponsored programs kept Americans involved in the war effort?

3. Close The war touched Americans at home in many ways. The next section describes how it dramatically changed the lives of many American women.

1941 OPA begins rationing auto tires	1941 Birthrate begins to rise from Depression levels	1942 Popular movies such as *Casablanca* combine patriotism and entertainment	1943 Point rationing begins	1943 All-American Girls' Softball League begins

1940	1942	1944

2 Daily Life on the Home Front

SECTION PREVIEW

Objectives

1 Describe some features of American popular culture during World War II.
2 Explain how shortages and controls affected everyday civilian life.
3 List some of the ways the government enlisted public support for the war.
4 *Key Terms* Define: Office of War Information; victory garden.

Main Idea

As the war economy brought both prosperity and shortages, the government worked to keep Americans at home involved in the war effort.

Reading Strategy

Formulating Questions Before you read, rewrite each of this section's main headings in the form of a question. Look for answers to the questions as you read.

Low traffic speeds helped save on fuel and rubber.

The daily life of most Americans during World War II was filled with constant reminders of the war. Nearly everyone had a relative or friend in the military, and people closely followed war news on the radio. The war uprooted families, too. Many soldiers' wives and children moved in with relatives. Other people moved to new places to take defense jobs. Although the wartime economy gave many people their first extra cash since the Depression, shortages and rationing limited what people could buy. Books, movies, and sports provided a chance to escape wartime worries. At the same time, many Americans of all ages took part in the war effort by buying bonds or recycling paper and tin.

Wartime Popular Culture

Americans' morale was quite high as wartime spending ended the Depression. In 1941, about 24 percent of all American families had incomes of less than $1,000 a year. By 1945,

new jobs created by the war brought that figure below 20 percent. One measure of people's optimism was an increase in the birthrate. The population grew by 7.5 million between 1940 and 1945, nearly double the rate of growth for the 1930s. The postwar "baby boom" that extended through the 1950s really began during World War II.

As the wartime economy expanded, many Americans suddenly found themselves earning more money than they needed for basic necessities. They were eager to spend this extra income on new cars, trucks, or home appliances. Since war production made those goods unavailable, they looked for other ways to spend their money.

Books and Movies People bought and read more books and magazines. The new Pocket Books company, founded by Robert de Graff in 1939, developed a market for small-size paperback books. De Graff believed that more Americans would read if books were less expensive, more widely available, and easy to carry. He published paperback versions of recent bestsellers at just 25 cents. In only two months,

---

 RESOURCE OPTIONS

Teaching Resources

 Reproducible Lesson Plan Lesson Plans folder, p. 136

Big Idea Graphic Organizer Big Idea Graphic Organizer folder, p. 108

Guided Reading and Review Units 7–8 folder, p. 59

Literature Activity How to Win Friends and Influence People, Units 7–8 folder, p. 68

Nystrom *Atlas of Our Country* People on the Move, pp. 34–35

34,000 copies of the first Pocket Book, Dale Carnegie's *How to Win Friends and Influence People,* were sold. Soldiers carried Pocket Books with them into combat. When the war was over, the market for paperbacks continued to grow.

Millions of Americans—about 60 percent of the population—also went to the movies every week. Hollywood, too, was doing its part for the war effort, making movies for both soldiers and civilians. Director Frank Capra, for example, who was known for warm-hearted comedies, made a series of films for the army called *Why We Fight.* Many wartime films were love stories, adventure tales, or light comedies that took audiences' minds off the serious business of war. Others, such as *Casablanca,* added themes of patriotism and confidence in an Allied victory. Movie newsreels also boosted patriotism.

With high spirits and money to spend, Americans on the home front were eager for entertainment. Pete Gray, a one-armed outfielder (above), did his part for the war effort by playing for the St. Louis Browns and giving the "troops" at home a lift. *Culture* Why were Americans so eager for diversions?

Baseball Although more than 4,000 of the 5,700 major and minor league baseball players were in the military services, Americans still flocked to baseball games during the war. Ball clubs had to scramble to find other players. To fill their rosters, some placed want ads in newspapers:

> **AMERICAN VOICES**
> ❝If you are a free agent and have previous professional experience, we may be able to place you to your advantage on one of our clubs. We have positions open on our AA, B, and D classification clubs. If you believe you can qualify for one of these good baseball jobs, tell us about yourself.❞
>
> —Sporting News, *February 25, 1943*

For the first time, women had a chance to play ball professionally. In 1943 Philip Wrigley founded the All-American Girls' Softball League, which became the All-American Girls' Baseball League in 1945. Women who played for teams such as the Rockford (Illinois) Peaches and the South Bend (Indiana) Blue Sox had to attend charm school and wear impractical skirted uniforms. They put up with such difficulties to play the sport they loved. Their games drew hundreds of fans.

Popular Music As in World War I, many popular songs encouraged hope and patriotism. Frank Loesser's "Praise the Lord and Pass the Ammunition" was based on a widely told story about a navy chaplain who took over an anti-aircraft gun at Pearl Harbor after the gunners had been killed. "There's a Star-Spangled Banner Waving Somewhere" was a best-selling record in 1942.

Other ballads, like "I'll Be Seeing You" and "You'd Be So Nice to Come Home To," reflected people's longing for loved ones who were far away. In the 1942 film *Holiday Inn,* Bing Crosby sang Irving Berlin's song "White Christmas." It quickly became a sentimental favorite, both for soldiers overseas and for civilians at home.

Main Idea CONNECTIONS

How did movies, sports, and songs help the war effort?

Shortages and Controls

Although they had money to spend, Americans lived with shortages throughout the war. Some familiar consumer items were simply unavailable "for the duration." Metal to make zippers or typewriters was used for guns, and rubber for girdles went into tires for army trucks. Nylon

From the Archives of
American Heritage

Swoon Song On December 30, 1942, New York's Paramount Theater was packed for Frank Sinatra —the young balladeer from across the river in Hoboken—when a young admirer did something provocative: she passed out from a combination of hunger and excitement. This shocked a second girl who screamed. In no time one teenager after another began standing and screaming as teenage hysteria surged through the house. Sinatra kept on singing until most of the audience was on its feet in wailing tribute. He had become a teenage idol. Sinatra played the Paramount for eight more weeks while the audience stood and squealed to the rafters around him. When he played again there in 1944, some thirty thousand of his army of bobby-soxers rioted outside. Nearly five hundred police were brought in to restrain the frenzied waves of girls. "Most kids feel I'm one of them," the skinny twenty-five-year-old crooner explained, "the pal next door, say. So maybe they feel they know me. And that's the way I want it to be." Source: Nathan Ward, "The Time Machine," *American Heritage* magazine, December 1992.

TEST PREPARATION

Have students read the passage from *Sporting News* on this page and then answer the question below.

From the ad, you can infer that—

A baseball managers were not satisfied with their current players.

B free agents were better than other players.

C managers were eager to recruit players with all levels of experience.

D there was a shortage of professional baseball players.

Answer to . . .

Viewing History They had extra money to spend; luxury items were unavailable so they spent their money on entertainment.
Main Idea Connections They boosted patriotism.

FACT Finder
Government Controls on Wartime Economy

Agency or Program	Function
Rationing (1941)	Limited consumption of goods such as rubber, gasoline, sugar, meat, butter, and cheese.
Fair Employment Practice Committee (1941)	Established to end racial discrimination in war production industries and government employment.
Office of Price Administration (1942)	Limited prices on all nonfarm commodities. Controlled rents in defense areas.
National War Labor Board (1942)	Used mediation and arbitration to settle labor disputes in defense industries.
Revenue Act of 1942	Raised the number of people who paid income taxes from 13,000,000 to 50,000,000 and raised the tax rate of the wealthiest Americans.
Labor Disputes Act (Smith-Connally Anti-Strike Act) (1943)	Gave the President more power to seize war production plants threatened by labor disputes. Made illegal any attempts to strike at plants the government had seized.

Interpreting Tables The government took firm control of the economy to keep the war effort afloat. *Culture How did these government controls affect people's attitude toward the war?*

authority to freeze rents and prices. In December 1941, the OPA began rationing, or distributing, auto tires. The goal of rationing was a fair distribution of scarce items.

Beginning in 1943, the OPA assigned point values to items such as sugar, coffee, meat, butter, canned fruit, and shoes. Consumers were issued ration books of coupons worth a certain number of points for categories of food or clothing. Once they had used up their points, they could not buy any more of those items until they got new ration books or traded coupons with neighbors. One young woman who grew up in California during the war remembered her mother's gatherings to trade coupons:

AMERICAN VOICES
❝My mother and all the neighbors would get together around the dining-room table, and they'd be changing a sugar coupon for a bread or a meat coupon. It was like a giant Monopoly game. It was quite exciting to have all the neighbors over and have this trading and bargaining. It was like the New York Stock Exchange. This was our social life.❞

—*Sheril Cunning, as quoted in* "The Good War" *by Studs Terkel*

made parachutes instead of stockings. To save cloth, government regulations changed fashions. Men's suits no longer had vests, patch pockets, or trouser cuffs. Women's skirts were cut shorter and narrower.

People got used to the shortages. Not only were great amounts of food being sent to the military, but supplies of some imported foods were cut off. Sugar, for example, became scarce when the Philippines, the major source of American imports, fell to the Japanese. Many shipping lanes were closed, making it hard to bring in tropical fruits or Brazilian coffee.

Worried that shortages would cause price increases, the government used tough measures to head off inflation. Early in the war, the Office of Price Administration (OPA) was given

Ration stamps

Gasoline for cars was rationed, too, on the basis of need. Signs asked, "Is this trip necessary?"

Enlisting Public Support

The government understood the need to maintain morale. It tried to create a sense of patriotism and participation in the war effort, while convincing citizens to accept rationing and to conserve precious resources. The **Office of War Information** was set up in June 1942 to work with magazine publishers, advertising agencies, and radio stations. It hired writers and artists to create patriotic posters and ads.

One unexpectedly popular idea was the **victory garden.** Shortly after the Japanese attack on Pearl Harbor, the Secretary of Agriculture suggested that families could plant home gardens to make up for the farm produce sent to feed the soldiers. Soon people in cities and suburbs were planting tomatoes, peas, and radishes in backyards, empty parking lots, and playgrounds. By 1943, victory gardens were producing about one third of the country's fresh vegetables.

The war became a part of everyday life in many ways. Periodically, people drew their shades for nighttime "blackouts," which tested their readiness for possible bombing raids. Men too old for the army joined the Civilian Defense, wearing their CD armbands as they tested air-raid sirens. Women knit scarves and socks or rolled bandages for the Red Cross.

Shortages produced efforts to recycle scrap metal, paper, and other materials. In one drive, people collected tin cans, pots and pans, razor blades, old shovels, and even old lipstick tubes. In Virginia, volunteers raised sunken ships from the James River; in Wyoming they took apart an old steam engine to use the parts. At home, people were asked to save kitchen fats because the glycerin could be used to make powder for bullets or shells. Some historians have questioned whether the items collected were ever really used in the war. Whether they were or not, the collection drives kept adults and children actively involved in the war effort.

"Play your part." "Conserve and collect." "Use it up, wear it out, make it do or do without." These slogans echoed throughout the United States and reminded people on the home front of their part in the war.

Children, too, did their part for the war effort. These boys in New York City used their powers of persuasion—and noise-making—to urge their neighbors to contribute to an aluminum drive. *Economics* *How did the government handle the shortages of consumer items?*

SECTION 2 REVIEW

Comprehension

1. **Key Terms** Define (a) Office of War Information; (b) victory garden.

2. **Summarizing the Main Idea** What direct effects did wartime shortages have on the everyday lives of Americans at home?

3. **Organizing Information** Create a web diagram showing the ways in which civilians on the home front had to interact with the government and government agencies during World War II.

Critical Thinking

4. **Analyzing Time Lines** Review the time line at the start of the section. Identify the events that you think would have come to an end once the war was over.

5. **Identifying Assumptions** What did the government hope to achieve by such efforts as scrap metal drives?

Writing Activity

6. **Writing a Persuasive Essay** How could you motivate a group of people to organize a scrap metal drive? Write an editorial for your community newspaper in which you persuade people to organize and cooperate in the war effort.

ON THE HOME FRONT

Focus Review the ways in which the United States government attempted to bolster morale and enlist support for the war effort during World War II. Recall the ways in which the government appealed to the conscience of every American.

Instruct Using the images and captions on these pages as a basis for discussion, ask why propaganda campaigns were important and necessary for American victory in World War II. Have students identify the messages and targeted groups for the various artifacts. Ask students about the role of television in advertising today, and how "infomercials" help create images for political campaigns.

Extend You might want to have students bring to class examples of advertisements from today. What is the target audience of the advertisement, and what propaganda techniques are used?

① Wartime Posters

At work, on the street, at the movies, these posters reminded people that their way of life depended on the outcome of the war. The posters used images of happy families to personalize the war and stir up even more support for the war effort.

② Hitler and Uncle Sam

This button used gallows humor to ask everyone to "pull" together to win the war. The need to put aside disagreements among Americans was a common wartime message.

③ Dogs for Defense

The armed forces needed dogs to sniff out explosives, and for many other tasks. Citizens who donated dogs to the military could proudly wear this button.

④ Victory Button

The letter "V, " for victory, was the most common symbol of the war effort. Many businesses used the V and the American flag to send a patriotic and promotional message.

⑤ Ration Cards and Stamps

Notice the initials OPA, which stood for Office of Price Administration. This agency distributed the ration books and also had the authority to set prices for items in short supply.

▶ **RESOURCE OPTIONS**

Teaching Resources

American History Block Scheduling Support Air Raid! Pearl Harbor and the United States Declaration of War, found in the Prosperity, Depression, and War folder, includes interdisciplinary lesson suggestions and activities for Geography and History, Primary Sources, Biography, and Literature.

6
Label on Milk Bottle

This label conveyed the message that conserving resources was every American's patriotic duty.

RETURN WHEN EMPTY
and you'll help
WIN THE WAR

Each Milk Bottle lost or destroyed means precious material and man-hours wasted. Speed Victory by speeding empty bottles back to the dairy.

★★ Milk consumers in every State are urged to help lengthen the life of MILK BOTTLES by using them carefully and returning them promptly when empty.

7
Sleeve for U.S. War Bonds

The government borrowed an incredible $135 billion from individual Americans to finance the war effort.

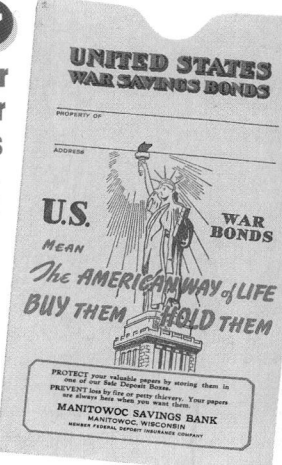

UNITED STATES
WAR SAVINGS BONDS

PROPERTY OF

ADDRESS

U.S.
WAR BONDS
MEAN
The American Way of Life
BUY THEM — HOLD THEM

PROTECT your valuable papers by storing them in one of our Safe Deposit Boxes.
PREVENT loss by fire or petty thievery. Your papers are always here when you want them.

MANITOWOC SAVINGS BANK
MANITOWOC, WISCONSIN
MEMBER FEDERAL DEPOSIT INSURANCE COMPANY

VIEWING HISTORY

1. **Summarize** What do the objects tell you about daily life during the war?

2. **Connecting to Today** In peacetime as well as wartime, government and other organizations conduct public relations campaigns to persuade people to support some policy or change their behavior. Report on the following to your class: (a) examples of recent campaigns; (b) what, in your view, makes such campaigns successful or unsuccessful.

American ARTIFACTS

FROM EXHIBITIONS AND COLLECTIONS AT THE SMITHSONIAN INSTITUTION'S NATIONAL MUSEUM OF AMERICAN HISTORY

ON THE HOME FRONT

During World War II, colorful posters papered the windows of American businesses. Pleas rang out across the radio, urging Americans to sacrifice and band together. Everywhere there were reminders that the nation was in a life-or-death struggle against totalitarian dictatorships. *See* **1** *and* **2**.

Every life was affected by the war. If you didn't have a family member in the armed forces, you knew someone—a neighbor or friend—who was serving in the armed forces or working in a defense plant. Even the family dog was a possible recruit. The army used dogs as sentries on the battlefront and in other ways. *See* **3**.

The steady stream of patriotic messages kept Americans focused on the job at hand—putting individual disagreements aside to work together for the good of the country. People showed their support by wearing victory buttons, marked by the letter "V." *See* **4**.

Supporting the war effort also meant putting up with shortages. The government rationed certain items that were scarce or needed by the armed forces. Ration books restricted things like gasoline and sugar. Conserving and recycling were also necessary. The recycling effort included hundreds of everyday products. *See* **5** *and* **6**.

In addition to working hard, Americans contributed their own money to pay for the war effort. They did this by purchasing war savings bonds. Savings bonds gave thousands of Americans a personal and financial stake in the outcome of the war. *See* **7**.

1942
"Rosie the Riveter" becomes a symbol for women war workers

1942
National War Labor Board backs "equal pay for equal work"

1944
Number of women working exceeds 19 million

1940   **1942**   **1944**

Women and the War

Objectives

You may wish to call students' attention to the objectives in the Section Preview. The objectives are reflected in the main headings of the section.

Bellringer

Have students list their after-school activities and responsibilities at home. Then ask them how their lists might change if they were of the opposite sex. How might expectations of parents and others be different?

Reading Strategy

Outlining Information Refer students to the Reading Strategy in the Section Preview. You may wish to have volunteers help you model the outline on the chalkboard, which students can copy on a piece of paper.

LESSON PLAN

Connecting to the Main Idea

1. Focus Explain that during the war, women responded to the urgent demand for workers in factories and shipyards. They quickly adapted to their new status. Just as quickly, most gave up their jobs when the war ended. Ask students what impact the war had on their lives.

2. Instruct Ask students to explain why women went to work during the war. Have them provide examples of how women felt about their experience, such as working conditions, attitudes, stresses of family life, salaries, and discrimination. Ask if these issues are still valid today. Discuss why some women were ambivalent about giving up their jobs after the war.

3. Close World War II changed the lives of American women who went to work outside their homes for the first time or moved into jobs previously held by men. The next section describes how other groups were affected by World War II.

3 Women and the War

SECTION PREVIEW

Objectives

1. Explain why new kinds of jobs opened up for women in World War II.
2. Compare the benefits and problems that women workers experienced.
3. Describe what happened to women workers at the end of the war.
4. *Key Terms* Define: Rosie the Riveter; seniority.

Main Idea

During World War II, more American women went to work in nontraditional, war-industry jobs, but they were discouraged from keeping those jobs after the war ended.

Reading Strategy

Outlining Information As you read this section, create an outline that includes the headings from the section. Fill in at least two main ideas for each heading.

The motto of the women's Auxiliary Reserve Pool (ARP) during World War II was Prepared and Faithful.

A popular song in 1942 told the story of a fictional young woman called **Rosie the Riveter,** who worked in a defense plant while her boyfriend Charlie served in the marines. The government used images of Rosie the Riveter in posters and recruitment films of the 1940s to attract women to the work force. The government image of Rosie was young, white, and middle class. Patriotism was her main motive for taking a war job—she wanted to do her part on the home front while her boyfriend was fighting. In reality, American women of all ages and ethnic and economic backgrounds went to work in the wartime economy. Patriotism was only one of many reasons they took new and different jobs.

Changes for Working Women

Before the war, most women who worked for wages were single and young. Even during the hard times of the Depression, most people disapproved of married women working—that is, holding paying jobs outside the home. Social disapproval was reinforced by the fear that working women would take jobs away from unemployed men. According to a poll taken in 1936, 82 percent of Americans believed that a married woman should not work if her husband had a job. Nonetheless, by 1940 more than 15 percent of all married women were working.

New Kinds of Jobs Except for teaching and nursing, few women entered professional careers. They often had to take low-paying jobs such as sales clerks or household servants. Women with factory jobs usually worked in industries that produced clothing, textiles, and shoes, while men dominated the higher-paying machinery, steel, and automobile industries. Almost everywhere, women earned less than men.

Like World War I, World War II brought women into different parts of the work force. As men were drafted into the armed forces, many factory jobs fell vacant. News of these better-paying job openings attracted women who were working in traditional women's jobs. They moved into manufacturing, particularly the

RESOURCE OPTIONS

Teaching Resources

Reproducible Lesson Plan Lesson Plans folder, p. 137

Big Idea Graphic Organizer Big Idea Graphic Organizer folder, p. 109

Guided Reading and Review Units 7–8 folder, p. 61

Media and Technology

 AmericanHeritage® CD-ROM

Time Tour Prosperity, Depression, and War: World War II

defense industries. Like the fictional Rosie, women worked in airplane plants and shipyards as riveters, steelworkers, and welders.

Recruiting Women Workers Still there was a labor shortage. To fill those jobs, the Office of War Information launched a recruitment campaign. It was aimed at women who normally would not have considered working outside the home: older and married women.

Posters and advertisements told women that it was their patriotic duty to work for their country. "An American homemaker with the strength and ability to run a house and raise a family . . . has the strength and ability to take her place in a vital War industry," one ad declared. As a result of this campaign, the number of working women rose by almost one third, from 14.6 million in 1941 to about 19.4 million in 1944. (See the graph on the next page.) Women at one point made up about 35 percent of the total civilian labor force.

The campaign brought married women workers into the labor force. They soon accounted for almost three quarters of the increase. For the first time in American history, they outnumbered single working women. More than 2 million women over the age of 35 found jobs, and by the end of the war, half of all women workers were over age 35.

Benefits of Employment

Despite their resistance in the past, employers were usually pleased to have women workers during the war. Some of their reasons seem misguided today. Employers assumed, for instance, that women could do simple, repetitious tasks more effectively than men. They thought that women were better suited for certain welding jobs because they could squeeze into smaller places.

Women and Work On the whole, women were pleased to be employed. The money they earned made a difference in their lives. For example, Josephine McKee, a Seattle mother of nine who worked at the Boeing Aircraft Company, was able to pay off debts from the Depression. Leola Houghland, also from Seattle, used her shipyard earnings to pay for her family's home.

Other women found the work more interesting and challenging than what they had done before. Evelyn Knight left a job as a cook to work in a navy yard. She explained, "After all, I've got to keep body and soul together, and I'd rather earn a living this way than to cook over a hot stove." Many women took jobs for patriotic reasons. One rubber plant worker declared, "Every time I test a batch of rubber, I know it's going to help bring my three sons home quicker."

Women were eager to prove that they could do whatever their jobs required. Beatrice Morales Clifton, a mother of four, had never worked outside the home. At first, she found that other workers at Lockheed Aircraft in

VIEWING HISTORY

These women welders at the Kaiser shipyard in Richmond, California, are working on the Liberty ship *S.S. George Washington Carver.* *Economics How did wartime job recruitment change the kinds of jobs women filled?*

Main Idea CONNECTIONS

What benefits did women experience as a result of wartime employment?

Los Angeles resented working women. Her confidence grew, however, as she mastered one skill after another:

 AMERICAN VOICES 66 I felt proud of myself and felt good [because] I had never done anything like that. I felt good that I could do something, and being that it was war, I felt that I was doing my part. I went from 65 cents to $1.05 [an hour]. That was top pay. It felt good and, besides, it was my own money. I could do whatever I wanted with it. 99

—*Beatrice Morales Clifton*

Clifton left her wartime job after the war, then returned to Lockheed in 1951. By the time she retired in 1978, she was a supervisor for about 50 other workers.

Jobs for African Americans Black women had long worked in greater proportion than white women. Generally, though, only domestic work such as cleaning and child care was open to them. When they applied for defense jobs, African American women often faced both gender prejudice and racial discrimination. Some women fought back. Through lawsuits and other forms of protest, African American women improved their chances in the work force. Between 1940 and 1944, the proportion of African American women in industrial jobs increased from 6.8 percent to 18 percent. The number working in domestic service dropped from 59.9 percent to 44.6 percent.

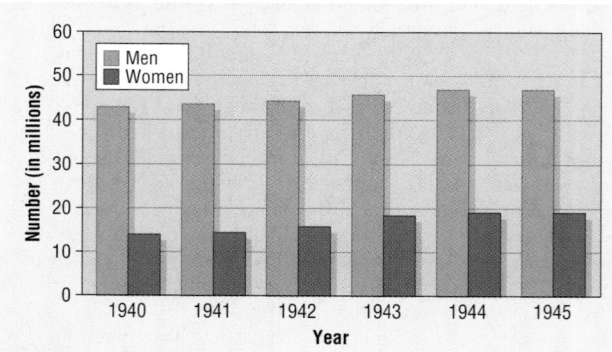

Labor Force, 1940–1945

Interpreting Charts Wartime production created a demand for workers, both male and female. *Economics Compare the overall trend in women's employment during World War II with the ratio of women to men in the labor force during the war.*

Problems for Working Women

In spite of the benefits of working, women faced a number of problems in the workplace. Some faced hostile reactions from other workers, particularly in jobs previously held only by men. Many managers were uneasy about mixing the sexes, and so set up strict rules. General Motors, for example, fired male supervisors and female employees found "fraternizing," or socializing with one another.

Working women also worried about leaving their children alone. More than half a million women with children under the age of 10 worked during the war, and day-care centers were scarce. Even when care was available, most women preferred to have family members or friends care for their children. This often required making complicated arrangements. Women were encouraged to work, but at the same time they continued to also be responsible for their children and their homes.

Women also earned much less than men doing the same jobs. The National War Labor Board declared in the fall of 1942 that women who performed "work of the same quality and quantity" as men should receive equal pay. This policy was widely ignored. Women began at the bottom, with the lowest-paying jobs. Because they had less **seniority,** or status that is derived from length of service, they commonly advanced more slowly. Their wages reflected these patterns. At the Willow Run plant in 1945, women earned a yearly average of $2,928, compared with $3,363 for men. Conditions improved toward the end of the war, but the gap never disappeared.

After the War

The government drive to bring women to defense plants assumed that when the war was over, women would leave their jobs and return home. War work was just "for the duration." While many women wanted to continue working at the war's end, the pressures to return home were intense. Returning servicemen expected to get their jobs back. They also longed

Sisters under the apron—Yesterday's war worker becomes today's housewife.

What's Become of Rosie the Riveter?

Government campaigns aimed at women did an about-face once the war was over. Posters such as this one tried to persuade women to give up their factory jobs and return to full-time homemaking. *Culture* *Why were women being urged out of the work force?*

ACTIVITY
LEARNING STYLES

Ask students to read interviews with women in Studs Terkel's book *The Good War: An Oral History of World War II* or pertinent chapters in Richard R. Lingeman's *Don't You Know There's a War On? The American Home Front, 1940–1945.* Have them summarize what they read. *(Verbal/Linguistic)*

to return to the kind of family life they had known before the war. A new campaign by industrialists and government officials now encouraged women to leave their jobs. Articles in women's magazines changed their emphasis after the war, too. They focused on homemaking, cooking, and child care, starting a trend that would continue into the 1950s and 1960s.

As the economy returned to peacetime, twice as many women as men lost factory jobs. Some women were tired of their defense jobs, which in many cases were not very fulfilling once the wartime sense of urgency ended. They looked forward to returning home. Others, however, had discovered new satisfactions in the workplace that made them want to keep on working. As one woman stated, "For the first time in their lives, they worked outside the home. They realized that they were capable of doing something more than cook a meal." Some women also continued to work part time to bring in additional income.

Answers to
SECTION 3 REVIEW

1. (a) Rosie the Riveter, see p. 726; (b) seniority, see p. 728.

2. Women over 35 and married women entered the work force, taking jobs previously reserved for men. Married women outnumbered single working women for the first time in American history.

3. Benefits: Extra money, interesting and challenging work, chance to learn new skills. Drawbacks: discrimination, necessity of keeping job and caring for children, lower earnings than men.

4. 1942—National War Labor Board backs "equal pay for equal work"; though the pay gap between the genders has narrowed over the years, it is still an issue today.

5. Sample answers: Women really belonged in the home; it was more important for men to have jobs than for women.

6. Essays will vary but should address themes introduced in the section.

SECTION 3 REVIEW

Comprehension

1. *Key Terms* Define: (a) Rosie the Riveter; (b) seniority.

2. *Summarizing the Main Idea* How did employment patterns for women change during World War II?

3. *Organizing Information* Make a two-column chart comparing the benefits of war work for women with the problems and disadvantages they faced. Label one column *Benefits*, the other *Drawbacks and Problems*.

Critical Thinking

4. *Analyzing Time Lines* Review the time line at the start of the section. Choose one event and relate it to present-day conditions for working women.

5. *Recognizing Bias* Although women workers were recruited during the war, once it ended they were pressured to leave their jobs and return to domestic work. What underlying beliefs does this series of events suggest?

Writing Activity

6. *Writing a Persuasive Essay* How would you prepare an all-male work force to accept women workers? Write a short guide that will convince the workers to accept the newcomers as equals.

 RESOURCE OPTIONS

Teaching Resources

 Quiz Units 7–8 folder, p. 6

Student Performance Pack

 Guide to the Essentials Chapter 25, Section 3 (English and Spanish)

Answer to . . .

Viewing History To accommodate the employment needs of men returning from the war.

SKILLS FOR LIFE

Critical Thinking

Identifying Assumptions

Focus Identify and evaluate assumptions in historical sources such as editorials, speeches, or works of art.

Instruct Ask students to list adjectives that describe "Rosie the Riveter," the symbol of women workers during World War II. Have them work in groups to identify the assumptions that underlie their lists. Compare their assumptions to those of Norman Rockwell's magazine cover.

Extend See the Skills for Life Activity in the Resource Options below.

Answers

1. (a) Taking a break from work to eat lunch. (b) American women during World War II. (c) Women in the workplace. (d) Women are capable of doing traditional men's work.

2. (a) To show support for women in the workplace. (b) He seems to admire these women workers. (c) The woman looks strong, capable, and confident. (d) The woman's muscular body contrasts with her childish face. The artist may be suggesting a contradiction in a young woman doing a "man's" job.

3. (a) That the work is physically demanding and "men's" work. The American flag background suggests that she had patriotic reasons. (b) That women have had to give up their femininity. (c) Some students may think that a muscular appearance signals physical labor or that a person who wears a dress or suit must work in an office; others, that appearances are not reliable indicators. (d) Read about or interview women who lived during World War II.

TEST FOR SUCCESS

Answers should show an understanding of the steps in the skill.

SKILLS FOR LIFE

Identifying Assumptions

Identifying assumptions means recognizing the unstated beliefs that may underlie a statement or action. An assumption is an idea that a person takes for granted as true. In fact, it may prove either true or false, but in order to determine the accuracy of an assumption, you must first be able to recognize it as such.

Editorials, opinion pieces, and illustrations frequently contain many assumptions. Magazine covers, such as the one shown here, are often excellent sources of information about public attitudes toward historical events. At the same time, illustrations may be drawn in such a way that they also reveal assumptions of the artist.

By the time artist Norman Rockwell's portrayal of "Rosie the Riveter" appeared on the cover of *The Saturday Evening Post* in 1943, American women by the thousands were already making history. They were working in nontraditional factory jobs, assembling ships and airplanes for the country's war effort.

To examine the accuracy of the image portrayed in this illustration, use the following steps to identify and evaluate the assumptions on which it may be based.

1. Determine the subject of the cover illustration. Study the illustration carefully and answer the following questions. (a) What is the woman in the illustration doing? (b) Who is "Rosie the Riveter" supposed to represent? (c) What general subject or issue does the illustration address? (d) What is the overall message of the illustration?

2. Define the artist's point of view. To help determine if the artist is presenting a particular viewpoint, answer the following questions. (a) What seems to be the artist's purpose in creating this illustration? (b) How would you describe the artist's attitude toward the subject? (c) What aspects of the illustration clearly express this point of view? (d) Are there any elements in the illustration that seem to contradict each other? If so, what might the artist be trying to convey through these contradictions?

3. Identify the assumptions on which the artist's viewpoint is based and decide whether they are valid. To help decide if the artist's assumptions can be supported by facts, answer the following questions. (a) What assumptions, if any, does the artist make about the nature of the work performed by the woman in the illustration? Does the artist make any assumptions about why she holds this job? (b) What assumptions, if any, does the artist make about the women who work in nontraditional jobs?

(c) Can any aspects of a person's physical appearance, such as clothes or posture, be reliably linked to his or her occupation? Explain. (d) How can you find out if the artist's apparent assumptions are valid?

TEST FOR SUCCESS

Choose an advertisement from a current magazine and analyze it by determining (a) the assumptions made by the advertiser about the audience for this product; (b) the purpose of the ad; and (c) the artist's or photographer's point of view.

RESOURCE OPTIONS

Teaching Resources

Skills for Life Activity Units 7–8 folder, p. 69, uses a recruitment brochure for the United States Air Force to help students apply this skill.

Media and Technology

Color Transparencies Critical Thinking, I–9

1941	1942	1942		1945
Executive Order 8802 outlaws race discrimination in war plants	FDR authorizes the internment of Japanese Americans	CORE is founded to work for racial equality	1943 Race riots in Detroit, New York, and Los Angeles	Japanese Americans are released from internment camps

1941	1942	1943	1944	1945

4 The Struggle for Justice at Home

SECTION PREVIEW

Objectives

1 Describe the kinds of discrimination that African Americans faced and the steps they took to counter them.
2 Compare the experiences of Mexican Americans and Native Americans at home during World War II.
3 Explain why Japanese Americans were interned during the war.
4 *Key Terms* Define: "Double V" campaign; Nisei; internment camp.

Main Idea

While the war brought new job opportunities for some racial and ethnic minorities, Japanese Americans were the victims of widespread intolerance.

Reading Strategy

Organizing Information As you read, create a graphic organizer including information about the experiences of African Americans, Mexican Americans, Native Americans, and Japanese Americans during the war.

President Roosevelt, in his 1942 Columbus Day speech, expressed the need to overcome bigotry for the sake of the wartime effort: "In some communities employers dislike to hire women. In others they are reluctant to hire Negroes. We can no longer afford to indulge such prejudice."

In fact, the war did bring greater opportunities for some groups of Americans. Nevertheless, racial and ethnic prejudices did not disappear during the war years. Instead, the pressures of wartime made some of those injustices more obvious. Japanese Americans in particular faced hardship and hostility because of Japan's part in the war.

Discrimination Continues Against African Americans

When the war began, the struggle to end discrimination against African Americans had been under way for decades. Yet the Jim Crow system, which established the strict legal separation of the races, was still strong in the South. The North had fewer laws enforcing segregation. In reality, however, African

Americans in the North faced discrimination in employment, education, and housing.

Economic Discrimination African American unemployment was high in 1941, with one out of five potential workers jobless. Even government agencies set up to help workers during the Depression honored employers' requests for "whites only." Such attitudes allowed old patterns to continue.

During the 1940s, more than 2 million African Americans migrated from the South to cities in the North. (See the map on the next page.) They found new job opportunities but also encountered new problems. Segregation severely limited the houses and apartments where African Americans were welcome. In addition, many could not afford good housing. As a result, many ended up living in urban ghettos, neighborhoods where members of a minority group are concentrated. A survey taken in 1941 showed that 50 percent of all African American homes were substandard, versus only 14 percent of white homes.

The "Double V" campaign urged victory over enemies overseas and over racial discrimination at home.

SECTION 4

The Struggle for Justice at Home

Objectives

You may wish to call students' attention to the objectives in the Section Preview. The objectives are reflected in the main headings of the section.

Bellringer

Write the words *injustice* and *inequality* on the chalkboard. Have students describe an incident that they associate with these words.

Reading Strategy

Organizing Information Refer students to the Reading Strategy in the Section Preview. You may wish to have students show their graphic organizer to the class.

LESSON PLAN

Connecting to the Main Idea

1. Focus Point out that just as women were mobilized to support the war effort, Americans of different ethnic groups were also recruited. Ask what impact the war had on these Americans.

2. Instruct Although the war provided opportunities for African Americans, it did not end discrimination. Have students list examples of continued discrimination and describe efforts to promote racial equality.

Ask students what new job opportunities opened for Mexican Americans and Native Americans. How did both groups face cultural challenges as their interaction with the dominant society increased? Discuss why Japanese Americans were treated so harshly during the war. What civil rights were violated by their internment?

3. Close World War II hastened the demand for and the rate of social change on the home front. Although minority groups overcame some racial barriers during the war, many Americans continued to face discrimination and injustice.

The 99th Fighter Squadron, formed in 1942, were the first African Americans to fly in the Army Air Corps. They were known as the "Black Eagles" because of their success in escorting all-white bomber crews over Europe. The 99th was commanded by Benjamin O. Davis, Jr., the son of the man who became the first African American general. In 1991, Davis wrote about the exploits of the Black Eagles in his autobiography. By the early 1990s, 5,527 African American officers made up 5.6 percent of the officers in the United States Air Force.

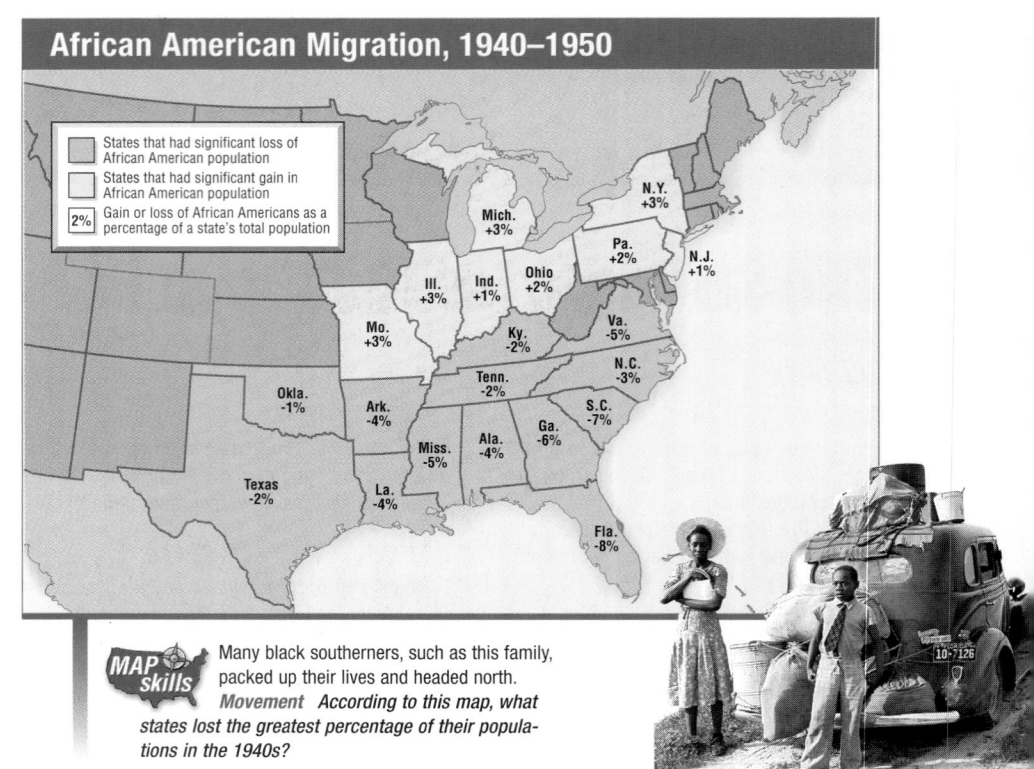

African American Migration, 1940–1950

States that had significant loss of African American population

States that had significant gain in African American population

2% Gain or loss of African Americans as a percentage of a state's total population

N.Y. +3%

Mich. +3%

Pa. +2%

N.J. +1%

Ill. +3%

Ind. +1%

Ohio +2%

Va. -5%

Mo. +3%

Ky. -2%

N.C. -3%

Okla. -1%

Tenn. -2%

S.C. -7%

Ark. -4%

Miss. -5%

Ala. -4%

Ga. -6%

Texas -2%

La. -4%

Fla. -8%

MAP Skills Many black southerners, such as this family, packed up their lives and headed north. *Movement According to this map, what states lost the greatest percentage of their populations in the 1940s?*

To make things worse, white workers and homeowners often feared and resented the newcomers in their workplaces and neighborhoods. In some places, resentments escalated into violence and riots. In June 1943, riots in Detroit killed 34 people and did millions of dollars worth of damage. Later that summer, riots broke out in New York City.

Soldiers and Segregation Even in the American military, where men were risking their lives for their country, white and African American troops were strictly segregated. At home, an army uniform was no block to prejudice. Alexander J. Allen, who worked for the Baltimore Urban League during the war, remarked, "It made a mockery of wartime goals to fight overseas against fascism only to come back to the same kind of discrimination and racism here in this country." In Kansas, for instance, the owner of a lunch counter refused to serve a group of African American GIs. One of them told this story:

AMERICAN VOICES ❝ 'You know we don't serve coloreds here,' the man repeated. . . .We ignored him, and just stood there inside the door, staring at what we had come to see—the German prisoners of war who were having lunch at the counter. . . .We continued to stare. This was really happening. It was no jive talk. The people of Salina would serve these enemy soldiers and turn away black American GIs. ❞

—*Lloyd Brown*

Divided Opinions In a 1942 poll, six out of ten whites felt that black Americans were satisfied with existing conditions and needed no new opportunities. Government attitudes mirrored this lack of concern. Franklin Roosevelt was not willing to disrupt the war effort to promote social equality. "I don't think, quite frankly," he said in late 1943, "that we can bring about the millennium [a period of human perfection] at this time."

Answer to . . .

Map Skills Virginia, South Carolina, Florida, Georgia, and Mississippi.

TEST PREPARATION

Have students read the quotation by Lloyd Brown on this page and then answer the question below.

The main reason the writer is disturbed by what he sees is that—

(A) the restaurant refused black soldiers but would serve enemy prisoners.

B he hates German soldiers.

C he is angry because the man isn't giving him the proper respect as a soldier.

D he is disturbed that the Germans aren't in jail.

African Americans, however, worked for change on their own. *The Pittsburgh Courier,* an African American newspaper, launched a **"Double V" campaign.** The first V was for victory against the Axis powers, the second for victory in winning equality at home.

Another step was the founding of the Congress of Racial Equality (CORE) in Chicago in 1942. CORE believed in using nonviolent techniques to end racism. In May 1943 it organized its first sit-in at a restaurant called the Jack Spratt Coffee House. Groups of CORE members, including at least one African American, filled the restaurant's counter and booths. They refused to leave until everyone was served. The sit-in technique ended Jack Spratt's discriminatory policies and quickly spread to CORE groups in other cities. These efforts paved the way for later civil rights actions.

A. Philip Randolph

AMERICAN BIOGRAPHY While organized labor won better working conditions for many people in the early 1900s, many unions did not accept African American members. Through two world wars, A. Philip Randolph worked to overcome that discrimination. He made a place for black Americans in the labor movement.

While working his way through college in New York and later as a ship's waiter, Randolph began work as a union organizer. He also entered politics and became a lecturer. Starting in 1925, Randolph gradually won recognition for the Brotherhood of Sleeping Car Porters, a railway union. At the time, most railroad maids and porters were African Americans. For years, railway companies had stopped them from unionizing. The new union won its first major victory in 1937, getting higher wages and cuts in working hours and travel requirements.

Even as war production grew, many factories still turned away African Americans. To protest, Randolph planned a massive march on Washington for July 4, 1941. Worried about the effect on national unity, President Roosevelt tried to talk Randolph out of the march. Finally, on June 25, 1941,

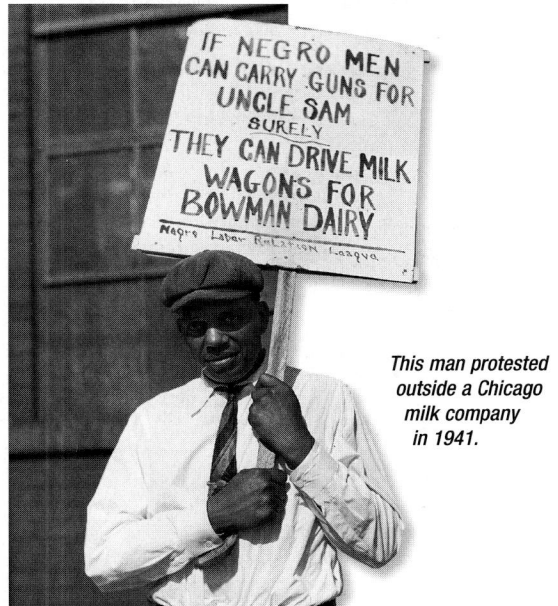

This man protested outside a Chicago milk company in 1941.

A. Philip Randolph (1889–1979)

the President signed Executive Order 8802 and Randolph called off the march. The order opened jobs and job training programs in defense plants to all Americans "without discrimination because of race, creed, color, or national origin." The order also created the Fair Employment Practices Committee (FEPC) to hear complaints about job discrimination in defense industries and government. Though this law was weakly enforced, it was still a beginning.

After the war, Randolph continued as a labor leader. He became a vice president of the combined AFL and CIO labor union in 1955. When the civil rights movement got under way, the march that Randolph had wanted to hold years before finally took place. In August 1963, he directed the March on Washington, D.C. There, more than 200,000 people gathered to call for jobs and freedom. Randolph, then 74 years old, stood beside Martin Luther King, Jr., as King gave his famous "I Have a Dream" speech. ▪

Graphing the Main Idea

To make sure students understand the main idea of this section, you may wish to use the double web graphic organizer below.

Tell students that a double web is used to compare and contrast information. Ask students to use it to compare how Japanese Americans were treated during the war with how other racial and ethnic minorities were treated.

Teaching Tip A template for this graphic organizer can be found in the Color Transparencies, G-2.

ACTIVITY
LEARNING STYLES

Ask students to suppose that they are writing for a magazine distributed to the armed services during World War II. Ask them to write an editorial about the Zoot Suit riots, expressing an opinion about the actions of sailors before and during the riot. (*Verbal/Linguistic*)

Main Idea CONNECTIONS

How did the wartime economy benefit Mexican Americans?

Mexican Americans

Like African Americans, both Mexican American citizens and Mexicans working in the United States faced discrimination during the war. On the other hand, the wartime economy brought Mexican Americans new job opportunities in defense industries. By 1944, about 17,000 had jobs in the Los Angeles shipyards, where none had worked three years before. Mexican Americans also found jobs in shipyards and aircraft factories elsewhere in California and in Washington, Texas, and New Mexico. Some headed for other war production centers such as Detroit, Chicago, Kansas City, and New York.

The Bracero Program In agriculture, a shortage of farm laborers led the United States to seek help from Mexico. In 1942 an agreement between the two nations provided for transportation, food, shelter, and medical care for thousands of *braceros* (Spanish for "workers"), Mexican farm laborers brought to work in the United States. Between 1942 and 1947, more than 200,000 braceros worked on American farms and, occasionally, in other industries. The program brought a rise in the Latino population of Los Angeles and other cities in southern California. Many lived in Spanish-speaking neighborhoods called *barrios*. Crowded conditions and discrimination caused tensions to rise within the *bracero* communities.

Zoot Suit Riots In the 1940s some young Mexican Americans in the Los Angeles barrio began to wear a style known as the "zoot suit." It had a long draped jacket and baggy pants with tight cuffs. "Zoot-suiters" often wore a slicked-back "ducktail" haircut. This look offended many people, especially sailors who came to Los Angeles on leave from nearby military bases. Groups of sailors roamed the streets looking for "zoot-suiters," whom they beat up and humiliated for looking "un-American." One Spanish newspaper, *La Opinión*, urged the Mexican American youths not to respond with more violence, but some took revenge on the sailors when they could.

Early in June 1943, the street fighting turned into full-scale riots. Local newspapers usually blamed Mexican Americans for the violence. Police often arrested the victims rather than the sailors who had begun the attacks. Army and navy officials finally intervened, restricting soldiers' off-duty access to Los Angeles.

Native Americans

The war also changed the lives of Native Americans. About 25,000 Native Americans joined the armed forces (as you read in the previous chapter). Many others migrated to urban centers to work in defense plants. Roughly 23,000 Native Americans worked in war industries around the country.

Life in the military or in the cities was a new experience for Native Americans who had lived only on reservations. They had to adapt quickly to white culture. At the end of the war, those who had moved away often did not return to reservation life. For some, the cultural transition brought a sense of having lost their roots.

Japanese Americans

Japanese Americans suffered the worst discrimination during the war. In late 1941, they were a tiny minority in the United States, numbering only 127,000 (about 0.1 percent of the entire population). Most lived on the West Coast, where prejudice against them had

Mexican American "zoot-suiters" were the targets of attacks in 1943, but they themselves were often blamed by police for the violence. **Diversity** Why do you think soldiers and police were set against zoot-suiters?

▶ RESOURCE OPTIONS

Teaching Resources

📁 **Biography** Daniel K. Inouye, Units 7–8 folder, p. 65

🗔 **American History Block Scheduling Support** The Internment of Japanese Americans During World War II, found in the Prosperity, Depression, and War folder, includes interdisciplinary lesson suggestions and activities for Geography and History, Primary Sources, Biography, and Literature.

Answer to . . .

Main Idea Connections It brought them new job opportunities in defense, shipyards, and aircraft factories.

Viewing History Fear, and suspicion of foreigners heightened by the war.

always been strong. About two thirds of the Japanese Americans were **Nisei,** or people born in the United States of parents who had emigrated from Japan. Although they were native-born citizens, they still often met hostility from their white neighbors.

Hostility grew into hatred and hysteria after Japan attacked Pearl Harbor. Rumors flew about sabotage on the West Coast. The press increased people's fears with headlines such as "Jap Boat Flashes Message Ashore" and "Japanese Here Sent Vital Data to Tokyo." Americans were left with the feeling that Japanese spies were everywhere.

Japanese Relocation As a result of these fears and prejudices, the government decided to remove all "aliens" from the West Coast. On February 19, 1942, President Roosevelt signed Executive Order 9066. It authorized the Secretary of War to establish military zones on the West Coast and remove "any or all persons" from such zones. For a few months, foreign-born Italians and Germans were also told to move away from the coast, but those orders were soon changed. The War Relocation Authority was then set up to move out everyone of Japanese ancestry—about 110,000 people, both citizens and noncitizens. They would go to **internment camps** in remote areas inland. (Internment means confinement, especially during wartime.)†

Relocation took place so fast that Japanese Americans had little time to secure their property before they left. Many lost their businesses, farms, homes, and other property. Henry Murakami, a resident of California, remembers losing the $55,000 worth of fishing nets that had been his livelihood:

AMERICAN VOICES ❝When we were sent to Fort Lincoln [in Bismarck, North Dakota] I asked the FBI men about my nets. They said, 'Don't worry. Everything is going to be taken care of.' But I never saw the nets again, nor my brand-new 1941 Plymouth, nor our furniture. It all just disappeared. I lost everything.❞

—*Henry Murakami*

Japanese Americans had no idea where they were going when they boarded the buses for the internment camps. Monica Sone, who lived in Seattle, imagined her camp would be

---

† Similar fears swept Canada, which interned Japanese Canadians.

 At assembly centers for Japanese Americans, tags with family identification numbers were attached to each piece of luggage and likewise to each family member. Permitted to take only a few possessions with them, many were forced to abandon what they could not carry or sell. *Government Why do you think the Supreme Court failed to uphold the rights of Japanese Americans?*

"out somewhere deep in a snow-bound forest, an American Siberia. I saw myself plunging chest deep in the snow, hunting for small game to keep us alive." She and her family packed their winter clothes, only to end up in Camp Minidoka, on the sun-baked prairie of central Idaho where the normal July temperature is about 90 degrees Fahrenheit.

All the internment camps were in desolate areas, with wooden barracks covered with tar paper. Inside the barracks, families had a room equipped with only cots, blankets, and a light bulb. People had to share toilet, bathing, and dining facilities. Barbed wire and armed guards surrounded the camps.

Legal Challenges A few Japanese Americans challenged the internment policy in the courts. Four cases eventually reached the Supreme Court, which ruled that the wartime relocation was constitutional. In one case, California resident Fred Toyosaburo Korematsu, a defense-plant worker, was arrested for refusing

 BACKGROUND

Geography in History

Japanese Americans provided most of California's fresh produce in 1940, although they were less than 1% of the state's population. The internment of Japanese American farmers and grocers after Pearl Harbor threw parts of California's agricultural sector into chaos. While the government scrambled to feed its troops and encouraged Americans to start victory gardens, California had lost its primary supply of fruits and vegetables.

BACKGROUND

Recent Scholarship

The decision to relocate Japanese Americans in internment camps has been debated for over 50 years. In *All the Laws but One: Civil Liberties in Wartime* by Chief Justice of the United States William H. Rehnquist, the legacy of that complex decision is ". . . that the courts will pay more careful attention to the basis for the government's claims of necessity as a reason for curtailing civil liberty. The laws will thus not be silent in time of war, even though they will speak with a different voice."

▶ **RESOURCE OPTIONS**

Teaching Resources

📁 **Comparing Primary Sources** On Japanese American Internment, Units 7–8 folder, pp. 66–67

📁 **Primary Source Activity** Anti-Japanese Sentiment, Learning with Documents folder, p. 31

Answer to . . .

Viewing History Sample answer: The Supreme Court is not immune to politics or public opinion.

INTERNMENT OF JAPANESE AMERICANS

The forced internment of Japanese Americans produced strong feelings on both sides of the issue. Two views are given below. How does each of these viewpoints address the issue of constitutional rights?

For Internment	Against Internment
"It is a fact that the Japanese navy has been reconnoitering [investigating] the Pacific Coast . . . . It is [a] fact that communication takes place between the enemy at sea and enemy agents on land. The Pacific Coast is officially a combat zone: some part of it may at any moment be a battlefield. Nobody's constitutional rights include the right to reside and do business on a battlefield." —*Walter Lippmann, American columnist, February 12, 1942*	"Racial discrimination in any form and in any degree has no justifiable part whatever in our democratic way of life. . . . All residents of this nation are kin in some way by blood or culture to a foreign land. Yet they are primarily and necessarily a part of . . . the United States [and are] . . . entitled to all rights and freedoms guaranteed by the Constitution." —*Supreme Court Justice Frank Murphy's dissenting opinion,* Korematsu v. United States, *1944*

ANALYZING VIEWPOINTS What different assumptions does each of these writers make about Japanese Americans on the West Coast?

---

to report to a relocation center. Korematsu appealed, saying his civil rights had been violated.

The Supreme Court ruled in *Korematsu v. United States* (1944) that the decision was not based on race. The majority opinion said that "the military urgency of the situation demanded that all citizens of Japanese ancestry be segregated from the West Coast temporarily." The dissenting opinion, however, labeled the policy "an obvious racial discrimination."

Early in 1945, Japanese Americans were allowed to leave the camps. Some returned home and resumed their lives, but others found that they had lost nearly everything. As time passed, many Americans came to believe that the internment had been a great injustice. In 1988 Congress passed a law awarding each surviving Japanese American internee a tax-free payment of $20,000. More than 40 years after the event, the United States government also officially apologized.

Nisei Soldiers Despite injustices against the Japanese Americans, more than 20,000 of them served in the armed forces. About 1,200 of the Japanese Americans who volunteered did so from relocation centers. Many other volunteers came from Hawaii, where there had been no internment.

The 442nd Regimental Combat Team was made up entirely of Japanese Americans. Fighting in France and Germany, its soldiers won more medals for bravery than any other unit in United States history.

SECTION 4 REVIEW

Comprehension

1. *Key Terms* Define: (a) "Double V" campaign; (b) Nisei; (c) internment camp.

2. *Summarizing the Main Idea* Did the wartime economy make workplace discrimination worse or just create more of it?

3. *Organizing Information* Make a tree-map chart comparing and contrasting the wartime experiences of the four different ethnic and racial groups discussed in this section.

Critical Thinking

4. *Analyzing Time Lines* Review the time line at the start of the section. Which of those events do you think had the greatest impact on conditions for minorities after the war? Write a short paragraph explaining your choice.

5. *Recognizing Bias* The government acted more harshly against Japanese Americans than against people of Italian and German ancestry. Why do you think this discrimination occurred?

Writing Activity

6. *Writing a Persuasive Essay* Imagine that you are an adviser to Franklin D. Roosevelt and have been asked to give the President your opinion about A. Philip Randolph's idea for a protest march. Are you in favor of or against the march? Write a memo to FDR persuading him that your opinion is right.

Answers to

SECTION 4 REVIEW

1. (a) "Double V" campaign, see p. 733; (b) Nisei, see p. 735; (c) internment camp, see p. 735.

2. Sample answer: It gave minority groups new job opportunities, but their influx into the cities for jobs led to the formation of ghettos and sparked conflict with whites.

3. African Americans: new jobs but forced to live in ghettos, discriminated against socially and economically. Mexican Americans: new jobs but forced to live in barrios, suffered from violence and riots. Native Americans: assimilated culturally in new military jobs. Japanese Americans: suffered intense discrimination, relocated to internment camps.

4. Answers will vary but should be supported with facts from the section.

5. Possible answers: The government feared Japanese spies; public outrage against Japan had been stirred up by a direct attack on American soil; it was easy to make them scapegoats; they had endured prejudice for many years.

6. Essays will vary but should be supported with facts from the section.

Answer to . . .

Comparing Primary Sources
Lippmann: They live in a military zone and therefore can have their rights abridged. Murphy: They are U.S. citizens and deserve their full rights.

RESOURCE OPTIONS

Teaching Resources

Quiz Units 7–8 folder, p. 64

Chapter Tests Forms A and B Chapter Test folder

Student Performance Pack

Guide to the Essentials Chapter 25, Section 4 (English and Spanish)

Standardized Test Preparation Handbook

Media and Technology

Guided Reading Audiotapes Chapter 25 Summary (English and Spanish)
Student Edition on Audiotape Chapter 25

Test Bank CD-ROM; Interactive Student Tutorial CD-ROM Chapter Test

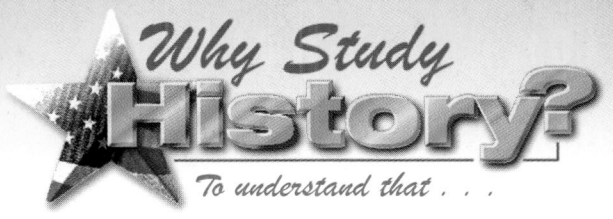

Why Study History?

To understand that . . .

Most Women Are in the Work Force

Working women in the United States today are facing some of the same challenges that confronted working women during World War II.

The alarm clock rings at 5:30 A.M. Ann Bogar makes breakfast and packs lunches for her husband and children before leaving the house at 6:15. Bogar is an executive assistant in an oil and gas company based in Houston, Texas.

Millions of American women like Bogar

Woman assembling aircraft during World War II

begin each weekday by preparing breakfast and helping children get ready for school. They also work outside the home—as teachers, bankers, lawyers, secretaries, doctors, computer programmers, sales associates, rabbis or ministers, waitresses, or business executives.

The Impact Today

During World War II, about 6 million American women joined the work force. They took jobs in factories and offices to help the war effort and replace the men who were fighting overseas. After the war, most women returned to their jobs as homemakers—some by choice, others as a result of pressure by government and industry. Still, women's work experience helped shape the expectations of later generations.

In 1940 only about 15 percent of married women worked outside the home. Today more than 60 percent do. Many women work to meet the challenges and reap the rewards of a career. Others work out of necessity, to help meet the living expenses of their families.

In the 1940s, working women earned significantly less money than men who performed the same jobs. Although women have made strides toward greater economic equality, they still experience wage discrimination. In 1999, full-time women wage and salary earners earned 76 percent of men's median weekly earnings. This wage gap exists for women at all educational levels. Even female college graduates earn roughly 16 percent less than their male peers.

Women make up about 61 percent of employees in the nation's top 500 companies but only 2.4 percent of corporate executives. Why? In seeking to move up the corporate ladder, many women encounter a "glass ceiling" of gender-based barriers to advancement. Women often start in areas such as personnel and staff support, which do not generally lead to top management positions. Also, there are few women executives to act as sponsors to younger women, helping them to rise in the corporation. An important challenge for American corporations is to ensure that women have equal opportunity for advancement.

Office worker

The Impact on You

Create a typical daily schedule that shows the responsibilities of two working parents. You can base this schedule on your own family or that of a neighbor. Your schedule should show what each parent's typical day is like and how the parents divide household responsibilities.

Class Discussion

Discuss with the class women's roles and challenges in the work force. For a more thorough examination of the issue, see the activity folder in the Resource Options below.

ACTIVITY
STUDENT PARTICIPATION

Making a Comparison Chart

Ask students to read the text. Then divide them into small groups to compare and contrast the responsibilities of working men and working women in American society today. Each group should consider and discuss together one of the following areas:
- **household**
- **child care**
- **finances**
- **employment**

Use the information to create a class chart showing the similarities and differences in men's and women's responsibilities.

Follow up Discuss whether students' findings help to explain the "wage gap" and "glass ceiling" phenomena.

Using the Internet

Students can learn more about women in the work force by exploring links in the *America: Pathways to the Present* Web site at

http://www.Pathways.phschool.com

Assessment

See the Lesson Plans folder, pp. 24–27, for rubrics on assessing Class Participation Projects.

RESOURCE OPTIONS

Teaching Resources

Why Study History? Activity Most Women Are in the Work Force, found in the Why Study History? folder, p. 26, provides an activity to help students better understand women's roles in the work force.

Media and Technology

Prentice Hall United States History Video Collection™ Volume 19 *World War II*

737

Chapter 25 Review

Key Terms

Students should refer to the definitions of key terms in the chapter to write sentences that show an understanding of how the government mobilized people and resources for war and how people at home were affected.

Comprehension

1. The economy was boosted by the massive production of goods to supply the Allied forces.

2. They stopped producing consumer goods, converting to weapons and other wartime production. They built new factories and developed new mass production techniques.

3. It raised taxes and witheld taxes from paychecks; it launched bond drives to encourage Americans to buy war bonds.

4. To limit prices on all non-farm commodities; to control rents in defense areas.

5. Sample answer: gasoline, sugar, coffee, meat, clothing. These shortages forced people to buy ration books, conserve, and recycle.

6. Before the war most women worked as sales clerks, teachers, or domestic servants. During the war many women took jobs in manufacturing, especially in the defense industry.

7. Making their own money; more challenging work; feelings of accomplishment.

8. They launched the "Double V" campaign to win equality at home, founded CORE, and used activism to try to end discrimination.

9. Prejudice that had existed for years on the West Coast, rumors suggesting that Japanese Americans were spies, and outrage over Pearl Harbor.

Chapter Summary

The major concepts of Chapter 25 are presented below. See also **Guide to the Essentials of American History** or **Interactive Student Tutorial CD-ROM,** which contains interactive review activities, time lines, helpful hints, and test practice for Chapter 25.

Reviewing the Main Ideas

Wartime production ended the Depression, bringing prosperity and high employment. As factories stopped producing consumer goods and converted to making military equipment, government programs worked to keep popular support behind the war effort. War jobs brought new opportunities for women and members of most minorities, but discrimination continued.

Section 1: The Shift to Wartime Production
At the beginning of World War II, the government mobilized industries and workers to produce materials for the war.

Section 2: Daily Life on the Home Front
As the war economy brought both prosperity and shortages, the government worked to keep Americans at home involved in the war effort.

Section 3: Women and the War
During World War II, more American women went to work in nontraditional, war-industry jobs, but they were discouraged from keeping their jobs after the war ended.

Section 4: The Struggle for Justice at Home
While the war brought new job opportunities for some racial and ethnic minorities, Japanese Americans were the victims of widespread intolerance.

Working women today face many of the same challenges that confronted working women during World War II. Today about 61 percent of married women work outside the home.

Using Graphic Organizers

- Economy: Stimulated by government mobilization of industries and workers to boost production of war materials.
- Daily Life: People had money but were confronted with shortages; the government used programs to get all citizens involved in the war effort.
- Women: Job opportunities opened up as women were needed to take over men's jobs; married women joined the work force.

Key Terms

For each of the terms below, write a sentence explaining how it relates to the chapter.

1. Liberty ship
2. wildcat strike
3. war bond
4. deficit spending
5. rationing
6. Office of War Mobilization
7. Office of War Information
8. victory garden
9. "Double V" campaign

Comprehension

1. How did World War II end the Depression?
2. What changes did American businesses make at the start of the war?
3. In what two ways did the government finance war costs and war production?
4. What were the responsibilities of the Office of Price Administration?
5. Name five items that were in short supply during the war. How did these shortages affect people at home?
6. What changes took place in the kinds of jobs women held before and during World War II?
7. Describe some of the benefits that women got from war work.
8. What strategies did African Americans use to gain equal rights during World War II?
9. What attitudes led to the internment of Japanese Americans during World War II?

Using Graphic Organizers

On a separate sheet of paper, copy the tree-map organizer below. Using your own words, fill in the main ideas for each category.

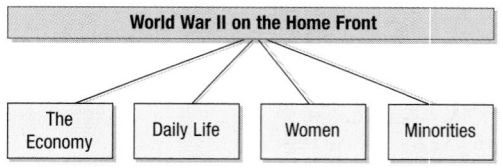

World War II on the Home Front

| The Economy | Daily Life | Women | Minorities |

- Minorities: New job opportunities opened up for Native Americans, African Americans, and Mexican Americans, though these groups still faced job discrimination; Japanese Americans were the victims of racial intolerance and were sent to internment camps.

Analyzing Political Cartoons ▶

1. What does the woman in the cartoon symbolize?
2. What is the significance of her having her own "man-size" pay?
3. What point does the man's speech make?
4. Examine both figures. What message is conveyed by the woman's huge size and the man's clothing?

Critical Thinking

1. *Applying the Chapter Skill* What assumptions did employers and society as a whole make about the women who took new jobs during World War II? How were these like or unlike those that were made about "Rosie the Riveter"?
2. *Perceiving Cause-Effect Relationships* Why were there shortages of sugar, coffee, and tropical fruits during World War II?
3. *Drawing Conclusions* Why did Americans generally accept rationing, bond drives, and other government programs to involve them in the war effort?
4. *Predicting Consequences* How might the changes that the war brought for African Americans have affected the later civil rights movement?

INTERNET ACTIVITY

For your portfolio:
CREATE A DIARY ENTRY

Access Prentice Hall's *America: Pathways to the Present* site at **www.Pathways.phschool.com** for the specific URLs to complete the activity. Additional resources and related Web sites are also available.

Read several interviews with women who experienced life on the home front in World War II. Create a fictional diary entry of a week in the life of one such woman. Choose a typical week or a week during which a major event happened. How did the war affect the lives of the people at home?

ANALYZING DOCUMENTS ◀▶ INTERPRETING DATA

Turn to the map on page 732.

1. One of these statements about this map is *not* true. Which is it? (a) Every state in the South lost population in the wartime migration. (b) Florida, Georgia, and South Carolina lost the greatest percentage of their populations. (c) Every state in the industrial Northeast gained population in the African American migration.
2. Which statement best reflects the information shown on this map?

(a) African Americans moved mainly to northern industrial areas. (b) Wartime job opportunities were available to African Americans throughout the United States. (c) West Coast war industries did not draw African Americans.

3. *Writing* In one paragraph, summarize the events shown by this map and what they meant for African Americans.

Connecting to Today

Essay Writing Choose one of the groups whose wartime experiences are discussed in Section 4. Then research and write an essay about the changes that have taken place in that group's position in American society in the 50-plus years since World War II.

INTERNET ACTIVITY

Diary entries will vary, but students should address issues such as jobs outside the home, participating in rationing and recycling programs, descriptions of meals and shopping trips, and letters from friends and relatives overseas.

Analyzing Political Cartoons

1. Women who entered the labor force in support of the war effort.
2. It is an incentive to enjoy working in traditionally male jobs and to remain in the labor force.
3. Women were expected to give up their new jobs once men returned home from the war.
4. Women empowered by gainful employment are threatening to men.

Critical Thinking

1. They assumed that women, like "Rosie," were working for patriotic reasons and would turn over their jobs to men at the end of the war. Unlike "Rosie," who was young, white, and single, many of the women entering the work force were older, married, and non-white, and were working for a variety of reasons.
2. The sugar supply was cut off when the Philippines, the major source of American imports, was taken by the Japanese. Coffee and tropical fruits became scarce when shipping lanes were closed during the war.
3. The government promoted war programs to involve citizens. People were stirred by patriotism to do whatever they could on the home front to support the war effort, especially as most people had friends or relatives fighting in the war.
4. The war highlighted that the ideals Americans were fighting for were not being realized at home. African Americans used this contradiction as an opportunity to rally for equal rights, paving the way for later activisim.

Interpreting Data

1. c
2. a
3. Answers should be based on the map and on facts from the chapter.

Connecting to Today

Essays will vary but should be supported with research and examples.

CHAPTER 26

The Cold War, 1945–1960

Managing Time and Instruction

INSTRUCTION SUPPORT

These materials for instruction are provided for **each section** in the **Teaching Resources.** See **Units 7–8 folder for Enrichment Support:**

- Reproducible Lesson Plans in Lesson Plans folder • Learning Styles Lesson Plans in Learning Styles Lesson Plans folder • Big Idea Graphic Organizers in Big Idea Graphic Organizer folder
- Guided Reading and Review • Quizzes • Test Preparation Practice booklet

DAILY LESSON	ENRICHMENT SUPPORT
1 **Origins of the Cold War** *(pp. 741–746)*	• Primary Source Activity, "Uncle Joe," Learning with Documents folder, p. 32 • Visual Learning Activity, What They Fear Most, Learning with Documents folder, p. 68 • Biography, George F. Kennan, Units 7–8 folder, p. 76 • Skills for Life Activity, Units 7–8 folder, p. 80
2 **The Cold War Abroad and at Home** *(pp. 748–755)*	• Comparing Primary Sources, On Joining NATO, Units 7–8 folder, pp. 77–78 • Critical Thinking Activity, Identifying Central Issues: Cold War Policy, found on **Resource Pro** • Primary Source Activity, The Rise of Joseph McCarthy, found on **Resource Pro**
3 **The Cold War Expands** *(pp. 756–762)*	• Biography, Marguerite Higgins, found on **Resource Pro** • Key Documents, General Douglas MacArthur, Address to Congress, Learning with Documents folder, p. 98 • Visual Learning Activity, Civilian Control of the Military, found on **Resource Pro** • Literature Activity, The Hunt for Witches and Communists, found on **Resource Pro** • Literature Activity, *The Ugly American,* Units 7–8 folder, p. 79 • Defense Spending Affects You, Why Study History? folder, p. 27

Running Out of Time?

- Use Tape 4, "Hot and Cold War, 1939–1960," from **Visions of America** videotapes series.
- Use Chapter 26 Summary from **Guide to the Essentials of American History (English and Spanish).**

Companion Web Site

The companion Web site offers online links for all chapter review activities. It also provides key content links and structured support for this chapter for both teachers and students.

http://www.Pathways.phschool.com

Media and Technology

For the Student

Interactive Student Tutorial CD-ROM Chapter 26

Student Edition on Audiotape Chapter 26

American Heritage® CD-ROM

Guided Reading Audiotapes (English and Spanish) Chapter 26

For the Teacher

Resource Pro CD-ROM Chapter 26

Test Bank CD-ROM Chapter 26

Listening to Literature Audiotapes *Timeless Voices, Timeless Themes* Inaugural Address by John F. Kennedy

 ## Assessment Options

Chapter Test Forms A&B Test Bank CD-ROM booklet

Test Bank CD-ROM Chapter 26

Standardized Test Preparation Handbook

 ## Block Scheduling

Pacing Suggestions

For 90-minute Blocks

- Teach sections 1 and 2 using Transparencies I-13, E-8, J-8, K-8, and F-10 and the Extended Class Periods Activity on p. 743.
- Teach section 3 using the Big Idea Graphic Organizer from Teaching Resources and the Background note on p. 758 for class discussions.

Additional Resources

- Prentice Hall's **American History Block Scheduling Support File** covers over 40 major topics in American history.
- **Prentice Hall United States History Video Collection™** contains 20 videotapes covering American history from beginnings to present.
- **Decision America Videotapes and Videodiscs**

 ## Connections to American Literature

from Prentice Hall

Prentice Hall Literature *Timeless Voices, Timeless Themes: The Crucible* by Arthur Miller, p.1069

Additional Resources

For the Student

Aleksandr I. Solzhenitsyn. *One Day in the Life of Ivan Denisovich.* Bantam, 1984.

Theodore H. White. *In Search of History: A Personal Adventure.* Harper and Row, 1978.

For the Teacher

George F. Kennan. *Memoirs: 1925–1959.* Pantheon, 1983.

 American Heritage®

Prentice Hall brings into the classroom the vast archives and scholarship of the nation's premier American history magazine. See "From the Archives of American Heritage®" and "About the Presidents" teaching notes in this chapter.

 ## History Alive!

Teacher's Curriculum Institute, in partnership with Prentice Hall, provides unique materials that engage students with diverse learning styles. See History Alive!® unit on The Cold War.

 ## Student Performance Pack

Ensures success in the three critical areas of Reading, Test Taking, and English Language Development with the following materials:
- Guide to the Essentials of American History in English and Spanish
- Guided Reading Audiotapes in English and Spanish
- Interactive Student Tutorial CD-ROM
- Test Preparation Handbook
- Test Preparation Practice booklet

Introducing the Chapter

American foreign policy after World War II remained consistent with the nation's wartime activities: force would be used to oppose authoritarian regimes that the United States considered a threat to the free world. At home the federal government would use strong, and sometimes questionable, measures to counter what it perceived to be threats to the nation's internal security.

Themes in American History

The theme for this chapter, Foreign Policy, is listed at the beginning of this unit. An alternate theme for the chapter is Geography. To teach this unit thematically, you may wish to use The Nation After World War II folder in American History Block Scheduling Support.

Why Study History?

Have students explore suggested ways of connecting the past to the present on page 763.

Answer to . . .

Viewing History Students should use this question as an aid in reading the chapter. The artist depicts the "chill" of the cold war, reflected in the ice blocks, and a sense of hope evoked by the people using the ice blocks to rebuild.

CHAPTER
26 The Cold War
1945-1960

CHAPTER FOCUS

This chapter examines the post–World War II hostility between the United States and the Soviet Union that played out in large and small conflicts across the globe.

 The Why Study History? page at the end of this chapter explores the connection between defense spending before and after the cold war.

VIEWING HISTORY
Artist Ben Shahn's 1945 painting entitled *Reconstruction* portrays the rebuilding process after World War II. *Culture* **What feelings does the artist seem to depict?**

RESOURCE OPTIONS

Teaching Resources

 Big Idea Graphic Organizer folder Graphic summary of the main idea of the chapter.

Learning Styles Lesson Plans folder Alternate lesson plans for diverse learning styles for each chapter.

Media and Technology

 AmericanHeritage® CD-ROM
Time Tour The Nation Today and Tomorrow: The Fifties

 Prentice Hall United States History Video Collection™ Volume 20
Post-War USA

1945	1946	
Yalta Conference (February); UN founded (April); FDR dies, Truman becomes President (April); Potsdam Conference (July)	Stalin predicts triumph of communism (February); Churchill gives iron curtain speech (March); Kennan article on containment (July)	**1947** Truman Doctrine

1945   **1946**   **1947**

1 Origins of the Cold War

SECTION PREVIEW

Objectives

1. Explain why 1945 was a critical year in international relations and how it was followed by conflicting postwar goals.
2. Describe how the Soviet Union tightened its control over Eastern Europe.
3. Identify the iron curtain and how it led to containment policy and the Truman Doctrine.
4. *Key Terms* Define: satellite nation; iron curtain; cold war; containment; Truman Doctrine.

Main Idea

At the end of World War II, conflicting goals for Europe led to growing hostility between the United States and the Soviet Union.

Reading Strategy

Arranging Events in Order As you read, make a list of events that led to the development of the cold war. List the date of each event. Then, arrange them in chronological order.

Objectives

You may wish to call students' attention to the objectives in the Section Preview. The objectives are reflected in the main headings of the section.

Bellringer

Write the following questions on the chalkboard and ask students to write an answer: What do you think a "cold war" is? Why was this war considered "cold" and not "hot"? What made it a war?

Reading Strategy

Arranging Events in Order Refer to the Reading Strategy in the Section Preview. You may wish to ask volunteers to contribute to a list of events that you write on the chalkboard.

"I know you will not mind my being brutally frank when I tell you that I can personally handle Stalin," President Roosevelt told Winston Churchill during World War II. "He thinks he likes me better, and I hope he will continue to." By 1944, Roosevelt was so sure of Stalin's cooperation that he began calling the Soviet dictator "Uncle Joe."

A Roosevelt adviser later wrote that the President did not have "any real comprehension of the great gulf that separated [their] thinking." Churchill, however, clearly understood the situation. "Germany is finished," he told an adviser. "The real problem is Russia. I can't get the Americans to see it."

1945—A Critical Year

The wartime cooperation between the United States and the Soviet Union was a temporary arrangement. The two nations had a history of bad feelings following the Russian Revolution. During the revolt, President Wilson had dispatched American troops to Russia to support anti-Communist resistance. The United States

did not recognize the legal existence of the Soviet government until 1933.

As wartime allies, the Soviets disagreed bitterly with their American and British partners over battle tactics and postwar plans. As the end of the war approached, relations grew increasingly tense.

Differences at Yalta In February 1945, Roosevelt met with Stalin and Churchill at Yalta

Churchill, Roosevelt, and Stalin, (left to right) met at Yalta to discuss postwar Europe.

LESSON PLAN
Connecting to the Main Idea

1. Focus Having defeated a common enemy in World War II, the United States and the Soviet Union then became enemies themselves. Ask students what both sides sought to gain after World War II.

2. Instruct Discuss how the United States and the Soviet Union became bitter rivals after World War II. Was the cold war the result of a mistake, or were there powerful forces at work that made the conflict inevitable? Point out the differing views of Joseph Stalin held by Roosevelt and Churchill, and discuss what effect the personalities of western leaders might have had on Soviet policy.

3. Close Deep and bitter divisions emerged between the United States and the Soviet Union after World War II. The next section describes how the Soviets' dream of spreading communism soon fueled a massive American effort to stop it.

RESOURCE OPTIONS

Teaching Resources

📁 **Reproducible Lesson Plan** Lesson Plans folder, p. 139

📁 **Big Idea Graphic Organizer** Big Idea Graphic Organizer folder, p. 111

📁 **Guided Reading and Review** Units 7–8 folder, p. 70

📁 **Primary Source Activity** "Uncle Joe," Learning with Documents folder, p. 32

Media and Technology

 AmericanHeritage® CD-ROM

Time Tour The Nation Today and Tomorrow: The Fifties

At its birth, the United Nations was hailed by President Harry Truman as "a victory against war itself." In this photograph, Truman and representatives from other member nations look on as Secretary of State Edward Stettinius signs the UN charter in June 1945. *Government* Why do you think Congress agreed to United States membership in the United Nations, even though it had not supported the League of Nations?

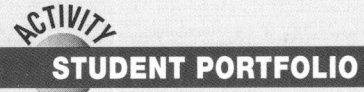
to work out the future of Germany and Poland. They agreed on the division of Germany into American, British, French, and Soviet occupation zones. (Later, the American, French, British zones were combined to create West Germany. The Soviet zone became East Germany.) Roosevelt and Churchill rejected Stalin's demand that Germany pay the Soviet Union $10 billion in war damages.

Roosevelt pressed Stalin at Yalta to declare war on Japan. The atomic bomb had not yet been tested, and the President wanted Soviet help if an invasion of Japan became necessary.

Poland proved the most difficult issue to address at Yalta. The Red Army had occupied that country and supported the Communist-dominated government. Stalin opposed the return of Poland's prewar government. Historically, Poland was an invasion route into Russia. The Polish government, Stalin insisted, must be sympathetic to Soviet security needs.

The meeting stalled until Stalin agreed on elections to let Poles choose their own type of government. Disputes over Poland would continue to strain American-Soviet relations.

The United Nations One item on which the leaders all agreed at Yalta was creation of the United Nations (UN), a new international peacekeeping organization. The League of Nations, founded after World War I, had failed largely because the United States refused to join. This time, policymakers got congressional support for the UN.

In April 1945, delegates from 50 nations met in San Francisco to adopt a charter, or statement of principles, for the UN. The charter stated that members would try to settle their differences peacefully. It vowed to try to stop wars from starting and to end those that did break out.

All member nations belonged to the UN's General Assembly. Representatives of 11 countries sat on a Security Council. The United States, the Soviet Union, Great Britain, France, and China had permanent seats on the council and a veto over proposed policies.

Truman Takes Command Roosevelt never lived to see his dream of the United Nations fulfilled. On April 12, 1945, just two weeks before the UN's first meeting, the President died while resting at Warm Springs, Georgia. Although he was in poor health and noticeably tired, his unexpected death shocked the nation. No one was more surprised than Vice President Harry S. Truman, who suddenly found himself President.

Few Vice Presidents have been less prepared to become President. While he had spent 10 years in Congress, Truman had been Vice President for just 82 days. Roosevelt had never involved him in major foreign policy discussions. Truman at first adopted FDR's willingness to compromise with the Soviets. But before long his attitude hardened.

The Potsdam Conference Truman's first meeting with Stalin came in July 1945 in the Berlin suburb of Potsdam. The Allies continued to debate the issues that had divided them at Yalta, including the future of Germany and of Poland. Stalin renewed his demand for war payments from Germany, and Truman insisted on the promised Polish elections.

At Potsdam, Truman got word that the atom bomb had been tested in New Mexico. Hoping to intimidate Stalin, Truman told him that America had a new weapon of extraordinary force. Stalin, who already knew of the bomb from Soviet spies, simply nodded and said that he hoped it would be put to good use. Stalin's casual manner hid his concern over America's new strategic advantage.

Conflicting Postwar Goals

Shortly after Truman took office he scolded Soviet Foreign Minister Vyacheslav Molotov for the Soviet Union's failure to allow Polish elections. Molotov was offended by Truman's bluntness. "I have never been talked to like that in my life," Molotov protested. "Carry out your agreements and you won't get talked to like that," Truman snapped.

The American View Tensions over Poland illustrated American and Soviet leaders' differing views of the world. Americans had fought to bring democracy and economic opportunity to the conquered nations of Europe and Asia. The United States hoped to see these goals achieved in the postwar world. An economically strong and politically open world also served American interests by providing markets for its products.

The Soviet View After losing more than 20 million people during the war and suffering widespread destruction, the Soviet Union was determined to rebuild in ways that would pro-

tect its own interests. One way was to establish **satellite nations,** countries subject to Soviet domination, on the western borders of the Soviet Union. These governments would be friendly to Communist goals.

Stalin thus refused to cooperate with new agencies such as the World Bank and the International Monetary Fund, intended to help build strong, capitalist economies. Instead, he installed or supported totalitarian Communist governments in Eastern Europe.

Soviets Tighten Their Hold

The Soviet Union quickly gained control over Eastern European nations freed from the Nazis. The promised elections in Poland did not take place for nearly two years. Meanwhile, Poland's Soviet-installed government eliminated all political opposition.

Albania and Bulgaria In Albania, Communist guerrilla forces had driven out the Germans by 1944. When elections were held the following year, all anti-Communist leaders had been silenced. Soviet troops rolled into Bulgaria in 1944, and the Communists secured their hold on the country by 1948.

Main Idea
CONNECTIONS

How did American and Soviet goals for postwar Europe differ?

ACTIVITY
EXTENDED CLASS PERIODS

Time: 90 minutes.
Activity: Reenact a meeting between President Truman and Soviet foreign minister Molotov.
Grouping: Four to six students.
Purpose: Each group should assign two students to role-play the officials, and two students to act as coaches. Each official/coach team should develop a list of overall goals and specific demands for the meeting. Students should consider the desires, fears, and political system of their respective countries.
Roles: Officials, coaches, researchers, moderator.
Outcome: Students will understand the political perspective of each official and nation.

A Divided Europe

MAP Skills

This map shows the nations controlled by Communist and non-Communist countries. After World War II, the Soviet Union was highly concerned about protecting its national security.
Location How does this map illustrate the policy pursued by the Soviet Union to protect itself from its non-Communist rivals in Europe?

RESOURCE OPTIONS

Teaching Resources

Visual Learning Activity What They Fear Most, Learning with Documents folder, p. 68

Answer to . . .

Main Idea Connections The United States wanted to open markets by spreading democracy. The Soviet Union wanted to secure markets by creating satellite nations.
Map Skills The map shows how the Soviet Union secured satellite nations along its European borders.

Winston Churchill (left) is shown making the 1946 speech in which he introduced the idea of the iron curtain. In the cartoon (right), United States Secretary of State James Byrnes is portrayed as a determined suitor. **Foreign Relations** *Whom is he courting? How does the cartoonist rate his chances of success?*

East German resources and installed a brutal totalitarian government there. In 1949, under the Communist government, the country became known as the German Democratic Republic.

Finland and Yugoslavia Two other countries managed to maintain a degree of independence from the Soviet Union. Finland signed a treaty of cooperation with the Soviets in 1948. The treaty required Finland to remain neutral in foreign affairs but allowed it to manage its domestic affairs. In Yugoslavia, Communists gained control in 1945 under the leadership of Josip Broz, better known as Tito. A fiercely independent dictator, Tito refused to take orders from Stalin, who unsuccessfully tried to topple him in 1948. For the next three decades Tito would pursue his own brand of communism relatively free from Soviet interference.

Czechoslovakia The Czechs desperately tried to hold on to their democratic multiparty political system. The Communist candidate won 40 percent of the vote in free elections in 1946, but Communist repression in neighboring nations weakened the Czech Communists' popularity. They plotted to take power, therefore, by replacing all non-Communist police officers with party members. By 1948 Czechoslovakia was a Soviet satellite nation.

Hungary and Romania After Communist candidates lost elections in Hungary in late 1945, Soviet troops remained in that country and demanded Communist control of the police. The arrest of anti-Communist leaders allowed the Communists to win new elections held in 1947. The Red Army also stayed in Romania, and in 1945 the Soviets forced the Romanian king to name a Communist as prime minister. Less than two years later, the prime minister forced the king to resign.

East Germany While the Western Allies wanted a strong, rebuilt Germany at the center of Europe, Stalin was determined that the Germans would never threaten his nation again. He established national control of all

The Iron Curtain

In a February 1946 speech, Stalin predicted the ultimate triumph of communism over capitalism. Yet he knew that it would be years before the Soviets were strong enough militarily to directly confront the United States.

In the meantime, Stalin called on Communists to spread their system by other means. He soon established Cominform, a Soviet agency intended to direct the activities of Communist parties throughout the world.

The month after Stalin's speech, Winston Churchill responded. Although he had recently been defeated for reelection as prime minister by Clement Attlee, Churchill remained a powerful voice of opposition to the Soviet Union. Speaking at Westminster College in Fulton, Missouri, he condemned the division of Europe that Stalin had already accomplished:

 "From Stettin in the Baltic to Trieste in the Adriatic, an iron curtain has descended across the Continent. Behind that line lie all the capitals of . . . Central and Eastern Europe. . . . The Communist parties, which were very small in all these Eastern States of Europe, have been raised to pre-eminence and power far beyond their numbers and are seeking everywhere to obtain totalitarian control. . . . This is certainly not the Liberated Europe we fought to build up. Nor is it one which contains the essentials of permanent peace.**"**

—*"Iron Curtain" speech, Winston Churchill,*
March 5, 1946

In his speech, Churchill called on Americans to help keep Stalin from closing the **iron curtain** of Communist domination and oppression around any more nations.

These two speeches set the tone for the **cold war,** the competition that developed between the United States and the Soviet Union for power and influence in the world. For nearly 50 years, until the collapse of the Soviet Union in 1991, the cold war was characterized by political and economic conflict and military tensions. The rivalry stopped just short of a "hot" war—a direct military engagement—between the two competing nations. However, United States military forces did engage in combat in other nations in efforts to defeat Soviet-supported uprisings and invasions.

Containment

In a secret telegram to the State Department in early 1946, George Kennan, a top American diplomat stationed in Moscow, analyzed Soviet behavior and policy. Like Stalin, Kennan saw the Soviet Union's weaknesses. Soon thereafter, he publicized his observations in an anonymous magazine article.

Soviet policies show "no real faith in the possibility of a permanently happy coexistence of the Socialist and capitalist worlds," Kennan warned. The Soviets believed the triumph of communism was inevitable. Therefore, Kennan concluded:

AMERICAN VOICES

❝[The Soviet Union] cannot be easily defeated or discouraged . . . but only by intelligent long-range policies . . . no less steady in their purpose . . . than those of the Soviet Union itself. In these circumstances, it is clear that the main element of any United States policy toward the Soviet Union must be that of a long-term, patient but firm and vigilant containment of Russian expansive tendencies.❞

—*American diplomat George Kennan, article in* Foreign Affairs *magazine, July 1947*

From Kennan's analysis, the policy of **containment** emerged. This policy recognized the possibility that Eastern Europe was already lost to communism. It called for the United States to resist Soviet attempts to form Communist governments elsewhere in the world.

CAUSE AND EFFECT: The Cold War

CAUSES
- United States and USSR clash over the postwar administration of Poland.
- USSR's totalitarian government is increasingly at odds with Western ideals.
- Stalin pledges to ensure the survival of the Soviet system, while Churchill urges the West to oppose it.

THE COLD WAR

EFFECTS
- United States adopts a policy to "contain" communism.
- Truman Doctrine offers U.S. aid to countries opposing communism.
- NATO and Warsaw Pact are formed.
- Fear of communism at home leads to a climate of suspicion in American culture.

Interpreting Charts The cold war affected life in the United States, as people began to fear communism within the nation. *Foreign Relations* **What effect did the cold war have on United States foreign policy?**

Critics saw containment as too moderate an approach to Soviet-American relations. They called for action to push the Communists out of Eastern Europe, Russia, and anywhere else. Kennan, however, argued that the Soviet system "bears within it the seeds of its own decay" and would eventually crumble. Thus, although containment remained controversial, it became the cornerstone of America's cold war foreign policy.

The Truman Doctrine

President Truman soon had a chance to apply the policy of containment. Since 1945 the Soviet Union had been making threats against Turkey. Stalin wanted control of the Dardanelles, a narrow strait in Turkey that would give Soviet ports on the Black Sea access to the Mediterranean. In addition, a civil war had broken out in nearby Greece in the closing days of the war. There Communists fought to overthrow the government that had returned to power after the Axis invaders withdrew.

Still suffering from the economic devastation of WWII, Britain announced in February

Main Idea
CONNECTIONS

What was the policy of containment?

Naming the New War On April 16, 1947 Bernard Baruch gave a name to something that had been developing for several years but was still inchoate in the public mind: the Cold War. In a speech before the legislature of his native South Carolina, on the occasion of the unveiling of his portrait, the venerable financier, humanitarian, and presidential adviser said: "Let us not be deceived—we are today in the midst of a cold war. Our enemies are to be found abroad and at home. Let us never forget this: Our unrest is the heart of their success." The phrase was not original with Baruch. In his autobiography he attributed it to his longtime friend the journalist Herbert Bayard Swope. As early as October 1945 George Orwell had used the same words to refer to a hostile peace, and the following March the *London Observer* employed them to describe Soviet policy toward Britain. Neither one drew much attention, so commentators made do with references to "current world events" or "Russia's actions in Europe" until Baruch crystallized the situation in a compact, convenient form. Source: Frederic D. Schwarz, "The Time Machine," *American Heritage* magazine, April 1997.

Answer to . . .

Interpreting Charts It led to the containment policy, the Truman Doctrine, and NATO.

Main Idea Connections A call for American resistance to communism around the world.

President Truman was named Man of the Year by Time in 1949.

In March 1947, in a speech before a joint session of Congress, Truman called on the United States to take a leadership role. In a statement of principles known as the **Truman Doctrine,** he established another major policy that guided American actions in the cold war.

KEY DOCUMENTS "Nearly every nation must choose between alternative ways of life. The choice is too often not a free one. One way of life is based upon the will of the majority. . . . The second way of life is based upon the will of a minority forcibly imposed upon the majority. . . . I believe that it must be the policy of the United States to sup-port free peoples who are resisting attempted subjugation [conquest] by armed minorities or by outside pressures. I believe that we must assist free peoples to work out their own des-tinies in their own way."

—*Truman Doctrine,*
speech by President Harry S. Truman
to Congress, March 12, 1947

1947 that it could no longer afford to provide aid to Greece and Turkey. The British suggested that the United States take over responsibility for defending the region. Undersecretary of State Dean Acheson report-ed that at that moment Great Britain "handed the job of world leadership, with all its burdens and all its glory, to the United States."

State Department officials developed a plan to provide American aid to Greece and Turkey. To head off congressional opposition, Acheson warned of grave dangers if the United States failed to act. "Only two great powers remain in the world," he observed, "the United States and the Soviet Union."

Responding to Truman's plea, Congress approved $400 million in aid for Greece and Turkey. In addition, the United States soon established military bases in both countries.

During the next four decades, the Truman Doctrine and the policy of contain-ment continued to guide United States foreign policy. These principles would lead the United States into controversial involve-ments in "hot" and "cold" conflicts around the world.

SECTION 1 REVIEW

Comprehension

1. *Key Terms* Define: (a) satellite nation; (b) iron curtain; (c) cold war; (d) containment; (e) Truman Doctrine.

2. *Summarizing the Main Idea* How did post-war hostility develop between the United States and the Soviet Union?

3. *Organizing Information* Create a time line to show how the Soviets tightened their hold on Eastern Europe.

Critical Thinking

4. *Analyzing Time Lines* Refer to the time line at the start of the section. Why was 1945 a crucial year in history?

5. *Drawing Conclusions* What effects do you think the Stalin and Churchill speeches of 1946 had on American public opinion?

Writing Activity

6. *Writing an Expository Essay* How did the idea of containment and the Truman Doctrine affect cold war policy?

Recognizing Cause and Effect

History is more than a list of events; it is a study of relationships among events. Recognizing cause and effect means examining how one event or action brings about others. If you can understand how events or ideas relate to and affect each other, you can begin to formulate workable solutions to problems.

Follow the steps below to practice recognizing cause and effect.

1. Identify the two parts of a cause-effect relationship. A cause is an event or action that brings about an effect. As you read, look for key words that signal a cause-effect relationship. Words such as *because, due to,* and *on account of* signal causes. Words such as *so, thus, therefore,* and *as a result* signal effects. Read statements A through C at right, and answer the following questions. (a) Which statements contain both a cause and an effect? (b) Which is the cause and which is the effect in each statement? (c) What words, if any, signal the cause-effect relationship?

2. Remember that an event can have more than one cause and more than one effect. Several causes can lead to one event. So, too, can a single cause have several effects. Read statement D at right, and respond to the following. (a) Find an example of a cause that has more than one effect. (b) Find an example of an effect that has more than one cause.

3. Understand that an event can be both a cause and an effect. A cause can lead to an effect, which in turn can be the cause of another event. In this way, causes and effects can form a chain of related events. You can diagram the following statements to show such a chain: The United States feared Soviet expansion in Europe. →The United States began a military buildup. →The Soviet Union began a military buildup. →An arms race between the two countries began. Now read statement D below. Draw a diagram showing the chain of related events.

TEST FOR SUCCESS

Use the information in the preceding section under the heading "The Soviet View" to write a statement in one or two sentences that shows cause and effect.

Statements

A Because President Roosevelt believed that postwar cooperation with the Soviet Union was necessary, he viewed Stalin as a partner—if not an ally—in formulating a peace.

B Unlike Roosevelt, President Truman was persuaded by advisers that the Soviet Union would become a "world bully" after the war. As a result, he adopted a "get tough" policy whose aim was to block any possibility of Soviet expansion.

C The Soviets, for their part, believed that the United States was intent on global domination and meant to encircle the Soviet Union with anti-Communist states.

D Due to mounting distrust between the United States and the Soviet Union, each power came to view the postwar peace negotiations as an opportunity to test the other's global objectives. Thus, negotiating the status of Poland became the first such test. Other tests included the plans for former German satellite states and the policies for the occupation of Germany. Each power regarded its own positions in these negotiations as essentially defensive, but each viewed the other's stances as aggressive and expansionist. Together these tests and stances produced the cold war, an armed and dangerous truce that lasted for 45 years.

RESOURCE OPTIONS

Teaching Resources

 Skills for Life Activity Units 7–8 folder, p. 80, helps students apply this skill by focusing on the end of the cold war.

Media and Technology

 Color Transparencies Cause and Effect, F–10; Critical Thinking, I–13

SKILLS FOR LIFE

Critical Thinking

Recognizing Cause and Effect

Focus Students distinguish between causes and effects and recognize multiple causes and effects.

Instruct Present this quotation from Harry Truman: "There is nothing new in the world except the history you do not know." Why, then, is it important to study the causes and effects of historical events?

Ask students to cite causes of the cold war. Discuss events in the world today that are similar to those that caused the cold war.

Answers

1. (a) A and B. (b) A: Cause—Roosevelt believed that postwar cooperation with the Soviet Union was necessary; Effect—he viewed Stalin as a partner in formulating peace. B: Cause—Truman was persuaded that the Soviet Union would become a "world bully"; Effect—he adopted a tough policy to block Soviet expansion. (c) *Because* signals cause. *As a result* signals effect.

2. (a) Cause: mounting distrust between the U.S. and the Soviet Union. Effects: negotiations on Poland, the satellite states, and the occupation of Germany used as ways to test global objectives. (b) Effect: the cold war. Causes: mounting distrust; negotiations viewed as tests; defensive positions seen as aggressive stances.

3. Distrust between the U. S. and the Soviet Union. → Peace negotiations viewed as tests of global objectives. → Negotiations used as tests. → Defensive positions viewed as aggression. → Cold war begun.

TEST FOR SUCCESS

Statements will vary but should follow the steps listed.

Objectives

You may wish to call students' attention to the objectives in the Section Preview. The objectives are reflected in the main headings of the section.

Bellringer

Write on the chalkboard, "The buck stops here." Ask students if they know what this famous quotation means. Tell them that President Truman kept it on his desk, and ask how it reflected his political style.

Reading Strategy

Organizing Information Refer to the Reading Stategy in the Section Preview. You may wish to have students record the challenges and solutions in the form of a chart.

LESSON PLAN

Connecting to the Main Idea

1. Focus Fearing the further spread of communism, the United States developed a new foreign policy called containment. Ask students how this policy was enacted.

2. Instruct Explain that the events in Berlin, Germany, in 1948–49 highlighted cold war tensions. Discuss why the blockade of one city caused so much anxiety to people around the world. What might the Soviets have hoped to gain by such a move? Why is the incident a good example of the cold war and of the policy of containment?

3. Close Over the course of just a few years in the late 1940s, United States opposition to communism shaped a foreign policy that would dominate the nation for decades. With the subsequent fall of the Soviet Union, such policies can be seen as successful. However, as the next section explains, the costs of the cold war were high.

1947 Hollywood Ten hearings	1948 Marshall Plan enacted	1948 Berlin airlift begins	1948 HUAC probes Hiss spy case	1949 Communists take China; Soviets test atom bomb; NATO created	1953 Rosenbergs executed for spying	1955 Warsaw Pact created

1947 **1951** **1955**

2 The Cold War Abroad and at Home

SECTION PREVIEW

Objectives

1. Explain how the Marshall Plan, the Berlin airlift, and the creation of NATO helped achieve American goals in postwar Europe.
2. Assess the impact of two Communist advances on American foreign policy.
3. Summarize the effects of the cold war on American life.
4. *Key Terms* Define: Marshall Plan; Berlin airlift; North Atlantic Treaty Organization (NATO); collective security; Warsaw Pact; HUAC; Hollywood Ten; blacklist; McCarran-Walter Act.

Main Idea

As the cold war intensified, American policy focused on rebuilding and unifying Western Europe. At home, emotionally charged spy cases raised fears of Communist infiltration into American society and government.

Reading Strategy

Organizing Information As you read, list major challenges the United States faced in its efforts to oppose communism. Then describe the solutions carried out.

Truman's decision to send aid to Turkey and Greece was only a down payment on rebuilding Europe. World War II had devastated the continent to a degree never before seen. About 21 million people had been made homeless. In Poland, some 20 percent of the population had died. Nearly 1 of every 5 houses in France and Belgium had been damaged or destroyed. Across Europe, industries and transportation were in ruins. Agriculture suffered from the loss of livestock and equipment. In France alone, damage equaled three times the nation's annual income.

Turning Point: The Marshall Plan

American policymakers were determined not to repeat the mistakes of the post–World War I era. This time the United States would help restore the war-torn nations so that they might create stable democracies and achieve economic recovery. The Truman Doctrine was one of two fundamental shifts in postwar foreign policy intended to fulfill these goals. The other was the **Marshall Plan,** which called for the nations of Europe to draw up a program for economic recovery from the war. The United States would then support the program with financial aid.

The plan was unveiled by Secretary of State George C. Marshall in 1947. The Marshall Plan responded to the concern of American policymakers that Communist parties were growing stronger across Europe, and the Soviet Union might intervene to support more of these movements. The plan also reflected the belief that United States aid for European economic recovery would create strong democracies and open new markets for American goods.

Marshall described his plan in a speech at Harvard University in June 1947:

KEY DOCUMENTS ❝It is logical that the United States should do whatever it is able to assist in the return of normal economic health in the world, without which there can be

RESOURCE OPTIONS

Teaching Resources

📁 **Reproducible Lesson Plan** Lesson Plans folder, p. 140

📁 **Learning Styles Lesson Plan** Learning Styles Lesson Plans folder, p. 54

📁 **Big Idea Graphic Organizer** Big Idea Graphic Organizer folder, p. 112

📁 **Guided Reading and Review** Units 7–8 folder, p. 72

no political stability and no assured peace. Our policy is directed not against any country or doctrine but against hunger, poverty, desperation, and chaos. Its purpose should be the revival of a working economy in the world so as to permit the emergence of political and social conditions in which free institutions can exist. **"**

—Marshall Plan speech at Harvard University by Secretary of State George C. Marshall, June 5, 1947

The Soviet Union was invited to participate in the Marshall Plan, but it refused the help and pressured its satellite nations to do so as well. Soviet Foreign Minister Vyacheslav Molotov called the Marshall Plan a vicious American scheme for using dollars to "buy its way" into European affairs. In fact, Soviet leaders did not want outside scrutiny of their country's economy. Seventeen Western European nations joined the plan: Austria, Belgium, Denmark, France, Greece, Iceland, Ireland, Italy, Luxembourg, the Netherlands, Switzerland, Norway, Portugal, Sweden, Turkey, the United Kingdom, and West Germany.

In 1948 Congress approved the Marshall Plan, which was formally known as the European Recovery Program. Over the next four years, the United States sent some $13 billion in grants and loans to Western Europe. The region's economies were quickly restored, and the United States gained strong trading partners in the region.

The Berlin Airlift

One of the nations that benefited from the Marshall Plan was West Germany. By 1948 American, British, and French leaders had become convinced that Stalin was not going to allow the reunification of Germany. Therefore the Western Allies prepared to merge their three occupation zones to create the Federal Republic of Germany, or West Germany.

Main Idea CONNECTIONS

What was the purpose of the Marshall Plan?

BACKGROUND

The Berlin Airlift

The Berlin airlift remains one of the most dramatic and unforgettable events of the long cold war between the Soviet bloc and the western allies. During these months American and allied cargo planes flew in a constant stream to West Berlin, bringing in supplies to a population cut off from the West by a Soviet blockade. Yet this tense, dangerous mission had its brighter side, too. One American pilot, Gail Halvorsen, began to make airdrops of chocolate bars and chewing gum to crowds of West Berlin's children. "Uncle Wigglywings" as he was called, signaled the children by rocking his plane's wings as he approached the city.

TURNING POINT: *The Marshall Plan*

Since the announcement of the Marshall Plan, the United States has sent economic help to countries facing a variety of challenges.

1948
The Marshall Plan provides aid to Western Europe.

1961
President Kennedy creates the Peace Corps, a program of volunteers to help developing nations.

1997
The United States sends food shipments to North Korea to help ease a severe famine.

1940 **1960** **1980** **2000**

1973
United States sends famine relief to Bangladesh after its bloody war for independence.

1992
The United States begins helping Russia's transition to a market economy.

ACTIVITY
LEARNING STYLES

Ask students to identify the major United States foreign policy efforts discussed in this section. Then have them analyze those actions and decide whether each was aimed more at confrontation or at peacemaking. Students should support their analysis with specific facts from the text. (*Logical*)

RESOURCE OPTIONS

Media and Technology

 Prentice Hall United States Video Collectionᴛᴍ Volume 20
Post-War USA

Answer to . . .

Main Idea Connections To help rebuild Europe's economy, and ultimately lead to political stability.

Recent Scholarship

The cold war dominated post–World War II American life. In *A Preponderance of Power: National Security, the Truman Administration, and the Cold War,* published after the cold war had ended, Melvyn P. Leffler describes developments in politics, economics, and diplomacy that led to the hostility between the Soviet Union and the United States. American officials, he argues, wanted to create a viable international economy, but insisted that the Soviets follow their lead. They were prepared to do everything necessary to preserve their nation's power and were as responsible as Soviet leaders for the struggle that ensued.

Partitioning of Berlin, 1949

EAST GERMANY

French Zone

Havel R.

British Zone

American Zone

East Berlin

West Berlin

Spree R.

0   5   10 Miles
0   5   10 Kilometers

 MAP Skills After the partitioning of Berlin (above), the Soviet Union blockaded West Berlin. Rather than risk a military engagement, Truman responded by ordering an airlift (top) to bring supplies to the city. *Movement* **Why did Stalin blockade West Berlin?**

The western part of Berlin, which lay in the Soviet zone, was to become part of West Germany. The Soviets responded in 1949 by forming the German Democratic Republic, or East Germany.

Capitalist West Berlin and Communist East Berlin became visible symbols of the developing cold war struggle between the Soviet Union and the Western powers. Hundreds of thousands of Eastern Europeans left their homes in Communist-dominated nations, fled to East Berlin, and then crossed into West Berlin. From there they booked passage to freedom in the United States, Canada, or Western Europe.

Stalin decided to close this escape route by forcing the Western powers to abandon West Berlin. In June 1948, when a dispute developed over using West German money in that city, the Soviets used it as an excuse to block Allied access to West Berlin. All shipments to the city through East Germany were banned. The blockade threatened to create severe shortages of food and other supplies needed by the 2.5 million people in West Berlin.

Truman did not want to risk starting a war by using military force to open the transportation routes. Nor did he want to give up West Berlin to the Soviets. Instead Truman began the **Berlin airlift,** moving supplies into West Berlin by plane. During the next 15 months, British and American military aircraft made more than 200,000 flights to deliver food, fuel, and other supplies. At the height of the Berlin airlift, nearly 13,000 tons of goods arrived in West Berlin daily.[†]

The Soviets finally gave up the blockade in May 1949, and the airlift ended the following September. By this time the Marshall Plan had

---

[†] In May 1998, a reunified Germany celebrated the 50th anniversary of the Berlin airlift. President Bill Clinton and German Chancellor Helmut Kohl participated in the ceremonies. They honored the courage of the pilots, who had showered the city with food, medicine, and even chocolate, and the city's residents, who endured a frightening year at the center of superpower conflict.

Answer to . . .

Map Skills To stop people from fleeing Communist nations via West Berlin.

helped achieve economic stability in the capitalist nations of Western Europe, including West Germany. Berlin, however, remained a focal point of East-West conflict.

NATO

In the early postwar period, the international community pinned its hopes on the United Nations to protect nations and maintain world peace. However, the Soviet Union's frequent use of its veto power in the Security Council prevented the UN from effectively dealing with a number of postwar problems.

This development soon made it clear that Western Europe would have to look beyond the UN in protecting itself from Soviet aggression. In 1946 Canadian Foreign Minister Louis St. Laurent proposed creating an "association of democratic peace-loving states" to defend Western Europe against attack by the Soviet Union.

American officials expressed great interest in St. Laurent's idea. Truman was determined that the United States not return to pre–World War II isolationism. The Truman Doctrine and the Marshall Plan soon demonstrated his commitment to making America a leader in postwar world affairs.

Yet Truman did not want the United States to be the only nation in the Western Hemisphere pledged to defend Western Europe from the Communists. For this reason, Canada's role in any proposed organization became vital to American support.

In April 1949, Canada and the United States joined Belgium, Britain, Denmark, France, Iceland, Italy, Luxembourg, the Netherlands, Norway, and Portugal to form the **North Atlantic Treaty Organization (NATO).** Member nations agreed that "an armed attack against one or more of them . . . shall be considered an attack against them all."†

---

† NATO provided the model for similar alliances with nations in other parts of the world. In 1954, the United States joined Britain, France, Australia, New Zealand, Pakistan, the Philippines, and Thailand in creating the Southeast Asia Treaty Organization (SEATO). Five years later, the United States joined an existing alliance of Britain, Iran, Pakistan, and Turkey to form the Central Treaty Organization (CENTO). These regional alliances and other collective security arrangements became key elements of America's policy of containment.

This principle of mutual military assistance is called **collective security.** Having dropped its opposition to military treaties with Europe for the first time since the Monroe Doctrine, the United States became actively involved in European affairs.

In 1955, the Soviet Union responded to the formation of NATO. It created the **Warsaw Pact,** a military alliance with its satellite nations in Eastern Europe.

Communist Advances

In 1949, two events heightened American concerns about the cold war. The first was President Truman's terrifying announcement that the Soviet Union had successfully tested an atomic bomb. Then, just a few weeks later, Communist forces took control of China.

The Soviet Atomic Threat "We have evidence that within recent weeks an atomic explosion occurred in the USSR," Truman told

Using the Internet

Write a Documentary

Objective Use the Internet to write a description of the buildings, art, or architecture of the United Nations. Have students follow these instructions:

1. See the *America: Pathways to the Present* Web site at

http://www.Pathways.phschool.com

for the URL of the United Nations.

2. Follow the link to the UN Headquarters On-Line Tour. Use the links to explore the headquarters, taking notes about interesting sights and features.

3. Write a description of UN Headquarters, including any supplemental historical information that you have found. Present your description in the format of a television documentary.

RESOURCE OPTIONS

Teaching Resources

Comparing Primary Sources On Joining NATO, Units 7–8 folder, pp. 77–78

Answer to . . .

Comparing Primary Sources Connally's argument in favor of joining NATO is based on the fear that Western Europe and North America are vulnerable to attack; Taft's argument against joining NATO conveys the fear that an arms buildup will inevitably lead to another war.

ACTIVITY
HETEROGENEOUS GROUPS

Have students trace the steps that the United States took to counter communism from 1945 to 1949. Then have them discuss as a group how the nation's foreign policy began to shift after Truman's announcement in 1949 that the Soviet Union had developed nuclear weapons technology. *(Reteach)*

BACKGROUND

Civil Defense

Successful Soviet development of a nuclear bomb created widespread fear of a "sneak" attack by the Soviets. The Civil Defense Administration (CDA) was set up to oversee warning, evacuation, and communications systems. Thousands of Americans built backyard bomb shelters, while schoolchildren learned to "duck and cover." In 1955, the CDA staged the first nationwide nuclear air raid drill, dubbed "Operation Alert '55," in which 60 cities underwent mock hydrogen-bomb attacks and were evacuated.

Answer to . . .

Interpreting Tables Because the Soviet Union often used its veto power at the UN.

NATO and Warsaw Pact Members, 1955

NATO

Belgium	Italy	United Kingdom
Canada	Luxembourg	United States
Denmark	Netherlands	Greece
France	Norway	Turkey
Iceland	Portugal	West Germany

Warsaw Pact

USSR	Czechoslovakia	Poland
Albania	East Germany	Romania
Bulgaria	Hungary	

Interpreting Tables After World War II, the world began squaring off again. Alliances formed between non-Communist nations and between Communist nations. *Foreign Relations Why did Western Europe feel that the United Nations was inadequate to protect against Soviet aggression?*

reporters in September 1949. The news jolted Americans. New York, Los Angeles, and other American cities now risked the horrible fate of Hiroshima and Nagasaki.

Truman's response to the Soviet atomic threat was to forge ahead with a new weapon to maintain America's nuclear superiority. In early 1950, he gave approval for development of a hydrogen, or thermonuclear, bomb, which was many times more destructive than the atomic bomb. The first successful thermonuclear test occurred in 1952, reestablishing the United States as the world's leading nuclear power.

At about the same time, Truman organized the Federal Civil Defense Administration. The new agency flooded the nation with posters and other information about how to survive a nuclear attack. These included plans for building bomb shelters and instructions for holding air raid drills in schools. Privately, however, experts ridiculed these programs as almost totally ineffective. Not until the late 1950s did civil defense truly become a federal government priority.

China Falls to the Communists The struggle between China's government and Communist revolutionaries had been a long one. It began in the 1920s, after the Chinese government under Jiang Jieshi began to imprison and kill

Communists. Mao Zedong and a handful of other Communist leaders escaped to southern China. From there they organized poor, discontented rural peasants and started a civil war.

During World War II, Mao and Jiang grudgingly cooperated to resist the invading Japanese. The war enabled Mao to strengthen his forces, and by its end his army had grown to about 700,000. Mao also launched popular political, social, and economic reforms in the regions he controlled.

As World War II drew to a close, the fighting between the Communists and government forces resumed in China. The Truman administration at first provided economic and military assistance to Jiang. Despite this aid, by 1947 Mao's forces had occupied much of China's countryside, and its northern cities had begun to come under their control.

When Jiang asked for more American help, Truman and his advisers concluded that Mao's takeover of China probably could not be prevented. Instead they decided to focus on saving Western Europe from Soviet domination.

In early 1949 China's capital of Peking (now Beijing) fell to the Communists. A few months later, Mao proclaimed the creation of the People's Republic of China. The defeated Jiang and his followers withdrew to the island of Taiwan, off the Chinese mainland. There they continued as the Republic of China, claiming to be the legitimate government of the entire Chinese nation. With American support, the Republic of China also held on to China's seats in the UN's General Assembly and Security Council.

Many Americans viewed the "loss of China" as a stain on the record of the Truman administration. It led to calls from members of Congress and others for greater efforts to protect the rest of Asia from communism. It also caused some Americans to suspect the loyalties of those involved in making military and foreign policy.

The Cold War at Home

Throughout the Great Depression, tens of thousands of Americans had joined the Communist party, which was a legal organization. Many were desperate people who had developed serious doubts about the American capitalist system, partly because of the economic collapse of the 1930s. Others were intellectuals who were attracted to Communist ideals. After World War II, however, improved eco-

---

RESOURCE OPTIONS

Media and Technology

RESOURCE⊙PRO

Critical Thinking Activity Identifying Central Issues: Cold War Policy, found on Resource Pro, uses a speech by Christian A. Herter, Undersecretary of State in 1957, to help students apply this skill.

nomic times, as well as the increasing distrust of Stalin, caused many people to become disappointed with communism.

Most American Communists quit the party, but some of these citizens remained members, whether active or not. Now, as a new red scare began to grip America, their pasts came back to haunt them.

During the presidencies of Truman and his successor, Dwight D. Eisenhower, concern about the growth of world communism raised fears of a conspiracy to overthrow the government, particularly when a number of spies were caught and tried. These fears launched an anti-Communist crusade that violated the civil liberties of many Americans. Anyone who had ever had Communist party ties and many who had never even been Communists were swept up in the wave of persecutions.

The Loyalty Program As the Truman administration pursued its containment policy abroad, government officials launched programs to root out any element of communism that might have infiltrated the United States. Exposure of a number of wartime spy rings in 1946 increased Americans' anxiety. (In recent years, evidence of Soviet infiltration has come to light. It is known, for instance, that Soviet spies gathered information on the United States nuclear program that helped the USSR advance its own atomic development.)

When Republicans made big gains in the 1946 congressional elections, Truman worried that his rivals would take political advantage of the loyalty issue. To head off this possibility, he began his own investigation, establishing a federal employee loyalty program in 1947.

Under this program, all new employees hired by the federal government were to be investigated. In addition, the FBI checked its files for evidence of existing government employees who might be engaged in suspicious activities. Those accused of disloyalty were brought before a Loyalty Review Board.

While civil rights were supposed to be safeguarded, in fact those accused of disloyalty to their country often had little chance to defend themselves. Rather than being innocent until proven guilty, they found that the accusation alone made it difficult to clear their names.

The Truman program examined several million government employees, yet only a few hundred were actually removed from their jobs. Still, the loyalty program added to a climate of suspicion taking hold in the nation.

Early Cold War Crises, 1944–1950

Year	Crisis	Significance
1944–1948	Poland, Albania, Bulgaria, Czechoslovakia, Hungary, Romania, and East Germany become Soviet satellite nations.	Communist power grows with the Soviet Union's domination of Eastern Europe.
1948–1949	Soviet Union blockades West Berlin. Truman initiates Berlin airlift to supply the city with food, fuel, and other necessities.	Tensions increase between the United States and the Soviet Union, with Berlin a focal point of East-West conflict.
1949	Soviet Union develops nuclear weapon technology.	The United States no longer has the upper hand in weapons technology.
	China falls to Communist dictator Mao Zedong.	China is no longer the "anchor" of democracy in Asia.

Interpreting Tables A series of early cold war crises stepped up demands on the government to deal effectively with the spread of communism. *Foreign Relations* **Why was the fall of China to communism seen as a crisis?**

HUAC As the Loyalty Review Board carried out its work, Congress pursued its own loyalty program. The House Un-American Activities Committee, referred to as **HUAC,** had been established in 1938 to investigate disloyalty on the eve of World War II. Now it began a postwar probe of Communist infiltration of government agencies and, more spectacularly, a probe of the Hollywood movie industry.

Claiming that movies had tremendous power to influence the public, in 1947 HUAC charged that numerous Hollywood figures had Communist leanings that affected their filmmaking. In fact, some Hollywood personalities were or had been members of the Communist party. Others in the industry had openly supported various causes and movements with philosophical similarities to communism.

With government encouragement, Hollywood had also produced some movies

> *Main Idea*
> **CONNECTIONS**
>
> Why did Truman create a loyalty program?

Graphing the Main Idea

To make sure students understand the main idea of this section, you may wish to use the double web graphic organizer below.

Tell students that a double web compares information about two main ideas or topics. Ask students to use it to record details about how the cold war affected American policies at home and abroad.

Teaching Tip A template for this graphic organizer can be found in the Color Transparencies, G-2.

Answer to . . .

Interpreting Tables Because of China's influence in Asia.

Main Idea Connections To guard against the possibility of Communist infiltration of the federal government; also, to prevent the Republican party from using loyalty as an issue in political campaigns against the Democrats.

HETEROGENEOUS GROUPS

In the late 1940s and early 1950s, the film and television industries were often a target of investigation by the House Un-American Activities Committee (HUAC). Have students work in small groups to list three activities by the film and television industry today that might be considered un-American, and three activities that would be considered "good" for Americans. **(Enrichment)**

▼ BACKGROUND

Connections to Today

The Alger Hiss controversy was refueled in 1992 when the chairman of the Russian Military Intelligence Archives announced that, based on his review of Soviet archives, the espionage charges against Hiss were groundless. The official subsequently admitted that he could not fully clear Hiss; given the size and complexity of Soviet archives, perhaps no one could. The debate thus remains very much alive.

favorable to the Soviet Union and its people. This had been during the war, when the United States and the Soviet Union had been allies.

Many stars protested HUAC's attitude and procedures. Actor Frederic March asked Americans to consider where it all could lead:

> **AMERICAN VOICES** "Who's next? . . . Is it you, who will have to look around nervously before you can say what's on your mind? . . . This reaches into every American city and town."
>
> —*Actor Frederic March, 1947*

The Hollywood Ten In September and October 1947, HUAC called a number of Hollywood writers, directors, actors, and producers to testify. They were a distinguished lot, responsible for some of Hollywood's best films of the previous decade.

Facing the committee, celebrities who were accused of having radical political associations had little chance to defend themselves. The committee chairman, Republican representative J. Parnell Thomas of New Jersey first called witnesses who were allowed to make accusations based on rumors and other flimsy evidence. Then the accused were called.

Over and over the committee asked, "Are you now or have you ever been a member of the Communist party?" When some attempted to make statements, they were denied permission.

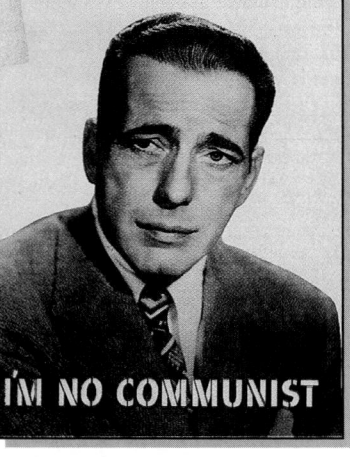

I'M NO COMMUNIST

Actor Humphrey Bogart (right), who protested HUAC's actions against other actors, ended up having to clear his own name. Red Channels (above) was an index of blacklisted actors published in 1950.

Invoking their Fifth Amendment rights, 10 of the accused declined to answer the committee's questions. The **Hollywood Ten** were cited for contempt of Congress and served jail terms ranging from six months to a year.

The HUAC investigations had a powerful impact on filmmaking. Nervous motion picture executives denounced the Hollywood Ten for having done a disservice to their industry. The studios compiled a Hollywood **blacklist,** a list of people whom employers agree not to hire. Many other entertainment figures were added to the blacklist simply because they seemed subversive or they opposed the idea of a blacklist. The list included actors, screenwriters, directors, and broadcasters.

In the past, Hollywood had been willing to make movies on controversial subjects such as racism and anti-Semitism. Now studios resisted all films dealing with social problems and concentrated on pure entertainment.

The McCarran-Walter Act While HUAC carried out its work, Democrat Pat McCarran headed a Senate hunt for Communists in the movie industry, labor unions, the State Department, and the UN. Senator McCarran became convinced that the most disloyal Americans were immigrants from Communist-dominated parts of the world.

At his urging, in 1952 Congress passed the **McCarran-Walter Act.** This law established a quota system for each country, discriminating against potential immigrants from Asia and Southern and Central Europe. President Truman vetoed McCarran's bill, calling it "one of the most un-American acts I have ever witnessed in my public career." Congress, however, passed the bill over the President's veto.

Spy Cases Inflame the Nation Two famous spy cases helped fuel the suspicion that a conspiracy within the United States was aiding the Communists overseas in their military and political successes. In 1948, HUAC investigated Alger Hiss, who had been a high-ranking State Department official before he left government service. Whittaker Chambers, a former Communist who had become a successful *Time* magazine editor, accused Hiss of having been a Communist in the 1930s. Hiss denied the charge and sued Chambers for slander. Chambers then went one step further and declared that Hiss had been a Soviet spy.

Too much time had passed for the spying charge to be pressed. After two trials, Hiss was

▶ RESOURCE OPTIONS

Media and Technology

 Color Transparencies Time Lines, E-8; Links Across Time, J-8; Political Cartoons, K-8

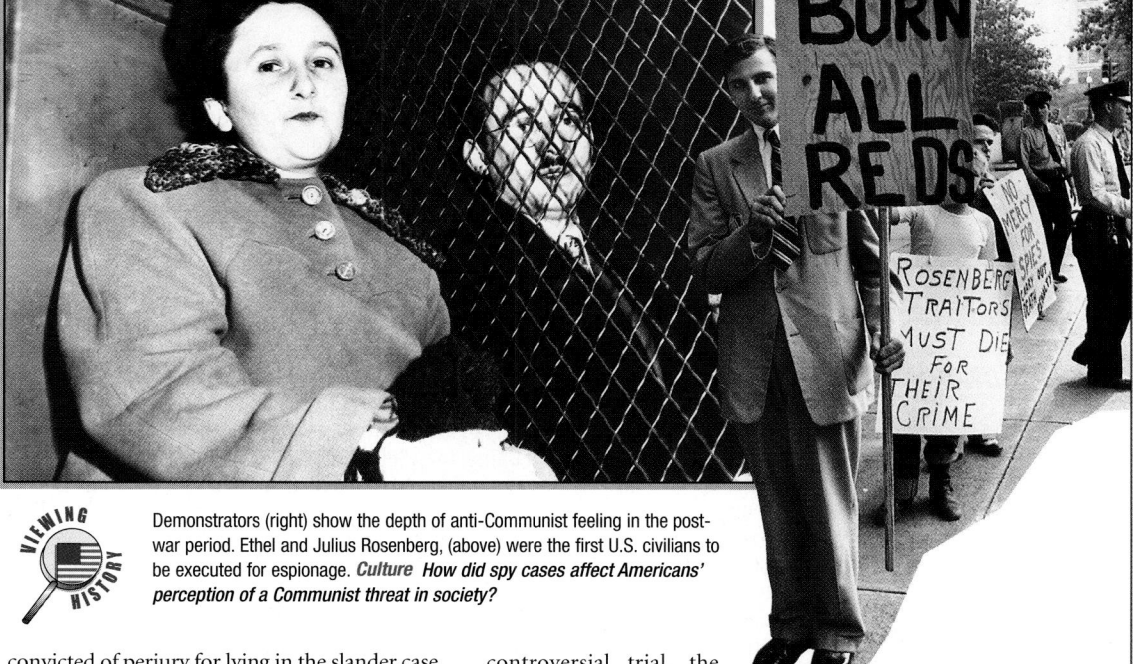

Demonstrators (right) show the depth of anti-Communist feeling in the post-war period. Ethel and Julius Rosenberg, (above) were the first U.S. civilians to be executed for espionage. *Culture How did spy cases affect Americans' perception of a Communist threat in society?*

convicted of perjury for lying in the slander case. In 1950 he went to prison for four years.

Not all Americans were convinced he was guilty, and for many years thereafter the Hiss case was hotly debated. For most people, however, the case seemed to prove that there was a real Communist threat in the United States.

Several months after Hiss's conviction, Julius and Ethel Rosenberg, a married couple who were members of the Communist Party, were accused of passing atomic secrets to the Soviets during World War II. After a highly controversial trial, the Rosenbergs were convicted of espionage and executed in 1953. The case was another event that inflamed anti-Communist passions and focused attention on a possible internal threat to the nation's security.

Like the Hiss case, the Rosenbergs' convictions were debated for years afterward. Careful work by historians in once-classified American records and in secret Soviet records opened at the end of the cold war indicate that both Alger Hiss and Julius Rosenberg were guilty.

SECTION 2 REVIEW

Comprehension

1. **Key Terms** Define: (a) Marshall Plan; (b) Berlin airlift; (c) NATO; (d) collective security; (e) Warsaw Pact; (f) HUAC; (g) Hollywood Ten; (h) blacklist; (i) McCarran-Walter Act.

2. **Summarizing the Main Idea** What events abroad and at home in the late 1940s and early 1950s helped raise Americans' fears of communism?

3. **Organizing Information** Construct a cause-and-effect chart showing the origins and impact of the Truman Doctrine.

Critical Thinking

4. **Analyzing Time Lines** Refer to the time line at the start of the section. How was 1949 a key year in the development of the cold war?

5. **Determining Relevance** How does America's pre–World War II isolationism relate to a discussion of the Marshall Plan, the Berlin airlift, and NATO?

Writing Activity

6. **Writing a Persuasive Essay** Did Americans have reason for concern about Communist infiltration of government and society? Consider the events going on in the world.

RESOURCE OPTIONS

Teaching Resources

Quiz Units 7–8 folder, p. 73

Student Performance Pack

Guide to the Essentials Chapter 26, Section 2 (English and Spanish)

| 1950 | 1950 | 1953 | 1956 | 1957 | 1957 | 1960 |
| Korean War begins | McCarthy launches anti-Communist campaign | Soviet Union tests hydrogen device | Suez crisis | Eisenhower Doctrine | Soviet Union launches Sputnik satellite | U-2 incident |

1950   **1955**   **1960**

SECTION 3

The Cold War Expands

Objectives

You may wish to call students' attention to the objectives in the Section Preview. The objectives are reflected in the main headings of the section.

Bellringer

Set up a row of dominos in the front of the classroom. Knock over the first domino so that it causes the whole line to fall. Ask students to explain what this "domino effect" has to do with containing communism in the 1950s.

Reading Strategy

Outlining Information Refer to the Reading Strategy in the Section Preview. You may wish to have students share examples of the key facts they add to their outlines.

LESSON PLAN

Connecting to the Main Idea

1. Focus The momentum of the cold war carried the United States into troubled political waters. The Korean War, the arms race, and the domestic suppression of communism all proved costly in varying ways. Discuss whether there was any precedent in United States history for the ideological warfare of the 1950s.

2. Instruct Explain that in its efforts to fight Communist aggression, the United States engaged in its own aggressive policies, both at home and abroad. Discuss whether those actions were justified in order to oppose communism. Encourage students to support their opinions with facts and reasoning.

3. Close Despite the cold war, the 1950s are remembered as a settled and prosperous time. Students will learn more about this side of the decade in the following chapter.

3 The Cold War Expands

SECTION PREVIEW

Objectives

1 Describe General Douglas MacArthur and his role in the Korean War.
2 Analyze the effects of Senator Joseph McCarthy's anti-Communist campaign.
3 Trace the development of the cold war and the arms race in the 1950s.
4 *Key Terms* Define: Korean War; 38th parallel; domino theory; arms race; brinkmanship; ICBM; *Sputnik;* U-2 incident.

Main Idea

During the 1950s, the cold war spread to new locations around the world. At home, a senator's anti-Communist crusade ruined many people's careers but ultimately failed.

Reading Strategy

Outlining Information Copy the headings in this section on a sheet of paper. As you read, add two or three key facts under each heading to create an outline.

Koreans hoped their nation would be restored after Japan withdrew. However, in 1945 the Allies agreed to divide the nation temporarily into a Soviet-occupied northern zone and an American-occupied southern zone. Soon a pro-American government formed in South Korea and a Communist regime in North Korea. Occupying forces withdrew from both zones in 1948 and 1949.

In June 1950, the **Korean War** broke out when North Korean troops streamed across the **38th parallel,** the latitude line dividing the two nations, aiming to reunite Korea by force. Because the USSR was boycotting the Security Council at the time to protest the exclusion of Communist China, the UN was able to act. It called on its members to defend South Korea.

anti-Communist, General Douglas MacArthur was Truman's choice to lead the UN forces in Korea. For MacArthur, the command capped a long, distinguished, and controversial career.

The son of an army officer, MacArthur graduated from the United States Military Academy at West Point in 1903 at the top of his class. He was cited seven times for bravery in World War I and by 1918, at age 38, had attained the rank of general. After serving in the Philippines during the 1920s, he returned to the United States in 1930 to become Army Chief of Staff.

At the start of World War II President Roosevelt appointed MacArthur to be commander of American forces in Asia. From this post he organized the defense of the Philippines and, later, the three-year island-hopping campaign against the Japanese in the Pacific.

As virtual dictator of Japan during the postwar occupation period, MacArthur was responsible for establishing Western democracy

Douglas MacArthur

 AMERICAN BIOGRAPHY A hero of two world wars and a strong

General Douglas MacArthur (1880–1964)

▶ RESOURCE OPTIONS

Teaching Resources

📁 **Reproducible Lesson Plan** Lesson Plans folder, p. 141

📁 **Learning Styles Lesson Plan** Learning Styles Lesson Plans folder, p. 55

📁 **Big Idea Graphic Organizer** Big Idea Graphic Organizer folder, p. 113

📁 **Guided Reading and Review** Units 7–8 folder, p. 74

Media and Technology

 AmericanHeritage® CD-ROM

Time Tour The Nation Today and Tomorrow: The Fifties

there and for creating Japan's new democratic constitution. He was less successful in implementing democracy in South Korea, where he also commanded American occupation forces. There MacArthur supported South Korean president Syngman Rhee, despite Rhee's brutal elimination of his opponents.

Although a hero to those he commanded and to much of the American public, MacArthur was disliked by many political leaders, who viewed him as overly ambitious. MacArthur, in turn, had little respect for either Roosevelt or Truman, both of whom he viewed as soft on communism. His attitude made MacArthur an anti-Communist hero. Yet his characteristic contempt for anyone with authority over him led him to take actions that undermined his otherwise brilliant career. ■

The Korean War

Despite his difficult personality, MacArthur was an excellent military strategist, and he developed a bold plan to drive the invaders from South Korea. With Soviet tanks and air power, the North Koreans had swept through South Korea in just weeks. Only a small part of the country, near the port city of Pusan, remained unconquered.

MacArthur suspected that the North Koreans' rapid advance had left their supply lines stretched thin. He decided to strike at this weakness. After first sending forces to defend Pusan, in September 1950 he landed troops at Inchon in northwestern South Korea, and attacked enemy supply lines from behind.

MacArthur's strategy worked. Caught between UN forces in the north and south, and with their supplies cut off, the invaders fled back across the 38th parallel. UN troops pursued them northward. American and South Korean leaders began to boast of reuniting Korea under South Korean control. Such talk alarmed the Chinese Communists, who had been in power less than a year and who did not want a pro-Western nation next door.

As UN troops approached North Korea's border with China, the Chinese warned them not to advance any farther. MacArthur ignored the warning. On November 24, 1950, the general announced his "Home by Christmas" offen-

Main Idea CONNECTIONS

In what way was the Korean War a cold war conflict?

BACKGROUND

Geography in History

A few months before North Korea launched the Korean War, Secretary of State Dean Acheson gave a speech on American postwar military commitments at Washington, D.C.'s National Press Club. In the case of Soviet attack, Acheson said, the United States would only defend countries within its Pacific defense perimeter. Because China had recently fallen to the Communists, Acheson drew this line off the coast of Asia. The islands of Japan, the Philippines, and Okinawa fell under American protection, but South Korea did not. Although American historians have found no proof, many suspect that Acheson's speech encouraged Communist leaders to invade South Korea.

The Korean War, 1950–1953

June 1950 North Korea captures South Korea's capital.

Sept. 1950 UN forces hold Pusan Perimeter.

Sept. 1950 Inchon landing

Nov. 1950 Farthest UN advance

Nov. 1950 China enters the war in an effort to repel UN forces.

Dec. 1950 North Korea attempts to re-invade South Korea.

July 1953 Truce Line is established near the original division between North and South Korea.

North Korean troop movements / Chinese troop movements / United Nations troop movements

These maps show the back-and-forth nature of the fighting in the Korean War. *Movement* Examine the maps and the movements of the UN troops. Why do you think China entered the war when it did?

RESOURCE OPTIONS

Teaching Resources

■ **American History Block Scheduling Support** Korea: The Unknown War, found in The Nation After World War II folder, includes interdisciplinary lesson suggestions and activities for Geography and History, Primary Sources, Biography, and Literature.

Media and Technology

RESOURCE PRO

Biography Marguerite Higgins, found on Resource Pro, profiles a female journalist who overcame discrimination to become a war correspondent in Korea.

Answer to . . .

Main Idea Connections It grew out of ideological differences, with a Communist government on one side and an anti-Communist government on the other.
Map Skills To stop the northward progression of UN troops.

Have students work in small groups to analyze the conflict between President Truman and General MacArthur. Have them list two or three beliefs held by each. What goals did they have in common? Why did they come into conflict? Whose views do students favor more? (*Verbal/Linguistic*)

BACKGROUND

Antiradicalism

Joseph McCarthy was not solely responsible for the wave of anti-Communist hysteria that swept the nation in the 1950s. A long tradition of antiradicalism in the United States goes back to the late nineteenth and early twentieth centuries. This tradition surfaced in the red scare of 1919. It also fueled the decision not to grant formal recognition to the Bolshevik regime of the new Soviet Union until 1933, a decade and a half after the Russian Revolution. Thus Joseph McCarthy was not the first to prey on and magnify fears and suspicions about Communists, though he created perhaps the most serious upheavals with his irresponsible charges. Journalist Walter Lippmann, a relentless critic, called McCarthy's charges a "cold, calculated, sustained and ruthless effort to make himself feared."

Answer to . . .

Viewing History Korea remained divided almost exactly as it had been before the war, despite the high number of American casualties.

---

sive, designed to drive the enemy across the North Korean border at the Yalu River into China and end the war.

Chinese troops poured across the Yalu to take the offensive. The Chinese and North Koreans pushed the UN forces back into South Korea. A stalemate developed.

MacArthur favored breaking the stalemate by opening a second front in the war. He urged that the Chinese opposition forces of Jiang Jieshi on the island of Taiwan be returned to the mainland to attack the Chinese Communists. Truman opposed this strategy, fearing it could lead to a widespread war in Asia.

Unable to sway Truman, MacArthur sent a letter to House Minority Leader Joseph Martin in March 1951, attacking the President's policies. Martin made the letter public. On April 11, Truman fired MacArthur for insubordination.

MacArthur returned home to a hero's welcome. In an address to a joint session of Congress on April 19, he made an emotional farewell:

AMERICAN VOICES ❝Since I took the oath at West Point, the hopes and dreams [of youth] have all vanished. But I still remember the refrain of one of the most popular barracks ballads of that day, which proclaimed most proudly that old soldiers never die, they just fade away. And like the old soldier of that ballad, I now close my military career and just fade away, an old soldier who tried to do his duty as God gave him the light to see that duty. Good-bye.❞

—*General Douglas MacArthur, speech to Congress, April 19, 1951*

Once tempers cooled, MacArthur did, in fact, fade from view, and Truman was able to keep the war limited. However, the struggle dragged on for over two more years. Finally, a truce was signed in 1953, leaving Korea divided at almost exactly the same place as before the war, near the 38th parallel.

The Korean War caused enormous frustration at home. Americans wondered why about 55,000 of their soldiers had been killed and 103,000 wounded for such limited results. They wondered if their government was serious about stopping communism.

The McCarthy Era

The events in Asia seemed to many Americans to support sensational charges made in 1950 by Republican senator Joseph McCarthy of Wisconsin. During a speech in Wheeling, West Virginia, McCarthy held up a paper that he claimed was a list of 205 known Communists in the State Department.

In fact, McCarthy's list was nothing more than the names of people still in their jobs, who had been accused of disloyalty under Truman's federal employee loyalty program. When pressed for details, the senator reduced the number from 205 to 57.

McCarthy's Rise to Power McCarthy soon took on larger targets. He attacked former Secretary of State George Marshall, a national hero and a man of unquestioned integrity, saying he was involved in "a conspiracy so immense and an infamy so black as to dwarf any previous venture in the history of man."

Communist aggression in Korea was already heightening Americans' fear of communism when McCarthy aired his accusations. In this atmosphere, his charges gained support.

McCarthy's Fall In early 1954, McCarthy charged that even the army was full of Communists. Finally, political and military leaders decided that he had to be stopped.

VIEWING HISTORY

More than 5.8 million military personnel and more than 1.6 million draftees served in the Korean War. *Culture* Why were Americans frustrated by the outcome of the war?

RESOURCE OPTIONS

Teaching Resources

📁 **Key Documents** General Douglas MacArthur, Address to Congress, Learning with Documents folder, p. 98

Media and Technology

RESOURCE⊙ PRO

Visual Learning Activity Civilian Control of the Military, found on Resource Pro, uses a cartoon to present one view of Truman's controversial firing of General MacArthur during the Korean War.

Meanwhile, army officials charged McCarthy with seeking special treatment for an aide who had been drafted. As charges and countercharges flew between McCarthy and the army, the senator's subcommittee voted to investigate the claims.

The Army-McCarthy hearings began in late April 1954. Democrats asked that the hearings be televised, hoping that the public would see McCarthy for what he was. Ever eager for publicity, the senator fell into the trap by agreeing to the coverage. For the next several weeks, Americans remained riveted to their TVs. Most were horrified by McCarthy's bullying tactics and baseless allegations.

By the time the hearings ended in mid-June, the senator had lost even his most hard-core supporters. The Senate condemned him for his reckless actions. Unrepentant, the senator charged his accusers with being tools of the Communists. However, he no longer had credibility. Although McCarthy remained in the Senate, his power was gone. He died three years later, a broken man.

Eventually this second red scare, much like the one that followed World War I, subsided. But the nation was damaged by the era's suppression of free speech and open, honest debate.

The Cold War in the 1950s

When Republican and World War II hero Dwight Eisenhower succeeded Truman as President in 1953, American cold war policy entered a new phase. Eisenhower's Secretary of State, John Foster Dulles, was a harsh anti-Communist who considered winning the cold war to be a moral crusade. Dulles believed Truman's containment policy was too cautious. Instead, he called for a policy to roll back communism where it had taken hold.

As a military leader, Eisenhower recognized the risks of confronting the Soviets. He acted as a brake on Dulles's more extreme views. Eisenhower realized that the United States could not intervene in the affairs of the Soviet Union's Eastern European satellite nations. So when East Germans revolted in 1953, and Poles and Hungarians in 1956, the United States kept its distance as Soviet troops crushed the uprisings.

Eisenhower understood that any other response risked war with the Soviet Union. He wanted to avoid that at all costs. Thus the policy of containment remained in effect during the 1950s.

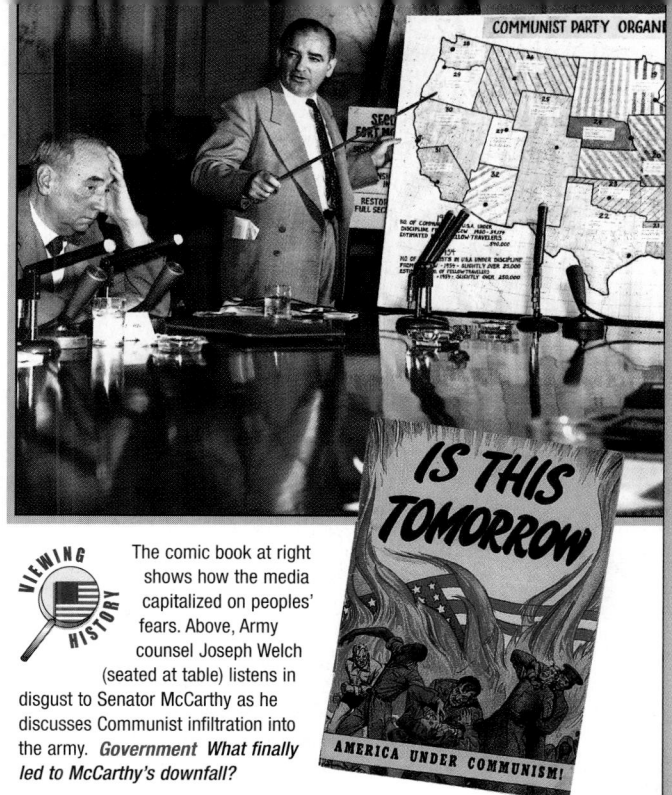

The comic book at right shows how the media capitalized on peoples' fears. Above, Army counsel Joseph Welch (seated at table) listens in disgust to Senator McCarthy as he discusses Communist infiltration into the army. **Government** *What finally led to McCarthy's downfall?*

Southeast Asia In July 1953, Eisenhower fulfilled a campaign promise to bring the Korean War to an end. He was aided in this effort by the sudden death of Stalin in March and by the rapid rise of more moderate Soviet leaders.

Meanwhile, another conflict had developed. This one was in Vietnam, a French colony in Southeast Asia that had fallen to Japan during World War II. Just after the Japanese surrender in 1945, Ho Chi Minh, head of the Vietnamese Communist party, had declared the colony's independence. France rejected Ho's declaration and sent troops to reassert its authority in Vietnam. An ugly war began to unfold.

Eisenhower subscribed to what became known as the **domino theory.** This belief held that if one country fell to the Communists, its neighbors soon would follow, like a toppling row of dominos. By 1954 the United States was providing substantial military aid to support France in its Southeast Asian war.

After a major defeat in May 1954, France withdrew its forces. An international conference divided Vietnam, like Korea, into a

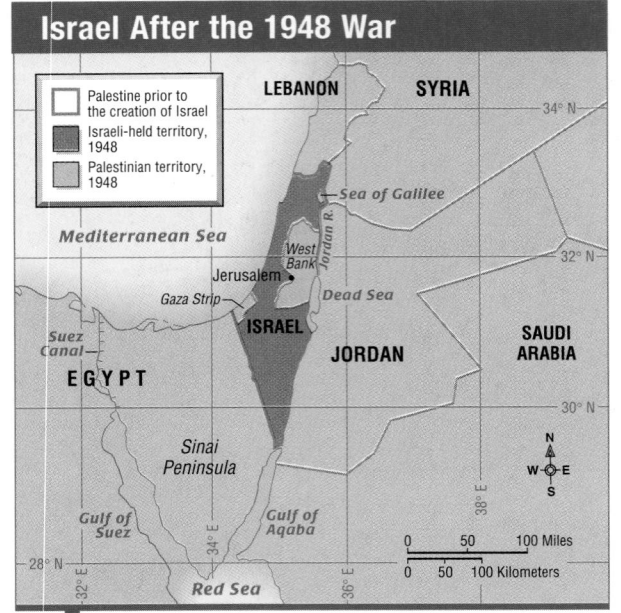

Israel After the 1948 War

Palestine prior to the creation of Israel

Israeli-held territory, 1948

Palestinian territory, 1948

MAP skills Following the 1948 war, the new state of Israel controlled most of what had once been Palestine. *Regions* What regions were still held by Palestinians after the 1948 war?

Communist north and anti-Communist south. The United States provided aid to South Vietnam but resisted greater involvement. That course would change in the 1960s.

The Middle East The cold war was also played out in the historic tensions of the Middle East. Britain and France were given control over much of this region after World War I. The British area included Palestine, a region on the Mediterranean coast and biblical home of the Jewish people.

In the 1930s, anti-Semitism in Germany and Eastern Europe forced many Jews to seek safety in Palestine. Calls for a Jewish state followed. In 1947 the British turned the question over to the UN, which called for the creation of two states in the area, one Jewish and one Arab. In May 1948 the Jews in Palestine proclaimed the new nation of Israel. (See map above.)

Conflict soon erupted between Israel and its Arab neighbors, who also viewed Palestine as their ancient homeland. The United States supported Israel. The Soviet Union generally backed the Arab opposition.

While supporting Israel, the United States worked to prevent oil-rich Arab nations from falling under the influence of the Soviet Union. In 1952, a pro-Communist leader gained control in Iran. The next year the United States Central Intelligence Agency (CIA) organized his overthrow and restored to power the pro-American Shah of Iran.

The next cold war clash in the Middle East was the Suez crisis of 1956. When Egypt's ruler, Gamal Abdel Nasser, sought Soviet support, America and Great Britain cut off their aid. Nasser responded by seizing the British-owned Suez Canal, a vital waterway that passed through Egypt and allowed Middle East oil to reach Europe via the Mediterranean.

In late 1956, British and French forces attacked Egypt to regain control of the canal. Reacting to Soviet threats of "dangerous consequences," Eisenhower persuaded his NATO allies to withdraw from Egypt, which retained control of the canal.

Eisenhower then acted to combat further Soviet influence in the Middle East. In January 1957, the President announced the Eisenhower Doctrine. This policy stated that the United States would use force "to safeguard the independence of any country or group of countries in the Middle East requesting aid against [Communist-inspired] aggression." Eisenhower used his doctrine in 1958 to justify landing troops in Lebanon to put down a revolt against its government.

Latin America The cold war likewise affected Latin America. Since the mid-1920s, the United States had exercised control over the economies of some 10 Latin American nations. In Central America, United States troops had invaded Nicaragua and Honduras to prop up leaders who supported American interests.

After World War II, the United States became concerned about the possible spread of communism to other Latin American nations, especially where American companies had large investments. In 1947, the United States signed the Rio Pact, a regional defense alliance with 18 other nations in the Western Hemisphere. The following year the United States led the way in forming the Organization of American States (OAS) to increase cooperation among the nations of the hemisphere.

Main Idea CONNECTIONS

How did the cold war affect the Middle East?

In 1954 the CIA helped overthrow the government of Guatemala on the grounds that its leaders were sympathetic to radical causes. The CIA takeover restored the property of an American corporation, the United Fruit Company, which had been seized by the Guatemalan government. Such actions fueled a Soviet perception that America was escalating the cold war.

In 1958 another crisis began as revolutionary leader Fidel Castro overthrew the corrupt Cuban dictator Fulgencio Batista. Batista, who fled the country on January 1, 1959, had ties to American organized crime. Yet Eisenhower would not support Castro after the CIA reported that his movement had been infiltrated by Communists.

When Castro seized American property in Cuba, Eisenhower responded by cutting diplomatic ties and halting exports to the island. Castro then turned to the Soviet Union for economic and military aid, which it would rely on for the next three decades.

The Arms Race

Throughout the 1950s the United States and the Soviet Union waged an increasingly intense struggle for world leadership. Whenever one side appeared to be gaining the upper hand in the cold war, the other would respond with new programs and policies. Nowhere was this competition more dangerous than in the **arms race,** the struggle to gain weapons superiority.

The Growth of Nuclear Arsenals In August 1953, less than a year after the United States exploded its first thermonuclear device, the Soviet Union successfully tested a hydrogen device of its own. In part to publicize that the United States still led in nuclear technology, in December 1953 Eisenhower announced an Atoms for Peace Plan at the United Nations. The President's proposal called for the world's nations to work together under UN supervision to find peaceful uses for nuclear technology. The Soviet Union, which did not want to give the UN any of its nuclear material, refused to participate.

At the same time, Eisenhower stepped up the American weapons development program to counter the new Soviet nuclear threat. Between 1954 and 1958 the United States conducted 19 hydrogen bomb tests at Bikini Island in the Pacific.

The first of these explosions, in March 1954, was over 750 times more powerful than the atomic bomb that was dropped on Nagasaki in World War II. Japanese fishermen some 90 miles from the blast suffered severe radiation burns, and residents of an island nearly 200 miles away had to be evacuated. The test chillingly revealed that nuclear war could threaten the entire world with radioactive contamination.

A 1959 Newsweek illustration showed Soviet leader Khrushchev (left) and Eisenhower (right) using arms to maintain a balance of power.

Brinkmanship American policymakers used the fear of nuclear war to achieve their cold war objectives. In 1956, Secretary of State John Dulles made it clear that the United States was prepared to risk war to protect its national interests. Dulles explained this policy of **brinkmanship** in an interview in *Life* magazine:

U.S. Defense Spending, 1940–1960

Source: *Historical Statistics of the United States, Colonial Times to 1970*

Interpreting Graphs The competition for world leadership led to an arms race between the United States and the Soviet Union.
Government Describe the pattern of American defense spending in the post–World War II era. What was the cause of the sharpest rise?

AMERICAN VOICES

❝The ability to get to the verge without getting into the war is the necessary art. If you cannot master it, you inevitably get into war. If you try to run away from it, if you are scared to go to the brink, you are lost.❞

—Secretary of State John Foster Dulles, interview in Life *magazine*, 1956

Many Americans agreed with the reaction of Illinois senator Adlai Stevenson: "I am shocked that the Secretary of State is willing to play Russian roulette with the life of our nation." Still, the Eisenhower administration employed the policy a number of times.

Cold War in the Skies To carry hydrogen bombs to their targets, American military planners relied mainly on the United States Air Force. Unable to match this strength, the Soviets instead focused on long-range rockets known as intercontinental ballistic missiles, or **ICBMs,** as their primary delivery system.

Americans also worked to develop ICBMs. However, in part because of its dependence on conventional air power, the United States lagged behind the Soviet Union in missile development.

The size of this technology gap became startlingly apparent in 1957, when the Soviets used one of their rockets to launch *Sputnik,* the first artificial satellite to orbit Earth. Most Americans, who had viewed their country as the world's foremost scientific power, were mortified.

Main Idea CONNECTIONS

Why did the launch of Sputnik shock Americans?

Worse yet, the United States' own satellite and rocket, rushed to the launching pad before it was ready, came crashing to the ground. Another fear prompted by *Sputnik* was the realization that the rocket used to launch it could also carry a hydrogen bomb to American shores.

In May 1960, the Soviet military again demonstrated its capabilities by shooting down an American spy plane over Soviet territory with a guided missile. The plane, called a U-2, flew more than 15 miles high. At such altitudes, American officials had assumed that the spy planes were immune to attack. The **U-2 incident** shattered this confidence.

One of the legacies of the cold war was the creation of what Eisenhower called a "permanent armaments industry of vast proportions." He warned that the existence of this "military-industrial complex," employing millions of Americans and having a financial stake in war-making, could become a threat to peace:

KEY DOCUMENTS

❝Our arms must be mighty, ready for instant action. . . . We recognize the imperative need for this development. Yet we must not fail to comprehend its grave implications. . . . [In] government, we must guard against the acquisition of unwarranted [unnecessary] influence, whether sought or unsought, by the military-industrial complex. The potential for the disastrous rise of misplaced power exists and will persist.❞

—Farewell Address, President Dwight D. Eisenhower, January 17, 1961

SECTION 3 REVIEW

Comprehension

1. *Key Terms* Define: (a) Korean War; (b) 38th parallel; (c) domino theory; (d) arms race; (e) brinkmanship; (f) ICBM; (g) *Sputnik;* (h) U-2 incident.

2. *Summarizing the Main Idea* Where and how was the cold war carried out during the 1950s?

3. *Organizing Information* Using the Korean War maps as a guide, create a time line of the major events of the war.

Critical Thinking

4. *Analyzing Time Lines* Refer to the time line at the start of the section. Choose three entries and summarize their causes and effects.

5. *Determining Relevance* What overstatements did Senator McCarthy make in his accusations about Communists?

Writing Activity

6. *Writing an Expository Essay* Trace the development of the arms race in the 1950s. What effect did the policy of brinkmanship have on the arms race?

▶ RESOURCE OPTIONS

Teaching Resources

 Quiz Units 7–8 folder, p. 75

Chapter Tests Forms A and B Chapter Test folder

Student Performance Pack

 Guide to the Essentials Chapter 26, Section 3 (English and Spanish)

Standardized Test Preparation Handbook

Media and Technology

🎧 **Guided Reading Audiotapes** Chapter 26 Summary (English and Spanish)

Student Edition on Audiotape Chapter 26

💿 **Test Bank CD-ROM; Interactive Student Tutorial CD-ROM** Chapter Test

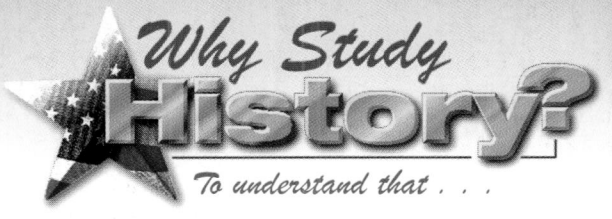
Defense Spending Affects You

High defense spending in recent decades has had a major impact on American society that continues to this day.

Bomber assembly line, 1950s

In 1971, one Huey helicopter cost the United States as much as 66 units of low-income housing. In 1998, the estimated cost of one B-2 Stealth bomber was roughly half the yearly expenses of the National Park Service. The more that the nation spends on weapons, the less it has available for domestic needs. Yet, while many Americans support cuts in defense spending, others warn of the military risks and economic consequences.

The Impact Today

During the cold war, as you have read, the United States sought to contain communism around the world. To achieve this goal, the United States devoted a high proportion of the federal budget to defense. Billions of dollars were spent building weapons, training troops, and establishing military bases.

In 1950, the United States spent approximately $13 billion on defense, which amounted to a little less than one third of the federal budget. By 1961, defense spending had soared to $47 billion, or roughly one half of the total budget. Many Americans became concerned. In 1961, outgoing President Dwight Eisenhower warned the nation about the "military-industrial complex," or the growing alliance of business and military leaders who worked together to keep defense spending high.

Defense spending continued to increase in dollar amounts in the 1970s, 1980s, and early 1990s. At the same time, it slowly declined as a percentage of the total federal budget, averaging about 25 percent between 1975 and 1990.

Since the collapse of the Soviet Union in 1991, American defense spending has decreased significantly as a percentage of the federal budget. Today defense spending represents only about 16 percent of the total budget. This is the lowest percentage since before World War II.

Cutting defense spending can create problems. For example, the United States must maintain the military strength it needs not only to defend itself but also to meet its commitments to other nations. In addition, high defense spending produces jobs. In 1971, the Pentagon employed 3.8 million workers, including men and women in the armed forces. An additional 2.2 million people worked in defense-related private industries. Although these numbers have decreased in recent years, millions of Americans still owe their jobs to defense spending.

The Impact on You

Imagine that you have been assigned to write an editorial on future defense spending. What information would you need before deciding whether defense spending should increase, decrease, or remain the same? List five questions that you would want to research.

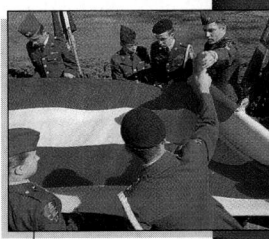

Ceremony at closing of army base, 1996

Class Discussion

Discuss with the class the impact of defense spending on society and the economy. For a more thorough examination of the issues, see the activity folder in the Resource Options below.

ACTIVITY

STUDENT PARTICIPATION

Writing a Proposal

Ask students to read the text. Then divide the class into two groups to brainstorm ways in which defense plants and bases might be converted to the following peacetime uses:
- **business**
- **industry**
- **housing**
- **recreation**

Have each group write a proposal explaining its best idea in detail.

Follow up Ask students to investigate real-life examples of defense conversions to peacetime use.

Using the Internet

Students can learn more about defense spending by exploring links in the *America: Pathways to the Present* Web site at

http://www.Pathways.phschool.com

Assessment

See the Lesson Plans folder, pp. 24–27, for rubrics on assessing Class Participation Projects.

RESOURCE OPTIONS

Teaching Resources

Why Study History? Activity Defense Spending Affects You, found in the Why Study History? folder, p. 27, provides an activity to help students better understand defense spending.

Media and Technology

Prentice Hall United States History Video Collection™ Volume 20 *Post-War USA*

Decision America Videotapes and Videodiscs Issue 6 *A New Role for the Military?*

Key Terms

Students should refer to the definitions of key terms in the chapter to write sentences that show an understanding of the cold war and the conflicts that arose from it.

Comprehension

1. Germany had been divided into four occupation zones following World War II. The USSR increasingly took charge of their zone, installing a totalitarian government and turning it into a separate nation.

2. People convicted of being Soviet spies in the 1950s. Hiss served a prison term, the Rosenbergs were executed.

3. NATO was formed by western countries to provide security against Soviet aggression. The Warsaw Pact, a military alliance between the USSR and its satellites, was the Soviet response to NATO.

4. The partition of Germany by the Soviet Union, the flight of East Germans into West Germany, and the Soviet decision to block Allied access to West Berlin.

5. McCarthy gained popularity by crusading against communism and using exaggeration and half-truths to inflame the populace. He lost power when he accused the army of housing Communists.

6. Yalta was a meeting among the United States, the Soviet Union, and Britain to decide the future of Germany and Poland. Potsdam was a meeting between Truman and Stalin to try to resolve issues that were not decided at Yalta.

7. MacArthur was a general renowned for his heroism and anti-Communist stance. He was commander of American forces in Asia, a key player in reshaping Japan's government after the war, and leader of UN forces in Korea.

8. It set the tone of the cold war.

Chapter Summary

The major concepts of Chapter 26 are presented below. See also *Guide to the Essentials of American History* or *Interactive Student Tutorial CD-ROM,* which contains interactive review activities, time lines, helpful hints, and test practice for Chapter 26.

Reviewing the Main Ideas

After World War II, the United States and the Soviet Union entered a period of intense hostility known as the cold war. The conflict was mostly indirect, taking place in countries where the two superpowers competed for influence and in a nuclear arms race. The cold war inflamed anti-Communist fears and suspicions at home.

Section 1: Origins of the Cold War

At the end of World War II, conflicting goals for Europe led to growing hostility between the United States and the Soviet Union.

Section 2: The Cold War Abroad and at Home

As the cold war intensified, American policy focused on rebuilding and unifying Western Europe. At home, emotionally charged spy cases raised fears of Communist infiltration into American society and government.

Section 3: The Cold War Expands

During the 1950s, the cold war spread to new locations around the world. At home, a senator's anti-Communist crusade ruined many people's careers but ultimately failed.

High defense spending in recent decades has had a major impact on American society that continues to this day.

Key Terms

Use each of the terms below in a sentence that shows how it relates to the chapter.

1. domino theory
2. *Sputnik*
3. Truman Doctrine
4. U-2 incident
5. Hollywood Ten
6. cold war
7. iron curtain
8. Berlin airlift
9. containment
10. NATO
11. HUAC
12. Marshall Plan
13. brinkmanship
14. satellite nation
15. blacklist
16. Warsaw Pact

Comprehension

1. How did Germany come to be a divided nation?
2. Who were Alger Hiss and the Rosenbergs?
3. Why were NATO and the Warsaw Pact created?
4. What events led to the Berlin airlift?
5. Describe the rise and fall of Senator Joseph McCarthy.
6. What were the Potsdam and Yalta conferences?
7. Who was Douglas MacArthur, and what is his historical significance?
8. What was the importance of the Iron Curtain speech?

Using Graphic Organizers

Using information from the chapter, fill in the ovals to identify the causes and effects of the cold war.

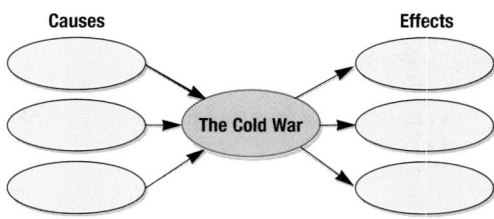

Using Graphic Organizers

- Causes: Disagreements between the Soviet Union and the United States over what kind of government to allow in Poland; different economic and political systems; conflicts with the governing and partitioning of Germany; the Truman Doctrine.
- Effects: American involvement in the Korean War and other conflicts in Southeast Asia; entanglements in the Middle East and Latin America; hysteria in American society and the curtailing of rights.

Analyzing Political Cartoons ▶

"FIRE!"

1. Examine the images in this 1949 cartoon. (a) What is the flame that the man is about to douse? (b) What does it represent?
2. (a) What does the man represent? (b) How do you know?
3. What is the cartoonist's message?

Critical Thinking

1. *Reviewing the Chapter Skill* Write a cause-and-effect statement about the Korean War.
2. *Arranging Events in Order* List three or four major events that preceded Churchill's declaration that an "iron curtain" had divided Europe.
3. *Recognizing Ideologies* How did differing ideologies lead to the development of the cold war?
4. *Analyzing Primary Sources* Reread the Key Documents quotation from Eisenhower at the end of Section 3. Restate the main point in your own words.

INTERNET ACTIVITY

For your portfolio:
PREPARE A SUMMARY

Access Prentice Hall's *America: Pathways to the Present* site at **www.Pathways.phschool.com** for the specific URL to complete the activity. Additional resources and related Web sites are also available.

Read about the history and organization of the United Nations. Choose one branch or suborganization of the United Nations and prepare a summary of the work carried out by that branch.

ANALYZING DOCUMENTS ◀ INTERPRETING DATA

Turn to the excerpt from the Truman Doctrine at the end of Section 1.

1. What was the main purpose of Truman's speech? (a) to frighten the Soviet government (b) to make clear how the United States would respond to Communist aggression (c) to win congressional approval of the containment policy (d) to expand the cold war.

2. Who did Truman promise to help? (a) subjugated minorities (b) armed resistance movements (c) majorities whose freedom was threatened (d) all of the above.

3. *Writing* Do you think the Truman Doctrine would be a good model for conducting American foreign policy today? Why or why not?

Connecting to Today

Essay Writing Since the breakup of the Soviet Union and the end of the cold war around 1991, relations between the United States and Russia have changed. Research and write an essay explaining the changes. Compare American and Russian goals today. Do you think Russia is still a threat to American interests?

INTERNET ACTIVITY

Summaries should be supported with specific examples from the Web site and include relevant quotes.

Analyzing Political Cartoons

1. (a) The torch held by the Statue of Liberty. (b) Liberty.
2. (a) Cold war hysteria; exaggerated fear of communism. (b) The date of the cartoon, the label "hysteria" on the man.
3. Cold war hysteria is threatening American civil liberties.

Critical Thinking

1. The seeds of the Korean War were planted by the division of the country at the 38th parallel. North Korean troops attempted to unify the country by crossing the line, leading to war. The war resulted in loss of American life, little change in the Korean peninsula, and disillusionment on the part of Americans.
2. The Yalta Conference, the formation of the United Nations, the death of Roosevelt and ascension of Truman to the presidency, the Potsdam conference, the Soviet establishment of satellite nations.
3. The Soviet Communist ideology had as its goal the collapse of capitalism worldwide. This was in direct conflict with the ideology of western nations to preserve open markets and promote democracy.
4. Students' answers will vary but restatements should reflect the main point of the quotation.

Analyzing Documents

1. c
2. c
3. Answers will vary, but might cite examples of current foreign policy.

Connecting to Today

Essays will vary but should explore themes introduced in the text and provide strong examples.

The Postwar Years at Home, 1945–1960

Managing Time and Instruction

INSTRUCTION SUPPORT
These materials for instruction are provided for **each section** in the **Teaching Resources. See Units 7–8 folder for Enrichment Support:**

- Reproducible Lesson Plans in Lesson Plans folder ● Learning Styles Lesson Plans in Learning Styles Lesson Plans folder ● Big Idea Graphic Organizers in Big Idea Graphic Organizer folder ● Guided Reading and Review ● Quizzes ● Test Preparation Practice booklet

DAILY LESSON	ENRICHMENT SUPPORT
1 **The Postwar Economy** (pp. 767–771)	• Biography, Ray A. Kroc, Units 7–8 folder, p. 89 • Visual Learning Activity, The Miracle of Television, Learning with Documents folder, p. 69
2 **The Mood of the 1950s** (pp. 774–777)	• Literature Activity, Conformity in the 1950s, Units 7–8 folder, pp. 92–93 • Nystrom *Atlas of Our Country,* People on the Move, pp. 34–35 • Critical Thinking Activity, Determining Relevance: Wages, Hours, and Unions, found on **Resource Pro** • Literature Activity, Noncomformity in the 1950s, found on **Resource Pro** • Comparing Primary Sources, On Rock and Roll, Units 7–8 folder, pp. 90–91
3 **Domestic Politics and Policy** (pp. 779–784)	• Skills for Life Activity, Units 7–8 folder, p. 94 • Visual Learning Activity, Auto Strike, 1950, found on **Resource Pro** • Primary Source Activity, Harry Truman: Off the Record, found on **Resource Pro**
4 **Demands for Civil Rights** (pp. 785–788)	• Primary Source Activity, Enforcing *Brown* v. *Board of Education,* Learning with Documents folder, p. 33 • Decision-Making Activity, Integrating the University of Georgia, Decision-Making Activities folder, pp. 20–21 • Key Documents, *Brown* v. *Board of Education,* Learning with Documents folder, p. 100 • Biography, Maria Latigo Hernando and Pedro Hernandez, found on **Resource Pro** • Health Care Is a Growing Concern, Why Study History? folder, p. 28

Running Out of Time?

- Use Tape 4, "Hot and Cold War, 1939–1960," from **Visions of America** videotapes series.
- Use Chapter 27 Summary from **Guide to the Essentials of American History** (English and Spanish).

Companion Web Site

The companion Web site offers online links for all chapter review activities. It also provides key content links and structured support for this chapter for both teachers and students.

http://www.Pathways.phschool.com

Teaching in the Information Age

Media and Technology

For the Student

Interactive Student Tutorial CD-ROM Chapter 27

Student Edition on Audiotape Chapter 27

American Heritage® CD-ROM

Guided Reading Audiotapes (English and Spanish) Chapter 27

For the Teacher

Resource Pro CD-ROM Chapter 27

Test Bank CD-ROM Chapter 27

Listening to Music CD "Rock Around the Clock" by Bill Haley

Listening to Literature Audiotapes *Timeless Voices, Timeless Themes* "The Unknown Citizen" by W. H. Auden

Assessment Options

Chapter Test Forms A&B Test Bank CD-ROM booklet

Test Bank CD-ROM Chapter 27

Standardized Test Preparation Handbook

Block Scheduling

Pacing Suggestions

For 90-minute Blocks

- Teach sections 1 and 2 using Transparencies L-5 and I-4 and the Extended Class Periods Activity on p. 776.
- Teach sections 3 and 4 using the Big Idea Graphic Organizers from Teaching Resources and the Recent Scholarship note on p. 783 for class discussions.

Additional Resources

- Prentice Hall's **American History Block Scheduling Support File** covers over 40 major topics in American history. Included are lesson plans, strategies, primary sources, literature, biographies, Great Debates, art history, simulations, and songs.
- **Prentice Hall United States History Video Collection™** contains 20 videotapes covering American history from beginnings to present.

Connections to American Literature

from Prentice Hall

Prentice Hall Literature *Timeless Voices, Timeless Themes* "The Brown Chest" by John Updike, p. 904

Additional Resources

For the Student

Ralph Ellison. *Invisible Man.* Random House, 1989.

Time-Life Books editors. *This Fabulous Century. Vol. 6, 1950–1960.* Time-Life Books, 1969.

For the Teacher

David Halberstam. *The Fifties.* Villard Books, 1993.

Prentice Hall brings into the classroom the vast archives and scholarship of the nation's premier American history magazine. See "From the Archives of American Heritage®" and "About the Presidents" teaching notes in this chapter.

 History Alive!

Teacher's Curriculum Institute, in partnership with Prentice Hall, provides unique materials that engage students with diverse learning styles. See History Alive!® unit on Contemporary American Society.

 Student Performance Pack

Ensures success in the three critical areas of Reading, Test Taking, and English Language Development with the following materials:
- Guide to the Essentials of American History in English and Spanish
- Guided Reading Audiotapes in English and Spanish
- Interactive Student Tutorial CD-ROM
- Test Preparation Handbook
- Test Preparation Practice booklet

The Postwar Years at Home 1945–1960

Introducing the Chapter

As it emerged from World War II, the American Dream of having a secure job, owning a house, and using labor-saving appliances came within reach of many Americans. Fueled by the postwar baby boom, the economy rocketed forward in the late 1940s and 1950s. The dividends of the triumph of democracy eluded many Americans, however, and the civil rights movement gained momentum as it brought into focus the democratic principles that the United States had fought for in World War II.

Themes in American History

The theme for this chapter, Diversity, is listed at the beginning of this unit. An alternate theme for the chapter is Culture. To teach this unit thematically, you may wish to use The Nation After World War II folder in American History Block Scheduling Support.

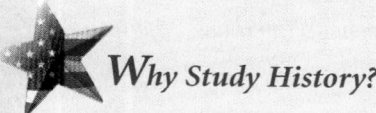

*W*hy Study History?

Have students explore suggested ways of connecting the past to the present on page 789.

Answer to . . .

Viewing History Students should use this question as an aid in reading the chapter. The picture shows that some Americans were thriving economically. The family shown here has a large house, probably in the suburbs, and a variety of material possessions.

CHAPTER 27 The Postwar Years at Home

1945–1960

CHAPTER FOCUS

*T*his chapter describes the years following World War II, during which time Americans began to enjoy the benefits of their new standing as a military and economic superpower. While not all groups shared in the prosperity, most Americans now were able to buy the homes, cars, and other items that they had once only dreamed of owning.

The Why Study History? page at the end of this chapter explores the connection between President Truman's efforts to provide health care to Americans and the continued demands on the health care industry today.

VIEWING HISTORY This image of 1950s suburban life is on the cover of a 1958 issue of *The Saturday Evening Post.* **Culture** *What does this picture tell you about life in the United States in the 1950s?*

▶ RESOURCE OPTIONS

Teaching Resources

📁 **Big Idea Graphic Organizer** folder Graphic summary of the main idea of the chapter.

📁 **Learning Styles Lesson Plans** folder Alternate lesson plans for diverse learning styles for each chapter.

Media and Technology

 AmericanHeritage® **CD-ROM Time Tour** The Nation Today and Tomorrow: The Fifties

💿 **Prentice Hall United States History Video Collection**™ Volume 20 *Post-War USA*

Timeline

1944
GI Bill offers veterans low-interest loans and a college education

1947
Invention of the transistor allows computer industry to grow

1954
Dr. Jonas Salk successfully tests polio vaccine

1955
AFL and the CIO merge

1956
Interstate Highway Act provides money for an interstate highway system

1944 — 1950 — 1956

1 The Postwar Economy

SECTION PREVIEW

Objectives

1 Understand that following World War II rapid economic growth encouraged businesses to reorganize.
2 Describe how technological advances transformed life in the United States.
3 Explain how changes in the working lives of Americans influenced the growth of suburbs, highways, and consumer credit.
4 *Key Terms* Define: per capita income; conglomerate; franchise; transistor; baby boom; GI Bill.

Main Idea

The American Dream, characterized by a home in the suburbs and a car in the garage, came true for many people in the postwar years.

Reading Strategy

Reading for Evidence Note the statement below that, after the war, the United States "embarked on one of its greatest periods of economic expansion." As you read the section, look for evidence to support this statement.

Objectives
You may wish to call students' attention to the objectives in the Section Preview. The objectives are reflected in the main headings of the section.

Bellringer
Have students think of inventions that would be totally new to a person from the 1930s who was suddenly transported to the present.

Reading Strategy
Reading for Evidence Refer students to the Reading Strategy in the Section Preview. You may wish to have students organize their information into a chart.

When American soldiers returned from the battlefields, they wanted to put the horrors of the war behind them and enjoy the comforts of home. During the war, when most items were rationed or not produced at all, many people had simply put their money into savings. Now most Americans were eager to acquire everything the war—and before that, the Depression—had denied them.

Businesses Reorganize

During the postwar years, the United States embarked on one of its greatest periods of economic expansion. The gross national product (GNP) more than doubled, jumping from $212 billion in 1945 to $504 billion in 1960. **Per capita income,** the average income per person, increased from $1,526 to $2,788.

Major corporate expansion accompanied economic growth. In the 1950s a few huge firms dominated many industries. General Motors, Ford, and Chrysler overshadowed all competitors in the automobile industry; General Electric and Westinghouse enjoyed similar positions in the electrical business. Giant corporations, fearful after the Great Depression of investing all their resources in a single business, became **conglomerates.** (A conglomerate is a large corporation that owns many smaller companies that produce entirely different goods and services.) They reasoned that if one area of the economy failed, their investments in another area would be safe. International Telephone and Telegraph, for example, purchased Avis Rent-a-Car, Sheraton Hotels, Hartford Fire Insurance, and Continental Baking.

At the same time, another kind of expansion took place. In 1954 Ray Kroc, who sold milk-shake machines called Multimixers, was amazed when two brothers who owned a restaurant in San Bernardino, California, ordered their tenth Multimixer. With ten

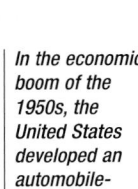

In the economic boom of the 1950s, the United States developed an automobile-centered culture.

LESSON PLAN
Connecting to the Main Idea

1. Focus The nation's economy boomed during the postwar years. Ask students how this boom changed American life.
2. Instruct Explain that after World War II, people wanted to enjoy the comforts that war had denied them. Ask students to explain why the economy expanded after World War II. What new ways of organizing businesses developed in response to the growing economy?

Ask students for examples of new technology after World War II that changed American culture and work. How did the widespread use of the automobile lead to the growth of consumer credit? Why does a credit-driven economy move faster than a cash-only economy? Have students describe the relationship between the growth of white-collar jobs, the creation of the suburbs, and "car culture."
3. Close After World War II, the nation's economy boomed. Many Americans enjoyed a comfortable lifestyle, with a new house in the suburbs and a car to drive to work. In the next section, students will learn why some critics claimed that conformity was the cost of comfort.

RESOURCE OPTIONS

Teaching Resources

📁 **Reproducible Lesson Plan** Lesson Plans folder, p. 142

📁 **Learning Styles Lesson Plan** Learning Styles Lesson Plans folder, p. 56

📁 **Big Idea Graphic Organizer** Big Idea Graphic Organizer folder, p. 114

📁 **Guided Reading and Review** Units 7–8 folder, p. 81

Media and Technology

 AmericanHeritage® CD-ROM

Time Tour The Nation Today and Tomorrow: The Fifties

Today we take business franchises for granted, but after World War II the franchise was a new concept, designed to address the growing consumer demand in the United States. Divide students into small groups and have them list as many franchises as possible in five minutes. Discuss how the increasing number of franchises contributed to the growing economy after World War II. Then have the groups list two positive and two negative effects of franchises. *(Reteaching)*

You may wish to have students add the following to their portfolios. To assess student work, refer to the generic rubrics in the Program Overview in the Teaching Resources.

Have students watch episodes from some children's television series of the 1950s, such as *Kukla, Fran, and Ollie; Howdy Doody; The Lone Ranger; Hopalong Cassidy;* or *The Mickey Mouse Club.* Some of these programs are broadcast on cable networks, and some are available on video. Ask students to write a paper comparing the subject matter, format, types of people and groups represented, and level of sophistication of these programs with current children's television programs.

Answer to . . .

Interpreting Graphs It probably encouraged buying, since TV shows were funded by advertising.

This sign at the original fast-food restaurant in San Bernardino, California, advertised the McDonald brothers' mass-produced hamburgers.

machines, the restaurant could make 50 milk shakes at once. Because of the restaurant's fast, efficient service and its prime location along a busy highway, it was enjoying great success. Intrigued by the possibilities, Kroc purchased the two brothers' idea of assembly-line food production. He also acquired the name of the brothers' restaurant: McDonald's. Kroc built a nation-wide chain of fast-food restaurants. Others quickly saw the benefits in selling **franchises,** or the right to open a restaurant using a parent company's brand name and system, to other eager entrepreneurs. Hundreds of other restaurant franchises followed.

The franchise system flourished in the 1950s. It worked so well that it was applied to other kinds of businesses, such as clothing stores and automobile muffler shops. The system's advantage lay in the fact that an individual with only a few thousand dollars could own a small business that enjoyed the support of a multimillion-dollar parent company. With the growth of the franchise system, unique stores with ties to the local community were replaced by nationwide chains that were the same everywhere in the country.

Technology Transforms Life

Developments in technology spurred industrial growth. Rushing to keep up with demand, businesses produced hundreds of new and improved products, such as dishwashers and gas-powered lawnmowers, that would save the consumer time and money. Eager Americans filled their homes with the latest inventions.

Television In the 1950s Americans fell in love with television. Developed in the 1930s, television became enormously popular after World War II. By 1953 two thirds of all American families owned TVs.

In 1955 the average American family watched television four to five hours a day. Children grew up on such programs as *Howdy Doody* and *The Mickey Mouse Club.* Teenagers danced to the rock-and-roll music played on *American Bandstand,* a predecessor of today's MTV. Other viewers followed situation comedies like *I Love Lucy* and *Father Knows Best.*

Three large networks controlled television programming. They raised the money to broadcast their shows by selling advertising time. Television commercials constantly bombarded Americans with advertisements for the latest consumer products. Companies got their money's worth from advertising dollars; millions of viewers were persuaded to buy the items they saw on television commercials.

The Computer Industry Television was not the only machine that changed American culture. Wartime research led to the development of ever more powerful calculators and computers. During the 1950s, American businesses reached out to embrace the computer industry. Grace Hopper, a research fellow at Harvard University's computation laboratory, pioneered the creation of the software that runs computers. She also introduced the term *debugging,* which was born when she removed a moth caught in a relay switch that had caused a large computer to shut down. Today the term means "ridding a computer program of errors."

In 1948 scientists at Bell Telephone Laboratories invented the **transistor,** a tiny circuit device that amplifies, controls, and generates electrical signals. The transistor could do the work of a much larger vacuum tube, but took up less space. Because of the transistor, giant machines that once filled whole rooms could now fit on a desk. Calculations that had taken hours could now be computed in fractions of a second. The Census Bureau purchased one of the first computer systems to tally the 1950 census.

Households with Televisons, 1950–1960

Number of Households (in millions) vs. *Year*

Source: *Historical Statistics of the United States, Colonial Times to 1970*

Interpreting Graphs Notice how many households acquired televisions during the 1950s. *Economics How do you think television influenced economics?*

Nuclear Power An entirely new industry, the generation of electrical power through the use of atomic energy, resulted from the research that had produced the atomic bomb. In 1956 film producer Walt Disney voiced Americans' hopes and fears about atomic power in his book and film *Our Friend the Atom*. Disney began with a story about a fisherman who found a sealed bottle. When the fisherman opened the bottle, a genie escaped and threatened to kill him. The fisherman got the genie back into the bottle and would only open it again when the genie promised to grant him three wishes. "The story of the atom is like that tale," Disney explained:

AMERICAN VOICES ❝The fable . . . has a happy ending; perhaps our story can, too. Like the Fisherman we must bestir our wits [think carefully before we act]. We have the scientific knowledge to turn the Genie's might into peaceful and useful channels.❞

—*Walt Disney*

The next year, navy captain Hyman G. Rickover oversaw the development of the first commercial nuclear power plant in Shippingport, Pennsylvania. The new plant promised the peaceful use of atomic energy that Walt Disney had imagined.

Advances in Medicine Americans also found hope in developments made in medicine. In 1954, Dr. Jonas Salk and Dr. Thomas Francis conducted a successful field test of a vaccine to prevent one of the most feared diseases—poliomyelitis. Before the vaccine, the disease, known commonly as polio, killed or disabled more than 20,000 children in the United States every year. Salk's injected vaccine, together with an oral version developed later by Dr. Albert Sabin, effectively eliminated the threat of polio.

Research in the development of drugs that could fight bacterial infections had been under way long before the start of World War II. By 1944, advances in the production of antibiotics, such as penicillin, saved countless lives. During the 1950s, doctors discovered other antibiotics effective against penicillin-resistant bacteria.

Doctors who had served during the war saving the lives of wounded soldiers came home to a new era of surgical advances. They made great strides in the growing specialty of heart surgery. Lessons learned in war allowed doctors to operate to correct heart defects.

These Chicago-area commuters display the conformity that has come to characterize the 1950s. *Culture* **What role did the changes in the economy play in the growing uniformity of the culture?**

Changes in the Work Force

In earlier years, most Americans made a living as blue-collar workers, or those who produce goods. After the war, however, new machines performed many of the jobs previously done by people. By 1956 a majority of all American workers held white-collar jobs, in which they no longer produced goods but instead performed services for others, working at counters or in offices.

The growth of the service industry had a great effect on the lives of Americans. The new white-collar workers felt encouraged by the working conditions they found: clean, bright offices. But they soon realized that office jobs had drawbacks as well. Work in large corporations was often impersonal. White-collar workers had little connection with the products that their companies made. Employers might pressure employees to dress, think, and act alike. Sociologist C. Wright Mills had this scathing comment: "When white-collar people get jobs, they sell not only their time and energy but their personalities as well."

For those who kept their blue-collar jobs, working conditions and wages improved during the 1940s and 1950s. During this period, workers in

Main Idea
CONNECTIONS
How did the growing service industry affect the lives of Americans?

some unions won important gains, such as guaranteed cost-of-living increases. By 1955 nearly 33 percent of the total labor force in the United States was unionized. In that year, the two largest unions, the American Federation of Labor (AFL) and the Congress of Industrial Organizations (CIO) merged. The AFL-CIO, a new and more powerful organization, remains a major force today.

Suburbs and Highways

With so many people working and making a better living than ever before, the **baby boom** that had begun during World War II continued. The birthrate, which had fallen to 19 births per 1,000 people during the Depression, soared to more than 25 births per 1,000 in its peak year of 1957.

Moving to the Suburbs Growing families retreated from aging cities and sought new houses in suburbs that ringed the urban areas. World War II veterans enjoyed the benefits of the Servicemen's Readjustment Act of 1944, commonly known as the **GI Bill,** which gave them low-interest mortgages to purchase their new homes.†

Developers like William J. Levitt began to cater to the demand for housing. Levitt built new communities in the suburbs, pioneering mass-production techniques in home building.

Levitt and other developers offered not just houses, but entire communities. *Culture What were the benefits and drawbacks of Levittowns?*

He bought precut and preassembled materials and built houses in just weeks instead of months. Proud of his creations, Levitt gave his name to the new towns. Soon there was a Levittown in New York, another in Pennsylvania, and a third in New Jersey. Others adopted Levitt's techniques, and new communities sprang up all over the United States.

For the first time, average Americans could easily afford to buy their own home. While most fully enjoyed life in their new houses, others complained that the developments all looked too much alike. Folk singer Malvina Reynolds expressed her distaste for the new communities with these words from "Little Boxes," a popular song of the era:

> Little boxes on the hillside
> Little boxes made of ticky-tacky
> Little boxes on the hillside
> Little boxes all the same.
> There's a green one and a pink one
> And a blue one and a yellow one
> And they're all made out of ticky-tacky
> And they all look just the same.

Cars and Highways Suburban growth brought with it other changes. Stores began to move from cities to shopping centers located in

---

Birth Rate, 1930–1960

Year	Live Births (per 1,000 people)
1930	21
1935	18.5
1940	19.5
1945	20.5
1950	24.5
1955	25
1960	23.5

Source: *Historical Statistics of the United States, Colonial Times to 1970*

Interpreting Graphs A healthy postwar economy encouraged people to have larger families. *Culture What was the difference in the birth rate between 1945 and 1955?*

†Nearly half of all eligible veterans took advantage of another provision in the GI Bill that offered money for college tuition.

Left margin sidebar

▼ BACKGROUND

Connections to Today

While the houses of Levittown, New York, were commonly criticized as "little boxes" and as symbols of a cheapened mass culture, many commentators think they look better as time goes on. Historian Alexander O. Boulton, for instance, has pointed out that far from being "made of ticky-tacky," the Levittown houses were unusually well-designed and built. In addition, Levittown residents have modified their homes in so many ways through the years that those homes still in original condition are sought after as rarities. In Boulton's words, Levittown "now seems not the model of mass conformity but a monument to American individualism."

*C*ustomize for
More Advanced Students

The baby boom was both a result of increased economic growth and the cause of more growth. Ask students to write one sentence explaining how the huge increase in births caused what syndicated economics writer Sylvia Porter called "the biggest, boomiest boom ever known in history."

Answer to . . .

Viewing History Benefits: low costs, fast construction, built-in communities. Drawbacks: uniformity.
***Interpreting Graphs** It increased dramatically.*

TEST PREPARATION

Have students read the excerpt from the song "Little Boxes" on this page and then answer the question below.

The main reason the songwriter dislikes the new housing developments is that—

A the houses resemble boxes.

Ⓑ all the houses look the same.

C the houses are in poor taste.

D she dislikes pastel colors.

the suburbs. Americans, at the same time, depended more on automobiles and less on public transportation. To meet the demand, auto makers started introducing new car designs every year. People eagerly awaited the unveiling of the latest models. During the 1950s American auto makers produced up to 8 million new cars each year.

Growth in the car industry created a need for more and better roads. The 1956 Interstate Highway Act provided $26 billion to build an interstate highway system more than 40,000 miles long. The project provided a national web of new roads and allowed for the evacuation of major cities in the event of nuclear attack.

The car culture inspired the development of many new businesses. Americans, especially teenagers, flocked to drive-in movies and restaurants. Families, encouraged by car advertisements that urged them to "See the USA," headed off on vacations at national parks, seaside resorts, and amusement parks.

The Growth of Consumer Credit

Eager to cash in on the increasing number of cars on the road, gasoline companies began offering credit cards to loyal customers. These cards allowed people to charge gas purchases when they were on the road. Americans found the cards easy and convenient to use.

After years of depression and war, Americans willingly went into debt to purchase the products they wanted. (See the graph on this page.) Lending agencies picked up the credit card idea and made borrowing easy. The Diner's Club credit card appeared in 1950, followed at the end of the decade by the American Express card, and then by the BankAmericard (later called Visa).

Advertisers persuaded consumers that only by buying new products could they attain status and success. Americans responded by using their credit to purchase washing machines, vacuum cleaners, and television sets. The United States had become, in the words of economist John Kenneth Galbraith, "the affluent society."

Consumer Credit Debt, 1946–1960

Source: *Historical Statistics of the United States, Colonial Times to 1970*

Interpreting Graphs Consumer debt included far more than just credit card debt. The consumer credit debt shown in this graph includes installment payments, home loans, and other loans as well as credit card debts. *Economics* By how much did consumer credit debt increase between 1946 and 1960?

SECTION 1 REVIEW

Comprehension

1. **Key Terms** Define: (a) per capita income; (b) conglomerate; (c) franchise; (d) transistor; (e) baby boom; (f) GI Bill.
2. **Summarizing the Main Idea** How did the growth of the United States economy after World War II help many people achieve the American Dream?
3. **Organizing Information** Create a two-column chart that shows how conglomerates and the franchise system changed the American economy after World War II.

Critical Thinking

4. **Analyzing Time Lines** Review the time line at the start of the section. In your opinion, which entry had the greatest impact on American society in the postwar years?
5. **Identifying Central Issues** What technological advances had an important impact on Americans in the decade after World War II?

Writing Activity

6. **Writing a Persuasive Essay** Changes in the workplace influenced the growth of suburbs, highways, and consumer credit. Write an ad convincing people to move to the suburbs, buy a car, or apply for a credit card.

Customize for Less Proficient Readers

Ask students to write one or two sentences showing how each of the following developments changed American life during the postwar period: corporate expansion, technological advances, changes in the work force, changes in farm work and life, the move to the suburbs, and consumer credit.

Answers to SECTION 1 REVIEW

1. (a) per capita income, see p. 767; (b) conglomerate, see p. 767; (c) franchise, see p. 768; (d) transistor, see p. 768; (e) baby boom, see p. 770; (f) GI Bill, see p. 770.

2. More people were working, and per capita income rose. Average Americans could afford to buy homes and own small businesses, paying on credit.

3. Conglomerates: led to giant corporations that owned businesses in many areas of the economy. Franchise system: created chains that often pushed out local businesses.

4. Answers will vary. Sample: 1954—polio vaccine, because it prevented 20,000 deaths a year due to polio.

5. New and improved products; television; computers; transistors; the use of atomic energy.

6. Advertisements will vary but should point out the benefits of a white-collar job, a move to the suburbs, buying a car, or applying for a credit card.

Answer to . . .

Interpreting Graphs By about 50 billion dollars.

GEOGRAPHY AND HISTORY

The Suburban Explosion

Focus Explain that before the post-war building boom, only the wealthy could afford to live in the suburbs. After the war, prosperity and government programs to finance mortgages started a suburban building spree that changed the way many Americans lived.

Instruct Show students a detailed map of the nearest large city and its surrounding suburbs. Ask students to point out the core city, beltways, and "edge cities."

Ask students to list ways in which the development of suburban housing changed American life. Ask them to consider:

• The family: How did suburban housing encourage nuclear, as opposed to extended, families?

• The environment: What impact did the growth of suburbs have on wildlife, quality of air and water, and amount of farmland?

• Integration: Did the growth of suburbs encourage or discourage integration of housing and schools?

Extend Many observers thought that the shopping mall would become the "community center" of the suburbs, filling the roles of Main Street, the town common, the city square, and the neighborhood playground. Ask students how successful they think shopping malls have been in creating a sense of community. What activities other than shopping, such as eating meals, taking an exercise class, or going to a movie, are available in shopping malls?

GEOGRAPHY AND HISTORY

The Suburban Explosion

The geographic theme of location explores where a place is, not only in absolute terms but in relation to other places. After World War II, American cities rapidly expanded outward as people moved into the suburbs—places defined by their location near cities. What factors contributed to this suburban explosion?

A 1950s' game piece reflects the suburban ideal.

In the decades following World War II, the location of people's homes and jobs changed. Millions of people moved to the suburbs, leveling the land, building homes, highways and stores. The suburbs that housed them soon became major centers for shopping, working, and recreation. But this change did not come without a price.

The Expansion of Waterfront Centers

In the 1700s, the largest cities in the United States were commercial centers located on waterfronts. This was because goods and people could travel more easily and quickly over water than on land. Workplaces in these cities were clustered near the waterfront, with homes located nearby, so people could walk between home and work.

In the decades before and after the Civil War, railroads grew, cutting paths outward from these waterfront centers. The compact, circular-shaped cities began to expand. Small residential communities sprouted around railroad stations situated six or more miles from the central cities. These small communities provided quiet settings and appealing neighborhoods for those who could afford to make the daily rail trips to and from their jobs in the city.

> In 1956, the nation's first enclosed, climate-controlled shopping center opened. The suburban mall became increasingly popular for suburban consumers.

People Leave the Cities

After the late 1880s, electric-powered streetcar lines reached into the surrounding countryside. This enabled even more urban residents to move out of city centers. Many of the homes they built were bigger and had more land around them.

By the time the United States entered World War I in 1914, some of the larger cities extended ten miles out from their centers, where most people still worked and shopped. Streetcar lines did not extend as far in some directions as in others, and thus the overall shape of the cities was star-like.

Relocation After World War II

During the Great Depression and World War II, most Americans put their desire for better surroundings on hold. Once the war ended, however, millions of

---

 RESOURCE OPTIONS

Teaching Resources

📁 **Geography and History Activity** Edge Cities, Geography and History folder, pp. 16–17

📘 **Nystrom *Atlas of Our Country*** Land Use, Population, and Ethnicity, pp. 46–47 people returned to the nation's cities, where they married, had children in record numbers, and then began to search for bigger homes. Also, in the first decade after the war ended, the number of automobiles owned by city dwellers increased dramatically.

Housing in cities filled quickly. Because many veterans now owned automobiles, they had more options as to where they might live. Now they could consider living in locations outside cities.

The GI Bill made money readily available for housing. The result was construction at a rate unprecedented in the nation's history. Between 1947 and 1965, at least 1.25 million new houses were built each year, with more than one half of those in the suburbs.

The Growth of Edge Cities

In 1956 the federal government established an interstate highway system to connect major cities. In addition to highways radiating out from city centers, engineers constructed "beltways" that circled cities at distances of six to twenty miles from the core. But as people moved to the suburbs, they found it inconvenient to travel back into the city for things they needed. In 1956, the nation's first enclosed, climate-controlled shopping center opened. The suburban mall became increasingly popular for suburban consumers.

A major reason for the success of the mall was that people could easily get to it from the freeway. Such mall locations were also ideal sites for offices, factories, service providers, and other businesses. These businesses were grouped in low buildings located on either side of heavily traveled freeways and streets. All this new construction formed what journalist Joel Garreau called the "edge city."

The rapid growth of edge cities was not without its problems. As suburbs became more densely settled, pollution, crime, and other problems that had plagued the central cities began to creep in. Of greatest concern to the people who worked, shopped, and lived in edge cities was the increasing traffic congestion. The easy access that attracted people to the suburbs was becoming a memory. Urban observers today wonder how new forms of transportation will change the geography of American cities.

Detroit, 1920

- –·– Detroit city limits
- ☐ Developed areas
- — Streetcar and bus lines

0   1.5   3 Miles
0   1.5   3 Kilometers

New forms of public transportation led to development away from urban centers.

GEOGRAPHIC CONNECTIONS

1. Choose three forms of transportation mentioned in the passage and describe how each affected the growth of cities.

2. What factors contributed to the boom in suburban housing construction after World War II?

Themes in Geography

3. *Location* The earliest large cities were located on waterfronts. How might new changes in transportation affect the location of cities?

RESOURCE OPTIONS

Media and Technology

  Prentice Hall United States History Video Collection™
Volume 20 *Post-War USA*

The Mood of the 1950s

Objectives

You may wish to call students' attention to the objectives in the Section Preview. The objectives are reflected in the main headings of the section.

Bellringer

Ask students to decide what they consider to be the "proper" roles for men and women in today's society. How do their views of gender-based roles differ from those of their parents or grandparents?

Reading Strategy

Reinforcing Main Ideas Refer students to the Reading Strategy in the Section Preview. You may wish to have students discuss whether conformity was more prevalent in the 1950s than in their lives today.

LESSON PLAN

Connecting to the Main Idea

1. Focus In the 1950s, many Americans enjoyed unprecedented prosperity and security. Ask students if this comfort was worth the price of conformity.

2. Instruct Ask students how people behave when they want to fit into a group. How did the Great Depression and World War II affect Americans' need for security? Discuss other factors, such as the fear of communism, that led to increased conformity. Remind students that not everyone wanted to conform. Ask how rock and roll challenged middle-class mores in the 1950s. What distinguished the beatniks?

Discuss men's and women's roles in the postwar era. Ask students to define those roles and to compare them with the roles of men and women today.

3. Close Middle-class Americans prized comfort and security in the 1950s, and most valued conformity. The next section focuses on the attempts of government to maintain prosperity and security.

1946
Dr. Spock publishes The Common Sense Book of Baby and Child Care

1953
Alan Freed begins playing rock and roll on a Cleveland, Ohio, radio station

1955
The film Rebel Without a Cause released

1957
Jack Kerouac publishes his best-selling novel On the Road

1945   1950   1955   1960

2 The Mood of the 1950s

SECTION PREVIEW

Objectives

1. Explain why most Americans valued comfort and security during the 1950s.
2. Describe the expectations about the proper roles for men and women in society.
3. Identify some ways in which people challenged conformity during the 1950s.
4. *Key Terms* Define: rock and roll; beatnik.

Main Idea

After World War II, many Americans were blessed with wealth, success, and leisure. Conformity seemed the order of the day, although some groups made it their business to avoid the popularly accepted lifestyles of the 1950s.

Reading Strategy

Reinforcing Main Ideas Write two headings on a piece of paper: *Conformity* and *Nonconformity*. As you read the section, note relevant information in the appropriate column. Then write a sentence explaining whether conformity or nonconformity was more prevalent in the 1950s than in American life today.

The hula-hoop craze was one of many 1950s fads.

Most Americans were comfortable during the 1950s. They valued security over adventure, reflecting the mood of a nation still recovering from years of depression and war. They applauded the apparent harmony that minimized differences between individuals and groups in the United States. Compromise, rather than conflict, was the way disagreements could be settled. People wanted to enjoy their newly won prosperity and provide even better opportunities for their children.

Comfort and Security

In the past, sociologist David Riesman observed, Americans had valued individuality. Now most preferred to conform. Riesman cited *Tootle the Engine,* a children's story in the popular Little Golden Book series. Tootle, a young train engine, found it was more fun to play in the fields than it was to stay on the tracks. His fellow citizens in "Engineville" worked hard to break him of the habit. Tootle finally absorbed the lesson of his peers: "Always stay on the track no matter what." The story, Riesman believed, was a powerful parable for the young people of the 1950s.

Youth Culture Some called the youth of the 1950s the "silent generation." The silent generation seemed to have little interest in the problems and crises of the larger world. The strong economy allowed more young people to stay in school rather than leave early to find a job. With more leisure time, some teenagers appeared to devote their energies to organizing parties and pranks, joining fraternities and sororities, and generally pursuing entertainment and fun.

American businesses seized the opportunity to market products directly to this youth culture. Advertisements and movies helped to

▶ RESOURCE OPTIONS

Teaching Resources

 Reproducible Lesson Plan Lesson Plans folder, p. 143

Big Idea Graphic Organizer Big Idea Graphic Organizer folder, p. 115

 Guided Reading and Review Units 7–8 folder, p. 83

Literature Activity Conformity in the 1950s, Units 7–8 folder, pp. 92–93

ATLAS **Nystrom** *Atlas of Our Country* People on the Move, pp. 34–35

build an image of what it meant to be a teenager in the 1950s. The girls were shown in bobby socks and poodle skirts and the boys in letter sweaters. These images created a greater sense of conformity in style.

A Resurgence in Religion In the 1950s Americans, who had drifted away from religion in earlier years, flocked back to their churches or synagogues. The new interest in religion was a response in part to the cold-war struggle against "godless communism." Some looked to religion to find hope in the face of the threat of nuclear war.

Evidence of the newfound commitment to religion was everywhere. In 1954 Congress added the words "under God" to the Pledge of Allegiance, and the next year it required the phrase "In God We Trust" to appear on all American currency. Like other aspects of American life, religion became more commercial. Those in need could call Dial-a-Prayer for the first time, and new slogans such as "The family that prays together stays together" became commonplace. Evangelists used radio and television to carry their messages to more people than ever before. By the end of the 1950s, 95 percent of all Americans felt linked to some formal religious group.

Billy Graham

AMERICAN BIOGRAPHY One evangelist who gained a wide following in the 1950s was Billy Graham. Born in Charlotte, North Carolina, William Franklin Graham, Jr., was the son of a prosperous dairy farmer. After declaring his faith as a teenager, Graham attended fundamentalist institutions in Tennessee and Florida. In 1939 he was ordained as a Southern Baptist minister. He continued his education at Wheaton College in Illinois, graduating in 1943.

After leaving Wheaton, Graham joined Youth for Christ, an organization founded to minister to young soldiers during World War II. Following the war, his reputation grew as a result of appearances at tent revivals and at Youth for Christ rallies in the United States and Europe.

Thousands of Americans flocked to hear Graham preach at large-scale crusades, or tours, in major cities throughout the United States. In 1949, Graham gained widespread recognition at a crusade in Los Angeles, California. Originally scheduled to last for three weeks, the crusade was extended as crowds filled the tent every night for more than eight weeks. More crusades followed, with a 1957 meeting in New York City's Madison Square Garden lasting for 16 weeks.

Graham's direct style of speaking made religion accessible, and he became known as fundamentalism's chief spokesperson. In addition to his televised crusades, Graham published his sermons and started the magazine *Decision*. He has also written 18 books. Graham's prominence continued to grow and he was a frequent guest at the White House. In 1996, he was awarded the Congressional Gold Medal. ∎

Billy Graham (b.1918)

Men's and Women's Roles

Americans in the post–World War II years were keenly aware of the roles that they were expected to play as men and women. Men were supposed to go to school and then find jobs to support wives and children. Theirs was the public sphere, the world away from home where they earned money and made important political, economic, and social decisions. Men of this time often judged themselves and others by what they could buy with the money they earned.

Women in the 1950s were expected to play a supporting role for their husbands' lives in the public sphere. They kept house, cooked meals, and raised children. Many women had enjoyed working outside the home during World War II and were reluctant to give up good jobs. But many young couples wanted to start families, and most Americans at that time expected mothers to stay at home with their children. Moreover, there were no day-care centers. In 1947 *Life* magazine recorded women's frustration in a photo essay titled "The American Woman's Dilemma."

By the 1950s the dilemma seemed solved. Most middle-class women settled into the demands of raising children and maintaining their suburban homes. In 1956 *Life* produced a special edition on women that carried a very different message from the issue of nine years before. In a story titled "Busy Wife's Achievements," *Life* profiled Marjorie Sutton, a happy housewife who had married at the age

Main Idea CONNECTIONS

How did the traditional role of women in the 1950s support the ideals of postwar America?

Prepare a Report

Objective Use the Internet to write a report about the recollections and attitudes of men who turned 50 years old in the 1950s. Have students follow these instructions:

1. See the America: *Pathways to the Present* Web site at

http://www.Pathways.phschool.com

for the URL of the *Wall Street Journal* article "Turning 50 in 1950: Harvard Men Reflect on Lives Between the Wars."

2. Read the article, taking detailed notes. Write a report on these men's experiences of life in the 1950s. Be sure to address these questions in your report: What do these men's recollections say about conformity in the 1950s? What do they infer about the role of women? What kind of work did they do and what were their hobbies? Do you think the fact that they were Harvard graduates made them more or less likely to conform?

3. Share your report with your classmates.

Answer to . . .

Main Idea Connections Their role of managing their families and maintaining their homes supported the ideals of stability and security.

EXTENDED CLASS PERIODS

Time: 90 minutes.

Activity: Prepare questions and select potential subjects for interviews about life in the 1950s.

Grouping: Groups of four to six students.

Purpose: Have students work in groups to brainstorm topics concerning life in the 1950s, write questions for potential interviews, and select possible subjects to interview. Students may focus their interview questions on a specific population, for example, women.

Roles: Topic specialists, writers, editors, interviewers, spokesperson.

Outcome: Students will identify significant aspects of life in the 1950s and learn about them through first-person accounts.

Customize for

More Advanced Students

Ask students to consider this statement by Annie Dillard about her early life in *An American Childhood:* "Every woman stayed alone in her house in those days, like a coin in a safe. Amy [Dillard's sister] and I lived alone with our mother most of the day." What is the mood of Dillard's statement? What image does she create of a woman's life in the 1950s?

Answer to . . .

Interpreting Charts More and more married women were entering the labor force, while the number of single working women remained about the same.

The "happy housewife" portrayed in the 1950s media looked glamorous as she used state-of-the-art appliances to cook and clean.

of 16, had four children, and now kept busy with the PTA, Campfire Girls, and charity causes. She served as "home manager, mother, hostess, and useful civic worker," and even found time to exercise twice a week "to help preserve her size 12 figure."

The pediatrician Dr. Benjamin Spock assured American families that mothers should stay home with their young children. In *The Common Sense Book of Baby and Child Care,* published in 1946 and still selling today (in revised form), he advised a mother to remain with her children if she wanted them to grow up stable and secure. Adlai Stevenson, Democratic candidate for President in 1952 and 1956, reinforced this message when he told a group of female college students that "the assignment for you, as wives and mothers, you can do in the living room with a baby in your lap or in the kitchen with a can opener in your hand."

In 1963 Betty Friedan published an explosive critique of the 1950s' ideal of womanhood. Friedan had graduated with top honors from Smith College in 1942, but had given up her career as a journalist to become a full-time homemaker and mother. In her book *The Feminine Mystique,* Friedan lashed out at the culture that denied creative roles to women:

AMERICAN VOICES ❝It was unquestioned gospel [in the 1950s] that women could identify with nothing beyond the home—not politics, not art, not science, not events large or small, war or peace, in the United States or the world, unless it could be approached through female experience as a wife or mother or translated into domestic detail!❞

—*Betty Friedan,* The Feminine Mystique

Millions of women, Friedan charged, were frustrated with their roles in the 1950s.

The situation was not as simple as Friedan claimed, however. In fact, more women than ever before—many of them married with children—held paying jobs in the 1950s. Besides the satisfaction of earning their own money, women wanted to be able to buy the items that were part of the media image of "the good life"—automobiles, electric appliances, and so on. In 1950, 24 percent of all married American women had jobs; by 1960 the figure had risen to 31 percent. Married women with jobs had first begun to outnumber unmarried women with jobs near the end of World War II; in the postwar years, the gap grew even larger. The graph at left shows these trends.

Challenges to Conformity

Occasionally, challenges to 1950s' society erupted. Some young people rejected the values of their parents and felt misunderstood and alone. A few films, such as *Rebel Without a Cause,* released in 1955, captured these feelings of alienation. The movie's young star, James Dean, became a teen idol and a film legend.

Holden Caulfield, the main character in J. D. Salinger's 1951 novel *The Catcher in the Rye,* was troubled by the hypocrisy of the "phonies" he saw at boarding school and in the world around him. Throughout the book, Holden struggles to preserve his own integrity despite the fierce pressure to conform. Many readers could relate to this experience.

Young people sought a style they could call their own. In 1953, Alan Freed, a radio disc jockey in Cleveland, Ohio, began playing a new type of music that had grown out of the rhythm-and-blues tradition. He called this

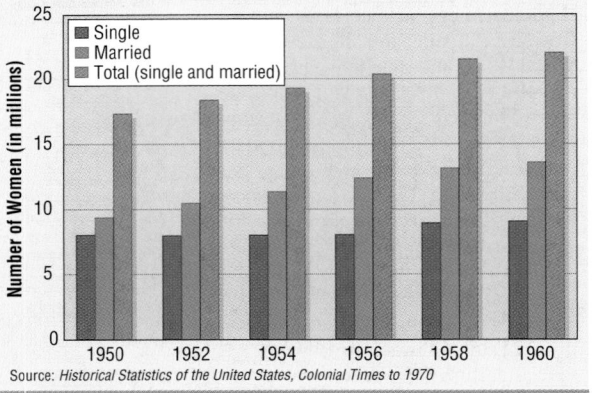

Female Labor Force, 1950–1960

(Bar graph)
- Single
- Married
- Total (single and married)

Y-axis: Number of Women (in millions), 0 to 25

X-axis: 1950, 1952, 1954, 1956, 1958, 1960

Source: *Historical Statistics of the United States, Colonial Times to 1970*

Interpreting Charts More and more women continued to join the labor force throughout the 1950s. *Culture According to the graph, what change was taking place in the female labor force?*

▶ ## RESOURCE OPTIONS

Media and Technology

RESOURCE ⊙ PRO

Critical Thinking Activity Determining Relevance: Wages, Hours, and Unions, found on Resource Pro, uses graphs of American work statistics between 1900 and 1960 to help students apply this skill.

Literature Activity Noncomformity in the 1950s, found on Resource Pro, features a passage from the novel *On the Road* by Jack Kerouac, the author whose work and life are often considered synonymous with the "Beat Generation."

new music **rock and roll.** Teenagers across the nation quickly became fans of the driving beat and simple melodies that characterized rock and roll. They rushed to buy records of their favorite performers, such as Chuck Berry, Bill Haley and the Comets, and Little Richard.

One of the most popular rock-and-roll singers was Elvis Presley. Presley's performances showcased his flamboyant style and good looks. He attracted hordes of screaming teenage girls everywhere he went. Presley released many records that became huge hits, including "Don't Be Cruel," "Hound Dog," and "Heartbreak Hotel." Many adults disliked the new music, fearing it would cause a rise in immorality. Despite some efforts to ban rock concerts and keep records out of stores, rock and roll's popularity soared.

Members of the "Beat Generation," called **beatniks,** launched a different kind of challenge. Beatniks, some of them writers, some artists, some simply participants in the movement, stressed spontaneity and spirituality instead of apathy and conformity. They challenged traditional patterns of respectability and shocked other Americans with their more open sexuality and their use of illegal drugs.

Author Jack Kerouac, the spiritual leader of the beatniks, gathered with others in coffee houses in San Francisco, California, to share ideas and experiences. The unconventional Kerouac typed his best-selling novel *On the Road*, published in 1957, on a 250-foot roll of paper. The novel's lack of standard punctuation and paragraph structure was meant to

reflect an open approach to life. One of Kerouac's friends, Allen Ginsberg, used the unstructured and chaotic style of the Beat Movement to write his powerful and moving poem "Howl."

COMPARING PRIMARY SOURCES

ROCK-AND-ROLL MUSIC

When the defiant beat of rock and roll burst onto the American scene in the mid-1950s, few people remained impartial about its sound or its impact.

Opposed to Rock and Roll	In Favor of Rock and Roll
"Rock 'n' roll . . . is sung, played and written for the most part by [mentally deficient] goons and by means of its almost imbecilic repetition and sly, lewd, in plain fact, dirty lyrics . . . it manages to be the [warlike] music of every sideburned delinquent on the face of the earth." —*Singer Frank Sinatra,* The New York Times, January 12, 1958	"If my kids are home at night listening to my radio program, and get interested enough to go out and buy records and have a collection to listen to and dance to, I think I'm fighting delinquency." —*Radio disc jockey* *Alan Freed,* The New York Times, January 12, 1958

ANALYZING VIEWPOINTS What does each viewpoint above say about the relationship between rock music and delinquency?

SECTION 2 REVIEW

Comprehension

1. *Key Terms* Define: (a) rock and roll; (b) beatnik.
2. *Summarizing the Main Idea* In what aspects of American life was conformity most visible during the period between 1945 and 1960?
3. *Organizing Information* Use information from the section to create a web diagram that shows ways in which Americans expressed the values of comfort and security.

Critical Thinking

4. *Analyzing Time Lines* Review the time line at the start of the section. Choose one event

that you think best illustrates the mood of the 1950s. Explain why you chose that entry.

5. *Identifying Central Issues* What social and economic roles were men and women expected to play in the 1950s?

Writing Activity

6. *Writing an Expository Essay* Research and write a brief essay on a person or group of people that challenged conformity in the 1950s. You might want to write on a rock-and-roll artist, a movie star, or a writer involved in the Beat Movement.

Answers to SECTION 2 REVIEW

1. (a) rock and roll, see p. 777; (b) beatnik, see p. 777.

2. Students may discuss the following: life in suburbs; dress; commitment to religion; children's stories that stressed conformity; men assuming roles in the public sphere while women played a supporting role.

3. Webs may contain the following: lived in homes in suburbia, joined organized religion, men and women assumed traditional roles.

4. Sample entry: 1946—Dr. Spock's book, because it encapsulated the traditional female role of the time and, according to feminist views, further subjugated women.

5. Men assumed the public sphere. They worked outside the home and brought in money to support the family. Women played a supporting role, working within the home, raising children and managing the family.

6. Essays will vary but should be supported with facts from the section.

Answer to . . .

Comparing Primary Sources Sinatra implies that only delinquent people are attracted to rock music. Freed argues that the music gives kids something wholesome to do and keeps them out of trouble.

SKILLS FOR LIFE

Historical Evidence

Evaluating Magazine Advertisements

Focus Evaluate for historical accuracy the view of American life presented in a magazine advertisement.

Instruct Explain that in 1957 Vance Packard published a bestseller about the advertising industry called *The Hidden Persuaders*. Packard outlined how advertisers "help" consumers make choices by investing their ads and packages with ideas and symbols. Packard quotes an advertising executive who says that women will pay ten times more for skin cream that promises to make them beautiful than they will pay for plain soap that promises only to make them clean.

Extend See the Skills for Life Activity in the Resource Options below.

Answers

1. (a) It advertises a sweepstakes and encourages readers to enter.
(b) Wheaties (or General Mills); breakfast cereal. (c) A power boat, a pool, a grill, a badminton set, a lawn-mower, and a bicycle. (d) Families.

2. (a) Using the products shown, being outside and active, and being together as a family. (b) Suburban life; people living in cities would not need such products.

3. (a) Material wealth and happiness seem to go hand in hand. (b) No.
(c) Most students will probably say that this ad reinforces what they have already learned about the shift to the suburbs and consumerism in the 1950s.

TEST FOR SUCCESS

The "good life" as promoted by the ad includes owning many consumer goods, living in the suburbs, and being part of a traditional family.

Evaluating Magazine Advertisements

Magazine advertisements can be a rich and colorful source of evidence about the past. Because popular weekly or monthly magazines are aimed at a broad audience, advertisements frequently reflect a society's prevailing attitudes and values. Remember, though, that every ad also reflects the purpose of the company whose products are being advertised—namely, to sell its products. Therefore, an ad may present a slanted or false view of the desirable American life, designed to make consumers want to buy certain products.

Use the following steps to evaluate the advertisement at right, which appeared in the *Saturday Evening Post* in April 1958.

1. Identify the nature of the advertisement. Carefully review the entire advertisement, then answer the following questions. (a) What is the point of this advertisement? What does it encourage readers to do? (b) What company created this ad? What product does the company make? (c) What other products are shown in the ad? (d) Who do you think is the intended audience for the advertisement?

2. Study the advertisement to evaluate the underlying messages it contains. Look closely at the image in the ad. (a) What things seem to make the people shown in the advertisement happy? (b) Does this ad suggest a preference for suburban life or city life? Explain why you think so.

3. Study the advertisement to learn more about the historical period. Use the information in the ad to help you answer the following questions. (a) Based on what you see in this ad, how closely linked were happiness and material wealth in the minds of many Americans in the 1950s? (b) Would everyone in the 1950s have been able to afford to buy the items shown in the ad? (c) Are your conclusions consistent with what you already know about the United States in the 1950s? Explain.

TEST FOR SUCCESS

What does this ad suggest is the "good life" toward which Americans should strive?

RESOURCE OPTIONS

Teaching Resources

Skills for Life Activity Units 7–8 folder, p. 94, encourages students to apply this skill in a modern setting, using a magazine ad for the sporting goods retailer L. L. Bean.

1946 The government eases economic controls and prices soar	1947 Congress passes Taft-Hartley Act	1948 Truman wins upset victory in presidential election	1952 Republicans capture the White House and both houses of Congress	1958 Congress passes National Defense Education Act

1946   1952   1958

3 Domestic Politics and Policy

SECTION PREVIEW

Objectives

1 Describe Truman's domestic policies as outlined in his Fair Deal.
2 Describe how Truman won the election of 1948.
3 Explain the highlights of Dwight Eisenhower's Republican presidency.
4 *Key Terms* Define: Taft-Hartley Act; modern republicanism; National Defense Education Act.

Main Idea

Presidents Harry S. Truman and Dwight D. Eisenhower used two very different styles of leadership to meet the challenges they faced during the postwar period.

Reading Strategy

Problem Solving Evaluate how Presidents Truman and Eisenhower handled domestic affairs. As you read, note positive and negative points about the administration of each President. Then write a brief analysis of each President and use them to give each a grade.

The 1950s were a conservative time politically as well as culturally. Most Americans pressured the government to help maintain the nation's newly won prosperity. Democrat Harry S. Truman first struggled with the problems of reconversion to a peacetime economy, then fought for a reform program blocked repeatedly by Congress. Republican Dwight D. Eisenhower took a more low-key approach to the presidency. His genial, reassuring manner made him one of the most popular Presidents in the years following World War II.

Truman's Domestic Policies

Harry Truman wanted to follow in Franklin Roosevelt's footsteps, but he often appeared ill-prepared for the presidency. He seemed to have a scattershot approach to governing, offering a new batch of proposals in every speech. People wondered where his focus lay.

Moving to a Peacetime Economy Truman's first priority was reconversion—the social and economic transition from wartime to peace-

time. Soldiers wanted to return home, and politicians were flooded with messages that warned, "No boats, no votes." Truman responded quickly and got most soldiers home by 1946.

Lifting the economic controls that had kept wartime inflation in check proved a more difficult challenge. Most Americans had done without consumer goods during World War II. Now they wanted those goods, and they wanted them right away. The government eased the controls in July 1946, and prices soared almost 25 percent. One political cartoonist quipped that prices had gone "Over the moon!" Since wages failed to keep up with prices, many people still could not enjoy the fruits of their years of sacrifice.

In some ways, the economic issues facing the United States at the end of World War II

This sign, which sat on Truman's desk, expressed both his responsibility and authority.

Truman on TV On October 5, 1947, Harry S. Truman became the first President to address the nation on television from the White House. The subject of his speech was the need for Americans to conserve food in order to feed Europe. Truman declined the opportunity to hog the cameras. Instead he appeared as the last of five speakers, coming on after rousing talks from the Secretaries of Agriculture, State, and Commerce and the Chairman of the Citizens Food Committee. With only a few hundred thousand television sets in the entire country, the vast majority of Americans listened to the program on radio. In 1951, Truman made another accommodation to technology that would have far-reaching results. He let reporters use recording machines to tape his remarks at press conferences, not for broadcast, but so they could check their notes. In 1955, his successor, Dwight D. Eisenhower, allowed his conferences to be filmed for broadcast, with the understanding that his press secretary could edit them first. From there it was only a short step to live broadcasts, sound bites, one-liners, and all the fulsome vapidity that characterizes American politics in the information age.
Source: Frederic D. Schwarz, "The Time Machine," *American Heritage* magazine, October 1997.

Main Idea
CONNECTIONS

Why did Truman oppose labor's demand for higher wages?

were similar to those at the end of World War I. Workers demanded wage increases that they had forgone for the sake of the war effort. In 1946, 4.6 million workers went on strike, more than ever before in the United States. Strikes hit the automobile, steel, electrical, coal, and railroad industries and affected nearly everyone in the country.

Though Truman agreed that workers deserved high wages, he thought that their demands were inflationary. He feared that such increases would push the prices of goods still higher. In his view, workers failed to understand that big wage increases might destroy the health of the economy.

In the spring of 1946, a railroad strike caused a big disruption in the economy. In response, Truman asked Congress for the power to draft the striking workers into the army. He would then be able to order them as soldiers to stay on the job. Truman's request was soundly rejected by the Senate.

Truman's White House took other steps against labor as well. When John L. Lewis and his United Mine Workers defied a court order against a strike, the Truman administration asked a judge to serve Lewis with a contempt of court citation. The court fined Lewis $10,000 and his union $3.5 million.

Congress went even further than Truman. In 1947 it passed the **Taft-Hartley Act.** This act allowed the President to declare an 80-day cooling-off period when strikes hit industries that affected the national interest. During this period, strikers had to return to work while the government conducted a study of the situation. Reflecting the widespread anti-Communist feelings gripping the United States at the time, the measure also required union officials to sign non-Communist oaths. Furious union leaders complained bitterly about the measure, and Truman vetoed it. Congress, however, passed the act over Truman's veto.

Truman's Fair Deal Truman had supported Roosevelt's New Deal, and now, playing on the well-known name, he devised a program he called the Fair Deal. The Fair Deal extended the New Deal's goals.

Truman agreed with FDR that government needed to play an active role in securing economic justice for all American citizens. As the war ended, he introduced a 21-point program that included legislation designed to promote full employment, a higher minimum wage, greater unemployment compensation for workers without jobs, housing assistance, and a variety of other items. Over the next ten weeks, Truman added more proposals to the Fair Deal. By early 1946 he had asked for a national health insurance program and legislation to control atomic energy.

Truman ran into tremendous political opposition in Congress. A coalition of conservative Democrats and Republicans opposed him at every turn. They rejected the majority of the Fair Deal initiatives, passing only the Employment Act of 1946. In this act they created a Council of Economic Advisers to advise the President.

As the 1946 midterm elections approached, Truman seemed little more than another bungling bureaucrat. Some people commented, "You just sort of forget about Harry until he makes another mistake." Others adapted a well-known saying: "To err is Truman." Truman's support in one poll dropped from 87 percent just after he assumed the presidency to 32 percent in November 1946. The results of the 1946 elections reflected many people's feelings that

Harry S. Truman became the first President ever to campaign in Harlem, the heart of New York City's African American population. *Government How did Truman's support of civil rights cause a split in the Democratic party?*

▶ RESOURCE OPTIONS

Media and Technology

(RESOURCE○**PRO**)

Visual Learning Activity Auto Strike, 1950, found on Resource Pro, illustrates the continuing rift between workers and management in a photograph of United Auto Workers members preparing for a strike.

Answer to . . .

Main Idea Connections He thought higher wages would ultimately hurt the economy.
Viewing History Segregationist southern Democrats formed a separate party, the States' Rights party.

Truman was not an effective leader. Republicans won majorities of both houses of Congress.

The 80th Congress battered the President for the next two years. Under the leadership of the conservative Republican senator Robert A. Taft of Ohio, commonly known as "Mr. Republican," the Republican party did whatever it could to reduce the size and the power of the federal government, to decrease taxes, and to block Truman's liberal goals.

The Election of 1948

Truman decided to seek another term as President in 1948. He had no reason to expect victory, however, because even in his own party, his support was disintegrating. The southern wing of the Democratic party, protesting a moderate civil rights plank in the party platform, split off from the main party. These segregationists formed the States' Rights, or Dixiecrat, party and nominated Governor J. Strom Thurmond of South Carolina for President.

Meanwhile, the liberal wing of the Democratic party deserted Truman to follow Henry Wallace, who headed the Progressive party ticket. Wallace had been Franklin Roosevelt's second Vice President, and many Democrats believed that he was the right person to carry out the measures begun by Roosevelt. Most recently Wallace had served as Truman's Secretary of Commerce. Wallace had resigned, however, because he did not support Truman's cold war policies.

Running against Republican Thomas E. Dewey, governor of New York, Truman crisscrossed the country by train. He campaigned not so much against Dewey as against the Republican Congress, which the President repeatedly mocked as the "do-nothing" 80th Congress. Truman's campaign style was electrifying. In off-the-cuff speeches, he challenged all Americans: "If you send another Republican Congress to Washington, you're a bigger bunch of suckers than I think you are." "Give 'em hell, Harry," the people yelled as Truman got going. And he did.

Among other things, Truman vehemently attacked Congress's farm policy. In the past, a federal price-support program permitted farmers to borrow money to store surplus crops until someone bought the produce. Recently, however, Congress had failed to provide additional storage bins, just as a good harvest loomed on the horizon. Truman told the farmers:

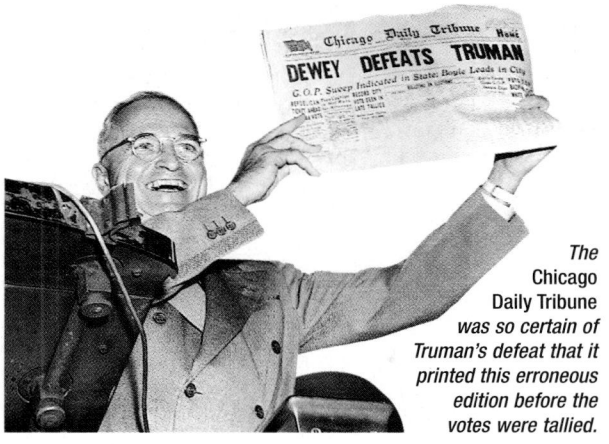

The Chicago Daily Tribune was so certain of Truman's defeat that it printed this erroneous edition before the votes were tallied.

AMERICAN VOICES "The Republican Congress has already stuck a pitchfork in the farmers' backs. . . . When you have to sell your grain below the support price because you have no place to store it, you can thank this same Republican Congress."

—*Harry Truman*

On election day, although virtually all experts and polls picked Dewey to win, Truman scored an astounding upset. With this victory, he stepped out of FDR's shadow to claim the presidency in his own right.

Truman looked forward to a chance to push further for his legislative goals. Over the next four years, however, the Fair Deal scored only occasional successes. Instances of corruption among federal officials further hurt Truman's image.

After at first toying with the idea, Truman decided not to run for reelection in 1952. Instead, the Democrats chose Adlai Stevenson, governor of Illinois, as their presidential candidate.

Dwight Eisenhower and the Republican Approach

Running against Stevenson for the Republicans was Dwight Eisenhower, former commander-in-chief of the Allied forces, president of Columbia University, and head of NATO. As a public figure, Eisenhower's approach to politics differed from that of Harry Truman. Whereas Truman was a scrappy fighter, Ike—as the people affectionately called Eisenhower—had always been a talented diplomat. During World

ACTIVITY
STUDENT PORTFOLIO

You may wish to have students add the following to their portfolios. To assess student work, refer to the generic rubrics in the Program Overview in the Teaching Resources.

Intelligent and witty, Adlai M. Stevenson, governor of Illinois from 1949 to 1953, ran for President against Eisenhower in 1952 and 1956. Ask students to research Stevenson's life and career, focusing on his bids to occupy the Oval Office, and to write and perform a monologue to convey the information.

▶ RESOURCE OPTIONS

Media and Technology

RESOURCE PRO

Primary Source Activity Harry Truman: Off the Record, found on Resource Pro, uses excerpts from the private papers of the former President to provide students with an additional perspective on the issues of that era.

 AmericanHeritage® CD-ROM

Presidents Harry S. Truman

Graphing the Main Idea

To make sure students understand the main idea of this section, you may wish to use the double web graphic organizer below.

Tell students that a double web compares information about two main ideas, topics, groups, or individuals. Ask students to use it to compare and contrast the leadership styles and domestic policies of Presidents Truman and Eisenhower.

Teaching Tip A template for this graphic organizer can be found in the Color Transparencies, G-2.

Answer to . . .

Viewing History A wholesome image of the politician as a trustworthy family man.

Richard Nixon thanked the voters who had shown their support after his "Checkers" speech with this postcard. *Culture What image of Nixon does this photograph promote?*

The "I Like Ike" message was seen everywhere in 1952, even on cosmetics containers.

War II, Eisenhower forged agreements among Allied military commanders. His easy-going charm gave Americans a sense of security.

By 1952 Americans across the land chanted, "I Like Ike." The Republicans devised a "K_1C_2" formula for victory, which focused on three problems: Korea, communism, and corruption. Eisenhower promised to end the Korean War, and the Republican party guaranteed a tough approach to the Communist challenge. Eisenhower's vice-presidential running mate, Californian Richard M. Nixon, hammered on the topic of corruption in government.

The Checkers Speech In spite of his overwhelming popularity, Eisenhower's candidacy hit a snag in September 1952. Newspapers accused Richard Nixon of having a special fund, set up by rich Republican supporters. "Secret Nixon Fund!" and "Secret Rich Man's Trust Fund Keeps Nixon in Style Beyond His Salary," screamed typical headlines. In fact, Nixon had done nothing wrong, but the accusation that he had received illegal gifts from political friends was hard to shake.

Soon, cries arose for Eisenhower to dump Nixon from the ticket. Eisenhower decided to allow Nixon to save himself, if he could. On September 23, Nixon went on television to explain the situation in his own words. He emotionally denied wrongful use of campaign funds. Nixon also gave a detailed account of his personal finances. In response to the charge that he was living above his means, he described his wife, Pat, as wearing a "good old Republican cloth coat."

The emotional climax of the speech came when Nixon admitted that he had, in fact, received one gift from a political supporter:

AMERICAN VOICES "It was a little cocker spaniel dog. . . . Black and white spotted. And our little girl—Tricia, the 6-year-old—named it Checkers. And you know the kids love that dog and I just want to say this right now, that regardless of what they say about it, we're going to keep it."

—*Richard Nixon*

At the end of his speech, Nixon requested that the American people contact the Eisenhower campaign to register their opinions as to whether or not he should stay on the Republican ticket. People from all across the nation called, wired, and wrote to Eisenhower, demanding that Nixon continue as his running mate. Nixon had turned a political disaster into a public relations bonanza.

Support for Eisenhower continued to grow through the fall. Democratic candidate Adlai Stevenson never had a chance. Ike got 55 percent of the popular vote and swept into office with a Republican Congress as well.

Eisenhower as President Ike's natural inclination was to work behind the scenes. One writer has described his style as the "hidden hand." "I am not one of those desk-pounding types that likes to stick out his jaw and look like he is bossing the show," Eisenhower said. Critics misinterpreted his apparent lack of leadership, joking about an Eisenhower doll—you wound it up and it did nothing. Eisenhower defended his approach, declaring:

TEST PREPARATION

Have students read the quotation by Richard Nixon on this page and then answer the question below.

From the passage, you can infer that—

A Nixon feels guilty about accepting the gift.

B Nixon secretly blames his daughter for making him take the gift.

C Nixon knows that his emotional story will win public approval.

D Nixon doesn't understand why anyone would get angry over him accepting a dog as a pet for his children.

"Now, look, I happen to know a little about leadership. I've had to work with a lot of nations, for that matter, at odds with each other. And I tell you this: you do not lead by hitting people over the head. . . . I'll tell you what leadership is. It's persuasion—and conciliation—and education—and patience. It's long, slow tough work. That's the only kind of leadership I know or believe in—or will practice."

—*Dwight Eisenhower*

The American people approved of Ike's style. In 1956, Eisenhower once again faced Stevenson and easily won reelection. This time he gathered an even greater margin of victory, with almost 58 percent of the vote. The Democrats, however, retained control of Congress in the 1956 election.

Modern Republicanism In domestic matters, Eisenhower was determined to slow the growth of the federal government. He also wanted to limit the President's power and increase the authority of Congress and the courts. Eisenhower was not, however, interested in completely reversing the New Deal.

Ike's priorities included cutting spending, reducing taxes, and balancing the budget. He called this approach to government "dynamic conservatism" or **modern republicanism.** He intended to be "conservative when it comes to money, liberal when it comes to human beings."

In the tradition of past Republican Presidents such as Coolidge and Hoover, Eisenhower favored big business. His Cabinet was composed mostly of successful businessmen, plus one union leader. Critics charged that the Cabinet consisted of "eight millionaires and a plumber." For Secretary of Defense he chose Charles E. Wilson, former president of General Motors, who claimed that "what was good for our country was good for General Motors, and vice versa."

Modern republicanism sought to encourage and support corporate America. It transferred control of about $40 billion worth of offshore oil lands from the federal government to the states so that the states could lease oil rights to corporations. The administration worked to end government competition with big business.

Ike's attempt to balance the budget backfired. His cuts in government spending caused the economy to slump. When that happened, tax revenues dropped, and the deficit grew larger instead of smaller. Economic growth, which

Notable PRESIDENTS

Dwight Eisenhower

1953–1961

"I am no politician as you well know."
—Eisenhower as he prepared to assume the presidency.

Born in Texas in 1890, Dwight Eisenhower grew up in Abilene, Kansas. After high school he attended the U. S. Military Academy at West Point and began a long and distinguished military career. That career peaked during World War II when Eisenhower, as supreme commander of the Allied Expeditionary Force, oversaw the D-Day landings in France and the final defeat of Germany. After the war Eisenhower served as Army Chief of Staff, president of Columbia University, and then head of NATO, the North Atlantic Treaty Organization.

Though "Ike" had no formal political experience, both major parties courted him as a presidential candidate because of his enormous wartime prestige. In 1952 he ran as a Republican and won a landslide victory in the general election. His wide grin, folksy manner, and proven leadership abilities gained him support around the country.

Eisenhower helped bring peace by negotiating a truce in 1953 that ended the fighting in Korea. He was a strong defender of American interests abroad, yet he also feared that high military spending would harm the economy. Thus Eisenhower endorsed a military strategy of relying on nuclear weapons, rather than more costly conventional armies, in conflicts around the world.

At home, Eisenhower generally favored restraint in government actions and spending. He did, however, strongly support the Interstate Highway Act of 1956, which created a nationwide network of roads. Also, in 1957 Eisenhower sent federal troops to enforce school desegregation in Little Rock, Arkansas.

Eisenhower's critics sometimes complained about his low-key approach to the presidency and blamed him for lacking strong leadership. Yet he provided the nation with stability and reassurance during a dangerous period of the cold war.

Connecting to Today

How might experience as a military leader help a President? Can you think of any ways in which such experience might not be helpful? Explain.

About the Presidents

Dwight David Eisenhower (1953–1961) often spoke out against the idea of a welfare state—one that gives handouts to those in need. Nevertheless, New Deal policies were continued during his administration. The National Defense Education Act of 1958 made student loans available. The Department of Health, Education, and Welfare was created. Ten million more people joined the Social Security rolls while Eisenhower was President. Source: Charles L. Mee, Jr., "Dwight David Eisenhower," *The American Heritage® Pictorial History of the Presidents of the United States,* vol. 2, 1968.

BACKGROUND

Recent Scholarship

The decade of the 1950s was peaceful and prosperous on the surface. Most Americans seemed comfortable with the conservative patterns of their lives. Beneath this calm exterior, however, lay the seeds of the turbulence that unfolded in the 1960s. In *The Fifties,* David Halberstam describes the cold war anti-Communist fervor that culminated in the war in Vietnam, assesses the growing impact of television on American life, and highlights the social and sexual tensions festering beneath the surface that helped create the lively and colorful counterculture of the 1960s.

RESOURCE OPTIONS

Media and Technology

 AmericanHeritage® CD-ROM

Presidents Dwight D. Eisenhower

1954, from 1957 to 1958, and again from 1960 to 1961.

Despite occasional economic troubles, Eisenhower helped maintain a mood of stability in America. He also underscored the basic commitment the government had made during the New Deal to ensure the economic security of all Americans. For example, in 1954 and 1956 Social Security was extended to make eligible 10 million additional workers. In 1955 the minimum wage was raised from 75 cents to one dollar an hour.

Meeting the Technology Challenge When the Soviet Union launched *Sputnik* in 1957, as described in the previous chapter, many Americans feared a nuclear attack would soon follow. Others grew concerned that the United States was losing its competitive edge. In response, less than a year later Congress passed and President Eisenhower signed into law the **National Defense Education Act** of 1958. The measure was designed to improve science and mathematics instruction in the schools so that the United States could meet the scientific and technical challenge from the Soviet Union. The act provided millions of dollars in low-cost loans to college students and significant reductions in repayments if they ultimately became teachers. The federal government also granted millions to state schools for building science and foreign language facilities.

BACKGROUND

Global Connections

After World War II, as demands for independence increased, European countries gradually began to quit colonial possessions in Asia and Africa. In 1947, the former British colony of India was partitioned into two independent countries, India and Pakistan, signaling the dissolution of the British Empire, the largest in history. As two centuries of British world dominance ended, the United States rose to superpower status in the West.

"Wonder Why We're not Keeping Pace?"

The author of this cartoon blamed U.S. government and education for the nation's failure to keep pace with Soviet technology. *Government What steps did the government take to improve American education?*

had averaged 4.3 percent between 1947 and 1952, fell to 2.5 percent between 1953 and 1960. The country suffered three economic recessions during Eisenhower's presidency, from 1953 to

---

SECTION 3 REVIEW

Comprehension

1. **Key Terms** Define: (a) Taft-Hartley Act; (b) modern republicanism; (c) National Defense Education Act.

2. **Summarizing the Main Idea** How did Truman's and Eisenhower's approaches to the role of the federal government in solving domestic problems differ?

3. **Organizing Information** Create a web diagram that organizes information about Eisenhower's policies known as modern republicanism. In the center circle write *Eisenhower's Modern Republicanism.* Include details from the section for at least five surrounding circles.

Critical Thinking

4. **Analyzing Time Lines** Review the time line at the start of the section. Choose one event that relates to domestic policies or politics in the postwar years and write a paragraph explaining why you think that event was important to the nation.

5. **Expressing Problems Clearly** What was the main problem that President Truman faced in the election of 1948?

Writing Activity

6. **Writing a Persuasive Essay** Reread the section on the Checkers speech. Then write a letter to President Eisenhower either in support of or opposition to keeping Richard Nixon on the Republican ticket. Include specific examples to support your opinion.

RESOURCE OPTIONS

Teaching Resources

 Quiz Units 7–8 folder, p. 86

Student Performance Pack

 Guide to the Essentials Chapter 27, Section 3 (English and Spanish)

1946	1947	1948	1954	1955	1956
Truman appoints Committee on Civil Rights	Jackie Robinson is first African American to play major league baseball	Truman orders desegregation of armed forces	Brown v. Board of Education of Topeka, Kansas	Bus boycott begins in Montgomery, Alabama	Supreme Court declares segregation on buses illegal

1946   **1951**   **1956**

4 Demands for Civil Rights

SECTION PREVIEW

Objectives

1 Describe the progress made in the struggle for equality during the Truman years.
2 Understand such highlights of the 1950s as the *Brown* decision, the Montgomery bus boycott, and the confrontation in Little Rock.
3 Describe how other minorities began to follow the example set by the African American movement.
4 *Key Terms* Define: *Brown* v. *Board of Education of Topeka, Kansas;* Montgomery bus boycott; integration.

Main Idea

Following World War II, African Americans began to push harder in the civil rights movement and brought about significant results.

Reading Strategy

Formulating Questions Reread the main idea above. Then rewrite it as a question. As you read the section, write down possible answers to your question.

Before and during World War II, African Americans were not treated as equals by a large portion of American society. After the war, however, the campaign for civil rights began to accelerate. Millions of people believed that the time had come to demand that the nation live up to its creed that all are equal before the law.

The Struggle for Equality

The story of the postwar struggle for racial equality begins with President Truman. While holding in private many of the racial prejudices he had learned growing up in the South, Truman recognized that as President he had to take action. In a letter to a friend, he wrote, "I am not asking for social equality, because no such things exist, but I am asking for equality of opportunity for all human beings."

Truman's Actions Truman had publicly supported civil rights for many years. In September 1946 he met with a group of African American leaders to discuss the steps that needed to be taken to achieve their goals. They asked Truman to support a federal anti-lynching law, abolish the poll tax as a voting requirement, and establish a permanent board to prevent discriminatory practices in hiring. Congress refused to address any of these concerns, so in December 1946, Truman appointed a biracial Committee on Civil Rights to look into race relations. This group produced a report demanding action on the concerns listed above. In addition they also recommended that a permanent civil rights commission be established.

Once more Congress failed to act. In July 1948 Truman took action and banned discrimination in the hiring of federal employees. He also ordered an end to segregation and discrimination in the armed forces. Real change came slowly, however. Only with the onset of the Korean War in 1950 did the armed forces make significant progress in ending segregation.

This 1948 campaign button proclaimed Truman's commitment to civil rights.

Objectives

You may wish to call students' attention to the objectives in the Section Preview. The objectives are reflected in the main headings of the section.

Bellringer

Ask students to consider the role of sports in American life. Ask if sports stars should be considered heroes. What qualities does a "hero" possess? Ask students who their heroes are. Why?

Reading Strategy

Formulating Questions Refer students to the Reading Strategy in the Section Preview. You may wish to write students' questions on the chalkboard and have volunteers answer them.

LESSON PLAN

Connecting to the Main Idea

1. Focus The civil rights movement took on a new momentum in the years following World War II. Ask what methods Americans used in the struggle to attain racial justice.

2. Instruct Discuss why African Americans began to step up their demand for equality after World War II. Have students compare the Supreme Court's rulings in the 1896 *Plessy* v. *Ferguson* and the 1954 *Brown* v. *Board of Education* decisions. How do social factors affect the Court's decisions?

Discuss the factors that might have motivated other groups to follow the lead of African Americans in the 1950s.

3. Close The civil rights movement accelerated quickly following World War II. African Americans worked for their rights through the courts and on the streets in nonviolent protests, and other minority groups began to demand equal rights.

Racism on the Gridiron On November 5, 1946, Penn State and the University of Miami canceled a football game scheduled for the end of the month over the presence of two black players on the Penn State team. The president of Miami had banned the pair on grounds of good fellowship, saying that he hoped to avoid "unfortunate incidents" and "not catapult very important, not-well-understood inter-racial problems into a football game." The dean of athletics at Penn State insisted that the boys were regular members of the Penn State team and declined to place any conditions on their participation. Similar disagreements were cropping up elsewhere. Earlier in the season a pair of smaller colleges had worked out a solution to the American dilemma: Fresno State's black players sat out a game at Oklahoma City but would be allowed to play in a return match at Fresno.

Source: Frederic D. Schwarz, "The Time Machine," *American Heritage* magazine, November 1996.

After his brilliant first season with the Brooklyn Dodgers, Jackie Robinson was featured on baseball cards such as the one above, issued in 1951.
Diversity How did Robinson's career serve the cause of civil rights?

Jackie Robinson The battle against racial segregation was taken up not only in the military but on the professional baseball diamond as well. For years, major league baseball had refused to allow African Americans to participate, forcing them to play in the separate Negro Leagues. In the mid-1940s, Branch Rickey, the general manager of the Brooklyn Dodgers, decided to challenge the ban.

Rickey selected an athlete named Jackie Robinson to be the first African American to break the color line. Robinson had grown up in Pasadena, California, and attended the University of California in Los Angeles. In college Robinson earned letters in football, basketball, baseball, and track.

Robinson had a record of standing up against racial injustice. While he was in the army during World War II, a bus driver had snarled at him, "Get in the back where you belong or there'll be trouble." Robinson knew that buses on the army post were not segregated, so he stood his ground. Although he had not broken any rules, Robinson had to undergo a court-martial before clearing his name.

The mental toughness that Robinson acquired from such experiences and his ability to rise above the injustices he encountered served him well during his baseball career. In August 1945, Branch Rickey called Robinson into his office and told the ballplayer of his plan to integrate baseball. Then, in a calculated move to test how Robinson would respond to the pressure he was likely to face, Rickey acted the part of those who might try to discourage him. He roared insults at Robinson and threatened him with violence. "Mr. Rickey," Robinson finally said, "do you want a ballplayer who's afraid to fight back?" Rickey answered, "I want a player with guts enough not to fight back."

Robinson played first for the Montreal Royals, a minor league team, during the 1946 season. Then in 1947 he joined the Brooklyn Dodgers, becoming the first African American to play in the major leagues. Despite many instances of prejudice, Robinson behaved with dignity and had a sparkling first season. He was named Rookie of the Year in 1947. In 1949 he was voted the league's most valuable player. Just as important, Robinson fostered pride in African Americans around the country and opened the way for other African Americans to follow him into professional sports.

Brown v. Board of Education

Perhaps the greatest civil rights victory in the early postwar period took place in the courts. For years the NAACP had tried to get the 1896 *Plessy* v. *Ferguson* decision overturned. That decision held that segregation of the races in public institutions and accommodations was constitutional as long as facilities were "separate but equal." In practice, that was rarely—if ever—the case.

In 1951 Oliver Brown sued the Topeka, Kansas, Board of Education to allow his 8-year-old daughter Linda to attend a school that only white children were allowed to attend. She passed the school on her way to the bus that took her to a distant school for African Americans. After appeals, the case reached the Supreme Court. There a lawyer named Thurgood Marshall argued on behalf of Brown and against segregation in America's schools.

On May 17, 1954, in **Brown v. Board of Education of Topeka, Kansas,** the Supreme Court issued its historic ruling. It declared unanimously that "separate facilities are inherently unequal." The "separate but equal" doctrine was no longer permissible in public education.[†] President Eisenhower, who privately disagreed with the *Brown* ruling, said only that "the Supreme Court has spoken and I am sworn to uphold the constitutional processes in this country; I will obey." A year later, the Court ruled that local school boards should move to desegregate "with all deliberate speed."

[†] The Supreme Court's decision struck down laws in Kansas, Delaware, South Carolina, and Virginia that required or allowed separate schools for blacks and whites.

Main Idea
CONNECTIONS

What was the principle behind the Supreme Court's ruling in Brown v. Board of Education?

Answer to . . .

Viewing History He publicly broke a professional race barrier and was an inspirational role model.

Main Idea Connections That separate facilities are inherently unequal.

RESOURCE OPTIONS

Teaching Resources

American History Block Scheduling Support Martin Luther King, Jr.'s Nonviolent Way to Civil Rights, found in the Nation After World War II folder, includes interdisciplinary lesson suggestions and activities for Geography and History, Primary Sources, Biography, and Literature.

Primary Source Activity Enforcing *Brown* v. *Board of Education,* Learning with Documents folder, p. 33

Media and Technology

 AmericanHeritage® CD-ROM

History Makers Thurgood Marshall

The Montgomery Bus Boycott

In 1955 the nation's attention shifted from the courts to the streets of Montgomery, Alabama. In December Rosa Parks, a seamstress who had been secretary of the Montgomery NAACP for 12 years, took a seat in the middle section of a bus, where both African Americans and whites usually were allowed to sit. When a white man got on at the next stop and had no seat, however, the bus driver ordered Parks to give up hers. She refused. Even when threatened with arrest, she held her ground. At the next stop, police seized her and ordered her to stand trial for violating the segregation laws.

Civil rights leaders in Montgomery quickly met and, after Jo Ann Robinson of the Women's Political Council (WPC) suggested the idea, decided to organize the **Montgomery bus boycott.** The plan called for African Americans to refuse to use the entire bus system until the bus company agreed to change its segregation policy. Robinson and other members of the WPC wrote and distributed leaflets announcing the boycott. Martin Luther King, Jr., the 26-year-old minister of the Baptist church where the original boycott meeting took place, eventually became the spokesperson for the protest movement. He proclaimed:

 AMERICAN VOICES ❝There comes a time when people get tired . . . tired of being segregated and humiliated, tired of being kicked about by the brutal feet of oppression. We have no alternative but to protest.❞

—*Martin Luther King, Jr.*

The morning of the first day of the boycott, King walked the streets of Montgomery. He was anxious to see how many African Americans would participate. Here are excerpts from his account of that morning:

AMERICAN VOICES ❝During the rush hours the sidewalks were crowded with laborers and domestic workers, many of them well past middle age, trudging patiently to their jobs and home again, sometimes as much as twelve miles. They knew why they walked, and the knowledge was evident in the way they carried themselves. And as I watched them I knew that there is nothing more majestic than the determined courage of individuals willing to suffer and sacrifice for their freedom and dignity.❞

—*Martin Luther King, Jr.*

 These participants in the Montgomery bus boycott seemed not to mind getting a little wet as they walked to work. *Culture How did the boycott demonstrate the effectiveness of applying economic pressure to promote social change?*

Over the next year, 50,000 African Americans in Montgomery walked, rode bicycles, or joined car pools to avoid the city buses. Despite losing money, the bus company refused to change its policies. Finally, the Supreme Court ruled that bus segregation, like school segregation, was unconstitutional.

The Montgomery bus boycott produced a new generation of leaders in the African American community, particularly Martin Luther King, Jr. In addition, it introduced nonviolent protest as a means of achieving equality for minority groups in the United States.

Resistance in Little Rock

The protests in Montgomery, as well as the ruling in *Brown* v. *Board of Education,* caused many southern whites to react with fear and angry resistance. The worst confrontation came at Central High School in Little Rock, Arkansas. Just before the start of the 1957 school year, Governor Orval Faubus declared that he could not keep order if he had to enforce **integration,** or the bringing together of different races. He posted Arkansas National Guard troops at the school who turned away nine African American students.

Eisenhower could no longer avoid the issue of segregation. Faubus's actions were a direct

Graphing the Main Idea

To make sure students understand the main idea of this section, you may wish to use the multiflow map graphic organizer below.

Tell students that a multiflow map shows causes and effects. Ask students to use it to show the causes and effects of African Americans' push for civil rights after World War II.

Teaching Tip A template for this graphic organizer can be found in the Color Transparencies, G-5.

Answers to
SECTION 4 REVIEW

1. (a) *Brown* v. *Board of Education,* see p. 786; (b) Montgomery bus boycott, see p. 787; (c) integration, see p. 787.

2. Marches and boycotts.

3. Charts may include: the governor declared he could not keep order if he had to enforce integration; he posted the National Guard; Eisenhower placed the National Guard under federal command.

4. Sample entry: 1946—Truman appoints Committee on Civil Rights, which resulted from Truman's meeting with African American leaders.

5. Mexican Americans used peaceful protest to demand equal rights. Native Americans petitioned the federal government's termination policy. Eventually the policy was abandoned.

6. Posters will vary but content should reflect issues discussed in the section.

African American students like Elizabeth Ekford of Little Rock, Arkansas, had to endure the insults of white students who disagreed with the Court's *Brown* v. *Board* decision. *Government* What finally forced Eisenhower to support desegregation?

Arkansas to protect the nine students, the long, slow process of school integration began.

Other Voices of Protest

African Americans were not the only group to demand equal rights after World War II. Mexican Americans, for instance, also worked for their rights. In one case a funeral home in Texas refused to bury Felix Longoria, a Mexican American war hero. Protests in the Mexican American community over the refusal led to the soldier's burial in Arlington National Cemetery in Washington, D.C. Groups like the Community Service Organization and the Asociación Nacional México-Americana found that peaceful protest could slowly bring about some of the results Mexican Americans desired.

Native Americans faced a unique situation. The federal government managed the reservations where most Native Americans lived in terrible poverty. In 1953, however, the government adopted a new approach, known as "termination," which sought to eliminate reservations altogether. The goal of the policy was to assimilate Native Americans into the mainstream of American life.

Termination met with resistance. In time the federal government discarded the termination policy. Yet the problems of the Native Americans remained: poverty, discrimination, and little real political representation. For Native Americans, the civil rights advances of the 1950s were mere tokens of the real gains that were needed.

challenge to the Constitution and to his own authority as President. Eisenhower acted by placing the National Guard under federal command. With paratroopers and other soldiers on guard in

SECTION 4 REVIEW

Comprehension

1. *Key Terms* Define: (a) *Brown* v. *Board of Education of Topeka, Kansas;* (b) Montgomery bus boycott; (c) integration.

2. *Summarizing the Main Idea* What avenues of protest did civil rights activists use in their struggle?

3. *Organizing Information* Create a flowchart that organizes information about the events that took place in Little Rock, Arkansas.

Critical Thinking

4. *Analyzing Time Lines* Review the time line at the start of the section. Chose one entry and explain how it was a result of increased demands for equality from African Americans following World War II.

5. *Identifying Central Issues* How did Mexican Americans and Native Americans assert their rights in the 1950s?

Writing Activity

6. *Writing an Expository Essay* Use information from the section to create a poster that explains the issues in *Brown* v. *Board of Education* or describes the Montgomery bus boycott.

RESOURCE OPTIONS

Teaching Resources

📁 **Quiz** Units 7–8 folder, p. 88

📁 **Chapter Tests Forms A and B** Chapter Test folder

Student Performance Pack

Guide to the Essentials Chapter 27, Section 4 (English and Spanish)

Standardized Test Preparation Handbook

Media and Technology

🎧 **Guided Reading Audiotapes** Chapter 27 Summary (English and Spanish)
Student Edition on Audiotape Chapter 27

💿 **Test Bank CD-ROM; Interactive Student Tutorial CD-ROM** Chapter Test

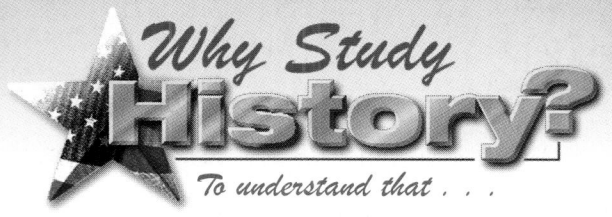

To understand that . . .

Health Care Is a Growing Concern

Providing quality health care, an issue during President Truman's administration, remains an important challenge for the United States.

First polio vaccine is given in 1955

A house in the suburbs, a two-car garage, a television set, a refrigerator, and a washing machine—these items were a part of the American Dream in the 1950s. Thanks to improvements in medicine, good health care also became available to many more Americans. New operations extended the lives of people with heart disease, for example, and millions of Americans benefited from newly developed antibiotics and other medicines.

The Impact Today

In 1950, the average life expectancy of Americans was about 67 years. By 2000, it had increased to about 76 years. The change occurred partly from advances in health care and greater access to quality care. In the 1950s and afterward, Americans began to expect better and more affordable health care.

Yet as the demand for health care increased, the costs soared. Between 1960 and 1998, total health care costs in the United States grew from $27 billion to more than $1 trillion. As health care became more expensive, the number of Americans too poor to afford health insurance grew. By 1999 an estimated 43 million Americans lacked health insurance.

For many years, most Americans received health care under insurance plans for which they,

or their employers, paid. Traditional "fee for service" insurance allowed individuals to choose their own doctors. It also gave health care providers flexibility in treating patients.

In recent years, efforts to reduce health care costs have prompted the rise of "managed care" plans like health maintenance organizations (HMOs). These organizations seek to "manage" health care closely to keep costs down.

Today roughly 150 million Americans are enrolled in managed-care plans. Many are unhappy with their plans, however. In a 1997 study, three fifths of those surveyed said that managed care causes doctors to spend less time with patients and makes it harder to get specialized care. Only one fourth of the people surveyed believed that managed-care plans make health care more affordable. Thus, many Americans question whether managed care can provide quality care at a lower cost. Other critics, focusing on the large number of Americans without health insurance, are calling for an effort to provide health care for all Americans.

The Impact on You

Ask your parents, grandparents, or other adults what type of health care plans they have. Ask how satisfied they are with their health care and why. Then write three paragraphs giving the pros and cons of each plan.

New medical technology is beneficial but expensive

Class Discussion

Discuss with the class health-care costs and options. For a more thorough examination of the issue, see the activity folder in the Resource options below.

ACTIVITY
STUDENT PARTICIPATION

Creating Debate Posters
Have students read the text. Then divide the class into two groups. Have each group create a poster to be used in a debate on this question: Which type of health-care plan would you choose—managed care or traditional health insurance? (Students can use their findings from interviews conducted in The Impact on You activity on this page.) Posters should address:
- **cost**
- **coverage**
- **time with doctors**
- **expertise of doctors**
- **choice of doctors**

Have the groups present their posters. Encourage debate.

Follow up Discuss which factors contribute to the trend toward greater enrollment in managed-care plans.

Using the Internet
Students can learn more about health care by exploring links in the *America: Pathways to the Present* Web site at

http://www.Pathways.phschool.com

Assessment
See the Lesson Plans folder, pp. 24–27, for rubrics on assessing Class Participation Projects.

▶ RESOURCE OPTIONS

Teaching Resources

 Why Study History? Activity Health Care Is a Growing Concern, found in the Why Study History? folder, p. 28, provides an activity to help students better understand health-care options.

Media and Technology

AmericanHeritage® CD-ROM

Time Tour The Nation Today and Tomorrow: The Fifties *and* A Time of Turmoil

 Prentice Hall United States History Video Collection™ Volume 20 *Post-War USA*

Key Terms

Students should refer to the definitions of key terms in the chapter to write sentences that show an understanding of the social and political issues facing post-World War II American society.

Comprehension

1. The conglomerate system led to the formation of giant corporations that owned businesses in many different areas of the economy. The franchise system meant that local businesses were sometimes pushed out of business by chains that were uniform throughout the country.

2. Suburbs developed because of urban decay, an increase in population due to the postwar baby boom, cheap, plentiful housing, improved roads, and availability of automobiles and fuel.

3. *Life* magazine produced a special edition featuring a happy housewife. Benjamin Spock advised mothers to remain home with their children. Adlai Stevenson told female college students that their "assignment" was to care for children and to cook.

4. Beatniks challenged traditional patterns of respectability. Authors J. D. Salinger and Jack Kerouac wrote novels whose themes challenged 1950s conformity.

5. Releasing the American economy from wartime price controls, which created postwar inflation.

6. He wanted to cut spending, reduce taxes, and balance the budget. He was largely unsuccessful in achieving these goals, because his cuts in government spending caused the economy to slump.

7. The NAACP launched a series of court cases that culminated in the Supreme Court's *Brown* v. *Board of Education* decision overturning the "separate but equal" doctrine. African Americans also successfully used nonviolent protest in the Montgomery bus boycott.

Chapter Summary

The major concepts of Chapter 27 are presented below. See also *Guide to the Essentials of American History* or *Interactive Student Tutorial CD-ROM,* which contains interactive review activities, time lines, helpful hints, and test practice for Chapter 27.

Reviewing the Main Ideas

Americans had dreamed of peace and prosperity through 16 grueling years of economic depression and world war. After the war, they embraced a wide array of technological developments that promised to make their lives easier, and they relished the chance to live more comfortably than their parents had. Minorities began to speak more loudly for equality of civil rights.

Section 1: The Postwar Economy

The American Dream, characterized by a home in the suburbs and a car in the garage, came true for many people in the postwar years.

Section 2: The Mood of the 1950s

After World War II, many Americans were blessed with wealth, success, and leisure. Conformity seemed the order of the day, although some groups made it their business to avoid the popularly accepted lifestyles of the 1950s.

Section 3: Domestic Politics and Policy

Presidents Harry S. Truman and Dwight D. Eisenhower used two very different styles of leadership to meet the challenges they faced during the postwar period.

Section 4: Demands for Civil Rights

Following World War II, African Americans began to push harder in the civil rights movement and brought about significant results.

Providing quality health care, an issue during Harry Truman's administration, remains an important challenge for the United States. Yet as the demand for care increases, the costs also soar.

Key Terms

Use each of the terms below in a sentence that shows how it relates to the chapter.

1. Taft-Hartley Act
2. conglomerate
3. GI Bill
4. beatnik
5. integration
6. baby boom
7. modern republicanism
8. rock and roll
9. National Defense Education Act
10. Montgomery bus boycott

Comprehension

1. How did the conglomerate and the franchise system change the American economy after World War II?
2. What factors contributed to suburban development from 1945 to 1960?
3. Give examples showing how the media fostered expectations about the proper role of women.
4. What challenges to the rigid expectations of the period arose in the 1950s?
5. What problem did Harry Truman face as the nation converted to a peacetime economy after World War II?
6. What were Dwight Eisenhower's goals for the presidency? How successful was he in achieving these goals?
7. How did African Americans use the courts and nonviolent protest in their battle for equality?

Using Graphic Organizers

On a separate sheet of paper, copy the web diagram to organize information about the culture and politics of postwar America. Provide at least six supporting details in the surrounding circles.

Culture and Politics in Postwar America

Using Graphic Organizers

Details may include the following: modern republicanism, the Fair Deal, growth of the service industry, civil rights activism, beatniks, the American Dream, conformity in schools, traditional gender roles, and suburban explosion.

Analyzing Political Cartoons ▶

1. A cartoonist drew this view of suburban life in 1952. (a) What is most striking about this community? (b) What do you know about such communities?

2. Read the caption. What is the cause of the woman's dilemma?

3. What is the cartoonist saying about life in a 1950s suburb?

"I'm Mrs. Edward M. Barnes. Where do I live?"

Critical Thinking

1. *Applying the Chapter Skill* Review the Evaluating Magazine Advertisements skill on page 778. Find an advertisement in a modern magazine that shows a family and evaluate it to see if it reveals information about life in the United States today.

2. *Recognizing Cause and Effect* In what ways did the Depression and World War II contribute to the postwar economic boom of the 1950s?

3. *Demonstrating Reasoned Judgment* Which technological advance of the 1950s—atomic energy, computers, or television—do you think has had the most far-reaching impact on the way Americans live? Explain why you think so.

4. *Identifying Central Issues* What was the principle behind the Supreme Court's ruling in *Brown* v. *Board of Education*?

INTERNET ACTIVITY

For your portfolio:
CREATE A DIARY ENTRY

Access Prentice Hall's *America: Pathways to the Present* site at **www.Pathways.phschool.com** for the specific URL to complete the activity. Additional resources and related Web sites are also available.

Follow the links to learn about Harry S. Truman by looking at the photographs and reading some of his campaign speeches. Then write a diary entry from Truman's point of view about life during the 1948 campaign. What issues was Truman concerned about? How did people respond to Truman?

ANALYZING DOCUMENTS ◀ ▶ INTERPRETING DATA

Turn to the "Birth Rate, 1930–1960" graph on page 770.

1. After what year did the birth rate rise higher than its 1930 level?
(a) 1940 (b) 1945 (c) 1955 (d) 1960

2. According to the graph, the birth rate was the lowest in (a) 1930. (b) 1935. (c) 1945. (d) 1960.

3. *Writing* Research and write a brief essay describing the impact of the baby boom generation on American culture.

Connecting to Today

Essay Writing Reread the section on pages 775–776 that describes the *Life* photo essay. Then write the text for a *Life* photo essay about a working mother's life today. Include activities from a typical working mother's day.

791

INTERNET ACTIVITY

Diary entries will vary but should be supported with specific facts and quotes from the Web site. Students may also address themes introduced in the chapter.

Analyzing Political Cartoons
1. (a) Its uniformity.
(b) Prefabricated communities were built in the postwar years by Levitt and other developers. The affordable, mass-produced houses created such uniformity.
2. She cannot distinguish her home from the rest.
3. It is lacking individuality and originality.

Critical Thinking
1. Answers will vary but students should apply the steps outlined in the skill.
2. People who had put their money into savings were eager to buy everything that the war and the Depression had denied them. The economy was driven by the needs and wants of consumers who had more real purchasing power. In addition, new technological advances spurred the economy.
3. Answers will vary. Students may point out that television has been blamed for such problems as obesity, violence, and consumerism; computers have become elements of ordinary daily life, changing the nature of work and recreation; and atomic energy has raised concerns about waste disposal, accidents, and terrorism.
4. There can be no such thing as "separate but equal"; segregated facilities are by definition not equal.

Interpreting Data
1. b
2. b
3. Essays will vary but should be based on facts from the chapter.

Connecting to Today
Students' essays should show an awareness of the complexity and stresses in the lives of many women today as they struggle to balance work and family responsibilities.

My Brush with History

Focus Have students find the meaning of each of these words in a dictionary before they begin to read: *transmission, meteorologist, keen, court-martial, insubordination.* Ask them to think, as they read, about the responsibilities that Roddewig had despite his young age.

Instruct Explain that the work of radio operators was critical during World War II. After World War I, the U.S. Navy led the world in radio innovation. (Unlike telegraph and telephone, radio was developed mainly for military use.) The interception of radio transmissions became routine during World War II. When decoded, such transmissions significantly influenced the movements of all naval forces. Discuss Roddewig's responsibilities as a radio operator during the war.

Analyzing the Document

Use this additional question to generate class discussion:

CRITICAL THINKING: IDENTIFYING ASSUMPTIONS Why did Roddewig think that his naval career was sure to end in disgrace? *(Because he, a lowly third-class radioman, had told a four-star admiral to "shut up.")*

My Brush with History

BY ROBERT RODDEWIG

INTRODUCTION In the passage below, Robert Roddewig, a sailor on the battleship U.S.S. *Missouri* in the final months of World War II, describes a terrifying experience in the waters near Japan. As you read, think about the responsibilities that Roddewig had despite his young age.

The year was 1945. As an eighteen-year-old eligible for the draft, I had enlisted in the Navy before graduation from high school in Davenport, Iowa. After boot camp and radio school, at Farragut, Idaho, I was assigned to the staff of Adm. William F. "Bull" Halsey aboard the *Missouri,* an *Iowa*-class battleship.

I felt honored to pull duty as a staff member with a four-star admiral. Halsey usually selected the *New Jersey,* another *Iowa*-class ship, but the *Jersey* had steamed stateside for some badly needed maintenance and repair. The *Missouri* got the call.

There were seven radio transmitting-and-receiving stations aboard the *Missouri,* and I usually spent my four hours handling routine communications among ships of the fleet. I had been onboard several weeks and had not even seen the admiral. Then I was transferred to the radio station just behind the ship's bridge. I would be copying coded messages from several military shore stations. When decoded, these transmissions would help our meteorologists map weather conditions over possible Japanese bombing targets. I quickly came to realize the importance of my work. The safety of our carrier pilots might well depend upon the accuracy and thoroughness of the radiomen on duty behind the bridge.

To obtain weather information I usually copied station NPG Honolulu or an Army station from Andrews Air Force Base on Guam. These were clear stations with little interference of any kind. But station KCT from Vladivostok, U.S.S.R., was different.

If our planes were to raid the Japanese islands of Hokkaidō or Honshū, we needed the weather

Battleship "Missouri"

Launched in 1944, the Missouri **was nearly 900 feet long and had a crew of 1,900.**

TEST PREPARATION

Have students use the excerpt above to answer the following question.

From what you read, which statement best describes Admiral Halsey?

A He understood the importance of the contributions of all his staff members.

B He hated war.

C His nickname came from the way he bullied his staff.

D He had little interest in the task that Roddewig was carrying out.

report from KCT. The Japanese, knowing this, constantly jammed the KCT frequency with music, loud laughter, foreign languages—anything and everything to drown out the signal. It required keen concentration to find our signal and stay on it while totally ignoring all the "trash."

One evening I was copying KCT with the usual Japanese garbage jamming my frequency. I had my eyes closed, and I was concentrating totally on that faint but distinctive signal: Dit dah dit. I automatically hit the R key on the typewriter (or mill, as the Navy called it). Dah dit dit dit, B. Dit dit dit, S.

Then a loud voice behind me asked, "Are they jamming our station?"

"Yes, sir," I replied, my concentration broken. I hit the space bar of the mill several times to indicate missed letters. I found the signal once again.

"Are you able to copy it?" The voice again. I hit the space bar several more times before finding my signal once more. "Will you be able to get enough for us?" And the space-bar routine again. But this time I blurted out, "Shut up!"

When the transmission was complete, I pulled the message from my machine. Wondering if the blank spaces would ruin our mapmaking effort, I turned in my seat—and looked up at four stars on each lapel of a brown shirt. I had just met Admiral Halsey.

Oh my…, I thought. I was an insignificant radioman, third class, and I had told an admiral to shut up.

At nineteen years my life would end. I would be fortunate to get a court-martial for insubordination along with a dishonorable discharge from the Navy.

"Sir, are you the one I told to 'shut up'?"

This tough-looking admiral was standing there with arms folded and legs apart in a mild inverted Y, brown naval field cap pulled to his brow, jaw jutting menacingly with lips pressed firmly together. I could see now why they called him Bull Halsey.

"Yes, lad," he blared.

"I apologize, sir. I did not know it was you. I have no excuse, sir."

The admiral broke his stance and began to pace the floor. "Lad," he bellowed, "when I come into this radio shack and speak to you while you are on that radio, you do not tell me to shut up! Do you understand?"

His voice boomed like the nine 16-inch guns attached to the ship's three main turrets.

"Yes, sir, I understand." I was frozen at attention and, I am certain, tears were welling in my eyes.

Then, stopping in front of me and looking me straight in the eye, he went on in a very calm and friendly voice. "If I or anyone else ever bothers you while you are on that radio, you do not tell them to shut up. What you tell them is to stay out of here and that's an order. Do you understand, lad?"

I could only look at him and stammer, "Yes, sir."

We saluted. Admiral Halsey went on his way. I never met him again.

Source: *American Heritage* magazine, September 1997.

General Douglas MacArthur called Admiral Halsey the "greatest fighting admiral" of World War II.

ADDITIONAL READING

To learn more about the topics discussed in this selection, you might want to read the following books:

- *Battleship Missouri,* by Valerie Drogues (New York: Crestwood House, 1994)
- *Combined Fleet Decoded: The Secret Story of American Intelligence and the Japanese Navy During World War II,* by John Prados (New York: Random House, 1995)
- *Eagle Against the Sun: The American War with Japan,* by Ronald H. Spector (New York: Free Press, 1985)
- *The Two-Ocean War: A Short History of the United States Navy in the Second World War,* by Samuel Eliot Morison (Boston: Little, Brown, 1963)

793

TEST PREPARATION

Have students use the excerpt on these pages to answer the following question.

What is the main idea of this document?

A Insubordination is never acceptable.

B The Japanese jammed the weather reports from station KCT.

Ⓒ Robert Roddewig was performing an important job and had the right not to be bothered, even by a four-star general.

D Admiral Halsey had no right to be in the radio cabin.

The Upheaval of the Sixties 1960–1975

Introducing the Unit

Using Historical Evidence

The 1960s and early 1970s were years of unrest and change. Many Americans, determined to reform the nation, worked to bring change quickly; other Americans resisted their efforts. The energy and confidence of the marchers in the photograph on the right reflect the spirit and determination of the civil rights movement, one of the most controversial social struggles of the sixties.

Ask students to think of a title for this photograph that appropriately conveys its mood and feeling. Who are the people in the march? What sort of appearance do they project and what message does this send?

Themes in American History

Direct students' attention to the Unit Themes. Point out that each chapter in this unit has its own theme. To teach this unit thematically, you may wish to use The Nation After World War II folder in **American History Block Scheduling Support.**

Using the Time Line

To provide students with practice in using a time line to connect key events in the United States with key events in the world, ask questions such as these: (1) Who was President during the Cuban Missile Crisis? *(Kennedy)* (2) How many years passed between the signing of the Vietnamese peace agreement and the fall of South Vietnam? *(2 years.)* (3) What civil rights leader was killed in 1968? *(Martin Luther King, Jr.)*

---

unit NINE

The Upheaval of the Sixties

1 9 6 0 – 1 9 7 5

*W*hen John F. Kennedy became President in 1961, many Americans felt a sense of optimism. Buoyed by the promise of change, African Americans pushed hard to claim their civil rights. The civil rights movement also inspired women, Latinos, Native Americans, and others to seek equality. Although great strides were made in the 1960s, the hope that began this turbulent decade was shattered by a series of assassinations, a wave of urban riots, and a controversial war in Southeast Asia.

Chapter 28	The Kennedy and Johnson Years *1961–1968*	
Chapter 29	The Civil Rights Movement *1954–1968*	
Chapter 30	Other Social Movements *1960–1975*	
Chapter 31	The Vietnam War and American Society *1960–1975*	

UNIT THEMES

Government President Lyndon Johnson pushed through Congress the most ambitious social program since FDR's New Deal.

Culture A mood of change and protest characterized the 1960s.

Foreign Relations Attempts to stop the spread of communism led to costly foreign entanglements.

EVENTS IN THE UNITED STATES

1962	1963	1964	1966	1968
Cuban missile crisis	President Kennedy assassinated	Turning Point: Civil Rights Act (p. 833)	National Organization for Women formed	Martin Luther King, Jr., assassinated

Presidents Kennedy Johnson

1960 **1965**

EVENTS IN THE WORLD

1961	1963	1966	1967	1968
Berlin wall built	South Vietnam leader Diem assassinated	Chinese Cultural Revolution	Six-Day War in Middle East	Tet Offensive in Vietnam

▶ RESOURCE OPTIONS

Teaching Resources

📁 **Units 9–10 folder** Contains instructional materials organized by chapter.

VIEWING HISTORY Civil rights workers march toward a better future in this 1965 voter registration drive in Selma, Alabama. *Culture* Why were such public demonstrations so successful in bringing about change?

1969 Woodstock music festival poster

1970	1972	1973
Environmental Protection Agency established	Gloria Steinem founds MS. magazine	• Vietnam peace agreement signed • Roe v. Wade decision

Nixon

1970   **1975**

1971	1972	1975
India and Pakistan go to war	Martial law declared in Philippines	Fall of South Vietnam

---

▶ RESOURCE OPTIONS

Media and Technology

 Color Transparencies Specific transparencies are referenced at points of use. See American Photo, B-9; Our Multicultural Heritage, C-15; Fine Art, D-20; Links Across Time, J-9; and Political Cartoons, K-9.

 Visions of America "Scenes of an Era: The Upheaval of the Sixties" located on videodisc side 4 and on videotape 5. Lesson plans for "Scenes of an Era" can be found in the Visions of America Guidebook.

Side 4, Chapter 32

Listed below are the technology resources that *America: Pathways to the Present* offers:

RESOURCE PRO

America: Pathways to the Present Teaching Resources on CD-ROM offers lesson planning flexibility, test generation capability, and additional enrichment support.

🖥 Using the Internet
Prentice Hall's *America: Pathways to the Present* companion Web site offers student-appropriate Internet activities and links as well as resources for teachers. Visit us at
http://www.Pathways.phschool.com

◉ AmericanHeritage®
History of the United States CD-ROM This interactive, multimedia exploration of the American experience provides a journey through historical, political, and social aspects of American history. Includes Time Tours, Presidents, and History Makers.

◉ ▄ *Visions of America*
This award-winning integrated multimedia package offers Scenes of an Era, Turning Point stories, and historians' viewpoints on core content.

◉ *Our Times Multimedia Encyclopedia of the 20th Century* CD-ROM

◉ INTERACTIVE STUDENT TUTORIAL CD-ROM

🎧 GUIDED READING AUDIOTAPES

🎧 STUDENT EDITION ON AUDIOTAPE

◉ PRENTICE HALL LISTENING TO MUSIC THE AMERICAN EXPERIENCE AUDIO CD

Answer to . . .

Viewing History A large, orderly group is difficult to repress. Marches presented a sympathetic image to the world.

The Kennedy and Johnson Years, 1961–1968

Managing Time and Instruction

INSTRUCTION SUPPORT

These materials for instruction are provided for **each section** in the **Teaching Resources.** See **Units 9–10 folder for Enrichment Support:**

• Reproducible Lesson Plans in Lesson Plans folder • Learning Styles Lesson Plans in Learning Styles Lesson Plans folder • Big Idea Graphic Organizers in Big Idea Graphic Organizer folder • Guided Reading and Review • Quizzes • Test Preparation Practice booklet

DAILY LESSON	ENRICHMENT SUPPORT
1 **The New Frontier** (pp. 797–800)	• Visual Learning Activity, Creating Images of the Candidates, Learning with Documents folder, p. 70 • Biography, Dr. Frances Kelsey, found on **Resource Pro** • Literature Activity, A Grieving Nation, Units 9–10 folder, pp. 12–13 • Skills for Life Activity, Units 9–10 folder, p. 14
2 **The Great Society** (pp. 802–806)	• Primary Source Activity, President Johnson's Thanksgiving Address, Learning with Documents folder, p. 34 • Nystrom *Atlas of Our Country,* People on the Move, pp. 34–35; The Fourth Wave of Immigration, pp. 36–37 • Visual Learning Activity, The Job Corps, found on **Resource Pro** • Critical Thinking Activity, Recognizing Cause and Effect, found on **Resource Pro** • Key Documents, Lyndon B. Johnson, The Great Society, Learning with Documents folder, p. 102 • Literature Activity, The Invisible Poor, found on **Resource Pro**
3 **Foreign Policy in the Early 1960s** (pp. 807–814)	• Key Documents, John F. Kennedy, Inaugural Address, Learning with Documents folder, p. 101 • Biography, Robert F. Kennedy, Units 9–10 folder, p. 9 • Primary Source Activity, Cuban Missile Crisis, found on **Resource Pro** • Comparing Primary Sources, On the Cold War, Units 9–10 folder, pp. 10–11 • Welfare Remains a Controversial Issue, Why Study History? folder, p. 29

Running Out of Time?

• Use Tape 5, "The Upheaval of the Sixties, 1960–1975," from **Visions of America** videotapes series.
• Use Chapter 28 Summary from **Guide to the Essentials of American History (English and Spanish)**.

Companion Web Site

The companion Web site offers online links for all chapter review activities. It also provides key content links and structured support for this chapter for both teachers and students.

http://www.Pathways.phschool.com

Teaching in the Information Age

Media and Technology

For the Student

Interactive Student Tutorial CD-ROM Chapter 28
Student Edition on Audiotape Chapter 28
American Heritage® CD-ROM
Guided Reading Audiotapes (English and Spanish) Chapter 28

For the Teacher

Resource Pro CD-ROM Chapter 28
Test Bank CD-ROM Chapter 28
Listening to Literature Audiotapes *Timeless Voices, Timeless Themes* "Frederick Douglass" by Robert Hayden
Color Transparencies The Way It Works, H-20

Assessment Options

Chapter Test Forms A&B Test Bank CD-ROM booklet
Test Bank CD-ROM Chapter 28
Standardized Test Preparation Handbook

Block Scheduling

Pacing Suggestions

For 90-minute Blocks

- Teach sections 1 and 2 using Transparencies C-3, I-13, and K-9 and the Extended Class Periods Activity on p. 799.

- Teach section 3 using the Big Idea Graphic Organizers from Teaching Resources and the Recent Scholarship note on p. 814 for class discussions.

Additional Resources

- Prentice Hall's **American History Block Scheduling Support File** covers over 40 major topics in American history.

- **Prentice Hall United States History Video Collection**™ contains 20 videotapes covering American history from beginnings to present.

- **Decision America Videotapes and Videodiscs**

Connections to American Literature

from Prentice Hall

Prentice Hall Literature *Timeless Voices, Timeless Themes* From *The Mortgaged Heart* by Carson McCullers, p. 994

Additional Resources

For the Student

Claude Brown. *Manchild in the Promised Land.* Macmillan, 1965.
Robert F. Kennedy. *Thirteen Days.* Norton, 1971.

For the Teacher

Merle Miller. *Lyndon: An Oral Biography.* Ballantine, 1987.

Prentice Hall brings into the classroom the vast archives and scholarship of the nation's premier American history magazine. See "From the Archives of American Heritage®" and "About the Presidents" teaching notes in this chapter.

History Alive!

Teacher's Curriculum Institute, in partnership with Prentice Hall, provides unique materials that engage students with diverse learning styles. See History Alive!® unit on Contemporary American Society.

Student Performance Pack

Ensures success in the three critical areas of Reading, Test Taking, and English Language Development with the following materials:
- Guide to the Essentials of American History in English and Spanish
- Guided Reading Audiotapes in English and Spanish
- Interactive Student Tutorial CD-ROM
- Test Preparation Handbook
- Test Preparation Practice booklet

Introducing the Chapter

The contrast between the presidencies of John Kennedy and Lyndon Johnson is striking. While Kennedy articulated plans for domestic reform, few of his programs actually advanced through Congress, perhaps because of his pre-occupation with foreign affairs. When Johnson took office after Kennedy's death, he used his legislative skills to push through Congress some of the most significant social programs in the nation's history.

Themes in American History

The theme for this chapter, Government, is listed at the beginning of this unit. An alternate theme for the chapter is Foreign Policy. To teach this unit thematically, you may wish to use The Nation After World War II folder in American History Block Scheduling Support.

Why Study History?

Have students explore suggested ways of connecting the past to the present on page 815.

Answer to . . .

Viewing History Students should use this question as an aid in reading the chapter. Kennedy's New Frontier programs included encouraging a strong economy through tax cuts, attempting to provide federally funded aid to the poor, and developing the space program.

CHAPTER 28
The Kennedy and Johnson Years

1961–1968

CHAPTER FOCUS

A spirit of optimism energized the United States during the early 1960s. John F. Kennedy, the youngest President ever elected, focused on cold war politics. His successor, Lyndon B. Johnson, rallied the Congress and the country behind the most ambitious social program since the New Deal of the 1930s.

The Why Study History? page at the end of this chapter explores the connection between government assistance to the poor during the Kennedy and Johnson years and today.

▲
VIEWING HISTORY
President John F. Kennedy delivers an inspiring address at his inauguration.
Government **What were Kennedy's plans for the country?**

RESOURCE OPTIONS

Teaching Resources

📁 **Big Idea Graphic Organizer** folder
Graphic summary of the main idea of the chapter.

📁 **Learning Styles Lesson Plans** folder
Alternate lesson plans for diverse learning styles for each chapter.

Media and Technology

 AmericanHeritage® CD-ROM
Time Tour The Nation Today and Tomorrow: A Time for Turmoil

 Prentice Hall United States History Video Collection™ Volume 20
Post-War USA

1960
John F. Kennedy
elected President

1961
Alan Shepard
becomes first
American to
travel in space

1962
John Glenn
becomes first
American to
orbit Earth

1962
Michael Harrington
publishes The
Other America

1963
President Kennedy
assassinated

1960   1962   1964

1 The New Frontier

SECTION PREVIEW

Objectives

1 Describe the election of 1960 and its outcome.
2 Summarize Kennedy's domestic programs.
3 Explain Americans' reaction to President Kennedy's assassination.
4 *Key Terms* Define: mandate; New Frontier; Warren Commission.

Main Idea

Before his assassination in 1963, President John F. Kennedy proposed a number of domestic programs to improve the economy and to address issues of inequality, including poverty and civil rights. Most of Kennedy's proposals were defeated in Congress.

Reading Strategy

Reinforcing Main Ideas As you read the section, create a list of the programs that Kennedy proposed.

On September 26, 1960, millions of Americans turned on their televisions to watch as two presidential candidates squared off in the country's first televised debate. The two candidates were Republican Richard Nixon (Eisenhower's Vice President) and Democrat John F. Kennedy. With studio lights glaring, Nixon appeared tired and hot. Kennedy, in contrast, looked polished and relaxed. He had hired consultants to help him with makeup and clothes. This debate and the three that followed had a major impact on the outcome of the election. The debates also changed forever the role that television would play in American politics.

The Election of 1960

Kennedy, a Massachusetts Democrat who had served in the United States House of Representatives and Senate, faced serious obstacles in his quest for the presidency. He was only forty-three years old, and many questioned whether he had the experience needed for the nation's highest office. In addition, Kennedy was a Roman Catholic, and no Catholic had ever been elected President. Kennedy put an end to the

religion issue when he won the primary in the largely Protestant state of West Virginia. With that hurdle behind him, he campaigned hard, with promises to spur the sluggish economy.

During the last years of the Eisenhower administration, the Gross National Product (GNP) had grown very slowly. In addition, the economy had suffered several recessions. During the campaign, Kennedy proclaimed that it was time to "get America moving again."

In the election, Kennedy won by an extraordinarily close margin.[†] Though the electoral vote was 303 to 219, Kennedy won by only 120,000 popular votes out of more than 34 million cast. If but a few thousand voters in Illinois or Texas had cast ballots for Nixon, the Republicans would have won. As a result of

Presidential candidates Richard Nixon and John F. Kennedy squared off in a series of televised debates in 1960.

[†] Although the youngest person ever to be elected President, Kennedy was not the youngest ever to hold the office. Theodore Roosevelt, who became President when McKinley was assassinated, was the youngest to hold the office.

RESOURCE OPTIONS

Teaching Resources

📁 **Reproducible Lesson Plan** Lesson Plans folder, p. 146

📁 **Learning Styles Lesson Plan** Learning Styles Lesson Plans folder, p. 58

📁 **Big Idea Graphic Organizer** Big Idea Graphic Organizer folder, p. 118

📁 **Guided Reading and Review** Units 9–10 folder, p. 3

📁 **Visual Learning Activity** Creating Images of the Candidates, Learning with Documents folder, p. 70

Jacqueline and John F. Kennedy dazzled the nation with their beauty, youth, and glamour. *Government* Why was Kennedy's administration later nicknamed Camelot?

this razor-thin victory, Kennedy entered office without a strong **mandate.** A mandate is a set of wishes expressed to a candidate by his or her voters. Without such a mandate, Kennedy would have difficulty pushing his more controversial measures through Congress.

No matter how slim his margin of victory, Kennedy was now President. In ringing phrases he declared in his Inaugural Address:

> **KEY DOCUMENTS** "Let the word go forth from this time and place, to friend and foe alike, that the torch has been passed to a new generation of Americans, born in this century, tempered by war, disciplined by a hard and bitter peace. . . . And so, my fellow Americans, ask not what your country can do for you; ask what you can do for your country."
>
> —*John F. Kennedy,* Inaugural Address

The new administration was buoyant, energetic, and full of optimism. Jacqueline Kennedy, the President's wife, charmed the country with her grace. Nobel Prize winners visited the White House. The Kennedys and their friends loved to play touch football on the lawn or take long hikes.

The administration, which seemed full of idealism and youth, later earned the nickname "Camelot" after a 1960 Broadway musical. The musical portrayed the legendary kingdom of the British King Arthur. Arthur dreamed of transforming medieval Britain from a country in which "might makes right," or the strong always get their way, into one where power would be used to achieve right.

Kennedy's Domestic Programs

In a speech early in his administration, Kennedy said that the nation was poised at the edge of a **New Frontier.** The name stuck and was used to describe Kennedy's proposals to improve the economy, give aid to the poor, and breathe new life into the space program.

The Economy Concerned about the continuing recession, Kennedy hoped to work with the business community to restore prosperity to the nation. Often, however, he faced resistance from executives who were suspicious of his plans. The worst fears of business leaders were realized in the spring of 1962. When the U.S. Steel Company announced that it was raising the price of steel by $6 a ton, other firms did the same. Worried about inflation, Kennedy called the price increase unjustifiable and charged that it showed "utter contempt for the public interest." He ordered a federal investigation into the possibility of price-fixing. Under that pressure, U.S. Steel and the other companies backed down. Business leaders remained angry, and the stock market fell in the steepest drop since the Great Crash of 1929.

On the larger issue of ending the economic slump, Kennedy proposed cutting taxes. In 1963 the President called for a $13.5 billion cut in taxes over three years. The measure would reduce government income and create a budget deficit at first. Kennedy believed, however, that the extra cash in taxpayers' wallets would stimulate the economy and bring added tax revenues in the end. The tax-cut proposal was soon bottled up in a congressional committee and stood little chance of passage.

Combating Poverty and Inequality Kennedy also was eager to take action against poverty and inequality. In his first two years in office, Kennedy hoped that he could help the poor simply by stimulating the economy. In 1962 author Michael Harrington described the situation of the poor in his book, *The Other America.* Harrington's book revealed that while many Americans were enjoying the prosperity of the

1950s, a shocking one fifth of the population was living below the poverty line. Kennedy began to believe that direct aid to the poor was necessary.

Despite his concern, Kennedy rarely succeeded in pushing legislation through Congress. Kennedy's ambitious plans for federal aid for education and medical care for the aged both failed. Kennedy did succeed, however, in raising the minimum wage and passing the Housing Act of 1961. This act provided $4.9 billion for urban renewal. Congress also approved the Twenty-Fourth Amendment to go to the states for ratification. This amendment outlawed the poll tax, which was still being used in five southern states to keep poor African Americans from voting.

The Space Program Kennedy was more successful in his effort to breathe life into the space program. Following the Soviet Union's launch of *Sputnik* in 1957, numerous government agencies and industries had been working furiously with NASA, the National Aeronautics and Space Agency, to place a manned spacecraft in orbit around Earth. As part of the Mercury program, seven test pilots were chosen to train as astronauts in 1959. Government spending and the future of NASA seemed uncertain, however, when a task force appointed by Kennedy recommended that NASA concentrate on exploratory space missions without human crews.

All of this changed in April 1961. The Soviet Union announced that Yuri Gagarin had become the first human to travel in space and had circled Earth on board the Soviet spacecraft *Vostok*. Gagarin's flight rekindled Americans' fears that the United States was falling behind the Soviet Union.

Twenty-three days later, on May 5, 1961, the United States made its own first attempt to send a person into space. Astronaut Alan Shepard made a 15-minute suborbital flight that reached an altitude of 115 miles. Though this flight did not match the orbital flight of the Soviets, its success did convince Kennedy to move forward. On May 25, Kennedy issued a bold challenge to the nation. He said the United States "should commit itself to achieving the goal, before this decade is out, of landing a man on the moon."[†]

Both the nation and the government accepted the challenge, and funding for NASA

---

† For the remainder of the decade, succeeding NASA flights brought the country closer and closer to its goal. On July 20, 1969, United States astronaut Neil Armstrong became the first person to set foot on the moon.

Federal Funding of NASA, 1950–1965

Dollars (in billions) / Year

Launching of *Sputnik*, 1957

*National Aeronautics and Space Administration
Source: *Historical Statistics of the United States, Colonial Times to 1970*

 Interpreting Graphs NASA grew out of the National Advisory Committee for Aeronautics, which was established in 1915. Alarmed by the launching of *Sputnik*, in 1958 Congress authorized the new federal agency to promote the research and development of air and space. *Economics How does the graph illustrate the influence of the Soviet Union's* Sputnik *on United States policy?*

was increased. Less than a year later, on February 20, 1962, John Glenn successfully completed three orbits around Earth and landed in the Atlantic Ocean near the Bahamas. Later that year Kennedy spoke at Rice University in Houston, Texas:

**Main Idea
CONNECTIONS**

Why did Kennedy's space program succeed while most of his other domestic programs did not?

AMERICAN VOICES ❝We set sail on this new sea because there is new knowledge to be gained, and new rights to be won, and they must be won and used for the progress of all people. . . . [O]nly if the United States occupies a position of preeminence can we help decide whether this new ocean will be a sea of peace or a new, terrifying theater of war.❞

—*John F. Kennedy*

Kennedy Is Assassinated

On November 22, 1963, as Kennedy looked ahead to reelection the following year, he traveled to Texas to mobilize support. Texas Governor John Connally and his wife Nelly met Kennedy and his wife at the airport in Dallas. Together they rode through the streets of Dallas in an open limousine. Thousands of supporters lined the route of the motorcade. Suddenly shots rang and bullets struck both Connally and the President. While Connally

---

Customize for
More Advanced Students

Have students write a paragraph comparing JFK's handling of business interests such as U.S. Steel with Teddy Roosevelt's handling of the trusts.

A sad and solemn-looking Lyndon Johnson is sworn in as President aboard Air Force One shortly after President Kennedy's assassination. A grief-stricken Jacqueline Kennedy (right) looks on. *Culture* What was the nation's reaction to Kennedy's death?

Answers to
SECTION 1 REVIEW

1. (a) mandate, see p. 798; (b) New Frontier, see p. 798; (c) Warren Commission, see p. 800.

2. Successes: the space program, passage of the 24th Amendment, Housing Act of 1961. Failures: the stock market decline, inability to push through education, medical care, or tax-cutting plans.

3. Time lines should include: 1959—Mercury program; 1961—Shepard's suborbital flight; 1962—Glenn's orbital flight.

4. He planned programs for direct aid to the poor; though many proposals were rejected by Congress, he did succeed in getting some legislation passed.

5. The youth and idealism of the Kennedy adminstration reminded Americans of the reign of the legendary King Arthur. The dream ended when Kennedy was assassinated, although President Johnson carried out many of Kennedy's plans.

6. Essays will vary but should be supported with facts from the section.

---

was only wounded, President Kennedy was pronounced dead soon after his arrival at a nearby hospital. The country was shattered. Millions of Americans remained glued to their television sets for the next four days as the impact of the tragedy sank in.

Shortly after Kennedy's death, a commission headed by Chief Justice Earl Warren was formed to investigate the crime. The prime suspect in Kennedy's assassination was Lee Harvey Oswald, a former marine and supporter of Cuba's Fidel Castro. Two days after Kennedy's assassination, Oswald was transferred from one jail to another. While the nation watched on television, Dallas nightclub owner Jack Ruby stepped through the crowd of reporters and

fatally shot Oswald. After months of investigation, the **Warren Commission** declared that Oswald had worked alone in shooting the President. Since then, however, some people have argued that Oswald was involved in a larger conspiracy, and that he was killed in order to protect others who had helped plan Kennedy's murder.

Lyndon Johnson, who had also traveled to Dallas with Kennedy, took the presidential oath of office on board Air Force One just ninety minutes after Kennedy's death. Johnson went on to make good use of the spirit of hope and the desire for change that Kennedy had inspired. He saw enacted much of the legislation that his predecessor had tried to push through Congress.

SECTION 1 REVIEW

Comprehension

1. **Key Terms** Define: (a) mandate; (b) New Frontier; (c) Warren Commission.

2. **Summarizing the Main Idea** What were some of the successes and failures of Kennedy's domestic policies?

3. **Organizing Information** Create a time line of the major events in the space program between 1959 and 1962.

Critical Thinking

4. **Analyzing Time Lines** Review the time line at the start of the section. How did President Kennedy respond to Michael Harrington's book, *The Other America*?

5. **Drawing Inferences** Why was the Kennedy administration nicknamed "Camelot"? How did the dream of Camelot end?

Writing Activity

6. **Writing an Expository Essay** Write an essay describing the role of television in the election of 1960 and its role today.

Answer to . . .

Viewing History It was shocked and devastated.

RESOURCE OPTIONS

Teaching Resources

📁 **Quiz** Units 9–10 folder, p. 4

📁 **Literature Activity** A Grieving Nation, Units 9–10 folder, pp. 12–13

Student Performance Pack

 Guide to the Essentials Chapter 28, Section 1 (English and Spanish)

Historical Evidence

Critical Thinking

Geography

Graphs and Charts

Exploring Oral History

Oral history is made up of people's verbal accounts and recollections of former times and events. As historical evidence, it is one of the oldest and most universal methods by which people have acquired information about the past.

Today, historians preserve oral history by interviewing people and recording their words on audio- or videotape or in written transcripts. Historians may gather oral history at the time an event takes place or at some later date, perhaps years or even decades later.

Historians often seek out oral histories because they give a unique perspective on the past. Oral histories are a type of primary source and therefore are more valuable to historians than secondary sources. Oral histories record not only facts about the past, but also people's opinions, feelings, and impressions—all important to a historian in putting together a picture of the past.

The excerpt at right is taken from a 1983 interview with John Lewis, an Atlanta city council member, on the twentieth anniversary of President Kennedy's death. In 1963 Lewis was chairperson of the Student Nonviolent Coordinating Committee and one of the leaders of the civil rights March on Washington.

Read the oral account at right and then use the following steps to analyze its content.

1. Identify the nature of the oral account. (a) Who was interviewed? (b) When did the interview take place? (c) What was Lewis's attitude toward Kennedy at the time of his death? (d) Did that attitude change in any way over time?

2. Determine the reliability of the evidence. (a) How might Lewis's role in the events being recollected affect his interpretation of those events? (b) How might events after Kennedy's death have affected the account? (c) What do Lewis's views reveal about his political perspective?

3. Study the evidence to learn more about the historical event. (a) What impact does Lewis think Kennedy's presidency had on government policy and the nation? (b) What can you learn about Kennedy's presidency from Lewis's account?

TEST FOR SUCCESS

Why must historians be cautious when using oral history accounts as resources?

An Interview with John Lewis: Remembering President Kennedy's Assassination

"I was living in Atlanta then, but I had gone back to Nashville for a trial. I was getting into a car to go to the Nashville airport when I heard it on the radio. And to me, it was the saddest moment in my life. I had grown up to love and to admire President Kennedy. I remember crying on the plane.

I saw him as a sort of guy that listened. Sincere. Caring. People argue and say that he didn't really do anything. But he did listen, and during that period from 1961 to 1963, I'll tell you, I think probably for the first time in modern American history, we felt, "Well, we have a friend in the White House." On some things we disagreed. We'd call them up and argue and debate with them on some issue, and we said a lot of different things, and sometimes it was harsh. But we saw the Kennedy administration during that period as a sympathetic referee in the whole struggle for civil rights.

His campaign had created a sense of hope, a sense of optimism for many of us. When someone asked him about the civil rights sit-ins that year, he said, 'By sitting down, these young people are standing up for the very best in American tradition.'"

—*Newsweek,* November 28, 1983

RESOURCE OPTIONS

Teaching Resources

Skills for Life Activity Units 9–10 folder, p. 14, provides an example of what oral history can reveal about public affairs in a *U.S. News & World Report* interview with President Clinton.

1963
Johnson becomes
President

1964
Johnson
elected
President

1965
Immigration Act
of 1965

1966
Miranda v.
Arizona

1962 · 1964 · 1966

Objectives

You may wish to call students' attention to the objectives in the Section Preview. The objectives are reflected in the main headings of the section.

Bellringer

Ask students what they think is great about American society. Was it as great in Johnson's time? What differences are evident?

Reading Strategy

Organizing Information Refer students to the Reading Strategy in the Section Preview. You may wish to list Great Society legislation on the chalkboard for students' reference.

2 The Great Society

SECTION PREVIEW

Objectives

1. Describe Johnson's path to the White House.
2. List some of the programs and effects of Johnson's Great Society.
3. Identify some of the landmark cases handed down by the Supreme Court under Chief Justice Earl Warren.
4. *Key Terms* Define: Great Society; Volunteers in Service to America (VISTA); Medicare; Medicaid; Immigration Act of 1965; Miranda rule; apportionment.

Main Idea

The goals of Johnson's Great Society program were to improve the economy, education, and the environment, as well as to offer government assistance to the poor.

Reading Strategy

Organizing Information As you read, create a chart describing the key elements of Johnson's Great Society program.

LESSON PLAN

Connecting to the Main Idea

1. Focus Taking office after Kennedy's assassination, Lyndon Johnson moved many reform bills through Congress as part of his goal of achieving a "Great Society." Ask what Johnson's most important reform bills were. Why did some Americans criticize Johnson's program?
2. Instruct Discuss why LBJ was able to succeed where Kennedy had failed. Remind students that Congress, as well as LBJ, wanted to pass legislation proposed by the slain President as a memorial and as a way of reassuring the country. Ask to what extent LBJ's political experience helped him move legislation through Congress.

Ask students to describe the impact of Chief Justice Earl Warren on the Supreme Court. What were some landmark cases handed down by the Court under Warren?
3. Close Lyndon Johnson moved an astonishingly comprehensive reform program through Congress in an attempt to build a "Great Society." The next section discusses foreign affairs during the Kennedy and Johnson administrations.

Lyndon Johnson used his forceful personality to forge a Great Society.

Speaking to the nation for the first time after John F. Kennedy's death, President Johnson expressed his grief at the loss. "All I have," he declared in this address, "I would have given gladly not to be standing here today." He went on to convey his determination to carry on where the slain President had left off. Johnson's theme was "Let us continue." Once in office, he used all the talents he had developed as Senate Majority Leader to push through Congress an extraordinary program of reforms on domestic issues.

LBJ's Path to the White House

Lyndon B. Johnson arrived in the United States House of Representatives in 1937 as a New Deal Democrat from Texas. In 1948 he won a seat in the Senate, but only by a tiny margin of 87 votes. He was promptly dubbed "Landslide Lyndon"—a nickname that stuck for the rest of his career. In the Senate,

Johnson demonstrated both his talent and his ambition by winning leadership posts. In the six years from 1954 to 1960, he became famous for his ability to work within the political system to accomplish his goals.

When Johnson's bid for the Democratic nomination failed in 1960, he accepted Kennedy's invitation to run for the vice presidency. Once elected, however, Johnson was frustrated with the powerlessness of the office. He was also unhappy being away from Congress, where he had been so effective. Then came the assassination, and suddenly he was President.

Building the Great Society

Like LBJ, Congress was aware that the American people needed some action that would heal the wound caused by the loss of their President. Swift passage of Kennedy's civil rights (see the next chapter) and tax-cut bills followed. Soon Johnson branched out and sought laws to aid public education, provide

RESOURCE OPTIONS

Teaching Resources

Reproducible Lesson Plan Lesson Plans folder, p. 147

Big Idea Graphic Organizer Big Idea Graphic Organizer folder, p. 119

Guided Reading and Review Units 9–10 folder, p. 5

Primary Source Activity President Johnson's Thanksgiving Address, Learning with Documents folder, p. 34

Nystrom *Atlas of Our Country* People on the Move, pp. 34–35; The Fourth Wave of Immigration, pp. 36–37

medical care for the elderly, and eliminate poverty. By the spring of 1964, he had begun to use the phrase **Great Society** to describe his goals. In a speech at the University of Michigan in May 1964, he told students:

 ❝Your imagination, your initiative, and your indignation will determine whether we build a society where progress is the servant of our needs, or a society where old values and new visions are buried under unbridled [unrestrained] growth. For in your time we have the opportunity to move not only toward the rich society and the powerful society, but upward toward the Great Society.**❞**

—*Lyndon B. Johnson*

The Election of 1964 Johnson's early successes paved the way to a true landslide victory over Republican Barry Goldwater in the election of 1964. Goldwater, a senator from Arizona, held conservative views that seemed radical to many Americans. For example, he opposed civil rights legislation, and he believed that military commanders should be allowed to use nuclear bombs as they saw fit on the battlefield. The Johnson campaign took advantage of voters' fears of nuclear war. They aired a television commercial in which a little girl's innocent counting game turned into the countdown for a nuclear explosion. Johnson received 61 percent of the popular vote and an overwhelming 486 to 52 tally in the Electoral College. Democratic majorities were established in both houses of Congress: 295 Democrats to 140 Republicans in the House of Representatives and 68 to 32 in the Senate. Landslide Lyndon now had the mandate to move ahead even more aggressively.

The Tax Cut Like Kennedy, Johnson believed that a budget deficit could be used to improve the economy. Not everyone agreed. To gain conservatives' support for Kennedy's tax-cut bill, which was likely to bring about a deficit, Johnson also agreed to cut government spending. Once that was done, the measure passed and worked just as planned. When the tax cut went into effect, the Gross National Product (GNP) rose 7.1 percent in 1964, 8.1 percent in 1965, and 9.5 percent in 1966. The deficit, which many people feared would grow, actually shrank. This was because the revival of prosperity generated new tax revenues. Unemployment fell, and inflation remained in check.

The War on Poverty Next, LBJ pressed for the antipoverty program that Kennedy had begun to consider. In his 1964 State of the Union message Johnson vowed, "This administration today, here and now, declares unconditional war on poverty in America." The Economic Opportunity Act, passed in the summer of 1964, was created to combat several causes of poverty including illiteracy, unemployment, and inadequate public services. Almost $950 million was set aside to fund 10 separate programs, including work training programs and **Volunteers in Service to America (VISTA)**. VISTA sent volunteers to help people in poor communities. The act also gave the poor a voice in defining housing, health, and education policies in their own neighborhoods.

Main Idea **CONNECTIONS**

What was the Economic Opportunity Act of 1964?

Aid to Education Johnson was equally successful in his effort to provide funds for education. He endorsed the Elementary and Secondary Education Act to provide aid to states based on the number of children from low-income homes. That money, totalling $1.3 billion, would be distributed to public as well as private schools, including parochial schools. When the Education Act was passed, Johnson signed it into law in the small Texas school he had attended as a child. The graph below shows federal aid to schools from 1959 to 1972.

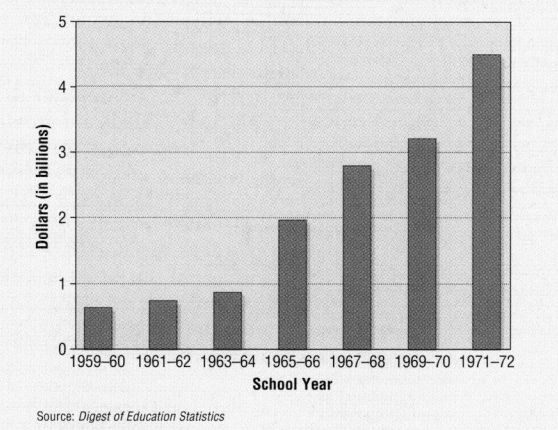

Federal Dollars to Public Schools, 1959–1972

(y-axis: Dollars (in billions), 0 to 5; x-axis: School Year: 1959–60, 1961–62, 1963–64, 1965–66, 1967–68, 1969–70, 1971–72)

Source: *Digest of Education Statistics*

 Interpreting Graphs Congress passed President Johnson's Elementary and Secondary Education Act in 1965. *Economics How does the graph illustrate the overall effect of this legislation?*

Answer to . . .

Main Idea Connections An act that allocated money to fund programs intended to combat the causes of poverty. *Interpreting Graphs* It shows that the overall effect of the law was to increase federal spending for public schools.

Rush to Judgment By 1967, theories about the assassination of President Kennedy were many. One magazine offered a review of twenty-five alternative theories grown up since the Warren Commission's report. They included the suggestion that original autopsy pictures had been destroyed to arguments over how many shots had been fired to the assertion that the killer's killer had been injected with cancer while in prison. But the most spectacular theory belonged to New Orleans district attorney Jim Garrison, who arrested respected New Orleans businessman Clay Shaw. According to Garrison, Shaw was part of a conspiracy funded by a rightist Cuban anti-Castro group that was angry at Kennedy for the failed Bay of Pigs invasion. After a trial filled with ever-widening charges and shadowy figures, Shaw was acquitted in 1969. Source: Nathan Ward, "The Time Machine," *American Heritage* magazine, May/June 1992.

Ask students to draw a political cartoon illustrating either a criticism of Johnson's Great Society legislation or a response to LBJ's critics. (*Visual*)

Answer to . . .

Interpreting Graphs Asian immigrants.

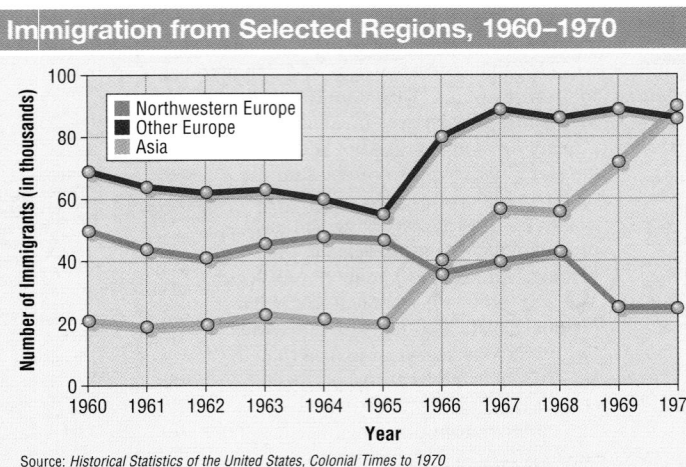

Immigration from Selected Regions, 1960–1970

Legend:
- Northwestern Europe
- Other Europe
- Asia

(Y-axis: Number of Immigrants (in thousands), 0 to 100; X-axis: Year, 1960–1970)

Source: *Historical Statistics of the United States, Colonial Times to 1970*

Interpreting Graphs Congress eased the strict restrictions on immigration with the more generous Immigration Act of 1965. *Diversity On which group of immigrants did this legislation have the greatest effect?*

Medicare and Medicaid Johnson also focused attention on the increasing cost of medical care. Twenty years before, Harry Truman had proposed a medical assistance plan as part of his Fair Deal program. It had never been passed into law. Johnson used his leadership skills to push two new programs through Congress, Medicare and Medicaid. **Medicare** provided hospital and low-cost medical insurance for most Americans age 65 and older. "No longer will older Americans be denied the healing miracle of modern medicine," Johnson declared. "No longer will illness crush and destroy the savings that they have so carefully put away." **Medicaid** provided low-cost health insurance for poor Americans of any age who could not afford their own private health insurance. These broad-based health care programs were the most important pieces of social welfare legislation since the passage of the Social Security Act in 1935. They demonstrated the government's commitment to provide help to those Americans who needed it.

Immigration Reform The Great Society also revised the immigration policies that had been in place since the 1920s. The immigration laws passed in 1921 and 1924 had set quotas, or numerical limits, for each foreign nation. The laws set low quotas for immigrants from southern and eastern Europe and banned Asian immigration altogether. The **Immigration Act of 1965** eliminated the quotas for individual countries and replaced them with more flexible limits. These included 170,000 people from the Eastern Hemisphere and 120,000 from the Western Hemisphere.[†] Family members of United States citizens were exempted from the quotas, as were political refugees. In the 1960s approximately 350,000 immigrants entered the United States each year; in the 1970s the number rose to more than 400,000 a year.

Earl Warren

AMERICAN BIOGRAPHY Earl Warren earned his law degree at the University of California, Berkeley, and went on to serve as district attorney and then attorney general in California. While serving as the governor of that state, Warren ran as the Republican candidate for Vice President in 1948. Warren left his office as governor of California when he was appointed Chief Justice of the United States by President Eisenhower in 1953. Warren served as Chief Justice until he retired in 1969.

Under Earl Warren, the Supreme Court took action to overturn many old laws and court rulings and to establish new legal precedents. For example, just one year after Warren's appointment, the Court outlawed segregation in public schools with its decision in *Brown* v. *Board of Education* (1954). (See the previous chapter.) In 1965 the Court struck down a Connecticut law that prohibited the use of birth control. In another area, the Court ruled that religious prayer in public schools was unconstitutional according to the First Amendment principle of separation of church and state. In yet another significant decision, the Court decreed that obscenity laws could not restrict material that might have some "redeeming social value." Many of the Court's other far-reaching decisions were made in the areas of criminal procedure and legislative apportionment.

[†] The 1965 law did place a maximum of 20,000 immigrants from any one country.

Criminal Procedure Earl Warren and other members of the Supreme Court were concerned with safeguarding the constitutional rights of the individual against the power of the state. In particular, the Warren Court handed down several decisions protecting the rights of persons accused of crimes.

The case of *Mapp* v. *Ohio* (1961) established the exclusionary rule, which stated that evidence seized illegally could not be used in a trial. The court's decision in *Gideon* v. *Wainwright* (1963) ruled that suspects in criminal cases who could not afford a lawyer had the right to free legal aid. In the case of *Escobedo* v. *Illinois* (1964), the justices stated that accused individuals had to be given access to an attorney while being questioned.

Earl Warren
(1891–1974)

The Court's decision in *Miranda* v. *Arizona* (1966) stated that a suspect must be warned of his or her rights before being questioned. As a result of the **Miranda rule,** police must inform accused persons that they have the right to remain silent, that anything they say can be used against them in court, that they have a right to an attorney, and that if they cannot afford an attorney one will be appointed for them.

Congressional Reapportionment
The Warren Court also handed down a series of decisions having to do with **apportionment,** or the distribution of a legislative body's seats among electoral districts. At the time that Warren came to the Court,

Great Society Legislation, 1964–1966

Legislation	Purpose
Economic Opportunity Act, 1964	Created to combat causes of poverty such as illiteracy and unemployment.
Volunteers in Service to America (VISTA), 1964	Sent volunteers to help people in poor communities and set up community action programs to give the poor a voice in defining local housing, health, and education policies.
Medicare, 1965	Provided hospital and low-cost medical insurance for most Americans age 65 and older.
Medicaid, 1965	Provided low-cost health insurance for poor Americans of any age who could not afford their own private health insurance.
Elementary and Secondary Education Act of 1965	Provided education aid to states based on the number of children from low-income homes.
Immigration Act of 1965	Eliminated strict quotas for individual countries and replaced them with more flexible limits.
The Department of Housing and Urban Development (HUD), 1965	Established to oversee the nation's housing needs and to develop and rehabilitate urban communities. HUD also provided money for rent supplements and low-income housing.
The National Foundation of the Arts and Humanities, 1965	Offered grants to artists and scholars.
Water Quality Act, 1965; Clean Water Restoration Act, 1966	Brought about water and air quality standards and provided funding for environmental research.
The National Traffic and Motor Vehicle Safety Act, 1966	Established safety standards for all vehicles to protect consumers.

Interpreting Tables Great Society legislation addressed a wide range of topics. *Economics Which legislation attempted to combat poverty?*

GOVERNMENT CONCEPTS

judicial review: **the power of federal courts to decide whether laws are constitutional**

▼ **The Historical Context:** The Supreme Court first assumed the power to decide whether laws were constitutional in the case of *Marbury* v. *Madison* (1803). In the 1950s and 1960s the Supreme Court made a number of major rulings that overturned state laws in such areas as school segregation and apportionment of congressional districts. Critics charged that the Supreme Court was interfering in questions that the U.S. Constitution declared should be decided by legislatures.

▼ **The Concept Today:** While specific Supreme Court decisions still cause controversy, Americans generally accept the Court's right to judge the constitutionality of state and federal laws. In recent years the membership and rulings of the Supreme Court have been more conservative than during the 1960s.

most state governments had not reapportioned or redistributed their electoral districts to reflect population shifts. Over the years, many people in the United States had moved from rural to urban areas. Because the electoral districts were not redrawn, rural citizens were overrepresented and urban citizens were underrepresented. The Warren Court's decision in the case of *Baker* v. *Carr* (1962) declared that congressional districts had to be apportioned on the basis of "one person, one vote." This decision prevented the party in power from drawing district lines in unfair ways to give themselves more votes.[†] In *Reynolds* v. *Sims* (1964) the Supreme Court held that state legislative districts not based on the "one person, one vote" formula violated the equal protection clause of the Fourteenth Amendment.

Many of the Warren Court's decisions were controversial. Some people argued that the justices had gone too far in their "loose construction" of the Constitution. The opponents hoped to see more conservative judges appointed to the Court so that the new rulings could be overturned.

Effects of the Great Society

At first the Great Society seemed enormously successful. Opinion polls taken in 1964 after Johnson introduced his vision of the Great Society showed him to be more popular than Kennedy had been at a comparable point in his presidency. Pressed by Johnson, Congress had passed Kennedy's tax-cut bill early in 1964, and the state of the economy improved.

Soon, however, criticisms began to surface. New programs raised expectations, and disillusionment followed when not all demands could be met. Some Americans complained that too many of their tax dollars were being spent on poor people. Other critics argued that Great Society programs put too much authority in the hands of the federal government. Despite such criticisms, the number of people living in poverty in the United States was cut in half during the 1960s and early 1970s.

Michael Harrington, who wrote about poverty in his book *The Other America,* argued that the amount of money the government spent was not nearly enough. He wrote, "What was supposed to be a social war turned out to be a skirmish and, in any case, poverty won." Before long it was a war in Southeast Asia that began to consume the resources that Johnson had hoped to spend on his programs at home.

[†] Today each of the 435 seats in the United States House represents an average of 665,000 persons.

SECTION 2 REVIEW

Comprehension

1. *Key Terms* Define: (a) Great Society; (b) Volunteers in Service to America (VISTA); (c) Medicare; (d) Medicaid; (e) Immigration Act of 1965; (f) Miranda rule; (g) apportionment.

2. *Summarizing the Main Idea* Summarize the goals of Johnson's Great Society.

3. *Organizing Information* Create a graphic organizer listing and describing the Warren Court cases relating to protecting the rights of the accused.

Critical Thinking

4. *Analyzing Time Lines* Review the time line at the start of the section. Why do you think Johnson won the election in 1964?

5. *Demonstrating Reasoned Judgment* Do you think Johnson's Great Society programs were a success? Why or why not?

Writing Activity

6. *Writing an Expository Essay* Write an essay outlining Johnson's qualities as an effective legislator.

| 1961 Peace Corps established | 1961 Kennedy announces the Alliance for Progress | 1961 Bay of Pigs invasion | 1961 Berlin Wall erected | 1962 Cuban Missile Crisis | 1963 Limited Nuclear Test Ban Treaty signed | 1965 United States involvement in Vietnam intensifies |

1961   **1963**   **1965**

3 Foreign Policy in the Early 1960s

SECTION PREVIEW

Objectives

1 Describe the United States' role in the Bay of Pigs invasion.
2 Analyze the events leading to the building of the Berlin Wall and the Cuban Missile Crisis.
3 Outline the goals of Kennedy's Alliance for Progress and the Peace Corps.
4 Summarize Johnson's foreign policy.
5 *Key Terms* Define: Bay of Pigs invasion; Berlin Wall; Cuban Missile Crisis; Limited Test Ban Treaty; Alliance for Progress; Peace Corps.

Main Idea

President Kennedy acted boldly in response to a series of dramatic cold war crises in Cuba and Berlin. Johnson continued many of Kennedy's foreign policies.

Reading Strategy

Formulating Questions Before you read the section, write one question for each of the main headings. As you read, look for answers to those questions.

In his Inaugural Address, Kennedy proclaimed that the United States would do anything to uphold freedom throughout the world:

 "Let every nation know, whether it wishes us well or ill, that we shall pay any price, bear any burden, meet any hardship, support any friend, oppose any foe to assure the survival and the success of liberty.**"**

—*John F. Kennedy,* Inaugural Address

As President at the height of the cold war between the Soviet Union and the United States, Kennedy spoke boldly. Three crises during Kennedy's short time in office gave him the opportunity to prove that he would also act boldly.

The Bay of Pigs Invasion

Kennedy's first serious foreign crisis arose in Cuba, an island approximately 90 miles off the Florida coast. The United States had worried about Cuba ever since revolutionary Fidel Castro had seized power. Castro had overthrown the United States-backed dictator Fulgencio Batista in 1959. Some Cubans had supported Castro because he promised to improve the lives of poor people. Castro claimed that the poor were being exploited by wealthy Cubans and by United States companies operating in Cuba.

Once in power, Castro had taken over private property, including property owned by United States corporations in Cuba. The United States broke diplomatic relations with Cuba and refused to accept Castro as the country's legitimate leader. When Castro developed ties to the Soviet Union, United States officials began to fear that he could become a model for revolutionary upheaval throughout Latin America.

After Kennedy became President, he learned of a plan that President Eisenhower had approved in 1960. Under this plan, the Central Intelligence Agency (CIA) was training

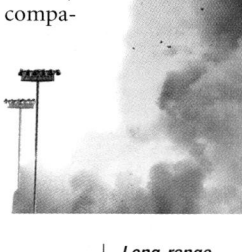

Long-range missiles capable of carrying nuclear explosives heightened cold war tension.

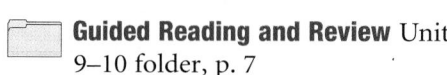
RESOURCE OPTIONS

Teaching Resources

📁 **Reproducible Lesson Plan** Lesson Plans folder, p. 148

📁 **Learning Styles Lesson Plan** Learning Styles Lesson Plans folder, p. 59

📁 **Big Idea Graphic Organizer** Big Idea Graphic Organizer folder, p. 120

📁 **Guided Reading and Review** Units 9–10 folder, p. 7

📁 **Key Documents** John F. Kennedy, Inaugural Address, Learning with Documents folder, p. 101

Foreign Policy in the Early 1960s

Objectives
You may wish to call students' attention to the objectives in the Section Preview. The objectives are reflected in the main headings of the section.

Bellringer
Ask students to think about the way the United States pursues relationships with other countries. Ask them to list what they think should be the goals of our foreign policy.

Reading Strategy
Formulating Questions Refer students to the Reading Strategy in the Section Preview. You may wish to have students use their questions to quiz each other as a way to review the section content.

LESSON PLAN
Connecting to the Main Idea

1. Focus The foreign policies of Presidents Kennedy and Johnson were grounded in the cold war. Ask how Kennedy reacted to Communist challenges. How did Johnson continue many of Kennedy's foreign policies?

2. Instruct Discuss the Bay of Pigs fiasco. Why was the United States concerned about Castro? Why did Kennedy agree to support the invasion? Have students make a time line of the Cuban Missile Crisis events on the chalkboard. Ask them to identify the most critical time period of the crisis.

Ask students to explain the underlying political goal of the Alliance for Progress and the Peace Corps. How successful were these programs?

3. Close President Kennedy acted boldly to maintain United States strength in the cold war, at times bringing the nation perilously close to war. President Johnson maintained a similar foreign policy.

Cuba and the United States

Since the Communist revolution in 1959, Cuban leader Fidel Castro has insisted that the small United States naval base in Guantanamo Bay on the eastern coast of Cuba is "a dagger plunged into Cuban soil." It has been there since 1903—five years after the end of the Spanish-American War—and some 70,000 United States military personnel and their families live and work at the base.

Cuban opponents of Castro. The training took place in Guatemala, a nearby Central American country. When it was complete, the Cubans planned to invade Cuba. Kennedy and his advisers expected that the Cuban people would use the opportunity to help overthrow Castro.

Resistance to the plan soon surfaced, however. When Senator J. William Fulbright, Democratic chairman of the Foreign Relations Committee, learned of the scheme, he called it an "endless can of worms." In a memorandum to the President, he declared:

AMERICAN VOICES "To give this activity even covert [secretive] support is of a piece with the hypocrisy and cynicism for which the United States is constantly denouncing [condemning] the Soviet Union in the United Nations and elsewhere. This point will not be lost on the rest of the world—nor on our own consciences. . . . The Castro regime is a thorn in the flesh; but it is not a dagger in the heart."

— *Senator J. William Fulbright*

Despite such reservations and those of some military leaders, Kennedy accepted the advice of the CIA, Joint Chiefs of Staff, and Secretary of Defense. He reluctantly pushed ahead.

The **Bay of Pigs invasion,** depicted in the map below, took place on April 17, 1961. It was a total disaster. An air strike failed to destroy Cuba's air power. Castro was therefore able to stop the United States-backed troops from coming ashore. When advisers urged Kennedy to use United States planes to provide air cover for the 1,500 Cuban soldiers, he refused. Rather than continue a hopeless effort, he chose simply to accept defeat.

The United States lost a great deal of prestige in the disastrous attack. To begin with, the invasion was clumsy and incompetent. Furthermore, the nation's support of an effort to overthrow another nation's government was exposed to the world. The United States faced anger from other countries in Latin America for violating agreements not to interfere in the Western Hemisphere. European leaders, who had high hopes for the new President, were concerned about the kind of leadership he planned to provide.

Bay of Pigs Invasion, 1961

CIA training camp for Cuban exile recruits

Large Cuban exile population from which Cuban Brigade recruited most of its invasion force

3. Cuban Brigade lands on two beaches, Apr. 17.

4. Cuban forces led by Fidel Castro sink two ships and capture 1,200 men of the invasion force, Apr. 17.

CIA advanced training base for more than 1,400 Cuban exiles

1. Six B26 bombers, flown by Cuban exiles, attack Cuban airfields and assist invasion force on beaches, Apr. 15.

2. Seven U.S. Navy ships and planes assist landing of Cuban Brigade but take no part in the fighting, Apr. 17.

CIA-constructed air base used to train Cuban exile pilots

Staging area for invasion force

U.S. naval forces
Transport ships with Cuban invasion troops
Flight path of B26 bombers
Cuban airfields bombed
Battle

Gulf of Mexico • Florida • Miami • Homestead • BAHAMAS • Bay of Pigs • Havana • CUBA • ATLANTIC OCEAN • HAITI • DOMINICAN REP. • JAMAICA • Puerto Rico • MEXICO • BR. HONDURAS • GUATEMALA • HONDURAS • Caribbean Sea • EL SALVADOR • Puerto Cabezas • NICARAGUA • PACIFIC OCEAN

0   200   400 Miles
0   200   400 Kilometers

UNITED STATES • CUBA • Area of main map

MAP Skills

This map traces the ill-fated Bay of Pigs invasion authorized by President Kennedy in 1961.
Location How does the map show why the United States would want to maintain friendly governments in Latin American nations?

The Berlin Crisis

Upset by the failure at the Bay of Pigs, Kennedy was now even more determined to respond firmly to growing Communist threats. When Soviet leader Nikita Khrushchev took action again to increase Soviet power, Kennedy responded boldly.

This time the issue was Germany. After World War II, the Allies had divided Germany into zones. The United States, Great Britain, the Soviet Union, and France each controlled one sector of the country. While the original intention was that the zones would be temporary, the lines had hardened as cold war tensions increased among the former Allies. In time the western regions had been combined into one, creating the nation of West Germany. The sector controlled by the Soviet Union became East Germany. The city of Berlin, although located completely inside East Germany, had also been divided among the World War II victors.

The Soviet effort to cut off access to Berlin in 1948 had failed as a result of President Truman's successful Berlin airlift. Now the Soviets made another effort to resolve problems in Berlin on their own terms. They demanded a peace treaty that would make the division of the city permanent. Their goal was to cut off the large flow of East Germans who frequently escaped to West Germany, particularly through Berlin.

Kennedy feared that the Soviet effort in Germany was part of a larger plan to take over the rest of Europe. Kennedy's first conversation with Khrushchev in Vienna, Austria, in June 1961 went poorly. When Khrushchev made a public ultimatum regarding Germany, Kennedy felt bullied by the Soviet leader.

Upon returning home, Kennedy decided to show the Soviets that the United States would not be intimidated. He asked Congress for a huge increase of more than $3 billion for defense. He doubled the number of young men being drafted into the armed services, and he called up reserve forces for active duty. At the same time, he sought over $200 million for a program to build fallout shelters across the country. He argued that the United States had to be prepared if the crisis led to nuclear war.

Kennedy appeared on television to tell the American people that West Berlin was "the great testing place of Western courage and will, a focal point where our solemn commitments . . . and Soviet ambitions now meet in basic confrontation." The United States, he said, would not be pushed around: "We do not want to fight—but we have fought before."

The Berlin Wall began as a series of concrete and barbed wire barriers. Over the years it grew into a heavily fortified wall separating West Berlin from East Berlin over a stretch of 28 miles. It also extended for 75 miles around West Berlin, separating it from the rest of East Germany. **Foreign Relations** Why was the Berlin Wall an appropriate symbol of the cold war?

The Soviets responded by building a wall in Berlin beginning in August 1961. The **Berlin Wall** became a somber symbol of the cold war. Still, by stopping the flow of East Germans to the West, the Soviet Union had found a way to avoid a showdown over East Berlin. Although the immediate crisis was over, the tensions of the cold war continued. Standing near the Berlin Wall in June 1963, Kennedy spoke to a cheering crowd saying that the United States "will risk its cities to defend yours because we need your freedom to protect ours." He concluded his speech with the rousing words, *"Ich bin ein Berliner."* I am a Berliner.

Main Idea
CONNECTIONS

How did President Kennedy respond to Khrushchev's ultimatum regarding Germany?

The Cuban Missile Crisis

Kennedy had a chance to restore his prestige in another crisis with Cuba. The Soviet Union, disturbed by the attempted invasion at the Bay of Pigs, had pledged to support Cuba. On October 16, 1962, photographs taken from a United States spy plane revealed that the Soviets were building missile bases on Cuban soil. Khrushchev may have been trying to bolster Soviet power by positioning missiles so close to the United States. The missiles did not alter the overall strategic balance between the United States and the Soviet Union. The Soviets could already inflict serious damage on the United States from bases within their own country. Nevertheless, Kennedy was convinced that the missiles in Cuba presented a direct challenge to which he must respond.

The President quickly convened his top advisers in a series of secret meetings. His brother Robert, serving as the nation's Attorney General, argued against an air strike to knock out the missiles. It seemed, he said, too much like the Japanese attack on Pearl Harbor that had started World War II. President Kennedy ordered United States forces on full alert. Bombers and missiles were armed with nuclear weapons. The fleet was ready to move. Soldiers were prepared to invade Cuba at a moment's notice.

Kennedy's advisers in the National Security Council realized the danger of the situation. Throughout this **Cuban Missile Crisis,** nuclear warheads on both sides were poised and ready for use. At one point former Secretary of State Dean Acheson joined the deliberations and declared that the United States had to knock out the Soviet missiles. He was then asked what would happen next. His response points out the very real danger of a local conflict escalating, or expanding, into a widespread war:

Acheson: I know the Soviet Union well. I know what they are required to do in the light of their history and their posture around the world. I think they will knock out our missiles in Turkey.

An NSC Adviser: Well, then what do we do?

Acheson: I believe under our NATO treaty . . . we would be required to respond by knocking out a missile base inside the Soviet Union.

Another Adviser: Then what do they do?

Acheson: That's when we hope that cooler heads will prevail, and they'll stop and talk.

After preparing the armed forces, Kennedy went on television on Monday, October 22, to tell the public about the missiles. During the

Cuban Missile Crisis, 1962

1. **Oct. 16** CIA provides President Kennedy with evidence of Soviet missile bases under construction in Cuba.

2. **Oct. 24** President Kennedy announces a naval "quarantine" of Cuba.

3. **Oct. 24** Soviet ships reverse course upon learning of the blockade.

4. **Oct. 26** Premier Khrushchev offers to withdraw missiles from Cuba in exchange for removal of the quarantine and a U.S. pledge not to invade Cuba.

5. **Oct. 27** President Kennedy accepts the offer. Soviet missile bases are dismantled by mid-November.

MRBM LAUNCH SITE 1
SAN CRISTOBAL, CUBA
23 OCTOBER 1962

Soviet missile bases
U.S. naval quarantine

MAP Skills Khrushchev, in what Robert Kennedy described as a "very long and emotional" letter, offered to withdraw the missile bases from Cuba (photograph) in exchange for assurances that the United States would not invade Cuba. *Location* What advantages and disadvantages would the missile bases have given the Soviet Union?

exploring TECHNOLOGY

1960s Bomb Shelter

- House
- Control panel (water, electricity, air)
- Geiger counter
- 550-gallon water tank
- Water heater
- Hot plates
- Air blower and filter
- 5 feet
- Wall (16-inch cement)
- Earth
- Earth
- Toilet
- Television Radio
- Tool storage
- Fire extinguisher
- Oil burner
- Food storage
- Generator
- Oxygen cylinders
- Escape hatch
- Battery charger and battery

After an atomic explosion, radioactive particles attach themselves to dust in the atmosphere, which continues to rain down upon the earth for as long as two weeks. Many Americans hoped they could survive a nuclear war in a basement fallout shelter. In the shelter shown above, an air filter protects people from breathing radioactive dust, and a Geiger counter tells them when the radioactivity outside has returned to a safe level. *Foreign Relations How were bomb shelters a symbol of the cold war era?*

speech he demanded that the Soviets remove the missiles. The United States, he said, would not shrink from the risk of nuclear war. He then announced that he had authorized a naval "quarantine" around Cuba. The quarantine would prevent the Soviets from transporting more missiles to Cuba. Kennedy was careful not to call the action a "blockade," because a blockade is an act of war.

For the next two days the two most powerful nations in the world stood teetering on the brink of disaster. The naval quarantine was put into effect on Wednesday, October 24. United States forces were ready to respond as soon as the line was crossed. On October 25 a Soviet

ship crossed the line and was stopped by the Navy. Because it was carrying only oil it was allowed to proceed. At the same time several other Soviet ships were headed toward Cuba. To everyone's great relief, the Soviet ships suddenly reversed their direction. Khrushchev had called the ships back, though work on the missile sites inside Cuba continued.

On October 26 Khrushchev sent Kennedy a long letter in which he pledged to remove the missiles if Kennedy promised that the United States would end the quarantine and stay out of Cuba. A second letter delivered the next day demanded that the United States remove its missiles from Turkey in exchange for the

About the Presidents

John Fitzgerald Kennedy (1961–1963) won rave reviews for the first three months of his presidency. He announced the formation of the Peace Corps to send volunteer workers to developing countries. His administration continued Eisenhower's Food for Peace Program, helping to solve the problem of agricultural surplus while winning friends abroad. He also launched the Alliance for Progress for Latin-American economic cooperation and social development. Kennedy's live press conferences only added to his glamour. Some commentators suggested that Kennedy's first 100 days might surpass FDR's. Then came the Bay of Pigs. The disaster cost him prestige abroad and the support of liberals at home. Source: Joseph L. Gardner, "John Fitzgerald Kennedy," *The American Heritage® Pictorial History of the Presidents of the United States,* vol. 2, 1968.

COMPARING PRIMARY SOURCES

THE COLD WAR

The United States and its allies continued to battle against Communist expansion in the 1960s.

For Civility in the Cold War	For Aggressiveness in the Cold War
"The issues called the cold war . . . must be met with determination, confidence, and sophistication. . . [C]hannels of communication should be kept open. . . . Our discussion, public or private, should be marked by civility; our manners should conform to our own dignity and power and to our good repute throughout the world."	"[I]t is really astounding that our government has never stated its purpose to be that of complete victory over the tyrannical forces of international communism. . . . And we need an official act, such as the resumption of nuclear testing, to show our own peoples and the other freedom-loving peoples of the world that we mean business."
Secretary of State Dean Rusk in a speech at the University of California, Berkeley, California, March 20, 1961	*Senator Barry Goldwater of Arizona in an address to the United States Senate, July 14, 1961*

ANALYZING VIEWPOINTS **What strategy did each of the speakers want to pursue during the cold war?**

withdrawal of Soviet missiles in Cuba. The United States accepted the terms of the first note and ignored the second. With that, the crisis was over. As Secretary of State Dean Rusk observed to President Kennedy, "We have won a considerable victory. You and I are still alive."

In the Cuban Missile Crisis, the world was closer than ever before to nuclear war. Far more powerful hydrogen bombs had replaced the first atomic weapons, and this was the closest the superpowers had come to using them. For a time, Kennedy emerged from the confrontation as a hero. He had stood up to the Soviets and shown that the United States would not be pushed around. His reputation, and that of the Democratic party, improved. This popular support helped with mid-term congressional elections just weeks away.

The Cuban Missile Crisis did lead to a number of efforts to reduce the risk of nuclear war. Once the confrontation was over, Kennedy and Khrushchev established a "hot line" between their two nations to allow for immediate discussion in the event of a future crisis. In the summer of 1963, they also signed the first nuclear

treaty since the development of the atomic bomb. The **Limited Test Ban Treaty** banned nuclear testing above the ground. By doing so it eliminated the radioactive fallout that was threatening to contaminate human, animal, and plant life. It still permitted underground testing, however, and scientists continued to create bigger and bigger bombs. Nonetheless, as Kennedy noted, the treaty was, "an important first step toward peace, a step toward reason, a step away from war."

The Alliance for Progress

The Limited Test Ban Treaty reflected Kennedy's hopes for a peaceful and better world. So too did his establishment of the **Alliance for Progress** in 1961. In addition to his bold stands against communism, Kennedy tried to promote "peaceful revolution" in developing countries around the world. Through his efforts, Kennedy hoped to encourage countries to ally themselves with the democratic countries of the West rather than with the Soviet Union.

To counter pro-Communist revolutionary movements, the United States wanted to help countries in Latin America, Asia, and Africa. To do so, Kennedy believed that modern transportation and communication systems and stable governments sympathetic to the United States were necessary. Two months after taking office, Kennedy called on all the people of the Western Hemisphere to join in a new Alliance for Progress or *Alianza para Progreso.* The Alliance would be a vast cooperative effort to satisfy the basic needs of the North, Central, and South American people for homes, work, land, health, and schools.

The task was a huge undertaking. The administration pledged $20 billion from the United States over ten years. The money would be spent to promote economic development and social reform and to sidetrack revolution before it occurred. All citizens in the Western Hemisphere, Kennedy declared, had "a right to social justice," and that included "land for the landless, and education for those who are denied

▶ RESOURCE OPTIONS

Teaching Resources

📁 **Comparing Primary Sources** On the Cold War, Units 9–10 folder, pp. 10–11

Media and Technology

 AmericanHeritage® CD-ROM

Presidents John F. Kennedy

Answer to . . .

Comparing Primary Sources Rusk favored encouraging civil dialogue among nations throughout the world; Goldwater sought a stated policy of armed aggression to crush communism.

education." Soon, however, Latin Americans began to question the benefits of the Alliance. Some viewed it simply as a tool of the United States to stop the spread of communism. Because of such doubts, the Alliance for Progress never lived up to Kennedy's expectations.

The Peace Corps

Kennedy's hope for a world in which nations worked together peacefully to solve problems was also reflected in his establishment of the Peace Corps in 1961. This new program would send volunteers abroad as educators, health workers, and technicians to help developing nations around the world.

Paul Cowan was typical of many **Peace Corps** volunteers. After graduating from college in 1963, he worked in the civil rights movement tutoring African American children in Maryland. In 1965 Cowan and his wife, Rachel, joined the Peace Corps and prepared to work in South America. After a training program at the University of New Mexico, they went to the city of Guayaquil in Ecuador to do community development work. Their job was to raise the standard of living in poor areas and to work with local governments to provide services such as garbage removal and clean water. Today Peace Corps volunteers throughout the world continue to work for Kennedy's vision of a peaceful world.

Johnson's Foreign Policy

The Alliance for Progress and the Peace Corps, while worthwhile efforts, could not erase the tensions of the cold war. When Johnson came to the presidency in 1963, he too faced threats of Communist expansion.

The Dominican Republic In 1965 Johnson heard that the military-backed government in the Dominican Republic, a Caribbean nation close to Cuba, had been attacked by rebels. Johnson feared that the disruption might endanger United States citizens living there. Arguing (wrongly, it turned out) that Communist elements were causing the disruption, Johnson sent 22,000 marines to the Dominican Republic. Their presence tipped the balance away from the rebels.

Peace Corps volunteers live alongside the citizens of the countries which they are sent to, doing the same work, eating the same food, and speaking the same language. This Peace Corps volunteer (left) is teaching sewing skills to women in Sri Lanka. *Culture How does the Peace Corps contribute to Kennedy's vision of a peaceful world?*

Answer to . . .

Viewing History Sample answer: By promoting understanding among nations and cultures.

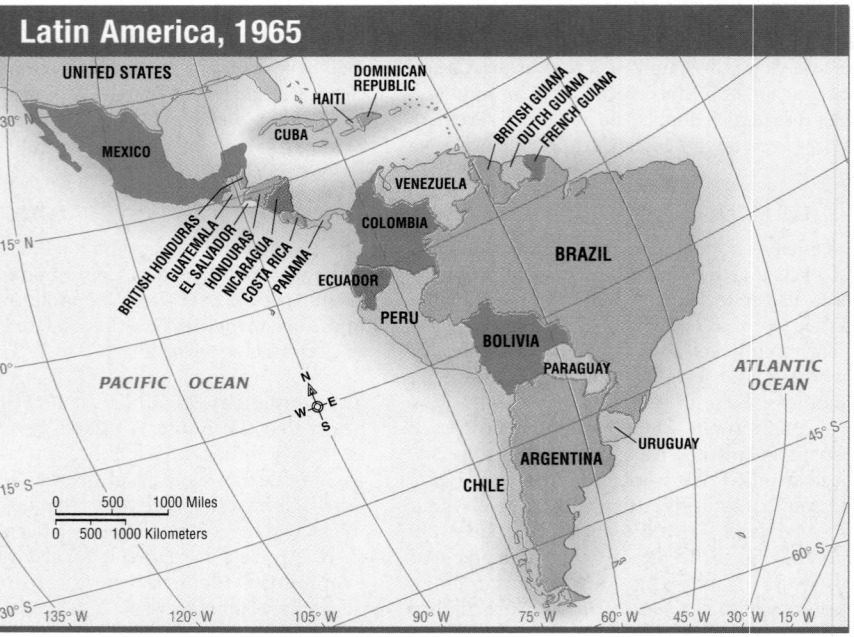

Latin America, 1965

President Johnson often felt annoyed when problems in Latin America took his attention away from domestic policy. *Location* In the context of the cold war, why did United States leaders consider it important to maintain a strong presence in this part of the world?

Within a few months a provisional government backed by the United States was put in place. Elections were held the following year.

Vietnam Johnson's administration was also deeply involved in the ongoing conflict between Communist North Vietnam and non-Communist South Vietnam in Southeast Asia. (You will read about this war in an upcoming chapter.) Like Kennedy, Johnson was determined to prevent the spread of communism. By 1963 about 16,000 military advisers were already in South Vietnam. The United States was also contributing economic aid to the South Vietnamese government. Johnson opposed more direct United States involvement in the war in his 1964 campaign for President. Before long, he could not tolerate simply letting the Communists take over South Vietnam. During 1965, American involvement in the conflict deepened as more and more troops and money were sent to prop up the South Vietnamese government.

SECTION 3 REVIEW

Comprehension

1. *Key Terms* Define (a) Bay of Pigs invasion; (b) Berlin Wall; (c) Cuban Missile Crisis; (d) Limited Test Ban Treaty; (e) Alliance for Progress; (f) Peace Corps.

2. *Summarizing the Main Idea* Was President Johnson's approach to foreign affairs similar to or different from Kennedy's? Explain your answer.

3. *Organizing Information* Create a time line of events leading up to and during the Cuban Missile Crisis.

Critical Thinking

4. *Analyzing Time Lines* Review the time line at the start of this section. Why was the Berlin Wall built in 1961?

5. *Determining Relevance* Why do you think Kennedy established the Alliance for Progress and the Peace Corps?

Writing Activity

6. *Writing an Expository Essay* Write an essay outlining the basic events leading up to and during the Bay of Pigs invasion.

RESOURCE OPTIONS

Teaching Resources

Quiz Units 9–10 folder, p. 8

Chapter Tests Forms A and B Chapter Test folder

Student Performance Pack

Guide to the Essentials Chapter 28, Section 3 (English and Spanish)

Standardized Test Preparation Handbook

Media and Technology

Guided Reading Audiotapes Chapter 28 Summary (English and Spanish)
Student Edition on Audiotape Chapter 28

Test Bank CD-ROM; Interactive Student Tutorial CD-ROM Chapter Test

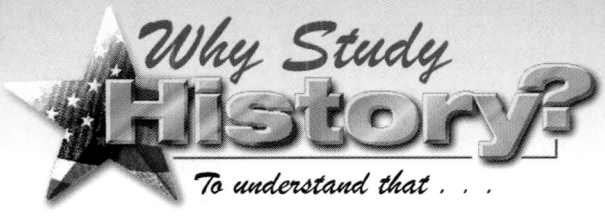

Why Study History?

To understand that . . .

Welfare Remains a Controversial Issue

Many Americans' views on social welfare programs have changed in the decades since President Johnson declared his war on poverty.

President Johnson passing out Medicare checks, 1968

Low-income preschoolers attend Head Start to ensure that they will be ready for grade school. VISTA volunteers live and work on Indian reservations and among the homeless to help poor people help themselves. These images of social welfare programs date from the 1960s, when the federal government launched a massive effort to help poor, elderly, and disabled Americans.

Today discussions of social welfare programs bring different images to many Americans' minds. Many Americans worry that the programs are not fighting poverty effectively. Why have Americans' views on social welfare changed?

The Impact Today

For a number of years, the Great Society programs initiated by President Johnson distributed aid to poorer Americans. Between 1970 and 1992, federal spending on social welfare programs increased dramatically, from about $1.5 billion to $1.3 trillion. Tens of millions of Americans received some form of assistance through programs such as Medicare and Medicaid, Head Start, food stamps, school lunches, low-income housing assistance, job training, and Aid to Families with Dependent Children.

By the 1980s, however, many Americans were angry about the large amounts of money spent on federal anti-poverty programs. Critics argued that federal spending had created a cycle of dependency in which generations of poor families chose to remain on public assistance rather than become self-sufficient.

Presidents Reagan and Bush shared this view. In the 1980s and early 1990s, they persuaded Congress to make cuts in Medicare and Medicaid, federal pensions, food stamps, and government-guaranteed home mortgages.

President Clinton promised to "end welfare as we have known it." Congress called for sweeping reforms as well. In 1996 Clinton signed the Personal Responsibility and Work Opportunity Reconciliation Act. This new welfare law made dramatic cuts in spending. It set a lifetime limit of five years of receiving welfare benefits and required welfare recipients to work in exchange for help.

Supporters of the welfare reform law saw the "welfare to work" provision as a way to encourage individual effort. Critics pointed out that many welfare recipients are single mothers who have no safe place to leave their children while at work. The full effects of the law will not be known for years.

The Impact on You

In your view, what responsibility, if any, does the government have toward the unemployed? (For example, should the government support people until they find work? Should it provide public jobs when other jobs are unavailable?) Present your conclusions in an essay. Give reasons to support your views.

Participant in state "welfare to work" program

RESOURCE OPTIONS

Teaching Resources

 Why Study History? Activity Welfare Remains a Controversial Issue, found in the Why Study History? folder, p. 29, provides an activity to help students better understand social welfare programs.

Media and Technology

AmericanHeritage® CD-ROM

Time Tour The Nation Today and Tomorrow: A Time of Turmoil *and* New Directions

 Prentice Hall United States History Video Collection™ Volume 20 *Post-War USA*

Why Study History?

Class Discussion

Discuss social welfare programs with the class. For a more thorough examination of the issue, see the activity folder in the Resource Options below.

ACTIVITY
STUDENT PARTICIPATION

Presenting Reports

Ask students to read the text. Then divide the class into three groups. Have each group find out about the costs and benefits of one of the following assistance programs, using the library, the Internet, or an almanac:

- **Medicaid (medical care)**
- **housing subsidies**
- **Head Start**

Have students present their findings in short reports.

Follow up Ask students to discuss the consequences of cutting off any of these support programs.

Using the Internet

Students can learn more about the welfare system by exploring links in the *America: Pathways to the Present* Web site at

http://www.Pathways.phschool.com

Assessment

See the Lesson Plans folder, pp. 24–27, for rubrics on assessing Class Participation Projects.

Key Terms

Students should refer to the definitions of key terms in the chapter to write sentences that show an understanding of social programs and cold war politics under Presidents Kennedy and Johnson.

Comprehension

1. In the legendary kingdom of Camelot, King Arthur wanted to transform Britain into a country where strength was used for the good of the people. Americans saw the Kennedy administration as symbolizing a similar idealism.

2. A tax cut to stimulate the economy and aid the poor indirectly, a direct aid program for the poor, and the space program.

3. He lacked a mandate and was unable to push his programs through Congress. He addressed the problem of poverty too late in his presidency.

4. The Warren Commission was formed to investigate the crime.

5. A tax cut combined with a cut in government spending, legislation to help the poor, education laws, Medicare and Medicaid, and immigration reform.

6. *Gideon* v. *Wainwright* upheld the right to free legal aid. *Escobedo* v. *Illinois* guaranteed defendants access to an attorney during questioning. *Miranda* v. *Arizona* held that a suspect must be informed of his or her rights before questioning.

7. The United States lost prestige; Kennedy tackled communist threats even more forcefully.

8. Khrushchev gave an ultimatum regarding the division of Germany; Kennedy responded by building up American defenses; the Soviets built the Berlin Wall.

9. To help people in developing nations and encourage democracy.

10. He was militantly anticommunist and ready to send troops to fight Latin American rebels backed by communists.

Chapter Summary

The major concepts of Chapter 28 are presented below. See also *Guide to the Essentials of American History* or *Interactive Student Tutorial CD-ROM,* which contains interactive review activities, time lines, helpful hints, and test practice for Chapter 28.

Reviewing the Main Ideas

Kennedy's New Frontier program and Johnson's Great Society program both aimed at bringing about domestic reforms in education, the economy, and poverty. The foreign policies of both Presidents were largely influenced by the dynamics of the cold war.

Section 1: The New Frontier

Before his assassination in 1963, President John F. Kennedy proposed a number of domestic programs to improve the economy and to address issues of inequality, including poverty and civil rights. Most of Kennedy's proposals were defeated in Congress.

Section 2: The Great Society

The goals of Johnson's Great Society program were to improve the economy, education, and the environment, as well as to offer government assistance to the poor.

Section 3: Foreign Policy in the Early 1960s

President Kennedy acted boldly in response to a series of dramatic cold war crises in Cuba and Berlin. Johnson continued many of Kennedy's foreign policies.

Americans' views on social welfare have changed since President Johnson declared war on poverty. Some Americans argue that instead of ending poverty, federal spending created a cycle of dependence.

Key Terms

For each of the terms below, write a sentence explaining how it relates to this chapter.

1. mandate
2. New Frontier
3. Great Society
4. Medicare
5. Medicaid
6. Immigration Act of 1965
7. Miranda rule
8. apportionment
9. Limited Test Ban Treaty
10. Peace Corps
11. Alliance for Progress

Comprehension

1. Explain why the Kennedy administration was compared to the Broadway musical *Camelot.*
2. What domestic programs did Kennedy propose?
3. Why was Kennedy's domestic program largely unsuccessful?
4. What actions were taken to investigate Kennedy's assassination?
5. What domestic programs did Johnson propose?
6. Describe three landmark decisions handed down by the Supreme Court under Earl Warren.
7. What were some of the consequences to the United States of the failed Bay of Pigs invasion?
8. Describe the Berlin Crisis of 1961.
9. Why did Kennedy establish the Peace Corps?
10. What was Johnson's approach to foreign policy?

Using Graphic Organizers

On a separate sheet of paper, copy the tree map below. Fill in at least two facts or main ideas for each of the headings on the tree.

Foreign Policy, 1961–1962		
Bay of Pigs	Berlin Crisis	Cuban Missile Crisis

Using Graphic Organizers

- Bay of Pigs: Castro stops American-backed troops from coming ashore; United States loses prestige.
- Berlin Crisis: JFK sees Berlin as testing ground for United States resolve; Soviets build Berlin Wall.
- Cuban Missile Crisis: JFK tries to regain respect; United States and Soviet Union come to brink of nuclear war; Soviets back down.

Analyzing Political Cartoons ▶

1. This cartoon was printed in November 1962. Examine the figures. (a) Who is the man on the left? (b) Who is the man on the right? (c) What are they trying to do?

2. Examine the box. What does the monster represent?

3. What is the overall message of the cartoon?

4. What event do you think inspired the cartoon?

Critical Thinking

1. *Applying the Chapter Skill* Interview an adult who remembers Kennedy's assassination. Ask him or her to describe their reaction to the news as well as the impact of the assassination on the nation.

2. *Making Comparisons* Describe the programs you would implement if you were to create a Great Society today. In what ways would they be similar to the programs of Johnson's Great Society?

3. *Predicting Consequences* How did the beliefs of Presidents Kennedy and Johnson about the spread of communism influence their foreign policy decisions?

4. *Drawing Inferences* In what ways did the Warren Court help to uphold the principle that a person is "innocent until proven guilty"?

"LET'S GET A LOCK FOR THIS THING"

NUCLEAR WAR

HERBLOCK
Nov. 1, 1962

INTERNET ACTIVITY

For your portfolio:
WRITE AN ARTICLE

Access Prentice Hall's *America: Pathways to the Present* site at **www.Pathways.phschool.com** for the specific URL to complete the activity. Additional resources and related Web sites are also available.

Write an article on Lyndon Johnson's presidency. Analyze the "American Covenant" portion of Lyndon Johnson's 1965 Inaugural Address. Identify the issues Johnson refers to in each paragraph. Then identify the Great Society policies or programs that address each issue. How did Johnson attempt to fulfill the American Covenant? Why did he say that America must end its isolationism?

ANALYZING DOCUMENTS ◀▶ INTERPRETING DATA

Turn to the graph of immigration on page 804.

1. In which year did the number of immigrants from Asia equal about 40,000? (a) 1960 (b) 1965 (c) 1966 (d) 1967

2. Which of the following groups experienced the greatest increases in immigration between 1965 and 1970? (a) Asians

(b) Northwestern Europeans (c) Other Europeans (d) North Americans

3. *Writing* How did the Immigration Act of 1965 affect overall immigration to the United States? How did it reflect the other liberal reforms of the era?

Connecting to Today

Identifying Central Issues Although the cold war has ended, the threat of nuclear war remains. Conduct research to learn more about nuclear disarmament and nuclear proliferation in the post-cold war era.

INTERNET ACTIVITY

Students' articles will vary. Students should connect the issues to each of the Great Society programs described in the chapter. Students should also show an understanding of Johnson's willingness to end isolationism in order to contain communism.

Analyzing Political Cartoons

1. (a) President Kennedy. (b) Premier Khrushchev. (c) Keep a monster from escaping from a box.
2. Nuclear war.
3. The threat of nuclear war is near and almost out of control; Kennedy and Khrushchev are having trouble preventing war.
4. The Cuban Missile Crisis.

Critical Thinking

1. Answers will vary. Students' questions should pursue themes introduced in the chapter.
2. Students may propose a variety of social welfare programs to combat such contemporary problems as homelessness and unemployment. They may mention that while the focus has shifted somewhat, many issues of the 1960s, such as civil rights and medical care, are still unresolved.
3. Both Kennedy and Johnson were convinced that communism needed to be fought wherever it appeared, or else the Soviet Union and its allies would take control of the world. Thus they were willing to send American troops to fight the forces of Ho Chi Minh in Vietnam.
4. It oversaw four decisions—*Mapp* v. *Ohio, Gideon* v. *Wainwright, Escobedo* v. *Illinois,* and *Miranda* v. *Arizona*—to protect the rights of the accused.

Interpreting Data

1. c
2. a
3. Sample answer: It eliminated some of the restrictions on immigration from places outside of northwestern Europe.

Connecting to Today

Answers will vary, but research results should be clearly presented.

The Civil Rights Movement, 1954–1968

Managing Time and Instruction

INSTRUCTION SUPPORT

These materials for instruction are provided for **each section** in the **Teaching Resources**. See **Units 9–10 folder for Enrichment Support:**

- Reproducible Lesson Plans in Lesson Plans folder ● Learning Styles Lesson Plans in Learning Styles Lesson Plans folder ● Big Idea Graphic Organizers in Big Idea Graphic Organizer folder
- Guided Reading and Review ● Quizzes ● Test Preparation Practice booklet

DAILY LESSON	ENRICHMENT SUPPORT
1 Leaders and Strategies (pp. 819–824)	• Biography, Thurgood Marshall, Units 9–10 folder, p. 23 • Visual Learning Activity, Passive Resistance, Learning with Documents folder, p. 71 • Comparing Primary Sources, On School Integration, Units 9–10 folder, pp. 24–25 • Literature Activity, SNCC Workers, Units 9–10 folder, pp. 26–27
2 The Struggle Intensifies (pp. 826–830)	• Skills for Life Activity, Units 9–10 folder, p. 28 • Primary Source Activity, Protecting the Freedom Riders, Learning with Documents folder, p. 35 • Biography, Sidney Poitier, found on **Resource Pro** • Lasting Impact Activity, The Lasting Impact of Nonviolent Confrontation, History's Lasting Impact folder, pp. 18–19
3 The Political Response (pp. 831–835)	• Key Documents, Martin Luther King, Jr., "I Have a Dream," Learning with Documents folder, p. 103 • Primary Source Activity, Registering to Vote in Mississippi, found on **Resource Pro** • Visual Learning Activity, A White House Demonstration, found on **Resource Pro**
4 The Challenge of Black Power (pp. 836–840)	• Literature Activity, Sins of the Father, found on **Resource Pro** • Critical Thinking Activity, Demonstrating Reasoned Judgment: How to Respond, found on **Resource Pro** • You Can Help Achieve Racial Equality, Why Study History? folder, p. 30

Running Out of Time?

- Use Tape 5, "The Upheaval of the Sixties, 1960–1975," from **Visions of America** videotapes series.
- Use Chapter 29 Summary from **Guide to the Essentials of American History (English and Spanish).**

Companion Web Site

The companion Web site offers online links for all chapter review activities. It also provides key content links and structured support for this chapter for both teachers and students.

http://www.Pathways.phschool.com

Teaching in the Information Age

Media and Technology

For the Student

Interactive Student Tutorial CD-ROM Chapter 29

Student Edition on Audiotape Chapter 29

American Heritage® CD-ROM

Guided Reading Audiotapes (English and Spanish) Chapter 29

For the Teacher

Resource Pro CD-ROM Chapter 29

Test Bank CD-ROM Chapter 29

Listening to Literature Audiotapes *Timeless Voices, Timeless Themes* "For My Children" by Colleen McElroy

Assessment Options

Chapter Test Forms A&B Test Bank CD-ROM booklet

Test Bank CD-ROM Chapter 29

Standardized Test Preparation Handbook

Block Scheduling

Pacing Suggestions

For 90-minute Blocks

- Teach sections 1 and 2 using Transparency B-9 and the Extended Class Periods Activity on p. 828.
- Teach sections 3 and 4 using the Big Idea Graphic Organizers from Teaching Resources and the Background note on p. 834 for class discussions.

Additional Resources

- Prentice Hall's **American History Block Scheduling Support File** covers over 40 major topics in American history.
- **Prentice Hall United States History Video Collection™** contains 20 videotapes covering American history from beginnings to present.
- **Visions of America Videotapes and Videodiscs**

Connections to American Literature

from Prentice Hall

America: Pathways to the Present "Letter from the Birmingham Jail" by Martin Luther King, Jr.

Prentice Hall Literature *Timeless Voices, Timeless Themes* "Who Burns for the Perfection of Paper" by Martín Espada, p. 979

Additional Resources

For the Student

Eyes on the Prize. PBS Video.

Howell Raines. *My Soul Is Rested: Movement Days in the Deep South Remembered.* Penguin, 1983 edition.

For the Teacher

Taylor Branch. *Parting the Waters: America in the King Years, 1954–1963.* Simon & Schuster, 1988.

Flora Davis. *Moving the Mountain: The Women's Movement in America Since 1960.* Simon & Schuster, 1991.

Prentice Hall brings into the classroom the vast archives and scholarship of the nation's premier American history magazine. See "From the Archives of American Heritage®" and "About the Presidents" teaching notes in this chapter.

 History Alive!

Teacher's Curriculum Institute, in partnership with Prentice Hall, provides unique materials that engage students with diverse learning styles. See History Alive!® unit on The Civil Rights Movement.

 Student Performance Pack

Ensures success in the three critical areas of Reading, Test Taking, and English Language Development with the following materials:
- Guide to the Essentials of American History in English and Spanish
- Guided Reading Audiotapes in English and Spanish
- Interactive Student Tutorial CD-ROM
- Test Preparation Handbook
- Test Preparation Practice booklet

Introducing the Chapter

The 1960s were a time of great progress and great frustration for African Americans. Through nonviolent protests and an extremely focused civil rights struggle, African Americans ended institutional segregation and secured voting rights in the South. Lack of progress on economic issues, especially in urban areas, however, drove some to vent their anger through bitter violence.

Themes in American History

The theme for this chapter, Diversity, is listed at the beginning of this unit. An alternate theme for the chapter is Government. To teach this unit thematically, you may wish to use The Nation After World War II folder in American History Block Scheduling Support.

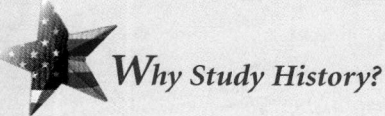

*W*hy Study History?

Have students explore suggested ways of connecting the past to the present on page 841.

Answer to . . .

Viewing History Students should use this question as an aid in reading the chapter. The marchers are committed to nonviolent change. They are determined, but perhaps somewhat apprehensive about the violence that has been directed against them.

CHAPTER 29
The Civil Rights Movement

1954–1968

CHAPTER FOCUS

*T*his chapter examines the civil rights movement of the 1960s, the historic battle to desegregate America and win equal treatment for African Americans. Challenged by violent opposition and internal divisions, the civil rights movement nonetheless won significant victories on the road to freedom.

The Why Study History? page at the end of this chapter explores how far the United States has come in achieving racial equality, and how far the nation still has to go.

▲
VIEWING HISTORY
Civil rights leader Martin Luther King, Jr. (center) leads a protest march from Selma to Montgomery, Alabama, in 1965. *Culture* **Describe the attitude of the marchers.**

 RESOURCE OPTIONS

Teaching Resources

 Big Idea Graphic Organizer folder
Graphic summary of the main idea of the chapter.

 Learning Styles Lesson Plans folder
Alternate lesson plans for diverse learning styles for each chapter.

Media and Technology

AmericanHeritage® CD-ROM
Time Tour The Nation Today and Tomorrow: A Time for Turmoil

◉ **Prentice Hall United States History Video Collection™** Volume 20
Post-War USA

1954 Brown v. Board of Education strikes down "separate but equal"	1955 Bus boycott in Montgomery, Alabama, begins	1957 Southern Christian Leadership Conference founded	1960 Student Nonviolent Coordinating Committee founded

1954   **1956**   **1958**   **1960**

1 Leaders and Strategies

SECTION PREVIEW

Objectives

1. Explain how the activities of existing civil rights organizations laid the groundwork for the movement of the 1960s.
2. Describe the philosophy that Martin Luther King, Jr., brought to the movement.
3. Explain why some students formed their own civil rights organization.
4. *Key Terms* Define: interracial; Congress of Racial Equality (CORE); Southern Christian Leadership Conference (SCLC); nonviolent protest; Student Nonviolent Coordinating Committee (SNCC).

Main Idea

The civil rights movement of the 1960s consisted of many separate groups, whose leaders and methods differed while sharing the same goal of securing equal rights for all Americans.

Reading Strategy

Problem Solving Civil rights workers faced violence, even death, from opponents of change. List techniques you might use when confronted with this problem. Then read on to see what actually happened.

The civil rights movement of the 1950s and 1960s was a grassroots effort of ordinary citizens determined to end racial injustice in the United States. Although no central organization directed the movement, several major groups formed to share information and coordinate civil rights activities. Each of the groups described in this section had its own goals, priorities, and strategies. In different ways, they all helped to focus the energies of thousands of Americans committed to securing civil rights for all citizens.

Laying the Groundwork

Although the civil rights movement spread nationwide in the 1960s, the struggle had been going on for decades. World War II spotlighted much of the racism that existed throughout the United States.

In the postwar era, several landmark events occurred as both African Americans and white Americans reacted against obvious injustices in the South. These events set the stage for the civil rights battles of the 1960s.

As you read previously, one turning point was the Supreme Court's 1954 decision in the Topeka, Kansas, case of *Brown* v. *Board of Education*. The Court's ruling struck down the doctrine of "separate but equal" that had kept African Americans in segregated—and usually inadequate—public schools. Despite resistance, the integration of public schools moved forward from then on.

Civil rights marchers drew the nation's attention to issues of racial equality.

NAACP Behind the case of *Brown* v. *Board of Education* was the National Association for the Advancement of Colored People (NAACP), one of the oldest civil rights organizations in the United States. In 1909, a number of people

RESOURCE OPTIONS

Teaching Resources

📁 **Reproducible Lesson Plan** Lesson Plans folder, p. 149

📁 **Big Idea Graphic Organizer** Big Idea Graphic Organizer folder, p. 121

📁 **Guided Reading and Review** Units 9–10 folder, p. 15

📁 **Biography** Thurgood Marshall, Units 9–10 folder, p. 23

Media and Technology

🦅 **AmericanHeritage® CD-ROM**

Time Tour The Nation Today and Tomorrow: A Time of Turmoil

SECTION 1

Leaders and Strategies

Objectives

You may wish to call students' attention to the objectives in the Section Preview. The objectives are reflected in the main headings of the section.

Bellringer

Ask students to think of ways that people can protest without resorting to violence. What advantages do these tactics have?

Reading Strategy

Problem Solving Refer to the Reading Strategy in the Section Preview. You may wish to offer a sample answer to the problem offered there before students give their answers.

LESSON PLAN

Connecting to the Main Idea

1. **Focus** Explain that the civil rights movement was not a monolithic organization under the sway of a single leader. The groups were as diverse as the people in the movement. Ask students to note in what ways the movement was diverse and in what ways it was united.
2. **Instruct** Ask students to read the first quotation by Martin Luther King, Jr., under the subheading "SNCC Breaks Away." Then discuss these questions: Do you agree with King's view that the failure to fight oppression made African Americans guilty of cooperating with evil? What values and beliefs did King hold that caused him to view the struggle this way?
3. **Close** The civil rights movement was made up of many groups that differed on tactics but agreed on the urgent need to halt segregation. As the next section describes, the first battle lines were drawn on the whites-only buses and lunch counters of the South.

BACKGROUND

Biography

In a 1955 meeting in Atlanta, Georgia, NAACP leaders met with African American leaders from southern states to discuss the *Brown v. Board of Education* ruling. Seated at the table (second from left) is Thurgood Marshall, NAACP chief counsel. **Government** What was the goal of the NAACP?

Main Idea CONNECTIONS

What approach did the NAACP take toward ending discrimination?

associated with the Niagara Movement founded this **interracial** organization, one with both African Americans and white Americans as members.

The NAACP worked to secure full legal equality for all Americans and to remove barriers that kept them from voting. W.E.B. Du Bois, a prominent African American scholar, was a founding member. He summarized the NAACP's goals in a memo to the organization's board of directors:

AMERICAN VOICES

❝The main object of this association is to secure for colored people, and particularly for Americans of Negro descent, free and equal participation in the democracy of modern culture. This means the clearing away of obstructions to such participation, effort toward fitting these people for this participation, and it means also the making of a world democracy in which all men may participate.❞

—*W.E.B. Du Bois*

Du Bois, who was the first African American to receive a doctoral degree from Harvard University, served as director of pub-

licity and research. He also edited the NAACP magazine, *Crisis*.

From the start, the NAACP focused on challenging the laws that prevented African Americans from exercising their full rights as citizens. The group worked for new laws and brought lawsuits.

In the 1920s and 1930s, lynching was still a threat to African Americans, particularly in the South. Working to end such violence, the NAACP succeeded in getting two anti-lynching bills passed by the House of Representatives in the 1930s. Southern leaders in the Senate prevented the bills from becoming law, but the NAACP kept the issue of lynching in the public eye.

The NAACP was more successful in its lawsuits that challenged segregation laws. In the 1920s and 1930s, it had won a number of legal battles in the areas of housing and education. The *Brown* decision on school segregation was another major legal victory.

The NAACP appealed mainly to educated, middle- and upper-class African Americans and some liberal white Americans. It emphasized achieving legal equality for all races. Critics, however, charged that it was out of touch with the basic issues of economic survival faced by many African Americans.

National Urban League One organization that took on the economics issue was the National Urban League, founded in 1911. It sought to assist people moving to major American cities. It helped African Americans moving out of the South find homes and jobs and made sure that they received fair treatment at work.

Urban League workers looked for migrant families on ship docks and at train stations. They placed them in apartments they had inspected. They also insisted factory owners and union leaders teach African American workers the skills that could lead to better jobs.

CORE Founded by pacifists in 1942, the **Congress of Racial Equality (CORE)** was dedicated to bringing about change through peaceful confrontation. It, too, was interracial, with both African American and white members. During World War II, CORE had organized demonstrations against segregation in

Answer to . . .

Viewing History To secure legal equality.
Main Idea Connections It challenged unfair laws and strove to get new legislation passed.

cities including Baltimore, Chicago, Denver, and Detroit.

In the years after World War II, CORE director James Farmer worked without pay in order to keep the organization alive. The growing interest in civil rights in the 1950s gave him a new base of support and allowed him to turn CORE into a national organization. It would play a major role in the confrontations that lay ahead.

The Philosophy of Nonviolence

The successful Montgomery bus boycott led to the founding of a new and significant civil rights organization. In 1957 Martin Luther King, Jr., and other African American clergymen organized the **Southern Christian Leadership Conference (SCLC).** SCLC introduced the concept of **nonviolent protest,** a peaceful way of protesting against policies. Nonviolent protesters did not resist even when attacked by opponents.

In its first official statement, SCLC set out this principle:

AMERICAN VOICES ❝To understand that nonviolence is not a symbol of weakness or cowardice, but as Jesus demonstrated, nonviolent resistance transforms weakness into strength and breeds courage in the face of danger.❞

—*SCLC statement*

SCLC shifted the focus of the civil rights movement to the South. Earlier organizations had been dominated by northerners. Now southern African American church leaders moved into the forefront of the struggle for equal rights. Among them, Martin Luther King, Jr., became a national figure.

Martin Luther King, Jr.

AMERICAN BIOGRAPHY When the Montgomery bus boycott began, Martin Luther King, Jr., was a young, small-town Baptist preacher. Within a few years he would become one of the most loved and admired—and also one of the most hated—people in the United States. King became not only a leader in the African American civil rights movement but also a symbol of nonviolent protest for the entire world.

Born in Atlanta, Georgia, in 1929, King grew up amid all the symbols of southern segregation—separate schools, stores, churches, and public places. Though he had white playmates as a child, that ended when he reached school age. King's father, Martin Luther King, Sr., and his grandfather were both prominent and respected Baptist preachers. He was raised with a sense of personal pride and dignity that went beyond the limitations of segregation.

Even in high school, young Martin was an inspiring and eloquent public speaker. Graduating early from high school, he went to Morehouse College in Atlanta. He earned a divinity degree at Crozer Theological Seminary in Pennsylvania, then a doctorate in theology at Boston University in 1955. There he met and married Coretta Scott.

 On the night of April 26, 1960, burning crosses—the symbol of the Ku Klux Klan—appeared in the front yards of many African American residents of Atlanta. Above, Martin Luther King, Jr., calmly removes a cross from his lawn as his young son looks on. *Culture* How did King move to the forefront of the civil rights movement?

Graphing the Main Idea

To make sure students understand the main idea of this section, you may wish to use the tree map graphic organizer below.

Tell students that a tree map records a main idea, main topics, and supporting details. Ask students to use it to record the groups, leaders, and methods of civil rights movement.

Teaching Tip A template for this graphic organizer can be found in the Color Transparencies, G-3.

▼ BACKGROUND

A Diverse Nation

After the death of Martin Luther King, Jr., in 1968, his widow, Coretta Scott King (b. 1927), remained active in various civil rights issues. In the 1993 edition of her book, *My Life with Martin Luther King, Jr.,* she wrote: "One reason so many young people became involved in the Movement was television. The Movement began in Montgomery just when the electronic era was beginning. Students were educated about social issues through the nightly news."

COMPARING PRIMARY SOURCES

Integrating Schools

In parts of the Deep South, the battle for equal rights continued to be fought at the nation's schoolhouse doors each September, long after the Supreme Court ordered schools to desegregate in 1954.

For School Integration	Against School Integration
"Nearly nine years have elapsed since the Supreme Court ruled that state laws requiring or permitting segregated schools violate the Constitution. . . . Since that time it has become increasingly clear that neither violence nor legalistic measures will be tolerated as a means of thwarting court-ordered desegregation." —*President John F. Kennedy, message to Congress, February 28, 1963*	"I draw the line in the dust and toss the gauntlet before the feet of tyranny and I say segregation today, segregation tomorrow, segregation forever." —*Alabama governor George Wallace, Inaugural Address, January 14, 1963*

ANALYZING VIEWPOINTS **How do these two speeches, made about a month apart, reflect the divisions in the country?**

It was at Morehouse College that Martin Luther King, Jr., was first influenced by the beliefs of Mohandas K. Gandhi. Gandhi had been a leader in India's long struggle to gain independence from Great Britain, which finally succeeded in 1947.

Gandhi preached a philosophy of nonviolence as the only way to achieve victory against much stronger foes. Those who fought for justice must peacefully refuse to obey unjust laws, Gandhi taught. They must remain nonviolent, regardless of the violent reactions such peaceful resistance might provoke. The tactic required tremendous poise and courage.

King's first job as pastor was in Montgomery, Alabama. Though only 27 years old, he was chosen to lead the year-long boycott of the city's segregated bus system that began in December 1955.

Martin Luther King, Jr. (1929–1968)

Once the Montgomery boycott ended, King began training volunteers for what they might expect in the months ahead. Films, songs, and skits showed Gandhi's activities and demonstrated the success of passive resistance in India. Bus boycotters were advised to follow 17 rules for maintaining a nonviolent approach as they prepared to ride newly desegregated vehicles through the South. These are some of those rules:

AMERICAN VOICES ❝Pray for guidance and commit yourself to complete nonviolence in word and action as you enter the bus. . . . Be loving enough to absorb evil and understanding enough to turn an enemy into a friend. . . . If cursed, do not curse back. If pushed, do not push back. If struck, do not strike back, but evidence love and goodwill at all times. . . . If another person is being molested, do not arise to go to his defense, but pray for the oppressor and use moral and spiritual force to carry on the struggle for justice. . . . Do not be afraid to experiment with new and creative techniques for achieving reconciliation and social change. . . . If you feel you cannot take it, walk for another week or two [rather than ride the bus].❞

—*Leaflet distributed in black churches*

For his role in the Montgomery boycott, King gained national prominence. For the next 11 years, he would play a key role in almost every major civil rights event. His work earned him the Nobel Peace Prize in 1964.

King's opponents would attack him physically and verbally, and he would often go to jail for his beliefs. Death threats were frequent. As King had sometimes predicted, he did not live to see the success of the movement. He was assassinated in Memphis, Tennessee, in April 1968, at the age of 39.[†] King's accused killer, a white southerner named James Earl Ray, was convicted in 1969 and sentenced to 99 years in prison. [††] ■

[†] To honor the slain leader, Congress voted to make King's birthday a federal holiday beginning in 1986. It is observed on the third Monday of January each year.

[††] Ray confessed to the crime, but three days later retracted his story. In the 1990s the King family, convinced that Ray was not the killer and hoping to find the real one, supported his attempt to have the case reopened. Ray died in prison in 1998. Later that year the Justice Department began a review of the case.

▶ RESOURCE OPTIONS

Teaching Resources

📁 **Comparing Primary Sources** On School Integration, Units 9–10 folder, pp. 24–25

Answer to . . .

Comparing Primary Sources
Kennedy expresses frustration at the slow course of change in the area of school integration; Wallace symbolizes the intransigence of the South.

SNCC Breaks Away

Nonviolent protest was a practical strategy in the civil rights struggle. It also represented a moral philosophy.

"To accept passively an unjust system is to cooperate with that system; thereby the oppressed become as evil as the oppressor," King said. "Noncooperation with evil is as much a moral obligation as is cooperation with good." King's message was that African Americans would ultimately win. At the same time, his philosophy of nonviolence won the support of many white Americans for the growing movement for change.

An offshoot of SCLC took a somewhat different approach. The **Student Nonviolent Coordinating Committee,** usually known as **SNCC** (pronounced "snick"), was originally part of SCLC. It began in 1960 at a meeting in Raleigh, North Carolina, for students active in the struggle. SCLC executive director Ella Baker thought that the NAACP and SCLC were not keeping up with the demands of young African Americans. She wanted to give them a way to play an even greater role in the civil rights movement.

More than 200 students showed up for the first SNCC meeting. Most came from southern communities, but some northerners attended as well.

Baker delivered the opening address. "The younger generation is challenging you and me," she told the adults present. "They are asking us to forget our laziness and doubt and fear, and follow our dedication to the truth to the bitter end."

Martin Luther King spoke next to the young audience, calling the civil rights movement "a revolt against the apathy and complacency of adults in the Negro community. . . ."

At the end of the meeting, the participants organized a temporary coordinating committee. A month later, student leaders met with Baker and other SCLC and CORE leaders and voted to maintain their independence from other civil rights groups. By the end of the year, the Student Nonviolent Coordinating Committee was a permanent and

separate organization. It was interracial at first, though that changed in later years.

SNCC filled its own niche in the American civil rights movement. It gave young activists a chance to make decisions about priorities and tactics. It also shifted the focus of the civil rights movement away from church leaders alone. SNCC also sought more immediate change, while most of the older organizations were committed to gradual change.

One of SNCC's most influential leaders was Robert Moses, a former mathematics teacher in Harlem. As the civil rights movement developed, he wanted to be involved. He first went to work for SNCC in Atlanta, and later headed for Mississippi to encourage other African American students to come to SNCC meetings.

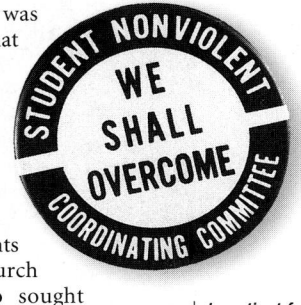

Impatient for change, young NAACP members founded their own activist group, SNCC.

Police arrested SNCC member Eddie Brown at a 1962 protest in Albany, Georgia. *Culture How do Brown's actions reflect the philosophy of nonviolent protest?*

Customize for
Less Proficient Readers

Have students list the key organizations and people mentioned in this section and describe the contributions of each to the civil rights movement.

BACKGROUND

Biography

The turmoil of the 1960s gave rise to various protest movements. It also sparked sharp reactions against those movements. George Wallace (1919–1998), governor of Alabama and presidential candidate, galvanized the angriest elements of that reaction during the 1960s and early 1970s. In 1963, Wallace stood in a doorway at the University of Alabama at Tuscaloosa, blocking entrance to the school's first African American students. Later he turned his defiant rhetoric on the counterculture, antiwar protesters, and others. Shot and paralyzed in an assassination attempt during his 1972 run for the presidency, Wallace returned to Alabama where he served as governor again in the 1980s. This time, however, he used his position to build bridges to the state's African Americans, apologizing, sometimes tearfully, for his earlier support of segregation, and appointing African American officials.

RESOURCE OPTIONS

Media and Technology

 Prentice Hall United States History Video Collection™ Volume 20
Post-War USA

🎧 **Listening to Literature** Colleen McElroy, "For My Children"

Answer to . . .

Viewing History He remains nonviolent even when police officers are carrying him away.

Answers to
SECTION 1 REVIEW

1. (a) interracial, see p. 820; (b) CORE, see p. 820; (c) SCLC, see p. 821; (d) nonviolent protest, see p. 821; (e) SNCC, see p. 823.

2. World War II spotlighted racism; *Brown* v. *Board of Education* struck down segregation; organizations such as the NAACP, CORE, and SCLC had been working for equal rights.

3. NAACP: interracial organization with W.E.B. Du Bois as a founding member; worked primarily for full legal equality and for the removal of voting barriers; appealed to upper middle class Americans. National Urban League: helped African Americans find homes and jobs in cities; encouraged businesses and unions to teach African Americans skills. CORE: interracial organization; main tactic was peaceful confrontation; headed by James Farmer. SCLC: organization of clergymen founded by Martin Luther King, Jr.; introduced concept of nonviolent protest; shifted focus of movement to South.

4. Sample answer: The NAACP did not meet the needs of poor migrant workers and farmers, whose plight began to be recognized only in later years.

5. SNCC was made up of young people, and was much more radical than the SCLC.

6. Agendas will vary but should be supported with facts from the section.

Answer to . . .

Viewing History It provided a place for young activists outside the church to make decisions about priorities and tactics.

Gitlin went on to describe Moses's style of oratory:

AMERICAN VOICES ❝He liked to make his points with his hand, starting with palm downturned, then opening his hand outward toward his audience, as if delivering the point for inspection, nothing up his sleeve. The words seemed to be extruded [thrust forth], with difficulty, out of his depths. What he said seemed earned. . . . To teach his unimportance, he was wont [accustomed] to crouch in the corner or speak from the back of the room, hoping to hear the popular voice reveal itself.❞

—*Todd Gitlin*

One young civil rights worker faced resistance from a most difficult source: her own family. Anne Moody joined the NAACP in college in Mississippi and worked with CORE and SNCC. She endured humiliation, physical violence, and jailing for her participation in civil rights protests. But the toughest test came when her brother was beaten and nearly lynched in her hometown of Centreville, Mississippi. The local sheriff warned that Moody should never return home. Her frightened mother begged her to stop her civil rights work, and her sister angrily told her that her work was threatening the life of every African American in Centreville. Still, Moody continued. She was one of many who would sacrifice deeply for her beliefs.

VIEWING HISTORY

Anne Moody and her family suffered terribly because of her civil rights activities. *Diversity* What niche did SNCC fill in the civil rights movement?

While Martin Luther King, Jr., spoke with eloquence and passion, Moses was more soft spoken. He took time to gather his thoughts, and then he spoke slowly. Todd Gitlin, a white student activist leader, later noted that Moses was loved and trusted "precisely because he seemed humble, ordinary, accessible."

SECTION 1 REVIEW

Comprehension

1. *Key Terms* Define: (a) interracial; (b) Congress of Racial Equality (CORE); (c) Southern Christian Leadership Conference (SCLC); (d) nonviolent protest; (e) Student Nonviolent Coordinating Committee (SNCC).

2. *Summarizing the Main Idea* What events of the 1940s and 1950s laid the groundwork for the civil rights movement of the 1960s?

3. *Organizing Information* Make a two-column chart showing the prominent civil rights organizations working in the early 1960s and their goals and/or characteristics.

Critical Thinking

4. *Analyzing Time Lines* Review the time line at the start of the section. How would you explain the long gap in time between the founding of the NAACP and the start of CORE and SCLC?

5. *Making Comparisons* In what important ways did SNCC and its goals differ from the SCLC?

Writing Activity

6. *Writing an Expository Essay* As a student in the 1960s you have been asked to help organize a local chapter of SNCC. Write an agenda for organizing such a group, explaining how you would recruit members and work for change.

 RESOURCE OPTIONS

Teaching Resources

📁 **Literature Activity** SNCC Workers, Units 9–10 folder, pp. 26–27

📁 **Quiz** Units 9–10 folder, p. 16

Student Performance Pack

✦ **Guide to the Essentials** Chapter 29, Section 1 (English and Spanish)

Using Autobiography and Biography

Autobiography and biography are two major sources of evidence about a historical period. An autobiography is an account of a person's life as written by that person. A biography is an account of a person's life written by someone else.

Both sources offer clues—revealed in the narrative—of what society was like at the time the person lived. As well as describing the person's life, an autobiography or biography also describes the kind of conditions under which people lived, how they reacted to those conditions, and the attitudes and values prevailing at that time.

An autobiography can be especially helpful in capturing a moment in time because it is a firsthand account. But both autobiography and biography must be judged on their reliability. How objective is the writer about the facts presented? Do the facts seem colored by the writer's desire to cast the person profiled in a good or bad light? Or do the facts seem straightforward and believable?

Use the following steps to analyze an excerpt from *And the Walls Came Tumbling Down*, by Ralph Abernathy. Abernathy was a civil rights leader who worked with Martin Luther King, Jr., in organizing the Montgomery bus boycott and who later founded SCLC with King.

1. *Identify the kind of account and the subject of the profile.* (a) Is the excerpt from an autobiography or a biography? How can you tell? (b) What events is Abernathy describing? How can you tell?

2. *Analyze the source's reliability as historical evidence.* (a) How well acquainted is the writer with the facts he describes? (b) What is his point of view toward them? (c) How accurate do you judge his report to be? Explain.

3. *Search for clues that tell what the historical period was like.* (a) What groups are in conflict and why? (b) What can you learn about the level of violence that exists in some parts of society? (c) What is the attitude of certain whites to the struggle? (d) What is the attitude of the African Americans involved?

TEST FOR SUCCESS

What are the advantages and the drawbacks of using autobiography as a historical reference source?

> ❝Though we knew that our people could follow the path of nonviolence while in control of themselves, we also knew that in moments of sudden anger almost anybody could be tempted to strike back—and one injured policeman could nullify the work of weeks. So we took particular care to teach our people to count to ten before they responded in any way to verbal or physical abuse.
>
> We also showed them how to march along bent over, elbows guarding their stomachs and hands covering their ears and temples. We devised this technique for use in the event that we were bombarded with rocks and bottles while demonstrating. We also taught a modified version of the same maneuver for use while being beaten with fists or billy clubs.
>
> Then, too, we told everyone to go limp when anyone laid hands on them during an arrest. In the first place, it signaled to the arresting officer that he would encounter no active resistance; hence there was no need for excessive force. But equally important, a limp body was harder to handle, took more time to haul into a paddy wagon, and therefore limited the efficiency of the police. . . .
>
> It is surprising how many of the situations we would later face were actually anticipated and discussed in these Saturday workshops. By the time we reached the end of our years together, Martin and I had seen people assaulted with fists, clubs, bottles, and rocks and were moved by the manner in which they endured such abuse. Almost without exception they behaved exactly as we taught them to behave. They protected themselves from the full force of blows, but they didn't strike back, even when their lives were endangered; and for the most part they replied with courtesy and charity.❞
>
> —And the Walls Came Tumbling Down,
> *the Rev. Ralph David Abernathy, 1989*

RESOURCE OPTIONS

Teaching Resources

Skills for Life Activity Units 9–10 folder, p. 28, provides students with further practice in this skill with a passage written by Elizabeth Dole in 1988.

SKILLS FOR LIFE

Historical Evidence

Using Autobiography and Biography

Focus Use autobiography and biography as sources of clues about society at a given time.

Instruct Ask students to work through the questions and discuss their responses. Then have groups use the library to choose a biography and an autobiography of an important figure in American history. Suggest that they focus on one important event in the person's life. Ask them to use the questions in the feature as a guide to decide which source is more reliable.

Extend See the Skills for Life Activity in the Resource Options below.

Answers

1. (a) An autobiography; the use of the first person. (b) The events surrounding the nonviolent struggle for civil rights; his references to nonviolence, arrests, and Martin [Luther King, Jr.].

2. (a) He was on the scene, training the protesters in nonviolent tactics. (b) He operates from a firm belief in the justice of the civil rights cause. (c) Quite accurate; he was an eyewitness, his tone is matter-of-fact, and his presentation does not seem exaggerated.

3. (a) Whites who resist the civil rights movement and African Americans who support it. (b) Physical attacks with billy clubs, fists, rocks, and bottles attest to a high degree of violence. (c) They are willing to act violently in the midst of it. (d) They are willing to withstand physical abuse to further their cause.

TEST FOR SUCCESS

Sample answer: Autobiography provides a firsthand account, but may be unreliable.

1960	1961	1962	1963	1963
CORE holds lunch counter sit-ins	Freedom Riders challenge segregation on interstate buses	James Meredith enrolls at University of Mississippi	Protests in Birmingham	King writes "Letter from the Birmingham Jail"

1960   **1961**   **1962**   **1963**

Objectives

You may wish to call students' attention to the objectives in the Section Preview. The objectives are reflected in the main headings of the section.

Bellringer

Read aloud the quotation by John Lewis on this page. Then ask students to weigh carefully this question: Could you have endured what the lunch-counter protesters did without either fleeing or defending yourself? Ask what motivated Lewis and the other protesters to suffer the abuse of the white segregationists.

Reading Strategy

Analyzing Outcomes Refer to the Reading Strategy in the Section Preview. You may wish to offer students the example of a single protest and its outcome.

LESSON PLAN

Connecting to the Main Idea

1. Focus Explain that as civil rights activists put the philosophy of nonviolence into action, protests began to sweep the South. Ask students to describe what happened as a result of these protests.

2. Instruct Discuss what issues made the civil rights movement so unstoppable. Ask students to consider the following factors in their examination of the movement: the people involved; the tactics; the moral philosophy of the movement; the reactions of whites; television and newspaper images of the violence.

3. Close Nonviolent protests sparked violent responses but caught the attention and sympathy of the nation. In the next section students will read about how politicians, slow to take up the civil rights issue, finally were forced to take action.

2 The Struggle Intensifies

SECTION PREVIEW

Objectives

1 Describe the goals of sit-ins and Freedom Rides and the reactions they provoked.
2 Summarize civil rights protests in Albany, Georgia, and at "Ole Miss."
3 Explain how violence against protesters in Birmingham affected attitudes throughout the nation.
4 *Key Terms* Define: sit-in; Freedom Ride; Albany Movement.

Main Idea

The tactics of nonviolent protest, including sit-ins and boycotts, challenged segregation and brought change, but also generated violent confrontations.

Reading Strategy

Analyzing Outcomes As you read, make a list of the civil rights protests mentioned and their outcomes. Write a sentence summarizing the effectiveness of these protests.

This protester picketed a restaurant in Georgia.

"We Shall Overcome," sang civil rights protesters. As they had anticipated, angry white segregationists met many peaceful protests with violence. But the civil rights protesters remained committed to nonviolence.

Sit-Ins Challenge Segregation

As you read in a previous chapter, the Congress of Racial Equality (CORE) created the **sit-in** in 1943 to desegregate the Jack Spratt Coffee House in Chicago. In this technique, a group of CORE members simply sat down at a segregated lunch counter or other public place. If they were refused service at first, they simply stayed where they were.

This tactic was a popular form of protest in the early 1960s. It often worked because it forced business owners to decide between serving the protesters or risking a disruption and loss of business. In some places, sit-ins brought strong reactions. John Lewis, a SNCC activist, participated in sit-ins in Nashville, Tennessee, in 1960s. He remembered the experience:

> **AMERICAN VOICES** "It was a Woolworth in the heart of the downtown area, and we occupied every seat at the lunch counter, every seat in the restaurant. . . . A group of young white men came in and they started pulling and beating primarily the young women. They put lighted cigarettes down their backs, in their hair, and they were really beating people.
>
> In a short time police officials came in and placed all of us under arrest, and not a single member of the white group, the people that were opposing our sit-in, was arrested."
>
> —*John Lewis*

Soon thousands of students were involved in the sit-in campaign, which gained the support of SCLC. Martin Luther King, Jr., told students that arrest was a "badge of honor." In 1961, some 70,000 students participated in sit-ins, and 3,600 served time in jail. The protests began a process of change that could not be stopped.

 RESOURCE OPTIONS

Teaching Resources

📁 **Reproducible Lesson Plan** Lesson Plans folder, p. 150

📁 **Learning Styles Lesson Plan** Learning Styles Lesson Plans folder, p. 60

📁 **Big Idea Graphic Organizer** Big Idea Graphic Organizer folder, p. 122

📁 **Guided Reading and Review** Units 9–10 folder, p. 17

Media and Technology

🖥 **Color Transparencies** American Photo, B-9

Signs like the one at the right were clear indications of how institutionalized segregation was in the South. Above, John Salter, Jr., Joan Trumpauer, and Anne Moody (left to right) held a sit-in at a Jackson, Mississippi, lunch counter in May 1963. A hostile crowd registered their response by mocking and pouring food on the three activists. *Economics Why was the sit-in often a successful tactic?*

The Freedom Rides

In *Boynton* v. *Virginia* (1960), the Supreme Court expanded its earlier ban on segregation on interstate buses. As a result, bus station waiting rooms and restaurants that served interstate travelers could not be segregated, either.

In 1961 CORE, with aid from SNCC, organized and carried out the **Freedom Rides.** They were a tactic designed to test whether southern states would obey the Supreme Court ruling and allow African Americans to exercise the rights newly granted to them.

Violence Greets the Riders The first Freedom Ride departed Washington, D.C., on May 4, 1961. Thirteen freedom riders, both blacks and whites, boarded an interstate bus heading south. (See the map of the route on the next page.) At first the group encountered only minor conflicts. In Atlanta the group split into two buses headed for the Deep South. It was there that the trip turned dangerous.

In Anniston, Alabama, a heavily armed white mob met the first bus at the terminal. The bus attempted to flee. CORE director James Farmer described what happened next:

AMERICAN VOICES "Before the bus pulled out, however, members of the mob took their sharp instruments and slashed tires. The bus got to the outskirts of Anniston and the tires blew out and the bus ground to a halt. Members of the mob had boarded cars and followed the bus, and now with the disabled bus standing there, the members of the mob surrounded it, held the door closed, and a member of the mob threw a firebomb into the bus, breaking a window to do so. Incidentally, there were some local policemen mingling with the mob, fraternizing with them while this was going on."

—*James Farmer*

The riders escaped before the bus burst into flames, but many were beaten by the mob as they stumbled out of the vehicle, choking on the smoke. They had anticipated trouble, since they meant to provoke a confrontation. However, the level of violence took them by surprise.

As a result of the savage response, Farmer considered calling the project off. SNCC leaders, though, begged to go on. Farmer warned, "You know that may be suicide." Student activist Diane Nash replied, "If we let them stop us with violence, the movement is dead! . . .

Answer to . . .

Viewing History It forced business owners to decide between serving the protesters or risking a disruption of business.

ACTIVITY

EXTENDED CLASS PERIODS

Time: 90 minutes.

Activity: Make a collage depicting the civil rights movement.

Grouping: Groups of three students.

Purpose: Have each student in the group find or make three images relating to the civil rights movement to include in the collage. The group should decide on a title for the artwork, perhaps borrowing a film or television series title (such as *Mississippi Burning* or *Eyes on the Prize*), using a line from a speech (such as "I have a dream"), or making up a title. One student from each group should present the finished collage to the class.

Roles: Art designers, caption writers, presenters.

Outcome: Students will identify images that express the goals, attitudes, controversies, and sentiments surrounding the civil rights movement in the 1960s.

Answer to . . .

Map Skills Six states; beatings and a firebombing.

Viewing History Attorney General Robert Kennedy sent federal marshals to protect the Freedom Riders and pressured the Interstate Commerce Commission to issue a ruling prohibiting segregation in all interstate transportation. The Justice Department sued local communities that did not comply.

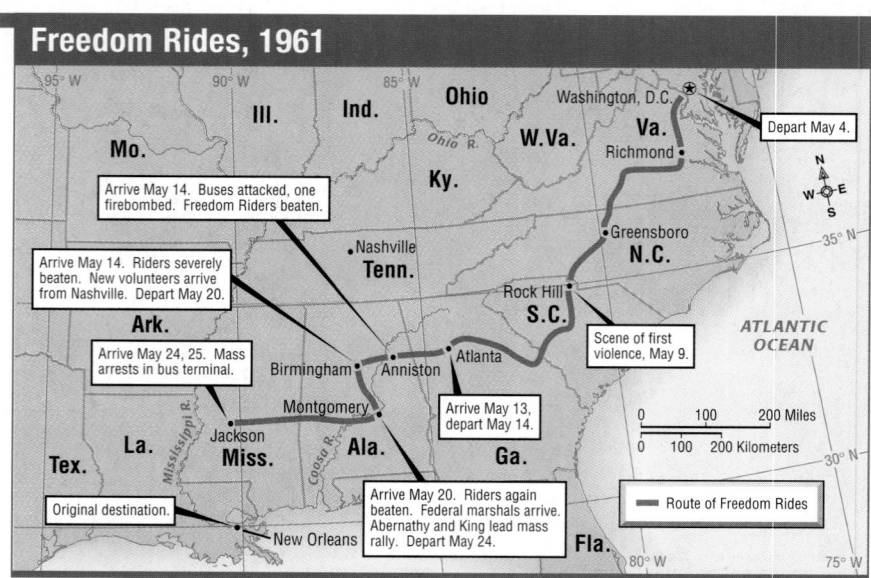

Freedom Rides, 1961

MAP skills

The Freedom Riders left Washington, D.C., for New Orleans, Louisiana, to test southern compliance with desegregation laws.

Movement
Through how many states did they pass? What kinds of opposition did they face?

Arrive May 14. Buses attacked, one firebombed. Freedom Riders beaten.

Arrive May 14. Riders severely beaten. New volunteers arrive from Nashville. Depart May 20.

Arrive May 24, 25. Mass arrests in bus terminal.

Arrive May 13, depart May 14.

Scene of first violence, May 9.

Arrive May 20. Riders again beaten. Federal marshals arrive. Abernathy and King lead mass rally. Depart May 24.

Original destination.

Depart May 4.

Route of Freedom Rides

Your troops have been badly battered. Let us pick up the baton and run with it."

National Reactions Photographs of the smoldering bus in Anniston, horrified the country. Burke Marshall, the Assistant Attorney General who headed the Justice Department's Civil Rights Division, was astonished "that people—presumably otherwise sane, sensible, rational—would have this kind of reaction simply to where people were sitting on a bus."

The violence intensified in Birmingham and Montgomery. Upon their arrival in Jackson, Mississippi, the riders met no mobs but were arrested immediately. New volunteers arrived to replace them and were also arrested, This first Freedom Ride died out in Jackson, but about 300 Freedom Riders continued the protest throughout that summer. Attorney General Robert Kennedy had at first been reluctant to lend federal support to the protest, but now he sent federal marshals to protect the Freedom Riders.

Kennedy took further measures. He pressured the Interstate Commerce Commission to issue a ruling prohibiting segregation in all interstate transportation—trains, planes, buses. The Justice Department sued local communities that did not comply.

The Albany Movement

In October 1961, a group of black Americans in Albany, Georgia, known as the **Albany Movement,** began a year-long campaign of protest marches. They called for desegregation of bus terminals and talks with white community leaders. Martin Luther King, Jr.,

On May 14, 1961, a group of white men in Anniston, Alabama, attacked a busload of Freedom Riders. They tossed a bomb into the bus and beat the fleeing activists. Local hospitals refused to treat the wounded Freedom Riders.
Government How did the federal government respond?

▶ RESOURCE OPTIONS

Media and Technology

◉ 📼 **Visions of America: Turning Point Story** "Nonviolent Solutions," a story about the role of nonviolent action in the civil rights movement. Located on videodisc side 4 and videotape 5. Includes lesson plan in the Visions of America Guidebook.

◉ 📼 **Visions of America: Roundtable Discussion** Play all or part of the Roundtable Discussion on "Nonviolent Solutions," remarks by respected historians and social commentators. Located on videodisc side 4 and videotape 5.

Side 4, Chapter 33

Side 4, Chapter 34

went to Albany to help. His presence inspired many blacks to join, yet it irritated some local civil rights leaders, who resented outside involvement.

The Albany police chief, Laurie Pritchett, kept police violations of civil rights out of public view. His tactic of "nonviolent opposition" to the protests deprived the Albany Movement of the nationwide sympathy that the Freedom Riders had gained. The movement largely fizzled out by the end of 1962.

Integration at "Ole Miss"

In September 1962, James Meredith, a black Air Force veteran, fought a personal battle for equal rights. Meredith was a student at Jackson State College but wanted to transfer to the all-white University of Mississippi, known as "Ole Miss." After being turned down on racial grounds, Meredith got legal help from the NAACP.

The Supreme Court upheld Meredith's claim. Mississippi governor Ross Barnett declared that Meredith could not enroll, whatever the Court said. Barnett personally blocked the way to the admissions office.

The issue became a standoff between the governor and the Justice Department. Crowds of angry white protesters destroyed vehicles bringing marshals to campus. As violence erupted on campus, tear gas covered the grounds. Two bystanders were killed and hundreds of people hurt. Finally, President Kennedy sent army troops to restore order, and federal marshals escorted Meredith to class.

Clash in Birmingham

Elsewhere, civil rights leaders looked for chances to protest segregation nonviolently. The Rev. Fred Shuttlesworth, head of the Alabama Christian Movement for Human Rights, in Birmingham, invited Martin Luther King, Jr., to visit the city in April 1963. Birmingham's population was 40 percent African American, but King had called it "the most segregated city in the country." Victory there could be a model for resistance.

King planned boycotts of downtown stores and attempts to integrate local churches. Business leaders, fearing disruptions and lost sales, tried to negotiate with Shuttlesworth to call off the plan, without success.

When reporters wanted to know how long King planned to stay, he drew on a biblical story and told them he would remain until "Pharaoh

Mississippi's Lieutenant Governor, Paul Johnson (left), is shown reviewing a court order admitting James Meredith (right) to the University of Mississippi. Johnson disobeyed the court order and refused to admit Meredith. *Government To what lengths did the government have to go in order to force Mississippi to comply with the Court's decision?*

let his people go." Birmingham police commissioner Eugene "Bull" Connor, a determined segregationist, replied, "I got plenty of room in the jail."

Main Idea CONNECTIONS

How did local police often treat non-violent protesters?

From Birmingham Jail The campaign began nonviolently with protest marches and sit-ins. City officials declared that the marches violated a regulation prohibiting parades without a permit. Connor arrested King and other demonstrators. When a group of white clergy criticized the campaign as an ill-timed threat to law and order by an "outsider," King responded from his cell.

In his "Letter from the Birmingham Jail," King defended his tactics and his timing:

> **KEY DOCUMENTS** "Frankly, I have yet to engage in a direct-action campaign that was 'well timed' in the view of those who have not suffered unduly from the disease of segregation. For years now I have heard the word 'Wait!' It rings in the ear of every Negro with piercing familiarity. This 'Wait!' has almost always meant 'Never.' "
>
> —"Letter from the Birmingham Jail," Martin Luther King, Jr., 1963

Answers to
SECTION 2 REVIEW

1. (a) sit-in, see p. 826; (b) Freedom Ride, see p. 827; (c) Albany Movement, see p. 828.

2. The nation was shocked by the violence; the federal government began to support the protesters.

3. Webs may include sit-ins, the Freedom Rides, the Albany Movement, boycotts, attempts to integrate churches and schools, and protest marches.

4. Sample entry: 1960—CORE holds lunch counter sit-ins. Sample sentence: The sit-ins mobilized students in the movement; they also generated tremendous publicity throughout the country, which helped the larger movement gain momentum.

5. Answers will vary but may include working through established political channels, voting for candidates who supported their cause, or letter-writing campaigns.

6. Essays will vary but should be supported with facts from the section.

Police in Birmingham, Alabama, used high-powered hoses to break up civil rights marches in 1963. Television coverage of this brutal treatment of peaceful demonstrators prompted widespread sympathy for the movement. **Government** *How did the Birmingham crisis end?*

dren. Police used high-pressure fire hoses, which could tear the bark from trees, on the demonstrators. They also brought out trained police dogs that attacked marchers' arms and legs. When protesters fell to the ground, policemen beat them with clubs and took them off to jail.

The Nation Watches Television cameras brought the scenes of violence to people across the country. Even those unsympathetic to the civil rights movement were appalled.

As reporter Eric Sevareid observed, "A newspaper or television picture of a snarling police dog set upon a human being is recorded in the permanent photo-electric file of every human brain."

In the end, the protesters won. A compromise arranged by Assistant Attorney General Burke Marshall led to desegregation of city facilities and fairer hiring practices. An interracial committee was set up to aid communication.

The success of the Birmingham marches was just one example that proved the effectiveness of nonviolent protest. Sometimes the technique did not work, or worked only slowly. Nevertheless, nonviolent protest as a means to social change had earned itself a place of honor in the history of civil rights in the United States.

After more than a week, King was released on bail. Soon after, he made a difficult decision: to let children join the campaign. Though dangerous, it would test the conscience of the Birmingham authorities and the nation.

As they marched with the adults, "Bull" Connor arrested more than 900 of the chil-

---

SECTION 2 REVIEW

Comprehension

1. *Key Terms* Define: (a) sit-in; (b) Freedom Ride; (c) Albany Movement.

2. *Summarizing the Main Idea* How did the violent response to the Freedom Rides and the Birmingham boycott aid the civil rights movement?

3. *Organizing Information* Create a web diagram with *Nonviolent Protest* at the center, showing events and examples of this technique.

Critical Thinking

4. *Analyzing Time Lines* Review the time line at the start of the section. Write a sentence that explains the broader effect of each event.

5. *Identifying Alternatives* If student protesters had not chosen nonviolent protest, what other options might they have used, for example, in ending lunch-counter segregation?

Writing Activity

6. *Writing a Persuasive Essay* In May 1961, an article in *The New York Times* urged the Freedom Riders to call off their plans, saying, "Non-violence that deliberately provokes violence is a logical contradiction." Write an essay explaining why you agree or disagree with this opinion.

RESOURCE OPTIONS

Teaching Resources

📁 **Quiz** Units 9–10 folder, p. 18

Student Performance Pack

Answer to . . .

Viewing History City facilities were desegregated, fairer hiring practices were instituted, and an interracial committee was established to aid in communication.

⭐ **Guide to the Essentials** Chapter 29, Section 2 (English and Spanish)

American Literature

Connections to American Literature Martin Luther King, Jr., "Letter from the Birmingham Jail"

| 1963 King delivers "I Have a Dream" speech | 1964 Freedom Summer voter registration drives | 1964 Congress passes Civil Rights Act | 1965 March from Selma to Montgomery, Alabama | 1965 Congress passes Voting Rights Act |

1963 **1964** **1965**

3 The Political Response

SECTION PREVIEW

Objectives

1 Analyze how President Kennedy's policies on civil rights changed between 1961 and 1963.
2 Describe the political impact of the March on Washington.
3 Summarize the progress in civil rights made under Lyndon Johnson.
4 **Key Terms** Define: March on Washington; cloture; Civil Rights Act of 1964; Voting Rights Act of 1965.

Main Idea

Continuous civil rights protests in the 1960s gradually made politicians respond to public opinion and move forward with strong civil rights legislation.

Reading Strategy

Analyzing Cause and Effect As you read, analyze how effective the civil rights movement was by making a list of all the major cause-and-effect relationships you can find.

As a senator from Massachusetts, Kennedy had voted for civil rights measures but never actively pushed the issue. During his presidential campaign, however, Kennedy had sought and won many African American votes with bold rhetoric. In 1960 he proclaimed, "If the President does not himself wage the struggle for equal rights—if he stands above the battle—then the battle will inevitably be lost."

Kennedy on Civil Rights

In October 1960, just weeks before the election, Senator Kennedy had a chance to make a powerful gesture of goodwill toward African Americans. Martin Luther King, Jr., had been arrested in Alabama and sentenced to four months of hard labor. His family feared for his life in the prison camp. Kennedy called King's wife, Coretta Scott King, and offered his help. Robert Kennedy then persuaded the Alabama sentencing judge to release King on bail.

Word of the Kennedys' actions raced through the black community. Many switched their votes from Nixon to Kennedy. The votes were crucial in Kennedy's slim margin of victory.

Once in office, however, Kennedy moved slowly on issues such as fair housing. He did not want to alienate southern Democratic senators whose votes he needed on foreign policy issues. Yet, Kennedy did appoint a number of African Americans to prominent positions.

The violent response to the Freedom Rides in 1961 embarrassed the President when he met with Soviet leader Nikita Khrushchev. Observers around the world watched the brutality in Birmingham early in 1963. Aware that he had to respond, Kennedy spoke to the American people on television:

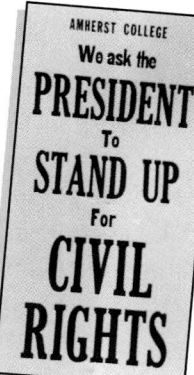

AMERICAN VOICES "We preach freedom around the world, and we mean it, and we cherish our freedom, here at home, but are we to say to the world, and much more importantly, to each other that this is a land of the free except for the Negroes? . . . The time has come for this nation to fulfill its promise."

—*President John F. Kennedy, television address*

Students demanded leadership from President Kennedy.

RESOURCE OPTIONS

Teaching Resources

📁 **Reproducible Lesson Plan** Lesson Plans folder, p. 151

📁 **Learning Styles Lesson Plan** Learning Styles Lesson Plans folder, p. 61

📁 **Big Idea Graphic Organizer** Big Idea Graphic Organizer folder, p. 123

📁 **Guided Reading and Review** Units 9–10 folder, p. 19

Objectives

You may wish to call students' attention to the objectives in the Section Preview. The objectives are reflected in the main headings of the section.

Bellringer

Ask students if they plan to vote when they reach voting age. Why or why not? How many students would vote if it meant facing possible harassment or violence? Explain that protection of voters' rights was an important aspect of the civil rights movement.

Reading Strategy

Analyzing Cause and Effect Refer to the Reading Strategy in the Section Preview. You may wish to have students contribute to a composite list that you write on the chalkboard.

LESSON PLAN

Connecting to the Main Idea

1. **Focus** Explain that few politicians of the early 1960s were willing to risk taking a strong stand for civil rights. Ask students to note what forced them to change their minds.
2. **Instruct** Tell students that John Kennedy was from Massachusetts and Lyndon Johnson was from Texas. Discuss Kennedy's and Johnson's reactions to the civil rights crisis. How might each man's origins have played a role in his handling of civil rights issues?
3. **Close** Politicians belatedly joined the cause of civil rights. Their efforts left many wrongs unrighted, and some African Americans became disillusioned with nonviolence as a solution to continuing discrimination. The next section describes the reactions of those African Americans.

"Jobs and Freedom" was the official slogan of the March on Washington in 1963. Thousands turned out to show their support for the civil rights movement.
Government Why was President Kennedy at first opposed to the march?

About the Presidents

Lyndon Baines Johnson (1963–1969) served in Congress from 1937 to 1961, when he became JFK's Vice President. After Kennedy's assassination, President Johnson used his skills as a legislative leader to push his domestic programs through Congress. Under his influence, Congress passed a strong civil rights act, laws that provided federal aid to mass transportation and to education, and the anti-poverty bill. This all occurred within a nine-month period. At the time, one commentator said, "LBJ has been hurling himself about Washington like an elemental force." Source: Wilson Sullivan, "Lyndon Baines Johnson," *The American Heritage® Pictorial History of the Presidents of the United States,* vol. 2, 1968.

Customize for
English Language Learners

Ask students to reread the passage from the speech by Martin Luther King, Jr., on this page. Have them rephrase the speech in their own words, then write a sentence summarizing King's main point. Explain why the speech is regarded as one of the most powerful in American history.

Answer to . . .

Viewing History He feared it would alienate Congress and attract violence.

Main Idea Connections To focus attention on Kennedy's civil rights bill.

Earlier in his term, Kennedy had proposed a modest civil rights bill. After the crisis in Birmingham, he introduced a far stronger one. It would prohibit segregation in public places, ban discrimination wherever federal funding was involved, and advance school desegregation. Powerful southern segregationists in Congress, however, kept the bill from coming up for a vote.

The March on Washington

To focus national attention on Kennedy's bill, civil rights leaders proposed a march on Washington, D.C. Kennedy feared it would alienate Congress and might cause racial violence. Yet when he could not persuade organizers to call off the march, he gave it his support.

The **March on Washington** took place in August 1963. More than 200,000 people came from all over the country. Labor leader A. Philip Randolph directed the march. Participants included religious leaders and celebrities, such as writer James Baldwin, entertainer Sammy Davis, Jr., and baseball player Jackie Robinson.

The march was peaceful and orderly. After many songs and speeches, Martin Luther King, Jr., delivered what was to become his best-known address. With power and eloquence, he spoke to all Americans:

Main Idea
CONNECTIONS
What was the purpose of the March on Washington?

KEY DOCUMENTS
❝I have a dream that one day this nation will rise up and live out the true meaning of its creed, 'We hold these truths to be self-evident, that all men are created equal.' I have a dream that one day on the red hills of Georgia, sons of former slaves and the sons of former slave owners will be able to sit down together at the table of brotherhood. . . . I have a dream that my four little children will one day live in a nation where they will not be judged by the color of their skin, but by the content of their character. . . . When we allow freedom to ring, when we let it ring from every village and every hamlet, from every state and every city, we will be able to speed up that day when all of God's children, black men and white men, Jews and Gentiles, Protestants and Catholics, will be able to join hands and sing in the words of the old Negro spiritual: 'Free at last. Free at last. Thank God Almighty, we are free at last.' ❞

—*"I Have a Dream" speech, Martin Luther King, Jr., August 28, 1963*

Johnson on Civil Rights

The new President, Lyndon Johnson, was a Texan who had voted against civil rights measures early in his congressional career. As Senate majority leader, however, he had worked suc-

---

▶ RESOURCE OPTIONS

Teaching Resources

📁 **Key Documents** Martin Luther King, Jr., "I Have a Dream," Learning with Documents folder, p. 103

🔲 **American History Block Scheduling Support** Presidential Power: Changes in the Twentieth Century, found in The Nation After World War II folder, includes interdisciplinary lesson suggestions and activities for Geography and History, Primary Sources, Biography, and Literature.

cessfully to get a civil rights bill passed in 1957. Now Johnson used his political skills to pass Kennedy's bill. In his first public address, he told Congress and the country that nothing "could more eloquently honor President Kennedy's memory than the earliest possible passage of the civil rights bill."

After the House of Representatives passed the bill, civil rights opponents in the Senate started a lengthy filibuster, exercising their right of unlimited day-and-night debate. Johnson finally enlisted his former colleague, Republican minority leader Everett Dirksen, to support the rarely used procedure called **cloture**—a three-fifths vote to limit debate and call for a vote. In June 1964 the Senate voted for cloture. Soon after, the bill passed with support from both Democrats and Republicans.

Turning Point: The Civil Rights Act

The **Civil Rights Act of 1964** had an impact in many areas, including voting, schools, and jobs.

It gave the Justice Department authority to act vigorously in school segregation and voting rights cases. The law's major sections (called "titles") included these provisions:

(1) Title I banned the use of different voter registration standards for blacks and whites.

(2) Title II prohibited discrimination in public accommodations, such as motels, restaurants, gas stations, theaters, and sports arenas.

(3) Title VI allowed the withholding of federal funds from public or private programs that practice discrimination.

(4) Title VII banned discrimination on the basis of race, sex, religion, or national origin by employers and unions. †

(5) Title VII also created the Equal Employment Opportunity Commission (EEOC) to investigate charges of job discrimination.

---

† A last-minute change, which was meant to make it harder for the bill to pass, changed the wording of Title VII to forbid sex discrimination as well as racial discrimination in employment. When the 1964 Civil Rights Bill passed anyway, it was the first law to call for equal hiring opportunities for women.

TURNING POINT : The Civil Rights Act of 1964

Following the Civil Rights Act of 1964, other federal laws and Supreme Court decisions dealt with the issue of discrimination.

1964
Civil Rights Act of 1964 outlaws discrimination in a variety of areas

1968
Civil Rights Act of 1968 bans discrimination in housing

1990
Americans with Disabilities Act guarantees disabled Americans equal opportunity in employment and public accommodations

| 1960 | 1970 | 1980 | 1990 | 2000 |

1967
Age Discrimination in Employment Act prohibits job discrimination against people age 40 or older

1978
In the Bakke case, the Supreme Court rules that race may be a factor (though not the only one) in school application decisions

1995
In the Adarand case, the Supreme Court limits government in giving preferences to minority groups

RESOURCE OPTIONS

Media and Technology

AmericanHeritage® CD-ROM

Presidents Lyndon B. Johnson

STUDENT PORTFOLIO

You may wish to have students add the following to their portfolios. To assess student work, refer to the generic rubrics in the Program Overview in the Teaching Resources.

Encourage interested students to examine the book or video version of *Eyes on the Prize* or another source of firsthand information on the civil rights movement. Then ask them to write a short essay addressing these questions: Was it right for "outsiders" (northern African Americans and whites) to come to southern towns to spark confrontations over civil rights? Were some southern whites and African Americans justified in accusing these activists of igniting violence with their nonviolent actions?

BACKGROUND

"Building a New South"

Southerners were caught off guard when Representative Charles Weltner (D–Georgia) voted in favor of the Civil Rights Act of 1964, arguing, "We can offer resistance and defiance, with their harvest of strife and tumult. We can suffer continued demonstrations, with their wake of violence and disorder. Or, we can acknowledge this measure as the law of the land. We can accept the verdict of the Nation. . . . I would urge that we at home now move on to the unfinished task of building a new South. We must not remain forever bound to another lost cause."

Answer to . . .

Viewing History They were peaceful; they challenged laws; they urged desegregation.

FACT Finder

Major Civil Rights Protests, 1954–1965

Year	Event	Outcome
1954	*Brown* v. *Board of Education*	Supreme Court ruled that separate educational facilities for whites and African Americans are inherently unequal.
1955–1956	Montgomery Bus Boycott	Bus company was forced to desegregate its buses. Martin Luther King, Jr., emerged as an important civil rights leader.
1961	Freedom Rides	Interstate Commerce Commission banned segregation in interstate transportation.
1963	James Meredith sues University of Mississippi for admission	Supreme Court upheld Meredith's right to enter the all-white institution.
1963	Protest marches in Birmingham, Alabama	Violence against peaceful demonstrators shocked the nation. Under pressure, Birmingham desegregated public facilities.
1963	March on Washington	More than 200,000 people demonstrated in an impressive display of support for civil rights.
1965	Selma March	State troopers attacked marchers. Johnson used federal force to protect route from Selma to Montgomery, and thousands joined march.

Interpreting Tables The visibility of civil rights protests led to advances in civil rights on both the local and national level. *Culture* **What did most of these protests have in common?**

Over the years, the Civil Rights Act of 1964 has helped millions of Americans and affected the nation's political and business life. The lasting impact of the legislation is shown in the Turning Point feature on the previous page.

Fannie Lou Hamer

Freedom Summer Even with a strong new law, change came slowly. Protests continued, and segregationists often answered them with violence. In 1964, leaders of the major civil rights groups organized a voter registration drive in Mississippi. About a thousand African American and white volunteers, mostly college students, joined in what came to be called Freedom Summer. Many white Mississippians were already angry about the new Civil Rights Act. The Ku Klux Klan held rallies to intimidate the volunteers.

Soon three young civil rights workers were reported missing: James Chaney, Andrew Goodman, and Michael Schwerner. Later in the summer, FBI agents found their bodies buried in a new earthen dam a few miles from where their burned-out station wagon had been found. These three murders were only part of the turbulence reported that summer. Civil rights leaders also reported 80 mob attacks. Volunteers were beaten up and a few wounded by gunfire. About a thousand were arrested. African American churches and homes were burned or fire-bombed.

The Democratic Convention Newly registered Mississippi voters, along with members of SNCC, organized the Mississippi Freedom Democratic party (MFDP). The MFDP sent delegates to the Democratic National Convention in the summer of 1964. The delegates argued that they, not politicians from the segregated party organization, were the rightful representatives.

One delegate was Fannie Lou Hamer, who had lost her job on a cotton plantation when she tried to register to vote. She told the convention about her experiences in one voter drive:

> **AMERICAN VOICES** "I began to scream, and one white man got up and began to beat me on my head and tell me to 'hush.' . . . All of this on account we want to register, to become first class citizens. [If] the Freedom Democratic Party is not seated now, I question America."
>
> —*Fannie Lou Hamer*

The MFDP rejected an offer by President Johnson to seat two MFDP delegates of his choosing and to change the rules for the 1968 convention to eliminate discrimination. Johnson was reelected in a landslide in 1964, but he knew he had to do something about the issue of voting rights.

RESOURCE OPTIONS

Media and Technology

RESOURCE PRO

Primary Source Activity Registering to Vote in Mississippi, found on Resource Pro, uses the testimony of Fannie Lou Hamer to show why hundreds of civil rights workers volunteered to spend the summer of 1964 in Mississippi.

The Selma March Many black southerners still had trouble obtaining one basic right: voting. In Selma, Alabama, police and sheriff's deputies were arresting people just for standing in line to register to vote. To call attention to the voting rights issue, King and other leaders decided to organize a protest march. They would walk from Selma to the state capital, Montgomery, about 50 miles away.

As the marchers set out on a Sunday morning in March 1965, armed state troopers on horseback charged into the crowd with whips, clubs, and tear gas. TV pictures of the attack again shocked many viewers. In response, President Johnson put the Alabama National Guard under federal control. He sent them, along with federal marshals and army helicopters, to protect the march route. When the Selma marchers started out again, supporters from all over the country flocked to join. By the time the march reached Montgomery, the ranks had swelled to about 25,000 people.

The Voting Rights Act Reacting to Selma, Johnson also went on national television, promising a strong new law to protect voting rights. Raising his arms, Johnson repeated, "And . . . we . . . shall . . . overcome!" That summer, despite another filibuster, Congress passed the **Voting Rights Act of 1965.**

Under the act, federal officials could register voters in places where local officials were blocking registration by African Americans. The act also effectively eliminated literacy tests and other barriers. In the year after the law passed, more than 400,000 African Americans registered to vote in the Deep South.

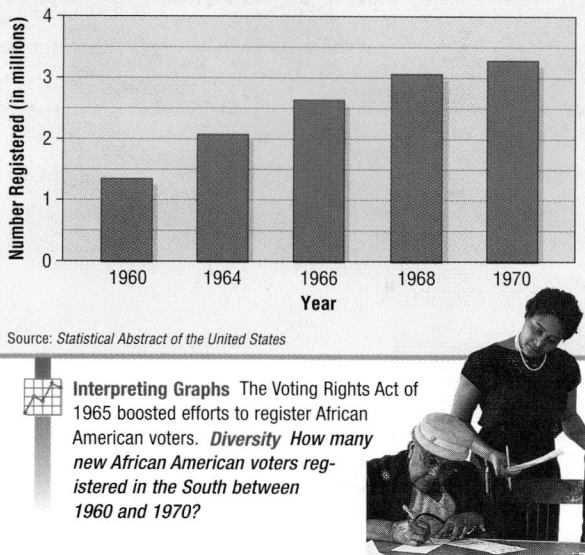

Southern Black Voters, 1960–1970

Source: *Statistical Abstract of the United States*

Interpreting Graphs The Voting Rights Act of 1965 boosted efforts to register African American voters. *Diversity* How many new African American voters registered in the South between 1960 and 1970?

Legal Landmarks Together, the Civil Rights Act of 1964 and the Voting Rights Act of 1965 created an entirely new voting population in the South. That meant that more black Americans would be elected to political office. Another legal landmark was the Twenty-fourth Amendment to the Constitution, ratified in 1964. It barred the use of the poll tax in federal elections.

For some African Americans new laws were not nearly enough. Impatient with the slow pace of progress, they were ready to listen to more militant leaders.

SECTION 3 REVIEW

Comprehension

1. **Key Terms** Define: (a) March on Washington; (b) cloture; (c) Civil Rights Act of 1964; (d) Voting Rights Act of 1965.

2. **Summarizing the Main Idea** What events forced both Kennedy and Johnson to move ahead with civil rights legislation?

3. **Organizing Information** Create a two-column chart comparing the provisions of the Civil Rights Act and the Voting Rights Act.

Critical Thinking

4. **Analyzing Time Lines** Review the time line at the start of the section. Explain how each event is related to the one after it.

5. **Tracing Cause and Effect** How did President Johnson's previous experience in Congress help to achieve passage of the Civil Rights Act?

Writing Activity

6. **Writing an Expository Essay** Write a short news story explaining the reasons for the March on Washington.

 RESOURCE OPTIONS

Teaching Resources

 Quiz Units 9–10 folder, p. 20

Student Performance Pack

Guide to the Essentials Chapter 29, Section 3 (English and Spanish)

Media and Technology

Visual Learning Activity A White House Demonstration, found on Resource Pro, uses a 1965 photo of a civil rights demonstration to enrich students' understanding of the pressure on Washington to pass the Voting Rights Act.

Answer to . . .

Interpreting Graphs About 2 million voters.

Objectives

You may wish to call students' attention to the objectives in the Section Preview. The objectives are reflected in the main headings of the section.

Bellringer

Ask students what kinds of activities go on in school that are officially against the rules. Then explain the difference between the terms *de jure* and *de facto*.

Reading Strategy

Outlining Information Refer to the Reading Strategy in the Section Preview. You may wish to have volunteers share their facts, and make a composite outline on the chalkboard.

LESSON PLAN

Connecting to the Main Idea

1. Focus Explain that nonviolent protests resulted in early gains, but that progress subsequently seemed to stall. Ask students how African Americans reacted to continuing discrimination.

2. Instruct Discuss the alternatives to nonviolent confrontation that evolved in the civil rights movement. How did the views of Malcolm X differ from those of Martin Luther King, Jr.?

Point out President Johnson's comment on the last page of the section. Then discuss the answers to his and the following questions: Why, after so much progress on civil rights, did so much anger and violence erupt? Why did African Americans become cynical about the goal of nonviolent integration pursued by Martin Luther King, Jr.?

3. Close Delays in achieving full equality caused increasing frustration among some African Americans, whose anger boiled over into violence.

4 The Challenge of Black Power

SECTION PREVIEW

Objectives

1 Compare the ways that James Baldwin, Malcolm X, and other African Americans expressed anger at the pace of progress toward civil rights.
2 Explain the principles and tactics used by advocates of black power.
3 Summarize the legacy of the civil rights movement.
4 *Key Terms* Define: Nation of Islam; black nationalism; black power; de jure segregation; de facto segregation.

Main Idea

Gains in civil rights came so slowly that some African Americans rejected nonviolence, calling for black power and more militant actions.

Reading Strategy

Outlining Information On a separate sheet of paper, copy the headings and subheadings in this section. As you read, add at least two key facts under each subheading to create on outline.

Author James Baldwin wrote movingly of the black experience.

The passage of two civil rights acts represented enormous progress. Over time, African Americans would use these statutes to win court battles that would tear down segregation. But in the meantime, African Americans still faced economic and social discrimination. Many were angry at this slow pace of change.

In 1964, Martin Luther King, Jr., whom the world admired for nonviolent protest, won the Nobel Peace Prize. Yet some Americans in the civil rights movement questioned his approach.

The movement was becoming deeply divided. Younger leaders rejected the ideas of both nonviolence and integration with white society. The simmering anger of many African Americans against continuing injustices was reflected in more militant rhetoric, sometimes exploding into urban riots.

James Baldwin

In 1963, in the bestseller *The Fire Next Time*, writer James Baldwin told how generations of oppression and suffering had set African Americans apart but had also made them stronger. Now, he said, African Americans were tired of promises. Their anger was ready to erupt. As Baldwin put it, "the Negro himself no longer believes in the good faith of white Americans—if, indeed, he ever could have."

Baldwin's essays and novels were powerful descriptions of the African American experience that touched both black and white Americans deeply. He was a strong voice for the civil rights movement. In *Notes of a Native Son* (1955), Baldwin wrote about the damaging effects of segregation in the United States. He recounted "the Negro's past, of . . . death and humiliation; fear by day and night; fear as deep as the marrow of the bone; doubt that he was worthy of life, since everyone around him denied it. . . ."

▶ RESOURCE OPTIONS

Teaching Resources

📁 **Reproducible Lesson Plan** Lesson Plans folder, p. 152

📁 **Big Idea Graphic Organizer** Big Idea Graphic Organizer folder, p. 124

📁 **Guided Reading and Review** Units 9–10 folder, p. 21

Media and Technology

(R E S O U R C E ◉ **P R O**)

Literature Activity Sins of the Father, found on Resource Pro, uses an essay from Eldridge Cleaver's *Soul on Ice* to show Cleaver's view that there could be mutual respect between the races if "white youth" could repudiate the evils of the past.

Malcolm X

Outside the mainstream civil rights movement, more militant political leaders emerged. The best known was Malcolm X, born Malcolm Little in Omaha, Nebraska, in 1925. His father, a Baptist minister who spread the "back-to-Africa" message of Marcus Garvey, died when Little was a child. Growing up in ghettos in Detroit, Boston, and New York, Little turned to crime. At age 20, he was arrested for burglary and served seven years in prison. While in jail he joined the **Nation of Islam,** a group often called the Black Muslims. Viewing white society as oppressive, it preached black separation and self-help.

Black Nationalism The Nation of Islam was founded in 1933 in Chicago by Elijah Muhammad. He taught that Allah (the Muslim name for God) would bring about a "Black Nation," a union among all nonwhite peoples. According to Elijah Muhammad, one of the keys to self-knowledge was knowing one's enemy. For him, the enemy of the Nation of Islam was white society.

Members of the Nation of Islam did not seek change through political means but waited for Allah to create the Black Nation. In the meantime, they tried to lead righteous lives and worked hard to become economically self-sufficient.

Released from prison in 1952, Malcolm Little changed his name to Malcolm X. (The other name, he said, came from slaveowners.) He spent the next 12 years as a minister of the Nation of Islam, winning followers with his fiery speeches. He spread the ideas of **black nationalism,** a belief in the separate identity and racial unity of the African American community.

Opposition to Integration Malcolm X disagreed with both the tactics and the goals of the early civil rights movement. He called the March on Washington the "Farce on Washington," and voiced his irritation at "all of this non-violent, begging-the-white-man kind of dying . . . all of this sitting-in, sliding-in, wading-in, eating-in, diving-in, and all the rest." Instead of preaching brotherly love, he rejected ideas of integration. Asking why anyone would want to join white society he noted:

AMERICAN VOICES

"No sane black man really wants integration! No sane white man really wants integration! No sane black man really believes that the white man ever will give the black man anything more than token integration. No! The Honorable Elijah Muhammad teaches that for the black man in America the only solution is complete separation from the white man. . . . The American black man should be focusing his effort toward building his own businesses, and decent homes for himself. As other ethnic groups have done, let the black people, wherever possible, however possible, patronize their own kind, hire their own kind, and start in those ways to build up the black race's ability to do for itself. That's the only way the American black man is ever going to get respect."

—*Malcolm X*

Malcolm X and Elijah Muhammad came to disagree about many things, including political action. In 1964 Malcolm X left the Nation of Islam and formed his own religious organization, called Muslim Mosque, Inc. He

Main Idea CONNECTIONS

Why did black nationalists such as Malcolm X believe the civil rights desegregation movement was doomed to fail?

Elijah Muhammad (left) called African Americans "the lost-found Nation of Islam in the wilderness of North America." Malcolm X (right) was a leading minister of the Nation of Islam until 1964. *Diversity How did black nationalism differ from other civil rights activism?*

ACTIVITY
LEARNING STYLES

Ask students to locate protest poems, prose, songs, and art from the 1960s and to include several in a notebook. Suggest that they begin by examining the writings of James Baldwin and Malcolm X. (*Verbal/Linguistic*)

ACTIVITY
HETEROGENEOUS GROUPS

Stage a mock panel debate between supporters of nonviolent protest, such as Martin Luther King, Jr., and Black Power advocates, such as Malcom X or Stokely Carmichael, in 1966. Panel members on both sides should become familiar with the moral, social, and political arguments of their positions and try to refute the arguments of the opposition. (*Reteaching*)

TEST PREPARATION

Have students read the quotation by Malcolm X on this page and then answer the question below.

What does Malcolm X advocate for blacks in American society?

A Total segregation.

B Social segregation, but integration in business pursuits.

C Integration with other ethnic groups but segregation from whites.

D Total integration.

Answer to . . .

Main Idea Connections They believed that only segregation could bring African Americans autonomy and respect.
Viewing History It was segregationist, and its leaders were opposed to nonviolent protest. It was a Nation of Islam–led, rather than a Christian-led, movement.

Members of the Black Panthers marched through the streets of New York City in 1968 to protest the trial of Huey P. Newton. Newton had been convicted of voluntary manslaughter in the death of a police officer. His conviction was later overturned. *Economics What efforts did the Black Panthers make to improve the quality of life in black communities?*

soon involved in protests. At Howard University in Washington, D.C., he and other students took over the Washington chapter of SNCC.

As Carmichael rose to SNCC leadership, the group became more militant. After being beaten and jailed for his participation in demonstrations, he was tired of nonviolent protest. He called on SNCC workers to carry guns for self-defense. He wanted to make the group exclusively black, rejecting white activists.

The split in the civil rights movement became obvious in June 1966. At a protest march in Greenwood, Mississippi, while King's followers were singing, "We Shall Overcome," Carmichael's supporters drowned them out with "We Shall Overrun." Then Carmichael, just out of jail, jumped into the back of an open truck to challenge the moderate leaders:

AMERICAN VOICES "This is the twenty-seventh time I have been arrested, and I ain't going to jail no more! . . . The only way we gonna stop them white men from whuppin' us is to take over. We been saying freedom for six years—and we ain't got nothin.' What we gonna start saying now is 'black power!' "

—*Stokely Carmichael, public address, June 1966*

then made a pilgrimage (a religious journey) to Mecca, the holy city of Islam in Saudi Arabia.

Seeing millions of Muslims of all races worshipping together peacefully had a profound effect on Malcolm X. It changed his views about separatism and hatred of white people. When he returned, he was ready to work with other civil rights leaders and even with white Americans on some issues. It seemed as if Malcolm X might become one of the leaders in a unified civil rights movement. His change of heart, however, earned him some enemies.

A month later, in February 1965, he was shot to death at a rally in New York. Three members of the Nation of Islam were charged with the murder.

Malcolm X's message of black nationalism lived on. He particularly influenced younger members of SNCC, the Student Nonviolent Coordinating Committee.

The Black Power Movement

One SNCC leader who heard Malcolm's message was Stokely Carmichael. Born in Trinidad, in the West Indies, in 1941, Carmichael came to the United States at the age of 11 and was

As he repeated "We . . . want . . . black . . . power!" the audience excitedly echoed the new slogan. Carmichael's idea of **black power** called on African Americans "to unite, to recognize their heritage, to build a sense of community . . . to begin to define their own goals, to lead their own organizations and support those organizations."

The Black Panthers In the fall of 1966, a new militant political party, the Black Panthers, was formed by activists Bobby Seale and Huey Newton. The Panthers wanted African Americans to lead their own communities. They demanded that the federal government rebuild the nation's ghettos to make up for years of neglect. Newton repeated the words of Chinese Communist leader Mao Zedong: "Power flows from the barrel of a gun." Though the Panthers had violent encounters with police, they also set up community programs such as day-care centers and free breakfast programs.

Black power gave rise to the "Black is beautiful" slogan, fostering racial pride. It also led to a serious split in the civil rights movement. More radical groups like SNCC and the Black Panthers moved away from the NAACP and other more moderate organizations.

Riots in the Streets The early civil rights movement focused on battling **de jure segregation,** racial separation created by law. Changes in the law, however did not address the tougher issue of **de facto segregation,** the separation caused by social conditions such as poverty. De facto segregation was a fact of life in most American cities, not just in the South. (See map below right.)

There were no "whites only" signs above water fountains in northern cities, yet discrimination continued in education, housing, and employment. African Americans were kept out of well-paying jobs, job training programs, and suburban housing. Inner-city schools were run-down and poorly equipped.

Residents of ghetto neighborhoods viewed police officers as dangerous oppressors, not upholders of justice. James Baldwin remarked that a white police officer in one of these neighborhoods was "like an occupying soldier in a bitterly hostile country." Eventually, frustration and anger boiled over into riots and looting. In 1964, riots ravaged Rochester, New York; New York City; and several cities in New Jersey.

One of the most violent riots occurred in the Los Angeles neighborhood of Watts. On August 11, 1965, police in Watts pulled over a 21-year-old black man for drunken driving. At first the interaction was friendly among the police, the suspect, and a crowd of Watts residents that had gathered. When the suspect resisted arrest, however, one police officer panicked and began swinging his riot baton. The crowd was outraged, and the scene touched off six days of rioting.

Thousands of people filled the streets, burning cars and stores, stealing merchandise, and sniping at firefighters. When the national guard and local police finally gained control, 34 people were dead and more than a thousand were injured.

Violence spread to other cities in 1966 and 1967. Cries of "Burn, baby, burn" replaced the gentler slogans of the earlier civil rights movement.

Another serious blow to believers in nonviolence was the assassination of Martin Luther King, Jr., in 1968 (which you will read about in a later chapter). Sorrow and anger again caused riots across the country.

A concerned federal government set up a special National Advisory Commission on Civil Disorders, headed by former Illinois Governor Otto Kerner, to investigate. In 1968 the Kerner Commission report declared flatly that the riots were an explosion of the anger that had been smoldering in the inner-city ghettos. It declared that "our nation is moving toward two societies, one black, one white—separate and unequal."

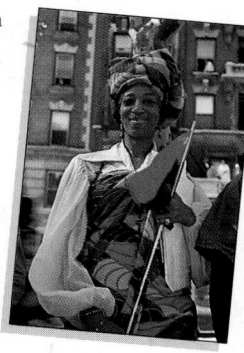

One result of the civil rights movement was the wearing of ethnic African clothing as a symbol of black pride.

Legacy of the Movement

At times, both black and white Americans wondered whether real progress in civil rights was possible. Many young activists felt frustrated and discouraged when the movement failed to bring changes quickly. Lyndon Johnson was devastated by the violence that

De Facto Segregation in the North

Area of city more than 70% African American
- · - · Cleveland city limits

Cleveland, c.1965

Lake Erie

0   2.5   5 Miles
0 2.5   5 Kilometers

SUPERIOR AVE.
EUCLID AVE.
CARNEGIE AVE.
LORAIN AVE.
PEARL RD.
BROADWAY
KINSMAN BLVD.
MILES AVE.
90 71 77

This map shows the areas of Cleveland, Ohio, with the highest concentrations of African Americans in the mid-1960s. *Place What social and economic factors may have contributed to this pattern of settlement?*

RESOURCE OPTIONS

Media and Technology

RESOURCE PRO

Critical Thinking Activity Demonstrating Reasoned Judgment: How to Respond, found on Resource Pro, presents passages from four of America's most powerful civil rights leaders to help students apply this skill.

Using the Internet

Write an Article

Objective Use the Internet to write an article on the ideals and motives of SNCC. Have students follow these instructions:

1. See the *America: Pathways to the Present* Web site at

http://www.Pathways.phschool.com

for the URL of The Sixties Project.

2. Read the SNCC position paper. Keep in mind questions that you will answer in your article, such as: What myths is SNCC trying to combat? What is its view of white and black power? What are its views of the roles of various Americans?

3. After articles are completed, collect them into a "newspaper" about black power.

Customize for

Less Proficient Readers

Have students make a chart illustrating the key occurrences in the chain of events that led from nonviolent protests to the ghetto riots.

Answer to . . .

Map Skills Job discrimination resulting in low wages and thus the need to live in low-income areas; prejudice on the part of realtors and residents in white neighborhoods.

Answers to

SECTION 4 REVIEW

1. (a) Nation of Islam, see p. 837; (b) black nationalism, see p. 837; (c) black power, see p. 838; (d) de jure segregation, see p. 839; (e) de facto segregation, see p. 839.

2. Segregation was illegal, African Americans had full voting rights, and the stage was set for African Americans to take leadership roles in politics and government.

3. James Baldwin: writer who attacked legal and social segregation; appealed to whites and blacks. Malcolm X: spread ideas of black nationalism; called for segregation; opposed mainstream civil rights movement; died at time when he was modifying his views and was ready to rejoin the mainstream movement. Stokely Carmichael: moved SNCC into a more militant position; advocated black power; rejected whites.

4. Sample entry: 1964—King receives Nobel Peace Prize. Many who disagreed with King's tactics were motivated to make their ideas known.

5. Sample answer: It is an opinion. There were many different solutions proposed, and Malcolm X's was only one of them.

6. Essays will vary but should be supported with facts from the section.

The rallying cry "Burn, Baby, Burn" became a nightmarish reality in the streets of Los Angeles in 1965. After firefighters quenched the flames in buildings all over Watts, crowds of looters moved in to carry off the spoils. *Culture* **What set off the Watts riot?**

they wielded changed the nature of American political life.

Between 1970 and 1975, the number of African American elected officials rose by 88 percent. Black mayors were elected in Atlanta, Detroit, Los Angeles, and Newark, N.J. Others served in Congress and state legislatures. In 1966 Barbara Jordan became the first African American elected to the Texas state Senate since Reconstruction. Six years later she was elected to the United States Congress. Jordan noted what made the movement necessary:

 "The civil rights movement called America to look at itself in a giant mirror. . . . Do the black people who were born on this soil, who are American citizens, do they really feel that this is the land of opportunity, the land of the free? . . . America had to say no.**"**

—*Texas Representative Barbara Jordan*

exploded near the end of his presidency. "How is it possible," he asked, "after all we've accomplished?" Still, the measures passed by his administration had brought tremendous change. Segregation was now illegal. Because of voter registration drives, thousands of African Americans could now vote. The power

Trying to change the answer to that question spurred the civil rights movement. It was the first step toward making the United States a fairer society for all.

SECTION 4 REVIEW

Comprehension

1. *Key Terms* Define: (a) Nation of Islam; (b) black nationalism; (c) black power; (d) de jure segregation; (e) de facto segregation.

2. *Summarizing the Main Idea* What was the lasting impact of the civil rights movement of the mid-1960s?

3. *Organizing Information* Create a two-column chart to compare the basic ideas of the leaders discussed in this section. Put people's names in the left column, with summaries of their ideas in the right column.

Critical Thinking

4. *Analyzing Time Lines* Review the time line at the start of the section. Choose three events and explain how each played a part in the division of the civil rights movement.

5. *Distinguishing Fact from Opinion* Malcolm X once said that for African Americans, "the only solution is complete separation from the white man." Explain the factors that make this statement either a fact or an opinion.

Writing Activity

6. *Writing a Persuasive Essay* Black nationalists believed that African Americans should establish communities separate from white society. Do you think this was a desirable goal? Explain.

Answer to . . .

Viewing History Police brutality against an African American motorist enraged an already frustrated community.

RESOURCE OPTIONS

Teaching Resources

Quiz Units 9–10 folder, p. 22

Chapter Tests Forms A and B Chapter Test folder

Student Performance Pack

 Guide to the Essentials Chapter 29, Section 4 (English and Spanish)

Standardized Test Preparation Handbook

Media and Technology

Guided Reading Audiotapes Chapter 29 Summary (English and Spanish)

Student Edition on Audiotape Chapter 29

Test Bank CD-ROM; Interactive Student Tutorial CD-ROM Chapter Test

You Can Help Achieve Racial Equality

In years following the civil rights movement, the United States has made progress toward equal access to education and jobs.

James Meredith, who integrated the University of Mississippi in 1962

The civil rights movement of the 1960s achieved tremendous victories in ending legal discrimination based on race. Are there segregated public schools in your community? No. Today public schools educate boys and girls of any race in the same classrooms. Are there segregated public hospitals in your community? No. African American and white physicians treat patients of different races side by side.

Still, the United States is not a colorblind society. Much remains to be done to ensure that all American children have the opportunity to realize their dreams.

The Impact Today

Since the civil rights movement, many African Americans have achieved a higher standard of living. In 1970 only 10 percent of black families had incomes above $50,000 dollars per year. In 1993, the figure had risen to nearly 18 percent. Greater educational opportunities, the result of school integration, helped create these economic gains. In 1960 only about 20 percent of African Americans age 25 or older had completed high school. A mere 3 percent had finished four years of college. By 1994 those numbers had increased to 73 percent and 13 percent, respectively.

Affirmative action policies have also created greater opportunities for African Americans.

Affirmative action gives preference to racial minorities in such areas as job hiring and college admissions. Almost all institutions doing business with or receiving funds from the federal government have practiced affirmative action since the 1960s. Many private institutions and businesses have also adopted affirmative action policies.

Affirmative action has been controversial from the beginning. Many Americans argue that giving preference to some groups amounts to "reverse discrimination" that is unfair to other groups. In recent years, opponents of affirmative action have mobilized to eliminate it. For example, in 1996, California voters passed Proposition 209, which outlaws racial preferences in education and employment. The law has dramatically affected admissions to schools in the University of California system. At one school, African American acceptance fell by 66 percent two years after Proposition 209 was passed.

Supporters of affirmative action fear that laws like Proposition 209 will worsen racial inequality. Opponents of affirmative action claim that outlawing all racial preferences is the only way to achieve true racial equality.

The Impact on You

Do you think affirmative action is a good way to achieve racial equality? Discuss the issue with your classmates. Then generate lists of arguments for and against affirmative action.

Racially mixed campus in New York State

Key Terms

Students should refer to the definitions of key terms in the chapter to write sentences that show an understanding of the 1960s civil rights movement.

Comprehension

1. Sample answer: The NAACP had many legal successes including *Brown* v. *Board of Education* and the passage of two anti-lynching laws. CORE had organized many demonstrations against segregation and had become a national organization by the 1950s.

2. King's approach of nonviolent protest was influenced by Mohandas Gandhi's ideas, espoused during India's struggle for independence from Britain.

3. A group of CORE members, both black and white, would sit down at a segregated lunch counter or other public place and simply stay seated if they were refused service.

4. To ride buses and stop at terminals to test the new decision *Boynton* v. *Virginia,* which disallowed segregation on interstate buses and in interstate facilities.

5. Johnson used his political skills and played on the nation's sorrow over the death of Kennedy to ensure passage of the Civil Rights Act of 1964 and the Voting Rights Act of 1965.

6. Violence against protesters during Freedom Summer and particularly following the Selma March.

7. That white society was oppressive, and that African Americans should create a separate society based on self-knowledge and self-help.

8. He saw millions of people from all races worshiping together.

9. It changed from a mainstream movement guided by the nonviolent views of Martin Luther King, Jr., to a collection of splinter groups advocating various degrees of militancy. It also became younger and less church-influenced.

Chapter Summary

The major concepts of Chapter 29 are presented below. See also *Guide to the Essentials of American History* or *Interactive Student Tutorial CD-ROM,* which contains interactive review activities, time lines, helpful hints, and test practice for Chapter 29.

Reviewing the Main Ideas

In the early 1960s, new groups and new leaders emerged in the fight for civil rights for African Americans. Continuing pressure from those groups, plus growing public sympathy, forced political action and the passage of strong new legislation. Though Martin Luther King, Jr., and his supporters carried on nonviolent protest, other African Americans took a more militant position.

Section 1: Leaders and Strategies

The civil rights movement of the 1960s consisted of many separate groups whose leaders and methods differed while sharing the goal of securing equal rights.

Section 2: The Struggle Intensifies

The tactics of nonviolent protest, including sit-ins and boycotts, challenged segregation and brought change, but also generated violent confrontations.

Section 3: The Political Response

Continuous civil rights protests in the 1960s gradually made politicians respond to public opinion and move forward with strong civil rights legislation.

Section 4: The Challenge of Black Power

Gains in civil rights came so slowly that some African Americans rejected nonviolence, calling for Black Power and more militant actions.

In the years following the civil rights movement, the United States has made progress toward equal access to education and jobs. Yet much remains to be done to ensure that all American children have the opportunity to realize their dreams.

Key Terms

For each of the terms below, write a sentence explaining how it relates to this chapter.

1. interracial
2. black nationalism
3. de jure segregation
4. sit-in
5. Freedom Ride
6. cloture
7. Civil Rights Act of 1964
8. Voting Rights Act of 1965
9. de facto segregation

Comprehension

1. Name two groups that were working for African Americans' rights *before* the 1960s. What did they accomplish?
2. What new approach did Martin Luther King, Jr., bring to the civil rights movement? What was the inspiration for his philosophy?
3. What happened during a typical sit-in?
4. What were the goals of the Freedom Rides?
5. What was Johnson's role in passing civil rights legislation?
6. What events spurred the passage of the Voting Rights Act?
7. What were the beliefs of the Nation of Islam?
8. How did Malcolm X's pilgrimage to Mecca change his thinking?
9. What major changes occurred in the civil rights movement in the mid-1960s?

Using Graphic Organizers

On a separate sheet of paper, copy the tree map below. Fill in the boxes with major protests and descriptions of their outcomes. Each section of the tree map should focus on one event or tactic of nonviolent protest, such as sit-ins.

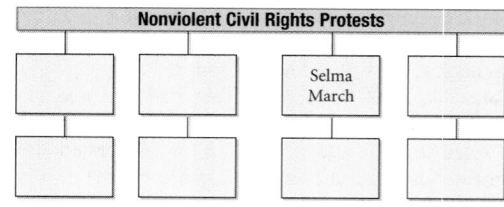

Nonviolent Civil Rights Protests

Selma March

Using Graphic Organizers

- Sit-ins: test limits of segregation; put business profits at risk; was an effective way to integrate businesses.
- Freedom rides: travel on interstate buses to test laws; responded to with violence in South; resulted in segregation being prohibited on interstate transportation.
- Selma march: march to protest lack of voting rights; troopers attack protesters; Johnson protects route with National Guard.
- Birmingham: activists challenge discriminatory hiring practices and segregated city facilities; violence erupts; results in the desegregation of city facilities, fairer hiring practices, and creation of a biracial committee.

Analyzing Political Cartoons ▶

1. Examine both panels of the cartoon. What does the man represent?

2. (a) What does the first pit represent? (b) What does the second pit represent?

3. What is the man's overall goal, and what obstacles does he face?

4. What point is the cartoonist trying to make?

Critical Thinking

1. *Applying the Chapter Skill* Reread the excerpt on the Skills for Life page. (a) Why was Ralph Abernathy a reliable source for information about the civil rights movement? (b) How might his association with Martin Luther King, Jr., have affected his point of view toward those events?

2. *Analyzing Cause and Effect* Why did the violent reactions of segregationists to nonviolent protests such as the Freedom Rides actually help those protests become more effective?

3. *Formulating Questions* Make a list of three to five questions that you could ask a student activist from the 1960s in order to find out his or her reasons for taking part in the civil rights movement.

4. *Drawing Conclusions* Voter registration drives greatly increased African Americans' political power in the South. What are the potential results of increased political influence for a certain group?

INTERNET ACTIVITY

For your portfolio:
WRITE AN ESSAY

Access Prentice Hall's *America: Pathways to the Present* site at **www.Pathways.phschool.com** for the specific URL to complete the activity. Additional resources and related Web sites are also available.

Use the links provided to read about Martin Luther King, Jr., and the civil rights movement. Write an essay on a particular aspect of King's life or the civil rights movement.

ANALYZING DOCUMENTS ◀ ▶ *INTERPRETING DATA*

Turn to the excerpt from King's "I Have a Dream" speech in Section 3.

1. Which of the following phrases best *summarizes* King's dream? (a) that Americans of all religions will be free at last (b) that all Americans will achieve true equality and freedom (c) that African Americans will form a brotherhood (d) that children will not be judged by their color.

2. King hopes that his dream will be fulfilled (a) in the long run. (b) in his children's lifetime. (c) in the 20th century. (d) today.

3. *Writing* King said that he hoped the nation would "live out the true meaning" of the statement "all men are created equal." Write two or three paragraphs that explain what you think is the meaning of that phrase.

Connecting to Today

Essay Writing Reread the list of provisions of the 1964 Civil Rights Act in Section 3. Research current newspapers and news magazines. Then write an essay showing how these laws and regulations have affected American life and politics today.

INTERNET ACTIVITY

Essays will vary but should demonstrate an understanding of the goals and ideals of the civil rights movement and of King's place in it.

Analyzing Political Cartoons

1. African Americans.
2. (a) Racial inequality. (b) Economic inequality.
3. He is seeking equality in American society, but racism and lack of economic opportunity prevent him from achieving it.
4. Economic inequality is as effective as racism in preventing equality between blacks and whites.

Critical Thinking

1. (a) He was a firsthand observer, his tone seems matter-of-fact, and he doesn't seem to exaggerate. (b) He was a strong partisan of King's views and worked closely with him, meaning that his views would be favorable.
2. The violence shocked average Americans and drew them to the cause; they also prodded the government to take action on civil rights.
3. Sample questions: Why did you join the civil rights movement? What was your family's response to your participation in it? Did your opinions of race relations change as a result of your participation? Do you agree that the use of nonviolent confrontation is the most effective way of achieving equality?
4. Sample answer: It allows the groups' views and goals to have a voice; it ensures that members of the group take leadership roles and can be seen as role models.

Analyzing Documents

1. b
2. b
3. Paragraphs should draw on examples and quotes from the text.

Connecting to Today

Essays will vary but should include current cases of discrimination and show how the focus was widened to include gender and other types of discrimination; essays may also allude to affirmative action.

CHAPTER 30

Other Social Movements, 1960–1975

Managing Time and Instruction

INSTRUCTION SUPPORT

These materials for instruction are provided for **each section** in the **Teaching Resources**. See **Units 9–10 folder for Enrichment Support:**

• Reproducible Lesson Plans in Lesson Plans folder • Learning Styles Lesson Plans in Learning Styles Lesson Plans folder • Big Idea Graphic Organizers in Big Idea Graphic Organizer folder • Guided Reading and Review • Quizzes • Test Preparation Practice booklet

DAILY LESSON	ENRICHMENT SUPPORT
1 The Women's Movement (pp. 845–850)	• Primary Source Activity, The Equal Rights Amendment, Learning with Documents folder, p. 36 • Great Debates, What Are "Equal Rights"?, Decision-Making Activities folder, pp. 42–43 • Comparing Primary Sources, Units 9–10 folder, pp. 38–39 • Skills for Life Activity, Units 9–10 folder, p. 41
2 Ethnic Minorities Seek Equality (pp. 852–856)	• Nystrom *Atlas of Our Country,* Later Expansion of the United States, pp. 32–33; The Fourth Wave of Immigration, pp. 36–37 • Biography, Dolores Huerta, Units 9–10 folder, p. 37 • Literature Activity, Perspectives of Women of Color, found on **Resource Pro**
3 Native American Struggles (pp. 857–861)	• Visual Learning Activity, Changing Attitudes Toward Native Americans, found on **Resource Pro** • Biography, Vine Deloria, Jr., found on **Resource Pro** • Critical Thinking Activity, Identifying Assumptions: The Beeah Tribe, found on **Resource Pro** • Literature Activity, Native American Voices, Units 9–10 folder, p. 40
4 The Environmental Movement (pp. 862–866)	• Visual Learning Activity, Preserving the Environment, Learning with Documents folder, p. 72 • Primary Source Activity, The Desecration of America, found on **Resource Pro** • Crime Victims Have Rights, Why Study History? folder, p. 31

Running Out of Time?

• Use Tape 5, "The Upheaval of the Sixties, 1960–1975," from **Visions of America** videotapes series.
• Use Chapter 30 Summary from **Guide to the Essentials of American History** (English and Spanish).

Companion Web Site

The companion Web site offers online links for all chapter review activities. It also provides key content links and structured support for this chapter for both teachers and students.

http://www.Pathways.phschool.com

Media and Technology

For the Student

Interactive Student Tutorial CD-ROM Chapter 30
Student Edition on Audiotape Chapter 30
American Heritage® CD-ROM
Guided Reading Audiotapes (English and Spanish) Chapter 30

For the Teacher

Resource Pro CD-ROM Chapter 30
Test Bank CD-ROM Chapter 30
Listening to Literature Audiotapes *Timeless Voices, Timeless Themes* "Bidwell Ghost" by Louise Erdrich
Color Transparencies Critical Thinking, I-10; Time Lines E-9

 ## Assessment Options

Chapter Test Forms A&B Test Bank CD-ROM booklet
Test Bank CD-ROM Chapter 30
Standardized Test Preparation Handbook

 ## Block Scheduling

Pacing Suggestions

For 90-minute Blocks

- Teach sections 1 and 2 using Transparencies D-20 and C-15 and the Recent Scholarship note on p. 853 for class discussions.
- Teach sections 3 and 4 using the Big Idea Graphic Organizers from Teaching Resources and the Extended Class Periods Activity on p. 863.

Additional Resources

- Prentice Hall's **American History Block Scheduling Support File** covers over 40 major topics in American history. Included are lesson plans, strategies, primary sources, literature, biographies, Great Debates, art history, simulations, and songs.
- **Prentice Hall United States History Video Collection™** contains 20 videotapes covering American history from beginnings to present.

 ## Connections to American Literature

from Prentice Hall

Prentice Hall Literature *Timeless Voices, Timeless Themes* "Mirror" by Sylvia Plath, p. 1050

Additional Resources

For the Student

Rachel Carson. *Silent Spring.* Houghton Mifflin, 1962.
Betty Friedan. *The Feminine Mystique.* Dell, 1984.
N. Scott Momaday. *House Made of Dawn.* New American Library, 1969.

For the Teacher

Voices From Wounded Knee. Akwesasne Notes, 1973.

Prentice Hall brings into the classroom the vast archives and scholarship of the nation's premier American history magazine. See "From the Archives of American Heritage®" and "About the Presidents" teaching notes in this chapter.

 History Alive!

Teacher's Curriculum Institute, in partnership with Prentice Hall, provides unique materials that engage students with diverse learning styles. See History Alive!® unit on The Civil Rights Movement.

 Student Performance Pack

Ensures success in the three critical areas of Reading, Test Taking, and English Language Development with the following materials:
- Guide to the Essentials of American History in English and Spanish
- Guided Reading Audiotapes in English and Spanish
- Interactive Student Tutorial CD-ROM
- Test Preparation Handbook
- Test Preparation Practice booklet

Introducing the Chapter

Inspired by the civil rights movement, women, Latinos, Asian Americans, and Native Americans struggled to achieve equality in the 1960s and 1970s through protests. The movement for social change affected almost every aspect of American society from the environment to consumer awareness.

Themes in American History

The theme for this chapter, Culture, is listed at the beginning of this unit. An alternate theme for the chapter is Diversity. To teach this unit thematically, you may wish to use The Nation After World War II folder in American History Block Scheduling Support.

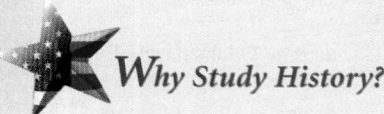 *Why Study History?*

Have students explore suggested ways of connecting the past to the present on page 867.

844

CHAPTER FOCUS

This chapter describes the social revolution of the 1960s and early 1970s. The civil rights movement of the 1960s spurred other groups, such as women, Latinos, Asian Americans, and Native Americans, to work for their own goals of equality. Activists adapted civil rights tactics to launch movements to protect the environment and to improve the quality and safety of consumer goods.

 The *Why Study History?* page at the end of this chapter explores the connection between social activists of the 1960s and early 1970s and activists today who are working to secure rights for victims of crimes.

▲
VIEWING HISTORY
The first Earth Day rallies helped bring environmental issues to the public's attention. *Culture **What other social movements were competing for the nation's attention?***

 RESOURCE OPTIONS

Teaching Resources

 Big Idea Graphic Organizer folder
Graphic summary of the main idea of the chapter.

 Learning Styles Lesson Plans folder
Alternate lesson plans for diverse learning styles for each chapter.

Media and Technology

AmericanHeritage® **CD-ROM**
Time Tour The Nation Today and Tomorrow: A Time for Turmoil

Prentice Hall United States History Video Collection™ Volume 20
Post-War USA

1963	1966	1971	1972	1973
Betty Friedan publishes The Feminine Mystique	National Organization for Women formed	National Women's Political Caucus organized	Gloria Steinem founds Ms. magazine	Roe v. Wade decision

1962   1966   1970   1974

1 The Women's Movement

SECTION PREVIEW

Objectives

1 Summarize the background of the women's movement and analyze the impact of the civil rights movement on it.
2 Describe how feminist leaders organized groups to advocate for women's rights and explain the impact of feminism.
3 Understand that the feminist movement was opposed by some who wanted to preserve traditional roles.
4 *Key Terms* Define: feminism; National Organization for Women (NOW); *Roe v. Wade;* Equal Rights Amendment (ERA).

Main Idea

Encouraged by the gains of the civil rights movement, a women's movement arose in an effort to end discrimination based on gender.

Reading Strategy

Organizing Information Write the following three column headings on a piece of paper: *Social Conditions for Women in the 1950s, Steps Taken by Feminists to Change Conditions,* and *Opposition to the Feminist Movement.* As you read the section, note relevant information in the appropriate column.

The African American struggle for civil rights made other groups aware of other inequalities in American life. Women, though not a minority in numbers, recognized that certain aspects of society placed them at a disadvantage. They became determined to elevate their status.

The quest for women's rights was not new to the nation's history. In the late 1800s, particularly, women had worked for the right to vote and for equality in education and in jobs. The term **feminism** first came into recorded use in 1895 as a word to describe the theory of political, economic, and social equality of men and women. Feminists were those who believed in or acted on behalf of this theory.

Background of the Women's Movement

The women's movement of the 1960s sought to change aspects of American life that had been accepted for decades. Mainstream society expected women to put home and family first.

The stereotype of women in the 1950s placed them in the home, married and raising children. During and after World War II, however, more and more women entered the labor force. By the beginning of the 1960s, about half of all women held jobs.

In addition, an increasing number of women were going to college. In 1950 only 25 percent of all Bachelor of Arts degrees were earned by women. Twenty years later, in 1970, it was 41 percent. Better-educated women had high hopes for the future, but often were discouraged by the discrimination they faced when they looked for jobs or tried to advance in their professions. Many people thought it was appropriate for young women who entered the work force to leave after only a few years in order to start families. In many cases, employers were reluctant to invest training in women because they were not expected to stay on the job for very long. Other employers

The new women's movement chose symbols of power to represent its cause.

RESOURCE OPTIONS

Teaching Resources

Reproducible Lesson Plan Lesson Plans folder, p. 153

Big Idea Graphic Organizer Big Idea Graphic Organizer folder, p. 125

Guided Reading and Review Units 9–10 folder, p. 29

Media and Technology

 AmericanHeritage® CD-ROM

Time Tour The Nation Today and Tomorrow: A Time of Turmoil

SECTION 1

The Women's Movement

Objectives

You may wish to call students' attention to the objectives in the Section Preview. The objectives are reflected in the main headings of the section.

Bellringer

Write the terms *feminist* and *women's libber* on the chalkboard. Ask students to list five words that help describe each. Have them rank the words in order from most positive to most negative.

Reading Strategy

Organizing Information Refer to the Reading Strategy in the Section Preview. You may wish to provide students with an example of information relevant to each column.

LESSON PLAN

Connecting to the Main Idea

1. **Focus** Women were among the first groups to note the successes of the civil rights movement and to apply them to the inequalities of their own lives. Ask students how the women's movement affected American society.
2. **Instruct** Discuss the conditions in American society that feminists wanted to change. Ask students to list the ways in which employers discriminated—and in some cases continue to discriminate—against women.

Ask students to list the kinds of action taken by feminists to improve conditions for women. Which were most successful?
3. **Close** American women were encouraged by the successes of the civil rights movement to work for greater equality for their sex. The women's rights movement made some significant gains but produced a backlash among those who wished to preserve traditional roles. As students will read in the next section, other groups also learned from the civil rights movement.

Graphing the Main Idea

To make sure students understand the main idea of this section, you may wish to use the web graphic organizer below.

Tell students that a web shows a main idea with its supporting details. Ask students to use it to show details to support the idea that the women's movement grew out of the civil rights movement.

Teaching Tip A template for this graphic organizer can be found in the Color Transparencies, G-1.

Answer to . . .

Interpreting Graphs It decreased slightly.

Main Idea Connections They were significantly lower.

Incomes of Men and Women, 1950–1975

Source: *Statistical Abstract of the United States*

Interpreting Graphs Women's incomes continued to lag behind men's earnings, partly because many low-paying fields were traditionally considered "women's work." *Economics Did the gap increase or decrease between 1950 and 1975?*

Main Idea CONNECTIONS

How did women's salaries compare to men's salaries?

completely denied women job opportunities for which they were qualified because they believed that home and family should be a woman's only responsibility.

Women who did enter the work force often found themselves underemployed, performing jobs and earning salaries below their abilities. Working women earned less than working men doing similar or even identical jobs. In 1963, women, on average, were paid only 63 cents for each dollar that men earned. By 1973 this figure had dropped to 57 cents. The graph above shows median incomes of men and women from 1950 to 1975. This financial inequality created a growing sense of frustration among women and led to demands for change.

The Impact of the Civil Rights Movement

While social conditions set the scene for the women's movement, the civil rights movement provided a model for techniques and an inspiration for action. Black and white women joined in the struggle for civil rights and gained valuable skills from their work in the movement.

As they worked to bring racial discrimination to an end, many women in the civil rights movement were discouraged. They were expected to make coffee and do clerical work while men made most of the policy decisions. Frustrated over their assigned roles, they applied the techniques they had learned in the

civil rights movement to address their own concerns.

The civil rights movement also provided women with legal tools to fight discrimination. One important piece of legislation was the 1964 Civil Rights Act.

Originally, the section of the act called Title VII prohibited discrimination based on race, religion, or national origin. When Congress debated the bill, however, some opponents of civil rights added an amendment to outlaw discrimination on the basis of gender. This action was a strategy to make the entire bill look ridiculous, so that it would fail in the final vote. To the dismay of its opponents, both the amendment and the bill passed. The new Civil Rights Act now had a provision that gave women a legal framework to fight discrimination.

Even with the added boost of the new legislation, progress took time. Women soon discovered that the Equal Employment Opportunity Commission (EEOC) set up by the bill did not take women's discrimination claims seriously. Nevertheless, Title VII would be tremendously important as the women's movement gained strength.

Women's Groups Raise Consciousness

As the 1960s unfolded, women began to meet together to compare experiences. Women civil rights workers met to look for ways in which they could play a larger role in the struggle. Soon they went beyond politics, exploring other aspects of their lives. The growing movement drew women who were active in other forms of protest and reform. They included student radicals, opponents of the draft, and workers for welfare rights and other social issues.

Another important influence was Betty Friedan's 1963 book *The Feminine Mystique.* Friedan described the cultural patterns that prevented women from achieving their full potential. Many readers recognized what she called "the problem that has no name"—the disillusionment that came from trying to be the perfect wife and mother, the only roles for women that society valued.

Women Form Support Groups Meeting in kitchens and living rooms, women in consciousness-raising groups began to talk about their lives in new ways. One participant, Nancy Hawley, a community activist in Boston, Massachusetts, was troubled by patterns she saw

---

in her work. "Though many of us were working harder than the men," she noted, "we realized we were not listened to and often ignored."

Throughout the country, growing numbers of women recognized the negative attitudes directed toward them. In New Orleans, Louisiana, civil rights activist Cathy Cade mentioned that her boyfriend had made fun of her for going to a "women's meeting." Others in her group told stories of being teased or ridiculed for coming to a women's group. Such lack of support outside the group made their bond stronger within the group. As Cade put it:

> **AMERICAN VOICES** ❝One thing became clear: that in the black movement I had been fighting for someone else's oppression and now there was a way that I could fight for my own freedom, and I was going to be much stronger than I ever was.❞
>
> —*Cathy Cade*

In San Francisco, California, Mimi Feingold, also a veteran of the civil rights and draft resistance movements, felt the same sense of exhilaration at her group's first meeting:

> **AMERICAN VOICES** ❝It was something that we had all been waiting for, for a long time. It was a really liberating experience for all of us. . . . This was finally permission to look at our own lives and talk about how unhappy we were.❞
>
> —*Mimi Feingold*

Women Organize NOW In 1966 a small group of women decided to form an organization to pursue their goal of achieving equality with men. These women were frustrated that existing women's groups were unwilling to pressure the Equal Employment Opportunity Commission to take women's grievances more seriously. Twenty-eight professional women, including Betty Friedan, established the **National Organization for Women (NOW).** Their goal was "to take action to bring American women into full participation in the mainstream of American society now."

NOW sought fair pay and equal job opportunities. It attacked the "false image of women" in the media, such as advertising that used sexist slogans or photographs. In one such ad in the 1960s, for example, an oven manufacturer asked, "Can a woman ever feel right cooking on a dirty range?" In so doing the ad reinforced the popular notion that a woman's sole contribution was to be a homemaker. NOW also called

Betty Friedan voiced many women's feelings in her influential book *The Feminine Mystique.* **Culture** *What was "the problem that has no name"?*

for more balance in marriages, with men and women sharing parenting and household responsibilities. A year after NOW was founded, it had 1,000 members. Only four years later some 15,000 women had joined.

For some women, NOW seemed too extreme; for others it was not extreme enough. Some saw NOW—and the women's

Women from different backgrounds shared their stories in informal meetings and found they had common experiences. **Culture** *What role did consciousness-raising groups play in the feminist movement?*

Changing attitudes expanded job opportunities for women by allowing them to work in traditionally male fields. *Culture How was this changing attitude reflected in higher education?*

movement in general—as mainly for the benefit of white, middle-class women. Nonetheless, NOW served as a rallying point in the movement to end sex discrimination and to promote equality for all women.

The Impact of Feminism

This cover from the first edition of Ms. magazine shows the many roles women had to fill.

The women's movement came of age in the early 1970s. Songs helped to express the energy of the struggle. In 1971 pop singer Helen Reddy recorded a song that was soon broadcast on radio stations around the country. Delivered in the ringing, forceful style of an anthem, Reddy's hit song proclaimed:

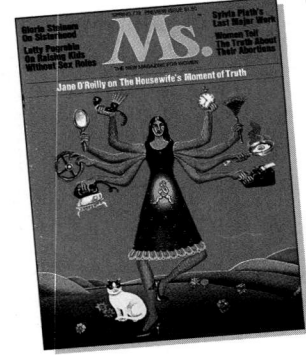

> I am woman, hear me roar
> In numbers too big to ignore,
> And I know too much to go back and pretend. . . .
> Yes, I've paid the price
> But look how much I gained.
> If I have to, I can do anything.
> I am strong, I am invincible,
> I am woman.

Reddy's lyrics reflected a sense of women's self-confidence and a strength that drove the movement on.

Literary Impact Books and magazines likewise promoted the cause. *Our Bodies, Ourselves,* a handbook published by a women's health collective in Boston, encouraged women to understand their own health issues. It sold 200,000 copies in the first several years after its publication and three million by 1990. In 1972 journalist Gloria Steinem and several other women founded *Ms.* magazine. Devoted to feminist issues, *Ms.* provided women with viewpoints that were decidedly different from those in *Good Housekeeping, Ladies' Home Journal,* and other women's magazines of the day. All 300,000 copies of the preview issue sold out in eight days. Only one year later, *Ms.* had nearly 200,000 subscribers. While not all readers considered themselves feminists, the magazine familiarized them with the arguments and issues of the women's movement.

A Shift in Attitudes Slowly the women's movement brought a shift in attitudes. For example, a survey of first-year college students revealed a significant change in career goals. In 1970, men interested in fields such as business, law, engineering, and medicine outnumbered women by eight to one. Five years later, the margin had dropped to three to one. More women entered law school and medical school. They were finally admitted to military academies and trained as officers. In 1971 the National Women's Political Caucus was formed to expand women's participation in politics. By working from within the system, women were able to gain broader support for the goals of the women's movement.

Many women did not actively participate or support the women's movement. Still, most agreed with NOW's goal to provide women with better job opportunities. Many were also pleased to see that the women's movement brought with it a greater recognition of issues important to women. These concerns included the need for child-care facilities, shelters for homeless women, more attention to women's health concerns, and increased awareness of harassment.

Despite many shared concerns, the women's movement continued to be divided as to its goals. In 1972 *Time* magazine observed, "The aims of the movement range from the modest, sensible amelioration [betterment] of the female condition to extreme and revolutionary visions." Radical feminists emphasized the need to end male domination, sometimes rejecting men, marriage, and childbearing. Other women rejected the strong opinions of the radicals, fearing they would cause a split in the women's movement.

Roe v. Wade One issue that had the potential to divide the movement was abortion. NOW and other groups worked to reform the laws governing a woman's decision to choose an abortion instead of continuing an unwanted pregnancy. Many states outlawed or severely restricted access to abortion. Women who could afford to travel to another state or out of the country could usually find legal medical services, but poorer women often turned to abortion methods that were not only illegal but unsafe.

A landmark social change came in 1973, when the Supreme Court legalized abortion in the controversial **Roe v. Wade** decision. The justices based their decision on a constitutional right to personal privacy and struck down state regulation of abortion in the first three months of pregnancy. However, the ruling still allowed states to restrict abortions during the later stages of pregnancy. The case was, and remains, highly controversial, with radical thinkers on both sides of the argument.

The Equal Rights Amendment Many women also took part in the campaign for a change to the Constitution that would make discrimination on account of sex illegal. In

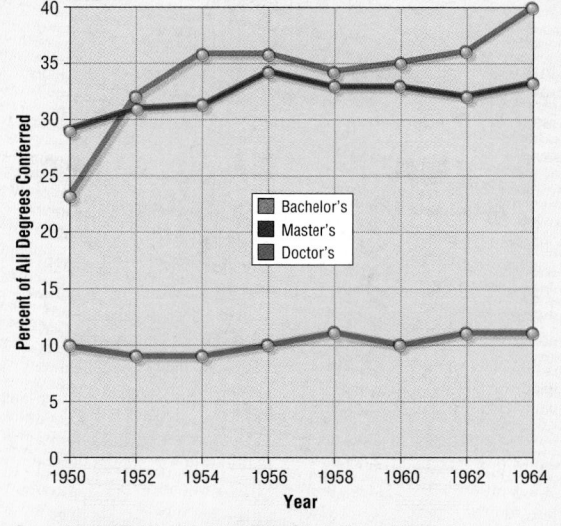

Women Earning College Degrees, 1950–1964

Source: *Historical Statistics of the United States, Colonial Times to 1970*

Interpreting Graphs As women's educational levels rose, so did their expectations of good jobs and fair salaries. *Diversity* At which degree level—bachelor's, master's, or doctoral—did women gain the least?

1972 Congress passed the **Equal Rights Amendment (ERA)** to the Constitution:

KEY DOCUMENTS "Equality of rights under the law shall not be denied or abridged by the United States or by any State on account of sex."

—*Equal Rights Amendment, 1972*

To become law, the amendment had to be ratified by thirty-eight states. Thirty states complied quickly, then a few others, and approval at first seemed certain. Strong opposition surfaced, however, and the struggle for ratification limped along until 1982 and then died.

Opposition to the Women's Movement

Conservative political activist Phyllis Schlafly led a national campaign to block ratification of the ERA, saying:

Phyllis Schlafly

From the Archives of

American Heritage

E.R.A. On March 22, 1972, by a vote of 84 to 8, the Senate passed the Equal Rights Amendment, a goal of feminists for half a century. Since the House had given equally lopsided approval the previous fall, the amendment went to the states for ratification. Thirty-two minutes after the Senate vote, Hawaii became the first to ratify; New Hampshire and Nebraska followed the next day. Support for the idea of equality quickly swept the country, with both major parties endorsing the amendment. Within a year of the Senate vote, 30 of the required 38 states had passed the E.R.A. Boosters confidently predicted a quick completion of the process. Over the remainder of 1973, though, no more states added their names to the list. In 1974, even as polls showed three quarters of Americans in favor, just three states gave their consent. One state ratified in 1975 and one in 1977, raising the total to 35, but that was all. The E.R.A.'s time limit expired in 1982, and since then, there has been no serious attempt to get it through Congress again. Source: Frederic D. Schwarz, "The Time Machine," *American Heritage* magazine, February 1997.

Answer to . . .

Interpreting Charts Doctoral.

1. (a) feminism, see p. 845; (b) National Organization for Women, see p. 847; (c) *Roe* v. *Wade*, see p. 849; (d) Equal Rights Amendment, see p. 849.

2. They formed support groups to share ideas and plan the movement; organized NOW to fight for equal jobs and equal pay; fought for abortion rights and for the ERA.

3. Webs may include: fair pay, equal job opportunities, the addressing of women's health concerns, improved child-care facilities, shelters for homeless and abused women, the legalization of abortion, passage of the ERA.

4. Sample answer: 1966—NOW formed, because this organization spearheaded most of the women's rights initiative, including the fight for abortion and equal rights.

5. That women should fight discrimination just as African Americans had in the civil rights movement; that the Civil Rights Act applied to women as well; that women were doing work equal to men but not being compensated equally.

6. Essays will vary but should be supported with facts from the section.

COMPARING PRIMARY SOURCES

ON WORKING MOTHERS

In the early years of the women's movement, experts on both sides voiced their opinions in the debate over the issue of working mothers.

In Favor of Working Mothers	Opposed to Working Mothers
"At the present time, one can say anything—good or bad—about children of employed mothers and support the statement by some research finding. But there is no definitive evidence that children are less happy, healthy, adjusted, because their mothers work. The studies that show working women to be happier, better, more mature mothers do not get much publicity."	"To work or not to work? Some mothers have to work to make a living. Usually their children turn out all right, because some reasonably good arrangement is made for their care. But others grow up neglected and maladjusted. . . . It doesn't make sense to let mothers go to work making dresses in a factory or tapping typewriters in an office, and have them pay other people to do a poorer job of bringing up their children."
—*Betty Friedan*, The Feminine Mystique, *1963*	—*Benjamin Spock, M.D.,* Baby and Childcare, *1957 edition, first published in 1945*

ANALYZING VIEWPOINTS What argument does each author use to support his or her opinion?

 AMERICAN VOICES "It won't do anything to help women, and it will take away from women the rights they already have, such as the right of a wife to be supported by her husband, the right of a woman to be exempted from military combat, and the right . . . to go to a single-sex college."

—*Phyllis Schlafly*

Women already had legal backing for their rights, Schlafly argued. ERA supporters contested Schlafly's charges about the supposed effects of the ERA, such as coed bathrooms and the end of alimony. Such arguments prevented the ERA from being ratified within the time limit.

Schlafly was not alone in her opposition. Many men at first were hostile to the feminist movement, which became known as "women's liberation" or "women's lib." Nor were all women sympathetic. Some responded by stressing their desire to remain at home and raise children and voicing their satisfaction with traditional roles.

Some African American women felt that combatting racial discrimination was more important than battling sex discrimination. In 1974, NOW's African American president Aileen Fernandez acknowledged that "Some black sisters are not sure that the feminist movement will meet their current needs."

Many working-class women felt removed from the movement, too. They believed they were being encouraged to give up homemaking in order to take up the unpleasant paid labor their husbands endured.

SECTION 1 REVIEW

Comprehension

1. *Key Terms* Define: (a) feminism; (b) National Organization for Women (NOW); (c) *Roe* v. *Wade;* (d) Equal Rights Amendment (ERA).

2. *Summarizing the Main Idea* Name at least three ways in which women tried to fight discrimination.

3. *Organizing Information* Create a web diagram that shows the issues supported by organized women's groups such as NOW. Write *Issues Supported by the Women's Movement* in the center circle. Include at least six supporting details in circles surrounding the center circle.

Critical Thinking

4. *Analyzing Time Lines* Review the time line at the start of the section. In your opinion, which event had the greatest impact on the women's movement? Explain your reasoning.

5. *Identifying Assumptions* What beliefs prompted many women to join the women's movement in the 1960s?

Writing Activity

6. *Writing an Expository Essay* Research and write an essay about the opposition to the women's movement. Focus your essay on the battle to stop the ratification of the ERA.

Answer to . . .

Comparing Primary Sources Spock argues that some children are harmed because their mothers work. Friedan argues that there is no proven cause-and-effect relationship between working mothers and maladjusted children.

▶ RESOURCE OPTIONS

Teaching Resources

 Comparing Primary Sources On Working Mothers, Units 9–10 folder, pp. 38–39

Quiz Units 9–10 folder, p. 30

Student Performance Pack

 Guide to the Essentials Chapter 30, Section 1 (English and Spanish)

Media and Technology

 Color Transparencies Fine Art, D-20

Recognizing Bias

Recognizing bias means being aware of information and ideas that are one-sided or that present only a partial view of a subject. Knowing how to recognize bias is important because this skill helps you to better understand not only historical events, but also current issues. Campaign speeches, debates on controversial topics, and opinions expressed in the media all contain elements of bias. The ability to spot bias will help you analyze information.

Bias often is attached to issues that have emotional impact. One such issue is the women's movement, which questions the role of women in American life. Both of the excerpts on this page were taken from articles written during the women's movement in the late 1960s and early 1970s. Use the following questions to help you determine whether either of these writings is biased.

1. *Decide whether or not the excerpt presents only one side of an issue while suggesting it covers all sides.* Writing from a single viewpoint signals imbalance—and bias. Read both passages and then answer the following questions. (a) What is the overall message of each excerpt? (b) Which presents only one side of the issue while suggesting that it presents a complete picture?

2. *Determine whether the issue as described is supported by opinions or verifiable facts.* Sometimes what appear to be facts are actually

opinions disguised as facts. (a) Which details presented in the excerpts can be checked for accuracy? (b) Are any opinions presented as though they were facts? Give an example from the excerpts.

3. *Examine the excerpts for hidden assumptions or generalizations that are not supported by facts.* What hidden assumptions or general-

izations do you find in Excerpt A? Excerpt B?

TEST FOR SUCCESS

Analyze the excerpts below for bias. Which excerpt is the least biased? Explain your answer.

A "What do black women feel about Women's Lib? Distrust. It is white, therefore suspect. They don't want to be used again to help somebody gain power—a power that is carefully kept out of their hands. They look at white women and see them as the enemy—for they know that racism is not confined to white men. . . . The faces of those white women hovering behind that black girl at the Little Rock school in 1957 do not soon leave the retina of the mind."

—*Toni Morrison,*
"What the Black Woman Thinks About Women's Lib,"
The New York Times Magazine, *August 22, 1971*

B "The 14th and 15th amendments, written in 1868 and 1870, said: 'All persons born or naturalized in the U.S. are citizens and have the right to vote.'

Susan B. Anthony, considering herself to be a person, registered and voted in 1872. She was arrested, brought to trial, convicted of the crime of voting—because she was a woman, and the word *persons* mentioned in our Constitution did not mean women. . . . If she were alive today, Susan B. Anthony might vote, but she would still see 1000 legal discriminations against women upon various state statute books. . . .

The solution of the problem of giving women 100 per cent protection of the Constitution . . . is the adoption of the Equal Rights for Women Amendment which reads: *Equality of rights under law shall not be denied or abridged by the United States or by any state on account of sex.*"

—*Marjorie Longwell,*
"The American Woman—Then and Now,"
Delta Kappa Gamma Magazine, *Fall 1969*

Focus Students will practice recognizing bias in two written selections.
Instruct After students have read the selections, ask them to analyze the following quotation using the steps in this feature.
"As radical feminists we recognize that we are engaged in a power struggle with men, and that the agent of our oppression is man insofar as he identifies with and carries out the supremacy privileges of the male role. For while we realize that the liberation of women will ultimately mean the liberation of men from their destructive role as oppressor, we have no illusion that men will welcome this liberation without a struggle."
Extend See the Skills for Life Activity in the Resource Options below.

Answers

1. (a) A: Black women distrust women's lib and see white women as a racist enemy. B: Passing the ERA will solve the problem of legal discrimination. (b) Both A and B.

2. (a) A: The phrase "faces of those white women hovering behind that black girl at the Little Rock school in 1957." B: The text of the amendments; Anthony's arrest, trial, and conviction; the number of discriminations against women in state statutes. (b) Yes, A's opinions of black women's attitudes toward women's lib, white feminist organizations, and white women.

3. A: All black women have the same distrustful view of women's lib, white feminist organizations, and white women; all white women are racist. B: Women are not now protected by the Constitution.

TEST FOR SUCCESS

B, as it is more verifiable.

Ethnic Minorities Seek Equality

Objectives

You may wish to call students' attention to the objectives in the Section Preview. The objectives are reflected in the main headings of the section.

Bellringer

Ask students to consider the dilemma faced by all ethnic Americans from the early days of mass immigration: whether to assimilate or to try to retain their native culture. Ask students to note what is gained and lost by assimilation.

Reading Strategy

Outlining Information Refer to the Reading Strategy in the Section Preview. You may wish to provide the first heading, subheading, and details as a model for students.

LESSON PLAN

Connecting to the Main Idea

1. Focus Inspired by the civil rights movement, other ethnic minorities such as Latinos and Asian Americans began to struggle for greater equality. Ask how their struggles differed.

2. Instruct Discuss how cultural differences among different groups of Latinos have led to many Latino movements rather than a single unified effort for equality in American society. Read this comment by Daniel Villanueva, a TV executive: "We need a Spanish Bobby Kennedy or Martin Luther King. Right now he's just not there." Discuss what a "Spanish Martin Luther King" might have been able to do that Cesar Chavez did not do.

3. Close Latinos and Asian Americans both used the techniques of the civil rights movement to overcome racial discrimination. The next section describes the struggle of Native Americans for self-determination.

Timeline

1959 Hawaii becomes a state	**1967** Cesar Chavez organizes boycott of grapes	**1968** Mexican American students protest inferior quality schools	**1970** La Raza Unida formed

1959 — **1965** — **1971**

2 Ethnic Minorities Seek Equality

SECTION PREVIEW

Objectives

1 Describe the Latino population.
2 Explain how Cesar Chavez and others protested discrimination.
3 Describe the ways in which Asian Americans fought against racial discrimination and made economic and political gains in the 1960s and 1970s.
4 *Key Terms* Define: Latino; migrant farm worker; United Farm Workers (UFW); Japanese American Citizens League (JACL).

Main Idea

Inspired by the civil rights movement, Latinos and Asian Americans launched their own movements to overcome discrimination.

Reading Strategy

Outlining Information Skim the section and use the headings and subheadings to create an outline. As you read, fill in appropriate details in your outline of the section.

Inspired by the civil rights and women's movements, other ethnic and racial groups began to fight for equality during the 1960s and 1970s. In May 1970, journalist Rubén Salazar predicted the future of the Chicano movement in Los Angeles, California. "We are going to overthrow some of our institutions," he said. "But in the way Americans have always done it: through the ballot, through public consensus. That's a revolution." Three months later, Salazar was killed when rioting broke out after police tried to stop a Chicano anti-Vietnam War demonstration. Although Salazar was not an activist, after his death he became a martyr to the movement.

The Latino Population

People whose family origins are in Spanish-speaking Latin America, or **Latinos,** come from many places. They share the same language and some elements of culture. But whether they come from Puerto Rico, Cuba, Mexico, or other parts of the Americas, Latinos often have been seen as outsiders.

They have been denied equal opportunities in many aspects of life, including employment, education, and housing.

In the late 1960s and early 1970s, more and more people arrived from Central America and South America. Between 1970 and 1980, census figures for people "of Spanish origin" rose from 9 million to 14.6 million. Specific groups tended to settle in certain areas. Cubans moved to Florida, Puerto Ricans moved to the Northeast, and Mexicans moved to the West and Southwest.

Mexican Americans, often known as Chicanos, always have been the most numerous Latinos in the United States. In the 1960s, they began to organize against discrimination in education, jobs, and the legal system, leading to *el Movimiento Chicano*—the Chicano movement.

Cultural Identity Activists began encouraging pride in Mexican American culture and its dual heritage from Spain and the ancient cultures of Mexico. In 1967 Rodolfo "Corky" Gonzales, a Denver, Colorado, activist, wrote a

---

 RESOURCE OPTIONS

Teaching Resources

 Reproducible Lesson Plan Lesson Plans folder, p. 154

Learning Styles Lesson Plan Learning Styles Lesson Plans folder, p. 62

Big Idea Graphic Organizer Big Idea Graphic Organizer folder, p. 126

Guided Reading and Review Units 9–10 folder, p. 31

long poem that raised Mexican Americans' self-awareness nationwide. *Yo Soy Joaquin* ("I am Joaquin") expresses the importance of cultural identity. It begins:

> I am Joaquin
> lost in a world of confusion
> caught up in the whirl of a gringo [white] society,
> confused by the rules,
> scorned by attitudes,
> suppressed by manipulation
> and destroyed by modern society.

Gonzales' claim was that the Anglos—white, English-speaking non-Latinos—had undermined Mexican Americans' control over their lives through economic pressure and through institutions such as the schools, the Roman Catholic Church, and the media.

Education Schools in the barrios, or Latino neighborhoods, were crowded and run-down, with high dropout rates. In March 1968, 10,000 Mexican American students walked out of five such Los Angeles high schools to protest their unequal treatment. Students in other parts of California, and in Colorado and Texas, followed their example. Students demanded culturally sensitive courses, better facilities, and Latino teachers and counselors.

Cesar Chavez

 AMERICAN BIOGRAPHY The students were not, however, the only people protesting in the Latino community. Throughout the 1960s organizers struggled to unite Latino farm workers. Cesar Chavez, founder of the United Farm Workers, became a hero to millions of Americans, both Latino and Anglo. He was born in Yuma, Arizona, where his family had farmed for three generations. During the Great Depression, they lost their adobe farmhouse because they could not afford the taxes. Relocating to California, they made their living as **migrant farm workers,** moving from farm to farm to provide the labor needed to plant, cultivate,

Cesar Chavez (1927–1993)

and harvest crops. Chavez later remembered how his family fostered a powerful sense of independence:

AMERICAN VOICES "I don't want to suggest we were that radical, but I know we were probably one of the strikingest families in California, the first ones to leave the fields if anyone shouted "Huelga!" — which is Spanish for *Strike!*"

—*Cesar Chavez*

As he grew up among farm workers, Chavez came to believe that unions offered the best opportunity to gain bargaining power and resist employers' economic power. Migrant farm workers were some of the most exploited

 FACT Finder

United Farm Workers Achievements

Financial	• First collective bargaining agreements between workers and growers
	• First contracts requiring hiring out of union halls
	• First pension plan for retired farm workers
	• First functioning credit union for farm workers
	• Extension of unemployment compensation for farm workers
Health and Safety	• First union contracts requiring rest periods, clean drinking water, hand washing facilities, and protection against exposure to pesticides
	• First comprehensive union health benefits for farm workers and their families
	• First union contracts regulating safety and sanitary conditions of farm labor camps
	• Abolition of the crippling short-handled hoe
	• Extension of disability and workers' compensation to farm workers

Interpreting Tables Labor activists Cesar Chavez and Dolores Huerta founded the United Farm Workers Association (UFWA) in Fresno, California, in 1962. *Economics* **What do you view as the UFWA's most important achievement, and why?**

RESOURCE OPTIONS

Teaching Resources

📁 **Biography** Dolores Huerta, Units 9–10 folder, p 37

Media and Technology

AmericanHeritage® CD-ROM

History Makers Cesar Chavez

 BACKGROUND

Recent Scholarship

The movement for Latino rights followed on the heels of the African American struggle for civil rights and women's campaign for equality. Today, Latinos, like members of other groups, are trying to define their own role in American society. In *Mexican Americans: The Ambivalent Minority,* Peter Skerry argues that the Mexican American population faces different challenges from those faced by other groups. Focusing on San Antonio and Los Angeles and drawing on recent history, he suggests that assimilation will occur, but only within the context of radical changes in American institutions.

 BACKGROUND

Art History

In the tradition of early 20th-century Mexican muralists, Mexican-American artists of the 1960s and 1970s applied their skills to the public walls of Los Angeles. Influenced by Catholicism, Mexican history, and contemporary issues, these murals inspired pride in Chicano culture. Many murals illustrate the problems of migrant farm workers. Others commemorate the 1984 Olympics or tell the history of California from the point of view of women and people of color. Today, the murals testify to the city's diversity of cultures and artistic talent.

Answer to . . .

Interpreting Tables Sample answer: The first union contracts, as they paved the way for later achievements.

workers in the country. They had to spend long hours doing backbreaking work for little pay. In the 1960s Chavez began to organize Mexican field hands into what became the **United Farm Workers (UFW).** He and a group of loyal followers went from door to door and field to field. By 1965 the union had 1,700 members.

The UFW's first target was the grape growers of California. Chavez, like Martin Luther King, Jr., believed in nonviolent action. In 1967, when growers refused to grant more pay, better working conditions, and union recognition, Chavez organized a successful nationwide consumer boycott of grapes picked on nonunion farms. Later boycotts of lettuce and other crops also won consumer support.

Chavez's efforts created many angry enemies and even brought him death threats. He responded by saying:

Main Idea
CONNECTIONS

What methods did Cesar Chavez use to gain rights for migrant farm workers?

AMERICAN VOICES ❝It's not me who counts, it's the Movement. And I think that in terms of stopping the Movement—this one or other movements by poor people around the country—the possibility is very remote. . . . The tide for change now has gone too far.❞

— *Cesar Chavez*

In 1975 California passed a law that required collective bargaining between growers and union representatives. Workers now had a legal basis to ask for better working conditions. Chavez's efforts not only made him a national hero but also brought migrant farm workers into the movement for civil rights. ■

Other Latino Protests

Mexican Americans had other heroes, too. Some formed organizations that took a militant approach, while others used political action. In

 Mexico's northern neighbors, California and Texas, receive the majority of immigrants from Mexico. This mural in Los Angeles illustrates Mexican American pride. *Culture How did Chicano activists use their cultural heritage in the Chicano movement?*

1961 voters in San Antonio, Texas, elected Henry B. González to Congress. Another Texan, Elizo "Kika" de la Garza, went to the House of Representatives in 1964, while Joseph Montoya of New Mexico was elected to the Senate.

New political groups formed to support Latino interests. For example, José Angel Gutiérrez brought together Latino groups in Crystal City, Texas, leading to the formation of the political party *La Raza Unida* in 1970. The new party worked for better housing and jobs and backed Latino political candidates.

Another leader, Reies López Tijerina, argued that the Anglo culture had stolen the Chicanos' land and heritage. To call attention to broken treaties, in 1966 his *Alianza Federal de Mercedes* (Federal Alliance of Land Grants) marched on the New Mexico state capital, Santa Fe.

At about the same time, the Mexican American Legal Defense and Educational Fund (MALDEF) was founded. It has provided legal aid to help Mexican Americans defend their rights and encouraged Mexican American students to become lawyers.

Asian Americans Fight Discrimination

Ever since their arrival in the United States, Americans of Chinese and Japanese ancestry have faced racial discrimination. Prejudice against Japanese Americans reached a peak during World War II, while the Communist takeover of China in 1949 influenced attitudes toward Chinese Americans. Still, the years after the war brought many hopeful and positive changes for Asian Americans.

Japanese Americans After the War A major issue for Japanese Americans was compensation for the losses they had suffered during their wartime internment in the 1940s. As previously discussed, Japanese American citizens living along the West Coast were forced to relocate to internment camps. The government had feared that they were a risk to American security following Japan's attack on Pearl Harbor. Not only had their lives been disrupted, but they had lost

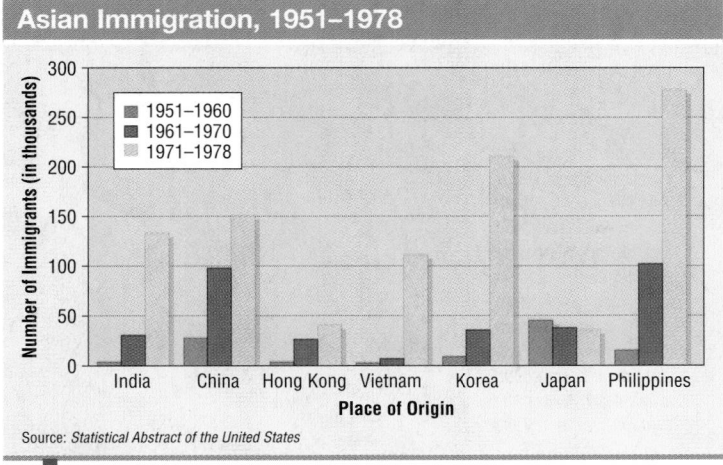

Asian Immigration, 1951–1978

Legend:
■ 1951–1960
■ 1961–1970
□ 1971–1978

Y-axis: Number of Immigrants (in thousands) — 0, 50, 100, 150, 200, 250, 300
X-axis: Place of Origin — India, China, Hong Kong, Vietnam, Korea, Japan, Philippines

Source: *Statistical Abstract of the United States*

 Interpreting Graphs Patterns of immigration from Asia changed dramatically in the 1950s, 1960s, and 1970s. *Diversity From which two countries came the greatest number of people in the 1950s? In the 1970s?*

hundreds of millions of dollars in homes, farms, and businesses. The main voice for Japanese Americans, the **Japanese American Citizens League (JACL),** in 1948 won passage of the Japanese American Claims Act. Under the act, Congress eventually paid relatively small amounts for property losses.[†]

About two thirds of Japanese Americans who had been relocated returned to the Pacific Coast. Others moved to cities east of the Rockies. Their new communities were more a part of mainstream society than the prewar *nihonmachis*—"Japantowns"—had been.

Economic Changes Although Asian Americans as a group were well educated, in 1960 they earned less than white Americans. In California, for example, for each $51 a white male was paid, a Chinese man would earn $38 and a Japanese man, $43. College graduates faced prejudice in attempting to move into management jobs.

As a group, Asian Americans in the 1960s and 1970s made economic gains faster than other minorities. Nonetheless, they still faced

---

[†] The United States did not officially apologize for the losses and injuries suffered by interned Japanese Americans until 1988. In that year Congress passed legislation that provided some monetary compensation to the approximately 60,000 surviving Japanese Americans who had been interned.

LEARNING STYLES

Ask students to research the Congressional Hispanic Caucus. Who are its members? What are its goals? How successful has the caucus been in reaching its goals? Have students present their information in a three-paragraph paper, with appropriate details covering each question above. (*Verbal/Linguistic*)

BACKGROUND

Interdisciplinary

The 1983 Nobel prize in physics was won by an Indian American, Subrahmayan Chandrasekhar. As a student at Cambridge University in England, he questioned the existing theory that stars become "white dwarfs," very old stars that no longer make much light, because they lack hydrogen gas. Chandrasekhar, who moved to the United States in 1937, agreed that the theory applied to small stars, but not to big ones. Gravity, he argued, would make big stars shrink until they were much smaller than white dwarfs and turned into what would later be called "black holes."

 RESOURCE OPTIONS

Teaching Resources

[ATLAS] **Nystrom *Atlas of Our Country*** Later Expansion of the United States, pp. 32–33; The Fourth Wave of Immigration, pp. 36–37

Answer to . . .

Interpreting Graphs Japan and China; the Philippines and Korea.

Answers to
SECTION 2 REVIEW

1. (a) Latino, see p. 852; (b) migrant farm worker, see p. 853; (c) United Farm Workers (UFW), see p. 854; (d) Japanese American Citizens League (JACL), see p. 855.

2. Latinos launched the UFW to improve working conditions, while Asian Americans formed the JACL and pushed for political representation.

3. Latinos—Reasons: poor treatment of migrant workers, poor housing and jobs. Results: legislation passed to facilitate employer and union compromise, Latino political parties formed and candidates elected. Asian Americans—Reasons: no compensation for wartime losses, wage discrimination, lack of political representation. Results: Japanese American Claims Act passed, economic gains made, several Asian American politicians elected.

4. Sample entry: 1959, Hawaii becomes a state—Asian Americans were given political influence in Congress.

5. He formed the UFW in order to win better conditions for migrant workers. By succeeding in having legislation passed in California, he drew national attention to the cause.

6. Pamphlets will vary but should be supported with facts from the section.

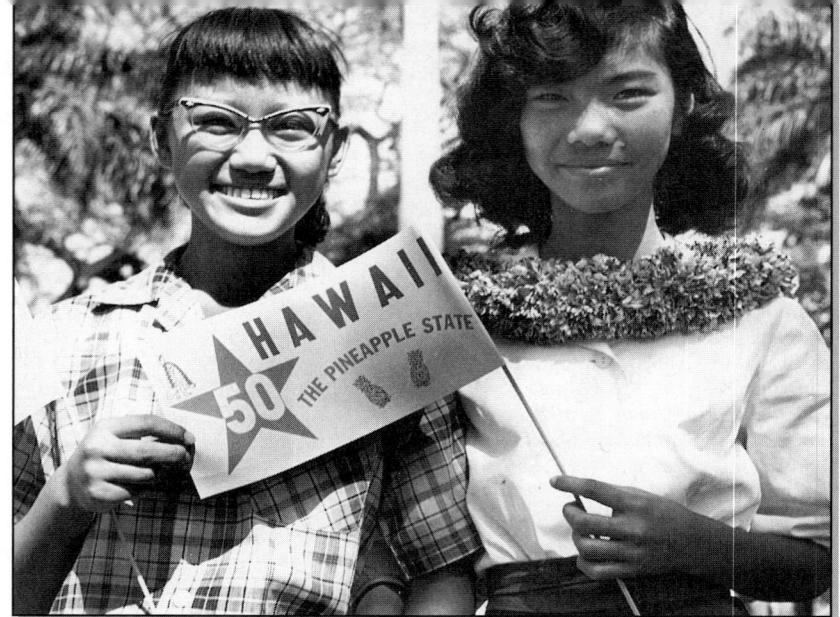

These girls are celebrating Hawaii's new status as the nation's fiftieth state in 1959. Statehood for Hawaii created, for the first time, a state in which most voters were of Asian or part-Asian ancestry. *Diversity How did Hawaii's statehood affect Asian Americans throughout the nation?*

discrimination and relied on the example of the civil rights movement to push for gains. Some Chinese American community activists in the 1970s asked for federal help in overcoming problems of unemployment, health, and language barriers. The 1970s also saw an increase in immigration from other Asian countries, especially Korea, India, and Vietnam, as illustrated by the graph on the previous page.

Political Representation In 1959 Asian Americans' self-image took a major step forward with the granting of statehood to Hawaii. The new state sent Hiram Leong Fong, a Chinese American, to the Senate, and Daniel K. Inouye, a Japanese American, to the House of Representatives. Other Asian American lawmakers have since been elected to various positions in local and state governments as well as in the federal government.

SECTION 2 REVIEW

Comprehension

1. *Key Terms* Define: (a) Latino; (b) migrant farm worker; (c) United Farm Workers (UFW); (d) Japanese American Citizens League (JACL).

2. *Summarizing the Main Idea* What were the main movements launched by Latinos and Asian Americans to overcome racial discrimination?

3. *Organizing Information* Create a two-column chart to organize information about Latino and Asian American protests. Label the two vertical columns *Latinos* and *Asian Americans.* Label the two horizontal rows *Reasons for Protest* and *Results of Protest.*

Critical Thinking

4. *Analyzing Time Lines* Review the time line at the start of the section. Choose one entry and explain its role in expanding the rights of Latinos or Asian Americans.

5. *Identifying Central Issues* What role did Cesar Chavez play in the Chicano struggle for equal rights?

Writing Activity

6. *Writing a Persuasive Essay* Write a pamphlet urging consumers to support the grape boycott organized by Cesar Chavez and the United Farm Workers.

RESOURCE OPTIONS

Teaching Resources

Quiz Units 9–10 folder, p. 32

Student Performance Pack

Guide to the Essentials Chapter 30, Section 2 (English and Spanish)

Answer to . . .

Viewing History It gave them a positive self-image.

1968	1969		1972	1973		1975
American Indian Movement (AIM) formed	Occupation of Alcatraz begins		Congress passes Indian Education Act	AIM takes over reservation at Wounded Knee		Indian Self-Determination and Education Assistance Act passed

1968		**1972**		**1976**

3 Native American Struggles

SECTION PREVIEW

Objectives

1 Describe the unique problems Native Americans faced.
2 Summarize the roots of Native American activism.
3 Understand how Native Americans confronted the government with protests and legal challenges to win more self-determination.
4 *Key Terms* Define: American Indian Movement (AIM); autonomy.

Main Idea

Native Americans in the 1960s also took their cue from the civil rights movement to work to improve their living conditions.

Reading Strategy

Formulating Questions Write the main headings from the section on a piece of paper. Formulate at least two questions for each heading and look for answers to your questions as you read the section.

Native Americans made up another minority group that was inspired by the civil rights movement to seek equality and control over their own lives. Shifting government policies had caused Native Americans great suffering over the years. Activists began using legal challenges and direct action to reach their goals.

Native Americans Face Unique Problems

As the original inhabitants of North America, Native Americans occupied a unique social and legal position. Although Indian cultures and languages varied among peoples, white society viewed them as one group. By 1871 the United States no longer recognized Indian nations as independent powers. It did not, however, extend Native Americans full citizenship.

From the 1800s on, government agencies limited self-government for Native Americans and often worked to erase their traditional lifestyles. Not until the Snyder Act of 1924 was citizenship granted to all Native Americans

born in the United States. After 1924 Native Americans were recognized as citizens of both the United States and their own nations or tribal groups.

As a whole, Native Americans have routinely been denied equal opportunities. Many states refused to give them the vote until pushed by Native American communities. It was not until 1948 that Arizona and New Mexico granted Indians the right to vote. Native Americans have higher rates of unemployment, alcoholism, and suicide, as well as a shorter life expectancy, than white Americans. Many communities have suffered from poverty and poor living conditions. Like other nonwhite groups, Native Americans have been the victims of centuries-old stereotypes reinforced by the images in movies and other media.

Native Americans also have had some grievances unique to their situation. Dennis Banks, a Chippewa, explained why he became an activist:

A Sioux woman joins a protest against federal policies for Native Americans.

Graphing the Main Idea

To make sure students understand the main idea of this section, you may wish to use the flow map graphic organizer below.

Tell students that a flow map shows a sequence of events unfolding. Ask students to use it to record the events of the Native American movement of the 1970s.

Teaching Tip A template for this graphic organizer can be found in the Color Transparencies, G-4.

Answer to . . .

Viewing History Lack of equal opportunities, loss of land.

AMERICAN VOICES ❝It was a question of this government being responsible to me, and not seeing to it that I had an opportunity to lead a decent life, or to own a piece of land, or to find a good job, like they had promised my ancestors in all these treaties. They broke all of those promises. They stole everything from them and wrecked their way of life—which was a good way.❞

—*Dennis Banks*

Roots of Native American Activism

An important part of the Native Americans' way of life was their ties to the land and what it stood for. "Everything is tied to our homeland," declared D'Arcy McNickle, a Native American anthropologist, in 1961. Yet, many years after pioneers first moved onto Native American territory, state and federal governments continued to take over traditional tribal lands. Protecting what was left became a major goal of Native Americans.

 Native Americans living on reservations, like the Navajo reservation above, suffer a rate of poverty far higher than that of the rest of the United States. *Economics* What are some of the historical reasons behind this poverty?

Land Claims A government project in New York State triggered one early protest. According to rights originally granted in a 1794 treaty, the Seneca Nation owned the land on its Allegany reservation. The federal government, however, wanted to build a dam there as part of a flood control project. The Kinzua Dam would affect 10,000 acres of hunting and fishing land, as well as homes and sacred sites.

In 1956 Congress held hearings, which did not include the Seneca, and appropriated funds for the dam. After legal appeals failed, the Seneca in 1961 went to President John Kennedy to ask that the project be halted. The President supported the government claim to the lands, and the dam was built. After construction was completed, Congress agreed to pay $15 million in damages to the Seneca, but this did not restore the land.

Other Native Americans responded to this decision by bringing lawsuits for violations of treaty rights and failure to make promised payments. Court rulings supported many claims. For example, in 1967 the Court of Claims ruled that the federal government had forced the Seminole to give up Florida lands in 1823 for an unreasonably low price. The court directed the government to pay more to the Seminole community.

The American Indian Movement One of the primary activist movements was started in Minneapolis in 1968 by Dennis Banks and George Mitchell, both Chippewa. At a meeting of 250 people representing 20 Native American organizations, Banks set forth the goals: "Let's get a new organized effort going, a new coalition that will fight for Indian treaty rights and better conditions and opportunities for our people."

The new organization came to be called the **American Indian Movement (AIM).** It originally focused on the special problems of Native Americans living in cities. Following the example of militant black groups, AIM set up Native American patrols to monitor street activity. It also began survival schools to encourage racial and cultural pride in young people. Eventually AIM's goals broadened to include the protection of Native American legal rights. They began to fight for **autonomy,** or self-government, with respect to local matters, especially natural resources on Native American lands. They also sought the restoration of lands that they believed had been illegally taken from them.

AIM leader Dennis Banks leads a protest march in South Dakota. Mount Rushmore looms in the background as a powerful symbol of the changes wrought on America by white Americans of European descent. *Government How did the federal government respond to Native American activism?*

Many people, both white and Native American, criticized AIM's militant approach. On the group's second anniversary, however, Banks repeated its goals:

> **AMERICAN VOICES** ❝The government and churches have demoralized, dehumanized, massacred, robbed, raped, promised, made treaty after treaty, and lied to us. . . . We must now destroy this political machine that man has built to prevent us from self-determination.❞
>
> —*Dennis Banks*

Confronting the Government

To call attention to issues long ignored, Native Americans staged several standoffs with the federal government. In 1972, demonstrators protesting the violation of treaties between the United States and various Indian groups formed the Broken Treaties Caravan. They traveled to Washington, D.C., and occupied the Bureau of Indian Affairs' offices for six days. Other protests were even more dramatic.

The Occupation of Alcatraz In 1969, seventy-eight protesters from several Native American groups landed on Alcatraz, an island in San Francisco Bay on which stood an abandoned federal prison. They claimed the 13-acre rock under the terms of the Fort Laramie Treaty of 1868, which allowed male Native Americans to file homestead claims on federal lands.

Others joined the group, planning to turn the deserted island into an educational and cultural center. In March 1970, author Vine Deloria, Jr., a Standing Rock Sioux, wrote hopefully about the project in *The New York Times:*

> **AMERICAN VOICES** ❝By making Alcatraz an experimental Indian center operated and planned by Indian people, we would be given a chance to see what we could do toward developing answers to modern social problems. . . . Perhaps we would not succeed in the effort. . . . It just seems to a lot of Indians that this continent was a lot better off when we were running it.❞
>
> —*Vine Deloria, Jr.*

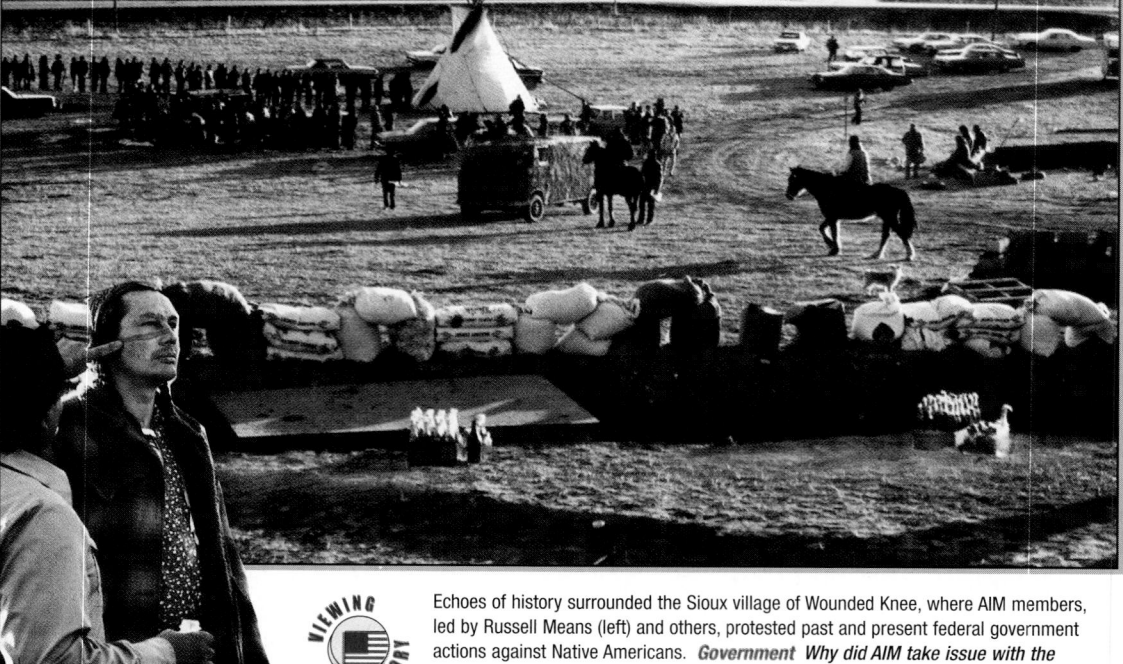

Echoes of history surrounded the Sioux village of Wounded Knee, where AIM members, led by Russell Means (left) and others, protested past and present federal government actions against Native Americans. **Government** *Why did AIM take issue with the federal government?*

The occupation failed. Federal marshals eventually removed the last protesters after a year and a half. But the episode succeeded in drawing national attention to Native American grievances.

Confrontation at Wounded Knee An even more dramatic confrontation came in 1973 at the Oglala Sioux village of Wounded Knee, South Dakota. There, in 1890, the army's Seventh Cavalry had massacred more than 200 Sioux men, women, and children.

The Pine Ridge reservation around the village was one of the country's poorest, with half its families living on welfare. In February 1973, AIM leaders Russell Means and Dennis Banks and some 200 AIM members took over the village. AIM refused to leave the reservation until the United States government agreed to investigate the treatment of Indians and the poor conditions on the reservation. AIM members also demanded that the United States review 371 treaties they said the government had broken over the years.

Main Idea
CONNECTIONS

What did AIM leaders demand during their confrontation at Wounded Knee?

Other Native American leaders came out in support of the occupation. Onondaga Chief Oren Lyons, speaking for the Iroquois, said:

AMERICAN VOICES "We support the Oglala Sioux Nation or any Indian Nation that will fight for its sovereignty. . . . The issue here at Wounded Knee is the recognition of the treaties between the United States Government and the sovereign nations that were here before."

— *Onondaga Chief Oren Lyons*

Federal marshals and FBI agents surrounded the village, allowing only occasional shipments of supplies. From time to time, gunfire broke out. As the siege went on, agents arrested some 300 people, including news reporters and outside supporters.

The standoff finally came to an end in May, when AIM agreed to surrender their weapons and leave the reservation. In exchange, the government consented to reexamine treaty rights. During the siege, two AIM members had been killed and about a dozen people hurt, including two federal marshals.

Government Response Native American activism brought some responses from the government. The Kennedy and Johnson administrations in the 1960s tried to bring jobs and income to some reservations by encouraging industries to locate there. They also encouraged the leasing of reservation lands to energy and development corporations. But many Native Americans worried about the effects of these projects on the land. In the 1970s, the Navaho, Crow, Northern Cheyenne, and others sought to renegotiate or cancel many of the leases.

Pressure by Indians also led to their inclusion in Great Society programs dealing with housing, health, and education. Government agencies made resources available and let Native Americans plan and run their own programs and, in some places, their own schools.

A number of laws passed in the 1970s favored Native American rights. The Indian Education Act of 1972 gave parents and tribal councils more control over schools and school programs. The Indian Self-Determination Act of 1974 upheld Native American autonomy and let local leaders administer federally supported social programs for housing and education.

Native Americans also continued to win legal battles to regain land, mineral, and water rights. For example, in 1971 the Alaska Federation of Natives was given $1 billion and 40 million acres of land. In 1970, after reject-

ing a cash settlement, the Taos in New Mexico won back Blue Lake, a religious shrine, as well as 48,000 acres of land.

Wearing traditional ceremonial dress, George Crows Fly High and Martha Grass seek a meeting with Supreme Court justices. *Government* *What sorts of issues did Native American groups seek to settle in the courts?*

SECTION 3 REVIEW

Comprehension

1. **Key Terms** Define: (a) American Indian Movement (AIM); (b) autonomy.

2. **Summarizing the Main Idea** How did the African American civil rights movement influence the tactics of Native American groups?

3. **Organizing Information** Create a web diagram that organizes information about the various Indian protests and legal challenges. In the center circle write *Native Americans Seek Equality Through Protest.* Provide details in surrounding circles.

Critical Thinking

4. **Analyzing Time Lines** Review the time line at the start of the section. Choose one entry and explain its significance in the struggle for Native American rights.

5. **Expressing Problems Clearly** What problems were typical of Native American communities in the 1960s?

Writing Activity

6. **Writing an Expository Essay** Write a brief essay about the goals of the American Indian Movement. Be sure to include answers to the following questions: How did AIM try to achieve its goals? In your opinion, was the group successful? Why or why not?

1962	1966	1970	1970	1972	1974
Rachel Carson publishes Silent Spring	National Traffic and Motor Vehicle Safety Act	First Earth Day celebrated on April 22	Environmental Protection Agency established	Congress passes Clean Water Act	Nuclear Regulatory Commission established

1962 **1966** **1970** **1974**

SECTION 4

The Environmental Movement

Objectives

You may wish to call students' attention to the objectives in the Section Preview. The objectives are reflected in the main headings of the section.

Bellringer

Ask students to recall how many decisions they made on each day of the past week that affected the environment. Discuss how and why they made these decisions. How many of their decisions were good for the environment?

Reading Strategy

Reading for Evidence Refer to the Reading Strategy in the Section Preview. You may wish to discuss the meanings of the terms *attitudes* and *public policies* before you begin.

LESSON PLAN

Connecting to the Main Idea

1. Focus Inspired by other protest movements, environmentalists and consumer advocates demanded action to preserve the environment and protect the buyers and users of products in America. Ask students what triggered these movements. How successful were they?

2. Instruct Explain that many environmental problems grew out of the rapid development of technology, industry, and transportation after World War II. Have students list some voluntary measures that people undertake to preserve the environment. What role should the federal government play in regulating the environment? Should it determine how communities dispose of trash, or how manufacturers package items?

3. Close The environmental and consumer movements of the 1960s borrowed the techniques of the civil rights movement to change attitudes and public policy.

4 The Environmental Movement

SECTION PREVIEW

Objectives

1 Describe the efforts begun in the 1960s to protect the environment.
2 Explain how the government has tried to balance economic development with environmental protection.
3 Understand that a movement for consumers' rights grew out of other protest movements of the 1960s.
4 **Key Terms** Define: Nuclear Regulatory Commission (NRC); Environmental Protection Agency (EPA); Clean Air Act; Clean Water Act.

Main Idea

The mood of protest in the 1960s energized movements to preserve the environment and to ensure the safety of consumer products.

Reading Strategy

Reading for Evidence The text below states that the efforts of environmentalists and consumerists "brought lasting changes in public attitudes and public policy." As you read the section, look for evidence to support this statement.

People showed their support for the environmental movement by wearing buttons such as this one.

In the 1960s and the early 1970s, the mood of protest surrounding the civil rights movement inspired several other movements. Environmentalists demanded actions that would preserve and restore the earth's environment and resources. Consumer advocates used proven protest techniques to ensure that industry would be accountable to their customers and workers. These efforts brought lasting changes in public attitudes and public policy.

Protecting the Environment

Like the women's movement, the environmental movement of the 1960s had roots in the American past. In the late 1890s and early 1900s, Progressives had worked to make public lands and parks available for the people. New Deal programs of the 1930s included tree-planting projects in an effort to put people back to work—and to conserve forests and farmlands. The modern environmental movement, however, stemmed even more directly from the work of one woman.

Rachel Carson Marine biologist Rachel Carson grew up wanting to become a writer. Her mother taught her to appreciate nature and encouraged Carson's growing interest in zoology. In the 1930s and 1940s Carson combined her talents and began to write about scientific subjects for general audiences. In 1951 she published *The Sea Around Us*, which was an immediate bestseller and won the National Book Award. This book, and her next, *The Edge of the Sea*, made her famous as a naturalist. A main theme in Carson's work was the notion that human beings are part of nature. Furthermore, she believed that humans carried a great responsibility because they had the

RESOURCE OPTIONS

Teaching Resources

📁 **Reproducible Lesson Plan** Lesson Plans folder, p. 156

📁 **Learning Styles Lesson Plan** Learning Styles Lesson Plans folder, p. 63

📁 **Big Idea Graphic Organizer** Big Idea Graphic Organizer folder, p. 128

📁 **Guided Reading and Review** Units 9–10 folder, p. 35

Media and Technology

 AmericanHeritage® CD-ROM

Time Tour The Nation Today and Tomorrow: Toward a New Century

power to change the environment. Her most influential book, *Silent Spring,* warned against the abuse of that power.

In *Silent Spring,* published in 1962, Carson attacked the use of chemical pesticides, particularly DDT. She argued that DDT had increased agricultural productivity but killed various plants and animals along with the insect pests that were its target. She stated:

AMERICAN VOICES ❝The most alarming of all man's assaults upon the environment is the contamination of air, earth, rivers, and sea with dangerous and even lethal materials. This pollution is for the most part irrecoverable. . . . In this now universal contamination of the environment, chemicals are the sinister and little-recognized partners of radiation in changing the very nature of the world.❞

—*Rachel Carson in* Silent Spring

As Carson explained, chemicals sprayed on crops entered into living organisms and moved from one to another in a chain of poisoning and death. Specifically, the lingering effects of DDT threatened to destroy many species of birds and fish, including the national symbol, the bald eagle.

Silent Spring caused a big stir. The chemical industry fought back vigorously, arguing that Carson confused the issues and left readers "unable to sort fact from fancy." The public was not persuaded by this attack. So great was national concern that a special presidential advisory committee was appointed. It called for continued research and warned against the widespread use of pesticides. Eventually DDT was banned in the United States, and other chemicals were controlled more strictly. (For more information about the impact of *Silent Spring,* see the "Geography and History" feature that follows this section.)

It was not only DDT that worried people. They became more conscious of poisonous fumes in the air, oil spills on beaches, and toxic wastes buried in the ground. In the mid-1960s, President Lyndon Johnson addressed environmental concerns as part of the Great Society. Johnson hoped for "an environment that is pleasing to the senses and healthy to live in." Environmental legislation was part of his broader reform program.

Nuclear Power During the 1960s, concern about the overuse of nonrenewable resources, such as oil and gas, had encouraged the development of nuclear power plants built to generate electricity. Many people considered nuclear plants to be better than coal-burning plants because they caused less air pollution. Nuclear plants, however, produced steam that was then discharged into local waterways. The steam raised water temperatures, killing fish and plant life.

People were also worried about the possibility of nuclear plant accidents. People feared that in the event of an accident, radioactivity would be released into the air, causing serious damage to all plant and animal life in the surrounding area. In response to these fears, the government created the **Nuclear Regulatory Commission (NRC)** in 1974. The NRC became responsible for overseeing the use of nuclear materials in civilian life. Its chief goal was to ensure that nuclear power plants and facilities were operated safely.

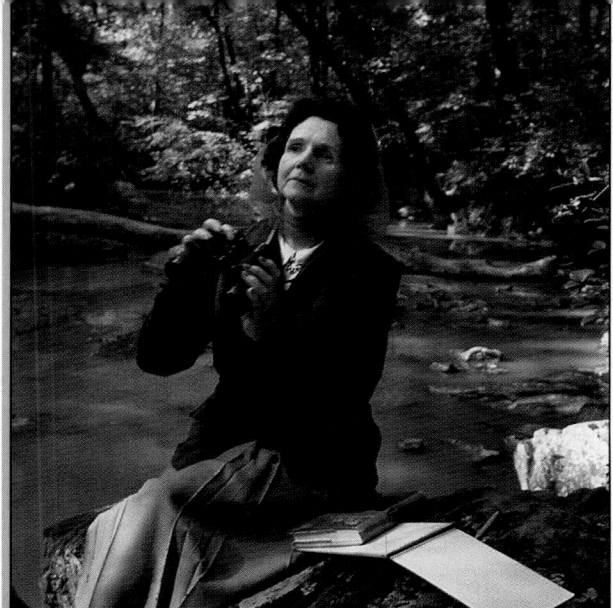

Disturbed by the changes she saw in the environment, biologist Rachel Carson sounded a trumpet call to action in her book *Silent Spring,* inspiring others to join a strong environmental movement. *Science and Technology According to Carson's book, how was science and technology working against the public interest?*

Environmental activists battled for a variety of issues in the 1960s, including the banning of nuclear power.

Concern about Earth and its resources prompted Earth Day rallies and mass clean-up activities. **Geography** What earlier efforts at environmental protection produced the new environmental movement?

Public Response Besides Rachel Carson, other scientists were alarmed by environmental problems. They too began to publicize their concerns. For example, in his 1971 book *The Closing Circle,* biologist Barry Commoner warned about rapid increases in pollution.

Grassroots environmental movements sprang up in many places as a result of increased awareness. Groups supporting conservation efforts and opposing actions such as the building of new nuclear plants gained attention. In 1969, Senator Gaylord Nelson of Wisconsin announced plans to hold a national day of discussion and teaching about the environment. The following year, on April 22, 1970, Americans celebrated the first Earth Day. Organizers stressed the important role Americans could play in improving awareness of environmental issues and bringing an end to environmental damage. Earth Day would become a yearly observance. Its aim was to heighten concern for the environment, to increase awareness about environmental issues, and to clean up pollution and litter.

Government Actions The efforts of environmentalists helped spur the federal government to create a new agency that would set and enforce national pollution-control standards. In 1970, President Nixon established the **Environmental Protection Agency (EPA).** The EPA was formed by combining existing federal agencies concerned with air and water pollution.

One of the EPA's early responsibilities was to enforce the **Clean Air Act.** Passed by Congress in 1970 in response to public concerns about air pollution, the Clean Air Act was designed to control pollution caused by

Main Idea
CONNECTIONS

How did Americans respond to the environmental concerns of scientists?

industries and car emissions. The EPA forged an agreement with car manufacturers to install catalytic converters (devices that convert tailpipe pollutants to less dangerous substances) in cars to reduce harmful emissions.

In 1972 the EPA gained further responsibilities when Congress enacted the **Clean Water Act** to regulate the discharge of industrial and municipal wastewater. The act also provided for grants to build better sewage-treatment facilities. As the nation's watchdog against polluters, the EPA continues to monitor and reduce air and water pollution. It regulates the disposal of solid waste and the use of pesticides and toxic substances.

Balancing Jobs and the Environment

Efforts to clean up and preserve the environment did not come without a cost. Many industry leaders worried that the new regulations would be confusing to follow and overly costly to businesses. They raised concerns that the increased costs associated with cleaning up the air and water would result in the loss of jobs. Government and industry worked to balance the demands of economic development and environmental protection.

The development of oil fields in Alaska provides an example of how the government tried to achieve this balance. Construction began in 1974 on an 800-mile long pipeline designed to carry oil across the frozen landscape to ice-free ports in the southern part of Alaska. Growth in the oil industry created new jobs and expanded revenues for the state.

Development brought with it increased concern over the welfare of the Alaskan wilderness and the rights of native Alaskans. The Alaska Native Claims Settlement Act of 1971 set aside millions of acres of land for the state's native groups, to be used partly for conservation purposes. In 1978 and again in 1980 additional land was added to the state's protected conservation areas.

The Consumer Movement

The consumer movement was yet another outgrowth of the 1960s protests. It too had earlier roots. The Pure Food and Drug Act of 1906, for example, was one early effort to maintain standards and protect the public. In the 1960s and early 1970s, however, the consumer movement grew far stronger and larger.

Attorney Ralph Nader spearheaded the new consumer effort. Nader had been a serious activist all his life. While a student at Princeton University in the early 1950s, Nader protested the spraying of campus trees with DDT. His interest in automobile safety began at Harvard Law School. In 1964 Daniel Patrick Moynihan, then Assistant Secretary of Labor, hired Nader as a consultant on the issue of automobile safety regulations.

FACT Finder

Major Environmental Legislation, 1964–1976

Year	Legislation	Description
1964	Wilderness Act	Designated lands to be maintained and preserved for public enjoyment.
1966	Rare and Endangered Species Act	Established protection for rare, endangered, and threatened plants and animals.
1970	Environmental Protection Agency	Created as an independent federal agency to administer the laws that affect the environment.
1970	Clean Air Act	Instituted a research and development program to prevent and control air pollution.
1972	Clean Water Act	Established regulations for preventing urban and industrial water pollution.
1974	Resource Conservation and Recovery Act	Established guidelines for storage and/or disposal of existing hazardous waste.
1974	Safe Drinking Water Act	Established guidelines for safe drinking water.
1976	Toxic Substance Control Act	Enacted to regulate the commercial manufacture, processing, and distribution of chemical substances.

Interpreting Tables The government responded to environmental activism by enacting a series of legislation, including the formation of the Environmental Protection Agency. *Government How do these acts affect both individuals and industry?*

TEST PREPARATION

Have students read the quotation by Ralph Nader on the next page and then answer the question below.

The word *inestimable* in the passage means—

A extreme.

(B) impossible to calculate.

C unexplained.

D unexpected.

Answer to . . .

Interpreting Tables Individuals: They provide for clean air and water, and protect people from toxic substances. Industries: They regulate their production of pollutants, subject their products to safety tests, and protect wild animals and ecosystems.

Answers to

SECTION 4 REVIEW

1. (a) Nuclear Regulatory Commission (NRC), see p. 863; (b) Environmental Protection Agency (EPA), see p. 864; (c) Clean Air Act, see p. 864; (d) Clean Water Act, see p. 865.

2. People formed awareness groups, began grassroots movements, and organized protests to bring about government regulation.

3. Causes: offshoot of 1960s protest movements to protect public health; crusade of activist Ralph Nader, who had been involved in other protests. Effects: National Traffic and Motor Vehicle Safety Act passed; Wholesome Meat Act of 1967 passed; consumer awareness groups begun.

4. Rachel Carson's book influenced later activists such as Ralph Nader and the people who established Earth Day, and prompted government regulation.

5. Its awakening of public concern over pesticides led people to consider a host of other environmental concerns and to act on them.

6. Essays will vary but should be supported with facts from the section.

Attorney and consumer activist Ralph Nader shed a light on consumer health and safety issues not seen since the Progressive era. *Government What was the government's response to Nader's accusations against the auto industry?*

ago reflecting new and unexpected ravages by the motor vehicle. A 1959 Department of Commerce report projected that 51,000 persons would be killed by automobiles in 1975. That figure will probably be reached in 1965, a decade ahead of schedule.**"**

—*Ralph Nader in* Unsafe at Any Speed

Like the muckrakers of the Progressive era, Nader drew attention to the facts with passionate arguments. He called many cars "coffins on wheels," pointing to dangers such as a tendency to flip over. The industry, he charged, knowingly continued to build over one million cars before confronting the safety problems.

Nader's book was a sensation. In 1966 he testified before Congress about automobile hazards. That year, Congress passed the National Traffic and Motor Vehicle Safety Act. The *Washington Post* noted that, "Most of the credit for making possible this important legislation belongs to one man—Ralph Nader. . . . A one-man lobby for the public prevailed over the nation's most powerful industry."

Nader broadened his efforts and investigated the meatpacking business, helping to secure support for the Wholesome Meat Act of 1967. He next looked into consumer problems in other industries. Scores of volunteers, called "Nader's Raiders," signed on to help. They turned out report after report on such issues as the safety of products such as baby food and insecticides and inspired consumer activism. As ordinary Americans began to stand up for their rights, consumer protection offices began to respond to their many complaints.

The government report Nader wrote soon became a book, *Unsafe at Any Speed: The Designed-in Dangers of the American Automobile.* It began:

AMERICAN VOICES **"**For over half a century the automobile has brought death, injury, and the most inestimable sorrow and deprivation to millions of people. . . . [T]his mass trauma began rising sharply four years

SECTION 4 REVIEW

Comprehension

1. *Key Terms* Define: (a) Nuclear Regulatory Commission (NRC); (b) Environmental Protection Agency (EPA); (c) Clean Air Act; (d) Clean Water Act.

2. *Summarizing the Main Idea* In what ways were the environmental and consumer movements similar to other protest movements of the 1960s and 1970s?

3. *Organizing Information* Create a cause-and-effect chart on the consumer movement. Be sure to include how the movement began, by whom it was led, and some of its effects.

Critical Thinking

4. *Analyzing Time Lines* Review the time line at the start of the section. Explain how the first entry caused one of the later entries to occur.

5. *Recognizing Cause and Effect* Describe how Rachel Carson's *Silent Spring* initiated the environmental movement.

Writing Activity

6. *Writing a Persuasive Essay* Balancing jobs and the environment often involves tradeoffs. Research and write an essay in support of or in opposition to the development of oil fields in the Alaskan wilderness.

Answer to . . .

Viewing History It passed the National Traffic and Motor Vehicle Safety Act.

 RESOURCE OPTIONS

Teaching Resources

Quiz Units 9–10 folder, p. 36

Chapter Tests Forms A and B Chapter Test folder

Student Performance Pack

Guide to the Essentials Chapter 30, Section 4 (English and Spanish)

Standardized Test Preparation Handbook

Media and Technology

Guided Reading Audiotapes Chapter 30 Summary (English and Spanish)
Student Edition on Audiotape Chapter 30

Test Bank CD-ROM; Interactive Student Tutorial CD-ROM Chapter Test

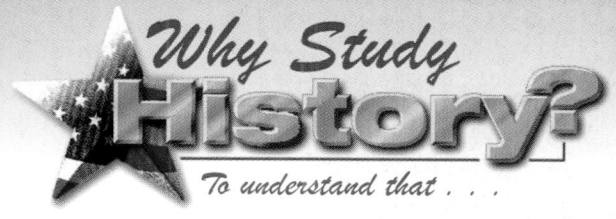

Why Study History?

To understand that . . .

Crime Victims Have Rights

A social movement of recent years has been the effort to secure fair treatment for crime victims and to protect potential victims.

Les Thomas shakes his head as he reads the news. A convicted sex offender has been paroled after only three years in jail. Thomas believes that the nation's courts pay more attention to the rights of people accused of committing crimes than to the rights of their victims. Many Americans share Thomas's viewpoint. They are demanding that judges and legislators get tough on crime.

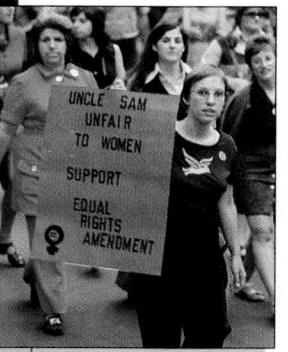

Women's rights march, 1970s

The Impact Today

Social activists in the 1960s and early 1970s sought equal rights for people who suffered discrimination because they were born into a particular group—for example, women. Today many Americans are mobilizing to secure rights for the millions of people who are victims or potential victims of crime. According to FBI figures, nearly 14 million crimes were committed in the United States in 1995 alone.

New laws have helped protect crime victims' rights. One such law allows crime victims to speak in court during the sentencing portion of trials. In this way, victims can influence the punishment of their offenders.

Victims' rights has also become a constitutional issue. By 1998, victims' rights amendments had been added to 27 state constitutions. President Clinton endorsed a victims' rights

amendment to the United States Constitution in 1996.

Alongside the victims' rights movement, a movement has emerged to protect potential victims of sexual assault. In 1994, public outrage over the murder of Megan Kanka, a seven-year-old New Jersey girl, led to the passage of a law popularly known as Megan's Law. It requires that law enforcement officials and communities in New Jersey be notified when a convicted sex offender moves into the area.

A number of states passed similar laws. Congress followed suit in 1996, requiring law enforcement agencies in all 50 states to notify schools, day-care centers, and parents about the presence of sexual offenders in the community.

Laws designed to protect victims and potential victims have drawn some criticism. Most criticism focuses on whether such laws violate the rights of people accused of committing crimes.

The Impact on You

List the rights that you believe crime victims should have. Then examine the Fourth, Fifth, Sixth, and Eighth amendments to the Constitution. Consider whether your list of rights violates the rights listed there. Finally, write an essay on how best to ensure victims' rights in a free society.

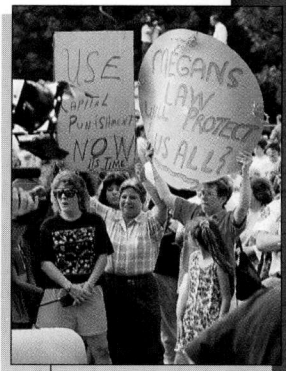

Demonstration in support of Megan's Law

RESOURCE OPTIONS

Teaching Resources

 Why Study History? Activity Crime Victims Have Rights, found in the Why Study History? folder, p. 31, provides an activity to help students better understand victims' rights.

Media and Technology

AmericanHeritage® CD-ROM

Time Tour The Nation Today and Tomorrow: A Time of Turmoil

 Decision America Videotapes and Videodiscs Issue 8 *Revenge or Deterrent?*

Class Discussion

Discuss with the class the rights of crime victims. For a more thorough examination of the issue, see the activity folder in the Resource Options below.

ACTIVITY
STUDENT PARTICIPATION

Drafting an Amendment

Ask students to read the text. Then have students work in small groups to write an amendment to the U.S. Constitution that both:

- **ensures crime victims' rights**
- **preserves rights of the accused**

Have groups share their ideas and discuss strengths and weaknesses of each.

Follow up Ask students to compare the amendments they wrote with amendments that have been added to state constitutions.

Using the Internet

Students can learn more about victims' rights by exploring links in the *America: Pathways to the Present* Web site at

http://www.Pathways.phschool.com

Assessment

See the Lesson Plans folder, pp. 24–27, for rubrics on assessing Class Participation Projects.

GEOGRAPHY AND HISTORY

The Environmental Movement

Focus Tell students that when *Silent Spring* appeared in 1962, *ecology* was not a familiar word to most Americans. There was virtually no way for Americans to recycle glass, paper, metal, or plastic. The Environmental Protection Agency did not exist. Most Americans did not know about the ozone layer, and store clerks would have cast strange looks at a shopper who wanted to reuse grocery bags. The publication of *Silent Spring* marks the moment when the American public began to learn about the choices required to safeguard life on Earth.

Instruct Divide the class into small groups. Ask students to discuss the information on DDT presented in the feature and to brainstorm as many groups as possible who were hurt by restrictions on the use of DDT. *(Farmers who lost crops, manufacturers, suppliers, stockholders, employees.)* Make a list of these groups and ask students to decide if the benefit to the world as a whole from the banning of DDT outweighed the cost to the groups on the list. Ask who makes such cost-benefit decisions. *(Individuals; federal, state, and local governments; the courts.)*

Extend Ask students to monitor the local news for reports on an environmental issue in your community. Have students outline the persons or groups involved, the environmental problem, and the potential costs to individuals. Students may present this information in a chart.

GEOGRAPHY AND HISTORY

The Environmental Movement

The geographic theme of human-environment interaction examines ways in which people affect their natural environment. Rachel Carson's book Silent Spring *blamed the disappearance of songbirds from America's towns and cities on the widely used pesticide DDT. Why did Carson's book have such an impact?*

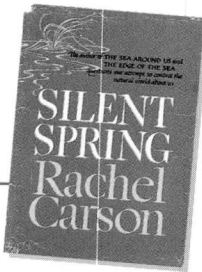

The book that launched the environmental movement

The publication of *Silent Spring* in 1962 is usually described as a landmark event in the history of the environmental movement. Author Rachel Carson planted an important concept in the public's mind: that humans are a part of a living ecological system, not outside of or dominant over it.

Humans and the Environment

Until the 1960s, most Americans believed that humans should use nature for their own ends. Science was seen as a tool for this use.

However, scientists had long been interested in the concept that people, plants, and animals all depend on one another to survive. Progress in science and technology that made humans' lives easier might have unintended outcomes. Cars, for example, enabled people to live outside the cities in which they worked. Yet cars caused pollution. By the end of the 1960s, cars and trucks were the source of more than half the air pollution in the United States.

Like cars, insecticides had both positive and negative consequences. Scientists began to weigh the environmental costs of insecticides, such as DDT, against their proven benefits in fighting insects. Chemical companies and the agricultural lobbies, however, favored continued use of DDT.

> *Progress in science and technology that made humans' lives easier might have unintended outcomes.*

The Use of DDT

For many years, DDT had been used by large-scale commercial farmers. Many American farm crops had come originally from Europe and Asia, bringing their own insect pests with them. By the early 1900s, farmers were ready to use any easy-to-use, inexpensive method to kill insects that gobbled up corn, wheat, and other crops.

Farmers turned enthusiastically to chemical insecticides, but many of these poisons contained metals such as lead or arsenic that were deadly to humans. DDT, which was apparently not toxic to humans even in massive doses, seemed like a wonderful solution.

New Research

By the 1960s, however, new research findings caused some people to question the assumption that humans

---

 RESOURCE OPTIONS

Teaching Resources

Geography and History Activity The Costs of Environmental Protection, Geography and History folder, pp. 18–19

Nystrom *Atlas of Our Country* Land Use, Population, and Ethnicity, pp. 46–47

A Shift in Public Opinion: The Environment

"Which of these problems would you like to see government devote most of its attention to in the next two years?" – Gallup poll question

Issue	Percent of Public Mentioning Item		
	1965	1970	Five-Year Change
Reducing amount of crime	41	56	+15%
Reducing pollution of air and water	17	53	+36%
Improving public education	45	31	-14%
Helping people in poor areas	32	30	-2%
Conquering "killer" diseases	37	29	-8%
Improving housing, clearing slums	21	27	+6%
Reducing racial discrimination	29	25	-4%
Reducing unemployment	35	25	-10%
Improving highway safety	18	13	-5%
Beautifying America	3	5	+2%

Source: *The Politics of Environmental Concern*, by Walter A. Rosenbaum

should freely exploit nature. Rachel Carson brought some of that new research to light.

In *Silent Spring*, Carson pointed out that DDT not only poisoned insects, but also killed birds that ate the poisoned insects. She based her book on observations of the negative effect of DDT caused by massive spraying in American urban areas in an attempt to protect Dutch Elm trees from insect pests. As it turned out, DDT remained in the ecosystem long after it had destroyed insect pests. It built up in the fatty tissues of birds and fish that ate the poisoned insects, and its long-term effects could be fatal. In birds, for example, DDT weakened shell formation so that young birds did not hatch. Predator birds high in the food chain, such as hawks and eagles, reached the crisis stage first because they ate smaller birds, fish, and rodents containing DDT. The more food the birds ate, the higher their concentration of DDT became.

The Environmental Movement

After the publication of *Silent Spring*, a growing public awareness of the theme of interaction between humans and the environment led to a national environmental movement. The movement continued to grow throughout the 1960s, partly because of court cases against the use of DDT brought by the Environmental Defense Fund, one of many activist groups. At

the close of the decade, the movement won official government recognition with the founding of the Environmental Protection Agency in 1970.

Silent Spring sparked a debate that in 1972 resulted in the banning of almost all uses of DDT in the United States. Even more significantly, by questioning the belief that nature exists for the benefit of humanity, Carson and other scientists and historians helped introduce a new ideology. Within a decade, environmentalism grew from something that interested only a small number of geographers and scientists to a nationwide movement embraced by a majority of citizens.

GEOGRAPHIC CONNECTIONS

1. Why were American crops such as wheat and corn susceptible to insect pests?

2. How did farmers' use of DDT affect other parts of the environment?

Themes in Geography

3. *Human-Environment Interaction* How did the belief that humans should use the natural world for their own ends change during the 1960s?

Key Terms

Students should refer to the definitions of key terms in the chapter to write sentences that show an understanding of the many social movements that grew out of the civil rights movement of the 1960s.

Comprehension

1. Fair pay, equal job opportunities, overcoming sexism in the media, equal domestic responsibilities, legalization of abortion.
2. Many men disliked feminism and many women saw no need for an expanded role; African American women were more concerned with civil rights; conservative groups opposed the movement.
3. He organized the UFW and led the movement, drawing on the 1960s tactic of nonviolent confrontation.
4. Japanese Americans were paid some compensation for the property losses they incurred because of internment during World War II, Asian Americans in general made economic gains and had their pride boosted by Hawaii's statehood.
5. They wanted to protect what was left of tribal lands and Native American customs, and gain autonomy and a political voice.
6. AIM set up patrols to monitor street activity and began survival schools to encourage racial and cultural pride.
7. They began grassroots environmental movements, participated in Earth Day, and called for government regulation.
8. Automobile safety and the meat-packing industry.

Chapter Summary

The major concepts of Chapter 30 are presented below. See also **Guide to the Essentials of American History** or **Interactive Student Tutorial CD-ROM,** which contains interactive review activities, time lines, helpful hints, and test practice for Chapter 30.

Reviewing the Main Ideas

Change. Upheaval. Action. These words describe the social revolution of the late 1960s and early 1970s. The 1960s civil rights movement breathed new life into other issues. Women, Latinos, Asian Americans, and Native Americans adapted civil rights tactics to achieve their own goals of equality. Similar tactics helped launch movements to protect the environment and improve the quality and safety of certain consumer goods.

Section 1: The Women's Movement

Encouraged by the gains of the civil rights movement, a women's movement arose in an effort to end discrimination based on gender.

Section 2: Ethnic Minorities Seek Equality

Inspired by the civil rights movement, Latinos and Asian Americans launched their own movements to overcome discrimination.

Section 3: Native American Struggles

Native Americans in the 1960s also took their cue from the civil rights movement to work to improve their living conditions.

Section 4: The Environmental Movement

The mood of protest in the 1960s energized movements to preserve the environment and to ensure the safety of consumer products.

In recent years social activists have worked to secure fair treatment of victims of crime. New laws have been passed to protect crime victims' rights, and many states have added victims' rights amendments to their constitutions.

Key Terms

Use each of the terms below in a sentence that shows how it relates to the chapter.

1. Equal Rights Amendment (ERA)
2. United Farm Workers (UFW)
3. autonomy
4. Environmental Protection Agency (EPA)
5. feminism
6. migrant farm worker
7. Latino
8. Clean Air Act
9. National Organization for Women (NOW)
10. American Indian Movement (AIM)

Comprehension

1. What were some of the goals of NOW?
2. What opposition did the women's movement encounter?
3. What role did Cesar Chavez play in the Chicano struggle for equal rights?
4. What positive changes did the years after World War II bring for Asian Americans?
5. Why did Native American activists confront the federal government?
6. Describe some of the tactics used by the American Indian Movement.
7. How did people show their support for the environmental movement?
8. What were two of the targets of Ralph Nader's consumer movement?

Using Graphic Organizers

On a separate piece of paper, copy the tree map to organize information about some of the major protest movements in the 1960s and 1970s. Provide at least two supporting details describing each movement.

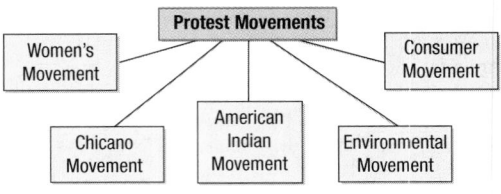

Using Graphic Organizers

- Women's movement: formed NOW and other protest groups; used direct action and political pressure to achieve goals.
- Chicano movement: protested working conditions and education; formed UFW to better condition of migrant workers.
- American Indian Movement: organized protests in several highly publicized events; lobbied for autonomy, the improvement of reservation conditions, and the review of broken treaties.
- Environmental movement: initiated by the publication of *Silent Spring;* public responded with environmental groups and lobbying of government.
- Consumer movement: begun by Ralph Nader; succeeded in passing vehicle safety and food safety legislation.

Analyzing Political Cartoons ▶

1. Examine the images in the cartoon. What do the ships represent?
2. Who are the people, and what do they represent?
3. Explain the humor in the dialogue, and the serious point it is making.

Critical Thinking

1. *Applying the Chapter Skill* Review the Recognizing Bias skill on page 851. Then turn to the quote by author Vine Deloria, Jr., on page 859. Are any opinions presented as though they were facts? Give an example from the excerpt.
2. *Drawing Conclusions* During the 1960s and 1970s, Cesar Chavez's United Farm Workers organized buyer boycotts of grapes, lettuce, and other produce. Explain the purpose of these boycotts.
3. *Demonstrating Reasoned Judgment* Think of a local concern that affects your community, for example, the need for increased recycling in your neighborhood. Following the examples of any of the activists you have read about in the chapter, such as Gloria Steinem, Cesar Chavez, Rachel Carson, or Ralph Nader, what could you do to champion your cause?

INTERNET ACTIVITY

For your portfolio:
Prepare a Report

Access Prentice Hall's *America: Pathways to the Present* site at **www.Pathways.phschool.com** for the specific URLs to complete the activity. Additional resources and related Web sites are also available.

Read about Rachel Carson and prepare a report about her efforts to warn people about the dangers of pesticides. How was Carson's book *Silent Spring* received? Who opposed her findings? What was Carson's legacy to the environmental movement?

ANALYZING DOCUMENTS ◀ ▶ INTERPRETING DATA

Turn to the first "American Voices" quotation on page 859.

1. Which of the following was one of AIM's goals as expressed by Dennis Banks? (a) to join the government (b) to make no changes to Native American lifestyles (c) to make radical changes in order to gain self-determination (d) to enter into a new treaty with the government

2. How did Banks suggest that AIM achieve its goals? (a) through peaceful demonstration (b) by destroying the political machine built by the government and churches (c) by joining churches (d) by ignoring the problem

3. *Writing* Do you think Banks's speech would have been successful at persuading other people to join AIM in their efforts? Explain why or why not.

Connecting to Today

Essay Writing Earth Day, first celebrated in 1970, is still observed every year. Research and write an essay on some of the most recent Earth Day activities in or near your community. Then create a list of activities you could plan to celebrate the next Earth Day.

INTERNET ACTIVITY

Reports will vary but should be supported with specific facts or quotes and mention environmental groups and legislation that Carson's book influenced.

Analyzing Political Cartoons

1. The arrival of Europeans to the Americas.
2. They are Native Americans, representing the original inhabitants of the Americas.
3. The words are a play on the sentiment that one generation hands down all it has achieved to the next. The cartoonist is saying that Native Americans lost all they had achieved with the arrival of the Europeans.

Critical Thinking

1. Sample answer: When the author says, "It just seems to a lot of Indians that this continent was a lot better off when we were running it," he assumes that the continent was an entity run by Native Americans, and that it had no problems.
2. Boycotts were organized to show support for the goals of the UFW; namely, more pay, better working conditions, and union recognition.
3. Sample answers: Speak and write to inform people about the issue, organize boycotts, propose legal challenges, and carry out more militant actions such as sit-ins.

Analyzing Documents

1. c
2. b
3. Sample answer: No, because his approach was too militant and exclusionary.

Connecting to Today

Essays will vary but should be supported with specific examples or quotes, and address themes introduced in the chapter.

CHAPTER 31

The Vietnam War and American Society, 1960–1975

Managing Time and Instruction

These materials for instruction are provided for **each section** in the **Teaching Resources**. See **Units 9–10 folder for Enrichment Support:**

- Reproducible Lesson Plans in Lesson Plans folder • Learning Styles Lesson Plans in Learning Styles Lesson Plans folder • Big Idea Graphic Organizers in Big Idea Graphic Organizer folder
- Guided Reading and Review • Quizzes • Test Preparation Practice booklet

DAILY LESSON	ENRICHMENT SUPPORT
1 **Deepening American Involvement** (pp. 873–877)	• Biography, Bob Kerrey, Units 9–10 folder, p. 52
2 **The Brutality of the War** (pp. 878–881)	• Literature Activity, Experiences of a Young Soldier in Vietnam, Units 9–10 folder, pp. 55–56 • Primary Source Activity, An Army Nurse Remembers, Learning with Documents folder, p. 37
3 **Student Protest** (pp. 882–885)	• Key Documents, The Port Huron Statement, Learning with Documents folder, p. 104 • Visual Learning Activity, Antiwar Demonstations, Learning with Documents folder, p. 73 • Great Debates, Should the U.S. Have Stayed in Vietnam? Decision-Making Activities folder, pp. 44–45
4 **The Counterculture** (pp. 887–889)	• Skills for Life Activity, Units 9–10 folder, p. 57 • Literature Activity, The Flower Children, found on **Resource Pro** • Visual Learning Activity, Reflection of the Counterculture, found on **Resource Pro**
5 **The End of the War** (pp. 890–894)	• Primary Source Activity, LBJ Withdraws from the Race, found on **Resource Pro** • Comparing Primary Sources, On the Tragedy of Kent State, Units 9–10 folder, pp. 53–54 • Decision-Making Activity, Helping to Heal a War-Torn Nation, Decision-Making Activities folder, pp. 22–23 • Critical Thinking Activity, Drawing Conclusions: Military Spending, found on **Resource Pro** • Draft Registration Is Required Today, Why Study History? folder, p. 32

Running Out of Time?

- Use Tape 5, "The Upheaval of the Sixties, 1960–1975," from **Visions of America** videotapes series.
- Use Chapter 31 Summary from **Guide to the Essentials of American History (English and Spanish).**

Companion Web Site

The companion Web site offers online links for all chapter review activities. It also provides key content links and structured support for this chapter for both teachers and students.

http://www.Pathways.phschool.com

Teaching in the Information Age

Media and Technology

For the Student

Interactive Student Tutorial CD-ROM Chapter 31

Student Edition on Audiotape Chapter 31

American Heritage® CD-ROM

Guided Reading Audiotapes (English and Spanish) Chapter 31

For the Teacher

Resource Pro CD-ROM Chapter 31

Test Bank CD-ROM Chapter 31

Listening to Literature Audiotapes *Timeless Voices, Timeless Themes:* "Camouflaging the Chimera" by Yusef Komuyakaa *and* "Ambush" by Tim O'Brien

Color Transparencies Critical Thinking, I-7

Assessment Options

Chapter Test Forms A&B Test Bank CD-ROM booklet

Test Bank CD-ROM Chapter 31

Standardized Test Preparation Handbook

Block Scheduling

Pacing Suggestions

For 90-minute Blocks

- Teach sections 1, 4, and 5 using Transparencies I-13 and J-9 and the Recent Scholarship note on p. 891 for class discussions.
- Teach sections 2 and 3 using the Big Idea Graphic Organizer from Teaching Resources and the Extended Class Periods Activity on p. 883.

Additional Resources

- Prentice Hall's **American History Block Scheduling Support File** covers over 40 major topics in American history.
- **Prentice Hall United States History Video Collection**™ contains 20 videotapes covering American history from beginnings to present.
- **Decision America Videotapes and Videodiscs**
- **Visions of America Videotapes and Videodiscs**

Connections to American Literature

from Prentice Hall

Prentice Hall Literature *Timeless Voices, Timeless Themes:*
- "In a Classroom" by Adrienne Rich, p. 1051
- "Camouflaging the Chimera" by Yusef Komunyakaa, p. 1080
- "For What It's Worth" by Stephen Stills, p. 487

Additional Resources

For the Student

Ron Kovic. *Born on the Fourth of July.* McGraw-Hill, 1976.

Larry Rottman, Jan Barry, and Basil T. Paquet, eds. *Winning Hearts and Minds: War Poems by Vietnam Veterans.*

For the Teacher

Frances Fitzgerald. *Fire in the Lake: The Vietnamese and the Americans in Vietnam.* Random House, 1989 edition.

Prentice Hall brings into the classroom the vast archives and scholarship of the nation's premier American history magazine. See "From the Archives of American Heritage®" and "About the Presidents" teaching notes in this chapter.

History Alive!

Teacher's Curriculum Institute, in partnership with Prentice Hall, provides unique materials that engage students with diverse learning styles. See History Alive!® unit on The Cold War.

Student Performance Pack

Ensures success in the three critical areas of Reading, Test Taking, and English Language Development with the following materials:
- Guide to the Essentials of American History in English and Spanish
- Guided Reading Audiotapes in English and Spanish
- Interactive Student Tutorial CD-ROM
- Test Preparation Handbook
- Test Preparation Practice booklet

Introducing the Chapter

The 1960s and 1970s were decades of deep division and turmoil in the United States. Under Presidents Kennedy and Johnson, the country became increasingly involved in trying to stop a Communist takeover in Vietnam. As the war continued to cost more and more lives and money while achieving little apparent success, many Americans began to question their government's role there. At the same time, a youthful counterculture arose, criticizing the traditional values of many Americans.

Themes in American History

The theme for this chapter, Foreign Relations, is listed at the beginning of this unit. An alternate theme for the chapter is Culture. To teach this unit thematically, you may wish to use The Nation After World War II folder in American History Block Scheduling Support.

Why Study History?

Have students explore suggested ways of connecting the past to the present on page 895.

Answer to . . .

Viewing History Students should use this question as an aid in reading the chapter. American policymakers believed that if Vietnam fell to the Communists, the way would be paved for a Communist takeover of the rest of the free world.

872

CHAPTER

31 The Vietnam War and American Society

1960-1975

CHAPTER FOCUS

The Vietnam War was one of the most tragic events of the cold war. Hundreds of thousands of soldiers served in Vietnam, and billions of dollars were spent on the war effort. Over time, many Americans questioned the extent of United States involvement in this faraway conflict. In this chapter you will read about the war and other issues that caused deep divisions within American society.

The *Why Study History?* page at the end of this chapter explores the connection between the use of a military draft during the Vietnam War and the all-volunteer military forces in existence today.

VIEWING HISTORY
American soldiers like this one endured extreme fighting conditons in Vietnam. *Foreign Relations* *Why were American soldiers sent to fight in Vietnam?*

 RESOURCE OPTIONS

Teaching Resources

Big Idea Graphic Organizer folder
Graphic summary of the main idea of the chapter.

Learning Styles Lesson Plans folder
Alternate lesson plans for diverse learning styles for each chapter.

Media and Technology

 AmericanHeritage® CD-ROM
Time Tour The Nation Today and Tomorrow: A Time for Turmoil

 Prentice Hall United States History Video Collection™ Volume 20
Post-War USA

1955 Diem becomes president of South Vietnam	1961 Kennedy takes office	1963 Military coup overthrows Diem	1964 Gulf of Tonkin Resolution	1965 War in Vietnam escalates	1968 Tet Offensive

1955   **1960**   **1965**   **1970**

1 Deepening American Involvement

SECTION PREVIEW

Objectives

1. Describe the background events leading up to war between North and South Vietnam.
2. Describe the Vietnam policies of President Kennedy and Robert McNamara.
3. Explain how President Johnson changed the course of the war.
4. *Key Terms* Define: Geneva Conference; Viet Cong; Gulf of Tonkin Resolution; escalation; Ho Chi Minh Trail; Tet Offensive.

Main Idea

The United States entered the Vietnam War to defeat Communist forces threatening South Vietnam.

Reading Strategy

Structured Overview Write the following column headings on a sheet of paper: *Background of the War, Kennedy's Vietnam Policy, Johnson's War.* As you read the section, take notes in the appropriate column.

A merican involvement in Vietnam began during the early years of the cold war. It ended in defeat and disappointment more than twenty years later.

Background of the War

Vietnam had a history of nationalism that extended back nearly 2,000 years. The Vietnamese spent much of that time resisting attempts by neighboring China to swallow their small country. In the 1800s France established itself as a new colonial power in Vietnam, and it met similar resistance.

After World War II Ho Chi Minh, a nationalist who sympathized with Communist ideas, led the Vietnamese independence movement. He aroused his people's nationalism in order to repel the French. Policymakers in the United States, however, saw Ho merely as a Communist, and therefore an enemy.

While France and Vietnam fought, an international conference met in Geneva, Switzerland. Representatives of Ho Chi Minh, Vietnamese emperor Bao Dai, Cambodia, Laos, France, the United States, the Soviet Union, China, and Britain discussed the situation in Indochina. After the French defeat at Dien Bien Phu in May 1954, the conference tried to settle the conflict.

As a result of the **Geneva Conference,** Vietnam was divided into two separate nations in July 1954. Ho Chi Minh controlled northern Vietnam. Ngo Dinh Diem, a former official in Bao Dai's government, became the premier of southern Vietnam. Diem, who had lived in exile in the United States, gained the backing of the United States. In 1955, Diem became the president and declared South Vietnam a republic. Thus began United States involvement in the Vietnam War. The war lasted from 1955 to 1975 and was fought to protect South Vietnam from being taken over by Communists.

The Geneva agreements provided for elections to be held in 1956 to unify the country. South Vietnam refused to support this part of the agreement, and the United States government backed this decision. The elections never took place.

The fates of three nations—Vietnam, the United States, and France—became interwoven in the struggle for control over Vietnam.

RESOURCE OPTIONS

Teaching Resources

📁 **Reproducible Lesson Plan** Lesson Plans folder, p. 157

📁 **Big Idea Graphic Organizer** Big Idea Graphic Organizer folder, p. 129

📁 **Guided Reading and Review** Units 9–10 folder, p. 42

Media and Technology

AmericanHeritage® CD-ROM

Time Tour The Nation Today and Tomorrow: A Time of Turmoil

Objectives

You may wish to call students' attention to the objectives in the Section Preview. The objectives are reflected in the main headings of the section.

Bellringer

Ask students to brainstorm words, phrases, and images that come to mind when they hear the word *Vietnam.*

Reading Strategy

Structured Overview Refer to the Reading Strategy in the Section Preview. You may wish to write a sample note under one of the suggested headings as an example for students.

LESSON PLAN

Connecting to the Main Idea

1. Focus Explain that in the 1960s, Presidents Kennedy and Johnson were determined to maintain South Vietnam under an anti-Communist government. Ask how the United States became involved in Vietnam. How did the American presence in Vietnam escalate?

2. Instruct Discuss Eisenhower's decision to support Diem and Kennedy's decision to increase United States support for Diem's regime. What other decisions might those Presidents have made? Ask students to list the most probable results of those other decisions. Could the nation accept those results today? Why would the results have been unacceptable in the late 1950s and early 1960s?

3. Close Attempting to keep communism out of Vietnam, Presidents Kennedy and Johnson supported dictatorships and sent thousands of American troops to Southeast Asia. The next section describes the brutality of the Vietnam war.

Ask each student to create a chart to illustrate the buildup of American forces in Vietnam as described in the section, starting with the 675 military advisers provided by President Eisenhower before 1960. Have students continue to add to the chart to reflect the progress of the war. *(Visual/Spatial)*

BACKGROUND

Biography

By the early 1990s, Brigadier General Sherian Grace Cadoria, born in 1940 in Marksville, Louisiana, was the highest-ranking African American woman in the United States armed forces. She served in Vietnam from January 1967 to October 1969. She remembers her arrival: "I interviewed for a protocol job. When I got there, the colonel told me I couldn't do the job. He said, 'You can't travel, you can't carry luggage, it's too heavy. Women can't do this.' And I said, 'Nobody said I couldn't carry those hundred-pound bags of cotton when I was just a child.'"

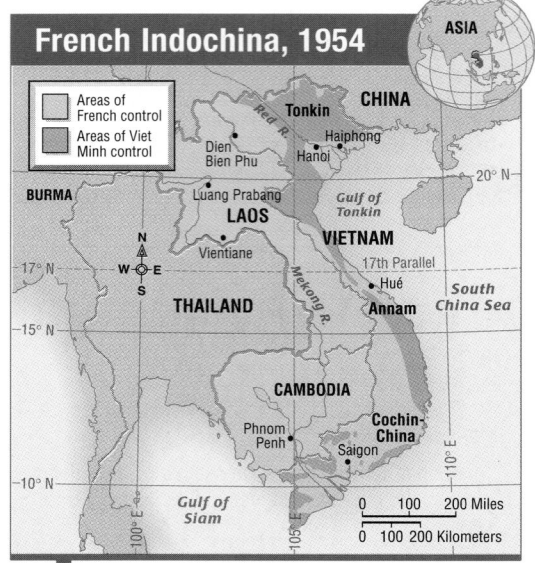

French Indochina, 1954

- Areas of French control
- Areas of Viet Minh control

Events in Southeast Asia caught the attention of the United States in 1954, as France struggled to maintain control in this region. **Regions** *Where was the largest region of Viet Minh (Ho Chi Minh's) control?*

Kennedy's Vietnam Policy

President Eisenhower pledged his support to Diem's South Vietnamese government. In 1960 he provided some 675 United States military advisers to assist in the struggle against the North. When President Kennedy took office in 1961, he did even more. Kennedy was determined to prevent the spread of communism at all costs. This meant strengthening and protecting the government that the United States had helped create in South Vietnam.

Kennedy sent Vice President Lyndon Johnson to Vietnam to assess the situation there. Diem told him that if South Vietnam was to survive, it would need even more aid. In response, Kennedy increased the number of American military advisers to Vietnam. By the end of 1963, that number had grown to more than 16,000.

Military aid by itself could not ensure success. Diem lacked support in his own country. He imprisoned people who criticized his government and filled many government positions with members of his own family. United States aid earmarked for economic reforms went instead to the military and into the pockets of corrupt officials.

In addition, Diem launched an unpopular program to move peasants from their ancestral lands to "strategic hamlets." These government-run farming communities were intended to isolate the peasants from Communist influences seeping into South Vietnam.

In addition, Diem was a Catholic in a largely Buddhist country. When Diem insisted that Buddhists obey Catholic religious laws, serious opposition developed. In June 1963 a Buddhist monk burned himself to death. Photographs showing his silent, grisly protest appeared on the front pages of newspapers around the world. Other monks followed the example, but their martyrdom did not budge Diem.

Kennedy finally realized that Diem would never reform and acknowledged that the struggle against communism in Vietnam could not be won under Diem's rule. United States officials told South Vietnamese military leaders that the United States would not object to Diem's overthrow. With that encouragement, military leaders staged a coup in November 1963. They seized control of the government and, to Kennedy's dismay, assassinated Diem on November 2 as he tried to flee.

Robert McNamara

AMERICAN BIOGRAPHY One of the American officials who gave up on Diem was Robert McNamara, Kennedy's Secretary of Defense. A Republican with a strong business background, McNamara became one of Kennedy's closest advisers on Vietnam. Later he would help shape the policies that drew the United States deeper into the war.

Robert McNamara was born June 9, 1916, in San Francisco, California. He grew up across the bay in Oakland. McNamara attended the University of California at Berkeley and went on to earn a graduate degree at Harvard Business School in 1939. He used his degree to land a job at the Ford Motor Company. Through hard work and solid business decisions, McNamara moved quickly up the corporate ladder. He took over the

Robert McNamara (b. 1916)

RESOURCE OPTIONS

Teaching Resources

American History Block Scheduling Support Vietnam: The War at Home, found in The Nation After World War II folder, includes interdisciplinary lesson suggestions and activities for Geography and History, Primary Sources, Biography, and Literature.

Media and Technology

Color Transparencies Critical Thinking, I-13

presidency of Ford Motors in November 1960. This rising star caught the eye of President Kennedy, who offered him a position in his Cabinet just one month later.

As Secretary of Defense, McNamara applied his business knowledge, managing to cut costs while modernizing the armed forces. He turned the Pentagon's thinking away from reliance on the threat of nuclear bombs toward the development of a "flexible response" to military crises. He also began to focus his attention on how to handle the conflict in Vietnam.

Later, under Lyndon Johnson, McNamara would push for direct American involvement in the war. But in 1963 he still questioned whether a complete withdrawal was not the better alternative. Looking back on that period later, McNamara revealed his and Kennedy's feelings:

 AMERICAN VOICES " I believed that we had done all the training we could. Whether the South Vietnamese were qualified or not to turn back the North Vietnamese, I was certain that if they weren't, it wasn't for lack of our training. More training wouldn't strengthen them; therefore we should get out. The President agreed."

—*Robert McNamara*

As you will read, the United States did not withdraw. It continued to back South Vietnam and the coup leaders who took over the government.

Johnson's War

Three weeks after Diem's assassination, Kennedy himself fell to an assassin's bullet in Dallas, Texas. By then the new military government in South Vietnam was already in trouble. The ruling generals bickered among themselves and failed to direct the South Vietnamese army effectively.

The Viet Cong Meanwhile Communist guerrillas in the south, known as **Viet Cong,** gained control of more territory and earned the loyalty of an increasing number of South Vietnamese. Ho Chi Minh and the North Vietnamese aided the Viet Cong throughout the struggle.

Lyndon Johnson, the new United States President, was suspicious of Ho's Communist sympathies, as Kennedy had been. He believed strongly in the need for containment:

 AMERICAN VOICES " The Communists' desire to dominate the world is just like the lawyer's desire to be the ultimate judge on the Supreme Court. . . . You see, the Communists want to rule the world, and if we don't stand up to them, they will do it. And we'll be slaves. Now I'm not one of those folks seeing Communists under every bed. But I do know about the principles of power, and when one side is weak, the other steps in."

—*Lyndon Johnson*

Just after he assumed office, Johnson met with Henry Cabot Lodge, United States ambassador to South Vietnam. Lodge told the new President that if he wanted to save Vietnam, he faced some tough choices. Johnson was determined to do whatever was necessary to win the war. "I am not going to lose Vietnam," he said. Referring to the Communist takeover of China in 1949, he went on: "I am not going to be the President who saw Southeast Asia go the way China went."

In his campaign for President in 1964, Johnson tried to keep the war from becoming an issue. "We are not about to send American boys nine or ten thousand miles away from home to do what Asian boys ought to be doing for themselves," he declared. He called Barry Goldwater,

 VIEWING HISTORY Buddhist monks protested Ngo Dinh Diem's government by burning themselves to death on the streets of Saigon. *Government How does this picture symbolize the difficult problems Johnson inherited in Vietnam?*

Graphing the Main Idea

To make sure students understand the main idea of this section, you may wish to use the tree map graphic organizer below.

Tell students that a tree map presents an outline of a topic, main ideas, and supporting details. Ask students to use it to outline deepening United States involvement in Vietnam.

Teaching Tip A template for this graphic organizer can be found in the Color Transparencies, G-3.

Customize for
More Advanced Students

As students read this section, have them create two lists. In the first, they should name the strengths the United States brought to the war. In the second, they should list the factors that might have undercut those strengths in the actual war effort.

Answer to . . .

Map Skills It allowed the North Vietnamese government to provide the Viet Cong with ammunition and other supplies for the Tet Offensive.
Main Idea Connections The Tonkin Gulf incident and Johnson's reelection.

Vietnam War, 1964–1968

The Ho Chi Minh Trail, shown in the map above, was a supply route from North Vietnam through Laos and Cambodia into South Vietnam.

Movement How might the Ho Chi Minh Trail have contributed to the execution of the Tet Offensive?

his Republican opponent in the election, an extremist who would lead the nation into nuclear war. Even when the Viet Cong attacked an airfield outside of Saigon, killing four Americans, Johnson declined to retaliate.

Intensifying the War In August 1964, during the presidential campaign, Johnson made a dramatic announcement. North Vietnamese torpedo boats, he said, had attacked United States destroyers in the international waters of the Gulf of Tonkin, 30 miles from North Vietnam. Those attacks would change the course of the war.

Details about the attacks were sketchy, and some people doubted that they had even taken place. In any case, Johnson used the Tonkin Gulf incident to deepen American involvement in Vietnam. Johnson asked Congress for and obtained a resolution giving him authority to "take all neces-

Main Idea
CONNECTIONS

What events led to an increase in American involvement in Vietnam in 1964?

sary measures to repel any armed attack against the forces of the United States and to prevent further aggression."

Congress passed this **Gulf of Tonkin Resolution** on August 7 by a vote of 414 to 0 in the House of Representatives and 88 to 2 in the Senate. Johnson had been waiting for some time for an opportunity to propose the resolution, which, he noted, "covered everything." The President now had nearly complete control over what the United States did in Vietnam, even without an official declaration of war from Congress.

After winning the election in 1964, Johnson started a gradual military **escalation,** or expansion, of the war, devoting ever more American money and personnel to the conflict. Enemy gains in South Vietnam led to this course of action.

Initially, United States soldiers had gone to Vietnam to advise the South Vietnamese. Now they took on the task of propping up the South Vietnamese government. The leader of that government in 1965 was military officer Nguyen Cao Ky. In 1967 Nguyen Van Thieu succeeded him as president. Ky and Thieu were more effective leaders than Diem had been, but they remained authoritarian. More important, they were unable to put together an army that could successfully defend the country.

By 1965 the Viet Cong were steadily expanding within South Vietnam. North Vietnamese troops and supplies poured into the south via the **Ho Chi Minh Trail,** a supply route that passed through Laos and Cambodia. The Communists appeared close to victory.

In February 1965 a Viet Cong attack at Pleiku in South Vietnam killed 8 Americans and wounded 126. President Johnson responded by authorizing the bombing of North Vietnam. Two weeks after the Pleiku attack, General William Westmoreland, the commander of United States forces in Vietnam, requested more soldiers. He asked Johnson for two battalions of marines to protect the American airfield at Da Nang.

Johnson heeded the request, beginning a rapid buildup of American combat troops. At the start of 1965 some 25,000 American soldiers were stationed in Vietnam. By the end of the year the number had risen to 184,000. The Americans brought with them advanced weaponry and new tactics and did achieve some successes. But they still failed to drive out the Viet Cong, who were masters at jungle warfare.

RESOURCE OPTIONS

Teaching Resources

Biography Bob Kerrey, Units 9–10 folder, p. 52

Media and Technology

Prentice Hall United States History Video Collection™ Volume 20

Post-War USA

Month after month the fighting continued. United States planes bombed North Vietnam, and the flow of American soldiers into the south increased. Their number climbed to 385,000 by the end of 1966, to 485,000 by the end of 1967, and to 536,000 by the end of 1968. Despite the large United States presence in South Vietnam, the Communist forces only intensified their efforts.

The Tet Offensive Those efforts reached a climax in 1968, during Tet, the Vietnamese New Year. On January 30 the Viet Cong and North Vietnamese launched a major offensive. The **Tet Offensive,** shown in the map on the previous page, included surprise attacks on major cities and towns and American military bases throughout South Vietnam. In Saigon, the South Vietnamese capital, the Viet Cong boldly attacked the American embassy and the presidential palace. Fierce fighting continued in Saigon for several weeks. The siege of Khe Sanh, an American base near the border with North Vietnam, lasted until April.

Even though they were turned back with heavy losses, the Viet Cong had won a psychological victory. The Tet Offensive demonstrated that the Viet Cong could launch a massive attack on targets throughout South Vietnam. Furthermore, as images of the fighting flooded American television, many people at home began to express reservations about United States involvement in Vietnam. Many were discouraged, believing that once

there the troops had not been allowed to win the war. In spite of the vocal "pro-peace" protesters, a majority of Americans supported a policy tougher than the one pursued by the administration. President Johnson, caught in the middle, saw his popularity plunge.

FACT Finder — The War in Vietnam Escalates

Year	Event
1964	Gulf of Tonkin Resolution passes. Gradual military escalation begins.
1965	President Johnson responds to attacks against American troops by authorizing the bombing of North Vietnam and by rapidly increasing the number of American combat troops in South Vietnam.
1966–1967	The number of American soldiers in South Vietnam continues to increase.
1968	The Viet Cong and North Vietnamese launch the Tet Offensive.

Interpreting Tables The Gulf of Tonkin Resolution gave President Johnson increased authority over troops in Vietnam. *Government* *What was the Tet Offensive?*

SECTION 1 REVIEW

Comprehension

1. *Key Terms* Define: (a) Geneva Conference; (b) Viet Cong; (c) Gulf of Tonkin Resolution; (d) escalation; (e) Ho Chi Minh Trail; (f) Tet Offensive.

2. *Summarizing the Main Idea* Why did the United States get more and more involved in the conflict in Vietnam?

3. *Organizing Information* Draw a line graph to show the changes in the number of American soldiers in Vietnam between 1960 and 1968. Write notes to describe events that influenced United States policy toward Vietnam, and connect them to points on the graph.

Critical Thinking

4. *Analyzing Time Lines* Review the time line at the start of the section. Which event do you think affected Kennedy's viewpoint on Vietnam the most? Explain.

5. *Identifying Assumptions* What do you think Johnson hoped to gain by authorizing the bombing of targets in North Vietnam in 1965?

Writing Activity

6. *Writing a Persuasive Essay* Imagine that you are Robert McNamara in 1963. Write an essay presenting President Kennedy with two options—withdraw from Vietnam or fully support Diem.

Answers to SECTION 1 REVIEW

1. (a) Geneva Conference, see p. 873; (b) Viet Cong, see p. 875; (c) Gulf of Tonkin Resolution, see p. 876; (d) escalation, see p. 876; (e) Ho Chi Minh Trail, see p. 876; (f) Tet Offensive, see p. 877.

2. Fearing that communism was in danger of spreading throughout the region, various Presidents used real and alleged incidents to step up American involvement in the war.

3. Graphs should include: 1960—675 advisers sent by Eisenhower; 1963—16,000 advisers sent by Kennedy after Johnson's visit; 1965—25,000 troops in place after Viet Cong attack; end of 1965—184,000 troops; 1967—485,000 troops; 1968—536,000 troops.

4. Sample answer: 1963—military coup overthrows Diem, because Kennedy then realized that the struggle against communism could not be won under Diem's rule.

5. Sample answer: The escalation of the war and increased American involvement.

6. Essays will vary but should be supported with facts from the section.

Answer to . . .

Interpreting Tables A series of North Vietnamese surprise attacks on major cities and American military bases in South Vietnam.

The Brutality of the War

Objectives

You may wish to call students' attention to the objectives in the Section Preview. The objectives are reflected in the main headings of the section.

Bellringer

Ask students to consider how they would define a "just" war. Is any war just? Does the way the war is waged, including the types of weapons and damage inflicted, determine whether or not it is just?

Reading Strategy

Reading for Evidence Refer to the Reading Strategy in the Section Preview. You may wish to ask students to define the word *evidence* in order to make sure that all students in the class understand the exercise.

LESSON PLAN

Connecting to the Main Idea

1. Focus American soldiers were not prepared for the brutality of the fighting in Vietnam, and Americans at home were shocked by the violence they witnessed on their television screens. Ask why American forces had little success in Vietnam. How did the war affect Vietnamese civilians?

2. Instruct Ask students to explain how a guerrilla war differs from a conventional war. Discuss why the superior firepower of the American forces was not more successful against the Viet Cong. Ask students whether the Vietnam War meets the definition of "total war," one in which destruction of property and civilian life is carried out to persuade the enemy that continuing the conflict is not worth the cost.

3. Close The Vietnam War took an enormous toll on both American soldiers and Vietnamese civilians. The next section describes how the brutality of the war helped turn the student protest movements of the time into the antiwar movement.

1966 B-52 bomber first used in Vietnam	1968 My Lai massacre	1969 Americans first learn of My Lai massacre	1971 Calley sentenced to life in prison
1966	**1968**	**1970**	**1972**

2 The Brutality of the War

SECTION PREVIEW

Objectives

1 Describe the conditions under which American soldiers fought in Vietnam.
2 Identify the effects of the war on Vietnamese civilians.
3 Summarize the impact of the massacre at My Lai.
4 *Key Terms* Define: saturation bombing; napalm; My Lai massacre.

Main Idea

The violence and brutality of the Vietnam War affected civilians as well as soldiers.

Reading Strategy

Reading for Evidence Read the section that summarizes the effects of the war on American soldiers and Vietnamese civilians. As you read, list the different ways in which the soldiers and the civilians suffered.

Images of brutality and bloodshed made American television viewers question U.S. involvement in Vietnam.

When Americans first started arriving in Vietnam in large numbers, they encountered all the frustrations of guerrilla warfare. American forces had superior arms and supplies. The Communists, however, had advantages of their own. For one thing, the swamps and jungles of Vietnam offered them protection. Sanctuaries across the border in Cambodia and Laos were valuable too. Finally, the Communists could often count on the support of the local population. At times that support was gained through terrorist methods. But it was often genuine, especially in the early 1960s.

Battlefield Conditions

Many American soldiers went to war enthusiastic about the job they were being asked to do. Some, like Ron Kovic of Long Island, worried about the Communist threat. Kovic was afraid that Communists "were infiltrating our schools, trying to take over our classes and control our minds." After high school, he joined the marines to do his part to defend his country. He proudly served a tour in Vietnam and signed up for a second tour. This second tour of duty would take a terrible toll on Kovic's body and mind.

He and other soldiers were finding the war confusing and disturbing. They were trying to defend the freedom of the South Vietnamese, but the people seemed indifferent to the Americans' effort. The dishonest and inept government in Saigon may have caused that indifference. "We are the unwilling working for the unqualified to do the unnecessary for the ungrateful," Kit Bowen of the First Infantry Division wrote to his father in Oregon.

Fighting conditions were also different from those they had seen in films. Carrying 60-pound packs, they had to walk through jungles of 10-foot-tall elephant grass and across flooded rice paddies. Much of the time they fought leeches, fever, and jungle rot—a tropical fungus that infected the skin.

American troops never knew what to expect next, and they never could be sure who was a friend and who was an enemy. The

RESOURCE OPTIONS

Teaching Resources

Reproducible Lesson Plan Lesson Plans folder, p. 158

Big Idea Graphic Organizer Big Idea Graphic Organizer folder, p. 130

Guided Reading and Review Units 9–10 folder, p. 44

Literature Activity Experiences of a Young Soldier in Vietnam, Units 9–10 folder, pp. 55–56

Vietnamese woman selling soft drinks by the roadside might be a Viet Cong ally, counting government soldiers as they passed. A child peddling candy might be concealing a live grenade.

The Viet Cong lacked the sophisticated equipment of the United States troops, so they avoided head-on clashes. Instead they used guerilla warfare tactics, working in small groups to launch sneak attacks and practice sabotage. They often frustrated American search parties by hiding themselves in elaborate underground tunnels. Some of these were equipped with running water and electricity. The largest contained hospitals, stores, and weapons storage facilities.

The various booby traps of the guerrilla fighters posed constant hazards to the Americans. There were animal snares, camouflaged holes filled with razor-sharp punji stakes that were sometimes poisoned, carefully hidden land mines, and grenades triggered by concealed trip wires. GIs could go weeks without making contact with the enemy—in fact, most never did—but there was always the possibility of sudden danger.

In the face of the uncertain situation, a GI wrote home:

AMERICAN VOICES "The VC [Viet Cong] are getting much stronger, so I think this war is going to get worse before it gets better. . . . I try and take great pride in my unit and the men I work with. A lot of the men have been in a lot of trouble and have no education or money. But I feel honored to have them call me a friend."

—*Letter home from an American soldier*

Ron Kovic confronted his fears by making an aggressive effort to be a good soldier. But the horrors of war came to haunt him after he accidentally killed a United States corporal. Later he shot at shadowy figures in a village hut, only to learn that his unit had killed and wounded innocent children.

The final blow for Ron Kovic came when a sniper's bullet entered his spine. As his spinal column was severed and he lost the feeling in his legs, all he could think of was "the worthlessness of dying right here in this place at this moment for nothing." Kovic survived the bullet wound but was paralyzed from the chest down. The injury caused him to feel, in his words, "like a big clumsy puppet with all his strings cut."

Effects on Civilians

The war was also devastating for Vietnamese civilians in both the north and the south. Because American soldiers were never sure who might be sympathetic to the Viet Cong, civilians suffered as much as soldiers. As the struggle intensified, the destruction worsened.

In April 1966 the Americans introduced the huge B-52 bomber into the war to smash roads and heavy bridges in North Vietnam. During air raids these planes could drop thousands of tons of explosives over large areas. This **saturation bombing** tore North Vietnam apart.

Many of the bombs used in these raids threw pieces of their thick metal casings in all directions when they exploded. These fragmentation bombs were not confined to the north alone. They were also used in the south, where they killed and maimed countless civilians.

United States forces also used chemical weapons against the Vietnamese. Pilots dropped an herbicide known as Agent Orange on dense jungle landscapes. By killing the leaves and thick undergrowth, the herbicide exposed Viet Cong hiding places. Agent Orange also killed crops, and later it was discovered to cause health problems in livestock and humans, including civilians and American soldiers.

Main Idea CONNECTIONS

How were Vietnamese civilians affected by the war?

In addition to killing and injuring many civilians, the war also forced many Vietnamese to flee their homes. *Culture What impact did the war have on Vietnamese culture?*

VIEWING HISTORY

From the medic trying in vain to save a dying comrade (above), to the soldier finally giving in to anguished tears in a lonely barracks (right), the war left few untouched. *Culture How did the nature of the fighting add to the frustrations of American soldiers?*

Another destructive chemical used in Vietnam was called **napalm.** This jellylike substance, when dropped from planes as a "firebomb," burned uncontrollably. It stuck to people's bodies and seared off their flesh.

The war affected everyone in Vietnam. Le Thanh, a North Vietnamese, recalled the horrors he had witnessed as a child in the 1960s:

> ❝Nobody could get away from the war. It didn't matter if you were in the countryside or the city. While I was living in the country I saw terrible things. . . . I saw children who had been killed, pagodas and churches that had been destroyed, monks and priests dead in the ruins, schoolboys who were killed when schools were bombed.❞
>
> —*Le Thanh*

The situation was similar in the south. Near the village of My Thuy Phuong, the war suddenly intruded on the life of a peasant who later described the frightening incident:

> ❝One day I was walking back home from the ricefield, carrying tools on my shoulder. Then behind me I heard a large, loud noise. A very bad noise. I looked back and saw an American helicopter following me, shooting down the path toward me. I was very scared, so [I] jumped into the water by the side. Just one moment later, the bullets went right by. So scary.❞
>
> —*Vietnamese peasant*

The My Lai Massacre

In March 1968 the brutality of the war came into sharp focus at My Lai, a small village in South Vietnam. In response to word that My Lai was sheltering 250 members of the Viet Cong, a United States infantry company moved in to clear out the village. Rather than enemy soldiers, the company found women, children, and old men. The American troops already had suffered heavy combat losses. They were worn down by the tensions, terrors, and frustrations of fighting a guerrilla war. Some lost control.

Lieutenant William L. Calley, Jr., was in charge. First he ordered, "Round everybody up." Then he gave the command for the prisoners to be killed. One soldier, Private Paul Meadlo, later described what happened to one group of Vietnamese:

> AMERICAN VOICES
>
> ❝We huddled them up. We made them squat down. . . . I poured about four clips [about 68 shots] into the group. . . . Well, we kept right on firing. . . . I still dream about it. . . . Some nights, I can't even sleep. I just lay there thinking about it.❞
>
> —*Private Paul Meadlo*

At least 175 and perhaps more than 400 Vietnamese died in the **My Lai massacre.** Even more would have perished without the heroic actions of a helicopter crew who stepped in to halt the slaughter. The pilot, Hugh Thompson, saw at least 10 villagers racing for a bunker, with a group of American soldiers in pursuit. From the air, he had already seen bodies piled in ditches and had witnessed the killing of a wounded woman by an American officer. So he knew what would happen if he did nothing.

At great risk to himself and his crew, Thompson landed the helicopter between the soldiers and the fleeing Vietnamese. He ordered his door gunner, 18-year-old Lawrence Colburn, to fire his machine gun at the American troops if they began shooting the villagers. Thompson got out, confronted the leader of the soldiers, and then arranged to evacuate the civilians. Thompson's crew chief, Glenn Andreotta, pulled a child from a ditch full of dead bodies.[†]

Despite Thompson's testimony about My Lai, his superiors covered up the incident. When the story finally came out, late in 1969, it shocked Americans at home. In 1971, for his role in the massacre, Lieutenant Calley began serving a sentence of life in prison with hard labor. Many Americans saw him as a scapegoat, however, and the public outcry was such that President Nixon reduced his life sentence to twenty years. He was released on good behavior three years later.

The publicity surrounding the My Lai massacre was so great that news accounts of atrocities in the city of Hué, also just coming to light, were completely overshadowed. During the Tet Offensive, the Communists had been uncommonly brutal, slaughtering anyone they labeled an enemy. This included harmless minor officials, teachers, and doctors. While the

The helicopter was first widely used in warfare during the Vietnam War. *Science and Technology Why did American troops with superior equipment fail to defeat the enemy?*

Communists had control of Hué, they ordered all civil servants, military personnel, and those who had worked for the Americans to report to special locations. Of those who obeyed, some 3,000 to 5,000 were killed. Their bodies were found in mass graves after American and South Vietnamese forces retook the city.

[†] The heroics of the helicopter crew did not surface until much later. Finally, in 1998 the United States honored all three men with the Soldier's Medal, the highest award for bravery unrelated to fighting an enemy.

SECTION 2 REVIEW

Comprehension

1. *Key Terms* Define: (a) saturation bombing; (b) napalm; (c) My Lai massacre.

2. *Summarizing the Main Idea* Why was the Vietnam War particularly brutal for American soldiers?

3. *Organizing Information* Create a chart to compare the effects of the war on American soldiers and Vietnamese civilians.

Critical Thinking

4. *Analyzing Time Lines* Review the time line at the start of the section. What evidence do you see of a cause and an effect in the time-line events?

5. *Drawing Conclusions* Do you think that the United States made every effort to win the Vietnam War? Why or why not?

Writing Activity

6. *Writing a Persuasive Essay* Write an essay either condemning or forgiving the actions of Lieutenant Calley at My Lai.

1960
Students for a Democratic Society organized

1964
Free speech movement begins

1965
First teach-in

1968
More than 200 demonstrations at U.S. colleges and universities

1969
Weathermen clash with police in Chicago

1971
Publication of Pentagon Papers

1960   1965   1970   1975

Objectives

You may wish to call students' attention to the objectives in the Section Preview. The objectives are reflected in the main headings of the section.

Bellringer

Ask students whether the decade in which they are living seems to have a particular theme or identity. Ask them to suggest adjectives that might describe its general tone and compare these adjectives to descriptions of the 1960s and early 1970s.

Reading Strategy

Structured Overview Refer to the Reading Strategy in the Section Preview. You may wish to point out the difference between student activism and resistance to war, since these terms often overlap.

LESSON PLAN

Connecting to the Main Idea

1. Focus Explain that during the 1960s, college campuses erupted in student protest. The most dramatic, and perhaps the most effective, protests were against the war in Vietnam. Ask why college students became activists during the 1960s.

2. Instruct Note that the Port Huron Statement on the next page begins with a generational identification: "We are people of this generation." Ask students why they think Hayden began the statement with those words. Discuss how the civil rights movement strengthened students' belief in their ability to bring about change. Ask why student activists, trained in the civil rights movement, worked to change their schools and to stop the Vietnam War.

3. Close Student protesters demanded many changes during the 1960s, but the primary focus of their protest became the Vietnam War. The next section describes the development of the counterculture.

3 Student Protest

SECTION PREVIEW

Objectives

1. Describe student activism in the 1960s.
2. Identify actions some people took to resist the Vietnam War.
3. *Key Terms* Define: Pentagon Papers; New Left; teach-in; conscientious objector; deferment.

Main Idea

Students in the 1960s demonstrated in support of free speech and other issues and protested against the Vietnam War.

Reading Strategy

Structured Overview Write the main headings *Student Activism* and *Resistance to War* on a sheet of paper. As you read the section, write important details in the column under each heading.

This 1969 poster advertised one of many antiwar demonstrations during the Vietnam War era.

In June 1971 *The New York Times* began publishing articles based on a classified government study of United States involvement in the Vietnam War. The study came to be called the Pentagon Papers. The **Pentagon Papers** revealed that government officials had lied to Congress and the American people about the war. Presidents had made secret policy decisions, such as giving military aid to France and waging an undercover war against North Vietnam in the early 1960s.

Such revelations shocked the public and gave a boost to the growing antiwar movement. Popular support for the war began to drop. Still, many loyal and patriotic Americans defended their country's actions in Vietnam, and the issue created deep divisions within the United States.

Student Activism

Students stood at the forefront of the antiwar movement. In the early 1960s members of the baby-boom generation started graduating from high school. Postwar prosperity gave many of these students opportunities unknown to previous generations. Instead of going directly into the working world after high school, these young men and women could afford to continue their education. College enrollments swelled with more students than ever before.

Change was in the air. It had been building for a while, even through the conformist years of the 1950s. The popular culture of that decade, including rock-and-roll music and rebellious youths on the movie screen, indicated that many young Americans were not satisfied with the values of their parents. The early 1960s saw a widening of this generation gap.

The civil rights movement, discussed in an earlier chapter, also became a steppingstone to other movements for change. Civil rights activists helped organize Students for a Democratic Society (SDS) in 1960. SDS's declaration of principles and goals, called the Port Huron Statement, appeared in 1962. Written largely by Tom Hayden, a student at the University of Michigan, the statement explained some of the feelings behind the antiwar movement:

 RESOURCE OPTIONS

Teaching Resources

Reproducible Lesson Plan Lesson Plans folder, p. 159

Learning Styles Lesson Plan Learning Styles Lesson Plans folder, p. 64

Big Idea Graphic Organizer Big Idea Graphic Organizer folder, p. 131

Guided Reading and Review Units 9–10 folder, p. 46

Key Documents The Port Huron Statement, Learning with Documents folder, p. 104

" We are people of this generation, bred in at least modest comfort, housed now in universities, looking uncomfortably at the world we inherit. When we were kids the United States was the wealthiest and strongest country in the world. . . . As we grew, however, our comfort was penetrated by events too troubling to dismiss. . . . We would replace power rooted in possession, privilege, or circumstance by power and uniqueness rooted in love, reflectiveness, reason, and creativity. As a social system we seek the establishment of a democracy of individual participation."

—*Port Huron Statement*

SDS was a tiny organization at the start. Still, it had a major influence on the development of a new political movement that came to be called the **New Left.** Members of the New Left believed that problems such as poverty and racism called for radical changes.

The Free Speech Movement The first confrontation of the student revolution came at the University of California at Berkeley in September 1964. Students became angry when the university administration refused to allow them to distribute leaflets outside the main gate of the campus.

The students, who had fought for equal rights in the South, argued that their right to free speech was being challenged. They resisted the university's effort to restrict their political activity. When police came to arrest one of their leaders, students surrounded the police car and kept it from moving. The free speech movement was under way.

The university administration tried to find a compromise. But then the university governing board stepped in. The board had the final word over university policy. It decided to hold student leaders responsible for their actions and filed charges against some.

On December 2, 1964, thousands of irate students took over Sproul Hall and shut down the university administration. That night police moved in. They arrested more than 700 students in the hall. Other students, supported by some faculty members, went on strike. They stopped attending classes to show their support for the free speech demonstrators.

Berkeley remained the most radical campus, but the agitation there spread to other campuses across the United States. In the spring of 1965, activists at several schools launched

In October 1964, Berkeley student Mario Savio stood atop a police car to address a crowd of protesters demanding free speech. The building in the background is Sproul Hall. *Culture How had the civil rights movement influenced the antiwar movement?*

protests against regulations they thought unfairly curbed their freedom. Students at Michigan State University and elsewhere challenged social restrictions, such as the hours when women and men could visit each others' dormitories. Students also sought greater involvement in college affairs. Others left their campuses to work in campaigns to improve conditions in the inner cities.

The Teach-in Movement As American involvement in the Vietnam War grew, students were among the first to protest the war. Some opposed what they regarded as American imperialism. Others viewed the conflict as a civil war that should be resolved by the Vietnamese alone.

As escalation began (see the graphs on the next page), antiwar activists used new methods to protest the war. The first **teach-in** took place at the University of Michigan in March 1965. When a small

Main Idea CONNECTIONS
What was a teach-in?

U. S. Military Forces and Battle Deaths in Vietnam, 1965–1972

Source: *Statistical Abstract of the United States*

Source: *Statistical Abstract of the United States*

 Interpreting Graphs United States involvement in Vietnam peaked in 1968. *Foreign Relations How many United States soldiers were in Vietnam in 1968? How many United States soldiers died in battle in 1968?*

Dr. King Decries the War April 1967 brought proclamations, draft-card burnings, and mass demonstrations against the United States's continuing grim entanglement in Vietnam. In New York City's Riverside Church on April 4, the Reverend Dr. Martin Luther King, Jr., encouraged conscientious objection to the draft on a nationwide scale, called the U.S. government the "greatest purveyor of violence in the world today," and offered a five-point plan for a peaceful American withdrawal. It was Dr. King's strongest statement yet on the war, in which "twice as many Negroes as whites" were serving. "If America's soul becomes totally poisoned," he warned, "part of the autopsy must read Vietnam." Source: Nathan Ward, "The Time Machine," *American Heritage* magazine, April 1992.

Customize for

English Language Learners

Ask students to create a list of the goals of the free-speech, draft-resistance, and antiwar movements.

Answer to . . .

Interpreting Graphs Over 500,000; over 14,000.

group of faculty members planned a strike to protest the war, the Michigan legislature threatened to fire them. Instead, an even larger group decided to make a public statement. Some 50 or 60 professors decided to teach a special night session in which issues concerning the war could be aired.

To their surprise, several thousand people showed up and made the evening a monumental success. Soon other teach-ins followed at colleges around the country. Supporters as well as opponents of the war appeared at the early teach-ins, but soon antiwar voices dominated the sessions.

Resistance to War

A Selective Service Act allowing the government to draft men between the ages of 18 and 26 had been in place since 1951. Relatively few people refused to be drafted in the first half of the 1960s. Most who did were **conscientious objectors.** They opposed fighting in the war on moral or religious grounds.

In July 1965 President Johnson doubled the number of men who could be drafted into the armed forces. By the end of the year he had doubled the number again. These moves led to the rise of a draft-resistance movement that urged young men not to cooperate with their local draft board.

As more and more young men were called into service and sent to fight in Vietnam, Americans began to question the morality and fairness of the draft. College students could receive a **deferment,** or official postponement of their call to serve. Usually this meant they would not have to go to war. Those who could not afford college did not have this avenue open to them. In 1966 the Selective Service System announced that college students who ranked low academically could be drafted.

In 1967 resistance to the military draft began to sweep the country. Many young men tried to avoid the draft by claiming that they had physical disabilities. Others applied for conscientious-objector status. Still others left the country. By the end of the war more than 50,000 were believed to have gone to countries such as Canada.

Antiwar groups grew by leaps and bounds around the country. During demonstrations, marchers chanted "Hey, hey, LBJ. How many kids did you kill today?" In April 1967 some 200,000 opponents of the war marched in New York City. In October more than 50,000 protesters gathered in Washington, D.C., for a March on the Pentagon, home of the Defense Department.

In 1969 the National Chicano Moratorium Committee staged its own antiwar demonstrations. These protesters argued that Vietnam was a racial war, with black and brown Americans being used against their brothers and sisters in developing nations. In the first six months of 1968, more than 200 major demonstrations erupted at colleges and universities around the country.

Despite the widespread discontent, not all students agreed with the antiwar protesters. Some firmly supported American involvement in Vietnam. Others questioned the war but were troubled by the lawlessness and radicalism of many antiwar protests. These students did not receive the press coverage of their more outspoken classmates. But they did make their opinions known by writing letters to campus newspapers or by challenging the actions of antiwar groups in court. Many other Americans expressed their patriotism by putting flag decals on their car windows or attaching bumper stickers that read "My Country, Right or Wrong" and "Love It or Leave It."

The most dramatic confrontation of 1968 came in April at Columbia University in New York City. Students there linked the issues of civil rights and the war. An SDS chapter sought to get the university to cut its ties with a research institute that did work for the military. At the same time, an African American student organization tried to halt construction of a gymnasium that would encroach upon a nearby minority neighborhood.

Together these two groups took over the president's office. Finally the president of Columbia called the police, and hundreds of students were arrested. A student sympathy strike followed, and the university closed early that spring.

Sometimes the radical movement turned violent. Activists in one SDS faction called themselves the Weathermen, after a line in a Bob Dylan song—"You don't need a weather-

As President Johnson dramatically stepped up the draft, antiwar sentiment stepped up, too. Antiwar protests, like this one in San Francisco in 1967, received much press coverage. Still, many Americans supported the war effort—some with bumper stickers like the one below. *Diversity How else did students who supported the administration make their views known?*

My Country
Love It or Leave It

man to know which way the wind blows." They were determined to bring about a revolution immediately.

In October 1969 the group converged on Chicago. Members dressed in hard hats, boots, and work gloves rampaged through the streets wielding pipes, clubs, rocks, and chains. They tangled with police (as they had planned), regrouped, and came back for still another confrontation. This kind of violence alarmed most Americans and turned some against the antiwar movement.

SECTION 3 REVIEW

Comprehension

1. **Key Terms** Define: (a) Pentagon Papers; (b) New Left; (c) teach-in; (d) conscientious objector; (e) deferment.

2. **Summarizing the Main Idea** What forms did student protest take in the 1960s?

3. **Organizing Information** Use a flowchart to show the sequence of important events related to student protests in the 1960s. You might start with the civil rights movement of the 1950s.

Critical Thinking

4. **Analyzing Time Lines** Review the time line at the start of the section. Which event do you think had the strongest effect on American public opinion about the war? Explain.

5. **Determining Relevance** Do you think that the war protests of the 1960s could have taken place if there had never been a civil rights movement? Explain.

Writing Activity

6. **Writing an Expository Essay** Write an essay about the forms of protest Americans used to express their views on the war in Vietnam.

Answers to
SECTION 3 REVIEW

1. (a) Pentagon Papers, see p. 882; (b) New Left, see p. 883; (c) teach-in, see p. 883; (d) conscientious objector, see p. 884; (e) deferment, see p. 884.

2. The organization Students for a Democratic Society; the development of the New Left; the free-speech and teach-in movements; the draft-resistance movement.

3. Civil Rights movement of the 1950s—college enrollment booms in the 1960s—SDS formed and New Left grows—students organize antiwar demonstrations and teach-ins—students begin draft resistance movement.

4. Sample answer: 1969—clash with Weathermen, because seeing this kind of violence against Americans at home turned many people against the war.

5. Sample answer: Not as likely, because people would have been less likely to question the government, and would be unfamiliar with the techniques of resistance.

6. Essays will vary but should be supported with facts from the section.

▶ RESOURCE OPTIONS

Teaching Resources

📁 **Quiz** Units 9–10 folder, p. 47

📁 **Great Debates** Should the U.S. Have Stayed in Vietnam?, Decision-Making Activities folder, pp. 44–45

Student Performance Pack

⭐ **Guide to the Essentials** Chapter 31, Section 3 (English and Spanish)

Answer to . . .

Viewing History By writing letters to the editors of their college newspapers; challenging the actions of antiwar groups in court; distributing leaflets and displaying bumper stickers.

Critical Thinking

Checking Consistency

Focus Students check for consistency between what they have read about the Vietnam era and the passages provided. **Instruct** Have students work with partners to answer the questions. Ask for a show of hands to indicate how many students find the passages in Item A and Item B inconsistent. Then ask for volunteers to explain the inconsistency they find. Ask those who find the passages consistent to explain their reasoning. **Extend** See the Skills for Life Activity in the Resource Options below.

Answers

1. (a) The First Amendment, which guarantees freedom of the press. (b) That his objectives were geared toward peaceful settlement. (c) His policy objectives and attitudes can be compared with his policy objectives and attitudes on the same subject at a later date.

2. (a) It turned down the government's request to keep two newspapers from publishing "The Pentagon Papers." (b) The newspapers probably published the material. (c) His depiction of the North Vietnamese in harsh, threatening terms suggested policy objectives geared toward a military victory rather than a peaceful settlement.

3. (a) It agreed with the First Amendment that no law interfere with the freedom of the press. (b) No. In 1965 Johnson's policy objective was peaceful settlement with the North Vietnamese. In 1966 it was a military victory over them.

Statements will vary but should be consistent or inconsistent with Johnson's 1965 statement.

886

Checking Consistency

Checking consistency means determining whether ideas that should agree, or follow logically one from the other, actually do. Government actions, for example, should always agree with the Constitution. Where no such overriding rules apply—in the creation of foreign policy, for instance—policy objectives are expected to be consistent with past decisions on similar issues.

Use the following steps to check for consistency in the examples at right.

1. *Identify the principle or other factor to be used as the baseline for checking consistency.* You should expect certain facts, ideas, or actions to agree, either with one another or with an overriding principle. Read the information in Items A and B, at right. (a) What rule or principle serves as the baseline for checking consistency in Item A? (b) In Item B, what did Johnson's description of the North Vietnamese in 1965 suggest about the goals of his policy in Vietnam at the time? (c) How can Johnson's statement serve as the baseline for checking his consistency in other statements about Vietnam?

2. *Note the corresponding action or idea to be checked for consistency.* (a) In Item A, what action did the Supreme Court take? (b) What probably happened as a result of this action? (c) In Item B, what did Johnson's description of the North Vietnamese (the "Communists") in 1966 suggest about the goals of his policy in Vietnam?

3. *Check for consistency between the principle or baseline factor and the corresponding action or idea.* In the examples below, compare the second action or idea against the baseline you have identified to see if the two ideas are consistent with or contradict each other. (a) In Item A, did the action taken by the Supreme Court agree or conflict with the First Amendment? Explain your answer. (b) In Item B, was Johnson's statement of his policy objective in 1966 consistent with the statement he had made in 1965? Explain your answer.

Compose a statement that Johnson might have made after the Tet Offensive. Label the statement either consistent or inconsistent with the statement he made in 1965. Explain your reasoning.

A

"Congress shall make no law . . . abridging the freedom of speech, or of the press. . . ."

—First Amendment, United States Constitution

In 1971 the United States Supreme Court denied the government's request to prohibit two newspapers from publishing the Pentagon Papers, a highly classified documentary history of United States involvement in Vietnam through May 1968.

B

"This war, like most wars, is filled with terrible irony. For what do the people of North Vietnam want? They want what their neighbors also desire: food for their hunger, health for their bodies, . . . an end to the bondage of material misery. . . . Neither independence nor human dignity will ever be won by arms alone. It also requires the works of peace."

—President Lyndon B. Johnson, address at Johns Hopkins University (April 7, 1965)

"Aggression is on the march and the enslavement of free men is its goal. . . . If we allow the Communists to win in Vietnam, it will become easier and more appetizing for them to take over other countries in other parts of the world. . . . That is why it is vitally important to every American family that we stop the Communists in South Vietnam."

—President Lyndon B. Johnson, Honolulu Conference (February 6, 1966)

RESOURCE OPTIONS

Teaching Resources

Skills for Life Activity Units 9–10 folder, p. 57, provides passages in which students can practice this skill by determining whether words and actions follow a given principle.

Media and Technology

Color Transparencies Critical Thinking, I-7

| 1963 | | 1966 | |
| Two Harvard researchers fired for LSD experiments | 1965 Miniskirt introduced | Masters and Johnson publish Human Sexual Response | 1969 Woodstock festival |

1963 | **1965** | **1967** | **1969**

4 The Counterculture

SECTION PREVIEW

Objectives

1 Identify the social changes promoted by members of the counterculture.
2 Describe the music world in the 1960s and how it both reflected and contributed to cultural changes.
3 *Key Terms* Define: counterculture; Woodstock festival.

Main Idea

In the 1960s a youth culture arose that promoted freedom and individuality. Its new attitudes about personal relationships, drugs, and music shocked many Americans.

Reading Strategy

Reinforcing Key Ideas As you read the section, note details that support the following sentence from this page: "In the 1960s many Americans began to look for alternatives to traditional patterns of living."

In the 1960s many Americans began to look for alternatives to traditional patterns of living. Young people, in particular, adopted values that ran counter to, or against, the mainstream culture. Drawing on the example of the Beat Generation of the 1950s, members of this **counterculture** rejected most of the conventional social customs. They experimented with new forms of dress, different attitudes toward sexual relationships, and the recreational use of drugs. Their rejection of accepted ways of life in favor of change and individual choice still affects society today.

A Time of Change

People's appearances reflected the social changes that were taking place. Hippies—people who were "hip," or aware of the latest styles—wanted to look different. Some women wore their hair long and chose freer fashions, such as loose-fitting dresses. Others chose to wear tight miniskirts, which were introduced by British designer Mary Quant in 1965. Men often let their hair grow long and wore beards.

Many hippies adopted the dress of working people, which seemed somehow more "authentic" than the school clothes of middle-class youth. Both men and women wore blue jeans (often with bell bottoms), plain cotton shirts, and other simple garments that were intended to look natural.

The Sexual Revolution The new views of sexual behavior advanced by the counterculture were labeled "the sexual revolution." The young people who led this revolution demanded more freedom to make personal choices. Some argued that sex should be separated from its traditional ties to family life.

The sexual revolution in the counterculture led to more open discussion of sexual subjects. Newspapers, magazines, and books published articles that might not have been printed just a few years earlier. The 1962 book by Helen Gurley Brown, *Sex and the Single Girl*, became a bestseller. In 1966 William H. Masters and Virginia E. Johnson shocked

Some 1960s youth expressed themselves by turning their possessions into works of art.

RESOURCE OPTIONS

Teaching Resources

 Reproducible Lesson Plan Lesson Plans folder, p. 160

Learning Styles Lesson Plan Learning Styles Lesson Plans folder, p. 65

Big Idea Graphic Organizer Big Idea Graphic Organizer folder, p. 132

Guided Reading and Review Units 9–10 folder, p. 48

BACKGROUND

The War's Opponents

The common belief during this period was that antiwar sentiments were held exclusively by the young and the highly educated. But a May 1971 Gallup Poll found that 75 percent of those with only a grade-school education opposed the war, against 66 percent of college graduates. "A careful review of public opinion data over the last seven years [1965–72]," stated a 1972 University of Michigan Survey Research Center study, "shows that on most war-related issues, the greatest opposition to continued American involvement has come from the least educated parts of the population."

Customize for
More Advanced Students

Ask students to analyze what ultimately happened to the 1960s counterculture. Why did most hippies melt back into the middle class, and why had many who protested against capitalistic values in the 1960s become business executives by the 1980s? What aspects of American life were permanently changed by the counterculture?

Answer to . . .

Viewing History By living together as couples without getting married.
Main Idea Connections Its rejection of traditional values and embracing of what many Americans saw as lax morals frightened them.

888 Chapter 31 • Section 4

This group of hippies lived together in the New Buffalo Commune. They turned out for the 1968 Fourth of July parade in El Rito, New Mexico, in their outrageously painted bus. *Culture In what other ways did people reject traditional social customs?*

many people when they published *Human Sexual Response,* a report on their scientific studies of sexuality.

Many men and women also experimented with new living patterns. Some hippies rejected traditional relationships and lived together in communal groups, where they often shared property and chores. More and more people simply lived together as couples, without getting married.

The Drug Scene Some members of the 1960s counterculture also turned to psychedelic drugs. These powerful chemicals cause the brain to behave abnormally. Users of psychedelic drugs experience hallucinations and other altered perceptions of reality. The beatniks had experimented with drugs a decade before, but they had been relatively few in number. Now the use of drugs, especially marijuana, became more widespread among the nation's youth.

One early proponent of psychedelic drug use was researcher Timothy Leary. Leary worked at Harvard University with Richard Alpert on the chemical compound lysergic acid diethylamide, commonly known as LSD. The two men were fired from their research posts in

Main Idea
CONNECTIONS

Why do you think the counterculture disturbed many Americans?

1963 for using undergraduates in experiments with the drug. Leary then began to preach that drugs could help free the mind. He advised listeners, "Tune in, turn on, drop out."

Soldiers who had used drugs in Vietnam brought them home when their tours of duty were completed. Marijuana became common among middle-class college students. Todd Gitlin, a radical activist who became president of SDS, explained that "the point was to open up a new space, an inner space, so that we could space out, live for the sheer exultant point of living."

This view presented just one side of the drug scene. On the other side lay serious danger. The possibility of death from an overdose or from an accident while under the influence of drugs was very real. Three leading musicians—Janis Joplin, Jim Morrison, and Jimi Hendrix—died of complications from drug overdoses. They were not the only ones. Their deaths represented the tragic excesses to which some people were driven by their reliance on drugs as an escape.

The Music World

Music both reflected and contributed to the cultural changes. The rock and roll of the 1950s and the folk music of the early 1960s gave way to a new kind of rock. The Beatles heavily influenced the music of this period, taking first their native England and then the United States by storm. Mick Jagger of the Rolling Stones was a dramatic and electrifying showman on stage. Janis Joplin was a hard-drinking singer whose powerful interpretations of classic blues songs catapulted her to superstardom.

Woodstock The diverse strands of the counterculture all came together at the Woodstock Music and Art Fair in upstate New York in August 1969. About 400,000 people gathered for several days in a large pasture in Bethel, New York, to listen to the major bands of the rock world. Despite brutal heat and rain, those who attended the **Woodstock festival** recalled the event with something of a sense of awe for the fellowship they experienced there. Police avoided confrontations with those attending by choosing not to enforce drug laws. The crowd remained under control. Tom Law, one participant at Woodstock, commented on the mood:

❝The event was so much bigger than the music. It was a phenomenon. It was absolutely a phenomenon. And it was also the most peaceful, civilized gathering that was probably happening on the planet at the time.❞

—Tom Law

Other Americans, however, viewed both the festival and the mood it reflected with disgust. Even as some older people began growing their hair longer and wearing "hipper" clothing, they were alarmed at the changes they saw around them. These changes also disturbed many young people. In particular, people in the mainstream culture deplored the drugs, sex, and nudity they saw at the Woodstock festival and around the country. To them the counterculture represented a rejection of morals and honored values and seemed a childish reaction to the problems of the era.

Altamont The fears of those who criticized Woodstock came true at another rock festival that took place at the Altamont Speedway in California in December 1969. There, 300,000 people gathered for a concert by the Rolling Stones.

When promoters of the concert failed to provide adequate security, the Stones hired a band of Hell's Angels, an infamous and lawless motorcycle gang, to keep order. The cyclists ended up beating one man to death when he

The young people who attended the Woodstock Music and Art Fair in 1969 reflected the new fashions and social values of their times. *Culture What were some of these values?*

ventured onstage. The ugly violence at Altamont contradicted the values preached by the counterculture. It also signaled that the era of "peace and love" would not last forever.

Despite their celebration of simple lifestyles, most hippies were children of the comfortable middle class. American corporations marketed items such as blue jeans and stereo equipment to them, and they eagerly bought the products. When the counterculture fell apart, the hippies melted right back into the mainstream. By the 1980s many baby boomers who had protested the values of the 1950s and 1960s would hold executive positions in the same corporations they had once denounced.

SECTION 4 REVIEW

Comprehension

1. **Key Terms** Define: (a) counterculture; (b) Woodstock festival.

2. **Summarizing the Main Idea** What values did the counterculture reject in the 1960s and what did it embrace?

3. **Organizing Information** Create a web diagram to organize information related to the counterculture of the 1960s.

Critical Thinking

4. **Analyzing Time Lines** Review the time line at the start of the section. Which event do you think reflected the sharpest break with the culture of the 1950s?

5. **Identifying Assumptions** What assumptions did members of the counterculture make about mainstream culture?

Writing Activity

6. **Writing an Expository Essay** Write an essay describing the traditional values that members of the counterculture rejected.

 RESOURCE OPTIONS

Teaching Resources

 Quiz Units 9–10 folder, p. 49

Student Performance Pack

Guide to the Essentials Chapter 31, Section 4 (English and Spanish)

Media and Technology

 Color Transparencies Links Across Time, J-9

The End of the War

1968	1969	1970	1973		1982
Johnson quits race for President	Nixon takes office	Kent State protest	Peace agreement signed	1975 South Vietnam falls	Vietnam Memorial completed

1965	1970	1975	1980	1985

Objectives

You may wish to call students' attention to the objectives in the Section Preview. The objectives are reflected in the main headings of the section.

Bellringer

Ask students whether it is possible for a United States President to continue a course of action strongly opposed by most of the American people. In what ways can the people make their opinions known to the President?

Reading Strategy

Predicting Content Refer to the Reading Strategy in the Section Preview. You may wish to have students make their predictions in light of previous sections in this chapter as a whole.

LESSON PLAN

Connecting to the Main Idea

1. Focus Explain that antiwar protests grew in strength and frequency until President Nixon finally managed to bring the war to a close. Ask how opposition to the war affected the election of 1968. How did the war finally end?

2. Instruct Ask students to list the reasons for growing opposition to the war. Ask why Lyndon Johnson could not end the war. What steps finally led to the cease-fire and withdrawal of American forces? Why did Nixon's escalation of the bombing and the invasion of Cambodia cause such outrage? Tell students that Nixon's adviser Henry Kissinger hoped that "jugular diplomacy" would force the North Vietnamese into making some concessions at the negotiating table.

3. Close The Vietnam War finally ended in 1973, but the war left deep scars in both the United States and Vietnam.

5 The End of the War

SECTION PREVIEW

Objectives

1 Explain how opponents of the Vietnam War helped force Johnson's departure, and describe how they reacted to Nixon's policies.
2 Describe how the American troop withdrawal came about and what it meant for South Vietnam.
3 Identify elements that make up the legacy of the Vietnam War.
4 *Key Terms* Define: Paris peace talks; Vietnamization; Vietnam Veterans Memorial.

Main Idea

The end of the Vietnam War involved slow-moving peace negotiations, the gradual withdrawal of American troops, and the fall of South Vietnam.

Reading Strategy

Predicting Content Skim the section, reading headings and the first sentence of each paragraph. Then list the main headings on a sheet of paper. Under each heading, write a sentence or phrase predicting the content of that part of the section. When you have finished reading, compare your predictions with the actual content.

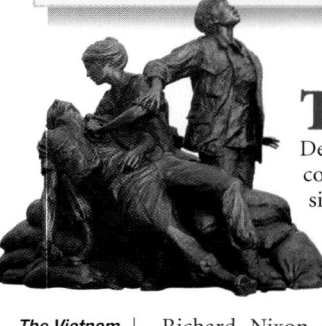

The Vietnam Women's Memorial in Washington, D.C., honors the thousands of women who served in Vietnam.

The Vietnam War created deep divisions in the Democratic party and in the country as a whole. These divisions forced Lyndon Johnson to leave the presidency at the end of his term and paved the way for the election of Republican Richard Nixon in 1968. Nixon pledged to withdraw the United States from the Southeast Asian struggle. He succeeded, but only after expanding the war outside Vietnam, which led to even more violent protest at home.

Johnson's Departure

By 1968 the antiwar movement was in full swing. Political activists drew on all of their resources to mount the most extensive resistance campaign in American history. Marchers took to the streets, while artists, authors, and musicians contributed their talents to the antiwar crusade.

Years of protests and a growing list of American casualties had steadily increased public opposition to Johnson's handling of the war. By 1967 Robert McNamara, Johnson's Secretary of Defense, had lost faith in the war effort. Privately, he urged the President to turn more of the fighting over to the South Vietnamese and to stop the bombing of North Vietnam. Johnson, fearful of risking defeat on the battlefield, ignored the proposal. He continued to increase American troop levels and to authorize bombing raids on North Vietnam. Still, after the Tet Offensive, Johnson recognized that American public opinion had turned against him. He rarely left the White House near the end of his presidency for fear of being assaulted by angry crowds of protesters. He felt like "a jackrabbit in a hailstorm, hunkering up and taking it."

In early 1968 Johnson watched the campaign of antiwar candidate Eugene McCarthy gain momentum. On March 12 McCarthy almost beat the President in the New

RESOURCE OPTIONS

Teaching Resources

📁 **Reproducible Lesson Plan** Lesson Plans folder, p. 161

📁 **Big Idea Graphic Organizer** Big Idea Graphic Organizer folder, p. 133

📁 **Guided Reading and Review** Units 9–10 folder, p. 50

Media and Technology

 AmericanHeritage® **CD-ROM**

Time Tour The Nation Today and Tomorrow: A Time of Turmoil

Hampshire Democratic primary. Four days later another critic of the war, Robert Kennedy, joined the race for the Democratic nomination.

Johnson realized that he had lost his base of support. On March 31, 1968, he declared dramatically in a nationally televised speech that he would not run for another term as President:

❝I do not believe that I should devote an hour or a day of my time to any personal partisan causes or to any duties other than the awesome duties of this office—the presidency of your country. Accordingly, I shall not seek, and I will not accept, the nomination of my party for another term.❞

—*Lyndon Johnson*

Earlier in the same speech, Johnson had ordered a pause in the relentless bombing of Vietnam to open the possibility of peace talks. In this way he hoped to end the war and so restore unity to the United States as he left public life. In April the North Vietnamese agreed to begin formal negotiations with the United States in Paris. A month later the **Paris peace talks** began.

Nixon's Policies

McCarthy's campaign for the presidency faltered, and on June 5 Robert Kennedy was assassinated. The Democrats eventually nominated Johnson's Vice President, Hubert Humphrey, at their party's convention in Chicago (see the next chapter). For the Republicans, Richard Nixon ran for the presidency with the claim that he had a secret plan to end the war in Vietnam. He never divulged the details, and critics doubted that a plan really existed, but his pledge still helped secure his election over Humphrey.

Vietnamization Once in the White House, Nixon dedicated himself to a policy of **Vietnamization.** This involved removing American forces and replacing them with South Vietnamese soldiers. Between 1968 and 1972 American troop strength dropped from 536,000 to 24,000, and opposition to the war among people in the United States declined. †

Even as he moved to bring American soldiers home, Nixon himself became caught up in the war. As much as he wanted to defuse anti-

---
† In January 1973 Nixon announced the end of the military draft, which further defused antiwar protests.

war sentiment at home, he was determined not to lose the war. Therefore, as he withdrew American troops, he resumed bombing raids, keeping his actions secret from his critics. The map later in this section shows the major targets of the bombing raids.

Invading Cambodia President Nixon also widened the war beyond the borders of Vietnam. Hoping to avoid more antiwar protests, Nixon ordered secret bombings in Cambodia. Later, in April 1970, Nixon publicly announced that United States and South

---

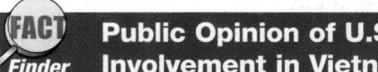

Public Opinion of U.S. Involvement in Vietnam

"Do you approve or disapprove of the way President Johnson is handling the situation in Vietnam?"

	Approve	Disapprove	No opinion
December 1965	56%	26%	18%
May 1966	41%	37%	22%
April 1967	43%	42%	15%
July 1967	33%	52%	15%
December 1967	39%	49%	12%
February 1968*	35%	50%	15%

"In view of the developments since we entered the fighting in Vietnam, do you think the United States made a mistake sending troops to fight in Vietnam?"

	Yes, made mistake	No, did not	No opinion
May 1966	36%	49%	15%
April 1967	37%	50%	13%
July 1967	41%	48%	11%
February 1968†	49%	41%	10%

* During Tet Offensive †After Tet Offensive
Source: *The Gallup Poll: Public Opinion 1935–1971,* by George H. Gallup

Interpreting Tables Public opinion of U.S. involvement in Vietnam changed over the course of the war. *Culture What percentage of those polled in 1965 approved of Lyndon Johnson's handling of the war? What percentage approved in 1968?*

Customize for
English Language Learners

Ask students to make time lines, beginning with 1960, identifying the major dates in the Vietnam War.

COMPARING PRIMARY SOURCES

THE TRAGEDY OF KENT STATE

In May 1970 the National Guard opened fire on a crowd of antiwar protesters at Kent State University and killed four students.

Opposed to National Guard's Actions	In Support of National Guard's Actions
"Nixon acts as if the kids had it coming. But shooting into a crowd of students, that is violence. They say it could happen again if the Guard is threatened. They consider stones threat enough to kill children. I think the violence comes from the government." —*Mother of Jeffrey Glenn Miller, a student killed at Kent State, quoted in* Life *magazine, May 15, 1970*	"He told me they didn't fire those shots to scare the students off. He told me they fired those shots because they knew the students were coming after them, coming for their guns. People are calling my husband a murderer; my husband is not a murderer. He was afraid." —*Wife of a member of the National Guard, quoted in* Newsweek *magazine, May 18, 1970*

ANALYZING VIEWPOINTS How do these viewpoints reflect the issues that tore apart American society at that time?

Vietnamese ground forces were moving into neighboring Cambodia. Their goal was to clear out Communist camps there, from which the enemy was mounting attacks on South Vietnam. The United States, he asserted, would not stand by like "a pitiful helpless giant" while the Viet Cong attacked from Cambodia:

 AMERICAN VOICES "We take this action not for the purpose of expanding the war into Cambodia but for the purpose of ending the war in Vietnam and winning the just peace we all desire. We have made and we will continue to make every possible effort to end this war through negotiation at the conference table rather than through more fighting on the battlefield."

—*Richard Nixon*

Main Idea CONNECTIONS

Why did the United States invade Cambodia?

Nixon knew that invading Cambodia would not win the war, but he thought it would help at the bargaining table. He was willing to intensify the war in order to strengthen the American position at the peace talks. Nixon's actions, however, brought chaos and civil war in Cambodia and a fresh wave of protests at home.

Kent State and Jackson State Nixon's invasion of Cambodia in 1970 reignited the protest movement on college campuses in the United States. At Kent State University in Ohio, students reacted angrily to the President's action. On the weekend following his speech, they broke windows in the business district downtown. They also burned the army ROTC building on campus, which had become a hated symbol of the war.

In response, the governor of Ohio ordered the National Guard to Kent State. Tension mounted. When students threw rocks and empty tear-gas canisters at them, the guardsmen loaded their guns and donned gas masks. They knelt down and aimed their rifles at the students, as if warning them to stop. Then the guardsmen retreated to another position. At the top of a hill, they suddenly turned and began firing on the students below.

Seconds later, four students lay dead, with nine others wounded. Two of the dead had been demonstrators more than 250 feet away from the guardsmen. The other two were bystanders, almost 400 feet away.

Similar violence flared at Jackson State, a nearly all-black college in Mississippi. A confrontation between students and police left two students dead and eleven wounded.

These attacks horrified Americans. In a sign of the deep divisions in the nation, 100,000 construction workers marched in an angry demonstration in New York City in support of the President.

American Withdrawal

The war dragged on, as did the Paris peace talks. In January 1972, while running for a second term as President, Nixon announced that North Vietnam had refused to accept a proposed settlement. At the end of March, the North Vietnamese began a major assault on South Vietnam. This led Nixon to order the most intensive bombing campaign of the war. The United States bombed Hanoi, the North Vietnamese capital, and mined North Vietnamese harbors.

"Peace Is at Hand" Just days before the 1972 election, National Security Adviser Henry Kissinger announced, "Peace is at hand." As it turned out, the settlement was not actually final.

But after Nixon's reelection in November and another round of B-52 bombings of North Vietnam in December, peace finally did arrive. In January 1973 the United States, South Vietnam, North Vietnam, and the Viet Cong signed a formal agreement in Paris. Among the provisions in the agreement were these:

(1) The United States would withdraw all its forces from South Vietnam within 60 days.

(2) All prisoners of war would be released.

(3) All parties to the agreement would end military activities in Laos and Cambodia.

(4) The 17th parallel would continue to divide North and South Vietnam until the country could be reunited.

South Vietnam Falls United States involvement in the war came to an end, but the fighting between North and South Vietnam continued for another two years. After the withdrawal of American forces, South Vietnamese soldiers steadily lost ground to their North Vietnamese enemies. In the spring of 1975, the North Vietnamese launched a campaign of strikes against strategic cities throughout South Vietnam, the final objective being the seat of government in Saigon.

South Vietnamese forces crumpled in the face of this campaign. On April 29, 1975, with Communist forces surrounding Saigon, the United States carried out a dramatic last-minute evacuation. American helicopters airlifted more than 1,000 Americans and nearly 6,000 Vietnamese from the city to aircraft carriers waiting offshore. On April 30 North Vietnam completed its conquest of South Vietnam, and the Saigon government officially surrendered. After decades of fighting, Vietnam was a single nation under a Communist government.

Legacy of the War

The Vietnam War was the longest and least successful war in which the United States had ever participated. Its costs were enormous.

Counting the Costs The Vietnam War resulted in more than 58,000 Americans dead and 300,000 wounded. It cost at least $150 billion in direct expenses and produced a huge national debt and growing inflation.

The costs of the war were even higher for the Vietnamese. More bombs rained down on Vietnam than had fallen on all Axis powers during World War II. The number of dead and wounded Vietnamese soldiers ran into the millions, with countless civilian casualties. The landscape itself would long bear the scars of war.

Southeast Asia After the War One of the reasons for American involvement in Vietnam was the belief in the domino theory. This was the assumption that the entire region would collapse if the Communists won in Vietnam. With the North Vietnamese victory, two dominoes did topple—Laos and Cambodia. The rest of the region, however, did not fall.

The suffering of the Cambodian people was one of the most tragic effects of the war in Vietnam. In April 1975, Cambodia fell to the Khmer Rouge, a force of Communists led by the fanatical Pol Pot. In five years of fighting, Cambodia had already suffered as many as a

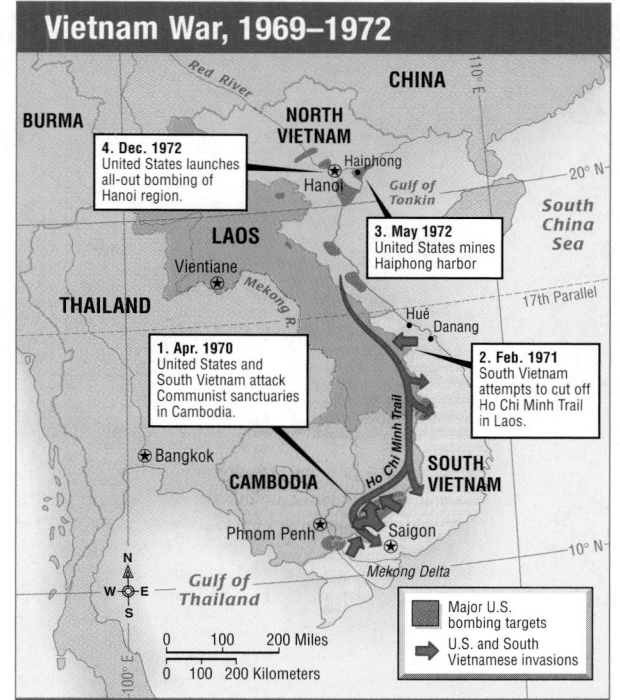

Vietnam War, 1969–1972

4. Dec. 1972 United States launches all-out bombing of Hanoi region.

3. May 1972 United States mines Haiphong harbor

1. Apr. 1970 United States and South Vietnam attack Communist sanctuaries in Cambodia.

2. Feb. 1971 South Vietnam attempts to cut off Ho Chi Minh Trail in Laos.

Major U.S. bombing targets

U.S. and South Vietnamese invasions

MAP skills Although Nixon began withdrawing troops from Vietnam in 1969, he stepped up bombing raids. *Location According to this map, in what areas were United States bombing raids concentrated during the later years of the war?*

Prisoners of War (POWs) and soldiers missing in action (MIAs) were also part of the enormous costs of the Vietnam War.

BACKGROUND

Connections to Today

One of the lasting images of the war in Vietnam for Americans is the scene of the final hours of the United States presence in Saigon (now Ho Chi Minh City). Helicopters that swooped down to the roof of the U. S. embassy were immediately filled with diplomatic and military personnel, then jammed to overflowing with frantic refugees before flying off to safety. For nearly 25 years afterward, the massive building was a reminder of the war, but no longer. The State Department decided in 1997 to demolish the old building and replace it with a sleek new consulate, designed to foster commercial ties. Many people in the city see the change as symbolic of a new era. As one Vietnamese said, "The relationship between the United States and Vietnam is different now. We are doing trade, not fighting a war."

RESOURCE OPTIONS

Media and Technology

Critical Thinking Activity Drawing Conclusions: Military Spending, found on Resource Pro, charts the increase in military spending that many people thought was prolonging the Vietnam War.

 AmericanHeritage® CD-ROM

History Makers Maya Lin

Answer to . . .

Map Skills On the Vietnam-Cambodia border and in the Hanoi area.

Graphing the Main Idea

To make sure students understand the main idea of this section, you may wish to use the flow map graphic organizer below.

Tell students that a flow map is useful for showing a sequence of events unfolding. Ask students to use it to record the events that led to the end of the Vietnam War.

Teaching Tip A template for this graphic organizer can be found in the Color Transparencies, G-4.

Answers to

SECTION 5 REVIEW

1. (a) Paris peace talks, see p. 891; (b) Vietnamization, see p. 891; (c) Vietnam Veterans Memorial, see p. 894.

2. Nixon widened the war; peace talks dragged on; fighting between North and South Vietnam continued after the U. S. withdrawal.

3. Led to end: Vietnamization, peace talks, public protest. Kept war going: invasion of Cambodia, stalled peace talks, continued fighting between North and South Vietnam.

4. Sample answer: Violence against antiwar protesters may have been averted, and the peace agreement may have been signed much earlier.

5. South Vietnam could not stand up to the forces of the North, and inevitably was forced to surrender.

6. Essays will vary but should be supported with facts from the section.

Answer to . . .

Viewing History North Vietnam.

In 1975 Nha Trang in South Vietnam was evacuated just before Communist troops took over. The man above was punched by an American official as he tried to board the last plane out, which was already overcrowded with fleeing refugees. *Foreign Relations* Who finally won the Vietnam War?

half million civilian casualties, mostly by American bombs. Worse was to come. The Khmer Rouge in effect declared war on anyone "tainted" with Western ways. They killed as many as 1.5 million Cambodians—a quarter of the population. Many were shot, while the rest died of starvation, disease, mistreatment in labor camps, or on forced marches.

Although not so extreme, Vietnam's new leaders also forced hundreds of thousands of South Vietnamese soldiers, civil servants, and other professionals into "re-education camps." Meanwhile, more than 1.5 million Vietnamese fled their country by boat, leaving behind all personal possessions in their determination to escape. In addition to these refugees, hundreds of thousands of Cambodians and Laotians also fled their homelands, many making their way to the United States.

The United States After the War In the United States the war splintered the foreign policy that had guided the nation during and after World War II. Americans had believed that they could defend the world from communism anywhere, at any time. American technology and money, they assumed, could always bring victory. Vietnam proved that assumption to be false. Many people called for a reassessment of America's global mission.

The impact of the war in the United States lingered on long after the last bomb had been dropped. Soldiers came home to a different reception from the ones their fathers and grandfathers had following World War II. There were no welcoming ticker-tape parades. Many veterans complained that Americans did not appreciate what they had gone through.

In 1979 a group of veterans began making plans for a **Vietnam Veterans Memorial.** They wanted to recognize the courage of American GIs during the Vietnam ordeal and to help heal the wounds the war had caused. The memorial was completed in 1982. In 1994 the United States announced an end to the long-standing American trade embargo against Vietnam. The next year the United States agreed to restore full diplomatic relations with its former enemy.

SECTION 5 REVIEW

Comprehension

1. *Key Terms* Define: (a) Paris peace talks; (b) Vietnamization; (c) Vietnam Veterans Memorial.
2. *Summarizing the Main Idea* Why did the end of the Vietnam War come so slowly?
3. *Organizing Information* Create a chart to show the events or other factors that led to an end to the war and the factors that kept the war going.

Critical Thinking

4. *Analyzing Time Lines* Review the time line at the start of the section. How might the period 1968–1975 have been different if Johnson had been willing and able to end the war?
5. *Recognizing Cause and Effect* What did the complete withdrawal of American troops mean for South Vietnam?

Writing Activity

6. *Writing an Expository Essay* Write an essay about the legacy of the Vietnam War.

RESOURCE OPTIONS

Teaching Resources

📁 **Quiz** Units 9–10 folder, p. 51

📁 **Chapter Tests Forms A and B** Chapter Test folder

Student Performance Pack

Guide to the Essentials Chapter 31, Section 5 (English and Spanish)

Standardized Test Preparation Handbook

Media and Technology

🎧 **Guided Reading Audiotapes** Chapter 31 Summary (English and Spanish)
Student Edition on Audiotape Chapter 31

💿 **Test Bank CD-ROM; Interactive Student Tutorial CD-ROM** Chapter Test

Why Study History?

To understand that . . .

Draft Registration Is Required Today

Registration for the military draft, which provoked fierce opposition during the Vietnam War, is in effect today.

Young men burning draft cards to protest the Vietnam War

One of the issues that divided the country during the Vietnam War was the military draft, or conscription. More than a million young American men were drafted into the army to fight in Southeast Asia. As the war dragged on and casualties increased, public support for the war declined. Increasing numbers of Americans began to question conscription.

The Impact Today

Since the Civil War, the United States has used a draft in wartime to meet its military needs. Reacting to the start of World War II in Europe, President Franklin Roosevelt initiated the nation's first peacetime draft in 1940. About 10.1 million American men were drafted into the military between 1940 and 1946. After the war, the number of men drafted each year declined dramatically—except during the Korean War. Some 1.5 million men were drafted between 1950 and 1953 as a result of that conflict.

The manpower needs of the armed forces increased again with deepening American involvement in Vietnam. Between 1964 and 1973, about 1.8 million men were drafted into military service. College students, however, could receive draft deferments that exempted them from service as long as they remained in school. This meant that a high number of those drafted were young men too poor to afford college. Following complaints about the system, Congress eliminated the deferment in 1971.

In another effort to make the draft fairer, in 1969 the government instituted a lottery system. In a random drawing, all eligible men ages 18 and over were assigned a number according to their birth date. A person's number told him the likelihood that he would be called for service.

Despite these changes, opposition to the draft remained. Thousands even left the country to avoid the draft. In 1973 Congress ended conscription, and the United States converted to an all-volunteer military force. A law requiring 18-year-olds to register at local draft boards was suspended in 1975. It was resumed, however, in 1980 and remains in effect today. Male United States citizens ages 18 through 25 must register with the Selective Service System. In a national crisis, if the country needs more soldiers than an all-volunteer service can provide, the draft can be resumed.

Army soldiers leave for Middle East, 1990

The Impact on You

List two arguments in support of maintaining the current all-volunteer system in the armed forces. Next to these, list two arguments in support of returning to a system of conscription. Then, below these two sets of arguments, write a paragraph explaining which position you favor and why.

Class Discussion

Discuss the military draft with the class. For a more thorough examination of the issue, see the activity folder in the Resource Options below.

ACTIVITY
STUDENT PARTICIPATION

Making an Issues Chart
Have students read the text. Then divide the class into two groups. Have each group create a chart with arguments in favor of or opposed to draft registration. Charts should address these issues:
- **responsibility to country**
- **service to country**
- **needs of country**
- **fairness**
- **opportunity**

Have the groups present their charts. Encourage debate.

Follow up Have students discuss whether their ideas would change if the United States were involved in a war that they supported, or in a war that they opposed.

Using the Internet
Students can learn more about draft registration by exploring links in the *America: Pathways to the Present* Web site at

http://www.Pathways.phschool.com

Assessment
See the Lesson Plans folder, pp. 24–27, for rubrics on assessing Class Participation Projects.

RESOURCE OPTIONS

Teaching Resources

 Why Study History? Activity Draft Registration Is Required Today, found in the Why Study History? folder, p. 32, provides an activity to help students better understand the military draft.

Media and Technology

AmericanHeritage® **CD-ROM**

Time Tour The Nation Today and Tomorrow: A Time of Turmoil

American ARTIFACTS

THE VIETNAM VETERANS MEMORIAL

Focus Recall that United States involvement in the Vietnam War divided the country into two angry camps: those who opposed the war and those who supported it. Many Americans were indifferent or hostile to returning soldiers, but a change in attitude was evident when the Vietnam Veterans Memorial was unveiled in Washington, D.C., in 1982.

Instruct Ask students to focus on the various images in the feature and discuss the significance of each to a combat soldier or a soldier's family. Ask students to compare the items belonging to soldiers in Vietnam with the artifacts they studied from the Civil War. Then ask students to list experiences common to veterans of both conflicts.

Extend Ask students to suppose that they had lost a friend or family member in the Vietnam War. Students may wish to write a letter examining their feelings toward that individual, the United States government, and the Vietnamese people.

Personal Memorials

1 Visible in this photo are some of the names on the Vietnam Veterans Memorial.

Mementos

2 People leave objects, such as these stuffed animals, in memory of their loved ones.

Boots and Helmet

3 The National Park Service collects items left at the wall, such as these boots and helmet that once belonged to a soldier.

▶ RESOURCE OPTIONS

Teaching Resources

American History Block Scheduling Support Vietnam: The War at Home, found in The Nation After World War II folder, includes interdisciplinary lesson suggestions and activities for Geography and History, Primary Sources, Biography, and Literature.

896

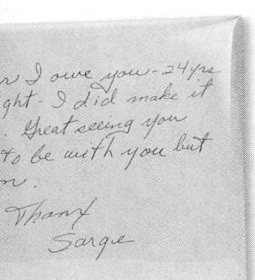

④

Letters

Family and friends have left letters for the soldiers whose names are on the wall.

⑤

Dog Tags

Listing information such as name, identification number, and blood type, "dog tags" were issued to each soldier. Many have been left at the wall.

VIEWING HISTORY

1. **Summarize** What do the objects tell you about Americans' feelings about the Vietnam War?

2. **Connecting to Today** What can the Vietnam Veterans Memorial and the objects that have been left there teach us about the war and the people whose lives it affected?

American ARTIFACTS

FROM EXHIBITIONS AND COLLECTIONS AT THE SMITHSONIAN INSTITUTION'S NATIONAL MUSEUM OF AMERICAN HISTORY

THE VIETNAM VETERANS MEMORIAL

The United States' involvement in the Vietnam War divided the country into two angry camps: those who supported it and those who opposed it. This division continued even after the American withdrawal from Vietnam in 1973. Returning veterans, instead of being honored for their service, were sometimes greeted with indifference or even hostility.

In 1982 the Vietnam Veterans Memorial was unveiled in Washington, D.C. Unlike most other monuments in the city, the wall is built on a small, human scale. Its two polished, black-granite walls hold the names of more than 58,000 Americans killed and missing in the war. *See* **①** .

With the dedication of the Vietnam Veterans Memorial, a healing of the war's bitter divisions seemed to begin. People began leaving personal tokens at the base of the monument to honor and remember the soldiers who fought in the war. These tokens ranged from stuffed animals, favorite magazines, beverages, and items of clothing to the everyday items of a soldier in Vietnam, such as helmets and combat boots. *See* **②** *and* **③** .

A few visitors have written notes to their loved ones and left those notes at the wall. Others have left dog tags and driver's licenses. Such items carry memories of the bond between soldier and mourner. *See* **④** *and* **⑤** .

This practice continues today. The National Park Service collects and preserves the artifacts. In 1992 the Smithsonian Institution put some of these items on display, where thousands of Americans view them each year.

VIEWING HISTORY

Answers to . . .

1. Many people lost friends and relatives in the fighting in Vietnam. Although the war divided Americans, the Vietnam Veterans Memorial serves as a common focus for their grief.

2. The objects left at the Vietnam Veterans Memorial remind us that each casualty touched many other lives, and that the pain of war continues long after the fighting has ended.

Key Terms

Students should refer to the definitions of key terms in the chapter to write sentences that show an understanding of the issues of the Vietnam War.

Comprehension

1. Johnson used the Gulf of Tonkin incident as an excuse to devote increasing amounts of American money and personnel to the war and to bomb North Vietnam.
2. The guerrilla warfare in the jungle was confusing and frightening, and soldiers never knew who their friends or enemies were.
3. Their primary demand was for an end to the Vietnam War. They also called for free speech and an end to poverty and racism.
4. They formed organizations such as SDS, organized antiwar protests such as teach-ins, and began movements such as draft resistance and the free-speech movement.
5. They saw the counterculture as a rejection of traditional morals and values; they were shocked by the new attitudes toward sex and drugs.
6. In order to destroy the North Vietnamese bases located there.
7. Vietnam suffered millions of casualties and the destruction of its land. The United States lost 58,000 soldiers and would never again feel as confident about its ability to defeat communism around the world.

Chapter Summary

The major concepts of Chapter 31 are presented below. See also *Guide to the Essentials of American History* or *Interactive Student Tutorial CD-ROM,* which contains interactive review activities, time lines, helpful hints, and test practice for Chapter 31.

Reviewing the Main Ideas

Under Presidents Kennedy and Johnson, the country became deeply involved in stopping a Communist takeover in South Vietnam. As the war dragged on, many Americans began to question American participation in the war. At the same time a youthful counterculture arose, criticizing the traditional values of many Americans.

Section 1: Deepening American Involvement

The United States entered the Vietnam War to defeat Communist forces threatening South Vietnam.

Section 2: The Brutality of the War

The violence and brutality of the Vietnam War affected civilians as well as soldiers.

Section 3: Student Protest

Students in the 1960s demonstrated in support of free speech and other issues and protested against the Vietnam War.

Section 4: The Counterculture

In the 1960s a youth culture arose that promoted freedom and individuality. Its new attitudes about personal relationships, drugs, and music shocked many Americans.

Section 5: The End of the War

The end of the Vietnam War involved slow-moving peace negotiations, the gradual withdrawal of American troops, and the fall of South Vietnam.

Registration for the draft, which provoked fierce opposition during the Vietnam War, is still in effect today.

Key Terms

Use each of the terms below in a sentence that shows how it relates to the chapter.

1. counterculture
2. Viet Cong
3. deferment
4. Gulf of Tonkin Resolution
5. Vietnamization
6. conscientious objector
7. Pentagon Papers
8. escalation
9. Tet Offensive
10. teach-in
11. Woodstock
12. Ho Chi Minh Trail
13. My Lai massacre
14. napalm

Comprehension

1. How did the Vietnam War escalate under President Johnson?
2. Why was the war so hard on American soldiers fighting in Vietnam?
3. What were some of the changes that student activists demanded during the 1960s?
4. What methods did activists use during the 1960s?
5. Why did many Americans view the counterculture with shock and dismay?
6. Why did Richard Nixon authorize the invasion of Cambodia in 1970?
7. What was the lasting impact of the war on Vietnam and on the United States?

Using Graphic Organizers

On a separate sheet of paper, copy the web diagram below. Create additional circles to show (1) shifts in United States policy, from Kennedy to Nixon; (2) major events related to the war; and (3) main effects of the war on American soldiers, Vietnamese civilians, and American society.

Using Graphic Organizers

1. Circles might include: increasing involvement in Vietnam; the concealment of secret policy decisions from the public; the use of government force to put down protest; the extension of the war to Cambodia.
2. Circles might include: the Gulf of Tonkin incident; the Gulf of Tonkin Resolution; the Pleiku attack; the Tet Offensive; the My Lai massacre; the Vietnamization policy; the invasion of Cambodia, and the Paris peace talks.

3. Circles might include: Soldiers—58,000 dead and 300,000 wounded; psychological trauma; cold reception by the American public after the war. Vietnamese civilians—countless civilian casualties; the destruction of land; the creation of a refugee population; "reeducation camps." American society—questioning the nation's global mission and methods; disruption of society.

Analyzing Political Cartoons ▶

1. Examine the images in the cartoon. Who are the two men?

2. What is the occasion shown in the cartoon?

3. (a) What is the significance of the documents held by the man on the right? (b) What does the gravestone refer to?

4. What point is the cartoonist trying to make?

Critical Thinking

1. *Applying the Chapter Skill* President Nixon promised to end the war in Vietnam. Yet he authorized the heaviest bombing raids of the war and he expanded the war into Cambodia. Were these actions consistent with his promise? Explain.

2. *Demonstrating Reasoned Judgment* If you had been a student during the Vietnam War, do you think that your views of the conflict would have changed or remained the same throughout the course of the war? What factors might have influenced your views?

3. *Expressing Problems Clearly* Since the end of the Vietnam War, government officials have advised caution in global affairs so that the United States does not get involved in "another Vietnam." Explain what is meant by this warning.

©1972 HERBLOCK

INTERNET ACTIVITY

For your portfolio:
WRITE AN ARTICLE

Access Prentice Hall's *America: Pathways to the Present* site at **www.Pathways.phschool.com** for the specific URLs to complete the activity. Additional resources and related Web sites are also available.

Use the links provided to read about the Kent State shootings on May 4, 1970. Write a newspaper article describing the incident. How did Americans react to the event? In what ways did the incident reflect the deep divisions in the nation?

ANALYZING DOCUMENTS ◀ ▶ INTERPRETING DATA

Turn to the map titled "Vietnam War, 1969–1972" on page 893.

1. About how long was the Ho Chi Minh Trail? (a) 150 miles (b) 300 miles (c) 600 miles (d) 3,000 miles

2. What action would have helped prevent Soviet war supplies from reaching North Vietnam? (a) mining Haiphong harbor

(b) attacking Communist bases in Cambodia (c) cutting off the Ho Chi Minh Trail (d) bombing Saigon

3. *Writing* Write an essay explaining how the neighboring countries of Laos and Cambodia became involved in the Vietnam War.

Connecting to Today

Although we call it the Vietnam War, Congress never officially declared a war against North Vietnam. Write an essay about how American involvement in Vietnam might have changed if Congress had pursued its right to declare war.

899

INTERNET ACTIVITY

Articles will vary, but should be supported with specific facts and quotes about Kent State from the Web site, and explore themes introduced in the chapter.

Analyzing Political Cartoons
1. A man representing the American voter; President-elect Richard Nixon.
2. The 1972 presidential election.
3. (a) Nixon was elected President in 1968 by claiming that he had a secret plan to end the war in Vietnam; he is making the same claim in 1972. (b) The number of U.S. soldiers killed in Vietnam despite Nixon's secret plan to end the war.
4. Nixon was only claiming to have a plan to end the war in order to get elected, then reelected; meanwhile, U.S. citizens are being killed.

Critical Thinking
1. Inconsistent—Though Nixon seemed to be pulling the United States out of the war with his policy of Vietnamization, his attack on Cambodia showed that he planned to keep the war going.
2. Students' answers should show an understanding that many people's views changed from acceptance to strong disapproval. Factors that influenced this shift included television coverage of the war and student protests.
3. The warning cautions against becoming involved in distant conflicts that are difficult to pull out of, that consume great amounts of money and numbers of lives, and that are probably doomed to failure.

Interpreting Data
1. c
2. c
3. Essays will vary but should mention the North Vietnamese formation of bases in those countries and subsequent American bombing.

Connecting to Today
Essays will vary. Students might suggest the role of the public in influencing Congress's decision to declare war, and that Congress may have taken into account potential expenses and deaths.

Focus Have students find the meaning of each of these words in a dictionary before they begin to read: *defunct, premise, freestanding, sparse, Jim Crow.* Ask them to consider, as they read, how a greater understanding of segregation might have changed white Americans' attitudes toward civil rights.

Instruct Have students role-play Bruce Killebrew and Joan W. Musbach talking to each other, as adults, about their childhood experiences of race. Have students work in pairs to outline conversations and choose roles. Tell them to construct conversations so that they give information in a manner that is consistent with both characters. Then have them perform their conversations for the class.

Analyzing the Document

Use this additional question to generate class discussion:
CRITICAL THINKING: MAKING COMPARISONS How were Bruce Killebrew's and Joan W. Musbach's experiences alike? How were they different? (*They were alike in that both students became aware of current issues dealing with race through personal experience. They were different in that Killebrew was inspired by integration, whereas Musbach was shocked and saddened by segregation.*)

My Brush with History

BY BRUCE KILLEBREW & JOAN W. MUSBACH

INTRODUCTION The two passages below describe how two white Americans became aware of the system of racial segregation that existed in many parts of the country. In the first account, Bruce Killebrew recalls the integration of his third-grade class. In the second account, Joan W. Musbach remembers the day that she, as a high school student, came face to face with her own ignorance of segregation.

In 1954 my father was stationed at the Pentagon in Washington, D.C., and we lived on the now-defunct South Post of Fort Myer. My friends and I had a grand time romping through the nearby Civil War battlefields, taking turns being Yankee and Rebel. I couldn't decide whether to favor the Blue or the Gray. At the age of eight I'd really never thought about the issues that fueled the fighting.

Then, one day in the first week of September 1954, at the beginning of the year for our small military elementary school at Fort Myer, there were new faces in my class—and reporters from United Press and *Army Times* taking pictures. They were photographing the class while I led the Pledge of Allegiance for the first integrated class in the formerly Confederate state of Virginia. The two new students were black, and to me and the rest of my third-grade classmates they did not seem any different from the rest of us kids. But I was very proud to have been chosen to lead the Pledge of Allegiance on that day.

The event would help shape this nation's future, and my own. It brought home to me the idea that all men are created equal and have the right to equal opportunity. Much of my life as an individual and a social worker has been based on the premise I learned in that classroom in 1954.

—*Bruce Killebrew*

On a crisp, cool, sunny Saturday in January, a Midwestern café—a freestanding building with one counter, stools in front, grill behind—became the site of the most memorable experience of my high school years.

Bruce Killebrew appears in the far left of this photo.

TEST PREPARATION

Have students use the excerpt on these pages to answer the following question.

Why did newspaper reporters appear in Bruce Killebrew's class in the first week of school?

A Newspaper reporters in every town cover the beginning of the school year.

B Killebrew's school was particularly newsworthy because it was located on a military base.

C The reporters expected violence in the newly integrated school.

D Killebrew's was the first integrated class in Virginia.

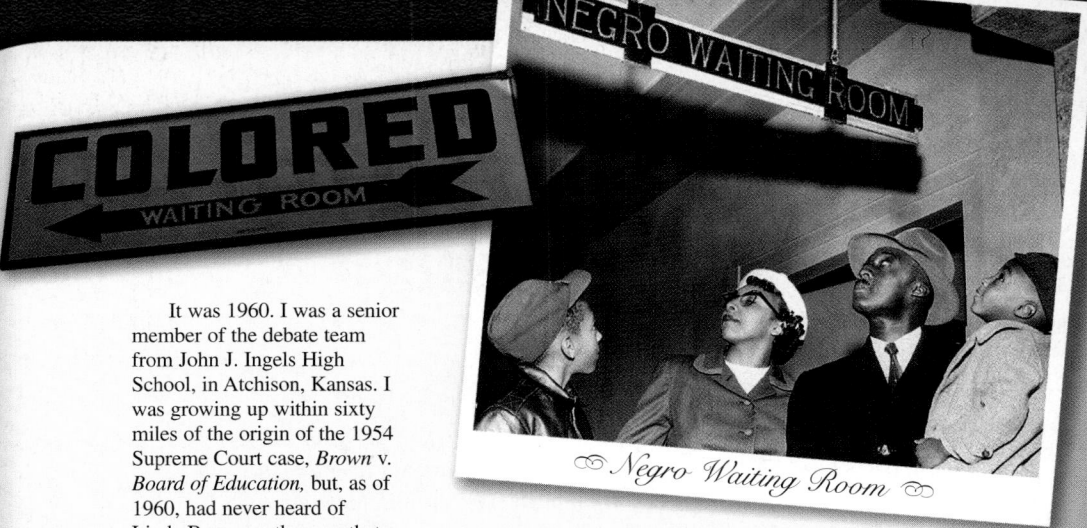

Negro Waiting Room

It was 1960. I was a senior member of the debate team from John J. Ingels High School, in Atchison, Kansas. I was growing up within sixty miles of the origin of the 1954 Supreme Court case, *Brown* v. *Board of Education,* but, as of 1960, had never heard of Linda Brown or the case that bears her name. I was soon to discover that there was a great deal about which I was unaware.

Segregation, announced in some places by signs like this, was practiced more quietly in other places.

We finished the Saturday-morning rounds and then went out for lunch before returning to the college to hear the semifinalists announced. We chose an appealing-looking cafeteria near the college. I was the only girl on the trip, and I was still just entering when Mr. Phipps and the boys turned around and came back out. I was busy talking and didn't ask why we had left. I assumed the cafeteria was too crowded. We got into Mr. Phipps's old car and drove a few blocks to a café. Business was sparse, and we spread out down the red-plastic-covered stools along the counter. John, my partner, was seated beside me. The waitress came down the counter distributing menus. John did not get one. We called this to her attention, and she quickly informed us that blacks were not served in there. I was shocked. I had never heard of such a thing. We all got up and went to the car, and Mr. Phipps went to a nearby hamburger stand and bought hamburgers and sodas for us all to eat in the car.

John wouldn't eat. He sat in the corner of the back seat, speechless. We didn't know what to say either. We just ate our hamburgers and went back to the college.

As I thought about the incident, I realized that John was the victim of our ignorance as well as of the prejudice of the management of the cafeteria and the café. He had probably never been exposed to such humiliation before, protected by parents or other adults who would have avoided such an incident. Strange as it may seem, a carful of high school students and their teacher were unaware of the segregation of public services just across the river from where they lived.

The look on John's face as we ate our hamburgers ensured that I would never forget that crisp January Saturday or the Kansas City café where I met Jim Crow.

—*Joan W. Musbach*

Source: *American Heritage* magazine, April 1991 and April 1994.

ADDITIONAL READING

To learn more about the topics discussed in this selection, you might want to read the following books:

- *The Children,* by David Halberstam (New York: Random House, 1998)
- *The Color Line: Legacy for the Twenty-first Century,* by John Hope Franklin (Columbia: University of Missouri Press, 1993)
- *Parting the Waters: America in the King Years, 1954–1963,* by Taylor Branch (New York: Simon & Schuster, 1989)
- *The Strange Career of Jim Crow,* by C. Vann Woodward (New York: Oxford University Press, 1974)

TEST PREPARATION

Have students use the excerpt on these pages to answer the following question.

Of what two things was John a victim?

A Affirmative action and poverty.

B Ignorance and prejudice.

Ⓒ Segregation and integration.

D The debate team and the business community.

Continuity and Change

1968–Present

Introducing the Unit

Using Historical Evidence

Discuss the concept of continuity and change in American government. Explain that although Americans elect new leaders at regular intervals, government continues in an orderly manner according to the Constitution and the traditions of government.

Direct students' attention to the photograph on the right. Ask them to suppose that they are one of the new citizens in the photo. Have volunteers explain why, as new immigrants, they decided to become American citizens. What do they hope to contribute to the United States as citizens? What do they most appreciate about the American system of government? What concerns, if any, do they have about the future of their new country?

Themes in American History

Direct students' attention to the Unit Themes. Point out that each chapter in this unit has its own theme. To teach this unit thematically, you may wish to use The Nation After World War II folder in **American History Block Scheduling Support.**

Using the Time Line

To provide students with practice in using a time line to connect key events in the United States with key events in the world, ask questions such as these: (1) What major international event occurred during the same year as the Persian Gulf War? (*The Soviet Union broke up.*) (2) What international crisis occurred during Nixon's presidency? (*OPEC oil embargo.*) (3) When was the first woman appointed to the Supreme Court? (*1981*)

unit TEN

Continuity and Change

1 9 6 8 – P r e s e n t

By 1968 many Americans were tired of the turmoil of the 1960s. The election of Richard Nixon as President that year marked the emergence of a Republican majority that lasted, with one brief exception, for more than twenty years. A recession following the election of George Bush in 1988, however, created growing dissatisfaction with Republican policies. When Democrat Bill Clinton defeated Bush in the 1992 presidential election, and was reelected in 1996, Americans seemed ready to head in a new direction.

Chapter 32 The Nixon Years *1969–1974*

Chapter 33 The Post-Watergate Period *1974–1980*

Chapter 34 The Conservative Revolution *1980–1992*

Chapter 35 Entering a New Era *1992–Present*

UNIT THEMES

Government The public lost confidence in the government as scandal forced President Nixon to resign from office.

Economics President Reagan embarked on major program of deregulation in order to spur business growth.

Foreign Relations In the mid- to late-1990s, the nation found itself trying to promote peace abroad while at the same time avoiding costly foreign entanglements.

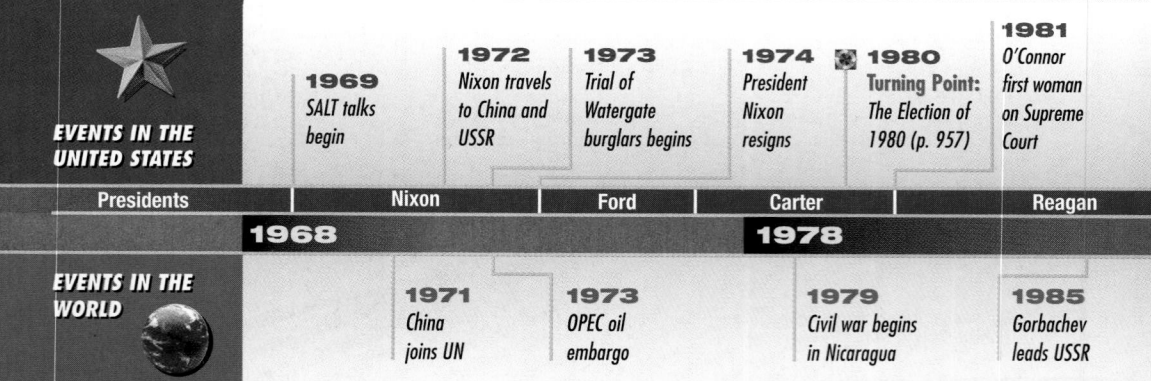

EVENTS IN THE UNITED STATES

1969 SALT talks begin

1972 Nixon travels to China and USSR

1973 Trial of Watergate burglars begins

1974 President Nixon resigns

1980 Turning Point: The Election of 1980 (p. 957)

1981 O'Connor first woman on Supreme Court

| Presidents | Nixon | Ford | Carter | Reagan |

1968 **1978**

EVENTS IN THE WORLD

1971 China joins UN

1973 OPEC oil embargo

1979 Civil war begins in Nicaragua

1985 Gorbachev leads USSR

 ### RESOURCE OPTIONS

Teaching Resources

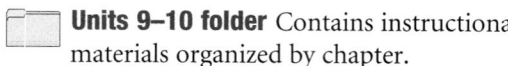 **Units 9–10 folder** Contains instructional materials organized by chapter.

VIEWING HISTORY These recently sworn-in citizens are symbolic of the cultural diversity that is one of the United States' greatest strengths. *Culture* What impact has recent immigration had on American society and politics?

1991 Persian Gulf War	1994 Senate ratifies NAFTA	1998 Clinton announces a federal budget surplus	2000 Clinton hosts Camp David Accords

George H. Bush	Clinton	George W. Bush

1988   **1998**

1988 Poland's Communist government falls	1991 Soviet Union breaks up	1995 Israeli leader Rabin assassinated	1998 U.S. embassies bombed in Kenya and Tanzania	1999 NATO goes to war over Kosovo

▶ RESOURCE OPTIONS

Media and Technology

Color Transparencies Specific transparencies are referenced throughout the chapters at appropriate points of use. For this unit, see American Photo, B-10; Our Multicultural Heritage, C-3; Links Across Time, J-10; Political Cartoon, K-10; and Historical Maps, L-5.

Visions of America "Scenes of an Era: Republican Revival and Decline" located on videodisc side 4 and on videotape 5. Lesson plans for "Scenes of an Era" can be found in the Visions of America Guidebook.

Side 4, Chapter 38

Answer to . . .

Viewing History While many Americans have welcomed diversity, others have worried about effects on jobs, education, and national unity.

903

The Nixon Years, 1969–1974

Managing Time and Instruction

INSTRUCTION SUPPORT

These materials for instruction are provided for **each section** in the **Teaching Resources**. See **Units 9–10 folder for Enrichment Support**:

- Reproducible Lesson Plans in Lesson Plans folder • Learning Styles Lesson Plans in Learning Styles Lesson Plans folder • Big Idea Graphic Organizers in Big Idea Graphic Organizer folder
- Guided Reading and Review • Quizzes • Test Preparation Practice booklet

DAILY LESSON	ENRICHMENT SUPPORT
1 The Crises of 1968 *(pp. 905–908)*	• Primary Source Activity, "Selling" Candidate Nixon, found on **Resource Pro** • Lasting Impact Activity, The Lasting Impact of the Year 1968, History's Lasting Impact folder, pp. 20–21
2 The Nixon Administration *(pp. 909–914)*	• Visual Learning Activity, The Imperial President, found on **Resource Pro** • Critical Thinking Activity, Predicting Consequences: Wage-Price Freeze, found on **Resource Pro** • Biography, Maggie Kuhn, found on **Resource Pro**
3 Nixon's Foreign Policy *(pp. 915–919)*	• Primary Source Activity, The Trip to China: Diplomacy and Publicity, Learning with Documents folder, p. 38
4 The Watergate Scandal *(pp. 920–925)*	• Visual Learning Activity, Wanted, Learning with Documents folder, p. 74 • Biography, John J. Sirica, Units 9–10 folder, p. 66 • Literature Activity, Unraveling the Story of Watergate, Units 9–10 folder, pp. 69–71 • Comparing Primary Sources, On Nixon's Impeachment, Units 9–10 folder, pp. 67–68 • Skills for Life Activity, Units 9–10 folder, p. 72 • Government Requires Checks and Balances, Why Study History? folder, p. 33

Running Out of Time?

- Use Tape 5, "Republican Revival and Decline, 1968–Present," from **Visions of America** videotapes series.
- Use Chapter 32 Summary from **Guide to the Essentials of American History (English and Spanish).**

Companion Web Site

The companion Web site offers online links for all chapter review activities. It also provides key content links and structured support for this chapter for both teachers and students.

http://www.Pathways.phschool.com

Teaching in the Information Age

Media and Technology

For the Student

Interactive Student Tutorial CD-ROM Chapter 32

Student Edition on Audiotape Chapter 32

American Heritage® CD-ROM

Guided Reading Audiotapes (English and Spanish) Chapter 32

For the Teacher

Resource Pro CD-ROM Chapter 32

Test Bank CD-ROM Chapter 32

Listening to Literature Audiotapes *Timeless Voices, Timeless Themes* "The Adamant" by Theodore Roethke

Block Scheduling

Pacing Suggestions

For 90-minute Blocks

- Teach sections 1 and 4 using Transparencies E-9 and K-10, and the Recent Scholarship note on p. 923 for class discussions.
- Teach sections 2 and 3 using the Big Idea Graphic Organizers from Teaching Resources and the Extended Class Periods Activity on p. 918.

Additional Resources

- Prentice Hall's **American History Block Scheduling Support File** covers over 40 major topics in American history.
- **Prentice Hall United States History Video Collection**™ contains 20 videotapes covering American history from beginnings to present.
- **Decision America Videotapes and Videodiscs**
- **Visions of America Videotapes and Videodiscs**

Assessment Options

Chapter Test Forms A&B Test Bank CD-ROM booklet

Test Bank CD-ROM Chapter 32

Standardized Test Preparation Handbook

Connections to American Literature

from Prentice Hall

Prentice Hall Literature *Timeless Voices, Timeless Themes* "Antojos" by Julia Alvarez, p. 966

Additional Resources

For the Student

The Right Stuff. Warner Communications, 1983.

All the President's Men. Warner Home Video, 1976.

For the Teacher

S. M. Hersh. *The Price of Power: Kissinger in the Nixon White House.* Summit Books, 1983.

Garry Wills. *Nixon Agonistes: The Crisis of the Self-Made Man.* Houghton Mifflin, 1970.

Prentice Hall brings into the classroom the vast archives and scholarship of the nation's premier American history magazine. See "From the Archives of American Heritage®" and "About the Presidents" teaching notes in this chapter.

 History Alive!

Teacher's Curriculum Institute, in partnership with Prentice Hall, provides unique materials that engage students with diverse learning styles. See History Alive!® unit on Contemporary American Society.

 Student Performance Pack

Ensures success in the three critical areas of Reading, Test Taking, and English Language Development with the following materials:
- Guide to the Essentials of American History in English and Spanish
- Guided Reading Audiotapes in English and Spanish
- Interactive Student Tutorial CD-ROM
- Test Preparation Handbook
- Test Preparation Practice booklet

The Nixon Years
1969–1974

Introducing the Chapter

A series of tumultuous events in 1968 helped pave the way for the presidency of Richard Nixon and a 24-year era of almost uninterrupted Republican control of the White House. The new President's domestic and foreign policies marked a shift in national politics. But Nixon's leadership style led to scandal and his own shattering downfall.

Themes in American History

The theme for this chapter, Government, is listed at the beginning of this unit. An alternate theme for the chapter is Foreign Relations. To teach this unit thematically, you may wish to use The Nation After World War II folder in American History Block Scheduling Support.

Why Study History?

Have students explore suggested ways of connecting the past to the present on page 927.

Answer to . . .

Viewing History Students should use this question as an aid in reading the chapter. Presidential visits are a sign of trust and an opportunity to express appreciation for another culture. They also give leaders a chance to speak directly to one another, thus uniting nations in common interests.

904

CHAPTER
32 The Nixon Years
1969-1974

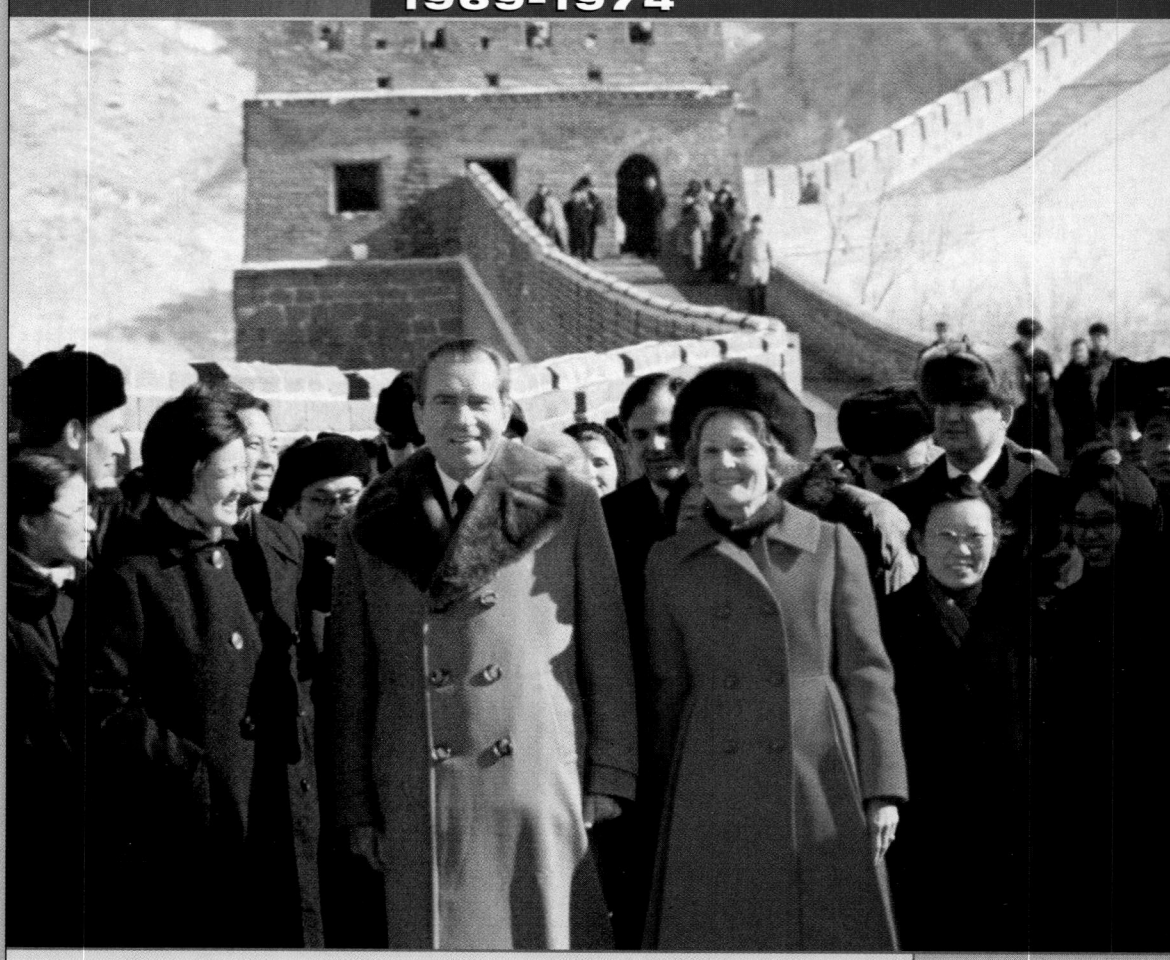

CHAPTER FOCUS

This chapter examines the accomplished and ill-fated presidency of Richard M. Nixon. It looks at the bold policies for which he is remembered and the scandal that finally brought him down.

 The **Why Study History?** page at the end of this chapter explores the connection between Nixon's use of presidential power and the balance of power today.

▲
VIEWING HISTORY
President Richard Nixon and his wife Pat tour the Great Wall of China in a historic visit to China in 1972. *Foreign Relations* **How do presidential visits help diplomatic relations?**

▶ RESOURCE OPTIONS

Teaching Resources

📁 **Big Idea Graphic Organizer** folder
Graphic summary of the main idea of the chapter.

📁 **Learning Styles Lesson Plans** folder
Alternate lesson plans for diverse learning styles for each chapter.

Media and Technology

 AmericanHeritage® **CD-ROM**
Time Tour The Nation Today and Tomorrow: A Time for Turmoil

 Prentice Hall United States History Video Collection™ Volume 20
Post-War USA

January	April	June	August	November
Tet Offensive begins	Martin Luther King, Jr., assassinated	Robert F. Kennedy assassinated	Democratic National Convention	Richard M. Nixon elected President

Jan. 1968   **June 1968**   **Dec. 1968**

1 The Crises of 1968

SECTION PREVIEW

Objectives

1 Explain how the Tet Offensive increased antiwar sentiment.
2 Explain the impact of the assassinations of Martin Luther King, Jr., and Robert Kennedy.
3 Describe the impact of the 1968 Democratic convention on that year's presidential election.
4 *Key Terms* Define: Middle America; Poor People's Campaign.

Main Idea

The year 1968 was a turbulent and painful time for the country that resulted in the election of Richard Nixon as President.

Reading Strategy

Finding Evidence As you read the section, jot down facts to support the idea, stated on this page, that 1968 was "the most shattering year" of the 1960s.

I n the troubled decade of the 1960s, perhaps the most shattering year was 1968. A series of tragic events hit with such force that, month by month, the nation seemed to be coming apart. Amid the turmoil, and partly because of it, the way was paved for the election of Richard Nixon.

Nixon's win marked the start of a Republican hold on the presidency that would last, with one interruption, for the next 20 years. This political shift reflected how distressing the 1960s had become for mainstream Americans, a group sometimes called **Middle America.** In an era of chaos and confrontation, Middle America turned to the Republican party for stability.

Antiwar Sentiment Increases

The Vietnam War reached a crucial turning point in 1968. Beginning in January, as you have read, the Viet Cong launched the Tet Offensive. This massive surprise attack against South Vietnam ended in military defeat for the Viet Cong and their North Vietnamese allies. But it caused more and more Americans to question whether victory in the Vietnam War was possible.

The Johnson administration had been escalating the war for three years before the Tet Offensive. Many Americans wondered what had been achieved if the enemy could still mount such a blistering offensive. From a military perspective, Tet was a major defeat for the Viet Cong. But from a political perspective, it was a major defeat for the United States—and for Lyndon Johnson.

After Tet, polls showed for the first time that a majority of Americans opposed the war. Television news coverage of Tet increased the impact that the attack had on the public. Millions watched as news anchor Walter Cronkite, known for his objectivity, said in February, "It now seems more certain than ever that the bloody experience in Vietnam is to end in stalemate." President Johnson heard Cronkite's assessment of the war and reacted with dismay. Reportedly he said, "If I've lost Cronkite, I've lost Middle America."

LBJ's political career is crushed in this 1967 British cartoon, "The Time Machine."

RESOURCE OPTIONS

Teaching Resources

📁 **Reproducible Lesson Plan** Lesson Plans folder, p. 162

📁 **Big Idea Graphic Organizer** Big Idea Graphic Organizer folder, p. 134

📁 **Guided Reading and Review** Units 9–10 folder, p. 58

Media and Technology

🦅 **American**Heritage® **CD-ROM**

Time Tour The Nation Today and Tomorrow: A Time of Turmoil

SECTION 1

The Crises of 1968

Objectives
You may wish to call students' attention to the objectives in the Section Preview. The objectives are reflected in the main headings of the section.

Bellringer
Present students with the following situation: The United States is losing a war and violence is breaking out in many cities. How might the nation react under such circumstances? Who would be held responsible for the state of affairs?

Reading Strategy
Finding Evidence Refer students to the Reading Strategy in the Section Preview. You may wish to offer a definition of the word *evidence,* using an example from the text.

LESSON PLAN
Connecting to the Main Idea

1. Focus Explain that in 1968 Americans endured a series of shocks, shaking the nation's faith in itself. As a result, many voters seemed interested in changing political direction. Ask students how the Republicans took advantage of these changing attitudes.

2. Instruct Explain that the 1960s was a time of great political and social upheaval. Discuss the impact of the Tet Offensive. Ask students why Tet made many Americans feel that they had been misled about the war in Vietnam.

Have students explain why the deaths of Robert Kennedy and Martin Luther King, Jr., led many people to feel that their hopes for the future were disappearing.

3. Close The traumatic events of 1968 revealed deep divisions in the nation and helped clear the way for a Republican victory. The next section examines the domestic policies introduced by President Nixon as he sought to steer the nation on a more conservative path.

King Assassinated

For most Americans, the memory of President John F. Kennedy's assassination in 1963 was still vivid and haunting five years later. They looked to other leaders to carry on the spirit and idealism of the Kennedy years.

Main Idea
CONNECTIONS

How did the nation react to the murder of Martin Luther King, Jr.?

One such leader was Martin Luther King, Jr. By the mid-1960s King had led the civil rights movement to several major political victories in battles ranging from integration to voting rights.

In 1968 King turned his attention to economic issues. Convinced that poverty bred violence, he broadened his approach to attack economic injustice. Calling his new crusade the **Poor People's Campaign,** King began planning a Poor People's March on Washington. Traveling around the United States to mobilize support, he went to Memphis, Tennessee, in early April. There he offered his assistance to striking garbage workers who were seeking better working conditions.

King spoke eloquently, referring to threats made against his life:

AMERICAN VOICES 66 We've got some difficult days ahead. But it doesn't matter with me now, because I've been to the mountain top. And I don't mind. Like anybody, I would like to live a long life. . . . But I'm not concerned about that now. I just want to do God's will. And He's allowed me to go up to the mountain. And I've looked over. And I've seen the promised land. 99

—*Martin Luther King, Jr.*
April 3, 1968

The next day, as King stood on the balcony of his motel, a bullet fired from a high-powered rifle tore into him. An hour later, King was dead.

King's assassination sparked violent reactions across the nation. In an outburst of rage and frustration, some African Americans rioted, setting fires and looting stores in 124 cities. The riots, and police responses to them, left 45 people dead. President Johnson ordered flags on federal buildings to be flown at half-mast to honor King, but it took more than 5,500 troops to quell the violence. For many Americans of all races, King's death eroded faith in the idea of nonviolent change.

Robert Kennedy Assassinated

In March 1968 the battle for the Democratic presidential nomination intensified. Senator Eugene McCarthy, a vocal antiwar candidate, challenged President Johnson in the New Hampshire primary on March 12. McCarthy did well, losing by just 6 percentage points.

Senator Robert F. Kennedy, who had served his brother John as Attorney General, realized that Johnson was vulnerable. On March 16 Kennedy entered the campaign himself. His candidacy received a critical boost on March 31, when Johnson stunned the nation by announcing that he would not run for a second term as President.

VIEWING HISTORY Assassinations in 1968 shocked the nation. Above, Martin Luther King lies mortally wounded, while companions point frantically to the direction from which shots were fired. At right, busboy Juan Romero is the first to reach Robert Kennedy after he was shot in a hotel kitchen just after winning the California primary. *Culture What effect did these murders have?*

In the years since his brother's death, Robert Kennedy had reached out to many Americans, including Chicanos in the California farm fields, Native Americans in the Southwest, African Americans in the Mississippi delta, and poor white families in New York tenements. Opposed to the Vietnam War, he condemned the killing of both Americans and Vietnamese. He criticized the Johnson administration for financing a war instead of funding the programs needed to help the poor and disadvantaged at home.

Kennedy spent the spring of 1968 battling McCarthy in the Democratic primary elections. On June 5 he won a key victory in California's primary. But just after midnight, after giving his victory speech in a Los Angeles hotel, Robert Kennedy was shot by an assassin. He died later that day.

When the shooting was reported, several campaign workers who had watched the speech on TV were waiting for Kennedy in his hotel room. One of them, civil rights leader John Lewis, later said, "We all just fell to the floor and started crying. To me that was like the darkest, saddest moment." Looking back on Kennedy's death, Lewis said,

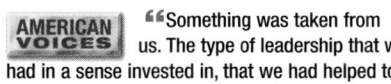

66Something was taken from us. The type of leadership that we had in a sense invested in, that we had helped to make and to nourish, was taken from us.**99**

—*Civil rights leader John Lewis, 1987*

Kennedy's death ended many people's hopes for an inspirational leader who could heal the nation's wounds.

The 1968 Democratic Convention

Delegates to the Democratic convention met in Chicago that summer to nominate candidates for President and Vice President. By the time the Democrats convened, their party was in shreds. Many of them backed McCarthy for

Violence seemed to follow the Democratic party in the turbulent year 1968. At the Democratic National Convention, Chicago police and National Guardsmen used nightsticks, tear gas, and rifles against demonstrators and others caught up in the violence. *Government Why did the Democrats lose the 1968 presidential election?*

President, but party regulars thought he was too far out of the mainstream. They supported Vice President Hubert Humphrey, longtime advocate of social justice and civil rights. Humphrey, however, was hurt by his defense of administration policies on Vietnam. In the face of growing antiwar protest, he hardly seemed the one to bring the party together.

Groups of radicals, peace activists, and hippies all vowed to descend on Chicago in August for the convention. The prospect of thousands of demonstrators in his city enraged Chicago mayor Richard J. Daley. He had the convention hall protected by barbed wire and chain-link fencing. He also ordered police to clear out protesters gathered in Lincoln Park, along the shore of Lake Michigan. As the police went in with tear gas and clubs, several violent confrontations took place.

The climax came when the convention delegates voted down a peace resolution and seemed ready to nominate Humphrey. As thousands of protesters gathered for a rally near the convention hotel, the police moved in, using their nightsticks to club anyone on the street, including bystanders, hotel guests, and reporters.

Answer to . . .

Viewing History Division and disillusionment within and outside of the party, voter apathy, a third party candidate, a Republican candidate who boasted a plan to end the Vietnam war.

Customize for
More Advanced Students

Ask students to examine the election of 1968 and explain how the Republicans benefited from the events taking place in the United States and in the Democratic party.

Answers to
SECTION 1 REVIEW

1. (a) Middle America, see p. 905; (b) Poor People's Campaign, see p. 906.

2. By showing that the Vietnam War had reached a stalemate, it turned American public opinion against the war and against Johnson.

3. Sample events: Tet Offensive; McCarthy does well in New Hampshire primary; Robert Kennedy joins race for President; Johnson quits race; Kennedy assassinated; violence at Democratic convention; Republicans nominate Nixon; Democrats nominate Humphrey; Wallace runs as third-party candidate; Nixon wins presidency.

4. Students should support their answers with details from the text.

5. Sample answers: If the Tet Offensive had not happened, Johnson might have run for President, he might have won, and the war might have continued longer. If Robert Kennedy had not been assassinated, he might have won the presidency, and the war might have ended sooner.

6. Essays should draw conclusions about American society during the 1960s. Some students might paint a picture of a violent society; others might offer a portrait that reflects King's, Kennedy's, and other individuals' pursuit of peace.

Historian Theodore H. White, chronicler of presidential elections, recorded the scene:

> **AMERICAN VOICES**
> "Slam! Like a fist jolting, like a piston exploding from its chamber, comes a hurtling column of police . . . into the intersection, and all things happen too fast: first the charge as the police wedge cleaves through the mob; then screams, whistles, confusion. . . . And as the scene clears, there are little knots in the open clearing—police clubbing youngsters, police dragging youngsters, police rushing them by the elbows, their heels dragging, to patrol wagons. . . ."
>
> —*Theodore H. White*

Much of the violence took place in front of television cameras, while crowds chanted "The whole world is watching." As convention delegates voted, Senator Abraham Ribicoff of Connecticut denounced the "Gestapo tactics on the streets of Chicago," provoking an angry scene with Daley. Humphrey was nominated, but the party had been further torn apart.

George Wallace created trouble for the Democrats in 1968 by running as a third party candidate.

The Election of 1968

The Republicans had already held their convention, in early August. They had chosen Richard M. Nixon, who had narrowly lost to John Kennedy in 1960. In his campaign Nixon backed law and order and boasted of a secret plan to end the war in Vietnam.

Nixon was determined to stay "above the fray" and act presidential during the campaign. So he let his running mate, Governor Spiro Agnew of Maryland, make harsh accusations, such as calling Humphrey "squishy soft" on communism. With a well-run and well-financed campaign, Nixon quickly took the lead in public-opinion polls.

Adding to the Democrats' problems was a third-party candidate for President. Alabama governor George C. Wallace, a lifelong Democrat, had gained national fame for playing on racial tensions among southerners. In 1968, representing the American Independent party, he appealed to blue-collar voters in the North who resented campus radicals and anti-war activists. Wallace won support by attacking "left-wing theoreticians, briefcase-totin' bureaucrats, ivory-tower guideline writers, bearded anarchists, smart-aleck editorial writers, and pointy-headed professors."

Late in the campaign, Humphrey began to catch up to Nixon in the public-opinion polls. But even though President Johnson stopped the bombing of North Vietnam on October 31, it was too late. Many disillusioned Democrats stayed home on election day, voting for no one.

The election, held on November 5, was close. Nixon won 43.4 percent of the popular vote—less than one percentage point more than Humphrey's 42.7 percent. Nixon gained 302 electoral votes to 191 for Humphrey and 45 for Wallace. Although Democrats kept control of both houses of Congress, the Republicans had regained the White House.

SECTION 1 REVIEW

Comprehension

1. *Key Terms* Define: (a) Middle America; (b) Poor People's Campaign.

2. *Summarizing the Main Idea* Why did the Tet Offensive have such a strong impact on American politics?

3. *Organizing Information* Create a flowchart to show the sequence of events that led to the election of Richard Nixon as President.

Critical Thinking

4. *Analyzing Time Lines* Review the time line at the start of the section. Which event do you think had the greatest impact on Americans? Explain your reasoning.

5. *Predicting Consequences* Choose one important event from 1968 and explain how history might have been different if the event had never happened.

Writing Activity

6. *Writing an Expository Essay* Write an essay about the assassinations of Martin Luther King, Jr., and Robert F. Kennedy. In your essay explore what these killings said about American society at the time.

▶ RESOURCE OPTIONS

Teaching Resources

📁 **Quiz** Units 9–10 folder, p. 59

📁 **Lasting Impact Activity** The Lasting Impact of the Year 1968, History's Lasting Impact folder, pp. 20–21

Student Performance Pack

 Guide to the Essentials Chapter 32, Section 1 (English and Spanish)

Media and Technology

 Color Transparencies Time Lines, E-9

1969	1969	1970	1971	1971	1973
Warren Burger becomes Chief Justice	America lands astronauts on the moon	Student protesters killed at Kent State U.	Supreme Court rules in favor of busing	Nixon imposes wage and price controls	OPEC oil embargo

1969 **1971** **1973**

2 The Nixon Administration

SECTION PREVIEW

Objectives

1 Describe how Nixon's personality might have affected his choice of staff members.
2 Describe how Nixon's domestic policy differed from that of his predecessors.
3 Explain how Nixon applied his "southern strategy" to the issue of civil rights and to his choice of Supreme Court justices.
4 *Key Terms* Define: deficit spending; Organization of Petroleum Exporting Countries (OPEC); embargo; silent majority.

Main Idea

As President, Richard Nixon relied on several close advisers to help him move the country in a new direction.

Reading Strategy

Reinforcing Key Ideas Create a two-column chart with the headings *Nixon's Personality* and *Nixon's Domestic Policies*. As you read the section, write details describing Nixon's personal traits and his policies in the proper column.

The Nixon Administration

Objectives

You may wish to call students' attention to the objectives in the Section Preview. The objectives are reflected in the main headings of the section.

Bellringer

Write the word *leadership* on the chalkboard. Ask students to list ideas they associate with this term. Explain that Nixon, upon taking office, exercised a new type of leadership.

Reading Strategy

Reinforcing Key Ideas Refer students to the Reading Strategy in the Section Preview. You may wish to model the activity by suggesting one detail under each column.

Richard Nixon's victory in 1968 was, for him, particularly sweet. His earlier bid for the presidency, in 1960, had failed. Two years later he had lost another election, for governor of California. Deeply unhappy, Nixon had vowed to retire from politics. Instead he came back from those bitter defeats to win the nation's highest office at a time when the country sorely needed strong leadership.

Nixon in Person

Unlike most politicians, Richard Nixon was a reserved and remote man. Uncomfortable with people, he often seemed stiff and lacking in humor and charm. He overcame these drawbacks by using modern campaign techniques to get his message across.

Many Americans looked beyond these personal disadvantages. They respected Nixon for his experience and for his skillful handling of the vice presidency under Eisenhower. But many others neither trusted nor liked him.

Nixon grew up in a low-income family in Whittier, California. He never got over his sense of being an outsider. In 1963 he described how that feeling drove him to achieve:

AMERICAN VOICES "What starts the process really are laughs and slights and snubs when you are a kid. Sometimes it's because you're poor or Irish or Jewish or Catholic or ugly or simply that you are skinny. But if you are reasonably intelligent and if your anger is deep enough and strong enough, you learn that you can change those attitudes by excellence, personal gut performance."

—*Richard Nixon, 1963*

According to Patrick Buchanan, then a Nixon speech writer, there was "a mean side to his nature." He was willing to say or do any-

Although he was a private man, Nixon loved the applause of a crowd.

LESSON PLAN
Connecting to the Main Idea

1. **Focus** Explain that as President, Nixon employed a closed, secretive style in his effort to steer the nation in a more conservative direction than had his Democratic predecessors. Ask how Nixon's style influenced his presidency.
2. **Instruct** Explain that domestically, Nixon favored the existing power structure. This proved difficult in the realm of economics, where inflation caused by war spending forced Nixon to act contrary to his stated goals. Explain that the oil crisis further aggravated the nation's economic problems. Discuss the nation's dependence on petroleum. Ask students what might happen if fuel prices rose suddenly today. Point out Nixon's greater success in instituting conservative policies in the area of social programs and law and order.
3. **Close** In the domestic sphere, Nixon tried to take the nation in a new, more conservative direction. The next section examines his foreign policy efforts.

▶ RESOURCE OPTIONS

Teaching Resources

📁 **Reproducible Lesson Plan** Lesson Plans folder, p. 163

📁 **Big Idea Graphic Organizer** Big Idea Graphic Organizer folder, p. 135

📁 **Guided Reading and Review** Units 9–10 folder, p. 60

Media and Technology

RESOURCE ⊙ PRO

Visual Learning Activity The Imperial President, found on Resource Pro, depicts what some people termed Nixon's "imperial presidency" in two humorous posters from the early 1970s.

To make sure students understand the main idea of this section, you may wish to use the web graphic organizer below.

Tell students that a web graphic organizer shows a main idea and its supporting details. Ask students to use it to illustrate the idea that Nixon relied on several advisers to help him move the country in a new direction.

Teaching Tip A template for this graphic organizer can be found in the Color Transparencies, G-1.

Customize for
English Language Learners

Ask students to read the American Voices quotation on the previous page. Ask how Nixon's personal characteristics and the qualities he valued in his aides are reflected in this quote. In the discussion, have students chose specific words or phrases from the quotation that best reveal Nixon's sensibility.

The Oval Office in the White House saw many meetings of Nixon and his inner circle of close advisers. Left to right in this photo are Kissinger, Ehrlichman, the President, and Haldeman. *Government What role did his advisers play in Nixon's presidency?*

Main Idea
CONNECTIONS

How did Nixon's personality affect his administration style?

thing to defeat his enemies. Those enemies included his political opponents, the government bureaucracy, the press corps, and leaders of the antiwar movement.

Nixon was fully prepared to confront these forces. He wrote, "I believe in the battle, whether it's the battle of the campaign or the battle of this office, which is a continuing battle. It's always there wherever you go."

Nixon had few close friends, insulating himself from people and the press. He took support and security from his family: his wife, Pat, and their two daughters. He also established lasting associations with several activists in his political campaigns. Away from the White House, he secluded himself at his estates in Florida and California.

Nixon wanted the executive branch to dominate the other branches of government. When he took office, he gathered a close circle of trusted advisers around him to pursue that goal.

Nixon's Staff

Cabinet members, who represent the major departments of government, have historically been a President's top advisers. They have tended to be independent-minded people. More than most other post–World War II Presidents, Nixon avoided his Cabinet and preferred to rely on his White House staff to develop broad policies. Staff members were team players. They gave him unswerving loyalty.

Two key appointees had direct access to the President. They shielded Nixon from the outside world and carried out his orders. One was H. R. Haldeman, an advertising executive who had campaigned tirelessly for Nixon. He became chief of staff. Haldeman once summarized how he served the President: "I get done what he wants done and I take the heat instead of him." The other key staffer was lawyer John Ehrlichman. Ehrlichman served as Nixon's personal lawyer and rose to the post of chief domestic adviser.

Haldeman and Ehrlichman framed issues and narrowed options for the President. They also stood between the President and anybody else who wanted to speak to him. Together they became known as the "Berlin Wall" for the way they protected Nixon's privacy.

A third trusted adviser was John Mitchell, a lawyer. Mitchell had worked with Nixon in New York and managed his presidential campaign. Nixon asked him to be Attorney General just after the 1968 election. Mitchell exerted great influence on the President, often speaking with him several times a day.

Another of Nixon's closest advisers did not fit the mold of Haldeman, Ehrlichman, and Mitchell. Henry Kissinger, a Harvard government professor, had no previous ties to Nixon. Still, he acquired tremendous power in the Nixon White House. Kissinger joined the administration as head of the National Security Council. In 1973 he became Nixon's Secretary of State. Kissinger played a major role in shaping foreign policy, both as an adviser to the President and in behind-the-scenes diplomacy.

Domestic Policy

The Vietnam War and domestic policy had both been important in the 1968 political campaigns. On domestic issues, Nixon broke with many of the policies of his Democratic predecessors.

Answer to . . .

Viewing History They analyzed information for him, provided advice, carried out his orders, protected him from criticism, and guarded his privacy.

Main Idea Connections His shyness and remoteness fostered an administration that was closed and secretive.

TEST PREPARATION

Have students read the quotation by Nixon in the first paragraph on this page and then answer the question below.

From the quote, you can infer that Nixon—

A believed the three branches of government should work together.

B was prepared to take a passive role in government.

C thought that he could trust most people in the government.

D was suspicious of people and took an aggressive stance as President.

OPEC Nations, c. 1970

OPEC brought together the world's major oil producers. **Regions** *In what region of the world are many of these nations concentrated?*

ACTIVITY

LEARNING STYLES

Have students reread Nixon's views and statements on student protests quoted on these pages. Then ask students to respond in a brief essay explaining whether or not they share Nixon's views. Students' essays should explore their understanding of the proper role of protest in a democratic society. *(Logical)*

Inflation The economy was shaky when Nixon took office. Largely because of spending for the Vietnam War, inflation had doubled between 1965 and 1968. The budget had also gone out of balance, with government spending exceeding revenues. Meanwhile, unemployment continued to grow. Nixon's first priority was to halt inflation. He wanted to get federal spending under control, even if it led to further unemployment.

At the same time, Nixon was determined to avoid government control of wages and prices. He had seen such controls in action while working for the Office of Price Administration during World War II. "I will not take the nation down the road of wage and price controls, however politically expedient they may seem," he said in 1970.

During his first few years in office, however, controlling spending proved difficult. Unemployment and inflation both continued to rise. Although Republicans traditionally aimed for a balanced budget, Nixon began to consider **deficit spending.** By spending more money than the government received in revenues, he hoped to stimulate the economy.

This was the approach that Franklin Roosevelt had used during the Depression, following the advice of British economist John Maynard Keynes. "I am now a Keynesian in economics," Nixon announced in 1971, to the surprise of many people.

To slow the high rate of inflation, shown in the graph to the right, he imposed a 90-day freeze on wages, prices, and rents. Pressure from business and labor, however, led him to lift these controls, and inflation again soared.

Oil Crisis Unrest in the Middle East brought more disruptions to the troubled economy. Americans depended on cheap, imported oil for about a third of their energy needs. But in 1973 Israel and the Arab nations of Egypt and Syria went to war. The United States backed its ally Israel. In response, the Arab members of the **Organization of Petroleum Exporting Countries (OPEC)** imposed an **embargo,** or ban, on the shipping of oil to the United States.

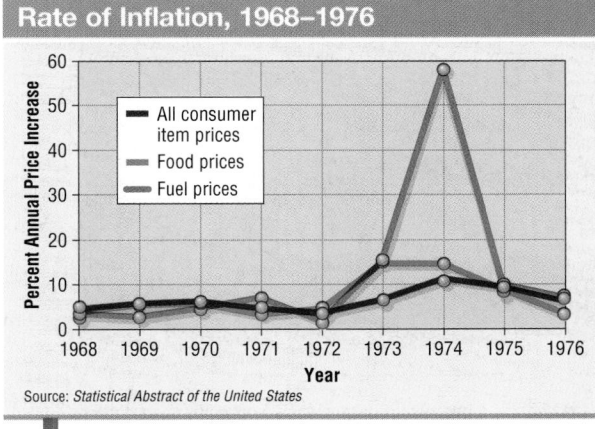

Rate of Inflation, 1968–1976

Percent Annual Price Increase

- All consumer item prices
- Food prices
- Fuel prices

Year

Source: *Statistical Abstract of the United States*

Interpreting Graphs Rising oil prices in the 1970s had a strong impact on all parts of the American economy. *Economics When did fuel prices reach their peak?*

BACKGROUND

Connections to Today

When Richard Milhous Nixon died on April 22, 1994, at age eighty-one, biographer Garry Wills wrote of him: "In some areas of politics, he seemed to know almost everything about anything—except about himself. His strengths and weaknesses fed upon each other. He was a small bitter man and a very grand diplomat. Who can read that riddle? Some of us have spent much of our lives trying to read it, with little better success than his own."

RESOURCE OPTIONS

Media and Technology

RESOURCE PRO

Critical Thinking Activity Predicting Consequences: Wage-Price Freeze, found on Resource Pro, presents an excerpt from President Nixon's televised national address announcing a 90-day wage and price freeze.

Answer to . . .

Map Skills *Africa and the Middle East.*
Interpreting Graphs *1974*

OPEC, a group of nations that cooperates to set oil prices and production levels, also quadrupled its prices. The cost of oil skyrocketed. The map on the previous page shows the nations that belonged to OPEC.

Higher oil prices added to inflation, which affected everyone. A loaf of bread that had cost 28 cents earlier in the 1970s now cost 89 cents. Americans who were used to paying 25 cents a gallon for gas now paid 65 cents. Inflation, in turn, led consumers to cut back on spending. The result was a recession. Unemployment reached 9 percent, the highest rate since the 1930s.

Social Programs Nixon hoped to halt the growth of government spending by redirecting or shutting down some of the social programs that had mushroomed under Johnson's Great Society. Critics claimed that these programs were wasteful, encouraged "welfare cheaters," and discouraged people from seeking work.

Nixon had exploited those complaints in his campaign, but he now faced a dilemma. On the one hand, he wanted to please conservative voters who demanded cutbacks. On the other hand, he hoped to appeal to traditionally Democratic blue-collar voters, who wanted to keep the programs that benefited them.

In 1969 the administration suggested a Family Assistance Plan that would give needy families a basic minimum income. In return, heads of families would have to register for job training and accept a job when one was found. The plan failed to pass the Senate but did gain Nixon political points with some voters.

Law and Order Another important campaign pledge had been to restore "law and order" in the country. Nixon recognized that student radicals, antiwar protesters, and the counterculture in general had begun to lose their appeal among the general public. Many blue-collar and middle-class Americans held those groups responsible for rising crime, growing drug use, and permissive attitudes toward sex. In a speech in 1969 Nixon referred to this large group of Americans as the **silent majority.**

To strengthen his position on law and order, Nixon aimed to discourage protest, especially against the war. In his "silent majority" speech he declared, "If a vocal minority, however fervent its cause, prevails over reason and the will of the majority, this nation has no future as a free society."

Tensions between antiwar activists and law-and-order supporters reached a peak in 1970. At a demonstration at Kent State University in Ohio, National Guardsmen opened fire on the crowd. Four student protesters were shot dead. Nixon implied that the students themselves had caused the tragedy:

> **AMERICAN VOICES** "The time has come for us to recognize that violence and terror have no place in a free society. Whatever the purported [supposed] cause of the perpetrators may be . . . no cause justifies violence."
>
> —*Richard Nixon, speech at Kansas State University, 1970*

Other members of the administration backed up the President. Attorney General Mitchell stepped up the Justice Department's campaign against crime. Unhappy with press coverage of the White House, Vice President Spiro Agnew also accused television reporters of distorting administration actions.

This famous photo of the shooting of a student at Kent State University horrified the nation. *Government How did President Nixon regard such antiwar protests?*

The "Southern Strategy"

Nixon believed that he had little to gain by supporting advances in civil rights. Few African Americans had voted for him in the 1960 race against John Kennedy, and in 1968 he had won just 12 percent of the black vote. Besides, he reasoned, any attempt to court the black electorate could threaten the white southern vote in a reelection bid.

Explaining his position, Nixon once observed that "there are those who want instant integration and those who want segregation forever. I believe that we need to have a middle course between those two extremes." In effect, this meant a slowdown in desegregation.

Nixon's aim was to find the proper "southern strategy" to win over white southern Democrats. Republican senator Strom Thurmond of South Carolina, who had left the Democratic party in 1948, became Nixon's strongest southern supporter. To keep him and his colleagues happy, Nixon sought to cut funding for the enforcement of fair housing laws. He also made it easier to comply with desegregation guidelines.

The Justice Department, headed by John Mitchell, tried to prevent the extension of the Voting Rights Act of 1965. This law had greatly increased the number of African Americans who could vote in the South. Congress went ahead with the extension, but Nixon had made his point to white southern voters.

Another controversial issue was the use of busing to end school segregation. In several cities, federal courts ordered school systems to bus students to other schools in order to end the pattern of all-black or all-white schools. Particularly in northern cities, such as Detroit and Boston, some white students and their parents met incoming black students with boycotts or violent protests.

In 1971 the Supreme Court issued guidelines for busing that went against Nixon's views. A federal judge in North Carolina had ruled that voluntary integration was not working. In *Swann* v. *Charlotte-Mecklenburg Board of Education*, the Court agreed, saying that busing was one possible option for ending school desegregation.

Nixon had long opposed busing. He now went on national television to say that he would ask Congress to halt it.[†] He also allowed the Department of Health, Education, and Welfare to restore federal funding to school districts that were still segregated. Nixon's

 These demonstrators expressed their unhappiness with busing by burying a school bus. *Government How did Nixon's views on busing influence efforts to desegregate the schools?*

refusal to enforce the Court ruling did not halt busing in the country but did limit it.

Nixon's Supreme Court

During the election campaign, Nixon had criticized the Supreme Court as too liberal and soft on criminals. In his first term, four of the nine justices died, resigned, or retired. This gave him the extraordinary opportunity to name four new justices and thus reshape the Court. Nixon first named Warren Burger as Chief Justice, replacing Earl Warren. Burger, a moderate, was easily confirmed by the Senate in 1969.

Later nominations reflected Nixon's southern strategy and conservative views. The Senate rejected his first nominees from the South. Opponents charged that both men showed racial bias. Eventually Nixon successfully appointed Harry A. Blackmun (1970), Lewis F. Powell, Jr. (1972), and William H.

[†] One of Nixon's often-repeated lines was: "I think it is the job of the courts to interpret the law and not make the law."

BACKGROUND

Geography in History

Despite the introduction of busing, the desegregation movement rapidly lost relevance for northern cities. Many middle-class white Americans abandoned city schools for suburban school districts and private schools in the 1960s and 1970s. This exodus, sometimes called "white flight," created de facto segregation in states like New Jersey and New York. A Harvard Graduate School of Education study noted in the late 1990s that the most drastic shift toward resegregation since 1954 took place between 1991 and 1994. By 1997, the ten largest inner-city school districts in the United States had black and Hispanic majorities.

Answer to . . .

Viewing History His opposition did little to halt busing.

Answers to

SECTION 2 REVIEW

1. (a) deficit spending, see p. 911; (b) OPEC, see p. 911; (c) embargo, see p. 911; (d) silent majority, see p. 912.

2. It was an attempt to gain the votes of white southern Democrats. He did not push for African Americans' civil rights; he tried to undermine some civil rights laws, including those calling for busing; he nominated southerners to fill Supreme Court vacancies.

3. Webs should include Nixon's personality, his staff, his domestic policies, and his dealings with the Supreme Court.

4. Sample answer: 1973—OPEC oil embargo. This caused widespread inflation, economic recession, and the highest unemployment rate since the 1930s.

5. Sample answer: A shy man who thought of his political opponents as enemies, Nixon preferred a close group of loyal staffers whom he could trust and over whom he could maintain control.

6. Essays should draw on details in the section and on students' knowledge of the Vietnam war and the student protest movement.

Astronaut Buzz Aldrin takes a walk on the moon. *Government* *Why was the government so committed to the space program?*

achieve the goal, "before this decade is out, of landing a man on the moon." That man was *Apollo 11* astronaut Neil A. Armstrong.

On July 20, 1969, at 10:56 P.M. Eastern Daylight Time, Armstrong descended from the *Eagle* lunar landing craft and set foot on the moon's surface. As a TV camera aboard the *Eagle* captured the event, Armstrong radioed back the famous message: "That's one small step for man, one giant leap for mankind."

TV viewers around the world witnessed this triumph of the *Apollo* program, carried out by the National Aeronautics and Space Administration (NASA). The *Apollo 11* crew included Edwin E. "Buzz" Aldrin, Jr., who landed with Armstrong in the *Eagle,* and Michael Collins, who remained in the *Apollo 11* Command Module circling the moon.

Aldrin joined Armstrong in the two-hour moon walk, during which they collected rock and soil samples and set up scientific instruments to monitor conditions on the moon. They also photographed the landing area, a dusty plain in an area called the Sea of Tranquillity.

Rehnquist (1972). All three were respected jurists who generally tilted the Court in a more conservative direction.

The First Moon Landing

The Nixon years witnessed the fulfillment of President Kennedy's commitment in 1961 to

The *Eagle* and its crew stayed on the moon for 21 hours and 36 minutes before lifting off to rejoin Collins in the Command Module for the return trip. After a safe splashdown, the astronauts were quarantined for 18 days to ensure that they had not picked up any unknown lunar microbes. They emerged to a hero's welcome.

SECTION 2 REVIEW

Comprehension

1. *Key Terms* Define: (a) deficit spending; (b) Organization of Petroleum Exporting Countries (OPEC); (c) embargo; (d) silent majority.

2. *Summarizing the Main Idea* What was Nixon's "southern strategy," and how did it affect his domestic policies?

3. *Organizing Information* Create a web diagram to organize text information about the Nixon administration.

Critical Thinking

4. *Analyzing Time Lines* Review the time line at the start of the section. Which event do you think may have had the greatest effect on the American people? Explain.

5. *Determining Relevance* Do you think that Nixon's use of his staff, rather than his Cabinet, as policy advisers reflected the President's personal traits? Explain.

Writing Activity

6. *Writing a Persuasive Essay* Write an essay that might have appeared in 1970 either supporting or opposing the Nixon administration's position on antiwar protests.

RESOURCE OPTIONS

Teaching Resources

Quiz Units 9–10 folder, p. 61

Student Performance Pack

Guide to the Essentials Chapter 32, Section 2 (English and Spanish)

1969 Strategic Arms Limitation Talks open	1971 United States ends trade embargo with China	1972 Nixon travels to China	1972 Nixon visits Soviet Union	1972 SALT I treaty signed	1973 Kissinger appointed Secretary of State

1969   **1971**   **1973**

3 Nixon's Foreign Policy

SECTION PREVIEW

Objectives

1. Analyze Henry Kissinger's role in relaxing tensions between the United States and the major Communist powers.
2. Outline Nixon's new approach toward the People's Republic of China.
3. Describe how the Nixon administration reached an agreement with the Soviet Union on limiting nuclear arms.
4. *Key Terms* Define: *realpolitik;* détente; proliferation; SALT I.

Main Idea

President Nixon's foreign policy led to more positive relationships with China and with the Soviet Union.

Reading Strategy

Notetaking As you read the section, take notes on the following topics: (a) Henry Kissinger and American foreign policy, (b) United States relations with China, and (c) United States relations with the Soviet Union.

Objectives

You may wish to call students' attention to the objectives in the Section Preview. The objectives are reflected in the main headings of the section.

Bellringer

Present students with the following situation: The United States is locked in a costly competition with powerful enemies for influence around the world, and neither side is winning. How should the United States break the stalemate? Explain that Nixon faced a similar dilemma during his presidency.

Reading Strategy

Notetaking Refer to the Reading Strategy in the Section Preview. You may wish to make a composite outline of students' notes on the chalkboard.

As President, Richard Nixon's greatest achievements came in the field of foreign policy. "I've always thought this country could run itself domestically without a President," he observed. Nixon's creative approach to foreign affairs helped ease cold war tensions. Aided by the skillful diplomacy of Henry Kissinger, Nixon opened the way to establishing ties with China and crafted stronger relations with the Soviet Union.

Henry Kissinger

AMERICAN BIOGRAPHY

While Nixon had a keen understanding of foreign policy, he still relied heavily on Henry Kissinger in charting his course. Kissinger quickly gained the President's confidence. By the time Nixon appointed him Secretary of State in 1973, he was a dominant figure in the administration.

Henry Kissinger (b.1923)

Kissinger came from a Jewish family that fled Nazi Germany in 1938, when he was 15, and settled in New York City. During the day, the young immigrant worked at a shaving brush company. At night he completed high school courses. Kissinger attended City College of New York and later transferred to Harvard. There he completed both undergraduate and graduate degrees.

Kissinger wrote his doctoral dissertation on Klemens von Metternich, an Austrian statesman and diplomat in the nineteenth century who helped maintain stability in Europe amid liberal change. Kissinger's studies in European history gave him an admiration for *realpolitik,* a German term for "practical politics." Nations that follow this policy make decisions based on maintaining their own strength rather than clinging to rigid moral principles. Kissinger would later apply this approach to dealing with China and the Soviet Union.

LESSON PLAN

Connecting to the Main Idea

1. Focus Tell students that Nixon hoped to have an especially powerful impact as President in the field of foreign policy. Ask students to evaluate the success of Nixon's efforts.

2. Instruct Discuss the role of Henry Kissinger in shaping Nixon's foreign policy. What skills made Kissinger such a valued aide? What did he offer Nixon that other advisers could not? Tell students that relations with China were tense during Nixon's presidency. Ask how Nixon's reputation as a strong anti-Communist enabled him to approach China.

3. Close Nixon's efforts in foreign policy marked a significant shift in direction for the nation and helped reestablish relationships between the United States and its most powerful enemies. The next section discusses the events that overshadowed Nixon's success and helped lead to his downfall.

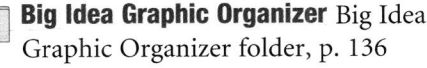

RESOURCE OPTIONS

Teaching Resources

 Reproducible Lesson Plan Lesson Plans folder, p. 164

Learning Styles Lesson Plan Learning Styles Lesson Plans folder, p. 66

Big Idea Graphic Organizer Big Idea Graphic Organizer folder, p. 136

Guided Reading and Review Units 9–10 folder, p. 62

Media and Technology

 AmericanHeritage® **CD-ROM**

Time Tour The Nation Today and Tomorrow: A Time of Turmoil

Main Idea
CONNECTIONS

How did Kissinger gain influence with Nixon?

As a Harvard professor, Kissinger became a recognized expert on foreign relations. Nixon lured him away from Harvard in 1969 by offering him a job as his national security adviser.

Nixon liked to be flattered, and he liked people who could talk tough. Kissinger understood these things, and soon he became the man Nixon talked to most. "Henry, of course, was not a personal friend," Nixon later said, but the two spoke five or six times a day, sometimes in person, sometimes by phone, and often for hours at a time.

Both men were suspicious and secretive. They tended not to seek consensus, but to keep information to themselves. "They tried not to let anyone else have a full picture, even if it meant deceiving them," noted Lawrence Eagleburger, a State Department official.

Kissinger's actual influence in shaping American foreign policy was broader than his official role as Secretary of State. He knew how to frame questions in ways the President wanted. He could distill foreign policy issues into briefing papers that gave Nixon clear options for making decisions. In his memoirs, Kissinger wrote:

AMERICAN VOICES

" Nixon could be very decisive. Almost invariably during his Presidency, his decisions were courageous and strong and often taken in loneliness against all expert advice. But wherever possible Nixon made these decisions in solitude on the basis of memoranda or with a few very intimate aides. "

—*Henry Kissinger,*
The White House Years, 1979

In addition to his intellectual skills, Kissinger understood the power of the press. He had a remarkable ability to use the media to shape public opinion. Journalists depended on him for stories, so they refrained from antagonizing him. "You know you are being played like a violin," a *Time* magazine reporter observed, "but it's still extremely seductive."

Kissinger's efforts in ending the Vietnam War and easing cold war tensions made him a celebrity. He shared the 1973 Nobel Peace Prize with North Vietnam's Le Duc Tho (who refused it); he appeared on 21 *Time* magazine covers; and in a 1973 Gallup Poll he led the list of the most-admired Americans. Kissinger's efforts in the Nixon administration left a lasting mark on American foreign policy. ■

Relaxing Tensions

Nixon's and Kissinger's greatest accomplishment was in bringing about **détente,** or a relaxation in tensions, between the United States and the two Communist giants. China and the Soviet Union were sworn enemies of the United States. Nixon's willingness to negotiate peacefully with them stunned many observers. In the 1950s Nixon had been one of the most bitter and active anti-Communists in government. He had made his reputation by demanding that the United States stand firm against the Communist threat.

As President, however, Nixon dealt imaginatively with both China and the Soviet Union. Nixon distrusted government bureaucracy, so he kept much of his diplomacy secret. Bypassing Congress, and often bypassing his own advisers, he and Kissinger reversed the direction of postwar American foreign policy.

Nixon drew on Kissinger's understanding that foreign affairs were more complex than a simple standoff between the United States and communism. Kissinger pointed out that the Communist world itself suffered from serious rifts, noting, "The deepest international con-

President Nixon owed the success of much of his foreign policy to his Secretary of State, Henry Kissinger.
Foreign Relations **Why did Nixon rely so heavily on Kissinger's advice?**

TEST PREPARATION

Have students read the quotation by Henry Kissinger on this page and then answer the question below.

Kissinger means by the phrase "taken in loneliness" that—

A Nixon had no one to help him.

(B) Nixon's decisions went against the advice most people gave him.

C Nixon was a lonely man.

D Nixon insisted on making decisions wth no outside help or advice.

flict in the world today is not between us and the Soviet Union but between the Soviet Union and Communist China."

A New Approach to China

The most surprising policy shift was toward China. In 1949 the Communist revolution had resulted in the establishment of the People's Republic of China. Americans saw all Communists in Asia as part of a united plot to dominate the world. As a result, the United States did not extend formal diplomatic recognition to the new Chinese government. In effect, the United States officially pretended that it did not exist.

Even when a Chinese-Soviet alliance crumbled, the United States clung to its rigid position. It insisted that the government of Jiang Jieshi, which was set up on the island of Taiwan when the Nationalists fled the Chinese mainland, was the rightful government of all China.

Quietly, Nixon began to prepare the way for a new policy of *realpolitik*. In his Inaugural Address in 1969, he referred indirectly to China when he declared, "We seek an open world . . . a world in which no people, great or small, will live in angry isolation." His first foreign policy report to Congress in 1970 began:

AMERICAN VOICES ❝The Chinese are a great and vital people who should not remain isolated from the international community. . . . United States policy is not likely soon to have much impact on China's behavior, let alone its ideological outlook. But it is certainly in our interest, and in the interest of peace and stability in Asia and the world, that we take what steps we can toward improved practical relations with Peking [Beijing].❞

—*Richard Nixon*,
report to Congress, *1970*

The administration undertook a series of moves designed to open a better relationship with China:

(1) In January and February 1970, American and Chinese ambassadors met in Warsaw, Poland.

(2) In October 1970, in a first for an American President, Nixon referred to China by its official title, the People's Republic of China.

(3) In March 1971, the United States government lifted restrictions on travel to China.

 Chinese premier Zhou Enlai and President Richard Nixon congratulate each other on the new ties between their nations. *Culture* Why was it important for the press to capture such moments?

(4) In April 1971, the American table-tennis team accepted a Chinese invitation to visit the mainland, beginning what was called "ping-pong diplomacy."

(5) In June 1971, the United States ended its 21-year embargo on trade with the People's Republic of China.

In July 1971, after extensive secret diplomacy by Kissinger, Nixon made the dramatic announcement that he planned to visit China the following year. He would be the first United States President ever to travel to that country.

Nixon understood that the People's Republic was an established government that would not simply disappear. Other nations had recognized the government, and it was time for the United States to do the same. Similarly, other countries wanted to give China's seat in the United Nations to the People's Republic. The United

 Mao Zedong

President Nixon shakes hands with Egyptian President Anwar Sadat in front of Egypt's famous pyramids. Nixon's administration faced difficult diplomatic challenges in the Middle East, particularly during the 1973 Arab-Israeli war. *Foreign Relations* *What do you think was Nixon's greatest foreign policy success?*

Intercontinental Ballistic Missile (ICBM)

States could no longer muster international opinion against this change.

Nixon had other motives as well. He recognized that he could use Chinese friendship as a bargaining chip in his negotiations with the Soviet Union. Press coverage of the trip would give him a boost at home. Also, he believed that he could take this action without suffering political damage, because of his past reputation as a strong anti-Communist.

Nixon traveled to China in February 1972. He met with Mao Zedong, the Chinese leader who had spearheaded the revolution in 1949. He spoke with Premier Zhou Enlai about international problems and ways of dealing with them. He and his wife, Pat, toured the Great Wall and other Chinese sights, all in front of television cameras that sent the historic pictures home.

When he returned to the United States, Nixon waited in his plane until prime time so that his return would be seen by as many television viewers as possible. Formal relations were not yet restored—that would take a few more years—but the basis for diplomatic ties had been established.

Limiting Nuclear Arms

Several months after his 1972 China trip, Nixon visited the Soviet Union. He received as warm a welcome in Moscow as he had in Beijing. In a series of cordial meetings between Nixon and Premier Leonid I. Brezhnev, the two nations reached several decisions. They agreed to work together to explore space, eased longstanding trade limits, and completed negotiations on a weapons pact.

Nixon viewed arms control as a vital part of his foreign policy program. Like many Americans, he was worried about the widespread **proliferation,** or growth, of nuclear weapons. The Limited Test Ban Treaty of 1963 had ended atmospheric testing of new bombs, but underground testing continued. The two superpowers were making bigger and better bombs all the time. Some people feared that the world might be destroyed unless these weapons were brought under control.

Nixon was determined to address the nuclear threat and to deal creatively with the Soviet Union at the same time. He had taken office intent on building more nuclear weapons to keep ahead of the Soviet Union. But he came to recognize that this kind of arms race made little sense. Each nation already had more than enough weapons to destroy its enemy many times over. The nuclear age demanded balance between the superpowers.

To address the issue, in 1969 the United States and the Soviet Union began Strategic Arms Limitation Talks. The talks produced a 1972 pact to limit offensive nuclear weapons, ready to be signed when Nixon went to Moscow.

The first Strategic Arms Limitation Treaty, known as **SALT I,** included a five-year agreement that held the number of intercontinental ballistic missiles (ICBMs) and submarine-launched ballistic missiles (SLBMs) at 1972 levels. Ballistic missiles ascend in a controlled manner, and descend in free-fall. The treaty also included an agreement restricting the development and deployment of antiballistic missile defense systems.

SALT I was a diplomatic triumph for the Nixon administration and an important step forward. But it did little to limit the number of warheads the two nations possessed or to stop them from improving nuclear weapons systems in other ways.

The practical Kissinger called for respecting the limits imposed, but he also urged the American military to improve its defenses. "The way for us to use this freeze is for us to catch up," he said soon after the summit. "If we don't do this, we don't deserve to be in office." Still, SALT I showed that arms control agreements were possible, paving the way for more progress in the future.

About a year before the signing of SALT I, Nixon pointed out that the potential benefits of negotiating with the Soviet Union went beyond the issue of limiting nuclear arms:

The cold war warmed slightly as Soviet premier Leonid Brezhnev (center, left) and President Nixon (center, right) met and SALT I was signed. *Government How was SALT I both a success and a failure?*

AMERICAN VOICES

"Perhaps for the first time, the evolving strategic balance allows a Soviet-American agreement which yields no unilateral [one-sided] advantages. The fact [that] we have begun to discuss strategic arms with the USSR is in itself important. Agreement in such a vital area could create a new commitment to stability, and influence attitudes toward other issues."

—*Richard Nixon*

SECTION 3 REVIEW

Comprehension

1. **Key Terms** Define: (a) *realpolitik*; (b) détente; (c) proliferation; (d) SALT I.

2. **Summarizing the Main Idea** Why were Nixon's policies toward China and the Soviet Union so surprising?

3. **Organizing Information** Create a web diagram to organize information about Nixon's foreign policy.

Critical Thinking

4. **Analyzing Time Lines** Review the time line at the start of the section. Do you think these events support the idea that in foreign relations change comes slowly? Explain.

5. **Demonstrating Reasoned Judgment** Considering its weaknesses, how important was the SALT I treaty? Why?

Writing Activity

6. **Writing an Expository Essay** Write an essay that Henry Kissinger might have prepared to explain the importance of relaxing tensions between the United States and both China and the Soviet Union. Try to refer to *realpolitik* and détente in your essay.

1969
Nixon White House wiretaps government employees

1971
Pentagon Papers released

1972
Watergate break-in; Nixon wins reelection

1973
Trial of Watergate burglars; Senate Watergate hearings; "Saturday Night Massacre"

1974
House committee recommends impeachment; Nixon resigns

SECTION 4

The Watergate Scandal

Objectives

You may wish to call students' attention to the objectives in the Section Preview. The objectives are reflected in the main headings of the section.

Bellringer

Ask students how they would feel if they discovered that the President might have broken the law. Ask them to discuss the impact of such a piece of news, and the symbolic role of the President.

Reading Strategy

Taking Notes Refer to the Reading Strategy in the Section Preview. You may wish to model a visual scheme by which to organize the notes using the suggested headings.

LESSON PLAN

Connecting to the Main Idea

1. Focus Tell students that Nixon's suspicious nature and his willingness to use his presidential power for partisan political ends set in motion a series of events that compromised the presidency itself. Ask students how the people of the United States reacted to presidential wrongdoing.
2. Instruct Discuss the atmosphere in the White House as described in this section. What does the existence of the "enemies list" reveal about Nixon's view of the world? Ask how students view the fact that Nixon harassed those he perceived as hostile by arranging income tax investigations of them. Are such actions an abuse of power? Why or why not?
3. Close Nixon's White House was characterized by suspicion and abuse of power. His efforts to use the presidency for his own political gain led to scandal—and to the end of his presidency.

4 The Watergate Scandal

SECTION PREVIEW

Objectives

1 Explain how the siege mentality at the White House led to illegal and unethical actions during Nixon's reelection campaign.
2 Describe the Watergate break-in and how the story of the Watergate scandal unfolded.
3 Describe the events that directly led to Nixon's resignation.
4 *Key Terms* Define: Watergate scandal; special prosecutor; impeachment.

Main Idea

The break-in at the Watergate apartment complex started a scandal that led to President Nixon's resignation.

Reading Strategy

Taking Notes As you read, take notes on the various events related to the Watergate scandal. Use the terms *Who, What, When, Where,* and *Why* to help you organize each piece of information.

L ooking toward the 1972 election, Nixon was determined to win an overwhelming victory. With such a mandate he would be in a position to move his programs through Congress. Fiercely loyal aides concocted various schemes to help ensure that the President would win. Some of them committed crimes in the process. When Nixon tried to hide their illegal actions, he involved himself in a scandalous series of events that ended his presidency and shook the foundations of American government.

MR. PRESIDENT:
RELEASE the TAPES!

A series of secret Oval Office recordings became the center of controversy.

Siege Mentality

The President's suspicious and secretive nature caused the White House to operate as if it were in a state of siege, surrounded by political enemies. Nixon's staff responded to the President's attitude by trying to protect him at all costs from anything that might weaken his political position.

The Enemies List One result of this mind-set was what became known as the "enemies list."

Special counsel Charles W. Colson helped develop a list of prominent people unsympathetic to the administration. It included politicians such as Senator Edward Kennedy, members of the media such as reporter Daniel Schorr, and a number of outspoken performers such as comedian Dick Gregory and actors Jane Fonda and Steve McQueen. Aides then considered how to harass these White House "enemies." One idea, for example, was to arrange income tax investigations of people on the list.

Wiretaps Despite his dedication to a domestic policy of law and order, Nixon was sometimes willing to take illegal actions. In 1969 someone in the National Security Council appeared to have leaked secret information to *The New York Times.* In response, Nixon ordered Henry Kissinger to install wiretaps, or listening devices, on the telephones of several of his own staff. He also ordered wiretaps on some news reporters' phones. These wiretaps, installed for national security reasons, were legal at the time. But they would lead to a flurry of illegal wiretapping, much of it done for political purposes.

RESOURCE OPTIONS

Teaching Resources

Reproducible Lesson Plan Lesson Plans folder, p. 165

Learning Styles Lesson Plan Learning Styles Lesson Plans folder, p. 67

Big Idea Graphic Organizer Big Idea Graphic Organizer folder, p. 137

Guided Reading and Review Units 9–10 folder, p. 64

At the same time, Nixon sought tighter coordination of intelligence activities. The FBI, under director J. Edgar Hoover, was already illegally monitoring radical activists by tapping their phones and opening mail. In mid-1970 Nixon's staff proposed a plan for wiretaps and other probes that was so far outside the law that even Hoover rejected it.

The Plumbers In the spring of 1971 Daniel Ellsberg, a former Defense Department official, handed *The New York Times* a huge, secret Pentagon study of the Vietnam War. In June 1971, as you have read, *The New York Times* began to publish this study, which became known as the Pentagon Papers. The documents showed that previous Presidents often had deceived Congress and the American people about the real situation in Vietnam and had deliberately escalated the conflict.

Nixon was upset that Ellsberg could get away with leaking secret government information. He was even more upset when leaks to the press continued. He and Kissinger were in the midst of secret discussions with China and the Soviet Union, and he did not want those delicate negotiations undermined.

Nixon approved a plan to organize a special White House unit to stop government leaks. The group, nicknamed the Plumbers, included E. Howard Hunt, a spy novelist and former CIA agent, and G. Gordon Liddy, a former FBI agent. In September 1971, with approval from White House chief domestic adviser John Ehrlichman, the undercover unit broke into the office of Ellsberg's psychiatrist. To punish Ellsberg for leaking the Pentagon Papers, they hoped to find and disclose damaging information about his private life.

Nixon's Reelection Campaign

Determined to ensure Nixon's victory in 1972, the Committee to Reelect the President used other questionable tactics. Headed by former Attorney General John Mitchell, the Committee launched a special fund-raising campaign. It wanted to collect as much money as possible before a new law made it necessary to report such contributions. The money would fund both routine campaign activities and unethical stunts hidden from the public.

The Committee funded a variety of questionable actions. For example, in 1972 people on its payroll made up a letter attempting to

Nixon's downfall began when burglars paid by the Committee to Reelect the President broke into Democratic party headquarters in Washington's Watergate apartment complex. *Government* *What did Nixon do to become ensnared in the scandal?*

discredit Edmund Muskie, a Democratic senator from Maine who was a leading presidential contender. Then they leaked the letter to a conservative New Hampshire newspaper.

Charging Muskie with making insulting remarks about French Canadians living in the state, the letter was timed to arrive two weeks before the New Hampshire primary. The letter also claimed that Muskie's wife was an alcoholic. The normally composed Muskie broke down in tears in front of TV cameras, which seriously damaged his candidacy.

Attempts such as this to sabotage Nixon's political opponents came to be known as "dirty tricks." They included sending hecklers to disrupt Democratic campaign meetings and assigning undercover "spies" to join the campaigns of major candidates.

The Watergate Break-In

Within the Committee to Reelect the President a group was formed to gather intelligence, or secret political information. It included "Plumbers" Liddy and Hunt. The group masterminded several outlandish plans.

One scheme called for wiretapping top Democrats to try to compromise delegates at their convention. Twice Mitchell

Security guard Frank Willis discovered the Watergate break-in.

Graphing the Main Idea

To make sure students understand the main idea of this section, you may wish to use the flow map graphic organizer below.

Tell students that a flow map shows a sequence of events unfolding. Ask students to use it to show the chain of events that began with the Watergate scandal and ended with Nixon's resignation.

Teaching Tip A template for this graphic organizer can be found in the Color Transparencies, G-4.

BACKGROUND

The Youth Vote in 1972

The 1972 Republican campaign was not without support from young people, as might be assumed from Nixon's and Agnew's criticisms of youth in general and the still-fresh memories of Kent State. Young Republicans, according to *Life* magazine in September 1972, comprised "the nation's largest bloc of first-time voters, 2.5 million of them, mostly 18–24-year-olds." By early fall 1972, "Young Voters for the President" claimed 10,000 college volunteers on more than 90 campuses—many established far ahead of McGovern's youth workers. On election day Nixon got 52 percent of the votes cast by those under 30.

▶ RESOURCE OPTIONS

Teaching Resources

📁 **Visual Learning Activity** Wanted, Learning with Documents folder, p. 74

📁 **Biography** John J. Sirica, Units 9–10 folder, p. 66

Answer to . . .

Viewing History He ordered the CIA to persuade the FBI to stop the Watergate investigation.

About the Presidents

The presidency of **Richard Nixon** (1969–1974) defies simple assessments. While his presidency was scandal-ridden, and Nixon stands as the only President ever forced to resign from office, his historic legacy is complex. Nixon had acute political intelligence and a knack for innovative policy making. In domestic policy he oversaw the creation of the Occupational Safety and Health Administration and the Environmental Protection Agency. In foreign policy he pursued détente with the Soviet Union and opened relations with the People's Republic of China. In doing so, Nixon laid the foundation for stable relations between the United States and the world's dominant Communist powers. Source: Adapted from Henry F. Graff's *The Presidents,* Scribner's, 1984, by the editors of *American Heritage* magazine.

refused to go along, not because the plan was illegal, but because it was too expensive.

Finally, in March 1972, he approved a different idea. Liddy would oversee the wiretapping of phones at Democratic National Committee headquarters in the Watergate apartment complex in Washington, D.C.

The first break-in to install illegal listening devices failed. A second attempt, begun late at night on June 16, 1972, ended with the arrest of the five men involved. One suspect was James McCord, a former CIA officer working as a security officer for the Committee to Reelect the President. The Watergate burglars carried money that could be traced to the Committee. Thus they tied the break-in directly to Nixon's reelection campaign.

When the FBI traced the money carried by the Watergate burglars to the reelection committee, Nixon contacted the CIA. He authorized that organization to try to persuade the FBI to stop its investigation on the grounds that the matter involved "national security."

This action would come back to haunt the President. Although he had not been involved in planning the break-in, Nixon was now part of the

Main Idea
CONNECTIONS

What was the purpose of the Watergate break-in?

illegal coverup. The break-in and the coverup are now known as the **Watergate scandal.**

In the months following the Watergate break-in, the incident barely reached the public's notice. Behind the scenes in the White House, some of the President's closest aides worked feverishly to keep the truth hidden.

In the summer of 1972, Haldeman, Ehrlichman, Mitchell, and others launched a scheme to bribe the Watergate defendants. They distributed hundreds of thousands of dollars in illegal "hush money" to buy their silence. Also, to shield the President, Mitchell and other top officials committed perjury by lying under oath in court.

Their efforts paid off in the November presidential election. Nixon trounced Democratic liberal Senator George McGovern of South Dakota by 520 to 17 electoral votes and a sizable majority of the popular vote. He had the mandate he wanted, though he did not get a Republican majority in either house of Congress.

The Watergate Scandal Unfolds

Despite Nixon's victory in the election, the Watergate story refused to go away. Newspapers such as the *Washington Post* continued asking probing questions of administration officials. Nixon himself had proclaimed publicly that "no one in the White House staff, no one in this administration, presently employed, was involved in this very bizarre incident." Not everyone believed him.

The Watergate Trial The trial of the Watergate burglars began in January 1973, with Judge John J. Sirica presiding. All the defendants either pleaded guilty or were found guilty. Meanwhile the White House and the President himself were becoming more deeply involved. In March 1973, just before the judge handed down the sentences, Nixon personally approved the payment of "hush money" to defendant E. Howard Hunt.

At sentencing time Judge Sirica was not convinced that he had gotten to the bottom of the matter. Criticizing the prosecution, he said:

Washington Post investigative reporters Bob Woodward (right) and Carl Bernstein (left) persisted in tracking down information to uncover the Watergate story. *Culture How do you think their reporting affected the official investigation?*

AMERICAN VOICES ❝ I have not been satisfied, and I am still not satisfied that all the pertinent facts that might be available—I say *might* be available—have been produced before an American jury. . . . I would hope that the Senate committee is granted the power by Congress . . . to try to get to the bottom of what happened in this case.**"**

—*Judge John J. Sirica*

To prompt the burglars to talk, Sirica sentenced them to long prison terms, up to 40 years. But he suggested that their sentences could be reduced if they cooperated with the upcoming Senate hearings on Watergate.

Woodward and Bernstein Meanwhile, two *Washington Post* reporters were following a trail of leads. Bob Woodward and Carl Bernstein, both young and eager, sensed that the trail would lead to the White House.†

Even before the election, Woodward and Bernstein had learned about the secret funds at the Committee to Reelect the President. They had written about the political spying and sabotage. As they began to realize who was involved, they called John Mitchell and asked him to verify their story. He denied it angrily.

The Senate Investigates In February 1973 a Senate Select Committee on Presidential Campaign Activities had begun to investigate the Watergate affair. James McCord, one of the convicted Watergate burglars, responded to his lengthy prison sentence by testifying before the committee in secret session. He gave members a vague sense of what had gone on, and he suggested that Nixon staffers were involved. The stories by Woodward and Bernstein helped the probe. In turn, leaks from the Senate committee aided these and other reporters.

As rumors of White House involvement grew, Nixon tried to protect himself. In April 1973 he fired Haldeman and Ehrlichman, his two closest aides. On national television he proclaimed that he would take final responsibility for the mistakes of others, for "there can be no whitewash at the White House."

The investigation ground on. In May 1973 the Senate committee, chaired by Senator Sam Ervin of North Carolina, began televised public hearings on Watergate. Millions of Americans watched, fascinated, as the story unfolded like a mystery thriller. John Dean, the

---

†The reporters received key clues from a shadowy informant whose identity remains a secret today. The cloak-and-dagger story of the investigation became a popular book and movie, *All the President's Men.*

Watergate Chronology

June 1972	Five men linked to Nixon's reelection campaign arrested for breaking into Democratic National Committee headquarters.
April 1973	Nixon denies knowledge of the break-in.
May 1973	Senate Select Committee on Presidential Campaign Activities begins hearings.
June 1973	Former Nixon counsel John Dean tells the committee that Nixon authorized a coverup.
July 1973	Committee discovers that Nixon had been secretly recording presidential conversations since 1971 and orders Nixon to release certain tapes. Nixon refuses.
Aug. 1973	Special Prosecutor Archibald Cox sues Nixon for the tapes.
Oct. 1973	Nixon offers summaries of the tapes, which Cox rejects. Nixon fires Cox, setting off a series of firings known as the "Saturday Night Massacre." The House takes steps to impeach Nixon. Nixon releases all but two of the requested tapes.
Nov. 1973	An 18 1/2-minute gap is found on one of the tapes.
Jan. 1974	Nixon claims "executive privilege."
April 1974	Nixon is ordered to surrender more tapes and related documents. Nixon supplies 1,254 pages of edited transcripts. Special Prosecutor Leon Jaworski sues Nixon for the originals.
July 1974	Supreme Court orders Nixon to surrender the tapes and documents. The House Judiciary Committee recommends impeachment.
Aug.1974	Nixon releases transcripts that prove he learned of the break-in as early as June 23, 1972, and ordered the coverup. Nixon resigns August 9.

 Interpreting Charts As the investigation unfolded, it became increasingly clear that Nixon had something to hide. **Government** *How was the investigation an example of the federal system of checks and balances?*

 RESOURCE OPTIONS

Media and Technology

 Listening to Literature Theodore Roethke, "The Adamant"

ACTIVITY

EXTENDED CLASS PERIODS

Time: 90 minutes.
Activity: Have students debate whether or not Nixon should be impeached for his involvement in Watergate.
Groupings: Groups of four students.
Purpose: To explore the Constitution's guidelines for impeachment, as well as the charges and evidence against President Nixon.
Roles: Proponents and opponents of impeachment.
Outcome: Students will learn about the issues surrounding the decision to impeach a high official.

 BACKGROUND

Recent Scholarship

Richard Nixon's complicity in the Watergate affair led him to become the first President of the United States ever to resign his office. That step became necessary when tape recordings of presidential conversations demonstrated beyond the shadow of a doubt that he had been involved in a massive coverup attempt. In *Abuse of Power: The New Nixon Tapes,* Stanley I. Kutler provides transcripts of recordings released only after a lengthy court case in which Nixon sought tenaciously to keep the tapes from getting a public airing.

Answer to . . .

Interpreting Charts *The judicial branch checked the abuses of the executive branch of the federal government.*

STUDENT PORTFOLIO

You may wish to have students add the following to their portfolios. To assess student work, refer to the generic rubrics in the Program Overview in the Teaching Resources.

Suggest that students research and prepare a biographical file of the major figures in Watergate, their roles, and what happened to them in the aftermath of the scandal. The file could include figures in the Nixon administration, in the press, and in Congress.

▼ BACKGROUND

Biography

Senator Samuel Ervin, Jr., (1896–1985) of North Carolina headed the seven-member Senate committee on Watergate. He won praise not only for his easy southern manner but for his doggedness in pursuing evidence against Nixon and resisting the President's claims to "executive privilege." Ervin, who called the United States Constitution "the finest thing to come out of the mind of man," served in the United States Senate for more than 20 years until he retired in 1974. He wrote two books, *The Whole Truth: The Watergate Conspiracy* (1980) and *Humor of a Country Lawyer* (1983).

Answer to . . .

Comparing Primary Sources Jordan points to the constitutional basis for impeachment; Hutchinson argues that legislative grounds for impeachment have not yet been established.

COMPARING PRIMARY SOURCES

SHOULD NIXON BE IMPEACHED?

In July 1974 the House Judiciary Committee debated the possible impeachment of President Richard Nixon.

In Favor of Impeachment	Opposed to Impeachment
"My faith in the Constitution is whole, it is complete, it is total. I am not going to sit here and be an idle spectator to the diminution [lessening], the subversion [overthrow], the destruction of the Constitution. . . . The Framers confided in the Congress the power if need be to remove . . . a President swollen with power and grown tyrannical." —*Texas Representative Barbara Jordan, Democrat*	"As the trust is placed in Congress to safeguard the liberties of the people through the . . . powers to remove a President, so must Congress's vigilance be fierce in seeing that the trust is not abused. . . . Not only do I not believe that any crimes by the President have been proved beyond a reasonable doubt, but I do not think the proof even approaches the lesser standards of proof which some of my colleagues . . . suggested we apply." —*Michigan Representative Edward Hutchinson, Republican*

ANALYZING VIEWPOINTS **Compare the views of the two speakers toward impeachment of Nixon.**

President's personal legal counselor, sought to save himself by testifying that Nixon knew about the coverup. Other staffers described illegal activities at the White House.

The most dramatic moment came when one aide revealed the existence of a secret taping system in the President's office that recorded all meetings and telephone conversations. The system was set up to provide a historical record of Nixon's presidency. Now those audiotapes could show whether or not Nixon had actually been involved in the coverup.

The "Saturday Night Massacre" In an effort to prove his honesty, Nixon agreed in May 1973 to the appointment of a special Watergate prosecutor. A **special prosecutor** works for the Justice Department but conducts an independent investigation of alleged wrongdoing by government officials. Archibald Cox, a Harvard law professor, took the post and immediately asked for the tapes. Nixon refused to release them. When Cox persisted, Nixon ordered him fired during the weekend of October 20, 1973. This action triggered a series of resignations and firings that became known as the "Saturday Night Massacre."

An Administration in Jeopardy By this time, Nixon was in serious trouble. His public approval rating plummeted. After Cox's firing, *Time* magazine declared "The President Should Resign."

Cox's replacement as special prosecutor, Leon Jaworski of Texas, also asked for the tapes. Nixon then tried to show his innocence by releasing edited transcripts of some of his White House conversations. He carefully cut out the most damaging evidence. Still, many people were angry and disillusioned when they read even the edited comments of some of the conversations in the Oval Office.

Meanwhile, a subplot emerged in the troubled White House. Vice President Spiro Agnew stood accused of evading income taxes and taking bribes. Early in October 1973, just 10 days before the "Saturday Night Massacre," he resigned in disgrace. To succeed Agnew, Nixon named Gerald R. Ford, the House minority leader. For nearly two months, until the Senate confirmed Ford, the nation had a President in big trouble—and no Vice President.

Impeachment Ahead? Nixon had to do something. After the "Saturday Night Massacre," Congress had begun the process that could lead to **impeachment**—bringing charges of misconduct against a government official.

In July 1974 the House Judiciary Committee, which included 21 Democrats and 17 Republicans, began to hold hearings to determine if there were adequate grounds for impeachment. This debate, like the earlier hearings, appeared on national television. The country watched anxiously as even Republicans deserted the President. Representative M. Caldwell Butler of Virginia spoke for many of them when he said:

> **AMERICAN VOICES** ❝For years we Republicans have campaigned against corruption and misconduct. . . . But Watergate is our shame. Those things have happened in our house and it is our responsibility to do what we can to clear it up. . . . It is a sad chapter in American history, but I cannot condone what I have heard; I cannot excuse it; and I cannot and will not stand for it.❞
>
> —*Representative M. Caldwell Butler, 1974*

▶ RESOURCE OPTIONS

Teaching Resources

 Comparing Primary Sources On Nixon's Impeachment, Units 9–10 folder, pp. 67–68

Media and Technology

 Color Transparencies Political Cartoons, K-10

By sizable tallies, the House Judiciary Committee voted to impeach the President on charges of obstruction of justice, abuse of power, and refusal to obey a congressional order to turn over his tapes. To remove him from office, a majority of the full House of Representatives would have to vote for impeachment, and the Senate would then have to hold a trial. The outcome seemed obvious.

Nixon Resigns

On August 5, after a brief delay, Nixon finally obeyed a Supreme Court ruling and released the tapes. They contained a disturbing gap of 18 1/2 minutes, during which the conversation had been mysteriously erased. Still, the tapes gave clear evidence of Nixon's involvement in the coverup.

Three days later Nixon appeared on television and painfully announced that he would leave the office of President the next day. On August 9, 1974, Nixon resigned, the first President ever to do so.

That same day, in a smooth constitutional transition, Vice President Gerald Ford was sworn in. "Our long national nightmare is over," he said. Many Americans wanted Nixon to face the charges against him in court. Ford, however, believed that a long, public trial might divide the country and draw the focus away from vital issues. A month after Nixon resigned, Ford granted him a presidential pardon.

The Watergate scandal still stands as a low point in American political history. It revealed how trusted government officials could abuse

In this famous photograph, former President Richard Nixon offers the crowd his familiar salute as he leaves Washington, D.C., following his resignation. *Government* *Why did President Ford pardon Nixon?*

the power granted to them by the people. The scandal also proved the strength of the United States' constitutional system, especially its balance of powers. The judicial and legislative branches of government forced the members of the executive branch to answer for their criminal actions.

SECTION 4 REVIEW

Comprehension

1. **Key Terms** (a) Watergate scandal; (b) special prosecutor; (c) impeachment.

2. **Summarizing the Main Idea** Why was the Watergate break-in such an important event?

3. **Organizing Information** Create a cause-and-effect chart to organize information about the Watergate scandal.

Critical Thinking

4. **Analyzing Time Lines** Review the time line at the start of the section. Which events do you think are related to the siege mentality that gripped the Nixon White House? Explain.

5. **Formulating Questions** Imagine that you are a member of the House Judiciary Committee, preparing for impeachment hearings. What three questions would you want to ask President Nixon?

Writing Activity

6. **Writing a Persuasive Essay** Write an essay either in favor of or opposed to President Ford's pardon of Nixon.

RESOURCE OPTIONS

SKILLS FOR LIFE

Historical Evidence

Analyzing Presidential Records

Focus Examine the transcript of a presidential conversation to analyze its value as historical evidence.

Instruct Ask for student volunteers to read and act out the transcript. After the performance, ask students to discuss what strikes them as interesting or important about the conversation. Was it what they expected of a "presidential" conversation? Why or why not? What does the conversation reveal about Nixon and his leadership style? Ask students how they think American citizens might benefit by reading such presidential records.

Extend See the Skills for Life Activity in the Resource Options below.

Answers

1. (a) Chief of Staff H. R. Haldeman and President Richard Nixon. (b) Pat Gray of the FBI, John Mitchell of CREEP, and Vernon Walters of the CIA. (c) On June 23, 1972. (d) The Oval Office. (e) How to stop the investigation of the Watergate break-in.

2. (a) They have traced the money the burglars were carrying to people who contributed to CREEP. (b) He describes Mitchell's recommendation that the CIA tell the FBI to stop the investigation because it involves the CIA. (c) He agrees to it.

3. (a) Nixon obviously believes that he can order one government agency to lie to another if it is expedient for his needs. (b) He must believe that protecting his administration and getting himself reelected take precedence over honesty and proper use of government agencies.

TEST FOR SUCCESS

Sample answer: His influence was probably strong, as Nixon seems to agree with all of his actions and ideas.

926

Analyzing Presidential Records

Presidential papers record a President's time in office. They include letters, memoranda, notes on meetings, speeches, transcripts of press conferences, and more. They provide a valuable source of historical evidence.

In more recent times technology has added new forms of "papers" as historical evidence, such as audio- and videotapes. President Nixon's audiotapes, recorded in the Oval Office, loomed large in the Watergate affair. In fact, one of these tapes finally ended the affair. It was a recording of a conversation that took place just a few days after the Watergate break-in on June 16, 1972. Not released until August 5, 1974, it proved that Nixon knew of the cover-up all along.

1. *Identify the source by asking who, when, where, and what.* (a) Who are the speakers on the tape? (b) Who else is mentioned in it? (c) When did the conversation take place? (d) Where? (e) What is the major topic?

2. *Identify the main points of information in the excerpts.* (a) Why is Haldeman concerned about the FBI? (b) What recommendation does he put forward about using the CIA to end the investigation? (c) How does President Nixon respond to the recommendation?

3. *Study the tape to find clues to the historical period.* (a) What can you infer about the extent of the powers that Nixon believed he had over FBI and CIA operations? (b) What can you infer about Nixon's sense of priorities at the time the recording was made?

TEST FOR SUCCESS

What can you infer about the extent of Haldeman's influence on Nixon?

June 23, 1972
Speakers
President Nixon
H. R. Haldeman, Chief of Staff

Haldeman Now, on to the investigation, you know the Democratic break-in thing. We're back in the problem area because the FBI is not under control, because [acting FBI director L. Patrick] Gray doesn't exactly know how to control it and . . . their investigation is now leading into some productive areas—because they've been able to trace the money [that was found on the Watergate burglars]. . . . [John] Mitchell's recommendation [is] that the way to handle this now is for us to have [deputy CIA director Vernon] Walters call Pat Gray and just say, "Stay . . . out of this—this is ah, business here we don't want you to go any further on it." That's not an unusual development, and ah, that would take care of it.

Nixon What about Pat Gray—you mean Pat Gray doesn't want to?

Haldeman Pat does want to. He doesn't know how to, and he doesn't have any basis for doing it. Given [Walters's call], he will then have the basis.

Nixon Yeah.

Haldeman [Gray will] say, "We've got this signal from across the river [the CIA] to put a hold on this." And that will fit rather well because the FBI agents who are working the case, at this point, feel that's what it is.

Nixon They've traced the money? Who'd they trace it to?

[Haldeman describes various people who contributed to the Committee to Reelect the President, and Nixon wonders if these people will say that the burglars, not the committee, asked for the money.]

Haldeman Well, if they will. But then we're relying on more and more people all the time. That's the problem, and they'll stop if we could take this other route.

Nixon All right.

Haldeman And you seem to think the thing to do is get [the FBI] to stop?

Nixon Right, fine.

—Excerpted from The New York Times, *Tuesday, August 6, 1974*

▶ RESOURCE OPTIONS

Teaching Resources

📁 **Skills for Life Activity** Units 9–10 folder, p. 72, focuses on the Inaugural Address of President Clinton for further examination of presidential documents as historical evidence.

Why Study History?
To understand that . . .

Government Requires Checks and Balances

The issue of presidential power, keenly reflected in the Watergate scandal, continues to shape American politics today.

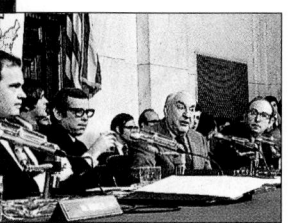

Senate Watergate hearings, 1973

The United States in 1968 seemed to be slipping into chaos. Protests against the Vietnam War multiplied after the Tet Offensive. The assassination of Martin Luther King, Jr., abruptly halted the Poor People's Campaign. Another assassin's bullet killed presidential candidate Robert F. Kennedy. Outside the Democratic Convention in Chicago, police wielded tear gas, nightsticks, and rifles against demonstrators as a horrified nation watched on television.

In November 1968, Richard Nixon won the presidency on the promise to restore law and order. Yet behind the scenes, President Nixon violated the standards that he publicly upheld. The Watergate scandal revealed the extent to which he abused his power as President.

The Impact Today

Vast executive power was not what the Founding Fathers had in mind when they wrote the Constitution, with its system of checks and balances. The Constitution lists the powers of the executive, legislative, and judicial branches. But the language of the Constitution is sometimes general, and thus the extent of the three branches' powers is open to interpretation.

The balance of power between Congress and the President has shifted over time. In the cold war era, for example, presidential power

expanded, especially in the area of military affairs. Though the Constitution gives Congress the power to declare war, Presidents deployed American military forces abroad on several occasions without a formal declaration of war.

In 1950, President Truman sent troops to South Korea. In 1965, President Johnson sent troops to Vietnam. In 1970, President Nixon launched an invasion of Cambodia. All these actions undermined Congress's war power. In response, in 1973 Congress passed the War Powers Act, which required congressional approval for sending troops overseas.

In recent years, the budget has become a battleground for disputes over presidential and congressional powers. In 1996, Congress passed the Line-Item Veto Act. It gave the President the power to veto specific items in the federal budget. (In the past, Presidents had to approve or veto the budget bill as a whole.) Yet two years later, the Supreme Court ruled the line-item veto unconstitutional.

The Impact on You

Make a two-column table titled "Executive Versus Legislative Power." In the first column, list powers that you think the President should have. In the second column, list powers that should reside with Congress. Give a brief reason why each power on your table should belong to the President or to Congress.

President Clinton addresses Congress, 1997

Why Study History?

Class Discussion

Discuss with the class governmental checks and balances. For a more thorough examination of the issue, see the activity folder in the Resource Options below.

ACTIVITY
STUDENT PARTICIPATION

Predicting Consequences

Ask students to read the text. Then divide the class into three groups. Have each group focus on one branch of government and discuss the possible consequences of having no checks and balances. Each group should consider the potential for:
- **abuse of power**
- **dictatorship**
- **lack of leadership**
- **weak government**
- **general confusion**

Ask groups to write down their ideas and share them with the class.

Follow up Ask students to find historical examples showing what happens when the balance of power is upset.

Using the Internet

Students can learn more about the system of checks and balances by exploring links in the *America: Pathways to the Present* Web site at

http://www.Pathways.phschool.com

Assessment

See the Lesson Plans folder, pp. 24–27, for rubrics on assessing Class Participation Projects.

RESOURCE OPTIONS

Teaching Resources

📁 **Why Study History? Activity**
Government Requires Checks and Balances, found in the Why Study History? folder, p. 33, provides an activity to help students better understand the system of checks and balances.

Media and Technology

 AmericanHeritage® CD-ROM

Time Tour The Nation Today and Tomorrow: A Time of Turmoil

  Decision America Videotapes and Videodiscs Issue 5 *How Are We Represented?*

Key Terms

Students should refer to the definitions of the key terms in the chapter to write sentences that show the relation of each term to the events of 1968 or the Nixon years.

Comprehension

1. Many Americans began to question whether the Vietnam War was winnable because the Viet Cong could still mount a widespread attack on South Vietnam, despite continuing escalation.

2. President Johnson quit the race early; Robert Kennedy was assassinated; protests and violence marred the Democratic convention; George Wallace's independent candidacy drained votes from the Democrats; Richard Nixon's campaign was well-run and well-financed.

3. They gave him unswerving loyalty and support; he relied on them to develop broad government policies; they shielded Nixon from the outside world.

4. To try to win white southerners over to the Republican party, he slowed civil rights reforms and opposed busing; he tried to appoint southerners to the Supreme Court.

5. He pressed for a policy of *realpolitik* and used his diplomatic skills to help ease tensions with China and the Soviet Union.

6. It opened diplomatic contact and eased travel and commercial restrictions.

7. It used lies to discredit Edmund Muskie, sent hecklers to disrupt Democratic campaign meetings and assigned undercover "spies" to join the campaigns of major candidates; engineered the Watergate break-in.

8. Nixon tried to get the FBI to halt its investigation of the break-in; he personally authorized payment of "hush money" to E. Howard Hunt, a Watergate defendant.

Chapter Summary

The major concepts of Chapter 32 are presented below. See also *Guide to the Essentials of American History* or *Interactive Student Tutorial CD-ROM,* which contains interactive review activities, time lines, helpful hints, and test practice for Chapter 32.

Reviewing the Main Ideas

In 1968 a fateful series of events helped Richard Nixon win the presidential election. Relying on his close advisers to help develop domestic and foreign policy, Nixon tried to shift the country in a new direction. The Watergate scandal forced Nixon to resign in 1974.

Section 1: The Crises of 1968

The year 1968 was a turbulent and painful time for the country that resulted in the election of Richard Nixon as President.

Section 2: The Nixon Administration

As President, Richard Nixon relied on several close advisers to help him move the country in a new direction.

Section 3: Nixon's Foreign Policy

President Nixon's foreign policy led to more positive relationships with China and the Soviet Union.

Section 4: The Watergate Scandal

The break-in at the Watergate apartment complex started a scandal that led to President Nixon's resignation.

The issue of presidential power, reflected in the Watergate scandal, continues to shape American politics today.

Key Terms

Use each of the terms below in a sentence that shows how it relates to the chapter.

1. SALT I
2. Poor People's Campaign
3. deficit spending
4. special prosecutor
5. *realpolitik*
6. Watergate scandal
7. détente
8. silent majority
9. proliferation
10. embargo
11. Organization of Petroleum Exporting Countries (OPEC)

Comprehension

1. What effect did the Tet Offensive have on American public opinion in 1968? Why?
2. What factors hurt the Democrats' chances for victory in the presidential election of 1968?
3. Why were President Nixon's key staff members so important to him?
4. What was Nixon's "southern strategy"?
5. How did Henry Kissinger affect American foreign policy under President Nixon?
6. How did the Nixon administration change United States' policy toward China?
7. What measures did the Committee to Reelect the President take to win the 1972 election?
8. What illegal actions did Nixon take in attempting to cover up the Watergate break-in?

Using Graphic Organizers

On a separate sheet of paper, copy the flowchart to organize the main ideas of the chapter. Fill in the blank boxes with important details.

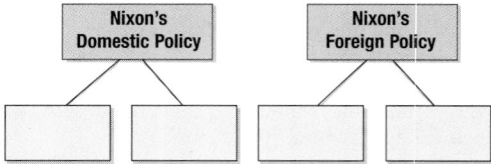

Using Graphic Organizers

Possible details:
- Wage and price controls, Family Assistance Plan, law and order campaign.
- Break-in at Watergate complex, coverup of crime, threat of impeachment, Nixon resignation.
- Kissinger's diplomacy.
- Nixon visits China, SALT I.

Analyzing Political Cartoons ▶

1. This cartoon appeared during the Watergate scandal. (a) What is the building shown? (b) How has it been modified?

2. What does this modification represent?

3. What is the cartoon's message?

Critical Thinking

1. *Applying the Chapter Skill* Compile a brief presidential record for one of the earlier American Presidents. The record may be a letter, speech, notes on a meeting, a memorandum, or the transcript of a press conference. It should focus on a critical issue or event. Other details might suggest the time period, the mood of the President, and the importance of the issue or event. Use your textbook as an aid.

2. *Testing Conclusions* Some observers have concluded that only a Republican veteran of the cold war like Richard Nixon could have reestablished relations with China. Do you agree, or do you believe that a Democratic President could have been equally successful? Explain.

3. *Predicting Consequences* What kind of President do you think Americans were looking for after Watergate and the Nixon resignation?

ANALYZING DOCUMENTS ◀▶ INTERPRETING DATA

Turn to the line graph titled "Rate of Inflation, 1968–1976," in Section 2.

1. When did consumer prices reach their peak? (a) 1968 (b) 1971 (c) 1974 (d) 1976.

2. What is the best description of the rate of inflation through the period from 1968 to 1972? (a) stayed about the same (b) rose steadily (c) dropped steadily (d) rose and dropped wildly from year to year.

3. *Writing* Imagine that you are the manager of a grocery store in 1973. Customers have been complaining about rising food prices. Write a notice to your customers explaining why food prices go up when fuel prices rise. Think about the grocer's costs and how they might be affected by changes in fuel prices.

INTERNET ACTIVITY

For your portfolio:
PREPARING A SUMMARY

Access Prentice Hall's *America: Pathways to the Present* site at **www.Pathways.phschool.com** for the specific URLs to complete the activity. Additional resources and related Web sites are also available.

Use the links provided to prepare a summary of the short- and long-term effects of the Watergate scandal. What impact did the scandal have on Nixon and his administration? What lasting impact did the scandal have on the presidency and the American public?

Connecting to Today

Essay Writing Today, in part because of the Watergate scandal, Congress and the press keep a watchful eye on top government officials. They eagerly probe any questionable activity, past or present, public or private. Is this level of watchfulness good for the country, or bad? Explain your answer in an essay.

Analyzing Political Cartoons

1. (a) The White House. (b) It has been converted into a tape recorder.
2. Nixon's secret taping of presidential conversations; the Watergate scandal.
3. The White House has been overwhelmed by the secrecy and scandal.

Critical Thinking

1. Records should seem authentic and focus on a recognizable event.
2. Students' responses should demonstrate an awareness that a hard-liner like Nixon was less likely to encounter conservative opposition than a Democrat.
3. Possible answer: Americans were probably looking for a President who could restore Americans' trust in the government.

Interpreting Data

1. c
2. a
3. Notices should state that when fuel prices climb, food and other prices climb with them. This may be explained by increased energy and transportation costs related to the fuel rise. Higher costs for petroleum-based fertilizers might also add to the inflation rate for food.

Connecting to Today

Essays might consider the benefit or harm to the government of continuing investigations, the rights of high government officials, and whether such a mood of suspicion encourages or discourages people from entering politics.

INTERNET ACTIVITY

Summaries will vary but should demonstrate a valid interpretation of the data, and be supported with specific facts or quotes wherever possible.

The Post-Watergate Period, 1974–1980

Managing Time and Instruction

INSTRUCTION SUPPORT

These materials for instruction are provided for **each section** in the **Teaching Resources**. See **Units 9–10 folder for Enrichment Support**:

- Reproducible Lesson Plans in Lesson Plans folder • Learning Styles Lesson Plans in Learning Styles Lesson Plans folder • Big Idea Graphic Organizers in Big Idea Graphic Organizer folder • Guided Reading and Review • Quizzes • Test Preparation Practice booklet

DAILY LESSON	ENRICHMENT SUPPORT
1 **The Ford Administration** (pp. 931–935)	• Literature Activity, A Search for Roots, Units 9–10 folder, pp. 84–86 • Primary Source Activity, 1976: The Bicentennial Year, Learning with Documents folder, p. 39
2 **The Carter Transition** (pp. 936–939)	• Key Documents, Barbara Jordan, Keynote Address to the Democratic National Convention, Learning with Documents folder, p. 105 • Biography, Patricia Roberts Harris, Units 9–10 folder, p. 81 • Primary Source Activity, A Crisis of Confidence, found on **Resource Pro**
3 **Carter's Foreign Policy** (pp. 940–944)	• Biography, Andrew Young, found on **Resource Pro** • Visual Learning Activity, The Hostage Crisis as a Media Event, Learning with Documents folder, p. 75 • Skills for Life Activity, Units 9–10 folder, p. 87
4 **Carter's Domestic Issues** (pp. 946–950)	• Critical Thinking Activity, Formulating Questions: Prices at the Pump, found on **Resource Pro** • Visual Learning Activity, Responding to the Energy Crisis, found on **Resource Pro** • Comparing Primary Sources, On Nuclear Energy, Units 9–10 folder, pp. 82–83 • Americans Are Skeptical About Government, Why Study History? folder, p. 34

Running Out of Time?

- Use Tape 5, "Republican Revival and Decline, 1968–Present," from **Visions of America** videotapes series.
- Use Chapter 33 Summary from **Guide to the Essentials of American History (English and Spanish)**.

Companion Web Site

The companion Web site offers online links for all chapter review activities. It also provides key content links and structured support for this chapter for both teachers and students.

http://www.Pathways.phschool.com

Teaching in the Information Age

Media and Technology

For the Student

Interactive Student Tutorial CD-ROM Chapter 33
Student Edition on Audiotape Chapter 33
American Heritage® CD-ROM
Guided Reading Audiotapes (English and Spanish) Chapter 33

For the Teacher

Resource Pro CD-ROM Chapter 33
Test Bank CD-ROM Chapter 33
Listening to Literature Audiotapes *Timeless Voices, Timeless Themes* "Average Waves in Unprotected Waters" by Anne Tyler

Block Scheduling

Pacing Suggestions

For 90-minute Blocks

- Teach sections 3 and 4 using Transparencies H-21 and I-11 and the Connections to Today note on p. 943 for class discussions.
- Teach sections 1 and 2 using the Big Idea Graphic Organizers from Teaching Resources and the Extended Class Periods Activity on p. 933.

Additional Resources

- Prentice Hall's **American History Block Scheduling Support File** covers over 40 major topics in American history.
- **Prentice Hall United States History Video Collection™** contains 20 videotapes covering American history from beginnings to present.
- **Decision America Videotapes and Videodiscs**

Assessment Options

Chapter Test Forms A&B Test Bank CD-ROM booklet
Test Bank CD-ROM Chapter 33
Standardized Test Preparation Handbook

Connections to American Literature

from Prentice Hall

Prentice Hall Literature *Timeless Voices, Timeless Themes* "Onomatopoeia" by William Safire, p. 996

Additional Resources

For the Student

Anne Colby and William Damon. *Some Do Care: Contemporary Lives of Moral Commitment.* The Free Press, 1993.
Tracy Kidder. *The Soul of a New Machine.* Little, Brown, 1981.

For the Teacher

Neil Sheehan. *After the War Was Over: Hanoi and Saigon.* Vintage, 1993.

Prentice Hall brings into the classroom the vast archives and scholarship of the nation's premier American history magazine. See "From the Archives of American Heritage®" and "About the Presidents" teaching notes in this chapter.

History Alive!

Teacher's Curriculum Institute, in partnership with Prentice Hall, provides unique materials that engage students with diverse learning styles. See History Alive!® unit on Contemporary American Society.

Student Performance Pack

Ensures success in the three critical areas of Reading, Test Taking, and English Language Development with the following materials:
- Guide to the Essentials of American History in English and Spanish
- Guided Reading Audiotapes in English and Spanish
- Interactive Student Tutorial CD-ROM
- Test Preparation Handbook
- Test Preparation Practice booklet

Introducing the Chapter

Watergate profoundly shook Americans' faith in their leaders. Coming on the heels of the turbulence of the 1960s, the scandal's reach into the highest, most trusted offices of government seemed to confirm the country's worst fears about the abuse of power. It was no surprise, then, when an outsider to Washington politics, Jimmy Carter, was elected President.

Themes in American History

The theme for this chapter, Economics, is listed at the beginning of this unit. An alternate theme for the chapter is Culture. To teach this unit thematically, you may wish to use The Nation After World War II folder in American History Block Scheduling Support.

Why Study History?

Have students explore suggested ways of connecting the past to the present on page 951.

Answer to . . .

Viewing History Students should use this question as an aid in reading the chapter. People were able to forget the Watergate scandal and economic recession as they became involved in nationwide celebrations, parades, and concerts.

930

CHAPTER 33 The Post-Watergate Period

1974–1980

VIEWING HISTORY The fireworks shown here at Independence Hall in Philadelphia were part of the country's 200th birthday celebration. *Culture* **How did the bicentennial celebration help revive a sense of optimism in the United States?**

CHAPTER FOCUS

This chapter describes the years of the post-Watergate period when upheaval from the scandal continued to disrupt American society. Gerald Ford, the man who assumed the presidency after Nixon, tried to revive the confidence that had sustained the United States through past troubles. He was replaced after two years in office by a newcomer to national politics, Jimmy Carter, who promised the country honesty and morality.

The *Why Study History?* page at the end of this chapter explores the issue of trust in government, in the 1970s and today.

▶ RESOURCE OPTIONS

Teaching Resources

 Big Idea Graphic Organizer folder
Graphic summary of the main idea of the chapter.

Learning Styles Lesson Plans folder
Alternate lesson plans for diverse learning styles for each chapter.

Media and Technology

 AmericanHeritage® CD-ROM
Time Tour The Nation Today and Tomorrow: A Time for Turmoil

 Prentice Hall United States History Video Collection™ Volume 20
Post-War USA

| 1974 | 1974 | 1974 | 1975 | | 1976 |
| Gerald Ford becomes President after Nixon resigns | Ford grants Nixon presidential pardon | Ford presents WIN economic program | U.S. Marines rescue Mayaguez crew | 1975 Helsinki Accords | United States celebrates bicentennial |

1974   **1975**   **1976**

1 The Ford Administration

SECTION PREVIEW

Objectives

1. Describe how Gerald Ford became President and why he pardoned Richard Nixon.
2. Summarize the economic problems faced by the Ford administration.
3. Explain the foreign policy challenges that faced Ford.
4. Describe the importance of the nation's 200th birthday celebration.
5. *Key Terms* Define: stagflation; recession; War Powers Act; Helsinki Accords; bicentennial.

Main Idea

After becoming President, Gerald Ford worked to reunite the country. He faced economic problems at home as well as foreign policy challenges abroad.

Reading Strategy

Outlining Information Skim the section and use the headings and subheadings to create an outline for the section. As you read, fill in appropriate supporting details under each heading.

Objectives

You may wish to call students' attention to the objectives in the Section Preview. The objectives are reflected in the main headings of the section.

Bellringer

Ask students to think of a time when they excused, or forgave, a friend, classmate, or family member. What does offering a pardon imply about the guilt or innocence of the person pardoned?

Reading Strategy

Organizing Information Refer to the Reading Strategy in the Section Preview. You may wish to point out the first heading and subheadings to help students begin.

The new President, Gerald R. Ford, faced a difficult job. He had to help the United States emerge from its worst political scandal. At the same time, the economy was in trouble and the war in Vietnam had ended in defeat. At the start, Ford lost considerable support with a well-meant pardon for Richard Nixon. In the months that followed, he never recovered from the loss of support.

Ford Becomes President

"Jerry" Ford was one of the most popular politicians in Washington when he was appointed Vice President in October 1973. (Vice President Spiro Agnew had resigned in disgrace for accepting bribes.) Ford had been in the House of Representatives since 1948, rising to become Minority Leader in 1965. He was an unassuming Republican from Michigan who believed in traditional American virtues like hard work and self-reliance. Ford had been a football star at the University of Michigan. He played on the national championship teams of 1932 and

1933, then with the College All-Stars. After earning a law degree and serving in the navy during World War II, he entered politics.

Ford described himself as "conservative in fiscal affairs, moderate in domestic affairs, internationalist in foreign affairs." His stands on issues reflected those points of view. Over the years, he had opposed much government spending—federal aid to education, the antipoverty program, and spending for mass transit. He supported measures for law and order and defense spending.

Nixon chose Ford as a noncontroversial figure who might bolster his own support in Congress. When Ford was confirmed as Vice President, Congress and the public were interested mainly in his reputation for honesty, integrity, and stability. Some, however, questioned whether he was qualified to take over the presidency if that became necessary.

Vice President Gerald Ford became President after Richard Nixon resigned in August 1974.

LESSON PLAN

Connecting to the Main Idea

1. Focus Explain that when Vice President Ford stepped up to the presidency after Nixon resigned in 1974, Americans were cheered by his honesty. However, Ford's administration failed to provide strong leadership. Ask what problems it faced.

2. Instruct Review the constitutional requirements for the office of President and discuss Ford's qualifications. What about Ford made him suitable as Nixon's Vice President, but less suitable as President? Discuss Ford's reasons for pardoning Nixon. Then review the public reaction to Ford's well-intentioned action.

Discuss the efforts of the Ford administration to control inflation and increase productivity. Ask students to consider the results of these efforts. Why did the WIN program fail?

3. Close Since President Ford's administration failed to develop and carry out coherent policies, Ford was not perceived as a strong leader. The next section describes the 1976 presidential campaign.

▶ RESOURCE OPTIONS

Teaching Resources

📁 **Reproducible Lesson Plan** Lesson Plans folder, p. 166

📁 **Big Idea Graphic Organizer** Big Idea Graphic Organizer folder, p. 138

📁 **Guided Reading and Review** Units 9–10 folder, p. 73

Media and Technology

 AmericanHeritage® CD-ROM

Time Tour The Nation Today and Tomorrow: A Time of Turmoil

About the Presidents

Gerald Ford (1974–1977) became the first President to reach the White House by way of the Twenty-fifth Amendment and provided the nation with a "time to heal" after the Watergate scandal. Raised in a modest Midwestern home, he used his athletic ability to gain entrance into the University of Michigan, where he not only starred on the football team, but received good enough grades to enter the Yale Law School. After earning his law degree, he joined the Navy in the dark days of 1942 and fought in the Pacific, serving until 1946. Upon entering politics, he rose quickly through Republican ranks. All these experiences shaped Ford, who would always be essentially conservative, optimistic, and loyal to the institutions under which he thrived. Source: Adapted from Henry F. Graff's *The Presidents,* Scribner's, 1984, by the editors of *American Heritage* magazine.

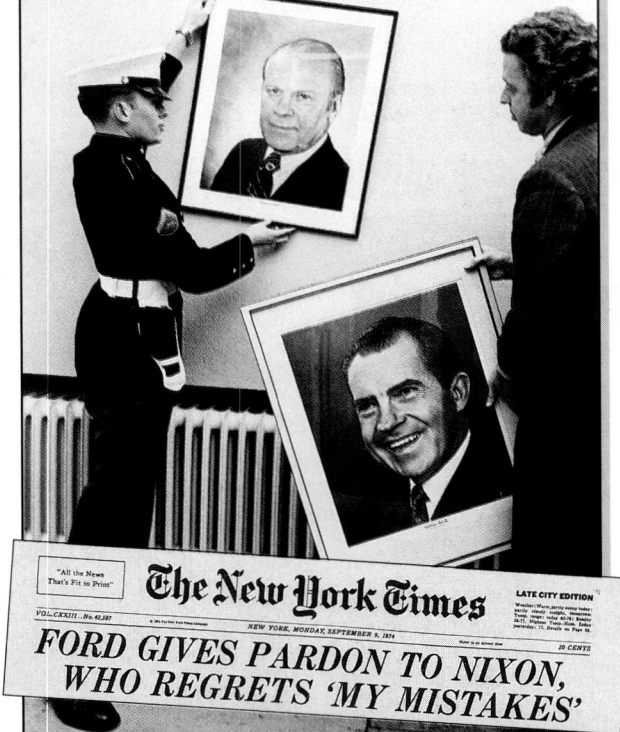

THE NEW YORK TIMES

FORD GIVES PARDON TO NIXON, WHO REGRETS 'MY MISTAKES'

Betty Ford described her husband as "an accidental Vice President, and an accidental President, and in both jobs he replaced disgraced leaders." *Culture* What was the popular reaction to Ford's pardoning of Richard Nixon?

Despite Ford's long experience in Congress, he had little experience as an administrator or in foreign affairs. Ford acknowledged his own limitations when he was sworn in, saying, "I am a Ford, not a Lincoln."

When Nixon resigned in August 1974, Ford became the first nonelected President. Other Vice Presidents who had moved into the White House had been elected to the vice presidency as part of the national ticket. To fill the vice-presidential vacancy, Ford named former New York governor Nelson Rockefeller. This created the unique situation of having both a President and a Vice President who had been appointed, not elected.

The Nixon Pardon

Ford became President in the midst of what he called "our long national nightmare." The nation was disillusioned by Watergate. During the scandal, many Americans had wondered whether the Constitution would survive their leader's actions. Few people looked forward to the prospect of an impeachment trial. It would have been only the second in United States history, after that of Andrew Johnson in 1868. When Ford assumed the presidency, the nation needed a leader who could take it beyond the ugliness of Watergate.

In response to this public mood, President Ford declared that it was a time for "communication, conciliation, compromise and cooperation." Americans were on his side. *Time* magazine noted "a mood of good feeling and even exhilaration in Washington that the city had not experienced for many years."

All too quickly, Ford lost some popular support. On September 8, barely a month after Nixon had resigned, Ford pardoned the former President for "all offenses" he might have committed, avoiding further prosecution. On national television, Ford explained that he had looked to God and his own conscience in deciding "the right thing" to do about Nixon and "his loyal wife and family":

AMERICAN VOICES 66Theirs is an American tragedy in which we have all played a part. It could go on and on and on, or someone must write the end to it. I have concluded that only I can do that, and if I can I must. . . . My conscience tells me that only I, as President, have the constitutional power to firmly shut and seal this book. My conscience tells me that it is my duty not merely to proclaim domestic tranquillity but to use every means that I have to ensure it.99

—President Ford

Ford expected criticism of the pardon, but he underestimated the widespread negative reaction. Many of Nixon's loyalists were facing prison for their role in Watergate. The former President, however, walked away without a penalty. Although some people supported his action, Ford's generous gesture backfired. Some people suggested that a bargain had been made when Nixon resigned. Many also criticized the new President's judgment. Ford occasionally was booed when he made public speeches, just as Johnson and Nixon had been. To counter the reactions, he went before a House committee in October to explain his reasons. Still angry, the public voted a number of Republicans out of office in the 1974 congressional elections.

Answer to . . .

Viewing History Widespread disapproval.

TEST PREPARATION

Have students read the quotation by President Ford on this page and then answer the question below.

The word *tranquillity* in the passage means—

(A) calm.

B happiness.

C power.

D tragedy.

"Stagflation," 1970–1979

UNEMPLOYMENT

INFLATION

Source: *Statistical Abstract of the United States*

 Interpreting Graphs Upon assuming office President Ford declared war on inflation, calling it "Public Enemy No. 1." Ford's administration, however, saw the worst economic slump in the United States since the Great Depression. *Economics In what year were consumer prices highest in the 1970s? When did unemployment peak in this decade?*

Economic Problems

The aftermath of Watergate was not the only difficult issue Ford faced. While focused on the scandal, the nation seemed to have stood still. Some conditions had grown worse. Now, facing a hostile Congress, the new administration found it hard to provide direction.

The Economy Stalls Months of preoccupation with Watergate had kept President Nixon from dealing with economic difficulties. By 1974 inflation was at about 11 percent, significantly higher than it had been in the past, while unemployment climbed to 5.6 percent. Home building, usually a sign of a healthy economy, slowed as interest rates rose. The fears of worried investors brought a drop in stock prices.

Usually, federal policymakers had to deal with either inflation—due to a rapidly growing economy—or unemployment, due to a slow economy. Most economists believed that each of those trends could balance out the other. For example, a moderate rise in inflation would help lower the rate of unemployment. Now, however, inflation and unemployment both rose, while the economy remained stalled and stagnant. Economists named this new situation **stagflation.**

By the time Ford assumed the presidency, the country was in a **recession,** a period of slow business activity. Not since Franklin Roosevelt took office during the Great Depression had a new President faced such harsh economic troubles.

Ford's approach (like Herbert Hoover's in the early 1930s) was to try to restore public confidence. Early in October 1974, he sent Congress an economic program called "WIN," or "Whip Inflation Now." The President asked Americans to wear red and white "WIN" buttons, to save instead of spending, conserve fuel, and plant vegetable gardens to counter high grocery store prices. The WIN campaign depended on people voluntarily changing their everyday actions, but had no real incentives. It soon faded away.

Eventually, Ford recognized the need for more direct action. The Federal Reserve tightened the money supply to control inflation, but that made the recession worse. There were widespread job layoffs. Unemployment soared to almost 8 percent in 1975. Congress then backed an anti-recession spending program. Despite his belief in less government spending, Ford backed an increase in unemployment benefits and a multibillion dollar tax cut. The economy recovered slightly, but inflation and unemployment remained high.

Main Idea CONNECTIONS

What economic problems did the Ford administration face?

Conflicts with Congress In spite of his long experience as a congressional leader, President Ford was often at odds with the Democratic-controlled Congress. He basically believed in limited government, while Congress wanted more government action in the economy.

ACTIVITY EXTENDED CLASS PERIODS

Time: 90 minutes.
Activity: Create a public relations campaign for a presidential program.
Grouping: Groups of four students.
Purpose: To create a program designed to increase public acceptance of Ford's WIN campaign and then rate the campaign's potential effectiveness.
Roles: Planners, writers, editors, media and marketing specialists.
Outcome: Students will identify key aspects of Ford's WIN program and analyze its potential.

Customize for
Less Proficient Readers

Ask students to find evidence in the text to help them assess President Ford's effectiveness in healing the wounds of Watergate, restoring the health of the economy, and maintaining peace and good relationships with other nations. Have them work together create a report card to record their assessments, including comments.

▶ RESOURCE OPTIONS

Teaching Resources

American History Block Scheduling Support Presidential Power: Changes in the Twentieth Century, found in The Nation After World War II folder, includes interdisciplinary lesson suggestions and activities for Geography and History, Primary Sources, Biography, and Literature.

Media and Technology

 AmericanHeritage® CD-ROM

Presidents Gerald Ford

Answer to . . .

Interpreting Graphs 1979; 1975.
Main Idea Connections Inflation, high unemployment, economic recession.

Jerold F. terHorst, Ford's first press secretary, noted how Ford's own sense of decency came into conflict with his view of government:

 AMERICAN VOICES ❝If he saw a schoolkid in front of the White House who needed clothing, he'd give him the shirt off his back, literally. Then he'd go right in the White House and veto a school-lunch bill.❞

— *Jerold F. terHorst*

Ford vetoed bills to create a consumer protection agency and to fund programs for education, housing, and health care. Congress responded by overriding a higher percentage of vetoes than it had since the presidency of Franklin Pierce in the 1850s.

Foreign Policy Actions

In foreign policy Ford generally followed Nixon's approach, working for détente. He kept Henry Kissinger on as Secretary of State. In 1974 and 1975 Ford made a series of trips abroad. He met with European leaders and

 Continuing Nixon's policy of détente, President Ford (right), shown with Soviet General Secretary Leonid Brezhnev (left), signed the Helsinki Accords in Finland in 1975. *Government What were the Helsinki Accords?*

was the first American President to visit Japan. Ford also visited China in order to continue to improve the political and trade ties that Nixon had initiated. As revolutions in Africa and elsewhere around the world toppled colonial governments, the administration acted to develop relationships with the new regimes.

War Powers Act Ford bore the legacy of Nixon's relationship with Congress. Irritated at the growth of the "imperial presidency," Congress had passed the **War Powers Act** in 1973 over Nixon's veto. Under this law, a President can send troops overseas only if there is a declaration of war, a specific law is passed, or if there is a national emergency. There are limits on his emergency powers:

(1) The President can send troops but must notify Congress within 48 hours.

(2) Troops may not stay overseas more than 60 days without congressional approval.

(3) Congress can demand that the President bring troops home by passing a concurrent resolution.

Southeast Asia The involvement of the United States in Vietnam was officially over. In the spring of 1975, however, North Vietnam began a new offensive against the South. Ford asked for military aid for South Vietnam, but Congress used the War Powers Act to say no. Most Americans also had no wish to become involved in Vietnam again. By late April, the South Vietnamese capital, Saigon, was about to fall. Ford agreed to an American airlift that helped evacuate thousands of people, both Americans and Vietnamese.

Southeast Asia remained a foreign policy problem. In May 1975, soldiers from Communist Cambodia (which had fallen to the Khmer Rouge) captured the *Mayaguez,* an American merchant ship cruising in Cambodian waters. When protests went unanswered, Ford sent the marines to recapture the ship. Although the rescue succeeded, 41 Americans were killed. Later investigations showed that the Cambodian government apparently was preparing to return both ship and crew. For the administration, however, the incident was a chance to counteract the impression of American weakness in Southeast Asia.

Europe and the Soviet Union On another foreign policy front, President Ford signed the

Helsinki Accords, a series of agreements on European security made at a 1975 summit meeting in Finland. The United States, Canada, the Soviet Union, and about 30 European countries pledged to cooperate economically, respect existing national boundaries, and promote human rights. Ford also continued Strategic Arms Limitation Talks (SALT) with the Soviet Union, holding out hope for further limits on nuclear weapons.

The Nation's Birthday

Looking for a way to forget Watergate and the recession, Americans held a nationwide birthday party. July 4, 1976, marked the **bicentennial,** or the 200th anniversary, of the Declaration of Independence. Throughout the summer, people in small towns and great cities across the country celebrated with parades, concerts, air shows, political speeches, and fireworks.

The climax of the national party was the Fourth of July itself. In New York City, more than 200 sailing ships, including majestic "tall

A parade of majestic tall ships during the nation's bicentennial celebration reminded the country of its long and glorious past. *History What image do these tall ships portray of the nation's past?*

ships," sailed into the harbor while millions watched from the shore. Other cities competed to have the most spectacular fireworks display or the longest parade. Many observers saw the bicentennial mood as an optimistic revival after years of gloom.

SECTION 1 REVIEW

Comprehension

1. **Key Terms** Define: (a) stagflation; (b) recession; (c) War Powers Act; (d) Helsinki Accords; (e) bicentennial.

2. **Summarizing the Main Idea** What were the major issues facing Gerald Ford when he became President?

3. **Organizing Information** Create a web with *U.S. Economy* at the center, showing the different problems and pressures that affected the economy during the 1970s.

Critical Thinking

4. **Analyzing Time Lines** Review the time line at the start of the section. Write a sentence that explains the broader effect of each event.

5. **Predicting Consequences** Should Gerald Ford have pardoned Richard Nixon? What might have happened if he had not done so?

Writing Activity

6. **Writing an Expository Essay** Imagine that you are the editorial writer for a local newspaper in 1976. Write the lead editorial for the bicentennial edition of the paper, explaining the historical background of this event and why it is still important.

Answer to . . .

Viewing History Dignity and strength.

February 1976	August 1976	November 1976	January 1977
Jimmy Carter wins New Hampshire primary	Gerald Ford wins Republican nomination	Carter wins presidential election	Jimmy Carter is sworn in as President

1976　　　　　　　　　　　　　　　　　　**1977**

SECTION 2

The Carter Transition

Objectives

You may wish to call students' attention to the objectives in the Section Preview. The objectives are reflected in the main headings of the section.

Bellringer

Ask students how they would rate the honesty of the current President and administration. Ask if they can envision any situation in which a President should be less than completely open and honest with the public.

Reading Strategy

Outlining Information Refer to the Reading Strategy in the Section Preview. You may wish to draw a sample web diagram on the chalkboard as a model for students.

LESSON PLAN

Connecting to the Main Idea

1. Focus Explain that in 1976, Jimmy Carter, former governor of Georgia, was elected President. Ask what promises Carter made to the American people.

2. Instruct Discuss how Ford's failure to convey a "presidential" image on television affected the election of 1976. Ask students which recent President they think had the strongest "presidential" image, and whether that President was also a good leader.

Discuss how Carter's outsider status, and his choice of other outsiders as his key advisers, hampered his ability to work with Congress.

3. Close In 1976 American voters selected Jimmy Carter, a Washington outsider, as the nation's new President. Carter, who had a small-town background and strong religious beliefs, vowed to bring honesty to government. The next section focuses on Carter's foreign policy.

2 The Carter Transition

SECTION PREVIEW

Objectives

1 Explain the background and outcome of the 1976 presidential election.
2 Describe Barbara Jordan's political career.
3 Summarize the changes that Carter brought to the office of the presidency.
4 *Key Terms* Define: incumbent.

Main Idea

Partly in reaction to Watergate, voters in 1976 elected a little-known Democrat, Jimmy Carter of Georgia, who stressed trust and honesty in his campaign for the presidency.

Reading Strategy

Outlining Information Write *Jimmy Carter* in the center of a web diagram. As you read the section, note major details about Carter in surrounding circles.

One writer described Jimmy Carter's famous smile as "the biggest grin of any President since TR."

The 1976 party conventions brought surprises for both political parties. Even though Ford was the **incumbent**—the current office holder—he faced strong opposition from conservatives inside his own Republican party. At the beginning of the campaign, few Americans even recognized the name of Jimmy Carter, a former governor of Georgia. "Jimmy who?" they asked. By the time of the convention, though, James Earl Carter, Jr., easily won the Democratic nomination.

The Election of 1976

Gerald Ford had initially said that he would not seek election to the office he had inherited, but by 1976 he had changed his mind. A number of qualities, however, continued to hurt his chances. While most people liked him, they said that Ford did not appear "presidential,"

and he never fully won the people's confidence. The press joked about his supposed clumsiness. Ford faced a strong challenge in the primaries from Ronald Reagan, an affable former actor and governor of California, who was backed by conservative Republicans. At the convention in August, Ford won the nomination by a close vote. He chose Kansas senator Robert Dole as his vice-presidential running mate.

Carter's Campaign The Democratic candidate, Jimmy Carter, was a relative newcomer to politics. Nationally, he began as a virtual unknown with a broad smile and soft southern accent. After taking the New Hampshire primary in February, he kept up a skillful campaign and appealed to a wide audience. A white southerner, Carter had the support of civil rights leaders because of his stand against racial discrimination in Georgia. His running mate was Walter Mondale, a senator from Minnesota.

Carter's campaign played on the distrust of politicians that followed Watergate. He

▶ RESOURCE OPTIONS

Teaching Resources

📁 **Reproducible Lesson Plan** Lesson Plans folder, p. 167

📁 **Big Idea Graphic Organizer** Big Idea Graphic Organizer folder, p. 139

📁 **Guided Reading and Review** Units 9–10 folder, p. 75

Media and Technology

💿📼 **Decision America Videotapes and Videodiscs** Issue 4 *Who Tells Us What to Think?*

stressed that he was not a lawyer and not part of the Washington establishment. He said he would bring a new perspective to the nation's capital. Carter emphasized the themes of honesty and straightforwardness.

Carter's appeal succeeded. The basic issue in 1976 was trust, and he used it well. His status as an outsider was another advantage. Patrick Caddell, a public opinion pollster, noted that people "had no reason to distrust him [Carter] and he didn't give them one." In addition, the state of the economy hurt Ford's chances.

Election Results Carter took an early lead in the campaign. He then nearly lost it as voters wondered whether he could be a national leader. Ford hurt his own cause with a number of embarrassing mistakes. During a television debate, for instance, he declared that the Soviets did not dominate Eastern Europe.

In the end, Carter gained the support of most factions of the old Democratic coalition. He was successful with blue-collar, African American, and some Catholic voters. Also, as the map at right shows, he won back most of the South. Though Democrats in races for Congress and local contests generally swept the election, Carter had only a narrow margin of the popular vote. The electoral vote, 297 to 240, was also close.

Barbara Jordan

AMERICAN BIOGRAPHY Jimmy Carter's nomination was not the only exciting event of the 1976 Democratic National Convention in New York City. Another highlight was the stirring keynote speech by Representative Barbara Jordan of Texas. Jordan was both the first woman and the first African American to address a national convention. In a rich, deep speaking voice, she pointed out that there was "something special about tonight":

Presidential Election of 1976

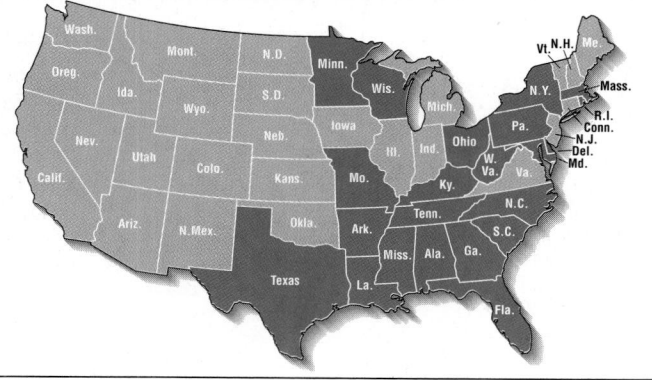

Candidate/Party	Electoral Vote	Popular Vote	% Electoral Vote	% Popular Vote
Jimmy Carter (Democrat)	297	40,827,394	55.3	49.9
Gerald R. Ford (Republican)	240	39,145,977	44.7	47.9
Minor parties		1,577,333		2.2

 Notice the regional voting pattern shown in this map. *Regions* What do you know about each candidate's background that might help to explain it?

AMERICAN VOICES **"A lot of years have passed since 1832 [the first Democratic convention] and during that time it would have been most unusual for any national political party to ask that Barbara Jordan deliver a keynote address, but tonight here I am. And I feel notwithstanding the past that my presence here is one additional bit of evidence that the American Dream need not forever be deferred."**

—*Barbara Jordan*

Barbara Jordan's political career included many "firsts." Born in Houston in 1936, she grew up in a segregated southern society. She graduated from Texas Southern University, where she led the debating team, then earned a law degree from Boston University in 1959. She considered staying in the North but returned to Houston to practice law. She was elected to the Texas state legislature in 1966—the first African American in the state senate since Reconstruction. People

Barbara Jordan (1936–1996)

RESOURCE OPTIONS

Teaching Resources

 Key Documents Barbara Jordan, Keynote Address to the Democratic National Convention, Learning with Documents folder, p. 105

ACTIVITY
STUDENT PORTFOLIO

You may wish to have students add the following to their portfolios. To assess student work, refer to the generic rubrics in the Program Overview in the Teaching Resources.

To help students understand the central issues of the 1976 presidential campaign, ask them to write a brief press release. Present to the class one of the broad themes of either the Carter or Ford campaign. Members of the class, acting as the press, may address questions to each "press official."

Answer to . . .

Map Skills Ford, a midwesterner, carried most of the Midwest and the West, while Carter, a southerner, carried the South.

Abandoning the traditional limousine ride, President Jimmy Carter takes an inaugural stroll with his wife, Rosalynn, and daughter, Amy. **Government** *How did Carter hope to be a different kind of President?*

Graphing the Main Idea

To make sure students understand the main idea of this section, you may wish to use the web graphic organizer below.

Tell students that a web records a main idea with its supporting details. Ask them to use it to record details about Carter's presidency.

Teaching Tip A template for this graphic organizer can be found in the Color Transparencies, G-1.

soon recognized Jordan as an outstanding leader and an inspiring speaker. In June 1972, fellow members of the state legislature named her "Governor for a Day," a traditional honor for outstanding state legislators.

Winning election to the House of Representatives that fall, Jordan was again "first"—the first woman and the first African American from Texas. As a member of the House Judiciary Committee, Jordan took part in the Watergate hearings in July 1974. Her strong opinions were based on her belief that Nixon's actions threatened the Constitution.

Jordan was reelected to the House for two more terms, in 1974 and 1976. Retiring from politics in 1978, she taught political ethics at the Lyndon B. Johnson School of Public Affairs (University of Texas). Jordan was again the keynote speaker at the Democratic convention in 1992. She died in 1996. ■

Carter's Presidency

Jimmy Carter, a southerner with no national political experience, was different from his recent predecessors in the White House. His family had lived for generations in the rural South. A 1946 graduate of the United States Naval Academy, Carter served as an engineering officer on nuclear submarines. When his father died, he took over management of the family's prosperous peanut farm and warehouse. He did not enter politics until 1962, and was elected governor of Georgia in 1970.

Main Idea
CONNECTIONS

How did Carter's background shape his approach to the presidency?

Carter was a born-again Baptist who noted that his life had been "shaped in the church." His deeply felt religious faith was central to his view of the world. His faith, he believed, would keep him from taking on "the same frame of mind that Nixon or Johnson did—lying, cheating, and distorting the truth."

While holding his own strong religious beliefs, Carter respected those of others. In campaigning he emphasized his belief in the "absolute and total separation of church and state." In Georgia, for instance, he had opposed prayer in the public schools.

Approach to the Presidency In the first months of Carter's presidency, he appeared to be a strong supporter of social programs and political activism. When he accepted his party's nomination, he demanded "an end to discrimination because of race or sex." He also challenged the established "political and economic elite" and suggested new welfare and health care programs.

The new President appointed significantly more women and minorities to his staff than previous administrations had done. Of about 1,200 full-time appointees, 12 percent were women, 12 percent were African American, and another 4 percent were Hispanic. In nominating federal judges, he chose four times as many women as had all previous Presidents combined.

In other areas, especially the economy, Carter moved away from Democratic stands. He supported spending cuts, which were meant to reduce inflation but which hit social programs. As a result, support from his own party began to

RESOURCE OPTIONS

Teaching Resources

Biography Patricia Roberts Harris, Units 9–10 folder, p. 81

Answer to . . .

Viewing History He hoped to have an administration free of dishonesty and cheating.

Main Idea Connections He was determined to lead an honest presidency, and he respected the religious beliefs of others.

dwindle. Since he had won by only a narrow margin, other Democrats felt they owed him less than if he had had a sweeping victory. The press, too, became more critical as the Carter presidency seemed to lose its momentum.

Staff Problems The "Washington outsider" role turned out to have disadvantages. The White House staff and other close advisers were also southerners, mostly Georgians. They had little sense of how crucial it was for the President to work with Congress. Carter himself was uneasy with Congress's demands and found it difficult to get legislation passed. He had no experience or former colleagues in Congress. He lacked Lyndon Johnson's ability to win over reluctant politicians.

Carter also suffered from hints of scandal in an administration that took pride in being pure. Banker Bert Lance, the director of the Office of Management and Budget, was an old friend from Georgia. When Lance was accused of having allowed large bank overdrafts and other irregularities in his bank, Carter at first strongly defended him. Finally Carter had to conclude that Lance must resign.

Carter's brother Billy posed another problem. He was an irreverent character who relished the attention he received as part of the presidential family. His careless comments were embarrassing. When he accepted $200,000 in "loans" from friends in Libya, it looked as if family business was entwined with foreign affairs.

Personal Style At first, people responded warmly to Carter's "down home" approach.

The Carters brought a folksy style to the presidency. In spite of the President's low-key image, he was known among friends as a "super-achiever." One friend called Carter "the most disciplined person I've ever seen." **Government** *Why do you think Carter's style appealed to many people?*

They loved it when he and his wife, Rosalynn, dismissed their limousine after the inauguration and strolled down Pennsylvania Avenue with their young daughter. He spoke to the nation on television wearing a cardigan sweater instead of a business suit. He cut out many of the ceremonial details of White House life, such as trumpets to announce his entrance at official receptions. Some critics, however, began to complain about a lack of dignity and ceremony.

Carter finally moderated his low-key approach. After a while, he let the band play "Hail to the Chief" on "special occasions," noting, "I found it to be impressive and enjoyed it."

SECTION 2 REVIEW

Comprehension

1. **Key Terms** Define: incumbent.
2. **Summarizing the Main Idea** What were the major issues that won the presidency for Jimmy Carter?
3. **Organizing Information** Create a two-column chart to compare the two candidates in the 1976 election.

Critical Thinking

4. **Analyzing Time Lines** Review the time line at the start of the section. Write a sentence or phrase that explains the significance of each event.

5. **Identifying Central Issues** What was special about having Barbara Jordan as the keynote speaker at the 1976 Democratic convention?

Writing Activity

6. **Writing a Persuasive Essay** Imagine that you are the chairperson of a political rally for either Jerry Ford or Jimmy Carter during the 1976 campaign. Write the speech in which you will introduce your candidate, stressing ideas and issues that will make the audience welcome and support him.

1977	1978	1979	1979	1979	1981
Carter signs Panama Canal treaties	Egypt and Israel work toward peace in the Camp David Accords	U.S. establishes diplomatic relations with People's Republic of China	Carter and Brezhnev sign SALT II agreement	Iranian revolutionaries take Americans hostage	Iranian hostages return home

1977　　　**1979**　　　**1981**

SECTION 3

Carter's Foreign Policy

Objectives

You may wish to call students' attention to the objectives in the Section Preview. The objectives are reflected in the main headings of the section.

Bellringer

Ask students to list the rights that they would include in a definition of the term *human rights*.

Reading Strategy

Formulating Questions Refer to the Reading Strategy in the Section Preview. You may wish to have students offer sample questions derived from the main idea as models for their classmates.

LESSON PLAN
Connecting to the Main Idea

1. Focus Point out that President Carter's greatest successes were in foreign policy. Ask what those successes were. How did Carter's stand on certain issues create tensions with other nations?

2. Instruct Ask students to use their list from the Bellringer activity to create a definition of human rights. Have them compare their definitions with that of the Carter administration.

Ask why boycotting the Olympic Games was a serious demonstration of dissatisfaction with the Soviet invasion of Afghanistan. How did the grain embargo hurt the Soviet Union?

Review the events leading up to the Iran hostage crisis. Ask what other measures Carter might have taken to free the hostages. Why was the situation so frustrating for Americans?

3. Close Carter tried to emphasize human rights and peacemaking in his foreign policy, but his actions complicated United States relationships with the Soviet Union and Iran. The hostage crisis in Iran cost Carter much support in the United States.

3 Carter's Foreign Policy

SECTION PREVIEW

Objectives

1　Explain Carter's support for human rights and his accomplishments in the Middle East.
2　Discuss the new policy directions Carter took in foreign affairs and the complex relationship between the United States and the Soviet Union.
3　Describe how the Iran hostage crisis began and ended.
4　*Key Terms* Define: shuttle diplomacy; Camp David Accords; dissident.

Main Idea

Carter's religious beliefs and principles led him to emphasize peacemaking and human rights in foreign affairs. This approach brought some notable results but caused disagreements with the Soviet Union and a crisis with Iran.

Reading Strategy

Formulating Questions Reread the main idea above. Then rewrite it as a question. As you read the section, look for answers to your question.

Although Jimmy Carter had little diplomatic experience when he took office, his personal high standards greatly influenced decisions he made about foreign affairs. During the campaign he had declared, "Peace is the unceasing effort to preserve human rights . . . a combined demonstration of strength and goodwill." The emphasis he placed on human rights brought notable achievements, but complicated the relationship of the United States with some nations.

Human Rights Diplomacy

Support for human rights was the cornerstone of Carter's foreign policy. In his inaugural speech, he declared, "Our commitment to human rights must be absolute. . . . We can never be indifferent to the fate of freedom elsewhere."

Later Carter wrote, "Our country has been strongest and most effective when morality and a commitment to freedom and democracy have been most clearly emphasized in our foreign policy." Since the Truman era the country had not kept to that standard, he went on:

 AMERICAN VOICES

"Instead of promoting freedom and democratic principles, our government seemed to believe that in any struggle with evil, we could not compete effectively unless we played by the same rules or lack of rules as the evildoers. . . . When I announced my candidacy in December 1974, I expressed a dream: 'That this country set a standard within the community of nations of courage, compassion, integrity, and dedication to basic human rights and freedoms.'"

—*Jimmy Carter*

A Step Toward Middle East Peace

Carter's commitment to finding ethical solutions to complicated problems was most visible in the Middle East. In that unstable region, conflicts between Israel and the Arab nations had existed for nearly 30 years, most recently in 1967 and 1973. After the last Arab-Israeli war, Henry Kissinger had undertaken **shuttle diplomacy,** traveling back and forth between

 RESOURCE OPTIONS

Teaching Resources

📁 **Reproducible Lesson Plan** Lesson Plans folder, p. 168

📁 **Learning Styles Lesson Plan** Learning Styles Lesson Plans folder, p. 68

📁 **Big Idea Graphic Organizer** Big Idea Graphic Organizer folder, p. 140

📁 **Guided Reading and Review** Units 9–10 folder, p. 77

Media and Technology

 AmericanHeritage® **CD-ROM**

Time Tour The Nation Today and Tomorrow: New Directions

nations in an attempt to arrange peace. Differences still remained.

At first, Carter hoped to call an international conference on the Middle East. Then Egypt's president Anwar el-Sadat made a historic visit to Israel to begin negotiations with Prime Minister Menachem Begin. The two men had such different personalities, however, that they had trouble compromising. Carter intervened, sending Secretary of State Cyrus Vance to invite them to Camp David, the rustic presidential retreat in the Maryland hills. In such a setting, he hoped that he could smooth their differences and move the peace process forward.

Carter knew it was a bold step. In his diary entry for July 31, 1978, he wrote, "We understand the political pitfalls involved, but the situation is getting into an extreme state." He and the two Middle Eastern leaders maintained tight secrecy about the coming conference.

At Camp David in September 1978, Carter assumed the role of peacemaker. He practiced highly effective personal diplomacy to bridge the gap between Sadat and Begin. They finally agreed on a framework for peace that became known as the **Camp David Accords.** Under the resulting peace treaty, Israel would withdraw from the Sinai peninsula, which it had occupied in 1967. Egypt, in return, became the first Arab country to recognize Israel's existence as a nation.

The Camp David Accords, of course, did not solve all the problems of the Middle East. Among the remaining problems was the question of what to do about the Palestinians. Many had fled their homes when Arab nations declared war on Israel immediately after that country was established in 1948. Still, as Secretary of State Vance noted:

 AMERICAN VOICES "The Camp David Accords rank as one of the most important achievements of the Carter administration. First, they opened the way to peace between Egypt and Israel, which transformed the entire political, military, and strategic character of the Middle East dispute. Genuine peace between Egypt and Israel meant there would be no major Arab-Israeli war, whatever the positions of [other Arab groups]."

—*Cyrus Vance*

Moreover, Vance pointed out, the agreement also let negotiators focus on the Palestinian question. It established a process for future talks.

VIEWING HISTORY

A jubilant President Carter congratulates Egypt's President Sadat (left) and Israel's Prime Minister Begin (right) on the signing of the Camp David Accords. *Foreign Relations What were the major achievements of the accords?*

New Policy Directions

Carter's foreign policy team took new steps in other parts of the world as well. Often these reflected the President's own philosophy. In Latin America, for example, the United States had for years backed military dictators against Communist or leftist rebels. Now the United States stopped helping regimes that seriously abused human rights, such as those in Nicaragua and Chile.

Main Idea CONNECTIONS

How did Carter's principles influence his policies regarding Latin America?

The Panama Canal Another diplomatic milestone was Carter's successful fight to have the Senate ratify treaties that would return the Panama Canal to Panama. In the early 1900s, President Theodore Roosevelt was proud of the way he had gained control of land for the canal. Now, however, many Latin Americans resented the continuing United States presence. For Carter, the treaties were a way to show that the United States could deal fairly with smaller nations.

The canal treaties, signed in 1977, caused bitter debate in Congress. In 1978 the Senate

Customize for
More Advanced Students

Have students analyze to what extent a President's personal beliefs should affect administration policy and presidential actions. Ask whether or not Carter's insertion of his own morality into his foreign policy was appropriate. Responses can take the form of a speech either defending Carter's use of personal morality in formulating policy, or criticizing it.

ACTIVITY
HETEROGENEOUS GROUPS

To emphasize the importance of the Carter administration in bringing stability to the Middle East, divide students into groups of three to form peace negotiation teams. Each group should assign one student to play Anwar el-Sadat of Egypt, another to be Menachem Begin of Israel, and the third to play President Carter. Have each group then role-play the Camp David peace negotiations. *(Enrichment)*

TEST PREPARATION

Have students read the quotation by Cyrus Vance on this page and then answer the question below.

From the passage, you can infer that Vance believed—

A that peace was instantly enacted with the signing of the Accords.

B that the Accords were a minor achievement for Carter.

C that Israel and Egypt were the key players in maintaining peace in the Middle East.

D that the Accords would have no real effect on the region.

Answer to . . .

Viewing History Israel withdrew from the Sinai peninsula, and Egypt recognized Israel.

Main Idea Connections His determination to deal fairly with smaller nations compelled him to work out treaties favorable to both sides.

President Carter and Soviet president Leonid Brezhnev sign SALT II in Vienna, Austria. Carter believed that the arms limitation agreement would "make the world a safer place for both sides." *Foreign Relations Why did relations with the Soviets worsen, despite SALT II?*

Main Idea CONNECTIONS

What were the main provisions of the Panama Canal treaties?

approved them by a margin of one vote. One treaty was an agreement to return the canal to Panama by the year 2000. The other gave the United States the right to take military action to keep it open. The pacts protected American interests while improving relations with Latin America.

Recognition of China Building on Nixon's initiative in Asia, Carter took the next step. He established diplomatic relations with the People's Republic of China as of January 1979. The Chinese wanted American technology and expertise in modernizing their country. The United States hoped that closer ties with China would provide an advantage in dealing with the Soviet Union. Businesses in the United States also were eager to open the Chinese market of nearly a billion people.

Africa Great changes were taking place in Africa, where independent nations that had once been European colonies were struggling to create prosperity. Carter had named civil rights leader Andrew Young as the U.S. ambassador to the

United Nations. Young played a large role in policies toward Africa.

Carter called for rule by the black majority in South Africa and in Rhodesia. He also declared that Cuba and the Soviet Union should stop interfering in African nations. When Carter visited Nigeria and Liberia in March 1978, the popularity of this approach was evident as thousands cheered him in the streets.

Soviet-American Relations

Several issues complicated the relationship between the United States and the Soviet Union. Détente—a relaxation of the tensions between the superpowers—was at a high point when Carter took office. In his first year, he declared optimistically that the United States and Soviet Union would forge even closer ties.

Then Carter's stand on human rights alienated Soviet leaders, undermining efforts to work together. The Soviets were annoyed when the President spoke in support of Soviet **dissidents**—writers and other activists who criticized the actions of their government.

SALT II The discord directly affected further agreements on arms control. Negotiations were already under way for a second round of Strategic Arms Limitation Talks (SALT II). Misjudging the Soviets, Carter offered new weapons reduction proposals that went further than earlier agreements. The Soviets were already suspicious of Carter and balked at the proposals.

Nevertheless, in June 1979, Carter and Soviet leader Leonid Brezhnev signed a new treaty in Vienna. More complicated than SALT I, it limited the number of nuclear warheads and missiles each power retained. SALT II still needed Senate approval. Its backers said it would slow the arms race. Opponents claimed it would weaken American defenses.

Afghanistan Late in 1979, before the Senate could ratify SALT II, the Soviet Union invaded Afghanistan, a country on its southern border. It sent troops to end agitation against the Soviet-supported government there.

Carter quickly called Brezhnev on the "hot line," the open telephone line between

Washington and Moscow, and told him that the invasion was "a clear threat to the peace." He also added, "Unless you draw back from your present course of action, this will inevitably jeopardize the course of United States–Soviet relations throughout the world." A United Nations resolution also called for Soviet withdrawal.

Carter halted grain shipments and took other steps to show disapproval of Soviet aggression. Realizing that SALT II surely would be turned down, he did not send it to the Senate. He also imposed a boycott on the 1980 summer Olympic Games to be held in Moscow. Eventually, some 60 other nations joined the Olympic boycott.[†] Détente was effectively dead.

The Iran Hostage Crisis

Iran, Afghanistan's neighbor to the west, was the scene of the worst foreign policy crisis of the Carter administration. For years the United States had supported the rule of Muhammed Reza Shah Pahlevi, who had taken many steps to modernize Iran. Americans overlooked the corruption and harsh repression of the shah's government because he was a reliable supplier of oil and a pro-Western force. Carter himself praised the shah on a visit to Tehran, Iran's capital, in late 1977.

In January 1979, revolution broke out in Iran. It was led by Muslim fundamentalists, who wanted to bring back traditional ways, and by liberal critics of the shah, who wanted more political and economic reforms. As the revolution spread, the shah fled the country. He was replaced by an elderly Islamic leader, the Ayatollah Ruholla Khomeini, who had been in exile.[††] Khomeini and his followers were aggressively anti-Western, determined to make Iran a strict Islamic state.

In October, in what was intended as a humanitarian gesture, Carter let the exiled shah enter the United States for medical treatment. Many Iranians were outraged. On November 4, 1979, angry followers of Khomeini seized the American embassy in Tehran. They took 66 Americans hostage, mostly embassy workers.

[†] In retaliation, the Soviet Union and several other Communist nations boycotted the 1984 Olympic games hosted by the United States in Los Angeles, California.

[††] Ayatollah is a title given to a Shiite Muslim religious leader.

More than 50 men and women were held for over a year. The situation caused bitter animosity between the United States and Iran.

The Hostages' Ordeal For 444 days, revolutionaries kept the hostages prisoner in different locations. The prisoners were blindfolded and moved from place to place. Some were tied up and beaten. Others spent time in solitary confinement and faced mock executions intended to keep them constantly afraid.

Kathryn Koob, a cultural exchange official, described part of her experiences:

 AMERICAN VOICES "And the sounds outside the embassy were nerve-wracking. . . . There seemed to be a continuous crowd of people shouting anti-American slogans, listening to the exhortations [cries] of the students and mullahs [clergymen] who were always on hand. In addition to the crowd noises, there were three or four loudspeakers blaring newscasts. . . . As I sat confined in my chair I thought, I can't take this, I just can't take this."

—*Kathryn Koob*

Meanwhile, the American public became increasingly frustrated and impatient for the hostages' release. Nightly newscasts made the crisis a national issue.

 In spite of the sentiments of anti-American Iranians, personnel from the United States embassy in Tehran, Iran, were freed after being held hostage for more than a year. *Foreign Relations How did Carter try to resolve the hostage crisis?*

Jubilant Americans returned home after being held hostage by Iranians. *Foreign Relations How did Carter's handling of the hostage crisis affect his career?*

in the United States. Khomeini held out, insisting that the shah be sent back for trial. Under pressure, in April 1980, Carter authorized a risky commando rescue mission. It ended in disaster when several helicopters broke down in the desert sands and eight American soldiers were killed. The government was humiliated, and Carter's popularity dropped further. Even after the shah died in July, the standoff continued. The unending crisis damaged Carter's chances for reelection.

Carter himself was torn apart by the crisis. At one point, just weeks after the Americans had been taken prisoner, he confided his feelings to Hamilton Jordan, one of his closest aides:

> **AMERICAN VOICES** ❝You know, I've been worried all week about the hostages as a problem for the country and as a political problem for me. But it wasn't until I saw the grief and hope on the faces of their wives and mothers and fathers that I felt the personal responsibility for their lives. It's an awesome burden. ❞
>
> —*President Carter*

After months of secret talks, the Iranians agreed to release the 52 remaining hostages in early 1981. Not until the day Carter left office, however, were they allowed to come home. The new President, Ronald Reagan, sent Carter to greet the freed hostages as they arrived at a United States military base in West Germany.

The End of the Crisis People expected the President to secure the hostages' freedom. He tried many approaches. He broke diplomatic relations with Iran and froze all Iranian assets

SECTION 3 REVIEW

Comprehension

1. *Key Terms* Define: (a) shuttle diplomacy; (b) Camp David Accords; (c) dissident.

2. *Summarizing the Main Idea* What ideals guided foreign policy during the Carter administration?

3. *Organizing Information* Create a flowchart tracing the progress of Soviet-American diplomatic relations during the Carter administration.

Critical Thinking

4. *Analyzing Time Lines* Review the time line at the start of the section. Write a sentence that explains the broader effect of each event.

5. *Making Comparisons* Give examples of the positive and negative results of Carter's approach to foreign policy.

Writing Activity

6. *Writing a Persuasive Essay* How much should human rights influence foreign policy? Write an editorial setting out your ideas on when it is and is not appropriate to ignore human rights concerns in dealing with other nations.

SKILLS FOR LIFE

- Critical Thinking
- Geography
- Graphs and Charts
- Historical Evidence

Recognizing Ideologies

An ideology is a set of beliefs that guide a person, a group, or a culture. If you can recognize ideologies, you can better understand why certain actions are taken or statements are made. Use the following steps to help you recognize the ideologies behind two opposing statements in the debate over the Panama Canal treaties.

1. *Identify the main topic of the statements and the people who made them.* (a) What is the subject in these statements? (b) Who made each statement? (c) In which branch of government does each speaker serve? (d) To what party does each belong?

2. *Locate the major points that each speaker makes.* (a) What reasons does Speaker A give for rejecting the proposed change? (b) What reasons does Speaker B give for accepting it?

3. *Identify the beliefs that underlie the reasons given.* (a) What does Speaker A believe about the rights of property with regard to the Panama Canal? (b) What attribute of the national character does he believe should guide American foreign policy? (c) What does Speaker B believe about the role of fairness with regard to the canal? (d) What attributes of national character does he think should guide American foreign policy?

TEST FOR SUCCESS

Choose a current issue before Congress and find speeches or articles expressing different points of view about it. Identify (a) the background of each person in the debate and (b) the beliefs that underlie his or her opinion.

A

The case for rejecting the proposed treat[ies] . . . begins with one crucial point: The Panama Canal is United States property, and the Canal Zone is United States territory. According to the terms of the 1903 treaty with Panama, we acquired sovereign rights over the Canal Zone "in perpetuity" [forever]. The Supreme Court upheld our exercise of sovereignty in 1907. . . . Moreover, the maps of the world show the Canal Zone as part of the United States.

Thus, it is clear that the burden of proof rests on those who favor the treaties; those who oppose them are merely standing up for American rights. Proponents must show that it is in the national interest to dispose of American property which, in addition to its strategic and economic value, represents a cumulative investment of roughly $7 billion.

. . . Would we give up Alaska to the Russians if they were suddenly to demand it? Such weakness is entirely contrary to our national character and heritage.

—Strom Thurmond, Republican (South Carolina), "Why the U.S. Should Keep the Panama Canal," The Christian Science Monitor, September 13, 1977

B

The most important reason, the only reason, to ratify the treaties is that they are in the highest national interest of the United States and will strengthen our position in the world. Our security interest will be stronger; our trade opportunities will be improved. We will demonstrate that as a large and powerful country we are able to deal fairly and honorably with a proud but smaller sovereign nation.

. . . We Americans want a more humane and stable world. We believe in goodwill and fairness as well as strength. This agreement with Panama is something we want because we know it is right.

. . . If Theodore Roosevelt were to endorse the treaties, as I'm quite sure he would, it would be mainly because he could see the decision as one by which we are demonstrating the kind of great power we wish to be. . . . In this historic decision, he would join us in our pride for being a great and generous people with a national strength and wisdom to do what is right for us and what is fair to others.

—President Jimmy Carter, televised speech, February 1, 1978

RESOURCE OPTIONS

Teaching Resources

 Skills for Life Activity Units 9–10 folder, p. 87, helps students apply this skill by analyzing two opposing viewpoints on taxing America's richer people to lower the federal deficit.

Media and Technology

 Color Transparencies Critical Thinking, I-11

SKILLS FOR LIFE

Critical Thinking

Recognizing Ideologies

Focus Students will learn the importance of recognizing the ideology of a speaker or writer.

Instruct After students have read and discussed the feature, recall that Theodore Roosevelt said, "Speak softly and carry a big stick." Ask whether Senator Thurmond or President Carter shared this ideology.

Ask students to work in small groups to identify several current issues and to draft a list of questions about those issues designed to reveal a presidential candidate's ideologies.

Extend See the Skills for Life Activity in the Resource Options below.

Answers

1. (a) Whether or not treaties should be ratified that would turn control and operation of the Panama Canal over to the Panamanians. (b) Passage A: Senator Strom Thurmond; Passage B: President Jimmy Carter. (c) Thurmond: legislative; Carter: executive. (d) Thurmond: Republican; Carter: Democratic.

2. (a) The Panama Canal belongs to the United States, so it is our right to retain it. It would show weakness to give it up. (b) It is in our national interest, and it is the right and fair thing to do.

3. (a) They take precedence over everything else. We bought the canal, and therefore it is ours. (b) Strength, with never a sign of weakness. (c) It should take precedence—Panama should be respected as a sovereign country. (d) Fairness, honor, and generosity, as well as strength.

TEST FOR SUCCESS

Answers will vary but should show an understanding of the steps outlined in this skill.

Carter's Domestic Issues

Objectives
You may wish to call students' attention to the objectives in the Section Preview. The objectives are reflected in the main headings of the section.

Bellringer
Ask students to think of four or five reasons why saving energy is important. Discuss whether their arguments are convincing.

Reading Strategy
Reading for Evidence Refer to the Reading Strategy in the Section Preview. You may wish to remind students of the connection between the word *domestic* and the term *programs at home.*

LESSON PLAN
Connecting to the Main Idea

1. Focus Explain that President Carter was largely unsuccessful in creating and passing legislation on domestic issues. Ask how historians have assessed Carter's presidency.

2. Instruct Discuss Carter's various attempts to regulate the economy and their results. Ask students to find a clear relationship among the attempts they have listed.

Ask why energy conservation became especially important during the Carter presidency. Discuss Carter's various energy proposals and ask students to identify those that became law.

Discuss the *Bakke* case and ask students to define reverse discrimination in their own words. Ask them if the Supreme Court decision in this case is consistent with their own ideas of fairness.

3. Close President Carter was largely unsuccessful at proposing and carrying out a clear economic program. Neither was he successful at creating or passing other domestic legislation.

1977 Carter grants amnesty to Vietnam War draft evaders	1977 Carter presents energy conservation program	1977 Department of Energy created	1978 Supreme Court decides Bakke case	1978 Airline deregulation begins	1979 Nuclear accident at Three Mile Island, Pennsylvania

1977 **1978** **1979**

4 Carter's Domestic Issues

SECTION PREVIEW

Objectives

1. Describe the economic instability facing the Carter administration.
2. List the elements of Carter's energy policy.
3. Summarize other domestic issues that weakened Carter's presidency and the outcome of the 1980 presidential election.
4. *Key Terms* Define: deregulation; amnesty; affirmative action.

Main Idea

Facing problems with the economy, Carter had trouble getting legislation through Congress and winning strong public support for his energy program and other policies.

Reading Strategy

Reading for Evidence As you read the section, look for evidence to support the statement below that President Carter "had little success in programs at home."

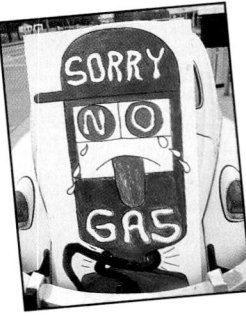

Oil shortages caused American drivers to face long lines at the gas pumps—when gas was available.

Jimmy Carter had little success in programs at home. He could not find a way to work effectively with Congress, which blocked his plans in many areas, especially energy and the economy. Looking back, he wrote, "I quickly learned that it is a lot easier to hold a meeting, reach a tentative agreement, or make a speech than to get a controversial program through Congress."

That was not the only problem. As *The New York Times* columnist Tom Wicker observed, Carter "never established a politically coherent administration." His strategies were not clearly defined. Public support faded as his programs floundered.

More Economic Instability

Carter inherited an unstable economy. Like his predecessors, he had trouble controlling inflation without hurting growth. Inflation had also been a problem for Ford, but had seemed under control after the recession in 1974–1976. Carter tried to prevent another recession by stimulating growth with government deficit spending. As deficits grew, the Federal Reserve Board increased the money supply, but inflation then rose to about 10 percent.

Spending Cuts In an attempt to stop inflation, slow the economy, and reduce the deficit, Carter cut spending. The cuts fell mostly on social programs, which angered liberal Democrats. At the same time, the slowdown in the economy increased unemployment and the number of business failures. Things got worse in 1980, when the new federal budget called for continued high spending. In reaction, bond prices fell and interest rates soared. Borrowers were angry at having to pay high interest rates—sometimes over 20 percent—for mortgages and other loans.

People lost confidence in Carter and his economic advisers. The administration's back-and-forth efforts—trying first one approach, then another—gave the impression that it had no idea what was happening or how to fix it.

Deregulation Another economic move was toward **deregulation**—the reduction or

---

RESOURCE OPTIONS

Teaching Resources

📁 **Reproducible Lesson Plan** Lesson Plans folder, p. 169

📁 **Learning Styles Lesson Plan** Learning Styles Lesson Plans folder, p. 69

📁 **Big Idea Graphic Organizer** Big Idea Graphic Organizer folder, p. 141

📁 **Guided Reading and Review** Units 9–10 folder, p. 79

Media and Technology

 AmericanHeritage® CD-ROM
Time Tour The Nation Today and Tomorrow: New Directions

Comparison of Energy Sources

Source	Advantages	Disadvantages
Oil	• Currently widely available to consumers. • Relatively affordable.	• Nonrenewable resource. • Supplies are concentrated in relatively few regions. • Oil exploration, production, and transportation risk oil spills and other environmental damage. • Significant source of air pollution.
Natural Gas	• Low emission levels of air pollutants, carbon monoxide, and solid wastes such as sludge and ash.	• Nonrenewable resource. • Majority of gas reserves located in just a few countries. • Difficult to transport.
Coal	• Most abundant nonrenewable energy source. • Least expensive of the fossil fuels.	• Nonrenewable resource. • Major source of air pollution. • Contributes to chronic and acute respiratory conditions. • Strip mining causes extensive erosion.
Nuclear Energy	• Uses uranium, a naturally occurring element. One ton of uranium can be used to produce more than 10,000 times the amount of electricity of a ton of oil.	• Produces hazardous radioactive waste that is difficult to dispose of safely. • Mechanical or human error could have serious or fatal results for workers and the general population.
Solar Energy	• Unlimited resource. • Produces no pollutants.	• Present equipment too expensive to put into general usage.
Wind Energy	• Unlimited resource. • Produces no pollutants. • Considered most environmentally safe energy source.	• Location has direct bearing on the productivity of the plant. • Wind doesn't always blow at adequate speeds.
Hydroelectric Power	• Renewable resource. • Produces no pollutants.	• Hydroelectric dams alter the environment. • Large dams can occasionally flood acres of productive land or wilderness area.

Interpreting Tables Oil shortages caused by United States dependence on foreign oil fueled the search for alternative forms of energy. **Geography** Which alternative source seems to have the most advantages? The fewest?

Using the Internet

Prepare a Report

Objective Use the Internet to prepare a report on state energy resources. Have students follow these instructions:

1. See the *America: Pathways to the Present* Web site at

http://www.Pathways.phschool.com

for the URL of the U.S. Geological Survey.

2. Choose a state to research. Each student should choose a different state.

3. Follow the link to the state you selected. Read the summary, taking detailed notes. Follow any additional links to add supplementary information to your report.

4. As a class, make a composite list from your reports of information about state energy resources.

removal of government controls in several industries. In the late 1800s and early 1900s, agencies such as the Interstate Commerce Commission had been established to regulate rates and business practices. Over the years, regulations had multiplied. Carter now argued that they hurt competition and increased consumer costs.

To encourage greater energy production, Carter proposed removing controls on prices for oil and natural gas. He also took steps to deregulate railroads, trucking, and airlines. While consumer groups and many liberal Democrats opposed deregulation, it continued during the next two administrations, both Republican.

A Program to Save Energy

Carter made energy conservation a major goal, but he had trouble winning support from Congress and the public. Despite earlier embargoes and shortages, Americans still depended heavily on imported oil. In the late 1970s, more than 40 percent of the oil used in the United States came from other countries. Some thought the country should be more energy self-sufficient. Others urged cutting down overall energy use, warning that oil reserves were limited.

Main Idea
CONNECTIONS

How did oil price increases and shortages affect Carter's popularity?

RESOURCE OPTIONS

Media and Technology

Critical Thinking Activity Formulating Questions: Prices at the Pump, found on Resource Pro, helps students practice this skill by analyzing the 1970s oil shortage.

Visual Learning Activity Responding to the Energy Crisis, found on Resource Pro, illustrates one solution to the problem of dwindling natural resources in a poster issued by the Hawaii Department of Planning and Natural Resources.

Answer to . . .

Interpreting Tables Answers will vary but students should be able to defend their choices.
Main Idea Connections They decreased his popularity.

About the Presidents

Having been a successful governor in Georgia, **Jimmy Carter** (1977–1981) ran for President as a Washington outsider at a time when national politics was in disrepute. This was a shrewd campaign strategy and won him the office, but once in Washington, Carter found it difficult to engage the machinery of government in a productive way. Despite his successes—the Camp David Accords were a major breakthrough in Middle East relations—Carter's failure to articulate and execute an appealing program left frustrated voters scrambling for an alternative by the end of his first term. He lost badly in his race for reelection to Ronald Reagan in 1980. Source: Adapted from Henry F. Graff's *The Presidents*, Scribner's, 1984, by the editors of *American Heritage* magazine.

exploring TECHNOLOGY — Nuclear Power Plant

- Turbogenerators
- Containment building
- Steam generators
- Reactor
- Control room
- Unused fuel storage
- Water pumps
- Steam lines
- Condenser
- Unused fuel storage

Inside the reactor, uranium or plutonium atoms are split in half, releasing energy in the form of heat and radiation. The heat is used to heat water and generate steam. Steam pipes carry the steam to the plant's turbogenerators, which produce electricity. *Science and Technology* *What are the drawbacks of nuclear energy production?*

OPEC, the Organization of Petroleum Exporting Countries, had been raising oil prices steadily since 1973. People grumbled about rising prices, shortages, and long lines at the gas station. Although the President was not responsible for oil prices or shortages, he often was the focus of people's complaints.

In April 1977, Carter presented his comprehensive energy program to Congress and the public. He asked people to save fuel by driving less and by using less fuel to heat or cool their homes and offices. He also created a new Cabinet department, the Department of Energy. It would coordinate various federal programs promoting conservation and looking for new energy sources. Carter took energy problems seriously, calling the need for conservation the "moral equivalent of war." Critics, however, created the acronym MEOW (from the first letter of each word) to make fun of it.

Representatives from states that produced oil and gas fiercely opposed the energy proposals. Many proposals were stalled in Congress for months. In 1978, though, the National Energy Act finally passed. It included these provisions:

(1) taxes on inefficient "gas-guzzling" cars

(2) conversion of new utilities to fuels other than oil or natural gas

(3) deregulation of prices for domestic oil and natural gas

(4) tax credits or loans to homeowners for using solar energy and improving insulation

(5) research funds for alternative energy sources such as solar energy and synthetic fuels.

Three Mile Island Nuclear power seemed to be one exciting alternative energy source. Serious questions persisted about its costs and safety, however. Since the 1960s, grassroots activists and some scientists had been criticizing the

---

Answer to . . .

Exploring Technology Plants are costly to build, and the radiation produced is extremely hazardous.

RESOURCE OPTIONS

Teaching Resources

 American History Block Scheduling Support Fueling the Nation: Energy and the Environment, found in The Nation After World War II folder, includes interdisciplinary lesson suggestions and activities for Geography and History, Primary Sources, Biography, and Literature.

Media and Technology

 AmericanHeritage® **CD-ROM**
Presidents Jimmy Carter

Color Transparencies The Way It Works, H-21

nuclear power industry. In March 1979, people's doubts seemed to be confirmed by an accident at the nuclear power plant at Three Mile Island, near Harrisburg, Pennsylvania.

A small leak through a faulty seal in the cooling system stopped the pumps that circulated the coolant. Temperatures in the reactor core rose, but plant operators misread the symptoms and shut down an emergency cooling system. A partial meltdown of the core occurred, releasing some radiation. People near the plant were terrified by the idea of a radioactive leak, and 140,000 people fled their homes. The story made headlines around the world.

The Future of Nuclear Power Carter named a commission to investigate the accident at Three Mile Island. Its report identified operator errors that had made the initial problem worse. In his response to the report, Carter noted "very serious shortcomings in the way that both the government and the utility industry regulate and manage nuclear power." He proposed reorganizing the Nuclear Regulatory Commission, the agency in charge of nuclear power. He also called on utility companies to improve standards.

In spite of Carter's efforts, the nuclear industry fell on hard times. People were angry at cost overruns in building new plants, which often increased their electric bills. Protesters blocked building sites. Orders for new plants were canceled, and some construction was halted.

Other Domestic Issues

Carter's concern for moral and humanitarian values influenced his approach to domestic questions as well as foreign policy. Some of his actions were controversial. Soon after taking office, he carried out his promise to grant **amnesty**—a general pardon—to those who had evaded the draft during the Vietnam War. Because that war still divided Americans, reactions were mixed.

Civil Rights As governor of Georgia, Carter had had a good civil rights record. During the 1976 campaign, he won African American support with what columnist David Broder called "an eloquence, a simplicity, a directness that moved listeners of both races."

Carter tried to move beyond the civil rights battles of the 1950s and 1960s. As a white southerner himself, he understood the South's need to overcome the negative images of the past decades:

COMPARING PRIMARY SOURCES

ON NUCLEAR ENERGY

The need to reduce the dependence on foreign oil prompted viewpoints strongly for and against nuclear power.

In Favor of Nuclear Energy	Opposed to Nuclear Energy
"When you debate the issue of nuclear energy, you are actually debating the issue of growth. Growth will be the key issue for the remainder of this century, and it is the resolution of that issue which will determine the lifestyles of most Americans for generations to come. . . . Economic growth has been inextricably linked to the growth of the supply of energy throughout history." —Senator James A. McClure (Idaho), address before the National Conference on Energy Advocacy, February 2, 1979	"If this country . . . continues to rely more and more on nuclear power a meltdown disaster is almost predictable. . . . For years now, the utilities and nuclear power industry have refused to listen to scientific logic and reasoning concerning the dangers of this technology. . . . Perhaps it is time for emotion and for passion and for commitment to stir our souls and our hearts and our minds once again into action." —Dr. Helen Caldicott, in Nuclear Madness, What You Can Do! 1980

ANALYZING VIEWPOINTS **What are the main concerns of each of these speakers?**

AMERICAN VOICES ❝The most important [message] was that we in the South were ready for reconciliation, to be accepted as equals, to rejoin the mainstream of American political life. This yearning for what might be called political redemption was a significant factor in my successful campaign.❞

—*Jimmy Carter*

Many of Carter's staff appointments, such as the United Nations ambassadorship for Andrew Young, won the approval of black Americans. On the other hand, his weak support of social programs disappointed many African Americans.

Affirmative Action In 1978 the Supreme Court ruled on a civil rights case that had important implications for **affirmative action** policies. Such policies give special consideration to women and members of minorities to make up for past discrimination against them. Allan Bakke, who was white, applied to the medical school at the University of California

---

Answers to

SECTION 4 REVIEW

1. (a) deregulation, see p. 946; (b) amnesty, see p. 949; (c) affirmative action, see p. 949.

2. The nation depended heavily on imported oil, oil-producing states opposed regulation, and Carter was often blamed for the shortages.

3. Rising inflation caused Carter to impose spending cuts; cuts affected social programs, angering Democrats; a new budget increased spending, raising interest rates.

4. Sample event: 1977, Carter grants amnesty to draft evaders—Carter's impulse was humanitarian but led to public disapproval in many sectors of society, as the Vietnam War was still highly controversial.

5. Sample answers: It has helped consumers by stimulating competition and lowering costs; or, it has hurt consumers by subjecting them to market fluctuations.

6. Letters will vary but should be supported with facts from the section.

Allan Bakke (above center) sued to gain a spot at the University of California. His case caused some people to march in support of affirmative action. **Culture** What was the outcome of the trial?

wrote six separate opinions. While the Court ordered Bakke's admission to the California medical school, it also upheld the school's right to consider race as one factor in admission decisions. It did not, however, allow actual quotas. The Court decision supported the concept of affirmative action, but the case signaled the start of a backlash against the policy.

The 1980 Election

Despite Carter's notable foreign policy achievements and his commitment to serious goals, his administration lost many people's confidence. Rising inflation in early 1980 dropped his approval rating to 21 percent in public opinion polls. Unemployment was still over 7 percent. At times Carter himself seemed to have lost confidence. In two speeches in July, he spoke of a national "crisis of confidence" and a "national malaise."

In the Democratic primaries leading up to the 1980 elections, Massachusetts Senator Edward M. Kennedy won a large number of delegate votes. Kennedy withdrew, however, just as the Democratic National Convention began, and Carter was nominated again. Nonetheless, many people were ready for the optimism and hopeful rhetoric of the Republican candidate, Ronald Reagan.

(Davis) in 1973 and 1974. After being turned down twice, he sued the school for "reverse discrimination." Bakke charged that the policy of reserving 16 of 100 class spaces for minority group applicants violated both the Civil Rights Act of 1964 and the Constitution.

In a complex ruling in *Regents of the University of California* v. *Bakke,* the justices

SECTION 4 REVIEW

Comprehension

1. **Key Terms** Define: (a) deregulation; (b) amnesty; (c) affirmative action.

2. **Summarizing the Main Idea** Why was it difficult for Carter to win public and congressional support for his energy program?

3. **Organizing Information** Create a flow map to show the causes and effects of the Carter administration's economic decisions.

Critical Thinking

4. **Analyzing Time Lines** Review the time line at the start of the section. Write a paragraph explaining how each event relates to Carter policies.

5. **Demonstrating Reasoned Judgment** Many politicians since 1980 have continued Carter's policy of deregulation. In what ways do you think this policy has helped or hurt consumers?

Writing Activity

6. **Writing a Persuasive Essay** President Carter had trouble getting Americans to support his efforts to conserve energy. Write a letter to the editor in which you support or oppose such efforts.

Why Study History?
To understand that . . .

Americans Are Skeptical About Government

Since the early 1970s, distrust of government has become widespread, and Americans have become more cynical about their leaders.

Vietnam protest march, 1969

Whom do you trust to make big decisions that affect your life? What about decisions that affect the entire nation? Whom can you trust to make such decisions wisely?

During and after World War II, most Americans trusted the nation's leaders in Washington to solve enormous problems. However, public trust in government plummeted after the Vietnam War and the Watergate scandal. Presidents Ford and Carter tried but largely failed to restore public trust. Today, many Americans do not trust the federal government to solve problems. They believe that the government itself is the problem.

The Impact Today

In 1964, a national poll showed that 76 percent of Americans trusted Washington to do what is right "always" or "most of the time." By 1997, however, only 22 percent of Americans expressed confidence in the federal government. (State and local governments fared somewhat better in the 1997 poll.) Some Americans resent the cost and size of government or its interference in their lives. Others see a lack of political leadership as the greatest problem.

Despite these bleak statistics, most Americans still believe that government has important responsibilities in areas such as foreign relations, civil rights, environmental protection, health, and safety. Public mistrust of government could make it difficult for government to perform these tasks.

Such mistrust might even threaten the nation's democratic institutions. A cynical public is less likely to vote and participate in other ways in the political process. (Indeed, during the 1950s and 1960s more than 60 percent of Americans usually voted in presidential elections. That percentage has since dropped, falling below 50 percent in 1996.) Mistrustful citizens are also less willing to support their government by paying taxes, obeying laws, and entering public service.

How can government improve its performance to restore Americans' trust? Some suggest that the government draw on the talents of business leaders to improve management of the public sector. Others say cynicism will persist as long as public officials serve their own interests rather than the nation's good.

The Impact on You

Take a poll of your classmates to find out what they trust about the federal government and what they mistrust about it. Compile the answers into a list. Then use the list to make a bar graph of the top five answers.

DON'T VOTE, IT ONLY ENCOURAGES THEM

Bumper sticker with a modern message

RESOURCE OPTIONS

Teaching Resources

Why Study History? Activity Americans Are Skeptical About Government, found in the Why Study History? folder, p. 34, provides an activity to help students better understand Americans' attitudes about government.

Media and Technology

AmericanHeritage® CD-ROM

Time Tour The Nation Today and Tomorrow: A Time of Turmoil

Decision America Videotapes and Videodiscs Issue 3 *Why Vote?*

Why Study History?

Class Discussion

Discuss with the class Americans' trust in government. For a more thorough examination of the issue, see the activity folder in the Resource Options below.

ACTIVITY
STUDENT PARTICIPATION

Taking an Opinion Poll
Ask students to read the text. Then have students work together to create an opinion poll on reasons for skepticism about government. Their poll might ask respondents about a variety of issues, such as:
- **cost of government**
- **size of government**
- **lack of leadership**
- **out-of-touch leadership**
- **influence peddling**
- **undue influence of the rich**
- **corruption**
- **scandals**

Have students discuss their findings. Use the information to create graphs and/or charts.

Follow up Ask students to brainstorm strategies for restoring public trust in government.

Using the Internet
Students can learn more about Americans' attitudes toward government by exploring links in the *America: Pathways to the Present* Web site at

http://www.Pathways.phschool.com

Assessment
See the Lesson Plans folder, pp. 24–27, for rubrics on assessing Class Participation Projects.

Key Terms

Students should refer to the definitions of key terms in the chapter to write sentences that show an understanding of the domestic and foreign policies of the Ford and Carter administrations.

Comprehension

1. The economy faced inflation and high unemployment; he first encouraged voluntary actions, then had the Federal Reserve limit the money supply.

2. He wanted to end the Watergate scandal and focus the nation on the future; the public widely censured his action.

3. The authority to bring back troops sent by the President in a war if congressional approval is not given.

4. Distrust over Washington politics and the sagging economy. Carter had the advantage of being a Washington outsider and of presenting an image of honesty.

5. He was largely unable to get his legislation passed.

6. Carter's humanitarian gesture to allow the exiled shah of Iran into the United States for medical treatment propelled angry followers of the new Iranian leader to seize the American embassy in Tehran.

7. Carter's support of Soviet dissidents, and economic sanctions the United States adopted against the Soviet Union after the invasion of Afghanistan.

Chapter Summary

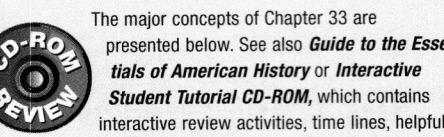

The major concepts of Chapter 33 are presented below. See also *Guide to the Essentials of American History* or *Interactive Student Tutorial CD-ROM,* which contains interactive review activities, time lines, helpful hints, and test practice for Chapter 33.

Reviewing the Main Ideas

Gerald Ford, who took over as President after Nixon's resignation, also inherited a troubled economy and foreign policy challenges. After two years, he lost the presidency to a little-known Democrat, Jimmy Carter, who campaigned on issues of trust and morality. Along with the aftereffects of Watergate, controlling inflation and unemployment remained problematic for political leaders throughout the 1970s.

Section 1: The Ford Administration

After becoming President, Gerald Ford worked to reunite the country. He faced economic problems at home as well as foreign policy challenges abroad.

Section 2: The Carter Transition

Partly in reaction to Watergate, voters in 1976 elected a little-known Democrat, Jimmy Carter of Georgia, who stressed trust and honesty in his campaign for the presidency.

Section 3: Carter's Foreign Policy

Carter's religious beliefs and principles led him to emphasize peacemaking and human rights in foreign affairs. This approach brought some notable results but caused disagreements with the Soviet Union and a crisis with Iran.

Section 4: Carter's Domestic Issues

Facing problems with the economy, Carter had trouble getting legislation through Congress and winning strong public support for his energy program and other policies.

Since the early 1970s, distrust of government has become widespread, and Americans have become much more cynical about their leaders.

Key Terms

Use each of the terms below in a sentence that shows how it relates to the chapter.

1. stagflation
2. recession
3. War Powers Act
4. Helsinki Accords
5. bicentennial
6. incumbent
7. Camp David Accords
8. deregulation
9. amnesty
10. affirmative action

Comprehension

1. What problems did the economy face during the Ford administration? What programs did Ford propose to solve them?

2. What were Ford's reasons for giving a pardon to former President Nixon? What was the public reaction?

3. What authority does Congress gain from the War Powers Act?

4. What were the main issues of the 1976 election? What gave Carter an advantage?

5. How did Carter's lack of Washington experience hurt his administration?

6. What brought about the Iran hostage crisis?

7. What factors made relations with the Soviet Union worse in the late 1970s?

Using Graphic Organizers

On a separate sheet of paper, copy the tree map to organize the main ideas of the chapter. Each section of the tree map should focus on developments in one political issue in the Ford and Carter administrations: economic policy, foreign policy, civil rights, energy. Supply in your own words the main ideas and supporting details for each section.

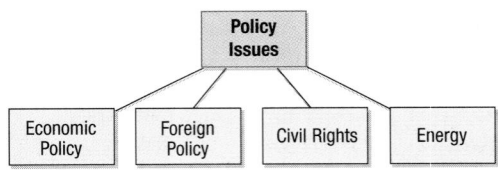

Using Graphic Organizers

- Economic Policy: Ford—encouraged voluntary actions to boost economy; Carter—supported spending cuts.
- Foreign Policy: Ford—continued Nixon's policy of détente, initiated trade with Africa, and continued SALT negotiations; Carter—humanitarian policies led to conflict with USSR and Iran; Camp David Accords; Panama Treaty.
- Civil Rights: Ford—little civil rights initiative; Carter—appointed civil rights leaders to posts in administration, called for majority rule of blacks in South Africa and Rhodesia.
- Energy: Ford—called for voluntary conservation; Carter—created Department of Energy, pushed through National Energy Act.

Analyzing Political Cartoons ▶

1. Examine the images in the cartoon. What is the significance of the two people being seated at the back of the bus?

2. Who is the man on the left?

3. Explain the woman's comment. What is her perspective?

4. What point might the cartoonist be trying to make?

Critical Thinking

1. *Applying the Chapter Skill* Trying to make peace in the Middle East was a risky move politically. Identify the beliefs that led President Carter to step in as peacemaker between Israel and Egypt.

2. *Checking Consistency* Although people complained about fuel shortages during the 1970s, many did not support Carter's energy program or try to conserve oil and gas. How do you explain this inconsistent behavior?

3. *Drawing Conclusions* Which do you think played a larger role in Congress's refusal to send military aid to South Vietnam in 1975—the War Powers Act or public opinion about involvement in Vietnam?

4. *Identifying Central Issues* In the 1976 election, trust was one of the most important issues. What do you think are the most important issues for voters today when electing a President?

INTERNET ACTIVITY

For your portfolio:
ORGANIZE A DEBATE

Access Prentice Hall's *America: Pathways to the Present* site at **www.Pathways.phschool.com** for the specific URLs to complete the activity. Additional resources and related Web sites are also available.

Follow the links to find information that supports a pro- or anti-nuclear position. Then organize a debate on the future of nuclear power as an energy source, considering its benefits and drawbacks.

ANALYZING DOCUMENTS ◀▶ INTERPRETING DATA

Turn to the 1976 election map on page 937.

1. Ford won the votes of all the states in the (a) Midwest. (b) West and Southwest. (c) South. (d) Northeast.

2. Why would Carter's winning margin of electoral votes be greater than his margin of the popular vote? (a) He won more states than Ford. (b) He won states with more electoral votes.

(c) He won states with smaller populations. (d) He lost only states in the West.

3. *Writing* Using this map and the rest of the chapter, write two paragraphs that explain why each candidate appealed to different groups of voters and different regions of the country.

Connecting to Today

Essay Writing Reread the account of the 1979–1981 Iranian hostage crisis. Then research newspapers and news magazines and write an essay explaining how that event has affected U.S.-Iran relations since that time.

INTERNET ACTIVITY

Debaters should support their positions clearly and solidly with facts from the Web sites.

Analyzing Political Cartoons

1. It signals that they are being discriminated against on the basis of race.

2. Allan Bakke, the white man who challenged affirmative action when he was not admitted to the University of California.

3. As an African American, she has endured a legacy of discrimination and offers sympathy, probably ironically, to Bakke.

4. Answers may vary. Students might suggest that the discrimination faced by Bakke doesn't compare in scale with the discrimination experienced by African Americans throughout U.S. history.

Critical Thinking

1. His firm belief in human rights and commitment to find ethical solutions to diplomatic problems.

2. Sample answers: Carter did not effectively promote his energy policies; Americans with their great dependence on fuel might have been unwilling to make sacrifices, despite high prices and shortages.

3. Sample answer: Public opinion. Congress would have been more likely to invoke authority given under the Act in the face of strong public disapproval of further actions in Southeast Asia.

4. Sample answer: The ability to solve economic and social problems.

Interpreting Data

1. b
2. b
3. Essays will vary but might mention Carter's southern background, Ford's midwestern background, and Carter's appeal to blue-collar workers and African Americans.

Connecting to Today

Essays will vary but should be supported with specific facts and quotes from the articles.

CHAPTER 34

The Conservative Revolution, 1980–1992

Managing Time and Instruction

INSTRUCTION SUPPORT

These materials for instruction are provided for **each section** in the **Teaching Resources**. See **Units 9–10 folder for Enrichment Support**:

- Reproducible Lesson Plans in Lesson Plans folder • Learning Styles Lesson Plans in Learning Styles Lesson Plans folder • Big Idea Graphic Organizers in Big Idea Graphic Organizer folder
- Guided Reading and Review • Quizzes • Test Preparation Practice booklet

DAILY LESSON	ENRICHMENT SUPPORT
1 **Roots of the New Conservatism** (pp. 955–958)	• Primary Source Activity, Speaking for the President, Learning with Documents folder, p. 40
2 **The Reagan Revolution** (pp. 959–963)	• Great Debates, How Should We Deal with Environmental Dangers?, Decision-Making Activities folder, pp. 46–47 • Visual Learning Activity, "Passing the Economic Buck," found on **Resource Pro** • Key Documents, Ronald Reagan, "These Are the Boys of Pointe du Hoc," Learning with Documents folder, p. 106
3 **Reagan's Second Term** (pp. 964–968)	• Comparing Primary Sources, On the Legacy of the Civil Rights Movement, Units 9–10 folder, pp. 97–98 • Literature Activity, Masters of the Universe, Units 9–10 folder, p. 99 • Visual Learning Activity, Wages for Housework, Learning with Documents folder, p. 76 • Biography, Sandra Day O'Connor, found on **Resource Pro** • Primary Source Activity, An Explanation of Iran-Contra, found on **Resource Pro** • Critical Thinking Activity, Recognizing Ideologies: The Bork Nomination, found on **Resource Pro**
4 **The Bush Presidency** (pp. 970–974)	• Skills for Life Activity, Units 9–10 folder, p. 100 • Nystrom *Atlas of Our Country,* People on the Move, pp. 34–35 • Biography, Melissa Rathbun-Nealy, Units 9–10 folder, p. 96 • Literature Activity, Operation Desert Storm, found on **Resource Pro** • Government Efficiency Can Be Improved, Why Study History? folder, p. 35

Running Out of Time?

- Use Tape 5, "Republican Revival and Decline, 1968–Present," from **Visions of America** videotapes series.
- Use Chapter 34 Summary from **Guide to the Essentials of American History (English and Spanish).**

Companion Web Site

The companion Web site offers online links for all chapter review activities. It also provides key content links and structured support for this chapter for both teachers and students.

http://www.Pathways.phschool.com

Teaching in the Information Age

Media and Technology

For the Student

Interactive Student Tutorial CD-ROM Chapter 34

Student Edition on Audiotape Chapter 34

American Heritage® CD-ROM

Guided Reading Audiotapes (English and Spanish) Chapter 34

For the Teacher

Resource Pro CD-ROM Chapter 34

Test Bank CD-ROM Chapter 34

Listening to Literature Audiotapes *Timeless Voices, Timeless Themes* "Coyote v. Acme" by Ian Frazier

Color Transparencies I-17, E-10, B-10, J-10

Block Scheduling

Pacing Suggestions

For 90-minute Blocks

- Teach sections 2 and 3 using Transparencies I-3 and I-11 and the Recent Scholarship note on p. 960 for class discussions.
- Teach sections 1 and 4 using the Big Idea Graphic Organizers from Teaching Resources and the Extended Class Periods Activity on p. 972.

Additional Resources

- Prentice Hall's **American History Block Scheduling Support File** covers over 40 major topics in American history.
- **Prentice Hall United States History Video Collection™** contains 20 videotapes covering American history from beginnings to present.
- **Decision America Videotapes and Videodiscs**

Assessment Options

Chapter Test Forms A&B Test Bank CD-ROM booklet

Test Bank CD-ROM Chapter 34

Standardized Test Preparation Handbook

Connections to American Literature

from Prentice Hall

Prentice Hall Literature *Timeless Voices, Timeless Themes* From *The Woman Warrior* by Maxine Hong Kingston, p. 958

Additional Resources

For the Student

Arthur Ashe and Arnold Rampersad. *Days of Grace: A Memoir.* Random House, 1993.

Marian Salzman and Ann O'Reilly. *War and Peace in the Persian Gulf: What Teenagers Want to Know.* Peterson's Guides, 1991.

For the Teacher

Charlayne Hunter-Gault. *In My Place.* Vintage, 1993.

Prentice Hall brings into the classroom the vast archives and scholarship of the nation's premier American history magazine. See "From the Archives of American Heritage®" and "About the Presidents" teaching notes in this chapter.

 History Alive!

Teacher's Curriculum Institute, in partnership with Prentice Hall, provides unique materials that engage students with diverse learning styles. See History Alive!® unit on Contemporary American Society.

 Student Performance Pack

Ensures success in the three critical areas of Reading, Test Taking, and English Language Development with the following materials:
- Guide to the Essentials of American History in English and Spanish
- Guided Reading Audiotapes in English and Spanish
- Interactive Student Tutorial CD-ROM
- Test Preparation Handbook
- Test Preparation Practice booklet

Introducing the Chapter

After the political, social, and cultural upheavals of the 1960s and 1970s, many Americans felt change had gone too far and wanted to return to smaller government and more conservative ideas. The policies of Ronald Reagan and his successor, George Bush, carried out the social and economic goals of "New Right" conservatives.

Themes in American History

The theme for this chapter, Government, is listed at the beginning of this unit. An alternate theme for the chapter is Economics. To teach this unit thematically, you may wish to use The Nation After World War II folder in American History Block Scheduling Support.

Why Study History?

Have students explore suggested ways of connecting the past to the present on page 975.

Answer to . . .

Viewing History Students should use this question as an aid in reading the chapter. After so many years of turmoil and change, a majority of voters was ready for a more patriotic, positive message from their leaders. Also, growing skepticism surrounded current government social programs.

954

CHAPTER
34 The Conservative
Revolution

1980-1992

CHAPTER
34 The Conservative
Revolution

1980-1992

CHAPTER FOCUS

This chapter examines the rise of conservatives to power in the 1980s, beginning with the election of President Ronald Reagan. It looks at the shift in values and policies that occurred in government during the Reagan and Bush presidencies and details the key events of their combined 12 years in office.

The Why Study History? page at the end of this chapter explores the connection between Reagan's efforts to reduce the size and scope of the federal government and such efforts today.

▲
VIEWING HISTORY
Ronald Reagan's genial personality helped make him a popular President. His wife, Nancy, strongly influenced his decision making. *Government Why do you think Americans chose a conservative President in 1980?*

▶ RESOURCE OPTIONS

Teaching Resources

 Big Idea Graphic Organizer folder
Graphic summary of the main idea of the chapter.

Learning Styles Lesson Plans folder
Alternate lesson plans for diverse learning styles for each chapter.

Media and Technology

 AmericanHeritage® CD-ROM
Time Tour The Nation Today and Tomorrow: New Directions

 Prentice Hall United States History Video Collection™ Volume 20
Post-War USA

1964	1965	1968	1973	1980
In setback for conservatives, Johnson crushes Goldwater in presidential race	Great Society program expands government's role	Nixon elected President, restoring Republican power	Roe v. Wade legalizes abortion, mobilizes conservatives	Conservatives triumph as Reagan elected President

1960	1965	1970	1975	1980

1 Roots of the New Conservatism

SECTION PREVIEW

Objectives

1. Outline the major events in Ronald Reagan's political career.
2. Trace the rise of modern political conservatism.
3. Evaluate the significance of the election of 1980.
4. **Key Terms** Define: New Right; televangelism.

Main Idea

After decades of government growth and social and cultural change, a conservative backlash grew during the 1970s. In 1980 it brought Ronald Reagan to power.

Reading Strategy

Arranging Events in Order As you read, make a list of dates that mark major events in the development of the conservative movement from the 1930s to 1980.

The inauguration of Ronald Reagan in early 1981 marked a major shift in American politics. The new President voiced the growing frustrations of voters around the country who believed that government had grown too large and had lost touch with the needs of the people. Reagan's own political journey reflected the growing conservatism of millions of Americans.

Reagan's Political Career

Reagan was originally a Democrat and voted for Franklin D. Roosevelt, architect of the New Deal, in 1932. When Reagan began his career as a movie actor in Hollywood, he became actively involved in the political affairs of the actors' union.

After World War II, Reagan found himself less comfortable with the Democratic party and joined the Republican party. In the 1950s he served as a spokesman for General Electric, making speeches praising capitalism and attacking government regulation. He also spoke out strongly against Communists in the United States. Ronald Reagan was now clearly in the conservative camp.

Reagan gained national attention in 1966, when he was elected governor of California. Likeable, photogenic, genial—and committed to conservative values—he gained support for cutbacks in social programs in his state. He also called for the same approach in the federal government.

The Rise of Conservatism

Americans have debated the proper size and scope of government since the nation's founding. That debate greatly intensified with Franklin Roosevelt's New Deal, which greatly enlarged the federal government.

New Deal Opponents New Deal agencies, which furnished banking regulation, assistance to farmers, aid for the unemployed, and a great deal more, changed the role of the President and the federal government. Critics argued that in a capitalist country, government should not undertake these tasks. They said

With this 1980 campaign poster, Ronald Reagan appealed to voters' patriotism.

▶ RESOURCE OPTIONS

Teaching Resources

📁 **Reproducible Lesson Plan** Lesson Plans folder, p. 170

📁 **Big Idea Graphic Organizer** Big Idea Graphic Organizer folder, p. 142

📁 **Guided Reading and Review** Units 9–10 folder, p. 88

Objectives
You may wish to call students' attention to the objectives in the Section Preview. The objectives are reflected in the main headings of the section.

Bellringer
Ask students what the terms *conservative* and *conservatism* mean to them. Ask them to identify two issues in the 1990s that would fit their definitions of the terms.

Reading Strategy
Arranging Events in Order Refer to the Reading Strategy in the Section Preview. You may wish to write a composite list of students' dates on the chalkboard.

LESSON PLAN

Connecting to the Main Idea

1. Focus Explain that many Americans had long opposed the expansion of the federal government. This opposition came to a head in the 1980s with a well-organized conservative rebellion. Ask students what issues the New Right targeted.

2. Instruct Explain that the conservative movement of the 1980s was part of an ongoing opposition to government growth after the 1930s. Review the shift in the role of government brought by the New Deal.

Discuss the aims of the various government programs that had been instituted over the years. Did critics argue with those aims, with the methods, or with both? Have students discuss the social issues that helped bring the New Right together.

3. Close For decades, federal programs had expanded, despite the objections of many Americans. This growing discontent, combined with unhappiness about social changes, brought together a powerful coalition that elected a conservative President, Ronald Reagan, in 1980.

Have students analyze the approaches to government growth taken by different Republican leaders: Eisenhower, Goldwater, Nixon, and Reagan. How did each one's philosophy reflect the times? What factors made Reagan's viewpoint "an idea whose time had come"? Have students answer these questions in a brief essay.

BACKGROUND

Biography

The title "Father of the New Right" may belong to former senator Barry M. Goldwater (1909–1998) of Arizona. He was a transport pilot in World War II, then ran for the Senate in 1952. There he became a critic of the Eisenhower administration and leader of conservative Republicans. Goldwater lost the presidential race in 1964 by 16 million votes, partly because his tough promilitary rhetoric frightened many people. So did his famous quote: "Extremism in the defense of liberty is no vice." He was reelected to the Senate in 1968 and served until his retirement in 1987.

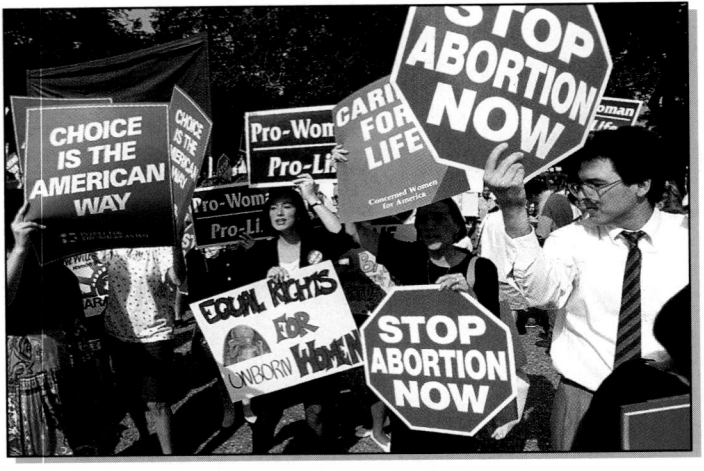

Pro-choice and anti-abortion activists gathered at this rally.

the nation could not afford the high federal spending that resulted.

Some of these critics joined together in the American Liberty League. Established in 1934, this organization included both industrialists and disgruntled politicians. The Liberty League sought to teach respect for the rights of individuals and property and to underscore the importance of individual enterprise. All of these values, members claimed, were being undermined by FDR's large government programs.

In 1937 an attempt by Roosevelt to "pack" the Supreme Court by adding new justices caused a backlash. Opponents formed a bipartisan coalition that opposed any further New Deal legislation.

From Eisenhower to Goldwater The election of Dwight D. Eisenhower as President in 1952 began eight years of Republican rule. Ike called his approach to government "modern Republicanism." He accepted the basic outlines of the New Deal. He never attempted to dismantle the federal bureaucracy. There was even occasional bureaucratic expansion, as in the 1953 creation of a new Department of Health, Education, and Welfare, headed by Oveta Culp Hobby.

In 1964 the Republican candidate for President, Senator Barry Goldwater of Arizona, ran on a staunchly conservative platform. Facing Democrat Lyndon B. Johnson, Goldwater opposed government activism, including civil rights laws and antipoverty

Main Idea
CONNECTIONS

What was Eisenhower's approach to government?

programs. He also demanded a military buildup against an expected Soviet attack.

Johnson portrayed Goldwater as a dangerous extremist and crushed him in the 1964 election. Some analysts concluded that Goldwater's conservatism would never gain wide support.

The Great Society Conservatives found themselves silenced for a time following Goldwater's decisive defeat in 1964. The Democratic landslide in the election gave liberals the political upper hand in the mid-1960s. Congress cooperated as President Johnson pushed ahead with his Great Society program, an extension of the New Deal, starting in 1965.

"Is a new world coming?" Johnson asked. "We welcome it, and we will bend it to the hopes of man."

The Great Society promised something for everyone. The Office of Economic Opportunity helped the poor and gave them a voice in handling their own affairs. Medicare ensured medical care for the elderly, while Medicaid gave similar aid to the poor. The Great Society included the most far-reaching school support program in American history. In 1965 a new Department of Housing and Urban Development gave Cabinet-level visibility to the effort to revive the nation's cities.

Nixon and the Welfare State In 1968 Richard Nixon won the presidency, bringing Republicans back into power. Nixon wanted to trim social welfare programs, which he claimed encouraged people not to work, and to bring the budget under control.

Yet in fact, the federal government continued to grow during Nixon's presidency. The Occupational Safety and Health Act (OSHA) of 1970 provided for employee rights in the workplace and demanded that safety standards be maintained, with federal enforcement regulation. Also in 1970 the Environmental Protection Agency (EPA) was created to oversee federal antipollution laws. Opponents of government growth bridled at these efforts.

Social Issues Many conservatives were deeply troubled by rapid cultural changes of the time. Rock music was becoming increasingly shocking, its lyrics more openly sexual

Answer to . . .

Main Idea Connections "Modern Republicanism," in which he accepted the basic outlines of the New Deal.

 ## RESOURCE OPTIONS

Media and Technology

 AmericanHeritage® CD-ROM

Time Tour The Nation Today and Tomorrow: New Directions

Color Transparencies Time Lines, E-10

and drug-oriented. Illegal drugs became widespread on college campuses.

The sexual revolution was another source of conservative concern. The use of the new birth control pill encouraged promiscuity, critics said. Also, after the 1973 Supreme Court ruling in *Roe* v. *Wade* legalized abortion, anti-abortion forces launched a campaign to overturn that ruling. The movement for gay and lesbian rights further angered many conservative Americans.

The women's movement caused still another rift. As women worked for equal rights and began to gain new opportunities, some conservatives reacted vigorously. A woman's place was at home, they argued. Phyllis Schlafly, who campaigned against ratification of the Equal Rights Amendment, echoed the desire to retain women's traditional roles.

Another controversy involved affirmative action. This is a policy whereby employers try to make up for past discrimination by giving special consideration to the hiring of women and minority applicants. When the government and private companies adopted affirmative action, some critics called the policy "reverse discrimination." This issue attracted some Democratic blue-collar workers to the Republican ranks, where they would help elect Ronald Reagan to the presidency.

Turning Point: The Election of 1980

In 1976, Ronald Reagan had challenged President Gerald Ford for the Republican nomination. He lost by a narrow margin. In 1980 Reagan again sought the nomination. Republican moderates claimed that he, like Goldwater in 1964, was too conservative to defeat the Democratic President, Jimmy Carter. Yet in fact, social changes were under way that would prove this prediction wrong.

The New Right Coalition By 1980, conservative groups had formed a powerful political

 TURNING POINT: *Election of 1980*

Ronald Reagan's election as President in 1980 reflected a growing public demand for smaller, less expensive government.

1980
Ronald Reagan, promising to reduce the size and cost of government, is elected President.

1994
Congress defeats President Clinton's plan for comprehensive health care.

1998
The federal budget deficit is eliminated.

1980 **1990** **2000**

1981
Congress approves cuts in taxes and domestic spending.

1988
George Bush wins the presidency on a pledge of "no new taxes."

"...Read my lips NO New Taxes.."

1996
President Clinton declares that "the era of big government is over."

RESOURCE OPTIONS

Teaching Resources

📁 **Primary Source Activity** Speaking for the President, Learning with Documents folder, p. 40

Media and Technology

 Decision America Videotapes and Videodiscs Issue 4 *Who Tells Us What to Think?*

Customize for
English Language Learners

Ask students to write the heading "Roots of the New Conservatism" on a sheet of paper and list at least six issues that helped to unite conservatives in forming the New Right.

ACTIVITY
LEARNING STYLES

Have students take on the role of a journalist covering a political campaign. Have each student prepare six questions to ask as he or she interviews one candidate from the New Right and one with liberal views. Some students can take the candidates' role and answer the questions. (*Auditory*)

ACTIVITY
HETEROGENEOUS GROUPS

Ask students to do research to find the strategies, slogans, and advertisements used by the three candidates in their 1980 presidential campaigns. Have them demonstrate or read samples from each campaign in class. (*Enrichment*)

Graphing the Main Idea

To make sure students understand the main idea of this section, you may wish to use the flow map graphic organizer below.

Tell students that a flow map shows a sequence of events unfolding. Ask students to use it to show the events that brought Ronald Reagan to power in 1980.

Teaching Tip A template for this graphic organizer can be found in the Color Transparencies, G-4.

Answers to
SECTION 1 REVIEW

1. (a) New Right, see p. 958;
(b) televangelism, see p. 958.

2. Rock music, the increase in drug use, the birth control pill, legalized abortion, the movement for gay and lesbian rights, the women's movement, and affirmative action.

3. Roosevelt: expand government with New Deal; Eisenhower: adhere to New Deal; Johnson: expand government with Great Society; Nixon: enact new programs.

4. (a) 1964, 1968, 1980. (b) Sample answer: People unhappy with an administration might vote for a different party in the next election.

5. He used television effectively; he used humor and acting techniques.

6. Essays will vary but should be supported with facts from the section.

Jerry Falwell and other televangelists helped change the way political candidates portrayed themselves and their opponents in the media. *Culture What were some of the issues addressed by the New Right?*

coalition known as the **New Right.** A key concern of many conservatives in the New Right was the size of government and its role in the economy. They proposed cutting government-funded social programs.

Other groups in the New Right wanted to restore what they considered Christian values to society. Members of the Moral Majority, led by the Reverend Jerry Falwell of Virginia, wanted to follow the dictates of the Bible and revive the traditional values they believed had strengthened the country in the past.

Falwell and other evangelists used the power of television to reach millions of people. In a format that became known as

televangelism, they appealed to viewers to contribute money to their campaign. They delivered fervent sermons on specific political issues and used the money they raised to back conservative politicians.

A Reagan Landslide The growing strength of conservatives in the Republican party gave Ronald Reagan the GOP presidential nomination in 1980. During the campaign, Reagan seized on growing discontent. His attacks on incumbent Jimmy Carter's handling of the economy were particularly effective. Criticizing Carter's economic record, he poked fun at the President's use of technical language:

> **AMERICAN VOICES** "I'm talking in human terms and he is hiding behind a dictionary. If he wants a definition, I'll give him one. A recession is when your neighbor loses his job. A depression is when you lose yours. A recovery is when Jimmy Carter loses his."
>
> —*Ronald Reagan, 1980*

The continuing hostage crisis in Iran, as well as other issues, hurt Carter, and Reagan won in a landslide. He gained 51 percent of the popular vote to Carter's 41 percent. (Illinois Representative John Anderson ran as a third-party candidate.) Carried along by Reagan's popularity, the Republicans gained control of the Senate for the first time in 25 years.

Conservatism now controlled the nation's agenda. The effects of this power shift are shown in the Turning Point on the previous page.

SECTION 1 REVIEW

Comprehension

1. *Key Terms* Define: (a) New Right; (b) televangelism.

2. *Summarizing the Main Idea* What types of social changes in the 1960s and 1970s led to a conservative backlash in 1980?

3. *Organizing Information* Create a table listing all the Presidents mentioned in this section and summarizing their approaches to government.

Critical Thinking

4. *Analyzing Time Lines* Refer to the time line at the start of the section. (a) Identify entries that show a shift in political power. (b) Why do you think power tends to swing between liberalism and conservatism?

5. *Recognizing Cause and Effect* How did Reagan use modern technology and new political techniques to increase his popularity?

Writing Activity

6. *Writing an Expository Essay* Many political analysts at first disregarded candidate Reagan as too conservative to win widespread support. Write an essay explaining how he was able not just to win the election, but to win in a landslide.

 RESOURCE OPTIONS

Teaching Resources

 Quiz Units 9–10 folder, p. 89

Student Performance Pack

Guide to the Essentials Chapter 34, Section 1 (English and Spanish)

Media and Technology

Prentice Hall United States History Video Collection™ Volume 18 *Depression and the New Deal;* Volume 20 *Post-War USA*

Answer to . . .

Viewing History The size and role of the government; following dictates of the Bible; reviving traditional values.

1981	1981		1983	1983	1983
5 percent tax cut; severe recession begins	Reagan wounded in assassination attempt	1982 10 percent tax cut	Strategic Defense Initiative announced	Inflation and unemployment drop below 10 percent	Bombing in Lebanon kills 241 marines; American victory in Grenada

1981   **1982**   **1983**

2 The Reagan Revolution

SECTION PREVIEW

Objectives

1 Describe how Reagan sought to change the economy and the government.
2 List the major initiatives and key foreign policy crises during Reagan's first term.
3 Describe the economic recession of the early 1980s.
4 *Key Terms* Define: supply-side economics; New Federalism; Strategic Defense Initiative (SDI).

Main Idea

Ronald Reagan aimed to boost the nation's pride and prosperity by cutting taxes, shrinking the federal government, and increasing defense spending.

Reading Strategy

Outlining Information On a separate sheet of paper, copy down the headings and subheadings in this section. As you read, add at least two key facts under each subheading to create an outline of the section.

During the 1980 campaign, Ronald Reagan stressed three broad policies that he would pursue if elected President: slashing taxes, eliminating unnecessary government programs, and bolstering the defense capability of the United States. In his first term, he moved aggressively to implement those policies.

Changing the Economy

President Reagan brought to Washington a plan for economic change that conservatives had long sought to put into action. In simple terms, he wanted to put more money back into people's paychecks instead of into tax coffers.

Supply-Side Economics Reagan's main goal was to spur business growth. His economic program, dubbed "Reaganomics," rested on the theory of supply-side economics. This theory reversed earlier policies based on the ideas of English economist John Maynard Keynes.

In the 1920s and 1930s, Keynes had argued that the government could best improve the economy by increasing consumers' demand for goods. This meant giving people more money—either directly, through government aid, or indirectly, by creating jobs. Once people had more money to spend, Keynes argued, they would purchase more goods and services, which would cause the economy to grow.

Keynesian theory had helped explain the Great Depression and the recovery that took place as the United States began a massive military spending program during World War II. In the postwar years, most economists accepted Keynesian arguments.

In contrast to Keynesian theory, **supply-side economics** focused not on the demand for goods but on the supply of goods. It predicted that cutting taxes would put more money into the hands of businesses and investors—those who supplied the goods for consumers to buy.

The theory assumed that businesses would then hire more people and produce more goods and services, making the economy grow faster. The real key, therefore, was encouraging business leaders to invest. Their individual actions would create and promote greater national economic abundance. Prosperity would

RESOURCE OPTIONS

Teaching Resources

Reproducible Lesson Plan Lesson Plans folder, p. 171

Learning Styles Lesson Plan Learning Styles Lesson Plans folder, p. 70

Big Idea Graphic Organizer Big Idea Graphic Organizer folder, p. 143

Guided Reading and Review Units 9–10 folder, p. 90

Objectives

You may wish to call students' attention to the objectives in the Section Preview. The objectives are reflected in the main headings of the section.

Bellringer

Ask students to suggest their own ideas for a fair method of taxing people to pay for government services. What kinds of income or purchases would they tax? How would they make sure the tax was fair?

Reading Strategy

Outlining Information Refer to the Reading Strategy in the Section Preview. Using the first heading, you may wish to offer examples of key facts and less important facts to help students distinguish between the two.

LESSON PLAN

Connecting to the Main Idea

1. **Focus** Explain that Reagan's actions and policies in his first term as President were intended to carry out the conservative ideas and principles on which he had campaigned. Ask students to name those principles.
2. **Instruct** Explain the two competing theories of economics that modern U.S. governments have followed: Keynesian and supply-side. Explore ways that tax policies and other actions, such as deregulation, are outgrowths of the economic policy that an administration is following. Discuss how the military buildup, increased spending on weapons, and overseas military expeditions such as the invasion of Grenada fit in with Reagan's agenda.
3. **Close** In his first term, Ronald Reagan worked steadfastly to carry out conservative policies. His successes—and the many voters who approved of them—would carry him into a second term.

eventually "trickle down" from the top to those at the lower levels of the economy.

George Bush, a rival candidate for the Republican presidential nomination, called Reagan's economic plan "voodoo economics." Only later, when he became Reagan's running mate, did Bush change his stand.

Cutting Taxes Reagan's first priority was a tax cut. In October 1981, a 5 percent cut went into effect, followed by 10 percent cuts in 1982 and 1983. In 1986, during Reagan's second term, Congress passed the most sweeping tax reform in history. The law closed loopholes that had allowed some people to avoid paying their fair share of taxes. It simplified the tax system by reducing the number of income brackets that determined how much tax a person paid. While all taxpayers benefited from these measures, the wealthy Americans benefited most. The tax rate on the highest incomes dropped from 50 percent to 28 percent.

Main Idea CONNECTIONS

What was the effect of Reagan's tax cuts?

Changing the Government

As you read in the previous section, for generations conservatives had criticized government

growth. Now, however, they had a Chief Executive committed to limiting both the size and the role of the federal government.

Cutting Regulations Reagan embarked on a major program of deregulation. Like President Carter before him, Reagan wanted to eliminate government regulations that he said stifled free market competition.

By the time of Reagan's presidency, regulation had been expanding for nearly a century. The Interstate Commerce Commission, established in 1887, was the first step. Government regulations grew during the Progressive era of the early 1900s and in the New Deal years of the 1930s. Regulation was intended to protect companies from unfair competition, workers from unsafe working conditions, and consumers from ineffective or unsafe products.

Reagan continued and expanded the deregulation of the energy, transportation, and banking industries begun under the Carter administration. He cut the number and size of regulatory agencies like the Environmental Protection Agency, which had its budget, and therefore its functions, reduced. Reagan argued that regulations made life difficult for producers, which meant fewer jobs for workers and higher prices for consumers. The more

In 1981, the Professional Air Traffic Controllers Association (PATCO) went on strike. Citing that federal employees were prohibited from striking, Reagan fired 11,500 strikers and banned them from their careers. **Government** Why do you think Reagan felt there was the need for decisive action?

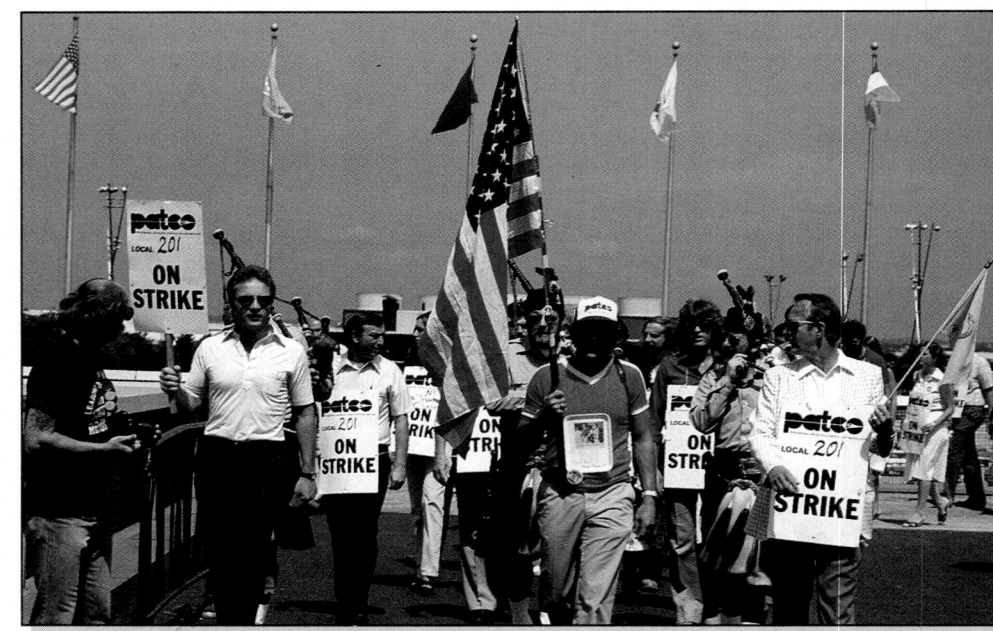

that businesses spent to comply with government rules, he charged, the less they could spend on new factories and equipment.

Slowing Federal Growth Reagan also attempted to cut the size of the federal government. The President believed that any American could succeed through individual effort. This belief ran counter to the argument on which welfare was based: that government should help people who could not help themselves. Reagan charged that the government had become too intrusive in people's lives:

 ❝It is . . . my intention . . . to make [government] work—work with us, not over us; to stand by our side, not ride on our back. Government can and must provide opportunity, not smother it; foster productivity, not stifle it.❞

—President Ronald Reagan, First Inaugural Address, 1981

Drawing support from opponents of the programs created by Lyndon Johnson's Great Society, Reagan attacked these programs head-on. The administration eliminated public service jobs that were part of an employment training program. It reduced unemployment compensation. It lowered welfare benefits and reduced allocations for food stamps. It raised fees for Medicare patients. Despite cuts in specific programs, total federal spending on social welfare rose between 1980 and 1982.

While he cut back the role of the federal government, Reagan sought to give more responsibility to state and local governments. Borrowing a term from the Nixon administration, he called his plan the **New Federalism.** Under this plan, the federal government would no longer tell states exactly how federal aid had to be used. Rather it would let states create and pay for programs as they saw fit.

The New Federalism program never worked as planned. A recession early in Reagan's presidency left a number of cities and states nearly bankrupt. They now had responsibility but not enough money for programs formerly funded by the federal government.

Reagan's Foreign Policy

While taking decisive measures to change the direction of domestic policy, Reagan was equally determined to defend American interests in the cold war. He believed in a tough approach toward the Soviet Union, which he called an "evil empire." He favored large defense budgets to strengthen both conventional military forces and the nuclear arsenal.

Military Buildup The costs of the buildup were enormous. Over a five-year period, the United States spent an unprecedented $1.1 trillion on defense. By 1985, the nation was spending half a million dollars every minute on defense. These expenditures contributed to the growing budget deficits.

Much of this money went into new weapons. The United States continued to develop new missiles, such as the intercontinental MX, as well as new bombers and submarines that could carry nuclear weapons. Reagan also explored ways to protect Americans against nuclear attack. In 1983 Reagan announced the **Strategic Defense Initiative (SDI),** popularly known as "Star Wars," after the 1977 film. SDI proposed the creation of a massive satellite shield in space to intercept and destroy incoming Soviet missiles.

Federal Defense Spending, 1976–1992

Source: *Statistical Abstract of the United States*

Interpreting Graphs Notice the change in defense spending in the early 1980s. *Economics* By how much did the defense budget increase during President Reagan's two terms in office?

President Reagan (left) reviews an honor guard at a Pentagon ceremony in 1987.

Using the Internet

Prepare a Report

Objective Use the Internet to prepare a report on the role of Reagan's Strategic Defense Initiative. Have students follow these instructions:

1. See the *America: Pathways to the Present* Web site at

http://www.Pathways.phschool.com

for the URLs for President Reagan's Address to the Nation on National Security and the *Atlantic Monthly* article on Gorbachev and SDI.

2. Read the speech and the article, taking detailed notes. Compare Gorbachev's and Reagan's views on the role of SDI and its causes and effects.

3. Write a report, including specific facts and quotes. Be sure to include your views on which document is more persuasive, and why.

 RESOURCE OPTIONS

Teaching Resources

American History Block Scheduling Support Presidential Power: Changes in the Twentieth Century, found in The Nation After World War II folder, includes interdisciplinary lesson suggestions and activities for Geography and History, Primary Sources, Biography, and Literature.

Media and Technology

 RESOURCE⊙PRO

Visual Learning Activity "Passing the Economic Buck," found on Resource Pro, reveals two cartoonists' suggestions of why successive administrations were unable to control government waste and inefficiency.

Answer to . . .

Interpreting Graphs *It nearly doubled, from approximately $150 billion to $290 billion.*

BACKGROUND

Geography in History

The outcome of the invasion of Grenada, the Western Hemisphere's smallest nation, was never in doubt. At 133 square miles in area, the island republic is less than one-tenth the size of Rhode Island. Grenada's principal ally, Cuba, lay at the other end of the Caribbean, while Grenada's neighbors supplied soldiers and police for the invasion. The United States landed 7,000 troops within one week, and Cuban and Marxist troops who survived the initial fighting retreated into the island's jungles. Resistance was so light that the United States began withdrawing its troops after less than a month.

Notable PRESIDENTS

Ronald Reagan

"I find no national malaise. I find nothing wrong with the American people."
—Ronald Reagan, 1980

1981–1989

Ronald Reagan was born in rural Tampico, Illinois, in 1911. The first in his family to go to college, Reagan became a radio sportscaster after graduating. The Iowa radio station could not afford to send him to Chicago to broadcast the Chicago Cubs baseball games, so Reagan used the wire service's running accounts and dramatized the rest. His ability to spin dramatic stories from a few dry facts helped him become known in later years as the "Great Communicator." During a business trip to California in 1937, Reagan took a screen test at the Warner Brothers studio. He spent the next ten years building a film career.

In 1947, Reagan became president of the film actors' union, the Screen Actors' Guild. He used his position to fight communism. In the mid- and late 1950s, he became the spokesman for General Electric. He spoke against communism and the "containment" policy. During the 1964 presidential campaign he gave a nationally televised speech, which outlined major conservative views. The speech made Reagan a national political figure.

In 1966 Reagan was elected governor of California. Likable and articulate, Reagan was a natural politician who appealed to any audience. In the presidential election of 1980, he asked the voters, "Are you better off today than you were four years ago?" The answer was apparent in his landslide victory over President Carter.

In 1984, Reagan was reelected, becoming the third Republican President to win reelection since the Depression. His aggressive defense policy helped bring about the end of the cold war and reshaped postwar politics.

Americans remember Reagan for his presidential style—unassuming, personable, candid, and optimistic. A later President, Bill Clinton, summed it up: " [Reagan's] unwavering hopefulness reminded us that optimism is one of our most fundamental virtues."

Connecting to Today

Ronald Reagan reminded Americans how important the role of the President is in helping overcome national self-doubt.
How has the United States' self-confidence changed since 1980? Explain.

Trouble Spots Abroad Relations with the Soviet Union remained frosty during Reagan's first term. The Soviets criticized the American defense buildup. They also complained when the United States stationed new intermediate-range nuclear missiles in Western Europe.

The United States was active in the Middle East as well. The country of Lebanon had become a battleground for a variety of armed political groups. In 1982, Reagan sent several thousand marines to Beirut, the Lebanese capital, as part of a peacekeeping force. In October 1983 a terrorist truck loaded with explosives crashed through the gates of a marine barracks, killing 241 Americans.

The attack horrified the nation. Many Americans demanded an immediate withdrawal from Lebanon, and by the following February, all the troops had left.

In Latin America, Reagan feared that Communist forces would gain power and threaten American interests. In El Salvador, the United States supported a repressive military regime in resisting guerrillas, some of whom were Marxists. Reagan increased military aid to El Salvador to the level of about $1 million a day. In Nicaragua, as you will read in the next section, the United States helped guerrillas who were fighting to overthrow that nation's leftist government.

Reagan claimed a victory on the tiny Caribbean island of Grenada. He ordered United States military forces to Grenada in October 1983, after a military coup installed a government sympathetic to Communist Cuba. The official aim of the invasion was to safeguard several hundred American medical students on the island. However, United States forces also overthrew the Grenadian government and remained in Grenada to oversee free elections.

Recession and Recovery

During Reagan's first two years in office, the United States experienced the worst recession since the Great Depression. High interest rates discouraged Americans from borrowing to purchase goods or invest in new equipment. Foreign competition cost thousands of American jobs. By 1982 several hundred businesses were going bankrupt each week.

The 1981–1982 recession did, however, pave the way for an economic recovery. The high interest rates cooled down inflation, and as Reagan's tax cuts took effect, consumer

TEST PREPARATION

Have students reread the paragraphs under the subheading "Trouble Spots Abroad," and then answer the question below.

A fact from this selection is that—

A Americans were unconcerned with the actions taking place in Lebanon.

B the United States supported a repressive military regime in El Salvador.

C Communist forces gained power in Latin America and threatened American interests there.

D in Grenada, the United States intervened only to safeguard American medical students.

spending began to rise. By 1983, both inflation and unemployment had already dropped below 10 percent. Business leaders gained new confidence, and increased their investments. The stock market pushed upward. Republicans claimed that the recovery demonstrated the wisdom of supply-side economics.

Yet an important prediction of the supply-side theorists had not come true. Cuts in tax rates were supposed to generate so much economic growth that the government's tax revenues would actually increase. As a result, the federal deficit, or the amount by which the government's spending exceeds its income in a given year, was supposed to decrease.

During the 1980 campaign, Reagan had vowed to balance the federal budget if elected. But, the combination of the Reagan tax cuts and defense spending pushed the deficit up, not down. The deficit ballooned from nearly $80 billion in 1980 to a peak of $221 billion in 1986.

While the rising deficits did help the government cut back on domestic spending, they drove the nation as a whole deeper into debt. The national debt, the total amount of money owed by the government, rose from $909 billion in 1980 to $3.2 trillion in 1990. Future generations would have to bear the burden of interest payments on this monumental debt.

Yet in spite of these problems, most Americans supported Reagan. They shared his values and principles.

In 1981, Reagan was wounded in an assassination attempt. The courage and humor with which he faced the situation ("Please tell me you're all Republicans," he quipped to the doctors treating him) only reinforced Americans' respect for their President.

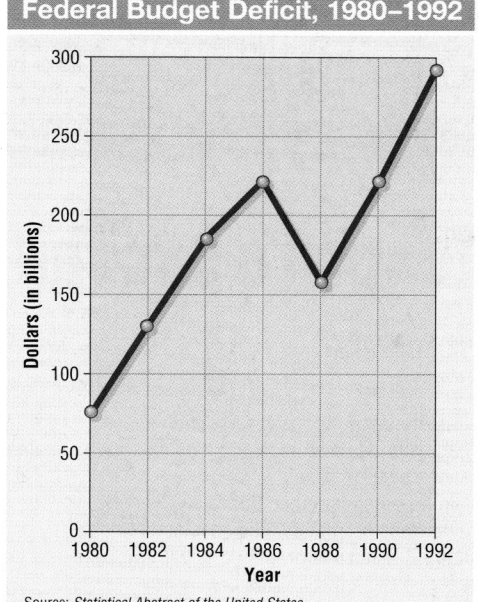

Federal Budget Deficit, 1980–1992

Source: *Statistical Abstract of the United States*

Interpreting Graphs Examine the graph above showing the federal deficit from 1980 to 1992. *Economics What happened to the federal deficit during Reagan's years in office? How did Reagan's policies contribute to that trend?*

SECTION 2 REVIEW

Comprehension

1. *Key Terms* Define: (a) supply-side economics; (b) New Federalism; (c) Strategic Defense Initiative (SDI).

2. *Summarizing the Main Idea* What major shifts in philosophy and policies did Reagan bring to the government?

3. *Organizing Information* Create a three-column table entitled *Changes Under Reagan.* The columns should have the headings *Economy, Government,* and *Foreign Policy.* Fill in at least three entries under each column.

Critical Thinking

4. *Analyzing Time Lines* Refer to the time line at the start of the section. Why was 1983 an active year for foreign policy in Reagan's first term?

5. *Drawing Conclusions* What consequences could result from cutting regulations enforced by the federal government?

Writing Activity

6. *Writing a Persuasive Essay* Take a stand for or against the theory of supply-side economics. Use specific details and examples to argue your position.

RESOURCE OPTIONS

Teaching Resources

 Quiz Units 9–10 folder, p. 91

 Key Documents Ronald Reagan, "These Are the Boys of Pointe du Hoc," Learning with Documents folder, p. 106

Student Performance Pack

Guide to the Essentials Chapter 34, Section 2 (English and Spanish)

Reagan's Second Term

Objectives

You may wish to call students' attention to the objectives in the Section Preview. The objectives are reflected in the main headings of the section.

Bellringer

Ask students to think about the American belief that all people are "created equal." In what ways is this belief reflected in social and economic policies?

Reading Strategy

Organizing Information Refer to the Reading Strategy in the Section Preview. You may wish to model a summary of a key event from the text under the first heading.

LESSON PLAN
Connecting to the Main Idea

1. Focus Explain that Ronald Reagan was personally popular with the majority of Americans, in large part because he made Americans feel good about themselves and their country. What difficulties became apparent during his second term?

2. Instruct Discuss the economic, social, and judicial issues that developed during the Reagan era, such as the growing gap between rich and poor, the recession, the defeat of the Equal Rights Amendment, conservative appointments to the Supreme Court, and the extension of the Voting Rights Act of 1965. Did these events help or hurt the conservative cause?

Explain the rapid changes going on in the Soviet Union in this period. Discuss the effects of these changes on Reagan's relationship with Mikhail Gorbachev.

3. Close Reagan's continuing popularity helped maintain support for conservative policies throughout his two terms and enabled George Bush to "inherit" the presidency. However, Reagan's shoes would prove hard to fill.

1981 O'Connor becomes first woman on Supreme Court	1982 Equal Rights Amendment defeated	1984 Reagan wins reelection	1985 Gorbachev takes power in Soviet Union	1986 Iran-contra affair revealed	1987 Reagan, Gorbachev sign INF Treaty

1980	1982	1984	1986	1988

3 Reagan's Second Term

SECTION PREVIEW

Objectives

1. Contrast the patriotic renewal inspired by Reagan with the unequal distribution of wealth increased by his policies.
2. Explain how Reagan used Supreme Court appointments to influence key social debates.
3. Describe Reagan's approach to governing, and summarize the legacy of his presidency.
4. *Key Terms* Define: AIDS; Sandinista; contra; Iran-contra affair; INF Treaty; entitlement.

Main Idea

After a decisive reelection victory in 1984, Reagan continued his conservative policies on economic and social issues. In domestic and foreign affairs, the administration had key successes but also serious missteps.

Reading Strategy

Organizing Information As you read the section, list the key events and crises described. For each event, summarize the significance or outcome.

Campaigning for reelection in 1984, Ronald Reagan asked voters if they were better off than they had been four years before. As they roared their approval, he told them, "You ain't seen nothing yet." His campaign advertisements, such as one depicting "Morning in America," heralded a new day of optimism.

Reagan faced Democrat Walter Mondale, former Vice President under Carter. Mondale's running mate was New York Representative Geraldine Ferraro, the first woman ever on a major party's presidential ticket.

The relative strength of the economy and Reagan's popularity gave the President a landslide victory over Mondale. Reagan took 59 percent of the popular vote and all the electoral votes except those of the District of Columbia and Mondale's home state of Minnesota. It was the second largest electoral-vote margin in history.

Ronald Reagan's charisma appealed to many voters.

Patriotic Renewal

Reagan wanted to re-create the sense of community he had known in his youth and to help revive the virtues that had made America strong. The nation had endured turbulence in the years following the Vietnam War. The 1980s offered several occasions to celebrate patriotic renewal.

1984 Olympic Games The 1984 Olympic Games were held in Los Angeles, the first time the Summer Games had come to the United States in half a century. The ceremonies, televised worldwide to hundreds of millions of viewers, were festive, patriotic affairs.

Some Communist countries, including the Soviet Union and East Germany, boycotted the games. The move was in retaliation to an American-led boycott of the 1980 Moscow games to protest the Soviet invasion of Afghanistan in 1979. As a result of the boycott, the United States won an unusually high number of medals.

Statue of Liberty Centennial Two years later, in 1986, the nation celebrated the centennial of the Statue of Liberty in New York harbor. This monument, the first structure many immigrants had seen as they entered the United

▶ RESOURCE OPTIONS

Teaching Resources

📁 **Reproducible Lesson Plan** Lesson Plans folder, p. 172

📁 **Big Idea Graphic Organizer** Big Idea Graphic Organizer folder, p. 144

📁 **Guided Reading and Review** Units 9–10 folder, p. 92

Media and Technology

 AmericanHeritage® CD-ROM

Time Tour The Nation Today and Tomorrow: New Directions

States, was a symbol of freedom around the world. But the copper lady in flowing robes had deteriorated over the course of 100 years. Now, after a massive campaign to refurbish the statue, the nation held a spectacular centennial celebration.

Bicentennial of the Constitution The following year the United States celebrated the 200th anniversary of the Constitution, drafted in 1787. Government and private groups sponsored lectures, workshops, and meetings focusing on the features of the Constitution that made the nation strong. This observance helped renew public appreciation of such enduring ideas as balanced government and separation of powers.

Unequal Wealth

The truly wealthy, more than anyone else, flourished under Reagan. The net worth of *Forbes* magazine's 400 richest Americans nearly tripled in the Reagan years. Political analyst Kevin Phillips described this new class of "upper America":

> **AMERICAN VOICES**
> ❝The truth is that the critical concentration of wealth in the United States was developing at higher levels— decamillionaires, centimillionaires, half-billionaires and billionaires. Garden variety millionaires had become so common that there were about 1.5 million of them by 1989.❞
>
> —*Political analyst Kevin Phillips,*
> New York Times Magazine, *June 24, 1990*

By the late 1980s, wealth was more unevenly distributed than at any time since the end of World War II. Many families increased their total income by having both husband and wife work outside the home. Individual wages, however, declined. For the poorest one fifth of the population, total family income dropped.

Continuing Social Debates

In the years leading to Reagan's election, conservatives gained public support with their stands on social issues as well as economic ones. In the 1980s, conservative policies on social issues made these "hot" issues even hotter.

Civil Rights The federal commitment to extend voting rights had given the vote to millions of African Americans who had been denied it for decades. These new voters elected an increasing number of African American candidates to local, state, and national offices.

Resistance to civil rights initiatives was growing, however, as critics complained that many of these policies trampled on the rights of state and local governments. Reagan tried to prevent the extension of the Voting Rights Act of 1965, backing off only after intense criticism. He appointed federal judges who were less sympathetic to civil rights goals. The administration also worked to end some affirmative action programs.

The Women's Movement As women gained access to jobs and other opportunities previously denied to them, the women's movement met with a backlash. One sign of this backlash was the defeat in 1982 of the proposed Equal Rights Amendment, which failed to gain the approval of enough state legislatures to be ratified.

Anti-abortion groups took aim at the right to abortion granted in the 1973 *Roe* v. *Wade*

COMPARING PRIMARY SOURCES

THE LEGACY OF THE CIVIL RIGHTS MOVEMENT

Decades after the civil rights movement, Americans disagreed on how much progress had been made.

Substantial Progress	Little or No Progress
"Before the civil rights movement, there was a very wide separation between blacks and whites. I don't think the separation is as great today. There has been more speaking out. Blacks now let themselves open up and say how they feel in no uncertain terms. I think there are friendships between blacks and whites that didn't exist before. In spite of everything, I think the racial situation is healthier than it was before. Blacks are no longer invisible."	"The country is more segregated today than it was when [Martin Luther] King and [Robert] Kennedy were alive. What Dr. King and Bobby were fighting was segregation and discrimination imposed by law, by the state. . . . All of that has changed. . . . But in the North, everybody knows what's happened in the cities. At universities, there's much more black withdrawal into separate communities. I grew up thinking we were going to have an integrated society, not just an end to official racism."
—*Eileen Barth, retired social worker, quoted in Studs Terkel's* Race, *1992*	—*New York Times* columnist *Anthony Lewis, April 1993*

ANALYZING VIEWPOINTS Compare the main arguments in the two quotations above.

From the Archives of

American Heritage®

About the Presidents

With his political identity forged in Barry Goldwater's presidential campaign of 1964, **Ronald Reagan** (1981–1989) was thought to be far too conservative to be a viable candidate for the presidency. But Reagan's call for a reduced federal role in domestic affairs and his projection of American force and ideals abroad won him a handy victory in the campaign of 1980. Despite a sharp recession in his first term, Reagan's popularity soared as he won his race for a second term in a landslide. Reagan was widely admired for his optimistic temperament and unwavering patriotism. Yet the true legacy of his presidency was to oversee a substantial shift in public opinion toward the conservative end of the spectrum. Source: Adapted from Henry F. Graff's *The Presidents,* Scribner's, 1996, by the editors of *American Heritage* magazine.

RESOURCE OPTIONS

Teaching Resources

 Comparing Primary Sources On the Legacy of the Civil Rights Movement, Units 9–10 folder, pp. 97–98

 Literature Activity Masters of the Universe, Units 9–10 folder, p. 99

Media and Technology

American Heritage® CD-ROM

Presidents Ronald Reagan

Listening to Literature Ian Frazier, "*Coyote* v. *Acme*"

Answer to . . .

Comparing Primary Sources Barth thinks that African Americans are more hopeful and more visible in society in the 1990s; Lewis sees less promise of integration than when Dr. King was alive.

Supreme Court decision. Opponents lobbied to halt federal funding of abortions for the poor.

Sexual Orientation The campaign for homosexual rights caused similar polarization. Contributing to the backlash was the discovery in 1981 of acquired immuno-deficiency syndrome, known simply as **AIDS.** At first, most of its victims were intravenous drug users and homosexual men. Some Americans therefore viewed AIDS as a curse that punished certain people for their habits and lifestyles. Even as AIDS spread into the larger community, the resistance to gay rights grew more vocal.

Conservatives on the Supreme Court

Many of these social issues wound up in the courts. Reagan used his years in office to appoint conservative federal judges. In 1981 he selected Arizona judge Sandra Day O'Connor as the nation's first woman Supreme Court justice. In 1986 Reagan chose another conservative, Antonin Scalia, for the Supreme Court.

While O'Connor and Scalia won Senate confirmation, Reagan's next Supreme Court appointment, conservative judge and former law professor Robert Bork, did not. Liberal groups joined together in 1987 to convince the Senate to reject Bork's nomination. The nominee whom the Senate finally approved, Anthony Kennedy, was known as a moderate conservative. He joined the Court in 1988.

Sandra Day O'Connor

 Among the conservatives on the Court, Sandra Day O'Connor emerged as someone who went her own way and often helped to reconcile differences. These were skills that she *had* to learn—a long time ago.

Born in El Paso, Texas, in 1930, Sandra Day grew up on her parents' ranch in Arizona. Graduating early from Austin (Texas) High School, at age 16 she entered Stanford University in California, where she earned an economics degree and high honors in 1950. Two years later she graduated third in her class at Stanford Law School and made the prestigious Law Review.

Sandra Day O'Connor (b.1930)

These credentials should have landed the young lawyer an excellent job. However, as she later recalled, "When I graduated from law school in 1952, there were still only a handful of women lawyers in the United States. None of the larger law firms had ever hired a woman attorney. I was unable to get a job on graduation as a lawyer in a law firm, although I did get a job as an attorney in a county government office."

Day married Stanford classmate John Jay O'Connor III in 1952. They eventually settled in Arizona, where Sandra Day O'Connor opened her own law firm, serving as a court-appointed attorney for impoverished clients. She discontinued her practice with the birth of the first of her three children in 1957 and began working for the Republican party in Arizona.

In 1965 she returned to full-time work, serving in a variety of roles: assistant attorney general, state senator (and the first woman majority leader), and superior court judge. In 1979, Arizona governor Bruce Babbitt appointed O'Connor to the state appeals court. Just 18 months later, in 1981, President Reagan nominated her to become the first woman justice of the United States Supreme Court. She was sworn in on September 26, 1981.

In her years on the Court, which included a battle with cancer, O'Connor gained the respect of both conservatives and liberals. Her opinions in several landmark cases showed a tendency to look for practical solutions instead of ruling along strictly ideological lines. She broke ranks with her fellow conservatives to support the Equal Rights Amendment and took a leadership role on women's issues. ▪

Reagan's Hands-off Style

Ronald Reagan favored less government regulation of the economy. A decade later, neither party—the Republicans or the Democrats—would argue with that. Reagan also followed a hands-off style in running the government. He delegated authority to those who worked for him rather than be involved in every decision. Several times this approach led to notable problems.

The S & L Scandal "Thrift institutions" or savings and loan banks, often called S&Ls, made home mortgage loans to individuals. The Reagan administration, with the help of Democrats in Congress, pressed for the deregulation of S&Ls to permit them to make riskier but more profitable investments.

Officials at some deregulated S&Ls took advantage of the new laws to make huge fortunes for themselves. Many made risky investments in an overheated real estate market. When the market cooled down in the late 1980s, many S&Ls collapsed, taking with them about $2.6 billion in depositors' savings.

Because bank accounts are insured by the federal government, taxpayers had to make up the billions of dollars lost when hundreds of S&Ls failed. A number of banking officials were prosecuted for their role in the scandal and their efforts to cover it up.

The Iran-contra Affair In Nicaragua, the Reagan administration sought to undermine the Marxist government that had seized power in 1979. The ruling group, the **Sandinistas,** was named after a Nicaraguan freedom fighter from the 1920s. Reagan feared that the Sandinistas' revolution would spread Marxist upheaval to other Latin American countries.

Working through the Central Intelligence Agency, the United States trained and armed Nicaraguan guerrillas known as **contras** (Spanish for "counterrevolutionaries"). This policy, however, violated American neutrality laws.

Congress discovered these secret missions and in 1984 cut off military aid to the contras. Some members of the Reagan administration still believed that aid to the contras was justified. These officials took the profits from secret arms sales to Iran and then sent those profits to the contras. (The arms sales were meant to encourage the release of American hostages held in Lebanon by pro-Iranian terrorists.)

When the secret actions became public in the fall of 1986, Oliver North, the marine colonel who had made the arrangements, took the blame. The **Iran-contra affair,** as this scandal came to be called, caused the most serious criticism that the Reagan administration ever faced. The President himself claimed no knowledge of North's operations.

The Reagan Legacy

The Iran-contra affair did not damage Ronald Reagan's personal approval ratings. When he

Relations between the United States and the Soviet Union warmed during Reagan's second term. Here, Reagan and Soviet leader Mikhail Gorbachev meet outside St. Basil's Cathedral in Moscow. *Foreign Relations Why do you think glasnost and perestroika helped smooth relations between the two countries?*

left office in 1989, polls showed that over 60 percent of the American people gave him high marks for his overall performance.

Foreign Policy Success One reason for the President's continued popularity was the improvement in relations between the United States and the Soviet Union during Reagan's second term. Despite his fierce anti-Communist stance, Reagan developed a close relationship with Mikhail Gorbachev, who became the Soviet leader in 1985.

To reform the ailing Soviet system, Gorbachev proposed a program of *glasnost,* a Russian word meaning "political openness." He also initiated *perestroika,* or "restructuring," an economic policy to allow limited free enterprise.

These moves paved the way toward better relations between the United States and the Soviet Union. Reagan and Gorbachev signed the Intermediate-Range Nuclear Forces (INF) Treaty in 1987. The **INF Treaty** provided for

Main Idea
CONNECTIONS

What changes did Gorbachev bring to the Soviet Union?

ACTIVITY
LEARNING STYLES

A President's ability to choose Supreme Court justices can have long-term effects. Have students research the biographies and judicial histories of the justices named by Reagan, tracing their votes and influence from their appointment to today. Have students share their findings with the class in an oral presentation. *(Verbal, Auditory)*

BACKGROUND

Global Connections

Nicaragua had been controlled by the wealthy Somoza family for 40 years when the Sandinista National Liberation Front led the overthrow of the government in 1979. The Sandinistas nationalized industry and took land from the rich to give to the peasants. Nicaraguans who were unhappy with some of these reforms joined with Somoza supporters to fight the Sandinista government. These guerrillas—known as contras, which means "against"—attacked from bases across the border in Honduras and Costa Rica. Thousands in Nicaragua and neighboring countries died as fighting raged through the 1980s. A negotiated cease-fire in 1990 let Nicaraguans choose their first democratically elected government.

RESOURCE OPTIONS

Media and Technology

RESOURCE PRO

Primary Source Activity An Explanation of Iran-contra, found on Resource Pro, uses an excerpt from President Reagan's televised address to demonstrate how he defended his involvement in the scandal.

Critical Thinking Activity Recognizing Ideologies: The Bork Nomination, found on Resource Pro, helps students apply this skill by analyzing the Senate debate about one of Reagan's nominees to the Supreme Court, Robert H. Bork.

Answer to . . .

Viewing History Because they were moves away from communism and toward democracy.
Main Idea Connections He restructured the economy and the political system.

FACT Finder
Arms Control Agreements, 1979–1993

Date	Legislation	Purpose
1979	SALT II (Strategic Arms Limitation Treaty)	• Reinforcement of SALT I Treaty between the United States and the USSR. Required reduction of strategic offensive weapons systems, specifically nuclear arms. Set limits on the types and numbers of weapons each side could acquire.
1987	INF (Intermediate-Range Nuclear Forces) Treaty	• Treaty between the United States and the USSR that required each party to destroy ground-launched and ballistic cruise missiles and their launchers within three years.
1993	START II (Strategic Arms Reduction Treaty)	• Treaty between the United States and former Soviet republics. The treaty parties reserved the right to conduct annual inspections at former INF missile sites to ensure that no missiles are being manufactured.

Interpreting Tables Soviet leader Mikhail Gorbachev's policy of glasnost helped slow the arms race between the United States and the USSR. *Foreign Relations* Why do you think arms control agreements were still necessary in the post-Soviet era?

the destruction of 2,500 Soviet and American missiles in Europe.

Domestic Policy Initiatives Another reason for Reagan's popularity was his stated commitment to reducing government. Actually Reagan's policies did not succeed in dramatically reducing Washington bloat. Payments for **entitlements**—programs like Social Security, Medicare, and Medicaid, which guarantee payments to a particular group of recipients—grew faster than policymakers expected. Social Security expenditures, for example, skyrocketed as the nation's elderly population continued to rise. Reagan failed to restrain the growth of these programs.

Economic turmoil erupted near the end of Reagan's presidency. Investor fears about the huge budget deficits and rising national debt prompted a stock market crash in 1987. Following six weeks of falling prices, the market suffered a huge 22.6 percent drop on October 19. The speculative bubble of the 1980s had burst.

While the stock market did recover, Reagan's successor, George Bush, inherited many economic problems. By the end of the decade the nation found itself in the midst of another recession.

For most Americans, Ronald Reagan's two-term presidency was marked by his vigorous emphasis on national pride and the force of his own optimistic personality. Reagan's presidency made many Americans feel confident for the first time since the Kennedy years.

SECTION 3 REVIEW

Comprehension

1. *Key Terms* Define: (a) AIDS; (b) Sandinista; (c) contra; (d) Iran-contra affair; (e) INF Treaty; (f) entitlement.

2. *Summarizing the Main Idea* List some successes and failures of Reagan's second term.

3. *Organizing Information* Make a web diagram called *Results of Reagan's Style of Governing*. Fill in entries that show the effects of Reagan's administrative approach.

Critical Thinking

4. *Analyzing Time Lines* Refer to the time line at the start of the section. Identify three events seen as successes for the Reagan administration, and explain why.

5. *Analyzing Cause and Effect* Despite some failures and scandals, Reagan was a highly popular President. Analyze Reagan's legacy and the effect of his patriotism on public opinion.

Writing Activity

6. *Writing an Expository Essay* In an essay, explain how the influence of conservatives was felt during the Reagan years, both in social issues and in changes in the Supreme Court.

RESOURCE OPTIONS

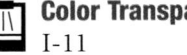

SKILLS FOR LIFE

Demonstrating Reasoned Judgment

Making connections between ideas is the basis for reasoned judgment. This critical thinking skill enables you to analyze the merits of a statement or opinion and thus to reach your own conclusions about its validity.

The passage below is an analysis of the effects of Reagan's economic policies. In order to decide whether you agree with the analysis, you must first evaluate the reasoning process the writer used to make his judgments.

Read the passage. Then use the following steps to analyze the response and to test the reasonableness of both the writer's judg-

ment and your own. Keep in mind that you do not have to agree with the viewpoint expressed in order to find that the reasoning is valid.

1. Examine the source and nature of the evidence by asking who, when, where, *and* what. (a) Who is the writer? (b) Is he qualified to speak on the subject? (c) Might he have any biases that affected his view of Reagan's economic policies or Republican policies in general?

2. Identify the major points in the argument. (a) What is the writer's main point? (b) What other points does he make?

3. Evaluate the evidence offered and the speaker's reasoning. (a) How does the writer support his points? (b) How convincing do you find his arguments? Explain. (c) What grade—from A down to F (failing)—would you give the speaker on how well he demonstrates reasoned judgment? Why did you choose that grade?

TEST FOR SUCCESS

Turn to Section 3 and reread the Comparing Primary Sources quotation by Anthony Lewis. Does the quotation show reasoned judgment? Why or why not?

" Of the many self-inflicted wounds suffered by America in the last thirty years, none was as deep, corrosive, and enduring as the series of huge, chronic federal budget deficits created by the policies of Ronald Reagan in his eight years in office. During that period, the average budget deficit was $211 billion, with the result that the federal debt (which had been less than $1 trillion over the entire course of the nation's history until then, including two world wars) nearly tripled to a total of $2.7 trillion, while the size of the nation's economy increased barely by half.

Bush went Reagan one better: in his four years, the deficit averaged $355 billion, adding another $1.4 trillion to the debt, for a total of more than $4 trillion. . . .

Over the sixteen-year period covering Johnson, Nixon, Ford, and Carter, the federal debt had risen only an average of $35 billion a year, for a total of $579 billion. Thus, in any three years of the Reagan-

Bush twelve, the budget deficit expanded more than it had in the sixteen years of the four prior administrations.

Reagan presided over an economy in which investment and savings stagnated and real wages declined, transforming America from the world's number one creditor nation to the number one debtor. Incredibly, America's foreign debt began to exceed that of Mexico or Brazil. . . . If Reagan was right to suggest in [his] 1980 [campaign for President] that Americans were "worse off" than they were in 1976, at the beginning of the Carter years, Bill Clinton could rightly argue during the 1992 presidential campaign that they had made no gains in the entire decade of the 1980s."

—*Hobart Rowen, economics columnist of* The Washington Post, *in his 1994 book* Self-Inflicted Wounds: From LBJ's Guns and Butter to Reagan's Voodoo Economics

---

RESOURCE OPTIONS

Teaching Resources

Skills for Life Activity Demonstrating Reasoned Judgment, Units 9–10 folder, p. 100, helps students apply this skill by analyzing Reagan's criticism of big government.

Media and Technology

Color Transparencies Critical Thinking, I-17

Critical Thinking

Demonstrating Reasoned Judgment

Focus Analyze a passage on American economics under Reagan and Bush to judge its validity.

Instruct After students have read the passage, have them identify the main idea of the statement. Then have them list key pieces of evidence that support the main message. Ask students if the writer includes any information that does not necessarily support his argument. Point out the importance of analyzing a statement in this way when making reasoned judgments.

Extend See the Skills for Life Activity in the Resource Options below.

Answers

1. (a) Hobart Rowen. (b) Yes, as he is the economics columnist of *The Washington Post.* (c) If he is a Democrat that could be a bias.

2. (a) That during the Reagan/Bush administrations, the United States economy took a downturn unprecedented in the history of the nation. (b) That the United States went from being a creditor to a debtor nation; that Clinton's economic campaign arguments against Bush were justified.

3. (a) With facts, figures, and quotes. (b) Convincing, because he relates a number of figures that can easily be verified. (c) Answers will vary, but grades should be on the high side.

TEST FOR SUCCESS

Sample answer: Yes, as a writer for the *New York Times,* he is qualified to speak on the subject.

1988	1988	1989	1990	1991	1991	1991
Bush elected President	Poland's Communist government falls	Berlin Wall opened	Germany reunified	Persian Gulf War	Bush and Gorbachev sign arms treaty; Soviet Union breaks up	Economic recession hits

1988   **1989**   **1990**   **1991**

SECTION 4

The Bush Presidency

Objectives

You may wish to call students' attention to the objectives in the Section Preview. The objectives are reflected in the main headings of the section.

Bellringer

Ask students when, in their opinion, the cold war really ended. What actions and attitudes have changed with the end of the cold war?

Reading Strategy

Analyzing Cause and Effect Refer to the Reading Strategy in the Section Preview. Use the example of the "nasty" turn in the 1988 election and its fallout to give an example of a cause-and-effect relationship.

LESSON PLAN

Connecting to the Main Idea

1. Focus Emphasize that it is very difficult to follow a popular President. What challenges did George Bush face in this respect? Explain that Bush found his greatest strength in foreign policy. What major world events took place during the Bush administration?

2. Instruct Explain that, as President, Bush inherited a varied assortment of policies from his popular predecessor. Bush concentrated on foreign policy—where his own background and strengths lay—but also had to deal with economic problems inherited from the Reagan administration. How successful was he domestically and in the sphere of foreign affairs?

3. Close While George Bush never rivaled Reagan in popularity, history was made during his administration as the cold war came to a close. With the end of the cold war, the United States and other world leaders had to rethink their policies and their nations' roles in the new era ahead.

4 The Bush Presidency

SECTION PREVIEW

Objectives

1. Evaluate the outcome of the 1988 presidential election.
2. Analyze President Bush's foreign policy successes, including the end of the cold war and victory in the Persian Gulf War.
3. Describe the effect of domestic issues on Bush's popularity.
4. *Key Terms* Define: Strategic Arms Reduction Treaty (START); Persian Gulf War; downsizing.

Main Idea

George Bush achieved notable foreign policy successes, including a popular victory in the Gulf War. However, his record on domestic issues, the economy in particular, eroded his public support.

Reading Strategy

Analyzing Cause and Effect As you read, identify as many cause-and-effect relationships as you can. List them in a chart.

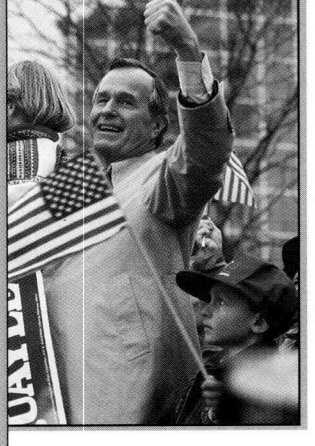

George Bush remained in Reagan's shadow throughout his presidency.

It is not easy to follow a legendary President. George Bush had the same problem as William Howard Taft, who succeeded Theodore Roosevelt in 1909. So did Harry S. Truman, who inherited the presidency upon the death of Franklin D. Roosevelt in 1945. Ronald Reagan remained enormously popular as he left office in 1989, and Bush sought to continue the revolution his predecessor had begun. But he lacked Reagan's charismatic appeal and found that it was not always easy to measure up.

The 1988 Election

Son of a well-to-do Connecticut senator, Bush served in World War II as a bomber pilot in the Pacific and was awarded the Distinguished Flying Cross. After the war he had a profitable career in the Texas oil industry.

In 1966 he entered a long and brilliant political career, serving in many roles: congressman from Texas; ambassador to the United Nations under Nixon; chairman of the Republican National Committee; American envoy to China under President Ford; and head of the Central Intelligence Agency (CIA) until 1977. He was well connected, with a reputation as a moderate and loyal Republican.

Despite these impressive credentials, Bush lacked the support of conservatives in the Republican party. Some Republicans, whose hero was Ronald Reagan, questioned Bush's commitment to their cause. They were concerned about his apparent early sympathy for abortion rights. They never truly forgave him for calling Reagan's economic plans "voodoo economics" in 1980. Bush's loyal service as Reagan's Vice President for eight years failed to ease their fears.

Bush began the 1988 campaign far behind his Democratic opponent, Governor Michael Dukakis of Massachusetts. Dukakis had revived his state after years of economic distress and promised to do the same thing nationally.

Bush took the offensive in what became a nasty contest. One part of his campaign was a pledge that there would be "no new taxes."

RESOURCE OPTIONS

Teaching Resources

 Reproducible Lesson Plan Lesson Plans folder, p. 173

Learning Styles Lesson Plan Learning Styles Lesson Plans folder, p. 71

Big Idea Graphic Organizer Big Idea Graphic Organizer folder, p. 145

Guided Reading and Review Units 9–10 folder, p. 94

Media and Technology

 AmericanHeritage® CD-ROM

 Presidents George H. W. Bush

Reagan's popular tax cuts had contributed to the huge budget deficit and national debt. Reagan's successor would be under great pressure to raise taxes in order to reduce the deficit. Yet Bush publicly committed himself to holding the line on taxes.

Bush also attacked Dukakis as soft on crime. He launched attack ads that apparently alienated many voters. Americans complained that neither candidate addressed the major issues facing the country. Nearly half of all eligible voters stayed home in frustration.

Bush won a solid 54 percent of the popular vote and carried 40 states in a 426-111 electoral vote win. But he failed to gain the mandate Reagan had enjoyed, as Democrats now controlled both houses of Congress.

The Cold War Ends

Bush's major triumphs came in foreign policy. Even more than Reagan, Bush benefited from the historic changes in the Communist world unleashed by Mikhail Gorbachev.

The Soviet leader started a chain reaction that would eventually bring down Europe's "Iron Curtain" and dissolve the Soviet Union. It began with Gorbachev's public statements encouraging Eastern European leaders to adopt perestroika and glasnost. The suggestion was unthinkable in a region where police states efficiently smothered all opposition. Yet it was enough to give hope and inspiration to anti-Communist movements throughout Eastern Europe that had worked for decades, at great risk, to keep a democratic spirit alive.

Poland In Poland the stage was set for the downfall of Soviet communism. The story had begun in 1970, when severe food shortages provoked riots in the city of Gdansk. A witness to those riots was a young electrician named Lech Walesa, who worked in the huge Lenin Shipyard at Gdansk. Walesa became involved in anti-Communist organizing and lost his job after helping to lead a protest in 1976.

When shipyard workers at Gdansk launched a strike in 1980, Walesa climbed over the fence of the facility and joined them, becoming

Main Idea
CONNECTIONS
What events led to the fall of the USSR?

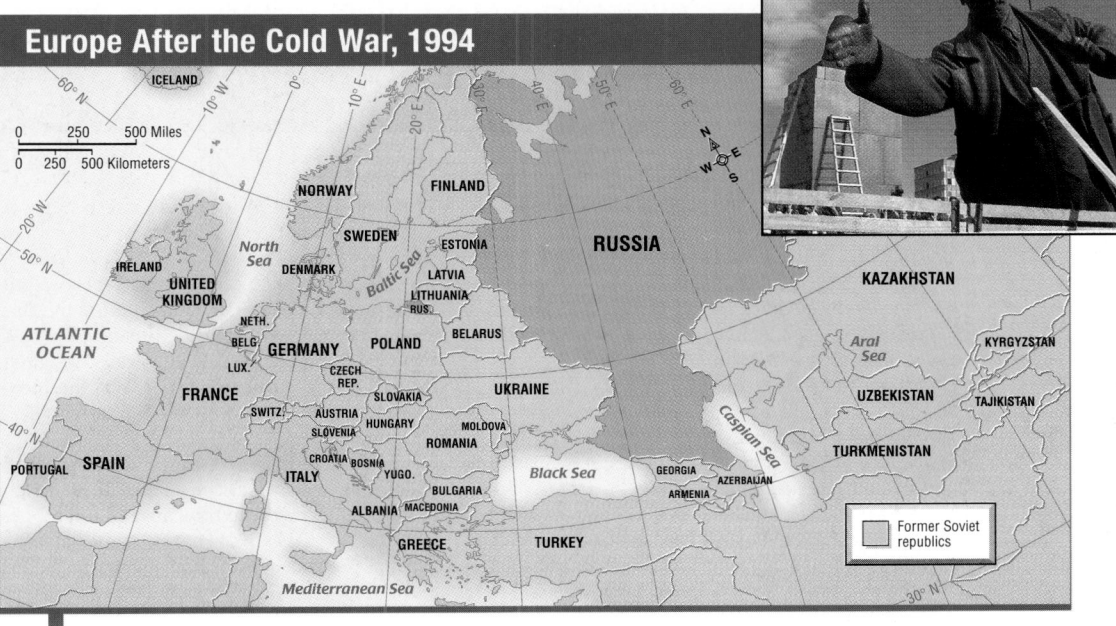

Europe After the Cold War, 1994

0 250 500 Miles
0 250 500 Kilometers

ICELAND · NORWAY · SWEDEN · FINLAND · IRELAND · UNITED KINGDOM · North Sea · DENMARK · NETH. · BELG. · LUX. · GERMANY · FRANCE · SWITZ. · AUSTRIA · SLOVENIA · CROATIA · BOSNIA · ITALY · YUGO. · PORTUGAL · SPAIN · ALBANIA · MACEDONIA · GREECE · Mediterranean Sea · Baltic Sea · ESTONIA · LATVIA · LITHUANIA · RUS. · POLAND · BELARUS · CZECH REP. · SLOVAKIA · UKRAINE · HUNGARY · MOLDOVA · ROMANIA · BULGARIA · TURKEY · Black Sea · RUSSIA · KAZAKHSTAN · KYRGYZSTAN · Aral Sea · UZBEKISTAN · TAJIKISTAN · TURKMENISTAN · GEORGIA · AZERBAIJAN · ARMENIA · Caspian Sea

ATLANTIC OCEAN

Former Soviet republics

MAP Skills In the late 1980s the Eastern bloc shattered into a jigsaw puzzle of diverse republics (above). Above right, a giant statue of Vladimir Lenin, founder of the Russian Communist party, is removed from Moscow in pieces. *Place What kinds of problems do you think might follow the breakup of such a large nation as the Soviet Union?*

TEST PREPARATION

Have students reread the two paragraphs under the subheading "The Cold War Ends" and then answer the question below.

What gave hope to anti-Communist movements in Eastern Europe?

A The election of George Bush as President.

B The concessions made by the police states of Eastern Europe.

C Gorbachev's assumption of leadership of the Soviet Union in 1985.

(D) Gorbachev's public statements about his policies and his encouragement of Eastern European nations to adopt them.

Answer to . . .

Main Idea Connections Gorbachev's policies; the collapse of communism in Poland; the spread of anti-Communist protest throughout Eastern Europe.
Map Skills Sample answer: Ethnic conflicts might arise between groups vying for power in the new governments; groups might fight over economic resources.

ACTIVITY
EXTENDED CLASS PERIODS

Time: 90 minutes.
Activity: Research some of the nations that underwent major changes in the period 1988–1992.
Grouping: Groups of four students.
Purpose: Have each group research one of the countries that underwent major upheavals between 1988 and 1992. One student per group should research each of these aspects: political system and leaders, economy, culture. The fourth person will collect data, summarize it in chart form, and present it in class.
Roles: Three research "experts," recorder/spokesperson.
Outcome: Students will gain an understanding of world events in the 1980s.

Customize for
More Advanced Students

Ask students to look at the Bush administration and several previous administrations and analyze what makes a President choose to emphasize either foreign or domestic policies. Is the main reason the course of world events? Or are some leaders naturally more interested in either one or the other? Have students illustrate their answers with solid biographical and historical details.

Answer to . . .

Viewing History Gorbachev's encouragement of *glasnost and* perestroika *throughout Eastern Europe.*

VIEWING HISTORY

Berliners celebrated the fall of the Berlin Wall with joyous, all-night celebrations. *Foreign Relations* What set off the end of the cold war?

head of a movement that grew with great speed. After two tense weeks, the government gave in to workers' demands for the right to form a free and independent trade union.

Union activity spread throughout Poland, forming an alliance called Solidarity. The Communist government launched a crackdown in 1981, banning Solidarity and jailing its leaders, including Walesa.[†] But support for Solidarity remained alive.

In 1988, further economic collapse in Poland sparked a new round of protests and strikes that brought down the government. The next year, Poland held its first free elections in half a century. It chose as its president the electrician from Gdansk, Lech Walesa.

[†] The Western world watched in admiration as events unfolded in the Gdansk shipyard. In 1983, Walesa, a plain-speaking man with minimal education, won the Nobel Peace Prize for his acts of courage.

The Wall Falls Throughout Eastern Europe, anti-Communist revolts broke out. Each had its own stories of courage and its own heroes. In Czechoslovakia, a poet and playwright once persecuted by the Communists, Vaclav Havel, was elected president. Eventually, new regimes took charge in Bulgaria, Hungary, Romania, and Albania as well. But the most dramatic events of 1989 took place in East Germany.

In East German cities, nonviolent protests pressured the country's dictator, Erich Honecker, to institute reforms and open border crossings. On November 9, the government announced that East Germans could travel freely to West Germany.

East Germans flooded around and over the hated Berlin Wall. Germans scaled it from both sides and stood atop the structure, cheering and chanting and waving signs. They came with sledgehammers and smashed it

▶ RESOURCE OPTIONS

Teaching Resources

Nystrom *Atlas of Our Country* People on the Move, pp. 34–35

American History Block Scheduling Support The Berlin Wall: Past and Present, *and* The End of the Cold War, found in The Nation After World War II folder, includes interdisciplinary lesson suggestions and activities for Geography and History, Primary Sources, Biography, and Literature.

with glee. The wall, the most potent symbol of the cold war, had been breached. Within a month the Communist party was in collapse. A year later East and West Germany reunified.

The Soviet Union By the end of 1991 the Soviet Union no longer existed. It had been replaced by a loose alliance of former Soviet republics called the Commonwealth of Independent States. Russia's new president, Boris Yeltsin, emerged as the dominant leader in this fragmented land.

As the Soviet Union disintegrated, Bush continued arms-control talks with Gorbachev and later with Yeltsin. The Soviets and Americans signed a number of pacts that signaled the end of the cold war. Agreements in 1989 and 1990 limited the buildup of nuclear and chemical weapons. The first **Strategic Arms Reduction Treaty,** known as START I, called for dramatic reductions in the two nations' supplies of long-range nuclear weapons. It was signed in 1991.

"The cold war is now behind us," Gorbachev declared. "Let us not wrangle over who won it." But clearly the United States was now the world's lone superpower.

The Persian Gulf War

In August 1990 the Arab nation of Iraq, headed by a brutal dictator, Saddam Hussein, launched a sudden invasion of neighboring Kuwait. Saddam justified the assault by citing centuries-old territorial claims. But in fact he had his sights on Kuwait's substantial oil wealth. The conquest promised to yield new riches and stir up patriotic support for Saddam's impoverished regime.

Of concern to the Bush administration was the flow of Kuwaiti oil to the West. Bush viewed the protection of those oil reserves as an issue of national security. The administration was also concerned for the security of Saudi Arabia, a key Arab ally in the region. Bush responded strongly:

AMERICAN VOICES "There is much in the modern world that is subject to doubts or questions—washed in shades of gray. But not the brutal aggression of Saddam Hussein against a peaceful, sovereign nation and its people. It's black and white. The facts are clear. The choice is unambiguous—right versus wrong."

—*President George Bush, 1990*

U.S. army helicopters hover over the Kuwaiti desert, as oilfields bombed by Iraq blaze in the background. (above) American soldiers (right) fought a brief, victorious war, aided by the open terrain, which provided no cover for Saddam's armies. *Foreign Relations Why did the Bush administration decide to intervene militarily in this regional conflict?*

Customize for

English Language Learners

Ask students to write two headings: World and United States. Under each heading have them list the major events that took place in each region during the Bush administration.

Answers to
SECTION 4 REVIEW

1. (a) Strategic Arms Reduction Treaty (START), see p. 973; (b) Persian Gulf War, see p. 974; (c) downsizing, see p. 974.

2. Successes: the end of the cold war; the signing of the Strategic Arms Reduction Treaty; leadership in the Persian Gulf War. Failures: lack of clear domestic policies; economic recession; breaking promise of no new taxes.

3. Gorbachev elected Soviet leader; encourages Eastern European nations to adopt his policies; economic protests in Poland lead to downfall of communism and free elections; anti-Communist protests lead to fall of Berlin Wall; Soviet Union dissolves and Yeltsin elected new leader of Russia; START signed, officially ending cold war.

4. Sample answer: 1989, Berlin Wall opened—The Berlin Wall had long been a symbol of the cold war; its destruction symbolized the opening up of a new political order in Eastern Europe.

5. He enjoyed moderate popularity during the 1988 presidential election. Though his approval rating soared during the Persian Gulf War, it dropped by the end of his term as people grew angry with his domestic policies.

6. Essays will vary but should be supported with facts from the section.

Americans at first seemed reluctant to get involved in a territorial matter between Arab nations. As the weeks passed, however, reports of rampaging Iraqi soldiers and atrocities against Kuwaiti civilians drew increasing concern.

Months of diplomatic efforts failed to persuade Saddam to withdraw. Finally, the United States, working through the United Nations, mobilized an alliance of 28 nations to launch the **Persian Gulf War.** It was a limited military operation to drive Iraqi forces out of Kuwait.

To organize military operations, President Bush turned to General Colin Powell. Powell had risen quickly through the ranks of the military. In 1979, at age 42, he had become the Army's youngest brigadier general. He was the first African American to serve as national security adviser. In 1989, he had been named the nation's top military officer, Chairman of the Joint Chiefs of Staff, the youngest ever.[†]

Powell's battle plan was simple. He would use airpower to destroy Iraq's ability to wage war and then smash the Iraqi forces occupying Kuwait. UN forces, directed by General Powell and led by General Norman Schwarzkopf, did just that. A series of massive air strikes, known as "Operation Desert Storm," was launched on January 16–17, 1991. In a war that lasted just 42 days, UN forces liberated Kuwait. The allies lost fewer than 300 soldiers, while tens of thousands of Iraqi troops died.

_____

[†] After the war, both Republicans and Democrats wooed Powell as a possible candidate for Vice-President in the 1992 election. Powell declined, but did not rule out a future political career.

Bush opted not to extend the war by sending troops into Iraq to oust Saddam, expecting Saddam's opponents to soon overthrow the weakened regime. Yet Saddam proved stronger and his opposition weaker than Bush's advisers thought. Saddam remained in power in Iraq.

Domestic Issues

Bush's leadership during the Persian Gulf War drove his approval rate up to an astounding 91 percent. Yet while his handling of foreign policy generally won him praise, Americans began to believe that Bush did not have a clear plan for handling domestic problems. In the end, this perception helped usher him out of office.

Bush angered many moderates and liberals with his nomination of Clarence Thomas, a conservative black judge, to the Supreme Court in 1991. Thomas faced grilling about his views on civil rights and about charges of past sexual harassment. Thomas won confirmation after stormy televised Senate hearings that ignited public debate on the issue of sexual harassment.

Bush's real undoing was a recession, with roots in the Reagan years, that began in the early 1990s. Unemployment climbed again. Companies laid off workers to cut costs in a process called **downsizing.** By 1991 the jobless rate reached 7 percent, the highest level in nearly five years.

Bush countered by slowing spending for social programs. Finally, he agreed to a deficit reduction plan that included new taxes. The tax hike broke Bush's 1988 campaign promise and generated public fury.

SECTION 4 REVIEW

Comprehension

1. *Key Terms* Define: (a) Strategic Arms Reduction Treaty (START); (b) Persian Gulf War; (c) downsizing.

2. *Summarizing the Main Idea* What were the major successes and failures of the Bush administration?

3. *Organizing Information* Create a cause-and-effect chart on the end of the cold war. Include information about the Soviet Union and Eastern Europe.

Critical Thinking

4. *Analyzing Time Lines* Refer to the time line at the start of the section. Choose a year that you think had historic significance, and explain your choice.

5. *Making Comparisons* Compare public opinion in the 1988 presidential election with public opinion of Bush near the end of his term.

Writing Activity

6. *Writing a Persuasive Essay* Is it fair to characterize Bush's successes and failures as largely the result of Reagan-era policies? Write an essay to support your views.

RESOURCE OPTIONS

Teaching Resources

📁 **Quiz** Units 9–10 folder, p. 95

📁 **Chapter Tests Forms A and B** Chapter Test folder

Student Performance Pack

Guide to the Essentials Chapter 34, Section 4 (English and Spanish)

Standardized Test Preparation Handbook

Media and Technology

🎧 **Guided Reading Audiotapes** Chapter 34 Summary (English and Spanish)
Student Edition on Audiotape Chapter 34

💿 **Test Bank CD-ROM; Interactive Student Tutorial CD-ROM** Chapter Test

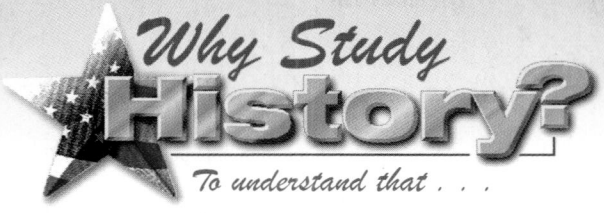

Why Study History?

To understand that . . .

Government Efficiency Can Be Improved

President Reagan's vision of a government that is less expensive and more efficient appeals to many Americans today.

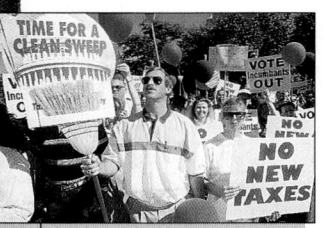

Anti-tax demonstration

What's the scariest day of the year? Most adults would say it's April 15, when tax returns are due at the Internal Revenue Service. The happiest? Some might choose "Tax Freedom Day," the day by which the average taxpayer has earned enough money to pay his or her taxes for the year. In 1998, for example, May 10 was Tax Freedom Day. That means that the average taxpayer's total taxes for 1998 amounted to his or her total income from January 1 to May 10.

Many taxpayers complain that their taxes are high because the federal government is wasting money. Republicans controlled the presidency through the 1980s by appealing to public complaints about bloated and ineffective federal programs.

The Impact Today

In his First Inaugural Address, President Reagan promised to make government "work with us, not over us; to stand by our side, not ride on our back." Reagan's speech reflected his views about the federal government: It was too big, too costly, and too involved in regulation.

During his presidency, Reagan made cuts in a number of federal programs and reduced federal regulations. Yet total federal spending actually increased during Reagan's two terms because of

growth in defense spending and in programs such as Social Security and Medicare.

Many Americans still want to "reinvent" government, making it more efficient. In 1993 President Clinton named Vice President Al Gore as head of the National Performance Review (NPR). The NPR sought to create a government that "works better, costs less, and gets results Americans care about."

The NPR, later renamed the National Partnership for Reinventing Government, made impressive gains. It recommended about $177 billion in savings over a five-year period and helped cut the federal civilian work force by 348,000. Federal agencies eliminated unnecessary regulations, adopted innovative practices, and raised customer service standards. President Clinton even ordered all federal agencies to use "plain language" rather than bureaucratic jargon when communicating with the public.

Still, many people still see the federal government as too costly. Others view the government more favorably and support programs to protect the environment, help the poor, and improve education.

The Impact on You

"The federal government is too large, too costly, and inefficient." Write a letter to the editor either agreeing or disagreeing with this statement.

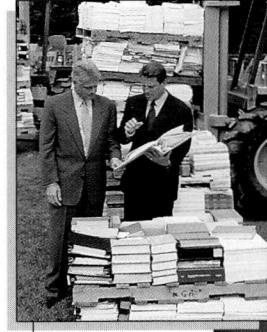

Clinton and Gore present report on reforming government, 1993

RESOURCE OPTIONS

Teaching Resources

 Why Study History? Activity
Government Efficiency Can Be Improved, found in the Why Study History? folder, p. 35, provides an activity to help students better understand the issue of efficiency in government.

Media and Technology

 AmericanHeritage® CD-ROM

Time Tour The Nation Today and Tomorrow: New Directions

 Decision America Videotapes and Videodiscs Issue 5 *How Are We Represented?*

Class Discussion

Discuss government efficiency with the class. For a more thorough examination of the issue, see the activity folder in the Resource Options below.

ACTIVITY STUDENT PARTICIPATION

Making a Chart

Ask students to read the text. Then point out that state and local governments fund or help fund many services, such as:

- **police protection**
- **fire protection**
- **infectious-disease control programs**
- **schools**
- **libraries**

Have students brainstorm a list of services that the government does not fund, such as gas, electricity, television, telephone, and the Internet. Ask students to compare funded services with those that are not funded. Encourage them to debate whether more services should be funded by the government.

Follow up Have students carry out a survey on the issue of what services the government should fund.

Using the Internet

Students can learn more about government efficiency by exploring links in the *America: Pathways to the Present* Web site at

http://www.Pathways.phschool.com

Assessment

See the Lesson Plans folder, pp. 24–27, for rubrics on assessing Class Participation Projects.

Key Terms

Students should refer to the definitions of key terms in the chapter to write sentences that show an understanding of the rise of the conservatives to power and the policies of the Reagan and Bush administrations.

Comprehension

1. To reduce the size of the federal government and its role, to cut government-funded social programs, and to restore traditional values to American society.

2. Because of the Iraqi invasion of Kuwait, which threatened American security and was met with a United Nations military intervention.

3. Reagan signed the Intermediate-Range Nuclear Forces (INF) Treaty, and Bush signed the Strategic Arms Reduction Treaty (START).

4. It wanted the contras to undermine the Marxist government, the Sandinistas, which had taken control of the nation in 1979.

5. A positive effect was a drop in inflation and unemployment; a negative effect was the skyrocketing of the federal budget deficit.

6. Sandra Day O'Connor was the first woman to be appointed to the Supreme Court. Her accomplishments include opinions in several landmark cases, leadership in women's issues, and a reputation for practical solutions.

7. It encouraged anti-Communist movements throughout Eastern Europe to pursue democracy.

8. He hoped to effect conservative policy through the justices of the Supreme Court. During his presidency, he appointed conservatives Sandra Day O'Connor and Antonin Scalia, and moderate conservative Anthony Kennedy.

Chapter Summary

The major concepts of Chapter 34 are presented below. See also *Guide to the Essentials of American History* or *Interactive Student Tutorial CD-ROM*, which contains interactive review activities, time lines, helpful hints, and test practice for Chapter 34.

Reviewing the Main Ideas

This chapter examines the rise of conservatives to power in the 1980s, beginning with the election of President Ronald Reagan. It looks at the shift in values and policies that occurred in government during the Reagan and Bush presidencies and details the key events of their combined 12 years in office.

Section 1: Roots of the New Conservatism

After decades of government growth and social and cultural change, a conservative backlash grew during the 1970s. In 1980 it brought Ronald Reagan to power.

Section 2: The Reagan Revolution

Ronald Reagan aimed to boost the nation's pride and prosperity by cutting taxes, shrinking the federal government, and increasing defense spending.

Section 3: Reagan's Second Term

After a decisive reelection victory in 1984, Reagan continued his conservative policies on economic and social issues. In domestic and foreign affairs, the administration had key successes but also serious missteps.

Section 4: The Bush Presidency

George Bush achieved notable foreign policy successes, including a popular victory in the Gulf War. However, his record on domestic issues, the economy in particular, eroded his public support.

Reagan's vision of a less expensive, more efficient government appeals to many Americans today.

Key Terms

Use each of the terms below in a sentence that shows how it relates to the chapter.

1. downsizing
2. entitlement
3. AIDS
4. supply-side economics
5. televangelism
6. Sandinistas
7. START
8. Iran-contra affair

Comprehension

1. What were some of the goals of the New Right?
2. Why did the United States go to war with Iraq?
3. What arms-control treaties were signed during the Reagan and Bush administrations?
4. Why did the United States government support the contras in Nicaragua?
5. Name one positive effect and one negative effect of Reagan's economic policies.
6. Who is Sandra Day O'Connor, and what were her major accomplishments?
7. What was the impact of Gorbachev's call for perestroika and glasnost?
8. What role did Supreme Court appointments have in Reagan's conservative strategy?

Using Graphic Organizers

On a separate sheet of paper, copy the chart below. In each box fill in key facts from the chapter.

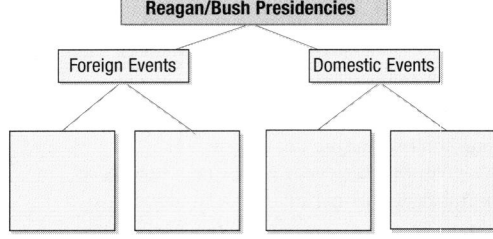

Using Graphic Organizers

- Foreign events: Reagan—military troops sent to Grenada, Iran-contra affair. Bush—Persian Gulf War.
- Domestic events: Reagan—tax cut, deregulation, New Federalism program, conservative justices appointed to Supreme Court, S & L scandal. Bush—nomination of Clarence Thomas to Supreme Court, economic recession, institution of new taxes.

Analyzing Political Cartoons ▶

1. Analyze the images in the cartoon. (a) Who is the man? (b) What does the ship symbolize? (c) How do you know?

2. (a) Where is the ship headed? (b) What is the man's attitude about the ship's course?

3. Summarize the cartoonist's message.

Critical Thinking

1. *Applying the Chapter Skill* Reread the American Voices quotation of President Bush in Section 4. Do you think this is an example of reasoned judgment? Why or why not?

2. *Recognizing Ideologies* (a) How did conservative beliefs affect Reagan's policies? (b) How did they affect Bush's policies?

3. *Analyzing Cause and Effect* How did the policies of the Reagan administration influence the outcome of the Bush presidency?

4. *Drawing Conclusions* During his first term, Reagan called the Soviet Union "the evil empire." In his second term, he developed a working relationship with Gorbachev. What do you think accounts for this change in strategy?

INTERNET ACTIVITY

For your portfolio:
CREATE A TIMELINE

Access Prentice Hall's *America: Pathways to the Present* site at **www.Pathways.phschool.com** for the specific URL to complete the activity. Additional resources and related Web sites are also available.

Use the links provided to read about the START treaties. Create a time line of important events relating to the treaties. Provide a caption to your time line. What is the importance of START?

ANALYZING DOCUMENTS ◀▶ INTERPRETING DATA

Turn to the Federal Budget Deficit graph in Section 2.

1. During the Reagan years, what happened to the overall course of the budget deficit? (a) It rose steadily. (b) It fell. (c) It increased by about $210 billion. (d) It increased, then fell back to its original level.

2. What was the major cause of deficit increases during the period shown in the graph? (a) the cost of the Persian Gulf War

(b) the Strategic Defense Initiative (c) increased defense spending and tax cuts under Reagan (d) Bush's pledge not to raise taxes.

3. *Writing* Do you think the government should be allowed to spend more money in any given year than it earns in revenues from taxes and other sources? Why or why not?

Connecting to Today

Essay Writing Is the conservative revolution alive and well today? Write an essay to explain your answer. Include examples of issues from the Reagan/Bush era that have either continued to be debated today or have faded in significance.

977

INTERNET ACTIVITY

Time lines will vary, but should include all relevant dates. Answers should demonstrate an understanding of START as a historical marker of the end of the cold war.

Analyzing Political Cartoons

1. (a) President Reagan. (b) His economic policies. (c) The life preserver gives the name of the ship as "SS Reaganomics."

2. (a) For an iceberg. (b) He is oblivious to the disaster ahead.

3. The cartoonist believes Reagan is leading the nation into disaster with his economic policies.

Critical Thinking

1. Sample answer: It is a reasoned judgment in that Bush, as President of the United States, is qualified to judge aggression, and is supported not only by the American people but by the United Nations as well.

2. (a) His beliefs caused him to end many government regulations and programs that he believed inflated the federal government. His "hands-off" approach also meant that he delegated authority freely, which resulted in the S & L scandal and the Iran-contra affair. (b) Bush was unable to translate his conservative beliefs into decisive domestic policy, though in foreign policy these beliefs led him to take a strong stance in the Persian Gulf War.

3. Reagan's economic policies began the recession that would harm the economy during Bush's presidency. Reagan's relations with Gorbachev and the Soviet Union set the stage for continuing good relations between the two nations under Bush.

4. Sample answer: Gorbachev's willingness to cultivate good relations with the United States helped change Reagan's opinion.

Interpreting Data

1. c
2. c
3. Answers will vary but should be based on reasoned judgment.

Connecting to Today

Essays will vary but might mention prominent Republican politicians today, and current conservative causes and movements.

Entering a New Era, 1992–Present

Managing Time and Instruction

INSTRUCTION SUPPORT

These materials for instruction are provided for **each section** in the **Teaching Resources**. See **Units 9–10 folder** for Enrichment Support:

- Reproducible Lesson Plans in Lesson Plans folder • Learning Styles Lesson Plans in Learning Styles Lesson Plans folder • Big Idea Graphic Organizers in Big Idea Graphic Organizer folder
- Guided Reading and Review • Quizzes • Test Preparation Practice booklet

DAILY LESSON	ENRICHMENT SUPPORT
1 **Politics in the 1990s** *(pp. 979–984)*	• Nystrom *Atlas of Our Country,* People on the Move, pp. 34–35 • Comparing Primary Sources, On Immigration Policy, Units 9–10 folder, pp. 108–109 • Biography, Ron Brown, Units 9–10 folder, p. 107 • Primary Source Activity, Defining Economic Goals, found on **Resource Pro** • Critical Thinking Activity, Drawing Conclusions: Comparing Budget Categories, found on **Resource Pro** • Visual Learning Activity, "Campaign Strategies '96," Learning with Documents folder, p. 77
2 **The United States in a New World** *(pp. 988–993)*	• Skills for Life Activity, Units 9–10 folder, p. 113 • Visual Learning Activity, Clinton's Foreign Policy, found on **Resource Pro** • Decision-Making Activity, Building an International Manned Space Station, Decision-Making Activities folder, pp. 24–25
3 **Twenty-First Century Americans** *(pp. 996–1000)*	• Nystrom *Atlas of Our Country,* The Fourth Wave of Immigration, pp. 36–37 • Primary Source Activity, Trying to Break the Cycle of Crime, Learning with Documents folder, p. 41 • Biography, Amy Tan, found on **Resource Pro** • Literature Activity, Living in a New World, Units 9–10 folder, pp. 110–112 • You Need to Stay Informed, Why Study History? folder, p. 36

Running Out of Time?

- Use Tape 5, "Republican Revival and Decline, 1968–Present," from **Visions of America** videotapes series.
- Use Chapter 35 Summary from **Guide to the Essentials of American History (English and Spanish)**.

Companion Web Site

The companion Web site offers online links for all chapter review activities. It also provides key content links and structured support for this chapter for both teachers and students.

http://www.Pathways.phschool.com

Media and Technology

For the Student

Interactive Student Tutorial CD-ROM Chapter 35

Student Edition on Audiotape Chapter 35

American Heritage® CD-ROM

Guided Reading Audiotapes (English and Spanish) Chapter 35

For the Teacher

Resource Pro CD-ROM Chapter 35

Test Bank CD-ROM Chapter 35

Listening to Literature Audiotapes *Timeless Voices, Timeless Themes* "Straw into Gold: The Metamorphosis of the Everyday" by Sandra Cisneros

Color Transparencies I-14, E-10

Assessment Options

Chapter Test Forms A&B Test Bank CD-ROM booklet

Test Bank CD-ROM Chapter 35

Standardized Test Preparation Handbook

Block Scheduling

Pacing Suggestions

For 90-minute Blocks

- Teach section 3 using Transparencies L-5, C-8 and C-14 and the Extended Class Periods Activity on p. 998.
- Teach sections 1 and 2 using the Big Idea Graphic Organizers from Teaching Resources and the Connections to Today note on p. 981 for class discussions.

Additional Resources

- Prentice Hall's **American History Block Scheduling Support File** covers over 40 major topics in American history.
- **Prentice Hall United States History Video Collection**™ contains 20 videotapes covering American history from beginnings to present.
- **Decision America Videotapes and Videodiscs**

Connections to American Literature

from Prentice Hall

Prentice Hall Literature *Timeless Voices, Timeless Themes* "For the Love of Books" by Rita Dove, p. 1010

Additional Resources

For the Student

Brent Ashabranner. *An Ancient Heritage: The Arab American Minority.* HarperCollins, 1993.

Esmeralda Santiago. *When I Was Puerto Rican.* Addison-Wesley, 1993.

For the Teacher

Derrick Bell. *Faces at the Bottom of the Well: The Permanence of Racism.* Basic, 1993.

Ronald Takaki. *A Different Mirror: A History of Multicultural America.* Little, Brown, 1993.

 Prentice Hall brings into the classroom the vast archives and scholarship of the nation's premier American history magazine. See "From the Archives of American Heritage®" and "About the Presidents" teaching notes in this chapter.

 History Alive! Teacher's Curriculum Institute, in partnership with Prentice Hall, provides unique materials that engage students with diverse learning styles. See History Alive!® unit on Contemporary American Society.

 Student Performance Pack Ensures success in the three critical areas of Reading, Test Taking, and English Language Development with the following materials:
- Guide to the Essentials of American History in English and Spanish
- Guided Reading Audiotapes in English and Spanish
- Interactive Student Tutorial CD-ROM
- Test Preparation Handbook
- Test Preparation Practice booklet

Introducing the Chapter

Sweeping changes in world affairs in the early 1990s changed the face of world politics. Although the cold war was over, these developments offered new challenges to the United States, now the only superpower, and to its President. The United States also faced challenging issues at home, as immigration and an aging population changed the demographics of American society.

Themes in American History

The theme for this chapter, Economics, is listed at the beginning of this unit. An alternate theme for the chapter is Diversity. To teach this unit thematically, you may wish to use The Nation After World War II folder in American History Block Scheduling Support.

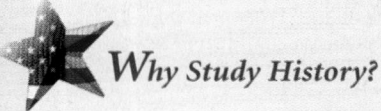

Have students explore suggested ways of connecting the past to the present on page 1001.

Answer to . . .

Viewing History Students should use this question as an aid in reading the chapter. Sample answer: People, communities, and businesses around the world are linked through the Internet; the growth of "high-tech" industries is demanding advanced education and skills from workers.

CHAPTER 35 Entering a New Era

1992-Present

CHAPTER FOCUS

I n 1993 Democrat Bill Clinton ended twelve years of Republican control of the White House when he became the forty-second President. In 1996, he won a second term. In this chapter you will read about the challenges that Clinton and the American people faced in the post–cold war era abroad and in a changing cultural climate at home.

The Why Study History? page at the end of this chapter explores the connection between the computer revolution and the public's access to information on the Internet.

▲
VIEWING HISTORY The map above shows the National Science Foundation's Internet network. *Culture* **How are telecommunication advances changing the ways Americans live, learn, work, and play?**

RESOURCE OPTIONS

Teaching Resources

Big Idea Graphic Organizer folder
Graphic summary of the main idea of the chapter.

Learning Styles Lesson Plans folder
Alternate lesson plans for diverse learning styles for each chapter.

Media and Technology

 AmericanHeritage® CD-ROM
Time Tour The Nation Today and Tomorrow: New Directions

 Prentice Hall United States History Video Collection™ Volume 20
Post-War USA

1992	1994	1995	1996	1998	1999
Bill Clinton elected President	Republicans promote Contract with America	Republicans take control of House and Senate	Clinton reelected President	Clinton announces a federal budget surplus	Bill Clinton impeached

| 1992 | 1994 | 1996 | 1998 | 2000 |

1 Politics in the 1990s

SECTION PREVIEW

Objectives

1 Describe Clinton's path to the presidency.
2 List the reforms that Clinton tried to accomplish during his first term.
3 Describe the goals of the Republicans' Contract with America.
4 Summarize the challenges Clinton faced during his second term.
5 *Key Terms* Define: Contract with America; Whitewater affair.

Main Idea

American voters, concerned with a sluggish economy, elected Bill Clinton to the presidency in 1992. Despite showing strong support for Republicans in the 1994 midterm elections, voters reelected Clinton in 1996. His second term, although filled with scandal, was marked by a strong, rapidly growing economy.

Reading Strategy

Organizing Information As you read the section, create a graphic organizer to record the proposed reforms that did and did not take effect during Clinton's two terms as President.

An earnest young man named Bill Clinton reached out and firmly grasped President John F. Kennedy's hand. At just 17, this high school student from a small town in Arkansas was actually shaking hands with the President! Clinton was in Washington as a member of Boys Nation, a program that teaches young people about government. Later, the experience contributed to Clinton's decision to pursue a career in politics. In 1993, some three decades after this meeting, Clinton was back in the White House. This time he stayed, for he was now the forty-second President of the United States.

Clinton's Path to the Presidency

Bill Clinton's political career got off to a fast start. In 1976, just three years after earning his law degree at Yale, he was elected Attorney General of Arkansas. Two years later, at age 32, Clinton won election as the state's governor. Though he was defeated in his reelection bid in 1980, Clinton

made a remarkable comeback. He was returned to office in the 1982 election and remained governor of Arkansas through the 1980s.

One of Clinton's closest advisers was his wife, Hillary Rodham Clinton, whom he had met at law school. Mrs. Clinton became a leader in efforts to reform education in Arkansas during the 1980s. She was praised by many for her intelligence and energy. Others criticized her active role in government, arguing that a governor's wife should confine herself to ceremonial duties.

After meeting President Kennedy at age 17, Bill Clinton decided to pursue a career in politics.

The 1992 Campaign The 1992 presidential campaign was a three-way race. Not since 1912, when President Taft faced both Woodrow Wilson and former President Theodore

RESOURCE OPTIONS

Teaching Resources

📁 **Reproducible Lesson Plan** Lesson Plans folder, p. 174

📁 **Big Idea Graphic Organizer** Big Idea Graphic Organizer folder, p. 146

📁 **Guided Reading and Review** Units 9–10 folder, p. 101

Media and Technology

 AmericanHeritage® **CD-ROM**

Time Tour The Nation Today and Tomorrow: New Directions

SECTION 1

Politics in the 1990s

Objectives
You may wish to call students' attention to the objectives in the Section Preview. The objectives are reflected in the main headings of the section.

Bellringer
Ask students to suppose that they are making a decision about how to vote in the 2000 presidential election. What factors and issues would influence their decision? How would they have voted?

Reading Strategy
Organizing Information Refer to the Reading Strategy in the Section Preview. You may wish to offer sample graphic organizers to students in preparation for the chapter.

LESSON PLAN

Connecting to the Main Idea

1. Focus Explain that American voters chose Democrat Bill Clinton after 12 years of Republican Presidents. Two years later, however, they chose a record number of Republican congressmen. Ask students to compare the two parties—where they have moved closer together, and where they still strongly differ.

2. Instruct Discuss the different attitudes toward the economy shown by the three candidates in the 1992 election. Explain how extreme political differences between a President and Congress—like those after the 1994 midterm elections—can affect the passage of legislation and frustrate political goals. Ask students to think about the role of partisanship in relation to Clinton's impeachment.

3. Close Rapid technological innovation helped the U.S. economy to grow at unprecedented levels during Clinton's second term—overshadowing major national scandals. The next section describes United States foreign policy in the 1990s.

Roosevelt, did a third candidate play such a major role in a presidential election.

On the Republican side, President George Bush sought a second term. Discouraged by Bush's high approval ratings, several prominent Democrats chose not to seek their party's nomination. This created an opening for the likable and eloquent Bill Clinton, who decided to run for the presidency.

Some critics charged that Clinton would say whatever was necessary—regardless of the truth—to get what he wanted. When a woman claimed to have been Clinton's mistress, and produced evidence that seemed to support her story, the candidate denied her charges. In addition, Clinton's statements about how and why he had avoided the draft during the Vietnam War seemed evasive to some. Clinton supporters praised his refusal to quit and called him the "comeback kid."

The third candidate was H. Ross Perot, a billionaire Texas businessman. He entered the race out of frustration over the government's policies on the federal budget and the economy. As an independent, however, Perot had no party base. So he organized a large network of volunteers who collected enough signatures on petitions to get his name on the ballot in each of the 50 states.

Campaign Issues The Republicans tried to focus the election on what they perceived to be a decline in family values. In addition, President Bush had won wide praise for his role in ending the cold war and winning the Gulf War. However, the recession of the early 1990s continued, and economic issues dominated the campaign.

Clinton promised to use government measures to end the recession and deal with the nation's other nagging economic problems. He also pledged to address the federal budget deficit and the problems in the health care system. Like his hero, President Kennedy, Clinton believed that government was necessary "to make America work again." At the same time, he called himself a "New Democrat," meaning he would look for new ways to make government more efficient and responsive. Clinton's message appealed to Americans who were frustrated at the seemingly endless bickering and deadlock between Democrats and Republicans in Congress. These voters were eager for action and change.

Like Clinton, Perot also focused on the economy. As a successful businessman, he argued, he had the necessary skills to cut costs, balance the budget, and restore prosperity. Perot ran as a Washington "outsider." He noted that he had no ties to special interest groups, and he pledged that he would consider the needs of the country as a whole.

Clinton Wins the Election Television played an important role in the campaign. In addition to the usual political ads and debates, all three candidates appeared on talk shows and interview programs in an effort to shape public opinion.

On election day, Clinton received 43 percent of the votes, while Bush polled nearly 38 percent. Perot's strong showing of about 19 percent meant that Clinton became President with less than a majority of the popular vote. Republicans claimed that Perot had prevented Bush's reelection by attracting support from conservative voters that otherwise would have chosen Bush. In the electoral college

Even before he ran for President of the United States, Bill Clinton had a reputation as a brilliant campaigner. Here he greets a crowd of supporters during his successful 1992 presidential campaign. *Culture How does this photo illustrate some of the challenges of campaigning for President?*

Clinton won 370 votes versus 168 for Bush. Perot won no electoral votes.

Clinton's First Term

Bill Clinton began his first term as President in January 1993. He recognized that the voters wanted a change from the politics of the past:

AMERICAN VOICES ❝Thomas Jefferson believed that to preserve the very foundations of the nation we would need dramatic change from time to time. Well, my fellow Americans, this is our time. Let us embrace it. . . . Today we pledge an end to the era of deadlock and drift, and a new season of American renewal has begun.❞

— *Bill Clinton, First Inaugural Address*

Clinton was buoyed by the fact that Democratic majorities existed in both the House and the Senate. For the first time in more than a decade, the executive and legislative branches would be in the hands of the same political party. The new President looked forward to working with Congress to fulfill the pledges he had made during the campaign. However, these promises proved difficult to accomplish.

Economic Reform In dealing with the economy, Clinton tried to follow a middle course. He wanted to end the lingering recession by raising spending or cutting taxes. At the same time, he needed to reduce the budget deficit, which meant cutting spending or raising taxes. Stimulating the economy and reducing the deficit involved contradictory actions. It was like a driver putting one foot on the gas pedal and the other on the brake, some said. Following this course proved more challenging than Clinton had realized.

Over and over, the President talked of the need to "grow the economy" with new government programs to create jobs and to provide job training. However, even with Democratic majorities in Congress, he could not muster the necessary support. Legislators sensed a conservative mood in the country and refused to pass his package.

Congress did approve Clinton's first budget, but just barely. The House passed the measure by only two votes, while in the Senate, Vice President Al Gore of Tennessee had to break a 50-50 tie. To reduce the deficit, the budget included both spending cuts and tax increases.

Neither action was well received by the public. The tax increases fell most heavily on the wealthiest Americans, but still irritated people with lower incomes.

The Battle over Health Care An estimated 37 million Americans had no health insurance in 1993. For years, this number had been rising, as were the costs of health care. Many Americans were finding it increasingly difficult to afford medical care. Soon after taking office, Clinton appointed his wife Hillary to head a task force to analyze health care and propose reforms.

"This health care system of ours is badly broken, and it is time to fix it," Clinton declared

From the Archives of
American Heritage®

About the Presidents

For most of his career **Bill Clinton** (1992–) has been a remarkably successful politician. He successfully campaigned for the Arkansas governor's seat in 1978, becoming the nation's youngest governor in decades. Through much of the 1980s and early 1990s, he won repeated reelection to the office and became a national leader of the Democratic party. He was elected twice to the presidency, breaking a 12-year Republican run in the office. Yet Clinton's career must also be seen in light of his losses. As a political apprentice, he fought on a number of failed campaigns, most notably that of George McGovern in 1972, and Clinton himself also suffered a stinging loss running for reelection after his first term as governor. In the second term of his presidency scandal engulfed Clinton and the White House, leaving his ultimate legacy in doubt. Source: Adapted from Henry F. Graff's *The Presidents*, Scribner's, 1996, by the editors of *American Heritage* magazine.

to a national TV audience in September 1993. "We must make this our most urgent priority." The proposal he presented to Congress called for creation of a government-supervised health insurance program that would guarantee affordable coverage to every American.

Although the public at first seemed to favor Clinton's plan, it was vigorously opposed by a number of insurance, professional, and small-business groups. Congressional Republicans charged the program would be expensive to taxpayers, and they attacked it as an example of big government.

The debate continued for about a year. During this time, lobbyists representing groups opposed to the President's plan lined up congressional support against it. In the end Clinton's plan for health care reform failed to gain the necessary support in Congress.

The Republicans' Contract with America

The failure of his health care plan signaled trouble for the President. During the 1994 midterm elections, Georgia representative Newt Gingrich called on Republican candidates to endorse what he called a **Contract with America.** This was a pledge, in writing, to scale back the role of the federal government, eliminate bothersome regulations, cut taxes, and balance the budget.

Many voters, feeling that the Democratic-controlled Congress had lost touch with their concerns, responded enthusiastically. In November 1994, voters elected Republicans in large numbers, giving them a majority in both houses of Congress for the first time in more than four decades.

Congress Versus the President The first-term Republicans quickly became a potent force in the House. For leadership they looked to Newt Gingrich, who was elected Speaker of the House. There was talk of a new era in American politics in which Congress, not the President, set the nation's course.

The Republicans in Congress moved quickly to keep the pledges they had made during the campaign. They demanded that the budget be balanced in seven years and proposed cuts in virtually all social services. Recalling the achievements of the "hundred days" of the New Deal in 1933, Gingrich demanded action on these items within the session's first hundred days. In most cases, approval was given.

Many of the bills approved by the House never became law, however. Some were rejected by the Senate, while others were vetoed by Clinton. Even so, Gingrich claimed that he had "changed the whole debate in American politics." That is, Americans were no longer debating whether to cut government and balance the budget, but rather *how* to do so.

The Budget and Welfare Reform The budget remained a point of contention. At the end of 1995, Clinton and Gingrich clashed over the size of budget cuts and the timetable for balancing the budget. When they were unable to compromise, government offices and operations temporarily shut down, disrupting services to millions of Americans. Not until the spring of 1996 did Congress and the President come to a permanent agreement on the budget.

The battle over the budget marked the start of yet another Clinton comeback. Many Americans blamed congressional Republicans for the government shutdown and began to regard them as uncompromising and extreme. By labeling proposed Republican cuts as mean-spirited and presenting himself as one who could make needed reforms, Clinton raised his approval rating in national polls.

Answer to . . .

Viewing History It changed the debate from whether to cut spending to how to cut spending.
Main Idea Connections Gingrich's call for a reduction of the federal government coupled with people's feelings that the Democratic Congress had lost touch with them.

In August 1996 Congress and Clinton did agree on a sweeping reform of the nation's welfare system. Affected were 12.8 million people receiving Aid to Families with Dependent Children (AFDC) and 25.6 million people receiving food stamps. The new law eliminated federal guarantees of cash assistance and gave states authority to run their own welfare programs with block grants of federal money. It also established a lifetime limit of five years of aid per family and required most adults to work within two years of receiving aid. The historic policy change reversed six decades of social welfare legislation dating back to the New Deal in the 1930s.

Clinton's Second Term

When the Republicans took control of Congress in 1995, Clinton's chances for reelection had seemed slim. The Republican message seemed to have great appeal to voters. In the months that followed, Clinton worked hard to counter that message and to show that he was not a "tax-and-spend liberal."

The 1996 Campaign The Republican candidate in 1996 was Bob Dole, Senate Majority Leader and a respected member of Congress for 35 years. Ross Perot again entered the race, this time as the nominee of the newly created Reform Party.

As the election approached, Clinton successfully maneuvered several popular bills through Congress, including a higher minimum wage. In addition the economy, which had been an important factor in the 1992 campaign, was now strong. Thus it again worked in Clinton's favor.

On election day, voters returned Clinton to office with 49 percent of the popular vote. Dole received 41 percent while Perot dropped off to 8 percent. In the electoral college, Clinton gathered 379 votes to 159 for Dole.

Scandal and the Second Term Charges of scandal in Clinton's first term, which Bob Dole emphasized in the 1996 election, continued into his new administration.

In what came to be known as the **Whitewater affair,** Clinton was accused of having participated in fraudulent loans and land deals in Arkansas and of having used his influence as governor to block investigation of his business partners. Attorney General Janet Reno appointed a special prosecutor to look into

these charges. As a result, some of Clinton's friends and former associates were convicted of various crimes and jailed. Yet no evidence was found to link the President to any wrongdoing.

Another charge was made by Republicans, shortly after Clinton's reelection, that he had accepted illegal campaign donations in return for political favors. A Senate committee found violations of campaign finance laws by members of both political parties, but Clinton was not directly implicated.

Clinton Impeached Clinton's sixth year in office, 1998, began with better news: the historic announcement that the government had achieved its first budget surplus since 1962. The moment was short-lived, however. Later that month a scandal erupted that engulfed the President and the Congress and led to only the second impeachment in the nation's history.

The crisis arose when the special prosecutor, Kenneth Star, began to investigate the relationship between Clinton and a young White House intern. Under oath in a separate sexual harassment lawsuit, Clinton denied having had sexual relations with the intern. He repeated this denial again to a grand jury convened by Starr in August. Finally, Clinton did admit to having had an "inappropriate relationship" and to having "misled" his family and the country.

In September, Starr sent a report listing numerous grounds for impeachment to the

Wall Street traders celebrate in 1999 as the Dow Jones reaches its highest levels ever (inset). The rising stocks reflected the explosion of the U.S. economy in the late 1990s. *Government* *How might the economic boom have influenced the public's attitude toward the Clinton scandals?*

Answers to
SECTION 1 REVIEW

1. (a) Contract with America, see p. 982; (b) Whitewater affair, see p. 983.

2. Democratic: Clinton elected President in 1992, Clinton's budget plan agreed to by Congress, Clinton elected for second term in 1996. Republican: failure of Clinton's health-care plan, Gingrich's Contract with America, the election of a majority of Republicans to both houses in 1994, Bush elected President in 2000.

3. Organizers may vary but should show a presidential Democratic victory in 1992 and 1996, and a presidential Republican victory in 2000.

4. Factors leading to Clinton's election included Perot's candidacy, which split the race three ways, and Clinton's strong personal appeal. After 1996, he faced charges of corruption in the Whitewater affair and other financial and sexual accusations.

5. Its approval by the American public meant that people were no longer debating whether to cut government, but instead how to do so.

6. Essays will vary but should be supported with facts from the section.

George W. Bush, shown here with his wife Laura, emerged the victor in one of the closest presidential elections in United States history in 2000.

House of Representatives. This led to a bitterly partisan debate in the House and throughout the country.

Polls showed that while most did not approve of Clinton's actions, a majority of Americans believed that he was doing a good job as President and should not be impeached. However, on December 19, 1998, the full House voted to impeach Clinton on charges of perjury and obstruction of justice. Most Republicans voted yes, and most Democrats voted no.

The Senate trial that followed opened on January 7, 1999. Many senators believed that Clinton had committed offenses, but debate centered around whether these offenses qualified as "high crimes and misdemeanors," the constitutional requirement for conviction of a President.

On February 12, 1999, the trial ended as most people expected, with the Senate voting to acquit Clinton on both charges. The episode, while raising serious constitutional issues, also fueled more partisan debate throughout the country.

Support for Clinton throughout the process may have been bolstered by an unprecedented economic boom. The Clinton presidency marked the longest period of economic expansion in American history. As the economy continued to grow, the nation maintained low levels of unemployment and inflation.

The 2000 Election The mixture of a strong economy and a scandal-ridden presidency would make for an interesting presidential election in 2000. Partisan debate and battles began anew throughout the campaign process. For months leading up to the election, national polls showed that the Republican candidate, Texas governor George W. Bush, was virtually tied with the Democratic nominee, Vice President Al Gore.

On election night the votes in several states were too close to call and neither candidate captured the 270 electoral votes needed to win the presidency. One undecided state, Florida, would give either candidate the electoral votes needed to win. A recount of the votes there was then ordered by law. Florida became a battleground for the presidency as lawyers, politicians, and the media swarmed there to monitor the recount.

Democrats and Republicans argued bitterly over how the recount process should proceed. Charges were made on both sides that the recounts were not fair or accurate. For 36 days, the nation waited and watched as a variety of court battles ensued between the two parties.

Eventually, matters reached the U.S. Supreme Court in *Bush* v. *Gore*. The nine justices were sharply divided about how to remedy the election crisis. By a majority of five to four, they issued a ruling that discontinued all recounts in Florida. This decision overturned a Florida Supreme Court decision to allow recounts to proceed, and effectively secured the presidency for George W. Bush. Although Gore won the national popular vote, Bush won 271 electoral votes to Gore's 266. President-elect Bush promised to bridge partisan gaps and find a common ground for renewed progress.

SECTION 1 REVIEW

Comprehension

1. *Key Terms* Define: (a) Contract with America; (b) Whitewater affair.

2. *Summarizing the Main Idea* Describe the election outcomes in 1992, 1996, and 2000.

3. *Organizing Information* Create a graphic organizer that summarizes the results of the elections of 1992, 1996, and 2000.

Critical Thinking

4. *Analyzing Time Lines* Review the time line at the start of the section. What factors led to Clinton's election in 1992? What challenges did Clinton face after his reelection in 1996?

5. *Recognizing Ideologies* Describe the impact of the Contract with America.

Writing Activity

6. *Writing a Persuasive Essay* Write an essay urging Congress to either accept or reject Clinton's proposal for health care reform.

RESOURCE OPTIONS

Teaching Resources

 Quiz Units 9–10 folder, p. 102

Student Performance Pack

 Guide to the Essentials Chapter 35, Section 1 (English and Spanish)

Critical Thinking

Geography

Graphs and Charts

Historical Evidence

Predicting Consequences

Many social scientists, especially those who work for the government, try to look into the future. They study what has happened in the past, and on the basis of that, they try to predict what might happen next.

Every ten years the government takes a census of the national population. Social scientists study the data from the census to see what they can predict from it. For example, what has the rate of population growth been over the past decades? What does this suggest about the rate of population growth in the next few years? Which groups are likely to grow faster and which slower?

The table at right focuses on census information on the changing number of families in three ethnic groups in the United States and family income in those groups over a fifteen-year period. Use the following steps to analyze the information in the table. Draw on your understanding of history to predict possible trends for the twenty-first century.

1. Identify the kinds of information in the table. (a) What does this table tell you about the number of families in various ethnic groups in the United States? (b) By what percentage did the number of Latino families increase between 1990 and 1995? (c) The median income for a given group represents the center of the income distribution—in each group,

exactly half of the families earn more and half earn less than the median income. What does it mean if one group has a lower median income than another group?

2. Analyze the rate of change. (a) Which group of families is growing at the fastest rate? (b) Which group's median income has grown at the fastest rate? (c) Which group seems the most economically vulnerable—that is, which has the least stable median income?

3. Use your knowledge of history to predict the consequences that your findings might have in the future. The Immigration Act of 1965 allowed more people from places other than Europe to immigrate to the United States. The Immigration Act of 1990

further increased immigration quotas by 40 percent. (a) How might the table illustrate the consequences of the 1965 law? (b) What consequences might the 1990 law have by the year 2005? (c) If an economic recession began in the first years of the twenty-first century, which group's median income would you expect to drop the most? (d) What changes in the trends shown on the table would have to take place in order to alter your predictions?

TEST FOR SUCCESS

Given the data on percent changes in median income, do you think the median income of Latino families will be higher or lower than the median income of African American families in the near future?

Change in Number of Families and Median Income,* by Selected Ethnic Groups, 1980—1995

	Year	Number of Families (in thousands)	Percent Change (from preceding figure)	Median Income (dollars)	Percent Change (from preceding figure)
White Families	1980	52,710	—	40,561	—
	1990	56,803	+7.8	43,044	+6.1
	1995	58,872	+3.6	42,646	−1.0
African American Families	1980	6,317	—	23,469	—
	1990	7,471	+18.3	24,980	+6.4
	1995	8,055	+7.8	25,970	+4.0
Latino Families	1980	3,235	—	27,251	—
	1990	4,981	+54.0	27,321	+0.3
	1995	6,287	+26.2	24,570	−10.0

* In 1995 dollars
Source: *Statistical Abstract of the United States*

SKILLS FOR LIFE

Critical Thinking

Predicting Consequences

Focus Students will use the statistics in a table to predict patterns of population growth and median income for three ethnic groups.

Instruct Have students examine the title and headings in the table. Make sure that they understand what the numbers in the Percent Change columns mean. Explain, for example, that the percentage in the 1995 row covers the period from 1990 to 1995. Ask students to compare the percentages for the three ethnic groups and to note any differences among them.

Extend See the Skills for Life Activity in the Resource Options below.

Answers

1. (a) That the number of white families in the United States greatly outnumbered African American and Latino families. (b) 26.2 percent. (c) More than half of the families in that group earn less than the median income for the other group.

2. (a) Latinos. (b) African Americans. (c) Latinos.

3. (a) The rapid increase in the number of Latino families between 1980 and 1995 reflects the continuing rise in the number of immigrants coming from Latin America after 1965. (b) The number of Latino families in the United States will continue to grow at a much faster rate than the number of white or African American families. (c) Latino families. (d) Sample answer: If the number of Latino families dropped significantly or if the Latino median income stabilized.

TEST FOR SUCCESS

It will probably be lower.

The Rise of the Sunbelt

The Rise of the Sunbelt

The geographic theme of movement explores ways in which people, goods, and ideas travel from one place to another. By 1990, large numbers of people had flocked to one region of the United States—the Sunbelt. What caused this? How did it affect politics and the economy?

Atlanta, Georgia

Focus Point out that until the mid-twentieth century, the South was mainly agricultural. The cities of the Northeast and North Central regions dominated business, banking, and manufacturing.

Instruct Ask students to describe economic and political changes they have observed in their own communities. They may consider:

- **Population** Has the population of the community grown or declined since the 1970s? What factors have caused the change? What effects have population changes had on services such as schools and libraries?

- **Business and industry** Have new firms and factories located in the area? Or have businesses closed or downsized? Has the number of jobs increased? What about service businesses such as supermarkets or video rental stores?

- **Politics** Is the community traditionally Democratic or Republican? What political issues are important in the community?

- **Environment** Have air and water quality improved or declined? Do growing populations put pressure on water supplies and other resources?

Extend The rise of the Sunbelt has had far-reaching ramifications. Have small groups research the growth of recreational attractions in the Sunbelt—e.g., Disney World, new sports franchises—as well as increased sales of sportswear and recreational equipment. What other effects on popular culture or consumer buying habits can they identify?

In the years after World War II, the southern states—mainly agricultural, often poor—suddenly exploded into growth and prosperity. Writers in the 1970s used the term "Sunbelt" to describe this change. Generally, the Sunbelt included the warm-weather states south of the 37th parallel, from North Carolina to Arizona. Neighboring states such as California and Colorado are often included as well.

Moving for New Jobs

The key reason for Sunbelt growth was jobs, both new and transplanted. New manufacturing industries were started in the South or moved there from other areas. Sunbelt cities such as Houston, Dallas, and Atlanta grew quickly, with more room to spread out than crowded metropolitan areas in the North. People flocked to the area, leaving behind hard times and cold weather. They turned their backs on the decaying industries and cities in northern states, which soon acquired unflattering nicknames, like "Frost Belt" and "Rust Belt."

Other factors attracted businesses to the Sunbelt. Hydroelectric power was inexpensive and widely available. Warmer weather reduced the expense of heating fuels. And lower taxes and costs of living attracted both workers and industry. As the Sunbelt economy grew, so did defense industries and aerospace and electronics companies.

While manufacturing jobs increased, other types of businesses grew. Newcomers built homes and offices, bringing a boom in construction and building supplies. Service businesses opened, from realtors to supermarkets to video rentals. Southern cities won franchises for expansion of professional team sports, even for that most wintry sport, ice hockey.

In addition to jobs, good weather and mild winters drew retired people and families. For younger families, quality of life was a big attraction.

Quality of Life

In addition to jobs, good weather and mild winters drew retired people and families. For younger families, quality of life was a big attraction. This meant a slower-paced way of life, clean air, a friendlier and safer atmosphere, and more outdoor recreation.

For the first time in decades, many new southerners were African American. Earlier in the century, many had left the South to escape racial prejudice and find jobs in industry. Now, many returned, deciding that racial attitudes and quality of life were better in the South than in many northern cities.

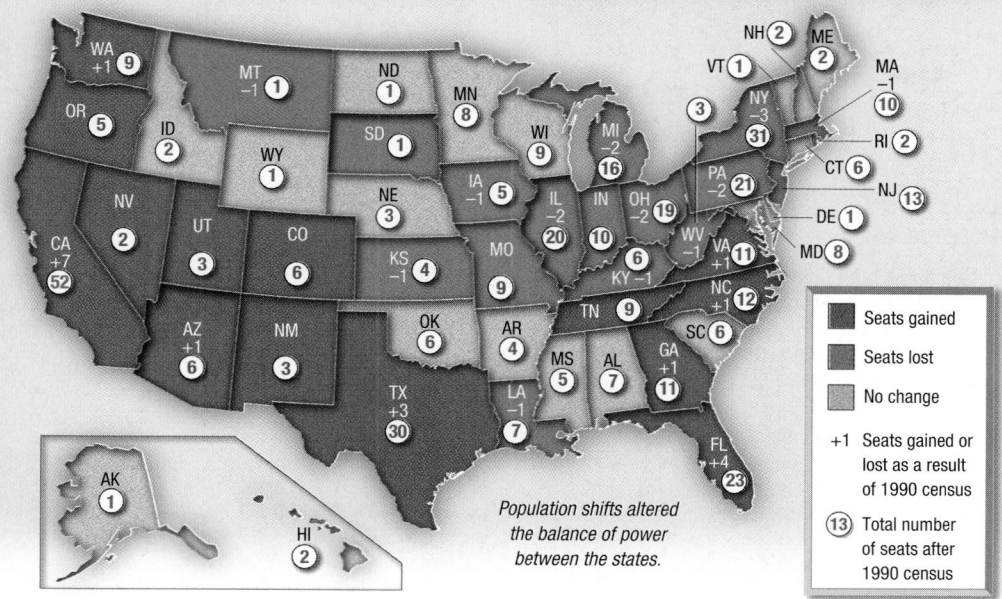

1990 Reapportionment

WA +1 (9)
OR (5)
MT -1 (1)
ND (1)
MN (8)
NH (2)
ME (2)
VT (1)
MA -1 (10)
NY -3 (31)
RI (2)
ID (2)
SD (1)
WI (9)
MI -2 (16)
CT (6)
NJ (13)
WY (1)
IA -1 (5)
IL -2 (20)
IN (10)
OH -2 (19)
PA -2 (21)
DE (1)
MD (8)
NV (2)
UT (3)
CO (6)
NE (3)
KS -1 (4)
MO (9)
KY -1 (6)
WV -1 (3)
VA +1 (11)
CA +7 (52)
AZ +1 (6)
NM (3)
OK (6)
AR (4)
TN (9)
NC +1 (12)
SC (6)
MS (5)
AL (7)
GA +1 (11)
TX +3 (30)
LA -1 (7)
FL +4 (23)
AK (1)
HI (2)

Population shifts altered the balance of power between the states.

Legend:
- Seats gained
- Seats lost
- No change
- +1 Seats gained or lost as a result of 1990 census
- (13) Total number of seats after 1990 census

New Political Influence

The shift of people to the Sunbelt has brought a dramatic shift in national political power. Every ten years, after the census, the 435 seats in the U.S. House of Representatives are reapportioned among the states on the basis of population changes. As the map shows, after the 1990 census, many southern and western states added congressional seats, while the Northeast lost representatives. These shifts have given the South and West greater influence on both politics and social issues.

The Sunbelt's voting strength is reflected in presidential politics. Since the mid-1960s, most Presidents have been from Sunbelt states. In 1996, for the first time, southern Republicans led both houses of Congress: Speaker of the House Newt Gingrich of Georgia and Senate Majority Leader Trent Lott of Mississippi.

Southern voting patterns have also changed. Once a stronghold for Democrats, the South has become more strongly Republican and conservative.

Sunbelt population growth is expected to continue. Of the 20 cities expected to grow the most between 1995 and 2005, 15 are in Sunbelt states, and 11 are in just three states: Texas, Florida, and California.

Eighteen of the 20 cities with the fastest projected job growth for the same period are also in the South and West. Whether the rest of the country can keep up with the growth of the Sunbelt remains to be seen.

GEOGRAPHIC CONNECTIONS

1. What were some factors that attracted people and businesses to the Sunbelt?

2. What political changes took place as a result of the growth of the Sunbelt?

Themes in Geography

3. *Movement* What could northern states and communities do to keep businesses and people from moving to the Sunbelt?

| 1993 Peace agreement between Israel and Palestinians | 1994 United States–led intervention in Haiti | 1994 Senate ratifies NAFTA | 1995 Bosnian peace agreement | 1996 Boris Yeltsin reelected Russian president | 1998 Northern Ireland peace accord | 1999 NATO goes to war over Kosovo |

1992   **1994**   **1996**   **1998**   **2000**

SECTION 2

The United States in a New World

Objectives
You may wish to call students' attention to the objectives in the Section Preview. The objectives are reflected in the main headings of the section.

Bellringer
Ask students what countries they have heard about in news in the last few weeks. What problems there are making news? Do they involve the United States or not? What is the responsibility of the United States to those countries?

Reading Strategy
Organizing Information Refer to the Reading Strategy in the Section Preview. To reinforce geography skills you may wish to have students name the regions of the world as you highlight them.

LESSON PLAN

Connecting to the Main Idea

1. Focus Explain that for 50 years American foreign policy had been based on cold-war philosophy. Now the nation had to find new ways of dealing with many nations around the world. Ask students how this "new world" offered both hopes and challenges.

2. Instruct Explain that Americans have always been ambivalent about involvement in foreign affairs. Ask if students think that isolationism is possible today. How does isolationist sentiment affect policies and positions on trade? Discuss the position of the United States as the world's remaining superpower. What are the responsibilities of that position?

3. Close Changes around the world in the 1990s challenged American foreign policymakers to take new approaches. At the same time, as discussed in the next section, the United States was facing major changes in its own society.

2 The United States in a New World

SECTION PREVIEW

Objectives

1. Summarize the Clinton administration's efforts to promote peace and freedom abroad.
2. Describe the role the United States played in helping nations torn by conflict in the 1990s.
3. Analyze the impact of an expanding global economy on the United States.
4. *Key Terms* Define: apartheid; economic sanction; North American Free Trade Agreement (NAFTA); General Agreement on Tariffs and Trade (GATT); World Trade Organization (WTO).

Main Idea

The collapse of communism and an increase in ethnic tensions in various parts of the world caused Americans to examine their nation's political and economic role in the post–cold war era.

Reading Strategy

Organizing Information Before you read the section, sketch a rough outline map of the world. As you read, highlight areas of United States involvement and write a brief note explaining the region's connection to the United States.

F. W. de Klerk and Nelson Mandela shared the 1993 Nobel Peace Prize for their work in ending apartheid.

Witnessing the collapse of communism in the Soviet Union and Eastern Europe, President Bush had spoken hopefully of the dawn of a "New World Order." By this, he meant a more stable and peaceful world, in which "the strong respect the rights of the weak." However, President Clinton found that in some ways the world was becoming less stable. While some nations had thrown off repressive governments and become more open and democratic, others were being torn apart by racial, cultural, or religious tensions. A few observers joked grimly of a "New World Disorder." Meanwhile, economic ties between nations continued to expand.

The Search for Peace and Freedom

In the 1980s, communism in the Soviet Union, racial oppression in South Africa, and conflict in the Middle East had seemed like permanent world problems. For decades they had been considerations in shaping American foreign policy. By the late 1990s, however, historic events had changed conditions in these and other regions.

Russia and Eastern Europe As the old Soviet empire crumbled, the United States tried to promote the move toward Western-style democracy in many of the former Soviet republics. It applauded the election of Boris Yeltsin as president of Russia.

To help that nation create a free market economy, the United States offered a $2.5 billion aid package. Yet even that was not enough. Goods remained in short supply, and the Russian economy remained unstable. In the fall of 1993 the Russian parliament resisted reforms that Yeltsin argued were necessary. In response, he dissolved the parliament and tightened censorship in a bid to silence his political opponents.

Russian reformers, angry at these curbs on freedom, soon grew angrier. In 1994, Yeltsin

▶ RESOURCE OPTIONS

Teaching Resources

📁 **Reproducible Lesson Plan** Lesson Plans folder, p. 175

📁 **Learning Styles Lesson Plan** Learning Styles Lesson Plans folder, p. 72

📁 **Big Idea Graphic Organizer** Big Idea Graphic Organizer folder, p. 147

📁 **Guided Reading and Review** Units 9–10 folder, p. 103

ordered troops into Chechnya, a self-governing republic that sought independence from Russia. After 21 months of fierce fighting, a cease-fire was finally reached, and the Russian troops were withdrawn. Although Yeltsin postponed the crisis, the bloody conflict had already taken thousands of lives. It cost Yeltsin much of his public support.

In 1999, this same conflict would be the source of great public support for newly appointed Russian Prime Minister Vladimir Putin. A series of Chechnyan terrorist attacks in Russia late in the year prompted Putin to assault the republic with air raids and a full-scale ground invasion. This act made Putin a popular figure in Russia. Political parties aligned with Putin won great support in the December parliamentary elections. Many people saw this as a mandate for Putin and at the end of the year, Yeltsin resigned his post, making Putin the acting president of Russia.

Great political change also continued to occur in other parts of Eastern Europe. In the early 1990s Poland, led by Solidarity hero Lech Walesa, had undertaken bold economic reforms to create a free market. Economic progress was initially slow and many people were quick to worry. In 1995, Polish voters elected Aleksander Kwasniewski as president. Despite his communist background, Kwasniewski continued the push for a free market economy and eventually the economy began to rebound.

In a clear sign that there was no returning to the past, in 1999, Poland, Hungary, and the Czech Republic all became members of NATO. The NATO allies also held out hope of membership to other former Communist nations in the region if they continued to make progress toward democracy.

South Africa The United States and nations around the world hailed South Africa's effort to overturn **apartheid,** the systematic separation of people of different racial backgrounds. South Africa's white minority, which made up only about 15 percent of the population, had long denied equal rights to the black majority. The United States and other nations had used **economic sanctions,** or trade restrictions and other economic measures intended to punish another nation, to encourage reform. Finally, in 1990, Prime Minister F. W. de Klerk released anti-apartheid leader Nelson Mandela from jail. Mandela had been held prisoner for 27 years.

Former rivals de Klerk and Mandela worked together to end apartheid. In 1994, South Africa held its first elections in which blacks as well as whites voted. These elections produced a new government, led by a new president, Nelson Mandela, and his anti-apartheid organization, the African National Congress (ANC). Although the world watched in fear that a civil war might erupt, South Africa made a peaceful transition to black majority rule. From 1996 to 1998, a government-appointed Truth and Reconciliation Commission investigated the atrocities of the apartheid era. Its final report, published in 1998, won international praise as it addressed wrongdoings on both sides and continued the nation's move toward peace.

The Middle East In September 1993, Palestine Liberation Organization (PLO) leader Yasir Arafat and Israel's prime minister Yitzhak Rabin signed the historic peace

Israel

- Final status of West Bank and Gaza Strip to be negotiated.
- 1993 agreement between Israel and the Palestine Liberation Organization called for Israeli military withdrawal from the Gaza Strip and gradual takeover of administration by Palestinians.
- Under the 1993 agreement between Israel and the Palestine Liberation Organization, Jericho was turned over to Palestinian administration.

LEBANON · SYRIA · Golan Heights · Haifa · Nazareth · Nablus · Amman · Tel Aviv · West Bank · Jericho · Jerusalem · Dead Sea · Hebron · Gaza Strip · Gaza · Beersheba · ISRAEL · JORDAN · EGYPT · Mediterranean Sea · Elath · Gulf of Aqaba

0 25 50 Miles
0 25 50 Kilometers

☐ Land occupied by Israel following the 1967 war
✿ Major Israeli settlements in the West Bank

MAP Skills The map above shows the effects of the peace accord between Israel's Yitzhak Rabin (left) and the PLO's Yasir Arafat (right), presided over by President Clinton (center) in 1993. *Regions How did the accord affect the West Bank and the Gaza strip?*

BACKGROUND

A Diverse Nation

"[A]frica is] where we came from, it's where civilization started. How can we turn our backs on it?" said George Curry, editor of the African American magazine *Emerge.* He spoke for many African Americans for whom South African history has been painfully relevant. One South African who attracted worldwide admiration was Nelson Mandela (b. 1918). Despite years of imprisonment under apartheid, Mandela emerged as a consummate peacemaker. For working to end apartheid, he shared the 1993 Nobel Peace Prize with the white South African leader F. W. de Klerk. In 1994 Mandela became South Africa's President after a landslide victory in its first democratic, all-race election.

RESOURCE OPTIONS

Teaching Resources

American History Block Scheduling Support The End of the Cold War, found in The Nation After World War II folder, includes interdisciplinary lesson suggestions and activities for Geography and History, Primary Sources, Biography, and Literature.

Media and Technology

AmericanHeritage® CD-ROM

Explorer Activity 29 A Changing World, CD-ROM Guidebook, pp. 77–78, helps students create a poster about the world after the cold war.

Answer to . . .

Map Skills It provided for self-rule in the Gaza Strip and part of the West Bank, and opened up negotiations on the rest of the West Bank.

The Former Yugoslavia

MAP skills

This map shows the regions of Bosnia-Herzegovina controlled by various groups. *Regions* How does it *demonstrate the problems in many former Communist nations after their governments collapsed in the late 1980s and early 1990s?*

agreement in Washington, D.C. It was a difficult step for both sides. However, as Rabin noted, "Peace is not made with friends. Peace is made with enemies."

The pact provided for Palestinian self-rule in the Gaza Strip (between Israel and the Sinai Peninsula) and in the town of Jericho on the West Bank of the Jordan River. The agreement also set the stage for negotiations on the status of the rest of the West Bank. Israel had seized these areas in the Six-Day War of 1967. At the same time, the PLO recognized Israel's right to exist.

The Middle Eastern peace process had other successes. In 1994, Israel and Jordan signed a treaty ending the state of war that had existed between them. Israel and Syria began talks as well. Extremists on both sides, meanwhile, tried to destroy prospects for peace through terrorist attacks. In 1995 a Jewish extremist assassinated Rabin.

Benjamin Netanyahu became the next prime minister and was more reluctant than Rabin to grant concessions to the Palestinians. The peace process faltered under his leadership, but in 1999, moderate leader Ehud Barak, touted as a soldier for peace, was elected prime minister of Israel by a landslide. Under Barak, the 1998 Wye River Accords between Israel and Palestine were implemented, in which both sides made concessions to further the peace process. The 2000 Camp David Summit between Barak and Arafat sought to build on the peacemaking efforts of the Wye River Accords.

Haiti Several other nations likewise took steps toward stability. In Haiti, military leaders had overthrown that country's first freely elected president, Jean-Bertrand Aristide, in 1991. Three years later, a United States–led military intervention forced Haiti's military to give up power. U.S. troops stayed in Haiti for many months, helping to restore democracy.

Northern Ireland In Northern Ireland, the United States encouraged renewed efforts in the 1990s to end decades of violence between Protestants and Catholics. In 1996, Clinton asked former U.S. senator George Mitchell to lead talks that included representatives of the warring factions and the British and Irish governments.

After 22 months of tense negotiations, Mitchell's efforts paid off. In 1998, all parties signed the Good Friday Accords, agreeing to major reforms in the government of the British province. The agreement was approved by a vast majority of voters in both Northern Ireland and Ireland. It stopped short of providing for unification of the two Irelands, which Catholics had desired. However, it offered the best hope yet for ending the shootings and bombings that in 30 years had taken over 3,000 lives.

Nations Torn by Conflict

For the United States, promoting peace and the spread of democracy were satisfying foreign policy challenges. Far less satisfying was the task of trying to stop the terrifying violence that erupted within several disintegrating countries. President Clinton had to balance Americans' desire to help other nations against Americans' fear of costly commitments. This fear was magnified by memories of the Vietnam War.

The Balkan Nations The nation of Yugoslavia had long been burdened with deep-rooted ethnic and religious tensions. Under communism, following World War II, these tensions remained below the surface. With the end of the cold war, however, these underlying problems erupted, resulting in a decade of violent conflict.

Some of the Yugoslav republics wanted to separate and become independent nations. Serbia, and its leader, Slobodan Milosevic, wanted to preserve a unified Yugoslavia, dominated by Serbia. When the Muslim and Croatian majority in Bosnia declared its independence in 1991, Bosnian Serbs, backed by Milosevic and Serbia, attacked. They began a siege of Sarajevo, Bosnia's major city, and carried on a ferocious "ethnic cleansing" campaign to remove non-Serbs from the republic. Millions were forced to flee their homes and 300,000 people were killed in the worst atrocities seen in Europe since World War II.

When Clinton campaigned for President in 1992, he promised strong action in Bosnia. Once in office, however, he hesitated when America's European allies resisted the use of force. Finally, in mid-1995, an American-led NATO bombing campaign pushed the Bosnian Serbs into peace talks. These talks, held in Dayton, Ohio, produced a cease-fire and the commitment of foreign peacekeeping troops, thousands of whom were U.S. troops.

Steps toward peace had been made, but none of the underlying problems had gone away. New troubles began in Kosovo, another part of the former Yugoslavia. As a part of Serbia, Kosovo was subject to Serbian rule. Much like Bosnia, however, Kosovo's majority population was not Serbian. Most people living there were ethnic Albanians and they had demanded more self-rule. This led to another brutal round of violence, this time between the Serbs and the Kosovars.

Thousands of ethnic Albanian refugees fled Kosovo as the fighting became more widespread throughout 1998. By July, the Kosovo Liberation Army (KLA) occupied 40 percent of Kosovo before being defeated by the Serbs. Following this victory, the Serbians took control and began a violent campaign closely resembling their actions in Bosnia.

In early 1999, the U.S. and NATO threatened airstrikes if both sides would not commit to a Kosovo peace conference. While Kosovo Albanians signed a peace deal authorizing the stationing of a NATO peacekeeping force there, the Serbs refused. After the failure of Serbs to commit to NATO peacekeeping efforts, NATO launched a series of airstrikes

which forced them to reconsider. Eventually, Milosevic agreed to the international peacekeeping force in Kosovo and the Albanian refugees were able to return home.

Somalia In the early 1990s the East African nation of Somalia had suffered from a devastating famine, made worse by a civil war. In 1992 President Bush sent American troops to assist a United Nations relief effort. The food crisis eased, but Somalia's government remained unable to control the armed groups that ruled the countryside. The following year, after several United States soldiers were killed in a battle with Somali rebels, Clinton recalled the troops without order having been restored. By 1998, the end of the long civil war seemed to be in sight after leaders of the rival factions signed a peace agreement. It remained to be seen whether a functioning government could be formed.

Main Idea CONNECTIONS

What role did the United States play in ending the conflicts in Bosnia and Kosovo?

VIEWING HISTORY

The war in Kosovo tore apart cities and towns throughout the region. Here, U.S. soldiers patrol through the village of Cuernica as part of a NATO peacekeeping operation. NATO played an integral role in rebuilding the infrastructure in villages such as these. *Foreign Relations* *Why did the U.S. support sending troops into Kosovo?*

Secretary of State Madeleine Albright, seen here during a trip to China, worked hard to establish a new leadership role for the United States in the post–cold war era. *Government What issues faced the Secretary of State during the Clinton administration?*

Rwanda and Zaire In 1994 the death of Rwanda's president in a suspicious plane crash wrecked an uneasy peace that had existed between the nation's two main ethnic groups, the Hutus and Tutsis. The Hutus, blaming the Tutsis for the crash, embarked on a massive genocidal campaign, slaughtering hundreds of thousands of Tutsis. Later that year, Tutsi rebels countered and overthrew the Hutu government prompting an estimated one million Hutus to flee the country.

Many of the Hutus fled to neighboring Zaire, one of Africa's largest nations. Zaire was then under the leadership of longtime dictator and U.S. ally Mobutu Sese Seko, whose power had recently been weakened. From Zaire, the Hutu refugees staged raids on the Tutsi-dominated Rwandan government. The ethnic Tutsis in Zaire responded by rebelling against Zaire's government.

In 1997, supported by Rwanda and other nearby countries, the rebels forced Sese Seko to resign. Rebel leader Laurence Kabila became president and renamed Zaire to the Democratic Republic of Congo. Since then, Kabila has failed to initiate basic reforms and has turned against the Tutsi and Rwandan influences that once supported him. A new rebellion formed, followed by a violent civil war, which by 2000 claimed an estimated 1.7 million lives.

India, Pakistan, and China At the same time that tensions were easing in Northern Ireland, Asia suddenly became less stable. In 1998, India exploded nuclear weapons for the first time in a series of underground tests. India's neighbor and rival, Pakistan, quickly responded with its first nuclear tests. A border dispute between the two nations had already embroiled them in three wars in the past half-century. The United States feared that their long-standing territorial and religious tensions would touch off nuclear war in the region.

Much of the world, including nearby China, viewed the developments in India and Pakistan with alarm. China's economic growth, combined with its size, made it an increasingly important power in the 1990s. As a result, the United States began working more closely with China on various issues, including trade and regional security.

Trade and the Global Economy

Despite dramatic events within countries, the most important world development of the mid- and late-1990s may have been one that took place between countries. That development was the continuing growth of global trade. The United States was active in promoting closer economic ties with other countries.

The European Union In 1957 six European nations set up the Common Market to coordinate economic and trade policies. Over time, new nations joined the Common Market. In 1986, member nations agreed to dismantle all tariffs on one another's exports, thereby creating a single market.

In 1993, the Common Market nations formed the European Union (EU) to provide political and monetary coordination as well. The EU, now with more than a dozen members, has a parliament and a council in which all member nations are represented. In the late 1990s member nations agreed to gradually replace their individual monetary systems with a single new currency called the eurodollar, or euro, by 2001.

The EU's goal is to create an economic unit that rivals the size and strength of the American economy. The United States has generally supported Europe's progress toward economic cooperation. As a Clinton administration official stated, "Close partnership between the United States and the European Union is essential to our common agenda of democratic renewal." The EU is today the largest trading partner of the United States.

NAFTA Meanwhile, the United States also sought to encourage greater economic cooperation in its own backyard. **The North American Free Trade Agreement (NAFTA)** called for removal of trade restrictions among the United States, Canada, and Mexico. The resulting free trade zone created a single market similar to the market of the European Union.

The NAFTA measure aroused tremendous controversy in the United States. NAFTA opponents worried that American factories would relocate to Mexico, where wages were lower and government regulations, such as environmental controls, were less strict. Supporters of NAFTA claimed that it would instead create more American jobs by increasing exports to Mexico and Canada. In 1994 the United States Senate ratified NAFTA, but only after a bruising battle. Three years later, the government's first study of NAFTA revealed it to be only a limited success. The report cited a "modest" increase in United States exports to Mexico and estimated that perhaps 90,000 to

160,000 new, NAFTA-related jobs had been created. However, some 128,300 American jobs had disappeared. Even with these mixed results, Clinton and others continued their efforts to expand the NAFTA agreement to include other countries in the Western Hemisphere.

International Agreements Clinton's support for NAFTA reflected his foreign policy goal of expanding United States trade throughout the world. As part of this effort, the United States joined many other countries in adopting a revised version of the **General Agreement on Tariffs and Trade (GATT)** in 1994.[†] The goal of GATT, originally established in 1948, was to reduce tariffs and expand world trade. In 1995 the **World Trade Organization (WTO)** was established to ensure compliance with GATT, to negotiate new trade agreements, and to resolve trade disputes.

[†] The GATT agreement was revised between 1986 and 1994 at a conference known as the Uruguay Round.

ECONOMICS CONCEPTS

tariffs: **taxes on foreign goods imported into a country**

▼ **The Historical Context:** In the 1980s and 1990s, a number of governments worked together to reduce tariffs in the hope that expanded trade would stimulate economic growth. These efforts produced regional trade agreements, such as NAFTA, and the formation of the World Trade Organization to resolve trade disputes.

▼ **The Concept Today:** Tariffs remain a controversial issue in the United States. Some Americans worry that as American tariffs are lowered, jobs will shift from the United States to less-developed nations. Other Americans, in contrast, argue that lower tariffs worldwide will boost American exports and create new jobs.

SECTION 2 REVIEW

Comprehension

1. *Key Terms* Define: (a) apartheid; (b) economic sanction; (c) North American Free Trade Agreement (NAFTA); (d) General Agreement on Tariffs and Trade (GATT); (e) World Trade Organization (WTO).

2. *Summarizing the Main Idea* What questions did Americans raise about their nation's political and economic role in the post–cold war era?

3. *Organizing Information* Create a chart summarizing the United States' role in conflicts in the following places: Bosnia, Kosovo, Somalia, and Rwanda.

Critical Thinking

4. *Analyzing Time Lines* Review the time line at the start of the section. Select one event on the time line and tell how it reflects the Clinton administration's efforts to promote peace and freedom abroad.

5. *Identifying Central Issues* Why have efforts to reduce tariffs and expand free trade been controversial in the United States?

Writing Activity

6. *Writing a Persuasive Essay* Write an essay to your senator either in support of or against the expansion of NAFTA to other countries in the Western Hemisphere.

THE INFORMATION AGE

Focus Explain that today's era is often called the "information age." Point out that many people believe that we are in the midst of an Information Revolution that is transforming the ways we work and live in the same way that the Agricultural and Industrial revolutions changed people's lives in the past.

Instruct Discuss how new computer and information technology will continue to change Americans' lives. Point out that a revolutionary invention such as the computer usually fosters the rapid development of other inventions and products. Ask students to list other recent products used to send or process information and to explain how each works.

Extend You may wish to ask students to suggest ways in which new information technology of the future will change their daily lives. What invention will have the strongest impact on the next decade, and why?

1 Communications Satellite

Telstar was the world's first communications satellite. On the day it was launched, July 10, 1962, it transmitted the first live television pictures from the United States to Europe.

4 Bar Codes

Mad Magazine makes fun of bar codes—lines of varying thickness carrying information that can be read by laser light.

2 Fiber-Optic Cable

Hair-thin glass fibers can carry sound and data long distances using coded light pulses.

5 Silicon Chip

The miracle of the information age is this chip of impure silicon—a microprocessor. Computers with silicon chips are more complex, faster, and can handle many times more information than the original room-sized computers that used vacuum tubes and transistors.

Laser Head

Theodore Maiman developed this early laser in 1960. Laser light can carry more information than radio waves.

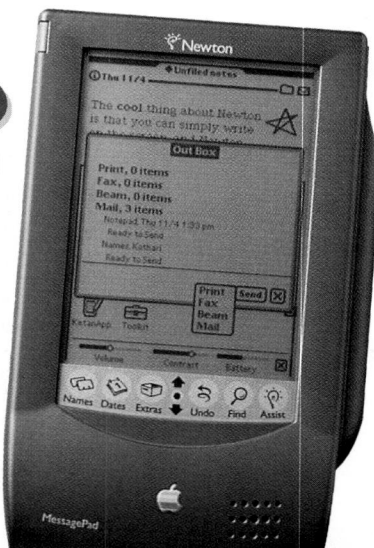

6 Hand-Held Computer

The ability of a single silicon chip to store and process great amounts of information has shrunk the size of the computer. A person can carry this computer anywhere and operate it at any time with a small stylus.

RESOURCE OPTIONS

Teaching Resources

American History Block Scheduling Support The Age of Affluence, found in The Nation After World War II folder, includes interdisciplinary lesson suggestions and activities for Geography and History, Primary Sources, Biography, and Literature.

Early Computer

The very first computers had no keyboards with which to enter information, no screens to view what was entered, and no storage devices. The Osborne, shown here, was a personal computer that offered all these improvements.

Watergate Bugs

The burglars who broke into the Democratic National Committee headquarters at the Watergate apartment complex in Washington, D.C., carried these "bugs."

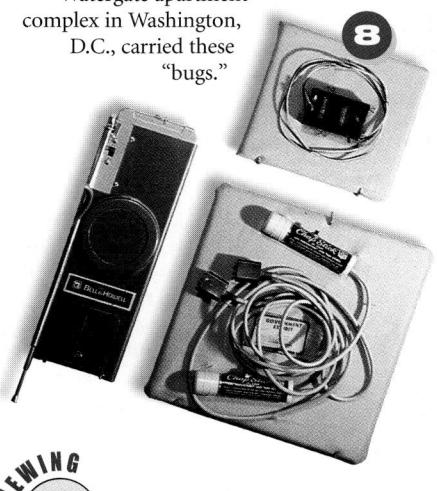

VIEWING HISTORY

1. Summarize What do the objects tell you about technological changes over the years?

2. Connecting to Today Think about how new technology affects our daily lives. Report the following to your class: (a) several ways in which computers have changed everyday activities; (b) what changes might take place as a result of technological advances in the next five to ten years.

FROM EXHIBITIONS AND COLLECTIONS
AT THE SMITHSONIAN INSTITUTION'S NATIONAL
MUSEUM OF AMERICAN HISTORY

THE INFORMATION AGE

You may not believe this, but there was a time before computers, before hand-held video games and CD-ROMs. The fact is that people have always needed ways to store and keep track of information. Do you know how people did this in the days before computers? You're probably holding the answer right in your hands—a book.

Technology has come a long way in a short period of time. In fact, the present era is called the Information Age because so many changes are happening so rapidly. Starting in the last century, people began to develop new forms of communication—the telegraph, the telephone, and the radio. In the last few decades, the invention of many more ways to store, retrieve, and transmit information has created an information explosion.

Developed in 1962, the first communications satellite transmitted television pictures across the globe. Today, fiber-optics technology is improving telephone and Internet service. Cables made of these optical fibers are lighter, cost less to use, and can carry more information than can metal cables. *See* **1** *and* **2**.

Laser light is used to decode information stored on CD-ROM and compact audio disks. Lasers have also made shopping easier. Using lasers that "read" the bar codes printed on consumer goods, store cashiers can add up a consumer's purchases far more efficiently. *See* **3** *and* **4**.

The centerpiece of the Information Age, of course, is the computer. Originally the size of a room, computers have shrunk in size as they grow in their ability to store information. *See* **5**, **6**, *and* **7**.

Many people worry that such huge technological strides have not come without a price. The ability to listen in on private conversations and invade privacy is seen by some as just one unwelcome by-product of the Information Age. Still, most people feel the benefits far outweigh the costs. We can only guess how far technology will take us. After all, who ever would have believed that some day you could talk on the phone while walking your dog? *See* **8**.

995

VIEWING HISTORY

Answers to . . .

1. Communications technology has rapidly become increasingly sophisticated. Computers, in particular, have become smaller and more efficient over time.

2. (a) Students may mention using computers to complete schoolwork, research their interests, talk to distant friends, or play games rather than using pen and paper, going to the library, talking on the telephone, or playing board games. (b) Answers will vary, but should be based on knowledge of recent developments in information technology.

RESOURCE OPTIONS

Media and Technology

 Prentice Hall United States History Video Collection™ Volume 20
Post-War USA

 AmericanHeritage® CD-ROM

 Time Tour The Nation Today and Tomorrow: Toward a New Century

| 1986 Immigration Reform and Control Act | 1990 Immigration Act increases quotas | 1992 Carol Moseley Braun elected to Senate | 1996 California passes Proposition 209 | 2000 Federal judge orders breakup of Microsoft |

1985   **1990**   **1995**   **2000**

SECTION 3

Twenty-First Century Americans

Objectives

You may wish to call students' attention to the objectives in the Section Preview. The objectives are reflected in the main headings of the section.

Bellringer

Ask students to take a poll of their classroom. What ethnic and national groups are represented? Do they belong to the "old" immigrants, who came in the 1800s and early 1900s (or earlier)? Or are they part of the newer immigrations?

Reading Strategy

Organizing Information Refer to the Reading Strategy in the Section Preview. Before beginning the section, you may wish to ask students about their views on the changes the United States faces.

LESSON PLAN

Connecting to the Main Idea

1. Focus The face of America was changing in the late 1990s. More Americans were immigrating from places outside Europe, especially from Asia and Latin America. Americans were also growing older. Ask what challenges these changes pose for the United States in the early years of the twenty-first century.

2. Instruct Explain that, while nearly all Americans are immigrants or descendants of immigrants, it has often been difficult for the newest group to be accepted. Discuss the various ways in which Americans have tried to make diversity work.

Have students discuss their views of the coming decade. For example, how might the "aging of America" affect family relationships?

3. Close The United States, part of a changing world, was itself changing as it faced the challenges of immigration, an aging population, and new technologies.

3 Twenty-First Century Americans

SECTION PREVIEW

Objectives

1 Describe the changing makeup of the nation's diverse population.
2 List the differences of opinion that emerged as Americans struggled to make diversity work.
3 Summarize the economic and political impact of the nation's aging population.
4 Analyze the impact of the computer revolution on the future of the United States.
5 *Key Terms* Define: multiculturalism, Internet.

Main Idea

In the 1990s, the United States sought new ways to create unity out of its ethnic and cultural diversity and to deal with the consequences of an "aging" population and a technological revolution.

Reading Strategy

Organizing Information As you read the section, create a graphic organizer summarizing the many changes facing the United States.

This California road sign warns drivers to be on the lookout for undocumented aliens who might have crossed the border from Mexico.

The Latin motto of the United States, found on American coins, is *"E pluribus unum"* meaning in English, "From many, one." This brief phrase reflects the patterns of the nation's past and the possibilities for its future. The United States was created when 13 separate colonies agreed to form a single union. Since then, people from an astonishing variety of lands have come to the United States and have enriched the culture of the nation. That process continued in the 1990s, and new priorities emerged as the nation matured. Creating unity out of diversity remains one of the nation's biggest challenges and a key to its future prosperity.

A Nation of Diversity

In the 1990s, as a result of another wave of immigration, the United States became more diverse than ever before. Throughout American history, each wave of immigration has been characterized by people from a different part of the world. Most immigrants in the 1600s came from England. Great numbers of German and Irish immigrants arrived in the mid-1800s. In the late 1800s and early 1900s most immigrants were from southern and eastern Europe. By the late 1900s, close to 90 percent of all legal immigrants came from Asia and Latin America. As points of origin shifted away from Europe, Los Angeles became the major port of entry, just as New York City had been a century before.

In 1996 an all-time high of 28 percent of the nation's people were African American, Hispanic, Asian American, or Native American. This expanding diversity meant that the United States was becoming, in the words of writer Ben J. Wattenberg, "the first universal nation."

Changing Immigration Policies American immigration policy contributed to the nation's growing diversity. Laws passed in the 1920s had strictly limited immigration and had given preference to immigrants from northern and western Europe. The Immigration Act of 1965 eliminated the bias that favored European

RESOURCE OPTIONS

Teaching Resources

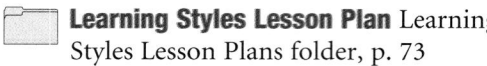

Reproducible Lesson Plan Lesson Plans folder, p. 176

Learning Styles Lesson Plan Learning Styles Lesson Plans folder, p. 73

Big Idea Graphic Organizer Big Idea Graphic Organizer folder, p. 148

Guided Reading and Review Units 9–10 folder, p. 105

Nystrom *Atlas of Our Country* The Fourth Wave of Immigration, pp. 36–37

immigrants. In 1986 the Immigration Reform and Control Act sought to curb illegal immigration, in part by forbidding employers to hire illegal aliens. At the same time, however, it permitted illegals who had lived in the United States since 1982 to register to become citizens. The Immigration Act of 1990 increased immigration quotas by 40 percent. It also erased restrictions that had denied entrance to many people in the past.

Changing Population Patterns
Changes in immigration caused changes in the nation's demographics, or population characteristics and patterns. While earlier immigrants had settled mainly on the East Coast, many of the new arrivals chose the Sun Belt. (The Sun Belt stretches from Florida to California.) Like their predecessors, most immigrants of the late 1900s settled in urban areas.

In 1990 minorities made up at least half the population in 15 of the nation's 28 largest cities. African Americans predominated in Detroit, Chicago, New Orleans, and Washington, D.C. Latinos were most heavily concentrated in Phoenix, El Paso, and San Antonio. Large numbers of Asian Americans settled in San Francisco. Los Angeles experienced the most dramatic variety of all. Korean, Vietnamese, Cambodian, Samoan, and Taiwanese newcomers joined established groups of Mexican Americans, African Americans, and European Americans. Like the many nationalities that had crowded into New York City a century earlier, these groups competed for jobs and housing. Similar competition occurred in other cities with large immigrant populations.

Minorities in Politics As minority groups grew in size, they also gained a new voice in the nation's political system. In 1992 Carol Moseley Braun, an Illinois Democrat, became the first African American woman to win election to the United States Senate. Also in 1992 Ben Nighthorse Campbell, a Republican from Colorado, became the first Native American to win election to the United States Senate. The 1994 midterm election sent 40 African Americans and 17 Latinos to the House. As Representative Nydia Velázquez of New York State observed, "Many of the new members were elected on [the promise of] changing 'business as usual.'" Minority political partici-

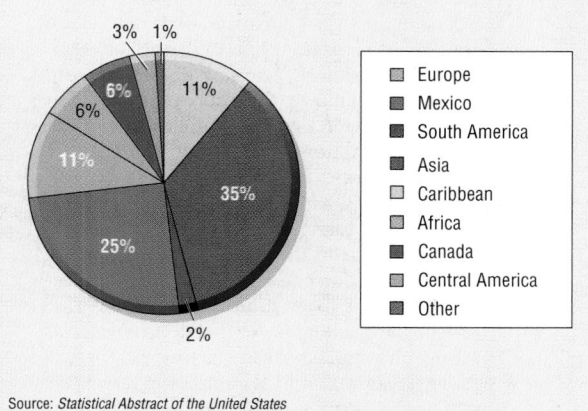

Origin of Immigrants, 1981–1995

- Europe — 35%
- Mexico — 25%
- South America — 2%
- Asia — 11%
- Caribbean — 11%
- Africa — 6%
- Canada — 6%
- Central America — 3%
- Other — 1%

Source: *Statistical Abstract of the United States*

Interpreting Graphs Immigration continues to keep the American population diverse. *Diversity* Which group comprised the largest percentage of immigrants to the United States between 1981 and 1995? How would you expect these statistics to affect the overall ethnic composition of the United States over several decades?

pation continued to grow as the century drew to a close. The House that took office at the start of Clinton's second term boasted 39 African Americans, 21 Latinos, and 5 Asian Americans.

Making Diversity Work

As American society became more diverse, government, private organizations, and individual citizens all undertook efforts to make diversity work. Some of these efforts aroused controversy.

Affirmative Action One of the most heated debates concerned affirmative action. President Johnson had introduced affirmative action policies under the Civil Rights Act of 1964 and an executive order in 1965. Its purpose was to improve employment and educational opportunities by giving preferences to African Americans and later to other minorities and women. Supporters of affirmative action argued that it succeeded in giving increased opportunities to tens of thousands of women and minorities. Opponents claimed that giving preferential treatment to some groups was unfair to everyone else. Americans should not "trample individual rights" in this way, argued California governor Pete Wilson.

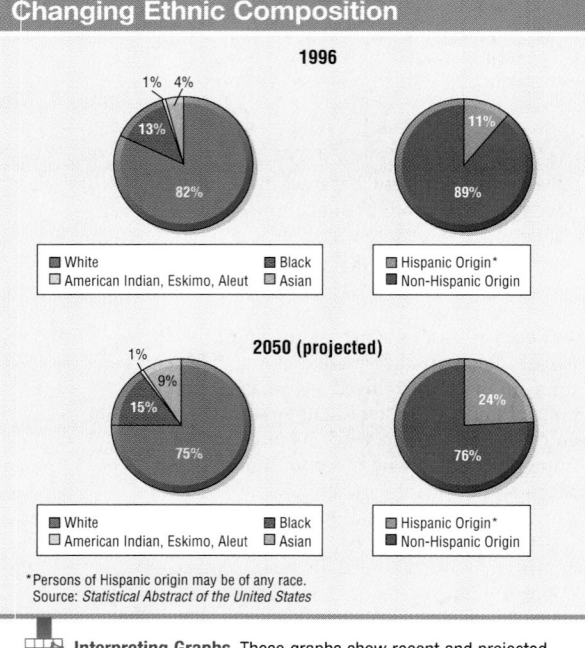

In 1996, California voters passed Proposition 209, ending affirmative action in state hiring and education. That same year, a federal court struck down an affirmative action admissions program at the University of Texas. The state's attorney general decided not to appeal the ruling to the Supreme Court. His decision reflected a growing public mood about affirmative action throughout the nation. Among the critics of the policy were some well-known African Americans, including Supreme Court Justice Clarence Thomas.

The courts in the 1990s heard a variety of affirmative action cases. However, the complexity of the issue made it difficult to decide. Can race be the deciding factor in a decision such as hiring, or just one of many factors? Is it proper for an organization to set numerical targets for selecting minorities or women? Should a less-qualified applicant ever be selected over a more-qualified one, simply because he or she belonged to a group discriminated against in the past? While both supporters and opponents of affirmative action agreed on the *idea* of fairness, fairness was not always easy to define.

Multiculturalism Another effort to make diversity work was **multiculturalism.** Multiculturalism was a movement that called for greater attention to non-European cultures in such areas as education. For example, advocates of multicultural education argued that school textbooks should include information on the contributions of people from all groups. Professor of education Jaime S. Wurzel explained the thinking behind this belief:

> **AMERICAN VOICES** "The multicultural person questions the arbitrary nature of his or her own culture and accepts the proposition that others who are culturally different can enrich their experience."
>
> —*Jaime S. Wurzel*

Others disapproved of this approach. History professor Arthur M. Schlesinger, Jr., referred to multiculturalism as "ethnic cheerleading." He criticized the use of history to make people feel good about themselves rather than to discover the truth about the past. Other critics worried that extreme versions of multiculturalism could damage the unity of society. They argued that the approach emphasized differences between groups rather than the shared values and experiences of all Americans.

The Future of Immigration In addition to debates over diversity, concerns about the economy in the 1990s caused some people to question government immigration policies. Some citizens proposed lowering the number of immigrants admitted each year. Other proposals included requiring schools to teach children only in English and limiting the rights of illegal immigrants.

In 1994, for example, California voters approved Proposition 187. This law required teachers and clinic doctors to deny assistance to illegal aliens and to report them to police. Supporters of the measure argued that states that were home to a large number of immigrants, like California, were unfairly burdened by heavy social welfare costs. The welfare reform passed by Congress in 1996 recognized this argument. It cut off food stamps for nearly all needy immigrants. In 1997 Congress reconsidered this drastic action and restored benefits to most immigrants who were legal residents of the United States. Also in 1997 a federal judge overturned Proposition 187, ruling it unconstitutional. It seemed likely that the public debate over immigration would continue.

Changing Ethnic Composition

1996

- White
- American Indian, Eskimo, Aleut
- Black
- Asian

82%, 13%, 1%, 4%

- Hispanic Origin*
- Non-Hispanic Origin

89%, 11%

2050 (projected)

- White
- American Indian, Eskimo, Aleut
- Black
- Asian

75%, 15%, 1%, 9%

- Hispanic Origin*
- Non-Hispanic Origin

76%, 24%

*Persons of Hispanic origin may be of any race.
Source: *Statistical Abstract of the United States*

Interpreting Graphs These graphs show recent and projected ethnic makeup of the United States. *Diversity According to the graphs, which group in the United States will experience the most dramatic rate of growth between 1996 and 2050?*

America's Aging Population

As the United States approached the turn of the century, its population was older than ever before. Elderly people made up the fastest-growing age group in the country. The number of people age 65 and over increased nearly elevenfold between 1900 and 1995. At the same time the nation's total population only tripled. Advances in medical care increased average life expectancy for newborns from 47 to 76 years. Between 1980 and 1995 alone, the number of people age 75 and over grew by 48 percent. An "aging revolution" was clearly under way.

The "graying of America" had important political and economic effects. Many older Americans pushed successfully for legislation that prohibited forced retirement at a given age. In addition, because older Americans were growing in number and living longer, entitlement payments increased greatly.

The Social Security system, for example, faced difficulties because the number of retirees receiving benefits was rising faster than the number of workers. In 1983, Congress tried to deal with the problem by raising taxes for workers and setting a later age for retirement benefits to begin. However, experts warned that more radical steps would have to be taken before the huge baby boom generation began retiring in the twenty-first century.

In the mid-1990s polls showed that many young Americans doubted that the Social Security system would exist when they reached retirement age. Some of them also indicated that they resented paying high taxes to provide benefits for people who were already retired. Some observers suggested that inter-generational conflict could become another tension in American society. Clearly, a solution to the Social Security problem needs to be found.

There was similar pressure on the medical care system. Medicare, established during the Great Society of the 1960s, provided many of the medical expenses of older Americans. As the number of recipients and health care costs rose, however, Medicare payouts exploded from $7.5 billion in 1970 to over $200 billion in the 1990s. As with Social Security, Congress agreed that long-term changes were needed. Clinton appointed a panel of Republicans and Democrats to study the future of Medicare.

The Computer Revolution

The pace of change today is increasing, and the computer is perhaps the best symbol of this change. Between 1983 and 1995, the percentage of American households with a computer jumped from 7 percent to 37 percent. Computers navigate spacecraft, route telephone calls, and assist in all kinds of scientific research. The **Internet,** a computer network that links millions of people around the world, is revolutionizing American education and business.

How will these changes affect employment? While computers have replaced some human workers, the growth of "high tech" industries has created thousands of new jobs. These jobs demand a high level of education and skills. One feature of the emerging economy is the lack of stable, well-paying jobs for unskilled workers. Education, therefore, has become more important than ever before.

Main Idea
CONNECTIONS

How will the computer revolution affect employment opportunities?

The computer's ability to store, manipulate, and transfer information with astonishing speed will continue to transform the American economy and society in the new century. *Culture Describe some of the ways in which the computer and the Internet have influenced American culture in recent years.*

Bill Gates

AMERICAN BIOGRAPHY In 1975, Bill Gates envisioned the future of computers and set to work turning that vision into reality. That year, at the age of 19, Gates dropped out of Harvard University to join his high school friend Paul Allen in establishing a new company. During high school Bill had used his computer knowledge to help create a company that sold traffic data to local governments. In 1975 the two friends first read about a kit computer in *Popular Electronics* magazine. "Paul and I didn't know exactly how it would be used, but we were sure it would change us and the world of computing."

Bill Gates (b.1955)

At first, people couldn't make the kit computer do much. Gates and Allen changed that by writing software, or the coded instructions for performing specific tasks, to run on the computer. Their efforts transformed it from a device with limited uses into a general-purpose computer similar (though much less powerful) to those we use today.

The company that the two friends started for marketing their software, later named Microsoft, grew to become a giant in the computer industry. Located in Seattle, Washington, where Gates was born, its success made Gates a billionaire by the age of 31. By 1998 Microsoft had become the world's second most valuable company, worth some $200 billion. Gates had become the richest person on Earth, with a personal fortune of about $45 billion.

Microsoft's size and success resulted in problems for Gates. In 1998 the Justice Department sued the company for violating the Sherman Antitrust Act of 1890. The suit was the biggest antitrust action since the government broke up the telephone company AT&T in 1984. The government accused Microsoft of using its power to gain a monopoly over software needed to browse the Internet. In 2000 a federal judge agreed and ordered that Microsoft be split into two smaller companies. Microsoft then began an appeals process in an effort to reverse this decision. ■

Facing the Future

In the future lie our hopes and dreams, as well as the struggles that bind us together as a nation. The next seven chapters focus on issues of our common future. By tackling these issues, we will make our own future together.

Near the end of his life, Thomas Jefferson wrote, "If a nation expects to be ignorant and free . . . it expects what never was and never will be." True as this statement was nearly 200 years ago, it is all the more true as we enter a century whose advances we can scarcely imagine.

SECTION 3 REVIEW

Comprehension

1. *Key Terms* Define: (a) multiculturalism; (b) Internet.

2. *Summarizing the Main Idea* Describe some of the major changes facing the United States at the end of the twentieth century.

3. *Organizing Information* Create a cause-effect graphic organizer showing the effects of the aging of the country's population.

Critical Thinking

4. *Analyzing Time Lines* Review the time line at the start of the section. How is the diverse nature of the nation's population reflected in the events shown?

5. *Drawing Inferences* How are economic issues related to questions about the country's immigration policies?

Writing Activity

6. *Writing an Expository Essay* Write an essay describing different points of view on affirmative action or multiculturalism.

Why Study History?
To understand that . . .

You Need to Stay Informed

As the world's supply of information explodes, learning how to obtain the information you need is becoming more important than ever.

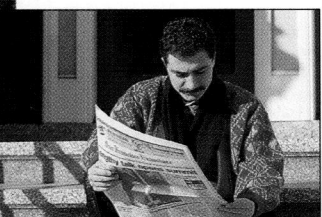

Traditional source of information, the newspaper

Katherine Chiao reads a daily newspaper and a weekly news magazine. She listens to news programs on the radio and watches documentaries on television. In addition, Chiao regularly uses the Internet, checking her favorite Web sites to find information on current topics of special interest. In short, she has learned to take advantage of the many sources of information that are available today.

The Impact Today

The 1990s represented the beginning of a new era in the United States. The end of the decades-long cold war prompted Americans to focus on domestic issues and challenges. At the same time, advances in communication technology produced a flood of information directed every day at average Americans.

Traditional forms of media, such as television, radio, and newspapers, remain the primary sources of news and information for most Americans. In the 1990s some 190 million Americans watched television regularly, while roughly 85 million listened to the radio and about 83 million read newspapers.

The Internet, however, has the potential to surpass all of these traditional forms in importance. Tens of millions of Americans are now connected to the Internet, which provides access to thousands of online magazines and newspapers. The Internet also has millions of articles, documents, and pictures from governments, businesses, and individuals.

With so much information becoming available, our challenge today lies not in obtaining information but in sorting through it to find what is both useful and reliable. Anyone can post materials on the Internet, and thus the quality of information there varies enormously. Many materials come from respected sources, such as universities and government agencies. Other materials are placed on the Internet by groups or individuals who have little expertise but want to express a certain point of view. Some materials are designed to deceive or to spread hatred. Internet users must therefore become intelligent "information consumers," distinguishing between reliable and unreliable sites.

The Impact on You

Watch the TV news coverage of an important event. Read about the same event in newspapers and magazines. Listen to radio accounts of the event. Search for documents about the event on the Internet, and read those as well. Discuss in class how the presentation of the event is similar or different in the various media. Then create a media report card that shows which medium you think is best for obtaining reliable information.

A dizzying array of information available on the Internet

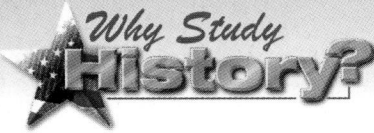

Why Study History?

Class Discussion

Discuss with the class information sources and their reliability. For a more thorough examination of the issue, see the activity folder in the Resource Options below.

ACTIVITY
STUDENT PARTICIPATION

Taking a Poll
Ask students to read the text. Then have them take a poll on sources people use to get their news, including:
- **newspapers**
- **magazines**
- **television**
- **radio**
- **Internet**

Each student should question at least three people.

Follow up Ask students to use the information from their poll to create charts and graphs.

Using the Internet
Students can learn more about staying informed by exploring links in the *America: Pathways to the Present* Web site at

http://www.Pathways.phschool.com

Assessment
See the Lesson Plans folder, pp. 24–27, for rubrics on assessing Class Participation Projects.

▶ RESOURCE OPTIONS

Teaching Resources

📁 **Why Study History? Activity** You Need to Stay Informed, found in the Why Study History? folder, p. 36, provides an activity to help students better understand how to stay informed.

Media and Technology

AmericanHeritage® CD-ROM

Time Tour The Nation Today and Tomorrow: Toward a New Century

  Decision America Videotapes and Videodiscs Issue 4 *Who Tells Us What to Think?*

Key Terms

Students should refer to the definitions of key terms in the chapter to write sentences that show an understanding of the domestic and foreign policy challenges that the United States faced during the 1990s.

Comprehension

1. It faced strong opposition from Republicans in Congress, as well as from lobbyists representing insurance, small-business, and professional groups who opposed the plan.

2. Republicans had won a majority in both houses of Congress in the midterm elections, and many backed Gingrich's Contract with America, a conservative plan for cutting government.

3. It took part in the NATO bombing campaigns and committed troops to NATO peacekeeping forces stationed in the area.

4. Supporters said that NAFTA would create new jobs by increasing exports to Canada and Mexico. Opponents argued that manufacturers would move factories to Mexico, resulting in a loss of American jobs.

5. Asia and Latin America.

6. The Immigration Act of 1965 eliminated the bias in favor of European immigration, increasing the number of immigrants from Asia, Africa, and Latin America. The 1986 Immigration Reform and Control Act allowed immigrants who had been living in the United States since 1962 to become citizens, and the Immigration Act of 1990 increased immigration quotas.

Chapter Summary

The major concepts of Chapter 35 are presented below. See also *Guide to the Essentials of American History* or *Interactive Student Tutorial CD-ROM,* which contains interactive review activities, time lines, helpful hints, and test practice for Chapter 35.

Reviewing the Main Ideas

Despite opposition from Congress and charges of political and personal scandal, Clinton remained a popular President. Throughout the 1990s, the country struggled to find its way through uncharted waters in post–cold war international relations. The country also worked to maintain a strong sense of unity and economic well-being in the face of demographic and technological changes.

Section 1: Politics in the 1990s

American voters, concerned with a sluggish economy, elected Bill Clinton to the presidency in 1992. Despite showing strong support for Republicans in the 1994 midterm elections, voters reelected Clinton in 1996. His second term, although filled with scandal, was marked by a strong, rapidly growing economy.

Section 2: The United States in a New World

The collapse of communism and an increase in ethnic tensions in various parts of the world caused Americans to examine their nation's political and economic role in the post–cold war era.

Section 3: Twenty-First Century Americans

In the 1990s, the United States sought new ways to create unity out of its ethnic and cultural diversity and to deal with the consequences of an "aging" population and a technological revolution.

Why Study History?

As the world's supply of information explodes, learning how to obtain the information you need is becoming more important than ever. Internet users must become intelligent "information consumers," distinguishing between reliable and unreliable sites.

Key Terms

For each of the terms below, write a sentence explaining how it relates to the chapter.

1. Contract with America
2. Whitewater affair
3. apartheid
4. economic sanctions
5. NAFTA
6. GATT
7. World Trade Organization
8. multiculturalism
9. Internet

Comprehension

1. Why did Clinton's health care plan fail to win passage in Congress?

2. After 1994, why did Republicans believe that they had a mandate to reduce the size of the federal government?

3. What role did the United States play in producing cease-fires in Bosnia and Kosovo?

4. Give reasons why some people supported NAFTA and others opposed it.

5. Which two regions of the world sent the most immigrants to the United States during the 1990s?

6. How did federal policy add to the diversity of the United States?

Using Graphic Organizers

On a separate sheet of paper, draw a web diagram similar to the one below. In each circle summarize an international event that occurred during the Clinton administration.

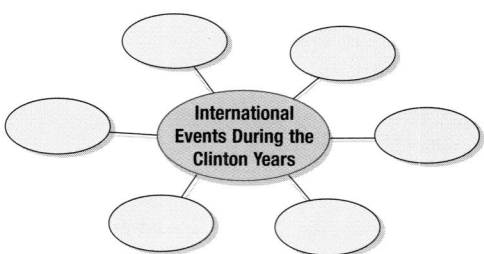

International Events During the Clinton Years

Using Graphic Organizers

- In Russia, Yeltsin was elected president, troops were sent to Chechnya, and independence was postponed.
- In South Africa, apartheid was overturned and the nation held its first free elections.
- In the Middle East, a settlement was worked out between Israel and the PLO.
- In Haiti, the U.S. intervened to restore democracy.
- In the Balkans, the U.S. led bombing raids and hosted a peace agreement between Serbs and Bosnians.
- In Africa, the U.S. sent troops on relief missions in Somalia.
- In India and Pakistan, nuclear weapons were detonated.

Analyzing Political Cartoons ▶

1. Read the title of the cartoon. What do you normally associate with vacations?

2. Examine the scene. (a) What do you traditionally associate with a trip to the beach? (b) How is this scene different?

3. What comment is the cartoonist making about 1990s lifestyle?

Critical Thinking

1. *Applying the Chapter Skill* Describe the consequences of the nation's aging population.

2. *Demonstrating Reasoned Judgment* The United States intervened in some world conflicts during the 1990s. What do you think should be the role of the United States in future conflicts throughout the world?

3. *Identifying Assumptions* What reasons do people who oppose affirmative action cite in support of their position?

4. *Drawing Inferences* President Clinton gave his speech regarding the need for health care reform to a national TV audience in 1993 as a way of rallying public support for reform. What benefits and drawbacks does television offer to Presidents?

INTERNET ACTIVITY

For your portfolio:
PREPARE A REPORT

Access Prentice Hall's *America: Pathways to the Present* site at **www.Pathways.phschool.com** for the specific URLs to complete the activity. Additional resources and related Web sites are also available.

Use information and trade data from the links provided to prepare a report on the purpose and goals of the European Union. Include a graph or chart in your report using data on trade.

ANALYZING DOCUMENTS ◀▶ **INTERPRETING DATA**

Turn to the ethnic composition graphs on page 998.

1. Which of the following groups made up 13 percent of the United States population in 1996? (a) White (b) Black (c) American Indian, Eskimo, and Aleut (d) Asian.

2. Which of the following groups will more than double its percentage of the United States population by 2050? (a) White (b) Black (c) Asian (d) Hispanic Origin.

3. *Write* What will happen to the white population as a percent of the total population?

Connecting to Today

Making Inferences
Reread the statement by Thomas Jefferson on page 1000. Describe in your own words how education and freedom are related. Why will education be so important to workers of the twenty-first century?

INTERNET ACTIVITY

Reports will vary, but should present information clearly and accurately, and include quotes and specific facts.

Analyzing Political Cartoons

1. Relaxation; freedom from work or school.

2. (a) Blankets and towels; coolers; swimming; looking for sea shells; sunbathing; making sand castles. (b) Instead of engaging in these activities, the family shown is surrounded by portable, mostly business-related, technology, which they are using.

3. Americans no longer know how to relax. The array of communications technology we have created does not free us from work, but enables us to do more of it.

Critical Thinking

1. Older Americans succeeded in getting legislation in their areas of interest passed; the number of people entitled to Social Security was increasing faster than payments, threatening a crisis; Medicare costs increased.

2. Sample answers: The United States, as the world's lone superpower, has an obligation to take on the role of peacekeeper. Or, becoming involved in dangerous situations such as Bosnia or Somalia may be too costly in money and lives.

3. That preferential treatment robs people of their dignity or self-worth; that it is unfair to other groups.

4. Answers will vary. Benefits might include reaching out to all people. Drawbacks might include appearing unpersuasive if the individual lacks "television appeal."

Interpreting Data

1. b
2. c
3. It will decline as a percentage of the total.

Connecting to Today

Answers will vary, but should mention that the technological revolution requires advanced education and skills.

My Brush with History

American Heritage®

My Brush with History

BY CRAIG B. GREENFIELD

INTRODUCTION The cold war decades were a boom time for the American defense industry. The billions spent each year to develop and produce modern weapons not only helped protect the nation, but boosted its economy. In the passage below, Craig B. Greenfield, whose father worked for a defense contractor, describes a visit to see his father's handiwork in action.

⊷ *Poseidon Missile Test* ⊷

A Poseidon missile submarine (left) launches one of its missiles (right).

It was 1974. As your average twelve-year-old, my world was one of mischievous after-school activities, mixed with the usual sandlot sports, awkward encounters with girls, and homework. With the exception of the trendy peace-sign belt buckle and fingers-gesturing peace-sign T-shirt that I owned, I had only a faint familiarity with the politics of peace and war in faraway Vietnam. In fact, my only real exposure to those events came from those television voices that came between "Gilligan's Island" and "Adam 12," who spoke of the specter of nuclear holocaust that losing to communism in Asia might invite. All that changed one winter with a brief but profound encounter with the inner workings and realities of the Cold War.

My family had taken a vacation that December. With my father employed as an electrical engineer by the Sperry Corporation, a leading Long Island defense contractor, and my mother keeping busy with her family at home, we set out for Fort Lauderdale to combine some sunshine with the duty of visiting all our recently retired relatives. A much-anticipated highlight of this trip for me was to be a visit to the newly opened Disney World. But compared with the show I was to see, that children's mecca turned out to be just a roadside attraction.

We were relaxing in the cool comfort of my uncle's condominium when my father proudly announced that he had arranged for a side trip to Cape Canaveral for what he called, in the acronymistic vernacular of the defense industry, a DASO, or "daytime at sea operation," wherein a Poseidon missile would be launched from an actual submarine. Although I viewed this development as one more dreaded lengthy car ride full of slap fighting with my brother, to my father, who had worked hard on developing submarine navigation systems, it was a rare and valuable chance to see his engi-

---

TEST PREPARATION

Have students use the excerpt on these pages to answer the following question.

Which statement best describes the speaker's feelings about weapons development and production during the cold war?

A He feels that U.S. military preparedness helped end the cold war and is grateful.

B He feels proud of his father and is grateful to have seen his achievement.

C He feels that high defense spending prevented the United States from adequately addressing problems such as poverty and infant mortality.

D He feels that the nation should have done more to prepare militarily.

Cape Canaveral

neering achievement at work—a demonstration otherwise possible only in an apocalyptic armed launch situation.

With a quick good-bye we set off on our three-hour journey to Port Canaveral, neighboring the cape, where so many televised space shots originated, my father's excitement manifesting itself in driving at a clip that ultimately got him ticketed.

We arrived at Cape Canaveral and were processed in true Cold War fashion: security clearance, identification cards, and a short, sharp admonishment to stay only in certain areas of the host Navy ship during our day at sea. Then we proceeded up the gangplank and onto the huge auxiliary ship *Compass Island* (EAG 153), which had seen action over the years as a part of the U.S. Military Sealift Command.

I spent the hours-long voyage out to sea exploring the ship and listening to a succession of lectures about this and that capability, guidance system, and the like on both the *Compass Island* and the day's feature attraction, the five-hundred-foot long Poseidon submarine USS *Lafayette* (SSBN 616), which rode regally beside us until it majestically submerged into the sparkling Atlantic water, trailed only by its perfect wake and the indiscreet presence of an antenna-laden Soviet "fishing trawler."

At dusk, with the Florida sun low on the horizon, everyone aboard became aware of the countdown that had actually been going on all day. With fifteen seconds left and our formidable companion well hidden under the sea, the boat buzzed with anticipation and excitement.

At about five seconds to launch, our immense host ship began to rock to and fro, despite the relative tranquillity of the Atlantic shortly before. At four seconds to launch the boat was heaving so violently that all of us had to brace ourselves. At three seconds to launch the rumbling became so loud that I imagined myself being in the center of a thunderclap. At two seconds to launch, with the blocks-long ship in its turbulent pitch and roll and the noise of eruption becoming ever louder, the inside missile hatch of the submarine blew open explosively far below. Finally, rising on a column of fire, the thirty-four-foot body of the C-3 Poseidon missile emerged from the boiling sea and, with a zig right and a zag left, rocketed skyward and headed toward its destination in the Indian Ocean, nearly three thousand miles away. As I gazed awestruck, my jaw opened wide, that image implanted itself indelibly in my memory.

Today, more than twenty years later, with the disintegration of soviet communism receding into history, what occurred on that winter day at sea seems almost to have been staged for a movie rather than the profound and scary reality that it was.

However, that vivid childhood memory allows me as an adult to appreciate fully the magnitude of the resources involved in that endeavor called the Cold War. Having personally lived with the practical realities of the Cold War —and having been fed, clothed, and educated with the money that the employment of thousands like my father in the defense industry brought—I greet these new historical developments with both a sense of hope for a peaceful future and a sense of what brought them about.

Source: *American Heritage* magazine, July 1995.

ADDITIONAL READING

To learn more about the topics discussed in this selection, you might want to read the following books:

- *The Cold War: A History,* by Martin Walker (New York: Henry Holt, 1994)
- *Grand Expectations: The United States, 1945–1974,* by James T. Patterson (New York: Oxford University Press, 1996)
- *The Nuclear Question: The United States and Nuclear Weapons, 1946–1976,* by Michael Mandelbaum (Cambridge: Cambridge University Press, 1979)
- *The Wizards of Armageddon,* by Fred Kaplan (New York: Simon & Schuster, 1983)

American Heritage®

Customize for
English Language Learners

Students may need help with the following words and phrases:

sandlot sports games such as baseball, kickball, softball, and soccer that children played on vacant lots

nuclear holocaust destruction of the world by a nuclear accident or by nuclear weapons

defense contractor firm that produces weapons and other supplies for the military

gangplank movable bridge used to board or leave a ship

a clip that ultimately got him ticketed a speed above the legal limit that resulted in a police officer issuing a ticket

Customize for
Less Proficient Readers

Have students use their textbooks to make a time line of key events in the cold war, from 1947 to 1991. Completed time lines should include events such as the establishment of NATO (1949), the House Un-American Activities Committee hearings (late 1940s and early 1950s), the Cuban Missile Crisis (1962), and the escalation of the Vietnam War (1964).

Customize for
More Advanced Students

How does hindsight affect our understanding of historical events? Have students analyze Greenfield's observation that his "vivid childhood memory allows [him] as an adult to appreciate fully the magnitude of the resources involved in that endeavor called the Cold War." How does Greenfield's upbringing influence his perceptions of the cold war?

TEST PREPARATION

Have students use the excerpt on these pages to answer the following question.

Based on the passage you can tell that—

A Greenfield was a rebel who, despite his father, opposed the war in Vietnam.

B Greenfield's father used the trip to Disney World as a means to get his family to Cape Canaveral.

C Greenfield grew up in a typical middle-class family of the 1970s.

D Greenfield was an exceptional child.

Pathways to the Future

Managing Time and Instruction

INSTRUCTION SUPPORT
These materials for instruction are provided for **each section** in the **Teaching Resources.** See **Unit 11 folder for Enrichment Support:**

- Reproducible Lesson Plans in Lesson Plans folder • Learning Styles Lesson Plans in Learning Styles Lesson Plans folder • Big Idea Graphic Organizers in Big Idea Graphic Organizer folder
- Guided Reading and Review • Quizzes • Test Preparation Practice booklet

DAILY LESSON	ENRICHMENT SUPPORT
36 **Immigration and the Golden Door** (pp. 1008–1015)	• Debating the Future, The Debate on Immigration, Unit 11 folder, pp. 4–5 • Literature Activity, Immigrant Dreams, Unit 11 folder, pp. 6–7
37 **Gun Control and Crime** (pp. 1016–1022)	• Debating the Future, The Debate on Gun Control and Violence, Unit 11 folder, pp. 9–10 • Literature Activity, Roots of the Brady Law, Unit 11 folder, pp. 11–12
38 **The Minimum Wage** (pp. 1023–1029)	• Debating the Future, The Debate on the Minimum Wage, Unit 11 folder, pp. 14–15 • Literature Activity, No Work Till Spring, Unit 11 folder, pp. 16–17
39 **Rethinking Entitlements** (pp. 1030–1038)	• Debating the Future, The Debate on Entitlements, Unit 11 folder, pp. 19–20 • Literature Activity, Responsibility, Not Entitlement, Unit 11 folder, p. 21 • Literature Activity, For the First Time, Unit 11 folder, p. 22
40 **The Debate over Trade** (pp. 1039–1047)	• Debating the Future, The Debate over NAFTA, Unit 11 folder, pp. 24–25 • Literature Activity, The Banana Republics, Unit 11 folder, pp. 26–27
41 **Foreign Policy After the Cold War** (pp. 1048–1055)	• Debating the Future, The Debate over Foreign Policy After the Cold War, Unit 11 folder, pp. 29–30 • Literature Activity, Toward a New Century, Unit 11 folder, pp. 31–32
42 **Technology and You in the Next Century** (pp. 1056–1065)	• Debating the Future, Should Funding Technology Be a Priority? Unit 11 folder, pp. 34–35 • Literature Activity, The Information Revolution, Unit 11 folder, pp. 36–37

Running Out of Time?

- 🔘 📼 **Decision America Videotapes and Videodiscs.**
- Use Chapters 36–42 Summaries from **Guide to the Essentials of American History (English and Spanish).**

AMERICA
PATHWAYS TO THE PRESENT

Companion Web Site

The companion Web site offers online links for all chapter review activities. It also provides key content links and structured support for this chapter for both teachers and students.

http://www.Pathways.phschool.com

Teaching in the Information Age

Media and Technology

For the Student

Interactive Student Tutorial CD-ROM Unit 11
Student Edition on Audiotape Unit 11
American Heritage® CD-ROM
Guided Reading Audiotapes (English and Spanish) Unit 11

For the Teacher

Resource Pro CD-ROM Unit 11
Test Bank CD-ROM Unit 11
Listening to Literature Audiotapes *Timeless Voices, Timeless Themes* "Mother Tongue" by Amy Tan
Color Transparencies Fine Art, D-4, D-7, D-12, D-15; Cause and Effect, F-7, F-8, F-10

Assessment Options

Chapter Test Forms A&B Test Bank CD-ROM booklet
Test Bank CD-ROM Unit 11
Standardized Test Preparation Handbook

Block Scheduling

Pacing Suggestions

For 90-minute Blocks

- Teach chapters 36, 38, 39, and 42 using Transparencies B-7, C-2, C-3, F-9, H-8 and K-7 and the Connections to Today notes on pp. 1025, 1032, and 1062 for class discussions.
- Teach chapters 37, 40, and 41 using the Big Idea Graphic Organizers from Teaching Resources and the Extended Class Periods Activities in each chapter.

Additional Resources

- **Our Times Multimedia Encyclopedia of the 20th Century CD-ROM** contains *The Columbia Encyclopedia* and over 2,500 images, charts, maps, and graphs. Teacher's guidebook with lesson plans is included.
- **Decision America Videotapes and Videodiscs**

Connections to American Literature

from Prentice Hall

America: Pathways to the Present "Straw into Gold: The Metamorphosis of the Everyday" by Sandra Cisneros, p. 1090; from *My American Journey* by Colin Powell, p. 1092
Prentice Hall Literature *Timeless Voices, Timeless Themes* "Who *Is* Here?" by Joyce Carol Oates, p. 349

Additional Resources

For the Student
Our Times Multimedia Encyclopedia of the 20th Century CD-ROM. Vicarious, 1996.

For the Teacher
Haynes Johnson. *Divided We Fall.* W.W. Norton, 1994.

Prentice Hall brings into the classroom the vast resources from the archives and scholarship of the nation's premier American history magazine.

History Alive!

Teacher's Curriculum Institute, in partnership with Prentice Hall, provides unique materials that engage students with diverse learning styles. See History Alive!® unit on Contemporary American Society.

Student Performance Pack

Ensures success in the three critical areas of Reading, Test Taking, and English Language Development with the following materials:
- Guide to the Essentials of American History in English and Spanish
- Guided Reading Audiotapes in English and Spanish
- Interactive Student Tutorial CD-ROM
- Test Preparation Handbook
- Test Preparation Practice booklet

Pathways to the Future:

Themes for the Twenty-first Century

Introducing the Unit

Using Historical Evidence

Have students look at the photo on the right and suggest reasons for this celebration—perhaps a new year, or a new century. Point out that the twentieth century was marked by American achievement and success. The late 1990s, however, found many Americans uncertain about the future.

Establishing Chronology

The chapters in this unit focus on national issues. Some are part of an ongoing national debate about the role of government. Others reflect changes in society and technology.

Teachers may wish to set these specific issues in the context of broader historical themes:

Economics

Budgetary constraints raised questions about entitlement programs.

Unity and Conflict

Some Americans charged that immigration hurt national unity.

Americans disagreed sharply about controls on gun ownership.

Diversity

Immigration from different cultures increased diversity in American society.

The United States and the World

The end of the cold war meant a reshaping of American foreign policy.

Trade changed the United States's relationships with Latin America.

Technology

The spread of computer networks raised questions about their use in education.

unit ELEVEN

Pathways to the Future

Themes for the Twenty-first Century

Chapter 36

Immigration and the Golden Door

In the 1990s, immigrants had a profound impact on the nation. Both the sheer numbers of immigrants and their cultural diversity are reshaping American society.

Chapter 37

Gun Control and Crime

In recent years, America has experienced a wave of violent crime, with a significant percentage of these crimes involving the use of guns. The Second Amendment to the Constitution protects the right to "keep and bear arms." But does it refer only to states' needs for security, or does it include individuals' needs as well?

Chapter 38

The Minimum Wage

In the 1990s the gap between the rich and the poor continued to widen. To narrow this gap, President Clinton proposed an increase in the minimum wage. While economists and politicians debated the effect of such a raise on the economy, others questioned whether the federal government should be setting a minimum wage at all.

Chapter 39

Rethinking Entitlements

In the 1990s increasing numbers of people receiving assistance in the form of cash benefits, food stamps, and medical care put a strain on the federal budget. Balancing the needs of the poor and the elderly against the needs of the budget is a challenge facing all Americans.

Chapter 40

The Debate Over Trade

With the end of the cold war and the rise of democratic institutions in the Western Hemisphere, trade has become a major concern of the United States and its neighbors. The North American Free Trade Agreement (NAFTA) is the lightning rod for the debate over what the model should be for relations among the countries of the Americas.

Chapter 41

Foreign Policy After the Cold War

What is the proper role of the United States in the world today? Should it continue its role of world leadership? Should it seek to be a peacekeeper or a humanitarian relief agency? These and other questions on the nation's role in world affairs will be debated into the next century.

Chapter 42

Technology and You in the Next Century

Technology has always had a profound effect on American society. Today it is the computer industry that is changing the way Americans live and work. What is the role of schools in preparing students to use and understand this technology, which will dominate the next century?

Ticker tape parade, New York City

RESOURCE OPTIONS

Teaching Resources

Unit 11 folder Contains instructional materials organized by chapter.

Listed below are the technology resources that *America: Pathways to the Present* offers:

RESOURCE PRO

America: Pathways to the Present Teaching Resources on CD-ROM offers lesson planning flexibility, test generation capability, and additional enrichment support.

Using the Internet

Prentice Hall's *America: Pathways to the Present* companion Web site offers student-appropriate Internet activities and links as well as resources for teachers. Visit us at http://www.Pathways.phschool.com

AmericanHeritage®

History of the United States CD-ROM This interactive, multimedia exploration of the American experience provides a journey through historical, political, and social aspects of American history. Includes Time Tours, Presidents, and History Makers.

Visions of America

This award-winning integrated multimedia package offers Scenes of an Era, Turning Point stories, and historians' viewpoint on core content.

Our Times Multimedia Encyclopedia of the 20th Century CD-ROM

INTERACTIVE STUDENT TUTORIAL CD-ROM

GUIDED READING AUDIOTAPES

STUDENT EDITION ON AUDIOTAPE

PRENTICE HALL LISTENING TO MUSIC THE AMERICAN EXPERIENCE AUDIO CD

RESOURCE OPTIONS

Media and Technology

 Decision America Videotapes and Videodiscs Issue 4 *Who Tells Us What to Think?* Issue 7 *Is America Still the Free-World Leader?*

AmericanHeritage® CD-ROM

Explorer Activity 31, Civics Overview: American Democracy, CD-ROM Guidebook, pp. 81–82, allows students to explore different branches of the government and search the Internet for additional resources.

Time Tour Toward a New Century

Objectives

Help students to explain the challenges presented by the increasing numbers and diversity of immigrants to the United States, understand historic patterns of immigration, and identify the arguments for and against tighter controls on immigration.

Bellringer

Ask students why they think people want to come to the United States. What do they think is the most common reason?

Reading Strategy

Reading for Evidence Ask students to look for evidence as they read supporting both sides of the question posed in the debate: Should we continue to welcome people from other lands, or do we need to restrict immigration?

LESSON PLAN

Connecting to the Main Idea

1. Focus Remind students of the waves of immigration that have contributed to building the United States. How are immigration patterns today different from those in the past? Have these new patterns influenced attitudes toward new immigrants?

2. Instruct Discuss how people's points of view about immigration may be influenced by personal factors such as their employment or economic status. Ask students to suggest other possible factors and discuss how these factors might influence attitudes.

3. Close As the twentieth century drew to a close, immigrants came from new parts of the world, increasing cultural diversity but challenging some elements of society. The next chapter discusses another current issue: gun control and crime.

CHAPTER 36 Immigration and the Golden Door

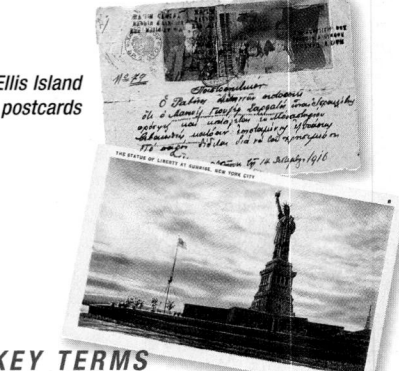

Ellis Island postcards

INTRODUCING THE THEME

A poem inscribed at the base of the Statue of Liberty begins: "Give me your tired, your poor, Your huddled masses yearning to breathe free...." Emma Lazarus wrote these lines in 1883, during a new wave of immigration to the United States. More than a hundred years later, immigration is again on the rise. Both the sheer numbers of immigrants and their cultural diversity are profoundly reshaping American society—everything from foods and phone books to schools and politics.

 DEBATE

Should we continue to welcome people from other lands, or do we need to restrict immigration?

KEY TERMS

undocumented immigrant, political asylum, green card, nativist, bilingual education

---

VIEWING THE PRESENT

Ovidiu Colea spent five years in a Romanian labor camp as punishment for trying to escape to the United States. He finally emigrated in 1978 and settled in New York. In 1985 he won the only contract to make replicas of the Statue of Liberty for the centennial celebration the next year. With the help of about two dozen other immigrants in his factory in Blissville, Queens, Colea and his business became very successful, manufacturing the very symbol of the American dream.

Not all immigrant stories end so happily. For example, in El Monte, California, 72 immigrants from Thailand lived and worked locked inside an apartment complex surrounded by razor wire. They sewed garments for up to 115 hours a week in cramped sweatshops. From their meager wages, their employer deducted the nearly $5,000 cost of transportation to the United States. "Living in there was like death, never able to see the world outside," said one woman. Eventually a worker escaped and notified authorities, who freed the others.

Rising Immigration

Between the extremes of these two experiences lie the stories of millions of newcomers to the United States. In the 1980s immigration skyrocketed. During that decade, the number of newcomers soared to about 7.3 million, more than one and a half times what it had been in the previous decade. This surge continued into the 1990s. In 1991, the number of official immigrants entering the United States totaled 1,827,200 people. The figures

Ovidiu Colea with a replica of the Statue of Liberty

 RESOURCE OPTIONS

Teaching Resources

Reproducible Lesson Plan Lesson Plans folder, p. 177

Learning Styles Lesson Plan Learning Styles Lesson Plans folder, p. 74

Big Idea Graphic Organizer Big Idea Graphic Organizer folder, p. 149

Guided Reading and Review Unit 11 folder, p. 3

dropped in succeeding years, with 660,447 arriving in 1998—the lowest numbers since 1988.

To appreciate the full impact of recent immigration, however, one must add to these figures the number of **undocumented immigrants.** (These are immigrants who have entered the United States illegally.) The Immigration and Naturalization Service estimated that in 1996 some 5 million people were living in this country illegally.

Reasons for Immigration

Immigrants can legally enter the United States for the following reasons:
1. They have relatives who are American citizens.
2. They possess needed job skills.
3. They are refugees from war or are seeking **political asylum** to escape persecution.

The principal reason immigrants come to the United States is family ties. In 1998, about 72 percent of legal immigrants were family members of American citizens. Another 12 percent were granted entry because they had specialized work skills. About 8 percent were refugees and asylum seekers. The rest fell into special categories of the immigration law.

Sources of Immigration

The largest group of immigrants in 1998—about 38 percent—came from North America and the Caribbean, with Mexico in the lead. Approximately one third of all immigrants in that year came from

You only need go as far as your local grocery store to see that immigration affects American culture. *Economics Which of the foods in this photograph can you find in your local grocery store? Do those foods reflect the background of the people who live in your area? How do they reflect the diversity of America as a whole?*

Asia, with the largest contingent from China. About 14 percent came from Europe, 7 percent from South America, and 6 percent from Africa. All in all, more people are coming to the United States from more countries than ever before.

Finding Homes

Once they arrive, newcomers face seemingly endless challenges, the first of which is finding a place to live. Immigrants move to every state of the Union, with the greatest concentrations in California, New York, Florida, and Texas. Most settle in cities with ethnic neighborhoods where they can find familiar food, language, and customs, as well as a network of people to help them learn the American way of life.

Nur Emirgil, a Turkish immigrant to Queens, New York, describes how her neighborhood

works: "Somebody calls or knocks on the door and asks, 'Can this person stay on your couch for a few days?' 'Do you know any job they can get, someplace that doesn't care about **green cards** [work permits for foreigners]?' 'Can you go with them to the doctor to translate?'"

Adjusting to America

For immigrants, striking a balance between preserving old ways and learning new ones can be difficult. Many immigrants discover they have to give up their old line of work and take the lowest-paying unskilled jobs just to be employed at all. While they want their children to learn English, they also want them to maintain their heritage.

Just as immigrants have changed to adjust to America, this nation has changed to adjust to them. New products and services

ACTIVITY
HETEROGENEOUS GROUPS

Divide students into groups to compile a "Who's Who" list of immigrants to the United States who have made notable contributions. Have groups focus on a specific discipline such as Science, Technology, Business, Arts, or Entertainment. Ask groups to provide brief biographies and, if possible, pictures for a display. To help students begin, suggest historical figures such as Enrico Fermi, Alexander Graham Bell, Nikola Tesla, Andrew Carnegie, Baron von Steuben, and Irving Berlin. **(Enrichment)**

ACTIVITY
STUDENT PORTFOLIO

You may wish to have students add the following to their portfolios. To assess student work, refer to the generic rubrics in the Program Overview in the Teaching Resources.

Suggest to students that they use the Internet or reading lists to find and read a first-person account, biography, or novel based on the immigrant experience. Ask students to write a review of the piece that both summarizes and comments on the account.

Answer to . . .

Viewing History Often with opposition and nativist sentiment.

have appeared to appeal to the nearly 10 percent of Americans who are foreign-born. Television and radio now broadcast in several dozen languages. Yellow pages have been published for different ethnic groups. Foods imported from places as different as Southeast Asia and Mexico line the shelves of grocery stores in small towns like Garden City, Kansas.

Caring for Immigrants

The arrival of so many immigrants of such diverse origins has placed a strain on the United States. Areas with large foreign-born populations must provide ballots in one or more languages besides English. Big-city school systems like those in Chicago and Los Angeles must devise ways to teach classes representing dozens of different languages. Public hospitals must treat poor immigrants who cannot

afford to pay for health care. All of these services cost money at a time when federal, state, and local governments have less to spend.

REVIEWING THE PAST

We are, as President Kennedy put it, a "nation of immigrants." With the exception of Africans, who were brought to the Americas against their will, all other immigrants have come here in search of a better life. They see America as a land of opportunity. But opportunity has always involved risk, loss, and change.

Coming to the United States has meant wrenching changes for immigrants, who had to leave their homelands behind and adapt to new circumstances. It has also meant the growth of a unique American culture. Some call it a melting pot. Others describe it as a

 This Russian family came to the United States in the early 1900s. In those years, thousands of new arrivals passed through the Ellis Island immigration center each day. ***Government** How did Americans respond to this wave of immigration?*

salad bowl or a mosaic. But whatever the metaphor, American society is indeed the product of many people from many nations.

Early Diversity

Archaeologists estimate that perhaps as long as 40,000 years ago, people began migrating to the Americas across a land bridge from Asia. Their descendants, today's Native Americans, disagree. They claim instead that their people have lived in the Americas since Earth's creation. In either case, Native Americans had formed about 500 nations by the time Europeans began colonization in the sixteenth and seventeenth centuries.

The European countries that colonized North America had a variety of goals and thus a variety of immigration patterns. The Spanish set up colonies to extract wealth from the land and to convert Native Americans to Christianity, but not primarily to relocate Spaniards. The French, similarly, did not emphasize settlement. They too wanted the riches of the land, and in the 1600s and 1700s that meant trapping and trading with Native Americans for furs.

The English and Dutch, on the other hand, did want to settle North America. The Dutch settlement of New Amsterdam advertised to recruit people. The Dutch were so successful in drawing people from many places that as early as 1644, 18 languages were spoken in New Amsterdam. William Penn also advertised throughout Europe for people to come to Pennsylvania. In 1750, in fact, more than half the people of the English colonies were non-English. Almost 20 percent were African, and the rest were Scotch-Irish, German, Irish, Scottish, Welsh, Dutch, French, and Swedish.

⏵ RESOURCE OPTIONS

Media and Technology
American Heritage® CD-ROM

Time Tour The Nation Today and Tomorrow: Toward a New Century

◎ **Our Times Multimedia Encyclopedia of the 20th Century CD-ROM** Helps students of all abilities to link the past to the present. Students can access the time line, listen to and read about immigration in the early part of the century, review the interactive essays in the Encyclopedia, and watch the Decade Video, 1900–1909.

Immigration and Backlash

In his 1782 *Letters from an American Farmer*, J. Hector St. John de Crèvecoeur wrote, "I could point out to you a family whose grandfather was an Englishman, whose wife was Dutch, whose son married a French woman, and whose present four sons have now four wives of different nations." As the new nation, founded on principles of equality, grew, so did its immigration from many nations. Until 1846 those nations were mostly in western and northern Europe, and almost all their emigrants were Protestant. In America there were jobs and land enough for all.

Starting in 1846 the immigrant population changed rapidly as the potato famine in Ireland sent hundreds of thousands of Irish Catholics to America. Most settled in northeastern cities, taking jobs in factories or on canals or railroads. Joining them were hundreds of thousands of German immigrants fleeing political oppression. This new wave of immigrants settled largely in the cities of the Northeast or bought farmland in the Midwest.

The Irish and many of the Germans were Catholic. Some native-born Americans, fearing control by the Pope and loss of jobs to newcomers, were hostile toward the foreign-born. Many of these **nativists** formed the Know-Nothing party, which became an important political force in 1854. The Know-Nothings wanted to keep Catholics and foreigners out of public office and to require 21-years of residence before an immigrant could qualify for citizenship.

Although the Know-Nothing party fell apart, nativist feelings grew as Chinese immigrants arrived in the mid-1800s. Fearing competi-

THE ONLY WAY TO HANDLE IT.

 This cartoon refers to a 1921 law that restricted immigration from European countries. That law set quotas based on national origin. Immigration from a particular country could not exceed 3 percent of the number of people of the same nationality living in the United States in 1910. *Culture How does the cartoon portray immigrants?*

tion for jobs, nativists succeeded in passing the Chinese Exclusion Act of 1882. This federal law cut off all immigration from China. Anti-Asian sentiment also curtailed Japanese immigration with the Gentlemen's Agreement of 1907.

The New Immigration

Beginning in the 1880s, immigration to the United States increased rapidly. Between 1870 and the end of the 1880s, immigration doubled. This new wave of immigrants was different from the ones before. Instead of coming from western and northern Europe, as earlier, they came from southern and eastern Europe. Instead of being mainly Protestant, they were Catholic and Jewish. Instead of spreading out over the farmlands of the Midwest and Great Plains, they settled in cities, where they found work in factories and mills.

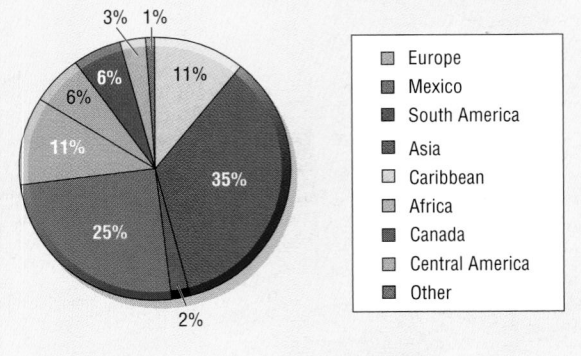

Origins of Immigrants to the U.S., 1981–1995

- 3%
- 1%
- 11%
- 6%
- 6%
- 11%
- 35%
- 25%
- 2%

Legend:
- Europe
- Mexico
- South America
- Asia
- Caribbean
- Africa
- Canada
- Central America
- Other

Source: *Statistical Abstract of the United States*

Interpreting Charts As the 1990s drew to a close, immigration was helping to create an increasingly diverse American population. Look at the graphs on pages 280 and 804. *Diversity How did immigration in those eras compare with immigration in the 1980s and early 1990s?*

Even as these newcomers were becoming part of the country's mainstream, opposition to immigrants continued to flourish. During World War I, government propaganda fanned nativist sentiment.

Immigration Laws

After the war, America went through a period of intense fear of foreigners. Believing political radicals were spreading communism and revolution, the Justice Department jailed or deported hundreds of innocent people between 1919 and 1921. Wanting no part of European politics, American foreign policy became isolationist.

In this spirit, Congress passed the Immigration Law of 1921, which limited immigration to 350,000 people per year and set up quotas for nationalities. The Immigration Law of 1924 went even further. It capped immigration at 164,000, banned all Asians, and limited the number of immigrants from each country to 2 percent of the number of people of the same nationality living in the United States in 1890. This last provision aimed to halt immigration from southern and eastern Europe.

With these laws in place, immigration slowed to a trickle. During the next 30 years, only about 100,000 people came to the United States each year. Then, in 1965, Congress passed a new law lifting all immigration quotas, thus opening the Golden Door to more non-Europeans. As a result, the number of immigrants has greatly increased, and their countries of origin have changed. Between 1930 and 1960, about 80 percent of all immigrants came from Europe or Canada. Since 1960, about 80 percent have come from Asia, Latin America, and the Caribbean.

As the number of legal immigrants has grown, so has the number of illegal, or undocumented, immigrants. To combat this problem, Congress passed the Immigration Reform and Control Act of 1986. This law punished employers who knowingly hired illegals. It also granted amnesty to illegals who had lived in the United States since 1982, to enable them to register to become citizens. The Immigration Act of 1990 raised immigration totals and removed certain restrictions on people who had been denied entry in the past.

The impact of these laws is reflected in the changing composition of American society. At nearly 10 percent of the total population, America's foreign-born population is at its highest level since 1940. This greater diversity has, in turn,

Some Americans today believe that immigration to the United States should be restricted or even stopped completely.

sparked intense debate about the future of American immigration policy.

DEBATING THE FUTURE

Massive immigration will destroy America, says author Lawrence Auster. "As whites lose their numerical, political, and cultural dominance, American civilization with all its constituent virtues will also come to an end." Not so, counters Julian L. Simon, a professor at the University of Maryland. He believes that "Talented young immigrants help us achieve every one of our national goals. They make us richer and not poorer, stronger and not weaker." Arguments such as these are representative of much of the national debate about immigration policy.

Arguments Against Immigration

Opponents of current policy argue that high levels of immigration hurt the American economy. Because immigrants are willing to work for low wages, many fear they will take jobs away from native-born Americans. "How can we keep bringing people into this country when our own people don't have jobs?" asks Clark Yates, an auto mechanic in Chicago, Illinois.

Illegal immigrants, in particular, will work for less than minimum wage, which drives down other workers' pay. "Undocumented immigrants tend to compete unfairly for low-skilled jobs, and they can sometimes bring down the level of wages and working conditions," according

to Charles Wheeler, executive director of the National Immigration Law Center.

There are political arguments against immigration as well. The federal government sets immigration policy, but it does not pay for all the services immigrants require. By and large, state and local governments must cover the costs of welfare, health care, and education for immigrants and for their children, who are citizens if born in the United States.

Many Californians oppose immigration because their state receives the largest number of immigrants, both legal and illegal. The costs for the state are enormous. Said a California state assembly aide in 1993:

AMERICAN VOICES "The state is broke. We've had a multibillion-dollar deficit three years in a row, and yet we continue to pay medical benefits for these illegal immigrants. We take better care of them than of our own people."

—*California State assembly aide*

In 1994 Governor Pete Wilson asked the President to declare an emergency in California and repay the state the $2.4 billion it spends each year on undocumented immigrants. Also that year, by a margin of 59 to 41 percent, California voters approved Proposition 187, which denied public services to illegal immigrants.

Finally, immigration opponents see the new immigrant groups as fragmenting American society, dividing it into ethnic enclaves rather than adapting to American culture. Language has become a rallying point, with campaigns for "English only" as the official language. In 1975, Congress amended the voting rights act to require bilingual ballots. English-only advocates point out that naturalized citizens are supposed to know the language and claim that many have cheated to pass the naturalization exam. John Silber, former chairman of the Massachusetts State Board of Education, argues:

AMERICAN VOICES "Citizens who are not proficient in English cannot, in most cases, follow a political campaign, talk with candidates, or petition their representatives. They are citizens in name only and are unable to exercise their rights. Providing them with bilingual ballots does not enable them to exercise those rights in any meaningful way."

—*John Silber*

Time magazine created this computer-generated portrait by combining the characteristics of all the races present in the United States in 1993. **Culture** What are some arguments in favor of immigration?

SPECIAL ISSUE

TIME

Take a good look at this woman. She was created by a computer from a mix of several races. What you see is a remarkable preview of...

THE NEW FACE OF AMERICA
How Immigrants Are Shaping the World's First Multicultural Society

Using the Internet

Create a Graph

Objective Use the Internet to research and graph data on United States immigration and emigration. Have students follow these instructions:

1. See the *America: Pathways to the Present* Web site at

http://www.Pathways.phschool.com

for the URL of the United States Immigration and Naturalization Service.

2. Follow the links and use the data to create a bar graph showing immigration to and emigration from the United States, by decade, since 1900.

3. Create a bar graph to compare the foreign-born population with the total United States population since 1900.

4. Use the graphs to answer these questions: (a) In which decade did immigration to the United States increase most? (b) In which year was the percentage of the foreign-born population the highest?

TEST PREPARATION

Have students read the quotation by John Silber on this page and then answer the question below.

From the passage you can infer that, according to Silber, people can only be good citizens if—

A they speak perfect English.

B they talk to every candidate.

C they make use of bilingual ballots.

D they take an active role in the political process.

Answer to . . .

Viewing History Arguments include immigrants' many contributions to the American economy and culture.

Bilingual education is another source of frustration for those who want to limit immigration. In bilingual programs, students are taught in their native language as well as English while their English-language skills improve. Opponents of bilingual education argue that these programs only perpetuate separateness rather than promote assimilation into the American mainstream. Without a common language, they believe, our common culture is in danger.

Opponents received a boost from voters in California. In 1998 Californians approved Proposition 227, which severely limits bilingual education in that state. The law gives all children with limited English skills just one year to learn English before joining regular classes. Proposition 227 ended 30 years of full-scale bilingual instruction in the nation's largest school system.

Arguments for Immigration

Immigrants help, not hurt, the economy, claim immigration supporters. They come highly motivated to work, with strong family units that promote discipline and high standards.

Immigrants contribute to the economy as consumers, small-business owners, and taxpayers. They also take jobs few native-born Americans want. As Chicago carpenter Eddy Jerena explains:

 AMERICAN VOICES ❝My brother . . . has a business, and the Mexicans work hard for him 12 hours a day and they don't complain. You get these American-born guys, they don't work like that. This country was built by immigrants. The Mexicans deserve to be here.❞

—*Eddy Jerena*

Immigration supporters point out that most immigrants do not receive public assistance. Most legal immigrants have to wait five years to be eligible for welfare. Illegal immigrants are not eligible for any social services except emergency Medicaid and vital programs related to child welfare. A study in 1997 showed that 4.9 percent of immigrants receive help, in contrast to 3.3 percent of the native-born population. But many of those immigrants are refugees or the elderly, who do not qualify for Social Security as older Americans do.

Finally, supporters say immigration is an investment that will pay off in a trained work force and future taxpayers. To those who would deny education to the children of illegal immigrants, Indianapolis Superintendent of Schools Esperanza Zendejas replies:

 AMERICAN VOICES ❝These kids are going to be here for a long time. So the question is whether we want to educate these kids now or pay for increased social welfare costs later down the line. I think it's an easy choice.❞

—*Esperanza Zendejas*

The Statue of Liberty was what many immigrants first saw when they arrived in the United States. For some, trunks like the one below carried all the possessions they were able to bring from home.

The Debate Continues

Although both supporters and opponents of immigration believe it is necessary to exert greater control over illegal immigrants, they disagree over how to do it. They also disagree over the level of legal immigration and whether legal immigrants should be eligible for social services. Voters will need to weigh the Statue of Liberty's promise against their perception of America's ability to keep that promise.

Key Terms

1. undocumented immigrant
2. political asylum
3. green card
4. nativist
5. bilingual education

Portfolio Activity

7. Think about your own attitude toward immigration and the services to which immigrants are entitled. Then consider how you can best express this opinion: for instance, a newspaper editorial, a pictorial essay, a series of interviews, a poem, a cartoon or drawing, a poster. When you have chosen a presentation that is acceptable to your teacher, put it in an appropriate format.

Creating a Time Line

6. To set the events of this chapter in context, construct a time line that includes eight to ten significant milestones in the modern history (since colonial times) of immigration to the United States. Include both events and legislation. You can refer to previous chapters of this textbook for information.

INTERNET ACTIVITY

For your portfolio:
PREPARE A SUMMARY

8. Access Prentice Hall's *America: Pathways to the Present* site at **www.Pathways.phschool.com** for the specific URL to complete the activity. Additional resources and related Web sites are also available.

   Use the link provided and choose a bill related to immigration that is currently pending in Congress. Summarize the bill and explain two arguments for and against passing it.

Using Graphic Organizers

9. Review the arguments in the Debating the Future section of the chapter. Then fill in the blanks in the graphic organizer below that show political movements and legislation affecting immigration between the mid-1800s and the 1990s. Large boxes show the major developments or laws. Specific details or effects appear in the smaller boxes. You can copy the organizer on another sheet of paper.

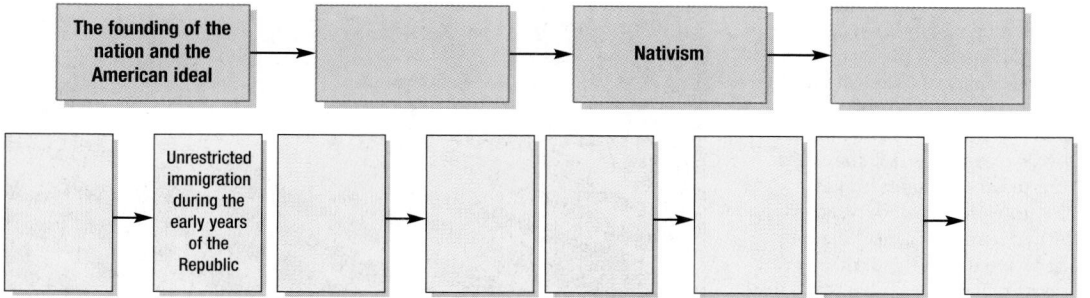

The founding of the nation and the American ideal → ☐ → Nativism → ☐

☐ → Unrestricted immigration during the early years of the Republic → ☐ → ☐ → ☐ → ☐ → ☐ → ☐

The major concepts of Chapter 36 are presented in *Guide to the Essentials of American History* and *Interactive Student Tutorial CD-ROM,* which contains interactive review activities, time lines, and test practice for Chapter 36.

Key Terms
1. undocumented immigrants, see p. 1009
2. political asylum, see p. 1009
3. green card, see p. 1009
4. nativist, see p. 1011
5. bilingual education, see p. 1014

Creating a Time Line
6. Students' time lines should include events such as the Irish potato famine and World War I, as well as major pieces of legislation.

Portfolio Activity
7. Student presentations should show both creativity and a thoughtful approach to the issue.

Internet Activity
8. See below.

Using Graphic Organizers
9. Large boxes: German/Irish wave of immigration; New era of open immigration. Smaller boxes: Prehistoric Native American immigration; Fears of job competition; Religious prejudice; Know-Nothingism and the Chinese Exclusion Act; Immigration law of 1921; Immigration Act of 1965; New immigration debates (e.g., bilingual education).

INTERNET ACTIVITY

Students' summaries should be clear and to the point, and be supported with specific facts from the Web site where applicable.

Objectives

Help students to understand the changing patterns of violent crime in the United States, trace the growth of American attitudes toward gun ownership since frontier days, and identify the arguments for and against gun control.

Bellringer

Ask students how crime or the fear of crime affects them in their daily lives. Do they, like many Americans, rank violent crime as one of the things that frighten and worry them the most?

Reading Strategy

Predicting Content Have students read the introductory paragraph and the headings and subheadings in the chapter. Ask them to predict the content of the chapter and then read to confirm or change this prediction.

LESSON PLAN
Connecting to the Main Idea

1. Focus Explain that violent crime is one of the issues that Americans worry about the most. Americans disagree, however, on ways to combat crime. One major point of contention is the question of gun control. Why is this issue so "hot," or charged with emotion, for many Americans?

2. Instruct Discuss the national debate about gun control and why those who resist controls feel so strongly. What issues—besides actual gun ownership—are involved in the resistance by the National Rifle Association and those who agree with it? How do these issues relate to attitudes toward government regulation in general?

3. Close Crime remains a major issue for Americans, although they are divided on the question of increasing controls on private gun ownership. The next chapter focuses on the minimum wage.

CHAPTER 37 Gun Control and Crime

Colonial woodcut

INTRODUCING THE THEME

Violent crime and the criminal use of guns have become part of life in the United States. At the same time, more private citizens are arming themselves in self-defense. Since the earliest days of this nation, Americans have debated the right to private ownership of guns. At the heart of this debate is the Second Amendment to the Constitution, which protects the right to "keep and bear arms." The meaning of this amendment is highly controversial and the subject of lawsuits. Some advocate an interpretation that guarantees all Americans the right to bear arms without restrictions from any government. Other experts believe that the amendment is important for its guarantee of the right of the states to maintain a militia.

DEBATE

Given the widespread public concern over violent crime, is stiffer gun control an effective way to restore tranquillity?

KEY TERMS

homicide, militia,
Second Amendment,
National Rifle Association (NRA)

VIEWING THE PRESENT

Under a Chicago railroad bridge the police found "Yummy" in a mud puddle. His face was torn apart by bullets fired through the back of his head. Eleven-year-old Robert "Yummy" Sandifer had been gunned down by members of his own gang. He was supposed to shoot members of a rival gang, but killed an unrelated 14-year-old girl instead. When police went after him, Yummy became too big a risk and fell victim to gang violence himself.

In Collingswood, New Jersey, Amy Fleming practices loading her handgun in the dark. She can do it in five seconds flat. Amy lives with her son, Justy, her dog, and

her fear of her ex-husband, Ed. A drug user who has been convicted of two violent assaults and theft of a firearm, Ed has repeatedly

Some people, like this woman, find that owning a handgun makes them feel more secure.

RESOURCE OPTIONS

Teaching Resources

 Reproducible Lesson Plan Lesson Plans folder, p. 178

Learning Styles Lesson Plan Learning Styles Lesson Plans folder, p. 75

Big Idea Graphic Organizer Big Idea Graphic Organizer folder, p. 150

 Guided Reading and Review Unit 11 folder, p. 8

threatened to kill Amy. No help is available from the police, who can only recommend that she run away and hide. Since Ed has no trouble finding out where she lives, Amy believes that her gun is the only protection she has.

Public Fears About Crime

How typical are these two stories? While they don't give the full picture, they do put human faces on some startling statistics. Every two minutes someone is shot in this country. The Federal Bureau of Investigation reports that Americans are much more likely to be the victim of a violent crime than to be hurt in a traffic accident. Violent crime includes murder, rape, robbery, and aggravated assault. Crime rates increased in the 1980s and through the recession years of the mid-1990s.

Crime has declined significantly in recent years, however. In fact, violent crime decreased about 19 percent from 1994 to 1999, reaching the lowest levels of violent crime ever recorded in this country. Despite this decline, public concern about crime remains high. Crime consistently placed one or two among the nation's leading concerns in Gallup polls conducted since 1959. People continue to think of crime as a more serious problem than other concerns like unemployment or taxes. Why?

Crime Trends

Criminologists (social scientists who study crime) cannot say for certain what makes crime rates increase or decrease. Still, they can identify historical trends. During

Murder Weapons, 1995

- Handguns
- Other guns
- Cutting or stabbing
- Blunt objects
- Personal weapons (fists etc.)
- Other

Source: *Statistical Abstract of the United States*

Interpreting Graphs In 1995, 20,220 murders were committed. Handguns were used in more than half of these killings. *Culture How do you think the statistics presented in this graph influence the debate on handgun control?*

Western frontier myths turned the sheriff's badge into a symbol of frontier justice in the popular imagination.

the 1940s and 1950s the United States enjoyed relatively low crime rates. Things began to change in

the mid-1960s, as a look at the rate of **homicide,** or murder, reveals. In 1965 the murder rate was about 5 per 100,000 people. By 1974 it had doubled. After falling in the mid-1970s, the murder rate rose to 10 per 100,000 people in 1980. Then it dropped again until the late 1980s. According to the FBI, the murder rate in 1998 was about 6 per 100,000 people.

There are no clear-cut explanations of these ups and downs. Still, Professor Lawrence M. Friedman of Stanford University suggests that crime rates may be connected with larger social, economic, and cultural trends. For example, the rise in murder rates in the late 1960s took place during a period of great social and political turmoil. The increase in murder rates in the late 1980s coincided with high inner-city unemployment and poverty and the get-rich-quick appeal of the crack cocaine trade.

A Cause of Crime

There is a direct link between drugs and violent crime. Reasons for the relationship between drug trafficking and violence include the following: competition for drug markets and customers, disputes among individuals involved in the illegal drug market, and the tendency toward violence of those who participate in drug trafficking.

The number of drug-related homicides, however, has been decreasing in recent years. In 1991, 6.2 percent of all homicides were drug-related, whereas in 1998, this figure dropped to 4.8 percent. Despite this decrease, drug-related homicides remain the fourth most documented type of murder.

During the American Revolution, volunteers organized themselves into militias, or small defense forces, known as minutemen. They got their name because they were ready to respond in a minute's notice to fight British troops. *Government Why did American colonists believe in their right to own guns?*

Guns and Crime: A Deadly Combination

Crime, especially murder, is reported widely in newspapers, magazines, and on television and radio. Major television networks tripled the time allotted to their news coverage of murder stories in 1993. These broadcasts draw attention to the fact that crime increasingly involves young people. Between 1987 and 1996 the rate of juvenile arrests for violent crime rose 60 percent. During the same period the rate of violent crime for all ages dropped by 5 percent.

An overwhelming proportion of violent crimes, whether juvenile or adult, are committed with a gun. In 1998 about 69 percent of all homicides involved firearms, and four out of five of these were handguns. Many Americans wonder if stiffer gun control is an effective way to reduce crime.

REVIEWING THE PAST

Foreign visitors are often surprised by the number of guns—some 230 million—owned by civilians in the United States. In many other countries, guns are banned or tightly controlled. For example, Britain strictly limits gun ownership, and it completely banned handguns in 1997. Since the assassinations of President Kennedy, Martin Luther King, Jr., and Robert F. Kennedy, there have been a number of attempts to pass gun-control laws in the United States. Each bill has met with heated debate because of the history of gun ownership in this country.

The English Tradition

Guns have been part of the American way of life since the first Europeans came to North America.

There were as many guns as colonists in early Jamestown. In the new setting, people needed guns to hunt and to protect themselves.

The colonists also had English tradition to support their ownership of weapons. That tradition gave them the right to defend themselves and their homes and the duty to have weapons to protect the public peace. Dating back to the Middle Ages, the English chose to arm themselves for defense rather than have an army under the direction of a monarch. They recognized that the monarch could become a tyrant and use the army against them.

Over time, tensions increased as the English kings sought more power. After the Glorious Revolution of 1688 overthrew James II, Parliament placed limits on the monarchy through the Bill of Rights. For one thing, it established the right to keep arms for the common defense. Thus English people, both before and after the Glorious Revolution, brought to the American colonies their strongly held belief in their rights to own guns and to protect themselves from absolute government power.

Colonists Fight for Their Rights

When American colonists believed that the British were trying to limit their rights, they fought back. The colonists had enjoyed a fair amount of self-government until Britain began to tighten its control after the French and Indian War. The British wanted to maintain their vast new North American empire, so they kept a standing army in the colonies. They expected the colonists to help pay for it.

Resistance to the British grew after passage of the Stamp Act. **Militias** began to form in 1774 and 1775. Militias are bands of citizens armed to defend themselves. One such group, known as minutemen, fought the British to protect supplies of ammunition at Lexington and Concord in Massachusetts. This "shot heard round the world" touched off the American Revolution.

The Second Amendment

After the American Revolution, the new nation had to form a stable, unified government. The result was the Constitution. That document, however, met with stiff resistance from those who feared it would not protect individuals' and states' rights. In order to get the Constitution ratified, its sponsors agreed to add a Bill of Rights. These are the first 10 amendments of the present-day Constitution.

Americans had fought the British to preserve their rights to self-defense and self-taxation. They had been able to resist the British because they had had their own militias. Following the war, Americans were not about to give up that protection. After all, who knew how the new government would turn out?

During the debate on ratifying the Constitution, many delegates demanded that the right to bear arms be included in a Bill of Rights. As a result, James Madison drafted the **Second Amendment.** In its final form it states, "A well-regulated militia being necessary to the security of a free state, the right of the people to keep and bear arms shall not be infringed."

An American Symbol

Thus guns were present at the creation of this country and became part of the law of the land. Firearms have also become the stuff of American legend. Think of the early pioneer, the mountain man, and the cowhand. These are strong, independent, free, and rugged individuals, symbols of an American ideal. Take away their guns, and what happens to those symbols?

Today the United States is far more urban than rural, and gun violence is alarmingly high. These are facts. So, should the right to have a gun continue to be part of the American way of life? Americans have wrestled with that question and have put some restrictions on the books.

Thousands of laws regulate firearms in the United States. Most of these are state and local laws that license gun dealers, provide permits for gun buyers, and, in some places, ban certain types of guns. On the federal level, the 1968 Gun Control Act (GCA) prohibits criminals, minors, the mentally ill, and illegal aliens from owning guns.

A 1993 amendment to the GCA known as the Brady Law required a five-day waiting period, as well as a police background check, before someone could purchase a gun. (This law was named for James Brady, who was paralyzed by a gunshot aimed at President Reagan.) In 1997 the Supreme Court struck down the requirement that police do a background check. Still, in 1998 every state was conducting voluntary background checks on gun purchasers.

Yet another federal law, the Assault Weapons Act of 1994, bans certain types of semiautomatic firearms. In 1998 President Clinton, through an executive order, also banned the importation

Frederic Remington's 1902 painting, *The Cowboy,* illustrates the popular notion of Americans' rugged individualism.
Culture *What American ideals did the cowboy represent?*

Graphing the Theme

To make sure students understand the theme of this chapter, you may wish to use the web graphic organizer below.

Tell students that a web is useful for showing a main topic with its supporting details. Have students use it to present the issues that relate to the interpretation of the Second Amendment.

Teaching Tip A template for this graphic organizer can be found in the Color Transparencies, G-1.

Answer to . . .

Viewing History Individualism, democracy.

1020 Chapter 37

---

of semiautomatic assault-style weapons that have been modified for sporting purposes. With so many regulations on firearms, what more is necessary?

DEBATING THE FUTURE

Natisha Campbell, whose friend Hank Lloyd was shot and killed in Washington, D.C., asks, "Why should you be able to have a gun laying under your pillow so that a baby can pick it up and shoot themselves?" "I say all guns are good guns," counters Joe Foss, former president of the **National Rifle Association (NRA),** the leading organization working against gun control. "There are no bad guns. I say the whole nation should be an armed nation. Period."

Against Gun Control

The National Rifle Association's members cite the Second Amendment phrase, "the right of the people to keep and bear arms shall not be infringed," as the basis for their belief that individuals have the right to own guns. Gun prohibition, besides being unconstitutional, would endanger society, says the NRA. Members believe that people must have guns to protect themselves against criminals. They point out that most gun owners are law-abiding citizens.

Says Mary Sue Faulkner of the NRA, "We know criminals fear armed citizens more than they do the police." Statistics support this statement: handguns are used more often in repelling crimes than in committing them. As one Florida rifle association member put it, "If I want to mug someone, I'll avoid a person who may have a handgun."

NRA members say that gun

Some Americans believe that the right to keep and bear arms, without federal or state regulations, is part of their constitutional rights as stated in the Second Amendment. *Culture* **What arguments does the NRA make opposing gun control?**

control is not the answer to the crime problem. "Gun control is a cop-out," said NRA lobbyist James Jay Baker, "an easy solution to a complex problem. And it doesn't work." People bent on committing

crime will find a way, says the NRA. So will people intent on getting a gun. "There is absolutely no way the legislation is going to stop the bad guys from getting guns," says a veteran Maryland police officer.

A 1991 Justice Department study showed that only 27 percent of state-prison inmates had bought their guns legally. The others got them from family or friends, stole them, or purchased them on the black market. Commented one gun-shop customer, "It's easier to get a firearm delivered in the Washington area than it is to get a pizza."

Many members of the NRA believe that any attempt to regulate firearms will lead to total gun prohibition. Before the 1994 federal laws were passed, former NRA president Jim Reinke said:

AMERICAN VOICES "If we give in on the gun waiting period and assault rifles, we'd lose half our membership, and six months later the anti-gunners will want our long guns."

—Jim Reinke

If gun control is not the answer to violent crime, what is? The NRA's J. Warren Cassidy, an executive vice president, responded to that question in 1990 this way:

AMERICAN VOICES "Tough laws designed to incarcerate violent offenders offer something gun control cannot: swift, sure justice meted out with no accompanying erosion of individual liberty."

—J. Warren Cassidy

For Gun Control

Supporters of gun control focus on the first phrase of the Second Amendment, "A well-regulated militia being necessary to the security of a free state." They emphasize that the purpose of the amendment is to provide protection for the entire community.

Restricting criminals' access to guns is absolutely essential to reduce violent crime, argues Dewey Stokes, national president of the Fraternal Order of Police. "The police are definitely outgunned in this country." Criminals are carrying more dangerous weapons and are more willing to use them. Al Baker of the Houston Police Department says:

 AMERICAN VOICES ❝Just about everybody committing a crime has a gun. Not cheap Saturday-night specials, but guns they can count on. And they're willing to shoot it out rather than go to jail.❞

—*Al Baker*

Gun-control advocates point out that in 1939 the Supreme Court upheld a law against short-barreled shotguns because their use could not "contribute to the common defense." In 1983, the Court refused to hear a case challenging the first ban on handguns in the nation.

Far from making society safer, gun-control advocates say, guns kept for defense against criminals make life more dangerous. A 1993 study appearing in *The New England Journal of Medicine* supported that claim. It showed that the risk of homicide in the home is three times greater in households with guns.

Children are often the victims of firearms both inside and outside the home. In 1997, according to the National Center for Health Statistics, 12 children were killed with guns every day in the United States.

Some of these incidents have shocked the nation. In 1998 five were killed by a student in a Jonesboro, Arkansas high school. One year later, two students armed with semi-automatic guns and bombs killed twelve classmates, a teacher, and later themselves at Columbine High School in Littleton, Colorado.

The Debate Continues

A Gallup survey in 1999 showed that 89 percent of Americans favor requiring a five-day waiting period on the purchase of guns. Another Gallup survey found that 68 percent support a ban on semi-automatic assault weapons. Yet according to another poll, also conducted by Gallup in that same year, 62 percent of Americans oppose a ban on the possession of handguns. Given these mixed feelings, Americans will need to look more closely and considerately at both sides of the gun-control issue to develop effective public policy in combatting crime.

James Brady, White House press secretary during President Reagan's first term, was paralyzed by a gunshot wound during an assassination attempt on President Reagan in 1981. Brady and his wife, Sarah, became strong advocates of gun control. Their efforts brought about the 1994 passage of the Brady law.

Using the Internet

Write an Essay

Objective Use the Internet to research political party platforms. Have students follow these instructions:

1. See the *America: Pathways to the Present* Web site at

http://www.Pathways.phschool.com

for the URLs of the Democratic and Republican parties.

2. Use links to learn about each party's position on gun control.

3. Write an essay describing each party's position on gun control. Cite information from the parties' current platforms.

4. Do you agree with the position taken by either party? Write a paragraph outlining your position on gun control and comparing it to those of the major political parties.

Customize for

English Language Learners

Have students create a chart with two columns: For More Gun Control and Against Gun Control. In each column have them list people who hold that view and two reasons why.

 RESOURCE OPTIONS

Teaching Resources

📁 **Chapter Tests Forms A and B** Chapter Test folder

Student Performance Pack

 Guide to the Essentials Chapter 37 (English and Spanish)

Standardized Test Preparation Handbook

Media and Technology

🎧 **Guided Reading Audiotapes** Chapter 37 Summary (English and Spanish)
Student Edition on Audiotape Chapter 37

💿 **Test Bank CD-ROM; Interactive Student Tutorial CD-ROM** Chapter Test

The major concepts of Chapter 37 are presented in *Guide to the Essentials of American History* and *Interactive Student Tutorial CD-ROM,* which contains interactive review activities, time lines, and test practice for Chapter 37.

Key Terms
1. homicide, see p. 1017
2. militia, see p. 1019
3. Second Amendment, see p. 1019
4. National Rifle Association (NRA), see p. 1020

Creating a Time Line
5. Students' time lines should trace the traditions of gun ownership and include the historic tensions between people and government that English settlers brought to the colonies and reinforced on the frontier.

Portfolio Activity
6. Students' presentations should be creative and relevant, and show a thoughtful approach to the issue.

Internet Activity
7. See below.

Using Graphic Organizers
8. Answers will vary, but should reflect an understanding of the debate. Possible answers may include: (left side blank)—Sees link between guns and violent crime; (bottom blank)—In favor of civil liberties; (right blank)—Focuses on long traditions of free gun ownership.

Key Terms
1. homicide
2. militia
3. Second Amendment
4. National Rifle Association (NRA)

Portfolio Activity
6. Think about your own opinions about crime and the role of gun control in reducing violent crime. Express the opinions in your own way. Consider the following: a poster or drawing, a letter to the editor, a poem or personal essay, a photo essay. When you have chosen a presentation that is acceptable to your teacher, put it in an appropriate format.

Using Graphic Organizers
8. Review the arguments in the Debating the Future section of the chapter. Then fill in the blank webs in the graphic organizer below, which compares and contrasts views on gun control. You can copy the web on a separate sheet of paper.

Creating a Time Line
5. To place the issue of gun control in context, construct time line that traces the English and American traditions toward gun ownership from the Middle Ages to the inclusion of the Second Amendment in the Constitution (from the Reviewing the Past section). Use your textbook as a reference.

INTERNET ACTIVITY

For your portfolio:
WRITE AN ESSAY

7. Access Prentice Hall's *America: Pathways to the Present* site at **www.Pathways.phschool.com** for the specific URL to complete the activity. Additional resources and related Web sites are also available.

   Review the constitutions of two nations other than the United States for information on firearms. Write an essay comparing their stance on firearms to the one presented in the Second Amendment to the United States Constitution. Which nation do you think handles the issue the best?

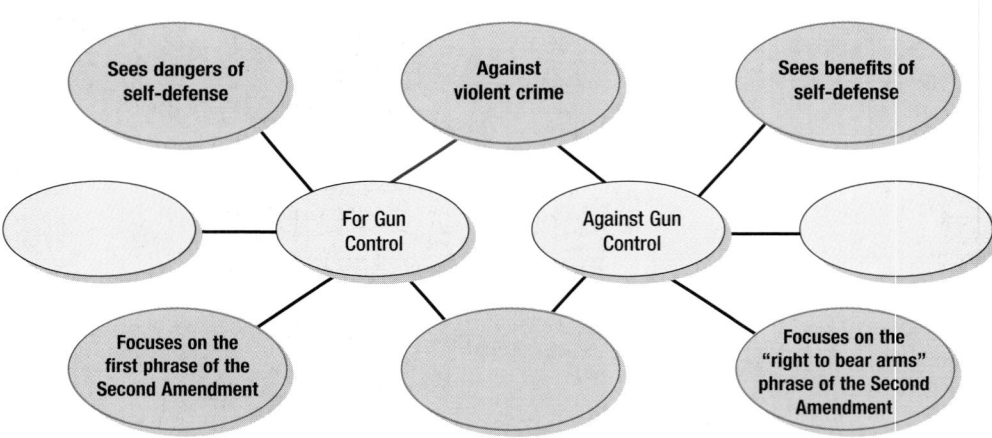

INTERNET ACTIVITY

Students' essays should be clear and to the point, and should be supported with specific facts or quotes from the Web site when applicable.

CHAPTER 38 The Minimum Wage

INTRODUCING THE THEME

For the last century, Americans have debated the role of the federal government in the economy. Should government have any control over industries in a free enterprise system? Americans continue to argue about agencies and laws regulating business, monitoring product safety, and assuring a safe workplace. A related issue is the government-mandated minimum wage. Most Americans agree that the government has the right to set a minimum wage. They disagree, however, over what that wage should be and how often it should change to reflect increases in the cost of living.

 DEBATE

What is the proper role of the federal government in protecting workers' incomes?

KEY TERMS

progressive,
New Deal,
work ethic

Objectives

Help students to understand the current situation for minimum-wage workers, trace the historic development of government regulations and standards protecting workers, and identify the arguments for and against a higher minimum-wage standard.

Bellringer

Ask students to list the kinds of jobs available to them and others their age. What do they think is a fair hourly wage?

Reading Strategy

Problem Solving Ask students, "What would you do if you worked full time but still did not earn enough to live on? Is it strictly your problem, or should the government help?" Then ask them to look for answers to these questions as they read.

VIEWING THE PRESENT

Jacqueline Barnes wants to be a doctor. To pay her way through medical school, she works eight-hour shifts at a sandwich shop in Washington, D.C., between semesters. The minimum-wage raise of 1996 promised to increase her earnings by 15 cents an hour. Does she turn her nose up at such a small raise? Not at all. "Fifteen cents might not sound like much, but you know what? Even after taxes that's enough to buy me at least one extra textbook at college."

Barnes works for a large chain of sandwich shops, but across town Karen Audia Shannon runs her own restau-rant. She worries that an increase in the minimum wage will have a ripple effect, forcing her to increase wages to her lowest-paid employees, even though they earn slightly more

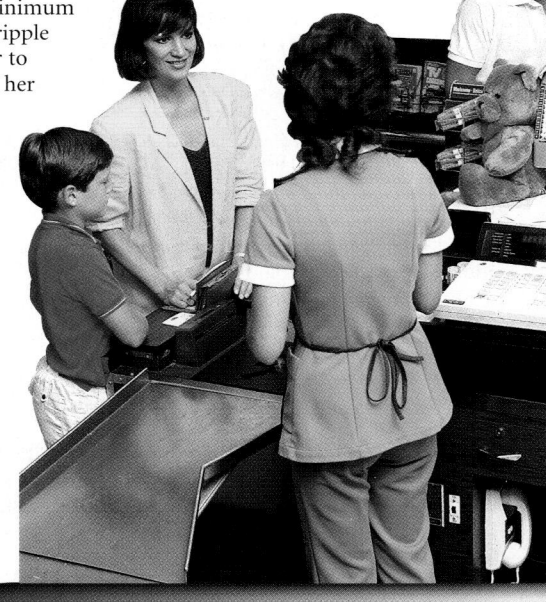

The majority of minimum-wage workers are adults. *Economics Why do some Americans oppose increases in the minimum wage?*

LESSON PLAN

Connecting to the Main Idea

1. Focus Explain that many people today question the proper role of government in the economy. One part of that debate is the minimum wage, which Congress sets by law. Advocates succeeded in raising the minimum wage in the summer of 1996, but the issue is far from settled. Discuss why raising the minimum wage is controversial.

2. Instruct Discuss the consequences of the growing gap between the rich and the poor in the United States. Have students think about what this development means for society as a whole and especially for those at the lower end of the wage scale.

3. Close The economy is an ongoing concern among Americans. Raising the minimum wage is part of that concern, with advocates on both sides of the issue. The next chapter discusses issues surrounding entitlements.

▶ RESOURCE OPTIONS

Teaching Resources

📁 **Reproducible Lesson Plan** Lesson Plans folder, p. 179

📁 **Learning Styles Lesson Plan** Learning Styles Lesson Plans folder, p. 76

📁 **Big Idea Graphic Organizer** Big Idea Graphic Organizer folder, p. 151

📁 **Guided Reading and Review** Unit 11 folder, p. 13

Workers toil away in this Progressive Era factory. During the Progressive Era, reformers tried to make factories less dangerous and improve overall working conditions. *Government* *What role did progressive reformers believe government should play in protecting workers?*

than the minimum now. Said Shannon, "It would put my business in serious jeopardy, so much so that I almost feel I'd be forced to close. I would be put in a position where operating as a profitable restaurant would no longer be a possibility." If the restaurant closed, she and her 26 employees would be out of a job.

Minimum-Wage Workers

In 1997 the minimum wage rose to $5.15 per hour for most jobs. Of the 130 million workers in the United States, some 2 million earn the minimum wage. Another 4 million, whose jobs are not covered by the law, earn less than the minimum wage. Who are these workers? What kinds of jobs do they have? Where do they live?

When you think of someone making minimum wage, you probably picture a teenager flipping hamburgers at a fast-food restaurant. As with many stereotypes, this picture is partly accurate. But the reality of minimum-wage work is much more complex.

1. A quarter of the people who are paid the minimum wage or less are food-service workers.
2. Only a small percentage of these are teenagers. The majority of workers earning up to minimum wage—about 70 percent—are adults.
3. The majority are also women—about 60 percent.
4. Just under half of the workers paid minimum wage or less work full time, and another third work 20 to 34 hours per week.
5. About 12 percent are the sole breadwinners in families with children.

Jobs paying the minimum wage include retail sales in shops and malls, restaurant work, gardening, farm work, motel cleaning, dry cleaning, child care, and garment work. These jobs can be found all over the country. Some, however, are more concentrated in particular areas. They include farm work in California; garment work in the Northeast, San Francisco, and Los Angeles; and textile jobs in the Southeast. Overall, the South has the highest concentration of minimum-wage workers.

REVIEWING THE PAST

The idea of government legislation to protect workers began with a group of political and social reformers in the late 1800s and early 1900s. These **progressives,** largely well-educated middle-class people, were appalled by the effects of rapid industrial growth. They saw corrupt politicians lining their own pockets and captains of industry amassing great wealth.

Meanwhile, workers labored long hours in unsafe conditions for low wages. To improve society, various progressive groups sought to end corruption in government. They tried to limit the abuses of power by giant corporations. They also worked to improve the living and working conditions of the poor, starting at the state level.

State Regulations

Instead of counting on public opinion or private charity to bring about social reform, the progressives looked to government to solve problems. They believed government had to increase its responsibility for the well-being of its citizens.

To protect workers, progressives pushed for state laws regulating workplace conditions, maximum hours, and minimum wages. They met with stiff resistance, however. At that time, such laws were considered restrictions on personal liberties. In 1905, for example, the Supreme Court overturned a New York law setting a maximum 10-hour workday for bakers. Wrote Supreme Court Justice Rufus W. Peckham, "[Statutes] limiting the hours in which grown and intelligent men may labor to earn their living, are mere meddlesome interferences with the rights of the individual."

It took a terrible tragedy to awaken public demand for more legislation to protect workers. On March 25, 1911, fire swept through the Triangle Shirtwaist Factory in New York City. As a result of locked doors and an inadequate fire escape system, many young women workers were trapped inside. More than 140 were killed. Some plunged to their deaths from the eighth, ninth, and tenth floors. As a result, the New York State legislature formed the Factory Inspection Commission.

The Commission recommended legislation on factory safety, workers' accident insurance, protection for women and children in industry, and minimum wages. The commission's work led to the adoption of a new Industrial Code in New York. This code became a model for legislation in other states.

First Minimum-Wage Law
Progressives like Frances Perkins, who had worked to set up the Factory Inspection Commission, believed that the minimum wage was essential. In 1912 Massachusetts became the first state to pass a minimum-wage law. That year Theodore Roosevelt made the minimum wage a part of his Progressive party platform. In 1913 eight additional states passed minimum-wage laws.

When the United States entered World War I, the federal government took on a larger role. To ensure defense production, it regulated wages, hours, and working conditions through the War Labor Policies Board. After the war, however, the military need for regulation ended, and public interest in workers' conditions dropped off.

Depression and New Deal
When the glamour of the Roaring Twenties gave way to the grim realities of the Great Depression, interest in protecting workers revived. As more and more people lost their jobs, those still employed often saw their wages drop. Between 1928 and 1932, for example, the average weekly earnings for factory workers dropped from $27.80 to $17.05.

When he took office in 1933, President Franklin D. Roosevelt made good on his campaign promise of a **New Deal** for Americans. He offered programs to provide relief, create jobs, and stimulate the economy. He also appointed Frances Perkins to be Secretary of Labor, the first woman to hold a Cabinet post. Perkins, who had fought tirelessly for worker protection in New York, continued her crusade in Washington.

The New Deal's first attempt to set minimum wages and shorter hours was part of the National Industrial Recovery Act of 1933. When the Supreme Court declared that law unconstitutional, workers renewed their demands for protection. With Perkins's help, FDR sent the Fair Labor Standards bill to Congress in 1937. He said, "A self-supporting and self-respecting democracy can plead no justification for the existence of child labor, no economic reason for chiseling workers' wages or stretching workers' hours."

The fire at the Triangle Shirtwaist Factory in New York City in 1911 brought national attention to the issue of workplace safety and workers' rights. *Government* *What impact did the fire have on government legislation?*

Many of the labor laws to which we have become accustomed were either enacted or proposed during FDR's New Deal. *Government How many familiar workplace laws and guarantees can you identify in this painting?*

The Works Progress Administration (WPA) was a New Deal agency set up in 1935. It lasted for eight years and provided work for more than eight million Americans.

Recent Developments

Since 1938 the minimum wage has become part of American working life. Following the New Deal came Harry Truman's Fair Deal, during which Congress raised the minimum wage to 75 cents an hour. Six years later it rose to $1 an hour, and another six years took it to $1.25. It has inched upward since then until it reached $4.25 in 1991.

Congress considered raising the minimum wage in the election year of 1996. Although many members opposed it, the bill finally passed, and President Clinton signed it. As the new law provided, the rate went to $5.15 on September 1, 1997. Three years later Clinton asked Congress to raise the minimum wage further—to $6.15. Other Democrats called for an even greater hike. Any attempt to raise the minimum wage again is sure to provoke heated debate.

DEBATING THE FUTURE

Jill Mattioli could no longer afford an apartment in Telluride, Colorado. She had to move to the outskirts of town. "If I wait [tables] and serve these people," she says, "I should be able to live here and have a decent standard of living." But to do so would involve raising the minimum wage. That is something Atlanta radio talk show host Sean Hannity opposes. "How much more can you pay someone

Congress passed the Fair Labor Standards Act the next year. It banned child labor and set the minimum wage at 25 cents per hour, increasing to 40 cents per hour over seven years. The maximum work week was set at 44 hours, to drop to 40 hours in the next three years. When the law took effect in 1938, it immediately helped about 300,000 workers earning less than 25 cents an hour and 1,384,000 others working more than 44 hours a week. The next year, when the minimum wage went up to 30 cents and maximum hours went down to 42, some 3 million more workers benefited.

who flips burgers for a living? Are you willing to pay more for a hamburger?" he argues.

A national poll taken by the *Los Angeles Times* in 1999 showed that more than three fourths of Americans favored increasing the minimum wage. Moreover, more than half of the people surveyed in every Gallup poll taken on this topic since 1945 have supported a higher minimum wage. Yet despite public opinion and congressional action, debate continues to swirl around the minimum-wage issue.

In Favor of Raising the Minimum Wage

In 1997 the average chief executive officer (CEO) of a corporation earned 326 times as much as the average factory worker. Proponents of increasing the minimum wage point to the vast gap between the rich and poor in America to argue their case. "It's a moral issue," says Representative John Lewis of Georgia. "Raising the minimum wage is the right thing to do."

It is the right thing to do, argue those in favor, because in 1998 a minimum-wage earner working full time earned $10,700. If that worker had three dependents, his or her earnings fell far below the federal poverty line of $16,450. Said Philadelphian John Trendler of the $4.25 minimum wage:

AMERICAN VOICES ❝I don't know of anyone trying to support a family who can get by on that.❞

—*John Trendler*

For most minimum-wage earners with families, getting by at that level has required government assistance. This means food stamps and even welfare.

Inflation is one reason often cited for continuing increases in the minimum wage. As prices rise, people with fixed incomes find it harder and harder to support a family. Reduced buying power means minimum-wage earners must skimp on everything.

That skimping, in turn, has far-reaching consequences for society as a whole. For example, an uninsured driver who gets into an accident forces someone else to pay and pushes up everyone else's premiums. Pregnant women who do not get adequate medical care are more at risk for having babies with birth defects. Caring for these children drives up everyone's medical costs.

Opposed to Raising the Minimum Wage

Restaurant owner Robert Bobbitt, Sr., of Canton, Ohio, argues that wages are not a matter of "employer whim." Mr. Bobbitt worked a second job at night to get enough training to qualify for ownership of a McDonald's franchise. Now he owns four of the restaurants. He opposes a wage increase. "Before, I would have thought of the minimum wage as a social issue. Then you start working for yourself, and all the risk and responsibilities are on you. Raising the minimum wage will

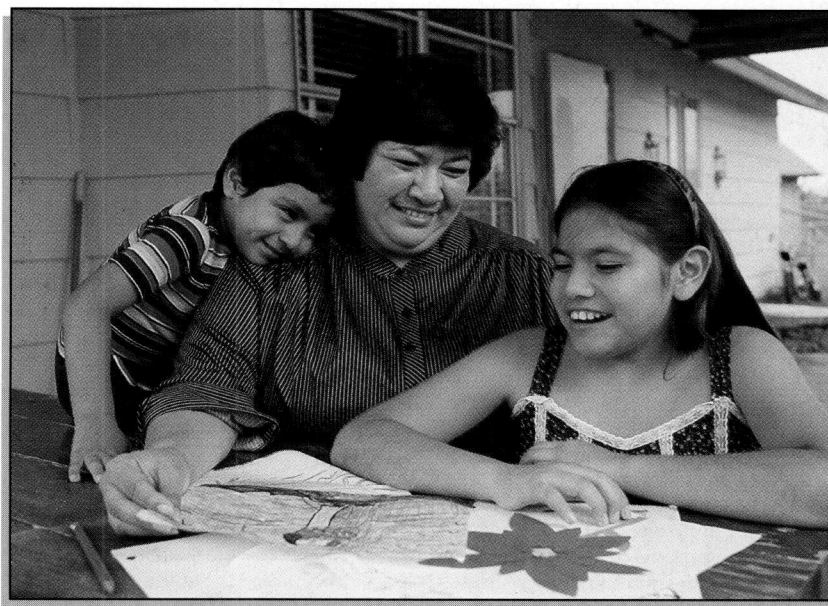

VIEWING HISTORY Those who support a rise in the minimum wage say that most families cannot support themselves on a low minimum wage. Families who cannot support themselves increase the burden on public assistance programs. *Economics What are the main arguments of those who favor raising the minimum wage?*

TEST PREPARATION

Have students read the paragraphs under "Opposed to Raising the Minimum Wage" and then answer the question below.

The term *whim* in the passage means—

A necessity.

B random impulse.

C right.

D morality.

Answer to . . .

Viewing History Inflation, to redress the gap between rich and poor.

BACKGROUND

Interdisciplinary

Many writers helped raise the public's perceptions of the poverty and unsafe conditions endured by American workers. Upton Sinclair, a leading progressive, exposed the horrors of the meat-packing industry in his novel *The Jungle* (1906), while muckraking investigative journalists such as Ida M. Tarbell and Lincoln Steffens urged government action. During the Depression, books like *The Grapes of Wrath* (1939), by John Steinbeck, and *Let Us Now Praise Famous Men,* by James Agee, with photographer Walker Evans, made people's hardships vividly real.

Robert Bobbitt, Sr., of Canton, Ohio, is a restaurant owner. He, like many small-business owners, fears that a rise in the minimum wage cannot be absorbed by a small business like his. He thinks the rise will result in worker layoffs. *Economics How do higher wages affect consumers?*

take money out of the entrepreneur's pocket," Bobbitt claims. In other words, the level of wages can make or break a small business.

Opponents of an increase say holding the minimum wage steady is also important to consumers. Typically, a producer of goods or services passes along any increase in costs to customers. "Businesses simply don't absorb increased wage costs," according to presidential adviser Rob Shapiro. "They pass them on in the form of higher prices, which are regressive [hardest on the poor] because they're borne equally by all." Higher prices hurt those least able to pay. They can also trigger inflation.

Consumers aren't the only ones who will suffer from raising the minimum wage, opponents say. Workers on the lowest rungs of the economic ladder will be hurt, too. When employers must raise the minimum wage, they often have to cut employee hours or drop employees from the payroll. Like Robert Bobbitt of Ohio, Maryland restaurant owner Chris Gallant says,

 ❝These people need their jobs. Congress would only be hurting us, and our employees, if they raised the minimum wage.❞

—*Chris Gallant*

So, what is the value of the minimum wage? The laws of supply and demand in the marketplace, not the government, should determine wages, according to these opponents of the minimum wage.

The Debate Continues

The majority of Americans favor increasing the minimum wage. Yet the debate among politicians over the minimum wage is intense because it pits two deeply held American values against each other. Americans hold fast to their belief in the **work ethic**—the idea that hard work will produce a decent life. The American dream, after all, is based on the notion that anyone who tries hard enough can achieve a comfortable standard of living. The minimum wage, therefore, should meet that standard.

On the other hand, Americans also believe in free enterprise. Government regulation that restricts free enterprise interferes with the workings of the marketplace and will ultimately hurt the economy. The challenge to Americans, then, is to find a way to reconcile these two beliefs in an era when government regulation is mistrusted but poverty is increasing.

Key Terms

1. progressive
2. New Deal
3. work ethic

Portfolio Activity

5. Review the issues of the debate about the minimum wage in the Debating the Future section of the chapter. How do they affect you personally and the country as a whole? Choose a way to express your opinion. Draw a cartoon, write a letter to a member of Congress, or construct a poster. When you have chosen a presentation that is acceptable to your teacher, put it in the appropriate format.

Creating a Time Line

4. To set the issues of this chapter in context, construct a time line that includes major events and legislation in twentieth-century United States history related to worker protection and the minimum wage. Begin with the Triangle Shirtwaist Factory fire. You may use your textbook as a reference.

INTERNET ACTIVITY

For your portfolio:
CREATE A GRAPH

6. Access Prentice Hall's *America: Pathways to the Present* site at **www.Pathways.phschool.com** for the specific URL to complete the activity. Additional resources and related Web sites are also available.

   Use the data provided to graph the change in wages between 1973 and 1997 for workers of various education levels. Describe the trend in wages for each category of education level. Have wages increased or decreased during this time period? Which group of workers has fared the best? The worst?

Using Graphic Organizers

7. Review the arguments in the Debating the Future section of the chapter. Fill in the blank circles in the web diagram below, which shows the connections among employers, wage earners, and the government.

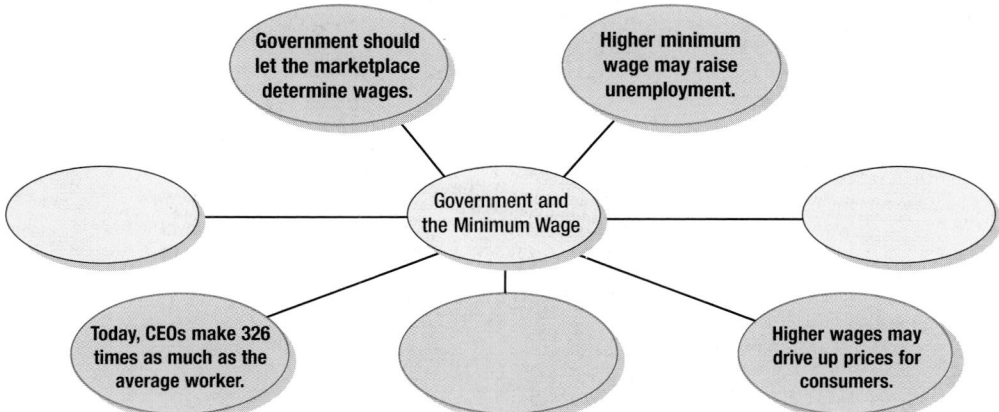

Government should let the marketplace determine wages.

Higher minimum wage may raise unemployment.

Government and the Minimum Wage

Today, CEOs make 326 times as much as the average worker.

Higher wages may drive up prices for consumers.

INTERNET ACTIVITY

Graphs should present information clearly and accurately. Descriptions should should reflect a thorough understanding of the data.

The major concepts of Chapter 38 are presented in *Guide to the Essentials of American History* and *Interactive Student Tutorial CD-ROM,* which contains interactive review activities, time lines, and test practice for Chapter 38.

Key Terms

1. progressive, see p. 1024
2. New Deal, see p. 1025
3. work ethic, see p. 1028

Creating a Time Line

4. Time lines should include: the Factory Inspection Commission formed by the New York State legislature; the adoption of the Industrial Code of New York; the 1912 passage of the minimum-wage law in Massachusetts; the regulation of labor by the federal government during World War I; various pieces of legislation passed during the New Deal; the raising of the minimum wage during the Truman and Clinton administrations.

Portfolio Activity

5. Student presentations will vary but should be creative and demonstrate a thoughtful approach to the issue.

Internet Activity

6. See below.

Using Graphic Organizers

7. Answers will vary but should show an understanding of minimum wage issues. Sample answers: (left blank)—At minimum wage, workers need federal support; (bottom blank)—Three out of four Americans support raising the minimum wage; (right blank)—Raising the minimum wage may stifle entrepreneurs.

CHAPTER 39 Rethinking Entitlements

CHAPTER 39 Rethinking Entitlements

Objectives

Help students to define the major social welfare programs known as "entitlements," understand the growth of social welfare programs beginning with the New Deal, and identify the different plans for changing or eliminating welfare programs.

Bellringer

Ask students for their own suggestions about ways to help people who live in poverty. What government or private programs do they know about? What does "promote the general welfare" mean to them?

Reading Strategy

Question Writing Ask students to read the chapter headings and subheadings and write *how, what, when,* and *why* questions about each. As they read, have them look for answers to those questions.

LESSON PLAN

Connecting to the Main Idea

1. Focus Explain that some social welfare programs have been in effect since the 1930s, while others were started in the 1960s. What factors have forced a reappraisal of those programs today? What criticisms are due to changes in the programs themselves?

2. Instruct Discuss the main entitlement programs—welfare and Medicare—and the different aims of each. What problems does each face? Discuss why these programs have become major budget issues. Discuss arguments for and against deep budget cuts.

3. Close Questions about entitlement programs pose major dilemmas for the American public, as the costs of such programs soar and government budgets remain tight, but the needs continue.

INTRODUCING THE THEME

Millions of people in the United States receive some form of government assistance, such as food stamps, health insurance, or medical care. While federal social welfare programs have existed since the 1930s, the rising cost of such programs has raised controversy in recent years. Critics of social welfare programs argue that they encourage dependency and unfairly burden taxpayers. Defenders of social welfare programs counter that such programs are needed to protect vulnerable groups, such as the elderly and children.

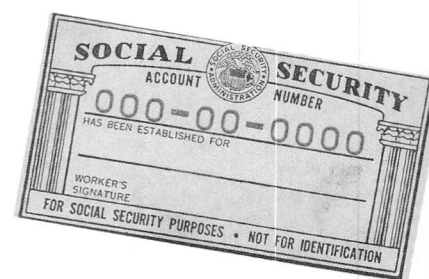

Social Security card

DEBATE

How do we balance the needs of the poor and the elderly against the needs of the budget, both for the present and for the future?

KEY TERMS

Medicare, entitlement, AFDC, federal deficit, national debt, food stamp, block grant

VIEWING THE PRESENT

When she was in the tenth grade in Milwaukee, Wisconsin, Keyola Lackey dropped out of school because she was pregnant. A year after her first baby was born, she had another child. Without a husband and without job skills, Lackey got by on welfare, or public assistance. She fit the welfare stereotype almost exactly: an unwed teenage

A welfare reform law passed in 1996 brought about sweeping changes in social welfare programs. *Economics What was one of the major goals of the law?*

RESOURCE OPTIONS

Teaching Resources

Reproducible Lesson Plan Lesson Plans folder, p. 180

Learning Styles Lesson Plan Learning Styles Lesson Plans folder, p. 77

Big Idea Graphic Organizer Big Idea Graphic Organizer folder, p. 152

Guided Reading and Review Unit 11 folder, p. 18

The United States' elderly population is the fastest-growing segment of American society. Almost all Americans aged sixty-five and over are insured by Medicare. *Economics What challenges does the Medicare system face?*

mother with several children and no way to support them.

When 75-year-old J. S. Russell learned that he needed heart surgery, his family worried a lot about how to pay for it. The costs of a pacemaker, the operation itself, and a week of care at Stanford University Hospital seemed enormous. As it turned out, the family had to pay much less than they feared. **Medicare,** a federal health-insurance program for elderly and disabled Americans, paid for almost everything except Russell's medications.

What Are Entitlements?

Welfare and Medicare are two examples of federal programs called entitlements. **Entitlements** are social welfare programs that people are "entitled to" by being at a certain income level or age. The federal government guarantees assistance for all those who qualify. As the number of people who qualify increases, so do the costs. As a result, managing costs has become a major concern.

In the 1990s politicians were quick to attack the idea of welfare but reluctant to question the need for Medicare. A 1995 *Time*/CNN poll reflected this split. Some 65 percent of those surveyed favored cutting welfare benefits, while 81 percent opposed cuts in Medicare. Yet despite these differences in public opinion, most Americans agreed that both programs needed to be reformed. There was little agreement, however, on how to do so.

Welfare

Welfare is a broad term that covers many forms of public assistance.

Yet when most people hear the word "welfare," they think of Aid to Families with Dependent Children (**AFDC**). Before major reform of the welfare system in 1996, AFDC was the largest and best-known program of public assistance. Federal outlays to AFDC families made up roughly 4 percent of the national budget. Medicaid, which provides health care services to more than 36 million Americans receiving public assistance, accounted for about 6 percent of the budget in 1996.

The federal government set the guidelines for who could receive AFDC and Medicaid and how money would be distributed. Slightly more than half of the costs of AFDC were paid for by the federal government. The rest was paid by the states. The federal government also paid at least half of each state's Medicaid expenses.

In 1996, roughly 12.8 million people received AFDC, about two thirds of them children. Approximately one in seven American children was on AFDC, and of these AFDC children, nearly 60 percent were African American or Hispanic.

Some people have been able to stop receiving welfare aid after a short time. Many others, however, have remained on the welfare system for extended periods. According to Ladonna Pavetti of the Urban Institute, about 63 percent of those receiving welfare in the past eventually spent nine years or more on public assistance. Critics of welfare point to such figures as proof that people have abused the system or at least have become dependent on it.

Medicare

Medicare provides health insurance for Americans over 65 and for people with disabilities—over 40 million people in 2001. Medicare pays for both hospital care and doctors' visits, but it does so in different ways. Money for Part A of Medicare, which covers hospital expenses, comes from a payroll tax paid for by workers and employers. About one fourth of the money for Part B, which covers doctors' visits, comes from premiums paid by Medicare recipients themselves. The other three fourths comes from congressional outlays. In 2001, government Medicare payments accounted for 12 percent of the federal budget.

Medicare faces several problems, but the biggest is financial. The hospital insurance fund, which had a surplus in the mid-1990s, is expected to run out of money by 2008 because of soaring costs. The main reason for the rising costs of medical care is the expense of new technology.

The number of people eligible

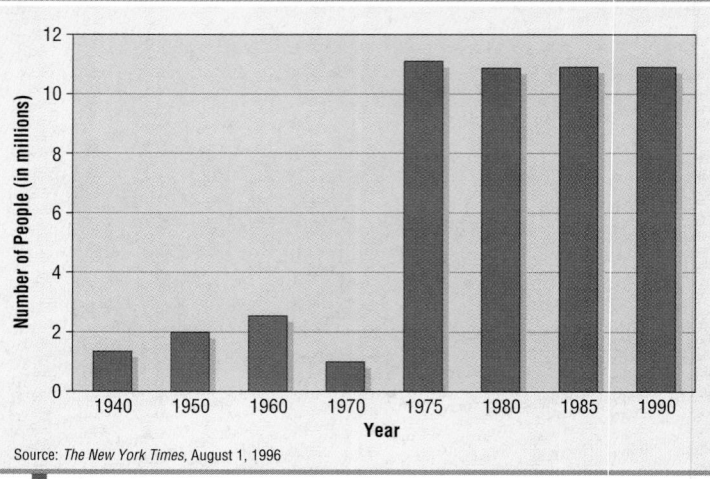

People on AFDC, 1940–1990

Source: *The New York Times*, August 1, 1996

Interpreting Charts The number of people receiving AFDC grew rapidly after 1970. *Culture* What connection is there between these figures and the public's view of social welfare?

for Medicare is growing steadily. By 2010, when baby boomers start to retire, the number of Americans over 65 will be about 40 million. Adding to the problem is the fact that the fastest-growing population group is also the group needing the most medical care. This is the group over age 85.

Unlike welfare, the main requirement for receiving Medicare is not income but age. In 1995, there were four people paying Medicare taxes for every Medicare recipient. By the middle of the next century there will only be two people paying taxes for every recipient.

Rethinking Entitlements

Every year from 1970 to 1996 the United States spent more money than it took in through taxes. This meant that in each of those years there was a **federal deficit.** Each year's deficit adds to the **national debt**—all the money that the fed-

eral government owes. By mid-1998 the national debt had reached around $5.5 trillion.

Like anyone who borrows money, the federal government must pay interest on this debt. For the fiscal year ending in September 1997, that interest totaled more than $244 billion. This amount represented about 14 percent of the entire federal budget.

Reducing the national debt would lower the government's annual interest payments. To do this, Congress either has to cut federal spending in another area or raise more money from the taxpayers. Because no one wants a tax increase, the government looks to make budget cuts. Entitlements have become a logical target for those cuts.

Tensions over budget cuts eased somewhat in 1998 when the U.S. recorded a budget surplus—the first one since 1969. The government's interest payments towards the national debt decreased to 11

Answer to . . .

Interpreting Charts The dramatic rise in people receiving AFDC made people worry about the costs and rethink entitlements.

percent of the federal budget in 2001. As a result, the budget gains flexibility and there is less pressure to slash spending in other areas.

To most people the "American Dream" is the belief that through hard work and determination, anyone can become successful in America. For most of this nation's history, people did not believe it was the government's responsibility to help the poor or the needy.

By the end of the nineteenth century, however, many people seemed to find it much more difficult to make it on their own. The Industrial Revolution had drawn people from the farm to the city. As working and living conditions in the growing cities became harsh, progressives worked for government regulation of some aspects of private industry. Passage of these laws signaled a shift in public opinion. It paved the way for greater government involvement in solving social problems.

FDR's New Deal

The economic crisis of the Great Depression motivated President Franklin D. Roosevelt (FDR) to set up a number of social welfare programs in the United States. Under his New Deal, work-relief projects like the Works Progress Administration provided billions of dollars for jobs for the poor. Such programs kept many families from starving.

Social Security was another New Deal program. The Social Security Act provided retirement pensions for workers over 65 and unemployment benefits for those who lost their jobs. Social Security was funded by deductions from workers' paychecks as well as by contributions from employers.

Added to the original Social Security Act was a section to provide Aid to Dependent Children (ADC)—direct payments to children whose fathers had died or deserted the family. Money for ADC was to come from both the federal government and the states, with the federal government handling a larger share. ADC became Aid to Families with Dependent Children (AFDC) in 1950. In that year, Congress broadened its coverage to include mothers in its benefits.

During the prosperous 1950s, most Americans thought little about the poor. Unknown to them, pockets of poverty existed in the midst of national prosperity—in Appalachia, in the Deep South, and in the big cities of the Northeast and Midwest. Michael Harrington brought these problems to light in his 1962 book, *The Other America*.

In response, President John Kennedy asked Congress for laws to eliminate poverty. One direct result was the food stamp program to help feed the poor. Under this

This photograph of a family during the Depression was taken by Dorothea Lange in 1936. The Social Security Act of 1935 provided direct payments to children whose fathers had died or deserted the family. ***Government** How did the role of government change during the New Deal?*

Graphing the Theme
To make sure students understand the theme of this chapter, you may wish to use the tree map graphic organizer below.

Tell students that a tree map is useful for showing a topic with its main ideas and supporting details. Have students use it to outline the topic of rethinking social welfare programs.

Teaching Tip A template for this graphic organizer can be found in the Color Transparencies, G-3.

Customize for
More Advanced Students

Have students research the sources of revenue and the expenditures of the current federal budget, including specific amounts or percentages for each major entitlement program. Ask students to make two pie graphs—one titled *Revenue* and one titled *Expenditures*—showing those figures and display their findings on the chalkboard or bulletin board.

Answer to . . .

Viewing History *It expanded to sponsor a number of social welfare programs.*

program, people receive **food stamps,** which are printed slips of paper that can be used like money to purchase groceries.

Johnson's Great Society

After Kennedy's assassination, President Lyndon Johnson enlarged Kennedy's ideas into his own vision of "The Great Society." To create it, he declared "an unconditional war on poverty in America." In 1964 and 1965 Congress passed laws that raised AFDC payments and broadened eligibility, increased Social Security

The food stamp program in the United States came about in part because of the publication of The Other America, *by Michael Harrington. Shown here is the original cover of the 1962 book.*

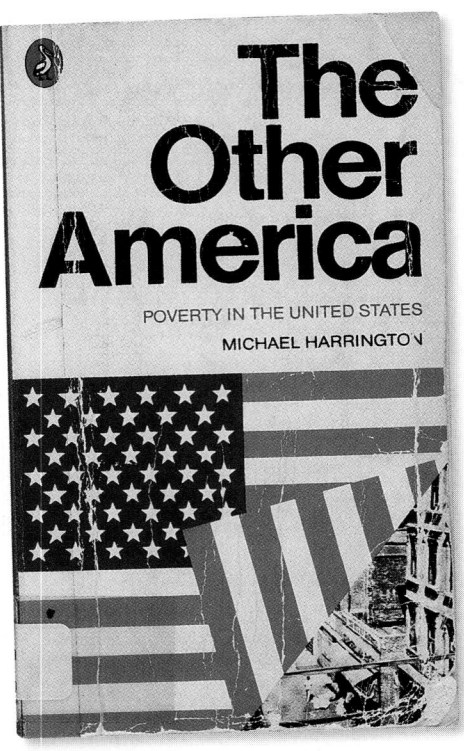

benefits, set up Medicare and Medicaid, and established job training and education programs like Head Start. Johnson, who had begun his political career as a strong New Dealer, believed that the federal government could and should solve the problems of poverty in America.

During the Johnson administration, federal welfare spending increased each year. It continued to grow during the Nixon, Ford, and Carter administrations as well. One reason for the increase was the growing number of people on welfare. Yet spending more money on more people did not create a Great Society. It did, however, generate a major backlash against federal anti-poverty programs.

Reagan's Revolution

Ronald Reagan was elected President in 1980, declaring that "government is not the solution to our problem. Government is the problem." Reagan wanted to reduce the size of government in most areas. Social welfare programs were a prime target. Welfare payments robbed people of their dignity and of their drive to work, Reagan believed. Promising to maintain a "safety net" for the neediest, he made dramatic cuts in social welfare budgets. For example, during the Reagan years, funding for food stamps dropped 18.8 percent and funding for AFDC decreased 17.7 percent. About 600,000 people found themselves excluded from Medicaid.

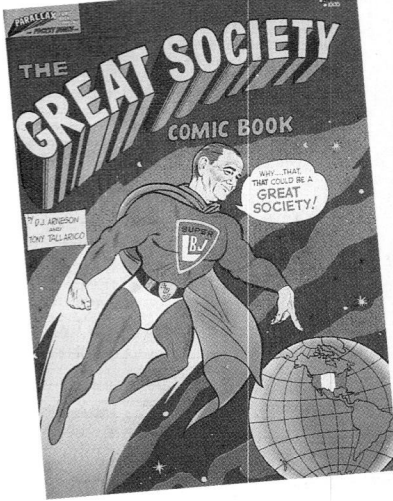

This comic book cover shows the energy with which President Johnson rallied Congress and the country behind his ambitious social programs. **Government** *What programs were established during Johnson's Great Society program?*

After Reagan

George Bush, elected President in 1988, carried on Reagan's legacy and continued to cut spending for social programs. Although Bush was defeated in 1992, the conservative desire to spend less on social programs gained momentum. Democrat Bill Clinton promised to "end welfare as we have known it" in his campaign for the presidency in 1992. When conservative Republicans won control of Congress in 1994, their "Contract with America" called for basic welfare reform.

1996 Welfare Reform

In 1996 President Clinton signed the Personal Responsibility and Work Opportunity Reconciliation

Act. This welfare reform law made sweeping changes in the welfare system. It eliminated AFDC. No longer will needy people receive cash assistance for an indefinite period of time.

Instead, the federal government makes funds available to the states in the form of **block grants.** By distributing these lump sums of money, which are intended to stay about the same from year to year, the federal government may be better able to control its budget.

The block grants carry some restrictions. To continue to receive the grants, states must devise programs to remove people from the welfare rolls. By the year 2002 at least 50 percent of a state's welfare recipients must have a job.

Even without welfare reform, the number of people receiving assistance began to drop in the mid-1990s. In 1994 the welfare rolls reached their highest level, and then they started declining. By 2000 they had fallen by nearly 59 percent. Part of the reason for the decline was the booming economy during this period, which tamed inflation, increased employment, and also helped produce a balanced budget. Another reason was the establishment of reform programs, at both the state and the federal level. Still another reason, some suggest, was that the old-fashioned work ethic had been restored.

Since passage of the federal welfare reform law, welfare cases did shrink at a faster pace. This suggests that the law is working. But President Clinton did not like all the provisions in the law. He promised to revise some of those provisions to make them less severe, especially on children. His voice joined those of others in the debate about the future of welfare.

DEBATING THE FUTURE

Clinton signed the welfare reform law in part because most people agreed that the welfare system needed to be overhauled. As Andrew Cuomo, Clinton's Assistant Secretary of Housing and Urban Development, said, "Nobody likes welfare. Nobody thinks it works."

There is similar agreement on the need to revamp Medicare. According to Frank Luntz, a Republican pollster:

AMERICAN VOICES "When the public realizes and personalizes the financial situation of Medicare, they end up backing significant reform."

—Frank Luntz

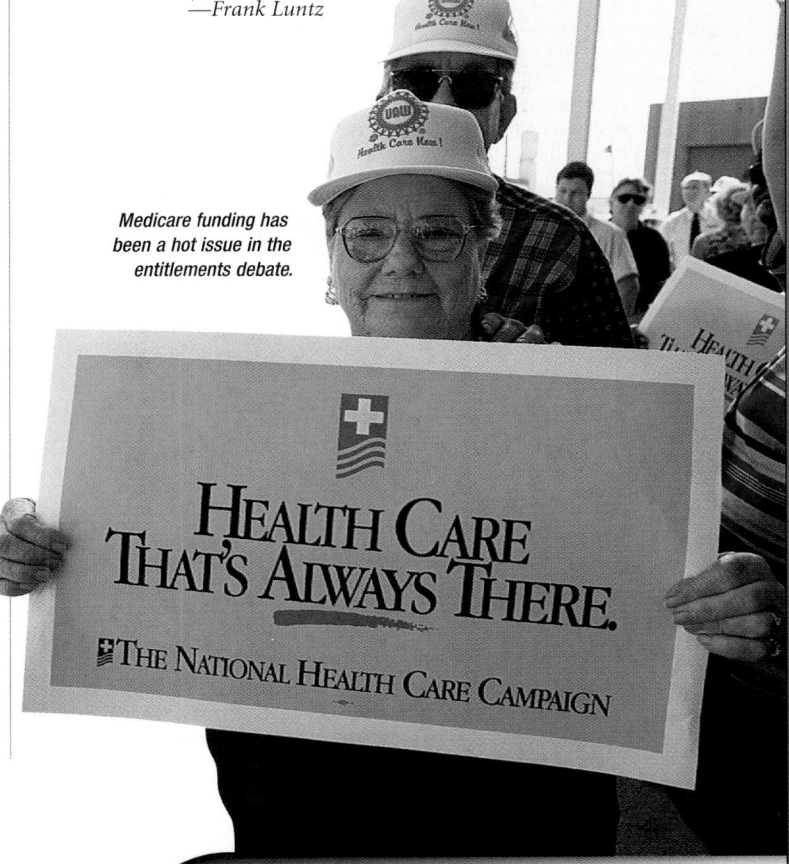

Medicare funding has been a hot issue in the entitlements debate.

Yet that is about as far as agreement goes. When it comes to actually cutting welfare and Medicare, the debate centers on one question: "How deep?"

In Favor of Deep Cuts

Welfare is by no means the largest item in the federal budget, but it provokes some of the sharpest attacks. Many people see welfare as a threat to the American belief in individual effort. They believe welfare recipients would rather take a handout than work. They see people getting something for nothing while the rest of America works hard and pays high taxes.

Global Connections

A study of health-care costs in Canada and Germany showed that operating costs there were 25 percent to 33 percent less than in the United States, mainly because fewer hospitals had expensive high-tech equipment or did certain highly specialized procedures. For every one million people, at least twice as many U.S. hospitals have units for open-heart surgery, organ transplants, and MRIs as do Canadian hospitals. Of Canada's 68 teaching hospitals, only 37 have open-heart surgery units.

Customize for

Less Proficient Readers

Have students write the headings Deep Cuts and Moderate Cuts in two columns on a sheet of paper. As they read the text, ask them to fill in information under each heading.

Answer to . . .

Viewing History *As being unwilling and unable to handle the responsibility.*

Tom DeLay, Republican whip in the House of Representatives, summed up this argument:

AMERICAN VOICES
❝The current welfare system undermines incentives to work, encourages expansion of the underclass, breaks up families, and promotes welfare as a way of life.❞

—*Tom DeLay*

DeLay and others have argued that sharply limiting the time people can receive assistance will get them out into the work force. The 1996 welfare reform law gives new welfare recipients two years to find work.

Some states already have programs in place to train welfare recipients. Wisconsin's Learnfare requires young people to stay in school or lose their benefits. Teenage mother Keyola Lackey supports Learnfare because it made her return to school to prepare for a job. "The people who

criticize it want the money free and do nothing for it. But nothing comes free," she says.

Welfare critics have also suggested that Congress allocate a fixed amount of money for welfare each year. To promote efficiency, reformers of welfare believe that the states, not the federal government, should administer welfare programs. The 1996 welfare reform bill, with its block grants, accomplished both of these goals.

Those who want to make stiff cuts in Medicare believe that it, too, must be more efficient and less generous. They point out that Medicare covers everyone, even those who could afford to pay for their own health care. Clyle Dwyer, retired truck driver in Fargo, North Dakota, believes that Medicare is too generous. "I know guys who have stuff done that they shouldn't because Medicare will pay for it."

To rein in the growth of Medicare, former Speaker of the House Newt Gingrich advocated

several cost-cutting measures.

1. Raise Part B premiums (which help cover doctors' visits) for people with higher incomes.
2. Promote the establishment of medical savings accounts, in which older Americans could deposit funds for use when they needed them.
3. Turn health care for older Americans over to private insurers such as health maintenance organizations (HMOs).

Gingrich believed that the private sector can do a better job than the government, especially at cutting costs. He predicted that the Health Care Financing Administration, which handles Medicare, "will wither on the vine because we think people are voluntarily going to leave it."

In Favor of Moderate Cuts

In the early 1990s the welfare population skyrocketed. Increasing poverty accounted for this growth far more than individual laziness. So said those who favor moderate welfare cuts. Rebecca Blank, a leading poverty economist, explained that the increase did not come about because of generous benefits or because single mothers were working less. In fact, she said, they were working more. The reason, according to Blank, was that inflation had decreased the value of food stamps and AFDC 26 percent between 1972 and 1992.

Those who favor moderate cuts also point out that most people who receive benefits want to work but cannot find jobs that pay a decent wage. Many of them lack job skills. According to Christopher Jencks, a professor at Northwestern University:

As this political cartoon shows, the federal government is making the states take more responsibility for public-assistance programs. ***Government*** *How does the cartoonist portray the ability of state governments to handle this responsibility?*

AMERICAN VOICES

❝ For a very large proportion of single mothers, it's impossible to find a job that pays as well as being on welfare. ❞

—*Christopher Jencks*

Removing these women from the welfare rolls will send them into minimum-wage jobs, observers point out. There they will earn less. They will also lose Medicaid coverage for themselves and their children.

Deep welfare cuts would harm children the most, say the moderates, and block grants will remove the federal guarantee of protection for all. Since each state can administer its money as it chooses, there may be areas where people completely lose their safety net. Reverend Sam Myskens of Wichita, Kansas, gives this illustration: "If the wheat crop is bad one year or Boeing lays off 5,000 people, there will be more hungry children but no more money available to feed them."

Moreover, cutting back welfare will not result in great savings, say the moderates. A better long-term solution would include child care services and job training or re-training. While these programs would cost money, they would be investments in a better-educated work force and healthier children in the future.

Some specialists who want moderate cuts in Medicare claim that privatizing this program will not produce the desired savings. They cite studies showing that private insurers are no more cost-effective than Medicare.

Furthermore, they say, shifting additional responsibilities for financing Medicare Part B to older Americans does nothing to stop the pressures that are driving health care inflation. Among those pressures is the soaring cost of new medical technology. In addition, this scheme does not rescue Part A, the hospital insurance fund.

The Debate Continues

The need to reduce the national debt is very real. Entitlements are one area of spending that can be cut to help keep the federal budget balanced. Like a household budget, the federal budget is more than a list of numbers. It is also a statement of priorities. The statement would have to consider what is most important to the household at the present time and how it will affect the household in the future. How America's leaders ultimately rethink and revise entitlements will reflect the nation's priorities for the future.

VIEWING HISTORY

In 1994 Republicans in Congress under the leadership of Speaker of the House Newt Gingrich (above), proposed a "Contract with America" to reduce the role of federal government. *Government How did Speaker Gingrich believe health care should be handled?*

Customize for
English Language Learners

Have students write down the terms *welfare* and *Medicare*. Ask them to first write a sentence explaining what each program does, and then one or two sentences giving some of the criticisms of each program.

ACTIVITY
EXTENDED CLASS PERIODS

Time: 90 minutes.
Activity: Prepare a photo essay on a social-welfare program.
Grouping: Groups of four to six students.
Purpose: To explore the facets of a social-welfare program by presenting the government view and the opinions of people served by the program. Students may choose either Medicare or welfare to research, providing documentation on the goals and history of the program, with statistical information. For the human side, they might interview welfare or Medicaid recipients or providers such as doctors or welfare workers.
Roles: Director, photographer, caption writer, researcher, entitlement recipients and providers of varying ages and situations.
Outcome: Students will present a photo essay including captions and interviews.

RESOURCE OPTIONS

Teaching Resources

📁 **Chapter Tests Forms A and B** Chapter Test folder

Student Performance Pack

Guide to the Essentials Chapter 39 (English and Spanish)

Standardized Test Preparation Handbook

Media and Technology

🎧 **Guided Reading Audiotapes** Chapter 39 Summary (English and Spanish)
Student Edition on Audiotape Chapter 39

💿 **Test Bank CD-ROM; Interactive Student Tutorial CD-ROM** Chapter Test

Answer to . . .

Viewing History He believed that the private sector, rather than the government, should handle health care.

Chapter 39 Review

The major concepts of Chapter 39 are presented in *Guide to the Essentials of American History* and *Interactive Student Tutorial CD-ROM*, which contains interactive review activities, time lines, and test practice for Chapter 39.

Key Terms

1. entitlement, see p. 1031
2. AFDC, see p. 1031
3. Medicare, see p. 1031
4. federal deficit, see p. 1032
5. national debt, see p. 1032
6. food stamp, see p. 1034
7. block grant, see p. 1035

Creating a Time Line

8. Time lines should include the passage of the Social Security Act; the establishment of AFDC, food stamps, Medicare, and Head Start; and the 1996 Personal Responsibility and Work Opportunity Reconciliation Act.

Portfolio Activity

9. Presentations should be creative and should demonstrate a thoughtful approach to the issue.

Internet Activity

10. See below.

Using Graphic Organizers

11. Answers will vary, but should reflect a coherent argument in favor of deep cuts in entitlement spending. Answers may include:
• Financing the national debt takes 11 percent of the federal budget.
• The national debt must be radically reduced.
• Citizens don't want higher taxes.
• The federal government has too many obligations.
• Welfare depresses individual initiative.
• Welfare may break up families.

Key Terms

1. entitlement
2. AFDC
3. Medicare
4. federal deficit
5. national debt
6. food stamp
7. block grant

Portfolio Activity

9. Think about the history of social welfare programs in the United States. What events or legislation do you think were the most important in creating the system of entitlements that exists today? Choose one or two of these landmarks and describe them in your own way. You may make a poster, an album of magazine or newspaper photographs, or choose another format acceptable to your teacher.

Using Graphic Organizers

11. Review the arguments in the Debating the Future section of the chapter. Study the web diagram below, and then create a new web that shows arguments for making *deep* cuts in entitlements. (Include information from elsewhere in the chapter as needed.)

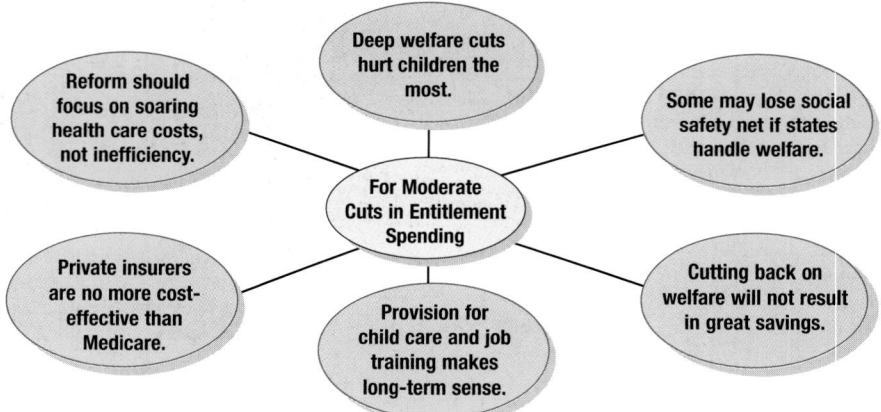

Creating a Time Line

8. To set a background for the entitlement debate, construct a time line that includes six to ten significant milestones related to social welfare programs. Include events and legislation from the New Deal to the present.

INTERNET ACTIVITY

For your portfolio:
PREPARE A REPORT

10. Access Prentice Hall's *America: Pathways to the Present* site at **www.Pathways.phschool.com** for the specific URL to complete the activity. Additional resources and related Web sites are also available.

Use the links provided to research debate on Social Security. Write a report on the current debate. What are seen as the problems with Social Security? What are the proposed solutions?

INTERNET ACTIVITY

Students' reports should be clear and to the point, and should be supported with specific facts or quotes from the Web site when applicable.

The Debate over Trade

CHAPTER 40

INTRODUCING THE THEME

When the North American Free Trade Agreement (NAFTA) took effect on January 1, 1994, the economy of the United States became more closely linked with the economies of Canada and Mexico. Since then, NAFTA has been a lightning rod for debate over free trade. While supporters of NAFTA argue that free trade will increase jobs and exports in the United States, opponents believe that it will result in a loss of American jobs. NAFTA may become the model for a trade agreement proposed for 2005 that would include all of North and South America.

DEBATE

How well has NAFTA worked? How good a model is it for our dealings with the other countries of the Americas?

KEY TERMS

NAFTA, tariff, trade deficit, trade surplus, Helms-Burton Act, Monroe Doctrine, Roosevelt Corollary, Good Neighbor Policy, *maquiladora*

Objectives

Help students to describe the trade ties the United States has with Canada and Mexico, trace the changes in the economic relationship between the United States and Latin America since the Monroe Doctrine, and identify arguments for and against NAFTA.

Bellringer

Ask students to identify anything they commonly use, eat, or wear that was imported from Canada or Mexico. Are there any items from elsewhere in Latin America? Ask them to check labels and packages in their home and list the exporting countries.

Reading Strategy

Reading for Evidence Ask students, as they read, to look for answers, both positive and negative, to the question posed in the Debate: How well has NAFTA worked?

VIEWING THE PRESENT

Nelson Silva used to operate a forklift at a TV-assembly plant in Elmwood Park, New Jersey. When the factory shut down and moved to Tijuana, Mexico, in 1995, he lost his job. "I'm bitter that we lost these people, lost these jobs, not just at JVC but all over America," he says. "We invented the television in the

Some American companies have their products assembled in Mexican factories, such as the one at right. *Economics How has this phenomenon been both good and bad for American workers?*

LESSON PLAN
Connecting to the Main Idea

1. Focus Point out that because of its size and wealth, the United States has a unique economic and political position in the Western Hemisphere. How is the United States important to its neighbors? In what ways does the United States in turn depend upon its neighbors?

2. Instruct Discuss the basic disagreements between people who favor free trade and those who favor protective tariffs and other limits. Is there a common thread that links people who are pro-NAFTA or anti-NAFTA?

3. Close Trade relationships between the United States and the world continue to change. The United States must reconsider not only the NAFTA debate, but its trade policies in the hemisphere as a whole.

RESOURCE OPTIONS

Teaching Resources

📁 **Reproducible Lesson Plan** Lesson Plans folder, p. 181

📁 **Learning Styles Lesson Plan** Learning Styles Lesson Plans folder, p. 78

📁 **Big Idea Graphic Organizer** Big Idea Graphic Organizer folder, p. 153

📁 **Guided Reading and Review** Unit 11 folder, p. 23

United States, and they're going to take it completely out of the country."

Key Tronic Corporation used to manufacture computer keyboards in Spokane, Washington. It too moved to Mexico. Although Key Tronic had to lay off workers, chief financial officer Ronald F. Klawitter points out that the move turned out to be good for Spokane. Lower labor costs for his company meant lower prices for the keyboards. Lower prices, in turn, meant more sales, which increased the demand for keyboard components made in Spokane. A greater number of people in Washington ended up with jobs making parts that are then assembled in Mexico.

What Is NAFTA?

Both of these factories relocated as a result of **NAFTA,** the North American Free Trade Agreement, which took effect on January 1, 1994. Their stories illustrate two sides of the argument over NAFTA.

The main purpose of NAFTA is to stimulate economic growth in the United States, Canada, and Mexico. To this end NAFTA

Ross Perot was the Independent candidate for president in 1992 and 1996. *Economics Why did he oppose the North American Free Trade Agreement?*

removed **tariffs,** or import taxes, and other barriers to trade. In this way it created a continent-wide free-trade zone. Without tariffs, companies can sell their goods more cheaply to a larger market. Since lower prices will bring higher sales, companies like JVC and Key Tronic moved some of their plants to Mexico, where labor costs less. They no longer have to pay tariffs if they want to sell such foreign-made goods in the United

States.

Before 1994, when NAFTA took effect, opponents argued that it would mean an enormous loss of American jobs to Mexico. In 1992, H. Ross Perot described the potential disaster as a "giant sucking sound" that would be heard as American jobs drained south of the border. Supporters of NAFTA like Presidents Bush and Clinton countered that the increased demand for American goods to Canada and Mexico would create more higher-skilled, higher-paying jobs in the United States, as well as more investment opportunities.

NAFTA and Canada

Trade between the United States and Canada has been strong for many years. President Kennedy summed up this relationship: "Geography made us neighbors. History made us friends. And economics made us partners."

Even before NAFTA, Canada and the United States were each other's largest trading partner. In 1988, the two countries agreed to the Free Trade Agreement. This pact, signed 6 years before NAFTA,

The North American Free Trade Agreement (NAFTA), 1994

The Agreement	The Result	The Controversies
The United States, Canada, and Mexico will remove tariffs and most other mutual trade restrictions over the next 15 years.	The resulting free-trade zone formed a single market similar to, but much larger than, the European Community.	Despite NAFTA's "side agreements" and other provisions, concern remains over its potential effects on the environment and the United States job market.

Interpreting Tables This table provides an overview of the NAFTA agreement and its consequences. *Economics What controversies were created by NAFTA?*

Opponents of NAFTA argued that many of the new jobs created in Mexico would pay low wages. They also argued that Mexican workers would take work that otherwise would be performed by Americans. *Economics How was trade between Mexico and the United States affected by NAFTA?*

was designed to eliminate tariffs over a 10-year period.

Since NAFTA took effect, both countries have greatly increased exports to each other. The United States, however, buys more than it sells to Canada, thus producing a **trade deficit** in the United States.

NAFTA and Mexico

The effect of trade with Mexico since NAFTA is more complicated. On the one hand, fewer jobs disappeared than had been predicted. Instead of the 6 million jobs that Perot claimed would be lost, the Labor Department reported in 1997 that 128,300 job losses were NAFTA-related.

On the other hand, not as many new jobs were created as had been anticipated. Supporters of NAFTA had predicted that it

would bring about 200,000 new jobs in its first year. That did not happen. While the number of people employed in the United States has risen steadily since NAFTA, it is impossible to say how many of the new jobs are directly a result of the free-trade agreement.

Mexican Debt Crisis

Overall, the two-way trade between the United States and Mexico rose nearly 93 percent between 1993 and 1997. But the balance of trade was not always in favor of the United States. During NAFTA's first year, 1994, exports from the United States to Mexico rose from $41.6 billion to $50.8 billion and also produced a **trade surplus.** This meant that the United States sold more to Mexico than it bought from Mexico.

During 1995, however, United States exports dropped to $46.3 billion, but imports soared, leaving a trade deficit.

This shift in balance of payments resulted from a drop in the value of the Mexican peso in December 1994. With that drop, a severe recession hit Mexico. Foreign investors became nervous. It did not help that an uprising for land reform and a scandal involving Mexico's president happened at the same time.

Loan to Mexico

To promote stability, in 1995 the United States granted Mexico a loan of $12.5 billion. With this help, Mexico was able to start to recover from its recession.

Much to the surprise of the loan's critics, by January 1997

Mexico had paid back the entire loan, three years ahead of schedule. Mexico also began making political reforms in 1996. Even so, the Mexican recession left many Americans wondering whether it was wise to be so closely tied economically to an unstable neighbor.

Balancing Economics and Politics

With the signing of NAFTA, the United States established a special economic relationship with its immediate neighbors. But what impact does the agreement have on political relations? What happens, for example, if Mexico or Canada wants to trade with a country to which the United States has restricted its trade?

In 1996 Congress passed the **Helms-Burton Act.** That act penalizes foreign companies that do business with Cuba. Canada and Mexico, as well as other nations of Latin America, loudly objected to it. They claimed that it violated NAFTA and international law. They saw the Helms-Burton Act as an abuse of United States power and the latest example of Uncle Sam's muscle-flexing in the Western Hemisphere.

John M. Hay, future Secretary of State, wrote his friend Teddy Roosevelt that the 1898 Spanish-American War was "a splendid little war." It marked the beginning of United States involvement in Latin America for the next century. Shown here are the African American soldiers of the Tenth United States Cavalry who fought in Cuba. *Foreign Policy How has trade influenced foreign policy?*

This 1901 political cartoon suggests how the United States applied the Monroe Doctrine.

REVIEWING THE PAST

The history of relations between the United States and Latin America shows how hard it is to separate economics and politics. In 1995 Deputy Secretary of State Strobe Talbott stated the government's two main goals in the Americas. He said, ". . . one is to support the growth of democratic institutions; the other is to advance prosperity through open markets and free trade." These objectives, democracy and trade, have shaped American foreign policy in the Western Hemisphere from the nation's earliest days. However, the ways the United States has chosen to pursue these goals have often made its neighbors wary of American power.

The Monroe Doctrine

In the early 1820s, independence movements rocked Spain's and Portugal's American colonies.

1042 Chapter 40

Several European monarchies seemed poised to help these countries regain their former colonies. To head them off, the United States issued the **Monroe Doctrine.** Remembering its own recent colonial status, the United States warned, "The American continents, by the free and independent condition which they have assumed and maintain, are henceforth not to be considered as subject for future colonization by any European powers."

Behind this hands-off message was the desire to promote trade. One enterprising American, Minor C. Keith, built banana plantations and a railroad in Costa Rica in the late 1800s. Keith and his partners made their business, the United Fruit Company, the largest employer in Central America. With its vast economic power, United Fruit also had enormous political influence. In the independent republics of Costa Rica, Guatemala, and Honduras, the company's power was especially strong. For this reason, some people called these nations "banana republics."

In most of the new Central American nations, a small number of families controlled the wealth, leaving the rest of the population in poverty. This ruling class generally backed military dictatorships that would defend their wealth and privilege. Dictators often replaced each other in rapid succession. Yet political stability was essential to maintain the profitability of American investments in the region.

Gunboats and Dollars

Extending the Monroe Doctrine, President Theodore Roosevelt announced in 1904 that the United States would exercise "international police power" to promote stability in Latin America. He called this policy the **Roosevelt Corollary.** It aimed to prevent European interference in the weak and unstable governments of the region. In practice, it meant that the United States sent troops to the Dominican Republic, Cuba, Nicaragua, and Haiti to keep the peace and protect American property.

In contrast to this style of "gunboat diplomacy," Roosevelt's successor, William Howard Taft, favored "dollar diplomacy." This term meant building regional stability through American investments in Latin America. Mexico, for example, attracted American investors. In time, Americans owned a large share of that nation's oil, railroads, mines, and rubber plantations. Yet dollar diplomacy just masked gunboat diplomacy. The United States continued to wield military power in Latin America to protect its interests, and many Latin Americans resented it bitterly.

Good Neighbors

After World War I the United States no longer needed to warn European nations away, and during the Depression it could no longer afford military occupation in Latin America. Instead of direct intervention, President Franklin D. Roosevelt promoted the **Good Neighbor Policy.** Stability would come from a higher standard of living, Roosevelt believed, and so his policy was to encourage trade by lowering tariffs. The United States also loaned money to Latin American governments to build public works such as bridges, roads, schools, hospitals, and water systems.

Latin America sorely needed economic development. A number of corrupt dictators still controlled countries in which the majority of people lived in poverty.

Teddy Roosevelt's vigorous policies set the course for the United States as a world power. The campaign pin (right) consists of a "teddy" bear with a soldier's hat and rifle.

After World War II

Protecting American interests after World War II meant opposing communism. Americans worried that the masses of poor people in Latin America might be attracted to communism's philosophy.

In 1959 Fidel Castro took control of Cuba. Within two years he had nationalized American property in Cuba and allied his country with the Soviet Union. Americans feared that Castro would export communism to the rest of Latin America. To gain support in blocking the spread of communism, the United States backed a number of governments headed by military strongmen.

▼ **BACKGROUND**

Global Connections

Free trade among Spanish-speaking Mexico, English- and French-speaking Canada, and the English-speaking United States posed new language problems. Directions for cooking, washing, or assembling a product made in one country now had to be written in three languages so that the others could understand them. Alternatively, manufacturers would have to stock three separate inventories of goods for each market. One solution proposed by clothing manufacturers is a nonverbal label for washing instructions. It uses icons and symbols for information such as "wash in cold water" and "do not bleach."

While these leaders tightly controlled their countries, they mismanaged the finances. Many had borrowed huge sums from foreign banks. By the early 1980s the loans could not be paid off, and Latin America plunged into a debt crisis. To get out of it, governments had to agree to plans that led to the restructuring of their economies. In time, better economic management brought new foreign investment.

In the course of these economic changes, governments were changing, too. Democracy was spreading throughout Latin America, given an added boost by the collapse of the Soviet Union. By 1995, all of the governments of the Western Hemisphere except Cuba had democratic institutions. As economies improved, political stability grew. So too did the potential for increased trade among the nations of the region.

DEBATING THE FUTURE

Opponents of NAFTA argue that the agreement is not fair to the United States. Politician Pat Buchanan believes the American people were misled by NAFTA supporters because none of the promises made about it have been kept. He says, "NAFTA should be canceled. A contract negotiated in deceit is no contract at all." President Clinton, on the other hand, says "NAFTA . . . is working superbly." What does our experience with NAFTA teach us about free trade and international relations?

In Favor of NAFTA

"The premise of NAFTA is that trade is not a zero-sum game," says former Secretary of Labor Robert B. Reich. In other words, both players win. Benefits for the United States include a net increase in jobs and a 57 percent growth in exports to Mexico and Canada in NAFTA's first four years. Both Canada and Mexico have enjoyed an increase in exports, too. NAFTA has also created jobs in those countries, particularly in the *maquiladoras,* Mexican border factories that assemble parts imported from the United States.

Some might say that these short-term gains are small. But those who support free trade also claim that NAFTA will build long-term confidence in the economy. As Professor Edward Leamers of Yale and UCLA explains:

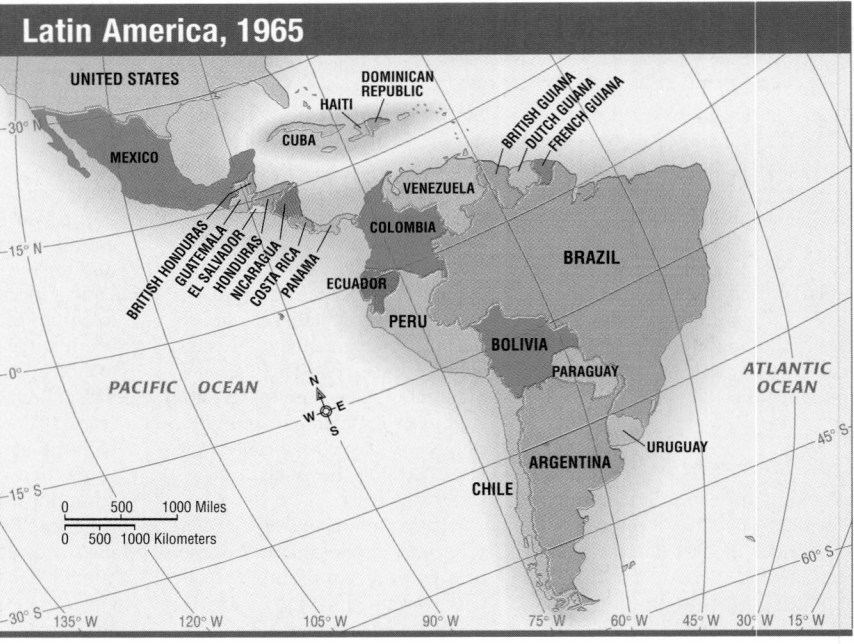

Latin America, 1965

After the missile crisis in Cuba in 1962, the United States was determined to stop the spread of communism in Latin America. By 1995, all of the governments of the Western Hemisphere except Cuba had democratic institutions.

Economics Today the region's political leaders are working to create a Free Trade Area of the Americas (FTAA). How is political stability related to a country's economy?

RESOURCE OPTIONS

Teaching Resources

Debating the Future The Debate over NAFTA, Unit 11 folder, p. 24–25

Media and Technology

Our Times Multimedia Encyclopedia of the 20th Century CD-ROM Helps students of all abilities to link the past to the present. Students can access the time line and listen to and read about the North American Free Trade Agreement. Encyclopedia articles have interactive links.

Value of U.S. Exports, 1994–1998

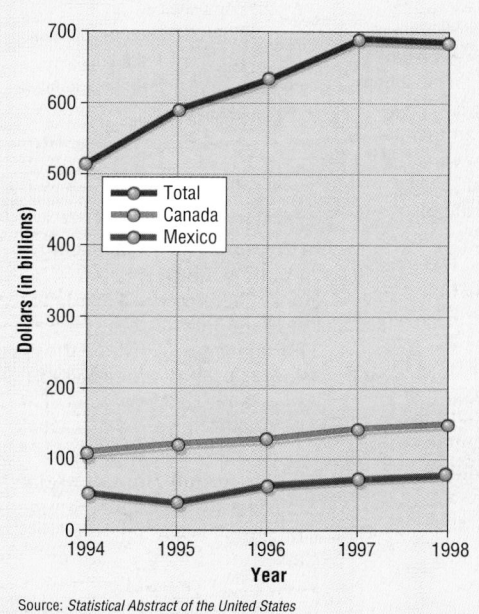

Value of U.S. Imports, 1994–1998

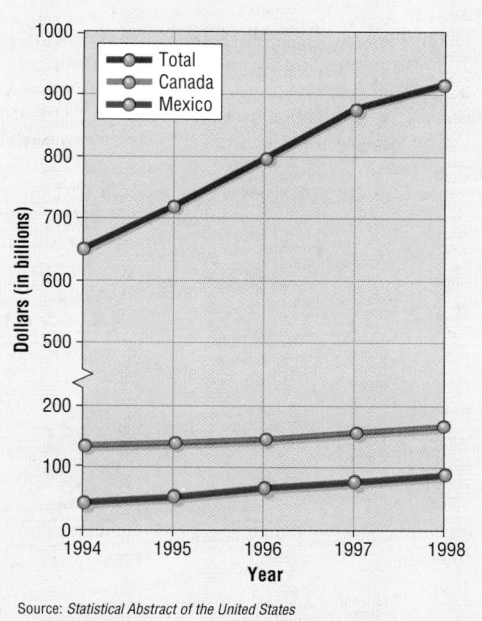

Source: *Statistical Abstract of the United States*

Source: *Statistical Abstract of the United States*

Interpreting Graphs Although the value of United States exports to Mexico and Canada increased between 1994 and 1998, so too did the value of its imports from these countries. *Economics* *Compare the value of United States imports from Canada for each year on the graph. Which country experienced a trade deficit with the other?*

AMERICAN VOICES "NAFTA guarantees that tariffs won't suddenly be raised. It is a major risk reduction document for investors. If your time clock is year by year, then NAFTA was definitely oversold. If your clock runs decade by decade, this is a more important event."

—*Edward Leamers*

Advocates of free trade believe that it will improve the Mexican economy over time. This, they say, is the best way to build political stability in Mexico. A more stable and economically successful Mexico will also mean fewer illegal immigrants to the United States in the years ahead.

Based on NAFTA, supporters believe that free trade is the wave of the future. Free trade "is simply going to happen, and no President or Congress can stand in the way of it or they will be eaten alive," predicts former Congressman Bill Frenzel. A free-trade agreement is essential, says G. Philip Hughes, former ambassador to Barbados, because "we simply cannot afford to be left behind."

Against NAFTA
NAFTA has been a bad deal, say opponents of free trade. It has not increased trade to the levels that were promised. It has mostly benefited large multinational corporations and has hurt workers. Public Citizen, a lobbying group, says:

AMERICAN VOICES "NAFTA is causing the loss of existing jobs, while the new jobs that were promised aren't being created."

—*Public Citizen*

To make matters worse, NAFTA is pushing down wages for some existing jobs. For these reasons, labor unions have vigorously opposed NAFTA.

TEST PREPARATION

Have students read the quotation by Edward Leamers on this page and then answer the question below.

The main point that Leamers is making in the passage is that—

A NAFTA has immediate positive results.

B NAFTA should be judged only from year to year.

C NAFTA has important, long-term effects.

D NAFTA is a risky proposition.

Answer to . . .

Interpreting Charts The United States.

NAFTA has not been uniformly good for Mexico either, opponents say. Mexican workers are still paid too little and work in unsafe conditions. Factory and job growth is strong only in the north. Investment in the rest of the country has dried up. Small businesses find it very hard to compete. For example, Mexican farmers suffer when American crops like corn undersell theirs. With these economic woes, NAFTA has not made good on its promise to stem the tide of illegal immigration into the United States.

Opponents like Ross Perot claim that the United States is making a great mistake by tying its economy to that of an unstable country. A crisis in that country could cost thousands of jobs in the United States. It could also wipe out billions of dollars in investments.

Other critics say that free trade is not unavoidable. Nor should it be the driving force in government policy. Lori Wallach of Public Citizen says:

Most American labor unions have strongly opposed NAFTA because they fear that companies will move American factories to Mexico, where wages are lower and where there are fewer environmental restrictions. *Economics What do these demonstrators mean when they say "Fighting for Good Jobs"?*

AMERICAN VOICES

"The notion that free trade is inevitable is just not right; trade is a conscious choice. The problem is, recently, trade has become an end in itself. . . . Public policy should not be determined solely by the global marketplace."

—*Lori Wallach*

The Debate Continues

In December 1994 the leaders of 34 nations in the Western Hemisphere met in Florida for the first Summit of the Americas. They agreed to work for the creation of a Free Trade Area of the Americas (FTAA) by 2005. This area would become the world's largest free-trade zone.

The second Summit of the Americas took place in Santiago, Chile, in April 1998. Since the earlier meeting, the economies of Latin America had begun to boom. The United States wants access to those fast-growing markets before European or other nations step in.

The main stumbling block for the United States involves labor and environmental issues. As with NAFTA, opponents fear that FTAA will lower wage rates. They also fear that businesses outside the United States will not meet American environmental standards. Democrats in Congress, especially, insist that these issues be addressed in any agreement.

Clearly, economic isolationism is no longer possible in the age of multinational corporations. But just what form the new trade pact will take remains to be seen. Congress must ratify it, and they will look closely at the effects of NAFTA before agreeing to FTAA. The debate is sure to be lively.

Key Terms

1. NAFTA
2. tariff
3. trade deficit
4. trade surplus
5. Helms-Burton Act
6. Monroe Doctrine
7. Roosevelt Corollary
8. Good Neighbor Policy
9. *maquiladora*

Portfolio Activity

11. Decide whether you agree with those who favor NAFTA or those who oppose it, and why. Then choose a way to express your opinion, such as an editorial, a cartoon, a photo essay, a letter to the President or your representatives in Congress, or another format that is acceptable to your teacher.

Using Graphic Organizers

13. Review the arguments in the Debating the Future section of the chapter. Then fill in the blank portion in the graphic organizer below, which shows the different major stages in the policies of the

United States toward its neighbors. You should provide at least three supporting details. Copy the organizer on another sheet of paper.

Creating a Time Line

10. To see the pattern of United States relations with Latin America, construct a time line tracing major events and developments from the Monroe Doctrine to NAFTA. Include at least six items and be sure you can explain the significance of each event on the time line.

INTERNET ACTIVITY

For your portfolio:
ORGANIZE A DEBATE

12. Access Prentice Hall's *America: Pathways to the Present* site at **www.Pathways.phschool.com** for the specific URL to complete the activity. Additional resources and related Web sites are also available.

Organize two debate teams. Furnish one with the Global Trade Watch anti-NAFTA report and the other with the Executive Summary from the U.S. Trade Representative site. Have teams use the data provided to debate the success of NAFTA.

U.S. Foreign Policy in the Western Hemisphere

Monroe Doctrine	Dollar Diplomacy	Good Neighbor Policy	NAFTA
• Anti-colonialism • Pro-democracy • Trade encouraged	• Regional stability promoted • United States corporate investment • Military enforcement of stability		

INTERNET ACTIVITY

Teams should demonstrate a thorough understanding of the contents of their reports, and support their positions with specific facts and quotes. Debates should be well-organized and compelling.

 (CD-ROM REVIEW)

The major concepts of Chapter 40 are presented in *Guide to the Essentials of American History* and *Interactive Student Tutorial CD-ROM,* which contains interactive review activities, time lines, and test practice for Chapter 40.

Key Terms
1. NAFTA, see p. 1040
2. tariff, see p. 1040
3. trade deficit, see p. 1041
4. trade surplus, see p. 1041
5. Helms-Burton Act, see p. 1042
6. Monroe Doctrine, see p. 1043
7. Roosevelt Corollary, see p. 1043
8. Good Neighbor Policy, see p. 1043
9. *maquiladora,* see p. 1044

Creating a Time Line
10. Time lines should include the Monroe Doctrine, the Spanish-American War, and the Roosevelt Corollary.

Portfolio Activity
11. Presentations should demonstrate creativity, careful reasoning, and a thoughtful approach to the issue.

Internet Activity
12. See below.

Using Graphic Organizers
13. Answers will vary. Sample answers may include: Good Neighbor Policy—Encourage trade by lowering tariffs; lend money to Latin American governments; oppose corrupt and Communist dictators. NAFTA—remove all tariffs and trade obstructions in 15 years; pro-growth, pro-investment for the region's economy; support Mexican stability through economic growth; fears of regulatory leveling.

Objectives

Help students to describe the new challenges brought by the end of the cold war, understand the philosophies and events that have guided American foreign policy since the 1790s, and identify the arguments for and against maintaining defense commitments to other nations.

Bellringer

Ask students to name some countries in the news. Where are those countries? What events are taking place there? How, if at all, do those events involve the United States?

Reading Strategy

Predicting Content Ask students to skim the chapter, list the main headings and subheadings, and write a sentence or phrase that predicts the content under each one. Then have them test their predictions against the content.

LESSON PLAN

Connecting to the Main Idea

1. Focus Recall that for some 50 years the United States dealt with the rest of the world mainly in terms of whether they were "with us" or "with them"—the Soviet Union. With the end of the cold war, what did people hope for?

2. Instruct Discuss the changes that have occurred in the world since the collapse of the Soviet Union in late 1991. Which had the most troubling effects on the United States? Ask students to consider whether military superiority is the only way the United States can maintain its position as a superpower.

3. Close The end of the cold war removed the issue that had been the focus of American foreign policy and began a debate about the country's future role in the world.

INTRODUCING THE THEME

From Theodore Roosevelt's "big stick diplomacy" to Ronald Reagan's talk of the Soviet Union as an "evil empire," the question has remained the same: What role should the United States play in the world? Since the end of the cold war, America's role as a world leader has continued to be a source of debate. While some argue that the United States should end the foreign alliances forged during the cold war, others argue that the United States must always maintain a leadership position in world affairs.

 DEBATE

What should be the American role in world affairs now that the cold war is over?

KEY TERMS

cold war,
Truman Doctrine,
NATO, Warsaw Pact

VIEWING THE PRESENT

In Woodside, California, Stephen Shapiro slices vegetables for a Malaysian gourmet dinner he's preparing. Shapiro was formerly an equipment operator in the Missile and Space Division of Lockheed Corporation, one of the nation's leading weapons manufacturers. Shapiro was laid off after Lockheed began receiving fewer and fewer government contracts. Now he works as a cook in an artists' colony.

Some 3,000 miles away, in Valley Forge, Pennsylvania, Sally Kain looks out her office window at a crab apple tree she planted in a company ceremony in 1971. Employed for the past 28 years by Martin Marietta Corporation, another major weapons producer, Kain is losing her job as well. Her layoff is one part of a company-wide reorganization announced after Lockheed and Martin Marietta merged in 1995, creating a new company called Lockheed Martin.

The Defense Boom Busts

Shapiro and Kain are two unlikely victims of the end of a decades-long conflict between the United

During the cold war the United States built an enormous military force to defend itself against the Soviet Union.

 ### RESOURCE OPTIONS

Teaching Resources

Reproducible Lesson Plan Lesson Plans folder, p. 182

Learning Styles Lesson Plan Learning Styles Lesson Plans folder, p. 79

Big Idea Graphic Organizer Big Idea Graphic Organizer folder, p. 154

Guided Reading and Review Unit 11 folder, p. 28

Media and Technology

Color Transparencies Cause-and-Effect, F-7, F-8, F-10

One of the roles the United States played during the 1990s was that of peacekeeper. United States troops were sent to Somalia in 1993 to distribute truckloads of food and other vital supplies in the famine stricken East African nation. *Economics* What role did the cold war play in the defense industry?

States and the Soviet Union. The two superpowers never actually fought each other on the battlefield. This was a **cold war,** marked by the buildup of arms and armies for use, if necessary, in "hot" combat. The United States spent billions each year on defense—as much as $300 billion a year by the late 1980s. Companies that made weapons thrived.

As cold war tensions began to ease, defense spending fell. Defense contractors reacted in three ways. First, they laid off workers. Employment in airplane manufacturing,

for example, fell from around 905,000 to around 585,000 between 1989 and 1994. Lockheed cut more than 10,000 jobs in its San Francisco–area plants alone.

Second, defense contractors negotiated mergers and takeovers with their competitors. Stronger companies swallowed weaker ones, and troubled companies sought stability by growing larger. Combining companies made more job cuts necessary to eliminate duplication of services. The merger of Lockheed and Martin Marietta resulted in the closing of 12 plants

and the layoffs of 12,000 workers, some 7 percent of the companies' combined work force.

The defense contractors' third response to the budget cuts was to move into non-defense areas of production. They believed that companies less dependent on the size of the government's military budget would be more stable over the long run. Lockheed's Missiles and Space Division (Stephen Shapiro's former employer) worked on the Hubble space telescope. It also signed a large contract with Motorola to build a string of com-

RESOURCE OPTIONS

Media and Technology

RESOURCE◉PRO

Provides classroom management at your fingertips. Access all Teaching Resources material on CD-ROM. Includes Planning Express for extended class period lesson planning and Test Bank.

Our Times Multimedia Encyclopedia of the 20th Century CD-ROM Contains *The Columbia Encyclopedia* and over 2,500 images, charts, maps, and graphs. Provides an interactive time line with search capabilities. Teacher's guidebook with lesson plans is included.

ACTIVITY
HETEROGENEOUS GROUPS

Divide students into groups and have each one prepare a short illustrated report on one of the recent missions in which U.S. military forces have carried out military, humanitarian, or peacekeeping efforts, including (but not limited to) the Persian Gulf War, Operation Provide Comfort (Kurdish refugees), Haiti, Somalia, Bosnia, and Kosovo. Have them locate the country or countries on a map of the world. *(Enrichment)*

BACKGROUND

Isolationism

American isolationism reached a peak in the 1930s, when the mood of Congress supported "Fortress America." One congressman, for example, predicted that a state visit by the king and queen of England would return America to colonial status. When President Franklin D. Roosevelt suggested a global "quarantine" of aggressors (meaning Germany and Japan), people protested heatedly. In 1938 an Indiana congressman introduced a bill requiring Congress to get majority approval in a nationwide referendum before declaring war. Though a poll suggested that 73 percent of Americans supported this idea, it never passed the House of Representatives.

munications satellites. Still, more than half of Lockheed Martin's sales come from defense contracts, which have declined significantly since their peak in the late 1980s.

Future Security
The health of the defense industry changes with the size of the military budget. In the same way, the size of the military budget changes with the extent of threats to American security. Cuts in the military budget have taken place because the collapse of the Soviet Union eliminated the most dangerous rival of the United States and ended the cold war.

Now the world, like the American defense industry, is in a state of transition. Will the next century be more dangerous, less dangerous, or simply dangerous in a different way from the cold war era? How will the United States deal with this new world? These questions lie at the heart of the present debate over the future of American foreign policy.

George Washington advised in his Farewell Address in 1796, "The great rule of conduct for us in regard to foreign nations is, in extending our commercial relations, to have with them as little political connection as possible." In other words, while trade with other nations would benefit Americans, entanglements in foreign conflicts could only threaten American democracy.

Most American leaders of the 1800s followed Washington's advice. Events during the first half of the twentieth century, however, changed that policy. The United States felt compelled to enter into foreign wars, permanent alliances, and involvement around the globe.

World War I
Millions of Americans had ties to the nations involved in World War I. Yet when the war started in 1914, most Americans wanted to stay out of it, just as they had stayed out of earlier European conflicts.

About 2 million American soldiers served "Over There" in World War I. The use of poisonous gases as weapons forced soldiers to wear masks such as this.

For three years the United States remained neutral. Still, the government and a majority of the people sympathized more with Britain and France than with Germany. German submarine attacks on American ships inflamed American anger at Germany. In 1917 those attacks drew the United States into the war on the side of Britain and France.

American soldiers helped turn back the last great German offensive in 1918. By November 1918, Germany was ready to sign an armistice.

Having played a key role in the war, the United States was in a position to help shape Europe's future. President Woodrow Wilson looked forward to a strong American presence in the League of Nations, the newly created international peacekeeping body. Still, the war had not converted Americans to the cause of global involvement. Americans worried that the League might dictate American foreign policy and even drag the United States into future European wars.

In 1919 the United States Senate rejected American participation in the League of Nations. For the next two decades the United States returned to its eighteenth-century approach to foreign policy. It would seek trading partners around the world while avoiding political entanglements.

World War II
The American people opposed involvement in World War II at first, just as they had in World War I. The United States had entered World War I with the goal of creating lasting peace in Europe. Many Americans saw the outbreak of World War II in 1939 as proof that no good could come of American participation in European wars. Nor did Americans favor war

RESOURCE OPTIONS

Teaching Resources

 Literature Activity Toward a New Century, Unit 11 folder, pp. 31–32

American Literature

Connections to American Literature Colin Powell, *My American Journey*

Media and Technology

 Decision America Videotapes and Videodiscs Issue 6 *A New Role for the Military?*

against Japan, despite Japanese aggression in East Asia.

Congress reflected the people's desire to keep out of the war. In August 1941, for example, a proposal to extend the service of Army draftees passed the House of Representatives by only one vote.

That attitude changed in a single day. On December 7, 1941, Japanese war planes attacked the American naval base at Pearl Harbor, Hawaii. Shocked and angered, Americans of all backgrounds rallied in defense of their nation and the Congress declared war. Three days later the other Axis powers—Germany and Italy—declared war on the United States.

To a far greater degree than World War I, World War II was a global war. Involvement in that war helped make the United States a truly global power. American troops, alongside Allied troops from Britain and Russia, fought battles from the Philippines to Morocco to France. American ships confronted German U-boats in the North Atlantic and Japanese aircraft carriers in the South Pacific. American bombers and supply planes crossed tens of thousands of miles of land and sea.

The war ended with an Allied victory in 1945. The United States now had the power to shape events nearly everywhere on the globe. It had done more than any other nation to defeat the Axis powers, and its economy was bigger than that of all other nations combined. Finally, only the United States possessed the awesome

The Japanese attack on Pearl Harbor pushed American sentiment in favor of entering World War II (below). Photographer Joe Rosenthal's study of victorious marines hoisting the American flag on the Pacific island of Iwo Jima (above) is one of the most famous photographs of the war. *Geography How did involvement in World War II help make the United States a global power?*

destructive power of the atomic bomb.

All these factors meant that the United States would not return to a policy of isolationism, as it had after World War I. Like Wilson, President Franklin Roosevelt set out to create an international peacekeeping body, to be called the United Nations. He wanted the United States to be a strong member, and this time most Americans agreed.

The Cold War

Between 1945 and 1950 the United States and Soviet Union changed from wartime allies to bitter rivals. As a result, a new American foreign policy took shape. The Communist government of the Soviet Union was aimed at world conquest, American leaders said, and only the United States had the

strength to lead the free world against it. From roughly 1947 to 1991, the cold war was the centerpiece of American foreign policy.

In 1947 President Harry Truman announced a bold new foreign policy. Known as the **Truman Doctrine,** this policy committed the United States to defend "free peoples who are resisting attempted subjugation by armed minorities or by outside pressures." The United States, in other words, would intervene wherever communism threatened to expand.

Under this commitment, the United States helped create **NATO** (the North Atlantic Treaty Organization), and promised to defend Western Europe against attack. The United States also signed agreements with other allies, such as Japan, and made large commitments to small and distant countries that faced a Communist threat.

Wars in Korea and Vietnam

Twice in Asia, the United States joined wars within divided nations to stop the spread of communism. In Korea, American forces rushed to defend South Korea after an invasion by Communist North Korea in 1950. Three years of bloody fighting brought stalemate on the battlefield and frustration within the United States. Still, American intervention had saved South Korea.

The United States would not manage to save South Vietnam. Despite American military involvement from 1961 to 1973, Communist North Vietnam overran South Vietnam and reunified the country in 1975.

The Vietnam War cost the United States some 58,000 lives and more than $150 billion. It also convinced most Americans that the United States should reduce its foreign commitments. The United States, more and more Americans argued, could not afford to be what some called "the world's policeman."

The Collapse of Communism

Whether and when to intervene in foreign countries remained controversial issues throughout the 1970s and 1980s. Americans still feared Communist expansion. But they

The Vietnam Women's Memorial in Washington, D.C.

did not think that they alone could, or should, fight it.

American defense spending declined after the Vietnam War, but then rose sharply in the 1980s under President Ronald Reagan. Reagan won election in 1980 on a promise of a stronger anti-Soviet policy. Americans supported the defense increases but remained wary of military intervention abroad.

During the late 1980s Americans began to question their commitment to the cold war, with its huge defense budgets. At the same time the list of America's cold war enemies began to shrink. One by one the nations of Eastern Europe, fed up with the brutalities and inefficiencies of communism, rejected their Communist leaders.

The Soviet Union tried to hold itself together in the face of this rejection of communism. Mikhail Gorbachev, who became leader of the Soviet Union in 1985, tried to improve the Soviet system. But his reforms only quickened the pace of communism's decline. On December 31, 1991, the Soviet Union officially ceased to exist. The cold war was over.

DEBATING THE FUTURE

E-mail messages raised the spirits of American troops stationed in Bosnia in 1996. A student in the 6th grade in Melbourne, Florida, wrote, "I would like to thank you for putting your life on the line for our country." From Jackson, Mississippi, came this message: "Being a Vietnam vet, I know how hard it is being away from family and friends." Another American wrote, "It seems that having U.S. troops abroad has become a traditional part of the holiday season. Please know that we miss you guys and are proud of the commitment that you have made to serve your country. . . . Hurry Home!"

While these letters used the new technology of the Internet, they contained a message that is as old as American commitments abroad. Americans are proud of their country's global role. Yet they also hope that Americans serving overseas will soon be able to return home.

As you have read, during the cold war the United States promised to protect other countries in case of attack. To meet these many foreign commitments, the United States spent hundreds of billions of dollars each year on defense. As the nation approaches the next century, it must confront two basic foreign-policy questions:

1. Now that the Soviet Union has collapsed, what are the benefits to the United States of maintaining its foreign commitments?
2. Now that the national debt has skyrocketed and other nations have become stiff trading competitors, can the United States afford the high cost of its foreign commitments?

Benefits of Foreign Commitments

Some foreign-policy analysts argue that the United States should cancel cold war–era alliances such as NATO and defense treaties with other nations, including Japan and South Korea. "It is time to recognize that with the disintegration of the Soviet Union, the mission of America's cold war alliances has been accomplished," writes Ted Galen Carpenter, a foreign-policy analyst at a research organization called the Cato Institute.

NATO, for example, was created to defend Western Europe against attack by the Soviet Union and the Eastern European countries

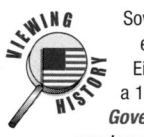

Soviet and American leaders Khrushchev and Eisenhower balanced on a 1959 *Newsweek* cover. *Government* How did cold war tensions influence American foreign policy?

under its influence. The danger increased when those Communist countries became allies under the **Warsaw Pact** in 1955.

Carpenter and others point out that the nations that once made up the Warsaw Pact are now joining NATO rather than attacking it. Recently, three former Soviet allies: Poland, the Czech Republic, and Hungary accepted membership into the organization. Also, for the first time, Russian ground combat troops joined a NATO peacekeeping exercise. Russia, NATO's long-time foe joined the Partnership for Peace, a NATO program designed to ensure security throughout Europe. There is no reason, critics like Carpenter argue, to defend Western Europe against an enemy that no longer exists. Thus, the NATO alliance is unnecessary.

Many analysts disagree with this assessment. Some believe that NATO's role should change from that of a strictly military organiza-

tion to one that can help solve global crises. Others prefer to keep the alliance focused on military defense.

Former President Richard Nixon favored keeping NATO a military alliance. In his book *Seize the Moment: America's Challenge in a One-Superpower World*, he also warned of any withdrawal from our global responsibilities:

AMERICAN VOICES **"**For many on the American left and right, the knee-jerk response to the decline of the Soviet Union . . . is to withdraw into a new isolationism. But in fact American world leadership will be indispensable in the coming decades. . . . The real world revolves not around wishful thinking about 'peace breaking out all over' but around the enduring realities of geopolitics. . . . In a world of competing states, clashing interests and national conflicts are inevitable.**"**

—*Richard Nixon*

Put most simply, Nixon's point is that nations will always need friends because they will always have enemies. Although the collapse of the Soviet Union removed the chief rival of the United States, Nixon argued, other rivals will surely emerge. The United States will need the help of allies against those new rivals. As Caspar Weinberger, who was Secretary of Defense under President Reagan, wrote:

AMERICAN VOICES **"**Clearly, no nation is strong enough alone to keep its own freedom. Every nation requires alliances, friendships or associations of one kind or another with other countries who share its goals and ideals.**"**

—*Caspar Weinberger*

Using the Internet

Create a Time Line

Objective Use the Internet to create a time line on the roles of the United States and the United Nations in the war in the former Yugoslavia. Have students follow these instructions:

1. See the *America: Pathways to the Present* Web site at

http://www.Pathways.phschool.com

for the URL of CNN's "Mission: Peace" page.

2. Use links to explore the history of the conflict in the former Yugoslavia.

3. Take notes on United States and United Nations involvement in the Bosnian crisis.

4. Create an annotated time line of significant events in the crisis. Highlight events in which the United States and United Nations played a role. Include in your notes your opinion on whether the United States and the UN should always be involved in the peace process.

TEST PREPARATION

Have students read the quotation by Richard Nixon on this page and then answer the question below.

The term *knee-jerk response* in the passage means—

(A) an automatic reaction.

B a surprising reaction.

C a thoughtful reaction.

D a worried reaction.

Answer to . . .

Viewing History They shaped American policy on increased defense spending, and influenced the Truman Doctrine, the formation of NATO, and American decisions to get involved in wars.

Customize for
Less Proficient Readers

Ask students to write short answers to these questions, based on information in the chapter:
• What was the cold war, and what brought it to an end?
• What was American foreign policy during the Reagan and Bush administrations?
• Why do some people think the United States should end its defense commitments to other nations?

ACTIVITY
EXTENDED CLASS PERIODS

Time: 90 minutes.
Activity: Prepare guidelines for future policies in various world regions as members of a State Department advisory team.
Grouping: Groups of four students.
Purpose: To prepare policy guidelines for five world regions: Eastern Europe, the Middle East, southern Africa, Central America, East Asia. Guidelines should include a brief overview of countries in the region, trouble spots, past policies, and current recommendations.
Roles: Policy advisers, note takers, writers, reporters.
Outcome: Students present oral reports demonstrating their understanding of world policy.

Answer to . . .

Viewing History It has opened a debate on whether to maintain foreign commitments and how to do so.

One of the most prominent symbols of the cold war was the barbed wire and concrete of the Berlin Wall. Shown here is the celebration of the wall's destruction in 1989. *Government How has the end of the cold war influenced American foreign policy?*

Cost of Foreign Commitments

"Today there is not, as some argue, a single superpower, the United States," columnist William Pfaff wrote in the quarterly *Foreign Affairs.* "There are none." Pfaff and others claim that the United States, with a national debt of more than $5 trillion, is not wealthy enough to try to control world events.

The Cato Institute's Ted Galen Carpenter agrees. He writes, "We cannot afford to maintain alliances for the sake of having alliances." Carpenter continues:

AMERICAN VOICES ❝The NATO commitment alone cost American taxpayers more than $120 billion a year during the latter stages of the cold war. . . . Washington's obligation to defend Japan, South Korea, and other East Asian allies costs another $40 billion. . . .The United States currently spends nearly seven times as much on the military as does any other member of the [major] industrial powers. Indeed, it spends some 60 percent more than all of the other [major industrial] countries combined.❞

—*Ted Galen Carpenter*

A nation that faces serious domestic problems cannot afford this burden, Carpenter concluded. High American defense spending does not only take money away from domestic programs like education, Carpenter and others argue. It also enables trading competitors of the United States, such as Germany and Japan, to spend less on defense, because those countries can rely on American military protection.

A number of other analysts believe that the United States can indeed afford the cost of remaining a superpower. Caspar Weinberger, for example, writes that "the United States could obviously afford larger defense budgets, provided that sacrifices were made elsewhere." Former President Nixon argued that in the long run, reducing foreign commitments would cost the United States even more money than maintaining them:

AMERICAN VOICES ❝The security of our home in this . . . interdependent world is affected by changes everywhere. Walking away from global challenges will carry a dangerous price. History may once again produce nations aspiring to regional or global dominance. . . . With imports and exports comprising over 20 percent of our economy, our prosperity depends on international stability.❞

—*Richard Nixon*

The Debate Continues

The questions outlined here have no simple or permanent answers. The United States' need for foreign commitments is influenced by events around the world. These can create or remove threats to American security almost overnight. The ability of the United States to afford foreign commitments depends on the continually changing health of the American economy. Each generation of Americans, therefore, must decide for itself the role its nation will play in the world.

Key Terms

1. cold war
2. Truman Doctrine
3. NATO
4. Warsaw Pact

Portfolio Activity

6. Decide which point of view on foreign policy you generally agree with. Then choose a way to express it: a magazine or newspaper article, a poster or cartoon, a letter to your representatives in Congress, an editorial, or some other format acceptable to your teacher.

Creating a Time Line

5. To see this chapter in context, construct a time line showing 6 to 12 major events of the twentieth century that had an important impact on American foreign policy.

INTERNET ACTIVITY

For your portfolio:
PREPARE A SUMMARY

7. Access Prentice Hall's *America: Pathways to the Present* site at **www.Pathways.phschool.com** for the specific URL to complete the activity. Additional resources and related Web sites are also available.

Use the State Department links to read about "Hot Topics" in U.S. foreign policy. Select a topic and summarize current policy. What is the issue? Why is the United States concerned? What is the government's official stance on the issue?

Using Graphic Organizers

8. Review the arguments in the Debating the Future section of the chapter. Then fill in the blank webs in the graphic organizer below. This web diagram shows the connection between various issues and arguments that have affected United States foreign policy in the years after the cold war. Copy the diagram on a separate sheet of paper.

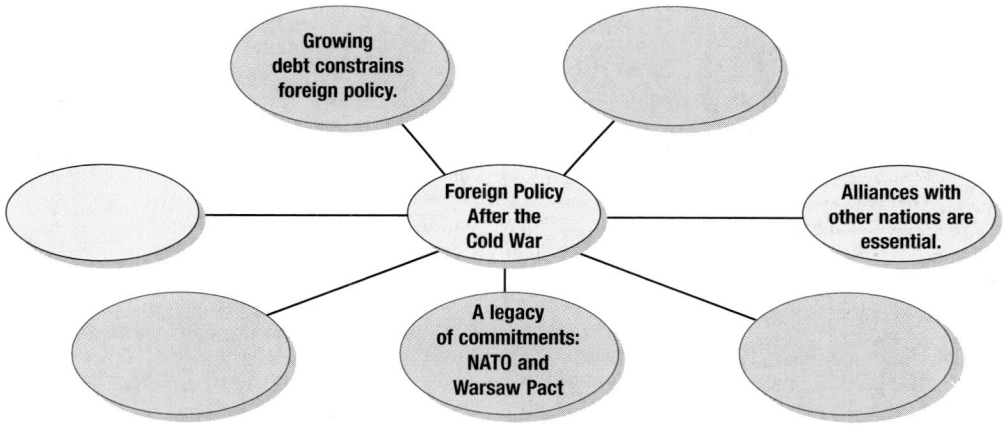

INTERNET ACTIVITY

Summaries will vary, but should reflect an understanding of the issue, and clearly articulate the position of the United States.

The major concepts of Chapter 41 are presented in *Guide to the Essentials of American History* and *Interactive Student Tutorial CD-ROM,* which contains interactive review activities, time lines, and test practice for Chapter 41.

Key Terms
1. cold war, see p. 1049
2. Truman Doctrine, see p. 1051
3. NATO, see p. 1052
4. Warsaw Pact, see p. 1053

Creating a Time Line
5. Time lines should include World War I, World War II, the Korean War, the Vietnam War, and the cold war.

Portfolio Activity
6. Presentations should demonstrate creativity and a thoughtful approach to the issue.

Internet Activity
7. See below.

Using Graphic Organizers
8. Answers will vary, but should reflect an understanding of the role of the United States in world affairs. Sample answers may include: Maintaining a large defense budget gives trading competitors an advantage; The cold war threat has ended; Defense can cause economic difficulties; New threats may emerge in formerly Communist areas of the world.

CHAPTER 42 Technology and You in the Next Century

Objectives
Help students to understand the trends of globalization, transition from a manufacturing to a service economy, and computer networking; describe the development of the computer age; and identify the arguments for and against more emphasis on computers in schools.

Bellringer
Ask students to describe when they most recently came into contact with computer technology. Remind them of not-so-obvious sources such as store scanners. How often during a single day do they use computer technology?

Reading Strategy
Structured Overview Ask students to skim the chapter for key terms and concepts. Then have them create an outline using the main headings and subheadings as they read.

LESSON PLAN
Connecting to the Main Idea

1. Focus Point out that rapidly changing technology is influencing almost everyone, every day, everywhere. While some of these changes are desirable, there is debate about whether all of them are necessary. Ask why the Internet has become a controversial issue.

2. Instruct Discuss the interplay of three trends in American society and industry: globalization, the change from a manufacturing base to an information base, and the importance of computer networks. Ask students to suggest ways in which these trends affect them.

3. Close Computer technology has brought profound changes in all aspects of American life, including education. Its role in schools is still a question for debate.

INTRODUCING THE THEME

Technological advances have changed the face of America many times. The cotton gin made possible the rise of King Cotton. Following the Bessemer steelmaking process came the expansion of the railroads and the rise of modern industry. The automobile revolutionized not only how people traveled, but also where they lived and how they spent their time. The computer, however, may prove to be the most impressive technological advance of them all.

DEBATE

How can schools best prepare students to use and take advantage of the technology of the next century?

KEY TERMS

e-mail, globalization, modem, telecommunications, software, productivity, automation, World Wide Web

VIEWING THE PRESENT

"**B**uy American," the principal told the school librarian, so she ordered a computer from a California company. Yet when she opened the boxes, she was surprised. She found a monitor made in Japan, a mouse made in China, a keyboard manufactured in Mexico from American parts, and a computer assembled in Taiwan. The memory chips were from Malaysia, the floppy disk drive from Korea, and the hard disk drive, central processing unit, and power supply from the United States.

It took many countries to create this finished product. It also took many computers to deliver it.

To order this computer, the librarian sent a fax to a dealer. The dealer's computerized inventory system noted the sale and kept track of how many more computers to buy.

Each month the dealer places orders by electronic mail, or **e-mail,** with the computer's California manufacturer. From the company's computerized order department, the information goes electronically to the billing department, the shipping department, and also the manufacturing department. There, computers automatically tally the demand and send orders to each of the suppliers in Asia. With computers talking to computers, this information can travel within the company and halfway around the globe in seconds.

The Global Economy

How typical is this computer use for the average American product? It is more typical than you might think. It illustrates an economic trend called **globalization.** This refers to a system of producing and selling goods that involves many countries. It also highlights the increasing importance of computer networks.

Reflecting this trend, administrators at Boeing, an American aerospace company, advertised, "It takes the entire world to pay our bills. . . . 70% of all our airplanes are sold outside the U.S." Foreign trade, which includes the exporting and importing of all kinds of goods, occupies a larger and larger position in the American economy.

▶ RESOURCE OPTIONS

Teaching Resources

📁 **Reproducible Lesson Plan** Lesson Plans folder, p. 183

📁 **Learning Styles Lesson Plan** Learning Styles Lesson Plans folder, p. 80

📁 **Big Idea Graphic Organizer** Big Idea Graphic Organizer folder, p. 155

📁 **Guided Reading and Review** Unit 11 folder, p. 33

As the computer example shows, the Asian countries of the Pacific Rim have become important trading partners of the United States. The computer also illustrates another side of globalization: the blurring of national boundaries in making products. Says Jeffrey Garten, dean of the Yale School of Management, "An increasing number of the goods we make are composed of both foreign and American components, and multinational companies, with plants all over the world, are responsible for an increased portion of international trade."

American companies not only buy foreign parts but also own factories in other countries. For example, Ford makes cars on every continent except Antarctica. Likewise, foreign companies like Honda build their cars in the United States. In some places, such as the NUMMI plant in Fremont, California, foreign and domestic companies team up to manufacture cars.

Shift to Service Jobs

Why are American companies buying foreign parts and building factories overseas? One reason is lower labor costs. Since the 1970s foreign countries such as Japan and Korea have been able to sell their products in the United States at lower prices than American products. To be competitive, American companies have had to reduce their costs, the largest of which is labor. So they have looked around the world for places with cheaper labor. As a result, more and more traditional manufacturing jobs have left the United States for other countries.

Meanwhile, service industries have grown strong in the American economy. Gaining importance within the service sector are jobs

Computers have made many tasks easier. Students often use computers in classrooms and libraries for research projects. They also use computers at home for both school projects and for their own entertainment. *Culture How are e-mail and the Internet likely to influence American culture?*

that involve managing information. Think of what happened when the librarian ordered the computer. Workers in California handled the flow of information that generated the bill, directed shipping, regulated the supply of parts, and determined levels of production. Most of the manufacturing was done abroad. Still, it was American engineers, highly skilled and well paid, who had designed these complex computer systems.

As the economies of the world grow more interconnected, countries are starting to specialize in what they do well. Countries with low labor costs are specializing in manufacturing, while the United States is specializing in managing information. For example, large American corporations with plants around the world still centralize their accounting in the United States.

Computer Networks

What makes these two trends possible is the widespread use of computer networks. A network enables one computer to send information to another through a central computer called a server. Although a single computer can store massive amounts of data, it is much more valuable when it can share data with other computers. Some businesses and schools have local area networks that link their computers. As a result, they can exchange data and e-mail.

Picture a network linking computers around the world. This is the Internet. The Internet is a global network that connects computers by sending electronic information from one to another. Most of this information travels over telephone wires, but it also can follow television cables or even travel as radio waves. Each computer needs a device called a **modem** to transmit its data.

The Internet makes it possible to use a computer to conduct research all over the world. It also makes it possible for anyone to send and receive information instantly.

Using this global computer network is a prime example of **telecommunications,** which is the sending of information over long distances. Says one California executive, "A modern company operating globally can't do anything without telecommunications."

For example, his company uses workers on opposite sides of the globe to prepare a new computer product. The company has computer programmers in India writing **software**—instructions telling the computer what to do. At the end of the day, the programmers can send their work via the Internet to California to be tested. While the programmers are sleeping, technicians half a world away test the program and send it back over the Internet, in time for the next workday in India.

Computers and Education

In this increasingly high-tech world, schools face the question of how best to prepare students for the next century. How much should they use computers to teach? How much should they teach students about using computers? Or should schools concentrate on traditional writing, computation, and thinking skills? Computers are, after all, only as smart as the people using them.

Some people argue that computers are the answer to preparing America's students for the future. But are they really?

REVIEWING THE PAST

The computer has brought American society to the turning point of a new age. Yet it is only the latest in a series of inventions that have changed the way Americans live, work, and learn. The

Byte traffic into the ANS/NSFNET T3 backbone (Dec. '94)
0   1 trillion
Copyright 1996 Donna Cox and Robert Patterson

Not only do computers have the power to do many complex operations at lightning speed, they can also share the information with other computers almost instantly. This telecommunications network map of the United States illustrates the idea. *Economics How have telecommunications helped bring about a global economy?*

automobile, electric power, and the telephone are probably the only other technologies that have had such a profound effect on American life.

Before the Industrial Revolution, the United States was a land of farmers and independent artisans. In today's terms, they would be considered "small-business people," owning their own tools and working for themselves. An artisan like Paul Revere would make his products in his own workshop, fashioning each piece of silver by hand from start to finish. Learning these skills took many years.

The Production Revolution

Making goods by machine began in the United States in 1793 when Samuel Slater built the first successful mill to spin cotton. Soon, New England had a number of factories to spin and weave cotton, each built beside a river.

Water powered the machines, and workers kept them running smoothly. Many of these workers were young women who had left small family farms to move near the factories. Unlike their mothers, who had to know all the steps of carding, spinning, and weaving wool to make cloth, these workers had to learn only one job: how to run their machine.

Manufacturing grew rapidly in the early 1800s, especially in the Northeast. In addition to textiles, factories turned out guns, shoes, and other goods. However, most American goods in this era were still made by skilled craftsworkers.

Not until the Civil War did industry really take off. After the war, cities grew rapidly as new factories attracted workers, both native-born and immigrant. In the 1870s and 1880s factories replaced workshops in the production of goods.

In this industrial transformation, workers no longer made all parts of a product. Instead, they performed only one step in the production process. Craftsworkers' skills learned through long years of apprenticeship were no longer needed. Industrial workers typically had to know only one task, and they learned it on the job.

Through his use of the assembly line, automobile maker Henry Ford ushered in the age of mass production. Now workers stood beside a moving conveyor belt to assemble a product. Each worker added one part, performing the same step over and over at a steady pace. This innovation greatly increased **productivity,** the amount of goods or services each worker produces in a given period of time.

Productivity grew even faster following World War II, with the coming of automation. **Automation** is the use of sophisticated machines in place of human labor. Automation is used in farming, mining, and manufacturing. In some cases a single worker, at the controls of such a machine, could now produce as many goods or services as 100 people had in the past.

Automation reduced the number of workers needed in manufacturing. More and more Americans turned to sales and service for employment. The service sector included not only jobs like auto

exploring TECHNOLOGY

A Textile Mill

Overhead shaft

Dressers

Looms

Spinning frames

Main shaft

Main drum

Mill wheel

Water flow

In the early 1800s, the textile mills of the Northeast had plenty of rivers and streams suitable for mill sites, busy ports for shipping, and an abundance of people in search of work. *Science and Technology How did the advent of factories change the nature of work?*

repair and dry cleaning but also office work. These jobs involved reading, writing, and calculating, which are skills learned in school rather than on the job. Tools that increased productivity among office workers included the typewriter and the telephone. But these improvements pale beside the achievements of the computer.

The Information Age

The workplace of the 1990s changed profoundly because of the computer. The American inspiration for it came not from a car factory or law office, but from the United States census. Herman Hollerith, an 1890 census agent, devised a time-saving machine that used punch cards to tabulate data.

By 1946, scientists had developed the Electronic Numerical Integrator and Computer, or ENIAC for short. ENIAC could do 5,000 addition problems per second. But its tremendous size and weight made it impractical for most uses.

Since ENIAC, transistors have replaced vacuum tubes, and computers have become much smaller, faster, and more sophisticated. In the 1960s and 1970s most computers in universities, businesses, and government offices were still just large calculating machines. Only a handful of people in any organization knew how to operate them. Some offices had a central computer, with connections to terminals beside a few workers' desks. But computer skills were limited to specially trained employees.

During the 1980s several breakthroughs in computer technology revolutionized the workplace. The first was the personal computer. After it appeared, early in the decade, millions of workers had a computer on their desk. Once they learned how to use it to write, calculate, and sort data, workers found that their productivity increased.

Another time-saver of the 1980s was the fax (facsimile) machine. The fax machine used computer technology to scan a page, turn its contents into electronic signals, and transmit them over telephone lines. Another fax machine received and decoded the electronic signals. An even faster way to send information was through computer networks, which were operating in many businesses by the end of the decade.

The Internet became the world's hottest telecommunications tool in the 1990s. Begun in the 1960s as a government project to link university science departments, the Internet grew to include millions of business, governmental, educational, and individual computers.

To help users find what they're looking for, the Internet has a system called the **World Wide Web.** Using software called a Web browser, users can retrieve electronic files to get information and use links to jump to related files.

Access to the Internet has spread to schools, businesses, libraries, homes, and even some cafés, where "Net-surfing" has replaced video games as a way to attract customers. With a global audience of millions, businesses scrambled to find ways to use the Internet.

Advances in Technology, 1775–Present

1793
Eli Whitney invents the cotton gin.

1775
James Watt perfects his invention of the steam engine.

1793
Samuel Slater builds first successful mill to spin cotton.

1876
Alexander Graham Bell invents the telephone.

1877
Thomas Edison invents the phonograph.

Industrial Revolution

Electric Age

A high school junior in a tiny town in Alaska is writing a term paper on the migration of gray whales. The nearest public library is more than a hundred miles away, but she is able to do research at school. Using a computer and modem, she browses the World Wide Web and within a few hours finds the most up-to-date information. Her teacher is very pleased with her paper, because her research far exceeded what the library has to offer.

At a high school in California, two seniors create a multimedia presentation on the stegosaurus for a geology assignment. They scan pictures into the computer, color them, and add sound clips downloaded from the Internet. While their presentation amuses their classmates, the teacher is not impressed. He says it's too little information dressed up in a flashy package.

How much do computers really add to a student's educational experience? Stories such as these fuel the debate over what place computer technology should have in school.

High-Tech Is the Answer

One of the most important jobs of the schools is to prepare students for work. Computer skills have become absolutely essential in the workplace, say advocates of educational technology. To support this position, they point to "What Work Requires of Schools," a 1991 report from the Department of Labor. The report states that understanding and applying technology and using computers to process information are essential requirements for workers.

1974
The first fax machine transmits one page in six minutes.

1983
The Federal Communications Commission issues a license for the first cellular phone system.

1984
Philips and Sony develop the compact disc read-only memory (CD-ROM)

1992
The World Wide Web is released by the European Laboratory for Particle Physics.

1896
Henry Ford builds his first car.

1969
American astronauts complete the first moon walk.

Electronic Age

Information Age

Using the Internet

Write a Report

Objective Use the Internet to research current technology initiatives of the United States Department of Education. Have students follow these instructions:

1. See the *America: Pathways to the Present* Web site at

http://www.Pathways.phschool.com

for the URL of the U.S. Department of Education.

2. Access the links under "The Technology Literacy Challenge. . . " for background information on the department's goals. Research at least three government initiatives to promote technology literacy. Take notes.

3. Create a report that outlines the initiatives you chose. Include information on the status of the programs; an analysis of the initiatives in your report, describing whether you think the programs are or will be effective; and one idea of your own that would promote technology literacy.

RESOURCE OPTIONS

Teaching Resources

Debating the Future Should Funding Technology Be a Priority?, Unit 11 folder, pp. 34–35

Colleges have already recognized the importance of computer skills. Some even require freshmen to bring their own computer to school with them.

Like today's mechanic who analyzes a car's problems electronically instead of poking around under the hood, more and more jobs of the future will rely on computers. In fact, the three fastest-growing occupations are in computer-related fields, according to the Labor Department. Labor economist Audrey Freedman says:

AMERICAN VOICES ❝The jobs that are being created are computer-using jobs. They're service, white-collar types of work.❞

—Audrey Freeman

Moreover, computer users earn more money than workers without computers in similar jobs—about 15 percent more in 1995. To prevent widening the gap between the rich and poor in this country, high-tech boosters argue, all students must learn how to use computers.

The ability to adapt to change is a key characteristic of the successful worker of the future. Computer skills provide that adaptability, supporters claim. They cite examples like Lizanne Gottung, a manager in a Connecticut factory. She says, "When we hire now, we're thinking about how easily a person can be trained to do different jobs." Mike Thomas, one of her employees, knows how adaptable workers need to be. "I'm an old dog who's adjusted to three product changes in the last year," he reports. He monitors computers that control production. Without his computer skills, he would have been out of a job.

Using computers and the Internet in schools not only prepares students for the future, advocates say, but also improves the quality of education. Computer-assisted learning gives students a chance to advance at their own pace. It gives them immediate feedback and the opportunity to repeat a lesson as many times as necessary. Computer programs such as word processing, spreadsheets, and databases let students write, calculate, and do research more efficiently than ever before. In addition, computers enable disabled students to complete many educational tasks that they could not perform in the past.

Computers with access to the Internet can connect students to a huge global pool of information. Says Jim Dunnigan, a high school teacher in Seattle, Washington:

In 1946, the University of Pennsylvania's Electronic Numerical Integrator and Computer (ENIAC) took up a huge room, weighed 30 tons, and had 17,000 vacuum tubes. *Science and Technology How has computer technology changed since 1946?*

FACT Finder **An Introduction to the Internet**

What is the Internet?	The Internet is a global network of computers that are linked together. It was set up as a government project to connect university science departments in the 1960s. Today individuals, businesses, schools, and many other groups use the Internet.
What is the World Wide Web?	The World Wide Web (WWW) is a group of electronic documents (called Web pages) and links that lead from one document to another. Documents on the Web can contain text, pictures, audio clips, and video clips.
Who uses the Web?	Millions of people use the Web every day. Hundreds of thousands of companies and individuals have Web sites, called home pages.
How do you get on the Web?	To get on the Web, you need a computer, a modem, and a computer application called a browser. The modem provides the link between your computer and the other computers on the Web. The browser helps you find and read Web pages.
What does the future hold?	Today people can do everything from grocery shopping to medical research on the Internet. Over time it will have even more uses. Almost any use you can think of for the Internet may someday become a reality. You could even be the one to make your idea come true.

Interpreting Tables Although the Internet is a product of fairly recent technology, use of the Internet skyrocketed during the 1990s. *Science and Technology* *What do you think will be the long-term significance of the Internet?*

AMERICAN VOICES "We have students in my school district who know no bounds to the classroom walls. They use electronic mail to talk with archaeologists in South America; they publish Civil War history research projects on the Internet; and they maintain e-mail correspondence with other students in the Czech Republic."

—*Jim Dunnigan*

Learning how to use computers and the Internet has enriched these students' education in ways that no one could have predicted. Students will be well prepared when they enter the increasingly global and increasingly computerized workplace. They will know how to find information and communicate internationally.

Good Teaching Is the Answer

Good teaching is far more important than electronic gadgets, say critics of computers in education. Clifford Stoll, an astrophysicist and one of the best-known critics of educational technology, describes the most important thing in a classroom:

AMERICAN VOICES "A good teacher interacting with motivated students. Anything else that separates them—filmstrips, instructional videos, multimedia displays, e-mail, TV sets, interactive computers—is of questionable educational value."

—*Clifford Stoll*

Stoll and others would have school districts spend their limited funds on more teachers rather than on computers.

Computer-assisted instruction sugarcoats the learning process, opponents argue. Learning takes hard work, concentration, and self-discipline. This calls for far more sustained effort than zapping an alien on a computer screen to get a correct answer. Critics argue that computer-assisted instruction promotes short attention spans among students rather than dedicated study and critical thinking skills.

Moreover, computer simulations are no substitute for real life. Students need to know how to conduct experiments and perform calculations in the real world, not just on the computer.

Those who favor a more traditional approach to education claim that students need basic skills more than computer skills. By focusing on technology, they say, computer lovers have missed the main point of the "What Work Requires of

 BACKGROUND

Interdisciplinary

Computer-generated imaging has brought new magic to movies and video, giving film animators a powerful new tool. To create the images of T-rex, velociraptors, and the other scary inhabitants of *Jurassic Park* and *Lost World,* animators used dinosaur models to draw wire mesh skeletal outlines that were recorded on a computer screen. The computer added color, shadow, texture, and other elements, and the dinosaur images were then processed into live-action scenes. Another software program created the dinosaurs' realistic movements. Filmmakers also have produced films entirely with computer animation. *Toy Story,* for example, won a Special Achievement Award from the Academy of Motion Picture Arts and Sciences.

TEST PREPARATION

Have students read the quotation by Clifford Stoll on this page and then answer the question below.

Stoll's main objection to educational technology is that—

A it cannot motivate students.

Ⓑ it limits teacher-student interaction.

C it is too difficult for many students.

D it causes students' attention to wander.

Answer to . . .

Interpreting Tables Sample answer: An increase in the speed and efficiency of communications should make the country and the world more interconnected.

Schools" report. The Labor Department report pays far more attention to other requirements, which call for fundamental academic skills, thinking skills, and personal qualities.

Critics of educational technology believe that emphasizing computer skills is not the best way to prepare students for the workplace. Even more than computer literacy, jobs of the future will require educated workers who can reason well, express themselves clearly, and work well with others.

Indeed, computer skills are easy to acquire and can be learned outside of school. Critics point out that computers can be found in many public libraries and in more than 40 percent of American households. Free time, they say, is better than school time for developing computer expertise. Moreover, school assignments that require high-tech delivery distract

students from the subject matter that they should be studying. Students end up spending more time using the software than they spend researching and thinking.

Turning students loose on the Internet to do research makes a lot of data available to them but gives them no organization or context for it, say opponents. It is also easy for students to download a file from the Internet and then cut and paste parts of it into their own work. Missing is any critical thought about the value of the source or any understanding of the true purpose of doing research.

The Debate Continues

Computers have become an essential part of American society, but their place in schools is still being determined. Some school systems are resisting the computer revolution. Many others are trying to deal

with it in a way that makes sound educational sense for their students.

A big challenge for schools will be to find the right balance between traditional teaching and new technology. This may mean limiting the role of the computer to tasks for which it is most useful. Alternately, it may mean adapting the computer to reinforce traditional skills. An even bigger challenge will be to find enough money to fund the new technology and all the changes that come with it.

Technology alone cannot solve the problems of education. The answer lies instead in studying the issues, communicating points of view, and working together to find solutions. As computers continue to play a larger role in daily life, we must ensure that everyone will be able to understand and use them. In this way the new technology can most effectively help people learn, communicate, and work together.

Using computers is a requirement in many colleges today. Computers are even more common in the workplace. *Diversity Why is equal access to computers for all students important?*

Key Terms

1. e-mail
2. globalization
3. modem
4. telecommunications
5. software
6. productivity
7. automation
8. World Wide Web

Portfolio Activity

10. From your experience and from the information in this chapter, decide what you think about how useful computers are and could be in schools. Then choose a way to express your point of view: a selection of magazine or newspaper articles, a poster or cartoon, a letter to the editor, or another format acceptable to your teacher. If possible, use a computer to prepare or present your project.

Using Graphic Organizers

12. The multiflow chart below gives an example of the ways that information travels today. On a separate sheet of paper, construct a similar chart to show how you might gather information from different sources to present a paper on why and how schools use computers.

Creating a Time Line

9. Using information in the Reviewing the Past section, construct a time line that shows the progress and changes in American technology. Include six to eight major developments, and be ready to explain why each step was important.

INTERNET ACTIVITY

For your portfolio:
WRITE AN ARTICLE

11. Access Prentice Hall's *America: Pathways to the Present* site at **www.Pathways.phschool.com** for the specific URL to complete the activity. Additional resources and related Web sites are also available.

Read about evaluating the quality of Internet resources. Write an article explaining how Internet resources differ from printed resources. Outline the necessity and methods of evaluating Web sites.

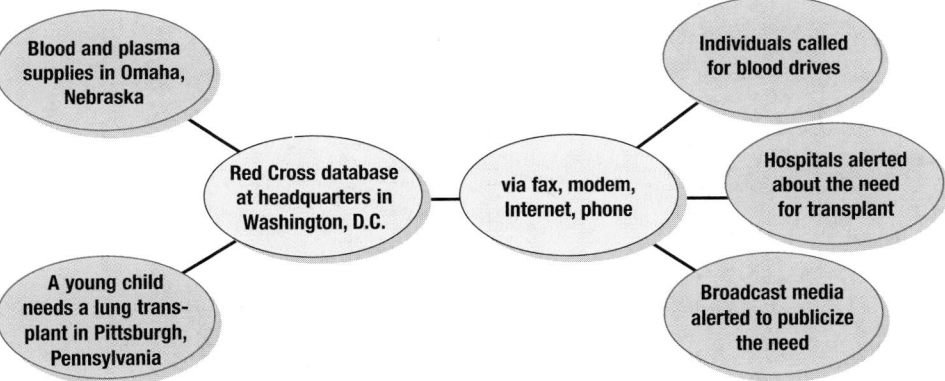

- Blood and plasma supplies in Omaha, Nebraska
- A young child needs a lung transplant in Pittsburgh, Pennsylvania
- Red Cross database at headquarters in Washington, D.C.
- via fax, modem, Internet, phone
- Individuals called for blood drives
- Hospitals alerted about the need for transplant
- Broadcast media alerted to publicize the need

INTERNET ACTIVITY

Articles will vary but should be supported with specific facts from the Web site and show a clear understanding of the issue.

The major concepts of Chapter 42 are presented in *Guide to the Essentials of American History* and *Interactive Student Tutorial CD-ROM,* which contains interactive review activities, time lines, and test practice for Chapter 42.

Key Terms

1. e-mail, see p. 1056
2. globalization, see p. 1056
3. modem, see p. 1057
4. telecommunications, see p. 1058
5. software, see p. 1058
6. productivity, see p. 1059
7. automation, see p. 1059
8. World Wide Web, see p. 1060

Creating a Time Line

9. Time lines should include Slater's mill, the rise of factories, Henry Ford's assembly line, the invention of automation, ENIAC, and telecommunications tools such as the fax, the computer, and the Internet.

Portfolio Activity

10. Presentations should demonstrate creativity and a thoughtful approach to the issue of computers in schools.

Internet Activity

11. See below.

Using Graphic Organizers

12. Students' charts will vary. Sample chart: (top left)—Library at State U. has valuable information; (bottom left)—regional school system headquarters has proposed plan for bringing computers to the schools; (middle left)—via fax, modem, Internet, phone; (middle right)—student's e-mail address or fax number; (top right)—paper turned in to teacher in classroom; (middle right)—paper published in local newspaper; (bottom right)—paper sent to regional school system headquarters.

Why Study History?
A Nation Looks Ahead

Your textbook began with a question: Why Study History? As you studied each chapter, you learned that there are many answers to this question. Most can be summed up in a simple statement: The people and events of the past have created the world in which we live today. You can understand your world only by understanding the people whose vision of the future shaped our society. To do this you must study history and engage in an active, imaginative journey into the past. Although the people you encounter on this journey may have spoken, thought, and dressed differently from you, they, like you, were motivated by universal concerns and a wish for a better future.

Today, Americans look forward to a new century with a sense of hope. We have tremendous resources to use as we help shape tomorrow's world. Among these resources are our system of government, our vision of the future, and, of course, our history.

Foremost of America's strengths is the nation's unique system of government, which allows Americans to face the future with confidence. Our representative democracy strikes a balance between the rights of the people and the responsibilities that are assigned to the government. The tone of our various national debates might sometimes be shrill, but the discussion itself is a testament to the power of democracy as a means of settling disputes.

Americans have always tried their best to work together. Although at times separated by race, religion, and culture, all have played a part in building a strong nation. Now, as we face the challenges of the future we look, as always, to the lessons of the past.

On January 6, 1941, President Franklin D. Roosevelt delivered a famous speech before both houses of Congress. In that speech President Roosevelt outlined what he hoped would be goals for all Americans:

There is nothing mysterious about the foundations of a healthy and strong democracy. The basic things expected by our people of their political and economic systems are simple. They are:

★ *Equality of opportunity for youth and for others.*

★ *Jobs for those who can work.*

★ *Security for those who need it.*

★ *The ending of special privilege for a few.*

★ *The preservation of civil liberties for all.*

★ *The enjoyment of the fruits of scientific progress in a wider and constantly rising standard of living.*

These are simple and basic things that must never be lost sight of in the turmoil and unbelievable complexity of the modern world. The inner and abiding strength of our economic and political systems is dependent upon the degree to which they fulfill these expectations. . . .

Americans have built a nation that is unique. It is unique in its diversity, its exciting opportunities, and the ability of its citizens to meet new challenges.

In the future days, which we seek to make secure, we look forward to a world founded upon four essential human freedoms.

THE FIRST IS FREEDOM OF SPEECH and expression everywhere in the world.

THE SECOND IS THE FREEDOM OF EVERY PERSON TO WORSHIP GOD in his own way everywhere in the world.

THE THIRD IS FREEDOM FROM WANT which, translated into world terms, means economic understandings which will secure to every nation a healthy peacetime life for its inhabitants everywhere in the world.

THE FOURTH IS FREEDOM FROM FEAR which, translated into world terms, means a worldwide reduction of armaments to such a point and in such a thorough fashion that no nation will be in a position to commit an act of physical aggression against any neighbor—anywhere in the world. . . . Since the beginning of our American history we have engaged in change—in perpetual peaceful revolution—a revolution which goes on steadily, quietly adjusting itself to changing conditions. . . .

Freedom means the supremacy of human rights everywhere. Our support goes to those who struggle to gain those rights or keep them. Our strength is in our unity of purpose.

—Franklin Delano Roosevelt

Reference Section

AMERICAN LITERATURE

SPANISH GLOSSARY

STOP THE PRESSES!

ILLUSTRATED DATA BANK

BIOGRAPHICAL DICTIONARY

INDEX

ACKNOWLEDGMENTS

SUPREME COURT CASES

GLOSSARY

Connections to American Literature

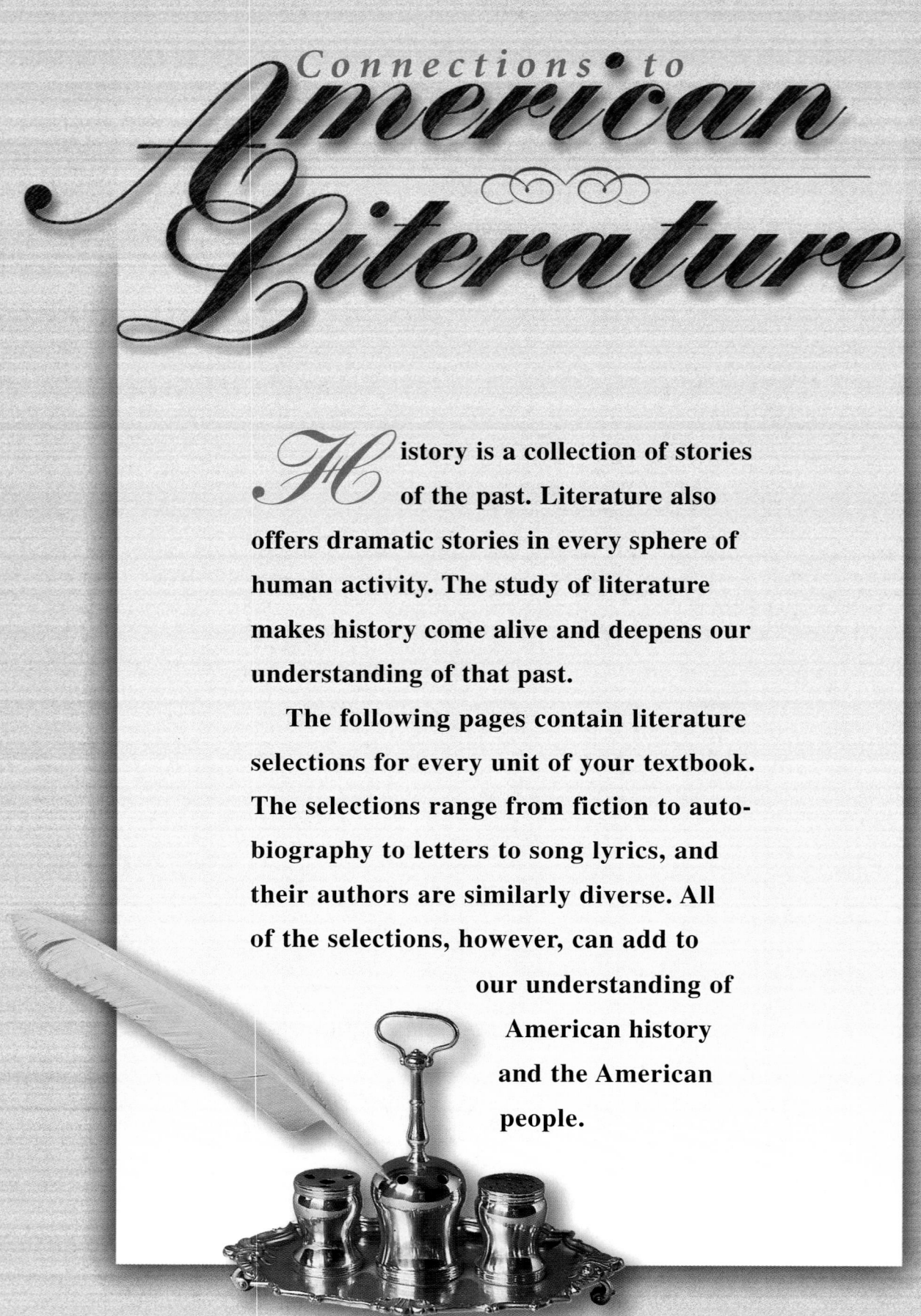

History is a collection of stories of the past. Literature also offers dramatic stories in every sphere of human activity. The study of literature makes history come alive and deepens our understanding of that past.

The following pages contain literature selections for every unit of your textbook. The selections range from fiction to autobiography to letters to song lyrics, and their authors are similarly diverse. All of the selections, however, can add to our understanding of American history and the American people.

American Literature

April Morning

Focus Have students read the Introduction and look up the meanings of the vocabulary words. Then explain that the excerpt from Howard Fast's *April Morning* dramatizes the tension of the Revolution by portraying the war's first battle through the eyes of a fictional young observer.

Instruct Ask students to recall facts about the Battles at Lexington and Concord based on their reading of Chapter 4. Then ask them to write a brief summary of the battles, labeled "historical writing." After students have read the selection, ask them to write another brief summary based on their reading, labeled "literary writing." Ask volunteers to read their summaries aloud. Discuss the differences between the two kinds of writing.

Extend Ask students to write the next chapter to *April Morning*, supposing that they are the boy in Fast's book. They should focus on the aftermath of the Battle at Lexington and draw on their knowledge of the events described in Chapter 4. Have volunteers read their chapters aloud to the class.

LITERATURE

April Morning
BY HOWARD FAST

INTRODUCTION The fighting at Lexington and Concord, Massachusetts, on April 19, 1775, marked the beginning of the American Revolution. In the following excerpt from his historical novel *April Morning*, Howard Fast captures the sights and sounds of the skirmish at Lexington Green.

VOCABULARY Before you read the selection, find the meaning of these words in a dictionary: *dissipate, jubilation*.

When the British saw us, they were on the road past Buckman's [Tavern]. First, there were three officers on horseback. Then two flag-bearers, one carrying the regimental flag and the other bearing the British colors. Then a corps of eight drums. Then rank after rank of the redcoats, stretching back on the road and into the curtain of mist, and emerging from the mist constantly, so that they appeared to be an endless force and an endless number. It was dreamlike and not very believable, and it caused me to turn and look at the houses around the common, to see whether all the rest of what we were, our mothers and sisters and brothers and grandparents, were watching the same thing we watched. My impression was that the houses had appeared by magic, for I could only remember looking around in the darkness and seeing nothing where now all the houses stood—and the houses were dead and silent, every shutter closed and bolted, every door and storm door closed and barred. Never before had I seen the houses like that, not in the worst cold or the worst storms.

And the redcoats did not quicken their pace or slow it, but marched up the road with the same even pace, up to the edge of the common; and when they were there, one of the officers held up his arm—and the drums stopped and the soldiers stopped, the line of soldiers stretching all the way down the road and into the dissipating mist. They were about one hundred and fifty paces from us.

The three officers sat on their horses, studying us. The morning air was cold and clean and sharp, and I could see their faces and the faces of the redcoat soldiers behind them, the black bands of their knapsacks, the glitter of their buckles. Their coats were red as fire, but their light trousers were stained and dirty from the march.

Then, one of the officers sang out to them, "Fix bayonets!" and all down the line, the bayonets sparkled in the morning sun, and we heard the ring of metal against metal as they were clamped onto the guns. . . .

British uniform jacket like those worn at Lexington

TEST PREPARATION

Have students use the excerpt on these pages to answer the following question.

On what date did the American Revolution begin?

A April 17, 1775

B April 18, 1775

C April 19, 1775

D April 17, 1776

Then another British officer—I discovered afterward that he was Major Pitcairn—called out orders: "Columns right!" and then, "By the left flank," and, "Drums to the rear!" The drummers stood still and beat their drums, and the redcoats marched past them smartly, wheeling and parading across the common, while the three mounted officers spurred over the grass at a sharp canter, straight across our front and then back, reining in their prancing horses to face us. Meanwhile, the redcoats marched onto the common, the first company wheeling to face us when it was past our front of thirty-three men, the second company repeating the exercise, until they made a wall of red coats across the common, with no more than thirty or forty paces separating us. Even so close, they were unreal; only their guns were real, and their glittering bayonets too—and suddenly, I realized, and I believed that everyone else around me realized, that this was not to be an exercise or a parade or an argument, but something undreamed of and unimagined.

I think the Reverend was beginning to speak when Major Pitcairn drove down on him so that he had to leap aside. My father clutched the Reverend's arm to keep him from falling, and wheeling his horse, Major Pitcairn checked the beast so that it pawed at the air and neighed shrilly. The Reverend was speaking again, but no one heard his words or remembered them. The redcoats were grinning; small, pinched faces under the white wigs—they grinned at us. Leaning over his horse, Major Pitcairn screamed at us:

"Lay down your arms . . . Disperse, do you hear me! Disperse, you lousy peasant scum! Clear the way, do you hear me! Get off the King's green!"

At least, those were the words that I seem to remember. Others remembered differently; but the way he screamed, in his strange London accent, with all the motion and excitement, with his horse rearing and kicking at the Reverend and Father, with the drums beating again and the fixed bayonets glittering in the sunshine, it's a wonder that any of his words remained with us.

Yet for all that, this was a point where everything appeared to happen slowly. Abel Loring clutched my arm and said dryly, "Adam, Adam, Adam." He let go of his gun and it fell to the ground. "Pick it up," I said to him, watching Father, who pulled the Reverend into the protection of his body. Jonas Parker turned to us and cried at us:

"Steady! Steady! Now just hold steady!"

We still stood in our two lines, our guns butt end on the ground or held loosely in our hands. Major Pitcairn spurred his horse and raced between the lines. Somewhere, away from us, a shot sounded. A redcoat soldier raised his musket, leveled it at Father, and fired. My father clutched at his breast, then crumpled to the ground like an empty sack and lay with his face in the grass. I screamed. I was two [persons]. One part of me was screaming; another part of me looked at Father and grasped my gun in aching hands. Then the whole British front burst into a roar of sound and flame and smoke, and our whole world crashed at us, and broke into little pieces that fell around our ears, and came to an end; and the roaring, screaming noise was like the jubilation of the damned.

I ran. I was filled with fear, saturated with it, sick with it. Everyone else was running. The boys were running and the men were running. Our two lines were gone, and now it was only men and boys running in every direction that was away from the British, across the common and away from the British.

ANALYZING LITERATURE

Use the passage on these pages to answer the following questions.

1. How did the British force at Lexington compare with the colonists' force?
A The two forces were roughly equal.
B The colonists' force was much larger.
C The British force was much larger.
D The mist made it impossible to compare the two forces.

2. What did the narrator mean by the use of such words as "dreamlike" and "unreal" to describe the events of that morning?
A He had not witnessed the events and was only imagining how they must have looked.
B He had arrived on the scene too late to understand what was happening.
C He was too young to understand what was happening.
D He had difficulty believing what was happening.

3. *Critical Thinking: Drawing Conclusions* Based on this account, what do you think caused the fighting at Lexington? Explain your answer.

Analyzing the Document

Use this additional question to generate class discussion:

CRITICAL THINKING: DEMONSTRATING REASONED JUDGMENT Do you think that the shooting and resulting death that occurred in Lexington was inevitable? *(Answers will vary. Students should point out that the British were provoking the colonists with their show of force and bravado.)*

Answers to . . .

Analyzing Literature
1. C
2. D
3. *The British taunted the colonists; a colonist fired a single shot and the British retaliated.*

Benjamin Franklin Campaigns for the Constitution

American Literature

Benjamin Franklin Campaigns for the Constitution

Focus Have students read the Introduction and look up the meanings of the vocabulary words. Then explain that the early days of the new United States government were filled with great uncertainty, with people not only from the United States but from around the world paying close attention to the proceedings. Point out that Benjamin Franklin's address to the delegates followed the close of the debates at the Constitutional Convention and the writing of the Constitution.

Instruct Ask a volunteer to read aloud Franklin's description of the President's chair at the end of the selection. When during the Convention might Franklin have viewed the carving as a setting sun? Why is he confident that he now sees a rising sun?

Extend Have groups of students create time lines of the events between the signing of the Treaty of Paris in 1783 and President Washington's inauguration in 1789. Suggest that they illustrate the various events with photocopied images or original drawings. Display the time lines in the classroom for students to use to review key events.

LITERATURE

INTRODUCTION "It is much easier to pull down a government . . . than to build up, at such a season as the present," wrote John Adams early in 1787. Yet on September 17, 1787, the completed Constitution of the United States was put before the delegates for their signatures. It was fitting that Benjamin Franklin, who for so long had been part of the revolutionary changes sweeping the nation, should rise at that point and give the delegates the benefits of his wisdom.

VOCABULARY Before you read the selection, find the meaning of these words in a dictionary: *sect, infallible, despotism, constituent, partisan, salutary, manifest, vicissitude.*

Monday, September 17, 1787: In Convention:

he engrossed [that is, formally written] Constitution being read, Doctor Franklin rose with a speech in his hand, which he had reduced to writing for his own conveniency, and which Mr. Wilson read in the words following.

Benjamin Franklin

Mr. President
I confess that there are several parts of this constitution which I do not at present approve, but I am not sure I shall never approve them: For having lived long, I have experienced many instances of being obliged by better information, or fuller consideration, to change opinions even on important subjects, which I once thought right, but found to be otherwise. It is therefore that the older I grow, the more apt I am to doubt my own judgment, and to pay more respect to the judgment of others. Most men indeed as well as most sects in Religion, think themselves in possession of all truth, and that wherever others differ from them it is so far error. Steele, a Protestant, in a Dedication tells the Pope that the only difference between our Churches in their opinions of the certainty of their doctrines is, the Church of Rome is infallible and the Church of England is never in the wrong. But though many private persons think almost as highly of their own infallibility as of that of their sect, few express it so naturally as a certain French lady, who in a dispute with her sister, said "I don't know how it happens, Sister but I meet with no body but myself, that's always in the right—*Il n'y a que moi qui a toujours raison.*"

In these sentiments, Sir, I agree to this Constitution with all its faults, if they are such; because I think a general Government necessary for us, and there is no form of Government but what may be a blessing to the people if well administered, and believe farther that this is likely to be well administered for a course of years, and can only end in Despotism, as other forms have done before it, when the people shall became so corrupted as to need despotic Government, being incapable of any other. I doubt too whether any other Convention we can obtain, may be able to make a better Constitution. For when you assemble a number of men to have the

TEST PREPARATION

Have students use the excerpt on these pages to answer the following question.

Why was Franklin willing to sign the Constitution?

A He thought that it was a perfect document.

Ⓑ He believed that despite its faults, it was the best document that could be produced.

C The Church of England is never in the wrong.

D It would only be approved if he signed it.

advantage of their joint wisdom, you inevitably assemble with those men, all their prejudices, their passions, their errors of opinion, their local interests, and their selfish views. From such an assembly can a perfect production be expected? It therefore astonishes me, Sir, to find this system approaching so near to perfection as it does; and I think it will astonish our enemies, who are waiting with confidence to hear that our councils are confounded like those of the Builders of Babel; and that our States are on the point of separation, only to meet hereafter for the purpose of cutting one another's throats. Thus I consent, Sir, to this

Philadelphia's Independence Hall, site of the Constitutional Convention

Constitution because I expect no better, and because I am not sure, that it is not the best. The opinions I have had of its errors, I sacrifice to the public good. I have never whispered a syllable of them abroad. Within these walls they were born, and here they shall die. If every one of us in returning to our Constituents were to report the objections he has had to it, and endeavor to gain partisans in support of them, we might prevent its being generally received, and thereby lose all the salutary effects & great advantages resulting naturally in our favor among foreign Nations as well as among ourselves, from our real or apparent unanimity. Much of the strength & efficiency of any Government in procuring and securing happiness to the people, depends, on opinion, on the general opinion of the goodness of the Government, as well as of the wisdom and integrity of its Governors. I hope therefore that for our own sakes as a part of the people, and for the sake of posterity, we shall act heartily and unanimously in recommending this Constitution (if approved by Congress & confirmed by the Conventions) wherever our influence may extend, and turn our future thoughts & endeavors to the means of having it well administered.

On the whole, Sir, I can not help expressing a wish that every member of the Convention who may still have objections to it, would with me, on this occasion doubt a little of his own infallibility, and to make manifest our unanimity, put his name to this instrument. . . .

Whilst the last members were signing it Doctor Franklin looking towards the President's Chair, at the back of which a rising sun happened to be painted, observed to a few members near him, that Painters had found it difficult to distinguish in their art a rising from a setting sun. I have, said he, . . . often in the course of the Session, and the vicisitudes [vicissitudes] of my hopes and fears as to its issue, looked at that behind the President without being able to tell whether it was rising or setting: But now at length I have the happiness to know that it is a rising and not a setting Sun.

The Constitution being signed by all the members except Mr. [Edmund] Randolph [of Virginia], Mr. Mason, and Mr. Gerry who declined giving it the sanction of their names, the Convention dissolved itself by an Adjournment *sine die*—

ANALYZING LITERATURE

Use the passage on these pages to answer the following questions.

1. Franklin believed that the Constitution should be approved because he
A thought no other convention could create a better one.
B agreed with all of its provisions.
C had complete confidence in his own judgment.
D had written the first draft.

2. Franklin's request that the delegates "doubt a little of [their] own infallibility" meant that he wanted them to
A trust their best judgment.
B recognize the errors in the Constitution.
C understand his objections to the Constitution.
D set aside their objections to the Constitution.

3. *Critical Thinking: Determining Relevance* How did Franklin's age and experience affect his thinking regarding whether or not to support the Constitution?

American Literature

Incidents in the Life of a Slave Girl

Focus Have students read the Introduction and look up the meanings of the vocabulary words. Point out that the autobiography of Harriet Ann Jacobs reveals both the subtle and the blatant abuses that even the kindest slave owners dealt the enslaved.

Instruct Divide the class into two groups and have each group make a list of the hardships described by Harriet Ann Jacobs. Then reconvene as a class and have the groups compare their lists. Use the lists as a basis for discussing the various challenges that African Americans faced in the mid-1800s.

Extend Have students research the daily life of an enslaved person on a southern plantation. Students might use such sources as *Six Women's Slave Narratives* by William Andrews. Then ask pairs of students to prepare a skit that demonstrates the daily life of the person chosen. Discuss with the class what the skit revealed about that person and the history of the times.

Incidents in the Life of a Slave Girl

BY HARRIET ANN JACOBS

INTRODUCTION Harriet Ann Jacobs was born into slavery in Edenton, North Carolina, in 1813. Her long and remarkable road to freedom began in 1835, when she and her two young children went into hiding in her hometown. In 1842, Jacobs escaped to New York with her son and daughter. There she made a home for her children and was eventually bought by the Colonization Society and freed in 1852. Shortly afterward she wrote her autobiography, which provides a personal account of what it was like to be enslaved in the 1800s.

VOCABULARY Before you read the selection, find the meaning of these words in a dictionary: *toilsome, bequeath, chattel, defraud.*

Antislavery logo linking the women's rights and abolitionist movements

I was born a slave; but I never knew it till six years of happy childhood had passed away. My father was a carpenter, and considered so intelligent and skillful in his trade, that, when buildings out of the common line were to be erected, he was sent for from long distances, to be head workman. On condition of paying his mistress two hundred dollars a year, and supporting himself, he was allowed to work at his trade, and manage his own affairs. His strongest wish was to purchase his children; but, though he several times offered his hard earnings for that purpose, he never succeeded.

I was so fondly shielded that I never dreamed I was a piece of merchandise, trusted to them for safe keeping, and liable to be demanded of them at any moment. . . .

Such were the unusually fortunate circumstances of my early childhood. When I was six years old, my mother died; and then, for the first time, I learned, by the talk around me, that I was a slave. My mother's mistress was the daughter of my grandmother's mistress. She was the foster sister of my mother; they were both nourished at my grandmother's breast. In fact, my mother had been weaned at three months old, that the babe of the mistress might obtain sufficient food. They played together as children; and, when they became women, my mother was a most faithful servant to her white foster sister. On her death-bed her mistress promised that her children should never suffer for any thing; and during her lifetime she kept her word. They all spoke kindly of my dead mother, who had been a slave merely in name, but in nature was noble and womanly. I grieved for her, and my young mind was troubled with the thought who would now take of me and my little brother. I was told that my home was now to be with her mistress; and I found it a happy one. No toilsome or disagreeable duties were imposed upon me. My mistress was so kind to me that I was always glad to do her bidding, and proud to labor for her as much as my young years would permit. . . .

TEST PREPARATION

Have students use the excerpt on these pages to answer the following question.

What skill did Jacobs learn from her mistress?
A Cleaning.
B Cooking.
C Sewing.
D Reading.

When I was nearly twelve years old, my kind mistress sickened and died. As I saw the cheek grow paler, and the eye more glassy, how earnestly I prayed in my heart that she might live! I loved her; for she had been almost like a mother to me. My prayers were not answered. She died, and they buried her in the little churchyard, where, day after day, my tears fell upon her grave.

I was sent to spend a week with my grandmother. I was now old enough to begin to think of the future; and again and again I asked myself what they would do with me. I felt sure I should never find another mistress so kind as the one who was gone. She had promised my dying mother that her children would never suffer for any thing; and when I remembered that, and recalled her many proofs of attachment to me, I could not help having some hopes that she had left me free. . . .

After a brief period of suspense . . . we learned that she had bequeathed me to her sister's daughter, a child of five years old. So vanished our hopes. My mistress had taught me the precepts of God's Word: "Thou shalt love thy neighbor as thyself." "Whatsoever ye would that men should do unto you, do ye even so unto them." But I was her slave, and I suppose she did not recognize me as her neighbor. I would give much to blot out from my memory that one great wrong. As a child, I loved my mistress; and, looking back on the happy days I spent with her, I try to think with less bitterness of this act of injustice. While I was with her, she taught me to read and spell; and for this privilege, which so rarely falls to the lot of a slave, I bless her memory. . . .

My grandmother's mistress had always promised her that, at her death, she should be free; and it was said that in her will she made good the promise. But when the estate was settled, Dr. Flint told the faithful old servant that, under existing circumstances, it was necessary she should be sold.

On the appointed day, the customary advertisement was posted up, proclaiming that there would be a "public sale of negroes, horses, &c." Dr. Flint called to tell my grandmother that he was unwilling to wound her feelings by putting her up at auction, and that he would prefer to dispose of her at private sale. My grandmother saw through his hypocrisy; she understood very well that he was ashamed of the job. She was a very spirited woman, and if he was base enough to sell her, when her mistress intended she should be free, she was determined the public should know it. She had for a long time supplied many families with crackers and preserves; consequently, "Aunt Marthy," as she was called, was generally known, and everybody who knew her respected her intelligence and good character. Her long and faithful service in the family was also well known, and the intention of her mistress to leave her free. When the day of sale came, she took her place among the chattels, and at the first call she sprang upon the auction-block. Many voices called out, "Shame! Shame! Who is going to sell you, Aunt Marthy? Don't stand there! That is no place for you." Without saying a word, she quietly awaited her fate. No one bid for her. At last, a feeble voice said, "Fifty dollars." It came from a maiden lady, seventy years old, the sister of my grandmother's deceased mistress. She had lived forty years under the same roof with my grandmother; she knew how faithfully she had served her owners, and how cruelly she had been defrauded of her rights; and she resolved to protect her.

ANALYZING THE DOCUMENT

Use this additional question to generate class discussion:

CRITICAL THINKING: PREDICTING CONSEQUENCES Why would it have been rare for slave owners to educate their slaves? *(Answers will vary, but students may suggest that education could have been a key to a slave's freedom. If slaves were educated, they may have refused to accept the system of slavery that many of them were born into and, as a result, revolt against it.)*

ANALYZING LITERATURE

Use the passage on these pages to answer the following questions.

1. How did Jacobs learn that she was born a slave?
A Her mother told her before she died.
B Her father told her when he purchased her freedom.
C Others mentioned it after her mother died.
D She was sold at a public auction.

2. Why did people not make bids for Jacobs's grandmother when she was put up for sale at an auction?
A Dr. Flint told people that he preferred not to sell her.
B People disapproved of the selling of human beings.
C People thought she was too old to be a useful worker.
D People knew that her mistress had wanted her to be freed upon the mistress's death.

3. *Critical Thinking: Identifying Central Issues* How does the passage show how little control slaves had over their lives?

Answers to . . .

Analyzing Literature
1. C
2. D
3. Students should point to the passages that describe Jacobs, and later her grandmother, being treated like merchandise that could be sold at any moment.

Classics from the Civil War

American Literature

Classics from the Civil War

Focus Have students read the Introduction and look up the meanings of the vocabulary words. Point out that Julia Ward Howe's "Battle Hymn of the Republic" and Abraham Lincoln's Gettysburg Address both unite patriotic ideals with strong religious belief. Explain that each has left an indelible mark on American history.

Instruct Before students read the selections, ask them what they already know about these two famous documents, including the circumstances under which they were written. List responses on the chalkboard. After students have completed the reading, have them add to and revise their responses.

Extend Ask students to consider how it might have affected the South's decision to secede from the Union if Southerners had read the text of the Gettysburg Address beforehand. Discuss the role of hindsight in our understanding of history and in our judgments about decisions made in the past.

INTRODUCTION Two of the best-known writings of the Civil War are presented below. After a tour of Union army camps in 1861, writer and reformer Julia Ward Howe wrote "The Battle Hymn of the Republic," to be sung to the tune of "John Brown's Body." Published in 1862, the song became a favorite of Union soldiers. President Lincoln's address at the November 19, 1863, dedication ceremony at the Gettsysburg cemetery was so short that a photographer who meant to take a picture of Lincoln did not have time to focus his camera. Yet Lincoln's message on the ideals of the war, and the nation, has been called the greatest address in the nation's history.

VOCABULARY Before you read the selections, find the meaning of these words in a dictionary: *contemners, consecrate, hallow.*

"The Battle Hymn of the Republic"
JULIA WARD HOWE

Mine eyes have seen the glory of the coming of the Lord:
He is trampling out the vintage where the grapes of wrath are stored;
He hath loosed the fateful lightning of His terrible swift sword:
His truth is marching on.

I have seen Him in the watch-fires of a hundred circling camps,
They have builded Him an altar in the evening dews and damps;
I can read His righteous sentence by the dim and flaring lamps:
His day is marching on.

I have read a fiery gospel writ in burnished rows of steel:
"As ye deal with my contemners, so with you my grace shall deal;
Let the Hero, born of woman, crush the serpent with his heel,
Since God is marching on."

He has sounded forth the trumpet that shall never call retreat;
He is sifting out the hearts of men before His judgment-seat:
Oh, be swift, my soul, to answer Him! be jubilant, my feet!
Our God is marching on.

In the beauty of the lilies Christ was born across the sea,
With a glory in his bosom that transfigures you and me:
As he died to make men holy, let us die to make men free,
While God is marching on.

TEST PREPARATION

Have students use the excerpts on these pages to answer the following question.

How does Abraham Lincoln describe the soldiers who fought at Gettysburg?
A Unprepared.

B Well-trained.

C Desperate.

D Brave.

The Gettysburg Address

ABRAHAM LINCOLN

Fourscore and seven years ago our fathers brought forth on this continent, a new nation, conceived in Liberty, and dedicated to the proposition that all men are created equal.

Now we are engaged in a great civil war, testing whether that nation, or any nation so conceived, and so dedicated, can long endure. We are met on a great battlefield of that war. We have come to dedicate a portion of that field, as a final resting place for those who here gave their lives, that that nation might live. It is altogether fitting and proper that we should do this.

But, in a larger sense, we can not dedicate—we can not consecrate—we can not hallow—this ground. The brave men, living and dead, who struggled here, have consecrated it far above our poor power to add or detract. The world will little note, nor long remember what we say here, but it can never forget what they did here. It is for us the living, rather, to be dedicated here to the unfinished work which they who fought here have thus far so nobly advanced. It is rather for us to be dedicated to the great task remaining before us—that from these honored dead we take increased devotion to that cause for which they gave the last full measure of devotion—that we here highly resolve that these dead shall not have died in vain—that this nation, under God, shall have a new birth of freedom—and that government of the people, by the people, for the people, shall not perish from the earth.

Abraham Lincoln

ANALYZING LITERATURE

Use the passages on these pages to answer the following questions.

1. In "The Battle Hymn of the Republic," the line "As he died to make men holy, let us die to make men free" compares the death of Jesus Christ to the death of
A Abraham Lincoln.
B Union soldiers.
C freedom.
D slavery.

2. In the Gettysburg Address, why, according to Lincoln, could the assembled crowd not consecrate the cemetery ground?
A History would not remember their words.
B They had not personally fought for freedom.
C The final victory had not yet been won.
D Those who fought there had already consecrated it.

3. *Critical Thinking: Determining Relevance* What are some of the ideals expressed in the Gettysburg Address that we still find relevant today?

Analyzing the Document
Use this additional question to generate class discussion:

CRITICAL THINKING: MAKING COMPARISONS What do "The Battle Hymn of the Republic" and The Gettysburg Address have in common? *(Answers will vary, but students should point out that both writings make reference to slavery and freedom and are intended to be inspirational.)*

Answers to . . .

Analyzing Literature
1. *A*
2. *D*
3. *Still relevant today are the ideals that everyone is created equal, that people who fight for their country should be honored, and that democracy and freedom are noble causes.*

Hungry Hearts

BY ANZIA YEZIERSKA

INTRODUCTION Like many other immigrants who flooded into the nation's cities during the late 1800s, Anzia Yezierska and her family came to New York to escape ethnic persecution in their homeland. In her autobiography, *Hungry Hearts*, Yezierska describes what it was like to leave her Russian village and begin a new life in the United States.

VOCABULARY Before you read the selection, find the meaning of these words in a dictionary: *Cossack, dilapidated, maw, galling.*

American Literature

Hungry Hearts

Focus Have students read the Introduction and look up the meanings of the vocabulary words. Explain that throughout American history, a vast difference has existed between the idealized, popular view of the United States and the reality that greets immigrants. Ask students to think about whether the people who painted such glorified pictures of the United States were lying or simply focusing only on some aspects of society and not on others.

Instruct Ask students whether they have ever undertaken a new experience, such as trying out for a part in a play, attending a new school, or going to a party where they know few people. Ask students to compare their expectations of the new experience to the reality. Then ask them to compare those feelings to those related by Anzia Yezierska. How are they similar? How are they different?

Extend Ask students to conduct further research on the immigrant experience, either for Europeans coming through Ellis Island or for Asians coming through Angel Island. Students may choose to concentrate on a period different from the time period of the selection, such as the present. Have students present the results of their research to the class. Discuss how the experiences described are both similar to and different from those in the selection.

Steerage—dirty bundles—foul odors—seasick humanity—but I saw and heard nothing of the foulness and ugliness around me. I floated in showers of sunshine. Vision upon vision of the new world opened before me. From everyone's lips flowed the golden legend of the golden country:

"In America you can say what you feel—you can join your friends in the open streets without fear of Cossack."

"In America is a home for everyone. The land is your land. Not like in Russia where you feel yourself a stranger in the village where you were born and lived—the village in which your father and grandfather lie buried." . . .

"Everybody can do what he wants with his life in America."

"There are no high or low in America. Even the President holds hands with Gedalyeh Mindel."

"Plenty for all. Learning flows free like milk and honey."

"Learning flows free."

The words painted pictures in my mind. I saw before me free schools, free colleges, free libraries, where I could learn and learn and keep on learning. . . .

"Land! Land!" came the joyous shout.

"America! We're in America!" cried my mother, almost smothering us in her rapture.

All crowded and pushed on deck. They strained and stretched to get the first glimpse of the "golden country," lifting their children on their shoulders that they might see beyond them.

Men fell on their knees to pray. Women hugged their babies and wept. Children danced. Strangers embraced and kissed like old friends. Old men and women had in their eyes a look of young people in love.

Age-old visions sang themselves in me—songs of freedom of an oppressed people. America! America! . . .

Between buildings that loomed like mountains, we struggled with our bundles, spreading around us the smell of the steerage. Up Broadway, under the bridge, and through the swarming streets of the ghetto, we followed Gedalyeh Mindel.

I looked about the narrow streets of squeezed-in stores and houses, ragged clothes, dirty bedding oozing out of the windows, ash cans and garbage cans cluttering the sidewalk. A vague sadness pressed down my heart—the first doubt of America.

"Where are the green fields and open spaces in America?" cried my heart. "Where is the golden country of my dreams?"

A loneliness for the fragrant silence of the woods that lay beyond our mud hut welled up in my heart, a longing for the soft, responsive earth of our village streets. All about me was the hardness of brick and stone, the stinking smells of crowded poverty.

"Here's your house with separate rooms like in a palace." Gedalyeh Mindel flung open the door of a dingy, airless flat.

TEST PREPARATION

Have students use the excerpt on these pages to answer the following question.

Where did Anzia Yezierska work after she came to America?

A On a farm.

B In a tenement.

C She was unable to find work.

(D) In a sweatshop, or factory.

"Oi weh!" my mother cried in dismay. "Where's the sunshine in America?"

She went to the window and looked out at the blank wall of the next house. "Gottuniu! Like in a grave so dark."

"It ain't so dark, it's only a little shady." Gedalyeh Mindel lighted the gas. "Look only." He pointed with pride to the dim gaslight. "No candles, no kerosene lamps in America, you turn on a screw and put to it a match and you got it light like with sunshine."

Again the shadow fell over me, again the doubt of America!

In America were rooms without sunlight, rooms to sleep in, to eat in, to cook in, but without sunshine. And Gedalyeh Mindel was happy. Could I be satisfied with just a place to sleep and eat in, and a door to shut people out—to take the place of sunlight? Or would I always need the sunlight to be happy?

And where was there a place in America for me to play? I looked out into the alley below and saw pale-faced children scrambling in the gutter. "Where is America?" cried my heart. . . .

"Heart of mine!" my mother's voice moaned above me. "Father is already gone an hour. You know how they'll squeeze from you a nickel for every minute you're late. Quick only!"

I seized my bread and herring and tumbled down the stairs and out into the street. I ate running, blindly pressing through the hurrying throngs of workers—my haste and fear choking each mouthful.

I felt a strangling in my throat as I neared the sweatshop prison [factory where she worked]; all my nerves screwed together into iron hardness to endure the day's torture.

For an instant I hesitated as I faced the grated window of the old dilapidated building—dirt and decay cried out from every crumbling brick.

In the maw of the shop, raging around me the roar and the clatter, the clatter and the roar, the merciless grind of the pounding machines. Half maddened, half deadened, I struggled to think, to feel, to remember—what am I—who am I—why was I here?

I struggled in vain—bewildered and lost in a whirlpool of noise.

"America—America—where was America?"

It cried in my heart.

The factory whistle—the slowing-down of the machines—the shout of release hailing the noon hour.

I woke as from a tense nightmare—a weary waking to pain.

In the dark chaos of my brain reason began to dawn. In my stifled heart feelings began to pulse. The wound of my wasted life began to throb and ache. My childhood choked with drudgery—must my youth too die—unlived?

The odor of herring and garlic—the ravenous munching of food—laughing and loud, vulgar jokes. Was it only I who was so wretched? I looked at those around me. Were they happy or only insensible to their slavery? How could they laugh and joke? Why were they not torn with rebellion against this galling grind—the crushing, deadening movements of the body, where only hands live and hearts and brains must die?

A touch on my shoulder. I looked up. It was Yetta Solomon from the machine next to mine.

"Here's your tea."

I stared at her, half hearing.

"Ain't you going to eat nothing?"

"Oi weh! Yetta! I can't stand it!" The cry broke from me. "I didn't come to America to turn into a machine. I came to America to make from myself a person. Does America want only my hands—only the strength of my body—not my heart—not my feelings—my thoughts?"

ANALYZING LITERATURE

Use the passage on these pages to answer the following questions.

1. Which statement best describes Anzia Yezierska's image of the United States before she arrived?
A It was her homeland.
B It was a land of freedom for all.
C It was a crowded and dark country.
D It was not a place of safety.

2. What was her biggest disappointment about the United States?
A It reminded her too much of her former home.
B It had too much open space.
C It had no jobs.
D It seemed to want her only as a laborer, not a complete person.

3. *Critical Thinking: Predicting Consequences* In what different ways might immigrants have reacted to disappointments in the United States?

Songs of World War I

Songs of World War I

Focus Have students read the Introduction and look up the meanings of the vocabulary words. Explain that new weapons used in combination with old fighting tactics resulted in huge casualties in World War I. Point out that the selection shows one way soldiers boosted their spirits during such a war.

Instruct Ask students to read the songs from the viewpoint of a World War I historian. As a historian, what information about World War I can you gain from the songs? How reliable are the songs as historical evidence? What questions would a historian need to answer before using the songs to learn about World War I?

Extend Ask students to find other World War I songs or songs from other wars. Have them write a brief essay that answers this question: How do the songs reflect the spirit of the times and American attitudes toward the war?

LITERATURE

INTRODUCTION Popular songs about World War I played an important role in boosting the morale of both American soldiers abroad and civilians at home. As one soldier said, "Music keeps us from getting blue. We all have a country, a home and a girl, and music talks about these things without making you say anything." George M. Cohan was perhaps one of the most famous songwriters of the time. His song "Over There" expressed the patriotic spirit of citizens on the home front. It was also a favorite marching song of the men in the American Expeditionary Force. Songs like Geoffrey O'Hara's "K-K-K-Katy," helped civilians and soldiers alike to rally their spirits and gave them hope for the future.

VOCABULARY Before you read the selections, find the meaning of these words in a dictionary: *hoist, gawk, foe.*

"Over There"

GEORGE M. COHAN

Johnnie get your gun, get your gun, get your gun,
Take it on the run, on the run, on the run;
Hear them calling you and me;
Every son of liberty.
Hurry right away, no delay, go today,
Make your daddy glad, to have had such a lad,
Tell your sweetheart not to pine,
To be proud her boy's in line.

Chorus:
Over there, over there,
Send the word, send the word over there,
That the Yanks are coming, the Yanks are coming,
The drums rum-tumming everywhere.
So prepare, say a prayer,
Send the word, send the word to beware,
We'll be over, we're coming over,
And we won't come back till it's over over there.

Johnnie get your gun, get your gun, get your gun,
Johnnie show the Hun [a derogatory term for Germans], you're a son-of-a-gun,
Hoist the flag and let her fly,
Like true heroes do or die.
Pack your little kit, show your grit, do your bit,
Soldiers to the ranks from the towns and the tanks,
Make your mother proud of you,
And to liberty be true.

Original cover of sheet music for "Over There"

TEST PREPARATION

Have students use the excerpts on these pages to answer the following question.

What continent does the song "Over There" refer to?
A Asia.
B Africa.
C Europe.
D North America.

"K-K-K-Katy"

GEOFFREY O'HARA

Jimmy was a soldier brave and bold,

Katy was a maid with hair of gold,

Like an act of fate,

Kate was standing at the gate,

Watching all the boys on dress parade.

Jimmy with the girls was just a gawk,

Stuttered every time he tried to talk,

Still that night at eight

He was there at Katy's gate,

Stuttering to her this lovesick cry:

"K-K-K-Katy, beautiful Katy,

You're the only g-g-g-girl that I adore;

When the m-moon shines over the cowshed,

I'll be waiting at the k-k-k-kitchen door."

No one ever looked so nice and neat,

No one could be just as cute and sweet.

That's what Jimmy thought,

When the wedding ring was bought;

Now he's off to France, the foe to meet.

Jimmy thought he'd like to take a chance,

See if he could make the Kaiser dance,

Stepping to a tune,

All about a silvery moon —

This is what they hear in far-off France:

"K-K-K-Katy, beautiful Katy,

You're the only g-g-g-girl that I adore;

When the m-moon shines over the cowshed,

I'll be waiting at the k-k-k-kitchen door."

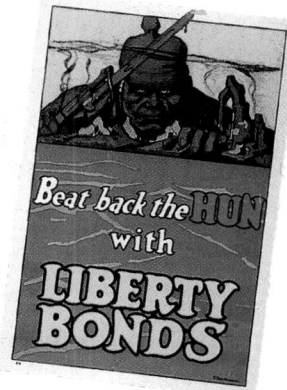

World War I patriotic poster

ANALYZING LITERATURE

Use the passages on these pages to answer the following questions.

1. In "Over There," the line "And we won't come back till it's over over there" means that the United States is committed to
A winning the war.
B staying out of the war.
C redrawing European boundaries.
D defending the United States from invasion.

2. In "K-K-K-Katy," what is meant by the lines "Jimmy thought he'd like to take a chance, /See if he could make the Kaiser dance"?
A Jimmy was in love with a girl named Kaiser.
B Jimmy thought there was a chance he could avoid overseas service.
C Jimmy had been drafted to fight against Germany's kaiser, or leader.
D Jimmy wanted to enlist to fight against Germany's kaiser, or leader.

3. *Critical Thinking: Recognizing Cause and Effect* How do you think these songs affected American soldiers serving in Europe?

Analyzing the Document
Use this additional question to generate class discussion:

CRITICAL THINKING: MAKING COMPARISONS What beliefs do "Over There" and "K-K-K Katy" demonstrate? *(Students should point out that both songs demonstrate a belief in patriotism, religious faith, liberty and freedom, love of family and home, and the honor of serving one's country.)*

Answers to . . .

Analyzing Literature
1. *A*
2. *D*
3. *These songs probably made American soldiers proud of serving their country. The songs could have boosted the morale of the troops by cheering them on. "K-K-K Katy" may have also made them think about their families back home.*

Growing Up

American Literature

Growing Up

Focus Have students read the Introduction and look up the meanings of the vocabulary words. Then explain that "going on relief" (what today would be called "going on welfare") has often been viewed as shameful in the United States. That is why President Franklin Roosevelt tried so hard to find work for the nation's unemployed, instead of giving them handouts. Some people were not eligible for any of Roosevelt's programs, however, and, like Baker's family, ended up on relief anyway, despite their best efforts.

Instruct Ask students to find evidence of how the Depression affected Baker and his family. What was Baker's attitude toward people who accepted government relief? How might his attitude toward accepting relief have been changed by his experience?

Extend Have students suppose that they are Baker or his mother. Ask them to write a letter to President or Mrs. Roosevelt that Baker or his mother could have written explaining their plight.

Growing Up

BY RUSSELL BAKER

INTRODUCTION Single parents rarely have an easy life, and during the Depression their families' very survival was threatened. Because they were the sole caregivers for their children, they could not travel to look for work. Many had no choice but to accept aid from the government. In the following excerpt from his 1982 autobiography, *Growing Up*, Russell Baker, a *New York Times* columnist, remembers those difficult days and one trying day in particular.

VOCABULARY Before you read the selection, find the meaning of these words in a dictionary: *dilapidation, appetizing, edible, incriminating, ostentatious.*

The paper route earned me three dollars a week, sometimes four, and my mother, in addition to her commissions on magazine sales, also had her monthly check coming from Uncle Willie, but we'd been in Baltimore a year before I knew how desperate things were for her. One Saturday morning she told me she'd need Doris and me to go with her to pick up some food. I had a small wagon she'd bought me to make it easier to move the Sunday papers, and she said I'd better bring it along. The three of us set off eastward, passing the grocery stores we usually shopped at, and kept walking until we came to Fremont Avenue, a grim street of dilapidation and poverty in the heart of East Baltimore.

"This is where we go," she said when we reached the corner of Fremont and Fayette Street. It looked like a grocery, with big plate-glass windows and people lugging out cardboard cartons and bulging bags, but it wasn't. I knew very well what it was.

"Are we going on relief?" I asked her.

"Don't ask questions about things you don't know anything about," she said. "Bring that wagon inside."

I did, and watched with a mixture of shame and greed while men filled it with food. None of it was food I liked. There were huge cans of grapefruit juice, big paper sacks of cornmeal, cellophane bags of rice and prunes. It was hard to believe all this was ours for no money at all, even though none of it was very appetizing. My wonder at this free bounty quickly changed to embarrassment as we headed home with it. Being on relief was a shameful thing. People who accepted the government's handouts were scorned by everyone I knew as idle no-accounts without enough self-respect to pay their own way in the world. I'd often heard my mother say the same thing of families in the neighborhood suspected of being on relief. These, I'd been taught to believe, were people beyond hope. Now we were as low as they were.

Pulling the wagon back toward Lombard Street, with Doris following behind to keep the edible proof of our disgrace from falling off, I knew my mother was far worse off than I'd suspected. She'd never have accepted such shame otherwise. I studied her as she walked along beside me, head high as always, not a bit bowed in disgrace, moving at her usual quick, hurry-up pace. If she'd given up on life, she didn't show it, but on the other hand she was unhappy about something. I dared to mention the dreaded words only once on that trip home.

TEST PREPARATION

Have students use the excerpt on these pages to answer the following question.

How would the neighbors know that the Bakers were on relief?
A The food had official government labels on it.
Ⓑ The food was not labeled.
C They would have seen them at the store.
D No one would want to buy grapefruit juice, cornmeal, prunes, and rice.

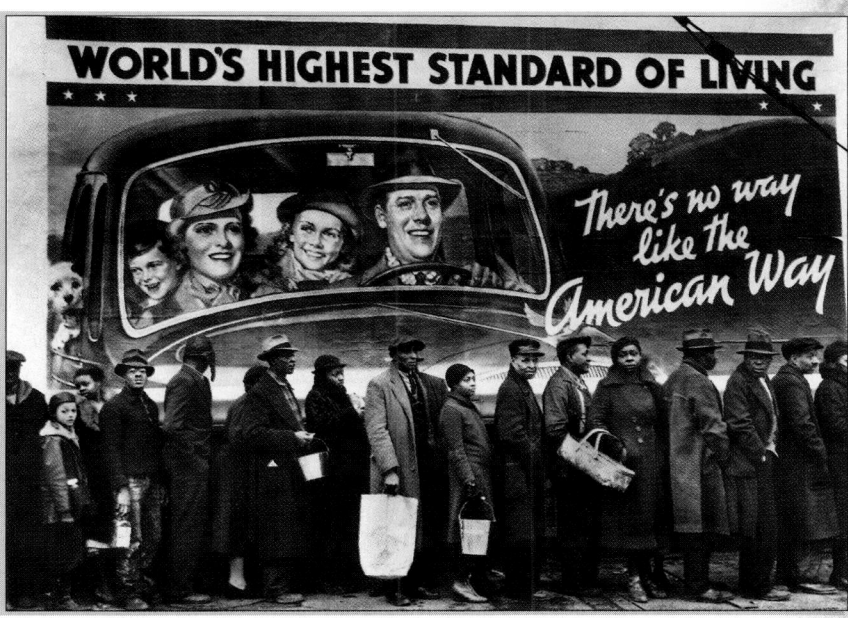

WORLD'S HIGHEST STANDARD OF LIVING

There's no way like the American Way

Taken at a relief center in Kentucky, this photograph offers an ironic comment on the Great Depression.

"Are we on relief now, Mom?"

"Let me worry about that," she said.

What worried me most as we neared home was the possibility we'd be seen with the incriminating food by somebody we knew. There was no mistaking government-surplus food. The grapefruit-juice cans, the prunes and rice, the cornmeal—all were ostentatiously unlabeled, thus advertising themselves as "government handouts." Everybody in the neighborhood could read them easily enough, and our humiliation would be gossiped through every parlor by sundown. I had an inspiration.

"It's hot pulling this wagon," I said. "I'm going to take my sweater off."

It wasn't hot, it was on the cool side, but after removing the sweater I laid it across the groceries in the wagon. It wasn't a very effective cover, but my mother was suddenly affected by the heat too.

"It is warm, isn't it, Buddy?" she said. Removing her topcoat, she draped it over the groceries, providing total concealment.

"You want to take your coat off, Doris?" asked my mother.

"I'm not hot, I'm chilly," Doris said.

It didn't matter. My mother's coat was enough to get us home without being exposed as three of life's failures.

ANALYZING LITERATURE

Use the passage on these pages to answer the following questions.

1. What conclusion did Baker draw from his mother's decision to accept government relief?
A His mother had given up on life.
B His mother no longer cared what others thought of her.
C His mother wanted him to quit his paper route.
D His mother was desperately poor.

2. Baker placed his sweater in the wagon because he was
A hot.
B ashamed of the government-surplus food.
C ashamed of his mother.
D ashamed of the wagon.

3. *Critical Thinking: Distinguishing False from Accurate Images* How might this experience have changed Baker's image of those who accepted government help?

Analyzing the Document

Use this additional question to generate class discussion:

CRITICAL THINKING: IDENTIFYING ASSUMPTIONS What did Russell Baker assume about people who accepted relief? (*Baker assumed that people on relief were shamefully lazy and didn't want to work to pay their own way. He also assumed that they had given up hope for their lives.*)

Answers to . . .

Analyzing Literature
1. *D*
2. *B*
3. *He probably realized that many people who accepted government relief were as hard-working and honest as his own family.*

Night

American Literature

Night

Focus Have students read the Introduction and look up the meanings of the vocabulary words. Then remind students that Nazi dictator Adolf Hitler imprisoned millions of European Jews and other "undesirables" in concentration camps as part of his extermination plan. One of these prisoners was Elie Wiesel, who has devoted his life to writing, teaching, and speaking out about the Holocaust.

Instruct Read aloud the first three paragraphs of the selection and point out how Wiesel repeats the word "never" to emphasize his point. Ask students to choose and read aloud the most memorable passages from the selection. Discuss the reasons for their choices.

Extend Have students read *Night* in its entirety, another of Wiesel's works, or an account of the Holocaust by another survivor. Ask students to give brief oral reports summarizing their readings. Then lead a discussion on the similarities and differences among the various accounts.

Night

BY ELIE WIESEL

INTRODUCTION Elie Wiesel, a Hungarian Jew, lost his parents and a sister in the Holocaust. Released from the Buchenwald concentration camp in 1945, he waited ten years before writing of his experiences. *Night,* the book he eventually wrote, is one of the most powerful memoirs written by survivors of the Nazi camps. The excerpt below recalls Wiesel's first night in the camp.

VOCABULARY Before you read the selection, find the meaning of these words in a dictionary: *nocturnal, antechamber, bestial, truncheon, crematory, lucidity, redemption, Talmud.*

Never shall I forget that night, the first night in camp, which has turned my life into one long night, seven times cursed and seven times sealed. Never shall I forget that smoke. Never shall I forget the little faces of the children, whose bodies I saw turned into wreaths of smoke beneath a silent blue sky.

Never shall I forget those flames which consumed my faith forever.

Never shall I forget that nocturnal silence which deprived me, for all eternity, of the desire to live. Never shall I forget those moments which murdered my God and my soul and turned my dreams to dust. Never shall I forget these things, even if I am condemned to live as long as God Himself. Never.

The barracks we had been made to go into was very long. In the roof were some blue-tinged skylights. The antechamber of Hell must look like this. So many crazed men, so many cries, so much bestial brutality!

There were dozens of prisoners to receive us, truncheons in their hands, striking out anywhere, at anyone, without reason. Orders:

"Strip! Fast! *Los*! Keep only your belts and shoes in your hands. . . ."

We had to throw our clothes at one end of the barracks. There was already a great heap there. New suits and old, torn coats, rags. For us, this was the true equality: nakedness. Shivering with the cold.

Some SS officers moved about in the room, looking for strong men. If they were so keen on strength, perhaps one should try and pass oneself off as sturdy? My father thought the reverse. It was better not to draw attention to oneself. Our fate would then be the same as the others. (Later, we were to learn that he was right. Those who were selected that day were enlisted in the Sonder-Kommando, the unit which worked in the crematories. Bela Katz—son of a big tradesman from our town—had arrived at Birkenau with the first transport, a week before us. When he heard of our arrival, he managed to get word to us that, having been chosen for his strength, he had himself put his father's body into the crematory oven.)

Blows continued to rain down.

"To the barber!"

Survivors of a Nazi concentration camp

TEST PREPARATION

Have students use the excerpt on these pages to answer the following question.

Elie Wiesel's friend Yechiel was weeping after they left the barber because—

A he no longer had any hair.

B he was still alive.

C he was exhausted.

D he knew how close they were to death.

Belt and shoes in hand, I let myself be dragged off to the barbers. They took our hair off with clippers, and shaved off all the hair on our bodies. The same thought buzzed all the time in my head—not to be separated from my father.

Freed from the hands of the barbers, we began to wander in the crowd, meeting friends and acquaintances. These meetings filled us with joy—yes, joy—"Thank God! You're still alive!"

But others were crying. They used all their remaining strength in weeping. Why had they let themselves be brought here? Why couldn't they have died in their beds? Sobs choked their voices.

Suddenly, someone threw his arms round my neck in an embrace: Yechiel, brother of the rabbi of Sighet. He was sobbing bitterly. I thought he was weeping with joy at still being alive.

"Don't cry, Yechiel," I said. "Don't waste your tears. . . ."

"Not cry? We're on the threshold of death. . . . Soon we shall have crossed over. . . . Don't you understand? How could I not cry?"

Through the blue-tinged skylights I could see the darkness gradually fading. I had ceased to feel fear. And then I was overcome by an inhuman weariness.

Those absent no longer touched even the surface of our memories. We still spoke of them—"Who knows what may have become of them?"—but we had little concern for their fate. We were incapable of thinking of anything at all. Our senses were blunted; everything was blurred as in a fog. It was no longer possible to grasp anything. The instincts of self-preservation, of self-defense, of pride, had all deserted us. In one ultimate moment of lucidity it seemed to me that we were damned souls wandering in the half-world, souls condemned to wander through space till the generations of man came to an end, seeking their redemption, seeking oblivion—without hope of finding it.

Toward five o'clock in the morning, we were driven out of the barracks. The Kapos beat us once more, but I had ceased to feel any pain from their blows. An icy wind enveloped us. We were naked, our shoes and belts in our hands. The command: "Run!" And we ran. After a few minutes of racing, a new barracks.

A barrel of petrol at the entrance. Disinfection. Everyone was soaked in it. Then a hot shower. At high speed. As we came out from the water, we were driven outside. More running. Another barracks, the store. Very long tables. Mountains of prison clothes. On we ran. As we passed, trousers, tunic, shirt, and socks were thrown to us.

Within a few seconds, we had ceased to be men. If the situation had not been tragic, we should have roared with laughter. Such outfits! Meir Katz, a giant, had a child's trousers, and Stern, a thin little chap, a tunic which completely swamped him. We immediately began the necessary exchanges.

I glanced at my father. How he had changed! His eyes had grown dim. I would have liked to speak to him, but I did not know what to say.

The night was gone. The morning star was shining in the sky. I too had become a completely different person. The student of the Talmud, the child that I was, had been consumed in the flames. There remained only a shape that looked like me. A dark flame had entered into my soul and devoured it.

So much had happened within such a few hours that I had lost all sense of time. When had we left our houses? And the ghetto? And the train? Was it only a week? One night—one single night?

How long had we been standing like this in the icy wind? An hour? Simply an hour? Sixty minutes?

Surely it was a dream.

ANALYZING LITERATURE

Use the passage on these pages to answer the following questions.

1. Prisoners who appeared stronger than others were
A killed immediately.
B given special privileges.
C assigned to work in crematories.
D beaten more severely.

2. The reference to fog on the first night describes the
A mental confusion of the prisoners.
B mental confusion of the guards.
C atmosphere surrounding the camp.
D atmosphere within the crowded barracks.

3. *Critical Thinking: Drawing Conclusions* Explain what Wiesel meant by the sentence, "Surely it was a dream."

LITERATURE

Analyzing the Document
Use this additional question to generate class discussion:

CRITICAL THINKING: FORMULATING QUESTIONS What questions might you ask of Elie Wiesel to learn more about his life? *(Questions might include: What sort of work were you forced to do at the concentration camp? How did you survive? Why did you wait ten years to write about your experiences? Do you think that the Holocaust could be repeated today?)*

Answers to . . .

Analyzing Literature
1. C
2. A
3. Wiesel was probably wondering how this nightmare could really be happening. He had lost all sense of time and everything felt foggy. He might have been asking himself how it was possible that this atrocity was not a dream.

Letter from the Birmingham Jail

Focus Have students read the Introduction and look up the meanings of the vocabulary words. Then remind students that before the civil rights movement, segregation was widely practiced in the United States, particularly in the South. Ask students to what extent they think racial tension is still evident in our society today, despite the gains made by the civil rights movement.

Instruct Discuss the various peaceful channels for effecting change in American society. *(Such as letters to elected officials, petition drives, letters to the editor.)* What methods for effecting change can Americans turn to if these methods fail? Discuss the various ways that Martin Luther King, Jr., tried to bring about change. *(Such as speeches, marches, mass protest.)* Ask students to list Dr. King's justifications for staging the mass protest that resulted in his being jailed.

Extend Ask students to look up articles on Martin Luther King, Jr., and the civil rights movement in issues of *Time, Newsweek,* or other news and popular magazines from the 1960s in the library or on the Internet. What can they learn from these sources about the civil rights movement and about what it was like for both white and African Americans to live during that time? You may wish to have students make photocopies of headlines, photos, and articles for a bulletin board display on civil rights.

UNIT 9 LITERATURE

LITERATURE

"Letter from the Birmingham Jail"

BY MARTIN LUTHER KING, JR.

INTRODUCTION In 1963 the Reverend Martin Luther King, Jr., and the Southern Christian Leadership Conference staged a mass protest in Birmingham, Alabama. King was arrested for his participation in the protest, and from his jail cell he wrote a letter, which is excerpted below. The letter was his answer to eight Birmingham clergymen who had condemned the civil rights demonstration and criticized King as an "outside agitator" coming to stir up trouble in Birmingham.

VOCABULARY Before you read the selection, find the meaning of these words in a dictionary: *deplore, unduly, ominous, complacency, manifest.*

My Dear Fellow Clergymen:

You deplore the demonstrations taking place in Birmingham. But your statement, I am sorry to say, fails to express a similar concern for the conditions that brought about the demonstrations. . . .

We know through painful experience that freedom is never voluntarily given by the oppressor; it must be demanded by the oppressed. Frankly, I have yet to engage in a direct-action campaign that was "well timed" in the view of those who have not suffered unduly from the disease of segregation. For years now I have heard the word "Wait!" It rings in the ear of every Negro with piercing familiarity. This "Wait!" has almost always meant "Never." We must come to see, with one of our distinguished jurists, that "justice too long delayed is justice denied." . . .

Perhaps it is easy for those who have never felt the sting-

TEST PREPARATION

Have students use the excerpt on these pages to answer the following question.

King criticizes the Birmingham clergy because they—

A advocate the black nationalist movement.

B support direct-action campaigns.

C are more concerned with the protests than their underlying causes.

D do not think that African Americans are oppressed.

ing darts of segregation to say, "Wait." But when you have seen vicious mobs lynch your mothers and fathers at will and drown your sisters and brothers at whim; when you have seen hate-filled policemen curse, kick, and even kill your black brothers and sisters; when you see the vast majority of your twenty million Negro brothers smothering in an airtight cage of poverty in the midst of an affluent society; when you suddenly find your tongue twisted and your speech stammering as you seek to explain to your six-year-old daughter why she can't go to the public amusement park that has just been advertised on television, and see tears welling up in her eyes when she is told that Funtown is closed to colored children, and see ominous clouds of inferiority beginning to form in her little mental sky, and see her beginning to distort her personality by developing an unconscious bitterness toward white people. . . then you will understand why we find it difficult to wait. . . .

You speak of our activity in Birmingham as extreme. At first I was rather disappointed that fellow clergymen would see my nonviolent efforts as those of an extremist. I began thinking about the fact that I stand in the middle of two opposing forces in the Negro community. One is a force of complacency, made up in part of Negroes who, as a result of long years of oppression, are so drained of self-respect and a sense of "somebodiness" that they have adjusted to segregation; and in part of a few middle-class Negroes who, because of a degree of academic and economic security and because in some ways they profit by segregation, have become insensitive to the problems of the masses. The other force is one of bitterness and hatred, and it comes perilously close to advocating violence. It is expressed in the various black nationalist groups that are springing up across the nation, the largest and best-known being Elijah Muhammad's Muslim movement. . . .

I have tried to stand between these two forces, saying that we need emulate neither the "do-nothingism" of the complacent nor the hatred and despair of the black nationalist. For there is the more excellent way of love and nonviolent protest. I am grateful to God that, through the influence of the Negro church, the way of nonviolence became an integral part of our struggle. . . .

Oppressed people cannot remain oppressed forever. The yearning for freedom eventually manifests itself, and that is what has happened to the American Negro. Something within has reminded him of his birthright of freedom, and something without has reminded him that it can be gained.

◁ *As his son looks on, Martin Luther King, Jr., removes a cross that had been burned in front of his home in Atlanta, Georgia, in 1960.*

Analyzing the Document
Use this additional question to generate class discussion:

CRITICAL THINKING: RECOGNIZING CAUSE AND EFFECT What effect did King see in his daughter after he explained that the amusement park was only for white families? *(King saw the first feelings of inferiority and resentment.)*

ANALYZING LITERATURE

Use the passage on these pages to answer the following questions.

1. Why, according to King, could African Americans not expect whites to grant them freedom?
A Those in power never give up power without a struggle.
B African Americans did not yet deserve full freedom.
C African Americans were too divided on the issue of segregation.
D "Do-nothingism" was too common among African Americans.

2. Between which two groups did King see himself as standing?
A blacks and whites
B black clergymen and white clergymen
C blacks who favored him and blacks who favored his enemies
D blacks who accepted segregation and blacks who advocated hatred

3. *Critical Thinking: Expressing Problems Clearly* Restate in your own words the message that "justice too long delayed is justice denied."

Answers to . . .

Analyzing Literature
1. *A*
2. *D*
3. *Sample answer: If people have to wait too long to be treated fairly, they are in fact not truly receiving justice.*

American Literature

"Straw into Gold: The Metamorphosis of the Everyday"

Focus Have students read the Introduction and look up the meanings of the vocabulary words. Then point out that in the selection, Sandra Cisneros describes her personal history as influenced by her family, her poverty, and her urban, Latin community. Explain that family, culture, and environment both helped shape Cisneros's career as a writer and helped her to discover herself.

Instruct Divide the class into groups and have each group list the various factors that influenced Sandra Cisneros's life. After students share their lists, encourage them to discuss the challenges that the author faced as a female of Mexican descent growing up in 1960s America. Do similar factors influence Hispanic American students today?

Extend Ask volunteers to read aloud Cisneros's descriptions of the influence of her family, of herself at age 11, and of her accomplishments. Then ask students to write a paragraph about either the influence of their own families, themselves at age 11, or their personal accomplishments.

"Straw into Gold:
The Metamorphosis of the Everyday"

BY SANDRA CISNEROS

INTRODUCTION Recent years have witnessed an explosive growth in the diversity of American literature. Works by women, African Americans, Hispanic Americans, and Asian Americans have been both critical and sales successes, and these works reflect themes as diverse as their authors. One member of the new generation of writers is Sandra Cisneros, who was born in Chicago in 1954. The following selection is taken from her essay "Straw into Gold: The Metamorphosis of the Everyday."

VOCABULARY Before you read the selection, find the meaning of these words in a dictionary: *threshold, taboo, vagabonding, sappy.*

I've managed to do a lot of things in my life I didn't think I was capable of and which many others didn't think me capable of either. Especially because I am a woman, a Latina, an only daughter in a family of six men. My family would've liked to have seen me married long ago. In our culture, men and women don't leave their father's house except by way of marriage. I crossed my father's threshold with nothing carrying me but my own two feet. A woman whom no one came for and no one chased away.

Sandra Cisneros

To make matters worse, I had left before any of my six brothers had ventured away from home. I had broken a terrible taboo. Somehow, looking back at photos of myself as a child, I wonder if I was aware of having begun already my own quiet war.

I like to think that somehow my family, my Mexicanness, my poverty all had something to do with shaping me into a writer. I like to think my parents were preparing me all along for my life as an artist even though they didn't know it. From my father I inherited a love of wandering. He was born in Mexico City but as a young man he traveled into the U.S. vagabonding. He eventually was drafted and thus became a citizen. Some of the stories he has told about his first months in the U.S. with little or no English surface in my stories in *The House on Mango Street* as well as others I have in mind to write in the future. From him I inherited a sappy heart. (He still cries when he watches the Mexican soaps [soap operas]—especially if they deal with children who have foreseken their parents.)

My mother was born like me—in Chicago, but of Mexican descent. It would be her tough, streetwise voice that would haunt all my stories and poems. An amazing woman who loves to draw and read books and can sing an opera. A smart cookie. . . .

What would my teachers say if they knew I was a writer? Who would've guessed it? I wasn't a very bright student. I didn't much like school because we moved so much and I was always new and funny-looking. In my fifth-grade report card, I have nothing but an avalanche of C's and D's, but I don't remember being that stupid. I was good at art and I read plenty of library books and Kiki [her brother] laughed at all my jokes. At

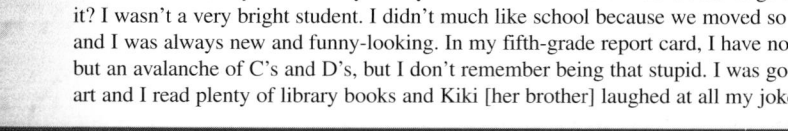

TEST PREPARATION

Have students use the excerpt on these pages to answer the following question.

As a Latina, for what reason was Cisneros expected to leave her father's house?
A She was expected to stay and take care of the family.
B She was expected to leave when she was married.
C She was expected to leave when she had a profession.
D She was expected to leave when her brothers needed her help outside the home.

home I was fine, but at school I never opened my mouth except when the teacher called on me, the first time I'd speak all day.

When I think how I see myself, it would have to be at age eleven. I know I'm thirty-two on the outside, but inside I'm eleven. I'm the girl in the picture with skinny arms and a crumpled shirt and crooked hair. I didn't like school because all they saw was the outside me. School was lots of rules and sitting with your hands folded and being afraid all the time. I liked looking out the window and thinking. I liked staring at the girl across the way writing her name over and over again in red ink. I wondered why the boy with the dirty collar in front of me didn't have a mama who took better care of him.

I think my mama and papa did the best they could to keep us warm and clean and never hungry. We had birthday and graduation parties and things like that, but there was another hunger that had to be fed. There was a hunger I didn't even have a name for. Was this when I began writing?

In 1966 we moved into a house, a real one, our first real home. This meant we didn't have to change schools and be the new kids on the block every couple of years. We could make friends and not be afraid we'd have to say goodbye to them and start all over. My brothers and the flock of boys they brought home would become important characters eventually for my stories—Louie and his cousins, Meme Ortiz and his dog with two names, one in English and one in Spanish.

My mother flourished in her own home. She took books out of the library and taught herself to garden, producing flowers so envied we had to put a lock on the gate to keep out the midnight flower thieves. My mother is still gardening to this day.

This was the period in my life, that slippery age when you are both child and woman and neither, I was to record in *The House on Mango Street*. I was still shy. I was a girl who couldn't come out of her shell.

How was I to know I would be recording and document-ing the women who sat their sadness on an elbow and stared out a window? It would be the streets of Chicago I would later record, but from a child's eyes.

I've done all kinds of things I didn't think I could do since then. I've gone to a prestigious university, studied with famous writers, and taken away an MFA [Master of Fine Arts] degree. I've taught poetry in the schools in Illinois and Texas. I've got-ten an NEA [National Endowment for the Arts] grant and run away with it as far as my courage would take me. I've seen the bleached and bitter mountains of the Peloponnesus. I've lived on a Greek island. I've been to Venice twice. In Rapallo, I met Ilona once and forever and took her sad heart with me across the south of France and into Spain. . . .

I've moved since Europe to the strange and wonderful country of Texas, land of polaroid-blue skies and big bugs. I met a mayor with my last name. I met famous Chicana/o artists and writers and politicos [politicians].

Texas is another chapter in my life. It brought with it the Dobie-Paisano Fellowship, a six-month residency on a 265-acre ranch. But most important Texas brought Mexico back to me.

Sitting at my favorite people-watching spot, the snaky Woolworth's counter across from the Alamo, I can't think of anything else I'd rather be than a writer. I've traveled and lec-tured from Cape Cod to San Francisco, to Spain, Yugoslavia, Greece, Mexico, France, Italy, and finally today to Seguin, Texas. Along the way there is straw for the taking. With a lit-tle imagination, it can be spun into gold.

LITERATURE

ANALYZING LITERATURE

Use the passage on these pages to answer the following questions.

1. How does Cisneros think her family and background affected her as a writer?
A   They shaped the kind of writer she became.
B   She became a writer in order to escape them.
C   They prevented her from becoming a serious writer.
D   They played no role in her career as a writer.

2. Cisneros's teachers would be surprised at her choice of occupation because she
A   always hated writing.
B   was not curious about the world around her.
C   got poor grades and participated little in class.
D   was constantly changing schools.

3. *Critical Thinking: Formulating Questions*   In this excerpt, Cisneros refers to accomplishing things she did not expect to accomplish. If you were interviewing Cisneros for a newspaper story on this topic, what questions might you ask her?

My American Journey

BY COLIN POWELL

American Literature

My American Journey

Focus Have students read the Introduction and look up the meanings of the vocabulary words. Then ask them to describe what "the American dream" means to them. Do they think most people still believe in the American dream? Tell students that this selection reflects the ideas of retired General Colin Powell about the national mood. Although he still believes strongly in the American spirit, he also realizes that we face challenge and change.

Instruct Point out that Americans have faced many difficult periods, notably after the Civil War, during the Great Depression, and during the unrest of the 1960s. Would students describe the present as one such difficult period? How would they describe the national mood today? Discuss what events and issues—political, economic, social—contribute to the national mood.

Extend Ask students to look for recent articles or books that make predictions about what the next decades will bring to the United States. Sources may focus on coming inventions and discoveries in science, technology, and communications. Then ask them to give short oral reports summarizing their findings.

INTRODUCTION The son of Jamaican immigrants, Colin Powell began his army career after college and served two tours of duty in Vietnam. In 1987 President Reagan appointed him national security adviser. Two years later Powell became Chairman of the Joint Chiefs of Staff. As Chairman he played a major role in planning and executing American strategy during the Persian Gulf War of 1991. Powell retired from the military in 1993 and became a prominent public speaker on issues related to public service.

VOCABULARY Before you read the selection, find the meaning of these words in a dictionary: *hyphenated, malcontent, fractious, resilience, hybrid.*

As I travel around the country, I invite questions from my audiences, which range from trade associations to motivational seminars, from prison inmates to the youngsters at my pride and joy, the Colin L. Powell Elementary School in Woodlands, Texas. What people ask gives me a good idea of what is on America's mind. . . .

American voters [are] looking, in my judgment . . . for a different spirit in the land, something better. How do we find our way again? How do we reestablish moral standards? How do we end the ethnic fragmentation that is making us an increasingly hyphenated people? How do we restore a sense of family to our national life? On the speech circuit, I tell a story that goes to the heart of America's longing. The ABC correspondent Sam Donaldson was interviewing a young African-American soldier in a tank platoon on the eve of battle in Desert Storm. Donaldson asked, "How do you think the battle will go? Are you afraid?"

Colin Powell

"We'll do okay. We're well trained. And I'm not afraid," the GI answered, gesturing toward his buddies around him. "I'm not afraid because I'm with my family."

The other soldiers shouted, "Tell him again. He didn't hear you."

The soldier repeated, "This is my family and we'll take care of each other."

That story never fails to touch me or the audience. It is a metaphor for what we have to do as a nation. We have to start thinking of America as a family. We have to stop screeching at each other, stop hurting each other, and instead start caring for, sacrificing for, and sharing with each other. We have to stop constantly criticizing, which is the way of the malcontent, and instead get

---

TEST PREPARATION

Have students use the excerpt on these pages to answer the following question.

Powell believes he knows what is on the nation's mind because he—

A travels throughout the country.

B was a soldier.

C was Chairman of the Joint Chiefs of Staff.

D was National Security Advisor.

According to Colin Powell, American voters are looking for "a different spirit in the land, something better."

Analyzing the Document
Use this additional question to generate class discussion:

CRITICAL THINKING: IDENTIFYING CENTRAL ISSUES What does Powell believe Americans need to do to improve the nation's spirit? *(Powell believes that Americans need to try to work together to solve problems instead of criticizing each other.)*

back to the can-do attitude that made America. We have to keep trying, and risk failing, in order to solve this country's problems. We cannot move forward if cynics and critics swoop down and pick apart anything that goes wrong to a point where we lose sight of what is right, decent, and uniquely good about America. . . .

We are a fractious nation, always searching, always dissatisfied, yet always hopeful. We have an infinite capacity to rejuvenate ourselves. We are self-correcting. And we are capable of caring about each other. . . .

We will prevail over our present trials. We will come through because our founders bequeathed us a political system of genius, a system flexible enough for all ages and inspiring noble aspirations for all time. We will continue to flourish because our diverse American society has the strength, hardiness, and resilience of the hybrid plant we are. . . . Jefferson once wrote, "There is a debt of service due from every man to his country, proportioned to the bounties which nature and fortune have measured to him." . . . My responsibility, our responsibility as lucky Americans, is to try to give back to this country as much as it has given to us, as we continue our American journey together.

ANALYZING LITERATURE

Use the passage on these pages to answer the following questions.

1. What lesson did Powell learn from the conversation between Sam Donaldson and the black soldier?
A Americans have too little faith in the news media.
B Americans need to ask each other fewer questions.
C Americans need to trust each other more.
D Americans need to work together more.

2. The quotation from Jefferson, cited by Powell, means that
A people who have more advantages owe more to their nation.
B all Americans owe their nation the same degree of service.
C Americans owe their success entirely to their nation.
D fortune, or luck, is more important than natural gifts.

3. *Critical Thinking: Drawing Conclusions* Two of the nation's strengths that Powell cited were its political system and its diverse society. Explain how each of these is a source of strength for the United States.

Answers to . . .

Analyzing Literature
1. *D*
2. *A*
3. *Answers will vary, but students may point out that the U.S. political system is a source of strength because it is based on ideas that are flexible enough not to become outdated. Diversity is a source of strength because it allows many voices and ideas to be heard.*

A Correlation to Prentice Hall Literature
The American Experience

AMERICA: PATHWAYS TO THE PRESENT	THE AMERICAN EXPERIENCE		
Chapter	**Author**	**Title and Page Number**	**Genre**
Unit 1: Origins of a New Society, to 1783			
1 The Atlantic World c. 700 B.C.–A.D. 1600	Michael J. Caduto and Joseph Bruchac	"The Earth on Turtle's Back" page 22	myth
2 European Colonization of the Americas 1492–1725	Alvar Núñez Cabeza de Vaca	"A Journey Through Texas" page 34	nonfiction
3 Growth of the American Colonies 1689–1754	Olaudah Equiano	from *The Interesting Narrative of the life of Olaudah Equiano* page 44	nonfiction
4 The Road to Independence 1754–1783	Benjamin Franklin	from *The Autobiography* page 131	nonfiction
Unit 2: Balancing Liberty and Order, 1776–1830			
5 The Constitution 1776–1800	Abigail Adams	"Letter to Her Daughter From the New White House" page 194	letter
6 The Origin of American Politics 1789–1820	Benjamin Franklin	"Speech in the Convention" page 172	speech
7 Life in the New Nation 1783–1830	Washington Irving	"The Devil and Tom Walker" page 236	short story
Unit 3: An Emerging New Nation, 1800–1860			
8 The Market Revolution 1812–1845	Ralph Waldo Emerson	from *Self-Reliance* page 366	nonfiction
9 Religion and Reform 1800–1850	Henry David Thoreau	from *Civil Disobedience* page 380	nonfiction
10 Beyond the Mississippi 1800–1860	Chief Joseph	"I Will Fight No More Forever" page 551	speech
Unit 4: Division and Uneasy Reunion, 1848–1877			
11 The Coming of the Civil War 1848–1861	Frederick Douglass	from *My Bondage and My Freedom* page 458	nonfiction
12 The Civil War 1861–1865	Ambrose Bierce	"An Occurrence at Owl Creek Bridge" page 468	short story
13 Reconstruction 1863–1877	Sojourner Truth	"An Account of an Experience With Discrimination" page 503	nonfiction
Unit 5: Expansion: Rewards and Costs, 1850–1915			
14 The Expansion of American Industry 1850–1900	Edwin Arlington Robinson	"Richard Cory" page 607	poem
15 Looking to the West 1860–1900	Bret Harte	"The Outcasts of Poker Flat" page 534	short story
16 Politics, Immigration, and Urban Life 1870–1915	Bernard Malamud	"The First Seven Years" page 892	short story
17 Daily Life in the Gilded Age 1870–1915	Kate Chopin	"The Story of an Hour" page 592	short story

AMERICA: PATHWAYS TO THE PRESENT	THE AMERICAN EXPERIENCE		
Chapter	*Author*	*Title and Page Number*	*Genre*
Unit 6: The United States on the Brink of Change, 1890–1920			
18 **Becoming a World Power** 1890–1913	William Carlos Williams	"This Is Just to Say" page 663	poem
19 **The Era of Progressive Reform 1890–1920**	Carl Sandburg	"Chicago" page 770	poem
20 **The World War I Era 1914–1920**	Ernest Hemingway	"In Another Country" page 731	short story
Unit 7: Boom Times to Hard Times, 1919–1938			
21 **The Twenties 1920–1929**	Zora Neale Hurston	from *Dust Tracks on a Road* page 830	nonfiction
22 **Crash and Depression 1929–1933**	F. Scott Fitzgerald	"Winter Dreams" page 670	short story
23 **The New Deal 1933–1938**	E.B. White	from *Here Is New York* page 822	nonfiction
Unit 8: Hot and Cold War, 1939–1960			
24 **World War II 1939–1945**	Randall Jarrell	"The Death of the Ball Turret Gunner" page 1045	poem
25 **World War II at Home 1941–1945**	Ezra Pound	"In a Station of the Metro" page 661	poem
26 **The Cold War 1945–1960**	John Hersey	"Hiroshima" page 1036	nonfiction
27 **The Postwar Years at Home 1945–1960**	W.H. Auden	"The Unknown Citizen" page 696	poem
Unit 9: The Upheaval of the Sixties, 1960–1975			
28 **The Kennedy and Johnson Years 1960–1968**	Robert Hayden	"Frederick Douglass" page 1053	poem
29 **The Civil Rights Movement 1954–1968**	Colleen McElroy	"For My Children" page 1060	poem
30 **Other Social Movements 1960–1975**	James Baldwin	"The Rockpile" page 1026	short story
31 **The Vietnam War and American Society 1960–1975**	Yusef Komunyakaa	"Camouflaging the Chimera" page 1080	poem
	Tim O'Brien	"Ambush" page 1082	short story
Unit 10: Continuity and Change, 1968–Present			
32 **The Nixon Years 1968–1974**	Theodore Roethke	"The Adamant" page 919	poem
33 **The Post-Watergate Period 1974–1980**	Anne Tyler	"Average Waves in Unprotected Waters" page 926	short story
34 **The Conservative Revolution 1980–1992**	Ian Frazier	"Coyote v. Acme" page 998	nonfiction
35 **Entering a New Era 1992–Present**	Sandra Cisneros	"Straw Into Gold: The Metamorphosis of the Everyday" page 1006	nonfiction
Unit 11: Pathways to the Future: Themes for the Twenty-First Century			
Chapters 36–42	Amy Tan	"Mother Tongue" page 1012	nonfiction

Illustrated Data Bank

The following maps, tables, and graphs that make up this Illustrated Data Bank are designed as reference materials to help you in your study of United States history:

- United States Population Density, 1790
- United States Ethnic Groups, 1790
- Enslaved Population of the United States, 1790
- United States Population Density, 1890
- United States Foreign-Born Population, 1890
- United States Territorial Growth
- United States Birth Rate, 1910–2000
- United States Gross Domestic Product, 1960–1996
- United States Median Age, 1840–2040
- United States Population by Race, 1995
- United States Latino Population, 1990
- United States Population Density, 1995
- Political Map of the United States
- Physical Map of the United States
- Natural Resources of the United States
- Political Map of the World
- Profile of the Fifty States
- Presidents of the United States

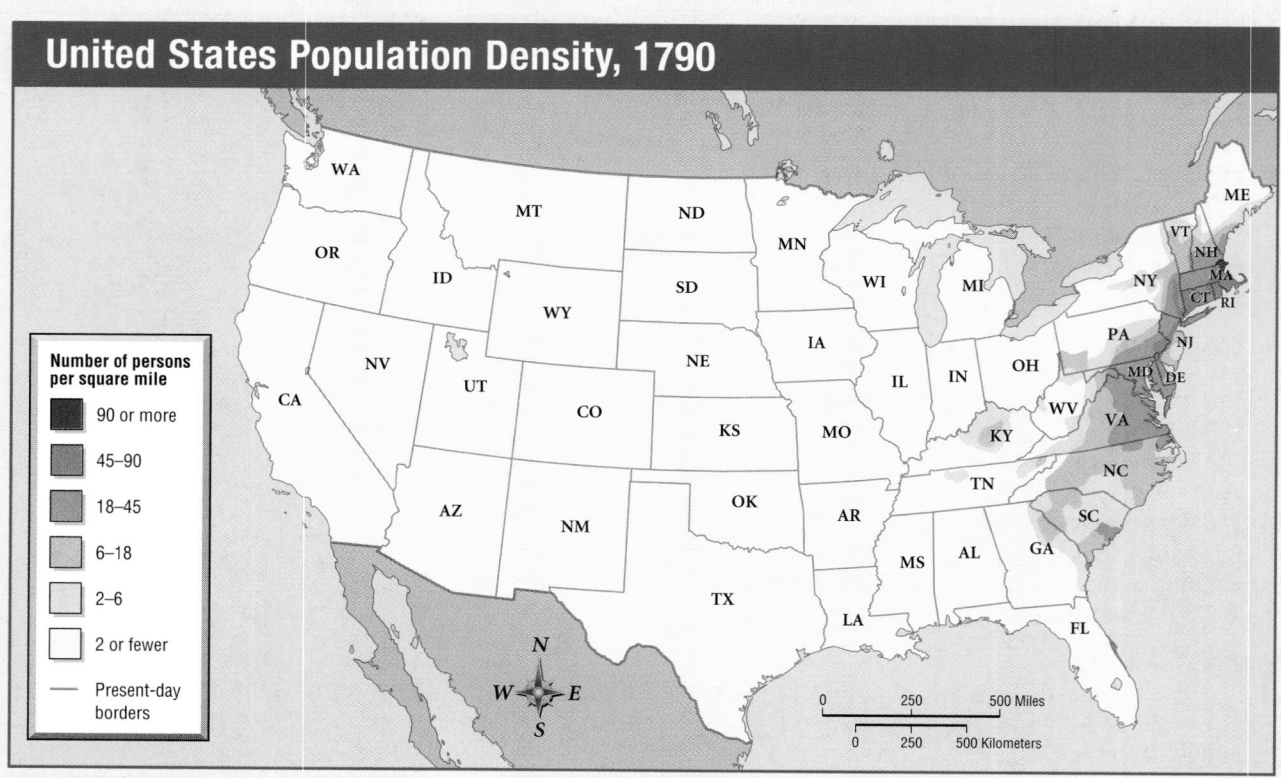

United States Population Density, 1790

Number of persons per square mile
- 90 or more
- 45–90
- 18–45
- 6–18
- 2–6
- 2 or fewer
- Present-day borders

United States Ethnic Groups, 1790

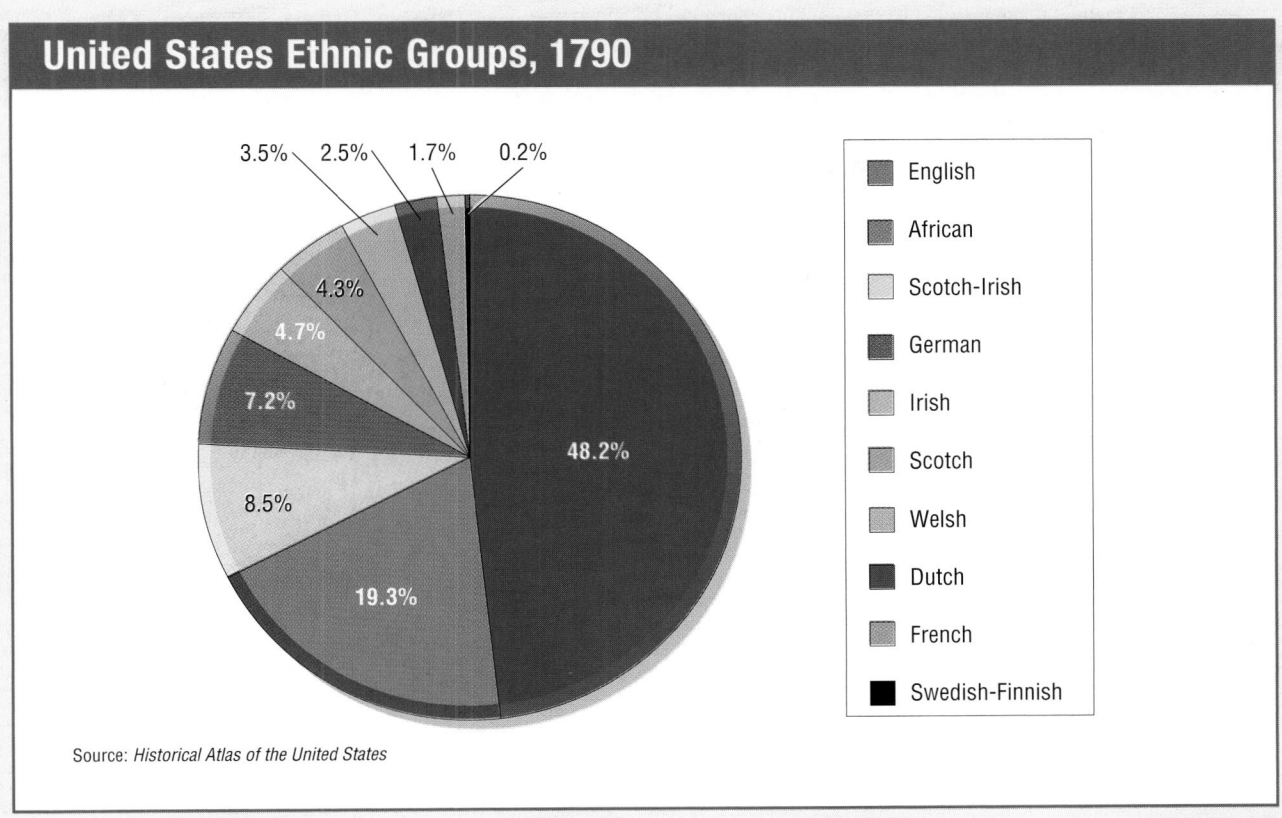

3.5% 2.5% 1.7% 0.2%

4.3%
4.7%
7.2%
8.5%
19.3%
48.2%

- English
- African
- Scotch-Irish
- German
- Irish
- Scotch
- Welsh
- Dutch
- French
- Swedish-Finnish

Source: *Historical Atlas of the United States*

Enslaved Population of the United States, 1790

State	Total Population	Enslaved Population	Percent Enslaved
Connecticut	237,946	2,648	1.11
Delaware	59,096	8,837	14.95
Georgia	82,548	29,624	35.89
Maryland	319,728	103,036	32.33
Massachusetts	475,307	0	0.00
New Hampshire	141,885	157	0.11
New Jersey	184,139	11,423	6.20
New York	340,120	21,193	6.23
North Carolina	393,751	100,783	25.60
Pennsylvania	434,373	3,707	0.85
Rhode Island	68,825	958	1.39
South Carolina	249,073	107,094	43.00
Virginia	747,600	292,627	39.14

Source: *Historical Statistics of the United States, Colonial Times to 1970*

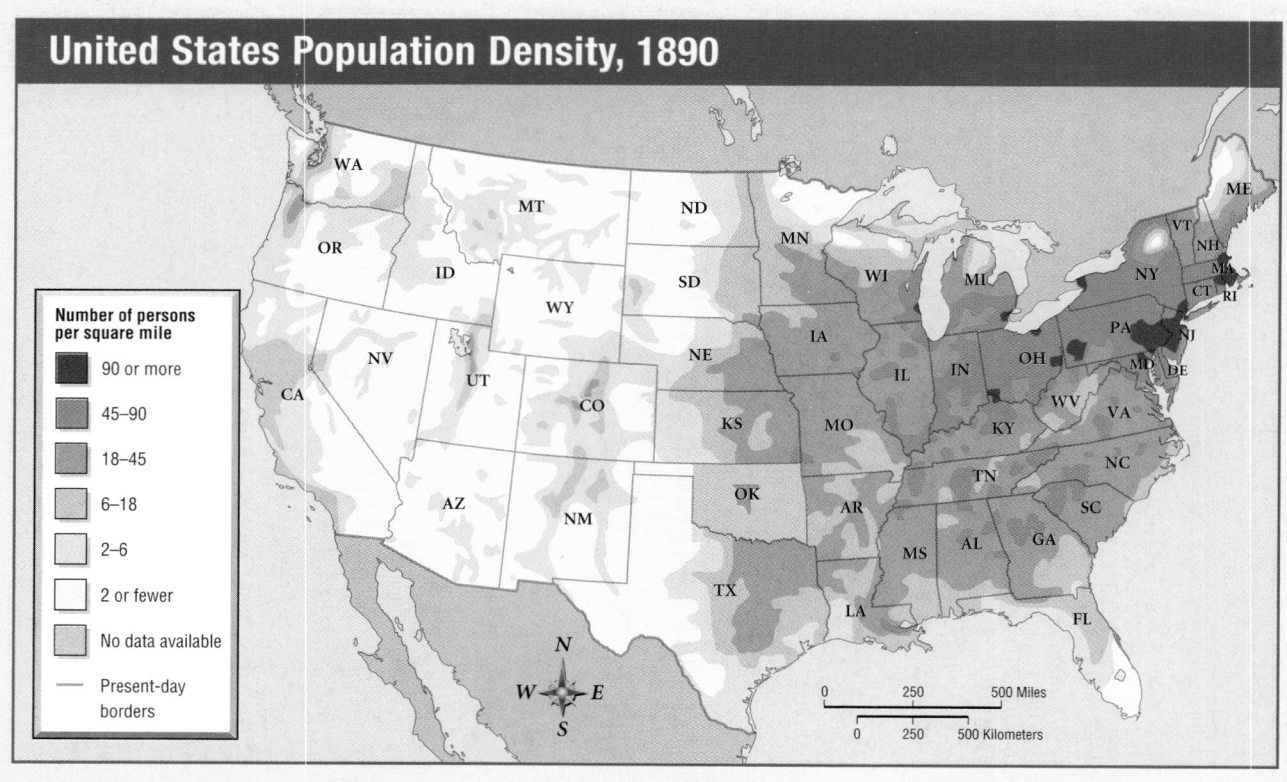

United States Population Density, 1890

Number of persons per square mile

- 90 or more
- 45–90
- 18–45
- 6–18
- 2–6
- 2 or fewer
- No data available
- Present-day borders

0   250   500 Miles

0   250   500 Kilometers

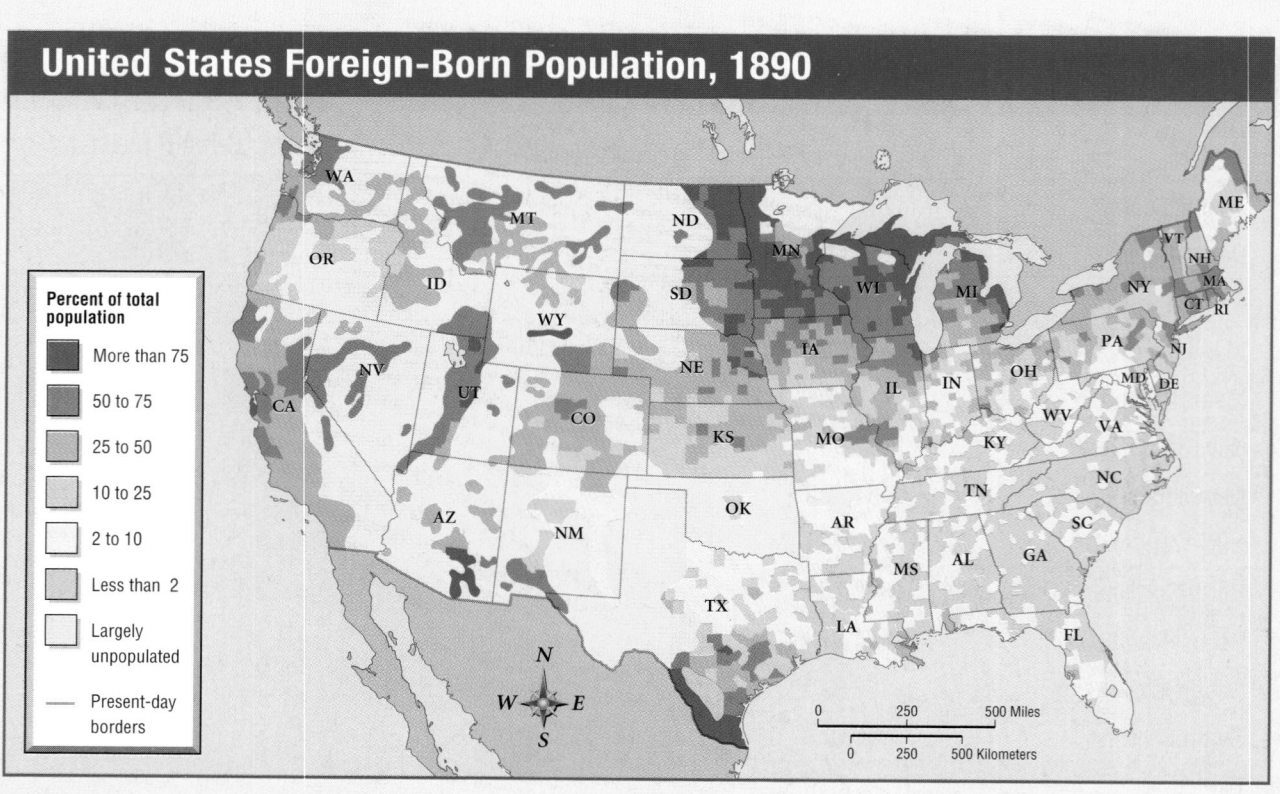

United States Foreign-Born Population, 1890

Percent of total population

- More than 75
- 50 to 75
- 25 to 50
- 10 to 25
- 2 to 10
- Less than 2
- Largely unpopulated
- Present-day borders

0   250   500 Miles

0   250   500 Kilometers

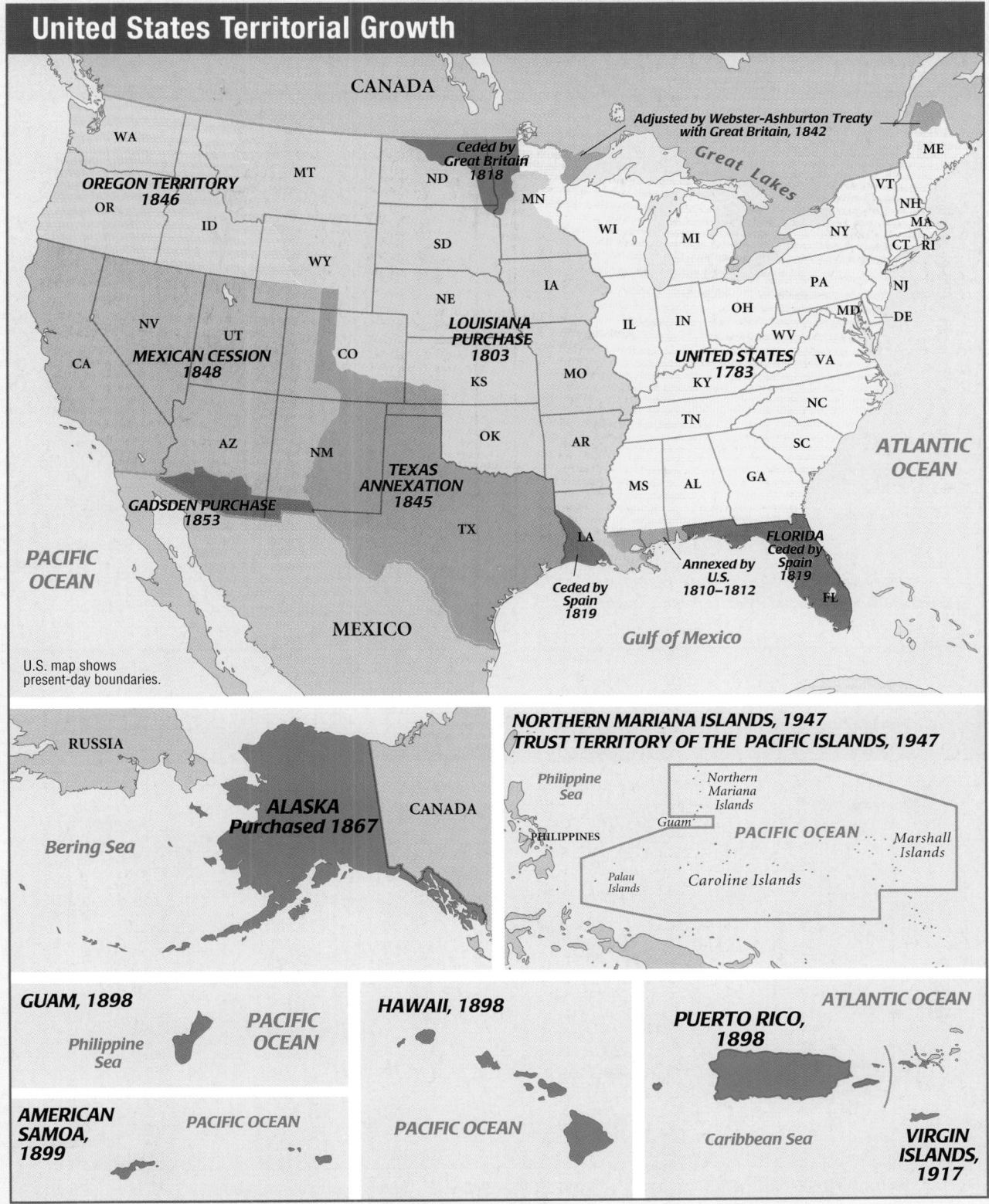

United States Territorial Growth

CANADA

WA

OREGON TERRITORY
1846

OR

ID

MT

ND

Ceded by
Great Britain
1818

MN

*Adjusted by Webster-Ashburton Treaty
with Great Britain, 1842*

Great Lakes

ME

VT

NH

MA

WY

SD

WI

MI

NY

CT RI

NV

UT

MEXICAN CESSION
1848

CA

CO

NE

IA

LOUISIANA
PURCHASE
1803

IL

IN

OH

PA

NJ

MD
DE

WV

UNITED STATES
1783

VA

KS

MO

KY

NC

AZ

NM

OK

AR

TN

SC

GADSDEN PURCHASE
1853

TEXAS
ANNEXATION
1845

MS

AL

GA

ATLANTIC
OCEAN

TX

LA

*Ceded by
Spain
1819*

*Annexed by
U.S.
1810–1812*

FLORIDA
*Ceded by
Spain
1819*

FL

PACIFIC
OCEAN

MEXICO

Gulf of Mexico

U.S. map shows
present-day boundaries.

RUSSIA

ALASKA
Purchased 1867

CANADA

Bering Sea

NORTHERN MARIANA ISLANDS, 1947
TRUST TERRITORY OF THE PACIFIC ISLANDS, 1947

*Philippine
Sea*

*Northern
Mariana
Islands*

PHILIPPINES

Guam

PACIFIC OCEAN

*Marshall
Islands*

*Palau
Islands*

Caroline Islands

GUAM, 1898

*Philippine
Sea*

PACIFIC
OCEAN

HAWAII, 1898

PACIFIC OCEAN

**PUERTO RICO,
1898**

ATLANTIC OCEAN

Caribbean Sea

**VIRGIN
ISLANDS,
1917**

**AMERICAN
SAMOA,
1899**

PACIFIC OCEAN

United States Birth Rate, 1910–2000

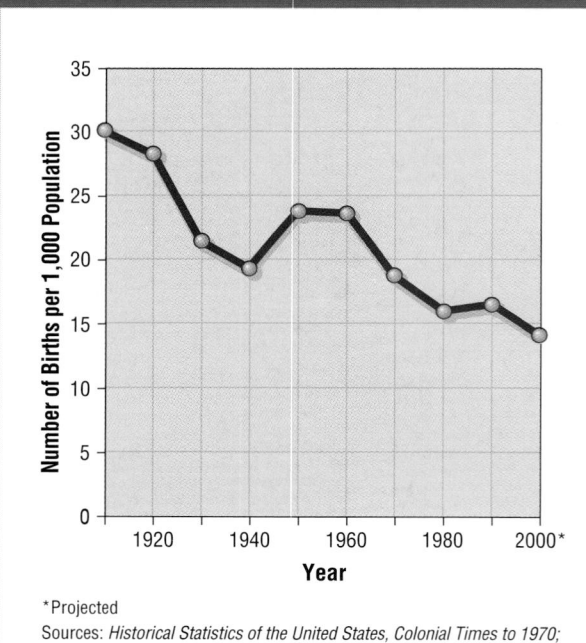

*Projected

Sources: *Historical Statistics of the United States, Colonial Times to 1970;*
Statistical Abstract of the United States; The Universal Almanac

United States Gross Domestic Product, 1960–1999

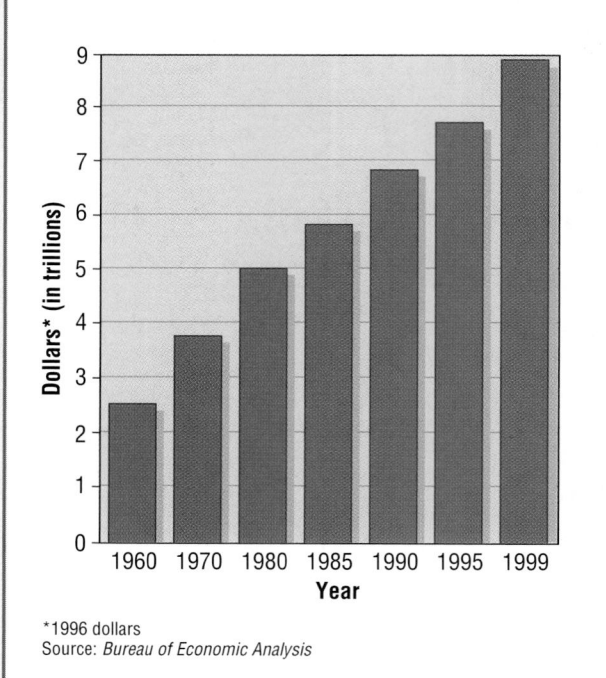

*1996 dollars
Source: *Bureau of Economic Analysis*

United States Median Age, 1840–2040

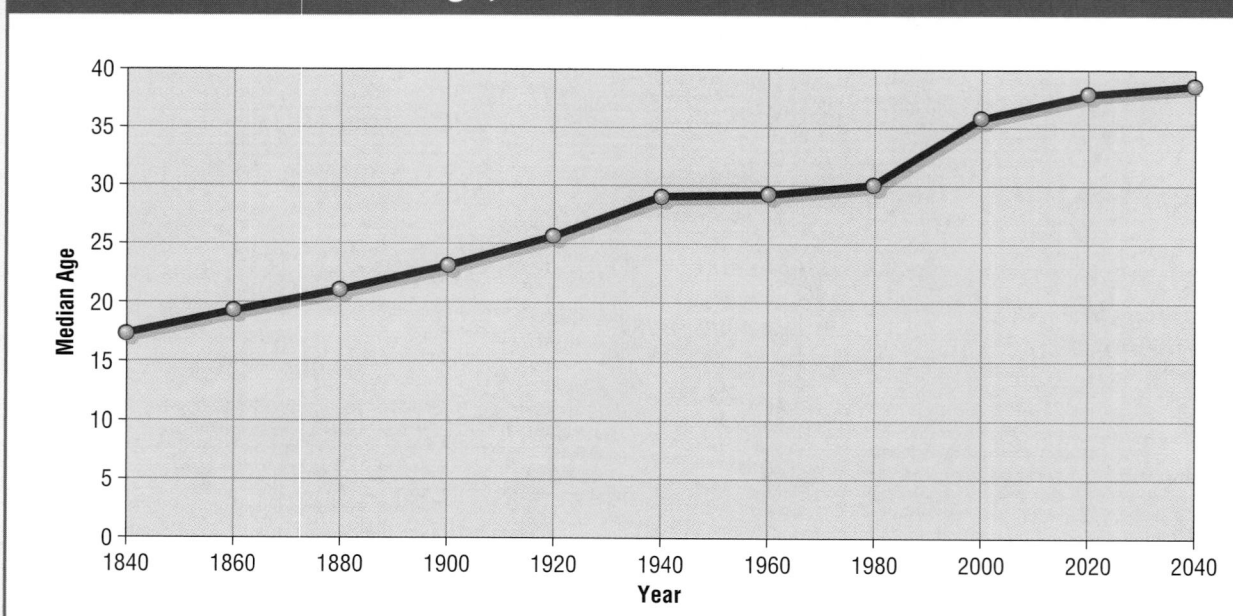

Sources: *Current Population Reports; Historical Statistics of the United States, Colonial Times to 1970;*
The Universal Almanac; World Almanac

United States Population by Race, 1995

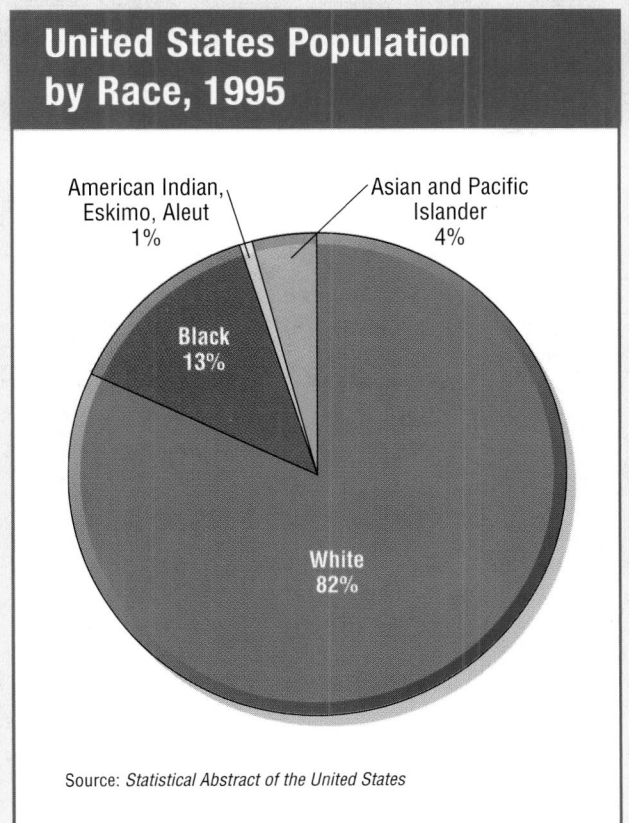

American Indian, Eskimo, Aleut 1%

Asian and Pacific Islander 4%

Black 13%

White 82%

Source: *Statistical Abstract of the United States*

United States Latino Population, 1990

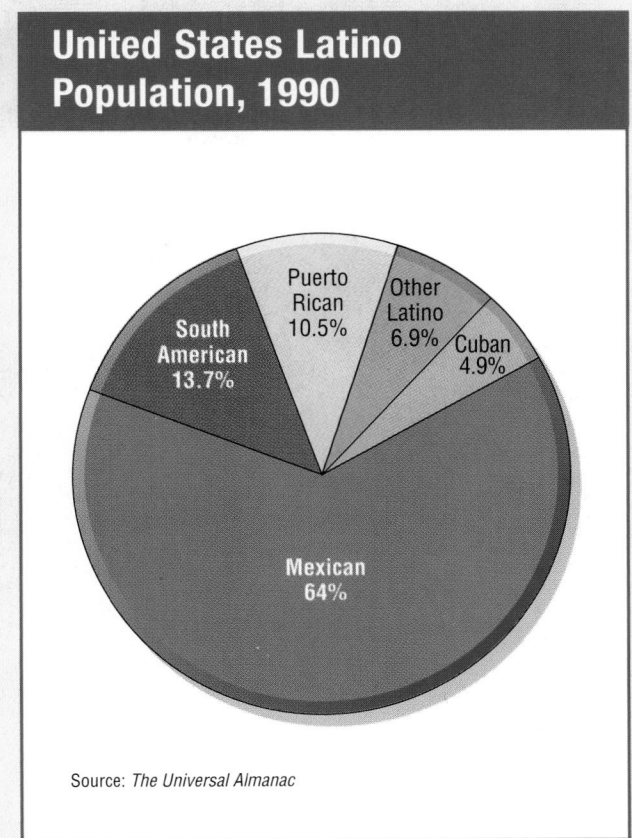

South American 13.7%

Puerto Rican 10.5%

Other Latino 6.9%

Cuban 4.9%

Mexican 64%

Source: *The Universal Almanac*

United States Population Density, 1995

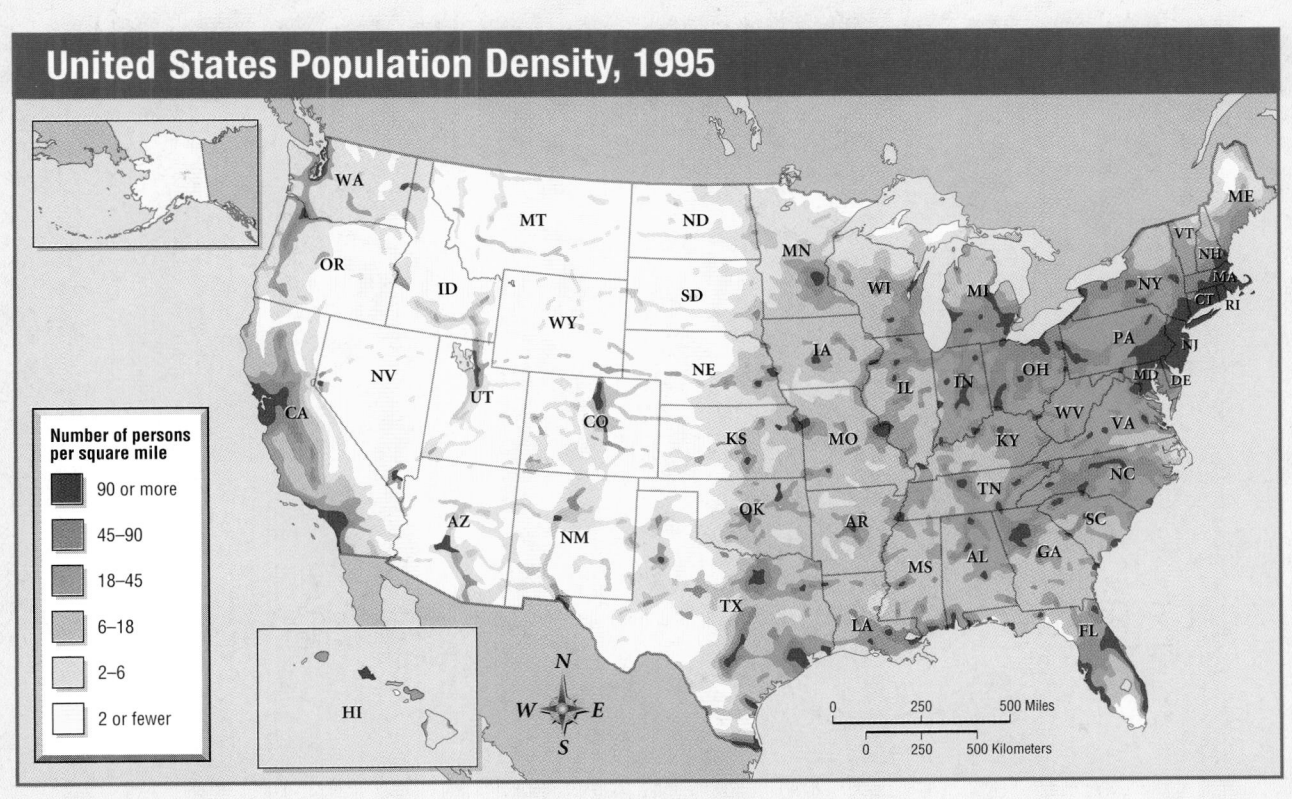

Number of persons per square mile

- 90 or more
- 45–90
- 18–45
- 6–18
- 2–6
- 2 or fewer

0   250   500 Miles

0   250   500 Kilometers

Political Map of the United States

Pacific Time Zone

Mountain Time Zone

CANADA

Central Time Zone

Washington 1889
- Seattle
- Spokane
- ★ Olympia

Montana 1889
- Great Falls
- ★ Helena
- Billings

North Dakota 1889
- Minot
- Grand Forks
- ★ Bismarck

Oregon 1859
- Portland
- ★ Salem
- Eugene

Idaho 1890
- ★ Boise
- Pocatello

Wyoming 1890
- ★ Casper
- Cheyenne ★

South Dakota 1889
- Rapid City
- ★ Pierre
- Sioux Falls

Nebraska 1867
- Omaha
- Lincoln ★
- Sioux City

Nevada 1864
- Reno
- ★ Carson City

Great Salt Lake
- Ogden
- ★ Salt Lake City

Utah 1896

Colorado 1876
- ★ Denver
- Colorado Springs

Kansas 1861
- Topeka ★
- Wichita

California 1850
- San Francisco
- Oakland
- San Jose
- Sacramento ★
- Las Vegas
- Los Angeles
- Long Beach
- Salton Sea
- San Diego

Arizona 1912
- ★ Phoenix
- Tucson

New Mexico 1912
- ★ Santa Fe
- Albuquerque
- Las Cruces
- El Paso

Oklahoma 1907
- Tulsa
- Oklahoma City ★

PACIFIC OCEAN

Texas 1845
- Dallas
- Fort Worth
- Austin ★
- San Antonio

Hawaii—Aleutian Time Zone

Hawaii 1959
- ★ Honolulu

PACIFIC OCEAN

0   50   100 Miles
0   50 100 Kilometers

Hawaii—Aleutian Time Zone

RUSSIA

Alaska Time Zone

Alaska 1959
- Fairbanks
- Anchorage
- ★ Juneau

Pacific Time Zone

Mountain Time Zone

CANADA

Bering Sea

Gulf of Alaska

PACIFIC OCEAN

MEXICO

0   200   400 Miles
0   200   400 Kilometers

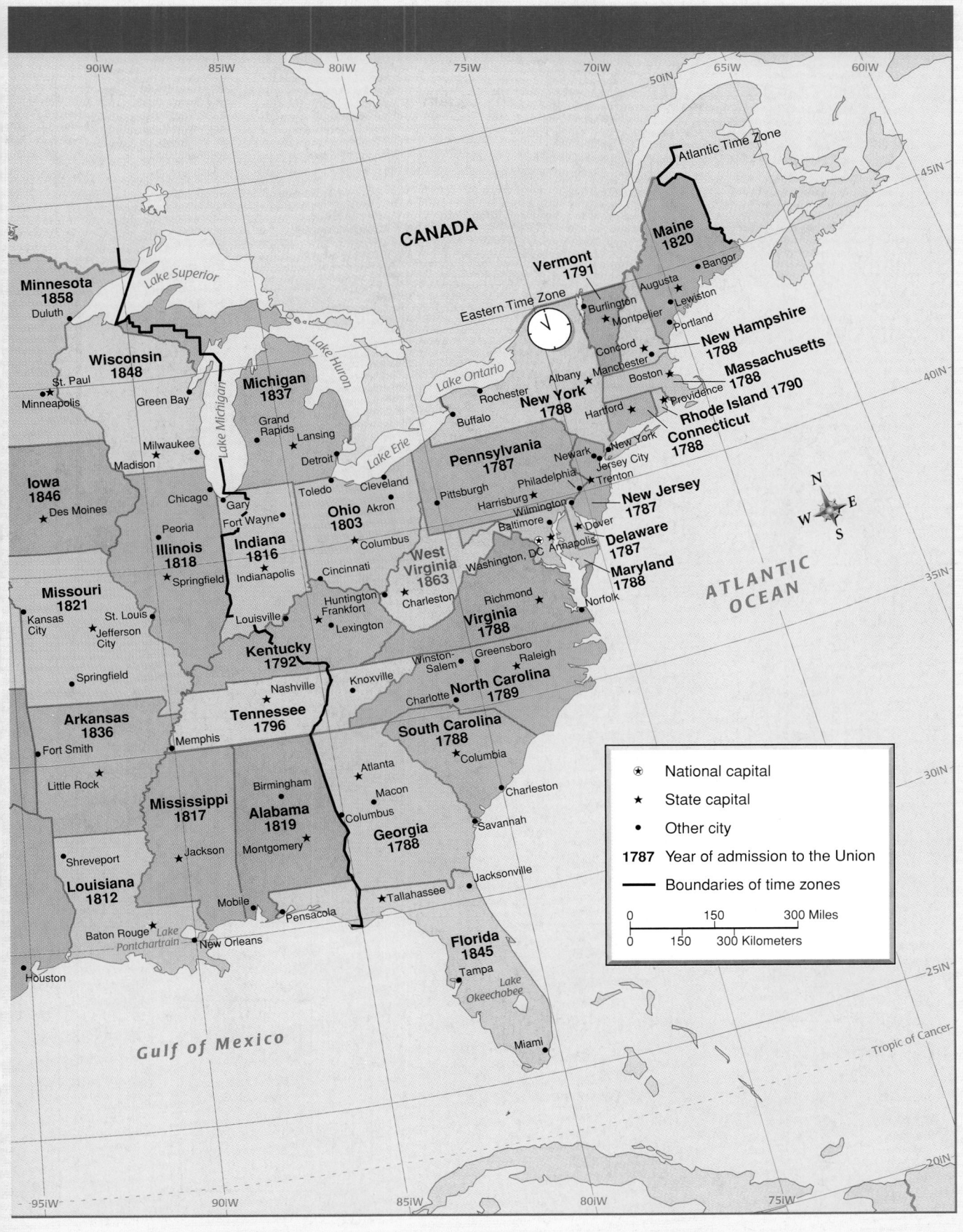

CANADA

Minnesota 1858
Duluth

Lake Superior

Wisconsin 1848
St. Paul
Minneapolis
Green Bay
Milwaukee
Madison

Iowa 1846
Des Moines

Missouri 1821
Kansas City
St. Louis
Jefferson City
Springfield

Arkansas 1836
Fort Smith
Little Rock

Mississippi 1817
Jackson

Louisiana 1812
Shreveport
Baton Rouge
Lake Pontchartrain
New Orleans

Houston

Gulf of Mexico

Michigan 1837
Grand Rapids
Lansing
Detroit

Lake Michigan
Lake Huron

Chicago
Gary
Peoria
Fort Wayne

Illinois 1818
Springfield

Indiana 1816
Indianapolis

Ohio 1803
Toledo
Cleveland
Akron
Columbus
Cincinnati

Lake Erie

West Virginia 1863
Charleston
Huntington
Frankfort
Lexington
Louisville

Kentucky 1792

Tennessee 1796
Nashville
Knoxville
Memphis

Alabama 1819
Birmingham
Montgomery
Columbus
Mobile
Pensacola

Georgia 1788
Atlanta
Macon
Columbus
Savannah
Jacksonville

Florida 1845
Tampa
Lake Okeechobee
Miami

Tallahassee

Eastern Time Zone

Vermont 1791
Burlington
Montpelier

Maine 1820
Bangor
Augusta
Lewiston
Portland

New Hampshire 1788
Concord
Manchester

Massachusetts 1788
Boston

Rhode Island 1790
Providence
Connecticut 1788
Hartford

Atlantic Time Zone

New York 1788
Albany
Rochester
Buffalo

Lake Ontario

Pennsylvania 1787
Pittsburgh
Harrisburg
Philadelphia

Newark
New York
Jersey City
Trenton

New Jersey 1787

Wilmington
Baltimore
Dover
Delaware 1787
Annapolis
Washington, D.C.
Maryland 1788

Virginia 1788
Richmond
Norfolk

West Virginia 1863

North Carolina 1789
Winston-Salem
Greensboro
Raleigh
Charlotte

South Carolina 1788
Columbia
Charleston

ATLANTIC OCEAN

N
W E
S

National capital
State capital
Other city
1787 Year of admission to the Union
Boundaries of time zones

0   150   300 Miles
0   150   300 Kilometers

Tropic of Cancer

90iW 85iW 80iW 75iW 70iW 65iW 60iW
50iN 45iN 40iN 35iN 30iN 25iN 20iN
95iW 90iW 85iW 80iW 75iW

ILLUSTRATED DATA BANK

1103

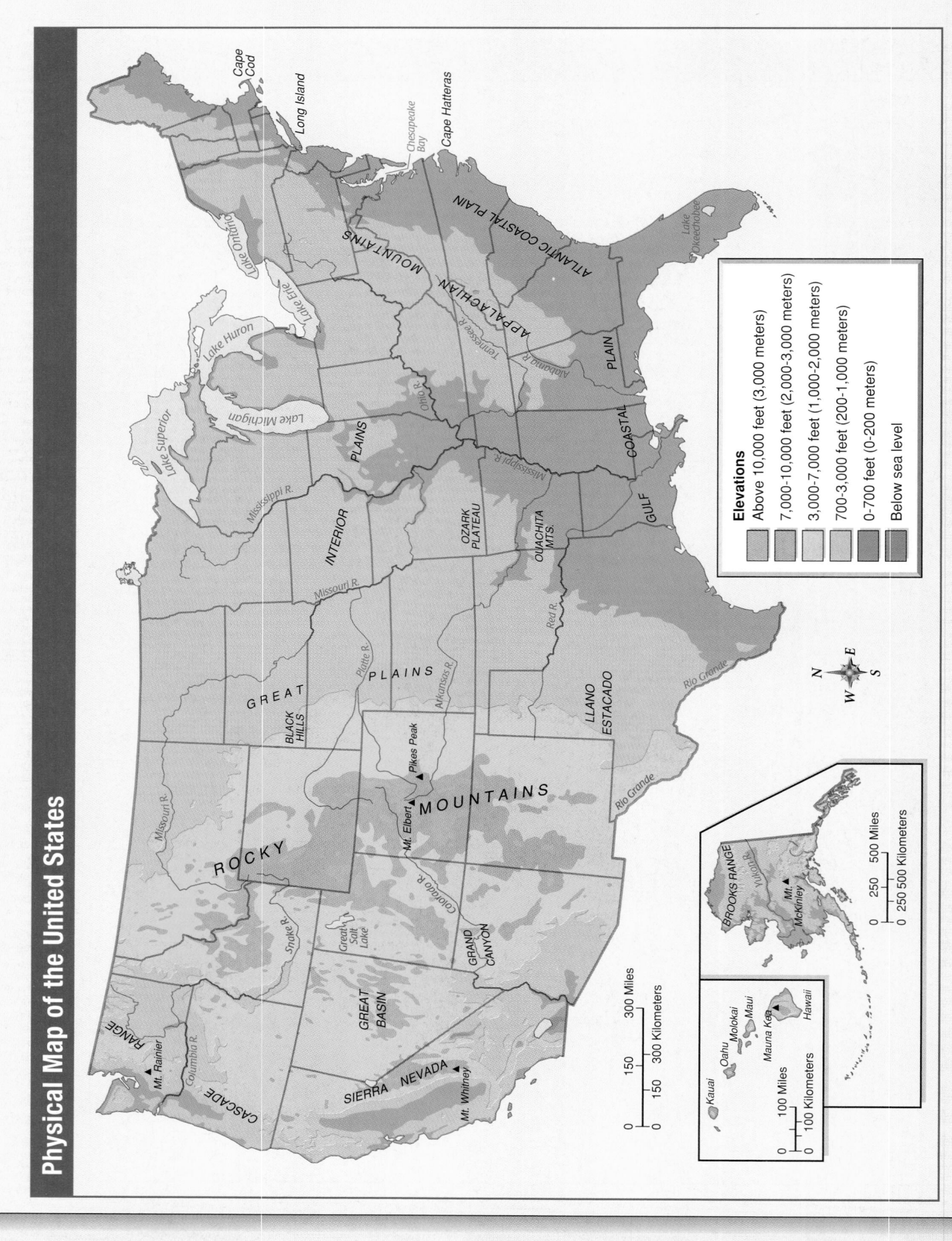

Physical Map of the United States

Elevations

- Above 10,000 feet (3,000 meters)
- 7,000-10,000 feet (2,000-3,000 meters)
- 3,000-7,000 feet (1,000-2,000 meters)
- 700-3,000 feet (200-1,000 meters)
- 0-700 feet (0-200 meters)
- Below sea level

Cape Cod
Long Island
Chesapeake Bay
Cape Hatteras
Lake Ontario
Lake Erie
Lake Huron
Lake Michigan
Lake Superior
Lake Okeechobee
APPALACHIAN MOUNTAINS
ATLANTIC COASTAL PLAIN
Tennessee R.
Alabama R.
COASTAL PLAIN
GULF
Mississippi R.
Ohio R.
Mississippi R.
PLAINS
INTERIOR
OZARK PLATEAU
OUACHITA MTS.
Missouri R.
Missouri R.
Red R.
Platte R.
PLAINS
Arkansas R.
LLANO ESTACADO
Rio Grande
GREAT
BLACK HILLS
Pikes Peak
MOUNTAINS
Mt. Elbert
ROCKY
Colorado R.
Rio Grande
GRAND CANYON
Great Salt Lake
Snake R.
Columbia R.
GREAT BASIN
CASCADE RANGE
Mt. Rainier
SIERRA NEVADA
Mt. Whitney

N E S W

BROOKS RANGE
Yukon R.
Mt. McKinley
0 250 500 Kilometers
0 250 500 Miles

Kauai
Oahu
Molokai
Maui
Mauna Kea
Hawaii
0 100 Miles
0 100 Kilometers

300 Miles
150
0
300 Kilometers
150
0

Natural Resources of the United States

	Aluminum		Copper		Magnesium		Natural gas		Sulphur
	Chromium		Gold		Manganese		Nickel		Tin
	Coal		Iron ore		Mercury		Oil		Uranium
	Cobalt		Lead		Molybdenum		Silver		Zinc

Political Map of the World

ARCTIC OCEAN

Greenland (Den.)

Yukon R.

Alaska (U.S.)

Reykjavik★ ICELAND

ALEUTIAN IS. (U.S.)

Mackenzie R.

60°N

CANADA

NORTH AMERICA

Montreal
Ottawa★

Chicago

New York

40°N

San Francisco●

UNITED STATES

Washington, DC

AZORES (Port.)

Mississippi R.

Colorado R.

Ohio R.

Bermuda (U.K.)

ATLANTIC OCEAN

CANARY IS. (Spain)

Midway I. (U.S.)

Houston●

New Orleans

BAHAMAS

Western Sahara (Mor.)

HAWAII (U.S.)

20°N

MEXICO

BELIZE

CUBA

Havana

Santo Domingo

DOMINICAN REP.

See inset map

Mexico City●

GUATEMALA

JAMAICA

Port-au-Prince

HAITI

Puerto Rico (U.S.)

ST. KITTS & NEVIS

ANTIGUA & BARBUDA

CAPE VERDE

HONDURAS

Guatemala★

Tegucigalpa

ST. LUCIA

DOMINICA

EL SALVADOR

NICARAGUA

TRINIDAD & TOBAGO

BARBADOS

San Salvador

Managua

COSTA RICA

Panama

GUYANA

San José

Caracas

VENEZUELA

SURINAME

PANAMA

Bogotá

Georgetown

Paramaribo

FRENCH GUIANA

Equator 0°

COLOMBIA

GALÁPAGOS IS. (Ecuador)

Quito●

Negro R.

ECUADOR

Amazon R.

Madeira R.

SOUTH AMERICA

PACIFIC OCEAN

São Francisco R.

SAMOA

AMERICAN SAMOA (U.S.)

Lima●

PERU

BRAZIL

Brasília★

TONGA

FRENCH POLYNESIA (Fr.)

COOK IS. (N.Z.)

BOLIVIA

La Paz

Sucre

20°S

Pitcairn I. (U.K.)

PARAGUAY

Rio de Janeiro

São Paulo●

Asunción

Uruguay R.

CHILE

N

Easter I. (Chile)

URUGUAY

W E

40°S

Santiago●

Buenos Aires

Montevideo

S

ARGENTINA

FALKLAND IS. (U.K.)

S. Georgia (U.K.)

Europe

0   200   400 Miles

0   400 Kilometers

FINLAND

Helsinki★

NORWAY

Oslo★   Stockholm★

Tallinn★

N. IRELAND

SWEDEN

ESTONIA

RUSSIA

Riga★

Dublin★

UNITED KINGDOM

DENMARK

LATVIA

IRELAND

NETHERLANDS

Copenhagen★

LITHUANIA

London★

Amsterdam★

Vilnius★

Minsk★

ATLANTIC OCEAN

Berlin★

Warsaw★

RUSSIA

BELARUS

Brussels★

GERMANY

POLAND

Kiev★

BELGIUM

Paris★

LUX.

Prague★

CZECH REP.

SLOVAKIA

UKRAINE

MOLDOVA

FRANCE

Bern★

LIECH.

Vienna★

Bratislava★

Budapest★

Chisinau★

SWITZ.

AUSTRIA

HUNGARY

ROMANIA

SLOVENIA

Ljubljana★

Zagreb★

CROATIA

Bucharest★

SAN MARINO

BOSNIA-HERZ.

Belgrade★

Danube R.

PORTUGAL

ANDORRA

MONACO

ITALY

Sarajevo★

SERBIA

BULGARIA

Lisbon★

Madrid★

Montenegro

Sofia★

MACEDONIA

SPAIN

Rome★

Tirana★

ALBANIA

Mediterranean Sea

GREECE

TURKEY

Rabat★

Algiers★

Tunis★

Athens★

MOROCCO

ALGERIA

TUNISIA

Africa

Nouakchott★

MAURITANIA

0   250   500 Miles

0   250   500 Kilometers

Dakar★

SENEGAL

MALI

Niamey★

NIGER

GAMBIA

Banjul★

Bamako★

Niger R.

BURKINA FASO

Bissau★

GUINEA-BISSAU

Ouagadougou★

GUINEA

BENIN

NIGERIA

Conakry★

Abuja★

Freetown★

SIERRA LEONE

CÔTE D'IVOIRE

GHANA

Porto-Novo★

Monrovia★

Yamoussoukro★

Lomé★

Lagos●

LIBERIA

Accra★

Abidjan★

TOGO

20°E 40°E 60°E 80°E 100°E 120°E 140°E 160°E

SVALBARD (Nor.)

See inset map

EUROPE

RUSSIA

Moscow

Ob R.
Volga R.
Lena R.

Novosibirsk

KAZAKHSTAN

ASIA

Astana
Ulanbaatar

MONGOLIA

Bishkek
KYRGYZSTAN
Dushanbe
TAJIKISTAN
AFGHANISTAN
Kabul Islamabad
PAKISTAN NEPAL BHUTAN
New Delhi Kathmandu Thimphu
INDIA
Dhaka

Beijing
N. KOREA
Pyongyang
Seoul
S. KOREA
JAPAN
Tokyo

Tianjin

CHINA
Chongqing

Huang He

Taipei
TAIWAN
Hanoi
Hong Kong

PACIFIC OCEAN

MYANMAR
Yangon
BANGLA-DESH
Bangkok
LAOS
Vientiane
THAILAND
VIETNAM
Ho Chi Minh City
CAMBODIA
Phnom Penh

Mekong R.

AFRICA

See inset map

SRI LANKA
Colombo

Manila
PHILIPPINES

NORTHERN MARIANA IS. (U.S.)
Guam (U.S.)
Wake I. (U.S.)

MARSHALL IS.

Bangui
CENTRAL AFRICAN REP.
Malabo
EQ. GUINEA
Yaounde
CAMEROON
UGANDA
Libreville
KENYA
GABON
DEM. REP. OF THE CONGO
CONGO RWANDA
SÃO TOMÉ & PRÍNCIPE
Brazzaville
Kinshasa
Kigali
Nairobi
Bujumbura
BURUNDI
Kampala

SOMALIA
Mogadishu

MALDIVES

SINGAPORE

BRUNEI
Bandar Seri Begawan

MALAYSIA
Kuala Lumpur

PALAU

FEDERATED STATES OF MICRONESIA

NAURU
KIRIBATI

Cabinda (Angola)
Luanda
MALAWI
TANZANIA
Dar es Salaam

SEYCHELLES

INDONESIA
Jakarta

PAPUA NEW GUINEA
Port Moresby

TUVALU

SOLOMON IS.

ANGOLA
ZAMBIA
Lusaka
COMOROS

Lilongwe
Harare
Zambezi R.

Réunion (Fr.)

VANUATU
FIJI

NAMIBIA
ZIMBABWE
MOZAMBIQUE
Antananarivo
MAURITIUS

Windhoek
BOTSWANA
Gaborone
Maputo
MADAGASCAR

New Caledonia (Fr.)

Pretoria
Mbabne
SWAZILAND
Maseru

INDIAN OCEAN

AUSTRALIA

Perth

Cape Town
SOUTH AFRICA
LESOTHO

National capital

Other city

0   1,000   2,000 Miles
0 1,000 2,000 Kilometers

Canberra
Adelaide
Sydney
Melbourne
Wellington
NEW ZEALAND

ANTARCTICA

Middle East

RUSSIA
KAZAKHSTAN

Istanbul
GEORGIA
Tbilisi
UZBEKISTAN

Ankara
ARMENIA
Yerevan
Baku
TURKMENISTAN
Tashkent

Tunis
TURKEY
AZERBAIJAN
Ashgabat

CYPRUS
Beirut
SYRIA
TUNISIA
LEBANON
Jerusalem
Damascus
IRAQ
Baghdad
AFGHAN.

Tripoli
ISRAEL
Amman
Tehran
IRAN

Cairo
JORDAN
Kuwait
KUWAIT
PAK.

LIBYA
EGYPT
BAHRAIN
Manama
QATAR
Doha
Riyadh
Abu Dhabi
Muscat
U.A.E.

Nile R.
Red Sea
SAUDI ARABIA
OMAN

NIGER
CHAD

Khartoum
Asmara
Sanaa
YEMEN
ERITREA
Aden
DJIBOUTI
Djibouti

0   300   600 Miles
0 300 600 Kilometers

SUDAN
ETHIOPIA
Addis Ababa
SOMALIA

INDIAN OCEAN

Profile of the Fifty States

State	Capital	Entered Union	Population (1998)	Population Rank	Land Area (Square Miles)	Land Area Rank
Alabama	Montgomery	1819	4,352,000	23rd	51,705	29th
Alaska	Juneau	1959	614,000	48th	591,004	1st
Arizona	Phoenix	1912	4,669,000	21st	114,000	6th
Arkansas	Little Rock	1836	2,538,000	33rd	53,187	27th
California	Sacramento	1850	32,667,000	1st	158,706	3rd
Colorado	Denver	1876	3,971,000	24th	104,091	8th
Connecticut	Hartford	1788	3,274,000	29th	5,018	48th
Delaware	Dover	1787	744,000	45th	2,044	49th
Florida	Tallahassee	1845	14,916,000	4th	58,664	22nd
Georgia	Atlanta	1788	7,642,000	10th	58,910	21st
Hawaii	Honolulu	1959	1,193,000	41st	6,470	47th
Idaho	Boise	1890	1,229,000	40th	83,564	13th
Illinois	Springfield	1818	12,045,000	5th	56,345	24th
Indiana	Indianapolis	1816	5,899,000	14th	36,185	38th
Iowa	Des Moines	1846	2,862,000	30th	56,275	25th
Kansas	Topeka	1861	2,629,000	32nd	82,277	14th
Kentucky	Frankfort	1792	3,936,000	25th	40,409	37th
Louisiana	Baton Rouge	1812	4,369,000	22nd	47,751	31st
Maine	Augusta	1820	1,244,000	39th	33,265	39th
Maryland	Annapolis	1788	5,135,000	19th	10,460	42nd
Massachusetts	Boston	1788	6,147,000	13th	8,284	45th
Michigan	Lansing	1837	9,817,000	8th	58,527	23rd
Minnesota	St. Paul	1858	4,725,000	20th	84,402	12th
Mississippi	Jackson	1817	2,752,000	31st	47,689	32nd
Missouri	Jefferson City	1821	5,439,000	16th	69,697	19th
Montana	Helena	1889	880,000	44th	147,046	4th
Nebraska	Lincoln	1867	1,663,000	38th	77,355	15th
Nevada	Carson City	1864	1,747,000	36th	110,561	7th
New Hampshire	Concord	1788	1,185,000	42nd	9,279	44th
New Jersey	Trenton	1787	8,115,000	9th	7,787	46th
New Mexico	Santa Fe	1912	1,737,000	37th	121,593	5th
New York	Albany	1788	18,175,000	3rd	49,108	30th
North Carolina	Raleigh	1789	7,546,000	11th	52,669	28th
North Dakota	Bismarck	1889	638,000	47th	70,703	17th
Ohio	Columbus	1803	11,209,000	7th	41,330	35th
Oklahoma	Oklahoma City	1907	3,347,000	27th	69,956	18th
Oregon	Salem	1859	3,282,000	28th	97,073	10th
Pennsylvania	Harrisburg	1787	12,001,000	6th	45,308	33rd
Rhode Island	Providence	1790	988,000	43rd	1,212	50th
South Carolina	Columbia	1788	3,836,000	26th	31,113	40th
South Dakota	Pierre	1889	738,000	46th	77,116	16th
Tennessee	Nashville	1796	5,431,000	17th	42,144	34th
Texas	Austin	1845	19,760,000	2nd	266,807	2nd
Utah	Salt Lake City	1896	2,100,000	34th	84,899	11th
Vermont	Montpelier	1791	591,000	49th	9,614	43rd
Virginia	Richmond	1788	6,791,000	12th	40,767	36th
Washington	Olympia	1889	5,689,000	15th	68,138	20th
West Virginia	Charleston	1863	1,811,000	35th	24,231	41st
Wisconsin	Madison	1848	5,224,000	18th	56,153	26th
Wyoming	Cheyenne	1890	481,000	50th	97,809	9th

Source: *World Almanac, Statistical Abstract of the United States*

Presidents of the United States

George Washington
(1732–1799)

Years in office: 1789–1797
No political party
Elected from: Virginia
Vice Pres.: John Adams

1

John Adams
(1735–1826)

Years in office: 1797–1801
Federalist
Elected from: Massachusetts
Vice Pres.: Thomas Jefferson

2

Thomas Jefferson
(1743–1826)

Years in office: 1801–1809
Democratic Republican
Elected from: Virginia
Vice Pres.: Aaron Burr,
George Clinton

3

James Madison
(1751–1836)

Years in office: 1809–1817
Democratic Republican
Elected from: Virginia
Vice Pres.: George Clinton,
Elbridge Gerry

4

James Monroe
(1758–1831)

Years in office: 1817–1825
National Republican
Elected from: Virginia
Vice Pres.: Daniel Tompkins

5

John Quincy Adams
(1767–1848)

Years in office: 1825–1829
National Republican
Elected from: Massachusetts
Vice Pres.: John Calhoun

6

Andrew Jackson
(1767–1845)

Years in office: 1829–1837
Democrat
Elected from: Tennessee
Vice Pres.: John Calhoun,
Martin Van Buren

7

Martin Van Buren
(1782–1862)

Years in office: 1837–1841
Democrat
Elected from: New York
Vice Pres.: Richard Johnson

8

ILLUSTRATED DATA BANK

William Henry Harrison*
(1773–1841)

Years in office: 1841
Whig
Elected from: Ohio
Vice Pres.: John Tyler

9

John Tyler
(1790–1862)

Years in office: 1841–1845
Whig
Elected from: Virginia
Vice Pres.: none

10

James K. Polk
(1795–1849)

Years in office: 1845–1849
Democrat
Elected from: Tennessee
Vice Pres.: George Dallas

11

Zachary Taylor*
(1784–1850)

Years in office: 1849–1850
Whig
Elected from: Louisiana
Vice Pres.: Millard Fillmore

12

Millard Fillmore
(1800–1874)

Years in office: 1850–1853
Whig
Elected from: New York
Vice Pres.: none

13

Franklin Pierce
(1804–1869)

Years in office: 1853–1857
Democrat
Elected from:
  New Hampshire
Vice Pres.: William King

14

James Buchanan
(1791–1868)

Years in office: 1857–1861
Democrat
Elected from: Pennsylvania
Vice Pres.:
  John Breckinridge

15

Abraham Lincoln**
(1809–1865)

Years in office: 1861–1865
Republican
Elected from: Illinois
Vice Pres.: Hannibal Hamlin,
  Andrew Johnson

16

Andrew Johnson
(1808–1875)

Years in office: 1865–1869
Republican
Elected from: Tennessee
Vice Pres.: none

17

Ulysses S. Grant
(1822–1885)

Years in office: 1869–1877
Republican
Elected from: Illinois
Vice Pres.: Schuyler Colfax,
  Henry Wilson

18

Rutherford B. Hayes
(1822–1893)

Years in office: 1877–1881
Republican
Elected from: Ohio
Vice Pres.: William Wheeler

19

James A. Garfield**
(1831–1881)

Years in office: 1881
Republican
Elected from: Ohio
Vice Pres.: Chester A. Arthur

20

Chester A. Arthur
(1830–1886)

Years in office: 1881–1885
Republican
Elected from: New York
Vice Pres.: none

21

Grover Cleveland
(1837–1908)

Years in office:
   1885–1889
Democrat
Elected from: New York
Vice Pres.:
   Thomas Hendricks

22

Benjamin Harrison
(1833–1901)

Years in office: 1889–1893
Republican
Elected from: Indiana
Vice Pres.: Levi Morton

23

Grover Cleveland
(1837–1908)

Years in office: 1893–1897
Democrat
Elected from: New York
Vice Pres.:
   Adlai Stevenson

24

William McKinley**
(1843–1901)

Years in office: 1897–1901
Republican
Elected from: Ohio
Vice Pres.: Garret Hobart,
   Theodore Roosevelt

25

Theodore Roosevelt
(1858–1919)

Years in office:
   1901–1909
Republican
Elected from: New York
Vice Pres.:
   Charles Fairbanks

26

William Howard Taft
(1857–1930)

Years in office: 1909–1913
Republican
Elected from: Ohio
Vice Pres.: James Sherman

27

Woodrow Wilson
(1856–1924)

Years in office: 1913–1921
Democrat
Elected from: New Jersey
Vice Pres.: Thomas Marshall

28

Warren G. Harding*
(1865–1923)

Years in office: 1921–1923
Republican
Elected from: Ohio
Vice Pres.: Calvin Coolidge

29

Calvin Coolidge
(1872–1933)

Years in office: 1923–1929
Republican
Elected from: Massachusetts
Vice Pres.: Charles Dawes

30

Herbert C. Hoover
(1874–1964)

Years in office: 1929–1933
Republican
Elected from: New York
Vice Pres.: Charles Curtis

31

Franklin D. Roosevelt*
(1882–1945)

Years in office: 1933–1945
Democrat
Elected from: New York
Vice Pres.: John Garner,
  Henry Wallace,
  Harry S. Truman

32

Harry S. Truman
(1884–1972)

Years in office: 1945–1953
Democrat
Elected from: Missouri
Vice Pres.: Alben Barkley

33

Dwight D. Eisenhower
(1890–1969)

Years in office: 1953–1961
Republican
Elected from: New York
Vice Pres.: Richard M. Nixon

34

John F. Kennedy**
(1917–1963)

Years in office: 1961–1963
Democrat
Elected from: Massachusetts
Vice Pres.:
  Lyndon B. Johnson

35

Lyndon B. Johnson
(1908–1973)

Years in office: 1963–1969
Democrat
Elected from: Texas
Vice Pres.: Hubert Humphrey

36

Richard M. Nixon***
(1913–1994)

Years in office: 1969–1974
Republican
Elected from: New York
Vice Pres.: Spiro Agnew,
  Gerald R. Ford

37

Gerald R. Ford
(1913–)

Years in office: 1974–1977
Republican
Elected from: Michigan
Vice Pres.:
  Nelson Rockefeller

38

Jimmy Carter
(1924–)

Years in office: 1977–1981
Democrat
Elected from: Georgia
Vice Pres.: Walter F. Mondale

39

Ronald W. Reagan
(1911–)

Years in office: 1981–1989
Republican
Elected from: California
Vice Pres.:
    George H.W. Bush

40

George H.W. Bush
(1924–)

Years in office: 1989–1993
Republican
Elected from: Texas
Vice Pres.:
    J. Danforth Quayle

41

William J. Clinton
(1946–)

Years in office: 1993–2001
Democrat
Elected from: Arkansas
Vice Pres.:
    Albert Gore, Jr.

42

George W. Bush
(1946–)

Years in office: 2001–
Republican
Elected from: Texas
Vice Pres.:
    Richard Cheney

43

ILLUSTRATED DATA BANK

* **Died in office**
** **Assassinated**
*** **Resigned**

Supreme Court Cases

These pages provide summaries of key Supreme Court rulings over the course of the nation's history. For additional material and links to Supreme Court cases, see America: Pathways to the Present *companion Web site at* http://www.Pathways.phschool.com

Baker v. Carr, 1962

(14th Amendment) Rapid population growth in Nashville and reluctance of the rural-dominated Tennessee legislature to redraw state legislature districts led Mayor Baker of Nashville to ask for federal court help. The federal district court refused to enter the "political thicket" of redistricting, and the case was appealed. The Court directed a trial to be held in a Tennessee federal court. The case led to the 1964 Westberry decision, which created the "one man, one vote" equal representation concept.

Bob Jones University v. United States, 1983

(14th and 1st amendments) Bob Jones University, a private school, denied admission to applicants in an interracial marriage or who "espouse" interracial marriage or dating. The Internal Revenue Service then denied tax-exempt status to the school because of racial discrimination. The university appealed, claiming that its policy was based on the Bible. The Court upheld the IRS ruling, stating that "Government has a fundamental overriding interest" in ending race discrimination in education.

Brown v. Board of Education of Topeka, 1954

(14th Amendment) Probably no 20th-century Supreme Court decision so deeply stirred and changed life in the United States as *Brown*. A 10-year-old girl from Topeka, Kansas, was not permitted to attend her neighborhood school because she was an African American. The Court found that segregation itself was a violation of the Equal Protection Clause, commenting that "in the field of public education the doctrine of 'separate but equal' has no place. . . . Segregation is a denial of the equal protection of the laws." The decision overturned *Plessy*, 1896.

The Civil Rights Cases, 1883

(14th Amendment) The Civil Rights Acts of 1875 included punishments for businesses that practiced discrimination. The Court ruled on a number of cases involving the Acts in 1883, finding that the Constitution, "while prohibiting discrimination by governments, made no provisions . . . for acts of racial discrimination by private individuals." The decision limited the impact of the Equal Protection Clause, giving tacit approval for segregation in the private sector.

Cruzan v. Director, Missouri Dept. of Health, 1990

(9th Amendment, right to die) A Missouri woman was in a coma from an automobile accident in 1983. Her family, facing astronomical medical bills and deciding that "her life had ended in 1987," directed the health care providers to end intravenous feeding. The State of Missouri opposed the family's decision, and the family went to court. The Court ruled that states could require "clear and convincing" evidence that Cruzan would have wanted to die. However, the Court did not require other states to meet the Missouri standard. At a subsequent hearing, "clear and convincing evidence" was presented. The intravenous feeding was ended, and Cruzan died on December 26, 1990.

Dennis v. United States, 1951

(1st Amendment) The Smith Act of 1940 made it a crime for any person to work for the violent overthrow of the United States in peacetime or war. Eleven Communist party leaders, including Dennis, had been convicted of violating the Smith Act, and they appealed. The Court upheld the Act. Much modified by later decisions, the Dennis case focused on anti-government speech as an area of controversy.

Dred Scott v. Sandford, 1857

(6th Amendment) This decision upheld property rights over human rights by saying that Dred Scott, a slave, could not become a free man just because he had traveled in "free soil" states with his master. A badly divided nation was further fragmented by the decision. "Free soil" federal laws and the Missouri Compromise line of 1820 were held unconstitutional because they deprived a slave owner of the right to his "property" without just compensation. This narrow reading of the Constitution, a landmark case of the Court, was most clearly stated by Chief Justice Roger B. Taney, a states' rights advocate.

Engel v. Vitale, 1962

(1st Amendment) The state Board of Regents of New York required the recitation of a 22-word nonsectarian prayer at the beginning of each school day. A group of parents filed suit against the required prayer, claiming it violated their First Amendment rights. The Court ruled New York's action unconstitutional, observing, "There can be no doubt that . . . religious beliefs [are] embodied in the Regents' prayer."

Escobedo v. Illinois, 1964

(6th Amendment) A person known to Chicago-area police confessed to a murder but had not been provided with a lawyer while under interrogation. The Court's decision in the case extended the "exclusionary rule" to illegal confessions in state court proceedings. Carefully defining an "Escobedo Rule," the Court said, "where . . . the investigation is no longer a general inquiry . . . but has begun to focus on a particular suspect . . . (and where) the suspect has been taken into custody . . . the suspect has requested . . . his lawyer, and the police have not . . . warned him of his right to remain silent, the accused has been denied . . . counsel in violation of the Sixth Amendment."

Everson v. Board of Education, 1947

(1st Amendment) In a case known as "the New Jersey School Bus Case," the Court considered New Jersey's use of public funds to operate school buses that carried some students to parochial schools. The Court permitted New Jersey to continue the payments, saying that the aid to children was not governmental support for religion. The decision, however, strongly stated that the wall separating church and state must be kept "high and impregnable." This was a clear incorporation of 1st Amendment limits of states.

Ex Parte Milligan, 1866

(Article II) An Indiana man was arrested, treated as a prisoner of war, and imprisoned by a military court during the Civil War under presidential order. He claimed that his right to a fair trial was interfered with and that military courts had no authority outside of "conquered territory." The Court ordered him to be released on the grounds that the Constitution "is a law for rulers and people, equally in war and peace" and covers all people "at all times, and under all circumstances." The Court held that presidential powers in time of war did not extend to creating another court system run by the military.

Furman v. Georgia, 1972

(8th Amendment) Three death penalty cases, including *Furman,* raised the issue of racial imbalances in the use of death sentences by state courts. Furman had been sentenced to death in Georgia. Overturning state death penalty laws, the Court noted an "apparent arbitrariness of the use of the sentence." Many states rewrote their death penalty statutes, and these were generally upheld in *Gregg,* 1976.

Gibbons v. Ogden, 1824

(Article I, Section 8) This case examined the power of Congress to regulate interstate commerce. Ogden's exclusive New York ferry license gave him the right to operate steamboats to and from New York. Ogden claimed that Gibbons's federal license did not give him landing rights in New York City. Federal and state regulation of commerce conflicted. The Court strengthened the power of the United States to regulate interstate business. Federal controls on television, pipelines, and banking are based on *Gibbons.*

Gideon v. Wainwright, 1963

(14th Amendment) Gideon was charged with breaking into a poolroom. He could not afford a lawyer, and Florida refused to provide counsel for trials not involving the death penalty. Gideon defended himself poorly and was sentenced to five years in prison. The Court called for a new trial, arguing that the due-process clause of the 14th Amendment applied to the 6th Amendment's guarantee of counsel for all poor persons facing a felony charge. Gideon later was found not guilty with the help of a court-appointed attorney.

Gitlow v. New York, 1925

(1st and 14th amendments) For the first time, the Court considered whether the 1st and 14th amendments had influence on state laws. The case, involving "criminal anarchy" under New York law, was the first consideration of what came to be known as the "incorporation" doctrine, under which, it was argued, the provisions of the 1st Amendment were "incorporated" by the 14th Amendment. Although New York law was not overruled in the case, the decision clearly indicated that the Court could make such a ruling. Another important incorporation case is *Powell,* 1932.

Gregg v. Georgia, 1976

(8th Amendment) In the 1970s activists tried to get the death penalty reinstated. Several test cases failed when the Court found the sentence had been motivated by racism, issued arbitrarily, or without due process. The case of Gregg, convicted of murdering two men, was considered to be free from such problems. Finding that his conviction and death sentence were fair and consistent with state law, the Court ruled that Georgia's death penalty did not violate the "cruel and unusual punishment" clause of the 8th Amendment. For the first time, the Court clearly affirmed that "punishment of death does not invariably violate the Constitution."

Griswold v. Connecticut, 1965

(14th Amendment) A Connecticut law forbade the use of "any drug, medicinal article, or instrument for the purpose of preventing conception." Griswold, director of Planned Parenthood in New Haven, was arrested for counseling married couples. After conviction, he appealed. The Court overturned the Connecticut law, saying that "various guarantees (of the Constitution) create zones of privacy" and asking, " would we allow the police to search the sacred precincts of marital bedrooms . . . ?" The decision is significant for examining the concept of "unenumerated rights" in the 9th Amendment, later central to *Roe*, 1973.

Heart of Atlanta Motel, Inc. v. United States, 1964

(Article I, Section 8) The Civil Rights Act of 1964 outlawed race discrimination in "public accommodations," including motels that refused rooms to blacks. Although local desegregation appeared to fall outside federal authority, the government argued that it was regulating interstate commerce. The Court agreed, declaring, "The power of Congress to promote interstate commerce also includes the power to regulate the local incidents thereof, including local activities . . . which have a substantial and harmful effect upon that commerce." Racial segregation of private facilities engaged in interstate commerce was found unconstitutional.

In Re Gault, 1966

(14th Amendment) Before *Gault*, proceedings against juveniles were generally handled as "family law," not "criminal law," and offenders received few due-process rights. Gault was sentenced to six years in state juvenile detention for an alleged obscene phone call. He was not provided counsel and not permitted to confront or cross-examine the key witness. The Court overturned the juvenile proceedings and required that states provide juveniles "some of the due process guarantees of adults," including a right to a phone call, to counsel, to cross-examine, to confront their accuser, and to be advised of their right to silence.

Katz v. United States, 1967

(4th Amendment) Arrested for illegal gambling after using a public phone to transmit information about betting, Katz claimed that the wiretapping of the phone, done without a warrant, was a violation of his 4th Amendment rights. The Court expanded the protections of the 4th Amendment, observing that people, not just property, are protected against illegal searches. Whatever a citizen "seeks to preserve as private, even in an area accessible to the public, may be constitutionally protected."

Korematsu v. United States, 1944

(5th Amendment) Two months after Japan attacked Pearl Harbor, President Roosevelt ordered the internment of more than 110,000 Japanese Americans living on the West Coast. Although many Japanese Americans were United States citizens, they had to abandon their property and live in primitive camps far from the coast. Korematsu refused to report to an assembly center and was arrested. The Court rejected his appeal, noting that "pressing public necessity [World War II] may sometimes justify the existence of restrictions which curtail the civil rights of a single racial group" but added that "racial antagonism" never can justify such restrictions. The *Korematsu* decision has been widely criticized, particularly since few Americans of German or Italian descent were interned.

Lemon v. Kurzman, 1971

(1st Amendment, Establishment Clause) In overturning state laws regarding aid to church-supported schools in this and a similar Rhode Island case, the Court created the Lemon test limiting "excessive government entanglement with religion." The Court noted that any state law about aid to religion must meet three criteria: (1) purpose of the aid must be clearly secular, not religious; (2) its primary effect must neither advance nor inhibit religion; and (3) it must avoid "excessive entanglement of government with religion."

Mapp v. Ohio, 1961

(4th and 14th amendments) Before *Mapp*, the admission of evidence gained by illegal searches was permitted by some state constitutions. Cleveland police raided Mapp's home without a warrant and found obscene materials. She appealed her conviction, saying that the 4th and 14th amendments protected her against improper police behavior. The Court agreed, extending "exclusionary rule" protections to citizens in state courts. The Court said that the prohibition against unreasonable searches would be "meaningless" unless evidence gained in such searches was excluded. The case developed the concept of "incorporation" begun in *Gitlow*, 1925.

Marbury v. Madison, 1803

(Article III) Chief Justice Marshall established "judicial review" as a power of the Supreme Court. After defeat in the 1800 election, President Adams appointed many Federalists to the federal courts, but the commissions were not delivered. New Secretary of State James Madison refused to deliver them. Marbury sued in the Supreme Court. The Court declared a portion of the Judiciary Act of 1789 unconstitutional, thereby declaring the Court's power to find acts of Congress unconstitutional.

Massachusetts v. Sheppard, 1984

(4th Amendment) A search in Massachusetts was based on a warrant issued on an improper form. Sheppard argued that the search was illegal and the evidence was inadmissible under *Mapp,* 1961. Massachusetts argued that the police acted in "good faith," believing that the warrant was correct. The Court agreed with Massachusetts, noting that the exclusionary rule should not be applied when the officer conducting the search had acted with the reasonable belief that he was following proper procedures.

McCulloch v. Maryland, 1819

(Article I, Section 8) Called the "Bank of the United States" case. A Maryland law required federally chartered banks to use only a special paper to print money, which amounted to a tax. McCulloch, the cashier of the Baltimore branch of the bank, refused to use the paper, claiming that states could not tax the federal government. The Court declared the Maryland law unconstitutional, commenting ". . . the power to tax implies the power to destroy."

Miller v. California, 1973

(1st Amendment) In *Miller,* the Court upheld a stringent application of California obscenity law by Newport Beach, California, and attempted to define what is obscene. The "Miller Rule" included three criteria: (1) That the average person would, applying contemporary community standards, find that the work appealed to the prurient interest; (2) that the work depicts or describes, in an offensive way, sexual conduct defined by state law; and (3) that "the work, taken as a whole, lacks serious literary, artistic, political or scientific value. . . ."

Miranda v. Arizona, 1966

(5th, 6th, and 14th amendments) Arrested for kidnapping and sexual assault, Miranda signed a confession including a statement that he had "full knowledge" of his legal rights. After conviction, he appealed, claiming that without counsel and without warnings, the confession was illegally obtained. The Court agreed with Miranda that "he must be warned prior to any questioning that he has the right to remain silent, that anything he says can be used against him in a court of law, that he has a right to . . . an attorney and that if he cannot afford an attorney one will be appointed for him. . . ." Although later modified, *Miranda* firmly upheld citizens' rights to fair trial in state courts.

Mueller v. Allen, 1983

(1st and 14th amendments) Minnesota law allowed taxpayers to deduct the costs of tuition, textbooks, and transportation for children in elementary and secondary schools. Several taxpayers sued to prevent parents with children in religious schools from claiming this deduction, arguing that this would constitute state sponsorship of religion. The Court disagreed, ruling that the deduction was not intended to promote religion and was available to all parents with school-age children. The Court argued that a law must have the advancement of religion as its primary purpose to be found unconstitutional.

New York Times v. United States, 1971

(1st Amendment) In June 1971 *The New York Times* published the first in a series of secret government documents known as the "Pentagon Papers," which detailed how the United States became involved in the Vietnam War. The Justice Department obtained a court order forbidding the newspaper from printing more documents. *The New York Times* and other newspapers challenged the order. The Court cited the 1st Amendment guarantee of a free press and refused to uphold the ban, noting that the government must prove that publication would harm the nation's security. The decision limited "prior restraint" of the press.

Nix v. Williams, 1984

(4th Amendment, illegal evidence) A man was convicted of murdering a 10-year-old girl after he led officers to the body. He had been arrested, but not advised of his rights, in a distant city, and in transit, he had conversed with a police officer. Williams agreed that the child should have a proper burial and directed the officer to the body. Later, on appeal, Williams's attorneys argued that the body should not be admitted as evidence because the questioning was illegal. The Court disagreed, observing that search parties were within two and one-half miles of the body. "Evidence otherwise excluded may be admissible when it would have been discovered anyway." The decision was one of several "exceptions to the exclusionary rule" handed down by the Court in the 1980s.

Plessy v. Ferguson, 1896

(14th Amendment, Equal Protection Clause) A Louisiana law required separate seating for white passengers and black passengers on public railroads. Plessy argued that the policy violated his right to "equal protection of the laws." The Court disagreed, saying that segregation was permissible if facilities were equal. It ruled that the 14th Amendment was "not intended to give Negroes social equality but only political and civil equality. . . ." The Louisiana law was seen as a "reasonable exercise of (state) police power. . . ." This "separate but equal" ruling allowed the segregation of public facilities throughout the South until *Plessy* was overturned by the *Brown* v. *Board of Education* case of 1954.

Powell v. Alabama, 1932

(6th Amendment, right to counsel) The case involved the "Scottsboro Boys," seven black men accused of rape. The men were quickly prosecuted without counsel and sentenced to death. The Court overturned the decision, stating that poor people facing the death penalty in state courts must be provided counsel, saying that "there are certain principles of Justice which . . . no [state] may disregard." The case was a step toward incorporating the Bill of Rights into state constitutions.

Regents of the University of California v. Bakke, 1978

(14th Amendment) Under an affirmative action program, the medical school of the University of California at Davis reserved 16 of 100 slots in each class for "disadvantaged citizens." When Bakke, who is white, was not accepted by the school, he claimed racial discrimination in violation of the 14th Amendment. The Court ruled narrowly, requiring Bakke's admission but not overturning affirmative action, preferring to review such questions on a case-by-case basis.

Roe v. Wade, 1973

(9th Amendment) A Texas woman challenged a state law forbidding the artificial termination of a pregnancy, saying that she "had a fundamental right to privacy." The Court upheld a woman's right to choose, noting that the state's "important and legitimate interest in protecting the potentiality of human life" became "compelling" at the end of the first trimester, but that before then "the attending physician, in consultation with his patient, is free to determine, without regulation by the state, that . . . the patient's pregnancy should be terminated." The decision struck down state regulation of abortion in the first three months of pregnancy and was modified by *Webster,* 1989.

Rostker v. Goldberg, 1981

(5th Amendment) In 1980, President Carter reinstated draft registration. For the first time both sexes were ordered to register. When Congress refused to fund the registration of women, several men sued, arguing that a selective draft violated their due process rights. The Court disagreed, noting that "the purpose of registration was to prepare for draft of combat troops" and that "Congress and the Executive have decided that women should not serve in combat."

Roth v. United States, 1957

(1st Amendment) A New York man named Roth operated a business that used the mail to invite people to buy materials considered obscene by postal inspectors. The Court, in its first consideration of censorship of obscenity, created the "prevailing community standards" rule, which required a consideration of the work as a whole. In its decision, the Court defined as obscene that which offended "the average person, applying contemporary community standards."

Schenck v. United States, 1919

(1st Amendment) Schenck, a member of an antiwar group, had urged men who were drafted into military service in World War I to resist and to avoid induction. He was charged with violating the Espionage Act of 1917, which outlawed active opposition to the war. The Court limited free speech in time of war, stating that Schenck's words presented a "clear and present danger. . . ." Although later decisions modified the decision, the Schenck case created a precedent that 1st Amendment rights were not absolute.

School District of Abington Township, Pennsylvania v. Schempp, 1963

(1st Amendment) Some Pennsylvania parents challenged a state law that required Bible readings each day at school. The Court agreed with the parents, saying that the Establishment Clause and Free Exercise Clause forbade states from engaging in religious activity. The Court ruled that if the purpose and effect of a law "is the advancement or inhibition of religion," it "exceeds the scope of legislative power."

Sheppard v. Maxwell, 1966

(14th Amendment) Sam Sheppard was convicted of murdering his wife in a trial sensationalized by the national media. Sheppard appealed, claiming that the pretrial publicity had made it impossible to get a fair trial. Rejecting arguments about freedom of the press, the Court overturned the conviction and ordered a new trial. Because of *Sheppard,* judges have issued "gag" orders limiting pretrial publicity.

South Dakota v. Dole, 1986

In 1984, Congress voted to withhold five percent of federal highway funds from any state which did not set a minimum drinking age at 21. South Dakota, which would lose money under the new law, challenged the government's right to coerce states to adopt specific policies through funding cuts. The Court ruled that highway funding was not an entitlement, and the national government could impose reasonable conditions upon the states in the interest of the "general welfare." All states that wished to continue to receive full federal highway aid were required to raise the legal age to purchase and consume alcohol to 21 years. In later years, the threat of spending cuts became a powerful tool of federal policy.

Tennessee Valley Authority v. Hiram G. Hill, Jr., et al., 1978

The Tellico Dam was nearly completed—and $100 million had been spent on it—when local residents succeeded in halting construction to save a tiny, nearly extinct fish called the snail darter. The fish's only habitat would have been flooded by the dam. The Court found the injunction against the TVA's completion of the nearly finished dam to be proper to prevent violation of the Endangered Species Act. Congress had declared the value of endangered species "incalculable." The Court refused to overrule Congress's judgment. The ruling affirmed the Environmental Protection Agency's power to protect the environment.

Texas v. Johnson, 1989

(1st Amendment) To protest national policies, Johnson doused a United States flag with kerosene and burned it outside the 1984 Republican National Convention in Dallas. He was arrested and convicted under a Texas law prohibiting the desecration of the Texas and United States flags. The Court ruled that the Texas law placed an unconstitutional limit on "freedom of expression," noting that ". . . nothing in our precedents suggests that a state may foster its own view of the flag by prohibiting expressive conduct relating to it."

Thompson v. Oklahoma, 1988

(8th Amendment, capital punishment) A 15-year-old from Oklahoma was convicted of murder and was sentenced to death at age 16. The Court overturned the death sentence, holding that "[t]he Eighth and Fourteenth Amendments prohibit the execution of a person who was under 16 years of age at the time of his or her offense." A death penalty was deemed cruel and unusual punishment for someone so young.

United States v. Nixon, 1974

President Nixon was widely suspected of participating in the coverup of the Watergate break-in. After journalists discovered that he had recorded all of his conversations in the White House, Congress demanded that Nixon hand over the tapes. The President cited executive privilege, arguing that his office placed him above the law. The Court overruled Nixon and ordered him to surrender the tapes. Limiting executive privilege, it ruled that the President's "generalized interest in confidentiality" was subordinate to "the fundamental demands of due process of law in the fair administration of criminal justice." The tapes implicated Nixon in the coverup and led to his resignation.

Walz v. Tax Commission of the City of New York, 1970

(1st Amendment, Establishment Clause) State and local governments routinely exempt church property from taxes. Walz claimed that such exemptions were a "support of religion." The Court disagreed, noting that such exemptions constituted a "benevolent neutrality" between government and churches, not a support of religion. Governments must avoid taxing churches, because taxation would give government a "control" over religion prohibited by the "wall of separation of church and state" noted in *Everson*, 1947.

Webster v. Reproductive Health Services, 1989

(9th Amendment) A 1986 Missouri law stated that (1) life begins at conception; (2) unborn children have rights; (3) public funds could not be used for abortions not necessary to save the life of the mother; and (4) public funds could not be used for abortion counseling. Health care providers in Missouri filed suit, challenging the law, claiming it was in conflict with *Roe*, 1973, and intruded into "privacy questions." A 5-4 Court upheld the Missouri law, stating that the people of Missouri, through their legislature, could put limits on the use of public funds. The *Webster* decision narrowed the *Roe* decision.

Weeks v. United States, 1914

(4th Amendment) A search without proper warrant was conducted in San Francisco, and the evidence collected was used by a postal inspector to prosecute Weeks. Weeks claimed that the evidence was gained by an illegal search, and thus was inadmissible. The Court agreed, applying for the first time an "exclusionary rule" for illegally gained evidence in federal courts. The decision stated ". . . if letters and private documents can thus be seized and used as evidence . . . his right to be secure against such searches . . . is of no value, and . . . might as well be stricken from the Constitution." See also *Mapp* v. *Ohio*, 1961; *Massachusetts* v. *Sheppard*, 1984; and *Nix* v. *Williams*, 1984.

West Virginia Board of Education v. Barnette, 1943

The beliefs of Jehovah's Witnesses forbid them to salute the United States flag. In the patriotic climate of World War II, thousands of children who refused to salute were expelled from public schools. The Court ruled that a compulsory flag salute violated the 1st Amendment's exercise of the religion clause and was therefore unconstitutional. "No official, high or petty, can prescribe what shall be orthodox in politics, nationalism, religion, or other matters of opinion."

Westside Community Schools v. Mergens, 1990

(1st Amendment, Establishment Clause) A request by Mergens to form a student Christian religious group at school was denied by an Omaha high school principal. Mergens took legal action, claiming that a 1984 federal law required "equal access" for student religious groups. The Court ordered the school to permit the formation of the club, stating, "a high school does not have to permit any extracurricular activities, but when it does, the school is bound by the Act of 1984. Allowing students to meet on campus and discuss religion is constitutional because it does not amount to a 'State sponsorship of a religion.' "

Glossary

This Glossary defines all key terms listed in section previews. The page number at the end of each entry indicates the text page on which the term appears in boldface. Key people are defined in the Biographical Dictionary.

Pronunciation Key

Pronunciations are provided for some of the entries in this Glossary. A syllable printed in SMALL CAPITAL LETTERS receives the greatest stress. The pronunciation key below lists the letters that will help you pronounce the word.

Symbol	Example	Respelling
a	hat	(hat)
ay	late	(layt)
ah	hot	(haht)
ai	air	(air)
aw	law	(law)
eh	met	(meht)
ee	eat	(eet)
er	learn	(lern)
ih	fit	(fiht)
ī	mile	(mīl)
ir	ear	(ir)
oh	no	(noh)
oi	boy	(boi)
oo	rule	(rool)
or	door	(dor)
ow	out	(owt)
u	book	(buk)
uh	fun	(fuhn)
yoo	few	(fyoo)
ch	reach	(reech)
g	go	(goh)
j	gently	(JENT lee)
k	cup	(kuhp)
ks	mix	(mihks)
kw	quick	(kwihk)
ng	bring	(brihng)
s	cent	(sehnt)
sh	she	(shee)
th	three	(three)
y	onion	(UHN yuhn)
z	always	(AWL ways)
zh	treasure	(TREH zher)

A

abolitionist movement   Movement to end slavery (p. 266)

abstinence   Refrain from some activity, such as drinking alcoholic beverages (p. 261)

Adams-Onís Treaty   1819 treaty between the United States and Spain in which Spain ceded Florida to the United States (p. 204)

administration   Term of office; also the members and agencies of the executive branch as a whole (p. 144)

AFDC   Aid to Families with Dependent Children, a public-assistance program commonly referred to as welfare (p.1031)

affirmative action   Policy which gives special consideration to women and members of minorities to make up for past discrimination (p. 949)

agenda   List of items to accomplish (p. 184)

AIDS   Acquired immuno-deficiency syndrome, a virus that killed many people starting in the 1980s (p. 966)

Albany Movement   Organization of African Americans formed in Georgia to promote civil rights (p. 828)

Albany Plan of Union   1754 proposal by Benjamin Franklin for the creation of a grand council of representatives from Britain's American colonies (p. 86)

alien   A noncitizen (p. 471)

Alien and Sedition Acts   Laws passed by Congress in 1798 that enabled the government to imprison or deport aliens and to prosecute critics of the government (p. 181)

Alliance for Progress   President Kennedy's proposal for cooperation among nations of the Western Hemisphere to meet the basic needs of their people (p. 812)

Allies   In World War I, Russia, France, Great Britain, and later the United States; in World War II, the alliance of Great Britain, the United States, the Soviet Union, and other nations (pp. 566, 688)

almanac   Book containing information such as calendars and weather predictions (p. 66)

amend   Revise (p. 133)

American Expeditionary Force (AEF)   Name given to American troops in Europe in World War I (p. 573)

American Indian Movement (AIM)   Organization formed in 1968 to help Native Americans (p. 858)

American Liberty League   Organization opposed to the New Deal (p. 668)

amnesty   General pardon for certain crimes (p. 949)

anarchist   Radical who violently opposes all government (p. 427)

annex   Join or attach (pp. 301, 516)

Antifederalist   An opponent of the Constitution during the debate over ratification; opposed the concept of a strong central government (p. 139)

anti-Semitism   Hostility or discrimination toward Jews (p. 707)

apartheid   (uh PAHRT hīt) South Africa's systematic separation of the white and black races (p. 989)

appeasement   Policy of giving in to someone's demands in order to preserve the peace (p. 687)

apportionment   Distribution of seats in a legislative body (p. 805)

apprentice   Person placed under a legal contract to work for another person in exchange for learning a trade (p. 66)

arbitration   Settlement of a dispute by a person chosen to listen to both sides (p. 519)

armistice   Cease-fire or truce (p. 576)

arms race   A contest between nations in which both expand their arms stockpiles in an effort to gain superiority (p. 761)

arsenal   Place where weapons are made or stored (p. 332)

Articles of Confederation   Plan of government under which the United States operated from 1781 until its replacement by the Constitution (p. 123)

assembly line   Manufacturing process in which each worker does one specialized task in the construction of the final product (p. 605)

assimilation   Process by which people of one culture merge into and become part of another culture (pp. 190, 488)

Atlantic Charter   Agreement signed by Roosevelt and Churchill in 1941 outlining the two nations' war aims (p. 692)

autocrat   Ruler with unlimited power (p. 567)

automation   The use of sophisticated machines in place of human labor (p. 1059)

autonomy   Self-government with respect to local matters (p. 858)

Axis Powers   In World War II, the alliance of Germany, Italy, and Japan (p. 686)

B

baby boom   Dramatic increase in birthrate during and after World War II (p. 770)

Bacon's Rebellion   Revolt in 1676 by Virginia colonists against the royal governor (p. 41)

balance of trade   Difference in value between imports and exports (p. 60)

banana republic   Term used to describe a Central American nation dominated by United States business interests (p. 517)

bank note   Piece of paper that a bank issues to its customers and that can be exchanged for gold or silver coin (p. 233)

barrio   Spanish-speaking neighborhood (p. 611)

barter   To trade goods or services without money (p. 7)

Bataan Death March   Brutal march of American and Filipino prisoners by Japanese soldiers in 1942 (p. 701)

Battle of the Alamo   Capture by Mexican troops of a Texas-held mission in San Antonio in 1836 (p. 295)

Battle of Antietam   Civil War battle in 1862 in Maryland (p. 348)

Battle of the Bulge   World War II battle in which German forces launched a final counterattack in the west (p. 698)

Battle of Bunker Hill   Revolutionary War battle in 1775 north of Boston (p. 107)

Battle of Chancellorsville   Civil War battle in 1863 in Virginia, won by the Confederacy (p. 361)

Battle of Cold Harbor   Civil War battle in 1864 in Virginia (p. 368)

Battle of the Coral Sea   World War II battle in 1942 between American and Japanese aircraft (p. 701)

Battle of Fredericksburg   Civil War battle in 1862 in Virginia, won by the Confederacy (p. 360)

Battle of Gettysburg   Civil War battle in 1863 in Pennsylvania, won by the Union and a turning point in the war (p. 362)

Battle of Guadalcanal   (gwahd uhl cuh NAL) World War II battle in 1942–1943 between the United States and Japan (p. 702)

Battle of Iwo Jima   World War II battle in 1945 between the United States and Japan (p. 703)

Battle of Little Bighorn   Sioux victory in 1876 over army troops under George Custer (p. 438)

Battle of Midway   World War II battle in 1942 between the United States and Japan, a turning point in the war in the Pacific (p. 701)

Battle of New Orleans   Battle in 1815 between American and British troops for control of New Orleans, ending in an American victory (p. 195)

Battle of Okinawa   World War II battle in 1945 between the United States and Japan (p. 703)

Battle of Saratoga   Revolutionary War battle in 1777 in New York, a turning point in the war (p. 110)

Battle of Shiloh   Civil War battle in 1862 in Tennessee (p. 345)

Battle of Spotsylvania   Civil War battle in 1864 in Virginia (p. 368)

Battle of Stalingrad   World War II battle in the Soviet Union that marked a turning point in the war in the east (p. 696)

Battle of Tippecanoe   Battle in the Indiana Territory in 1811 between American and Native American forces that led to the defeat of the Native Americans (p. 191)

Battle of Trenton   Revolutionary War battle in 1776 in New Jersey (p. 109)

Battle of the Wilderness   Civil War battle in 1864 in Virginia, won by the Confederacy (p. 367)

Battle of Yorktown   Revolutionary War battle in 1781 in Virginia, a decisive American victory (p. 113)

Battles of Lexington and Concord   First battles of the Revolutionary War, on April 19, 1775 (p. 96)

Bay of Pigs invasion   Failed invasion of Cuba by a group of anti-Castro forces in 1961 (p. 808)

beatnik   (BEET nihk) In the 1950s, a person who criticized American society as apathetic and conformist (p. 777)

Berlin airlift   Supply of West Berlin by American and British planes during a Soviet blockade in 1948–1949 (p. 750)

Berlin Wall   Barrier built by the East German government in 1961 to prevent East Germans from escaping to West Berlin (p. 809)

Bessemer process   New process, patented in 1856, for making steel more efficiently (p. 411)

bicentennial   200th anniversary (p. 935)

bilingual education   The teaching of students in their native language as well as in English (p. 1014)

Bill of Rights   First ten amendments to the Constitution (p. 141)

black codes   Laws that restricted freedmen's rights (p. 385)

blacklist   List that is circulated among employers, containing names of persons who should not be hired (p. 754)

black nationalism   Belief in the separate identity and racial unity of the African American community (p. 837)

black power   African American movement seeking unity and self-reliance (p. 838)

Black Tuesday   October 29, 1929, the day on which the Great Crash of the stock market began (p. 636)

Bland-Allison Act   1878 law requiring the federal government to purchase and coin more silver (p. 447)

blitzkrieg   (BLIHTS kreeg) Kind of warfare emphasizing rapid, mechanized movement (p. 687)

blockade   To isolate or close off a place from outside contact (p. 111)

block grant   Federal funds given to the states in lump sums (p. 1035)

blue law   Law that prohibits certain private activities, such as drinking alcohol on Sundays (p. 462)

Bonanza farm   Farm controlled by a large business and managed by professionals (p. 441)

Bonus Army   Group of World War I veterans and their families who in 1932 protested in Washington, D.C., to receive their pensions early (p. 651)

boomer   One of the settlers who rushed into Indian Territory upon its opening for settlement in 1889 (p. 439)

boom town   Town that has experienced rapid growth (p. 305)

bootlegger   During Prohibition, a supplier of illegal alcohol (p. 622)

Border States   In the Civil War, the states between the North and South: Delaware, Maryland, Kentucky, and Missouri (p. 333)

Boston Massacre   Incident on March 5, 1770, in which British soldiers in Boston killed five colonists (p. 94)

boycott   Refusal to buy a certain product or use a service (p. 92)

brinkmanship   Policy of risking war in order to protect national interests (p. 761)

Brown v. Board of Education of Topeka, Kansas   1954 case in which the Supreme Court outlawed racial segregation in public schools (p. 786)

buffalo soldier   Name given by Native Americans to black soldiers in the U.S. Army who served in the West during the late 1800s and early 1900s (p. 454)

bureaucracy   Departments that make up a large organization, such as a government (p. 184)

business cycle   Periodic growth and contraction of a nation's economy (pp. 418, 636)

buying on margin   Practice by which investors purchase a stock for only a fraction of its price, borrowing the rest (p. 633)

C

Cabinet   Leaders of the executive departments of the federal government (p. 143)

California Gold Rush   Mass migration to California following the discovery of gold in 1848 (p. 305)

Camp David Accords   1978 agreement between Israel and Egypt that made a peace treaty between the two nations possible (p. 941)

canister   A special type of shell filled with bullets (p. 344)

capital   Wealth that can be invested to produce goods and make money (p. 232)

carpetbagger   An insulting nickname for a Northern Republican who moved to the South after the Civil War (p. 390)

carpet bombing   Method of aerial bombing in which large numbers of bombs are dropped over a wide area (p. 697)

cartel   Loose association of businesses that make the same product (p. 416)

cash crop   Crop that is grown for sale (p. 23)

casualty   Person killed, wounded, or missing in battle (p. 342)

cede   (seed) To surrender officially or informally (p. 204)

centralized   Concentrated in one place (p. 231)

Central Powers   In World War I, Germany and Austria-Hungary (p. 566)

charter   Certificate of permission given by a government (p. 37)

checks and balances   System in which each of the branches of the federal government can check the actions of the other branches (p. 136)

Chinese Exclusion Act   Law passed in 1882 that prohibited Chinese laborers from entering the country (p. 470)

civil disobedience   Nonviolent refusal to obey a law in an effort to change the law (p. 557)

civil rights   Citizens' personal liberties guaranteed by law (p. 387)

Civil Rights Act of 1964   Law that outlawed discrimination in a number of areas, including voting, schools, and jobs (p. 833)

civil service   System of non-elected government workers (p. 463)

Civil War   War between the Union and the Confederacy from 1861 to 1865 (p. 341)

clan   Groups of families who are all descended from a common ancestor (p. 6)

Clayton Antitrust Act   1914 law passed to strengthen federal antitrust enforcement by spelling out business activities that were forbidden (p. 554)

Clean Air Act   Law passed in 1970 that aimed to control pollution caused by industrial and auto emissions (p. 864)

Clean Water Act   Law passed in 1972 that aimed to control pollution caused by the discharge of industrial and municipal wastewater (p. 865)

cloture   (CLOH cher) In the Senate, a three-fifths vote that permits the ending of debate on an issue (p. 833)

coalition   An alliance of groups with similar goals (p. 673)

cold war   The state of hostility, without actual warfare, that existed between the United States and the Soviet Union after World War II until the collapse of the Soviet Union (pp. 745, 1049)

collective bargaining   Process in which workers negotiate as a group with employers (p. 425)

collective security   Policy in which nations agree to protect one another against attack (p. 751)

colony   An area of land settled by immigrants who continue to be ruled by their parent country (p. 31)

Columbian Exchange   The transatlantic trade of crops, technology, and culture between the Americas and Europe, Africa, and Asia that began in 1492 with Columbus's first voyage to the Americas (p. 22)

Common Sense   Pamphlet written by Thomas Paine and published in January 1776, which called for American independence from Britain (p. 98)

communism   Official ideology of the Soviet Union, characterized there by complete government ownership of land and property, single-party control of the government, the lack of individual rights, and the call for worldwide revolution (p. 598)

Compromise of 1850   Agreement designed to ease tensions over the expansion of slavery into western territories (p. 322)

Compromise of 1877   Agreement in which the Democrats agreed to give Rutherford B. Hayes the victory in the presidential election of 1876 and Hayes, in return, agreed to remove the remaining federal troops from southern states (p. 397)

compulsory   Required (p. 535)

concentration camp   Place where prisoners of war and other prisoners are confined, usually under harsh conditions (p. 708)

concession   A grant for a piece of land in exchange for a promise to use the land for a specific purpose (p. 527)

Confederate States of America   Association of seven seceding Southern states, formed in 1861 (p. 334)

conglomerate   Large corporation that owns many smaller companies producing a variety of goods and services (p. 767)

congregation   The people of a church; a religious gathering (p. 219)

Congress of Racial Equality (CORE)   Organization founded in 1942 to promote racial equality through peaceful means (p. 820)

Congressional Union (CU)   Radical organization led by Alice Paul which campaigned for a constitutional amendment guaranteeing women's suffrage (p. 559)

conquistador   (kahn KEES tuh dor) Spanish conqueror (p. 29)

conscientious objector   Someone who opposes war on moral or religious grounds (p. 884)

conservationist   Person concerned with the care and protection of natural resources (p. 552)

constitution   Plan of government that describes the different parts of the government and their duties and powers (p. 124)

consumer economy   An economy that depends on a large amount of buying by individuals (p. 603)

containment   American policy of resisting further expansion of communism around the world (p. 745)

contra   Spanish for "counterrevolutionary," a rebel opposed to Nicaragua's Communist government in the 1980s (p. 967)

contraband   Items seized from the enemy during wartime (p. 354)

Contract with America   Pledge, made by Republican candidates in the 1994 election campaign, to scale back government, eliminate some regulations, cut taxes, and balance the budget (p. 982)

convoy   Group of armed and unarmed ships deployed to protect merchant shipping from attack (p. 574)

Copperhead   During the Civil War, an antiwar Northern Democrat (p. 352)

cotton gin Machine to separate the seeds from raw cotton fibers (p. 211)

counterculture Group of young Americans in the 1960s who rejected conventional customs (p. 887)

Crusades Series of military campaigns by European Christians from 1096 to 1291 to win the Holy Land from the Muslims (p. 10)

Cuban Missile Crisis 1962 crisis that arose between the United States and the Soviet Union over a Soviet attempt to deploy nuclear missiles in Cuba (p. 810)

Cumberland Road A federally built road that began in Cumberland, Maryland, in 1811 and was extended westward to Ohio and beyond (p. 212)

D

Dartmouth College* v. *Woodward 1819 case in which the Supreme Court ruled that states could not interfere with contracts (p. 245)

Dawes Act 1887 law that divided Native American land into private family plots (p. 438)

daylight saving time Turning clocks ahead one hour for the summer (p. 579)

D-Day Code name for the Allied invasion of France on June 6, 1944 (p. 698)

death camp In World War II, a German camp created solely for mass murder (p. 709)

Declaration of Independence Statement, issued by the Second Continental Congress in 1776, that explained why the colonies were seeking independence from Britain (p. 99)

de facto segregation Segregation based not on law but on poverty and ghetto conditions (p. 839)

deferment Official postponement of a person's call to serve in the armed forces (p. 884)

deficit spending Government spending of borrowed money (p. 719)

deflation Drop in the prices of goods (p. 447)

de jure segregation Segregation based on law (p. 839)

demagogue (DEHM uh gawg) A leader who manipulates people through such means as half-truths and scare tactics (p. 668)

demographics Statistics that describe a population, such as data on race or income (p. 610)

denomination A religious subgroup (p. 219)

department store Store that carries a variety of goods and sells in large quantities (p. 504)

depression A severe economic downturn marked by a decrease in business activity, widespread unemployment, and falling prices and wages (p. 195)

deregulation Reduction or removal of government controls (p. 946)

détente A relaxation in political tensions between nations (p. 916)

direct primary Election in which voters cast ballots to select nominees for upcoming elections (p. 548)

disarmament Program in which nations voluntarily give up their weapons (p. 600)

discrimination Unequal treatment of a group of people because of their nationality, race, sex, or religion (p. 280)

dissent Difference of opinion or belief (p. 80)

dissident Person who criticizes the actions of his or her government (p. 942)

diversity Variety (p. 51)

division of labor Way of producing in which different tasks are performed by different persons (p. 421)

dollar diplomacy President Taft's policy of encouraging American investment abroad (p. 531)

domestic affairs Issues relating to a country's internal affairs (p. 144)

domino theory Belief that if one country fell to communism, neighboring countries would likewise fall (p. 759)

"Double V" campaign An effort, launched by an African American newspaper, for victory against the Axis powers and victory in winning racial equality at home (p. 733)

Dow Jones Industrial Average Measure of average stock prices of major industries (p. 635)

downsizing Practice by companies of laying off workers in order to cut costs (p. 974)

draft Program of required military service (p. 349)

dry farming Techniques used to raise crops in areas that receive little rain (p. 440)

Dust Bowl A region in the Great Plains that had a period of drought and dust storms during the 1930s (p. 640)

duty A tax on imports (p. 60)

E

economic sanctions Trade restrictions and other economic measures intended to punish another nation (p. 989)

economies of scale Phenomenon that as production increases, the cost of each item produced is often lower (p. 417)

Electoral College Group of electors, chosen by the voters, who vote for President (p. 138)

e-mail Electronic mail transmitted via computer networks (p. 1056)

emancipation Freeing of enslaved people (p. 267)

Emancipation Proclamation Presidential decree, effective January 1, 1863, that freed slaves in Confederate-held territory (p. 353)

embargo Restriction on trade (pp. 188, 911)

emigrate To move out of one country or region to settle in another (p. 210)

Enlightenment 18th-century movement that emphasized science and reason to improve society (p. 99)

entitlement Government program that guarantees payments to a particular group, such as the elderly (pp. 968, 1031)

Environmental Protection Agency (EPA) Government organization formed in 1970 to deal with issues such as air and water pollution (p. 864)

Equal Rights Amendment (ERA) Proposed constitutional amendment, never ratified, to prohibit discrimination on account of sex (p. 849)

Erie Canal Canal in New York, completed in 1825, that linked the Hudson River with Lake Erie (p. 212)

escalation Expansion by stages, as from a limited or local conflict into a general, especially nuclear, war (p. 876)

evangelical (ee van JEHL ih cuhl) Focusing on emotionally powerful preaching, rather than formal ceremonies, and on the teachings of the Bible (p. 218)

executive branch Branch of government that enforces the laws (p. 124)

Exoduster One of a group of African Americans who migrated to the West following the Civil War (p. 435)

F

faction Group organized around a common interest and concerned only with furthering that interest (p. 139)

fascism Political philosophy that places the importance of the nation over that of the individual (p. 685)

federal Of or formed by a compact of a union of states that agree to divide power with a central government (p. 135)

federal deficit The sum of money lost when federal government expenditures exceed revenues (p. 1032)

Federal Reserve system Nation's central banking system, established in 1913 (p. 555)

Federalist Supporter of the Constitution during the debate over its ratification; favored a strong central government (p. 139)

feminism Theory favoring the political, economic, and social equality of men and women (p. 845)

feudalism Political and economic system in medieval Europe, in which lesser lords received lands from powerful nobles in exchange for service (p. 9)

Fifteenth Amendment Constitutional amendment, ratified in 1870, that guaranteed African Americans voting rights (p. 389)

filibuster Tactic in which senators take the floor, begin talking, and refuse to stop talking to permit a vote on a measure (p. 572)

First Battle of Bull Run First battle of the Civil War, won by the Confederates in July 1861 (p. 342)

First Continental Congress Assembly of representatives from the colonies that first met in Philadelphia in September 1774 (p. 95)

flapper Term coined during the 1920s to describe a young woman with a fondness for dancing and brash actions (p. 609)

food stamp Federal coupon given to qualifying low-income persons for use in purchasing food (p. 1034)

Fort Sumter Federal fort in the harbor of Charleston, South Carolina; the Confederate attack on the fort marked the start of the Civil War (p. 335)

Fourteen Points President Wilson's proposal in 1918 for a postwar European peace (p. 584)

Fourteenth Amendment Constitutional amendment, ratified in 1868, that guaranteed citizens equal protection of the laws (p. 386)

franchise Right to open a restaurant using a parent company's brand name and system (p. 768)

Freedom Rides Civil rights protest in which a racially mixed group of protesters challenged racially segregated bus terminals (p. 827)

free enterprise system Economic system in which companies compete for profits (p. 232)

free soiler Person dedicated to preventing the expansion of slavery into the western territories (p. 328)

French and Indian War War from 1754 to 1763 between France, with allied Indian nations, and Britain and its colonists, for control of eastern North America (p. 85)

Fugitive Slave Act Part of the Compromise of 1850, a law ordering all citizens of the United States to assist in the return of slaves (p. 322)

fundamentalism Set of religious beliefs including traditional Christian ideas about Jesus Christ, the belief that the Bible was inspired by God and does not contain contradictions or errors, and the belief that the Bible is literally true (p. 624)

G

Gadsden Purchase 1853 purchase by the United States of southwestern lands from Mexico (p. 303)

gag rule Rule passed by the House in 1836 prohibiting antislavery petitions from being read or acted upon (p. 271)

General Agreement on Tariffs and Trade (GATT) International agreement on reducing tariffs and expanding world trade (p. 993)

Geneva Conference An international conference in 1954 in which Vietnam was divided into two nations (p. 873)

genocide Deliberate murder of an entire people (p. 577)

Gentleman's Agreement 1907 agreement between the United States and Japan that restricted Japanese immigration (p. 471)

gentry In colonial America, men and women wealthy enough to hire others to work for them (p. 65)

Gettysburg Address A famous speech by President Lincoln on the meaning of the Civil War, given in November 1863 at the dedication of a national cemetery on the site of the Battle of Gettysburg (p. 366)

ghetto   Area in which one ethnic or racial group dominates (p. 475)

ghost town   Town that has been abandoned due to lack of economic activity (p. 305)

GI   Term used for American soldiers in World War II, derived from "Government Issue" (p. 692)

Gibbons v. Ogden   1824 case in which the Supreme Court ruled that states could not regulate commerce on interstate waterways (p. 245)

GI Bill   Law passed in 1944 that helped returning veterans buy homes and pay for college (p. 770)

Gilded Age   Term used to describe the period from 1877 to 1900 (p. 461)

globalization   Trend toward world-wide organization, such as in the manufacture and sale of goods (p. 1056)

Good Neighbor Policy   President Franklin D. Roosevelt's policy to promote good relations with Latin American nations (p. 1043)

graft   Use of one's job to gain profit (p. 477)

grandfather clause   Passage that exempts a group of people from obeying a law if they met certain conditions before the law was passed (p. 498)

Grange, the   Organization formed to help farmers cooperate economically and politically; also known as the Patrons of Husbandry (p. 448)

Great Awakening   Religious revival in the American colonies during the 1730s and 1740s (p. 79)

Great Compromise   Compromise at the Constitutional Convention calling for a two-house legislature, with one house elected on the basis of population and the other representing each state equally (p. 134)

Great Crash   Collapse of the American stock market in 1929 (p. 636)

Great Depression   Severe economic decline that lasted from 1929 until about 1939 (p. 636)

Great Migration   Migration of English settlers to Massachusetts Bay Colony beginning in the 1630s (p. 44)

Great Plains   Vast grassland between the Mississippi River and the Rocky Mountains (p. 287)

Great Society   President Lyndon Johnson's proposals to aid public education, provide medical care for the elderly, and eliminate poverty (p. 803)

Great White Fleet   A force of United States Navy ships that undertook a world cruise in 1907 (p. 536)

greenbacks   Name given the national paper currency created in 1862 (p. 351)

green card   Permit granting an alien permission to reside and work in the United States (p. 1009)

Gross National Product   Total annual value of goods and services that a country produces (p. 636)

guerrilla   (guh RIHL uh) A soldier who uses hit-and-run tactics (p. 371)

Gulf of Tonkin Resolution   1964 congressional resolution authorizing President Johnson to take military action in Vietnam (p. 876)

H

Harlem Renaissance   African American literary awakening of the 1920s, centered in Harlem (p. 619)

haven   A safe place (p. 53)

Hawley-Smoot Tariff   An especially high import tariff passed by Congress in 1930 (p. 650)

Haymarket Riot   1886 labor-related violence in Chicago (p. 427)

Helms-Burton Act   1996 act that penalizes foreign companies that do business with Cuba (p. 1042)

Helsinki Accords   Series of agreements on European security made in 1975 (p. 935)

hidalgo   (hih DAL goh) A Spanish noble (p. 29)

Ho Chi Minh Trail   Supply route that carried troops and supplies from North Vietnam to South Vietnam (p. 876)

holding company   Corporation that holds the stocks and bonds of numerous companies (p. 549)

Holocaust   Nazi Germany's attempt to murder all European Jews (p. 707)

Hollywood Ten   Group of people in the film industry who were jailed for refusing to answer congressional questions regarding Communist influence in Hollywood (p. 754)

home rule   System by which cities exercise a limited amount of self-rule (p. 542)

Homestead Act   1862 law that offered 160 acres of western land to settlers (p. 433)

Homestead Strike   1892 strike in Pennsylvania against Carnegie Steel (p. 427)

homicide   The killing of one human being by another (p. 1017)

Hooverville   Makeshift shelter of the homeless during the early years of the Great Depression (p. 639)

House of Burgesses   Virginia legislature formed in 1619 (p. 39)

horizontal consolidation   Process of bringing together many firms that are in the same business to form one large company (p. 417)

HUAC   House Un-American Activities Committee; congressional committee that investigated Communist influence in the United States in the 1940s and 1950s (p. 753)

hundred days   Period at the start of Franklin Roosevelt's presidency in 1933, when many New Deal programs were passed by Congress (p. 660)

I

ICBM   An intercontinental ballistic missile (p. 762)

immigrant   Person who enters a new country to settle (p. 77)

Immigration Act of 1965   Law that ended quotas for individual countries and replaced them with more flexible limits (p. 804)

impeach   Charge a public official with wrongdoing in office (pp. 388, 924)

imperialism   Policy by a stronger nation to create an empire by dominating weaker nations economically, politically, culturally, or militarily (p. 515)

impressment   Policy of forcing people into military or public service (p. 192)

inauguration   Official swearing-in ceremony (p. 143)

incumbent   Person already in office (p. 936)

indentured servant   Person who agrees to work for another person for a specified time in return for transportation, food, and shelter (p. 40)

Indian Removal Act   1830 law calling for the forced movement of Native Americans to west of the Mississippi River (p. 252)

indigo   Type of plant used in making a blue dye for cloth (p. 68)

industrialization   Growth of industry (p. 237)

Industrial Revolution   Effort, beginning in Britain in the late 1700s, to increase production by using machines powered by sources other than humans or animals (p. 209)

infant mortality rate   Rate at which babies less than one year old die in a population (p. 202)

inflation   A steady increase in prices over time, reducing the ability to buy (p. 112)

infrastructure   The public property and services that a society uses (p. 394)

initiative   Process by which citizens propose new laws by gathering signatures on a petition (p. 548)

injunction   Court order prohibiting some action (p. 542)

installment plan   A system that lets customers make partial payments (installments) at set intervals over a period of time (p. 603)

integration   Process of bringing together of different races (p. 787)

interchangeable parts   A system of manufacturing in which all parts are made to an exact standard for easy mass-assembly (p. 210)

interest   An extra sum of money that borrowers have to repay creditors in return for the loan (p. 176)

Intermediate-Range Nuclear Forces (INF) Treaty   1987 treaty between the United States and the Soviet Union calling for the destruction of 2,500 missiles in Europe (p. 967)

Internet   The network that links computers around the world (p. 999)

internment camp   A camp to which Japanese Americans were forcibly sent during World War II (p. 735)

interracial   Between, among, or involving people of different races (p. 820)

Interstate Commerce Act   1887 law that regulated railroads and other interstate businesses (p. 449)

Iran-contra affair   Scandal in the Reagan administration involving the use of money from secret Iranian arms sales to support the Nicaraguan contras (p. 967)

Irish Potato Famine   Famine in Ireland in the 1840s that led to a surge in immigration to the United States (p. 279)

iron curtain   Winston Churchill's term for the extension of Communist control over Eastern Europe (p. 745)

isolationism   Policy of avoiding political or economic alliances with foreign countries (p. 600)

isthmus   A narrow strip of land that joins two larger land areas (p. 29)

itinerant   (ī TIHN uhr uhnt) Traveling from place to place or on a circuit (p. 79)

J

Japanese American Citizens League (JACL)   Organization of Japanese Americans working to promote the rights of Asian Americans (p. 855)

Jay's Treaty   Treaty signed in 1794 between the United States and Britain in which Britain agreed to withdraw from forts in the Northwest Territory and which sought to improve trade relations (p. 177)

Jazz Age   Term used to describe the 1920s (p. 616)

Jim Crow   System of laws that segregated public services by race beginnning in the 1890s (p. 499)

jingoism   A feeling of intense national pride and a desire for an aggressive foreign policy (p. 521)

joint-stock company   Company funded and run by a group of investors who share the company's profits and losses (p. 37)

judicial branch   Branch of government that interprets and applies the laws (p. 124)

judicial review   Power of federal courts to decide whether laws are constitutional (p. 185)

K

kamikaze   (kah mih KAH zee) In World War II, a Japanese suicide plane (p. 703)

Kansas-Nebraska Act   1854 law that called on citizens in each territory to decide the issue of slavery there (p. 325)

Kellogg-Briand Pact   Agreement signed in 1928 in which nations agreed not to use war in their dealings with one another (p. 602)

King Philip's War   War, beginning in 1675, between English colonists and Native Americans (p. 49)

kinship   Family relationships (p. 6)

Korean War   Conflict over the future of the Korean peninsula, fought between 1950 and 1953 and ending in a stalemate (p. 756)

Kristallnacht The name given to the night of violence on November 9, 1938, when Nazi storm troopers attacked Jews in Germany and Austria (p. 708)

L

labor union Organization of workers formed to protect the interest of its members (p. 239)

laissez-faire (LES ay FAYR) A government policy of not interfering in private business (p. 461)

land speculator Person who buys up large areas of land in the hope of later selling it for a profit (p. 433)

Latino Person whose family origins are in Spanish-speaking Latin America (p. 852)

League of Nations International organization, formed after World War I, that aimed to promote security and peace for all members (p. 585)

legislative branch Branch of government that makes the laws (p. 124)

legislature A lawmaking assembly (p. 39)

Lend-Lease Act 1941 law that authorized the President to provide aid to any nation whose defense he believed was vital to American security (p. 690)

Lewis and Clark expedition Journey by Meriwether Lewis and William Clark through the Louisiana Territory during 1804–1806 (p. 188)

Liberty Bond Special war bonds sold to support the Allied cause during World War I (p. 578)

Liberty ship A large, sturdy merchant ship built during World War II (p. 717)

Limited Test Ban Treaty 1963 treaty in which the United States and the Soviet Union agreed not to test nuclear weapons above the ground (p. 812)

lineage Kinship groups that trace their origin to a common ancestor (p. 16)

literacy Ability to read and write (p. 487)

long drive Moving of cattle from distant ranges to busy railroad centers that shipped the cattle to market (p. 442)

loose construction Belief that the government can do anything that the Constitution does not say it cannot do (p. 176)

Lost Generation Group of writers of the 1920s who shared the belief that they were lost in a greedy, materialistic world that lacked moral values (p. 617)

Louisiana Purchase Purchase by the United States of the Louisiana Territory from France in 1803 (p. 187)

Lower South States of Texas, Louisiana, Mississippi, Alabama, Florida, Georgia, and South Carolina (p. 334)

Loyalist Person who remained loyal to Great Britain during the Revolution (p. 107)

lynching Illegal seizure and execution of a person by a mob (p. 499)

M

Magna Carta A "great charter" signed in 1215 that granted certain rights to English nobles (p. 11)

mail-order catalog Catalog advertising a wide range of goods that can be purchased by mail (p. 504)

mandate A set of wishes expressed to a candidate by the voters (p. 798)

Manhattan Project Secret American program during World War II to develop an atomic bomb (p. 704)

manifest destiny Argument that the United States was destined to expand across North America (p. 301)

manufacturing Making of goods by machinery (p. 231)

maquiladora Mexican factory located along the United States–Mexico border that assembles products for U.S. companies (p. 1044)

Marbury* v. *Madison 1803 Supreme Court case that established the principle of judicial review (p. 185)

March on Washington 1963 civil rights demonstration in Washington, D.C. (p. 832)

Market Revolution Shift from a home-based economy to one based on money and the buying and selling of goods (p. 231)

Marshall Plan Program of American economic assistance to Western Europe, announced in 1947 (p. 748)

martial law Emergency rule by military authorities (p. 352)

Massacre at Wounded Knee 1890 shooting by army troops of a group of unarmed Sioux (p. 438)

mass media Print and broadcast methods of communicating information to large numbers of people (p. 614)

mass production Manufacture of goods in great amounts (p. 411)

Mayflower Compact Agreement in which settlers of Plymouth Colony agreed to obey their government's laws (p. 44)

McCarran-Walter Act 1952 immigration law that discriminated against potential immigrants from Asia and Southern and Central Europe (p. 754)

McCulloch* v. *Maryland 1819 case in which the Supreme Court ruled that Congress has the authority to take actions necessary to fulfill its constitutional duties (p. 244)

median age Age that divides a population in half, with half the population above that age and half below it (p. 202)

Medicaid Federal program that provides medical benefits to poor Americans (p. 1031)

Medicare Federal program that provides medical benefits for older Americans (p. 804, 1031)

mercantilism Economic theory that a country should acquire as much bullion, or gold and silver, as possible, by exporting more goods than it imports (p. 59)

mercenary A foreign soldier who fights for pay (p. 108)

mestizo (mehs TEE zoh) A person of mixed Spanish and Native American heritage (p. 31)

Mexican War Conflict between the United States and Mexico from 1846 to 1848, ending with a United States victory (p. 302)

Middle Ages Era in European history from about A.D. 500 to 1300 (p. 9)

Middle America Term sometimes used to describe mainstream Americans (p. 905)

middle class A new class of merchants, traders, and artisans that arose in Europe in the late Middle Ages; in modern times, the social class between the very wealthy and the lower working class (p. 11)

Middle Colonies English colonies of New York, New Jersey, Pennsylvania, and Delaware (p. 51)

middleman Someone who buys items from one source and then sells them to others (p. 288)

Middle Passage Part of the triangular trade in which Africans were forcibly taken from Africa to slavery in the Americas (p. 72)

migrant farm worker Worker who moves from farm to farm planting and harvesting various crops (p. 853)

militarism Policy of aggressively building up a nation's armed forces in preparation for war (p. 565)

militia Armed citizens who serve as soldiers during an emergency (pp. 87, 1019)

Miranda Rule Rule that police must inform persons accused of a crime of their legal rights (p. 805)

missions Headquarters from which people from another country seek to spread their religion (p. 33)

Missouri Compromise 1820 agreement calling for the admission of Missouri as a slave state and Maine as a free state, and outlawing slavery in future states to be created north of 36° 30' N latitude (p. 196)

mobile society A society in which people are constantly moving about (p. 216)

mobilization The readying of troops for war (p. 566)

modem A device that converts data into signals that can be transmitted by telephone (p. 1057)

modern republicanism President Eisenhower's approach to government, described as "conservative when it comes to money, liberal when it comes to human beings" (p. 783)

monarch Someone who rules over a kingdom, such as a king or queen (p. 11)

monetary policy Federal plan for the makeup and quantity of the nation's money supply (p. 447)

monopoly Complete control of a product or service (p. 416)

Monroe Doctrine Declaration by President Monroe in 1823 that the United States would oppose efforts by any outside power to control a nation in the Western Hemisphere (pp. 245, 1043)

Montgomery bus boycott Protest in 1955–1956 by African Americans against racial segregation in the bus system of Montgomery, Alabama (p. 787)

Morrill Land-Grant Act 1862 law in which the federal government distributed millions of acres of western lands to state governments in order to fund state agricultural colleges (p. 433)

mountain man An American fur trader who explored the Rocky Mountains and regions farther west in the early 1800s (p. 297)

muckraker Journalist who uncovers wrongdoing on the part of politicians or corporations (p. 543)

multiculturalism Movement calling for greater attention to non-European cultures in such areas as education (p. 998)

municipal Relating to a city, as in municipal government (p. 542)

Munn v. Illinois 1877 Supreme Court decision that allowed states to regulate certain businesses within their borders (p. 464)

mutiny Revolt against superior authority (p. 73)

My Lai massacre Killing of several hundred Vietnamese by American soldiers in 1968 (p. 880)

N

napalm (NAY pahm) Highly flammable chemical used in firebombing attacks; dropped from U. S. planes during Vietnam War to burn away vegetation and expose Viet Cong hideouts (p. 880)

National American Woman Suffrage Association (NAWSA) Organization formed in 1890 to push for women's voting rights (p. 558)

National Association for the Advancement of Colored People (NAACP) Organization formed in 1909 to advance the cause of African Americans (p. 500)

national debt The total amount of money owed by the national government (pp. 672, 1032)

National Defense Education Act 1958 bill to improve science and math instruction in schools (p. 784)

nationalism Devotion to one's nation (p. 515)

nationalization Conversion to government ownership (p. 669)

National Organization for Women (NOW) Organization formed in 1966 to promote full participation of women in American society (p. 847)

National Rifle Association (NRA) Leading organization working against gun control (p. 1020)

Nation of Islam Organization, also called the Black Muslims, dedicated to black separation and self-help (p. 837)

nativism Movement to ensure that native-born

Americans received better treatment than immigrants (pp. 324, 479)

nativist Supporter of the policy of favoring native-born citizens over immigrants (p. 1011)

naturalize To apply for and be granted American citizenship (p. 280)

natural rights Rights which belong to people simply because they are human (p. 100)

neutral Not taking sides in a conflict or dispute (p. 177)

New Deal President Franklin Roosevelt's program of relief, recovery, and reform programs to combat the Great Depression (pp. 659, 1025)

New England Colonies English colonies which became the states of Connecticut, Rhode Island, Massachusetts, Vermont, New Hampshire, and Maine (p. 43)

New Federalism President Reagan's plan to give states more control over the use of federal aid (p. 961)

New Freedom Woodrow Wilson's 1912 campaign platform calling for antitrust action without threatening free competition (p. 554)

New Frontier President Kennedy's proposals to improve the economy, help the poor, and advance the space program (p. 798)

New Left New political movement of the late 1960s that called for radical changes to fight poverty and racism (p. 883)

New Nationalism Theodore Roosevelt's program of greater federal regulation of business and workplaces, income and inheritance taxes, and electoral reforms (p. 553)

New Right A coalition of conservative groups that emerged by 1980 (p. 958)

Niagara Movement Organization, founded in 1905 by W.E.B. Du Bois and other black leaders, that called for full civil liberties for African Americans, an end to racial discrimination, and recognition of human brotherhood (p. 491)

Nisei (nee SAY) A Japanese American whose parents were born in Japan (p. 735)

nomadic Moving regularly in search of food (p. 4)

nomad Person who continually migrates instead of living permanently in one place (p. 288)

nonviolent protest Form of protest in which protesters do not resist or fight back when attacked (p. 821)

North American Free Trade Agreement (NAFTA) Agreement calling for removal of trade restrictions among the United States, Canada, and Mexico (pp. 993, 1040)

North Atlantic Treaty Organization (NATO) Alliance between the United States, Canada, and Western European nations, formed in 1949 (pp. 751, 1052)

Nuclear Regulatory Commission Government organization formed in 1974 to oversee the civilian uses of nuclear materials (p. 863)

nullification A state's refusal to recognize a federal law (p. 181)

O

obsolete Outdated (p. 318)

Office of War Information Federal agency created in 1942 to enlist public support for the war effort during World War II (p. 722)

Office of War Mobilization Federal agency formed in 1943 to coordinate issues related to war production during World War II (p. 716)

Olive Branch Petition Plea by the American colonists to King George III in 1775 that he halt the fighting (p. 99)

Open Door Policy American approach to China around 1900, favoring open trade relations between China and other nations (p. 525)

oral history Traditions passed from generation to generation by word of mouth (p. 7)

Oregon Trail Trail linking Independence, Missouri, and Oregon, used by many pioneers during the 1840s (p. 298)

Organization of Petroleum Exporting Countries (OPEC) Group of nations that worked together to regulate the price and supply of oil (p. 911)

P

pardon An official forgiveness of a crime (p. 381)

Paris peace talks Negotiations between the United States and North Vietnam, beginning in 1968 (p. 891)

pass A low place in a mountain range that allows travelers to cross over to the other side (p. 298)

patent A license to make, use, or sell an invention (p. 408)

patronage Practice of hiring political supporters for government jobs (p. 250)

Peace Corps Federal program established to send volunteers to help developing nations around the world (p. 813)

Pendleton Civil Service Act 1883 law that created a Civil Service Commission and stated that federal employees could not be required to contribute to campaign funds and could not be fired for political reasons (p. 463)

Pentagon Papers Government study of United States involvement in the Vietnam War, made public in 1971 (p. 882)

Pequot War War between English settlers and Pequot Indians in 1637 (p. 48)

per capita income Average income per person (p. 767)

persecute To oppress someone because of his or her beliefs (p. 44)

Persian Gulf War 1991 war in which United Nations forces expelled an Iraqi occupation army from Kuwait (p. 974)

philanthropist Person who gives donations to worthy causes (p. 489)

Pickett's Charge   Unsuccessful charge by Confederate infantry during the Battle of Gettysburg (p. 363)

piecework   System in which workers are paid not by the hour but by what they produce (p. 420)

Pilgrim   One of the group of English Separatists who established Plymouth Colony in 1620 (p. 44)

Pinckney Treaty   Treaty between the United States and Spain in 1795 that set the southern boundary of the United States (p. 203)

placer mining   A method of mining used by individual prospectors (p. 441)

plantation   Large farm on which crops are raised mainly for sale (p. 23)

Plessy v. Ferguson   1896 Supreme Court ruling that racial segregation was legal as long as the separate facilities were equal for both races (p. 499)

political asylum   Protection given by one country to refugees from another (p. 1009)

political machine   Unofficial organization designed to keep a particular party or group in power and usually headed by a single, powerful boss (p. 476)

political party   Group of people who seek to win elections and hold public office in order to control government policy and programs (p. 178)

poll tax   Special fee that must be paid before a person can vote (p. 498)

Pontiac's Rebellion   1763 rebellion by Native Americans in the Great Lakes region (p. 90)

Poor People's Campaign   Crusade against economic injustice organized in 1968 by Martin Luther King, Jr. (p. 906)

popular sovereignty   Policy of letting the people in a territory decide whether slavery would be allowed there (p. 325)

population density   The average number of people living within a given area (p. 237)

Populist   Supporter of the Populist party, formed in 1891 to advocate a larger money supply and other economic reforms (p. 449)

precedent   (PREHS ih dehnt) Something done or said that becomes an example, rule, or tradition to be followed (p. 144)

prejudice   An unreasonable, usually unfavorable opinion of another group (p. 316)

presidio   (prih SEE dee oh) Fort built in Southwest by Spanish (pp. 32, 292)

price controls   System of pricing determined by the government (p. 579)

prime minister   Top official in a parliamentary government (p. 87)

privateer   Privately owned ship hired by a government to attack enemy ships (p. 37)

Proclamation of 1763   Order by the British king that closed the region west of the Appalachian Mountains to all settlement by colonists (p. 90)

productivity   Amount that a worker produces in a given period of time (pp. 408, 1059)

profiteering   Selling scarce items at unreasonably high prices (p. 111)

progressive   Political and social reformer of the late 1800s and early 1900s (p. 1024)

Progressive Era   Period from about 1890 to 1920, during which a variety of reforms were enacted at the local, state, and federal levels (p. 543)

progressive income tax   Tax in which the percentage of taxes owed increases with income (p. 449)

prohibition   A legal ban on the manufacture and sale of alcoholic beverages (p. 480)

proliferation   Rapid growth in number, spread (p. 918)

proprietary colony   Colony granted by a king or queen to an individual or group who have full governing rights (p. 52)

public works program   Government-funded project to build public facilities (p. 661)

Pueblo Revolt of 1680   Revolt by the Pueblo people in New Mexico against Spain (p. 33)

Pullman Strike   1894 railway workers' strike that spread nation-wide (p. 428)

Puritan   Person who favored the purification of England's Anglican Church (p. 44)

Q

Quaker   Member of a Protestant group that emphasizes equality (p. 53)

quarantine   A time of isolation to prevent the spread of a disease (p. 468)

quota   A numerical limit (p. 601)

R

racism   Belief that differences in character or intelligence are due to one's race and that asserts the superiority of one race over another or others (p. 534)

ragtime   Style of music consisting of melodies with shifting accents over a steady beat (p. 495)

ratify   Approve or sanction (p. 139)

rationing   Distributing goods to consumers in a fixed amount (p. 579)

realpolitik   (ray AHL poh lih teek) German for "practical politics," or a foreign policy based on interests rather than moral principles (p. 915)

recall   Process by which voters remove a public official from office before the next election (p. 548)

recession   Period of slow business activity (p. 933)

recognition   Official acceptance (p. 350)

Reconstruction   Federal government's effort between 1865 and 1877 to repair the damage to the South caused by the Civil War and to restore southern states to the Union (p. 379)

red scare   A period of intense fear of communism and other extreme ideas (p. 598)

referendum   Process by which citizens vote on a law passed by their legislature (p. 548)

Reformation   Revolt against the Catholic Church that began in 1517 (p. 14)

religious tolerance   Idea that people of different religions should live in peace together (p. 44)

Renaissance   Era of European history extending from the 1300s to the 1500s (p. 12)

reparations   Payment from an enemy for economic injury suffered during a war (p. 586)

republic   A government run by the people through their elected representatives (p. 125)

republican virtues   Virtues the American people would need to govern themselves, such as sacrificing individual needs for the good of the community, self-reliance, industry, and frugality (p. 209)

reservation   Area that the federal government set aside for Native Americans who had lost their homelands (pp. 190, 436)

restrictive covenant   Agreement among homeowners not to sell real estate to certain groups of people, such as African Americans or Jews (p. 475)

revenue   Income of a government (p. 672)

revival   A gathering where people are "revived", or brought back to a religious life (p. 219)

Revolutionary War   American colonists' war of independence from Britain, 1775 to 1783 (p. 96)

rock and roll   Music that grew out of rhythm and blues and that became popular in the 1950s (p. 777)

Roe v. Wade   1973 Supreme Court decision that legalized abortion (p. 849)

Roosevelt Corollary   President Theodore Roosevelt's 1904 extension of the Monroe Doctrine in which he asserted the right of the United States to intervene in Latin American nations (pp. 529, 1043)

Rosie the Riveter   Term used to symbolize the many women who worked in defense industries during World War II (p. 726)

royal colony   Colony with a governor appointed by the king (p. 39)

rural   Pertaining to the countryside (p. 240)

rural free delivery   Free delivery of packages to rural areas, begun in 1896 (p. 504)

Russian Revolution   Collapse of the czar's government in Russia in 1917, leading ultimately to the Bolshevik takeover (p. 572)

S

sachem   A Native American leader (p. 48)

Salem witch trials   The prosecution and execution of twenty women and men for witchcraft in Massachusetts in 1692 (p. 45)

SALT I   Strategic Arms Limitation Treaty, a 1972 agreement between the United States and the Soviet Union on limiting nuclear weapons (p. 918)

salutary neglect   Great Britain's policy in the early 1700s of not interfering in the American colonies' politics and economy as long as such neglect served British economic interests (p. 62)

Sandinista   Member of the group of Nicaraguans who took control of the government in 1979 (p. 967)

Santa Fe Trail   Trail linking Independence, Missouri, and Santa Fe, New Mexico in the mid-1800s (p. 293)

satellite nation   A country dominated politically and economically by another nation, especially by the Soviet Union during the cold war (p. 743)

saturation bombing   The dropping of a large concentration of bombs over a certain area (p. 879)

savanna   Region near the equator with tropical grasslands and scattered trees (p. 16)

scab   Worker called in by an employer to replace striking laborers (p. 426)

scalawag   An insulting nickname for a white southern Republican following the Civil War (p. 390)

scarce   In short supply (p. 18)

Scopes trial   1925 trial in Tennessee on the issue of teaching evolution in public schools (p. 624)

Scott v. Sandford   1857 Supreme Court decision that declared slaves not to be citizens and ruled the Missouri Compromise as unconstitutional (p. 329)

secede   To withdraw formally from membership in a group or organization (p. 251)

secessionist   Person who wanted the South to secede (p. 334)

Second Amendment   Amendment to the Constitution giving states the right to armed militias (p. 1019)

Second Continental Congress   Assembly of representatives from the colonies that first met in Philadelphia in May 1775 (p. 98)

Second Great Awakening   Religious movement of the early 1800s (p. 218)

Second New Deal   Period of legislative activity launched by President Franklin Roosevelt in 1935 (p. 664)

section   A geographic region (p. 236)

secularize   To put under the control of the government rather than the church (p. 293)

sedition   Speech or actions that encourage rebellion (p. 580)

segregation   Forced separation (pp. 263, 470)

Selective Service Act   1917 law authorizing a draft of young men for military service (p. 573)

self-determination   Power to make decisions about one's own future (p. 584)

self-sufficient   Having the necessary resources to get along without help (p. 68)

Seneca Falls Convention   The first women's rights convention in U.S. history, held in 1848 (p. 277)

seniority   Status derived from length of service (p. 728)

separation of powers   The Constitutional allotting of powers within the federal government among the legislative, executive, and judicial branches (p. 136)

settlement house   Community center organized to provide various services to the urban poor (p. 481)

sharecropping   System of farming in which a farmer farms some portion of a planter's land and receives a share of the crop at harvest time as payment (p. 392)

Shays' Rebellion   An uprising against taxes in Massachusetts in 1786 and 1787 (p. 127)

shell   Device that explodes in the air or when it hits a solid target (p. 344)

Sherman Antitrust Act   Law passed in 1890 that outlawed any combination of companies that restrained trade or commerce (p. 417)

shuttle diplomacy   Repeated trips by a mediator between disputing nations in order to reach an agreement (p. 940)

siege   Tactic in which an enemy is surrounded and starved in order to make it surrender (pp. 87, 364)

silent majority   Term used by President Nixon to describe Americans who disapproved of the counterculture (p. 912)

sit-down strike   Labor protest in which workers stop work but refuse to leave the workplace (p. 673)

sit-in   Form of protest in which protesters seat themselves and refuse to move; sometimes used as a means of peaceful protest (p. 826)

social Darwinism   Theory, derived from Darwin's theory of natural selection, that society should do as little as possible to interfere with people's pursuit of success (p. 416)

social gospel movement   Social reform movement that developed within religious institutions which sought to apply the gospel of Jesus directly to society (p. 481)

socialism   An economic and political philosophy that favors public (or social) control of property and income (p. 423)

Social Security system   Publicly run system that provides regular payments to people who cannot support themselves (p. 665)

social welfare program   Program designed to ensure a basic standard of living for all citizens (p. 544)

software Program for a computer (p. 1058)

solid South   Term used to describe the domination of post–Civil War southern politics by the Democratic party (p. 396)

sooner   Person who marked his or her claims in Indian Territory before it was legally opened to settlement (p. 439)

Southern Christian Leadership Conference (SCLC)   Civil rights organization formed in 1957 by Dr. Martin Luther King, Jr., and other leaders (p. 821)

Southern Colonies   The English colonies of Virginia, Maryland, the Carolinas, and Georgia (p. 53)

speakeasy   During Prohibition, a place where alcoholic drinks were served illegally (p. 622)

special prosecutor   An attorney appointed by the Justice Department to investigate wrongdoing by government officials (p. 924)

specie   (SPEE shee) Gold or silver coin (p. 127)

speculation   Making high-risk investments in hopes of getting a high gain (p. 633)

sphere of influence   Area of economic and political control exerted by one nation over another nation or other nations (p. 525)

spiritual   A folk hymn (p. 221)

spoils   Rewards gained by military victory (p. 585)

spoils system   System or practice of giving appointed offices as rewards from the successful party in an election; name for the patronage system under President Jackson (p. 251)

Sputnik   First artificial satellite to orbit Earth, launched by the Soviet Union in 1957 (p. 762)

stagflation   Combination of high inflation and high unemployment, with no economic growth (p. 933)

stalemate   Situation in which neither side in a conflict is able to gain the advantage (p. 566)

Stamp Act   1765 law passed by the British Parliament which taxed newspapers, legal documents, and other printed materials in the colonies (p. 91)

staple crop   A crop that is in constant demand, such as cotton, wheat, or rice (p. 62)

states' rights   Theory that holds that the Constitution divided power between the states and the federal government and that a strict interpretation of that division must be respected. (p.322)

steerage   Large open area beneath the ship's deck, in which many poorer immigrants traveled (p. 467)

stereotype   A fixed conception held by a number of people (p. 456)

Stono Rebellion   Slave revolt in South Carolina in 1739 (p. 76)

Strategic Arms Reduction Treaty   1991 agreement, known as START I, calling for dramatic reductions in Soviet and American nuclear weapons (p. 973)

Strategic Defense Initiative (SDI)   President Reagan's proposed defense system against Soviet missile attack, popularly known as "Stars Wars" (p. 961)

strict construction   Belief that the government should not do anything that the Constitution does not specifically say it can do (p. 176)

strike   A work stoppage intended to force an employer to meet certain demands, as for higher wages (p. 239)

Student Nonviolent Coordinating Committee (SNCC)   Student civil rights organization founded in 1960 (p. 823)

subsidy   Payment made by the government to encourage the development of certain industries (p. 462)

suburb   Residential community surrounding a city (p. 474)

suffrage   The right to vote (p. 277)

supply-side economics   Theory that tax reductions will increase investment and thereby encourage business growth (p. 959)

Sussex pledge   Pledge by the German government in

1916 that its submarines would warn ships before attacking (p. 571)

synagogue   Jewish house of worship (p. 52)

T

Taft-Hartley Act   1947 law that allowed the President to order striking workers in some industries back to work (p. 780)

tariff   Tax on foreign goods imported into a country (pp. 176, 1040)

Tariff of 1828   A high tariff on manufactured goods; called the "Tariff of Abominations" by southerners (p. 251)

teach-in   Special session of lecture and discussion on a controversial topic (p. 883)

Teapot Dome scandal   Scandal of the Harding administration involving the granting of oil drilling rights on government land in return for money (p. 601)

telecommunications   Communication over long distances by electronic means (p. 1058)

televangelism   Use by religious organizations of television, especially for fund-raising (p. 958)

temperance movement   An organized campaign to eliminate alcohol consumption (pp. 261, 480)

tenant farming   System of farming in which a farmer rents land to farm from a planter (p. 392)

tenement   Crowded apartment building with poor standards of sanitation, safety, and comfort (pp. 238, 474)

Tennessee Valley Authority (TVA)   A federal project to provide electricity, flood control, and recreational opportunities to the Tennessee River valley (p. 662)

Tet Offensive   1968 attack by Viet Cong and North Vietnamese forces throughout South Vietnam (p. 877)

Texas War for Independence   Successful revolt by Texans against Mexican rule in 1835–1836 (p. 294)

Thirteenth Amendment   Constitutional amendment, ratified in 1865, that abolished slavery (p. 370)

38th parallel   Latitude line that divided North and South Korea (p. 756)

Three-Fifths Compromise   Compromise at the Constitutional Convention calling for three fifths of a state's slave population to be counted for purposes of representation (p. 135)

totalitarian   Describing a form of government that controls every aspect of its citizens' lives (p. 685)

trade deficit   The money lost when a nation spends more on imports than it earns with exports (p. 1041)

trade surplus   The sum of money gained when a nation earns more with exports than it spends on imports (p. 1041)

Trail of Tears   The forced movement of Cherokees in 1838–1839 to land west of the Mississippi (p. 253)

trans-Appalachia   Area west of the Appalachian Mountains (p. 202)

transcendentalism   Philosophical movement of the mid-1800s that emphasized spiritual discovery and insight rather than reason (p. 260)

transcontinental railroad   Railway extending from coast to coast (p. 408)

transistor   Tiny circuit device that amplifies, controls, and generates electrical signals (p. 768)

Treaty of Ghent   Agreement, signed in 1814, that ended the War of 1812 (p. 195)

Treaty of Greenville   Treaty signed in 1795 by the United States and several Native American peoples in which the Native Americans gave up control of most of Ohio (p. 189)

Treaty of Guadalupe Hidalgo   Treaty signed in 1848 by the United States and Mexico, ending the Mexican War (p. 303)

Treaty of Paris (1763)   Treaty that ended the French and Indian War and in which France gave up its land claims in North America to Britain (p. 88)

Treaty of Paris (1783)   Treaty that ended the Revolutionary War and in which Britain acknowledged American independence (p. 113)

Treaty of Tordesillas   1494 treaty in which Portugal and Spain divided the non-Christian world (p. 23)

trek   A journey (p. 298)

Triangular Trade   Trade between the Americas, Europe, and Africa (p. 63)

Truman Doctrine   1947 declaration by President Truman that the United States would support nations that were being threatened by communism (pp. 746, 1051)

trust   A group of separate companies placed under the control of a single managing board (p. 417)

trustee   Someone entrusted to look after a business (p. 54)

Turner's Rebellion   Unsuccessful slave revolt led by Nat Turner in 1831 (p. 243)

Turner thesis   Argument, made by Frederick Jackson Turner in 1893, that the frontier had shaped American life (p. 454)

turnpike   A toll road (p. 212)

Twenty-first Amendment   Constitutional amendment, ratified in 1933, that ended Prohibition (p. 647)

U

U-boat   A German submarine (p. 570)

Underground Railroad   Network of escape routes that provided protection and transportation for slaves fleeing north to freedom (p. 270)

undocumented immigrant   Immigrant who has entered the United States illegally (p. 1009)

Union   The United States as a national unit; or, during the Civil War, the North (p. 315)

United Farm Workers (UFW)   Union organized by Cesar Chavez to organize Mexican field hands in the West (p. 854)

Upper South The states of Virginia, North Carolina, Tennessee, and Arkansas; designation used in the Civil War (p. 336)

urban Relating to a city (p. 237)

utopian community A small society dedicated to perfection in social and political conditions (p. 263)

U-2 incident The shooting down of an American spy plane over the Soviet Union in 1960 (p. 762)

V

vaudeville Variety show popular in the late 1800s and early 1900s (p. 492)

Versailles Treaty 1919 treaty that ended World War I (p. 586)

vertical consolidation Process of gaining control of the many different businesses that make up all phases of a product's development (p. 417)

veto To prevent from becoming law (p. 134)

vice Immoral or corrupt behavior (p. 480)

victory garden A home garden created to boost food production during World War II (p. 722)

Viet Cong Communist guerrillas in South Vietnam who, with North Vietnamese support, fought the South Vietnamese in the Vietnam War (p. 875)

Vietnamization President Nixon's policy of replacing American military forces with those of South Vietnam (p. 891)

Vietnam Veterans Memorial Monument in Washington, D.C., honoring those killed in the Vietnam War (p. 894)

vigilante Citizen who takes the law into his or her own hands (p. 580)

Virginia and Kentucky Resolutions Resolutions passed in 1798 that attacked the Alien and Sedition Acts as unconstitutional (p. 181)

Volunteers in Service to America (VISTA) Federal program organized to send volunteers to help people in poor communities (p. 803)

Voting Rights Act of 1965 Law aimed at reducing barriers to African American voting, in part by increasing federal authority to register voters (p. 835)

W

Wagner Act Law passed in 1935 that aided unions by legalizing collective bargaining and establishing the National Labor Relations Board (p. 665)

Wannsee Conference 1942 conference in Germany to plan the murder European Jews (p. 709)

war bond Government savings bond that is sold to raise money for a war (p. 719)

War of 1812 War between the United States and Great Britain (p. 192)

war of attrition A war in which one side inflicts continuous losses on the enemy in order to wear down its strength (p. 343)

War Powers Act 1973 law limiting the President's power to deploy troops abroad (p. 934)

War Refugee Board Federal agency created in 1944 to try to help people threatened with murder by the Nazis (p. 710)

Warren Commission Commission, headed by Chief Justice Earl Warren, that investigated the assassination of President Kennedy (p. 800)

Warsaw Pact Military alliance between the Soviet Union and nations of Eastern Europe, formed in 1955 (pp. 751, 1053)

Watergate scandal Scandal involving illegal activities that led ultimately to the resignation of President Nixon in 1974 (p. 922)

welfare capitalism An approach to labor relations in which companies met some of their workers' needs without prompting by unions (p. 632)

Whiskey Rebellion Unrest in 1794 caused by opposition to a tax on whiskey (p. 177)

Whitewater affair Charges that President Clinton had engaged in improper business transactions before becoming President (p. 983)

wildcat strike A strike organized by workers rather than union leaders (p. 718)

Wilderness Road Road built in the 1770s that became the main route across the Appalachians (p. 203)

Woodstock festival 1969 music festival in upstate New York (p. 888)

work ethic System of values stressing the importance of hard work (p. 1028)

World Trade Organization (WTO) International organization formed in 1995 to encourage the expansion of world trade (p. 993)

World Wide Web Organization of global computer networks (p. 1061)

writ of *habeas corpus* A legal protection requiring that a court determine if a person is lawfully imprisoned (p. 352)

X

XYZ Affair Controversy in 1798 over French demands for bribes from American negotiators (p. 180)

Y

Yalta Conference 1945 meeting between Churchill, Stalin, and Roosevelt in which the leaders discussed plans for the postwar world (p. 699)

yellow journalism Type of newspaper coverage that emphasized sensational stories (p. 494)

Z

Zimmermann note 1917 note by a German diplomat proposing an alliance with Mexico (p. 572)

Spanish Glossary

A

abolitionist movement (movimiento abolicionista) el movimiento para terminar con la esclavitud (p. 266)

abstinence (abstinencia) evitar alguna actividad, como beber bebidas alcohólicas (p. 261)

Adams-Onís Treaty (Tratado Adams-Onís) un tratado de 1819 entre Estados Unidos y España por el cual España cedió la Florida a los Estados Unidos (p. 204)

administration (administración) duración del cargo; también, los miembros y agencias del poder ejecutivo en su totalidad (p. 144)

AFDC Ayuda a Familias con Menores a Cargo, un programa de asistencia pública, popularmente conocido como welfare (p. 1031)

affirmative action (acción afirmativa) la política que da consideración especial a las mujeres y miembros de las minorías como compensación a la discriminación sufrida en el pasado (p. 949)

agenda (agenda) una lista de artículos que se quieren conseguir (p. 184)

AIDS (SIDA) síndrome de inmunodeficiencia adquirida, un virus que ha matado a mucha gente desde la década de 1980 (p. 966)

Albany Movement (Movimiento de Albany) una organización de afroamericanos formada en Georgia para promover los derechos civiles (p. 828)

Albany Plan of Union (Plan de Unión de Albany) una propuesta que Benjamin Franklin hizo en 1754 para la creación de un gran consejo formado por representantes de las colonias británicas en Norteamérica (p. 86)

alien (extranjero) una persona que no es ciudadano (p. 471)

Alien and Sedition Acts (Leyes de Extranjería y Sedición) leyes aprobadas por el Congreso en 1798 que permitían que el gobierno encarcelara o deportara a los extranjeros y procesara a sus críticos (p. 181)

Alliance for Progress (Alianza para Progreso) Propuesta para la cooperación entre las naciones del Hemisferio Occidental para satisfacer las necesidades básicas de sus pueblos (p. 812)

Allies (aliados) en la primera guerra mundial, Rusia, Francia, Gran Bretaña y, más tarde, los Estados Unidos; en la segunda guerra mundial, la alianza entre Gran Bretaña, los Estados Unidos, la Unión Soviética y otras naciones (pp. 566, 688)

almanac (almanaque) un libro que contiene información, como calendarios y predicciones meteorológicas (p. 66)

amend (enmendar) revisar (p. 133)

American Expeditionary Force (AEF) (Fuerza Expedicionaria Norteamericana) nombre que recibían las tropas norteamericana en Europa durante la primera guerra mundial (p. 573)

American Indian Movement (AIM) (Movimiento Indio Norteamericano) una organización formada en 1968 para ayudar a los nativos norteamericanos (p. 858)

American Liberty League (Liga Norteamericana de la Libertad) una organización que se oponía al Nuevo Trato

amnesty (amnistía) perdón general de ciertos crímenes (p. 949)

anarchist (anarquista) un radical que se opone violentamente a cualquier forma de gobierno (p. 427)

annex (anexar) juntar o unir (pp. 301, 516)

Antifederalist (antifederalista) opositor a la Constitución durante el debate para su ratificación (p. 139)

anti-Semitism (antisemitismo) hostilidad o discriminación contra los judíos (p. 707)

apartheid (apartheid; segregación racial) en Suráfrica, separación sistemática de las razas blanca y negra (p. 989)

appeasement (apaciguamiento) política de ceder a las exigencias de alguien para preservar la paz (p. 687)

apportionment (reparto) distribución de los escaños en un cuerpo legislativo (p. 805)

apprentice (aprendiz) una persona que está obligada por contrato a trabajar para otra a cambio del aprendizaje de un oficio (p. 66)

arbitration (arbitración) la solución de una disputa por una persona elegida para escuchar a ambas partes y llegar a una decisión (p. 519)

armistice (armisticio) alto el fuego o tregua (p. 576)

arms race (carrera armamentista) una competición entre dos naciones en la que ambas aumentan sus reservas de armas en un intento por conseguir la superioridad (p. 761)

arsenal (arsenal) un lugar en el que se hacen o almacenan armas (p. 332)

Articles of Confederation (Artículos de la Confederación) el plan de gobierno que siguió los Estados Unidos desde 1781 hasta su sustitución por la Constitución de los Estados Unidos (p. 123)

assembly line (cadena de montaje) un proceso de manufacturación en el que cada trabajador realiza un trabajo especializado para la construcción del producto final (p. 605)

assimilation (asimilación) el proceso por el que personas de una cultura se combinan y convierten en parte de otra cultura (pp. 190, 488)

Atlantic Charter (Acuerdo Atlántico) un acuerdo firmado por Roosevelt y Churchill en 1941 que perfilaba el objeto de los propósitos de guerra de las dos naciones (p. 692)

autocrat (autócrata) un gobernante con poder ilimitado (p. 567)

automation (automatización) el uso de máquinas sofisticadas en lugar de trabajadores (p. 1059)

autonomy (autonomía) autogobierno en los asuntos locales (p. 858)

Axis Powers (poderes del Eje) en la segunda guerra mundial, la alianza entre Alemania, Italia y Japón (p. 686)

B

baby boom (incremento de la natalidad) el dramático aumento del número de nacimientos durante y después de la segunda guerra mundial (p. 770)

Bacon's Rebellion (la rebelión de Bacon) revuelta de los colonos de Virginia contra el gobernador real (p. 41)

balance of trade (déficit comercial) la diferencia entre el valor de las importaciones y las exportaciones (p. 60)

banana republic (república bananera) un término que describe a una nación centroamericana dominada por los intereses económicos de los Estados Unidos (p. 517)

bank note (nota bancaria) un papel que un banco emite para sus clientes y que puede cambiarse por monedas de oro o plata (p. 233)

barrio (barrio) un vecindario en el que se habla español (p. 611)

barter (cambiar) cambio o trueque de bienes sin intervención de dinero (p. 7)

Bataan Death March (Marcha de la Muerte de Batán) la marcha brutal a la que fueron obligados los prisioneros norteamericanos y filipinos por los soldados japoneses en 1942 (p. 701)

Battle of the Alamo (batalla del Álamo) en 1836, la captura por las tropas mexicanas de una misión en San Antonio en poder de los texanos (p. 295)

Battle of Antietam (batalla de Antietam) una batalla de la guerra Civil en 1862, en Maryland (p. 348)

Battle of the Bulge (batalla de las Ardenas) la batalla de la segunda guerra mundial en la que las fuerzas alemanas lanzaron un contraataque final en el frente occidental (p. 698)

Battle of Bunker Hill (batalla de Bunker Hill) una batalla de la guerra de la Independencia que se libró en 1775 al norte de Boston (p. 107)

Battle of Chancellorsville (batalla de Chancellorsville) una batalla de la guerra Civil que ganaron los confederados en Virginia en 1863 (p. 361)

Battle of Cold Harbor (batalla de Cold Harbor) una batalla de la guerra Civil en Virginia (p. 368)

Battle of the Coral Sea (batalla del Mar de Coral) la batalla aérea que aviones norteamericanos y japoneses libraron en la segunda guerra mundial en 1942 (p. 701)

Battle of Fredericksburg (batalla de Fredericksburg) una batalla de la guerra Civil que ganó la Confederación en Virginia en 1861 (p. 360)

Battle of Gettysburg (batalla de Gettysburg) una batalla de la guerra Civil que ganó la Unión en 1863 en Pennsylvania, y que fue un momento crucial en la guerra (p. 362)

Battle of Guadalcanal (batalla de Guadalcanal) la batalla de la segunda guerra mundial en 1942–1943 entre Estados Unidos y Japón (p. 702)

Battle of Iwo Jima (batalla de Iwo Jima) la batalla de la segunda guerra mundial en 1945 entre los Estados Unidos y Japón (p. 703)

Battle of Little Bighorn (batalla de Little Bighorn) victoria de los siux en 1876 sobre las tropas del ejército bajo el mando de George Custer (p. 438)

Battle of Midway (batalla de Midway) la batalla de la segunda guerra mundial en 1942 entre los Estados Unidos y Japón, un momento crucial en la guerra del Pacífico (p. 701)

Battle of New Orleans (batalla de Nueva Orleans) la batalla por el control de Nueva Orleans en 1815 entre tropas norteamericanas y británicas, con victoria para los norteamericanos (p. 195)

Battle of Okinawa (batalla de Okinawa) la batalla de la segunda guerra mundial en 1945 entre los Estados Unidos y Japón (p. 703)

Battle of Saratoga (batalla de Saratoga) una batalla de la guerra de la Independencia en 1777 en Nueva York, un momento crucial en la guerra (p. 110)

Battle of Shiloh (batalla de Shiloh) una batalla de la guerra Civil en 1862 en Tennessee (p. 345)

Battle of Spotsylvania (batalla de Spotsylvania) una batalla de la guerra Civil en 1864 en Virginia (p. 368)

Battle of Stalingrad (batalla de Estalingrado) la batalla de la segunda guerra mundial en la Unión Soviética que marcó un momento crucial en la guerra en el este (p. 696)

Battle of Tippecanoe (batalla de Tippecanoe) la batalla en el territorio de Indiana en 1811 entre fuerzas norteamericanas e indias con derrota de los indígenas norteamericanos (p. 191)

Battle of Trenton (batalla de Trenton) una batalla de la guerra de la Independencia en 1776 en Nueva Jersey (p. 109)

Battle of the Wilderness (batalla de Wilderness) una batalla de la guerra Civil en 1864 en Virginia, ganada por la Confederación (p. 367)

Battle of Yorktown (batalla de Yorktown) una batalla de la guerra de la Independencia en 1781 en Virginia, una victoria norteamericana decisiva (p. 113)

Battles of Lexington and Concord (batallas de Lexington y Concord) las primeras batallas de la Guerra de la Independencia, el 19 de abril de 1775 (p. 96)

Bay of Pigs invasion (invasión de Bahía Cochinos) la fallida invasión de Cuba en 1961 por un grupo de fuerzas anticastristas (p. 808)

beatnik (beatnik) en la década de 1950, una persona que criticaba la sociedad norteamericana por ser apática y conformista (p. 777)

Berlin airlift (puente aéreo de Berlín) los suministros que los aviones norteamericanos y británicos lanzaron sobre Berlín Occidental durante el bloqueo soviético de 1948–1949 (p. 750)

Berlin Wall (Muro de Berlín) una barrera construida en 1961 por el gobierno de Alemania del Este para impedir que la gente escapara a Berlín Occidental (p. 809)

Bessemer process (proceso Bessemer) un nuevo proceso, patentado en 1856, para mejorar la fabricación del acero (p. 411)

bicentennial (bicentenario) ducentésimo aniversario (p. 935)

bilingual education (educación bilingüe) enseñar a los estudiantes en su lengua materna así como en inglés (p. 1014)

Bill of Rights (Declaración de Derechos) las primeras diez enmiendas a la Constitución (p. 141)

black codes (códigos negros) las leyes que restringían los derechos de los libertos (p. 385)

blacklist (lista negra) una lista que circulaba entre los patronos y que contenía los nombres de personas que no debían ser contratadas (p. 754)

black nationalism (nacionalismo negro) la creencia en una identidad separada y la unidad racial en la comunidad afroamericana (p. 837)

black power (poder negro) movimiento afroamericano que busca la unidad y la autosuficiencia (p. 838)

Black Tuesday (Martes Negro) el 29 de octubre de 1929, día en que empezó el Gran Crack de la bolsa (p. 636)

Bland-Allison Act (Acta Bland-Allison) una ley de 1878 que disponía que el gobierno federal comprara y acuñara más plata (p. 447)

***blitzkrieg* (guerra relámpago)** un tipo de conflicto bélico que enfatiza el movimiento rápido y mecanizado (p. 687)

blockade (bloqueo) aislar un lugar del contacto exterior (p. 111)

block grant (subvención en bloque) fondos federales entregados a los estados en un pago único (p. 1035)

blue law (ley azul) una ley que prohíbe ciertas actividades privadas, como tomar bebidas alcohólicas los domingos (p. 462)

Bonanza farm (granja bonanza) una granja controlada por una compañía grande y dirigida por profesionales (p. 441)

Bonus Army (ejército Bonus) un grupo de veteranos de la primera guerra mundial y sus familias, que en 1932 protestaron en Washington, D.C., por sus pensiones (p. 651)

boomer (boomer) uno de los colonos que se apresuraron en llegar al territorio indio después de que éste fuera abierto para su colonización en 1889 (p. 439)

boom town (ciudad de rápido desarrollo) una ciudad que ha experimentado un crecimiento rápido (p. 305)

bootlegger (contrabandista de alcohol) durante la prohibición, un suministrador de alcohol ilegal (p. 622)

Border States (estados fronterizos) los estados entre el Norte y el Sur: Delaware, Maryland, Kentucky y Misuri (p. 333)

Boston Massacre (la masacre de Boston) un incidente ocurrido el 5 de marzo de 1770 en el que los soldados británicos mataron a cinco colonos (p. 94)

boycott (boicó) la negativa a comprar cierto producto o a usar cierto servicio (p. 92)

brinkmanship (diplomacia arriesgada) la política de arriesgarse a ir a la guerra para proteger intereses nacionales (p. 761)

***Brown* v. *Board of Education* (*Brown* contra *la Junta de Educación*)** un caso por el que en 1954 el Tribunal Supremo declaró ilegal al segregación racial en las escuelas públicas (p. 786)

buffalo soldier (soldado "búfalo") nombre que los indios norteamericanos daban a los soldados negros del ejército de los Estados Unidos que sirvieron en el Oeste hacia finales de los 1800 y principios de los 1900 (p. 454)

bureaucracy (burocracia) los departamentos que componen una organización grande, como un gobierno (p. 184)

business cycle (ciclo económico) el crecimiento y la contracción periódicos de la economía de una nación (p. 418)

buying on margin (comprar por una fracción) la práctica por la que inversores compran acciones por sólo una fracción de su precio, tomando prestado el resto (p. 633)

C

Cabinet (gabinete) los líderes de los departamentos ejecutivos del gobierno federal (p. 143)

California gold rush (carrera del oro de California) emigración masiva a California en 1848 inmediatamente después del descubrimiento de oro (p. 305)

Camp David Accords (acuerdos de Camp David) en 1978, acuerdo entre Israel y Egipto que hizo posible el tratado de paz entre las dos naciones (p. 941)

canister (obús de metralla) un tipo especial de obús lleno de balas (p. 344)

capital (capital) riqueza que puede invertirse para producir bienes y hacer dinero (p. 232)

carpetbagger (carpetbagger) apodo insultante que recibían los republicanos del Norte que se mudaron al Sur después de la guerra Civil (p. 390)

carpet bombing (manto de bombas) un método de bombardeo aéreo por el que se suelta un gran número de bombas en una área extensa (p. 697)

cartel (cártel) una asociación informal de negocios que producen el mismo producto (p. 416)

cash crop (cultivo para la venta) una cosecha que se cultiva para ser vendida (p. 23)

casualty (baja) una persona muerta o herida (p. 342)

cede (ceder) rendirse oficialmente o informalmente (p. 204)

centralized (centralizado) concentrado en un lugar (p. 231)

Central Powers (poderes centrales) en la primera guerra mundial, Alemania y Austro-Hungría (p. 566)

charter (acuerdo) un certificado o permiso que da un gobierno (p. 37)

checks and balances (sistema de revisión) el sistema en el que cada una de las ramas del gobierno federal puede comprobar las acciones de las otras ramas (p. 136)

Chinese Exclusion Act (Acta de Exclusión de los Chinos) una ley aprobada en 1882 que prohibía la entrada en el país a los trabajadores chinos (p. 470)

civil disobedience (desobediencia civil) negativa no violenta a obedecer la ley en un esfuerzo por cambiarla (p. 557)

civil rights (derechos civiles) las libertades personales de los ciudadanos garantizadas por la ley (p. 387)

Civil Rights Act of 1964 (Ley de Derechos Civiles de 1964) una ley que declaraba ilegal la discriminación en varias áreas, incluidos el voto, las escuelas y el lugar de trabajo (p. 833)

civil service (servicio civil) el sistema de trabajadores gubernamentales no elegidos por votación (p. 463)

Civil War (guerra Civil) la guerra entre la Unión y la Confederación, desde 1861 a 1865 (p. 341)

clan (clan) grupos de familias en los que todos los miembros descienden de un antepasado común (p. 6)

Clayton Antitrust Act (Acta Antimonopolio Clayton) una ley aprobada en 1914 para fortalecer la política federal antimonopolio, en la que se detallan las actividades comerciales que estaban prohibidas (p. 554)

Clean Air Act (Ley del Aire Limpio) una ley aprobada en 1970 que pretendía controlar la polución causada por las emisiones industriales y automovilísticas (p. 864)

Clean Water Act (Ley del Agua Limpia) una ley aprobada en 1972 que pretendía controlar la polución causada por la descarga de aguas residuales industriales y municipales (p. 865)

cloture (limitación) en el Senado, una votación que cuenta con las tres quintas partes de los votos y que permite terminar el debate de un asunto (p. 833)

coalition (coalición) una alianza de grupos con objetivos similares (p. 673)

cold war (guerra fría) la competencia que hubo entre los Estados Unidos y la Unión Soviética a partir de la década de 1940 hasta el colapso de la Unión Soviética (pp. 745, 1049)

collective bargaining (negociación colectiva) un proceso en el que los empleados negocian en grupo con los propietarios (p. 425)

collective security (seguridad colectiva) una política por la que las naciones establecen un acuerdo para protegerse una a otra en caso de ataque (p. 751)

colony (colonia) un área establecida por inmigrantes que continúan siendo gobernados por el país del que provienen (p. 31)

Columbian Exchange (Intercambio colombino) el comercio trasatlántico de productos agrícolas, tecnología y cultura que se produjo entre las Américas y Europa, África y Asia, y que comenzó en 1492 con el primer viaje de Colón a las Américas (p. 22)

Common Sense (Sentido común) un panfleto escrito por Thomas Paine y publicado en enero de 1776, en el que se pedía la independencia norteamericana de Gran Bretaña (p. 98)

communism (comunismo) la ideología oficial de la Unión Soviética, caracterizada allí porque el gobierno poseía la total propiedad de la tierra y los bienes, control del gobierno por un solo partido, falta de derechos individuales y la llamada a la revolución en todo el mundo (p. 598)

Compromise of 1850 (Compromiso de 1850) un acuerdo designado para facilitar las tensiones producidas por la expansión de la esclavitud en los territorios del oeste (p. 322)

Compromise of 1877 (Compromiso de 1877) un acuerdo por el que los demócratas estaban de acuerdo en dar la victoria a Rutherford B. Hayes en la elección presidencial de 1876 y Hayes, a cambio, estaba de acuerdo en sacar de los estados del Sur las tropas federales que quedaban (p. 397)

compulsory (obligatorio) compulsivo (p. 535)

concentration camp (campo de concentración) un lugar en el que se confina a prisioneros de guerra y a otros prisioneros, usualmente en condiciones crueles (p. 708)

concession (concesión) cesión de una parcela de tierra a cambio de la promesa de usar la tierra para un propósito específico (p. 527)

Confederate States of America (Estados Confederados de Norteamérica) la asociación de siete estados secesionistas del sur, formada en 1861 (p. 334)

conglomerate (conglomerado) una corporación grande que es propietaria de muchas compañías pequeñas que producen variedad de bienes y servicios (p. 767)

congregation (congregación) los miembros de una iglesia; una reunión religiosa (p. 219)

Congress of Racial Equality (CORE) (Congreso para la Igualdad Racial) una organización fundada en 1942 para promover la igualdad por medios pacíficos (p. 820)

Congressional Union (CU) (Unión Congresional) una organización radical liderada por que hizo campaña a favor de una enmienda contitucional para garantizar el sufragio de la mujer (p. 559)

conquistador (conquistador) conquistador español (p. 29)

conscientious objector (objetor de conciencia) alguien que se opone a la guerra por razones morales o religiosas (p. 884)

conservationist (conservacionista) una persona pre-ocupada por el cuidado y protección de los recursos naturales (p. 552)

constitution (constitución) un plan de gobierno que describe las distintas partes del gobierno y sus deberes y poderes (p. 124)

consumer economy (economía de consumo) una economía que se basa en que los individuos com-pren muchas cosas (p. 603)

containment (contención) política norteamericana que se resiste a la expansión del comunismo en el mundo (p. 745)

contra (Contra) en español, "contrarrevolucionario" (p. 967)

contraband (contrabando) objetos confiscados al ene-migo durante la guerra (p. 354)

Contract with America (Contrato con Norteamérica) una promesa hecha por los candidatos republicanos en la campaña para la elección presidencial de 1994 en la que se comprometían a reducir el aparato de gobierno, eliminar algunas leyes, reducir los impuestos y equilibrar el presupuesto (p. 982)

convoy (convoy) un grupo de barcos armados y desarmados desplegados para proteger de los ataques a los barcos mercantes (p. 574)

Copperhead (Copperhead) durante la guerra Civil, un demócrata del Norte en contra de la guerra (p. 352)

cotton gin (desmotadora de algodón) una máquina para separar las semillas de las fibras de algodón en rama (p. 211)

counterculture (contracultura) en la década de 1960, un grupo de jóvenes norteamericanos que rechazaban las costumbres tradicionales (p. 887)

Crusades (Cruzadas) de 1096 a 1291, una serie de campañas militares de los cristianos europeos para arrebatarles la Tierra Sagrada a los musulmanes (p. 10)

Cuban Missile Crisis (crisis cubana de los misiles) la crisis que en 1962 se produjo entre los Estados Unidos y la Unión Soviética por el intento de los soviéticos de instalar misiles nucleares en Cuba (p. 810)

Cumberland Road (camino Cumberland) una carretera federal que se comenzó en Cumberland, Maryland, en 1811, y se extendió hacia el oeste hasta Ohio y más allá (p. 212)

D

***Dartmouth College* v. *Woodward* (*Dartmouth College* contra *Woodward*)** un caso en 1819 en el que el Tribunal Supremo falló que los estados no podían interferir en los contratos (p. 245)

Dawes Act (Acta Dawes) una ley de 1887 que dividió los territorios de los indígenas norteamericanos en parcelas familiares privadas (p. 438)

daylight saving time (cambio horario diurno) adelantar los relojes una hora en el verano (p. 579)

D-Day (día D) el nombre codificado para la invasión aliada de Francia, el 6 de junio de 1944 (p. 698)

death camp (campo de exterminio) en la segunda guerra mundial, un campo alemán creado con el único propósito de asesinar en masa (p. 709)

Declaration of Independence (Declaración de Indepen-dencia) la declaración, proclamada por el Segundo Congreso Continental en 1776, que explicaba por qué las colonias buscaban independizarse de Gran Bretaña (p. 99)

de facto segregation (segregación de facto) la segregación basada no en la ley sino en la pobreza y las condiciones de los guetos (p. 839)

deferment (aplazamiento) la prórroga oficial de la llamada de una persona al servicio militar en el ejército (p. 884)

deficit spending (gasto deficitario) cuando el gobierno gasta dinero prestado (p. 719)

deflation (deflación) una caída del precio de los bienes de consumo (p. 447)

de jure segregation (segregación de iure) segregación según la ley (p. 839)

demagogue (demagogo) un líder que manipula a la gente por medio de verdades a medias y tácticas alarmantes (p. 668)

demographics (demografía) las estadísticas que describen a la población, como información sobre la raza o los ingresos económicos (p. 610)

denomination (denominación) un subgrupo religioso (p. 219)

department store (grandes almacenes) un almacén que tiene gran variedad de productos y vende en grandes cantidades (p. 504)

depression (depresión) una recesión económica severa (p. 195)

deregulation (desregulación) la reducción o supresión de los controles gubernamentales (p. 946)

détente (détente) una relajación de la tensión entre naciones (p. 916)

direct primary (primaria directa) una elección en la que los votantes depositan sus votos para elegir a los candidatos de las futuras elecciones (p. 548)

disarmament (desarmamento) un programa en el que las naciones entregan sus armas voluntariamente (p. 600)

discrimination (discriminación) el trato desigual a un grupo de personas por su nacionalidad, raza, género o religión (p. 280)

dissent (disentir) diferencia de opinión o creencia (p. 80)

dissident (disidente) una persona que critica las acciones de su gobierno (p. 942)

diversity (diversidad) variedad (p. 51)

division of labor (división del trabajo) una forma de producción en la que diferentes personas realizan distintas tareas (p. 421)

dollar diplomacy (diplomacia del dólar) la política del Presidente Taft que fomentaba la inversión norteamericana en el extranjero (p. 531)

domestic affairs (asuntos domésticos) temas referentes a los asuntos internos del país (p. 144)

domino theory (teoría dominó) la creencia de que si un país se hace comunista, los países vecinos seguramente también se harán (p. 759)

"Double V" campaign (campaña "Doble V") un esfuerzo impulsado por un periódico afroamericano en favor de la victoria contra los poderes del Eje y la victoria en favor de la igualdad racial en el país (p. 733)

Dow Jones Industrial Average (Promedio Industrial Dow Jones) una medida promedio de los precios de las acciones de las principales industrias (p. 635)

downsizing (reducción de personal) la práctica empresarial de despedir a trabajadores para reducir los costos (p. 974)

draft (llamada a filas) un programa de servicio militar obligatorio (p. 349)

dry farming (cultivo en seco) las técnicas usadas para cultivar en áreas que reciben poca agua (p. 440)

Dust Bowl (Dust Bowl) una región de las grandes llanuras en la que hubo un periodo de sequía y tormentas de polvo durante la década de 1930 (p. 640)

duty (impuesto) una tasa (p. 60)

E

economic sanctions (sanciones económicas) restricciones en el comercio y otras medidas económicas con el propósito de castigar a otra nación (p. 990)

economies of scale (economías a escala) el fenómeno por el cual conforme la producción aumenta, el costo de cada objeto producido es frecuentemente menor (p. 417)

Electoral College (colegio electoral) el grupo de electores, elegidos por los votantes, que eligen al Presidente (p. 138)

e-mail correo electrónico transmitido por las redes informáticas (p. 1056)

emancipation (emancipación) liberación de esclavos (p. 267)

Emancipation Proclamation (Proclamación de Emancipación) el decreto presidencial, efectivo a partir del 1 de enero de 1863, que liberó a los esclavos en territorio confederado (p. 353)

embargo (embargo) una restricción del comercio (pp. 188, 911)

emigrate (emigrar) salir del propio país o región para establecerse en otro (p. 210)

Enlightenment (Ilustración) un movimiento del S. XVIII que enfatizaba la ciencia y la razón como claves para mejorar la sociedad (p. 99)

entitlement (tener derecho) un programa del gobierno que garantiza pagos a un grupo en particular, como a los ancianos (pp. 968, 1031)

Environmental Protection Agency (EPA) (Agencia para la Protección del Medio Ambiente) una organización gubernamental formada en 1970 para tratar asuntos como la polución del aire y del agua (p. 864)

Equal Rights Amendment (ERA) (Enmienda para la Igualdad de Derechos) una propuesta de enmienda constitucional, nunca ratificada, que propone la igualdad de derechos para ambos sexos (p. 849)

Erie Canal (Canal de Erie) un canal en el estado de Nueva York, acabado en 1825, que unía el río Hudson con el lago Erie (p. 212)

escalation (escalada) expansión (p. 876)

evangelical (evangélico) que consiste en sermones emocionalmente poderosos y en las enseñanzas de la Biblia, en lugar de en ceremonias formales (p. 218)

executive branch (poder ejecutivo) la rama del gobierno que hace cumplir las leyes (p. 124)

Exoduster (Exoduster) uno de un grupo de afroamericanos que emigró al Oeste a continuación de la guerra Civil (p. 435)

F

faction (facción) un grupo organizado en torno a un

interés común y preocupado únicamente por el progreso de dicho interés (p. 139)

fascism (fascismo) una filosofía política que sitúa la importancia de la nación por encima de la del individuo (p. 685)

federal (federal) un tipo de gobierno en el que el poder está dividido entre el gobierno central y gobiernos más pequeños (p. 135)

Federal Reserve System (Sistema Federal de Reserva) el sistema bancario central de la nación, establecido en 1913 (p. 555)

Federalist (federalista) partidario de la Constitución durante el debate sobre su ratificación; a favor de un gobierno central fuerte (p. 139)

federal deficit (déficit federal) la suma de dinero que se pierde cuando los gastos del gobierno federal superan a los ingresos (p. 1032)

feminism (feminismo) una teoría que favorece la igualdad política, económica y social de hombres y mujeres (p. 845)

feudalism (feudalismo) un sistema político y económico de la Europa medieval en el que los señores menos importantes recibían tierras de nobles poderosos a cambio de servicios (p. 9)

Fifteenth Amendment (Decimoquinta Enmienda) la enmienda constitucional, ratificada en 1870, que garantizaba el derecho al voto de los afroamericanos (p. 389)

filibuster (filibusterismo) una táctica en la que los senadores piden la palabra, empiezan a hablar, y se niegan a dejar de hablar impidiendo así la votación sobre una medida (p. 572)

First Battle of Bull Run (primera batalla de Bull Run) la primera batalla de la guerra Civil, que ganaron los confederados en julio de 1861 (p. 342)

First Continental Congress (Primer Congreso Continental) una asamblea de representantes de las colonias que se reunió por primera vez en Filadelfia en septiembre de 1774 (p. 95)

flapper (descocada) un término acuñado durante la década de 1920 que describía a una mujer joven de silueta erguida y delgada y gusto por el baile y las acciones atrevidas (p. 609)

food stamp (estampilla de comida) cupón federal para comprar alimentos que reciben las personas de bajos ingresos que tienen derecho a recibir asistencia (p. 1034)

Fort Sumter (Fuerte Sumter) un fuerte federal en la bahía de Charleston, Carolina del Sur; el ataque confederado al fuerte supuso el inicio de la guerra Civil (p. 335)

Fourteen Points (los Catorce Puntos) la propuesta del Presidente Wilson en 1918 para la paz europea de posguerra (p. 584)

Fourteenth Amendment (Decimocuarta Enmienda) la enmienda constitucional, ratificada en 1868, que garantizaba a todos los ciudadanos la misma protección de la ley (p. 386)

franchise (franquicia) el derecho a abrir un restaurante usando el nombre de marca y el sistema de una compañía principal (p. 768)

Freedom Rides (Marcha de la Libertad) una protesta a favor de los derechos civiles en la que un grupo racial mixto de manifestantes desafiaron a las estaciones de autobús que practicaban la segregación (p. 827)

free enterprise system (sistema de libre empresa) un sistema económico en el que las compañías compiten para conseguir beneficios (p. 232)

free soiler (antiesclavista) una persona dedicada a prevenir la expansión de la esclavitud hacia los territorios del oeste (p. 328)

French and Indian War (Guerra Franco-india) la guerra que, de 1754 a 1763, mantuvieron Francia, con naciones indias aliadas, y Gran Bretaña y sus colonos, por el control del este de Norteamérica (p. 85)

Fugitive Slave Act (Acta de Esclavos Fugitivos) parte del Compromiso de 1850, era una ley que ordenaba que todos los ciudadanos de los Estados Unidos ayudaran a la devolución de los esclavos fugitivos (p. 322)

fundamentalism (fundamentalismo) una serie de creencias religiosas que incluyen ideas cristianas tradicionales sobre Jesucristo, la creencia en que la Biblia fue inspirada por Dios y no contiene contradicciones o errores, y la creencia en que la Biblia es literalmente cierta (p. 624)

G

Gadsden Purchase (Compra Gadsden) la compra de las tierras del suroeste que en 1853 hizo los Estados Unidos a México (p. 303)

gag rule (regla de la mordaza) una regla aprobada por el Congreso que prohibía que se oyeran o se emprendieran acciones en favor de las peticiones antiesclavistas (p. 271)

General Agreement on Tariffs and Trade (GATT) (Acuerdo General sobre Aranceles Aduaneros y Comercio) un acuerdo internacional para la reducción de tarifas y la expansión del comercio mundial (p. 993)

Geneva Conference (Conferencia de Ginebra) una conferencia internacional en 1954 en la que Vietnam fue dividido en dos naciones (p. 873)

genocide (genocidio) el asesinato deliberado de todo un pueblo (p. 577)

Gentleman's Agreement (Acuerdo entre Caballeros) un acuerdo en 1907 entre los Estados Unidos y Japón que restringía la inmigración japonesa (p. 471)

gentry (aristocracia) en la Norteamérica colonial, hombres y mujeres suficientemente ricos como para contratar a otros para que trabajaran para ellos (p. 65)

Gettysburg Address (Discurso de Gettysburgh) famosa alocución del Presidente Lincoln en noviembre de 1863 sobre el significado de la guerra Civil, con motivo de la dedicación de un cementerio nacional en el sitio de la batalla de Gettysburg (p. 366)

ghetto (gueto) una área en la que domina un grupo étnico o racial (p. 475)

ghost town (ciudad fantasma) una ciudad que ha sido abandonada por falta de actividad económica (p. 305)

GI (Government Issued) (Aprobado por el Gobierno) él término que designaba a los soldados norteamericanos en la primera guerra mundial, derivado de "Government Issued" (p. 692)

Gibbons **v.** *Ogden* (*Gibbons* contra *Ogden*) un caso de 1824 en el que el Tribunal Supremo falló que los estados no podían regular el comercio en los cauces de agua interestatales (p. 245)

GI Bill (Ley del GI) una ley aprobada en 1944 para ayudar a los soldados veteranos a comprar casas y pagar estudios universitarios a su retorno (p. 770)

Gilded Age (edad de oro) término que describe el periodo comprendido entre 1877 y 1900 (p. 461)

globalization (globalización) tendencia a la organización mundial, como en la manufactura y venta de bienes (p. 1056)

Good Neighbor Policy (Política de buena vecindad) la política del Presidente Franklin D. Roosevelt para promover buenas relaciones con naciones latinoamericanas (p. 1043)

graft (cohecho) el uso del propio puesto para enriquecerse (p. 477)

grandfather clause (cláusula del abuelo) pasaje que exime a un grupo de gente de obedecer una ley si dicho grupo reúne ciertas condiciones antes de que se apruebe la ley (p. 498)

Grange (Grange) también conocida como Patrons of Husbandry (Protectores de la Economía Doméstica), una organización formada para fomentar la cooperación económica y política entre los agricultores (p. 448)

Great Awakening (Gran Despertar) un renacimiento religioso en las colonias norteamericanas durante las décadas de 1730 y 1740 (p. 79)

Great Compromise (Gran Compromiso) el compromiso adoptado en la Convención Constitucional que pedía una legislatura con dos cámaras, una de ellas elegida por la población y la otra justamente representativa de cada estado (p. 134)

Great Crash (Gran Crack) el colapso de la bolsa norteamericana en 1929 (p. 636)

Great Depression (Gran Depresión) el severo deterioro económico que duró desde 1929 hasta aproximadamente 1939 (p. 636)

Great Migration (Gran Migración) la emigración de colonos ingleses a la colonia de la bahía de Massachusetts que comenzó en la década de 1630 (p. 44)

Great Plains (Grandes Llanuras) las grandes praderas que se extienden entre el río Misisipí y las Montañas Rocosas (p. 287)

Great Society (Gran Sociedad) propuestas del Presidente Johnson para mejorar la educación pública, proveer cuidado médico a los ancianos y eliminar la pobreza (p. 803)

Great White Fleet (Gran Flota Blanca) una fuerza de barcos de la Marina de los Estados Unidos que emprendió un crucero mundial en 1907 (p. 536)

greenbacks (greenbacks) el nombre que recibe la moneda nacional en papel, creada en 1862 (p. 351)

green card (tarjeta verde) permiso de residencia y trabajo que se otorga a los extranjeros en los Estados Unidos (p. 1009)

Gross National Product (producto nacional bruto) el valor total de los bienes y servicios que produce un país en un año (p. 636)

guerrilla (guerrillero) un soldado que usas tácticas de ataque y huida (p. 371)

Gulf of Tonkin Resolution (Resolución del Golfo de Tonkin) resolución del Congreso que en 1964 autorizó al Presidente Johnson a emprender acción militar en Vietnam (p. 876)

H

Harlem Renaissance (Renacimiento de Harlem) el despertar literario afroamericano en la década 1920, centrado en Harlem, ciudad de Nueva York (p. 619)

haven (asilo) un lugar seguro (p. 53)

Hawley-Smoot tariff (tarifa Hawley-Smoot) una tarifa de importación especilmente elevada, aprobada por el Congreso en 1930 (p. 650)

Haymarket Riot (Revuelta de Haymarket) la violencia sindical en Chicago, en 1886 (p. 427)

Helms-Burton Act (Ley Helms-Burton) una ley de 1996 que penaliza a las compañías extranjeras que tienen negocios con Cuba (p. 1042)

Helsinki Accords (Acuerdos de Helsinki) una serie de acuerdos sobre seguridad europea, firmados en 1975 (p. 935)

hidalgo (hidalgo) un noble español (p. 29)

Ho Chi Minh Trail (Pista Ho Chi Minh) la ruta de suministros que llevaba tropas y materiales desde Vietnam del Norte a Vietnam del Sur (p. 876)

holding company (compañía de valores) una corporación que tiene acciones y contratos en numerosas compañías (p. 549)

Holocaust (Holocausto) El intento de la alemania nazi de asesinar a todos los judíos europeos (p. 707)

Hollywood Ten (los Diez de Hollywood) un grupo de personas de la industria cinematográfica que fueron encarceladas por negarse a responder preguntas del Congreso sobre la influencia comunista en Hollywood (p. 754)

home rule (autonomía) un sistema en el que las ciudades ejercen una cantidad limitada de autogobierno (p. 542)

Homestead Act (Acta de Protección a las Tierras de Colonización) una ley de 1862 que les ofrecía a los colonos 160 acres de tierra en el Oeste (p. 433)

Homestead Strike (huelga Homestead) la huelga contra los aceros Carnegie que hubo en Pennsylvania en 1892 (p. 427)

homicide (homicidio) el asesinato de un ser humano por otro (p. 1017)

Hooverville (Hooverville) un refugio para personas sin hogar durante los primeros años de la La Gran Depresión (p. 639)

House of Burgesses (House of Burgesses) la legislatura formada en Virginia en 1619 (p. 39)

House Un-American Activities Committee (HUAC) (Comité de Investigación de Actividades Anti-norteamericanas del Congreso) un comité del Congreso que investigó la influencia comunista en los Estados Unidos en las décadas de 1940 y 1950 (p. 753)

horizontal consolidation (consolidación horizontal) proceso de consolidación de muchas compañías que trabajan en el mismo ramo para formar una única gran compañía (p. 417)

hundred days (cien días) en 1933, el periodo al comienzo de la presidencia de Franklin Roosevelt, durante el cual el Congreso aprobó muchos programas del Nuevo Trato (p. 660)

I

ICBM un misil balístico intercontinental (p. 762)

immigrant (inmigrante) una persona que entra en un país nuevo para establecerse (p. 77)

Immigration Act of 1965 (Ley de Inmigración de 1965) una ley que terminó con las cuotas para países específicos y las reemplazó con restricciones más flexibles (p. 804)

impeach (inculpar) acusar a un funcionario público de corrupción en el cargo (pp. 388, 924)

imperialism (imperialismo) política de una nación más fuerte de crear un imperio basado en la dominación económica, política, cultural o militar de naciones más débiles (p. 515)

impressment (leva, enganche) política de forzar a las personas a hacer el servicio militar o civil (p. 192)

inauguration (inauguración) una ceremonia oficial de juramento (p. 143)

incumbent (titular) una persona que tiene el cargo oficialmente (p. 936)

indentured servant (aprendiz bajo contrato) una persona que está de acuerdo en trabajar para otra persona por un plazo de tiempo específico a cambio de transporte, alimento y cobijo (p. 40)

Indian Removal Act (Acta de Traslado de los Indios) una ley de 1830 que obligaba el traslado forzado de los indígenas norteamericanos al oeste del río Misisipí (p. 252)

indigo (índigo) una clase de planta usada para hacer un tinte azul para tela (p. 68)

industrialization (industrialización) el crecimiento de la industria (p. 237)

Industrial Revolution (Revolución Industrial) el esfuerzo que comenzó en Gran Bretaña a finales de los 1700 por aumentar la producción por medio de máquinas impulsadas por fuentes distintas de la fuerza humana o animal (p. 209)

infant mortality rate (tasa de mortalidad infantil) el porcentaje de niños menores de un año que mueren en una población (p. 202)

inflation (inflación) un aumento continuado del precio en un periodo de tiempo dado, que reduce la capacidad de compra (p. 112)

infrastructure (infraestructura) los servicios de propiedad pública que usa una sociedad (p. 394)

INF Treaty (Tratado INF) un tratado entre los Estados Unidos y la Unión Soviética firmado en 1987 que establece la destrucción de los misiles en Europa (p. 967)

initiative (iniciativa) un proceso por el que los ciudadanos proponen nuevas leyes por medio de la recogida de firmas en una petición (p. 548)

injunction (orden judicial) orden de un juzgado que prohibe alguna acción (p. 542)

installment plan (pago a plazos) un sistema que permite a los clientes hacer pagos parciales (plazos) a intervalos establecidos sobre un periodo de tiempo (p. 603)

integration (integración) el acercamiento de razas distintas (p. 787)

interchangeable parts (repuestos) un sistema de fabricación en el que se hacen todas las partes según un estándar exacto (p. 10)

interest (interés) una suma adicional de dinero que los que reciben dinero prestado deberán pagar al acreedor por el préstamo (p. 176)

Internet la red electrónica que une a los computadores por todo el mundo (p. 999)

internment camp (campo de internamiento) uno de los campos a los que se obligó a ir a los norteamericanos de origen japonés durante la segunda guerra mundial (p. 735)

interracial (interracial) que se realiza, contiene, o en el que participan gentes de razas diferentes (p. 820)

Interstate Commerce Act (Ley para el Comercio Interestatal) una ley de 1887 que regulaba los ferrocarriles y otros negocios interestatales (p. 449)

Iran-Contra affair (asunto Irán-Contra) el escándalo en la administración Reagan producido por la desviación de fondos hacia los contras nicaragüenses del producto de las ventas secretas de armas a los iraníes (p. 967)

Irish Potato Famine (Hambruna de la Patata en Irlanda) una epidemia de hambre en Irlanda en la década de 1840 que causó el aumento de la inmigración a los Estados Unidos (p. 279)

iron curtain (Telón de Acero) término con el que Winston Churchill describió la extensión del control comunista por Europa Oriental (p. 745)

isolationism (isolacionismo) la política de evitar alianzas políticas o económicas con países extranjeros (p. 600)

isthmus (istmo) una estrecha franja de tierra que une dos áreas de tierra más grandes (p. 29)

itinerant (itinerante) que viaja de un lugar a otro, o por un circuito (p. 79)

J

Japanese American Citizens League (JACL) (Liga de Ciudadanos Japonés-norteamericanos) una organización de japonés-norteamericanos formada para promover los derechos de los asiático-americanos (p. 855)

Jay's Treaty (Tratado de Jay) un tratado firmado en 1794 entre los Estados Unidos y Gran Bretaña por el que Gran Bretaña estaba de acuerdo en salir de los fuertes en los territorios del noroeste y ambos países en mejorar las relaciones comerciales (p. 177)

Jazz Age (Era del Jazz) un término usado para describir la década de 1920 (p. 616)

Jim Crow (Leyes Jim Crow) sistema de leyes que aplicaba la segregación en los servicios públicos a principios de la década de 1890 (p. 499)

jingoism (jingoísmo) un sentimiento intenso de orgullo nacional y deseo de una política exterior agresiva (p. 521)

joint-stock company (sociedad anónima) una compañía fundada y dirigida por un grupo de inversores que comparten las ganancias y pérdidas de la compañía (p. 37)

judicial branch (poder judicial) la rama del gobierno que interpreta y aplica las leyes (p. 124)

judicial review (revisión judicial) el poder de los tribunales federales para decidir qué leyes son constitucionales (p. 185)

K

kamikaze **(kamikaze)** en la segunda guerra mundial, un avión suicida japonés (p. 703)

Kansas-Nebraska Act (Decreto de Kansas-Nebraska) una ley de 1854 que pedía que los ciudadanos de cada territorio decidieran sobre el tema de la esclavitud en ellos (p. 325)

Kellogg-Briand Pact (Pacto Kellogg-Briand) un acuerdo firmado en 1928 por el que las naciones firmantes se ponían de acuerdo en no recurrir a la guerra para resolver sus diferencias (p. 602)

King Philip's War (guerra del rey Felipe) la guerra que empezó en 1675 entre los colonos ingleses y los indígenas norteamericanos (p. 49)

kinship (parentesco) las relaciones familiares (p. 6)

Korean War (guerra de Corea) el conflicto sobre el futuro de la península de Corea, que transcurrió entre 1950 y 1953 y acabó en punto muerto (p. 756)

Kristallnacht **(Noche de los cristales)** nombre que recibe la noche de violencia, el 9 de noviembre de 1938, en contra de los judíos en Alemania y Austria, en 1938 (p. 708)

L

labor union (sindicato) una organización de trabajadores formada para proteger los intereses de sus miembros (p. 239)

laissez-faire (liberalismo) la política gubernamental de no interferencia en los negocios privados (p. 461)

land speculator (especulador del suelo) una persona que compra grandes terrenos con la esperanza de venderlos después y obtener provecho (p. 433)

Latino (latino) una persona con orígenes familiares en la Latinoamérica hispanohablante (p. 852)

League of Nations (Liga de las Naciones) una organización internacional, formada después de la primera guerra mundial, que pretendía promover la seguridad y la paz para todos sus miembros (p. 585)

legislative branch (poder legislativo) la rama del gobierno que hace las leyes (p. 124)

legislature (legislatura) una asamblea legislativa (p. 39)

Lend-Lease Act (Ley de Préstamo-Alquiler) una ley de 1941 que autorizaba al Presidente a prestar ayuda a cualquier nación cuya defensa fuera, en su opinión, vital para la seguridad de los Estados Unidos (p. 690)

Lewis and Clark expedition (expedición de Lewis y Clark) el viaje de Meriwether Lewis y William Clark a través del territorio de Luisiana durante 1804–1806 (p. 188)

Liberty Bond (bonos de la libertad) unos bonos de guerra especiales que se vendían para apoyar la causa de los Aliados durante la primera guerra mundial (p. 578)

Liberty ship (barco de la libertad) un barco mercante grande y robusto construido durante la segunda guerra mundial (p. 717)

Limited Test Ban Treaty (Tratado para la Limitación de Pruebas Nucleares) en el tratado, firmado en 1963, los Estados Unidos y la Unión Soviética acordaron no probar armas nucleares por encima de la superficie terrestre (p. 812)

lineage (linaje) grupos familiares que trazan su origen hasta un antepasado común (p. 16)

literacy (alfabetismo) la capacidad de leer y escribir (p. 487)

long drive (gran travesía) la conducción de ganado desde las lejanas montañas a los bulliciosos centros ferroviarios que transportaban el ganado al mercado (p. 442)

loose construction (vaga interpretación) la creencia en que el gobierno puede hacer cualquier cosa que la Constitución no dice que no puede hacer (p. 176)

Lost Generation (generación perdida) un grupo de escritores de la década de 1920 que compartían la creencia de que estaban perdidos en un mundo codicioso y materialista que carecía de valores morales (p. 617)

Louisiana Purchase (adquisición de Luisiana) la compra por los Estados Unidos a Francia del territorio de Luisiana, en 1803 (p. 187)

Lower South (Bajo Sur) Los estados de Texas, Luisiana, Misisipí, Alabama, Florida, Georgia y Carolina del Sur (p. 334)

Loyalist (leal) una persona que permaneció fiel a Gran Bretaña durante la revolución (p. 107)

lynching (linchamiento) el secuestro y ejecución ilegal de una persona por una multitud (p. 499)

M

Magna Carta (carta grande) una "carta grande" firmada en 1215 que cedo ciertas derechas a los nobles ingleses (p. 11)

mail-order catalog (catálogo de pedidos por correo) un catálogo que anuncia una gran variedad de objetos que se pueden comprar por correo (p. 504)

mandate (mandato) una serie de deseos que los votantes piden a un candidato (p. 798)

Manhattan Project (Proyecto Manhattan) en la segunda guerra mundial, el programa secreto norteamericano para fabricar una bomba atómica (p. 704)

manifest destiny (destino manifiesto) el razonamiento que defendía que los Estados Unidos estaba destinado a expandirse por Norteamérica (p. 301)

manufacturing (manufactura) la fabricación de bienes por medio de máquinas (p. 231)

maquiladora (maquiladora) factoría mexicana instalada en las cercanías de la frontera entre los Estados Unidos y México, que produce y monta productos para compañías estadounidenses (p. 1044)

March on Washington (marcha sobre Washington) la manifestación en favor de los derechos civiles, en 1963, en Washington, D.C. (p. 832)

Marbury v. *Madison* (*Marbury* contra *Madison*) en 1803, un caso en el que el Tribunal Supremo estableció el principio de revisión judicial (p. 185)

Market Revolution (revolución de mercado) el cambio de la economía doméstica a la economía basada en el dinero y en la compra y venta de bienes (p. 231)

Marshall Plan (Plan Marshall) el programa de ayuda económica norteamericana a Europa Occidental,

anunciado en 1947 (p. 748)

martial law (ley marcial) gobierno de emergencia de las autoridades militares (p. 352)

Massacre at Wounded Knee (masacre de Wounded Knee) el asesinato a tiros por tropas del ejército de un grupo de siux desarmados, en 1890 (p. 438)

mass media (medios de comunicación) métodos para la comunicación de información a gran número de personas por medio de letra impresa o transmisión (p. 614)

mass production (producción en masa) producción de bienes en gran cantidad (p. 411)

Mayflower Compact (pacto del Mayflower) el acuerdo por el que los colonos de la colonia Plymouth se comprometían a obedecer las leyes de su gobierno (p. 44)

McCarran-Walter Act (Decreto McCarran-Walter) una ley de inmigración de 1952 que discriminaba en contra de potenciales inmigrantes de Asia y Europa Meridional y Central (p. 754)

McCulloch v. *Maryland* (*McCulloch* contra *Maryland*) en 1819, un caso en el que el Tribunal Supremo falló que el Congreso tiene la autoridad para llevar a cabo las acciones necesarias para cumplir sus deberes constitucionales (p. 244)

median age (edad mediana) la edad que divide a la población en dos mitades: una mitad por encima de esa edad y la otra por debajo (p. 202)

Medicaid un programa federal que provee ayuda médica para los norteamericanos pobres (p. 804, 1031)

Medicare un programa federal que provee ayuda médica para los ancianos norteamericanos (pp. 804, 1031)

mercantilism (mercantilismo) una teoría económica que razonaba que un país debía tratar de acumular tantos lingotes de oro y plata como le fuera posible, exportando más bienes de los que importa (p. 59)

mercenary (mercenario) un soldado extranjero que lucha por dinero (p. 108)

mestizo (mestizo) una persona de herencia mixta hispana e indígena americana (p. 31)

Mexican War (guerra Mexicana) el conflicto entre los Estados Unidos y México, de 1846 a 1848, que acabó con la victoria de Estados Unidos (p. 302)

Middle Ages (Edad Media) era de la historia europea que comprende desde el año 500 d. de C. hasta el año 1300 (p. 9)

Middle America (Norteamérica moderada) un término usado a veces para describir la tendencia principal entre los norteamericanos (p. 905)

middle class (clase media) una nueva clase de comerciantes, negociantes y artesanos que surgió en Europa al final de la Edad Media; en los tiempos modernos, la clase social entre los muy ricos y la clase trabajadora menos pudiente (p. 11)

Middle Colonies (colonias centrales) las colonias

inglesas de Nueva York, Nueva Jersey, Pennsylvania y Delaware (p. 51)

middleman (intermediario) alguien que compra objetos a un proveedor y luego los vende a otras personas (p. 288)

Middle Passage (paso medio) la parte del comercio triangular en la que los africanos eran sacados a la fuerza de África para ser llevados como esclavos a las Américas (p. 72)

migrant farm worker (trabajador agrícola migratorio) un trabajador que va de granja en granja sembrando y cosechando cosechas distintas (p. 853)

militarism (militarismo) la política de aumento de las fuerzas armadas de una nación, como preparación previa a la guerra (p. 565)

militia (milicia) ciudadanos armados que sirven de soldados durante una emergencia (pp. 87, 1019)

Miranda rule (Ley de Miranda) obligación que tiene la policía de informar de sus derechos legales a los acusados de cometer un crimen (p. 805)

mission (misión) la sede desde la cual personas de otro país pretenden la difusión de su religión (p. 33)

Missouri Compromise (Compromiso de Misuri) un acuerdo al que se llegó en 1820 que pedía la admisión de Misuri como estado esclavista y de Maine como estado libre, declarando ilegal la esclavitud en los futuros estados que se crearan al norte de los 36° 30' N de latitud (p. 196)

mobile society (sociedad móvil) una sociedad en la que las personas están constantemente yendo de lado a lado (p. 216)

mobilization (mobilización) la preparación de tropas para la guerra (p. 566)

modem (módem) un dispositivo que convierte datos en señales que pueden transmitirse por teléfono (p. 1057)

modern republicanism (republicanismo moderno) propuesta de gobierno del Presidente Eisenhower, descrito como "conservador en lo referente al dinero, liberal en lo referente a los seres humanos" (p. 783)

monarch (monarca) alguien que gobierna un reino, como un rey o una reina (p. 11)

monetary policy (política monetaria) el plan del gobierno federal para la fabricación y reserva del suministro de dinero de la nación (p. 447)

monopoly (monopolio) control completo de un producto o servicio (p. 416)

Monroe Doctrine (Doctrina Monroe) la declaración que hizo el Presidente Monroe en 1823 en la que decía que Estados Unidos se opondría a los esfuerzos de cualquier potencia extranjera que quisiera controlar a otra nación en el Hemisferio Occidental (pp. 245, 1043)

Montgomery bus boycott (boicó a los autobuses de Montgomery) la protesta que en 1955–1956 hicieron los afroamericanos contra la segregación racial en el sistema de autobuses de Montgomery, Alabama (p. 787)

Morrill Land-Grant Act (Acta Morrill de Concesión de Tierra) una ley 1862 por la que el gobierno federal distribuyó millones de acres de tierras en el oeste entre los gobiernos de los estados para fundar colegios agrícolas estatales (p. 433)

mountain man (hombre montañés) uno de los comerciantes de pieles norteamericanos que exploraron las Montañas Rocosas y otras regiones más al oeste en los 1800 (p. 297)

muckraker (reportero investigador) un periodista que investiga fechorías cometidas por políticos o corporaciones (p. 543)

multiculturalism (multiculturalismo) movimiento que pide más atención a las culturas no europeas en distintas áreas, como la educación (p. 998)

municipal (municipal) relativo a la ciudad, como el gobierno municipal (p. 542)

Munn v. *Illinois* (*Munn* contra *Illinois*) una decisión del Tribunal Supremo en 1877 que permitía que los estados regularan ciertos negocios dentro de sus fronteras (p. 464)

mutiny (motín) revuelta contra la autoridad superior (p. 73)

My Lai massacre (masacre de My Lai) la matanza de varios cientos de vietnamitas por soldados norteamericanos en 1968 (p. 880)

N

napalm una sustancia química muy inflamable usada en ataques con bombas incendiarias (p. 879)

National American Woman Suffrage Association (Asociación Nacional Norteamericana para el Sufragio Femenino) una organización formada en 1890 para impulsar el derecho de la mujer al voto (p. 558)

National Association for the Advancement of Colored People (Asociación Nacional para el Progreso de las Personas de Color) una organización formada en 1909 para el progreso de la causa de los afroamericanos (p. 500)

national debt (deuda nacional) la cantidad total de dinero que el gobierno federal ha tomado prestado y tiene que pagar (pp. 672, 1032)

National Defense Education Act (Ley Nacional para la Defensa de la Educación) una ley de 1958 para mejorar la enseñanza de ciencias y matemáticas en las escuelas (p. 784)

National Rifle Association (NRA) (Asociación Nacional del Rifle) organización destacada que está en contra del control de armas (p. 1020)

nationalism (nacionalismo) devoción hacia la propia nación (p. 515)

nationalization (nacionalización) conversión en

propiedad del gobierno (p. 669)

National Organization for Women (NOW) (Organización Nacional de Mujeres) una organización formada en 1966 para promover la participación total de las mujeres en la sociedad norteamericana (p. 847)

Nation of Islam (Nación del Islam) una organización, llamada también Musulmanes Negros, dedicada a la separación de las personas de raza negra y a la ayuda a sí mismos (p. 837)

nativism (indigenismo) un movimiento que promueve un mejor trato para los norteamericanos nacidos en el país que para los inmigrantes (pp. 324, 479)

nativist (natalista) que apoya la política de favorecer a los ciudadanos nacidos en el país y desfavorecer a los inmigrantes (p. 1011)

naturalize (naturalizar) solicitud y concesión de la ciudadanía norteamericana (p. 280)

natural rights (derechos naturales) derechos que tiene la gente simplemente por ser humanos (p. 100)

neutral (neutral) que no toma partido en un conflicto o disputa (p. 177)

New Deal (Nuevo Trato) los programas de ayuda, recuperación y reforma del Presidente Franklin Roosevelt para combatir la Gran Depresión (pp. 659, 1025)

New England Colonies (colonias de Nueva Inglaterra) las colonias inglesas que se convirtieron en los estados de Connecticut, Rhode Island, Massachusetts, Vermont, Nueva Hampshire y Maine (p. 43)

New Federalism (Nuevo Federalismo) el plan del Presidente Reagan para dar a los estados más control sobre el uso de la ayuda federal (p. 961)

New Freedom (Nueva Libertad) la plataforma de la campaña de Woodrow Wilson en 1912, en la que se pedía acción antimonopolio sin amenazar la libre competencia (p. 554)

New Frontier (Nueva Frontera) las propuestas del Presidente Kennedy para mejorar la economía, ayudar a los pobres y acelerar el programa espacial (p. 798)

New Left (Nueva Izquierda) un movimiento político nuevo de finales de la década de 1960 que pedía cambios radicales para luchar contra la pobreza y el racismo (p. 883)

New Nationalism (Nuevo Nacionalismo) el programa de Theodore Roosevelt para aumentar la regulación federal de los negocios y lugares de trabajo, los impuestos sobre la renta y las herencias y reformas electorales (p. 553)

New Right (nueva derecha) una coalición de grupos conservadores que surgió hacia 1980 (p. 958)

Niagara Movement (Movimiento Niágara) una organización fundada en 1905 por W.E.B. Du Bois y otros líderes negros que pedía libertades civiles totales para los afroamericanos, el fin de la discriminación racial y el reconocimiento de la hermandad de los seres humanos (p. 491)

Nisei (nisei) un japonés-americano cuyos padres nacieron en Japón (p. 735)

nomadic (nómada) que cambia de lugar regularmente en busca de alimento (p. 4)

nomad (nómada) una persona que emigra constantemente, en lugar de vivir permanentemente en un lugar (p. 288)

nonviolent protest (protesta no-violenta) una forma de protesta en la que los protestantes no se resisten o devuelven los golpes al ser atacados (p. 821)

North American Free Trade Agreement (NAFTA) (Zona de Libre Comercio del Atlántico Norte) un acuerdo por el que se suprimen las restricciones al comercio entre Estados Unidos, Canadá y México (pp. 993, 1040)

North Atlantic Treaty Organization (NATO) (Organización del Tratado del Atlántico Norte) (OTAN) la alianza entre Estados Unidos, Canadá y naciones de Europa Occidental, formada en 1949 (pp. 751, 1052)

Nuclear Regulatory Commission (Comisión para la Regulación Nuclear) una organización gubernamental formada en 1974 para supervisar los usos civiles de materiales nucleares (p. 863)

nullification (anulación) negativa de un estado a reconocer una ley federal (p. 181)

O

obsolete (obsoleto) anticuado (p. 318)

Office of War Information (Oficina de Información para la Guerra) una agencia federal creada en 1942 para conseguir apoyo público para el esfuerzo de guerra de la segunda guerra mundial (p. 722)

Office of War Mobilization (Oficina de Mobilización para la Guerra) una agencia federal creada en 1943 para coordinar asuntos relacionados con la producción de guerra durante la segunda guerra mundial (p. 716)

Olive Branch Petition (Petición de la Rama de Olivo) una petición que los colonos norteamericanos hicieron al rey Jorge III en 1775 para que él parara la lucha (p. 99)

Open Door Policy (política de puertas abiertas) la estrategia norteamericana con China hacia el 1900, que favorecía relaciones comerciales abiertas entre China y otras naciones (p. 525)

oral history (historia oral) tradiciones transmitidas por la palabra de generación en generación (p. 7)

Oregon Trail (Pista Oregón) una ruta que unía Independence, Misuri, y Oregón, usada por muchos pioneros durante la década de 1840 (p. 298)

Organization of Petroleum Exporting Countries (OPEC) (Organización de Países Exportadores de Petróleo) (OPEP) un grupo de naciones que colaboraban para regular el precio y suministro de petróleo (p. 911)

P

pardon (perdón) absolución oficial de un crimen (p. 381)

Paris peace talks (conferencias de París para la paz) las negociaciones entre los Estados Unidos y Vietnam del Norte, que comenzaron en 1968 (p. 891)

pass (paso) un lugar a poca altura en una cadena montañosa que permite el paso de viajeros al otro lado (p. 298)

patent (patente) una licencia para fabricar, usar o vender un invento (p. 408)

patronage (patrocinio) la práctica de contratar a partidarios políticos para puestos de trabajo en el gobierno (p. 250)

Peace Corps (Cuerpo de Paz) un programa federal establecido para mandar voluntarios para ayudar a las naciones en desarrollo en todo el mundo (p. 813)

Pendleton Civil Service Act (Acta Pendleton de Servicio Civil) una ley de 1883 que creó una Comisión para el Servicio Civil y declaró que a los empleados federales no se les podía exigir que contribuyeran a los fondos para las campañas electorales y no podían ser despedidos por razones políticas (p. 463)

Pentagon Papers (Papeles del Pentágono) un estudio del gobierno sobre la participación de los Estados Unidos en la guerra de Vietnam, hecho público en 1971 (p. 882)

Pequot War (guerra Pequot) la guerra entre los colonos ingleses y los indios pequot en 1637 (p. 48)

per capita income (renta per cápita) promedio de los ingresos por persona (p. 767)

persecute (perseguir) oprimir a alguien a causa de sus creencias (p. 44)

Persian Gulf War (guerra del Golfo Pérsico) la guerra en la que fuerzas de las Naciones Unidas expulsaron de Kuwait al ejército invasor iraquí en 1991 (p. 974)

philanthropist (filántropo) persona que hace donaciones a causas que lo merecen (p. 489)

Pickett's Charge (Carga de Pickett) la desafortunada carga de la infantería confederada durante la batalla de Gettysburg (p. 363)

piecework (trabajo a destajo) un sistema en el que a los trabajadores no se les paga por horas sino por lo que producen (p. 420)

Pilgrim (peregrino) un miembro del grupo de separatistas ingleses que establecieron la colonia de Plymouth en 1620 (p. 44)

Pinckney Treaty (Tratado Pinckney) un tratado entre los Estados Unidos y España en 1795 que estableció los límites de los Estados Unidos por el sur (p. 203)

placer mining (minería de lavadero) un método minero usado por buscadores particulares (p. 441)

plantation (plantación) una gran instalación agrícola en la que las cosechas se cultivan principalmente para la venta (p. 23)

***Plessy* v. *Ferguson* (*Plessy* contra *Ferguson*)** un caso de 1896 en el que el Tribunal Supremo falló que la segregación racial era legal siempre que las instalaciones separadas fueran iguales para ambas razas (p. 499)

political asylum (asilo político) protección que un país da a los refugiados de otro país (p. 1009)

political machine (maquinaria política) una organización no oficial diseñada para mantener en el poder a un partido o grupo en particular, dirigida normalmente por un único y poderoso jefe (p. 476)

political party (partido político) un grupo de personas que tratan de ganar las elecciones y los cargos públicos para controlar la política y los programas del gobierno (p. 178)

poll tax (impuesto por persona) una tarifa especial que se debe pagar antes de que una persona pueda votar (p. 498)

Pontiac's Rebellion (rebelión de Pontiac) una rebelión de los indígenas norteamericanos contra los británicos en la región de los Grandes Lagos, en 1763 (p. 90)

Poor People's Campaign (Campaña de los Pobres) una cruzada contra la injusticia económica organizada en 1968 por Martin Luther King, Jr. (p. 906)

popular sovereignty (soberanía popular) dejar que la gente de un territorio decida si se va a permitir la esclavitud en él (p. 325)

population density (densidad de población) el número de personas promedio que viven en un espacio dado (p. 237)

Populist (populista) un seguidor del partido populista, formado en 1891, que apoyaba la creación de una provisión mayor de dinero y otras reformas económicas (p. 449)

precedent (precedente) algo que se ha hecho o dicho que se convierte en un ejemplo, regla o tradición a seguir (p. 144)

prejudice (prejuicio) una opinión irracional, generalmente desfavorable, sobre otro grupo (p. 316)

presidio (presidio) fuerte construido en el Suroeste por los españoles (pp. 32, 292)

price controls (control de precios) un sistema de precios determinados por el gobierno (p. 579)

prime minister (primer ministro) el funcionario más alto de un gobierno parlamentario (p. 87)

privateer (corsario) un barco propiedad de un particular que es contratado por un gobierno para atacar a barcos enemigos (p. 37)

Proclamation of 1763 (Proclamación de 1763) una orden del rey británico que cerró la región al oeste de los Apalaches y prohibió el asentamiento de colonos (p. 90)

productivity (productividad) la cantidad que produce un trabajador en un periodo de tiempo (pp. 408, 1059)

profiteering (acaparamiento) venta de bienes escasos a precios irracionalmente altos (p. 111)

progressive (progresista) reformista político y social

de finales de los 1800 y principios de los 1900 (p. 1024)

Progressive Era (Era Progresista) el periodo entre 1890 y 1920 durante el cual se realizaron una serie de reformas a nivel local, estatal y federal (p. 449)

progressive income tax (impuesto progresivo sobre la renta) un impuesto en el que el porcentaje de tasas que se deben aumenta con la renta percibida (p. 449)

prohibition (prohibición) prohibición legal de manufacturación y venta de bebidas alcohólicas (p. 480)

proliferation (proliferación) aumento rápido del número, esparcimiento (p. 918)

proprietary colony (colonia propiedad) concesión de una colonia con plenos derechos de gobierno que el rey o reina hace a un individuo o grupo (p. 52)

public works program (programa de obras públicas) un programa financiado por el gobierno para construir obras públicas (p. 661)

Pueblo Revolt of 1680 (revuelta de los Pueblo de 1680) una revuelta de los indios pueblo de Nuevo México contra España (p. 33)

Pullman Strike (huelga Pullman) la huelga de trabajadores del ferrocarril que se extendió por toda la nación (p. 428)

Puritan (puritano) una persona a favor de la purificación de la Iglesia Anglicana de Inglaterra (p. 44)

Q

Quaker (cuáquero) un miembro de un grupo protestante que pone énfasis en la igualdad (p. 53)

quarantine (cuarentena) un periodo de aislamiento para prevenir la extensión de una enfermedad (p. 468)

quota (cuota) un número límite (p. 601)

R

racism (racismo) la creencia que sostiene que las diferencias en carácter o inteligencia se deben a la raza de la persona (p. 534)

ragtime (ragtime) un estilo de música que consiste en melodías con acentos sincopados sobre un pulso constante (p. 495)

ratify (ratificar) aprobar o sancionar (p. 139)

rationing (racionar) distribuir cantidades fijas de bienes entre los consumidores (p. 579)

realpolitik **(realpolitik)** en alemán, "política práctica," o política exterior basada en el interés en lugar de en principios morales (p. 915)

recall (retirar) un proceso por el que los votantes destituyen a un funcionario público de su puesto antes de la próxima elección (p. 548)

recession (recesión) un periodo de poca actividad económica (p. 933)

recognition (reconocimiento) aceptación oficial (p. 350)

Reconstruction (reconstrucción) el esfuerzo del gobierno federal entre 1865 y 1877 por reparar los daños causados al Sur y devolver los estados sureños a la Unión (p. 379)

red scare (miedo a los rojos) miedo al comunismo y a otras ideas extremas (p. 598)

referendum (referéndum) un proceso por el que los ciudadanos votan una ley aprobada por su legislatura (p. 548)

Reformation (Reforma) una revuelta contra la Iglesia Católica, que comenzó en 1517 (p. 14)

religious tolerance (tolerancia religiosa) la idea que mantiene que personas de religiones distintas deberían vivir juntas en paz (p. 44)

Renaissance (Renacimiento) una era de la historia europea, desde el año 1300 al 1500 (p. 12)

reparations (compensación) pago que un enemigo debe hacer por daños económicos sufridos durante una guerra (p. 586)

republic (república) gobierno del pueblo por medio de sus representantes electos (p. 125)

republican virtues (virtudes republicanas) las virudes que el pueblo norteamericano necesitaría para gobernarse a sí mismo, como sacrificar las necesidades individuales por el bien de la comunidad, autoconfianza, industria, frugalidad y armonía (p. 209)

reservation (reserva) una área que el gobierno federal reservó para los indígenas norteamericanos que habían perdido su tierra natal (pp. 190, 436)

restrictive covenant (pacto restrictivo) un acuerdo entre propietarios de viviendas para no vender propiedades inmobiliarias a ciertos grupos de personas, como a los afroamericanos o a los judíos (p. 475)

revenue (ingresos) renta (p. 672)

revival (renacer) una reunión en la que las personas "renacen," o son devueltas a una vida religiosa (p. 219)

Revolutionary War (guerra de Independencia) la guerra de los colonos norteamericanos por conseguir la independencia de Gran Bretaña, que duró de 1775 a 1783 (p. 96)

rock and roll un tipo de música que surge del rhythm and blues y que se hizo popular en la década de 1950 (p. 777)

Roe **v.** *Wade* **(***Roe* **contra** *Wade***)** en 1973, la decisión del Tribunal Supremo que legalizó el aborto (p. 849)

Roosevelt Corollary (Corolario de Roosevelt) la ampliación que el Presidente Theodore Roosevelt hizo en 1904 de la Doctrina Monroe, en la que Roosevelt afirmaba el derecho de los Estados Unidos a intervenir en naciones latinoamericanas (pp. 529, 1043)

Rosie the Riveter (Rosie "la remachadora") un término que simboliza a las muchas mujeres que trabajaron en la industria de defensa durante la segunda guerra mundial (p. 726)

royal colony (colonia real) una colonia con un gobernador nombrado por el rey (p. 39)

rural (rural) ambiente de campo, en vez de ambiente de ciudad (p. 240)

rural free delivery (reparto rural gratuito) la entrega gratuita de paquetes en las áreas rurales, que comenzó en 1896 (p. 504)

Russian Revolution (revolución Rusa) el colapso del gobierno del zar en Rusia en 1917, que finalmente llevó a la toma del poder por los bolcheviques (p. 572)

S

sachem (cacique) un líder indígena norteamericano (p. 48)

Salem witch trials (juicios por brujería de Salem) el procesamiento y ejecución de veinte mujeres y hombres acusados de brujería en Massachusetts, en 1692 (p. 45)

SALT I (Strategic Arms Limitation Treaty) (tratado para la limitación de armas estratégicas) el acuerdo firmado en 1972 por los Estados Unidos y la Unión Soviética sobre la limitación de armas nucleares (p. 918)

salutary neglect (negligencia saludable) la política británica a principios de los 1700 consistente en no interferir en la política y la economía de las colonias norteamericanas, siempre que dicha negligencia sirviera a los intereses económicos británicos (p. 62)

Sandinista (sandinista) un miembro del grupo de nicaragüenses que se hicieron con el gobierno en 1979 (p. 967)

Santa Fe Trail (Pista de Santa Fe) un camino que unía Independence, Misuri, con Santa Fe, Nuevo México, a mediados del siglo XIX (p. 293)

satellite nation (nación satélite) un país dominado política y económicamente por otro país, especialmente por la Unión Soviética durante la guerra fría (p. 743)

saturation bombing (bombardeo de saturación) arrojar grandes concentraciones de bombas sobre cierta área (p. 879)

savanna (sabana) una región cerca del ecuador con praderas tropicales y árboles dispersos (p. 16)

scab (esquirol) un trabajador contratado por un patrón para reemplazar a obreros en huelga (p. 426)

scalawag (republicano del Sur) un apodo insultante para un republicano blanco del Sur después de la guerra Civil (p. 390)

scarce (escaso) que hay poco (p. 18)

Scopes trial (juicio Scopes) un juicio en Tennessee en 1925 sobre la enseñanza de la teoría de la evolución en las escuelas públicas (p. 624)

Scott v. *Sandford* (*Scott* contra *Sandford*) una decisión del Tribunal Supremo en 1857 que declaró que los esclavos no eran ciudadanos y reguló que el Compromiso de Misuri era inconstitucional (p. 329)

secede (secesión) renunciar formalmente a ser miembro de un grupo u organización (p. 251)

secessionist (secesionista) una persona que quería que el Sur se separara (p. 334)

Second Amendment (Segunda Enmienda) enmienda a la Constitución de los Estados Unidos que concede a los estados el derecho a formar milicia armada (p. 1019)

Second Continental Congress (Segundo Congreso Continental) una asamblea de representantes de las colonias que se reunió por primera vez en Filadelfia en mayo de 1775 (p. 98)

Second Great Awakening (Segundo Gran Despertar) un movimiento religioso de principios del S. XIX (p. 218)

Second New Deal (Segundo Nuevo Trato) un periodo de actividad legislativa emprendido por el Presidente Franklin Roosevelt en 1935 (p. 664)

section (sección) una región geográfica (p. 236)

secularize (secularizar) poner bajo el control del gobierno en vez del de la iglesia (p. 293)

sedition (sedición) palabras o acciones que fomentan la rebelión (p. 580)

segregation (segregación) separación por la fuerza (pp. 263, 470)

Selective Service Act (Ley de Servicio Selectivo) una ley de 1917 que autorizaba la leva de hombres jóvenes para el servicio militar (p. 573)

self-determination (autodeterminación) el poder de tomar decisiones sobre el propio futuro (p. 584)

self-sufficient (autosuficiente) capaz de hacer todo lo necesario para mantenerse a sí mismo (p. 68)

Seneca Falls Convention (Convención de Seneca Falls) la primera convención sobre los derechos de la mujer en la historia de los Estados Unidos, celebrada en 1848 (p. 277)

seniority (antigüedad) estado derivado de la duración del servicio (p. 728)

separation of powers (separación de poderes) la separación de poderes en el gobierno federal entre el poder legislativo, executivo y judicial (p. 136)

settlement house (centro de residencia) un centro comunitario organizado para proveer varios servicios a los pobres de la ciudad (p. 481)

sharecropping (aparcería) un sistema de cultivo en el que un agricultor cultivaba una porción de tierra de otro propietario y recibía como pago parte de la cosecha en el momento de la recolección (p. 392)

Shays' Rebellion (Rebelión de Shay) una revuelta contra los impuestos en Massachusetts en 1786 y 1787 (p. 127)

shell (granada) un artefacto que explota en el aire o cuando choca contra un objetivo sólido (p. 344)

Sherman Antitrust Act (Acta Antimonopolios Sherman) una ley aprobada en 1890 que prohibía cualquier combinación de compañías que limitaran el comercio (p. 417)

shuttle diplomacy (diplomacia itinerante) viajes repetidos de un mediador entre naciones en disputa con la intención de llegar a un acuerdo (p. 940)

siege (asedio) una táctica en la que se rodea al enemigo y se le hace pasar hambre para que se rinda (pp. 87, 364)

silent majority (mayoría silenciosa) un término usado por el Presidente Nixon para describir a los norteamericanos que no estaban de acuerdo con la contracultura (p. 912)

sit-down strike (huelga de brazos caídos) una protesta laboral en la que los trabajadores dejan de trabajar pero se niegan a abandonar el lugar de trabajo (p. 673)

sit-in (sentada) forma de protesta en la que los protestantes se sientan y se niegan a moverse; los defensores de los derechos civiles las usaron a veces para protestar pacíficamente (p. 826)

social Darwinism (darwinismo social) una teoría, derivada de la teoría sobre la selección natural de Darwin, según la cual la sociedad debe interferir lo menos posible en la búsqueda de la felicidad de sus individuos (p. 416)

social gospel movement (movimiento del evangelio social) un movimiento de reforma social que se desarrolló en instituciones religiosas y que buscaba la aplicación directa de la palabra de Jesús en la sociedad (p. 481)

socialism (socialismo) una filosofía económica y política que favorece el control público (o social) de la propiedad y los ingresos (p. 423)

Social Security system (sistema de Seguridad Social) un sistema público que proporciona pagos regulares a personas que no pueden mantenerse a sí mismas (p. 665)

social welfare program (programa de bienestar social) un programa diseñado para asegurar un estándar de vida básico para todos los ciudadanos (p. 544)

software (software) programa para una computadora (p. 1058)

solid South (Sólido Sur) un término que describe la dominación ejercida por el partido demócrata en el Sur desde la guerra Civil (p. 396)

sooner (primer colono) una persona que señalaba su propiedad en territorio indio antes de que éste se abriera legalmente a la colonización (p. 439)

Southern Christian Leadership Conference (SCLC) (Conferencia de Liderazgo Cristiano del Sur) una organización en favor de los derechos civiles formada en 1957 por el Dr. Martin Luther King, Jr., y otros líderes (p. 821)

Southern Colonies (colonias del sur) las colonias inglesas de Virginia, Maryland, las Carolinas y Georgia (p. 53)

speakeasy (bar clandestino) durante la Prohibición, un bar donde se servían ilegalmente bebidas alcohólicas (p. 622)

special prosecutor (fiscal especial) un investigador nombrado por el Departamento de Justicia para investigar irregularidades cometidas por funcionarios del gobierno (p. 924)

specie (metálico) moneda de oro o plata (p. 127)

speculation (especulación) inversiones de alto riesgo con la esperanza de obtener mucha ganancia (p. 633)

sphere of influence (esfera de influencia) área de control económico y político que ejerce una nación sobre otra u otras naciones (p. 525)

spiritual (espiritual) un himno popular (p. 221)

spoils (botín) recompensa (p. 585)

spoils system (sistema de sinecuras) sistema o práctica por el que el partido ganador en una elección concede cargos oficiales como recompensa; el nombre del sistema de padrinazgo bajo la presidencia de Jackson (p. 251)

Sputnik el primer satélite artificial en orbitar la Tierra, lanzado por la Unión Soviética en 1957 (p. 762)

stagflation (estanflación) una combinación de alta inflación y alto desempleo, sin crecimiento económico (p. 933)

stalemate (punto muerto) una situación en la que ninguna de las partes en conflicto es capaz de conseguir ventaja (p. 566)

Stamp Act (Ley del Impuesto de los Sellos) una ley aprobada por el Parlamento británico en 1765 que exigía un impuesto sobre los periódicos, documentos legales y otros materiales impresos en las colonias (p. 91)

staple crop (cultivo básico) una cosecha que está en constante demanda, como el algodón, el trigo o el arroz (p. 62)

states' rights (derechos de los estados) la teoría que sostiene que la potencia dividida constitución entre los estados y el gobierno federal y que una interpretación terminante de esa división debe ser respetada

steerage (tercera clase) una área grande y espaciosa debajo de la cubierta del barco en la que viajaban muchos inmigrantes pobres (p. 467)

stereotype (estereotipo) una concepción fija en la que cree un grupo de personas (p. 456)

Stono Rebellion (rebelión Stono) una revuelta de esclavos en Carolina del Sur en 1739 (p. 76)

Strategic Arms Reduction Treaty (START) (tratado para la reducción de armas estratégicas) el acuerdo firmado en 1991 que establecía una reducción cuantiosa del armamento nuclear de norteamericanos y soviéticos (p. 973)

Strategic Defense Initiative (SDI) (Iniciativa de Defensa Estratégica) propuesta del Presidente Reagan para crear un sistema de defensa contra un ataque nuclear (p. 961)

strict construction (interpretación estricta) la creencia en que el gobierno no debería hacer nada que la Constitución no diga explícitamente que puede hacer (p. 176)

strike (huelga) parar de trabajar para forzar al patrón a cumplir ciertas exigencias, como un salario más alto o mejores condiciones de trabajo (p. 239)

Student Nonviolent Coordinating Committee (SNCC) (Comité No Violento de Coordinación Estudiantil) una organización estudiantil a favor de los derechos civiles fundada en 1960 (p. 823)

subsidy (subsidio) un pago del gobierno para fomentar el desarrollo de ciertas industrias clave (p. 462)

suburb (suburbio) una comunidad residencial que rodea una ciudad (p. 474)

suffrage (sufragio) derecho a votar (p. 277)

supply-side economics (economía de suministro indirecto) la teoría que defiende que las reducciones de impuestos aumentarán la inversión y por lo tanto fomentarán el crecimiento económico (p. 959)

Sussex pledge (la promesa de Sussex) en 1916, una promesa del gobierno alemán de que sus submarinos avisarían a los barcos antes de atacar (p. 571)

synagogue (sinagoga) casa judía de oración (p. 52)

T

Taft-Hartley Act (Ley Taft-Hartley) una ley de 1947 que permitía que el Presidente ordenara que volvieran al trabajo los trabajadores en huelga de ciertas industrias (p. 780)

tariff (tarifa) un impuesto sobre los bienes extranjeros importados en un país (pp. 176, 1040)

Tariff of 1828 (Tarifa de 1828) un impuesto elevado sobre bienes manufacturados; llamada la "Tarifa de la Abominación" por los sureños (p. 251)

teach-in (sesión de instrucción) una sesión especial de conferencia y debate sobre un tema polémico (p. 883)

Teapot Dome scandal (escándalo del Teapot Dome) un escándalo durante la administración Harding referente a la concesión de derechos de prospección petrolera en tierras del gobierno a cambio de dinero (p. 601)

telecommunications (telecomunicaciones) comunicación a larga distancia por medios electrónicos (p. 1058)

televangelism (televangelismo) el uso de la televisión por organizaciones religiosas, especialmente para recaudar fondos (p. 958)

temperance movement (movimiento de la templanza) una campaña organizada para eliminar el consumo de alcohol (pp. 261, 480)

tenant farming (agricultor arrendatario) sistema de labranza en el que un agricultor alquila tierras de cultivo a un hacendado (p. 392)

tenement (casa de vecindad) un edificio de apartamentos lleno de gente, con pobres condiciones sanitarias, de seguridad y de comodidad (pp. 238, 474)

Tennessee Valley Authority (Autoridades del Valle del Tennessee) un proyecto federal para proporcionar corriente eléctrica, control de inundación y oportunidades recreativas en el valle del río Tennessee (p. 662)

Tet Offensive (Ofensiva Tet) el ataque que en 1968 lanzaron fuerzas norvietnamitas y del Vietcong contra Vietnam del Sur (p. 877)

Texas War for Independence (guerra de la Independencia de Texas) la exitosa revuelta de los texanos contra el gobierno mexicano en 1835–1836 (p. 294)

Thirteenth Amendment (Decimotercera Enmienda) la enmienda constitucional, ratificada en 1865, que abolió la esclavitud (p. 370)

38th parallel (paralelo 38) la línea de latitud que dividía a Corea del Norte y Corea del Sur (p. 756)

Three-Fifths Compromise (Compromiso de las Tres Quintas Partes) el compromiso en la Convención Constitucional que establecía que las tres quintas partes de los esclavos de un estado contaran para propósitos de representación) (p. 135)

totalitarian (totalitario) que describe una forma de gobierno que controla todos los aspectos de la vida de sus ciudadanos (p. 685)

trade deficit (déficit comercial) la cantidad de dinero que se pierde cuando una nación gasta más en importación de lo que gana con la exportación (p. 1041)

trade surplus (excedente comercial) la cantidad de dinero que se gana cuando una nación gana más con la exportación de lo que gasta en importación (p. 1041)

Trail of Tears (Sendero de Lágrimas) el desalojo forzoso de los cheroquís en 1838-1839 y su traslado a tierras al oeste del río Misisipí (p. 253)

trans-Appalachia (transapalaches) el área al oeste de los Montes Apalaches (p. 202)

transcendentalism (trascendentalismo) un movimiento filosófico a mediados del S. XIX que enfatizaba el descubrimiento espiritual y la clarividencia en lugar de la razón (p. 260)

transcontinental railroad (ferrocarril transcontinental) un ferrocarril que iba de costa a costa (p. 408)

transistor (transistor) un pequeñísimo circuito que amplifica, controla y genera señales eléctricas (p. 768)

Treaty of Ghent (Tratado de Ghent) el acuerdo firmado en 1814 que puso fin a la guerra de 1812 (p. 195)

Treaty of Greenville (Tratado de Greenville) un tratado frimado en 1795 por los Estados Unidos y varios pueblos indígenas norteamericanos por el que los indios norteamericanos cedían el control de casi todo Ohio (p. 189)

Treaty of Guadalupe Hidalgo (Tratado de Guadalupe Hidalgo) un tratado firmado en 1848 por los Estados Unidos y México, que ponía final a la guerra Mexicana (p. 303)

Treaty of Paris (1763) (Tratado de París de 1763) el tratado que terminó la guerra Franco-india y por el cual Francia renunció en favor de Gran Bretaña a sus pretensiones sobre los territorios norteamericanos (p. 88)

Treaty of Paris (1783) (Tratado de París de 1783) el tratado que puso fin a la guerra de la Independencia y en el cual Gran Bretaña reconoció la independencia de Norteamérica (p. 113)

Treaty of Tordesillas (Tratado de Tordesillas) un tratado firmado por Portugal y España en 1494 en el que se repartían el mundo no cristiano (p. 23)

trek (traslado) una jornada (p. 298)

triangular trade (comercio triangular) el comercio entre las Américas, Europa y África (p. 63)

Truman Doctrine (Doctrina Truman) la declaración del Presidente Truman en 1947 que decía que los Estados Unidos apoyarían a las naciones amenazadas por el comunismo (pp. 746, 1051)

trust (sociedad de fidecomiso) un grupo de compañías independientes que se sitúan bajo el control de una junta directiva (p. 417)

trustee (depositario) alguien en quien se deposita la confianza para que se encargue de un negocio (p. 54)

Turner's Rebellion (Rebelión de Turner) una fracasada revuelta de esclavos dirigida por Nat Turner en 1831 (p. 243)

Turner thesis (Tesis de Turner) el razonamiento que hizo Frederick Jackson Turner en 1893, que decía que la frontera había dado forma al estilo de vida norteamericano (p. 454)

turnpike (carretera de peaje) una carretera en la que los usuarios deben pagar peaje (p. 212)

Twenty-first Amendment (Vigesimoprimera Enmienda) la enmienda constitucional, ratificada en 1933, que terminó con la Prohibición (p. 647)

U

U-boat un submarino alemán (p. 570)

Underground Railroad (Ferrocarril Subterráneo) una red de rutas de escape que facilitaba protección y transporte a los esclavos que huían hacia el norte en busca de libertad (p. 270)

undocumented immigrant (inmigrante indocumentado) inmigrante que ha entrado ilegalmente en los Estados Unidos (p. 1009)

Union (Unión) los Estados Unidos como entidad nacional; o, durante la guerra Civil, el Norte (p. 315)

United Farm Workers (UFW) (Trabajadores Agrícolas Unidos) un sindicato organizado por César Chávez para organizar a los braceros mexicanos en el oeste (p. 854)

Upper South (Alto Sur) los estados de Virginia, Carolina del Norte, Tennessee y Arkansas (p. 336)

urban (urbano) relativo a una ciudad (p. 237)

utopian community (comunidad utópica) una pequeña sociedad dedicada a la perfección de las condiciones sociales y políticas (p. 263)

U-2 incident (incidente U-2) el derribo de un avión espía norteamericano sobre la Unión Soviética en 1960 (p. 762)

V

vaudeville (vodevil) un espectáculo de variedades que presentaba números cómicos, musicales y de baile (p. 492)

Versailles Treaty (Tratado de Versalles) el tratado de 1919 que terminó la primera guerra mundial (p. 586)

vertical consolidation (consolidación vertical) hacerse con el control de los numerosos y distintos negocios que componen todas las fases del desarrollo de un producto (p. 417)

veto (veto) impedir que se convierta en ley (p. 134)

vice (vicio) comportamiento inmoral o corrupto (p. 480)

victory garden (huerta de la victoria) una huerta casera creada para incrementar la producción alimentaria durante la segunda guerra mundial (p. 722)

Viet Cong (Vietcong) fuerza formada por guerrillas comunistas en Vietnam del Sur que, con apoyo norvietnamita, luchó contra el gobierno de Vietnam del Sur en la guerra del Vietnam (p. 875)

Vietnamization (vietnamización) la política de reemplazar a las fuerzas militares norteamericanas por las de Vietnam del Sur (p. 891)

Vietnam Veterans Memorial (Monumento Conmemorativo de los Veteranos de Vietnam) el monumento en Washington, D.C., construido para honrar a los caídos en la guerra del Vietnam (p. 894)

vigilante (vigilante) un ciudadano que toma la ley en sus manos (p. 580)

Virginia and Kentucky Resolutions (Resoluciones de Virginia y Kentucky) resoluciones aprobadas en 1798 que atacaban la Ley de Extranjería y Sedición por ser anticonstitucionales (p. 181)

Volunteers in Service to America (VISTA) (Voluntarios en Servicio a Norteamérica) un programa federal organizado para mandar voluntarios a ayudar a las personas en las comunidades pobres (p. 803)

Voting Rights Act of 1965 (Ley de Derechos Electorales de 1965) una ley que se proponía reducir los impedimentos para el voto de los afroamericanos, en parte por medio del aumento de la autoridad federal para censar votantes (p. 835)

W

Wagner Act (Ley de Wagner) una ley aprobada en 1935 que ayudaba a los sindicatos al legalizar la negociación colectiva y establecer la Mesa Nacional de Relaciones Laborales (p. 665)

Wannsee Conference (Conferencia de Wansee) la conferencia celebrada en 1942 en Alemania relativa al plan para asesinar a los judíos europeos (p. 709)

war bond (bono de guerra) un bono de ahorro del gobierno que se vende para recaudar dinero para la guerra (p. 719)

War of 1812 (guerra de 1812) la guerra entre los Estados Unidos y Gran Bretaña (p. 192)

war of attrition (guerra de desgaste) una guerra en la que uno de los lados causa continuas pérdidas al enemigo para disminuir su resistencia (p. 343)

War Powers Act (Ley de los Poderes de Guerra) una ley de 1973 que limita el poder del Presidente para desplegar tropas en el extranjero (p. 934)

War Refugee Board (Oficina de Refugiados de Guerra) una agencia federal creada en 1994 para tratar de ayudar a las personas amenazadas de muerte por los nazis (p. 710)

Warren Commission (Comisión Warren) la comisión presidida por el juez presidente Earl Warren que investigó el asesinato del Presidente Kennedy (p. 800)

Warsaw Pact (Pacto de Varsovia) una alianza militar entre la Unión Soviética y naciones de Europa del este formada en 1955 (pp. 751, 1053)

Watergate scandal (escándalo Watergate) el escándalo que supuso el descubrimiento de actividades ilegales que finalmente produjeron la renuncia del Presidente Nixon en 1974 (p. 922)

welfare capitalism (capitalismo del bienestar) una estrategia laboral en la que las compañías satisfacen algunas de las necesidades de sus trabajadores sin intervención de los sindicatos (p. 632)

Whiskey Rebellion (rebelión del Whisky) los desórdenes de 1794 causados por la oposición a un impuesto sobre el whisky (p. 177)

Whitewater affair (asunto Whitewater) acusaciones contra el Presidente Clinton en las que se alegaba su participación en transacciones comerciales ilegales antes de convertirse en presidente (p. 983)

wildcat strike (huelga no autorizada) una huelga organizada por los trabajadores en vez de por los dirigentes sindicales (p. 718)

Wilderness Road un camino construido en 1770 que se convirtió en la ruta principal para atravesar los Montes Apalaches (p. 203)

Woodstock festival (festival de Woodstock) un festival de 1969 en el norte del estado de Nueva York (p. 888)

work ethic (ética del trabajo) sistema de valores que pone énfasis en la importancia del trabajo arduo para desarrollar la personalidad y conseguir el éxito (p. 1028)

World Trade Organization (WTO) (Organización Mundial del Trabajo) una organización internacional formada en 1995 para fomentar la expansión del comercio mundial (p. 993)

World Wide Web (Red Informática Mundial) organización de redes globales de computadores por medio de la cual los usuarios pueden acceder a la información (p. 1061)

writ of habeas corpus (orden de hábeas corpus) una protección legal que requiere que un tribunal determine si una persona ha sido encarcelada legalmente (p. 352)

X

XYZ Affair (Asunto XYZ) en 1798, la controversia causada por las exigencias de los franceses en recibir sobornos de los negociadores norteamericanos (p. 180)

Y

Yalta Conference (Conferencia de Yalta) la reunión en 1945 entre Churchill, Stalin y Roosevelt en la que los líderes hablaron de planes para el mundo de la posguerra (p. 699)

yellow journalism (periodismo amarillo) un tipo de información periodística que da importancia a relatos sensacionalistas de crimen y escándalo (p. 494)

Z

Zimmermann note (nota de Zimmermann) una nota de un diplomático alemán en la que en 1917 se proponía una alianza con México (p. 572)

Biographical Dictionary

A

Adams, Abigail First Lady, 1797–1801; as the wife of Patriot John Adams, she urged him to promote women's rights at the beginning of the American Revolution (p. 100)

Adams, John Quincy Sixth President of the United States, 1825–1829; proposed greater federal involvement in the economy through tariffs and improvements such as roads, bridges, and canals (p. 204)

Adams, John Second President of the United States, 1797–1801; worked to relieve increasing tensions with France; lost reelection bid to Jefferson in 1800 as the country moved away from Federalist policies (p. 94)

Addams, Jane Cofounder of Hull House, the first settlement house, in 1889; remained active in social causes through the early 1900s (p. 481)

Agnew, Spiro Vice President under President Richard Nixon until forced to resign in 1973 for crimes committed before taking office; known for his harsh campaign attacks (p. 924)

Allen, Richard African American religious leader; helped found the African Methodist Episcopal Church (AME) in 1816 (p. 222)

Anthony, Susan B. Political activist and women's rights leader in the late 1800s (p. 557)

Arthur, Chester A. Twenty-first President of the United States, 1881–1885; signed 1883 Pendleton Act, which instituted the Civil Service (p. 463)

Askia, Muhammad Ruler of the African empire of Songhai, 1493–1528; promoted Islamic culture (p. 17)

Austin, Stephen Leader of first American group of Texas settlers in 1822 (p. 294)

Susan B. Anthony

B

Bakke, Allan Student who won a suit against the University of California in 1978 on the grounds that the affirmative action program had kept him out (p. 950)

Baldwin, James African American author and spokesperson for the civil rights movement during the 1960s (p. 836)

Banks, Dennis Native American leader in 1960s and 1970s; helped organize American Indian Movement (AIM) and the 1973 Wounded Knee occupation (p. 858)

Beecher, Catharine Author whose 1841 book *A Treatise on Domestic Economy* argued that women should support reform from the home (p. 275)

Beecher, Lyman Revivalist during the Second Great Awakening; feared the rise of selfishness in the United States (p. 259)

Begin, Menachem Israeli leader during the 1970s; began the Middle East peace process by reaching the 1978 Camp David Accords with Egypt (p. 941)

Bell, Alexander Graham Inventor; developed the telephone in 1876; one of the founders of American Telephone & Telegraph (AT&T) (p. 410)

Bellamy, Edward Author of the novel *Looking Backward* (1888), which proposed nationalizing trusts to eliminate social problems (p. 541)

Bethune, Mary McLeod African American educator, New Deal worker; founded Bethune Cookman College in the 1920s, advised the National Youth Administration (p. 662)

Beveridge, Albert J. Indiana senator in the early 1900s; saw United States imperialism as a duty owed to "primitive" societies (p. 518)

Booth, John Wilkes Southern actor who assassinated President Abraham Lincoln in 1865 (p. 371)

Brady, James Press Secretary to President Reagan who was paralyzed by a gunshot during a 1981 assassination attempt; the 1994 law requiring a five-day waiting period before purchase of a gun was named for Mr. Brady (p. 1019)

Breckinridge, John C. Presidential candidate of the southern wing of the Democratic party in 1860 (p. 333)

Brown, John Abolitionist crusader who massacred proslavery settlers in Kansas before the Civil War; hoped to inspire slave revolt with 1859 attack on Virginia arsenal; executed for treason against the state of Virginia (p. 328)

Bruce, Blanche African American senator from Mississippi during Reconstruction (p. 389)

Bryan, William Jennings Advocate of silver standard and proponent of Democratic and Populist views from the 1890s through the 1910s; Democratic candidate for President in 1896, 1900, and 1908 (p. 450)

Buchanan, James Fifteenth President of the United States, 1857–1861; supported by the South; attempted to moderate fierce disagreement over expansion of slavery (p. 329)

Bush, George H. W. Forty-first President of the United States, 1989–1993; continued Reagan's conservative policies; brought together United Nations coalition to fight the Persian Gulf War (p. 970)

Byrd, William Wealthy plantation owner in colonial Virginia whose diary gives a vivid picture of colonial life (p. 66)

C

Calhoun, John C. Statesman from South Carolina who held many offices in the federal government; supported slavery, cotton exports, states' rights; in 1850 foresaw future conflicts over slavery (p. 246)

Carnegie, Andrew Industrialist who made a fortune in steel in the late 1800s through vertical consolidation; as a philanthropist, he gave away some $350 million (p. 415)

Carson, Rachel Marine biologist, author of *Silent Spring* (1962), which exposed harmful effects of pesticides and inspired concern for the environment (p. 862)

Carter, James Earl, Jr. Thirty-ninth President of the United States, 1977–1981; advocated concern for human rights in foreign policy; assisted in mediating the Camp David Accords (p. 936)

Castro, Fidel Revolutionary leader who took control of Cuba in 1959; ally of Soviet Union through the 1980s (p. 761)

Catt, Carrie Chapman Women's suffrage leader in the early 1900s; helped secure passage of Nineteenth Amendment in 1920; headed National American Woman Suffrage Association (p. 559)

Champlain, Samuel de French explorer who founded the city of Quebec in 1608 (p. 42)

Chavez, Cesar Latino leader from 1962 to his death in 1993; organized the United Farm Workers (UFW) to help migratory farm workers gain better pay and working conditions (p. 853)

Churchill, Winston Leader of Great Britain before and during World War II; powerful speechmaker who rallied Allied morale during the war (p. 687)

Clark, William Leader, with Meriwether Lewis, of expedition through the West beginning in 1804; brought back scientific samples, maps, and information on Native Americans (p. 188)

Clay, Henry Statesman from Kentucky; accused by Jackson of giving votes to John Q. Adams in return for post as Secretary of State; endorsed government promotion of economic growth; advocate of Compromise of 1850 (p. 247)

Cleveland, Grover Twenty-second and twenty-fourth President of the United States, 1885–1889, 1893–1897; supported railroad regulation and a return to the gold standard (p. 449)

Clinton, Bill Forty-second President of the United States, 1993–2001; defeated George Bush after overcoming numerous political obstacles; advocated economic and health-care reform (p. 979)

Columbus, Christopher Explorer whose voyage for Spain to North America in 1492 opened the Atlantic World (p. 19)

Coolidge, Calvin Thirtieth President of the United States, 1923–1929; promoted big business and opposed social aid (p. 599)

Coughlin, Father Charles E. "Radio Priest" who supported and then attacked President Franklin Roosevelt's New Deal; prevented by the Catholic Church from broadcasting after he praised Hitler (p. 669)

Coxey, Jacob S. Populist who led Coxey's Army in a march on Washington, D.C., in 1894 to seek government jobs for the unemployed (p. 465)

Custer, George Armstrong General who directed army attacks against Native Americans in the 1870s; commanded army forces killed in 1876 at Little Bighorn in Montana (p. 437)

D

Davis, Jefferson President of the Confederate States of America; ordered attack on Fort Sumter, the first battle of the Civil War (p. 334)

Dewey, George Officer in United States Navy, 1861–1917; led a surprise attack in the Philippines during the Spanish-American War that destroyed the entire Spanish fleet (p. 522)

Diem, Ngo Dinh Leader of South Vietnam, 1954–1963; supported by United States, but not by Vietnamese Buddhist majority; assassinated in 1963 (p. 874)

Dix, Dorothea Advocate of prison reform and of special institutions for the mentally ill in Massachusetts before the Civil War (p. 263)

Dole, Robert Senator from Kansas, 1969–1996; challenged Bill Clinton for the presidency in 1996 (p. 983)

Douglas, Stephen Illinois senator who introduced the Kansas-Nebraska Act, which allowed new territories to choose their own position on slavery; debated Abraham Lincoln on slavery issues in 1858 (p. 323)

Douglass, Frederick African American abolitionist leader who spoke eloquently for abolition in the United States and Britain before the Civil War (p. 268)

Du Bois, W.E.B. African American scholar and leader in early 1900s; encouraged African Americans to attend colleges to develop leadership skills (p. 491)

E

Edison, Thomas A. Inventor; developed the light bulb, the phonograph, and hundreds of other inventions in the late 1800s and early 1900s (p. 410)

Ehrlichman, John Adviser on domestic policy to President Richard Nixon; deeply involved in Watergate (p. 910)

Einstein, Albert Physicist who fled Nazi persecution and later encouraged President Roosevelt to develop the atomic bomb (p. 704)

Eisenhower, Dwight D. Thirty-fourth President of the United States, 1953–1961; leader of Allied forces in World War II; as President, he promoted business and continued social programs (p. 759)

Ellington, Duke African American musician, bandleader, and composer of the 1920s and 1930s (p. 616)

Ellsberg, Daniel Defense Department official; leaked Pentagon Papers to *The New York Times* in 1971, showing government lies to public about Vietnam (p. 921)

Dwight D. Eisenhower

Equiano, Olaudah Antislavery activist who wrote an account of his enslavement (p. 72)

F

Father Divine African American minister; his Harlem soup kitchens fed the hungry during the Great Depression (p. 642)

Fillmore, Millard Thirteenth President of the United States, 1850–1853; promoted the Compromise of 1850 to smooth over disagreements about slavery in new territories (p. 323)

Finney, Charles Grandison   Revivalist during the Second Great Awakening; emphasized religious conversion and personal choice (p. 259)

Fitzgerald, F. Scott   Novelist who depicted the United States and the world during the 1920s in novels such as *The Great Gatsby* (p. 618)

Fitzhugh, George   Southern author who criticized northern industrialists for exploiting workers in his 1857 book *Cannibals All!* (p. 317)

Ford, Gerald R.   Thirty-eighth President of the United States, 1974–1977; succeeded and pardoned Nixon; failed to establish strong leadership (p. 931)

Ford, Henry   Pioneering auto manufacturer in the early 1900s; made affordable cars for the masses using assembly line and other production techniques (p. 605)

Franklin, Benjamin   Colonial inventor, printer, writer, statesman; contributed to the Declaration of Independence and the Constitution (p. 66)

Frémont, John C.   Explorer, military officer, and politician; led United States troops in 1846 Bear Flag Revolt when the United States took California from Mexico; ran for President as a Republican in 1856 (p. 302)

Friedan, Betty   Feminist author; criticized limited roles for women in her 1963 book *The Feminine Mystique* (p. 776)

G

Garfield, James A.   Twentieth President of the United States, 1881; his assassination by a disappointed office seeker led to the reform of the spoils system (p. 463)

Garrison, William Lloyd   White leader of radical abolition movement based in Boston; founded *The Liberator* in 1831 to work for an immediate end to slavery (p. 267)

Garvey, Marcus   African American leader from 1919 to 1926 who urged African Americans to return to their "motherland" of Africa; provided early inspiration for "black pride" movements (p. 626)

Gates, Bill   Founder of Microsoft; revolutionized personal computing, investigated for questionable business practices (p. 1000)

George III   King of England during the American Revolution (p. 89)

George, Henry   Author of *Progress and Poverty* (1879) linking land speculation and poverty; proposed a single tax based on land value (p. 541)

Gingrich, Newt   Representative from Georgia, 1979–1998; called on Republican congressional candidates in 1994 elections to endorse "Contract with America" (p. 982)

Gorbachev, Mikhail   Soviet leader whose bold reforms led to the breakup of the Soviet Union in the late 1980s (p. 967)

Gore, Al   Senator from Tennessee; Vice President under President Bill Clinton, 1993– 2001 (p. 981)

Newt Gingrich

Graham, Billy   Evangelist and presidential adviser; known for leading large-scale crusades, or religious rallies (p. 775)

Grant, Ulysses S.   Eighteenth President of the United States, 1869–1877; commander of Union forces who accepted Lee's surrender in 1865 (p. 344)

H

Haldeman, H. R.   Chief of Staff under President Richard Nixon; deeply involved in Watergate (p. 910)

Hamilton, Alexander   Officer in the War for Independence: delegate to the Constitutional Convention; Federalist and first Secretary of the Treasury (p. 139)

Handsome Lake   Leader of Seneca in late 1700s; encouraged blending of Native American and white American cultures (p. 190)

Harding, Warren G.   Twenty-ninth President of the United States, 1921–1923; presided over a short administration marked by corruption (p. 600)

Harrington, Michael   Author; wrote *The Other America* in 1962, which described areas of poverty in the otherwise prosperous United States (p. 798)

Harrison, Benjamin   Twenty-third President of the United States, 1889–1893; signed 1890 Sherman Antitrust Act later used to regulate big business (p. 449)

Harrison, William Henry   Ninth President of the United States, 1841; died of pneumonia after only a month in office (p. 190)

Hayes, Rutherford B.   Nineteenth President of the United States, 1877–1881; promised to withdraw Union troops from the South in order to end dispute over his election; attacked spoils system (p. 396)

Hearst, William Randolph   Newspaper publisher from 1887 until his death in 1951; used "yellow journalism" in the 1890s to stir up sentiment in favor of the Spanish-American War (p. 494)

Hiss, Alger   Former State Department official investigated as a possible Communist spy by House Un-American Activities Committee after World War II; convicted of perjury in 1950 (p. 754)

Hitler, Adolf   German leader of National Socialist (Nazi) party 1933–1945; rose to power by promoting racist and nationalist views (p. 686)

Ho Chi Minh   Leader of the Communist party in Indochina after World War II; led Vietnamese against the French, then North Vietnamese against the United States in the Vietnam War (p. 873)

Hollerith, Herman   1890 census agent who devised a machine that used punch cards to tabulate data (p. 1059)

Hoover, Herbert   Thirty-first President of the United States, 1929–1933; worked to aid Europeans during World War I; responded ineffectively to 1929 stock market crash and Great Depression (p. 579)

Houston, Sam   Leader of Texas troops in war for independence from Mexico in 1836; elected first president of independent Texas (p. 294)

Humphrey, Hubert   Democratic presidential candidate in 1968; lost narrowly to Nixon in an election bid hurt by support for the Vietnam War and by third-party candidate George Wallace (p. 907)

Hutchinson, Anne   Critic of Puritan leadership of Massachusetts Bay Colony; banished for her religious beliefs (p. 46)

I

Isabella   Ruler of Spanish Christian kingdoms with Ferdinand in late 1400s; sponsored Columbus's voyage to North America (p. 14)

J

Jackson, Andrew   Seventh President of the United States, 1829–1837; supported minimal government and the spoils system; vetoed rechartering of the national bank; pursued harsh policy toward Native Americans (p. 250)

Jackson, Stonewall   Confederate general known for his swift strikes against Union forces; earned nickname Stonewall by holding his forces steady under extreme pressure at the First Battle of Manassas (p. 342)

Jefferson, Thomas   Third President of the United States, 1801–1809; main author of the Declaration of Independence; a firm believer in the people and decentralized power; reduced the federal government (p. 99)

Johnson, Andrew   Seventeenth President of the United States, 1865–1869; clashed with Radical Republicans on Reconstruction programs; was impeached, then acquitted, in 1868 (p. 381)

Johnson, Lyndon B.   Thirty-sixth President of the United States, 1963–1969; expanded social assistance with his Great Society program; increased United States commitment during Vietnam War (p. 800)

Jordan, Barbara   Member of Congress from Texas; first African American and woman to represent her state in Congress; gave keynote addresses at 1976 and 1992 Democratic National Conventions (p. 937)

Joseph, Chief   Leader of Nez Percé; forced to give up his home by United States army, fled toward Canada; captured in 1877 (p. 438)

K

Kamiakin   Yakima chief who led Native Americans in 1855 war against Northwest settlers (p. 306)

Kelley, Florence   Progressive reformer active from 1886 to 1920; worked in state and federal government for laws on child labor, workplace safety, and consumer protection (p. 544)

Kennedy, John F.   Thirty-fifth President of the United States, 1961–1963; seen as youthful and inspiring; known for his firm handling of the Cuban Missile Crisis; assassinated in 1963 (p. 797)

Kennedy, Robert F.   Attorney General under his brother, President John Kennedy, in the early 1960s; supported civil rights; assassinated while running for President in 1968 (p. 828)

Keynes, John Maynard   British economist who believed that government spending could help a faltering economy; his theories helped shape New Deal legislation (p. 651)

Khomeini, Ayatollah Ruholla   Islamic fundamentalist leader of Iran after the 1979 overthrow of the Shah;

approved holding of American hostages (p. 943)

Khrushchev, Nikita   Soviet leader from 1953 to 1964; opposed President Kennedy in the Cuban Missile Crisis (p. 809)

King, Martin Luther, Jr.   African American civil rights leader from the mid-1950s until his assassination in 1968; used nonviolent means such as marches, boycotts, and legal challenges to win civil rights (p. 821)

Martin Luther King, Jr.

Kissinger, Henry   Secretary of State under Presidents Richard Nixon and Gerald Ford; used *realpolitik* to open relations with China, to end the Vietnam War, and to moderate Middle East conflict (p. 915)

L

Lafayette, Marquis de   French officer who assisted American forces in the War for Independence (p. 112)

Lange, Dorothea   Photographed migrant farm workers during the Great Depression; inspired government aid programs and Steinbeck's *The Grapes of Wrath* (p. 640)

Lee, Jason   First Methodist missionary to Oregon Country in 1834; built a mission school in Willamette Valley (p. 298)

Lee, Robert E.   Brilliant general of Confederate forces during the Civil War (p. 347)

Lenin, Vladimir I.   Revolutionary leader in Russia; established a Communist government in 1917 (p. 574)

Levitt, William J.   Built new communities in the suburbs after World War II, using mass-production techniques (p. 770)

Lewis, John L.   Head of United Mine Workers through World War II; used strikes during the war to win pay raises (p. 718)

Lewis, Meriwether   Leader with William Clark of expedition through the West beginning in 1804; brought back scientific samples, maps, and information on Native Americans (p. 188)

Lincoln, Abraham   Sixteenth President of the United States, 1861–1865; known for his effective leadership during the Civil War and his Emancipation Proclamation declaring the end of slavery in Confederate-held territory (p. 351)

Lindbergh, Charles A.   Aviator who became an international hero when he made the first solo flight across the Atlantic Ocean in 1927 (p. 612)

Little Turtle   Native American leader of the late 1700s; adopted policy of accommodation (p. 190)

Lodge, Henry Cabot   Massachusetts senator of early 1900s; supported United States imperialism (p. 518)

Long, Huey   Louisiana politician in 1930s; suggested redistributing large fortunes by means of grants to families; assassinated in 1935 (p. 669)

M

MacArthur, Douglas   United States general during the Great Depression, World War II, and Korean War;

forced by Truman to resign in 1951 (p. 756)

Madison, James Fourth President of the United States, 1809–1817; called the Father of the Constitution for his leadership at the Constitutional Convention (p. 133)

Mahan, Alfred T. Author who argued in 1890 that the economic future of the United States rested on new overseas markets protected by a larger navy (p. 517)

James Madison

Malcolm X African American leader during the 1950s and 1960s; eloquent spokesperson for African American self-sufficiency; assassinated in 1965 (p. 837)

Mann, Horace School reformer and supporter of public education before the Civil War; devised an educational system in Massachusetts later copied by many states (p. 262)

Mao Zedong Leader of Communists who took over China in 1949; remained in power until his death in 1976 (p. 689)

Marshall, George C. Army Chief of Staff during World War II and Secretary of State under President Harry Truman; assisted economic recovery in Europe after World War II and established strong allies for the United States through his Marshall Plan (p. 696)

Marshall, John Chief Justice of the Supreme Court appointed by John Adams; set precedents that established vital powers of the federal courts (p. 185)

Marshall, Thurgood First African American Supreme Court justice; as a lawyer, won landmark school desegregation case *Brown* v. *Board of Education* in 1954 (p. 786)

McCarthy, Eugene Candidate in the 1968 Democratic presidential race who opposed the Vietnam War; convinced President Lyndon Johnson not to run again through his strong showing in the primaries (p. 890)

McCarthy, Joseph R. Republican senator from Wisconsin in the late 1940s and early 1950s; led a crusade to investigate officials he claimed were Communists; discredited in 1954 (p. 758)

McClellan, George Early Union army leader in the Civil War; careful organizer and planner who moved too slowly for northern politicians; ran against President Abraham Lincoln in the election of 1864 (p. 344)

McKinley, William Twenty-fifth President of the United States, 1897–1901; supported tariffs and a gold standard; expanded the United States by waging the Spanish-American War (p. 450)

McNamara, Robert Secretary of Defense under Presidents Kennedy and Lyndon Johnson; expanded American involvement in Vietnam War (p. 874)

Meade, George G. Union commander at Battle of Gettysburg in 1863; defended the high ground and forced Confederate army to attack, causing great casualties (p. 362)

Means, Russell Native American leader of 1960s and 1970s; helped organize American Indian Movement (AIM) and 1973 Wounded Knee occupation (p. 860)

Metacom Leader of Pokanokets in Massachusetts; also known by his English name, King Philip; led Native Americans in King Philip's War, 1675–1676 (p. 48)

Mitchell, John Attorney General under President Richard Nixon; deeply involved in Watergate scandal (p. 910)

Monroe, James Fifth President of the United States, 1817–1825; acquired Florida from Spain; declared Monroe Doctrine to keep foreign powers out of the Americas (p. 245)

Morse, Samuel F. B. Artist and inventor; developed telegraph and Morse code in the 1830s (p. 319)

Mott, Lucretia Women's rights leader; helped organize first women's convention in Seneca Falls, New York, in 1848 (p. 276)

Mussolini, Benito Italian fascist leader who took power in the 1920s; called *Il Duce* — "the leader"; known for his brutal policies (p. 685)

N

Nader, Ralph Consumer advocate; published *Unsafe at Any Speed* in 1965 criticizing auto safety and inspiring new safety laws (p. 865)

Nimitz, Chester Leader of American naval forces in World War II Battle of Midway, during which several Japanese aircraft carriers were destroyed (p. 701)

Nixon, Richard M. Thirty-seventh President, 1969–1974; known for his foreign policy toward the Soviet Union and China and for illegal acts he committed in the Watergate affair that forced his resignation (p. 909)

O

O'Connor, Sandra Day First woman Supreme Court justice; appointed by Reagan in 1981 (p. 966)

Oppenheimer, J. Robert Physicist who led American effort in World War II to develop first atomic bomb (p. 704)

P

Muhammed Reza Pahlevi, Shah, Leader of Iran, from 1941 until his overthrow in 1979; supported by the United States; brought modernization to his country along with repression and corruption (p. 943)

Paine, Thomas Author of political pamphlets during 1770s and 1780s; wrote *Common Sense* in 1776 (p. 98)

Paul, Alice Women's suffrage leader of early 1900s; her Congressional Union used aggressive tactics to push the Nineteenth Amendment (p. 559)

Penn, William English Quaker who founded the colony of Pennsylvania in 1681 (p. 52)

Perkins, Frances Secretary of Labor 1933–1945 under President Franklin Delano Roosevelt; first woman Cabinet member (p. 662)

Perot, H. Ross Billionaire businessman who challenged Bill Clinton and George Bush for the presidency in 1992; strong opponent of NAFTA (p. 980)

Pierce, Franklin Fourteenth President of the United States, 1853–1857; signed the Kansas-Nebraska Act, which renewed conflicts over slavery in the territories (p. 323)

Pinckney, Eliza Lucas South Carolina plantation manager in the 1740s; promoted indigo as a staple crop (p. 68)

Polk, James K. Eleventh President of the United States, 1845–1849; led expansion of United States to southwest through war against Mexico (p. 269)

Polo, Marco Venetian traveler to China in the late 1200s; his book about the journey helped make Europeans aware of trade opportunities in eastern Asia (p. 11)

Popé Medicine man who led Pueblos and Apaches against Spanish rule in the Pueblo Revolt of 1680 (p. 33)

Prosser, Gabriel Planned a slave revolt in Virginia in 1800; captured and executed after revolt failed (p. 181)

Pulitzer, Joseph Early 1900s newspaper publisher; used "yellow journalism" to stir up public sentiment in favor of the Spanish-American War (p. 494)

R

Randolph, A. Philip Civil rights activist from the 1930s to the 1950s; planned the Washington march that pressured President Franklin Delano Roosevelt into opening World War II defense jobs to African Americans (p. 733)

Reagan, Ronald Fortieth President of the United States, 1981–1989; popular conservative leader who promoted supply-side economics and created huge budget deficits (p. 955)

Riis, Jacob Reformer who wrote *How the Other Half Lives,* describing the lives of poor immigrants in New York City in the late 1800s (p. 476)

Robinson, Jackie Athlete who in 1947 became the first African American to play baseball in the major leagues (p. 786)

Rockefeller, Nelson Vice President appointed by President Gerald Ford in 1974; the nation's only nonelected Vice President to serve with a nonelected President (p. 932)

Roosevelt, Eleanor First Lady 1933–1945; tireless worker for social causes, including women's rights and civil rights for African Americans and other groups (p. 652)

Roosevelt, Franklin D. Thirty-second President of the United States, 1933–1945; fought the Great Depression through his New Deal social programs; battled Congress over Supreme Court control; proved a strong leader during World War II (p. 652)

Roosevelt, Theodore Twenty-sixth President of the United States, 1901–1909; fought trusts, aided progressive reforms, built Panama Canal, and increased United States influence overseas (p. 521)

Rosenberg, Julius and Ethel Husband and wife convicted and executed in 1953 for passing atomic secrets to the Soviet Union; their guilt is still debated (p. 755)

Rowson, Susanna Haswell Author of *Charlotte Temple* (1794), a popular moralizing novel that encouraged women to look beyond appearances when choosing a husband (p. 217)

S

Sacajawea Shoshone woman who served as guide and translator for Lewis and Clark on their exploratory journey through the West in the early 1800s (p. 188)

Sacco, Nicola Immigrant and anarchist executed, in a highly controversial case, for a 1920 murder at a Massachusetts factory (p. 598)

Sadat, Anwar el- Egyptian leader in the 1970s; began the Middle East peace process by reaching the 1978 Camp David Accords with Israel (p. 941)

Salinger, J. D. Author of 1951 novel *The Catcher in the Rye,* which criticized 1950s pressure to conform (p. 776)

Santa Anna, Antonio López de Mexican dictator who led government and troops in war against Texas; won the battle of the Alamo (p. 294)

Schlafly, Phyllis Conservative activist; led campaign during the 1970s and 1980s to block the Equal Rights Amendment (p. 849)

Seward, William Henry Republican antislavery leader during the 1860s; acquired Alaska in 1867 as Secretary of State (p. 516)

Sherman, William Tecumseh Union general in the Civil War; known for his destructive march from Atlanta to Savannah in 1864 (p. 367)

Sirica, John J. Washington judge who presided over the Watergate investigation in the 1970s; gave tough sentences to convicted participants and ordered President Richard Nixon to release secret tapes (p. 922)

Sitting Bull Chief Leader of Sioux in clashes with United States Army in Black Hills in 1870s (p. 437)

Slater, Samuel English textile worker who brought the Industrial Revolution to the United States by duplicating British textile machinery from memory (p. 210)

Smith, John Leader of the Jamestown, Virginia, colony in the early 1600s (p. 38)

Smith, Joseph Founder of Church of Jesus Christ of Latter-day Saints, or Mormons, in New York in 1830; killed by a mob in Illinois in 1844 (p. 220)

Spock, Benjamin Pediatrician and author of *The Common Sense Book of Baby and Child Care* (1946), which encouraged mothers to stay home with their children rather than work (p. 776)

Stalin, Joseph Leader of the Soviet Union from 1924–1953; worked with Roosevelt and Churchill during World War II but afterwards became an aggressive participant in the cold war (p. 696)

Stanton, Elizabeth Cady Women's rights leader in the 1800s; helped organize first women's convention; wrote the Declaration of Sentiments on women's rights in 1848 (p. 276)

Starr, Ellen Gates Cofounder of Chicago's Hull House, the first settlement house, in 1889 (p. 481)

Steinem, Gloria Journalist, women's rights leader since 1960s; founded *Ms.* magazine in 1972 to cover women's issues (p. 848)

Stevenson, Adlai Senator from Illinois and Democratic candidate for President in 1952 and 1956 against Eisenhower (p. 782)

Stowe, Harriet Beecher Author of the novel *Uncle Tom's Cabin* (1852), which contributed significantly to anti-southern feelings among Northerners before the Civil War (p. 316)

Harriet Beecher Stowe

Sumner, Charles Abolitionist and senator from Massachusetts; beaten badly in the Senate by a southern congressman after making an antislavery speech (p. 329)

T

Taft, William Howard Twenty-seventh President of the United States, 1909–1913; continued progressive reforms of President Theodore Roosevelt; promoted "dollar diplomacy" to expand foreign investments (p. 531)

Taney, Roger Chief Justice of the Supreme Court who wrote an opinion in the 1857 Dred Scott case that declared the Missouri Compromise unconstitutional (p. 330)

Taylor, Zachary Twelfth President of the United States, 1849–1850; tried to avoid slavery issues (p. 321)

Tecumseh Native American leader in the late 1700s and early 1800s; led a pan-Indian movement that tried to unite several groups despite their differences (p. 190)

Tenskwatawa Native American leader of the early 1800s known as the Prophet; he called for a return to traditional ways and rejection of white values (p. 190)

Thomas, Clarence Conservative African American Supreme Court justice appointed in 1991; during his confirmation hearings he was charged with sexual harassment (p. 974)

Thoreau, Henry David Transcendentalist author known for his work *Walden* (1854) and other writings (p. 260)

Travis, William Leader in Texas's bid for independence from Mexico in 1836; died at the Alamo after appealing to the United States for help (p. 294)

Truman, Harry S. Thirty-third President of the United States, 1945–1953; authorized use of atomic bomb; signed Marshall Plan to rebuild Europe (p. 742)

Truth, Sojourner Abolitionist and women's rights advocate before the Civil War; as a former slave, she spoke effectively to white audiences on abolition issues (p. 269)

Tubman, Harriet "Conductor" on the Underground Railroad, which helped slaves escape to freedom before the Civil War (p. 270)

Turner, Frederick Jackson Historian who wrote an essay in 1893 emphasizing the western frontier as a powerful force in the formation of the American character (p. 453)

Harry S. Truman

Turner, Nat African American preacher who led a slave revolt in 1831; captured and hanged after the revolt failed (p. 243)

Tweed, William Marcy Boss of the Tammany Hall political machine in New York City; convicted of forgery and larceny in 1873 and died in jail in 1878 (p. 477)

Tyler, John Tenth President of the United States, 1841–1845; accomplished little due to quarrels between Whigs and Jacksonian Democrats (p. 254)

V

Van Buren, Martin Eighth President of the United States, 1837–1841; Jacksonian Democrat; was voted out of office after the Panic of 1837 brought widespread unemployment and poverty (p. 254)

Vance, Cyrus Secretary of State under President Jimmy Carter; invited Israelis and Egyptians to Camp David in 1978 to begin Middle East peace process (p. 941)

Vanzetti, Bartolomeo Immigrant and anarchist executed, in a highly controversial case, for a 1920 murder at a Massachusetts factory (p. 598)

Vesey, Denmark African American who planned 1822 South Carolina slave revolt; captured and hanged after revolt failed (p. 242)

von Steuben, Friedrich Prussian officer who trained Washington's troops at Valley Forge (p. 110)

W

Walker, David African American author of *Appeal to the Colored Citizens of the World* (1829), which called for an immediate end to slavery (p. 266)

Walker, Madam C. J. African American leader and businesswoman in the early 1900s; she spoke out against lynching (p. 501)

Wallace, George C. Third-party candidate for President in 1968; focused his campaign on issues of blue-collar anger in the North and racial tension (p. 908)

Warren, Earl Chief Justice of Supreme Court 1953–1968; investigated President Kennedy's assassination; led in many decisions that protected civil rights, rights of the accused, and right to privacy (p. 804)

Washington, Booker T. African American leader from the late 1800s until his death in 1915; founded Tuskegee Institute in Alabama; encouraged African Americans to learn trades (p. 490)

Washington, George First President of the United States, 1789–1797; led American forces in the War for Independence; set several federal precedents, including the two-term maximum for presidential office (p. 145)

Webster, Noah Author of the best-known American dictionary in the early 1800s; promoted a standard national language and public support for education (p. 208)

Whitman, Narcissa Prentiss Missionary; one of the first white women to cross the Rocky Mountains to Oregon in 1836 (p. 298)

Whitney, Eli Inventor; developed the cotton gin in 1793, which rapidly increased cotton production in the South and led to a greater demand for slave labor (p. 210)

Wilhelm, Kaiser Emperor of Germany during World War I; symbol to the United States of German militarism and severe efficiency (p. 567)

Wilson, Woodrow Twenty-eighth President of the United States, 1913–1921; tried to keep the United States out of World War I; proposed League of Nations (p. 554)

Y

Yeltsin, Boris Leader of Russia in late 1980s and 1990s; took over from Mikhail Gorbachev as reforms continued and Communist party control ended (p. 988)

York, Alvin American soldier who was awarded the Congressional Medal of Honor for bravery during World War I (p. 575)

Young, Brigham Mormon leader who supervised migration to Utah beginning in the 1840s; first governor when Utah became a United States territory (p. 304)

Index

INDEX

minimum wage, 1023–1028
mining, 441–442, 441*p*, 442*m*
Minnesota, 1108
  farming in, 236
  gains statehood, 291
  Native Americans in, 7
  progressivism in, 668
  single-tax club in, 541
Minuit, Peter, 51
minutemen, 96
Miranda rule, 805
Miranda v. *Arizona,* 805
missionaries, 32–33, 291–292, 292*p*
Mississippi, 203, 473, 1108
  antiwar demonstrations in, 892
  civil rights movement in, 823, 827*p*,
    828*m*, 829, 834–835
  after Civil War, 380
  in Civil War, 344, 345, 364–365, 364*p*,
    365*m*
  economy of, 240
  election of 1860, 334
  farming in, 211
  Native Americans in, 191, 252
  secedes from the Union, 335*c*, 336*m*
  slavery in, 241
  Spain and, 31
Mississippian culture, 5*m*, 6
Mississippi Freedom Democratic
  party, 834
Mississippi River, 6, 43, 186, 345–346,
  449
  in Civil War, 365
Missouri, 333, 1108
  in Civil War, 352
  election of 1860, 334
  free soilers in, 328
  immigrants in, 280
  Missouri Compromise, 195–196, 196*m*
  Mormons in, 304
  slavery in, 329–330
Missouri, U.S.S., 792–793, 792*p*
Missouri Compromise, 195–196, 196*m*,
  320–321, 330
Mitchell, Billy, 575
Mitchell, George, 858
Mitchell, John, 910, 913, 922, 923
Mitchell, Maria, 278
modern republicanism, 783, 956
Mohawks, 108
monarchy, 11
Mondale, Walter, 936, 964
monetary policy, 447. *See also*
  economics.
money, 111, 231*p*, 233, 447–448, 447*c*
  economy, 11
  greenbacks, 351
Monitor (warship), 346, 346*m*
Monroe, James, 186, 1109
  election of 1816, 195
  foreign policy of, 245–246
Monroe Doctrine, 245–246, 518*c*,
  519–520, 529, 1042–1043, 1042*p*
Montana, 610, 1108
  gains statehood, 454*c*
  mining in, 305
  national parks in, 453
  Native Americans in, 437, 437*m*, 438
Montcalm, Marquis de, 87
Montgomery, Alabama, 787, 787*p*, 821,
  822, 834*c*

Montgomery, Bernard, 695
Montoya, Joseph, 855
Moody, Anne, 824, 827*p*
Moral Majority, 958
Morey, Samuel, 213*c*
Morgan, J. P., 607
Mormons, 220, 304
Mormon Trail, 298, 298*m*
Morrill Land-Grant Act (1862), 433
Morris, Gouverneur, 145
Morris, Margaret Hill, 118–119
Morrison, Toni, 851
Morse, Samuel F.B., 319, 409
Moseley-Braun, Carol, 399
Moses, Robert, 823–824
Mothers Against Drunk Driving
  (MADD), 283, 283*p*
motion pictures, 492, 614–615, 614*p*,
  615*p*, 674–675
  in 1950s, 776
  during World War II, 721
Mott, Lucretia, 276, 277
mountain men, 297
muckrakers, 543, 543*p*
Mugwumps, 464
Muhammad, Elijah, 837–838, 837*p*
Muir, John, 550
Muller v. *Oregon,* 549
multiculturalism, 55, 55*p*, 996–999,
  1008–1009
Munich Conference, 687
Munn v. *Illinois,* 464
Murray, Pauli, 488
Musbach, Joan W., 900–901
music, 494–495, 495*p*, 616–617, 616*p*,
  620–621*p*, 888–889, 889*p*
  conservatism and, 956–957
  jazz, 620–621*p*
  in 1950s, 776–777, 777*c*
  spirituals, 221
  during World War II, 721, 1082–1083
Muskie, Edmund, 921
Mussolini, Benito, 685–686
My American Journey (Powell),
  1092–1093
My Lai Massacre, 880–881

N

NAACP. *See* National Association for the
  Advancement of Colored People.
Nader, Ralph, 865–866, 866*p*
Nagasaki, 705
Naismith, James, 493
napalm, 880
Napoleon, 186
Nasser, Gamal Abdel, 760
Nast, Thomas, 477, 477*p*.
Natchez, 5*m*, 6
National Aeronautics and Space
  Administration (NASA), 307, 799, 799*c*
National American Woman Suffrage
  Association (NAWSA), 506, 558,
  559–560
National Association for the Advance-
  ment of Colored People (NAACP),
  491, 500, 556, 626, 819–820
National Bank, 244–245
National Defense Education Act
  (1958), 784
National Energy Act (1978), 948

National Foundation of the Arts and
  Humanities, 805*c*
National Industrial Recovery Act
  (NIRA), 661, 664, 1025
nationalism, 244–246, 515
  World War I and, 566
Nationalists, 125–127, 139–140
National Labor Relations Board
  (NLRB), 664*c*, 665
National Partnership for Reinventing
  Government, 977
National Organization for Women
  (NOW), 847–848
national parks, 453, 550, 551*m*
National Park Service, 549, 550*c*
National Reclamation Act (1902), 550,
  550*c*
National Recovery Administration
  (NRA), 661, 664*c*, 666
National Republicans, 248, 248*c*, 253
National Rifle Association, 1020
National Security League, 568, 580
National Trades Union, (NTU), 239,
  424
National Traffic and Motor Vehicle
  Safety Act (1966), 805*c*, 866
National Urban League, 501, 642, 820
National War Labor Board, 579, 728
National Women's Political Caucus,
  848–849
Nation of Islam, 837–838
Native Americans, 1010
  Alcatraz occupation and, 859–860
  American Indian Movement, 858–859,
    860*p*
  and Andrew Jackson, 252–253, 252*p*
  art, 34–35*p*
  Bacon's Rebellion and, 41
  Broken Treaties Caravan, 859
  citizenship for, 857
  civil rights movement and, 788
  Columbian exchange and, 22*c*, 22*p*
  Columbus and, 21–23
  conflicts with government, 859–861,
    859*p*, 860*p*, 861*p*
  cultures of, 5*m*, 7, 438
  diseases and, 22–23, 23*p*, 290, 292
  education and, 488, 861
  expansionism and, 189–191
  family life, 6, 7
  French and Indian War and, 85, 86, 87
  Gold Rush and, 305
  government and, 306
  horses and, 287–288, 287*p*, 288*p*, 289
  Indian Territory and, 439
  Jamestown and, 39
  King Philip's War and, 48–49, 49*m*, 50*p*
  land and, 6
  land claims of, 858
  Louisiana Purchase and, 188
  migration of, 43, 204–205, 205*m*, 288–
    290, 306
  New Deal and, 661
  nomads, 288–290, 289*p*, 306
  in Oregon Country, 297
  Pequot War, 48
  Plymouth Colony and, 44
  in politics, 997
  Pontiac's Rebellion, 89–90
  problems of, 857–858
  ranchers and, 444–445, 445*m*

INDEX

1179

INDEX

1185

INDEX

1187

Acknowledgments

Team Credits The people who made up the *America: Pathways to the Present* team include: Tom Barber, Joyce Barisano, Wendy Bohannan, Bruce Bond, Melinda Borosen, Todd Christy, Patrick Connolly, Anthony DeAngelis, Anne Falzone, Elizabeth Good, Mary Ann Gundersen, Ed Hagenstein, Mary Hanisco, Michal Howden, Linda Johnson, Lynne Kalkanajian, John Kelley, Russ Lappa, Marilyn Leitao, Dotti Marshall, Grace Massey, Kathy Maxcey, Efrat Metser, Gabriela Perez Fiato, Debra Reardon, Nancy Rogier, Luess Sampson-Lizotte, Suzanne Schineller, Angela Sciaraffa, Olena Serbyn Sullivan, Amit Shah, Carol Signorino, John Springer, Mark Staloff, Susan Swan, Kira Thaler-Marbit, Jean C. Thomas, Stuart Wallace.

Cover Design

Bruce Bond

Front Cover Painting

Original oil painting by William G.Muller, collection of Richard Hastings

Picture Research

Pembroke Herbert and Sandi Rygiel/Picture Research Consultants, Inc.

Geography and History Contributing Writers: Carol Barrett, Department of Geography, University of Wisconsin at River Falls, River Falls, WI; Tom Baerwald, Program Director of Geography and Regional Science, National Science Foundation, Washington, D.C.; Peter Hugill, Department of Geography, Texas A&M University, College Station, TX

Maps

Horizon Design/Sanderson Associates:
5, 13, 17, 30, 32, 37, 43, 48, 53, 62, 64, 86, 90, 108, 113, 183, 187, 194, 196, 205, 206, 212, 273, 295, 298, 302, 329, 336, 344, 346, 362, 368, 375, 384, 388, 396, 409, 413, 437, 442, 445, 450, 475, 516, 522, 526, 530, 533, 535, 551, 560, 566, 575, 576, 585, 611, 645, 652, 663, 687, 689, 690, 695, 702, 732, 743, 750, 757, 760, 773, 808, 810, 814, 828, 839, 874, 876, 893, 911, 937, 971, 987, 989, 1044

Olena Serbyn Sullivan: 71

Illustration

Precision Graphics:
24, 40, 80, 93, 112, 131, 135, 136, 195, 202, 238, 261, 263, 267, 280, 304, 306, 370, 393, 415, 417, 418, 419, 420, 426, 443, 456, 462, 468, 469, 488, 490, 517, 528, 599, 600, 605, 633, 637, 638, 662, 673, 698, 716, 718, 728, 745, 761, 768, 770, 771, 776, 799, 803, 804, 835, 846, 849, 855, 884, 911, 933, 961, 963, 997, 998, 1012, 1017, 1032, 1045

Matthew Pippin
6, 94, 211, 237, 365, 412, 434, 577, 587, 604, 605, 694, 811, 948, 1059, 1060

Photography

Abbreviation Key LOC = Library of Congress; RH/LS = photo by Rob Huntley/Lightstream; NA = National Archives; PRC = Picture Research Consultants, Inc.; FRENT = Collection of David J. and Janice L. Frent; BB = Brown Brothers; CP = Culver Pictures; WW = Wide World Photos; GL = Gamma Liaison; WC = Woodfin Camp & Associates; C&G = Chermayeff & Geismar/MetaForm photo by Karen Yamauchi; BS = Black Star; MP = Magnum Photos; CB = Corbis Bettman; TL = Time-Life.

Unit Openers Page 1 T, "Europeans Encountering Indians" artist unknown, ca 1700. (detail) Joslyn Art Museum, Omaha, Nebraska; **1 B**, Lexington Battle Drum. Lexington Historical Society; **121 T**, "Election Day in Philadelphia" by John Lewis Krimmel, 1815. Courtesy, Winterthur Museum; **121 B**, Wood Painted American Eagle, FE 37. Shelburne Museum; **229 T**, View of the Upper Village of Lockport Niagara Company, N.Y.", 1836. Library of Congress. Hand-colored by Sandi Rygiel/Picture Research Consultant & Archives; **229 B**, Woman at loom. Museum of American Textile History/ Photo by Rob Huntley, Lightstream; **313 T**, "Battle of Gettysburg". New Hampshire Historical Society #F1234; **313 B**, African-American regimental flag. National Museum of American History/Smithsonian Institution; **405 T**, "Excursion Parties at Devil's Gate Bridge, Utah" by A. J. Russell. (detail) The Oakland Museum History Department; **405 B**, Assiniboine war shirt. Addison Doty/ Morning Star Gallery/Santa Fe, NM; **513 T**, New York & Cuba Mail Steamship Company Dock scene. C/B; **513 B**,"Vote Yes" suffrage poster. Smithsonian Institution; **595 T**, Mother and Child during the Depression. LOC; **595 B**,"Kick Out Depression" button. FRENT; **683 T**, But War Bonds" painting by N.C. Wyeth. PRC; **683 B**, Army Medal of Honor. U.S. Department of Defense; **795 T**, Selma March. (detail) by James H. Karales; **795 B**, Woodstock poster. The Image Works Archive; **903 B**, Statue of Liberty. Elsa Peterson/Stock Boston; **903 T**, Newly sworn in immigrants in Brooklyn. Lynn Johnson/BS; **1007**, Flag and Confetti. C&G

American Artifacts:

Abbreviation Key: SI= Smithsonian Institution; OPPS=Office of Printing and Photographic Services, Smithsonian Institution; NPS=Courtesy of the National Park Service

The Changing Pueblo PUEBLO, Courtesy of the National Anthropological Archives, SI; JAR, Eric Long, SI, Courtesy of the Philbrook Arts Center, Tulsa, OK; BOWL, Eric Long, SI, courtesy of the Museum of Indian Arts and Culture, Laboratory of Anthropology Collection, Santa Fe; BELL, Laurie Minor-Penland, SI; ARCHANGEL, Diane Nordeck, SI, courtesy of Zuni Pueblo; ROCK PAINTING, Courtesy of the Texas Memorial Museum, Austin; BLANKET, Jeff Tinsley

Life After the American Revolution JUG, Eric Long, SI; ANVIL & HAMMER, Eric Long, SI; SUIT, Eric Long, SI; DAIRYING, Courtesy of Princeton University Library, Dept. of Rare Books & Special Collections; RESPECT, LOC; GRIDIRON, OPPS; TOYS, OPPS; GRAVESTONES, Diane Penland, SI

Engines of Change REVOLVER, LOCK, GOODS, HARVESTING MACHINE, all by Rick Vargas; SAFE, Eric Long, SI; REAPER, State Historical; Society of Wisconsin

Life at War UNIFORM, Diane Penland/SI; SHOULDER PLATE, KNIFE, TINS, CUTLERY, HARD TACK all by Rick Vargas and Richard Strauss, SI; MUSKETT, Rick Vargas, SI; FIELD HOSPITAL, OPPS; QUININE, Diane Penland, SI

The Growth of Sports FOOTBALL PLAYER, BASEBALL MUSIC, Larry Gates, SI; SKATING, Jim Wallace, SI; SKIING, FOOTBALL PANTS, BASEBALL, all by Rick Vargas, SI; BICYCLE, Alfred Harrell, SI; CYCLIST, Collection of Sally Fox

African Americans' Great Migration DOLL, Eric Long, SI; PLOW, Jeff Tinsley, SI; RECORD BOOK, Diane Penland, SI; HOME SCHOOLING, LOC; SUITCASE, Eric Long, SI; SOLDIERS, Courtesy of the National Archives & Records Administration; JOBS, Jeff Tinsley

The Jazz Age DUKE, Courtesy of John Hasse; TRUMPET, Jeffrey Ploskonka, SI; DRESS, Jeff Tinsley, SI; HYMIE, Danny Thompson, SI; SAXAPHONE, Diane Penland, SI; CLARINET, Diane Penland, SI; BAND, Missouri Historical Society, Block Brothers photo

On the Home Front Jeff Tinsley, SI all with exception of PROPAGANDA POSTERS, Richard Strauss, SI

The Vietnam Veterans Memorial VIETNAM MEMORIAL, Sandra Rogers, SI; STUFFED ANIMALS, Richard Strauss, SI; BOOTS, HELMET, LETTER , LETTER TO GARY, Eric Long, SI, NPS; DOGTAGS, Rick Vargas, SI

The Information Age SATELLITE, OPPS; FIBER-OPTIC, Courtesy of Intel Corporation, Jeff Tinsley, SI; LASER HEAD, OPPS; BAR CODES, MAD'S UPC, symbol cover is ©E.C. Publications, Inc. 1978. Used with permission from MAD Magazine; HAND HELD COMPUTER, Courtesy of Apple Computer, Inc. EARLY COMPUTER, Eric Long, SI; WATERGATE BUGS, Margaret McCullough, SI, courtesy of the National Archives & Records Administration

Chapter 1 Page 2, David David Gallery/Superstock; **3**, Courtesy of the National Museum of the American Indian/Smithsonian Institution #s:1514; **4**, Courtesy The Edward E. Ayer Collection, The Newberry Library; **7**, Etowah Indian Mounds Historic Site; **8**, Werner Forman/Art Resource, NY; **10**, Giraudon/Art Resource,NY; **12 L**, Orsanmichele, Florence, Italy/Art Resource, NY; **12 R**. Louvre, Paris, France/Art Resource, NY; **14**, Oronoz; **15**, Photograph by Jeffrey Ploskonka, National Museum of African Art, Eliot Elisofon Archive, Smithsonian Institution; **16**, Barth, Heinrich, Travels and Discoveries in North and Central Africa, London,1857. General Research Division. The New York Public Library, Astor, Lenox and Tilden Foundations.; **17**, Photograph by Jeffrey Ploskonka, National Museum of African Art, Eliot Elisofon Archive, Smithsonian Institution, Washington, D.C.; **19**, The Metropolitan Museum of Art, Gift of J. Pierpont Morgan, 1900 (10.18.2); **20**, Bry, Theodor de (America), Frankfurt, 1590, Part IV plate II ("Pisces in mari alati"),(detail) Rare Book and Manuscripts Division, The New York Public Library, Astor, Lenox and Tilden Foundations; **21**, London Science Museum. Photo © Michael Holford; **23**, London Science Museum. Photo © Michael Holford; **25 L**, Bibliotheque Nationale; **25 R**, Wide World Photos; **27**, Steve Kelley/Copley News Service.

Chapter 2 27, Vose Galleries of Boston, Inc.; **29**, Courtesy of South Florida Science Museum. Photo by Randy Smith; **36**, National Maritime Museum; **38**, Colonial National Historical Park; **40**, Fairholt, F.W., Tobacco: Its history, ... London. 1859 (detail) Arents Collection, The New York Public Library, Astor, Lenox and Tilden Foundations; **41**, LOC; **42**, Peabody & Essex Museum. Photo by Mark Sexton; **44**, Courtesy Plimoth Plantation, Plymouth, Massachusetts; **45**, Folger Shakespeare Library; **46 T**, "The Mason Children: David, Joanna, and Abigail" 1670 attributed to the Freake-Gibbs painter. Fine Arts Museums of San Francisco, Gift of Mr. & Mrs. John D. Rockefeller 3rd; **46 B**, CP; **49**, LOC; **51**, Chicago Historical Society; **52**, Museum of the City of New York. The J. Clarence Davies Collection; **54**, Methodist Collection of Drew University, Madison, New Jersey; **55 L**, Miriam and Ira D. Wallach Division of Art, Prints & Photographs. The New York Public Library. Astor, Lenox and Tilden Foundations; **55 R**, William Mercer McLeod; **57**, From *Divine Examples of God's Severe Judgments upon Sabbath-Breakers* (London 1671).

Chapter 3 58, Miriam and Ira D. Wallach Division of Art, Prints and Photographs, The New York Public Library. Astor, Lenox and Tilden Foundations; **61**, LOC; **63**, Houghton Library, Harvard University; **65**, Colonial Williamsburg Foundation; **66**, CIGNA Museum and Art Collection, photo by Joseph Painter; **67**, Connecticut Historical Society; **68 T**, Wethersfield Historical Society; **68 B**, Breton Littlehales © National Geographic Society; **69**, Massachusetts Historical Society; **70**, Wenham Museum, Wenham, MA; **72**, Royal Albert Memorial Museum, Exeter/ Bridgeman Art Library, London/ New York; **74**, Abby Aldrich Rockefeller Foundation, Colonial Williamsburg; **76**, Massachusetts Historical Society; **79 T**, LOC; **79 B**, Courtesy of the National Portrait Gallery, London; **81 L**, Bequest of Maxim Karolik/ Courtesy Museum of Fine Arts, Boston; **81 R**, Bob Daemmrich Photography; **83**, From *Divine Examples of God's Severe Judgments upon Sabbath-Breakers* (London, 1671).

Chapter 4 84, Abbot Hall, Marblehead, MA; **87**, LOC; **91**, Colonial Williamsburg Foundation; **94**, LOC; **95**, LOC; **99 TL**, Yale University Art Gallery; **99 TR**, Bob Daemmrich Photography; **99 B**, PRC; **100**, Massachusetts Historical Society; **105**, LOC; **107**, Gift of Edgar William and Bernice Chrysler Garbisch, © 1994 National Gallery of Art, Washington, D.C.; **109**, The Metropolitan Museum of Art, Gift of John S. Kennedy, 1897. (97.34); **115 L**, Private Collection; **115 R**, Bob Daemmrich Photography; **118**, Princeton University Libraries; **119**, David Schorsch.

Chapter 5 122, Collection of the Architect of the Capitol; **123**, Yale University Art Gallery, Mabel Brady Garven Collection; **124**, Chicago Historical Society; **126**, LOC; **128**, CP; **132**, Independence National Historic Park; **133**, LOC; **134**, Free Library of Philadelphia; **139**, Courtesy, American Antiquarian Society; **141**, Courtesy, American Antiquarian Society; **143**, Museum of American Political Life. Photo by Sally Anderson-Bruce; **144**, The Brooklyn Museum 39.536.1 Gift of the Crescent-Hamilton Athletic Club; **145**, LOC; **146**, LOC; **147 L**, Courtesy, American Antiquarian Society; **147 R**, SuperStock; **149**, LOC; **151**, Collection of the Architect of the Capitol; **173**, Locher/ The Chicago Tribune.

Chapter 6 174, Chicago Historical Society; **175**, Columbiana Collection,Columbia University; **177**, "An Exciseman" (detail) Atwater Kent Museum; **178**, Courtesy, Winterthur Museum; **180**, Henry Ford Museum and Greenfield Village; **181 L**, Courtesy, American Antiquarian Society; **181 R**, National Portrait Gallery, Smithsonian Institution, Washington, DC. Art Resource NY; **182**, © White House Historical Association/ Photo by National Geographic Society; **184**, PRC; **185**, Duke University Archives; **186 TL**, LOC; **186 TR**, LOC; **186 BL**, Courtesy of Bexar County & the Witte Museum, San Antonio; **186 BR**, Amon Carter Museum, Fort Worth, Texas; **189**, Ohio Historical Society; **190**, National Portrait Gallery, Smithsonian Institution,Washington, DC. Art Resource, NY; **192**, Division of Political History, Smithsonian Institution, Washington, DC #83-7221; **197 L**, C/B; **197 R**, Joe Travers/ GL; **199**, The New-York Historical Society.

Chapter 7 200, The New-York Historical Society; **201**, Peabody & Essex Museum; **203**, LOC; **204**, Colonial Williamsburg Foundation; **207**, National Museum of American History, Smithsonian Institution, Washington, D.C. Photo by Charles Philips; **208**, (detail) The Saint Louis Art Museum; **210**, CP; **212**, The New-York Historical Society; **217**, National Museum of American History, Smithsonian Institution, Washington, DC; **218**, Pennsylvania Academy of the Fine Arts, Gift of Paul Beck; **219 L**, New Bedford Whaling Museum; **219 R**, Dukes County Historical Society/ photo by Robert Schellhammer ©1994; **220**, The New-York Historical Society; **221**, LOC; **222**, LOC; **223 L**, Independence National Historic Park; **223 R**, Bob Daemmrich Photography; **225**, Courtesy, American Antiquarian Society; **226**, Prints Collection. Miriam and Ira D. Wallach Division of Art, Prints & Photographs. The New York Public Library. Astor, Lenox and Tilden Foundations; **227**, Private Collection.

Chapter 8 230, Museum of American Textile History; **231**, Lowell Historical Society; **233**, Old Sturbridge Village; **236**, Museum of American Textile History. Photo © Rob Huntely/Lightstream; **240**, LOC; **241**, LOC; **243**, LOC; **244**, Supreme Court Historical Society; **246**, LOC; **247**, The New-York Historical Society; **250**, Museum of the City of New York; **251**, City of Boston Art Commission; **252**, Woolaroc Museum, Bartlesville, OK; **254**, The New-York Historical Society; **255 L**, Private Collection; **255 R**, Courtesy, Burlington Industries, Inc.; **257**, The New-York Historical Society.

Chapter 9 258, Missouri Historical Society; **260**, Metropolitan Museum of Art, Rogers Fund, 1942; **262 T**, The Metropolitan Museum of Art Gift of I.N. Phelps Stokes, Edward S. Hawes, Alice Mary Hawes, Marion Augusta Hawes, 1937; **262 B**, Collection of Sue and Lars Hotham. Photo © Rob Huntley/Lightstream; **263**, Boston Athenaeum; **264**, Massachusetts Historical Society; **266**, Concord Museum; **267**, Massachusetts Historical Society; **268**, National Portrait Gallery, Smithsonian Institution, Washington D.C. Art Resource,NY; **269**, Women's Rights Collection, Sophia Smith Archives; **270 L**, Illinois State Historical Society; **270 R**, Sophia Smith Archives, Garrison Collection; **271 T**, LOC; **271 B**, Chicago Historical Society; **272**, ©Louis Pshoyos/Contact Press Images; **274**, Courtesy, American Antiquarian Society; **275**, Schlesinger Library, Radcliffe College; **276 L**, Courtesy National Women's Party, Washington, D.C. Photo by Jeff Mathewson; **276 R**, Seneca Falls Historical Society. Photo © Rob Huntley/Lightstream; **277 TL**, Seneca Falls Historical Society; **277 TM**, Collection of Bettye Lane. Photograph © Rob Huntley/Lightstream; **277 TR**, Fred Ward/Black Star; **277 BL**, C/B; **277 BR**, C/B; **279**, Mark Sexton; **281**, Museum of the City of New York; **283 L**, The Connecticut Historical Society; **283 R**, MADD (Mothers Against Drunk Driving); **285**, LOC.

Chapter 10 286, National Museum of American Art, Washington, DC/Art Resource, NY; **287**, Roberta Campbell Lawson Collection, Philbrook Museum of Art, Tulsa, Oklahoma; **288**, © Jerry Jacka; **289**, Collection of Western Americana, Beinecke Rare Book and Manuscript Library, Yale University; **290**, National Museum of American Art, Smithsonian Institution, Washington, D.C. Gift of Mrs. Joseph Harrison, Jr. Art Resource, NY; **291**, Courtesy of The Oakland Museum; **292 T**, Courtesy of the

Texas Memorial Museum, The University of Texas at Austin. #41VV343; **293**, Rare Books Division, New York Public Library; **294 T**, Archives Division-Texas State Library; **294 B**, The R.W. Norton Art Gallery, Shreveport, La. Used by permission; **297**, Boot Hill Collection, photo © Henry Groskinsky; **299**, Utah State Historical Society; **301**, Courtesy of the Texas Memorial Museum, The University of Texas at Austin; **305**, Amon Carter Museum Fort Worth, Texas; **307 L**, National Park Service; **307 R**, NASA; **309**, LOC; **310 L**, Cincinnati Art Mueum; **310 R**, Photograph from THE UNDERGROUND RAILROAD by Raymond Bial. Copyright © 1995 by Raymond Bial. Reprinted by permission of Houghton MIfflin Company. All rights reserved.

Chapter 11 314, Anne S. K. Brown Military Collection, Providence, RI; **316 T**, LOC; **316 B**, Radcliffe College Archives,Schlesinger Library; **317 L**, Chicago Historical Society; **317 R**, Chicago Historical Society; **319**, The Corcoran Gallery of Art, Mary E. Maxwell, Fund acc # 61.11; **321**, LOC; **323**, National Portrait Gallery, Smithsonian Institution, Washington, DC. Art Resource, NY; **324**, Chicago Historical Society; **326**, Ontario County Historical Society; **330**, Missouri Historical Society; **331**, LOC; **332**, Boston Athenaeum; **337 L**, Kansas State Historical Society; **337 R**, WW; **339**, LOC.

Chapter 12 340, West Point Museum; **341**, Collection of David & Kevin Kyle; **343**, LOC; **345**, Collection of Michael J. McAfee. Courtesy William Gladstone. Photo © Seth Goltzer; **347**, Museum of the Confederacy; **349**, West Point Museum Collections. Courtesy William Gladstone. Photo © Seth Goltzer; **351**, McLellan Lincoln Collection, John Hay Library, Brown University; **352**, LOC; **353**, Chicago Historical Society; **354**, LOC; **355**, LOC; **356**, Courtesy, American Antiquarian Society; **361**, Museum of the Confederacy; **363**, Photograph courtesy Historical Art Prints, Southbury, CT 06488; **364**, The Beverly R. Robinson Collection, U.S. Naval Academy Museum; **366**, Brown University Library; **371**, Virginia Historical Society; **372**, Anne S. K. Brown Military Collection, Brown University Library, Providence, RI; **373 L**, Artist: Douglas Volk, Minnesota Historical Society; **373 R**, Jay Syverson/Stock Boston; **374 T**, Museum of the Confederacy; **374 B**, Confederate Memorial Hall, New Orleans. From ECHOES OF GLORY; ARMS & EQUIPMENT OF THE CONFEDERACY. Photo by Larry Sherer © 1991Time-Life Books; **377**, CP; **378**, LOC.

Chapter 13 378, LOC; **380**, Chicago Historical Society; **382 TL**, Collection of William Gladstone. Photograph by Seth Goltzer; **382 BL**, Collection of William Gladstone. Photograph by Seth Goltzer; **382 BR**, Collection of William Gladstone; **383**, Collection of William Gladstone; **386 TL**, FRENT; **386 TR**, M. Abramson/BS; **386 BL**, Radcliffe College Archives, Schlesinger Library; **386 BR**, C/B; **389**, LOC; **390**, Collection of Nancy Gewirz, Antique Textile Resource, Bethesda, Maryland; **391**, Courtesy of the Decorative and Industrial Arts Collection of the Chicago Historical Society; Acc. No. 1920.53; Photographer: John Alderson; **392**, The New-York Historical Society; **395**, Collection of State Historical Museum/Mississippi Department of Archives and History; **397**, LOC; **398**, LOC; **399 L**, LOC; **399 R**, Rick Friedman/BS; **401**, LOC; **402**, LOC; **403**, NA.

Chapter 14 406, The Oakland Museum History Department; **407**, Division of Political History, Smithsonian Institution, Washington, DC. #89-6626; **408**, Division of Community Life, Smithsonian Institution, Washington, D.C. #86-2200; **409**, Lightfoot Collection; **411 T**, C/B; **411 BL**, LOC; **411 BR**, WW; **414**, Museum of American Textile History; **415**, LOC; **416**, LOC; **421**, Putman County Historical Society, Cold Spring, N.Y.; **422 L**, LOC; **422 R**, Urban Archives, Temple University; **423**, Collection of Ralph J. Brunke; **424 L**, LOC; **424 R**, PRC; **427**, C/B; **428**, BB; **429 L**, Hagley Museum and Library; **429 R**, Paul Chesley/Photographers/Aspen; **431**, LOC.

Chapter 15 432, National Cowboy Hall of Fame; **433**, The Oakland Museum History Department; **436**, © Justin Kerr; **438**, LOC; **440**, State Historical Society of Wisconsin; **441**, Western History Division, Denver Public Library, photo by L. C. McClure; **444**, The Oakland Museum History Department; **448**, East Carolina Manuscript Collection, J. Y. Joyner Library, East Carolina University; **449**, Kansas State Historical Society; **451**, LOC; **453**, Buffalo Bill Historical Center, Cody WY; **455 L**, Amon Carter Museum of Western Art; **455 R**, LOC; **457 L**, Denver Public Library; **457 R**, Bob Daemmrich Photography; **459**, LOC.

Chapter 16 460, CP; **461**, Puck March 10, 1897; **463**, LOC; **464**, Union Pacific Railroad Museum; **465**, New York Public Library. Astor, Lenox and Tilden Foundation; **466**, LOC; **467**, National Park Service Collection, Gift of Angelo Forgione; **468**, BB; **469**, LOC; **471 T**, C&G; **471 B**, C&G; **472**, California Department of Parks and Recreation, courtesy Fred Wasserman; **473**, PRC/RH/LS; **474**, LOC; **476 T**, Museum of the City of New York, Gift of Joseph Varner Reed; **476 B**, BB; **477**, The Granger Collection, New York; **479**, Division of Political History, Smithsonian Institution, Washington. D.C. #88-8676; **480**, C&G; **481**, LOC; **482**, California Museum of Photography WX5266; **483 L**, Courtesy George Eastman House; **483 R**, Bob Daemmrich Photography; **485**, Puck 1909.

Chapter 17 486, American Heritage; **488**, Nebraska State Historical Society; **489**, Sophia Smith Collection; **490**, BB; **491**, BB; **492**, Collection of Sally Fox; **493**, LOC; **494 L**, Chicago Historical Society; **494 TR**, Wood River Gallery, Mill Valley, California; **494 BR**, Wood River Gallery, Mill Valley, California; **495**, C/B; **498**, Frank Leslie's Illustrated Newspaper; **501**, National Portrait Gallery, Smithsonian Institution, Washington, DC. Art Resource, NY; **502**, Museum of American Political Life.Photo by Steve Laschever; **503**, Courtesy of The Maytag Company; **504**, PRC/RH/LS; **505**, Kansas State Historical Society; **507 L**, State Historical Society of North Dakota; **507 R**, Bob Daemmrich/Stock Boston; **509**, LOC; **510**, Kansas State Historical Society, **511**, Courtesy of Birmingham Public Library, Department of Archives & Manuscripts.

Chapter 18 514, Courtesy of the U.S. Naval Academy Museum; **515**, The Oakland Museum History Department; **518**, LOC; **520**, C/B; **521 TL**, NA; **521 TR**, Larry Burrows, Life Magazine; **521 BL**, NA; **521 BR**, Bill Gentile/SIPA Press; **523**, California Museum of Photography #24039; **524**, Courtesy of the Liliuokalani Trust and the Bishop Museum (detail); **525**, CP; **527**, PRC; **529**, BB; **530**, LOC; **531**, White House Historical Association; **532**, C/B; **534**, Courtesy of Fred and Kathryn Giampietro; **537 L**, LOC; **537 R**, WW; **539**, Puck, June 29, 1904.

Chapter 19 540, C/B; **542**, Labor-Management Documentation Center, Cornell University; **543**, CP; **544**, Courtesy George Eastman House; **545**, C/B; **548**, CP; **549**, LOC; **552**, National Portrait Gallery, Smithsonian Institution, Washington, DC. Art Resource, NY; **553**, Joseph Keppler from PUCK.Theodore Roosevelt Collection, Harvard College Library; **554**, Museum of American Political Life; **555 T**, C/B; **555 B**, FRENT; **556** FRENT; **557**, Meserve Collection; **559**, Sophia Smith College Archives; **561 L**, Chicago Historical Society; **561 R**, Corporation for National Service; **563**, Courtesy of the League of Women's Voters of the United States.

Chapter 20 564 C/B; **565**, Collection of Colonel Stuart S.Corning, Jr. Photo ©RH/LS; **567**, Bayerisches Hauptstaatsarchiv; **568**, CP; **570**, The Granger Collection; **571 L**, LOC; **571 R**, Boston Athenaeum; **572**, National Portrait Gallery, Smithsonian Institution, Washington, DC/Art Resource, NY; **573**, Collection of Colonel Stuart S.Corning, Jr. RH/LS; **574**, NA; **576**, BB; **578**, LOC; **580**, C/B; **581**, Wayne State University, Archives of Labor and Urban Affairs; **588**, LOC; **589 L**, Archive Photos/Lambert; **589 R**, C/B; **591**, Stock Montage; **592 T**, Collection of Colonel Stuart S. Corning, Jr.; **592 B**, U.S. Air Force; **593 T**, U.S. Air Force; **593 B**, C/B.

Chapter 21 596, John Sloan Sixth Avenue Elevated at Third Street, 1928 (detail). Collection of Whitney Museum of American Art, Purchase 36.154. Photograph 1998: Whitney Museum of American Art, NY; **598**, FRENT; **600**, LOC; **601**, FRENT; **602**, LIFE Magazine December 10,1925; **603**, PRC/RH/LS; **606**, Courtesy Ford Archives; **607**, Lake County (IL) Museum/Curt Teich Postcard Archives; **608**, Saturday Evening Post, June 30, 1928, Curtis Archives; **609**, C/B; **610**, LOC; **611**, Schomburg Center for Research in Black Culture, The New York Public Library, Astor, Lenox and Tilden Foundations; **612**, CP; **613 L**, C/B; **613 R**, C/B; **614**, SuperStock; **615**, Division of Electricity/Smithsonian Institution; **616 L**, Nipper's Choice Phonographs, Keene, New Hampshire. Photograph by Wright Studio; **616 R**, C/B; **617 T**, Purchased with funds from the Edmundson Art Foundation, Inc. Des Moines Art Center Permanent Collections, 1958.2; **617 B**, C/B; **618 L**, Cartier Bresson/ Magnum Photos; **618 TM**, Beinecke Library, Yale University; **618 BM**, C/B; **618 R**, C/B; **622**, The Michael Barson Collection/Past Perfect. RH/LS; **623**, Chicago Historical Society; **624**, BB; **625**, C&G; **626**, BB; **627 L**, LOC; **627 R**, PRC; **629**, The Granger Collection, New York.

Chapter 22 630, LOC; **631**, Courtesy of Speigel; **632**, Wood River Gallery, Mill Valley, California; **633**, Boston Athenaeum; **634**, C/B; **635**, LOC; **636**, C/B; **639**, Detroit News; **640**, Museum of the City of New York. Photograph by Bernice Abbott, Federal Arts Project; **641 L**, LOC; **641 R**, LOC; **642**, C/B; **644**, LOC; **647**, CP; **648**, C/B; **651**, C/B; **653 TL**, C/B; **653 TR**, FRENT; **653 BR**, Lyndon Baines Johnson Presidential Library; **654**, FDR Library; **655 L**, C/B; **655 R**, People Weekly © 1998 Steve Kagan; **657**, Reprinted from the Albany Evening News, 6/7/31 with permission of the Times Union, Albany, NY.

Chapter 23 658, LOC; **659**, C/B; **660**, C/B; **661 T**, U.S. Forest Service; **661 B**, LOC; **663**, Franklin D. Roosevelt Library; **665**, LOC; **667**, Margaret Bourke-White LIFE Magazine © Time Warner; **668**, ©1935, 1963 by the Condé Nast Publications, Inc.; **671**, National Portrait Gallery, Smithsonian Institution, Washington, DC. Art Resource, NY; **672**, The Oakland Museum History Department; **673**, C/B; **674**, LOC; **675**, James Prigoff; **677 L**, PTC; **677 R**, David Hurn/MP; **679**, Franklin D. Roosevelt Library; **680**, NA; **681**, National Baseball Hall of Fame and Museum.

Chapter 24 684, C/B; **685**, Collection of Chester Stott, RH/LS; **686**, Bilderdienst Suddeutscher Verlag; **687**, NA; **688**, LOC; **692**, Collection of Chester H. Stott, RH/LS; **693**, NA; **697 T**, National Portrait Gallery, Smithsonian Institution, Washington, DC. Art Resource. N.Y.; **697 B**, U.S. Army; **699**, U.S. Army; **701**, Navy Art Collection/ Gift of Abbott Laboratories; **702**, C/B; **704**, LOC; **705**, C/B; **706**, NA; **707**, US Holocaust Memorial Museum; **708 L**, Rijksinstituut voor Oorlogsdocumentatie, courtesy of U.S. Holocaust Memorial Museum Archives; **708 R**, Courtesy of U.S. Holocaust Memorial Museum Archives; **710**, US Holocaust Memorial Museum Archives; **711 L**, Yivo Institute for Jewish Research; **711 R**, C/B; **713**, Reprinted with permission of The Detroit News, a Gannett Newspaper, © 1993.

Chapter 25 714, © The Curtis Publishing Company; **715**, Private Collection, RH/LS; **716**, NA; **717 T**, The Bancroft Library, Kaiser Pictorial Collections; **717 B**, NA; **719**, NA; **720**, LOC; **721**, C/B; **722**, National Museum of American History,Smithsonian Institution, Washington, D.C.; **723**, WW; **726**, Collection of Col. Stuart S. Corning,Jr. RH/LS; **727**, NA; **729**, Ellen Kaiper Collection, Oakland; **730**, Courtesy of the Norman Rockwell Family Trust and Curtis Archives; **731**, Collection of Jeff Ikler, RH/LS; **732**, LOC; **733 T**, LOC; **733 B**, National Portait Gallery, Gift of the Harmon Foundation/ Art Resource, NY; **734**, LOC; **735**, NA; **737 L**, LOC; **737 R**, Bob Daemmrich/ Stock Boston; **739**, Des Moines Register.

Chapter 26 740, Collection of Whitney Museum of American Art, New York. Photography by Geoffrey Clements, NY; **741**, U.S. Army; **742**, Harry S. Truman Presidential Library; **744 L**, C/B; **744 R**, Courtesy of the J. N. Ding Darling Foundation; **746**, © 1949 Time Inc. Reprinted with permission; **749 T**, Bob Daemmrich/ Image Works; **749 BL**, C/B; **749 BR**, WW; **750**, Fenno Jacobs/BS; **754 T**, The Michael Barson Collection/Past Perfect, RH/LS; **754 B**, The Michael Barson Collection/Past Perfect. RH/LS; **755 L**, BB; **755 R**, Elliot Erwitt/MP; **756**, NA; **758**, C/B; **759 T**, C/B; **759 B**, The Michael Barson Collection/Past Perfect, RH/LS; **761**, © 1959 Newsweek Inc. All rights reserved. Reprinted by permission; **763 L**, Boeing Airplane Company; **763 R**, WW; **765**, From Herblock: A Cartoonist's Life (Macmillan Publishing, 1993).

Chapter 27 766, © The Curtis Publishing Company; **767**, PRC; **768**, The McDonald's Corporation; **769**, Dan Weiner, Courtesy Sandra Weiner; **770**, Van

Bucher/Photo Researchers; **772**, Collection of Robert and Bonnie Pope, RH/LS; **774**, Bill Ray LIFE Magazine © Time Warner ; **775**, Leo Chopin/BS; **776**, The Michael Barson Collection/Past Perfect, RH/LS; **778**, PRC, RH/LS; **779**, Harry S. Truman Presidential Library; **780**, C/B; **781**, C/B; **782 T**, FRENT; **782 B**; Division of Political History, Smithsonian Institution, Washington, D.C. #91-13778; **783**, Dwight D. Eisenhower Library; **784**, From The Herblock's Special for Today (Simon & Schuster, 1958); **785**, FRENT; **786**, The Michael Barson Collection/Past Perfect, RH/LS; **787**, Grey Vielet LIFE Magazine © Time Warner; **788**, WW; **789 L**, C/B; **789 R**, Lonnie Duke/Tony Stone Images; **791**, ©The New Yorker Collection, 1954, Robert J. Day from cartoonbank.com. All Rights Reserved; **792**, NA; **793**, U. S. Naval Historical Center; **795 T**, (detail) by James H. Karales ; **795 B**, The Image Works Archive.

Chapter 28 796, John F. Kennedy Library; **797**, FRENT; **798**, John F. Kennedy Presidential Library; **800**, John F. Kennedy Presidential Library; **802**, Lyndon Baines Johnson Presidential Library; **805**, Supreme Court Historical Society; **807**, Courtesy Boeing Defense & Space Group; **809**, C/B; **813 L**, Courtesy of the Peace Corps; **813 R**, Courtesy of the Peace Corps; **815 L**, Y. Okamoto/LBJ Library; **815 R**, WW; **817**, ©1962 Herblock in The Washington Post.

Chapter 29 818, Bob Adelman/MP; **819**, Dan Budnick/WC; **820**, C/B; **821**, C/B; **822**, WW; **823 T**, FRENT; **823 B**, Danny Lyon/MP; **824**, Dial Juvenile Books, 1968, a Division of Penguin Books USA, Inc.; **826**, Don Uhrbrock LIFE Magazine © Time Warner; **827 L**, Rapho/Photo Researchers; **827 R**, Danny Lyons/MP; **828**, C/B; **829**, WW; **830**, Charles Moore/BS; **831**, Robert Phillips LIFE Magazine ©Time Warner ; **832 L**, Fred Ward/BS; **832 R**, Steve Schapiro/BS; **833 TL**, WW; **833 TR**, Bob Daemmrich Photography; **833 BL**, Bob Daemmrich Photography; **833 BR**, Bob Daemmrich/The Image Works; **834**, C/B; **835**, Eve Arnold/MP; **836**, C/B; **837**, Eve Arnold/MP; **838**, C/B; **839**, Charles Moore/BS; **840**, AP/Wide World Photos; **841 L**, C/B; **841 R**, Bob Mahoney/ The Image Works; **843**, David Horsey/ The Seattle-Post Intelligencer.

Chapter 30 844, Ken Regan/Camera 5; **845**, Al Freni LIFE Magazine © Time Warner; **847 T**, Werner Wolff/ Black Star; **847 B**, © Bettye Lane; **848 T**, Bob Daemmrich Photography; **848 B**, Courtesy Lang Communications; **849**, C/B; **853**, Michael Nichols/MP; **854**, Craig Aurness/WC; **856**, George Bacon Collection, Hawaii State Archives; **857**, Eddie Adams/TIME Magazine; **858**, Jim Noelker/The Image Works; **859**, Rick Smolan/Against All Odds; **860 L**, Dirck Halstead/TIME Magazine; **860 R**, Dirck Halstead/TIME Magazine; **861**, C/B; **862**, FRENT; **862**, FRENT; **863 T**, Alfred Eisenstaedt/LIFE Magazine © Time Warner; **863 B**, FRENT; **864 L**, Collection of Michael McCloskey; **864 R**, Ken Regan/ Camera 5; **866**, C/B; **867 L**, M. Abramson/BS; **867 R**, Mike Orazzi; **868**, PRC; **871**, Mike Peters.

Chapter 31 872, Larry Burrows; **873**, Courtesy United Nations, RH/LS; **874**, Dennis Brack/BS; **875**, C/B; **878**, Philip Jones Griffiths/MP, Zenith Electronics Corporation; **879**, C/B; **880 L**, Catherine Leroy/AP, print courtesy Time Inc. Picture Collection; **880 R**, Larry Burrows LIFE Magazine © Time Warner; **881**, Harry Breedlove; **882**, FRENT; **883**, The Bancroft Library, University of California; **885**, ©Lisa Law/The Image Works; **887**, The Oakland Museum History Department; **888**, © Lisa Law/The Image Works; **889**, Michael Frederick/The Image Works; **890**, Brad Markel/GL; **893**, FRENT; **894**, Thai Khad Chuon/C/B; **895 L**, WW; **895 R**, Bob Daemmrich/Tony Stone Images; **899**, From Herblock on All Fronts (New American Library, 1980); **900**, C/B; **901 L**, LOC; **901 R**, WW.

Chapter 32 904, Nixon Presidential Materials Project; **905**, Courtesy of the Lyndon B. Johnson Presidential Library; **906 L**, Joseph Louw LIFE Magazine © Time Warner; **906 R**, Bill Eppridge LIFE Magazine © Time Warner; **907**, C/B; **908**, FRENT; **909**, Roddey E. Mims/C/B; **910**, Nixon Presidential Materials Project; **912**, John Filo; **913**, Ted Cowell/BS; **914**, NASA; **915**, Dennis Brack/BS; **916**, Steve Northup, Time Magazine © Time Inc. ; **917 T**, John Dominis LIFE Magazine © Time Warner; **917 B**, Sovfoto/Eastfoto; **918 T**, Rene Burri/MP; **918 B**, John T. Barr/GL; **919**, C/B; **920**, FRENT **921 T**, Richard Ellis/Sygma; **921 B**, Dennis Brack/BS; **922**, WW; **925**, Roland Freeman/MP; **927 L**, Mark Godfrey/Image Works; **927 R**, WW; **929**, Tony Auth. Reprinted by permission: Tribune Media Services.

Chapter 33 930, Robert Llewellyn; **931**, Dennis Brack/BS; **932 T**, WW; **932 B**, Copyright © 1974 by The New York Times Company; **934**, Gerald Ford Presidential Library; **935**, Hardin/BS; **936**, FRENT; **937**, Dennis Brack/BS; **938**, Jimmy Carter Presidential Library; **939**, Dennis Brack/BS; **941**, Jimmy Carter Presidential Library; **942**, C/B; **943**, Alain Mingam/GL; **944 L**, Peter Marlow/MP; **944 R**, FRENT; **946**, Dennis Brack/BS; **950 L**, WW; **950 R**, C/B; **951 L**, WW; **951 R**, PRC; **953**, Mike Peters/Dayton Daily News.

Chapter 34 954, Sygma; **955**, FRENT; **956**, Diana Walker/Time Magazine; **957 TL**, C/B; **957 TR**, WW; **957 B**, Ken Hawking/Sygma; **958**, Les Schofer/Sygma; **960**, Charles Steiner/Sygma; **961**, C/B; **964**, Dick Halstead/GL; **966**, Zimberhoff/Sygma; **967**, WW; **970**, Atlan/Sygma; **971**, WW; **972**, R. Bossu/Sygma; **973 L**, Abbas/MP; **973 R**, Langevin/Sygma; **975 L**, David Woo/Sygma; **975 R**, Larry Downing/Sygma; **977**, Bob Englehard/The Hartford Courant.

Chapter 35 978, National Center for Supercomputing Applications at the University of Illinois; **979**, John C. Sykes Jr.; **980**, Ira Wyman/Sygma; **982**, John Harrington/BS; **983** inset, The Liaison Agency Network; **983**, ©Garse/SIPA Press; **984**, AP Photo/ Eric Gay; **988**, C/B; **989**, Les Stone/ Sygma; **991**, AP Photo/Boris Grdanoski; **992**, WW; **996**, JB Pictures Ltd.; **999**, B. Kraft/ Sygma; **1000**, Rick Maiman/Sygma; **1001 L**, Doug Menuez/Stock Boston; **1001 R**, Bob Daemmrich/Stock Boston; **1003**, Mike Smith/Las Vegas Sun; **1004**, C/B.

Chapter 36 1008 T, C&G; **1008 B**, Rebecca Cooney/NYT Pictures; **1009**, Davies & Starr; **1010**, BB; **1011**, LOC; **1012**, David Butow; **1013**, ©1993 Time Inc., Reprinted by permission; **1014**, Elsa Peterson/Stock Boston.

Chapter 37 1016 T, The New-York Historical Society; **1016 B**, David J. Sams/Stock Boston; **1017**, Booy Hill Museum, photo by Henry Groskinsky; **1018**, North Carolina Museum of Art, Raleigh, Purchased with funds from the State of North Carolina; **1019**, "The Cowboy" by Remington, 1902. Amon Cater Museum of Western Art; **1020**, David Woo/GL; **1021**, Dennis Brack/BS.

Chapter 38 1023 B, John Zoiner/Uniphoto; **1024**, CP; **1025 T**, Stock Montage; **1025 B**, Museum of the City of New York; **1026 T**, FRENT; **1026 B**, LOC; **1027**, Bob Daemmrich/Tony Stone Images; **1028**, Barney Taxel/NYT Pictures.

Chapter 39 1030 T, PRC Archive; **1030 B**, Gilles Mingasson/GL; **1031**, David Hurn/MP; **1033**, "Mother and Child" by Dorothea Lange (detail) LOC; **1034 T**, FRENT; **1034 B**, Kingsport Press, Inc.; **1035**, J. Pat Carter/GL; **1036**, Leiderman/Rothco; **1037**, John Harrington/BS.

Chapter 40 1039 T, PRC Archive; **1039 B**, Lisa Quinones/BS; **1040**, Matthew McVay/Tony Stone Images; **1041**, William Campbell/Sygma; **1042 T**, NA; **1042 B**, LOC; **1043 T**, BB; **1043 B**, Museum of American Political Life; **1046**, Int'l Brotherhood of Teamsters.

Chapter 41 1048 T, Courtesy of Fred and Kathryn Giampietro; **1048 B**, © B. Thouanel/SIPA Press; **1049 T**, Christopher Morris/BS; Klaus Reisinger/BS; **1050 BOTH**, Collection of Col. Stuart S. Corning, Jr. RH/LS; **1027 T**, WW; **1027 B**, NA; **1052**, Brad Markel/GL; ©1959 Newsweek, Inc. All rights reserved. Reprinted by permission; **1054**, R. Bossu/Sygma.

Chapter 42 1056, David Chambers/Tony Stone Images; **1057**, David Young Wolff/Tony Stone Images; **1058**, National Center for Supercomputing Application at the University of Illinois; **1060 L**, Courtesy Picture Tel; **1060 M&R**, Div. of Political History, SI; **1061 BL**, Courtesy Ford Archives; **1061 BM**, NASA; **1062**, C/B; **1064**, Steve Dunwell/The Image Bank; **1067**, Stock Connection©1995 Joe Sohn/Chromosohm.

Reference Section 1068 TL clockwise, Jim Pickerell; Franklin D. Roosevelt Library; Van Bucher/Photo Researchers; Collection of the Architect of the Capitol; C/B; **1070**, Independence National Historic Park; **1072**, Nichipor Collection, Courtesy of Minuteman National Historical Park. Rob Huntley/ Lightstream; **1074**, Miriam and Ira D. Walsh Division of Art, Prints and Photographs, New York Public Library. Astor, Lenox and Tilden Foundations; **1075**, Free Library of Philadelphia; **1076**, Courtesy, American Antiquarian Society; **1079**, LOC; **1082**, PRC; **1083**, LOC; **1085**, Margaret Bourke-White LIFE Magazine © Time Warner; **1086**, US Holocaust Memorial Museum; **1088**, C/B; **1090**, WW; **1092**, Rick Reinhart/Impact Visuals; **1093**, Paul Conklin; **1113**, Corbis Sygma; **1114**, Jim Pickerell; **1156**, Meserve Collection; **1157**, Dwight D. Eisenhower Library; **1158**, John Harrington/BS; **1159**, WW; **1160**, LOC; **1161**, Radcliffe College Archives, Schlesinger Library; © 1949 Time Inc. Reprinted with permission.

Primary Source Bibliography

Chapter 1 Chief Joseph: McLuhan, T. C. *Touch the Earth: A Self-Portrait of Indian Existence.* Simon and Schuster, 1971, p. 54; **Leo Africanus:** Bennett, Jr., Lerone. *Before the Mayflower: A History of the Negro in America.* Johnson Publishing Company, 1966, p. 18; **Christopher Columbus:** Morison, Samuel Eliot. *Admiral of the Ocean Sea: A Life of Christopher Columbus.* Little Brown, 1942, p. 231.

Chapter 2 Fray Alonso de Benavides: Kupperman, Karen Ordahl, ed. *Major Problems in American Colonial History: Documents and Essays.* D.C. Heath, 1993, p. 43; **John Smith:** Lankford, John, ed. *Captain John Smith's America: Selections from His Writings.* Harper Torchbooks, Harper and Row, 1967, p. 105; **John Winthrop:** "A Modell of Christian Charity." *Collections of the Massachusetts Historical Society,* 3rd series, vol. 7, 1838, pp. 33–34, 44–48; **Mayflower Compact:** Caffrey, Kate. *The Mayflower.* Stein and Day, 1974, p. 340; **Miantonomo:** Cronon, William. *Changes in the Land: Indians, Colonists, and the Ecology of New England.* Hill and Wang, 1983, p. 162; **Adriaen Van der Donck:** Jennings, Francis. *The Ambiguous Iroquois Empire.* W.W. Norton & Company, 1984, p. 47.

Chapter 3 William Blackstone: Ulrich, Laurel Thatcher. *Good Wives.* Oxford University Press, 1982, p. 7; **Eliza Pinckney:** Ravenel, Harriott Horry. *Eliza Pinckney.* Charles Scribner's Sons, 1896, p. 6; **Olaudah Equiano:** Edwards, Paul, ed. *Equiano's Travels.* Heinemann Educational Books, 1967, p. 25; **Equiano:** Edwards, p. 32; **Charles Ball:** Bayliss, John F., ed. *Black Slave Narratives.* Macmillan, 1970, p. 52; **Jonathan Edwards:** Kupperman, Karen Ordahl, ed. *Major Problems in American Colonial History: Documents and Essays.* D.C. Heath, 1993, p. 369; **George Whitefield:** Gaustad, Edwin Scott. *The Great Awakening in New England.* Quadrangle Books, 1957, p. 27.

Chapter 4 Deputy Governor of Virginia: R. A. Brock, ed. *The Official Letters of Alexander Spotswood.* Richmond, VA: Virginia Historical Society, 1882, vol. II, p. 296; **Massachusetts militiaman:** Linda Monk, ed. *Ordinary Americans: U.S. History Through the Eyes of Everyday People,* Close Up Publishing, 1994, p. 24; **Declaration of Rights and Grievances:** Morgan, Edmund S., ed. *Prologue to Revolution: Sources and Documents on the Stamp Act Crisis, 1764–1766.* University of North Carolina Press, 1959, pp. 62–63; **Deborah Franklin:** Don Cook. *The Long Fuse: How England Lost the American Colonies, 1760–1785.* New York: Atlantic Monthly Press, 1995, p. 79; **John Dickinson:** Charles Dollar and Gary Reichard, eds. *American Issues: A Documentary Reader.* New York: Random House, 1988, p. 71; **Declaration and Resolves of the First Continental Congress:** Commager, Henry Steele, ed. *Documents of American History,* Eighth Edition. Appleton-Century-Crofts, 1968, p. 83; **Patrick Henry:** Commager, Henry Steele, and Richard B. Morris, eds. *The Spirit of 'Seventy-Six: The Story of the American Revolution as Told by Participants.* New York: Bonanza Books, 1983, pp. 108–109; **Thomas Paine, Common Sense:** Curti, Merle, et al., eds., *American Issues: The Social*

Record, 4th ed. rev. New York: J. B. Lippincott, 1971, vol. 1, pp. 82, 84; **John Locke:** *Two Treatises of Government,* Mark Goldie, ed. London, Orion Publishing Group, 1993, pp. 223–224; **Abigail Adams:** Brown, Richard D., ed. *Major Problems in the Era of the American Revolution, 1760–1791: Documents and Essays.* D. C. Heath, 1992, p. 302; **Thomas Paine:** Foot, Michael, and Isaac Kramnick, eds. *Thomas Paine Reader.* Penguin Books, 1987, p. 116; **Soldier at Princeton:** Commager and Morris, p. 519.

Chapter 5 Fisher Ames: Wood, Gordon S. *The Creation of the American Republic, 1776–1787.* W. W. Norton & Company, 1969, p. 411; **Richard Price:** Wood, p. 396; *The Federalist,* **No. 10:** *The Annals of America.* Vol. 3, *1784–1796: Organizing the New Nation.* Encyclopedia Britannica, 1968, p. 219; **Robert Yates and John Lansing:** Commager, Henry Steele, ed. *Documents of American History,* Eighth Edition. Appleton-Century-Crofts, 1968, p. 149; **Convention member:** Parton, James. *Life of Thomas Jefferson.* Da Capo, 1971, quoted in Barbash, Fred. *The Founding: A Dramatic Account of the Writing of the Constitution.* Simon and Schuster, 1987, p. 77.

Chapter 6 George Washington: Commager, Henry Steele, ed. *Documents of American History,* Eighth Edition. Appleton-Century-Crofts, 1968, p. 169; **Thomas Jefferson's First Inaugural Address:** Ravitch, Diane, ed. *The Democracy Reader.* HarperPerennial, 1992, p. 140; **Thomas Jefferson:** Peterson, Merrill D., ed. *Thomas Jefferson.* Library of America, 1984, p. 494; **Handsome Lake:** Wallace, Anthony F. C. *The Death and Rebirth of the Seneca.* Vintage Books, 1972, p. 268; **Tecumseh:** Edmunds, David R. *Tecumseh and the Quest for Indian Leadership.* Little, Brown and Company, 1984, p. 205.

Chapter 7 Morris Birkbeck: Birkbeck, Morris. "Notes on a Journey in America from the Coasts of Virginia to the Territory of Illinois." Philadelphia, 1817, p. 34; **Noah Webster:** Wood, Gordon S. *The Rising Glory of America, 1760–1820.* Northeastern University Press, 1990, p. 169; **Miss P. W. Jackson:** Kerber, Linda K. *Women of the Republic: Intellect and Ideology in Revolutionary America.* University of North Carolina Press, 1980, p. 229; **Zadoc Long:** Rothman, Ellen K. *Hands and Hearts: A History of Courtship in America.* Harvard University Press, 1984; **William Thacher:** Gorn, Elliot J., et al. *Constructing the American Past: A Source Book of a People's History.* HarperCollins, 1991, p. 185; **Richard Allen:** Hatch, Nathan O. *The Democratization of American Christianity.* Yale University Press, 1989, p. 107.

Chapter 8 millworker: Larcom, Lucy. *A New England Girlhood.* Corinth Books, 1961, pp. 145–156; **Harriet Robinson:** Davis, David Byron. *Antebellum American Culture: An Interpretive Anthology.* D. C. Heath, 1979, pp. 87–88; **Moses Grandy:** *Narrative of the Life of Moses Grandy Late a Slave in the United States of America.* Oliver Johnson Publishing Company, 1844, p. 11, quoted in Lerner, Gerda. *Black Women in White America, A Documentary History.* Vintage Books, 1973, p. 9; **James Monroe:** Commager, Henry Steele, ed. *Documents of American History,* Eighth Edition. Appleton-Century-Crofts, 1968, pp. 236–237; **John Quincy Adams:** Wilentz, Sean, ed. *Major Problems in the Early Republic, 1778–1848.* D. C. Heath, 1992, p. 341; **Cherokee:** Van Every, Dale. *Disinherited: The Lost Birthright of the American Indian.* William Morrow and Company, 1966, pp. 135–136; **President Jackson:** Commager, p. 260; **President Jackson:** Wilentz, p. 388.

Chapter 9 Henry David Thoreau: *Walden.* Princeton University Press, 1971, p. 326; **Horace Mann:** "Horace Mann." *Encyclopedia Britannica,* vol. 11, 1983, p. 455; **Germantown Mennonites:** Commager, Henry Steele, ed. *Documents of American History,* Eighth Edition. Appleton-Century-Crofts, 1968, p. 37; **William Lloyd Garrison:** Wilentz, Sean, ed. *Major Problems in the Early Republic, 1787–1848.* D. C. Heath, 1992, p. 477; **Martin Delany:** Wilentz, p. 514; **Catharine Beecher:** *A Treatise on Domestic Economy.* T. H. Webb, 1842, pp. 26–34, 36–38; **Elizabeth Cady Stanton:** Stanton, Elizabeth Cady, et al. *History of Woman Suffrage,* Vol. 1. Fowler and Wells, 1889, pp. 58–59; **Sojourner Truth:** *Anti-Slavery Bugle,* Salem, Ohio, June 21, 1851, 4: p. 81–82.

Chapter 10 James R. Walker: Walker, James R. *Lakota Society.* University of Nebraska Press, 1982, p. 74; **Wilkis:** Grinnell, George Bird. *When Buffalo Ran.* University of Oklahoma Press, 1966, p. 46; **William Travis:** Ramsdell, Charles. "The Storming of the Alamo," *American Heritage,* Vol. XII, No. 2, February 1961, p. 91; **Richard Henry Dana:** Dana, R.H., Jr. *Two Years Before the Mast and Twenty-Four Years After.* P. F. Collier, 1909, p. 394.

Chapter 11 Harriet Beecher Stowe: *Uncle Tom's Cabin.* New American Library, 1981, p. 32; **Harriet Beecher Stowe:** p. 93; **George Fitzhugh:** Gorn, Elliot J., et al. *Constructing the American Past: A Source Book of a People's History,* Vol. 1. HarperCollins, 1991, p. 259; **John C. Calhoun:** Wiltse, Charles M. *John C. Calhoun: Sectionalist, 1840–1850.* The Bobbs-Merrill Company, 1951, p. 461; **Daniel Webster:** Morris, Richard B., and Jeffrey B. Morris, eds. *Encyclopedia of American History.* Harper and Row, 1976, p. 1179. **Know Nothings:** Holt, Michael F. *The Political Crises of the 1850's.* John Wiley and Sons, 1978, p. 163; **Stephen Douglas:** Holt, p. 145; **Roger Taney:** Heffner, Richard D. *A Documentary History of the United States.* New American Library, 1976, p. 141; **Abraham Lincoln:** Angle, Paul M. *Created Equal? The Complete Lincoln-Douglas Debates of 1858.* The University of Chicago Press, 1958, p. 42; **Abraham Lincoln:** *Selected Speeches and Writings.* The Library of America, 1992, p. 131; **John Brown:** Oates, Stephen B. *To Purge This Land with Blood: A Biography of John Brown.* Harper Torchbooks, 1970, p. 351; **Augusta, Georgia, newspaper editor:** Holt, Michael F. *The Political Crisis of the 1850's.* John Wiley and Sons, 1978, p. 241; **Abraham Lincoln** (First Inaugural Address): Ravitch, Diane, ed. *The Democracy Reader.* HarperPerennial, 1992, p. 165.

Chapter 12 Mary Boykin Chesnut: Woodward, C. Vann, et al., eds. *Mary Chesnut's Civil War.* Yale University Press, 1981, pp. 326, 327, 330, 333, 339; **Abraham Lincoln:** Ward, Geoffrey C. *The Civil War: An Illustrated History.* Alfred A. Knopf,

1990, p. 110; **Louis Wigfall:** McPherson, James M. *Battle Cry of Freedom*. Oxford University Press, 1988, p. 430; **Abraham Lincoln:** McPherson, p. 510; **Emancipation Proclamation:** Boorstin, Daniel, ed. *An American Primer*. University of Chicago Press, 1968, p. 431; **Frederick Douglass:** *Douglass' Monthly*, August, 1863; **soldier at Gettysburg:** E. B. Long, *The Civil War Day by Day*. Da Capo Press, 1971, p. 377; **Abraham Lincoln:** *Selected Speeches and Writings*. First Vintage Books, Library of America, p. 449; **Abraham Lincoln:** Lincoln, p. 450.

Chapter 13 Abraham Lincoln: *Selected Speeches and Writings*. First Vintage Books, Library of America, p. 450; **Charlotte Forten:** "Life on the Sea Islands," *Atlantic Monthly*, Vol. 13 (May and June) 1864, pp. 588–589, 591–594, 666–667; **Lydia Child:** Foner, Eric. *Reconstruction: America's Unfinished Revolution 1863–1877*. Harper and Row, 1988, p. 473; **Ira Steward:** Levine, Bruce et al., eds. *Who Built America? Working People and the Nation's Economy, Politics, Culture, and Society*. Pantheon Books, 1989, p. 539.

Chapter 14 Andrew Carnegie: Carnegie, Andrew. *The Empire of Business*. Doubleday, 1902, pp. 138–140, quoted in Kirkland, Edward Chase. *Dream and Thought in the Business Community, 1860–1900*. Cornell, 1956, pp. 156–157; **Resident of Lynn, Massachusetts:** Bureau of Labor, *Fourth Annual Report*, 1873, p. 306; **Frederick Winslow Taylor:** Taylor, Frederick W. *The Principles of Scientific Management*. W.W. Norton and Company, 1911, p. 39; **Samuel Gompers:** *Labor and the Employer*. Ayer Company Publishers, 1971, p. 118; **August Spies:** Kogan, B. R. "The Chicago Haymarket Riot," 1959 (a reproduction of the circular in the Chicago Historical Society collection).

Chapter 15 newspaper reporter: Fite, Gilbert. *The Farmer's Frontier, 1865–1900*. University of New Mexico Press, 1974, p. 205; **newspaper report:** "Commercial and Financial Chronicle," September 21, 1879, quoted in Fite, p. 82; **Washington Gladden:** *The Annals of America*. Vol. 11, *1884–1894: Agrarianism and Urbanization*. Encyclopedia Britannica, 1968, p. 356.; **Tom Watson:** Woodward, C. Vann. *Tom Watson, Agrarian Rebel*. Oxford University Press, 1963, p. 220; **Frederick Jackson Turner:** Billington, Ray, ed. *Frontier and Section: Selected Essays of Frederick Jackson Turner*. Prentice Hall, 1961, p. 61; **Edward L. Wheeler:** *Deadwood Dick, The Prince of the Road*. Garland, 1979, p. 16.

Chapter 16 anonymous: Kutler, Stanley I. *Looking for America: The People's History*, Vol. 2. W. W. Norton & Company, 1979, p. 178; **Fiorello LaGuardia:** *The Making of an Insurgent*. J. B. Lippincott Co., 1948, pp. 64–65; **Sadie Frowne:** Adapted from "The Story of a Sweatshop Girl: Sadie Frowne," Katzman and Tuttle. *Plain Folk: The Life Stories of Undistinguished Americans*. Illinois, University of Illinois Press, 1982; **Emily Dinwiddie:** "Some Aspects of Italian Housing and Social Conditions in Philadelphia," *Charities and the Commons*, Vol. 12, 1904, p. 490; **Jacob Riis:** *How the Other Half Lives*. Penguin, 1997, p. 6; **Martin Lomasney:** *The Boston Globe*, December 2, 1923, quoted in Zink, Harold. *City Bosses in the United States. A Study of Twenty Municipal Bosses*. Duke University Press, 1930, p. 83.

Chapter 17 Pauli Murray: *Proud Shoes*. Harper and Row, 1956, pp. 269–270; **Booker T. Washington:** *Address of Booker T. Washington, principal of the Tuskegee Normal and Industrial Institute, Tuskegee, Alabama, delivered at the opening of the Cotton States and International Exposition, at Atlanta, Ga., September 18, 1895*. Daniel A. P. Murray Pamphlet Collection, Library of Congress, 1894, pp. 7–9; **W.E.B. Du Bois:** Du Bois, W.E.B. *The Negro Problem: A Series of Articles by Representative American Negroes of Today*. J. Pott & Company, 1903, pp. 33–75; **notice to performers:** Royle, Edwin Milton. "The Vaudeville Theatre," *Scribner's Magazine*, Vol. XXVI, October 1899, pp. 485–495.

Chapter 18 James G. Blaine: LaFeber, Walter. *The New Empire: An Interpretation of American Expansion, 1860–1898*. Cornell University Press, 1963, p. 165; **Theodore Roosevelt:** Hart, Albert Bushnell, and Herbert Ronald Ferleger, eds. *Theodore Roosevelt Cyclopedia*. Roosevelt Memorial Association, 1941, p. 407; **Theodore Roosevelt:** Commager, Henry Steele, ed. *Documents of American History*, vol. 2, Eighth Edition. Appleton-Century Crofts, 1968, p. 34; **Carl Schurz:** "The Policy of Imperialism," 1899 address by Carl Schruz to Anti-Imperialist Conference in Chicago, October 17, 1899; **Bishop Alexander Walters:** "Wisconsin Weekly Advocate," August 17, 1899, quoted in Gatewood, Willard B., Jr. *Black Americans and the White Man's Burden, 1898–1903*. University of Illinois Press, 1975, p. 200.

Chapter 19 Edward Bellamy: *Looking Backward*. River City Press, 1888, p. 56; **Upton Sinclair:** *The Jungle*. Doubleday, 1906, pp. 96–97; **Jane Addams:** "Why Women Should Vote." *Ladies Home Journal*, Vol. XXVII, January 1910, pp. 21–22; **Susan B. Anthony:** Sherr, Lynn. *Failure Is Impossible: Susan B. Anthony in Her Own Words*. Times Books, 1995, pp. 110–112.

Chapter 20 Arthur Zimmerman: Leckie, Robert. *The Wars of America*. Harper and Row, 1968, p. 628; **Woodrow Wilson:** Cooper, John Milton, Jr. *Pivotal Decades: The United States, 1900–1920*. W. W. Norton and Company, 1990, p. 265; **Corporal Elmer Sherwood:** Berger, Dorothy and Josef, eds. *Diary of America*. Simon and Schuster, 1957, p. 536; **Herbert Hoover:** "Gospel of the Clean Plate." *Ladies Home Journal*, August 1917, p. 25; **Woodrow Wilson:** Commager, Henry Steele, ed. *Documents of American History*, vol. II, Eighth Edition. Appleton-Century-Crofts, 1968, p. 138; **Alice Lord O'Brian:** *No Glory: Letters from France, 1917–1919*. Airport Publishers, 1936, pp. 8, 141, 152–153.

Chapter 21 Henry Ford: *My Life and Work*. Doubleday, 1923; **Preston Slosson:** *The Great Crusade and After, 1914–1928*. Macmillan, 1930, p. 157; **Edna St. Vincent Millay:** "First Fig." *Edna St. Vincent Millay: Selected Poems*. HarperCollins, 1991, p. 19; **Langston Hughes:** From COLLECTED POEMS by Langston Hughes Copyright (c) 1994 by the Estate of Langston Hughes reprinted by permission of Alfred A. Knopf, Inc.; **Alice Longworth:** *Crowded Hours: Reminiscences of Alice Roosevelt Longworth*. Charles Scribner's Sons, 1933, p. 324.

Chapter 22 Lincoln Steffens: Leuchtenberg, William. *The Perils of Prosperity, 1914–1932*. University of Chicago Press, 1958, p. 202; **Broadway show tune:** Words by E. Y. Harburg, music by Jay Gorney. Harms, Inc., 1932. Renewed, permission from Warner Brothers Music; **Gordon Parks:** *Voices in the Mirror: An Autobiography*. Doubleday, 1990; **Wilson Ledford:** "How I Lived During the Depression." Interview taped and transcribed by Reuben Hiatt, November 7, 1982. Quoted in Snell, William R. ed., *Hard Times Remembered: Bradley County and the Great Depression*. Bradley County Historical Society, 1983, pp. 117–121; **Gerald W. Johnson:** "The Average American and the Depression." *Current History*, February 1932; **Kitty McCulloch:** Terkel, Studs. *Hard Times: An Oral History of the Great Depression*. Pantheon Books, 1970; **William Saroyan:** *Inhale and Exhale*. Random House, 1936, p. 81; **Herbert Hoover:** Myers, William S., ed. *The State Papers and Other Public Writings of Herbert Hoover*. Doubleday, Doran and Company, Inc., Vol. II, 1934, pp. 408–413; **Franklin D. Roosevelt:** *The New York Times*, September 24, 1932; **Roosevelt's Inaugural Address:** March 4, 1933.

Chapter 23 Harry Hopkins: Dawley, Alan. *Struggles for Justice: Social Responsibility and the Liberal State*. Harvard University Press, 1991, p. 367; **federal official:** Markowitz, Gerald, and David Rosner, eds. "Slaves of the Depression." *Workers' Letters About Life on the Job*. Cornell, 1987, p. 154; **Franklin Roosevelt:** White, Walter. *A Man Called White: The Autobiography of Walter White*. Viking Press, 1948, pp. 179–180; **Sam E. Roberts:** Duram, James C., and Eleanor A. Duram. "Congressman Clifford Hope's Correspondence With his Constituents: A Conservative View of the Court-Packing Fight of 1937." *Kansas Historical Quarterly*, 37/1 (Spring 1971), p. 71; **Hiram W. Johnson:** Barnes, William R., and A. W. Littlefield. *The Supreme Court Issue and the Constitution, Comments Pro and Con by Distinguished Men*. Barnes & Noble, 1937, p. 49; **Walter Reuther:** Madison, Charles A. *American Labor Leaders, Personalities and Forces in the Labor Movement*. Ungar, 1950, p. 382; **Mrs. Renee Lohrback:** Blackwelder, Julia Kirk. *Women of the Depression: Caste and Culture in San Antonio, 1929–1939*. Texas A&M Press, 1984.

Chapter 24 Winston Churchill: Baldwin, Hanson W. *The Crucial Years: 1939–1941*. Harper and Row, 1976, p. 127; **Franklin D. Roosevelt:** Commager, Henry Steele, ed. *Documents of American History*, vol. II, Eighth Edition. Appleton-Century-Crofts, 1968, p. 452; **Franklin D. Roosevelt:** Commager, Henry Steele, ed. *Documents of American History*, vol. II, Eighth Edition. Appleton-Century-Crofts, 1968, p. 449; **American GI:** Martin, Ralph. *The GI War*. Boston: Little, Brown and Co., 1967, p. 338; **Hiroshima survivor:** Cook, Haruko Taya, and Theodore Cook. *Japan at War: An Oral History*. The New Press, 1992, p. 397; **Leon Bass:** *Holocaust and Human Behavior*. Facing History and Ourselves National Foundation, p. 414.

Chapter 25 Leonard Williamson: Hoopes, Roy. *Americans Remember the Home Front: An Oral Narrative*. Hawthorn Books, 1977, p. 115; **Want ad:** *Sporting News*, February 25, 1943; **Sheril Cunning:** Terkel, Studs. *"The Good War:" An Oral History of World War Two*. Ballantine Books, 1984, p. 234; **Beatrice Clifton:** Gluck, Sherna Berger. *Rosie the Riveter Revisited: Women, the War, and Social Change*. Twayne Publishers, 1987, pp. 211, 219; **Lloyd Brown:** Blum, John Morton. *V Was for Victory: Politics and American Culture During World War II*. Harcourt Brace Jovanovich, 1976, p. 191; **Henry Murakami:** Harris, Mark Jonathan, et al. *The Homefront: America During World War II*. G. P. Putnam's Sons, 1984, p. 113.

Chapter 26 Winston Churchill: *The Annals of America*. Vol. 16, *1940–1949: The Second World War and After*. Encyclopedia Britannica, 1968, p. 367; **George Kennan:** *The Annals of America*. Vol. 16, *1940–1949: The Second World War and After*. Encyclopedia Britannica, 1968, p. 444; **Harry Truman:** Commager, Henry Steele, ed. *Documents of American History*, vol. II, Eighth Edition. Appleton-Century-Crofts, 1968, p. 525; **George C. Marshall:** Commager, Henry Steele, ed. *Documents of American History*, vol. II, Eighth Edition. Appleton-Century-Crofts, 1968, p. 532; **MacArthur:** Phillips, Cabell. *The Truman Presidency: The History of a Triumphant Succession*. The Macmillan Company, 1966, p. 348; **John Foster Dulles:** Shafritz, Jay M. *HarperCollins Dictionary of American Government and Politics*. HarperCollins, 1993, p. 73; **Dwight D. Eisenhower:** Commager, Henry Steele, ed. *Documents of American History*, vol. II, Eighth Edition. Appleton-Century-Crofts, 1968, p. 667.

Chapter 27 Walt Disney: Winkler, Allan M. *Life Under a Cloud: American Anxiety About the Atom*. Oxford University Press, 1993, p. 140; **Malvina Reynolds:** Winkler, Allan M. *Modern America: The United States from World War II to the Present*. HarperCollins, 1985, p. 86; **Betty Friedan:** *The Feminine Mystique*. Norton, 1963; **Harry Truman:** Winkler, p. 70; **Richard Nixon:** Wicker, Tom. *One of Us: Richard Nixon and the American Dream*. Random House, 1991, p. 98; **Eisenhower:** Holbo, Paul S., and Robert W. Sellen, eds. *The Eisenhower Era*. Dryden Press, 1974, p. 113; **Martin Luther King, Jr.:** Sitkoff, Harvard. *The Struggle for Black Equality: 1954–1980*. Hill and Wang, 1981, p. 50; **Martin Luther King, Jr.:** *Stride Toward Freedom: The Montgomery Story*. Harper and Row, 1958, pp. 53–55; **Seminole petition to Eisenhower:** Josephy, Alvin M., Jr. *Now That the Buffalo's Gone: A Study of Today's American Indians*. Alfred A. Knopf, 1982, p. 28.

Chapter 28 John F. Kennedy's Inaugural Address: Commager, Henry Steele, ed. *Documents of American History*, Eighth Edition. Appleton-Century-Crofts, 1968, pp. 668–670; **John F. Kennedy:** Swenson, Lloyd S., James M. Grimwood, and Charles C. Alexander. *This New Ocean, A History of Project Mercury*. NASA, 1966. Frontispiece and p. 470; **Lyndon B. Johnson:** Speech at the University of Michigan, May 1964; **John F. Kennedy's Inaugural Address:** Commager, pp. 668–670; **Senator J. William Fulbright:** Schlesinger, Arthur M. *A Thousand Days: John F. Kennedy in the White House*. Houghton Mifflin, 1965, p. 251; **Dean Acheson:** Winkler, Allan M. *Life Under a Cloud: American Anxiety About the Atom*. Oxford University Press, 1993, pp. 173–174.

Chapter 29 W.E.B. DuBois: Aptheker, Herbert, ed. *Pamphlets and Leaflets by W.E.B. DuBois.* Kraus-Thomason Organization Limited, 1986, p. 116; **Southern Christian Leadership Conference:** Sitkoff, Harvard. *The Struggle for Black Equality.* Hill and Wang, 1981, p. 65; **SCLC leaflet:** Sitkoff, p. 59; **Todd Gitlin:** *The Sixties: Years of Hope, Days of Rage.* Bantam Books, 1987, pp. 148–149; **John Lewis:** Hampton, Henry, et al. *Voices of Freedom: An Oral History of the Civil Rights Movement from the 1950's Through the 1980's.* Bantam Books, 1990, p. 58; **James Farmer:** Hampton, p. 78; **Martin Luther King, Jr.:** "Letter From a Birmingham Jail." *Essay Series.* A. J. Muste Memorial Institute, p. 18; **John F. Kennedy:** *Radio and Television Report to the American People on Civil Rights,* June 11, 1963; **Martin Luther King, Jr.:** "I Have a Dream." Speech in Washington, D.C., August 1963. In Winkler, Allan M. *The Recent Past: Readings on America Since World War II.* Harper and Row, 1989, p. 275; **Fannie Lou Hamer:** Harley, Sharon, et al. *The African American Experience: A History.* Globe Book Company, 1992, p. 336; **Malcolm X:** *The Autobiography of Malcolm X.* Ballantine Books, 1990, pp. 245–246; **Stokely Carmichael:** Nash, Gary B., et al., eds. *The American People.* Harper and Row, 1986, p. 1001; **Barbara Jordan:** Harley, et al., p. 343.

Chapter 30 Cathy Cade: Evans, Sara. *Personal Politics: The Roots of Women's Liberation in the Civil Rights Movement and the New Left.* Alfred A. Knopf, 1979, p. 205; **Mimi Feingold:** Evans, p. 204; **Helen Reddy:** "I Am Woman." Words by Helen Reddy, music by Ray Burton. Irving Music, Inc. and Buggerlugs Music Co., 1971; **Phyllis Schlafly:** Nash, Gary B. *The American People: Creating a Nation and a Society.* Harper and Row, 1986, p. 1008; **Rodolfo Gonzales:** Gutierrez, Jose Angel, John C. Hammerback, and Richard J. Jensen. *A War of Words: Chicano Protest in the 1960's and 1970's.* Greenwood Press, 1985, p. 59; **Cesar Chavez:** Levy, Jacques E. *César Chávez: Autobiography of La Causa.* W. W. Norton, 1975; **Cesar Chavez:** Levy, p. 293; **David Sanchez:** Vigil, Maurilio. *Chicano Politics.* University Press of America, 1977, p. 173; **Dennis Banks:** Zimmerman, Bill. *Airlift to Wounded Knee.* Swallow Press, 1976, p. 117; **Dennis Banks:** Dewing, Rolland. *Wounded Knee: The Meaning and Significance of the Second Incident.* Irvington Publishers, Inc., 1985, p. 41; **Vine Deloria, Jr.:** "This Country Was a Lot Better Off When the Indians Were Running It." *New York Times Magazine,* March 8, 1970; **Onondaga Chief Oren Lyons:** *Voices from Wounded Knee: The People Are Standing Up.* Akwesasne Notes, 1974, p. 96; **Rachel Carson:** *Silent Spring.* Houghton Mifflin, 1962, p. 6; **Ralph Nader:** *Unsafe at Any Speed: The Designed-in Dangers of the American Automobile.* Grossman Publishers, 1972, preface.

Chapter 31 Robert McNamara: Shapley, Deborah. *Promise and Power: The Life and Times of Robert McNamara.* Little, Brown and Company, 1993, p. 263; **Lyndon B. Johnson:** Kearns, Doris. *Lyndon Johnson and the American Dream.* Harper and Row, 1976, p. 316; **Letter home from an American soldier:** Edelman, Bernard, ed. *Dear America: Letters Home from Vietnam.* New York Veterans Memorial Commission; **Le Thanh:** Chanoff, David, and Van Toai Doan. *Portrait of the Enemy.* Random House, 1986, pp. 62–63; **Vietnamese peasant:** Trullinger, James Walker, Jr. *Village at War: An Account of Revolution in Vietnam.* Longman, 1980, p. 118. **Private Paul Meadlo:** *The New York Times,* November 25, 1969, p. 16; **Port Huron Statement:** Hayden, Tom. Students for a Democratic Society. Quoted in Winkler, Allan. *The Recent Past: Readings on America Since World War II.* Harper and Row, 1989, pp. 218–219; **Tom Law:** Makower, Joel. *Woodstock: The Oral History.* Doubleday, 1989, p. 333; **Lyndon Johnson:** King, Larry L. "LBJ and Vietnam" from *A Sense Of History: The Best Writing from the Pages of American Heritage.* American Heritage/Houghton Mifflin Company, 1985, p. 801; **Richard Nixon:** Address to the Nation on the Situation in Southeast Asia. April 30, 1970.

Chapter 32 Martin Luther King, Jr.: Kaiser, Charles. *1968 in America: Music, Politics, Chaos, Counterculture, and the Shaping of a Generation.* Weidenfeld and Nicolson, 1988, p. 144; **John Lewis:** Morrison, Joan, and Robert K. Morrison. *From Camelot to Kent State: The Sixties Experience in the Words of Those Who Lived It.* Times Books, 1987, pp. 34–35; **Theodore White:** *The Making of the President 1968.* Atheneum, 1969, p. 298; **Richard Nixon:** Wicker, Tom. *One of Us: Richard Nixon and the American Dream.* Random House, 1991, p. 9; **Richard Nixon:** Ambrose, Stephen E. *Nixon: Volume Two: The Triumph of a Politician, 1962–1972.* Simon and Schuster, 1989, p. 376; **Henry Kissinger:** *White House Years.* Little, Brown and Company, 1979, p. 45; **Richard Nixon:** *The Memoirs of Richard Nixon.* Grosset and Dunlap, 1978, p. 545; **Richard Nixon:** *Public Papers of the Presidents of the United States: Richard Nixon,* p. 320; **John J. Sirica:** Bernstein, Carl, and Bob Woodward. *All the President's Men.* Warner Paperback Books, 1975, p. 268; **M. Caldwell Butler:** Burns, James MacGregor. *The Crosswinds of Freedom.* Alfred A. Knopf, 1989, p. 507.

Chapter 33 Gerald Ford: *A Time to Heal: The Autobiography of Gerald R. Ford.* Harper and Row, 1979, pp. 177–178; **Jerold F. terHorst:** "How Good a President?" *Newsweek,* October 18, 1976, p. 31; **Barbara Jordan:** Hine, Darlene Clark, ed. *Facts on File Encyclopedia of Black Women in America: Law and Government.* Facts on File, 1997; **Jimmy Carter:** Carter, pp. 142–143; **Cyrus Vance:** *Hard Choices: Critical Years in America's Foreign Policy.* Simon and Schuster, 1983, pp. 228–229; **Kathryn Koob:** *Guest of the Revolution.* Thomas Nelson Publishers, 1982, pp. 57, 64, 73; **Jimmy Carter:** Jordan, Hamilton. *Crisis: The Last Year of the Carter Presidency.* G. P. Putnam's Sons, 1982, p. 54; **Jimmy Carter:** Carter, p. 22.

Chapter 34 Ronald Reagan's Inaugural Address: "Putting America Back to Work," January 20, 1981. *Vital Speeches of the Day,* Vol. XLVII, No. 9, February 15, 1981. **Kevin Phillips:** "Reagan's America: A Capital Offense." *The New York Times Magazine,* June 24, 1990; **George Bush:** "Open Letter to College Students on the Persian Gulf Crisis," January 9, 1991.

Chapter 35 Bill Clinton's First Inaugural Address: *The New York Times,* January 22, 1993, p. A13; **Jaimie S. Wurzel:** *Toward Multiculturalism: A Reader in Multicultural Education.* Intercultural Press, Inc., 1988, p. 10.

Chapter 36 California state assembly aide: Church, George J. "Send Back Your Tired, Your Poor...." *Time,* June 21, 1993, p. 26; **John Silber:** "One Nation, One Language, One Ballot." *Wall Street Journal,* April 30, 1996, p. A14; **Eddy Jerena:** "Shutting the Golden Door." *U.S. News and World Report,* October 3, 1994, p. 39; **Esperanza Zendejas:** "To Make a Nation." *U.S. News and World Report,* October 4, 1993, p. 54.

Chapter 37 Jim Reinke: "Who is the NRA?" *Time,* January 29, 1990, p. 16; **J. Warren Cassidy:** "Who is the NRA?", p. 22; **Al Baker:** "Armed America." *Time,* February 6, 1989, p. 20.

Chapter 38 John Trendler: Silverstein, Stuart. "A Federal Pay Hike the Public Supports." *Los Angeles Times,* May 7, 1996, p. D1; **Robert Bobbitt:** Winerip, Michael. "Minimum Wage? As One Man Finds, It's Really a Matter of Perspective." *The New York Times,* May 10, 1996, p. A9.

Chapter 39 Frank Luntz: Ratan, Suneel. "The Most Unkindest Cut." *Time,* May 15, 1995, p. 37; **Tom DeLay:** Pear, Robert. "Ending Welfare as Americans Know It." *The New York Times,* July 21, 1996, Week in Review, p. 4; **Christopher Jencks:** Sancton, Thomas. "How to Get America Off the Dole." *Time,* May 25, 1992, p. 44.

Chapter 40 Edward Leamers: Sterngold, James. "Nafta Trade-off: Some Jobs Lost, Others Gained." *The New York Times,* October 9, 1995, p. A13; **Public Citizen:** Levinson, Marc. "Oh, No, Not NAFTA Again!" *Newsweek,* September 25, 1995, p. 59; **Lori Wallach:** "Free Trade Aftermath." *Christian Science Monitor,* January 3, 1996, p. 1.

Chapter 41 Richard Nixon: *Seize the Moment: America's Challenge in a One-Superpower World.* Simon and Schuster, 1992, p. 14; **Casper Weinberger:** *Fighting for Peace.* Warner Books, 1990; **Ted Galen Carpenter:** *A Search for Enemies: America's Alliances After the Cold War.* Cato Institute, 1992, p. 1; **Richard Nixon:** *Seize the Moment: America's Challenge in a One-Superpower World.* Simon and Schuster, 1992, p. 33.

Chapter 42 Audrey Freeman: Church, George J. "We're No. 1, and It Hurts." *Time,* October 24, 1994, p. 50; **Jim Dunnigan:** "Making the Internet Work For You and Your Students." *Using the Internet,* Prentice Hall, 1997, p. 5; **Clifford Stoll:** "Invest in Humanware." *The New York Times,* May 19, 1996, Op-ed.

Source Readings Acknowledgments/Literature

Unit 1 *April Morning:* From *April Morning* by Howard Fast. Copyright ©1961 by Howard Fast. Copyright renewed 1989. Reprinted by permission of Crown Publishers, Inc.

Unit 2 Benjamin Franklin Campaigns for the Constitution: Reprinted by permission from the Putnam Publishing Group from *Debates of the Constitutional Convention 1787* edited by Gaillard Hunt. Copyright ©1903.

Unit 3 *Incidents in the Life of a Slave Girl:* Harriet Ann Jacobs, *Incidents in the Life of a Slave Girl: Written by Herself.* (Cambridge, MA: Harvard University Press, 1987).

Unit 4 Gettysburg Address: Abraham Lincoln. Gettysburg Address, in Henry Steele Commager, ed. *Documents of American History,* 8th ed. (New York: Appleton-Century-Crofts, 1968).

Unit 5 *Hungry Hearts:* Anzia Yezierska. Permission granted by Ayer Company Publishers.

Unit 6 **"Over There":** From *Those Wonderful Years: 1900-1920,* Dick Stern (New York: Big Three Music Corp). Song by George M. Cohan ©1917, renewed 1945 by Leo Feist, Inc., New York; **"K-K-K-Katy":** by Geoffrey O'Hara © 1918, renewed by Leo Feist, Inc., New York.

Unit 7 *Growing Up:* From *Growing Up,* by Russell Baker. Reprinted by permission of Don Congdon Associates, Inc. Copyright ©1982 by Russell Baker.

Unit 8 *Night:* Excerpt from NIGHT by Elie Wiesel, translated by Stella Rodway. Copyright © by MacGibbon & Kee. Copyright renewed © 1988 by The Collins Publishing Group. Reprinted by permission of Hill and Wang, a division of Farrar, Straus & Giroux, Inc.

Unit 9 **"Letter from the Birmingham Jail":** Reprinted by arrangement with The Heirs to the Estate of Martin Luther King, Jr., c/o Writers House, Inc. as agent for the proprietor. Copyright 1963 by Martin Luther King, Jr., copyright renewed 1991 by Coretta Scott King.

Unit 10 **"Straw into Gold: The Metamorphosis of the Everyday":** "Straw into Gold," copyright ©1987 by Sandra Cisneros. First published in *The Texas Observer,* September 1987. Reprinted by permission of Susan Bergholz Literary Services, New York. All rights reserved.

Unit 11 *My American Journey:* From *My American Journey* by Colin Powell with Joseph E. Persico. Copyright ©1995 by Colin L. Powell. Reprinted by permission of Random House, Inc.

Stop the Presses!

Visit Prentice Hall on the Internet at

http://www.phschool.com

for the Prentice Hall Social Studies Update.

There you will find periodic updates in the following areas:

★ **United States History**

★ **World Studies**

★ **American Government**

Each update topic provides you with background information as well as carefully selected links to guide you to related content on the Internet.

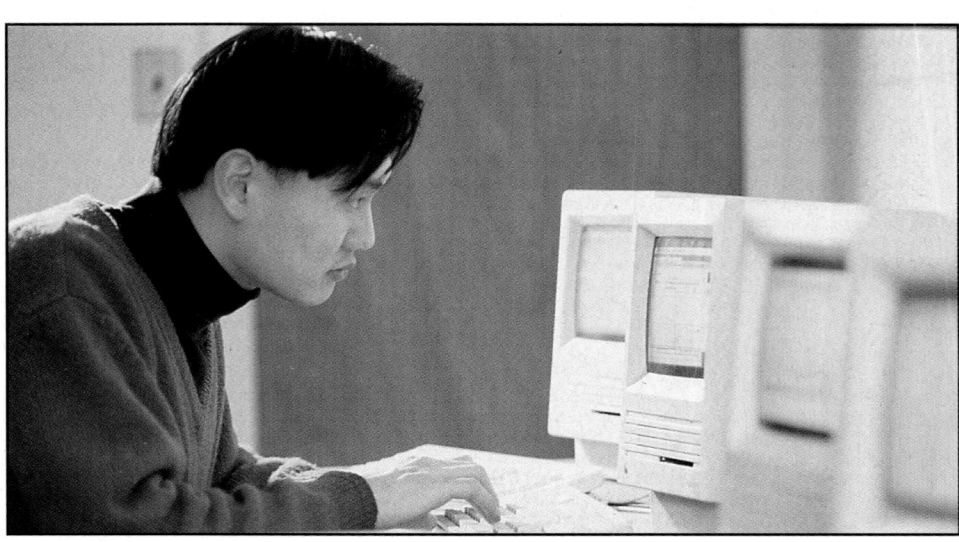